THE FEMINIST COMPANION TO LITERATURE IN ENGLISH

Editors

Virginia Blain, School of English and Linguistics, Macquarie University, Sydney

Patricia Clements, Department of English, University of Alberta, Edmonton

Isobel Grundy, Department of English, Queen Mary and Westfield College, University of London

Consulting Editors

Barbara Christian, Department of Afro-American Studies, University of California, Berkeley

Margaret Ferguson, Department of English and Comparative Literature, University of Colorado at Boulder

Margaret Homans, Department of English, Yale University

Elaine Showalter, Department of English, Princeton University

Contributing Editors

Julia Boffey, Queen Mary and Westfield College, London University
Charlotte Bruner, Iowa State University
Evelyn Haller, Doane College, Nebraska
Elaine Hobby, University of Loughborough
Helen Kidd, Wolfson College, Oxford University
Candida Lacey, Pandora Press, London
Aorewa McLeod, University of Auckland
Mary McCay, Loyola University, New Orleans
Lorraine McMullen, University of Ottawa
Susheila Nasta, Portsmouth Polytechnic
Emily Stipes Watts, University of Illinois at Urbana-Champaign
Elizabeth Webby, University of Sydney

THE FEMINIST COMPANION TO LITERATURE IN ENGLISH

Women Writers from the Middle Ages to the Present

Virginia Blain

Patricia Clements

Isobel Grundy

Yale University Press
New Haven and London

First published 1990 in the United Kingdom
by B. T. Batsford Ltd.

Published 1990 in the United States of
America by Yale University Press.

Typeset by J&L Composition Ltd, Filey, North
Yorkshire, Great Britain
and printed in Great Britain by
The Bath Press, Avon

Library of Congress catalog card number:
90–70515
International standard book number:
0–300–04854–8

10 9 8 7 6 5 4 3 2 1

For

Hettie Dorothea (Crisp) Blain

Alice Marjorie (Anderson) Clements

Nora Isobel Maclean (Henry) Grundy

Contributors

Debra Adelaide, University of Sydney
Linda Anderson, University of Newcastle-upon-Tyne
Susan Asbee, QMW, University of London
Diana Austin, University of New Brunswick
Susan Brown, University of Alberta
Margaret Cardwell, Queen's University, Belfast
Rachel Carr, King's College, University of London
JoAnn Castagna, University of Iowa
Dianne Chisholm, University of Alberta
Carla Contractor, Multi-Cultural Education Centre, Bristol
Barbara Christian, University of California, Berkeley
Cornelia Cook, QMW, University of London
Rosemary Curb, Rollins College, Florida
Patricia Demers, University of Alberta
Christine Devonshire, University of Newcastle-upon-Tyne
Maryanne Dever, University of Sydney
Ragnhild Eilkli, Oslo University
Maria Aline Ferreira, Universidade de Averio, Portugal
Kate Flint, Mansfield College, Oxford University
Shirley Foster, University of Sheffield
Yasmine Gooneratne, Macquarie University, Sydney
Elizabeth Grosz, University of Sydney
Eithne Henson, Wroxton College, Banbury, Oxfordshire
Coral Howells, University of Reading
Lorna Irvine, George Mason University, Virginia
Michelle Jones, University of Alberta
Smaro Kambourelli, University of Victoria, British Columbia
Joan Kirkby, Macquarie University, Sydney
Ann Larabee, Michigan State University
Betty Levitov, Doane College, Nebraska
Mary Loeffelholz, Northeastern University
Merja Makinen, Middlesex Polytechnic, London
Gina Mercer, University of Sydney
Rosemarie Morgan, Yale University
Arun Mukherjee, York University, Toronto
Laura Stempel Mumford, University of Wisconsin, Madison
Shirley Neuman, University of Alberta
Joanna Pappworth, Oxford University
Janet Paterson, University of Toronto
Lynn Penrod, University of Alberta
Jeanne Perreault, University of Calgary
Margaret Reynolds, University of Birmingham
Christine Salmon, QMW, University of London
Marion Shaw, University of Hull
Ann B. Shteir, York University, Toronto
Marni Stanley, St Hilda's College, Oxford University
Jane Thomas, University of Hull
Margaret Turner, University of Guelph
Sabine Vanacker, University of Hull
Jo-Ann Wallace, University of Alberta
Wendy Waring, University of Toronto
Margaret Whiteley, Shena Simon College, Manchester
Joanne Wilkes, University of Auckland
Dale Wilkie, University of Alberta
Susan Williams, University of Sussex
Janice Williamson, University of Alberta
Susan Wiseman, University of Kent at Canterbury
Jeanne Wood, York University, Toronto

Introduction

'All has vanished. No biography or history has a word to say about it.'
Virginia Woolf, *A Room of One's Own*, 1929

Literary history has long required an account of women's writing in English. For Virginia Woolf, when she addressed the young women of Newnham and Girton Colleges, women's past experience remained inaccessible, and the tradition of women's writing in English, as she sketched it for them, could be represented by the clear, rich, but very thin line from Margaret Cavendish, Duchess of Newcastle, to George Eliot. Now, nearly three generations later, the tight grip of a narrowly defined tradition of writing in English has been loosened and a broader figuring of women's contribution to the various literary cultures in English has been made possible by the development of feminist scholarship, whose powerful growth in the last two decades has opened works of history and reference to an adjusted focus and a renewed vision. This book is made possible by that scholarship; it grows from that rich ground.

Nevertheless, an account of women's writing in English is still a task of daunting proportion. The editors of this book have become acutely aware, in the years in which we have been preparing it, of a field far fuller, richer and more various than we could have dreamed at the outset of this work. We now know that any selection from this field is bound to be incomplete, choices occasionally misjudged, judgements never perfectly consistent, and that with whatever of good faith we approach the task of representing the un- and under-represented in our literary culture, we are bound, on occasion, to act in blindness. In this Introduction, we mean to give some indication of the grounds of our selection, a summary of our procedures, and a description of what we think the book (which has not ceased to grow into its present character since its conception) has become and to what futures it may contribute. (In this context, 'we' means the three editors, who, besides editing, have had chief responsibility for the shape of the book and for balance and emphasis, and have researched and written the largest proportion of entries. In other contexts, 'we' includes all of those other devoted feminist scholars who, with us, have selected, researched, written, and checked.)

First, to the shape of the book. It includes women writing from the beginning to the present (though not women writing wholly or mainly since 1985); not only English women, but women writing in English in several national traditions, including African, American, Asian, Australian, Canadian, Caribbean, New Zealand, South Pacific, the British Isles; not only works issuing from and reflecting the dominant ideologies of race, class, sexual practice; not only the canonized genres, but also diaries, letters, writing for children, and popular forms to which women have been relegated and which, often with joy, they have claimed. The women included are grouped by date on pp. 1210–1218. Another list, pp. 1219–1231, gives cross-references from their other names (many changed their name on marriage, some repeatedly; some sought the shelter of pseudonyms) and from the names of women whose writings are mentioned but who have no entry of their own – a reminder that this book's 2700-plus biographical entries reflect only a small fraction of a very large company.

To the biographical entries we have added topic entries (listed on p. 1209): sketches of genres, events, groupings, institutions important in the development of women's writing.

Some, like letter-writing or children's writing, have been practised particularly by women, recognized for centuries as areas of female specialization. Some, like early medical writing or slave narratives, cover significant corners which might easily be overlooked. Some, like education or the suffrage, are matters of history with vital connections for literature. Some, like theology, or black or lesbian criticism, have an important bearing on current efforts at re-vision of writing by women.

The slow retrieval of women's writing – never to be perfectly accomplished, since many works are lost – has so far been enabled by a host of readers and scholars with partial, complementary areas of knowledge and various focuses of enthusiasm. This book would have been impossible without several generations of predecessors of many kinds – archival, critical, theoretical, biographical. Since this project was conceived eight years ago, compilers of reference books and literary histories have become generally aware of the embarrassing gaps caused by the omission of women from the record. Such works, proliferating today, no longer exclude writing women or the uncanonized genres. Most, however, using an identical format for treatment of women and men, record likeness between the two almost to the exclusion of general differences. Most books also have limited space for women, and so their selection exerts a constricting effect on notions of a female canon, prematurely suggesting limits which this book hopes to hold open.

We have not included, as many Companions do, entries on characters in fiction or on particular works by title (except in the case of a very few anonymous works which demand inclusion). The reader will not find Elizabeth Bennet or *Uncle Tom's Cabin* or *The Second Sex* in our alphabetical sequence. The rationale for such entries is of course the common reader's knowledge of characters and titles: it supposes a companion to what is at least partly familiar, rather than to what is more unknown than known. We did not wish to reinforce existing criteria of 'the known' by entries on familiar characters and titles by women.

Then, to our procedures. The universally accepted way of making a reference book is to consult other reference books. This we have done when possible, but it has not been hard for us to avoid over-reliance on them, since for us they were often silent. We are writing here about knowledge and power and history, and against omission and exclusion: most of our women are not represented in the 'standard' reference books in the field. Furthermore, many reference works are more misleading than helpful in the case of women writers, both because they relay misinformation and because they have most usually issued from a set of (now well-known, but nevertheless still flourishing) stereotypes about women writers. To remedy omission and to counter error and stereotype, we have relied very heavily on freshly done research. In practice, this means that one or other of the writers of entries (editors and contributors) has read or at least examined almost every book written by the women included here. It does not mean that parish registers, publishers' archives, local feminist news-sheets, etc., have been consulted in any exhaustive manner: most of us have turned to such sources only when directed by a specific problem. Where scholarly biographies and editions of letters exist, we have used and cited them; bibliographies and such tools are usually noted. Where critical books or articles are sparse, they are cited even if also defective (few writings on women from more than a generation or so ago are unmarred by automatic condescension), with an occasional note of warning; where they abound, they have been very selectively cited. It is obvious that writers long recognized as important (Emily Brontë, for instance, still more Emily Dickinson) have generated a wealth of critical material far beyond what we have room for.

We have cast our entries biographically, aiming to emphasize the conditions in which these women lived and wrote. Their texts emerge from and intervene in conditions usually very different from those which produced most writing by men, and we have cast these entries as brief lives to provide the broad outlines of those conditions. These real women who made their entrance into history by writing lived widely different kinds of lives: until recently mostly auto-didacts, they earned livings by a range of non-literary means, bore, raised, and lost children, loved passionately, sorrowed, theorized about writing, travelled or stayed at home to cook and clean, wielded or felt the edge of political power. They also wrote for widely different reasons and for very different audiences: some for publication, some for social and political change, some for their intimates, some only for themselves. Every woman we have included, however, has been seen to have literary or historical significance: either her work has living appeal for readers of one stamp or another, or her life-experience has such appeal, or she has made a mark (sometimes still conspicuous, sometimes since forgotten) in the worlds beyond the boundaries of literary maps and charts. We have sought to bring out the relation of life to work which makes these women writers, in all of their variety, into participants in what we have come to recognize as a female tradition: to show them as writing, in whatever form, women's lives and women's selves. To any charge of heroinizing we should reply that struggle needs to be recorded as such and that women writers have from the beginning engaged in struggle – not yet done – to enter the dialectic of history.

No biographical entry in this book runs much above 500 words, so that coverage of major figures is comparatively summary. We have preferred to direct generosity towards finding or making space for the lesser-known. In casting our net widely, we hope to defer rather than to assist the gradual emergence of a canon of writing by women.

Literary history, and women's part in it, is of course part of the larger human history, and women's use of language and production of texts always relates on the one hand to currently dominant literary ideas and ideals and on the other to the currently dominant broader ideology and social practice concerning women. We see the development of feminist thought about literary history as part of a continuing process. A worldwide enterprise, the rapid accumulation and continual sifting of feminist scholarship, is still under way in English-speaking countries. To that enterprise this book contributes a good deal more information than has before been offered in reference books which are thought of as standard, or which are widely available to the common reader. The availability of this information will alter existing conceptions of literature in English in ways we cannot foresee.

Conscious of this intellectual history, and of the slow revolution in it to which we contribute, we are concerned not only that women should be represented, but also with the kind of representation they are given. In the presentation of this material – not limited to writers of our own time or our own several nationalities – we have been conscious of the specificity not only of gender but also of time, place, class, race and religion. Our selection gives preference to women whose works reflect awareness of their condition as women and as women writers. (Few indeed are works by women which do not do this: those of our writers who are not in some sense feminists are mostly anti-feminists.) We have shaped the entries to catch and transmit the signals of this awareness.

To read these signals sensitively is vital for both literary and political understanding. In such relatively short entries as we provide, much must be omitted: but to exclude the elements of what is in our day called feminist consciousness would be to suppress what has been for all of us engaged in this research the most striking and constant aspect discovered in discovering women's writing.

For this reason we name the mothers of writers wherever possible, normally before naming the father. (The number of cases where this is not possible, even down to the present day, tells its own story.) We point out women's connections with other women (often ignored by standard accounts in favour of connections with well-known men); we offer an integrated account of the personal and professional lives of our subjects (when the facts are traceable) in order to show how such personal factors both shaped and were shaped by material circumstances, sense of self, and opportunities as a writer. We avoid lists of titles to which we cannot afford some comment, and over-emphasis on official facts, such as posts held or honours awarded.

We have looked well beyond the canonized hierarchical genres and have included writers in the non-canonical modes: pamphleteers, letter-writers, diarists, memoirists, travellers, and so forth. Women who wrote only a small amount, or in so-called unliterary genres, are included if their texts are remarkable for their personal or historical situation; present-day, middle-class white women must win their place in competition with many others, by virtue of high literary ambition, or creative excellence, or feminist perception, or energetic output, or high profile.

This book is not about English literature, but literature in English. We have aimed to fracture the singularity of national viewpoints by gathering writers from the various traditions of writing in English as these have branched out and developed since the beginnings in England, primarily in North America and the Caribbean, Asia, Africa, and Australasia and the South Pacific. The breakdown of the national, however, is by no means exclusively a recent occurrence: Marie de France apparently came from France and wrote in England; Christine de Pizan came from Venice and wrote in Paris. The inter-nationality of the entries in this book confirms our sense both of a common literary inheritance differently managed in its several locations and of a tradition in women's writing based on common experience and spanning geographical and cultural boundaries.

We do not present women as icons of their nationalities (and have seldom identified entries with the national adjective). National classification cannot accurately render the experience of a woman passing from one culture to another, for one thing, and those whose writings are seen as a national asset become the subject of custody disputes. The United States has claimed Anne Bradstreet from England and Phillis Wheatley from Africa; Frances Brooke spent a few years in Quebec and became Canada's first novelist. The increasing fragmentation of national literatures (or ossification of national critical establishments, or pride in national heritage) can colour the reading of texts: Janette Turner Hospital reads differently as an Australian and as a Canadian, Dionne Brand as a Trinidadian and as a Caribbean Canadian.

We have tried to reflect women's experience of that imaginative internationalism which Ellen Moers noted between Harriet Beecher Stowe and Elizabeth Barrett Browning, and which flourishes today in, for instance, dialogue between French feminist thought and English-language practice. We have tried also to be sensitive to differences as we have gathered and presented information about other traditions than the three represented by the editors or the dozen or so represented by the contributors.

With all this multiplicity we have remained centred on the English language and its interactions with users of other languages, from Sappho to Monique Wittig: a kind of integrity, a relevance of independent parts to the understanding of a whole, can be modelled around an anglophone community or group of communities. We leave to the future the task of relating this linguistic communality to others among the polyglot literary voices of women around the world.

All entries, both topic and biographical, follow a narrative method which reflects our basically historical procedure and organization. Although we do not hold a progressivist view of women's writing, we believe that tradition is best formulated chronologically. Our cross-references within entries sketch lines of influence and dialogue radiating forward in time from, for instance, Madeleine de Scudéry or Mary Wollstonecraft or Margaret Fuller or Sojourner Truth.

The usual Companion format of individual entries precludes the presentation of an overall narrative. To arrange them chronologically (by birth? death? publication?) would be impossible, because of gaps in information, and unhelpful, because of the different rates at which writing lives develop. We considered the idea of three separate historical sections and rejected it, chiefly because of the impossibility of making satisfactory divisions. We are left with the pure randomness of the alphabet – especially arbitrary when applied to women, whose eventual names so often depended on the outcome of haggling between father and suitors. Writing pairs of mother and daughter, or of sisters, have sometimes been combined in one entry (when they used the same last name) and sometimes treated separately, whichever appears to offer more of clarity or of mutual illumination.

Beneath this randomness lies, we believe, a flexible, resilient, multiple tradition. The seventeenth century which nurtured Anne Bradstreet in England (first outstanding colonial poet of either sex) had already produced more than one self-conscious, purposeful alliance between literary women, and more than one project for revising or critiquing tales told by men. Its female radicals (in America as well as Britain) fused theology and social criticism in a crucible of feminist indignation; later its women-about-court attracted notoriety for theatrical writing, and, oddly, failed to attract it for pioneering prose fiction. These groups were often deeply divided, but seldom without some sense of writing sisterhood.

By the late eighteenth century Phillis Wheatley had used her oppressors' idiom to claim an audience and to win fame, though not material reward. Women had played an important part in the spread of British literary traditions in North America (poetry, plays, fiction, writings of self-analysis and imaginative public polemic). Women on two continents were earning their living by using the English language in the novel form, consumed chiefly though not only by women: using it for stories of courtship and social fashioning, of emotional extremity and psychological disturbance, of oppression and resistance, and of the forging of national consciousness (Irish, American, and Scottish). At the same time the female colonizer's viewpoint (in every case significantly differing from that of her male counterpart) had been applied to India, Australia, and other countries.

During the nineteenth century, women, long accustomed to publishing in periodicals, consolidated their position in the editing and managing of those periodicals and in other fields where writing meets the market-place. Many kept on writing through several marriages; many debated, both explicitly and implicitly, the issues of gender roles and separate spheres, of the educational, professional and political advancement of women, of solidarity with exploited sisters, and especially of the suffrage. These issues helped to create in our own century a strongly and consciously female tradition within new literatures based in colonial Africa and Australasia. Women of colour who entered, and altered the terms of, these debates included those of mixed inheritance: both genetically mixed, like the Grimké family, and culturally mixed, like the sisters Sui Sin Far and Winnifred Reeve. Women who stemmed from non-British traditions perforce adopted English literary conventions in order to publish in English, like the Bengali Sarojini Naidu in 1905; later, women educated in and appropriated by British culture delightedly rediscovered the traditions (often oral, as in the Caribbean) of their foremothers, and used those traditions to re-appropriate, re-shape, and transform the dominant culture.

In our own day, multiculturalism and multivalency provide a strong centripetal energy which matches the centrifugal forces of women's experience and of shared language. We hope here to have given some idea both of the inexhaustible variety of women's cultural resources and creative springs, and of the often surprising parallels, overlappings, and areas of dialogue.

This project has been a long collaboration: it began in a conversation between Virginia Blain and Tony Seward, our Batsford editor. Virginia mooted it to Pat and Isobel (all three, who had been graduate students at Oxford, were back there in 1982). The three of us planned the book together, persuading Tony (and Batsford) both to broaden its coverage and concentrate its focus to deal exclusively with women writers. We expected to invite a few contributors to help us. The book, however – from the beginning demanding, exacting, and wholly without regard for any *other* plans we might have had – rendered entirely inadequate our modest projections. Now we discover, when we count, that our feminist companion has gathered to this feast at least seventy-five scholars (who have served as research assistants, contributors, contributing editors, and consulting editors), together with very many helpful friends, not to mention sundry calming and invigorating children and cats and dogs.

Our procedures have included many detailed conversations continued from year to year in rooms and gardens in England, Canada, and Australia, punctuated by individual consultation both with our many collaborators and with specialists and friends of all kinds in the USA and other countries. These have been supplemented by letter, telephone, fax and thought-wave. Problems have been mulled over, and joint decisions taken and re-taken: we have argued, laughed, fought, forgiven, and feasted together at one another's tables.

After all this we are well aware of the plurality of much-debated feminisms that has fed into this book, ensuring that its 'feminism' remains multifarious and fruitfully fractured.

The editors of the book were responsible, overall, for selection of entries, and each has written a large number of entries in various areas. Isobel Grundy was responsible for entries on women who wrote from the beginning to *c.* 1830; Virginia Blain for those falling between *c.* 1830 and 1914 and for Australians, New Zealanders and South Pacific writers; Patricia Clements for those writing after *c.* 1914, and for Canadian and other colonial and post-colonial writers. The four consulting editors, who joined the project at a later stage, variously double-checked lists and provided helpful comment on, and sampling of, entries. Contributing editors helped – in some areas guided – selection: Charlotte Bruner with African women; Emily Stipes Watts with nineteenth-century Americans; Evelyn Haller, Candida Lacey, and Mary McCay with twentieth-century Americans; Carla Contractor with South Asian writers; Elizabeth Webby with Australians; Elaine Hobby with seventeenth-century British writers; Helen Kidd with twentieth-century British poets; Lorraine McMullen with Canadians; Susheila Nasta with Caribbeans; Julia Boffey with medieval writers; Aorewa McLeod with New Zealanders.

Main contributors worked, with the editors and contributing editors, in the following areas: pre-Victorian entries were written by Eithne Henson, Coral Ann Howells, Anne B. Shteir, and Margaret Whiteley; nineteenth-century British entries were written by Linda Anderson, Margaret Cardwell, Christine Devonshire, Kate Flint, Shirley Foster, Laura Stempel Mumford, Margaret Reynolds and Joanne Wilkes; nineteenth-century American entries were written by JoAnn Castagna, Joan Kirkby, Mary Loeffelholz, Rosemarie Morgan and Joanna Pappworth; Australian entries were written by Debra Adelaide, Maryanne Dever and Gina Mercer. African entries were written by Charlotte Bruner; twentieth-century British entries were written by Susan Asbee, Diana Austin, Rachel Carr, Dianne Chisholm, Cornelia Cook, Patricia Demers, Ragnhild Eilkli, Maria Aline Ferreira, Helen Kidd, Marja Makinen, Jane Thomas, Margaret Turner, Marion Shaw,

Sabine Vanacker, Susan Williams; twentieth-century American entries were written by Susan Brown, Michelle Jones, Candida Lacey, Ann Larabee, Betty Levitov, Lynn Penrod, Jeanne Perreault, Susan Wiseman; Canadian entries were written by Susan Brown, Lorna Irvine, Smaro Kamboureli, Lorraine McMullen, Dale Wilkie, Janice Williamson, Janet Patterson, and Wendy Waring; Caribbean entries were substantially researched by Christine Salmon and written by Susheila Nasta and the editors; South Asian entries were written by Carla Contractor, Yasmine Gooneratne, and Arun Mukherjee. Topic entries were written by the editors, Julia Boffey, Dianne Chisholm, Barbara Christian, Rosemary Curb, Patricia Demers, Elizabeth Grosz, Elaine Hobby, Maria Lauret, Betty Levitov, Shirley Neuman, Daphne Read and Jo-Ann Wallace.

While many contributors wrote a large number of entries, sometimes up to fifty, the following helped by writing a few entries: Moira Ferguson, Paul Hjartarson, Alexandra Kryworuchka, Janice Kulyk Keefer, Susie Meikle, Lee O'Brien, Janet Orr, Joanna Price, Daphne Read and Marni Stanley.

We are individually and collectively grateful for help afforded, often way beyond our expectation and their professional duty, by librarians and archivists: from probably every one of the substantial, internationally known collections of writings in English, to an amazing array of local records and repositories. Dr Iain G. Brown of the National Library of Scotland may well have answered more separate queries than anyone else, and the Interlibrary Loans librarians at the University of Alberta deserve special thanks, both for their professional zeal and for their patience.

We offer personal and heartfelt thanks, for commitment, scrupulousness, energy and ingenuity, to our research assistants: to Nina Burgis, whose encyclopaedic knowledge and wealth of research experience provided an invaluable resource; to Mary Allen, Nell Bernstein, Rachel Carr, Anne Cranny-Francis, Irene Cunningham, Marele Day, Elaine Filax, Michelle Jones, Diane Lichtenstein, Mary Loeffelholz, Jennifer McDonnell, Katherine Martin, Jan Merriman, Elizabeth Murray, Joanna Price, Margaret Reynolds, Christine Salmon, Gary Sherbert, Stephanie Tingley, and Catherine Waters; and most deeply and particularly to Jeanne Wood, whose fastidious work is silently present on every page of this book. Some of these assistants have also drafted entries.

Our further gratitude goes to individuals for advice, assistance, information, support: first and foremost to our Batsford editor Tony Seward for his share in planning from the very earliest stages, and for enthusiasm, patience and flexibility; to Oliver and Edward Steele, who cannot remember life without this book, for help of all kinds including housework and bringing endless cups of tea; then for help in many different areas to Christine Alexander, Ronald Ayling, John Baglow, Rosalind Ballaster, Candace Bamber, Douglas Barbour, Catherine Batt, Neville Blackburne, Julia Blazdell, Marilyn Brooks, Inge Brown, Susan Brown, Marilyn Butler, Barbara Caine, Judith Campbell, Warren Chernaik, Lorna Clark, Richard Clark, Eileen Mary Clarke and Geoffrey Clarke, Estelle Cohen, John Comyn, Susan Conley, Ed Copeland, Syndy M. Conger, Kathy Crowell, Michael Crump, Stuart Curran, Joanne Cutler, Charles Davidson, Margaret Anne Doody, A.C. Elias, Jr., John Fauvel, Jan Fergus, Moira Ferguson, Ra Foxton, Carole Gerson, Joel J. Gold, Phyllis Guskin, the late Robert Halsband, John Charles Hardy and Winnifred Ruth Hardy, Jocelyn Harris, Margaret Harris, Suzette Henke, Rachel Holmes, Bernard Jones, Margaret Jones, Siobhan Kilfeather, Paul Korshin, Donna Landry, Pamela Law, Sally Ledger, Gillion Lindsay, Joanna Lipking, Irma Lustig, William McCarthy, Alan McKenzie, Kerry McLeod, Juliet McMaster, Rowland McMaster, Angus Macnaghten, Peter Meekison, J. S. Mennell, Ann Messenger, Isabelle Meyer, Mary Nash, Pauline Nestor, Shirley Neuman, Susan O'Brien, Noel Parker-Servis, Linda Pasmore, Laura Payne, Michael Payne, Ruth Perry,

Mary Prior, Caroline Ralston, Helen Rankin, Malik Raza, Elizabeth Reid, Betty Rizzo, Jill Roe, Valerie Rumbold, Ashraf H.A. Rushdy, Peter Sabor, Dipti Saravanamuttu, Angela Smallwood, Margaret M. Smith, Gayatri Spivak, Sara Stambaugh, Judith Stanton, Lucy Sussex, John Sutherland, Janice Thaddeus, Dorothy Thompson, Martha Vicinus, Mary Waldron, Elizabeth Waterston, Howard Weinbrot, Linda Woodbridge, and Helen Yardley. In our widely scattered research, we have no doubt incurred other debts which we have failed to remember in time to record them here: we should like to include in our thanks every friend and supporter of the project over these years.

We have institutional debts as well: to the University of Alberta, the Australian Research Grants Scheme, the British Academy, the Humanities Research Centre at the Australian National University, the Leverhulme Trust, Macquarie University, Queen Mary College (now Queen Mary and Westfield College) in the University of London, and the Social Sciences and Humanities Research Council of Canada.

Without the generous help of these institutions – these communities of scholars – this book could not have existed; without the help of these generous people, it could not have existed in this form. We are fortunate to have had such help.

Sydney, Edmonton, and London VB
March 1990 PC
IMG

Editorial Conventions

Entries, biographical and other, follow in a single alphabetical sequence. Alphabeticization ignores blank spaces: Lathrop comes before La Tourette; the prefixes Mac, Mc, M', are, however, treated as if they were all Mac, forming a single sequence.

Entries are normally placed under the writing or best-known name ('Eliot, George', not Evans, Mary Ann). These names and headings of topic entries are given in boldface type. Pseudonyms are given in quotation marks. Birth names of married women appear in parentheses: though this is not universal cultural practice, it helps to distinguish the source of various names borne by the same woman. A writer's mother's name is normally given before her father's. Words in small capitals within entries signify the title of another entry. One index lists entries grouped by date. Another gives cross-references (alternative names and names of women who have no entries of their own but who are referred to in other entries). A third lists topic, or non-biographical, entries. Standard abbreviations are used sparingly, mostly in the preliminary part of the entry; abbreviations for journals and institutions are listed below. Frequently cited sources, sometimes given only by author's name in the entries, are listed from page 1205.

Abbreviations

AAS	American Antiquarian Society
ALR	*American Literary Realism*
AM	Member of the Order of Australia
AmQ	*American Quarterly*
ASSU	American Sunday School Union
ATS	Auxiliary Territorial Service, British WWII women's army corps., later the Women's Royal Army Corps (WRAC)
AWSA	American Woman Suffrage Association
BB	*Bulletin of Bibliography*
BL	British Library
BLC	*British Library Catalogue*
CanL	*Canadian Literature*
CBEL	*Cambridge Bibliography of English Literature*
CCF	Cooperative Commonwealth Federation (former Canadian socialist party)
CEAC	*College English Association Critic*
CFM	*Canadian Fiction Magazine*
CHR	*Canadian Historical Review*
CL	*Comparative Literature*
CLAQ	*Children's Library Association Quarterly*
CND	Campaign for Nuclear Disarmament
CritQ	*Critical Quarterly*
CSIRO	Commonwealth Scientific and Industrial Research Organization
CUNY	City University of New York
CWS	*Clearing-House on Women's Studies*
CWW	*Canadian Writers on their Work*
DR	*Dalhousie Review*
DLB	*Dictionary of Literary Biography*
DNB	*Dictionary of National Biography*
ECW	*English Canadian Writing*
ELN	*English Language Notes*
ELR	*English Literary Renaissance*
ERA	Equal Rights Amendment (USA)
ESA	*English Studies in Africa*
FRSL	Fellow of the Royal Society of Literature
FR	*Fortnightly Review*
FS	*Feminist Studies*
GLC	Greater London Council
GM	*Gentleman's Magazine*
HMC	Historical Manuscripts Commission
IJWS	*International Journal of Women's Studies*

IRA Irish Republican Army
JCF *Journal of Canadian Fiction*
JCS *Journal of Celtic Studies*
JCL *Journal of Commonwealth Literature*
JEGP *Journal of English and German Philology*
JML *Journal of Modern Literature*
JPC *Journal of Popular Culture*
JWIL *Journal of West Indian Literature*
LCC *Library of Congress Catalog*
LSE London School of Economics
MFS *Modern Fiction Studies*
MLA Modern Language Association of America
MLR *Modern Language Review*
MP *Modern Philology*
MRA Moral Rearmament
N&Q *Notes and Queries*
NAACP National Association for the Advancement of Colored People
NAWSA National American Woman Suffrage Association
NCF *Nineteenth Century Fiction*
NLH *New Literary History*
NLS National Library of Scotland
NOW National Organization of Women (USA)
NWSA National Woman Suffrage Association
NYPL New York Public Library
NYTR *New York Times Review*
NYTBR *New York Times Book Review*
NYTLR *New York Times Literary Review*
OED *Oxford English Dictionary*
OUP Oxford University Press
PAJ *Performing Arts Journal*
PBSA *Publications of the Bibliographical Society of America*
PMHB *Pennsylvania Magazine of History and Biography*
PMLA *Publications of the Modern Language Association of America*
Poetry R *Poetry Review*
PPE Politics, Philosophy and Economics (Oxford BA degree)
PRO Public Record Office
PW *Publishers' Weekly*
RADA Royal Academy of Dramatic Art (London)
RES *Review of English Studies*
RLF Royal Literary Fund
RN Royal Navy
RTS Religious Tract Society
SCanL *Studies in Canadian Literature*
SEL *Studies in English Literature*
SFS *Science Fiction Studies*
SoQ *Southern Quarterly*
SoR *Southern Review*
SP *Studies in Philology*
SPCK Society for the Promotion of Christian Knowledge
SR *Saturday Review/Sewanee Review*
TCL *Twentieth Century Literature*
TRSL *Transactions of the Royal Society of Literature*
TSWL *Tulsa Studies in Women's Literature*
UBC University of British Columbia
UMI University Microfilms International
UTQ *University of Toronto Quarterly*
VAD Voluntary Aid Detachment (an organization of amateur British women nurses during WWI and WWII)
VFRG *Victorian Fiction Review Guides*
WAL *Western American Literature*
WCTM Women's Christian Temperance Movement
WLT *World Literature Today*
WLWE *World Literature Written in English*
WRAC see ATS
WRB *Women's Review of Books*
WRNS Women's Royal Naval Service (Britain)
WSPU Women's Social and Political Union

Abbot, Eleanor Hallowell, 1872–1958, popular novelist and short-story writer, memoirist, b. in Cambridge, Mass., da. of Clara (Davis) and Edward A., and granddaughter of children's writer Jacob Abbott. Raised in a religious and literary household, EA early chose writing as her vocation. After a private school education, she took writing courses at Radcliffe, and taught English Composition at Lowell State Normal School, writing verse and fiction at night. 'On the verge of abandoning all hope of a literary career', she won three short-story prizes and became a bestseller, publishing dozens of short stories and 14 volumes of fiction, the best known of which is her novel *Molly Make-Believe*, 1910. She claimed never to have forgotten any 'emotionalized experiences': they are a staple of her romantic fiction which moves lively young heroines to happy endings through improbable plots. Her style is notable for its hectic pace and its unusual imagery. *Being Little in Cambridge When Everyone Else Was Big*, 1936, is an evocative memoir of her childhood.

Abbott, Margaret, English Baptist polemicist. Her *Testimony Against the False Teachers*, ?1659, says she became a Baptist after more than 30 years as 'a hearer of the Priests'. She celebrates the freedom which God promises to men and women and the Biblical promise that those who build and plant houses and vineyards shall not be ousted from them by others.

Abdullah, Mena, short-story writer, b. 1930 in Australia of Indian parents. Her father migrated from the Punjab at 15, and ultimately took up land in the New England district of NSW. She was educ. in Sydney, where she found the stimulation of books 'an absolute joy' after years of isolation and intellectual deprivation. MA believes that her family's experience of sharing the Depression and WWII with their neighbours made them 'Australian and not foreigners in the eyes of the community'. She worked for many years for the Commonwealth Government of Australia at the Commonwealth Scientific and Industrial Research Organization and has recently retired. Her stories have appeared in journals (e.g. *Quadrant* and *Hemisphere*) and anthologies (in e.g. Douglas Stewart and Beatrice Davis, eds., *Best Australian Short Stories*, 1971), as well as in *The Time of the Peacock* (with Ray Mathew, 1965). MA writes partly out of her experience as a migrant, partly for new Australians sharing her experience now. Most of her stories are set in the district where she grew up or in Sydney, and many probe areas of real or potential social and racial conflict.

Abdy, Maria (Smith), 'M.A.', *c.* 1797–1867, poet, b. London, da. of Maria (Smith), whose brothers James and Horace wrote *Rejected Addresses*, 1812, and influenced her early life. Her father was Richard S., solicitor. She began writing rhymes at the age of nine and m. 'at an early age' the Rev. John Channing A. (d. 1845), rector of St John's, Southwark, who encouraged her to contribute poems to the *New Monthly Magazine*. She also wrote for the *Metropolitan* while it was ed. by Thomas Campbell, and for the ANNUALS, particularly *The Keepsake* and the *Book of Beauty*. Her first small volume was printed for private circulation as *Poetry*, by Mrs Abdy, in 1834. Seven more privately-printed volumes with the same modest title appeared between 1838 and 1862. The BL has two copies with autograph inscriptions to friends. MA's longest poem, apparently called 'An Appeal on Behalf of Governesses', won a prize for the best poem on that subject. Written before 1856, it does not appear in any of her eight volumes. Allibone praises her 'religious spirit and grace of style', but most of her volumes are full of witty and sharply observant poems about modern situations and problems, with an intriguing strain of distinct but very gentle feminism: as in 'A Match of Affection' and 'The Chaperon's Complaint', sardonic pieces about the marriage market.

Abergavenny, Frances (Manners) Nevill, Lady, d. 1576, religious writer, da. of Eleanor (Paston) and the 3rd Earl of Rutland, m. by 1556 to Henry Nevill, Baron A. Her father was one of those who tried Anne Boleyn for treason; her husband tried Mary Queen of Scots. At her death she entrusted to her only daughter, Mary Fane, 'as a Jewell of health for the soule', her collection of prayers for every occasion (including childbirth, of which she ascribes the pain to sin, the deliverance to Christ's mercy), with acrostics on her name (in verse) and her daughter's (in prose). Thomas Bentley pub. them in the first and fifth parts of his *Monument of Matrones*, 1582. Horace Walpole was wrong in calling her aunt Joan, Lady Bergavenny, an author.

Abolition or Anti-slavery and Emancipation movements. Writing by women was an important influence towards these reforms. Aphra BEHN's *Oroonoko*, 1688, was remembered by abolitionists, though its royal slave-hero is deliberately unrepresentative. Slave-trading was banned among Quakers in 1761, became a *cause célèbre* in 1788, was prohibited by the British parliament in 1807 and made a capital crime in 1824. Writers for this ban included A. L. BARBAULD, Elizabeth BENGER, Elizabeth MONTAGU and other BLUESTOCKINGS, Hannah MORE, Charlotte SMITH, Priscilla WAKEFIELD, Susanna WATTS, Mary WOLLSTONECRAFT, and Ann YEARSLEY. *A Poem on the African Slave-Trade, Addressed to her Own Sex*, two parts, Dublin, 1792, by Mary Birkett, an Irish Quaker (a powerful work with modest prefaces), had several eds. In the USA Lydia CHILD's *Appeal in Favor of that Class of Americans called Africans*, 1833, was the first major anti-slavery document and brought her under damaging attack. Elizabeth CHANDLER was the first to aim abolitionist anger specifically against white women, while the most famous voice was that of H. B. STOWE, whose *Uncle Tom's Cabin*, 1852, had many imitators, both pro and con. The best-known of the latter is probably Mary H. EASTMAN's *Aunt Phillis's Cabin: or, Southern Life as it Is*, 1852. Mary B. CHESNUT's journal compares slavery with woman's oppression. Lucretia MOTT went as delegate in 1840 to the World's Antislavery Convention. Other writers became active abolitionists: Eliza FARNHAM, Frances HARPER, Frances GAGE, and the well-known GRIMKÉ sisters, who linked abolition with the Christian cause, and whose niece by marriage, C. F. Grimké, wrote movingly about the experiences of freed slaves in the north. Mary T. PUTNAM's 'Edward Colvil' fiction series suggests the double burden of the woman slave. Study by Moira Ferguson, forthcoming. See also SLAVE NARRATIVES.

Acker, Kathy, fiction-writer and playwright, b. 1948, a New Yorker now living in London. Her fifth book, *Kathy Goes to Haiti*, Toronto, 1978, opens: 'Kathy is a middle-class, though she has no money, American white girl, 29 years of age, no lovers.' Both narrative and descriptive styles remain deadpan through one voodoo and many sexual episodes. KA presents sexuality as a war zone between individual desires and society's imperatives and interdicts, but later said she wrote this naturalist book in painful boredom, 'just to show I could do it'. Later work is postmodernist and structurally alienating. *The Birth of the Poet* (written 1981, staged in Rotterdam 1984, NYC 1985, pub. *Wordplays 5*, 1986) calls itself 'a play in three acts'; but the acts are gratuitous, unconnected. Act 1 consists of a nuclear accident and the end of the world, act 2 of sex and violence in urban mean streets of simultaneously modern NYC and ancient Rome, act 3 of 'Ali Goes to the Mosque', with English as second language. KA claims that 'plagiarism became a strategy of originality': in *The Adult Life of Toulouse Lautrec by Henri Toulouse Lautrec* ('a deformed crippled beast'), 1978; *Hello, I'm Erica Jong*, 1982; *Great Expectations*, 1983 (she sees 'golden light' in Dickens's 'plurality of voices'); and *My Death, My Life by Pier Paolo Pasolini*. A section from this novel (of letters from the BRONTËS) with a letter to the US president from *Blood and Guts in High School*, 1984 (novellas), became a theatre event in Paris, 1985. *Don Quixote*, 1986, overlays Cervantes with surrealism and instability of genre and gender: 'Being dead, Don Quixote could no longer speak. Being born into and part of a male world, she had no speech of her own. All she could do was read male texts which weren't hers.' *Lulu*, a section of this novel in drama form, appeared in *Performing Arts Journal*, 30, 1987. In 1988 KA published both *Literal Madness* (three novels) and *Empire of the Senseless* (dedicated 'to my tattooist' and illustrated by herself: closing design of a dagger transfixing a rose, motto 'Discipline and Anarchy'). Its protagonists are male would-be pirate and female 'part robot, and part black' named Abhor; its fractured narrative(s) of torture and copulation end on a hope for 'a society which wasn't just disgust'.

Ackland, Valentine (Mary Kathleen McCrory Ackland), 1906–68, poet, short-story writer, autobiographer. She grew up unhappily in her Anglo-Catholic family in Norfolk and in London, where she was born, and was educ. at a convent school, later also in Paris. Her father, discovering an early sexual relationship with a schoolgirl friend, 'asked me if I realized that what I had done was the worst, the filthiest (a word reiterated constantly, shocking me each time afresh), the most unforgiveable thing that anyone could do' and became permanently estranged from her. She led a fashionable, daring, flashy life in London from about 1923, and was briefly married to Richard Turpin. She had written poetry from an early age; when she decided seriously to be a poet she gave herself the androngynous name, 'Valentine'. Nancy CUNARD became a friend; in 1930, novelist Sylvia Townsend WARNER became her lover. They lived together, mainly in Dorset, until VA's death, publishing together, without individual attribution, the separately-written poems in *Whether a Dove or Seagull*, 1934. VA's *Country Conditions*, 1936, admires improvements in Soviet Russia and exposes the harsh conditions in 'pretty' English villages for farm labourers, women, and children. During the thirties and forties VA published stories and poems in such journals as *Time and Tide*, *The New Statesman*, *News Chronicle*, *Women Today* (journal of the World Women's Committee Against Fascism and War) and *Left Review*. She attempted to organize medical support for Republicans in the Spanish Civil War, later joined an ambulance unit in Barcelona (with Warner). They joined the Communist Party in 1934 or 1935. During WWII, VA worked as a civil defence clerk, later in a doctor's dispensary. Her drinking problem, now of long term, grew worse. In 1947, VA's relationship with American Elizabeth Wade White separated her for a time from Warner; in 1949, she wrote *For Sylvia, An Honest Account*, published 1985, repr. 1989, about the relationship, her drinking, her sexuality and her guilt. In late years she became a Catholic and wrote non-fiction, short stories and poems about her wartime consciousness of intersecting politics, love, and quotidian sensuous pleasure: 'Who sees this, on a winter morning of war, and does not tremble with the same unchosen joy as the sun and the water?' Some poems were published in M. Elwin, ed., *The Pleasure Ground*, 1947, in a privately printed pamphlet, *Twenty-Eight Poems*, 1957, and, posthumously, in *The Nature of the Moment*, 1973. VA died of cancer, initially of the breast. Much unpublished work in Dorset County Museum. See Wendy MULFORD, *This Narrow Place: Sylvia Townsend Warner and Valentine Ackland: Life, Letters and Politics, 1930–1951*.

Acting. Female performers (while the stage proper was held by men and boys) included courtiers like Lady Mary WROTH and the 16-year-old Queen Henrietta Maria (in her own French masque, strongly disapproved). The amateur Mrs Coleman appeared in *The Siege of Rhodes* at William Davenant's house in 1656. Both theatre patents issued by Charles II in 1660 specified use of actresses. The stage remained for generations the only career open to a talented girl, though many had to supplement it with prostitution. Even the stars got only about half the men's pay. Many performers wrote plays (Catherine CLIVE, Sarah GARDNER, Elizabeth INCHBALD) or autobiographies (Charlotte CHARKE), and authors dabbled in acting (Henrietta BATTIER, Susanna CENTLIVRE). Theatrical lives are notoriously hard to ascribe: Alexander Bicknell wrote Sophia Baddeley's life as 'Elizabeth Steele', 1787, and had a hand in the classic stardom-and-exploitation story of George Anne Bellamy. Theatre families like the KEMBLES and SHERIDANS nourished several women writers: Sarah (Kemble) Siddons, 1755–1831, abridged *Paradise Lost*, 1822, and left brief *Reminiscences*, pub. 1942. In the early Victorian period, acting was not considered respectable in either sex: the theatre was seen as promoting immorality, and actresses especially faced prejudice as self-supporting, self-concerned, publicly on display, and sexually suspect because of their contact with men. In Britain from the late 1860s more 'polite' drama and better professional conditions raised the status of actresses and their proportion of all actors (from about 33 per cent to over 50 per cent). Instrumental in this change was Marie Wilton (later Bancroft), 1839–1921, a brilliant actress-manager, who brought in higher salaries for acting and began the vogue for drawing-room drama, adapting ideas of practicable scenery from Mme Lucia Vestris, 1797–1856, distinguished actress and theatre manager from the 1830s. (See Wilton's lively, perceptive *Mr and Mrs Bancroft, On and Off the Stage*, 1888.) Influential actresses in the USA included Charlotte Cushman (who met Matilda HAYS in London), noted during 1840–75 for male tragic roles (Hamlet, Romeo) and the well-born Anna Cora MOWATT, who also wrote the first durable US comedy, *Fashion*. Some women militantly refused to become respectable, like Ellen Terry, who nevertheless became the first Dame of the British Empire. Novels giving some attention to the actress's life include Geraldine JEWSBURY's *The Half Sisters*, 1848, Charlotte BRONTË's *Villette*, 1853, Maria GRANT's *Artiste*, 1871, actress Eliza Winstanley's *Shifting Scenes in Theatrical Life*, 1859, and works by Bertha BUXTON. Adelaide KEMBLE in *A Week in a French Country House*, 1867, and George ELIOT in *Daniel Deronda*, 1876, use successful women singers to explore predicaments facing female performers. The Actresses' Franchise League, founded 1908 at a meeting attended by Ellen Terry, Mrs Kendal, Violet Vanbrugh, and Eva and Decima Moore, and addressed by Cicely HAMILTON, engaged vigorously in the struggle for the vote, distributing *Votes for Women*, setting up speakers' classes, preparing political poems for recital at meetings. Edy CRAIG's woman's company, The Pioneer Players, founded 1911, mounted productions exploring issues in sexual politics. (See Julia Hollege, *Innocent*

Flowers: Women in the Edwardian Theatre, 1981.) See also THEATRE GROUPS.

Adam, Ruth Augusta (King), 1907–77, novelist, b. in Nottingham, da. of Annie (Wearing) and the Rev. Rupert William K. Writing at 12, she produced essays which much impressed her father; yet her socially-conscious parents, expecting her to marry because of her good looks, left her unqualified, unlike her sisters. After St Elphin's School, Matlock, 1919–26, and minimal teacher-training, she taught at a Notts. school for miners' children till 1932: she used the experience in *I'm Not Complaining*, 1938 (repr. 1983 with intro. by Janet Morgan), set in a town sharply divided on class lines. In 1932 she married Kenneth A., a Manchester journalist; after *Safety First*, 1934 (a children's play), she wrote a 'Family Page' for her local Anglican paper (chiefly out of loyalty to her father). She moved to Hampstead, London, in 1937 (the year of her *War on Saturday Week*, which draws on her childhood). She had four children, worked during WWII at the Ministry of Information, and wrote more novels, books for children (a book about the USA, 1944; fiction based on her 'Susan' series in *Girl* magazine), radio plays, and non-fiction. Q. D. LEAVIS, criticising Virginia WOOLF's *Three Guineas* in 1938, cited RA as a writer who truly understood the domestic pressures on women's mental lives. RA's novels depict, generally from her own life, a world which people strive to ameliorate, though their best intentions often go wrong; her younger female characters enjoy a stylish but insecure independence; older women have often abandoned ambition for the consolations of filling needs in family life; personal and communal relations are easily vulnerable to disruption, but the vision is finally comic. *A House in the Country*, 1957 (RA's only directly autobiographical work), is an amused account of an experiment in communal living near Harpenden, Herts., in which she (the only mother in the group) found it hard to protect her writing time. *Look Who's Talking*, 1960, was adapted for TV. RA's last works were a life of Beatrice WEBB, 1968, and *A Woman's Place*, 1975 (social history).

Adams, Abigail (Smith), 1744–1818, American patriot and letter-writer. B. at Weymouth, Mass., da. of Elizabeth (Quincy) and the Rev. William Smith, kept from school by poor health, she always felt badly educ. despite wide reading. She married, 1764, John A. (later second US President), and ran the family farm and repelled British soldiers during the Revolution. Women's patriotism, she noted, is heroic because unrewarded: 'even in the freest countries' women lack basic civil rights. Of her letters (first pub. 1840, selected to present a rosy view) those to Mercy Otis WARREN and other women deserve study; best-known are those to her husband in 1776, urging better status and more independence for women in the future US constitution. (He replied as to a joke; she fell back on quoting Pope on power through submission.) She wrote to him often as a lover, sometimes as 'Portia' (Brutus's wife, not Shakespeare's heroine). John A. relied on her acute political and economic analysis, though both subscribed to the idea of women as domestic and reserved; she continued her commentary to her son, John Quincy A. From 1784 to 1788 she reported travel in Europe. She regretted 'a little' that her first grandchild was a boy. See correspondence, complete 1963–73, selec. 1975 (both ed. L. H. Butterfield et al.); several recent lives: Paul C. Nagel, *The Adams Women*, 1987. Her daughter Abigail, 1765–1813, who married Col. William Stephens Smith (no relation), produced more intellectual but less vivid travel writings, pub. 1841–2.

Adams, Anna (Butt), poet and artist, b. 1926 at Richmond near London, da. of Dorothy (Till) and George B. She was educ. at Harrow School of Art and (after some teaching) Hornsey Art College, London (diploma in painting and sculpture). She married painter Norman A., and during the 1950s worked in ceramics and design at the Chelsea Pottery. She published essays in *Freedom*, 1951, then in the 1960s *Manchester Guardian*. She began writing poetry after a serious illness in 1960; first of a dozen volumes and pamphlets was *Journey Through Winter*, 1969. *A Reply to Intercepted Mail*, 1979, is a verse letter answering Auden's to Byron. Part I decides against writing a 'rhyming essay upon women' since 'In sexual fight / both adversaries are both wrong and right.' Part II describes her own life, and her writer-father's 'nadir' as a temporary clerk. Part III looks at the human desire to unify opposites: 'I cannot cast out Martha from my heart. / My family would starve, and garbage fill / the kitchen.' *Brother Fox and Other Relatives*, 1983, explores aspects of human society through animal analogies; *Dear Vincent*, 1986, uses Van Gogh's letters; *Trees in Sheep Country*, 1986, dedicated to her parents' memory, looks at the relation of humans to nature: 'even words / need scholar gardeners.' AA's poems are strongly visual (even painterly), closely observed from urban and rural, coastal and continental landscapes, and recreated characters from her past. Included in Trevor Kneale, ed., 1975, and later anthologies of women's poems, she has broadcast on TV and radio, and has taught art in schools in London and Manchester, where she lives.

Adams, Bertha Jane, 'Mrs Leith Adams' (Grundy) (later de Courcy Laffan), 1837?–1912, novelist, dramatist, song-writer, editor. Da. of Frederick Grundy, a solicitor from Cheshire, she married twice: first, Surgeon General Leith-Adams, Cheshire regiment; second, Rev. R. S. de Courcy Laffan, later Principal of Cheltenham College. She began publishing in the 1870s, with *Winstowe*, 1877, and *Madelon Lemoine*, 1879, producing novels regularly until the late 1890s. *Bonnie Kate: A Story from a woman's point of view*, 1891, asserts that the 'truest life-dramas' are played after marriage, while *A Garrison Romance*, 1892, more amusing and less sentimental, shows her knowledge of an army surgeon's life. In 1900 she published the famous song, 'Good-bye, Daddy', and from 1904, with *Their Experiment*, she turned her hand to plays and song writing. Her *Poems*, 1907, are slight but show talent. From 1880 she was on the staff of *All the Year Round*, having also edited *Kensington Magazine*, 1879–80. In 1910 she pub. *Dreams Made Verity*, memoirs and essays, including a lecture given at the Sesame Club: 'Fictional Literature as a Calling for Women', filled with down-to-earth advice. She was concerned to improve educational opportunities for women and the working classes.

Adams, Glenda (Felton), novelist and short-story writer, b. 1939 in Sydney, NSW, da. of Elvira (Wright) and L. H. F. Educ. at Sydney Girls' High School and Sydney Univ., she studied and taught Indonesian. In 1964 she went to the USA to study journalism at Columbia Univ., intending to stay only one year. While attending a fiction workshop there, she found that she was a natural story-teller. After divorce from her American husband, GA remained in NYC, teaching fiction writing at Columbia and at Sarah Lawrence College. Her first story to be pub. in the USA appeared in the first issue of *Ms* magazine; many stories in her first collection, *Lies and Stories*, 1976, point to the special powers of women. When these, and seven more stories, were pub. in Australia as *The Hottest Night of the Century*, 1979, GA was hailed as one of the first Australian women writers to attempt the 'new fiction'. Her first novel, *Games of the Strong*, 1982, concentrates on the interplay of truth and falsehood, love and loyalties, in a futuristic, totalitarian society. Her second, *Dancing on Coral*, 1986, won the Miles FRANKLIN Award.

Its witty, zany tale of a young Australian's travels to the USA clearly has some autobiographical basis.

Adams, Hannah, 1755–1831, historian, probably America's first professionally-writing woman, long the only female admitted to the Boston Atheneum. B. at Medfield near Boston, kept from school by illness, never taught how to hold a pen, shy and moody, she later learned Latin, Greek, geography and logic. Her mother died *c.* 1764, her father lost his money; during the War of Independence she set out to turn her hobby – research – to profit (having failed at lace-making). She published, 1784, an *Alphabetical Compendium* of Christian and (in an appendix) pagan sects, with a male friend's preface defending women's minds and citing Catharine MACAULAY. Her *Truth and Excellence of the Christian Religion*, 1804, includes extracts from works by three women (Mme de GENLIS, Hannah MORE, Jane WEST) whom she praises in notes though recounting male lives only. She published by subscription, with her name; a poor bargainer, she knew the need of later popularizations to squeeze profit from her scholarly reference works. A history by Dr Jedidiah Morse, 1804, being poised to damage both her *Summary History of New England*, 1799, and a projected abridgement for 'young persons' (pub. 1805), she said so, and the quarrel smouldered on into mutual printed accusation in 1814. Her *History of the Jews*, 1812, deplores 'oppression and persecution' but expects conversion. Her *Memoirs* of her life, 1832, quote Charlotte SMITH on the penalties of female authorship, which she always found hard.

Adams, Harriet (Stratemeyer), 'Carolyn Keene', 'Franklin W. Dixon', 'Laura Lee Hope', and other pseudonyms, 1892–1982, children's writer. She was b. at Pottersville, NJ, da. of Magdalene (Van Camp) and Edward S., whose many children's books included the openings of series on the Hardy Boys, the Bobbsey Twins, and the 16 year-old girl detective Nancy Drew. HSA was educ. at Wellesley College (BA 1914), married stockbroker Russel Vroom A., and began working for her father's Stratemeyer Syndicate, editing MSS, not writing, because 'he didn't feel women should work.' She later took over all his series, rewrote the three Nancy Drews he had published as Carolyn Keene, and added 53 more, making Nancy 18 so that she could be 'much more out on her own' and drive a car. Against a comfortable middle-class background (some adventures are HSA's, 'exaggerated'; she 'tried to bring up my daughters the same way'), Nancy's brains and courage inspired generations of readers (an 11-year-old girl outwitted a kidnapper by thinking what Nancy would have done). HSA accepted a link between Nancy and 'women's lib'; she disliked the violence of the TV version. The Syndicate continued the series after HSA's death; with the Hardy Boys (as Franklin W. Dixon), it has sold over 100 million copies; of the firm's more than 2000 books (including also the Dana Girls and Tom Swift), HSA wrote 170 'entirely myself', besides inventing plots and outlines. See Deirdre Johnson, ed., *Stratemeyer Pseudonyms and Series Books: An Annotated Checklist of Stratemeyer and Stratemeyer Syndicate Publications*, 1982; C. Keene in O. Prenzler, ed., *The Great Detectives*, 1978.

Adams, Jean, 1710–65, poet and schoolmistress. B. at Greenock, Renfrewshire, da. of a shipmaster, she was orphaned young, self-educated in the library of a minister she worked for, and well patronized. Her *Miscellany Poems*, Glasgow, 1734, had a strong local subscription list; her dedication, signed 'Jean Adams' (possibly anglicized from 'Adam'), apologizes for 'Weakness, and Want of Learning' but promises plain truth. The poems, vividly imaginative, many religious, all in standard English, include Milton imitations. JA ran a girls' school which added to the usual curriculum an emotional emphasis on Shakespeare. But the book sold badly, the school failed; she died the day after admission to the Glasgow hospital as a destitute wanderer. Her fame rests on contemporary local opinion that she wrote the fine Scots song 'There's nae luck about the house' (actually a celebration of a seafaring husband's return). Copied down by Burns after her death, often cheaply and anonymously repr. *c.* 1810–20, it was claimed too – less convincingly – for William Julius Mickle. See William Stenhouse, *Anthology of Scots Poetry*, 1853; pamphlet by Alexander Rodger, Greenock, 1866.

Adams, Léonie Fuller, 1899–1988, poet and translator, b. in Brooklyn, NY, where she grew up, da. of Henrietta (Rozier) and Charles Frederic A. She wrote her first poems as a student at Barnard College (AB, 1922): 'April Mortality' appeared in the *New Republic*, 1921. She worked in NYC (as a publisher's editor, 1922–6, and at the Metropolitan Museum of Art, 1926–8), then travelled to Mexico and Europe. She became an editor of *Poetry* magazine in 1924 and published her first book, *These Not Elect*, in 1925. In 1928, a Guggenheim Fellowship took her to Paris: there she shared a flat with Allen Tate and Caroline GORDON, met Gertrude STEIN and Ford Madox Ford and prepared *High Falcon and Other Poems*, 1929. In 1933, she published *This Measure* (a single poem) and a joint translation of Villon's lyrics and married critic William E. Troy (d. 1961). She taught at various colleges, including Sarah Lawrence, the NJ College for Women, Columbia, and NY Univ., 1947–68; in 1948–9 she was the Library of Congress Consultant in Poetry. *Poems: A Selection*, 1954, won the Bollingen Prize (with her long-time friend Louise BOGAN) and the Harriet MONROE Award. In a poetic life spent 'grappling with the limitations of the lyric', LA was influenced by seventeenth-century English metaphysical poetry, Jacobean drama, later by Mallarmé and Emily DICKINSON. Metrically sophisticated, formally traditional, never confessional, her poetry presents and elaborates an image, often natural, for a spiritual state. She is part of a cluster of women poets whose work, appearing around 1918, 'restored genuine and frank feeling', says Bogan (*Selected Criticism*, 1955), 'to a literary situation which had become genteel, artificial and dry'. See Babette Deutsch, *Poetry in Our Time*, 1952. Papers at Yale, Library of Congress, Univ. of Delaware.

Adams, Sarah Fuller (**Flower**), 'S.Y.', 1805–48, poet, magazine contributor, hymn writer, mountain climber, amateur actress, b. Great Harlow, Essex; later moved to London. Her teacher mother Eliza (Gould) gave up her Devon school rather than withdraw support for the radical *Cambridge Intelligencer*, whose editor, Benjamin Flower, she later married. She died when SFA, younger of their two daughters, was five. (SFA's sister, Eliza Flower, was a musician and composer.) After erratic education by village teachers and their father (d. 1829), the sisters were left in the guardianship of W. J. Fox, South Place Unitarian and editor of the *Monthly Repository*. Harriet MARTINEAU, a relation, supposedly based the Ibbotson girls in *Deerbrook* on them. SFA met her husband, engineer and inventor W. B. Adams, through Harriet TAYLOR; she married at 29 (no children). Always an independent thinker, she made a 'no housekeeping' pact with her husband, to avoid 'putting your mind into mahogany and rosewood, your capabilities into creams and custards, and your perceptions into pies and puddings'. Her own brand of Unitarian faith emerges in her letters and in her famous hymn, 'Nearer, my God, to Thee', written in a period of religious despair and later mutilated by editors' attempts to render it orthodox (see the account by John Julian, 1911). SFA aimed at a stage career, Macready rating her Lady Macbeth highly in 1837, but her health gave out. She contributed many articles to Fox's *Monthly Repository* (as 'S.Y.') and also wrote for the *Westminster Review*. Her chief work was *Vivia Perpetua*, 1841, a dramatic poem in five acts about an early Christian martyr. Forcefully written, it stresses that becoming a Christian under Roman patriarchal law was a defiant assertion of autonomy; slaves and women share a closer experience than do men and women of the same social standing. Another major poem, *The Royal Progress*, deals with the last Queen of the Isle of Wight. At 18 SFA broke the female record for the ascent of Ben Lomond, and she later wrote in a letter: 'As yet the power of woman is unknown ... [we should] enlarge [her] sphere of action to its *greatest possible extent* ... we would do away with that *mere dependence* which is only gratifying to man as it ministers to his love of power'. She died of tuberculosis at 43. See Richard Garnett's life of W. J. Fox, 1910, for family details, and Fox's 'Lectures to the Working Classes', iv, 9, for some unpublished political poems, many written for the Anti-Corn Law League.

Adcock, Karen **Fleur**, poet, b. 1934 in Papakura near Auckland, NZ, da. of Irene (Robinson) and Cyril John A., a psychology professor. She came to Britain in 1939 and (her father being an itinerant Workers' Educational Association lecturer) went to 11 English schools. She wrote poems about fairies and flowers at seven or eight and 'moved on to explorers, adventures and love'. Back in NZ as a teenager, she attended Wellington Girls' College, wrote of introspection, despair and 'seething ambition', and in 1952 married Alistair Campbell, poet and civil servant. ('Marrying was what we did in those days.') She had two sons, took a BA, 1955, and MA in Classics at Victoria Univ., and lectured at the Univ. of Otago. She was divorced at 24 and, after a brief second marriage and becoming a librarian, migrated to London in 1963. She worked at the Commonwealth Library until she became a full-time writer in 1979. She published her first poetry volume, *The Eye of the Hurricane*, in 1964; five more preceded *Selected Poems*, 1983, and *The Incident Book* followed in 1986. FA has also researched and translated medieval Latin secular poetry in *The Virgin and the Nightingales*, 1983, and edited *The Oxford Book of Contemporary New Zealand Poetry*, 1982, and *The Faber Book of Twentieth Century Women's Poetry*, 1987. She has won awards and held creative writing fellowships in Britain, NZ and Australia. Her economical, formal, ironic poetry is occasionally interrupted by glimpses of chaos or disquiet. She writes much about places, having in every place 'some residual feeling of being an outsider: a fruitful position for a writer, perhaps'. In her earlier poems 'the men and children were real', the women mostly herself; 'her more recent poems are full of women and girls, real or imaginary'. (They include potential victims of sex-murder, a little girl day-dreaming magically with a blue glass necklace, and Katherine MANSFIELD, with 'ragged lungs and work you burned to do'.) See her 'Women as Poets' in Dannie Abse, ed., *Poetry Dimension 2*, 1974, and piece on herself in Couzyn, ed., *Women Poets*, 1985 (quoted above); also Bill Ruddock in *Crit Q*, 26, 1984; *Poetry R*, 74, 1984.

Advice to women. A perennially popular genre in prose and verse, English superseding Latin and French in the thirteenth century, with the *Ancrene Riwle* and *Hali Meidenhad* addressed to nuns or female anchorites. Advice to laywomen began to appear in the next century. A work by CHRISTINE DE PIZAN was translated in 1521, and before 1641 a few Englishwomen wrote moral or religious advice (CRAMOND, GRYMESTON, Dorothy LEIGH; M. R.'s *The Mothers Counsell, or Live within Compasse*, 163[0], may be a man's). Despite Trotula (in Latin) on gynaecology (fifteenth century) and Lady LINCOLN on breast-feeding, 1622, practical advice (on dress, letter-writing, etc.) was still chiefly a male province (see study by Suzanne W. Hull, 1982). The following are particularly significant or egregious. *The Instruction of a Christen Woman*, 1541, which gives a few pages to what women should (and should not) read, was englished by Richard Hyrde (who also wrote a preface for a Latin work by Margaret ROPER) from Johannes Ludovicus Vives's Latin treatise, dedicated to Katherine of Aragon, written to train Mary Tudor for wifehood (facs. D. Bornstein, 1978). [?Richard Allestree]'s *The Ladies Calling*, 1673, ran to seven eds. by 1700 (see Lady PAKINGTON); *The Whole Duty of a Woman* followed in 1696. *The Lady's New-Year's Gift, or Advice to a Daughter*, by George Savile, Lord Halifax, 1688, prepares a beloved 12-year-old child to accept harshness or even cruelty from a future mate. Cotton Mather's *Ornaments for the Daughters of Zion*, 1692, counsels piety and submission. George Lord Lyttelton's verse *Advice to a Lady*, 1733, was wryly summarized by Lady Mary Wortley MONTAGU: 'In short, my dearee, kiss me and be quiet.' The so-called courtesy books include William Kenrick's biblically-styled *The Whole Duty of Woman*, 1753; John Gregory's unctuous *A Father's Legacy to his Daughters*, 1774 (attacked by Mary WOLLSTONECRAFT, it does not bear out its introductory claim to see women as equals); Thomas Gisborne's *Enquiry into the Duties of the Female Sex*, 1797 (less reactionary, though it cites bible authority for inequality in marriage). These had a long shelf-life and much influence on novel heroines (see Joyce Hemlow, *PMLA*, 65, 1950). A new practicality entered the advice market in the pamphlets *The Lawes Resolution of the Rights of Women* by I. L., 1632 but probably written earlier, facs. 1979 (on the age of consent – 12 – dowries, and status of the unmarried, who could be compelled to work or to face prison), and *Advice to the Women and Maidens of London*, 'By one of that Sex', 1678 (how to make a living by learning to keep accounts). Women moved gradually into both practical and theoretical fields. Mary ASTELL, breaking new ground in her *Christian Religion*, 1705, with 'Proper Directions for the due Behaviour of Women in every State of Life', had a host of followers a century later, most of whom also wrote novels; Maria EDGEWORTH, Elizabeth HAMILTON, Mary HAYS, Catharine MACAULAY, Hannah MORE, Lady PENNINGTON, Mary Ann RADCLIFFE, Clara REEVE, Priscilla WAKEFIELD, Jane WEST, Mary WOLLSTONECRAFT. *Woman's Mission*, 1839, by Sarah Lewis, was an enormously popular adaptation of Louis-Aimé Martin's work, showing women as moral regenerators of male profligacy. Often reprinted, it was also refuted by Marion (Mrs Hugo) Reid's *A Plea for Women*, 1843, and Ann Richelieu Lamb's 'Can Women Regenerate Society?', 1844, a book-length defence of spinsterhood's advantages against Lewis's claim that woman's sole purpose was to be mother of sons (and thus missionary among the barbarians). See Janet H. Murray, *Strong-Minded Women*, 1982. Sarah S. ELLIS was widely read in the late 1830s and 1840s: her separate addresses to the 'Wives', 'Mothers', 'Daughters' and 'Women' of England, all exhort long-suffering even while intimating a close understanding of the circumstances of women's oppression. Etiquette books were more popular in the USA than in Britain: Mary Elizabeth (Wilson) Sherwood, 1826–1903, NY lawyer's wife, was one of the most successful writers for this market. Her *Manners and Social Usages*, 1884, went through many eds., and (with novels, 1882 and 1889, on the initiation of uncouth western girls into polite society) helped fund her ambitious entertaining. Twentieth-century advice-writers have become increasingly specialized. Writers on the female role subdivide into those intending to keep society as it is (or put the clock back to some more or less fictional past) and those aiming at change. In the former category, Emily Post's *Etiquette: The Blue Book of Social Usage*, 1922, probably owed its success (facs. 1969, 86th printing in 1955) to its encyclopaedic comprehensiveness and detail. It was addressed chiefly to women, with chapters on 'The Débutante' and 'The Chaperon'; its longest chapter is one of five guiding from engagement through wedding, while 'The Code of a Gentleman' is among its shortest. Prefacing her ninth ed., Post opined that customs change but manners do not. Barbara CARTLAND's *Love and Marriage*, 1961, traces is lineage from her, as contemporary works of feminist counsel trace theirs from Margaret SANGER's *What Every Girl Should Know*, 1914 (parts of which had been banned as obscene), and Marie STOPES's *Married Love*, 1918, both intensely serious and idealistic. For listings of further kinds of advice, see Barbara Ehrenreich and Deirdre English, *For Her Own Good: 150 Years of the Experts' Advice to Women*, 1979; Nancy Armstrong and Leonard Tennenhouse, eds., *The Ideology of Conduct: Essays on Literature and the History of Sexuality*, 1987.

Aguilar, Grace, 1816–47, poet, novelist and historian, b. Hackney, London, only da. of Sarah (Diaz Fernandes) and Emanuel A., both of Spanish Jewish descent. Educ. chiefly by her mother, she kept a journal from the age of seven; an attack of measles left her permanently weakened. In 1828 they moved to Devon, where her father taught her Jewish history and she wrote a play, *Gustavus Vasu* (unpub.), and poems pub. 1835 as *The Magic Wreath*. After severe illness and her father's death (1835), she struggled to support herself by publishing several pioneering works on Judaism, including *The Women of Israel*, 1845. Most of GA's works were didactic novels which appeared posthumously, ed. by her mother, except for the often repr. *Home Influence; a tale for mothers and daughters*, 1847. Its moral theme, of the sister's self-sacrifice for a brother's misdeeds, was designed to appeal to all creeds, but can be seen to cloak a strong plea against rendering daughters invisible. Also popular was its sequel, *The Mother's Recompense*, 1851 (written 1836). Other works include *Woman's Friendship*, 1851, which values single women's existence and the support of female friends, despite the fashion 'to laugh at female friendship, to look with scorn on all those who profess it'. She died in Germany where her brother was studying music.

Aidoo, Christina **Ama Ata**, dramatist, short-story writer, poet. B. 1942 in Abeadzi Kyiakor, near Dominase, Ghana, she was educ. at Wesley Girls' High School, Cape Coast, and the Univ. of Ghana, Legon, where she won a short-story prize and her play *Dilemma of a Ghost* was presented by the Students' Theatre just before her graduation, 1964. She studied creative writing at Stanford Univ., and has taught literature in England, the USA, and Kenya, as well as the Univ. of Ghana, Cape Coast. She now lives in Zimbabwe and has one daughter, Kinna, to whom she dedicates recent poems. Her fiction often uses the material of her academic life: conflicts for a Ghanaian *been-to* scholar in *Dilemma*, student–teacher problems in her collected short stories, *No Sweetness Here*, 1970, and the shock of cultural difference as a Ghanaian high-school student visits Germany in *Our Sister Killjoy, or Reflections from a Black-Eyed Squint*, 1977. She treats the problems of African women as 'integral parts of the problems of colonial and post-colonial Africa'. Her frequently-produced play, *Anowa*, 1970, derives from a song-legend, learned from her mother, about a woman with a free spirit. In poetry and prose, she uses the Akan phraseology characteristic of the oral tradition in folk dramatic recitation. Her tone is sardonic, her characters frequently disillusioned by merely apparent change. Her article 'Unwelcome Pals and Decorative Slaves – Or Glimpses of Women as Writers and Characters in Contemporary African Literature' appeared in *Medium and Message*, 1, 1981. After long silence, she has published a collection of poems, *Someone Talking to Sometime*, 1985, in which, characteristically terse and ironic, she stresses illusory cross-cultural changes: 'I shuttle between two worlds.... / We grieve that in these days of / autobahns / motorways and / complex circles / it is still the / same'. See Charlotte Bruner in *Studies in the Humanities*, 7, 1979; Alice WALKER, *In Search of Our Mothers' Gardens*, 1984; Mildred H. Hill-Lubin and Chimalum Nwankwo in Davies and Graves, 1986; Molara OGUNDIPE-LESLIE, Brenda Berrian, and Arlene Elder in Jones, 1987; Berrian on AAA and Lorraine HANSBERRY in *African Literature Today*, 15, 1987.

Aiken, Joan, children's writer and novelist, b. in 1924 at Rye, Sussex, da. of Canadian Jessie (MacDonald) and poet Conrad A. She was educ. at home by her mother, who had degrees from McGill and Radcliffe, and at Wychwood School, Oxford. She married Ronald George Brown, 1945 (d. 1955) and had two children. In 1976, she re-married, to painter Julius Goldstein. After working for the BBC and the UN Information Centre and the magazine *Argosy*, she turned to writing, for children (full-length fiction, short-story collections, plays and verse) and later for adults. Her best-known children's book is the suspenseful *Wolves of Willoughby Chase*, 1962, an historical fantasy set in bleak Yorkshire countryside in 1832 during the reign of a mythical James III, which parallels the threat of wolves with that of a wicked governess. *The Stolen Lake*, 1981, transports its child-heroine to nineteenth-century Brazil, with such exotic touches as flying monsters and cats with clippings from Johnson's *Dictionary* in their collars. *Armitage, Armitage, Fly Away Home*, 1968, and *A Small Pinch of Weather*, 1969, deploy unicorns, witches, furies and wizards. She sets her romantic thrillers, *A Cluster of Separate Sparks*, 1972, and *Last Movement*, 1977, on Dendros, a Greek island, and the boudoir intrigues of *The Five-Minute Marriage*, 1977, in Regency London. Characterized as a hybrid of Iris MURDOCH and Agatha CHRISTIE, her dozen adult novels have the momentum but not the lyrical range or surprises of her children's work. See John R. Townsend, *A Sense of Story*, 1971, and Cornelia Jones and Olivia R. Way, *British Children's Authors*, 1976.

Aikin, Lucy, 1781–1864, woman of letters, da. of Martha (Jennings) and John A.: niece of Anna Laetitia BARBAULD, b. at Warrington, brought up at Yarmouth, living in or near London from 1792. Called 'Little Dunce' for not reading so early as others in the family, she soon showed her mettle, and pub. translations and articles in journals at 16, while also caring for her father from his retirement that year until his death in 1822. Her first book was an anthology, *Poetry for Children*, 1801; she wrote more children's books, edited writings by her aunt and father and did not class herself as a creative writer. Yet her *Epistles on Women*, 1810, prove her a fine poet in eighteenth-century style. This 'bold and arduous' study in women's history (with cautious introduction), opens by memorably re-telling the Adam and Eve story and closes on Rachel RUSSELL and Lucy HUTCHINSON. LA's one short novel, *Lorimer*, 1814, deals with a guilty secret. Her *Memoirs of the Court of Queen ELIZABETH*, 1818, was designed as a new genre: 'the manners of the age, the state of literature, arts, &c' interwoven with 'as slender a thread of political history as will serve to keep other matters in their places'. She went on to write works on James I, 1822 (comment on Lady Mary WROTH), and Charles I, 1833; lives of her father, 1823, and of Addison, 1843; brief memoirs of Elizabeth BENGER and Joanna BAILLIE (mentioning her privilege of 'personal acquaintance with almost every literary woman of celebrity' during her long life). *Memoirs*, ed. Philip Hemery Le Breton, 1864, include brief essays and many letters.

Akins, Zoë, 1886–1958, dramatist, poet and novelist, b. at Humansville, Mont., da. of Elizabeth (Green) and Thomas J. A. By 15 she had had a play produced by classmates at Monticello Seminary (Godfrey, Ill.) and published poems and essays, some in the *Mirror*, whose editor, William Marion Reedy, was a mentor to her. When her parents prevented her marrying him (he was much older), she moved to NYC to act. She collected early poems in *Interpretations*, 1912. Advised by Willa CATHER to write for the stage, she began with a verse play that flopped (*Magical City*, 1915) and a comedy, *Papa*, 1919. Her social melodrama *Déclassée*, 1919, written for Ethel Barrymore, has a foolish plot but a splendid aristocratic heroine who says, 'Englishwomen aren't educated, you know; our brothers are, but we aren't. My father used to say that my education cost him less than his oysters.' *Daddy's Gone A-Hunting*, 1921, is another tear-jerker with a failed marriage and a child's death. *The Texas Nightingale*, 1922, presents the reconciliation of an odd couple, an opera star and one of her four husbands, the reclusive novelist who first helped her to fame. As *Greatness – A Comedy* it was pub. with the previous two in 1923. ZA had a comedy hit with *The Greeks Had a Word for It*, 1930, about the Ziegfeld girls. Her screenwriting career, which began that year, included Edna FERBER's *Showboat*. She married Hugo Rumbold in 1932. Her dramatization of Edith WHARTON's *The Old Maid*, 1935, won a Pulitzer prize, raising a point of principle about the status of adapted work and causing the inauguration of the Circle Award. ZA is capable of witty, accurate, ironic social observation of women caught between traditional and 'advanced' mores. She wrote an all-woman biblical play in verse, *The Little Miracle*, 1936. Her Hollywood and Broadway careers flagged in the 1940s, but she kept writing until *The Swallow's Nest*, 1951 (unpub.). *Cake Upon the Waters*, 1919, and *Forever Young*, 1941, were novels. Scattered MSS include papers at the Huntington, plays etc. at UCLA, letters at Harvard.

Alcock, Mary (Cumberland), *c*. 1742–98, English poet, da. of Joanna (Bentley) and the Rev. Denison C.: granddaughter of Richard Bentley the scholar and younger sister of dramatist Richard C. His *Memoirs*, 1806, just mention her; lives of him and of her grandfather do not. Taken to Ireland in 1763, she was married and widowed there. She contributed to Lady MILLER's poetry contests and pub. an anonymous poem on ballooning, 1784, and 'The Confined Debtor' to raise money for debtors in Ilchester jail. These re-appeared in *Poems*, 1799, pub. by a niece, one of an orphaned family she had supported; subscribers included Elizabeth CARTER and Hannah MORE. MA is a versatile metrist (often best when least formal), a perceptive critic (a verse 'Receipt for Writing a Novel', prose essays on fiction, horror and sensibility) and a conservative supporter of social reform (e.g. for chimney-sweeping children).

Alcott, Louisa May, 'A. M. Barnard', 1832–88, novelist and story writer, b. Germantown, Penn., da. of Abigail (May) and Amos Bronson A., Transcendentalist and innovative educator. Though he encouraged his daughters' creative development, his erratic career kept the family in poverty; LMA's mother was the stabilizing centre of the family. By 1850 LMA was working at various jobs including teacher, seamstress and governess, to help support the family. Her first published work, the poem 'Sunlight', appeared in *Peterson's Magazine*, 1851, and she also pub. tales of violence and juvenile stories under pseudonyms for journals such as *The Liberator* and *Atlantic Monthly*. In 1862 as 'A. M. Barnard' she won a $100 prize from Frank Leslie's *Illustrated Newspaper* for the Gothic tale 'Pauline's Passion and Punishment'. The same year she began service as an army nurse, drawing on her experiences for *Hospital Sketches*, pub. in

The Commonwealth, 1863. In 1864 she pub. her first novel, *Moods*, and became editor of *Merry's Museum*, a girls' magazine. Her next novel, *Little Women*, 1868, was enormously successful, 38,000 copies being sold by the end of 1869. 'Amy' of *Little Women* was based on LMA's sister, Abigail May Nieriker, 1840–79, who wrote *Studying Art Abroad and How To Do It Cheaply*, 1879, a lively popular guidebook full of practical hints such as packing cheap underclothes for later use as paint rags. With *An Old-Fashioned Girl*, 1870, *Little Men*, 1871 and her last novel *Jo's Boys*, 1886, LMA continues the story of her tomboy heroine Jo which begins in *Little Women*. During the 1870s and 1880s she pub. 16 collections of stories and sketches for young people. Three novels, *Work*, 1873, *Eight Cousins*, 1875, and *Rose in Bloom*, 1876, deal with various reform movements such as temperance, dress reform and working conditions for women. A more sensational novel, *A Modern Mephistopheles*, 1877, appeared in the No Name series (repr. 1987); other sensational stories (all written as by Barnard) are coll. by Madeleine Stern, 1975, and Elaine Showalter, 1988. LMA was active in the suffrage and temperance movements and was the first woman in Concord to register to vote in 1879 when Massachusetts granted women limited suffrage. Her *Selected Letters* was pub. in 1987 and her papers are in the Houghton Library at Harvard, Concord Public Library and the LMA Association (Orchard House, Concord). See Ednah CHENEY, 1889, and Madeleine B. Stern, 1950, for her life, and the recent studies by Charles Strickland, 1985, and Sarah Elbert, 1987.

Alden, Isabella (Macdonald), 'Pansy', 1841–1930, novelist, children's writer, church worker, b. Rochester, NY, da. of Myra (Spafford) and Isaac M. She was educ. by her father and at upstate boarding schools. The novel *Helen Lester* 1866 (pub. under her pet name 'Pansy'), was awarded first prize by the Christian Tract Society; the same year she m. Presbyterian minister Gustavus R. A., and took up pastoral duties. For more than four decades she wrote, edited and organized over 120 books, mostly for children. From 1874, she edited the popular Sunday School magazine, *Pansy*, the *Presbyterian Primary Quarterly*, and contributed to other religious magazines. She was actively involved in the Young People's Society for Christian Endeavour and in the foundation of the Chautauqua movement. Her Chautauqua novels, beginning with *Four Girls at Chautauqua*, 1876, helped successfully establish the Christian summer camp. Her most popular novel, *Ester Reid*, 1870, portrays believable female characters, not afraid to stand up for their principles of Christian love in action. Though she sold over 100,000 copies a year, critics virtually ignored her. *Missent*, 1900, concerning a postcard (or is it the Lord working in mysterious ways?) which coincidentally unites several characters, is an example of her clean, readable style of storytelling. She was a friend of Frances WILLARD, and a member of the Women's Christian Temperance Union. At the time of her death she was writing her autobiography, *Memories of Yesterdays*, 1931, completed by her niece Grace Livingston Hill, 1865–1947, also a popular novelist. See also Sarah K. BOLTON, *Successful Women*, 1888.

Aldrich, Bess (Streeter), 'Margaret Dean Stevens', 1881–1954, novelist and short-story writer, b. in Cedar Falls, Iowa. Da. of pioneer settlers Mary (Anderson) and James S., she was educ. at the local High School and the State Teachers' College, then taught for six years in Iowa and Utah. In 1907 she married Charles S. A., a banker and lawyer with whom she had four children, and settled in Elmwood, Nebraska. She published stories under a pseudonym, 1911–18, but after her husband's death, 1925, wrote to support her family. *The Rim of the Prairie*, 1925, a novel recalling the settling of the prairies, was well received; *A*

Lantern in Her Hand, 1928, written as a tribute ('not in marble, but through the only medium I could use – the written word') to the pioneer mother, became a bestseller. In 1930, BSA became book editor for the *Christian Herald*. She published ten novels, including *Miss Bishop*, 1933 (filmed 1941, repr. 1986), about a school teacher, the remarkable *Song of Years*, 1939, charting the growth of Cedar Falls from a rural settlement to a prosperous, industrial city, and *The Lieutenant's Lady*, 1942, about an army wife on the Indian frontier in the nineteenth century. She wrote over 150 short stories, notable for detailed depiction of the middle-class family life of small-town America. Some are collected in *The Man Who Caught the Weather*, 1936, *Journey into Christmas*, 1949, *The BSA Reader*, 1950, and *A BSA Treasury*, 1959. She was awarded an Honorary D.Litt. from the Univ. of Nebraska, 1935, and elected to the Nebraska Hall of Fame, 1973. Papers in the Nebraska State Historical Society Collection and at Indiana Univ.

Aldrich, Mildred, 1853–1928, journalist, b. Providence, Rhode Island, da. of Lucy Ayers (Baker) and Edwin A. She contributed to the Boston *Home Journal* (as 'H. Quinn'), *Arena*, the *Boston Journal* and the *Boston Herald*, where her dramatic criticism gained notice. She also edited *The Mahogany Tree*, a journal of ideas. By 1904 she had moved to France where she supported herself by freelance writing for American magazines and became close friends with Gertrude STEIN and Alice B. TOKLAS. Although in a 1904 letter to Etta Cone, Stein noted that MA 'writes plays', no dramatic work survives. Her most important work, a bestseller in the USA, was *A Hilltop on the Marne*, 1915, an eyewitness account of the Battle of the Marne viewed from her hilltop garden in Huiry. She pub. three other books concerning WWI: *On the Edge of the War Zone*, 1917, *The Peak of the Load*, 1918, and *When Johnny Comes Marching Home*, 1919, and wrote the foreword to *The Letters of Thomasina Atkins (WAAC) on Active Service*, 1918. Her one work of fiction, *Told in a French Garden*, 1914, is a collection of stories recounted in the manner of the *Decameron*. For her war work (and particularly for her importance in influencing the USA to enter the war) she received the French Legion of Honour in 1922. Stein's *Autobiography of Alice B. Toklas*, 1932, and James L. Mellow's *Charmed Circle*, 1974, contain information and anecdotes concerning MA.

'Alexander, Mrs' Annie Hector (French), 1825–1902, novelist, b. Dublin, the only child of a solicitor. Educ. at home, she moved to England when she was 19. In 1858 she m. Alexander H., a wealthy merchant who disapproved of her writing. She had four children; her daughter Ida became Rider Haggard's secretary. When her husband died in 1875 she took his first name as her pseudonym and pub. over 40 books. Her heroines, often isolated and without family, struggle to attain status and security; though marriage within the novels is offered as the solution to their lives, the themes of suffering and insecurity are also strongly present. In *The Wooing O't*, 1873, Maggie, cruelly treated by her aunt and exploited in the shop where she works, becomes a lady's companion and then secretary to an 'authoress'. She eventually marries the man the authoress is in love with. In *Mona's Choice*, 1887, the orphan Mona faces a choice between two men and marries the man she at first rejected. Other novels include *Barbara: Lady's Maid and Peeress*, 1897 and *Kitty Costello*, 1902.

Alexander, Cecil Frances (Brown gives 'Cecilia') (Humphreys), 1818–95, hymn-writer and poet, b. Dublin, second da. of Elizabeth (Reed, sister of General Sir Thomas R.) and Major John H., landowner. 'Highly educated' (presumably at home: her brothers went to Oxford), she began writing verses and family newspapers from age nine. With her friend Lady Harriet Howard, she wrote 'An Old Man's Rambles' and contributed verse to the latter's tracts for the Oxford Movement, pub. sep. 1842–3; coll. 1848. Her *Verses for Holy Seasons*, 1846, dedicated to Keble, attempts 'to adapt the great principles of his immortal work to the exigencies of the school room'. In 1848, after she had met Charlotte YONGE and Keble, he prefaced her *Hymns for Little Children*, the profits going to a school for deaf and dumb children founded with her sister Annie. The *Hymns* include her famous 'All things Bright and Beautiful', 'Once in Royal David's City' and 'There is a Green Hill Far Away'. In 1850 she m. the Rev. William A., later Bishop of Derry and Raphoe, and had four children. After 1867, she organized district nurses and a home for fallen women. Apart from hymns, she pub. poetry on sacred and secular (often historical) subjects, in collections dated 1848, 1854 and 1859. Tennyson claimed to envy her lyric 'The Burial of Moses'. She also wrote N. Irish dialect poems, pub. posthumously in an 1896 coll. with a Preface by her husband. There is a life by Ernest Lovell (SPCK, 1970).

Alexander, Helen (later Umpherston, then Currie) of Pentland, *c.* 1654–1729, Covenanter and oral historian. B. at Linton, she m. Charles Umpherston *c.* 1673, became a Presbyterian, experienced conversion in 1678 and was raising money for the persecuted the next year when her husband died. Left with three small children, she was fined, dispossessed and imprisoned. Before her death she dictated her life story to her second husband, James Currie. He prepared it for print, for which it waited till Robert Simpson's *Voice from the Desert*, 1856; an earlier-written, shorter version was pub. at Belfast, 1869. It tells of unacceptable beliefs savagely suppressed. Soon after her second marriage the minister who had performed it was executed: she held the body 'in my arms till his cloathes were taken off'.

Alkali, Zaynab, novelist. B. 1950, in Borno State, northern Nigeria, da. of Auta Wawuta Jauni and Tembi Lindus Tura, she took her BA in English from Anmadu Bello Univ., 1973, and an MA in African literature in English, 1979. Married with six children, she lectures in English and African literature at the Univ. of Maiduguri in Borno State. Her award-winning first novel, *The Stillborn*, 1984, a humorous account of tempestuous family life, also deals with contemporary problems of broken marriages, urban dislocation and family loyalties. She published a second novel, *The Virtuous Woman*, 1986. 'I have earned a great responsibility of setting the pace for younger writers as the first woman novelist in Northern Nigeria. Here in the North there is a lot of material to write on which concerns the woman' – 'Bride-child and its consequences, forced marriages, polygamy, extended families, etc.'.

Allatini, Rose, also Scott, 'A. T. Fitzroy', 'Eunice Buckley', *c.* 1890–*c.* 1980, novelist. Little is known of her life. B. in Poland of a Polish mother and Italian father, she grew up in England and left home to live by writing. Her first book, *Happy Ever After*, Mills and Boon, 1914, was followed by two more romances, 1915 and 1917. *Despised and Rejected*, 1918, published (on the second attempt) as 'A. T. Fitzroy', reflects apparently first-hand knowledge of London pacifist and socialist circles during WWI. It also presents the self-discoveries of two homosexuals, a woman and a man, and links the persecution of pacifists, homosexuals, and Jews. Its publisher was tried and convicted for its anti-war stance (it was also asserted to be obscene). All unsold copies were destroyed: repr. 1975 and, with intro. by Jonathan Cutbill, 1988. The *Daily Herald* ran an appeal for funds: sympathizers included Ottoline MORRELL. RA published two more readable, non-controversial novels, and in 1921 married fellow-occultist and composer Cyril Scott. (His autobiography, 1969, says they had what occultists call 'an occult marriage' and praises her eagle eye in literary criticism.) RA had two children and published *White Fire*, 1933, as Mrs Cyril Scott. In 1941 she left him and settled in Rye, Sussex, with Melanie Mills, who is said to have written under various pseudonyms. Between then and 1978 RA issued 27 less remarkable novels as 'Eunice Buckley'. *Despised and Rejected* remains little discussed, and ignored by studies of literary opposition to WWI.

Alleine, Theodosia (Alleine), d. before 1685, Dissenting memoirist. B. at Ditcheat, Somerset, da. of a preacher, Richard A., she m. a kinsman, radical minister Joseph A., in 1659, and 'having alwayes been bred to work, undertook to teach a school' at Taunton with about 60 pupils, half of them boarders. He was ejected under Acts of 1662, often imprisoned, nursed by her in constant illness and died in 1668 aged 34. Her 'Narrative' of him, which she calls a draft expecting revision, went into the composite *Life*, 1671, as she wrote it, asserting contentment but revealing frustration at his all-consuming involvement in ministerial work.

Allen, Elizabeth Akers (Chase), 'Florence Percy', 1832–1911, poet and editor, b. Strong, Maine, da. of Mercy Fenno (Barton), who d. when she was four, and Thomas C., circuit rider, who soon remarried. Second of three surviving daughters, she was often beaten, locked in a cellar, then sent off alone to distant Farmington (Maine) Academy. M. in 1851 to Marshall Taylor, she later divorced him and moved to Portland, becoming assistant editor of the Portland *Transcript*. Her first book of poems, *Forest Buds, from the Woods of Maine*, 1856, which appeared under the name of 'Florence Percy', included 'By the Riverside', 'The Sunken Rock', and 'The Haunted River', in which questing women set out in boats to meet ambiguous fates. 'Both Sides of the Question' sharply satirizes male love poetry: the first sonnet, 'The Side Apparent', woos a woman in conventional terms of praise, while 'The Side Transparent' spells out the reality of the proposal: 'In short, my dear, by uttering one sweet word, / *Make me*, your humblest slave, *your master and your lord!*' Her most famous single poem, 'Rock Me to Sleep', appeared under her pseudonym in 1860. This sentimental hymn to motherhood later inspired a controversy over its authorship that EAA won only after a protracted struggle. She married Benjamin Akers in 1860; he died of TB a few months later. In 1865, she married Elijah A., eventually settling in Tuckahoe, NY. She collected her later magazine verse into *The Silver Bridge*, 1886, *The High Top Sweeting*, 1891, and *The Sunset Song*, 1902. Her papers, at Colby College, include three autobiographical essays, which reveal her bitterness about her financial exploitation by the men in her life, a view fiercely at odds with her sentimental poetry.

Allen, Hannah (Archer), Baptist autobiographer, da. of John Archer of Snelston, Derbyshire. She m. Hannibal A., merchant: her *Satan's Methods and Malice Baffled*, 1683, is a detailed account, based on her diary, of her melancholy in the mid 1660s after he died at sea. She became obsessed with death and attempted suicide in many ways, smoking a pipeful of spiders (believed to be venomous) and hiding in an attic to starve: 'but when I had lain there almost three days, I was so hungry and cold, it being a very sharp Season, that I was forced to call as loud as I could, and so was heard and released from that place'. Her family, especially her mother, supported her throughout, and despair ended on her remarriage to Charles Hatt.

Allen, Lillian, poet, b. 1951 in Jamaica, educ. there and in Canada, where she settled in 1969. In Toronto, as one of the first dub poets writing and performing there, she founded the performance group 'Domestic Bliss'. It published her volume,

Rhythm an' Hardtimes, 1982; she appears on a record with Clifton Joseph (*De Dub Poets*, Toronto Voice Spondence, 1984), and in the ORAL TRADITION part of Paula Burnett, ed., *The Penguin Book of Caribbean Verse in English*, 1986. LA uses insistent refrains, whether in patwah and singing rhythms ('The likkle seed / Jus a grow / Bloat her belly / It noh know / How it change / Mek life rearrange . . . Wey fe do! / / Anada heart / Start fe beat / anada mouth / Deh fe feed / Plant corn / Reap weed. / / Weh fe do!') or in jaggedly shaped standard English: 'ITT ALCAN KAISER / Canadian Imperial Bank of Commerce / these are privileged names in my country / but I am illegal here. . . . And I fight back . . . I FIGHT BACK.'

Allen, Paula Gunn, poet and novelist, b. 1939 in Cubero, New Mexico, of Laguna, Sioux, and Lebanese-American heritage. She earned a BA, MFA, and PhD from San Francisco State Univ., later directed Native American Studies there, taught at the Univs. of New Mexico and California (Berkeley), and won a post-doctoral fellowship in American Indian Studies at the Univ. of California, Los Angeles, 1981. She is Professor of Native American Studies / Ethnic Studies at Berkeley. A cousin of Leslie Marmon SILKO, she read Denise LEVERTOV and 'fell in love with' Gertrude STEIN at an early age, later learned from the Romantic poets and from Judy GRAHN, Adrienne RICH, and Audre LORDE. She is known as an activist for Indian and women's rights, an environmentalist, and a scholarly and imaginative proponent of the distinctness of tribal literature. Her poems, *The Blind Lion*, 1975, *Coyote's Daylight Trip*, 1978, *Starchild*, 1981, *A Cannon Between My Knees*, 1981, *Shadow Country*, 1982, *Skins and Bones*, 1985, and *Wyrds*, 1987, depict, in Adrienne RICH's words, a 'world of abandoned pueblos and modern cities, dreams and deserts, loneliness and tribal consciousness'. Her novel, *The Woman Who Owned the Shadows*, 1983, figures the ancient Spider Grandmother ('Thought Woman', who 'thinks the thoughts I write down'): she weaves traditional legends, songs, and rituals into the life of Ephanie, a contemporary woman of mixed blood who is struggling to survive. PGA's pioneering *Studies in American Indian Literature*, ed. 1983, includes a unit on women's writing; *The Sacred Hoop: Recovering the Feminine in American Indian Traditions*, 1986, gathers essays on spirit and myth, contemporary Indian literature (with special attention to women writers), lesbianism in American Indian cultures, and the 'Red Roots of White Feminism'. She sees American Indian traditions as 'fitting easily' into Western occult, Egyptian, and Tibetan spiritual traditions. She intends the stories in her anthology, *Spider Woman's Granddaughters*, 1989, to be read as 'tribal woman's literature, an old and honored literary tradition in its own right'. Biographical and bibliographical information in Tom Colonnese and Louis Owens's *American Indian Novelists*, 1985, and Rayna GREEN's *Native American Women*, 1983; criticism in Kenneth Lincoln's *Native American Renaissance*, 1983, and Judy GRAHN's *The Highest Apple*, 1985; interview in Joseph Bruchac, *Survival This Way: Interviews with American Indian Poets*, 1987. See also ORAL TRADITIONS.

Allfrey, Phyllis Byam (Shand), poet, novelist, journalist and politician, b. 1915 in Dominica. One of four das. of Elfreda (Nicholls) and Francis Byam Berkeley S., later Crown Attorney of Dominica, she descends from early settlers who formed the white Caribbean ruling class. Educ. at home by tutors and her scholarly Aunt Mags, she 'gobbled up scores of books', wrote poems at an early age, and sold her first story at 13, to *Tiger Tim's Weekly*. From 17 she studied in England, Belgium, Germany and France; in London she joined the Labour Party and Fabian Society, and m. Robert A. Her two children were born in the USA (later, in Dominica, she adopted three more). Back in London she worked for the Parliamentary Committee for West Indian Affairs, and published her first poetry book, *In Circles*, 1940. *Palm and Oak*, 1950, was named for 'the tropical and nordic strains in my ancestry'; a poem in it came second in the World Poetry Contest of the Society of Women Writers and Journalists (one judge was Vita Sackville-West). PA's novel *The Orchid House*, 1953 (French transl. 1954; repr. 1982 with intro. by Elaine Campbell), is 'a love story, by a woman in love with an island'. Its black servant-narrator (who has more of PA in him, she says, than any female character) reveals a post-colonial world lost in the past and afraid of the present; the only energy of the house 'empty of men ... a house of women' lies in its daughters, home from Europe or the USA with the power of money, sexuality, and in one case socialist politics. It shows parallels with Jean Rhys (later a correspondent of PA). Back in Dominica in 1954, PA was drawn into politics by the needs of poor workers: she founded the Labour Party (Dominica's first home-grown party), became an MP, then Minister for Labour and Social Affairs in the federal government in Trinidad, 1958–62. After the Federation ended she edited *The Dominica Herald*, and with her husband launched and still edits *The Dominica Star*. She issued more poems: *Contrasts*, Barbados, 1955, and *Palm and Oak II*, Roseau, Dominica, 1974 (including a poem for Rhys). Anthologized in *The Penguin Book of Caribbean Verse*, 1986, and elsewhere, her poems conjure up the secret, magical lushness of Dominica, and details like the humming-bird, the 'small one, the féerique ... hummer and fusser, darting untrapped spark'. Her own years of exile fuel the sense of dislocation in, e.g. 'The True-Born Villager' and 'Expatriates', about West Indians in Britain. Some of her many stories will appear in a forthcoming volume by Caribbean women, *The Whistling Bird*. Interrupted by politics, journalism, her daughter's death in 1977, and the loss of her house in a hurricane, 1979, she is still working on a second novel, *In the Cabinet*. See Kenneth Ramchand in *The West Indian Novel and Its Background*, 1970; Barrie Davis in *WLWE*, 11, 1972; and Evelyn O'Callaghan in *JWIL*, i, 1987.

Allingham, Margery Louise, 1904–66, mystery-writer, b. in London, da. of two journalists: ex-milliner Emily Jane (Hughes) and Herbert A. At eight she was paid for a story in a magazine her aunt edited; at school in Colchester, her narrative talent drew charges of plagiarism; at the Perse School, Cambridge, she wrote a play and a novel of period derring-do, *Blackkerchief Dick*, 1922, based on fragments she invented while table-turning. After a verse play written as a drama student (*Dido and Aeneas*, pub. 1922), she turned to magazine melodramas (many from silent films): one paid for the honeymoon when she m. artist-journalist Philip Youngman Carter, 1927. Her two dozen thrillers began with *The White Cottage Mystery*, 1928: most feature her gentlemanly, non-macho detective Albert Campion, launched in *The Crime at Black Dudley*, 1929 (*The Black Dudley Murder* in the USA), a TV series hero in 1989. At first, a 'silly ass', he pursues a courtship in *The Fashion in Shrouds*, 1938, and – after MA consulted Dorothy Sayers at a chance wartime meeting – in *Traitor's Place*, 1941 (*The Sabotage Murder Mystery* in the USA, about Nazi designs on the British currency). MA was a billetting officer in WWII, and wrote of its impact on village life in *The Oaken Heart*, 1941 (non-fiction written for US friends), and *Dance of the Years*, 1943 (an experimental non-murder novel). Her later mysteries probe further into psychological and social incongruities (many striking female characters), specialized milieus (e.g. the stage, fashion), precise and forceful use of words, and passages of controlled, cumulative power (e.g. the opening of *The Beckoning Lady*, 1955). Her admirers include Elizabeth Bowen and Jessica Mann. There are several recent reprints and a 1989 TV series. See her husband's memoirs, 1982 study by Susan Asbee, 1990.

Allnutt, Gillian, poet, b. 1949 in London. She was educ. at convent and grammar schools and Cambridge Univ. (philosophy and English). Involved in the women's movement since the 1970s, she has worked with alternative housing systems like co-operatives and squats. *The Rag and Bone Man's Daughter Imagines a Happy Family*, 1978, appeared in a limited edition. In 1981 GA and five others formed a feminist anti-nuclear group, 'Sister Seven': the seventh represents 'what we are together'. In *Spitting the Pips Out*, 1981, she looks at heterosexuality and writing as a 'way of exploring a dissatisfaction with "reality" and of trying to recover my "real" self'. *Lizzie Siddell: Her Journal*, 1986, gives a voice to the shop-girl who became the Pre-Raphaelites' favourite model, married D. G. Rossetti, and killed herself after bearing a still-born child. *Beginning the Avocado*, 1987, exemplifies GA's imagistic precision in poems about war, women writers (Virginia WOOLF, Sylvia PLATH) and the act of writing: 'All my life I / have collected / Stones or words / To weight the light.' She teaches adults in London and runs the poetry workshop of the Women's Arts Alliance, which she joined about 1976: she wants to 'help demystify writing', to open to 'other women (people)' the chance of doing it, and to serve women's present task, which she sees as 'to reject all the definitions of ourselves that have been offered / forced upon us by men and to re / discover and say who we are'. She is poetry editor of *City Limits*. Her poems appear in anthologies: Lillian Mohin, ed., *One Foot on the Mountain*, 1979; *No Holds Barred*, chosen by the Raving Beauties, 1985; and Sylvia Paskin, Jay Ramsay and Jeremy Silver, eds., *Angels of Fire*, 1986. With others, she has edited *The New British Poetry*, 1988, to collect non-mainstream (including feminist and black) work.

'Alta' Gerrey, poet, fiction writer, publisher, editor, journalist. B. 1942 and raised in Reno, Nevada, da. of a blind piano tuner, at four she 'started a newspaper and wrote down what the grownups were saying about each other. I got spanked'. She studied literature at the Univ. of California, Berkeley. After suburban housewifely existence, tranquilizer addiction, and three suicidal months in a mental hospital, A 'grew beyond the house, like Alice after eating too many cookies', emerging a shameless hussy. She has done various ill-paid jobs, taught at the Univ. of California, Berkeley, and elsewhere, and worked in TV film, and video. Her second husband, poet John Simon, published her first book, *Freedom's in Sight*, 1969; when they divorced, he took the house, she the press. Publishers refused her second, woman-centered book, so in 1969 A founded Shameless Hussy Press to publish the angry, loving *Letters to Women*, 1970, and otherwise unpublishable early works by writers such as Susan GRIFFIN and Pat PARKER. She also initiated women's poetry readings in the San Francisco Bay area, and has edited books and journals, including *The Shameless Hussy Review*. The 'Americanese' of A's 12 books is inspired by Gertrude STEIN. Whether punchy aphorisms – 'support the war, beat yr kid' (*I Am Not a Practicing Angel*, 1975) – longer poetry, or prose, her writing is ironic, irreverent, colloquial. Tillie OLSEN's challenge to write women's 'untold stories' sparked the short novel *Momma*, 1974, about the difficulties of watching 'the kids out the window while being immortal on paper'. Like another model, Dorothy PARKER, A makes te truth bearable with wit. New and collected poems, stories, and essays in *The Shameless Hussy*, 1980 (intro. by Judy GRAHN). See Juhasz, 1976.

Alther, Lisa (Reed), novelist, b. 1944 at Kingsport, Tenn., da. of Alice Margaret (Greene), and John Shelton R., a surgeon. She took a BA at Wellesley College, 1966, and that year m. painter Richard Philip A.; she has a daughter. Taking short, solitary vacations to write in a rooming house in

Montréal, she produced two unpub. novels and some stories before her first novel, *Kinflicks*, 1976, which attracted much attention. It combines a bleak overall vision (it opens, 'My family has always been into death') and matching political analysis with sardonic or hilarious depiction of the post-nuclear milieux through which its protagonist searches for meaning. She recapitulates her life since leaving Tenn. as she returns to visit her dying mother; first- and third-person narration build up the mother–daughter relationship: genetically and socially determined, escaped, re-chosen. LA wrote an introduction for a Flannery O'CONNOR reprint, 1980, and published stories and articles in magazines. *Original Sin*, 1981, again concerns people (at the outset a parodic version of the children's-book 'gang') who leave Tenn. for the north, coming together again for a funeral after extensive experience of the inadequacy and corruption of the people and institutions society offers as mentors. *Other Women*, 1984, is unexpectedly optimistic: a lesbian relationship brings creative strength (contrasting with a lesbian debacle in *Kinflicks*). Much good comment includes Mary Anne Ferguson in *SoQ*, 21, 1983.

Anderson, Ethel (Mason), 1883–1958, poet, essayist, short-story writer, b. Leamington, England, during a visit by her Australian parents Louise (Scroggie) and Cyrus M. She grew up on her grandfather's property near Picton, NSW, and was educ. by a governess, then at a Sydney private school. In 1904 she m. A. T. A., British army officer serving in India where they lived for the next ten years. Her experiences there are reflected in two collections of witty, keenly observed stories, *Indian Tales*, 1948, and *The Little Ghosts*, 1957. Despite her establishment connections, EA has been seen as a subversive writer who frequently questions the assumptions of patriarchy. This is particularly true of *At Parramatta*, 1956, a highly entertaining collection of interlinked stories set in 1854. Although she considered herself primarily a poet (her two volumes are *Squatter's Luck*, 1942, and *Sunday at Yarralumla*, 1947), her highly lyrical expression is at its best in her short stories and collections of essays, *Adventures in Appleshire*, 1944, and *Timeless Garden*, 1945. She also wrote frequently about art and, with others, painted frescoes in several Australian churches.

Anderson, Jessica (Queale), novelist, short-story writer, playwright, b. in a Queensland country town, da. of Alice (Hibbert) and Charles Q. She was educ. at Brisbane High School, then Brisbane Technical College Art School, and apart from time spent in London, has lived mostly in Sydney where she has written radio drama and literary adaptations. An avid reader, she began writing fiction as a child – 'it was my strongest intention, my strongest desire'. Her childhood is evoked in the first section of *Stories from the Warm Zone and Sydney Stories*, 1987. She pub. magazine stories under a pseudonym to earn money but did not become a novelist till her forties. Novels include *An Ordinary Lunacy*, 1963, *The Last Man's Head*, 1970, *Stories of the Warm Zone*, 1988, and the one she regards as her best, *The Commandant*, 1975, set in Queensland during the convict period. Her best known are the Miles FRANKLIN Award winners, *Tirra Lirra By the River*, 1978, which focusses on the life of an artist denied fulfilment by her prosaic environment, and *The Impersonators*, 1980, a perceptive, quietly ironic exposure of middle-class Sydney in its pursuit of money at the expense of morality and aesthetics. Though not a markedly feminist writer, JA is sympathetic to feminism and frequently portrays strong and independent women. See the articles by Alrene Sykes, *Southerly*, 1986, Roslynn Haynes, *Australian Literary Studies*, 1986, and P. Gilbert, *Coming Out from Under*, 1988. JA will not reveal her birthdate.

Anderson, Margaret Carolyn, 1886–1973, editor and founder of the *Little Review*, journalist, critic and autobiographer who proudly claimed to be 'no man's wife, no man's delightful mistress, and ... never, never, never ... a mother'. B. in Indianapolis, eldest of three daughters of Jessie (Shortridge) and Arthur Aubrey A., she attended Western College, Oxford, Ohio, then left for Chicago, 1906, accompanied by her sister Lois. She wrote reviews for Clara E. Laughlin (whom, eventually, she succeeded as literary editor of the religious weekly, *Interior*, later *The Continent*) and worked on *The Dial* and the *Chicago Evening Post*. In 1913, she decided to start her own magazine, to publish, as she recalled in *My Thirty Years War*, 1930, 'the best conversation.... the world has to offer'. The first issue of the *Little Review*, March, 1914, featured feminism, Nietzsche and psychoanalysis, and works by Chicago poets Eunice TIETJENS and Vachel Lindsay. MA published Imagist poetry as well as pieces on contemporary art and politics, including the writings of Emma GOLDMAN. In 1916, she was joined by Jane HEAP and, the following year, moved the magazine to NYC where it won notoriety for serializing the 'obscene' Nausicaa chapter of *Ulysses*. Turning the editorship over to Heap in 1922, MA went to Paris where she lived with singer Georgette Leblanc for nearly 20 years. In 1924 she began attending the philosophical lectures of George Gurdjieff and later recorded her experience in a book dedicated to Heap, 1962. Returning to the USA in 1942, she lived with Dorothy Caruso until the latter's death in 1955. She edited *The Little Review Anthology*, 1953, and wrote *The Fiery Fountains*, 1951, and *The Strange Necessity*, 1969, which was dedicated to her great friend Solita SOLANO, completing an autobiographical trilogy which is not only a moving account of her many friendships but also an important source of literary and musical history. MA was buried beside Georgette Leblanc in Notre Dame des Anges Cemetary in Cannes. Abby Ann Arthur Johnson in *South Atlantic Quarterly*, summer, 1976, and Shari Benstock, 1986, discuss the *Little Review* years. See also Jane RULE, *Lesbian Images*, 1975. Papers in the Library of Congress, Newberry Library, Univ. of Chicago, Harvard Univ. and private collections.

Andrews, Eliza Frances (Fanny Andrews), 'Elzey Hay', 1840–1931, novelist, poet, essayist and diarist, b. Washington, Georgia, da. of Annulet (Ball) and James Garnett A., judge. She was educ. at girls' schools and later taught at Wesleyan Female College, Macon, and Washington High School. She became Principal of Girls' High School, Yazoo City, Mississippi, and Girls' Seminary, Washington; and staff correspondent for Augusta *Chronicle*. A 'rebel' in opposition to her staunch Unionist father, she was best known for her Civil War diary, *War-Time Journal of a Georgia Girl 1865–1866*, 1908, where she pronounced 'I am never going to marry anybody' because 'Marriage is incompatible with the career I have marked out for myself'. Though a socialist and suffragist she believed in the natural superiority of the white races. Her novels include the bestseller, *A Family Secret*, 1876, *A Mere Adventurer*, 1879, and *Prince Hal*, 1882. Her best-known poem was 'Haunted'. *A Practical Course in Botany*, 1911, was transl. for use in French schools. Essays include 'Dress Under Difficulties' (*Godey's Ladies' Book*, July, 1866), 'Plea for the Ugly Girls' (*Lippincott's*), and 'Socialism in the Plant World' (*International Socialist Review*, July, 1916). Her papers are located in the Garnett Andrews Papers, Southern Hist. Colln., Univ. of N. Carolina Library.

Andrews, Mary Raymound (Shipman), 1860–1936, writer of magazine fiction, b. at Mobile, Ala., eldest child of Ann Louise Gold (Johns) and Jacob Shaw S. Educ. at Lexington school and by her father, she m. William Shankland A. in 1884 and lived at Syracuse, NY. She published stories from 1902, for a large magazine audience; sentimental in both plot and style, her work romanticizes parsonages (her father was an Episcopalian minister), courts (her husband became a Supreme Court judge), war and the Canadian wilderness (she canoed and hunted in Québec over 30 summers). Her most popular work, *The Perfect Tribute*, 1906 (in *Scribner's* before separate printing), pictures Lincoln's low spirits over public reception of the Gettysburg address, revived by a dying soldier's (apocryphal) tribute: it sold 600,000 copies. MA's stories were collected in volumes like *The Eternal Masculine*, 1913 (outdoor: less sentimental), *The Eternal Feminine*, 1916, and *Yellow Butterflies*, 1922. Her two dozen books include a novel of the Napoleonic wars (*The Marshal*, 1912), poems (*Crosses of War*, 1918) and a life of Florence NIGHTINGALE (*A Lost Commander*, 1929).

'Angelou, Maya' (Marguerite Annie Johnson), poet, playwright, actress, autobiographer, b. 1928 in St Louis, Missouri, da. of Vivian Baxter and Bailey J. She was raised in Stamps, Ark., by her grandmother, Anne Henderson, who helped her to develop a strong will to succeed. Of her childhood she says, 'I haven't stopped being angry at a number of things. I saw my mother once between the time I was three and thirteen.' She went to school in Arkansas and California and became a singer, dancer, composer and actor. She studied with Martha Graham: 'I loved to dance as much as I loved writing, but by twenty-two my knees were gone and so there was no chance of ever achieving the best I had to give in that.' After black political activism in the USA she lived in Ghana 1963–6, writing, acting (in *Mother Courage*, 1964) and editing *African Review*, 1964–6. Her important TV work began with *Black, Blues, Black*, 1968. She is best known for her multi-volume autobiography: *I Know Why the Caged Bird Sings*, 1969 (for which she later wrote a screenplay), tells of the rape that left her non-verbal for years. To Rosa GUY (long a close friend) MA said, 'I started writing when I was mute. I always thought I could write because I loved to read so much ... I had memorized so much of [Paul Laurence] Dunbar, Poe, Shakespeare.' To Claudia Tate she said she did 'envision young Maya as a symbolic character for every black girl growing up in America'. Of the later volumes, *Gather Together in My Name*, 1974, deals with her efforts to raise her son, *Singin' and Swingin' and Gettin' Merry Like Christmas*, 1976, with her first marriage, acting, and a European tour with *Porgy and Bess*; *The Heart of a Woman*, 1981, with her work with Martin Luther King and Malcolm X, and arrival in Africa; and *All God's Children Need Traveling Shoes*, 1986, with the complexities of her experience in Ghana where she had hoped to find a 'home'. Her first poetry volume, *Just Give Me a Cool Drink of Water 'fore I Diiie*, 1971, sounds many voices, from 'Soft you day, be velvet soft, / My true love approaches' to 'Too proud to bend / Too poor to break, / I laugh until my stomach ache / When I think about myself.' In further volumes, *Oh Pray My Wings are Gonna Fit Me Well*, 1975, *And Still I Rise*, 1978, *Shaker, Why Don't You Sing?*, 1983, *Now Sheba Sings the Song*, 1987, and *I Shall Not Be Moved*, 1990. MA writes for 'the Black voice and any ear which can hear it', in every mood: angry, dignified, comic. MA has taught from 1966: now at Wake Forest Univ., NC. See Regina Blackburn in Estelle Jelinek, ed., *Women's Autobiography*, 1980; interviews in Tate, ed., 1983, Mary Chamberlain, ed., 1988 (quoted above); Jeffrey M. Elliot, 1989; Christine Froula in *Signs*, 11, 1986; K. Kinnamon in Joe Weixlmann and Chester J. Fontenot, eds., *Studies in Black American Literature II*, 1986.

Anger, Jane, perhaps a pseudonym for the probably female author of a black-letter feminist pamphlet, *Jane Anger, her Protection for Women* 'by Ja: A. Gent', written 1588, pub. 1589 (for 1985 reprs. see DEFENCES). It has two dedications: to women and to gentlewomen. Only one copy survives (Huntington). In racy, rattling prose with some verse inserted, it defends 'mine owne sex' against 'untrue meaning men' and vengeful rejected lovers (probably against a particular printed attack). Men mistakenly 'think we wil not write to reprove their lying lips'; the gods gave men supremacy to prevent women becoming too proud of their 'wonderfull vertues'.

'Anna Livia', Anna Livia Julian (after JULIAN of Norwich) Brawn, lesbian fiction-writer, b. 1955 in Dublin, da. of Dympna Monica (Horsburgh-Porter), a secretary, and Patrick St John Tom Pavier B., a screen-writer. She grew up in multi-lingual Zambia and Swaziland and has found linguistic influences stronger than literary ones. After a multi-racial boys' boarding school in Swaziland and a South London girls' grammar school (from 14), she studied French and Italian at Bristol Univ., moving for her BA to Univ. College, London. She taught at Avignon Univ., and has worked as bus conductor, cabaret dresser and cleaner. Her fast-paced, zany *Relatively Norma*, 1982, has a wide range of characters and viewpoints (female: every male in it is called John). The heroine, disclosing her lesbianism to her mother, sister and foster-sister, finds them more interested in their own lives. *Accommodation Offered*, 1985, sets three disparate women striving for survival and identity against a backdrop of concern from tree-spirits or Boddesses of Hortus. The 'lesbian feminist love stories' 1980–5) in *Incidents Involving Warmth*, 1986, and *Saccharine Cyanide*, 1990, present every kind of fleeting or serious involvement, often between different ages or races: wrangles, cross-purposes, passion, loss, exhausting jobs (cashier, motorbike courier), fear and hatred of men. *Bulldozer Rising*, 1988, describes an imaginary, tightly-controlled youth culture where old women keep revolt alive. AL edits *Gossip*, a journal of lesbian feminist ethics: she is co-editor with leading lesbian anthologist Lilian Mohin of *The Pied Piper: Lesbian Feminist Fiction*, 1989.

Annuals or albums. Begun in the 1820s, all the rage in the 1830s and 1840s, albums like the *English Annual* contained extracts and original pieces in prose and verse, some by, as well as for, the English upper-class amateur, some solicited from well-known writers. They largely replaced ADVICE books as gifts for young ladies, and could be read without incurring the stigma of Bluestocking. Frequent contributors included A. L. BARBAULD, Mary SHELLEY, Maria JEWSBURY, Felicia HEMANS, Maria ABDY. The books were issued just before each new year, beautifully printed and bound, with fine steel engravings, often edited by ladies with aristocratic connections, like Lady Stuart-Wortley, Lady BLESSINGTON (editor of *The Keepsake*), and Caroline NORTON. (Mary Ann JEVONS's *Sacred Offering*, 1831–8, was exceptionally modest.) Adelaide PROCTOR contributed to Heath's *Book of Beauty* (where Camilla CROSLAND first published) and Isabel HILL to *Hood's Comic Annual*. They were equally popular in the USA and often imported under changed titles. Lydia SIGOURNEY edited *The Religious Souvenir* in the late 1830s. Christmas Annuals took over in England from about 1850 (1860 in the USA), and from the 1860s became linked inextricably with a tradition of ghost stories, in which Charlotte RIDDELL and Amelia EDWARDS were particularly adept. *Victoria Regina*, 1861, a display anthology beautifully printed at Emily FAITHFULL's all-woman VICTORIA PRESS, was in the album tradition. See Anne Renier's study, *Friendship's Offering*, 1964. Vita SACKVILLE-WEST introduced Dorothy WELLESLEY's selec., 1930.

Anon. Virginia WOOLF, who also wrote that 'Anon was often a woman', thus titled her last, unfinished work, in recognition of the corporate, untraceable sources of the stream of poetry in English. Among the earliest surviving texts in English (many are lost) no-one knows the date or identity of the first by a woman. After printing arrived, anonymity remained common for both sexes – many of the best-known writers used it on occasion – for several centuries. Mary ASTELL and Sarah SCOTT, to name but two, had widely differing reasons for choosing anonymity, but one factor for each was the ideal of silence and modesty enjoined on women. Valuable work remains unassigned, e.g. accomplished, passionate, early-eighteenth-century love-poems pub. in the *Barbados Gazette*, 1732–5 (see Roger Lonsdale, ed., *The Oxford Book of Eighteenth-Century Women Poets*, 1989), and *The Triumph of Prudence over Passion* [1781], an epistolary novel with political content by an unnamed Irishwoman. Aristocratic women like Lady Dufferin (Caroline NORTON's sister) sometimes wrote anonymously from inverted snobbery, while others flaunted their titles. Catherine GORE used anonymity for business reasons: on one occasion it allowed two of her novels to be billed as by rival authors. In the USA the 'No Name' series was popular with nineteenth-century women writers. Women still choose to write anonymously in certain societies (e.g. the Solomon Islands), or practise communal anonymity for various political reasons (in THEATRE GROUPS and South African protest writing). See also ORAL TRADITION, PSEUDONYMS.

Anspach, Elizabeth (Berkeley), Princess Berkeley and Margravine of, earlier Lady Craven, 1750–1828, writer in many genres, b. in London, youngest da. of Elizabeth (Drax) and Augustus 4th Earl of Berkeley. She disappointed her mother, who had set her heart on a boy, her father d. when she was five. She m. the future Lord Craven in 1767 and bore four daughters. Horace Walpole admired her early poems and printed a 75-copy edition of her comedy *The Sleep-Walker*, adapted from French, 1778. She dedicated to him her *Modern Anecdote ... A Tale for Christmas*, 1779, 'a little book no bigger than a silver penny' but inventive and experimental. In defiance of social class she had her comedy, *The Miniature Picture*, staged at Drury Lane, 1780, herself conspicuous in the audience. (Its sprightly heroine assumes men's clothes to fix up her own love-life and her scholarly brother's.) Both unfaithful, she and Craven parted in 1783. She crossed Europe and Russia to Constantinople, 1785–6, later printing (1789, 1814: some overlap, some rewriting) 'sisterly' travel-letters to the married Margrave of A. (They dismiss Lady Mary Wortley MONTAGU's letters from Turkey, on grounds of style, as male forgery.) Widowed in 1791, she married the (also widowed) Margrave 16 days later; they settled in England. Most of her nine more plays were acted privately, in Anspach and England, by herself and friends; many are lost. She pub. *Memoirs*, 1826: ed. A. M. Broadley and Lewis Melville, 1913, with a life and appendix of her poetry.

Anthologies. Two MS albums of lyrics and longer poems – the 'Findern Anthology' (Cambridge Univ. Library: facs. R. Beadle and A. E. B. Owen, 1977) and the 'Devonshire MS' (BL: described in Richard Harrison's work on Sir Thomas Wyatt, 1975) – were probably collected and transcribed chiefly by women; they include tales of women or in women's voices, and praise of female virtues. Female work is sparse in general printed collections of every date, though female editors (from e.g. Maria RIDDELL, Joanna BAILLIE) have been more likely than men to do their own sex justice. In 1582 Thomas Bentley compiled *The Monument of Matrones*, inspired by and dedicated to ELIZABETH I: it includes some of her work, along with chiefly religious writings all by, for, or about women, and lives of famous women. The all-female anthology appeared with letters ed. Du Bosque, 1638, and was popular late in the century: *The Triumphs of Female Wit*, 1683, Samuel Briscoe's catchpenny *Letters of Love and Gallantry ... All Written by Ladies*, 1693, and *THE NINE MUSES*, 1700. *Poems* *by Eminent Ladies*, ed. George Colman and Bonnell Thornton, 1755 (re-issued 1773, 1780), includes 18 well-known poets, but barely samples the riches tapped in recent volumes by Germaine GREER, Susan Hastings, Jeslyn Medoff and Melissa Sansome, 1988 (seventeenth century), and by Roger Lonsdale, 1989 (eighteenth century). Alexander Dyce's *Specimens of British Poetesses*, 1825, is committed, scholarly and wide-ranging. Of the more common form of nineteenth-century poetry anthology – retrospective, not contemporary – Frederic Rowton's *Female Poets of Great Britain*, London, 1848, is most enlightened (for instance, he eschews the term 'poetess'); George W. Bethune's *British Female Poets*, Philadelphia, 1848, is less conservative than Eric Robertson's *English Poetesses*, London, 1883, which claims that 'children are the best poems Providence meant women to produce.' The rarer contemporary collections include Sarah J. HALE's *The Ladies' Wreath*, Boston, 1837, compiled to convey her 'onward and upward' philosophy to young girls (Hale was both first woman and first US editor of women's poetry), and Henry Coppee's *Gallery of Distinguished Female Poets*, Philadelphia, 1860. In 1848–9 there were three collections of US female poets, by Caroline May, Thomas Buchanan Reid and the well-known Rufus Griswold. Later English anthologies include Elizabeth Sharp's *Women's Voices*, NY and London, 1889, and vol. 7 of Alfred Miles's monumental *Poets and Poetry of the Century*, London [1892]. Kate SANBORN put out *The Wit of Women* in 1885. Anthologies have played an important role in feminist writing in the twentieth century. They have identified communities, created and embodied collectivity, asserted multiplicity of voice, and explicitly linked the literary and the political (like Nancy CUNARD's *Negro*, 1934). Feminist anthologies, like those of other communities, have been 'the outgrowth of need and neglect' (James V. Hatch, ed., *Black Theatre, U.S.A.*, 1974). In the USA, Robin MORGAN broke important ground with *Sisterhood is Powerful: An Anthology of Writings from the Women's Liberation Movement*, 1970, writings by women of several races, classes, occupations, as did Toni Cade (later BAMBARA) with *The Black Woman, An Anthology*, 1970. In Australia Kate Jennings's poetry anthology, *Mother, I'm Rooted*, 1975, was a landmark in the women's movement. Louise Bernikow's *The World Split Open: Women Poets 1552–1950*, 1974 (UK, 1979) aimed to 'recover a lost tradition in English and American poetry', presenting, with biographical information, dozens of little known or lost poets; Honor MOORE's *The New Women's Theatre*, 1977, made available plays by ten contemporary US women and provided an outline of the exclusion of women from full participation in the theatre. Cherrie Moraga and Gloria Anzaldúa, eds., *This Bridge Called My Back, Writings by Radical Women of Color*, 1981, insisted on multiplicity of voice, printing works by Afro, Asian, Native American and Latina writers. Dexter Fisher, ed., *The Third Woman: Minority Women Writers of the U.S.*, 1981, is – like Elly Bulkin, ed. *Lesbian Fiction*, 1981, Bulkin and Joan Larkin, eds., *Lesbian Poetry*, 1981, Kate McDermott, ed., *Places, Please! The First Anthology of Lesbian Plays*, 1985, and Jill Davis, ed., *Lesbian Plays*, 1987, like Rosemary Sullivan, ed., *Poetry by Canadian Women*, 1982, like Diana Scott, ed., *Bread and Roses* [British poetry], 1982, like Rayna GREEN, ed., *That's What She Said, Contemporary Poetry and Fiction by Native American Women*, 1984, like Jeni COUZYN, ed., *The Bloodaxe Book of Contemporary [British] Women Poets*, 1985 – an anthology made 'In pursuit of our own history.' A landmark in the canonization of the long-lived female tradition is Sandra M. GILBERT and Susan Gubar, eds, *The Norton Anthology of Literature by Women, The Tradition in English*, 1985. See also BLACK FEMINIST CRITICISM, LESBIAN FEMINIST CRITICISM, NATIVE FEMINIST CRITICISM.

Anthony, Susan B. (Brownell), 1820–1906, suffragist, reformer and editor, b. at Adams, Mass., and educ. at district schools in Battenville, NY, and in 1837–8 at a Philadelphia Friends' Seminary. The second of eight children of Lucy (Read) and Daniel A., abolitionist, SBA was influenced by her father's Quakerism, which espoused religious equality for women, and she admired the mill girls who worked for him. She taught at various schools in NY 1839–49, met Elizabeth Cady STANTON in 1850, and from then until her death devoted herself to women's suffrage, temperance, abolitionism, labour reform (especially for women) and the rights of married women. From 1868–70 she ed. *Revolution*, a woman's suffrage weekly advocating liberalized divorce laws, equitable pay, and education for girls. She was prominent in groups such as the Woman's Loyal National League (abolition), American Equal Rights Association, and the National Woman's Suffrage Association. She carried her message nationwide on the lyceum circuit and as a lobbyist in Kansas, Michigan, California, and Colorado. Her many MSS are widely scattered (see study by Alma Lutz, 1959). With Stanton and Matilda Joslyn GAGE, SBA pub. Vol. I of *History of Woman Suffrage*, 1881; two more vols. appeared in 1882 and 1886; a fourth in 1902, ed. by Ida Husted Harper, who also pub. Vols. 5 and 6 in 1922. Called the 'Napoleon of the woman's rights movement' by William Henry Channing, SBA died before women's suffrage was achieved, but believed that 'Failure is impossible' (Lutz). See also the life by Ida Harper, 3 vols, 1898–1908, and by Kathleen Barry, 1988.

Antin, Mary, 1881–1949, autobiographer and journalist. Da. of Esther (Weltman) and Israel A., she was b. and grew up in Polotzk (variously spelt), Russia, in the 'prison' of the Pale of settlement, under the threat of pogroms, observing the educational privileges of boys and 'the pious burden of wifehood': 'It was not much to be a girl, you see.' The family migrated to the USA, was unsuccessful, and in 1894 reached the slums of Boston's South End. MA attended Girls' Latin School. While her sister went to work in a sweat-shop, she was taken up by Jewish philanthropists seeking to combat opposition to immigration. MA published a poem at 15 in the *Boston Herald*, and translated the Yiddish letters she had sent an uncle about the journey from Russia: they appeared in *The American Hebrew*, NY, then as *From Plotzk to Boston*, 1899. She married Columbia Univ. professor Amadeus W. Grabau in 1901, studied at Barnard and Teachers' College, and bore a daughter. She became interested in liberal Judaism, women's issues, and transcendentalism, and with the encouragement of essayist Josephine Lazarus wrote *The Promised Land*, 1912 (following serial printing), 'a genuine personal memoir ... illustrative of scores of unwritten lives'. Aspiring to assimilation in 'the land of freedom', it was used in Civics courses in US schools until 1949. Until 1918, when the assumption of authority and celebrity came to trouble her, MA 'crisscrossed the US as an itinerant preacher', lecturing on Jewish immigrant life and the country's 'spiritual mission'. She also wrote *Those Who Knock at Our Gates: A Complete Gospel of Immigration*, 1914, and periodical essays and stories until 1941. She separated from her husband in 1919 when his pro-German sympathies lost him his job.

Antrobus, C. L. (Clara Louisa) (Rogers), 1846–1919, novelist, da. of Margaret (Hannings) of a notable Lincs. family, and Newsome R., surgeon. B. at Grantham, Lincs., she grew up at Bowden, Cheshire; she m. Arthur John A. in 1871, but was widowed in 1872. She began writing late; her first and best-known novel, *Wildersmoor*, 1895, admired for its depiction of the clever wife of a conventional clergyman, makes use of Cheshire-Lancs. dialect and scenery. *Quality Corner*, 1901, concerns the doomed love of a morally reprehensible man for the strong woman whose father he wronged. Her next work, a story collection, *The Wine of Finvarra*, 1902, deals more directly with similar themes in village settings full of local colour. 'The Old Man's Daughter' treats a saddler's daughter whose ne'er-do-well husband spends all her money before shooting her father, whereupon she shoots him; protected by local loyalties at the trial, she lives calmly on, refusing to marry again. Reviewers often speculated as to CLA's sex, usually guessing correctly.

Arasanayagam, Jean (Solomons), Sri Lankan poet, short-story writer, artist. B. 1934 in the mountain country of Kandy, into a family of Dutch descent with roots in colonial Sri Lanka, she was educ. at the Univ. of Ceylon, Peradeniya. She is m. to a teacher, the younger son of a Sri Lankan Tamil family, and has two daughters. She has published her poems in journals in Sri Lanka and abroad, and in *Kindura*, 1973, *Poems of a Season Beginning and a Season Over*, 1977, *Apocalypse 83*, 1984, and *A Colonial Inheritance*, 1985. Her poetry combines her European and Asian heritages and explores her situation in a mixed marriage and as a woman both inside and outside her national life. Her early verse records her painterly impressions, especially of the mountain country of Kandy, her birthplace and home. Her early fiction focuses on characters in conservative Burgher and Tamil families, while her later work (both fiction and poetry) responds to the ethnic disturbances of 1983: the poems in *Trial by Terror*, 1987, record 'the beginning of alienation, and the polarization and purgation of pity. You can never be merely an observer in this context.' Study of Sri Lankan writing by Yasmine GOONERATNE forthcoming.

Archer, Robyn, performer, composer, dramatist, b. 1948 in Adelaide, South Australia, da. of Mary (Wohling) and Cliff Smith, club entertainer. Educ. at state schools and Adelaide Univ., she made TV appearances while still in her teens, then worked as a school teacher before becoming a full-time performer and writer. A committed feminist whose artistic expression is vigorous and pithy, she first achieved recognition for her songs, particularly 'Menstruation Blues', 1973, and settings of Australian poetry, recorded as *The Wild Girl in the Heart*, 1973, and *The Ladies' Choice*, 1977. *A Star is Torn*, 1986, her tribute to 11 famous but unhappy women performers, first produced in 1979, was a major success in Australia and London. She has written many other works for the stage, including *The Conquest of Carmen Miranda*, 1978, *Songs from Sideshow Alley*, 1980, and *Il Magnifico*, 1980, as well as a children's story, *Mrs Bottle Burps*, 1983, and *The Robyn Archer Songbook*, 1980. Her highly successful feminist cabaret, *The Pack of Women*, 1986, first produced in London in 1981, was also filmed for TV.

Archibald, Edith Jessie (Archibald), 1854–1936, miscellaneous writer and feminist. B. at St John's, Newfoundland, da. of Catherine (Richardson) and Sir Edward Mortimer A., she attended private schools in London and NYC. In 1874, she m. distant cousin Charles A., a prosperous mine-owner, later president of the Bank of Nova Scotia in Halifax. She was active in social welfare, the Red Cross (during WWI) and the suffrage movement: president of the Women's Christian Temperance Union (WCTU), 1892–6, and of Halifax Local Council of Women, 1896–1906. During the 1890s she advocated non-confrontational suffrage policies; in 1917 she headed a suffrage delegation to the legislature. She published periodical fiction, and a life of her distinguished diplomat father, 1924, giving humorous accounts of the Prince of Wales (later Edward VII) in NYC and an unusually interesting memoir of the US Civil War period. *The Token*, 1930, a novel revised from a play presented at the Majestic Theatre, Halifax, 1927, traces the adventures and misunderstandings of several romantic couples, most of them of Scots descent, against a well-drawn local background: a small Cape Breton mining community, the nearby French islands of St Pierre and Miquelon where smuggling was a way of life, St John's, and Boston.

Arendt, Hannah, 1906–75, philosopher, teacher, political activist. B. in Hanover, to middle-class Jewish parents, Martha (Cohn) and Paul A., she studied with Heidegger, then Jaspers, whose influence emerges in the existentialist formulation of the *vita activa* at the heart of her political philosophy. She fled Nazi Germany to Paris, where she organized Jewish emigration to Palestine, and moved to the USA, 1941, where she mobilized political conscience. She m. Gunther Stern, 1929 (divorced 1938), then Heinrich Bleucher, 1940. The first woman to be appointed to a full-time faculty position at Princeton, 1959, HA made her original contribution to philosophy in her argument that political activity has epistemological and ontological foundations. *The Human Condition*, 1958, upholds the Greek strategy of securing a privileged space or 'freedom from the necessities of life' for the operations of the *polis*, for public debate and the exercise of political power without the corruption of private interest. She advances the *polis* as a universal paradigm of the body politic. That its freedom and power is enjoyed by an elect minority, whose 'life necessities' are provided for by slave labour and by women's subjection and confinement to the private domain of the paterfamilias, is not, to her mind, essentially problematical. Women's oppression does not figure in her wide-ranging historical materialist analysis of anti-semitism, imperialism, racism, and totalitarianism in *The Origins of Totalitarianism*, 1958. *On Revolution*, 1963, discusses the historical corruption of the original, 'honorable', goal of 'revolution' (in particular, the French Revolution), namely, the restoration of power to the few 'free' enough to manage it with categorical disinterest and rational good faith. HA claims that this revolutionary ideal was lost before the advent of popular liberation fronts and the rise of utilitarian and socialist demands on the state to show immediate and expedient interest in 'the needs of the people'. Her notion that the 'human condition' deteriorates as the 'necessities of life' displace the bounds of 'freedom', precludes sympathy for a women's movement which pressures for improved material conditions. Her anti-materialism recalls Simone de BEAUVOIR's existentialist bias against woman's body as physically enslaving; and her liberalism precludes recognition of the autonomy of the women's movement or the specificity of women's needs. Accordingly, women should fight for equal access to men's public affairs but not sacrifice their 'femininity'. She also wrote *Rahael Varnhagen*, 1958, *Eichmann in Jerusalem*, 1963, *Men in Dark Times*, 1968, *On Violence*, 1970, and *The Life of the Mind*, 1978. Life by Elisabeth Young-Bruehl, 1982, includes bibliography; studies by Margaret Canovan, 1974, and Bikhu Parekh, 1981. Papers at the Library of Congress; correspondence with Jaspers at Deutches Literaturarchiv, Marbach, Germany.

'Ariadne', pseudonym of the 'Young Lady' whose didactic comedy *She Ventures, and He Wins* was acted Sept. 1695 at Lincoln's Inn Fields, London, pub. 1696. Her preface admits ignorance of the stage and 'the Error of a weak Woman's pen', but also an 'Inclination ... for Scribling from my Childhood': she had often thought of publishing before 1689. Her prologue invokes both Aphra BEHN and Katherine PHILIPS. Her female characters triumph acceptably: one, in male dress, seeks out, tests, and marries her man; the other entertains her husband by teasing and victimizing a would-be adulterer. *The Unnatural Mother*, 1697, second play of a

'Young Lady' whose lively female villain escapes execution by suicide, *may* be hers; critics have made other tenuous ascriptions.

Armour, Rebecca **Agatha**, 1846–91, novelist, local historian. She was b. at Fredericton, New Brunswick, eldest of four daughters of Margaret Hazlett and Joseph A., a grocer, both Irish immigrants. Educ. at teachers' college, AA taught in the Fredericton area for many years, 1864–73, then in southern NB and probably Lancaster. She was considered 'one of the best lady teachers in the service in New Brunswick'. She m. John G. Thompson, a carriage maker, 1885. Her 'Landmarks of Old Fredericton', historical sketches, appeared in the Fredericton *Capital* in 1880, and her four novels, also of historical interest, were published by the Saint John *Telegraph*. *Lady Rosamond's Secret*, 1878, gives a largely factual account of Fredericton society during the tenure of Sir Howard Douglas, Lieutenant-Governor of New Brunswick, 1824–9; *Marguerite Verne; or, Scenes from Canadian Life*, 1886, is set in Saint John, NB, at the time it was written.

Armstrong, Charlotte, 'Jo Valentine', 1905–69, novelist, b. at Vulcan, Mich., da. of Clara (Pascoe) and Frank Hall A. Educ. at the Univ. of Wisconsin and Barnard College, NYC (BA 1925), she worked in advertising and fashion reporting, m. Jack Lewi in 1928, and had three children. She published poems in the *New Yorker*, worked with a schools theatre group, and had two plays produced on Broadway: *The Happiest Days*, 1939, and *Ring Around Elizabeth*, 1940. Of her 30 suspense novels, beginning in 1942, the first three feature a traditional series detective, MacDougal ('Mac') Duff; when she dropped him her writing gained in emotional depth. She wrote screenplays for *The Unexpected*, 1947, and *Mischief*, 1951, repr. 1988, which features a deranged babysitter (film *Don't Bother to Knock*, 1952). Her film and TV work included the *Alfred Hitchcock Presents* series, 1955–61. She published one book as Jo Valentine (*The Trouble with Thor*, 1951, re-issued as *And Sometimes Death*) and two short-story volumes (*The Albatross*, 1957, and *I See You*, 1966). *The One-Faced Girl*, 1963, with female protagonist, focuses on the need for mutual help in overcoming suffering and evil. *A Little Less than Kind*, 1964, transplants the Hamlet story to contemporary California with an unstable central figure who ends by seeking psychiatric help. CA likes to reveal the identity of the criminal early in her books: she puts character, motivation and plotting to the fore, often delaying rescue of threatened innocents. *The Charlotte Armstrong Reader* appeared in 1970. MSS at Boston Univ.

Arnold, Ethel M., 1866–1930, writer, lecturer, photographer, sixth of seven children of Julia (Sorrel) and Thomas A. B. at Reading, Berks., she grew up at Harborne, Staffordshire, youngest sister of Mary WARD. She was educ. at home and at Oxford High School, leading a 'somewhat grey and melancholy childhood', enlivened by her friendship with Lewis Carroll, who taught her photography and encouraged her acting, which her family later vetoed; she cared for her mother until her death from cancer in 1888. Moving then to London, she began journalism, and despite life-long invalidism and a 30-year morphine addiction, wrote over 400 book reviews and some 20 news stories for the *Manchester Guardian* 1891–9, as well as a school history of the British Constitution and two short stories, 'Mrs Verrinder', June 1886, and 'Edged Tools', Aug.–Sept. 1887 (both in *Temple Bar*). In 1894 she published her only novel, *Platonics: A Study*, a portrait of an intense friendship between two women. EMA's own most important friendships were with women: with Agnes Williams Freeman, she translated a collection of Turgenev's letters from French in 1903, but wrote little after this beyond reminiscences of her friend Rhoda BROUGHTON, 1920, and Carroll, 1929.

Despite her sister's anti-suffrage role, EA actively supported women's enfranchisement, lecturing successfully throughout the USA between 1908 and 1912. She is barely mentioned in books about Ward or the Arnolds, but see life by Phyllis Wachter (diss. 1984).

Arnow, Harriette Louisa (Simpson), 1908–86, novelist, historian. She was b. in Wayne County, Ky., da. of Mollie Jane (Denney) and Elias Thomas S., schoolteachers who also farmed. She attended Berea College, 1924–6, then taught in a one-room schoolhouse in the hills of Southeast Kentucky before taking a BS at the Univ. of Louisville, 1930. After teaching several years in Kentucky public schools, she moved to Cincinnati in 1934 and began writing (except for casual jobs) full-time. She published short stories first (the best-known being 'The Washerwoman's Day'), then a novel about Kentucky hill people, *Mountain Path*, 1936. HA m. Harold B. A., 1939, had two children, and moved to Detroit, 1944, after farming in Southeast Kentucky. HA continued her Kentucky trilogy about the people of Appalachia with the 'subversive' *Hunter's Horn*, 1949, which, John Flynn says, she wanted to call 'The End of the Gravel' to refer to the coming of roads, and *The Dollmaker*, 1954, similarly changed by Macmillan from 'Dissolution'. Here HA referred to the end of 'hill life' caused by the great migration of what was to be seven million souls from Appalachia to big Northern cities. From 'an early age' HA saw her work 'as a record of people's lives in terms of roads' as well as 'a personal dream of community I'd had since childhood and have been trying ever since to recapture in my writings' (in Barbara L. Baer, *The Nation*, 222, 31 Jan. 1976). The latter novel, discussed by Joyce Carol OATES as 'our most unpretentious American masterpiece' (in David Madden, ed., *Rediscoveries*, 1971), is about a wood-carver who maintains some stability through her art when her family is uprooted to Detroit. Ronald Butler argues that Gertie Nevels' lack of strength to fight for what she wants is her tragedy and that the strong Gertie in Jane Fonda's televized production in 1983 is an interpretation against the text. HA's two works of social history, *Seedtime on the Cumberland*, 1960, and *Flowering of the Cumberland*, 1963, were well received. In *The Weedkiller's Daughter*, 1970, an adolescent aspiring to be a doctor maintains her integrity despite her parents, 'Bismark' and 'the Popsicle Queen', through a surreptitious relationship with her French-Canadian grandmother. *The Kentucky Trace: A Novel of the American Revolution*, 1974, has a significant sub-plot about a man undertaking the care of a stranger woman's rejected infant. *Old Burnside*, 1977, is documented family history about post-Revolutionary migration to a Kentucky town later submerged by the Cumberland River Project. HA lived latterly at Ann Arbor, Mich. The Univ. of Kentucky has her MSS; its press has reprinted most of her books; comment includes study by Wilton Eckley, 1974; Butler in *Appalachian Heritage*, 12, 1984; Glenda Hobbs in Emily Toth, ed., *Regionalism and the Female Imagination*, 1985; Joan Griffin in *Geography and Literature*, 1987.

Arrowsmith, Pat, political activist, editor, novelist, poet, b. 1930 in Leamington Spa, Warwicks., to Margaret Vera (Kingham) and George Ernest A. She studied at Newnham College, Cambridge, the Univ. of Ohio and Liverpool Univ. She lived with Wendy Butlin, 1962–76, and was married and separated in quick succession in 1979. She has done unskilled jobs and social work of many kinds, and been a reporter (*Peace News*, 1965) and researcher (Quakers' Race Relations Committee, 1969–71: see her study *The Colour of Six Schools*, 1972). She has worked for civil liberties and nuclear disarmament, and against the Vietnam War (see *To Asia in Peace: The Story of a Non-Violent Action Mission to Indo China*, ed. PA, 1972) and the British presence in

Northern Ireland. She has been jailed for political reasons a dozen times since 1958. Her novels fictionalize her own experience: *Jericho*, 1965, repr. 1983, about protest at a nuclear weapons factory; *The Prisoner*, 1982, about an elderly bedridden woman (from her casework and nursing jobs); *Somewhere Like This*, 1970, about a woman's prison. *Breakout*, 1975, contains poems and drawings done in prison; *On the Brink . . .*, 1981, is an anti-nuclear polemic, as are the poems in *Thin Ice*, 1984.

Ashbridge, Elizabeth (Sampson), 1713–55, Quaker autobiographer, only child of Mary and Thomas S., b. at Middlewich, Cheshire, and educ. by her mother, her father being at sea. She was a pious (Anglican) child, but in her teens ran away to marry. She was widowed in five months; her father never forgave her. She took refuge with a Quaker cousin in Ireland, then shipped as an indentured servant to America, 1732. Having flirted with Catholicism, atheism, and suicide, and dreamed 'a grave woman' summoned her to God, she still enjoyed reading plays and dancing; she married a schoolteacher called Sullivan who loved her gaiety. Living and teaching in various places, she suffered increasing religious torment, and despite strong feelings against the QUAKERS, especially women preachers, she was drawn at last to join them. (Her husband said he would rather see her dead; while she longed for his conversion, he joined the army; he died after corporal punishment.) She m. Aaron A. in 1746, followed a preaching call to Britain, 1753 (see Sarah STEPHENSON), and died in Ireland. Her vivid account of her early life, transcribed *c.* 1761 by Aaron A., was pub. 1774: many reprs., to 1927.

Ashford, 'Daisy', Margaret Mary Julia, later Devlin, 1881–1972, child writer, b. at Petersham, Surrey, da. of Emma Georgina (Walker) and William Henry Roxburghe A. She wrote fiction throughout her education (at home by a governess), dictating to her father 'The Life of Father McSwiney' (at four) and two more stories at eight (one now lost). Next year, 1890, she wrote out in her own hand the story that later made her famous, *The Young Visiters, or Mr Salteena's Plan*. Like all her work, it turns a sharp eye on the conventions of courtship and literature: the hero 'bit his lips rarther hard for he could hardly contain himself and felt he must marry Ethel soon' when she arrays herself as 'a dainty vishen' to visit his Cambridge 'pal' the Earl of Clinsham at his 'privite compartments . . . packed with all the Elite'. A play, 'A Woman's Crime', was performed but later lost; three more stories written from 11 to 14 were put away. After a year at a Haywards Heath convent and a secretarial course, 1904, DA worked in Switzerland. Sorting papers after her mother's death, 1917, turned up the stories; *The Young Visiters*, pub. 1919 with a preface by J. M. Barrie, was an instant hit and eventual best-seller: a play in 1920, a musical in 1968 and a film in 1984. In 1920, the year DA m. James Devlin, *DA: Her Book* added two more stories (with her sister Angela's 'The Jealous Governess, or The Granted Wish'); further selecs. in 1966 and 1983. DA and her husband ran a market garden; she wrote nothing as an adult. Life by her niece, R. M. Malcomson, 1984.

Ashton, Helen Rosaline, 1891–1958, novelist and biographer. B. in London, da. of Emma (Burnie) and barrister Arthur Jacob A., KC and judge, and sister of Leigh Ashton, later director of the Victoria and Albert Museum, she published 26 books spanning 43 years, from *Pierrot in Town*, 1913. The scepticism with which she treats marriage in *Almain*, 1914, and *Mackerel Sky*, 1931, is characteristic. She nursed as a VAD during WWI, then studied medicine at London Univ., took her MB and was house physician at Great Ormond Street Children's Hospital; but she was never in practice, 'in consequence of her marriage' (says her *Times* obituary) to barrister Arthur Jordan, 1927. She drew on her medical background for *Dr Serocold: A Page from His Day-Book*, 1930, and *Yeoman's Hospital*, 1944 (on which a film, *White Corridors*, 1955, was based). HA's lively novels (several repr. in large print for impaired eyes) were more successful than her literary (or fictional) biographies. In 1937 she published, with Katharine Davies, *I Had a Sister*, a study of Mary LAMB, Dorothy WORDSWORTH, Caroline HERSCHEL and Cassandra Austen. On her own she added *William and Dorothy*, 1938, a life of Henry Vaughan, 1940, and *Parson Austen's Daughter*, 1949 (told from Cassandra's point of view).

Ashton-Warner, Sylvia, 1908–84, novelist, teacher and educational theorist. B. in Taranaki, NZ, da. of Mary (a primary school teacher) and Francis (a permanent invalid) A-W. The middle child of nine, she was educ. wherever her mother taught. In 1932 she m. Keith D. Henderson; she taught with him in country schools 1937–58. They had three children. She 'always hated teaching', but her writings about education were radical, especially her 'key vocabulary' reading scheme. This was unappreciated by the NZ Education Dept. (which she described as 'the Permanent Solid Block of Male Educational Hostility'). She finally wrote it into a novel, *Spinster*, 1958, which uses much of her own experience in a story of a single woman teacher's romantic attractions. A more factual account of developing and teaching her reading program in an infant Maori class, *Teacher*, followed in 1963. Other novels include *Incense to Idols*, 1960, about a flamboyant cosmopolitan pianist who creates havoc in a small NZ town, a dream of passionate spontaneity in 'a sedated limited society'; *Bell Call*, 1964, a powerful account of a charismatic artist and mother of four, who tries to bring up her children as she pleases in opposition to the system; and *Greenstone*, 1966, partly realistic, partly romantic. Her works received limited or negative response. After her husband's death in 1969 she travelled widely and taught in Colorado, 1970, and was Professor of Education at Simon Fraser Univ., Vancouver, 1971–3, out of which experience she wrote *Spearpoint*, a book on experimental education. Her autobiography, *I Passed This Way*, 1979, is full and readable, but her novels, *Myself*, 1968, a record of the 'violent artist', and *Three*, 1971, tell more about her life as a highly emotional intelligent woman who in the 1950s managed to cope with marriage, teaching, writing and creating her own space. See Cherry Hankin's discussion in WLWE 14, 1975, and life by Lynley Hood, 1988.

Askew or Ayscough (variously spelt), **Anne**, 1520–46, Protestant controversialist and martyr. Da. of Elizabeth (Wrottesley) and Sir William A. of Lincs. (and ancestor of Margaret FELL), she was unusually well educ., but m. against her will, *c.* 1541, to the boorish Catholic squire Thomas Kyme (as substitute for an elder sister who died). He turned her out for Protestant practices; she resumed her birth name, went to Lincoln and then London seeking divorce, and became known for 'gospelling'. Arrested for heresy about the Mass (which she saw as religious *metaphor*), released and re-arrested, she was repeatedly interrogated (her sex being an issue throughout) and tortured, by the Lord Chancellor's own hands, in hopes of her incriminating Queen Katharine PARR, in whose circle she had been. She remained firm, and was burned alive (bound upright because of dislocated legs, keeping up the courage of her male fellow-victims). That year John Bale pub. at Marburg in Germany her full autobiographical account of her *First* and *Lattre Examinacyons*, statement of faith, prayer, and ballad: repr. in John Foxe, *Book of Martyrs*, 1563. 'Not oft use I to wryght, / In prose, nor yet in ryme', but her style is sinewy and vividly imagistic. She figures in a nephew's *History* of England and Scotland, 1607, pious lives, and novels (e.g. by Anne MANNING). See Derek Wilson, *A Tudor Tapestry*, 1972.

Asquith, Cynthia Mary Evelyn, Lady (Charteris), 1887–1960, diarist, journalist, anthologist, novelist, biographer, b. in Cheltenham, Glos., da. of Mary (Wyndham) and Hugo Charteris, later 11th Earl of Wemyss. She was educ. at home, chiefly by Miss Jourdain, about whom she felt intensely. After 'coming out' as a debutante ('an expression which aptly indicates a violently sudden change as though at a word of command a butterfly had to break her chrysalis and instantaneously spread her wings'), she m. Herbert A., second son of the Liberal Prime Minister, 1910. They had three sons. Discouraged in her childish literary ambitions, she later kept detailed accounts of her war experiences. These, her major work, were published posthumously, 1968, with a foreword by L. P. Hartley, repr. 1987. After the war, which left her husband seriously unwell, she became private secretary to J. M. Barrie, and, encouraged by him and Marie Belloc-Lowndes, 'most assiduous of literary midwives', began to write as 'breadwinner'. She wrote columns for *The Times*, collected several CHILDREN's Annuals, published a novel and other books for children, then moved to an adult audience with several collections of ghost stories. *The Ghost Book*, 1926, for which D. H. Lawrence wrote 'The Rocking-Horse Winner', had sequels, and there were other collections, such as *When Churchyards Yawn*, 1931. Her anthologies, which included work by, among others, Marghanita LASKI, Elizabeth TAYLOR, Elizabeth BOWEN, and Mary WEBB, sometimes masked her own work with PSEUDONYMS (e.g. 'Leonard Gray'); her novel *Spring House*, 1936, sets its female protagonist retrospectively in WWI, dramatizing her achievement of independence. CA also wrote bread-winning lives of members of the Royal Family. Her memoirs, *Haply I Remember*, 1950, and *Remember and Be Glad*, 1952, emphasize her struggle to achieve her own voice, a problem brilliantly sublimated in her story '"God Grante That She Lye Stille"', 1931. *Portrait of Barrie*, 1954, describes her working life with him. She wrote a life of Sonja Tolstoy, 1960. Harriet Blodgett writes on her diaries in *Turn-of-the-Century Women*, 2, 1985, Ruth Weston on her ghost stories in *TSWL*, 6, 1987. Life by Nicola Beauman, 1987. Papers with the Asquith Papers at the Bodleian Library.

Astell, Mary, 1666–1731, feminist, churchwoman, and polemicist, b. in Newcastle, da. of Mary (Errington) and Peter A. (a family once prominent in the coal trade). She studied with an uncle from about eight (her brother, though, had legal training), became a philosopher, and by 1683 was writing fine poetry on the struggles of faith. At perhaps 21 she settled alone at Chelsea near London, but found 'a liflyhood' hard to get. In 1689 she gave the non-juring Archbishop Sancroft (who had aided her) a hand-sewn booklet of her poems (Bodleian). *A Serious Proposal to the Ladies*, 'By a Lover of her Sex', 1694, laments 'Tyrant Custom', poor education, and husbands' exactions, and proposes college communities for short or permanent residence of unmarried women, financed by dowries; a second part, 1697, distils Cartesian thought for women. The work was received with respect (a man claimed authorship). She discussed belief, pain and evil with John Norris in *Letters Concerning the Love of God*, 1695. Perhaps best known today, *Some Reflections upon Marriage*, 1700, points out its pitfalls for women: enduring a bad marriage for good motives is 'a more Heroic Action than all the famous Masculine Heroes can boast of'; an appendix argues biblically that women are not created inferior. The preface to the 1706 ed. asks 'If all men are born free, how is it that all women are born slaves?' MA engaged freely in polemic: she answered James Owen in *Moderation Truly Stated*, Defoe in *A Fair Way with the Dissenters*, White Kennett in *An Impartial Enquiry into the Causes of Rebellion*, all 1704, Locke in *The Christian Religion, As Profess'd by a Daughter of the Church of England*, 1705, and Shaftesbury in *Bart'lemy Fair, or An Enquiry after Wit*, 1709. She ran a charity school from 1709, wrote a preface to Lady Mary Wortley MONTAGU's MS Embassy Letters, 1724, and befriended Elizabeth ELSTOB. A conservative radical, tempted by fame though publishing under pseudonyms, consistently intellectual, sharply witty and quotable, always ready to step out of her way for a feminist point, incalculably influential, she was attacked by Swift, Susanna CENTLIVRE, and Colley Cibber, and borrowed from by Defoe and *The Ladies Library*. Selecs. ed. Bridget Hill and life by Ruth Perry, both 1986.

Astley, Thea, novelist, short-story writer, critic, b. 1925 in Brisbane, Queensland, da. of Eileen (Lindsay) and Cecil A., journalist. She was educ. at All Hallows Convent, Brisbane, and Queensland Univ. She worked as a schoolteacher in small country towns, and, following her marriage to Jack Gregson in 1948, in Sydney. From 1968 until retirement in 1980 she taught English and Australian Literature at Macquarie Univ., Sydney. Though she pub. critical articles and a monograph, *Three Australian Writers*, 1979, TA's reputation rests on her ten very individual novels and her collection of stories, *Hunting the Wild Pineapple*, 1979. Her first two novels, *Girl with a Monkey*, 1958, and *A Descant for Gossips*, 1960 (TV adaptation 1989), draw wittily on her small-town experiences, though her studies of close-knit communities have now spread to the Pacific Islands, with *A Boat Load of Home Folk*, 1968, and *Beachmasters*, 1985, awarded the 1986 Gold Medal of the Australian Literature Society. Three times winner of the Miles FRANKLIN Award (for *The Well Dressed Explorer*, 1962, *The Slow Natives*, 1965, and *The Acolyte*, 1972), she began writing at a time when Australian fiction was dominated by male writers; yet, while most of her books use a male persona, the male ego has not escaped her pervasive irony. Racism is an additional target in *A Kindness Cup*, 1974, and *Beachmasters*, while the nuclear issue is central to *An Item from the Late News*, 1982. *It's Raining in Mango*, 1988, a series of interlinked stories tracing one family's progress against the history of North Queensland, won the inaugural Steele Rudd award for short fiction. For critical study, see Brian Matthews, *Southern Review*, 1973, and P. Gilbert, *Coming Out from Under: Contemporary Australian Women Writers*, 1988.

Aston, Katherine (Thimelby), *c.* 1619–58, Roman Catholic letter-writer and poet, vowed to Christ at nine years old, sister of Winefrid THIMELBY and sister-in-law of Constance FOWLER, whom her letters (now lost) made 'mad with love'. She quotes Donne and calls a couplet of her own 'Twang, but trew'. Her tone to Herbert A., whom she m. in 1638, is direct: 'I feel much shame. I think I never write so ill to any as I do to you'; 'Thus love for love will suply all other wants.' He and her friends called her 'Belamore' or 'Good Love'; she debates the nature of love in a late letter of religious and philosophical speculation. Her husband wrote a moving account of her death (after bearing her tenth child). He collected copies of poems, many by women; she gathered and transcribed *his* poems; few of hers and none of his survive. See *Tixall Poems*, 1813, *Tixall Letters*, 1815, ed. Arthur Clifford. The Huntington Library has poems exchanged with her cousin Lady Dorothy Shirley.

Atherton, Gertrude (Horn), 1857–1948, novelist, b. in San Francisco, eldest da. of a Southerner, Gertrude (Franklin), and a Northerner, Thomas H. Her mother's two broken marriages (the first unwillingly made) left GA an insecure child, educ. by her grandfather 'with a prayer-book in one hand and the *Atlantic Monthly* in the other', then at private schools: finally, after contracting TB, at Sayre Institute, Lexington, Ky. Sent home after twice becoming engaged, she eloped in 1876 to marry George H. Bowen A. (a suitor of her mother: d. 1887). One of her two children died young. To relieve tedium, she wrote for the San Francisco *Argonaut*, an anonymous *roman-à-clef*, 'The Randolphs of Redwoods', 1882, which caused family scandal (revised as *A Daughter of the Vine*, 1899). She called the melodrama of her several dozen novels, 'romantic realism'; her independent, thinking heroines often seek to transcend traditional roles, and are unashamed of directly-presented sexual desire. *Hermia Suydam*, 1889 (*Hermia, An American Woman* in London), was also pronounced immoral. GA finished her first Californian novel, *Los Cerritos*, 1890, in France; research on the Spanish missions produced *Before the Gringo Came*, 1894, and *The Doomswoman*, 1893. In England, where she moved in 1895, *Patience Sparhawk and her Times*, 1897, and *American Wives and English Husbands*, 1898, were praised for revealing 'the American character' (Henry James, though, said 'I abominate the woman'). Her 'biographical novels', from *Senator North*, 1900 (based on Eugene Hall of Maine), include her most popular book, *The Conqueror*, 1902 (on Alexander Hamilton). *The Gorgeous Isle*, 1908, presents the West Indian romance of a poet (drawn from Swinburne) and an Englishwoman. GA looked on facts as 'stimulants: each opens up a new vista'. She lost personal papers in the San Francisco fire, 1906. She wrote *Julia France and Her Times*, 1912 (about a glamorous suffrage campaigner in England), as a duty to her sex; she kept abreast of developing feminism till the 1930s, yet apparently regarded it as displacement of sexual energy. Work for hospital relief in WWI earned her the Légion d'Honneur: she wrote of Frenchwomen's war work in *The Living Present* (essays), 1917, and predicted in *The White Morning*, 1918, that German women would bring peace by overthrowing their government. That year she edited *The American Women's Magazine*, which ran for ten months. *Perch of the Devil*, 1914 (carefully researched working life in Butte, Montana), is notable for the relationship between the two heroines. *Black Oxen*, 1923, questions the lasting significance of even happy love. GA read 200 books on the ancient world to write of the woman philosopher Aspasia (a 'compelling interest') in *The Immortal Marriage*, 1927, of Alcibiades, 1928, and Dido, 1929. She pub. two memoirs, *Adventures of a Novelist*, 1932, and *My San Francisco*, 1946. See Emily Leider on her letters to Ambrose Bierce (*Calif. History*, 60, 1981–2); J. Bradley on her last works (*Women's Studies*, 12, 1985–6); critical life by Charlotte S. McClive, 1979; bibliog. by McClive in *American Literary Realism*, 9, 1976. Papers at Library of Congress and the Univ. of Calif., Berkeley.

Atkins, Mrs **Anna** (Children), 1799–1871, novelist and scientific writer, b. Tonbridge, Kent, to Hester Ann (Holwell), d. 1800, and scientist John George C., who m. twice more. AA's *Memoir* of her father (to whom she was very close), privately printed 1853, gives scattered information about her own upbringing, closeness to her nurse, removal from school after illness and her educ. by governess. In 1825, having survived her family's loss of money in a bank crash, she m. John Pelly A., of Halstead Place, near Sevenoaks, producing her first work in three vols. 1843–52, *Photographs of British Algae, Cyanotype Impressions*, dedicated to her father. Later she wrote several 'silver-fork' novels: *The Perils of Fashion*, 1852, a stilted and didactic tale of fashionable life pub. anon.; *The Colonel*, 1853; and *A Page from the Peerage*, 1863. *Murder Will Out: A Story of Real Life*, 1859, by the author of 'The Colonel', is extraordinarily different, dealing graphically with wife-murder and hanging, proceeding by flash-back technique. Purporting to be a plea against capital punishment, it ends by attributing all wrong-doing to going against one's father. AA was possibly a correspondent of Caroline CORNWALLIS.

Atkinson, Elizabeth, polemicist. Having left the Quakers, she attacked them in *A Breif and Plain Discovery*, 1669. Rebecca TRAVERS responded; so did Ann Travers and Elizabeth Coleman in Stephen Crisp's *Backslider Reproved*, calling EA's text 'a pack of lies, Feignedness, and Deceit, which discovers more Impudency, than Modesty or Sobriety'. She replied with *The Weapons of the People called Quakers*, 1669, attacking their theology, 'assured you have no more power to hurt me then you have to save your selves'.

Atkinson, Emma Willsher, *c.* 1826–1900, painter and novelist, b. Essex, one of eight children of Martha Cawston (or Causton) and John A., Willsher lecturer at Wethersfield church (a post endowed in 1634) and member of the minor landed gentry; later rector at Fishtoft, Lincs. Her two prose works are *Memoirs of the Queens of Prussia*, 1858, written after a sojourn in Germany and with some feminist sympathy, and a novel, *Extremes*, 1859, repub. in abridged form as Monthly Vol. of Standard Authors, 1866. Despite its conventional ending, it deals intelligently with the theme of mistaken zeal in religion, showing insight into complexities of village life as well as women's position. In 1888 she exhibited two paintings at the Society of Women Artists. She died in Kent possessed of considerable property.

Atkinson, Louisa (later Calvert), 1834–72, novelist, journalist, botanist, b. on the family property, Oldbury, NSW, da. of Charlotte (Waring, later Barton), author of the first Australian children's book, *A Mother's Offering to her Children*, 1841, and James A., Australia's first agricultural writer. She was educ. by her mother, who inspired LA's strong interest in botany and zoology. Some of her articles on Australian natural history have been reprinted in *A Voice from the Country*, 1978, and *Excursions from Berrima*, 1980. Her first novel, *Gertrude the Emigrant*, 1857 (originally pub. in threepenny weekly parts, each with a lively illustration by her), was the first to be published by an Australian-born woman. It relates life in the bush from the perspective of a newcomer and a woman, as an alternative to the better-known male adventure stories. Another pastoral novel, *Cowanda, the Veteran's Grant*, 1959, was followed by four others, serialized in the *Sydney Mail*: only one, *Tom Hellicar's Children*, 1983, has been pub. separately. She m. the explorer J. S. C. in 1869 and died in childbirth. See E. Lawson in D. Adelaide, ed., *A Bright and Fiery Troop*, 1988.

Attacks on women. What is often called the *querelle des femmes* stemmed from Juvenal and other ancient and medieval writers. It was re-activated, first in Europe and then in England, as a genre for women as well as men, by the work of CHRISTINE DE PIZAN, and ran strongly till the seventeenth century. Hundreds of published attacks on women as writers, or more generally as minds, provoked many rebuttals from writers of each sex, sometimes with deceptive pseudonyms. See Joan Kelly in *Signs*, 7, 1982; for attacks to 1568 see Francis Lee Utley, *The Crooked Rib*, 1944, repr. 1970; for Renaissance controversy see studies by Katharine M. Rogers, 1966; Linda Woodbridge, 1984; Katherine Usher Henderson and Barbara F. McManus, 1985. *A Lyttle Treatyse called the Image of Idlenesse*, 1558–9, reads like a burlesque of the debate. Notable attacks include those by Charles Bansley, 1548, John Knox, 1558, King James I, Joseph Swetnam, 1615 (answered by Rachel SPEGHT and others), John Taylor, 1639 (see 'Mary TATTLEWELL'), Robert Gould (answered by Sarah FYGE, 1686, and by 'SYLVIA', 1688), and the Rev. John Sprint (answered by Mary

CHUDLEIGH and 'EUGENIA', 1700 and 1701). The learned lady was a stock stage target (in Ben Jonson's *Volpone*, 1606, and many English versions of Molière's *Les Précieuses Ridicules*, 1659; as well as Aphra BEHN, 1678, and Susanna CENTLIVRE, 1705). So, from her emergence, was the female dramatist (MANLEY, PIX, and TROTTER attacked by W. M., 1697, and 'Phoebe Clinket', probably not intended for Anne FINCH, by Pope, Gay, and Arbuthnot, 1717). William Beckford, Elizabeth HERVEY's brother, savaged women novelists in 1796–7; Richard Polwhele savaged radicals in *The Unsex'd Females*, 1798. The old style of attack, reflecting full-blown masculinist ideology, haunts the margins of later works which are corrective, like George ELIOT's 'Silly Novels by Lady Novelists', or reactionary, like Eliza Lynn LINTON's 'The Girl of the Period', 1868, and other essays.

Atwood, Margaret Eleanor, poet, novelist, short-story writer, writer for children, critic, editor. B. 1939 in Ottawa, da. of Margaret (Killam) and entomologist Dr Carl Edmund A., whose research took the family in summers to the northern Ontario and Québec bush, 1939–61. The imprint of these years, during which MA was educated by her mother at home, then attended Leaside High School in Toronto, 1952–7, is evident in her preoccupation with 'metamorphosis' and the wilderness, explored in works like the novel *Surfacing*, 1972, and the poetry books *Power Politics*, 1971, *The Journals of Susanna MOODIE*, 1970, and *The Circle Game*, 1967 (her first book, winner of the Governor General's Award, like *The Handmaid's Tale*, 1985). She attended Victoria College, Univ. of Toronto (BA, 1961), where, influenced by Northrop Frye and Jay MACPHERSON, she 'discover[ed]' Canadian literature and won the E. J. Pratt Medal for Poetry for *Double Persephone*, 1961. She went as a Woodrow Wilson Fellow to Radcliffe College, Harvard (AM, 1962, in Victorian literature), and began doctoral studies, 1962–3, interrupted to work in Toronto for a market research company, 1963–4, and to teach at the Univ. of British Columbia, 1964–5. She returned to Harvard, 1965–7, intending to write a dissertation on the English metaphysical GOTHIC romance, a genre whose conventions she parodies, for the purpose of exposing contemporary society's threats to her predominantly female protagonists, in, for instance, the 'anti-gothic' *Lady Oracle*, 1976. At Harvard, she met and m. James Polk, 1967. They divorced, 1973, and she moved to a farm near Alliston, Ontario, with novelist Graeme Gibson. Their daughter was born in 1976. They have lived in Toronto since 1980. MA is one of the most astute critics of Canadian culture and literature. *Survival* is 'a diagram of Canadian literature' which explores the 'common themes' of Canadian aesthetic identity. Her publications have passed ten collections of poetry, six novels, two short-story collections (*Dancing Girls*, 1977, and *Bluebeard's Egg*, 1983), and two books for children (*Up in the Tree*, 1978, and, with her aunt Joyce Barkhouse, *Anna's Pet*, 1980). Her work has been translated into many languages. A full-time writer who often lectures in Canada and abroad, MA has been editor of Anansi Press in Toronto, 1971–3, and President of the Writers' Union of Canada, 1982–3. Wit, irony, and control of form, together with an interest in classical and popular mythologies, especially those concerning women, characterize both her fictional and poetic styles. Her vision of 'duplicity', whether sinister or oracular, distrusts the veneer of self – 'and I'm dragged to the mind's / dead-end, the roar of the bone- / yard' (*The Animals in That Country*, 1968) – a central theme in works like *Edible Woman*, 1969, *Lady Oracle*, 1976, *Life Before Man*, 1979, and *Bodily Harm*, 1981. The great impact of these novels on women readers comes partly from MA's daring exploration of the ramifications of feminism in political and social contexts together with her ability to keep in sight the tenacity of women's domestic roles as mothers and lovers. Her intricate and poignant novel, *The Handmaid's Tale*, treats a futuristic, bleak, totalitarian society where women are virtually denied all rights. Using the creative process as a recurring metaphor, but continually re-shaping the naming act of language, MA's aesthetics rely on questions – 'We know the names by now; / will that make anything better?' (*Two-Headed Poems*, 1978) – paradox, and the ambivalence of elliptical and aphoristic discourse – 'You can't take another poem of spring, not with the wound-up vowels, not with the bruised word green in it' (*Murder in the Dark*, 1983). *Cat's Eye*, 1988, explores the secrecies and cruelties of childhood from the point of view of a middle-aged painter, Elaine Risley, who does not want to taint her personal and artistic accomplishments with the labels of any feminist or aesthetic movements. The poems in *Interlunar*, 1988, question both myths and common life. No other Canadian author has generated such critical response in Canada and abroad. See Arnold E. Davidson and Cathy N. Davidson, eds., 1981, Frank Davey, 1984, and Jerome H. Rosenberg, 1984.

Aubin, Penelope, *c.* 1685–1731, novelist, poet, translator (publishing by name), friend of Elizabeth Rowe. B. in England, da. of a French émigré, she lavishly praised Queen Anne in Pindaric odes of 1707 and 1708. After a long silence, she hit in 1721 a high level of productivity: seven – shortish – novels in eight years (plus three translated from French), beginning with *The Strange Adventures of the Count de Vinevil and his Family* ('If this Trifle sells,' says the preface, 'you may be sure to hear of me again') and *The Life of Madam de Beaumount* [not, as often given, Beaumont], *a French Lady*, both facs. 1973. Vinevil gets to Constantinople and Greece; later works cover Madagascar (pirates), the Barbary coast and the West Indies (slavery) and China (missionaries and martyrdom). The support for Roman Catholicism (with many portraits of good priests) is bold and remarkable for its date. Virtue is always preserved from peril: Mme de Beaumount spends 14 years hidden in a Welsh cave, but it is well appointed and she is tended by servants. The lengthy, descriptive title-pages often open a new paragraph for a new generation: *Count Albertus*, 1728, is son to *The Lady Lucy*, 1726 (facs. 1973). The prefaces admit the need to make a living (though Elizabeth Griffith says PA's husband held a government post), while reflecting strong moral intent and High Tory patriotism. In 1729 she gave public orations and in 1730 spoke the epilogue on night two of her surprizingly bawdy and flippant comedy, *The Merry Masqueraders, or The Humorous Cuckold*. The Abbé Prevost, though influenced by her, attacked her in print in 1734; Samuel Richardson probably wrote the preface to her *Histories and Novels*, collected 1739 (some repr.).

Audland, Anne (Newby), later Camm, 1627–1705, Quaker preacher and pamphleteer, da. of Richard N., b. at Kendal and sent at 13 to school in London, where she joined a group of Seekers. She m. John A. about 1650; they had a daughter and son, were converted to Quakerism by George Fox in 1652 and both became preachers. She was imprisoned at Auckland, Co. Durham, in 1654 and at Banbury, 1655, for 18 months. She pub. from prison *A True Declaration*, 1655 (with Jane Waugh), which describes the trial of herself and others for blasphemy and asserts her right to argue face-to-face with her accusers (repr. the same year in the collectively written *The Saints Testimony*, in which she had a part). John A. died in 1664; two years later she m. Thomas C., with whose father and (probably) sister they had been closely connected. She contributed to his *Memory of the Righteous Revived*, 1689, a testimony and letter to John A., saying of her first marriage, 'our hearts being knit together in the unspeakable Love of Truth, which was our Life, Joy and Delight... made our days together exceeding comfortable'.

Aulnoy, Marie-Catherine La Mothe (Jumelle de Berneville), baronne d', 1649–1705, French writer of gothic, romantic and realistic fiction. English versions of her many works (some under varying titles) were highly influential. They were often repr. from 1691 to 1817, and some recently. She was a pioneer in several coming genres: travels, fictional letters, fairy stories, medieval tales and Court memoirs. A supposed autobiography, transl. 1699, which gave her feminist and scandalous repute, was actually written about someone else. Her lives of French poets were a model for Samuel Johnson. Her *Diverting Works*, 1707, includes new translations (some of tales not by her). See Melvin D. Palmer in *CL* 27, 1975, on her works in English, with a bibliog.

Austen, Jane, 1775–1817, novelist, b. at Steventon, Hants., youngest child but one of the prosperous, well-connected Cassandra (Leigh), whose cousins Cassandra COOKE and Cassandra HAWKE wrote novels, and the Rev. George A., who educated her at home. She read widely (many women, notably Mary BRUNTON, both BURNEYS, Maria EDGEWORTH, Anne GRANT, Elizabeth HAMILTON, L. M. HAWKINS, A. M. PORTER, Jane WEST, H. M. WILLIAMS) and wrote from an early age. The sparkling satires of her teens, pub. this century, show a practised hand; she began a draft of the later *Pride and Prejudice* in 1796. *Love and Freindship* parodies sentiment, *The History of England* pomposity, and *Lesley Castle* the epistolary form. *Lady Susan* may date from later. In 1803 she sold the MS of *Susan* (later *Northanger Abbey*) to Crosby, who dashed her hopes by deciding not to publish. Her father died in 1805 at Bath, where they had lived for four years, and after several moves JA, her sister Cassandra and her mother settled in 1809 in Chawton Cottage, Hants., to a life whose busy comings and goings are charted in her letters, but whose intimate details have been lost by Cassandra's censoring of the letters, and by her brother Henry's memoir, 1818. She fostered work on a novel by her niece Anna (Austen) Lefroy, later a children's writer. (Another niece was Catherine HUBBACK.) Having drafted two more novels and the unfinished *The Watsons*, JA pub. *Sense and Sensibility* at her own expense, 'by a Lady', 1811. Next came *Pride and Prejudice*, 1813 (earlier *First Impressions*), *Mansfield Park*, 1814, and *Emma*, 1816. *Northanger Abbey* and *Persuasion* appeared in 1818; *Sanditon* remained unfinished (for chronology see Brian Southam, 1964). JA's decorous social comedies of country gentry deal with women's training for life and the role expected of them. Her ironic narrative subjects systems of authority to damaging scepticism; she celebrates intellect, feeling, and moral sense in her heroines and ridicules their absence in others. With concerns close to Mary WOLLSTONECRAFT's, she adopts a conservative approach to accommodating women's aspirations to existing social structures. Walter Scott ranked her high, but Charlotte BRONTË found her passionless, and Victorian women novelists, except Harriet MARTINEAU, did not esteem her. Virginia WOOLF recognized her stature, 1922; R. W. Chapman ed. her *Works*, 1926, 1954, and letters, 2nd ed. 1952; Jo Modert her MS letters in facs., 1989. F. R. Leavis made her the cornerstone of *The Great Tradition*, 1948. Among a wealth of comment, see Mary Lascelles, 1939, Janet Todd, ed., 1983, Mary Poovey, 1984, Claudia L. Johnson, 1988; bibliog. by David Gilson, 1982; critics on JA ed. Southam, 1968, 1987; life by Deidre Le Faye, 1990.

Austen, Katherine, 1628–83, diarist, of London. Her husband Thomas (d. 1658) left her well off but barred from marrying for seven years. Her MS album (BL) dates chiefly from late in this time. Opening with a religious poem 'On the Birds Singing in my Garden', it includes notes of sermons heard, dreams and supernatural phenomena; 'Meditations in Poesy' (often on family deaths) and in prose; complaints of a sister-in-law's unkindness and of the pride and bad manners of academics; and debates with herself about re-marriage, which she decided against for reasons of past love and loyalty, her three children's interests and the prospect of legal extinction.

Austin, Jane (Goodwin), 1831–94, historical and children's novelist, short-story and prose writer. B. Worcester, Mass., probably only child of Elizabeth (Hammatt), poet, and Isaac G., lawyer, historian and *Mayflower* descendant, she was educated at Boston private schools. M. in 1850 to Loring Henry A., she had three children and lived in Boston. Family records inspired her early unpublished writing about her Pilgrim ancestors; she then ceased writing while caring for her children until, in 1859, she published her first work, *Fairy Dreams*; by 1892 she had written more than 20 books, mostly juvenile fiction recreating early American history. In her preface to *David Alden's Daughter and Other Stories of Colonial Times*, 1892, JA explains how through careful research she had noted some sturdy popular errors in accounts of history; through fiction she aimed to correct such errors by re-examining early events which had been recounted without recognition of the role of women; thus she gave prominence to the 'Pilgrim Mothers: the Anglo-British-Saxon-Norman woman perfected under an American sky ... the women who were not aware of their own importance' (*Standish of Standish*, 1889, Ch 1). JA's best known works are this and other Pilgrim novels for children: *A Nameless Nobleman*, 1881, *Dr Le Baron and his Daughters*, 1890, and *Betty Alden*, 1891. Earlier novels include *Dora Darling*, 1864, a children's civil-war fiction with a strong-minded, independent young heroine who joins the Union as a vivandière while her father and brother support the Confederacy, and *Cipher*, 1869, dedicated to her friend Louisa May Alcott for her ready sympathy and interest in the novel's construction, although there is no real evidence that Alcott collaborated with her. JA reproduced dialect, especially Negro, painstakingly and accurately. Some of her best writing is in *Nantucket Scraps*, 1882, where, losing her tendency towards sensationalism, she writes an informative and readable account of the day-to-day life of the 1880s inhabitants of Nantucket as well as relating local legends and history.

Austin, Mary (Hunter), 1868–1934, novelist, b. Carlinville, Ill., second da. of Susannah Savilla (Graham) and George H., barrister. She wrote poetry as a child and gained her BSc at Blackborn College in 1888, the year the family moved to a homestead on the edge of the Mojave Desert. In 1891 she m. Stafford Wallace A. (later divorced). They had one daughter, a congenital idiot. Her experiences crystallized in the ecologically sensitive books *The Flock*, 1906, and the Western classic, *The Land of Little Rain*, 1905 (repr. 1988), which present the desert ecosystem as a living force. MA's lifelong interest in Indian culture is reflected in *The Basket Woman*, 1904, *The American Rhythm*, 1923, and *The Children Sing in the Far West*, 1928. Feminist concerns are addressed in novels such as *Santa Lucia*, 1908, an examination of marriage through the stories of three women, and *A Woman of Genius*, 1912, a semi-autobiographical novel on competing claims of work and marriage. Lonely and neglected as a child, at age five she had a mystical experience, reflected later in works such as *The Lovely Lady*, 1913, *Outland* 1919 (with George Sterling; joint pen-name 'George Stairs'), and *Starry Adventure*, 1931. She recognized a more intuitive self, 'I-Mary', who wrote her novels in a trance-like state. She travelled to Rome while ill to perfect prayer techniques; recovered; and in London met Shaw, Yeats, Conrad and H. G. Wells. On her return to the USA in 1910 she lectured on her theories of Indian poetic rhythms. She campaigned for suffrage and birth control and joined the artistic circle of Mabel D. LUHAN; Willa CATHER wrote *Death Comes to the Archbishop* in the New Mexico house MA shared with her niece. Her autobiography, *Earth Horizon*, 1932, focuses on the constrictions faced by a gifted woman in a conventional world. See biographies by Augusta Fink, 1983, and Esther Lanigan Stineman, 1989. Some of her letters appear in T. M. Pearce, ed., *Literary America, 1903–1934*; her papers are in the Huntington Library.

Austin, Sarah (Taylor), 1793–1867, translator, b. Norwich, youngest of seven children of Susannah (Cook), a remarkable letter-writer, and John T., yarn-maker. Under her mother's supervision, she learnt German (which she later taught to J. S. Mill), French, Italian and Latin. Soon after her marriage in 1819, she began translating partly to support her husband and da. Lucie (later Lucie Duff GORDON). Her first notable effort was a rendering of French, Provençal and German medieval lyrics in *Lays of the Minnesingers*, 1825 (with Edgar Taylor). Her translation of Prince Pückler-Muskau's outspoken *Tour in England, Ireland and France*, 1832, led to a romantic correspondence with the author. She also transl. *Characteristics of Goethe*, 1833, and Leopold von Ranke's seminal *Ecclesiastical and Political History of the Popes*, 1840, and *History of the Reformation in Germany*, 1845, as well as *Fragments from German Prose Writers*, 1841, and F. W. Carove's popular children's tale, *The Story Without an End*, 1834. Translations from French included Guizot's *On the Causes of the Success of the English Revolution of 1640–1688*, 1850, and the Marquise d'Harcourt's memoir of the Duchess of Orleans, 1859. Keenly interested in working-class education, she pub. *On National Education* in 1839. Other original works were her *Life of Carsten Niebuhr*, 1833, and a social-intellectual history, *Germany from 1760 to 1814*, 1854. Although she supported girls' education, she thought it imprudent and unseemly to do so publicly. Her very cautious attitude to the WOMAN QUESTION is evident in her preface to the vol. of letters she ed. for Lady Holland's *Memoir of the Rev. Sydney Smith*, 1854. See her granddaughter Janet Ross's *Three Generations of Englishwomen*, 1888; and L. and J. Hamburger, *Troubled Lives: John and Sarah Austin*, 1985.

Autobiography. Marjery KEMPE composed the first one in English. Religious allegiance led many seventeenth-century women to set down what was for them the core of their lives: the spiritual tradition lasted well into the nineteenth century, while the secular genre, both subjective and domestic, held on through Anne HALKETT, Margaret NEWCASTLE and Alice THORNTON to Hester PIOZZI and M. A. RADCLIFFE (see Felicity Nussbaum, *The Autobiographical Subject: Gender and Ideology in Eighteenth-Century England*, 1989). Mary ROWLANDSON's first CAPTIVITY-NARRATIVE fed into sensation fiction. For the sensation autobiography of criminals or (often sexually) notorious women, see Nussbaum in her and Laura Brown, eds., *The New Eighteenth Century*, 1987. A few of her texts are probably male ventriloquism, though Charlotte CHARKE, Grace ELLIOTT, Laetitia PILKINGTON, and Lady STRATHMORE certainly, and T. C. PHILLIPS probably, wrote for themselves. Accounts of soldiers and sailors in male disguise – in Britain Christian (Cavenaugh) Davies, 1667–1739, and Hannah Snell, 1723–92 (Augustan Repr. 1988), in the US Almira Paul, b. 1790, and Emma Cole, 1775?–1829 – were fictionalized, some posthumously. Mary Ann (Thompson) Clarke, *c.* 1776–1852, took at least £1000 to suppress the story of her life as the Duke of York's mistress and illicit arbiter of army careers (her work was sighted at auction in 1930 but again lost sight of). Margaret (Moncrieff) Coghlan, born in America, raised in

Ireland, and Margaret (Plunket) Leeson, Irish, pub. memoirs in 1794 and 1797 which combine sentiment, moralizing, and scandal about eminent lovers. Minor writers like Ann CANDLER, Alison COCKBURN and Mary COLLIER, produced fine mini-life-stories in response to interest in their work. Full, imaginative yet secular self-depiction arrived with e.g. Elizabeth GRANT, M. A. SCHIMMELPENNINCK and M. M. SHERWOOD. Later in the nineteenth century much literary re-creation of female experience passed to the novel. Most autobiographers were attentive to propriety, though they included actresses like Mary ROBINSON and Annie Kemble, 1809–93, and Medora Leigh, 1814–49, thought to be the daughter of Byron and his half-sister, whose story of sexual abuse from her brother-in-law was published posthumously. Family history and the less personal forms of reminiscence and recollection were favoured by upper-class women (e.g. Lady Brownlow, pub. 1868, Lady Rose Graves Sawle, from diaries of 1833–96, and suffragette Adelaide Drummond, 1915). Sydney MORGAN apologized for writing; Margaret OLIPHANT explored the conflicting demands of family and career, but Harriet MARTINEAU, Annie BESANT and Beatrice WEBB wrote 'developmental' works about their careers which stem from the earlier tradition of spiritual conversion narratives; Elizabeth Cady STANTON wrote about her personal life and her activism. Lucy LARCOM, Margaret FULLER and Catharine SEDGWICK explored childhood. Rare records of working women include Mary Ann Ashford, 1844. Pioneer women like Susanna MOODIE wrote to cheer and inform prospective emigrant gentlewomen; TRAVEL autobiographies like that of Isabella BIRD had many readers. SLAVE NARRATIVES served the abolitionist cause and began a black tradition: Mary PRINCE in London and Martha BROWNE (d. 1906) in the USA dictated their narratives; Elizabeth KECKLEY's is probably ghostwritten; but Harriet JACOBS wrote her own. Mary Ann Loughborough, 1836–87, and Mary CHESNUT wrote about the US Civil War. Among non-literary women, Mary DOOLITTLE wrote as a Shaker, Mary Baker EDDY as Christian Science leader, and Clara BARTON as founder of the US Red Cross. This century the democratization process has accelerated, with thousands of life-stories by women in every conceivable occupation: artists Janet Scudder, 1869–1940, and Emily CARR; dancer Isadora Duncan, 1877–1927; activist Emmeline PANKHURST; socialist Ethel MANNIN (7 vols.); prostitute 'Madeleine', pub. 1919; blind-deaf Helen Keller, 1880–1968; migrants around the world, like Lorna SALVERSON in Canada and Mary ANTIN in the USA; minority members like Canadian métis Maria CAMPBELL; movie stars (hundreds of often ghost-written lives) and sportswomen; politicians like Emma GOLDMAN, Dorothy DAY, Golda Meir, and Eleanor ROOSEVELT, whose work Patricia Spacks sees as a 'female variant' on spiritual autobiography, which counters achievement by a self-denying 'rhetoric of uncertainty'. Translated autobiographies have been important to English-speaking readers: from German (Christa WOLF), and French (Flora Tristan, 1803–44, Simone de BEAUVOIR, Nathalie Sarraute, b. 1902, Marguerite DURAS). Portraits of the artist as child and young woman became prominent: Rebecca WEST's self-defining *Family Memories*; Virginia WOOLF's fragments about family, 'moments of being', and tedious social expectations of femininity; May SARTON's remembrance of herself as a child in relation to nature. Childhood milieus are recreated: working-class London by Angela Rodaway, b. 1918, Kenya by Elspeth HUXLEY, Beryl Markham, 1902–86, and (during the Emergency) Charity WACIUMA. Margaret MEAD records early experience of matriarchs; so does H. D., who like Rosamond LEHMANN and Mary AUSTIN treats intimations of vocation which make another variant on spiritual autobiography. Henry Handel RICHARDSON and Mary MCCARTHY each present a girls' school as formative; Janet FRAME's journey towards authorship leads through poverty-ridden childhood and years in a mental institution through misdiagnosis. Eudora WELTY discovers that a 'sheltered life can be a daring life as well. For all serious daring starts from within.' Gertrude ATHERTON, Mabel Dodge LUHAN and Edith WHARTON give more space to anecdotes of others than their proclaimed search for identity as writers, while others detail careers as well as personal lives (Beatrice WEBB, Charlotte Perkins GILMAN, Ella Wheeler WILCOX, Edna FERBER, Pearl BUCK, Margaret ANDERSON). Vera BRITTAIN chronicled the century. Zora Neale HURSTON 'translated' her black childhood for white readers, but is sketchy and inaccurate on her later career. Dramatic and fictional techniques are vital to Gertrude STEIN (in her *tour de force* in self-focalization through Alice TOKLAS' voice), Lillian HELLMAN, and Maxine Hong KINGSTON (whose self-reflexive narrative mimes the inscription on her body and her consciousness of Chinese and US gender identities). Since the 1960s the intersection of racial and feminist consciousness has joined that of class and gender as a favoured site for constructing an identity: see Maya ANGELOU, Gwendolyn BROOKS, Nikki GIOVANNI, Lorraine HANSBERRY, Nawal EL SAADAWI. Feminist and civil rights activism nourish each other in Shirley Chisholm, b. 1924, Anne Moody, b. 1940, Angela DAVIS, and Winnie Mandela. In a memoir 'of incest and healing' Sylvia FRASER recreated the 'Girl Who Knew' and the 'Girl Who Didn't Know'. Sexual experience is important in the self-scrutiny of Kamala DAS (heterosexual) and, among lesbians, Valentine ACKLAND, Rosemary MANNING (who added a second autobiographical work as she set her name to the first, previously pseudonymous), Barbara Deming, b. 1917, her friend and former lover Mary Meigs (3 vols. on her life as artist and lesbian), Sharon Isabell, b. 1942, and Kate MILLETT. See essays ed. Estelle Jelinek, 1980, Domna Stanton, 1984, 1987, Shari Benstock, 1988, Celeste Schenck and Bella Brodzki, 1988; studies by Jelinek, 1986, Sidonie Smith, 1987, Carolyn HEILBRUN, 1988. See also ORAL TRADITION.

Avery, Elizabeth (Parker), religious controversialist, da. of Dorothy and of Puritan divine Robert P., relation by marriage of Anne BRADSTREET: wife of a commissioner in Ireland. She suffered 'an horror, as if I were in Hell' at the deaths of her children, till religious guidance enabled her to 'bear it very well' and even 'rejoyce to be thus tryed'. Bereft of faith or hope for herself, she yet retained her love for 'Gods people', till she heard a voice saying 'sorrow thou shalt see no more.' Living at Newbury, Berks., she pub. with her name *Scripture-Prophecies Opened*, 1647 (originally three letters to friends). In unwieldy, quotation-stuffed but vigorous style she argues a close and technical case for expecting the end of the world and fall of Babylon. Since she means by Babylon both 'a State and a National Church', and since she finds the partly clay Kingdom superior to its head of gold, it is no wonder that churchmen attacked her: her brother Thomas P. of Newbury, New England, in *The Copy of a Letter*, 1650, in the name of her parents, husband, and other relations, berated her weak, presumptuous, fanciful 'attempt above your gifts and Sex'. The fifth-monarchy man John Rogers pub. her autobiographical testimony in *Ohel*, 1653.

Avison, Margaret, poet, reviewer, translator, social worker. B. in 1918 in Galt, Ont., da. of Mabel Clara (Kirkland) and minister Harold Wilson A., she spent part of her childhood in western Canada and now lives in Toronto, where she was educ. (Univ. of Toronto, BA 1940, MA 1964). She also studied creative writing at the Univs. of Indiana (1955) and Chicago (1956–7). She began writing in 1939 and was one of the important Canadian poets (including P. K. PAGE, Dorothy LIVESAY,

Miriam Waddington and Jay Macpherson) who were first published by Alan Crawley in the influential *Contemporary Verse*, 1940–52. Included in all major anthologies of Canadian poetry of the 1950s and 1960s even before she published her two books (1960, 1966), later collected together in *Winter Sun / The Dumbfounding: Poems 1940–66*, 1982, and also published in *Poetry* (Chicago) and *Kenyon Review*, MA was called 'the richest, most original, most fully and deeply engaged and therefore the most significant [poet] since the modern [Canadian] movement got under way'. Her metaphysical and modernist poetry, thought difficult and hermetic because 'what she experiences is "mysterious"', has also been associated with the 'projective verse' movement, especially after publication from 1957 by Cid Corman in *Origin*. She wrote many reviews of poets, including Edith Sitwell. Interested in paradox and language 'for both release and illumination', she centres the transfiguration of the self in the 'optic heart' which 'must venture: a jail-break / And re-creation. Sedges and wild rice / Chase rivery pewter'. Converted on 4 January 1963, she emerged as a deeply religious poet. In her latest book, *sunblue*, 1978, her ongoing attempt to rid the soul of 'undeathful technicalities' reveals to her 'Indoors promises / such creatureliness as disinhabits / a cold layered beauty / flowing out there', a vision informed by 'your all-creating stillness, shining Lord'. Recipient of the Governor General's Award, MA has worked at the Women's Missionary Society of the Presbyterian Church since 1968. See David Kent, ed., *'Lighting up the terrain': The poetry of MA*, 1987, Ernest Redekop, 1970, and Mia Anderson in *SCanL*, 6, 1981.

Ayres, Ruby Mildred, 1883–1955, popular novelist, author of 'good, clean love stories' whose sales are reported to have surpassed eight million. Da. of an architect, she was born in Watford, Herts., and m. London insurance broker Reginald William Pocock in 1909. She wrote about 150 books – 'First I fix the price. Then I fix the title. Then I write the book' – from *Castles in Spain*, 1912, to *Dark Gentleman*, 1953. Romantic fantasy peopled with stereotypical men and women, her plots are enlivened by misunderstandings, coincidence and other difficult circumstances that delay, but rarely prevent, the marriage of their generally well-to-do heroines to even wealthier heroes. Many were filmed and many serialized in newspapers, like the *Daily Chronicle* and *Daily Mirror*, and magazines. She also wrote short stories and a play, *Silver Wedding*, produced 1932. Brief mention in Alan Jenkins, *The Twenties*, 1974, quoted above.

'Ayrton, J. Calder', Mary F. Chapman, 1838–84, novelist, b. Dublin, where her father had a job in the custom house. She moved with her parents to England and was educ. at school in Staplehurst, Kent. Her first novel, *Mary Bertrand*, was partly composed when she was 15 and pub. under the pseudonym 'Francis Meredith' in 1860. As J. C. Ayrton she wrote three novels. The first, *Lord Bridgenorth's Niece*, 1862, shows a cool awareness of motives for marriage and uses the plot device of ambiguity about the identity of the heroine's intended husband. In 1869 she wrote an historical tale with her father, 'Bellasis; or, The Fortunes of a Cavalier', for *The Churchman's Family Magazine* and then, after a stay with her brother, a clergyman of the Scotch Episcopal Church, she wrote *A Scotch Wooing*, 1875 (the first of her books to attract attention). In her next three-vol novel, *Gerald Marlowe's Wife*, 1876, she focuses on the differences in female and male perception and self-awareness, since the whole story of the marriage of its strong heroine (with radical views on the Woman Question) is described through the diaries and journals of her governess and husband. Her last novel, *The Gift of the Gods*, 1879, was the only one pub. under her own name.

Ayscough, Florence (Wheelock), later MacNair, 1875–1942, sinologue, translator, biographer. B. in Shanghai, of an American mother and Canadian businessman father, she was educated privately there, then at school in Brookline, Mass. She returned to Shanghai, married Frank A., an English importer, and became a passionate student of Chinese language, literature and culture. In 1917 she took to the USA a collection of Chinese paintings, including some 'Written Pictures'. These sparked her collaboration with childhood friend Amy LOWELL. FA translated Chinese poetry, by analysis of characters and their 'ideogram mothers', and Lowell rendered them in 'unrhymed cadence'. Their work appeared in Harriet MONROE's *Poetry*, then in *Fir-Flower Tablets*, 1921, a 'cracker-jack book', whose title comes from the tale of a Chinese woman poet. It includes FA's account of her principles of translation. Widowed, she married H. F. MacNair in 1935 and returned to Chicago. She wrote eight other books about China, including *Chinese Women Yesterday and Today*, 1939, whose 'mandrel', the woman warrior Ch'iu Chin, wrote: 'We women love our freedom, / Raise a cup of wine to our efforts for freedom; / May Heaven bestow equal power on men, women. / Is it sweet to live lower than cattle?' H. F. MacNair ed. *Florence Ayscough and Amy Lowell: Correspondence of a Friendship*, 1945, and *The Incomparable Lady*, 1946. Harvard, the Library of Congress, and the Univ. of Chicago have some of her letters, books and rubbings.

B

Bâ, Mariama, 1929–81, Senegalese francophone novelist and feminist, b. in Dakar of prominent Muslim parents. Her civil servant and politician father was the first Minister of Health appointed in Senegal, 1956; her mother died when she was very young. Brought up by traditional, strict, maternal grandparents, she owes to her grandmother 'a sharp sense of virtue and honor' and to her father his insistence, against family opposition, that she have a good French education, which he gave her himself. She attended the Berthe Maubert elementary school and in 1943 was first in West Africa in the entrance examination to the Rufistique Ecole Normale. Two of the essays she wrote there were published. She m. a prominent Senegalese politician, Obéye Diop (later divorced), had nine children and worked as a secretary and primary school teacher. Active in several women's organizations – 'We do not have time to waste if we are going to bring something better to African women' – she wrote and spoke on feminist issues: women's legal rights in marriage and child custody, clitoridectomy, the need for women's education, and polygamy, a major subject of her fiction. MB won the first Noma Award for her first novel, 'a testimony of the female condition in Africa ... [of] true imaginative depth', *Une Si Longue Lettre*, 1980, immediately widely translated. *Le Chant Ecarlate*, 1981, followed, but MB died before its publication. Both the lyrical, epistolary *So Long a Letter*, and *Scarlet Song*, address the issue of polygamy: 'The fate of these two women', MB said, 'can be summed up in one word: suffering – having to keep quiet, suffering to the very last'. See Lauretta NGCOBO in *South African Outlook*, May 1984; Edris Makward in Davies and Graves, 1986 (which is dedicated to MB, 'Whose commitment and African feminism made works such as this one necessary'); Mbye B. Cham in Jones, 1987; Charles P. Sarvan in *MFS*, 34, 1988.

Bacon, Alice Mabel, 1858–1918, educator and author, b. New Haven, Conn., da. of Catherine and Rev. Leonard B., professor at Yale Divinity School and abolitionist, and niece of Delia BACON. Educ. at home, she passed three subject examinations in the 1881 Harvard examinations for women. During 1883–8 she taught at Hampton (Va.) Normal and Agricultural Institute and from 1888–9 at the Peeresses' School in Tokyo. She helped found Dixie Hospital, primarily in response to the denial of medical training to blacks. In 1891 she pub. *Japanese Girls and Women*, in which she describes Japanese women as 'the neglected half' (Preface) and chronicles their new life following feudalism. *A Japanese Interior*, 1893, contains her letters from Japan. She returned to Japan in 1900 to teach in the newly-opened Girls' English Institute (Tsuda College), which pioneered advanced education for Japanese women. In 1905 she pub. *In the Land of the Gods*, a collection of Japanese folk tales; she also edited an American edition of Sakurai's *Human Bullets: A Soldier's Story of Port Arthur*, 1907. After teaching in Miss Capen's School, Northampton, Mass., 1908–10, she devoted the remainder of her life to the Dixie Hospital.

Bacon, Ann (Cooke), Lady, 1528–1610, translator (best in the sixteenth century, said C. S. Lewis), puritan and letter writer, second of the learned daughters of Anne

(Fitzwilliam) and Sir Anthony C. (The others were Mildred, Lady Burghley, who had a 'Vein in Poetry' and wrote notable letters and a version of St Crysostom which she refused to print; Katharine, Lady Killigrew, a poet in Latin; and Elizabeth, Lady RUSSELL. Lady Burghley's daughter Anne, Lady Oxford, left four moving sonnet-epitaphs on a baby son: with John Soowthern's *Pandora*, 1584.) AB read Greek, Latin, Italian and French fluently, and is said to have helped tutor Edward VI. In probably 1550 appeared her versions of 14 sermons by the Italian Calvinist Bernardino Ochino (repr. in various collections), with her initials, emphasis on her sex and rank, and a dedication to her mother, who had thought her Italian studies not conducive to the glory of God. She became, probably 1557, second wife of Sir Nicholas B. (d. 1579), and added two sons to six step-children. In 1562 John Jewel, Bishop of Salisbury, wrote in Latin the first Anglican polemical manifesto; finding the English version defective, she produced her own, *An Apologie* for the Church of England, pub. 1564 (ed. J. E. Booty, 1963). Matthew Parker, Archbishop of Canterbury, prefaced it with high praise. In letters she upheld the rights of dissenting preachers, 1584, and advised (or over-ruled in all things, said one) her distinguished sons (corresp. in James Spedding's life of Sir Francis B., i, 1862). She became more fiercely puritan with age. See Ruth Hughey in *RES*, x, 1934.

Bacon, Delia Salter, 1811–59, author, lecturer and originator of the theory that Francis Bacon wrote Shakespeare's plays. Da. of Alice (Parks) and the Rev. David B., congregationalist missionaries to the Indians, DSB was b. at Tallmadge, Ohio, in her father's model community. At 14 she attended Catharine BEECHER's Hartford seminary, where she was a classmate of H. B. STOWE. During 1826–32 she taught school in Conn., New Jersey and NYC. In 1833 she began popular lectures and dramatic readings for women, and met Elizabeth PEABODY and Caroline W. H. DALL. *Tales of the Puritans*, 1831 (pub. anon.), consists of three stories set in seventeenth-century New England. In 1831 her story 'Love's Martyr', based on the murder of Jane McCrea by Indians, won a prize offered by the Philadelphia *Saturday Courier*. *The Bride of Fort Edward*, 1839, describes in blank verse and dialogue form an incident in the Civil War in which a Southern girl marries a British officer. The lengthy blank verse soliloquies are stilted, but the soldiers' dialogue is often lively and convincing. In 1845 an unfortunate friendship with Alexander MacWhorter, a Yale theologian, resulted in legal action by DSB's brother Leonard and became the subject of Catharine Beecher's *Truth Stranger than Fiction*, 1850. Her Shakespeare theory aroused interest in England, and Emerson's influence gained space for it in *Putnam's Monthly*, 1856. Although Hawthorne rejected her theory, he wrote a Preface and helped her publish *The Philosophy of the Plays of Shakespeare Unfolded*, 1857. In England DSB became poverty-stricken, isolated and obsessed with her thesis. In 1858 she was taken back to the USA and institutionalized at Hartford Retreat for the Insane. See Vivian C. Hopkins, 1959, for her life.

Badruddin, Gitaujali, 1961–77, teenage poet, b. in Meerut. She died of cancer in Bombay at barely 16; her mother, Khushi B., determined to publish the remarkably moving poems which GB had left hidden to spare pain (she knew she was dying before her mother did). A few appeared in journals, 1979, and the collection of 110 was pub. as *Poems of Gitaujali*, 1982, to warm response in India and Britain. Her free verse shows remarkable poetic maturity, courage and composure in the face of pain. She addresses her father and her brother ('I have a big brother / But he is only big / In name'. 'I am being used / by God like a /

harp', she wrote, and concluded 'Nothing is unimportant / Not even death.'

Bagnold, Enid, Lady Jones, 1889–1981, novelist, playwright, and autobiographer b. at Rochester in Kent, da. of Ethel (Alger) and army officer Arthur Henry B. She wrote from the age of nine, spent 1899–1902 in Jamaica and attended schools run by Aldous Huxley's mother and in Europe. She mixed with artists and studied painting with Walter Sickert. She nursed in 'a vast, weary military hospital' but was dismissed when she described it in *A Diary Without Dates*, 1917. *The Sailing Ships*, 1918, is a poetry book. *The Happy Foreigner*, 1920, records driving an ambulance in France. That year she m. Sir Roderick Jones, head of Reuters news agency; they had four children, but agreed she should have three undisturbed writing hours daily. *Serena Blandish, or The Difficulty of Getting Married*, 1924 (as 'A Lady of Quality', by her father's wish), was likened to upper-class, English Anita LOOS. EB's daughter illustrated *Alice and Thomas and Jane*, 1930, for children, and *National Velvet*, 1935. This tale of a girl in disguise winning the world's most gruelling horse-race (then barred to women) was a hit on stage and screen as well as in print. EB's two last novels were *The Squire*, 1938 (*The Door of Life* in the USA), portraying pregnancy in a traditional milieu where ladies were ladylike, and *The Loved and Envied*, 1951, whose equally old-world setting was popular. Her eight plays began with *Lottie Dundas*, pub. 1941, about a stage-struck girl. Best known (chiefly for its rich elaboration of language) is *The Chalk Garden*, 1956, which makes a symbol of the effort to grow plants in grudging soil. *The Chinese Prime Minister*, about old age, did well in NYC, 1964; EB condemned the London production, 1965, as sentimental. Her last play, *Call Me Jacky*, 1968, was revised as *A Matter of Gravity*, 1976, with Katharine Hepburn as the *grande dame* in 'ten-buttoned elbow-length kid gloves'. EB pub. her AUTOBIOGRAPHY (both flighty and profound), 1969, and poems, 1979; many works, including her first, recently reprinted; lives by Lenemaja Friedman, 1986, A. Sebba, 1987.

Bailey, Hilary, novelist, journalist, critic, b. 1936 and now living in London. She was educ. at ten schools and Newnham College, Cambridge (BA in English, 1958), worked in publicity, married and had three children. After two serious novels of middle-class life, *Polly Put the Kettle On*, 1975, and *Mrs Mulvaney*, 1978, she produced a racy, 400,000-word picaresque, *All the Days of My Life*, 1984, chronicling the adventures of Molly Flanders and a cast of modern rogues and vagabonds over 60 years, ending in the 1990s. *Hannie Richards, or the Intrepid Adventures of a Restless Wife*, 1985, parodies John Buchan and Rider Haggard, with a female international smuggler who has money, love, women friends, a liberal conscience and membership of a London club for women in D'Arblay Street, Soho; her big advantage, she says, 'is that I can disguise myself as a woman, which, in most societies, means that no one notices you'. As well as many stories, periodical articles, and fiction reviews for the *Guardian*, HB has written a life (to WWII) of Vera BRITTAIN, 1987. *As Time Goes By*, 1988, deals with the sexual and financial entanglements of West Londoners; the middle-aged female protagonist becomes a successful writer. In *A Stranger to Herself*, 1989, a woman researches the life of an earlier woman.

Bailey, Mary (Walker), 1792–1873, poet, b. Gestingthorpe, Essex, to Margaretta (Jones) and Edward W. Educ. at home, she was encouraged to study Greek and Latin as well as modern languages by her maternal grandfather, the Rev. William Jones, an eminent scholar. She m. the Rev. William B. and, after his conviction for forgery and transportation to Van Diemen's Land, followed him to Hobart in 1844. By then she had pub. several devotional works and volumes of poetry, including *The Months*, 1833, and *Musae Sacrae: A Collection of Hymns and Sacred Poetry*, 1835. Though no further volumes appeared in Australia, she continued to write prolifically, publishing over 80 poems between 1846 and 1849 in the *Colonial Times*, then Hobart's leading paper, as well as many others elsewhere. These ranged from lyrics such as 'A Mother's Love' to satirical attacks on such local issues as 'The State of the Roads!' and also included many translations from Greek, Latin and Italian. In the *Colonial Times* for 8 May 1849, she claimed to be the first in Australia to attempt to translate the odes of Anacreon into English verse. She also taught private pupils at her home in 1846 and opened a girls' school in Hobart the following year. In 1858 the Baileys moved to Sydney, where Mary died, after a long illness, in 1873.

Bailey, Irene **Temple**, 1869?–1953, writer of highly POPULAR FICTION. B. at Petersburg, Va., da. of Emma (Sprague) and Milo Varnum B., she grew up and lived very privately in Washington, DC. Her escapist fictions for girls and women were usually serialized in magazines like *McCall's* and *Cosmopolitan*, then published as books. They feature virginal heroines, young love, conventional morality and happy endings. Selling in millions, TB was among the best-paid magazine writers. Her more than two dozen books begin with *Judy*, 1907, and include *Adventures in Girlhood*, 1917, *Little Girl Lost*, 1932, *Fair as the Moon*, 1935, and *Red Fruit*, 1945.

Baillie, Lady **Grisell** or Grizel (Hume), 1665–1746, Scots patriot and song writer. B. at Redbrae Castle, Berwicks., eldest child of Grisell (Ker) and Sir Patrick Hume (later 1st Earl of Marchmont), persecuted Presbyterians, she carried a secret message to Robert B. of Jerviswood before she was 12 and later kept her father alive for a month in hiding in the family burial vault on smuggled food. She wrote prose and verse from earliest youth. After Robert B. was martyred by hanging in 1684, her family fled to Holland. Her mother being (after 18 children) an invalid, she ran the household, and later said she was happy in exile. In 1688 she turned down a Court post, and in 1692 m. B.'s son George. He was an MP, 1708–34, so she lived much in London society; but she is known for her Scots song 'And werena my heart licht I wad dee', pub. 1726 and admired by Burns. Her daughter Grisell MURRAY owned an MS volume of her songs (now lost), many 'interrupted, half writ, some broken off in the middle of a sentence'; anthologists like Allan Ramsay may have printed some anonymously. William Aikman painted her; Joanna BAILLIE wrote of her. Her *Household Book* (meticulous accounts, directions to servants, etc.) was pub. 1911.

Baillie, Joanna, 1762–1851, poet and dramatist, da. of Dorothea (Hunter) and James B. (later divinity professor at Glasgow): niece of Anne HUNTER. She was b. at Bothwell, Lanarkshire: a twin sister d. at birth. Taught by an elder sister, she was a tomboy, a late reader but early verse writer; at boarding school she loved maths and wrote plays. The family moved to England in 1784, settling at Hampstead. In 1790 she pub. *Poems ... of Nature and of Rustic Manners* (charming, sensitive, treating oddities and variations in human moods). Sewing one day by her mother's side, 'imprisoned by the heat', she thought of writing plays and planned a sequence of *Plays on the Passions* (perhaps in reaction against being early taught to suppress all emotion). Her system (one comedy and one tragedy for each passion) does not adequately realize the boldly original ideas in her preface. The anonymous debut, *A Series of Plays* (two on love and one on hate), 1798 (facs. 1976), caused a furore: Mary BERRY sat up with it all night after a ball, guessing the author's sex only later from the heroines' nobleness; Hester PIOZZI guessed from their age; Elizabeth CARTER 'felt a triumph' when she knew. Sarah Siddons starred in *De Monfort*, the tragedy on hate, 1800 (epilogue by Georgiana DEVONSHIRE). Further vols. and reprs. mainly stuck to the plan: *Miscellaneous Plays*, 1804, gathers some that did not. JB drew on history, imagination and recent events. *The Family Legend* (on the fifteenth-century clans) was a stage success at Edinburgh in 1810, but she was criticized (e.g. by Elizabeth INCHBALD) for lack of stage-craft: her sonorously-voiced passions float unanchored; her comedies are too sweet. A visit to Scotland produced *Metrical Legends*, 1821 (repr. with *Family Legend*, 1976), one about Lady Grisell BAILLIE. JB edited a verse anthology, 1823 (several women), and kept writing into old age: a book (Unitarian in approach) on the nature of Christ, 1831, more plays, fine ballads, *Fugitive Verses*, 1840 (mostly repr.), and *Ahalya Baee, A Poem*, 1849, about an actual Indian female ruler. Friends included Lucy AIKIN, A. L. BARBAULD, Maria EDGEWORTH and Walter Scott, who likened her to Shakespeare. Attack by Francis Jeffrey, 1803, signalled the decline of her great reputation. *Works*, 1851; life by Margaret S. Carhart, 1923; MSS in National Library of Scotland.

Bainbridge, Beryl Margaret, actress, novelist, b. in 1933 in Liverpool, da. of Winifred (Baines) and salesman Richard B. She was educ. there, at Merchant Taylors' School, then trained in ballet at Tring, Herts. 'All my childhood was spent with people who were disappointed. They'd married the wrong person, failed in business, been manipulated by others'. She began acting (repertory theatre, TV, radio), m. painter Austin Davies in 1954, had three children and divorced in 1959. After the birth of her first child she turned to writing. Her first novel was rejected: publishers found her central characters 'repulsive beyond belief'. It eventually appeared in 1972 as *Harriet Says* ... BB's first book was *A Weekend with Claude*, 1967 (revised 1981). For a decade she averaged a novel a year; she also produced short stories (*Mum and Mr Armitage*, 1985), TV plays including (with Philip Seville) *The Journal of Bridget Hitler*, 1980, and a TV series, *Forever England*, an idiosyncratic, impressionistic tour of localities and local people. She made a book of this, 1987; she has recently made film or TV scripts of several of her novels. These stylistically distinguished, controversial works, like *A Quiet Life*, 1976, look with detached irony on blighted suburban families. BB calls herself a socialist and lapsed Catholic. Her surface realism is often disturbed by comic or gruesome intrusions: by clumsy, possibly accidental murders in *The Dressmaker*, 1973 (*The Secret Glass* in NY ed.), and *The Bottle Factory Outing*, 1974 (about a plant where BB had worked). *Young Adolf*, 1978, which combines a portrait of BB's father with an improbable reconstruction of possible events during a visit by Hitler to his brother in Liverpool in 1912, exemplifies her quirky, often *risqué*, fictional concerns. *An Awfully Big Adventure*, 1989, looks at love for 'people who love someone else' and at the prospect of death. She claims to be 'not very good at fiction ... it is always me and the experiences I have had'.

Baker, Dorothy (Dodds), 1907–68, novelist and short-story writer, b. at Missoula, Mont., da. of Alice (Grady) and railroad dispatcher Raymond Branson D. The family moved to Calif. After studying music and taking a BA at UCLA, 1929, she tried, unsuccessfully, a writing career in France, where she m. poet Howard B. in 1930: she said her 'greatest advantage' was 'the constant chastening criticism' of Howard B. and Yvor Winters. She had two daughters, returned to UCLA for an MA, 1934, and taught Latin. Encouraged by acceptance of a short story about teaching, she published a best-selling novel based on the life of jazz musician Leon Beiderbecke, *Young Man with a Horn*, 1938 (filmed 1950).

Her second novel, *Trio*, 1943, details a love triangle between a woman professor, a female student and a young male suitor for the student. The older woman is presented as villain, who introduces her young lover to sadomasochistic sex and alcohol; she commits suicide and boy gets girl. Though critics objected to over-moralizing, the Broadway version, 1944, was censored. After *Our Gifted Son*, 1948, and *The Street*, 1951 (novels), magazine stories, and a TV drama, *The Ninth Day*, 1957 (with her husband), came DB's major work, the novel *Cassandra at the Wedding*, 1962. This treats the relation between twin sisters: one about to marry, one who has relationships with women and is cynical about 'the proper marriage, the fashionable career, the non-irritating thesis that says nothing new and nothing true'. Though much troubled, she is spared the retribution meted out in *Trio*; Jane RULE, 1975, says DB's work is deepened and humanized by its shift from moral to psychological.

Baker, Ella, 1859–88, essayist, poet, novelist, who wrote only 'on request' and not for print, taught herself French, German, Italian and was educ. at home in Kingscote, Wokingham, Surrey, mainly by her sister Amy (author of *A First History of the English People*, four vols. 1888). Da. of Maria Louisa (Watkins) and barrister Thomas B., who pub. her works in 1888 after she died (of a bee-sting). His autobiography, *A Battling Life*, 1885, tells more of his own outspoken radical views than of his family. EB only wrote (1876–7) *Kingscote Essays and Poems*; *Kingscote Stories*; and (1885) *Bertram de Drumont: A Medieval Tale*, a plotful novel with touches of spirited feminist protest in the heroine Claudine, who wishes to join the Crusades with Bertram: '"May we never be free as men are?"'. Her work is stilted but shows insight in its critiques of imperialism ('The Indian's Protest') and hypocrisy. EB is confused by Allibone and Bentley's List with American Ella Maria B.

Baker, Louisa Alice (Dawson), 'Alien', 1858–1926, novelist, b. in Otago, da. of Amelia (Troup) and William D., a farmer. She wrote in the *Otago Witness* as 'Alice'. In 1894 she settled in England where she m. a Mr Baker and had two children. Her early novels, set in NZ, are full of dialogue on women's rights. *A Daughter of the King*, 1894, is about a woman's right to free herself from an unhappy marriage and 'the dark and lonely way where women are groping, now the lamps of faith in men are extinguished.' The heroine studies her own sex – in the streets, prisons, asylums – searching for 'the secret of woman's power' and finding only their subjugation. *The Majesty of Man*, 1895, contains arguments for and against separatism: women must leave men for a time, it argues, but eventually, 'man and woman are indissolubly one.' Its heroine is strongly attracted to the leader of a celibate separatist sisterhood. After *In Golden Shackles*, 1896, and *Wheat in the Ear*, 1898, feminism becomes diluted in a stream of popular fictions: *Another Woman's Territory*, 1901, *Not in Fellowship*, 1902, *His Neighbour's Landmark*, 1907, and others.

Baldwin, Faith, later Cuthrell, 'Amber Lee', 1893–1978, POPULAR novelist, b. in New Rochelle, NY, da. of Edith Hervey (Finch) and Stephen Charles B. (a lawyer, son of missionaries). She began writing very young and had poems in the *Christian Advocate* as a child. She was educ. in Brooklyn and at the Leeterverein Housekeeping School in Berlin, spending the first two years of WWI in Germany. She m. Hugh Hamilton C. in 1920 and had four children. Magazines like *Good Housekeeping*, *Pictorial Review*, *McCall's* and *Woman's Home Companion* printed her stories and serials; the latter became a rapid stream of books, beginning with *Mavis of Green Hill*, 1921. *Alimony*, 1928, was a bestseller and established her as a successful sentimental novelist, often ranked with Kathleen NORRIS. Many works, like *Office Wife*, 1930, and

Weekend Marriage, 1932, became films. Titles like *White Collar Girl*, 1933, and *He Married a Doctor*, 1944, indicate her willingness to combine other themes with that of love. She based *The American Family*, 1934, on her grandfather's diaries. At the height of her fame during the Depression and WWII (because, she said, of the need for escape), she kept writing and publishing until her death. Her almost 100 titles include two under her pseudonym, two volumes of poetry, four children's books, and part-autobiographical sketches, e.g. *Testament of Trust*, 1960.

Baldwin, Louisa (MacDonald), 1845–1925, novelist and poet, b. Manchester, da. of Hannah (Jones) and George Browne M., a Methodist preacher. The family was poor and numerous but valued education and culture. Her sister Georgiana m. Burne Jones in 1860, and in 1862 Louisa m. businessman Alfred B., from 1892 Conservative MP. They lived in Wilden and had one son (Stanley, later PM), after whose birth LB was a semi-invalid for 16 years, travelling often to European spas. Her novels, such as *The Story of a Marriage*, 1889, and *Richard Dare*, 1894, take a sentimental view of marriage and centre on male characters. *Where Town and Country Meet*, 1891, juxtaposes country innocence with urban squalor. LB also wrote a book of ghost stories, *The Shadow on the Blind*, 1895, ded. to her nephew Rudyard Kipling, and several volumes of verse. There is no biography, but see her son's life by Middlemas and Barnes, 1969.

Balfour, Clara Lucas (Liddell), 1808–78, activist and writer, b. New Forest, Hants. An only child, she m. James B. in 1827. A temperance activist for 30 years, she began her career with an anti-socialist tract in 1837. By 1841 she was lecturing on temperance at the Greenwich Literary Institution and in 1877 was elected President of the British Women's Temperance League. Among her dozens of publications are *Moral Heroism*, 1846, *Women and the Temperance Revolution*, 1849, *Sketches of English Literature*, 1852, and *Working Women of the Last Half-Century*, 1854. She also wrote children's books and *The Victim*, 1860, a story warning working girls of the link between drink and prostitution. She edited temperance magazines and worked for the *London and Westminster Review*, through which she met the Carlyles and became friends with Jane Welsh CARLYLE. Her *Women Worth Emulating*, 1877, offers models of 'womanly worth and wisdom' such as Mary SOMERVILLE and Amelie OPIE. She also wrote sketches of Ann JUDSON and Hannah KILHAM. Caroline FOX was struck by hearing her lecture on women in 1849.

Balfour, Mary, 1755?–*c.* 1820, poet and dramatist, da. of a Church of Ireland clergyman, probably b. in Derry. After her parents died she ran schools with her sister at Newtown Limavaddy, then Belfast, where she pub. with her name *Hope*, 1810. The long, ambitious title poem, in heroic couplets, has notes on classical allusions, etc. Notes to 'Kathleen O'Neil', an equally lengthy ballad, explain Irish words, history, folklore: the princess of Ulster is abducted to a magic realm by the Banshee, a powerful female spirit whom her father has offended; she returns from eternal bliss to lament approaching family deaths. Odes, sonnets and Irish songs follow. MB's other *Kathleen O'Neil*, 'A Grand National Melo Drame', staged in Belfast, was anonymously pub. in 1814. This Kathleen, a famous deer-slayer combining boldness with 'all the timidity of my sex', is abducted (and rescued) only by suitors. The Celtic colour extends to a comic subplot, with songs.

Ball, Hannah, 1734–92, Methodist letter writer and diarist of High Wycombe, Bucks. One of 12 children, she grew up partly with relations, and accuses herself of pride at the age of five. From 1759 she brought up a brother's motherless children.

She had an intense religious experience during a thunderstorm in 1762; in 1765 she converted to Methodism, which she had previously abhorred. Next year she began her diary by recording how, sadly, she broke off her engagement to an irreligious man; in 1769 she opened a very early Sunday school. She wrote to John Wesley in 1770 'Christ is my husband, and I am his bride.' Some of her rather predictably pious diary and letters to Wesley and to female friends were pub. York, 1796; new ed. 1839.

Ballads. Although these share *motifs* with the *lais* of which the leading author was MARIE DE FRANCE, early twentieth-century theories of their origin (both communalist and individualist) mostly assumed all-male authors. (Virginia WOOLF did not, and Mary ROBINSON in 1902 claimed that the form was primarily woman's.) Women may indeed have played a leading part in fashioning as well as in performing and transmitting ballads. (This latter role is witnessed in the fourteenth century by John Barbour in *The Bruce*, 1375, and by a hostile preacher; in the eighteenth century by MSS collections, NLS and elsewhere.) Women are prominent and active in ballads: false sisters and lovers, murderers of their bastard babies, but also aggrieved, idealized or heroic women (for the last, see study by Dianne Dugaw, 1989). Plots turn on female sexuality, crimes of violence, heroines asserting themselves through perseverance or revenge, the independent girl who rejects suitors, the chaste woman falsely accused and vindicated, the loathly woman transformed to beauty by love and sexual courtesy ('King Henry': the same story as Chaucer's 'Wyf of Bath's Tale'). Women like Anna BROWN were leaders in the Scots eighteenth-century ballad revival. Individually famous pieces were written by Jean Elliott of Minto ('I've heard the lilting at our yowe-milking', *c.* 1756), Elizabeth Grant of Carron (new version of 'Roy's Wife o' Aldivalloch'), Janet Graham ('The Wayward Wife', pub. 1776), Jean ADAMS, Grisell BAILLIE, Anne BARNARD, Carolina NAIRNE and Elizabeth WARDLAW. Ballads and 'verse tales' often merged in the 1830s, e.g. in the work of Caroline BOWLES. Felicia HEMANS's 'Casabianca' was a famous example of the form. Charlotte BARNARD composed music for her own ballads. Other well-known nineteenth-century balladists were Jean INGELOW in England and the CARY sisters in the USA; Christina ROSSETTI also wrote them. In Australia, Mary H. FOOTT was famous in the 'bush ballad' tradition. Some, like Violet FANE, still wrote traditional ballads in the 1890s, as did the Irish Dora SIGERSON (George Meredith called her 'the best ballad-writer since Scott'); but the form had declined in popularity. See J. S. Bratton, *The Victorian Popular Ballad*, 1975. Woolf built *A Room of One's Own* around women's names from 'Mary Hamilton'. Louise POUND led the rediscovery of the American ballad.

Bambara, Toni Cade, writer of novels and short stories, self-described as 'a writer, an artist, a cultural worker ... whatever you want to call this vocation'. B. in 1931, da. of Helen Brent Henderson Cade, who 'read books', 'built book-cases', 'wanted to be a journalist' and 'gave me permission to wonder, to dawdle, to daydream'. She was raised with her brother in Harlem, Bedford-Stuyvesant and Queens, where she learned 'about the ORAL TRADITION and our high standards governing the rap', and educ. in literature, linguistics, dance and film at Queen's College (BA, 1959), in Italy and Paris, and at CUNY, 'Harlem University' (MA, 1964). She was director and advisor for the Theatre of the Black Experience, NY, 1965–9, and at various times has been a social worker, professor, women's studies co-ordinator and writing instructor. Self-naming (she added 'Bambara' to Cade when she found the name written on her grandmother's notebook in an old trunk), she has a daughter. She edited and contributed to *The Black Woman*, 1970, one of the early collections of feminist writing and *Tales and Stories for Black Folks*, 1971. The stories in her first collection, *Gorilla, My Love*, 1972, deal with the growing up of critical, sensitive, eight-year-old Hazel, a sprinter, 'Miss Quicksilver herself', in a world of racial, sexual and economic inequality. Those in *The Sea Birds are Still Alive*, 1972, portray intergenerational and political conflicts among women in black communities and in the male-dominated nuclear family. Here, and in her complex, dense, and thickly-populated novel, *The Salt Eaters*, 1980 (American Book Award), TCB probes the relationship of the individual and her communities. The novel began as a journal entry, a speculation on ways of fusing 'activists or warriors' and 'adepts or medicine people': it deals with the healing of emotionally-exhausted, attempted suicide, revolutionary Velma Henry, setting her in the centre of fragmented visions of a black activism bred in the 1960s but now attenuated in post-Vietnam USA, environmental poisoning, political corruption and female unity. 'I work to produce stories that save our lives', TCB says of herself; and of the writing of women of colour: 'The work: To make revolution irresistible'. With Leah Wise, she edited *Southern Black Utterances Today*, 1975. Interviews in Tate, 1983, and Evans, 1984. She makes important introductory comment to Moraga and Anzaldua, 1981. See Gloria T. Hull in Pryse and Spillers, 1985, and Susan Willis, *Specifying: Black Women Writing the American Experience*, 1987.

Bambrick, Winifred, c. 1892–1969, novelist and musician. B. in Ottawa, da. of Catherine (Corbett) and grocer Edward B., she made her debut as a harpist while still a child and later travelled with John Philip Sousa's band through N. America and Europe. After successful concerts as solo harpist in England, she joined a travelling revue which toured Europe in the late 1930s, apparently barely escaping Leipzig at the onset of WWII. *Continental Revue*, 1946, winner of the Governor General's Award, a novel based on this experience, realistically presents the intrigues, quarrels and everyday activities of a range of European, Asian and N. American characters in the shadow of impending war. War erupts; the troupe scatters; and the protagonists' romance ends tragically. After WWII WB continued her concert career. She returned to Montréal, 1960, and died there.

Bandler, Ida Lessing **Faith** (Mussing), Aboriginal activist and novelist, b. 1918 near Murwillumbah, NSW, da. of Ida (Kishdon) and Wacvie (Peter) M., Pacific Islander and indentured cane-cutter. She was educ. at Murwillumbah Public School and Cleveland Street Night School, Sydney, and m. Hans B. in 1952: she has one daughter. She has been active for many years in advancing the cause of Aborigines and Islanders and in working for peace and equality. She served on the Federal Council for the Advancement of Aboriginals and Torres Strait Islanders for over 20 years and was a central figure in the successful campaign to end legal discrimination against Aborigines. Her four books reflect these political and racial concerns. The first, *Wacvie*, 1977, tells the story of her father, kidnapped from his New Hebrides village to work in the Queensland canefields, from which he escaped 15 years later; this won the Braille Book of the Year Award in 1979. *Marani in Australia*, 1980, also based on the Islanders' role in the Queensland sugar industry, and *The Time was Right*, 1983, a history of Aboriginal-Australian fellowship (both with Len Fox), was followed by the biographical *Welou, My Brother*, 1984. In 1989 she pub. *Turning the Tide, a Personal History of the Federal Council for the Advancement of Aborigines and Torres Strait Islanders*.

Banks, Elizabeth L., 1870–1938, essayist and journalist, b. Taunton, NJ, da. of Sarah (Brister) and John B., and educ. at

Milwaukee-Downer College, Wis. Orphaned and raised by her aunt, she began work as society reporter for *St Paul's Globe* in 1889. Her first pub. essay, 'All about Typewriter Girls', recounts the first-hand experiences of a working woman. After editing the woman's column for the *Morning Herald*, Baltimore, 1891–3, she settled in England, where *The Times* pub. her patriotic 'American Girl's reply to Mr Kipling'. *Campaigns of Curiosity. Journalistic Adventures of an American Girl in London*, 1894, presents EB's witty and high-spirited account of her experiences, for which she gained 'copy' by working as a maidservant, laundry-girl, flower-girl and crossing-sweeper. Alternately vilified and acclaimed (each in turn, by Eliza Lynn LINTON), she became renowned for her 'unwomanly' self-assertion (see her *Autobiography of a 'Newspaper Girl'*, 1902). She also assumed the role of a US heiress to expose English aristocrats who sold introductions at court to Americans ('The "Almighty Dollar" in London Society', *St James's Gazette*, 1894). This led to Queen VICTORIA's rule, still effective, that such introductions should be made only by ambassadors. Proceeds from her animal stories went to help children, animals and the wounded of WWI. She attacked the US judicial system in *The Mystery of Frances Farrington*, 1909, and the class system in *School for John and Mary*, 1925. In *The Remaking of an American*, 1928, she describes how she turned her unsuspecting anti-suffrage newspaper into a leading supporter of the movement. Of her suffragist co-workers she writes: 'We women understand each other. We may disagree as to methods, but our solidarity is unquestioned'.

Banks, Isabella, 'Mrs G. Linnaeus Banks' (Varley), 1821–97, novelist and poet (she later wished she had kept her maiden name to write under). B. in Manchester, she was raised in an environment of freedom of thought and speech by her mother, Amelia (Daniels), mother's much older sister, Jane, and father, James V., small businessman and amateur artist. Educ. at Green Street School, Miss Hannah Spray's Ladies' Day School and Rev. John Weelden's Academy, with a good home library and wide cultural circle, she became a gifted teacher and from 18 ran a school in Cheetham for eight years. Her mother and aunt fostered her intense love of the past and provided much first-hand material for her fiction. Her first printed poem 'A Dying Girl to her Mother', appeared in the *Manchester Guardian*, 1837. Her first book of poems, *Ivy Leaves*, 1844, includes the very realistic 'Neglected Wife'. She m. G. Linnaeus B. in 1846 and thereafter led a nomadic life with this lecturer, orator, radical, journalist and drunkard, putting his work first until, aged 43, she began writing intensively to provide for their eight children (of whom five died). In 1865 she published a novel, *God's Providence House*, and, jointly with her husband, a selection of poems, *Daisies in the Grass* (27 are hers). Despite a breakdown in health in 1872, and while nursing her sick husband, she wrote her best-known novel, *The Manchester Man*. Of her more than 60 novels, about 12 have strong connections with Manchester; most include details of historical interest while proffering a strong moral message from a socially conservative viewpoint. Her poetry is more revealing of her views on the difficulties of women's role, particularly in marriages to selfish men, although many pompous and arrogant males people her novels. Highly skilled in the design of knitting and embroidery, she pub. an original fancy-work pattern every month for 50 years. See life by E. L. Burney, 1969.

Bannerman, Anne, 1765–1829, poet, b. at Edinburgh, eldest surviving child of Isobel (Dick) and William B. She pub. with her name *Poems*, 1800 (dating back to *c.* 1790: odes, translations, ten 'Sonnets from Werter'; 'The Nun' gives a Mme de GENLIS story a new unhappy ending). *Tales of Superstition and Chivalry*, 1802, are ballads of ghosts and female prophets, exclamatory in style, with scholarly historical notes. She contributed to *The Poetical Register*, 1802ff; its reviewer liked *Tales* but found them obscure. Her mother's and brother's deaths next year left her destitute (a friend applying to the RLF without her knowledge mentioned her infirm health and 'exquisite sensibility'). In 1807 she issued by subscription at Edinburgh a revised ed. of *Poems*, and became a governess at Exeter. Her subjects include religion, lost love, praise of her native land and of Joanna BAILLIE. She was much quoted by other women; as a 'shattered' invalid living at Portobello, Edinburgh, she impressed Anne GRANT with her intellect and piety.

Bannerman, Helen (Brodie Cowan Watson), 1862–1946, CHILDREN'S author-illustrator. B. in Edinburgh, da. of a minister in the Free Church of Scotland, she graduated from St Andrew's University (LLA) in 1887, gaining this title (Lady Literate in Arts) through external examinations two years before universities admitted women. She m. William Burney B., a surgeon in the Indian Medical Service, 1899; they had four children and lived in India for 30 years. She wrote ten children's stories, usually at the rate of one a year in time for the Christmas trade, but the source of her fame and notoriety is her first book, *The Story of Little Black Sambo*, 1899. Ironically, copyright to text and original illustrations was sold for £5. Thought racist from the 1960s, and banned from some libraries, this tale of a brave and resourceful lad outwitting four tigers attracted at least 12 different illustrators from 1925 to 1950 and was translated into French, Spanish, Arabic, Dutch, Hebrew, German and Danish. Simple and striking in style, it avoids moral didacticism, and makes an imaginary jungle a deliberate mixture of Indian scenery and African characters. The story's comedy lies in its unremitting logical matter-of-factness and appropriate and hilarious justice. More dramatic than the ring of melted butter which remains of the contesting tigers in *Black Sambo*, however, is the explosion of the two antagonists, 'a horrid cross old woman called Black Noggy' and the menacing crocodile Mugger, in *The Story of Little Black Mingo*, 1901, whose final scene captures the essence of HB's exotic mundanity. See Elizabeth Hay, *Sambo Sahib*, and Nicholas Tucker, *The Child and the Book*, both 1981.

Banning, Margaret (Culkin), 1891–1982, moralist, novelist and short-story writer, b. in Buffalo, Minnesota, da. of Hannah Alice (Young) and William C. She attended Vassar (AB, 1912) and the Chicago School of Civics and Philanthropy, 1913, then m. lawyer Archibald B., 1914. Divorced, she supported her two children by writing. In 1944, she m. LeRoy Salsick. A Catholic, she deals (in her more than 40 books, including several non-fiction works) with recurrent issues of birth-control, divorce, marriage and careers for women and women's political involvement. *This Marrying*, 1920, and *Path of True Love*, 1933, treat their heroines' conflicted progress towards marriage: the one, a university-educated journalist, initially resists but finally accedes to marriage; the other abandons independence, accepting her exclusion from life's 'drama', for 'a wife can't be an adventurer'. *Spellbinders*, 1922, depicts women who organize women's political participation, though they, too, are economically bound to marriage. *The Women of the Family*, 1926, fascinatingly treats a family history of supposedly hereditary insanity; Suzanne is rescued from her madness by a friend who encouragingly reinterprets its cause as the intellectual and emotional isolation of unsatisfying marriage, arguing that 'women need not wither because love and husbands fail them'. *The Case for Chastity*, 1937, is a moral tract; *Women for Defense*, 1942, and *Conduct Yourself Accordingly*, with Mabel Louise Culkin, 1944, are about women and the war effort. After WWII she worked in refugee camps in Germany and Austria and in the 1940s studied post-war conditions in England and Europe. As a Catholic, MB was concerned with the Church's views of birth-control and divorce. *The Vine and the Olive*, 1965, is a fictional treatment of the debate about birth-control in which MB, unable to commit herself explicitly to its use, couches her concessions in symbolic form. In *The Will of Magda Townsend*, 1973, thought fictionalized autobiography, a writer, revising her will, reflects on her past life and on Catholic values and the issues of remarriage and abortion.

Baptists. Radical sect whose congregations sprang up and split repeatedly, 1640–60 (briefly driven underground by the Clarendon Code in the early 1660s). Though their views on women's role (as on other issues) varied widely, they were a factor in the burgeoning of women's writing. Mary CARY and Anna TRAPNEL were early activists; many very radical Baptists became Quakers in the 1650s. They required confessions of faith from new church members and advocated DIARY records of God's grace; this encouraged many women to write autobiographically, while also imposing a pattern on the results. (Many in collections ed. John Rogers, 1653, and Henry Walker, 1652.) Some early works appeared in their authors' lifetimes, but most, of both sexes, appeared posthumously. Though the authors are usually presented as model good women, their records include unhappy marriages, deaths of children, travel in foreign lands and the effects of civil war. See J. F. McGregor in McGregor and Barry Reay, eds., 1984; studies by G. F. Nuttall, 1957, Owen Watkins, 1972, and M. R. Watts, 1978.

Barbauld, Anna Laetitia (Aikin), 1743–1825, Unitarian poet, educator, and critic, b. at Kibworth Harcourt, Leics., of eminent Dissenting stock, elder child of Jane (Jennings) and John A., schoolmaster and from 1758 classical tutor at Warrington Academy. Her early quickness at French and Italian persuaded her reluctant father to help her with Latin and Greek. By 1769 she was showing the MS of her fervent blankverse *Corsica*, pub. in 1773 in *Poems* (hymns, lyrics, tributes to Elizabeth ROWE and to her grandmother). Items by her and her brother John in *Miscellaneous Pieces in Prose*, 1773, included her 'On Romances'. A second joint work, the long-popular *Evenings at Home, or the Juvenile Budget Opened*, 1792–6, was mostly John's: he was always close, and supportive of her writing. In 1774, despite well-founded doubts, she m. Rochemont B., a Dissenting minister, clever but unstable. Declining his suggestion of an academy for women, she helped him start and run a boys' school in Suffolk, where till 1785 she taught (unusually) English, and produced plays and a 'weekly chronicle'. After a year in France they then lived at Hampstead and Stoke Newington. Childless, they adopted a nephew in 1777, for whom, as a new reader of two or three, ALB wrote her pioneering *Lessons for Children*, 1778. Her *Hymns in Prose for Children*, 1781, often reprinted, aim to link God in the child's mind with 'wonder or delight'. She wrote effective topical essays on religion (defending Dissenters, hoping for an end to sectarianism in *Civic Sermons*, 1790; defending public or social worship, hoping for an end to 'the gloomy perplexities of Calvinism', 1792) and against war, 1793. In poetry she combated the slave trade, 1791, and war in *Eighteen Hundred and Eleven* (repr. Warrington 1911), which pictures London laid waste, and brought cries of 'unfeminine'. Her valuable criticism lies in eds. of poets, 1794 and 1797, essayists, 1804, Samuel Richardson's letters, 1804, and 50 vols. of novels, 1810. Her husband became insane and violent (against her) and killed himself in 1808. She was friend and admiring critic to Joanna BAILLIE, Hester CHAPONE, Maria EDGEWORTH, Hannah MORE and the radical publisher Joseph Johnson. Her niece Lucy AIKIN edited her *Works*, 1825 (selec.; with memoir; including the well-known 'Rights of Women' – most unmilitant – and 'Life, I know not what thou art', admired by Frances BURNEY and Wordsworth), and *A Legacy for Young Ladies* (short pieces), 1826. Some odes have been repr., though ALB's formal poetry is somewhat stiff. Late-nineteenth-century lives are superseded by Betsy Rodgers, *Georgian Chronicle*, 1958, with fine unpub. letters.

Barber, Mary, 'Sapphira', 1690?–1757, poet, wife of Dublin clothier Jonathan B., friend of Jonathan Swift and Constantia GRIERSON. She says she began writing verse as an aid in teaching her children: many delightful poems purport to be spoken by her elder son, born about 1713. She is probably not the very similarly-named author of a MS book of Whig verse at Trinity College, Dublin, written in London 1711–14, but she pub. two poems, Dublin, 1725: a compliment to the Viceroy, Lord Carteret, and an anonymous 'Widow's Address' for a petitioner to Lady Carteret. In 1730 she visited England seeking help (she had gout, and despite or because of prominent friends her husband's business was failing). Swift provided introductions and matter for controversy: she passed off (knowingly or not) spurious letters as his, 1731, and two years later was arrested as a link (with Laetitia PILKINGTON's husband) between him and his publisher. Her *Poems on Several Occasions* (with some by Grierson and others), 1734, was lavishly subscribed for. In 1736 she was ill at Bath with her daughter to support; she gained a secure income in 1738 by printing by subscription the donated MS of Swift's *Polite Conversation*. Her best poems are racy and humorous. She pub. a poem in the *GM* in 1737, and later knew Mary DELANY in Ireland.

Barclay, Florence Louisa (Charlesworth), 1862–1920, novelist and best-selling phenomenon. Niece of Maria Charlesworth, 1819–80, CHILDREN'S writer (author of *Ministering Children*, 1854), she was born in a Surrey rectory, the middle sister of three. Moving to London at seven, she was taken by her mother to visit the poor and sing at revivalist meetings; in later life, m. to the Rev. Charles B., she ran village Bible readings and cricket clubs and toured the USA as a public speaker, to tell of her find, on her honeymoon in Palestine, of the true mouth of Jacob's Well. Of magnetic personality, she showed many instances of psychic powers – healing, finding lost objects and literally charming birds from the trees. During 1905, ill from 'heart-strain', she wrote *The Rosary* (pub. 1909), which sold 150,000 in a year, was translated into eight languages, carried to the trenches by countless young men and sold over a million copies by 1921 (she gave the proceeds away). A well-turned masochistic love story, it closes with 'the perfect happiness' of Jane's 'wedded home'. Other books, such as *The Following of the Star*, 1911, were only marginally less successful. There is an uncritical life by her daughter, 1923, which quotes FB's stated aim: 'Never to write a line which could introduce the taint of sin, or the shadow of shame, into any home' (240); but she saw herself as following E. B. BROWNING, whose favourite chair she bought at a sale (also the table at which *Aurora Leigh* was written).

'Barcynska, Hélène, Countess', 'Oliver Sandys', Marguerite Florence (Jervis) Barclay, later Evans, 1894–1964, POPULAR FICTION writer. Da. of Col. Henry J., who 'wasn't very fond of me because I wasn't a boy', she was b. in Henzada, Burma, came from India to England at five, attended private schools ('always scribbling' from seven) and the Academy of Dramatic Art, went on stage, and at about 15 published verse in *The Easy Chair* and a story in *Household Words* (final issue). She aimed to live by writing: 'strenuously opposed to marriage – the backwater oblivion where one spent the rest of one's life as Mrs

Someone'. Her 147 books (1911–64; several filmed) include 77 novels (from 1911: she called them 'goody goody and sweet') as 'OS' and 56 (more sophisticated) as the 'Countess', a version of her married name complete with fictional identity. She said she m. 'elderly' writer Armiger Barclay or Barcynsky (son of a Polish count), in 1911, for business reasons and made him unhappy. He housekept, supported her while she wrote, revised her stories and put his name on some. They co-authored books which began as serials. She broke down under the strain of his control, 1914, but kept writing during convalescence. She bore a son in 1915. *The Honey Pot*, 1916 (about two mutually supportive girls in comic opera), sold one million copies. HB favours the exotic (*Black Harvest*, 1960, has two convents, a circus, film stardom and debate over artificial insemination), romantic and semi-supernatural. Her heroines are memorable: a swindler in *Chicane*, 1912, a mother who defers to her son in *The Little Mother Who Sits at Home*, 1915, and an orphan flower-girl who becomes a film-star in *Rose o' the Sea*, 1920. She married another writer, Caradoc Evans, in 1933 and settled in Wales, where she set up and wrote for the Quarry Theatre. She describes her life in some novels (like *Calm Waters*, 1940) and in *Full and Frank*, 1941, *Unbroken Thread: An Intimate Journal of ... England's Best-Loved Woman Novelist*, 1948, and *The Miracle Stone of Wales*, 1957.

Barfoot, Joan, novelist and journalist. Da. of Helen (MacKinnon) and Robert B., she was b. in 1946 at Owen Sound, Ont., and educ. there and at the Univ. of Western Ontario (BA, 1969). Since 1976 she has worked on the London (Ont.) *Free Press*. Her novels explore women's domestic experiences – 'washing dishes, making meals and patching sheets and scrubbing floors and getting to the end of the day' – and the desire to 'be in control, that's freedom'. In *Abra*, 1979 (*Gaining Ground*, 1980, in English ed.), a woman abandons a safe city life as mother and wife and goes north to find a life that allows her body 'its own time, choosing when it wanted to move and how'. In *Dancing in the Dark*, 1982, a woman judged criminally insane for the murder of her husband continues in her journal her lifetime attention to detail, order, perfection. Having believed that her home, marriage and person met every demand of the 'women's magazines', she concludes with a vision of dancing 'all there is to be danced, as if there is no tomorrow – a free woman', but this freedom will be either death or further withdrawal. *Duet for Three*, 1985, taking up a mother–daughter motif introduced in *Abra*, depicts a dynasty of daughters striving to know themselves and their relationships, learning to stand together: 'if Aggie wavers or trips June will be right there behind her'.

Barker, Jane, 1652–*c.* 1727, 'Galesia' (variously spelled), poet and fiction writer, da. of Anne (Connock) and Thomas B., a tenant farmer. She grew up at Wilsthorpe (which she calls Wiltsthorp), Lincs., with friends at Cambridge Univ.; her brother taught her medicine. She began writing poetry *c.* 1674 (MSS at BL and Magdalen, Oxford); her *Poetical Recreations*, 1688, includes verses on 'A Virgin Life', medicine, nature, religion, her brother's death and the Muses' service (a fine ode). As a Catholic convert, her parents dead, she left London for St Germain near Paris on James II's flight. Over 12 years, despite severe eye trouble, she revised her poems and wrote, as 'FIDELIA', others still unpub., many political. Back at Wilsthorpe, she lived on a small inherited income; in 1718 she was employed as a Jacobite spy. Much of her prose – *Love Intrigues, or The History of ... Bosvil and Galesia* (pub. by Edmund Curll, 1713; rev. in *Novels*, 1719), *A Patch-Work Screen for the Ladies*, 1723, and *The Lining of the Patch-Work Screen*, 1726 – draws on her past life. Subordinate tales and poems (some already pub.) are inset:

Exilius [romance name of an actual friend], *or The Banish'd Roman*, 1715, is a collection of tales. Her recurrent courtship plots end in neither marriage nor seduction: Galesia at first wrestles with passion for a hurtfully vacillating suitor, later rejects unsatisfactory ones and leans increasingly towards poverty and chastity in emulation of SAPPHO and Katherine PHILIPS – whose annual coronation 'as Queen of Female Writers' JB describes in *The Lining*. Her last two works wittily justify her method – unity through variety – as widely symbolical of life and also as female: lacking sewing skill or fabric scraps, Galesia offers her MSS to the 'lady's' communal screen project. See Jane Spencer, *TSWL*, 2, 1984; three novels repr. 1973.

Barker, Mary Anne (Stewart), Lady, later Broome, 1831–1911, journalist and novelist, b. in Jamaica, where her father, W. G. S., was Island Secretary, and educ. in England. Having lived in Bengal in the 1850s with her first husband, Capt. George B. (later knighted), and their two sons, in 1865 she m. Frederick Napier Broome and accompanied him to NZ. They sheep-farmed at Canterbury 1866–9, then left for England. From 1875 they moved to colonial posts in Natal, Mauritius, Western Australia and Trinidad. She wrote *Station Life in New Zealand*, London, 1870, *Travelling Over Old and New Ground*, 1871, *A Christmas cake in four quarters*, 1872, *Station Amusements in New Zealand*, 1873, *Colonial Memories*, 1904, and many others (including children's books). Witty, humorous, totally sure of her equality with her husband or any men she meets, MAB provides a readable, lively record of three years in NZ. She finds pleasure in pig-hunts, 'burning-off' and tobogganing: 'I am afraid that it does not sound a very orderly and feminine occupation,' she writes of an expedition after wild cattle, 'but I enjoy myself thoroughly and have covered myself with glory and honor by my powers of walking all day.' She was too energetic, well-off and free (her only child with Broome died very young; the others were in England) to be a typical colonist, but she describes with sympathy the position of women settlers and servants. *Station Life* and *Station Amusements* were well received and remain in print as NZ classics.

Barker, Pat, novelist, b. 1943 at Thornaby-on-Tees to working-class parents, brought up by her grandmother, educ. at a local grammar school and the LSE (BSc 1965). She taught in further education and married David B., zoology lecturer, in 1978. She has two children. She had produced three 'sensitive and polite' novels (unpub.), when on a writing course Angela CARTER read a story about her grandmother and advised her to write about her past, not her present, class. The results, PB says, tap a women's ORAL TRADITION. *Union Street*, 1982 (Fawcett Prize), is a linked series of seven stories whose protagonists run from Kelly, angry about her mother's 'fancy man' and raped while 'nicking off' school, to Alice, 'returning in spirit to her beginnings' and to memory of her mother as she faces death. Vivid demotic style ('not if his arse was decked with diamonds') and individual resilience leave grim detail unmitigated: Kelly finds a dead baby under a pile of bricks, and defaces her headmaster's study with shit. *Blow Your House Down*, 1984, concerns another community of women: whores working from the same pub, living in fear of a Yorkshire-Ripper-like murderer. (After he is killed by a bereaved lesbian, a last episode presents the havoc he has caused to a loving heterosexual couple.) In *The Century's Daughter*, 1986, a woman born in 1990 relates the span of her life. In *The Man Who Wasn't There*, 1989, a young boy growing up in a female household looks to the – untrustworthy – media for masculine role models. PB is acclaimed in the USA; likeness between their work led to friendship with Gloria NAYLOR; *Union Street* was filmed as *Stanley and Iris*, set in Boston.

Barlow, Jane, 1857–1917, poet, novelist and story-teller, b. at Clontarf, elder da. of Mary Louisa (Barlow) and the Rev. James Barlow, history prof. at Trinity College, Dublin from 1866, Vice-Provost from 1899. An accomplished classical scholar and very popular author (*Irish Idyls*, 1892, went through eight editions), JB was so shy that she always preferred home (at Raheny, a village near Dublin) to meeting people. Yet her great sympathy with the Nationalist cause inspired all her work, beginning with anonymous contributions to the *Dublin University Review* (the editor advertized fruitlessly in 1885 for the author's name), through *Bog-land Studies*, 1892 (Irish dialect poetry, with Greek epigraphs), and other collections of stories and verse, and including her four novels, from *Kerrigan's Quality*, 1894, to *In Mio's Path*, 1917. *Flaws*, 1911, tells the story of a down-trodden daughter (a son was wanted), who unexpectedly takes the advice of a meek old spinster, to '"Keep a bit of your own will, my dear"' and defies her family to marry. JB had always wished to be a poet but felt she had 'nothing of the lyrical faculty'. She was awarded an honorary D. Litt. at Dublin in 1904. See articles by James MacArthur (*The Critic*, 21, 12 May 1894, pp. 325–6) and Katherine TYNAN Hinkson (in Miles, p. 433).

Barnard, Lady **Anne** (Lindsay), 1750–1825, balladist, letter and travel writer, eldest of 11 children of Anne (Dalrymple) and James Lindsay, Jacobite 5th Earl of Balcarres (who married at 60). (Her great-grandmother Anna (Mackenzie) Lindsay, 1621?–1707, Countess of Balcarres, then Countess of Argyll, had a tumultuous life – royalist during the Commonwealth, Whig during the Restoration – and wrote notable letters, some pub. in a life by her descendant Lord Crawford and Balcarres, 1868.) AB's birth confounded a prophecy that her parents' eldest (by implication, a boy) would restore the Stuart kings. She grew up in Fife with visits to Edinburgh, and wrote 'Auld Robin Gray' (new words for 'coarse and odious' ones to a loved ballad tune) in 1772. Printed anonymously, it had a great vogue and various metamorphoses; she hid her authorship till 1823, when she confided in Walter Scott (sending him also poems by two sisters), who said that old ladies already knew the secret. He published it, 1825, but at her wish suppressed a collection, *Lays of the Lindsays*. She called the ballad a 'little history of virtuous distress in humble life', written in loneliness after her sister Margaret's (reluctant) marriage and perhaps owing something to that event. A beautiful lunatic sings it in Mary WOLLSTONECRAFT's *Wrongs of Woman*. AB lived in London society from the 1770s and in 1793 'stood the world's smile', as she said, by rejecting other suitors to marry Andrew B., 12 years her junior. He became colonial secretary at the Cape of Good Hope, where she lived 1797–1802 and he died in 1807. Her S. African writings and superb drawings remain there and in Scotland; of her family memoirs, those of her father were pub. in *Lives of the Lindsays*, 1840, ii. Despite her prohibition, her papers have been used in many lives and collections of letters; that by A. M. Lewin Robinson, Cape Town 1973, has a wealth of her drawings.

Barnard, Charlotte Alington (Pye), 'Claribel', 1830–69, poet and song writer, b. Louth, Lincs., da. of Charlotte Mary (Yerburgh) and Henry Alington P. Musical from childhood, she was educ. at home and at day school, with lessons in drawing from a local artist and piano from the church organist. She m. the Rev. Charles Cary (b. 1854), for whose church she wrote hymns. They lived in London 1857–63, where she soon became widely known for her popular ballads by 'Claribel' ('Condor' was a less-favoured pseudonym). She was best known for her music, but wrote lyrics as well. Her works appeared under such titles as *Fireside Thoughts, Ballads, etc.*, 1865, and *Thoughts, Verses and Songs*, 1877, her best-known ballad being 'Come back to Erin'. She wrote musical settings for poems by Tennyson, whom she knew, and Arnold. Though advertised as 'the most popular Ballad composer of the day', she, and Mme Sainton Dolby who introduced many of her songs, were condemned by music critics for debasing the public taste. See Phyllis M. Smith, *The Story of Claribel*, 1965.

Barnard, Marjorie, 'M. Barnard Eldershaw', 1897–1987, novelist, short-story writer, historian, critic, librarian, b. Sydney, NSW, da. of Ethel Frances (Alford) and Oswald Holme B. In 1918 she graduated BA with First Class Honours from Sydney Univ. and was awarded a scholarship to England for postgraduate study, but her father prevented her going. She trained as a librarian and worked at Sydney Technical College Library, 1920–32, and the CSIRO, 1942–50. She pub. a collection of children's stories, *The Ivory Gate*, 1920, and began her literary collaboration with Flora ELDERSHAW. Between 1929 and 1947 they pub. five novels under a joint pseudonym, as well as three historical works and one of the first collections of essays on Australian literature, 1938, which discussed the work of Katharine PRICHARD, Henry Handel RICHARDSON, Christina STEAD and Eleanor DARK, among others. The first Barnard Eldershaw novel, *A House is Built*, 1929, shared first prize in the *Bulletin*'s novel competition of 1928 with PRICHARD's *Coonardoo.* A historical family saga set in nineteenth-century Sydney, it has remained the most popular of Barnard Eldershaw's novels. *Green Memory*, 1931, also set in nineteenth-century Sydney, *The Glasshouse*, 1936, and *Plaque with Laurel*, 1937, both dealing with contemporary subjects, have long been out of print. The last two have writers as their central characters and so look forward to their last novel, in part historical family saga, in part an examination of the nature of fiction. Though the exact nature of their collaboration is uncertain, it seems that MB did most of the writing and Eldershaw the planning and shaping. *Tomorrow and Tomorrow and Tomorrow*, not pub. in full till 1983, was, however, largely MB's work. (In 1947 it had appeared in a censored form and without its third 'Tomorrow', which the publisher could not fit on the cover.) Remarkable not only in its intellectual range and emotional depth but also in its experimental form, it anticipates many more recent developments in its use of futuristic settings and the novel-within-a-novel mode. Under her own name, MB pub. *The Persimmon Tree and other Stories*, 1943 (reissued with some additional stories, 1985). These fine pieces are influenced by Katherine MANSFIELD and share many of her concerns, such as the plight of the 'woman alone'. The highly resonant title story has often been anthologized. See also Robert Darby, ed., *But Not for Love, Stories of MB and M. Barnard Eldershaw*, 1989. MB also pub. seven historical works, most notably *Macquarie's World*, 1942, and *A History of Australia*, 1962, as well as a critical study of Miles FRANKLIN, 1967. The only major study of her work is by Louise E. Rorabacher, 1973. MSS are in the Mitchell Library, Sydney.

Barnes, Carmen Dee, novelist, b. in 1912 in Chattanooga, Tenn., da. of poet and folklorist Diantha Mills (Jackson) and James Neal, she took the name of her first stepfather, Wellington B. At 16, she wrote *Schoolgirl*, 1929, based on her boarding-school experiences: the novel led to her expulsion from Gardener School but became a Broadway play two years later. Here, as in subsequent novels, CDB treats sexual awakening, increasingly aware of the social exploitation of feminine desire and of the limited options open to women, limitations enforced in her fictions by the ROMANCE mode. The narrative of *Beau Lover*, 1930, framed by the romance convention of a girl's search for a 'beau lover', describes Gloria's early unquestioning feminine acculturation, her use of her lover quest to fend off marriage and sexual possession, her choice, instead, of art and her final recanting: 'All that mattered was that you two, Peter and Glory, might kiss some child's naked little body and smile across it at each other.' *Young Woman*, 1934, more bleakly depicts the plight of women: 'the depression was breeding a new class of young American women. Girls ... who were not strong enough to get along by themselves and seeking the old way of protection, sold themselves into bondage.' Here, the economics of the depression and the 'new world' of freedom for women comprize a double bind: 'Women had hanged themselves with their freedom.' *Time Lay Asleep*, 1946, describes its narrator's return to the landscape of her childhood, her development of identity in an environment consisting mainly of women (grandmother, maiden aunt, mother, etc., who provide conflicting models) and the legacy of narratives through which she, like the women before her, forms her femininity. CDB married Hamilton F. Armstrong, 1945; they collaborated on *A Passionate Victorian*, a play about Fanny KEMBLE.

Barnes, Charlotte Mary **Sanford**, 1818–63, playwright, actress and fiction writer, b. NYC, da. of Mary (Creenhill) and John B., well-known actors. CSB was introduced to the stage in her teens, receiving a thorough training, which contributed to her success as a playwright. Her first attempt, *The Last Days of Pompeii*, 1835, based on Bulwer Lytton's novel, was followed in 1837 by her most successful play, *Octavia Brigaldi or, The Confession*, a revenge drama set in fifteenth-century Milan but embodying contemporary class conflicts. CSB herself successfully took the leading role of tragic heroine. In 1846 she m. popular actor Edmond S. Connor. Other plays included *The Night of the Coronation*, 1837, inspired by the coronation of Queen VICTORIA: 'Woman is woman everywhere; on England's throne / Or tideless Mississippi's banks, she's still the same', and *The Forest Princess*, based on the story of Pocahontas. In some of her later works, CSB turned to contemporary settings and events as inspiration for romantic fiction. *The Heart? or the Soul? A Series of Tales*, 1848, an experiment in the literary contest genre, concerns a group of women who generate a school of romantic regionalist fiction for their own entertainment. The tales assert the central importance of the bonds between women. In 1848 CSB pub. a collection, *Plays, Prose and Poetry*, which included *Octavia Bragaldi*.

Barnes, Djuna, 'Lydia Steptoe', 1892–1982, novelist, short-story writer, poet, playwright, journalist, b. in Cornwall-on-Hudson, NY, da. of Elizabeth (Chappell) and Wald Barnes, who took his mother's rather than his father's name. DB was educ. by her father and grandmother, later attended the Pratt Institute, Brooklyn, 1911–12, and the Arts Students' League, NYC, 1915. (Later she illustrated her own books and drew portraits of, among others, Edna St Vincent MILLAY and Gertrude STEIN.) She began as a journalist for the *Brooklyn Daily Eagle*, 1913, and published stories, some pseudonymous, in the *Dial* and *Vanity Fair*. She was not a member of the Suffrage Movement; her anger at the 'brutal usurpation' of woman's functions, first expressed in a 1914 article on the force-feeding of suffragettes, nevertheless reappears throughout her work. Her early poems are lost, but her first collection of poems and drawings, *The Book of Repulsive Women*, privately printed in Greenwich Village in 1915, satirizes and grotesques the stock imagery of female sexuality. Married for two years (perhaps not legally) to Courtenay Lemon, DB left him in 1919, the year her first play, *Three From the Earth*, was produced by the Provincetown Players. (Two others, *Kurzy of the Sea* and *An Irish Triangle*, followed.) In 1920 she left for Paris, where she stayed for 12 years, living for most of that time, often unhappily, with US sculptor Thelma Wood in rue St Romain. A friend of Natalie BARNEY (who, with Peggy Guggenheim and Samuel

Beckett, gave her financial support), Janet FLANNER, Solita SOLANO and Mina LOY, she enjoyed the reputation of a writer close in stature to Joyce. *A Book*, 1923 (revised and reprinted as *A Night Among the Horses*, 1929), poems, short stories, and plays, drew attention to DB as a serious artist. Her best-selling *Ryder*, 1928, thought to be a fictional family chronicle, also a *tour de force* of stylistic parody, exposes 'the ways women are made to suffer for the patriarchy'. The privately-printed *roman à clef* to the Parisian lesbian community and to Natalie Barney's salon, *Ladies Almanack*, 1928 (which she called a 'slight satiric wiggling'), celebrates female sexuality and mocks eighteenth-century language, presenting Dame (subsequently Saint) Evangeline Musset and the community she has rescued from heterosexual patriarchy and to whom she has restored the sense of a place in history and the orders of meaning. *Nightwood*, 1936 (edited severely and introduced by T. S. Eliot), a densely allusive, metaphoric and autobiographical novel set in the homosexual underground of Paris, is a sustained, moving analysis of women's place in patriarchal culture. At first a cult book, it was quickly passed over: 'there is not a person in the literary world who has not heard of, read and stolen some from *Nightwood*,' DB wrote, 'not more than three or four have mentioned my name.' DB left Paris for London and NYC, settling in 1937 in Patchin Place, Greenwich Village, where she remained, largely in a seclusion devoted to writing, until her death. Here she published *The Antiphon*, 1958, a play in which mother and daughter act out their hatred of each other, a collection of stories, *Spillway*, 1962, and two essays based on Paris in the 1920s, *Vagaries Malicieux*, 1975. She spent her last 30 years writing a long poem (MS with her papers at the Univ. of Maryland). *Smoke and other early stories*, 1982, and Alyce Barry, ed., *I Could Never Be Lonely Without a Husband: Interviews by DB*, 1985, collect her juvenilia. Life by Andrew Field, 1983; study by Benstock, 1986 (quoted above); bibliog. by Douglas Messerli, 1975; Lynn DeVore in *JML*, 10, 1983; Erika Duncan, *Soul Clap its Hands*, 1984.

Barnes, Margaret (Ayer), 1886–1967, dramatist and novelist, b. in Chicago, sister of Janet Ayer FAIRBANK and youngest child of Janet (Hopkins) and Benjamin A. After the University School for Girls in Chicago, she took a BA in English and philosophy at Bryn Mawr College, 1907; she later helped set up the pioneering Bryn Mawr Working Woman's College, 1921. In 1910 she m. Cecil B., a lawyer; she had three sons. She began to write in 1926 while recovering from a back broken in a car accident in France: 'I held the paper above the casts covering my chest.' Her first stories appeared that year in the *Pictorial Review* (collected in *Prevailing Winds*, 1928). She was encouraged by playwright Edward Sheldon, a fellow orthopaedic patient. Her love of theatre and amateur acting prompted her to dramatize Edith WHARTON's *The Age of Innocence* (increasing its political content): produced by Katherine Cornell in 1928. She wrote two more plays, *Jenny*, 1929, and *Dishonored Lady*, 1930 (both with Sheldon), and five novels. *Years of Grace*, 1930 (Pulitzer prize), relates its heroine's well-to-do Chicago girlhood, her apprehension at the leadership role suggested by Bryn Mawr, her marriage and consequent compromises, and uneasy acceptance of her assertive daughter's decision to divorce and 'take my happiness'. MAB's next three novels focus on upper-class women whose near-feminist aspirations clash with their lifestyles as Chicago socialites and supporters of the careers of ambitious husbands. Her last novel, *Wisdom's Gate*, 1938, returns to the rebellious daughter of her first, to leave her at last 'helplessly' ready 'to put up with' the infidelities of her second husband. Study by Lloyd Taylor, 1974. MSS at Harvard and NY Public Library.

Barnett, Edith A., fl. 1879–1907, English novelist, pamphleteer. Nothing is known of her life; her first publication in the BL catalogue is *The National Health Society's Penny Cookery Book*, 1879, and the last is *A Wilderness Woman*, 1907. She published on many social welfare subjects, such as *Common-sense Clothing* [1882] and *The Training of Girls for Work*, 1894, as well as several novels. *Dr and Mrs Gold*, 1891, is a serious and carefully-written study of a woman anarchist visionary whose life is cynically exploited by a male intellectual. *A Champion of the Seventies*, 1898, is another drily written narrative of an intelligent girl's struggle between her wish for useful work, which she finds among women's causes in London, and her love for her family, who mindlessly oppose her freedom.

Barney, Natalie Clifford, 1876–1972, poet, playwright, novelist, essayist, epigrammatist and *salonnière* whose evenings at 20 rue Jacob, Paris, 'for over sixty years, brought together French and Americans, intellectuals and artists'. Eldest child of artist Alice (Pike) and railroad heir Albert Clifford B., she received a finishing school education in the USA and Europe, often in France while her mother studied painting. She 'came out' as a debutante in Washington (to please her father), then went to France, 1897, to study prosody, publishing her first verses, illustrated by her mother, *Quelques portraits-sonnets de femmes*, in 1900. These, which her father tried to suppress by buying the plates, and *Cinq petits dialogues grecs*, 1902, announce the sapphic theme which is central to her work. Made wealthy by her father's death, NCB settled permanently in Paris in 1902, launching the salon she continued for almost all of her life in 1909: 'And Miss Barney told me', said Berthe Cleyrergue, who cooked, 'you must always say that my literary salon was international' (interview in *Signs*, 4, 1979). Here, and in her Académie des Femmes, established by the late 1920s and wittily titled to counterpoint the reverend, exclusively-male Académie Française, she worked to create a sapphic circle and to make a forum for the presentation of writing by English- and French-speaking women. She translated STEIN's *The Making of Americans* for this. Her autobiographical 'Memoirs of a European American' is unpublished, but *Aventures de l'esprit*, 1929, *Souvenirs indiscrets*, 1960, and *Traits et portraits*, 1963, describe her literary acquaintance: Djuna BARNES, Mina LOY, Nancy CUNARD, Edith SITWELL, as well as Valéry, Proust and Rémy de Gourmont, whose late love for her inspired his *Lettres à l'Amazone* (pub. in the *Mercure de France*, 1912–13, and transl., 1931, by Richard Aldington). NCB's *Pensées d'une amazone*, 1920, and *Nouvelles Pensées de l'amazone*, 1939, appropriate the epigrammatic tradition of Pascal, La Rochefoucauld and Wilde for a female subject matter. *The One Who is Legion or A.D.'s After-Life*, with two illustrations by Romaine Brooks, 1930, a kind of gothic novel, probes NCB's own writing and the suicide of Renée VIVIEN, her early lover, in whose memory, for a time, she awarded a literary prize at her salon. Her relationship with Brooks – they met during WWI, spent WWII together in Italy, where NCB supported the Fascists, and lived together until a year before RB's death, 1970 – lasted nearly 50 years. A character in Barnes's *Ladies Almanack* and Radclyffe HALL's *The Well of Loneliness*, NCB 'wrote a prolific record of her own lesbianism', resolving early 'to live openly', asking 'why should they hold it against me for being a lesbian? It's a question of my nature: my queerness isn't a vice, isn't "deliberate", and harms no one.' Her view of her sexuality went against the orthodox grain, denying perversion and inversion. Life by George Wickes, *The Amazon of Letters*, 1976 (he also wrote the *NAW* and *DLB* accounts); Jean Chalon's *Portrait of a Seductress*, 1976, trans. 1979, situates NCB in the male erotic from which she is retrieved by Benstock, 1986. Papers, mostly letters, at the Fonds Littéraire Jacques Doucet, Paris (catalogue, *Autour de NB*, 1976); some letters to Pierre

Louys pub. in J.-P. Goudon, ed., *Correspondences croisées*, 1983; other letters and MSS at Yale Univ.

Barr, Amelia Edith (Huddleston), 1831–1919, novelist, b. Ulverston, Lancs., da. of Mary (Singleton) and William Henry H., a Methodist minister. AB attended private schools until her father lost his fortune; she then taught at a school in Norfolk for a year before attending the Normal School in Glasgow, Scotland, in preparation for working in the Methodist schools for the poor. In 1850 she m. Robert B. They migrated to the USA in 1853 following his bankruptcy and settled in Austin, Texas. After his death in 1867, AB took her three daughters (the only survivors of eight children) to NYC, where she wrote upwards of 60 novels and several vols. of short stories. Among the best-known are *Jan Vedder's Wife*, 1885, set in the Shetland Islands; *Friend Olivia*, 1889, which draws on the history of the Quakers in Cromwell's England; and *The Bow of Orange Ribbon*, 1886, set in pre-Revolutionary NY. At their best, these novels mingle romantic plots – larded with occult premonitions, in which AB firmly believed – with a vein of domestic realism. She wrote her autobiography, *All the Days of My Life*, 1913, 'mainly for the kindly race of women ... I have drank the cup of their limitation to the dregs'. It romantically recounts AB's childhood and ambivalent marriage; her writing career is a prosaic matter of dates and sales. Her papers are held at the State Archives Library, Austin, and the Univ. of Texas Library.

Barrell, Maria (Weylar), poet and reformer. She lived in London (where 'not one soul in twenty knows / How cellery or endive grows') and nearby rural Isleworth, and visited Europe. After some years of writing for periodicals as 'Maria', she pub. as Weylar *Reveries du Coeur, or Feelings of the Heart*, 1770 (the running head is 'Poems on Various and Select Occasions'), designed to save a relation brought to distress by compassion. General Paoli and John Wilkes (evidently a friend) subscribed; the *Literary Magazine*'s scorn may perhaps have been political. She writes many kinds of love poem (from burlesque to a rather distant imitation of SAPPHO), praises rural life (sometimes in vivid, down-to-earth style) and dwells on both the need for liberty and the threat of poverty ('bondage is a living death'). By about 1785, with a husband absent abroad and two children to feed, she fell prey to moneylenders, then debtors' prison, 'the sad regions of a living grave'. As Barrell she pub. a prose pamphlet, *British Liberty Vindicated, or A Delineation of the King's Bench Prison*, 1788, whose strong argument draws on slavery, the Bastille, US customs and wifely guilt at involving her husband. In *The Captive*, 1790, a highly-coloured drama with preface and prologue, a husband and father dies in jail despite the efforts of unlikely benevolists.

Barrell, Miss **P.**, (d. by 1811), obscure novelist and poet published in London. Her engaging short epistolary novel, *Riches and Poverty*, 1808, deals in misjudgements revised. Adversity reveals Amelia's confidante to be worldly and unfeeling, a woman supposed cold and reserved to be a model friend, her chosen suitor to be weak and snobbish and her harsh, unpredictable guardian to be the ideal lover. Inset poems include a tale of a black page falsely accused: 'Yahtah was poor, Indora rich, / And justice was not done.' The themes of violence, injustice and treachery, with unhappy love, dominate *The Test of Virtue, and Other Poems* (posthumous, 1811). PB's ballads are often disturbing: another page is unjustly framed for murder; an envious literary arbiter advances only bad poets; Rodolpho invites the poor and miserable to a feast and poisons them all; and Clarinda dons knightly armour to revenge the honour of a female friend, but when she finds the seducer is her lover she kills not him but herself.

Barrington, Emilie Isabel, 'Mrs Russell B.' (Wilson), 1840–1933, art critic, biographer and novelist, one of six das. of Elizabeth (Preston) and James W., businessman, MP, founder of the *Economist*. A close friend of Emily FAITHFULL from the mid 1860s, they fell out just before she m. Russell B. in 1868. Artistically gifted, she tried unsuccessfully to exhibit at the Royal Academy while pregnant with her second child, who died at four months. Later she turned to writing, editing the works of her brother-in-law, Walter Bagehot, as well as writing his life, 1914, and those of her friends G. F. Watts, 1905, and Frederick Leighton, 1906. It is owing to her that Leighton House is now a museum. She wrote several novels from 1890: *Lena's Picture*, 1892, and *Helen's Ordeal*, 1894, both have lonely heroines who find release from desire through submission to their lot. Despite EB's own considerable assertiveness, her fiction denigrates 'political and strong-minded ladies'. For her life, see Martha Westwater, *The Wilson Sisters*, 1984.

Bartlett, Elizabeth, poet, b. 1924 at Deal, Kent, 'near the coalfields'. She won a scholarship to grammar school but left at 15 to work in a factory. Twice married, she has two children and two stepchildren. She has worked as home help, secretary and teacher: for the Workers' Educational Association and in prisons and hospices. ('W. E. A. Course' mocks its teachers as 'persons with grave and tranquil eyes and great / Authority in our carriage and attitude.') *A Lifetime of Dying*, 1979, collects poems since 1942: anti-idealist, self-consciously working-class, combining the personal, social and political. 'Birth' likens a new-born daughter's skin to that of an old woman after a lifetime's wringing out laundry, and hopes the child will 'not live to curse your birth / As many have done before you, / And will do again'. 'Old Movies' juxtaposes teenage girls weeping at Greta Garbo with their cramped lives, 'a grandmother dying / Of cancer in the next room'. *Strange Territory*, 1983, deals much with disease, age, decay, and efforts to deny these unpleasant facts. 'Butterfly Rash' describes an elaborate wedding marred by an outbreak on the bride's face. Poems in response to others' work include answers to Marvell and Blake and 'Mistaken Identity', in which the author finds herself anthologized owing to a mix-up with E. B. BROWNING. *The Czar is Dead*, 1987, pursues the same theme of 'assaultability', but emotional rather than physical, in more introspective and philosophical style. EB has reached anthologies on her own merits and won regional awards for poetry. She belongs to the Labour Party and CND.

Barton, Clara (Clarissa), 1821–1912, diarist and founder of the American Red Cross, b. North Oxford, Mass., da. of Sarah (Stone) and Stephen B. She was educ. at public schools and taught 1839–50, followed by a year of study at the Liberal Institute in Clinton, NY. She founded New Jersey's first 'free' school and then became a clerk for the Patent Office, Washington, perhaps the first regularly appointed woman civil servant. She earned the title 'Angel of the Battlefield' when, after witnessing the Battle of Bull Run in the Civil War, she began raising money for medical supplies. With the help of President Lincoln and the War Department, in 1865 she established an office to trace missing soldiers. After the war she travelled to Europe and worked for the International Committee of the Red Cross during 1870–1. On returning to the USA she devoted herself to the establishment of an American Red Cross and in 1878 pub. her pamphlet *The Red Cross of the Geneva Convention*. Apart from a short period in 1883 serving as Superintendent of the Women's Reformatory Prison, Sherborn, she spent 1881–1904 working for the Red Cross in the USA and abroad. She pub. *The Red Cross*, 1898, and *A Story of the Red Cross*, 1904. Because of internal dissension she resigned as President of the American Red Cross in 1904. Her feminist achievements were recognized during her lifetime, as in Lucy LARCOM's *Our Famous Women*, 1884. The 35 vols. of her DIARIES, from 1866–1910, are in the Library of Congress. Her autobiographical *Story of my Childhood* was pub. in 1907. See life by Helen BOYLSTON, 1955.

Basset, Mary (Roper), *c.* 1522–72, translator. Eldest da. of Margaret ROPER, she m. Stephen Clarke, then (by 1557) her fellow-Catholic James B.; she had two sons. Between 1547 and 1553, as 'Mary Clarcke', widow, she translated from Greek the first five books of Eusebius's *Ecclesiastical History*, presenting it in a splendid MS copy (BL) to Mary Tudor, who in 1557 gave her a Court post. She also translated into English the later, Latin, part of her grandfather Sir Thomas More's *History of the Passion* – 'plainly and exquisitely', 'elegantly and eloquently', said scholars – with corrections of the unrevised original. Her version was pub. 1566 (by which time she was again a widow): repr. 1941, ed. P. E. Hallett. Each work, she said, was 'but for her own pastime and exercise.'

Bates, Katharine Lee, 1859–1929, educator and poet, b. Falmouth, Mass., da. of Cornelia Francis (Lee) and the Rev. William B. who d. one month after her birth. Her mother moved the family to Grantsville (now Wellesley) and in 1874 to Newtonville. KLB was educated at public schools and in 1876 entered Wellesley College, graduating in 1880. She taught from 1880, became Instructor in English Literature at Wellesley in 1885 and retired in 1925. She is best known for her patriotic lyric, 'America the Beautiful', which first appeared in 1895 in the *Congregationalist* and has since been pub. in the hymnals of many faiths. KLB thought of herself as a poet and pub. six collections, the most significant being *America the Beautiful and Other Poems*, 1911. She also wrote college textbooks on British authors, as well as the widely-used text *American Literature*, 1898. Her other works include travel books and juvenile fiction.

Bathurst, Anne, *c.* 1638–96/9, visionary autobiographer, of 'good' family, member of Jane LEAD's sect. As a child she loved praying with her sister; the only book for her was the Bible. She acquired a sense of sin at 14, asked serious questions at 17 and rejected the doctrine of Election. Her twenties were happy, her thirties troubled and consumed with hunger to know God. In 1678, visited by an angel, she began a diary of visions (Bodleian, with some of her letters). Day after day her 'Spiritual eye' showed her flowers, rivers, a 'Rock of wonder', a marble fountain: when she 'desired to see' persons or spirits she at once did so. Her prose, more than her few verses, is often sexual: 'O Love! Love! how am I imbellished sick with Divine Sweetness more than marrow or fatness. My Beloved has placed himself within me and made me too bigg for myself, as if the Earthen vessel were stretched beyond its wonted bigness.' She is not the AB who wrote in works by Elizabeth BATHURST (and who was probably Elizabeth's sister).

Bathurst, Elizabeth, *c.* 1655–85, Quaker apologist and feminist. Eldest child of Frances and Charles B. of London, she was sickly and could not walk alone till she was four. Pious very early, she became a Quaker at about 23, undertook a preaching tour to Bristol in a time of persecution, and was imprisoned in the Marshalsea by judges who 'thought her ... a Person of great Learning and Education'. She pub. *An Expostulatory Appeal* [1678] and *Truth's Vindication*, 1679 (begun some time earlier and 'swelled beyond my intention'). This defends the Quakers fervently yet rationally (point by theological point, with lavish bible quotation), draws on her own experience and ends with an epistle to recent converts. It was often reprinted, from 1691 as *Truth Vindicated*, with others' words of praise and assertions of authenticity and her own *Sayings of Women*, 1683, chosen from scripture to show that women 'receive an Office in the Truth as well as Men.'

Battier, Henrietta (Fleming), 'Patt. Pindar', 1751?–1813, poet and satirist, da. of John F. of Staholmock, Co. Meath. In 1768 she m. Major John Gaspard B. (d. 1794). Visiting London in 1783–4, she acted as an amateur at Drury Lane and sought subscribers (starting with Samuel Johnson) for a collection delayed by serious illness and the death of a child, pub. as *The Protected Fugitives*, Dublin, 1791. That year, under a name alluding to 'Peter Pindar' (John Wolcot), she attacked one of her subscribers (an ex-Catholic star preacher) in *The Kirwanade, or Poetical Epistle* (two instalments; another promised): magnificently controlled vituperation in vigorous, colloquial heroic couplets. She campaigned against the Union Bill in *The Gibbonade, or Political Reviewer* (3 nos., 1793–4), *The Terrors of Majesty* (untraced) and the anti-Orange, pro-Grattan *The Lemon* (1797; second part promised). These poems, fighting with unusual panache for reform, religious toleration and Irish liberty (with allusion to Swift), proudly emphasize the author's sex, independence and success. Her *Marriage Ode Royal* (the 'Royal' printed upside down), 1795, closely parodies Dryden's *Alexander's Feast* and lampoons the Prince of Wales. *An Address on ... the Projected Union, To the Illustrious Stephen III, King of Dalkey, Emperor of the Mugglins*, 1799, was written as poet laureate to a playful literary society described by Tom Moore, who met her – poor, 'acute, odd, warm-hearted, and intrepid' – in 1795.

Baughan, Blanche Edith, 1870–1958, poet, short-story writer, journalist and penal reformer, b. in Putney, London, da. of Ruth and John B. She was educ. at Brighton High School, Sussex, and Royal Holloway College, London Univ. (BA Hons in Greek). Having joined the suffragette movement, and done social work in the East End of London and pub. *Verses*, 1898, she emigrated to NZ in 1900. She founded the NZ Howard League for Penal Reform, 1924, and joined the staff of the Women's Reformatory at Addington, Christchurch. She pub. *Reuben*, 1903, *Shingle Short*, 1908, *Brown Bread from a Colonial Oven*, 1912, *Poems from the Port Hills*, 1923, and several brochures on NZ scenery, evidence of a passion for outdoor pursuits. Her poetry and stories experiment with colloquial NZ speech, and her poetry reads like a hybrid of Browning's dramatic monologue and the Australian ballad. In 'Red, Yellow and Ripe', an old woman says: '... out 'ere, the men'll let the women 'ave their share o' the say without a-shuttin' of 'em up'. BB believed that after an illness in 1910 her gift died: 'I did not desert it, it deserted me.' *People in Prison*, 1936, supports this opinion with its romantic and patronizing description of prison 'types'.

Bawden, Nina (Mabey), b. 1925, novelist for adults and children. Da. of Ellalaine Ursula (Cushing) and engineer Charles M., she was educ. at Somerville, Oxford (BA 1946, MA 1951). Married twice, to H. W. B. and to Austen Steven Kark, 1954, she has three children. She has been a JP, like the narrator of *Afternoon of a Good Woman*, 1976, who at 46 reviews her life with all its family disappointments and sexual betrayals, sees her good deeds stripped of power and influence and determines to pursue a career. NB's more than 30 novels for children and adults have many common features: multiple marriages and divorces, blended families, abusive and often drunken husbands, decidedly odd couples and chasms in understanding separating most adults from children. Her children's books stress cracking good adventures (apprehension of a child's murderer in *Devil by the Sea*, 1957, of a jewel thief in *The Witch's Daughter*, 1966) but their compassionate insight into the child's world (the lonely nine-year-old Perdita presumed to be a witch, the guilt-ridden Carrie in *Carrie's War*, 1973) is their most prominent aspect. Adults mistakenly disregard children in NB's adult as in her juvenile fiction. The child-narrator of *A Little Love, A Little Learning*, 1965, shows precocious children assessing their elders. *Anna Apparent*, 1972, stretches from the early memories of an illegitimate child evacuee during the blitz to the predicament she faces as a married woman and a mistress; *The Ice House*, 1983, perceptively examines a 30-year rivalry between girlhood friends.

Baxter, Annie Maria (Hadden), later Dawbin, 1816–1905, Australian diarist, b. Devon, da. of William H., army officer, who d. when she was five: her mother remarried and an uncle raised her. She was educ. at a boarding school. She m. Lieut. Andrew B. in 1834 and later that year went to Van Diemen's Land (later Tasmania) with his regiment. They lived in Sydney, then the Port Macquarie convict settlement and, after he left the army, on properties in NSW and Victoria. She left her husband in 1847, living with her brother in Hobart and later in England. After Baxter committed suicide in 1855, she returned to Melbourne, where she married Robert D. Her *Memories of the Past by a Lady in Australia*, 1873, based on diaries she kept 1834–65, gives insight into early colonial society. The original 32 volumes, now in the Dixson Library, Sydney, also reveal a well-educated, talented and spirited woman, probably Australia's best diarist. Extracts have appeared in *No Place for a Nervous Lady*, 1984, ed. by Lucy Frost, who is also writing a biography.

Bayfield, Mrs **E. G.**, d. after 1816, obscure poet and novelist publishing at London. Perhaps born Laura Cooper, she had known great matrimonial sorrow and had children of various ages by 1805, when Longman's paid six guineas for her *Fugitive Poems*. Lady HAWKE, Elizabeth INCHBALD and Jane PORTER subscribed. EGB's lively verses on family and love situations (some repr. from magazines) play with ideas like 'Man has pow'r enough already, / We need not grant him more' and (the volume's last line) 'MEN are BUTTERFLIES in LOVE.' An *Ode to Retirement* followed next year. A publisher, unauthorized, retitled her novel written as *Love as It May Be, and Friendship as It Ought to Be*, making it *A Winter at Bath* after Mrs E. M. FOSTER's *A Winter in Bath*, causing long-lived confusion between the two.

Baylor, Frances Courtenay (later Barnum), 1848–1920, novelist, short-story and sketch writer, b. Fort Smith, Ark., da. of Sophie (Baylor) and James Dawson. FB was educ. by her mother, who resumed her maiden name, and she lived in England with her sister's family for several years following the Civil War, visiting Europe again 1873–4. In 1896 she m. George Sherman Barnum. FB's first work, a play, *Petruchio Tamed*, pub. anon., was followed by two early sketches pub. together as *On Both Sides*, 1886, and a children's novel, *Juan and Juanita*, 1888. Other works include *Behind the Blue Ridge*, 1887, *A Shocking Example and Other Sketches*, 1889, *Claudia Hyde*, 1894, and *A Georgian Bungalow*, 1900. Despite her not marrying until nearly 50, and retaining her mother's name, FB's work does not challenge conventional attitudes about men and women. Her books combine US and British characters and settings, with vivid descriptions and exciting plots. Her articles and sketches, often more interesting, appeared in the Louisville *Courier-Journal*, London *Truth*, *Lippincott's*, *Atlantic Monthly* and others. See *Baylor's History of the Baylors*, 1914, for family history.

Baynton, Barbara (Lawrence), 1857–1929, short-story writer and novelist, b. Scone, NSW, youngest da. of Elizabeth (Ewart) and John L., carpenter; BB's own accounts of her background were more colourful. She was educ. at home and through her own reading. The day after divorcing Alexander Frater, who absconded with a servant, she m. Thomas B., gaining financial security and entry to Sydney intellectual circles. She became well known as a literary hostess in England and Australia, gaining a title in 1921 when she m. Lord Headley. Her first and best-known work, *Bush Studies*, 1902 (repr., with two additional stories, as *Cobbers*, 1917) was pub. in England after rejection in Australia. Her only novel was *Human Toll*, 1907. BB's fiction is notable for its uncompromising view of bush life, often focusing on the plight of isolated women, and its generally unheroic portraits of men. She was ahead of her time in her treatment of religion and sexuality and was perhaps the first Australian to use 'point-of-view' narration. See *The Portable BB*, 1980 (eds. Alan Lawson and Sally Krimmer); Kay Iseman in *Australian Literary Studies*, 1983; and Elizabeth Webby in *Southerly*, 1984; a life by her great-granddaughter, Penne Hackforth-Jones, 1989.

Beach, Sylvia Nancy Woodbridge, 1887–1962, publisher, editor and translator whose bookshop and lending library in Paris, Shakespeare and Company, attracted writers, or 'literary pilgrims', from all over the world. B. in Baltimore, da. of Eleanor (Orbison) and Presbyterian minister Sylvester B., she went to Paris, 1916, to study French poetry. Drawn into WWI, she farmed in Touraine for the *Volontaires Agricoles* and was made 'a regular feminist' by Red Cross work in Serbia. In 1917 she met French bookseller Adrienne Monnier, who was her lover, 1919–37, and was encouraged to open her own bookshop. Shakespeare and Company functioned, 1919–41, first in rue Dupuytren, then in rue de l'Odéon, as meeting place, club house, post office, money exchange and reading room for French, Irish, English and American writers, including Valéry, Gide, Eliot, Hemingway, Pound, STEIN, Alice TOKLAS, BRYHER, Djuna BARNES, Natalie Clifford BARNEY, Mina LOY, and Janet FLANNER. During the 1920s SB translated US authors, including Whitman and Eliot, into French and edited a collection of essays on *Finnegans Wake* (*Our Exagmination Round His Factification for Incamination of Work in Progress*), 1929. On 2 February 1922, Joyce's 40th birthday, she published *Ulysses*, though US courts had indicted Margaret ANDERSON and Jane HEAP in 1921 for serializing the 'obscene' Nausicaa chapter in the *Little Review*. SB organized its sales, distribution and even smuggling to the US, kept it in print throughout the 1920s and acted as the author's editor, publisher, secretary and banker. Her mother's death, 1929 (a suicide SB concealed), the recession and Joyce's increasing financial needs made her role difficult. In 1932, as she prepared the twelfth printing of *Ulysses*, Joyce negotiated with Random House for a test case in the Supreme Court: Judge Woolsey's famous 1933 ruling allowed US publication and sale of the novel, and SB relinquished publisher's rights. Over the next years, she helped Monnier edit *Mesures*, a new literary review, and sold books and manuscripts to carry Shakespeare and Company through the Depression. It was eventually closed by Nazis, 1941, and SB was interned at Vittel for six months. However, she managed to save her books, ran a library from her apartment after the war, translated several works, including BRYHER's *Beowulf*, 1948, and Henri Michaux's *Barbare en Asie*, 1933, in 1949 and contributed substantially to the 'Twenties Exhibition' in Paris, 1959. See her memoir, *Shakespeare and Company*, 1959, Noel Riley Fitch's 1983 life, and Benstock, 1986. Papers at Princeton Univ.

Beard, Mary (Ritter), 1876–1958, historian and feminist. B. Indianapolis, one of six children of Narcissa (Lockwood) and Eli Foster R., she was educ. at de Pauw Univ. (PhB, 1897). In 1900 she m. Charles Austin B.; they had two children. After a stay in England (her husband was doing research at Oxford), during which she was involved in the suffrage movement, she attended Columbia Univ. briefly, 1902–4, and became involved in labour and SUFFRAGE movements in NYC (interests reflected in her earliest publications, *Woman's Work in Municipalities*, 1915, and *A Short History of the American Labor Movement*, 1920). She edited the Woman Suffrage Party of New York's *The Woman Voter*, 1910–12, then worked for Alice PAUL's Congressional Union (later The Woman's Party), 1913–17. From the 1920s MRB left activism to work as historian, collaborating with her husband throughout their careers on works of US history (including *The Rise of American Civilization*, 1927, *America in Midpassage*, 1939, *The American Spirit*, 1942, and *A Basic History of the United States*, 1944) and working on her own on a variety of women's history projects. She was interested in documenting women's history in collections such as *America Through Women's Eyes*, 1933, and *Laughing Their Way: Women's Humor in America*, 1934 (edited with Martha B. Bruère), as well as in her unsuccessful attempt to establish a World Center for Women's Archives in the late 1930s. She also offered a fundamental feminist critique of historical scholarship in *On Understanding Women*, 1931, and *Woman as Force in History*, 1946. Challenging male scholars who 'confine their search for the truth to their own sex in history', she proposed the 'reopen[ing]' of 'the narrative of history ... to take in the whole course of civilization', challenging equally women who viewed their history as 'a blank or a record of defeat'. She attacked 'a sex education – masculine in design and spirit', outlining a syllabus for 'a genuinely equal education' in *A Changing Political Economy as it Affects Women*, 1934. She was invited by the *Encyclopaedia Britannica* to analyse its treatment of women – 'wholly fortuitous' – but most recommendations in her 1942 report were never adopted. Her final works were *The Force of Women in Japanese History*, 1953, and a biography of her husband, 1955. MRB and her husband destroyed the bulk of their papers, though Radcliffe and Smith Colleges and De Pauw Univ. have some. Many works reprinted; see Ann J. Lane, *MRB: A Sourcebook*, 1977, for biographical sketch, bibliog. and selected writings.

Beattie, Ann, novelist and short-story writer. B. in 1947 in Washington, DC, da. of Charlotte (Crosby) and James A. B., she was educ. at American Univ. (BA 1969) and the Univ of Conn. (MA 1970). Married in 1972 to David Gates (now divorced), and the mother of a son, she has taught at both Harvard, 1977–8, and the Univ. of Virginia, Charlottesville, where she lives. In 1976 she published a short-story volume, *Distortions*, and her first novel, *Chilly Scenes of Winter*, which established her as an acute observer of the foibles and delusions of the idealistic, 1960s, 'Woodstock generation' of upper-middle-class Americans. *Falling in Place*, 1980, portrays, largely from the point of view of the children, the eventful disintegration of a suburban Connecticut WASP marriage. *Love Always*, 1985, sketches a whole gallery of the phoney and the self-deluded, centred on an aunt and 14-year-old niece, both media people: the aunt writes, as 'Cindi Coeur', a parodic Miss Lonelyhearts column in a counter-culture magazine (and is lover of its editor); the niece is 'famous ... and difficult' star (as an abused, alcoholic teenager) in a preposterous soap opera with a Yeatsian title, *Passionate Intensity*. A deeper note interrupts the jostling, cinematically-presented adventures with the death on her lover's motorbike of the heroines' sister/mother. Social realism, wit, and black humour mingle; AB's eye for the grotesque has drawn comparison with the photographer Diane Arbus. She writes frequently for the *New Yorker*: further short-story volumes (*Secrets and Surprises*, 1979, *The Burning House*, 1982, *Where You'll Find Me*, 1986) illustrate her skilful, sensitive depiction of the small tragedies of daily life and relations. *Picturing Will*, 1990, is a novel.

Beauclerc, Amelia, author of eight novels pub. at London 1810–20 (*Eva of Cambria*, 1810, and *Ora and Juliet*, 1811, have been wrongly ascribed to Emma PARKER). She can be predictably gothic (castles, ghosts, ancient MSS), heavy-handed (the much-tried and constantly-fainting heroine of *Husband Hunters!!!*, 1816) or punitively moralizing (an over-indulgent mother in *Disorder and Order*, 1820, causes the deaths of *two* of her children). Her best work, though, is impressive, centring on relations between the sexes. *Alinda, or The Child of Mystery*, 1812, presents a female friendship begun when a 'handsome stranger' shockingly and comically sheds male disguise and vows sisterhood. *Montreithe, or The Peer of Scotland*, 1814, centres on a penniless noble who develops from 'turbulent, bold boy' into a tyrant who loves sport and despises women: his daughter, against all the odds, grows up strong and feeling, and turns the tables by rescuing him.

Beaumont or Beoment, **Agnes**, later Story, 1652–1720, religious memoirist. In 1672 she defied her father (John B. of Edworth, farmer) to join John Bunyan's Bedford congregation. In 1674, after gossip about her and Bunyan, her father turned her out, demanding a promise to attend no more meetings: she prayed all night in the barn in freezing weather, tried to win him round with her brother's counsel (which 'I thought I had noe need of') and suffered deeply after a reconciliation based on compromise. Two days later her father died (after a seizure in her arms) as she was running half-dressed through the snow for help. She was accused of poisoning him (by a former suitor who had withdrawn on her conversion), and tried for 'low treason': conviction would have meant burning alive. The coroner and jury acquitted her and rebuked her accuser, who still interfered with her inheritance, spread rumours of a confession (she publicly outfaced them on market day) and re-accused her of arson. She married twice; her second husband was rich and pious. Her *Narrative of the Persecution* is as spirited as her resistance. One of two BL MSS may be her own; pub. in Samuel James, *Abstract of the Gracious Dealings of God*, 1760 (poor text); G. B. Harrison's ed. [1929] is still the best.

Beauvoir, Simone de, 1908–86, French philosopher, novelist, essayist, autobiographer, feminist. B. in Paris, da. of fervently Catholic Françoise (Brasseur) and conservative lawyer Georges Bertrand de B., she was educ. at the Institut Catholique, the Institut Sainte-Marie and the Univ. de Paris. In 1929 she took her degree in philosophy and met Jean-Paul Sartre, with whom she pursued a self-examining intimacy until his death, 1980. She taught at *lycées* in Marseilles and Rouen, 1931–7, and Paris, 1938–43, thereafter devoting her life to writing and political activism. Her fiction features the existentialist anti-heroine, *'l'amoureuse'* – Elisabeth in *L'Invitée*, 1943 (*She Came to Stay*, 1954), Denise in *Le Sang des Autres*, 1944 (*The Blood of Others*, 1948), and Paule in *Les Mandarins*, 1954 (*The Mandarins*, 1960), awarded the Prix Goncourt. *'L'amoureuse'* abdicates autonomy and her capacity for 'authentic' engagement with others in favour of slavish attachments she falsely thinks she masters. *The Second Sex*, 1949, perhaps the century's most influential theoretical inquiry into women's condition, launches an existentialist account of woman's sexualization. It insists that 'a woman is made, not born', and exposes patriarchal ideology in the cultural construction of femininity. It exposes and denounces prevailing myths of womanhood perpetuated in men's literature and attacks both psychoanalysis (for representing women as 'lesser' men who 'lack' the phallus and men's full power of body, mind and spirit, and whose existence must be mediated by men to be fulfilled), and Marxism (for marginalizing and neglecting women's specific material history and needs). Her description of woman's biology is, however, ambiguous: her maternal body, an encumbering natural object threatening to engulf rational consciousness by subjecting it to the laws of nature (menstruation, gestation, lactation, etc.), betrays an Hegelian, if not Sartrean, idealist intolerance of the (female) body. But this is not misogyny so much as observation of women's need to be free of unwanted pregnancy in their struggle for self-determination. SdeB began the feminist section of *Les Temps Modernes*, 1973; as President of the Ligue du Droit des Femmes, 1974–85, she campaigned for pro-choice in abortion debates, pressed for support of victims of rape and domestic battery, and advocated a form of radical revolutionary feminism, which, while sharing some of socialism's concerns, would define itself and act autonomously. See her *Memoires d'une Jeune Fille Range*, 1958 (*Memoirs of a Dutiful Daughter*, 1959), *La Force de l'Age*, 1960 (*The Prime of Life*, 1962), *La Force des Choses*, 1963 (*Force of Circumstance*, 1964), *Tout Compte Fait*, 1972 (*All Said and Done*, 1974), and *Une Mort Très Douce*, 1964 (*A Very Easy Death*, 1966: on the death of her mother). In 1983 SdeB pub. Sartre's letters to her, 1926–63; her side of the corresp., unpub. till 1989, has raised a 'firestorm' of comment. Latest life by Deidre Bair, 1990. Bibliogs. include one in Claude Francis and Fernando Gontier, 1979, and one by Joy Bennett and Gabriella Hochman, 1988. See Michele Le Doeuff in *FS* 6, 1980, Judith Okely, 1986, Elaine Marks, ed., critical essays, 1987, and Toril Moi, 1990.

Beck, Lily Adams (Moresby), 'Louis Moresby' and 'E. Barrington', d. 1931, novelist and writer on the Orient, da. of Jane Willis (Scott) and John M. Her father was an admiral in the Royal Navy (whose memoirs, he said, 'could not have appeared without the collaboration of my daughter ... whose literary skill and judgment have given this volume whatever charm it may possess'). She spent many years in Asia before settling in Victoria, BC, 1919. She died in Japan. She began writing late, with short fiction and essays published in periodicals, and she produced about 30 books, beginning in 1921 with a joint translation from Japanese. She wrote a few novels and non-fiction works, many on religion, philosophy and the occult, like *The Splendour of Asia* (on Buddhism), 1926, and *The Story of Oriental Philosophy*, 1928, as L. Adams Beck. She also wrote historical romances (British and European) as 'E. Barrington' and (Oriental) as 'Louis Moresby': as all three she was well received. Her western historical romances are about love and adventure: *Glorious Apollo*, 1925, is about Byron, *The Divine Lady*, 1924, about Lady Hamilton and Lord Nelson, and *The Thunderer*, 1927, about Josephine and Napoleon. Her oriental stories deal with eastern mysticism and reincarnation: *A Romance of Reincarnation*, 1925, describes the effect of eastern mysticism on English men and women. *The Garden of Vision*, 1929, set in Japan, compares east and west.

Becker, Lydia Ernestine, 1827–90, political writer and suffragist, b. Manchester, eldest of 15 children of Mary (Duncuft) and Hannibal Leigh B. After a short stay at a boarding school in Everton, LB was educ. at home, learning German when she visited relatives in Thuringen Wald in 1844. She corresponded with Darwin and pub. *Botany for Novices* under her initials in 1864. In 1865 she began a short-lived Ladies Literary Society in Manchester to enable women to study scientific subjects and contributed an article on 'Female Suffrage' to *The Contemporary Review*, March 1867. *Some Supposed Differences in the Minds of Men and Women in Regard to Educational Necessities*, 1868, began the first of many lecture tours to northern towns. Though unmarried, she was Treasurer of the Married Women's Property Committee and the Vigilance Association for the Defence of Personal Rights. She edited the *Women's Suffrage Journal*, 1870–90. Her pamphlet on *The Political Disabilities of Women*, 1872, excoriates the inconsistencies and inhumanity of those who denied women emancipation and assumed the right to legislate on their affairs: 'those who compare the political status of women to that of minors, criminals, lunatics and idiots, give too favourable a view of the facts.' This was followed by *Liberty, Equality and Fraternity, a Reply to Mr Fitzjames Stephen's Strictures on the Subjection of Women*, 1873. LB became Secretary and later a parliamentary agent of the London Central Committee for Women's Suffrage. Much respected as a writer, speaker and organizer, she died in Geneva after contracting diptheria.

Bedford, Jean, novelist and short-story writer, b. 1946 in Cambridge, England, da. of Gladys (Green) and John B. She came to Australia as a young child and was educ. at Rosebud High School, Victoria, Monash Univ. and the Univ. of Papua New Guinea, then worked as a teacher, journalist and as literary editor of the *National Times*. She lived with novelist Peter Corris, with whom she had two daughters, and in 1987 m. Rod Parker. The feminist press, Sisters, pub. her first collection, *Country Girl Again*, 1979 (repr. 1985, with additional stories), based on her experiences growing up in the country. Her novel *Sister Kate*, 1982, presents the Ned Kelly legend from the perspective of his sister, while *Love Child*, 1986, is largely based on the life of her mother. *Colouring In*, 1986, subtitled 'A Book of Ideologically Unsound Love Stories', combines JB's stories with others written by her close friend, literary agent Rosemary Creswell. All focus on the same two women, who are clearly very close to their authors, and celebrate female friendship while casting an ironic eye on living and loving in contemporary Sydney. See P. Gilbert, *Coming Out from Under: Contemporary Australian Women Writers*, 1988.

Bedford, Sybille (Von Schoenebeck), novelist, travel writer, biographer, b. 1911 at Charlottenburg, in Brandenburg (now part of Berlin), da. of Elizabeth (Bernard) and Maximilian von S. After WWI (spent in Berlin) the money was gone; her mother left her with her father in remote Baden, living in a run-down *Schloss* and attending the village school, then took her to spend holidays in Italy and France and then to board with friends in London for (chiefly self-) education. By 1926 she was reading hard and frequenting the law-courts. She wrote 'contorted essays' then, at 19, while her mother was in a clinic for drug-addiction, an unpublished novel ('painful, hard work, and a great joy'). Having just met Aldous Huxley, she made it 'Huxley and water, not even soda-water ... it took me years to get away from it.' She m. Walter B. in 1935. As a journalist she covered the Auschwitz trial at Frankfurt, the *Lady Chatterley* trial and others; she also wrote on wine, food, travel and books. Her travel book, *The Sudden View: A Mexican Journey*, 1953, was repr. as *A Visit to Don Otavio*, from a ruined feudal landowner it portrays. *A Legacy*, 1956, is a novel comic, sharply satirical and coolly, analytically moral about wealthy pre-1914 Germany: a Catholic-Jewish marriage, a scandal provoked by army initiation rites. It draws on SB's own family, as she writes in *Jigsaw, An Unsentimental Education*, 1989, a 'Biographical Novel'. Her concern with justice produced books on the murderer John Bodkin Adams, 1958, and on famous British and European trials, 1961. *A Favourite of the Gods*, 1963, looks at three generations of women: a puritan New Englander, wife of a philandering Italian prince; their restless, sexually-active daughter; a granddaughter who destroys the two wills which embody and then revoke (in intention, not in law) her grandmother's rejection of her mother. In *A Compass Error*, 1968, the granddaughter, a successful 50-year-old writer, cannot quite absolve herself of complicity in the decisive error of her life: seduction by the wife of her mother's lover. (These two repr. 1984.) SB's life of Huxley, 1973–4, undertaken at his family's request, has been much praised. See Robert O. Evans in Jack I. Biles, ed., *British Novelists Since 1900*, 1987.

Beecher, Catharine Esther, 1800–78, educator and women's rights advocate. Sister of H. B. STOWE, she was b. at East Hampton, Long Island, NY, and briefly attended Miss Sarah Pierce's School, Litchfield, Conn. She began teaching in 1821 in New London, Conn., and, with her sister Mary, in 1823 opened a girls' school which was to become Hartford Female Seminary, where she revised the accepted curricula. Her 'Female Education' (*Am. J. of Education*, April and May 1827) and *Suggestions Respecting Improvement in Education*, 1829, advocated callisthenics as well as courses in teaching and domestic science. In 1831 she opened the Western Female Institute in Cincinnati, writing elementary textbooks, and when it closed in 1837 she wrote and lectured on the need for teachers in the West. In 1852 she founded the American Women's Educational Association. Not a suffragist, she fought against exploitation in home or factory (*The Evils Suffered by American Women and American Children*, 1846). She also wrote handbooks for housewives (most importantly *The American Woman's Home*, 1869, with her sister Harriet; repr. 1986); their *New Housekeeper's Manual*, 1873, advised a 'Pink and White Tyranny' in the home. CB wrote the autobiographical *Educational Reminiscences and Suggestions*, 1875; Mae E. Harveson's life of 1934 contains a complete bibliography. See also Milton Rugoff, *The Beechers*, 1981, and Jeanne Boydston et. al., 1988.

Beer, Patricia, poet, critic, novelist, b. 1924 in Exmouth, Devon, da. of Harriet (Jeffery), a teacher and Plymouth Brethren member, and Andrew William B., railway clerk. She began writing at about ten but 'was defeated from the start by having no idea that the real world could appear in literature'. She was taught at home by her mother, then went to council school, grammar school, Exeter Univ., London Univ. and St Hugh's College, Oxford (BLitt 1948). She was a lecturer at the Univ. of Padua ('A Street in Padua', written 25 years later, recalls the sensuous contrasts of the street the poet lived in, which now she cannot find), then worked in Rome, 1948–53, and lectured in English at Goldsmiths' College (London Univ.), 1962–8. Her marriage, 1964, to architect Damien Parsons was her second. Her first book of poems, *The Loss of the Magyar*, 1959, deals with her captain great-grandfather's death by shipwreck, *The Survivors*, 1963, with family and community history. Later volumes include *Just Like the Resurrection*, 1967, *The Estuary*, 1971, *Driving West*, 1975, *Selected Poems*, 1979, and *The Lie of the Land*, 1983. Her forms are various, measured, not always regular; in the 1970s she began experiments with free verse syllabics and half-rhyme. Her poems savour small experiences and yield small surprises: 'A cloud approaches the top / Of a mountain, surrounds it / Like a car-wash, then trundles / Onwards to the dry blue sea'. Present life often evokes earlier centuries. Jeni COUZYN says she has been 'a favourite ... for token woman, because she can be relied on never to embarrass the reader with anything too "female"'; yet gendered experience is teasingly interrogated in 'The Lost Woman', whose speaker contrasts the snappish, rebuking ghost of a mother, early dead, with the hero's or (male) poet's 'lost woman to haunt the home, / To be compensated and desired, / Who will not alter, who will not grow, / A corpse they need never get to know.' PB has written the autobiographical *Mrs Beer's House*, 1968; critical studies of the Metaphysical poets, 1972, and of nineteenth-century women novelists (*Reader, I Married Him*, 1974); and a novel, *Moon's Ottery*, 1978, of two sisters growing up just before the time of the Spanish armada. She has co-edited several modern anthologies and has been anthologized herself. See Anne STEVENSON in *Poetry R*, 70, 1980.

Behn, Aphra (Johnson?), 'Astrea', *c.* 1640–89, dramatist, poet and novelist, first professionally-writing Englishwoman, probably da. of Elizabeth (Denham) and Bartholomew J., Canterbury innkeeper. She complains of poor education but demonstrates wide reading. She was a covert Roman Catholic. She spent 1663–4 with her family in Surinam, later Dutch Guiana, already writing. In 1664, it seems, she m. Mr Behn, a merchant of Dutch descent; the marriage was over by July 1666, when she went to Holland to spy for Charles II. Her reports (including warnings – accurate but ignored – of Dutch invasion plans) survive (PRO). Her pay always in arrears, she returned to be jailed for debt, 1668. 'Forced to write for Bread, and not ashamed to own it', she wrote 18 plays, besides doubtfuls (coll. 1702): highly professional, sometimes recasting earlier works, they turn on rapid plotting as well as wit. Her characters voice the gamut of current anti-feminist attitudes but also of women's own views. Her first work, *The Forc'd Marriage*, Lincoln's Inn Fields 1670, has a deprecatory prologue and passive-victim heroine. Her third, *The Dutch Lover*, pub. 1673, has an 'Epistle to the Reader', which attacks prejudice against female writers and asks 'the privilege for my masculine part, the poet in me ... I value fame as much as if I had been born a hero.' *Abdelazar*, staged 1676, her only tragedy, deals with issues of racism and unbridled female passion. *The Rover, or The Banish't Cavaliers*, acted 1677 with prologue implying male authorship (soon amended), charts the relation between marriage, prostitution and women's subordination: it was a hit. *Sir Patient Fancy*, staged 1678, satirizes a learned lady. AB's partisan, pro-Stuart plays begin with *The Rover II*, staged 1681. *The Luckey Chance*, pub. 1687, renews her complaint of sexist prejudice. Her huge output includes snappy Tory versions of Aesop's fables, 1687, often repr.; poems on love and other topics, anthologized by others and by herself (including her verse-and-prose romance, *A Voyage to the Island of Love*, 1684); translations from Ovid, 1680, SAPPHO, 1681, several French authors, and from Latin by Cowley, 1689. She celebrated Charles II, James II and Mary II, but refused to celebrate William. Her 15 novels (short stories to us, another new form for an Englishwoman) often claim a factual basis for romantic plots: they treat unwilling marriage, financial malpractice, and women (either victimized or triumphantly reversing the sexual balance of power). In *Love-Letters Between a Nobleman and his Sister*[-in-law] (three parts, 1684–7) a woman submits first to incest, then to face-saving but degrading marriage. The immensely popular *Oroonoko*, whose royal-slave hero she claimed as a personal friend, appeared in *Three Histories*, 1688, the first of four collections (others 1689, 1696 and 1697). AB was generous and popular with her peers but often vilified in print. She had more than one lover; some poems hint at love between women. Her works (where sex is as central as in those of her friend Rochester and other contemporaries) often question expectations about women; the filth so long alleged is not to be found. She was arrested for political plain-speaking, 1682, injured in an accident, winter 1684–5, and constantly ill during her last year. Her name has been both inspiration and stumbling-block. See Montague Summers, ed., incomplete *Works*, 1915; recent reprs. and scholarly eds.; Germaine GREER, ed., *Uncollected Verse*, 1989; Patrick Lyons, ed., *Selected Writings*, forthcoming; lives by Vita SACKVILLE-WEST, 1927, Maureen DUFFY, 1977; bibliog. by Mary Ann O'Donnell, 1986; Catherine Gallagher in *Genders*, 1, 1988.

Bell, Deborah (Wynn or Winn), *c.* 1689–1738, Quaker preacher of 'great Authority' and autobiographer, only surviving child (of seven) of Deborah (Kitching) and John W. (d. 1699: he had left the army on becoming a pacifist). Piously educated, called to the ministry at about 18, she wrote *A Short Journal*, pub. 1762 (with a letter, 1711, defending women's preaching), of her tours round England, Scotland and Ireland, 1707–20, defying sometimes physical opposition. Whenever 'drawn in my Mind' to visit distant Friends, she would set off with a female companion, preferably old and experienced; she was on the road two months after marrying John B. in 1710. After 1720 he usually went with her; she was often ill with pleurisy. Minor writings were pub. 1715, 1736, [1738] and later.

Bell, Gertrude Margaret Lowthian, 1868–1926, travel writer and stateswoman, b. at Washington Hall, Co. Durham, da. of Mary (Shield), who d. when she was two, and industrialist Hugh B. (later knighted). Her step-mother, Florence Eveleen Eleonore (Olliffe), 1851–1930, published plays (from 1889), novels including *The Story of Ursula*, 1895 (whose sexually-liberated governess heroine gave offence), and non-fiction including the classic *At the Works: A Study of a Manufacturing Town*, 1907, repr. 1985. GB attended Queen's College, London; at Lady Margaret Hall, Oxford, she was the first woman to reach first-class degree level in history, 1888. In 1892 (forbidden by her family to marry Henry Cadogan, who died a year later), she visited Persia (having learned Persian), had essays on the trip published against her will (*Safar Nameh, Persian Pictures*, 1894, repr. as *Persian Pictures*, 1928) and translated poems by the fourteenth-century mystic Hafiz, 1897: 'a living flame / Transpiercing Death's impenetrable door'. She went twice round the world, learned Arabic in Jerusalem, 1899, climbed in the Swiss Alps, 1901, and in 1905 made a major exploration from Jerusalem through Syria and Asia Minor. She wrote of her journey and archaeological finds in *The Desert and the Sown*, 1907, repr. 1985, and three more erudite, humanly involving books. Often scornful of most women, afraid that militancy would jeopardize progress, she was a founder member of the Woman's Anti-Suffrage League, 1908. During 1914 she kept one diary for her family and another for 'Dick' Doughty-Wylie, a married man with whom she was passionately in love (he died in the Dardanelles). On her last trip before WWI – right across Arabia, an area hardly seen by Europeans – GB was detained for a month at the Emir's palace, where she gathered much useful information. In 1914 she went to work for the Red Cross, tracing missing persons; recruited in 1915 for an Arab intelligence office in Cairo, she later worked in India, Basra, and Baghdad, where after WWI she was director of antiquities, founding the national museum in 1923 and being influential in the setting up of the state of Iraq. Her writing range extends from revealing personal letters to *Review of the Civil Administration of Mesopotamia*, 1921. She died in Baghdad, a revered public figure, no longer at home in England, perhaps a suicide. Her stepmother edited her letters, 1927 (reviewed by Vita SACKVILLE-WEST as 'sincere, sharp, and discriminating'); Elsa Richmond edited *Earlier Letters*, 1937. Lives by H. V. F. Winstone, 1978, Susan Goodman, 1985. Papers at Newcastle Univ.

Bell, Vera, poet and short-story writer, b. in St Ann, Jamaica, and educ. at Wolmer's Girls' School. She became an executive officer in the Social Welfare Commission and editor of the *Welfare Reporter*, then left to study at Columbia Univ., NYC (library science), and London Univ. She writes unflinchingly of past and present scars on Caribbean life. In 'The Bamboo Pipe' the 11-year-old, 'very black', very poor Son-Son, whose eyes hold a 'perpetual question mark', is comforted by achieving a note on his home-made pipe after his baby brother dies in his care while their mother is at work (*14 Jamaican Short Stories*, 1950). VB's poems have appeared in various respected journals. In 'Ancestor on the Auction Block' she writes, 'Across the years your eyes seek mine...Is the mean creature that I see / Myself? / Ashamed to look...I stand / A slave' – until she sees the God within them both (Donald G. Wilson's anthology of Caribbean poetry for schools, *New Ships*, 1971, repr. 1975). VB has written a pantomime and contributed to *You Better Believe It: Black Verse in English from Africa, the West Indies and the US*, 1973.

Bellerby, Mary Eirene **Frances** (Parker), 1899–1975, poet and fiction-writer, younger child of Marion Eirene (Thomas), a trained nurse, and the Rev. F. Talbot P., socialist, Anglo-Catholic incumbent of a poor Bristol parish. She wrote poems at four and made her adored mother a little book of them at eight. The family was frugal and tightly-knit; her admired elder brother trained her to fight like a boy ('prettiness was for girls!'); she was sent to Mortimer House School, Clifton, at nine after knocking a boy down. Her brother's death in action, 1915, and her mother's physical and mental breakdown, ended intense early happiness and began a lifelong obsession with recovery of the past. Leaving school in 1918, FB trained in kennel care, taught at a girls' school in Berks., wrote articles for *The Bristol Times* and in 1927 became a drama critic for it in London, of which she later wrote, 'Heavens, how I loved it!' She published *Perhaps?* (essays) in 1927 and *The Unspoiled* (novella) in 1928. In 1929 she m. John Rotherford B., ex-soldier, Cambridge economist and member of an idealistic group who strictly limited their spending and paid the surplus towards the founding of a school in East London. FB wrote on the project: 'The Neighbours' (pamphlet), 1931, and *Shadowy Bricks* (novel), 1932, with contributions from her husband. In 1930 a fall on rocks made her a semi-cripple; in 1932 her mother killed herself. FB said she was 'temporarily insane' from these causes when in 1934 she arranged a short separation from her husband; but they finally parted eight years later. When in 1941 she settled at Upton Cross, Cornwall, she felt a 'tremendous, deep, still excitement', a freedom of her inner self as poetry returned after 'twelve lost years' and found herself writing down 'dictated words'. She had pub. a short-story volume, *Come To an End*, 1939; at 42 she began placing poems in periodicals, finished a half-written novel, *Hath the Rain a Father?*, and printed it and her first poetry volume, *Plash Mill*, in 1946. From then she kept writing and publishing stories and poems (some broadcast, some sent as greetings cards), despite a breast cancer operation, 1950, and some times of black depression. Later poems explore her feeling of having 'died' and risen again, as well as of epiphany and of timelessness: 'Merge, flow, Then and Now, / In my narrow breast.' She captures details of the Cornish natural world with delicacy and precision, her style becoming more succinct with time. Having failed for ten years to resolve 'August Night', on her brother's death, she recast it as '1915', 1968, now opening 'Never mourn the deathless dead'. From 1957 to 1968 she wrestled with an autobiography which was to 'pacify my entire living memory'; she found it 'dangerous work' and had to abandon it. Five more poetry volumes preceded *Selected Poems*, ed. Charles Causley, 1970; *Selected Poems*, ed. Anne STEVENSON, 1986 (Robert Gittings's intro. uses the MS autobiography); *Selected Short Stories*, ed. Jeremy Hooker, 1986.

Benedict, Ruth (Fulton), 'Anne Singleton', 1887–1948, anthropologist, poet, b. in NYC, da. of Bertrice Joanna (Shattuck) and Frederick Samuel F., who died when she was two. Left partly deaf by measles (undiagnosed until she entered school), she attended Vassar (graduated 1909), taught for some years in a California school, and saw marriage to Dr Stanley Rossiter B. as escape from becoming an 'old maid'. The marriage quickly showed strains; RB took refuge in her poetry and an uncompleted research project on the 'new women': Mary WOLLSTONECRAFT, Margaret FULLER and Olive SCHREINER. She studied with Elsie Clews Parsons at the New School for Social

Research from 1919, then at Columbia (Ph D 1923), with Franz Boas, who kept her, as a married woman, in low-paid posts. *Poetry* and *Nation* published her poems: she depicts marriage as captivity in 'Intimacies' ('All her quests / Had sailed but for this prize, this one note blown / To lead her captive') and as 'the treason in the blood' in writing on her parents. Finally separated in the late 1920s, she began work on her powerfully influential *Patterns of Culture*, 1934, a standard anthropological text for 25 years. She formed a 'lasting mutual dependence' with Margaret MEAD: RB wrote Mead poems; Mead published a brief life and selection of RB's writing, 1959. RB remained under-promoted; Columbia would not 'risk appointing a woman to head a department'. Her biographer Ruth Schacter Modell (1983) feels she 'anticipated current feminist thought precisely in her links between self and other in the conduct of inquiry'. Her work (like her book on Japan, *The Chrysanthemum and the Sword*, 1946) examines patterns of culture, not race; she was militant about racial equality during WWII, when this was not fashionable. MSS mostly at Vassar; life by Margaret Caffrey, 1989.

Benét, Laura, 1884–1979, poet, biographer, b. in Brooklyn, NY, da. of Frances (Rose) and James B.: sister of poets William Rose B. and Stephen Vincent B., whom she thought great where she was only good, sister-in-law of Elinor WYLIE. In *When William Rose, Stephen Vincent and I Were Young*, 1976, she remembered childhood as 'heavenly'. After Emma WILLARD School, 'Mother was criticized for letting me go' to Vassar (AB 1907), which 'never asked me to do a public reading. They asked my two brothers, but they never asked me.' She planned to be a missionary but became a social worker, Red Cross worker (1917–19) and newspaperwoman. She began writing after an astrologer told her she would do so whether she liked it or not, and produced 25 books. Her poems appeared widely, in, among other journals, *Poetry, The New Yorker* and the *Saturday Review of Literature*. Their figurative population is female: 'Spring, like a young woman who has borne her child', 'Night, the milky mother'. She won awards for *Basket for a Fair*, 1934 (dedicated to brother W. R.), and *In Love with Time*, 1959. *Come Slowly Eden*, 1942 (a novel about Emily DICKINSON, begun by Winifred Wells, completed by LB to soothe her grief over her mother's death), mentions her two lost loves. 'Portrait' presents herself, young, as 'a pest / A fluttering incessant bird' from whom 'Relatives run, those of more grace / Evade her queries as they may' (*Is Morning Sure?*, dedicated to brother Stephen Vincent, 1947). 'To Lola RIDGE' acknowledges a literary forebear: 'If poems born of some unconscious urge / Rise up like fountains on still days, / They mount on the approval of your tongue.' She wrote lives of Dickinson, 1974, and of Poe, P. B. Shelley, Washington Irving, Jenny Lind, ranked as children's books, though LB insisted 'I write for the rising adults, not for children ... I'm not a children's writer.' Believing prose easier to write, she considered herself primarily a poet, 'ecstatically happy' when the poetry came (five vols.). Papers at SUNY (Buffalo) and Brooklyn College. See Barbara Kaye Greenleaf in *Vassar Quarterly*, 73, 1977, quoted above.

Benger, or Benjays, **Elizabeth Ogilvy**, 1778–1827, feminist, biographer, and woman of letters, probably b. at West Camel, Somerset, only surviving child of Mary (Long) and John B. She grew up in naval towns (her father had enlisted when she was four), 'in the tormenting want of books', devouring open pages in bookshop windows. Her mother let her learn Latin at 12; she had read hugely in English by 1791, when out of 'zeal for the honour of my sex', she pub. with her name and age, dedicated to Lady CHAMPION DE CRESPIGNY, *The Female Geniad*, a poem with informative notes: an impressive roll-call of women writers from SAPPHO to contemporaries. In 1796 EOB's father died; in 1800 she settled in London and met on equal terms many of the women she had praised. (Friends included Elizabeth HAMILTON, Lucy AIKIN and Lady Caroline LAMB.) She wrote few more poems (one on ABOLITION, 1809) and found practical problems in drama. *Marian*, anon., 1812, first of two novels, ends not on the heroine's marriage but on a sketch of an eccentric, solitary female philanthropist; *The Heart and the Fancy, or Valsinore*, 1813, bears her name. EOB translated Klopstock's letters, 1814, then issued a series of lives, including Hamilton, 1818, Anne Boleyn, 1821 (the third ed., 1827, has a memoir by Aikin), and Mary Queen of Scots, 1823 (which judges ELIZABETH I without animus). Her work maintains a steady, searching interest in women's status and history; Germaine de STÄEL found her the most interesting woman in England.

Bennett, Anna (often miscalled Agnes) **Maria** (Evans), *c.* 1750–1808, novelist, b. at Merthyr Tydfil, Wales. The *European Mag.*, 1790, said her father and husband were customs officers, her brother a reputable City attorney; other stories give her a grocer father, David E., and tanner husband with whom she moved to the London area. She probably left him before working as shopkeeper, workhouse matron and then mistress ('housekeeper') to Admiral Sir Thomas Pye, whose name she gave to two of her children. He died the year of her first, anonymous, novel, *Anna, or Memoirs of a Welch Heiress*, 1785, which was said to have proved her notoriety by selling out in a day. Five more followed (*De Valcourt*, 1800, and two by 'Elizabeth B.' are probably not hers). *Juvenile Indiscretions*, 1786, is Fieldingesque, *Agnes De-Courci*, 1789, Richardsonian (see Isobel Grundy in Margaret Anne Doody and Peter Sabor, eds., essays, 1989). Prefacing *Ellen, or The Countess of Castle Howel*, 1794, AMB obliquely mentions the strain of simultaneously running the Edinburgh theatre and fighting legal battles over its lease, claimed by her and her actress daughter Harriet Pye Esten (subject of a poem by Susanna BLAMIRE). AMB's most popular book, *The Beggar Girl and her Benefactors*, 1797, is predictable in social attitudes, with mockery of a female gothic novelist; it made her a MINERVA best-seller. Her best work (featuring a whole gallery of female intellectuals and outcast children) bridges that of Fielding and Dickens in its verbal irony, robust satire and free range of low life, high life and the economic interactions between. But her fame (high with Scott and Coleridge) was brief: her vivid sexual comedy and strong handling of sexual exploitation quickly became equally unacceptable. Booklet by J. T. Fuller, 1913.

Bennett, Gwendolyn B., 1902–81, poet, short-story writer and artist, b. at Giddings, Texas. She spent her first years in Nevada, where her parents, Maime and Joshua B., taught on Indian reservations; in 1909 her father kidnapped her to live in Pa. and Brooklyn, NY, where she went to high school. She studied literature and fine art at Columbia Univ. and the Pratt Institute before teaching art at Howard Univ. Her first published poem, 'Heritage' (*Opportunity*, 1923), deals with blacks in the USA: 'sad people's soul / hidden by a minstrel smile'; it exemplifies GBB's painterly use of description and her interest in African roots, and pre-dates Countee Cullen's use of the same title. In May 1924 'To Usward', dedicated to Jessie FAUSET, appeared in both *Crisis* and *Opportunity*. After a year as a graphic artist in Paris, GBB returned in 1926 to teach at Howard and work on *Opportunity*; she provided an important account of the central Harlem Renaissance figures in her literary and fine-arts column, 'Ebony Flute'. As well as more poems, she also published stories: 'Wedding Day' (*Fire!!*, 1925) and 'Tokens' (Charles S. Johnson, ed., *Ebony and Topaz*, 1927) are strongly-voiced protests about the humiliations meted out to blacks by whites, controlling their bitterness through the use of male protagonists. In 1927 GBB was forced to resign from her post at Howard because the univ. disapproved of her planned marriage to Alfred Jackson, a medical student. They moved to the South then in 1930 to Long Island. An unfinished, untitled story apparently depicts in its alcoholic-doctor husband and near-suicidal wife GBB's own experience. She worked on federal government projects and as director of the new Harlem Community Center, but was suspended as a suspected Communist in 1941. Two schools where she taught were investigated for 'Un-American Activities'. GBB retired to Kultztown, Pa., with her second husband, Richard Crosscup. Her poems, often anthologized (the best known is 'To a Dark Girl'), have never been collected. Papers at the NY Public Library; PhD thesis by Sandra Yvonne Govan, Emory Univ., 1980.

Bennett, Louise Simone, MBE, 'Miss Lou', poet, performer, folklorist, b. 1919 in Kingston, Jamaica, only child of Kerene (Robinson), a dressmaker, and Augustus Cornelius B., a baker who 'went to bed rich and woke up poor' when a batch of bread made people ill. He d. when LB was seven. She early noted in clients of her mother (who supported her desire to write) the value of laughter, the way to express sadness without solemnity, and the contempt often felt by blacks for their own looks and dialect. After writing poems in standard English at school (Calabar Elementary, St Simon's College, Excelsior High School), she turned to patwah in 'On a Tramcar', which opens with a market-woman's words about LB dressed for a dance: 'Pread out yuhself, one dress-oman a come.' LB wondered others did not prefer this to 'writing in the same old English way about Autumn and things like that'. Attracted by Kingston 'yard' theatres, she began at school to perform her work at free concerts; comedian-impresario Eric 'Chalk Talk' Coverley engaged her for a Christmas concert in 1938; in 1943 her poems were read on ZQI, Jamaica's first radio station, and her weekly column began in *The Sunday Gleaner*. This had rejected poems until her performing fame grew: even after *Dialect Verses*, 1942, and *Jamaican Humour in Dialect*, 1943, she found it harder to publish than perform. Using patwah (although Claude McKay had preceded her) barred her from the Jamaica Poetry League and from *Focus*, 1943–60. After a correspondence course in journalism she went to London to study at Friends' College, Highgate (social work), then from 1945 at RADA. She launched her own radio programme and began studying folklore. Back in Jamaica in 1947, she taught and became active in developing a distinctively Jamaican pantomine. Need for money took her to England again to broadcast and work in repertory theatre, 1950–3, then to New York to perform in Greenwich Village and on radio. She m. Coverley in 1954 and co-directed the successful folk musical, *Day in Jamaica*; they returned home in 1955. As drama officer, then director, of the Social Welfare Commission LB travelled in rural areas, lectured, broadcast and wrote pantomime scripts. Her ten books include four *Anancy* titles (1944, 1950 and 1957, with others, and 1979); the well-known *Jamaica Labrish*, 1966, and *Selected Poems*, 1982, have useful introductions. Even in the 1970s a newspaper blamed the 'pernicious' linguistic influence of LB's radio programme 'Miss Lou's Views', but she is now much anthologized and influential with younger poets. Her work, often in ballad stanzas, uses literary and oral devices: repetition, rhetorical lists, catchy antitheses, onomatopoeia, contrasting voices in dialogue, invented aphorisms, traditional proverbs (of which she has collected 700) and allusions to the Bible, Jamaican folklore and English literature. Her speakers exposed through dramatic monologues evoke sympathy as well as comedy or satire; sorrow often lurks 'between the lines': 'Sun a shine an pot a bwile, but / Tings no bright, bickle no nuff. / Rain a fall, river dah flood, but / Water scarce and dutty tough.' Among critics see Mervyn Morris, *Jamaica Journal*, 1, 1967; interview with Dennis Scott, *Caribbean Quarterly*, 14, 1968.

Benson, Sally, Sara Mahala Redway (Smith), 'Esther Evarts', 1900–72, short-story writer, screenwriter. B. at St. Louis, Missouri, da. of Anna (Prophater) and Alonzo Redway S., she m. Reynolds B., 1919, had one daughter, and divorced. She wrote, sometimes as 'Esther Evarts', stories on modern life for *The New Yorker*, especially about women's manipulations of each other in competing for men. (She said her talent for malicious satire came from her mother, who told her: 'Go on to your party. You look terrible but maybe somebody will dance with you.') SB exposes rigid role expectations: *Junior Miss*, 1941 (her fourth collection), and *Meet Me in St Louis*, 1942, satirize petty, mean-minded, 'feminine' elder sisters who pressure the younger to become more like them. The former was chosen by the Book of the Month Club, dramatized in 1942 and later became a radio series. The latter, which draws on SB's elder sister's diary, became a movie with Judy Garland, 1944. *Women and Children First*, 1943, repr. 1976, focuses on women seeking to ignore the emptiness of their lives or to fill them by manipulating others. 'Suite 2049', in *People are Fascinating*, 1936, won an O. Henry Award. SB's screenplays include *National Velvet*, 1944, from Enid BAGNOLD, and *Anna and the King of Siam*, 1946, from Anna LEONOWENS.

Benson, Stella, 1892–1933, novelist, poet and travel writer, b. at Lutwyche Hall, Shropshire, da. of Caroline Essex (Cholmondeley) and Ralph Beaumont B.: niece of novelist Mary CHOLMONDELEY. Ill as a child (and frequently throughout her life), SB was educ. mainly at home but also in Freiburg and Switzerland. In 1912, on a convalescent voyage to Jamaica, she began her first novel, *I Pose*, 1915, the witty, accomplished tale of a 'militant suffragette' and a 'gardener'. A year later she moved to Hoxton, became a suffragette (she marched with Syliva PANKHURST to the House of Commons) and worked with women and the poor, in the Charity Organization Society, in a shop she ran with a Hoxton woman and as a 'jobbing gardener'. Her second novel, *This is the End*, 1917, is her account of the effects of war on the imagination. In 1918, she travelled across the USA to San Francisco, supported herself in a variety of jobs, and worked on *Living Alone*, 1919. Two years later, she sailed for China. There she worked in a US hospital, taught in a mission school, met and married, 1921, Shaemas O'Gorman Anderson and spent the rest of her life there, visiting England and the USA frequently. In the early 1930s, she campaigned successfully against the brutally abusive system of licensed brothels in Hong Kong. She wrote eight novels, including those mentioned above (which strikingly combine fantasy and realism) and *The Poor Man*, 1922, *Pipers and a Dancer*, 1924, *Goodbye, Stranger*, 1926, the unfinished *Mundos*, 1935, and *The Far-Away Bride*, 1930, republished in England as *Tobit Transplanted*, 1931, which won the Femina Vie Heureuse prize and the A. C. Benson silver medal of the Royal Society of Literature. Her *Poems* appeared in 1935, her *Collected Short Stories* in 1936, her travel writings, *The Little World* and *Worlds Within Worlds*, in 1925 and 1928, and *Pull Devil / Pull Baker*, an unusual collaboration, in 1933. Some letters are printed in R. Ellis Roberts, *Portrait of Stella Benson*, 1939, Naomi MITCHISON's *You May Well Ask*, and Cecil Clarabut, ed., *Some Letters of Stella Benson, 1928–1933*, 1978; the BL has others. Phyllis BOTTOME's appreciation was privately printed, 1934. See study by R. Meredith Bedell, 1983, and life by Joy Grant, 1987. SB's DIARIES, which she kept from childhood and throughout her life, are in Cambridge Univ. Library.

Benson, Theodora (the Hon. Eleanor Theodora Roby Benson), 1906–68, writer of fiction, travel books and humour, b. in Staffordshire, da. of writers Dorothea Mary Roby (Thorpe) and Godfrey Rathbone B., first Baron Charnwood. Her novels treat relationships between women and men in upper-class society where the ideal of love exists but becomes impossible. Beginning as romantics, her characters are stifled by rigid sex-role conventions, become jaded, then take lovers to relieve boredom. Clever, increasingly cynical, they learn by experience 'that where sustained mental effort and concentration are required they must be outclassed because of the bodily strength of men.... And that, however platitudinous, seems to be that'. The strong-minded protagonist of *Glass Houses*, 1929, attempts to evade marriage in platonic friendships, but convention overpowers her, and she concludes that though marriage is 'a cage', it is 'the only chance of great happiness.' The upper-class protagonist of *Lobster Quadrille*, 1930, marries a poor socialist, but cannot defeat class differences and abandons 'beauty and poetry' for a 'safe', 'steady' relationship. In *Facade*, 1933, women marry for social position. The *Best Stories of Theodora Benson*, 1940, short, ironic, often with a horrifying final twist, frequently centre on a woman travelling alone who loses her reputation and future by taking a risk on a man. *The Undertaker's Wife*, 1947, dedicated to Graham Greene, ends an unsuccessful marriage when the wife accidentally leaves windows open in her husband's sickroom, ensuring that she will live as she has wanted to. *In the East My Pleasure Lies*, 1938, is an account of TB's trip alone to Bali, Java and Sumatra in about 1936 (for which she learned Malay at the School of Oriental Languages in London): its observations on the position of women are trenchant ('a woman is not much better off in a matriarchate than anywhere else ... she gets bossed about by brothers and uncles instead of husband and father'). TB's popular comic works with Betty Askwith, *Foreigners of the World in a Nutshell*, 1935, and *Muddling Through; or Britain in a Nutshell*, 1936, now seem racist and unfunny.

Bentley, Catherine, nun of the Poor Clares at Aire, France, translator as 'Sister Magdalene Augustine' of Francis Hendriques' extracts from Luke Wadding's life of St Clare, pub. Douai, 1635. Dedicating to Queen Henrietta Maria, she calls herself a 'mortified Recluse', but takes pride in her subject, a saint 'of Feminine Sex, but Masculine Virtue', who left 'this Patrimonie to her children, that they might enjoy Nothing'. She praises poverty but insists on the right to beg a livelihood.

Bentley, Elizabeth, 1767–1839, of Norwich, labouring-class poet, only child of Mary and of Christopher B., a leather-worker brought down to odd jobs by a stroke. Two years after he died (1783), she discovered 'an inclination for writing verses, which I had no thought or desire of being seen'; her mother showed them about. In 1791 she pub. by subscription at Norwich *Genuine Poetical Compositions on Various Subjects*, with her portrait and brief account of her life written in 1790 (when a poem had appeared in the *GM*), and verse in various modes, all conventional in style and sentiments. With the proceeds she opened a small school to keep herself and her mother (twopence a week per child); she also made things to sell; the RLF helped her in 1799 and 1829. She pub. occasional poems in the *Norfolk Chronicle*, verses for children and a pamphlet ode on Trafalgar [1805]. A book of new poems, 1821, again by subscription, had a later portrait and memoir.

Bentley, Phyllis Eleanor, 1894–1977, novelist, journalist, autobiographer and critic. B. at Halifax, Yorks., da. of Eleanor (Kettlewell) and Joseph Edwin B., textile manufacturer, she was educ. at Halifax

Girls' High School and, from 1910, at Cheltenham Ladies' College, where she took an external London BA Pass degree, 1914. After brief spells of employment as teacher and Ministry of Munitions clerk, 1918–19, she returned to Halifax as a librarian, one of the million post-war 'surplus women', determined, as she records in her autobiography, *O Dreams, O Destinations*, 1962, 'to reform injustice, banish iniquities, dismiss hate. ... by presenting human character in story'. *Environment*, 1922, set in a West Riding town, was the first of more than 20 novels and volumes of short stories concerned with this region. The best known were *Carr*, 1929, and *Inheritance*, 1932, historical novels of the textile industry, and *A Modern Tragedy*, 1934, set in the slump. In *The English Regional Novel*, 1941, PB defines its chief strength as 'detailed faithfulness to reality, a conscientious presentation of phenomena as they really happen in ordinary everyday life on a clearly defined spot of real earth, a firm rejection of the vague, the high-flown and the sentimental'. She also wrote a study of narrative, 1946; three studies on the BRONTËS (1947, 1950, 1969), whose works she also edited, 1949; books and television plays for children; and contributions to *John O'London's*, the *Yorkshire Post* and US periodicals.

Beresford, Anne Ellen, poet, b. in 1929 in Redhill, Surrey, da. of Margaret (Kent), a musician, and Richmond B., a sales promoter for films. She grew up in London, where she was educ. privately and studied music, then attended the Central School of Speech Training and Dramatic Art. Involved in broadcasting and acting from 1948–70, AB has also taught drama in schools, 1969–73, and run a poetry workshop in the Cockpit Theatre. She m. poet Michael Hamburger, 1951, divorced him, 1970, and remarried him, 1974: they have three children and a grandchild. Since her first collection, *Walking Without Moving*, 1967, ed. by Edward Lucie-Smith, she has published several vols. of verse, radio plays (with her husband and alone) and a translation, *Alexandros*, 1974, selected poems by Romanian poet Vera Lungu. Earlier verses, as in *Footsteps on the Snow*, 1972, approach contemporary issues through their natural subjects. AB is deeply attracted to ancient myth and story, often making her impact in more recent work by attaching lived, particular experience to these, as in *The Curving Shore*, 1975, or in her poems about an Anglo-Saxon woman living in 'Silly [i.e. holy] Suffolk', *The Songs of Almut From God's Country*, 1980, in which the historically generalized woman voices her particular 'love, grown painfully / to hold the pheasants shining / the changing autumn winter land / and all unspoken passions'. Often she undoes cultural clichés by asserting a female viewpoint: '"I am the great law," said Orpheus. / And the woman turned her face to look at him.' 'The Great Man is Dead' plays its meanings from the difference between Anna Dostoievsky herself and her merely relational existence: 'She was his wife. Nothing more. / Nothing less' (*Love Songs a Thracian Taught Me*, 1980). A central understanding in AB's work is that her characters and animated natural objects live in language: 'How the rain beats down on the garden chairs, / What matters now is the revolving of the word-wheel.' MSS at the Univ. of Texas, Austin.

Beresford-Howe, Constance, novelist, short-story writer. B. in 1922 in Montréal, da. of Marjory (Moore) and Russell B.-H., she was educ. at McGill Univ. (BA, 1945, MA, 1946) and Brown (PhD in English, 1950), then taught at McGill and Ryerson Polytechnic, Toronto. Her first three novels, *The Unreasoning Heart*, 1946, *Of This Day's Journey*, 1947, and *The Invisible Gate*, 1949, treat contemporary young women at crucial stages in self-development; the fourth, *My Lady Greensleeves*, 1955, is an historical romance based on an actual sixteenth-century divorce in England, written 'as a deliberate experiment' in dealing with everyday middle-class lives. In 1960, CB-H m. Christopher W. Pressnell. After an 18-year silence, she wrote a trilogy whose protagonists represent three phases of woman's life. In *A Book of Eve*, 1973 (adapted for stage as *Eve*, produced at Stratford, Ont., 1976), the best of the three, CB-H interweaves biblical imagery with a quest motif, humorously and effectively presenting a protagonist who precipitately leaves her husband of 40 years and her life in comfortable Westmount the day she receives her first old-age-pension cheque, moving into a cheap east-end Montréal apartment to be 'neither wife, maid, nor mother.' 'But I'm myself,' she says, as she ekes out her pension by scavenging, takes a lover 20 years her junior and rejoices in new independence. *A Population of One*, 1977, treats an unmarried woman entering the academic world at 30, *The Marriage Bed*, 1981, a 24-year-old pregnant mother, both of whom also reject conventional expectations, but much less drastically than Eve. *Night Studies*, 1985, explores wittily and compassionately the loneliness and desperation of a motley group of night students and staff at an urban college. Though it suggests the possibility of love and companionship, it embodies a darker vision than do the earlier novels.

Bergé, Carol (Peppis), poet and fiction writer, b. 1928 in NYC, educ at NY Univ., 1946–52, and the New School for Social Research, 1952–4. She m. Jack B. in 1955 and has a son. From 1950 whe worked in journalism and public relations, from 1975 lectured at colleges and univs. She had edited *Center* magazine and Center Press for innovative fiction since 1970 (and other journals), written for journals on dance, film, theatre and painting, and published two accounts of the dealings of society with poetry, 1964, 1965. Her early poems in LeRoy Jones, ed., *Four Young Lady Poets*, 1962, show an eye for the pattern and fine detail of the natural world; her opening piece addresses Denise LEVERTOV: 'those moving near you, to remind / of roots and sources, of your own leaf'. First of a dozen poetry volumes was *The Vulnerable Island*, 1964. In 1969 came a story volume (*The Unfolding*) and *An American Romance, The Alan Poems, A Journal* – of a year of intimate living in a 'big new / old' country house and in 'the city alight with motion': charting the failures and frustrations of love as delicately as the pleasures. *From a Soft Angle: Poems About Women*, 1971, includes reprinted earlier work in sections on 'Women as Half the World', 'With Their Men', 'Portraits' (poems to individuals, e.g. Diane WAKOSKI, 'I was considering silk as being / a waiting substance, heavy as stone'), 'Love and Unlove' ('come darling / be my scapegoat') and 'One Woman's Life'. Since then CB has turned more towards prose. *A Couple Called Moebius, Eleven Sensual Stories*, 1972, depicts both sophisticates and primitives with a sharp, refined detachment; another 'American Romance' presents a couple choosing each other as connoisseurs, married at last in Cuernavaca, 'where they did not need to notice the ugly or the poor': a 'small wedding, with caviar and tropical fruits. . . .' In *The Unexpected, poems based in the elements*, 1976, CB's constant interest in zodiac signs spills over into the cover design. *Fierce Metronome*, 1981, includes 'One Page Novels'. *Secrets, Gossip and Slander*, 1984, her first novel (after one unpublished), turns the meticulous social and psychological probing of her stories on the academic world: love-affairs, a professor-student marriage and durable female friendship. CB has been working on another novel. MSS at the Univ. of Texas, Austin, and Washington Univ.

Berkeley, Eliza (Frinsham), 1734–1800, memoirist, b. Windsor Forest, daughter of Eliza (Cherry) and Henry F., friend of several BLUESTOCKINGS. In childhood a tomboy, at 11 a letter and sermon writer, she learned, with her father's approval, French, Spanish and Hebrew. When he died in 1746 her one year's schooling ended, her mother fearing piety and learning made old maids. In 1761 she m. George B., son of the philosopher-bishop and of Ann or Anne (Forster) B., d. 1786 (mystic and intellectual, who let her daughter study like a boy, and whose letters of pious admonition appeared as *The Contrast, or An Antidote* [to those of Lord Chesterfield], 1791). EB thenceforth centred her life on her family; the *GM*, 1796, carried her anonymous 'Singular Tale' of her husband's prior love for Catherine TALBOT, and their ideal three-way friendship. She pub. other *GM* and newspaper items and prefaces to her husband's *Sermons*, 1799, and (much longer) to her son George Monck B.'s *Poems*, 1797. Both had died within two years; her other son had died young. Sounding older than she is, she reminisces ramblingly, with dialogue, character-sketch, opinion (reactionary, non-feminist) – all tending to aggrandize her own connections but showing a sure touch with the small-change of life.

Berners, Dame **Juliana** ('Julyan Barnes'), supposed author of prose and verse treatises on hunting, hawking, heraldry and angling contained in *The Boke of St Albans*, 1486 (facs. J. Haslewood, 1810). She has been described as a noblewoman, daughter of Sir James B. of Essex, and as prioress of Sopwell Nunnery near St Albans; in fact her identity is obscure and her authorship doubtful (see R. Hands, 1975). At most she may have compiled some of the miscellaneous additions to the hunting and hawking material (mostly items of instruction for the 'courteous') in the book.

Berry, Mary, 1763–1852, woman of letters, b. in Kirkbridge, Yorks., da. of Elizabeth (Seton) and Robert B., wealthy merchant. After her mother's death (1767) her maternal grandmother brought up MB and her sister Agnes, 1764–1852, in Yorks. and then at Chiswick; chiefly self-educated, MB was inclined to disapprove of novels. In Florence on the first of many Continental trips, 1783, she began the journals ed., with letters, by Lady Theresa Lewis, 1865. The aged Horace Walpole met the sisters in 1788, called them his 'wives', dedicated books to them and left them MSS, ed. by MB but pub. in her father's name, 1798. In 1796 she broke off a brief engagement to General O'Hara, governor of Gibraltar, citing reluctance to live so far from her family. Literary friends included Anne DAMER, Harriet MARTINEAU and Joanna BAILLIE, who supplied prologue and epilogue for her comedy *Fashionable Friends*, given privately in 1801 and at Drury Lane in 1802, and blamed (from prejudice, said MB) for 'loose principles'. She expressed anti-revolutionary, pro-Malthusian opinions in *A Comparative View of the Social Life of England and France from the Restoration of Charles II* . . ., 1828–31; re-titled in her *Works*, 1844, which also repr. her annotated editions of letters by Mme du Deffand, 1810, and Lady Rachel RUSSELL, 1819. Corresp. of both sisters ed. 1914.

'Bersianik, Louky' (Lucile Durand), poet, novelist, playwright, essayist, children's writer. B. in Montréal in 1930, da. of Laurence Bissonet and Donat D., she took her pseudonym to sever ties to patriarchal lineage. She has a son. She spent five years in Paris, 1953–60, and a year in Greece, 1977–9. Her wide education includes literary studies in Montréal and at the Sorbonne (PhD, Université de Montréal), studies in radio and TV at the CERT in Issy-les-Moulineaux, France, as well as studies in music, library science and applied linguistics. She published four stories for children, 1964–6, and began work on her feminist triptych of novels and poetry, 1972: *L'Euguélionne*, 1976 (trans., 1981), is a picaresque novel of social satire and science fiction. *Le Pique-Nique sur l'Acropole*, 1979, parodies Plato's *Syposium* (the title means 'banquet'): women whose names occur in the margins of the 'great works' of Greek philosophy gather to picnic – they can't afford a banquet – and speak their minds. *Maternative: les Prè-Ancyl*, 1980, the third leaf of the triptych, is a collection of poetical and dramatic texts. Her feminist essay, 'Les Agénèsies du vieux monde', 1982 ('Agenesias of the old world', *Trivia*, 7, 1985), critiques our philosophical, phallocratic heritage. LB has also worked as a writer and researcher for Radio-Canada, collaborated in the feminist journals *La Nouvelle Barre du jour* and *Sorcières*, and organized and participated in writing workshops and colloquia. See interview in *Lettres Québecoises*, 26, 1982; Jennifer Waelti-Walters in *Atlantis*, 6, 1980, and Neuman and Kamboureli, eds, 1986.

Besant, Annie (Wood), 1847–1933, reformer, orator, theosophist, journalist and editor, b. London, only da. of Emily (Morris) and William W., businessman, scholar and dilettante. She was educ. by evangelist Ellen Marryat, with whom she visited the Continent in 1863. In 1867, she m. Frank B., clergyman; she had a son and a da. After a religious crisis she left her husband in 1873, taking her daughter. In 1874 she met Charles Bradlaugh, the crusading atheist, and under his influence started lecturing and writing for the National Secular Society, publishing *The Gospel of Atheism*, 1877, the same year they were prosecuted for publishing Knowlton's pamphlet on contraception. She lost custody of both her children in 1879, the year she started to read for a science degree. AB became a socialist in 1885, joining the Fabian Society. Known as the greatest woman public speaker of her time, she pub. her most important lectures on social issues in *Our Corner*, and was the magazine's general editor and science correspondent (1883–8). Other publications include *My Path to Atheism*, 1877, *Why I am a Socialist*, 1896 and *Why I Became a Theosophist*, 1889. In 1888, she led the first strike of match-girls, formed their union, and was elected to the London School Board. She became President of the Theosophical Society in 1907. Having visited India for the first time in 1893, she made it her home. She founded several schools there and in 1913 began her political work for India, launching the journals *Commonweal* and *New India* in 1914. She formed a Home Rule for India League in 1916 and had considerable influence on the growth of nationalist feeling, becoming President of India's National Congress in 1917. See her autobiography, 1893, life by Rosemary Dinnage, 1986, and study by Catherine L. Wessinger, 1988.

Betham, Mary Matilda, 1776–1852, diarist, scholar, poet and miniature painter, b. in Suffolk, eldest of 14 children of Mary (Damant), from Europe, and the Rev. William B. Self-educated in her father's library, sent to school for sewing 'to prevent my too strict application to books', she was torn between literary ambition, fear of public opinion, and need to make a living. If she failed to pursue fame, wrote her friend Lady Bedingfield, 'you deserve to have your *mental feet* cut off.' She settled in London, pub. *Elegies*, 1797 (sentimental ballads; praise of Ann Radcliffe and the ladies of Llangollen: facs. with 1808 *Poems*, 1978), exhibited, and researched for *A Biographical Dictionary of Celebrated Women* (1804, delayed from concern not 'to run a race with' Mary Hays). Her *Lay* of Marie de France, 1816, depicts a minstrel composing and reciting her own romantic life-story: she added notes on female minstrels and paraphrases from Marie. She knew A. L. Barbauld, Coleridge (who praised her), Charles and Mary Lamb, and Mary Anne Schimmelpenninck. When she had a breakdown in the 1820s, her family had her locked up and returned money paid her by the RLF; she wrote, only sometimes irrationally, of their disapproving her politics, religion and poverty. Later she sounds wholly coherent again. In a preface to *Crow-Quill Flights* she recalls her early feminism; she wrote verse on her brother aged 84 (and her mother at 81) and letters to a niece 'always about books and authors' (selec. corr. ed. Ernest Betham, 1905).

Betham-Edwards, Matilda Barbara, 1836–1919, novelist, poet and journalist, b. Westerfield Hall, Ispwich, Suffolk, where her father farmed; one of six children of Edward E.; cousin of Amelia Blandford EDWARDS. MB-E retained Betham because it 'was my mother's maiden name [with] literary associations'. She attended an Ipswich day school for two years, directed by a Miss Baker, to whom she attributed her love of French life and literature. Her mother died when she was 12 and thereafter MB-E educ. herself, borrowing books from the Ipswich Mechanics' Institute and serving briefly and unhappily as a pupil-governess at Peckham. Her first novel, *The White House by the Sea*, 1857, was an immediate success and was transl. into several languages, pirated in the USA and reprinted over the next 40 years. She maintained a prodigious literary output for over 60 years, her romantic best-sellers including *Kitty*, 1869, *Forestalled*, 1880, and *Love and Marriage*, 1884. She knew George ELIOT and Barbara BODICHON; she travelled widely in Europe, staying with Bodichon in Algeria and visiting France and Spain with her. On these travels are based *Dr. Jacob*, 1864, *A Winter with the Swallows*, 1866, *Through Spain to the Sahara*, 1867, her edition of *Murray's Handbook for Central France*, *French Men, Women and Books*, 1910, and *Twentieth Century France*, 1917. She contributed for many years to the *Daily News* on French topics, and the French Government made her *Officier de l'Instruction Publique de France*, the first Englishwoman to receive this honour. Her poetic output includes the hymn 'God make my life a little light' and 'The Golden Bee', a poem about a shipwreck. She was interested in women's movements, and attended a meeting of the International Working Men's Association where Karl Marx presided, later writing about it for *Fraser's Magazine*, 1875. *Six Life Studies of Famous Women*, 1880, included a portrait of her aunt, Mary Matilda BETHAM. Her *Reminiscences* were pub. in 1898 and *Mid-Victorian Memories* in 1919.

Bethell, Ursula, 'Evelyn Hayes', 1874–1945, poet, b. England, brought to NZ 1875, eldest da. of Isabel Anne (Lillie) and Richard B., a well-off sheep farmer. Educ at Rangiora primary school, Christchurch Girls High, Oxford, and Swiss finishing schools, she returned to NZ in 1892 and with an independent income undertook charitable work. From 1895 she studied painting in Geneva and music in Dresden, then joined an Anglican community, 'The Grey Ladies', and worked with boys' clubs in South London. She alternated between Europe and NZ until 1919 when she settled in the Cashmere Hills, near Christchurch, with Effie Pollen in 'our common home'. In 1925 she pub. her first poems, *From a Garden in the Antipodes*, by Evelyn Hayes. They are warm, witty, different poems, originally written for friends in England, about her garden, the flowers and plants, the contrast between the NZ and the English landscapes, and her life with Effie, of whom she wrote 'from her I have had love, tenderness and understanding for thirty years'. In the 1930s her poems were pub. in the *Christchurch Press* and the religious tone becomes stronger in *Time and Place*, 1938, and *Day and Night*, 1939. These are landscape poems, containing little of her personal life. In 1934 Effie died and she wrote six 'memorials' – poignant poems of love and loss, written for the anniversaries of Effie's death. Her collected poems were pub. in 1950. See the life by M. H. Holcroft, 1975.

Bethune, Mary (McLeod), 1875–1955, educator, civil rights politician, journalist,

b. at Mayesville, SC, da. of former slaves Patsy (McIntosh) and Samuel McLeod. She was educ. at a black mission school, Scotia Seminary, NC (graduated 1894 with teaching qualifications), and the Bible Institute for Home and Foreign Missions, but was unable to realize her ambition of working in Africa. Her marriage to Albertus B., 1898, was dissolved when she moved to Florida to open a mission school. Another such school which she began in 1904 with five girls and her son (an only child) grew into Bethune-Cookman College, 1929; MMB was its first president, until 1942. She also headed the National Association of Colored Women, 1924–8, advised F. D. Roosevelt and influenced Eleanor ROOSEVELT, and founded the Federal Council on Negro Affairs, the National Council of Negro Women, 1935, and its mouthpiece *Aframerican Women's Journal*. In 1939 she became Director of Negro Affairs within the National Youth Administration. Her writings, all reaffirming her race's struggle for dignity, include weekly columns for the *Pittsfield Courier* in the 1930s and later for the *Chicago Defender*; 'I'll Never Turn Back No More', 1938, 'Certain Unalienable Rights', 1944, 'My Last Will and Testament', 1955; and a short piece in Rabbi Louis Finkelstein, ed., *Spiritual Autobiographies*, 1948. Hers is the first memorial to either a black American or a woman in a Washington public park. Papers at Bethune-Cookman College and Dillard College, New Orleans; bibliog. by Dolores C. Leffall and Janet L. Sims in *Journal of Negro Education*, 45, 1976; life by Rackham Holt, 1964.

Beverley, Elizabeth, entertainer touring west-country England by 1814. Her pamphlets, some as 'Mrs. R. Beverley', aim not at 'a niche in Westminster Abbey' but at 'a much better purpose: – namely – of putting pence in her pocket to maintain life'. Princess Charlotte's death drew from her *Modern Times*, 1818, a 'sermon' on some 'very alarming words' of the prophet Jeremiah. *A Poetical Olio*, 1819, mixes piety with frisky satire (two pieces are repr. from the *Brighton Herald*): she laments a child's death, says it is male applause that women really value, and depicts an author beaten down by a publisher from £20 to £5, then getting £200 by subscription! *The Actress's Ways and Means, To Industriously Raise the Wind!* [*c.* 1820] claimed 12 eds. in a few years. It mentions business failure but success in her famous 'Dramatic Metamorphoses', largely verse recitation. She writes poems to a pawnbroker, to the public, on towns she has played in, and on 'my Child's being unfortunately burnt to death,' which hastened her husband's death. At least six more works include *The Indefatigable, bound on a Voyage to the Island of Liberality* and *Odd Thoughts on a Variety of Odd Subjects*, 1825. She calls herself a professor of elocution 'for the Pulpit, Bar, Stage, and Drawing Room', or 'that Odd Little Woman'; she repeats material, alludes increasingly to enemies, and writes in prose on charity schools, on 'The Fate of Genius', and on the need for 'some Charitable Institution for decayed Artists, Actors, &c.'

Bevington, L. S. (Louisa Sarah, later Mrs Ignatz Guggenberger), 1845–?95, journalist and poet, b. Battersea, London, to Louisa (De Hermes?) and Alexander B., 'gentleman', probably of Quaker family. The eldest of eight (seven girls), LSB pub. her first book of poems as 'Arbor Leigh' in 1876, followed by *Key-Notes*, 1879 (as L. S. Bevington), which shows signs of querying established Christian codes. Her article on 'Atheism and Morality' (*Nineteenth Century*, Oct. 1879) provoked a clerical essay in reply. After *Poems, Lyrics and Sonnets*, 1882, containing some interesting metrical experiments and laments for dead Christianity, in 1883 she m. Munich artist Ignatz G. By 1895 she was publishing with James Tochetti's 'Liberty' Press (a journal of 'Anarchist Communism') poems which, in Browningesque fable guise, offer a sharp critique of moral half-measures (e.g. 'The Spider and the Bee, A Tale for the Times').

Biddle, Hester or (the form used later) Esther, *c.* 1629–96, Quaker polemicist. Brought up an Anglican, she lived in Oxford before coming to London, where she applied herself day and night to reading. Initially disturbed at the king's execution, she found 'Peace of Conscience' on joining the QUAKERS. In May 1655 she pub. two broadsides proclaiming woe to Oxford and Cambridge for material and ideological domination; they closely link her voice and God's. Later, longer works develop her social analysis: *A Warning from the Lord* to London and its suburbs, dated 16 Dec. 1659; *The Trumpet of the Lord*, 1662, written from Newgate prison. She often uses images of women in labour: *The Trumpet* likens priestly robes 'unto a menstrous Cloth before the Eye of the pure Jehovah'. She attacks the usage of poor by rich and repeatedly threatens, in God's name, to set fire to her enemies. *A Brief Relation* of Quaker persecution, her last work, 1662, describes her, on trial for preaching, roundly rebuking the court: 'Christ is my husband, and I learn of him.' She published nothing after this.

Binchy, Maeve, journalist, short-story writer, novelist, b. 1940 in Dublin, educ. at the Holy Child Convent, Killiney, and University College, Dublin (BA in history). After teaching in girls' schools and writing travel articles, she joined the *Irish Times* in 1969; as its London correspondent she found her métier of explaining the English and Irish to each other. She had plays staged in Dublin (*End of Term, The Half-Promised Land*) and won awards in Ireland and Prague for her TV play *Deeply Regretted By*. Her journalism sold well in book form: *My First Book*, 1976, and *Maeve's Diary*, Dublin [1979], on London: good-humoured, light-hearted, sensitive. MB settled in London and married writer and broadcaster Gordon Snell. The stories in *Central Line*, 1978 (each titled from a London tube stop), capture a motley array of life-styles and women's love-lives, mostly disquieting and unresolved, like that of an Irishwoman seeking abortion: repr. with those in *Victoria Line*, 1980 (mostly on marriage, from 'yuppies' to a strong, silent black woman with a husband in jail for murder), as *London Transports*, 1983, and as *Victoria Line, Central Line*, 1987. MB explores her native city in *Dublin 4*, 1982 (longer, more complex stories), and *The Lilac Bus*, 1984 (which mediates between working lives and country weekends at home). Her first novel, *Light a Penny Candle*, 1982, traces a 20-year friendship between the only child of unexpressive English parents (later separated) and one of the turbulent Irish family who take her in, at ten, for WWII: each marries disastrously; an inquest on the English husband opens and closes the book. *Echoes*, 1985, set at the Irish seaside, also spans the years of growing up, and opens and closes on a death; in *Firefly Summer*, 1987, another sleepy Irish town awaits a cultural and economic revolution which accidents and violence prevent. Linked stories in *Silver Wedding*, 1988, depict varied, sometimes surprizing bids for personal autonomy.

Bingham, Sallie, later Ellsworth, playwright, fiction-writer, memoirist, b. 1937 at Louisville, Ky., da. of Mary (Caperton) and Barry B., powerful owner of 'liberal' local newspapers. Brought up to feel her family superior but with skeletons in its closet, she says she was 'saved' with warmth of love by 'Nursie'; she scorned the spinster teachers at her private girls' school. In 1958 she took a BA at Radcliffe College, m. A. Whitney E., and moved to Boston (she had three sons by her first two husbands). Her heroines, from the first, despairing one in *After Such Knowledge*, 1960 (novel), have been called self-portraits; but her stories (in periodicals, *The Touching Hand*, 1967, and *The Way It Is Now*, 1972), use a range of protagonists to depict painful family relations, the anguish of divorce or sudden bereavement: an old woman plots to kill her son's love-affair with kindness; a man seeks an unproblematic woman to take to lunch; a young mother is amazed to find in herself strength and optimism; and another nearly maims the baby she loves. Back in Louisville in 1977, SB joined the family board of directors, to find her consciousness raised by contact with 'male control and a male value system' and by working with the Women's Project THEATRE GROUP on the staging of her first play, *Milk of Paradise*, 1980. (Others followed, in NYC and Louisville.) In 1983 (the year she married businessman Tim Peters) she was told to resign (with her mother and sister) from the board. By selling her 15 per cent (reputedly making $60 million), she brought down the empire, and set up the Kentucky Foundation to help women artists. Wondering 'how I dared', she told the story in *Passion and Prejudice: A Family Memoir*, 1989. See *WRB*, June 1989.

Biography of women. Saints' lives preceded Chaucer on women famous for love, 1380s, and CHRISTINE DE PIZAN on women famous for virtue, 1390s. Still semi-fictional is Thomas Bentley's *Monument of Matrones*, 1582 (section on good and bad Biblical women). Thomas Heywood's three works – *Gunaikeion*, 1624 (goddesses, good and bad women, 'Learned Women, Poetresses, and Witches'); *The Exemplary Lives*, 1640 (nine female worthies); and *The General History of Women*, 1657 – were followed by books on 'Westerne Amazons' (James Strong, 1645), empresses, 1723, actresses, mistresses, 'Eminently Pious Women', 1777, etc. Meanwhile general works began to give space to women (e.g. Edward Phillipps on poets, 1675, John Wilford on the pious, 1741). George Ballard's pioneering, scholarly *Memoirs of Several Ladies of Great Britain Celebrated for their Writings*, 1752 (repr. 1985, ed. Ruth Perry) owed much to Sarah CHAPONE and Elizabeth ELSTOB, and had one-third female subscribers. It led the way for Mary BETHAM, Mary HAYS, Mary PILKINGTON, and Mary ROBERTS. Early biographers of their actual or spiritual mothers are various NUNS, Anne or Mary CARY and Griselda MURRAY. Elizabeth HAMILTON was followed in historical memoir by E. O. BENGER and Lucy AIKIN. WOLLSTONECRAFT's notoriety was fed by her husband's life of her. Nineteenth-century novelists continued to write the lives of other women writers; George SAND was a favourite subject. While some women made a living as biographers, they were predominantly biographers of men: Anna Stoddart, 1840–1911, a Scot, wrote lives of Hannah Pipe, Elizabeth P. Nichol, and of her friend Isabella BIRD, but was well-known only for her *Francis of Assisi*, 1903. Even historically researched biographies (by both men and women) were often anecdotal and indexless: the term still carries different meanings for historians and for literary critics or writers. Emily JUDSON wrote a life of her husband's previous wife, Sarah, in 1849. Elizabeth GASKELL's, *Life of Charlotte Brontë* 1857, broke new ground as the first truly personal biography of a woman writer. Jane WILLIAMS's *Literary Women of England*, 1861, carried on a tradition that extends into the present volume, and is always vulnerable to the charge of 'heroinizing'. Julia KAVANAGH, 1862, and Gertrude MAYER, 1894, each collected biographies into *Women of Letters* volumes. In the USA the tendency in the nineteenth century was towards making major statements about cultural achievements, most notably in Frances WILLARD and Mary Livermore's massive *Woman of the Century*, 1893 (repr. 1973 as *American Women: Fifteen Hundred Biographies*). Recent biographies of women by women tend to foreground the problematics of their enterprise: Margaret Doody on Frances BURNEY, several on Willa CATHER (who wished to have none), Wendy MULFORD on WARNER and ACKROYD, Anne Stevenson on PLATH, Joan Givner on Katherine Anne PORTER and Lucy Mand

MONTGOMERY. Carolyn HEILBRUN bought 73 new lives of women by women between 1970 (the year of Nancy Milford's life of Zelda FITZGERALD) and 1984. She suggests that anything approaching truth-telling is only now becoming possible, as female biographers acquire a theoretical framework enabling them to 'detach themselves from the bonds of womanly attitudes', and cope with 'unbearable discomfort in the face of' their subject-matter. See Phyllis Rose, *Writing on Women: Essays in a Renaissance*, 1985; Carol Ascher, Louise DeSalvo and Sara Ruddick, eds., *Between Women: Biographers, Novelists, Critics, Teachers and Artists Write about their Work on Women*, 1984; Heilbrun, *Writing a Woman's Life*. See also AUTOBIOGRAPHY.

Birchenough, Mabel Charlotte (Bradley), 1860–1936, novelist, third da. of Marian (Philpot) and the Rev. George Granville Bradley, Dean of Westminster; she married Sir Henry Birchenough, 1886, and had two children. Co-author with her sister Emily of *The Deanery Guide to Westminster Abbey*, 1885 (almost 20 eds.), MB also wrote occasional literary criticism for a variety of periodicals. Her novels have an anti-feminist bias; both *Disturbing Elements*, 1895, and *Potsherds*, 1898, focus on New Woman protagonists who eventually come to see love and marriage as more fulfilling than education or art. Her husband's position as head of several S. African and Rhodesian railway companies took her to Africa in 1910, and she opened her home to wounded soldiers during WWI.

Bird, Isabella Lucy (later Bishop), 1831–1904, travel writer, b. Boroughbridge Hall, Yorkshire, educ. by her mother, Dora (Lawson) and father, the Revd Edward Bird. She undertook a sea voyage to the USA, recording her experiences in *The Englishwoman in America*, 1856, and writing on the religious revival for the *Quarterly Review* and the *Patriot*. After her father's death in 1858 she made her home in Edinburgh with her mother and sister, Henrietta, giving practical help and considerable royalties from her first book to crofters forced to emigrate. In 1872, in a mood of kill-or-cure desperation after severe back pain, she set off for Australasia and, recovering her health, climbed an active volcano on the Sandwich Islands: she recorded the tour in *The Hawaiian Archipelago*, 1875. Returning home via North America, she discovered an 'inner world' among the inaccessible canyons, and published *A Lady's Life in the Rocky Mountains*, 1879, an immediate success. Back in Edinburgh she set up a cabmen's shelter and coffee house, and a training college for medical missionaries. Her trip to Japan, Indonesia and the Middle East in 1878 supplied material, in the form of long letters to Henrietta, for *Unbeaten Tracks in Japan*, 1880, and *The Golden Chersonese and the Way Thither*, 1883. These established her reputation and she became the first woman Fellow of the Royal Geographical Society. She m. her doctor, John Bishop, in 1881 after her sister's death. Of her nine books, works on Asia such as *Among the Tibetans*, 1894, and *The Yangtze Valley and Beyond*, 1899, are the most highly regarded. *Chinese Pictures*, 1900, containing her photographs, was her last book. A flamboyant courageous woman who lived life to the full, she died in Edinburgh, her bags packed for a return to China. See Pat Barr, *A Curious Life for a Lady*, 1970, and D. Middleton, *Victorian Lady Travellers*, 1965. See also her *Journeys in Persia and Kurdistan*, 2 vols., 1988–9.

Birdsell, Sandra (Bartlette), b. 1942, short-story writer, novelist and playwright. She was fifth of 11 surviving children of Louise (Schroeder), who had 19 pregnancies, and Roger Bartlette, town barker in Morris, Manitoba. A 'bad kid', she left school after Grade 10, worked as a waitress, then married, 1959 (divorced, 1984), and had three children. She kept journals in early married life and began writing after her father's death, 1976. Her backgrounds –

Mennonite ('something to push against') and Franco-Manitoban – show in her skill in balanced, intense observation of competing cultural and generational attitudes and loyalties. She published *Night Travellers*, 1982, at 40, with two grown children and a daughter at home. Here, and in *Ladies of the House*, 1984, both collections of linked stories, mostly female narrators explore alliances and rivalries with mothers, sisters, boyfriends and children. *Ladies of the House* – about 'the women women's lib forgot, for whom singleness is unthinkable and change is a new glaze on the ham' – depicts three generations of women, all wondering about themselves, 'sex and relationships and ambition and body and spirit.' Interview in *NeWest Review*, 13, 1987, and *Alberta Report*, 25 Feb. 1985, quoted above.

Birtles, Dora (Toll), poet, novelist, journalist, b. 1903 at Wickham, NSW, da. of Hannah (Roberts) and Albert Frederick T. She was educ. at Sydney Univ. where she met and m. (1923) Bert B. The controversy surrounding the appearance of their love poems in the university magazine, *Hermes*, led to her two-year suspension and his outright expulsion. She returned to obtain an honours degree in Oriental history and a Dip. Ed., and began a career as a schoolteacher. She travelled throughout Europe and Asia, including a voyage by cutter, an adventure captured in her best work, the unusual and compelling narrative *North-West by North*, 1935. Whilst travelling she contributed articles to English and Australian newspapers and was English correspondent for the *Newcastle Sun*, 1933–4. She has also pub. poetry, short stories, *Bonza the Bull*, 1949, and *Pioneer Shack*, 1947 (children's novels), *The Overlanders*, 1946 (the book of the film of that year), and *Exiles in the Aegean*, 1938 (with her husband), an important book based on their experiences in Greece prior to WWII.

Bishop, Claire (Huchet), French-American poet, story-teller, children's writer. She was b. 'more French than the "French"', in Brittany, where her grandfather and mother were village story-tellers. Although 'bored in school', she went on to the Sorbonne. After WWI she worked for *Nouvelle Revue Française*, published avant-garde poetry, and in 1924 founded 'L'Heure Joyeuse', the first children's library in France, where she told stories. She m. American pianist Frank B., moved to the USA in 1930, and began telling her stories in English at the NY Public Library. One became *Five Chinese Brothers* 1938, first of her books for many ages which introduce American children to those of other cultures. WWII figures in the award-winning *Pancakes-Paris*, 1947, about food deprivation and the dying custom of Mardi Gras, and *Twenty and Ten*, 1952, about French schoolchildren hiding and protecting Jewish class-mates. CHB has also written biographies for children (e.g. of Mozart and Bach), pieces in *Commonweal* and *Saturday Review*, and books for adults, including several about France and two looking at religion and flaws in its institutions: *Martin de Porres, Hero*, 1954 (about the sixteenth and seventeenth centuries), and *How Catholics Look at Jews*, 1974, on teaching methods in Italy, France and Spain.

Bishop, Elizabeth, 1911–79, poet, short-story writer, essayist, b. at Worcester, Mass., da. of Gertrude (Bulmer) and William Jones B., of the family firm that built the Boston Public Library. Eight months old when her father died, five when her mother suffered final, permanent mental breakdown, she lived with her mother's parents at Great Village, Nova Scotia (attending a one-room school), then her father's parents back at Worcester, then a maternal aunt in a South Boston tenement. Many of her stories are based on Great Village: 'Primer Class' describes her earliest school years. Owing to a combination of illnesses, she had little schooling until an inheritance took her to Walnut Hill

School in Nantick, Mass., 1927–30, and Vassar (AB in English, 1934). While there she met Mary MCCARTHY and Muriel RUKEYSER (they founded a paper to publish their work) and began a long friendship with the already eminent Marianne MOORE. She had read 'every poem . . . I could find, in back copies of *The Dial*', and later addressed Moore in verse. (See B. Costello in *TCL*, 30, 1984; L. Keller – on their letters – in *American Lit.*, 55, 1983.) Extensive and perceptive travel marks EB's life: 'More delicate than the historians' are the map-makers' colors', she observed. Her first trip abroad was to Paris, 1935; she moved to Key West, Fla., in 1939, to Mexico in 1943. She lived in Brazil, 1951–66, in a house called Casa Mariana after Moore, with her lover Lota de Macedo Soares. Winner of the Houghton Mifflin poetry award for her first book, *North and South*, 1946, and a Pulitzer Prize for *Poems: North and South – A Cold Spring*, 1955, she achieved high repute in her lifetime as a poet both naturalistic and inward. Her poems create contained idiosyncratic worlds, as do the small shadow box constructions of Joseph Cornell. (She made such boxes herself, despite jesting fears of being thought 'a witch', and translated an Octavio Paz poem about them.) Her '12 O'Clock News' transforms objects on her desk into apparitions from 'a small backward country': the ink-bottle may be 'a great altar' to a saviour-god, 'one last hope of rescue from their grave difficulties'. EB's translations include *The Diary of 'Helena Morley'*, 1957, repr. 1981, a popular Brazilian book about a girl of 12–15 in a mining town, 1893–5. Her essay-collection *Brazil*, 1962, was, she said, only 'two-thirds' her own after interference from the LIFE World Library editors, but it shows her epitomizing style and geographical sensitivity. (She notes centuries of female illiteracy and a paucity of Brazilian women writers.) After *Questions of Travel*, 1965, EB taught for years at several universities. She 'always' considered herself 'a strong feminist', but disliked dividing art by gender and refused to appear in all-women anthologies. She died in Boston. Her papers are at Vassar. Her *Complete Poems* appeared in 1983, *Collected Prose* in 1984. Life by Anne STEVENSON, 1966 (now out-dated), bibliog. by Candace MacMahon, 1980; essays ed. Lloyd Schwartz and Sybil P. Estess (who call her 'one of the major voices of our century'), 1983; Carolyn Handa in *SAQ*, 82, 1983 (who sees her as playing off dominant male poetic voices and reflecting a female sensibility in 'the formal aspects of her poetry'); concordance by A. M. Greenhaugh, 1985: Harold Bloom, ed., *Modern Critical Views: EB*, 1985 (especially Joanne Feit Diehl and Helen Vendler); life by David Kalstone, 1989.

Black, Clementina, 1855–1923, suffragist, trade-unionist and novelist, b. Brighton, the eldest of the eight children of Clara (Patten) and David B., coroner and Town Clerk; one of her sisters was Constance GARNETT. After her mother's death she moved to London where she studied in the British Museum and met Fabians and socialists. She also lived abroad for a time with her friend Amy LEVY. She worked to improve industrial conditions for women, leaving the Women's Provident and Protective League of which she had been Secretary (1886–8) to form the more militant Women's Trade Union Association. She ed. one of the League's (Women's Industrial Council from 1894) most famous reports, *Married Women's Work*, 1915 (repr. 1983), on enquiries of 1909 and 1910. It draws attention to the 'scandalous' low pay of married women. She inaugurated the SUFFRAGE petition of 1906, ed. the journal, *The Women's Industrial News* and wrote *Sweated Industry and the Minimum Wage*, 1907, and *Makers of Our Clothes*, 1909. Her first pub. fiction was *A Sussex Idyll*, 1877; six novels, and a collection of stories, *Mericas*, 1880, followed. Often using historical settings and focussing on male characters, her books (less important than her political work) trace the development from a state of dreams and isolation to the reality of commitment and relationship. In *Orlando*, 1880, her hero eventually outgrows his soulful solitude and his first unhappy love for a more mature and companionable relationship, whilst in *An Agitator*, 1894, her hero, 'entirely aloof, entirely unmoved, entirely just', learns about the importance of feeling. Her other novels are *The Princess Desiree*, 1896, *The Pursuit of Camilla*, 1899, *Caroline*, 1908, and *The Linleys of Bath*, 1911.

Blackborow, Sarah, English Quaker polemicist. Already seeking and striving at eight (as an Anglican), she recognized at last the QUAKERS' testimony as akin to her own internal spirit. Her signed pamphlets – *A Visit to the Spirit in Prison*, 1658, *The Gift and Good-Will of God to the World*, 1659, and *The Just and Equal Ballance Discovered*, 1660 – repeatedly stress that Christ's light, power and spirit 'was in the Male and in the Female'. Her language is richly biblical and moving: against priests who preach for hire, she says, there cries 'the blood of the innocent ones who have died in stinking holes and dungeons'. She longs – 'Oh woe is me for your souls!' – 'that into my Mother's house you all may come, and into the Chamber of her that conceived me'. *The Oppressed Prisoners Complaint*, 1662, attacks Old Bailey proceedings. The 'Sarah Blackberry', instrumental in founding an early Women's Meeting, whose short pieces appeared in works by James Nayler, 1657, and Richard Hubberthorne, 1663, has been identified with her, but also said to have died in 1655.

Blackburn, Helen, 1842–1903, editor, political activist, b. Knightstown, Valencia Island, Ireland, da. of Isabella (Lamb) and Bewicke B., slate-quarry manager. In 1859 the family moved to London and HB acted as Secretary of the National Society for Women's SUFFRAGE from 1874 to 1895. When a delegate to the TUC for the British National Union of Working Women she published *A Handbook for Women Engaged in Social and Political Work*, 1881; she later edited *A Handy Book of Reference for Irishwomen*, 1888. In 1885 she organized an exhibition of women's industries in Bristol and in 1893 a series of historical portraits of notable women for the International Exhibition at Chicago, later presenting these to the women's hall of Univ. College, Bristol. She edited *The Englishwoman's Review* 1881–90 and became a close associate of the proprietor Jessie BOUCHERETT, with whom she wrote *The Condition of Working Women and the Factory Acts*, 1896. With Nora VYNNE in *Women under the Factory Act*, 1903, HB distinguished between restriction and protection, and protested that the same measures did not apply to men. Despite giving up most public work in 1895 to look after her ailing father, she was involved in the production of *The Women's Suffrage Calendar*, 1896, 1897, and selected and edited Lydia BECKER's writings for *Words of a Leader*, 1897. Her most important work is the classic history, *Women's Suffrage. A record of the women's suffrage movement in the British Isles*, 1902. She bequeathed her library to Girton College, Cambridge, and after her death a scholarship fund was established for young women.

'Blackburne, E. Owens', Elizabeth Owens Blackburne Casey, 1848?–94, novelist, journalist, b. Slane, Co. Meath, da. of Andrew C., granddaughter of Richard Blackburne of Mulladillion House, Co. Meath. She lost her sight when about 11 but regained it after an operation at 18. She attended Trinity College, Dublin, taking the first medal and a certificate in the exam for women. In the early 1870s *The Nation* pub. some of her poetry and her first novel, *In at the Death* (afterwards the three-vol. *A Woman Scorned*, 1876). In 1874 she moved to London and became a journalist, apparently drawing on her experience for the heroine of *Molly Carew*, 1879, a young Irish writer seeking work in London and obsessed with a successful male writer who had befriended her as a child. The plot is sensational but unpredictable and is relentless in depicting the sacrifices the heroine makes to protect her ideal and in its refusal of a 'happy ending'. *A Bunch of Shamrocks*, 1879, is a lively collection of tales, some told in dialect and with a humour that knows and enjoys the credulity of the Irish peasantry without condescension. Many draw on superstition and depend on active women for their resolution. In 1877 she wrote *Illustrious Irishwomen. Being Memoirs of Some of the Most Noted Irishwomen from the Earliest Ages to the Present Century*. She ceased publishing with *The Heart of Erin: An Irish Story of Today*, 1882, and though she received assistance from the Royal Bounty Fund, she became almost destitute. She eventually returned to Dublin and was accidentally burned to death in her home. See Brown, *Ireland in Fiction*, 1916, and O'Donoghue, *Poets of Ireland*, 1892, for her life.

Blackett, Mary (Dawes), 'Marcia', poet and letter writer, publishing at London. Her husband died young; her daughter, against MB's will, was in a French convent; her brother died *en route* to India. She apparently never completed her first published poem, *The Antichamber* (first canto 1786), about the inadequacy of patrons. *Suicide*, 1789, dedicated to the painter Richard Cosway, laments, among others, a relation who died for unrequited love; it claims that women endure the unendurable better than men. In 1791 she pub. (besides a poem in the *European Mag.* and a tribute in the FALCONARS' *Poetic Laurels*) *The Monitress, or The Oeconomy of Female Life*, letters of advice to her daughter, which call chastity 'the very crown and glory of female virtue'.

Black feminist criticism, which was never monolithic, has evolved into a multiplicity of approaches which explore the ways in which black women (chiefly those in the USA) have affected and been affected by historical, sociological, literary, and cultural phenomena. It has challenged traditional definitions of race, class, and gender as separate categories, and has shown that these elements are always in relation to one another, for both dominant and minority groups. The term attained specific definition and wide circulation in Barbara Smith's landmark essay, 'Towards a Black Feminist Criticism' (*Conditions*, 1977). Claiming that the academic segments of the Black and Women's Movements of the 1960s and 1970s had failed to include African-American women's perspectives. Smith argued that critics needed to demonstrate how the literature of black and other Third World women exposes 'the complex systems of sexism, racism and economic exploitation' affecting the lives of African-American women. This approach was implicit in Anna J. COOPER's *The Voice From the South by a Black Woman of the South*, 1892, Jessie FAUSET's work, and the first thesis on African-American women's poetry (Frances Collier Durden, *Negro Women in Poetry, from Phillis* WHEATLEY *to Margaret* WALKER. Atlanta Univ., 1947), all early indicators of a developing black women's literary tradition.

More concentrated scholarly focus on black women writers developed in the seventies, with Toni Cade (later BAMBARA)'s far-ranging ANTHOLOGY, *The Black Woman*, 1970. Gerda Lerner's *Black Women in White America*, 1973, the first book-length history, stressed the distinctness of black women's history, shaped by intersections of sex, race, and class, from that of black men or white women. Alice WALKER's 'In Search of Our Mothers Gardens' (*Ms*, May 1974) traced the historical contexts for early African-American women writers from Wheatley to Zora Neale HURSTON, and emphasized black women's creative legacy in quilting, gardening, storytelling and folk forms. In August, 1974, the little-known

Hurston was also featured in *Black World*, then the most widely read African-American intellectual journal: poet June JORDAN contrasted her with Richard Wright, arguing that African-American *women* writers had been neglected; Mary Helen Washington analyzed recurring themes in contemporary African-American women writers, whom she saw as a distinct group. Jordan and Washington foreshadow the two directions of black feminist criticism during the next two decades.

The first challenge for black feminist critics was scholarly neglect of African-American women's history and literature, together with the inaccessibility of texts. Mary Helen Washington's anthology, *Black-Eyed Susans: Classic Stories By and About Black Women*, 1975, made selections available to a general public, and explored, in its introduction, the relationship between recurrent themes in contemporary writing and the experiences of African-American women. Another major anthology, Roseann Bell, Bettye Parker and Beverly Guy-Sheftall, eds., *Sturdy Black Bridges: Visions of Black Women in Literature*, 1979, included Caribbean and African writing.

During the 1970s, scholars explored the historical and social contexts within which to situate an African-American women's literary tradition. Sharon Harley and Rosalyn Terborg-Penn's collection of historical essays, *The African-American Woman*, 1978, analysed the roles African-American women played in the ABOLITIONIST and nineteenth-century Women's Movement, thus establishing the roots of black feminism. La Frances Rodgers Rose's *The Black Woman*, 1980, and Filomina Chiomka Steady's *The Black Woman Cross-Culturally*, 1981, social science anthologies, identified the complex social roles of African-American women and compared the societal contexts of black women in the Diaspora.

Barbara Christian's *Black Women Novelists, The Development of a Tradition*, 1980, the first book-length study of African-American women's writing, took an historical approach and claimed an identifiable tradition while focusing on contemporary novelists, Paule MARSHALL, Toni MORRISON, Alice Walker. She approached African-American women's novels as a means by which African-American women situated themselves as subjects within their cultural/artistic context even as they responded to the restrictions of sexism, racism, and class exploitation.

Deborah McDowell's essay 'New Directions for Black Feminism' (*Black American Literature Forum*, 1980) sought to distinguish between scholarship on black women and a specifically black feminist approach which could be applied to writings by groups other than African-American women. She suggested two parameters for black feminist criticism: it must be contextually informed and it must pay close attention to individual texts. Further criticism in the 1980s raised theoretical questions about the socio-political framework within which African-American women were being studied. Bell Hooks' *Ain't I A Woman: Black Women and Feminism*, 1981, and June JORDAN's *Civil Wars*, 1981, essays, emphasized challenges made by African-American women's history and politics to major tenets of black male and white female scholarship about race and gender. In popular culture, Michele Wallace's *Black Macho and the Myth of the Superwoman*, 1980, analysed both sexism in the Black Movements of the 1960s and African-American women's internalization of their oppression. Two historical works, Angela DAVIS's *Women, Race and Class*, 1981, and Bettina Aptheker's *Woman's Legacy: Essays on Race, Sex and Class in American History*, 1982, emphasized class as a necessary ingredient in the study of African-American women's history. Paula Giddings' *When and Where I Enter*, 1984, focussed on women's effect on the African-American historical process. In the area of higher education, Gloria Hull, Patricia Bell Scott, and Barbara Smith edited the first inter-disciplinary anthology of black women, *All the Women Are White, All the Blacks Are Men, But Some of Us Are Brave*, 1982: they provided a rationale for the new field, made necessary by the exclusion of African-American women from Black Studies and Women's Studies. Smith's anthology, *Home Girls*, 1983, included black lesbian writing. Dexter Fisher's anthology, *The Third Woman: Minority Women Writers of the US*, 1980, examined African-American women's writing within the context of American Women of Color literature, an approach buttressed by Gloria Anzaldúa and Cherrie Moraga, eds., *This Bridge Called My Back*, 1981, an anthology which, while acknowledging cultural differences, showed commonalities of racism, sexism and class exploitation affecting Women of Color.

Developments since 1985 include Barbara Christian's *Black Feminist Criticism*, Hortense Spillers' 'Afterword' to Marjorie Pryse and Spillers, eds., *Conjuring: Black Women, Fiction, and Literary Tradition*, 1985, and Hazel Carby, *Reconstructing Womanhood, The Emergence of the Afro-American Woman Novelist*, 1987. Christian stressed practice and process, located within and without the university; Spillers located the black women's writing community in the academy, responding to debates about canon formation and demonstrating how this writing could be integrated into American literary tradition; Carby focussed on conditions affecting production of nineteenth-century texts, argued the need to delineate a black female intellectual history that went beyond literature, and, challenging the view that there is a shared experience among black women writers, denied the existence of African-American literary tradition.

Carby's book indicates the increasing significance of nineteenth-century writing. Since the rediscovery of Harriet WILSON's *Our Nig*, 1858, in 1983 by Henry Louis Gates, female SLAVE NARRATIVES as well as nineteenth-century novels have received much attention. Two other previously ignored areas of black women's writing, poetry and drama, also began to be explored: see Erlene Stetson, *Black Sister: Poetry by Black American Women*, 1981, and Margaret Wilkerson, *Nine Plays by Black American Women*, 1986. Michael Awkward, *Inspiriting Influences*, 1989, studies Hurston as a precursor of Morrison, NAYLOR, and Walker, and of the Afro-American woman character's seeking for self in 'community'. Henry Louis Gates, Jr., ed., The Schomburg Library of Nineteenth Century Black Women Writers, 30 vols., 1988–, is making available much new material.

As these various works indicate, African-American women's writing is studied across a wide spectrum: as a distinct literary tradition, as central to African-American literature, as critical to interdisciplinary Black Women's and Lesbian Studies, as transforming Women's Studies as well as the study of race and/or class and/or gender. Not mutually exclusive, these approaches vary considerably in emphasis, some privileging race, class, or gender, and not focusing on their intersections. In its development, US black feminist criticism has challenged traditional definitions of these three and shown that they are always in relation to one another, for both dominant and minority groups.

Books by Black British women, often recent migrants, offer a stimulating range of approach to living and writing experience in the UK, the Caribbean, Africa and Asia. Their work (in several cases selected titles at London Feminist Book Fortnights) includes *Black Women Writers*, collaboratively written, 1983; Lauretta NGCOBO, ed., *Let It Be Told*, 1987; Rhonda Cobham and Merle COLLINS, eds., *Watchers and Seekers*, 1987; Kali for Women, ed., *Truth Tales*, 1987 (stories from India); the Asian Women's Workshop's *Right of Way*, 1988; Shabnam Grewal, Jackie Kay, Lilian Landor, Gail Lewis and Pratibha Parmar, eds., *Charting the Journey, Writings by Black and Third World Women*, 1988; and

Pamela MORDECAI, ed., *Women's Writing from the Caribbean, Her True-True Name*, 1989. The Women's Press has a catalogue of books by black and third-world women.

Blackwell, Alice Stone, 1857–1950, poet, biographer and feminist, b. Orange, NJ, only child of Lucy (STONE), publisher of the suffrage newspaper *Woman's Journal*, and Henry Browne B., and niece of Elizabeth B., the first US woman to receive a medical degree. ASB entered Boston Univ. in 1881, one of two women in a class of 26 males. After an early rebellion against her mother's cause, she became one of the movement's most distinguished reformers, editing the *Woman's Journal* for 35 years and writing editorials and pamphlets arguing for Women's Suffrage. From 1887 she edited the 'Woman's Column', a collection of suffrage news items sent weekly to 1000 US newspapers. She successfully united the American Suffrage Association led by her parents with the rival National Woman Suffrage Association of E. C. STANTON and S. B. ANTHONY. In 1893 she befriended Armenian theological student Johannes Chatschumian and after his death operated an employment service for needy Armenians and translated *Armenian Poems*, 1896, as a labour of love rather than skill. She also translated Yiddish, Hungarian, Spanish and Russian poetry and campaigned against Tsarist oppression, becoming a close friend and correspondent of Catharine Breshkouskuy. ASB helped start the League of Women Voters in Massachusetts and supported many causes including TEMPERANCE, anti-vivisection, and anti-race discrimination. The post-war period saw ASB becoming an avowed socialist radical, although her literary work remained entirely conventional. In 1930 she pub. a life of her mother.

Blackwell, Antoinette (Brown), 1815–1921, reformer, Congregational and Unitarian minister, author and lecturer, b. at Henrietta, NY, fourth da. of Abby (Morse) and Joseph B.'s large family. She was educ. at Monroe County Academy and co-ed Oberlin College where, despite opposition, she completed a theology course in 1850 but was initially refused a licence to preach on grounds of sex. In 1853, she became the first US woman to be ordained. In addition to her work as church minister in NY and New Jersey, she lectured on women's rights, TEMPERANCE and ABOLITION, worked in slums and prisons and was actively involved in the women's SUFFRAGE campaign. In 1856, she m. Elizabeth Blackwell's brother, Samuel. They had five daughters. She pub. 11 books, which, apart from two competent but unexceptional novels, are a religious and philosophical exploration of the universe, society and women's role, including *Shadows of our Social System*, 1856, *Studies in General Science*, 1869, and *The Sexes Throughout Nature*, 1875. AB tries to harmonize Christian beliefs and feminist principles with Darwinian theories of evolution: 'The great practical Creative plan will work out its own final justification' (*The Philosophy of Individuality*, 1893). Her own work testifies to her claim in an 1853 speech that the greatest injustice ever done to woman is that done to her intellectual nature. Lives are in WILLARD and Livermore's *Woman of the Century*, 1893 and L. Kerr's *Lady in the Pulpit*, 1951.

Blackwood, Caroline, b. 1931, novelist. Born Lady Caroline Maureen Hamilton-Temple-Blackwood in Ireland to the 4th Marquess and Marchioness of Dufferin and Ava–Maureen Constance (Guinness) and Basil Sheridan Hamilton-Temple-B. – she was educated in English boarding schools. Her first marriage was to the painter Lucian Freud, 1953 (dissolved 1957); she later m. US composer Israel Citkovitz, 1959, with whom she lived in NYC and had three daughters; she m. poet Robert Lowell in 1972 (died 1977), with whom she had a son. Her first book, short stories and articles, *For All That I Found There*, 1973, was followed by four novels (complex plot and psychology, bizarre characters, black humour). In *The Stepdaughter*, 1976, the heroine, whose husband has left her for another woman, develops affection towards the daughter from his first marriage only when she discovers that he is not actually her father. *Great Granny Webster*, 1977, is the story of the narrator's eccentric family. *The Fate of Mary Rose*, 1981, describes the effect of a girl's murder on a small country village and on the loveless marriage of a self-centred historian. In *Corrigan*, 1984, CB's most optimistic and subtle novel, a woman realizes that the criminal posing as a disabled charity worker has done more good than harm – by encouraging her passive and unhappy mother to raise money for a non-existent hospital. *Good Night Sweet Ladies*, 1983, collects short stories; *On the Perimeter*, 1984, is a journalistic account of CB's visit to Greenham Common. With Anna Haycraft (Alice Thomas ELLIS) she wrote a COOKERY BOOK, *Darling, You Shouldn't Have Gone to So Much Trouble*, 1980. See Crosland, 1981.

Blagden, Isa (Boase gives 'Isabella Jane'), 'Ivory Beryl', 1816?–73, novelist and poet. Little is known of her life before she made Florence her base for further travels from 1849; rumour said she was the (illegitimate?) da. of an English father and Indian mother, seemingly confirmed by her Eastern appearance. Enormously popular with the English community, she was particularly close to Elizabeth Barrett BROWNING and her husband, helping with Pen after Elizabeth's death. Inspired by the latter's *Aurora Leigh* and needing to write for money, IB overcame publishers' reluctance to accept her quirky and sometimes laboured novels, though she was forced to seek patronage from Browning and Trollope. Supposed to have been romantically involved with Robert Lytton (Rosina Bulwer LYTTON's son) after nursing him in 1857, she survived to nurse many more friends, always putting down her pen to help others, despite her slender means. Her first novel, *Agnes Tremorne*, 1861, is probably her best: dealing with the aspirations of a woman artist in the context of the struggle for Italian independence, secret societies and mesmerism, it ends with the heroine deciding to continue with her work after the death of her lover and to live with a dear woman friend: '... love is theirs in its purest impersonality, and yet in its closest sympathy ... seldom attained, even in the holiest and truest marriage'. Four other novels followed, including *The Woman I Loved, and the Woman Who Loved Me*, 1862 (narrated by a priggish male), *The Cost of a Secret*, 1863, *Nora and Archibald Lee*, 1867, and *The Crown of a Life*, 1869. She also wrote stories and articles as 'Ivory Beryl', while her MS poems were collected after her death by Mme Linda (White) Mazini and pub. in 1873 with a rather patronizing memoir by Alfred Austin. *Dearest Isa* (Robert Browning's letters to her), 1951, has an intro. by Edward McAleer; letters, ed. Sandra Donaldson, 1990.

Blais, Marie-Claire, novelist, short-story writer, poet and playwright, b. in 1939 in a working-class district of Québec City, da. of Véronique (Nolin) and Fernando B. Desiring to write from an early age and dissatisfied with school, she left the Convent Saint-Roch de Québec to work (in a shoe factory and various offices) before attending lectures at Laval University. For many years she lived in the USA, France and Québec with US sculptor Mary Meigs, who describes the relationship in *Lily Briscoe: A Self-Portrait*, 1981, and *The Medusa Head*, 1983. M-CB's *La Belle Bête*, 1959 (*Mad Shadows*, 1960), about a ten-year-old idiot, Patrice, the Beautiful, narcissistic, Beast, launched her career. *Tête Blanche*, also focussed on an adolescent boy, followed a year later (transl. 1961). M-CB spent a year in Paris as a Canada Council Fellow, then was a Guggenheim Fellow, sponsored by Edmund Wilson. She quickly won an international reputation as a voice of the new Québec. *Une Saison dans la vie d'Emmanuel*, 1965 (*A Season in the Life of Emmanuel*, 1966), a study of repressed rural Québec, opens unforgettably with its child's-eye description of Grandmother Antoinette's feet, seeming to 'dominate the room' as she 'Immense, souveraine ... semblait diriger le monde de son fauteuil.' It won the France-Québec and Médicis prizes and was translated into 13 languages. Her important trilogy followed: *Manuscrits de Pauline Archange*, 1968 (Governor General's Award), and *Vivre! Vivre!* 1969, were translated together in a single volume, *The Manuscripts of Pauline Archange*, 1970; *Les Apparences*, 1970, was translated as *Durer's Angel*, 1976. *Une Liaison parisienne*, 1975 (*A Literary Affair*, 1979), and *Un Joualonais, sa joualonie*, 1973 (*St. Lawrence Blues*, 1974), explore cultural colonialism and the France/Québec dynamic. Thematically an extremist ('I want to strip away the masks. What interests me in human beings is that element of dangerous freedom where they are saved or lost'), M-CB combines a dark vision of contemporary life (images of death, poverty, depravity) with lyricism, formal inventiveness, and compelling narrative style often reminiscent of Virginia WOOLF. She explores homosexuality (see especially *Le Loup*, 1972, transl. as *The Wolf*, 1974) and lesbian love. *Les Nuits de l'underground*, 1978, transl. as *Nights in the Underground*, 1979, is prefaced by Vita SACKVILLE-WEST's diary comment, 'I believe that the psychology of people like myself will be a matter of interest'. *Le Sourd dans la ville*, 1979, transl. as *Deaf to the City*, 1980, won the Governor General's Award. Here, as in *Visions d'Anna*, 1982 (*Anna's World*, 1985), and *Pierre, la guerre du printemps 81*, 1984, M-CB treats contemporary horrors: drugs, the nuclear threat, impending ecological disaster. She has published three volumes of poetry; her plays have been produced in Montréal and Québec. (She collaborated with Nicole BROSSARD and France THÉORET and others in *La Nef des sorcières*, 1976). In 1980, she was made a member of the Order of Canada. Interview with Lise Payette, in *Nous*, June 1973, with Giles Marcotte, in *Voix et Images*, 8, 1983 (also includes bibliog. by Aurelien Boiven, et al.). Much criticism: selecs. listed by Godard, 1987. See Edmund Wilson, *O Canada*, 1965; study by Philip Stratford, 1971; M. J. Green in Paula Gilbert Lewis, ed., *Traditionalism, Nationalism and Feminism: Women Writers of Quebec*, 1985, and P. G. Lewis in *Quebec Studies*, 1, 1984.

Blake, Lillie (Devereux) (formerly Umsted), 'Tiger Lily', 1833–1913, writer of novels and short stories, orator, essayist, journalist and feminist activist. B. at Raleigh, NC, she was elder da. of Sarah Elizabeth (Johnson) and George D., both descended from Jonathan and Sarah EDWARDS. She was educ. at a girls' school in New Haven and tutored by Yale professors. In 1855 she m. Frank Geoffrey Quay Umsted, lawyer, and moved to St Louis, Missouri, and then NYC. In 1859 her second daughter was born, her first novel *Southwold* published and her husband committed suicide. She supported her family by writing, acting as a Washington correspondent, 1861–2, and publishing hundreds of stories and articles, as well as *Rockford; or, Sunshine and Storm*, 1863, *Forced Vows; or, A Revengeful Woman's Fate*, 1870, and her last novel, *Fettered for Life; or, Lord and Master*, 1874. This is a feminist classic: a seduction/abduction story, the novel has politically sophisticated chapters dealing with women's issues – domestic violence, legal powerlessness, employment, prostitution – and the need for women to form strong bonds with each other across classes: 'We women ought to stand by each other, care for each other.' The 'hero' who frequently rescues the 'heroine' is revealed at the last to be a woman who has taken on male attire because 'No man insulted me, and when I asked for work, I was not offered outrage.' In 1866 LDB m. Grinfill Blake and after

1869 devoted her life to the women's movement; a brilliant orator and wit, she toured the USA speaking on women's rights. She was president of the NY Woman Suffrage Association, 1879–90, and of the NYC Woman Suffrage League, 1886–1900. Conflict with Susan B. ANTHONY led to her withdrawal from national activities, but she continued her work until her death. She also pub. *Woman's Place To-Day*, 1883, and the short stories *A Daring Experiment*, 1892. In her fiction, she wittily exposes the assumptions on which gender conventions are based. For her life, see Katherine Devereux Blake and Margaret Louise Wallace, 1943. Her MSS are held by Missouri Hist. Soc., St. Louis, and Smith College Library.

Blamire, Susanna, 1747–94, Cumberland poet, youngest child of Isabella (Simpson) and William B., yeoman. Brought up after her mother's death in 1754 by an aunt, educ. at the village school, she loved dancing, playing her guitar in the woods and amateur doctoring. From youth she wrote poems casually for others' pleasure, not keeping them. She visited London, Ireland and frequently a married sister in Scotland, whose dialect she used as well as Cumbrian for songs (some pub. in her lifetime singly and anon.). From her listening 'to the chat / Of country folks 'bout who knows what' came songs which dramatize partings, reunions, love and marital rows. She lived with her widowed sister from 1773, and later at Carlisle with Catherine Gilpin, 1738–1811, whose family were intellectual local gentry and who could match her in rhyming, as shown by the joint 'Cumberland Scold' and Gilpin's own 'Village Club'. SB wrote for Gilpin a spinning song: 'So twirl thee round wheely, I'll sing while I may; / I'll try to be happy the hale o' the day.' Her fine 'serious' poetry in various kinds shows the same attentive eye for nature and human life, moving or fanciful personification (most often Hope), a backbone of solid thought and a deep vein of feeling. The composite village portrait in 'Stoklewath' shows why her local fame still lives. She died after long illness: rheumatism and asthma. See her *Poetical Works*, Edinburgh, 1842; Henry Lonsdale, *Worthies of Cumberland*, 1873, iv.

Blaugdone, Barbara, *c.* 1609–1705, Quaker minister and autobiographer. Her *Account of the Travels, Sufferings, and Persecutions . . .*, 1691, tells how she was converted to Quakerism by Ann AUDLAND's first husband and future father-in-law while running a school, which failed when her public PREACHING put parents off. She travelled widely, was jailed in Devon, Marlborough, Bristol (where she went on hunger-strike and sang when whipped) and all over Ireland (once for interfering in a murder case; gentry acquaintances visited her in prison). She was accused of being a witch and knifed by a man when walking arm-in-arm with a woman. As she preached in a market-place 'a Butcher swore he would cleave my Head in twain; and had his Cleaver up ready to do it, but their came a Woman behind him and caught his Arms, and staid them till the Souldiers came and rescued me.' She wrote to James II in 1686.

Bleecker, Ann Eliza (Schuyler), 1752–83, poet and novelist. Youngest child of Margareta (Van Wyck) and Brant S. of NYC (who died before her birth), she wrote poetry vëy young and loved books but not school. On marriage to John J. B., a wealthy lawyer, in 1769, she destroyed all she had written so far. They settled at Tomhanick, near Albany – a frontier area – where she wrote poems in many kinds: verse for friends and children, natural description (she Americanizes the topographical genre to fit the Hudson River), meditations on death both grisly and pensive, religious self-analysis and comic satire. She suffered extreme shifts in mood and in depression would destroy light-hearted poems. In 1777 the approach of

British troops made the family flee on foot; her younger daughter died on the journey, her mother and sister within a few months; four years later she miscarried when her husband was captured; these shocks affected her health. She fictionalized the earlier experience of betrayal and horror (with some memory of CAPTIVITY-NARRATIVES) in 'The History of Maria Kittle, In a Letter' to her half-sister, begun 1779: more forceful than the sentimental 'Story of Henry and Anne', about German immigrants, which also treats of oppression. Her daughter Margaretta FAUGERES published her work first in the *New-York Magazine*, then in *Posthumous Works*, with her name and a memoir, 1793.

Blessington, Marguerite (Power), Countess of, 1789–1849, novelist, journalist, literary hostess, b. Co. Tipperary. Haphazardly educ. by her own reading and by her mother's friend Anne Dwyer, she was sold in marriage by her brutish father to Captain Maurice Farmer (1804), whom she left after three months. She lived under the protection of Captain Jenkins for five years, then with Charles, Viscount Mountjoy and Earl of B., in London. When her drunken husband fell from a window in 1817 she and Charles m. (1818). She was never considered respectable. She was beautiful ('most gorgeous'), luxurious, a charming, good-natured and accomplished hostess. She, her husband and Count Alfred d'Orsay travelled extensively on the Continent 1822–8: this gave her material which she used in her journalism, especially the association with Byron in Genoa in 1823. LB had no children and when her husband died of apoplexy in 1829 she found her circumstances much reduced. In 1831 she moved to Mayfair, becoming one of the greatest hostesses and meeting her increasing financial difficulties by editing ANNUALS, especially *The Keepsake* and the *Book of Beauty*, and by writing a number of genteel novels reflecting the social life of the times. Despite her industriousness, her life became increasingly burdened financially; bankrupt in 1849, she fled to Paris where she died after a month, worn out at 59 ('I have lost a mother', wept d'Orsay). The *Conversations of Lord Byron* remains her most sprightly and engaging work, but the novels have interest for their reflections of manners and social attitudes. Hers is an example of the kind of career a hard-working, fashionable woman of letters might make at this time and also of its unpredictability and suffering.

Blewett, Jean (McKishnie), 1862–1934, poet, essayist, journalist. B. at Scotia, Kent County, Ont., da. of Janet (McIntyre) and John M., Scottish immigrants, she was educ. at St Thomas Collegiate. She married Bassett B. and published her novel, *Out of the Depths?* 1879. Later a regular contributor to the Toronto *Globe* and editor of its Homemaker's Department, JB made her reputation with a series of pen portraits published in various newspapers and magazines. Her several vols. of poetry include *Between the Lights*, 1904, *Heart Songs*, 1897, *The Cornflower and Other Poems*, 1906, and *Heart Stories*, 1919. Mostly didactic, these range from narratives of farm life to nature poems and lyrical love poems (collected, 1922). Interested in suffrage and social reform, JB was popular in the late nineteenth and early twentieth centuries.

Blind, Mathilde, 'Claude Lake', 1841–96, poet, translator, literary critic and feminist, b. at Mannheim. After the death of her elderly father (Cohen, a banker), her mother m. Karl Blind, revolutionary leader, and the family fled to England in the early 1850s. MB was educ. at a London girls' school (where she knew Rosa CAREY), and later, at Zurich (where she tried unsuccessfully to gain entrance to univ. lectures).In 1860 she took a solitary walking-tour through the Swiss Alps: 'For once I felt truly free'. MB never married, forming all her closest ties with women. Influenced by George ELIOT (whose Life she wrote in 1883), George SAND, and above all, E. B. BROWNING's *Aurora Leigh*, MB staunchly supported the cause of improving women's education, asserting 'men might emigrate'. In 1867 she published, as 'Claude Lake', her first poems, dedicated to Mazzini, whom she knew well and always admired; although she continued to write, she also lectured, which led to the publication of her Shelley criticism (*Westminster Review*, July 1870). She translated Strauss's *Old Faith and the New*, 1873, travelled to Scotland in the same year and was inspired to write two long poems, *The Prophecy of St Oran*, 1881, dealing with religious questions, and *The Heather on Fire*, 1886, a protest against the treatment of the crofters during the Highland clearances. Between the two came MB's one novel, *Tarantella*, 1885 (a cross between fairytale and provincial realism), and a life of Madame Roland, 1886. She lived then with the Ford Madox Browns in Manchester, where she worked on her most ambitious poem, *The Ascent of Man*, 1889, a celebration of the theory of evolution. In 1890 she pub. her translation of *The Journal of Marie Bashkirtseff*, an important 'document about feminine nature, of which we as yet know so little ... [apart from] the theories of men with their cut-and-dried theories as to what women are or ought to be' (Intro.). *Dramas in Miniature* followed in 1891, asserting the miserable effects on women of the double standard. She also pub. articles in *Fraser's* (e.g. on Mary WOLLESTONECRAFT), *The Athenaeum* and the *Fortnightly Review* (on Mazzini). She knew and travelled with Mona CAIRD. She bequeathed her estate to Newnham College, Cambridge, to found a Scholarship for Language and Literature. Her poems were edited by Arthur Symons in 1900, with a memoir by Richard Garnett. Some letters are in the BL.

Bliss, Eliot, novelist. B. in 1903 in Jamaica to Eva (Lees) and Captain John Plomer B. of the West India Regiment, EB was educated in a series of British convent schools, returning to Jamaica in 1923 for two years before settling permanently in England. After completing a diploma in journalism at University College London, she named herself Eliot (after George ELIOT and T. S. Eliot) and worked at a series of publishing jobs while establishing important and influential friendships with Anna WICKHAM, Dorothy RICHARDSON, Jean RHYS, Romer WILSON (who provided financial support during the writing of her first novel) and Vita SACKVILLE-WEST. Her first novel, *Saraband*, 1931 (repr. with intro. by Paul Bailey, 1986), is the *Bildungsroman* of Louie, an imaginative young girl of genteel upbringing, conscious that 'she could not do anything' (in sharp contrast to her talented violinist-cousin), whose family's financial crises force her to train as a typist (an experience which makes her 'afraid of turning into a machine'), and who finally recognizes 'the personality of creative life' within her: her desire to write and its accompanying force 'that said: I'm damned if I'll die – the challenge thrown in the face of destruction.' Her second and last novel, *Luminous Isle*, 1934 (repr. 1984 with intro. by Alexandra Pringle), is the autobiographical tale of 'Em's' return, at 19, to Jamaica after her schooling in England. Although she has 'always wanted to come back' because 'the Island's my home,' she strains against the narrowness of colonial society, 'their social code with its hypocrisy and hidden indecencies' and also its racism.

Blondal, Patricia (Jenkins), 1926–59, novelist, b. at Souris, Manitoba, the 'Mouse Bluffs' of her first novel, da. of Pearl (Wark) and Nathaniel J. She attended the Univ. of Manitoba, where she occasionally wrote poetry, m. Henry B., 1946, had two children, then wrote, broadcast and worked in public relations. To escape the small towns later so effectively created in her fiction, PB travelled in Europe. By 1951, she had become interested in fiction, and in

1956 was circulating short stories and a play about Louis Riel. In 1959, *Chatelaine* serialized a version of what was to become her second novel, *From Heaven With a Shout*, 1982, about a marriage set in snobbish Vancouver society. Her first and best-known novel, *A Candle to Light the Sun*, 1959, new ed., 1976, describes the conflict between a small town and a city (Winnipeg) through the central male character's artistic and post-colonial cultural search for a father. Since 'Blondal clearly identifies with David's growing sensibility', the novel is also a woman's artistic statement. PB's early death from cancer abruptly terminated a potential distinguished literary career. See John Moss, 1981, quoted above, and L. R. Ricou, in *CanL*, 84, 1980.

Bloom, Valerie (Wright), poet, performer, b. 1956 at Clarendon, Jamaica, into a family of story-tellers, and brought up at Frankfield, where she attended primary and high schools. She learned and performed, with acclaim, the work of Louise BENNETT, but 'for fear of being ridiculed, I kept to myself the desire to create the same magic I had found in books from the minute I could read.' The few (Wordsworthian) poems she wrote made her sisters laugh. She worked a year as a librarian before training as a teacher at Mico College, and taught English, speech, drama and home economics at Frankfield, 1976–9. In 1978 came her first poem in the Bennett style, a comic monologue in what she now calls 'patois' or 'dialect' rather than 'Nation Language'. The speaker defends her theft of food (the cook was dangerously incompetent; it *needed* testing). This won a bronze medal at the National Festival. VB left for England in 1979, took a BA at the Univ. of Kent (English with African and Caribbean studies), m. Douglas B. (who is British) and has a daughter. Based in Manchester, she lectured and taught folk traditions in dance, song and poetry as a Multicultural Arts Officer. She made her London performing debut at the first Black Book Fair, 1982, and published a collection, *Touch Mi, Tell Mi*, next year. She has broadcast on radio in Britain (regularly on 'I'n'I Rule O. K.', Manchester) and Jamaica, where after several visits she has now returned to live and work. She wrote the lyrics for a musical on the history of cotton and slavery, has written for children, been much anthologized and is to publish a second volume soon. In an ORAL TRADITION derived from Africa, she mixes humour, irony and social protest, often in the iambic quatrain for its 'built-in sense of security, born of long familiarity'. In 'Yuh Hear 'Bout?' this phrase prefaces each item in a catalogue of British racism, ending 'Yuh no hear bout dem? / Me neida.' Another list – of reasons why a man shot by police was wholly to blame – uses the refrain, 'At leas' a soh dem sey.' The reader in 'Letter from Home' begins, 'Amy chile, pass mi specs', enumerates the detail of life from which she is absent, and ends, 'mi no know / Wha meck me dis feel soh depress.' VB feels the performance is 'fifty per cent of the poem'. She has told of her childhood in Lauretta NGCOBO, ed., *Let It Be Told, Black Women Writers in Britain*, 1987.

Bloomer, Amelia Jenks, 1818–94, suffragist, temperance reformer, and feminist editor, b. in Homer, NY; in 1840 she m. Dexter Chamberlain B., an attorney, anti-slavery reformer and editor of a Whig journal. At the July 1848 Seneca Falls Women's Rights convention she made friends with Lucretia MOTT and with E. C. STANTON, who contributed to her journal *Lily*. Begun in January 1849 as a TEMPERANCE paper, *Lily* was later a feminist journal. Although not originating the 'Bloomer' style, her early 1850s *Lily* articles defending the physical freedom of pantaloons for women created a national fad which spread to England (*Punch* satirized it). During the 1850s AJB toured the USA lecturing on SUFFRAGE and temperance, most notably in 1853 with S. B. ANTHONY. She continued to write and lecture until the end of her life, listing her goals as 'woman's right to better education, to a wider field of employment, to better remuneration for her labor, and to the ballot for the protection of her rights.' See *Life and Writings*, ed. D. C. Bloomer, 1895; repr. with intro. by Susan J. Kleinberg, 1975.

Blower, Elizabeth, 1757/63?–after 1816, poet, novelist and actress, b. at Worcester (a town notorious for election violence, where her father supported the unsuccessful independent candidate). Her first novel, *The Parsonage House* (1780, epistolary), turns a sharp satirical eye on current styles of fiction. In 1782 she published poems and the novel *George Bateman* (with a lively account of electioneering), went on stage and was well reviewed in both *métiers*. She then acted in Ireland for five years (with a younger sister) and probably in London, 1787–8. *Maria*, 1785, conducts its orphan heroine past various inset stories to carefully decorous marriage. In *Features from Life, or a Summer Visit* [1788] sentiment reigns: of the first scene, about a proffered self-sacrifice by wife to husband, the author says 'Nature beheld the graceful weakness of these her favourite children through tears of delight'; today it looks a convincing but repellent psychological study. (Betrayed and widowed, the heroine is left 'the most interesting object grief had ever made', entrancing 'the eye of sensibility'.)

Bluestockings. The name (from worsted stockings as against silk) had been used to abuse Puritans; Benjamin Stillingfleet's stockings led a group of female friends in the 1760s to apply the term to (chiefly male) intellectuals they knew; by the 1770s it meant the ladies rather than the gentlemen. Elizabeth MONTAGU, with her prestige as patron and as critic of Shakespeare, was dubbed 'Queen of the Blues'. Elizabeth VESEY, a gifted if whimsical hostess, campaigned for spending time at conversation not cards, and for seating guests in informal groups not a single large circle: to her Hannah MORE addressed her lighthearted, complimentary poem, *Bas Bleu*, 1786 (written 1784), which joins Frances BOSCAWEN to these two as leaders of the movement. Elizabeth CARTER, MARY DELANY, Hester CHAPONE, the younger Frances BURNEY and several men were their associates: gentlefolk of no mean talent, who favoured the cultivation of the mind, social decorum and high moral tone. Their horror at Hester PIOZZI's second marriage, with its clearly (though not solely) sexual motive, sadly reveals their insecurity and fear of contamination. See Sylvia H. Myers, 1990.

Blume, Judy (Sussman), children's novelist. B. in 1938 at Elizabeth, NJ, da. of Esther (Rosenfeld) and dentist Rudolph S., she was educ. at NY Univ. (BA 1960). She m. John B. in 1959 (divorced) and has two children. The outstanding popularity of her 15 novels for pre- and early-teen readers is largely due to her deliberate, though not always challenging, use of first-person narrators who desperately seek acceptance by their peers as well as understanding and affection from their parents. The 11-year-old speaker in *Are You There, God? It's Me, Margaret*, 1970, chats to and quizzes God about bras, menstruation and sex, all topics repeated in *Deenie*, 1973, and *Blubber*, 1974. Dealing with a first love affair, *Forever*, 1975, treats sexuality in a more overt but self-consciously talkative way. The family (where siblings quarrel, as in *The Pain and the Great One*, 1984, the neglected child vies for attention, as in *Tales of a Fourth Grade Nothing*, 1972, and *The One in the Middle is the Green Kangaroo*, 1981, and parents may divorce, as in *It's Not the End of the World*, 1972) is the core of JB's juvenile fiction. The comic *Wifey*, 1983, is for adults.

Blyton, Enid Mary (Carey), 1897–1968, children's writer. B. in London, da. of Theresa Mary (Harrison) and Thomas C., who left home when she was 12, she was educ. at St Christopher's Girls' School, Surrey, and Ipswich High School. She married Major Hugh Pollock, an editor, in 1924; they had two daughters. She secured a divorce to marry Kenneth Waters, a surgeon, in 1943. Before her publishing career began, she worked as a teacher and nursery governess. After over 400 books spanning four decades, EB enjoyed, and in some circles still enjoys, great popularity. Librarians and students of children's literature point to her clichés, class and race stereotypes and simplified vocabulary; children still enjoy her school, adventure and mystery series where snowballing action poses no challenge to the reader. One of her most successful creatures is Noddy, an animated wooden doll (male) in a series of nursery fantasies: Noddy is innocent, the Golliwog naughty, and their world untroubled. EB said of this formula that Noddy 'is like the children themselves, but more naive and stupid. Children like that – it makes them feel superior'. Her *Secret Seven* adventures follow a similarly logical appeal in their accounts of the exploits of three girls and four boys who often meet in 'the hols', share secret passwords and meeting places, and expose smugglers, spies and robbers, for which non-stop action they are usually rewarded with 'a thumping good tea, ice-creams and all'. She edited a children's magazine, *Sunny Stories for Little Folks*, 1926–52. Life by Barbara Stoney, 1974; memoir of her as a cold, 'emotionally crippled' mother by her daughter Imogen Smallwood, 1989; see also Sheila Ray, 1982.

'Boake, Capel', Doris Boake Kerr, 1889–1944, novelist, b. Sydney, da. of Adelaide Eva (B.), photographer, and Gregory Augustine K.: niece of poet Barcroft Boake. When she was four, the family moved to Melbourne, the city she was to write about in all of her novels. CB went from school to work, probably to help support the family as her father was an invalid. Her first short story appeared in the *Australasian*, 1916. Her first novel, *Painted Clay*, 1917, based on the author's own experience of shop and secretarial work, tells of a lonely girl facing life without family or financial support. Hers were urban novels, in great contrast to the bush tales so beloved in her time. A thriller, *The Romany Mark*, 1922, and a novel about a Jewish family, *The Dark Thread*, 1936, were followed by the posthumous *The Twig is Bent*, 1946, an historical novel of early Victorian times, and *Selected Poems*, 1949.

Bodichon, Barbara (Leigh-Smith), 1827–91, feminist, educational reformer, journalist, painter, b. Wathington, Sussex, eldest da. of the illegitimate family of Annie Longden and Benjamin L.–S., radical MP for Norwich, where she spent her childhood. Florence NIGHTINGALE and Hilary Bonham-Carter were her first cousins. Smith educ. his daughters and sons alike: taught by masters at home, they also attended Westminster Infant School. Her mother died when BB was seven, and her Aunt Julia became a powerful influence, introducing her to Harriet MARTINEAU, Mary SOMERVILLE and Amelia OPIE. In 1849, she and her aunt enrolled at the newly-formed Ladies' College in Bedford Square. Her father gave her an income of £300 p.a. when she came of age, ensuring her financial independence, and encouraged her philanthropic interests, giving her the deeds of the Westminster School for Infants, which led her to establish the Portman Hall non-denominational co-educational school. An energetic campaigner on women's issues, she pub. *A Brief Summary in Plain Language of the Most Important Laws Concerning Women*, 1854, which explains bluntly that 'a woman's body belonged to her husband; she is in his custody', and *Women and Work*, 1857, which argues the necessity of paid work for women: 'idleness, or worse than idleness, is the state of tens of thousands of young women in Britain today.' She helped draw up the petition for the Married Women's

Property Act and, with her childhood friend Bessie Rayner PARKES, helped set up the *English Woman's Journal* in 1858, writing for this and other periodicals. She was a founder of the Women's Suffrage Committee in 1866: her resolve that women should be entitled to higher education led to her involvement with the foundation of Girton College, Cambidge. She was a talented landscape artist, exhibiting in London and the provinces, and a regular contributor to the Society of Female Artists. In 1857, she m. Dr Eugène B.; they spent part of each year in their home in Algeria. On honeymoon in the USA, BB talked widely to slaves and slave-owners, recording her observations in *An American Diary, 1857–8*, 1972 (ed. by Joseph W. Reed). From 1877 she suffered from hemiplegia and was increasingly crippled. See the lives by Hester Burton, 1949, and Sheila R. Herstein, 1985.

Boesing, Martha, playwright. She wrote her first play, *Accent of Fools*, while a student at the Connecticut College for Women, before going on to a master's degree at the Univ. of Wisconsin and graduate work at the Univ. of Minnesota. She m. Paul B. and had three children. She worked with the Minneapolis Repertory Theater, the Moppet Players (co-founder) and Firehouse Theatre (as 'actress, fund-raiser and closet dramatist'). With Paul B. she wrote songs, then operas: *The Wanderer*, 1969, and *Earth Song*, 1970. With the feminist theatre group At-the-Foot-of-the-Mountain she wrote and co-wrote many plays and events. Her own include *Pimp*, *The Gelding*, both 1974, and *Love Song for an Amazon*. *Pimp* is a one-act play of mother, daughter and grandmother, their dreams and fantasies, all, until almost the end, of serving and pleasing men: 'Once upon a time there was a very wealthy and very handsome bachelor ... forever putting his most recent conquest carefully on his shelf and going off in gay pursuit of some new woman whom he had heard about from a friend or a prince' (in Rachel France, ed., *A Century of Plays by American Women*). With At-the-Foot she devised *The Story of a Mother. A Ritual Drama* (from 'Mourning' to 'Birthing' and 'Communion' – sharing bread with the audience), published in the form of outlines and notes for improvising in Helen Chinoy and Linda Jenkins, eds., *Women in American Theater*, 1981. *Raped*, 1976, is a feminist adaptation from Brecht; *Mad Emma*, 1977, depicts Emma GOLDMAN. MB's work avoids realism, which, she says, reflects and reinforces the status quo.

Bogan, Louise, 1897–1970, lyric poet, short-story writer, critic, translator. B. in Livermore, Maine, da. of working-class Irish parents, Mary Helen Murphy (Sheilds) and Daniel B., she was educ. at the Girls' Latin School and Boston Univ., leaving after a year (and declining a scholarship to Radcliffe) to marry army officer Curt Alexander, 1916. He died shortly after the death of their daughter. She wrote poems in high school and published first in *Poetry* in 1921, then in her collections *Body of This Death*, 1923, and *Dark Summer*, 1929. A perfectionist and slow writer, she was creatively fired by eroticism and simultaneously deterred by unequal relationships with men; a second marriage, to poet Raymond Holden in 1925, ended only after confrontations brought on by her two breakdowns. It was followed by a relationship with Theodore Roethke. *The Sleeping Fury*, 1937, is in part a record of the psychic demons which drove her to love but led her to expect betrayal. LB became poetry editor of *The New Yorker* in 1931; her reviews, collected in *A Poet's Alphabet*, 1970, are ambivalent about women poets. Early in her career, like many of the twenties generation, LB hated to be called a 'woman poet', but during the post-war 1940s she praised women's ability to bring 'heart' to poetry (as in her comments on Léonie Fuller ADAMS). Her own poems, like 'Women', carry her ambivalence into cold irony: 'Women have no wilderness in them, / They are provident instead, / Content in the tight hot cell of their hearts / To eat dusty bread.' In 1945–6, she was Poetry Consultant to the Library of Congress (cf. Elizabeth BISHOP, Josephine JACOBSEN); later she taught at various universities and colleges. Collected poems appeared in 1941 and 1954; *The Blue Estuaries*, 1969, contains the 105 poems LB considered good enough to be remembered. She was recognized in the 1950s as a 'poet's poet'. Her difficult modernist poems about female experience – romantic love, breakdown and betrayal – began to be discovered through the Pulitzer-prize-winning biography by Elizabeth Frank, 1985, and Gloria Bowles's critical study, 1987. LB was co-translator of Goethe, Valéry (with May SARTON) and Jules Renard. Her letters (to Harriet MONROE, Ruth BENEDICT, May Sarton and others, *What the Woman Lived*, 1973, and her moving autobiography, *Journey Around My Room*, 1980, both ed. by her executor Ruth Limmer, show her Irish humour and capacity for endurance. Papers in Amherst College Library.

Boland, Bridget, Irish playwright, screen and radio writer, novelist, memoirist. B. in 1913 in London, da. of Eileen (Moloney) and John Pius B., Nationalist MP, she was educ. at a Roehampton convent and at Oxford (BA in PPE, 1935). Her first novel, *The Wild Geese*, 1938, on eighteenth-century Irish mercenary soldiers (written at 21), was followed by *Portrait of a Lady in Love*, 1942, and *Caterina*, 1975, a novel based on the life of Caterina Sforza of Milan, who [illegible] in 14[illegible]7. Her first screen play, *Spies of the Air*, 1939, was followed by numerous others, mostly collaborative work: notable are *Gaslight*, 1940 (re-released as *Angel Street*, 1953), *War and Peace*, 1956, and the much-praised *Anne of the Thousand Days*, 1970. As a Senior Commander in the ATS, 1941–6, she wrote for the troops. Many stage plays since treat political topics, including women's rights, but avoid the 'domestic', which 'bores' her. *Cockpit*, 1948, a ground-breaking experiment in environmental theatre, is set in a Displaced Persons centre with symbolic resonance. *The Prisoner*, 1955, makes 'heavy drama' of a process of interrogation recalling that of the Hungarian Cardinal Mindszenty. BB has written for radio and TV, two books on gardening and 'Old Wives' Lore' (with her sister, Maureen, 1976 and 1977) and *At My Mother's Knee*, 1978, about her childhood.

Boland, Eavan Aisling, poet and reviewer. B. in 1944 in Dublin, da. of painter Frances (Kelly) and diplomat Frederick B., she went to school in Dublin, then to convents in London and NYC. She took a BA in English, 1966, at Trinity College, Dublin, where *Poetry*, with prose by J. O'Malley, was published, 1963, and where she lectured, 1967–8. In 1968 she began lecturing at the School of Irish Studies in Dublin and a year later m. novelist Kevin Casey; they have two daughters. Her second volume, *New Territory*, 1967, which stakes out her Irish subject-matter (legend, history, 'Dublin reverence and Belfast irony'), won an Irish Arts Council Macauley Fellowship. *The War Horse*, 1975, moves these subjects into tense, angry, grieving relation with the present Troubles: 'Yesterday I knew no lullaby / But you have taught me overnight to order / This song, which takes from your final cry / Its tune, from your unreasoned end its reason; / Its rhythm from the discord of your murder' ('Child of Our Time' *for Angus*). The rhythm she writes from this discord is a careful measure, formally impressive, as in 'Famine Road', which links the present with the past potato famines. In 1979, EB attended the International Writing Programme at the Univ. of Iowa. *In Her Own Image*, 1980, deals nakedly and forcefully with women's experiences. An 'attack on things like the mimic muse' and 'a belief that experiences which haven't been given a voice are degraded', it forces the categorical into the personal and the bodily into language, in such poems as 'Anorexic', 'Mastectomy', 'Menses' and 'Solitary'. 'In His Own Image' chillingly addresses marital violence. *The Night Feed*, 1982, aims to convey 'what is potent and splendid and powerful' about mothering. *The Journey*, Dublin 1986, NYC and Manchester (Poetry Book Society Choice), 1987, is dedicated to EB's mother. In its title piece, prompted by EB's infant daughter's serious illness, SAPPHO takes the poet, her dear daughter ('there are not many of us'), to visit an underworld of women dead with their children in epidemics and plague, and shows her 'the silences in which are our beginnings, / in which we have an origin like water'. *Introducing Eavan Boland*, 1981, prints selections; *Selected Poems*, 1989, includes several re-written versions. Article by Robert Henigan in *Concerning Poetry*, 18, 1985; splendid interview in *Northwest Rev.*, 25, 1987 (quoted above).

Bolt, Carol (Johnson), playwright, director, stage manager. B. in 1941 in Winnipeg, da. of schoolteacher and librarian Marjorie (Small) and miner and logger William J., she grew up in Manitoba, Ontario and British Columbia. At the Univ. of British Columbia (BA 1961), she studied play-writing and after a year in Britain helped to found, direct, and stage-manage a Montréal theatre. Later she moved to Toronto, where she lives with husband (m. 1969), actor David B., and one son. Since production, 1970, of her first comedy, *Daganawida*, she has written for adults and children, for radio, TV and stage. Like Sharon POLLOCK, she achieved success with politically committed historical dramas: *Buffalo Jump*, produced 1972, *Gabe*, produced 1973, and *Red Emma: Queen of the Anarchists*, produced 1974, a portrait of Emma GOLDMAN (collected in *Playwrights in Profile: Carol Bolt*, 1976). Her plays, often written collaboratively, are fast-paced, satiric and fluid in form. Since the mid 1970s, CB has shifted to more contemporary subjects: *Shelter*, produced 1974, a zany satire about a politician's widow running for Parliament, urged on by a friend who wants a perfect world ('Everybody tall and graceful. Without gender'); and *One Night Stand*, produced 1977, a 'comedy-thriller' which unsettles generic expectations by bringing a farcical pick-up scenario to a violent conclusion. *Escape Entertainment*, produced 1981, parodies the Canadian film industry. An advocate of Canadian national culture, CB is a founding member of the union Playwrights Canada. See Patricia Keeney Smith in *Canadian Forum*, 63, 1983.

Bolton, Sara (Knowles), 1841–1916, poet, novelist, biographer and reformer, b. Farmington, Conn., da. of Elizabeth (Miller) and John Segar K., of an old New England family. Growing up on a farm, she began writing early, publishing verses at 15. After her father's death in 1852 she moved with her mother to Hartford, where she met lifelong influences H. B. STOWE and Lydia SIGOURNEY. She graduated in 1860 from Hartford Female Seminary, founded by Catharine BEECHER, and taught school briefly in Natchez, Mississippi, and Meriden, Conn. In 1864 she pub. her first book, *Orlean Lamar and Other Poems*, and in 1865 her novel *Wellesley*, based on the insurrection under the Hungarian patriot Kossuth, was serialized in the *Literary Recorder*. In 1866 she m. Charles Edward B., active in the TEMPERANCE movement, for which she wrote *The Present Problem*, 1874, and assisted Frances E. WILLARD in the Women's Christian Temperance Union. During 1878–81 she worked on the editorial staff of the Boston *Congregationalist*. She travelled extensively, studying factory conditions and, in England, higher education for women. SKB pub. two other books of poetry, *From Heart and Nature* (with her son, Charles), 1887, and *The Inevitable*, 1895, as well as a book of short stories, *Stories of Life*, 1886. Her educational biographies include *Girls Who Became Famous*, 1886, *Some*

Successful Women, 1888, and *Famous Leaders Among Women*, 1895, as well as men's biographies. In later life she was active in the cause of animal welfare. *Sarah K. Bolton, Pages from an Intimate Autobiography*, ed. by Charles K. Bolton, was pub. in 1923.

Bolton, Sarah Tittle (Barrett), 1814–93, poet, was born in Newport, Ky., the da. of Esther (Pendleton) and Jonathan Barrett, farmer. She spent her early years in the wilderness near Vernon, Ind. In 1823, the family moved to Madison, Ind., where she attended the local schools. Her first poems were pub. in 1828 in the Madison *Banner*. In 1831 she m. Nathaniel B. of Indianapolis, later the first editor of the *Indiana Democrat*. They had two children. From 1836 to 1845 they were reduced to keeping a public tavern in their home near Indianapolis. STB became involved in the Woman's Rights movement and aided Robert Dale Owen 1850–1 in securing personal property rights for married women in Indiana. In 1851 her most famous poem 'Paddle Your Own Canoe' appeared – a poem which not only urged self-reliance but also spoke to the anti-slavery and women's rights causes: 'And to break the chains that bind / The many to the few – / To enfranchise slavish minds – / Paddle your own canoe.' For three years, until shortly before her husband's death in 1858, they lived in Europe – a source of inspiration for her poems as well as for a series of letters in the *Cincinnati Commercial*. In 1863 she m. Judge Addison Reese of Canton, Missouri, where she lived for two years until the marriage failed. She returned to Indianapolis and collected her verse as *Poems*, 1865. *The Life and Poems of STB*, 1880, contains biographical material. *Songs of a Lifetime*, 1892, ed. John Clark Ridpath, contains an introduction by Lew Wallace and a poem by James Whitcomb Riley, as well as a biography. Her final home, 'Beech-Bank,' five miles south-east of Indianapolis, has become the Sarah T. Bolton Memorial Park. In 1941 a plaque honouring her was placed in the Indiana state capitol building, Indianapolis. There is no biography or scholarly study of her work.

Bond, Elisabeth, playwright. B. in 1945 in Ceylon, of an English northern mother (from Lancaster) and Londoner father, she was educ. in Bristol. Many of her plays, from her first, *The Great War Show* and *Chalking the Flags*, both 1978, show northern awareness. Many have historical settings, like *Six Feet Apart* and *The Messiah of Ismir*, both 1979. *Love and Dissent* (Women's Theatre Group, 1983) moves between past and present, linking the ideas of Russian feminist Alexandra Kollontai and a woman teacher in present-day England. EB has lived since the early 1970s in an Asian community in Lancaster. Asian friends, visits to India, and her family's connection with the British Raj have greatly influenced her, most notably in *Minor Complications* (Royal Court Theatre, 1984) and her screenplay for *The Assam Garden*, directed by Mary McMurray, 1985, both portraying friendships between British and Indian women. Her community play *Sideways Down*, 1984 (given at the Riverside Studios, London, with a cast of 150), deals with the interaction of a foreign community with its host area. EB has written for radio (*Lily and Colin*, 1985) and TV (*The Partition Wallahs*, 1980).

Bonhote, Elizabeth (Mapes), 1744–1818, novelist and poet, da. of James M., baker, of Bungay, Suffolk. She grew up near the castle ruins, and m. solicitor Daniel B. between 1770 and 1774. A royalist, 'perfectly satisfied with our laws and constitution', she met with 'liberality and candour' in reviews. The hero of her anonymous *Rambles of Mr. Frankly*, 1772ff., learns contentment from sentimentally observing others (in the later series he sees high life before opting for rural retirement). Similar moralizing fills *The Fashionable Friend* (1773, epistolary), *Hortensia*, 1777, and *Olivia, or The Deserted Bride*, 1787. *The*

Parental Monitor, essays written in 1788 for her children, under fear of death, first bore her name: it says women should stay at home, but advises one censured for 'scribbling' to ignore this common trial and persevere. She became a MINERVA best-seller with three more novels. *Bungay Castle*, 1796, dedicated to the Duke of Norfolk, is an essentially eighteenth-century picture of the middle ages set at EB's own home: she had bought the ruins and converted them for modern use. She sold them to the duke about 1800 and moved to Bury. In 1810 she wrote a poem on the demise of Bungay's 1692 Corn Cross (in Ethel Mann, *Old Bungay*, 1934), and published anonymously, at Edinburgh, the ambitious *Feeling*, with other poems.

Bonner, Geraldine, 1870–1930, novelist, playwright and journalist, b. Staten Island, NY, da. of Mary Georgina (Sewell) and John B., and educ. by her father. GB lived for two years in mining camps in Colorado and then in San Francisco where she began her writing career, first as drama critic then as foreign correspondent for the *San Francisco Argonaut*, 1887–91. Her early novels are set in California in the years of the post-mining boom. *Hard Pan. A Story of Bonanza Fortunes*, 1900, contrasts the lives of two young women: Viola, who successfully markets her home preserves to supplement family funds, and Letitia, who prefers marriage as a solution to women's economic needs. *The Emigrant Trail*, 1910, details the experiences of a frontier woman, Susan Gillespie, who travels west with her physician father. Producing short stories for *Harper's*, *Collier's Weekly* and *Lippincott's* (as 'Hard Pan'), GB also wrote plays: *Sham* (with Elmer B. Harris, 1908) and *Sauce for the Goose* (with Hutcheson Boyd, 1909). Her later novels feature women in roles of exploration and discovery, as in *The Book of Evelyn*, 1913, whose heroine rebels against the 'superiority of countless generations of men who have ordered women's lives'. GB also wrote mysteries featuring women as 'discoverers': *The Black Eagle Mystery*, 1916, *Miss Maitland, Private Secretary*, 1919, and *The Leading Lady*, 1926.

'Bonner, Sherwood' (Katherine or Catherine, Sherwood Bonner McDowell), 1849–83, novelist and short-story writer, b. Mississippi, da. of Mary (Wilson) and Charles Bonner, doctor. She was educ. at the Holly Springs Female Institute, Miss., and at Hamner Hall, a private girls' school in Montgomery, Ala. In 1864 the Boston *Ploughman* pub. her story 'Laura Capello: a Leaf from a Traveller's Notebook', a melodramatic mystery with an illegitimate heroine. In 1871 she m. Edward McDowell, whom she left in 1873 to go to Boston, where she worked for Longfellow, who helped her publish numerous short stories, poems and articles in New England journals. Her novel *Like Unto Like*, 1878, presenting an analysis of the South during Reconstruction, angered Southern critics, who found her objectivity unsympathetic, but was admired in the North. (*The Story of Margaret Kent*, 1886, usually attributed to Ellen KIRK, may also have been written by SB; it is generally acknowledged to draw on her life, and Kirk's sister-in-law, Sophia Kirk, mentions a novel which has not yet been found). SB also wrote dialect stories which include exploration of negro life. 'The Volcanic Interlude', 1880, tells of three young Louisianans attending an exclusive girls' school, who discover that they are all daughters of their father's mistresses, including his black slave. The blunt language and the characters' attitudes caused many *Lippincott's* readers to cancel their subscriptions. SB's fiction became increasingly realistic, prefiguring the work of later writers such as Kate CHOPIN. There is a bibliography by Jean N. Bigline, *ALR*, 5, 1, and a life by Hubert H. McAlexander, 1981.

Booth, Mary Louise, 1831–89, translator and editor, b. Millville (Yaphank), Long Island, NY. Da. of Nancy (Mansell) and

William Chatfield B., she was educ. at public schools in Yaphank and Williamsburgh (now part of Brooklyn), where her father was principal of the first public school. After teaching for a brief period she moved to Manhattan, where she worked as a seamstress and wrote for journals including the *New York Times*. A friend of Susan B. ANTHONY, she was one of the secretaries at the Women's Rights Conventions in Saratoga, NY, 1855, and NYC, 1860. Her first book, *Marble-Workers' Manual*, 1856, was a translation from the French and was followed by nearly 40 further translations, including works such as de Gasparin's *Uprising of a Great People, The United States in 1861*, which was sympathetic to the Northern cause. She also wrote a *History of the City of New York*, 1859. In 1867 she became editor of *Harper's Bazaar*, a post she held until her death. During her lifetime her biography appeared in H. P. SPOFFORD's *Our Famous Women*, 1884, and S. K. BOLTON's *Some Successful Women*, 1888.

Boothby, Frances, 'Arcasia', dramatist staged before Aphra BEHN. *Marcelia, or The Treacherous Friend*, tragicomedy in blank verse, given by the King's Company in summer 1669 and pub. with her name, 1670, is probably the play which made Elizabeth (Thimelby) Cottington 'tremble for the poor wooman exposed among the critticks'. Her dedication to her kinswoman Lady Yate foresees censure 'upon this uncommon action in my Sex'; the prologue jokes about female authorship. *Marcelia* presents courtship from a woman's perspective: female solidarity looks a lot more attractive than the marriages finally contracted between both the king and his cast-off mistress, and the heroine and her untrusting, vengeful lover. To her cousin Anne (Aston) Somerset, FB says that a false charge of having 'prophan'd gainst heaven' damned the play: unfairly, since 'sure a woman's pen / Is not (like comets), ominous to men' – or to women (*Tixall Poetry*, 1813).

Borden, Mary, later Lady Spears, 'Bridget Maclagan', 1886–1968, novelist and journalist, b. in Chicago, Ill., da. of Mary (Whiting) and businessman William B. She was educ. at Vassar (BA). An early marriage to George Douglas Turner gave her three daughters and ended in divorce. During WWI, she equipped and ran, at her own expense, an award-winning field hospital for the French army. (She wrote of another such venture, in WWII, in *Journey Down a Blind Alley* [1946].) In 1918 she m. the distinguished English soldier Edward Spears, later baronet, MP and diplomat; they had one son. Her numerous works (many differently titled in the USA, first two pub. pseudonymously) are often thought merely intelligent fiction about the wealthy, but they also treat male-female communication. *Flamingo*, 1927, and *Passport for a Girl*, 1939, vividly present intersecting personal and socio-political stories, as do *For the Record*, 1950, an account of the psychology of a secret agent, and *Martin Merriedew*, 1952, about a pacifist tried for treason and the reactions of the female narrator who tells his tale. *The Forbidden Zone*, 1929, essays, stories and poems about her war experience, mixes the mundane with the powerfully lyrical, and *Sarah Gay*, 1931, a novel, treats the love-affair of a nurse for whom the war 'meant freedom, exhilarating activity and romance' as opposed to marriage. MB was awarded the Croix de Guerre and made a member of the Legion of Honour for her hospital work at the front. *Mary of Nazareth*, 1933, and *The King of the Jews*, 1935, are humanizing depictions of the Christian legend. MB's *The Technique of Marriage*, 1933 (social rather than sexual advice), was thought shockingly radical. See Nicola Beauman, *A Very Great Profession*, 1983.

Borson, 'Roo', Ruth Elizabeth, poet, b. 1952 in Berkeley, Calif., da. of physicians Josephine (Esterly) and H. J. B. She became an artist at four and made 'little lyrics' as soon as she could write, during the time 'when there was just one word for each object'. She 'grew up in my mother's garden', later recalling 'My father asleep inside a book, my mother among those loud tropicals which blossom.' At high-school she attended anti-Vietnam-war rallies. She was taught by Louise GLUCK at Goddard College, Vermont (BA 1973), and – very briefly – creative writing by Pat LOWTHER at the Univ. of British Columbia (MFA 1977). She was a librarian in Vancouver, 1974–5, and a lab technician in Toronto, 1977–9; she says her 'sensibility has been shaped by Canadian poetry', in which she has made her mark. After *Landfall*, 1977, she published in 1980 *In the Smoky Light of the Fields* and *Rain*, a sequence of linked poems making 'a vision of mortality', of things flowing away. RB's poems reflect landscapes and townscapes ('I am really excited by physical scenery') and, increasingly, 'interpersonal issues'. She creates atmospheric pictures from precise observation and often daring metaphor: 'Frost chains the pumpkins, / like planets run aground, or / buoys the dead hang onto, / their eyes lit in the loam' (*A Sad Device*, 1981). *The Whole Night, Coming Home*, 1984, moves from free verse to prose poems, 'often character sketches', about growing up in California. In *The Transparence of November / Snow*, 1985, jointly written, RB's work is indistinguishable from that of Kim Maltman (her male 'roommate'). At a pond when cows leave they note 'the stars reappearing / where no one can touch them.' Interview in Bruce Meyer and Brian O'Riordan, eds., *In Their Words*, 1984; article by Robert Billings in *CFM*, 56, 1986.

Bosanquet, Theodora, 1880–1961, poet, critic, biographer, editor, diarist, da. of Gertrude Mary (Fox) and Frederick B. She was b. at Sandown, Isle of Wight, where she grew up, and educ. at Cheltenham Ladies' College and the Univ. of London (BSc). From 1907 until his death, she was Henry James's secretary, an experience which informed her *Henry James at Work*, 1924. In 1916, she published *Spectators*, a novel, jointly with Clara Smith. She worked with the Department of War Trade Intelligence, later with the Ministry of Food. From 1920 to 1935, she was Executive Secretary of the International Federation of University Women. After WWI she met Lady RHONDDA, founder of *Time and Tide*. They became friends and subsequently lived together. TB was literary editor of the journal, 1935–43. Always interested in the spiritual, also in extra-sensory perception and paranormal phenomena, she was a member of the Society for Psychical Research, whose journal she edited. She printed Evelyn UNDERHILL in *Time and Tide*. In Harriet MARTINEAU, whose life she wrote, 1927, she found a congenial subject. She also wrote a study of Valéry, 1933. Her unpublished diaries are at the Houghton Library, Harvard.

Boscawen, Frances (Glanville), 1719–1805, letter writer and BLUESTOCKING, only child of Frances G. and William (Evelyn), who took his wife's name with her fortune. In 1742 she m. Edward B. (d. 1761), admiral and MP, had five children and remained gallant and cheerful through his long absences, and some infidelity, and her own long widowhood. Her letters (dating in print from 1737) to him, friends and relations sparkle with inventiveness, affection, chat, all in lively style and varied rhythms, reminding Hannah MORE and others of Marie de SÉVIGNÉ. Owned by her descendants, many unpub.; some among editions of her friends, some ed. by Cecil Aspinall-Oglander, 1940, 1942.

Boston, Lucy Maria (Wood), 1892–1990, children's writer, b. Southport, Lancs., fifth of six children in a wealthy but strict Wesleyan family. She spent most of her childhood with siblings and nurse in the third-floor nursery, playing at 'Christian soldiers' and reading the New Testament 'illustrated in colour, very nightgowny',

Bunyan and Foxe. Neither parent was close or warm. Educ. at Downs School, Seaford, Sussex, and Somerville, Oxford, she did not graduate but served as a nurse in France in WWI. She m. her cousin Harold Boston, an English officer, 1917; they had one son, Peter, who became the illustrator of her books. The marriage was dissolved in 1935. She began her best-known work, the six stories about Green Knowe, in her sixties; they were all inspired by her twelfth-century manor house at Hemingford Grey in Huntingdonshire, 'that sombre house standing in a perfect position' which she bought although it was unfit 'for rational habitation' because of 'the atmosphere that took [her] by the throat and filled [her] with a welcoming and headlong excitement' (*Memory in a House*, 1976). She did not set out to be a CHILDREN's writer but, because she insisted on including Peter's illustrations, her publisher, Faber, put *The Children of Green Knowe*, 1954, in its juvenile list. Only later did LB realize 'what a step down this was'. The stories are about the conjunction of past and present, with the house ('Green Noah') along with its sage occupant, Granny Oldknow, serving as a paradigm of endurance and incorporating 'all of human experience ... under its arklike roof'. Within the pastoral tradition, the series deals with a timelessness that transcends the passing of centuries. The fourth of these books, *A Stranger at Green Knowe*, 1961, won the Library Association's Carnegie Medal. LB's two adult books, *Yew Hall*, 1954, and *Persephone* (*Strongholds* in the USA), 1969, are mainly potboilers; in both the house is prominent as refuge and repository of ancestral history. In her 85th year, LB wrote *Perverse and Foolish; A Memoir of Childhood and Youth*, 1979, from which she emerges as a cosseted sister, a headstrong adolescent who refused to be formally received into the Wesleyan community and a surprisingly naive young wife. See Lynne Rosenthal (quoted above) and Jon Stott in *Children's Literature* 8, 1980, and 11, 1983.

Botsford, Margaret, poet, novelist, journalist. She called herself 'a lady of Philadelphia', where in 1816 she published *Adelaide* and wrote 'one of my first National pieces'; but in 1820 she pub. *Viola, Heiress of St Valverde*, with other poems, on a visit to Louisville, Kentucky; by 1829 (when a second ed. pub. at Philadelphia said she had lived long in the West) she had dated poems from many different towns in Pennsylvania, Kentucky, Virginia, Ohio and Missouri. *Viola* is a romantic verse tale set in Italy. *Adelaide*, an epistolary novel, called 'insufferably vulgar' by *Port-Folio*, has its action divided between England and Barbados, with tales interwoven; there is a pathetic, submissive heroine. Both favour stylistic and typographical overemphasis. MB's poems and prefaces reflect national pride; *The Reign of Reform, or Yankee Doodle Court*, Baltimore, 1830, a dialogue between two revolutionary patriots, attacks Andrew Jackson and reform, supports Henry Clay, and relates how she was snubbed and refused presidential patronage.

Botta, Anne Charlotte (Lynch), 1815–91, poet, literary historian, salon hostess, sculptor, b. in Bennington, Vt, da. of Charlotte (Gray) and Patrick L. (student participant in the 1798 Irish Rebellion; imprisoned; sailed for America at 18; d. at sea 1819). AB was sent by her mother to good schools, then from 16 supported herself at Albany Female Academy by writing and copying work. She won poetry prizes, graduated in 1834 and continued as a teacher before becoming a governess at Shelter Is., NY, where she wrote *The Diary of a Recluse* (first pub. in *The Gift*, 1843). Joining her mother in Providence, she took pupils and ed. a local writers' anthology, *The Rhode Island Book*, 1841. By 1843 her successful evening receptions were established. In Philadelphia she met Fanny KEMBLE and pub. an essay on her poems in *The Democratic Review*. In NYC by 1846, in 1849 she moved to Ninth Street, her famous salon visited by celebrities like Grace GREENWOOD, Margaret FULLER, Elizabeth OAKES SMITH, Emma EMBURY, Maria BROOKS, Frances OSGOOD and E. A. Poe. Kate SANBORN wrote about her salon; Helen J. HUNT wrote a poem to it. Believing in women's legal rights (though not their suffrage), AB fought fiercely and successfully for her mother's rights as daughter of a soldier, Lieut.–Col. G., who served under Washington. In 1848 she pub. *Poems*, with public pieces in exclamatory style but also some fine unassuming personal poems. In 1853 she visited Europe; in 1855 she m. philosophy professor Vincenzio B. (who pub. *Memoirs* of her in 1894). In 1860 she issued her ambitious *Hand-Book of Universal Literature*, from Hebrew classics to modern American, often reprinted as a teaching textbook. The posthumous *Memoirs* include selections from her correspondence and from her early diary.

Bottome, Phyllis, later Forbes-Dennis, 1884–1963, novelist, lecturer, b. Rochester, Kent, da. of Mary (Leatham) and the Rev. William MacDonald B., an American. She spent her childhood in the USA, England and Europe, especially Switzerland and Italy, where she went for treatment of tuberculosis. She met her future husband, Ernan F.-D., also afflicted with chest illnesses, in St Moritz, but did not marry him until several years later (1917), when he was an officer fighting in France. He was seriously wounded but cured by experimental drugs. Her writing, encouraged by her father ('the great thing was, my father now declared that I was going to be a writer') began early: *Life the Interpreter* was published when she was 18. After her father died, 1913, she looked after her mother for a time in London, where, at a party given by May SINCLAIR, she met Ezra Pound, who attempted to persuade her to live 'on and for my work', a course she declined: 'I should have lost the larger life I was to have in Europe; and the deepest of my human relationships.' She wrote what she thought one of her best stories, 'The Liqueur Glass', under his influence and also '*The Captive*, the first of my novels which really became mine'. During WWI, she worked for the Ministry of Information under John Buchan. Her novel 'Secretly Armed', published, like her other works, in *The Century Magazine*, became, as *The Dark Tower*, 1916, 'the book of the hour' in the USA. With its earnings, she employed her dearest friend Lislie Brock, with whom she had collaborated on *Crooked Answers*, 1911, as literary helper and advisor. In 1920, her husband took a position in passport control in Vienna, where she met Dorothy Thompson and Edna St Vincent MILLAY, and wrote the novel *Old Wine*, 1925, 'a personal record of what Vienna meant to the observer in 1920 to 1923.' There, with Valerie and Alfred Adler, she established welfare kitchens which fed 600 daily. In Munich from 1931–3, she 'was actually present when Hitler came to power, and could write of the Nazis as I saw them': she did, in *The Mortal Storm*, 1937, her extremely popular anti-war novel. *Private Worlds*, 1934, issued partly from her interest in Adler's psychology and partly from her visit to a State mental hospital. Adler appealed partly because he opposed male dominance. Later in her life, PB lectured in the USA (on 'Modern Literature' and 'The Seven Countries in Which I Have Lived'). Her autobiographies, *Search for a Soul*, 1947, *The Challenge*, 1952, and *The Goal*, 1962, are detailed descriptions of the important stages in her life. Her life of Adler, 1939, and *From the Life*, 1944, biographical sketches of Adler, Beerbohm, Sara Delano Roosevelt, Pound and others, supplement the story of her life. She was a close friend of Gertrude ATHERTON and wrote a memorial pamphlet on Stella BENSON, 1934.

Boucherett, Emilia **Jessie**, 1825–1905, feminist, editor, essayist, b. Willingham, Lincs., da. of Louisa (Pigou) and Ayscoghe

B., landowner. Educ. at the Miss Byerleys' ladies' school, Avonbank, Stratford-upon-Avon, she also read widely, including Harriet MARTINEAU's 'Industrial Position of Women in England' (*Edinburgh Review*, April 1859) and the *English Woman's Journal*, which prompted her interest in feminism. In 1859 she moved to London and became involved with the women who were active in the *Journal*, supported by a private income. With Barbara BODICHON and Adelaide PROCTER, she launched the Society for Promotion of Employment for Women in 1859 and financed a school where 20 women at a time were taught the rudiments of clerical work. She launched the *Englishwoman's Review*, 1866–1910, with which the *EWJ* was amalgamated, and was its first editor, 1866–70. She contributed essays concerning woman's right to paid employment to other periodicals and volumes on women's issues. She advocated a variety of careers for educated women: poultry and pig farming, telegraphy, wood engraving, photograph tinting, house decorating and nursing. For women too old for technical training, she advised a cookery course and domestic service. An active suffragist, she helped to organize the 1866 petition to Parliament, with the support of Harriet MARTINEAU, Frances COBBE and Mary SOMERVILLE, and campaigned for the Married Women's Property Act. Notable among her essays are 'The Condition of Women in France' (*Contemporary Review*, May 1867) and 'Provision for Superfluous Women' in Josephine BUTLER's *Essays*, 1868. Nonetheless, JB was politically conservative, and in 1899, she and Helen BLACKBURN founded the Freedom of Labour Defence League, which opposed protective legislation for women workers.

Boulbie or Boulby, **Judith**, d. 1706, Quaker polemicist who probably lived at Skipworth, Yorks. Her *A Testimony for the Truth*, 1665, and *To all Justices of the Peace*, 1668, short pamphlets crying out against persecution of QUAKERS, were followed (after distraint of her goods, 1671) by *A Few Words to the Rulers of this Nation*, broadside, 1673. After 1672 she came into conflict with the Quaker hierarchy, who repeatedly refused her leave to publish. She signed conservative pamphlets of the York Women's Meeting between 1686 and 1688, when she was jailed for non-payment of tithes.

Boulger, Dorothea (Dora) Henrietta (Havers), 'Theo Gift', 1847–1923, novelist, b. Norfolk, second da. of Ellen (Ruding) and Thomas H. Educ. at home, she spent much of her youth in Uruguay and the Falkland Islands, where her father was Colonial Manager, returning to England on his death in 1870. The following year she began publishing stories in British and US periodicals, and worked for a number of years at *All the Year Round* and *Cassell's*. She m. botanist George Simonds B. in 1879. *True to her Trust*, 1874, was her first novel, followed by her best-known: *Pretty Miss Bellew*, 1875, a tale of antagonistic love which provides an interesting portrait of a selfish, spendthrift son. Other novels include the semi-autobiographical *Lil Lorimer*, 1855. DB co-authored children's stories with her friend Edith NESBIT. Her year of death is incorrectly listed in most sources as 1889.

Bourke-White, Margaret, 1906?–71, photographer, social commentator and autobiographer, b. in NYC, da. of Minnie Elizabeth (Bourke), a teacher, and Joseph White, from whom came her 'love for industrial form and pattern'. As a child she wanted to be a scientist, to travel, to do 'all the things that women never do'. She studied at Columbia and the Univ. of Michigan, tried photography while at Cornell (at first simply to earn money after the break-up of her first marriage) and took up architectural photography. Her photos of Ohio steel mills were privately printed as *The Story of Steel*, and made her the first staff photographer on *Fortune* magazine, 1929–35. After a trip there she published *Eyes on Russia*, 1931, and with her second husband, Erskine Caldwell (m. 1939), *North of the Danube*, 1933, *Say, is this the U.S.A.*, 1941, and *You Have Seen Their Faces*, 1937, a study of the rural South in the Depression. Her long association with *Life* magazine began in 1936. The first woman war photographer, she covered WWII (on which she wrote three books), then (after a report on India, *Halfway to Freedom*, 1949) the Korean War for the UN. Persecuted by McCarthy anti-Communism in 1951 (see Robert E. Snyder in *Journal of American Studies*, 19, 1985), she later received various awards. Her autobiography, *Portrait of Myself*, 1963, describes her career (the advantages and hazards of being 'a woman in a man's world') and her fight against crippling Parkinson's Disease. Several of her books have been recently repr.; life by Jonathan Silverman, 1983. See also Carol Schloss in *Virginia Quarterly Rev.*, 56, 1980.

Bovasso, Julie, actress, director and playwright, b. 1930 in Brooklyn, NYC, da. of Angela Ursula (Padovini) and Bernard Michael B., a truck driver. She was on stage at 13 with the Davenport Free Theatre, and attended the City College of NY, 1948–51. Her two marriages (to artist George Ortman, 1951, and to actor Leonard Wayland, 1959) both ended in divorce. In 1953 she founded the Tempo Playhouse (hailed as NY's best experimental theatre at the first Obie ceremony, 1956), which introduced Genet, Ionesco, and de Ghelderode to the USA. After years of versatile acting JB wrote *The Moon Dreamers*, staged in NYC, 1967, first of a steady stream of plays; in it, disguised characters proliferate extravagantly around a central love triangle. She received a triple Obie for writing, directing and acting in her *Gloria and Esperanza*, a mock epic about an artist, reviewed as 'eccentric ... far out' (staged 1968, pub. in Albert Poland and Bruce Mailman, eds., *The Off Off Broadway Book*, 1972). In *Schubert's Last Serenade*, 1971 (pub. in Rochelle OWENS, ed., *Spontaneous Combustion*, 1972) a restaurant maître d'hôtel mediates to the audience a love-affair between a college girl and a hard-hat: when the script requires him to crack her across the jaw, all the actors rebel, causing an 'unscripted' happy ending. In 1972, with Maria Irene FORNÉS, Megan TERRY, Owens, Adrienne KENNEDY, and Rosalyn DREXLER, JP founded the Women's Theatre Council to support women's plays and combat the reductionism of 'masculine-oriented theatre'. That year saw the premiere at Providence, RI, of *Down by the River Where Waterlilies are Disfigured Every Day*, a zany tale of royalty and revolution. With La MaMa, NY, in 1975 she directed her own *The Nothing Kid*, set in a rowdy bar-room where bets are laid on a child beauty contest. JB has twice, in 1983 and 1985, found planned productions of her *Angelo's Wedding* (about an air-force veteran) unsatisfactory and called them off. She teaches drama at Sarah Lawrence College and the New School for Social Research.

Bowdler, Henrietta Maria, 'Harriet', 1753–1830, woman of letters, da. of Elizabeth Stuart (Cotton), *c.* 1718–97, who pub. a theological work (well reviewed as by a man, 1785; expanded with her name, 1800), and of Thomas B. Four of the family (educ. by their mother) wrote. HMB probably ed. the posthumous *Poems and Essays* (thoughtful, pleasant, predictable) of her invalid sister Jane, 1743–84, whose health was destroyed by smallpox and measles. Pub. in 1786 for the benefit of the hospital at Bath, where they lived, this ran to 16 eds. by 1830 there alone. Her own anonymous *Sermons on the Doctrines and Duties of Christianity*, 1801, were an equal success (nearly 50 editions); the Bishop of London contacted the publishers to offer a parish to the author, whoever he might be. She expurgated Shakespeare (four vols., Bath, 1807) *before* her brother Thomas's famous ten vols. (1818), and ed. her friend Elizabeth SMITH's works with a memoir, 1810. *Creation*, anon., 1818, claims to have been written without recalling Milton on this topic (with other poems and essays, one reprinted from the *Christian Observer*). Her novel *Pen Tamar, or The History of an Old Maid*, unpub. till 1831, gives a mixed message: ostensibly defending both virtue and single women, it excuses the hero's prejudice against old maids with one hateful example and harshly penalizes him and the heroine for their filial obedience. Friend of the BLUESTOCKINGS, HMB was censorious about Hester PIOZZI's marriage.

Bowen, Catherine (Drinker), 1897–1973, biographer and novelist. B. in Haverford, Pa., da. of Aimee Ernesta (Beaux) and Henry Sturgis D., president of Lehigh Univ., she was educ. at St Timothy's, a boarding school in Catonsville, Md, the Peabody Conservatory of Music, Baltimore (1915–17), and the Institute of Musical Arts (later the Julliard School) in NYC. Twice m. – to Ezra B., 1919, and to Dr Thomas McKean Downs, 1939 – she had two children but approved the remark she found in her ancestor Elizabeth DRINKER's diary, that 'woman's best years came after she left off bearing and rearing'. She taught music after marrying but felt most intimately connected to the musicians about whom she wrote, and 'Writing saved me. (Talk about rewards!)' She sold her first piece to a magazine, 1920, and wrote 'fairly steadily' thereafter, though she kept the fact a secret 'until I had two Books-of-the-Month' (1951), after which she signed her voter's registration *writer* instead of *housewife*. Her only novel, *Rufus Starbuck's Wife*, 1932, represents the difficulties besetting the artistic woman: its protagonist, an aspiring violinist attempting to achieve some independence from her dominant husband, turns briefly to feminism as escape but recognizes the dangerous subversiveness of 'the man-woman topic, the feminist topic', and turns 'from the tortuous trail of melodrama ... to the straightest, plainest path' of reconciliation. Chiefly a biographer, CDB evolved her method, which shapes its form to its subject, while working on *Beloved Friend*, 1937, about Tchaikovsky and his patron, Nadejda von Meck. (See her *Biography: the Craft and the Calling*, 1969, also other works on biography.) Her musical interest provided other subjects – for *Friends and Fiddlers* (with B. von Meck), 1935, and *Free Artist*, 1939 (about Anton and Nicholas Rubinstein) – but, prevented by WWII from doing European research for a book on Mendelssohn, she refocused her interest on US political figures, such as Oliver Wendell Holmes, John Adams and Benjamin Franklin. She reflects on writing, and on women writing, in 'Discipline and Reward: A Writer's Life', *Atlantic Monthly*, June, 1957, which sounds the note of Virginia WOOLF's *Room of One's Own*, with its emphasis on overcoming socially-obligatory female fear ('something to wrestle with': 'Women writers are notably tender in this regard, possibly because women are trained, from the cradle, to please').

Bowen, Elizabeth Dorothea Cole, 1899–1973, novelist, short-story writer, autobiographer. Da. of Florence (Colley) and Henry Cole B., barrister and landowner, she wrote of her Dublin childhood in *Seven Winters*, 1943; in *Bowen's Court*, 1942, repr. 1979, she related the history of her family (she was the last) and its County Cork home, built 1776. She was, she said 'a writer for whom places loom large'. She left familiar places as a child when her father was certified insane, and travelled with her mother, whose death in 1912 was 'total bereavement'. Last of her three schools was Downe House, Kent, 1914–17. She nursed wounded soldiers in Dublin, then studied art briefly in London, and married Alan Cameron in 1923 (the year of her first book, *Encounters*, stories). Thereafter she divided her time between England and Bowen's Court, which she inherited in 1930. She spent years at Headington, near Oxford, and worked for the government in

London during the WWII blitz (vividly recreated in *The Heat of the Day*, 1949). EB saw the novelist's aim as 'the non-poetic statement of a poetic truth'; she called the story 'a matter of vision rather than of feeling'. In both she depicts with psychological acuteness and delicate irony the painful and complex impinging of private worlds on one another; she can create a tone of 'atmospheric lyricism' even while mercilessly anatomizing the relations between people who dislike each other. EB's feel for a particular time and place is apparent from her first novel, *The Hotel*, 1927 (the English in Italy), and *The Last September*, 1929 (Irish scenes and weather, an Anglo-Irish great house destroyed in the Troubles of 1920). She writes much of children: in *The Death of the Heart*, 1939, an unhappy schoolgirl orphan ('child of an aberration') confronts a sister-in-law ('already half way through a woman's checked, puzzled life'). In EB's last novels, *The Little Girls*, 1964, and *Eva Trout*, 1968, the dangers and terrors sometimes glimpsed in her stories move into clearer focus. Other writings include a play, *Castle Anna*, 1945 (with John Perry, who also collaborated with her friend Molly KEANE); a book about a Dublin hotel, 1951; one on Rome, 1960; a nativity play whose staging was the first ecumenical event in Derry's Protestant Cathedral, 1970; and criticism, like her succinct and trenchant 'Notes on Writing a Novel' (first pub. 1945; repr. with fragments of a last novel and a longer work on her art in *Pictures and Conversations*, 1975). Widowed in 1952, she sold Bowen's Court in 1959; it was destroyed the next year. See *Collected Stories*, 1980; many recent reprints; studies by Harriet Blodgett, 1975, and Hermione Lee, 1981; lives by Victoria Glendinning, 1977, and Patricia Craig, 1986; bibliog. by J'nan M. Sellery and William O. Harris, 1981.

'Bowen, Marjorie', Gabrielle Margaret Vere Long (Campbell), 1888–1952, also 'Joseph Shearing', 'George R. Preedy' novelist; and 'John Winch' and 'Robert Paye', writer of children's books; also other pseudonyms. B. in Hayling, Hants., to Josephine Elizabeth (Ellis) and Vere C., whose marriage 'pleased no one, least of all themselves', she was brought up in their 'disquieting' doctrines of sin and punishment and in extreme poverty, became 'introspective and reserved', and was taught to read and write by her well-educated mother, who thought her dull and uncooperative. In her French name, she saw a 'sentimental flavour of faded romance passed almost furtively from one generation to another'. Her important literary experience, her reading of Wordsworth's 'Lucy Gray', 'gave her 'pleasure amounting to terror': 'I think I was different that day. Something in me must have changed or expanded.' After her parents separated, she was sent to the Slade School of Art, then to art school in Paris. In London, she began historical research (as a research assistant in the BL). This started her first novel: 'I was very particular as to the technique, as I was entirely self-taught and the grammar and spelling gave me a great deal of trouble'. But the self-teaching included wide reading (*Clarissa Harlowe* was her favourite novel), literary exercises (imitations of Chaucer, Spenser and Browning) and an attempt at Latin. (She was also 'decently proficient' in Italian and French.) She finished her first novel in Paris: rejected by 11 publishers ('not the kind of thing ... that a girl was expected to write'), *The Viper of Milan*, 1906, hugely successful, launched her massively productive, though not always happy, career. She wrote more than 90 books as 'MB' (her great-grandfather's name), mostly historical novels but also historical studies, biographies, plays and short stories. In 1928, 'George R. Preedy' published *General Crack*, the first of 30 works by that name, including *This Shining Woman: Mary* WOLLSTONECRAFT *Godwin*, 1937; in 1932, 'Joseph Shearing' pub. *Forget-me-not* (*Lucile Cléry* in the USA), the first of about 20.

In 1912, MB married Zefferino Emilio Costanza, lived with him and their one (of two) surviving child in Italy, writing to support them until he died, 1916. In 1917, she married Arthur L. Long; they had two children. MB came to see herself as a hack, supporting her mother's bank account, and recognized that she had been 'commercialized, inevitably of course': 'I felt abject, yet I could not retire from writing because we needed the money.' Her autobiography, *The Debate Continues*, written as Margaret Campbell, 1939, quoted above, is a full account of the early development of her literary/commercial career, quite conscious of the role her gender played in that; *Ethics in Modern Art*, 1939, takes up her concern with commercialization ('Providers of popular commodities always observe popular moralities') and reflects on the place of women in modern literature: 'The prose-writers of to-day have revealed, with a fullness unknown to any other civilization, the woman's point of view. [Here] you have a half of humanity made articulate for the first time.' She singles out Virginia WOOLF, Dorothy RICHARDSON, Elizabeth BOWEN, Rosamund LEHMANN and Storm JAMESON: 'already male novelists have been influenced by these feminine revelations'. See Crosland, 1981.

Bowen, Sue (Petigru), 1824–75, novelist and story writer, b. Charleston, S. Carolina, da. of James L. P. She m. Henry King. Her novels and stories are set in the deep South before the Civil War. *Busy Moments of an Idle Woman*, 1854, is a story collection. 'Old Maidism versus Marriage' concerns a group of young single women who vow to meet again after ten years, when the married ones amongst them must tell the truth about conditions in their 'prison-house'. Ten years on, all but one are married and have sad stories of disillusionment to recount to the only one still single; yet she marries anyway, leaving the reader in some doubt as to her future happiness. This theme is also expressed in her novels. *Lily*, 1855, has as heroine a young orphaned heiress who falls in love with a promiscuous man and is poisoned by his jealous mistress, while in *Gerald Grey's Wife*, 1864, the heroine is married for her fortune. SPB has strong views on woman's role in marriage, asserting that 'man is the superior power to whom [woman] must pay homage and deference ... he is her head and her master' (*Gerald Grey's Wife*). Her novels are notable for their depiction of life in the South before the Civil War, describing dress, hairstyles, furnishings, meals and social customs.

Bower, B. M., Bertha (Muzzy), 1871–1940, leading writer of Western novels, many of whose readers assumed she was a man. B. in Cleveland, Minnesota, da. of Eunice A. (Miner) and Washington M., she grew up in the Montana ranges with some home teaching and some schooling. She m. Clayton J. B. in 1890 and had three children. In 1904 she scored a success with her first adventure story, *Chip of the Flying U.*, whose heroine is a doctor and fearsome gunslinger (filmed 1939); the Flying U cowboys reappear in later titles, in a formula of brave, one-dimensional heroes and skilfully-evoked landscapes. Other books too were filmed; others too feature women of action, e.g. *Rim O'the World*, 1919, *Laughing Water*, 1932, and *Points West*, 1928: 'Mrs Harris picked up the hat and twirled it slowly upon a forefinger while she examined the telltale marks. ... "Son, you're a good shot," she said shortly.' BMB uses American Indian culture for plot rather than depth, as in *The Eagle's Wing*, 1924. She was married twice more: in 1906 to a Scot, Bertrand W. Sinclair, and later to a Texan, Robert Ellsworth Cowan. Last of 60 titles was *The Family Failing*, 1941.

Bowers, Bathsheba, *c.* 1673–1718, Quaker autobiographer from Philadelphia, one of 12 children of Elizabeth (Dunster) and Benanual B., who sent her there from

Mass., where Quakers were persecuted. From about six she suffered religious fears and torments; at 14 she craved luxury and loved reading romances. Terrors renewed when at 18 she caught smallpox (her brother died of it). Convalescent, she was 'overcome with a divine Sweetness' and took up pious meditation, but feared Quakerism since it would mean preaching. Torment and joy still alternated; after God spoke to her 'very Friendly ... as a Father or a Husband' she became a teetotaller and vegetarian. Her account of her life, *An Alarm Sounded to Prepare the Inhabitants of the World to Meet the Lord*, NY, 1709, describes her earlier terror of publication and her decreased but not vanquished pride; it mentions other writings, presumably lost. Her niece Ann Bolton wrote that she owned several works by a female visionary. She died a missionary in S. Carolina. See William John Potts in *PMHB*, 3, 1879.

Bowles, Caroline Anne (later Southey), 'C', 1787–1854, poet and essayist, b. Buckland, Hants., da. of Anne (Burrard) and Captain Charles B. Educ. at home, CB took up writing for love, not money, and pub. anon. for over 20 years, some of her work appearing in *Blackwood's* over the signature 'C'. Her poetry, mainly descriptive narrative, draws on her life in the New Forest region and has an easy, natural tone, often quietly humorous. However, it was less valued than her collection of prose tales, *Chapters on Churchyards*, 1829, which consolidated her reputation as a 'pathetic' writer after the earlier success of *Ellen FitzArthur: a metrical tale*, 1820. This had been recommended for publication by Robert Southey, with whom CB corresponded as a friend for 20 years (letters pub. 1881, ed. E. Dowden) before marrying him in 1839, when his health broke down and he lapsed into senility (d. 1843). She forfeited her annuity upon marriage and wrote nothing after it: 'The last three years have done upon me the work of twenty', she wrote to Lydia SIGOURNEY. She had pub. other verse volumes earlier, including *The Widow's Tale*, 1822, *Tales of the Factories*, 1833, and *The Birthday*, 1836. This last describes the feelings, thoughts and occupations of a lonely child and adolescent in a kind of poetic autobiography.

Bowles, Jane (Auer), 1917–73, fiction-writer. B. in NYC, da. of Claire (Stajer) and Sidney A., she learned French early from governesses then went to Mme Tisnée's (a Manhattan French school) and public schools in Woodmere, Long Island, and Stoneleigh. She had some private tutoring in Switzerland, where she was treated for tuberculosis of the knee, 1932–4. On her way home she met and fell in love with the writer Louis-Ferdinand Céline; in 1938 she m. Paul B., composer and writer, who receives more critical attention than she does. She said she 'always wanted to be a religious leader'; she found writing debilitatingly painful but pushed herself to the limits of her various fears, often taking irrational chances. Her only published novel (an unpublished one in French, *Le Phaéton hypocrite*, *c.* 1935, is lost) is *Two Serious Ladies*, 1943 (repr. 1978, with introduction by Francine du Plessix GRAY, and 1984); her most highly-regarded short stories are 'Camp Cataract', 1949, and 'A Stick of Green Candy', 1957. She travelled extensively, including time in Tangier, where she studied Arabic and tried to share the lives of Arab women (see her 'East Side; North Africa' in *Mademoiselle*, 1951). Her play, *In the Summer House*, was staged at Ann Arbor and NYC in 1953. A short puppet play, *A Quarrelling Pair*, about two middle-aged sisters, was pub. in 1966. JB's work, limited in quantity, has been much praised: John Ashbery called her 'a writer's writer's writer'; Millicent Dillon, in a biography of 1981, describes her as 'always trying to explore in fictional form what was mysterious in women'. While JB writes of a bisexual, nihilistic milieu, her pictures of isolation and indecision are widely recognizable. At 40 she suffered a stroke which severely reduced her ability to read and write. From 1967 she was often in hospital, including a psychiatric hospital in Malaga, where she died. *Collected Works*, 1966, with introduction by Truman Capote, were expanded as *My Sister's Hand in Mine*, 1978; fragments appear as *Feminine Wiles*, 1976, stories as *Plain Pleasures*, 1985; selected letters, ed. Dillon, 1985. See also Dillon in *Confrontation*, 1984, and Robert E. Lougy in *CEAC*, 49, 1986–7.

Bowne, Eliza (Southgate), 1783–1809, letter writer. B. at Scarborough, Maine, da. of Mary (King) and Robert S., she was taught by Susanna Rowson, m. Walter B. in 1803 and had two children. Her daughter kept her letters (a virtual diary from 1797 until Jan. 1809, eight months before her death), pub. as *A Girl's Life Eighty Years Ago*, 1887. She sent a male cousin into 'a kind of fury' by stepping 'out of my sphere' in a letter of 23 May 1802 which says that if a man she would be a lawyer: 'remember I desire to be thankful I am not a man . . . I do not feel that great desire of fame I think I should if I was a man.'

Bowra, Harriette, d. 1898, English novelist. Nothing is known of her life; she never married and no near male relatives can be traced. But she was well-off, leaving over £17,000 when she died in Nice, where she requested burial beside her 'dear friend Mary Ann Paynter', eldest da. of Revd S. Paynter. Her first two novels, *Redlands; or Home Temper* and *Una; or the Early Marriage*, both conventionally pious, appeared in 1872. *A Young Wife's Story*, 1877, is a surprisingly trenchant account of the tribulations of a second wife's interactions with her stepchildren.

Box, Muriel (Baker), dramatist, screenwriter, novelist, biographer, autobiographer, film director, publisher, b. in 1905 in New Malden, Surrey, da. of Beatrice (Tyler) and Charles Baker, who lived 'on the edge of poverty'. She was educ. at the local Board School, at Holy Cross Convent, which expelled her for her 'rebellious attitude', and at Regent Street Polytechnic. In childhood she admired G. B. Shaw and the cinema, later Joyce and Woolf, whose *A Room of One's Own* 'made such an impact on me in my twenties that I [was thereafter] possessed with a strong urge to support the cause of equality between the sexes.' In 1935 she m. Sydney Box, with whom she wrote numerous plays and screenplays, including *The Seventh Veil*, 1946 Academy Award winner for best screenplay. Their plays for all-woman casts, collected as *Ladies Only*, 1934, and *Petticoat Plays*, 1935, often satires of conventional sex roles, were widely played by amateur theatre societies. She began directing films in the 1950s: 'The film personally significant to me above all others was *The Truth About Women*', 'a comedy with serious undertones concerning the status of women in various societies from the turn of the century until today.' It was released 'without a press show' and 'denied a West end run.' MB's novel, *The Big Switch*, 1964, a fantasy of post-nuclear-holocaust matriarchy, combines feminist and CND politics. Founding Director of Femina Books, 1966, she published books 'with an original and interesting angle on women', including her own *The Trial of Marie Stopes*, 1967. In 1970, divorced, she m. Gerald Gardiner. She wrote her own life, *Odd Woman Out*, 1974, quoted above, and his, 1983.

Boyd, Elizabeth, 'Louisa', London poet and publisher. Her *Variety*, Nov. 1726, is a rapid, compressed, paradoxical poem full of new-coined words, which praises Eliza Haywood, Susanna Centlivre, Delarivier Manley and Aphra Behn. Her preface calls it ambitious but juvenile; an Ovidian epistle with it is strongly emotional, with a vivid description of birth. Less original is the long, crowded romance, *The Happy-Unfortunate, or The Female Page* (better known by its sub-title), pub. 1732, re-issued

1737, though written earlier (facs. 1972), set in Cyprus 'where Venus keeps her court'; its prose often slips into blank-verse rhythms. Lady HERTFORD was a dedicatee; 134 of the 332 subscribers were women: their help raised EB 'from almost the lowest Condition of Fortune' to open a pamphlet shop and support her aged mother, despite persistent ill-health. She printed and advertised some of her own later work, mostly separate verse pamphlets with her name. These celebrate royal and noble occasions and voice political views (calls for war in the 1730s, patriotic pride in [April 1744]). *The Humorous Miscellany*, 1733, with her initials (wrongly ascribed to Eustace Budgell), mixes compliments and laments for dead babies with the riddles promised in the sub-title. Her unstaged ballad-opera, *Don Sancho, or The Students Whim*, 1739 (with the masque *Minerva's Triumph*), conjures the mentor-ghosts of Shakespeare and Dryden. Her periodical, *The Snail, or The Lady's Lucubrations*, 1745, was short-lived.

Boylan, Grace (Duffie), 1862–1935, poet, novelist and journalist, b. Michigan, Ill., da. of Juliette (Smith) and Captain Phelix D. She was educ. at Kalamazoo, Ill., Harvard Annexe (later Radcliffe College) and NE Conservatory of Music, Boston. She worked for the *Chicago Journal* as a sketch writer and, in 1897, pub. a volume of poems, *The Old House*, later incorporated into *If Tam O'Shanter'd had a Wheel*, 1898. The poems exhibit polyphonic skills and versatility in adopting diverse personae, and strong multi-ethnic interests. Most notable is her epic poem 'The Cuban Amazon', which celebrates the fearless black leader of half-a-thousand women battling against the 'degrading yoke of Spain'. The sketches treat with pathos and compassion incidents in the lives of the unfortunate: convicts, vagrants and the destitute. In *The Kiss of Glory*, 1902, a novel based on the life of Joseph, son of Jacob, GB portrays strong, fearless warrior women. Her most popular work, *Thy Son Liveth: Messages from a Soldier to His Mother*, sold 31,407 copies by the year of her death. Pub. anon. in 1918 but later (1927) 'transcribed by Mrs Louis Napoleon Geldert' (GB), the book has a strong autobiographical flavour. The narrator's son, killed in battle in France, speaks to his mother on 'etheric waves' (telepathy).

Boyle, Kay, poet, writer of fiction and children's books, editor, translator. B. in 1902 in St Paul, Minnesota, da. of well-off parents, Katherine (Evans) and Howard P. B., she was educ. in wide travel, at home and at, among other schools, the Cincinnati Conservatory of Music. Later she studied architecture at the Ohio Mechanics Institute and m. French engineering student, Richard Brault, 1922. They went to Europe, where, even after divorce, she remained based (mainly in Paris) for nearly 30 years. KB was cured of tuberculosis shortly before bearing her first child, 1927. Active in the literary expatriate community, she knew all the 'Lost Generation', briefly worked for *Broom* and (with Ethel MOORHEAD) edited *This Quarter*, and wrote for *Poetry*, *Contact*, and later *Close-up* and *transition*. She now says the story of that 'miserable time' has 'all been very much twisted around': 'the people who accomplished everything [like Gertrude STEIN] did not sit around in cafés.' Her *Short Stories*, 1929, were followed in 1931 by *Landscape for Wyn Henderson* (poetry), *Don Juan* (translation) and *Plagued by the Nightingale* (a novel whose multiple plots centre on the heroine's wish to bear a child despite a threat of inherited disease, which symbolizes the corrupt nature of family tradition). Before WWII KB worked at helping Jews acquire US visas; her marriage to Laurence Vail ended in 'a monumental political split'. Back in the USA she wrote to combat ignorance about conditions in Europe; she returned there in 1946 as foreign correspondent for the *New Yorker* while her third husband, Joseph

Franckenstein (d. 1963; he had come to the US as an anti-Nazi Austrian refugee) served the USA in occupied Germany. McCarthyist accusations lost him his job in 1953, and they returned to teach in the USA. KB has reared six children and two stepchildren and taught at various univs. (including San Francisco State Univ., 1963–80). Her more than 40 books include poetry, novels, short fiction (from novellas to short-short stories), non-fiction, children's books, translations and editions; she supplemented Robert McAlmon's memoir, *Being Geniuses Together: 1920–1930*, 1968. She now 'prefers her poems to her short stories, and her short stories to the novels', on the grounds of the latter's autobiographical element: 'always this searching American woman' – who, however, has great feminist interest in her struggles to maintain identity and integrity in the face of cultural, political, and psychological turmoil in Europe and European marriages. KB wrote of the French Resistance in *Avalanche*, 1944, and in *The Smoking Mountain: Stories of Post War Germany*, 1951, of 'the day by day acts we accept as part of our routine, to indicate how these seemingly harmless acts can lead to official oppression.' *Words That Must Somehow Be Said*, 1985 (selected essays), charts the increasingly urgent convergence in her work of politics and art. She was active in Amnesty International and twice jailed in the 1960s for protest against the Vietnam War, experience which fed her latest novel, *The Underground Woman*, 1975. In recent poetry (*Collected Poems*, 1962: two more vols. have followed) she writes perceptively and defiantly of old age. 'Do not resort to / An alphabet of gnarled pain, but speak of the lark's wing / Unbroken, still fluent as the tongue.' See Roberta Sharp in *Bulletin of Bibliog.*, 35, 1978; life by Sandra Whipple Spanier, 1986 (with letters, MSS, and personal comment by KB); special issue of *TCL*, 34, 1988.

Boyle, Mary Louisa, 1810–90, author, fifth of six children of Caroline Emilia (Poyntz) and Vice-Admiral the Hon. Sir Courtenay B. (Her elder sister was 'The Hon.', not Mary as Dickens thought.) Educ. by governesses then at Miss Poggi's Brighton school, her chief love was the theatre. She published two rather wooden historical novels – *The State Prisoner*, 1837, and *The Forester*, 1839 – as well as poems (priv. printed, 1849) and a dramatic sketch in verse, *The Bridal of Melchior*, 1844. She met Dickens in 1849 and became a friend, contributing to *Household Words* and acting in his private theatricals. *Tangled Wefts*, two stories, appeared in 1865; so did *The Court and Camp of Queen Marian*, printed by Emily FAITHFULL at the Victoria Press. She met Tennyson in 1882 (her niece Audrey m. Hallam T. in 1884) and he became a good friend, sending her the poem 'To Mary Boyle' in 1888 after the death of her close friend Lady Marian Alford. Her reminiscences, which show a lively, likeable woman (but do not mention Tennyson), were pub. posthumously in 1901 by her cousin Sir Courtenay B.

Boyle, Nina, 1865?–1943, novelist, lecturer, journalist, suffragette, who was, according to Cicely HAMILTON, 'at her best' on the platform. After an extended period in S. Africa, where she served on the staff of the *Transvaal Leader* and with emergency hospitals in Johannesburg during the Boer War, she returned to England and became involved in the SUFFRAGE Movement, first as Political Organiser, then as Hon. Secretary of the Women's Freedom League. She lectured widely, engaged in several militant actions and went to prison a number of times. Her pamphlet, *The Traffic in Women*, 1913, published by the Women's Freedom League, argues for the protection of women of all colours in British colonies against sexual slavery, documenting its case with 'Unchallenged Facts and Figures'. *What is Slavery? An Appeal to Women*, [1932], expresses outrage that in none of the reports and recommendations which led to the League of Nations' Slavery Convention, 1925, was there the 'faintest allusion' to 'the Report on the Traffic in Women – the grossest form of slavery – already lying in the pigeon-holes of the Palais des Nations.' During WWI, she worked in the Anglo-Serbian Hospital in Macedonia and began to establish the first voluntary women's police force in Britain. In 1918 she became the first woman in Great Britain to be nominated for a seat in Parliament (though a procedural fault made her ineligible). After the war, she worked for years with the Save the Children Fund, travelling on its behalf to the Soviet Union in 1921. NB's novels, which she said were 'hobbies', do not address her political concerns directly: accomplished work in the adventure genre, they are sometimes witty, usually fast, always light, not – except for *How Could They*, 1932 – markedly autobiographical. But they plot glancing attacks on the circumstances of real life: the first, *Out of the Frying Pan*, 1920, sends its young woman protagonist on an identity quest which must begin by recovery of her lost parents; the second, *What Became of Mr Desmond*, 1922, places a number of female characters in complex relation to a father who suddenly goes missing (and for whom 'New Woman was the last word of reproach'). Cicely HAMILTON wrote a pamphlet for the Nina Boyle Memorial Committee (quoted above), n.d.; see Stella Newsome, *Women's Freedom League, 1907–1957*, 1960.

Boylston, Helen Dore, nurse, diarist, travel writer, novelist and biographer, b. in 1895 in Portsmouth, N.H., da. of Fannie D. (Wright) and physician Joseph B. She considered medical school but thought the training too long, graduating instead from Mass. General Hospital School of Nursing, 1915, then joined a Harvard Univ. medical unit and nursed in France, 1917–18. After a brief return to the USA ('I can't stand it here much longer, in this place where nothing ever happens and every day is like every other day'), she went to Albania and Poland with the Red Cross in 1920. Her letters to Rose Wilder LANE (signed 'Troub', for her nickname, 'Troubles'), first appeared in the *Atlantic Monthly*, 1925, as did excerpts from *Sister: The War Diary of a Nurse*, 1927. The letters reveal an exuberant personality equally moved by 'the horror and the pity' of the wounded soldiers and the 'wild joyous youth of us all'. She nursed and taught at Mass. General Hospital, 1921–3, then, in 1926, with Lane, travelled by car from Paris to Albania. Their letters to Lane's parents are published in *Travels with Zenobia: Paris to Albania by Model T. Ford*, ed. William Holtz, 1983. After a short stay in Albania, HDB returned to NYC and supported herself as a psychiatric nurse while she established her career as a children's writer. To dispel the 'wildly inaccurate pictures' of the nursing and acting professions, she wrote the seven 'Sue Barton' nursing books, 1936–52, and, with the help of her actress friend Eva Le GALLIENNE, the four 'Carol' novels, 1941–6. The Sue Barton books chart a career from student to superintendent of a nursing school, at which she succeeds more from natural aptitude and the force of personality than from any sense of herself as a professional. HDB also wrote a biography of Red Cross founder Clara BARTON, 1955.

Brackenbury, Rosalind Mary Hamilton (Crabtree), novelist, poet and teacher, b. in 1942 in London to Sylvia (Barrington-Ward) and William C. She was educ. at Sherborne Girls' School, Dorset, and Girton College, Cambridge (BA in History, 1963, MA, 1967), m. architect Michael B. in 1965, had two children and divorced in 1985. Her first novel shows the concerns and style of nearly all her work: an intense exploration of female experience, particularly involving love, and a kaleidoscopic presentation of consciousness. The cost of love for women in *A Day to Remember to Forget*, 1971, seems to be self-betrayal or madness, while in *A Virtual Image*, 1971, it becomes self-betrayal joined to sister-betrayal, or death. *Into Egypt*, 1973, deals with personal development, friendship and love against the political background of war in Israel; *A Superstitious Age*, 1977, examines the effects of separation on an unhappily married couple and their eventual reunion mediated by their child. *The Coelacanth*, 1979, depicts marriage as an achievement of willed self-sacrifice by women. *The Woman in the Tower*, 1982, a hauntingly evocative portrait of love from the painful female perspective, skilfully interweaves the lives of an older and a younger woman against the backdrop of social conventions. *Sense and Sensuality*, 1985, a semi-autobiographical account of intellectual and emotional growth as student, writer, wife and mother, and *Crossing the Water*, 1986, are increasingly self-conscious articulations of woman's search for self-identity. *Telling Each Other It Is Possible*, 1987, is RB's first volume of poetry.

Bradburn, Eliza Weaver, miscellaneous writer, da. of Sophia (Cooke), an early promoter of Sunday schools, and Samuel B., well-known Methodist preacher. She worked as a governess and was called the Methodist Maria Edgeworth. Apart from a brief preface to her father's sermons, 1817, and 'Memoirs' of him, 1816 (said to stress his inner conflicts and neglect his humour and oratory), she wrote mostly for children, notably *The Story of Paradise Lost*, 1828 (several English and US reprints), in the popular pedagogical-dialogue form. Eliza (nearly 11) dislikes Eve's exclusion from Raphael's talk with Adam, and concludes firmly, 'Whatever Milton may say about it', that Eve was not originally designed to obey. EWB edited the Methodist journal *Youth's Instructor*. Her contributions to the annual *Early Days* began in 1846 with 'Alphabetical Amusements' like 'The Flattering Fox and the Foolish Fowl. A Fable for forward Females', and include a happy ending for a sad poem by Jane Taylor, 1847.

Braddon, Mary Elizabeth (later Maxwell), 'Ada Buisson', 'Babington White', 1835–1915, novelist, b. London, youngest da. of Fanny (White) and Henry B., solicitor. Her parents separated in 1839, and MEB was educ. first at school, then largely by her Irish mother, who wrote occasionally for *Ainsworth's Magazine*. In 1857, as 'Mary Seyton', she began acting, an invaluable experience for her sensation fiction; she also wrote several plays, mostly unpub. She started writing in her teens, met publisher John Maxwell in 1860 and pub. stories in *The Welcome Guest*, *St James's Magazine*, *Robin Goodfellow* and *The Halfpenny Journal*. Enormous success came with her two 'bigamy' novels: *Lady Audley's Secret*, 1862 (repr. 1985), and *Aurora Floyd*, 1863 (repr. 1984), first serialized in *Temple Bar*. Both are notable for their subtle critique of patriarchal structures. MEB lived with Maxwell, whose wife was in a Dublin asylum, supporting his five children and then five of their own. They m. in 1874. She was mercilessly attacked for the immorality of her fiction (e.g. by Margaret Oliphant) and her private life but continued to produce subversive novels about 'the mysteries at our own doors'. She also wrote very different studies of society, like *The Lady's Mile*, 1866, and edited *Belgravia* from 1866. Upon her mother's death in 1868 she suffered a complete nervous collapse. Among her women friends were Rhoda Broughton, Lucy Clifford and Mary Tuttiet ('Maxwell Gray'). In 1878 she founded *The Mistletoe Bough*, at the same time continuing to experiment with fictional forms – historical, naturalistic, supernatural – producing over 70 novels in all. See the critical biography by Robert L. Wolff, 1979, who also ed. her letters to Edward Bulwer Lytton, *Harvard Library Bulletin* 22, 1 (Jan. 1974). Over 30 of her MSS are in the State Library of Tasmania; other papers are in Wolff's collection.

Bradley, Marion (Zimmer), science-fiction writer, b. in 1930 near Albany, NY, to farmers Evelyn Parkhurst (Conklin) and Leslie Raymond Z. She was enchanted early by the Arthurian legends, on which she began a novel at 14, and read *The Golden Bough* at 15. She attended NY State College for Teachers (now SUNY, Albany), 1946–8, writing prolifically the while (her Darkover idea developed then). She m. Robert Alden B. in 1949 and had a son. Her productive career as novelist and short-story writer (well over 50 titles) began in the early 1950s. With her early works, including romances, gothics and fantasies published under several pseudonyms – 'Lee Chapman', 'Morgan Ives', 'John Dexter', 'Valerie Graves', 'Miriam Gardner' and others – she supported both her family, when her husband was ill, and her own university study. Divorced in 1964, MZB m. Walter B. Breen that year (two children), and received her BA from Hardin-Simmons Univ., going on to graduate work at Berkeley, 1966–7. She is best known for her SCIENCE-FICTION, especially for her ongoing Darkover books, written at a rate of roughly one a year from *The Planet Savers*, 1962, to *Four Moons of Darkover*, 1988 (written by MZB and 'the Friends of Darkover'). The series pits the traditional, almost feudal Darkovans against the bureaucratic, technologically-advanced Terran colonizers. Some feature the Free Amazons or Renunciates, a group of Darkovan women who, renouncing 'the protections for women in the society,' form a community to replace learned sexist behaviour and assumptions with independence, self-sufficiency, and self-defence. *The Shattered Chain*, 1976, dramatizes an initiation (Magda, a Terran, meets Jaelle, a Renunciate, and herself takes the oath); *Thendara House*, 1983, elaborates their story (Magda undertakes the rigorous Free Amazon training, Jaelle lives and works with a Terran man, until his assumptions about the role of women, especially as wives, drive her back). In *The Ruins of Isis*, 1978 (antithetically read as either MZB's most 'feminist' novel or a warning to women to avoid power), a corrupt matriarchate crumbles. *The Mists of Avalon*, 1982, prodigiously popular, and *The Firebrand*, 1987, retell the Arthurian legends and the Trojan War respectively from the point of view of the women involved. See Rosemarie Arbur, bibliog., 1982, and study, 1985; Susan M. Schwartz in T. Staicar, ed., *The Feminine Eye*, 1982; and Sarah Lefanu, *In the Chinks of the World Machine*, 1988.

Bradshaw, Mary Ann Cavendish (Jeffereyes), 'Priscilla Parlante', *c.* 1758–1849, author of two rattling historical novels. Eldest da. of Arabella (FitzGibbon) and James St John J. of Blarney Castle, Co. Cork, she m. George Frederick Nugent, Earl of Westmeath, in 1784 and had several children; divorced in 1796, she at once m. Augustus C. B., MP. *Memoirs of Maria, Countess d'Alva ... Interspers'd with Historic Facts and Comic Incidents ... not altogether inapplicable to the Events of this Distracted Age*, 1808, illustrated by herself, makes its active, adventurous heroine wife of a villainous Spanish spy: it ends on the Armada's defeat, with allusion to the current war. MACB's dedication to 'The Man in the Moon' tells how she bought a bundle of MSS from an Edinburgh rag-dealer (cheated because of 'the helpless and defenceless state of our sex'), and has threaded into her story a letter from Mary Queen of Scots, a sexually suggestive lampoon, etc. *Ferdinand and Ordella, A Russian Story*, 1810, set in the reign of Peter the Great, combines travel-book material with adventure: again a heroine escapes from unhappy marriage. An introductory dissertation, on patrons, notes the superlative contempt of men for female abilities and argues the novel's right not to be a sermon (with detailed, damaging analysis of Hannah MORE's *Coelebs*, written assuming the author to be male).

Bradstreet, Anne (Dudley), 1612–72, first poet of America. B. English, da. of Dorothy

(Yorke) and Thomas D., steward to Lady LINCOLN's son, she was educ. by tutors, with use of the Earl's and her father's libraries. Her father, sister (Mercy Woodbridge) and later her son all wrote verse, as she did from her teens. Surviving smallpox at 16, she m. Simon B. soon afterwards and emigrated in 1630 with husband and parents. After living in Newtown (now Cambridge, Mass.) and Ipswich, she settled in North Andover. She had eight children and slowly developed tuberculosis. Her father and later her widower served as Governors of Mass. In 1650 her sister Mercy's husband, visiting London, pub. a volume of her work, apparently without her knowledge: *The Tenth Muse Lately Sprung Up in America*, 'By a Gentlewoman in Those Parts' (facs. 1965; more poems added in 1678 (Boston) and 1867; see ed. by Jeannine Hensley, 1967, with foreword by Adrienne RICH, repr. 1981). Two long composite works in heroic couplets stand out: the 'Exact Epitome of the Four Monarchies' (a verse chronicle of Assyria, Persia, Greece and Rome), and lively and imaginative 'Quaternions', written by 1642 and dedicated to her father, a four-fold structure of poems in groups of four: on the elements, the humours, the ages of man and seasons of the year, the whole based on a translation by Joshua Sylvester from the French Calvinist Guillaume Du Bartas. These have a humble prologue but ambitious structure and defiant praise of ELIZABETH I ('Let such as say our sex is void of reason, / Know 'tis a slander now but once was treason'). More often read today are the personal prefatory lines, and 'Contemplations' in seven-line stanzas. AB's more private lyrics (reflecting actual events, Puritan piety, marital and parental love) were mostly unpub. in her lifetime. In late years she both revised and wrote new poems and prose (meditations and an account, for her children, of her religious life). Praised by Bathsua MAKIN, she was later undervalued until Conrad Aiken, 1929, and John Berryman, 1956; life by Elizabeth Wade White, 1971 (for facts not views); study by Ann STANFORD, 1974; essays ed. Pattie Cowell and Stanford, 1983.

Bramston, Mary Eliza, 1841–1912, da. of Clarissa (Trant) and the Revd John B., Dean of Winchester 1872–83. Her mother d. 1844; her journals and papers were preserved and read. MB was influenced by the Oxford Movement, like her friends Christabel COLERIDGE and Charlotte YONGE, with whom she later collaborated in at least two light-hearted novels (*The Miz-Maze*, 1883 and *Astray*, 1886), contributing also to Yonge's *Monthly Packet*. She managed her brother's Winchester school house until his marriage, and was remembered by one Wykehamist as providing an education in herself (*The Times*, 10 Feb. 1912). Between 1869 and 1911 she wrote more than 70 tales and novels, many for children or young people, most revealing a sharp power of observation and lively humour. *The Carbridges*, 1874, contains a silly, charming heroine and her splendid spinster sister, determined to retrieve the family business; but *A Woman of Business* (pub. SPCK, 1885) is a much more conventional story of a young girl whose fortitude is rewarded with marriage. In 1899 she published the more complex *Apples of Sodom*, whose unusually gifted and outspoken heroine fascinates both sexes, with mixed results; *In Hiding*, 1889, treats women involved in intricate moral struggles.

Branch, Anna Hempstead, 1875–1937, poet and social worker, b. at New London, Conn., da. of Mary Lydia (Bolles), poet and author of children's stories, and John Locke B. She was educ. first at Froebel and Adelphi Academies in Brooklyn, then at Smith College and the American Academy of Dramatic Arts, NYC, taking a degree in dramaturgy in 1900. Here began her association with Christodora House, a settlement on the Lower East Side, where she helped sponsor poetry readings that led to the foundation of the Poet's Guild. Robert Frost, Carl Sandburg, Sara TEASDALE, and J. P. PEABODY all read there with AB. Her first vol. of poetry, *Heart of the Road*, 1901, was followed by *The Shoes that Danced*, 1905. *Rose of the Wind*, 1910, includes her most famous poem, 'Nimrod', a Miltonic epic, as well as several revisions of Romantic and Victorian poets, among them Keats, Robert Browning and Coleridge. These poems are derivative and occasionally opaque but are also metrically skilful and not without independent interest. *Sonnets from a Lock Box*, 1929, expounds AB's Christian mysticism in a sequence of 38 sonnets. Introducing her *Last Poems*, 1944, Ridgely Torrence compared AB to Emily BRONTË and Christina ROSSETTI. Her papers are at Smith College.

Brand, Dionne, poet, b. 1953 in Guayguayare, Trinidad. After Naporima Girls' School she left in 1970 to study at the Univ. of Toronto (BA in English and Drama). Except for a short time as an Information and Communications Officer in Grenada before the US invasion of October 1983, she has lived and worked in Toronto, where she is active in many aspects of black community work: education, advocacy and counselling women immigrants. She gives readings of her work, has broadcast on radio and TV, and writes for *Spear*, Canada's 'National Magazine of Truth and Soul', where her poems have often first appeared. Her first vol., *'Fore Day Morning*, 1978, was followed by *Earth Magic*, 1980, *Primitive Offensive*, 1982, *Winter Epigrams and Epigrams to Ernesto Cardenal in Defense of Claudia*, 1983, and *Chronicles of the Hostile Sun*, 1984; she has also been anthologized. DB's work often uses history: to apply to the present, to reveal hidden figures – black, female, or both – and to 'institute [her] people centrally in the poetic universe'. 'St Mary's Estate' evokes the haunted remains of an abandoned plantation: 'They left remnants of the holocaust / in two long barracks guarding the mud road.' 'Afro West Indian Immigrant' situates her own in the wider African Diaspora: 'I feel like a palm tree / at the corner of Bloor and Yonge in a wild snow storm.' Writing of Trinidad, she can focus on a single aspect of the natural world with haiku-like minimalism and exactitude ('A Green Flat Leaf') or capture everyday living: 'Rain fall yesterday, / it run up the hill. / We see it coming / we put a pot on the bed / where the galvanise roof had a hole. / Natural indoor plumbing actually. ... Rain loosened the air for twenty miles, / ten unsheathed toes gave thanks. / Bad day for market though.' Himani Bannerji finds her 'alternative feminist aesthetic' most apparent in *Winter Epigrams*: 'Have you ever noticed / that when men write love poems / they're always about virgins or whores / or earth mothers? / How feint-hearted' (in Daryl Cumber Dance, ed., *Fifty Caribbean Writers*, 1986). With Krisontha Sri Bhaggiyadata, DB pub. *Rivers Have Sources, Trees Have Roots: Speaking of Racism*, 1986, an educational book. *Sans Souci*, 1989, collects stories.

Brand, Hannah, d. 1821, actress and playwright, da. of Norwich harness-maker John B., intensely devoted to her elder sister, with whom she ran a respected school. She wrote a poem to Anne DAMER in 1790. Her stiff, declamatory historical tragedy of Christians and Turks, *Huniades*, was given at Norwich in 1791; at Drury Lane, 1792, she played the lead, expiring melodramatically of poison (her first stage appearance). Takings were respectable, but in the next fortnight she re-wrote it minus the title role and re-named for her own part, *Agmunda*. The change was ridiculed, as were her antiquated dress, self-taught style and provincial accent when she acted it at York and Liverpool, 1794 (John Nichols, though, recorded a favourable opinion). Numbers of women writers subscribed to her *Plays and Poems*, 1798, which added a heroic comedy (also blank verse), a prose comedy (a servant swaps her baby daughter for her mistress's: both nature and nurture produce elevated behaviour), and several poems, the last a 'Prayer to the Parcae' that she and her sister might die together. William Beloe, who disliked her as a 'great stickler' for women's rights, alleged that she lost heavily by overestimating sales of her book, split the family where she was a governess and had to leave England with the wife for a distant colonial island.

Brand, Mona, dramatist and poet, b. 1915 in Sydney, NSW, da. of Violet (Nixon) and Alexander B. She was educ. at North Sydney Girls' High, and m. Len Fox, poet and labour historian. During WWII she worked in industrial social welfare and later as research officer, Dept. of Labour and National Service. She travelled and worked in Europe 1948–54, and taught English in Hanoi. Her controversial play, 'Here Under Heaven', produced by Melbourne's New Theatre in 1948, deals with racism and class struggle against the background of WWII; it was widely translated and subsequently produced for theatre and TV in China and throughout Eastern Europe. Her later work includes *Strangers in the Land*, 1955, an anti-colonial drama first produced by London's Unity Theatre, and *Our 'Dear' Relations*, 1963, which won first prize in the NSW Arts Council Drama Festival. She also wrote revues and political satire, mainly for New Theatre audiences. Her work, characterized by a strong sense of justice and topicality, includes three volumes of poetry, 1938–46, her selected plays, 1965, a children's play, 1971, and *Here Comes Kisch*, 1983. She has also written educational books and TV and radio scripts.

Brassey, Anna 'Annie B.', (Allnutt) Lady, 1839–87, travel writer and charity campaigner (especially St John's Ambulance). B. London, da. of Elizabeth (Burnett) and John A.; after her mother's early death AB was sent to her grandfather in Clapham where she acquired her love of the countryside and studied botany. After her return to her father in London she received a more organized education, including languages. In 1860 AB m. Thomas B., 1st Baron B., heir of a railway contractor and later an MP. They had four daughters and one son, and lived near Hastings, then elsewhere in Sussex from 1870. Her first two books, *The Flight of the Meteor*, 1869, and *A Cruise in the Eöthen*, 1872, were privately circulated. *A Voyage in the 'Sunbeam' Our Home on the Ocean for Eleven Months*, 1878, was an instant success, going into 19 editions by 1896 and trans. into five languages. In diary form it deals with the daily details of circumnavigating the globe in a yacht with young children on board and reveals her great interest in fauna and flora and zealous specimen-collecting (including an albatross). Her remaining books – *Sunshine and Storm in the East* (1880: Cyprus and Constantinople), *In the Trades, the Tropics, and the Roaring 40's* (1885: the Caribbean), and *The Last Voyage* (1889: India and Australia) – were less successful and lack the freshness of the first's observations. *The Last Voyage* was ed. by Lady Broome, who had helped her with her first efforts, and it includes a memoir by her husband. She died at sea and was buried lat. 15°50′S., long. 110°35′E.

Bray, Anna Eliza (Kempe), 1790–1883, novelist, b. Newington, Surrey, da. of Ann (Arrow) and John K., bullion porter in the Mint. Educ. at home, taught Latin and Italian by a Cambridge friend of her brother's, she wanted to act, but lost her chance through illness. In 1818 she m. Charles Alfred Stothard (d. 1821), illustrator of sculptured monuments. For his work they travelled in England and France, and she first pub. her *Letters written during a tour through ... France*, 1818, with his illustrations. Their one child died. She laboured to complete his unfinished book, pub. 1832, then after her next marriage, to the Rev. Edward Atkyns B., vicar of

Tavistock, Devon, she began to publish historical romances. Her first was *De Foix*, 1826, a rather fusty story mugged up from Froissart (as she acknowledges in the preface, where she also explains her 'melancholy pleasure' in gleaning details of knightly equipment from her late husband's work). This was followed by *The White Hoods*, 1828 (transl. into French the same year), and many more, often set in Devon and Cornwall. These were her most popular, being often reprinted, and re-issued as a set, 1845–6, and again in 1884. Loving that region, she produced in 1836, as a series of letters to Robert Southey (whom she hero-worshipped), *A Description of the part of Devonshire bordering on the Tamar and the Tavy* (repr. 1838 as *Traditions, legends, superstitions and sketches of Devonshire*). She was also a correspondent of L.E.L., and helped pub. poems by Mary COLLING, a local working-class girl. She moved to London after Bray's death (1857), edited some of his poetry and sermons, 1860, then wrote further novels; her last years were clouded by a rumour (later dispelled in *The Times*) that in 1816 she had stolen a piece of the Bayeux tapestry. Her autobiography, ed. J. A. Kempe, 1884, gives detail about her childhood.

Brazil, Angela, 1869–1947, children's writer, b. in Preston, Lancs., da. of Angelica (McKinnel) and cotton mill manager Clarence B. (She changed pronunciation of his name to rhyme with 'dazzle'.) She was educ. at Miss Knowle's Select Ladies' School in Preston and at Ellerslie in Manchester. She did not marry, but lived with her older, unmarried brother and sister in Coventry until her death. Though she worked as a conservationist to preserve various monuments and as a committee woman for such causes as the YWCA and the City guild, she is most remembered for her 49 schoolgirl novels packed with slang which Gillian FREEMAN, in *The Schoolgirl Ethic*, 1976, considers 'incongruously at odds with the cultured and self-consciously correct hostess'. AB's novels did deteriorate to formula writing, but the earliest examples – *The Fortunes of Philippa*, 1906, *The Third Class at Miss Kaye's*, 1908, *The Nicest Girl in the School*, 1909, and *A Fourth Form Friendship*, 1912 – deal feelingly and romantically with the positive influences of peers and teachers on the middle-class schoolgirl's development. As a middle-aged woman AB admitted that she was 'still an absolute schoolgirl' in her sympathies; hence, such characters as Lesbia Carrington in *For the School Colours*, 1918, and Lesbia Farrars in *Loyal to the School*, 1920, both of whom enter strong but naïve schoolgirl friendships, belonging psychologically to AB's own world, just as the characters in Brigid BROPHY's *The Finishing Touch*, 1963, are part of her witty and psychologically different world. See her *My Own Schooldays*, 1926, and Gillian Freeman, *The Schoolgirl Ethic*, 1976.

Brereton, Jane (Hughes), 'Melissa', 1685–1740, poet. B. in Flintshire, Wales, younger da. (an elder died) of Anne (Jones) and Thomas H., who educ. her. In 1711 she married Thomas B., then a spoiled undergraduate, later a writer, who remained spendthrift and sometimes violent. She left him by advice in 1721; he was drowned next year, and she settled at Wrexham. A poet since before her marriage, with pieces printed in 1716 and 1720, she pub. as 'Melissa' in the *GM*, entered (vainly) its contest for a poem on the Five Last Things and joined its verse colloquy begun by 'FIDELIA' (whose work JB so admired that she thought it a man's). She is a skilled occasional versifier. Of her four children, Charlotte also placed poems in the *GM*, 1736–43, including some on her mother's death, and wrote a memoir for JB's *Poems on Several Occasions*, pub. by subscription, 1744, with letters to Elizabeth CARTER, praise of Elizabeth ROWE and Queen Caroline, and learned imitation of Chaucer.

Brett, Dorothy Eugénie, 1883–1977, artist and memoirist, b. in London, da. of

Eleanor (Van de Weyer), a Belgian, and Reginald Baliol B., 2nd Viscount Esher. She chose to call herself by one name only, B. She studied at the Slade School of Art, 1910–16, shared a house with Katherine MANSFIELD, and numbered among her friends Mark Gertler, D. H. Lawrence, Ottoline MORRELL and Virginia WOOLF. In 1924 she migrated with Lawrence and Frieda to found a utopian community at Taos, New Mexico (cf. Mabel Dodge LUHAN), whose scenery and people inspired much of her painting. He is the centre of her only book, *Lawrence and Brett: A Friendship*, 1933 (addressed in the present tense to him as 'Lord of us all', re-issued with epilogue, 1974): she treats her own ideas and feelings as he affected them, showing a painter's grasp of landscape, interiors, and figures. Life by Sean Hignett, 1984.

Breuer, Bessie, Elizabeth (Freedman), 1893–1975, journalist, novelist. B. in Cleveland, Ohio, da. of Julia (Bindley) and Samuel Aaron F., educ. at the Univ. of Missouri, she worked as a journalist (St Louis *Times*, NY *Tribune*, many journals). Three times married (lastly to Henry Varnum Poor, 1925), BB had two children; she wrote under her first husband's name. Her friend Kay BOYLE (whom she met in France) encouraged her to express in fiction her interest in women's issues: her first three heroines find that their sexuality does not conform to expectations and are rejected by men they love. The male narrator of *Memory of Love* (filmed as *In Name Only*), 1934, is given to comments on 'what women were'. In BB's greatest success, *The Daughter*, 1938, the protagonist's divorced mother drifts from resort to resort, affair to affair. The daughter, drifting alongside, feels she must establish 'contact with a man, and therefore with the world', but her 'intellectual and moral agonizing' proves alien to her lover's 'unmoral animal' nature; she finds no alternative to her first predicament. The heroine of *The Actress*, 1956, told by Hollywood that she lacks 'sex appeal', finally establishes a stage career and a marriage of 'complete and separate selves'. BB collected her magazine fiction in *The Bracelet of Wavia Lea*, 1947, and had a play, *Sundown Beach*, produced in 1948. Her last novel is *Take Care of My Roses*, 1961.

Brewster, Elizabeth, poet, novelist, short-story writer. Da. of Ethel (Day) and Frederick John B., she was b. 1922, and had a rural childhood in New Brunswick. In Grade 10 she won a poetry competition judged by, among others, P. K. PAGE. She attended the Univ. of New Brunswick (BA in English and Greek, 1946), Radcliffe College, Harvard (AM, 1947), King's College, London, and the Univs. of Toronto (BLS, 1953) and Indiana (PhD, 1962). Before becoming a professor of English at the Univ. of Saskatchewan, 1972, she worked in various locations as librarian. Her first book of poems, *Lillooet*, 1954, won the E. J. Pratt Medal. EB grew up on Shelley, Keats, Wordsworth, Robert Frost and Robert Lowell, whose influences, reflecting her desire 'to be a Romantic *and* a Classicist', pervade her poetry (*The Way Home*, 1982, *Sometimes I Think of Moving*, 1977, and *Sunrise North*, 1972). She encompasses the gamut of human emotions. 'If I could walk out into the cold country / And see the white and innocent dawn arise . . . / Perhaps I might find again my lost childhood'. EB also goes beyond her conventions with an ironic, modern sensibility emerging from memory and detached perception – 'I am the girl at the next table, raising vague eyes, / Flicking the ash from her cigarette, the thoughts from her mind' (*Passage of Summer*, 1969). That same detachment, coupled with an erudition subtly expressed through literary references or mythic contexts, characterizes her love poetry: 'Your hand, which has written these poems / . . . has also traced poems on my flesh. / The inside of my mouth / has flowered into lyrics; / my breasts are rhymed / couplets; / my belly is smoothed to a sonnet; / and the cave of my body / is a found poem' (*In Search of Eros*, 1974). EB often writes about gender roles especially in her prose works like *It's Easy to Fall on the Ice*, 1977 (short stories all about women), *The Sisters*, 1974 (a novel), and *a house full of women*, 1983 (tightly controlled, stylistically unostentatious short stories). *Entertaining Angels*, 1988, is her most recent collection of poems. See Desmond Pacey, in *Ariel*, 4, 1973; Paul Denham, in *ECW*, 18/19, 1980.

Brewster, Martha (Wadsworth), 1710–after 1759, poet, b. at Lebanon, Conn., youngest child of Lydia (Brown) and Joseph W. She m. her cousin Oliver B. in 1732 and moved to remote Columbia, Conn., in 1747. Her slim *Poems on Divers Subjects*, New London, 1757, Boston, 1758, facs. 1979, has a verse preface begging readers' clemency: she believes female bards are rare, almost unknown in print. She defeated a charge of plagiarizing from Isaac Watts (whom she admired) by writing a verse biblical paraphrase 'in a few Minutes Extempore'. Her work, dating back to 1741, is old-fashioned in style and shows Anne BRADSTREET's influence. It centres on religious emotions, with affectionate verses to husband, children ('delight in Reading', she urges her daughter) and grandsons, praise of publ c virtue (male) and American patriotism, and of a dream about her father (in prose).

'Bridge, Ann', Mary Dolling (Sanders), Lady O'Malley, 1889–1974, popular novelist, b. at Shenley, Herts., of an American mother and English father. Educ. privately and at the LSE, in 1913 she m. Owen O'M., a diplomat later knighted, and had three children. At the British Legation in Peking from 1925, she learned Chinese and spent spare time exploring the old Imperial city and countryside. She wrote for money (children's education, upkeep of their English home). Her first novels, *Peking Picnic*, 1932, repr. 1984, and *The Ginger Griffin*, 1934, repr. 1985, are set in China. These combine travelogue (she had a prodigious visual memory) and psychology, portraying isolated diplomats and their views on the Chinese character. The travel element remained constant (blended with romance or spying) as AB followed her husband's postings from China to Scotland. She closely guarded her pseudonym and accepted Foreign Office vetting. The Julia Probyn series of spy novels opens in Morocco. Julia, an ex-governess who typically displays discretion and resourcefulness ('despite' her good looks) in relatively undemanding adventures, searches for a lost cousin in *The Lighthearted Quest*, 1956. In *Emergency in the Pyrenees*, 1965, now married and pregnant, she deals with terrorists and premature birth; in *The Malady in Madeira*, 1970, she clears her dead husband's name by discovering a secret nerve gas. *Permission to Resign*, 1971, defends her own husband against allegations of involvement in currency speculation. See her *Facts and Fictions*, 1968.

Brink, Carol (Ryrie), 1895–1981, miscellaneous and children's writer, b. Moscow, Idaho, da. of Herietta (Watkins) and Alexander R. They d. early; a grandmother and aunt raised her. After the Univs. of Idaho and Calif., Berkeley, she m. Raymond B., 1918, and moved to St Paul, Minn. Among a prolific output (poems, stories, plays, articles) she is best known for the 16 children's books she began as mother of two. The classic *Caddie Woodlawn: A Frontier Story*, 1935 (Newbery Medal: rev. 1970), about a tomboy unwilling to be a young lady, re-tells her grandmother's tales of pioneer childhood. Its characters reappear in *Magical Melons* (stories), 1944. The comic fantasy *Baby Island*, 1937, strands two girls with four babies and requires them to cope. CB based *Two Are Better Than One*, 1968, and *Louly*, 1974, on her own youth. Her seven adult novels also use recent history and autobiography. In *Snow in the River*, 1964, the narrator fictionalizes her family's immigration in

1888 to a US town called Opportunity.

Briscoe, Sophia, author of two sentimental epistolary novels pub. at London, celebrating female friendship. *Miss Melmoth, or The New Clarissa*, 1771, anon., ends happily despite its subtitle: Caroline 'Melmoth' escapes an 'alarming situation' in an 'odious house', clears her reputation, and discovers her mother to be Lady Evelin. (The striking coincidence of name with Frances Burney's first novel is probably not significant.) *The Fine Lady*, 1772, closes on the heroine's saintly death, leaving her two friends to marry and weep together.

Bristow, Amelia, 1783–after 1845, novelist, Christian convert from Judaism, living in and near London. (A different AB published both together, with many Northern Irish subscribers, *The Maniac* – a poem about the recent rebellion – and 'The Merits of Women', from French, which equates those merits exactly with value to men: 1810.) AB married a clerk and wrote 'for the benefit of the lower classes', heavily Evangelical novels beginning anonymously with *The Faithful Servant, or The History of Elizabeth Allen*, 1824, by subscription. *Sophie de Lissau*, 1826, *Emma de Lissau*, 1828, *The Orphans of Lissau*, 1830, and *Miriam and Rosette, or The Twin Sisters* (3rd ed. 1847) offer information about the 'domestic and religious habits' of Polish Jews in England and at home, especially women; their overt message of 'interest and sympathy' is undermined by stress on 'bigotry', cruel husbands and fathers, and women in clear need of rescue. The central figure, committed at birth to a stern grandfather to atone for her mother's rebellion, is denied education and hated by her mother. A Christian convert, she wins family hearts by selfless love, suffers persecution and penury, publishes poems and hymns and marries a Christian. From 1827 AB received aid from the RLF, to which she mentions four titles of the 1830s, unpaid periodical work, unprofitable novels and sewing till her eyes failed.

Bristow, Gwen, 1903–80, writer of historical and genre fiction, b. at Marion, SC, da. of Caroline Cornelia (Winkler) and the Revd Louis Judson B. She began writing as a child. At Judson College, Ala. (AB, 1924), she wrote friends' assignments (for a fee) and a play produced by students. She put herself through journalism courses at Columbia, NY, by working as nursemaid and secretary and writing rags-to-riches lives of businessmen. She became a reporter on the *Times-Picayune*, New Orleans, in 1925, published a book of poems in 1926 and m. fellow-writer Bruce Manning in 1929. They co-authored *The Invisible Host*, 1930, a mystery novel (adapted for stage and film as *The Ninth Guest*), and three less successful mysteries. Moving to Hollywood, 1934, he became a scriptwriter, while she wrote her best-known work, *Plantation Trilogy* (*Deep Summer*, 1937, *The Handsome Road*, 1938, and *This Side Glory*, 1940), chronicle of a Louisiana settlement family, which runs in history through colonial days to WWI and in class through Southern aristocrats, poor whites and blacks. It was praised for 'firm sense of character', dramatic effects and emotional sincerity. After a war propaganda novel, *Tomorrow Is Forever*, 1943 (filmed 1946), she set *Jubilee Trail*, 1950 (filmed 1953), and *Calico Palace*, 1959, in the Calif. Gold Rush, and *Celia Garth*, 1959, in colonial SC. Their protagonists are women, some with children, who built independent lives.

Brittain, Vera Mary, 1893–1970, feminist, pacifist, writer. B. in Newcastle-under-Lyme, Staffordshire, da. of Edith (Bervon) and Thomas B., a prosperous paper manufacturer, she was educ. at St Monica's School, Surrey, and, in spite of parental opposition, at Somerville College, Oxford. She left in 1915 to become a VAD nurse during WWI. Her struggle for education, nursing experiences, and love for Roland Leighton, his death in action in France, 1915, and her brother's, 1918, form the material for her most famous book,

Testament of Youth, 1933, a record of 'the stark agonies of my generation ... from the years leading up to 1914 until about 1925'. Reprinted five times in five months, this book has been in print ever since, and was made a BBC–TV serial, dramatized by Elaine MORGAN, 1979. Returning to Oxford, 1918, VB met Winifred HOLTBY, with whom she lived in London after they graduated, 1921. Like Holtby, VB lectured for the League of Nations Union and for various feminist organizations, including the Six Point Group, founded by Margaret Haig, Lady RHONDDA. Her tribute to Holtby and 'the story of a friendship which continued unbroken and unspoilt for sixteen incomparable years' was given in *Testament of Friendship*, published in 1940, five years after Holtby's death. VB m. George Catlin, a political philosopher, 1925. In their 'semi-detached' marriage he spent much time in the USA while she remained in London with their two children, John Edward and Shirley (Williams, the politician), with Holtby as a member of the household. VB wrote five novels, but her reputation rests on her 'Testaments'. The third, *Testament of Experience*, 1957, an account of her life from 1925 to 1950, traces the development of her feminist and pacifist convictions. A prolific and outspoken journalist, she wrote for *Time and Tide* and *Peace News* for many years, as well as for the *Yorkshire Post* and the *Manchester Guardian*. She also wrote a number of non-fiction books, most notably *Lady into Woman*, 1953 (a history of women from Victoria to Elizabeth II), *The Woman at Oxford*, 1960, and *Radclyffe Hall: A Case of Obscenity*? 1968. Her uncompromising honesty and integrity of purpose (which combined with a nervous and possessive disposition to make her an exacting companion) were exemplified in *Seed of Chaos*, 1944 (US title, *Massacre by Bombing*), a pamphlet whose opposition to mass bombing of enemy cities earned her unpopularity in England and hostility in the USA. Her novels are worthy rather than entertaining. *The Dark Tide*, 1923, provides a useful if embittered account of post-war Oxford, and *Honourable Estate* is a fictionalized account of the Women's Movement from 1883 to 1933. Both are heavily autobiographical. Her journalism, letters and diaries have appeared in volumes of 1981, 1983, 1985, 1988 and 1989. See Muriel Mellown in *TSWL*, 2, 1983; and Hilary Bailey, *Vera Brittain*, 1987.

Brodber, Erna, fiction writer and sociologist, b. 1940 at Woodside, St Mary, Jamaica, da. of Lucy and Ernest, a teacher and farmer active in local community affairs and culture, sister of Velma POLLARD. She wrote stories from an early age and boarded with Kingston relatives for secondary educ. at Excelsior High School. She taught and did social work, took a BA at the Univ. of the West Indies (history, 1963), worked as a children's officer and did an MA on the socialization of Jamaican children. In Washington, DC, in 1967, on a Ford Foundation scholarship to study children psychology, she discovered the Black Power and Women's Liberation movements. Back in Jamaica she published two sociological books, *Abandonment of Children in Jamaica*, 1974, and *A Study of Yards in ... Kingston*, 1975. That year she joined the Institution of Social and Economic Research and won a National Festival award with a story, 'Rosa'. Her first novel, or stylistically adventurous prose poem, *Jane and Louisa Will Soon Come Home*, 1980, reflects her need to 'grapple with' and 'write out' the relation between her academic work and personal experiences. Its themes are alienation and historical trauma in Jamaican life, community influence on the individual and the dilemma posed by long-held stereotypes of Caribbean womanhood. EB explores the idea of *Kumbla*, a disguise or hiding place which both protects and imprisons (cf. Carole Boyce Davies and Elaine Savory Fido, eds., *Out of Kumbla: Womanist Perspectives on Caribbean Literature*, forthcoming). EB then published *Reggae and Cultural Identity in Jamaica*, 1981 (with J. Edward Greene), and *Perceptions of Caribbean Women, Towards a Documentation of Stereotypes*, 1982 (examples from the Press and Church rather than fiction). This finds that black women have often escaped white female stereotyping, but are more vulnerable to ideas of their own culture, especially that of the long-suffering, strong, enduring mother-figure (who may also encourage her children to move into 'the official image-making culture'). EB still combines academic life with fiction writing. A second novel, *Myal*, 1988, again inventive and exciting in language, evokes a many-layered world where 'the spirit of the past, subdued by spirit thieves, becomes submerged, yet lives on.' She deconstructs the colonial fiction of domesticated, docile blacks; her reclaiming of myth and history has been compared to Toni MORRISON. Article on *Jane and Louisa* by Carolyn Cooper in *New Beacon Review* 2/3.

Bromley, Eliza (Nugent), d. 1807, novelist. Her father owned large West Indian estates but was 'despoiled' after educating her (at a fashionable London boarding school) to expect a fortune. As a 'young lady' she pub. *Louisa and Augustus, An Authentic Story in a Series of Letters*, 1784, dedicated humbly to Georgiana DEVONSHIRE's mother. It abounds in hectic West Indian local colour, loyal negroes, savage Indians, cruel father, remorseless villain, destitution and long-drawn deathbeds: Jane AUSTEN mocked it in *Love and Freindship*. ENB married a half-pay subaltern who died in 1791. *The Cave of Cosenza*, 1803, is dedicated, with high-class subscription list, to the Duke of York. In the cave the hero, lovelessly married and seduced by a passionate Italian, lies in durance; he returns penitent after ten years; again a long-suffering wife is glorified. ENB mentioned another novel (*Charles Bentinck and Louisa Cavendish*), MS play (*Deeds of Other Times*) and MS opera to the RLF in a failed appeal for aid one month before she died.

Broner, Esther (Masserman), playwright, novelist, short-story writer, educator. B. in 1930 in Detroit, da. of Beatrice (Weckstein) and journalist and historian Paul M., she grew up in a close-knit traditional Jewish family and after finishing high school at 16 lived in NYC but returned to the Midwest to continue her education at Wayne State Univ. (BA, 1950, MFA, 1962). In 1978 she received her PhD from Union Graduate School. Married 1948, to artist Robert B., mother of four, EMB has taught at Wayne State and Sarah Lawrence College. She first gave serious attention to her writing career in her early thirties, publishing and producing her verse-drama, *Summer Is a Foreign Land*, 1966. Other produced plays include a musical drama, *Colonel Higginson*, 1968, *The Body Parts of Margaret FULLER*, 1976 (which won the National Bicentennial Contest), and a radio play, *Above the Timber Line*, 1984. She has also had staged readings of *Letters to My TV Past*, 1986, *The Olympics*, 1987, and *Half-a-Man*, 1988. EMB's first novel, *Her Mothers*, 1975, is a contemporary quest romance: searching for her missing adolescent daughter Lena, Beatrix Palmer, herself a writer, recalls her own younger years while continuing to gather material for her proposed book, *Unafraid Women*. EMB's other prose works – *Journal/Nocturnal and Seven Stories*, 1968, and *A Weave of Women*, 1978 – also interweave Jewish tradition, women's experience and communal history, and celebrate the female hero in a poetic fluid structure marked by rich word play and non-linear form. EMB has also edited, with Cathy Davidson, *The Lost Tradition: Mothers and Daughters in Literature*, 1980. Her work 'depicts a feminine vision, merges it with a masculine tradition, to create something new, a fully human tradition' (Marilyn FRENCH, intro. to EMB's *Her Mothers*, 1975 [repr. 1985]). See EMB in *Regionalism and the Female Imagination* 3, 1977–8.

Brontë, Anne, 1820–49, **Charlotte**, 1816–55, **Emily**, 1818–48. The Brontë sisters, all novelists and poets, wrote collaboratively as children (with their only brother, Branwell), and are often referred to collectively as 'the Brontës'. Their imaginative development began early: a gift to Branwell of wooden soldiers sparked the fantasy play which evolved into the complex sagas of Gondal and Angria (see Christine Alexander, 1983). But although their lives were intertwined, their mature works were highly individualized. B. at Thornton, near Bradford, Yorks., three of six children of Maria (Branwell, d. 1821), and Patrick Brontë. Three months after Anne's birth they moved to Haworth, where their father became perpetual curate. He and their Aunt Branwell supervised their education. Later the girls (except AB) went to the Clergy Daughters' School at Cowan Bridge, where the poor diet and conditions lastingly affected their health: their elder sisters Maria and Elizabeth died (1825). Next they attended Miss Wooler's school at Roe Head, EB only briefly because of illness and homesickness, AB staying to become proficient in governessing skills, including languages, and CB returning there as assistant teacher 1835–8. CB worked as a governess in 1839, and again in 1841, before she and EB went in Feb. 1842 as pupils to the Pensionnat Heger in Brussels. In 1843 CB returned there as teacher until her worsening relationship with Mme Heger drove her home in Jan. 1844. The sisters then tried unsuccessfully to set up a school at home, and in 1846 they pub. an almost unnoticed vol. of poems (by 'Currer, Ellis and Acton Bell'). After the remarkable success of CB's *Jane Eyre* (by 'Currer Bell') in 1847, she devoted herself to writing, remaining based at Haworth, loyal to her father's needs and combating the ill-health, depression and loneliness consequent upon the deaths of EB and AB. In June 1854 she m. Arthur Bell Nicholls, having finally overcome her father's opposition; her letters show an often painful effort to adjust to the demands of married life. In Mar. 1855 CB died from the combined results of chronic ill-health and complications in pregnancy. Her first novel, *The Professor*, pub. posthumously, 1857, explores sex-roles and attitudes towards women with the apparent detachment of a male narrator. It includes her only portrayal of a working wife. *Jane Eyre*, 1847, which brought her notoriety, is the narrative of a self-determined, strong-minded and articulate heroine, while *Shirley*, 1849, makes more specific social and political protest, linking the oppression of workers by tyrannical masters with that of women; it also argues for the needs of single women. Her last novel, *Villette*, 1853, shows the female narrator, Lucy Snowe, overcoming social disadvantages and emotional disappointment, achieving an independent, satisfying existence in which the demands of the heart, though imperious, do not obliterate female individuality. EB, 'Ellis Bell', was passionately attached to her home and the local environment at Haworth. Returning from Roe Head in 1835, she began to write poetry, having already established her creative ability in the Gondal stories which she composed with AB. She taught at Law Hill, near Halifax, from Sept. 1837, but only for about six months. For the next few years her life centred on domestic tasks and the world of the imagination embodied in Gondal and her poetry, briefly interrupted by her Brussels experience (Feb.–Nov. 1842). She died three months after Branwell, having been taken ill after his funeral and refusing all medical assistance. Her early work focuses on noble, courageous heroines. Her poetry (pub. complete ed. C. W. Hatfield, 1941) shows a close observation of nature, a longing for freedom, and a profound spiritual state of desire for union with a visionary spirit. Her novel *Wuthering Heights* was offered for publication in 1846, but was only finally pub. (by the unscrupulous Newby) in late 1847, after the success of *Jane Eyre*. CB apologized for the novel's intensity in her Preface to the 1850 edition, softening the dialect and re-arranging the punctuation. Early reviewers found it gloomy and disagreeable, despite its originality, but later opinion has established it as a classic. AB, 'Acton Bell', was governess to the Ingham family at Blake Hall, Mirfield, in 1839, and was unfairly dismissed after less than a year. Returning to Haworth, she fell in love with her father's new curate, Willie Weightman, who d. two years later. She was governess to the Robinson family at Thorpe Green Hall, near York, 1841–5, and then lived at home, writing and helping in the house, until she died at Scarborough. Her verses for the Gondal saga, written with EB (to whom she felt closest), express the bliss of freedom in nature, while her heroes and heroines voice the spirit of rebellion and passionate feeling. The 21 poems pub. with CB's and EB's in 1846 are more personal though less dramatic, and convey her delight in nature, nostalgia and lost love as well as her desire for religious assurance. The rest of her poetry was pub. posthumously. Her first novel, *Agnes Grey*, 1847, argues for female self-dependence and individual choice. *The Tenant of Wildfell Hall*, 1848, speaks even more directly for female freedom and defends a woman's right to flee from the torments of a brutal marriage. This novel also ends romantically, but its message of revolt remains clear, and it is – through a male narrator – one of the most outspoken portrayals of male oppression in the period. For CB's life, see Elizabeth GASKELL, 1857 (an immediate, if biased view); the admirable 1967 life by Winifred Gérin, who also wrote lives of EB, 1971, and AB, 1959, and most recent, Rebecca Fraser's life of CB, 1988. The best available edition of Brontë letters is in T. J. Wise and J. A. Symington, eds., *The Brontës: Their Lives, Friendships and Correspondence*, 1932; the letters are being re-edited by Margaret Smith (forthcoming OUP). For critical studies of CB, see particularly Helene Moglen, 1976 and S. GILBERT and S. Gubar, *The Madwoman in the Attic*, 1979. EB's *Wuthering Heights* has attracted a wide diversity of critical commentary, including mythical, sociological and structural interpretations.

Brook, Mary (Brotherton), *c.* 1726–82, Quaker pamphleteer, b. at Woodstock, Oxon, da. of Anglicans Mary and William Brotherton, brought up partly by a Presbyterian aunt at Warwick. Elizabeth ASHBRIDGE's preaching helped to make her a Quaker, about 1753; she was soon a minister. In 1759 she m. Joseph Brook, woolstapler, of Leighton Buzzard, Beds.; she had two daughters. She wrote many edifying epistles to Friends and others; her well-known work is *Reasons for the Necessity of Silent Waiting*, 1774 (22 reprints, including French and German versions). Quoting the Bible, using rhetorical questions to imply her readers' necessary consent, she defends a humble attendance on the Spirit within the heart, against set forms which make the mind 'agitated in a continual Practice of running over a Multitude of unfelt Expressions.'

Brooke, Charlotte, d. 1793, translator and poet, b. at Rantavan, Co. Cavan, one of the last of 22 children of Lettice (Digby) and Henry B., author. Educ. by her father, she later taught herself ancient Irish in two years. His success as a Dublin dramatist brought her literary and theatrical friends; she wrote poetry early but destroyed most of it. Her mother and last surviving sister died in 1772; she devoted herself, 'incapable of any other love', to her stricken father till his death late in 1783. She contributed an anon. translated poem to *Historical Memoirs of Irish Bards*, 1786; having weathered financial crisis, she pub. *Reliques of Irish Poetry ... translated into English verse, with ... the originals*, Dublin [1788], repr. with life, 1816, facs. 1970. Anna SEWARD, Charlotte SMITH, and Lady TUITE subscribed. CB aimed to rescue the Irish tradition from the damage done by James Macpherson's *Ossian*, to inform 'the

British muse' of her 'elder sister in this isle'. Her forceful, feeling narratives (most trans.; one original) and historical and critical notes were well reviewed, but their significance not fully grasped (see Kenneth F. Gantz in *Studies in English*, Texas, 1940). Her tragedy, *Belisarious*, was admired, *perhaps* plagiarized, and certainly lost for ever by actor Charles Kemble. Her rather sickly dialogues, *School for Christians*, 1791, were bought in bulk by subscribers for poor children. She lovingly edited her father's works, 1792, to replace a defective earlier edition. Though she had disapproved of novels, she left among many MSS that of *Emma, or the Foundling of the Wood*, pub. 1803.

Brooke, Elizabeth (Colepeper), Lady, 1601–83, religious writer, da. of Elizabeth (Cheney) and Sir Thomas, later Lord C., of Wigsale, Sussex. Orphaned young, brought up by her grandmother to be pious, she read tirelessly theology and (translated) ancient philosphers. In 1620 she m. Sir Robert B., and lived in London, then Herts., then Suffolk. He died in 1646; only one of her seven children survived her. She left MSS of Bible commentary and controversy; her *Observations, Experiences, and Rules for Practice*, pub. 1684 with a funeral sermon, include both formal aphorism and personal witness: 'I find trusting in God my most necessary Duty ... I find it comfortable to trust in God ... I find it *difficult to trust in God at all times*.'

Brooke, Emma Frances, 'E. Fairfax Byrrne', 1845–1926, novelist, b. Cheshire, descended from an old yeoman family on mother's side, an old Yorks. family on father's. She was educ. at Newnham College, Cambridge, and the LSE and belonged to the Fabian Society from its beginnings. Her first publication, *Milicent. A Poem*, 1881 (as 'Byrrne'), was followed by *A Fair Country Maid*, serialized in the *Manchester Examiner*, 1883. Secretary of the Karl Marx Club (started 1884) in Hampstead, she was also, like Edith ELLIS, a member of the Fellowship of the New Life commune in Doughty Street, moving in the 1880s to join a close-knit community of radicals and writers in Kent. A contributor to many periodicals, such as the *Cornhill, Guardian* and *New Review*, she wrote as 'Brooke' after 1887, but in 1894 pub. anon. her best-known novel, the strongly feminist and didactic *A Superfluous Woman. Transition*, 1895, basing its hero on Sydney Webb, was also issued anonymously: both novels treat the Socialist and sexual education of young women. Beatrice WEBB called EFB 'a bundle of sensibilities – not over-burdened with intelligence' (letter of ?25 March 1892), but in 1898 she pub. an impressive *Tabulation of the Factory Laws of European Countries* with special reference to women and children. Her papers are in Univ. College Library, London.

Brooke, Frances (Moore), 1724–89, journalist, playwright and novelist, b. Claypole, Lincs., da. of Mary (Knowles), who educ. her, and the Revd William M. (d. 1727), who left £1000 to come to her at 21. By 1748 she was in London; when she launched her periodical *The Old Maid* on 15 Nov. 1755, she was vainly urging both Garrick and Rich to produce her blank-verse classical tragedy *Virginia* (pub. 1756, with poems), and was possibly already m. to the Revd John B., 15 years her senior. *The Old Maid* ran till July 1756 (coll. 1764): as by Mary Singleton, 'on the verge of fifty', it includes trenchant comment on society, politics, and drama. She worked on a pastoral (MS with other papers at Harvard) and farce, bore a son (in 1757, about the time her husband left for Canada as an army chaplain) and translated from Marie-Jeanne RICCOBONI's French *Letters from Juliet, Lady Catesby*, 1760. Next came her own sentimental, epistolary *History of Lady Julia Mandeville*, 1763 (ten eds. by 1792, repr. 1930). In it, a jealous duel caused by misunderstanding destroys both hero and heroine; its gothic touches are remarkable for this date. That year FB sailed for Quebec. She stayed (with at least one break) till 1768 and considered settling. Her life there informs *The History of Emily Montague*, first North American novel (1769, ed. Mary Jane Edwards, 1985: some critical attention). Also epistolary, with happy ending, it has a setting and minor characters which outshine the heroine and hero. FB further translated from French *St Forlaix*, 1770, and Milot's *History of England*, 1771, with informed notes attentive to women's history. She met most of the female writers of her day, was always short of money and found her husband sometimes interfering. From 1773 to 1778, with her actress friend Mary Ann Yates, she managed the Haymarket opera house. Lorraine McMullen's life of her, 1983, supports the ascription to her of the anonymous, non-epistolary novel *All's Right at Last*, 1774 (set partly in Canada), and *Charles Mandeville*, 1790, sequel to *Lady Julia*, set partly in the utopian Youngland where, however, the status of women is not improved. (But *Eliza Beaumont and Harriet Osborne*, 1789, which praises women novelists, is by the otherwise unknown Indiana Brooks, not FB.) *The Excursion*, 1777, has a dark, sprightly heroine who seeks success in London with a novel, tragedy and epic poem; Garrick's management is attacked, and Maria and her fair, mild twin sister suddenly enriched at the end. In 1779 FB planned a life of Richardson; her tragedy *The Siege of Sinope* ran for ten nights in 1781; her musical *Rosina*, 1782, was a terrific hit in several countries (recorded 1966); and *Marion*, staged 1788, also did well (both set by William Shield).

Brooke-Rose, Christine, novelist, short-story writer, journalist, literary critic, translator. B. in 1923 in Geneva, Switzerland, da. of Evelyn Blanche Brooke and Alfred Northbrook Rose, CB-R was educ. at Oxford (BA, 1949, MA, 1953) and the Univ. of London (PhD, 1954). A freelance journalist in London during the 1950s and 1960s, she m. Jerzy Peterkiewicz, 1968 (divorced, 1975), moved to France, 1969, and was first lecturer, then Professor of American literature at the Univ. of Paris VIII, retiring in 1988. As a freelance journalist she was instrumental in introducing the French *nouveau roman* and new trends in French literary criticism (structuralism, post-structuralism) to the English-speaking public. As a creative writer she has produced strikingly original and witty metafictional narratives, which, like the *nouveau roman*, force outward the novel's generic boundaries. A radical departure from the conventional philosophical style of *The Sycamore Tree*, 1958, *Out*, 1964, inverts Alain Robbe-Grillet's *La Jalousie*, while *Thru*, 1975, would appear to be experimentally modelled on the Joyce of *Finnegans Wake*. *Such*, 1966, is the story of Lazarus, an astronomer who dies looking through his telescope but who, brought back to life by CB-R for three minutes (the time of the narrative), explores the problems of science and language as tools for judging human concerns. Language itself is the subject of *Between*, 1968. (See also *Amalgamemnon*, 1984, and *Xorander*, 1986.) Her major critical work, *A Grammar of Metaphor*, 1958, analyses 15 English poets from Chaucer to Dylan Thomas to consider the reaction of a metaphoric word on other words to which it is syntactically and grammatically related. She has also written two important books on Pound, 1971 and 1976, extending and applying Roman Jakobson's linguistic analysis to free verse. CB-R's *A Rhetoric of the Unreal*, 1981, collects studies in narrative and structure, covering a wide range of fiction and such topics as the fantastic, science fiction, the marvellous, metafiction and surfiction. CB-R won the Arts Council Translation Prize for her translation of Robbe-Grillet's *Dans le labyrinthe*, 1957 (*In the Labyrinth*, 1968). *The CB-R Omnibus*, 1986, collects four novels.

Brookner, Anita, art historian and novelist, b. in 1938 in London to Polish parents, singer Maude (Schiska) and businessman Newsom Bruckner, who changed their name because of anti-German feeling. AB calls them 'Exiles, Jews. Complicated people'; 'mismatched, strong-willed, hot tempered, with a great deal of residual sadness which I've certainly inherited'. Educ. at James Allen's Girls' School (Dulwich) and London Univ. (BA at King's College; MA and PhD, 1953, at the Courtauld Institute), she has 'never been at home here'. A distinguished scholar, she has published on French painters, including Watteau, Greuze, and David, and on art criticism by writers including Baudelaire, been the first woman Slade Professor at Cambridge, 1967–8, and lectured at the Courtauld, 1964–88. From 1980 to 1988 she wrote a novel each summer; she writes without revising. In *A Start in Life*, 1981 (*The Debut* in the USA), a university lecturer looks back and 'at forty, knew that her life had been ruined by literature'. She is the first of AB's heroines: intelligent, lonely, financially independent, no longer young but haunted by conventional, romantic patterns of aspiration, pictured with delicate irony as well as pathos, in elegantly fashioned prose. Those of *Look at Me*, 1983, and *Hotel du Lac*, 1984 (Booker Prize), are novelists. The former writes in a penitential mood which AB now regrets. The latter, Edith Hope, writes happy-ending romances for a living. Her life belies her name and metier; she twice rejects marriage (first fleeing, literally, in a taxi, leaving wedding guests gaping; undramatically at the end), and seems to move only from one limbo to another. In *Family and Friends*, 1986 ('basically my own family – I knew them all'), *A Misalliance*, also 1986, and *A Friend from England*, 1987, AB uses larger casts of characters to examine the quality of dutifulness; in the last the narrator realises with pain that she lacks 'the patience or the confidence to invent a life for myself'. *Latecomers*, 1988, again expands AB's range: her protagonists are two men, childhood refugees in London, and her climax a fearfully undertaken visit back to Berlin. *Lewis Percy*, 1989, has an unheroic male protagonist. See interview in *Paris Review*, 29, 1987; Olga Kenyon, *Women Novelists Today*, 1988.

Brooks, Gwendolyn, poet and novelist, b. in 1917 in Topeka, Kansas, to Keziah Corinne (Wims), a teacher who promised her she would be 'the lady Paul Laurence Dunbar', and David Anderson B. At about 13 she buried her poems in the back yard, to be dug up one day and save the world. Raised in Chicago (still her home), she graduated from Wilson Jr. College, 1936, and in 1939 m. a fellow-poet, Henry Blakely, whom she met at an NAACP meeting; she had two children. She studied writing at the South Side Community Art Center in the 1940s, and was soon published and recognized. Poems in *A Street in Bronzeville*, 1945, deal with 'chocolate Mabbie' losing her man to a 'lemon-hued lynx', and with abortions that 'will not let you forget'. GB won a Pulitzer Prize (first black poet to do so) and a Eunice TIETJENS prize for *Annie Allen*, 1949, a linguistically elaborate, formally rigorous (and sometimes formally satiric) narrative poem about black life and a black girl growing to womanhood: 'Think of sweet and chocolate, / Left to folly or to fate,/ Whom the higher gods forgot, / Whom the lower gods berate; / Physical and underfed / Fancying on the featherbed / What was never and is not' ('The Anniad'). Later poetry volumes to *In the Mecca*, 1968, are collected with *Maud Martha* (an innovative, semi-autobiographical novel), 1953, in *The World of GB*, 1971. She treats a 14-year-old black's murder from the horrified perspective of the white woman who had called him 'fresh', and invites blacks and whites to come together in 'a common peoplehood'. Later volumes, *Riot*, 1969, *Family Pictures*, 1970, *Beckonings*, 1975, *To Disembark*, 1981, *The Near-Johannesburg Boy*, 1986, express GB's steadily growing allegiance to black liberation: there 'is no Race Problem./ There is the white decision, the white and pleasant vow / that the white foot shall not release the black neck' ('In Montgomery'). The late 1960s, Toni Cade BAMBARA says, infused GB's poetry with 'new intensity, richness and power', giving extra pressure to her admired formal control, offering new experiments with voice, line, and theme, like the portentous gravity of 'The Boy Died in My Alley'. Her impressionistic autobiography, *Report from Part One*, 1972, describes her change from 'Negro to Black' in the context of her intellectual life, a visit to Africa, and the influence of radical black poets. In *Primer for Blacks*, 1980, GB says she aims to write 'poems I could take into a tavern, into the street, into the halls of a housing project'. She published poems for children, 1956, 1974, edited anthologies, taught creative writing at various colleges, and set up poetry workshops with Chicago street gangs. See Maria K. Mootry and Gary Smith, eds., *A Life Distilled*, 1987; studies by Harry B. Shaw, 1980, D. H. Melhem, 1987; interview in *Southwest Review*, 74, 1989; life by George E. Kent forthcoming 1990.

Brooks, Maria (Gowen), 'Maria del Occidente', 1794–1845, poet, b. Medford, Mass., da. of Eleanor (Cutter) and William G., a goldsmith. Early proficient in music, painting and languages, by nine she had read all of Shakespeare. After her father's death in 1809, she lived with her elderly brother-in-law John B., whom she m. in 1810, producing two sons. MB later fell passionately in love with a young Canadian officer who was to be a romantic model in her writing and figures as 'Ethelwald' in her novel *Idomen*. In 1820 she pub. *Judith, Esther and Other Poems*, which focuses on the Old Testament heroines from a psychological viewpoint. After her husband's death in 1823, MB lived in Cuba on her uncle's coffee plantation which she later inherited. She became engaged to the Canadian officer, but they were estranged, and she twice attempted suicide. From 1826 MB corresponded with Robert Southey; she was his guest in 1831, when she also met Wordsworth and Coleridge. Southey encouraged the writing of her epic *Zophiel* which she pub. in 1833 as by 'Maria del Occidente'. Its theme is the love of a fallen angel for a mortal maiden; it is notable for its erudition and sensuality, while its lyricism won MB critical acclaim. Her fictionalized autobiography *Idomen: or the Vale of Yumuri* was first serialized in the Boston *Saturday Evening Gazette*, 1838. Examining in depth a state of mental suffering in the heroine, its style is stilted and sentimental, falling well below her poetry in achievement. Probably only 100 copies were ever printed. MB returned to Cuba in 1843 and began work on another epic, *Beatrice, the Beloved of Columbus*, but died of typhoid fever before its completion. Her MSS are at Boston Public Library, Yale and the Library of Congress. For her life, see Ruth S. Grannis, 1913.

Brophy, Brigid Antonia, novelist and critic. B. 1929 in London, da. of headmistress Charis (Grundy) and novelist John B., she began writing 'poetic dramas' at three but at nine 'found out I couldn't write poetry'. She attended St Paul's Girls' School and read classics at St Hugh's College, Oxford, but was sent down in her second year for unspecified offences. (Later, she spoke frankly about her bisexuality.) She became a shorthand-typist (latterly for a pornography distributor). In 1953 she published *The Crown Princess* (short stories) and *Hackenfeller's Ape*, a novel reflecting philosophical and ethical concerns including fierce opposition to vivisection. She m. art historian Michael Levey, later Director of the National Gallery, in 1954, and has a daughter. Her later novels examine the complex connection between sex and death in heterosexual relationships: *The Finishing Touch*, 1963 (lesbian high camp), and *The Snow Ball*, 1964, are baroque tributes to Ronald Firbank, on whom she wrote a 600-page study, *Prancing Novelist*, 1973. *In Transit*, 1969, is a trans-sexual fantasy; *Flesh*, 1972, is a dispassionate but bizarre account of sexual awakening; *Place Without Chairs*, 1978, is a Kafkaesque comic nightmare framing the vitality of a lesbian survivor. BB's work is unevenly experimental and has provoked critical scepticism; it is often erudite, like the psychoanalytical essay *Black Ship to Hell*, 1962. She has written a play each for radio and stage, worked in journalism and written studies of Mozart, 1964, Aubrey Beardsley, 1968 and 1976, and censorship, 1972. With Levey and Charles Osborne she published the flippant *Fifty Works of ... Literature We Could Do Without*, 1967. With Maureen DUFFY, she organized a Pop-Art exhibition, 1969, and worked to produce the Public Lending Right Act, 1979, to which BB wrote a guide, 1983. She has done much other public work for writers. In 'A Case Historical Fragment of Autobiography' (in *Baroque-'n'-Roll and Other Essays*, 1987), and in *The Times* (12 Feb. 1987) she confronts her multiple sclerosis, diagnosed in 1984. She disapproves of 'separatist' books like this one.

Brossard, Nicole, poet, feminist, radical lesbian, and author of 'theory-fiction', b. in Montréal in 1943, da. of Marguerite (Matte) and Guillaume B., mother of one daughter. Co-founder of the cultural journal, *La Barre du jour*, 1965 (from 1977 *La Nouvelle Barre du jour*), she was central in the *nouvelle écriture* which emerged from the conjunction of French *modernité* and Québec's political ferment of the 1960s, which aimed to 'sabotage' poetic and social conventions. Her poetry of this period is collected in *Le Centre blanc*, 1978. Two volumes won Governor-General's Medals for poetry: *Mécanique jongleuse* suivi de *Masculin grammaticale*, 1974 (transl. as *Daydream Mechanics*, 1980), and *Double Impression*, 1984. Prominent as a feminist cultural activist since the 1970s, NB co-directed the National Film Board's *Some American Feminists*, 1976, participated in its *Firewords*, 1986, edited special issues on women and language of *La Barre*, 1975 and 1981, been a member of the feminist theatre collective production of *La Nef des sorcières*, 1976 (*A Clash of Symbols*, 1979), co-founded the radical feminist journal *Les Têtes de Pioche*, 1976–9 (all issues collected together, 1980), and founded the feminist press L'Intégrale, 1982. Her first 'theory-fiction', *Un livre*, 1970 (*A Book*, 1976) and her subsequent work revisions the political/writerly preoccupations of *nouvelle écriture* from the experience of inhabiting a woman's body. She enacts a Utopian project of discovering through writing the body / consciousness of the suppressed feminine 'E muet mutant', 1975. Several later 'theory-fictions', from *Sold-out*, 1973 (*Turn of a Pang*, 1976) to *Amantes*, 1980 (*Lovers*, 1986), *Picture Theory*, 1982, and *Le Désert Mauve*, 1987, develop a fragmented, plotless, poetic style in which the 'otherness' of English words disrupts the French text and metaphors of the spiral, of the city/body/body politic (*circulation* / circulation) and the hologram as a 'screen skin', lead the textual exploration. Her *écriture au féminin* undertakes discovery, through the process of writing female consciousness(es) of the 'feminine' enforced by fathers, heterosexuality and 'patriarchal' mothers. In oft-quoted statements such as 'To write *I am a woman* is full of consequences', NB deconstructs society's 'real' as a patriarchal 'fiction' which must be 'killed' to enable women to write *their* 'real' of their bodies, their experience. 'If it weren't lesbian, this text would make no sense at all', she insists, pointing to the process of writing outside patriarchal 'fiction' as the means to feminist self-knowledge. Widely recognized as Québec's leading avant-garde writer, NB's influence in English Canada has grown in the 1980s through translations of her work, her impassioned essays on lesbian writing and culture, collected in *La Lettre aérienne*, 1985 (*The Aerial Letter*, 1988), her presidency of the 1988 Third International Feminist Book Fair in Montréal, and her collaborative translation project, with Daphne

MARLATT. See special issue of *La Nouvelle barre du jour*, nos. 118–19, Nov. 1982; Barbara Godard in *Atlantis*, 9, 1984.

Brotherton, Mrs **Mary** Isabella Irwin (Rees), 1820–1910, English novelist, da. of John Melford R., Puisne Judge of the Calcutta Bench. She m. minor landscape painter Augustus Henry B. in Paris *c.* 1852–3, moving then to Rome, meeting the BROWNINGS, beginning to write stories and poems, and coping with her 'mad and tipsy and foolish' husband (Thackeray's description). She had known Thackeray's mother and stepfather in Devon as a girl and later knew his daughter, Anne Thackeray RITCHIE. She lived at Freshwater, Isle of Wight, where she knew Tennyson (and suggested to him the subject of his 'Rizpah'). Her first novel, *Arthur Brandon*, 1856, based on her Roman experiences, has sharply observed pictures of the British abroad but a sprawling plot, while *Respectable Sinners*, 1863, dedicated to her husband, has a very eighteenth-century flavour and a sub-Jane AUSTEN tone. Her poems, *Rosemary for Remembrance*, 1895, are mixed: some in stilted poetic diction, others more direct; 'The Mother's Story' is about a case of infanticide. Her health later declined and she stopped writing except for letters: Blanche WARRE-CORNISH called her 'One of the best letter-writers' ('Memories of Tennyson', *London Mercury*, V, 1921–2).

Broughton, Rhoda, 1840–1920, novelist, b. Denbigh, Wales, da. of Jane (Bennett) and the Revd Delves B. Brought up in Staffordshire, she was educ. by her father until 1863, after which she lived with her sisters, spending a long period in Oxford, where she became a notable character. Her admiration for A. T. RITCHIE first inspired her to write, and her first work, *Not Wisely but Too Well*, was pub. serially with the help of her uncle, Sheridan Le Fanu. It was then reissued together with the much more successful *Cometh Up as a Flower*, in 1867. She created in her bestsellers a new kind of heroine, tomboyish and plain-spoken, which her public at first adored, while critics (such as Margaret OLIPHANT) indignantly derided. But her work seemed less daring as woman's status improved, and she later commented: 'I began life as Zola and I finished it as Miss YONGE.' RB wrote 26 novels, notable for their witty, sometimes malicious, chronicle of 'county' life, and for their radical protest against marriage and women's economic oppression. She also wrote a fantasy story about precognition: *Behold, It Was a Dream*, 1873. Loyalty to Bentley's kept her from making more money, and her naturally succinct style was sorely tried by the tyranny of three-decker publication. Her later single-vol. works, such as *Mrs Bligh*, 1892, *Dear Faustine*, 1897, and *The Game and the Candle*, 1899, are often both more astringent and more sympathetic towards women. She was an important influence on younger writers: see Ethel ARNOLD's memoir, *Fortnightly* 108, 1920.

Broumas, Olga, poet and translator, b. in 1949 in Syros, Greece, da. of Claire (Pendell) and Nicholas B. She wrote poetry from an early age, spent the whole winter she was four reading *Jane Eyre* in Greek, and later studied mythology ('my earliest intimations of power and godliness'). In 1968, she migrated to the USA to study architecture, also an influence in her poetry, at the Univs. of Pennsylvania (BA 1970) and Oregon (MFA 1973), where she taught English and women's studies, 1972–6. She read Diane WAKOSKI and Louise BOGAN and was deeply influenced by Adrienne RICH. Her first book of poems, *Caritas*, appeared in 1976; her second, *Beginning with O*, 1977, was chosen by Stanley Kunitz for the Yale Younger Poets Award. Her political and feminist verse is powerfully revisionary: 'When I look at gods, fairy-tale figures, the raped women, the killed women, I feel them as lives I am possibly living. . .I don't speak for Artemis: I speak for the Artemis in myself.' She updates fairy tales and myths (as in 'Demeter', which famously salutes literary foremothers, 'Anne. Sylvia. Virginia. Adrienne'), explores the lesbian erotic and repeatedly asserts the political centrality of language: in a 'politics of transliteration ... we must find words / or burn'; 'speaking the truth as a lesbian feminist is a political art'. The milder *Pastoral Jazz*, 1983, treats family and love relationships. Among later volumes, *Black Holes, Black Stockings*, 1985, densely allusive, sensuous prose poems written jointly with poet Jane Miller, has been compared to the work of Monique WITTIG and Marie-Claire BLAIS, thought 'unlike anything' in American poetry. *Perpetua*, 1989, is a grave, moving volume much concerned with death and illness. Founder of Freehand, Inc., a community of women artists, OB lives in Provincetown, Mass. She translated Odyssesas Elytis's poems, *What I Love*, 1986. Interview in *Northwestern Review*, 18, 1980; see Er ka Duncan, *Unless Soul Clap its Hands*, 1984, and Adrien Oktenberg in *WRB*, April 1986.

Brown, Alice, 1857–1948, novelist, short-story writer, dramatist, b. Hampton Falls, NH, only da. of Elizabeth (Lucas) and Levi B., farmer. Graduating from Robinson Seminary, NH, in 1876, she became a schoolteacher, which she disliked. She moved to Boston, joining the literary group of Louise GUINEY. Her early collections of short stories and novels, including *Stratford-by-the-Sea*, 1884, *Meadow Grass*, 1895, and *Tiverton Tales*, 1899, vivid portraits of rural New England, are her best work, although her greatest popularity was during the first two decades of this century and some of her later work, such as *The Black Drop*, 1919, enters urban settings. In 1914, she won a $10,000 prize for her play *Children of Earth*, first produced in NYC. Its heroine, Mary Ellen, having spent years looking after her father, abandons her love for a former suitor and a married man, realizing 'I'm past lovin'.' The warm lyricism of AB's prose borders on verbosity, e.g.: 'here the wild rose lives and blooms, fed on manna brought by roving winds and fleeting sunlight, never unblest ...' (*Agnes Surriage*, 1894), but she is remarkable as a prolific writer whose career spanned 70 years. See article by S. A. Toth in *ALR*, 2 (Spring 1972) and life by P. Walker, 1974.

Brown, Anna (Gordon), 1747–1810, balladist, youngest da. of Thomas G., Aberdeen philosophy professor. Her mother was a Highlander; she learned most of her ballads by 11 years old, from an aunt (Mrs Farquhar), 'old women and maidservants'. She m. the Revd Dr B. and lived at Falkland. A major collector and transmitter, and a singer, she was also a poet (with baroque elements in her late style) who often feminized but seldom censored. MSS at Edinburgh Univ., Aldourie Castle, Inverness, and Harvard Univ.

Brown, Audrey Alexandra, poet and essayist. Born in 1904 and raised in Nanaimo, BC, da. of moderately wealthy Catholic parents, Rosa Elizabeth (Rumming) and Joseph Miller B., she attended convent school. Hailed as one of Canada's bright young poets, she developed a highly rhetorical, later romantic style. She has published five vols., of verse, among them *A Dryad in Nanaimo*, 1931 (new poems added in 1934), *Challenge to Time and Death*, 1943, and *All Fool's Day*, 1948. In the well-known 'Laodamia', she elaborately reconstructs the legends she loved. Her memoir, *The Log of a Lame Duck*, 1938, describes her treatment for rheumatic illness at a solarium on Malahat Beach. Silent during the second half of the century, in the 1930s and 1940s she published in *Canadian Poetry* and *Saturday Night*. She won the Canadian Women's Club Award, 1936, and addressed the Canadian Authors' Association, 1941 (publishing her comments as *Poetry and Life*, 1944). See L. A. Mackay in *Canadian Forum*, June 1932 (with her 'Record of a Pioneer', on her grandfather).

Brown, Beverley Elizabeth, poet, critic and painter, b. 1954 in Kingston, Jamaica, eldest da. of Rena and Roy B. Her musical mother was always an encouragement to her. Their house in Portland stimulated her poetry. She imagined the columns Doric, the rooms orange groves; 'forty steps at the back ... was Pluto's stairway.' She was educ. at Port Antonio Junior School, Kingston, and the Univ. of the West Indies (MA in English, 1977), where she began writing seriously. Poet and lecturer Mervyn Morris was an important influence, together with Edward Brathwaite: both have selected her work for anthologies. She published in John Hearne's *Arts Review*, and won bronze and silver medals in the National Festival, 1976. She taught English and history at Immaculate Conception and Kingston College, worked as painter and art-gallery adviser and writes regularly on the arts for the *Jamaica Daily News*. In the journal *Savacou* she published poems and scholarly articles (e.g. 'George Liele: Black Baptist and Pan-Africanist 1750–1826', 1975). Introducing *Dream Diary*, 1982, her first book of poems, EB mentions the importance to her of painting, classical architecture, literature and myth. She finds her 'greatest creative well' in 'the retrospective glance' and fills her poems with ghosts and memories. Sometimes the spectre seems an unnamed or other self: 'I sit and see / the double image / (dike-louper) / lover of strange things / and the pub at 7 o'clock / if only to discover / who are the two women / who stare back / from the crystal. ...'

Brown(e), Frances, 1816–79, poet, novelist, and children's writer, b. at Stranolar, Co. Donegal, seventh of village postmaster's 12 children. At 18 months FB had smallpox and lost her sight. Extraordinarily gifted, she struggled to educate herself vicariously through her siblings and began to write verse at seven. At 15 she discovered Pope's Homer and Byron's *Childe Harold*: she destroyed her own MSS in despair but began to write again in 1840, publishing first in the *Irish Penny Journal*, then the *Athenaeum*, whose editor (T. K. Hervey) greatly encouraged her. Her first vol. of poems, *The Star of Atteghei*, 1844, had a preface (by Hervey?) describing her character and circumstances, and it resulted in a literary pension (through Peel) of £20 a year. Probably its best poem is 'The Australian Emigrant': 'But why should WOMAN weep her land? / She has no portion there'. In 1847, with a younger sister as amanuensis, FB left Ireland 'which offered no encouragement to intellectual tastes' for Edinburgh, where she contributed stories and essays to *Fraser's*, *Chambers*, *Tait's*, *Leisure Hour* and others, in 1848 publishing *Lyrics and Miscellaneous Poems*. In 1852 she moved to London, where a gift of £100 from an admiring reader (the Marquess of Lansdowne) enabled her to write a novel, *My Share of the World*, 1861, the autobiography of a young (male) journalist, followed by *The Castleford Case*, 1862, and *The Hidden Sin* (anon.), 1866. She was granted a civil list pension of £100 a year in 1863. Her best-known children's book was *Granny's Wonderful Chair*, 1857; Frances Hodgson BURNETT was given this as a child, loved it, lost it and later retold it as 'Stories from the Lost Fairy Book', 1887. Promptly accused of plagiarism, she explained herself in a 1904 edition of *Granny's Wonderful Chair*. See 1844 preface, which draws on FB's own account of her education; introduction by Dollie Radford to the 1906 Everyman *GWC*.

Brown, Margaret Adeline (Porter), b. 1867, novelist. B. in western Ontario, da. of Margaret (McKee) and Richard P., she was educ. at Goderich High School and Toronto Normal School, then m. John Y. Brown, 1904. She began writing with newspaper and magazine sketches. Though she published *Life of Joseph Brant, Comprising in Part the Origin and History of the Iroquois or Six Nations Indians*, n.d., set in Ottawa during the last days of Sir John A. MacDonald's administration, she is best known for her political novel, *My Lady of the Snows*, 1908. Its central characters are cabinet ministers, senators and opposition party leaders, its society a wealthy élite. Despite living in a new country, characters speak of their centuries-old names and see themselves as born to govern. Most scenes entail political and philosophical discussion, with frequent references to Plato, Aristotle, Socrates and other classical writers as well as to Ruskin, Carlyle and other European thinkers and literary figures. The elegant protagonist enters this world of political power by means of her *salon* – 'Her politics are to her her life and religion, as they were to De STAEL' – and her romance with its complications is politically enmeshed.

Brown, Pamela, 'Pamela Cocabola Brown', poet and performer, b. 1948 in Seymour, Victoria, da. of Jeanette (Vinnicombe) and George B., army officer. Brought up by a great-aunt (who fostered her love of language) until seven, owing to her mother's TB, PB rejoined the family in many moves round Queensland bases, ending (like Janette Turner HOSPITAL) at Mitchelton High School, where she won the poetry prize. Involving herself in Vietnam War protest, she headed south at 20 and soon published the sassy *Sureblock*, 1972, first of nine poetry vols. Since then she has supported her writing by screenprinting, practising acupuncture, selling stamps and working at the Experimental Art Foundation, Adelaide, 1981–2. In 1989 she was playwright-in-residence at Sydney's Performance Space, following the production in 1988 of her co-written (with Jan McKemmish) *As Much Trouble as Talking*. Her *New and Selected Poems*, 1990, her first book since the poetic prose pieces of *Keep It Quiet*, 1987, updates her 1984 *Selected Poems*. Her earlier work celebrates the fragmentation of the self as speaking subject within an urban milieu, asserting a posture based on shared codes: 'all roads lead to album cover landscapes'; her recent work is more inward and contemplative.

Brown, Rita Mae, novelist, poet, activist, b. 1944 at Hanover, Penna., adopted da. of working-class Julia (Buckingham) and Ralph B., who took her to Florida at 11. She was educ. at the Univ. of Florida, NY Univ. (BA 1968, after being near starvation in 1965), and NY School of Visual Arts (certificate in cinematography, 1968). That year she brought up the issue of lesbian rights with her local chapter of NOW; in 1970 she co-authored *The Woman-Identified Woman*. She attended the Institute for Policy Studies, Washington, 1972–3, and became famous with the semi-autobiographical *Rubyfruit Jungle*, 1973 (at first rejected by publishers), joyously irresponsible lesbian erotics. Gloria STEINEM called it a 'good and true account of growing up un-American in America. For once a woman has been honest and vulgar and political and funny enough to write about her real life.' In her poetry (*The Hand that Cradles the Rock*, 1971, *Songs to a Handsome Woman*, 1973, *Poems*, 1987), RMB makes political points, contrasting an 'army of lovers' (in 'Sappho's Reply') with unwed pregnant women 'like / Dumb cargo ships . . . / Eyeless as their unborn'. *A Plain Brown Rapper*, 1976, a highly personal view of the feminist movement over ten years (its title and cover mockingly hinting at pornographic content), opens with SAPPHO, celebrates poor, lesbian and minority women, and is hard on stars and the well-dressed. RMB's stories include one of a 4-ft female snake in Lyn Lifshin, ed., *Ariadne's Thread*, 1982. Of later novels, *Southern Discomfort*, 1982, centres on an improbable love-affair between a white matron and black teenager in segregated Montgomery; *Sudden Death*, 1983, about the money-corrupted world of professional women's tennis, stems from a promise made to dying sports-writer Judy Lacy and from RMB's relationship with champion Martina Navratilova. *High Hearts*, 1986 (a researched, but anachronistic and fable-like 'feminist *Gone With the Wind*'), features a young Southern woman riding in the Confederate cavalry in male dress with her husband. RMB is not attentive to the texture of the past. She has written screenplays (including one for *Rubyfruit Jungle*) and TV scripts; her various teaching posts (beginning at Federal City College, Washington, DC), include the Women's Writing Center in Cazenovia, NY; she is a member of the National Gay Task Force. See Leslie Fishbein in *IJWS*, 7, 1984.

Brown, Rosellen, poet and fiction-writer, b. 1939 at Philadelphia, da. of Blossom (Lieberman) and David H. B. After a BA at Barnard College, NYC, in 1960 and MA at Brandeis Univ. in 1962, she m. Marvin Hoffman, had two children, and embarked on 'the profound and guilt-producing self-gratification of writing'. Her first book, *Some Deaths in the Delta*, 1970 (poems on Mississippi and Brooklyn), was largely written while teaching at Tougaloo College, Miss., during the civil rights movement and the babyhood of her first daughter (now a recently-launched novelist); she calls the poems 'a bill of damages' of the cost 'of living in perpetual opposition'. The stories in *Street Games*, 1974, also evoke the Brooklyn of 'hopeful yellow and green paint jobs over sour barnacled soot', 'unfresh ladies sunk in support stockings'. *The Autobiography of My Mother*, 1976, is a hard-hitting novel about an incompatible mother (left-wing campaigning lawyer who sees her apprentices as her children) and sexually laid-back daughter; each thinks the other's life all wrong. RB has been blamed for the ending of shock and despair; she says, 'I write my nightmares.' She likes best her *Cora Fry*, 1977, short poems in the person of a rural NH woman: children, parents, marital friction, domestic life against a background of snow and seasons. *Tender Mercies*, 1978, and *Civil Wars*, 1984, present exceptional pain: a husband who has made his wife a paraplegic in an accident leaves home, then reassumes his care of her; a liberal wife settled in the South in the 1960s departs reluctantly from the battle zone after witnessing the hysterical suffering of her bigoted 13-year-old niece (whose diary is a *tour de force*). RB has taught creative writing; living in NYC, Miss., Boston, San Francisco and NH, she often feels an outsider. A new novel will depict a fictional, silenced, Russian immigrant great-grandmother. See *WRB*, July 1989.

Browne, Martha (Griffith), d. 1906, novelist, poet, abolitionist, da. of Martha (Young) and Thomas G., slave owners. MGB freed her slaves and helped them establish themselves as free persons. She moved to Boston in 1860 and wrote for Boston and NYC anti-slavery publications. She also took part in William Lloyd Garrison's American Anti-Slavery Society. MGB's main work was her fictional *Autobiography of a Female Slave*, pub. anonymously in 1857. Despite a melodramatic plot, it is a serious attempt to redress the balance of representation of women in SLAVE NARRATIVES. In her depiction of the Yankee schoolmistress, tutor to the cruel slave-owner's daughters, MGB condemns the hypocrisy of women opposed to slavery who cannot find the courage to speak against it. MGB's *Poems*, 1853, pub. under the name 'Mattie Griffith', includes some unsuccessful attempts at the romantic genre of blank-verse meditation, influenced by Wordsworth and Coleridge. However, some of her lyrics of disappointed love such as 'The Deserted' and 'Thou Lovest Me No More', although somewhat clichéd are still powerfully expressive.

Browning, Elizabeth (Barrett) (Moulton-Barrett), 1806–61, poet, b. at Coxhoe Hall, Co. Durham, eldest of 12 children of Mary (Graham-Clarke) and Edward M-B., a Jamaican landowner. In 1809 the family moved to Hope End in Herefordshire. As a child, EBB was a precocious scholar, sharing, at her own request, her brother's lessons and overtaking him in Greek and

Latin; her later self-directed study included Hebrew. Her mother encouraged her literary efforts, copying out her poems, recognizing an anon. pub. poem as her daughter's (1824) and expressing pride in seeing her launched 'on the world as Authoress' (1825). She was also tolerant of (though unsympathetic to) EBB's early conversion to the principles of Mary WOLLSTONECRAFT. An illness in her teens (still not convincingly diagnosed) meant that EBB came to be regarded as 'delicate' and lived most of her life as a semi-invalid. Her mother's death in 1828, her father's jealous seclusion of the family, the sudden removal (owing to the loss of fortune) from her childhood home in 1832 and the deaths of two brothers in 1840 confirmed her physical debilitation and dependent emotional life. Yet she went on studying and writing with commitment and confidence; only writing, she said, made her feel 'alive'. Her earliest works, *The Battle of Marathon* (priv. pr.) 1820, and *An Essay on Mind*, 1826, are imitative epics. But with *The Seraphim*, 1838, her work matured – even the apparently innocuous 'Romaunts', ballads, and narrative poems of the 1830s, often written to order for ANNUALS such as *The Keepsake* or *Finden's Tableaux*, have recently been reassessed as subversive texts challenging feminine stereotypes. 'A Drama of Exile', 1844, self-consciously revises Milton to offer an explicitly female perspective on Eve. Her *Poems*, 1844, established her fame and led, indirectly, to her now well-known correspondence with, meeting and eventual marriage to Robert Browning (1846, one son b. 1849). In Italy, where they settled, she produced her finest works: *Poems*, 1850, *Casa Guidi Windows*, 1851, *Aurora Leigh*, 1856 (post-dated 1857; repr. 1978, with important intro. by Cora Kaplan), *Poems before Congress*, 1860, and posthumous *Last Poems*, 1861. Political and didactic, these works emphasized the right of a woman to speak and to act, in world affairs as in her private existence. Her best-known work, *Sonnets from the Portuguese*, 1850, while embodying a popular ideal of the loving woman, also revises (like Mary WROTH) the sonnet tradition of male poet and silent mistress. Her important, experimental first-person verse-novel, *Aurora Leigh*, offers discerning analysis of poetic theory and forceful criticism of contemporary morality and convention. In her friendships with other women writers (M. R. MITFORD, Anna JAMESON, Margaret FULLER, Matilda HAYS, Isa BLAGDEN, Eliza OGILVY), she maintained a private support network. Her work (especially *Aurora Leigh*) was admired by George ELIOT, Emily DICKINSON, Elizabeth GASKELL, Dinah M. CRAIK, Alice MEYNELL and Virginia WOOLF. Blake Taplin Gardner's 1957 life has not been superseded by Margaret Forster's, 1988. See Philip Kelley and Ronald Hudson's ed. of EBB's diary, 1969, and corresp. with RB, 1984–. Recent critical studies include Angela Leighton's, 1986; Helen Cooper's, 1988.

Bruce, Mary Grant, 1878–1958, Australian journalist and children's novelist, b. near Sale, Victoria, da. of Mary (Whittakers) and Eyre Lewis B., surveyor. She attended a Ladies' High School in Sale, where she edited the school magazine. Three times winner of the Melbourne Shakespeare Society's essay competition, she worked for over ten years in Melbourne, editing the children's page of the *Leader* and contributing to many other newspapers and magazines. In 1913 she went to London where she worked for the *Daily Mail* and m. a distant cousin, Major George B; subsequently she lived in Ireland, England, Europe and Australia. She pub. 37 children's novels, a book of Aboriginal legends, *The Stone Age of Burkamukki*, 1922, and a collection of radio talks, *The Power Within*, 1940, but is best known for her 'Billabong' books, beginning with *A Little Bush Maid*, 1910, and concluding with the fifteenth title, *Billabong Riders*, 1942. Her work has sold some two million copies, and the Billabong characters, Jim and Norah Linton, have passed into Australian bush mythology. Though some of her early journalism is feminist in tone, her novels uphold conventional gender roles and sexist attitudes (Brenda Niall's *Seven Little Billabongs*, 1979, compares her fiction with Ethel TURNER's). For her life see *Billabong's Author*, by Alison Alexander, 1979; her papers are in the LaTrobe Library, Melbourne.

Brunton, Mary (Balfour), 1778–1818, novelist. Da. of Frances (Ligonier) and army officer Thomas Balfour, she was b. on Barra, Orkney, which no doubt coloured her view of the sublime effects of solitude. Only spasmodically educ., she picked up French, Italian and music. She m., *c.* 1798, the Revd Alexander Brunton. They studied history and philosophy together, living at Edinburgh from 1803 and visiting London and south-west England in 1815. She dedicated the anonymous *Self-Control*, 1811 (repr. 1974, 1986), to Joanna BAILLIE: its heroine as a child covets Christian martyrdom, later struggles to earn money to support her aged father and suffers persecution culminating in escape by canoe from wilderness confinement near Québec. The Canadian scenes are a weakness among many strengths: Ellen Moers remarked critics' reluctance to accept Jane AUSTEN's debt to this work. *Discipline*, 1814 (repr. 1987), has a spoilt heroine who must be taught virtue by fearful misfortunes. *Emmeline*, unfinished, was to begin a series of domestic novels; it metes out savage social retribution to a well-meaning woman who has left a loveless marriage to wed again. MB's death in childbirth is movingly described in a letter by Anne GRANT; her husband pub. *Emmeline*, letters and other pieces (intelligent novel criticism from a didactic standpoint), with a life, 1819. See Sarah W. R. Smith in Mary Anne Schofield and Cecilia Macheski, 1986. Anna Ross, later B., who wrote or adapted *The Cottagers*, 1788, is no connection.

Bryan, Margaret, London science writer. A widow and schoolmistress, she based her books on lectures and experiments for her pupils and declared: 'I rejoice in the titles of Parent and Preceptress.' She adapted scientific learning for women and for children in *A Compendious System of Astronomy*, 1797; *Lectures on Natural Philosophy*, 1806 (praised by the *Critical Review* for 'spirit, copiousness, and ingenuity'); and *A Comprehensive Astronomical and Geographical Class Book*, 1815. In a frontispiece she sits with two daughters, pen in hand and surrounded by scientific instruments. Subscription lists for her books include many women (e.g. the aged Elizabeth CARTER) and reflect high female interest in science.

Bryan, Mary, poet, from Sedgemoor, Somerset, wife of Edward B., Bristol printer and bookseller. Her preface to *Sonnets and Metrical Tales*, Bristol, 1815, pub. as a widow with six children, writhes between expression and suppression: fearing blame for 'vanity and presumption', obliquely hinting at ambition and citing Charlotte SMITH, she rejects the usual claim to pity: 'superciliousness under the mask of compassion' is 'most humiliating towards its object'. She says she wrote many poems to her husband during separations early in her marriage; when circumstances changed he laid on her writing a total, painful prohibition which she claims to find wise and proper. She suffered financial calamity, his physical and mental collapse and death, and her own ill health; yet her 'amazed and delighted mind' was 'almost engrossed' in contemporary literature. Her poems are unusual: mostly plaintive, deliberately simple yet sometimes obscure, with some boldly irregular sonnets and blank verse. She writes discriminating praise of Wordsworth, and protest at a painting of military victory: 'Oh that gashed head! – I am the mother whose / Breast did pillow it!' Other topics are death, madness, rejected love, seduced innocence and remembered childhood. She abandoned another work of which some individuals might have disapproved. She ran the printing firm, 1815–24.

Bryan, Mary (Edwards), 1838?–1913, journalist, novelist and poet, b. Jefferson County, Fla., da. of Louise Crutchfield (Houghton) and Major John E., planter and member of the Florida legislature. MEB was educ. by her mother and at the Fletcher Institute in Georgia, and continued studying after her marriage to Iredell E. B. in 1854. She left her husband after one year, although the two eventually resumed living together. MEB began her journalistic career in 1858, contributing to the *Georgia Literary and Temperance Crusader* and becoming literary editor in 1859. Her essay 'How Should Women Write?', 1860, claims that men have restricted women by telling them how to write and what to write about and urges women to extend the 'influence of letters' and to write 'honestly and without fear'. Having lost the plantation after the war, the family moved to Natchitoches, Louisiana; in 1866 MEB became editor of its *Tri-Weekly* and (1874–84) of the *Sunny South* in Atlanta. In 1879 she pub. *Manch*, a successful first novel, which was subsequently both pirated and dramatized. Over 20 novels followed, including *The Bayou Bride*, 1886, *My Own Sin: A Story of Life in New York*, 1888, and *His Legal Wife*, 1894. *Poems and Stories in Verse* appeared in 1895. MEB's novels have conventional plots, although they contain some sharp political observation. Her career as a novelist was secondary to her prowess as an editor, which earned her a respectable living and reputation.

'Bryher', Annie Winnifred Ellerman, 1894–1983, poet, novelist, autobiographer, patron of the arts. B. at Margate, Kent, da. of Hannah (Glover) and Sir John E., a wealthy businessman, she later renamed herself after one of the Scilly Isles. She travelled extensively as a child but received no formal schooling until she went to Queenswood School, Eastbourne, at 15. Her first novel, *Development*, 1920, traces her psychological and literary maturation from an 'epic childhood' nurtured on *The Boy's Odyssey* to an adolescent's discovery of *vers libre* after several intervening years of intellectual confinement in an Edwardian girls' school. *Two Selves*, printed by Robert McAlmon's Contact Press along with Mina LOY's *Lunar Baedecker*, 1923, brings its heroine together with an H. D.–like poet. Though dedicated to such writers as H. D., COLETTE and Dorothy RICHARDSON, and author of *Amy LOWELL: A Critical Appreciation*, 1918, B in her own writing usually fails to question or subvert gender conventions. *Civilians*, 1927, an exception, presents a materialist feminist perspective on B's experience of British women's home labour during WWI. To escape her Victorian family, B contracted two marriages of convenience. The first, to Robert McAlmon, 1921, led her into the Parisian avant-garde and to her acquaintance with Gertrude STEIN, Natalie BARNEY and life-long friend Sylvia BEACH. With her second husband, Kenneth MacPherson (m. 1927), she started the first avant-garde English-language film periodical, *Close up*. Financially instrumental in bringing cinematography and psychoanalysis to Britain (she helped to found the *Psychoanalytic Review*), B also supported Anglo-French literary connections during WWII by contributing to the production of *Life and Letters Today*. Her autobiographies, *The Heart to Artemis*, 1962, and *The Days of Mars, 1940–1946*, 1972, describe her enduring literary and passionate attachment to H. D., to whose daughter, Perdita MacPherson, she was adoptive mother. See Noel Riley-Fitch, *Sylvia Beach and the Lost Generation*, 1983, Benstock, 1986, and Hanscombe and Smyers, 1987. Papers at Yale Univ.

Buck, Pearl Comfort (Sydenstricker), 'John Sedges', 1892–1973, novelist and biographer, first woman Nobel prizewinner for literature. B. in Hillsboro, W. Va, da. of missionaries Caroline (Stulting) and Absolom S., she was raised in China, becoming 'mentally bifocal', as she tells in *My Several Worlds*, 1954. Graduating from Randolph-Macon Woman's College, Va, in

1914, she returned to China and, in 1917, m. John Lossing B., a US agriculture expert. Their daughter, born in 1920, was mentally retarded. Back in the USA to begin an MA in Cornell in 1924, PB won the $200 Messenger Prize for an essay, 'China and the West', and adopted another child. In China again, she taught at Southeastern, 1925–7, Chung Yang, 1928–30, and Nanking, 1921–31, Univs. Her first book perished in Nanking's uprising in 1927; *East Wind: West Wind*, 1930, did well; *The Good Earth*, 1931, transformed her life. The first sympathetic, realistic portrayal in Western literature of a Chinese peasant family, it won the Pulitzer Prize, headed bestseller lists and inspired a Broadway play, 1932, and an award-winning film, 1937. Two sequels made a trilogy, *House of Earth*, 1935. *The Mother*, 1934, broke taboos with vivid childbirth and abortion scenes. PB also translated the Chinese classic *Shui Hu Chuan*, 1933, and wrote companion lives of her parents, *The Exile* and *Fighting Angel*, both 1936. Divorced, she m. her publisher, Richard Walsh, in 1935 and settled in the USA, issuing up to five books annually (some for juveniles) to support her children (eight adopted). These included *This Proud Heart*, 1938, based on her own conflict between work and marriage. The Nobel Prize, 1938, honouring her portrayals of China (and ungenerous response from intellectual critics), encouraged her to write, like Chinese novelists, for the masses. During WWII she supplied data for servicemen's guidebooks to Asia, wrote radio plays broadcast in China and publicized the war there in three novels (*Dragon Seed*, 1942, is the best known). Her essays, like *Of Men and Women*, 1941, and *American Unity and Asia*, 1942, prophesied that white imperialist, racist and sexist attitudes would damage both the Allied struggle and any future peace. Novels on inter-racial topics, like *Pavilion of Women*, 1946, and *The Hidden Flower*, 1952, continued to sell widely, as did those set in the USA, like *The Townsman*, 1945 (one of five books as 'John Sedges'), *The Child Who Never Grew*, 1950 (a moving account of her daughter's life), and *Command the Morning*, 1959 (about research for the atom bomb). In 1949 she founded the Welcome House, an adoption agency for Asian Americans, and in 1964 The Pearl S. Buck Foundation, to assist fatherless half-American children in Asia. She died of lung cancer, leaving over 25 MSS (now at the Foundation, Hillsboro, W.Va.), some since pub., like the poems in *Words of Love*, 1974. Other papers at Randolph-Macon Woman's College. See life by Theodore F. Harris, 1969; Lucille S. Zinn in *Bulletin of Bibliog.*, 36, 1929.

Buckmaster, Henrietta Henkle (Stephens), 1909–83, novelist and children's writer. B. in Cleveland, Ohio, da. of Pearl (Wintermute) and newspaper editor Rae S., she was educ. in NYC, at Friends Seminary and Brearly School, and in Europe. She published her first story at 12 and by 18 was writing book reviews for the *New York Times*. *Tomorrow is Another Day*, 1934, her first, autobiographical novel, is about Rebecca Starr, a novelist's daughter who goes to NYC to find herself as a writer. Other work addresses oppression. *Deep River*, 1944, set in Georgia in the 1850s, reaches back to her family's past as non-slaveholders in conflict with plantation slave owners. This, and her earlier historical study, *Let My People Go: The Story of the Underground Railroad and the Growth of the Abolition Movement*, 1941 (*Out of the House of Bondage*, 1943, in Britain), won her a Guggenheim Fellowship, 1944. (She also wrote, for children, *Flight to Freedom: The Story of the Underground Railroad*, 1958.) At the end of WWII, she travelled to Germany to write on concentration-camp survivors. *Bread from Heaven*, 1952, written after her return, is about two survivors of the Treblinka camp. Its narrative traces the working through of reactions of prejudice, self-doubt and self-questioning touched off by their arrival in a US village. HB's writing comes 'out of questions: how and why people *are*, individually, collectively, in terms of their own self-concepts, in terms of social change.' Much of her fiction is based on biography: on St Paul (*Walk in Love*, 1956), of whom she later wrote a life, 1965, and Shakespeare (*All the Living*, 1962). *Fire in the Heart*, 1948, based on actress Fanny KEMBLE's marriage to wealthy slaveholder Pierce Butler, shows her zeal for emancipation. *Women Who Shaped History*, 1966, for younger readers, underscores the idealism and courage of US women who challenged convention to contribute to the nineteenth-century struggle for human justice: Dorothy Dix, Prudence Crandall, Elizabeth Cady STANTON, Elizabeth Blackwell, Harriet Tubman, Mary Baker EDDY. (She also wrote for younger readers about *Rebel Congressmen*, 1971.) *The Lion in the Stone*, 1968, turns to the politics of world peace: like *The Walking Trip*, 1972, it presses a claim for international solutions to the problems of oppressed minorities and nations. From 1973, HB was literary editor of the *Christian Science Monitor*.

'Buckrose, J. E.', Annie Edith (Foster) Jameson, 1868–1931, novelist and magazine contributor. B. in Hull, Yorks., educ. there and at Dresden in Germany, she m. Robert Falconer J., Yorks. timber merchant. Her more than 40 novels and short-story collections are mostly set in Yorks. Paeans to, and victims of, stolid middle-class family values, they nevertheless question conventional attitudes towards women. *The Silent Legion* [1918] propagandistically praises middle-class stoicism in WWI but features as a minor figure an 'odd' (because bright) young girl who resists the traditional female role. Such a figure is seen also in *The Round-About* [1916] and *Young Hearts*, 1920: each novel suggests that social change must affect beliefs about women as well as class. The questioning female who disturbs the status quo becomes central in the sprightly *Because of Jane*, 1913, and the lighter *Susan in Charge*, 1924. A sympathetic fictional life of George ELIOT [1931] is JEB's most mature depiction of the problems faced by intelligent women.

Bulstrode, Cicely, 1584–1609, 'news'-writer. Da. of Cecily (Croke) and Edward B. of Hedgerley Bulstrode, Bucks.; lady-in-waiting to James I's queen, she was the centre of a circle (including Lady SOUTHWELL and Lady Anne CLIFFORD) which produced the writing repr. 1968 as by Sir Thomas Overbury and his friends, ed. James E. Savage: witty social comment turning largely on the nature of good and bad women, defined in terms of value to men. The second impression, 1614, names her as author of the moral 'Newes of my Morning worke'; other pieces may be hers too. Ben Jonson savaged her intellect and sexual morals in 'An Epigram on the Court Pucell'; after her death he (and John Donne) eulogized both.

Bunbury, Selina, 1802–82, Irish writer, mainly for older children, often confused with Selina Burbury, author of *Florence Sackville, or Self-Dependence*, 1851 (e.g. by Allibone; also LCC). B. probably in Kilsaran House, Louth, one of 15 children of Rev. Henry B., she lived at Beaulieu, writing prolifically for 50 years, often pub. by the SPCK. Some sources give her father's bankruptcy as reason for the family's move to Dublin in 1819, where SB taught primary school. Later she kept house for her twin brother in Liverpool. *Early Recollections*, 1825, dedicated 'to Christian Parents', is a stilted tale about the importance of Eustace's early moral training; but *Our Own Story*, 1856, is a lively first-person narrative by a girl, who, given the same education as her twin brother, grows up to be a writer. When her fiancé forbids writing after marriage, she says: '"Then I must get my book edited, if I can have no name."' SB's most successful work was *Coombe Abbey: an Historical Tale of the Days of James Ist* (Dublin, 1843). After the death of her parents (or her brother's marriage, 1845) she travelled widely in

Europe, recording her wanderings in many vols. Some were fictionalized: *Evelyn: or, the Maiden's Secret*, 1851, is a traveller's tale showing a strong consciousness of female oppression and a real love and respect for women. SB wrote at least 30 novels and travel books, many reaching several editions.

Bunn, Anna Maria (Murray), 1808–89, novelist, b. Balliston, Ireland, only da. of Ellen (Fitzgerald) and Terence M., army officer. Following her mother's death in 1814, she was sent to the Ursuline Convent, Cork, and later attended a private school in Limerick. She arrived in Sydney with her father and brother in 1827 and the following year m. George B., shipowner and whaler. After his death in 1834 she wrote *The Guardian*, 1838, the first novel to be printed on the mainland of Australia and the first by a woman to be written and printed in Australia. Originally pub. as by 'An Australian', its author's identity was not established until 1968. Though set in Ireland, *The Guardian* includes many passing references to Australia and is a delightful mix of genres, being by turn a novel in letters, a novel of manners and a gothic tale. See Gwendoline Wilson, *Murray of Yarralumla*, 1968, and S. McKernan in D. Adelaide, *A Bright and Fiery Troop*, 1988.

Burch, Dorothy, pamphleteer. A married woman of Stroud, Kent, she found herself and friends rejected by her local clergyman as 'poore, ignorant simple people', and published – unwillingly, she says, but 'to vindicate the honour of God', to help her fellow believers rebut criticism and to do good to her children – *A Catechisme of the severall Heads of Christian Religion*, 1646. It gives a strict Calvinist account of the nature of God, the Creation, Fall, selection of the Elect, and the Crucifixion, all supported from scripture.

Burges, Mary Anne, 1763–1813, polymath. Much youngest child of Anne (Somerville) and George B., she was b. at Edinburgh and learned ancient and modern languages, geology (editing work by J. A. De Luc), biology (writing and illustrating an unpub. account of British lepidoptera) and music (composing, performing). Living in Devon, she pub. anonynously the highly-successful *Progress of the Pilgrim Good-Intent, in Jacobinical Times*, 1800 (13 eds., British and USA, in two years). Her hero, great-great-grandson of Bunyan's Christian and Christiana, follows the Bunyan trail and encounters radical figures like Lord Love-Change, Mr Hate-Controul, Mr Philosophy and Mr Cosmopolitan. Her brother Sir James Bland B. (later Lamb) revealed her authorship after her death. She has been confused with his third wife, Margaret Ann, sister of Lady Anne BARNARD.

Burke, Anne, governess, who pub. eight novels at London, 1785–1805, with inflated prose and melodramatic action. The heroine of the epistolary *Eleanora: from the Sorrows of Werter*, 1785, turns to religion on her lover's suicide, and begs forgiveness for him. That of *Ela, or The Delusions of the Heart*, 1787, sees herself as a disciple of Rousseau, rejects a faithful suitor for a ne'er-do-well and dies still full of masochistic love: this had several English and US eds., and perhaps influenced Ann RADCLIFFE's *Romance of the Forest*. In *Emilia de St Aubigne*, 1788, hero and heroine are driven to death by a cruel father and uncle. Later works, too, blend sensationalism and sensibility. Between 1795 and 1799 (a widow nursing her son through smallpox in a shared room, borrowing clothes but hoping to set up a school) AB applied three times, humbly, to the RLF; she received 15 guineas in all before her claim was listed as 'questionable', 1806. The witty and stylish comic opera *A Ward of the Castle* (Covent Garden, 1793), by 'Miss Burke', is not hers.

'Burke, Barbara', Oona Howard Ball (Butlin), *c.* 1860–1941, author, of whom little is known. She lived her adult life in Oxford, after marrying (*c.* 1892) the

Oxford don and Fabian Sydney Ball, whom she met at country-house theatricals. An anti-feminist, she pub. *Barbara Goes to Oxford*, 1907, in which the heroine ends by marrying a don. In fact, it is really a guidebook to Oxford ways for the prospective don's wife. Her *Domestic Rhymes* by O. H. B., 1909, are jolly pieces on housewifely topics, designed 'to keep the feminine mind fixed' on proper subjects 'for the comfort of man'. She produced a vol. of memorial tributes to her husband, 1923, and a book on Dalmatia in 1932. She d. in Dubrovnik.

Burke, Colleen, poet, biographer, b. 1943 in Sydney, NSW, da. of Meryl (Glaister) and Francis Patrick B. Initially trained as a stenographer, she later received a BA, 1974, from the Univ. of Sydney. As a community worker she has run workshops on subjects from women writers to folk music. CB is the mother of a son and da., the inspiration for some of her best (refreshingly unsentimental) poetry. Her four vols. of poetry, *Go Down Singing*, 1974, *Hags, Rags and Scriptures*, 1977 (with L. Roche and N. Phillips), *The Incurable Romantic*, 1979, and *She Moves Mountains*, 1984, contain mostly brief, witty and conversational verses expressing ambivalent pleasures in motherhood, domesticity and suburban life. Within the poet's hazardous inner-city world ('In Newtown ... there is lead in the air') adult relationships are usually painful, but children, who seem independent, sagacious entities, are an endless source of amazement. CB has also written a sympathetic biography of the unjustly neglected poet Marie E. J. PITT, entitled *Doherty's Corner*, 1985.

Burkholder, Mabel Grace, 1881–1973, Canadian writer of fiction, poetry, local history and drama, descendant of a German settler in Pennsylvania who came to Ontario as a loyalist, da. of Peter B. and his second wife Dinah Ann (Street). B. at Mt Hamilton, Ont., she obtained a first-class teaching certificate from Hamilton Central Collegiate Institute. She did not marry, though she was proposed to weekly for seven weeks running on a visit to northern BC. She taught for two years, contributed poems and prose to many Canadian and American periodicals, and turned her hand to many genres in separate publications. Her fiction includes *The Course of Impatience Carningham*, 1911, a study of the problems of industrialization and the exploitation of young women in factories. She discussed strike action in a pamphlet and re-told Indian legends in *Before the White Man Came*, both 1923. Several of her short religious dramas or pageants were staged at Mt Hamilton and printed in the 1920s. Her historical works include biographies for schools, a life of the early Canadian newspaperwoman Kathleen COLEMAN, and accounts of Hamilton, 1938, and of its area, one in 1956. *Out of the Storied Past*, 1969, collects her weekly Hamilton *Spectator* articles on local history. See William F. E. Morley in *Douglas Library Notes* 20, 1971. Papers at Queen's Univ., Kingston, Ont.

Burnet, Elizabeth (Blake), also Berkeley, 1661–1709, religious writer and diarist. Eldest da. of Elizabeth (Bathurst) and Sir Richard Blake, she studied philosophy and geometry, and criticized religious books at 11. In 1678 she m. Robert Berkeley (d. 1693); they spent James II's reign abroad. As a charitable widow she was called the most 'considerable Woman in England'. Her *Method of Devotion*, drafted at 22 or 23 but revised and expanded for anonymous publication in 1708, is pious but down-to-earth: of 'those unhappy and wretched Women whose Beauty is set to Sale' she adds '(tho' at a miserable Price)'. In 1700 she became third wife of Gilbert Burnet, Scots historian and churchman, taking on five stepchildren (her own two died as infants). Her MSS (Bodleian Library, Oxford) include a Protestant-Catholic dialogue, 1688, discussion of marriage, 1700, and of the need for personal 'litle rooms or closets' for private thinking in a crowded household, and part of her lifelong diary: comments on European travel, 1707, reflect her wide intellectual interests. She was a friend of Sarah Duchess of MARLBOROUGH and John Locke, with whom she exchanged (self-doubtingly) views on writings and to whom she introduced Catharine TROTTER. Her *Method*, second ed., 1709, has her name and a memoir largely by her husband. See C. Kirchberger in *Church Quarterly Review*, 148, 1949.

Burnett, Frances Eliza (**Hodgson**), 1849–1924, novelist, short-story writer and playwright, b. Cheetham Hill, Manchester, da. of Eliza (Boond) and Edwin H., who d. when she was six. She was educ. at a neighbourhood dame school. In 1865 the family emigrated to Tennessee, and in 1868 her first story, 'Miss Carruthers', was pub. in *Godey's Lady's Book*. Because she wrote in Lancashire dialect, editors were slow to accept her work, but by 1872 she was contributing regularly to *Peterson's Ladies' Magazine* and *Scribner's*, in which her first novel, *That Lass o' Lowrie's*, was serialized, 1876–7. In 1873 she m. Dr Swan Moses B. *Louisiana*, 1880, was her first novel set in the USA, and by 1883 she was held to be in the 'front rank' of US writers. Her most famous novel, *Little Lord Fauntleroy*, 1886, set a fashion for the clothes worn by the young hero (based on her son Vivian), particularly after it was made into a play. Financially comfortable, she travelled often between England and the USA while producing a novel and a volume of short stories almost yearly between 1880 and 1922. Although Phyllis Bixler (1984) has noted feminist themes in *A Lady of Quality*, 1896, the heroine, Clorina Wildairs, is an exception to the independent woman of previous stories: Joan Lowrie (*That Lass o' Lowrie's*); Christian Murdoch (*Haworth's*, 1879); Sara Crewe (*Sara Crewe*, 1888). FHB always emphasized 'happiness' for women protagonists, much as she depicted the perfect child in *Fauntleroy*. In 1898 she divorced, and in 1900 m. Stephen Townsend, her English protégé and a physician, but she divorced him after one year, describing their break-up in *The Shuttle*, 1907. In 1910 she pub. *The Secret Garden*, a novel intended for adults but now a children's classic. Her autobiographical memoir, *The One I Knew Best of All*, 1893, deals with her first 18 years. Her son Vivian's biography of her, *The Romantick Lady*, 1927, quotes from many of her letters. Ann Thwaite's life, 1974, contains a bibliog. Study by Marghanita LASKI, 1950.

Burney, Frances 'Fanny' (later D'Arblay), 1752–1840, diarist, novelist, letter writer. Da. of Esther (Sleepe), who d. in 1762, and Charles B., music historian, she grew up in King's Lynn, Norfolk, and London, 'the Old Lady' among siblings and stepsiblings, mixing (not quite equally) with high society. At 15 she burned her 'Elegies, Odes, Plays, Songs, Stories, Farces, – nay, Tragedies and Epic Poems'; next year she began the DIARY pub. 1889, addressed with witty flourish to a female Nobody. Secrecy later gives way to social letter-journals: her sisters Esther, Susan and Charlotte all at times rival her in expressiveness (see catalogue by Joyce Hemlow, 1971). *Evelina*, 1778, sequel to the early 'Caroline Evelyn' (destroyed), was copied by night in a disguised hand, since publishers knew her scribal work for her father. Its immediate success, and the end of anonymity, delighted and alarmed her: 'I would a thousand times rather forfeit my character as a writer, than risk ridicule and censure as a female.' Evelina's story moves between the comic agony of social embarrassment and the romance longing for acceptance by an unjustly rejecting father. Friendship with the future Hester PIOZZI and her circle proved pure gold for FB's diary; but an irreverent comedy about BLUESTOCKINGS, *The Witlings*, was dropped under paternal pressure. *Cecilia*, 1782, centres on an heiress who is to keep her name on marriage, who desires moral independence but refuses full self-determination. (Her incompatible guardians stem from

Susanna CENTLIVRE's *Bold Stroke*.) In 1786 FB was appointed second Keeper of the Robes to Queen Charlotte; it took her five years to summon courage to confess that the court etiquette (which she fascinatingly describes) was stifling her and to arrange her resignation. Her marriage, at 41, to the aristocratic, penniless French Catholic refugee Alexandre D'Arblay, took another assertion of will. She bore a son, 1794, and earned £2000 from subscribers to *Camilla*, 1796, whose mentor-hero nearly kills the heroine by constant accusation before realizing her essential goodness. In France in 1802, seeking restitution for confiscated D'Arblay estates, she was caught by war and lived there ten years: her letters report history as well as an unanaesthetized mastectomy, 1811. *The Wanderer, or Female Difficulties* (begun by 1800, pub. 1814) again treats the unguided hiatus between father and husband: Juliet's very perfections block all possible ways of earning money. FB endured the deaths of her sisters, husband, 1818, and son, 1837, pub. *Memoirs* of her father, 1832, and battled editorially with seas of family papers: her last letters remain valiant and humorous. All her novels have modern eds. Of her four tragedies (written at Court) and four comedies (written after *Camilla*), only *Edwy and Elgiva* was staged, 1795 (and failed); Tara Ghoshal ed. *A Busy Day*, 1984; others in Berg Coll., NYPL. A niece, Frances B., 1776–1828, wrote poems and *Tragic Dramas*, 1818, for children to act. Another, Charlotte Barrett, pub. some of FB's journals, 1842–6. Hemlow's ed., 1972–84 (selec. 1986), runs from 1791; Lars Troide has begun, 1988, editing from 1768; lives by Hemlow, 1958, Margaret Doody, 1989; bibliog. by Joseph A. Grau, 1981.

Burney, Sarah Harriet, 1772–1844, novelist, half-sister of Frances BURNEY, da. of the hated second wife Elizabeth (Allen). Her anonymous, successful *Clarentine*, 1796, presents a blandly ideal orphan under-appreciated among richer cousins. In 1798 SHB left her father's house to live with her half-brother James (who had left his wife and children; he returned five years later). Her family slowly forgave and suppressed this variously-interpreted event. She wrote from need ('I must scribble, or I *cannot live*') and worked as a governess and companion (highly prized, 1822–9, among descendants of Frances GREVILLE). *Geraldine Fauconberg*, 1808, epistolary, makes good use of a priggish, superior hero. *Traits of Nature*, 1812, with her name, has lively childhood scenes: a male orphan turned lord marries a heroine terrorized by an unloving father. *Tales of Fancy*, 1816–20, pairs *The Shipwreck* (a mother strives to be self-sufficient Crusoe for herself and daughter, until male cast-aways herald a more conventional plot) and *Country Neighbours* (16-year-old heroine is eclipsed in interest by grand-parents and unmarried aunts, one the narrator: praised in a sonnet by Charles Lamb). *The Romance of Private Life*, 1839, begun during four years' European travel, pairs *The Hermitage*, a courtship story, and *The Renunciation*, which presents with convincing subjectivity the experience of a girl inexplicably kid-napped from humble English life to be brought up abroad as a lady. For some of SHB's letters, 1830–43, see Edith J. Morley, *MP*, 39, 1941–2. Her half-sister's achievement has too much overshadowed hers.

Burnford, Sheila (Every), 1918–84, writer of children's literature and non-fiction, autobiographer. B. in Scotland, da. of Ida Philip (MacMillan) and Wilfred E., and educated privately in Edinburgh, Yorks., France and Germany. During WWII, she was a VAD nurse and ambulance driver. In 1941, she m. David B., with whom she had three children and moved to Canada, 1951. Her children's writing, often about animals, responds to the new landscape. *The Incredible Journey*, 1960 (of which there are 16 translations and a film), is the tale of the trek of two dogs and a cat across northern Ontario. *Bel Ria, Dog of War*, 1977, which involves both humans and animals in WWII adventures set in France, Britain and at sea, has had similar wide exposure. *The Fields of Noon*, 1964, collects light autobiographical essays, many about childhood experience, several previously pub. in Britain and N. America. *Without Reserve*, 1969, and *One Woman's Arctic*, 1972, are accounts of SB's visit to northern Ontario Indian reservations and Eskimo settlements on Baffin Island. *Mr Noah and the Second Flood*, 1973, is a children's story of environmental pollution.

Burr, Anna Robeson (Brown), 1873–1941, author and editor, b. Philadelphia, da. of Josephine Lea (Baker) and Henry Armitt Brown, and educ. at private schools. She m. Charles Burr in 1899 and moved to England, where she wrote (as Anna Robeson Brown) her most powerful love story, *Truth and a Woman*, 1903. Her self-reliant heroine builds her own house, refusing her suitor when he wishes to impose his views upon her: 'Manlike, you want to hammer me into your ways of thinking'. *The Wine Press*, 1905, presents similar problems of male domination and supremacy. Two non-fiction works followed: *The Autobiography, a Critical and Comparative Study*, 1909, and *Religious Confessions and Confessants*, 1914. *The House on Charles Street*, 1921, set in war-time London with characters drawn from life, was the first of her novels of political intrigue. The young heroine, private secretary to an MP, who proves her heroism in her investigation of a political scandal, also appears in *The House on Smith Street*, 1923. *The Great House in the Park*, 1924, a suspense thriller, follows a similar theme: Jean Lang, private secretary to Lord Monckton, collaborates with a middle-aged woman of considerable power, Chief Inspector Byrd, in investigating fraud and murder. Here and elsewhere, themes of inheritance and illegitimacy supervene, as in *The Jessop Bequest*, 1907, and *St Helios*, 1925, in which the orphaned and illegitimate Nick (who also features in *The Wrong Move*, 1923, a mystery-thriller romance), recovers her titled father but is forced to pose as his secretary to prevent his public disgrace. ARB here criticizes both the contemporary bastardy laws and conventional marriage codes. In *Alice James. Her Brothers. Her Journal*, 1934, ARB presents the events, actions and conversations of the Jamesian circle with vivid detail and acute psychological insight, while acknowledging that Alice JAMES must, alone, tell her story.

Burr, Esther (Edwards), 1732–58, Puritan diarist, b. Northampton, Mass., third of 11 children of Sarah EDWARDS. She m. (1752) Aaron B., 16 years her senior, future founder of Princeton College. (Theodosia, later Alston, 1782–1813, her daughter-in-law, was to receive a gruelling education designed to prove female capacity, to live dominated by her male relations, and to be lost at sea leaving letters pub. 1929. Historical novels about her include one by Anya SETON; EB's alleged journal, 1903, is really another of these.) Her actual journal, from Oct. 1754 to Sept. 1757, up to her husband's death, was exchanged regularly with her friend Sarah Prince, later GILL, whom she calls 'FIDELIA'. It records in vivid prose her religious fears and struggles, detail of daily life, unabashed political opinion and vigorous vindications of female abilities and friendship: 'religion, work, and sisterhood', say her eds., Laurie Crumpacker and Carol F. Karlsen, 1984. She discusses work by Elizabeth ROWE, Annis later STOCKTON and Mary JONES (admiring her feminist views, deploring her religious ones).

Burrell, Sophia (Raymond), Lady, 1750?–1802, later Clay, amateur poet, dramatist and novelist, in both light and solemn modes. She was da. of Sarah (Webster) and wealthy Charles R., who was granted a baronetcy on her marriage, 1773, to lawyer and antiquary William B., to descend to her husband and male heirs. Most of her work circulated in MS before printing. *Poems* of

20 years appeared anonymously in 1793: *vers de société*, ballads and fables (some medieval), Ovidian and Ossianic imitation, a vindication of Goethe's Charlotte, and praise of Elizabeth MONTAGU and Georgiana DEVONSHIRE. The second vol. bore her name, as did the long poems *Telemachus* (couplets, from Fénelon, written 1779) and *The Thymbriad* (blank verse, from Xenophon), both 1794. Widowed in 1796, she next year m. the Revd William Clay, and pub. anonymously her only novel, *Adeline de Courcy*, a conventional but gripping distress story. In 1800 she pub. two tragedies, *Maximian* (from Thomas Corneille), and *Theodora, or The Spanish Daughter* (with happy ending), whose title has caused confusion of her with Ann MCTAGGART.

Burton, Catharine, 1668–1714, spiritual autobiographer, b. near Bury St Edmunds, da. of the Catholics Mary (Suttler) and Thomas B. (Her mother died of her tenth child when CB was eight.) She was wild and high spirited, 'yet when alone I had very serious thoughts'; she used to tell the others stories. At 17, having just passed from a worldly to a pious and abstinent phase, she fell violently ill and remained so for seven years. Her vow to become a nun if cured was, she believed, answered by a miracle. She joined the English Teresian nuns at Antwerp in 1694 as Mother Mary Xaviera of the Angels. Her Mistress of Novices, to whom she was deeply attached, died. About 1697 a vision of St Francis Xavier 'bade me write my life and the favours God had done me.' She was at first reluctant, pleading no talent and (as Novice Mistress) no time. Her director elaborately tested her, telling her first to write, then to burn her work, now slighting and insulting it, now praising it, but always keeping it secret. She took all 'with the same sedate calmness of mind' and found the actual writing very easy. She was elected Superior of the convent and died holily. Her work was ed. by H. J. Coleridge, 1876; re-told by Anne Hardman, 1939.

Burton, Katherine (Kurz), 1880–1969, biographer, essayist, editor, b. in Cleveland, Ohio, da. of Louise (Bittner) and John K. She was educ. at Western Reserve Univ., and taught for a year in Mt Pleasant, Penn., before returning to Cleveland to marry editor Harry Payne B., 1910. She had three children. After her husband's nervous breakdown, she moved to NYC and became an editor for *McCall's* magazine, 1928–30, then *Redbook*, 1930–3. There, she turned to the Anglo-Catholic church and the guidance of Dr Selden Delany: he became a Roman Catholic priest; she converted, 1930, and began to edit a woman's page for *Sign*, a Catholic monthly. Some of her pieces are collected in *Woman to Woman*, 1961. She 'wanted to read of American converts of the last century and of my own' but, finding few such books, turned to writing them. Her interest in Hawthorne and his daughter Rose, a Catholic convert, resulted in two books: *Sorrow Built a Bridge*, 1937 (new ed., 1956) and *Paradise Planters: The Story of Brook Farm*, 1939 (a utopian community at W. Roxbury, 1841–7). She also wrote on Elizabeth SETON, Mother Butler of Marymount, The Sisters of Mercy. *The Story of Dr. Agnes McLaren and the Society of Catholic Medical Missionaries*, 1946, exemplifies her interest in Catholic women doctors and the problems confronting women faced with the male Catholic hierarchy. Though she 'always detested the kind of biography which mixes fact and fiction', she 'did like the fictional form of writing': her biographies derive their information from letters, diaries and people who knew her subjects, adding to this fictionalized dialogue. Her life of Isaac Thomas Hecker, 1943, the Brook Farm baker and founder of the Paulists, was followed by her autobiography, *The Next Thing*, 1949.

Bury, Lady **Charlotte** Susan Maria (Campbell), 1775–1861, poet, novelist, memoirist, literary hostess. She was b. London to Elizabeth (Gunning) and the

5th Duke of Argyll. In 1796 she m. her impoverished cousin Col. John ('wild Jack') C. (d. 1809) by whom she had nine children (only two survived). She served as Lady-in-Waiting to the ill-reputed Princess of Wales, 1810–15, then in 1818 she m. the Rev. Edward B. (d. 1832), her son's tutor, with whom she had two children. As a young literary hostess in Edinburgh, she was admired by Sir Walter Scott, Susan FERRIER and Matthew Lewis, the heroine of whose novel *The Monk* was reputedly modelled on her. She pub. *Poems on Several Occasions*, anon., in 1797, and 17 novels, the last appearing posthumously in 1864. She also ed. Catherine GORE's *Memoirs of a Peeress*, but is best remembered for the anon. *Diary Illustrative of the Times of George IV*, 1838, comprising her journal notes, correspondence and other materials relating to the period 1810–20. A contemporary *succès de scandale*, with three editions in the first year, it provides an intimate and candid background to the 'Queen Caroline scandals', and a fascinating commentary on literary and political events of the era. It was both satirized and borrowed from by Thackeray. In 1837 she wrote to an old friend: 'It would all be well enough if one lived to write for fame and fancy, and to try to do good; but writing to coin money is slavery to body and mind. I am that slave.'

Bury, Elizabeth (Lawrence), 1644–1720, religious diarist and letter writer, da. of Elizabeth (Cutts) and Adams L., b. at Clare, Suffolk. Her father d. when she was four; three years later her mother m. a clergyman later ejected by Charles II. Widely read (French, Hebrew, philosophy, history, maths, music, medicine), EB left MS notes on philology but loved divinity best, and wished scholars to write in English for the sake of women. A witty talker and expert fund raiser, she always rose at 4 or 5 a.m. to study. In 1667 she m. Griffith Lloyd of Hunts, who died in 1682; having rejected three clergymen she re-married in 1697 Samuel B., a dissenting minister 19 years her junior. He published excerpts of her diary, begun in shorthand about 1661, in his *Account* of her, 1720, 'to the Honour of her Sex, Relation, and Profession'. She writes much self-examination and (in letters) advice, but also incident: frequent and dangerous house fires, walking 16 miles to a lecture, and women's meetings.

Bush, Olivia (Ward), later Banks, 1869–1944, poet and playwright, b. on Long Island, NY, da. of Eliza (Draper), who d. when she was a baby, and Abraham W., both of Indian-African descent. She was brought up by an aunt at Providence, Rhode Island, attended high school, m. Frank Bush in 1889 (later divorced) and had two daughters. She issued at Providence her *Original Poems*, 1899, and *Driftwood*, 1914 (already planned in 1900), containing extended prose pictures of the waterfront, and poems which address public figures (some black) and evoke private emotion through use of landscape and personified abstractions. OWB wrote for the *Colored American Mag.* and later directed plays for a community centre in Boston, publishing an Easter pageant, *Memories of Calvary*, Philadelphia [1915]. She married Anthony Banks, with whom she ran a drama school in Chicago. Back in NY, she continued to teach drama and foster black and interracial culture. But her plays, *Indian Trail* (about her ancestors the Montauks), *Shadows* (a dramatic monologue re-creating African art-forms) and *A Shantytown Scandal*, remained unpublished and unproduced. Also unpub. were her dialect 'Aunt Viney' stories and unfinished autobiography: see thesis by her great-great-grand-daughter Bernice F. Guillaume, Tulane Univ. 1983.

Butler, Josephine Elizabeth (Grey), 1828–1906, editor, political activist and writer, b. Glendale, Northumb., youngest child of Hannah (Annett) and John G., chief Whig agent in the North and radical agricultural reformer. Educ. principally at home, in

1852 she m. George B., educationalist and ecclesiastic. In 1864 she witnessed the fatal fall of her young daughter and in 1866, after moving to Liverpool, began her work for destitute women and prostitutes. She stressed the connection between prostitution and lack of education and employment for women. She also supported the movement for higher EDUCATION for women and edited *Woman's Work and Woman's Culture*, 1869 (including essays by F. P. COBBE, Jessie BOUCHERETT, et al.). Her major efforts went into her 'Great Crusade': the abolition of the Contagious Diseases Acts. She worked for an end to the regulation of prostitution in Europe and the Empire, arguing that it denied women's basic rights and ensured their enslavement to male lust. Secretary of the Ladies' National Association for Repeal from 1869, she argued the case, with others, in their manifesto (pub. in *The Daily News*, 31 Dec. 1869) and in many books and pamphlets, including *The Constitution Violated*, 1871, *Government by Police*, 1879, and *The Hour Before the Dawn*, 1881. When the Acts were finally repealed, JB set up and ed. her own periodicals, *The Dawn* (1888–96), and *The Storm Bell* (1898–1900), to ensure vigilance against re-introduction and to maintain international connections. *Personal Reminiscences of a Great Crusade*, 1896, is an account of the conflict. Her writing also includes lives of Jean Frederic Oberlin, 1882, and Catherine of Siena, 1879, as well as of her father, 1869, husband, 1896, and sister, Harriet Meuricoffre, 1903. See G. W. and Lucy A. Johnson, eds., *JEB: An Autobiographical Memoir*, 1909, and Glen Petrie, *A Singular Iniquity*, 1976. Her papers are in the J B Coll., Fawcett Library, London Polytechnic.

Butler, Octavia Estelle, science-fiction writer, b. 1947 at Pasadena, Calif., only child of black parents, Octavia M. (Guy) and Laurice B., who d. when she was very young. Raised a strict Baptist, she began writing for pleasure at about ten. She attended Pasadena City College and State Univ. (Los Angeles) and sold her first stories while at a SCIENCE-FICTION workshop, 1970. In her *Patternmaster*, 1976, two sons compete to succeed their dying father as head of a telepathic clan network which rules a rigidly hierarchical, polygamist, violently threatened future society. *Mind of My Mind*, 1977, and *Wild Seed*, 1980, trace the Pattern backwards: its 4000-year-old founder (who survives by killing and appropriating bodies of any colour or sex) is killed by a heroic daughter who brings freedom to all his psychically-linked descendants; he is then shown from 1690, at the height of the slave trade, multiplying and guarding his special offspring; in each book his ruthless superiority is matched by a female partner who is also abnormally gifted and more feeling than he. In *Survivor*, 1978 (written earliest), OEB turns to relations between human and extraterrestrial races: here and in *Dawn, Xenogenesis: 1*, 1987, a remarkable woman makes contact across the barrier, bearing hybrid children who bring cruel and blinkered humanity some hope for its future. In *Kindred*, 1979, a young woman is repeatedly snatched back 160 years, to a nightmare world of slavery and the power-poisoned mating of a white and a black ancestor. The novella *Bloodchild*, 1985 (more human-alien crosses, this time borne by males), won three awards. In *Adulthood Rites, Xenogenesis: 2*, 1988, the previous heroine's tentacle-covered son leads some scanty human survivors to a faint chance of new – if radically altered – life on Mars. See *Black American Literary Forum*, 18, 1984.

Butler, Sarah, obscure author said to be dead when the shady Edmund Curll published as hers *Irish Tales, or Instructive Histories for the Happy Conduct of Life*, 1716. This single novel in ten parts has a learned preface claiming historical accuracy about the kings of Ireland before its subjection to 'the heavy Yoke of [English] Bondage'. It celebrates 'Heroic Love, and all the Patriot

Virtues', but lets its 'Lovers die unmarried: since I could find no Authority to the contrary.' It is unusually well versed in Gaelic culture for its date: re-issued 1719, 1727 as *Milesian Tales*.

Butt, Beatrice May, 1856–1918, novelist, da. of Colonel Thomas Bromhead B. In 1876 she m. William Hutt Allhusen of Stoke Hall (mentioned in *Burke's Peerage*). Little else is known about her life. Her novels are often tragic, accept that dreams are better than reality and reject political solutions. In *Keith Deramore*, 1893, a woman lies about her artistic achievements (the sketches are her brother's) and is rejected for another woman by the hero. In *Dan Riach: Socialist*, 1908, the hero separates from the woman he has been living with and loses faith in socialism. Another short novel, *Ann*, 1907, has father falling in love with adopted daughter and her being killed by her lover. Other novels include *Miss Molly*, 1876, *Eugenie*, 1877, *Delicia*, 1879, *Geraldine Hawthorne*, 1882, *Alison*, 1883, *A Friend*, 1891, and *The Great Reconciler*, 1903, where two husbands die of drink and a woman is shot, mistaken for a man. BB was a minor novelist who was attracted by dark subjects and melodrama.

Butts, Mary Francis, 1890–1937, novelist, b. at a country house near Poole, Dorset, da. of Mary Jane (Briggs) and the much older naval captain Frederick John Butts. Her autobiography, *The Crystal Cabinet*, 1937, repr. 1988, very critical of her mother and stepfather, also shows her early awareness of the power of language: 'I could make words do things. But words could do things to me too. Words could make me use them.' She attended St Leonard's School in St Andrews, Scotland, 1906–09, then Westfield College, London Univ. 'The femininity of their minds irked me; nine out of ten of them only wanted to get married,' she wrote later, and she left after illegally attending a horse race with a young lecturer, taking no degree. She worked for the London County Council in East London, and during WWI moved in the literary circles of Ezra Pound, H. D., and others (including Rebecca WEST, Stella BOWEN, Nina HAMNET, May SINCLAIR), m. poet and publisher John Rodker in 1918 and had a daughter. She left him in 1920 to live with Cecil Maitland (a painter and writer with acute personal problems), with whom she was involved in Aleister Crowley's occult set, and moved to Paris. She lived on the Left Bank, associated with Sylvia BEACH and Djuna BARNES, among others, had affairs with men and women, experimented with drugs, kept a journal, and published stories and poems in little magazines. Her *Ashe of Rings* (excerpts in the *Little Review*, 1919; book form 1925), a mystical handling of ritual, witchcraft and the chaos of war, affirms 'a sense of living in at least two worlds at once'. Short stories in *Speed the Plough*, 1923, deal with unexpected manifestations of the unconscious. *Armed with Madness*, 1928, centres on the recurring image of a chalice imbued with different meanings according to characters' differing desires. *Imaginary Letters*, also 1928, is an epistolary novel of female involvement with male homosexuality. After a nervous breakdown in 1930, MB returned to England and m. painter and cartoonist Gabriel W. Aitken, from whom she separated in 1934. Her *Death of Felicity Taverner*, 1932, shows mechanization, alien to 'thought or art or love', defeated only by murder. She wrote three historical novels: *The Macedonian*, 1933, *Scenes from the Life of Cleopatra*, 1935, repr. 1974, retelling from a woman's perspective a 'tale only men have told', and *Julian the Apostate*, unpub. Further stories appeared in *Several Occasions*, 1932, and *Last Stories*, 1938, selec. by BRYHER, for whose *Life and Letters Today* she had written. She died of a burst appendix. See Hanscombe and Smyers, 1987.

Buxton, Bertha Henry (Leopold), 1844–81, novelist, da. of Germans settled in

London, Therese – a musician – and William Leupold. At 11 she wrote stories for schoolfellows at Queen's College, Tufnell Park. After travel in Europe and the USA, she m. club manager Henry B. in 1860; he paid to publish her *Percy's Wife*, 1867, as by 'B. H. Bee' (in which a faithful wife reclaims a faulty husband), and she translated a German operetta. In 1875 he lost his money and deserted her; keeping her youngest child, she won by writing a 'glorious independence'. After two anonymous novels, and children's stories as 'Auntie Bee', 1878 and 1879, she used her own name. She took a walk-on stage part at Exeter to prepare for *Jennie of 'The Prince's'*, 1876, dedicated to her mother, which argues that 'a right-minded woman' can preserve 'her purity and simplicity' on 'the much-abused stage'. Its heroine, a soldier's daughter, marries happily but perseveres in the career which her husband calls 'theatrical bondage'. This theme recurs, e.g. in *Nell – On and Off the Stage*, 1879, dedicated to 'My Ideal Ophelia': its model heroine (with snobbish mother, noble rejecting relations, and scene-painter step-father) reaches 'the first step of the steep ladder which leads to success', in the touring company of an actress she idolizes. (Strong women abound in BHB's stage world.) Other frequent themes are aristocratic disdain for artistic activity, English-European relations, and blindness. BHB collaborated with the blind W. W. Fenn, and wrote much for magazines: *Tinsley's* and the *Carisbrooke* were running her work when she died suddenly of heart failure.

Byatt, A. S., Antonia Susan (Drabble), novelist and critic. B. in 1936 in Sheffield, Yorks., da. of Quakers Kathleen Marie (Bloor) and John Frederick D., a barrister: sister of Margaret DRABBLE. She was educ. at Sheffield High School, The Mount, York (where her mother had taught), Newnham College, Cambridge (BA, in English, 1957), Bryn Mawr, USA (one year), and Somerville College, Oxford. There her research grant (contingent, for women, on single status) ended on her marriage, 1959, to economist Ian B. Her first novel, *Shadow of a Sun*, 1964, deals with the creative arrangements needed to combine marriage and career. She lectured at London Univ., extramurally, then at University College, 1972–81. Her scholarly publications include two critical studies of Iris MURDOCH, 1965 and 1976, an edition of George ELIOT, 1979, and introductions to Willa CATHER, yet she derives her 'sense of an order behind things from T. S. Eliot and Pound' and writes 'the way I do from James *via* T. S. Eliot': 'Literature has always been my way out, my escape from the limits of being female.' Her novels often portray relationships between sisters; 'creative tension' in her writing and Drabble's has been attributed to the complexity of their bond. ASB's *The Game*, 1967, repr. 1986, fictionalizes her childhood and student days: the novelist sister in it sees *her* fiction not as autobiography but as an attempt 'to understand events in her own life, and others'. She re-married Peter Duffy in 1969; she has two children by this marriage, two by her first. A quartet of novels, still in progress, began with *The Virgin in the Garden*, 1978 (see Juliet Dusinberre in *Critique*, 24, 1982), in a complex double time scheme which treats the 1950s as a 'second Elizabethan age'. The second part, *Still Life*, 1985, again explores the tension between two sisters, one committed to domesticity, the other to scholarship. ASB's short-story collection *Sugar and Other Stories*, 1987, includes 'July Ghosts', about a writer whose son has died: this draws on actual experience and aims to make it 'into something containable'. Parts three and four of the quartet are forthcoming. In *Possession*, 1989, two scholars investigate fictitious Victorian poets (one male, one female). See interview with Dusinberre in Todd, 1983.

'Byng, the Hon. Mrs **Julian',** Marie Evelyn (Moreton), Viscountess, 1870–1949, novelist and memoirist, b. in London, only child of the Greek Janie (Ralli) and the Hon. Richard M. (knighted in 1913), who both held court posts. Educ. by governesses, she grew up lonely, convinced of inferiority and of her conventional mother's wish that she was male, or at least prettier. In 1902 she m. Julian B., soldier, later Governor-General of Canada, 1921–6, Viscount B. of Vimy, and Field-Marshal. *Anne Inescourt* [1909], later rewritten as *Anne of the Marshland* [1914], and *Barriers*, 1912, apparently conventional romances, question the consequences of the constraints society puts on women. They sensitively depict emotional suffering amid material privilege; this is also true of her autobiographical *Up the Stream of Time*, 1945, written as a widow in Canada during WWII.

Byron, Catherine (Greenfield), poet. She was b. in 1947 in London, da. of Catholic Peggy (Duane), from Galway, Eire, and Protestant Englishman David G. She moved to Belfast, 1948, when her father became head of Physiology at Queen's University, and was educ. first at Rathmore Convent, Dunmurry, then at St Mary's Convent, Ascot. Later she read Classics and English at Somerville College, Oxford, moving on to graduate work in Medieval Studies. She married Ken B., a history student, in 1967, and had her first child in 1973. From 1974–8, she practised self-sufficiency farming in Strathaven, in the west of Scotland, then moved to Leicester, where she lives with Michael Farley, editor of Taxus Press, working as freelance journalist for Radio Eiran and teaching creative writing at the Loughborough College of Art and Design. Her first vol. of poetry, *Settlements*, appeared in 1985; *Samhain*, her second, in 1987. Her poetry interweaves women's lives with family history and Ireland's past, mixing a powerful nature imagery with scenes of neolithic sites and Celtic mythology, evoking Irish consciousness and topography. Dramatic emphasis falls on individual narratives, as in her 'Galway' sequence, 'Wedding at Aughrim,' which recalls the violence of a 'made-marriage', or 'The Black and Tans Deliver Her Cousin's Son', which compresses personal and national tragedy into a chilling keen for the dead. CB is working on a feminist reading of Seamus Heaney. See CB on her own verse in *Women's Review*, January 1986, and Carol RUMENS in *Poetry R.*, 76, 1986.

'Byron, Medora Gordon', novelist: the name appears in the 1816 MINERVA catalogue and probably stems from Medora in George Gordon, Lord Byron's *Corsair*, 1814, not Charlotte SMITH's *Young Philosopher*, 1798. MGB published several novels as 'Miss Byron' (the future Elizabeth STRUTT was Mrs Byron) and others as 'A Modern Antique', perhaps to prevent an impression of glut (she started out with three works dated 1809). She is fond of literary allusion, even in titles: her *Englishman*, 1812, follows her *English-Woman*, 1809; her *Celia in Search of a Husband*, 1809 (well reviewed), sets out directly to answer Hannah MORE's 'inimitable' *Coelebs*; *The Spinster's Journal*, 1816, uses one of MGB's names to answer *The Bachelor's Journal*, 1815, under the other. These two, her best work, turn away from upwardly-mobile love stories and pious pattern characters (condemning fashionable society, boosting domesticity) towards a sympathetic probing of the melancholy but good-hearted male and the nervous, self-defensive female solitary. MGB always writes self consciously, with much first-person, essay-like moralizing and heavily emphatic typography.

C

Cable, Mildred, 1878–1952, and **Francesca French**, 1871–1960, itinerant missionaries and travel writers. Da. of Eliza (Kindred) and master draper John C., MC was b. and educ. in Guildford and at the Women's Candidates Home of the China Inland Mission in North London. She undertook missionary work in Huochow, Shansi province, China in 1900, just after the Boxer rebellion. She joined Evangeline French (1869–1960), who had been working in women's education there since 1893. They took a school where the girls had to have unbound feet and developed it to a large, important venture. After seven years and a furlough, they were joined in 1909 by FF. The French sisters, das. of Elizabeth and John E. F., had been educated abroad, Evangeline in Algeria, Francesca in Belgium. Thereafter, the three enjoyed a life-long connection. In 1926 they obtained a 'roving commission' from the China Inland Commission. For 15 years, in Chinese dress and with acquired fluency in Chinese and Turkish, they travelled the trade routes of the Gobi Desert, crossing it several times (with Bibles and portable harmonium). At home, they were thought of as explorers and lectured extensively on their frequent visits to England and after their permanent return, in 1939. When their Asian work was no longer possible, they organized women's volunteer work for the British and Foreign Bible Society. In 1942, MC was awarded the Lawrence Memorial medal of the Royal Central Asian Society, and the following year the three were jointly awarded the Livingstone medal of the Royal Scottish Geographical Society. In 1947, they toured Australia and NZ for the Bible Society; in 1950, they toured S. America for the Evangelical Union of South America. MC and FF jointly wrote more than 20 books about their experiences: among the best known are *Through Jade Gate and Central Asia*, 1927, *Something Happened*, 1933, *The Gobi Desert*, 1942, repr. with intro. by Marina WARNER, 1984, *China: Her Life and Her People*, 1946, and *Journey With a Purpose*, 1950. *Desert Journal*, 1934, is letters written during their years in China. Their style is rich, detailed, leisurely: 'A rag of the rising sun touched the scalloped ridge of ice-fields in the Tibetan Alps and threw a veil of pink over their snowy slopes. . . .' See W. J. Platt, *Three Women*, London, 1964.

Caddell, Cecilia Mary, *c.* 1813–77, novelist and religious writer, second da. of Paulina (Southwell) and Richard O'Ferrall-Caddell of Harbourstown, Co. Meath, member of an old Catholic family that kept its religion and estates intact. Despite ill health, CMC wrote articles on Irish history and the Catholic faith for *The Irish Monthly* and other periodicals. Her prose fiction, exploiting similar interests, includes *Blind Agnese, or, The Little Spouse of the Blessed Sacrament*, 1855, written for 'little ones'. It is spoilt by bigotry, but in *Home and the Homeless*, 1858, a work of contemporary life, the enemy is no longer Protestantism but agnosticism. Despite protracted and repetitive religious arguments and a melodramatic plot, this novel has more interest. *Nellie Netterville, or, One of the Transplanted*, 1867, an unpretentious historical romance, has a basis in fact, as does *Wild Times, a Tale of the Days of Queen Elizabeth*, 1872, in which her early fervour about persecution of the Catholics is more restrained and effective.

Cadell, Violet **Elizabeth** (Vandyke), 'Harriet Ainsworth', popular novelist, b. 1903 in

Calcutta, da. of Elizabeth (Lynch) and colonial officer Frederick Reginald V. She was sent to England when judged old enough for boarding school and spent holidays with her mother's family in Ireland. In 1928 she m. banker Henry Dunlop Mallock C.; she had two children. She turned to writing as a widow; her 50 titles began with *My Dear Aunt Flora*, 1946 (about a family's reliance on the aunt who is 'born to look after somebody'). They include a children's book, *Sun in the Morning*, 1950, and three pseudonymous murder mysteries. An unpretentious writer and skilled plotter, whose closing pages usually bear the words 'I love you', she also questions assumptions about character with variations on stereotypes. A hateful old woman seems a proper murder victim in *Consider the Lilies*, 1955; a not dissimilar character, a *comtesse*, is outwitted but indomitable in *Bridal Array*, 1957 (a double love story in which a rich girl escapes exploitation). *The Stratton Story*, 1967, builds suspense round a widow making a hit with a first novel, and her sinisterly hostile sister-in-law; right lies on the unexpected side: 'How could I hope to convince? . . . I was old and odd; she was the very picture of womanly goodness and dutifulness and graciousness.' In *Out of the Rain*, 1987, a confirmed bachelor finds romance with a slapdash but old-fashioned widow with three children; a woman who rose from servant to mistress to second wife is engagingly presented. EC has been much reprinted (*Gay Pursuit*, 1950, became *Family Gathering*, 1979); she has lived latterly in Portugal.

Cadell, Jessie Ellen (Nash), 1844–84, novelist and Persian scholar, b. Scotland, da. of a city merchant. In 1859 she went to India with her mother and stepfather; at 16 she m. Henry Mowbray C., captain in the Bengal artillery. After his death, she moved to Edinburgh with her two sons in 1867 and to London in 1873. She had begun to learn Persian in India and became interested in Omar Khayam's poetry, which she aimed to translate more accurately than Fitzgerald. She wrote a well-received scholarly article on it for *Fraser's* (May 1879) but increasingly struggled with ill health and died in Florence just before completing what she had hoped would be the standard edition; it was eventually pub. by her friend Richard Garnett in 1899. She wrote two novels, enjoyable rather than subtle explorations of the complexity of sex relations. *Ida Craven*, 1876, set in India, treats the difficulties of a young girl who, resenting the lack of purpose in female lives, marries young and naïvely tries to become her husband's 'femme camarade'. *Worthy: a Study of Friendship*, 1895, deals with problems faced by a mature man and woman trying to live as friends and with a mother's determination not to engross her son's life. Independence in women is admired, up to a point, but 'advanced' ideas and radical socialism are criticized.

Caesar, Mary (Freeman), 1677–1741, memoirist. Da. of Ralph F. of Aspenden, Herts, she m. Charles C. of Benington in 1702 and had four children. A fervent Jacobite, she revered Queen Anne and collected an archive of Stuart portraits and political papers. She introduced Pope to the future Judith MADAN and raised subscribers for his *Odyssey*, as well as for Mary BARBER and for Matthew Prior. In 1724, moved by Lord Oxford's death to recall the changes she had seen, she began an irregular journal where current politics spark her comments on the past (now in the BL). Though shy about her problems with language ('Righting was Never my Tallent'), she at last showed her work to her husband, who proudly planned to have her painted with the volume. To Barber she confided the wish to write a history of her own times; what she did write re-shapes family and national history idealistically, ideologically and symbolically. She died soon after Charles C., after years of money troubles. Letters also survive, privately owned. See

Valerie Rumbold in essays ed. Isobel Grundy and Susan Wiseman, forthcoming.

Caffyn, Kathleen (Hunt), 'Iota', 1853–1926, novelist and short-story writer, b. Tipperary, da. of William H. of Waterloo House. Educ. by English and German governesses, she trained as a nurse in London. She m. surgeon and writer Stephen Mannington C. in 1879, arrived in Sydney the following year but soon moved to Melbourne, where she was one of the founders of the District Nursing Society of Victoria. She contributed to local magazines and, after returning to London in 1892, achieved great success with her first novel, *A Yellow Aster*, 1894. Condemned for its traces of Zola and Ibsen, this centres on a woman, brought up by scientific parents in an irreligious atmosphere, who discovers the power of love through the birth of her child. Though none equalled the success of her first, a further 16 novels appeared between 1894 and 1916.

Caillard, Emma Marie, 'M. C. E.', 1852–1927, poet, religious and scientific writer. Little is known of her life: she preserved the strictest privacy, often signing herself only with her initials (in various orders). She was a member of the London Literary Society, which published her first vol., *A Poem of Life*, 1884, divided into 'secular' and 'sacred' poems; in the same year, she published *Charlotte Corday and Other Poems*. In 1889 came *The Lost Life*, containing poems like 'Stolen Flowers' (a starving girl steals for her dying mother) and 'Tight-Rope Dancer' (daughter falls from the rope when her father dies), which the preface claims as 'true', as well as lighter poems like 'The City Pillar-Box'. EMC also wrote *Electricity: The Science of the Nineteenth Century*, 1891, and several vols., of religious essays.

Caird, Alice **Mona** (Alison), 'G. Noel Hatton', 1855–1932, novelist and feminist, b. Isle of Wight, only da. of Matilda (Hector) and inventor John A. In 1877 she m. James Alexander Henryson-C. who d. 1921; they had one son. She pub. a series of essays about marriage as a patriarchal institution which argue 'against that popular view that allows men to dictate to women', collected as *The Morality of Marriage*, 1897. Her novels often take the view that women should not allow themselves to be victims. In her best known, *The Daughters of Danaeus*, 1894, the heroine Hadria leaves her husband and children in order to study music. A later novel, *The Stones of Sacrifice*, 1915, also develops the idea that self-sacrifice can be unhealthy to both the woman and others, though this novel does end with marriage. Other novels include *The Wing of Azrael*, 1889, and *A Romance of the Moors*, 1891. MC travelled widely, and another novel, *The Pathway of the Gods*, 1898, is set in Italy; she also pub. a travel book, *Romantic Cities of Provence*, 1906. As well as being an important feminist polemicist, she was an active anti-vivisectionist in both her fiction and non-fiction, which includes *A Sentimental View of Vivisection*, 1895, *Beyond the Pale*, 1897, and *The Inquisition of Science*, 1903.

Cairns, Elizabeth, 1685–1741, Scots labouring-class preacher and autobiographer, b. to dissenting parents in time of persecution. As a child keeping her father's sheep on the rocks, taught to read by her mother, she loved solitude and had vivid religious experiences. During a seven-year famine she sometimes ate grass. At about 17, set to work chiefly indoors, she found her light darkened, and embarked on years of religious struggle, even facing temptation to suicide; a female 'experienced Christian' helped with counsel, likening Christ's love to a mother's. In her early 20s EC went to Stirling to work as a servant and preach, returning to care for her parents as needed. For four years in her late 30s she could not read or write because a single room served her to live, run a school and tend her paralysed, widowed mother. Such hardships troubled her only lest they shake her faith. Her remarkable account of 'the Lord's visits to my soul' was precious as manna to her; she was deeply anxious (though not ashamed of it) when unauthorized copies got out: ed. John Greig, Glasgow, 1762, repr. 1857.

Calderwood, Margaret (Steuart), 1715–74, diarist and novelist, da. of Anne (Dalrymple) and Sir James S. of Coltness. In 1735 she was painted by Allan Ramsay and m. Thomas C. of Polton near Edinburgh. In 1756 they took their two sons to Holland and Belgium to visit her brother the political economist Sir James S., Jacobite exile. Her travel narrative, drawn from her journal and letters home to her married daughter, was pub. by the Maitland Club, 1842, and ed. Alexander Fergusson, Edinburgh, 1884. It explores every possible topic – agriculture, manufacturing processes and social habits – salted with humour and racy dialect. MC excels herself in describing England, since there she could 'speak to the folks and ask questions', cross swords at will and exercise a sharp Scots eye for English insularity and self-regard. She left an unpub. novel, the first-person *Adventures of Fanny Roberts*, and another journal, kept for teaching her husband's tenants over eight years' 'factorship' of his estates, which puts her mathematical studies to good use. MSS privately owned, with Dundas of Arniston papers.

Calisher, Hortense, short-story writer, novelist, reviewer. B. in 1911 in NYC, where she spent her youth in museums, 'not learning art' but 'an attitude toward art,' she was da. of German-Jewish Hedwig (Lichtstern), to whom she dedicated *New Yorkers*, 1966, and English-Southern Joseph Henry C., a manufacturer. *Herself*, 1972, her autobiography, describes growing up in the Depression: she attended Hunter College High School; then her parents scraped together $400 and she worked in a restaurant to enable her to attend Barnard College. After graduation, 1932, she counselled poor families, and m. Heaton B. Heffelfinger, 'the only engineering grad of his class to get a job within the year', with whom she had two children. Describing herself as 'a secret artist (for I continue writing poems in between the housework)', she published her first story, composed while walking a child to school, 1947. (*Herself* discusses the difficult combination of writing and children.) After *In the Absence of Angels*, 1957, which includes 'The Middle Drawer', a memorable study of daughter-mother relationships, HC says, 'my work itself enters politics'. In 1959, she m. novelist Curtis Arthur Harnack, whom she met at an Iowa Writers' Workshop. More collections of stories followed: *Tale for the Mirror*, 1962, *Extreme Magic*, 1963, *Saratoga, Hot*, 1985, *The Railway Police and The Last Trolley Ride* (novellas), 1966. HC's mode is often satire, her subjects male-female relations, gender, androgyny and female sexuality. *Journal From Ellipsia*, 1965, is a SCIENCE FICTION akin to *Erewhon* and *Gulliver's Travels*; *Queenie*, 1971, is a bawdy, very funny sexual farce. The stories in *On Keeping Women*, 1977, deal with sex-role issues, and *The Bobby-Soxer*, 1986, the ribald tale of 'hermaphrodite Aunt Leo', with gender divisions in both society and individuals. HC's style is technically complicated, formally adventurous, intensely metaphorical, her diction at once poetic and colloquial. She has taught at several universities in the USA and Europe, contributed widely to newspapers and journals, including the *New York Times*, the *New Yorker* and *Harper's*. She was awarded an honorary D. Litt. by Skidmore College, NY, 1980. *Mysteries of Motion*, 1983, imagined the first civilian space shuttle; her most recent book is *Age*, 1987. See interview in *Saturday Review of Books*, July/Aug., 1985.

Callcott, Maria (Dundas), also Graham, 1785–1842, travel and children's writer, b. Papcastle, Cumberland, da. of an American loyalist refugee née Thomson, and of Scots Rear-Admiral George D. Taught by her mother, and at many schools, from one in a village to that of the Miss Brights at Draycot, Berks. (once friends of Samuel Johnson), she thought herself mainly self-educated from books (Pope's Homer at nine). She had to contend with warnings about learned ladies and the burning of her verse: 'I used to hear that it was a pity I was not a boy.' Her first extant diary, begun on leaving for India with her father, 1808, shows her alert to racial issues. She cut out pages relating her marriage to naval officer Thomas G., 1809. Returning in 1811, she published *Journal of a Residence in India*, 1812, and *Letters on India*, 1814, which reflect reading in Sanskrit and try to avoid 'the reproach of European prejudice'. Living in Scotland, she translated a work by A. J. M. de Rocca, 1815. In Italy, 1818–19, she did sketches (now in the BM) and prepared a travel book, 1820, focusing on the peasants whom other writers ignored; that year she also pub. a life of painter Nicolas Poussin. In 1821 she sailed to Brazil; in 1822 Thomas G. died between Brazil and Chile. After a year alone at Valparaiso she was briefly, by invitation, governess to the emperor's daughter. Her Chilean and Brazilian *Journals*, 1824, illustrated from her sketches, cover personal events, social structure and the independence struggle of 'the patriots of the New World': Spanish and Portuguese transls. 1902, 1974. Some reviewers were politically hostile. MC settled in London, knew many women writers, and read MSS and wrote articles for publisher John Murray; in 1828 the *North American Review* called her 'a sort of literary *redacteur*, or intellectual mechanic' when she edited a work critical of US missionaries in the Sandwich Islands. MC m. painter Augustus Wall C., 1827, and published more on painting and for children. The famous *Little Arthur's History of England*, 1835, aimed to 'satisfy the almost boundless inquiries of intelligent children': 70 eds. in 100 years; that of 1975 extends her coverage from George IV to 1973. Life by Rosamund Brunel Gotch, 1937, draws on letters and diaries.

Calthorpe, Mena (Field), novelist, b. 1905. Called Mena by her family, Calthorpe her married name, she was b. Ivy Bright F. in Goulburn, NSW, da. of Ivy Pearl (Anderson) and Francis Arthur F. After a basic education she worked as a clerk, secretary, and teacher, travelling and working throughout Australia. In Goulburn she was encouraged to write by newspaper editor T. J. Hebblewhite (who also encouraged Miles FRANKLIN); after moving to Sydney, she joined the Sydney Modern Writers' Club. Her two novels reflect political and social concerns, portraying the working and living conditions of labouring people. *The Dyehouse*, 1961, is set in an inner-city factory, while *The Defectors*, 1969, describes the power and corruption within union and labour politics.

Cambridge, Ada (later Cross), 1844–1926, novelist and poet, b. Norfolk, eldest da. of Thomasina (Emerson) and Henry C. She was educ. by governesses and through her own wide reading. In 1870 she m. Anglican clergyman George Cross, and shortly afterwards left for Melbourne. Intensely religious in her youth (she pub. three moral tales and two collections of hymns before leaving England), she began writing in Australia to supplement the family income. 'Up the Murray', serialized in the *Australasian*, 1875, has never appeared in book form. Following her first volume of poetry, *The Manor House*, 1875, and at a traumatic period of her life, she pub. (anon.) the controversial *Unspoken Thoughts*, 1887 (repr. 1988); some of its more orthodox poems were repr. in her last collection, *The Hand in the Dark*, 1913. Her later romance novels became more socially aware and critical, particularly of marriage and the materialism of urban Australia's middle classes. The best of these are her first success, *A Marked Man*, 1890 (repr. 1987, with intro. by D. Adelaide), in which youthful mistakes in love and marriage are played out on a grand and ironic scale, *The Three Miss Kings*, 1891 (repr. 1987), treating the dilemma of single women in patriarchal society, and the satirical *Materfamilias*, 1898, whose manipulative first person narrator exemplifies the limitations imposed on women. Exiles, artists and misfits feature in other novels, including *Not All in Vain*, 1892, *Fidelis*, 1895, *Path and Goal*, 1900, *Sisters*, 1904, and *A Platonic Friendship*, 1905, all of which dramatize conflict in middle-class female characters. Besides numerous stories and articles for newspapers and magazines, she wrote an autobiography, *Thirty Years in Australia*, 1903, and the childhood reminiscences *The Retrospect*, 1912. Despite some 26 published novels, three volumes of poetry, and her reputation as a well known and respected author, she died in poverty. See J. Rose, *Australian Literary Studies*, Oct. 1972, and P. Barton in D. Adelaide, ed., *A Bright and Fiery Troop*, 1988.

'Cambridge, Elizabeth', Barbara K. (Webber) Hodges, 1893–1949, novelist, b. at Rickmansworth, Herts., da. of Dr H. W. Webber. Educ. at English private schools and a Paris finishing school, she wrote short stories for publication from the age of 17. In 1914 she nursed briefly as a VAD and m. Dr G. M. Hodges. She had three children and began writing again only in 1930. Six novels, much-praised, sometimes patronizingly, rapidly followed, comprising a keen yet kindly chronicle of village and family life. Their easy style and low-key realism powerfully record sexual and social struggles in this milieu. *The Sycamore Tree*, 1934, and *The Two Doctors*, 1936, portray male victims of social injustice. *Susan and Joanna*, 1935, depicts wary sisterhood between a battered wife and a woman whose frail appearance belies her strength. In *Spring Always Comes*, 1938, various women defend their vocations. EC's strongest novels study a woman under stress: torn between art and family in *Hostages to Fortune*, 1933, and coping with social and personal change in *Portrait of Angela*, 1939. See Beauman, 1983.

Cameron, Caroline Emily Lovett, 'Mrs H. Lovett Cameron' (Sharp), 1844–1921, novelist, b. Walthamstow, Essex, da. of Ann (Hill) and Granvill S., a merchant. Educ. at a Putney boarding school, then in Paris, in 1867 she m. Henry L. C., Parliamentary agent to the treasury. Her first novel, *Juliet's Guardian*, 1877, was followed at the rate of two a year: *In a Grass Country*, 1885, was her best known. *A Sister's Sin*, 1893, treats a pregnant girl left to die by her lover, who has promised his dying father never to cross his mother's will. *The Man Who Didn't*, 1895, 'Dedicated to Married Men', a riposte to Grant Allen's *The Woman Who Did*, is a short comedy about the NEW WOMAN, suggesting that marriage needs reform and that children should be maintained by the nation. *An Ill Wind*, 1901, is another romance with a satiric twist.

Cameron, Eleanor (Butler), children's novelist. She was b. in 1912 in Winnipeg, Man., da. of Florence (Vaughan) and Henry B. She studied at UCLA, m. Ian Stuart C., 1934, had one child and worked as a librarian in public schools and businesses. She wrote 15 well-crafted books for children, including SCIENCE FICTION, fantasy and domestic adventures. The Mushroom Planet quintet, 1954–60, concerns space travel by a host of bizarre characters to the secret planet of Basidium. *The Court of the Stone Children*, 1973, and *To the Green Mountains*, 1975, more accomplished and subtle narratives, explore the 'strange intersections' of young female characters from different historical periods. Her well-known Julia sequence – *A Room Made of Windows*, 1971, *Julia and the Hand of God*, 1977, *That Julia Redfern*, 1982, and *Julia's Magic*, 1984 – works backwards in time to reveal the development of a young writer who was a highly-imaginative child always 'intertwangling' words. Her essays on CHILDREN'S literature, *The Green and Burning Tree*, 1969, 'written out of joy and in appreciation', treat many women authors. See Virginia Haviland, ed., *The Openhearted Audience*, 1980.

Campbell, Dorothea Primrose, 1793–1863, Shetland poet and novelist, eldest child of Eliza (or Betty) and Duncan C. Her grandfather crippled them with debt; her father died; she offered an Inverness publisher her poems written from 1803. He issued them by subscription, with her name, in 1811: they are remarkable for her age, including narratives rich in character and situation, occasional poems and personal lyrics. She wavers between desire and reluctance to leave 'rugged rocks and scanty rills' for richer, distant scenes. A teacher from 1812, she hoped to profit from an enlarged second edition, dedicated to Walter Scott, London, 1816, but the publisher crashed. Her school at Lerwick survived recurrent illness, near-destitution and her mother's opium addiction, with some support from Scott 1817–21 (letters in NLS). Her novel *Harley Radington*, 1821 (payment: 20 copies), quotes Anne BANNERMAN and Margaret CHALMERS. Its hero's mother has fled grinding poverty in Shetland, hidden her past and married well. The best scenes, succinct in style and thick with almost impenetrable dialect and notes, show him shipwrecked, slowly realizing that the barely human creatures around him are his nearest relations. Newman promised DPC *money* for a further 'Tale' (untraced). She migrated to England in 1842 to work for a family which also went bankrupt, received £30 from the RLF in 1844 and died at an Aged Governesses' Asylum in Kentish Town, London.

Campbell, Grace MacLennan (Grant), 1895–1963, novelist, short-story writer. She was b. Williamstown, Ont., the da. of Caroline (M.) and Alexander G., and educ. there and at Queen's Univ., where she won the gold medal in English, 1915. After a year in Education at Queen's, she taught for two years, then m. the Rev. Harvey C., 1919, and lived thereafter in Saskatchewan, Ont., and Québec. They had three children. Of her five novels, 1942–53, the two most popular celebrate pioneer farming communities of Glengarry, where her family had lived for generations. *Thorn-Apple Tree*, 1942, and *The Higher Hill*, 1944, rich in local colour, describe lives of early-nineteenth-century Highland settlers, their pleasures, hardships and community spirit. *The Higher Hill* depicts the near-impossibility of women succeeding in art: only by marrying a man who could offer study abroad could the protagonist develop her talent; instead, she chooses a farmer she loves, with whom she will have neither time nor opportunity to study. GC's short stories and articles appeared widely in Canadian magazines. *Highland Heritage*, 1962, is a historical work based on her travels with her husband in the Scottish Highlands. GC died in Niagara-on-the-Lake, Ont. See Royce MacGillivray and Ewan Ross, *A History of Glengarry*, 1979.

Campbell, Hazel D., short-story writer, b. and educ. in Jamaica; she works for the Jamaica Information Service. Her work has appeared in Edward Brathwaite's journal *Savacou* (which published her two books, *The Rag Doll and Other Stories*, 1978, and *Woman's Tongue*, 1985) and in *Focus*, ed. Mervyn Morris, 1983. Her subtle stories treat domestic relationships, the testing of female faith and strength, 'Survival Rhythms' (the things that people do or believe in order to negotiate their lives), and the co-option by Caribbean people, especially women, of dreams, visions and rituals from chapel, church or balm-yard. Everyday reality rules as a young girl in church with her mother resists the pressure to go up and be 'saved' or a wife discovers that she prefers her husband's absence in a live-in job (with one day off a week) to his demanding presence. HDC shifts into the surreal in 'The Ebony Desk': protagonist realizes that this heirloom from her mother sheds an inhibiting influence, quieting her children and colouring her writing towards a heroine named Rosebud and a happy-ever-after ending; she decides the heirloom must go. 'Princess Carla and the Southern Prince', longest item in *Woman's Tongue*, is a 'Caribbean Fairy Tale' of a dreaming princess who becomes a lucrative tourist attraction, and how those of her subjects still wedded to the old order play on her traditional female longing for love to banish enchantment and bring old age.

Campbell, Helen (Stuart), Helen C. Weeks, 'Campbell Wheaton', 1839–1918, essayist, reformer, novelist and home economist, b. Lockport, NY, da. of Jane (C.), whose surname she adopted from 1877, and Homer H. S., lawyer and president of the Continental Bank Note Company. Educ. at several schools, including Mrs Cook's Seminary, Bloomfield, NJ, in 1860 she m. Grenville Mellen W., surgeon, but they later divorced. In 1862 she began writing children's stories under her married name, pub. in the popular Ainslie Series 1868–71. In 1877 she wrote *His Grandmothers*, her first adult fiction, followed by *Unto the Third and Fourth Generations*, 1880, *Miss Melinda's Opportunity*, 1886, and *Mrs Herndon's Income*, 1886, prefaced by a letter from H. H. JACKSON. *Prisoners of Poverty*, 1887, a collection of her weekly articles from the *New York Tribune*, describes lucidly and forcefully real life exploitation, mainly in the NYC garment industry. 'The Case of Rosa Hughes' has a heroine forced into prostitution to support her family. Her other reformist works include *The Problem of the Poor*, 1882, and *Women Wage-Earners*, 1893, which received an award from the American Economic Association for its survey of the conditions of working women and its recommendations for improvements. From 1894 to 1912 she lived and worked with Charlotte P. GILMAN; they co-edited *Impress* in San Francisco. In 1897 her lectures at the Univ. of Wisconsin were pub. as *Household Economics*. Later that year she was appointed Professor of Home Economics at Kansas State Agricultural College.

Campbell, Jean, novelist, b. 1901 in Melbourne, Victoria, fourth child of Louise (Bollinger) and John McNeil C., manager of the London Bank. She attended the Presbyterian Ladies' College where she edited the school magazine, *Patchwork*. She taught English to migrants, worked in the censorship department of the Army during WWII and took an active interest in the stage, co-writing *Puritan Beware* (performed 1939) and acting with the Little Theatre. Her first novel, *Brass and Cymbals*, 1933, concerns the Jewish community in Melbourne at the turn of the century. An interest in the migrant population of Australia (attributed to her own mixed ancestry) is evident in her other novels, including *Greek Key Pattern*, 1935, *Lest We Lose Our Edens*, 1935, *The Red Sweet Wine*, 1937, and *The Babe is Wise*, 1939. During WWII she published a string of romantic novels designed to make money, which belie the merits of her earlier fiction.

'Campbell, Maria', June Stifle, autobiographer, dramatist, writer for juveniles, feminist, human-rights activist, of Scots, French and Indian ancestry, b. 1940 at Park Valley, Saskatchewan, eldest of eight children. At 12, on her mother's death, she left school to care for her siblings. She m. at 15, lived in Vancouver and Edmonton and then returned, 1981, to Saskatchewan. Since 1963 MC has been involved in social issues. She co-founded the Edmonton Women's Halfway House and Women's Emergency Shelter. She began writing in 1968 and published her best-selling autobiography, *Halfbreed*, 1973, a remarkable, understated account of her courageous struggle against poverty, racism, sexism, alcoholism and drug addiction to achieve self-realization as a woman and member of an ethnic minority. Her great-grandmother Cheechum was her model of wise, strong womanhood. MC has published children's books, has written radio and TV plays and feature films and has been writer-in-residence at the Univs. of Alberta, 1980, and Regina, 1982.

'Campion, Sarah' (Mary Rose Coulton), novelist, b. 1906 in Eastbourne, Sussex, da. of Rose (Ilbert) and George Gordon C. She taught in England, Germany and Canada before visiting S. Africa, NZ and Australia. She lived in north Queensland, 1938–40, before settling in NZ, where she m. writer Antony Alpers in 1949. Six of her 12 novels (pub. in London) have Australian settings or connections, the most important being the trilogy *Mo Burdekin*, 1941, *Bonanza*, 1942, and *The Pommy Cow*, 1944. Vivid, colloquial and often amusing, they reveal a keen understanding of the northern Australian landscape and its effect on human nature and fate. Other novels include *Makeshift*, 1940, *Turn Away No More*, 1940, concerning the return to Europe by Australians, and the dramatic *Dr Golightly*, 1946. SC also pub. a biography of her father, 1929, and stories in *Southerly*. J. Mackellar, 1950 (in *Southerly*), offers a useful commentary on her fiction.

Candler, Ann (More), 1740–1814, labouring-class poet and autobiographer, b. at Yoxford, Suffolk. Her father, William M., was a working glover; her mother died when she was 11, soon after a slide into poverty drove them to Ipswich. AC's writing was discovered when she repaid the parson's Christmas charity with a poem; to her surprise, he did not blame her for presumption, but became her patron. In 1762 she m. a man with a taste for drinking and the army: when he enlisted she reclaimed him, not easily; next time she had to put four of six children in the workhouse and live on charity. Having agreed to follow him to London, for which she later severely blamed herself, she came back destitute and distraught, pregnant with short-lived twins, to 20 years in the workhouse (broken only by a brief reconciliation and final parting). Here she wrote poems for the *Ipswich Journal* (some still unidentified). Patrons including Elizabeth COBBOLD procured her a cottage, 1802, and issued her *Poetical Attempts*, 1803, with an autobiographical letter. As 'a peasant' she 'supplicate[s] the muse' fearfully, yet with thought and skill: compliments, introspection, and an attack on war, on 'curst ambition', 'speculators, and oppressors'.

Cannan, Joanna Maxwell, 1896–1961, novelist and children's writer, b. in Oxford, youngest sister of M. W. CANNAN. Educ. at the future Wychwood School, she published magazine fiction and articles from girlhood, but meant to be an artist. In 1918 she m. infantry captain Harold James Pullein-Thompson. Many of her nearly 20 adult novels contrast suburban with country life, men (usually) of action with men and women of culture. In her first, *The Misty Valley*, 1922, an aspiring artist from Oxford marries an ex-soldier who 'knew that wives bought food and changed frocks and sat in the drawing-room looking pleased': she leaves him to paint, then returns out of duty to find him prepared to change his way of life for hers. *No Walls of Jasper*, 1930, dedicated to Georgette HEYER, traces its protagonist from conventional fretting over money troubles to murdering his father, then his wife's lover, and killing himself when discovery looms. In 1931 came *Ithuriel's Hour* (aristocratic he-man revealed as inhumanly ruthless) and *High Table*, repr. 1987, dedicated to Carola OMAN (dried-up Oxford don, product of loveless parents, hankers after the 'commonplace and heroic'). JC also wrote pleasing murder mysteries (up to *All is Discovered*, 1962) and virtually created the pony-book genre: schoolgirls develop into writers and illustrators in *I Wrote a Pony Book,* 1950, and *Gaze at the Moon,* 1957 (with satirical self-portrait). All her four children wrote: Josephine, Diana and Christine Pullein-Thompson co-authored a pony book, *It Began with Picotee,* 1946, in their teens, and in 1975 *Black Beauty's Clan* (re-issued as *Black Beauty's Family*) about collateral descendants, in the 1880s, WWI, and 1930s, of Anna SEWELL's equine hero. Their joint score is over 100 popular titles, mostly pony stories; Josephine has written thrillers, and one adult novel as 'Josephine Mann'.

Cannan, May Wedderburn, 1893–1973, poet, novelist and memoirist, middle surviving da. (her twin died a baby) of Scots parents who wanted sons: Mary (W.) and Charles C., then Dean of Trinity College, Oxford, a noted mountaineer. She had published poems in e.g. *The Scotsman* by 1908, when the sisters selected and issued *The Tripled Crown. A Book of English, Scotch and Irish Verse* for children, introduced by their friend Sir Arthur Quiller-Couch. She went to the future Wychwood School, Oxford (where she shared literary projects with Carola OMAN), and Downe House, Kent. WWI prevented her training as an actress; she nursed, ran a canteen in Rouen and worked with her father at the Oxford Univ. Press. Her fiancé survived the army to die of 'flu in 1919. Landscape, patriotism, male sacrifice and female loss ('all the best men die') fill her three poetry volumes, 1917, 1919, and 1934 (with an allegorical verse-drama, 'The Journey of Women'). Her pre-modernist mode was rapidly outdated, but she appears in Catherine Reilly, ed., *Scars Upon My Heart*, 1981 (see Judith KAZANTZIS). As one of the war's 'surplus two million', she was the first woman to work at the Athenaeum Club (not hard, she said, after Oxford), and president, through Margaret WOODS, of the female Writers' Club. She published nothing after *The Lonely Generation*, 1934 (idealized autobiography): it and her memoirs pub. as *Grey Ghosts and Voices*, 1976, end with her imminent marriage to P. J. Slater, army officer and admirer of her poems.

Cappe, Catharine (Harrison), 1744–1821, autobiographer and religious writer, b. in Craven, Yorks., da. of the Rev. Jeremiah H., who barred women from his own literary pursuits; her formidable, aristocratic maternal grandmother regaled her with stories of Mary II and Lady Rachel RUSSELL. CC was an ambitious child, longing for praise (only once given by her father), occupation and reading. After he died, 1763, she started a Sunday school at Catterick, then a benefit club for miners' wives and daughters. A dissenter by 1775, she rejected the idea of a smart school, but supported her mother by running one for poor children at York. In 1788 she m. Newcome C., a widower with six grown children who at once became her own. That year she abridged an advice manual by Jonas Hanway; later works include religious journalism, writings on charity schools and on Christ, and a prefatory life of her husband (d. 1799). Her remarkable *Memoirs* (pub. 1822, written 1812, appendix 1818), with clear memory, candour and penetration, recall early influences, frustrations, and an unhappy love-affair.

Cappiello, Rosa, novelist and poet, b. 1942 in Caivano (Naples), da. of Carmela (Vittorioso) and Vincenzo C. She migrated to Australia in 1971, and with no formal education has written two novels: *I Semi Neri,* 1977, and *Paese Fortunato,* 1981 (transl. as *O, Lucky Country,* 1984, by Gaetano Rando). This ironically titled second novel describes the experience of migrant women in Australia. Poverty, loneliness, sexual and economic exploitation in an atmosphere of distrust effectively preclude any sense of community, even within the ghetto. Winner of the prestigious Premio Calabria Prize in Italy, 1982, and the NSW Premier's Literary

Award for Best Ethnic Book, 1985, this book has caused controversy within both the migrant and Anglo-Australian communities with its outspokenness.

Captivity-narratives. American Indians carried off settler women and children more often than live males. Among the most vivid and observant recorders of such incidents are Mary ROWLANDSON (the first), Susannah JOHNSON, and Rachel Plummer (one of the last), who died a month after finishing her *Narrative*, 1839. Most of these books, printed on small remote presses, are now very rare; some, like those of Massy Harbison and Mary Kinnam, were written for, not by, their protagonists; some, like that of Elizabeth HANSON, had their authentic text progressively 'polished' (some repr. ed. Richard VanDerBeets, 1973). Frances Slocum told her rediscovered relations, who wanted her home after 59 years, 'The Indians are my people' (briefly reported in translation by the hostile John Todd, 1842). An English parallel is Mrs Crisp's *The Female Captive*, 1769 (pub. at a financial low ebb), about capture by Barbary pirates in 1756, sometimes classed as fiction.

Carey, Mary (Jackson), Lady, 1609/12–1680, religious writer, da. of 'tenderly loving parents'; her father was Sir John J. of Berwick. She lived fashionably, with theatre, cards and dancing, till a severe illness at 18 began a year of religious terror, ending in assurance of salvation. She says her first marriage, to Sir Pelham C., was good for her. Widowed, she m., by 1643, George Payler, a parliamentary paymaster with whom she moved around between garrison towns during the civil war. (She still called herself C.) In 1653 she began to collect her meditations, dedicated to him (MS privately owned: Bodleian Library scribal copy, 1681). Long prose treatises mix with verse on the deaths of babies: by 1657 she had borne and lost five who were 'sickly, weake, pained'; two more were still healthy and hopeful. She strives to accept God's will, as 'more deare to me, than any Child'. Even when an 'abortive Birth' ('my dead formlesse Babe', with, she insists, a soul) makes her ask God's reasons, she concludes that dead babies are his just return for her 'dead' service. She favours the dialogue form: in exchanges with her husband, with God or Satan, or between soul and body (1649).

Carey, Rosa Nouchette, 'Le Voleur', 1840–1909, novelist, b. Stratford-le-Bow, London, da. of Jane (Woodhill) and William Henry C., shipbroker. She was educ. at home in Hackney, writing little plays to amuse her family, and at the Ladies' Institute, St John's Wood, where she was friendly with Mathilde BLIND until her rigid high church views separated them. Later friends included Ellen WOOD. The first of her 39 novels, *Nellie's Memories*, 1868, sold over 52,000 copies and was followed by the popular *Wee Wifie*, 1869, *Wooed and Married*, 1875, *Not Like Other Girls*, 1884, *Uncle Max*, 1887, and *Only the Governess*, 1888. Often written for girls, these were 'wholesome' optimistic domestic romances stressing the moral value of work for middle-class women, but offering conservative resolutions. More exotic novels (pub. under 'Le Voleur') include *By Order of the Brotherhood*, 1895, *For Love of a Bedouin Maid*, 1897, and *In the Tsar's Dominions*, 1899. She also wrote religious essays and *Twelve Notable Good Women of the XIXth Century*, 1899, which includes studies of 'virtuous' women such as Queen VICTORIA, Florence NIGHTINGALE and Elizabeth Fry.

Carleton, Mary, 1634?–73, autobiographical writer, claiming to be a German lady well educ. in a convent. She m. John C. in 1663 (apparently thinking him rich, as he thought her), was arrested for bigamy (his family's move, it seems, to get rid of her) and subsequently acquitted. Three works of that year, *The Case* (addressed to Prince Rupert), *A True Account*, and *An Historical*

Narrative (all answered by John C., who also wrote two more of the many pamphlets on her case) are probably her own; John C. thought so, though later commentators have often doubted it, and preferred Francis Kirkham's semi-fictional life of her, 1673. She uses romance conventions to make her story convincing, writing of her youth 'I blindly wished I were (what my inclinations prompted me to) a man, and exempt from that tedious life, which yet was so much worse, because it was altogether passive and sedentary.' She possibly studied at the Inns of Court, perhaps acted the lead in Thomas Parker's play about her, 1664, was transported to Jamaica for theft in 1671, arrested for further theft in 1673, and hanged. See Elaine Hobby, 1988.

Carlisle, Isabella Howard (Byron), Countess of, 1721–95, advice-writer, da. of Frances (Berkeley) and William Lord B. She m., 1743, Henry H., 4th Earl of C. (Lady IRWIN's brother); Anna SEWARD wrote a dedication to her son, 1804. She answered Frances GREVILLE's 'Prayer for Indifference', by 1758, in jaunty but weakish stanzas arguing that indifference never goes with sense and beauty: pub. following the original in the *London Mag.*, 1771. Lady Louisa STUART said she was 'evermore scribbling' and that she rebelled against propriety once widowed, 1758. She m. the young Sir William Musgrave in 1759, parted from him ten years later, and lived much abroad, where the attention of a series of 'barons' worried her family. Her *Thoughts in the Form of Maxims Addressed to Young Ladies*, 1790, too late for her four daughters' use, is a slight thing.

Carlyle, Jane Baillie **(Welsh)**, 1801–66, memoirist, letter writer, b. Haddington, East Lothian, Scotland, only child of Grace W. and Dr John W. (no relation to Grace). Mercurial and precocious, she was educ. from age four at Haddington School, learning Latin from Edward Irving. Her father's death in 1819 left her emotionally devastated but financially secure, though in 1823 she transferred his estate to her mother. In 1826 she m. Thomas C., historian and essayist, and after some years they moved to London. Here she acted as a hostess to some of the most talented people of her time including J. S. Mill and Harriet TAYLOR, Mazzini, Macready, Thackeray, Dickens and JWC's great friend Geraldine JEWSBURY. Despite poor health, she was her husband's chief protector and critic, and wrote voluminous letters and memoirs, some of which were pub. by J. A. Froude, 1883; others have appeared in numerous selections since. Her writing demonstrates acute perceptions and considerable literary talent. Whilst not focusing specifically on issues of female emancipation, her witty observation of social behaviour is apparent: 'Women, they say, will always give a varnish of duty to their inclinations. I wonder whether men are any better in always giving to their disinclinations a varnish of justice.' See Lawrence and Elizabeth Hanson's life of JWC, 1952, John Stewart Collis, *The Carlyles*, 1971, and articles by Gail Kmetz, *Mass. Studies in English* 4 (1974–5) and Elizabeth Hardwick, *NYRB*, Dec. 4, 1972. An edition of her letters, ed. A. Sanders and K. Fielding, 1970–, is in progress.

Carmichael, Sarah Elizabeth (later Williamson), 1838–1901, poet, b. Setauket, NY, da. of Mary Anne and William C. The family joined the Mormons and in 1850 moved west from Illinois to Salt Lake City, Utah. There, SEC began publishing poems in the *Deseret News (sic)* and the *Women's Exponent*, a feminist newspaper put out by Mormon women. Her selected *Poems* were pub. in 1866. Though some of her poems, such as 'Lake Tahoe' and 'Moonrise on the Wasatch', praise the Western landscape, most are on general topics. Some, such as the often reprinted 'Allie's Prayer', typify the verse of the sentimental 'poetesses' parodied by Twain in *Huckleberry Finn*. She also wrote melodramatic narrative poems like 'Lucretia Borgia's Feast', and during the Civil War she pub. a series of poems based on battle scenes. Not a 'Mormon' poet, her marriage in 1866 to a non-Mormon, Jonathan M. Williamson, brought criticism, and she moved from Utah. She became mentally ill and wrote no more.

Carr, Emily, 1871–1945, painter and autobiographer. B. in Victoria, BC, to Emily (Saunders) and Richard C. (who died in 1888, two years after his wife), she attended school in Victoria. She began art lessons in early childhood, studied at California School of Design in San Francisco, 1891–3, Westminster School of Art, London, 1899–1901, and Académie Colarossi in Paris, 1910–11 (exhibiting at the 1911 Salon D'Automne). Her art studies in England were interrupted by serious illness treated by a lengthy stay at East Anglia Sanitorium, 1903–4 (described in *Pause: A Sketch Book*, 1953). EC's paintings, inspired by her visits to West Coast native settlements and her love of Canadian landscape (she fought against 'Old World' artists who told her 'our West was crude, unpaintable') gained wide acceptance only late in her life (particularly after a 1927 exhibition in Ottawa). She earned her living by giving art lessons in the 1890s and 1900s, and, from 1913, by running a boarding house in Victoria for 22 years (described in *The House of All Sorts*, 1944), selling pottery, and breeding dogs. Her first book, *Klee Wyck*, 1941 (winner of the Governor-General's Award), written during convalescence from a heart attack in 1937, is titled after the name, meaning 'Laughing One', given to EC during a visit to a Nootka Indian reserve in 1899. Her next, *The Book of Small*, 1942, describes her childhood – 'I was the disturbing element of the family' – and her father, 'a stern straight man.' After her death appeared her AUTOBIOGRAPHY, *Growing Pains*, 1946, *The Heart of a Peacock*, 1953, stories and sketches; and her journals, *Hundreds and Thousands*, 1966, describing her desire to write 'plain, straight, simple' prose. Much has been written on her life: see Paula Blanchard's biog. and Ruth Gowers's study, both 1987. Eva-Marie Kroller in *Can L.*, 109, 1986, surveys poems about EC by Florence MCNEIL, Susan MUSGRAVE, Dorothy LIVESAY; Adrienne RICH has based a poem on EC's life.

Carrie, Grace, prophet, living at Bristol. She had a series of visions in 1635 and described them in an account entitled *Englands Fore-Warning*.... She declined to print it, thinking 'very unfitt, that such divine and miracalous truth should be made common' or read by 'the meaner sort, of voulgar people', but she made copies (Cambridge Univ. Lib.).

Carrier, Constance, poet and translator. She was b. in 1908 in New Britain, Conn., da. of Lillian (Jost) and Lucius A. C., assistant to the Treasurer at Trinity College, Hartford. Educ. at public schools, Smith (BA, 1929) and Trinity College, Hartford (MA, 1940), she taught Latin in New Britain and West Hartford public schools, 1931–69, and lectured occasionally at Tufts Univ. Her poetry appeared first in journals such as *Atlantic Monthly*, *The New Yorker* and *Poetry*. Her first book, *The Middle Voice*, 1955, won the Lamont Prize, and John Ciardi praised her as a 'passionate formalist'. Her 'Fugue', a villanelle, declares an aesthete's allegiances in its impressionist, metaphoric rendering of a city scene, but draws away from surfaces in the end to cite 'the ancient argument / of bone and blood and brain'. She translated Sextus Aurelius Propertius, 1963, Tibullus, 1968, and two among the *Complete Comedies of Terence*, 1974 (in verse). Her second volume of poems, *The Angled Road* (a phrase from Emily DICKINSON), 1973, shows Dickinson's pervasive influence in its concern with mortality and with the relation between the infinite natural world (the Angled Road of experience) and the limited world of our minds. Of a child under a lilac tree she writes, 'O leaf and light, that can divide thus clearly / the world in two // and give the halves to a child ... that she may move in both.' 'Martha Carrier, 1669–1692' celebrates a namesake, 'short of temper and harsh-tongued', executed in the Salem witch trials.

Carrighar, Sally, nature writer, autobiographer, b. *c.* 1905 in Cleveland, Ohio, da. of Perle Avis Harden (Wagner) and George Thomas Beard C. Disfigured at birth, she lived under threat from her psychotic mother, who tried to strangle her and urged her to suicide, until her father entrusted her to her grandparents. From them she learned an appreciation of nature that saved her from breakdown. She attended Wellesley College. Her first study of nature, *One Day on Beetle Rock*, 1944, is written from the points of view of various species inhabiting the Sierra Nevada; its success led her to re-use the strategy in later books, notably *One Day at Teton Marsh*, 1947 (for which she wrote a screenplay, 1966). She went to Alaska on a Guggenheim, stayed nine years, and wrote *Icebound Summer*, 1953, about her studies there, *Moonlight at Midday*, 1958, about Eskimo villagers and the impact on them of 'civilization', and *Wild Voice of the North*, 1959, about her association with Bobo, a sled dog. *The Glass Dove*, 1963, a novel, depicts a young woman running a station on the Underground Railroad during the Civil War, torn between her political beliefs and love for a suspected Confederate spy. SC's moving, feminist AUTOBIOGRAPHY, *Home to the Wilderness*, 1973, chronicles her struggle to emerge whole and alive from her mother's and her own mental illness.

Carrington, Dora de Houghton, 1893–1932, artist, diarist, letter-writer, b. at Hereford to pious, prudish ex-governess Charlotte (Houghton) and 60-year-old Samuel C., Christian pacifist and ex-railway builder in India: 'I was devoted to my father. I hated my mother.' She grew up in Bedford, going to its high school but beginning a self-education in history and literature at the Slade School of Art, London, 1910–13. From then on she used her surname alone (plus nicknames: 'Doric', 'Cirod', 'Mopsa', etc.). She 'always hated being a woman', responding to men with both desire and shame (no shame, she wrote in 1925, with a woman). From 1915 she loved and devoted herself to the older homosexual writer Lytton Strachey. She did illustrations for Leonard and Virginia WOOLF, 1917; Virginia read her LETTERS with 'great relish' and parodied her punctuation (all dashes); C praised *Jacob's Room* as painterly. C lived with Strachey from 1917 in the Thames Valley (Tidmarsh, then Pangbourne). Her marriage, 1921, to Ralph Partridge (whom Strachey also loved) was unhappy: both were unfaithful (she with Gerald Brenan), and he furiously jealous. Her LETTERS, spiced with line-drawings and verse, are equally playful with language; her DIARY is keenly self-aware. She shot herself seven weeks after Strachey's death; poems written in those weeks begin 'I did not realize till now, that you / Made lovely all my fields and view', and 'Turn down the wick! / Your night is done.' An exhibition of her work was held in 1970. Memoir by her brother Noel C. in *Letters and Extracts From her Diaries*, patronizingly ed. by David Garnett, 1970, which opens on a dignified statement to painter Mark Gertler, 1915, that sex is impossible 'unless one does love a man's body'. Noel C. ed. her *Paintings, Drawings and Decorations*, 1978. Life by Gretchen Gerzina, 1989.

Carrington, Elaine (Sterne), 1892–1958, 'John Ray', scriptwriter, b. in NYC, da. of Mary Louise (Henriguez) and Theodore S. She sold her first story, 'King of the Christmas Feast', at 18, and at 19 won two scriptwriting contests. Educ. at Columbia Univ., she m. lawyer George Dan C. and had two children. She wrote, as 'John Ray', the movie script *Alibi*, 1929 (earlier version entitled *Nightstick*), and published a short-story volume, *All Things Considered*, 1939; but she specialized in radio serials, shaping the soap-opera genre which treats day-to-day middle-class family life with sentiment and occasional satire. A founder of the Radio Writers' Guild, she 'fiercely' retained independent choice of topics for her serials, in which she sought to give women psychological support and positive self-images. Her greatest hits were *Pepper Young's Family*, 1936–56 (begun with Burgess Meredith), which underwent several changes of title, *When a Girl Marries*, 1939–56, and *Rosemary*, 1944–55. Her patriotic scripts for the Treasury Department earned her a citation; her 'Carrington Playhouse' produced scripts by aspiring young writers during the 1940s. See M. Edmondson and D. Rounds, *From Mary Noble to Mary Hartman: The Complete Soap Opera Book*, 1976.

Carson, Rachel Louise, 1907–64, biologist, conservationist, environmental writer. B. in Springdale, Penn., da. of Maria (McLean) and Robert Warden C., she was determined, as a child, to become a writer. She majored in English at Pennsylvania College for Women, switched to biology in her junior year, and took her AM at Johns Hopkins, 1932. She taught at the Univ. of Maryland from 1932–6, then became one of the first women to occupy a non-clerical position in the Fisheries Bureau in Washington, DC, meanwhile caring for her mother and two orphaned nieces. Her first book, *Under the Sea*, 1941, went unnoticed in the furore following Pearl Harbor: reissued after publication of *The Sea Around Us*, 1951, it became a bestseller. Both books combine scientific knowledge and demystifying style. *Silent Spring*, 1962, her most controversial book, began the mobilization of pressure against irresponsible use of toxic chemicals. At her death, the *New York Times* wrote that 'the power of her knowledge and the beauty of her language combined to make [her] one of the most influential women of our time.' See study by Carol B. Gartner, 1983.

Carswell, Catherine Roxburgh (Macfarlane), also Jackson, 1879–1946, novelist, biographer, literary journalist. Da. of deeply religious Mary Anne (Lewis) and merchant George Gray M., she was b. and educ. in Glasgow, later travelled to Italy, studied music at the Frankfurt Conservatorium, *c.* 1897–9, and attended the Glasgow School of Art. Then, though women were not yet admitted to degrees, she studied English at Glasgow Univ. and launched her literary career by reviewing drama and fiction for the Glasgow *Herald*. In 1902, she m. Herbert J. who was dangerously insane by the end of their honeymoon. Since insanity was not yet a ground for divorce, CC's successful suit for annulment, 1908, made legal history. She moved to London and continued to review 'piles of novels' for the *Herald*, including, in 1911, D. H. Lawrence's *White Peacock*. They met, 1914, and 'From beginning to end I had for Lawrence, as he well knew, a special kind of love and admiration which I never knew for any other human being.' In 1915, she m. Donald Carswell: they had one son. She slipped her favourable review of *The Rainbow* past her editor, so losing her job in the same week as Lawrence's publisher was forced to withdraw the book from sale. Between 1916 and 1920, she and Lawrence exchanged MSS, corresponded, and planned to write a novel together, she to provide the female character, he the male. *Open the Door!*, which won the Melrose first novel prize, 1920, is, as Lawrence said, a 'real' and 'honest' treatment of female sexuality. *The Camomile*, 1922, named for the plant which 'the more it is trodden on, the faster it grows', is a deeply and sometimes comically ironic epistolary tale of the making of a woman writer. These clear-headed, powerful, feminist novels have a significant relation to male texts of their time: the *bildungsroman* of 1920 to Lawrence's necessary theme, the *kunstleroman* of 1922 to Joyce's *Portrait.* More notice, however, has been given to CC's later works on Burns, 1930, and Lawrence (*The Savage Pilgrim*, 1932, withdrawn in its first edition because J. Middleton Murry thought it libellous). CC wrote *The Tranquil Heart*, 1937, about Giovanni Boccaccio, because he was, she said, the first writer who 'dreamed of writing avowedly for women readers'. A friend of Susan TWEEDSMUIR, she helped prepare the memorial volume on John Buchan. Reprints of *Open the Door!*, 1986, and *The Savage Pilgrim*, 1981, have introductions by her son John, who collected her autobiographical writings in *Lying Awake*, 1950. See also his *Lives and Letters*, 1978. Her literary journalism is not collected.

Carter, Angela (Stalker), novelist, short-story writer, essayist, journalist, poet, playwright. B. 1940 in London, da. of Olive (Farthing) and Hugh Alexander S., she spent a working-class youth in S. Yorkshire. She worked as a journalist, 1958–61, then took her degree in English (Univ. of Bristol, 1965), held posts in creative writing at Sheffield and Brown Univs., and for two years lived in Japan, where she observed a 'concealed matriarchy' behind a 'prostitute society'. A 'neo-GOTHIC' or 'magic-realist', indebted to Isak DINESEN, Djuna BARNES and Jane BOWLES, she uses the gothic mad-doctor-in-his-castle-laboratory scenario to satirize Western patriarchy and capitalism. *The Magic Toyshop*, 1967, exposes, behind the scenes of a petit-bourgeois family business, the master craftsman at work in his funhouse of free enterprise, exploiting domestic labour and transforming female family members into fetish commodities. The post-apocalyptic *Heroes and Villains*, 1969, features a shaman-magus engineering a barbarous state of nature in which the heroine survives by abandoning deference and acquiring an autonomous, female will. In *The Infernal Desire Machines of Doctor Hoffman*, 1972, a Freudian Faust invades the sterile bureaucracy of civilization with an anarchic dream world designed by his pornographic imagination and generated by the libido of copulating couples harnessed to his 'desire machine'. *Love*, 1971, de-mythifies fatherly 'love', which controls the daughter's virginity, brotherly 'love', which bullies the sister into incestuous relations, and conjugal 'love', which serves masculine narcissism while it subjects the woman to abuse and neglect. The short stories and fairy tales of *The Bloody Chamber*, 1979, figure women's healthy, animal lusts against backgrounds of repressive civility or mutilating pornography. In its feathered heroine, a Winged Victory who achieves fame and notoriety on the flying trapeze, *Nights at the Circus*, 1984, allegorizes woman's transformation of her 'deformity' (being female in a man's world) into an extraordinary talent which she manages, successfully, for herself. *The Passion of New Eve*, 1977, analyses the art of gender construction in the quest for romance between a transsexual and a transvestite of the opposite sex. AC edited *Wayward Girls and Wicked Women* (stories), 1986. Other works are *Black Venus*, 1985, short stories, *The Sadeian Woman*, 1979, *Nothing Sacred*, 1982, *Don't Bet on the Prince: Contemporary Feminist Fairy Tales in North America and Europe*, 1987, and *Come Unto These Yellow Sands: Four Radio Plays*, 1987. Critical studies by Patricia Duncker in *Literature and History*, 10, 1984, and David Punter in *Critique*, 25, 1984. Interview in *Meanjin*, 44, 1985.

Carter, Elizabeth, 1717–1806, scholar, poet and letter-writer, elder da. of Margaret (Swayne) and the Rev. Nicolas C. of Deal, Kent, who found her slow but taught her Latin, Greek and Hebrew with her brothers, and planned a Court post for her. She added other languages (even Portuguese and Arabic) for herself, using aids to study like snuff, a wet towel round the head and chewing green tea. Always subject to severe headaches, she combatted ill health by strenuous country walking. Aged ten when her mother died, she ran the household till her father married again, educated a half-brother 21 years her junior, and cared for her father till he died in 1774. Cave's *Gentleman's Magazine* carried verse by her in 1734, then regular contributions: he pub. her slim *Poems on Particular Occasions*, 1738. That year she translated, with critical comment, Crousaz's French critique of Pope, and in 1739 Algarotti's Italian popularization of Isaac Newton's *Optics* 'for the use of Ladies'. Always outspokenly glad to be unmarried, she had a perhaps romantic friendship of almost 30 years with Catherine TALBOT, chiefly by letter. She was enchanted at first prospect ('I think of her all day, dream of her all night'), stilted in her first letter, then fond, ironic, hyperbolical and whimsical. A superlative letter-writer who dreaded print, she requires in her reader a keen sense of the ridiculous; her penetrating literary criticism convinced her nephew she was biased towards female writers. She contributed to others' works (e.g., like Talbot, to Johnson's *Rambler*); Talbot suggested the scholarly translation of Epictetus which EC worked at 1749–52 and pub. by subscription 1758, earning fame and nearly £1000. (An unknown 'Selina', translator of another ancient work, had challenged Epictetus's view of women in a version by J. W., 1707.) EC knew most of the outstanding women and men of her time; her sense and learning won deep respect from the BLUESTOCKINGS and others. Her *Remarks on the Athanasian Creed*, 1752, part of a debate raging at Deal, opens with a gesture of female politesse and proceeds to annihilate her antagonist. A larger *Poems*, 1762, expands her range from solemn and classical to include the emotional and comic; a third ed., 1776, added more. She refused a post as royal governess, and travelled in Europe with Elizabeth MONTAGU, another close friend, in 1763 and 1782. An unnamed female friend pub. a *Sketch* of her, Kelso, 1806; her nephew Montagu Pennington pub. *Memoirs* (with poems and essays), 1807 (facs. 1974), and some of her widely scattered letters (to Talbot and Elizabeth VESEY, 1809; to Montagu, 1817, facs. 1973). A. Gaussen's life, 1906, is poor.

Cartland, Mary **Barbara** Hamilton, also McCorquodale, b. 1901, popular novelist, 'Queen of Romance'. B. to Polly (Scobell) and Major Bertram C., who died in WWI, she attended Malvern Girls' College and Abbey House, debuted in London society, 1919, and was presented at Court, 1925. In 1927 she m. Alexander M. (divorced 1933), with whom she had a daughter, then, 1936, his cousin Hugh M., with whom she had two sons. She began writing in 1923 as a gossip columnist for the *Daily Express*, and published her first novel, *Jig-Saw*, 1925, while active in the London social life her novels depict, though most of these are set in the nineteenth century. Author of over 300 books (most dictated to a secretary), she is the 'top-selling authoress' in *The Guinness Book of (World) Records*: sales of 390 million. Her novels – 'an escape from the depression and boredom and lack of romance in modern life' – extol the virtues of 'home, love, and ... high ideals': her chaste, pure heroines marry wealthy, invariably titled, husbands. She has also written fictionalized 'biographies' of various women, like *Josephine, Empress of France*, 1961, ADVICE books on marriage and sex, like *Love, and Marriage*, 1961, and several vols. of autobiography.

Cartwright, Mrs **H.**, novelist and advice-writer, unknown except by the name on her works, pub. at London. She issued conservative *Letters on Female Education*, 1777 (dedicated to Elizabeth MONTAGU, on how to produce the ideal child), *Memoirs of Lady Eliza Audley*, 1779 (said by the *Monthly Review* to be from a French original of *c.* 1760), *Letters Moral and Entertaining*, 1780 (by subscription: imaginary ladies write on manners and religion), and epistolary novels beginning with *The Generous Sister*, 1780. Most are now rare; nothing, even date, is known of *The Vale of Glendor*. *Retaliation, or The History of Sir Edward Oswald and Lady Frances Seymour*, 1787, typically glorifies literary retirement in Wales, disdain for worldly titles (which come, however, to the heroine's father and future husband), and happiness found in charity and patronage. Mary WOLLSTONECRAFT condemned *The Platonic Marriage*, 1786, in *Mary*, 1788; E. O. BENGER praised HC in 1791 for her *Letters* and two novels.

Cartwright, Joanna, pamphleteer. B. in England, she was a widow living in Amsterdam in 1649 when she pub. with her son Ebenezer C. *The Petition of the Jewes* (well received, she says, when she presented it to Gen. Fairfax). It urges him and the Council of Officers to repeal laws banning Jews from England, so that they 'may again be received and permitted to trade and dwell amongst you', as in the Netherlands.

Cartwright, Mrs **Robert**, fl. 1850s, novelist, poet, essayist, *may* have been m. to Dr Robert C., who wrote five pieces on Shakespeare, 1859–77. Her extraordinary first novel, *Lamia: A Confession*, 1850 (pub. anon. and written in a mixed didactic, gothic and sentimental style) is almost viciously punitive towards its dying heroine, a brilliantly gifted young woman turned atheist: such women need special moral guidance (Mrs RC says) to slot them into conventional roles. After her next novel, *Christabelle*, 1855, came *The Royal Sisters, or, Pictures of a Court*, 1857, followed by *Pilgrim Walks: A Chaplet of Memories*, 1859, a conventional travel book with poems appended, one of which, 'The Amazon Attacked by a Tiger (Crystal Palace, 1851)', is again perversely interesting: 'This, *this* is glorious, – and I gazing now, / A poor weak woman of my century, / Haunted by dreams, and circled by my bonds . . .'.

Carver, Mrs, English novelist unknown but for her (MINERVA) works. In 1797 she pub. *Elizabeth* (whose humble preface claims some not entirely fictitious characters) and *The Horrors of Oakendale Abbey* (which horrors are finally dispelled for ever by the combined virtues of the heroine and her new husband). The whole of this novel's first page is a single sentence which revels in gloom and 'thick drippling rain'; the plot embraces romance and melodrama, corsairs and noble Greek ladies, but keeps a toehold in sober scepticism. *The Legacy*, 1799, mixes pathos with satirical humour: an uncle leaves his nephews Bibles with interleaved banknotes which remain long undiscovered. Last came *The Old Woman*, 1800.

Cary, Alice Patty Lee, 1820–71, poet, novelist, and **Phoebe,** 1824–71, poet, wit, editor. Both sisters were abolitionists. B. in Hamilton County, Ohio, fourth and sixth of nine children of Elizabeth (Jessup) and Robert C., they grew up on a poor farm with little access to literature or formal education. Their literary affinity sustained them, and from her early teens AC published highly popular poems (praised by Whittier and Poe) in Western journals and newspapers, while at 18, PC wrote the well-known hymn, 'Nearer Home'. Griswold included both in *Female Poets*, 1849, and helped them publish their *Poems*, 1850. Financed by her writings, AC moved to NYC in 1850, where, joined by PC, who nursed her and ran their household, she maintained a leading literary establishment for 20 years and was president of the first American women's club, 'Sorosis'. They both pub. poetry in leading periodicals as well as in volumes. AC produced *Lyra*, 1852, *Poems*, 1855, and *Ballads, Lyrics, Hymns*, 1866; while PC published *Poems and Parodies*, 1854 and *Poems of Faith, Hope, and Love*, 1868, and with the Rev. Dr C. F. Deems, edited *Hymns for All Christians*, 1869, and worked briefly as assistant editor for Susan B. ANTHONY's suffrage paper,

The Revolution. More varied in tone and voice, more worldly and sensuous than her sister's, PC's poetry is surprisingly mindful of the delights of physical passion – 'O for the time when I felt his caresses . . . Talk not of maiden reserve and of duty' – and its grim social consequences. She writes with perspicacity of passionate, wry, bitter women who show anger, not submission, at the vagaries of men's affections: 'And yielding to the blessed gush / Of my ungovernable spite, / Have risen up, the red, the old, / Scolding as hard as I could scold' ('Worser Moments'). AC, by contrast, focuses obsessively on dead, abandoned and ostracized women – dead maidens with heavy tresses, victims of male oppression, create a cumulative effect of despair, futility and wasted lives. Her more lasting achievement probably lies in her fiction: sketches and stories of the straitened lives of women in frugal farming communities. *Clovernook*, 1852, was a minor bestseller, particularly in England, and was followed by *The Clovernook Children*, 1855, *Married Not Mated*, 1856, *Pictures of Country Life*, 1859, and *Adopted Daughter and Other Tales* (ed. with PC), 1859, among other titles. See the coll. ed. Judith Fetterley, 1988. Phoebe died six months after AC, and a posthumous edition of their last poems appeared in 1873, followed by *Ballads for Little Folks*, 1874, and finally a complete *Poetical Works*, with a memorial, in 1877 (all ed. by M. C. Ames).

Cary, Anne, *c.* 1615–71, or **Mary**, *c.* 1622–93, biographer. One of Lady FALKLAND's four youngest daughters wrote her mother's life (normal for a saint, not for a woman writer) with piety, loving humour, and 'dry intelligence that puts to shame the effusive contemporary masculine biographers' (Donald A. Stauffer in *English Biography before 1700*). Most scholars think it was Anne, later Dame Clementia, some of whose letters of 1650 are in the Bodleian; but, either elusive or clumsy, she keeps herself unidentifiable. Having said that Lady Falkland, while still an Anglican, vowed her *last* daughter (Mary) to the Virgin, she then *implies* it was the same one whose desire to be a nun (awkward, since her mother was planning a Court place for her) is treated with the detail of inside knowledge. Both lived as Protestants with their Catholic mother after their father's death; converted in secret; refused to leave her for their elder brother's house until sent; and helped kidnap their (willing) little brothers into a Catholic environment. Mary joined the Benedictine convent at Cambrai in 1638, Anne in 1639; Anne led a colony to Paris. The MS life stayed with the nuns: now in Imperial Archives, Lille. Their brother Patrick 'erased several passages which he considered too feminine': part pub. 1857, the whole by Richard Simpson, 1861; see Patrick C., *Poems*, ed. Sister Veronica Delany, 1978.

Cary, Mary, *c.* 1621–after 1653, English gentlewoman, radical pamphleteer. She published (as Cary, though she apparently m. before 1651 a man named Rande) a series of prophecies foreseeing parliamentary victory in the Civil War and advising how to build God's kingdom on earth. In closely-argued, literary style she calls for alliances among the whole range of anti-monarchists. *The Resurrection of the Witnesses*, 1648, dates this event from the formation of the New Model Army, 1645. Her most visionary and expansive works are *The Little Horns Doom and Downfall* and *A New and Exact Mappe or Description of New Jerusalems Glory*, pub. together 1651, dedicated to three prominent women and prefaced by praise from three prominent radicals. She argues that the Saints must take arms against their oppressors: hierarchies will be overthrown, according to biblical promise, so that 'not onely men, but women shall prophesie . . . not only superiou[r]s but inferiours; not onely those that have University-learning, but those that have it not; even servants and handmaids'; schisms among the Saints will cease; 'old men and old women shall live till they come to a good old age' and 'no infant of days shall die; none shall die while they are young.' She considers but decides against vegetarianism. A postscript to this volume amends her *Resurrection* by borrowing from an anonymous male attack on her for lack of learning, 1649. In 1653 she amended that work further in a 2nd ed., and addressed *Twelve Humble Proposals* to the Barebones Parliament, calling on them to abolish tithes, promote preaching and attend to the needs of the poor, and advising in detail how to fund and administer her proposed changes.

Casely-Hayford, Adelaide (Smith), 1868–1960, educator, feminist, autobiographer, b. in Sierra Leone, the da. of Anne (Spilsbury) and William S., son of a Yorkshire father and Fanti mother. She moved with her family to England, 1872, settling in Jersey, where she was educ., first by a governess, then at the Jersey Ladies' College. At 17, she went to Germany for three years, studying music at a branch of the Stuttgart Conservatory. With her sister she established, *c.* 1898, the Girls' Vocational School in Freetown, for adult African women, 'the first private enterprise to establish girls' secondary education in Sierra Leone'. It was short-lived, however, and she went to England, where, in 1903, she m. Joseph Ephraim C-H, a prominent lawyer and activist. Their daughter Gladys CASELY-HAYFORD was born in Axim, Gold Coast, 1904. They separated in a few years. AC-H spent much time in England and lived in the US, 1920–3, soliciting support for her Industrial and Technical Training School for Girls, which began in 1923 and survived a chequered history until 1940. She wrote two widely anthologized short stories, 'Mista Courifer' and 'Savages', an article, 'A Girls' School in West Africa', and, as an old woman, *Memoirs*, quoted above, which appeared in the *West African Review*, Oct. 1953–Aug. 1954, later in Lucilda Hunter, ed., *Memoirs and Poems by Adelaide Casely-Hayford and Gladys Casely-Hayford*, 1983. Life by Adelaide M. Cromwell, 1986, who calls her 'An African Victorian Feminist'.

Casely-Hayford, Gladys May, 'Aquah Laluah', 1904–50, Sierra Leone poet and short-story writer. Da. of Adelaide CASELY-HAYFORD, she was born with a malformed hip, and went at a young age with her mother to England to seek treatment. Later, from about 1915, she attended Penrhos College in Wales. She returned to Freetown, 1926, to help her mother reopen her vocational school for girls, then, 1929, set off for the US via Europe, pausing to join a black jazz group in Berlin. About 1936, she m. Arthur Hunter. Their son was born in Accra, 1940, where GC-H died. Her poems in Krio, the English-based lingua franca of Sierra Leone, are collected in *Take Um So*, 1948. Poems characterized by her concern for ordinary people appeared in the *Atlantic Monthly* and in Lucilda Hunter's edition of her work and her mother's, 1983. See Langston Hughes, *An African Treasury*, 1960, Eustace Palmer in Bruce King and Kolanọle Ogunbesan, eds., *A Celebration of Black and African Writing*, 1975, and Adelaide Cromwell's life of her mother, 1986.

Caspary, Vera, novelist, journalist, screenwriter, b. 1899 in Chicago, da. of Julia (Cohen), 'a refugee from orthodoxy, a challenger of God', and unsuccessful businessman Paul C. She grew up in Chicago and Memphis, Tenn., later recalling that her bridge-playing family's 'extraordinary dullness' had propelled her to 'become a writer, a woman of the world, and independent'. After a brief business course, 1918, she worked as a stenographer, then overcame gender-bias to become an advertising copywriter. The *Tribune* published a 'few of my light verses'. Emotional strains in 1924 (her father's death, a notorious murder, fear of anti-semitic outbreaks) made her 'a writer of murder stories': her words for her complex psycho-thrillers using multiple narrators. She became a published novelist at her second attempt and supported her mother by writing plays, stories and screenplays. At the Chicago Council of Jewish Women, 1933, she made an 'impassioned plea for unity to replace the prejudice and snobbery of assimilated Jews' – an impulse which also produced *The White Girl*, 1929, whose fair-skinned black heroine, she said, she had shunned when younger. She became a friend of Gwen BRISTOW, then a Communist (influenced by Anna Louise STRONG) until the Stalin-Hitler pact disillusioned her. She did research on proletarian women (used later in *The Rosecrest Cell*, 1967), and visited Russia in 1939. During WWII she m. film producer Isidor Goldsmith, lived with him in London, and worked on documentary scripts; after the war she was blacklisted. A dead woman in *Laura*, 1943, repr. 1987 (begun as a play and an 'escape from political argument'), a murderer of several husbands in *Bedelia*, 1945 (serialized before book form), and an amnesiac in *Elizabeth X*, 1978, each arouse the voyeuristic fascination of several people, becoming 'an intensely personal symbol, the shadow of an unacknowledged need'. Many of VC's novels were filmed; she wrote over 20 screenplays. Of her many tales of young women in city jobs, she felt that *Evvie*, 1960, best 'defines the changing position of women' through the 1920s. *Thelma*, 1953, set in pre-WWI Wisconsin, depicts marriage between German and Slav, and the malign effects of the Cinderella happy-ever-after myth. *The Man Who Loved His Wife*, 1966, shows how a mutilation (laryngectomy) induces fears of lost masculinity, and loathing of self and other. VC's autobiographical *The Secrets of Grown-ups*, 1979, concludes 'Never have I regretted that I was born female.'

Catchpole, Margaret, 1762–1819, letter writer, da. of the unmarried Elizabeth C. B. in Suffolk, she was servant to several employers, lastly Elizabeth COBBOLD. In 1797 she was persuaded to abet the theft of a horse from Cobbold's husband, rode it to London, and was arrested trying to sell it. The Cobbolds supported her at her trials (a daring escape bid brought a second) with witness to her good character, her riding ability, and her heroic saving their children from accidental death. Transported in 1801, she settled in Richmond, NSW, and wrote artless, vivid letters home both to relations and to Cobbold, magnifying Australia's dangers but painting herself 'as young as ever', in high enough spirits 'to jump over' the first church built in the district, delighted at being among free people 'where they make much of me as if i was a Ladey'. Cobbold's son Richard pub. a very successful novel about her, 1845, which centres on an invented smuggler lover and ends happily on an invented husband. Its many editions gathered extra spurious 'facts'. See Richard Barber in 1979 reprint: letters at Suffolk Record Office.

Cather, Willa (christened Wilella) Sibert, 1873–1947, novelist, woman of letters, b. at Gore (also called Back Creek), Va., eldest of seven children of Mary Virginia (Boak) and Charles Fectigue C. They moved to Nebraska in 1883, where she discovered the pioneer West, growing up in Red Cloud from 1884. At the Univ. of Nebraska, Lincoln, 1890–5, she supported herself by literary and dramatic criticism, published short stories, and established friendships with Louise POUND and Dorothy Canfield FISHER. Already an 'experienced newspaperman' and respected drama critic, she went to Pittsburgh to work on *Home Monthly*, then the *Pittsburgh Daily Leader:* these writings collec. as *The World and the Parish*, ed. William M. Curtin, 1970. In 1900 she began high-school teaching (classics, then English); she published *April Twilights* (poems), 1903, and *The Troll Garden* (stories, 1905, ed. James Woodress,

1983). In NYC from 1906 she wrote for and later edited *McClure's* (she met Zoë AKINS when rejecting some of her poems), leaving to write full-time in 1911. She also began her lifelong residence with Edith Lewis. (The degree and nature of her lesbianism is still being debated.) Her first novel, *Alexander's Bridge*, 1912, began as a serial. She made her name with lyrical novels of Nebraska frontier women: *O Pioneers!*, 1913 (dedicated to her late friend Sarah Orne JEWETT), and *My Antonia*, 1918, which introduced her technique of dividing between two characters an essentially inner struggle. She often drew on her own dilemmas, notably in *The Song of the Lark*, 1915, where a future opera-singer emerges from a 'smug, domestic, self-satisfied provincial world of utter ignorance'; doubtful of the result, she pruned it hard for re-issue, 1937. She joined the Episcopalian church in 1922. She won the Pulitzer Prize for *One of Ours*, 1922, the Prix Femina Américaine for *Shadows on the Rock*, 1931 (set in Québec); Sinclair Lewis, receiving the Nobel Prize for Literature, 1930, said it should have gone to WC. Interested in artistic and religious striving, she treats a woman's rejection of Catholicism in *My Mortal Enemy*, 1926, and the self-scrutiny of committed churchmen in *Death Comes for the Archbishop*, 1927 (set in New Mexico). While working on *Lucy Gayheart*, 1935, she began to suffer from a painful wrist condition; she published only one more novel, *Sapphira and the Slave Girl*, 1940, plus stories and essays: *Not Under Forty*, 1936, has essays on JEWETT and Katherine MANSFIELD, and 'The Novel Demeublé', with WC's famous dictum that '*Selection* of detail is what matters.' She and Edith Lewis destroyed most of her letters, and her will stipulated no publication: survivors are listed in Sharon O'Brien's feminist study of WC's growth as a writer, 1987. See also lives by Lewis, 1953, Hermione Lee, 1989; bibliog. by J. Crane, 1982; study by J. Woodress, 1983; Jane RULE, 1975; Gelfant, 1984; A. S. BYATT's introductions to recent British reprints. WC's criticism, 1967, and uncollected stories, 1973, have been ed. by Bernice Slote; early stories by Virginia Faulkner, 1970, and Mildred R. Bennett, 1983; interviews, speeches and letters by L. Brent Bohlke, 1987.

Catherwood, Mary (Hartwell), 1847–1902, novelist and short-story writer, b. Luray, Ohio, da. of Phoebe (Thompson), d. 1857, and Marcus H., d. 1858, MHC was brought up by relatives and educ. in village schools and Granville Female College. In 1871, she won a $100 prize for 'Peter Snubby' and by 1874 was self-supporting. In 1877 she m. James C., salesman, but lived apart from him towards the end of her life. Her first novels, *A Woman in Armor*, 1875, and *Craque-O'-Doom*, 1881, were serialized in *Hearth and Home* and *Lippincott's* before appearing in book form. MHC's early novels and stories depict Midwestern life: 'Serena' (*Atlantic Monthly*, 1882) creates a picture of rural Ohio in the mid-nineteenth century. Beginning with *The Romance of Dollard*, 1889, based on the writings of Francis Parkman, MHC wrote historical romances, her most popular being *Lazarre*, 1901, about the alleged dauphin of France who was sent to the USA and raised by Indians. She also wrote some children's novels, including *The Dogberry Bunch*, 1879, and *Old Caravan Days*, 1884. She achieved national prominence, helped form the Western Association of Writers, and was important in the development of American historical romance.

Cato, Nancy Fotheringham, novelist, poet, and short-story writer, b. 1917 in Adelaide, South Australia, da. of Mab (Pearce) and Raymond C. She attended Presbyterian Girls' College, Glen Osmond, SA, then studied English literature at Adelaide Univ. Working as a journalist 1935–41, she m. Eldred de Bracton Norman in 1941 (d. 1971) and had children. She was art critic for the Adelaide *News* and *Mail*, assistant editor of *Poetry*, 1947–8, and ed. of the *Jindyworobak Anthology*, 1950. She achieved wide recognition only after re-writing the trilogy of historical novels, *All the Rivers Run*, 1958, *Time Flow Softly*, 1959, and *But Still the Stream*, 1962, which appeared simultaneously in Australia, England and USA as the best-selling one-volume *All the Rivers Run*, 1978, adapted for TV in 1983. Set in the River Murray region, it vividly brings to life the riverboat era through the story of 'Delie' Gordon and her love for the river. Other novels include *Green Grows the Vine*, 1960, *North West by South*, 1964, *Brown Sugar*, 1974, *Forefathers*, 1983, *A Lady Lost in Time*, 1986, and *A Distant Island*, 1986. As well as non-fiction she has written two vols. of poetry, *The Darkened Window*, 1950, and *The Dancing Bough*, 1957 (which deals with the nuclear issue); a collection of short stories; and a children's book. Member of the Order of Australia, 1984.

Cave, Jane, later Winscom, before 1757–1813, poet, da. of John C. of Talgarth, Brecon (exciseman, glover, nonconformist convert). Early inclined to 'books and poetry', though a working woman, she pub. *Poems on Various Subjects* ..., Winchester, 1783, with her name and many West Country and Oxford subscribers. The poems, grouped by genre, are lively, individual, and confident, though she feels outclassed by Anna SEWARD, Anne STEELE, and Hannah MORE: reasons of Fortune and Duty make her often decline the Muses' social calls. Her earnest piety (as an Anglican with Methodist sympathies) does not exclude playfulness: she reproves young men for flattery or conceit, and a lady for doubting her authorship. That year she married at Winchester a Bristol exciseman, Thomas W.; she re-issued her book at Bristol, 1786. Without comment, she dropped some poems (mainly low-comic ones) and added others. 'An Elegy on a Maiden Name' bids, with apology to her husband, 'Adieu, dear name, which birth and nature gave – / Lo! at the altar I've interr'd dear Cave'; she links the name with her dead mother. 'To my Dear [unborn] Child' offers advice to a potential son, but says she is powerless to help a daughter. 'For such the deep deceits of men, / And such their power o'er female hearts, / We cannot penetrate their arts.' Later eds. at Shrewsbury and Bristol add more poems, including attacks on the slave trade.

Cavendish, Lady **Jane**, later Cheyne, 1621–69, and Lady **Elizabeth,** 1626–63, poets and playwrights, das. of Elizabeth (Bassett) and William C., later Duke of Newcastle, who was involved with Court and public acting. With Elizabeth married to Lord Brackley (later Earl of Bridgewater) but still living at home, Jane took the lead in a handsome joint MS volume, *c.* 1643–5, now in the Bodleian Library, first titled *Poems Songs and a Pastoral*, with 'and a Play' added later. It begins and ends with eulogy of their absent father. He is 'the Accademy of all trueth'; their recently-dead mother is the 'quinticence [a favourite word] of best'; the royal family are also praised. The play, *The Concealed Fansyes* (pub. by Nathan Comfort Starr, *PMLA*, 1931), in supple and lively prose with verse passages, features two heroines who hold out for and get 'equall marryage', having trained the gallants, Courtley and Praesumption, who were intending to train them. 'Lady Tranquillity', in love with the heroines' father, must be the authors' future step-mother, Margaret NEWCASTLE, whom they had not yet met. Space left blank to list 'The Actors' suggests a hope of staging. The pastoral, a verse drama of which they wrote alternate parts, is more dated, but has dash and vigour. At a date close to this writing they underwent the siege and garrison of Welbeck, their family home, yet later urged mercy for their jailer as well as reprieve for exiled father and brothers. Jane lived in Chelsea after marrying Charles Cheyne in 1654; she left three children and a 'considerable Stock' of writings (untraced.). Her poem on Elizabeth's death in childbirth is extant; so are Elizabeth's prayers and meditations, many on marriage and the births and deaths of children, written from 1648 (BL scribal copy, 1663). See Margaret M. J. Ezell in *Huntington Library Quarterly*, 51, 1988.

Celesia, Dorothea (Mallet), *c.* 1738–90, poet and dramatist. Da. of the poet David M. and his first wife, Susanna, who d. in 1742, she grew up near London, her father having quickly re-married (to a distant connection of Elizabeth ELSTOB) and had two more daughters. DC's friends included Edward Gibbon and David Hume. On her marriage, 1758, to Pietro Paolo C., Genoese envoy to London, his ex-mistress, Mme de Fauques or Vaucluse, published a volume of furious complaint: it calls DC a staunch Protestant, author of 5000 lines of poetry (half written before '*l'âge de raison*'), and ill-treated by her stepmother. DC became a Catholic and lived in Genoa from 1759; her husband had diplomatic postings around Europe; her two daughters married Frenchmen. She received Garrick in Genoa, 1763, and in 1769 sent him her tragedy *Almida* (taken 'like a poet, not like an imitator' from Voltaire's *Tancrede*), a stage success in London, 1771. Its heroine, martyr to her father's politics, runs mad. DC's poem *Indolence*, 1722, aphoristically but thoughtfully condemns pride, ambition, war, and 'the tiresome task of being great', which Queen Christina of Sweden gave up for the Muses.

Cellier, Elizabeth (Dormer), London midwife and feminist, da. of well-connected Protestants; she turned Catholic in reaction against the Cromwellians, m. Peter C. (a Frenchman living in London), and had two children. Enlisted in Jan. 1678 to dispense charity to Catholic prisoners while on her rounds, she also compiled a dossier on torture, and organized political meetings. In Oct. 1679 occurred the 'Meal Tub Plot' (actually a plot to convict Catholics of plotting): incriminating papers were found in EC's kitchen and she was arrested. Acquitted in April and June 1680 of intent to destroy Church and King, she pub. and sold from her own house, in Aug., *Malice Defeated*, a fine polemical narrative of her 'Accusation and Deliverance', with *The Matchless Picaro* (re-issued alone as *The Matchless Rogue*), a satiric attack on her accuser Thomas Dangerfield. Both appear to be her own work (Augustan Repr. 249–50, 1988). *Malice Defeated* mentions her legal knowledge, quotes the psalms, calls herself 'not the most timorous of my Sex' and hopes her political activity will not be thought too 'Masculine'. It had nearly 20 answers and attacks, and was publicly burned; she was jailed for probably two years, and three times pilloried (she collected into her pocket those stones which fell close enough). In 1687 she submitted to James II a written scheme for a foundling hospital and midwives' corporation, repr. 1745 in the *Harleian Miscellany*. Both compassionate and businesslike (on statistics, finance and administration), it aims to put women professionally in control of a skill which was just being taken over by men. *To Dr —— an Answer to his Queries, concerning the Colledg of Midwives*, researched and written in four days, 1688, draws on biblical and Greek history, and notes better survival rates when the bishops did *not* license midwives, 1642–62. James II's flight that year killed the project; EC too may have gone into exile.

Centlivre, Susanna (Freeman), also Carroll, perhaps Rawkins, 1669–1723, dramatist, poet, journalist, and actress, b. at Whaplode, Lincs., da. of Anne (Marham) and William F., who seem both to have died during her childhood. Dubious tales of her early life abound: that she wrote a song at six, read Molière at 12, was m. at 14 and widowed at 16, m. once or twice more while very young, and studied at Cambridge dressed as a boy. She knew many writers of both sexes, contributed to (perhaps) THE NINE MUSES and to three collections of letters,

1700–1, exchanged verse with Sarah FYGE, Martha SANSOM and Eliza HAYWOOD, and in 1707 m. Joseph Centlivre, employee in the royal kitchen. She may have written (with Bernard Mandeville) the thrice-weekly *Female Tatler,* 1709–10, as well as complimentary poems (her Whig views landed her in Pope's *Dunciad*), verse letters (one about her life as a writer and wife), and anti-Catholic essays, 1720. Her fame rests on her plays: 14 new or adapted action-packed comedies, a few farces and tragedies. The first, *The Perjur'd Husband, or The Adventures of Venice,* 1700, bore her name (Carroll) and cited Aphra BEHN. Judged too *risqué,* she took to hiding her identity; she said her *Love's Contrivances,* 1703, from Molière, succeeded because it bore a man's initials; managers always 'treated her ... in the Masculine Gender'. *The Gamester,* 1705 (hero loses all, including her picture, to his mistress in male disguise), was a hit. Her later bullseyes (in repertory throughout the nineteenth century) play for laughter instead of sentiment: *The Busie Body,* 1709, repr. 1949 (lovers outwit fathers and guardian by stock means); *The Wonder: A Woman Keeps a Secret,* 1714, in Fidelis Morgan, ed., 1981 (jealous Don Felix, later a favourite Garrick role, learns to trust his beloved); *A Bold Stroke for a Wife,* 1718, repr. 1968 (suitor tricks heiress's ill-assorted guardians, one of them 'the real Simon Pure', one of SC's many Quaker characters). She *may* have written a lost autobiography. Coll. 1761 (life by anonymous woman), her plays have had recent revivals. Life by John Wilson Bowyer, 1952, study by F. P. Lock, 1979.

Chalmers, Margaret, poet, b. 1758 at Lerwick, Shetland, eldest child of Kitty (Irvine) and William C., customs officer and great men's steward. He was dead by 1806, when her only brother, master of a ship, fell at Trafalgar, leaving his sisters and blind old mother in want. In 1808 they vainly sought a government pension; her *Poems,* Newcastle, 1813, unadvertised, full of misprints and with many subscribers lost by delay, earned little. Like D. P. CAMPBELL later (she calls herself 'the first British Thulian quill'), MC looks ambivalently on her remote home, saying it lacks 'scope for the display of poetical talent' yet treating its landscapes with passion and sensitivity, and its crafts, beliefs and customs with delight and with informative notes. She writes of shipwreck, naval victories, female friendship, religion, and the royal family. She depicts her relations with the Muses as both romantic and comic, showing pride ('I'll drain Pieria's sacred spring / (By halves I hate to do a thing,) / What though it leaves the channel dry / To the next comer, what care I?') as going before a metaphorical fall. She sent letters and poems to Walter Scott, 1814–15 (NLS), and lines addressing 'the Powerful Benevolent' to the RLF, which paid her £10 in 1816.

Chambers, Jane, 1937–83, actress and playwright, b. in Columbia, SC, da. of book-keeper Clarice (Summerour) and engineer Carroll J. C. She attended Rollins College, 1953–4, acted off-Broadway and in 'coffee-house theatre', and wrote for periodicals, then for educational and network TV and theatre groups. She took a BA from Goddard College in 1971 and taught creative writing; she worked for many theatrical and gay organizations, and helped set up the NJ Women's Political Caucus and the Interart Theatre, NYC. She won awards for *Ejected,* 1971 (poem), and plays: *Christ in a Treehouse,* 1971, *Tales of the Revolution and Other American Fables,* 1972, and *Search for Tomorrow,* 1973. In her 'lesbian gothic suspense novel', *Burning,* 1978 (dedicated to her 'life-companion', Beth Allen), twentieth-century people are possessed by the spirits of tragic figures from 1691: two lesbians, one burned as a witch; the little son of one; the husband (later, against her will) of the other. The modern women's short-lived love-affair lays the spirits to rest. JC's lesbian plays (a minority of her output) are best known. *A*

Late Snow (recast from a screenplay of 1974, pub. in William Hoffman, ed., *Gay Plays*, 1979) presents varying lesbian attitudes: radicalism, denial, cautious hope for progress. *Last Summer at Bluefish Cove*, staged 1980, pub. 1982, uses eight women characters to range through humour (naïve ex-wife gradually realizes the others are all dykes) to intense love and impending death from cancer. *My Blue Heaven*, staged and pub. 1981, is a comedy about a couple coping with excessive sympathy and interest from straights. JC died of a brain tumour; *Warrior at Rest*, 1984, and *Chasin' Jason*, 1987, have been published since. See Penny M. Landau in *Women and Performance*, 1, 1984.

Chambers, Marianne, novelist and playwright, da. of Charles C. of the East India Company, whose death at sea she mentions on the title-page of her novel *He Deceives Himself*, pub. by subscription, 1799, and dedicated to her grandfather Thomas Powell of Bristol. Its heroine, living in a castle among apparently rich relations, finds they have usurped her rightful heritage; mysterious sounds she heard were those of the death and burial of her imprisoned mother. MC's two comedies, successful on stage and in print, are more convincing and accomplished. *The School for Friends*, 1805, has a wronged virtuous wife who reforms her husband and an ingénue who wins a worldly older man; yet it is also good-humoured and comic, full of characters combining goodness with eccentricity. The heroine of *Ourselves*, 1811, speaks fluently and imaginatively of the burden of marriage, before undertaking it with a sceptical and philosophical hero.

Champion de Crespigny, Mary (Clarke), Lady, 1748?–1812, miscellaneous writer, only da. of Joseph Clarke of Yorks. At 16 she m. Claude C. de C., Admiralty official, later baronet. Hostess to naval and intellectual notables, and later the Prince of Wales, she wrote *Letters of Advice from a Mother to her* [only] *Son* about 1780 but published it (with her name) in 1803. It stresses religion, details reasons against extramarital relationships, and advises on cautious reconnoitring of possible partners. She received many dedications from women writers, and staged at home plays by e.g. Mariana Starke. Her novel, *The Pavilion*, 1796, is named after a building consecrated to mark the scene of the exemplary heroine's eventual reunion with the noble mother who had reluctantly, mysteriously abandoned her in infancy. The stock tale, intelligently told (only Minerva novel to appear in two formats, de luxe and normal), was signed only by an elegant monogram device. MCdeC pub. a poem on Admiral Collingwood's death, 1810.

Chandler, Elizabeth Margaret, 1807–34, Quaker abolitionist, poet and essayist, b. at Centre, Delaware, only da. of Mary (Evans) and Thomas C. Orphaned at nine, she was raised in Philadelphia by her grandmother and aunts, attending the Friends' school until 12 or 13. She wrote poetry at nine and appeared anonymously in magazines at 16. Her poem 'The Slave Ship' (her first writing on slavery) won a prize (third) from *The Casket*. As editor from 1829 of 'The Ladies Repository' in *The Genius of Universal Emancipation*, she wrote, from deepening knowledge, poems (many later hymns for anti-slavery meetings), fictional correspondence, allegories, and praise of Felicia Hemans, L. E. L., and Hannah Kilham. Addressing the 'Christian mother ... daughter, sister, wife!' as consumers, she exhorts them not to buy the produce of slave labour. 'Looking at the Soldiers' and 'What is a Slave, Mother?' voice her doubts about patriotism and her passionate sympathy for (especially) 'our suffering sisters'. She denies that political women will lose precious domestic softness, and appeals to women 'bravely and nobly ... in the face of the world' to reject their brothers' institution and refuse to 'be tamely made the instruments of oppression'. In 1830 she moved with an aunt and brother to Lenawee County, 60 miles from Detroit: she described the wilderness, wrote for the Boston *Liberator,* and founded Michigan's first anti-slavery society. MSS at Univ. of Mich.; nine letters in *Yale Review,* 1926; *Poetical Works* (memoir by Benjamin Lundy) and *Essays, Philanthropic and Moral,* both 1836; Merton L. Dillon in *Mich. History,* 39, 1955.

Chandler, Mary, 1687–1745, poet, b. at Malmesbury, Wilts., da. and sister of dissenting ministers. Fond of poetry as a child, she admired Horace (in English) and George Herbert as not martial or heroic. Handicapped by a crooked spine, she was 'naturally eager, anxious, and peevish', but fought to subdue her passions and became 'firm and established', as well as vegetarian. She ran a milliner's shop in Bath from 1705, and circulated poems in MS among friends like Mary BARBER, Lady HERTFORD, and Elizabeth ROWE. James Ralph pub. one in an anthology, 1729; her *Description of Bath* [1733], dedicated to her brother John, ran to six editions in her lifetime, with 18 new poems added in 1734 and her name in 1736. 'My Wish' (for a modest income and country retirement) brought her a marriage proposal, as she tells in 'A True Tale' (written *c.* 1742, added 1744), but she knew herself too old and independent. Her most personal poems (several treat the marriage option) are the best. She left unfinished one on the attributes of God. Her brother Samuel wrote her life for 'Cibber's' *Lives of the Poets,* 1753. The possibility that she influenced Pope is unlikely.

Chandos, Cassandra Brydges (Willoughby), Duchess of, 1670–1735, family historian. Da. of Emma (Barnard) and naturalist Francis W. (d. 1672), she perhaps inherited his passion for work. Her travel journal, begun 1695 (cf. Celia FIENNES), pays close attention to country houses. She learned to read early MSS, and in 1702 began a carefully researched family history. Most of the letters she used (like those to her father which she gave William Derham to publish in 1718) are now lost. She catalogues, summarizes, and transcribes, showing an interest in changing styles of housekeeping, dress (on which she pens a 'long digression'), advice-giving and marital strife. Her two volumes (Nottingham Univ. Library) are pub. in HMC Reports, 69, 1911, and ed. Alfred Cecil Wood, 1958. After marrying, 1713, her rich cousin James Brydges, widower, patron of arts, later Duke of Chandos, she went on with this work and also transcribed and extended her mother-in-law's family 'Register', continued in turn by her two successors. Life by Joan Johnson, 1981; more MSS at Glos Record Office and North London Collegiate School (letter-books) and BL (genealogies). A diary of 'Lady Willoughby', pub. 1844, is a work of fiction by Hannah Mary RATHBONE.

Channel, Elinor, pamphleteer, wife of 'a very poor man' in Cranley, Surrey. He denied her desire to go to London (she had 'many small children') until she became 'speechless' and unable to sleep, when he consented. In the capital, seeking someone to write down and publish her message to Oliver Cromwell, she met Arise Evans, Royalist pamphleteer. He glosses her *Message from God (by a Dumb Woman),* 1654, as royalist (whereas it is clearly an appeal against tithing) and contrasts her with Anna TRAPNEL, of whom he disapproves.

Channon, Ethel **M**ary, 'Mrs Francis Channon', 1875–1951, novelist. She was b. in Rathdowney, Ireland, educ. at St Leonard's and Cheltenham Ladies' Colleges, and m. the Rev. Francis Granville C., an assistant master at Eton, with whom she had six children. She wrote 36 novels between 1910 and 1937, from *The Authoress,* 1909. *A Street Angel,* 1910, the story of a young heiress who evades a charming fortune hunter, then marries a worthy man, sets the pattern for her subsequent romances. She also wrote children's novels, like *The Honour of the House,* 1931, about a girl's experiences at boarding school, which appeared in several editions. *Miss King's Profession,* 1913, recounts the misfortunes of a naïve young woman determined to become a writer.

Chanter, Charlotte (Kingsley), 1828–82, miscellaneous writer, da. of Mary (Lucas) and the Rev. Charles K., aunt of 'Lucas MALET'. B. (in a haunted room) in Barnack, near Stamford, Lincs., she moved in 1832 to Clovelly, Devon, and in 1836 to Chelsea. She m. family friend the Rev. John Mill Chanter in 1849; her da. recalled her love of German (from which she translated for magazines) and 'endless stock of delightful German legends and fairy-tales' told to the children. Her descriptive power first showed in *Ferney Combes,* 1856, on the ferns of Devon, based on a driving tour with her husband, where she found a new species, named Lastreas Chanteriae. In 1858 she and her husband pub. children's rather bloodthirsty animal stories, *Jack Frost and Betty Snow,* followed in 1860 by her one novel, *Over the Cliffs.* Set in Cornwall during the Napoleonic Wars, and relishing the coastal wildness, it has a fearless heroine, Gratiana, who climbs cliffs and rides horses as well as defying her violent father who has killed her mother. There are refs. to CC in lives of her brothers; the main source is the memoir of her husband ed. by their daughter, Gratiana C. (priv. pr., Ilfracombe, 1887: copy in London Library).

Chapman, Esther, journalist, novelist, b. 1904 in England. At eight she published a poem (religious) and wrote a 'novel', with 'a corpse on every page', on linings from her father's cigar boxes. As an adolescent she published in periodicals, declined a publisher's offer on a first novel, and longed to qualify as a writer by mixing with 'people different from my middle-class English associates'. She found a job on a Jamaican weekly paper as 'the editor, the chief writer, the circulation manager and the advertisement salesman', on pay cut from £4 weekly to £3 10s. with higher commission (a deal that worked in her favour). She did not plan to stay long. Met at the boat by Lucille IREMONGER's mother (whose husband worked for her boss), EC overcame the shock of arrival and scored an 'outstanding success': the paper's size and circulation rocketed (see her autobiographical essay in her annual, *Jamaica, 1955* [1954]). She published four novels, from the 1920s; founded *The West Indian Review,* 1934, and the Arts and Crafts Committee of the Institute of Jamaica, 1941; and issued four books about the island, besides the annual and *Caribbean Album,* 1960 (a selec. of travel writings). EC looks at local race relations in *Study in Bronze,* 1952, and *Too Much Summer,* 1953, whose English protagonist, banished to Jamaica by her domineering husband for her children's safety in WWII, loves and sleeps with a rising coloured lawyer whose feelings for her include race hatred, is dropped by him and her husband, and drifts into promiscuity and rum.

Chapone, Hester (Mulso), 1727–1801, miscellaneous writer and BLUESTOCKING, only da. of Hester (Thomas) and Thomas M. of Twywell, Northants. (nicknamed 'Yes Papa' by her brothers; later strong in family feeling). She wrote a romance at nine (her mother allegedly disapproved), taught herself modern languages, music and drawing, and kept house, mostly in London, after her mother died. Her first poem, 1749, was an ode to peace; then came fictional letters for the *Rambler* (which she thought hard on women) and 'The Story of Fidelia' (a woman's fall through free-thinking and rescue by religion) in *Adventurers* 77–79, 1753. She influenced Richardson's novels (e.g. lessening Clarissa's guilt over her father's curse); he called her a spitfire and rebel when she argued that society subjects women to too much parental (though not husbandly) power. She wrote an ode for Elizabeth CARTER's *Epictetus*, was quoted in Johnson's *Dictionary*, corresponded with Gilbert White, and saw 'strong sense' (as well as vanity and indelicacy) in Mary WOLLSTONECRAFT. In 1760 she married, against her father's will, Sarah CHAPONE's son John, who died nine months later. HC mourned intensely: relations stoutly denied that the marriage was unhappy (said in life by Selina DAVENPORT's husband, who gave A. L. BARBAULD as his source). HC's later works are didactic: *Letters on the Improvement of the Mind,* 1773, written to a niece, dedicated to Elizabeth MONTAGU, which counsel submissiveness, and caution in friendship; *Miscellanies in Prose and Verse,* 1775, dedicated to Carter (more profitable); *A Letter to a New-Married Lady,* 1777. *Posthumous Works,* 1807, contains chiefly letters.

Chapone or Capon (her own spelling), **Sarah** (Kirkham), 1699–1764, feminist, da. of Damaris (Boyse) and the Rev. Lionel K. She m. the Rev. John C., 1725, had five children, and ran a school at Stanton near Chipping Campden, Glos; a son m. Hester (Mulso) CHAPONE. She corresponded (1730–1, as 'SAPPHO'), with John Wesley and the future Mary DELANY, with Samuel Richardson (who thought her one of the best women writers he knew), and George Ballard. She probably wrote the anonymous *Hardships of the English Laws in relation to Wives,* 1735, which takes a strong stand based on legal knowledge and recent cases: though her own marriage is happy, 'the Estate of Wives' – subject to beating or confinement, without rights in their property or children – 'is more disadvantagious than Slavery itself'. She introduced Ballard to Elizabeth ELSTOB, helped in his research on women writers, and tried to stiffen the feminist element in his views and expression (Ruth Perry's ed. of his work, 1985: see BIOGRAPHY). She addressed *Remarks* to T. C. PHILLIPS,, 1750 offering her 'as a most abused injured Woman ... my affectionate Compassion', as a talented one her esteem, but as an apologist for promiscuity a full rebuttal and call for repentance. Some letters at Glos. Record Office.

Charke, Charlotte (Cibber), 1713–60, actress, jill-of-all-trades, autobiographer. Final, eleventh child of Katherine (Shore) and Colley Cibber, actor-manager and Poet Laureate, she mimicked him in men's clothes at four, went to Mrs Draper's school, but preferred horses, guns, gardening and quack medicine. In 1729 or 1730 she m. Richard Charke, actor and musician. He was unfaithful, and she left, with her daughter; he remained a financial threat till his death about 1738. She acted roles of each sex (in 1734 Pistol, Macheath, and Lothario, each associated with some male relation, next year Harlequin in her own *The Carnival,* unpub.). Fired from Drury Lane for alleged immorality, she hilariously featured its manager in *The Art of Management, or Tragedy Expell'd,* 1735 (good roles for herself and her brother Theobald); its victim got most copies destroyed. She played in Henry Fielding's company till the Licensing Act, 1737, killed it, then tried the food trade, theatrical ventures and puppet-shows (the highly inventive *Tit for Tat,* staged 1743, was probably hers). With no help from her family, she understudied, was bailed on a debt charge by Covent Garden whores, and took to dressing as a man. She denied tales of melodramatic rebuffs to her father, even knocking down a man who spread one. In 1745 she secretly m. John Sacheverell, who then died. She knew farce and hardship as 'Mr Brown', strolling actor (accompanied by 'Mrs Brown' and for a time by her own daughter), as conjuror's assistant and printer. Back in London in 1755, she pub. in parts *A Narrative* of her life, begun *c.* 1750, which glories in her own oddity but kowtows to her father (often repr.: passages paraphrased by Maureen DUFFY in *The*

Microcosm, 1966; supplemented with comment to make a life by Fidelis Morgan, 1988). CC got 10 guineas for her novel *Henry Dumont and Charlotte Evelyn,* 1756, from a publisher who reported her as living in squalor with a dog and a parrot. Three undated novellas, *c.* 1758, bore her name. She died in poverty soon after her last stage appearance.

Charles, Elizabeth, 'Mrs Rundle Charles', 1828–96, novelist, da. of John Rundle, MP. She grew up in Devon, travelled on the Continent in her teens and began to write early, drawing praise from Froude and Tennyson. In 1848? she m. Andrew Paton C., owner of a soap and candle factory in Wapping, London. Of evangelical leanings, though unusually tolerant of other faiths, she worked among the slum-dwellers and wrote religious fiction and non-fiction. Modestly successful at first, she made her name with the enormously popular *Chronicles of the Schönberg-Cotta Family,* 1862, which tells the story of Martin Luther from the point of view of the family of one of his student friends: Charlotte YONGE, otherwise admiring, complained it was 'a lady's Luther, without his force or coarseness' (*Monthly Packet,* 1865). *The Bertrams,* 1875 (repr. 1977), another family story with a strong religious slant, uses the technique of alternating narrators. Although didactic, it is lively and insightful in its depiction of family politics, including the lot of spinsters. EC often pub. with the SPCK.

'Charles, Gerda' (Edna Lipson), novelist, b. in 1914 in Liverpool to Gertrude L. Her father died when she was nine. She received a minimal education in Liverpool schools until she was 15, then she and her mother moved to London and together ran a boardinghouse. Later, she took evening classes at London colleges. Her five novels, published between 1959 and 1971, examine 'the day-after-dayness' of ordinary lives, what GC describes as 'the job of maintaining sanity, dignity, and order' in suburban, middle-class society with strict conventions and few opportunities. The heroine of her first novel, *The True Voice,* 1959, rejects her sister's plea to become 'a married woman with a home of your own and security and a social position', instead searching (like George ELIOT's Dorothea) for 'some key to the universe which ... would open the world'. Not an unhappy affair, nor a disillusioning infatuation with two poets, nor an acquaintance with a stylish woman novelist provides the key, and the novel ends with Lindy's resignation to make the most of the opportunities within her reach. *The Crossing Point,* 1960 (winner of the James Tait Black Award) draws on GC's background to portray a Jewish community, focusing on a middle-aged rabbi's decision to marry – as in GC's other work, he compromises his desire to enlarge his experience because of the demands and limitations of his position and background. *A Slanting Light,* 1963, explores the unsatisfying private life of an American playwright. Other novels are *A Logical Girl,* 1966, and *The Destiny Waltz,* 1971 (Whitbread Award). GC has written a number of short stories, reviewed widely, been a TV critic, and edited the anthology *Modern Jewish Stories,* 1963.

Charlton, Mary, English author of probably ten novels from 1794 (plus versions from French, Italian and German). The first was *The Parisian, or Genuine Anecdotes of Distinguished and Noble Characters* (heroine's birthright revealed to be stolen by father of her favoured, unlikable friend). She became a MINERVA bestseller with *Andronica, or The Fugitive Bride,* 1797, set in early England, Greece and France, and *Phedora, or The Forest of Minski,* 1798, set in war-torn Europe a century earlier (opening in what became Estonia and Latvia, closing in Warsaw). Today her modern, satirical or humorous manner reads better: *Rosella, or Modern Occurrences,* 1799 (whose heroine, child of a brief disastrous marriage contracted under the influence of the sentimental novel, never manages to teach her mother sense), *The Wife and the Mistress,* 1802 (whose heroine is child of the feeling, anxious, guilty mistress ousted by a spoilt wife), *Grandeur and Meanness, or Domestic Persecution,* 1824 (opening with a brisk exposé of the stultifying education offered to each sex: sensible, poor-relation heroine). Her anthology *Pathetic Poetry for Youth,* 1815, has two Wordsworth poems among the expected tear-jerkers. A 'life' with heroine of her name, 1817 (recorded, untraced), is probably irrelevant fiction.

Charnas, Suzy McKee, science-fiction and fantasy writer. B. in 1939 in NYC to artists Maxine (Szanton) and Robinson McKee, she attended NY High School of Music and Art and Barnard College (BA in economic history, 1961). After teaching at a girls' school, 1961–2, and the Univ. of Ibadan, 1962–3, both in Nigeria, she completed a MA at NY Univ. in 1965, taught at New Lincoln School, NYC, until 1967, then worked for NYC's Community Mental Health organization until 1969, having m. lawyer Stephen C. in 1968 (two children). Her first novel, *Walk to the End of the World,* 1974, depicts the nightmare post-holocaust world of the 'Holdfast' in which history has been skewed to place the blame for the 'Wasting' upon women and so justify their enslavement as cruelly exploited labourers and child-bearers. In *Motherlines,* 1978, an escaper from this world moves between the Riding Women, a strong, self-sufficient community in which each woman has her own 'self-song' and belongs to a 'Motherline' forming her immediate kin group, and the 'Free Fems', a small group of other escapers whose social development has been stunted by their Holdfast legacy of master-slave relationships and struggle for power. SMC's later work integrates her fantasy into contemporary settings. Dr Weyland, a vampire disguised as an anthropology professor in *The Vampire Tapestry,* 1980, retreats into hibernation when human social contact causes him to sympathize with his prospective victims. The woman artist of *Dorothea Dreams,* 1986, recognizes the social irresponsibility of solitude when she is haunted by a figure from the French Revolution. SMC has also written for children. See Marleen S. Barr et al., eds., essays, 1986, Susan E. Howard in *Extrapolation,* 27, 1986, and Sarah Lefanu, *In the Chinks of the World Machine,* 1988. SMC's 'A Woman Appeared' in Marleen Barr, ed., *Future Females,* 1981, describes the origins of her feminist SCIENCE FICTION.

Chase, Ilka, 1907–78, actress, novelist, autobiographer, b. in NYC, da. of Edna (Woolman), editor of *Vogue,* and Francis D. C. Educ. at nine private schools (one in France) and initiated into society ('in the coming-out season one is apt to acquire a bright yellow view of femininity which fades but slowly through the years'), she promptly joined a theatre company. 'I played maids. I played more damn maids.' Her first two marriages (of three) ended in divorce. She acted on Broadway (e.g. in Claire Boothe LUCE's *The Women*) and in movies, ran radio shows, wrote a newspaper column, and published nearly 20 books, mostly novels. In *Past Imperfect: The Indiscretions of a Lady of Wit and Opinion,* 1943, she tried to strike a balance between interest and accuracy. 'I suppose I am a feminist ... I believe in careers and votes and independent incomes for women, but ... life without a man is no life at all.' *In Bed We Cry,* 1945, features a woman cosmetics executive (IC starred in her own stage version), *I Love Miss Tilli Bean,* 1946, a model, *The Sounds of Home,* 1972, a wealthy family, all constructed of wisecrack and stereotype. *Free Admission,* 1948, is chiefly theatre gossip. IC co-authored her mother's memoirs, *Always in Vogue,* 1954.

Chase, Mary Ellen, 1887–1973, regional novelist, literary critic, memoirist. B. in Blue Hill, Maine, da. of teacher Edith (Lord) and lawyer Edward E. C., she attended a local village school, then Blue

Hill Academy (studying Latin and Greek there and at home with her parents), later the Univs. of Maine (BA, 1909, MA, 1918) and Minnesota (PhD, 1922). Encouraged by her father, she taught at country schools midway through her BA, travelled to Europe, 1913, to study German; contracted, 1914, and recovered from, tuberculosis. She taught English at the Univ. of Minnesota, subsequently at Smith. MEC's introduction to Sarah Orne JEWETT's *The Country of the Pointed Firs,* 1968, recalls the childhood meeting when Jewett urged her to write 'good books', 'all about Maine'. She began her writing with juvenile stories and novels; her first story for adults appeared in *Harper's,* 1918; *Mary Christmas,* about a woman cycling the Maine coast, appeared in 1926. In 1927, MEC published both her doctoral dissertation on Thomas Hardy and *Uplands,* a novel about Maine. Other carefully researched historical novels followed, including *Mary Peters,* 1934, in which the protagonist, of Petersport, learns to reverence the past as a means of dealing with the future; *Silas Crocket,* 1935, in which a family, of Saturday Cove, comes to the humble present of the Depression from an adventuring maritime past; *The Edge of Darkness,* 1957, in which an unnamed fishing village is shown to have lost its connection with the energetic past and to have sunk to the edge of darkness. MEC wrote four volumes of reminiscences: *The Golden Asse,* 1929, essays; *A Goodly Heritage, c.* 1934, and *The White Gate,* 1954, about her childhood in Blue Hill, early education, and early teaching career; *A Goodly Fellowship,* 1939, 'the story of a life spent in teaching.' She also published textbooks, two biographies, four books on the Bible, and various introductions and essays. Perry D. Westbrook's study, 1965, includes a bibliography. See also his *The New England Town in Fact and Fiction,* 1982.

Chatterton, Georgiana, Lady (Henrietta Georgiana Marcia Lascelles Iremonger), 1806–76, English novelist and miscellaneous writer, da. of Harriett (Gambier; French aristocratic family) and the Rev. Lascelles I. She learnt little from a succession of governesses, and only when she went to school for a month in Winchester, aged ten, did she discover her aptitude for learning (see *Home Sketches,* 1841). She m. Sir William C. (d. 1855) and spent time in Ireland, Italy and Germany. In London she moved in literary circles, meeting Browning, Dickens, Anna JAMESON and Catherine GORE. *Aunt Dorothy's Tale,* 1837, pub. anon., was followed by *Rambles in the South of Ireland,* 1839, which was an enormous success, the first edition selling out in a matter of weeks. Some 25 other works followed, including *The Heiress and Her Lovers,* 1863, a story of illegitimacy, changelings, murder and narrowly-avoided incest; and *Leonore and Other Poems,* 1864. Her diary concentrates on social encounters (GC and her mother, whom she loved 'with a kind of exclusive devotion', met with the Duchess of Kent and Queen VICTORIA every day at Tunbridge Wells) and meetings with writers such as Wordsworth and Joanna BAILLIE, with passing reference to her works in progress. Her second husband, E. H. Dering, took over her diary, eulogizing GC to the point of sainthood, though she had doubts about her faith, finally converting to Catholicism the year before her death. See his *Memoirs* of her, 1878.

Chedid, Andrée (Saab), francophone feminist, poet, novelist, dramatist, writer of short stories, b. in 1920 in Cairo, da. of Alice Godel (Khoury-Haddad) and Selim S., who divorced when she was a child. She was educ. in boarding schools, spending summers in France, where she went to school from 14 to 17. Bilingual, she took her BA at the US Univ. in Cairo, and signed her first collection of poems, which she wrote in English, *On the Trails of My Fancy,* 1943, as 'A. Lake'. At 21, she married Louis C., who studied medicine in Lebanon, 1942–5. They moved to Paris, 1946. She has a da., painter Michèle Koltz-Chedid, a son, and six grandchildren. For ten years she wrote only poems, then moved to prose narratives which emphasize links between ancient Egypt and the present, portraying the consistent concern of women through the ages for a non-violent world. Her novels – 'double. Facts and the myth' – develop multivalent characters, 'rooted and uprooted' women. The protagonist of the first, *Le Sommeil délivré,* 1976 (*From Sleep Unbound,* 1983), is an Arab woman 'enslaved by husband and society ... in a world of whispers and fleeting emotions, expressed in a closed, walled-in realm of murmurs and half hints – of fear'. In *Le Sixième Jour,* 1960 (*The Sixth Day,* 1962), which became a film, a grandmother nurses her fatally-ill grandchild. *La Maison sans racines,* 1985, currently being translated, shows a woman and a young girl caught in the mad tragedy of war in Lebanon. AC turned to plays later in her career, finding that 'theatre gives one companionship'. She has occasionally written for children, light verse with absurd rhymes on the marks of punctuation, and her version of an ancient Egyptian fable, 'le coeur suspendu'. Her 20 volumes of poetry, nine novels, seven plays and three short-story collections have won many literary prizes, including the Grand Prix of Belgium for French literature, 1975. *Mondes, Miroirs, Magies,* 1988, comprises memoirs, fantasies and narratives from Paris, Lebanon, Egypt, and Florida. See Kamal Boullata, ed. and transl., *Women of the Fertile Crescent: An Anthology of Modern Poetry by Arab Women,* 1978, and Bettina Knapp, *Andrée Chedid,* 1984. Interview in Knapp's *French Novelists Speak Out,* 1976.

Cheney, Ednah Dow (Littlehale), 1824–1904, writer and reformer, b. Boston, da. of Ednah Parker (Dow) and Sargent Smith L., wholesale grocer, who supported women's rights and ABOLITION. EDC was educ. privately in Boston and at Joseph Hale Abbott's girls' school. She became associated with the Transcendentalist movement, attending Margaret FULLER's 'conversations' and lecturing at Bronson Alcott's Concord School of Philosophy, 1879–88. In 1853 she m. Seth Wells C., portrait artist (d. 1856). Her first pub. work was *Handbook for American Citizens,* 1864. Other works include novels, such as *Patience,* 1870, and *Sally Williams,* 1874; *Gleanings in the Field of Art,* 1881, a collection of her philosophy lectures; a translation of poems by Michelangelo, 1885, and *Nora's Return,* 1890, a sequel in novel form to Ibsen's *Doll's House.* Of particular note is her *Life, Letters and Journals of Louisa May* ALCOTT, 1889. She had a lifelong interest in reform and helped found the New England Hospital for Women and Children, serving as its president 1887–1902. From the Civil War she worked for abolition, and Harriet Tubman was amongst her friends. She was also active in SUFFRAGE reform, and worked with J. W. HOWE in the Association for the Advancement of Women, believing that 'the emancipation of women ... is the most important and far-reaching reform of the world ...' (*Reminiscences,* 1902). See also *Memoir of Seth W. Cheney,* 1881, for her life.

Cheney, Harriet Vaughan **(Foster)**, d. after 1854, North American novelist and religious writer, b. at Boston, da. of H. W. FOSTER. She and her sister Eliza (later CUSHING) share their themes. Soon after leaving school they published anonymously *The Sunday School, or Village Sketches,* 1820; a pirate 2nd ed. stole their profit. *A Peep at the Pilgrims,* 1824 (UK and US reprs.), calls HFC 'author of divers unfinished' MSS. It presents a young Englishman who in 1636 leaves 'all the refinements of polished life' and for love of 'the fairest maiden of New-England' (he hears her singing a psalm as he comes ashore), renounces episcopalianism. He 'became eventually a sincere, and liberal Puritan'; they 'hand down to their children's children ... principles of civil and religious freedom'. The background is Indian warfare: a feeling, intelligent Pequod woman saves the captured heroine from the rage of her husband, the chief, before the tribe (all but herself and her children) are killed. Anne Hutchinson makes an appearance. After the similar *Rivals of Acadia, An Old Story of the New World,* 1827, HFC, now living in Montréal, published no more till her husband died. Then came a work on Christ, 1844, *Confessions of an Early Martyr,* 1846 (her only book in her name), tales on US, Canadian and Indian topics in *The Literary Garland,* and joint-editorship of her sister's next magazine. She helped with Jane E. Locke's memoir of her mother, pub. 1855.

'Chesebro, Caroline', Caroline Chesebrough, 1825–73, novelist, short-story writer, teacher, b. Canandaigua, NY, da. of Betsey (Kimball) and Nicholas Goddard C., hatter, wool dealer and postmaster. She was educ. at Canandaigua Seminary. From 1865 until her death, CC taught English Composition at Packer Collegiate Institute, Brooklyn. In 1848 she began writing magazine stories and articles; her first book was a collection, *DreamLand by Daylight,* 1852; her fourteenth and final work was *The Foe in the Household,* 1871. Most of CC's books are novels with a didactic purpose; she worked 'in earnest-handedness, with a definite aim' (Dedication, *The Children of Light,* 1853). Despite her sermonizing propensity, she achieved worthwhile characterizations of able women whose potentials are restricted. For instance, Asia Phillips (*The Children of Light*) is ambitious, intellectually superior, idealistic and artistic but she comes to loathe the very name 'woman' as 'significant of weakness, folly and bondage'. In *Peter Carradine,* 1863, CC's major work, the educated heroine has learned from her cradle 'to conceal herself, to circumvent, connive, contrive, to have her own way, to conquer herself, to choose the will of another, to prefer another's pleasure to her own'. In the same work, CC claims a moral and spiritual superiority for women as compensation. She also used fiction to explore religious experience, attacking in *Victoria, or The World Overcome,* 1856, the Calvinist who bases religion only on justice, not mercy; but overall her writing suffers from biblical declamation, and her constant digressions cause her texts to appear as if she is avoiding decisions.

Chesnut, Mary Boykin (Miller), 1823–86, journal writer, b. Camden, SC, da. of Mary (Boykin) and Stephen Decatur M., governor of SC and US senator. She m. James C., lawyer and planter, in 1840. During the Civil War, MBC ran an informal salon for politicians, generals and their wives and kept a journal of her social activities, reading, reflections on the war news and views on slavery. Thackeray's social satire served as her literary model. Although MBC acknowledges the evils of slavery and the common ground of oppression shared by women and blacks in the South, these views are partly overshadowed by her recollections of violence offered to white women by blacks. Her conflictual feelings about slavery and the situation of women found expression in compulsive re-readings of *Uncle Tom's Cabin,* although she saw H. B. STOWE as a literary and social antagonist. After the War, MBC worked at translating to bring in money, and began three autobiographical novels, which, however, were never published. In the 1880s she revised the journal, her major work, and it was pub. in expurgated form as *A Diary from Dixie,* 1905. The complete journal was finally pub. as *Mary Chesnut's Civil War,* 1981. See Elizabeth Muhlenfeld, 1981, for her life.

Chidley, Katharine, Independent pamphleteer. She m. Daniel C., tailor, at Shrewsbury in Feb. 1626, and that year refused, with other women, to be churched after childbirth. In 1630 she moved to London with her family (one of her seven children, Samuel C., also became a prominent Independent). Her *Justification of the Independent Churches of Christ,* 1641, and *A New-Yeares-Gift, or A Brief Exhortation* *to Mr Thomas Edwards,* 1645, are extended attacks on Edwards (whose *Gangraena* calls her a 'brazen-faced, audacious old woman'). She mocks reactionaries in combative and entertaining style, while expounding a detailed defence of toleration and of separation from the national church, a position she further developed in *Good Counsel to the Petitioners,* 1645. She may have participated in Leveller women's petitioning for John Lilburne's release in 1649, and is commonly believed to have led the deputation of twelve who in June 1653 presented to parliament a PETITION signed by 6000 women calling for his trial to be stopped.

Chilcot, Harriet, later Meziere, 1754–84, sentimental poet and novelist of Bath, Somerset, probably da. of Ann and of jeweller Henry C. Her writing was known and respected there under her birth name, though she was married when she published *Elmar and Ethlinda,* 1783, a group of hectically emotional verse tales set in India, Persia and the middle ages, dedicated to Georgiana DEVONSHIRE. Subscribers included writers (Elizabeth CARTER, Elizabeth MONTAGU), and Drury Lane people (Sarah Siddons). HC left her sister MSS including an incomplete epistolary novel, *Moreton Abbey,* finished by an anonymous (male) hand and pub. [?1790], as overpoweringly pathetic as her poems.

Child, Lydia Maria (Francis), 1802–80, novelist, reformer and woman of letters, b. Medford, Mass., da. of Susannah (Rand) and David Convers F., baker and anti-slavery campaigner. She was educ. at the local dame school and Miss Swan's Seminary, and by her brother Convers, Unitarian clergyman and later Professor at Harvard Divinity School. She was a close friend of Margaret FULLER, whom she greatly influenced. In 1828 she m. David Lee C., lawyer and editor of the *Massachusetts Whig Journal* and a founder of the New England Anti Slavery Society. (She, however, was the main financial supporter of the marriage.) In 1824 she pub. her very successful first novel *Hobomok* (rep. 1988), a historical romance set in Salem in 1630, which contains a moving argument for racial and religious tolerance. She opened a private girls' school in Watertown, Mass. (1825) and in 1826 founded and edited *Juvenile Miscellany,* the first children's monthly in the USA. Its success ended in 1833 when she pub. the first anti-slavery document, *An Appeal in Favor of that Class of Americans called Africans.* While converting many, it also aroused condemnation, bringing its author financial ruin and social ostracism. Her *History of the Condition of Women in Various Ages and Nations,* 1835, is a plea for female equality which aims to give women a means of identification with their past. Her successful *Letters from New York,* 1843–5, contain her powerful letter on women's rights, with its scathing attack on male domination through 'brute force and animal instinct'. Her work on women's history led her to write the *Memoirs of Madame de* STAËL *and of Madame Roland,* 1847, a message to American women that being female and intellectual may result in social alienation and devaluation of their work and character. Her practical and advanced ideas may be seen in *The Frugal Housewife,* 1829, which sold in England and Germany as well as the USA; *The Mother's Book,* 1831, which instructs mothers to remedy 'the greatest evil in education' by telling their daughters about 'delicate matters', and *The Freedman's Books,* 1865, which cites black heroes as inspiring examples. She encouraged and ed. Harriet JACOBS's 1861 SLAVE NARRATIVE. *The Progress of Religious Ideas through Successive Ages,* 1855, attempted to place Christianity in the context of other religions. Regarding the future of women, she remarked: 'I have no sanguine hopes about anything' (Susan P. Conrad, *Perish the Thought,* 1976). Her papers are at Cornell University. See Helene G. Baer, 1964, for her life, and Meltzer and Holland, 1982, for her selected letters.

Children's Literature. Books written explicitly for children (as distinct from ballads, romances, etc.) were an outgrowth of the urge to save souls, later to improve and educate. Moralizing (Robert Crowley, 1577) and poems (John Bunyan, 1686, Isaac Watts, 1715) led on to tales (perhaps Elizabeth HARRISON, 1741; publisher John Newbery, 1744ff.). After Sarah FIELDING's *The Governess*, 1749, first full-length fiction for children, women took a leading role – probably to seize the market, since most women who wrote for children wrote other genres as well. High moral tone was urged by Sarah TRIMMER, Mary WOLLSTONECRAFT, Eliza FENWICK, M. M. SHERWOOD, Lady Eleanor Fenn, Dorothy and Mary Ann Kilner, and Mary PILKINGTON. Mary Anne Hedge wrote against slavery; Mary LAMB retold Shakespeare. A. L. BARBAULD and Maria EDGEWORTH, while no less moral, also fostered imagination and (like Jane MARCET and Priscilla WAKEFIELD) knowledge of the natural world. By the mid nineteenth century, significant changes in attitude and direction were at work, with women writers signalling much of the expansiveness and new imaginative spark. Mary Howitt's translations of Andersen's fairy tales contributed psychological deftness to her own moral tales, like *Strive and Thrive*, 1840. Catherine SINCLAIR's *Holiday House*, 1839, provided fresh air with its mischievous children and a fond, story-telling uncle, yet still concluded with a sobering death-bed scene.

Sprawling sagas of family life, extolling forbearance and service to others, were equally popular with bookish parents in England and the USA. Following an early example – the American Susan WARNER's three-volume chronicle of the orphaned Elizabeth Montgomery in *The Wide, Wide World*, 1850 – Charlotte YONGE set the standard for the middle-class family novel with *The Heir of Redclyffe*, 1853, and *The Daisy Chain*, 1856, placing 11 individualized children and their widower-physician father in a home utterly faithful to High Church ideals. Her influence pervades Margaret Murray ROBERTSON's stories about stout-hearted children and matriarchs in the Ottawa valley. The family setting (of juvenile mishap, adventure stories, science lessons or tales of vicarage life) was equally prominent in the exuberant *Katy* books by Sarah WOOLSEY, the Colorado adventure *Nelly's Silver Mine*, 1878, and California-based Indian novel *Ramona*, 1884, by Helen Hunt JACKSON, the instructive *Parables from Nature*, 1855–71, by Margaret GATTY, and the range of SPCK stories by her daughter Juliana Horatia EWING, especially *Mrs Overtheway's Remembrances*, 1869, and *Six to Sixteen*, 1876.

Another important late-nineteenth-century development headed by women was the socially conscious reformism of evangelical publications and street-arab tales, championed by Maria Louisa Charlesworth (notably in her unctuous *Ministering Children*, 1854), Charlotte TUCKER, Mrs O. F. WALTON, and Hesba STRETTON. The least cloyingly sentimental of these, Stretton produced many bestsellers for the RTS, with the engaging waif in *Jessica's First Prayer*, 1867, and the spunky ten-year-old heroine in *Little Meg's Children*, 1868, topping the list. (See Margaret Cutt's *Ministering Angels*, 1975, Jacqueline Bratton's *The Impact of Victorian Children's Fiction*, 1981, and Doreen Rosman's *Evangelicals and Culture*, 1984.) Women were less overtly didactic in fantasies and in animal, adventure and school stories. The Irish-born, blind Frances BROWNE is a neglected, important early fantasist: *Granny's Wonderful Chair*, 1857, features a magical, fairy-story-telling chair. Dinah CRAIK's 'parable' of a little lame prince flying above his realm on a carpet has all the elements of the conventional fairy story. Both Jean INGELOW's *Mopsa the Fairy*, 1869, and Christina ROSSETTI's *Speaking Likenesses*, 1874, contain more psychological symbolism, while Lucy CLIFFORD's *Anyhow Stories*, 1882, are page-turners full of such horror as a 'new mother' transformed to a witch-like creature with a wooden tail and glass eyes. Anna SEWELL made the animal story an enduring success in the horse's autobiography *Black Beauty,* 1877; Margaret Marshall SAUNDERS tugged unashamedly at heart strings in her tale of an abused mongrel, *Beautiful Joe,* 1894 (and sequel). In the adventure story (not a favourite of Victorian women), Catherine Parr TRAILL and Bessie MARCHANT frame the period. Traill's *Canadian Crusoes,* 1851, stresses the resourcefulness and Christian fortitude of three children fending for themselves in the Ontario wilderness; more incredible than their piety is the spring-like resilience of Marchant's host of plucky girls.

These women extended the whole range and audience of literature for children; by treating their readers as perceptive individuals, they forecast some of the liberating realism and wonderful gallimaufry of modern work. Rossetti and Laura RICHARDS used verse to open new areas in nonsense language and infant lyricism. As author-illustrators Kate GREENAWAY and Beatrix POTTER added stylized charm and miniaturism to the look of children's books. Jean Webster and Angela BRAZIL initiated female characters into the male domain of the school story and made the clannish dormitory world a moulding influence. Gatty's *Aunt Judy's Magazine* and Mary Elizabeth Dodge's *St Nicholas* established periodicals devoted to children's literature and serious criticism. M. L. MOLESWORTH and E. NESBIT focused loving attention on the adventure-filled nursery milieu, with only occasional intrusions by adults. Flora SHAW in *Castle Blair,* 1878, and Annie KEARY in *Father Phim,* 1879, depicted a remarkable toughness in children dealing with violence and murder. Frances Hodgson BURNETT stressed picturesque innocence in *Little Lord Fauntleroy,* 1886, but turned with great success to wizened or neglected child personalities in *The Secret Garden,* 1911, and many others.

Twentieth-century authors have developed specialized genres like the ballet story (e.g. Noel STREATFEILD) and the pony story (Joanna CANNAN, the Pullein-Thompson sisters, Monica Edwards), settings which offer heroines growth and achievement. Others (like Patricia Wrightson, who draws imaginatively on the Australian Aboriginal mythology) combine realistic portrayals or fanciful flights with determination to regard books for children as works of art. The perfectionism of such author-illustrators as Wanda Gag, Lois Lenski, Virginia Lee BURTON, Pat Hutchins, Ann Blades and Gail Haley – reflective of many art styles and ethnic backgrounds – has made the picture-book a treasured artefact. From the gently whimsical fairy tale (Eleanor FARJEON, Rumer GODDEN, Joan AIKEN) to the engrossingly realistic novel (Virginia Hamilton, Judy BLUME, Eleanor CAMERON, Jean LITTLE, Katherine PATERSON), the story has cast off overt didacticism in favour of imaginative involvement. Historical fiction has probed new depths of character analysis and narrative technique (Rosemary Sutcliff, Mollie Hunter, Paula Fox). P. L. TRAVERS's *Mary Poppins* octet, Mary Norton's *Borrowers* series, Lucy BOSTON's *Green Knowe* books, and Susan Cooper's *Dark is Rising* sequence anchor fantasy in reality; with varying degrees of success Catherine Anthony Clark, Madeleine l'Engle, Ruth Nichols, Penelope LIVELY and Janet Lunn have followed their lead. The animal story provides parables of social comment and criticism (Jean Craighead GEORGE; Australian writers with distinctively Australian animal protagonists). The quest tale has grown into a Jungian myth of re-birth and discovery (Ursula LEGUIN). Karla Kuskin has made children's poetry a participatory event; anthologists Lucille CLIFTON and Mary Alice Downie, and folklorist Edith Fowke have assembled fine collections of children's eclectic tastes. Complementary contributions have come from Francelia Butler and others, who founded the US annual *Children's Literature,* 1971–, Nancy Chambers, who worked with the British Journal *Signal,* and Iona and

Peter Opie, who researched children's oral traditions. See F. J. Harvey Darton, new ed. 1982.

In Africa, writers have worked to create African-based texts for schools where colonial influence hung on in British reading materials. Efua SUTHERLAND wrote rhythm plays for Ghanaian schools; Barbara KIMENYE has created a series of graded readers for East-African elementary and secondary schools, as has Florence NWAPE, who, excluded from that market for political reasons, established her own press to publish children's stories, including two by Ifeoma OKOYE. Buchi EMECHETA has written for children, juveniles, and adults. See Charlotte Bruner, *AfrSR,* 29, 1986.

Childress, Alice, playwright, novelist, actress, director, b. in Charleston, SC, in 1920, and raised in Harlem by her grandmother Eliza, who urged her to 'write that thought down on a piece of paper'. A high school dropout, she taught herself various literary and dramatic forms, learning 'to break rules and follow [her] own thought and structure.' Actor, director and writer with the American Negro Theatre, 1941–52, she was nominated for a Tony for her Broadway role in *Anna Lucasta,* 1944. *Florence,* 1949, introduces her strong female characters and show business theme; *Just a Little Simple,* 1950 (adapted from Langston Hughes) and *Gold Through Trees,* 1952, the US's first professionally produced play by a black woman, followed. Their success encouraged AC to work for Harlem actors' and stage hands' unions. In *Trouble in Mind,* 1955 (first by a woman to win an Obie Award for best off-Broadway play), black actors rebel against the stereotypes they are to represent. AC does not consider her writing controversial ('not at all contrary to humanism'), but *Wedding Band: A Love/Hate Story in Black and White,* about an interracial common-law marriage, waited several years to find a producer (first professional performance at Univ. of Michigan, 1966), and its New York Shakespeare Festival production, on ABC television, 1973, met with several refusals to broadcast. *Wine in the Wilderness,* 1969, rejects the 'African queen' image and the view that black women are responsible for the problems of black men. AC compares it to Shaw's *Pygmalion:* 'In both plays men fail to correctly evaluate another human being; because of the macho-ego, they are prejudiced in the assessment of womanhood.' The one act plays *String,* 1969, from de Maupassant's story, and *Mojo: A Black Love Story,* 1970, about a hard-drinking, hard-living couple, focus on life in black contexts. Playwright and scholar at the Radcliffe Institute for Independent Study, 1966–8, AC studied art and culture in the USSR and theatre arts in China in the 1970s. Her juvenile novels, *A Hero Ain't Nothin' But a Sandwich,* 1973 (award-winning film, 1977), *Rainbow Jordan,* 1983, *Those Other People,* 1989, and plays, *When the Rattlesnake Sounds,* 1975, and *Let's Hear it for the Queen,* 1976, treat subjects ranging from Harriet Tubman to adolescent drug addiction. She collaborated with her husband, composer Nathan Woodward (married 1957), on *Sea Island Song,* about the isolated Gullah-speaking people of Georgia Sea Island, produced in Charleston, 1979, and *Gullah,* 1984, produced at the Univ. of Mass. *Like One of the Family: Conversations from a Domestic's Life,* 1956, repr. 1986, collects satirical sketches from her column 'Here's Mildred' in *Freedom* and the *Baltimore Afro-American.* In the novel *A Short Walk,* 1979, Cora James, gifted card-sharp, show-business hustler, single mother, and survivor, encounters Marcus Garvey's black nationalist movement and rides on the Black Star Line. AC says, 'The Black writer explains pain to those who inflict it.' See Evans, 1984, and Gayle Austin in *So Q,* 25, 1987.

Chisholm, Caroline (Jones), 1808–77, social reformer and writer, b. near Northampton, da. of Sarah and William J., farmer. Educ. by governesses, at 22 she m. Captain

Archibald C. of the East India Company and converted to Catholicism. In 1832 they went to Madras where she founded the Female School of Industry for the Daughters of European Soldiers. They visited Sydney in 1838, where she began her work of assisting female immigrants, establishing the Female Immigrants' Home in 1841, and publishing *Female Immigration,* 1842. In order to promote family emigration schemes, she returned to England in 1846 and pub. more pamphlets, including *Emigration and Transportation,* 1847. By 1853 she had become one of the most famous (or infamous) women in England: see Dickens's satirical portrait of her as Mrs Jellyby in *Bleak House,* 1852–3; more sympathetic were poems by Robert Lowe and Henry Kendall, and George Landen Dann's play, 1943. She revisited Australia in 1854 and agitated for better conditions for goldseekers and for the release of land to small farmers. Impoverished, she opened a girls' school in Sydney in 1862 and on returning to England in 1866, received a small pension from the British government. See the biographies by Eneas Mackenzie, 1852, Margaret Kiddle, 1950, and Mary Hoban's *Fifty-One Pieces of Wedding Cake,* 1973.

Cholmondeley, Mary, 1859–1925, novelist, b. Hodnet, Shropshire, third child and eldest da. of Emily (Beaumont) and Richard Hugh C., clergyman; aunt of Stella BENSON. Her invalid sister Hester, poet, died aged 22. MC suffered from delicate health all her life, and was educ. privately. Until her late thirties, she lived in the country, helping her father with parish work; when he retired in 1896 she moved with him to a London flat. In later life she lived with another sister, moving between London and Suffolk. Her writing career began with short stories for the *Graphic* and other periodicals. Her first pub. novel was the detective story *The Danvers Jewels,* 1887, pub. by George Bentley, to whom she had been introduced by her friend Rhoda BROUGHTON. *Sir Charles Danvers,* 1889, *Diana Tempest,* 1893, and *A Devotee,* 1897, followed, but her major success came with *Red Pottage* in 1899. This mildly scandalous novel attacked middle-class hypocrisy and complacence, and highlights both the difficulties of the independent woman writer, and the issue of 'woman's friendship for woman', seen as a blessing which 'sustains the life of both, which is still young when life is waning, which man's love and motherhood cannot displace, nor death annihilate.' She pub. five further novels, and a book of memoirs, *Under One Roof: A Family Record,* 1918. She was a friend of the FINDLATER sisters. See life by Percy Lubbock, 1928, and the bibliog. by Jane Crisp, *VFRG* 6, n.d.

Chopin, Kate (O'Flaherty), 1850–1904, novelist, diarist, essayist and poet, b. St Louis, da. of Eliza (Faris) and Thomas O'F. She was educ. at the Sacred Heart Convent, where Mother O'Meara, her English teacher, urged her to write. She was deeply influenced by her maternal great-grandmother, Mme Victoria Charleville, who recounted spell-binding tales of local colour and fostered her compassionate and intelligent curiosity about life. The tragic deaths of her father, two brothers and later her husband Oscar C. (whom she m. in 1870), followed closely by the deaths of her mother and great-grandmother, left permanent scars, and on the advice of her physician she turned to writing. 'If It Might Be', an elegiac poem, appeared in 1889, but her Louisiana tales, pub. in *Vogue, The Century* and *The Atlantic,* brought her renown. Her first novel, *At Fault,* 1891, announced a number of future concerns, including the pitfalls of moral absolutism, and the modern woman's dilemma in confronting sexual passion. Her refusal to condemn divorce was a first in fiction, as was her unconventional characterization of a female alcoholic. Her reputation soared with the publication of *Bayou Folk,* 1894, tales of local colour in settings of sensual ambiance, focusing upon the psychology of the individual and including such themes as miscegenation ('Desiree's Baby'), love and marriage (repudiated by Paula in 'Wiser than a God' in favour of a musical career), female self-assertion and sexual desire ('A Shameful Affair') and the possibilities and perils of emancipation. Influenced by Darwinian theory, KC exposes the conflict between woman's search for self-authenticity and biological destiny in her collection, *A Night in Acadie,* 1897, deplored for its unabashed treatment of sensuality. She admired S. O. JEWETT for her technique, M. W. FREEMAN for her depiction of frustrated women and Germaine de STAËL and George SAND for their feminism. She had difficulties in getting her more unconventional stories published: 'The Storm', which deals with sex more freely and openly than either Flaubert or Zola, was not pub. in her lifetime, while *The Awakening,* 1899, her masterpiece, prompted such critical outrage that it ended her literary career. Her heroine, Edna Pontellier, leaves husband and children and attempts to redefine herself outside traditional female roles; awakening to sexual passion, and realizing the futility of the struggle for life beyond marriage, she chooses to take her own life rather than have it taken from her. See Per Seyersted, 1969, critical biography; diaries and letters ed. Seyersted and Toth, 1979; *The KC Companion*, ed. Thomas Bonner, 1988. Papers are at the Missouri Historical Society.

Christie, Agatha (Mary Clarissa Miller), DBE, 'Mary Westmacott', 1890–1976, crime novelist, playwright, short-story writer, youngest da. of Clarissa (Boehmer) and Frederick M. of Torquay, Devon. She grew up in a large, wealthy, matriarchal family, educ. after her father's death, 1901, by her mother, who encouraged her to write. After a year studying singing in Paris, she moved to Cairo. Her 1914 marriage to Archibald C. (divorced, 1928), a penniless officer by whom she had one daughter, made financial problems an important initial stimulus to her writing. An avid reader of detective fiction, she had moderate success with *The Mysterious Affair at Styles*, 1920. Its small, vain Belgian detective, Hercule Poirot, made a comic departure from the traditionally heroic, active sleuth, by sole reliance on observation and rationality, denominated 'little grey cells'. AC's more than 60 novels and more than 30 collections of stories shaped the 'Golden Age' of the classical English detective novel, the light-hearted, conventionalized clue-hunting game. Characterization was limited, style simple, unexpected twists of plot her major mark. *The Murder of Roger Ackroyd*, 1926, caused a sensation with its unprecedented narrator-murderer. AC herself staged a much-publicized, mysterious disappearance, when her mother's death and her impending divorce (1928) allegedly caused amnesia. *Unfinished Portrait*, 1934, is thought to be based on this: see Jessica Mann, *Deadlier than the Male*, 1981. In 1930 AC m. archeologist Max Mallowan, whose expeditions she often joined. *Come, Tell Me How You Live*, 1946, describes their Syrian expeditions. In *The Murder at the Vicarage*, 1930, an even less heroic sleuth appeared: benevolent, sympathetic Miss Marple, using the 'feminine' methods of sharp sight, intuition, gossip and practicality. The interbellum was AC's most creative period. The post-war world caused nostalgia: Poirot came full circle, returning to Styles for a final shocking adventure, *Curtain*, 1975, AC's famous play, *The Mousetrap* (adapted from *Three Blind Mice*, 1948), is currently (1990) in its 38th consecutive year. Other plays include *Ten Little Niggers*, 1944 (repr.as ... *Indians*, 1946), *Murder on the Nile*, 1946, and *Witness for the Prosecution*, 1953. AC revealed sparse personal information in *An Autobiography*, 1977. She had written romantic novels as 'Mary Westmacott'. At her death she was the world's second-most-translated author;

her work has been much filmed. See *Companion* to her work by Russell H. Fitzgibbon, 1980; study by Patricia B. Maida and Nicholas B. Spornick, 1982; Stephen Knight, *Form and Ideology in Crime Fiction*, 1980.

Christine de Pizan, or Pisa, 1363/4–?1429, European feminist and woman of letters, whose writings were influential in England from the fifteenth century on. B. at Venice, she was educ. and spent most of her life in Paris after her father, Tommaso da Pizzano, was invited to the French court. She married, *c.* 1379, Etienne de Castel, French royal notary and secretary, who died in *c.* 1389, leaving her poor, with a daughter and probably two sons. From about 1393 she lived by writing (see studies by Enid McLeod, repr. 1976, and Charity Cannon Willard, 1984) and working as a scribe. Many of her love-poems provide an unusual female response to the favourite situations of contemporary love poetry; other works (especially the *Cité des dames* and *Le Livre des trois vertus*) controversially discuss women's social position. *L'Epistre au dieu d'amours* gives an 'anti-anti-feminist view' of women's historical importance; her response to *Le Roman de la rose* led to a protracted epistolary debate with leading male French writers and intellectuals. Her contacts with England were close, and her reputation there quickly established through translations, beginning in 1402. Some works, French and English, have modern eds.; many remain unedited; the Bibliothèque National and BL have important MS collections.

Chudleigh, Mary (Lee), Lady, 1656–1710, poet, essayist, and feminist, da. of Richard L. of Winslade, Devon; in 1674 she m. George C. of Ashton, later a baronet. Her daughter's death was a great blow; two sons survived; she lived in Devon very quietly, studying and writing, with some winters in London. A savagely anti-feminist wedding sermon by the Rev. John Sprint, 1699 (which also angered 'EUGENIA' and Elizabeth THOMAS), provoked her to issue anonymously *The Ladies' Defence*, 1701 (repr. in Moira Ferguson, *First Feminists*, 1985), a verse debate about women's role among a bitter parson, brutal squire, vapid flattering ladies' man and Melissa the female mouthpiece (MC's own literary name is Marissa). Melissa is moderate in views, sometimes biting in tone; the male speakers are adeptly self-exposed. MC was angry when the poem was repr. with her name, though she set that to her other works, both of them 'chiefly design'd' for women: *Poems on Several Occasions*, with a biblical paraphrase, 1703 (the dedication to Queen Anne mentions MC's aspiring ambition), and *Essays upon Several Subjects*, 1710, with passages of verse embedded in their prose. She treats female friendship and writing talent (with romance names for her friends), mourns her mother and daughter, urges reason and the limitation of desire, praises country retirement, philosophy, religion, Mary ASTELL, and Eugenia. Her letters to Elizabeth Thomas, 1701–3, were pub. in *Pylades*, 1732. She left poems and dramatic works in MS.

Churchill, Caryl, playwright. B. in 1938 in London, an only child, her mother a secretary-film-actress, her father a cartoonist, she lived in the Lake District, then Montreal, 1948–55 (attending Trafalgar School), then took a BA in English at Lady Margaret Hall, Oxford, 1960. She began writing plays early: three at Oxford, beginning with *Downstairs*, staged 1958. She m. lawyer David Harter, 1961, and had three sons and a succession of difficult miscarriages. Need for time with her family made her concentrate on writing for radio: eight plays from 1962, when *The Ants* was broadcast. This set a theme for later work: the individual oppressed by capitalist and sexist society. *Owners* (Royal Court Theatre, 1972) followed some radio plays in exploring the effects of trying to own people as well as things. After this CC wrote, despite ill health and family pressure, almost always for the stage and TV. Prolific, polemical, basing much of her work on women's history, she is seen as Britain's leading female playwright. Her feminism, imagination and Brechtian style have developed through work with the THEATRE GROUPS Joint Stock and Monstrous Regiment. With each she wrote of the seventeenth century: *Light Shining in Buckinghamshire* (on women and millenialism) and *Vinegar Tom* (on witch-hunts), both produced 1976. Historical vision and experimental use of character 'transformations' appear in *Cloud Nine*, 1979, a commercial success, which juxtaposes sexual politics of the nineteenth century and 1970s. *Top Girls*, 1982, prefaces the struggles of a businesswoman and her domestic sister with the life stories of four women from history, the first a thirteenth-century Japanese courtesan. *Fen*, 1983, is 'an archetype of feminist drama as "landscape"'; *Softcops* (written 1978, produced 1983) examines government's 'soft' control of dissent. *Serious Money*, 1987, satirizes big business in rhyming couplets. *Plays: One*, 1985, has CC's introduction and a chronology of writing as well as staging. See Keyssar, 1984; Austin Quigley in Enoch Baxter, ed., *Feminine Focus, The New Women Playwrights*, 1989; *Casebook* on CC, ed. Phyllis R. Randall, 1988.

Circulating libraries. Bookshops began letting out as well as selling at the Restoration; the widow Page near London Bridge was doing it in 1674. The provinces seem to have been before London, which had a library in 1739. In the 1760s libraries were doing good business in Charleston (SC), Boston, and a small town in Pennsylvania; in London they were taking 400 of 1000-copy editions of new novels. They were run by Mary COLLYER, Ann YEARSLEY, Catherine HUTTON's father (who thus made a fortune), and the founder of the MINERVA Press, who also encouraged their spread in the provinces. By the 1780s every notable English market town had one, spas had several, and London 20. Bombay had one in 1806 and Jamaica several in 1808. J. Bell of the Strand had 10,000 books in 1776, 100,000 in 1786, and went bankrupt in 1793; William Garner of Margate went bankrupt three times between 1796 and 1824. The great municipal libraries often began as male societies: Bristol in 1782 had five times as many female authors as female members. *The Use of Circulating Libraries Considered*, 1797 (repr. in Devendra P. Varma, *The Evergreen Tree of Diabolical Knowledge*, 1972), claims various kinds of usefulness, and the credit for a marked increase in learning, especially among women (it opens with a parallel between prejudice against libraries and prejudice against women). Though it suggests that nearly 80 per cent of stock should be fiction, many surviving catalogues reverse that proportion. The popular view, however (given by Elizabeth GRIFFITH, Hannah MORE, Clara REEVE, and R. B. Sheridan), was that libraries pandered to escapist fantasy in girls; male periodical reviewers frequently voiced contempt (see Hilda M. Hamlyn in *The Library*, 1947). Mudie's Select Library, begun in London in 1842, held greater sway than any other over publishers, authors and readers, censoring doubtful works (Annie EDWARDES's *The Morals of Mayfair*, 1858, was banned) and virtually determining three-volume novels as the standard shape of British fiction until 1894 (see Guinevere Griest, *Mudie's Circulating Library and the Victorian Novel*, 1970). Cheap subscriptions (a guinea a year per exchangeable volume) ensured success, and large consignments were shipped to the country or abroad. Popular writers began to look for their public directly through the libraries; Margaret OLIPHANT, M. E. BRADDON and Ellen WOOD were among the most sought after; Rhoda BROUGHTON was unacceptable to Mudie's until the mid-1870s (and she chafed at the three-decker form). In the USA, three-deckers never took hold, books were much cheaper, and libraries did not turn into 'Leviathans'.

Cixous, Hélène, French writer, teacher, feminist, b. in 1937 in Oran, Algeria. Founder of the Paris Centre des Recherches en Etudes Féminines, 1974, HC has since 1968 been professor of English literature at the Univ. of Paris VII. Feminist critics attribute to her the prominence of *l'écriture féminine* in French cultural and political debates of the seventies. English-speaking audiences know her best through translations of *La Jeune Née*, with Catherine Clément, 1975 (transl. 1986), of 'Le Rire de la Méduse', 1975 (transl. 1976), and of the explorative psychological fictions, *Angst*, 1977 (transl. 1985) and *Dedans*, awarded the Prix Médicis, 1969 (transl. 1986), 'Le Rire' emerges from HC's sense of 'otherness' as an Algerian, a Jew, and a woman writing to displace the universal Voice of the White, Male, speaking subject. Taking her cue from Adrienne RICH, she stages an 'awakening of the dead [woman]' who inhabits malestream Western literature as sublimated or fetishized female 'other' and whose repressed self-love has never been articulated. HC urges women to inscribe their own pleasures and defeat the 'loathsome logic of anti-love [and] anti-narcissism', in a women's discourse privileging the materiality rather than the idea of speech, foregrounding the rhythms, tones, and affective richness, reminiscent of the Voice of the Good Mother. Her *écriture féminine* would tap the female imaginary and its phantasmic profusion without constraining it to the laws and categories of the patriarchal symbolic order. It appeals to the 'bisexuality' of every writer, prompting her/him to inscribe his/her Other, the repressed femininity of men and the repressed masculinity of women. HC's feminism is 'deconstructive': it entertains essentializing strategies but does not advocate campaigning under the banner of any political identity. She champions the hysteric, as a non-Oedipal heroine whose excessive, polyglottal, polyphonic, imagistic 'discourse' signifies woman's protest and escape from the oppressive order of the phallic signifier and the father's law. See also her 'Reading the Point of Wheat', *NLH*, 19, 1987, and interview in *Women's Review*, 7, 1986. Selections ed. Susan Sellers, 1988; critical study by Verena Conely, 1984. See also Toril Moi, *Sexual/Textual Politics*, 1985, and Nancy Miller, ed., *The Poetics of Gender*, 1986.

Clampitt, Amy, poet, b. 1920, and brought up in New Providence, Iowa, da. of Pauline (Felt) and Roy Justin C. She was educ. at Grinnell College (BA in English, 1941, DHL, 1984), Columbia Univ., the New School, and Hunter College. She has been Writer-in-Residence at the College of William and Mary and Visiting Writer at Amherst. From 1943 to 1982 she worked at various jobs in NYC – in publishing, freelance research and editing, and as a librarian. Her poems first began appearing in *The New Yorker* in 1978, later in many literary periodicals. AC's comment on the title poem of her first collection, *The Kingfisher*, 1983, aptly describes much of her work: 'The design here might be thought of as an illuminated manuscript in which all the handwork happens to be verbal, or (perhaps more precisely) as a novel trying to work itself into a piece of cloisonné'. Her keen sense of the natural world ('the Snow Queen's frore boudoir', 'the planar windowpanes of tidepools', the turtle described as 'domed repoussé leather with an underlip of crimson') and her almost uncanny ability to evoke the spirit of place (the limestone quarries of Le Grand, Iowa – in 'The Quarry' – the Mexican village of 'Tepoztlan', Italy's Lake Trasimene) appear also in *What the Light Was Like*, 1985. Women's experience as individuals and as a part of history is the central concern in *Archaic Figure*, 1987.

Daphne, the Virgin Mary, the Medusa, and the female deities associated with the oracle at Dodona all appear in these poems, as do Margaret FULLER, Dorothy WORDSWORTH, and George ELIOT. The book's epigraph (Virginia WOOLF on the heroines of ELIOT) is particularly apt: 'The ancient consciousness of women, charged with suffering and sensibility, and for so many ages dumb, seems, in them, to have brimmed and overflowed'.

Clappe, Louise Amelia Knapp (Smith), 'Dame Shirley', 1819–1906, writer and teacher, b. Elizabeth, NJ, da. of Lois (Lee) and Moses S., teacher. She was educ. at Charlestown (Mass.) Female Seminary and Amherst Academy. In 1848 or 49 she m. Fayette Clapp, doctor (she added the 'e' to her name); they divorced in 1857. She lived in San Francisco, then in frontier mining settlements near the unexplored Sierra Nevada mountains. In 1851, as 'Dame Shirley', she began a series of letters to her sister Mary Ann in New England, aiming to record 'a true picture of mining life and its peculiar temptations' (Letter 12). The 23 letters were pub. serially in *The Pioneer*, 1854–5, and in book form as *The Shirley Letters*, 1922. Simple and absorbing, they recount her residence on the diggings (7), a miners' 'Saturnalia' (12), and her reading of Shakespeare, Spenser, Coleridge, Burns and Shelley in her isolated log cabin. They offer an accurate account of mining equipment and activities, as well as vivid scenic description. Bret Harte drew heavily on *The Shirley Letters* in his writing. LC loved the frontier life and returned to San Francisco with regret. She taught until 1878 when she moved to NYC to live with her adopted niece, Genevieve Stebbins, and lectured to women's groups. Her letters are in the Californian State Library, Sacramento; the introductions to the four editions contain biographical information.

Clark, Eleanor, novelist, short-story and non-fiction writer, essayist, translator, memoirist. B. in 1913, in Los Angeles, Calif., da. of Eleanor (Phelps) and Frederick H. C., she grew up in Connecticut, then attended Vassar (BA, 1934), where she wrote for a short-lived 'rebel literary magazine', *Con Spirito*, with Mary MCCARTHY and others. She published short stories, essays, and reviews in periodicals, including the *Partisan Review, Kenyon Review* and *Nation*. She translated Ramon J. Sender's *The Dark Wedding*, 1943, and published *Song of Roland*, a retelling for juveniles, 1962. Her first novel, *The Bitter Box*, 1946, about a repressed bank teller who walks 'out of his cage' into revolutionary encounters and compassion for others, won her a Guggenheim fellowship and an American Academy grant, but she did not write another for almost 24 years. In 1952, she m. Robert Penn Warren. She had two children. 'Can a woman be a good writer (artist) and a good mother? I have no idea. Are the two in conflict? Of course – so is art and everything else.' Between her novels, she turned to non-fiction: Doris Grumbach called *Rome and a Villa*, 1952, new ed. 1975, 'one of the best books ever written on the Eternal City', and *The Oysters of Locmariaquer*, 1964, won the National Book Award. In her middle years, EC became blind: *Eyes, Etc., a Memoir*, 1977, a book she composed on large drawing pads using magic markers, documents and reflects on her battles with blindness, self-pity, and language; it declares, by parallel and allusion, her affinity with the blind poet of the *Odyssey*. Her second novel, *Baldur's Gate*, 1970, grapples fictionally, in its character Eve, with some of the issues of *Eyes*: traditional values, art, the *métier*, the place of the individual in society. The literary and allusive narrative of *Camping Out*, 1986, explores relationships (amorous, reproductive, triangular): two women (one is a lesbian writer, the other has tried to save her childless marriage by becoming pregnant by her brother) take a camping trip to a Vermont lake. A murderous psychotic, taking vengeance for, among other things, their education and literary pretensions, rapes one and kills their dog. The experience produces self-knowledge, a new understanding between the two, and a vision of sexual violence in contemporary America. EC's short stories are collected in *Dr Heart*, 1974. Interview in Roy Newquist, *Conversations*, 1967.

Clark, Emily Frederick, d. after 1833, novelist, poet and portrait-painter, 'granddaughter of the late Colonel Frederick, Son of Theodore, King of Corsica', as her title-pages say. Theodore reigned very briefly and died in debt in London, 1756; his self-styled natural son Frederick Vigliawischi (called by James Boswell 'a low-lifed being') educated his granddaughter and later shot himself in the porch of Wesminster Abbey, 1797. From an early age, EFC said, she published to help support her mother and sisters. Some titles are untraced. *Ianthé, or The Flower of Caernarvon*, 1798 (dedicated to the Prince of Wales), *Ermina Montrose*, 1800 (with subscribers including Maria EDGEWORTH and other writers), *The Banks of the Douro*, 1805, and *The Esquimaux*, 1819, follow the same pattern: high life, partly abroad; ideal heroines happily married after undeserved suffering; villains punished, and loyal lower orders (of whom the Esquimaux is one) thanked. *Poems*, 1810 (aristocratic subscribers), are mostly sentimental ballads. *Tales at the Fire Side*, 1819, are told by a father, though mother suggests she might contribute too. EFC was a fervent client of the RLF: 42 wheedling approaches, 1811–33, brought 24 payments. Accounts of her works (about 14 mentioned), illnesses, accidents, dealings with publishers, all become lures for that 'bread of dependance' which she calls 'bitter'.

Clarke, Edith **Doreen** (Joy), playwright, b. 1928 at Middleton, England, da. of Elsie (Clements) and Percy J. She left school at 14 to work in cotton mills, factories and government offices. In 1950 she m. Fred C., with whom she had four sons; the family moved to Australia in 1958. She has written poetry and short stories but only began writing plays in 1977. A committee member and writer with Troupe, Adelaide's alternative theatre group (1978–80), in 1981 she was playwright-in-residence with the State Theatre of S. Australia. Her plays include *Roses in Due Season*, 1978 (pub. 1982), *Missus Queen*, 1979, *Bleedin' Butterflies*, 1980 (pub. 1982), *Farewell Brisbane Ladies*, 1980 (pub. 1983), *The Sad Songs of Annie Sando*, 1981, and for radio, *The Name of Your Uncle*, 1981, and *Salt and Vinegar*, 1982. These present women's experience as a valid dramatic subject and deal with women in difficult domestic circumstances: *Roses in Due Season* shows alcoholism and violence within marriage. *Bleedin' Butterflies* provides an unusual account of the plight of women in the Depression.

Clarke, Gillian (Williams), poet, teacher, b. 1937 in Cardiff, da. of Ceinwin (Evans) and Penri W. Brought up with Welsh as her second language, she was educ. at St Clare's Convent, Porthcawl, and Univ. College, Cardiff (BA in English, 1958). After working as a news researcher she m. Peter C. in 1960; she has three children, and is divorced. She includes no work from her first collection, *Snow on the Mountain*, 1971, in her *Selected Poems*, 1985. Deeply involved in Welsh language and culture, she sometimes uses traditional Welsh metres in her English poetry, informed by acute awareness of Welsh landscape, history and folklore. She lectured as a freelance, then at Gwent College of Art and Design, 1975–84 (art history), while editing a leading poetry journal, *Anglo-Welsh Review*, and raising its proportion of poems by women. *The Sundial*, 1979 (complex poems with deceptively simple surfaces), was much reprinted; *Letter from a Far Country*, 1982 (title-poem written for radio), uses the ancestral memories of generations of women in a small Welsh village. 'The gulls grieve at our contentment. / It is a masculine question. / "Where" they call "are your great works?" / They slip their fetters and fly up / To laugh at land-locked women. / Their cries are cruel as greedy babies.' In 1984 GC held a Writing Fellowship at Univ. College, St David's; she now teaches children creative writing. A member of the Welsh Academy English-language executive committee, she has travelled on scholarships to Ireland, Yugoslavia, the USSR and the US. 'Neighbours' in *Letting in the Rumour*, 1989, notes 'each little town / in Europe twinned to Chernobyl'.

Clarke, Marion, 'Mrs Charles Montague Clarke' (Doake), (Brown gives pseud. 'Miriam Drake': not in BL catalogue), fl. 1872–87, Irish novelist; her husband also a writer. She wrote 14 tales and novels, two with her more conventional sister, Margaret Doake. Her first was *Oughts and Crosses*, 1872; others include *No Security*, 1873, *Strong as Death*, 1875, set in the Ulster uprising of 1798 and using dialect, and, lastly, *More True than Truthful*, 1887, with an interestingly spirited heroine. She writes with a good observation of country life and her women are life-like and lively.

Clarke, Mary Victoria **Cowden** (Novello), 1809–98, story writer, Shakespeare scholar, b. London, da. of Mary and Vincent N., organist and teacher. Educ. at home, in a household frequented by artists and poets (Mary Lamb taught her Latin) and later at Boulogne, preparing to be a governess; she m. Charles CC in 1828, and they lived with her parents for 20 years: 'Happy the girl whose letters from and to the man she prefers are conveyed by her own father' (*My Long Life*, 42). They were part of the circle including Keats (Charles CC's close friend) and Leigh Hunt. Her main output was educative: *The Complete Concordance to Shakespeare*, which took 16 years to prepare, appeared in monthly parts 1844–5, often reprinted; *The Girlhood of Shakespeare's Heroines*, 1851–2; *World-noted Women: or Types of Womanly Attributes*, 1858. She often worked in collaboration, either with her husband (d. 1877) – *Recollections of Writers*, 1878, *The Shakespeare Key*, 1879 – or, earlier, with women friends: *A Book of Stories for Young People*, 1847, with Mary Howitt, and Anna Maria Hall. She pub. other stories and some poems, a sketch of her husband (priv. printed 1887) and autobiographical reminiscences, *My Long Life*, 1896, in which she gives thanks for her 'rose-coloured spectacles'. See Richard Altick, 1948, and George Gross, *Victorian Studies* 16, 1 (1972), 37–58.

Clarke, Olivia (Owenson), Lady, 1785?–1845, Irish dramatist, much younger sister of Lady Morgan. She was sent very young to boarding-school after her mother's early death, worked as a governess, and in 1808 m. Dr Arthur C., soon to be knighted; she lived in Dublin, had three daughters, wrote constantly to her sister, and was known for mimicry and comic verse. She turned J. W. Croker's hostile *Quarterly* review of Sydney Morgan's *France*, 1817, into burlesque couplets, and pub. a dozen verse parodies, 1826, and magazine verse, 1831–5. Most notable is her rollicking, good-humoured comedy, *The Irishwoman* (acted Dublin and pub. London, 1819), in which language sparkles as the heroine and her disreputable old Irish nurse outplot a motley selection of males, including the nurse's long-lost, upwardly-mobile son.

Clausen, Jan, writer of poems, fiction and essays, b. 1950, who grew up in the Pacific North-West USA, 'lived by writing' from 15 or earlier, dropped out of college and moved to NYC in 1973. She 'came up in a very self-consciously and proudly female literary world': she self-published her first book, *After Touch*, 1975 (poems); founded *Conditions* and was on its editorial collective until 1981; and ran the Long Haul Press, publishing lesbian poetry and theory.

JC has helped mother a non-biological daughter to maturity, and writes much of lesbian mothering. Some of the finest stories in *Mother, Sister, Daughter, Lover*, 1980, evoke the plight of children caught between poor lesbian mother and absent or rich bourgeois father, as well as the 'infinite possible permutations and combinations' of love-affairs in lesbian circles. Her first novel, *Sinking, Stealing*, 1985, traces the steps by which a woman is provoked to go on the run with her dead lover's ten-year-old daughter, whose father has tried to part them. JC has published theoretical essays in *A Movement of Poets: Thoughts on Poetry and Feminism*, 1982, and *Books and Life*, 1988, and mixed poetry and prose in *Duration*, 1983. *The Proserpine Papers*, 1988 (influenced by Meridel LE SUEUR), personifies complex conflicts: the protagonist hunts the diaries of a pre-WWI lesbian feminist in Iron Range, Minn., who loved her more conventional grandmother; the radical voice is shockingly silenced, but not wholly. See JC on herself in *WRB*, July 1989.

Clayton or Cleaton, **Anne,** later Easton, Quaker pamphleteer. She worked as a servant in Margaret FELL's household, travelled and was imprisoned in England, visited Barbados in 1657 and 1659, and m. Nicholas E. of Rhode Island before 1672. In 1660 she published a broadside *Letter to the King*, describing her vision of Charles II's arrival, in which she saw his spirit as three people, 'and one was a Woman'; she calls on him to 'reject not the Counsel of the Lord spoken to thee by his Servants and Hand-maids.'

'Cleeve, Lucas', Adeline Georgina Isabella Kingscote (Wolff), d. 1908, novelist, only da. of Adeline (Douglas) and Sir Henry Drummond W., MP. In 1885, after attending Oxford Univ., she m. Howard K., Lt. Col. Oxfordshire Light Infantry. She pub. more than 60 novels 1895–1911. *The Woman Who Wouldn't*, 1895, is a riposte to Grant Allen's *The Woman Who Did*, while *What a Woman Will Do*, 1900, tells of a couple who agree to divorce so that he can marry a rich woman and support the four children. Strained plots mingle with feminist concerns in other novels: *Yolande the Parisienne: a Dream of the Twentieth Century*, 1900, begins with the bizarre suicide of Yolande who returns to haunt the lover who had tired of her, while *A Woman's Aye and Nay*, 1908, speculates on the results of female enfranchisement. *The Love Letters of a Faithless Wife*, 1911, argues for men appreciating their wives, and contains some nice portraits of female friendships. As Mrs Howard K., she pub. a collection of Indian tales, 1890, and *The English Baby in India and How to Rear It*, 1893, which gives sensible advice on confinement, nursing, etc., but is predictably opposed to Indian nurses.

Cleghorn, Sarah Norcliffe (Dalton), 1876–1959, poet, novelist, autobiographer, journalist, teacher and political activist, b. Norfolk, Va., da. of Sarah (Hawley) and John D. She and her brother Carl, the youngest and only survivors of six children, lived in Vermont with their aunts after their mother's death. SC was educ. first at home; she later attended Burr and Burton Seminary in Manchester, Vermont, and spent a year at Radcliffe College. SC's early verse was self-consciously 'old-timey', as she explained in her autobiography *Threescore*, 1936: 'a set of old figures and a gallery of old landscapes'. Not until she went to Europe in 1912 did she begin to write 'burning poems' out of her involvement in pacifism and socialism. *Portraits and Protests*, 1917, collects both the earlier sentimental verse and the later protest poetry. 'The Poltroon' infuriated readers by imagining Jesus as a conscientious objector. Four lines of protest became SC's most famous poem: 'The golf links lie so near the mill / That almost every day / The laboring children can look out / And see the men at play.' After WW1, SC could not find publishers for her pacifist writing, including a novel and a history of the US. She taught at a variety of experimental schools and wrote ballads about radicals like Harriet Tubman for her students, later collected in *Poems of Peace and Freedom*, 1945. *The Spinster*, 1916, is an autobiographical novel; while *Threescore*, 1936, reflects on her childhood with the honesty and insight of a radical teacher.

Clerke, Ellen Mary, 1840–1906, poet, b. Skibbereen, Co. Cork, da. of John William C., bank manager and classical scholar. Her mother's maiden name was Deasy. EMC was educ. at home by her parents. From 1867–76 the family travelled in Europe. EMC became a friend of Vernon LEE and Agnes Mary Frances ROBINSON. Her first publication was *The Flying Dutchman, and Other Poems*, 1881. She was an accomplished linguist and studied Arabic and Italian literature, some of her translations being chosen by Richard Garnett for his *History of Italian Literature*, 1898. She was a member of the Manchester Geographical Society and contributed to its journal. She also studied astronomy and wrote two monographs. (Her sister and companion Agnes Mary, 1842–1907, was a noted writer on astronomy.) EMC worked as a journalist and wrote a weekly letter for the *Tablet* for twenty years, filling in for the editor on request. She also wrote for the *Westminster Review*. *Fable and Song in Italy*, 1899, includes poems, translations and essays on Italian literature. Two short monographs followed: *Jupiter and Her Sister*, 1892, and *Vesuvius*, 1893. In 1901 EMC pub. *Flowers of Fire*, an implausible romantic novel about spies and revolutionaries, which contains a realistic description of the eruption of Vesuvius. See *AMC and EMC: an Appreciation* by Lady Huggins, 1907.

Cliff, Michelle, novelist, poet, editor, and teacher, b. in Kingston, Jamaica in 1946. She migrated with her family to NYC as a child. 'In the family I was called "fair" – a hard term. My sister was darker, younger. We were split: along lines of color and order of birth. This kind of splitting breeds insanity.' The split later emerged as the major subject of MC's writing. She studied European history at Wagner College, NYC (BA, 1969), then languages and comparative historical studies of the Italian Renaissance at the Warburg Institute in London (MPhil, 1974). Only after becoming involved in the women's movement did she fully realize that she had been raped by a man she had been dating, 'a white graduate of Oxford University, even though the bruises on [her] breasts, neck, and thighs took weeks to diminish'. Her first publication, an edition of Lillian SMITH's anti-racist writings, *The Winner Names the Age*, 1978, was followed by *Claiming an Identity They Taught me to Despise*, 1980 (quoted above), poetry and poetic prose which works to 'conjure a knowledge' wherein the 'obsolete geography' of her personal and political history 'conspire to make a past'. With Adrienne RICH, she co-edited the influential lesbian feminist journal, *Sinister Wisdom*, 1981–3. *The Land of Look Behind*, 1985, intensifies her anti-colonial feminist voice: 'They like to pretend we didn't fight back. We did: with obeah, poison, revolution. It simply was not enough' ('If I Could Write This in Fire, I Would Write This in Fire'). MC's novels, *Abeno*, 1984, and *No Telephone to Heaven*, 1987, are about Clare Savage, a light-skinned Jamaican, first as she becomes conscious of her status and privilege in relation to her darker friend, Zoe, and then as she becomes a revolutionary committed to the liberation of her country from neo-colonial forces. MC's account of the influence on her of Simone Weil appears in Carol Ascher, Louise De Salvo, and Sally Ruddick, eds., *Between Women*, 1984 (quoted above), her significant essay on Afro-American women visual artists in Myriam Diaz-Diocaretz and Iris M. Zavala, eds., *Women, Feminist Identity and*

Society in the 1980s, 1985. See reviews in *Conditions*, 13, 1986, and *WRB*, 5.2, Nov., 1987.

Clifford, Lady **Anne**, later Sackville, Countess of Dorset, later Herbert, Countess of Pembroke and Montgomery, 1590–1676, diarist and memoirist. She was b. at Craven Castle, Yorks., only surviving child of George C., 3rd Earl of Cumberland, explorer and sea-dog, who forbade her to learn Latin, and Margaret (Russell), to whom she was very close. She was tutored by the poet Samuel Daniel and 'much beloved' by ELIZABETH I; later she acted and wrote in Court circles. Her father died in 1605, leaving his brother the estates to which she believed her legal right absolute. Mistress of Knole, Kent, by her marriage in 1609 to the future 2nd Earl of Dorset, she pressed her claim despite opposition from him and later from James I. Letters to her mother about her first baby survive, and, from an eighteenth-century copy, a diary covering 1603 and (with gaps) 1616–19: ed. Vita SACKVILLE-WEST, 1923. Widowed in 1624, AC m. Lady PEMBROKE's second son in 1630; they soon separated, but she probably learned from his architectural activities. After Charles I's death, having come into her estates in 1643, she moved north and began to enjoy life: in six castles in turn, she built, restored, managed her little kingdom and far-flung, hugely-extended family, pinned her favourite quotations round the walls and from 1653 wrote her *Great Books*, distilling earlier writings on family genealogy and herself. She had several versions copied: part, on her life (from conception) and parents, ed. J. P. Gilson, 1916, from BL Harley MS; third-person version pub. 1846; others in Portland and Gower MSS. She kept a diary to the day before she died. Her funeral sermon called her 'this great wise Woman'; Virginia WOOLF wrote of her more than once and used her to mark the birth of the English common reader. Lives by George Williamson, 1922 (with autobiographical letter by her mother), and Martin Holmes, 1975.

Clifford, Sophia **Lucy**, 'Mrs W. K. Clifford' (Lane), *c.* 1853–1929, English novelist and dramatist, b. Barbados, where her grandfather, Brandford L., was Speaker of the House of Assembly. She spent her childhood with her maternal grandmother in the English countryside, described later in the story *A Flash of Summer. The Story of a Simple Woman's Life*, 1895. In 1875 she m. philosopher-mathematician Professor William Kingdon C.; he died in 1879, leaving her with two small children, and in 1882 she pub. two books of stories, followed in 1885 by her first and best-known novel, *Mrs Keith's Crime*, dealing with the controversial subject of infanticide. Equally praised and reviled, it was reprinted five times by 1893 and revised with a preface in 1925. She was a great friend of Henry James, and also an intimate of M. E. BRADDON and a friend of Elizabeth ROBINS. *Love-Letters of a Worldly Woman*, first pub. *Temple Bar*, Aug.–Dec. 1890, is a witty, perceptive and feminist account of a failed love-affair, written with the dramatic flair that was carried over into her subsequent play-writing career. Her most popular play, with 63 performances at St James's Theatre, London, was *The Likeness of the Night*, 1900 (founded on her earlier story, 'The End of Her Journey', pub. anon. in *Temple Bar*, 1887). It is a love story with a chilling twist. Other plays, like the farce *A Honeymoon Tragedy* (pub. 1904; first performed 1896), were less successful. See also CHILDREN'S LITERATURE.

Clift, Charmian, 1923–69, novelist, short-story writer, essayist, b. Kiama, NSW, da. of Amy (Curry) and Sidney C., mining engineer. She was educ. at Wollongong High School and in 1942 joined the Australian Women's Army Service. She then worked on the Melbourne *Argus*, and in 1947 m. writer George Johnston. With him she collaborated on three novels: the award-winning *High Valley*, 1949, a mystical, compelling novel set in Tibet, *The Big Chariot*, 1953, set in seventeenth-century China, and *The Sponge Divers*, 1956, describing life on the Greek islands, where the couple lived for over ten years. On Hydra they became a focus of literary and artistic life, particularly for expatriate Australians. Their relationship was plagued by drinking, ill-health and the collision of two literary talents. CC returned to Sydney in 1964 but despite success as a journalist (including her highly popular weekly column for the *Sydney Morning Herald*), she committed suicide in 1969. Other works include *Walk to the Paradise Gardens*, 1960, a novel about a middle-class couple enmeshed in the tension and violence of a small sea-side holiday resort; *Honour's Mimic*, 1964, concerning the love of an Australian woman for a poor Greek sponge diver; and the noteworthy essays collected in *Images in Aspic*, 1965, and *The World of Charmian Clift*, 1970 (repr. 1983, with intro. by her son, writer Martin Johnston). Further accounts of her life can be seen in *Mermaid Singing*, 1956, and *Peel Me a Lotus*, 1959, and in some of George Johnston's fiction as well as the biography of him by Garry Kinnane, 1986, who also ed. a collection of their stories, *Strong Man from Piraeus and Other Stories*, 1986.

Clifton, Lucille (Sayles), poet and children's writer, b. in 1936 in Depew, NY, da. of Thelma (Moore) and Samuel S. She grew up seeing 'reading as a natural part of life' and loving 'books and words' and family history. *Generations: a Memoir*, 1976, a powerful, loving 'family mythology', traces her family history from her great-great-grandmother, Caroline Sale, 'born free in Afrika in 1822 died free in America in 1910', to Lucille Sale, her great-grandmother, the 'First Black woman legally hanged in the state of Virginia' for murdering the white father of her son, through the rest of the generations. At 16, LC won a scholarship to Howard Univ., but left after two years. At Fredonia State Teachers' College in 1955, she met a group of black intellectuals (including writer Fred C., whom she married, 1958) and began to find her own voice, but 'what I was writing was not like the poems I'd been reading'. She won the Discovery Award for promising poets, 1969, and, when she was 33 'and had six children under ten years old', *Good Times*, 1969 (poems described by Sherley Anne WILLIAMS as 'created out of the collective experience which culminates in and is transformed by the inner city') was chosen by the *New York Times* as one of the year's best books. Rooted in racial and personal history, its 'compacted and memory-evoking' free-verse poems examine black and female experience: 'I came from a line / of black and going on women'. *Good News About the Earth*, 1972, includes poems about personal and public heroes; *An Ordinary Woman*, 1974, asserts solidarity: 'me and you / got babies / got thirty-five / got black . . . / be loving ourselves / be sisters. / only where you sing / i poet.' *Two-Headed Woman*, 1980, includes a cycle of poems on the life of Mary, mother of Christ: 'princes sitting on thrones in the east / studying the incomprehensible heavens. / joseph carving a table somewhere / in another place. / i watching my mother. / i smiling an ordinary smile.' LC celebrates family history, black and female pride (see 'homage to my hips'), in light, luminous, sometimes comic language, having 'shaped and jerked, patched and stitched everyday language in a way that few poets have been able to do.' She is author of several books for children, about mental illness, remarriage, death, black pride, and poverty. *Next*, poems, appeared in 1987, as did *good woman*, which collects poems and reprints *Generations*. See both her preface to, and Haki Madhubuti in, Mari EVANS, ed., *Black Women Writers (1950–1980)*, 1984, both quoted above, Harriet Jackson Scarupa in *Ms.*, October 1976, and Williams, 'The Roots of Contemporary

Afro-American Poetry', *Mass. Review*, 18, 1977.

Clipsham, Margery, joint author with fellow-Quaker Mary Ellwood of *The Spirit that Works Abomination*, 1685, an attack on Susanna Aldridge's *Abomination in Jerusalem Discovered* (now lost). They claim that Aldridge's visions and her unfeminine behaviour (travelling the country and arguing with male QUAKERS) stem from 'disorder[s] in her Head' after childbirth, a 'Distemper' prevalent in her family, of which her own mother died, 'as we have been credibly informed'.

Clive, Caroline (Meysey-Wigley), 'V', 1801–73, poet and novelist, b. Brompton Grove, London, second da. of Anna Maria (Meysey), heiress, and Edmund Wigley, MP for Worcester. She was educ. at home and was lame, ugly and unhappy as a child. As 'Paul Ferrol' she pub. religious *Essays of the Human Intellect*, 1828. On a tour of France in 1838 (where she scandalized the innkeepers by dining with her young maid) she renewed her friendship with Catherine GORE, for whom she felt 'nearly the strongest of my passions'. She pub. the first of her several vols. of verse, *Six Poems by V* (greatly admired by Caroline NORTON), in 1840 (repr. 1841), the year she m. Archer Clive. They kept a joint diary but most entries are CC's, including a graphic account of her first pregnancy. She contributed to *Blackwood's* though they refused her satire on the Oxford movement, *Saint Oldooman: A Myth of the Nineteenth Century*. She knew M. R. MITFORD and E. B. BROWNING (who thought her very 'peculiar'). She became famous for the sensation novel, *Paul Ferroll* (sic), 1855, which popularized a modern breed of villainous hero. Other novels include *Year After Year*, 1858, *Why Paul Ferroll Killed His Wife*, 1860, and *John Greswolde*, 1864, all challenging simplistic Victorian morality. Paralysed by a stroke, she died as a result of her dress catching fire. Her coll. poems were pub. 1890. See essay by Eric Partridge, *Literary Sessions*, 1932 (repr. 1970) and extracts from her diary ed. by Mary Clive, 1949.

Clive, Catherine or Kitty (Raftor), 1711–85, Irish singer, actress and playwright, b. Kilkenny into the large family of William R., lawyer. Stage-struck from childhood, largely uneducated, she sang at Drury Lane, 1728, and won fame in comic chambermaid roles. Her marriage to the barrister George C., 1733, ended quickly. She published newspaper skirmishes with Susannah Cibber, 1736, then her *Case ... Submitted to the Public*, 1744, repr. 1973, over what amounted to anti-union action by management. Her *Rehearsal, or Bayes in Petticoats*, acted 1750, pub. 1753, was a hit (in it a conceited female author makes a point of abusing the actress Mrs Clive). Of her other, unpublished farces, *Every Woman in her Humour*, 1760, has a majority of female parts; *The Sketch of a Fine Lady's Return from a Rout*, 1763, was expanded as *The Faithful Irish Woman*, 1765; *The Island of Slaves*, 1761 (perhaps hers), reverses social stations. She retired to a cottage on Horace Walpole's land; a life by Percy Fitzgerald, 1888, pub. some of her sprightly letters; better is P. J. Crean's unpub. London thesis, 1933.

Cluysenaar, Anne Alice Andrée, poet and critic, b. 1936 in Brussels of Irish and Belgian parents, Sybil (Hewat) and John C., both visual artists. She was educ. at Trinity College, Dublin (BA in English and French, 1957), began lecturing, and took a diploma in linguistics at Edinburgh Univ., 1963. She has taught at English, Scottish and Irish univs. and polytechnics: at Sheffield Polytechnic from 1976, when she married Walter Jackson, an engineer with three children. She judges her first important poetical work to be neither *A Fan of Shadows*, 1967, nor *Nodes: Selected Poems 1960–68*, 1971 (which rewrites classical myth: Orpheus as the poet searching 'for the dark / Centre which no song expresses'), but *Double Helix*, 1982, which juxtaposes her poems with her mother's memoirs and other family mementoes. This experimental exploration of personal history includes letters that AC's grandmother wrote while she 'could not see / her own fate, the years of forsaken madness / alien in her own country, in sombre houses / where no one is at home' or 'her baby's baby, writing at another window / in an England dark with rain'. It meditates on links and cleavages by time and culture, on the sources and silencing of writing. AC has also published *An Introduction to Literary Stylistics: A Discussion of Dominant Structures in Verse and Prose*, 1976, and *Verbal Arts: The Missing Subject*, 1987, and edited US poet Burns Singer, 1977.

'Clyde, Constance', Constance McAdam, novelist and journalist. B. in Scotland in 1872, she was taken to Otago, NZ in 1879, educ. at Dunedin, and employed on newspapers in Auckland and Christchurch before moving to Queensland. In her one novel, *A Pagan's Love*, pub. London, 1905, the heroine moves from a small South Island town to Sydney and confronts the problem of whether to live with the man she loves without marriage. A journalist with a career and an illegitimate child argues that women of her generation should be able to have both, although her mother's generation 'considered themselves advanced for recognizing that there must be two types of women – the bluestocking all brains, and the fireside slave all affection.' This evolutionary view of women's progression is put forward in a readable novel with vivid local description.

Cobbe, Frances Power, 1822–1904, philanthropist, feminist and philosopher, b. Ireland, only da. of Frances (Conway) and Charles C., landowner and magistrate. She was educ. by a succession of governesses, then at an expensive Brighton boarding school, whose stress on 'accomplishments' she censures in her autobiography, *The Life of FPC by Herself*, 1894. She produced her first book, an *Essay on the Theory of Intuitive Morals*, in 1855 while still living under the paternal roof. Her father died in 1857 and, reduced to relative poverty, she travelled in Europe and the Middle East before settling in Bristol where she worked with Mary Carpenter in her ragged schools. FPC took up other philanthropic causes, particularly workhouse visiting and the establishment of societies to help workhouse girls. In the early 1860s, she began to write about the WOMAN QUESTION, attacking problems women faced in marriage and suggesting celibacy and female friendships as a better alternative in 'Celibacy vs Marriage', 1862, and 'What Shall We do with our Old Maids?', 1862. She continued her discussion of the marital problems of women in 'Criminals, Idiots, Women and Minors: Is the Classification Sound?', 1868, 'The Little Health of Ladies', 1878, and 'Wife-Torture in England', 1878, and campaigned to reform the property laws. FPC was the first person to speak publicly (1862) about the need for women to have access to univ. examinations. Active in the SUFFRAGE campaign from the 1870s, she was unusual in attempting to persuade other suffragists to work through the Conservative Party. FPC devoted herself to the anti-vivisection movement from the 1870s until the mid-1880s when she retired to Wales. She continued to write on the woman question, and saw her autobiography as a contribution. Several of her early articles were coll. in *Essays on the Pursuits of Women*, 1863. Her lectures linking philosophical and moral issues with feminist concerns were pub. as *The Duties of Women*, 1881.

Cobbold, Elizabeth (Knipe), also Clarke, *c.* 1764–1824, poet and miscellaneous writer, b. London, da. of Robert K. of Liverpool; she grew up there and in Manchester, where she published *Poems on Various Subjects*, 1783. *Six Narrative Poems*, 1787, by subscription, dedicated to Sir Joshua Reynolds, won critics' praise. The one non-exotic tale is best, but all have dash and vigour. In 1790 she married – for love, a poem suggests – William Clarke of Ipswich, a much older invalid who died after six months. She pub. as Clarke a medieval novel, *The Sword, or Father Bertrand's History of his Own Times*, Liverpool, 1791; next year she m. John Cobbold, a wealthy brewer. His house contained 14 children (in time she added seven more) but, she said, no books but Bibles and account books. Student of many subjects, a flower painter of note, active in local society and charity, she continued to publish, chiefly at Ipswich: magazine verse (from 1809 for *The Ladies Fashionable Repository*), valentines for an annual party (pub. 1813, 1814), an ode on Waterloo, 1815. A one-woman entertainment, *Cassandra*, given in London, remained unpub.; she may be the (supposedly male) editor of *The Chaplet*, Ipswich 1807, an anthology including much women's verse. *The Mince Pye* by 'Carolina Petty Pasty', 1800, parodies C. S. Pybus's pompous *The Sovereign*, sends up jingoism and heroicizes 'the cook-maid' and Hannah GLASSE. EC helped Ann CANDLER and employed Margaret CATCHPOLE. Her *Poems* were collected 1825 with a memoir.

Cochrane, Elizabeth (later Seaman), 'Nellie Bly', 1865–1922, journalist, b. Cochrane's Mills, Armstrong Co., Pa., da. of Mary Jane (Kennedy) and Michael C., lawyer and mill-owner. She was educ. by her father, and at boarding school in Indiana for two years, after which her precarious health made further study impossible. After her father's death, EC moved with her mother to Pittsburgh. In 1885 she contributed a daring series on divorce to the Pittsburgh *Despatch*, followed by a series on the condition of Pittsburgh's working women, which attracted much attention. With her mother, EC toured Mexico, observing local manners and scenery, and wrote an account of her trip, including an exposé of exploitative social conditons in *Six Months in Mexico*, 1888. She then moved to New York, where Joseph Pulitzer, investigative journalist with the *World*, asked her to do an exposé on the infamous Blackwell's Island asylum. Masquerading as a Spanish woman who had lost her memory and sanity, EC's story made her an instant celebrity at 22, and led to the asylum being investigated and improved. A succession of 'stunt' articles followed, including a globe-circling tour for the *World* to beat the record of Jules Verne's fictional hero, Phileas Fogg. She made the journey, by ship, train, burro, sampan, carriage and cart in 72 days; see *Nellie Bly's Book: Around the World in Seventy-Two Days*, 1890, which also notes the condition of women in other countries and marks of sexual difference in dress. In 1895 she m. Robert L. Seaman, a wealthy industrialist, but on his death returned to journalism, writing a column on orphans for the New York *Journal*, 1919–22. When she died, the obituary in her paper called her 'America's best reporter'.

Cockburn (or, her spelling, Cokburne), **Alison** or Alice (Rutherford), 1713–94, poet and letter-writer, b. at Fairnalie, Selkirkshire, youngest da. of its laird, Robert R., and Alison (Ker), who died when she was ten; she was educ. by an elder 'mother-sister'. She m. Patrick C. in 1731, bore a son, and lived, she says, 20 years of happiness. Her occasional and personal poems (now mostly lost) include the famous 'I've seen the smiling of Fortune beguiling', a lament for the exploitation of her native Ettrick. Praised and imitated by Burns, unpub. till 1764, it eclipsed Jean Elliott's haunting, less genteel lament for 1745 to the same tune, 'The Flowers of the Forest'. Walter Scott, a distant relation, praised AC's 'play of imagination' and 'activity of intellect'. In 1750 came financial ruin, then the deaths of her husband and son, and multiple disasters to family and friends. She fought grief with physical exertion: gaiety shines in her letters (one autobiographical, some to David Hume) and songs (one on the wedding of Lady Anne BARNARD's parents, one a risky satire on Bonnie Prince Charlie, 1745): ed. T. Craig-Brown, 1900.

Coke, Lady Mary (Campbell), 1727–1811, letter writer, youngest da. of Jane (Warburton) and John C., 2nd Duke of Argyll, who both thought girls inferior and learned women deeply suspect: she still grew up versed in history, admiring Mary Queen of Scots and Lady Jane GREY. In 1747 she m., 'most unwillingly', the Earl of Leicester's heir, Edward, Viscount Coke (d. 1753). He ill-treated and imprisoned her; she refused to sleep with him but could not obtain a divorce, so left him and turned to gardening, travelling, socializing, an obscure intrigue with the much younger Duke of York and flamboyant quarrels with people from the Austrian Empress downwards. Horace Walpole dedicated *The Castle of Otranto* to her, 1764. From 1766 to 1791 she sent regular journal-letters to her sister Lady Strafford (later to her brother-in-law): ed. I. A. Home with memoir by Lady Louisa STUART, 1889–96, repr. 1970. Her Court gossip may pall, but not her energy or eccentricity. She worshipped Marie de SÉVIGNÉ.

Cole, Margaret Isabel (Postgate), 1893–1980, lecturer, historian, political analyst, biographer, novelist. B. in Cambridge, da. of Edith (Allen), 'the most *individual* person I have known', and John Percival P., lecturer at Cambridge Univ. and later Professor of Latin at Liverpool, she was educ. first at a small private school, then, on scholarship, at Roedean School, Brighton, which she loathed. At Girton College, Cambridge, 'next door to Utopia', she studied classics with Jane HARRISON, 'commenced a poet' (poems pub. 1914, 1918), 'slipped into Socialism ... as easily as a duck slips into water', and 'naturally became at the same time a feminist'. In 1914 (the year her brother Raymond was jailed for refusing to be conscripted) she took a job at St Paul's Girls' School, London, joined the Fabian Society and met G. D. H. Cole (m. 1918), to whom, she said, she was 'all but born married'. Leaving her job to work for the Labour movement, she began a long political and literary collaboration with him. Activists both, they worked with Bernard Shaw, Bertrand Russell, H. R. Orage, H. G. Wells, Sidney and Beatrice WEBB and other figures whose politics shaped the English 1920s and 30s. They also shared a 'remarkable passion for poetry', attended Harold Monro's readings at The Poetry Bookshop, knew Ezra Pound, T. S. Eliot, Henri Gaudier-Brzeska and Ford Madox Hueffer. G. D. H. C.'s prodigious output included more than 150 books and pamphlets on economics and politics. (He became Chichele Professor of Social and Political Theory at Oxford, 1944.) Together they wrote several works of history and political and economic commentary. Independently, MC wrote political polemic, several works on Fabian socialism (including a history, 1961), books on the Webbs, 1949 and 1955, her admired biography of Beatrice Webb, 1945, the life of G. D. H., 1971, and three books of feminist purpose: *The Road to Success*, 1936, essays on careers for women (including Storm JAMESON's 'The Writer'); *Women of To-Day*, 1938, 'heroines' (including Ethely SMYTH, Edith Cavell, Rosita FORBES and Annie BESANT); and *Marriage, Past and Present*, 1938, an analysis of the contemporary institution with a history of women in western culture. MC's main collaboration with G. D. H. was their DETECTIVE FICTION: they wrote 29 novels and four collects. of short stories. A member, with Dorothy SAYERS, of the Detection Club, MC wrote for both amusement and money. Her autobiography, *Growing Up Into Revolution*, 1949, gives not only a detailed account of her political and cultural experience of the 1920s and 1930s, but also advice on formulae for aspirants to the detective genre. Her study of 'The Case of Adelaide Barrett' (in *The*

Anatomy of Murder, 1936) exemplifies her feminist slant. An Honorary Fellow of the London School of Economics, MC was made DBE, 1970.

Coleman, Emily (Holmes), 1899–1974, novelist and poet, b. Oakland, Calif., but raised in Hartford, Conn., by her father, insurance executive John H. (her mother died after years of mental illness). EHC graduated from Wellesley College in 1920 and m. 'Deke' (Loyd Ring) C. a year later. After bearing a son, 1924, she suffered puerperal fever and mental collapse, and spent two months in Rochester State Hospital, NY. She went to Paris in 1926, where she worked for the *Chicago Tribune* and began publishing her poems in *transition*. In 1928 she became secretary to Emma GOLDMAN in St Tropez, where she met Peggy Guggenheim. Their long and turbulent friendship (see Guggenheim's autobiography, *Out of This Century*, 1979) also involved writer John Holms (d. 1934), who was latterly Guggenheim's lover. EHC's first novel, *The Shutter of Snow*, 1930 (repr. with intro. by Carmen Callil and Mary Siepmann, 1981), combines lyrical surrealism and witty social critique of the insane asylum to explore connections between the heroine's different confinements: in giving birth, in a strait-jacket, figuratively in her mother's grave, physically amid the snow. Divorced by 1931, she travelled in England and Europe, had various affairs, and visited Guggenheim with Antonia WHITE and Djuna BARNES (whose *Nightwood* she urged T. S. Eliot to publish). Back in the USA in 1939, she lived as common-law wife of an Arizona rancher whom she left soon after her conversion to Catholicism. She returned to England (to Rye, Sussex) in 1953, lived in retreat at Stanbrook Abbey, 1957–68, and spent her last years at Dorothy DAY's Catholic Worker Farm in Tivoli, NY. Her poetry, published in the 1920s and 30s in periodicals, is uncollected; her second novel, *The Tygon*, and other writings are unpub. See Jane Marcus in *WRB*, August 1986.

Coleman, Kathleen (Ferguson), 'Kit', 1856–1915, journalist. B. at Castleblakeney, Ireland, da. of Mary (Burke) and Patrick F., she was educ. in a Catholic boarding school in Dublin and at finishing school in Belgium. Left destitute on the death of her first husband, Thomas Willis, 1884, she migrated to Toronto, remarried philandering, drinking Thomas Watkins, had two children, and moved to Winnipeg. When the marriage ended, she returned to Toronto, wrote a weekly full-page 'Woman's Kingdom' for the *Mail* (later *Mail and Empire*), 1889, which went beyond recipes, fashion and deportment to topics of general interest, and attracted a wide readership. KC's assignments broadened: to articles in *Saturday Night*, 1890; to a series of articles on Charles Dickens's London in 1892; to the St Louis World's Fair in 1894; to Queen Victoria's Jubilee in 1897. In 1898 she became the first woman accredited correspondent to cover the Spanish–American War: asked by the American War Secretary to undertake a speaking tour, she reportedly replied: 'If I tell the women of the United States what I have seen, you'll have a riot on your hands.' She married physician Theodore C., and in 1904 became first president of the Canadian Women's Press Club. Her syndicated 'Kit's Column' appeared from 1911 until her death. She wrote short stories and poetry: 'A Pair of Gray Gloves', for instance, deals sensitively with an unmarried journalist's reaction to being left for a younger woman. Her reputation rests on her journalism; but though she dealt with controversial issues – prostitution, divorce, racism, pollution, abortion – she opposed SUFFRAGE and TEMPERANCE. Papers in National Archives of Canada MG29 D112 Inventory File. See Dorothy Turcotte in *Early Canadian Life*, May, 1979.

Colenso, Frances Ellen, 'Atherton Wylde', 1849–87, novelist, b. Norfolk, England, second da. of Frances Sarah (Bunyon) and John William C., Bishop of Natal 1853–83, where he worked to prevent the Zulu war, and later to restore Cetewayo. It was a lively, intellectual household, and FC's elder sister Harriette Emily (1847–1932) became a well-known humanitarian and polemicist. In 1879 FC published a novel, *My Chief and I*, told in the first person by a young officer, serving with Colonel Anthony Durnford, who tried to befriend the Zulu people. Anthony Trollope, reading proofs, told Chapman its criticism of the government's prosecution of the war might be considered libellous in the Colony, but it was well-received in England. Durnford (to whom she may have been engaged) was killed in the war; she collaborated with his brother Edward in a *History of the Zulu War*, 1880.

Coleridge, Christabel Rose, 1843–1921, novelist, story writer, b. Chelsea, London, da. of Mary (Pridham) of Plymouth and the Rev. Derwent C. (son of Samuel Taylor C.): niece of Sara COLERIDGE, who, with Hartley, disapproved of Derwent's High Church affectations. CC was named after STC's heroine. She always lived at home, a bookish household with a large library, first at Chelsea, then Hanwell, Middlesex, then Winchester, and from 1880, Torquay. Between 1869 and 1908 she wrote numerous tales, stories and novels, many for girls and young women as well as for a wider readership. Many of her novels, such as *Hanbury Mills*, 1872, *An English Squire*, 1881, and *Ravenstone*, 1896 (in which she collaborated with Helen SHIPTON), deal with complex family relationships. One of her best, *The Tender Mercies of the Good*, 1895, concerns a young man's dishonour and his subsequent misery under family surveillance; a sub-plot treats the unexpected bid for freedom by a middle-aged woman dominated by her aunt, 'good' Agatha, who tyrannizes the others 'in her softest and most deprecating voice'. A close friend of Charlotte YONGE and from early days a member of her circle, including Mary BRAMSTON (with whom she wrote *Truth With Honour', 1890*), CC co-edited the *Monthly Packet* from 1890, and in 1903 published a hagiographic life and letters of Yonge.

Coleridge, Mary Elizabeth, 'Anodos', 1861–1907, poet and novelist, b. London to Mary Ann (Jameson), one of two talented musical sisters, and Arthur Duke C., amateur musician, Clerk of the Assize and great-nephew of Samuel Taylor C. Educ. at home by W. J. Cory, poet, scholar and friend of her father, from 1895 MC taught at the Working Women's College. She lived at home all her life with her parents and sister and had a group of close women friends with whom she discussed her writing and her inner life. Extracts from her letters and diaries together with some prose were pub. posthumously as *Gathered Leaves*, 1910. Her first pub. work, *The Seven Sleepers of Ephesus*, 1893, a novel about a group of young men, has a dreamy quality and blurs fictional boundaries. Other novels are a historical romance, *The King with Two Faces*, 1897, *The Shadow on the Wall*, 1904, and *The Fiery Dawn*, 1901. All her novels take as their themes waiting, constancy and the coincidence of past and future, memory and hope. Her most interesting is *The Lady on the Drawing Room Floor*, 1906, where her solitary male narrator, who says that he 'cannot get on without a name', has to explore unnamed emotions and hazy memories. At the centre of the novel is a lost, unopened letter from the past. MC pub. few poems: the vol. *Fancy's Following*, 1896, appeared under her pseudonym, as did *Fancy's Garden*, 1897, which contained only seven new poems. More than 200 poems were collected by Henry Newbolt from letters and notebooks after her death and pub. in 1907, further poems being added, 1954. The poems are usually brief records of psychic states, of pain and loss, the distance of love and the fragility of identity. She is aware of a hidden place (see 'Gone') and an intimacy of response which is only possible in dream (see 'A Daydream'). Her most famous poem is 'The Other Side of the Mirror', which deals with self-alienation and which has been extensively discussed by Sandra Gilbert and Susan Gubar in *The Madwoman in the Attic*, 1979. A group of her poems has been anthologized in *The World Split Open*, ed. Louise Bernikow, 1974. She also pub. a collection of short prose sketches, *Non Sequitur*, 1900, and a life of Holman Hunt, 1908.

Coleridge, Sara, 1802–52, literary editor, poet and children's writer, b. Greta Hall, Keswick, Cumberland, da. of Sarah (Fricker) and Samuel Taylor C., the poet, who alternately adored and neglected her. She was largely self-educ., using Robert Southey's library. Her first publications were translations: Dobritzhofer's *An Account of the Abipones*, 1822; and memoirs of the Chevalier Bayard, 1825. In 1829 she m. her cousin, barrister Henry Nelson C., Samuel's literary executor. She wrote *Pretty Lessons in Verse for Good Children*, 1834, for their children; and the work for which she was best known, an extended fairy tale in verse and prose, *Phantasmion*, 1837. She co-edited her father's work with her husband, and after his death in 1843 continued alone. Her essays also contributed to Coleridge scholarship. Other literary work includes a long review of Tennyson's *The Princess* in *Quarterly Review* 82, 1847–8, which reveals her own conventional views on woman's role. Her autobiographical *Memoirs and Letters*, 1873, ed. by her da. Edith, comment on contemporary theological debates, the Oxford Movement, German metaphysics and her father's political theories, as well as domestic details of her own social circle. She knew Wordsworth, the BROWNINGS, Gladstone, Harriet MARTINEAU, Elizabeth GASKELL, Joanna BAILLIE, among others. In 1850 breast cancer was diagnosed. She died, leaving two lines: 'Father, no amaranths e'er shall wreathe my brow – / Enough that round thy grave they flourish now.' See lives of her by Earl Leslie Griggs, 1940, and Bradford Keyes Mudge, 1989; life of her mother by Molly Lefebure, 1986.

Colette, Sidonie-Gabrielle, 1873–1954, novelist, dramatist, short-story writer, journalist, *femme de lettres*. B. in Saint-Saveur-en-Puisaye, France, da. of Adèle-Eugénie-Sidonie Landoy (called 'Sido' by C) and Captain Jules-Joseph C., she moved to Paris after marrying, at 19, Henry Gauthier-Villars ('Willy') and began to write. Her first novels (the *Claudine* series, based on C's schoolgirl experience in her Burgundy village) were signed by her husband although written by C. In 1904 she began to sign her works 'Colette Willy' and continued to use this signature until 1923, thereafter signing simply 'Colette'. She separated from Willy, 1906, and divorced, 1910. From 1905–13 she studied mime and went on tour in mimodramas. *The Vagabond*, 1955 (*La Vagabonde*, 1911); *The Shackle*, 1964 (*L'Entrave*, 1931); and *Music-Hall Sidelights*, 1957 (*L'Envers du music-hall*, 1913) all originate in this period of her life. She began publishing articles in *Le Matin* and married the editor Henri de Jouvenel, 1912, and had a daughter, Colette de J. (caled 'Bel Gazou' by C). C divorced de J., 1924, and lived alone until she m. Maurice Goudeket, 1935. She was a member of both the Belgian Academy and the Académie Goncourt (first woman). Many of C's works are autobiographical and reflect her lifelong writerly preoccupations with the problematics of sexual politics (*La Retraite sentimentale*, 1907, transl. *The Retreat from Love*, 1974; *Mes Apprentissages*, 1936, transl. *My Apprenticeships*, 1978), the mother-daughter bond (*La Maison de Claudine*, 1922, transl. *My Mother's House*, 1953; *Sido*, 1929, transl. 1953), and the ambiguous nature of sexual orientation (*Le Pur et l'impur*, 1941, transl. *The Pure and the Impure*, 1968). C's enormous oeuvre (some 70 titles in all in two, soon to be three, Pléiade vols.) is remarkable for its lyricism and its extraordinary crossing and mixing of genders, genres, social classes and cultures. For C, women's writing is dual: 'a generation of self, a living fiction, and a projection of the self in writing, an auto-fiction' (Erica Eisinger and Mari McCarty, 1981). C 'alters the rules of literary play': whereas such rules 'require that the signs identifying male and female, fiction and biography or autobiography, social classes, and levels of style be unambiguous', these signs are always ambiguous in her works (Elaine Marks, in Eisinger and McCarty). Among her translators is Antonia WHITE. Studies by Michele Sarde, 1980, Joan Hinde Stewart, 1983, and Nicole Ward Jouve, 1987.

Collier, Jane, 1710–54/5, experimental writer, da. of Margaret (Johnson) and Arthur C., philosopher and parson, who taught Latin and Greek to her and Sarah FIELDING, a childhood neighbour in Salisbury. She wrote a critique of her friend Samuel Richardson's *Clarissa* for the *GM* but did not publish it, and defended Sarah's *The Governess* from his proposed corrections. Her anonymous *Essay on the Art of Ingeniously Tormenting*, 1753, ironically addresses both those who can hurt by power (husbands, but chiefly mistresses of servants) and those who can hurt by affection (wives, friends). Writing as a sufferer, not inflicter, of hurt, she explores 'labyrinths and inward turns of the mind', most frighteningly the power of women to sap women's confidence (repr. 1804 ed. 'The Invisible Girl') JC wrote *The Cry*, 1754, an allegorical tale whose title refers to public opinion, with Sarah (repr. as Sarah's, NY 1986) and perhaps her sister Margaret C., housekeeper to the widowed Henry Fielding: it defends his work. Margaret went with him on his last journey, and was upset when his *Journal of a Voyage to Lisbon* was ascribed to her; after JC's death she retired to the Isle of Wight, writing to Richardson sadly of her poverty and perceptively of women's concealing their talents.

Collier, Mary, 1679–after 1762, washerwoman and poet, b. Heyshott, Sussex, da. of the 'poor, but honest' Mary and Robert C. 'No Learning ever was bestow'd on me; / My Life was always spent in Drudgery'; yet they taught her early to read, which she kept up despite working both in the fields and at brewing and washing. *The Thresher's Labour*, 1730, by Stephen Duck, poet and ex-labourer, provoked her to write an answer. Since he now, lifted up by patrons, scorns women's 'little Work', she vividly itemizes the rigours of both washing and fieldwork: women, she says, work harder, as farmers know. Hearing her quote her poem 'to amuse myself and entertain my Company', her employers persuaded her to write more, then made her work known. She pub. *The Woman's Labour* at her own expense in 1739 (3 eds., in 2 years; facs. 1985), though 'others run away with the profit'. She became a housekeeper about 1753, and in 1762, living at Alton, Hants., published by subscription *Poems on Several Occasions*, Winchester, with autobiographical 'remarks' and work in several genres. She refused a request to write on disappointed old maids, saying she knew no such beings. See Donna Landry in *The Muses of Resistance*, 1990.

Colling, Mary Maria, poet, b. 1805 at Tavistock, Devon, da. of Anne and Edmund C., husbandman. Brought up for service, she was sent to dame school 'to be kept out of the way' and to learn sewing and knitting. But she longed to read, and taught herself (and later her illiterate father). Her love of reading alienated her fellow servants, but Anna BRAY spotted her 'expressive features and ... decorous behaviour' in church, took her into employment, and encouraged her writing. In 1831 Bray pub. MC's *Fables and Other Pieces in Verse*, with notes on her life, 'for the sole benefit' of the author. Subscribers included Wordsworth and Southey; the work was dedicated by the poet to the Marchioness of Tavistock. Much given to apology for her temerity in overstepping class boundaries: 'Heaven knows that respect with presumption's combined' ('To Mrs Bray'), she yet scores some hits: 'Death to the great pays no respect: / No substitute will be accept', ('The Vanity of Riches'). Whenever she felt 'hurt and angry', she encoded her feelings in a fable, many of which are wittily turned, expressing sharp observations under cover of flowers and animals.

Collins, An, Christian poet, who set her name thus to her *Divine Songs and Meditacions*, 1653 (part repr. 1961 as by 'Anne Collins'). Only one original copy survives (Huntington); an alleged 2nd ed. is not known. Long housebound by illness, she had 'little Hopes of worldly Gain', but loved knowledge. She wrote in many metres (some a little shaky) of theology, the Civil War, the soul's need for repentance and passage from 'the Ocean of Adversity' to the 'peacefull temper and spiritual calmnesse' which she claims as hers in a prose address to the 'Christian Reader'. She uses biblical imagery of dark and sunshine, drought and fruition. Unlike other fruitful women, she says, she has 'offspring of my mind'; she hopes that after a late spring 'Perhaps my Sommer-age may be, / Not prejudiciall, but benificiall / Enough for me.' See Elaine Hobby, 1988.

Collins, Merle, poet, performer and novelist, b. and brought up in Grenada under the post-Independence dictator E. M. Gairy. A teacher and researcher, she worked for the revolutionary government of Grenada after March 1979, and became well known as a performer of her poetry, often to large audiences at rallies or meetings of Workers' Parish Councils. Like other Grenadian artists she met the revolution, and new popular enthusiasm for distinctively Grenadian work, with an outburst of creative energy. After the US invasion of 1983 she left to live and work in Britain. A member of 'African Dawn', she performs a fusion of dramatic verse and Afro-Caribbean music: she also performs her own poetry. Her 'Callaloo', in Chris Searle's Grenadian anthology of that name, 1984, is titled from a 'hot / thick / Sweet' local dish: it celebrates the revolution as source of new national pride: 'No more hidin' you passport ... No more / Playin' you don hear / Or sayin' some shit like ... A island / Near by Trinidad / Or ... / A few mile / Off Venezuela / But out / Loud and bole / Like you make de name / Grenada!' Her own first volume, *Because the Dawn Breaks!*, 1985, is dedicated to the Grenadian people and named from the inevitability of revolution and from the influence of poetry in fostering revolutionary consciousness. In *Wasafiri*, 8, 1988, MC describes being writer-in-residence in Waltham Forest, London, 1986–7. She often blends humour and anger, as in 'The Lesson', a long, tragi-comic poem about colonial education: 'Great Grand-mammy ... Living proof / Of de power / of de word / Talked knowingly / Of William the Conqueror / Who was the fourth son / Of de Duke of Normandy ... Grannie / Din remember / No Carib chief / No Ashanti king ... Toussaint / Was a whispered curse / Her heroes / Were in Europe.' Other poems concern women's freedom and identity. 'Butterfly Born' uses childhood memories to examine the suppression of girls' energies before the revolution brought sharing. MC's novel, *Angel*, 1987, charts the post-colonial history of Grenada through three generations of women. Angel, an infant when the white landowners' houses are burned down and blacks hope for a leader from 'we own people', grows up rebellious, resisting her mother's imposition of girlishness, and returns from university a radical, disillusioned like many about Gairy's abuse of power. Political struggle reunites her with her community. The clock is not quite turned back by the loss of lives and hope following the US invasion. With Rhonda Cobham, MS has edited *Watchers and Seekers*, 1987, a volume of writing by black women in Britain; her own pieces there are notable.

Collyer, Mary (Mitchell), 1716/17–1762/3, novelist and (like her husband Joseph C.) translator: since she worked with him as bookseller and circulating-library owner, her writings – all anonymous – have often been ascribed to him. Her *Virtuous Orphan, or The Life of Marianne*, 1742, from Marivaux, mostly written before 1741, is anglicized, moralized, the unfinished original ended with reformation and happiness (see ed. by W. H. McBurney and M.F. Shugrue, 1965). It was both pirated and re-issued: a 'translator's preface' to a 1784 ed. sounds like the posthumous work of MC or her husband. After *Memoirs of the Countess de Bressol*, 1743 (called a transl.: original unknown), she pub. in 1744 her own romantic novel, *Felicia to Charlotte*, letters from a young Londoner who ecstatically discovers and settles in the country, and is wooed by the sentimental, philosophical Lucius Manly. A second ed., 1749, added a second vol. (both repr. 1974) in which the heroine bears a child, as her author had just done (she had seven). Rousseau is strongly foreshadowed in the discussions of pedagogy and the influence of nature; Charlotte joins the rural retreat. The work brought MC to BLUESTOCKING notice; she may have planned a third vol., but produced only her popular and influential versions of Salomon Gessner's *The Death of Abel*, 1761, and Klopstock's *Messiah*, 1763 (completed by Joseph C.). See Helen S. Hughes in *JEGP*, 15, 1916.

Comden, Betty, writer for stage and screen, performer, b. 1919 in Brooklyn, NYC, da. of Rebecca (Sadvoransky) and Leo Cohen, lawyer. She was educ. at Brooklyn Ethical Culture School, Erasmus Hall High School, and NY Univ. (BS 1938), and in 1939 joined the Revuers, a group (including Adolph Green and Judy Holliday) who wrote and performed their own material. In 1942 she m. Steven Kyle; they had two children. She and Green co-authored many musicals and screenplays. BC acted in their *On the Town*, 1944 (music by Leonard Bernstein: revived London 1963, NY 1971), and other shows. By 1950 they were 'pioneers in bicoastal living', working on Hollywood films and Broadway musicals, as vividly related in their introduction to *Singin' in the Rain*, 1952, pub. 1972 (about a silent-screen star; admired by François Truffaut and Pauline KAEL). *The Band Wagon*, 1953, draws on 'our own real-life experiences': pub. 1986. Musicals like *Bells are Ringing*, 1956, pub. [1965], provide a sharp index to current sex roles: the hero tells his girl (who works, in many guises, at an answer-phone service) to stop spreading love 'around all over the place, give it to me. I need it. I want it.' *A Doll's Life*, 1982, pub. 1983, which follows Ibsen's Nora out of her home into a series of lessons learned in relationships with men, is more ideological but less closely observed. In 1971 they appeared together as themselves. BC has won many awards, and written for TV.

Compton, Jennifer, playwright, poet, short-story writer, b. 1949 in Wellington, NZ, da. of Dorothy (Lee) and William C. An artist's model before enrolling at Central Theatre Drama School in Auckland, she m. actor–director Matthew O'Sullivan in 1971. Two years later she moved to Australia and joined the Playwright's Studio at the National Institute of Dramatic Art in Sydney. *Crossfire*, which was also produced as *No Man's Land* in 1975, shared first prize in a 1974 Newcastle playwriting competition with John Romeril's *The Floating World*. Also produced in 1975 was *They're Playing our Song* (pub. in the collection *Can't You Hear Me Talking to You?*, 1978, ed. Alrene Sykes). These, and other plays such as *Adolf*, *All good Children Go To Heaven* and *Stream of Consciousness*, are concerned with women's issues. *Crossfire* proved controversial in its exploration of the problems women encounter both in relation to feminism and in relation to conventional roles within marriage and motherhood. By using two different time settings within the play, one in 1910 and one in 1975, she is able to question the gains made by women in the intervening period. JC has also written for radio and TV.

Compton-Burnett, Ivy, 1884–1969, DBE, novelist. She was b. at Pinner, Middx., eldest of seven children of Katharine (Rees) and James C-B, a homeopathic doctor and author who had five children by his first wife: 'a booky family' where she made with her nearest siblings a private world with its own invented deity. At 14 came a school 'for the Daughters of Gentlemen' at Hove, later another at Bedford; at 16 or 17 she rejected the 'nonsense' of religion. Her mother subjected them to the oppression of rigid mourning from the father's death, 1901, to her own in 1911. ICB's closest brother died the year before she took her BA in classics at Royal Holloway College (now of London Univ.) in 1906; she came home to teach the little ones. In 1915 it was her sisters who broke from her sway to live in London; the other brother died in WWI; in 1918 the two youngest committed suicide and ICB nearly died of influenza. From 1919 she lived with freelance writer Margaret Jourdain. She later disowned her first novel, *Dolores*, 1911. Her second, *Pastors and Masters*, 1925, was reviewed as a 'work of genius': it set the pattern for 18 more, dealing with extended families, claustrophobic relationships ('I do not feel that I have any real or organic knowledge of life later than about 1910'), centres of tension, abuse of power, financial tangles and manipulations, and hovering death. In *Brothers and Sisters*, 1929, a family unknowingly based on incest (after a concealed illegitimate birth) lives in a context of intensely-feeling sister-and-brother pairs: 'this devotion to each other will end in our not marrying'; 'We understand each other. How seldom can that be said of two human beings!' In *More Women than Men*, 1933, set in a girls' school, a male homosexual relationship (broken) is openly compared to marriage; feelings among women are guardedly expressed: 'I have cared in my way for the women whom one by one I have tried to care for'; 'my happiness depends on women'. Dialogue (unusually predominant for fiction) suggests or reveals character and motive in minimalist style: penetrating insights, and also surface banalities with encoded implications of pressure, complicity or rage, in what has been called 'the most brilliant and sustained verbal comedy in English'. Hierarchy extends downwards in *Manservant and Maidservant*, 1947, where the butler and cook, seen 'in awe and almost incredulity' by their underlings, love pomp in routine and in words: 'It is not a matter the inexperienced would be conversant with.' Younger writers like Rosamond LEHMANN, Elizabeth BOWEN and Sybille BEDFORD admired ICB's originality. There are many recent reprints and memoirs; two-part life by Hilary Spurling, 1974, 1984; Robert Liddel on ICB and Elizabeth TAYLOR, 1986; critical studies include Mary MCCARTHY in *The Writing on the Wall*, 1970. MSS at Univ. of Texas.

Comyns, Barbara (Bayley), novelist, b. 1912 at Bidford-on-Avon, Warwicks., da. of Margaret Eva (Fenn) and businessman Albert Edward B. Educ. privately by governesses and at Heatherly's Art School, London, she began writing at ten, and worked at various jobs through necessity: advertising, antique furniture and cars, dog breeding, property management. She m. in 1935, and had two children. In 1945 she m. Richard Comyns-Carr, a journalist. Her first novel, *Sisters by a River*, 1947, in loosely connected chapters narrated by a child, draws on details of her own childhood: the deaf mother to whom the children spoke in sign language, the older, violent father, the river which provides adventures as well as putrefying bodies. Its chaotic household, irregularly educated children, and parade of governesses and servants of declining social status, figure again in *The Skin Chairs*, 1962 (titled from chairs covered in human skin from Africa), narrated by a young daughter. Both books combine quirkiness and humour with the frighteningly macabre; the starkly innocent child sees this grotesque horror as characteristic of the adult world. The same innocence defines the young adult, Sophia, whose supposed autobiography, *Our Spoons Came from Woolworths*, 1950, draws on BC's first marriage. It presents the desperately poor and eventually unhappy marriage of a woman who supports her artist husband by work as an artist's model. *The Vet's Daughter*, 1959, BC's best-known novel (adapted for radio and as a musical, *The Clapham Wonder*), is a bizarre tale of a lonely young girl trampled to death at an exhibition of her power of levitation arranged by her abusive and violent father. *Out of the Red Into the Blue*, 1960, describes years spent by BC and her husband in Spain. *The Juniper Tree*, 1985, called by Margaret DRABBLE an example of 'English magical realism', powerfully retells a Brothers Grimm fable, following the life of its narrator, Bella, from independence through a 'travesty' marriage to reconciliation with her mother and a new life. *The House of Dolls*, 1989, is a breezy account of ageing prostitutes. There are many recent reprints.

Conan, Laure, Marie-Louise-Félicité Angers, 1845–1924, journalist, Québec's first woman novelist. B. at La Malbaie, she studied at the Ursuline Convent in Québec City. Her pseudonymous story 'Un Amour Vrai' appeared in *La Revue de Montréal*, 1878 (repr. 1899, as *Larmes d'Amour*). Her best-known work, *Angéline de Montbrun*, 1884 (transl. 1974), introduced the psychological novel to Québec literature. Formally innovative, combining letters, narrative and diary, it is thematically traditional, curiously bound to an oppressve patriarchal and religious social order. Inspired by LC's unrequired love for politician Pierre-Alexis Tremblay, it develops a theme of personal sacrifice and pious resignation to repress sexual desire, as does *A l'Oeuvre et à l'épreuve*, 1891 (*The Master-motive: a tale of the days of Champlain*, 1909). LC's perspective underwent a significant change, however, as a result of her years at the Convent of the Precious Blood in Saint Hyacinthe, 1893–8, when, while editing the convent's journal, to which she contributed many articles, she became acquainted with the *Relations of the Jesuits*, which galvanized her interest in history. Thereafter she wrote several historical novels (e.g. *L'Oublié*, 1900, about a garrison sergeant-major killed by Iroquois in 1662) and a biography of Elizabeth SETON, 1903, and many articles and essays encouraging women to participate more fully in life. Today, LC is considered one of nineteenth-century Québec's most original writers. Her fiction has been reprinted and annotated by Roger Le Oloine in *Oeuvres romanesques*, three vols., 1974–5. See E. D. Blodgett in Neuman and Kamboureli, 1986.

Conway, Anne (Finch), Viscountess, 1631–79, philosopher, younger da. of Elizabeth (Cradock), formerly a rich widow, and Sir Heneage F., who d. a week before her birth. A fever at 12 brought on lifelong excruciating, almost perpetual headaches. Tutored in Latin, with some Greek and Hebrew, she discovered philosophy early, and corresponded with Henry More from 1650. In 1651 she m. Edward, later Viscount C.: her only child died young. From Ragley, Warwicks., she kept up a lively intellectual corrrespondence (though she writes to her husband about his shirts), ed. Marjorie Hope Nicolson, 1930 (only about 30 of the letters are hers; she also wrote to Joseph Glanvill from Ireland, 1663, about apparitions). Her thought is essentialist, rationalist, monistic, attentive to Descartes but arguing against him; she strongly influenced Leibnitz; her close friendship with More was shaken by her joining the Quakers, 1677. She left 'some Remains', probably religious, which friends considered publishing, and a treatise dating chiefly from her last two years, of which a Latin version appeared in 1690, re-englished 1692 as *The Principles of the Most Ancient and Modern Philosophy* and sometimes wrongly ascribed to van Helmont: both ed. Peter Loptson, 1982. See Carolyn Merchant in *Journal of the Hist. of Philosophy*, 17, 1979.

Conway, Katharine St John, Katharine Bruce Glasier, 1867–1950, short-story writer and lecturer, da. of Samuel C., radical Congregational minister in Walthamstow, Essex. Educ. at Newnham College, Cambridge, she signed her first book as a 'B.A.': two stories, 'Husband & Brother: A Few Chapters in a Woman's Life of To-Day', and 'From Key-Note to Dominant' (n.d.) dedicated 'To Lizzie, Sister and Comrade', and published while she was teaching at Redcliffe High School, Bristol. Both stories are strongly feminist; the first treats warm friendship between women in erotic terms. In 1893, she m. John Glendower Bruce Glasier, whom she met through her work for the Independent Labour Party, of which she was a lifelong member from its inception, being elected to its first national administrative council. Attractive, impassioned and self-assured, she was always a platform success in addressing working women. *Tales from the Derbyshire Hills,* 1907 (proceeds to the ILP), are rather sentimental and much more floridly written then her earlier work. In WWI she edited the *Labour Leader*, and firmly supported her husband's pacifist stand.

Cook, Ann, cookery writer. Born, probably late seventeenth century, 'in a homely Cottage', perhaps a Roman Catholic, she worked as cook and housekeeper in several families before marrying John C., *c.* 1725, and keeping, with him and her daughters, the Black Bull at Hexham, Northumberland. A feud arose with a local gentleman, Hannah GLASSE's brother; despite extra work during the Jacobite rebellion, a move to Morpeth and then to Newcastle, they went bankrupt. Glasse's anonymous *Art of Cookery*, 1747, provoked her to write *The Professed Cook* (1st ed. not known; 2nd, Newcastle, 1755; 3rd [1760], sold by herself from London lodgings), whose title and argument set her own professionalism against her 'Lady' rival's alleged incompetence. Spirited prefatory heroic couplets say she is untaught but 'free-born', and accuse Glasse of 'fleec[ing] the poor low Servants to get Wealth'. She criticizes in minute detail before giving her own recipes. Her mistitled 'A Plan of House-Keeping', after some advice on poultry management and other matters, is devoted to the exchange of life-stories with a friend, in the style of vivid, low-life, realistic fiction. See selecs. ed. Regula Burnet, 1936; Madeleine Hope Dodds in *Archaeologia Aeliana*, 15, 1938.

Cook, Eliza, 1817–89, poet and journal editor, b. in Southwark, London, youngest of 11 children of Joseph C., tinman and brazier, who retired to a small Sussex farm when EC was nine. Though her father discouraged reading, her intelligent mother, who d. when EC was 15, encouraged her gifted child. Mostly self-educated, she wrote many of her best poems before she was 15, including 'Star of Glengarry', 'Lines to My Pony', 'I'm Afloat' and 'Charlie O'Ross'. Her first volume, *Lays of a Wild Harp*, was pub. in 1835. From about 1836 EC's poems appeared in the *Weekly Despatch, Metropolitan Magazine, New Monthly Magazine* and *Literary Gazette*, signed only with initials. Thought by many to be written by a man, they were compared to the works of Robert Burns and praised for their originality, optimism and flow. She edited *Eliza Cook's Journal*, 1849–54, a weekly which greatly appealed to the middle classes with its emphasis on their values and mores. A popular and populist poet, EC also published *Melaia*, 1838 (repub. 1840 with additional poems), *New Echoes*, 1864, *Jottings from My Journal*, 1860 and *Diamond Dust*, 1865. In 1864 she was awarded a Civil List pension of £100 p.a.; in later years ill health prevented her from writing.

Cook, Fannie (Frank), 1893–1949. Missouri novelist and painter, b. at St Charles, da. of Jennie and Julius F. She took a BA at the Univ. of Missouri, 1914, m. Jerome E. C. in 1915, and had two sons. Until 1935 (when she won a *Reader's Digest* new writers' competition) she taught English part-time at Washington Univ. (where she did an MA, 1916), edited the state League of Women Voters *Bulletin*, and published only a few magazine stories and poems. *The Hill Grows Steeper*, 1938, offers its heroine a choice between independence and marriage. A white woman with strong commitment to racial harmony, FC chaired the Missouri Committee for Rehabilitation of Sharecroppers, 1940; from this came the novel *Boot-Heel Doctor*, 1941. She sat on the Mayor's Race Relations Committee during WWII, became an adviser to the NAACP, lectured on race, laws, and literature, wrote for the *St Louis Post-Dispatch*, and supported the cause of unions in her short fiction. Her most successful novel, *Mrs Palmer's Honey*, 1946 (George Washington Carver award), follows the growth of Honey ('I've been a maid for a long time. I got feelings like a maid') into the role of union organizer. Other works, like *Storm Against the Wall*, 1948, reinforce the message that reality can be changed by people's will. *The Long Bridge*, 1949, draws on FC's experience as a painter.

Cook, Frances, autobiographer. She m. John C. (barrister executed as a regicide, 1660) and went with him when he was appointed Chief Justice to the Court of Munster in Ireland, 1650. Their ship almost sank in a storm, and she published an account of this event, with related thoughts, as *Meditations*, Cork and London, 1650. (John C. also recorded it in *A True Relation*, 1650, 1652.) She justifies her boldness in writing: 'they which have a heart to bless God for his mercies, ought to have a tongue to prayse him for the same, and a pen to record them.'

Cooke, Cassandra (Leigh), 1744–1826, novelist, da. of Ann (Bee) and Theophilus L., master of Balliol College, Oxford. Her husband, the Rev. Samuel C., was thought by Jane AUSTEN (her cousin, his god-daughter) a 'disagreable, fidgetty' man; her sons became Oxford dons. In 1798 she meant her anonymous historical novel *Battleridge*, 1799, not to be her last; but no more are known. With a preface praising Fanny BURNEY and Ann RADCLIFFE, and a disproportionate inset Scots tale of the crusading era, it brings to imaginative life a divided family under Charles I (admirable Royalists, hateful but *almost* credible Puritans), and leaves a new generation growing up under the aegis of Lady Rachel RUSSELL (their relation) and Lady Anne CLIFFORD. Living first at Great Bookham, Surrey, then chiefly at Bath, CC knew Burney and followed Austen's work with discriminating interest.

Cooke, Marjorie Benton, 1876–1920, novelist, monologuist. B. in Richmond, Ind. to Jessie (Benton) and Joseph Henry C., she received a PhB from the Univ. of Chicago in 1899. Her earliest publications, satiric, humorous monologues and plays for children (collections include *Modern Monologues*, 1903, *Dramatic Episodes*, 1905, *Plays for Children*, 1905, *More Modern Monologues*, 1907) expose ignorance and pretence: in *On Woman's Rights*, 1903, for instance, the speaker considers that women should have the right to 'manage yer [home], yer children, an' yer husband to suit yerself'. In MBC's first novel, *The Girl Who Lived in the Woods*, 1917, a woman attempts to gain control of her family after a financial disaster; in *The Threshold*, 1918, a young woman graduate charged with the education of a 17-year-old boy due to inherit his uncle's factories and fortune decides that rather than make an 'aristocrat' of him, she will alert him to the lives and concerns of the factory workers. *Bambi*, 1915, humorously presents a young woman's marriage to an eccentric playwright whose female characterization 'is all man psychology. You don't know your woman.' She writes her own novel and with its success wins 'her independence, and it was sweet'. In *Cinderella Jane*, 1917, a woman undertaking a 'business arrangement' marriage gains the cooperation of her narrowly traditional husband and continues her writing career after their child is born. Central to MBC's later novels is the issue of women combining marriage, family and career. One character explains why her family life should not end her writing: 'Being a woman, the fact that I am married, that I have a child, gives me more to say. Everything that enriches my life makes it more impossible for me to be dumb.' Her last novel was *The Cricket*, 1918. For a brief discussion of *The Threshold* see Nan Bauer Maglin, 'Discovering Women's Activist Fiction' in *University of Michigan Papers in Women's Studies*, 2, 1976.

Cooke, Rose (Terry), 1827–92, short-story writer and poet, b. on a farm near Hartford, Conn., da. of Anne Wright (Hurlbut) and Henry Wadsworth T., wealthy banker and Congressman. She was educ. at Catherine BEECHER's Hartford Female Seminary and by her parents. She taught for three years until a legacy enabled her to concentrate on writing (though still housekeeping for the family and caring for her deceased sister's children). Her first story was pub. in *Graham's Magazine*, 1845, and her first poem, signed in tribute with her mother's initials, was pub. in 1851 in the *New York Herald Tribune*. Her first important short story, 'The Mormon's Wife', appeared in *Putnam's*, 1855. Her stories provide realistic regional backgrounds and authentic dialect, and she was the precursor of local colour realists S. O. JEWETT and M. W. FREEMAN. They often feature strong-minded spinster heroines, explore the power relations of male/female roles and examine the realities of married life. In 'How Celia Changed her Mind' (*Huckleberries*, 1891; repr. 1988), Celia's fear of being an old maid – 'They ain't nothing or nobody' – leads her to marry the tyrannical Deacon Everts, thereby becoming a household drudge; however, Everts dies, leaving Celia well-off, and she adopts female children to rear them as 'dyed-in-the-wool old maids'. RTC also pub. two collections of poems, in 1861 and 1888, and one novel, *Steadfast*, in 1889. In 1873 RTC m. Rollin H. C., whose financial incompetence and depletion of her savings forced her by 1885 to resort to hack-work for economic support. H. P. SPOFFORD included her in *Our Famous Women*. She wrote over 100 sketches for *Atlantic*, *Harper's*, *Putnam's* and *Galaxy*, and her collected short stories include *Rootbound*, 1885, *Sphinx's Children and Other People*, 1886, and *Somebody's Neighbours* and *Huckleberries Gathered from New England Hills*, 1891. Her significance lies in her open criticism of Puritan hypocrisy, her sympathetic and innovative portrayal of women and her honest portrayal of a region she knew first-hand, while her conscious rejection of romantic conventions influenced twentieth-century writers. There is a recent story selection with bibliography and excellent introduction by Elizabeth Ammons, 1986.

Cookery Books or cookbooks, printed, began as a male preserve: women's MS recipe-books, handed down the generations, survive in numbers from the seventeenth century. Elinor Fettiplace's, 1604, ed. Hilary Spurling, 1986, covers food and medicaments; many recipe compilers, like the Countess of Kent, 1653, concentrated on MEDICAL WRITING. The virtuoso Hannah

WOLLEY exemplifies the early literary and feminist interest of the genre. E. [?Eliza] Smith, 2nd ed. 1728, was repr. at Williamsburg, Va., 1742 (first cookery book pub. in America: see Genevieve Yost in *William and Mary Quarterly*, 1938), facs. from later eds. 1968. Sarah Harrison of Devon, prefacing a book in 1733, ranks the 'Feminine Arts of Government', which men despise, above 'some admired Branches of Literature'. Early cookery writers included ladies (Hannah GLASSE, Maria RUNDELL) and working women (Ann COOK, Elizabeth RAFFALD). The first American to publish in the genre was 'orphan' Amelia Simmons, 1796. Eliza Leslie, 1787–1858, published an early and successful US cookbook in 1828 (often repr.), and Lydia M. CHILD published the very popular *Frugal Housekeeping* in 1829. Isabella Beeton, 1837–65, who helped her publisher husband Samuel to edit *The English-Woman's Domestic Magazine* and compiled *Mrs Beeton's Book of Household Management*, 1861, often repr., remains a household name. US equivalents were by S. J. HALE (*The Good Housekeeper*, 1839) and the BEECHER sisters in 1869. In the twentieth century, while specialized recipe books have proliferated, a sub-genre of literary cookery books has emerged; and while many women have written about the problematics of female relation to the preparation and consumption of food, others have celebrated it, often moved by pleasure in the cooking of other cultures or periods, like M. F. K. FISHER. Elizabeth David, OBE, an Englishwoman who lived with a French family while studying French history and literature at the Sorbonne, in 1950 published *Mediterranean Food*, the first of an influential output mixing marketing and cooking instructions with travel impressions, her own and anthologized. *The Alice B. TOKLAS Cookbook*, 1954, whose author claimed to believe a cookbook has nothing to do with writing, is also a 'mingling of recipe and reminiscence'. Fisher's foreword to the 1984 edition of Toklas expresses faith in its power to 'feed my soul abundantly'. The genre has also been variously reshaped, alluded to and played with by writers of fiction and poetry: Maura LAVERTY's autobiographical novels were first sparked by memories of a cookery book; Marion HALLIGAN writes fiction and essays about food; Nora EPHRON scatters recipes through the pages of a personal fiction *à clef*; Sandra GILBERT gives her poetry collections titles which suggest cookbooks; and Joyce Carol OATES calls one of hers *Woman Whose Lives are Food, Men Whose Lives are Money*, 1978. Merle COLLINS expresses her national, social and sexual identity through a poem, 'Callaloo', which incorporates a recipe: this word is also the title of an anthology and an important Caribbean literary journal.

Cookson, Catherine (McMullen), OBE, 'Catherine Marchant', romance novelist and autobiographer, b. 1906 at Tyne Dock, South Shields, da. of Catherine (Fawcett) domestic servant and alcoholic, and a 'gentleman'. Brought up a Catholic, educ. at local schools, she went into service at 14, spent two years 'pen-painting', then worked as laundry checker in a workhouse, 1924-9, managed a laundry at Hastings, Sussex, 1929–39, and m. Thomas Henry C., teacher, in 1940: unwillingly childless, she had three miscarriages. She joined the Hastings Writers' Circle in the late 1940s. Despite nervous breakdowns and debilitating vascular disease, she has written, besides children's books, over 50 sprawling, immensely POPULAR novels, some as 'Catherine Marchant'. The first, *Kate Hannigan*, 1950, draws on her own experience of childhood hardship (see 'My First Book' in *The Author*, Spring 1987). After *Our Kate*, an autobiography, 1969, she wrote of herself again in *CC Country*, 1986, and *Let Me Make Myself Plain* (meditations and poems), 1988. The popular Mary Ann series (seven novels, 1954–67, omnibus ed., 1981) chronicles the growth of a strong-minded girl bent on saving her alcoholic father from self-destruction. CC's characters tend to overcome against odds, attaining respectability through determined hard work. *The Round Tower*, 1968, won the Winifred HOLTBY prize for regional novels. CC sees her work as regional, not romantic; her women characters are strong 'because they are me. I have had to be strong all my life.' She moved back north in 1975 and now lives at North Shields. In *The Cultured Handmaid*, 1988, the heroine feels 'Of late she had been inclined to be pessimistic. She'd have to get out of that way of thinking ... the future promised to be bright': right-minded attitude brings its own reward. CC's work has been adapted for TV (e.g. *The Mallens*, 1979–80, from four novels, 1973–4), screen, stage (e.g. *The Fifteen Streets*, 1988), and radio (e.g. by Michelene WANDOR: *The Dwelling Place*, 1989). MSS at Boston Univ.

Coolbrith, Ina Donna (Smith), 1842–1928, poet, b. Nauvoo, Ill., da. of Agnes (C.) and Don Carlos S., printer and brother of Joseph S., founder of the Mormon church. After his death when IC was four months old, her mother remarried and renounced Mormonism. In 1849 the family moved to Los Angeles where IC attended local schools but was educ. mainly by her own reading. Her first poems appeared in local papers in the 1850s under 'Ina'. In 1859 she m. Robert Carsley, iron works partner, but divorced in 1861 following his attempt to kill her, and after the death of her only child, moved to San Francisco in 1865, adopting her mother's maiden name. Here she wrote for the *Californian* and became co-editor with Bret Harte of *Overland Monthly* in 1868. From 1874 she made a home for a niece and nephew as well as the Indian daughter of the poet Joaquin Miller. She was librarian at various San Francisco libraries 1874–1906, and influenced many young readers including Jack London and Isadora Duncan. By the 1870s her poetry was acclaimed in England (by Meredith, Tennyson and the ROSSETTIS) as well as the USA. In 1871 she pub. her most famous poem, 'California', commissioned as commencement ode for the Univ. at Berkeley, which invokes heroic male truth. In 1881 her first collection *A Perfect Day*, appeared; others are *The Singer by the Sea*, 1894, *Songs from the Golden Gate*, 1895, and the posthumous *Wings of Sunset*, 1929, which includes the dramatic and erotic 'Concha', portraying a woman's sly struggle with religious and political orthodoxy. Her poetry celebrates nature and offers timeworn but sincere advice which attracted a large reading public. She, Bret Harte and George Stoddard became known as the 'Golden Gate Trinity', and in 1915 she was made California's poet laureate. Her mother was a lifelong support and her poem 'A Last Word' is an unsentimental, fine appreciation of a mother / daughter bond. See J. Rhodehamel and R. Wood, 1973, for her life.

Cooper, Anna Julia (Haywood), 1859?–1964, educator, b. Raleigh, N.C., da. of Hannah (Stanley), a slave, and a white father, George Washington H. She was educ. at St Augustine's Normal School and Collegiate Institute, Raleigh, where she became a pupil-teacher at eight. In 1877 she m. the Rev. George C. C., a former slave who had become an Episcopalian minister (d. 1879). She was admitted to Oberlin College in 1881, receiving her BA in 1884 and her MA in 1888. In 1887 she began a 40-year career at Washington High School (Principal from 1901), and was soon embroiled in controversy with those who advocated only a vocational training for blacks. Her essay 'A Voice from the South by a Black Woman of the South', 1892, argued that aptitude, not race or sex, should be the criterion for higher education. She also advocated a special role for women in her essay, 'Womanhood: a Vital Element in the Regeneration and Progress of a Race': 'Only the BLACK WOMAN can say "When and where I enter ... without violence and without suing or special patronage, then and there the whole Negro race enters with me".' In 1893, she addressed the World's Congress of Representative Women and, in 1900, the Pan African Congress Conference in London; she helped establish the Colored Women's YMCA in 1905. From 1914–17 she studied for a doctorate in French language and literature at Columbia University, and her dissertation, a college edition of *Le Pélerinage de Charlemagne*, was pub. in Paris in 1925. She completed a Sorbonne doctorate in 1925, a pioneering work concerning the attitude of post-revolutionary France towards slavery in Haiti, and in the same year pub. her autobiographical work, *The Third Step*. In 1930 she retired and became president of the Freylinghuysen Group of Schools for Employed Coloured Persons (later Freylinghuysen University). She pub. the two-volume *Life and Writings of the Grimké Family*, 1951. Her papers are at the Moorland-Springarn Research Center, Howard University. See Leona Gabel's study, 1982, for her life, as well as Mary Helen Washington's article in *Legacy*, Fall 1987.

Cooper, Elizabeth, dramatist, actress and scholar. Her comedy *The Rival Widows, or Fair Libertine* (dedicated to the Duchess of MARLBOROUGH) was 'the first publick Tryal of my Muse', pub. and acted 1735, after her auctioneer husband's death. On benefit nights she played the lead, a young widow 'capable of thinking for herself, and acting on the Principles of Nature and Truth', who gets her man and triumphs over her wicked rival. *The Nobleman, or The Family Quarrel*, staged 1736 and puffed by herself in the *Daily Advertiser*, 17 May, is lost. In 1737 she pub. *The Muses Library*, a pioneering historical anthology of poems from Edward the Confessor to Samuel Daniel, with brief lives and a scholarly and critical preface. An intended second vol. never appeared; later editions did; it was an important influence on Thomas Chatterton. William Oldys, who lent her old books, has been credited with the work. It criticizes enthusiastically and perceptively, not afraid to make original judgements, but ignorant of women writers (mentioning only 'the great' Lady Anne CLIFFORD, and her as patron, not author). Mary SCOTT, however, mentions EC with praise.

Cooper, Katherine (Saunders), 1841–94, novelist, b. London, eldest da. of 12 children of Katherine (Nettleship) and John S., novelist and playwright. She m. 1876, Rev. Richard C. Her first published story, 'Old Matthew's Puzzle', was written at 16 and appeared in her father's collection, *Martin Pole*, 1863. Her lucid, often evocative style and the subtle, sympathetic treatment of characters from 'humble life' in her collection *The Haunted Crust*. 1871, and her novel *Sebastian*, 1878, led reviewers to compare her to George ELIOT. Although also possessing these qualities, other novels like *The High Mills*, 1875, and especially *Margaret and Elizabeth*, 1873, have the implausible plots and melodramatic scenes common in contemporary sensation novels. After an uneven collection of short stories, *Heart Salvage by Sea and Land*, 1884, KC turned to writing religious tracts.

Cooper, Lettice Ulpha, OBE, novelist, b. 1897 at Eccles, Lancs., da. of Agnes Helena (Fraser) and Leonard C. At seven she was writing a historical novel (unfinished) in the family laundry book. After St Cuthbert's School, Southbourne, and Lady Margaret Hall, Oxford (graduating in classics, 1918), not wanting to teach, she worked some years in her father's engineering firm in Leeds. Social work for the unemployed began her lifelong Labour Party activity. Her first novels, from *The Lighted Room*, 1925, were historical, local, and highly intelligent. She turned to the present in *The Ship of Truth*, 1930, which won (anonymously) a £1,000 prize for a religious novel. *We Have Come to a Country*, 1935, is set in a centre for unemployed men. Freudian psychoanalysis (for severe phobias) fed into her books. *The New House*, 1938, repr. 1987, traces a removal which ends traditional family life; half unwillingly, the heroine accepts independence and responsibility for herself. Maureen DUFFY notes its emotional clarity and political and psychological insight. LC's best-known novel, *National Provincial*, 1938, repr. 1987, uses Leeds ('Aire') as microcosm of a world where a younger socialism battles to win power from the old. As associate editor of *Time and Tide*, 1939–40, LC refused Lady RHONDDA'S request to use a male pseudonym. She worked during WWII for the Ministry of Food, writing nothing; success proved hard to regain, though some think her best work is *Fenny*, 1953, repr. 1987, set in Florence, where she was a regular visitor. It deals with living in fantasy: not, she says, the frustration in life but the life in frustration. LC was President of International PEN, 1979–81. She has written biographies (some for children, like some of her fiction): of e.g. George ELIOT, 1951, and Florence NIGHTINGALE, 1960. After about 20 novels, 'written for delight', she remains alert to the topical: the 1971 miners' strike in *Snow and Roses*, 1976 (dedicated to Brigid BROPHY and Maureen Duffy); squatters in *Desirable Residence*, 1980 (where the meshing of chance-met lives, and a study of old age are especially fine); IRA bombing in *Unusual Behaviour*, 1986. MSS at Eccles Public Library.

Cooper, Maria Susanna (Bransby), 1738–1807, novelist and poet. Eldest da. and heiress of Anna Maria (Paston) and James B. of Shottisham, Norfolk, she m. the Rev. Samuel C. and lived at nearby Brooke Hall. Of ten children, her five daughters all died young of consumption. From writing children's stories, she moved to sentimental, didactic, epistolary novels which posed as actual letters till she became popular and set her name to revisions. *Letters between Emilia and Harriet*, 1762, features an awful warning and 'a perfect pattern of filial obedience, and female delicacy', re-worked more earnestly once she was a mother herself as *The Daughter*, 1775; *The Exemplary Mother, or Letters between Mrs Villars and Her Family*, 1769, was similarly revised in 1784. *The History of Fanny Meadows*, 1775, has a heroine of apparently low birth and forcibly threatened virtue. MSC's verse epistle *Jane Shore to her Friend*, 1776, dedicated to Soame Jenyns, was faintly praised by reviewers for its moral purpose. She moved to Great Yarmouth in 1781. A grandson printed a few of her letters, and suspected that her too-obsequious submission fostered her husband's self-importance (life of her eminent doctor son Astley C., 1863). Another son collected ten *Moral Tales* from the 1770s and 80s (1811) and added further revision to *The Wife, or Caroline Herbert*, 1813.

Cooper, Susan Fenimore, 1813–94, novelist, nature writer and editor, b. Mamaroneck, NY, da. of Susan Augusta (DeLancey) and the novelist James Fenimore C. She was educ. by tutors and at private schools in NYC and Europe, where she travelled with her family 1826–33, then settled in Cooperstown, NY, where SC acted as her father's copyist until his death in 1851. SC pub. her first novel, *Elinor Wyllys*, 1845, under the pseudonym 'Amabel Penfeather', with a preface by her father; the title character, a plain, dark, sweet orphan, triumphs after mild romantic tribulations. *Rural Hours*, 1850, a journal of natural observations, was more successful both in the US and in England. SC compiled and introduced *Pages and Pictures, from the Writings of James Fenimore Cooper*, 1861. After the Civil War she turned to philanthropic work, founding Thanksgiving Hospital and a house for orphans in Cooperstown.

Cope, Wendy, poet and journalist. B. in 1945 at Erith, Kent, she was educ. at private schools at Ashford and Chislehurst, and St Hilda's College, Oxford (BA in History, 1966). She became a teacher and music specialist in a London primary school, then a Deputy Head. She began writing poetry in 1973 after analysis for severe depression after her father's death, and published a small pamphlet, *Across the City*, 1980. In 1981 she became Arts and Books editor of the Inner London Education Authority magazine *Contact*, then taught again part-time till 1986, when she became a freelance writer. The sometimes rowdy but always accomplished, witty parodies and poignant lyrics in her best-selling *Making Cocoa for Kingsley Amis*, 1986 (Poetry Book Society choice), dextrously handle traditional, often recherché verse forms such as villanelle, triolet, rondeau, sonnet and haiku. Her pithy, cynical verses on love, sex and men invite comparison with Dorothy PARKER, and critics have welcomed her into the predominantly male preserve of commercial poetry and parody. WC has also written a book of hand rhymes for children, *Twiddling Your Thumbs*, 1988. She edited *Is That the New Moon?*, poems by women, 1989.

Corbett, Elizabeth Burgoyne, 'Mrs George Corbett', 1846–*c.* 1922, novelist and dramatist. Nothing is known of her life except that she lived in Suffolk towards the end. The BLC lists a dozen novels, but she specialized in commissioned serial-writing, producing over 70, including society, nautical, DETECTIVE and adventure stories, as well as several dramas and comedies, such as *A Bit of Human Nature* (staged June, 1899) and *On the Threshold* (April, 1900). *Mrs Grundy's Victims*, 1893, is a novel about two sisters alone in London; one is trapped by the White Slave Trade and never found. *When the Sea gives up its Dead*, 1894, a detective thriller, is much stronger than *The Marriage Market*, 1905. EBC rises well above the 'hack' level in *New Amazonia* [1899], a witty Utopian fantasy about a future community of giant women, where illegitimate fathers are punished by exile and only the unmarried can hold public office. The Preface expresses her rage at the women's Anti-Suffrage movement. She must be the Elizabeth T. Corbett whose story 'My Visit to Utopia', 1869, was repr. from *Harper's New Monthly* in Carol F. Kessler's *Daring to Dream*, 1984.

Corbett, Elizabeth Frances, 1887–1961, novelist, b. at Aurora, Ill.; her parents, Isabelle Jean (Adkins) and Richard W. C., ran a home for army veterans. She took a BA at the Univ. of Wisconsin, 1910, and moved to NYC with her mother in 1927. She wrote magazine pieces (*Poet Lore*, 41, 1930, printed her play *The Hanger Back*), lives of Walt Whitman, 1928, and Ulysses S. Grant, 1930, and more than 50 novels, from *Cecily and the Wide World*, 1916, to *Sunday at Six*, 1971. Most are set in a nostalgic, ordered, changeless present where men wield benign authority and women happily submit. The best-known mediator of her vision appears in *The Young Mrs. Meigs*, 1931, as an 80-year-old evaluating with kindly irony the marriageability and other qualities of children and grandchildren while braced to keep her independence; in *Mrs. Meigs and Mr. Cunningham*, 1936, she finds a twilight romance; in *She Was Carrie Eaton*, 1938, she is a 30-year-old novel-reader angling for her chosen husband. *Our Mrs Meigs*, 1954, combines three abridged texts. Another series, 1936–9, presents a nineteenth-century family in the fictional Mount Royal, Ill. The heroine of *The Langworthy Family*, 1937, is typical: 'a creature born and trained to attract attention, and to enjoy attracting it'. EC's memoirs, *Out at the Old Soldiers' Home*, 1941, regret that 'American life is poorer and thinner' for the passing of ceremonies like Decoration Days (replaced by the start of the golf season) and of strong and simple men unmatched in later generations. *The Red-Haired Lady*, 1945, is an autobiographical novel. Papers at the Univ. of Oregon include a dramatized *Young Mrs Meigs*.

'Corelli, Marie', Mary Mackay, 1855–1924, best-selling novelist, spiritualist, musician. Though she invented her own version of her background (see e.g. *Who's Who*, 1903), it now seems certain she was the illegitimate da. of Ellen, or Mary Elizabeth, (Kirtland, later Mills, later Mackay) and Charles M., Scottish song writer, who were unable to marry till MC was nine. Educ. at home by governesses and briefly in a convent school, she first enjoyed a career as a pianist, but prompted by a 'psychical experience' and a need for money, changed to writing. She later supported both her hypochondriacal father and profligate stepbrother. Her first novel, *A Romance of Two Worlds*, 1886, met with popular, but not critical, approval; *The Sorrows of Satan*, 1895, was the first English bestseller, and *The Treasures of Heaven*, 1906, sold 100,000 copies on its first day. Her popular success is attributed to several recurring themes and practices: *Ardath*, 1889, and *The Soul of Lilith*, 1892, combine spiritual and scientific phenomena in bizarre narratives about the meaning of life; *Barabbas*, 1893, *The Sorrows of Satan*, *Ziska*, 1897, *The Masterful Christian*, 1900, and *The Devil's Motor*, 1910, focus on characters from Christian mythology, the Christian churches and other religions. Others, such as *Wormwood*, 1890, and *Holy Orders*, 1908, focus on contemporary problems such as alcohol addiction, while her attack on critics and publishers in *The Silver Domino*, 1892, alienated almost all her professional contacts. In 1899 she and her life-long companion, Bertha Vyver (who wrote a *Memoir* of MC, 1930), moved from London to Stratford-upon-Avon, where she cultivated a reputation as an eccentric, became embroiled in various civic controversies, and took up public speaking. She disapproved of female SUFFRAGE ('Speaking personally as a woman, I have no politics, and want none'), but believed in female superiority and her own genius. There are several lives, including Brian Masters's, 1978. See also Richard Kowalczyk's article in the *JPC* 7 (Spring 1974).

Corke, Helen, 1882–1978, poet, novelist, autobiographer, historian, b. in Hastings, Sussex, to Louisa (Gallop) and Alfred C., a shopkeeper. She left school at 14, later qualified as a teacher, and met D. H. Lawrence in 1908 while both were teaching in Croydon. Her journal describing her love affair with her violin teacher – an older married man who committed suicide – formed the basis of Lawrence's *The Trespasser*, 1912. HC's account of the affair, and of her relationship with Lawrence, appears in Part One of her autobiography, *In Our Infancy* (Whitbread Award), 1975, and in a disguised fictional version, *Neutral Ground*, 1933. Intelligent and unconventional, not in awe of Lawrence though she respected his work, HC rejected absolutely the idea of marrying him or bearing his children. 'It is not for me to be either wife or mistress.' She lost touch with him after 1912, but several of her later writings (of 1933, 1951, 1965) concern his work and their early relationship. Information about HC's life after Lawrence is scarce. She became headmistress at a school in Kelvedon, Essex, 1919–28, experimented in the teaching of international human history at Aylett's Foundation in Essex, and wrote several history textbooks, as well as two volumes of economic history and *Songs of Autumn*, 1960 (poems; some, dating from the Croydon period, heavily autobiographical). She died in Kelvedon, Essex, after completing a second vol. of autobiography.

Cornford, Frances Crofts (Darwin), 1886–1960, poet and translator, b. and d. in Cambridge, only child of Ellen (Crofts), who d. when FC was 17, and Francis D., son of Charles D. and Reader in Botany at Cambridge University. Educ. at home, she grew up in conditions described by her cousin, Gwen Raverat, in *Period Piece*, 1952. In 1908 she m. Francis M. Cornford, classical scholar (who was much influenced by Jane HARRISON, a friend of FC's mother). Their poet son John was killed in Spain in 1936. She published eight books of poetry between 1910 and 1960. Her *Collected Poems* was the choice of the Poetry Book Society in 1954, and in 1959 she won the Queen's Medal for Poetry. She translated some Russian poems with Esther Polianowsky Salaman, 1943, and, with Stephen Spender (who said she was 'one of the best translators living'), Paul Eluard's *Le Dur Désir de Durer*, 1950. Other translations from the French were published posthumously in 1976. Initially derided by Chesterton, her poems have since been superficially read as modest and picturesque. (See, e.g., John Galassi, ed., *Understand the Weapon Understand the Wound, Selected Writings of John Cornford with Some Letters of FC*, 1976, which represents the son as struggling 'to overcome the tradition of the personal, unsocial lyric which he had learned from his mother'.) It has often been noted that she evokes the beauties of Cambridge, but not that she confronts the experience of war more directly than her friend Rupert Brooke, nor that she records with barely subdued pain the division between male and female in that pretty academic scene. She writes frequently about unnamed women, and motherhood is one of her major subjects. Her verse conveys a strong sense of isolation (as in her triolet 'To a Fat Lady Seen From the Train') and it is often elegaic. FC is intensely aware of an exclusively masculine Cambridge literary tradition: 'Milton and Chaucer, Herbert, Herrick, Gray,/ Rupert, and you forgotten others'. Virginia and Leonard WOOLF published *Different Days*, 1928, and Gwen Raverat illustrated some of her books. Bibliography by Alan Anderson, 1975. The BL has her papers.

Cornwallis, Caroline Frances, 1786–1858, scholar and popularizer of scientific and technical knowledge, b. Wittersham, Kent, younger child of Mary (Harris), theological writer, and Rev. William C. At 15, on the death of her sister, she resolved to devote her life to scholarship and to helping her often-ailing parents. She taught herself Latin, Greek, Hebrew, German, Anglo-Saxon, and ancient Egyptian, and read history, philosophy, theology, and the sciences, but seldom met anyone who knew 'a book from a hedgehog' (*Letters*, 35). A lifelong friend of her one-time suitor Sismondi, historian, she spent two years in Italy studying mineralogy and law. Anxious to present her years of research in accessible form, and to show that scholarship was not an exclusively male domain, she wrote, anon., most of a well-received 22-vol. series, *Small Books on Great Subjects*, 1841–54, covering grammar, organic chemistry, geology, physiology, the treatment of insanity, and criminal law. Her main concern, however, was to present Christianity as a rationally-based philosophical system, as in *A Brief History of Greek Philosophy*, 1844, *On the State of Man Before the Promulgation of Christianity*, 1848, and the novel *Pericles*, 1846. *On the State of Man Subsequent to the Promulgation of Christianity*, 4 vols. 1851–4, traces Christianity's decline into a system of superstitions. She advocated better educational and career opportunities for women, particularly in two *Westminster Review* articles, 1856 and 1857. See *Selections from the Letters of CFC*, ed. M. C. Power, 1864.

Corp, Harriet (usually miscalled Hannah), religious novelist, who plays with that term in more than one preface. She and her sister ran a school at Stoke Newington, London, from c. 1791. Her anonymous *Antidote to the Miseries of Human Life*, 1807, had many eds. Countering a book by James Beresford which 'burlesque[d] the petty troubles of life', it has a stage-coach-journey setting, male narrator, and as heroine the Widow Placid – who caused the otherwise admiring *Evangelical Magazine* to question 'the propriety of making a Quaker Lady so profoundly wise, so truly liberal in her sentiments, or so very communicative, when a scholar [who praises Marianne CHAMBERS's *School for Friends*] and an author are present. Such a character is a *rara avis* indeed.' HC's *Sequel*, 1809, and four more didactic works (some reissued after serial publication, the last dated 1829) remain evangelical but also humorous, ironical, inventive and quietly feminist. She favours a single life for women with intellectual and charitable interests; her hero–narrator in *Coelebs Deceived*, 1817, remains single, unlike Hannah MORE's. Mary LEADBEATER admired her. She applied to the RLF in 1831, mentioning her small profits and two bankrupt publishers.

Cortez, Jayne, jazz poet, b. 1936 in Arizona, raised in Calif. She had a son and settled in the late 1960s in NYC, which is a frequent, scatological, hostile presence in her work. She has done printing and etching: a poem for a printmakers' exhibition celebrates 'a ceremony of rakes and rollers crosshatching / into a gel of artificial light'. Her typical mood is a highly political anger, though she recognizes the danger that 'you will disappear into your own rage'; she argues that the oppressors of humanity have always known what they were doing. *Pisstained Stairs and the Monkey Man's Wares*, 1969, and four more books went into *Coagulations, New and Selected Poems*, 1984; her three records, 1975–82, include *Unsubmissive Blues*, 1980. She writes on actual events, like two notorious rapes (a poem she judges 'definitely finished' where most are 'never finished'), and for individuals like Christopher Okigbo, Duke Ellington, Michael Smith. She has read her work with and without music in the USA, West Africa, the Caribbean and Europe (the US publishing industry 'is not yet desegregated enough for an African–American poet to take for granted equal access'). Often her words on the page evoke music: 'i sure would like to write a blues . . . you know / a serious blues / you know', or 'if your drum is a woman / don't abuse your drum'. 'Expenditures. Economic Love Song I' consists wholly of the repeated capitals: 'MILITARY SPENDING HUGE PROFITS & DEATH'. See D. H. Melhem, ed., *Heroism in the New Black Poetry, Introductions and Interviews*, 1990.

Costello, Louisa Stuart, 1799–1870, miniature painter, poet and novelist, b. in Ireland, only da. of Colonel James Francis C. After the death of her father in 1814 she supported her mother and brother in Paris by painting miniatures and by governessing, and in 1815 pub. her first poems, *Maid of the Cyprus Isle*. She was also one of the earliest copyists of illuminated manuscripts (some of her work is in the British Museum). Her first volume to attract attention was *Songs of a Stranger*, 1825, and she was well known as a song writer. She wrote picturesque descriptions of France, and histories of French and English celebrities, which were as popular as her poems and novels. Other works include *The Queen's Poisoner*, 1841, and *Clara Fane*, 1848, a novel dedicated to 'my close friend Miss Janet Wilkinson in memory of a visit to LLANGOLLEN'; its heroine a governess and school teacher who eventually finds her long-lost father. Her *Memoirs of Eminent Englishwomen*, 1844, is illustrated with her own engravings from portraits in the Duke of Devonshire's collection. She became friendly with the Burdett family who awarded her a liberal pension. In 1852 she was given a Civil List pension of £75 p.a. LSC retired to Boulogne where she died of cancer.

Cotton, Priscilla, d. 1664, Quaker pamphleteer living at Plymouth. She m. Arthur C., merchant (who died in 1708 at over 80), and had one daughter. *To the Priests and People of England*, 1655, written from Exeter prison with Mary Cole, includes the earliest known extended female defence of women's PREACHING, arguing that inspired women are duty-bound to speak, and that church ministers are 'weak women' who should be silent. She also published *As I Was in the Prison-House*, 1656, *A Briefe Description*, 1659, *A Visitation of Love*, 1661 (all remarkable for their confident tone), and testimonies to dead Friends.

Cottrell, Dorothy (Wilkinson), 1902–57, novelist, b. Picton, NSW, da. of Ida (Fletcher) and Walter W., mine manager. Confined to a wheelchair from polio at five, she was educ. by governesses, then with sculptor Theodore Cowan, and painter Dattilo Rubbo. In 1920 she lived on her uncle's station in Queensland and two years later m. his book-keeper, Walter C. She moved to America after achieving international success with her first novel, *The Singing Gold*, 1928 (serialized in *Ladies' Home Journal*, 1927). This is a comico-tragic tale narrated in a condensed, ironical manner, with reticence and jocularity muffling the poignant moments of the heroine's life. *Earth Battle*, 1930 (pub. as *Tharlane* in USA), much gloomier, is also set in Queensland, while *The Silent Reefs*, 1953 (film version 1959), is an adventure mystery set in the Caribbean. She has also pub. children's books and numerous uncollected articles and short stories. MSS are in the National Library, Canberra.

Couani, Anna, prose writer, poet, publisher, of Polish and Greek ancestry, b. 1948 in Sydney, NSW, da. of Dr Stefania Siedlecky and Dr John C. Her informal educ. included four years studying painting at the John Ogburn Studio and one year studying Chinese painting with Maurice Lin. She was also educ. at the Univ. of Sydney (BSc, Architecture) and Sydney Teachers' College (Dip. Ed.), and has trained as a teacher of English as a Second Language. She has pub. the collections *Italy*, 1977, *Were All Women Sex-Mad? and Other Stories*, 1982, and *Leaving Queensland and The Train*, 1983 (with Barbara Brooks), and has appeared in many literary journals and most anthologies of migrant or women's writing since the late 1970s. Her prose, episodic and questioning, challenges realism and the purpose of fiction. Voices and themes, not characters and events, dominate AC's fiction; personal and national identity are particular themes. Influential as a feminist, AC has run writing workshops for women and migrant writers, has been a major force in the Poet's Union for many years, and operates the small publishing house Sea Cruise Books (dedicated to experimental fiction). See Brenda Walker and David Brooks, eds, *Poetry and Gender: Issues in Australian Women's Poetry*, 1989, for AC's poet's statement.

Courtney, J. E. (Janet Elizabeth) (Hogarth), 1865–1954, essayist, editor, feminist, b. at Barton-on-Humber, Lincs., one of 14 children of Jane (Uppleby) and the Rev. George H. Educ. at school in Grantham and at Oxford, where she gained the equivalent of a first in Philosophy, 1888, she tried teaching, but preferred managerial work, and in 1894 became the first superintendent of women clerks at the Bank of England. Although she was an anti-suffragist, her writing focused on women, beginning with *The Higher Education of Women*, 1903. She helped to start the *Times Book Club*, 1906, and to edit the *Encyclopedia Britannica*, 1910. In 1911 she m. William Leonard C., journalist (d. 1928); she served as an advisor on staff welfare to the Ministry of Munitions 1914–18, returning to editorial work after the war, including acting editor of *The Fortnightly Review*, 1928–9. *The Adventurous Thirties: A Chapter in the Women's Movement*, 1933, expresses her anxiety that modern feminism may be eclipsed like that of a century earlier (MARTINEAU, NORTON). Other books include *The Women of My Time*, 1934, and an autobiography, *Recollected in Tranquillity*, 1926.

Couzyn, Jeni, poet, editor, b. 1942 in South Africa. She grew up in Johannesburg, reading little but writing poems in secret from about ten, solitary, 'rebellious and defiant ... yet always – as I remember, afraid'. She attended the Univ. of Natal (BA Hons. in Drama and English, 1963), published poems in a magazine ed. by Lionel Abrahams, taught drama in Rhodesia and produced for the African Music and Drama Association. She migrated to London in 1965, worked in special schools, the Camden Arts Centre and Loughton College of Higher Education, and first read her poems in Dublin. She felt she faced an impossible choice: '"happiness" (i.e. home, husband and children) or poetry.' In the late 1960s she discovered women's poetry (Anne SEXTON was 'a revelation'), and directed poetry workshops and readings. She published *Flying*, 1970, *Monkeys' Wedding*, 1972, and *Christmas in Africa*, 1975. That year she moved to Canada, where she 'tried marriage (briefly)', taught creative writing at Victoria Univ., BC, and became a Canadian citizen. In 1978 she published *House of Changes*, and returned to Britain. In 1985 she revised *Life by Drowning: Selected Poems*, first pub. 1983, and edited *The Bloodaxe Book of Contemporary Women Poets*. After bearing a daughter she 'was forced to die to the idea of myself as a poet'; later it became one of a 'wardrobe of identities ... if I am a poet, then I am a feminist, a therapist, and a mother. But I am none of these things. They are clothes the Jeni puts on, as I put on the Jeni.' Her poems, too, are much preoccupied with shifting identities, grounding the metaphysical in the physical. She becomes 'a wide house / a commune / of bickering women, hearing / their own breathing / denying each other' (named e.g., Vulnerable, Commendable, Equivocal, Harmful, and the one who watches). A dying friend 'takes her speech and returns it / syllable by syllable / she unpicks it thoughtfully, like knitting / unravels it, one plain, one purl / meaning by meaning'. *Tom-Cat-Lion*, 1987, is a children's story, *Singing Down the Bones*, 1989, an anthology of women's poetry for young adults.

Coventry, Anne (Somerset), Countess of, 1673–1763, religious writer. Da. of Mary (Capell) and the 1st Duke of Beaufort, close friend and patron of Mary ASTELL, heiress, Tory, perhaps Roman Catholic, she m. Thomas, 2nd Earl of Coventry, in 1691. Her tiny book, *Meditations and Reflections, Moral and Divine,* 1707, 1726, bore her name. Addressed to both sexes, it has both piety and good sense. Its final item was premature: 'I do now seriously think it is time to put my self into a fit Posture of Dying.' Outliving husband and two sons, she sued their heirs, 1724, for rich jointure lands, won, and verified her own 'Wealth ought not to be desirable, but as an Instrument of doing good.' Ruth Perry's life of Astell, 1986, prints catalogues of her extensive library.

Covey, Elizabeth (Rockfort), 'Elizabeth Fremantle', b. 1873, novelist. Little is known about her life. Da. of an English army officer, she m. Arthur C., 1907, who worked in government in Northern Nigeria, and she lived for some years in the Canadian North-West Territories. She was one of the few women writing in the Canadian west in the 1890s. (See also Kate HAYES.) Her *Comrades Two: A Tale of the Qu'Appelle Valley,* 1907, a tale 'more idyllic than realistic', appeared also as *The One, and I*, [1908]. Underlying its lively, journalistic account of day-to-day experience is its protagonist's reluctance to marry the fiancé she loves ('The One'), since she wants freedom to write and experience life. But when he nearly dies of typhoid fever, she eagerly renounces her freedom for marriage.

Coward, Rosalind, feminist critic, journalist and semiologist. *Language and Materialism*, with J. Ellis, 1977, a pioneering, critical history of semiology, reviews the structuralist foundations of semiology, demonstrating the residual idealism in structural linguistics and anthropology. Criticizing both on historical materialist grounds, it points to the implied presence of a transcendental subject, a universal speaking 'I' or a transhistorical, transcultural 'mind', whose symbolic and communicative function may be determined simply through a formal, synchronic systems analysis. It then turns to Julia KRISTEVA's revolutionary semiotics as the most adequate contemporary response to psychoanalytical and Marxist critiques of 'the sign', hailing her revaluation of the subject as the real, material, site of signifying practices and meaning-production. *Patriarchal Precedents*, 1983, examines the history of the study of sexual relations since the emergence of 'patriarchal theory' in the nineteenth century. RC analyses social sciences sprung from debates between adherents of mother-right and father-right, initiated by students of comparative law and furthered by social evolutionists; traces deconstruction of 'patriarchal theory' in empirical anthropology, as well as its persistence in Marxism and psychoanalysis; and criticizes cultural relativism no less than biological determinism for presupposing the naturalness of sexual difference, the traditional historiographic justification for the division of labour between the sexes and the removal of women from public life. RC criticizes Marxism for assuming the naturalness of man's psychological need to dominate, possess and accumulate, and psychoanalysis for confining its problematisation of sexuality to family structuration. Finally, RC abandons the concept 'patriarchy' in favour of an historical analysis of the construction of sexual identity, 'that mechanism by which men and women combine in a unit which subordinates women.' *Female Desire*, 1984, analyses the marketing and reproduction of women's sexual identity in clothing, food, and fitness fashions, women's pages, romantic fiction, and anthropomorphic discourse on the sex instinct in nature. *The Whole Truth: The Myth of Alternative Health*, 1989, charts the abuses of self-heal medicine.

Cowley, Hannah (Parkhouse), 1743–1809, dramatist and poet, b. at Tiverton, Devon, da. of Philip P., a scholarly bookseller later proud of her work. In ?1772 she m. Thomas C. and moved to London. A memoir of 1813 says that having 'never before written a literary line' she drafted a first act one morning after her husband had laughed at a casual boast of what she *might* do. This first play, *The Runaway*, 1776, mocks a pompous 'Female Student'. She tried tragedy (*Albina*, 1779, written earlier) and farce (*Who's the Dupe*, 1779) but was best at comedy, holding her place in the repertoire for a century. *The Belle's Stratagem*, acted 1780, and *A Bold Stroke for a Husband*, 1783, reverse predecessors' titles. *A School for Greybeards*, acted 1786, remakes BEHN's *Luckey Chance*. Her lively, ingenious, perfectly virtuous heroines dominate other rather stock characters and fast-moving, complex plots; she draws on CENTLIVRE as well as Behn. She is credited with a Gothic novel, *The Italian Marauders*, 1810. Her *Works*, 1813, include the 11 of her 13 plays to reach print (repr. from early eds., 1979), and poems: the long, separately-published *Maid of Arragon*, 1780, *Scottish Village*, 1786, and *Siege of Acre*, 1801 (epic on a topical theme), and her 'Anna Matilda' poems to Robert Merry, already coll. from *The World* in 1788. She claimed to write rapidly, not revising, leaving many short poems to perish, ignoring intellectual and theatrical life and finding politics unfeminine; but she cared enough to enter into debate with theatre managers and to accuse Hannah MORE of plagiarism, 1779. Her husband went to India for the East India Company in 1783 and died there in 1797; the eldest of their four children, a girl, died at 16. HC retired to Devon in 1801. See J. E. Norton in the *Book Collector*, 7, 1958.

Cowley, Joy (Summer), novelist, short-story and children's writer, b. Levin, NZ, 1913, da. of Cassia Katharina (Gedge) and Peter S. Was m. 1956–71 to Ted C., farmer; four children; in 1971 m. Malcolm Mason, accountant. Her first novel, *Nest in a Falling Tree*, 1968, is about a 43-year-old spinster who boards and ends up in an affair with an opportunistic teenage boy. *Man of Straw*, 1970, is a lucid and tragic story of a girl growing up in a constricting family and community. *Of Men and Angels*, 1972, concerns an older single woman in a small NZ town who fosters a pregnant girl for the pleasure of vicariously nursing her child. The novels focus on the limited and repressive life of NZ pakeha (white) society, both in the relationship of parent and child, and of man and woman. More recently she has moved to writing prolifically for children (over 300 titles) – picture books, stories, plays, and a novel, *The Silent One*, 1980, which won the NZ book of the year award and was filmed.

Cowper, Mary (Clavering), Countess, 1685–1724, diarist. Da. of John Clavering of Co. Durham, she was living near London in 1706 when she became (at first secretly) second wife of William, son of Sarah COWPER, later Earl C. and Lord Chancellor: Delarivier MANLEY portrays her as subduing him by guile. MC had several children. An outstanding harpsichordist, she annotated erudite books in her library, patronized the writer John Hughes, and corresponded with the future Queen Caroline. When the latter made her a Lady of the Bedchamber, she began a private diary of memorable events to offset the 'perpetual Lies that One hears'; she also turned her husband's political reports into French for the non-English-speaking monarch. The diary gives a penetrating account of Court rivalries and hypocrisies, and her own dealings with her relations, some of whom were place-hunters (through her) and some Jacobites. She wrote it up about once a week, but destroyed a large part early in 1723 during a crisis in Lord C.'s career; what survives, from 1714–16 and 1720, was pub. 1864. She died four months after him, seeming deranged by grief and probably in disgrace with the princess.

Cowper, Sarah, Lady (Holled), 1644–1720, diarist, da. of Anne and of Samuel H., merchant of Eastcheap, London; they both died by 1664, when she married the future Sir William C. (d. 1706). Her sons included Mary COWPER's husband and Judith MADAN's father. Her daily journal entries, 1700–16, fill seven 300-page vols. (Herts Record Office). She leavens pious introspection with some informed and lively comment on public affairs, but sees these and events in her own life chiefly as matters for religious response. On the worst of terms with her husband, she regularly and robustly blames his actions and his 'difficult humour to live at Ease with'.

Craig, Christine (Linch), poet and writer of short stories, scripts, and children's books, b. 1943 at St Andrew, Jamaica, da. of Linda and Winston L. Educ. in Jamaica, she worked in London from 1964 and trained as a journalist on the *Guardian* from 1967. She published *Emmanuel and his Parrot*, 1970, and *Emmanuel Goes to Market*, 1971, married Karl C. (who illustrated them), and had two daughters. A freelance writer from 1972, she published poems and stories in journals like *Savacou* and anthologies like Pamela MORDECAI and Mervyn Morris, eds., *Jamaica Woman*, 1980. Back in Jamaica, working from 1975 at the government Women's Bureau (Acting Director 1977–8), she published a career booklet for women, a text on family life, radio and TV scripts, and a film script (*Women in Crisis*). She took a BA at the Univ. of the West Indies in 1980, and after other jobs returned there to work on research into fertility management. Her poetry volume, *Quadrille for Tigers*, 1984, shows her concern with identity and with the problems of reporting herself and others accurately. She sees black writers as 'Rushing to see, / separately, whatever speaks of our warm, / black roots. Still the cold creeps up / through our careful behaviour ... want to push past the cool that we are', or herself as voyeur peering into the fenced garden of an unmarried neighbour who cares for a blind mother: 'She keeps the half-drawn shutters of her life / Open just so, and mocks my greed and restlessness / With a calm refusal to be other than she seems.'

Craig, Edith, 'Edy', 1869–1947, actress, suffragist, 'creator of a political theatre for the women's suffrage movement'. She was b. in Gusherd Wood Common, Herts., da. of Ellen Terry and Edward Godwin C.; sister of theatre designer Gordon Craig. She lived in Harpenden until her mother's retirement, then in London. She was educ. in Earl's Court, then in Glos. at a school run by an early pioneer of Women's SUFFRAGE, and later in Berlin. She first appeared on stage in 1878 and became a member of the Lyceum Company in 1890. She became a suffragist in 1905, and a member of the Actresses' Franchise League. She directed Cicely HAMILTON's and Christopher ST JOHN's *How the Vote Was Won*, and *The Pageant of Good Women*. In 1911, she formed a women's company, The Pioneer Players: its first matinee presented St John's *The First Actors* and Hamilton's *Jack and Jill and a Friend*, both about exclusion of women from the artistic establishment. Until 1925, the company produced plays about marriage and prostitution, including Margaret Wynn Nevinson's *In the Workhouse*, Laurence Housman's *Pains and Penalties*, Jess Dorynne's *The Surprise of His Life*, Antonia William's *The Street*, Gwen John's *Luck of War* and works by Susan GLASPELL. Later, unable to find work in London because, Julia Holledge suggests in *Innocent Flowers*, 1981 (quoted above), of her relationship with St John, EC worked in various locations (Leeds, Letchworth, York) in the Little Theatre Movement. In 1928, she retired to Small Hythe, where she created the Barn Theatre, mounted luminous Shakespeare productions in memory of her mother, and organized pageants on English history for villages and towns around the country: Holledge thinks her the model for Virginia WOOLF's Miss LaTrobe. See *Ellen Terry's Memoirs*, ed. by EC and Christopher St John, 1933; Edward Percy, *Remember Ellen Terry and Edith Craig*, 1948, and *Edy*, ed. Eleanor Adlard, 1949. Holledge's excellent study gives much detail on EC together with a history of women in the Edwardian theatre.

Craig, Isa, 1831–1903, poet, essayist, feminist, b. Edinburgh, da. of a hosier; she m. her cousin John Knox, iron merchant, in 1866. Poor and largely self-educ., she began writing for periodicals at an early age, serving on the staff of *The Scotsman*. In 1856 she won the Burns Centenary Festival poetry competition and, moving to London in 1857, she was part of the newly formed Langham Place Circle and other feminist groups. A protegée of Bessie PARKES, she was an original staff member of the *English Woman's Journal* and the first woman Assistant Secretary of the National Association for the Promotion of Social Science (an appointment that drew public scorn). Politically active till about 1870, she then withdrew from public life; her essays and pamphlets supported the abolition movement and a strictly academic curriculum for women's education, while her poetry often treated feminist issues. Publications include *Poems*, 1856, *Esther West, a Story*, 1870, *The Little Folks History of England*, 1872, and *Songs of Consolation*, 1874.

Craik, Dinah Maria (**Mulock**), 1826–87, novelist, essayist, poet, b. Stoke-on-Trent, eldest child and only da. of Dinah (Mellard) and Thomas M., feckless and eccentric Irish Baptist preacher committed as a pauper lunatic in the 1830s. DMC was educ. at home with her two younger brothers, and after her mother's death in 1845 was left to provide for the family. Living independently in London, she wrote for *Chambers Magazine*, and produced her first novel, *The Ogilvies*, in 1849. In *A Woman's Thoughts About Women*, 1858, she protests against marriage as the sole female career and demands better education and more professional opportunities for women. She also insists that female independence must include personal financial responsibility. She knew Elizabeth GASKELL, Jane CARLYLE, Anna Maria HALL and Margaret OLIPHANT. In 1865, she m. George Lillie C., the son of old friends and 11 years her junior, and in 1869 adopted a da., Dorothy. Though happily married, she still expressed her belief in the value of self-reliant womanhood. She pub. over 20 novels, several collections of short stories, articles in *Macmillans* and other periodicals, books of poetry, and tales for children. Beneath its veneer of romantic sentimentality, DMC's fiction subverts conventional ideologies about women. Though her best-known work is *John Halifax, Gentleman*, 1858, a study of a self-made man, other novels are enlivened by unconventional female characters. The heroines of *Olive*, 1850, and *The Little Lychetts*, 1855, for example, are artists, while in *The Head of the Family*, 1852, one of the main characters is an actress. DMC's portrayal of matrimony is particularly trenchant: *Agatha's Husband*, 1853, and *Christian's Mistake*, 1865, show how marriage can crush womanly individuality. *A Brave Lady*, 1870, was written in support of the Married Women's Property Act. Her most perceptive discussion of women's attitudes towards love and marriage is in *A Life for a Life*, 1859, in which the double narration of hero and heroine expresses her own questioning of stereotyped sexual roles. See Elaine Showalter's article, *FS* 2 (1975), Sally Mitchell's study, 1983, and Shirley Foster's *Victorian Women's Fiction*, 1985. Her sister-in-law, Georgiana Craik, 1831–95, pub. some 30 undistinguished sensation novels and books for children, as well as periodical contributions, mostly hack-work, but at least one singled out for praise by George ELIOT (*Letters*, IV, 69).

Craik, Helen, 1750?–1825, poet and *MINERVA* novelist, da. of William C. of Arbigland, Dumfries, friend of Maria RIDDELL, said to be sister of Catherine CUTHBERTSON (possibly owing to similar titles). Robert Burns admired her poetry in 1790 and advised on her long *Helen* in 1792 (not now known); her verse praise of him heads the Glenriddell MS of his poems (facs. 1973). *Julia de Saint Pierre*, 1796, written in 'peculiarly painful circumstances', is dedicated to a supportive female friend, anonymous like herself: heroine survives victimization by her degraded but finally penitent mother, her mother's lover, and a young man whose betrayal comes as a surprise. *Henry of Northumberland, or The Hermit's Cell*, 1800, with a strong, gloomy medieval atmosphere, purports to be a fair copy of a 'torn and defaced' MS found in a friend's trunk; *Adelaide de Narbonne, with Memoirs of Charlotte de Cordet*, 1800, makes Corday into a rational republican but omits mention of Marat's bath. *Stella of the North, or The Foundling of the Ship*, 1802, presents *two* mysterious babies, one dead, the other the heroine; last came *The Nun and her Daughter*, 1805. HC draws character well, even (unlike others) the lower classes.

Cramond, Elizabeth Richardson (Beaumont), Baroness of, d. 1651, ADVICE-writer. Da. of Catherine (Farnham) and Sir Thomas B. of Stoughton, Leics., she m. Sir John Ashburnham, had six children, and was left poor when he died in 1620. At Chelsea during plague, 1625, she wrote a letter of advice to her daughters, with prayers and meditations in place of the wealth not now to be theirs. Next year she became second wife of Sir Thomas R., and in 1628 Baroness of C., nominally in her own right, really because his position as a judge barred him from the award. Widowed again in 1634, she sought consolation in writing prayers for each day of the week; a third collection marks a later serious illness. She agreed to publish all three in 1645 as *A Ladies Legacie to her*

Daughters, saying that although a woman's 'endeavour may be contemptible to many', yet 'devotions and prayers ... surely concernes and belongs to women, as well as the best learned men'; daughters (she now adds her sons' wives) 'will not refuse your Mothers teaching'; she does not address her sons 'lest being men, they misconstrue my well-meaning'. (*CBEL* lists the work under 'Advice to a Son').

Crapsey, Adelaide, 1878–1914, poet, teacher, scholar, b. Brooklyn, NY, da. of Adelaide (Trowbridge) and Algernon Sidney C. The third of nine children, AC was educ. first at Kemper Hall, an Episcopal boarding school in Kenosha, Wisconsin, and later at Vassar College, where she was for three years class poet, graduating with Honours in 1901. She taught at Miss Lowe's preparatory school in Stamford, Conn., from 1906 to 1908, when she quit with the onset of TB. Returning to Europe, AC embarked on a wide-ranging programme of reading, then taught poetry at Smith College 1911–13. Both her *Verse*, 1915, and her unfinished *Study in English Metrics*, 1918, were pub. posthumously, although she had earlier tried to publish both. AC invented the cinquain, a five-line poetic form often compared both to Japanese *haiku* and to the short poems of the Imagists. Her collected poems mingle traditional with experimental forms, Christian with classical themes. The cinquain 'Fate Defied' sets forth her reserved and modestly sensual poetic persona: 'As it / Were tissue of silver / I'll wear, O Fate, thy grey, / And go mistily radiant, clad / Like the moon.' *The Complete Poems and Collected Letters of Adelaide Crapsey*, ed. Susan Sutton Smith, 1977, includes biographical and critical essays. See life by Mary E. Osborn, 1933; Karen Alksley-Gut, 1988; study by Edward Butscher, 1979. Papers in the Univ. of Rochester Library and Vassar College Library.

Crawford, Isabella Valancy, 1850?–87, poet, novelist, writer of short stories and fairy tales. One of 12 or 13 children (of whom three survived to adulthood) of Sydney (Scott) and Dr Stephen Dennis C., she was b. in Dublin and educ. at home. The family migrated first to Wisconsin, USA, then, *c.* 1857, to Paisley, Ontario, moving to North Douro (Lakefield, Ont.), 1863, where IVC became acquainted with Catherine Parr TRAILL, and to Peterborough, 1870. They endured poverty and hardship largely because Dr C. (d. 1875) was an alcoholic; much of IVC's writing was deliberately commercial, necessary support for herself and her family. In 1876, her remaining sister died, and about 1880 she moved with her mother to Toronto, where her mother died. She reportedly began writing in childhood; her stories and poems appeared from 1872, first in Canadian, then in American journals. Her only book, *Old Spookses' Pass, Malcolm's Katie, and Other Poems*, 1884, was a critical, not a commercial, success. Influenced by Tennyson, the beautiful natural setting of her early years, and her acquaintance with native peoples, IVC's lyric and narrative poetry incorporates Indian legend, anthropomorphic imagery, and mythic elements in a variety of metrical forms, energetic and incantatory rhythms. A poetry of metaphysical and cosmological significance, it opposes light and dark, summer and winter, life and death, good and evil. Its powerful, original vision of Canadian landscape and its significance in Canadian literature have been recently recognized: *Collected Poems*, 1905 (incomplete and questionably edited), repr., with introduction by James Reaney, 1972; *Hugh and Ion*, part of an unpub. narrative poem, ed. Glenn Clever, 1977; *Selected Stories*, ed. Penny Petrone, 1975; *Fairy Tales*, ed. Petrone and Susan Ross, 1977. *The Halton Boys*, ed. Frank Tierney, 1979, an unpub. boy's adventure set in Canada, includes a checklist of her writings; the Univ. of Ottawa's *Crawford Symposium*, ed. Tierney, 1979, prints essays by Dorothy LIVESAY and Penny Petrone on her life and Fred

Cogswell on her feminism. See also Mary F. Martin's 'Short Life' in *Dalhousie Review* 52, 1972. Papers at Queen's Univ., Kingston, Ont.

Crawford, Mabel Sharman, Irish novelist, probably da. (or granddaughter) of Mabel Fridiswid (C.), heiress, and radical Irish MP William S., later Crawford (by Royal Licence). Her *Life in Tuscany*, 1859, was followed in 1863 by *Through Algeria*, a sharp, forthright and humorous travel book with a strongly-worded feminist preface, 'A Plea for Lady Tourists'. 'The butt of wit and witlings ... the "unprotected" lady looms before the popular gaze as a synonym for ... Gorgon'. Like Isabella BIRD, she 'found buoyant health to which I had long been a stranger' on her travels, undertaken with a female friend. Her novel *The Wilmot Family*, 1864, is disappointing: a wooden, old-fashioned didactic story of a family unexpectedly inheriting wealth, written from a high Tory standpoint.

Cristall, Ann Batten, 1769–after 1816, poet and teacher, b. at Penzance, Cornwall, da. of Elizabeth (Batten) and Alexander C., ship's captain and later sailmaker. He was often away; her mother, who loved literature and classical mythology, taught the family (ABC's brother Joshua was a noted water-colourist). They moved to Rotherhithe and then Blackheath, near London, and ABC published *Poetical Sketches*, Joseph Johnson, 1795. Subscribers included A. L. BARBAULD, Ann JEBB, A. M. PORTER and Mary WOLLSTONECRAFT (a personal friend). ABC says she is young, solitary, inexperienced, not very well-read – but original, a claim she justifies. Her longer narratives achieve the uncanny ('Holbain') or horrific ('The Triumph of Superstition', whose heroine is burned for witchcraft after rejecting the lust of a wicked priest). Characters in her irregular-verse pastoral sketches include a traditional Lysander, the ill-matched couple of Hebe and 'shallow Ned', Urban with his 'soft-breathed flute; / Whose notes, when touch'd with art, / Steal to the inmost heart, / And throw the tyrannizing spirit down', and the Blakean poet Eyezion. She writes ardent lyrics, nature description (of Devon), and lament for genius dying: 'When fled by base delusive gold'. George Dyer, who wanted her to join with Mary HAYS in a novel with inset poems, in 1800 linked her as well-known with e.g. Charlotte SMITH and Hannah MORE.

Crocker, Hannah (Mather), 1752–1829, Boston polemicist, seventh child of Hannah (Hutchinson) and Samuel M., descended from Anne Hutchinson (see PREACHING). She m. Joseph C. in 1779 (having already founded a female Masonic lodge for the purposes of education) and had ten children. As a widow she wrote a *Series of Letters on Free Masonry*, repr. 1815 as by 'a Lady of Boston', from a newspaper of 1810. In 1816 came *The School of Reform* (a TEMPERANCE tract for sailors), and in 1818 (delayed a year by sickness) *Observations on the Real Rights of Women, with their Appropriate Duties, Agreeable to Scripture, Reason and Common Sense*, with her name, dedicated to Hannah MORE. She opens in a scripture context, hoping to avoid dispute about superiority or inferiority but to prove that God gave women 'powers and faculties' equal with men, and 'the same right of judging and acting for themselves'; woman's 'original right and dignity', lost at the Fall, has been restored by Christianity. She defends female learning, tellingly quotes Lucy AIKIN and other British and US women, yet stresses the need to please men. An unpub. work on Boston history is in the New England Historic Society.

Croker, B. M. (Bithia May or Mary) (Sheppard), *c.* 1849–1920, Irish novelist, eldest da. of the Rev. William S. of Gilgefin, Co. Roscommon, writer and controversialist, who d. when she was seven; her family on both sides were old Irish Puritans. Educ. at Rockferry, Cheshire, and Tours, France, she was a famous horsewoman, hunting with the Kildares. She m. very young and with her husband, L. Col. John C., spent 14 years in Burma and India, where in 1880 she began writing as distraction from the hot season. Written in secret, then read aloud to other women with encouraging response, her first novel, *Proper Pride*, 1881?, had good reviews (three eds. in six weeks; 12 by 1896) and was thought to be by a man. Entertainingly written, in a sophisticated style ('I need scarcely tell the astute reader'), it shows open sympathy with the male viewpoint and metes out punishing treatment to its spirited, horse-riding heroine, whose distrustful pride separates her from her devoted husband. *Pretty Miss Neville*, 1883, even more successful, was followed by more novels dealing with life in India or Burma, including *The Road to Mandalay*, 1917, full of upright men and calculating women, and later made into a film. Other novels treated upper-class life in Ireland, where she and her husband retired, and were visited at Bray by Helen Black, who wrote on BMC in 1896.

Croker, Margaret Sarah, poet and novelist, b. 1773 at Holbeton, Devon, da. of Mary and Capt. Richard C. Just before his death in 1816 she contacted the RLF and began to think of earning by her pen (a brother's education had cost a lot). Her poems are well-written, feeling, but not remarkable: memorial tributes to Princess Charlotte, 1817, Sir Samuel Romilly, 1818, and Queen Victoria's father, 1820 (with hopes for his baby's future reign), and a volume by subscription, *Nugae Canorae*, 1818. Her extant novel, *The Question, Who is Anna?*, 1818, is extraordinary. Without excitement or condemnation, with understated ironic sympathy, it presents the heroine's birth to under-age, unmarried parents; the baffled, reluctant kindness this meets from father-figures and the cheerful amorality of servants (fine portrait of the uneducated, strong, loving Ruth); and her mother's later, faithless, grand marriage. Despite some slippage into melodrama, it subtly penetrates the difficulty of understanding one's own motives or governing one's own actions. MC mentions her *Henry de Courtenay* and *The Widow of Wingfield* (untraced), and a novel unpub. in 1825.

'Cromarty, Deas', Elizabeth Sophia Fletcher (later Mrs Robert Addison Watson), d. 1918, regional novelist. Da. of Elizabeth Sophia (Holmes), an artistic and cultivated woman, and the Rev. John F., a Wesleyan minister, she m. Robert Addison W., minister of the Free Church of Scotland. Her works written from 1873 until 1911 under Fletcher included religious studies as well as some tales, such as *Crabtree Fold*, 1881. Under Cromarty, she wrote five novels from *This Man's Dominion*, 1894, to *Lauder and her Lovers*, 1902, as well as *Scottish Ministerial Miniatures*, 1892, tales collected from hundreds which appeared in *British Weekly* and other periodicals, and *Picturesque Lancashire*, 1906, in the Shire series. Her dark and moody Yorkshire novels, including *A High Little World*, 1892, and *Under God's Sky*, 1895, make use of dialect and have a strong sense of place: wild moorland, smoky manufacturing towns, and small enclosed communities of narrow religious persuasion, where the surviving women are strong. See her husband's memoir prefaced to *The Heir of All Things* [1919].

Crommelin, May, Maria Henrietta de la Cherois, *c*. 1850–1930, Irish novelist and traveller, second da. of Anna-Maria (Thompson) and Samuel de la Cherois Crommelin of Carrowdore Castle, Co. Down, whose mother Elizabeth (Mullins) had been to the Bath school kept by Hannah More's sisters. MC was educ. at home, and later travelled widely (N. and S. America, W. Indies, Syria, Palestine, Japan), producing travel books, e.g. *Over the Andes*, 1896, and some 40 novels. Her first, *Queenie*, 1874, has a girl narrator who is aware of the gulf her intelligence puts between her and most young men she meets: 'Fatally gifted as I was by nature with a keen insight into failings and weakness of intellect' (3, 83). Her later novels often have unusual plots and settings (e.g. *For the Sake of the Family*, 1892, set on ship to S. Africa; *Half Round the World for Love*, 1896, in which an English girl marries a Chilean by proxy), but their style became increasingly clichéd. There is an autograph family history by MC's aunt Maria de la C. C., 1853, in Sydney University Library.

'Crompton, Richmal' (Richmal Crompton Lamburn), 1890–1969, novelist. B. at Bury, Lancs., da. of Clara (C.) and the Rev. Edward L., she was educ. at the Clergy Daughters' boarding school in Warrington (later at Darley Dale, Derbyshire; she was also a pupil-teacher there) and Royal Holloway College, London Univ. (BA in classics, 1914). She taught classics at Darley Dale, then Bromley High School, but retired in 1924, soon after contracting polio which left her lame (though mobile). As a teacher, needing anonymity for her first writings, she used her Christian names (one her mother's birth name). She depicted her schooldays, early relationships and experiences in her third novel, *Anne Morrison*, 1925. Feminism is a tenuous thread throughout RC's fiction: Anne is relieved when war exempts her from total commitment to the suffragist cause; women have a problem over independence, often solved by inheritance from distant unknown relations. RC's famous 'William' writings (first magazine story, 1919; 39 books, 1922–70) feature four pre-pubescent boy 'outlaws' inventively disrupting their stuffy middle-class milieu. (The only little girl around is a stooge for adult authority.) Intended for adults, acclaimed by children, adapted for radio, films and TV, these books brought RC financial security and her own house, 1928; but she saw as more important her 50 other novels (many middle-class family chronicles) and short-story volumes. *Frost at Morning*, 1950, demonstrates anew her skill at depicting childhood. The stories in *A Monstrous Regiment* [1927] exemplify the possessive, life-denying, self-deceived women who recur (along with more attractive specimens of womanhood) in the novels. Her portraits of men tend to be less vivid. Kay Williams's biography is more informative than Mary Cadogan's (both 1986).

Crosby, 'Caresse', Mary Phelps (Jacob), 1892–1970, poet, memoirist, journalist, b. in NYC, da. of well-to-do Mary (Phelps) and William J. (who shaped, she said, her 'indestructible idealism'). She was educ. privately, at home (where she wrote a first poem beginning 'O wonderful, beautiful Springtime', and her *Madison Avenue Gazette* reached a print-run of 20) and at NY schools. In her early twenties she earned $1,500 by patenting the unwired brassière. She 'stepped right into a bonded circle of Boston hierarchs' by marrying Richard Rogers Peabody in 1915, and had two children. After an attempt at film acting and a notorious divorce, both 1921, she 'became a rebel' by marrying her lover, the writer Harry C., in 1922; they settled in Paris. Her poem 'Harry' opens *Crosses of Gold*, her first poetry volume, printed in a limited ed. with her own watercolours, and a larger edition, both 1925. After her *Graven Images*, 1926, she and Harry C. published under their own imprints: from Editions Narcisse (4 vols. by CC, 1927–8, including a limited ed. of her epic poem *The Stranger*); from The Black Sun (a joint translation of Proust letters, 1930; CC's *Poems for Harry Crosby*, 1931; papers at Southern Ill. Univ.). CC says the presses, of which she took primary charge, were 'born of Necessity and Desire' ('the simplest way to get a poem into a book was to print the book'), but they published others like Joyce, Lawrence, Hart Crane, Ezra Pound and Kay BOYLE (a friend who dedicated two books to CC). In 1929 Harry C. (always erratic and unfaithful, mystically obsessed with death since WWI, which had left CC's first husband a near-alcoholic) died in a suicide pact with a lover. CC continued the Black Sun and Crosby Continental Editions, an avant-garde paperback house. Except *The Stranger*, her own work avoids experiment: she called it 'easeful cliché and well-worn rhyme'. During WWII she ran the Crosby Gallery of Modern Art (Washington, DC), combated racial segregation, and staged the dramatic version of BEHN's *Oroonoko*. She founded *Portfolio: An International Review*, 1945 (published in four countries, always giving the original with its translations), and headed international bodies like Women Against War and Citizens of the World. *The Passionate Years*, 1953, rev. 1955, describes, 'the way they live in my memory', her happy childhood and enthusiastic maturity, ending on a plea for ensuring to 'unborn citizens' the means to personal life and individual expression. See Boyle and Harry T. Moore in *Icarus* 3, 1977; life by Anne Conover, 1989. Papers at Southern Ill. Univ., Carbondale.

Crosland, Camilla Dufour (Toulmin), 'Mrs Newton Crosland', 1812–95, poet and novelist, b. London, da. of William T., solicitor. Her mother was a Wright, related to Mary BERRY. Camilla had two half-brothers from her father's first marriage, and a younger brother. Despite lacking systematic education, she was a precocious child with a love of reading. Her father died when she was young; to provide income she made jewellery, and worked as a teacher and governess; she was also an expert on heraldry. Though one or two early pieces were pub. anon., she first appeared in print with verses in the *Book of Beauty*, 1838. She continued publishing in periodicals, including *Chambers*, to which she contributed for 54 years. Editor of the *Ladies Companion* and sub-editor of *Friendship's Offering*, she wrote stories for the latter under the names 'Emma Grey', 'Mrs Macarthy' and 'Helena Herbert'. She knew many literary women including Mary Cowden CLARKE, Mary HOWITT, Mary MITFORD, Geraldine JEWSBURY, Catherine CROWE, Lady BLESSINGTON, Frances BROWNE, and formed a close relationship with the young Dinah Mulock CRAIK, who was bridesmaid when she m. Newton C. in 1848 (he was at first uncertain which to marry). *Lydia, A Woman's Book*, 1852, depicts life from a woman's point of view, while *Mrs Blake: A Story of Twenty Years*, 1862, advocates the necessity of a 'room of one's own' for young women. In 1854 she became interested in spiritualism, discussing this with the Brownings in Italy in 1857. *Landmarks of a Literary Life 1820–1892*, 1893, is remarkably feminist in tone and includes portraits of Grace AQUILAR, and of her American friends and acquaintances such as Charlotte Cushman, Hawthorne, H. B. STOWE, Madame Le Vert, Grace GREENWOOD and Margaret FULLER. Included in her husband's autobiography, *Rambles Round My Life*, 1898, are extracts from her autobiographical MS which reflect her enterprising spirit in the hardship years following her father's death.

Cross, Zora, 1890–1964, poet and novelist, b. Eagle Farm, Queensland, da. of Mary (Skyring) and Ernest C., accountant. Educ. at Sydney Girls' High and Sydney Teachers' College, she taught for three years before becoming an actress and, later, a journalist. She scandalized the literary establishment by her long *de facto* relationship with the editor of the *Bulletin*'s 'Red Page', David McKee Wright. She had two children with him and two by previous lovers. Her work was as controversial as her life, particularly the love sonnets in *A Song of Mother Love*, 1916, *Songs of Love and Life*, 1917, and *The Lilt of Life*, 1919, which give an unusually frank expression of woman's sexuality. Other works include *Elegy on an Australian Schoolboy*, 1921, about the death of her young brother in WWI, a lyrical collection of children's verse, *The City of Riddle-me-Ree*, 1918, and the critical pamphlet,

An Introduction to the Study of Australian Literature, 1922. Novels *Daughters of the Sun*, 1924, and *The Lute Girl of Rainyvale*, 1925, are romances set in the Queensland bush, while *This Hectic Age*, 1944, tells of a country girl's experiences in the big city; 'The Victor' was serialized in the *Sydney Morning Herald*, 1933. Her MSS and papers are in the Univ. of Sydney Library, Mitchell Library and Latrobe Library.

'Cross(e), Victoria', Vivian Cory, d. 1930s, English novelist, da. of Fanny (Griffin) and Arthur Cory, Colonel in the Indian army: sister of 'Laurence HOPE' (Adela Nicolson) and Isabell Tate, who became editor of the *Sind Gazette* in India. Very little is known of VC's life; she never married, and after many years in India, as well as world travel with her uncle after her father's death, retired to Monte Carlo to live among women friends. She wrote many popular novels with a frankness about female sexual desire regarded as shocking at the time; the most successful was *Anna Lombard*, 1901, whose heroine persuades her new husband to let her continue her pre-marital affair. Others include *The Woman who Didn't*, 1895 (a riposte to Grant Allan's bestseller *The Woman Who Did*) and *Life of My Heart* (19th ed. 1905), about a woman who is spurned by her father for running away with a native Indian. Most of her novels employ male narrators; all were castigated by reviewers. Her last was *Martha Brown, M.P.*, 1935. There is a brief account of her in Sewell Stokes's *Pilloried*, 1928. She dropped the 'e' from her pseudonym after Queen VICTORIA's death.

Crothers, Rachel, 1878–1958, playwright and screen-writer, b. Bloomington Ill., youngest child of Marie Louise (DePew) and Eli Kirk C. Both parents were doctors (her mother, who in 1878 had just begun training, became the first woman to practise in Illinois), but RC (who had 'transcendent ambition') never considered a life outside the theatre. She wrote and produced a family melodrama at 12, graduated from high school in 1891, studied elocution briefly in Boston, settled in NYC at 16, took a one-term acting course ('Not that I needed it at all') at the Stanhope-Wheatcroft school, where she then taught and directed students in her own plays (some at minor theatres from 1899: several on New Women who are admired but not loved by men). She acted from 1897. *The Three of Us*, 1906, began a group of plays she called a 'Dramatic History of Women'. Its heroine, with the habit of freedom and 'the courage of belief in herself', saves and manages her family; critics approved because by the end her 'sphere is narrowed down . . . her view smilingly fixed upon a wedding ring'. RC began directing with *Myself Bettina*, 1908. The reforming feminist heroine of *A Man's World*, 1909, declares 'I am a natural woman because I am a free one'; she is deeply disappointed when the man she loves upholds the double moral standard; they separate. *He and She*, 1911 (also called *The Herfords*), was less successful at first, but often revived, e.g. 1920, 1980. In it a dual-career couple (sculptors) resolve their problems when the wife, out of perceived duty to her daughter, turns over her prize commission to her husband. In 1912 RC warned, 'Watch women. Their evolution is the most important thing in modern life.' But after *Ourselves*, 1913, about prostitution, she moved from social problems towards comedy and satire on women's follies: in 1914 came *Young Wisdom*, on 'extreme' feminism, and *The Heart of Paddy Whack*, Irish romance. RC set up and ran Stage Women's War Relief in WWI, and similar projects in the Depression and WWII. Her heroines range from flappers (*Nice People*, 1921) to those in middle age (*When Ladies Meet*, 1932, which gently rules out extramarital love) or old age (*Old Lady 31*, 1916). Her pictures of women's lives are ironic and double-sided: in *Susan and God*, staged 1937 as her last play, the protagonist gives up an alleged religious calling for that of wife and mother. RC lost money directing Zoë AKINS's *Thou Desperate Pilot*, 1927, wrote of her work in the joint *Art of Playwriting*, 1928, and did some Hollywood screenwriting. In 1945 and 1950 she withdrew plays from rehearsal. Study by Lois C. Gottlieb, 1979, lists archives.

Crowe, Catherine (Stevens), 1790(?1800)–1872, novelist, essayist, dramatist, translator, short-story writer, b. Borough Green, Kent, da. of John S. Educ. at home, she m. in 1822 Lt Col. John C. (d. 1860), and they moved to Edinburgh. CC's morbidity and passion for spiritualism and the supernatural culminated in a brief but violent attack of insanity *c.* 1859, when she was arrested and jailed. She was a pioneer of domestic realism in her concern with simple characters in domestic environments, but much of her writing (novels and stories) is a curious combination of the mundane, sensational and sentimental, mingled with conventional morality. *Lilly Dawson*, 1847, contains ghosts, brutal murders, criminal activities, and amazing coincidences, plus social commentary about poverty and female oppression. CC's novels also take up issues such as the inadequacy of female EDUCATION and the evils of forced marriages; her women are frequently tough-minded and courageous. The eponymus heroine of *Susan Hopley*, 1841, determines to discover and expose her brother's murderer, and triumphs over male treachery; in *Men and Women*, 1844, the heroine boldly sets out alone to solve the problems created by male cowardice; *Linny Lockwood*, 1854, portrays an abandoned wife who establishes a liaison with her husband's deserted mistress, and resolutely refuses to pardon him despite his pleas for forgiveness. CC also wrote stories for children, two plays, a treatise, *Spiritualism and The Age We Live In*, 1859, and a collection of ghost stories, *The Night Side of Nature*, 1848; she also adapted *Uncle Tom's Cabin* for young readers. Chambers's *Vestiges of Creation*, 1844, was mistakenly attributed to her.

Cruger, Mary, 1834–1908, novelist, b. Westchester Co., NY, da. of Eliza (Kortright) and Nicholas C. A strong advocate of self-sufficiency, MC built herself a house and took up writing after both parents died. Notable in her five novels for addressing social problems with sympathetic understanding, MC's reformist zeal gains force from her acute psychological insights. Her first, *Hyperaesthesia*, 1885, set in an exclusive New York health resort, concerns the morbid invalidism of a leisured class of women. Despite the inertia of the central characters and the prevalence of the fragile, pallid, shrinking women with 'whims', dialogues reveal a latent female power only thinly disguised by enforced idleness. *A Den of Thieves*, 1886, a TEMPERANCE novel, features a strong reformist woman rejecting traditional female roles. MC's fearless and indomitable heroine, Ruth, in *The Vanderheyde Manor-House*, 1887, exemplifies most of the strong qualities that MC herself upholds in her autobiographical work, *How She Did It. Or, Comfort on $150 a Year*, 1888. Renovation of the decaying mansion rests solely in Ruth's capable hands; her skills with chisels, saws and hammers are matched by a keen intuitive sense and a sharp intelligence that invariably outwits her menfolk. More sympathetic, in all her novels, to the bonds of affection between sister and brother than to industrial brotherhood, in *Brotherhood*, 1891, MC takes a stand against labour unions. Her heroine, Meta, urges that true brotherhood should be cemented 'with love and kindly deeds', not 'violence and wrong'. Repudiating dependency, Meta also demands the right to work. 'A woman had best work, be it ever so hard, than to accept the support of another's labor. That is charity . . .'.

Cullwick, Hannah, 1833–1909, diarist, maid-of-all-work, pot-girl, b. Shifnal, Shropshire, da. of a housemaid and saddler: chiefly remembered for her relationship with upper-middle-class Arthur Munby, poet and barrister, kept secret during their 54 years together. They married in 1873, but HC refused the role of 'lady', seeing more dignity in remaining his servant. The story emerged when Munby's will was published in 1910, and caused a furore. A significant part of the Munby collection at Trinity College, Cambridge, is by HC. Her 17 diaries run from 1854 to 1873, giving details of daily life for Victorian servants and revealing an intelligent, forthright observer. Initially written for him, detailing her jobs, later they were for herself. Although he encouraged her to write, he did not want her to educate herself by reading or 'be anything higher'. Selections have been edited by Liz Stanley, 1984. See also Derek Hudson's life of Munby, 1972.

Cummins, Maria Susanna, 1827–66, novelist, b. Salem, Mass., da. of Mehitable (Cave) and David C., judge, of Norfolk County. She was educ. by her father, who encouraged her interest in literature, and at Mrs Charles Sedgwick's School, Lenox, Mass. Her magazine stories were pub. in the *Atlantic Monthly* when she was 20. In 1854 she pub. anon. her first novel, *The Lamplighter* (repr. 1988), an instant best-seller which sold 40,000 copies in two months. Pious and moralistic, it inspired Hawthorne's famous letter to his publisher protesting about the 'damned mob of scribbling women' who were dominating sales of American books with 'trash' (*Letters to Tickner*, 1, 75). MC's second novel, *Mabel Vaughan*, 1857, was a similar smug, sentimental formula-novel, whose heroine is a symbol of proper feminine virtue. She pub. two more novels, *El Fureidis*, 1860, and *Haunted Hearts*, 1864, but none had the success of her first. Her characterization, although potentially realistic, is weakened by her artificial melodramatic style. After her father's death she settled in Dorchester, where she died at the age of 39. See Nina Baym, 1978, for a discussion of her work.

Cunard, Nancy, 1896–1965, poet, publisher, journalist, political activist. B. in Leics, only child of Maud Alice (Burke), an American-born hostess and patron of the arts in England, and Sir Bache C., of the shipping family, she was educated by governesses and at exclusive schools in London and abroad. She left her mother's fashionable, establishment circle to conduct a sexually and socially unorthodox life. During the 1920s (of which, to her distress, she became an emblem), she knew, among many others, Pound, Lewis, T. S. Eliot, Aldous Huxley, Virginia WOOLF in England, the dadaists and Surrealists, expatriate Americans in Paris (where she moved in 1920). Her poems first appeared in Edith SITWELL's *Wheels*, 1916, then in her collections, *Outlaws*, 1921, and *Sublunary*, 1923. Leonard and Virginia Woolf published *Parallax*, 1925. In 1928, she established The Hours Press, publishing Aldington, Pound, Beckett, Aragon, Laura RIDING. Her mother's reaction to her relationship with black musician Henry Crowder provoked her *Black Man and White Ladyship*, 1931, a bridge-burning attack on her mother and the British aristocracy. Her ANTHOLOGY, *Negro*, 1934, presented a record of 'the struggles and achievements, the persecutions and the revolts against them, of the Negro people'. Having begun as an aesthete, NC now sought to politicize writers and artists, working for the Scottsboro Boys, Ethiopia and Republican Spain. Her diary notes the 'three main things' as 'Equality of races. Of sexes. Of classes.' Her later memoirs of Norman Douglas, 1954, and George Moore, 1956, as well as *These Were the Hours*, 1969, give information on her life as do Hugh Ford, 1968, and Ann Chisholm, 1979. Papers and letters at the Univs. of Texas and Southern Illinois, and Library of Congress. See Benstock, 1986, and Patricia Clements in *DR*, 66, 1986.

Cuney-Hare, Maud, 1874–1936, biographer, folklorist, music historian and pianist, b. at Galveston, Texas, da. of

Adeline (Dowdie), musician, and Norris Wright Cuney, businessman and politician: both highly cultured offspring of slaves and slave-owners. After Central High School, Galveston, the New England Conservatory, Boston, and private teaching by eminent musicians, she became director of two Texas colleges. Back in Boston in 1906, she m. William P. Hare, and published much music journalism, an evocative life of her father as 'A Tribune of the Black People', 1913, and a poetry anthology, 1918. She set up a Musical Art Studio and a black theatre group where she directed her own *Antar*, about a seventh-century Arab poet (pub. in Willis Richardson, ed., 1930). A collector and performer of folk songs from the Caribbean, Mexico, Africa and USA, she was first to popularize New Orleans music in *Six Creole Folk-Songs* [1921], and in Nancy CUNARD's *Negro*, 1934 (which also has a piece by her on Puerto Rican music). Her last work was the learned and fascinating *Negro Musicians and Their Music*, 1936, repr. 1967.

Cunningham, Lady **Margaret**, d. after 1622, Scots memoirist and letter-writer, da. of Margaret (Campbell) and James C., Earl of Glencairn. She m., 1598, Sir James Hamilton of Crawfordjohn, also called Master of Evandale, who was publicly 'unkind, cruell and malicious', refused her money for food, 'gave credit to misreports' and turned her out naked in the middle of the night. A keen Protestant, she wrote to him in prose and 'unformall' verse while reconciled, rejoicing in the prospect of his salvation from iniquity and 'that most detestable idollatrie of the papists', and reporting her own 'many strong and dangerous conflicts with my spirituall adversaries'. After bearing her fifth child, however, she refused to sleep with him becuse of his adultery and 'excommunication for slaughter'; by 1608, when she wrote out her story (NLS; pub. Edinburgh, 1827), she had left him. Widowed, she found a loving husband in Sir James Maxwell of Calderwood. Widowed again, with six more children and near death in 1622, she sent her sister-in-law an impassioned plea to see justice and charity done them all; she mentions her love for her mother, and godly women's influence for good.

Curwen, Alice, d. 1679, Quaker minister and writer of an autobiography pub. with many letters as part of the *Relation of ...*, 1680. About 1641 she m. Thomas C. In 1660 when God, she said, told her to go to Boston, Thomas contested the validity of the command and refused to accompany her; but 'the Lord made me willing to leave all (that was near and dear to me) and ... having got my Bed and Clothes on board the Ship, it pleased the Lord (in whom was and is my Trust) to send my Husband to go along with me.' They travelled widely in America and the West Indies, and were beaten and imprisoned. In Barbados 1676–7, she argued the right of black slaves to attend Quaker meetings regardless of the opinions of their owners. She mentions Ranter disruptions, and attempted to alter the system of Women's Meetings.

Curzon, Sarah Anne (Vincent), 1833–98, poet, journalist, feminist. B. in Birmingham, England, da. of Mary Amelia (Jackson) and George Philips V., she was educ. at home and private school. She m. Robert C., 1858, migrating with him to Canada, 1862. A contributor to many journals, including the *Canada Monthly, Dominion Illustrated, Grip* (a brilliant satirical weekly), *The Week*, and *Canadian Magazine*, for two years she wrote a column in *Canada Citizen* on women's issues. Throughout her career, she spoke out strongly on women's rights, including SUFFRAGE and university EDUCATION. SC wrote much patriotic poetry and prose, often celebrating the United Empire Loyalists and the heroes of 1812. *Laura Secord, the Heroine of 1812: A Drama, And Other Poems*, 1887, joins her patriotism and feminism. A carefully researched presentation of Secord's heroic crossing of enemy lines to warn the British of impending attack (as is also SC's narrative account, *The Story of Laura Secord, 1813*, 1891), it made Secord's name a household word. The 1887 volume also includes *The Sweet Girl Graduate*, a comic play requested by *Grip*. This tells of a young woman who, disguising herself as a man, graduates as Gold Medallist at the Univ. of Toronto. SC was first president of the Women's Canadian Historical Society and an active lecturer on historical subjects.

Cusack, Ellen **Dymphna**, 1902–81, novelist, dramatist and travel writer, b. Wyalong, NSW, da. of Beatrice (Crowley) and James C. She attended St Ursula's College, Armidale, then Sydney Univ., graduating in 1926. A teacher for more than 20 years, she also broadcast on education and women's issues, and worked for women's groups and the peace movement from the 1930s. She gave up teaching in 1944 and was forced to dictate most of her work because of a neuralgic disease. A prolific writer whose work was translated into 15 other languages (in Eastern Europe she sold millions of copies), she is best remembered for her socialist-realist novel set in wartime Sydney, *Come in Spinner*, 1951 (with Florence James, who ed. and introduced the first unexpurgated edition, 1989), and her assistance in the autobiographical *Caddie*, 1953, based on the life of a barmaid and popularized as a film, 1976. She wrote 11 other novels between 1936 and 1971, seven published plays, including the popular *Pacific Paradise*, 1963, dealing with the nuclear issue, three travel books, including *Chinese Women Speak*, 1958, and a book for children. Her work often focuses on the alienation of individuals in their social contexts, and is harshly critical of the racism, sexism, and general complacency of post-war Australian society. *Jungfrau*, 1936, examines the plight of the unmarried pregnant woman; *Say No To Death*, 1951, written to dispel ignorance of TB, proved highly influential in improving hospital conditions; others deal with racism or neo-Nazism. Even her humorous fiction has its serious aspect: *Pioneers on Parade*, 1939 (with Miles FRANKLIN; repr. 1988), satirizes the snobbery and vain posturing of the 1938 sesquicentenary celebrations. Notable amongst her plays is *Morning Sacrifice*, 1943, remarkable for its all-female cast and its moving denunciation of sexual double standards in a girls' school. Her books received many awards, and DC herself received the Queen's Silver Jubilee Medal, 1977, and the AM, 1981. See the life by her husband, Norman Freehill, 1975 (with DC's assistance). Papers and MSS are in the National Library, Canberra.

Cushing, Eliza Lanesford (**Foster**), 1794–after 1854, novelist, sister of Harriet CHENEY, with whom she shared her first publication. Next came two novels about the clash and later resolution between parties and generations in the infant USA. In *Saratoga, A Tale of the Revolution*, 1824, the heroine, daughter of an English soldier in America, differs from him in favouring the cause of independence. She picks her American suitor (her loyalist one settles for her cousin). Scenes are set in military and Indian camps; the father at last becames 'an American in heart' and tells his grandchildren stories of courage on both sides. In *Yorktown, An Historical Romance*, 1826, dedicated to Lafayette (who appears on page one) the clash between young idealists (two English/American, one French) and a vicious, corrupt, loyalist uncle is complicated by a tale of concealed parentage and usurped inheritance. EFC m. Montréal physician Frederick C. (d. 1846). She was associate editor of *The Literary Garland*, 1838–51, variously subtitled *Canadian* or *British North American Magazine*, which pub. much prose and verse by her (mainly religious narrative or dialogue), as well as by her sisters Cheney and T. D. Foster, later Gibson, and Susanna MOODIE and *her* sisters: see index by Mary Markham Brown, 1962. She and Cheney also ed. *The Snow-Drop*, for children, 1847–51. Most notable of her later works is *Esther, a Sacred Drama, with Judith, a Poem*, 1840, on biblical heroines able with 'frail woman's hand' to 'dare a desperate deed'.

Cushing, Enid Louise, detective writer publishing under her mother's name, 'Mabel Louise Dawson'. Between 1953 and 1957 she published at least five lively romantic mysteries set in Canada and published in New York. *Blood on My Rug*, 1956, is set in Montréal (her home town), its protagonist a bookstore owner who finds a man's body in her office and becomes romantically involved with the police inspector she helps resolve the murder. Like the others, it uses realistic dialogue, intriguing plots, happy endings.

Custer, Elizabeth (Bacon), 1842–1933, journalist and memoirist, b. Monroe, Michigan, only da. of Eleanor Sophia (Page) and Judge Daniel S. B., who d. when she was 12. She was educ. at Boyd Seminary in Monroe and the Young Ladies' Institute in Auburn, NY. In 1864 she m. George Armstrong (later General) C., officer in the Union army. After the Civil War, EBC followed Custer's regiment through Kansas and Texas, later writing about her experiences of military life. After her husband died in battle with the Sioux at Little Big Horn, EBC had to support herself and her husband's parents. Moving to NYC, EBC became secretary to the Society of Decorative Arts, then turned to writing, both to uphold her husband's posthumous reputation and for money. *Boots and Saddles*, 1885, recalls the years 1873–6 spent on the Dakota frontier, while *Tenting on the Plains*, 1887, covers the aftermath of the Civil War and praises the cameraderie of regimental life in which she was frequently the only woman. *Following the Guidon*, 1890 (repr. 1960), which covers the years 1867–9, includes the story of two white women ransomed from the Indians. When one of them is later blamed by her husband for being raped in captivity, EBC shows an awareness of the idiocy of blaming the victim. After 1890 EBC spent her life overseeing the placement of monuments to Custer, lecturing and travelling. She spent summers at Onteora, an artists' colony in the Catskills, and was friendly with Mary Mapes DODGE, Susan COOLIDGE and Ella Wheeler WILCOX. See Laurence A. Frost, 1976, for her life.

Cuthbertson, Catherine, novelist in Ann RADCLIFFE style. She has been called sister to Helen CRAIK; but the comedy *Anna* (staged 1793, unpub.) is listed as by *Miss* Cuthbertson. It presents its heroine (confined in an ancient castle by a wicked stepmother) with wit and levity; a prologue canvasses antifeminist prejudice. CC's seven heavily moralized, romantic adventure stories employ foreign and conventual settings, arresting openings (often, like *Rosabella*, 1817, by the seaside at night), flowery style, and complicated family situations extending over several generations. The brother-and-sister hero and heroine of the anonymous *Romance of the Pyrenees*, 1803, begin their tribulations 'as faultless as nature and education can make them'. Later title-pages go on describing her as author of this and *Santo Sebastiano, or The Young Protector*, 1806. *Adelaide, or The Countercharm*, 1813, full of persecuting father-figures, gives its heroine at last 'complete and permanent' felicity; *The Hut and the Castle*, 1823, foregrounds a bandit-villain; *Sir Ethelbert, or The Dissolution of the Monasteries*, 1830, has footnotes which reflect wide historical reading.

Cutts, Mrs (but unmarried), moral writer, friend of Sarah SCOTT, perhaps model for a *Millenium Hall* character. She subscribed to Mary LEAPOR's poems, 1751, was pursued by Sterne, 1765, and addressed her didactic poem *Almeria, or Parental Advice*, 1775, 'By a Friend to the Sex' to 'the Daughters of

Great Britain and Ireland'. Everyone subscribed (to benefit 'Two Worthy Persons'): 240 men, over 560 women, BLUESTOCKINGS, BOWDLERS, Samuel Johnson, many Yorkshire people (Doncaster appears with London on the title-page). In elegant heroic couplets a father offers his daughter conservative advice, praising Scott, Barbara Montagu, and Georgiana DEVONSHIRE. He counsels independence in religion – 'Judge for thyself; nor idly rest thy faith / On what another, tho' a Parent, saith' – but submission in marriage: 'let it be the purpose of thy life / To please at home.'

D

Dacier, Anne (Lefevre), 1654–?1720, French critic and scholar, da. of Tanneguy Le Fèvre, professor of Greek at Saumur. She m. her fellow-scholar André D. in 1683; her published work helped establish a female presence in academic studies. (Her horoscope at birth was said to have caused consternation by predicting 'a fortune and fame quite foreign to a woman'.) Her scholarly French prose versions of the *Iliad*, 1711, and *Odyssey*, 1716 (which Pope found useful), and her *Remarks* on his poetic version (englished in 1724), were the basis of her British fame.

Dacre, Barbarina Brand (Ogle), Lady, later Wilmot, 1768–1854, playwright and translator. Youngest of three daughters of Hester (Thomas) and Admiral Sir Chaloner Ogle, she was privately educ. with emphasis on French and Italian, m., 1789, Valentine Wilmot, a Guards officer, but later separated and moved to Hampton Court, where she devoted herself to educating her da. Arabella (b. 1796), writing plays, and translating Italian poetry. M. 1819 Thomas B., Baron D., a Whig peer. Two years later her *Dramas, Translations and Occasional Poems* appeared. One of the four dramas, *Ina*, set in Anglo-Saxon times, ran for one night (22 April 1815) at Drury Lane. More admired were her translations from Petrarch, which were reprinted by Ugo Foscolo in his *Essays on Petrarch*, 1823, and in her own *Translations from the Italian*, 1836. Belonging to a 'blue' circle, she knew many of the leading artistic, literary, theatrical and political figures of her day, and was noted for her modelling in wax and her talent as a letter-writer. Her occasional verse too shows skill and wit. She revised and ed. the two colls. of stories by her daughter, Arabella Sullivan, *Recollections of a Chaperone*, 1831, and *Tales of the Peerage and Peasantry*, 1835 (both pub. anon.); the latter's death in 1839 darkened her last years, as did her own increasing deafness. See also Barbarina, Lady Grey, *A Family Chronicle*, ed. G. Lyster, 1908.

Dacre, Charlotte (King), later Byrne, 'Rosa Matilda', b. *c.* 1782, sensational novelist and poet, da. of the notorious London Jewish money-lender, blackmailer and radical writer John K. (or Jacob Rey) and his first wife, Deborah (Lara), divorced by Jewish law in 1785 on his marriage to a countess. In 1798 (the year he went bankrupt and was arrested on the evidence of whores) CD and her sister Sophia KING dedicated to him by name their juvenile *Trifles from Helicon* (sentiment, mouldering skulls, ghosts), to show 'the education you have afforded us has not been totally lost'. As 'Rosa Matilda' she visited R. F. A. Le DESPENSER and dedicated *The Confessions of the Nun of St Omer*, 1805, to M. G. Lewis; later title-pages often name her both thus and as Dacre; Byron disparaged her by the pseudonym in 1809. The verse *Hours of Solitude*, 1805 (facs. 1978), adds new poems to others pub. in 1798 and in her sister's 1801 novel; lyrics for music accompany *George the Fourth*, 1822. Most popular was her melodramatic *Zofloya, or The Moor*, 1806, a fifteenth-century GOTHIC romance owing much to Lewis's *Monk* and Jacobean drama. Presented as a moral warning against the passions, it sets illicit love and revenge amid the sublime scenery of the Appennines: the female protagonist ends in the arms of the Moorish slave, who reveals himself as the devil and flings her over a precipice. It influenced P. B. Shelley's

Zastrozzi, 1811, and became a chapbook, *The Daemon of Venice*, 1810. *The Libertine*, 1807, had three eds that year; *The Passions*, 1811, is epistolary. Little is known of CD's later life. She was Mrs Byrne by 1806, having married 'the *Morning Post*'; this leaves her (presumably second) husband's precise identity uncertain. Facsimiles of four novels, NY, 1972, 1974.

Dahlgren, Madeleine (Vinton), 'Corinne', 1825–98, novelist, poet, translator, essayist, short-story and etiquette writer. B. at Gallipolis, Ohio, da. of Romaine Madeleine (Bureau) and Samuel Finley V., a Congressman, she was educ. at Picot's boarding school in Philadelphia and at a convent in Georgetown, DC. When her mother died, she became her father's Washington hostess. She m. Daniel Goddard in 1846 and had two children. After his death, she earned money by submitting short stories and poems to magazines. Her first book, *Idealities*, 1859, collected these under the pen name 'Corinne'. She also translated religious and political works from Spanish, French and Italian. In 1865 she m. John D., with whom she had three children; she took up writing again after his death in 1870. Her pamphlet *Thoughts on Female Suffrage*, 1871, and the melodramatic novel *Divorced*, 1887, testify to MD's conservative Catholic views on woman's place in law and marriage. In *Divorced*, as in *Lights and Shadows of a Life*, 1887, ostensibly written to uphold the 'distinctively American' animus against interracial marriages, MD's convoluted Gothic plotting is often at odds with her simplistic moralizing. *South Mountain Magic*, 1882, a collection of historical and ghostly anecdotes about MD's home in Maryland, foregrounds her lifelong interest in the occult.

Dall, Caroline Healey, 1822–1912, biographer, essayist, lecturer and women's-rights advocate, b. Boston, Mass., da. of Caroline (Foster) and Mark H. She was educ. at private schools and became vice-principal of Miss English's school for young ladies, Georgetown, Md, in 1840. Her early writings, *The Liberty Bell*, 1847, and *Essays and Sketches*, 1849, which deal with social, moral and religious issues, bear none of the marks of her later feminism. In 1844 she m. the Rev. Charles Henry Appleton D.; they separated in 1855, and with Pauline Wright Davis, she organized a woman's rights convention in Boston, 1855, and pub. *Nine Lectures* which the *New York Evening Post* praised for their force and eloquence on the woman question. In *A Woman's Right to Labor*, 1860, she pays tribute to the intrepid Marie E. Zakrzewska, whose story 'inspires the reformer'. *Woman's Rights under the Law*, 1861, includes a comprehensive study of British/French laws on marriage, divorce, franchise and labour and their effect on women. In *The College, the Market and the Court*, 1867, CHD develops her favourite theme, woman's control of her own destiny, and emphasizes three basic tenets: that education for women is a God-given right; that it involves the right to a vocation; and that protection of that vocation by legislative action involves the right to vote. In 1877 she gained the degree of LL.D at Alfred Univ., NY. Drawing upon real-life models of exceptional women (*The Romance of the Association*, 1875, *Margaret and her Friends*, 1895), she calls for educational and legal reforms for the maximization of *every* woman's potential.

'Dallas, Ruth' (Mumford), poet and writer of children's fiction, b. 1919 at Invercargill, NZ, youngest of three das. of Minnie Jane (Johnson) and Francis Sydney M., petrol station proprietors. Educ. at Waihopai School, Invercargill, Southland Technical College and informally at public libraries, she wrote stories and poems from age 12 for the *Southland Daily News* children's page. In 1946 some poems were published in the *Southland Times* and from then on she used the pen-name Ruth D., after her maternal grandmother. She lived with her invalid mother (d. 1961) – 'my one close intellectual companion' – and pub. her poems from 1947 in *Landfall*, a NZ literary quarterly. Her first collection, *Country Road*, was 1953; the last, *Steps of the Sun*, 1979. She has eight vols of poetry, and her *Collected Poems*, 1987. She was a Burns Fellow at Otago Univ. (D. Litt., 1978) where she wrote three children's books. Her poetry – precise, clear, songlike – is about Southland – the countryside, seasons and gardens. People are often absent or peripheral. Few of her poems are explicitly personal, but she has written about her grandmother's death, her mother, and a poem to her sister – 'Singing in the Backyard'. Her last volume contains haiku and more surreal poems. She believes 'whether [poetry] is written by men or women [is] irrelevant'.

d'Alpuget, Josephine **Blanche**, novelist, biographer, journalist, b. 1944 in Sydney, NSW, da. of Josephine (Curgenven) and Lou d'A., Sydney journalist. She was educ. at a private girls' school, then worked as a journalist. After her marriage to A. K. Pratt in 1965, she spent several years in England, Indonesia and Malaysia. Her first novel, *Monkeys in the Dark*, 1980, concerns the affairs of journalist Alexandra Wheatfield as she tries to reconcile personal, political and sexual conflict amid the chaos and unease of Sukarno's Indonesia. *Turtle Beach*, 1981, describes the experiences of a journalist involved in the bizarre political and diplomatic life of Kuala Lumpur, whose successful career is threatened by a demanding husband. This political thriller won three prizes, including the *Age* Book of the Year Award, 1981. *Winter in Jerusalem*, 1986, the story of a scriptwriter's professional assignment and personal odyssey, consolidated her reputation as a fiction writer. Her non-fiction includes *Mediator*, 1977, a biography of Sir Richard Kirby; *Robert J. Hawke*, 1982, a frank life of the prominent trade union leader and Prime Minister of Australia, which won the NSW Premier's Award for non-fiction, 1983; and *The Workers*, 1987.

Daly, Elizabeth, 1878–1967, mystery writer, producer of amateur theatre, and poet, b. into a New York literary family, da. of Emma (Barker) and Supreme Court Justice Joseph Francis D. She read avidly in the library of her uncle, Augustin D., which included a Shakespeare First Folio, and attended Miss Baldwin's School, Bryn Mawr (BA, 1901) and Columbia (MA, 1902). She returned to Bryn Mawr, 1904, as a reader in English and a producer of plays and pageants. She wrote poems and stories as a girl, and began experimenting in mystery in the late thirties, publishing her first novel, *Unexpected Night*, 1940, at 61. It introduces Henry Gamadge who, over the next 12 years, appeared in 15 more novels. A gentleman and a scholar, whom ED 'snatched out of the air', he became so popular that several people wrote to him at her address. In *The Book of the Dead*, 1944, he detects his way through clues provided by Shakespeare's plays. The Council on Books in Wartime selected *Evidence of Things Seen*, 1943, for a special overseas reprint series; *Murders in Vol. 2*, 1941, established her popularity in Britain. ED's only non-mystery, *The Street has Changed*, 1941, follows 40 years in the lives of several turn-of-the-century NYC theatrical families. ED's *New York Times* obituary quotes her as saying 'I suppose it's simply awful for a little old lady to go around bopping people off, so to speak, but I do so enjoy this type of writing.' See Frances O. Wallace in *Wilson Library Bulletin*, 19, 1944.

Daly, Mary, feminist theorist and theologian, b. in 1928 in Schenectady, NY, da. of Anna Catherine (Morse) and Frank X. D., a salesman. Educ. at the College of St Rose in Albany, NY (BA, 1950), Catholic Univ., Washington, DC (MA, 1952), the Univ. of Fribourg, Switzerland, (PhDs in theology,

1963, and philosophy, 1965), MD has taught in the USA and at the Univ. of Fribourg, settling as a professor of theology at Boston College, Chestnut Hill, Mass., since 1969. Early writing, *Natural Knowledge of God in the Philosophy of Jacques Maritain*, 1966, was quickly and consistently followed by challenges to Roman Catholic conservatism, from the perspective of 'new' Catholicism and of feminist analysis of church and society. In 1968, her writing appeared in *The New Day: Catholic Theologians of the Renewal* and in *Controversial Conversations with Catholics*. Her influential feminist book *The Church and the Second Sex*, 1968, repr. 1975 and 1985 with MD's 'post-christian' comments, is a critique of the status of women in the church. *Beyond God the Father*, 1973, signals her shift towards a female spirituality with its potential for a new language of 'Be-ing' in which the nouns that paralyse spirituality are replaced by verbs spinning 'gynergy'. *Gyn/Ecology: The Metaethics of Radical Feminism*, 1978, claims patriarchy as the primary source of oppression, citing female abuse in various cultures. Its elaborate word-play embodies MD's earlier insistence that 'women have had the power of *naming* stolen from us' that to 'exist humanly is to name the self, the world, and God' and that this reclaiming demands a revision of language. *Pure Lust*, 1984, proposes a 'Breakthrough to Metamorphospheres' in which 'Wild Weird women' are 'Metapatriarchal Mutations' of Self-creation. This serious language play is the subject of *Websters' First New Intergalactic Wickedary of the English Language*, with Jane Caputi, 1987, whose definitions index MD's analysis of patriarchy: 'fembot n: female robot: the archetypal role model forced upon women throughout fatherland: the unstated goal/end of socialization into patriarchal womanhood: the totaled woman.' See Carol P. Christ, *Laughter of Aphrodite*, 1987, Wanda Warren Berry in *Ultimate Reality*, 11, 1988, and Emily Culpepper's (much quoted in MD) 1983 Harvard ThD dissertation.

Damer, Anne (Seymour Conway), 1748–1828, sculptor, scholar, book-collector, amateur actress, diarist and novelist, only child of Lady Caroline (Campbell) and Field Marshal Henry S. C.; cousin of Lady Mary COKE. She m., 1767, John D., who ran up huge debts and shot himself in 1776. AD won fame with her sculpture; her friends included Georgiana DEVONSHIRE, Joanna BAILLIE, Horace Walpole (who said she wrote 'Latin like Pliny' and bequeathed Strawberry Hill to her), and Mary BERRY, with whom she travelled in France, and whom her notebooks show that she loved. (Hester PIOZZI remarked her 'suspected' lesbianism in 1790.) She published *Belmour*, 1801, an intelligent didactic novel whose hero marries a girl with parents resembling Jane AUSTEN's Bennets. AD's papers were, at her direction, mostly burned. Charlotte SMITH ascribed to her *Letters of Miss Riversdale*, a novel strong in piety as well as sentiment, 1803. Some papers at Lewis Walpole Library, Farmington, Conn.

'Danby, Frank', Julia Davis Frankau, 1861–1916, novelist and art historian, b. Dublin, da. of Hyman Davis. Her family, of Jewish origin, were all writers, but lost contact with Judaism. She was raised by Mrs Paul Lafargue, da. of Karl Marx; around 1883 she m. Arthur F., merchant; one of their four children was the novelist Gilbert Frankau. She became a journalist in her teens, and found success with her first novel, *Dr. Phillips, a Maida Vale Idyll*, 1887. She then turned to the study of engravings, producing three extremely successful art histories: *Eighteenth-Century Colour Prints*, 1900, *The Life of John Raphael Smith*, 1902, and *The Lives of James and William Ward*, 1904. In her own words, she 'relapsed' into novel-writing, which brought her great popularity, although critics saw her art books as more enduring. She was also a great horsewoman and bicyclist, ran two businesses, and co-founded a theatre (The Independent). Four of her 15 novels attack Jewish materialism. They were characterized as 'very shrewd and very unpleasant studies of ill-behaved and disagreeable people' (*Times* obit., 18 March 1916), an apt description of the two most famous, *Dr. Phillips* and *Pigs in Clover*, 1903. The former depicts a Jewish doctor's clandestine affair with a Gentile woman, and offers a stereotyped portrayal of Jewish social life, while the latter created a sensation because of its relatively frank picture of the affair between an unscrupulous man and a naive but unconventional woman writer, set against the Jameson Raid and the beginning of the Boer War. See Linda Gertner Zatlin's discussion in *The Nineteenth-Century Anglo–Jewish Novel*, 1981. P. FRANKAU was a granddaughter.

'Dane, Clemence', Winifred Ashton, 1888–1965, novelist, essayist, writer of plays and screenplays. B. in Greenwich, London, da. of Florence (Bentley) and Arthur Charles A., a commission merchant, she was educ. at private schools in England, Germany and Switzerland, but trained in independent thinking by 'having to go to church too often'. She studied art in Dresden and at the Slade School, London, went on stage in 1913 as 'Diana Cortis', and later taught in a girls' school in Ireland. Her first novel, *The Regiment of Women*, 1917, published under the name she took from the Church of St Clement Danes in the Strand, examines lesbian relations (not called that) in girls' schools, a subject she returns to in *The Woman's Side*, 1926. Occasionally bold, as in its debate on marriage, the novel resolves its conflicts in a cliché of the rescuing male. *Legend*, 1919, an unflinching inquiry into the nature of the writing woman, poses as problem its antithetical characterizations of a dead 'romantic' novelist of impeccably sexually submisive views – 'Can "literature" fill my emptiness? Are the books I write children to love me with your eyes?' – and a living, truth-telling biographer, given as perhaps evil and certainly emotionally deficient – 'I can record – but I can't create.' CD's first play, *A Bill of Divorcement*, 1921 (not, as has been said, an adaptation of *Legend*), confronted the serious subject of divorce and the wife's duty (though its sad theme of inherited insanity was more noticed). She wrote several other plays, including *Will Shakespeare*, 1921, a crashing failure with the critics, in which the strong figures are Ann Hathaway and Queen ELIZABETH I, and *Wild Decembers*, 1932, about the BRONTËS. *Broome Stages*, 1931, transposes Plantagenet history into a novel about an English stage family. She adapted Rostand, Schiller and Shakespeare, based a play on Max Beerbohm's *The Happy Hypocrite*, 1936, and wrote seven filmscripts. Her essays in *The Woman's Side*, 1926, outline her feminist politics: 'Canute and the Marriage Laws' maintains that the bill reforming divorce law 'is one of the most important scraps of paper in the history of women, in the history, at any rate, of English women'. *Tradition and Hugh Walpole*, 1929, gives her views of the modern English novel. *London Has a Garden*, 1964 (quoted above), an impressionist history of the Covent Garden area in which she lived, includes some reminiscences.

Daniels, Sarah, London playwright, b. 1957, who 'did not fall out of my pram wanting to be a writer', became a clerical assistant, then wrote three plays produced in 1981: *Penumbra*, *Ma's Flesh is Grass* and *Ripen Our Darkness*, the last at the Royal Court Theatre. In 1983 'ferocious comment' greeted *The Devil's Gateway*, about a working-class woman who leaves the family she has spent years caring for, for the Greenham Common women's peace camp, and *Masterpieces*, which links pornography with male violence. (*The Devil's Gateway* was pub. with *Ripen our Darkness*, 1986.) In *Neaptide* (National Theatre, 1986) SD examines lesbians living with prejudice. *Byrthrite* (Royal Court, 1986), set in seventeenth-century England, presents male attempts to take control of women's reproductive capacity (cf. Jane SHARP). *Gut*

Girls (Albany Empire, 1988) explores the intersection of class and gender in the late nineteenth century: despite their refusal of traditional feminine roles, the hard-living, self-reliant workers in London's slaughter-houses must confront a philanthropic lady's efforts to convert them to domestic servants when their jobs become obsolete. SD has won several awards, been writer-in-residence at the Royal Court, 1984, and often worked with women directors. See SD in *Drama*, 152, 1984 (quoted above); Carole Woddis in *Plays and Players*, 368 (May 1984); interview in *The Stage*, 11 Sept. 1986.

Danquah, Mabel (Dove), 'Marjorie Mensah', Ghanaian short-story writer, journalist, the first woman to be elected to a government assembly in Africa. B. *c.* 1910, in the Gold Coast, she was educ. in local schools, later studied in England and travelled in Europe and the US, returning to edit the *Accra Evening News*, which began publication under Nkrumah in 1948. She m. scholar, newspaper editor and plawright J. B. D., as his second wife, and worked with him for independence. She was elected to the pre-independence Ghanaian parliament, 1952. As 'Marjorie Mensah' she contributed a column to the *West African Times*. She is known for urging her people to take pride in their cultural traditions as they moved toward independence. Her short stories deal with the place of women in contemporary Ghana; her husband also addressed the question in his analysis of marriage customs of the matrilineal Akan and in his play *The Third Woman*. (He died in a detention camp in 1965.) Three of her short stories – 'Anticipation', 'Payment', and 'The Torn Veil' – are frequently anthologized, by, for instance, Langston Hughes in *An African Treasury*, 1960, A. J. Shelton in *The African Assertion*, 1968, and Charlotte Bruner in *Unwinding Threads*, 1983. See Phebean Itayemi and MDD, *The Torn Veil and Other Stories*, 1975.

D'Anvers, Alicia (Clarke), 1667/8–1725, poet, da. of Oxford University's learned printing director Samuel C. She m. lawyer Knightley D. before publishing *A Poem upon His Sacred Majesty* ..., 1691, dedicated to Queen Mary. This presents a debate, finally reconciled, between Belgia (as mother) and Britannia (wife) over their emotional claims to Albion (King William). *Academia, or The Humours of the University of Oxford*, 1691 (repr. 1716, 1730), recounts in hudibrastics Oxford's mistreatment of the Muses ('Nine handsome bonny Girls'), the college progress of a bashful country boy to dissolute debtor, and (central in the poem), the tourist's Oxford as seen by a yokel servant (at Queen's College, he assumes, the 'Queen was once a Schollar'). Next came *The Oxford-Act*, 1693 (anonymous: a contemporary note says it is AD's), 'Comprizing an immortal Sing-Song / How all th'old Dons were at it Ding-dong' in an annual July ceremony with a licensed burlesque speaker. Well versed in literature and college politics, she pokes fun at academic personages, often through their presumed or imagined sex lives.

D'Arcy, Ella, 1851–1939, short-story writer and novelist, about whom there is little biographical information. B. London, of Irish parents, she was educ. in France and Germany, and also lived in the Channel Islands. She trained as an artist at the Slade, then turned to writing because of defective eyesight. Her first story, 'Irremediable', and two others were pub. in *The Yellow Book*, of which she was also assistant literary editor. She pub. two vols. of short stories, *Monochromes*, 1895, and *Modern Instances*, 1898, and one novel, *The Bishop's Dilemma*, 1898, and a translation of *Ariel* by Maurois, 1924. She later lived in Paris, remaining unmarried. Her stories examine romantic idealism with a certain astringency: her view of women was harsh. In 'The Pleasure-Pilgrim', Lulie Thayer could be interpreted both as whore and devoted lover; in 'The Elegie' the woman dies for love and the male artist uses the experience to enhance his painting. Her novel laments the division between spirituality and sensuality, ironically undercutting the opinion that death is better than endangering the soul. Her output was small. Her friend Netta Syrett considered her, though 'clever and amusing', 'the laziest woman I ever met' (*The Sheltering Tree*, 1939, p. 98). See also Katharine Mix, *A Study in Yellow*, 1960.

Dargan, Olive (Tilford), 'Fielding Burke', 1869–1968, playwright, poet, novelist. B. near Litchfield, Grayson County, Kentucky, da. of schoolteachers Rebecca (Day) and Elisha Francis T., she was educ. at Peabody College, Nashville, and at Radcliffe, where she met Pegram D. She m. him in 1898, after years of teaching. He published one book at his own expense; she won quick success with two vols. of verse plays (*Semiramis*, 1904, and *Lords and Lovers*, 1906) and one of poems. This, and her left-wing political views, strained the marriage; she stopped writing. She had a premature daughter in 1907, who died; in 1911 she left for England alone. Here she resumed her writing (*The Mortal Gods and Other Dramas*, 1912; *The Welsh Pony*, 1913) and her political interests. Sympathizing with the militant WSPU, she hoped that WWI would 'settle the suffrage question anyhow' and that 'there would be no more superior males'. A year after her return to the US, in 1914, Pegram drowned himself; OTD retired to Kentucky. *The Cycle's Rim*, 1916, a sequence of commemorative poems, was likened to the work of Elizabeth Barrett BROWNING. In her sixties, after writing fairly traditional rural sketches, she at last gave literary expression to her socialism (she was never a Communist) and feminism. *Call Home the Heart*, 1932 (pub. pseudonymously, repr. 1983, a highly successful proletarian novel based on the 1929 Gastonia textile strike), was 'like a sword fresh from the scabbard' to 'stick in the public mind' (see Joseph R. Urgo in *the minnesota review*, 24, 1985). She made her beliefs equally clear in two more novels, *A Stone Came Rolling*, 1935, and *Sons of the Stranger*, 1947. Late works include *The Spotted Hawk*, 1958 (poetry), and *Innocent Bigamy*, 1962 (stories). Despite suspected attempts to destroy political papers by fire, she left many letters: most at Princeton, Harvard, Amherst and the Univs. of NC and Kentucky.

Dark, Eleanor (O'Reilly), 'Patricia Rane', 1901–85, novelist, b. in Burwood, Sydney, da. of Eleanor Grace (McCullough) and writer Dowell O'R. She was educ. at private schools, including Redlands, Sydney, and in 1922 m. Eric Payten D., medical practitioner, then settled in Katoomba, NSW. Under her pseudonym she pub. poems, articles and stories in magazines such as *Triad* and the *Bulletin*, 1921–46. She pub. her first novel, *Slow Dawning*, concerning a woman doctor in a country town, in 1932, but became known with her second, *Prelude to Christopher*, 1934, a psychological study focusing on the complexities of time, a characteristic theme. Her nine novels include *Return to Coolami*, 1936, an actual and emotional journey of four people; *Sun Across the Sky*, 1937, and *Waterway*, 1938, each with a time span of one day; and the trilogy of Australian historical novels: *The Timeless Land*, 1941 (ABC TV adaptation, 1980); *Storm of Time*, 1948; and *No Barrier*, 1953. These are noted for their democratic characterization – convicts, blacks, settlers and governors are treated alike – and powerful evocation of clashes between and within different cultures. *The Little Company*, 1945, demonstrates ED's concern with political and feminist issues, and *Lantana Lane*, 1959, based on her experiences of rural Queensland, is an amusing collection of related short stories. ED always avoided publicity, but awards include the Australian Literary Society's Gold Medal, 1934 and 1936, Officer of the Order of Australia (AO) in 1977, and the Society of Women Writers' Alice Award in 1978. Her papers are in the Mitchell Library, Sydney. See A. Grove Day, 1977, M. BARNARD Eldershaw in *Essays in Australian Fiction*, 1938.

Darwall, Mary (Whateley), 1738–1825, poet, youngest child of Mary and of William W., gentleman farmer, of Beoley, Worcs. She read widely, wrote poetry by 1759, and kept house for a brother at Walsall from 1760. Her *Original Poems on Several Occasions*, 1764, went through several issues at London, Dublin and Walsall; Shenstone praised it; Mary DELANY and Elizabeth TOLLET's nephew and heir, subscribed. Attracted by 'smart satire', and the topics of 'War and Arms' or 'the Park and Play', fearful of the 'Happy Valley' of confinement, MD yet laments her lack of learning and opts mainly for pastoral; her best work centres on this conflict. The *Monthly Review* called her one of the 'British Nine', 1774; Dorothea DU BOIS and Maria RIDDELL reprinted poems by her. She m. John D., vicar of Walsall (1766), added to six stepchildren six of her own, ran a printing press with him, and wrote songs for his congregation and poems for the theatre. She also published in the *GM* as 'Harriot Airy'. Widowed in 1789, she moved to Newtown in Wales, 1793. Her *Poems on Several Occasions*, Walsall, 1794, includes work by two of her daughters, one of whom published *The Storm*, 1810. See Ann Messenger in *Bulletin of Research in the Humanities*, 1986.

Daryush, Elizabeth (Bridges), poet, 1887–1977, da. of Mary Monica (Waterhouse) and Robert B., Poet Laureate. She grew up in rural Berks., was privately educ., and moved to Boar's Hill near Oxford in 1907. She later suppressed her first three books of poems, 1911, 1916, and 1921. She m. Ali Akbar D. in 1923, and lived three years with him in Persia, where she studied Persian poetry and made a free translation of the thirteenth-century mystic Sufi poet Jalal ad Din, or Rumi. From 1929 she again lived on Boar's Hill near her father, whose metrical experiments were the starting-point for her own. After three more poetry volumes she was praised by US critic Yvor Winters in *American Review*, 8, 1937; after one more volume, he prefaced her *Selected Poems*, 1948, with more prominent appreciation. Further volumes were *Selected* in 1972; *Collected Poems*, 1976, ed. Donald Davie, with ED's note on syllabic metres. She later rejected the early archaism which had been one ground of hostile comment. She has been overshadowed by her father, dismissed as a mere technician, and perhaps devalued on grounds of over-championing by Winters. Roy Fuller calls her 'a pioneer technical innovator' whose poems 'grapple with life's intensest issues'; but she has had comparatively little attention and few readers. She writes on three rhythmical systems: the usual one in English poetry, usually called syllabic; the accentual, associated with Old English and with G. M. Hopkins; and what ED herself called syllabic, in which she aimed 'to build up subtler and more freely-followed accentual patterns' than either of the other forms allows. Her work encompasses a wealth of moods and subjects: 'Children of wealth in your warm nursery . . . you cannot tell / What winter means'; 'I have followed a sky-filled river, whose flickering throe / Leapt from its actual nodes, to a moon-tide gave / Its might.'

Das, Kamala (Nair), 'Madhavi Kutty', poet, short-story writer, autobiographer. She was b. 1934 at Punnayurkulam in Malabar, S. India, da. of Balamani Amma (a Nalapati by community, with a strong matrilinear tradition; a poet in Malayali) and V. M. N., who sold luxury cars. 'I grew up watching my mother write her poems lying on her stomach on an old four poster bed. I knew that the time would come for me to begin writing too.' Her various schools included a Catholic one. Her arranged marriage, at 15, to banker K. Madhava D. was unhappy; she had three sons, and also a breakdown. She treated sexual love in *Summer in Calcutta: Fifty Poems*, 1965, and wrote in 'Substitute' (*The Descendants*, 1967), 'love became a swivel door, / When one went out, another came in.' *The Old Playhouse*, 1973 (33 poems), deals with the search for love as an aspect of that for selfhood. KD writes, apparently of herself, 'You called me wife, / I was taught to break saccharine into your tea and / To offer at the right moment the vitamins. Cowering / Beneath your monstrous ego I ate the magic loaf and / Became a dwarf.' Her essay 'Why Not More Than One Husband?' (*Eve's Weekly* 26, 1972) drew much notice. She translated into English her confessional, frankly sexual autobiography (written 'during my first serious bout of heart disease', serialized in *The Current Weekly*, Bombay, 1974): *My Story*, New Delhi 1976, London 1978. Other books include *Driksakshi Panna*, 1973 (for children), *A Doll for the Child Prostitute*, 1977 (stories), *Alphabet of Lust*, 1977 (novel), and *Heart of Britain*, 1983 (novel-cum-travelogue). Her many Malayali stories (as Madhavi Kutty) in periodicals include the celebrated 'Thanuppu' (Cold). In English she is valued for urging self-fulfilment and new roles for Indian women, for her lovingly recreated Malabar scenes, for expressions of nostalgia and loneliness. Having lived in coastal cities, she often uses the sea as indicator of mood. 'I am Indian, very brown. ... Don't write in English, they said, / English is not your mother-tongue. ... The language I speak / Becomes mine, its distortions, its queernesses / All mine, mine alone.' She edited the *Illustrated Weekly of India*, 1971–2, and has held public posts furthering the interests of writers and artists. Studies include Devindra Kohli, 1975. She won the 1986 Sahitya Akademi Award in English. See Mohamed Elias in *WLWE*, 25, 1985.

Davenport, Selina (Wheler), 1779–after 1856, author of 11 effective if stereotyped novels, da. of Capt. Charles Granville W. of Kent. (Robert Surtees's Wheler pedigree gives that name only for a bachelor.) She m. writer Richard Alfred D. in 1800, left him for 'sufficient reasons', and wrote to support her two daughters. (He said she saddled him with debts of £150 incurred in running a school; his life of Hester CHAPONE for Ballatyne suggests dislike of educated women.) SD's *Sons of the Viscount, and the Daughters of the Earl*, 1813, has a typical title and plot (Dorothy Blakey calls them 'fatuous'): a generation earlier, a fiancé's seduction of his betrothed (even though he did not blame her and still wished to marry her) has produced deadly family enmity: two sisters meet and love two forbidden brothers; the good and gentle pair achieve married bliss; the others are separated by her 'giddiness' and – providential! – death. SD later published, by name, with MINERVA. *Italian Vengeance and English Forbearance*, 1828, contrasts 'good' and 'bad' women; the avenger, in male dress, shoots her seducer dead in a duel. SD's last, *Personation*, 1834, ends with a complaint of long illness and 'blighted hopes'. Her friend Jane PORTER helped her with money, Elizabeth GASKELL with a letter to the RLF, 1850. (SD's husband, a beneficiary of the fund, tried to prevent its paying her; she supported widowed daughters on under a shilling a day from a tiny shop at Knutsford, Cheshire, which was Gaskell's Cranford.)

Davidson, Margaret (Miller), 1787–1844, and her daughters **Lucretia Maria Davidson**, 1808–25, and **Margaret Miller Davidson**, 1823–38, poets. Margaret senior m. Oliver D. of Plattsburgh on Lake Champlain, NY, brought up all her large family on poetry, and herself wrote religious and family poems, a fictional account of a brush with Indians, 1814, and a versification of *Fingal*. Lucretia was writing verse at 13, though ambivalent about parental praise. Her longest poem, *Amir Khan*, 1829, is a romantic tale about a Christian maiden whose Muslim wooer narrowly averts her suicide. Others are biblical, domestic, patriotic; a violent note appears in prophecies of doom for imagined women, and descriptions of volcanoes and of the day of judgment. Her mantle fell to the infant Margaret, who early identified with her dead sister: she wrote poems and letters to her mother and female friends, a tragedy and a prophetic prose tale of a girl's early death, and judicially admired Felicia HEMANS. Like Lucretia, she died of tuberculosis; in 1841 Washington Irving ed. her *Poetical Remains* and Catharine SEDGWICK ed. Lucretia's, both often repr.; Margaret senior's followed in 1843.

Davie, Elspeth, short-story writer, novelist, b. in Edinburgh, where (after childhood in England) she went to school and the College of Art. She taught painting, returned to Edinburgh after some years in Ireland, m. George D., philosophy lecturer, and had a daughter. Her first of many writing awards came from the *Observer* newspaper. Stories like 'A Woman of Substance' (*Cornhill*, 1959) already broach her favourite themes, here a lonely woman in a park, haunted by feelings of insubstantiality, 'the immense loss and waste which went with every day'. *The Spark*, 1968, repr. 1984, *The High Tide Talker*, 1976, *The Night of the Funny Hats*, 1980, and *A Traveller's Room*, 1985, collect stories (many repr. from journals) which illuminate apparently trivial oddities (the effect on a concert when someone is carried out in a faint, or on a criminally self-indulgent dabbler in astronomy when he grasps that not even the latest book can remain accurate) with complex, concentrated, often painful intensity. 'Lines', in the last, finely exemplifies ED's qualities: again in a public park, gender-conscious adolescents are baffled by an encounter with a solitary, unreadable woman. Of ED's novels, *Providings*, 1965, repr. 1984, is comic in tone: a young man vainly pursues 'his notion of free beings ... continually on the move', while dogged by his mother's ceaseless, excessive gifts of homemade jam. *Creating a Scene*, 1971, repr. 1984, takes a broader canvas: a male art teacher of 'rigid, limited, and consciously self-sacrificing talent', works to enable others to reach for freedom; a male pupil unconcernedly accepts the creative vandalizing of his masterpiece; a female pupil learns of her descent from a long line of loved and hated models – goddesses, Eves, Virgins. *Climbers on a Stair*, 1978, traces the web of disparate lives in an Edinburgh tenement block. Central is a feisty, self-aware old woman who would have liked to compose but glories in teaching the piano, 'bringing talent to light': these words and themes echo in *Coming to Light*, 1989. ED fruitfully pursues her aim: to 'strike in at an angle to experience rather than going along parallel to it'. She is interested in film and has written for radio.

Davies, Arabella (Jenkinson), 1753–87, religious diarist, da. of Eleanor (Deane) and Richard J., b. at Hoxton, London. At about nine conviction of sin gave her 'spiritual distress', and her diary at 14 is earnestly pious, yet she says she was 'naturally lively', loved novels and satires as well as Elizabeth ROWE and Edward Young, turned to 'dress and folly', and 'seemed to make a tacit agreement with the Almighty, to repent hereafter'. She m., 1774, the Rev. Edward D., a widower with four children. She prayed before childbirth, 'Bless us as a family', and felt a 'strong desire of being a friend to my children', but two of her own died young; she suffered much ill-health. Her *Diary* and *Letters from a Parent to Her Children*, both pub. 1786, are painfully conscientious, focused on death and judgment. Her last diary entry, on her birthday, prays 'Bless the dear unborn!' – of whom, four days later, she died.

Davies, Sarah **Emily**, 1830–1921, feminist activist and educational reformer, b. Southampton, fourth child of Mary (Hopkinson) and John D., rector of Gateshead, near Newcastle. Educ. at home, she longed for the univ. education her brothers received. She met Barbara BODICHON in Algiers in 1859 and learned of the Langham Place Circle; visiting London, she was impressed by the Society for the Employment of Women, and set up a branch at Gateshead. After her father died in 1862, she moved to London, briefly ed. the *English Woman's Journal* and the *Victoria Magazine*; campaigned with Elizabeth Garrett and others for women to be admitted to London Univ. and the medical profession; and pressed for girls' EDUCATION to be included in the Schools Enquiry Commission, in 1865 giving evidence before them. She pub. *The Higher Education of Women*, 1866 (repr. 1988), the year she formed the London Schoolmistresses' Association. She wrote of the need of women for occupation, for the variety of their abilities to be more fully recognized, and for the modernization of their EDUCATION. Her essays are collected in *Thoughts on Some Questions Relating to Women, 1860–1908*, 1910. ED helped organize the first women's suffrage petition, but directed her main energies to educational reform, particularly to establishing a college which opened with five students at Hitchin in 1867, moved to Cambridge in 1873, and was renamed Girton College. Wishing to prepare students for the existing Cambridge degree examination, she opposed all plans to treat women separately. Later in life, she returned to suffrage campaigning, joining the Executive Committee of the London Society of Women's Suffrage; she was shocked, however, by the more militant suffragette activities. See Barbara Stephen, *Emily Davies and Girton College*, 1927.

Davis, Angela Yvonne, revolutionary, autobiographer, writer, b. in 1944 in Birmingham, Ala., da. of Sallye B. D., a primary school teacher and activist whose work with whites to free the Scottsboro Boys (cf Nancy CUNARD) led her to teach AYD that whites could 'walk out of their skins and respond with the integrity of human beings', and Frank D., who left his low-paying job as a high school history teacher to invest in a service station. She remembers the sound of bombings as the Ku Klux Klan destroyed the homes of black families who moved into white areas. Rejecting the 'purely social' life of the middle-class black girl, AYD went to an experimental high school in NYC sponsored by the American Friends Service Committee. There she discovered the *Communist Manifesto* ('What had seemed a personal hatred of me ... became the inevitable consequence of a ruthless system') and joined Advance, a Marxist-Leninist youth organization that supported the anti-nuclear and civil rights demonstrations. After Brandeis Univ. and the Sorbonne (BA, 1964, in French literature), AYD went to the Univ. of Frankfurt, 1965–7, to study philosophy but, hungering for an active liberationist role, she arranged to work with Herbert Marcuse at the Univ. of California, San Diego (MA, 1968). She joined the Communist Party in 1968 and was fired from her teaching position at UCLA in 1969. AYD's 'political' autobiography, *With My Mind on Freedom*, 1974, details her role as organizer in the black power movement, 'simply following in the footsteps of her foremothers'. It describes systematic murder or imprisonment of black leaders and her own arrest on charges of conspiracy and murder when 17-year-old Jonathan Jackson used her gun in a courtroom shootout (acquitted, 1972). *If They Come in the Morning*, 1971, collects AYD's prison letters and essays, with pieces from other black activists, including Erika Huggins, Bobby Seale, and Soledad prisoner George Jackson, who was later murdered. After release AYD worked to keep the 'Free Angela' movement alive as 'the only hope to our sisters and brothers behind walls', helped form the National Alliance Against Racist and Political Repression, and ran for vice-president of the USA, 1980, as a Communist. *Women, Race and Class*, 1981, relates the anti-slavery movement to the sometimes racist women's rights campaigns, and gives a brief history of individual Communist women. No longer believing that 'the revolution was going to arrive tomorrow', AYD studies the 'role of Black women in forging the blues tradition for the purpose of uncovering the social implications of their music'. Artists are needed to 'nourish our hearts, to refine our consciousness, and to arouse our collective action'. See AYD and June JORDAN, 'On Poetry and Politics,' *WRB*, July/Aug. 1987. Biography by Regina Nadelson, 1972, unfavourably reviewed by Toni MORRISON, *NYTBR*, 29 Oct. 1978.

Davis, Mary Evelyn (Moore), 1852–1909, novelist, poet and short-story writer, b. Talladge, Atlanta, da. of Marian Lucy (Crutchfield) and Dr John M.; educ. privately. MD always lived in the South, first in Alabama and Texas, then in New Orleans. She pub. her first volume of poetry, *Minding the Gap*, in 1867. Her poems include 'Père Dagobert', a light-hearted account of a well-loved but less than saintly priest, and 'Throwing the Wonga', in which a crone casts a voodoo spell on a young Creole woman who has gone off with the crone's husband, utilizing Creole patois dialogue. In 1874 she married Thomas Edward D., editor of the New Orleans *Daily Picayune* from 1879. In 1888 MD published her first prose work, *In War Time at La Rose Blanche*, a semi-autobiographical group of stories. Her first novel, *Under the Man-Fig*, 1895, was set in Texas, as was *The Wire Cutters*, 1899. Other novels set in New Orleans or Louisiana include *The Queen's Garden*, 1900, and *The Little Chevalier*, 1903. MD also wrote a history of Texas for children, *Under Six Flags*, 1897. Many of her novels and stories use dialect and Creole patois, and her portrayal of blacks is less condescending than that of many Southern writers. Her short stories appeared in magazines such as *Harper's* and *Atlantic Monthly*, and in 1896 she collected them in *An Elephant Track*. 'The Love-Stranche' deals implicitly with incest and miscegenation, a theme also found in *The Price of Silence*, 1907. She does not address women's issues in a controversial way, accepting the prescribed roles for Southern women both in her life and in her fiction.

Davis, Natalie (Zemon), historian and feminist. B. in 1928 in Detroit, Mich., da. of Helen (Lamport) and Julian Leon Z., she was educ. at Smith (BA, 1949), Radcliffe (MA, 1950) and Michigan (PhD, 1959). In 1948 she m. Chandler D., a professor of mathematics, whom she credits with urging economy and persuasiveness on her naturally 'Talmudic cast of mind'. They have three children. She has taught at Brown and the Univs. of Toronto and California at Berkeley, at the *Ecole des Hautes Etudes en Sciences Sociales* and, since 1978, at Princeton, where she is the Henry Charles Lea Professor of History. She has been president of the Society for French Historical Studies and became president of the American Historical Association, 1987. Her over-40 articles and two books show special interest in sex roles and sexual symbolism as reflected in popular ritual. The eight essays about peasants and artisans in *Society and Culture in Early Modern France*, 1975, see sexual symbolism as 'statements about social experience' and stress particularly the 'multivalent image' of the disorderly woman as one that widened 'behavioral options' and sanctioned 'riot and political disobedience'. Recognizing, in her collaboration on the screenplay of *Le Retour de Martin Guerre*, an opportunity 'to reflect upon the significance of identity in the sixteenth century', she devoted her second book, *The Return of Martin Guerre*, 1983, to the 'stubborn vitality' of invention, probing the motives of a cuckolding impostor-husband and his shrewdly conniving, adulterous wife, who after a slippery legal process are actually reconciled.

Davis, Rebecca (Harding), 1831–1910, social-protest novelist and editor, b. in Washington, Penn., and aged 5 moved to

Wheeling, W. Va. Eldest of five children of Rachel Leet (Wilson), granddaughter of the first white settler in Washington, and Richard H., she was educ. by her mother, private tutors and at Washington Female Seminary. In 1863, after the success of her first novel, she married Lemuel Clarke D., journalist and law clerk of Philadelphia, producing a daughter Nora and two sons Richard Harding Davis and Charles Belmont Davis, both writers. Preceding the naturalism of Zola, Crane and Dreiser, *Life in the Iron Mills*, hailed as the first American proletarian novel, was published in *The Atlantic* in 1861. Visiting Henry James, also Annie FIELDS with whom she maintained an intimate correspondence, she met Oliver Wendell Holmes, L. M. ALCOTT, Emerson, the Hawthornes, Bronson Alcott – experiences which are recorded in *Bits of Gossip*, 1904. Fields rejected her second novel, *A Story of Today* (finally pub. as *Margaret Howth*, 1862) – 'It assembles the gloom too depressingly'. RHD reluctantly took up 'cheerful', 'popular' serial writing for *Peterson's*, but continued to write stories concerned with contemporary social issues, earning the label 'the poet of the poor people'. She wrote prolifically for money in oppressive circumstances, and in 1868 pub. the massive, complex *Waiting for the Verdict*: it explores the fate of blacks and those of mixed blood after the Civil War. In 1869 she joined the editorial staff of the *NY Tribune* for several years. Fanny KORTRIGHT's anti-feminist *Pro Aris et Focis – A Plea for Our Altars and Hearths*, 1870, was long attributed to RHD, despite her denials. Yet 'The Wife's Story', 1864, like *Earthen Pitchers*, 1873–4, acknowledges conflict between work and commitment to others. Espousing Margaret FULLER's motto, 'The only object in life is to grow', the narrator notes that her marriage is 'Two middle-aged people with inharmonious intellects ... my role was outlined plain to the end – years of cooking, stitching, scraping together of cents: it was the fate of thousands of married women without means.' Other novels include *Dallas Galbraith*, 1868, *Berrytown*, 1872, *Kitty's Choice*, 1874, *A Law Unto Herself*, 1878, *Natasqua*, 1886, *Silhouettes of American Life*, 1892, and *Doctor Warrick's Daughters*, 1896. For her life, see Tillie Olsen, 1972.

Davy, Sarah (Roane), *c.* 1639–70, spiritual autobiographer. She gives an extraordinary account of her conversion to Independency, applying the vocabulary of romance to her love for an unnamed woman friend. She finds peace in God's new commandment to 'love one another, with a pure unbounded love ... as I have loved you, or to love thy friend, as thou lovest thy self'. She married *c.* 1660 and fell silent. The editor of her work (*Heaven Realiz'd*, posthumous, 1670) calls on others to imitate her godliness.

Davys, Mary, 1674–1732, novelist and playwright. B. in Dublin, she m. the Rev. Peter D., headmaster and friend of Jonathan Swift. Widowed in 1698, she moved to England to live by her writing, which is outstanding in intelligence and humour. She sold an MS for 3 guineas in 1700 (pub. 1704 as *Amours of Alcippus and Lucippe*, it became 'The Lady's Tale' in 1725: story delightfully confided by one female friend to another). She dedicated to Esther Johnson *The Fugitive*, 1705 (re-written as 'The Merry Wanderer', 1725: praise of Ireland and Swift introduces rambling, sometimes earthy tales). Fifteen years' experience of life at York went into *The Northern Heiress, or The Humours of York*, a comedy; she came south for its staging, 1716. It scored a success with the Ladies in particular' for its main plot of heiress testing suitor, with background detail of crude, self-satisfied, bourgeois past Lady Mayoresses. With the profits MD opened a coffee-house at Cambridge, supplementing her income with subscriptions to *The Reform'd Coquet, or Memoirs of Amoranda* (1724, facs. 1973: novel with mentor-hero) and *Works*, 1725. This has a thoughtful critical preface, revisions of earlier work, *The Self-Rival* (unacted comedy), 'The Modern Poet' (satirical poem), *The Cousins* (melodramatic fiction pirated 1732 as *The False Friend, or The Treacherous Portuguese*), and *Familiar Letters Betwixt a Gentleman and a Lady* (facs. 1955), between a politically opposed pair, evasive about their personal feelings yet likely at last to marry. In *The Accomplish'd Rake, or Modern Fine Gentleman*, 1727 (repr. ed. W. H. McBurney, 1963) a self-conscious narrator demonstrates women's resilience in face of damage done by rapacious men: a likely influence on Hogarth. MD's poems may include a lost reply to one by Susanna CENTLIVRE, pub. 1717. Attacked for bawdy in *The Grub-Street Journal*, she replied with vigour (1731). Some works repr. 1752, 1756, 1785.

Dawbarn, Elizabeth (Saltonstall), d. 1839, trained nurse and pamphleteer of Wisbech, Cambs. (called 'the elder' because one of her six children also wrote). She came from Alford, Lincs.; in 1782 she m. Richard Bunbury D., later a Baptist pastor. She published at Wisbech. Her anonymous *Dialogue between Clara Neville and Louisa Mills, on Loyalty*, 1794, is strongly conservative: silly Louisa, who admires liberty, Tom Paine and the USA, is lectured by Clara on God's approval of monarchy, the comforts of the poor, and the influence women may have on men. (Women's relation to public life is an issue with both speakers.) ED published with her name an anthology of anti-theatrical writings, 1805, in reply to a Mrs Robertson (mentioning her 'former pamphlet' on this topic). Other pamphlets treat the nature of Christ (1800?); the Old Testament (in letters to her children, 1806, 2nd ed. 1816); and *The Rights of Infants, or ... Nursing of Infants*, 1805 (title alluding, without hostile irony, to Mary WOLLSTONECRAFT). Following on a similar (lost?) work of ten years earlier, addressing a daughter 'now likely to be a *mother*', it urges with kindly commonsense the importance of infant care: a baby, if female, may live to be a Catharine MACAULAY, a Sarah TRIMMER, or a Lady Mary Wortley MONTAGU, if male an Edward Jenner.

Dawson, Jennifer, novelist, b. 1929. She grew up in South London, attended Mary Datchelor School, then studied history at St Anne's College, Oxford (MA, 1952) and philosophy at University College, London. She is married to Michael Hinton. She has worked in publishing and as a teacher, a social worker in a psychiatric hospital, and a welfare worker in East London. The first of her five novels, *The Ha-Ha*, 1961 (repr. with a new afterword by the author, 1985, 'a minor classic', winner of the James Tait Black Memorial Prize), portrays a young woman's recovery from mental illness. Here, as in subsequent novels, JD writes from the 'unstable', richly fantastical perspective of the schizophrenic protagonist, whose askew vision breaks through repressive social forms, overcoming the imprisoning external with intense sensory awareness. The novel was adapted for radio, 1964, for stage, 1968, and for TV, 1969. *Fowler's Snare*, 1962, and *The Cold Country*, 1965, return to JD's theme of imaginative madness in deadly conflict with repressive social norms. Her tone darkens as she develops her theme. Active in the Campaign for Nuclear Disarmament and a lover of music, JD presents, in *A Field of Scarlet Poppies*, 1979, a cellist whose waning of interest in his music measures his disaffiliation from society. JD is co-author, with Elizabeth Mitchell, of *The Queen of Trent*, 1961, a children's book, and *Hospital Wedding*, 1978, a collection of short stories. *Judasland* and *The Upstairs People*, each about a middle-aged woman assuming a role of warmth and charm, are to appear in 1990. See Crosland, 1981, quoted above, and Alasdair MacIntyre, *TLS*, 1967, 657.

Day, Dorothy May, 1897–1980, journalist, activist, founder and editor of *The Catholic Worker*. Da. of Grace (Satterlee) and John

D., a journalist, she was b. in Brooklyn, NYC, and raised in San Francisco and Chicago. At school she wrote diaries, stories and poems. After two years at the Univ. of Illinois at Urbana-Champaign, she joined the Industrial Workers of the World (the 'Wobblies'), and became an outstanding reporter for the socialist *Call*, then *The Masses* (suppressed during WWI), and later the *Liberator*. Her first of many political jail sentences was 30 days in 1917, for suffragist picketing of the White House; she was arrested in 1973, demonstrating in support of Cesar Chavez. She trained as nurse, had a 'fatal passion' and an abortion, and an equally unhappy (and brief) marriage. After travel in Europe, she worked in several cities, then bought a cottage on Staten Island with money from her autobiographical novel, *The Eleventh Virgin*, 1924. Her relationship with anarchist Forster Batterham produced a daughter, but ended as she moved steadily towards baptism as a Catholic, 1927. She had a stint as a Hollywood scriptwriter, 1929, then six months in Mexico writing for *Commonweal*. She founded *The Catholic Worker* with Peter Maurin in 1933, edited it until her death (bibliog. by Anne and Alice Klejment, 1986), and set up 'houses of hospitality' for the poor and unemployed, living in voluntary poverty as a leader of the Worker Groups. Her books (which she ranked below practical work, but which have lastingly influenced US Catholicism) include *From Union Square to Rome*, 1938, her conversion story; several accounts of her ongoing work (from *House of Hospitality*, 1939, to *On Pilgrimage: The Sixties*, 1972); and books about Maurin, 1950, and St Thérèse of Lisieux, 1960. She wrote an autobiography, *The Long Loneliness*, 1952 (often repr. and transl.), because 'if you love you want to give'. It explains her related Catholicism, radicalism and pacifism (Communism was incompatible with her faith though she accumulated a fat FBI dossier) and the effects of her belief and work on her personal life. She died at a Catholic Worker hospice in NYC. MSS at Marquette Univ.; selected writings ed. Robert Ellsberg, 1983; life by William D. Miller, 1982, study by Mel Piehl, 1982.

Daye, Eliza, Lancaster poet, educ. by her father. In 1798 she pub. *Poems on Various Subjects*, Liverpool, Lancaster, and London, with a strongly north-country subscribers' list. She likes fable, allegory, and personification, and often treats charitable or reforming and occasionally feminist subjects. 'The Laurel' tells how the poet Colin, crowned by Hannah and Eliza, gives the crown to Eliza instead. In 1812–13 she was editing her father's sermons for print, suffering ill health, 'continual depressions and anxiety', and corresponding with M. A. JEVONS's father, who helped her with money despite a quarrel over leases. She has been confused with three others. First: Eliza (Nichols) Day, b. in rural Hunts. *c.* 1735 (wife of Thomas Day, d. 1807), a Methodist; she pub., as 'Eliza', elegies on five deaths in 1789, and *Poems on Various Subjects*, 1814 (all pious, many funerary), culled from her whole span after her conversion in 1757. Second: a more worldly 'Eliza', who pub. sentimental, sometimes amorous poetry in *The Star* and collected it in *Poems and Fugitive Pieces*, 1796; she cannot be Daye since she writes on the unhealed 'recent anguish' of her mother's death, while Daye tells how in 'thoughtless youth' she made visits with her father to her mother's tomb. Third: Esther (Milnes) Day (d. 1792), wife of Thomas Day (d. 1789: author, eccentric, and enemy of female learning); she died broken-hearted after her husband's death, and had early poems and letters (earnest, remarkable work for the age of 11–16) pub. in *Select Miscellaneous Productions* of the couple, 1805, dedicated to 'Fair Females' with warm but patronizing praise.

D'Costa, Jean Constantine (Creary), poet, scholar, children's writer, da. of two teachers, b. 1937 at St Andrew, Jamaica, living 1942–5 in a small farming community in St James. She was educ. at St Hilda's diocesan and St Hugh's high schools, the Univ. College of the West Indies, then from 1955 at University College, London (English with some French). She did research in Jacobean drama at the Univs. of Oxford and Indiana. Back in Jamaica as a lecturer in English (Univ. of the West Indies) and government consultant on English teaching, she published scholarly articles on Caribbean literature and dialect (e.g. in Louis James, ed., *The Islands In Between, Critical Essays*, 1968), and sat on the editorial board of *Jamaica Journal* (now the *Journal of Afro–West Indian Studies*). Her first children's book, *Sprat Morrison* (finished 1968, unpub. till 1972), was disapproved of for using 'patois' (actually idiomatic yet 'correct' Jamaican English in a middle-class setting). Undeterred, JD'C broadened her social scope in two more books: adventures of orphaned or abandoned children from a 'home', 1975, and rural St James in WWII, 1978. Often reprinted, they present vivid, precise natural settings, and a children's fantasy world with folklore elements, which may have to yield in part to the constraints of the 'real' world, but is never wholly invalidated. JD'C is now praised for the sense of Jamaican identity which her linguistic variety conveys (see Joyce Johnson in *Wasafiri*, 5, 1986). She edited children's stories, with Velma POLLARD, in *Over Our Way*, 1981. Her poems (in journals, and anthologies like Pamela MORDECAI and Mervyn Morris, eds, *Jamaica Woman*, 1980) catch the grim contradictions of Caribbean history, as in 'On Reading the Life of Mr Silas Todd: Slave-trader, sailor, teacher and saint'. Today's places (like a village now bisected by a road) are haunted by 'laughter of the fieldhands' or 'Particular incidents, clear as newsprint', which 'Glint from the edge of sight'. JD'C published a study of Kingston novelist Roger Mais, 1978; she used her own experience in 'The West Indian Novelist and Language: A Search for a Literary Medium' (Lawrence D. Carrington *et al.*, eds, *Studies in Caribbean Literature*, 1983). She has planned a novel of eighteenth-century Jamaica. See study of her children's books by Joyce Johnson in *Wasafiri*.

Deamer, Dulcie (later Goldberg), 1890–1972, poet, novelist, dramatist, journalist, b. Christchurch, NZ, da. of Mabel (Reader) and George D., physician. She was educ. by her mother, a former governess, and learnt elocution and ballet in Wellington, first appearing on stage at age nine. She m. actor Albert G. in 1907 and toured Asia with a theatre company. Between 1908 and 1924 she bore six children and published a collection of short stories and four popular novels. After separating in 1922, she lived at King's Cross, Sydney, where she was crowned 'Queen of Bohemia' in 1925. During the 1930s she wrote for the stage and published another novel and two vols. of poetry. Her work demonstrates a fascination with religion, mythology and classical culture (typical of her associates such as Norman Lindsay and Hugh McCrae) and is characteristically ornamental in style. Highly romantic novels such as *Revelation*, 1921, and *The Street of the Gazelle*, 1922 (both set in Jerusalem at the time of Christ), embrace antiquity, while *Holiday*, 1940, has a theme of reincarnation. The collection of poetry, *Messalina*, 1932, includes 'Nine Women', portraits of famous women from the past. An unpublished autobiography, 'The Golden Decade', was written in the 1960s. Her MSS are in the Mitchell Library, Sydney, and in the Bellamy Archive, Bredbo.

de Cleyre (formerly De Claire), **Voltairine**, 1866–1912, poet, essayist, journalist and feminist, b. Leslie, Michigan, da. of Harriet Elizabeth (Billings) and Hector De Claire (*not* Liza and Gustave as some sources claim). She was educ. at the Convent of Our Lady of Lake Huron, Sarnia, Ont., and then wrote essays and short stories for (and later edited) *The Progressive Age* (Grand Rapids), as 'Fanny Fern' and 'Flora Fox' (later 'Fanny Forester'). Converted to anarchism by the Haymarket bombing trials of 1887, she started lecturing under the auspices of the American Secular Union and the Woman's National Liberal Union. She made her living by private teaching, beginning with Jewish immigrants in 1891. In 1892 she helped found the Ladies Liberal League and her speech 'In Defense of Emma GOLDMAN', 1893, was published the next year. She was a major contributor to *The Rebel*, and later to Goldman's *Mother Earth*. Her poems and essays on social oppression, women's liberation, education and corporate industrialism were published in numerous periodicals and translated into several languages. In revolt against male domination, strongly anti-Church (see her long poem 'The Gods and the People') and anti-marriage, as reflected in 'Sex and Slavery', 'Love and Marriage' and 'Those Who Marry Do Ill', she not only attacked stereotyped sex-roles but herself rejected the 'regular program of marriage', preferring free-love unions with men. She bore a son to James B. Elliot, but her most enduring bond was with fellow activist and poet, Dyer Lunn. In 1897 she left for France and Britain, addressing the Women's Labour Party and the Independent Labour Party in Scotland on issues of anarchy and the WOMAN QUESTION. Returning to the USA, she suffered an attempt on her life in 1902, and, although never regaining full health, she refused to press charges against her assassin, asserting that violence and brutality are a product of government itself. Her views are expressed in *Crime and Punishment*, 1903. Paying tribute to Mary WOLLSTONECRAFT, she says: 'If we must have hero worship, let us have a little she-ro worship to even things up.' To Emma Goldman she was 'the poet-rebel, the liberty-living artist, the greatest woman Anarchist of America'. See Paul Avrich, 1978, for her life.

Deevy, Teresa, 1903–63, dramatist, b. in Waterford, educ. at its Ursuline Convent and the National Univ. of Ireland, Dublin: a devout Catholic, from her teens totally deaf and dependent on lip-reading. She lived in Dublin during the 1930s and 1940s. Its Abbey Theatre produced her plays, from *The Reaper*, 1930, and *A Disciple*, 1931, and awarded her, jointly, a prize for new playwrights, 1932; but its always qualified enthusiasm for her work waned, and latterly she lacked a forum. *The King of Spain's Daughter*, staged 1935, was her earliest piece to be printed (in *Three Plays*, 1939, with *Katie Roche*, her best-known work, and *The Wild Goose*, both staged 1936). She also wrote for religious orders, and for radio (e.g. *Polinka*, 1946, from Chekhov; *Going Beyond Alma's Glory*, 1949, and *Wife to James Whelan*, 1956, both the latter much admired). Despite her deafness she used sound and the nuances of talk to great effect. She portrays complex psychological motivation, especially that of women; her poetic plays are demanding for both actors and audiences. She writes of romantic, imaginative young women whose life in remote, unchanging parts of Ireland offers no chance of the greatness to which they aspire: often, in some tragi-comic episode, they inherit a more prosaic adult reality. The old, no longer romantic, are powerfully portrayed as well. She also published a children's story, 'Strange People' (in *Lisheen at the Valley Farm and Other Stories*, 1945), and pieces in *The Dublin Magazine, Theatre Arts Monthly*, and *Irish Writing* (on children's author Patricia Lynch, 5, 1948). See J. D. Riley in *Irish Writing*, 32, 1955, Robert Hogan in *After the Irish Renaissance*, 1968. TD died in Waterford.

Defences of women were often a response to written ATTACKS: medieval defences were often conceived as a joke, palpably inadequate, with ironical intent. CHRISTINE DE PIZAN's serious one (drawing on Boccaccio) was translated into English before those of

Sir Thomas Elyot (perhaps alluding to the disgraced – and learned – Katherine of Aragon), 1540. Edward Gosynhyll (a mercenary on both sides of the controversy), [1542?], and dozens more sixteenth- and seventeenth-century male authors. In 1985 two new collections were issued of early defences by or allegedly by women e.g. Rachel SPEGHT: ed. Katherine U. Henderson and Barbara F. McManus; and ed. Simon Shepherd. Other defenders tended to take their stand on three categories: models of chastity, models of exceptional or martyred love for men, and women sharing manly virtues. The more intellectually rigorous Henri Cornelius Agrippa von Nettersheim reached English during the sixteenth century, and Anna Maria van SCHURMAN and François Poulain de la Barre during the seventeenth; Marie de Jars de Gournay remained in French only. The Civil War period brought more popular female voices, many of them QUAKERS, to the genre in English. The forceful generation of Mary ASTELL and Sarah FYGE drew in such obscure contributors as M. B., a 'City Lady' who published *The Ladies Answer* [1703]. Mid-eighteenth-century women mostly make more limited claims, but misogynist lines in Pope and Swift found answerers in Lady Mary Wortley MONTAGU and Lady IRWIN (and in 'Mrs. I. Robinson, chambermaid at an inn at Bath', 1741). By the time of Mary WOLLSTONECRAFT, defenders were formulating more systematic positions; they now had the submissive of their own sex to answer, as well as repressive male advisers who no longer assumed the guise of ATTACK. See also WOMAN QUESTION.

De Fleury, Maria, French-descended Protestant polemicist living in London. After the Gordon riots she pub., by name, an anti-Catholic vindication of their leader: *Unrighteous Abuse Detected and Chastised*, 1781, sold from her own house, depicts her enemies baying against Truth like village curs at the moon. The same year came *Poems* on Gordon's imprisonment and release. She dedicated to him the masque-like *Henry, or The Triumph of Grace*, 1782, blank verse with lyrics inset (Henry is protected from the wiles of Syren by his guardian angel, Religion and Grace). *Hymns for Believers' Baptism*, 1786, is less remarkable. In 1787 MDF plunged again into pamphlet war, with the eccentric preacher William Huntington. He countered her *Letter*, Nov. 1787, with personal abuse from the pulpit and in a pamphlet by his daughter, 1788, denying women's place in the public arena and calling her 'Mother Abbess'. Her *Answer*, 1788, stresses women's God-given liberty of speech. Her *Antinomianism Unmasked and Refuted*, 1791, drew further fire from him, answered in *Falsehood Examin'd*. That year she collected *Divine Poems and Essays* from as early as 1773 (on her brother's wedding). Her most striking poem is the Miltonic *British Liberty Established and Gallic Liberty Restored, or The Triumph of Freedom*, 1789, in powerful couplets. She likens herself to Deborah celebrating Jael, praises (from English history) Alfred, Magna Charta, Cromwell, William III and (with qualifications) George III, welcomes the French Revolution, including women's 'Amazonian' share, and looks forward to Christ's reign on earth.

De Groen, Alma (Mathers), playwright, b. 1941 at Foxton, NZ, da. of Eileen (Vertongen) and Archibald M. She attended Magakino District High School till age 16, then worked in libraries before moving in 1964 to Australia, where she was one of the first contemporary women dramatists to have plays performed. Her four years in Europe and Canada with husband, Geoffrey De G., informed her best-known play, *Going Home*, 1977 (first produced 1970), a study of the tensions among a group of expatriates. They returned to Australia in 1973 and have since separated. While some of her plays have been concerned with eccentric individuals such as the Sydney dress and sex reformer William Chidley, most of her work has focused on women, particularly women under pressure. *Perfectly All Right* (first performed 1973) traces a link between sexual frustration and compulsive housework, while *The Joss Adams Show,* 1970, uses a TV show format to examine the reasons why women batter their babies. Her most recent play, *The Rivers of China*, 1987, returns to the less naturalistic style of these earlier plays, combining scenes dealing with the last days of Katherine MANSFIELD, with scenes set in a future dominated by women. In 1988 it won both the Louis Esson Prize for Drama and the NSW Literary Award for Drama.

'Delafield, E. M.', Edmée Elizabeth Monica (de la Pasture), later Dashwood, 1890–1943, novelist, short-story writer, playwright, journalist. She was born in Llandogo, Mon., da. of Catholics Elizabeth (Bonham), 'Mrs Henry DE LA PASTURE', novelist, and Count Henry de la P. Educated privately by a series of governesses whose characteristics inform the 'Mademoiselle' of *The Diary of a Provincial Lady*, 1931, repr. 1984, her most celebrated work, she spent eight months as postulant in a Belgian convent (described 20 years later in *Brides of Heaven*), served as a VAD in Devon during WWI, 1914–17, then worked at the Ministry of National Services until the end of the war. Her first novel, *Zella Sees Herself*, appeared 1917 and *The War Workers*, 1918. She had published four novels, when, in 1919, she m. Major Arthur Paul Dashwood, OBE. She had two children. Advised by her mother to write about what she had experienced, EMD based a number of her novels, including her best, *Thank Heaven Fasting*, 1931, repr. 1988, on the society she had known as an Edwardian debutante, later drawing on upper-middle-class life in a modernizing Georgian world both in novels (*The Way Things Are*, 1927, repr. 1988; *Late and Soon*, 1943) and in the *Diaries*. She also studied criminology, and based a novel, *Messalina of the Suburbs*, 1924, on a famous murder. Writing from experience for EMD meant observing closely and critically her own life and those of other women. The observation which produced her telling satire also became her motif of self-observation, reflected in many of her works. She reveals the frustrations, desires, evasions and vanities through which women's complicity in their subjugation is exposed. For her, self-awareness is the strength by which women become shrewd critics of their society and responsibilities: 'intelligent women can perhaps best perform their duty towards their own sex' by 'devastating process of telling them the truth about themselves'. In 1931 Margaret Haig Thomas, Lady RHONDDA, editor of the feminist weekly *Time and Tide*, asked EMD to write a series which became the Provincial Lady's *Diary*, an acute, witty register of the habits, mores, and idiom of the English 'county' from the perspective of the Lady – wife, mother, and household administrator (significantly atypical of her class in politics). Succeeding vols. took the Lady out of the provinces to America, Russia and the wartime experience of the 1940s. EMD, who contributed significantly to her family's support, continued to produce numerous works of fiction including *Faster! Faster!*, 1936, satirizing the tensions besetting the successful woman, and *Nothing is Safe*, 1937, excoriating the harm to children consequent on divorce. Social criticism of a milder kind is always present in EMD's fictions which in simple, precise style capture an era in its material tokens, its societal totems, and in the understated tensions of its women's private, inward lives. Life by Violet Powell, 1988.

Deland, Margaret, Margaretta Wade (Campbell), 1857–1945, novelist, short-story writer and poet, b. Allegheny, Pa., da. of Margaretta (Wade) and Sample C. Brought up by her aunt and uncle and educ. at local schools and at Pelham Priory near New Rochelle, NY, she studied design at Cooper Union, NYC, and taught drawing and design at Girls' Normal School (now Hunter College) before her marriage to Lorin Fuller D., publisher and advertising executive, in 1880. They housed and helped find employment for unwed mothers in Boston. MD first tried poems, published in *The Old Garden and Other Verses*, 1886. Her controversial first novel, *John Ward, Preacher*, 1888, deals with the heroine's disbelief in hell and her husband's withdrawal of love to bring her to the 'truth'. (This novel appeared six weeks after Mary A. WARD's *Robert Elsmere*.) Subsequent novels, such as *The Awakening of Helena Richie*, 1906, are less controversial and emphasize the 'rightness' of marriage. Her series of essays, 'Studies in Great Women', *Harper's Bazaar*, 1900–1, praises women like Cleopatra and Joan of Arc, but suggests that the 'modern feminine ideal' is changing too quickly and questions the effect of 'individualism' on society. In her autobiography, *Golden Yesterdays*, 1940, MD reflects little on her identity as a woman, except to comment on J. W. HOWE's efforts for women's rights: 'a movement in which it took all the courage I had not to follow her like a worshipping puppy'. Her view that the right to vote should depend upon the intelligence of the voter, man or woman, made her 'disliked by both Suffragists and Antis', yet she received honorary doctorates from Rutgers, Tufts, Bates and Bowdon and was one of the first women elected to the National Institute of Arts and Letters, 1926. Maud Howe ELLIOTT discusses her friendship with MD in her autobiography.

Delaney, Shelagh, dramatist and short-story writer. B. in 1939 in Salford, Lancs, da. of Elsie and of Joseph D., bus-inspector, she failed the eleven-plus and attended a secondary modern (non-academic-stream) school before transferring to a grammar school and passing exams at 16. She then found various jobs, but 'all the time I intended to write'. She is still best-known for her first play, *A Taste of Honey* (written at 18, produced 1958, pub. 1959, repr. 1982, filmed with SD's award-winning screenplay, 1961). It treats, with 'a pronounced, authentic local accent', the pregnancy of a working-class Manchester schoolgirl whose 'semi-whore' mother has left her for a man, and her alliance with a nurturing male homosexual. SD has a daughter and lives in London. Later work includes *Sweetly Sings the Donkey*, 1964 (short stories, autobiographically based), radio and stage plays, and filmscripts such as *Charlie Bubbles*, 1968, the account of an author's unsuccessful return to his northern working-class background; and *Dance With a Stranger*, 1985, a carefully researched examination of the 'actual case' leading to the hanging of Ruth Ellis, last woman executed in England.

Delany, Mary (Granville), also Pendarves, 1700–88, BLUESTOCKING, artist and letter writer, b. at Coulston, Wilts., da. of the poor but well-connected Mary (Westcombe) and Bernard G., who had her brought up at school and by an aunt; a Court job fell through at Queen Anne's death. Her father disliked intellectual or 'intrepid' women; her uncle, poet and diplomat Lord Lansdowne, m. her at 17 to his nearly 60-year-old political crony Alexander Pendarves. 'I was married with *great pomp*. Never was woe drest out in gayer colours.' Her husband became 'hardly ever sober'; he died in 1724. When independent she turned to friends, religion, and many kinds of exquisite handwork. She wrote as 'Aspasia' to Sarah CHAPONE and John Wesley, and befriended writers from Mary BARBER to Frances BURNEY. In 1743 she stepped out of her class to marry Swift's friend Patrick Delany. George Ballard dedicated part of his work (see BIOGRAPHIES) to her. She wrote occasional verse; a libretto from *Paradise Lost* for Handel (untraced), 1744; a moral romance, *Marianna* (unpub.), 1759; a translation of a Latin flower treatise, 1762; and succinct advice on propriety to a great-niece, 1777. The BM has her beautiful and botanically exact 'paper mosaick' flower pictures, *Flora*

Delanica, made 1772–82. Letters to Swift were pub. 1766, some on Court life 1820; more, with her account of her first marriage, ed. Lady Llanover, 1861–2; life by Ruth Hayden, 1980. MSS at Central Library, Newport, Gwent.

De la Pasture, Elizabeth Lydia Rosabelle (Bonham), CBE, 'Mrs Henry de la P.', 1866–1945, novelist, playwright, writer for children. B. in Naples, da. of diplomat Edward B., she m. in 1887 Count Henry de la P. (d. 1908) of Llandogo Priory, Mon. (priories, abbeys and manors are common in her books), and in 1910 Sir Hugh Clifford (d. 1941), colonial governor and friend of Joseph Conrad. She began writing with short stories for *The World*. The elder of her two daughters became the novelist 'E. M. DELAFIELD'; she does not mention her mother in her own *Who's Who* entry. E de la P's most popular novels, *The Little Squire*, 1894, and *Deborah of Tod's*, 1897, were both dramatized (*Deborah* at Boston, 1909), as was *Peter's Mother*, 1905 (acted 1906; given at Sandringham by royal command). *Catherine of Calais*, 1901, is historical romance; *The Man from America*, 1905, is 'sentimental comedy'; other plays are *The Lonely Millionaires* and *Grace the Reformer*, both 1906. One of her children's books, *The Unlucky Family*, 1907, was repr. 1980; Auberon Waugh's preface calls it 'one of the great classics of its genre'. Other novels – like *The Lonely Lady of Grosvenor Square*, 1907, *The Grey Knight: An Autumn Love-Story*, 1908, and *Michael Ferrys*, 1913 – concentrate on young women's problems in marriages (often arranged) to usually much older, tyrannical men, on mother daughter relations, on mothers turning to their children to compensate for unfulfilled or empty lives, and on fear of ageing. A pervasive aura of sentimental romance is sometimes mitigated by successfully displayed comic sense. Between 1912 and 1929 E de la P lived in the then Gold Coast (editing an album there, 1918), Nigeria, Ceylon, the Malay States and Borneo.

De la Roche, Mazo, Maisie, 1879–1961, novelist, short-story writer, dramatist, da. of Alberta (Lundy) and William Richmond Roche, who was Irish, not (as widely believed) of aristocratic French descent. B. in Newmarket, Ont., she lived there and in Toronto and Galt before moving with her family to a southern Ontario farm. She was educ. at Parkdale College, Toronto, and spent most of her writing life in a rural cottage with her beloved secretary, Carolyn Clement, who was adopted by the family as a child. MDR's autobiography, published at 78 (though far from self-revealing), mentions their decades of shared private story-telling ('our Play'). The first of her public fictions, *Possession*, 1923, and *Delight*, 1926, set in rural Ontario, were read as realist. So successful was *Jalna*, 1927, the story of the rural gentry Whiteoaks family, which won the Atlantic–Little Brown $10,000 fiction award, that it led to 15 further volumes in the Whiteoaks chronicle. Dramatic and vivid, with strong characterization (its most notable figure is its matriarch), the series made gothic romance seem plausible and created a lasting myth of a Canadian gentry. Selling in the millions with several foreign-language editions, it made MDR one of the most internationally popular of Canadian novelists. See Joan Givner, *MDR: The Hidden Life*. 1989.

Delaval, Lady **Elizabeth** (Livingston), 1649–1717, memoirist, da. of Catherine (Howard), 'a woman of very good wit' (d. 1650) and James L., Viscount Newburgh, Royalists who soon 'forsoke' their baby and fled abroad. Brought up at Nocton, Lincs., by a stern aunt and beloved grandmother, she learned French, tried hard to learn 'subjection', loved reading (especially Madeleine de SCUDÉRY and other ROMANCE-writers), and at 14 began writing meditations on events of her life, with related prayers and some verse (early 'scater'd paper's' gathered when she lost her lover, *c*. 1670; all re-copied after 1700: MS in Bodleian, ed. Douglas G. Greene, 1978). The first tells how, before 11, she was flattered and fooled by a woman servant she loved. Employed at Catherine of Braganza's court, *c.* 1663–5, she ran up debts for clothes; this added to her guilt about her lukewarm religion and anger at her father, whose financial demands drove away her lover. Her resistance to the 'shakells' of marriage to the debauched and sickly Robert D. sank into apathy; she renounced gaiety and mirth; the last meditation, 1671, confesses her 'wicked revengefull spirit' towards new husband and newly dead father. As a childless widow she married the much younger Henry Hatcher, 1682. Business interests of the 1670s gave way to Jacobite ones on her political exile in 1689.

Dell, Ethel May, 1881–1939, popular novelist and short-story writer, da. of Irene (Parrott), a Protestant, and Victor D., an ex-Catholic who worked in life assurance. B. in Brixton, she lived at various places near London. She wrote tales (of knights errant) while her mother was teaching her and her dominating elder sister at home, then for schoolmates at Streatham College for Girls, 1893–8; her father had some privately printed. She sent work to magazines in 1900; next year she tried to place a novel, rejected an inadequate offer for three stories, and had her first acceptances from *Red Magazine* and the *Universal and Ludgate Magazine*. (Some cousins at once began counting her uses of 'passion', 'tremble', 'pant', and 'thrill'.) Her characteristic first novel, *The Way of an Eagle*, collected 13 rejections (probably as too risqué for a woman) in many drafts before appearing in 1912, an instant bestseller, repr. 27 times by 1915. Its scapegrace hero promises the heroine's father (commander of an Indian frontier fort where whites are about to be overwhelmed by 'a host of dark') that he will save her honour by shooting her if necessary, but instead rescues her and wins her after many vicissitudes. Disturbed by her 'sudden wealth', EMD gave most of it to her family. She wrote about 20 more novels (*The Knave of Diamonds*, 1913, was dramatized in 1921), eight books of stories, and one of verse, and married Lt.-Col. G. T. Savage in 1922. Her code is simple (courage, Empire, and protection of women, 'the first primaeval instinct of human chivalry') and classbound (heroines bear 'the unmistakable stamp of high breeding in every delicate movement'), her style cliché-ridden. Male sexuality is steamily hinted at (she was forbidden to nice girls like Nancy MITFORD) and often violent ('great purple welts crossed and re-crossed each other on the livid features'), but idealizing love triumphs. By critics she was 'much derided', as Stevie SMITH wrote in defending her, 1958. Many works were condensed by Barbara CARTLAND in the 1970s and 1980s. Life by her adoptive niece Penelope D., 1977.

Dempster, Charlotte Louise Hawkins, 1835–1913, novelist, b. Forfar, Scotland, fourth of five children of Charlotte D. and James Whitshed H., who were 'more or less cousins' and descendants of the same landowner. She was educ. at home by masters, including a professor of anatomy who taught her science. She spent her late teens in Paris, later travelled in Italy and settled in Cannes in 1880 with her sister. Her novels use a variety of settings to treat potentially serious subjects in a superficial way. In *Vera*, 1871, Colonel St John, in love with Vera, is almost thwarted by his injury and the fact that he killed Vera's cousin in the Crimean War. *Marjory's Husband*, 1888, is about two middle-class sisters' involvement with a working-class couple but remains safely within middle-class perspective. She also wrote *Essays*, 1872, on European art and literature and an autobiography, *The Manners of My Time*, 1920 (pub. posthumously, ed. Alice Knox), which is factual and external, eschewing 'things that belong to the sanctuary of the soul'. It also comments negatively on her spinsterhood:

'A spinster can only look at life through the windows'.

Denison, Mary (Andrews), 'Clara Vance', 1826–1911, novelist, b. Cambridge, Mass., da. of Jerusha (Robins) and Thomas Franklin A. She was educ. in public and private schools and in 1846 she m. Rev. Charles Wheeler D., editor of *The Emancipator*, a New York anti-slavery paper, and the Boston *Olive Branch*, and later a consul. They lived in many places, including British Guiana and London. Her novel *Gertrude Russell*, a crusade against alcohol, was published by the American Baptist Publication Society in 1849. She contributed to *Godey's Ladies' Book, Harper's Weekly* and *People's Home Journal*, and wrote over 60 novels. Although popular in their time, her novels about pure, sweet, noble heroines soon dated. Novels such as *Chip, the Cave Child*, 1860, offer stereotypical situations and stock formulas and *Out of the Prison*, 1864, and *Victor Norman, Rector*, 1873, reinforce religious conservatism. Her most popular and famous novel, *That Husband of Mine*, 1877, promoted the virtues of marriage. *The Romance of a School Boy*, 1893, was for young readers.

De Pratz, Claire, d. 1934, novelist, teacher and journalist, b. London, of partly French parentage on both sides. She was educ. in London, an Associate of Queen's College and a graduate of the Sorbonne. She worked as professor of English Language and Literature at the Lycée Racine, Paris, and for the General Inspectorship of the Public Charities of France at the Ministry of the Interior. A regular contributor to the *Westminster Gazette, Daily News, Athenaem*, she worked more notably on the staff of *La Fronde*, the Paris daily managed and written entirely by women. In 1890, she transl. Pierre Loti's *Pêcheurs d'Islande*. Her first novel, *Eve Norris*, 1907, was followed by *Elizabeth Davenay*, 1909, a semi-autobiographical novel dealing with teaching and women's journalism in Paris. Its heroine proclaims, 'I want to feel myself free to owe nothing to man's help or dominion'. *The Education of Josephine*, 1910, and *Pomm's Daughter*, 1914, present a more moderate message of the need to temper feminism with femininity. She also wrote on France in and out of wartime, and compiled a much-reprinted French cookery book.

Desai, Anita (Mazumdar), novelist, short-story writer, b. 1937 at Mussoorie, N. India, da. of German Toni (Nime) and Bengali D. N. M. She wrote in English from early childhood, and had her Indian education in that language at Queen Mary's School, Miranda House (a women's college) and Delhi Univ. (BA in English). She began publishing stories before marrying Ashvin D. in 1958; she has four children. (Unusually among Indian authors, she has published three fine children's books, 1974, 1976, 1982.) Her themes are Indian, middle-class, feminist and psychological. Her heroines, from Maya in *Cry, the Peacock*, 1963, struggle silently, heroically, to retain a sense of order, integrity and dignity. Maya, driven insane, kills her husband; most feel rather than act, enduring lost years of suppression and misery, seldom fighting, suffering in any battle, winning no wars. Well-travelled, AD sets almost all her fiction in N. India (though she places an Indian heroine in England in *Bye-Bye, Blackbird*, 1971). In a story in *Games at Twilight*, 1978, an American woman yearns for the simple Indian life, with vegetarian food, meditation, perhaps Buddhism. Though she denies being a political writer, AD's historical political vision can be sharp. In *Fire on the Mountain*, 1977, an account of an old house ends in an evocation of 1947, when maiden ladies were 'Quickly, quickly ... packed onto the last boats and shipped back to England – virginity intact, honour saved, natives kept at bay.' AD's essay 'Indian Women Writers' (a moving paper given in 1982: Maggie Butcher, ed., *The Eye of the Beholder*, 1983) remarks that 'criticism is an acquired faculty' and Indian women have been discouraged all their lives 'from harbouring what is potentially so dangerous'. *Clear Light of Day*, 1982, looks at the Independence struggle and post-colonial India through the eyes of two ageing, contrasted sisters; *In Custody*, 1984, sees the last great Urdu Muslim poet as overcome by age, decline – and modern India. *Baumgartner's Bombay*, 1988, on another decline, brilliantly fuses an obliterated Jewish past, conflicting models of German identity, and kaleidoscopic Indian present. AD delights in polishing her cool, clear style: 'the conscious labour of uniting language and symbol, word and rhythm'. She is reticent about herself; her many awards include the Winifred HOLTBY Prize, 1978. Much comment includes study by M. Prasad, 1981; special number of *Journal of Indian Writing in English*, 9, 1981; Malashri Lal in N. S. Pradhan, ed., *Major Indian Novels*, 1986. Interview in *Mass. Review*, 29, 1988.

Deshpande, Shashi, short-story writer, novelist, journalist, born in Dharwar, India, daughter of the Kannada playwright, Shri Adya Rangacharya. She took a degree in economics from Elphinstone College, Bombay, and later won two gold medals for academic standing in law at Mysore Univ. After marriage (to Dr D. H. D.) and the birth of two sons, she studied journalism, again with high distinction. One of today's most promising and prolific Indian women writers, SD has published three volumes of short stories, five novels and four children's books. *The Legacy*, 1978, short stories, describes the multifarious lives of Indian women and their compromises with patriarchy. 'The Intrusion', for instance, is narrated by a woman on her honeymoon who married only because of her father's entreaties ('I have two more daughters to be married'). Finding her husband's sexual advances offensive because 'we scarcely know each other', she wants to say, 'what you think, what you feel and why did you agree to marry me ... and do you like the things I do and will we laugh together at the same jokes, enjoy the same books?' The story ends with the husband raping her. Though complicit in their oppression, SD's women articulate their frustrations in an ironic voice that subverts the cultural legitimations of patriarchy, and her novels portray the restricted lives of educated Indian women from the point of view of highly self-critical narrators. *Roots and Shadows*, 1983, winner of the Best Indian Novel Award, is the story of an emancipated Indian woman, who, having left her family home to marry a husband of her choice, finds that she has sacrificed her autonomy to comply with her husband's wishes. An earlier version of *If I Die Today*, 1982, appeared serially in *Eve's Weekly*. *Come Up and Be Dead*, 1983, which reads like a most unusual DETECTIVE fiction, is about a high-walled women's college and its ambitious principal, who wishes to suppress the pregnancy and suicide of one of the students. *That Long Silence*, 1988, is narrated by an upper-middle-class housewife who suddenly finds the even pattern of her life and 17-year-old marriage shockingly disrupted when her business executive husband is accused of corruption.

Desjardins, Marie Catherine Hortense, also de Villedieu (1632–83), French playwright, poet and novelist. She is said to have eloped from her parents' home, borne an illegitimate son, donned male dress to issue a challenge, and made two bigamous marriages. She had great success in 1662 with her first tragedy, *Manlius*, and a prose-and-verse work, *Le Carousel [du] Daufin*. Her third marriage was to a cousin. Like Marie Madeleine de LA FAYETTE, she set her fictions in the sixteenth-century French court and was popular in translation. She published mostly by name (de Villedieu): half a dozen novels appeared in English versions, from *Loves Journal*, 1671, through *The Disorders of Love*, 1677 (*Les Désordres de l'amour*, 1675: ed. Micheline

Cuenin, 1970), to *The Unfortunate Heroes*. 1679. She claimed to write realistically, presenting wickedness in order to inculcate disapproval. Oeuvres, 1702; study by Bruce A. Morisette, 1947.

Despard, Margaret **Charlotte** (French), 1844–1939, novelist and activist, b. at Ripple Vale, Kent, da. of wealthy heiress Margaret (Eccles), who went mad in 1860, and Capt. John Tracey William F., RN (d. 1854), of a Co. Roscommon family. Educ. by governesses with a spell at school after running away from home, she calls her childhood 'repressive' but its 'playworld ... irrepressibly happy'. She m. Maximilian Cardan D., an Anglo–Irish merchant and invalid, in 1870; they spent the winters travelling, and he urged her to literary effort. CD's first novel, *Chaste as Ice, Pure as Snow*, 1874, is forceful though overwritten: a woman unjustly cast off by her husband struggles to survive with her child. *A Voice from the Dim Millions*, 1884, professes to be written by a 'Working-Woman', merely edited by CD: its protagonist's family succumb in turn (all but two sisters) to the evils of London. *The Rajah's Heir*, 1890, based on Indian travel, describes a synthesis of Hindu spirituality and western know-how. Widowed in 1890, CD rejected literature, moved to the Battersea slums, set up mother and baby health centres, and became a vegetarian, a Catholic, and a social and political campaigner. Believing that women and labour, the two great twentieth-century movements, should come together, she published in *The Vote* and *Women's Franchise* ('Why I became a Suffragette', 1907), suffrage pamphlets, 1908–13, and, jointly, *Outlawed*, 1908, a novel drawing on prison experience. Joint secretary of the WSPU in 1906, she later founded the Women's Freedom League. A friend of Maud GONNE from 1918 (the year her brother became Viceroy of Ireland), she moved to Dublin in 1921 and Belfast in 1934, campaigned strongly (into old age) as a Sinn Feiner, and died a bankrupt. MSS at PRO, Belfast; lives by Andro Linklater, 1980, Margaret Mulvihill, 1989.

Despenser, Rachel Fanny Antonina (Dashwood) Lee, self-styled Baroness Le D., 1773–1829, political and polemical writer, da. of Francis Dashwood, Baron Le D. (who d. when she was seven, leaving her £40,000), and his mistress Mrs Barry, who married on his death. Sent to a French convent at ten, RFAD deduced her father's family wanted her out of the way. A studious, emotional child, used to writing down her opinions 'almost from infancy', educated chiefly by a young woman with classical knowledge, she returned from France (at the Revolution) a democrat. Courted by several men, she eloped in 1794 with Matthew Allen Lee, but left him next year to live alone pursuing her already eccentric studies. De Quincey likened her, *c.* 1796, to Shelley for atheistical fervour and debating skill. In 1804 she was abducted for her money (her story) or else eloped (their story) with two brothers Gordon, who were tried, acquitted, and fêted. Shaken by mob hostility, accused of insanity, exiled from London (till her husband's suicide, 1808), she nevertheless published a balanced *Vindication*, 1807. Her *Essay on Government*, 1808 (as 'Philopatria'), learnedly expatiates on the social contract, lower-class rights, administrative detail and the role of women. Wordsworth admired it. But her *Memoirs* [*c.* 1812], *Epistle* in Hebrew with English version by H. V. Bolaffey [1822], and pamphlets on family quarrels, [1823]–8, show increasing paranoia (implicitly admitted), extending to charges of 'indirect attempted murder'. She laid claim to her father's title in 1809; her last pamphlet impugns the legitimacy of her brother's sons.

Detective fiction. Some elements of this genre – mystery, 'backward intuition' or 'had-I-but-known', the unmasking of villains – go back to the GOTHIC novel. In Australia, 'WANDER Waif' wrote successful detective stories in the 1860s, drawing her sources from her policeman husband. In the USA, Metta VICTOR (as 'Seeley Regester') published *The Dead Letter* in 1866 in nine issues of *Beadle's Monthly*, then in a 50-cent edition, 1867. This was long overlooked, and Anna Katherine GREEN's *Leavenworth Case*, 1878 (preceding Conan Doyle), was called 'the first American detective novel'. The first detective bestseller, it gave its police protagonist a female assistant, forerunner of the spinster detective. Mary CHOLMONDELEY's first novel, 1887, was a detective story. Baroness ORCZY's *Lady Molly of Scotland Yard*, 1910, belonged to one distinct type among those kinds of female sleuth introduced by early crime-writers of both sexes: genteel ladies, often redoubtable elderly spinsters, teenagers headed by Harriet Stratemeyer ADAMS's Nancy Drew, 'female auxiliaries', proto-feminists (see Patricia Craig and Mary Cadogan, *The Lady Investigates*, 1986). US and British mystery writers in the first decades of this century followed classic formulas of ratiocination in the 'teacake' or 'vicarage' style – clues, puzzles, suspects in the drawing-room – associated with Mary Roberts RINEHART, Mignon EBERHART, Mabel SEELEY, Agatha CHRISTIE, and Ngaio MARSH. Their detectives are generally male: Christie's Miss Marple, a classic amateur, draws on skills as unobtrusive observer and good listener which have developed from her middle-class spinster status (socially respected but not personally held of any account); it is always sweetly and quietly that she tells the experts what they have missed. These writers' settings, though sometimes exotic, preserve the social structure familiar to their readers; the plot vanquishes disorder as well as evil. P. D. JAMES remains close to this school today, while Ruth RENDELL and Patricia HIGHSMITH explore the darker reaches of the psyche, and Emma LATHEN the jungles of high finance. Edith Pargeter ('Ellis Peters'), b. 1913, who writes several genres, is best known for her Brother Cadfael mysteries set in twelfth-century Shrewsbury, their hero a monastic apothecary, herbalist and ex-crusader; other forays into history have been made by 'Lillian De La Torre' (from *Dr. Sam. Johnson: Detector*, 1948) and Margaret Anne Doody (*Aristotle Detective*, 1978). In the USA the 'hard-boiled' school – action story with tough-talking cop (epitomized by Raymond Chandler and Dashiell Hammet) – was joined in the 1960s and early 70s by two New York female cops: Dorothy UKNAK's Christie Opara and Lillian O'DONNELL's Norah Mulcahaney. Recent women series detectives braving the 'mean streets' come from Sara PARETSKY, Sue GRAFTON, and Marcia MULLER, in books which project a feminist aesthetic because their controlling intelligence and moral values come from a female point-of-view and because they are subversive, 'implicitly questioning, and undermining, received wisdom about gender-specific traits'. The Kate Fansler novels of 'Amanda Cross' (Carolyn HEILBRUN) serve as a transition between traditional and more centrally feminist works, written to classical formulas, but focusing as much on social conditions, particularly those of women, as on mystery. (They are set in an academe much changed from that of Dorothy SAYERS's pre-WWII Oxford in *Gaudy Night*, where Harriet Vane was independent in mind but auxiliary in action.) More self-consciously feminist mysteries emerged in the USA with M. F. Beal's *Angel Dance*, 1977, which prompted a steadily growing list of titles, mostly from small, 'left-leaning' presses, like Valerie MINER's *Murder in the English Department*, Sarah Schulman's *Sophie Horowitz Story*, 1984, and Sarah Dreher's Stoner McTavish mysteries. Maureen T. Reddy calls these books 'sometimes a bit preachy', but 'sophisticated in their social/political analyses', challenging dominant values and focusing on 'the mystery of human character' and 'the development of women's character in patriarchal culture'. She includes in her comment the flourishing sub-genre of lesbian detection, which builds on the tradition of sleuth as crusader-outlaw. Katherine V. Forrest, Lauren Wright Douglas and Vicki P. McConnell (whose *Mrs Porter's Letters*, 1982, is a mystery/coming-out story) offer 'soft-centred butch' lesbian cops; Barbara Wilson's *Murder in the Collective*, 1984, and *Sisters of the Road*, 1986, posit 'lesbianism as a strategy for dealing with evil and disruption'; Sarah Schulman unmakes truth into ambiguity and contradiction; Mary Wings (who projected, to her publisher's dismay, a whole series of ambiguous *She Came*... titles) has become a cult success through her sexual openness. See Sally Munt's personal readings of 'Inverstigators' in Susannah Radstone, ed., *Sweet Dreams, Sexuality Gender and Popular Fiction*, 1988 (quoted above). See also Bobbie Ann Mason, *The Girl Sleuth*, 1975; Michelle Slung, *Crime on Her Mind*, 1975; Dilys Winn, *Murderess Ink*, 1979; Barbara Lawrence, 'Female Detectives: The Feminist–Anti-Feminist Debate' in *Clues*, Fall/Winter 1979; Jill Dunbar and Catherine Sapinsky, 'Nancy Drew for Grown-ups' in *Ms*, xiii, 10, April 1985; Kathleen Gregory Klein, *The Woman Detective*, 1988; Maureen T. Reddy, *Sisters in Crime: Feminism and the Crime Novel*, 1988; Barbara Godard, 'Sleuthing: Feminist Re/writing the Detective Novel' in *Signature*, 1, Summer 1989. Sara PARETSKY writes about female stereotypes in detective fiction by men in *WRB*, November 1988.

Deutsch, Babette, 1895–1982, poet, critic, novelist and translator, b. in NYC, da. of Melanie (Fisher) and Michael D. She wrote a surviving poem at five. She was educ. at the Ethical Cultural School and Barnard College, where she began publishing in *New Republic* and the *North American Review*. After graduating, 1917, she worked for Thorsten Veblen. Her first of seven poetry volumes, *Banners*, 1919, whose title poem celebrates the Russian Revolution, was well received. Having co-translated Alexander Blok's *The Twelve* with scholar Avrahm Yarmolinsky, she m. him, 1921. They had two sons, travelled widely in western and eastern Europe, and translated poetry together from Russian and German. BD's *Honey out of the Rock*, 1925, focused on marriage and motherhood: some critics, expecting from the title a 'rich warm emotional essence', blamed its imagist style as self-conscious. She won the *Nation* poetry prize, 1926, for 'Thoughts at the Year's End', and was acclaimed for *Epistle to Prometheus*, 1931, a book-length poetic survey of all human history: she omitted both from her selected poems, 1959, and collected, 1963, 1969. Her work, centrally concerned with wars and 'the victim's pain', also celebrates 'Love, as the old know love. / Fibred with grief, it is strong.' An acrostic ingeniously celebrates Marianne MOORE at 75 as 'Mischievous moralist'. BD also wrote fiction: *A Brittle Heaven*, 1926, whose protagonist, juggling roles as writer, wife and mother, is clearly a self-portrait; *In Such a Night*, 1927, a stream-of-consciousness portrayal of guests' reactions to a woman giving birth at a dinner party (badly reviewed); and novels about Socrates (*The Mask of Silenus*, 1933) and François Villon (*Rogue's Legacy*, 1942). She taught at the New School for Social Research, 1933–5, and Columbia Univ., 1944–71, and wrote tales from Shakespeare, 1946, important critical studies like *This Modern Poetry*, 1935, and *Poetry in Our Time*, 1952 (a standard text which, however, treats only 18 women among 226 poets), and a handbook of poetic terms, 1957. She wrote, translated, and edited for children (including a life of Walt Whitman, 1941). Late poems in periodicals remain uncollected. See Jean Gould, *American Women Poets*, 1980.

Devanny, Jean (Crook), 1894–1962, Australian novelist and socialist, b. Ferntown, NZ, da. of Jane (Appleyard) and William C., boilermaker. She had little formal education but read widely. In 1911 she m. radical trade unionist Francis

Harold (Hal) D.; she had two daughters and a son. Before leaving NZ she published four novels: *The Butcher Shop*, 1926, banned for its frank treatment of sexuality and violence, *Lenore Divine*, 1926, *Dawn Beloved*, 1928, and *Riven*, 1929; and a collection, *Old Savage*, 1927. She joined the Communist party when she moved to Australia in 1929 and despite expulsion, 1940–4, for her forthright feminist attitudes, was a prominent member until 1950. She played an active part in the Popular Front, and helped form the Writers' League and the Queensland branch of the Fellowship of Australian Writers. Novels of this period include *All for Love*, 1932, *Paradise Flow*, 1935, *The Ghost Wife*, 1935, and *Roll Back the Night*, 1945. Best known is *Sugar Heaven*, 1936 (also transl. into Russian), which deals with the 1935 Queensland canefields strikes and the politicization of the heroine, Dulcie. Her only extant play, *Paradise Flow*, 1985, also deals with the struggles of canefield workers in the 1930s. Non-fiction includes a volume on the history of the Queensland sugar industry, *Cindie* 1949, *By Tropic Sea and Jungle*, 1944, *Bird of Paradise*, 1945, and *Travels in North Queensland*, 1951. Her work deals with the role of women in the family, and the need to struggle against sexual and class oppression. Her papers (including four unpub. novels) are held in the James Cook Univ. Library in Townsville. Her autobiography, *Point of Departure*, was pub. 1986, ed. Carole Ferrier, whose extensive research into JD also appears in other publications. See *Hecate* 13, 1 (1987) for a bibliography.

Devas, Nicolette (Macnamara), painter and novelist, b. in 1911 in Co. Clare, Ireland, da. of Frenchwoman Yvonne (Majolier) and painter Francis M., who left his wife with their three young children (one of whom, Caitlin, m. Dylan Thomas). Yvonne moved to Dorset to be near Augustus John. ND 'elected' him as 'second father', became a keen bird-watcher, and met his visitors – Bernard Shaw, Lady Ottoline MORRELL, Henry Lamb, T. E. Lawrence, Yeats, Lady GREGORY and Stanley Spencer. Her father believed in free love but not in education for women ('and quoted Jean-Jacques Rousseau'), and her mother could not afford to send her to school. She learned to read at 12, after begging to be taught: it was a 'major event in my life'. Later her godfather sent her to school in Cannes, then to art school in Paris. She entered the Slade School of Art, London, 1928, where she met Anthony Devas (m. 1931). They had two children. She began her first novel, *Bonfire*, 1958, during WWII, while living with her family in quarters too cramped for painting. It conveys the emotional intensity of childhood alliances, figuring a seducing 'witch' as destroyer of family solidarity. *Nightwatch*, 1961, derives from her experience of the art world (modelling one character on Stanley Spencer), *Black Eggs*, 1970, from her bird-watching. Her sharply observed novels suggest ironic readings for their conventional resolutions, which restore order in the essential pair. *Two Flamboyant Fathers*, 1966, repr. 1985, is 'my personal fable, my truth', also an account of the men in her life. *Susannah's Nightgales*, 1978, explores her mother's family history: visiting France with her second husband, Rupert Shephard (m. 1965, after Devas's death), ND enacts 'a link between the past and the present – a clasping of hands after death between mother and daughter'. *Pegeen Crybaby*, 1986, is a novel about the invasion of comfortable, conventional lives by a sexually free spirit.

Deverell, Mary, b. ?1731/4, 'plebeian' essayist and poet, one of the large family of a clothier near Minchinhampton, Glos. Self-educ., she was dared by a clergyman friend to write a sermon for him to preach; in 1774, after delay by 'sickness and misfortunes', she pub. at Bristol, with mainly local subscribers, *Sermons on Various Subjects*. (Her title-pages still mention Glos. after her move to London a few years later.) The *Sermons*' challenging title, disapproved by many clergymen, was, she said, the only one that fitted. Her repeated claims to humility mask a combative feminism: the sermon on mercy, suggested by an action of the queen in 1770, says that the story of Christ and the woman taken in adultery (who faces trial while her lover does not) shows the Pharisees' 'vile partiality ... in favour of their *own sex*'. Famous subscribers to the second edition, 1776, and to MD's later works, included Elizabeth Montagu and Samuel Johnson. MD's epistolary *Miscellanies in Prose and Verse*, 1781, ostensibly 'a light kind of summer reading' for the young, ranges widely and displays much learning. She notes the unlikelihood of anyone poor becoming a writer, details her own search for patrons, prints an MS poem by Anne Finch, and imagines switching sex-roles in the verse 'Epistle to a Divine, on the united merits of the Pen and the Needle'. *Theodora and Didymus*, 1784, is a poetic tale of the 'female heroism' of a Christian martyr under Diocletian; *Mary Queen of Scots, An Historical Tragedy or Dramatic Poem*, 1792, has stilted language but a strong dramatic grasp of the complex minds of Mary and Elizabeth I.

Devi, Mahasveta, short-story writer, novelist, educator. B. in 1926 in Dhaka, East Bengal (now Bangladesh), da. of well-known Bengali writer Manish Ghatak, she was educ. at the famous experimental university, Shantiniketan, established by major Bengali novelist and poet Rabindranath Tagore, and at Calcutta Univ. (MA in English). She teaches at Bijaygarh College for Women in Jadavpur Univ. A self-consciously political novelist, MD writes about the most oppressed sections of the Indian population: the urban working poor, the dispossessed tribals and the young men and women who joined the Naxalite movement in the 1970s and were ruthlessly exterminated by the government. Author of several novels in Bengali, she became known outside Bengal upon translation into Hindi and English of *Hajar Churashir Ma* ('No. 1084's Mother'), 1979, which describes the agony of the middle-class mother of Number 1084, or Brati, a Naxalite brutally killed by right-wing street toughs working in complicity with the police. The novel is a gruesome account of political repression in West Bengal in the 1970s when lost young men and women often turned up in the morgue, their bodies brutalized beyond recognition. MD's other well-known works are the short-story collections, *Agnigarbha* ('Womb of Fire'), 1978, and *Aranyer Adhikar* ('The Right to the Forest'), published serially in 1979. MD won a Sahitya Akademi Award, 1979. See English versions of two short stories and critical analysis in Gayatri Spivak, *In Other Worlds: Essays in Cultural Politics*, 1987.

Devlin, Anne, dramatist and short-story writer, b. in 1951 in Belfast, da. of socialist politician Paddy D. Raised as a Catholic, active in the early civil rights movement, she has lived experience of her frequent topic, the impact of political on personal lives. She taught English at a Protestant school (which caused 'tremendous pressure'), and began writing only on leaving Ireland for Germany with her first husband in 1976. Her story 'Passages' relates a girl's spooky, misunderstood glimpse of class and sex violence, repressed and emerging to haunt her at a time of polictical unrest (*Threshold*, 32, 1982; repr. as the first piece in *The Way-Paver*, 1986): recast as a TV play, *A Woman Calling*, shown in 1984. Its emphasis on dream and on memory is typical of AD'S work. The play appeared in a volume of 1985 with *The Long March* (also TV 1984: people involved with the hunger strike at the Maze prison in Belfast, 1979–80, both political activists and those who feel 'Your causes are destroying us!'). The volume's title piece, named from a not-quite-accurate translation of the Irish 'Sinn Fein', is *Ourselves Alone*, staged 1985. This centres on three young women involved in the Provisional IRA of Belfast (sisters and a sister-in-law, one 'funny', one 'serious', one 'listening') and their involvements with men and politics. AD settled in Birmingham in 1984 with her second husband, English producer Chris Parr, and son. *The Way-Paver* collects nine stories, written over five years: almost all with female narrators whose lives are buffeted by men, and the past, and politics. AD co-wrote *Heartlanders*, a Birmingham centenary drama for 300 actors, staged 1989.

Devonshire, Georgiana and **Elizabeth** Cavendish, Duchesses of, miscellaneous writers. Georgiana (Spencer), 1757–1806, wrote two fine epistolary novels. Her mother, Georgiana (Poyntz), Countess Spencer, 1738–1814, was also a letter-writer (*Corresp.* with David Garrick pub. 1960); Sarah Duchess of MARLBOROUGH was an ancestor. Before her marriage, 1774, to the 5th Duke of D., GD wrote, besides poems and letters, her anonymous *Emma, or The Unfortunate Attachment*, 1773, confessedly sentimental, also powerful, observant, and humorous (see Isobel Grundy in Margaret Anne Doody and Peter Sabor, eds., 1989). After marriage, GD dazzled society, knew everyone (Mary DELANY, Elizabeth MONTAGU, Johnson, Charles James Fox, for whom she pioneered the art of political publicizing), gambled rashly, and (like her mother and sister) patronized women writers. *The Sylph*, 1779, racily pictures the pressures of high society on an attractive naive heroine who has an unpleasant husband and two mentors: the male, anonymous one turns out, once she is widowed, to be an earlier, faithful lover. From 1782 GD and the Duke formed a *ménage à trois* with Lady Elizabeth (Hervey) Foster, 1757–1824, who was separated from her husband and two sons. The women exchanged fervent letters ('the first instant I saw you, my heart flew to your service'); Georgiana's much-longed-for first baby, born 1783, was spoken of as the child of three people. While she had two more by the Duke (one, Lady Granville, was a writer and mother of Lady Georgiana FULLERTON), Elizabeth also had two by him, born secretly abroad but educated all together, by Sarah TRIMMER's sister-in-law. When Georgiana had a baby by a lover, both women were packed off abroad for two years: Elizabeth wrote *A Journey through Switzerland*, Georgiana a poem to her children, *Passage of the St Gothard*, both pub. without their authors' consent. Elizabeth, widowed 1796, m. the Duke three years after Georgiana died; he died in 1811, and she lived in Rome, commissioned sumptuous Italian versions of Latin classics, and re-issued her *Journey* with her name and Georgiana's poem. Lord Dormer and the Duke of Devonshire own rich MSS hoards. By Elizabeth have appeared *Anecdotes*, 1863; letters, 1898, 1955, and (in French, to Germaine de STAËL) 1980; by Georgiana, letters, 1898 (with verse), 1955; diary (in a life of R. B. Sheridan), 1909. Many lives, some fictional.

De Witt, Susan (Linn), 1778–1824, religious writer, da. of the Rev. William L. of NY. In 1810 she became third wife of Simeon De W., distinguished surveyor, scientist, Elder of the Dutch Reformed Church, and widower with six children. Her *Father Rowland* seems not to survive; *The Pleasures of Religion*, 1820, in verse, was widely reprinted and admired; *Justina*, 1823 (a title already used by Harriet Ventum in 1801), was subtitled in the NY edition *The Will. A Domestic Story*, but in London *Religion Pure and Undefiled. A Moral Tale*. Its heroine is likeable even today, despite a childhood spent collecting biblical texts against scepticism (printed in notes): back in New York after education in London, she says she will always love the land of Cowper, Milton, Hannah MORE, and Maria EDGEWORTH; she is pressed to marry a spendthrift on the grounds that he *needs* her money, and loves the hero (who is likened to Dr Johnson) long in vain before he ceases to love her less serious sister. SDW's *Letters to Ada from her brother-in-law*, also fiction, was published in 1834, the year her husband died.

Diaries. Margaret HOBY began hers in 1599. Puritan advocacy of daily self-monitoring led women to record their lives, but so did secular motives (see Sara Heller Mendelson on the Stuart age in essays ed. Mary Prior, 1986): in America Sarah KNIGHT comes before Esther Edwards BURR, while Elizabeth DRINKER combines pious and worldly interests. Most early diaries are partial or irregular; some are deeply absorbed in the prescribed technical stages of religious progress; others, with broader emotional or factual base, can still bring their writers' experience to life. Later on, leisure, especially for well-to-do unmarried girls, produced thousands of non-religious diaries of every degree of value. Survival is chancy: before her death in 1697, Susanna WESLEY's sister Elizabeth Dunton destroyed a shorthand diary of 20 years, fearing to seem vainglorious (her husband John published excerpts); Dionysia Fitzherbert, b. 1608, deposited two copies of her diary and meditations in the Bodleian. Testimony of witnesses to history (like Elizabeth Byrom, 1722–1801, on the Pretender at Manchester in 1745: first pub. with her diarist-father John Byrom's *Remains*, ii, 1857) gains a dimension from distinctively female viewpoints like those of Mary CAESAR or Anne LISTER. Nineteenth-century diaries took many forms, mostly by middle- and upper-class women (Caroline Fox and Emily SHORE in England, Alice JAMES in the USA), while from Australia, Canada and elsewhere came diaries of diplomats' wives, pioneering women and travellers. Pioneer women's diaries have been ed. by Lillian Schlissel, 1982 (American), and Lucy Frost, 1984 (Australian). US frontier journals include those of missionary Narcissa WHITMAN, Sarah ROYCE, Mary Dodge Woodward, 1826–90 (about a Dakota farm in the 1880s: pub. 1937), Martha Farnsworth, 1867–1924 (engaging, alternately clipped and sentimental; ed. Marlene and Haskell Springer, 1986), and Elinore Pruitt Stewart, b. 1878 (epistolary homesteader diary pub. 1914).

The best-known female Civil War diarist is Mary Boykin CHESNUT, abolitionist but Southern sympathizer: 'God forgive us, but ours is a *monstrous* system.' Other Southern participants were Phoebe Yates Levy Pember, 1823–1913 (pub. 1879), Kate Cummings, 1828?–1909 (pub. 1866, repr. 1959), and Mary Ann Webster Loughborough, 1836–87 (siege journal, 1864); Judith McGuire, 1867, and Sarah Dawson, 1913, were Southern refugees. More recent Civil War discoveries include Hattie Wisdom Tapp (ed. Emma Inman Williams, *West Tenn. Historical Soc. Papers*, 1982), Virginia Davis Gray (ed. Carl H. Moneyhon, *Arkansas Historical Quarterly*, 1983), Annie Harper (refugee, pub. 1983) and Emma LeConte, later Furman (wonderfully clear and direct, pub. 1957). Free blacks Elizabeth KECKLEY and Harriet Tubman (see SLAVE NARRATIVES) wrote in the North and, unlike many others, for publication, as did Sarah MACNAUGHTAN on the WWI seige of Antwerp, 1915. Edith SIMCOX's secret (unpub.) *Diary of a Shirt-maker* chronicles her love for George ELIOT; Hannah CULLWICK, Victorian maid-servant, and Beatrice WEBB, socialist and reformer, in different ways provided a mine for social and political historians; Hannah RATHBONE caused a stir with an allegedy seventeenth-century diary; suffrage workers left fine accounts of their struggles. Historical studies drawing heavily on diary material include M. E. Massey, 1964 and 1966, Anne F. Scott, 1970, Nancy F. Cott, 1979 (New England, 1780–1835), Catherine Clinton, 1982 (the US South), K. K. DYSON (Anglo–Indian), Margo Culley, 1985 (the USA), Harriet Blodgett, 1988 (Britain), and Margaret Conrad (the maritime provinces of Canada 1750–1950), 1982. Cynthia Huff's bibliog., 1985, specializes in nineteenth-century British women's

MS diaries. In this century Anaïs NIN made her diary her literary life's work; May SARTON saw hers as a branch of her writing, Virginia WOOLF hers as ancillary to her fiction. All are of equal interest to literary critics and feminists. Many diary-keepers are marginally authors, like Edna Manley (diaries ed. 1989 by Rachel Manley, a granddaughter: she writes as an insider of artistic creativity and Jamaican politics). Cheryl Cline, in her (intermittently and briefly) annotated bibliography, 1989, rather depressingly observes that 'An unreadable diary may be useful to social historians, psychologists, and linguists', but opens her introduction by quoting Nin, who said her diary 'helped me to make the separation between my real self and the role-playing a woman is called upon to do . . . the diary kept my other self alive.' (It is also true that Nin in time became taken over by the role of diary-keeper.) Cline confines herself to printed sources, and so misses e.g. Stella BENSON and Frances CORNFORD. Margo Culley, ed., *A Day at a Time: The Diary Literature of American Women from 1764 to the Present*, 1985, writes that the 'unique specificity of most journals' makes special demands on the reader 'for active participation'. Having begun with Mary Vial Holyoke writing 'First wore my new Cloth riding hood', she ends with Barbara Smith wondering 'how many Black women have *ever* had the chance to do the simple thing that I have just done. To go away by oneself to write.' See also Nin, 'The Diary Versus Fiction' in Jeanette Webber and Joan Grumman, eds., *Woman as Writer*, 1978; Suzanne Juhasz, 'The Journal as Source and Model for Feminist Art: the Example of Kathleen Fraser' in *Frontiers*, 8, 1984.

Diaz, Abby Morton, 1821–1904, educator, reformer, essayist, children's writer, b. at Plymouth, Mass., only child of Patty (Weston) and Ichabod M. She was educ. at Farm in 1843. She taught in the infants' school there until 1847; an unsuccessful marriage in 1845 to Manuel D. left her with two sons to support. She published educational children's stories (best known: *The Willian Henry Letters*, 1870) and tales of village life for adults. In *The Schoolmaster's Trunk*, 1874, she comments on women's lives from the perspective of a boarding-school teacher. Housework, she declared flatly, was 'woman-killing'; she searches for solutions in *A Domestic Problem*, 1875. She helped found the Women's Educational and Industrial Union of Boston in 1877, and worked for women's suffrage.

Dick, Anne (Mackenzie), Lady, d. 1741, comic poet living in Edinburgh. Da. of Elizabeth and Sir James M. (law lord), granddaughter of an earl, she m. William Cunyngham (from 1728 a wealthy baronet under his mother's name of Dick), who had a mansion below Arthur's Seat. Her 'coarse lampoons and epigrams' and 'many unseemly pranks' (i.e. going out dressed as a boy) drew the censure of the *DNB*. Her few extant poems, pub. 1824, include raillery against fickle lovers: 'For I can kilt my coats as high, / And curl my red toupee.'

Dickens, Mary Angela, 1862–1948, novelist and short-story writer, b. in London, da. of Elizabeth (Evans) and Charles D. She first published serially in her famous grandfather's *All the Year Round*, and later 'retold' for children parts of his novels. Her first, most popular, book, *Cross Currents*, 1891, depicts the price in lost love paid by an actress of 'striving, consuming genius' to reach 'the head of her profession'. Several later novels deal with miserable marriages and disrupting passions. The title of *The Wastrel*, 1900, can apply to either of two cousins: a streetwise opportunist first seen in a western US 'flashy drinking saloon', or a rich, indolent Englishman who eventually achieves moral will) and divorce (by perjury). Among MD's stories, 'An Unprincipled Woman' (in *Some Women's Ways*, 1896) shows a moral and tactical victory by a young widow, 'unusually clever ... a born leader' (misread and disliked by her neighbours) over a power-hungry parson. The title piece of *Unveiled*, 1906, depicts the preternatural exposure of a woman's murderer. MD must have been a Catholic by 1912, when *The Debtor* related, with tact and wide sympathy, the steps towards conversion of a woman whom disastrous marriage, early widowhood, and business success have taught the joy of 'using all her faculties – making the most of her powers'. The religious musings in *Sanctuary*, 1916, question 'the Spirit of the Age' and the value of women's higher education.

Dickens, Monica Enid, novelist, journalist, and autobiographer. B. in 1915 in London, da. of Fanny (Runge) and barrister Henry Charles D., great-granddaughter of *the* Charles D., she was educ. at St Paul's Girls' School, London, which expelled her for destroying her uniform, at a French finishing school and, briefly, at drama school, and was presented at Court as a debutante. Her early, very popular, books describe her own experiences 'exaggerated a bit': *One Pair of Hands*, 1939 (on 20 jobs below stairs in two years as a cook-general), *One Pair of Feet*, 1942 (on WWII nursing training), and *My Turn to Make the Tea*, 1951 (on cub reporting with the *Herts. Express*). She wrote a column for *Woman's Own*, for 20 years. On marriage in 1951 to US naval commander Roy O. Stratton (d. 1985), she settled in the USA until 1980, but continued to visit Britain regularly, feeling it important for the column to remain a local 'everyone's Monica'. MD has two adopted daughters, and has published children's books. Her prolific writings, still mainly English-based, translated into many languages, turned increasingly to in post-war cutbacks. She founded the first American branch of the Samaritans, the organization for helping the suicidal, which she wrote of in *The Listeners*, 1970. Still aiming 'to entertain, rather than instruct', she treated alcoholism in *The Heart of London*, 1961, and child abuse (after going on rounds with case-workers) in *Kate and Emma*, 1964. *Enchantment*, 1989, is an account of the making of a mass killer. Her autobiography, *An Open Book*, 1978, deals with 'the parts of my life that lay behind the books'. Her non-fiction includes *Miracles of Courage*, 1985, about families coping with a child's critical illness.

Dickinson, Emily, 1830–86, poet and letter writer, b. at Amherst, Mass., da. of Emily (Norcross) and Edward D., a congressman and treasurer of Amherst College. She was educ. at Amherst Academy and Mt Holyoke Female Seminary, run by Mary Lyons. Here she resolved to dedicate her life to 'the unknown', which she called 'the largest need of the intellect.' Valuing female friendships, she became passionately involved with Susan Gilbert ('I am glad there's a big *future* waiting for me and you') who became her sister-in-law. Her chosen life was contemplative and increasingly secluded: she read widely, including the 'gigantic' Emily BRONTË, E. B. BROWNING, George ELIOT; wrote; and formed friendships, literary and otherwise. Her circle included Elizabeth and Josiah Holland, who founded *Scribner's*, Samuel Bowles, flamboyant editor of *The Springfield Republican*, her cousins Fanny and Louise Norcross, Otis Lord, a family friend with whom she had a romance in her forties; and after Bowles's death, another of his friends, the free-thinker Maria Whitney. ED wrote at a prodigious rate, sometimes 2–300 poems a year; nearly 1800 survive, as well as 1000 letters – only a fraction of those she wrote – often rivalling the poems in brilliance and intensity.

beneath the superficial to expose the darker side of nature, death and love: temporality and decay. The poems attempt to restore the sense of the abyss before it is domesticated by the word. Most startling are the gothic poems in which the speakers encounter an unknown self or address the reader relentlessly from death bed or grave. ED celebrates 'The Fact that Earth is Heaven – / Whether Heaven is Heaven or Not'. In 1862 she sent a selection of her poems to T. W. Higginson, editor of *The Atlantic Monthly*, who recommended modification of her 'spasmodic' use of grammar and rhyme. ED continued in her own practice, sending poems to friends. H. H. JACKSON urged her to publish: 'You are a great poet – and it is a wrong to the day you live in, that you will not sing aloud.' After ED's death, her sister Lavinia persuaded M. L. TODD to undertake the editing of the poems, and a small selection was pub. in the 1890s, later supplemented by selections by Todd's daughter, Millicent Todd Bingham, and the poet's niece, Martha Dickinson Bianchi. Family feud prevented publication of the complete poems until 1955, ed. Thomas Johnson, who also edited the letters, 1958; the poet's MS books were pub. in 1983. For the life see Richard Sewall, 1974, Cynthia Griffin Wolff, 1986. Recent critical studies include Wendy Barker's, 1987, Cristanne Miller's, 1987 and Joan Kirkby's, 1990.

Didion, Joan, novelist, journalist, b. 1934 in Sacramento, Calif., in an area where nothing now is constant but 'the rate at which it disappears', da. of Eduene (Jerrett) and Frank D. She began early 'to perceive the world in terms of things read about it'. Moving often between army bases during WWII, she later attended Sacramento public schools. She took a BA in English at the Univ. of Calif. at Berkeley, 1956, and won *Vogue*'s Prix de Paris and a job on the magazine: caption-writer, copywriter, then associate features editor, also writer of articles freelance, a hectic time described in 'Goodbye to All That'. Her novel *Run River*, 1963, about a disintegrating, morally muddled Sacramento family, was critically admired for technical skill and coolness. In 1964 JD married writer John Gregory Dunne, and they soon left NYC ('a city only for the very young') for southern Calif. They adopted a daughter in 1966; JD wrote freelance and sought to 'come to terms with disorder'. Her vision of 1960s turmoil, *Slouching Towards Bethlehem*, 1968, collects devastatingly apt comment on 'atomization, the proof that things fall apart', Calif. lifestyles (e.g. the famous title essay on Haight-Ashbury in 1967), and personal history. JD wrote columns for the *Saturday Evening News* (with her husband) and *Life* (bi-weekly). The protagonist's restless wanderings in *Play It As It Lays*, 1970, show the transience and lack of connection of the modern soul, but imply its eventual survival. The prose is broken and jagged, some chapters only a few lines long (screenplay, one of several by JD and her husband, 1972). *A Book of Common Prayer*, 1977, concerns two female outsiders in imaginary Boca Grande: an alienated, unconnected 'norteamericana', and her 'witness', a 'student of delusion', who realizes at last that they are more alike than she had supposed. JD sees this novel, which 'aged me a good deal', 'almost as a chant . . . an attempt to cast a spell or come to terms with certain contemporary demons'. Essays in *The White Album*, 1979, less extreme than before in despair and disconnection, provide vivid topical snapshots (the Manson family, the Black Panthers) and comment on e.g. a shopping mall, Hollywood, Georgia O'Keefe. *Salvador*, 1983, is a nightmarish personal account of that country's civil war: 'no ground is solid, no depth of field reliable.' *Democracy*, 1984, calls the life of its woman protagonist 'a hard story to tell'. JD's style is cold, spiky, incantatory, repeating key phrases with minute, significant variation: 'Colors, moisture, heat, enough blue in the air'; 'Imagine my mother dancing.' JD has been praised by feminists for opposing delusionary romance, blamed for creating passive or masochistic characters. In the *NY Times Book Review*, 1972, she attacked the women's movement as obsessed with trivia and with victimization, denying female heterosexuality, unhelpful to those committed 'to the exploration of moral distinctions and ambiguities'. She reviles political interpretations of art, believes in individualism, is sceptical of social activism. In 'Why I Write' she sees her novels as cautionary tales for herself. See Ellen G. Friedman, ed., interviews, 1984; and for controversy, study by Katherine Usher Henderson, 1980; Patricia Merivale in *Gender Studies*, 1986.

Diehl, Alice Georgina (Mangold), 1844–1912, novelist, musician, b. at Aveley, Essex, da. of Eliza (Vidal) and German pianist Carl M. Educ. by private tutors in English, classics, languages and, in London and Germany, music, she first performed in public as a pianist in Paris, 1861. In 1863, she m. composer Louis D.; they had six children. Highly praised by Berlioz, she performed in London until 1872, and taught for much of her life. But literature was her first love, and she wrote reviews for *Musical World* in the 1870s, later contributing critical essays and short stories to many publications. From the early 1880s she wrote nearly 50 novels, among which are *Griselda*, 1886, a heavy-handed story of womanly self-sacrifice (although AD described herself as 'deeply interested in all schemes to render females women, instead of dolls'), and a number of mysteries and sensation novels. Other books include *The Story of Philosophy*, 1881 (by 'Aston Leigh'), *The Life of Beethoven*, 1907, and two vols., of autobiography, *Musical Memories*, 1897, and *The True Story of My Life*, 1907.

Dike, Royline **Fatima**, playwright, b. in Cape Town, South Africa, in 1948. She attended Moshesh High Primary School and boarding-school at Rustenburgh in the Transvaal, then worked in butcher shops, book stores and supermarkets. She turned to writing to express outrage at her discovery behind the garbage of a Cape Town store of the body of a raped seven-year-old. She worked as manager of the Space Theatre and studied Xhosa history of the British massacre of the Gcaleka nation to make her first play, 'The Sacrifice of Kreli', like traditional folk-drama. She wrote dialogue and praise-songs in Xhosa, later translated them into English and set them to tribal music to keep the rhythms and declamatory style authentic, as a ritualistic political parable based on the oral history of the Kreli resistance to the British in the late nineteenth century. She also designed and sewed the costumes. The play was published in *Theatre One: New South African Drama*, ed. Stephen Gray, Johannesburg, 1978, the year she became resident playwright at the Space Theatre in Cape Town. Her second play, *The First South African*, pub. 1979, is about a mixed-race child. Winner of the Papillon Rising Star Award for women who excel in their professions, she has also written unpublished children's plays. 'The Glass House', produced in NYC, 1980, stresses women's roles in the apartheid struggle, emphasizing the idea that a black and a white girl can become friends and that 'it is not harmful for a white to help a black'. Miriam Tlali, commenting on the difficulty for women writing in South Africa, calls her the only 'really good' playwright. Admitting increasing constraints on her work, FD says: 'I have actually been frustrated to a point where I thought, "What is the point of sitting here and writing these plays?" but, on reflection, "We have suffered for a long time. I don't see why I should give up now. I must just carry on talking until I can talk no more."' See Mineke Schipper, *Unheard Words*, 1985, and Val King and Paul Roberts in *Bond*, Jan. 1980, and *Drum*, Oct. 1979.

Dilke, Emilia Francis (Strong), 1840–1904, art historian and trade-union activist, b. Ilfracombe, Devon, fourth of five children of Emily (Weedon) and Major Henry S., bank manager. Educ. by a governess, she later studied at the South Kensington Art School, 1859–61, then learnt Latin, French and German under the guidance of her first husband, Mark Pattison, Rector of Lincoln College, Oxford. Her friend George ELIOT is thought by some to have based Dorothea and Edward Casaubon in *Middlemarch* on the Pattisons. After his death in 1884 she m. prominent Liberal MP Sir Charles Dilke. From the 1860s she wrote art and literary criticism for the *Saturday* and *Westminster Reviews, Portfolio* and *Academy*, becoming art editor for the latter in 1873; and from 1879 wrote on art, archaelogy and politics for the *Annual Register*. She pub. numerous authoritative books on French art. In the 1870s she joined the Women's Suffrage Society and became actively involved in campaigns for better wages and conditions for female industrial workers. She also pub. two collections of allegorical stories, *The Shrine of Death*, 1886, and *The Shrine of Love*, 1891, as well as *The Book of the Spiritual Life*, 1905, a series of religious musings much influenced by à Kempis. See life by Betty Askwith, 1969.

Dillard, Annie (Doak), poet, b. 1945 and raised ('fiercely anti-Catholic') in Pittsburgh, educ. at Hollins College (BA 1967, MA 1968). She studied theology, m. poet and novelist Richard Henry Wilde Dillard, settled in the Blue Ridge Mountains, Va., 1965, and wrote a column for *Living Wilderness*, 1973–5. In 1974 she published *Pilgrim at Tinker Creek* (prose) and *Tickets for a Prayer Wheel* (poetry). The poems confront transcendence, showings of divine spirit through living things and objects, violence and surreal transformations. The title poem is narrated by one of a family frantically 'looking for someone who knows how to pray', trying out strange rites: 'We baited our hooks / with burnt pigeons / and papers of prayers on a string.' In 'Feast Days', Thanksgiving recalls 'A thousand tipi doors lashed back / void, like riven graves'; at Christmas 'the soil and freshwater lakes / also rejoice, / as do products / such as sweaters / (nor are plastics excluded / from grace).' *Tinker Creek* (Pulitzer Prize) records AD's urgent, vivid, disturbing response to the natural world: 'We wake, if we ever wake at all, to mystery, rumors of death, beauty, violence.' Divorced in 1975, she m. novelist Gary Clevidence in 1980. *Holy the Firm*, 1977, contains religious musing centred on a child burn victim, Julie [JULIAN?] Norwich. *Living by Fiction*, 1982, is criticism 'attempt[ing] to do unlicensed metaphysics' in the 'teacup' of contemporary fiction. *Teaching a Stone to Talk: Expeditions and Encounters*, 1982, continues AD's 'personal narratives' of 'the fringes and hollows in which life is lived' and death is rife: the killer weasel 'choosing the given with fierce and pointed will', a trussed and flailing deer, another burn victim. One piece alternates tales of heroic polar explorers with chaotic contemporary church-going. AD's trip to China with a US delegation and later meeting with Chinese counterparts, both 1982, produced *Encounters with Chinese Writers*, 1985, 'a purified nonfiction narrative ... coupled with humor in the American tradition and no comment': good on women writers in China. AD's latest books (with jointly ed. essays, 1987) are *American Childhood*, 1987, and *The Writing Life*, 1989. See William J. Scheick in Catherine Rainwater and Scheick, *Contemporary American Women Writers: Narrative Strategies*, 1985; E. H. Peterson in *Theology Today*, 43, 1986.

Dillwyn, E. A., Elizabeth Amy, 1845–1935, diarist, novelist, industrialist, b. Swansea, Glamorgan, da. of the moneyed, unconventional, Elizabeth (de la Beche) and Lewis Llewelyn D., later a Liberal MP. A tomboy whom her brother called 'cleverer than us', educ. by disapproving governesses, she kept a diary from her teens. Her fiancé died of smallpox in 1864, her mother in 1866; running the household with seasons in London, she felt like a driverless steam engine ready to run away or explode. Ministering to the deprived, epidemic-ridden village of Killay, she longed for 'actual real work' (perhaps in a religious Sisterhood) and succumbed to invalidism. She wrote 'as a *pis-aller*': stories, religious allegories, a chapter of a novel, 1872, a rejected first book she called 'rubbish', reviews for the *Spectator*, and six social-reform novels treating crime, melodrama, and intelligent women's quest for a place in society. *The Rebecca Rioter, A Story of Killay Life*, 1880, deals with west-Wales unrest which EAD's father had helped put down; it nicely catches its working-man hero's viewpoint (how would the rich take do-gooding intrusions from the poor?) though not attempting his 'Welshy, and somewhat uncouth' language. EAD called *Chloe Arguelle*, 1881, 'Caricatures of the [London society] Humbugs'. The heroine of *A Burglary*, 1883, rejects marriage; that of *Jill*, 1884, and *Jill and Jack*, 1887, working below her station as a maid, burns the whiskers of a valet who harrasses her: *Maggie Steele's Diary*, 1892, juxtaposes a likably priggish young lady and a governess-adventuress. That year EAD inherited a bankrupt zinc-making works: 'becoming a man of business', she paid off the £100,000 deficit and found 'the press have rather gone in for taking me up'. As a public figure she supported the SUFFRAGE and a women's strike of 1911. Life by David Painting, 1987.

di Michele, Mary, poet, b. in 1949 at Lanciano, Abruzzo, Italy, da. of Cancetta (Andrea Cola) and Vincenzo di M., who migrated to Toronto in 1955. A Canadian citizen, MDM lives in Toronto. Married to Bryan Newson (now separated), she has a daughter. Despite an 'unhappy' childhood because of her alienation as an immigrant and her family's 'patriarchal' pressure on her to 'conform ... to a limited and very female role', she found 'a kind of happiness' in the world of books. Her bilingual experience of language, together with her reading of writers such as Christina ROSSETTI, Emily DICKINSON, Simone de BEAUVOIR, Adrienne RICH, Margaret ATWOOD and Erin MOURÉ, led her to writing. She found 'intellectual self-confidence' as an 'immigrant woman' in her education (BA in English, Univ. of Toronto, 1972; MA in English and Creative Writing, Univ. of Windsor, 1974). From Joyce Carol OATES in Windsor, she learned 'to dive into her own experience', and write from a 'woman's sensibility'. Her poetry has enjoyed popularity and praise since *Tree of August*, 1978. She writes in spite of 'the indolent / lips of our Father, / poet without a word'. Her awards include the CBC Poetry Prize, 1980, for 'Mimosa', a long narrative poem which, influenced by Cesare Pavese, explores family relations, but from an ethnic and feminist perspective. MDM edited *Anything is Possible*, 1984, an anthology of Canadian women poets. *Immune to Gravity*, 1986, reinforces her 'double jeopardy', the ethnic and female selves giving voice, without sentimentality, to the silence of margins. Interview in *Vice Versa*, 1, 1983. See Robert Billings in *ECW*, 27, 1983–4.

Dinesen, 'Isak', Karen Christentze Dinesen, 'Karen Blixen', 'Pierre Andrezel', 'Tania B.', 'Osceola', 1885–1962, writer of stories, memoirs, plays; broadcaster. B. in Rungstead, Denmark, da. of Ingeborg (Westenholz) and Wilhelm D., who committed suicide, 1895. She was educ. by tutors, her maternal grandmother, Mary W., and her aunt, Mary Bess W., a women's rights campaigner. She studied painting in Copenhagen, Paris and Rome. As a child she wrote stories, poems and plays which, like her later writings, exploited the fantastic, first publishing stories (in Danish) in 1907 and 1909. In January 1914 ID m. her Swedish cousin Baron Bror von

Blixen-Finecke; they divorced 1925. She managed a coffee plantation in British East Africa (Kenya) with him and then alone, after their separation, 1921. In 1918, she met Denys Finch Hatton, her lover until his death in a plane crash, 1931. In that year financial difficulties forced her return to Denmark. As 'Karen Blixen' she re-created and interpreted her African experience in *Out of Africa*, 1937 (filmed 1985); the modern European saw in the life of primitive peoples and of nature the survival of a lost pre-Enlightenment, pre-industrial past. She had begun to write stories in Africa, and in Denmark completed her first collection, *Seven Gothic Tales*, 1934: like all her major ensuing works, written and published first in English and subsequently written in a Danish parallel version. Its art is an impersonal one, of highly patterned narratives, detached and uniform in style, calling attention to their character as stories, often through the devices of inset tales and multiple narrators. The pseudonym 'Isak (signifying 'laughter') Dinesen' constituted the mask of the storyteller who, controlling god-like the order of the world of story, can mirror the invisible order of God's framing, all-embracing story. The title alludes to the tales' conscious extravagant exploitation of fantasy to display the decadence of old virtue and the limitations of new values. ID's tales present a quest for enduring value, and art becomes a paradigm for the patterns of a life recognized 'as a twined and tangled design, complicated and mazy', wherein the individual discovers fulfilment not in the inaccessible 'secret which connects all the phenomena of existence', but in embracing 'his destiny' (*Winter's Tales*, 1942). ID published three articles written in 1940 after visiting Berlin ('Letters from a Country at War', *Heretica*, 1948) critical of Nazi totalitarianism; she became a public figure and well-known radio broadcaster in Denmark and was honoured abroad. In her seventies, despite the ravages of syphilis caught from her husband, she returned to writing stories and, with undiminished technical skill, renewed the exploration of the themes of imagination and design, of desire, and of destiny. Her story 'The Blank Page' (in *Last Tales*, 1957) has excited stimulating feminist commentary by Susan Gubar and Christine Froula (*Critical Inquiry*, 8, 1981, and 10, 1983). *Last Tales* and *Anecdotes of Destiny*, 1958, develop the familiar influences of folk-tale, Norse saga, the Arabian Nights and the Bible, along with moods and echoes of Shakespeare's late romances. They enhance a debate with Kierkegaard concluded in the posthumously published fairy-tale *Ehrengard*, 1963. *Shadows in the Grass*, 1961, is a collection of reminiscences recreating the world of *Out of Africa*. The final story, 'Echoes from the Hill', recognizes that that world, not only in its romantic-mythical character but even in its historical character, has passed. ID's *Letters from Africa, 1914–1931*, transl. by Anne Born and ed. by Frans Lasson, were pub. 1981. Authorized biography by Parmenia Migel, 1968. See also Judith Thurman's substantial, scholarly, informative life, 1982; Robert Langbaum, 1964; and Sara Stambaugh's feminist reading, 1988.

Di Prima, Diane, poet, playwright, and publisher, b. in 1934 in NYC, da. of Emma (Mallozzi) and Francis DP. After a rebellious youth in Brooklyn, she attended Swarthmore College for two years, then became one of the few women writers among the Beats – Jack Kerouac, Allen Ginsberg and others – described in *Memoirs of a Beatnik*, 1969 (much 'nondescript orgy'). *This Kind of Bird Flies Backward*, 1958, collects poems 1951–6. *Dinners and Nightmares*, 1961, rejects the 'bourgeois' in a stream-of-consciousness (shopping, dinners, guests) cut across with nightmares. DDP edited *Kulchur*, 1960–1 and, 1961–9, co-edited, with LeRoi Jones, *Floating Bear* (nos. 1–37, collected 1973), which printed news, gossip, survival tips and avant-garde poetry: its editors were arrested for mailing obscene material. Her Poets Press, 1964–9, published many '"first books" by writers, often third world people', as well as Timothy Leary, and DDP's anthology, *War Poems*, 1968. Her Eidolon Editions, San Francisco, 1972–6, produced her *Loba Part II*, 1976, and works by Audre LORDE and Jane Augustine. After marriage (to actor Alan Marlowe, 1962; to poet Grant Fisher, 1972) and five children, DDP wrote frequently of childbearing, motherhood, and relations between the sexes: 'I write. I do not / often / like what I write. / dont dont mommy the child says / reaching the desk the pen' (*Earthsong*, 1968). *Revolutionary Letters*, 1968, 1971, a briskly selling underground press publication, chronicles acts of revolution 'like a million earthworms / tunnelling under this structure / till it falls'. *Selected Poems*, 1975, new ed. 1977, tracks DDP's evolving politics, experience, and Buddhist faith, describing her 'ping-ponging back & forth across America' as a mother and poet. 'Yes, I sound like / my mother, yes my face / is lining in the same places ... feel shame / that I still desire / food, sex, soft cloth, feel ludicrous, a fat / old lady'. In poems for Audre Lorde and H.D. DDP salutes 'my mirror image and my sister'. DDP originally typeset her own *Selected Poems* with her family and friends because 'The macho guys in New York publishing don't think I match their image for the Lady Poet.' *Loba, Parts I–VIII*, 1978, enfolds Iseult, Mary, Eve, Persephone, Lillith into a myth of power: 'she laughs, her fangs / flash white and red, they are set with rubies.' DDP has directed the New York Poets' Theatre, 1961–5, and taught at Naropa Institute in Boulder, Colorado, and the New College of California in San Francisco since 1980. Her work includes eight plays produced in NYC or San Francisco, more than 25 books of poetry (many out of print or in limited editions), novels, short stories, translations of Genet and Middle Latin love poems, and several anthologies. Interview in Arthur Knight, ed., *The Beat Road*, 1984.

Diver, Katharine Helen **Maud** (Marshall), 1867–1945, journalist and novelist, b. India, da. of Col. C. H. T. M. She was educ. in England, returning to India when she was 16. She m. Lt-Col D., Royal Warwickshire Regiment, and settled in England in 1896. She shows awareness of the problems of cultural difference in *The Englishwoman in India*, 1909, 'the failure to recognize and allow for the racial differences between East and West'. The book also includes sections on Indian female pioneers. Her novel *Candles in the Wind*, 1909, examines with psychological realism the difficulties encountered by a woman who marries a Eurasian doctor and comes to live in India. In *Lilamani: a Study in Possibilities*, 1911, the situation is reversed: an Indian woman studying medicine in England marries an English artist but finds she cannot adjust to English manners and particularly her husband's fear of a dark child. *Far to Seek*, 1921, continues her story, centring on the experiences of her son Roy, whom she advises not to marry an Indian. *The Lonely Furrow*, 1923, explores Colonel Challoner's love of India which he does not wish to leave. She also wrote a biography of her aunt Honoria Laurence in 1936.

Dix, Beulah Marie, 1876–1970, novelist, dramatist, screenwriter, b. Kingston, Mass., da. of Marie and Henry D. She was educ. at Radcliffe College. After her marriage to George Flebbe, she worked in Hollywood, writing scripts for silent films. This career is reflected in her action-packed novels, many of which, e.g. *Hugh Gwyeth*, 1899, and *Blithe McBride*, 1916, are set in the seventeenth century, testing the courage and maturity of their young protagonists. In *Hands Off!*, 1920, Ned Amory and Sarita Graves rebel against the compromises and wrongdoings of their parents. Her most interesting work (she published nearly 40) is the short play, *Across the Border*, 1915, which underlines the futility and brutality of WWI. Its hero, an unnamed junior lieutenant, is transported 'across the border' into death, where he is forced to revisit the scenes of his military violence: 'All we ask is that a man should take a quiet look at what he's done.' See also M. S. Logan, *American Women: Images and Realities*, 1972.

Dixie, Lady **Florence** Caroline (Douglas), 1855–1905, novelist, journalist, travel writer and feminist, b. London (*DNB* wrongly gives 1857), da. of Caroline Margaret (Clayton) and Archibald William Douglas, 7th Marquess of Queensberry. FD had a twin brother, James, with whom she identified as male companion, and three other brothers, the eldest, John, being the notorious father of Lord Alfred. Her mother converted to Roman Catholicism when FD was seven, and fled to Paris (and the Emperor's protection) with the children. FD's sister Georgina also wrote (as 'George DOUGLAS'). FD was educ. at home in Scotland, then in a convent. By 12 she had met every crowned head in Europe. She was deeply affected as a child by the violent deaths of both her father and of her brother Francis; also by separation from her beloved twin (whose 1891 suicide prostrated her). A great rider (she pioneered the cross-saddle for British women), in 1875 she m. keen horseman Sir Alexander Beaumont Dixie of Leics. She had two sons. She explored Patagonia 1878–9, returning with a pet jaguar acquired in Brazil, and publishing *Across Patagonia*, 1880, an immediate bestseller. In 1881 she worked as war correspondent for the *Morning Post* in South Africa, an experience which transformed her into an ardent Liberal and anti-imperialist. She passionately supported the cause of the Zulu King Ceteswayo, petitioning successfully for his return. Though opposed to Parnell, she supported Home Rule for the Irish, which led to an attempt being made upon her life. FD's works include autobiographical novels such as *The Story of Ijain; or, The Evolution of a Mind*, 1903, which express her growing atheism, her dress reform arguments and her opposition to the marriage service. This last theme also runs through *Isola; or, The Disinherited: a Revolt for Women and All the Disinherited*, 1903. *Redeemed in Blood*, 1889, is partly autobiographical, while *Gloriana; or, The Revolution of 1900*, 1890, is a feminist fantasy in which the heroine decides to ameliorate the condition of women, and succeeds in passing the Women's Suffrage Bill. An epilogue set in 1999 describes a peaceful and prosperous England under female rule. After several more novels, she wrote a feminist introduction to Joseph McCabe's *Religion of Woman*, 1905. For her life, see Brian Roberts, *Ladies in the Veld*, 1965 (marred by sexism); Catherine Barnes Stevenson, *Victorian Women Travel Writers*, 1982. There is a forthcoming biography by Nan Bowman Albinski.

Dixon, Ella Nora **Hepworth**, 'Margaret Wynman', 1857–1932, novelist and journalist, b. London, seventh of eight children of Marian (MacMahon) and William Hepworth D., editor of the *Athenaeum*; she was educ. privately. She wrote a book of short stories, *One Doubtful Hour*, 1904, and a collection of short comic pieces, *My Flirtations*, 1892, under her pseudonym. Her extraordinary novel, *The Story of a Modern Woman*, 1894, deals with an independent young woman art student, art critic and novelist, and her decision to give up her own emotional happiness in order not to betray another woman: 'All we modern women mean to help each other now. If we were united, we could lead the world.' Part of the *Yellow Book* circle, she knew prominent literary figures, including Oscar Wilde, fictionalized as the corrupt Gilbert Vincent in 'The World's Slow Stain' (in *One Doubtful Hour*). Her early journalism included work for publications such as *Woman's World*, and she ed. *The English-Woman*, 1895–1900, an entertaining rather than radical publication which also operated an employment bureau. She served as

Vice-President of the Femina Vie Heureuse and Northcliffe Prizes for Literature. Her autobiography, *As I Knew Them*, 1930, reveals a mellowing of her scathing criticisms of *fin de siècle* society.

Dixon, Sarah, poet, of Canterbury: very likely b. 1671 at Rochester, da. of Elizabeth (Southouse) and James D. Devoted to writing during 'a Youth of much Leisure' (but earliest surviving dated poem 1716), she never thought to publish till pressed by financial need. Though an unnamed benefactor met the need, printing went ahead, through a niece's husband, of her anonymous *Poems on Several Occasions*, Canterbury, 1740: Lady COVENTRY, Elizabeth CARTER, and Alexander Pope subscribed. The BL copy has extra poems written mostly later and bound in. 'The Ruins of St Austin's, Canterbury' (the oldest British Christian site) was written at 73 and published in the *Kentish Gazette*, 1774. Tory, perhaps Jacobite, SD calls her work 'all artless, uninformed', her reason only such 'as by Heaven / To weaker Woman in its Wrath was given', but is well-read and versatile. Her personal tone is often moving, in religious poems and lines to female friends: 'I, from Wave to Wave, have long been tost; / My Tackling shatter'd, my Sheet Anchor lost'. She is also a mordant satirist of both sexes: her love poems, through dramatic pastoral characters, run the gamut from rejoicing to pathos to scoffing.

Dobson, Rosemary, poet, b. 1920 in Sydney, NSW, da. of Marjorie (Caldwell) and Austin D.; granddaughter of English poet and essayist Austin D. She was educ. at Frensham, Mittagong, NSW, later studied art, and worked for a time as an art teacher. The visual arts, especially painting, have remained a strong interest and are invoked in many of her better known poems, such as those in *Greek Coins*, 1977. During WWII she worked as an editor for publishers Angus & Robertson. She later spent several years in England and Europe with her husband, A. T. Bolton, editor and private press owner, and in 1972 settled in Canberra. She has pub. five collections of poetry since her first, *In A Convex Mirror*, 1944. Though the title poem of her second volume, *The Ship of Ice*, 1948, won the *Sydney Morning Herald* poetry prize, she has not achieved widespread recognition, perhaps because she has written few poems on obviously Australian subjects. Her latest collection, *The Three Fates*, 1985, contains some of her best work. A particularly fine sequence celebrates the memory of poet David Campbell with whom she translated two volumes of Russian poetry. Recipient of the Robert Frost Award in 1979, she has also published two selections from her poetry, 1973 and 1980, and edited four anthologies, including *Sisters Poets*, 1979. See P. Carter, *Meanjin*, 1985, and J. Tulip, *Southerly*, 1985.

Dobson, Susannah (Dawson), d. 1795, historical writer. B. in southern England, she m. the medical writer Matthew Dobson of Liverpool, where she wrote the popular *Life of Petrarch*, 1775, which brought her £400. Rendering down the Abbé de Sade's massive French original, she probes the actions and feelings of another age: six eds. by 1805, praised by Clara REEVE, Elizabeth BENGER, and Donald A. Stauffer, 1941. Later came two works based on Sainte-Palaye: *The Literary History of the Troubadours*, 1779, a collection of lives including some women, and *Memoirs of Ancient Chivalry*, 1784, a vivid picture of the knighthood system reading like a source-book for historical novelists. Its preface defends ROMANCE writers, including Madeleine de SCUDÉRY, and stresses medieval chivalry towards women. In London in 1783 Samuel Johnson called SD 'the Directress of rational conversation' (he thought she translated a life of Théodore Agrippa d'Aubigné, 1772, usually given to Sarah SCOTT); Frances BURNEY found her 'coarse, low-bred, forward, self-sufficient, and flaunting', her 'strong and masculine understanding' untempered by modesty. She translated Petrarch's *View of Human Life* [1790]; probably hers too are the didactic *Dialogue on Friendship and Society* [1777] and the original, scholarly *Historical Anecdotes of Heraldry and Chivalry*, 1795.

Docwra, Anne (Waldgrave), *c.* 1624–1710, religious polemicist (Anglican during the interregnum, Quaker from about 1663), b. at Bures, Suffolk, da. of William W. She m. James D. of Fulbourne near Cambridge by 1655; he d. in 1672. Her vigorous, effective writings (seven known) begin with the prose-and-verse *Looking-Glass for the Recorder and Justices of the Peace ... of Cambridge* [1682], bold instruction to those in authority. *An Epistle of Love and Good Advice* to AD's 'Old Friends' the old Royalists, 1683, argues that God's power and spirit 'is tendred to all mankind, as well Women as Men', cites gospel licence for women to prophesy, and ends with a poem. Having been attacked in print, she wrote *The New Projecting Formalist*, 1685, which embroiled her in battle with the ex-Quaker Francis Bugg, who claimed, to her disgust, to be her nephew (accepted by the *DNB*), and printed as hers letters which she also denied. Her 1699 attack on him, *An Apostate Conscience Exposed* ('He writes the same thing over and over again'), drew several vituperative replies styling her Jezebel; by November she had written a *Second Part* of her attack, published with her *Treatise concerning Enthusiasm*, which vindicates the word by means of its Greek derivation. She left her estates to poor Quakers.

Dodd, Catherine Isabel, 1860–1932, educationalist and novelist, b. Birmingham, only da. of Christian (Kelly) and Thomas Milner D., businessman; she had three brothers. She was educ. at a private girls' school, and attended science and art lectures. Though she had hoped to read medicine at Cambridge, her family could not afford the expense. She studied elementary school teaching at Swansea Training College, then taught in several schools, a teacher training college in Manchester from 1892, and at Manchester Univ., 1897–1905. In 1902, she opened a school based on her Froebel-derived principles, pioneering school trips and nature study. From 1906–20, she was Principal of Cherwell Hall teacher training college in Oxford. On retiring to London, she wrote 12 novels, including *A Vagrant Englishwoman*, 1905, *The Farthing Spinster*, 1925, *Three Silences*, 1927, *Ming and Magnolia*, 1931, and *Paul and Perdita*, 1932, which mingled mysticism and an idealized historical past. A Fabian and a feminist in her younger days, she became progressively more conservative. Non-fiction includes various educational works, such as *The Child and the Curriculum*, 1906, numerous articles on teaching methods, and *Eagle Feather*, 1933, a biography of Mary SHELLEY. See the life by Edith Caroline Wilson, 1936.

Dodge, Janet, perhaps also known as **Theodora**, d. probably by 1936, novelist and musicologist, living in Chipping Campden, Glos. A specialist in Elizabethan lute music, she edited songs in 1902 and contributed to her friend Arthur Henry Bullen's *Thomas Campion*, 1903, to periodicals, and to *Grove's Dictionary of Music and Musicians*, 1927. Her two novels deal with women's conflicts with social convention. The artist heroine of *Tony Unregenerate*, 1912, is 'always championing people who do unconventional not to say worse things'. Her lover, a married composer, betrays her, and she loses her baby, but despite social disapproval she rejects a safe marriage and remains 'thoroughly unregenerate ... I don't consider I did wrong'. In *An Inn upon the Road*, 1913, a young woman terrified of the physical abandons her lover; her assertive friend, champion of spinsterhood, tries in vain to teach her 'what a mistake most women make in thinking of love as the end of desire'. The unhappy ending is somewhat melodramatic. JD may have died in NYC.

Dodge, Mary Abigail, 'Gail Hamilton', 1833–96, essayist, journalist and fiction writer, b. Hamilton, Mass., da. of Hannah (Stanwood), former schoolteacher, and James Brown D., farmer. She was educ. at the village school, at a boarding-school and at Ipswich Female Seminary, graduating in 1850. She taught at Ipswich, the Hartford Female Seminary and Hartford High School, then in 1858 moved to Washington to establish herself as a writer. Her early essays were published in *The National Era* (an anti-slavery journal), the *Independent*, the *Congregationalist* and the *Atlantic Monthly*. She saw authorship as a means of attaining independence and in 'Men and Women' exhorts women to 'Write .... The more a man tells you not to write, the more do you write', a theme she continued in *Woman's Wrongs, a Counter Irritant*, 1868, and *Woman's Worth and Worthlessness*, 1872. In 1865–7, with Lucy LARCOM, she edited *Our Young Folks* and in 1870 she managed *Wood's Household Magazine* and published *A Battle of the Books*, about authors' rights. Her other works include children's books, one novel, *First Love is Best*, 1877, a travel book, *Wool Gathering*, 1867 and several books on religion such as *Sermons to the Clergy*, 1876. In 1871 she began spending winters at the Washington, DC, home of her cousin's husband, Representative James G. Blaine, and assisted him in writing *Twenty Years of Congress*, 1884–6. She worked on his biography until she suffered a stroke, when her friend H. P. SPOFFORD completed the work, pub. 1895. Her sister, H. Augusta D., edited *Gail Hamilton's Life in Letters*, 1901; and Spofford's *A Little Book of Friends*, 1916, contains other biographical information. See also Judith Fetterley in *Provisions*, 1985, and Susan Coultrap-McQuinn in *Legacy* (Fall 1987). MAD's papers are at the Essex Institute, Salem, Mass., and other material is held at the Library of Congress and at Smith College.

Dodshon, Frances (Henshaw), later Paxton, 1714–93, Quaker minister. B. near Leek in Staffs., orphaned young, brought up Anglican by an uncle, she learned at boarding-school to read, write, and sew, also music and dancing, which later 'cost me great sorrow to lay aside'. After two years of 'unspeakable afflictions' during which she wrote out a statement of her beliefs, her relations let her join the QUAKERS about 1736. Her *Serious Call ... to the Sinners in Sion*, written as Henshaw, appeared at Kendal in 1744. She married William Paxton (d. 1753) of Durham, 'one of the most amiable of his sex', who left her with four sons; she m. William D. in 1755. A minister for about 56 years, she made PREACHING journeys in England, Scotland and Wales before settling with a son in Warrington. She presented an address to George III in 1775. Her *Brief Narrative* of her Convincement, 1794, was suppressed after proof-readers detected in it 'a certain kind of spiritual pride'; later eds. (as *Some Account*, Warrington, 1803 ff.) are incomplete.

Doherty, Ann (Holmes Hunter), 'St Ann', b. 1786, novelist, da. of Thomas Holmes (who changed his name on inheriting money). As a 15-year-old of 'very superior intellect', accomplishment and wealth, she m. Hugh D., an Irish ex-dragoon twice her age, after a long stream of excited love-letters ('If there is nothing left, we will die, but let me die first'), laced with verse. In 1806 she left him and her baby (alleging his extravagance and cruelty); next year he published *The Discovery*, with her letters, telling how she had eloped with him from a private mad-house where her parents had confined her. In 1811 he sued her lover for £20,000 damages, and got £1,000. She used the name 'Mrs St Anne' privately, and 'St Ann' as an author. *Ronaldsha*, 1808, *The Castles of Wolfnorth and Mont Eagle*, 1812, and *The Knight of the Glen, An Irish Romance*, 1815, tend towards Ossianic, flowery šyle, ghosts, and heroines with 'for those warlike [medieval] times ... a great degree of feminine softness'.

Dole, Dorcas, Quaker pamphleteer whose work shows how female sectaries after the Restoration withdrew to their 'proper concerns'. Where earlier QUAKERS in jail had discussed affairs of state, her *Salutation and Seasonable Exhortation to Children*, written in Bridewell prison, Bristol, in 1682 and published the next year (2nd ed. 1700), calls on disobedient Quaker children to reform 'for though you are Young and Tender in Years, you know not how soon the Messenger of Death may come to call you.' *Once more a Warning to Thee O England*, from Newgate prison, Bristol, 1683 (2nd ed. 1684), describes her prison conditions and urges obedience to the king. She contributed to Elizabeth STIRREDGE's *A Salutation of my Endeared Love*, 1683, and pub. her own work of the same name in 1685 (2nd ed. 1687).

D'Oliviera, Evadne, poet, dramatist, story writer and journalist, b. 1942 in Guyana. She began writing early, based plays and children's stories on local folk myths, wrote with five others in *Stories from Guyana*, 1967 (for the Canadian Expo), and as a PEN member in Donald Trotman, ed., *Voices of Guyana*, 1968, lamenting that 'man is burdened by the brutal bite / Of Tyranny: battered to bits upon / The harsh anvil / Of someone's will.' That year the BBC broadcast her short story 'Drama at Turkeit' as 'The Choice'; others followed it. Living partly in London, she has produced and directed her (unpub.) plays for radio (*The Female of the Species* and *If Freedom Fails*) and the highly successful stage fantasy for children, *The Scattered Jewels*, 1969. Her long ballad, 'Seraphon, or The Passionate Mermaid', based on legend, won a poetry prize; she appeared (with Shana YARDAN) in *Guyana Drums*, Georgetown, 1972.

Doolittle, Mary Antoinette, 1810–86, Shaker journalist and autobiographer, b. New Lebanon, NY, da. of Esther (Bennett) and Miles D. From 10 to 13, she lived with her strongly religious maternal grandmother; she joined the Shaker community, in spite of her parents' objections, at 15. MD worked for ten years at the Shakers' major community at Mt Lebanon, and at 38 attained the highest office of eldress. In 1873 she became co-editor of *The Shaker and Shakeress*, having changed the title from *The Shaker*. In a letter to the *Brooklyn Eagle*, 1881, she complained that 'the voice of woman is not heard in legislative halls', and that 'male rulers alone preside, judge and decide'. Her AUTOBIOGRAPHY was published in 1880 after MD had been among the Shakers 55 years. In it she compares Shakerism with primitive Christianity, which 'lacked ... the recognition of woman's rights'. This defect, she claimed, was remedied in the organization of the Shaker hierarchy, where 'woman was no longer a slave in bounds ... but she became a coworker with her brother man in every department of life'.

Dorr, Julia Caroline (Ripley), 'Caroline Thomas', 1825–1913, poet and novelist, b. Charleston, SC, da. of Zulma De Lacy (Thomas) and William Young R., merchant. Her mother d. when she was two and she and her father moved to Vermont, where she was educ. at Middlebury Seminary and Middlebury College, graduating as Litt. D. She was a founder of Rutland Library. In 1847 she married Seneca M. D., businessman. Her first novel, *Farmingdale*, 1854, was published as by 'Caroline Thomas' but thereafter she used her married name. She pub. at least ten volumes of undistinguished sentimental verse, although poems such as 'Weaving the Web' speak immemorially to women: 'This morn I will weave my web, she said ... / Whose pattern is known to none but me ...', but the day's tasks, as well as Love, tangle her threads and by night she is too tired and falls asleep longing for a 'longer day'. JD's novels, which include *Lanmere*, 1856, and *Sibyl Huntingdon*, 1869, with heroines who apply themselves to their educational opportunities and thus rise above their impoverished beginnings, offered role models to young, poor and uneducated girls. Mary Lester in *Farmingdale*, for example, goes from extreme poverty to become principal of a female seminary 'to do credit to the sisterhood'. The novels contrast the beauty of Vermont with the harsh, unending toil of the men and women who live there. JD also wrote travel books and a book of advice to young married couples.

Dorsey, Anna Hanson (McKenney), 1815–96, novelist, poet and short-story writer, b. Georgetown, DC, da. of Chloe Ann (Lanigan) and Rev. William M. Educ. at home, she m. Lorenzo D. in 1837. Her being a Unionist was less significant for AD's writing than Catholicism, to which she converted in 1840. One of her most popular novels, *Coaina, The Rose of the Algonquins*, 1866/7? (transl. into German and Hindustani and twice dramatized), which AD claimed was true, tells of a young Algonquin Catholic woman, martyred because of her relatives' scheming. Though interesting for its descriptions of Indian life, its main function is to present an idealized model of Catholic womanhood. Another, *The Flemings*, 1869, chronicles the conversion of a Protestant New England family in the early days of America. As well as several other novels, she wrote short stories and poems, some of which were published in magazines. She received two papal benedictions, and was awarded the University of Notre Dame's Laetare Medal. Her daughter, Ella Loraine Dorsey, 1853–1935, wrote Catholic light fiction.

Dorsey, Sarah (Ellis), 1829–79, novelist, journalist and biographer, b. Natchez, Mississippi, da. of Mary (Routh) and Thomas George Percy E. She was educ. at home and finished her schooling with a European tour. SD was active in scientific and intellectual circles and wrote for various periodicals before the Civil War; *The Churchman* published her account of developing services for her slaves. In 1853 she m. Samuel Worthington D. Her first novel, *Agnes*, was serialized during the Civil War, and in 1866 she pub. a biography of Henry Watkins, Confederate governor of Louisiana. *Lucia Dare*, 1867, includes a self-portrait recounting her wartime tribulations, and shows her pro-slavery sympathies, slaves being described as 'inferior organizations' with 'strong animal attachments'. Two other novels followed, *Athalie*, 1872, and *Panola*, 1877, which features a bizarre and convoluted plot, poisonings and miracle cures, and a heroine who is part Cherokee Indian. After the war SD opened her home to Jefferson Davis and acted as his amanuensis until her death.

Doudney, Sarah, 1843–1926, novelist and story writer, b. Portsmouth, younger child of G.E.D. She was educ. by Mrs Kendall of Southsea, and at 18 pub. with Dickens in *Churchman's Family Magazine*. She was a prolific writer of improving stories for girls (for example, 'The Whisperer' in *Eighteen Stories for Girls*, pub. by the RTS). Her novels often end tragically but look forward to happiness beyond death. In *Janet Darney*, 1873, an old woman surveys her life, working through pain and loss towards an acceptance of death. In *Anna Cavaye: or The Ugly Princess*, 1882, a dying child is comforted by the fact her life has brought others together. SD's religious viewpoint, conventionally and superficially applied, often seems like an evasion of the painful emotions she is treating. Other novels include *A Woman's Glory*, 1883, *Where Two Ways Meet*, 1891, *A Child of the Precinct*, 1892, and *Pilgrims of the Night*, 1897. She also published *Psalms of Life*, 1871, and *Drifting Leaves*, verse, 1889.

Dougall, Lily, 1858–1923, novelist, poet and theological writer, b. in Montréal, da. of Elizabeth (Redpath) and John D., religious publisher. She was educ. at home, at private school, and at the Univs. of Edinburgh (separate classes for women) and St Andrews. She divided her time between Britain and Canada from 1880. Her lifelong friend Mary Sophia Earp (Cambridge graduate, teacher and lecturer in political science), whom she met in 1887, acted as her critic, proof-reader, business manager, secretary and adviser. LD published a dozen novels, 1891–1908, original in their unexpected plotting and in the ethical, philosophical and feminist dilemmas with which they confront their characters. Her first, *Beggars All*, 1891, caused a sensation by questioning current moral assumptions, when a well-bred young woman, responsible for her elderly mother and crippled sister, unprepared by education or upbringing to earn a living, answers a newspaper advertisement for a wife. *What Necessity Knows*, 1893, portrays the social, psychological and intellectual diversity of British immigrants in a small Canadian town: it may be read as a story of spiritual regeneration, or of strong, effective women, or of migrants adapting (or not) to a new land. Perhaps the best of her increasingly didactic later novels is *The Mormon Prophet*, 1899, which relates the early years of Joseph Smith through the eyes of a spirited, intelligent young woman who becomes involved with his sect. LD's anonymous *Pro Christo et Ecclesia*, 1900, challenged Christian churches to confront contemporary ethical issues and scientific knowledge; it pointed to pharisaical attitudes, to sectarianism, inflexibility and hypocrisy, and urged love as the basis of religious thought and action. It was widely assumed to be the work of some eminent cleric who preferred his controversial views to be unidentified. LD's later theological works continued in the same vein. From 1911, when she settled at Cumnor near Oxford, she made her home a centre for religious discussion among men and women of varying background, profession, and denomination. Four volumes of essays, in which she was the guiding force, resulted from these conferences. LD made a deep study of spiritualism, and interested herself in the relation between physical, mental and spiritual health. She published *Arcades Ambo* (poems), 1919, jointly with Gilbert Sheldon.

Douglas, Amanda Minnie, 1831–1916, novelist and short-story writer, b. NYC, da. of Elizabeth (Horton) and John D. She was educ. at the City Institute and by private tutors, and as a child met Thackeray and Poe. She began writing stories for the New York *Ledger*, *The Saturday Evening Post*, and *The Lady's Friend*. From the age of 18, she wrote in order to contribute to the family income, and was active in local literary societies. Her first novel, *In Trust*, 1866, sold 20,000 copies, and from then till her death, she published at least one novel a year. She produced three series for children; *Larry*, 1893, won the $2,000 *Youth's Companion* award for children's fiction. AD was a friend of Louisa May ALCOTT and Hon. Vice-President of the New Jersey Women's Press Club. Despite lip service to the NEW WOMAN, most of her novels, like *Sydnie Adriance*, 1869, and *A Sherburne Inheritance*, 1901, embody conventional values of hearth and home, her favourite theme being the suddenly impoverished heroine who regains a home by honest work (in *Home Nook*, 1874, she becomes an architect). More boldly, in *Out of the Wreck*, 1885, the central character, Mrs Marshall, leaves her alcoholic husband and becomes a successful businesswoman. AD's last book was *Children at Grafton*, 1913.

Douglas, Lady **Eleanor** (Audeley or Touchet), also Davies, 1590–1652, prophet, youngest da. of Lucy (Mervyn) and George Touchet (Baron Audeley and later Earl of Castlehaven): sister of Maria THYNNE. Learnedly educ., she m., 1609, Sir John Davies, poet and statesman of nearly 50. In July 1625 (later remembered as the first emperor's month, in the first year of Charles I's reign, herself the daughter of the first peer, wife of the king's first sergeant, living in Berks., the first county) she first heard God's voice, and pub. *A Warning to the Dragon and All His Angels*. In a riot of anagrams, 'masking' her name (Davies) as 'A Snare O Devil' and (Audeley) as 'Reveale O Daniel', claiming 'the Spirit of God' and of the biblical Daniel, she excoriated Charles I and Bishop Laud, and announced the end of the world. On Davies's death, 1626 (foretold by her), she m. Sir Archibald Douglas: God punished each husband, she said, for burning one of her works. She was admired for forecasting Buckingham's death in 1628; in 1633 she visited Amsterdam and published works including an attack on the accusers of her brother (executed for homosexuality and rape), and an elaborate application of the Belshazzar's Feast story to the king. She was undeterred by prison, public burning of her works, a fine of £3000, and a counter-anagram ('Never so mad a ladie'). Her daughter, Lucy Hastings, Countess of Huntingdon ('your mother's Copartner', 'her alone and sole supporter under the Almighty'), published *The New Proclamation, In Answer To A Letter*, 1649, backing ED's interpretation of a text though admitting others as possible. C. J. Hindle's bibliography (*Papers of Edinburgh Bibliog. Soc.*, 1935 – incomplete) lists 42 works. Notable are *A Star to the Wise*, 1643, which finds emblematic meaning for Knightsbridge (where ED is writing), Hyde Park, and Oxford alongside Bethlehem; *The Restitution of Reprobates*, 1644, against the dogma of eternal hell-pains; attacks on Gerrard Winstanley, 1650; and *The Restitution of Prophecy*, 1651, repr. 1978. Eloquent even in incoherence, she loves word-play, double meanings, and confused and gorgeous imagery of beasts and shipwrecks.

'Douglas, George', Gertrude Georgina Douglas, 1842–93, novelist, elder sister of Lady Florence DIXIE. Her novel *Brown as a Berry*, 1874, in which the 17-year-old heroine marries a 52-year-old Calvinist minister, brings out the restrictions of her marriage and of provincial Scottish society, also described in *The Red House by the River*, 1876. *Linked Lives*, 1876, tells of the orphaned Mabel Forrester and the Glasgow slum child Katy Mackay, whom Mabel takes into service. The strongest section of the story is the grimly realistic description of Katy's life in the slums with her sister Maggie. In 1882 GD married Thomas Henry Stock and they set up a baker's shop in Kensington. At her death Stock was serving with the Bechuanaland police in South Africa. GD's other works include *Mar's White Witch*, 1877, and *Nature's Nursling*, 1885.

'Douglas, O.', Anna Buchan, 1877–1948, novelist. The da. of Helen (Masterton) and the Rev. John B., she was b. at Porthead, Fife, and educ. chiefly in Glasgow, at Hutcheson's Grammar School and Queen Margaret College, though 'the only real education I ever had was listening to Father and the boys talking'. Having abandoned as incompatible with her role as daughter of a Presbyterian minister an early desire to act, she spent most of her life as mistress of the house of her brother Walter, town clerk of Peebles. As a young woman she travelled to India, where her brother William was a civil servant; later she went to Canada, where her brother John, the writer of adventure novels, was Governor-General, 1935–40. She began to write when sitting up at night with her sick mother, choosng her pseudonym and her subject-matter to avoid John's shadow. *Olive in India*, 1913, 'a book in which practically all the incidents were true and in which the characters could all recognise themselves and each other', discovered her method. Later, she made conventional claims about 'fictitious characters', as in *Priorsford*, 1932, but *The Setons*, 1917 (originally to be titled 'Plain Folks'), fictionalizes her ordered, hierarchical, provincial family life, and *Anna and Her Mother*, 1922, is 'my mother's Life'. OD disparaged her work as 'mild domestic fiction', but her subject-matter made her a best-seller. 'I'm a Glasgow man myself', wrote a soldier from the trenches in 1917, 'and it's pure Balm of Giliad to me.' *Unforgettable, Unforgotten*, 1945, OD's autobiography (quoted above), describes the development of her writing; *Farewell to Priorsford*, 1950, includes an essay by her sister-in-law Susan TWEEDSMUIR. See also Janet Adam Smith's *John Buchan*, 1965.

Dowdall, Mary Frances Harriet (Borthwick), the 'Hon. Mrs Dowdall', 1876–1939, novelist and non-fiction writer. B. in London to Harriet Alice (Day) and Cunninghame, 16th Baron Borthwick, she was privately educ. and m. Judge Harold Chaloner D., KC, in 1897. They had four children. A contributor to a number of periodicals including *Time & Tide*, she published five volumes of light, humorous non-fiction about the perils of housekeeping, marriage and socializing, from *The Book of Martha*, 1913 (frontispiece by Augustus John), to *Questionable Antics*, 1927. Her four astutely critical novels, 1915–22, address the subject of marriage: *Susie Yesterday, To-Day, and Forever*, 1919, exposes a calculating young woman whose suspect motives backfire when she marries unhappily. *Three Loving Ladies*, 1921, anatomizes the lack of communication between men and women ('I have to treat what I want to say as if it were to a foreigner and had to be translated into his language'), attributing it to radically different sexual characteristics: 'He wants to preserve his own qualities; you want to preserve yours; they are wholly contradictory, and one side or the other must impose its will.' *The Tactless Man*, 1922, describes Frances bargaining with her husband in order to be recognized as a complete person, not 'the wretched button-faced, bird-happy, soap-spirited fool', 'the woman in the white dress under the trees, his little girl, the mother of his children' that he wants for a wife.

Dowie, Menie Muriel, 1866–1945, novelist and traveller, b. Liverpool, second da. of Annie (Chambers) and Muir D. Educ. in France and Germany, she was fluent in both languages. At 20, she travelled alone in the Karpathians and published a lively travel book, *A Girl in the Karpathians*, 1891, the year she m. Henry Norman. Her controversial novel, *Gallia*, 1895, advocated the separation of love and motherhood, with 'splendid, beautiful, healthy, accredited' women bearing children to healthy males irrespective of emotional bonds between them, in order to produce 'finely-bred children growing up happily'. She also wrote short stories, a novel about an Englishwoman in London and Constantinople, *The Crook of the Bough*, 1898, which reveals late nineteenth-century Turkish attitudes to women; and contributed rural vignettes to *Country Life*, reprinted as *Things About Our Neighbourhood*, 1903. Divorced in 1903, she then m. Major Edward Fitzgerald, spent some years in India with him, and returned to England to become a successful breeder of sheep and cattle.

Downing, Harriet, d. by 1852, poet and fiction writer. She grew up (probably) in Dorset, m. a freemason, and for the benefit of her children pub., with an impressive subscription list but 'extreme dread at her own temerity', a 12-book poem, *Mary, or Female Friendship*, 1816, dedicated to a clergyman uncle, 'the kind preceptor of my youth'. Orphan Mary, selflessly devoted to the cousin whose mother oppresses her, proves that woman can be heroic in a 'narrow sphere'. *The Child of the Tempest*, 1821, includes other lyrics, some hectically romantic; in two 'dramatic poems', *The Bride of Sicily*, 1830, and *Satan in Love*, 1840, pious women, by their love, convert first a noble Moor, then Lucifer himself. In 1836 HD published a children's book and (in *Fraser's Magazine*) began the remarkable prose sketches reprinted 1852 as *Remembrances of a Monthly Nurse*. Her narrator, a widow of good family earning her living among a wide range of mothers and babies (rich and poor, Quakers and

Jews), deals matter-of-factly with social climbing, niceties of dress, murder and suicide. Tales in *Bentley's*, 1837, maintain an interest in Satan, the grotesque, and female redemptiveness.

Dowriche, Anne (Edgecombe), poet. Da. of Margaret (Lutterell) and Peter E. of Mount Edgecombe, Devon, she m. Hugh D., rector of Honiton. She spent her leisure time for several years composing *The French Historie, A Lamentable Discourse of Three of the Cheife and most Famous Bloodie Broiles that have happened in France for the Gospel of Jesus Christ*, 1589: a handsome volume, with signed dedication to her brother, a couplet playing on their two names, and an acrostic on his. A preface says the French martyrs are not, like the English, known, and wishes 'the excellent and rare wits that now flourish in England' would devote their gifts to the glory of God. The poem, in alexandrines, recounts at some length events in France since 1557: leading characters (including a crafty Satan) make extended heroic speeches, Protestants are burned and the agents punished by God. AD contributed verses with her initials to a religious pamphlet by her husband, 1596. Later, it seems, he died and she married Richard Trefusis. See Elaine Beilin, 1987.

Drabble, Margaret, CBE, novelist, biographer, editor, lecturer, writer of plays, stories, children's books, essays, b. in 1939 in Sheffield, da. of Kathleen (Bloor) and John Frederick D., and sister of A. S. BYATT. Her maternal grandparents were from the Potteries, and she retains an affinity with that region and its most significant writer, Arnold Bennett, whose biography, 'partly an act of self-exploration', she wrote. Educ. at the Mount School, York (Quaker), and Newnham College, Cambridge, she m. actor Clive Swift, 1960, worked for a year as a member of the Royal Shakespeare Company, had three children, and divorced, 1975. She m. Michael Holroyd, 1982. She describes herself as 'provincial in background, brought up in and inclined to admire traditional realism and social concern in literature'. *A Summer Birdcage*, 1962, *The Garrick Year*, 1964, and *The Millstone*, 1965 (filmed as *A Touch of Love*, 1969), explore the psychology and sexuality of the educated young woman, marriage and motherhood. Her next novels, bracketed by *Wordsworth*, 1966, and *Arnold Bennett*, 1974, reflect admiration for these writers who 'hold on to the ordinary human emotions, the ordinary human duties, the ordinary common human experiences'. Sensitive characterization of the heroine in the semi-autobiographical *Jerusalem the Golden*, 1967, leads to more experimental treatment of woman's subjectivity and subjection, sexual being and expressive power in *The Waterfall*, 'the most female of all my books'. Its successor, *The Needle's Eye*, 1972, scrutinizes patriarchy, of which a stronger condemnation is enacted in *The Realms of Gold*, 1975. Self-reflexiveness in this and her next fiction signals a conflict between 'visions of perfection' and 'the real world' (*Wordsworth*). In *The Ice Age*, 1977, the 'monstrous' patriarchal values of the male protagonist secure practical survival; the feminist alternative remains unrealized, as the openness of earlier endings permitting a sense of liberation and of future is denied: 'Her life ... will not be imagined.' The journalist heroine of *The Middle Ground*, 1980, re-examining her life in her forties, may, says MD, be 'an analogy for the novelist who is fed up with the feminist critics'. Examining modes of survival in women, the book continues an emergent dialogue with feminism in MD's fictions, in which 'The truth' – or 'ordinary common human experience' – is 'more important than ideology'. Reaching for the 'common', MD reflects the 'inclusive' view she admired in George ELIOT: 'the writers that I most admire are those who strive to retain their links with the community'. *The Radiant Way*, 1987, and its sequel, *A Natural*

Curiosity, 1989, examine links with an original community which become entry points to the radiating complexities of family relationships and personal psyches, and points of comparison with the changed social and political conditions of a wider national community. MD edited *The Oxford Companion to English Literature* (5th ed.), 1985. See Ellen Cronan Rose, 1980 (study), and in *Studies in the Novel*, 20, 1988; interview in *Twentieth Century Literature*, 33, 1987; Jane Campbell (on her stories) in *Critique*, 25, 1983; Joanne V. Creighton (on MD and Byatt) in *Mosaic*, 20, 1987; bibliog. by Joan Garret Packer, 1988; studies by Mary Hurley Morin, 1983, Creighton, 1985; critical essays ed. Rose, 1985.

Drake, Judith, medical practitioner and probable author of an anonymous *Essay in Defence of the Female Sex*, 1696 (repr. *c.* 1750; NY, 1970), dedicated to the future Queen Anne; it refers to unnamed earlier works; the 2nd ed. has a commendatory poem by JD's brother James, doctor and Tory pamphleteer. Bolder than her contemporaries publishing by name, she writes to a female friend to pursue ideas which arose in mixed conversation, and 'by Arguments to raise' her sex 'to an Equality' with men, who keep women ignorant on purpose to preserve their advantage. She draws biting character-sketches of feeble males (beau, pedant, etc.). The *Essay* has been ascribed to others like Mary ASTELL or Jane BARKER (both more Christian, less sharp in tone). *A Farther Essay* . . ., the same year, is not, as has been said, merely a translation from French. On JD's brother's death, 1707, she completed the preface to his great anatomical work *Anthropologia Nova* (calling herself 'a Retir'd Disconsolate Woman'). In 1723, after years practising medicine 'among my own Sex and Little Children', she was summoned before the Royal College of Physicians by an aggrieved patient; her son, another James D., wrote a letter in her support.

Drake-Brockman, Henrietta (Jull), 'Henry Drake', 1901–68, playwright, novelist, historian, b. Perth, Western Australia, da. of Roberta (Stewart), medical practitioner and campaigner for women's health, and Martin Edward J., public service commissioner. She was educ. at Frensham in Mittagong, NSW, but lived most of her life in WA, where she was active in the literary world, establishing the WA branch of the Fellowship of Australian Writers, 1938, and serving on the committee of *Westerly*. In 1921 she m. Geoffrey D-B. Her outback travels provided material for her *West Australian* articles (pub. under her pseudonym), and for her fiction and drama, which focuses on the individual shaped by environment. Among her many successful plays are *The Man from the Bush*, 1934, *Dampier's Ghost*, 1937, *The Lion Tamer*, 1948, and the winner of the NSW sesquicentenary competition, *Men Without Wives*, 1938, which contrasts a hardened bushwoman, Ma Bates, with a weaker white woman to explore the limitations of the role of white women in the outback. Her novels include *Blue North*, 1934, *Sheba Lane*, 1936, both set in Broome, WA, *Younger Sons*, 1937, set in pioneering days, and *The Fatal Days*, 1947, about US servicemen in Australia during WWII. *The Wicked and the Fair*, 1957, and *Voyage to Disaster*, 1963, are, respectively, fictional and historical accounts of the wreck of the *Batavia*. She edited several collections of short stories as well as publishing her own, *Sydney or the Bush*, 1948, and her critical study of K. S. PRICHARD, 1967. Her MSS are held in the Battye Library, Perth, and significant appreciations of her appear in Geoffrey D-B's *The Turning Wheel*, 1960, and Alexandra Hasluck's *Of Ladies Dead*, 1970.

Draper, Muriel (Sanders), 1886–1952, memoirist, b. at Haverhill, Mass., one of eight children of Susan Bradley (Howe) and Thomas S., breeder of horses and cattle. She m., 1909, Paul D., musician, brother of the *diseuse* Ruth D. After living in Europe, and from 1911 in London, they settled in 1912 in Chelsea, where MD ran a chiefly musical salon; she had two sons, and divorced after WWI. In 1929 she edited black US singer Taylor Gordon's *Born To Be* (sensitively translating 'the crescendoes and diminuendoes of his ... richly patterned' MS into 'ordered rows of words in nice white spaces') and published her own *Music at Midnight*, written from memory, which moves from her 'two enchanted Italian years', through anecdotes of friends like Artur Rubinstein and Henry James, to leaving for the US in 1914: 'The golden era was at an end.' Living in NYC, she was co-founder and president of the Congress of American Women, and defended it against the charge of being pro-Communist.

Drexler, Rosalyn (Bronznick), playwright, novelist, artist, b. 1926 in the Bronx, NY, da. of Hilda (Sherman) and George B. She was writing at six or seven (with her mother transcribing), and at 14 to 16 producing poems about sex and death. She was 'kicked out of high school [of Music and Art, NYC]' and had a brief career wrestling, as 'Rosa Carla' (used in her third novel, *To Smithereens*, 1972, and a play, *Delicate Feelings*, 1984). She m. artist Sherman D. in 1946, had two children, and educated herself. Her sculpture and painting of the 1950s and 1960s was retrospectively exhibited in 1986 (catalogue, *Intimate Emotions*, 1986); she has taught both art and writing. Her first play, *Home Movies*, staged in 1964, won an Obie; later awards include one from *Paris Review* for a story, 'Dear'. Six early plays were pub. with *The Line of Least Existence*, 1967; *Transients Welcome*, 1984, prints three one-acters; but most of her 20 plays remain unpub. Her novels favour female narrators, from *I Am the Beautiful Stranger*, 1967 (the funny, sensitive diary and fantasies of a girl growing up and negotiating with boys), to *Bad Guy*, 1982 (an egotistical psychiatrist ends by composing her own obituary). Most being out of print, RD set out to save *Starburn, The Story of Jenni Love*, 1979 (whose heroine 'evolved a new female-funk/punk-American idiom'), in 1983. (Her four novels as 'Julia Sorel', 1976–8, are for teenagers or from screenplays.) With her 'exceptional peers' in drama, chiefly women, RD founded NY Theatre Strategy, 1972. Her dramatic parodies take genres which have boded ill for women and drive them crazy: bedroom farce in *The Bed Was Full*, staged 1972, Freudian analysis in *Vulgar Lives or Burlesque as a Way of Life*, staged 1979 (alluding particularly to Freud's *Dora*). She likes to implicate the audience by emphasizing its voyeurism. In *She Who Was He*, staged 1973, RD handles 'a bigger subject than women are normally given credit for': Hatshepsut, peace-loving queen of ancient Egypt. She is raped (as, symbolically, is her country), killed and erased from the records by her husband the next pharoah, a war-maker. Sometimes likened to Kafka, RD wrote of him in *The Heart That Eats Itself*, staged 1987. She calls herself a super-realist, because 'Life is now more absurd than fiction'; incest, rape and death loom large in her work because 'I'm a newspaper and TV addict. It's addled my brains.' '*People* make art. Gender is only part of the artist's experiential stockpile' (Betsko and Koenig, 1987). See Rosette C. Lamont in *Theater*, 17, 1985.

Drinker, Elizabeth (Sandwith), 1734–1807, Philadelphia Quaker diarist. Da. of Sarah (Jervis) and merchant William S., educ. (like Hannah GRIFFITTS) at Anthony Benezet's outstanding girls' school, she m. Henry D. (who left interesting letters) in 1761 and had 8 children and 25 grandchildren. Her DIARY, secular not religious, makes occasional use of lively doggerel verse. She says keeping it is a mere habit; but she is a born writer, with a mind which orders experience by means of words; the habit lasted from 1758 till a few days before her death, her final entry still paying careful attention to language. She is a mine of fascinating detail and shrewd political and personal judgements, fullest during the revolution (a pacifist with loyalist leanings, she coped in her husband's absence with the arrival of British soldiers) and in the yellow fever epidemic of 1793. She read voraciously (though inclined to disapprove of fiction): Lady Rachel RUSSELL, Lady Mary Wortley MONTAGU, Rousseau, Thomas Paine, Mary WOLLSTONECRAFT (who, she finds, 'often speaks my mind'), and H. M. WILLIAMS. See Elaine F. Crane in *PMHB*, cvii, 1983. Of 36 vols. (Hist. Soc. of Penna), extracts were pub. 1889; others (of MEDICAL interest), 1937. Her great-great-granddaughter Catherine (Drinker) BOWEN, 1897–1973, biographer and historian, learned from her work.

Drummond, May, *c.* 1710–72, Quaker preacher and pamphleteer, da. of George D. of Newton. In 1731, while her brother George was Lord Provost of Edinburgh, she 'found Strength to own the [QUAKER] Truth in a publick Manner' there, 'to the Grief and Trouble' of her Church of Scotland family. Called to the ministry, she preached in 1735 at Chester, Bath, Bristol and London, where 'many Thousands flocked to hear her'. Her birth and manner drew the upper classes and even Queen Caroline; she raised money for the Edinburgh Royal Infirmary scheme of George D. (whose fourth wife, married after 1742, was a Quaker). In 1736 MD pub. *Internal Revelation the Source of Saving Knowledge*: three letters of 1733 and 1735, which question Shaftesbury's concept of reason and advise awaiting the dictates of the inner light: also in the *Salisbury Journal* [*c.* 1737]. Returning to Edinburgh about 1756, she was banned from preaching in 1764–5, as she related in [1766]. She failed to pacify the Friends by shifting her ministry back to London, and died still under a cloud. Pope praised her (mistakenly) as 'a Quaker's wife', and an anonymous 'Young Lady' as a champion of her sex.

Drury, Anna Harriet, fl. 1846–79, novelist, possibly b. late 1820s in Brussels. Her grandfather (Rev. Mark D.) and father (Rev. William D.) both taught at Harrow, and left a mass of debts when they quitted the school in 1826. Her father then became chaplain to the Belgian King, and in 1833 in Brussels AD first met Frances TROLLOPE (the Trollopes were family friends). AD knew Greek and some Hebrew, and began her own writing as a child. Later living in London, and from 1866 at Torquay (where she became a close friend of Frances PEARD), AD wrote conventional romances, with a few sharp observations on the role of unattached women in their relatives' households, as in *The Story of a Shower*, 1872, and *The Normans; or, Kith and Kin*, 1870, where the heroine asks Papa: 'What becomes of clergymen's daughters when their fathers die, and their homes are broken up?' (1, 29). Bentley Papers (46619) record an agreement for *Gabriel's Appointment*, April 1877.

Du Bois, Lady **Dorothea** (Annesley), 1728–74, poet and autobiographer, b. in Ireland, eldest child of the perhaps bigamous marriage of Ann (Simpson) and Richard A., later Earl of Anglesey, who 'never scrupled to marry any woman whom he pursued'. She grew up in Ireland, with boarding-school in Dublin, till about 1740 when her father 'set up another wife against' her mother and cut off support. She m. Peter Du B., French musician, had six children, and wrote for much-needed money. *Poems on Several Occasions* 'by a Lady of Quality', by subscription, Dublin 1764, stimulatingly mixes 'Tales, Fables, Songs and Pray'rs', including comment on women's writing and martial spirit. Later works bear her name. In 1766 she wrote the *Case* of her mother, recently dead, in measured legal style; its emotional introduction features a scene (given with variants in *Poems*, and in *Theodora*, 1770, DD's autobiographical novel) in which she confronts her father to demand his blessing at pistol-point. The novel, melodramatic about her own love-life, brilliantly catches her roles as her mother's champion, her father's adversary and passionate admirer. In 1771 appeared two slight musical dramas (*The Divorce*, which makes a cheery romp from her favourite topic, and *The Magnet*) and *The Lady's Polite Secretary, or New Female Letter Writer*, which includes, as a section on verse letters, an anthology of poems by women: Elizabeth CARTER, Mary DARWALL, and especially Irish writers.

Du Bois, Shirley (Graham), 1906–77, playwright, biographer, composer, b. at Indianapolis, da. of Etta (Bell) and the Rev. David Andrew G.: 'one hundred per cent All-American: Indian-Negro-French-Scotch. This is the rich heritage my father cultivated in his children.' She was educ. at both black and mixed schools (where she began writing to explain 'Negroes or Indians' to white children), and at Oberlin College (BA, 1934). The Cleveland Opera staged her *Tom-Tom* (music drama) in 1932; while with the Federal Theatre, Chicago, she composed, designed and directed the children's opera *Little Black Sambo*, 1938 (cf. H. BANNERMAN); her plays (chiefly for colleges and THEATRE GROUPS: unpub.) include *Track Thirteen*, 1940, and *I Gotta Home*, 1942. She did graduate work at Yale (in drama, 1939–41), NY Univ., 1944–6, and the Sorbonne, 1946–7, and had two sons by her first marriage. She became known for her lives of black Americans: the first, on George Washington Carver, 1944, written jointly with George D. Lipscomb, is one of several for children. She wrote of Phillis WHEATLEY in 1949 (juvenile) and Pocahontas in 1953. In 1951 she m. W. E. B. Du Bois, founder of the NAACP. His career overshadowed hers, though her *NY Times* obituary remarked that she 'won fame on her own many years before' the marriage. She wrote for periodicals like *Black Scholar* and was founding editor of *Freedomways*, 1960–3. In 1961 she migrated with her husband to Ghana, whence they fled in 1967. She published books about him in 1971 and 1976, about Nasser of Egypt in 1972 and Nyerere of Tanzania in 1975. In her novel, *Zulu Heart*, 1974, a male Afrikaner is converted to the cause of a united multi-racial South Africa after receiving the heart as a transplant. SGDB died in Beijing, China.

Duckworth, Marilyn (Adcock), novelist, b. 1935 in Auckland, NZ, da. of Irene (Robinson), writer, and Cyril John A., Professor of Psychology: sister of Fleur ADCOCK, poet. She was educ. at 12 English primary schools, Queen Margaret's College for Girls, Wellington, and for two years part-time at Wellington Univ. Married four times since 1955, she has four daughters and a number of step-children; she has worked as psychiatric nurse aid, factory worker, mother's help, public relations clerk, editor of giveaway newspaper, library assistant and waitress. Her early novels create an almost gothic sense of entrapment in women's roles and sexuality. In *A Gap in the Spectrum*, 1959, a SCIENCE FICTION novel, a young woman finds herself in an alien world, like England, where her only role seems to lie in the search for love, leading to trapped dependency. *The Matchbox House*, 1960, focuses on the sexually obsessive closeness of the family, while *A Barbarous Tongue*, 1963, is about a love-affair and pregnancy, complicated by incest. The power games, violence and domination of marriage reach a peak in *Over the Fence is Out*, 1969. In 1975 she published *Other Lovers' Children: Poems 1958–74*. After a lengthy silence – 'writing just couldn't compete with the children' – *Disorderly Conduct* appeared in 1985, set during the 1981 Springbok tour protests, and figuring a 40-year-old mother of four children by three different fathers. *Married Alive*, 1985, treats the effects of an infected serum which drive part of the population insane as a metaphor for the dangers of close personal relationships. *Rest for the*

Wicked, 1986, and *Pulling Faces*, 1987, were followed by the award of OBE, 1987.

Dudeney, Alice (Whiffin), 'Mrs Henry E. Dudeney', 1866–1945, novelist and short-story writer. B. at Brighton, Sussex, she was educ. locally and in 1884 m. Henry Ernest D., whom she called 'the greatest [mathematical] puzzlist of his age'. They had a daughter, and lived in the castle precincts at Lewes. Her popular fiction (50 titles) is set in rural Sussex or contrasted suburbs. She began in 1898, with *A Man with a Maid* and *Hagar of Homerton*, which recounts an attempt to make a lower-middle-class girl into a lady: after two suicides come two downbeat marriages, one putting 'her neck under Young Bill's heel ... perfectly, riotously happy in the prospect of life-servitude', one 'the best that could be done with the fag-end of a life that had always been perversely twisted.' In *The Maternity of Harriott Wicken* and *Folly Corner*, both 1899, one protagonist bears a defective child and comes belatedly and tragically to love it; the other finds happiness only on her ne'er-do-well lover's death. *The Head of the Family*, 1917, and *Candlelight*, 1918 (at first titled *Round the Corner*), each trace over a generation the tangled love-lives of a group of characters. In *Manhood End*, 1921, a turbulent clergy marriage is introduced by a later generation's fantasy of it as idyllically tranquil; in *Seed Pods*, 1927, a penniless foundling and ex-strolling actress marries a pompous mayor of Lewes. Widowed in 1930, AD edited volumes of her husband's puzzles. Her stories share the themes of heredity, sexual mores, marriage both happy and painful, violence, childlessness, and retrospect in age; they include *A Baker's Dozen*, 1922, and *Petty Cash*, 1937, her last book.

Dudley, Mary (Stokes), 1750–1823, Quaker preacher and autobiographer, b. at Bristol, da. of Methodist-inclined Anglicans Mary and Joseph S. She loved school, despite ill health, and was vain of her learning. Though warned against it by John Wesley, she became a QUAKER on the advice of women friends, *c.* 1773, conquering first her dread of speaking in public at all, then of entering the ministry. She married Robert D., 1777, and lived at Clonmel in Ireland, often leaving her beloved family of children (the youngest at ten weeks) and stepchildren for preaching tours in Britain and Europe. Widowed in 1807, she moved to Peckham near London in 1810. An *Extempore Discourse* she gave at Epping in 1812 was taken down by a non-Quaker 'previously informed of the distinguished station she held as a minister'; published at Coventry [1812?] and London, 1823, it displays unforced eloquence and the authority of long experience. Two of her daughters and a son were writers: Elizabeth D.'s life of her, 1825, draws largely on her own letters and memoranda.

Duffy, Carol Ann, poet, playwright, b. 1955 in Glasgow, da. of Mary (Black) and Francis D., brought up in Staffs. She published her first poetry volume, *Fleshweathercock*, in 1973, before taking her BA (philosophy, 1977) at Liverpool Univ. In 1982 she had a play, *Take My Husband*, produced in Liverpool, and began a series of awards and appointments with a C. Day Lewis writers' fellowship, and a writership-in-residence in East London schools. Of later plays, *Cavern of Dreams* was produced at Liverpool, 1984, *Loss* on radio, 1986, and *Little Women, Big Boys* in London, 1986. Seven more books of poems include *Standing Female Nude*, 1985 (praised by, e.g., Gillian ALLNUTT in *Writing Women*, 4), *Selling Manhattan*, 1987, and best-selling *Thrown Voices*, 1988. She is best known for dramatic monologues in alienated voices: a dispossessed Indian, an unfulfilled wife, an ethnic child in Anglo-Saxon society. 'The Dolphins', on captured animals, 'Shooting Stars', on concentration camps, and 'Too Bad', on a political hit-man, use poetic form to control material of violence and horror. After his completed assignment, the killer, one of the 'hard men knocking back the brandy, each of us / wearing revenge like a badge on his heart', regrets only that it has kept him from pursuing a fancied barmaid. CAD has been criticized as prosaic, didactic or voyeuristic, but she often makes irony or epigrams both moving and shocking. *The Other Country*, 1990, is newly, vividly personal.

Duffy, Maureen Patricia, novelist, poet, playwright, activist, teacher. B. in 1933 in Worthing, Sussex, to Grace Rose Wright and Cahia Patrick D., she was educ. at Trowbridge and Sarah Bonnell Girls' High School, then King's College, London (BA in English, 1956). She was writing both poetry and plays before finishing university, and soon added novels. Co-founder of the Writers' Action Group, 1972, she has held responsible positions in many organizations concerned with the arts. The semi-autobiographical novel *That's How It Was*, 1962, depicting a powerful relationship between an impoverished mother and illegitimate daughter, and the daughter's despair when the mother dies, foreshadows the themes and style of much work. Sexual identity and the politics of gender are intrinsic to MD's work. Marginalized because of social or sexual alienation, her characters desperately desire love, often experiencing this desire as sexual hunger. Her intense, fragmented style bizarrely blends realism and fantasy. *The Microcosm*, 1966, one of several works about London, draws on writing by Charlotte CHARKE as it eloquently portrays a lesbian underworld. MD describes *Love Child*, 1971, as 'a psychological statement, an elaboration of the Freudian theory of primal relationships with a subtext from classical mythology'. *I Want to Go to Moscow*, 1973, about anti-vivisection terrorists, articulates MD's concern for animal rights, as does *Gor Saga*, 1982 (TV film, 1988), about the extreme outsider (an experimental half-man, half-gorilla) and scientists playing God. *The Change*, 1987, explores in fragmented episodes the effects on socially diverse characters of WWII: pre-war innocence and the 'falling' into the knowledge of suffering are paralleled by a theme of sexual and emotional maturation. MD's highly regarded plays, *Rites*, 1969, and *Solo* and *Olde Tyme*, 1970, form a trilogy based on Greek myth. In *A Nightingale in Bloomsbury Square*, 1974, Virginia WOOLF muses over her achievements as she prepares to die. *The Venus Touch*, 1971, includes MD's love poems. Her provocative *The Erotic World of Faery*, 1972, is a Freudian study of British literature. She has done much work on Aphra BEHN: a life, 1977, an edition of *Oronooko*, 1986, and an introduction to the full text of *Love Letters*, 1987. Papers at King's College, London. See RULE, 1975, and MD in *Women's Review*, 20 June 1987.

du Fresne, Yvonne, short-story writer and novelist, b. 1929 at Takaka, near Nelson, NZ, da. of Alma Elle (Kerr) and Harold Andreas du F., farms dairy adviser. After attending Christchurch Teachers' College and Canterbury Univ. she was a music teacher for 40 years. She had a story published when she was 20, but as a result of trying to write NZ–English stories 'in a second generation effort to become a New Zealander' she mostly gave up writing until in the late 1970s she began again, from her own ethnic (Danish Huguenot French) roots. Her first two collections, *Farvel*, 1980, and *The Growing of Astrid Westergaard*, 1985, are amusing poignant stories about a young girl growing up in a small Danish Huguenot community in the Manawatu in the 1930s and the cultural clashes that occur with her schooling and the wider community. They are a celebration of being different – a cultural minority – and parallels are made to the Maoris. *The Book of Ester*, 1982, is narrated by a 50-ish widowed Danish French Huguenot living in the Manawatu, trying to come to terms with her loss and the loss of her cultural heritage, while *Frederique*, 1987, tells of an emigrant in NZ in 1864.

Duggan, Eileen, 1894–1972, poet and journalist, b. at Tua Marina in Marlborough Province, NZ. Youngest of four das. of Julia (Begley) and John D., Irish railway worker, she won a scholarship to Marlborough High School. After being a pupil teacher at Tua Marina school she got her teacher's certificate in Wellington and in 1918 graduated MA from Victoria Univ. College. Ill health led to her giving up teaching, and she lived a secluded life with her widowed sister and Julia McLeely, a close friend for almost 50 years. She wrote the woman's page of *The Tablet*, NZ's Catholic paper, under the pen name of 'Pippa' from 1927 to 1972, and stories and features for the NY national Catholic weekly *American*. Some of her five small vols. of poetry published between 1921 and 1951 (one, *Poems*, 1937, with intro. by Walter de la Mare) sold well, and she was then the best known NZ writer. In 1937 she was awarded the OBE, and in 1942 was granted a government annuity. Since then, her literary reputation has declined. Hers is the first NZ poetry to aim at a sense of national identity. She writes of the landscape, 'the bushwoman', 'the milker', 'fencing', and makes use of Maori life and terms. She celebrates childbearing – 'The swaying crib upon the firelit floor / Ah, how could you these gentle things forgo?' ('Rosa Luxembourg').

Duley, Margaret, 1894–1968, novelist and suffragette. She was b. in St John's, Newfoundland, da. of Tryphena Chancey Soper (with whom, later, she co-authored *A Pair of Grey Socks*, poems, 1917) and Thomas D., a jeweller. She was educ. at the Methodist College in St John's, then at the London Academy of Music and Dramatic Art. In the 1920s she was active in the Newfoundland suffrage movement; though she began to write for money, her feminism is an element in all her work. She published four novels: *The Eyes of the Gull*, 1936, repr. 1976, *Cold Pastoral*, 1939, repr. 1977, *Highway to Valour*, 1941 (new ed. 1977, with intro. by Margo Duley Morrow), and *Novelty on Earth*, 1942. The protagonists of the first three, women in the harsh life of the Newfoundland outports, experience a double growth, learning acceptance of this difficult land, but moving, through their relations with men, to self-aware independence. The first, superficially romantic, plots the destruction of a young woman crushed by conflicting demands of her mother and her patronizing ex-lover; the last culminates the movement to independence, its protagonist rejecting her married lover since to accept him on his terms would be 'subduing myself to your wish, because I was aching for your unhappiness, and that would be death to the feeling I had before'. See Alison Feder, 1983.

Du Maurier, Daphne, 1907–89, DBE, novelist and miscellaneous writer, b. in London, da. of Muriel (Beaumont) and actor-manager Sir Gerald D. M. Privately educ. in London and Paris, she was strictly brought up but encouraged to write (her grandfather was a novelist). She published articles and stories, then a novel, *The Loving Spirit*, 1931, with strong female protagonist. Next year she m. Frederick Arthur Montague Browning, army officer and courtier; they had three children. Their sailing honeymoon took them to Frenchman's Creek, later the title of a novel; her Cornish home (loved but not owned; sorrowfully relinquished in 1969) was the original of Manderley in her hugely successful *Rebecca*, 1938. The idea for this book (a second wife haunted by the memory of her charismatic predecessor, who turns out at last to have been hated, not loved) was said to have come to her on reading old love-letters of her husband's. DDM's 17 novels and 12 vols. of stories deal much in Cornish backgrounds, in suspense or GOTHIC elements (though she disliked being classed as a mystery writer) and archetypes or stereotypes connected with gender. (She often uses male narrators.)

My Cousin Rachel, 1951, never reveals whether its central, compelling female figure was good or evil. The austere community of mysterious priestesses in 'Monte Verita', the pathetically unfulfilled and unappreciated wife in 'The Apple Tree', touch deep chords, though both their concept and their symbolic embodiments may be crude. DDM also published a life of her father, 1934, a selection of his letters, 1951, a fictionalized family history, 1937, historical novels featuring her ancestors (like *Mary Anne*, 1954, and *The Glass-Blowers*, 1963), a life of Branwell Brontë, 1960, *Vanishing Cornwall*, 1967, and *The Rebecca Notebook and Other Memories*, 1981. *Rebecca* was memorably filmed by Alfred Hitchcock, as were 'The Birds' and *Don't Look Now*. She herself dramatized *Rebecca*, 1940, and wrote two more plays, a screen-play (jointly) and a TV play. DDM lived as a recluse in her last years. See Jane S. Bakerman, ed., *And Then There Were Nine*, 1985.

Dumbrille, Dorothy, 1897–?1983/4, poet, novelist. B. at Crysler, Ont., da. of Winnie (Fulton) and Rupert John D., she was educ. at Kemptville High School and Business College in Philadelphia, worked for the Department of Defense, 1916–20, and for a life insurance company in Philadelphia, 1921–4, then m. James Travers Smith in 1924, and lived in Alexandria, Ont. She published stories, poems and articles in many Canadian journals, and wrote radio plays. Her novels are lively social history. *Up and Down the Glens*, 1954, and *Braggart in My Steps*, 1956, recount early Scottish settlement history, giving brief sketches of prominent community members. *All This Difference*, 1945, set in the area DD lived in, weaves wartime romance and tragedy together with local history, recounting the misunderstandings, prejudices, and conflicts between Scottish settlers and more recently arrived French Canadians. DD also published five books of poems, one with G. V. Thompson, 1964. Her *Memories of My Father* appeared in 1980.

Dunbar, Andrea, b. 1961, playwright. At her local comprehensive school in Bradford, Yorks. (where she still lives), she wrote her first play, *Arbor*, for an exam in drama (CSE). Encouraged by a teacher, she sent it to the Royal Court Theatre in London: it had a great success there in 1981. AD writes with wit and humour about her surroundings on a large council housing estate. Her plays brim with working-class female resilience in face of male dominance and economic depression. Never married, AD has three children, whom she supports alone. She used her experience of early pregnancy in *Rita, Sue and Bob Too*, 1982 (commissioned by the Royal Court). She based a screenplay, filmed in Bradford, 1986, on her first two works. *Shirley* (Royal Court, 1986) depicts a girl's tumultuous relationship with her mother. AD says she meant to write 'about Shirley and John but, you know, I wrote the mother in and she bloody took over the whole play'. Interview in *Time Out*, 23–9 April 1986.

Dunbar-Nelson, Alice (Moore), 1875–1935, poet, short-story writer, journalist, educator, b. New Orleans, La., da. of Patricia (Wright) and Joseph M. The second of two daughters, AD-N was educ. at public schools and Straight College in New Orleans. She m. gifted poet Paul Laurence Dunbar in 1889, separated from him in 1902, and returned to teaching English; in 1916 she m. Robert John Nelson. During WWI, AD-N mobilized black women's support for the US Council of National Defense. Her first book, *Violets, and Other Tales*, 1895, combined poems, stories and essays. *The Goodness of St Rocque, and Other Stories*, 1899, centres on life in and around New Orleans; the sketches draw on AD-N's knowledge of Creole dialects and appreciation for the port city's diversity. The anthologies she edited while teaching – *Masterpieces of Negro Eloquence*, 1914, and *The Dunbar Speaker and Entertainer*, 1920 – provided students with oratorical models in both standard and non-standard English, including Creole, as AD-N tried to educate readers to the range and depth of black linguistic culture. Included in *The Dunbar Speaker* is the poem of the most interest to current feminist critics, 'I Sit and Sew', in which AD-N compares 'My hands grown tired, my head weighed down with dreams –' to the lives of men caught up in the 'panoply of war'. See Gloria T. Hull, *Color, Sex and Poetry*, 1987, and Roger Whitlow in Emily Toth, ed., *Regionalism and the Female Imagination*, 1985.

'Duncan, Jane', Elizabeth Jane Cameron, 'Janet Sandison', 1910–76, novelist and children's writer. B. in Dunbartonshire to Janet (Sandison), who died when JD was ten, and Duncan Cameron, a policeman, she received her MA in English from Glasgow Univ. in 1930, held various secretarial jobs through the 1930s, and in WWII served in the Photographic Intelligence Unit of the Women's Auxiliary Air Force (WAAF). After the war she worked as office manager for a small Scottish engineering firm, where she met her common-law husband, Sandy (his wife refused to divorce him), with whom she lived in the West Indies. There he worked as an engineer from 1948 until his death in 1958, when she returned to Scotland. The 19 novels of the 'My Friend' series, 1959–76, draw upon these experiences: at their centre is the intelligent, unconventional Janet Sandison. *My Friend Annie*, 1961, focuses on her childhood and her rocky relationship with her conventional stepmother. The five Cameron books, 1963–8, for children, draw on JD's own nieces and nephews, the youngest of whom had Down's syndrome. *Camerons at the Castle*, 1964, describes the children's journey with their aunt to a Scottish castle being restored as a hotel. Three illustrated children's books, 1975–8, and the four Jean Robertson books, 1969–75, for adults, are also set in Scotland. JD's memoir, *Letter from Reachfar*, 1975, casts light on the relationship between the events of her life and her fiction.

Duncan, Sara Jeanette (christened Sarah Janet), 'Garth Grafton', 1861–1922, novelist, journalist and travel writer. Eldest of ten surviving children of Jane (Bell) and Charles D., merchant, she was b. in Brantford, Ont. and educ. at the Collegiate, Ladies College, and County Model School (teachers' college), then at Toronto Normal School, 1879. She wanted to write from childhood and published short pieces from 1880. She taught for nearly four years, worked on a local newpaper, then wrote for the Toronto *Globe*, the London, Ont., *Advertiser*, and the Washington *Post*. In 1886 she became the first full-time woman in the editorial department of a Canadian paper (the *Globe*); in 1887 she moved to the Montréal *Star*, where she was one of two women in the Parliamentary Press Gallery. She also wrote for the *Week* (Toronto). 'Careers, if possible', she wrote in 1886, 'and independence anyway, we must all have, as musicians, artists, writers, teachers, lawyers, doctors, ministers, or something.' Her first novel, *A Social Departure: How Orthodocia and I Went Round the World by Ourselves*, 1890 (based on *Star* articles), is a lively, humorous fictionalized account of her round-the-world trip with fellow journalist Lily Lewis, which ended with two years in England. In late 1890 SJD returned to Calcutta, m. Everard Cotes, 1890, an English-born civil servant, later a journalist. She remained in India for 25 years, travelling frequently to Canada and England, where she spent her last years. She published 22 books. *The Simple Adventures of a Memsahib*, lightly critical of British colonial attitudes in India, 1893, and *A Pool in the Desert*, 1903, short stories, repr., 1987, 1984. Influenced by W. D. Howells, Henry James, and her journalistic experience, SJD is an acute, ironic observer of the political, social, and cultural scene, in Canada, India, or England. Her protagonists are usually perceptive, independent-minded young women. Best known today are *The Imperialist*, 1904, which portrays religious and political small-town Canada, and *Cousin Cinderella; or A Canadian Girl in London*, 1908, which records the reactions of a brother and sister to experiences in British high society. Several of SJD'S novels are 'international': *A Daughter of Today*, 1894, about a young US woman struggling to succeed as a self-styled NEW WOMAN in the artistic and literary worlds of Paris and London, explores the difficulties of an unconventional (female) life and of friendship between competitive women. Later, SJD became interested in theatre; several of her plays had brief runs. The autobiographical works, *On the Other Side of the Latch*, 1901, and *Two in a Flat*, 1908, deal with her English life and reflections while under treatment for tuberculosis, 1900. See *Selected Journalism*, ed. Thomas Tausky, 1978, study by Tausky, 1980, and life by Marian Fowler, 1983.

Duncombe, Susanna (Highmore), 1725–1812, poet and artist. Da. of Susanna (Hiller), who pub. several poems in magazines, and of painter Joseph H. – well-educ. and travelled, 'the Muses' pupil from her tend'rest years' – she belonged to Samuel Richardson's circle, and made a famous drawing of them in 1751. Her best-known poem, an allegory, told how Fidelio and Honoria settled for content in lieu of happiness. John D. (whom she m. in 1761) praised it in his *Feminiad*, 1754, repr. 1981. He hoped his poem (in which she or Elizabeth CARTER may have had a hand) would induce more ladies to publish; yet her allegory is now lost, and of 16 extant poems written over 30 years, those which reached print did so in antholgies or the works of others (e.g. Hester CHAPONE's, a sonnet for Mary LEAPOR's works was rejected). SD lived in Canterbury, had four children (only one survived), became a close friend of Eliza BERKELEY, and pub. a note on Catherine TALBOT in the *GM*, 1772. The *DNB* entry is particularly faulty, giving her a novel by Mrs A. Duncombe, 1808: see Warren Mild in *Proceedings of the Amer. Philosophical Soc.*, 122, 1978.

Dunham, Bertha Mabel, 1881–1957, Ontario historical writer, novelist and librarian. B. on a farm near Harriston, Ont., da. of Magdalena (Eby) and Martin D., she was educ. at Kitchener public schools and Normal School. After several years of teaching, she attended the Univs. of Toronto (BA, 1908) and McGill (Library School), became a prominent librarian (Kitchener Public Library, 1908–44), and lectured in library science at the present Waterloo Univ. and elsewhere. Her novels are remarkable chiefly for well-researched historical detail. *The Trail of the Conestoga* (intro. by W. L. Mackenzie King), 1924, and *Toward Sodom*, 1927, feature Dutch Mennonite emigrants to Waterloo County, Ont., in the early nineteenth century. Her maternal great-grandfather, Sam Bricker, one such emigrant, was the model for the protagonist of her first novel (foreword by Prime Minister Mackenzie King). In *The Trail of the King's Men*, 1921, the United Empire Loyalist hero settles in Montréal after the American Revolution. MBD also published local history (an account of Trinity United Church, 1941, *Grant River*, 1945, and *Mills and Millers of Ontario*, 1946) and a children's book, *Kristli's Trees*, 1948, about a young Mennonite boy on an Ontario farm. Bibliography of works by and about her by Ryan Taylor in *Waterloo Historical Society*, 69, 1981.

Duniway, Abigail Jane (Scott), 1834–1915, novelist, poet, and journalist, b. near Groveland, Ill., da. of Anne (Roelofson) and John Tucker S. She was educ. by her mother, at an academy, and later self-taught. *Captain Gray's Company*, 1859 (supposedly the first novel printed west of the Rockies) and *From the West to the West*, 1905, are fictionalized accounts of her family's journey from Illinois to Oregon in 1852, describing the harsh conditions and cholera that killed her mother, as well as AD's views on women's rights. In 1853 she m. Benjamin C. D. In 1870, with Martha Foster and Martha Dalton, she formed the

State Equal Suffrage Association, and the following year founded the suffragist newspaper *The New Northwest*, writing serialized novels, editorials, ADVICE columns, and general news stories. Volumes of poetry include *My Musings*, 1875, and *David and Anna Matson*, 1876, a feminist version of a story by John G. Whittier. Her career in public speaking began in 1871, when she toured with Susan B. ANTHONY. Although personally believing in temperance, she felt that Prohibition sat oddly with women's suffrage. She was forbidden to speak in churches and had eggs thrown at her. Her autobiography, *Path Breaking*, 1914, reveals an outspoken, dauntless fighter and concludes: 'The young college women of today ... should remember that every inch of this freedom was bought for them at a great price.... The debt that each generation owes to the past it must pay to the future.' See D. N. Morrison's study, 1977.

Dunlap, Jane, Boston poet, just widowed, poor and 'in an obscure station of life' when in 1771 she published *Poems*, a pamphlet in 'homely stile', on George Whitefield's preaching visit to Boston several years before. She calls herself 'a Daughter of Liberty and lover of Truth', inspired by the example of Phillis WHEATLEY ('a young Afric damsel'), though fearing 'some may sneer and others laugh'. She laments a decline in New England religion in favour of cards, dice and plays, and calls for conversion of both whites and blacks ('Your colour's no exception'). With encouragement, she says, she will write more; but no more is known.

Dunlop, Eliza (Hamilton), 1796–1880, poet, b. County Armagh, Ireland. Her mother appears to have died at the birth; her father, Solomon H., a lawyer, left for India soon afterwards, so she was raised and educated by her grandmother. She m. James Law and, after his death, David D., with whom she travelled to Australia in 1838. She began writing poetry in her teens and contributed to many Irish magazines. Her poems also appeared in *The Dark Lady of Doona*, 1834, a novel by her cousin William Hamilton Maxwell, a best-selling author. Her best-known Australian poem, 'The Aboriginal Mother', based on the infamous Myall Creek Massacre of 1838, was published in the *Australian* newspaper on 13 December 1838. Later, while living at Wollombi in the Hunter Valley of NSW, where her husband was Police Magistrate and Protector of Aborigines, ED developed a strong interest in Aboriginal customs and languages. She was the first Australian poet to attempt transliterations of Aboriginal songs, some of which were published in local newspapers and magazines, along with many others on themes as various as her continuing love for Ireland and the exploits of Australian explorers. A manuscript collection of poems, 'The Vase', is in the Mitchell Library, Sydney. A few of her poems have been published as *The Aboriginal Mother and other poems*, 1981.

Dunmore, Helen, poet, b. 1952 at Beverley, Yorks., educ. at York Univ. (BA in English, 1973). She is married, with a son and stepson, and works as a nursery teacher. Her first book, *The Apple Fall*, 1983, includes poems on Greenham Common, Zelda FITZGERALD, rewritten stories ('Mary says to the angel: "Come. / My husband is sleepy. / You're rapid and warm-winged"'), the way male poems categorize women and leave female experience unvoiced, and the different feelings of mother and father for their baby. Of Virginia WOOLF she writes 'I am a stone and the world falls from me / I feel untouchable – a new planet / where life knows it isn't safe to begin ... my loose pips ripen ... The black tread of my husband on the lawn / as he goes from the house to the loft / laying out apples' ('Rodmell Garden'). *The Sea Skater*, 1986, includes poems on Mary SHELLEY and Lady Macduff. Gillian CLARKE praised the way it suggests how 'women spend their lives in uncertainty':

domestic settings and relationships are shadowed, uneasy; distant international aggression and ecological threats loom behind familiar yet estranging snowy landscapes, 'muddy horizons', 'the rainy village'. Topics of *The Raw Garden*, 1988, range from wild strawberries to 'The Peach House', artichokes to American bases; HD says they are closely related, like strands in the DNA helix, to question human interventions in nature: 'What does it take to disturb the sense of naturalness held by the human being in his or her landscape?'

Dunn, Nell, journalist, novelist and playwright, b. 1936 to well-to-do London parents. She left her convent school at 14, married writer Jeremy Sandford in 1956 (later separated) and had three sons. In Battersea, London, from 1959 as a 'refugee' from her own class and milieu, she wrote terse, vivid, documentary-style stories of working-class life: pub. in the *New Statesman*, then much discussed as *Up the Junction*, 1963, televised 1965. She published interviews as *Talking to Women*, 1965, then a best-selling first novel, *Poor Cow*, 1967 (filmed 1967, repr. with Margaret DRABBLE's introduction, 1988), whose resilient heroine, Joy, seen through both first- and third-person narrative, is young mother, barmaid, model and factory hand (as ND had also been) while her husband is in gaol, quite happy for him to go back there if he gets her some money first. ND next issued a children's book, then *The Incurable*, 1971, whose housewife-protagonist's life begins to unravel as her husband's body physically decays in a well-organized hospital. She co-wrote with Liverpool poet Adrian Henri *I Want*, 1972 (staged 1982), a 50-year love-affair in letters. In *Tear the Head Off His Shoulders*, 1974, two middle-aged women bolster each other up until one finds a man, when the other kills herself. ND's own life-style prompted her to compile from others' words 'a book about alternative families', *Different Drummers* (title changed from *Living Like I Do*), 1977. *The Only Child*, 1978, fictionalizes the oppressive, obsessive ties of a conventional, prosperous nuclear family. ND scored a West End hit with *Steaming*, 1981, a play set in a women's Turkish bath under the threat of closure, whose users are mutually supportive and eventually politicized (see Michael Coren, *Theatre Royal*, 1984). In 1988 came another play, *The Little Heroine*, and her first original TV film, *Every Breath You Take*. See Keyssar, 1984.

Dupuy, Eliza Ann, 'Annie Young', 1814–?80, novelist and short-story writer, b. Petersburg, Va, da. of Mary Anne Thomson (Sturdivant) and Jesse D., merchant and shipowner. She spent her whole life in the South and worked for a period as governess to Sarah DORSEY. Financial difficulties forced her father to emigrate to Kentucky, and prompted her first work, *Morton: A Tale of the Revolution* (pub. date unknown; possibly as early as 1828). After her father's death, ED became a teacher, but with the successful publication of *The Conspirator*, 1843, she was able to support herself. This novel is a melodramatic fictional treatment of Aaron Burr's attempt to rule over a vast area of the Southwest. *The Huguenot Exiles: or, The Times of Louis XIV*, 1856, is more convincing, because of its obviously heartfelt purpose. ED apparently wrote the novel, with its strong anti-Catholicism, to explain the plight of her Huguenot ancestors. She wrote over 20 novels, many of which were serialized in the NY *Ledger*, to which she also contributed short stories under the name 'Annie Young'.

Durack, Mary, historian, novelist, children's writer, b. 1913 in Adelaide, South Australia, da. of Bessie Ida Muriel (Johnstone) and Michael Patrick D., of a well-known pioneering and pastoralist family. She was educ. at Loreto Convent, Perth, then helped manage the family properties in the Kimberleys before settling in Perth. She m. Horrie Miller in 1938 and had four das. (two deceased) and two sons. She began her career as a journalist writing a column for countrywomen in the *West Australian*, then wrote children's books, illustrated by her sister, the artist Elizabeth D. Many of these contain Aboriginal tales and legends, including *Chunuma*, 1936, *Son of Djaro*, 1940, and *Kookanoo and Kangaroo*, 1963. The sisters also wrote *All About: The Story of a Black Community on Argyle Station*, 1935. MD wrote Australian non-fiction such as *The Rock and the Sand*, 1969, and *To Be Heirs Forever*, 1976, a biography of pioneer Eliza Shaw. However her reputation rests with the book tracing the lives and achievements of the Durack family, *Kings in Grass Castles*, 1959, and its sequel, *Sons in the Saddle*, 1983, and her novel, *Keep Him My Country*, 1955, a passionate and moving story of a station manager's relationship with an Aboriginal woman. MD has received an OBE, 1966, DBE, 1978, and an honorary D. Litt. from the Univ. of WA, 1978.

Duras, Marguerite, novelist, playwright, screenwriter, film-maker, b. in 1914 in Indochina, da. of teacher Marie and mathematics professor Henri Donnadieu. She studied in Saigon, then in Paris at the Faculté de Droit and the Ecole Libre des Sciences Politiques. Since *Les Impudents*, 1943, she has published more than 35 plays, novels and filmscripts (almost half translated into English, many filmed). For years thought a major writer in France, she drew attention in the English-speaking world with renewed interest in psychoanalysis and French theory. In a writing marked by spare narrative complexity, she investigates representation of the female body and the relation between female desire and violence, language and experience. Her filmscript *Hiroshima mon amour*, 1960, meditates on memory and human suffering; it centres on interracial love, like the hauntingly erotic autobiographical novel, *L'Amant*, 1984 (*The Lover*, 1985), an account of an adolescent French girl's affair with an older Chinese businessman in Indochina. *Un barrage contre le Pacifique*, 1950 (*The Sea Wall*, 1985), maps out a similar Indonesian autobiographical landscape. *Le Ravissement de Lol V. Stein*, 1964 (*The Ravishing of Lol Stein*, 1966) produces a shifting, often uncertain narrative perspective to enact the doubleness of voyeuristic desire. In the heat of India, *Le Vice-Consul*, 1966 (*The Vice Consul*, 1968), falls obsessively in love with a *Lol Stein* character: the languid film *India Song*, 1973, replays this obsession and loss in discontinuous visual and aural terms. The fragmentary novel *Détruire dit-elle*, 1969 (*Destroy, She Said*, 1970), is published in English together with an interview in which MD says she doesn't 'think there are any sentences left'. *La Douleur*, 1985 (*The War: A Memoir*, 1986), written in 1944 during MD's participation in the Resistance, is punctuated with her retrospective words: 'I give you the torturer along with the rest of the texts. Learn to read them properly, they are sacred.' *Les Yeux Bleus Cheveux Noirs*, 1987 (*Blue Eyes, Black Hair*, 1987), returns to the scopophilic relation between looking and reading, and recounts the obsessive longing of one man for another misread in his substitute sexual encounters with a look-alike woman. See *Marguerite Duras*, 1979 (*Duras by Duras*, 1987), interview with Xavière Gauthier in *Les Parleuses*, 1974 (*Woman to Woman*, 1987), and studies by Sharon Willis, *Marguerite Duras: Writing on the Body*, 1987, and Trista Selous, *The Other Woman: Feminism and Femininity in the Works of Marguerite Duras*, 1988.

Dutt, Toru, 1856–77, poet, novelist, translator, b. in Calcutta, youngest child of well-to-do writers combining Bengali, Hindu and Christian culture: Kshetramoni (Mitter), who translated from English to Bengali for a Tract Society, and poet Govind Chunder D. (who edited a *Family Album* of verse, 1870). She was baptized in 1862, educ. at home in English (intellectual and drawing-room skills) by tutors and parents. In 1869 she was taken to France (learning fluent French in four months), in 1870 to

England. She attended Cambridge 'Higher Lectures for Women' and read French Romantic poets in the BM. The family returned to Calcutta in 1873. Next year TD's sister and fellow-poet, Aru, died, and TD's work began to appear in the *Bengal Magazine*: essays on and translations from French writers (poems collected in *A Sheaf Gleaned in French Fields*, 1876) and English poems. A sonnet on 'Baugmaree', her garden house, describes 'the ranges / Of bamboos to the eastward, when the moon / Looks through their gaps, and the white lotus changes / Into a cup of silver. One might swoon / Drunken with beauty then.' TD died of pulmonary tuberculosis. Other works were a French novel, *Le Journal de Mlle D'Arvers*, 1879, which uses an epilogue to wind up its romantic, tragic plot; an unfinished English novel, *Bianca or The Young Spanish Maiden* (already a *Bengal Mag.* serial); and *Ancient Ballads and Legends of Hindustan*, 1882 (intro. by Edmund Gosse; repr. 1941, 1969, with critical memoir by Amaranatha Jha). This, thought her best work, stems from her mother's early reciting, and develops a mystical vein perhaps connected with studying Sanskrit: TD's 'The Tree of Life' owes much to the mythical Hindu speaking tree. *Life and Letters* by Harinar Das, 1921; studies by Padmini Sen Gupta, 1968, and A. N. Dwivedi, 1977.

Dutton, Anne (King), Lady, 1621–after 1678, possibly a significant though lost poet, da. of Joan (Freeman) and John K., Bishop of London. The name of her brother the poet Henry K., 1592–1669, is linked with several MS volumes of unascribed family poetry; he mentions a loving verse reproof from her. James Howell called her the tenth muse (a title too for SAPPHO, Anne BRADSTREET, and many others) in 1637. She married the rich, elderly John D. in 1648, and in the 1650s belonged to 'a kinde of Collage' of High Church friends at Richings in Bucks. Widowed in 1657, she married Sir Richard Grobham Howe of Great Wishford near Salisbury in 1671. Only two slight pieces are known, one on a sister's death (in anthology ed. Germaine Greer *et al.*, 1988).

Dutton, Anne (Williams), 1692–1765, religious pamphleteer. B. at Northampton, piously educ. but 'airy and proud', she acquired acute sense of sin after a serious illness. At 22 she m. a Mr Coles, and after his death Benjamin D., Baptist minister. She settled at Great Gransden, Hunts., in 1732. Her desire to do some 'service to the Cause of Christ' gradually conquered nagging ill health and the avid humility which her sect decreed for all but especially for women. Criticized as unwomanly, she was a tough critic herself. In 30 years she issued nearly 50 'little Tracts' and letters to George Whitefield and others, not all anonymous, beginning with two long Calvinist poems and 61 HYMNS: 2 eds. 1734. Her 13 titles of 1743 include *A Brief Account to the Negroes Lately Converted to Christ in America* (non-ABOLITIONIST), a *Letter* to opponents of printing women's work, and the opening of an autobiography. She seems today clumsy in verse and tedious in prose; a leaflet by J. C. Whitebrook [1921] is violently hostile; but a reader of 1884 praised 'such savoury meat ... given me in answer to prayer' (BL 1578/4520). Widowed in 1747, she pub. as 'An Old Woman' and masqueraded as male editors and proprietors of *The Spiritual Magazine*, 1761–3. See Stephen J. Stein in *Church History*, 44, 1975.

Du Verger, Susan, translator, who pub. with her surname and initial in 1639 *Admirable Events ... Together with Morall Relations*, consisting of 'severall Histories culled out of' two vols., 1628 and 1638, by Jean Pierre Camus, Bishop of Belley. Her dedication to Queen Henrietta Maria vigorously defends 'Histories' as storehouses, armouries and mirrors of virtue, 'the only monuments of Truth'; she slightly softens both her original's self-righteous prefatory indignation against 'Romants', and the Christian or Catholic colouring he gives his tales of love, jealousy, passion and prudence. Several tales feature heroic women; one, 'The Waking Man's Dream', about a drunken tradesman transformed for a single day to Duke of Burgundy, is a version of Shakespeare's frame story in *The Taming of the Shrew*.

Dworkin, Andrea, radical feminist, critic, novelist, short-story writer, b. in 1946 in Camden, NJ, da. of Jewish parents, secretary Sylvia (Spiegal), and teacher and civil libertarian Harry D. AD lived in Crete, 1965–6, and Amsterdam, where her 1969 marriage to a batterer ended after three years, then studied literature and philosophy at Bennington College (BA, 1968). Active in the civil rights and anti-war movements, she was arrested at 18 for demonstrating and subjected to an internal examination which caused 15 days of hemorrhaging and which she later publicly denounced. In *Woman Hating*, 1974 – 'This book is an action where revolution is the goal. It has no other purpose' – and *Our Blood*, 1976, AD delineates the artificiality and destructiveness of sex roles and male dominance and, as in her later non-fiction, relentlessly connects the values embodied in literature, fairy tales, and pornography with cultural practices. *Pornography*, 1981, argues that 'Male power is the raison d'être of pornography; the degradation of the female is the means of achieving this power.' In 1983 with feminist lawyer Catherine MacKinnon, AD drafted a controversial civil rights ordinance which defines pornography as sex discrimination (overruled, 1986, as a violation of the First Amendment guarantee of freedom of speech). Further analyses of sexual politics (*Right-Wing Women*, 1983, *Intercourse*, 1987, and *Letters from a War Zone, 1976–87*, 1989) continue to insist on damage done by male sexuality. Her fiction, autobiographical and stylistically experimental, reflects the concerns of her polemical works. Stories in *the new womans broken heart*, 1980, set wry, intelligent humour against women's painful lives: 'laugh to death or starve to death. Ive always been pro choice'. The narrator of *Ice and Fire*, 1986, struggles through prostitution and a violent marriage to become a dedicated writer who asserts, 'I am a feminist, not the fun kind.' An epistolary novel, *Ruins*, is in progress. Interview in *WRB*, May 1986.

Dyer, Mary, d. 1660, Quaker preacher. In 1635 she migrated from England with her husband, William D., a rich milliner; in Rhode Island she became a close friend and follower of Anne Hutchinson, and he became Attorney General, 1650. They had six children. They visited England in 1652; she stayed on, became a QUAKER, and in 1657 sailed to Boston, where she was repeatedly imprisoned for PREACHING. After a trial in 1659 she was conditionally reprieved on the scaffold when two men were executed (as she recounts in a brief passage in *A Call from Death to Life*, 1660). Eight months later she was hanged for preaching again. Her story probably inspired Alice CURWEN to go to Boston. Life by Horatio Rogers, 1896.

Dykeman, Wilma, Appalachian novelist, historian, biographer, b. at Asheville, Tenn., da. of Bonnie (Cole) and Willard J. D. She took a BA at Northwestern Univ., m. James R. Stokely, Jr, had two children, lectured at colleges and univs., and travelled worldwide. Though she feels that the regional label has dimmed critical response to her work, her fiction and non-fiction alike are nourished by local knowledge and passion. She won awards for her first two books: *The French Broad*, 1955 (Rivers of America series), and *Neither Black nor White*, 1957 (with her husband). She has written three novels (*The Tall Woman*, 1962, *The Far Family*, 1966 – both recently repr. – and *Return the Innocent Earth*, 1972), and three lives: of Will Alexander, Methodist minister turned race-relations reformer (with her husband, 1962), of W. D. Weatherford, scholar, social reformer and 'gadfly of the South', 1966, and of Edna Rankin McKinnon, trail-blazer of international birth-control, 1974. WD wrote a column for the Knoxville *News-Sentinel* and collected essays in *Look to this Day*, 1968. Of her historical books (including *Tennessee*, a bicentennial portrait, 1975, and an account of a famous battle, 1978), the best is probably *Highland Homeland, The People of the Great Smokies*, also 1978 (with her son); the first of its riveting photos shows an old woman in a rocking chair, with caption noting her man's shoes and strongly-developed hand and arm.

Dyson, Ketaki (Kushari), poet, translator, critic, b. 1940 in Calcutta, da. of Amita and of civil servant Abanimohon Kushari. She was educ. at St John's Diocesan girls' high school, Lady Brabourne College, and Presidency College, Calcutta (BA in English, 1958), then at St Hilda's, Oxford (BA first class, 1963). She taught for a year at Jadavpur Univ. Back in England, she m. teacher Robert D. in 1974 and completed her D. Phil. in 1975 with a thesis on male and female British diarists in India, 1765–1856 (pub. as *A Various Universe*, 1978, repr. 1980). She taught at Burdwan Univ., 1976–7, but is now settled near Oxford; she has two sons. Her poetry uses both Bengali and English. She has published a novel in Bengali, translated Anglo-Saxon poetry, D. M. Thomas and David Constantine into Bengali, and essays by Sudhindranath Datta into English. Her three English books of poems are *Sap-Wood*, 1978, *Hibiscus in the North*, 1979, and *Space I Inhabit*, 1983. They focus on women's lives in a world governed by patriarchal assumptions, expressing anger at issues from the fetishization of Sylvia PLATH's suicide ('Myths and Monsters') to the infibulation of Middle Eastern women. KD's richly layered language is studded with vivid images: 'Sun dripped / like margarine / from sky's enamelled / *sauté*-pan' ('Lumb-Bank, May 1980'). By applying Bengali perspectives to English society and landscape, she produces an impressive critique of both patriarchal and western culture. She has worked on an edition of letters between Indian Rabindranath Tagore and Argentinian Victoria Ocampo.

E

'Earle, Jean', Doris (Stanley) Burge, poet, b. 1909 in Bristol and raised in the Rhondda Valley, da. of Ella (Wilks) and William S. She was educ. at the Institute of Science and Technology, Cardiff, m. William Edward B. in 1937 and had two das. While still young she published articles, stories and poems in magazines such as *Good Housekeeping, The Lady*, the *Anglo-Welsh Review* and *Poetry*. After years of silence she began writing poetry again in her late sixties, and won a Welsh Arts Council prize with *A Trial of Strength*, 1970. *The Intent Look*, 1984, and *Visiting Light*, 1987, followed; she appears in Raymond Garlick and Ronald Mathias, eds., *Anglo-Welsh Poetry 1480–1980*, 1984, in RUMENS, ed., 1985, and in the Welsh *Poets against Apartheid*, 1986. JE uses free verse to narrate personal and community history, and evoke landscapes of coastline and mountainside and Welsh mining community. Often an arresting visual image leads back to wider experience the image recalls. Recreated childhood is juxtaposed with the processes of memory. 'The Arch Rock' strings together repetitions of intense remembered moments with unexplained gaps in the record. See articles by Kenneth R. Smith and Diane Davies in *Poetry Wales*, 24, 1988.

Easdale, Joan Adeney, poet, b. 1913, living at Sevenoaks, Kent. During WW1 her father became jealous and left her mother, Gladys Ellen (Adeney), whose artless, self-centred, anonymous autobiography, *Middle Age*, 1935, says JAE's conception was marked by an apparition; as a baby she had septic pneumonia and at eight wanted to be a ballet dancer. By January 1930 she had sent Virginia WOOLF 'piles of dirty copy books written in a scrawl without any spelling'; the Woolfs published her books. *A Collection of Poems*, 1931 (written 1927–30), is sharp-eyed on love, sadness, the end of relationships, family life, and authority: 'Wisdom laid his hand on me, / "Now just look and you will see." / And I looked, but did not see. / Wisdom shook his head at me.' In July 1931 she performed her work to music by her brother. The title poem of *Clemence and Clare*, 1932, addresses Woolf; a poem to JAE's mother describes a lost but remembered vision. She later worked in London and published in the *Adelphi*. In 1938 she married James Meadows Rendel, relative of the STRACHEY family. *Amber Innocent*, a portentous verse narrative couched in symbols, was written 1932–9, pub. 1939. JAE bore a child in 1940.

Eastman, Elaine (Goodale), 1863–1953, novelist, poet and editor, b. S. Egremont, Mass., da. of Dora Hill (Read) and Henry Stirling G., and educ. by her 'feminist' mother and language tutors. A precocious scholar, she and her sister Dora (beloved sole companion for 17 years) wrote journals for family entertainment, and in 1878 astonished the world with their book of poems *Apple Blossoms. The Journal of a Farmer's Daughter*, 1881, describing life in an isolated mountain home. In 1886 EGE established a reservation school for Sioux Indians where she learned the Dakota tongue and wrote songs of Indian life. Appointed Supervisor of Education in the Dakotas, 1890, she was nursing victims of the Wounded Knee massacre when she met a young Sioux physician, Dr Charles A. E., whom she m. in 1891. While raising six children, collaborating with her husband on lectures and books of Indian culture such as *Wigwam Evenings*, 1909, EGE also pub. books for young readers, including *Little Brother O'Dreams*, 1910, and *Indian Legends Retold*, 1919. Her marriage ended in 1921. A strong advocate of educating and Christianizing the Indians, she was aware of the hazards of assimilation. The Sioux orphan in *Yellow Star*, 1911, returns to the reservation, following her assimilation to a white community to whom Indians are 'savages', to find herself 'pulled in two directions'. A similar disorientation shapes Ellen Strong's life in *A Hundred Maples*, 1935; this novel also implicitly endorses the Filiation Act to ensure that men are made responsible for their illegitimate offspring. In 1930 EGE published her collected poems, *The Voice at Eve*. Her deep regard for the Sioux is expressed in 'Songs of Nature and the Red Man', which tell, with emotional intensity and crisp clarity, of love and death and of fearless courage ('One Woman's Story').

Eastman, Mary (Henderson), 1818–87, novelist, poet and chronicler of Indian life and legends, b. Warrenton, Va, da. of Anna Maria (Truxton) and Thomas H., US army surgeon. She m. Seth E., army officer and drawing instructor at West Point, in 1835, and had four children. In 1841 she accompanied her husband to Fort Snelling, Minn., and there began studying and recording Sioux customs and legends. In *Dahcotah: or, Life and Legends of the Sioux around Fort Snelling*, 1849 (said to have inspired Longfellow's *Hiawatha*), and *The American Aboriginal Portfolio*, 1853, MHE presents a great deal of factual material as well as Sioux beliefs and tales. She points out that the 'civilized' white Americans have brought alcohol and disease to the Indians and taken away their land, although she also reminds her readers that Sioux mothers are not Christian women. *The Romance of Indian Life*, 1853, contains poems; she also wrote a pro-slavery novel, *Aunt Phillis's Cabin; or, Southern Life as it Is*, 1852, which sold 18,000 copies within a few weeks. Written hastily in response to H. B. Stowe, the novel relies on sentimental characters and plot to convey MHE's opinions about evil abolitionists, benevolent slave-holders and happy slaves. In her novel *Fashionable Life*, 1856, she argues for women's right to teach and to write.

Eaton, Charlotte Anne (Waldie), 1788–1859, novelist and travel writer, da. of Maria Jane (Ormston) and George W. of Roxburghshire. In 1814 she dropped her 'Unfashionable Novel' *At Home and Abroad* on finding plot parallels to Maria Edgeworth's *Patronage*; she revised and pub. it in 1831. Her brief 'Circumstantial Detail' by 'a near Observer' appeared in her *Battle of Waterloo*, with her sister's sketch of the terrain: both had been in Brussels at the time. This had ten editions by 1817, when her family pub. her longer *Narrative of a Residence in Belgium*, by 'an Englishwoman', which recreates suspense, horror, yet delight in English greatness and glory. It was reprinted under varying titles as late as 1888; *Rome in the Nineteenth Century*, 1820, was also popular. In 1822 she married Stamford banker Stephen E.; she had four children. *Continental Adventures*, 1826, also anonymous, combines real travel experience 'with a fictitious story and imaginary characters'. Her adventurous, intelligent, humane women often see men as 'subordinate things'. She died in London.

Eaton, Evelyn Sybil Mary (Vernon), novelist and poet, b. 1902 in Montreux, Switzerland, of partly Indian descent, da. of Myra (Randolph) and Daniel Isaac V., a Canadian army colonel who was killed at Vimy in 1917. After early educ. in Canada and England, she went to univ. in New Brunswick, England and at the Sorbonne, 1920–21; m. 1928, Ernst Paul R. Vredt (d. 1942). *Every Month Was May*, 1947, describes her early years, schooling, society 'coming out', work as secretary and translator, life in Paris, marriage to 'a penniless foreigner ... with love, courage, and 500 francs', divorce,

1934, and the rise of Hitler in Europe. She had a daughter, moved to NYC, 1937, became a war correspondent in the China–Burma–India area in 1945, and later a frequent lecturer and visiting professor at US universities. She published several collections of lyric and reflective poems, many of which have been set to music, and short stories in *The New Yorker*. *Quietly My Captain Waits*, 1940, a novel set in the last years of the French regime in Québec and the Maritimes, has had 17 foreign eds.: its exotic setting, suspense, adventure, and, for its time, sexual explicitness account for its success, despite stereotypical characters and stilted dialogue. Papers at Boston Univ. See her autobiographical *The North Star is Nearer*, 1949.

Eberhart, Mignon (Good), writer of more than 60 popular mystery novels, the second woman, after Agatha CHRISTIE, to win a Mystery Writers of America Grand Master Award, 1970, for her contribution to the genre. Daughter of Margaret Hill (Bruffey) and William Thomas G., she was b. in 1899 in Lincoln, Neb., where she attended public schools, then, 1917–20, Nebraska Wesleyan Univ., which made her D.Litt., 1935. In 1923, she m. Alanson C. E., a civil engineer whose work took them to several locations which provided detail for her books. She divorced him, 1946, to marry John H. Perry, then divorced him, 1948, to remarry Eberhart. 'In the heyday of magazines', says Dorothy B. HUGHES, 'ME's name on the cover of *The Saturday Evening Post* and *The Ladies Home Journal* ensured a sell-out', and during the Depression, ME said, 'the writing was a godsend'. Her first book, *The Patient in Room 18*, 1929, introduces series character Nurse Sarah Keate, a descendent of Mary Roberts RINEHART's Hilda Adams. A self-described 'old maid' resolved to reject stereotypical spinsterhood, she survived in ME's novels until the 1950s. Subsequent novels are also much influenced by the Rinehart 'Had I But Known' school of DETECTIVE writing, with its first person-female narrator, heavy atmosphere, and romance. *While the Patient Slept*, 1930, won the $5000 Scotland Yard Prize. *The Cases of Susan Dare*, 1934, introduced another series character, a writer of crime stories with a talent for finding 'real' murder mysteries. Translated into at least 16 languages, ME's books have appeared serially in Europe and the USA in most major mystery and espionage magazines. A past President of Mystery Writers of America, she has also written filmscripts, and several of her novels have been filmed ('The White Cockatoo', 1935; 'While the Patient Slept', 1935; 'Murder by an Aristocrat', 1935, to name only three). She also wrote two plays, *320 College Avenue*, with Fred Ballard, 1938, and *Eight O'Clock Tuesday*, with Robert Wallsten, 1941. Marcia MULLER finds the heroine of *The Patient in Cabin C*, 1983, not very different from ME's heroines of the 1940s. More than 30 books in print reflect her continuing popularity. Papers at Boston Univ. Interview in *Publisher's Weekly*, September 1974. See Patricia Craig and Mary Cadogan, *The Lady Investigates*, 1981, and Dilys Winn, *Murderess Ink*, 1979 (quoted above).

Eccles, Charlotte O'Conor, 'Hal Godfrey' d. 1911, journalist, essayist, novelist. B. Roscommon, Ireland, eldest surviving da. of Alexander O'C. E., she was educ. at Upton Hall, near Birkenhead, and in convents in Paris and Germany. She worked for the provincial press, then the *New York Herald* in London where she lived with her mother and sister. In 'The Experience of a Woman Journalist', *Blackwood's Magazine*, June 1893, she comments on 'the immense difficulty a woman finds in getting into an office in any recognised capacity' and the restrictions on her movements and subject-matter. She was interested in the housing of the poor. She lectured in Ireland for the Board of Agriculture and Technical Instruction and wrote an article on 'Irish Housekeeping and Irish Customs in the Last Century' for *Blackwoods*, December

1888. *Aliens of the West*, 1904, depicts life in the imaginary Irish town of Toomevara, a place rent by class and religious antagonism. The book is composed of six stories reprinted from the *American Ecclesiastical Review* and the *Pall Mall Magazine*. Her translation from the Polish, *Peasants in Exile*, 1899, by Sienkiewicz, was also pub. in the USA. She travelled to Vienna to report on nursing conditions in teaching hospitals. Her article on 'The Hospital Where the Plague Broke Out' for *The Nineteenth Century*, October 1899, expresses her indignation at the brutal treatment of patients, particularly women. Her characteristic sense of humour is most apparent in *The Rejuvenation of Miss Semaphore*, 1897, by 'Hal Godfrey'. This hilarious novel tells of a middle-aged woman who drinks too much of an elixir of youth, causing pandemonium in the pretentious boarding-house where she lives with her sister. Her last novel, written under her own name, was *The Matrimonial Lottery*, 1906.

Echlin, Elizabeth (Bellingham), Lady, 1704?–?83, amateur critic. Da. of Elizabeth (Spencer) and William B. of Westmorland, she m., ?1727, Sir Robert E., Irish baronet; of her three children, two died young. Reading Richardson's *Clarissa* and finding the rape both vile and unlikely, she at once wrote her own (shorter) version of its later stages (read by Richardson in 1755: MS in NY Public Library; pub. in Switzerland, 1982, ed. Dimiter Daphinoff). Her Clarissa sees through Lovelace's plots while at Hampstead; her approach to death renders her lover and brother penitent; her sister is punished by a bad marriage to a Mr Cabbage. Critical notes (better than the story) stress EE's improving purpose and her horror at the rape. Her sister Dorothy, Lady Bradshaigh, wrote her detailed and sensitive criticism to Richardson in notes (*N. and Q.*, 1877) and letters which she planned to publish, but did not.

Eddy, Mary Baker, 1821–1910, author of religious tracts and founder of the Church of Christ, Scientist, b. near Bow, NH. Her father, an orthodox Congregationalist, was firm with his family but Mary, the sixth and last child, was influenced by her mother's and grandmother's less austere faith. Educated at district schools and Sanbornton Academy, NH, she m. three times, outliving one husband and divorcing another. Always a semi-invalid, she was 'cured' in 1862 by Phineas Parkhurst Quimby, 1802–66, and immediately espoused his theory of the mental basis of disease and health. In 1875 she established the Christian Scientists' Home in Lynn, Md, and published *Science and Health, with Key to the Scriptures* (16 eds. by 1886). She then began a series of lectures proclaiming her new faith, and in 1879 the Church of Christ, Scientist, was chartered. She founded the monthly *Christian Science Journal*, 1883, the weekly *Christian Science Sentinel*, 1898, and the daily *Christian Science Monitor*, 1908. She prayed to 'Our Father-Mother God', and her church and its philosophy of health and healing have spread worldwide. Her other important writings are her autobiography, *Retrospection and Introspection*, 1895; *Manual of the Mother Church*, 1895; and *Miscellaneous Writings*, 1896. Two reliable studies are by Robert Peel, 1966, and Julius Silberger, Jr, 1980, who also quotes a portion of her poetry.

Eden, Emily, 1797–1869, novelist, artist, traveller, political hostess, b. London, twelfth of 14 children of Eleanor (Eliot) and William E., 1st Baron Auckland. Spurning marriage, she devoted herself to her family, acting as hostess for her brother George till his death in 1849. She spent six years in India when he was appointed Governor-General in 1835, and published a selection of excellent paintings, *Portraits of the People and Princes of India*, 1844, and travel notes, *Up the Country*, 1866, which suffer from her lack of real interest in the country and its politics. The success of *The*

Semi-Detached House, 1859 (anon.), led to the publication of the 30-year-old *The Semi-Attached Couple* the following year (both repr. 1979). Though conventionally plotted, her novels have clever dialogue and biting satire. Like her travel writing and paintings, they are better at particulars than at the larger vision. In spite of carefully arranged happy endings, marriage seems a bleak affair, with husband and wife knowing little of each other's lives and communicating poorly: 'it is better that the love should be most on the husband's side; and then he is afraid of you, and that is not amiss when the wife is cleverer than the husband'. Her letters were pub. 1919, ed. Violet Dickinson.

Edgell, Zoe, novelist and journalist, b. in Belize, a colony not fully independent till 1981. Educ. there in the 1940s and 1950s, she learned no Belizean history: her novel *Beka Lamb*, 1982 (co-winner of the Fawcett Society Prize; first Belizean novel to reach an international audience), sets out to provide some of this missing knowledge. In the early 1960s ZE was a reporter on the *Daily Gleaner* in Kingston, Jamaica; back in Belize, she edited a small newspaper and taught at St Catherine Academy, 1966–8. She then travelled widely with her husband and children, living in Nigeria, Britain, Afghanistan, Bangladesh, the USA, Belize again (where she returned to St Catherine and was director of the Women's Bureau), and from 1982 in Somalia. *Beka Lamb* centres on a 14-year-old black schoolgirl in 1950, looking back on the interweaving of her personal story and the early decolonization struggle; it develops a strong cultural language and imagery with which to confront the influences which marginalize the young, the black, the female, and the citizens of small countries. See Fr Charles Hunter, SJ, in *Belizean Studies*, 10, 1982; Roger Bromley in *Wasafiri*, 2, 1985.

Edgeworth, Maria, 1768–1849, novelist and CHILDREN's writer, b. and largely brought up in England, second surviving child of Anna Maria (Elers), who d. 1773, and Anglo-Irish Richard Lovell E., landowner, scientist, author and father of 22 children. Severely treated on high-minded principles by her first stepmother, at boarding-school 1775–81, ME hungered for approval, sought it both by writing and by submissiveness, and began to receive it from her father on his third marriage. She probably had herself in mind when she set an early heroine to unlearn virtues 'such as were more estimable in a man than desirable in a female'. From 1782 she lived in and studied Ireland as her father's 'agent and accountant' at Edgeworthstown, Co. Longford. She translated Mme de GENLIS's *Adelaide and Theodore* (one vol. printed, 1783, but now untraced), and visited England, 1791–3 and 1799. Her informal style first emerged in letters, unpublished plays, and stories for children of unprecedented immediacy in *The Parent's Assistant*, 1796. *Letters for Literary Ladies*, 1795, is for adults, *Moral Tales*, 1801, for adolescents. She also worked with her father: on the treatise *Practical Education*, 1798, and *Early Lessons*, 1801 (projects begun by him), and, against her grain, on *Essays on Professional Education*, 1809. Her adult novels began with the comic Irish microcosm *Castle Rackrent, An Hibernian Tale*, 1800, and the anti-fashionable *Belinda*, 1801 (re-written in 1810 to make more decorous the heroine whom she called 'that stick or stone'); her novellas blossomed with *Tales of Fashionable Life*, 1809 and 1812. These, on wider public themes, include the very funny *Ennui*, another of the Irish tales which influenced Turgenev and Scott. ME visited France, 1802–3 (where she rejected a marriage proposal), and was lionized in London in 1813. She corresponded with A. L. BARBAULD, Elizabeth INCHBALD, Elizabeth HAMILTON and Jane MARCET, and wrote notes and preface for Mary LEADBEATER's *Cottage Life*, 1811. *The Absentee*, 1812, was dramatized by Marianne MOORE. ME's father died in 1817, just as *Harrington* (whose Christian hero loves a Jewish woman) and *Ormond* appeared. Devastated by grief, missing him not as helper but as motive, ME completed his *Memoirs*, pub. 1820, then gradually began to move in and enjoy English society. Besides children's stories she wrote one more work, *Helen*, 1834, with a new emphasis on plot rather than moral. She destroyed the draft of *Taken for Granted*, 1838. Publishers used her surname for works by others, 1806ff. See life by Marilyn Butler, 1972; several recent reprints.

Edginton, May, 1883–1957, popular novelist publishing in London. She wrote over 50 novels, 1909–55, all firmly within the popular ROMANCE genre, and collaborated with Rudolph Besier on two plays, *The Prude's Fall*, produced 1920, and *Secrets*, produced 1929. In *The Sin of Eve*, 1913, a pretty suffragette worker leaves 'the Cause' to marry. Some of ME's novels propose escapes or solutions for their heroines trapped in unhappy domestic relationships. *Married Life or The True Romance*, 1917, describes the disintegration of the relationship between newlyweds living on a small income. Forced to depend completely on her husband for money and housebound by the arrival of their three children, the wife loses all power and independence. When her husband takes an extended business trip, she uses his absence, the increased income from his larger salary, and an inheritance from her recently deceased mother to gain control of the household affairs and her own life; he returns to discover his 'power ... broken' and that his wife wants him back only on her terms. *Woman of the Family*, 1936, describes the metamorphosis of another 'household drudge' when Eve, supporting her family on a meagre secretarial salary, takes a glamorous job as dance club hostess. But while 'The man breadwinner is flattered and obeyed and waited upon ... the girl is supposed to do a man's job and a woman's job combined', and has 'no right to her own money. She is supposed to sacrifice and sacrifice and all the time to be under her parents' authority.' Eve escapes from that to marriage to one of her club's wealthiest clients. ME m. novelist Francis Bailey in 1912 and had one son. Her last novel was *Two Lost Sheep*, 1955.

Edmonds, Elizabeth Mayhew (Waller), fl. 1881–1910, English scholar, translator, poet and novelist. Her first pub. work, *Fair Athens*, 1881, recounts her unaccompanied excursions there, offering astute social observation and domestic and culinary details. In 1883 she pub. a volume of poetry, *Hesperas, Rhythm and Rhyme*, including a dramatic monologue, 'The Poet's Wife' (once the source of his inspiration, now neglected). Over the next 20 years she pub. numerous works on, and translations of, Greek literature and history, including *Greek Lays, Idylls, Legends: A Selection*, 1885, *Rhigas Pheraios, The Protomartyr of Greek Independence*, 1890, and *Stories from Fairyland* by George Drosines, 1892. Her first novel, *Mary Myles, A Study*, 1888 (written at the request of her husband), tells of a heroine who takes the highest honours in classics at Cambridge (while managing to retain her subtle beauty) and later becomes the respected headmistress of a school before marrying a young suitor with whom she goes to India, where her language skills in Hindustani make her his invaluable secretary. EME pub. two more novels, *Amygdala. A Tale of the Greek Revolution*, 1894, and *Jabez Nutyard, Workman and Dreamer*, 1898.

Education. Most early books of 'instruction' or 'learning' for women fall under the heading of ADVICE. In 1405–6 the Statute of Artificers guaranteed parents' rights to send sons and daughters to school. In the mid sixteenth century a number of men urged admission of girls to grammar schools: specifically excluded from many such schools, a few girls were admitted, as a few were apprenticed to trades. The norm was merely primary schooling for middle-class girls and some teaching of skills in workhouses, while a few potential Court ladies received advanced tutoring in the new humanities, and an intellectual tradition lingered among upper-class women. Deptford had the first public school for girls, 1619. By the late seventeenth century Bathsua MAKIN had made good education a controversial issue, but boarding schools (chiefly middle-class) often catered to parents' desire for accomplishments instead of learning. The Bar convent, York (house bought 1686), had a unique run as a girls' school for almost 300 years. Charity schools spread fast in London, but for girls were strictly job oriented except for religious teaching fostered by the SPCK (founded 1699). What was deemed appropriate learning for girls depended on conflicting views of the nature and purpose of Woman; theoretical debate tended to remain divorced from women's experience of generally low-level teaching for subsistence, even when the same woman was both governess and educational writer, like Mary WOLLSTONECRAFT. In the late eighteenth century Sarah TRIMMER helped politicize the issue of working girls' education, while for their 'betters' a demand was growing among parents for serious reading and science (of which the leading text-book writers at this time were women). The Young Ladies' Academy, Philadelphia, opened 1787 (following Anthony Benezet but preceding S. H. ROWSON), quoted Vicesimus Knox on the covers of its exercise books: 'The superior advantages of boys' education are perhaps the sole reason of their subsequent superiority.' In London in the late 1840s, Queen's College for governesses (later a school) and the more ambitious Bedford College (later part of London Univ.; merged in 1986 with Royal Holloway, also an ex-women's college) were established for women. The next decade saw the birth of some girls' secondary schools emphasizing intellectual attainment: North London Collegiate School, 1850, founded by Mary Buss, 1827–84, and Cheltenham Ladies' College, 1858, founded by Dorothea Beale, 1831–1906. The sisters Maria GREY and Emily SHIRREFF set up the National Union for the Education of Girls in 1871; the Girls' Public Day School Trust was founded to build schools in 1872. In the 1860s Frances Power COBBE began the campaign for women's higher education, which proceeded by first gaining access to London, Cambridge and Oxford matriculation examinations, then establishing women's university colleges. Emily DAVIES pressed it through with the founding of Girton in 1869; Newnham, 1871, and Somerville, 1879, followed. Women received degrees at London from 1878, and Oxbridge women were granted degrees by Trinity College, Dublin; but Oxford graduated women only from 1920, 'the total number of women candidates being carefully regulated'. At Cambridge women first became full university members in 1947. In the USA, girls' public secondary schools comparable to boys' grammar schools began in New England in the 1820s. Lydia Huntley, later SIGOURNEY, ran a school in Norwich and Hartley, Conn., 1811–19. Other influential voices were those of Frances WRIGHT (in public lectures of the 1820s), Catharine BEECHER, and Emma WILLARD, who faced a storm of ridicule when a girl was publicly examined in geometry in 1829. Progress was slow until after the Civil War. Education remained largely restricted to whites; in most Southern states slaves were forbidden to learn reading or writing. University admission of women began with Oberlin College in 1837, Hillsdale in 1844, Antioch in 1853; many women's colleges, including Vassar, were established in these years. After the war their number greatly increased; Dr Elizabeth Blackwell, 1821–1910, and Dr Emily Blackwell, 1826–1910, opened the first medical college for women, NYC, 1868; a number of state universities began admitting women; by 1870 there were around 70 women's colleges as well as some 180 co-educational ones (which became increasingly popular). Unlike their English contemporaries, US women were granted degrees from the first. In Australia, girls' state education began in the 1880s; women could gain degrees at the Univ. of Melbourne from 1879, and were admitted to Adelaide in 1880 and Sydney in 1881. In New Zealand women had access to both secondary schools and universities from the 1870s. The first woman BA from the new Univ. of Auckland (which was induced to admit women on the same terms as men) graduated in 1877. See books by Dorothy Gardiner, 1929, Josephine Kamm, 1965; Vera BRITTAIN, *The Women at Oxford*; Susan Leonardi, *Dangerous by Degrees: Women at Oxford and the Somerville College Novelists*, 1989. Even after the explosion of women's studies courses in the 1970s, research still shows women in education to be disadvantaged in comparison with men in almost every area and every country: the inequality is always greatest at the most advanced levels, both of learning and teaching. See, merely as a sample, on the UK, Dale Spender and Elizabeth Sarah, eds., *Learning to Lose: Sexism and Education*, 1980; Rosemary Dean, ed., *Schooling for Women's Work*, 1980 (essays on race, mixed or single-sex schools, maths, science); Pat Mahony, *Schools for the Boys? Co-education reassessed*, 1985 (arguing from research 'that mixed-sex groupings constitute a disaster area for girls'); Mary Hughes and Mary Kennedy, eds., *New Futures, Changing Women's Education*, 1985; Felicity Hunt, *Lessons for Life: The Schooling of Girls and Women, 1850–1950*, 1987; on the USA, Madeleine R. Grumet, *Bitter Milk: Women and Teaching*, 1988; Elizabeth K. Minnich, et al., eds., *Reconstructing the Academy: Women's Education and Women's Studies*, 1988 (essays repr. from *Signs*).

Edward(e)s, Annie (Jones), *c.* 1830–96, English novelist. Nothing is known of her life, except that she m. John E. (not T. L. E.) and had one son, b. 1859. Reviewed in the *Spectator* and *Athenaeum*, well paid (she got £170–180 for one vol., £350–500 for three), she had one novel banned by Mudie's Library. She published 21 novels between 1858 and 1899, changing the spelling of her name after 1871 (to distinguish herself from Amelia EDWARDS). Her early novels (*A Point of Honour*, 1863; *Steven Lawrence*, 1868) are more moralistic and less sympathetic to women than her later works, which often portray unworthy society men and frank young women. Her best known, *Ought We To Visit Her?*, 1871, treats social inequality in marriage in saucy style. But *A Girton Girl*, 1885, set on Guernsey (AE spent time in Jersey), is ambivalent about women's role: the bright and independent heroine ends by marrying her tutor: 'I need no other life, no other wisdom, no other ambition than yours' (3, 298).

Edwards, Amelia Ann Blandford, 1831–92, novelist, travel writer, and Egyptologist, b. London, educ. at home in Islington. Her mother was a lively theatre-loving Irish woman, her father an ex-army officer who worked in a City bank. She supported the family when her father's bank failed, by writing stories for magazines such as *Household Words* and *All the Year Round*. She also became a staff member of *The Saturday Review* and *The Morning Post*. *Miss Carew*, 1865, was a collection of tales, and her sensation stories such as *The 4.15 Express*, 1867, and *The Tragedy in Bardello Place*, 1868, were very popular. Her first novel was *My Brother's Wife*, 1855, and her earliest success, *Barbara's History*, 1864, a 'bigamy' novel, had three editions and was translated into German, Italian and French. *Half a Million of Money*, 1865, *Debenham's Vow*, 1870, and *In the Days of My Youth*, 1873, were all well received. *Lord Brackenbury*, 1880 (with illustrations based on her water-colour sketches), was her last and most popular novel. She wrote poetry, summaries of English and French history, and the letterpress for Caldesi's *Photographic Historical Portrait Gallery*, 1860. *Sights and Stories*, 1862, is an account of a tour through Belgium, while *Untrodden Peaks and Unfrequented Valleys*, 1873, illustrated with her own sketches, describes the Dolomites. A trip to Egypt and Syria in 1873 began a lifelong passion: she learnt hieroglyphics and became England's foremost Egyptologist, fighting to preserve Egypt's heritage, founding and becoming Secretary of the Egypt Exploration Fund. She wrote *A Thousand Miles up the Nile*, 1877, and published numerous articles in British, US and European journals. A brilliant tour of America in 1889 (lectures pub. in *Pharaohs, Fellahs and Explorers*, 1891), was marred by an accident from which she never fully recovered. She died a few months after the friend with whom she had shared her home for the previous 28 years. She left her Egyptian collection and library to University College, London, together with a fund to establish the first Chair in Egyptology in Britain. The rest of her books were left to Somerville College, Oxford.

Edwards, Sarah (Pierrepont), 1710–58, religious memoirist, da. of Mary (Hooker) and James P., minister at New Haven and one of the founders of Yale. From the age of five or six she held to 'the religion of joy'; at 13 she loved solitude. In 1727 she m. the famous preacher and theologian Jonathan E. of Northampton, Mass.; she had seven children in 13 years. Her duties included managing his poor health and heavy workload, dispensing hospitality, and running women's meetings. In 1738 and 1740 (as the Great Revival began in Northampton) she solemnly re-dedicated herself to Christ. In January 1742, Jonathan E.'s hint that in talking to a rival preacher she had 'failed' in 'prudence' showed her her vulnerability to any threat of 'ill treatment of the town, or ill will of my husband', and awoke an acute sense of sin and 'desire to be alone with God'. She powerfully relates (quoting Elizabeth ROWE) the following two weeks of intense religious experiences, chiefly in her husband's absence (printed in life of him by Sereno E. Dwight, 1830; his version, calling her 'the person', 1743, repr. in his *Great Awakening*, ed. C. C. Goen, 1972). She had four more children and lived through his dismissal, financial hardship, his death and that of her daughter Esther BURR.

'Egerton, George', Mary Chavelita (Dunne), 1859–1945, Irish short-story writer, playwright, novelist, b. Australia. Her Welsh-born mother d. 1875, leaving GE as eldest da. of John J. D., talented but incompetent Irishman, and in charge of younger siblings, coping with bailiffs and other distresses. She spent part of her childhood in Chile, and in 1875 taught and studied in Germany, then worked in New York, Dublin and London. In 1887 she went to Norway with bigamist Henry Higginson. There she read deeply in Ibsen, Strindberg, Nietzsche and others, and met Knut Hamsun, whose novel *Hunger* she began to translate in 1890 (pub. 1899). Higginson died, and in 1891 she m. George Egerton Clairmonte, lived in Ireland, but soon had to support him by writing. Her first volume of stories, *Keynotes*, was published by John Lane to begin his 'Keynote' series, 1893. Sensationally successful in its outspoken treatment of the NEW WOMAN, it was followed within a year by a sequel, *Discords* (repr. together, 1983). In 1895 she had a child, her marriage broke up, but she refused to compromise her style for the increasingly pusillanimous Lane in *Symphonies*, 1897. *The Wheel of God*, 1898, her semi-autobiographical novel, caused her feckless husband to complain. In 1901 she divorced him and m. Reginald Golding Bright, a theatre agent 15 years her junior. She pub. the novel *Rosa Amorosa*, 1901, and stories *Flies in Amber*, 1905, but became more interested in the stage, translating French plays and writing four (three were staged in the US). See her nephew's rather gossipy biographical account and selection of her correspondence, *A Leaf from the Yellow Book*, ed. Terence de Vere White, 1958. Her work has received most attention in Scandinavia and Germany, but see M. D. Stetz, *Turn-of-the-Century Women* 1, 1 (Summer 1984).

Elaw, Zilpha, autobiographer calling herself an 'American Female of Colour', one of three survivors in a religious Pennsylvania family of 22 children, 'of a very lively and active disposition', with some schooling. Orphaned in her teens, she worked for Quakers whose lack of outward observance shocked her. After warnings in dreams and teaching by Methodists, she was converted at 14 by a vision of God: real, she says, not merely of 'the eye of my mind', since the cow she was milking saw it too and bowed down. She m. Joseph E., a non-religious fuller, in 1810, had a daughter, and lived near Philadelphia, then at Burlington, NJ. She prefaces with a homily on woman's duty of submission to fathers and husbands ('the dictate of nature') her refusal to let her husband turn her from religion to dancing. After great success PREACHING to a local magnate, she became a minister (with much doubt and struggle) two months before her husband knew of it. When he died in 1832 she opened a school for children barred from white schools. Later she made preaching tours in the slave states, the North, and from 1840 in England, where she gave more than 1,000 sermons, and strongly refuted the case against female preaching. About to return home, she pub. her *Memoirs*, 1846, partly to explain the USA to English friends.

Elder, Anne (Mackintosh), 1918–76, poet, b. Auckland, NZ, da. of Rena (Bell) and Norman M. She moved to Australia at the age of three and became a noted soloist with the Borovansky Ballet Company before marrying John E. in 1943. Occasional short stories and poems began appearing in newspapers and journals in the 1950s, but her first collection, *For the Record*, was not pub. till 1972. Her second volume, *Crazy Woman and Other Poems*, 1976 (pub. posthumously), received wide acclaim. The title poem blends subtle rhymes with lyrical, sometimes humorous, word-play and a straightforward first-person narrative to describe the crazy woman in the public gardens: 'the poet, who has first to find / the spangled fern, the gift, then grow it / bedded in the heart's ground'. Her most striking poems are those which deal with subjects close to her: her mother and family, and places where she lived. Her vision, however, is dark and violent. The Anne Elder Trust Fund Award is made annually for the best book of poetry published that year in Australia.

Eldershaw, Flora Sydney Patricia, 1897–1956, novelist, critic, b. Sydney, NSW, da. of Margaret (McCarroll) and Henry E. She was educ. at Wagga Wagga and Sydney Univ., where she was secretary of the Women's Union. From 1923 to 1940 she was Senior Mistress at the Presbyterian Ladies' College, Croydon. Best known for her collaboration in novels written with university friend Marjorie BARNARD under the pseudonym 'M. Barnard-Eldershaw', she also wrote non-fiction such as her address to the English Association, *Contemporary Australian Women Writers*, 1931. She edited the *Australian Writer's Annual*, 1936, for the Fellowship of Australian Writers (FAW) and *The Peaceful Army*, 1938 (repr. 1988), a collection of essays and poems by contemporary women writers on famous Australian women of the past, in honour of Australia's sesquicentenary. During WWII she worked in the Department of Reconstruction and the Department of Labour and National Service, before becoming an industrial consultant in 1948. She was President of the Sydney branch of the FAW 1935 and 1943, instrumental in the expansion of the Commonwealth Literary Fund and a member of its advisory board, 1939–53. She was also a member of the Women's

Advisory Council. Among her literary friends were Vance and Nettie PALMER and Katharine Susannah PRICHARD.

Elgin, Patricia Anne **Suzette Haden** (Wilkins), science-fiction writer and linguist, b. in 1936 in Louisiana, Missouri, to teacher Hazel (Lewis) and lawyer Gaylord Lloyd W. She attended the Univ. of Chicago, 1954–6, m. Peter H., 1955, and had three children. During the 1960s she taught music and languages and performed as a folk singer. After Haden's death she m. George E., 1964: they have one child. She completed her BA in 1967 (Calif. State Univ., Chico), did graduate work in linguistics at the Univ. of Calif., San Diego (MA, 1970, PhD, 1973), where she taught, 1972–80. She is a specialist in American Indian languages and transformational grammar. She financed her return to study by beginning her four Communipath novels featuring Coyote Jones of the Tri-Galactic Intelligence Service (a 'rather bumbling mind-deaf superspy' who can send but not receive telepathic messages), 1970–9, then wrote the Ozark Fantasy Trilogy, 1981, which mixes American folklore and magic with interplanetary action to create a world of power struggles among magicians. Her latest series, *Native Tongue,* 1984, and *The Judas Rose*, 1987, creates a dystopia in which women, deprived by the US Congress of legal rights and status, are exploited as workers and childbearers. (See Mary Kay Bray in *Extrapolation*, 27, 1986.) In a world in which interplanetary economics makes language skills empowering, these women create their own language, Láadan (to which SHE published *A First Grammar and Dictionary* in *SF* 3, 1984) to express 'the perceptions of women rather than those of men': 'The hypothesis was that if we put the project into effect it would *change reality*.' SHE founded *The Lonesome Node* (newsletter for the Ozark Center for Language Studies), 1980. Her *Gentle Art of Verbal Self Defense*, 1980, and its sequels, discuss techniques for coping with verbal aggression by others. Papers at San Diego State Univ.

'Eliot, George', Mary Anne (Evans), later Lewes, then Cross, 1819–80, novelist, b. Arbury, Warwicks., youngest da. of Christiana (Pearson) (d. 1836) and Robert E. (d. 1849), land agent and overseer. Chilvers Coton Parish Register records her name as Mary Anne; in 1837 she adopted the form Mary Ann and, in 1850, Marian, reverting to Mary Ann in 1880. She grew up in a large pleasant farmhouse at Griff. Not intellectually precocious, she was educated at various boarding-schools from age five. Her father arranged for her to have lessons in Italian and German; she later learnt Latin and Greek. At 15 she entered a protracted Evangelical phase, characterized by a combination of priggishness and theatricality ('I used to go about like an owl'). Her relationship with family members was close, but often antagonistic; of her feelings for her mother we know nothing. Her early work was as a translator and journalist. She transl. Strauss's *Das Leben Jesu*, 1846, and contributed articles anon. to the *Coventry Herald*. Her translation of Feuerbach's *Das Wesen des Christenthums*, 1854, uniquely, carried her name, Marian Evans, on the title-page. She was, in all but name, the editor of *The Westminster Review*, 1851–3, re-establishing its liberal intellectual eminence. After a series of unsatisfactory and often painful relationships she entered into a long, stable, happy union with G. H. Lewes, a married man unable to divorce his wife. Their decision to live openly together caused considerable scandal, and even some of her closest friends were alienated. Her family ceased corresponding with her. She continued to make major contributions to *The Westminster Review*, and in 1856 began to write fiction as 'George Eliot'. *Scenes of Clerical Life*, 1857, was well received, and was followed by the sensationally successful *Adam Bede*, 1859, then *The Mill on the Floss*, 1860, *Silas Marner*, 1861, *Romola*, 1863, *Felix Holt*,

1866, *Middlemarch*, 1871–2, *Daniel Deronda*, 1876. Her financial, critical, and popular success was phenomenal. It was widely recognized that her novels introduced a new realism and psychological seriousness into English fiction. Her delineation of the coercive nature of social, cultural and familial structures, for men and women alike, gives her work a feminist significance even though she eschewed commitment to 'the Cause', and despite the conservative bias of the philosophical and deeply moral discourse of the 'George Eliot' persona. Other prose works are *The Lifted Veil*, 1859, *Brother Jacob*, 1864, *The Impressions of Theophrastus Such*, 1879. Her vols. of poetry are *The Spanish Gypsy*, 1866, and *The Legend of Jubal*, 1874, which included the verse drama *Armgart*, a poignant delineation of the dilemmas of the nineteenth-century woman artist. GE was devastated by Lewes's death in 1878. In 1880 she m. J. W. Cross, 20 years her junior; she died suddenly in December of that year. The standard life is by Gordon Haight, 1968; see also Ruby Redinger, 1975. Feminist critical accounts include: S. GILBERT and S. Gubar, *The Madwoman in the Attic*, 1979; Margaret Homans, *Bearing the Word*, 1986; and Gillian Beer, 1986.

Eliza's Babes, *or The Virgins-Offering*, 1652, dedicated to 'my [probably metaphorical] Sisters' by 'a Lady, who onely desires to advance the glory of God, and not her own'. Her poetic 'babes' explore a relationship with God which makes writing and publishing necessary, marriage irrelevant: 'Give me a Soule, give me a Spirit, / That flyes from earth, heaven to inherit. / But those that grovell here below, / What! I love them? I'le not do so.' They set out the emotions and issues at stake to a woman considering wifehood: if they are autobiographical, she married after several years of happy singleness. A poem to Charles I, 1644, calls on him to compromise; one to Elizabeth of Bohemia celebrates the fact that the Civil War has driven the poet abroad, enabling her to 'see that Queen, so much admir'd'. See Elaine Hobby, 1988.

Elizabeth I, 1533–1603, Queen of England, writer of poems, prayers, letters, speeches and translations, da. of Ann Boleyn and Henry VIII. Her mother and aunts MARGARET Tudor and Mary of France are remembered for their letters. An apt Renaissance pupil, she could speak fluently in Greek, Latin and modern languages, and was rated very highly by her tutors William Grindal and Roger Ascham. In 1544 she sent her stepmother Katharine PARR, in a cover embroidered by herself, her prose translation from Marguerite de NAVARRE, 'The Glasse of the Sinful Soul': printed as *The Godly Medytacyon*..., 1548; facs. as *The Mirror*..., 1897. She translated further texts, and perhaps wrote her own *Devotions* (a tiny book – cf. Elizabeth TYRWHIT – now lost: facs. 1893, pub. 1970; see William P. Haugaard in *Sixteenth-Century Journal*, 12, 1981). She was a mistress of prose styles designed to rouse patriotism, confidence and personal devotion or respect (see Allison Heisch in *Signs*, 1, 1975). After coming to the throne, 1558, she often mentions her sex in a tone that cloaks pride with surface humility: 'thoughe I be a woman, yet I have as good a corage awnsuerable to my place as evere my father had ... I thanke god I am in deed indued with suche qualytes, that yf I were turned owte of the Realme in my pettycote, I were hable to lyve in any place of Chrystendon.' Lives by e.g. Edith SITWELL, 1946, repr. 1988; Neville Williams, 1967; Susan Bassnett (feminist), 1988; Allison Heisch in *Feminist Review*, 4, 1980. Poems ed. Leicester Bradner, 1964; letters ed. G. B. Harrison, 1935, and E. I. Kouri, 1982 (an earlier ed. was reviewed by Virginia WOOLF); speeches ed. George P. Rice, Jr., 1951 (authorship contested by Felix Barker in *History Today*, 1988). E's literary flatterers were men; but women (Diana PRIMROSE, Anne BRADSTREET) wrote of her in a tone of personal delight. Her usage of Mary

Queen of Scots cast her as villain for many later novelists like Sophia LEE.

Ellet, Elizabeth Fries (Lummis), 1812?–77, poet, essayist and historian, b. at Sodus Point, NY, da. of Sarah (Maxwell) and William Nixon L., educ. at a girls' school in Aurora, NY. Her first book was a translation of Silvio Pellico's *Euphemio of Messina*, 1834. In 1835 she published *Poems, Translated and Original*, and m. William Henry E. From 1839 to 1857 she published poems and essays in leading American journals and seven books ranging in subject from Schiller to housekeeping. Her most important writing is historical, primarily documentation of women's roles, as in *The Women of the American Revolution* (3 vols., 1848 and 1850, repr. 1969) and *Domestic History of the American Revolution*, 1850. In *Pioneer Women of the West*, 1852, and *Women Artists in All Ages and Countries*, 1859, as well as social histories of federalist and early nineteenth-century USA, she recognized the validity of studying 'minor' art forms created by women: 'From the early ages of the world ... spinning and weaving were feminine employments, in which undying germs of art were hidden' (*Women Artists*). See Anne Hollingsworth Wharton's introduction to *The Women of the American Revolution*, 1900 ed., and Sydney P. Moss, *Poe's Literary Battles*, 1963.

Elliot, Anne, novelist, about whose life little is known. She published at least 12 novels between 1883 and 1912, most anon. with Bentley (who also pub. novels by her sister Emma, 'Margery Hollis', whose first was *Anthony Fairfax*, 1885). AE's first novel, *Dr Edith Romney*, 1883, casts its heroine as a GP in a country town, while later works also show women in roles usually occupied by men. *Evelyn's Career*, 1891, set among realistic scenes of London poverty, has another strong-minded heroine who begins by thinking for herself, but in the end 'returned to her child's faith'. In *A Woman at the Helm*, 1892, Claire Thurston takes over the management of her father's dye-works. AE's novels are long and her plots over-complicated, but her writing is not without talent. She and her sister appear to have lived together, with a series of addresses (boarding-houses?) on the coast and in the London suburbs.

Elliot, Lady **Charlotte** (Carnegie), 1839–80, poet, da. of Charlotte (Lysons; d. 1848) and Sir James C. In 1860 she m. Thomas Fotheringham, d. 1864. In 1867, as 'Florenz', she published *Stella and other Poems*, including 'The Pythoness', about the distress of being a prophet and an instrument of the gods. In 1868 she married Frederick Boileau E. (d. 1880), a barrister and earl's son. Ten years later, she dedicated *Medusa and other Poems* to him. It reprints 'The Pythoness' and adds more poems on women caught in extreme situations: Medusa's face 'gleam'd out mid the sulphurous gloom / All pallid with passions long-perish'd', while Mary Magdalene talks with Salome and repents 'For sins that were my joys'. In 1880, 50 copies of *Mary Magdalene and other Poems* were printed for the Earl of Southesk – CE's brother, and himself a poet – in fulfilment of her dying wish for a small vol., to be distributed among friends.

Elliott, Miss, epistolary novelist 'in genteel life' (said to be sister of a novelist Mrs Hall, untraced). She pub. *The Relapse*, London and Dublin, anon., 1780, then *The History of the Hon. Mrs Rosemont and Sir Henry Cardigan* and *The Masqued Weddings*, 1781 (plenty of action, even fighting; heroine and confidante nicely combine dash with moralizing). Of *The Orphan* and *The Portrait*, both 1783, the *European Magazine* preferred the former: both have courtship plots with some Continental scenes; in the latter, Maria is eager to experience life in Russia, 'attended by half a hundred freezing beaux, whose only chance of being thawed is by the fire of my bright eyes'. *Fancy's Wreath*, 1812, moral fables and allegories for children, bears the same name.

Elliott, Charlotte, 1789–1871, hymn writer and poet, da. of Eling (Venn) and Charles E. She was third of eight children and suffered ill-health from an early age. Her parents were the centre of the Clapham Sect, a coterie of evangelical, philanthropic and religious activists. CE's early writings are witty and lively: they include a poem in which an anti-feminist is taken to Saturn, whose dull appearance is supposed to be due to an absence of women. After a spiritual crisis in 1821 she confined her reading to scripture and devoted her poetical talents solely to religion. Her famous hymn 'Just as I Am' was published in the *Invalid's Hymn Book*, 1834, followed by *Hours of Sorrow*, 1836, and the often reprinted *Hymns for a Week*, 1837. In 1843 CE's mother and sister, with whom she had been living at Brighton, died. *Poems by Charlotte Elliott* was published in 1863. Her brother Henry's death in 1865 was a severe blow and after 1867 she became a complete invalid. See the memoir by her sister, Eleanor Babington, prefacing *Selections from the Poems*, 1873, and Eleanor's ed. of *Leaves from the Unpublished Journals, Letters and Poems*, 1874, which gives a picture of daily and family life in letters to CE's beloved friend Jane Scott Moncrieff and to her sisters and nephew.

Elliott, Grace (Dalrymple), 1754–1823, courtesan and memoirist, youngest da. of Hew D., an Edinburgh lawyer who abandoned her mother before her birth. Educ. at a French convent, she was m. in 1771 to John E., a wealthy doctor and later knight, eloped from him in 1774 and was divorced with damages of £12,000. Her lovers included the Prince of Wales (who contended paternity of her daughter, born around 1782) and Philippe Egalité. She was in Paris from about 1786: her *Journals of my Life during the French Revolution* cover 1789–93 and were allegedly written at the request of George III on her return to England in 1801. Parts read like fiction (the king's gamekeepers dying for grief at the treatment of him) but others have the ring of personal experience, including the whole account of prison life with its instant intimacy, its lack of a future, its detail of food items given, procured, pilfered. Pub. in 1859 by a granddaughter against her family's wishes: reprints, English and French, up to [1955].

Elliott, Janice, novelist, b. 1931 at Derby, da. of Dorothy (Wilson) and advertising executive Douglas John E. After St Anne's College, Oxford (BA, 1953), she worked as a journalist, 1954–62, m. Robert Cooper in 1959 and had a son. Since *Cave With Echoes*, 1962, she has been a prolific full-time writer. *The Somnambulists*, 1964, treats a sister and brother lastingly alienated by their parents' early deaths. She centres many plots on the ups and downs of basically good marriages (a wife is surprised to realize that her husband 'genuinely liked women, enjoyed them, was interested in them'), with slightly offbeam politics at the periphery: international-leaning left-wing sympathies of the comfortably placed in her 'England trilogy' (*A State of Peace*, 1971, *Private Life*, 1972, *Heaven on Earth*, 1975). *Secret Places*, 1981, is set in a girls' boarding-school during WWII, *The Country of Her Dreams*, 1982, in a Balkan city picked as a site for a nuclear bunker for European masterworks of art. JE has developed lately: works like *Magic*, 1983, *Dr Gruber's Daughter*, 1986, *The Sadness of Witches*, 1987, blend studies of fringe politics or the occult with those of old age and human ties to animals.

Elliott, Maud (Howe), 'Maud Howe', 1854–1948, novelist, journalist, lecturer, art critic and suffragist, b. Boston, da. of Julia Ward Howe and Samuel Gridley H., physician. MHE was educ. at private schools and by her parents. Her first story, 'May Blossom', appeared in *Godey's Ladies'*

Magazine and her first novel, *A Newport Aquarelle*, pub. anon. in 1883, was an immediate success. Other novels include *San Rosario Ranch*, 1884, *Atalanta in the South*, 1886, and *Honor*, 1893, interesting for its depiction of American 'types'. In the 1880s MHE befriended Margaret DELAND, whose autobiography has a description of her. In 1887 she married John E., painter, and for several years they lived in Chicago where MHE lectured on literary subjects. They travelled extensively in Europe and MHE wrote letters describing her life there for a newspaper syndicate. She studied painting and wrote art reviews for the *Boston Transcript*, and in 1912 or 1913 she founded the Art Association of Newport. With her sister Laura E. RICHARDS (prolific children's novelist), MHE wrote a biography of their mother in 1915, for which they received the Pulitzer Prize. Like her mother, MHE was committed to women's suffrage, and was active in the Equal Suffrage League. She was also involved in war work during WWI. MHE corresponded with Henry James, a lifelong friend, and knew many other literary figures. In 1940 Brown University made her a Doctor of Letters. Her autobiography, *Three Generations*, 1923, paints a vivid picture of her life.

Elliott, Sarah Barnwell, 1848–1928, novelist, short-story writer, playwright, essayist and suffragist, birthplace uncertain, da. of Charlotte Bull (Barnwell) and Stephen E., leading liberal Episcopal bishop. SBE grew up in Sewanee and Savannah. She was educ. privately and at Johns Hopkins Univ. Her first novel, *The Felmeres*, 1879, has a Southern setting and shows atheism leading to tragedy. Her popular novel *Jerry*, 1891, deals with the poor whites of the Tennessee mountains and presents an early example of naturalism. In 1871 she wrote her brother, 'When a woman gives up all idea of matrimony, she either turns saint or woman's rights.' Though she threatened the former, by 1895 SBE was supporting herself by writing in New York, where she became a suffragist. Other novels include *John Paget*, 1893, *The Durket Sperrett*, 1898, and *The Making of Jane*, 1901. Her play, *His Majesty's Servant*, was produced in London in 1904. In 1912 she was elected first president of the Tennessee Equal Suffrage Association and she wrote an Equal Rights Manifesto which was used as a petition for legislators and politicians. In 1913 she joined a national suffrage march in Washington, DC, and was the first woman to address the Tennessee legislature. SBE openly criticized the position of blacks in the South, and her story 'An Incident', *Harper's*, 1897–8, describes a valiant sheriff holding off a lynch mob. In 1910–11 she was assistant editor of the *Forensic Quarterly Review*, for which she wrote 'A Study of Women in Civilization', 1910. She received an honorary doctorate of Civil Law from the Univ. of the South, 1913. See Clara Childs Mackenzie, 1980, for her life and work.

'Ellis, Alice Thomas', Anna (Lindholm) Haycraft, novelist, b. 1932 in Liverpool, da. of Alexandra and John L., educ. at Bangor Grammar School and Liverpool School of Art. In 1956 she m. London publisher Colin H., who features as 'Someone' in her *Spectator*, later *Tablet*, column (selecs. as *Home Life* series, 1986–9: domesticity teetering on the edge of chaos). She has five surviving children. Her married name appears on two cookery books, 1977 and (jointly) 1980, her pseudonym on other writings. Characters express both love and hatred through cooking in *The Sin Eater*, 1977 (Welsh Arts Council Award), a funny and shocking story exposing the hidden, violent rancours of Irish, Welsh, upper-class English, and Midlanders: Catholics, dissenters, and Anglicans. *The Birds of the Air*, 1980, features a hideous family Christmas. ATE contrasts characters of extreme conventionality with resolute eccentrics: Ukrainian forebears of Aunt Irene in *The 27th Kingdom*, 1982, left the Orthodox church when it introduced confession – for Catholicism. She often includes supernatural touches, echoes from ancient and bloody legend or 'the manless irrelevance of prehistory', and gibes at modern trendy religion. Her style is an integral part of her macabre, brilliant comedy. *The Other Side of the Fire*, 1983, provides alternative readings of intense emotions: a wife who has watched other women's rebellion 'from the battlemented safety of an incurious mind' falls in love with her husband's son; another character is writing a romance in which agony is wont to seize the heart in a vice-like grip; a feminist notes that 'Certainly women were better suited to coping with infidelity and misery. They were used to it, and they had each other.' *The Clothes in the Wardrobe*, 1987, *The Skeleton in the Cupboard*, 1988, and *The Fly in the Ointment*, 1989, make up a trilogy. ATE is a fiction editor with her husband's firm.

Ellis, Edith Mary Oldham, Mrs Havelock Ellis (Lees), 1861–1916, essayist, novelist, story writer, b. in Cheshire to Mary Laetitia (Bancroft) – who died soon after her premature birth – and landed proprietor Samuel Oldham L. Brought up by her brutal hypochondriac father and unsympathetic stepmother, she had a 'violent and irrational' (said her husband) prejudice against men. Her father withdrew her from a Manchester convent and sent her to a London school kept by German freethinker Mme Thesma, which gave her a love of literature. On her father's death she taught, then started a school in Sydenham, had a breakdown, and was rescued by Stopford Brook's daughter, Honor. She went into politics, lecturing successfully, and joined the Fellowship of the New Life, an experiment in communal living; but concluding that 'Fellowship is Hell', she resigned as secretary and m. Havelock E., 1891, maintaining close ties with him even after she left him. Her later relationships were with women. Her major novel was the controversial and highly regarded *Seaweed: A Cornish Idyll*, 1898, set in a Cornish fishing village and rendering local speech. Janet, a strong and deeply sensual woman, is married to the devoted but paralysed miner Kit, who comes to accept her sexual relations with another man. *Kit's Woman*, 1907, supposedly a revised version, is little changed (pub. in the USA as *Steve's Woman*, 1909). *My Cornish Neighbours*, 1906, has skilful local colour sketches, while *Attainment*, 1909, and *Love-Acre*, 1914, draw on her own childhood and youth. EE's essays, treating her interest in eugenics and in open marriage, were published as *The New Horizon in Love and Life*, 1921 (pref. by Edward Carpenter; intro. by Marguerite Tracy), and *Stories and Essays*, 1924. She also wrote a play, *The Subjection of Kezia*, 1908 (adapted from a story in *My Cornish Neighbours*), long used in several London theatres as a curtain-raiser. See H. Ellis's *My Life*, 1940, and Goldberg's *Havelock Ellis*, 1926.

Ellis, Ellen E. (Colebrook), 1829–95, NZ novelist, b. at Guildford, Surrey, England. The second eldest of 17 children, she was educ. at a local girls' 'seminary' and m. Oliver E., businessman, in 1852. They had two sons and emigrated to Auckland in 1859. In 1882 she pub. in London an autobiographical novel, *Everything is Possible to Will*. It is a clumsily written but vivid portrayal of life with an alcoholic husband, a plea for women's education and equal rights and an attack on male drunkenness and the availability of alcohol. Its heroine settles for passive resistance: 'gradually I perceived that although I was worthless in law, I was not in fact powerless. With faltering courage I came to a decision. I would not have a large family. I would not consent to have a child every year. I believed I had a moral right to refuse to allow my body so to be used at the will of another person.' The novel was not reviewed in NZ, and her son destroyed most copies of it to protect his father's reputation. See life by Vera Colebrook, 1980.

Ellis, Sarah (Stickney), 1799–1872, writer of ADVICE manuals for women, b. near Hull, youngest da. of Esther (Richardson) and William S., farmer. Brought up in a Quaker family, she was taught to read by her mother, who d. 1803, then educ. privately. Her early writings were moral tales, including 'The Negro Slave', 1831; many of these were collected in *Pictures of Private Life*, 1833–7. In 1837 she became a Congregationalist and m. William E., who was a missionary in Madagascar. Although she continued to write poetry and fiction, she is best known for her popular, conservative vols. of advice to women, such as *The Women of England*, 1838, *The Daughters of England*, 1842, *The Mothers of England*, 1843 and *The Wives of England*, 1843. She recommended that all action should be based on Christian principles and faith, and saw women as supportive, loving, uncomplaining wives and mothers: 'inferior to men – inferior in mental power, in the same proportion that you are inferior in bodily strength'. Yet her writing reveals a strong fellow-feeling for women's domestic trials. Her other interests included Sunday School administration, TEMPERANCE, work among the poor, and curative mesmerism, and she also organized and directed a girls' school near her home in Hoddesdon, Herts. *The Home Life and Letters of Mrs Ellis*, compiled by her nieces in 1893, gives a full, if entirely uncritical, picture of her life.

El Saadawi, Nawal, b. 1931, Egyptian novelist, doctor, and militant writer on Arab women's struggle for liberation. She has two children with her second husband, Sherif Hatala (m. 1964), translator of some of her work, who served 13 years as a prisoner of conscience. Egypt's Director of Public Health, 1966–72, Deputy General of the Egyptian Medical Syndicate, and editor of *Health* magazine until 1972, she was stripped of these duties because of her controversial scientific work on women's relation to traditional Arab society: see *Women and Sex*, 1972. As consultant to the UN on women and development, 1978–80, she observed: 'In the United Nations, men of the upper classes and of the rich First World countries reign supreme and women of the Third World sink to the bottom.' She was arrested under Sadat, 1981, and held until his assassination three months later. *Memoirs from the Woman's Prison*, 1985, deals with her experiences; the *Index on Censorship*, 4, 1985, reprints her account of her interrogation. She participated in a London conference on censorship, 1985. Her discussion of the physical and psychic trauma she and other Arab women experienced when excised called international attention to clitoridectomy at the UN conference for women, Copenhagen, 1983. She has published six novels – *Memoirs of a Woman Doctor*, first pub. serially and incomplete in 1957, transl. 1988, *Woman at Point Zero*, 1975, transl. 1983, and *God Dies by the Nile*, 1974, transl. 1985, are available in English – and five books on women's issues, including *The Hidden Face of Eve: Women in the Arab World*, trans. 1980. Though the complete manuscript of her first novel, *Memoirs of a Doctor*, is lost, NES regards it as her 'first daughter'. The title story in the collection *Death of an Ex-Minister*, 1987, examines male anger at a woman's refusal to defer. The outstanding voice for Muslim women, NES combines psychiatric acuity, the authority of personal experience, and political courage, speaking out to an international audience against the abuse of women. *The Fall of the Imam*, transl. 1989, has been compared to Margaret ATWOOD's *Handmaid's Tale*. See Mona N. Mikhail, ed., *Images of Arab Women*, 1979.

Elstob, Elizabeth, 1683–1756, scholar and feminist, b. at Newcastle, da. of Jane (Hall) and Ralph E. Her mother, 'a great admirer of learning, especially in her own sex', d. 1691: her father being also dead, she went to live with an uncle who thought one 'Tongue enough for a Woman'. She mastered eight, however, and found Germanic studies more open to women than 'the Greek and Latin Stores'. She lived with her brother, perhaps from 1696 at Oxford, certainly from 1702 in London. She translated Madeleine de SCUDÉRY's *Essay upon Glory*, 1708, and in 1709 *An English-Saxon Homily on the Birthday of St Gregory ...* (facs. 1974, in Univ. of Michigan Papers in Women's Studies), with many female subscribers and her own decorations, dedicated to Queen Anne, whom she praises in feminist prefaces to both works. Her plan to continue with the complete homilies of Aelfric (with a life of him) resulted in collected *Testimonies of Learned Men* in its favour, 1713, and *Proposals*, 1715, but only two gatherings printed of the work itself, 1715. That year she dedicated to Princess Caroline her first-ever Old English grammar, begun to help a female student: *Rudiments of Grammar for the English-Saxon ... with an Apology for the Study of Northern Antiquities*, with her name. Its title-page quoted a bishop on the suitability of women as critics of our 'Mother-Tongue' (facs. 1968). Mary ASTELL helped find subscribers. The *Apology* (repr. ed. Charles Peake, 1956) refutes Swift's strictures on antiquarians and on English monosyllables; it perhaps influenced his later views. Good as linguistic and as church historian, better as literary critic, EE cites among poetic examples Anne FINCH, Katherine PHILIPS, and Anne WHARTON. In 1715, too, her brother died; so did her academic patron Dr Hickes; she vanished from records, leaving books and MSS with a woman friend who never restored them. By 1735, when she became a friend and adviser of George Ballard (see BIOGRAPHIES), she was running (as 'Frances Smith') a school at Evesham, which failed from her inadequacy at spinning and knitting. Through Sarah CHAPONE and Mary DELANY she was made governess to the Duchess of Portland's children; but, often ill, she published no more. MSS in BL and Bodleian (brief lives of herself and her brother, *c.* 1738; lists of famous women begun 1709); Caroline A. White in A. M. HALL, ed., *Sharpe's London Mag.*, 1869–70; recent philological and feminist comment includes thesis by Sarah Huff Collins, Indiana, 1970.

Elwood, Anne Katharine, travel writer and biographer, m. in England, *c.* 1823/5, Col. Charles William E. of the Bombay Army, who had already had 25 years in India. She travelled there overland in 1825, wrongly thinking herself the first Englishwoman to do so. Back in England after his retirement in 1828, she pub. her *Narrative of a Journey* in 1830. Though sometimes nervous, she loved travel: on the Nile she allows 'the thoughts to assume a romantic, tropical colouring, unlike – oh! how unlike our European coldness and frigidity'. She wrote vividly, had some sympathy for Hinduism, read Indian literature in translation, and was keen for the British to work to abolish female infanticide. In 1843 she published *Memoirs of the Literary Ladies of England from the Commencement of the Last Century*. See K. K. DYSON's study of Anglo-Indian journals, *A Various Universe*, 1978.

Embury, Emma Catherine (Manley), 1806–63, poet, journalist and story writer, b. NYC, da. of Elizabeth (Post) and James M. In 1828 she m. Daniel E., President of the Atlantic Bank in Brooklyn, where she established a salon, and became a prolific writer of poems, tales and sketches which she contributed to the leading popular magazines of the day. EE was on the editorial staff of *Godey's*, *Graham's*, and *The Ladies' Companion*. Her first collection, *Guido: a Tale, Sketches from History and Other Poems*, 1828, uses dramatic or historical personae to explore the cultural origin of female melancholy, transposed onto 'Guido' in the title poem, and the androgynous 'Shepherd Boy' (really a girl) in another. Other poems, however, show a diffidence about competing with the male poets of the day, and those on the theme of de STAËL's Corinne explore the moral ambiguities of a woman's assuming poetic power in her own right. In 'Madame de Staël' EE asserts that

'They who climb Fame's mountain steep / Must mourn their own high doom'. EE's prose fiction includes *Pictures of Early Life; or Sketches of Youth*, 1839, and *The Blind Girl. With Other Tales*, 1845, and consists for the most part of moralistic tales with less sense of the social contradictions which are sometimes acknowledged in her poetry. 'Constance Latimer, or The Blind Girl', 1838, is interesting as an allegory of the formation of the woman poet. Her collected poems were published in 1869.

Emecheta, Buchi, novelist, scriptwriter, writer for children, publisher. An Ibo, she was b. in 1944 in Yaba, Nigeria, da. of Alice Ogbanje and Jeremy Nwabudike E., 'who came right out of their innocent and yet sophisticated and exotic bush culture'. Both died when she was very young. She was educ. on scholarship in a Methodist Girls' High School (where she was made to ask God's forgiveness for wanting to be a writer), married immediately after, had her first child by 17, then accompanied her student husband to London, 1962, where they lived in council housing and had four more children. He burned the manuscript of her first novel, *The Bride Price*, rewritten and published, 1976, 'And I felt the native, bush, independent woman in me come to the fore. I packed my dripping four siblings and pregnant self and faced the streets of London.' She worked at odd jobs, writing in the morning before work, finally gaining recognition for her column in the *New Statesman*, 'Observations of the London Poor', which became *In The Ditch* (on the dole), 1972, her own story of struggles and loneliness. *Second-Class Citizen*, 1974, another thinly veiled autobiographical novel, gives a compelling account of her marriage breakup and of her determination to write, despite living in an alien country and writing in a foreign tongue. BE has since studied sociology at the Univ. of London, and lectured in universities in England and Nigeria. *The Slave Girl*, 1977, won the Jock Campbell Award for Britain's most promising writers. The ironic *Joys of Motherhood*, 1979, portrays BE's Nigerian mother-in-law with warmth and compassion for all women with traditional values caught up in changing urban life. She fictionalizes the war in *Destination Biafra*, 1981, drawing on first-hand accounts from her home in Ibuza where many of her friends and relatives died, including her niece-namesake, who perished of starvation. She also writes children's books. *Titch the Cat*, 1980, was inspired by her daughter Alice's diary, *Nowhere to Play*, 1981, by her daughter Christy's story of their life in a London County Council housing project. BE named her own publishing house Ogwugwu Afor Co., after a strong Ibo goddess. *Double Yoke*, 1982, is based on her lecture-stay at Calaba Univ., and *The Rape of Shavi*, 1983, SCIENCE-FICTION satire. She has written plays for the BBC and scripted a photographic book on Third World women, *Our Own Freedom*, 1981. Her best work treats contemporary Nigerian women and their victimization at home and abroad, and she is keenly aware that 'the world, especially the African world, still regards the premise of serious writing as a masculine preserve'. She has won several major awards. Sections of autobiography appeared in *Kunapipi*, 3 and 4, 1981, 1982 (quoted above), the whole, *Head Above Water*, in 1986. *Gwendolen*, 1989, follows a sexually-abused girl from Jamaica to 1970s London. See interview in *Ba Shiru*, 12, 2, and Charlotte H. and David Bruner in *WLT*, Winter, 1985.

Emerson, Eleanor (Read), 1777–1808, New England religious autobiographer. B. at Northbridge, one of 12 children of Martha and Thomas R., with 'an ardent thirst for knowledge' and very poor health, she had little educ. because her father died early. At 14 she began 'school-keeping' at various places: she taught English (all branches), religion, and plain sewing but disapproved of embroidery. Her 'Account' of her religious life (pub. Boston, 1809, with letters and a funeral sermon) captures the nuances of feeling: shame at denying her belief; paranoid anger and 'rankling envy' that grew with her growing conviction that she was damned and her sister saved; attack on those around for 'mock kindness, as it then appeared'; then religious joy transforming her view of other people: 'I recognized the finger of God in every feature of every face'. On marrying, 1803, the widower of her friend Nancy (Eaton) Emerson (both were close friends also of Hannah ADAMS), she returned to the voracious reading of her childhood (after her death her husband thought women should strictly limit their studies) and published poems and biographical sketches in the *Massachusetts Missionary Magazine*. She died of consumption, leaving a baby daughter.

Engel, Marian (Passmore), 1933–85, novelist. B. in Toronto, da. of Mary (Fletcher) and Frederick Searle P., both teachers, she later attended McMaster and McGill Univs. (where she was taught by Constance BERESFORD-HOWE). She m. Howard Engel, 1962 (divorced, 1977), and gave birth to twins, an experience which is reflected in several works. Her first novel, *No Clouds of Glory*, 1968 (repub. as *Sarah Bastard's Notebook*, 1974), is marked by intelligent, witty dialogue, strong female narrators, and complex family relationships, characteristics also of *The Honeyman Festival*, 1970, and *Lunatic Villas*, 1981. Her first collection of stories, *Inside the Easter Egg*, 1975, deals with marriage and women's ongoing relationships with their mothers as they bear children of their own. ME had a strong sense of the difference of women's experience from men's in a 'completely sexually divided' society where men's and women's roles have been 'worked out very clearly according to a pattern that was laid down a thousand years ago'. Her controversial novel *Bear*, 1976, winner of the Governor General's Award, plays against William Faulkner's story 'Bear' to show a woman's relationship to nature as loving rather than aggressive. In *The Glassy Sea*, 1978, the female protagonist creates a family among a group of Protestant nuns, where sisterhood allows her to escape her marriage and to reflect on the death of her hydrocephalic child. *The Tattooed Woman* (of which Timothy Findley writes, 'when you come away from her, you have not been disfigured – just transformed') was published posthumously, 1985: its stories focus on female bodies which, often scarred in sexual battles, survive to talk and write. The first Chair of the Writer's Union of Canada, 1973–4, ME was awarded the Order of Canada, 1982. See interviews in Graeme Gibson, *Eleven Canadian Novelists*, 1973, and Alan Twigg, *For Openers*, 1981. Critical studies by Lorna Irvine, *Sub/Version*, 1986, and Christl Verduyn in *The New Quarterly*, 1987.

'Ephelia', name used most notably by the unidentified author of the following: an anonymous verse paean to the king [1678]; *Female Poems on Several Occasions*, 1679; an unpublished elegy [1679] (Nottingham Univ.); a verse broadside, *Advice to his Grace* [1681–2]; and a lost play, *Pair Royal of Coxcombs*, c. 1678. Of the play only the prologue (which hopes critics will not demean themselves by noticing even such a daring work by a woman), epilogue and songs survive (in *Poems*). This work of 'an Infant Muse' reprints the eulogy of [1678] and explores each stage of an unhappy love story. The writer's Strephon, *alias* J. G., a captain in the Tangier trade, is scorchingly arraigned for inconstancy. The risqué 'Maidenhead' is balanced by attack on other women's unfeeling lovers (E doubts whether 'Sacred Friendship can / Dwell in the Bosom of inconstant Man'), and praise of both Aphra BEHN and Katherine PHILIPS. Some of these poems have been ascribed to others, notably George Etherege; guesses at E's identity include Philips's daughter Joan (unlikely); Carey (Fraser) Mordaunt, after 1660–1709, later Countess of Peterborough; and a cabal of men. A re-issue of 1682 adds poems (unascribed) by libertines like Rochester. The powerful *Advice* praises the future James II and urges Monmouth to 'lay betimes Your mad *Ambition* down'.

Ephron, Nora, journalist, novelist, screen-writer, b. 1941 in NYC, da. of Hollywood filmwriters and comedy co-authors Phoebe (Wolkind) and Henry E. She grew up in Beverly Hills, feeling in fifth and sixth grade not 'at all like a girl' because 'athletic, ambitious, outspoken, competitive, noisy, rambunctious'. Her parents are said to have based their *Take Her, She's Mine*, 1961, on her letters from Wellesley College, where she took a BA in 1962; she too uses her life in her work. She m. writer Dan Greenburg in 1967, and divorced in 1972, the year she moved from the *New York Post* to *Esquire*. She took an LHD at Briarcliffe College in 1975, m. reporter Carl Bernstein in 1976, had two sons, and divorced. After *Wallflower at the Orgy*, 1970 (interviews), she issued two volumes of *Esquire* pieces. *Crazy Salad*, 1975 (titled from W. B. Yeats on 'fine women'; dedicated to her three sisters), comes from a column about women, 1972–4, and *Scribble Scribble*, 1978, from one on the media, 1975–7, with one piece ('Gentle-men's Agreement', on a libel suit) which *Esquire* refused. She co-authored with Alice Arlen the screenplay for *Silkwood*, 1983. Her novel, *Heartburn*, 1983, relates a marriage breakup said to reflect her own with Bernstein. Its cookbook-author heroine says (exaggerating) that she has 'hidden the anger, covered the pain', but made it 'into a story' because 'if I tell the story, I control the version'. Recipes are interspersed. Her much-praised script for *When Harry Met Sally*, 1989, comically explores the feasibility of male–female non-sexual friendship.

Ercole, Velia, 'Margaret Gregory', 1903–78, novelist, b. White Cliffs, NSW, da. of Adele Margaret (Veron) and Dr Quinto E., a political refugee (1898) from Italy. Brought up in Grenfell, she was educ. at the Dominican Convent, Moss Vale, NSW. After working as a journalist for the *Sunday Sun*, she m. Eric Gregory, then travelled in France before settling in England. *No Escape*, 1932, which won the *Bulletin* novel competition for that year, is especially attentive to the dull triviality of country town society early in this century. Dedicated to VE's father, it concerns Leo Gherardi, an Italian doctor and political exile strugg-ling with alienation and frustration amidst public ignorance and prejudice in the town of Banton in 1905. Its real story, however, tells of his wife Theresa, haunted by loneliness, whose derangement leads to suicide. VE's second novel, *Dark Windows*, 1934, is also a tale of intense alienation; Julie Purvis is a stranger in a French family and culture that should by rights be hers, but somehow mutual accommodation of values and feelings cannot be achieved. Her eight other novels, including *Marriage Made on Earth*, 1939, *Marriage by Ordeal*, 1941, and *This Life to Live*, 1944, are mostly concerned with family and marital relationships.

Erdrich, Louise, short-story writer, novel-ist and poet, b. 1954 at Little Falls, Minn., da. of Rita (Gourneau), a Chippewa Indian, and Ralph E., a German-born teacher with the Bureau of Indian Affairs. She grew up near Turtle Mountain Chippewa Reserva-tion, N. Dakota, where her maternal grandparents lived. After taking her BA at Dartmouth, 1976, and MA at Johns Hopkins, she married Michael Dorris, also part-Indian. They have five children and live at Dartmouth, where he directs the Native American Studies Program. LE won awards from 1982 with the stories 'The World's Greatest Fisherman', 'Scales', and 'Saint Marie'; the last two were inclu-ded in important anthologies. Her poetry appeared in *Jacklight* in 1984. She draws on her Chippewayan roots in *Love Medicine*, 1984, 14 linked short stories told by seven members of the Kashpaw and Lamartine families. The complex form suggests the interwoven heritage and cross-cultural pressures the narrators have endured. The characters have been called insufficiently distinct, but also 'stubbornly alive and magnificently self-possessed because they are not self-obsessed'; this mode strengthens the work's tribal basis. *The Beet Queen*, 1986, next in LE's projected Northern Plains series, is a story of survival against odds. It uses several narrators, some partly Indian, one crippled by war wounds. The Beet Queen parade is attended by a dead body and an apparition of another dead woman. The novel uses dark humour, ORAL techniques, existential philosophy, and characters who lean to their old traditions under stress, showing the wounds of uprooting by a government seeking to turn them from fishermen to farmers. *Tracks*, 1988, opens earliest of the series, in 1912; among tribes riddled with tuberculosis and swindled out of their land, one woman is raped and drowned, another takes refuge in alien Catholic mysticism; a third survives. In the nun-narrator's mind are juxtaposed a copper-scaled male lake spirit and a weeping statue of the Virgin Mary. LE has taught at several places and published in various journals. See Elaine Jahner in *Parabola*, 10, 1985, quoted above; and Louis Owens in *WAL*, 22, 1987.

Escoffery, Gloria, poet, painter and critic, b. 1923 in Kingston, Jamaica. She attended St Hilda's High School (already active in Kingston's literary and artistic life), McGill Univ., Montréal, and the Slade School of Art, London. After some years in England she returned to Jamaica to paint, write, and teach at a rural community college. She has had exhibitions of her painting. Her poems (not a high output) have appeared in journals and anthologies like *BIM* (Barbados, from the 1950s), *Focus*, 1956, 1960, 1983, and *Jamaica Journal* (now the *Journal of Afro-West Indian Studies*), where GE also publishes art criticism. In 1976 she received the Order of Merit for services to the arts, and published a collection, *Landscape in the Making*. She writes of her childhood, her development, of women as wives, mothers and artists, of ordinary people like the speaker in 'The Shoemaker'. In 'Sign of the Ripening Fruit' she writes as one in the line of Caribbean painters: 'It is time to remember the artists who made this sign for their shop / front. . . . May my son, who repainted it according to my design, / Grow sweet in the ripening and in season take the orange for his / emblem. . . .' 'No Man's Land' exactly paints but also recoils from the sight of a boy 'caught playing politics' and shot: 'Wai oh! Eheu! mourns the camera shot matron / Whose stringy son, like a sucked mango seed, / Lies there no more use to anyone. . . . Why this pieta needs to be enacted in our land / No one can explain: / It clearly belongs within the pieties of a museum frame. / Is there no way but through this scene?' Interview in *Jamaica Journal*, 1, 1971.

Escombe, Edith, 1865–1950, story writer and essayist, b. Manchester, third in a family of six sisters and two brothers, da. of Eliza (Fergusson) and William E., shipping and insurance agent, d. 1882. She lived in or near Bishopstoke, near Winchester, with her mother (d. 1930) and sisters, and well provided for by the family firm. Her first book, *Bits I Remember*, by 'A Grown-Up', 1892, gives a delightful account of her childhood, including education by governesses and at boarding-school. Three of her later stories, written with subtlety and humour, are about women and marriage; *A Tale that is Told*, 1893, and *Stucco and Speculation*, 1894, are novellas about 'experimental' marriages. Two other stories, *Love's Ghost and 'Le Glaive'*, appeared in 1903. She also published essays: *Old Maids' Children*, 1906, on child-rearing from an aunt's point of view, and *Phases of Marriage*, 1907, casting a distinctly cool eye on the institution, especially the damage it can do to women, who need education and independent minds and interests to survive it.

Esler, Erminda (Rentoul), *c.* 1852–1924, novelist, b. Co. Donegal, second da. of the Rev. Alexander R. of Manorcunningham. She was educ. at home, on the Continent, and then at Queen's University where she took an Honours degree in 1879. In 1883 she married Robert E., MD, scientific writer, and moved to England; in 1888 she published her first work, the tale *Almost a Pauper*. Novels and a history of the Rentouls followed. Her fiction draws on her knowledge of the narrow intensities of Irish Presbyterian life in small communities, particularly in her stories *The way they lived at Grimpat*, 1893, and her novel *The Wardlaws*, 1896. Sympathetic to the plight of Irish peasant women, she also reveals special insight into the lives of middle-aged and elderly women in *A Maid of the Manse*, 1895 and *The Awakening of Helena Thorpe*, [1902], in which one character says: 'If one graduated Mrs. as one graduates Mr. through mere lapse of time, celibacy would lose one of its terrors for women.'

'Eugenia', name assumed by the 'Lady of Quality' who pub. *The Female Advocate, or A Plea for the Just Liberty of the Tender Sex, and Particularly of Married Women*, 1700 (another undated ed. as *The Female Preacher*), in reply to John Sprint's sermon *The Bride-Woman's Counsellor*, 1699. Some thought E was male. One contemporary reader, and others later, thought she was Mary CHUDLEIGH, another answerer of Sprint; but Chudleigh's own *Poems*, 1703, include praise of E's 'ingenious Pen'.

Evans, Anne, 1820–70, poet, b. at Sandhurst, Berks., eldest da. of Anne (Dickinson) and the Rev. Arthur Benoni E., linguist, musician, artist and schoolmaster, and professor of classics and military history at the Royal Military College until 1822. AE was educ. at home. In the 1850s she became a companion to Thackeray's daughters, including Anne Thackeray (later RITCHIE), travelling abroad with them. However, in 1854 her father died and she moved with her family to Kensington Square where she subsequently had long periods of illness. Her favourite brother Sebastian also wrote poetry and edited the *Birmingham Gazette*, 1867–70. AE felt sorrow deeply, and said: 'If anyone expects to find poetry without susceptibility, let him look in the sky for a rainbow without rain.' Her poems include sonnets; 'Maurice Clifton', a verse drama; and two ballads, 'Sir Ralph Duguay' and 'Orinda'. She was adept at epigrams and the witty definition. She was also an accomplished composer. Her *Poems and Music* was prefaced by A. T. Ritchie in 1880.

Evans, Augusta Jane (later Wilson), 1835–1909, novelist, b. Columbus, Ga., eldest of eight children of Sarah Skrine (Howard) and Matt Ryan E., storekeeper. She was educ. at home. From 1845 to 1849 the family lived in Texas in poverty, moving then to Alabama. In 1855 her first novel, *Inez : A Tale of the Alamo*, an attempt to show that women have minds as well as hearts, was pub. anon. *Beulah*, 1859, rejected by one publisher, sold 22,000 copies in nine months. Its heroine, reminiscent of Jane Eyre, is 'impatient of dependence'; she struggles for an education and questions conventional religious beliefs. However, AJE had conflicting feelings about the role of women, and the ending of the book, in which Beulah returns to the church and marries her guardian, is disappointing. Beulah's valedictory address, while affirming that women's intellect is capable of the most exalted attainment, asserts that her highest role is that of 'angel guardian of the sacred hearthstone'. Although AJE's heroines are tempestuous, proud and alienated, they are also moral, virtuous and pious, and her novels are anti-suffrage. *St Elmo*, 1866, also featuring an independent but anti-feminist heroine, was one of the most successful nineteenth-century novels, selling more copies than any other novel by a woman. It was parodied in *St Twel'mo* by William Webb and was adapted to the stage

(1909–15) and to silent film (1923). In 1869 AJE m. Col. Lorenzo Madison Wilson, who d. 1891. Her letters are at UCLA. See William P. Fidler, 1951, for her life, and studies by Nina Baym, 1978, and Anne Goodwyn Jones, 1981.

Evans, Katherine, d. 1692, Quaker missionary and pamphleteer, wife of the wealthy John E. of near Bath, who d. in jail, 1664. She travelled widely in Britain in the 1650s, being stripped and whipped at Salisbury; in 1658 or 1659 she and Sarah Chevers (of Slaughterford, Wilts.) left husbands and children to sail for the East, and were imprisoned for three years in Malta by the Inquisition. *This is a Short Relation*, 1662 (expanded after their release as *A True Account*, 1663), with Daniel Baker's introduction defending women's PREACHING, mixes hymns, letters, prophecies, and narratives of their sufferings by both women. Accused of witchcraft, they steadfastly refused to convert or to kiss the Cross, continued to trust each other's courage through two years' solitary confinement, 'did knit Stockins, and gave to them that were made serviceable to us, and did make Garments for the poor prisoners, and mended their Clothes'. Hunger-strike, prophesying God's vengeance, a nearby explosion, and negotiations in England brought release. They then visited Tangier (being well received by the Governor). KE added further facts and defence in *A Brief Discovery*, 1663 (with an account by Chevers of her visions), and was imprisoned in Newgate, 1682, and in Bristol with 116 Friends.

'Evans, Margiad', Peggy Eileen Arabella (Whistler) Williams, 1909–58, novelist, short-story writer, poet and autobiographer. B. near Uxbridge, Middx, da. of Katharine (Wood) and Godfrey Whistler, a clerk in an insurance firm, she was educ. at Ross-on-Wye High School; like the heroine of her second novel, *The Wooden Doctor*, 1933, she left at 16. She attended Hereford School of Art, 1926, and worked as teacher, guest-house keeper, and book illustrator. She wrote under her paternal grandmother's surname (emphasizing her link with Wales), but her first book, the novel *Country Dance*, 1932, pub. as ME, was illustrated under her birth name. Like *Creed*, 1936, it is set in the remote Herefordshire she loved. *The Wooden Doctor*, one of her early 'bitter, passionate cries of protest' against personal frustrations, features a violent childhood (the heroine's father is a drunkard), anger at the coming of puberty, and mysterious gynaecological pains 'like a fox in a bag scratching and rending to get out'. ME m. Michael Mendus Williams, 1940, and published (in periodicals and an unconventional AUTOBIOGRAPHY, 1943) poems, stories and journals reflecting her intense feeling for nature. She idolized the BRONTËS, who were thought unhappy but 'had all that *I* wanted of this world'. She published an essay on Emily; a projected book remained unfinished. From 1948 ME was in England, in exile, and bitterly so, from the Welsh border. In 1951 she bore a daughter, after the onset of serious epileptic fits caused by an inoperable brain tumour. The little more she published included *A Candle Ahead*, 1956 (her second poetry volume), and *A Ray of Darkness*, 1952. This examines her epilepsy: as punishment for insufficient devotion to writing, as linked with creativity but also with lack of structure – the mind expanding 'in all directions at once'. MSS (including journals) divided between Yale and ME's family; several recent reprints. See D. S. Savage in *The Withered Branch*, 1950; critical biography by Moira Dearnley, 1982.

Evans, Mari, poet, children's writer, and dramatist, b. in 1923 in Toledo, Ohio, and educ. at the Univ. of Toledo. Her father saved her first printed story and showed her 'the importance of the printed word'. She 'drifted into poetry' by writing about the 'intuited drama and poignancy' of her housing project. Her discovery, at ten, of

Langston Hughes and the black literary tradition committed her to writing. At university, she wrote a column in a black-owned weekly. While she was a producer-director-writer for the TV show 'The Black Experience', 1968–73, she published *Where Is All the Music*, 1968: 16 of its 21 poems appear also in *I Am a Black Woman*, 1970. These poems refuse submission ('I don't / get on my knees'), attack complacent notions about progress towards equality ('the Beads were / mine / before you stole them'), and move to personal and political affirmation ('Who can be born / black / and not exult!'). The arresting, explosive poems in *Nightstar*, 1981, explore family history, personal visions, themes of the death of dreams and the waste of lives ('On the Death of Boochie by Starvation', 'The Expendables'). ME writes 'reaching for what will nod Black heads over common denominators', believing that language is 'a political force'. She uses ORAL TRADITION and visual design to 'be as explicit as possible while maintaining the integrity of the aesthetic'. Her extensive, pioneering work on US black writers includes *Black Women Writers (1950–1980)*, 1984, an important critical evaluation of Alice WALKER, Toni MORRISON, Gwendolyn BROOKS, and others. She has taught at Northwestern, Purdue, and Washington Univs., and worked for prison reform. She was distinguished writer at Cornell Univ.'s African Studies and Research Center, 1981–4, later writer-in-residence at SUNY, Albany. Her poetry has been recorded, choreographed, used in off-Broadway productions, and widely anthologized. Three of her plays have been produced: *River of My Song*, 1977, *Portrait of a Man*, 1979, and *Bacchie*, 1979. She also adapted Zora Neale HURSTON's *Their Eyes Were Watching God*. She has written six children's books. Divorced with two sons, she continues to write plays and has a novel in progress. See *Black Women Writers*, quoted above.

Evans, Sarah Anne, author of the evangelical *Resignation, An American Novel*, Boston, 1825. Her patriotic preface expresses diffidence because she has neither softened her view of a world where 'man is a mourner by inheritance' nor attempted strict historical accuracy. She dwells much on death ('the victory of the grave, lost in the interminable triumphs of heaven') and on exploring US identity: the heroine, orphan child of an Independence hero, leaves the Bay State to grow up in Virginia, her story woven with those of a British loyalist, Scots missionary, poor Irish immigrant, and sentimentally presented black slave.

Evelyn, Mary, 1665–85, and **Mary** (Browne) **Evelyn**, *c*. 1634–1709, moral writers, da. and wife of diarist John E. ME senior grew up in French exile and m. John E. at 13. Her surviving letters (selec. with his diary ed. William Bray, 1818) begin in 1667 with disparagement of Margaret NEWCASTLE: 'Never did I see a woman so full of herself, so amazingly vain and ambitious.' She praises Katherine PHILIPS as contrast. She pertinently analyses the letter-writing genre, but resists advice to expand her literary activity (some prose and verse mentioned in E. S. de Beer's ed. of John E.). Her modesty ('Hope not for volumes or treatises; raillery may make me go beyond my bounds, but when serious, I esteem myself capable of very little') fits her orthodox view of women's role. Her daughter, educated in history, French, Italian, music, and ancient and modern poetry, enjoyed the company both of children and of learned men, and wrote with surprising 'maturitie of judgement, and exactnesse of the periods'. After her death from smallpox John E. published her conservative satirical poem *Mundus Muliebris* [Women's World], *or The Ladies Dressing-Room Unlock'd*, 1690, with a 'Fop-Dictionary' of trendy terms presumably also hers: often reprinted with and without her father's works. The Evelyn MSS (on deposit at Christ Church, Oxford) include her 'Rules for Spending my Pretious Tyme Well', and letters from both women.

Everett-Green, Evelyn, 'Cecil Adair', 1856–1932, popular novelist and children's writer, b. London, da. of Mary Anne Everett (Wood), scholar and historian, and G. B. E–G., artist. Her mother (1818–95) edited historical texts, such as *Letters of Royal and Illustrious Ladies of Great Britain*, 1846, *Diary of John Rous*, 1856, *Letters of Queen Henrietta Maria*, 1857, and also pub. *Lives of Princesses of England*, 6 vols., 1849–55, and her main work, *Calendars of State Papers*, 1857–93. EEG was educ. at Gower Street Prep. School and Bedford College, studied music at the London Academy, and nursed in a London hospital for two years. In 1883 she moved to Somerset and began her writing career, producing over 300 titles, mostly for children but some for adults, under her own name, and from 1911, many more as Cecil Adair. Family sagas or romancсs with a historical adventure setting were her speciality.

Ewing, Juliana Horatia (Gatty), 1841–85, children's writer, b. Ecclesfield, nr Sheffield, second da. of Margaret GATTY. She received 'somewhat desultory, if intellectual home education' from her mother and her own reading and later taught her younger siblings. JE was an energetic parish worker and was responsible for establishing Ecclesfield village library. In 1867 she m. Major Alexander E. of the Army Pay Department and resided at Fredericton, New Brunswick, where he was posted; see her letters, ed. Margaret and Thomas Blom as *Canada Home*, 1983. They returned to England in 1869, living subsequently at Aldershot, Manchester, and York; ill-health prevented her accompanying him on later postings. She was reunited with him in 1883 and lived in Taunton. JE's creative imagination first revealed itself in stories made up for the home nursery, and she started to publish to help family finances; after marriage she wrote to pay off her husband's debts. Her complete stories, later collected in 17 vols., were almost all published initially in periodicals, the earliest in Charlotte YONGE's *Monthly Packet*, the others in her mother's *Aunt Judy's Magazine*. These stories, addressed mainly to young people, deal with children, animals and fairies, and many draw on her memories of childhood and army life. Sentiment and religion mix with strong social comment on, e.g., the danger of poor sanitation. The best-known include 'The Brownies', 1865 (which provided the name for the Girl Guides' junior branch), 'Flat-Iron for a Farthing', 1871, and 'Jackanapes', 1879, the tale of a young soldier who sacrifices himself for his friend; the lively and altruistic heroine of 'Madam Liberality', 1873, is said to be a self-portrait. See the memoirs by her sisters, Horatia Eden, 1885, and Christabel Maxwell, 1949; study by Marghanita LASKI, 1950. Her MSS are in Sheffield Central Library.

Eyles, Margaret **Leonora** (Pitcairn), 1889–1960, novelist, journalist, feminist and memoirist. B. at Tunstall near Stoke-on-Trent, Staffs., da. of Sir A. Tennant P., owner of a pottery works, she attended private day school, then at 14 became a pupil-teacher at a nearby Board School. At 18, an orphan with no money, she went to London and found a job addressing envelopes. She m. first A. W. Eyles, by whom she had three children, and, in 1928, after divorce, David Leslie Murray, editor of the *TLS*, 1938–44. Her painful early struggles are evident in *For My Enemy Daughter*, 1941 (reminiscences addressed to a daughter living in Italy during WWII), and *The Ram Escapes*, 1953 (memoir of a traumatic childhood). Both make clear the origins of the fierce battle for female dignity and independence that LE waged in her personal and professional life. She attacked the social, economic, and sexual subjugation of women in the many practical books for which she is best known, like *The Woman in the Little House*, 1922, *Careers for*

Women, 1930, and *Commonsense about Sex*, 1933, and in novels like *Margaret Protests*, 1919, and *Strength of the Spirit*, 1930. Her strongest fictional expression of the chains that bind women, body and soul, comes in *Captivity*, 1922, which has obvious autobiographical elements. She also wrote successful crime fiction. Nicola Beauman, *A Very Great Profession*, 1983, discusses her treatment of abortion, birth-control, and desire.

F

Fage, Mary, wife of Robert F. the younger, gentleman: author of *Fames Roule, or The Names of Our Dread Soveraigne Lord King Charles* [and of the queen, nobility, bishops, privy counsellors, knights, and judges] *Annagramatiz'd and Expressed by Acrosticke Lines on the Name*, 1637, with her own name. As this implies, she is fulsome about rank: her dedication to all the British and some foreign Protestant royalty begins 'Pardon powerfull Princes and potent Potentates, my presumption, in pressing into your presence.' Her short acrostic poems on each name are equally strained, partly because they often allude to the meaning of an also strained anagram. (She shares this passion with Eleanor DOUGLAS and other contemporaries.) RARA AVIS METT for MARIA STUARTE (the queen) and A MERRY STATU for MARY STUARTE (the princess) are among her better efforts. No non-royal women qualify.

Fainlight, Ruth Esther, poet, short-story writer, translator, b. in NYC in 1931, da. of Austro-Hungarian Fanny (Nimhauser) and British Leslie Alexander F. She was educ. at schools in the USA and England and at Birmingham and Brighton Colleges of Art. In 1958 she published *A Forecast, A Fable* (poems) and in 1959 m. novelist Alan Sillitoe, with whom she has a son and adopted daughter. With at least eight more poetry books, she has adapted (with Sillitoe) a play from Lope de Vega, 1967; published short stories, *Daylife and Nightlife*, 1971; joined with Sillitoe and Ted Hughes in *Poems*, 1971; and translated the Portuguese poet and political activist Sophia de Mello Breyner Andresen. Other stories and translations have appeared in anthologies. RF's poetry examines conflicts and compatibility between the roles of poet and woman, a perceived antagonism between the domestic and the intellectual. Technically and metrically accomplished, rooted in lived experience, it expresses 'a specifically female anger' in feminist iconography: heroines from scripture (RF's religion is Jewish) or classical mythology (*Sibyls and Others*, 1980), or her own ambivalent relationship with her mother (*Fifteen to Infinity*, 1983). She also writes 'the "negative capability" of the poet extends beyond / below/above gender' (in her account of female poetics in Jeni COUZYN, ed., *The Bloodaxe Book of Contemporary Women Poets*.

Fairbairns, Zoe Ann, novelist, short-story and pamphlet writer, journalist, b. 1948. Da. of Isabel (Dippie) and John Joshua F., she studied at the College of William and Mary, Virginia, 1969–70, and at the Univ. of St Andrews (MA, 1972). Her concerns are political, and she sees 'the first weapon' of understanding and politically aware action as *'information'*. (See her CND pamphlet, *Study War No More*, 1974; and her contributions to 'No Place to Grow Up', 1977, a Shelter report on the effect of bad housing on children, and *Women's Studies in the UK*, 1975.) Her novels equally highlight aspects of contemporary living and of women's experience in ways which inform judgement, complementing historical, social and political understanding with significant use of fictional form. Two short novels, *Live as Family*, 1968, and *Down: an Exploration*, 1969, use first-person narrative to explore personal responsibility, relationship with the community and alternative impulses in middle-class youth. *Benefits*, 1979, makes a fantasy extending into the twenty-first century a thoughtful criticism of the present, while *Stand We at Last*, 1983, 'a family saga with a feminist background', recounts the ordinary and extraordinary experiences of women, the forgetfulnesses and renewed struggles of the women's movement and of their context in public history from the mid nineteenth century to the present. This novel, with its extended historical perspective, complements ZF's earlier contributions to the concise, more personal orientation of *Tales I Tell My Mother*, 1978, with Sara MAITLAND, Valerie MINER, Michèle ROBERTS, and Michelene WANDOR. *Here Today*, 1984, and *Closing*, 1987, explore tensions in the lives of ordinary women between survival in an exploitative society and feminist awareness, between needs for personal achievement and fulfilment and the alienating and competitive practices of capitalist society. Dramatizing social existence, anatomizing social structures, these fictions promote ZF's consistent project, entertainingly to document and inform.

Fairbank, Janet (Ayer), 1878–1951, novelist. Sister of Margaret Ayer BARNES (for whom, wrote Barnes in 1931, she 'Blazed the Trail'), she was b. in Chicago and educ. at private schools and the Univ. of Chicago. In 1900 she m. lawyer Kellogg F.; she had three children. The 13 years' publishing silence between her first novel, *Home*, 1910, and her next were busy with public service. She held important posts on women's committees of the Progressive Party (before WWI), and for fund-raising and National Defense during the war, and continued as a committee-woman from 1919 for the campaign for woman SUFFRAGE and the Democratic Party, and on the board of the Chicago Lying-In Hospital. *The Cortlandts of Washington Square*, 1923, a historical novel, uses its somewhat idealized young heroine, Ann, to present a compelling woman's-eye-view of the Battle of Gettysburg. Two later novels, *The Smiths*, 1925 (runner-up for the Pulitzer Prize in 1926 when Sinclair Lewis refused it), and *Rich Man, Poor Man*, 1936 (see Mary Jean De Marr in *Midamerica*, 12, 1985), make up a trilogy coming forward to Ann's granddaughter-in-law, the suffrage movement, and reforms of the early Progressive Party. *Idle Hands*, 1927, is a short-story volume. *The Lion's Den*, 1930, follows a congressman's career, and *The Bright Land*, 1932, the life of a woman (see De Marr in *Midamerica*, 11, 1984). Each shows characters caught up in the political issues of their times. In their completion of Henry Kitchell Webster's unfinished *The Alleged Aunt*, 1935, JAF's and her sister's hands are indistinguishable.

'Fairless, Michael', Margaret Fairless Barber, 1869–1901, religious writer and mystic, b. Castle Hill, Yorks., youngest da. of Maria (Musgrave) and Fairless B., lawyer and antiquarian. She was educ. at home, then briefly at schools in Torquay and outer London. She trained as a nurse and worked in a London slum, earning the title the Fighting Sister. Forced into retirement by a chronic spinal condition, she made a crucifix for a London church. When deteriorating health made modelling impossible, she wrote or dictated the works for which she is now remembered. Her first, *The Gathering of Brother Hilarius*, 1901, is a tract focusing on the Black Death; her most famous is a series of meditations, *The Roadmenders*, 1902 (repr. 31 times in ten years), which first appeared in *The Pilot*. Her other works were a book of Christmas writings, *The Child King*, 1902; a collection of verse and prose fragments, *The Grey Brethren*, 1905; and *Stories Told to Children*, 1914. In her work she combined minute descriptions of natural beauty with didactic fantasy and abstract meditation on the nature of God or the path to heaven (of which she was 'roadmender'). A mystic agnostic, she wrote: 'We can never be too Pagan if we are truly Christian'. See the life by W. Scott Palmer and A. M. Haggard, 1913.

Faithfull, Emily, 1835–95, publisher, writer, activist, b. Headley Rectory, near

Epsom, Surrey, youngest da. of Rev. Ferdinand F. Educ. at a girls' school in Kensington, she became a founding member of the Society for Promoting the Employment of Women. Although her interest was 'industrial rather than political', the guidelines she established for the employment of women (in the pamphlet *Woman's Work*, 1871) incorporate a recognition of women's intelligence and systematic exclusion from occupational training. In 1860 she established the VICTORIA PRESS, which provided in-service training to women compositors. Its first book, the anthology ed. Adelaide PROCTER, *Victoria Regia*, 1861, was dedicated to the Queen, who appointed EF 'Printer and Publisher in Ordinary to her Majesty' in 1862, the same year EF opened a steam printing office. She then founded the *Victoria Magazine* (1863–80) and in 1865 the weekly penny magazine, *Work and Women*. Her one novel, *Change upon Change*, 1868 (issued in America as *A Reed Shaken With the Wind*), ran to a second edition in a month: it deals with 'woman's work' in the context of upper-class life. Very little is known of EF's own life, although she was a key figure in a network of writers and activists such as Matilda HAYS, F. P. COBBE, Mary BOYLE, Mary TAYLOR and Isa CRAIG, and her reputation survived her involvement in the infamous Codrington divorce case 1864–5. She toured America 1872–83, lecturing on topics such as the WOMAN QUESTION and Queen VICTORIA, and meeting suffragists Elizabeth STANTON and Lucretia MOTT: see her *Three Visits to America*, 1884. Back in England she founded the Women's Printing Society, 1874, and the International Musical, Dramatic, and Literary Association in 1881, to protect the rights of composers and artists. She received a grant from the Royal Bounty in 1886, an inscribed, engraved portrait from the Queen in 1888, and a Civil List pension in 1889. See William E. Fredeman's account of the Victoria Press in *The Library*, 29, 2 (June 1974).

Falconar, Maria and **Harriet**, juvenile poets, das. of Jane (Hicks) and the Scots poet William F. Since he died in 1769, the condescendingly laudatory preface to their *Poems*, 1788, stretched a point in giving their ages as about 16 and 14. Maria had already published in the *European Magazine* in 1786. They were living in London. The poems, with their names, joint portrait, and subscribers including Elizabeth CARTER, Catharine MACAULAY and Helen Maria WILLIAMS, are sentimental ballads, pastoral lyrics, addresses to Candour, Friendship, etc., and very early *jeux d'esprit* written to order. *Poems on Slavery* (one by each), also 1788, enliven their abstract approach with some personal feeling: Harriet is compelled to picture 'the tortur'd wretch implore / Eternal vengeance on Britannia's shore'. *Poetic Laurels*, 1791, addressed to the Prince of Wales, includes verse exchanges with Mary BLACKETT and other women.

Falconbridge, Anna Maria, later DuBois, TRAVEL writer from Bristol. Having disobeyed her family by marrying Alexander F. (who had been a surgeon in the slave trade and exposed it in a book of 1788), she sailed with him, 1791, to reclaim and reorganize a colony in Sierra Leone, and sent home vivid letters intended for print: *A Narrative of Two Voyages ...*, 1794, facs. 1967. A lukewarm opponent of slaving, she tried 'to new fashion' the black princess Clara and was outraged at the plight of prostitutes kidnapped in Wapping and shipped out to service the settlers; she noted the hard labour of women in the native culture, the extreme piety of free blacks from America, and the slovenly hoggishness of Europeans in Gambia. Her husband died disappointed and drunken in 1792; she quickly m. Isaac DuBois and returned home to financial battles with the Sierra Leone Company (via Jamaica, where her opinion of slavery improved, facilitating a 2nd ed. of her book, 1802).

'Falconer, Lanoe', Mary Elizabeth Hawker, 1848–1908, short-story writer, b. Inveraray, Aberdeenshire, da. of Elizabeth (Fraser) and Col. Peter H.; she had a younger brother and sister. After her father died in 1857, her mother m. Herbert Fennell and the family lived for several years in France. Educ. at home, she wrote for a family chronicle as a child, and began to publish short stories and articles in magazines in 1882. Never prolific, she largely produced character sketches and atmospheric pieces, some of which are collected in *The Hôtel d'Angleterre*, 1891. She achieved considerable popularity with *Mademoiselle Ixe*, 1891, the story of a Russian governess in an English country house and her political struggles on behalf of her people, 'crushed beneath a tyranny so monstrous that their souls, like their bodies, are but half alive'. The novel was banned in Russia; LF gave her royalties to help Russian exiles. She soon followed the work with a ghost story, *Cecilia de Noël*, 1891; but then declining health prevented her from writing more than personal religious meditations. See the life by Evelyn March Philips, 1915.

Falkland, Elizabeth Cary (Tanfield), Viscountess, *c.* 1585–1639, dramatist, translator, and historian, only child of Elizabeth (Symondes), who 'was never kind to her', and wealthy Oxford lawyer Sir Lawrence T. According to her daughter and biographer Anne or Mary CARY, she mastered Latin, Hebrew and modern languages almost unaided, translated Seneca, criticized Calvin, and ran up a £100 bill to servants for illicit candles. At ten she saved a 'witch' who, she realized, was confessing lies out of fear. At 15 she was m. to Henry C., later Lord F. Locked up without books by his mother, she wrote a verse life of Tamburlaine, a play now lost, and *The Tragedie of Mariam, The Faire Queene of Jewry* (written 1603–4; imitated 1611 by ?Middleton in *The Second Maiden's Tragedy*; pub. 1613; ed. A. L. Dunstan and W. W. Greg, 1914). This well-researched Senecan work, in varying rhyme-schemes expressing intellect and passion, centres on Mariam's inner conflicts over wifely submission. (Salome, meanwhile, claims for women a right to 'hate as well as men'.) EF was mentioned by John Davies of Hereford, 1612, with Lady PEMBROKE and Lucy Russell, Countess of Bedford, as patrons *and* writers. She gave up her inheritance to her husband (angering her father). For years 'either with child or giving suck' to 11 babies born alive, she oversaw their education, taught them to love their father best, and strove against her natural absent-mindedness. Twice while pregnant she suffered depression verging on madness. In 1622, while her husband as Lord Deputy of Ireland militantly enforced Protestantism, she learned Irish and began a project to boost Dublin manufacture by setting up 60 orphans as apprentices. Back in England, 1626, she acted on her early study of the Church fathers and embraced Catholicism. Her husband renounced her in bitter letters, took her children and left her destitute but writing. Debate goes on over her authorship of the 'mature and melancholy' *History of Edward II*, said to be rapidly written in 1627, with dramatic verse speeches, pub. as her husband's, 1680 (Donald A. Stauffer in Hardin Craig, ed., 1935; D. R. Woolf in *Bodleian Library Record*, xii, 1988). Her translation of Cardinal Perron's reply to King James (464 pp., Douai, 1630, dedicated as 'a Catholique, and a Woman' to Henrietta Maria) was publicly burned; Yale Univ. has a copy revised in her hand, with two poems added. Her version of the rest of Perron (finished 1636) stayed unpublished, as did saints' lives, 'innumerable slight things in verse', and hymns to the Virgin (now lost). She tended her dying husband, 1633, and later became steadily poorer and more eccentric. See Elaine Beilin, 1988. Two nineteenth-century lives follow her daughter's.

'Fallon, Mary', Kathleen Mary Berriman (Denman), writer, b. 1951 in Monto,

Queensland, da. of Hilma (Rasmussen) and Philip Denman, surveyor and Brisbane Council alderman. Her pen-name is her beloved grandmother's name. MF grew up in Bundaberg, Isis and (mainly) Brisbane, where she was expelled from Brisbane Girls' Grammar, which she hated (her working-class background clashed). Between 1969 and 1973 she began a social work degree, studied art, travelled alone round Queensland, completed an arts degree, and worked in a handicapped children's home, where she met Henry Phineasa, an Indonesian/Thursday Island boy. In 1973 she m. Rodney B., undertook the foster-care of Henry, and also became a lesbian. The houshold moved to Sydney in 1975 (Queensland was hostile to lesbian foster-mothers), then to London for three years from 1976. In 1978 MF wrote *Explosion/Implosion* (self-published in Sydney, 1980) and exhibited her art; in 1979 she returned to Australia alone. In 1981 she published the highly experimental *Sexuality of Illusion* under her own imprint, 'Working Hot', which she later took as title for her lyrical, zany, outrageous postmodern prose poem pub. by the avant-garde women's press, Sybilla, in 1989. Her major work so far, it is an erotic lesbian fantasy: comic, celebratory and elegiac. While writing *Working Hot* (begun in 1982 while living in Paris and Vienna), MF also developed her talent for the theatre. She has had two pieces performed, 'Laying Down the Law' (about Lindy Chamberlain) in 1985, and 'Spill', a black comedy about fashion magazines and media pornography, 1987. Since 1982 she has had numerous short stories published in magazines and anthologies of experimental and women's writing. She won the Victorian Premier's Award for fiction, 1989.

Fane, Elizabeth, Lady, d. 1568, writer or compiler, wife of Sir Ralph Fane or Vane, knight. Robert Crowley, who published her collection of 21 *Certaine Psalmes of Godly Meditation*, with 102 proverbs, 1550, and dedicated a book to her next year, calls her 'ryght worthy Patrones' of Protestants – a dangerous role. Her husband was hanged for conspiracy, 1552; Crowley went into exile; she remained, 'a liberal benefactor' of those persecuted in Mary's reign, and died at Holborn.

'Fane, Violet', Mary Montgomerie Lamb, later Singleton, then Currie, 1843–1905, poet, novelist, essayist, b. Beauport, Littlehampton, Sussex, eldest da. of Anna Charlotte (Grey) and Charles James Saville Montgomerie L., gentleman. Educ. privately, she began to write early, first using her pseudonym to avoid parental disapproval. In 1864 she m. Henry Sydenham S. (d. 1893), Irish landowner, had four children, and became involved in London society. Her first vol. of poetry, *From Dawn to Noon*, 1872, was followed by six more, ending with *Under Cross and Crescent*, 1896 and *Betwixt Two Seas*, 1900, written in Constantinople and Rome, where her second husband, Sir Philip Henry Wodehouse Currie (later Baron C. of Hawley), was ambassador. Her work is really that of a skilled amateur: fluent, assured; emotionally honest, but worldly (sometimes cynical, sometimes sentimental). Some better pieces are in ballad form; some were set to music. Her verse novel, *Denzil Place*, 1875, takes after E. B. BROWNING's *Aurora Leigh*. Her novels are in similar style, and include *Sophy, or the Adventures of a Savage*, 1881, *Thro' Love and War*, 1886, and *The Story of Helen Davenant*, 1889. She also translated *Memoirs of Marguerite de Valois*, 1892. Her several volumes of essays, collected from journal publication, include *Edwin and Angelina Papers*, 1878, and *Two Moods of a Man*, 1901, in which the title essay is a perceptive observation of the emotional blackmail used by men to manipulate women.

Fanshawe, Ann (Harrison), Lady, 1625–80, memoirist, b. in London, da. of John H.

and Margaret (Fanshawe: first cousin of Ann's future husband). A wild and active child, she sobered down at her mother's death, 1640. Serving the Stuarts brought her father to poverty two years later. M. in 1644 to Sir Richard F., diplomat and writer 17 years her senior, AF shared his life of under-rewarded royalist devotion. Their souls, she wrote, 'were wrapped up in each other'; she bore 14 live children, few of whom survived; her six miscarriages included triplets. She went with him on royal service to France, Ireland and Spain, and visited him in an English prison when he was captured after the Battle of Worcester. They were abroad again in time to share Charles II's triumphal return. They went on embassy in 1662–3 to Portugal and in 1664 to Spain, where Sir Richard's death, 1666, left her destitute. Refusing Spanish overtures, she sold enough to bring his body home. Her *Memoirs* (reaching to 1672, completed 1676 for her only surviving son, still a child; known to the ladies of LLANGOLLEN) were pub. 1829, 1907 (heavily annotated; reviewed by Virginia WOOLF), and 1979, with Anne HALKETT's. AF is best at narrating adventures: seeing an Irish apparition, donning cabin-boy's clothes, concealing secret papers. She left her own and her daughters' writings to one of them, Katherine.

Fanshawe, Catherine Maria, 1765–1834, poet and letter writer. Da. of Penelope (Dredge) and John F., who held a post in George III's household, she lived with her two sisters in genteel and cultured society in or near London (friend of Mary BERRY and – by letter – Anne GRANT), visiting Italy because of poor health. Joanna BAILLIE and M. R. MITFORD printed some of her poems in publications of 1823 and 1859; an edition, 1865, was repr. 1876. Mitford sees her as rightly not aspiring to fame, but content with 'the very finest qualities, mental and moral; – feminine, modest, generous, pure'. Yet CF's poems sparkle with irony. She mimics political voices she disagrees with; as herself she defends the spelling of her name in elaborate, ingenious argument on two fronts: C is Anglo-Saxon, not classical; and Katherine is a name for shrews – 'such as still with ceaseless clamour, / Dance round the anvil and the hammer. ... No females louder, fiercer, worse.' She kept a journal (untraced); Walter Scott, who admired her poems, says she and her sisters first published Ann FANSHAWE's *Memoirs*.

Fanthorpe, U. A., Ursula, poet, b. 1929 at Lee Green, London, of 'middle-class but honest parents'. After 'inadequate schooling' she 'came to life' at St Anne's, Oxford (BA in English, 1953), and London Univ. (Diploma of Education, 1954), taught at Cheltenham Ladies' College, 1962–70, took a diploma in school counselling at University College, Swansea, 1971, and lived some time on the dole and as a hospital clerk in Bristol. 'Observations of a Clerk' (*Poetry Review*, 75, 1985) tells how 'the irresponsibility of a really low-status job set me free to write' poems 'on the backs of old clinic lists', voicing 'anger, at the hierarchical system'. Her first volume, *Side Effects*, 1978, unsentimentally recovers the invisible lives and voices of psychiatric patients. 'Case-Histories' records 'These were not lovely in their lives, / and when they died, they were instantly forgotten'. 'Julie' selects snatches of conversation with an encephalitic patient groping for continuity after loss of memory: snatches of Ophelia's songs provide continuity; sympathy is made touching yet robust and honest. A first award for poetry (third in an important London competition) came in 1980; others, and writer-in-residence posts, followed. *Standing To*, 1982, draws on experiences at work 'exposed to extremes' with soldiers. It applies restrained irony, and feeling for the ordinary, to warfare and, in 'Only here for the Bier', to 'the masculine world of Shakespeare's tragedies ... from the woman's angle'.

Voices Off, 1984, deals with student life, with learning critical vocabulary and finding that 'naming / is power'. *Selected Poems*, 1986, includes 'From the third storey', a history of women's writing (novels as well as poetry) and the benefits of past struggles: 'Now at last I know / why I was brought here / and what I have to do.' *A Watching Brief*, 1987, includes 'Three Women WORDSWORTHS' and a poem setting 'the record straight' on Mary's and Martha's solidarity in face of Christ's praise of one, blame of the other.

Farjeon, Eleanor, 1881–1965, children's writer, b. in London, second of four children and only da. of Margaret (Jefferson), and novelist Benjamin F., who travelled to the Australian goldfields and ceased to practise his orthodox Judaism as a young man. EF's upbringing was Bohemian and unconventional: attending neither church nor school, she prayed daily and read uncontrollably. *A Nursery in the Nineties*, 1935 (*Portrait of a Family* in the US), charms by remembered detail: her father's bargain-addicted extravagant purchases (of books, clothes, shoes); her mother's encouragement of the children's role-playing; her own half-absorption in 'multitudinous Other Selves' in the game of Tar. This innocent yet addictive clubbishness comprised 'a harmful check on life itself': 'I was never aware of my own sex till I was nearly thirty years old, and it took at least ten years more for emotional crudeness to get abreast of mental ripeness.' Shortly before WWI she met and fell in love with Edward Thomas, grieving deeply at his death, 1917. (She wrote a memoir of him, 1958.) About 1921, EF began her 30-year liaison with unhappily married scholar George Earle (her beloved 'Pod'). An extended friendship with actor Denys Blakelock, 20 years her junior, followed. She converted to Roman Catholicism in her seventieth year. EF's stories, poems, re-tellings, fables, saints' lives and prayers are marked by ingenuous, childlike trust and hope. Her traditional sources were never 'blunted by habitual familiarity', and her narrative persona is like that of the title character in *The Old Nurse's Stocking-Basket*, 1931, loved by her charges because 'she'd always been with them' and with their mother and grandmother. EF fervently believed in the closing observation of her rhymed legend of St Christopher (*Ten Saints*, 1936): 'Our strength is our gift for the good of mankind.' *The Little Bookroom*, 1955, won the Carnegie Medal and the Hans Christian Andersen Award. The Children's Book Circle makes an annual award in her name. Life by her niece, Annabel Farjeon, 1986.

Farmer, Beverley, short-story writer, b. 1941 in Melbourne, Victoria, da. of Maude Ruby (Thomas) and Colin Stewart F. Educ. at MacPherson High School and Melbourne Univ., she ran a restaurant and worked as a secondary school teacher before becoming a full-time writer. Her first work, the autobiographical novella *Alone*, 1980, a reworking of a story that appeared in *Westerly*, 1968, was pub. by the feminist press Sisters, and gives a sensitive portrayal of the breakup of a lesbian relationship. The experience described in *Alone* had such an effect on BF that she was labelled a schizophrenic. Many of the stories in her award-winning first collection *Milk*, 1983, draw on the three years she spent in Greece, following her marriage to a Greek man. (They are now divorced.) While several of the stories in *Home Time*, 1985, have similar themes and settings, others show a greater awareness of the relationship between life and fiction, writers and readers. Like Marjorie BARNARD whom she admires, BF focuses her work on women, presenting a sensitive view of them and their world. See Cassandra Pybus, *Island Magazine*, 1986.

Farnham, Eliza Woodson (Burhams), 1815–64, suffragist, novelist, journalist, essayist, b. Renselaerville, NY, fourth of five children of Mary (Wood), a Quaker, and Cornelius B. After her mother's death in 1812, she lived with relatives (an unhappy period described in the autobiographical novel *My Early Days*, 1859), who sent her to a Quaker boarding-school for a year, then to Albany Female Academy. She m. Thomas Jefferson Farnham (d. 1848), and in 1844 became matron at Sing Sing Prison, where she implemented progressive reform, editing a US edition, 1846, of M. B. Sampson's *Rationale of Crime*. One of her assistants was Georgiana Kirby, 1818–87, to whom she had been introduced earlier by Margaret FULLER (who met Kirby at Brook Farm: see Kirby's semi-fictionalized autobiography, *Years of Experience*, 1887). EF worked for a time at the Perkins Institute with Maud Howe ELLIOTT's father, helping to educate Laura Bridgman. Her journey to the West was chronicled in *California, In-doors and Out*, 1856. She returned to NYC, divorced her second husband, William Fitzpatrick, and began campaigning for women's rights. Through the Women's Loyal National League, she worked for abolition. Her best-known work, *Woman and Her Era*, 1864, presents 'organic, religious, esthetic and historic' arguments (vol. I) for women's superiority, and vol. II concludes: '... it follows that the grandest Era of Humanity must be that which is dominated by the Feminine qualities'. A novel, *The Ideal Attained*, 1865, has the heroine, Eleanor Bromfield, moulding the hero into a worthy mate. In 1863, EF nursed wounded soldiers in Gettysburg; she died the following year of consumption.

Farr, Florence Beatrice, also Emery, 1860–1917, actress, occultist, novelist, playwright, b. in London, much youngest child of Mary Elizabeth (Whittal) and William F., self-made apothecary and reformer, associate of Florence NIGHTINGALE (whence, probably, FF's name). Educ. at Cheltenham Ladies' College and Queen's College, London (till 1880), she 'failed' at teaching, trained for the stage, and acted as 'Mary Lester'. Her marriage, 1884, to actor Edward Emery, was quickly over; G. B. Shaw and W. B. Yeats were among her lovers and felt her influence. From 1894 she managed the Avenue Theatre, vital force in modern drama, and was Scribe to the occultist Golden Dawn. In fiction she treats a philandering actor and card-sharper who is shot by the New Woman he has rejected (*The Dancing Faun*, 1894), and a woman who flees from a violent second marriage (made for love) to find new friendship and 'mutual charity' with her divorced first husband (*The Solemnization of Jacklin*, 1912). After two plays set in ancient Egypt (with Olivia Shakespear, *c.* 1895), she wrote a masque, *The Mystery of Time*, 1905. Of her tracts, those on the occult include *Egyptian Magic*, 1896, repr. 1982 (not really serious Egyptology). *Modern Woman: Her Intentions*, 1912, pictures women 'rousing themselves from their former deadly attitude of quiescent acceptance' over the vote, sex, marriage (to be mended, not ended), and economic independence. FF kept a diary from 1904, defended prostitutes in *The New Age* in 1907, and in 1912 left England for Ceylon, to become principal of Ramanathan College for girls, Jaffna. There she experimented with translation from High Tamil; she died five months after a mastectomy. Her scattered MSS include the closing passage of *Life Among the Supermen*, probably autobiographical. Yeats planned a book on her; letters *to* her ed. Clifford Bax, 1946; life by Josephine JOHNSON, 1975.

Faugeres, Margaretta V. (Bleecker), 1771–1801, poet, playwright, and essayist, b. in Brooklyn, NY, da. of Ann Eliza BLEECKER. As a child she saw the horrors of war and her mother's death. She disobeyed her rich, cultivated father to marry (Bastille Day, 1792) a Jacobin French physician, Peter F. She included a memoir and some of her own early poems and essays (the first on 'Benefits of Scolding') in editing, 1793, works by her mother, whom she resembles in elegiac tone, classical poetic diction, and subject-matter ranging through Nature, piety, patriotism and social occasions. Her topographical-historical poem 'The Hudson' addresses its Miltonic 'adventurous song', with female 'trembling', to a river which 'never hath been sung'; she dwells on ghosts and storms. Her blank-verse tragedy *Belisarius*, 'intended for the closet', pub. by subscription, NY, 1795, leans to sentiment rather than the Roman heroism of M. O. WARREN; it expresses radical idealism through a hero placed between the equal inhumanity of ruling class and revolutionaries. MF published further short pieces both in magazines and separately: a poem against US adoption of capital punishment [1797], a commissioned Fourth of July ode, 1798. Her husband proved unkind and extravagant; after his death in 1798 she supported herself and infant daughter by teaching, but died poor and obscure (see Ann HATTON).

Faulding, Gertrude Minnie, 1875–1961, children's writer and novelist. B. in London, she was educ. in Switzerland, Germany, and, in modern languages, at Somerville College, Oxford. She published two books of illustrated fantasies for children, *Old Man's Beard and other Tales*, 1909, and *Nature Children*, 1911, then *Fairies*, 1913, an affectionate study of the magical elements in such tales. With Lucy (Hanson) Dale, a writer of history textbooks and also a Somerville graduate, she wrote two novels of romance and marriage with unusually independent heroines. *Time's Wallet*, 1913, is cast as letters between Somerville graduates working in the deprived East End of London; one of them ends her engagement rather than give up thinking for herself. In *Merely Players*, 1917, an unconventional playwright goes through the disintegration of her marriage to a civil-servant husband.

Fauset, Jessie Redmon, 1882–1961, novelist, poet and literary editor, b. in Camden County, NJ, da. of Annie (Season) and Redmon F., an African Methodist Episcopal minister: reared in Philadelphia after her mother's death. She was the first black woman to attend Cornell Univ., graduating Phi Beta Kappa in 1905; she later took an MA at the Univ. of Pennsylvania, and studied at the Sorbonne. She taught at a black high school in Washington, DC, joined the NAACP, and as literary editor of W. E. B. Du Bois's *The Crisis*, 1919–26, was influential in the discovery of writers later prominent in the Harlem Renaissance. Her own poems, stories and essays also appeared in it. She is best known for her novels, which break new ground in portraying the new black middle class. She wrote *There is Confusion*, 1924, because T. S. Stribling's *Birthright*, 1922, made her feel 'better qualified to present the truth than any white writer'. JRF went back to teaching in 1927 and m. Herbert E. Harris, insurance broker, three years later. *Plum Bun*, 1929 (like her stories 'Emmy', 1912, and 'The Sleeper Wakes', 1920), exposes cultural structures enforcing fantasies of romantic love, and efforts by those of mixed race to evade that half of their heritage which denies them 'happiness, prosperity and respect'. (It was at first to have been called *Market*.) In *The Chinaberry Tree*, 1931, furtive sexual relations between white and black lead, romance-wise yet plausibly, to the threat of incest; *Comedy, American Style*, 1933, centres on a mixed-race woman self-hatingly obsessed with skin shades. Critics have only recently perceived the subversive aspects of these 'vapidly genteel lace-curtain romances'. See critical biography by Carolyn Wedin Sylvander, 1981; Deborah E. MacDowell in Marjorie Pryse and Hortense J. Spillers, eds., 1985.

Fawcett, Millicent (Garrett), 1847–1929, feminist and suffragist, b. at Aldeburgh, Suffolk (portrayed in her one novel, *Janet Doncaster*, 1875), one of ten children of Louisa (Dunnell) and Newson G., merchant and shipowner: sister of pioneering doctor Elizabeth G. She was educ. at home, and from 12 to 15 at a school in Blackheath run by Robert Browning's aunt. Her sister's struggle for medical training strongly influenced her. In 1867 she m. the blind radical MP, Henry F., who was also Professor of Political Economy at Cambridge. Acting as his secretary until 1871, she familiarized herself with political and social debate, publishing *Political Economy for Beginners*, 1870. She was a member of the first women's SUFFRAGE committee in 1867, and argued that granting the vote to women was 'the only means of cleansing the Statute Book from the Laws that are oppressive to their sex'. She also campaigned for the Married Women's Property Act. After her husband's death in 1884, she became involved in the protection of young girls, having been greatly influenced by W. T. Stead's *Maiden Tribute* of 1885. She made many speeches in Ireland opposing Home Rule; and, whilst anti-Boer, she visited South Africa in 1901 heading a commission enquiring into conditions in concentration camps. In 1897, she became President of the National Union of Women's Suffrage Societies, which maintained its belief in a lawful and constitutional route to reform. She retired from the NUWSS presidency in 1918 but continued to take an active interest in women's issues. Her autobiography, *What I Remember*, appeared in 1925, the year she was awarded a DBE. See the life by Ray STRACHEY, 1931.

Fay, Eliza, 1756–1816, TRAVEL writer. Leaving England for India in 1779 with her new husband, Anthony F., an Irish lawyer, she wrote splendid letters home describing with gusto the journey through France and Egypt, imprisonment at Calicut by Hyder Ali, arrival at Madras, her husband's plunge into debt and anti-government politics, their legal separation (August 1781), her return, and later travels. She observes that suttee is not, as some Englishmen think, a proof of feeling, but 'is entirely a political scheme intended to insure the care and good offices of wives to their husbands', comparable to other countries' 'rules to render the weaker sex subservient to [male] authority'. Needing now to earn her living, she considered printing her letters, but since a 'female author' was 'an object of derision' went back to Calcutta to set up a millinery business. Misfortunes kept her on the move, pursuing new schemes. She was charged at St Helena with selling a woman as a slave. She wrote up these later adventures at Blackheath, London, in spring 1815; in Calcutta next year she was preparing the whole for the press, but died leaving her tale (at New York, 1797) incomplete. *Original Letters from India*, Calcutta, 1817, was reprinted there; by Leonard and Virginia WOOLF with notes by E. M. Forster, 1925; and 1986. Barbara HOFLAND used a few details from EF's (apparently oral) account for *The Captives in India*, 1834. See Ketaki Kushari DYSON, *A Various Universe*, 1978.

Fearon, Jane (Hall), *c.* 1656–1737, Quaker controversialist of northern England. After a godly education, she became a minister about 1688, and preached in the Isle of Man (where she was jailed) and round Britain. She m. Peter F. in 1693, had two sons, and continued to travel. Her works, pub. with her name, all combat the idea that anyone is predestined to Hell. Despite her first title, *Universal Redemption in Jesus Christ*, 1698, she did believe in Hell, but not that 'from Eternity, God did predestinate or fore-ordain' any individual to go there. Having heard Independents maintaining the contrary at Cockermouth in 1704, she quickly drafted *Absolute Predestination not Scriptural*, pub. 1705 (repr. Concord, NH, 1813, as *A Plain Refutation* ...). In answers to 48 queries about biblical passages, it aims to prove that the choice of salvation lies with ourselves. An answer by John Atkinson drew a *Reply* to him, 1709, her most notable work. She uses colloquialism ('No, it's not the same'), sarcasm (when he rebukes Quakers as 'these Men' she retorts that victory would bring him no glory, since ''Tis but a Woman he hath to Answer'), learning (confutation by syllogism), and history (the persecuted, she says, become persecutors in New England).

Feinstein, Elaine (Coolin), poet, novelist, short-story writer, radio and TV writer, biographer, translator, b. in 1930 in Bootle, Lancs., da. of Fay (Compton) and Isidore Coolin. She was educ. at Wyggeston Grammar School, Leics., and Newnham College, Cambridge (BA in English, 1952; MA, 1955). In 1956, she m. immunologist Arnold F.; they had three children. An editor with Cambridge Univ. Press, 1960–2, then a lecturer at Bishops Stortford Training College and the University of Essex, she wrote poetry from the early 1960s, influenced by Emily DICKINSON and other US poets. She published *In a Green Eye*, 1966, selections from John Clare, 1968, and translations from Marina TSVETAYEVA, 1971 (further selec. 1981). Translating, a crystallizing experience, 'opened the way to a wholeness of self-exposure which my English training would otherwise have made impossible'; under Tsvetayeva's 'spell', EF began to write novels, 'allowing myself to say *not* what I knew was expected'. These goals, and a search for harmony in personal relationships and between the human and natural worlds, inform EF's own five poetry volumes (including a selection, *Some Unease and Angels*, 1977), nine spare, intensely felt, highly wrought novels, and two volumes of stories. Her first novel, *The Circle*, 1970, is a study of a marriage, mostly through the wife's mind: talking, illnesses trivial and serious, childbirth, bills, failure and rediscovery of desire, infidelity, and the necessary refuge in separate 'circles of interest': his laboratory, her books. *The Glass Alembic*, 1973, was re-issued as *The Crystal Garden*. Several novels reflect EF's Russian-Jewish roots: *The Survivors*, 1982, spans the generations before and after the Holocaust; in *The Border*, 1984, an old woman in Sydney, Australia, on the Day of Atonement, tells the painful, mysterious story of her escape from Vienna with her husband in 1939, his affair with a Communist and his death, to her scholarly Californian grandson whose interest springs only from their link with Walter Benjamin. *Mother's Girl*, 1988, treats the responses of two widely separated sisters to their dominating, promiscuous father's death. *All You Need*, 1989, uses its heroine's isolation in London for a sharp critique of current politics and values. EF has written radio and TV plays, lives of Bessie Smith, 1985, and Tsvetayeva, 1987, and translated poetry by other Russian women, 1979 and (with Antonia Bovis) 1988. Interview in *Literary Review*, 1, 1982.

Fell, Alison, journalist, poet, novelist, children's writer, b. 1944 at Dumfries, Scotland, da. of Doris F., part-time office-worker, and Andrew F., motor mechanic. After urban poverty at Hamilton, Lanarks., she moved gladly to Kinloch Rannoch in the central Highlands, 1949–53 (which made her 'some kind of pagan pantheist'), then to Lochmaben in the Borders, attending a Lockerbie secondary school, then Dumfries Academy and Edinburgh Art College. She began to write for *Scotland Magazine* in 1962. In 1967 she married an academic at Leeds Univ.; she bore a son. After joining a THEATRE GROUP and a women's liberation group she moved (separated) to London in 1970 'in search of all-woman theatre'. She co-founded the Women's Street Theatre Group (later Monstrous Regiment), and was arrested in 1971 for performing in protest at the moral-majority Festival of Light. Her press release on this to underground papers led to writing for *Ink*, then the Marxist-feminist *Red Rag* and *Islington Gutter Press*, and, after a breakdown in 1974, for others, including *Spare Rib*. Her poems, much anthologized, speak for women, activists, and political victims. 'Border Raids' describes gifts offered her grandmother: 'the merry gods / of the midsummer garden / who dance among the columbines / who fib and fart', and a flower basket made as a child: 'cupped like a jewel or a robin's egg / It will lie, perfect, in her wrinkled palm / I will cross the grass and give it'. AF also writes for Greenham Common wire-cutters ('The Hallowe'en Witch'). She has been a writer-in-residence in London. Her children's books, *Grey Dancer*, 1981, and *The Bad Box*, 1987, deal with growing up in left-wing working-class families: myths, models, and sexual politics. In 1984 she published *Every Move You Make* (autobiographical novel) and *Kisses for Mayakovsky* (poems). In 1988 she edited *The Seven Deadly Sins*, a book of stories by women writers (Kathy ACKER does lust, Zoe FAIRBAIRNS covetousness, Sara MAITLAND GLUTTONY, MICHÈLE ROBERTS anger). AF writes about herself in Liz Heron, ed., *Truth Dare or Promise: Girls Growing up in the Fifties*, 1985. She lives in a council flat on the site of Mary WOLLSTONECRAFT's school.

Fell, Margaret (Askew), 1614–1702, Quaker, b. at Marsh Grange, Lancs, da. of Margaret (?Pyper) and John A., descended from Anne ASKEW. In 1632 she m. barrister Thomas F., later MP and judge. She had eight daughters (many also leading QUAKERS, especially Isabel YEAMANS, Sarah Meade and Rachel Abraham) and a son, who caused her misery in legal property battles. MF and her household were converted to Quakerism by George Fox in 1652, while her husband was away; once he accepted the change (though he never converted) their home, Swarthmore Hall, became vital to the movement, communicating news and reprimanding 'unruly' Friends. MF visited London many times, wrote to and called on Cromwell, Charles II, James II, and William, and wrote for publication from 1655. Many of her pamphlets are very long, with extensive use of Bible learning; several are addressed to Jews, attempting to convert them (Spinoza translated *A Loving Salutation*, 1656, into Hebrew). A rich crop written in prison in Lancaster Castle, 1664–8, includes *Womens Speaking Justified*, 1666 (facs. Los Angeles, 1979): not, as often said, the first Quaker defence of women's PREACHING, but a learned, conservative assertion of selected women's right to activity in limited circumstances. St Paul, she says, 'did not say that such Women should not Prophesie as had the Revelation and Spirit of God poured upon them; but their Women that were under the Law, and in the Transgression, and were in strife, confusion & malice in their speaking'. MF married George Fox in 1669, though they continued to live apart for many years. Her family pub. most of her writings, including her autobiography, as *A Brief Collection*, 1710. See lives by Helen Crosfield, 1913, and Isabel Ross, 1949.

Female Advocate, The, title whose users include Sarah FYGE, 1686, 'EUGENIA', 1700, William Woty, 1770, Mary SCOTT, 1774, an anonymous writer to *The Morning Post*, 1780–1, Mary Ann RADCLIFFE (her publisher's choice), 1799, and an 'aged matron' of New Haven, Conn., 1801: her strong polemic against the contempt meted out to women cites Noah, St Paul (since women may not preach unveiled, it follows that they may preach), Lord Chesterfield, Hester CHAPONE, Elizabeth GRIFFITH, Catharine MACAULAY, Lady Mary Wortley MONTAGU, Elizabeth ROWE, and Phillis WHEATLEY.

Feminist theory can be characterized in terms of its different relations to male-dominated theory, since feminists have only recently considered what autonomous, self-determined female types of discourse, knowledges and cultural practices would be like. Four types of relation between feminist and malestream knowledges describe both a chronology of development (late 1960 to late 1980s) and a range of competing positions.

'Feminist critique' denounces the elisions and prejudices of patriarchal knowledges, focusing on women's exclusion, as both subjects and objects, from theoretical analysis. It remains committed to the basic precepts and values governing mainstream knowledges. A largely negative project, it points to the ways male knowledges denigrate women or participate in sexist discrimination. It presents overwhelming evidence of women's subordinate status within theory (e.g. Germaine GREER, Shulamith Firestone, Betty FRIEDAN, Kate MILLETT and others) and aims to eliminate barriers to women's inclusion alongside men as objects worthy of even-handed investigation.

A second project can be described as 'feminist extensions'. It is committed to re-writing, extending and supplementing existing knowledges, adding and suitably altering history, Marxism, psychoanalysis, and literary theory, so that women may be included where previously ignored, their positions explained instead of presumed (e.g. Juliet Mitchell, Michele Barrett, and liberal, Marxist and psychoanalytic feminists). Since women have been 'hidden from history' (Sheila Rowbotham), the task now is to include them. Such archaeological retrieval from patriarchal silence reveals a wealth of newly-gathered or previously neglected information about women's lives and contributions to history and culture. Women have in the past contributed in unacknowledged ways to the production of knowledge, much work by women has never been adequately circulated or made public: a counter- or alternative HISTORY waits to be written.

But feminists soon recognized that knowledges did not simply 'neglect' or 'forget' women. This strategic amnesia legitimizes and neutralizes the patriarchal foundations of existing knowledges. Male knowledges could accommodate women only if they were regarded as variations of male-defined categories: women writers and artists judged by male canons of greatness, women who contributed to public life as men do. For example, Mitchell's reading of Freudian and Lacanian psychoanalysis showed that, even if these Great Men were not aware of it, their work *could* be used to explain how patriarchal social relations function; feminists, like Barrett, relied on Marxist categories of economic production to include women in an account of social and productive life. The project of feminist extension cannot criticize and reorganize the key discourses it attempts to extend: psychoanalysis can neither distinguish between patriarchy and civilization nor see female sexuality in positive or autonomous terms; Marxism can neither account for women's private, unpaid work (which could not be classified as labour) nor explain the role of domestic and familial life in the class organization of society. The frameworks of patriarchal knowledges pose inherent limits on what feminists can achieve within them.

A third form of feminist theory can be described as 'feminist deconstructions'. Based on dual or duplicit reading, it uses a theory's or system's own techniques, concepts and arguments to question its explicit pronouncements and implicit ideals. It uses a theory's language against its own proposals, inhabiting a theoretical position to move beyond it, provisionally accepting it to signal its limits and points of excess (e.g. Gayatri SPIVAK, Barbara Johnson, Jane Gallop, Luce IRIGARAY, Josette Feral, Hélène CIXOUS). Feminist deconstructions subvert the logical oppositions (e.g. identity/difference, mind/body, subject/object, reality/representation) which structure all theoretical texts: its double procedure consists in a reversal of the relations between binary terms and a displacement of the subordinated terms to the dominant. It meets the violence and coercion at stake in the production of knowledges with a kind of counter-violence of its own. It demonstrates both the historical tenacity of structures of thought and writing and their logically arbitrary status. Taken together, reversal and displacement demonstrate the necessary but *impossible* or unfounded privilege of dominant concepts in patriarchal thought. They are neither forms of critical destruction of theories and knowledges nor attempts to 'correct' them. It is neither possible nor necessarily desirable to eliminate the historical effects of problematic yet prevailing knowledges. This would efface the power of such discourses to affect current theories, including those used by deconstruction itself.

Deconstructive feminism retriangulates the relation of feminist politics and malestream knowledges: it is no longer a question of *either* patriarchal *or* feminist models. There is no other heritage than the one patriarchy provides, and feminist theory is not derived from a 'pure' feminist, or woman-produced history, but is the effect of patriarchal discourses and their subversions. This recognition need not cause lament: feminists do not need continually to reinvent the wheel. Feminism's 'debt' to the models it criticizes is also its strength. Feminism is able to know not only the strength and power of patriarchal discourses, but also their greatest vulnerabilities, which, if pressed, will effect major transformations in the structure of knowledges. This view abandons an ideal of feminist revolution: a dramatic transformation of the social and intellectual order is impossible if the tools one uses, the criteria one develops, the alternatives one poses are still derived from patriarchy. It is thus not a question of either starting afresh to rewrite knowledge and reformulate political and social life, or accepting patriarchal frameworks as they stand.

This awareness may explain why a fourth category of theory, 'feminist explorations', has focused on language. This feminism, like the pioneering one which sought to highlight and transform sexist language (e.g., Robin Lakoff, Kate Swift and Casey Miller, Dale Spender), does not see that creation of sexually neutral language (eliminating 'he' or 'chairman') will have any overall effect on the patriarchal functioning of language. Such changes remove evidence of women's social and linguistic subordination without transforming the underlying linguistic structure. For these feminists, language *per se* is not patriarchal, for it contains the possibility of saying any and everything: the problem comes from the models and norms of dominant discourses, which are incapable of expressing woman-centred utterances. This view holds that feminists need not construct a new woman's language – indeed, cannot, since language is not the construct of, but rather itself constructs individuals, as such. The task ahead is not to create a new language but to experiment with new kinds of writing, models of coherence and types of theory. The goal of this work is exploratory – to play with, to construct, different types of texts, arts, knowledges by blurring the boundaries between the traditional disciplines, questioning the norms of grammar, syntax and sentence-construction, and developing criteria for assessment which both contest patriarchal constraints and develop autonomous or woman-defined categories and forms of utterance.

Fenton, Elizabeth 'Bessie' Sinclair (Knox), also Campbell, d. 1875, TRAVEL diarist, da. of the Rev. John Russel K. of Lifford, Co. Donegal, later of Inishmagrath, Co. Leitrim. In 1826 she m. the Scots Capt. Niel (sic) C., sailed with him for India, and began a series of journal letters home, aiming to give 'a familiar picture of the everyday ... habits' of ordinary – chiefly European – people. She dwells on the picturesque, on pains and pleasures of travel, quotes poets including HEMANS ('the SAPPHO of English poetry') and herself ('Formerly I could express my feelings better in verse than in prose'). The death of her adored husband of less than a year turned her perceptions inward to chart the progress of her own anguish. Most sensitive and efficient of those at his deathbed was the Irish Capt. Michael F.; after a year's courtship by letter she married him. They migrated to Van Diemen's Land (Tasmania) in 1828 with three little orphanage children; EF bore a daughter (first of six children) in Mauritius in 1829. Her text (ed. and abridged by Sir Henry Lawrence as *The Journal ... A Narrative ...*, 1901) ends with her settled like 'Hagar in the desert' at a house later called Fenton Forest, a difficult journey from Hobart, thinking 'home' a word 'of sorrowful import', appreciative as never before of common duties and comforts. Later journals are lost. Michael F. became a rich landowner and Tasmanian statesman.

Fenwick, Eliza, 1760s–1840s, novelist and children's writer: not the EF who was Emily CLARK's sister (RLF MSS). Her friends included Mary LAMB; she m. radical author John F. Her powerful, perpetually surprising, tragic novel, *Secresy, or The Ruin on the Rock*, 'By a Woman', 1795, repr. 1989, opens on passionate female friendship and revolt against a 'system' of education which forbids thinking. Sibella, 'wood nymph', idealist, and unusually convincing child of nature, gradually sees through the unworthy object of her innocent but fully sexual love; Caroline, hated for her intellect and 'far-fetched ideas', unhappy that her wealth comes from the 'depredating practices' of the so-called protectors of India, loses both the man and the woman she loves (see Isobel Grundy in Margaret Anne Doody and Peter Sabor, eds., 1989). EF tended the dying Mary WOLLSTONECRAFT. In 1800 she left her alcoholic husband to support her two children by various kinds of 'slavery' (recounted in 30 years of letters to Mary HAYS, ed. Annie Wedd, 1927), such as writing earnest little children's books. Her *Visits to the Juvenile Library*, 1805, tells how a horrid family from the West Indies (and their slave nurse) are reclaimed by discovering the joys of learning: a facs., 1977, lists others, including an ambitious anthology pub. as 'the Revd. David Blair'. She later ran such a library (Godwin's), governessed in Ireland, and taught in London, Barbados (where she joined her actress daughter in 1814), New Haven and New York.

Ferber, Edna, 1885–1968, fiction writer and playwright, 'probably the most popular Jewish American author in history'. B. in Kalamazoo, Mich., second da. of Julia (Neumann) and Hungarian-born storekeeper Jacob Charles F., she grew up in Chicago, Iowa and Wisconsin, observing localized anti-semitism as effect, not cause, of general social problems. First woman reporter on the *Appleton Daily Crescent* (later with the *Milwaukee Journal*), she began writing fiction after a breakdown. Her first story, 'The Homely Heroine', in *Everybody's Magazine*, 1910, was followed by a novel, *Dawn O'Hara: The Girl Who Laughed*, 1911, and four volumes of stories: *Buttered Side Down*, 1912, and the highly popular series about divorcée saleswoman Emma McChesney: *Roast Beef, Medium*, 1913, *Personality Plus*, 1914, and *Emma McChesney and Company*, 1915, illustrating the viewpoint of EF's 'Joy of the Job', 1918. Based chiefly in NYC from 1912, she belonged to the famous Algonquin literary circle. From *Fanny Herself*, 1917, her most autobiographical novel, about a Jewish family in an anti-Semitic Midwest town, she set herself to write 1000 words a day. Often studies of 'a distinct region' of the USA, her novels depict 'human stuff' and tend to show women as 'the stronger sex': *The Girls*, 1922, deals with the unmarried of three generations; the best-selling *So Big*, 1924 (Pulitzer Prize; films 1925, 1953), centres on a woman dirt farmer and her wayward son; Sabra Venable in *Cimarron*, 1929 (films 1931, 1961), who becomes Oklahoma's first US congresswoman, stands out among her accomplished, ambitious, pioneering women. The plays EF co-wrote with

George S. Kaufmann include *Minick*, 1924, from one of her own stories, and *The Royal Family*, 1927 (in which she fulfilled her childhood acting ambition). *Show Boat*, 1926 ('whose actual writing was the nearest I ever came to enjoyment of my particular craft'), became a famous musical. Many books were screen hits, notably *Saratoga Trunk*, 1941 (film 1943), about vengeance exacted on a prosperous family by its illegitimate daughter, and her two last novels, *Giant*, 1952 (film 1956), and *Ice Palace*, 1958 (film 1960): a critique of Texan chauvinism and parochialism, and a study of Alaska's past and present. Her autobiographies, *A Peculiar Treasure*, 1939, and *A Kind of Magic*, 1963, are breezy, sometimes reticent, but insightful about her work. Papers at Wisconsin State Historical Society. EF is championed in a life by her great-niece Julie Goldsmith Gilbert, 1978, which works backwards from death to birth; see too V. J. Brenni and B. L. Spencer in *Bulletin of Bibliog.*, 22, 1958; Steven P. Horowitz and Miriam J. Landsman in *Studies in American Jewish Literature*, 2, 1982.

Ferguson, Elizabeth (Graeme), 1737–1801, Pennsylvania woman of letters. Of Scots Jacobite stock, youngest child of Ann (Diggs), who died in 1764 leaving, like Elizabeth ROWE, posthumous letters, and of Dr Thomas G., she grew up on an estate near Philadelphia. An album dating from 1752 (earlier pages cut out) includes occasional poems, pastorals, burlesques, ambitious longer pieces, and a pre-*Rasselas* 'The Choice of Life'; later notes and index proclaim her serious emulation of Elizabeth CARTER, Hannah MORE, Anna SEWARD. Her heroic-couplet *Telemachus* (from Fénelon, with criticism both translated and original, and notes still ongoing until 1799) was said to have been therapy after her fiancé, a natural son of Benjamin Franklin, married another. EGF visited England and Scotland, 1764 (a social and literary success yielding a now lost diary, 'a feast to all who read it'), and at home presided over a cultural salon. Her next work was a metrical version of the psalms with thoughtful critical introduction. In 1772 she married a younger Scot, Henry Hugh F., which brought trouble in 1775–7, he being a British officer and she a patriot; she attempted mediation between the two sides. She wrote for periodicals as 'Laura' and 'Arachne': the *Columbia Magazine* printed her well-known 'Spring Song', for women's communal labour. She exchanged work with Susanna WRIGHT, addressed some to Annis STOCKTON, and fostered that of her niece Ann SMITH. Her letters were admired. Poor and alone in old age, she owned 400 books. MSS, lavishly bound with book-plates, at Library Company of Philadelphia and elsewhere; see Martha Slotten in *PMHB*, 1984.

Ferland, Barbara, poet, b. 1919 in Jamaica. Educ. at Brompton and Wolmer's Girls' School, she began her working life in Jamaica, then moved to England (where she now lives), joined the British Council, and contributed regularly to 'Caribbean Voices', a BBC radio programme begun by Una MARSON. BF is an accomplished musician, versed in Caribbean folklore. Her poems have appeared in *Caribbean Quarterly* (e.g. 5:3, 1958); Edna Manley's *Focus* anthologies; the Jamaican *Independence Anthology*, 1962; John Figuerola, ed., *Caribbean Voices*, 1 and 2; Paula Burnett, ed., *The Penguin Book of Caribbean Verse in English*, 1986. BF can be romantic, as in 'Hibiscus' ('I see her walking in her garden in the morning, / Her feet follow her eyes to where / hibiscus grows / Her hair falls like the night behind her'); dramatic, as in 'Orange' ('You must learn how to peel, man . . . ring it round, / like a ball . . . . Then / Bite. And when the juice sweets your tongue, / Man, let the seed fall'); or detailed: 'From a church across the street / Children repeat / Hail Mary, full of Grace; / Skipping the syllables, Follow-the-leader pace. // A little girl (the Lord is with Thee).

White in organdy, / Lifts her starched, black face / Towards the barricaded altar / Meadowed in lace.'

'Fern, Fanny', Sara Payson (Willis) Parton, 1811–72, essayist, novelist and newspaper columnist, b. Portland, Maine, fifth of nine children of Hannah (Parker) and Nathaniel W., newspaper publisher (who founded the *Youth's Companion*, 1827, to which FF contributed). She was educ. at Catharine BEECHER's Seminary. She m. M. C. H. Eldredge in 1837, and had three children. In 1844 her mother, husband and daughter Mary all died. She m. S. P. Farrington in 1849, but was divorced three years later. After failing to support herself by teaching and sewing, FF lost her daughter Sara to the Eldredge family. She began writing for *The Mother's Assistant* and other small Boston magazines, and when her pieces were collected as *Fern Leaves from Fanny's Port-Folio*, 1853, the volume was an immediate bestseller. A second series of *Fern Leaves* appeared in 1854, as well as the juvenile *Little Ferns for Fanny's Little Friends*. These books were so outstandingly successful that Robert Bonner, owner of the New York *Ledger*, offered FF $100 for a regular weekly column, making her the USA's leading woman columnist. She moved to NY and remained with the *Ledger* for the rest of her life. In 1856 she married James Parton, well-known biographer, and over the next 15 years collected many of her *Ledger* pieces, including *Fresh Leaves*, 1857, *Ginger Snaps*, 1870, and *Caper-Sauce*, 1872. She also wrote two novels, *Ruth Hall*, 1855 (repr. 1988), a roman à clef admired by Hawthorne, and portraying an unusually independent woman, and *Rose Clark*, 1856. Although much of FF's work is sentimental, it can also be satirical and humorous, particularly in the second *Fern Leaves* series, as in her comment on marriage: 'It is only the privileged few who can secure a pair of corduroys to mend, and trot by the side of' ('Who Is It?'). She dealt increasingly with social issues such as poverty and exploitation of workers in NYC, and her 'Soliloquy of a Housemaid' sympathetically depicts the overworked servant girl's gruelling routine. Her work was critical of conventional religion and focused on women's issues, including the double standard, excessive housework and large families. In the 1850s she moved to active support of women's rights movements, women's SUFFRAGE and better EDUCATION. With Jane C. Croly she was a founder, in 1868, of NYC's pioneering women's club, Sorosis. See the study by F. B. Adams, 1966.

Fernando, Chitra Elaine, b. 1935, Sri Lankan writer of short stories and children's literature. She was educ. at Balika Vidyalaya, Kalutara, and at the Univ. of Ceylon in Peradeniya, and later took her MA and PhD in Australia, at the Univs. of Sydney and Macquarie, where she lectures in linguistics. She has written several vols. of stories for children, all set in Sri Lanka, among them *Glass Bangles*, 1968, *The Adventures of Senerat Bandara* and *Bempi Appu*, both 1972, a collection of adult stories, *Three Women*, 1983, and a novella, *Between Worlds*, 1988. She is co-editor with Ranjini Obeyesekere of *An Anthology of Modern Writing from Sri Lanka*, 1981. She observes life at various social levels, pinpointing inconsistency and religious hypocrisy, particularly as these warp female lives. *Between Worlds*, a work concerned with East–West tensions and the search for individual and national identity, focuses on the traditional woman, the rebel, and the young Asian who has migrated to the West and is, as a result, completely westernized and modern in her outlook. Other stories, especially those for children, draw with ironic humour on the characters and themes of the Asian and European folk-tale, giving these new life in a Sri Lankan, generally Sinhalese domestic, setting. Sinhala folk-tales usually illustrate the national sense of humour, which delights in the ridiculous, in the pretentious brought low, and in richly pithy expressions, characteristics which appeal to CF's temperament and her linguistic training and which appear in her best work.

Ferrar, family (apparently) of religious writers. In 1625 the widowed Mary (Woodnoth) F., 1550–1634, moved with her son Nicholas F. from London to set up at the manor of Little Gidding, Hunts., a family-monastic Anglican community. Along with church services, hospitality, charity, teaching, music, embroidery, bookbinding and concordance-making, the 'Little Academy' practised both discussion and 'storying'. Four MSS survive (Clare College, Cambridge; BL), written 1631–2, some in Nicholas F.'s absence: pub. 1899 (ed. E. Cruwys Sharland); 1938 (ed. B. Blackstone); and 1970 (ed. A. M. Williams). Scholars no longer see Nicholas F. as sole, certain author. Many hands, many speakers, many sharply distinguished viewpoints appear: Mary F. ('the Mother, Founder, or Grandmother'); her daughter Susanna (F.) Collett, 1581–1657 ('the Moderator'), and Susanna's husband ('the Resolved'); six of *their* daughters and a granddaughter. Most likely part-author is the able and learned Mary Collett, 1601–80 ('the Chief' and after her grandmother's death 'the Mother'): she says 'Let us not blame either our sex or our condition, as disabled for the advancement of Gods Kingdome', and 'neither Forme nor Substance of Mans Vertue is complete without the Consortship of Woman's Excellencie.' Martha (F.) Peckard, 1729–1805, collateral descendant, left a few much admired poems.

Ferrier, Susan Edmonstone, 1782–1854, novelist, b. at Edinburgh, youngest of ten children of Helen (Coutts) and James F.: friend of Sir Walter Scott and Lady Charlotte Bury. As only unmarried daughter, she cared for her father from her mother's death, 1797, till his, 1829. Her lively social life, based in Edinburgh, took in London and Inveraray, home of her lifelong friend Charlotte Clavering, 1790–1869, who was instrumental in bringing to birth her first novel, *Marriage*, 1818 (repr. 1977 and later). Popular, praised by Scott (who either respected or had not penetrated the anonymity which she fanatically retained till two years before her death), it mixes sententious moralizing with detailed, wry, caustic observation of the 'thrice-told tale' of factors which make unions happy or unhappy. *The Inheritance*, 1824, repr. 1984, and *Destiny*, 1831, dwell on similar issues: the heroines are rewarded, morally and materially, when they learn 'how much of moral deformity may be veiled beneath the mask of worldly refinement'. Both were praised, but not so warmly as *Marriage*; Joanna Baillie admired *Destiny*, which, more than earlier works, quotes poets like Felicia Hemans. In age, developing eye problems, SF became reclusive. *Temple Bar* magazine pub. her 'Recollections' of Scott, 1874. NLS has film of privately owned MSS (diaries, memoirs, two novels and unfinished *Maplehurst Manor*). See letters ed. John A. Doyle, 1929; Nancy L. Paxton in *Women and Lit.*, 4, 1976; study by Mary Cullinan, 1984.

Fetherstonhaugh, Hon. Mrs **Maria** Georgiana (Carleton), 1847–1918, novelist. Known as Minna Carleton, she was the youngest da. of Anne (Wauchope) and Guy, 3rd Baron Dorchester. She m. Timothy F. of Kirkoswald, Cumberland, late captain 13th Hussars, 1865. MF and her sister were readers for Bentley, her publisher. *Kilcorran*, 1877, *Kingsdene*, 1878, *Robin Adair*, 1879, *Alan Dering*, 1880, *For Old Sake's Sake*, 1882, and *Dream Faces*, 1884, when not marred by over-wrought sentiment and effusive verse quotation, have vitality, particularly in their outdoor scenes. Her women characters are often more resolute, noble and practical than the men: she had a fondness for lively, outspoken, unusual heroines as well as for self-sacrifice as woman's role.

Fiamengo, Marya, poet. B. in 1926 in Vancouver, where she still lives, da. of Yugoslav immigrants, Matija and Jack F., she m., and subsequently divorced, sculptor and printmaker Jack Hardman, with whom she had a son. She attended the Univ. of British Columbia (BA, and MA in creative writing, 1961). Now Senior Instructor in English there, she is not 'a terribly prolific writer', but one who craftily composes 'a debris mosaic of sadness and splendour' out of the rich imagery of her heritage and the West Coast. She observes and criticizes the world with rhetorical flair, caustic wit and irony: 'The defeat of the heart in a syllable's quiet / Is like snow falling in a frozen forest.' Excerpts from her four collections, 1958–61, have been reprinted, with new poems, in *North of the Cold Star*, 1978. Especially interested in the conditions of immigrant women and the marriage of politics and culture, MF shows her strong politics in her poetry – 'O, the anarchist / liberal American academic / is a sight to see! / ... on the humble supinely grateful soil / of the Canadian university' – often bordering on racial hatred against the Islamic world or Germans. Her honest account of her perceptions, however, and her tight control of language and rhythm, make her fascinating reading. Her most accomplished book, *In Praise of Old Women*, 1976, condemns as contrived and decadent American women's resistance to old age for the sake of men: 'Smooth-skinned at sixty, / second debuts at fifty / renascent / they never grow old in America / ... I will wrinkle adamantly in America / ... and I will liberate all women / to be old in America'. See Leona GOM in *Event*, 5, 1976.

'Fidelia', perhaps the eighteenth century's favourite female pseudonym: used (for a 'fallen' protagonist) by Hester CHAPONE, and (for themselves) by Mary ASTELL, Jane BARKER, Sarah GILL, Hannah GRIFFITTS, Sukey VICKERY, and various newspaper writers. A sparkling Lincoln poet of this name printed in the *GM*, 1734–5, may be Susanna WESLEY's daughter Keziah, d. 1742. She judges an offered poetry prize of £50 too skimpy ('Sir, you forget the price of candle') and proposes instead the award of Swift's hand in marriage. Ensuing verse exchanges involved Jane BRERETON and Elizabeth CARTER.

Field, Kate, 1838–96, journalist, lecturer, actress and dramatist, b. St Louis, Missouri, da. of theatrical parents Eliza Lapsley (Riddle) and Joseph M. F. She arranged her own schooling, informing her parents afterwards, and had her first article published when she was eight. She admired Charles Dickens, and, after reading his 1867–8 tour, pub. *Pen Photographs of Dickens's Readings*, 1871. Friends included Trollope and the BROWNINGS; her interest in SPIRITUALISM resulted in *Planchette's Diary*, 1868, 'planchette' being both the female character, and a type of ouija board. She made her stage debut in New York, 1874, as Peg Woffington, and in 1877 toured England with her 'Extremes Meet', a successful but lightweight play, also produced in NY, 1878. KF travelled in the USA and Europe, and lectured on a variety of topics, including John Brown's body and Mormonism. Her articles appeared in leading journals, and after 'Telephone' was published in the London *Times* she sang to Queen VICTORIA through this new medium. In 1890, she established *Kate Field's Washington*, a literary and political journal. Its feminism is self-satisfied and patriotic. KF was awarded the Order of the French Legion of Honour. See the eulogizing account of her life by L. Whiting, 1899, who also wrote *After her Death*, about her psychic communication with the spirit of KF.

'Field, Michael', Katharine Harris Bradley, 1864–1914, and Edith Emma Cooper, 1862–1913, collaborative poets and dramatists. KB was b. in Birmingham, da. of Emma (Harris) and Charles B., tobacco manufacturer. Her niece EC was b. at Kenilworth, da. of Emma (Bradley), elder sister of KB, and James Robert C., merchant. After the death of her father KB and her mother moved in with EC. KB helped with EC's education and upbringing. Both were educated at home, and KB attended Newnham College, Cambridge, and Collège de France. Both classical scholars and linguists, they attended courses at Univ. College, Bristol. They saw their collaboration as a spiritual partnership, 'closer married' than their friends the BROWNINGS. KB pub. poems *The New Minnesinger*, 1875, as Arran Leigh; they first collaborated in a volume of poems, *Bellerophon*, as Arran and Isla Leigh. The first 'Michael Field' play, *Callirrhoe*, 1884, was widely acclaimed. Sensitive to the importance of male pseudonyms, they warned Browning against disclosure: 'we have many things to say that the world will not tolerate from a woman's lips'. After their identities were discovered they received little critical attention. Enjoying a private income, they wrote 27 dramas, all poetic tragedies, often pub. in limited editions. They drew on a wide range of historical material and legend, but their plays usually involved an intense exploration of intertwining death and love. In *Callirrhoe*, drawn from classical legend, the heroine is converted to the cult of Dionysus through her lover's death and her own self-sacrifice. *The Tragic Mary*, 1890, shows Mary Stuart as a victim of her own capacity for love. *Julia Domna*, 1903, examines pathological emotions between a mother and two sons, while *Queen Mariamne*, 1908, dramatizes Herod's wife's acceptance of her condemnation and death. They also pub. vols. of poems: *Underneath the Bough*, 1893, *Long Ago*, 1889, which is a re-writing of SAPPHO, *Sight and Song*, 1892 and *Poems of Adoration*, 1912, mainly EC's work, and *Mystic Trees*, 1913, KB's. Their work includes love poems to each other. Excerpts from their journal *Work and Days*, 1933, ed. T. and D. C. Moore, give a greater sense of their feminist consciousness and engagement. In 1907 they converted to Catholicism. Their relationship has been treated extensively in Lillian Faderman's *Surpassing the Love of Men*, 1981. See also Mary Sturgeon's study, 1922. They lived together all of their lives and died of cancer within months of each other.

Fielding, Sarah, 1710–68, novelist, b. East Stour, Dorset, da. of Sarah (Gould) and Edmund F. Her mother d. in 1718; her father m. a Roman Catholic; SF and her sisters were brought up by her grandmother. Her Salisbury boarding-school was non-academic, but she was later extremely well-read in Greek, Latin, French, and English. Jane COLLIER was an early friend, Samuel Richardson a later one; she lived in London with her widowed brother Henry's family, 1744–7. Having, probably, contributed to two of Henry's works, 1742 and 1743, she pub. her *Adventures of David Simple in Search of a Faithful Friend*, 1744, anonymously in his absence from London, pleading financial distress as motive. (Its 2nd ed. has his preface, praising, dissociating himself, helpfully correcting grammar; it was repr. as his as late as 1822.) A 'moral romance', it brings together four young people each outcast or disinherited by wicked relations and a cruel world. Both heroines make important points about the stifling of women's intellect and the barriers against a gentlewoman's earning her living. *Familiar Letters* between these characters, 1747, is somewhat static (fine subscription list; contributions from Henry); more exciting is a new ed. adding *Volume the Last*, 1753, preface probably by Collier (ed. Malcolm Kelsall, 1969), which kills off most of those left improbably happy in 1744. (SF's sisters had all died in 1750–1.) She wrote the first, outstanding critique on *Clarissa*, 1749 (repr. 1985, ed. Peter Sabor). *The Governess, or Little Female Academy*, 1749 (still in print 1903; facs. 1968 ed. Jill E. Grey) makes of moral tales by 'Mrs Teachum' and others the first full-length

English CHILDREN's fiction. Having worked with Collier on *The Cry*, 1754 (repr. as hers, NY 1986), SF lived near Bath from at least 1758, still very poor, producing *Lives* of Cleopatra and Octavia (bad woman and, more briefly, good), 1757; *The ... Countess of Dellwyn*, 1759 (also schematized: a fall from natural goodness to forced marriage, corruption, feigned repentance); probably *Histories of ... Penitents in the Magdalen House* [1759] (fiction aimed at softening the cruel effects of moral condemnation); and *Ophelia*, 1760 (heroine, a child of nature, finally enforces reform in her abductor). The last of SF's unfailingly intelligent and ground-breaking works was a translation of Xenophon's *Memoirs of Socrates*, pub. by subscription at Bath, 1762, repr. 1910. Several facs. 1974; dissertation by Carolyn Woodward, 1988.

Fields, Annie (Adams), 1834–1915, biographer, editor, poet, diarist and social worker, b. Boston, sixth of seven children of Sarah May (Holland) and Dr Zabdiel Boylston A. She was educ. at home and at George B. Emerson's School. In 1854 she m. James T. F., renowned publisher, and after his death in 1881 formed a 30-year 'Boston marriage' with Sarah Orne JEWETT, whose story 'The Queen's Twin' reflected and predicted this relationship. AF participated fully in her husband's publishing activities, making editorial decisions and presenting the woman's point of view, though her own writing was frustrated by her responsibilities as hostess. She ran a successful literary salon, and edited collections of letters and biographical sketches of Celia THAXTER, H. B. STOWE, and Jewett; and gave literary advice and emotional support to other writers like Rebecca DAVIS, J. W. HOWE, Elizabeth PHELPS, Louise GUINEY, Mary MURFREE, M. W. FREEMAN, Edith WHARTON and Willa CATHER. She published three vols. of poetry: *Under the Olive*, 1881, poems to the ancient Greeks, in which the evocative imagery is often marred by forced rhythms, *The Singing Shepherd*, 1895, and *Orpheus*, 1900; her handbook on charity work, *How to Help the Poor*, 1883, sold 22,000 copies in two years. She also wrote literary reminiscences of J. T. Fields, Whittier and Hawthorne, and *A Shelf of Old Books*, 1894, which reminisces, in a flowery, kid-glove manner, on English men of literature, and the 'sacred' books which inspired them. AF supported female emancipation; her most interesting writing is her DIARY, which is in the Mass. Hist. Soc., and was the main source for Mark A. De W. Howe's *Memories of a Hostess*, 1922.

Fiennes (pronounced *fines*), **Celia** or Cecilia, 1662–1741, TRAVEL writer, b. at Newton Toney near Salisbury, da. of Frances (Whitehead) and Nathaniel F., both of leading anti-monarchical families. She covered every English county between 1685 and *c.* 1712. At first (with her mother) and in later life she used a coach, but she rode her longest journeys, 1697 and 1698, on horseback. Her journal (written later, not daily) vividly describes towns, roads, the shortcomings of inns, the treasures of great houses, industries and improvements, local life and religion. In a preface she addresses her MS to none but 'near relations' yet promises to correct errors in a supplement to her 'Book'; she urges the gathering of information but fears gentlemen have better sources than her work. Robert Southey quoted it as by a lady, 1812; her collateral descendant Emily Griffiths pub. part, 1888; see Christopher Morris, ed., 1947, 1982.

Figes, Eva (Unger), b. 1932 in Berlin, novelist and social critic. She was da. of Irma (Cohen) and Emil Edward U., who was imprisoned in Dachau in 1938; the whole family escaped to England in 1939. She was educ. at Kingsbury Grammar School in London and Queen Mary College, London Univ. (BA in English, 1953), and worked as a publishers' editor. She m. John George F. in 1954 and had two children; divorced in 1963. Her first novel, *Equinox*,

1966, chronicles the breakup of the protagonist's marriage and her attempts to build a new life. *Konek Landing*, 1969, treats the subject of the Holocaust. EF's rejection of parochial English realism for the 'European', experimental, modernist structuring of her interior monologues has kept her readership small though appreciative. *B*, 1972, is the self-reflexive monologue of a male writer. *Days*, 1974 (which she adapted for radio, 1981), distils the significant experiences of an imagined lifetime; *Waking*, 1981, focuses on seven moments of awaking during the female narrator's life; *The Seven Ages*, 1986, interprets 1000 years of history through the eyes of specifically located women protagonists. *Ghosts*, 1988, is praised by Fay WELDON as 'half poetry, half prose'. EF made a lasting mark with *Patriarchal Attitudes: Women in Society*, 1970, published just a few months before Germaine GREER's *The Female Eunuch* and Kate MILLETT's *Sexual Politics*. It examines power in theology, commerce, education, psychology and philosophy, and attacks 'the cult of Freudian femininity': 'the remedy lies in our own hands, and it will be found in social change, not on the analyst's couch'. *Tragedy and Social Evolution*, 1976, sets Greek and Renaissance dramas in their historical periods; *Sex and Subterfuge: Women Novelists to 1850*, 1982, investigates 'female structures' and the constrictions caused by male expectations of suitability. EF has also published stories in anthologies, children's books, and translations of half a dozen French and German novels. An autobiography, *Little Eden*, 1978, deals with her childhood war experience. Her edited volumes include *Women their World* (jointly), 1982; her radio plays include *The True Tale of Margery KEMPE*, 1985.

Film theory. Women have written about film from the earliest days of the industry, frequently dominating criticism and review. In spite of overlap, it is useful to distinguish between women film critics, feminist film critics, and feminist film theorists. Early women film critics include Iris Barry (*Let's Go to the Pictures*, 1926; *D. W. Griffith: American Film Master*, 1940), founder of the NY Museum of Modern Art Film Department; BRYHER (*Film Problems of Soviet Russia*, 1929), founder and assistant editor of *Close Up*, 1927–33, the first journal devoted to film; and C. A. (Caroline) Lejeune (*Cinema*, 1931), reviewer for the *Manchester Guardian*, 1922–8, and the *Observer*, 1928–73. H. D., Dorothy RICHARDSON, Gertrude STEIN, and Marianne MOORE also contributed regularly to *Close Up*. Later women film critics include the influential *New Yorker* writers, Pauline KAEL (*I Lost It At the Movies*, 1965; *Kiss Kiss Bang Bang*, 1968) and Penelope GILLIATT (*Three-Quarter Face*, 1980).

Many women film critics, early and late, were attracted by the medium's accessibility and mass appeal; others fought for its recognition as a valid 'high' art. Although some (such as Richardson, who saw film as 'essentially feminine') foreshadowed feminist approaches, an explicitly and consistently feminist criticism waited for the women's movement of the late 1960s and early 1970s. Concentrating on character and narrative, feminist film criticism offers a critique of the marginalization and stereotyping of women's experience in the dominant cinema. Critics like Molly Haskell (*From Reverence to Rape*, 1973), Marjorie Rosen (*Popcorn Venus*, 1973), and Joan Mellen (*Women and Their Sexuality in the New Film*, 1973), largely descriptive, focus on the correspondence of cinematic images of women to social and psychological reality.

Feminist film theory, on the other hand, less concerned with film's reflection of an assumed prior social or psychological reality, poses two different questions: how has film, as a system of representation, contributed to the construction of gendered subject positions within patriarchal ideology? and can alternative film practices effectively disrupt the patriarchally constructed subject, substituting other as yet still tentative subject positions? Thus the agenda of feminist film theory is both analytic and prescriptive. Feminist film theorists have drawn heavily on semiotics, psychoanalysis and Marxism as these fields have been reformulated by such theorists as Roland Barthes (*Mythologies*, 1957, transl. 1972), Jacques Lacan (*Écrits*, 1966, transl. 1977), and Louis Althusser (*Lenin and Philosophy*, 1968, transl. 1971).

Claire Johnston's early, influential essay, 'Women's Cinema as Countercinema' (*Notes on Women's Cinema*, 1973) established the terms of continuing debates. Building on Barthes' definition of myth as a form of speech which appropriates and renders invisible a prior sign (in this case the sign of 'woman', who is mythologized in cinema as 'what she represents for man'), Johnston argues that the classical narrative (Hollywood) film has more to offer a feminist countercinema than does the European art film which, because it is less iconographic, is 'more open to the invasion of myth'. The blatant iconography of the Hollywood film provides opportunities for 'internal criticism' (as evidenced in the films of Ida Lupino and Dorothy Arzner) and thus 'a strategy for the subversion of ideology in general'. Johnston further argues that 'women's cinema must embody the working through of desire: such an objective demands the use of the entertainment film'.

Theorist and filmmaker Laura Mulvey also addresses desire in her important essay, 'Visual Pleasure and Narrative Cinema' (*Screen*, 16, 1975). Working from a psychoanalytic model – Freud's discussion of scopophilic pleasure and voyeurism and Lacan's discussion of the mirror phase and the construction of the ego ideal – she outlines the ways in which classical narrative cinema, structured by 'the unconscious of patriarchal society', reflects and reinforces the patriarchal unconscious both in its fetishization of the female form (which 'speaks castration and nothing else') and in its construction of man as active bearer of the look and woman as passive image. Mulvey calls for a 'break with normal pleasurable expectations in order to conceive a new language of desire'.

Extensive response to Mulvey's essay has focused on the problematics of and possibilities for female spectatorship. In 'Film and the Masquerade: Theorising the Female Spectator' (*Screen* 23, 1982), Mary Ann Doane discusses the ways in which 'an excess of femininity', the adoption of a female masquerade (by, for example, the *femme fatale* figure in film) creates an enabling distance from the cinematic image of the female, rendering the image readable and manipulable by the woman spectator. In *Women and Film*, 1983, E. Ann Kaplan asks 'Is the gaze male?' and borrows from KRISTEVA to argue that Motherhood – which (as non-symbolic, pre-linguistic, pre-Oedipal) has been repressed by patriarchal representation – offers the possibility of a 'mutual gazing' outside of patriarchal patterns of opposition. In *Technologies of Gender*, 1987, Teresa de Lauretis suggests that a film like Chantal Akerman's *Jeanne Dielman, 23 Quai du Commerce, 1080 Bruxelles*, 1975, or Lizzie Borden's *Born in Flames*, 1983, 'addresses its spectator as a woman', marking a shift to an 'aesthetics of reception' and an engagement in 'the project of transforming vision by reinventing the forms and processes of a social subject, women, that until now has been all but unrepresentable'.

Other major contributions to feminist film theory include E. Ann Kaplan, ed., *Women in Film Noir*, 1978, Annette Kuhn, *Women's Pictures*, 1982, Kaja Silverman, *The Subject of Semiotics*, 1983, and *The Acoustic Mirror*, 1988, Mary Ann Doane, *The Desire to Desire*, 1987, and Tania Modleski, *The Women Who Knew too Much*, 1987. Major journals include *Women and Film*, 1972–75, and *Camera Obscura*, 1976–.

Finch, Anne (Kingsmill), later Countess of Winchilsea, 'Ardelia', 1661–1720, poet, b. near Newbury, Berks., da. of Anne (Haselwood) and Sir William K., of old county families, who both died soon after her birth. All we know of her childhood is her enduring fondness for her sister. In 1683 she became (with Anne KILLIGREW) Maid of Honour to Mary of Modena; next year she married Heneage F. (an active antiquarian after 1688, Lord W. in 1712), who delighted in her poetry and in later years transcribed it. After James II's flight they left the court and settled at their nephew's estate, Eastwell Park, Kent. AF's recurring depression has been ascribed to the ruin of her political allegiance; but country life appealed to her, and she longed to make Eastwell famous in literature. Her poems circulated in MS from the 1680s; a few appeared in print, for instance an elegy on James II and 'The Spleen' (a Pindaric ode often repr. and much admired), both 1701. Her *Miscellany Poems on Several Occasions*, 1713, was reissued next year with variant title-pages both with and without her name. Its 'prefatory poem' suggests that women must write for their own satisfaction only; AF's MS albums, which include more controversial work than what she printed, have an introduction which, while disclaiming any aim of publication, strongly opposes the restrictions women endure. She encompasses metaphysical wit, strong satire, fervent religious feeling, imaginative response to the natural world (fables are a favourite form), subtle and complex feminist argument, translation from Italian and French, neo-classical plays, humour and burlesque. Her very productiveness and versatility may have contributed to the underestimating of her achievement. Swift and Nicholas Rowe praised her; Pope expressed ambivalent feelings but probably did not aim his satire on women writers at her; Wordsworth anthologized her; Anna SEWARD learned at her mother's knee a poem which she only later found to be by AF. *Poems*, ed. Myra Reynolds, 1903, repr. 1974; full ed. still needed, despite useful selecs., and Wellesley College MS ed. J. M. Ellis d'Alessandro, Florence, 1988; much good comment includes Ann Messenger in *Restoration*, 5, 1981.

Findlater, Mary, 1865–1963, and **Jane Helen**, 1866–1946, Scottish novelists and short-story writers, who wrote separately and together. Their mother, Sarah (Borthwick), was also a writer, who with her sister Jane wrote and edited religious works. Their father, Eric F., was a minister of the Free Church at Lochearnhead. They were educ. by governesses (one being Annie Lorrain Smith, 1854–1937, later a distinguished botanist and ardent suffragette). Their cook was 'a gifted horror-monger' and their mother often took them to local death-beds as part of a pious education. The sisters enjoyed an extremely close relationship, described by Mary (who broke her engagement rather than part with Jane) as 'halves of one whole'. Jane's first novel, *The Green Graves of Balgowrie*, 1896, treats just such a relationship between sisters raised by an eccentric socialist-atheist mother. Its success made subsequent publication easy. Mary had already pub. *Songs & Sonnets*, 1895, and went on to write six novels of her own and four with Jane, including *Crossriggs*, 1908 (repr. 1986), and a story collection, 1901. Jane pub. four more novels and several story collections, and they both joined in two other novels with their friends 'Allan MacAulay' (Charlotte Smith) and American Kate Douglas WIGGIN. These were *The Affair at the Inn*, 1904, where each author took a different character, and *Robinetta*, 1911. In 1905 the sisters visited America, where they made sharp comments to their diaries (F. H. BURNETT had 'an evil eye, dyed hair ... like a nightmare dream') and several lasting friends, including Alice James (William's wife). Back in England, they became friends with Mary CHOLMONDELY and her sisters from 1906, moved to Rye after the war, and then in 1940 returned to Scotland. Their best works have an acerbic realism; their weakest sentimentalize. There is a life by Eileen Mackenzie, 1964.

Finley, Martha, 'Martha Farquharson', 1828–1909, novelist, b. Chillicothe, Ohio, da. of strongly Presbyterian parents, Maria Theresa (Brown) and James Brown F., a physician. The family eventually settled in South Bend, Ind. Educ. at private schools, MF taught school near home, then in Pennsylvania, moving in 1853 to Philadelphia. Here she struggled to make ends meet as a writer of sentimental Sunday School stories for the Presbyterian Publications Committee. She finally struck gold with her invention during the Civil War years of the Elsie Dinsmore series, set in the South, which became a publishing phenomenon from the early 1870s. Elsie is figured as a tender-hearted and courageous goody-goody, much misunderstood, whose main mission in life is to win and keep her stern father's love. The first Elsie manuscript was divided by the publisher into *Elsie Dinsmore*, 1867 and *Elsie's Holidays at Roselands*, 1868; 26 more titles followed, earning MF one-quarter of a million dollars. MF also wrote other series, e.g., the Mildred Keith series and the Do-Good Library, but these were less successful. After more than 20 years in Philadelphia, MF moved to Elkton, Md., in 1876, settling in a house she built there.

First, Ruth, 1925–82, journalist, political commentator, activist and martyr. B. in Johannesburg, da. of radical socialist parents, she studied social science at Witwatersrand Univ., and worked briefly for the Social Welfare Department of Johannesburg City Council, leaving in outrage over the miners' strike, 1946, to begin her career in journalism. She edited a series of newspapers, notably *Fighting Talk*, in which she wrote against apartheid. All of her papers were eventually banned. A member of the banned African National Congress, she organized protests in South Africa, England, and Mozambique, and was tried for treason in the 1950s. 'She and her husband, advocate Joe Slovo, were at the heart of the liberation struggle', says Winnie Mandela (*Part of My Soul Went with Him*, 1985). Detained without charge, 1963, she was held in solitary confinement under the Preventive Detention Act, an experience she describes in *117 Days*, 1965, repr. 1982. After her release, she went with her family into political exile, first in London then in Mozambique, where she joined the Centre of African Studies, and wrote *Black Gold: the Mozambican Miner, Proletarian and Peasant*, 1983. She also wrote *South West Africa*, 1963, *Power in Africa* (also called *The Barrel of the Gun*), 1970, and, with Ann Scott, a biography of Olive SCHREINER, 1980. She was killed in Mozambique by a letter bomb. Her daughter Shawn Slovo wrote the script for the anti-apartheid film, *A World Apart*, 1988, about RF; her other daughters, Gillian and Robyn, write thrillers and plays.

Fisher, Ann, 1719–78, educationalist, da. of Henry F. of Oldscale, Cumberland: she published in this name even after marrying Newcastle publisher and bookseller Thomas Slack. She partnered his business, bore nine daughters (eight survived) and opened a school in 1745. Early copies of her extremely popular works are now rare. Of *A New Grammar: Being the Most Easy Guide to Speaking and Writing the English Language Properly and Correctly*, advertised 1745, the earliest edition known is the 2nd, Newcastle, 1750 (over 30 eds. by 1800: facs. 1968). From the 6th ed., 1759, it was called *A Practical New Grammar*. . . . It mentions an earlier *Child's Christian Education*, and is ascribed to AF although a prefatory letter by 'a Friend' calls the author 'Sir'. (No woman had written such a work before.) Remarkably, it does not downgrade English in relation to classical tongues; it influenced the language reformers Thomas Sheridan and Thomas Spence. English teaching continued to benefit from AF's elementary school-books. *The Pleasing Instructor or Entertaining Moralist*, 1756, is an anthology of short pieces (including Elizabeth CARTER), also much reprinted, with a prefatory 'New

Thoughts on Education'. Of *The New English Tutor*, 1763, nothing before the 3rd ed., 1774, is known; *The Young Scholar's Delight* and *New English Exercise Book* date from 1770; *Fisher's Spelling Dictionary*, 1774, survives from a later date, differently titled. AF has been wrongly credited with works by mathematician George F. See P. M. Horsley in *Héaton Works Journal*, 6, 1951.

Fisher, Dorothy (Dorothea) Frances (**Canfield**), 1879–1958, writer of fiction (as Dorothy Canfield) and non-fiction (as Dorothy Canfield Fisher), and educationalist. Da. of artist Flavia (Camp) and economics professor James Hulme Canfield, she was b. in Lawrence, Kan., and educ. there (with a year in Paris) and in Nebraska: she and her lifelong friend Willa CATHER co-authored a ghost story, 'The Fear that Walks by Noonday', in the Univ. of Nebraska Yearbook, 1894. Deafness thwarted DCF's musical aspirations. She studied languages at Ohio State Univ., the Sorbonne, and Columbia, turned down, at her parents' wish, a post at Western Reserve Univ., and became secretary at the nearby Horace Mann School. Here she began writing stories. In 1907 came her first novel, *Gunhild*, set in Norway, and marriage to John Redwood F., with whom she had two children. They moved to Arlington, Vt, the home of DCF's ancestors and subject for much of her writing from *Hillsboro People*, 1915 (stories, with poems by Sarah CLEGHORN), to *Vermont Tradition: The Biography of an Outlook on Life*, 1953. In 1911 (on money for *The Squirrel Cage*, 1912, which attacks the entrapping, infantilizing 'labyrinth' which society prescribes for wives), she visited Maria Montessori's Italian school, and returned to expound its method in several books, the first *A Montessori Mother*, 1912. In France with her family, 1916–19 (having longed to help during WWI), she founded a braille press and a home for refugee children. Her novels (nine were best-sellers) supported her family. She discussed such role-reversal in *The Home-Maker*, 1924 (repr. 1983), and wrote an article for the *Los Angeles Examiner* on 'Marital Relations'. In *The Brimming Cup*, 1921, a woman is torn between her family and her love for another man. In *Her Son's Wife*, 1926, another conquers her deep dislike for, and assertion of power over, her daughter-in-law. DCF suspected that men, notorious for 'melting away out of the house' in moments of tension, would 'melt away from [this novel] at about the third chapter' but hoped that women would read it with 'a certain horrified interest' (see intro. to repr., 1986). DCF wrote 11 vols. of stories, a play, poetry, children's books, translations from Italian, and non-fiction including the patriotic *American Portraits*, 1946, and *Our Independence*, 1950. She was the first woman on Vermont's board of education and for 25 years the only woman on the selection board of the Book-of-the-Month Club. Ida H. Washington's life, 1982, draws on DCF's papers, mostly at the Univ. of Vermont, Princeton and Columbia.

Fisher, M. K. V., Mary Frances (Kennedy), writer of gastronomy and memoirs, b. 1908 in Albion, Mich., and raised in Whittier, Calif., elder da. of Edith Oliver (Holbrook) and Rex K. (who owned the Whittier *News*), some of the few non-Quakers in town. She was 'a very happy little girl' and a 'Wild Indian' with her sister. She attended Illinois College, Occidental College, UCLA and the Univ. of Dijon; she has lived much in France and cultivated a vineyard in Switzerland. She m. Alfred Young F. in 1929 (divorced 1938), and in 1934 sold a story, 'Pacific Village', for $10, and three illustrations (the last she ever did) for $25: 'I spent the money, all of it, on riotous living', by which she meant lavish presents for her family. Much of her writing appeared in the name of Parrish, from her second husband, who died in 1942. Her first five books, from *Serve It Forth*, 1937, *Consider the Oyster*, 1941, and *How to Cook a Wolf*, 1942, were collec. as *The Art of Eating*,

1954, subtitled 'Gastronomical Works'. MKVF writes with passion and precision of the arts of cooking and living: her first restaurant visit at six, the 'avidity' of hunger in adolescence: 'Anything can be a lodestar in a person's life, I suppose ... the Kitchen serves well.' She had two daughters by her third husband (divorced 1951), and has also written novels, poetry, a screenplay and a book on Marseilles. Recent works are introspective, never without humour. *As They Were*, 1982, is 'a report about some first days'. *Sister Age*, 1983, tells of years studying the art of ageing, filling boxes with clippings on old age but then giving them away, because some of her earlier notes 'sound like fabrications'. Scrupulously seeking the truth, she finds age 'not a nagging harpy but a teacher'.

Fisher, Mary, *c*. 1623–98, Quaker prophet of almost mythical status, owing to her walk of 500 or 600 miles to Turkey. B. near York, she worked as a servant to Richard and Elizabeth Tomlinson of Selby, Yorks. In 1652, having met George Fox and become a Quaker, she was imprisoned for 16 months in York Castle with Elizabeth HOOTON and four others; they collectively published *False Prophets and Teachers Described*, 1652, calling on people to leave the state church and rely on the Inner Light: 'they that are taught of the Lord deny all teaching without'. MF travelled throughout England to preach, being repeatedly jailed and whipped. In 1657–8 she visited the West Indies, and then went on foot to meet Mohammed IV and explain her beliefs to him. She m. William Bayly in 1662 and had three children. Widowed in 1675, she m. John Cross in 1678 and in 1686 moved with him to Charleston, SC, where she outlived him by probably 11 years. Property she left her heir included a black slave.

Fitzgerald, Penelope Mary (Knox), novelist and biographer, b. 1916 in Lincoln. Da. of graduate and moderate suffragette Christine (Hicks), d. 1935, and Edmund George Valpy (E. V.) Knox ('Evoe', later editor of *Punch*), she grew up in London and attended Wycombe Abbey, Glos., and Somerville College, Oxford (BA in English, 1939). She m. Desmond F. (d. 1976) in 1941, had three children, and worked for the BBC and in a bookshop, and tutored. Her scholarly, accessible biographies convey the period and milieu of their subjects: Edward Burne-Jones, 1975, *The Knox Brothers*, 1977 (her father and uncles: her aunt Winifred PECK, whom they classed in 'an inferior species', gets scant mention), and Charlotte MEW, 1984 (evoked in rich detail, not evaluated). Her swift, spare, ironic novels present – often from observation – enclosed worlds with special routines and thought-patterns. *The Golden Child*, 1977, recalls the Tutankhamen exhibition, 1971–2, with freezing queues, children's school projects, and an alleged curse – as well as faked exhibits and murderous skulduggery for gain. *The Bookshop*, 1978, miniaturizes such intricate plotting, as Suffolk small-town feuds kill the project of a middle-aged widow mindful of a 'duty to make it clear to herself, and possibly to others, that she existed in her own right'. *Offshore*, 1979 (Booker Prize), is set in a heterogeneous community living on Thames barges (as PF had with her young family), *Human Voices*, 1980, in the early wartime BBC, *At Freddie's*, 1982, in a London drama school whose proprietress looks an 'old wreck' but has everyone just where she wants them. Her pupils, whose professionalism can crack hilariously, are notable among a gallery of inscrutable children. *Innocence*, 1986, set in Italy, ends in failed suicide. In *The Beginning of Spring*, 1988, set in ramshackle, bureaucracy-ridden, emotional pre-revolution Moscow, with an English print-shop owner abandoned (temporarily) by his wife, surface detail masks the undertow of love-relationships not fully understood. In each, different nationalities think they can read each other, and the present thinks it understands the past. PF has ed. an unpub. novel by William Morris, 1982.

Fitzgerald, Zelda (Sayre), 1900–48, fiction writer and artist, b. in Montgomery, Ala, youngest da. of Minnie (Machen) and Anthony S., later a Supreme Court Judge. By 1918 a tearaway and verse writer, she m. novelist F. Scott F. in 1920 and had a daughter in 1921. Before they moved to France in 1924 ZF had published a couple of magazine articles. She then took ballet training (some of her weird, powerful paintings are of dancers). In 1928 two articles by her appeared as joint work with Scott F., so did five of her stories (sketches of young girls' lives) in *College Humor*, 1929; a sixth, in *The Saturday Evening Post*, bore his name only, which brought better pay. The pair were competitive as writers, each seeking to rewrite the other's version of their lives. Of his fiction's appropriation of her letters and diaries (now lost: he is said to have vetoed publication), she wrote in a strenuously flippant review, 'plagiarism begins at home'. (He then joked about 'the famous author my wife'.) From then on she wrote mostly while in mental-breakdown clinics: a ballet libretto, stories, some admired by *Scribner's* in 1931 but thought (except one) too 'curious' for print, now lost; her *roman-à-clef, Save Me the Waltz*, 1932, repr. 1967. Scott found it both hostile and parasitic; ZF was by turns placating and defiant. Revised but not proof-read, cheaply printed, it had mixed reviews and sold poorly; Linda W. Wagner sees it as moving from 'Ornamental, rococo' to 'somber, spare, direct' (in *Notes on Contemporary Literature*, 12, 1982). In 1933 Scott sought ZF's promise to 'give up the idea of writing anything'; she wrote and produced a farce, *Scandalabra*, pub. 1980 (see Wagner in *Journal of Narrative Technique*, 12, 1982), and exhibited paintings in NYC. She continued to be in and out of clinics (with a brief respite after Scott's death, 1940, while living with her mother). She had another exhibition, 1942, then further breakdowns, and died in a hospital fire, with nine other women. She left an incomplete novel, *Caesar's Things*. The huge dossier on the F. marriage is still growing. See her daughter, 'Scottie' Fitzgerald Smith, et al., eds., *Bits of Paradise ... Uncollected Stories*, 1973; life of ZF by Nancy Milford, 1970. Papers at Princeton Univ.

Flanner, Janet, 'Genêt', 1892–1978, journalist, novelist and translator. Da. of Mary-Ellen (Hockett), a Quaker, and businessman Francis F., she was b. and educ. in Indianapolis. After a year in Germany and expulsion from the Univ. of Chicago, she was a pioneer FILM critic in Indianapolis. She was briefly married, 1920–2. Hopes of writing full-time took her to New York, then Paris, 1922, with her lover Solita SOLANO. Her novel *The Cubical City*, 1926 (repr. 1974 with her afterword), criticizes US sexual mores. She translated COLETTE's *Chéri* in 1929. In 1925 *The New Yorker* published her first 'Letter from Paris', growing from her 'newsy letters' to Jane Grant, wife of its founder, 'about anything except fashion'. JF kept writing these fortnightly, under her pseudonym, for 50 years (except during WWII). They bear the mark of her vivid personality and strong interest in work done by women (especially the expatriate Americans, who were mostly her friends), which is 'described, promoted, and analysed at length'. Her topics embrace writing, publishing, theatre, films, photography, visual arts, French feminism – and fashion, in terms of exploited garment workers. The 1930s letters reflected the rise of fascism by a deepening, anxious concentration on political and military matters. In the USA, 1939–44, JF wrote on France for *The New Yorker* under her own name. The post-war letters have been ed. as *Paris Journal* i and ii, 1965 and 1971, the earlier ones as *Paris was Yesterday*, 1979. JF also wrote a 'Letter from London', 1934–9 (sampled in *London was*

Yesterday, 1975); a study of Pétain as 'The Old Man of France', 1944; and other journalistic pieces, gathered in *An American in Paris: Profile of an Interlude between Two Wars*, 1940 (material often revised or expanded), *Men and Monuments*, 1957, and *Janet Flanner's World: Uncollected Writings*, 1979. See Natalia Danesi Murray, ed., *Darlinghissima*, 1985, letters from JF to her written between 1945 and 1975, with extensive commentary by Murray; also Benstock, 1986. Papers at Library of Congress.

'Fleming, George', Julia Constance Fletcher, 1853–1938, US novelist, short-story writer and translator, da. of James C. Fletcher, Presbyterian missionary and author on Brazil. She spent her most productive years in Europe, settling in Rome. She translated the sonnets of Venetian poet Gaspara Stampa, 1881, and Edmond Rostand's *The Fantasticks*, 1900. Her first success, *A Nile Novel*, 1876 (repub. as *Kismet*, 1877), tells of a self-willed Midwesterner travelling in Egypt who is granted the man she loves only when she has extricated herself from a previous engagement. Oscar Wilde said, 'she writes as cleverly as she talks', and in 1878 dedicated his prize-winning Newdigate poem 'Ravenna' to her. Woman's thwarted passion is explored in *The Truth about Clement Ker*, 1889, which sensitively portrays a loveless marriage. Other works include *Mirage*, 1877, set in the Middle East, and containing a probable portrait of Wilde as the aesthete Claude Davenant, *The Head of Medusa*, 1880, and *Vestigia*, 1884, both set in Italy, *Andromeda*, 1885, *For Plain Women Only*, 1885 and *Little Stories about Women*, 1897. GF's story-telling skills are matched by her incisive characterization and cosmopolitan wit: 'We treat our fellow countrymen as the old Florentines did their saints, and only recognize them against golden backgrounds' (*A Nile Novel*) is her comment on US materialism.

Fleming, Marjory, 1803–11, child diarist, da. of Elizabeth (Rae) and James F. of Kirkcaldy, Fife: youngest person to have a *DNB* entry (its shortest, by Leslie Stephen). She began her journal in spring 1810 under the eye of her elder cousin Isabella Keith, mixing scraps of fact, morality, and observation: 'The Monkey gets as many visitors as I or my cousins'; 'I like to here [sic] my own sex praised but not the other'; 'I am thinking how I should Impro[ve] the many talents I have'; 'I never read Sermons of any kind but I read Novelettes and my bible.' Her poems deal with turkeys, a pug, and Mary Queen of Scots: MSS in NLS: first pub. 1858; ed. Frank Sidgwick, 1934.

Fleming, May Agnes (Early), 'Cousin May Carleton', 1840–80, Canada's first best-selling novelist and short-story writer. Da. of Mary (Doherty) and Bernard Early, she was b. in Saint John, New Brunswick, where she was educ. at the Sacred Heart Convent. The story papers were coming into their own; she was 15 when the NY *Mercury* published her first story. A prolific writer, for a time she wrote for four papers. In 1865, after an acquaintance of three weeks, she m. John F., a machinist. From 1868 she wrote three novels a year exclusively for the Philadelphia *Saturday Night*. Five years later she transferred to the *New York Weekly*, then the most widely circulated story paper, and began publishing her serials in the *London Journal* as well (hardback eds. pub. by G. W. Carleton). The family, which now included four children, moved to Brooklyn, NY, about 1875. Shortly thereafter, she separated from her dissolute husband. Now a prosperous woman – she made $15,000 a year in the 1870s – she made a will excluding him from her estate with instructions for guardianship and education of her children. MAF's early serialized novels were gothic ROMANCES, but usually include humorous elements. She soon mastered the complex, suspenseful, ingeniously twisting serial plot. Several contrast a villainess of passion, initiative, and determination with a virtuous, submissive heroine, both perhaps reflecting her own personality. Her later novels lessen the GOTHIC element while retaining mystery and romance. The last, *Lost for a Woman*, 1880, breaks new ground: its protagonist faces psychologically complex problems and demonstrates the initiative and courage heretofore evident only in her villainous women. It also includes a perceptive portrait of a woman trapped in an unhappy marriage, who, like MAF herself, has the courage to escape and make an independent life. Compared at times to Mary E. BRADDON on one side of the Atlantic and Emma SOUTHWORTH on the other, she was one of the most popular and successful writers of her day and genre.

Fletcher, Eliza (Dawson), 1770–1858, autobiographer. B. in Yorks, a yeoman's daughter, she was much influenced in childhood by female relations and an unhappily married friend of her dead mother (*née* Hill). On leaving boarding-school she was given £20 to buy books; she wrote for her family a 'sentimental journal' of a Highland tour, 1786. She enlisted 500 subscribers for Ann YEARSLEY, responding to 'a case of direct attempt by the strong to oppress the weak'. In 1791 she married, despite her beloved father's disapproval, the much older Archibald F., advocate and radical sympathizer (who called her 'Sophia' after *Tom Jones*). She had six children. She knew most of the female and male writers in Edinburgh (where she lived) and London; Margaret FULLER left an account of her. Her blank verse *Elidure* and *Edward*, 'historical dramatic sketches' written in 1820, privately printed 1825, show the influence of Joanna BAILLIE and were admired by her, Anne GRANT and Lucy AIKIN. Her surviving daughter published letters from them and others with her autobiography (begun at nearly 68, ending in journal form), Carlisle, 1874; Edinburgh, 1875. See Mona Wilson in essays, 1938, repr. 1966.

Fletcher or de La Flechere, **Mary** (Bosanquet), 1739–1815, Methodist autobiographer, da. of wealthy Anglicans. B. at Leytonstone near London, she cared about prayer at four, clashed with her father over fashionable dress in her teens, and at 21 left home rather than promise not to try to convert her brothers. In lodgings at Hoxton she began a religious revival; back at Leytonstone she founded an orphanage which grew into a religious community. She pub. several evangelical pamphlets: *Jesus, Altogether Lovely* (advice to single Methodist women: 2nd ed. Bristol, 1766); *An Aunt's Advice to a Niece*, 1780, with letters to the condemned forger Dr Dodd; letters (one to John Wesley) on her husband's death in 1785. (He was John F., Swiss-born vicar of Madeley, Yorks.: they m. in 1781, she deeply frightened, but were ideally happy.) Her richest work was pub. by Henry Moore, Birmingham, 1817, as a life: early narrative, later journal entries, it records personal ups and downs and a warm, constant meeting of the needs of others: sweet little seven-year-old thief, confused old woman, middle-aged man who insists on confiding his whole life story.

Flexner, Anne, 1874–1955, playwright, b. Kentucky, da. of Susan (Farnum) and Louis Crawford. She was educ. at Vassar College and after graduation, 1895, returned to Kentucky and supported herself by tutoring. In 1897 she moved to NYC and began writing plays. She m. noted educator Abraham F., 1898, and they had two daughters, one of whom, Eleanor, became historian of women's suffrage in the USA. Seven of AF's plays were produced. Her first successful production, *Miranda of the Balcony*, 1901, received excellent reviews and helped her obtain the rights to Alice Hegan Rice's popular novel *Mrs Wiggs of the Cabbage Patch*, which had a very successful Broadway run in 1904. *The Marriage Game*, 1913, a semi-farce, features a woman who has chosen to live outside conventional marriage, teaching three 'foolish' wives how to 'work' at their marriages.

Florence, Lella (Secor), 1887–1966, journalist, memoirist, activist for peace and for birth-control. She was b. at Battle Creek, Mich., da. of Loretta Reynolds (Sowle) and William Secor, who deserted the family when she was a child. Wanting to write after high school (her mother wanted her to teach), she got a job on the Battle Creek *Journal*. She homesteaded in Coulee, Washington, then in 1915 joined Henry Ford's Peace Ship as a journalist and felt 'the sublime sort of certainty that I shall be able to fight my way, however difficult the obstacles'. Her memoir of this appeared in Julian Bell, ed., *We Did Not Fight: 1914–18 Experiences of War Resisters*, 1935. She m. Philip Sargant F. in 1917 and found it hard to continue her journalism career while raising two sons; when the family moved to England, writes Eleanor Flexner, LSF, despite her working-class background, 'learned to accept servants as a way of life, which gave her back her independence while not, in her own mind at least, causing the loss of any of her democratic ideals'. She wrote two books on birth-control as a means of freeing women, 1930 and 1956; one on her WWII experiences, *My Goodness! My Passport!* 1942; and two 'to tell the plain American American about Britain and British achievement, and the plain Briton about America and American achievement' to serve 'the task of reconstruction' after WWII: *Only an Ocean Between*, 1943, and *Our Private Lives*, 1944. Her daughter-in-law B. M. Florence ed. her *Diary in Letters 1915–1922*, 1978 (foreword by Flexner quoted above).

Flowerdew, Alice, 1759–1830, schoolmistress and poet, sometimes wrongly called Anne. Her work dates from 1779 (written at Lowestoft, Suffolk, her lamented early home); some was written for relief 'under the severe Pressure of Misfortune'. She married in youth the Baptist widower Daniel F. (d. 1801); his government post took them to slave-owning Jamaica, which she left with relief. She wrote thoughtful blank verse, fine hymns, poems to her daughters and stepson, praise of Lady Mary Wortley MONTAGU for her fight to establish smallpox inoculation: collected in *Poems on Moral and Religious Subjects*, 1803, whose many subscribers included Edward Jenner and Sarah AIKIN's mother. AF was then running a school in Islington, London; it moved to Bury St Edmunds between 1806 and 1811, when her third edition added new poems and a preface on female education. Quoting Elizabeth HAMILTON, she argues that women are thought intellectually inferior only because untaught; to remedy this could benefit the human race more than any other step. The curriculum she then sets out is disappointingly limited.

Flynn, Elizabeth Gurley, 1890–1964, political activist and writer, journalist, autobiographer, b. in Concord, NH, da. of Annie (Gurley), an early 'advocate of equal rights for women' who 'rebelled against the endless monotony of women's household tasks', and Thomas F., a stonecutter and often unemployed engineer, both active socialists. She dropped out of school in the Bronx to work for the Industrial Workers of the World. She gave her first speech at 16, to the Harlem Socialist Club, on 'What Socialism will do for Women'. She married labour co-worker John Archibald Jones, 1908, but differences over her role (as wife and political organizer) led to separation, 1910, and divorce, 1920. She had one child. Convinced that 'full opportunity for women to become free and equal citizens with access to all spheres of human endeavor cannot come under capitalism', she joined the Communist Party, 1936, and became its first woman national chair, 1961. Organizing the Lawrence, Mass., textile workers' strike, she met Carlo Tresca, an Italian political activist she lived with, but left for the same reason she had divorced Jones. Throughout her career, she worked for the legal defence of strikers and immigrants threatened with deportation for political activities; she wrote for women's rights: in *Women in the War*, 1942, *Women Have a Date with Destiny*, 1944, and *Women's Place in the Fight for a Better World*, 1947. In 1951 she was arrested under the Smith Act for subversive activities. *The Alderson Story: My Life as a Political Prisoner*, 1963, describes her trial and imprisonment at the women's prison at Alderson, W Va, 1955–7. *I Speak My Piece: Autobiography of 'The Rebel Girl'*, 1955 (repr. as *The Rebel Girl*, 1973), describes her life as US radical and feminist, 1906–26. She died in Moscow, leaving a second autobiographical volume incomplete. She also wrote for the *Daily* and *Sunday Worker*. Most of her papers are at the American Institute for Marxist Studies, NYC. See Corliss Lamont, ed., *Trial of EGF*, 1969, and Joyce Maupin, *Labor Heroines: Ten Women Who Led the Struggle*, 1974.

'Foley, Helen', Helen Rosa (Huxley) Fowler, novelist, b. 1917 at Birkenhead, Cheshire, da. of Olwen (Roberts) and Thomas Hugh H. She was educ. at Newnham, Cambridge (BA, 1939), taught medieval English literature at Cambridge, m. Brigadier-Gen. Arthur Laurence Fowler in 1945 and had three children. She later worked in school examinations and in planning. Her eight novels (from *Between the Parties*, 1958, to *Come to Grief*, 1976) appeared under a name which also belonged to an earlier Newnham student, Helen Foley, 1896–1937, who m. H. A. St George Saunders in 1924 and worked for the League of Nations, whose poems (many written very young) were posthumously published, 1938, and discussed in C. J. Eustace's study of five women's religion and art, *An Infinity of Questions*, 1946. The later HF's novels are small-scale, sensitive explorations of the lives of educated girls and women, including relations between different generations. *The Traverse*, 1960, treats a woman's relationship with her stepchildren; *The Grand-Daughter*, 1965, is a sensitive treatment of an adolescent girl's last year at school. HF and her husband published an anthology about Cambridge, 1984.

Foote, Mary (Hallock), 1847–1938, illustrator, novelist and short-story writer, b. Milton, NY, da. of Ann (Burling) and Nathaniel H., Quakers and farmers. She was educ. at the Poughkeepsie Female Seminary and the Cooper Institute School of Design for Women (later Cooper Union) in NYC. She illustrated such famous works as Longfellow's *Skeleton at the Feast* and Hawthorne's *Scarlet Letter*. In 1876 she m. Arthur De Wint F., civil and mining engineer, and they moved to California. Her first publications, *A California Mining Camp* and *A Sea-Port on the Pacific*, appeared with her own illustrations in *Scribner's*, 1878. Encouraged by H. H. JACKSON, she pub. her first novel, *The Led-Horse Claim*, in 1883, followed by *John Bodewin's Testimony*, 1886, and *The Last Assembly Ball*, 1889, all based upon her experiences in the boomtown of Leadville, Colo. With an increasingly alcoholic husband, she supported the family with her writing and illustrating. Due largely to editorial influence, her novels tended to follow a romance formula. But her semi-autobiographical novel, *The Cup of Trembling*, 1895, catches with grim power the loneliness and desperation of women in frontier society. Isolated in the West and frustrated by her marriage, she wrote to her friend Helena De Kay Gilder in 1887: 'There *is* no *art* for a woman who marries.' She wrote and illustrated 12 novels in all, and four short-story collections. Her *Reminiscences* have been pub. as *A Victorian Gentlewoman in the Far West*, 1972. There is a critical biography by Lee Ann Johnson, 1980. MHF's letters are in Stanford Univ. Library.

Foott, Mary Hannay (Black), 1846–1918, poet, journalist, b. Glasgow, Scotland, da. of Margaret (Grant) and James B., brought to Melbourne in 1853. Educ. at a private school, she trained as a teacher at the Model School and the National Gallery

Art School, then taught from 1862 and began contributing poems and articles to Melbourne newspapers and magazines. In 1874 she m. Thomas F., a stock inspector; she moved to western NSW and later to his Queensland station. There she wrote most of the poems published, a year after her husband's death, in *Where the Pelican Builds*, 1885. The title poem is one of the best-known nineteenth-century bush ballads, though MHF's poetry is much more varied than one would gather from anthologies of Australian verse. She wrote sonnets, *in memoriam* poems on famous people, verse on biblical topics and on local events such as 'The Melbourne International Exhibition'. Her earlier poems were reprinted with some additions in *Morna Lee*, 1890. She also wrote extensively for the *Queenslander*, where she was literary editor for several years from 1887.

Forbes, Esther, 1891–1967, novelist, children's writer, biographer, b. in Westborough, Mass., da. of lawyer and judge William T. F. and Harriette (Merrifield), who wrote local history and studied New England gravestone art. She graduated from Bradford Academy, Haverhill, Mass., 1912, studied writing at the Univ. of Wisconsin, 1916–18, and was a farmhand in Virginia during WWI. Her story 'Breakneck Hill', 1920, won an O. Henry Award. In 1926, she m. lawyer Albert Learned Hoskins. They lived briefly in NYC, but she divorced him in 1933 because he blocked her pursuit of a writing career, and returned to her family home. She wrote eight historical novels, 1926–58. The first, *O Genteel Lady*, 1926, identifies as a major strand in her fiction confrontation with an unrepressed demonic female sexuality. Its heroine runs away to Boston to write and paint. Encouraged by her feminist cousin (in a mentor–protégée relationship which recalls *The Bostonians*), she realizes at a women's meeting that 'Women suddenly hurt her, and she wished to do something for them, but hardly knew what.' She supports herself by writing, has a love-affair in which she learns that her sexuality is not 'evil', but is haunted by images of witches. She visits Salem, sees the gallows, then exorcizes her demons by writing about them. Accused by her cousin of betraying her own talent and the original potency of women, she concludes that 'There is something wrong with women and I can't put my finger on it – only feel it in myself and in others', deciding (as she is accepted into a literary milieu which includes Thoreau and the Alcotts) that 'It is through my children I will now see life.' *A Mirror for Witches*, 1928, recreates the trial of a seventeenth-century New England 'witch-woman', presenting Dolly Bilby, who 'wanted no other God than Lucifer' and for whom 'Hell was her true home', as a rebellious outsider seeking escape from the tyranny of New England divines, such as Cotton Mather (whom her demon lover almost strangles), and refusing to submit to the patriarchal community. The protagonist of *Miss Marvel*, 1935, writes passionately to non-existent lovers. EF's biography, *Paul Revere and the World He Lived In*, 1942 (researched with her mother), won the Pulitzer Prize; her children's novel, *Johnny Tremaine*, 1943, won the Newbery Medal and became a Walt Disney movie. *Mirror* became the basis of a Sadler's Wells ballet, London; the novel *Rainbow on the Road*, 1955, was the basis for a musical, *Come Summer*, 1969. EF was working on a study of witchcraft in New England when she died. Life by Margaret Erskine, 1976. Papers at Clark Univ., Worcester, Mass.

Forbes, Joan **Rosita** (Torr), 1890–1967, TRAVEL writer and novelist, b. at Riseholme Hall, Lincoln, eldest child of Rosita (Graham), who had Spanish blood, and Herbert James T., landowner. As a girl, with a classical education begun by a governess, she had an article on bird life accepted, and drafted but burned a novel. She m. Col. Ronald Foster F., 1911, travelled to India and Australia with him, then divorced. She was twice decorated for ambulance driving in WWI; her first book, *Unconducted Wanderers*, 1919, relates a world tour with a woman friend, from the USA to China, ending on her first meeting with Arabs. That year she left for Cairo; in Palestine over the Easter riots, she went on to Kufra (only once reached by Europeans), disguised as a Muslim woman, 'Khadija'. She took up King Feisal's cause, met Gertrude BELL, and described the trip in *The Secret of the Sahara*, 1921. That year (wearing black for the demise of 'RF') she married Col. Arthur Thomas McGrath, then of the War Office; from a London base, they travelled together and alone. In 1923 RF explored the Atlas mountains and made her first US lecture tour, 'far more exhausting than any amount of desert travel'. She was prolific in both articles and books, in fiction, biography (a sultan, 1924, a pirate, 1948; assorted leaders – Hitler, F. D. Roosevelt, Gandhi – all from personal encounters, 1940) and autobiography: *Gypsy in the Sun*, 1944, and *Appointment with Destiny*, 1946, abridged together as *Appointment in the Sun*, 1949. Her early novels, like *The Jewel in the Lotus*, 1922, provide love, adventure, and significant female friends for heroines who move like RF between fashionable and nomadic society. Later novels are more noteworthy: *One Flesh*, 1930, and *The Extraordinary House*, 1934, for instance, present the complex and contradictory experience of unusual heroines partly through experimental techniques. RF found a new orientation in South America in 1931, was impressed by Russia in 1933, made 'the last of my heedless journeys' in 1934 (S. America), met Sarojini NAIDU in India in 1936, gave official lectures for the War Office in the Caribbean, USA, and Canada, 1940–5, and was strenuously brave in the London blitz. She settled with her husband in the Bahamas, and died in Bermuda, having seen and vividly recreated most of the world. She is the subject of a chapter in Margaret Postgate COLE's *Women of Today*, 1938. See Billie Melman, *Women and the Popular Imagination in the Twenties*, 1988.

Forché, Carolyn (Sidlosky), poet and activist, eldest of seven children of Louise and Michael S., a die-maker. Raised in Detroit, then rural Michigan, she studied languages at Justin Morell College (Mich. State Univ.), graduating the same year as her mother. At 19 she married a man 'deeply scarred' by fighting in Vietnam. After living in the Mohave desert and New Mexico mountains, she celebrated in *Gathering the Tribes*, 1976, her Slovak grandmother ('hands ... like wheat rolls. ... Heavy sweatered winter woman' whose refugee experience – 'When time come / We go quick' – gave CF her 'dark sense that the world is at risk'): also a birth in an Okanogan tipi, nature in many moods and places, tribal rituals, kitchen routines, and a love-encounter with a woman at the sea's edge. Next, with a writing 'block', she turned to translating; in 1977 she visited Spanish poet Claribel Alegría, whose cousin next year persuaded her to take her Guggenheim award to El Salvador ('your country's next Vietnam'): 'do you want to write poetry about yourself the rest of your life?' She 'stayed two years, off and on, back and forth', until 1980, and wrote of it (not as submission of 'art to ideology' but as 'the impassioned voice of witness' to 'a private grief and a dark vision of historical repetition') in poems she thought she might never publish. Margaret ATWOOD helped her to do so, in *The Country Between Us*, 1982: 'You will fight / and fighting, you will die. I will live / and living cry out until my voice is gone / to its hollow of earth.' They evoked both praise and controversy about the relation of poetry and politics; CF is amazed that 'issues which I view as essentially moral and ethical are treated as if they are merely political in the narrowest sense'. She spent years teaching, reading, and reporting (with her husband, a war photographer) from tortured places of the world, writing 'fragments and notes' which never grew to a poem. She returned to the USA from S. Africa to bear her son; she sometimes fears the world may not have 'enough time to finish another book of poems'. She has been seeking ways to avoid the privileging that comes from use of the first person; she has forthcoming a translation, with William Kulik, of poems by Robert Desnos, and a book of six voices, about our century and modern memory, tentatively called *The Angel of History*. See her statements in *TriQuarterly*, 65, 1986, and *The American Poetry Review*, Nov.–Dec. 1988.

Ford, Cathy Diane, poet. B. in 1952 in Lloydminster, Sask., da. of Mary Magdalene (White) and Gerald James F., she m. Dwain Anton Ruckle, 1974, and was educ. at the Univ. of British Columbia (BFA, 1976, MFA, 1978). She has worked as teacher and editor, and co-founded Caitlin Press, Vancouver, 1979, for 'new writers and writing by the labors of love entailed in the works of a small literary press'. She lives on Maine Island, BC. Her poems, ranging from a 'sparse, spare, minimalist style' to jagged lines that fully engage the page, are set predominantly in the lush BC landscape and often become the mythscape of goddesses and women. At once sensuous and meditative – 'structure / of a bone graft / you / touched bone deep / the bleached white thigh of me / they said / must be driftwood' (*Blood Uttering*, 1976) – intimate and political, CF's imagery reflects her ongoing concern with language ('you askt where / is it changing / I said / on the page', *Affaires of the Heart*, 1982) and women's issues. *The Womb Rattles Its Pod Poems*, 1981, beginning with the title line from Sylvia PLATH, includes a series of 'poetic biographies' of women including SAPPHO, George SAND and Zelda FITZGERALD: 'and I choose my pens that way / with admiration / the ink testimony to your beauty'. *By Violent Means*, 1983, expresses her belief that 'writing about crime and violence is the taskwork that needs to be done in women's literature, in our literature as a world literature. This writing is a public work, documentation work; it's a refusal to be silent.' *Saffron, Rose and Flame* was published in 1988. See also Marya FIAMENGO in *CanL*, 101, 1984.

Forman, Charlotte, 1715–87, journalist and letter writer, da. of Mary and Charles F. (he an Irish Jacobite pamphleteer). 'Probus's' knowledgeable, moralizing essays on national and international affairs in various newspapers, 1756–60, are probably hers. Though 'not brought up to any business', she wrote as an exploited professional from 1764, when a supportive brother died. Autobiographical letters to John Wilkes, 1768–70, describe with force and some humour her grinding poverty (prison for debt, 1766–7), ill health, fears of madness, and gruelling anonymous TRANSLATION work (books and foreign news reports). CF calls the Muses jilts and whores who favour only men; she earns less with her pen than she would if skilled with a mop. She sends passionate sentimental reproaches to another, uncaring brother and dignified rebuke to an unhelpful noble patron; she inveighs against the slavery women suffer in marriage. Further 'Probus' essays of 1773–5, sympathetic to American freedom, probably hers, suggest she had become more radical. See Joel J. Gold in *Eighteenth-Century Life*, viii n.s., 1982.

Fornès, Maria Irene, playwright, writing in both English and Spanish, and director. B. in 1930 in Havana, Cuba, da. of Carmen (Collado) and Carlos Luis F., she went to school in Cuba, then migrated with her mother and sister to the USA in 1945, just before the end of WWII. She became a painter at 19 and went to Europe to paint, 1954–7. In Paris she was profoundly influenced by Samuel Beckett's *Waiting for Godot*: 'When I returned from Europe, I started writing.' (She shared an apartment with Susan SONTAG.) She wrote her first play (*Tango Palace*, produced 1963) not out of desire to be a playwright, but out of obsession with an idea, writing steadily for 19 days. Her first produced play was *The Widow*, published in Cuba, 1961. MIF won an Obie Award (she has had several) for the avant-garde *Successful Life of 3* and *Promenade*, both 1965. *Vietnamese Wedding*, produced 1967, and the musical *The Red Burning Light*, produced 1968, protest the Vietnam war. MIF became a founding member of the Women's Theatre Council in 1971; she was President of the New York Theatre Strategy, 1972–9 ('I was the office, the fundraiser, the production co-ordinator, the bookkeeper, the secretary, the everything'). Her chilling, galvanizing *Fefu and Her Friends*, 1977, explicitly debates the place of women in patriarchal culture, powerfully rejecting the political/emotional pattern of woman as victim. It marks a breakthrough to an iconic realism linked by its bareness to surrealism which has given MIF a reputation as a major voice in US drama. Her contributions to INTAR, a NY native Spanish theatre, include *Cap-a-Pie*, 1975, *Lolita in the Garden*, 1977, *Eyes on the Harem*, 1979, and *Sarita*, 1983. *The Danube*, produced 1982, an anti-nuclear play, evokes the unnamed, 'unspeakable horror of nuclear death'. MIF is more interested in female protagonists ('Even women are not aware of how important that is') than feminist statements. *Mud*, 1983, focuses on the struggle for autonomous understanding of the partly literate Mae, *Abingdon Square*, a Women's Project production at the American Place Theatre, 1987, on the sexuality and gender role development of Marion, an American at the turn of the century. MIF has written adaptations of Garcia Lorca, Calderón and Chekhov. Collections include *Four Plays*, 1986, *Plays* (with preface by Susan SONTAG), 1986, and *Promenade and Other Plays*, 1987. Interviews in *PAJ*, 2, 1978, and Betsko and Koenig, 1987 (quoted above); studies by Beverley Byers Pevitts in Helen Krich Chinoy and Linda Walsh Jenkins, eds., *Women in American Theatre: Careers, Images, Movements*, 1981; Bonnie Marranca in *PAJ*, 8, 1984 (quoted above); William Worthen in Enoch Baxter, ed., *Feminine Focus, The New Woman Playwrights*, 1989. Papers at Lincoln Center Library.

Forrest, Helena **Mabel** Checkley (Mills), 1872–1935, poet, novelist, short-story writer, b. Yandilla, near Toowoomba, Queensland, da. of Margaret Nelson (Maxwell) and James Checkley M., station manager. She attended an Anglican school in Parramatta, NSW, for a year but was otherwise taught by her literary mother. In 1901 MF divorced her first husband, John Burkinshaw, for desertion, and turned to writing, sewing, and teaching dancing to support herself and her da. In 1902 she m. John F., but his death in 1921 again forced her to write professionally. Her first volume was the short-story collection *The Rose of Forgiveness*, 1904. Her work appeared in magazines and newspapers, such as the *Age*, which in 1914 originally pub. *The Wild Moth*, 1924, a story of an ingenuous bush girl from Queensland, said to be her best novel. A series of romantic novels appeared between 1914 and 1929, among them *Gaming Gods*, 1926, *Hibiscus Heart*, 1927, and *White Witches*, 1929; while the plots hold interest, the characters remain unconvincing. Her collections of verse include *Alpha Centauri*, 1909, *Streets and Gardens*, 1922, and *Poems*, 1927. A writer of varied talents, she wrote drama and two cantatas (performed in NZ) and won several prizes for her poetry and fiction.

'Forrester, Helen', June or Jamunadevi Bhatia, also 'June Edwards', 'J. Rama', novelist and autobiographer, b. 1919 at Hoylake, Cheshire, eldest of seven children. She left private school early on her middle-class father's bankruptcy. Her four volumes of autobiography (*Twopence to Cross the Mersey*, 1974, *Minerva's Stepchild*, 1979 – later *Liverpool Miss – By the Waters of Liverpool*, 1981, *Lime Street at Two*, 1985) detail her struggle to escape being the unpaid family housekeeper, 'prizing a sliver of soap, a pennyworth of jam', and mourn her mother's 'bright and intelligent mind' stifled first in 'wild, superficial gaiety', then 'disaster'. HF had a classic breakdown at 20, but survived the 'deadly routine of night school [seven years at Liverpool Evening Institute], of being an exact and obedient employee, an inoffensive helper at home'. She married, 1950, Avadh Behari Bhatia, settled in Canada where he was a physics professor, and had a son. Her first novel, *Alien There Is None*, 1959 (repr. as *Thursday's Child*, 1985), and *The Money-Lenders of Shahpur*, 1987, draw on time spent in India; like her other fiction, both depict women striving to balance claims of self, others, and restricting tradition. The protagonist of *Liverpool Daisy*, 1979, supports her extended Irish family and becomes its acknowledged head, or Mam, through rape-initiated prostitution; that of *Yes, Mama*, 1988, escapes by marriage and emigration from sacrificing energy, intellect and emotional life in dutiful care for uncaring parents. HF lives in Edmonton and ed. *The Alberta Diamond Jubilee Anthology*, 1980.

Forrest-Thomson, Veronica, 1948–75, poet and theorist, b. and brought up in Glasgow. She was educ. at Liverpool and Cambridge Univs. (PhD on science in modern poetry), and taught at Cambridge, and elsewhere. Her Cambridge friends included Wendy MULFORD and Denise RILEY. Her poetry volumes or pamphlets are *Identikit*, 1967, *Twelve Academic Questions*, 1970, *Language-Games*, 1971, *Cordelia* (love poems), 1974, and *On the Periphery*, 1976; her critical articles include one on *Tel Quel* in *Language and Style*, 6, 1975. She outlined in *Poetic Artifice*, 1977, the theory which her poems exemplify, stressing poetry's autonomy as a distinct form of utterance. 'To those who kiss in fear that they shall never kiss again / To those that love in fear that they shall never love again / To such I dedicate this rhyme and what it may contain. / None of us will ever take the transiberian train / Which makes a very satisfactory refrain / Especially as I can repeat it over and over again / Which is the main use of the refrain.' By exploring poetry's artificiality, obscurity and irrationality VFT proposes to construct radical new ways of thinking about the world outside the poem. The poet Edwin Morgan, who calls her 'spiky, difficult ... engaging, vulnerable and lonely', valued her part in the Scottish, especially Glaswegian, poetry revival, and commemorated her in a sequence of ten 'Unfinished Poems' (Morgan, *The New Divan*, 1977).

Forshaw, Thelma, short-story writer, book reviewer, b. 1923 at Glebe Point, Sydney, NSW, da. of Mary Winifred (Burke) and Leslie Alfred F. She was educ. at Catholic and state schools in Sydney, then served with the WAAF in WWII before working as a secretary and in advertising. She writes a column for *Quadrant*, as well as frequent book reviews for major newspapers. Her fiction appears in most anthologies of Australian short stories, though she has published only one collection, *An Affair of Clowns*, 1967, which features the autobiographical sketches, 'Some Customs of my Clan'. The title is a good indication of the quirky, humorous eye she turns on many aspects of contemporary Australia.

Forster, Margaret, novelist and critic, b. in 1938 in Carlisle, da. of working-class parents Lilian (Hind) and Arthur George F. She was educ. at Carlisle Girls' High School and Somerville College, Oxford (open scholarship; BA in modern history, 1960). She m. journalist and broadcaster Hunter Davies in 1960, and taught at Barnsbury Girls' School, London, 1961–3. She has three children. Since 1964 she has published 12 novels, beginning with *Dames' Delight* and including the popular success *Georgy Girl*, 1965, later a film. With gentle irony these dissect love, divorce, and the problems inherent in family life, in growing up and growing old. MF turns a sharp eye on the dilemmas of middle-aged women: over their marriages (*Marital Rites*, 1981) and their adolescent children (*Private Papers*, 1986). She has sat on a BBC TV advisory committee, become a Fellow of the Royal Society of Literature, 1975, and been chief non-fiction reviewer for the *Evening Standard* (London), 1977–80. Her several historical and literary studies include *Significant Sisters: The Grassroots of Active Feminism 1839–1939*, 1984 (chapters on Caroline NORTON, Elizabeth Blackwell, Florence NIGHTINGALE, Josephine BUTLER, Elizabeth Cady STANTON, Margaret SANGER, and Emma GOLDMAN). Her life of Elizabeth Barrett BROWNING, 1988, examines the poet's responses to the nineteenth century's crushingly male, and her own limitingly middle-class, culture.

Forster, Mary, 1620?–87, Quaker polemicist, wife of Thomas F. (d. 1660), to whose *Guide to the Blind*, 1671 ed., she wrote a preface. Her style is impassioned exhortation. She composed and signed the address 'To the Reader' published with the text of a PETITION to parliament, 20 May 1659, by women 'against the oppression of Tithes'. She begins 'Friend, it may seem strange to some that women should appear in so publick a manner', but says it is God's way to use 'weak means to bring to pass his mighty work'; 7000 listed names take up 60 pages. She provided 'A Few Words' in an account of the 'young and beautifull' Mary Harris's death-bed conversion, 1669, repr. 1693, and a testimony on Ann WHITEHEAD in *Piety Promoted*, 1686. She tackled persecution of QUAKERS in *Some Seasonable Considerations*, 1684, and prejudice against women in *A Living Testimony from ... Our Faithful Women's Meeting*, 1685, signed by herself and five others: 'we are not to put our Candles under a Bushel, nor to hide our Talents in a Napkin'; 'we which have been Mothers of Children, and Antient Women in our Families, do know, in the Wisdom of God, what will do in Families'.

Foster, Mrs E. M., obscure novelist publishing in London, usually as 'E. M. F.' (14 books known between 1795 and 1810, many for MINERVA); a publisher, copying one of her titles, has confused her with Mrs E. G. BAYFIELD. *The Duke of Clarence*, 1795, presents the fifteenth century in incongruous style. The hero, an illegitimate child advised in youth to seek out and reclaim his unhappy mother, finds it hard to keep his vow to lay down his arms for ever after Bosworth Field. 'Thrice he essayed'; a 'tear fell upon the glittering steel. The hero blushed; and hastily wiped away the clouded moisture.' EMF's technique improved as she turned to modern subjects. *Frederic and Caroline, or the Fitzmorris Family*, dedicated to the Princess of Wales, one of four titles dated 1800, has a scene set in the Minerva CIRCULATING LIBRARY. Her views were conservative: *The Corinna of England*, 1809, wreaks retribution on a travesty of Germaine de STÄEL's heroine.

Foster, Hannah (Webster), 1758–1840, Massachusetts novelist. B. at Salisbury, eldest da. of merchant Grant W., she m., 1785, the Rev. John F. of Brighton. She wrote for periodicals, then scored an immense success with her anonymous, epistolary *The Coquette, or The History of Eliza Wharton*, 'founded on fact', 1797 (13 eds. in 40 years; ed. Cathy N. Davidson, 1986). For generations, comment on it centred on its relation to fact (HWF's husband was by marriage a remote cousin of the real-life victim); this does no justice to its many-angled, perceptive view of a young woman poised between equally rigid 'good' and 'bad' roles. Her high-minded clerical wooer coldly rejects her *before* she allows herself to be seduced, is abandoned, bears a child and dies alone. *The Boarding School, or Lessons of a Preceptress to her Pupils*, 1798, uses non-narrative, didactic letters. The widow Mrs Williams aims to 'domesticate' her pupils through needlework and letter-writing, and warns against the dangers of novel-reading; but each day one of them produces a piece of prose or verse for discussion. HWF's six children included the novelists Eliza CUSHING (with whom as a widow she lived, in Montréal) and Harriet CHEYNEY. See Robert L. Shurter in *AML*, iv, 1932.

Fothergill, Caroline, novelist, younger sister of Jessie FOTHERGILL. CF's work is much less known. Her first novel, *Put to the Proof*, 1883, discomfited reviewers with its heroine who behaved like a man, passionately loving a woman friend and forming a ménage à trois with her and her husband. Its witty literate style belies its apparent sexual naivety. *A Question of Degree*, 1896, tells of a wealthy independent woman who almost marries, but is repelled by her fiancé's mother's obsessively dependent love for her son. *A Matter of Temperament*, 1897, treats a man's impatience at his future wife's putting the needs of her dying sister before his. Most of CF's novels employ Yorkshire settings, a cool tone, and witty dialogue. Her last was pub. in 1898.

Fothergill, Jessie, 1851–91, novelist, b. Manchester, eldest child of Anne (Coultate) and Thomas F., businessman in the cotton trade and former Quaker. She attended private school in Bowdon, and boarding-school in Harrogate. After her father's death in 1866, the family moved to Littleborough, where she loved 'the strange uncouth people, the out-of-the-worldness of it all', material reflected in her first novel, *Healey*, 1875, and in *The Lasses of Leverhouse*, 1878–9. The Lancashire cotton famine of 1863 is the background of *Probation*, 1879, which like *Kith and Kin*, 1881, and *Peril*, 1884, ran serially in *Temple Bar*. Though she lived most of her life within 20 miles of Manchester she spent time abroad, including 15 months in Dusseldorf with her sister Caroline and two friends. There she studied German and began *The First Violin*, 1876, her first successful novel (stage versions were produced after her death). After a trip to the USA in 1884 to recover her failing health, she pub. 'Some American Recollections' in *Temple Bar*, Feb. 1886. Novels also appeared in Indian and Australian journals. Having taught herself Italian, she visited and wrote on Florence, and set her last novel, *Oriole's Daughter*, 1893, in Rome. This tells of an illegitimate daughter's relationship with her Republican father. JF's heroines are strong-minded and socially aware. She is notable as a regional novelist whom contemporary critics compare to the BRONTËS and Elizabeth GASKELL. See the bibliography by Jane Crisp, *VFRG* 2, 1980.

Fowke, Martha, later Sansom, 'Clio', 1690–1736, poet, b. in Herefordshire, da. of a Catholic mother and of army officer Thomas F. (murdered in 1708). With William Bond she wrote the prose and verse *Epistles of Clio and Strephon*, published anonymously by Edmund Curll, 1720 (re-issued under different titles, [1728]–32; repr. 1971). Clio, living in France, is by turns coy, flattering, submissive, manipulative, erotic. She begins the friendship with a poem praising Strephon's work; she says she has an 'unpleasing Person' (from smallpox) and 'Peasant Air'; though she has 'been what *others called beloved*', she now shuns men for solitude and writing. Later, however, she says *he* has inspired her with desire of fame: he urges her to emulate SAPPHO, Aphra BEHN, Katherine PHILIPS; she says she is turning from them to Shakespeare. Other poems appeared in miscellanies or the works of others. MF exchanged compliments with male poets James Thomson, Richard Savage, John Dyer, and Aaron Hill, insults with Eliza HAYWOOD; she praised Mary CHUDLEIGH. Her autobiographical *Clio*, 1752, has a preface dated 1723: it must have circulated in MS, perhaps with erotic material later excised. She married, by 1726, the wealthy

Arnold S. of Leics. See Karen E. Davis in *ELN*, 1986.

Fowler, Constance (Aston), letter writer and collector of MS verse, one of the large, literary Roman Catholic family of Gertrude (Sadleir), godmother to Anne HALKETT, and Sir Walter, later Lord A., of Tixall, Staffs. (patron of Michael Drayton). She was in Spain as a child, 1620–5. Betrothed in 1629 to Walter F., d. 1681, of nearby St Thomas's Priory, she m. him when of age, and left four children. *Tixall Letters*, 1815, prints her letters to her brother Herbert (from 1636, some carried to Spain by Ann FANSHAWE's future husband), which juggle dexterously with conceits like that of exchanged hearts. The most striking extols her future sister-in-law Katherine ASTON: 'ther was never any more passionat afectionat lovers then she and I'; 'you never knew two cretures more truely and deadly in love'; 'Never creture lov'd two with more aquell afection then I dote on you both.' The relationship grew, as she relates, largely through letters now apparently lost.

Fowler, Ellen Thorneycroft (later Felkin), 1860–1929, poet and novelist, elder da. of Ellen (T.) and Sir Henry Hartley Fowler, Wesleyan MP and 1st Viscount Wolverhampton. Her sister, Edith Henrietta Hamilton, also wrote novels, and a biography of their father, 1912. ETF began her writing career with *Verses Grave and Gay*, 1891, followed by *Verses Wise and Otherwise*, 1895, but was best known for her novels: *Concerning Isabel Carnaby*, 1898, *A Double Thread*, 1899, and *The Farringdons*, 1900, which won popular, if not critical, acclaim for their lively and piquant style. Unusually combining themes of Methodism and high life, her novels are mostly conventional romances, with a strong heroine who, though converted and repentant, still keeps a sophisticated, half-flippant tone. In 1903 ETF left home to marry Alfred Felkin, schoolmaster. *Miss Fallowfield's Fortune*, 1908, shows a serious concern for the lot of single women not evident in a later work, *Her Ladyship's Conscience*, 1913, which, in presenting the unconventional case for love between a younger man and older woman, earned her writing a feminist reputation. She was a member of the Writers' Club, the Women's Athenaeum Club, and a Fellow of the Royal Society of Literature.

Fox, Caroline, 1819–71, diarist and letter writer, b. at Falmouth, Cornwall, one of five children of Quakers Maria (Barclay), a very pious woman, and Robert Were F., a successful scientific inventor and amateur geologist. Educ. at home, surrounded by some of the most progressive thinkers of the day, such as J. S. Mill, John Sterling, Jane Welsh CARLYLE and Thomas C.; she also knew Elizabeth Fry, Wordsworth, and Hartley Coleridge. Her lively journals (extracts ed. Horace N. Pym, 1882; repr. 1972, ed. Wendy Monk) contain accounts of her varied travels, acquaintances and friends, and of her spiritual life (though struggles with religious doubt were censored by Pym). She termed herself a 'Quaker-Catholic' (meaning an inclusive Quaker). Some of her comments are extremely candid. She taught and cared for the poor ('My mind, I fear, is a Republic') and gives a full account of hearing Clara BALFOUR speak, in 1849, on women's topics. Widely read, she admired Emerson and Elizabeth GASKELL in particular. See Robert J. Tod, 1980.

Frame, Elizabeth, Eliza, 1820–1913, author of fiction, local history, poetry, sketches. She was b. in Shubenacadie, NS, da. of Janet (Sutherland) and John F. After studying at J. S. Thompson's private school, Halifax, Truro Academy, and Normal School (Truro), she taught school for 38 years. Her *Descriptive Sketches of Nova Scotia in Prose and Verse*, 1864, published as 'by a Nova Scotian', are colourful stories of the landscape and events and figures of the past. She contributed widely to newspapers and periodicals; the *Halifax Herald* printed her essays, 'Pioneer Heroines of the Past', June 1897, and papers to the Nova Scotia and Massachusetts Historical Societies. *The Twilight of Faith*, 1871, is a short, admonitory fiction written chiefly as a journal and letters: it urges pious acceptance of a husband's death. *A List of Micmac Names of Places, Rivers, etc. in Nova Scotia*, 1892, compiled with the assistance of a Micmac Indian, gives pronunciations and meanings.

Frame, Janet Paterson, novelist, short-story writer, poet, b. 1924 in Dunedin, NZ, da. of Lottie Clarice (Godfrey) and George Samuel F., railwayman. Third child of five, of whom two sisters drowned in separate accidents in their adolescence, she was educ. at small South Otago and Southland towns, the first of the children to reach high school. Her mother idolized Katherine MANSFIELD and wrote poems, stories and songs – 'in my family writing was an accepted pastime'. In 1943 she went to Dunedin Teachers College and attended univ. courses in English, French and psychology. She walked out of the classroom in her first year of teaching, never to return. In 1947 she voluntarily entered Seacliff Psychiatric Hospital, and remained in psychiatric hospitals for the next eight years. *The Lagoon*, containing stories of childhood faced with the incomprehensibility and threat of adult life, was pub. in 1951. *Owls Do Cry*, 1957, is a poetic re-creation of her childhood. The narrator Daphne rebels against her parents' marriage, its extinction of her mother as a person, and the sterility of materialistic NZ society. In 1957 JF left NZ on a State Literary Fund grant, visited Ibiza, and lived in London where doctors confirmed that she was not in fact schizophrenic. *Faces in the Water*, 1961, is a fictionalized account of her time in NZ mental hospitals. After this her novels and stories move increasingly into the 'room two inches behind the eyes' – symbolic poetic works of loneliness, tragedy, fantasy and dream which have little to do with being a woman or being a New Zealander. A series of novels from the 1960s, including *The Edge of the Alphabet*, 1962, *Scented Gardens for the Blind*, 1963, *The Adaptable Man*, 1965, *The Rainbirds*, 1968 and *Intensive Care*, 1970, examine the place of death, violence and war, including nuclear war, in contemporary society, while experimenting with different narrative voices and modes. Woman's fear is powerfully imaged in *A State of Siege*, 1967. JF turned to North American settings with *Daughter Buffalo*, 1972, and *Living in the Maniototo*, 1979, exploring the role of the writer and the relationship between life and fiction. During the 1970s she worked at the Yaddo Foundation and the McDowell Colony in the USA – 'it was a rich experience for me to feel for the first time in my life among my own kind'. She has pub. 12 novels, three collections of short stories, and a vol. of poetry, *The Pocket Mirror*, 1967. Only since the publication of her three vols. of autobiography, *To the Island*, 1982, *An Angel at my Table*, 1984 and *The Envoy from Mirror City*, 1985, has she received much public recognition in NZ. They give a realistic, lucid and very readable account of the loneliness, despair and final success of an unusual and unworldly girl and woman in NZ and England. Returning to fiction in *The Carpathians*, 1988, JF also returns to many earlier preoccupations, particularly the function of memory, language and the imagination in a consumerist society. For critical discussion see Patrick Evans, 1971 and 1977, and Jeanne Delbaere, 1978.

'Franc, Maud Jeanne', Matilda Jane Evans (Congreve), 1827–86, novelist, b. Peckham Park, Surrey, elder da. of Henry C., schoolmaster. Orphaned, she was left to support the family soon after their voyage to South Australia in 1852. She worked as a governess, then opened her own school where she wrote *Marian, or the Light of Some One's Home*, 1861. Other novels featuring life in the Australian bush are *Emily's Choice*, 1867, and *John's Wife*, 1874. She m. Baptist minister Ephraim Evans in 1860, but his death three years later again left her with young children to support through teaching. In 1868 she became a Baptist deaconess, and devoted herself to writing and religious work, publishing 14 novels as well as many short stories and articles. Her books, such as *Minnie's Mission: An Australian* TEMPERANCE *Tale*, 1869, contained strong moral and religious messages and were favoured for Sunday School prizes.

France, Ruth Helena (Henderson), 'Paul Henderson', 1913–68, NZ novelist, poet, short-story writer, b. Leithfield, Canterbury, da. of Helena (Hayes) and Francis H. (Her mother wrote many unpub. stories and plays, and pub. essays, poems and stories in local papers.) Educ. at Christchurch Girls' High School, she worked as a librarian until in 1934 she m. Arnold F.; she had two sons. She pub. two vols. of poetry, *Unwilling Pilgrim*, 1955, and *The Halting Place*, 1961, both as Paul Henderson. Both looked at the idea of life as imprisonment, and the theme of impermanence. Critics at the time suggested that the male pseudonym led to her success in poetry, and gave it a freedom from 'poetess mannerisms'. Her first novel *The Race*, 1958, breaks from the NZ tradition of writing about 'Man Alone' to writing about New Zealanders as 'creatures of small groups'. It alternates between the struggle for survival of a yacht crew in a storm, and the experiences and emotions of the group of women waiting for them. *Ice Cold River*, 1962, sets the emotional turmoil in a family gathered to celebrate Christmas against the fury and destructiveness of a river in flood. A third novel, *The Tunnel*, remained unpublished at her death.

'Frances, Sophia', pseudonym (unlikely to be either the prolific Francis Lathom or a Sophia L. Frances: gender not certain). 'Her' four 'romances' (three for MINERVA), set in Continental Europe, portray tortured family relationships. The Neopolitan hero of *Vivonio, or The Hour of Retribution*, by a 'Young Lady', 1806, supposedly murdered (with his mother) as a baby, 'flourishe[s] like the flower in the sequestered glade, cherished by the Universal Parent', to reap ideal happiness at last with his sister and their spouses. The heroine's father in *The Nun of Miserecordia, or The Eve of all Saints*, 1807, is murdered in revenge for seduction; that in *Angelo Guicciardini, or The Bandit of the Alps*, 1809, turns out himself to be the bandit. In each, virtue triumphs over revenge, violence and terrors.

Francis, Anne (Gittins), 1738–1800, scholar and poet, da. of Jane (Sapp) and the Rev. Daniel G. of South Stoke, Arundel, Sussex, who fed her 'rip'ning genius' with Latin, Greek and Hebrew. When very young she wrote on Frederick the Great, but gave up verse on her father's death. Having m. the Rev. Robert Bransby F. of Edgefield, Norfolk, she pub. by subscription, with her name, 1781, a powerful Pindaric translation of the *Song of Solomon*, with scholarly notes and a preface which foresees that this 'may perhaps be thought an *improper* undertaking for a *woman*'. *The Obsequies of Demetrius Poliorcetes*, 1785, re-tells Plutarch's story of a hero's ashes making a triumphal sea progress home to Greece, with lavish description – flowers, gems, sky, sea – and evocation of history, geography, and battles (footnotes provided) in couplets with artfully interspersed lyric measures. In *Charlotte to Werther. A Poetical Epistle*, 1787, written to follow the lovers' last meeting, Charlotte prays for the return of Reason: AF defends Goethe's work, with some evasions, against mounting criticism (see Syndy M. Conger in *Goethe Yearbook*, 3, 1986). *Miscellaneous Poems*, 1790, adds another *Werther* piece to odes, elegies, and praise of AF's mother, sister, sons and Elizabeth ROWE. She pub. a ballad on fears of a French invasion, 1798.

'Francis, M. E.', Mary Blundell (Sweetman), *c.* 1858–1930, novelist and story writer, b. in Ireland, da. of Michael James S. of Lamberton Park, Queen's Co., educ. by governesses, then masters at Brussels. With her sisters Eleanor and Agnes (later Castle, d. 1922, who pub. sentimental romances), she wrote a family periodical, and later contributed to the *Irish Monthly*. In 1879 she m. Francis Nicholas B. (d. 1884), of a well-known Lancashire Catholic family, and settled at Crosby, Lancs., later moving to Dorset, and writing mostly regional novels of farming communities. Her first success came with the selection of *A Daughter of the Soil*, 1895, to open a new series of novels in *The Times Weekly*. Over 20 titles appeared by Mary Blundell 1886–1928; but many more under her pseudonym, adopted from 1892. *Fiander's Widow*, 1901, depicts a young widow wooing her elderly husband's friend for the sake of the farm, which she can't work alone. Close observations of country customs, mixed with dialect and sentiment, inform books like *Dorset Dear*, 1905 and *Mossoo*, 1927, though *The Story of Mary Dunne*, 1913, ventures into the white slave trade theme.

Frankau, Pamela, 1908–67, novelist, journalist, short-story writer, memoirist, granddaughter of Julia Frankau ('Frank DANBY'): younger da. of Dorothea (Drummond-Black) and novelist Gilbert F., who wanted sons. They divorced and she grew up in Windsor, Berks., an Anglican with Jewish blood. In *I Find Four People*, 1935, she depicts earlier selves (a favourite theme), beginning with the naive, ambitious Sussex boarding-school pupil. By 16 she had drafted a novel about a 'lady tennis-champion'; one with her father as villain was abandoned, and two more rejected. She declined a university place and, after a year at home writing, worked in journalism and advertising. *Marriage of Harlequin*, 1927, written on commuter trains, was a runaway success. Its boyish novelist-heroine reclaims her scapegrace husband when he reads of her love in a self-revealing novel. PF was likened to Michael Arlen and befriended by Rebecca WEST. About 30 more titles aim with varying success at greater depth; most draw on her own life, especially *Letters from a Modern Daughter to her Mother* (written 1928, serialized, book form 1931). From 1931 PF was the lover of poet and civil servant Humbert Wolfe (d. 1940). Her *Jezebel*, 1937 (first woman in a series of biblical lives), vividly realizes (more from imagination than research) the 40-year ruler of Israel who is wrongly labelled a harlot. *A Democrat Dies*, 1939 (*Appointment with Death* in the US), deals with fathers and sons, and a secret society fighting fascism and Communism. PF rose from private to major in WWII, became a Roman Catholic in 1942, and in 1945 married Marshall Dill, Jr (later divorced). Her only child died a baby. Her biggest earner in the USA (where she lived seven years) was 'The Duchess and the Smugs', a *Harper's* story which later opened *A Wreath for the Enemy*, 1954, repr. 1988. She often juxtaposes countries, nationalities, and conflicting identities. The protagonist of *The Willow Cabin*, 1949, repr. 1988, on the point of maturity and stage success, falls consumingly in love with an older man; after his death she turns towards his widow. *The Offshore Light*, 1952 (pub. as 'Eliot Naylor'), centres on a 'mad' political idealist and his fantasy post-atomic society. *Pen to Paper, A Novelist's Notebook*, 1961, discusses writing technique and PF's life, notably her dealings with her father. Her CND leaflet *Letter to a Parish Priest* [1962] attacks the atomic bomb. *Slaves of the Lamp*, 1965, and its sequel *Over the Mountains*, 1967, both end in WWII. *Colonel Blessington*, 1968 (finished from PF's MSS by her novelist cousin Diana Raymond), presents a mystery figure discovered (once dead) to have been a woman.

Franken, Rose (Lewin), later Meloney, POPULAR short-story writer, novelist and playwright, b. ?1895 at Gainesville, Texas, youngest child of Hannah (Younker) and Michael L. Her mother, almost an invalid from her birth, soon decamped with her children to her native NYC; RF adored her largely absent and heavily criticized father. At 17 she enrolled at Barnard College, but next day m. Dr Sigmund Walter Anthony F., who almost at once fell ill with tuberculosis. They had three sons. Her first story, written at 19 (rejected by *Good Housekeeping*, which 20 years later paid $5,000 for it, unrevised), deals with two old ladies observed at a shop window. Her chatty, self-deprecating autobiography, *When All is Said and Done*, 1962, ascribes all her early success to luck and her husband; in 1969 she wrote that she began as an intellectual writer but quickly became 'too readable and coherent' for critics. Her first novel, *Pattern*, 1925, a bestseller, was a study of psychoanalysis. Her first play, *Fortnight*, 1926, was rejected; *The Hallam Wives*, produced 1929, became the hit *Another Language*, 1932. (Her last play, *The Hallams*, 1949, returns to the same family.) Widowed in 1933, she m. William Brown Meloney in 1937; they wrote filmscripts and magazine serials together; she was prolific in stories. Her heroine in *Of Great Riches*, 1937 (*Gold Pennies* in UK), finds happiness in renouncing literary success to please her would-be masterful husband. Her Claudia, who begins as 'a little nobody from Virginia', eager for her Ivy League spouse to tell her what to do and think, developed from story to novel, 1939, play, 1941, two films, and omnibus embodying eight retooled novels, 1962. RF's work celebrates the joys of marriage; the best acknowledges too its problems and constraints. The maternal relationship is also important, usually as a threat. *Twice Born*, 1935 (withdrawn in the UK, revised 1969 with RF's introduction), traces a bisexual male musician to the point at which his wife leaves him. RF directed her own plays, published as 'Margaret Grant' and 'Franken Meloney', and was much translated. MSS at Columbia.

Franklin, Stella Maria Sarah **Miles**, 1879–1954, novelist and feminist, b. Talbingo, NSW, eldest child of Margaret Susannah (Lampe) and John F., of Brindabella Station. She was educ. at home and at Thornford Public School. Her precocious first novel, *My Brilliant Career*, 1901 (with a preface by Henry Lawson), brought instant notoriety even though its strongest criticisms of religion, marriage and the place of women in Victorian society had been toned down by the publisher. He also omitted the question mark after 'Brilliant' and, against her wishes, revealed that the novel had been written by a young girl rather than a man. Consequently, it was read as autobiography and many of MF's friends and relatives were offended by it. Its success, however, led to her being taken up by Sydney literary and feminist circles, and to friendships with Joseph Furphy, Rose SCOTT, and Vida GOLDSTEIN. After a literary liaison with the poet Banjo Paterson, in 1906 she left for the USA, where she worked with Alice HENRY for the National Women's Trade Union League until 1915. In 1909 she pub. *Some Everyday Folk and Dawn* (repr. 1986 with useful intro. by Jill Roe), a novel showing increased awareness of feminist issues. Despite her anti-war sentiments, she served as a nurse in the WWI Serbian campaign. Returning to Australia in 1927, she began publishing her chronicle novels of pioneering days under the male pseudonym 'Brent of Bin Bin'. Six eventually appeared in this series, and a further five novels under her own name, including the sequel to *My Brilliant Career*, *My Career Goes Bung*, 1946, originally rejected because of its satirical portraits of literary figures such as Paterson. A later satirical work, *Pioneers on Parade*, 1939, was written with Dymphna CUSACK. An ardent nationalist, MF actively promoted Australian literature and published two critical works, *Joseph Furphy* (with Kate Baker), 1944, and *Laughter, Not for a Cage* (posthumously), 1956. She left her estate to found a prize for Australian fiction, the now prestigious

Miles Franklin Award. Works published posthumously include an autobiography, *Childhood at Brindabella*, 1963, and an early novel, *On Dearborn Street*, 1981. Her MSS, including many unpublished novels and plays, are held in the Mitchell Libary, Sydney. See the good introductory account of her life and work by Marjorie BARNARD, 1967; Verna Coleman, 1981, for her years in America; Colin Roderick, 1982, is a misogynist study.

Fraser, Lady **Antonia** (Pakenham), biographer, historian and novelist, b. in 1932, eldest da. of Elizabeth (Harman) – author, as Elizabeth Longford, of lives of Queen VICTORIA and others – and of Francis Aungier P., Labour MP, later Lord Longford. She was educ. (like Naomi MITCHISON) at the Dragon [boys'] School, Oxford, at Catholic and Anglican girls' schools and Lady Margaret Hall, Oxford (BA in history, 1963). She worked in publishing, wrote children's books on King Arthur and Robin Hood, m. Hugh F., wealthy Conservative politician, in 1956, and had six children. Her *Mary, Queen of Scots*, 1969, a full, sound and lively biography, was a best-seller; lives of other rulers followed. In 1977 AF was divorced, and published a mystery novel, *Quiet as a Nun*: TV reporter returns to the convent of her schooldays to investigate a murder. Her series detective, Jemima Shore, pleasingly if improbably combines expensive elegance, social concern, and unusual sexual independence. She appears in four more novels (up to *Your Royal Hostage*, 1987, about animal rights kidnappers and a princess), TV series, 1978 and 1983, and short stories, 1986. AF has edited anthologies, written TV plays, and served literary public life, lately working against apartheid with the British PEN club. She m. Harold Pinter in 1980. She looks at women's HISTORY in *The Weaker Vessel*, 1984 (a detailed, accessible overview of every kind of seventeenth-century woman, including writers), and *Boadicea's Chariot: The Warrior Queens*, 1988 (those women who have, exceptionally, wielded power).

Fraser, Gilly or Gillian (Emmett), playwright, b. in 1940 at Hunslet, Leeds, da. of working-class Olga (Blacker) and George Stanley E. She left West Leeds Girls' High School at 16 to work with Esmee Church's Northern Theatre School, 1956–7. After a scholarship to the Guildhall School of Music and Drama, London, 1958–60, she acted in repertory and on TV, playing 'dumb dollies' (she was in Nell DUNN's *Up the Junction*). At 30, married with two children, she began courses in English and script-writing, and since 1973 has had work regularly on TV, radio and stage. 'You write what it feels like to be that dumb dolly and you write for the women who haven't been written for'; 'The people I want to reach most ... wouldn't dream of going to the theatre.' Her first play was *A Quick Visit Home*, about tensions between mother, married daughter and career-girl daughter after father's funeral (Manchester radio; pub. in A. Bradley and A. Leake, eds., *Family Circles*, 1984). Other radio plays include the early *Playmates* (a bunny finds liberation), *Bracelet*, 1980, and *Somewhere Else*, 1983. GF wrote episodes for popular 1980s TV series (*Angels*, on nurses 'as they really are', and *East Enders*, on Cockneys of various races); also for TV was *Not For the Likes of Us*, 1980, about a 40-year-old, 14-stone working-class woman 'finding joy' and the riches of her own mind. GF's *Do a Dance for Daddy*, 1976, and *A Bit of Rough*, 1977, appeared at the Soho Poly, London, and *I Can Give You a Good Time*, 1981, at the Royal Court. *Blame it on the Boogie*, 1980, and *Domestic Affair*, 1981, are for young people.

Fraser, Mary (Crawford), 'Mrs Hugh Fraser', 1851–1922, novelist, travel writer and autobiographer, b. Rome, da. of US sculptor Thomas C.; she had one sister, Marion, also a novelist. Educ. at Bonchurch by Elizabeth SEWELL and in Rome, she later

m. a diplomat, Hugh F. and accompanied him to China, South America and Japan; after his death, 1894, she lived in Italy. She drew on her travels for exotic settings of novels which are conventionally romantic. In *The Looms of Time*, 1898, set in South America, the heroine, Gilda, must be rescued by the hero from a cave in which she has been trapped by her brother, an archetypal villain, who turns out luckily not to be related to her at all. In *Marna's Mutiny*, 1901, set in Japan, Marna's objections to her father's remarriage dissolve when she falls in love herself. Other novels are *Palladia*, 1896, and *The Splendid Posenna*, 1899. The TRAVEL and autobiographical writings are more interesting. In *A Diplomatist's Wife in Japan*, 1899, she records her three-year residence in Japan in the form of letters, and sensitively details her own reactions to cultural difference. *Storied Italy*, 1915, written from a woman's point of view, is equally impressive in the way it moves between inner and outer reality. Other travel books include *A Diplomatist's Wife in Many Lands*, 1911, and *Further Reminiscences of a Diplomatist's Wife*, 1912.

Fraser, Sylvia (Meyers), novelist, b. 1935 in Hamilton, Ont., da. of Gladys (Wilson) and steel inspector George Nicholas M. Her childhood (from six) and teenage years were warped by paternal incest which her memory wholly suppressed. Markedly successful at school, she took her BA at the Univ. of Western Ont., 1957, worked for the *Toronto Star Weekly*, 1957–68, and m. lawyer Russell James F. in 1959 (divorced 1977). Her first novel, *Pandora*, 1972, traces a working-class girl in wartime Hamilton ('Steeltown') from birth to nearly eight, relating the family (rage-driven father, long-suffering hymn-singing mother) to social, sexual and international political structures. Its total recall (on one level) of childhood events was noted and admired. SF further anatomized gender relations in *The Candy Factory*, 1975, and *A Casual Affair: A Modern Fairytale*, 1978, whose unnamed heroine, herself a tale-teller, finds her own love-affair a bitter parody of fairy story. After *The Emperor's Virgin*, 1980, about an ancient Roman woman buried alive for breaking her vow of chastity, SF shifted her scene to Germany of 1923–45 in *Berlin Solstice*, 1984, whose male protagonist becomes important in the SS and Gestapo, a destroyer of Jews. Though a work of imagination, it adheres closely to a historical record which makes, says SF, 'the seemingly most far-fetched incidents and dialogue ... the most authentic'. SF's father's death in 1984 gradually opened her mind to her own past. *My Father's House: A Memoir of Incest and Healing*, 1987 (begun as fiction, bravely recast as AUTOBIOGRAPHY which she felt might be her last book), relates her own division into the Girl Who Knows and the Girl Who Doesn't Know, and marks recently recovered memories by italics.

Fraser-Tytler, Christiana Catherine, Mrs Edward Liddell, 1848–1927, poet and novelist, b. in Morayshire, da. of Harriet Jane (Pretyman) and Scottish landowner Charles Edward F-T, ex-Indian Civil Service. She was educ. at home, but visited Germany and Italy with her sister Mary in 1870, after her father's second marriage. In 1869, CF-T had published *Sweet Violet*, a book of short stories and poems illustrated by her other sister, Margaret. In 1870 she pub. *A Rose and a Pearl*, partly set in the Tyrol, which treats the suffering of a peasant girl after the thoughtless attention of a young Englishman. Her best-known work was *Jasmine Leigh*, 1871, about the abduction, forced marriage and effective rape of a saintly 16-year-old heiress, strongly protested by her free-thinking governess, who calls it 'murder'. In Rome, CF-T met Edward Thomas L., whom she married in 1871 (no children, which she regretted); in 1876 he gave up his comfortable Cambridgeshire living to accept a poor parish at Jarrow, leading to years of difficulties for both of them. She added, or used alone, 'Mrs Edward Liddell' for her poetry and other works, but retained her maiden name for her novels. *Margaret*, 1872, tells of an artist who sacrifices her career to the demands of a selfish brother: *Mistress Judith*, 1873, and *Jonathan*, 1876, both employ local dialects and deal with working people. *Making or Marring*, 1879, her last novel, treats the dilemma of the idle middle-class woman. In 1881 CF-T pub. a poetry collection, *Songs in Minor Keys*, mainly religious or pastoral, and *The Other Half of the World*, stories of her experiences among Jarrow parishioners. Her later works include a biography of her husband, 1916.

Freeman, Gillian, novelist and miscellaneous writer, b. 1929 in London, da. of Freda (Davids) and Jack F. Educ. at Reading Univ. (BA in English and philosophy, 1951), she worked as copywriter, teacher, reporter and literary secretary. In 1955 she turned to full-time writing and m. Edward Thorpe: they had two daughters. *The Liberty Man*, 1955, repr. 1986, a story of a love-affair, established her interest in matters of class. Nine more novels highlight issues like young male homosexuality (*The Leather Boys*, 1961, as 'Eliot George'; filmed with GF's script, 1963), high-pressure fund-raising for churches (*The Campaign*, 1963), a racist, populist 'Britain First Party' (*The Leader*, 1965), abortion and anti-Semitism repeatedly. *The Alabaster Egg*, 1970, intercuts the story of a young, Jewish, socialist woman in 1930s Munich and her careerist, Nazi-sympathizing lover, with the diary of his uncle who, just as unwisely, loved Ludwig of Bavaria. Diaries figure in later novels: *Nazi Lady*, 1978 (*The Confessions of Elisabeth von Stahlberg* in the US, wrongly taken at first for non-fiction), and *An Easter Egg Hunt*, 1981, where a diary belatedly reveals the cause (death after an abortion) for which a French refugee teacher vanished in WWI. *Termination Rock*, 1989, is a psychological study flirting with the supernatural. GF has written plays for the stage, radio and TV, ballet scenarios (including *Isadora*, 1981), and non-fiction (*The Undergrowth of Literature*, 1967, on pornography; a life of Angela BRAZIL, 1976). MSS at Reading Univ.

Freeman, Mary Eleanor (**Wilkins**), 'Mary E. Wilkins', 1852–1930, short-story writer, novelist and children's poet, b. Randolph, Mass., da. of Eleanor (Lothrop) and Warren E. W., builder. She was educ. at Brattleboro High School, Mt Holyoke Seminary and Mrs Hosford's Glenwood Seminary. Her lifelong friend, Evelyn Sawyer, shared her love of literature, especially the work of S. O. JEWETT. In 1902 she m. Charles M. F., business manager; she lived in Metuchen, NJ, until her death. In 1921 they were legally separated. She concentrated on adult fiction after her first adult story won a prize from the Boston *Sunday Budget* in 1882. Her stories and novels are concerned with relationships between women. Many of her characters never find love with men, but live contentedly, apparently passionlessly, with other women or alone. Her first two collections, *A Humble Romance*, 1887, and *A New England Nun*, 1891, established her reputation as an acute observer of rural life, particularly from a female point of view, but the universality of her themes makes her more than a 'local-colorist'. Her most famous story, 'The Revolt of Mother' (*A New England Nun*), has as protagonist an oppressed wife, Sarah Penn, who eventually asserts her will against her husband and wins. MWF's insight into the pressures of feminine life is starkly manifest in 'Old Mother Magoun' (*The Winning Lady*, 1909), a forceful and heart-rending comment on the degeneracy of men and the desperation of women. Her novels *Jane Field*, 1893, *Pembroke*, 1894 and *The Portion of Labor*, 1901, also explore the dilemma of women without men in the late nineteenth century, but her perceptive and telling portrayal of the constricted, unfulfilled but stoic lives of women is best seen in her stories. Her letters are at Columbia Univ., the Univ. of Virginia and the NYPL. See Edward Foster, 1956, for her life, and Josephine Donovan's feminist study in *New England Local Color Lit.*, 1983.

Freke, Elizabeth (Freke), 1641–1714, autobiographer and poet, eldest da. of royalists Cecily (Culpeper) and Ralph F.: sister of Frances NORTON; godmother of Grace GETHIN. B. in London, she was brought up chiefly in Kent (by an aunt after her mother died in 1650). In 1671, after seven years' courtship (letters from it destroyed), she m. an Irish second cousin, Percy F., 'withoutt my deer Fathers Consentt or knowledg, In A most dreadfull Raynie day, A presager of all my sorrows & Misfortunes'. In the next two years Percy F. issued a duel challenge and was cheated out of £1500; they were on bad terms in 1682; she was more often in Norfolk without him than with him at Rathbarry in Ireland. She wrote many letters and journals, mentioning a 'Brown Book' and 'my White Vellum Book of Remembrances'. After his death (1706: they were by then happy together but at odds with their only son) she compiled an autobiography which becomes fuller for her widowed years, with copies of letters (a row with her bishop ended in excommunication, 1714), accounts, inventories (including books), recipes, and four poems (three of them dialogues of great dramatic verve, one between Eve and the serpent). Pub. as *Diary*, Cork, 1913.

French, Lucy Virginia (Smith), 1825–81, poet, novelist and editor, b. in Accomac County, Va., da. of Elizabeth (Parker) and Mease W. S., educator and lawyer. After her mother's death, LVF and her sister lived with their grandmother in Washington, Pa., and were educ. at Miss Hannah's school. Unhappy with their father's second wife, the sisters moved in 1844 to Memphis, Tenn., where they both taught. LVF's first published work appeared in the *Louisville Journal* under 'L'Inconnue'. In 1852 she became associate editor of the *Southern Ladies' Book* and the following year she m. John Hopkins F., a wealthy stockman, who had been attracted to her because of her poetry and who encouraged her in her career. From 1856–79 she was literary editor of various journals: *The Crusader, Ladies' Home Journal* and *Southern Literary Messenger*. She also pub. two books of poems, *Wind Whispers*, 1856 and *Legends of the South*, 1867; a blank-verse tragedy, *Istalilxo, the Lady of Tula*, 1856; and two novels, *My Roses: The Romance of a June Day*, 1872 and *Darlingtonia*, 1879, which are of interest for their exploration of women's lives, including a prostitute's in *My Roses*. LVF occasionally wrote isolated passages in both her poetry and prose which depict suffering womanhood, e.g., the mother of the lost child who raises 'the cry of Woman / . . . the *really* lost and wandering soul' ('The Lost Soul' in *Legends of the South*); yet her heroines also embody the traditional female of nineteenth-century sentimental fiction. Istalilxo states, 'The empire I crave is one sweet home / With two hearts dwelling in it: I do not seek / *To sway but one, for that is all the world.*'

French, Marilyn (Edwards), 'Mara Solwoska', fiction writer, scholar and social critic. B. 1929 in NYC, da. of Isabel (Hazz) and E. C. E., she worked her way through Hofstra College (BA and MA, 1951, 1964), choosing English with some regret for philosophy (she sees herself as more a philosophical than a political feminist). She m. Robert M. F., Jr, in 1950 and supported him through law school. MF wrote seriously from 1957 but was almost unpublished; she read Simone de BEAUVOIR in 1958, and taught at Hofstra 1964–8. Divorced in 1967, she received her PhD from Harvard in 1972, with a thesis on James Joyce which became her first book, 1976. *The Women's Room*, 1977, a hugely popular bestseller, uses a narrative voice with a mediumistic quality to tell the jostling composite story (which 'has no ending') of many women who studied together at Harvard: televised 1980. *The Bleeding Heart*, 1980, continues this narrative voice, dwelling on the traditional, societally induced role of women as sufferers grieving for humankind (men, 'legitimate' bearers of anger and power, are relatively exempt from the burden of suffering). These themes receive further treatment in MF's scholarly *Shakespeare's Division of Experience*, 1981, which also examines his 'horror at female sexuality'. The encyclopaedic *Beyond Power: On Women, Men, and Morals*, 1985, provides an extensive philosophical and historical view. *Her Mother's Daughter*, 1987, illustrated with black-and-white snapshots, treats four generations of women and gives an acute sense of female experience lived through extended memory. MF says, 'To me feminism is not just about women ... it's about moral values, identified with women, though I don't think women have a gene for them.' Her polemical style produces painful fictional dialogues filled with sex-antagonism; but in fiction and non-fiction (including stories and articles) she tries to follow 'a truth about how [life] should be led'. She has written introductions to several recent Edith WHARTON reprints.

Frere, Mary Eliza Isabella, 1845–1911, traveller and collector of oral tales, b. at Bitton Rectory, Glos., eldest of five children of Catherine and Sir Henry Bartle F., Governor of Bombay and High Commissioner of South Africa. She was educ. at Wimbledon, and as her father's hostess travelled widely, collecting southern Indian fairytales. *Old Deccan Days*, 1865 (reissued as *Eastern Fairy Tales*, 1874), was well reviewed and went through many editions and translations, but her 'pastoral play' *Love's Triumph*, 1869, and occasional verse were less popular. MEF's 'Collector's Apology' to *Old Deccan Days* describes her project as the rescue of the tales 'from the danger of oral transmission', and her treatment of Indian beliefs and traditions is respectful and serious. She visited the Holy Land (1906–8), and the MEF Library at Girton College, Cambridge, includes a collection of Semitic and Jewish MSS.

Freytag-Loringhoven, Baroness **Elsa** (Ploetz), 'the Baroness', 1874–1927, Dada poet and artist. B. Else Hildegard in 1874 in Swinemünde, Pomerania, eldest da. of Eva-Marie and Adolf P., 'a prosperous contractor and businessman', she was largely self-taught both as poet and artist. Although EF-L began writing poetry and painting in her early teens, she did not offer her work to the public until she was in her forties. She married three times: first to August Endell, an architect and designer, in Berlin in 1901; several years later to Felix Paul Greve, the German translator of Oscar Wilde and André Gide (who pub. two novels based on her life, *Fanny Essler*, 1905, and *Maurermeister Ihles Haus*, 1906); lastly to Baron Leopold von Freytag-Loringhoven in NYC in 1913. When he left for Germany at the outbreak of WWI, EF-L moved from the Ritz Hotel to Greenwich Village, where she earned a meagre living as an artists' model and began associating with members of the NY Dada group. In the ten years between her arrival in New York and her return to Germany in 1923 she completed much of her published work and made a name for herself both as the 'queen of New York Dada', and as perhaps the most colourful of Greenwich Village eccentrics. She frequently used her own body as her medium: at various times, she shaved, painted and shellacked her head, wore postage stamps on her cheeks, metal tea balls on her breasts as jewellery, and an inverted coal scuttle or a peach basket as a hat. When in 1921 Man Ray and Duchamp published the first and only issue of *New York Dada*, they featured the poetry and body art of EF-L. Several major pieces of her artwork survive, including the famous mitre box and plumbing trap assemblage,

GOD, ca. 1916, Philadelphia Museum of Art, which she created, possibly in collaboration with Morton Schamberg. EF-L's poetry was championed by Margaret ANDERSON and Jane HEAP, who published her extensively in *The Little Review*, and by Djuna BARNES, who corresponded with EF-L once the latter returned to Germany in 1923; her writing also appeared in *Broom*, *The Transatlantic Review*, and *transition*. EF-L died in Paris in 1927. Papers at the Univ. of Maryland, College Park. On her relation to Barnes and others, see Lynn DeVore in *JML*, 10, 1983; for a preliminary assessment of her artwork, see Robert Reiss in Rudolf E. Kuenzli, ed., *New York Dada*, 1986.

Friedan, Betty Naomi (Goldstein), b. 1921, feminist: founder (1966) and first president of NOW, original convener of the National Women's Political Caucus, 1971. She was b. at Peoria, Ill., da. of Miriam (Horowitz) and jeweller Harry G., and was educ. at Smith College (AB in psychology, 1947), the Univ. of California (Berkeley), and Esalen Institute. She m. Carl F. in 1947 and had three children (divorced in 1969). *The Feminine Mystique*, 1963, her first book, is the most important single source of the modern feminist movement in the USA: many reprints. It highlights the emotional emptiness felt by women trying to live through their husbands' and children's lives, and reactivates issues which previous generations had laboured for – pointing out, for instance, how the suffragists' goals and achievements were discredited by ridicule of them as TEMPERANCE fanatics. It urges equal relations between the sexes (to their mutual benefit), not superiority for women, nor separatist policies. BF's later positions are even more controversial. *'It Changed My Life': Writings on the Women's Movement* (1976, repr. with BF's new introduction, 1985) evaluates progress and issues politically pragmatic warnings. *The Second Stage*, 1981, combats a *'feminist* mystique': to 'deny the part of one's being as woman that has, through the ages, been expressed in motherhood' and nurturing is to deny 'part of one's personhood as woman'. *The Nation* published four responses as 'The Feminist Papers', 14 and 28 Nov. 1981, arguing against privileging of the nuclear family and a 'politics of puritanism' and in favour of keeping practical strategies informed by 'utopian dreams'. BF has held many teaching posts (*The Second Stage* discusses the first women at the US Military Academy), and lectured and published in popular periodicals in support of the ERA and of reforms in divorce, abortion law, housing, employment and education. She became a director of the First Women's Bank and Trust Co., NYC, 1974. Radcliffe College has her papers. M. Meltzer published a life of her for children, 1985.

Fugard, Sheila (Meiring), poet and novelist. She was b. in Birmingham, England, in 1932, of an Irish mother and a South African doctor father. They took her to South Africa at eight. She studied drama at the Univ. of Cape Town, became an actress, met, 1956, and shortly m. Athol F., whose work she has since been involved in and with whom she has shared house confinement, searches, and ostracism in South Africa. She directed and acted in his first play, *The Cell*, 1956, in an amateur theatre they founded. They moved to England, 1959, where she typed and he wrote and did house cleaning, but Sharpeville brought them back, 1960. Their daughter was born in South Africa. Kept there by government order, 1967, Athol F. wrote *Boesman and Lena*, dedicated to and partly inspired by SF. Her first novel, *The Castaways*, 1972, a fantastical narrative about a patient in a mental hospital, won the Olive SCHREINER Prize. *Threshold*, 1975, and *Mythic Things*, 1981, poems, declare her concerns as political (poverty, oppression in South Africa, India and the USA) and historical ('See history afresh / The dinosaurs looming as a mountain / The ant

/ Insect and real.'). In her second novel, *Rite of Passage*, 1976, two white men enter a pre-scientific, pre-psychiatric tribal culture to confront barriers between races, cultures, sexes. In India for the filming of *Gandhi*, 1981 (Athol F. played Smuts), SF was deeply impressed by Indian history and beliefs. These appear in *A Revolutionary Woman*, 1983: set in the Karoo district, in 1920, it presents a South African of English descent who teaches coloured students in a Boer neighbourhood. A disciple of Gandhi and an advocate of passive resistance, she likens apartheid to the traditional Indian caste system. The novel examines the psychologies of damaged Boer War veterans, of the teacher who clings unavailingly to her principles, and of the coloured youth whose fantasies of crossing the line end tragically. In the figure of Kasturbai, Gandhi's willingly subservient wife, SF raises questions of women's power, sexual equality, and a double standard in education. SF lives with her husband in Port Elizabeth and NYC.

Fuller, Anna, 1853–1916, novelist and short-story writer, b. Cambridge, Mass., da. of Mary L. (Bent) and Robert Henry F. She was educ. at Abbot Academy, Andover, Mass. In *A Literary Courtship under the auspices of Pike's Peak*, 1893, AF adopts a male persona, John Brunt, who in turn adopts a female persona, Lilian Leslie Lamb, to prove that it is not a disability to write as a woman. Lauded for its 'virile strength', tempered by 'true feminine delicacy of feeling', Brunt's book is an instant success and appears to prove his point. The question of persona is complicated, however, when Brunt meets the true Lilian Leslie Lamb whose volume of poems had led him to expect a misanthropic older woman. Widely popular and noted for the originality of her plots, AF collected in *Pratt Portraits. Sketched in a New England Suburb*, 1893, her stories from *Harper's Bazaar*. Featuring unconventional heroines, the tales treat of the vagaries of married life, slavery issues, homeopathy and gender roles: on Old Lady Pratt's observation that no daughter of her 'highly respectable house' had ever 'worked for a living', AF comments, 'an unprejudiced observer might have thought that Old Lady Pratt herself had worked ... harder than any school-teacher, all through the childhood of her six boys and girls'. Stories in *Peak and Prairie. From a Colorado Sketch Book*, 1894, portray strong mountain women who prefer to befriend rather than shoot wild bears, and who empower men to change their lives. AF covers issues of wife-beating (*The Rumpety Case*), and child-battering (*The Lame-Gulch Professor*), and presents a vivid picture of prairie life, its hardships and joys. *The Thunderhead Lady*, 1913, written with Brian Reed, tells of a 'Mere Man' who advertises 'for a permanent position as husband ... used to female domination ...' who 'can trot in double-harness or money refunded'.

Fuller, Anne, d. 1790, author of three novels pub. in Dublin and London. In *The Convent, or The History of Sophia Nelson*, by a 'young Lady' [1786], the rich, orphaned heroine (whose opinion of women is low) avoids a clodpole suitor for a nobleman and joins an epistolary circle of idyllic couples. The most sentimental lover has fled his tyrannical French aristocrat father for life in a cave recalling Sophia LEE's *The Recess*. Broad satire includes a bookshop scene where *Cecilia* and *Tom Jones* draw the scorn of stupid readers. AF prefaces her first 'historical romance', *Alan Fitz-Osborne*, 1786, by swearing by the Muses to serve truth through fiction: yet its hero, a knight of Henry III, ends as a hermit after two women, one vilely slandered, have died for love of him. A ghost visits her murderer, pulls a dagger from her breast and lets her blood drip on him. *The Son of Ethelwolf*, 1789 (about Alfred's resistance to the Danes), summons an anachronistic Druid priest to sacrifice the defiant heroine. It had 568 subscribers; the *Monthly Review* called it 'prose run mad'. AF died of consumption near Cork in Ireland.

Fuller, Jean Violet Overton (Middleton), poet, biographer, thriller writer, b. 1915 at Iver Heath, Bucks., da. of Violet Overton (Smith) and Indian Army captain John Henry M. After the Royal Academy of Dramatic Art, 1930–1, JF had two years as an actress, then studied painting in Paris. Having contributed (with Dylan Thomas and Pamela Hansford JOHNSON) to the *Sunday Referee*'s 'Poet's Corner' and 'Comment', she worked during WWII in government jobs and as an examiner in French and Italian. At London Univ. she took a BA in English, 1945, and certificate in phonetics, 1950, in which she then lectured. She became known for her life of her friend Noor Inayat Khan, resistance heroine: *Madeleine*, 1952, re-issued as *Born for Sacrifice*, 1957, and as *Noor-an-nisa Inayat Khan*, 1971. JF also wrote four books on WWII spies and double agents in France (beginning with *The Starr Affair*, 1954), and more lives (including Swinburne, 1967, and P. B. Shelley, 1968). She writes of herself in *The Magical Dilemma of Victor Neuberg*, 1965. After astronomy at Goldsmiths' College, London, 1962–4, she studied Tibetan, oriental and theosophical metaphysics, was Vice-President of the Theosophical Society, 1968, and co-founded the publishing firm Fuller D'Arch Smith. Her poetry includes *Venus Protected*, 1964, *Carthage and the Midnight Sun*, 1966 (one long poem relating ancient myth to modern atrocities, one relating in visionary mode a journey to Iceland), *African Violets*, 1968 (for her mother), *Darun and Pitar*, 1970, *Tintagel*, 1970, *Conversations with a Captor*, 1973 (a prose-poem on the relation of oppressed to oppressor, based on actual interviews between Inayat Khan and an SS officer), and *Shiva's Dance*, 1979 (translated from her friend Hélène Bouvard's French, influenced by Krishnamurti). Sometimes portentous about mysticism, she deals precisely and delicately with human relations. She has contributed to poetry workshops and radio programmes. *The New Arrival*, 1987, is a single poem.

Fuller, Sarah **Margaret**, later Marchesa d'Ossoli, 1810–50, journalist, critic and pioneer feminist, b. Cambridgeport, Mass., da. of Margaret (Crane) and Timothy F., lawyer, politician and rationalist. Educ. by her father, who insisted on a masculine education, at 13 she developed a passionate attachment for an artistically cultivated Englishwoman at Cambridge. At 14 she went to Groton as a boarder: her autobiographical story 'Mariana' records these as unhappy years. In 1827 she met Lydia CHILD, whose early work preceded MF's feminist theory. Her father d. in 1835 and she took over the education of her brothers and sisters. In 1836, after visiting Emerson, she became associated with the Transcendentalists; she taught at Bronson Alcott's Temple School 1836–7, and 1837–9 at Greene Street School, Providence, where she translated Eckermann's *Conversations with Goethe* and began work as a critic. Moving to Boston in 1839, she began her famous Conversations at Elizabeth PEABODY's bookshop: women's meetings designed to combat the myth that the female mind was deficient. In 1840, with Emerson and others, she produced the Transcendentalist journal *Dial*. Her first book, *Summer on the Lakes*, 1844, followed research at Harvard where she was the first woman to study and so impressed Horace Greeley on the NY *Tribune* that he invited her to become his literary critic. Her collected criticism is in *Papers on Literature and Art*, 1846, and forms a major contribution to American cultural history. With Poe, MF is the first of America's major critics. Her chief work, *Woman in the Nineteenth Century*, 1845 (repr. 1980), stresses that men have deliberately kept women in a subordinate position, and that women must help themselves towards independence. In 1846 she went to Europe as foreign correspondent for the *Tribune*, and met Carlyle, Wordsworth, De Quincey and George SAND, of whom she wrote: 'She has bravely acted out her nature.' During the revolution in Rome she met the Marchese d'Ossoli, with whom she lived and had a son, marrying him 1849 or 1850, while writing a history of the revolution. She knew E. B. BROWNING. Throughout her life MF was stereotyped by James and others as an archetypal 'ugly' feminist. She died in a shipwreck while returning to NYC. See Bell Gale Chevigny, 1976, for her biography, and S. P. Conrad, 1976 and M. M. O. Urbanski, 1980, for feminist studies. Her letters are pub. in five vols., 1983–8. Her papers are in the Boston Public Library and Houghton Library, Harvard.

Fullerton, Lady **Georgiana** (Leveson-Gower), 1812–85, novelist and philanthropist, b. Tixall Hall, Staffs., youngest da. of Lady Harriet ('Hary-O') Elizabeth (Cavendish; da. of Georgiana, Duchess of DEVONSHIRE) and 1st Earl Granville. Her mother's letters (rakish when young, pious when old), pub. 1944, were reviewed by Virginia WOOLF. Much of GF's early life was spent in Paris where her father was ambassador. In 1833 she m. Alexander George F., embassy attaché; she lived in France, Italy, and Germany, before finally settling in Bournemouth. She converted to Catholicism in 1846. After the death of her only child, Granville, in 1855, she dedicated her life to charity, enrolling in the third order of St Francis, co-founding a religious community, and devoting the profits of her writing to the poor. Her first and best-known novel, *Ellen Middleton*, 1844, is a melodramatic yet psychologically powerful story of a young woman's anguish after unintentionally causing the death of her disagreeable cousin. Themes of religion and conscience are present in GF's other fiction: *Grantley Manor*, 1847, contrasts an Anglican and a Catholic heroine and discusses the human damage wrought by religious prejudice; in *Lady-Bird*, 1852, the passionate high-reaching heroine, thwarted in love, eventually turns to a life of self-sacrificial ministry; *Mrs Gerald's Niece*, 1869, is a kind of sequel to *Grantley Manor* and takes up themes of religious differences and conversion. Many of her later novels are historical, including one about Margaret of Anjou, and a supposedly true account of the flight to Canada of Peter the Great's daughter-in-law, to escape the clutches of her insane, brutal husband. She also wrote (or adapted) a life of Lady FALKLAND. See the life (in French) by her friend Mme Augustus Craven, 1888 (whose novels GF trans. from French); English version by H. J. Coleridge, 1888.

Fullerton, Mary, 1868–1946, poet and novelist, b. Glenmaggie, Victoria, da. of Eliza (Leathers) and Robert F., selector. She was educ. by her mother, at the local state school, and by her own avid reading, particularly of poetry, which she began writing at an early age. Active in the women's SUFFRAGE movement during the 1890s, she later wrote articles on feminist issues for magazines, as well as stories and poems. Some of the latter were collected in *Moods and Melodies*, 1908, and *The Breaking Furrow*, 1921. In 1922 she moved to England to live with a friend, Mabel Singleton, and there met Miles FRANKLIN, who greatly encouraged her literary work. She published five novels, some under male pseudonyms, a book of childhood reminiscences, *Bark House Days*, 1921 (repr. several times), and two further volumes of poetry under the pseudonym 'E': *Moles Do So Little With Their Privacy*, 1942, and *The Wonder and the Apple*, 1946, which both feature lucid, succinct lyrics, some satirical and quite modern in subject. A Gippsland writer whose work mainly identifies with that distinctive region of north-eastern Victoria, MF's childhood experience of hardship and poverty is reflected in the insular, remote families of her fiction, in, for example, *The People of the Timber Belt*, 1925. *A Juno of the Bush*, 1930, is also located in Gippsland. *Rufus Sterne*, 1932, is dedicated to 'Brent of Bin Bin' (Miles Franklin), and, like *The Murders at Crabapple Farm*, 1933, published under a pseudonym. MSS are in the Mitchell and LaTrobe Libraries.

Fulton, Mary, English novelist of the 1920s whose work treats of SUFFRAGE, class, and gender. *Blight*, 1919, examines 'the deadlock of this problem of women's work', in the counterpointed lives of wealthy, socially conscious Irene, who breaks with her charming fiancé in hope of making a useful life, and working-class Grace, who marries her wealthy, titled employer: both fail. Irene comes to believe that desire for independence through work and suffrage is misguided: 'If woman, who creates man, who carries him helpless in her womb, blood of her blood, who feeds him at her breast, who guides and trains him until his maturity, cannot inspire him to vote for what is fine, what is true, how can she hope to do anything with a vote of her own?' *The Plough*, 1919, depicts social change wrought by WWI. Its protagonist Patricia, refusing the life of her wealthy, titled parents, marries a soldier. When he is killed in the war, she retreats with her child for solace and recovery to the country, wishing to throw off 'the mere unreasonable objection of class' and to 'try without prejudice to determine what was right'. *Grass of Parnassus*, 1923, imagines a sterile, upper-middle-class marriage disrupted by an adulterous affair which concludes when English Viola is strangled by her Italian lover.

Furlong, Alice, b. ?1875, Irish poet and story writer, da. of James Walter F. (d. 1897), and sister of Mary, 1866–98, who died of typhus while nursing, and pub. verse which was never collected. AF wrote poems and serial stories for *Irish Monthly*, *United Ireland*, *Sinn Fein Weekly* and other periodicals such as *Chambers's Journal*. She published a volume of musical 'Celtic twilight' poems, *Roses and Rue*, London, 1899, dedicated to 'My Dead Mother'; and *Tales of Fairy Folks, Queens and Heroes*, Dublin [1907], Irish legends well and simply told, dedicated to Douglas Hyde, George Sigerson and Eleanor Hull. She was a friend of the poet Dora SIGERSON.

Furlong, Monica, novelist, journalist and Christian feminist, b. 1930 at Harrow near London, da. of Freda (Simpson) and Alfred Gordon F. From early childhood she was 'puzzled about the status of women', feeling equal but observing from junior school that she was not. After Harrow County Girls' School and Univ. College, London, she m. William John Knights in 1953 and had two children: divorced 1977. She worked on newspapers from 1956 and for the BBC, 1974–8. Her poetry volume, *God's a good man*, 1974 (title – absurd but moving, she says – from Shakespeare's Dogberry), traces patterns in her life: of JULIAN of Norwich she asks 'Be with us still, who bear our cells so badly. . . . And like a mother touch us in the night.' MF's half-dozen books on Christian issues are trenchant, tolerant, and feminist. *Christian Uncertainties*, 1976, which reprints articles from the Anglican *Church Times*, treats prayer, suffering, and 'hot potatoes' like 'the almost total masculinisation of our churches', abortion, divorce, and homosexuality (the 'acid test of whether Christians *really* believe in the goodness of sex'). Her biographies of Christians range from John Bunyan, 1975 (another work on him reprints Agnes BEAUMONT, 1978), to Thérèse of Lisieux, 1987 (whose sweet, self-abnegating femininity, MF is embarrassed at finding fascinating). Her novels, *Cat's Eye*, 1976, and *Cousins*, 1983, present webs of sexual and emotional relationships during shorter or longer periods of crisis for her narrators: a woman leaving her marriage, and a female sculptor. MF was Moderator of the Movement for the Ordination of Women, 1982–5, and has edited two sets of essays on this topic, *Feminine in the Church*, 1984, and *Mirror to* *the Church, Reflections on Sexism*, 1988 (timed to coincide with the Anglican Lambeth Conference). Her novel for children, *Wise Child*, 1987, presents a charismatic 'witch' in the seventh-century Isle of Man.

Fyge, Sarah, later Field and **Egerton**, 1670–1723, feminist poet, da. of Mary (Beacham) and physician Thomas Fyge. She grew up in London, evidently well educ., and wrote (at hardly 14, she says) *The Female Advocate*, a verse reply to the violently misogynist *Love Given O're*, 1682, by Robert Gould (who later savaged Aphra BEHN; see also *SYLVIA'S REVENGE*). Pub. without her consent but with her initials, 1686, her poem brought paternal anger and banishment from London. She revised for a 2nd ed., 1687 (repr. in *Satires on Women*, ed. Felicity Nussbaum, 1976), expanding and polishing without losing any bite; her preface argues that Gould's obscenity was an argument for, not against, reply. Soon afterwards SF m. Edward Field, an attorney near London; later poems tell of her growing love and her bereavement. In 1700 she wrote probably four anthology poems on Dryden's death (three in *The Nine Muses*), and in 1701 passages for John Froud's *The Grove*, a survey of the London literary scene where she now had a place. After, apparently, falling in love with an attorney's clerk, 'Alexis', she married, 1700, her much older widower cousin the Rev. Thomas E., but petitioned (vainly) for divorce on grounds of cruelty, 1703. In *Poems on Several Occasions*, the same year (dedicatory verses probably by Mary PIX and Susanna CENTLIVRE), she rejects all kinds of restraint, especially of her 'daring Pen', which treats her own loves, marriages, retirement and mental suffering, and touches on the occult. After a quarrel in 1704–5, Delarivier MANLEY printed some of her letters, 1707, and wrote a lurid account of her second marriage. Her later life is obscure; the Huntington has a MS address to the Duke of Marlborough, 1708. See Jeslyn Medoff in *TSWL*, 1, 1982.

Fytche, Maria Amelia (Fitch except for publication), 1844–1926, novelist. Da. of Margaret Ross (Paddock) and Dr Simon Fitch, she was b. and lived mostly in Saint John, New Brunswick, though the family spent some time in Portland (Maine), NY, and Halifax, and MAF spent some years in England. She taught, probably privately, contributed short fiction to periodicals, and wrote two novels. *Kerchiefs to Hunt Souls*, 1895, repr. 1980, explores through its protagonist the difficulties of women seeking educational and professional opportunities, and the internal division caused by incompatible objectives of self-expression and professional success, traditional marriage and family life. Like her contemporaries Sara Jeanette DUNCAN and Alice JONES, she develops the international theme, taking her protagonist to Europe for the purpose of weighing and contrasting Canadian, US and European characteristics.

G

Gage, Frances Dana (Barker), 'Aunt Fanny', 1808–80, journalist, temperance novelist and women's rights activist, b. Marietta, Ohio, da. of Elizabeth (Dana) and Joseph B., farmer. Both parents were concerned with social issues. In 1829 she m. lawyer James L. G.; she had eight children. She moved to St Louis in 1853, where her outspoken anti-slavery opinions brought social ostracism and threats of violence, while journals refused her articles. In 1854 she lectured in Iowa on women's SUFFRAGE; she addressed the Nebraska Legislature on the same topic the following year. When war broke out she went to the front to urge Northerners to give help to the freed slaves. She also lectured to TEMPERANCE organizations, and her first novel, *Elsie Magoon*, 1867, shows how men's drinking can victimize women in the particular context of Ohio frontier life. Elsie protests: 'The law is a barbarism ... it is *monstrous*, to give a man *all* the property of his wife, *all her labour, all her mind and soul*' (146). FG's next two novels pursue the temperance theme. *Gertie's Sacrifice*, 1869, describes the degradation of society women who take to drink, while *Steps Upward*, 1870, illustrates the dilemma of the heroine whose father is a drunkard and to whom marriage offers the only possibility of improving her social situation. FG's *Poems*, 1867, treat homely topics alongside contemporary political issues; 'The Perplexed Housekeeper' complains with acute insight about 'doing the work of six; / *For the sake of being supported!*' As 'Aunt Fanny', her contributions to Amelia BLOOMER'S *The Lily* and other feminist papers intersperse practical household advice with witty reflections on women's position in society and satirical treatment of anti-suffrage correspondents. See L. P. Brockett and Mary Vaughn, *Woman's Work in the Civil War*, 1867, for an account of her life.

Gage, Matilda (Joslyn), 1826–98, feminist activist, editor, and journalist, b. Cicero, NY, da. of Helen (Leslie) and Hezekiah J. Her father, a physician and advocate of reformist movements, directed her education at home until, at 15, she was sent to the Clinton (NY) Liberal Institute. In 1845 she m. Henry G. and they settled in Fayetteville, NY, where she had five children. In 1852 she gave a speech at the National Woman's Rights Convention at Syracuse, NY. In 1869 she became a founding member of the National Woman Suffrage Association and a contributor to the *Revolution*, its newspaper; she was also Vice-President and Secretary of the NY Woman Suffrage Association. During the 1870s and 1880s MJG pub. several pamphlets, and 1878–81 ed. the *National Citizen and Ballot Box*. With S. B. ANTHONY and E. C. STANTON she produced the first three vols. of the *History of Woman Suffrage*, 1881–6. MJG's controversial *Woman, Church, and State*, 1893 (repr. 1980), attacked the idea that Christianity, in collaboration with the modern state, has historically improved woman's lot. Drawing on anthropological discoveries, she argued that 'in many ancient nations woman possessed a much greater degree of respect and power than she has at the present age'. MJG also served on the Revising Committee of Stanton's *Woman's Bible*, 1895. Her interest in matriarchies, witchcraft, and laws regulating female sexuality anticipated many of the concerns of today's radical feminists. Her tombstone reads: 'There is a word sweeter than Mother, Home, or Heaven; that word is

Liberty.' See *A Woman of the Century*, 1893, ed. by WILLARD and Livermore. Valuable sources for study are the MJG Suffrage Scrapbooks, four vols., Library of Congress, and other materials in the Schlesinger Library, Radcliffe College; the Public Library, Fayetteville, NY; and the Onondaga Historical Society, Syracuse, NY.

Gagnon, Madeleine, poet, novelist, short-story writer. She was b. in 1938 in Amqui in the Gaspésie region of Québec, one of ten children of Jeanne (Beaulieu) and Jean-Baptiste G., and educ. at the Univs. of St Joseph du Nouveau-Brunswick, Montréal, and Aix-Nice, in France. Before concentrating exclusively on writing, she taught literature at the Univ. de Québec à Montréal. She is divorced, with two boys. Though best known as a poet, she first published short stories, *Les Morts-vivants*, 1969. A member of the editorial collective of the journal *Chroniques*, 1974–6, she has also published in other feminist journals, including *La Nouvelle Barre du jour*, *Room of One's Own*, and *Sorcières*. Much of her politicized prose and collage poetry appeared during the political and social upheaval in Québec in the 1970s: *Pour les femmes et tous les autres*, 1974, *Retailles*, prose poems, 1977, and *Les fées ont soif* (*The fairies are thirsty*, 1978) with playwright Denise Boucher. Her involvement with radical feminism took a new turn in her collaboration with Annie Leclerc and Hélène CIXOUS on the well-known collection of feminist essays, *La venue à l'écriture*, 1977. Her growing interest in the articulation of a woman's voice is evident here, in her essay 'Mon corps dans l'écriture', in *Antre*, 1978, and in *Lueur*, 1979, her best-known novel, an archaeological exploration of woman, her/self, her images, her fragmented language. Her more recent poetry (*Pensées du Poème*, 1983, *La lettre infinie*, 1984, *Les Fleurs du Catalpa*, 1986, *L'infante immémoriale*, 1987) explores a blend of lyrical voice and theoretical reflection. She also writes short stories for radio (Vidéo-Presse, 1985). See special issues of *La Barre du jour*, 1977 (on 'Le corps, les mots, l'imaginaire', by MG, Nichole BROSSARD, Louky BERSIANIK, and others), and *Voix et Images*, 8, 1982; also K. Gould in Paula Gilbert Lewis, ed., *Traditionalism, Nationalism, and Feminism: Women Writers of Quebec*, 1985.

Gale, Zona, 1874–1938, novelist, playwright, short-story writer, only child of Eliza (Beers) and railroad engineer Charles Franklin G., b. at Portage, Wis., a small frontier town where she later lived and set most of her work. (*When I Was a Little Girl*, 1913, deals with her childhood; *Portage, Wisconsin, and Other Essays*, 1928, mixes memoirs and literary essays.) She sold her first story, to a Milwaukee newspaper, early in her time at the Univ. of Wisconsin (BL 1895; MA 1899, during six years as a Milwaukee reporter). She made contact with women's organizations and met Jane Addams, a lifelong friend who prompted her activity in suffrage compaigns and the Women's Peace Party. (ZG was involved in drafting the Wisconsin Equal Rights Law, 1923.) In 1901 she moved to NYC, as journalist and secretary to the writer Edmund Clarence Stedman, who fostered her literary ambitions. By 1903 her stories were appearing regularly in popular magazines; by 1906, date of her first novel, *Romance Island*, she was self-supporting. Her success grew with *The Loves of Pelleas and Etarre*, 1907 (stories repr. from magazines), and *Friendship's Village*, 1908, and its sequels (including a one-act play, *The Neighbors*, 1914, for the expanding community theatre movement). The series, with a caring, resourceful heroine modelled on ZG's mother, belongs to a tradition of sentimental, happy-ending, small-town fiction. ZG wrote as a feminist in *Heart's Kindred*, 1915, and *A Daughter of the Morning* (about women's working conditions), 1917. *Miss Lulu Bett*, 1920, repr. 1976, on a young woman's revolt against family values and custom, won the Pulitzer

Prize for drama in her adaptation, 1921. She also dramatized her *Birth*, 1918 (as *Mister Pitt*), and *Faint Perfume*, 1923 (acted 1934). Her many other works include *The Secret Way* (poems), 1921, *What Women Won in Wisconsin*, 1922, a foreword to Charlotte Perkins GILMAN's autobiography, 1935, and late, mystically oriented novels. In 1928 she m. Portage widower William L. Breese. Papers at Wis. Hist. Soc.; letters to Ridgely Torrence (her fiancé in 1904) at Princeton. See life by August Derleth, 1940; study by Harold P. Simonson, 1962; Virginia Cox in *The Feminist Connection*, 5, 1984.

Gallant, Mavis, Mavis de Trafford Young, writer of short fiction, novels, essays, plays, b. in 1922 in Montréal, Québec. She began her education at the age of four in a Jansenist boarding-school and after her father's premature death was sent to some 17 schools in Canada and the USA. She never attended university. Bilingual and literate in French and English from an early age, she returned to Montréal from NYC at 18. Her brief marriage to pianist Johnny G. ended in divorce; she has not remarried. Her commitment to anti-fascism and her discovery of Nazi genocide had a formative effect on her development as a writer. (A satirical view of the political experience open to women in wartime Canada is found in her play *What is to be Done?*, produced 1982, pub. 1983. She wrote for *The Montreal Standard*, 1944–50, analysing economic, cultural, political and social issues, then, after publishing a handful of stories in Canadian journals, sold a story to *The New Yorker* (where she has published throughout her career), quit her job, and gave herself three years to establish herself as a writer in Europe. She has been there since 1950, travelling widely and living in Paris. MG's mastery of narrative voice, her attention to the troubled lives of women and children and the equally unhappy men involved with them are as evident in her first collection of short fiction, *The Other Paris*, 1956, as in her latest, *In Transit*, 1988. Her profound concern with history as the lived experience of the powerless and her delineation of the ambiguous role of memory in both revising and uncovering truth are best revealed in what is arguably the finest of her nine short-fiction collections, *From the Fifteenth District*, 1979, although they also inform such other European-centred works as *The Pegnitz Junction*, 1973, and *Overhead in a Balloon*, 1985. Her novels, *Green Water, Green Sky*, 1959, and the comic *tour de force*, *A Fairly Good Time*, 1970, deal with the complex experiences of women trapped in the feminine mystique. The 'Linnet Muir' sequence collected in *Home Truths* (Governor-General's Award, 1981) is one of her rare portrayals of a woman who refuses imprisonment inside the female 'kitchen in a slum' (*Green Water, Green Sky*) and who attains MG's *sine qua non*, personal independence. Her comprehensive, acute intelligence and incisive social and political sense inform *Paris Notebooks*, 1986, which contains superb analyses of Marguerite Yourcenar's fiction, of the 1968 student uprising in Paris, and the case of Gabrielle Russier. Both a consummate stylist and a creator of powerfully disturbing fictions, MG is working now on a study of the Dreyfus affair, on her memoirs, and on a series of new fiction. See Neil K. Besner, *The Light of Imagination*, 1988, and Janice Kulyk Keefer, *Reading Mavis Gallant*, 1989.

Galloway, Grace (Growden), d. 1789, Philadelphia diarist who also left verse and some letters, da. of Hannah and Lawrence Growden, a rich man who brought her home from an extended English visit in 1751 to end a love-affair. In 1753 she m. Joseph Galloway, lawyer, political power like her father, and loyalist. Left 'friendless & alone' in the American-occupied city, she kept a diary (begun as mere notes) June 1778–Sept. 1779: Historical Soc. of Penna, pub. *PMHB*, 1931, 1934. She counters anxiety ('shou'd I not live to get to my dear

Child and Mr Galloway let this be shown them'; 'I am Not well and am Not happy – know not how I shall do this winter') with indomitable spirit: evacuated, she calls a soldier to witness 'I do not leave my house of My own accord or with my own inclination but by force', and adds 'it was not in their power to humble Me'. Her husband became Speaker of the colonial assembly, but she never regained her estates.

'Gardener, Helen Hamilton', Alice Chenoweth, 1853–1925, novelist, short-story writer, essayist, lecturer, free thinker, magazine editor. Youngest child of Katherine (Peel), a strict Calvinist, and Alfred Griffith Chenoweth, a Methodist circuit rider, she was b. in Winchester, Virginia; the family moved to Washington, DC, in 1853 when her father freed his slaves, and to Indiana in 1855. She was educ. at Cincinnati Normal School. In 1875 she m. Charles Selden Smart, state school commissioner of Ohio, moving to NYC where she studied biology and lectured in sociology. Associated with agnostic Robert Ingersol and his wife, she lectured against Christianity which 'teaches disrespect, abject slavery and oppressive degradation for woman'; and pub. *Men, Women and Gods* in 1884. Of the Bible HG wrote: 'That Book I think degrades and belittles women ...'. She challenged neurologist Dr William Hammond's argument against equality of the sexes in 'Sex in Brain', a lecture read before the International Council of Women in 1888. She helped Elizabeth Cady STANTON prepare the *Woman's Bible*, 1895, and published essays and short stories concerned with social issues, many collected in *Pushed by Unseen Hands* and *A Thoughtless Yes*, 1890. Two popular protest novels concerned with women's issues were *Is This Your Son, My Lord*, 1890, which she intended to be the *Uncle Tom's Cabin* for women's issues, and *Pray You, Sir, Whose Daughter?*, 1892. *An Unofficial Patriot*, 1894, the story of her father's life, has been considered her best novel. Smart died in 1901; HHG m. Col Selden Allen Day and, after a six-year world tour, resumed feminist political activities at the urging of Anna Howard SHAW. At the age of 67 she was the first woman appointed to the US Civil Service Commission, a position she held for five years. Her papers are in the Schlesinger Library, Radcliffe College.

Gardner, Isabella Stewart, 1915–81, poet, b. at Newton, Mass., of rich parents, Rose Phinney (Grosvenor) and George Peabody G. She wrote poetry from her youth, wanted to act (she was often taken to plays by her famous art-collector aunt, also ISG), attended the Leighton Rollins and Embassy drama schools and worked in the theatre until 1943, the year of her second marriage. She published nothing until her third, 1947, to Robert H. McCormick, Jr (divorced 1957), who encouraged her writing. She was assistant editor of *Poetry*, 1952–5, and in 1955 published her first volume, *Birthdays from the Ocean*, which quotes Martin Buber as epigraph and bears out her comments: 'My poems celebrate and affirm life, but they are also elegiac'; their central theme is 'the contemporary failure of love ... the specific and particular recognition of one human being by another'. She called herself 'woman first and poet second'; Edith SITWELL and Sylvia PLATH admired her. Her fourth husband (m. 1959) was her fellow-poet Allen Tate (previously married to Caroline GORDON). ISG's three last volumes – *The Looking Glass*, 1961, *West of Childhood: Poems 1950–65*, 1965, and *That was Then: New and Selected Poems*, 1980 – dwell much on death (a son lost at sea; a daughter, 'my beautiful bountiful womanful child', a drug addict), as well as sexual desire and the passage of time. Looking in the mirror, 'I see and fear the girl you were'. ISG's technical experiments include inserted Yiddish phrases (after a summer among East European Jews), and variants of rhyme, punctuation and line length ('Uneasy in the drafty shade I rock on the verandah reminded of Europa Persephone Miranda'). She writes of poetry as a game with high stakes, 'love fame life and sanity', and of the poet as a lover of disguises: 'For women Quaker bonnets wimples coifs and sun-shades / long blue stockings hawking gloves a fan a hobnailed boot.' She received the first Walt Whitman Citation of Merit, 1981. See Ralph J. Mills, Jr, in *Contemporary American Poetry*, 1966; ISG's friend Jean Gould in *Modern American Women Poets*, 1984.

Gardner, Sarah (Cheyney), d. after 1798, playwright, poet and actress. She began acting in London in 1763 and continued after she m., 1765, the struggling actor William G. In 1774 the marriage broke up; in 1777, harassed by the expense of educating her several children, she wrote a comedy, *The Advertisement, or A Bold Stroke for a Husband*. (The sub-title reverses Susanna CENTLIVRE.) After much prodding the manager George Colman agreed to put it on for one night, her benefit – in a manner designed, she later wrote, to cause it to fail. Though weak in plot, it features distinctive female revisions of several stock types: a spirited young widow picking out a second mate, a courageous female hack writer, a physician obsessed with women and childbirth. Inadequately acted, it was applauded, though Colman ascribed this to sheer gallantry; his anger having made London untenable, SG spent 18 years acting (and lecturing and giving concerts) mostly in Jamaica, Dublin (a row with the manager over refusal to stage one of her plays), St Kitts (a row over remuneration), S. Carolina (a brush with a swindler) and NYC. She last acted in London, 1795, in a lampoon on herself. She copied out as if for publication her poems, political essay, a later comedy and a farce on her St Kitts visit (not equal to *The Advertisement*): the album (now privately owned) was found in 1952 at Colyton, Devon, where she seems to have retired. See Isobel Grundy in *TSWL*, 7, 1988.

Gare, Nene (Wadham), novelist, short-story writer and painter, b. 1919 in Adelaide, South Australia, da. of Mary (Hounslow) and John Henry W. She attended East Adelaide Public School, Adelaide School of Arts and, later, Perth Technical College. She m. Frank Ellis G. in 1941 and had two daughters and a son. An interior designer in Adelaide, she moved to Perth where she became active in literary affairs, and had several successful exhibitions (winning the Canning Art Awards four times). She is best known for *The Fringe Dwellers*, 1961, one of the first novels from the Aboriginal standpoint. Concerned with the problems of cultural identification for half-caste Aborigines, it was filmed by Bruce Beresford in 1986. Her other three novels are: *Green Gold*, 1963, about banana-growing in Canarvon; and the humorous episodic books describing the domestic problems of women, *A House with Verandahs*, 1980, based on her childhood in Adelaide, and *An Island Away*, 1981, set in Papua New Guinea, where her husband was a patrol officer. *Bend to the Wind*, 1978, is a collection of short stories about Aborigines in Western Australia.

Gargill, Ann, religious pamphleteer. Ejected (with other women) by the Quakers for Ranter principles, she sailed in 1655 from Plymouth, Devon, to preach in Portugal; the Inquisition examined and banned but did not otherwise punish her. In 1656 she pub. *A Warning to all the World* and *A Briefe Discovery of that which is called the Popish Religion*, which addresses its Ranter-like word-play to Catholics and in part to the Pope: 'even as a child is nourished by the mother, so doth the Lord tender those that feed on him'.

Garner, Helen (Ford), novelist, short-story and scriptwriter, b. 1942 in Geelong, Victoria, da. of Gwen (Gadsen) and Bruce F. After graduating from Melbourne Univ. she worked as a high school teacher for five years but was dismissed in 1972 for giving frank answers to students' questions about sex. Her experiences of the counter-culture of the 1970s, acting in fringe theatre and living in collective households, produced her first novel, *Monkey Grip*, 1977 (filmed 1982). Written while she was living on a supporting mother's benefit, it was a controversial winner of the National Book Award because of its frank presentation of female sexuality and heroin addiction. After spending a year in Paris, HG published the novellas *Honour and Other People's Children*, 1980, and *The Children's Bach*, 1984, which examine family life and relationships in the light of feminism and the sexual revolution of the 1970s. Both *The Children's Bach* and her collection of stories, *Postcards from Surfers*, 1985, have won major literary prizes. Most recently she has been writing filmscripts: in 1987 her script for Jane Campion's prize-winning telemovie *Two Friends* won the NSW Premier's Award for scriptwriting. See the article by Peter Craven, *Meanjin*, 1985, and P. Gilbert in *Coming Out from Under: Contemporary Australian Women Writers*, 1988.

Garnett, Constance (Black), 1862–1946, translator of Russian literature. She was da. of Clara (Patten), who d. when she was 14, and David B., who came from Russia to study law in London and was later Brighton Coroner. Her sister was novelist Clementina Black. Educated at home by her brothers, then at boarding-school in Brighton, she won a scholarship to Newnham College, Cambridge, where she occasionally saw 'the great Miss Harrison' and took a First in classics, 1883. Afterwards, she tutored girls (in a family that sent its boys to school), m. Edward G., 1889 (the editor Frieda Lawrence later called 'midwife' to her husband's genius), joined the Fabian Society, and took a job in the People's Palace in East London. About 1891, she met exiled Russian revolutionary Felix Volkovsky, who urged her to learn Russian. She never looked back, and in the years between 1894 and 1928 translated, she thought, about 70 vols. of Russian literature. The first translator into English of much of Chekhov and Dostoyevsky, she also made available works by Gogol, Tolstoy, Gorky, and others, and the complete works of Turgenev. She travelled twice to Russia, alone in 1894, to deliver relief money collected in England after the 1892 famine, and with her son David in 1904. She met Tolstoy on the first visit. CG did not write herself, leaving prefaces and introductions to her husband or her son, but Katherine Mansfield wrote of her translations, 'These books have changed our lives, no less.' Carolyn Heilbrun, who thinks her 'largely responsible for the part Russian literature had played in the transition from Victorian letters to twentieth-century realism', devotes a chapter of *The Garnett Family*, 1961, to her. See also David Garnett, *The Golden Echo*, 1954.

Garrigue, Jean, 1914–72, poet, b. Evansville, Ind., da. of Gertrude (Heath) and Allan Colfax Garrigus (she chose an earlier French form). She was educ. at the Univs. of Chicago (BA, 1937) and Iowa, where she also taught English literature (MA, 1943). A series of academic posts followed, latterly as poet-in-residence. She published in periodicals, in *Five Young American Poets*, 1944, and collections from *The Eagle and the Centaur*, 1947; she travelled a good deal in Europe in the decade from 1953. In *A Water Walk by Villa d'Este*, 1959, she writes often of birds: in the Himalayas she sees a caged grackle; her grandmother fed migrants arriving 'so sudden here / By roads exact of wind and light / I call invisible'. Dreams are another link between visible and invisible: 'Where are my long hills? Who took my horse, / And who my apparels of green?' In a pamphlet on Marianne Moore, 1965, JG names some of her own virtues in invoking the care of the 'god of all-powerful detail' to preserve 'rich indigenous honesties'. Later works include a novella (*The Animal Hotel* 1966), two volumes of 'prose poems' (*Chartres*, 1958, *Essays*, 1970), and editions: *Translations by American Poets*, 1970 (a Bollinger project; good female presence), and love poetry, 1975. JG's translations from Andrei Voznesensky focus on abused and battered women, meticulously observed. Her poetry volumes include *New and Selected Poems*, 1967, and *Studies for an Actress*, 1973, which embraces political topics ('Might's still right / In this our swollen pigsfoot of a state'), and past love: 'the wind now makes a storm / Of leaf-loss, old rue / Of autumn's monotone, / And all is masked by flying rain.' See Mary Anne Shea, ed., symposium in *Twentieth-Century Literature*, 29, 1983.

Gaskell, Elizabeth Cleghorn (Stevenson), 1810–65, novelist, b. Chelsea, London, eighth and, apart from one brother apparently lost at sea, only surviving child of Elizabeth (Holland) and William S., ex-Unitarian minister, writer, and Treasury employee. After her mother's death (1811), EG was brought up in Knutsford, Cheshire by her mother's sister, Mrs Lumb, educ. by aunts and private tutors till 12, then went to boarding-school in Warwicks. Themes of motherless girls and paternal shortcomings pervade her fiction, which also draws on her experiences of the enclosed, genteel rural society of Knutsford. In 1832 she m. William G., Unitarian minister; she had four daughters, and a son who died in infancy. Her marriage was essentially happy and she accepted the primacy of wifehood and motherhood, but refused to ignore her writing. Her literary career began with tales for *Howitt's Journal*, but she moved to longer works, partly to assuage the sorrow of her son's death. Her complete output includes several volumes of short stories, seven novels, and an excellent *Life* of Charlotte BRONTË, 1857, whom she first met in 1850. Her wide-ranging fiction focuses particularly on the tensions and dualities of womanhood. Though not an ardent feminist, EG was a strong and independent-minded woman, active in her support of her sister authors and in schemes for the improvement of the position of women such as the Establishment for Invalid Gentlewomen and projects for the promotion of women's emigration. Similarly, her works often boldly tackle 'unorthodox' subjects: *Ruth*, 1853, deals sympathetically and uncompromisingly with 'the fallen woman'; *Cranford*, 1855, depicts a community of spinsters, glorying in their freedom from male interference; *Sylvia's Lovers*, 1863, gives a penetrating portrayal of sexual jealousy and wifely matrimonial suffering; *Cousin Phillis*, 1864, traces a young girl's sexual awakening and the proprietorial nature of father–daughter relationships; short stories like 'The Grey Woman' and 'Half a Life-Time Ago' explore the strength of bonding between women; and in her two 'industrial novels', *Mary Barton*, 1848, and *North and South*, 1855, the heroines play major roles in helping to reconcile men and masters. See *Letters*, ed. 1966; life by Winifred Gérin, 1976; essay on *Cranford* in Nina Auerbach's *Communities of Women*, 1978; EG section of Margaret Homans's *Bearing the Word*, 1986; Pauline Nestor's *Female Friendships and Communities*, 1985; and Patsy Stoneham's critical study, 1987.

Gaskin, Catherine Majella Sinclair, novelist, b. 1929 in Dundalk, Ireland, da. of Mary (Harrington) and James G., engineer. The family emigrated to Australia when CG was a young girl; she was educ. at Holy Cross College, Sydney, causing a sensation when, at 15, she pub. her first novel, *This Other Eden*, 1945. Following her second novel, *With Every Year*, 1947, she travelled widely, living in London and NYC before settling in Ireland and the Isle of Man. She m. Sol Cornberg in 1955, the year *Sara Dane* was published. It sold over two million copies in Australia and later became a successful TV series: based partly on the life of Mary Reiby, it follows the rapid rise to fortune of a young woman wrongly convicted and transported to

NSW in 1792. She puts to use knowledge which had been called 'quite useless to a woman' and proves that 'what one woman can do, so may another'. CG has produced 20 best-selling modern and historical romances, including *Blake's Reach*, 1955, *Corporation Wife*, 1960 (which follows the lives of four women in a small community engulfed by a large company), *Promises*, 1982, and *The Charmed Circle*, 1988.

Gates, Susa (Young), 1856–1933, novelist, biographer and editor, b. Salt Lake City, Utah, second da. of Lucy (Brigelow) and Brigham Y., territorial governor and Mormon Church leader. She grew up in Lion House, Brigham Young's polygamous household, and was educ. in her father's private school, Brigham Young Univ. and at Deseret Univ. SYG began her literary career at 14 editing the Univ. of Deseret's magazine. She taught at Brigham Young Academy and in 1880 m. Jacob G., a church official. She edited the Mormon *Young Women's Journal*, 1889–1919, and *Relief Society Magazine*, 1915–22, and also wrote for non-Mormon periodicals including the *North American Review*. SYG participated in the successful campaign for universal suffrage in the Utah constitution, 1896, and her involvement with the International Council of Women took her to London, 1889, and Copenhagen, 1902. She strongly supported the patriarchal and polygamous family structure of the Mormon church, which she defended in an essay, 'Family Life Among the Mormons', *North American Review*, 1890, claiming that polygamy enabled a woman to 'launch out into her chosen vocation' when she was past childbearing. Her novel *John Steven's Courtship*, 1909, is moralistic and didactic. She thought that a woman should be as morally strong as a man but also 'sympathetic', her first responsibility being to home and family. *The Life Story of Brigham Young*, 1930, was written with her daughter, Leah D. Widtsoe, as was her novel *The Prince of Ur*, pub. posthumously, 1945. Although set in Old Testament times, it comments on contemporary society and warns of the 'swift destruction' following the abandonment of traditional ideals.

Gatty, Margaret (Scott), 1809–73, children's writer and naturalist, b. Burnham, Essex, younger da. of Mary Frances (Ryder) (d. 1811) and the Rev. Alexander John S., Nelson's chaplain on *Victory*. Educ. mainly by her father, she also studied in the BM print room, learned German and Italian and became an accomplished painter and calligraphist. In 1839 she m. Alfred G., who obtained the living of Ecclesfield, near Sheffield, soon after marriage. She had four daughters, including Juliana EWING, and six sons, and worked at parish affairs; all her literary earnings went into the family budget. Her first pub. work was a joint biography (with her husband) of her father, in 1842. Of her many tales for children, the best known include *The Fairy Godmothers*, 1851, *Parables from Nature*, 1855–71 (five series), *Aunt Judy's Tales*, 1859, *Aunt Judy's Letters*, 1862, and *Domestic Pictures and Tales*, 1865. Most are simple accounts of everyday life and natural history and contain matter-of-fact unobtrusive morality. In 1866 she established *Aunt Judy's Magazine*, and also contributed to Charlotte YONGE's *Monthly Packet*. She was essentially conservative, believing that women should not air grievances in public. Her *History of British Seaweeds*, 1863, embodies 15 years' research and was a valuable contribution to the subject. See her daughter Christabel Maxwell, *Mrs Gatty and Mrs Ewing*, 1949. MSS are in Sheffield Central Library.

Gaunt, Elizabeth, d. 1685, political speaker. Executed by burning for her involvement in the aftermath of Monmouth's rebellion, she left with her jailer for publication her *Last Speech*, defending her decision to hide Monmouth followers. She leaves vengeance to Christ, 'who will tread upon the Princes as upon mortar, & be terrible to the Kings of the earth'.

Gaunt, Mary, 1861–1942, novelist, short-story and travel writer, b. Chiltern, Victoria, da. of Elizabeth Mary (Palmer) and William Henry G., police magistrate and later judge. She was educ. at Grenville College, Ballarat, and in 1881 was one of the first women students to enrol at Melbourne Univ., studying arts. With the support of her husband, Dr Hubert Lindsay Miller, she wrote her first four novels and, after his death in 1900, went to London and wrote three successful books with John Ridgewell Essex, resulting in commissions from her publishers for books such as *Alone in Africa*, 1912, *A Woman in China*, 1914, and *A Broken Journey*, 1919, based on her own extensive travels. Five of her 20 novels and collections of short stories are set in Australia, the most exceptional being *Kirkham's Find*, 1897 (repr. 1988 with intro. by Kylie TENNANT), the story of a young woman apiarist's struggle for independence, with a sub-plot of gold-prospecting. *Dave's Sweetheart*, 1894, and *Deadman's*, 1898, are also set in the goldfields; *As the Whirl-Wind Passeth*, 1923, in the early days of NSW. She pub. a number of other stories and novels, often with foreign settings, including *Joan of the Pilchard*, 1930, which touches on Bligh's voyage in the *Bounty*. In the early 1920s she settled in Italy, but fled to France in 1940, where she died. A versatile and cosmopolitan writer, she was particularly skilled at the short story; many of these, plus numerous articles and reviews, appeared in magazines and journals in Australia and England. See S. Martin in D. Adelaide, ed., *A Bright and Fiery Troop*, 1988.

Gawthorpe, Mary, 1881–*c*. 1960, suffragist and autobiographer, b. in Leeds, da. of Annie Eliza (Mountain), mill-worker and dressmaker, and John G., employee in a leather factory. From 13 she was a pupil-teacher for four years at St Michael's National School, later turning down an opportunity to go to teachers' training college because she needed to support her mother. (Her father was no longer doing this; the family split from him in 1901.) MG became an assistant teacher at St Luke Boys' School at 19, and qualified for teaching certification in 1904. With her fiancé, she became involved in the labour movement; for a time she edited the Women's Page of *Labour News*, the Independent Labour Party's 'propaganda sheet'. In 1905–6 she worked for the Leeds Women's Suffrage Society, and in 1906 became secretary of the National WSPU. She was briefly imprisoned in Holloway, 1906, for protest activities. Her suffragette pamphlet, *Votes for Men* [1910], rallies support for women's SUFFRAGE in a retrospective argument about the achievement of men's. MG was joint editor with Dora Marsden of *The Freewoman* for its first 16 issues, though illness prevented her from doing much. She later worked as a journalist in Canada. Her *Up Hill to Holloway*, 1962, gives details of her life only to 1906. See Carol Barash in *Princeton Univ. Chronicle*, 49, 1987.

Gearhart, Sally Miller, feminist utopian novelist, professor of speech and communication studies. B. in 1931 in Pearisburg, Va., to Sarah and Kyle G., she graduated BA from Sweet Briar College, 1952, MA from Bowling Green State Univ., 1953, and PhD from the Univ. of Illinois, 1956. She has taught at several institutions: since 1972 at San Francisco State Univ. Her only novel, *The Wanderground: Stories of the Hill Women*, 1979 (several reprs.), illustrates her 'hefty motivation' for creating: 'love of myself as a woman and my love of other women'. It gives an essentialist picture of Mother Earth in revolt against male domination and technology, and the Hill Women, a group who have escaped the city and work to counteract its violence. As one character states it: 'It is not in his nature not to rape. It is not in my nature to be raped.

We do not co-exist.' SMG edited, with William R. Johnson, *Loving Women/Loving Men: Gay Liberation and the Church*, 1974. See Sarah Lefanu, *In the Chinks of the World Machine*, 1988, Natalie M. Rosinsky, *Feminist Futures: Contemporary Women's Speculative Fiction*, 1987.

Gedge, Pauline, novelist. Though born (1945) in Auckland, NZ, PG spent much of her childhood in England, then, at 14, moved to Canada where her father studied for the Anglican priesthood. She studied for a year at the Univ. of Manitoba, taught briefly in NZ, then returned to Canada, where she lives in rural Alberta. Having given herself until 30 to become successful as a writer, PG established her reputation and popularity with her first novel, *Child of the Morning*, 1977, a lively historical novel based on the life of Hatshepsut, only woman pharaoh of Egypt and, says PG, 'the first liberated woman' (cf. Rosalyn DREXLER). It won Alberta Culture's New Novelist Competition, 1978. *The Eagle and the Raven*, 1978, about Celtic Britain, had advance sales, reportedly, of 500,000. *Stargate*, 1982, is SCIENCE-FICTION; *Twelfth Transforming*, 1984, returns to ancient Egypt.

Gee, Maggie, novelist, b. 1948 at Poole, Dorset, da. of Aileen (Church) and Victor Gee, educ. at Horsham High School for Girls and Somerville College, Oxford (BA in English, 1969, M.Litt. on surrealism), and Wolverhampton Polytechnic (PhD on the modern novel, 1980). As creative writing fellow at the Univ. of East Anglia, 1982, she edited *For Life on Earth* ('ephemeral' anti-war writings). She m. Nicholas Rankin in 1983, and has a daughter. Her first three books, she says, rework the thriller, family saga, and romance genres. *Dying, in Other Words*, 1983, the most experimental, opens on the violent death of a woman (who is later said to be writing the book) which is played with, journalistically slanted, recapitulated, made the centre of other stories tending to sinister dying, and seen to be not suicide or murder but accident while trying to survive. The work moves towards a post-nuclear ending: 'The last great story was death: someone failed to tell it, or else no-one wanted to hear.' *The Burning Book*, 1983, brings directness and passion to this theme: 'bird-cries' from the '*hibakusha*, atomic victims' haunt the margins of a text about a family mostly 'quite the same as everyone else', wiped out with everyone else on the brink of their happy ending. Three blackened pages precede a return to the present: 'Our bright lives beat against ending ... Always beginning again, beginning against ending'. Later works show more hope: in *Light Years*, 1985, 12 months run from a marriage's breakup to its rebirth, from the death of a rare, exploited animal to the preservation of others, against a backdrop of infinitesimal cosmic time; *Grace*, 1988, presents the narratives of an anti-nuclear campaigner, the detective watching her, and her aunt, who at 85 is still caring for the future. MG has written a TV play, *Handfast*, and is working on a novel called *Where Are the Snows*.

Gee, Shirley, playwright living in London. She was b. in 1932 and educ. at Frensham Heights School, Surrey (to which she credits her 'certain sense of fascination with, empathy with outsiders'), and the Webber–Douglas Academy of Dramatic Art, London. She spent 12 years acting, m. actor Donald G., and had two sons. After writing classes she had a play, *Stones*, broadcast in 1974. *Moonshine*, 1977, and *Bedrock*, 1979, followed on radio. *Typhoid Mary*, 1979, about an Irish immigrant who carries typhus to America, and *Never in My Lifetime*, 1983, about love amid Ulster violence, both award-winners, were both adapted from radio for the stage (and both printed in *Best Radio Plays*, 1979 and 1983). SG values highly support from, and solidarity with, theatre women and women friends. Her first commissioned stage play, *Ask for the Moon* (Hampstead Theatre,

1986) exposes past and present exploitation of female labour, and the system which causes it.

Gellhorn, Martha, novelist and war correspondent, b. 1908 in St Louis, only da. of suffragist and reformer Edna (Fischel) and physician George G. She attended Bryn Mawr for a year before going to Paris as a reporter on *The New Republic* and the *Hearst Times Union*. There she became 'involved in [Europe's] politics the way a tadpole is involved in a pond'. She returned to the USA in 1934, the year of her part-autobiographical novel *What Mad Pursuit*. A job reporting on the Federal Emergency Relief Program resulted in her highly praised set of four novellas set in the Depression, *The Trouble I've Seen*, 1936. She lived with Ernest Hemingway in Spain (m. 1940, divorced 1945), and began a career as war correspondent in 1937 by sending *Collier's* an unsolicited piece describing life under siege in Madrid. She reported on Czechoslovakia before and after the Munich Pact. Her 'afterword' to the 1986 reprint of *A Stricken Field*, 1940, about a US woman journalist in refugee-filled Prague in 1938, says she wrote it to 'show what history is like for people who have no choice except to live through it or die from it'. She also described Finland under Russian invasion, the British presence in China, the Normandy landings, VE day in Dachau, the Nuremberg and Eichmann trials, and the Six Day and Vietnam wars. Further collections of stories and novellas, from *The Heart of Another*, 1941 (stories often of US journalists in the Spanish Civil War and WWII), to *The Weather in Africa*, 1978 (about the damage caused by poverty), illustrate her recurring concerns. Among six novels, *Liana*, 1944, ends on the suicide of a mixed-race Caribbean woman whose husband strives to make her 'like a white lady'. *The Wine of Astonishment*, 1948, is a novel of WWII. Best known is her non-fiction and collected journalism, including *The Face of War*, 1959 (rev. 3rd ed., 1986), *Vietnam: A New Kind of War*, 1966, *Travels With Myself and Another*, 1978, 'On Apocryphism' in *Paris Review*, 79, 1981 (rebuking inaccurate memoir-writers), and *The View from the Ground*, 1989. She married Thomas Matthews in 1953, divorced in 1963, has an adopted son, and lives in Wales. Critical biography by Jacqueline Orsagh as Michigan State Univ. thesis, 1978: many recent reprints, three with her afterwords.

Gems, Pam (Price), playwright. B. in 1925 at Bransgore in the New Forest, da. of Elsie (Annetts) and Jim P. (who died in the workhouse when she was four), she was bought up by her mother and two widowed grandmothers, and educ. at Brockenhurst Grammar School. WWII service with the WRNS gave her a place at Manchester Univ. (BA in psychology, 1949). That year she m. Keith Gems, a model-manufacturer; they settled in the Isle of Wight. Of PG's four children, the elder son writes plays; the younger daughter was a Down's syndrome child, which helped to bring PG to London and the women's movement. After writing several TV screenplays (*A Builder by Trade* was produced, 1961), she had a children's play staged in London, 1972. Half a dozen productions followed, at theatres there and elsewhere, including two monologues about women alone, 1973 (*My Warren* and *After Birthday*, about 'an older lady living in a bed-sitter who is sent a vibrator as a mean joke', and 'a girl who shoves her baby [miscarried] down the lav'), and a play for the Almost Free's first Women's Theatre Season, 1974. *Dusa, Fish Stas and Vi* (originally *Dead Fish*), which reached both the West End and print in 1977, Los Angeles in 1978, was PG's first big success. (Four women variously scarred by patriarchal society help Dusa recover the children her husband kidnapped.) PG has treated historical figures: Christina of Sweden, seventeenth-century ruler, intellectual and cross-dresser (acted 1977, pub. 1982); Fritz Perls, *gestalt* psychologist (acted 1977); Edith Piaf (opened 1978, pub. 1979). In 1982 she wrote of women in a brothel (*The Treat*) and male transvestites (*Aunt Mary*). *Loving Women* played at the Arts Theatre, 1984, the year of PG's version of Chekhov's *Cherry Orchard* and her Royal Shakespeare Company *Camille* (after Dumas). She favours a synoptic approach, loose in structure but rich in dramatic images, with strong female roles and tough, often subversive, humour. She has translated Marianne Auricoste's play about Rosa Luxembourg, and work by Marguerite DURAS, Chekhov and Ibsen. See *Three Plays*, 1986; Catherine Itzin, *Stages in the Revolution*, 1980; Keyssar, 1984.

Genlis, Stéphanie-Félicité (du Crest de Saint-Aubin), marquise de Sillery, comtesse de, 1746–1830, French educator and fiction writer with great influence in England. Married at 16, she became governess to the daughters of the Duc de Chartres, later Philippe-Egalité (she was also, like Grace ELLIOTT, his mistress); in 1785 she was made *Gouverneur* (masculine form) to the boys as well, including the future Louis-Philippe. Both her husband and lover were guillotined. In 1785–6 and 1791 she visited England, where she was admired for pedagogy more than the ROMANCES among her 100 books. *Theatre of EDUCATION* (1781, original 1779) consists of little plays, many for girls only. *Adelaide and Theodore, or Letters on Education*, 1784, and *Tales of* [more accurately Evenings at] *the Castle, or Stories of Instruction and Delight*, 1785, tell improving tales of children in the country whose mother has full control and submerges her own life in theirs. Adelaide and Theodore are presented on marriage with copies of the book about them, and reading lists (male writers, plus Lady Mary Wortley MONTAGU): carefully selected novel-reading is recommended. Life by Violet Wyndham, 1958.

George, Jean (Craighead), children's writer and naturalist. B. in 1919 in Washington, DC, da. of Carolyn (Johnson) and entomologist Frank C., she was educ. at Pennsylvania State Univ. (BA, 1941) She m. John L. G. in 1944 (divorced 1963), and had three children. Her nearly 30 books focus on ecological balance and the lessons of respect and insight which humans can learn from animals. She shared the writing of the first six with her husband, but illustrated them herself. Details of habitat, diet and movement are precise and unsentimentalized; the style is staccato and powerful, as when a single gun shot ends *Vulpes, the Red Fox*, 1948: 'Buck never missed. The hunt was done.' JCG often shows children's greater understanding of themselves as a result of time in the wilderness. In *Julie of the Wolves*, 1972, being befriended by a pack of Arctic wolves shows a lost Eskimo girl, Miyax/Julie, parallels between her situation on the mountain slope and the Eskimo's place in an English world. A city girl's chance landing of a great fish is similarly a learning experience in *Hook a Fish, Catch a Mountain*, 1975. Contact with animals provokes discovery in *The Wendletrap Trap*, 1978 (a picture book set in Bimini), *The Cry of the Crow*, 1980 (an Everglades adventure), *Water Sky*, 1987 (Alaskan whaling). JG's settings often become characters. In *One Day in the Alpine Tundra*, 1984, a monolith breaks away from a cliff face: as a breeze drops a fragment of lichen on to the exposed 'scar', 'the healing began'.

Gerard, Jane **Emily**, 1849–1905, novelist and critic, and **Dorothea**, 1855–1915, novelist, daughters of Euphemia (Robinson) and Archibald G. EG was b. in Jedburgh, Roxburghshire, and educ. at home. At 15 she shared lessons in Venice with Princesse Marguerite to whom *A Sensitive Plant*, 1891, was dedicated; she also spent three years at a convent in the Tyrol. In 1869 she m. Chevalier Miecislas de Laszowski, officer in the Austrian army. They lived in Galicia, then Transylvania, and died in Vienna within weeks of each other. DG was

b. in Rocksoles, Lanarks, educ. at home, then spent four years at a convent in Graz, Austria. After their mother's death in 1870, she joined EG. In 1886 she m. Julius Longard de Longgarde, Austrian army officer, and lived in Galicia, then Vienna. Their experience of life in Eastern Europe and their understanding of Austrian aristocracy contribute to their fiction. They wrote independently and collaborated (under the initials E. D. or E. and D. Gerard) on four novels: *Reata*, 1880, about a Mexican girl unaccustomed to European ways; *Beggar My Neighbour*, 1882, a cleverly plotted novel of family relationships in which brother beggars brother; *The Waters of Hercules*, 1885, in which comic, but not unfeeling, observation supplies background for a story of logical heroine and unheroic hero; and *A Sensitive Plant*, the tale of a shy heroine whose happiness is threatened by an ambitious mother and her beautiful wayward daughter. Their independent works are on occasion referential: the heroine of EG's *A Foreigner*, 1896, meets the central character from DG's *A Queen of Curds and Cream*, 1892. The novels, particularly those of EG, successfully combine humour and pathos as in her *The Extermination of Love*, 1901. The Gerards wrote for pleasure and did not set out to write thesis novels (DG sub-titled one of hers 'A Novel without a purpose'). Their attitudes are traditionally conservative. EG's non-fiction includes a record of her time in Transylvania, *The Land Beyond the Forest*, 1888, and reviews of German and French literature for *The Times* and *Blackwood's*. The more prolific DG reveals fertility of invention, ranging from the short but moving *Angela's Lover*, 1895, which exposes the inadequacy of conventional views of romantic love, to studies of the gulf between Jewish and Christian communities in *Orthodox*, 1888. EG and DG well deserve the composite tribute paid by the *SR* to 'one of the most fascinating of our lady novelists'.

Gerould, Katherine Elizabeth (Fullerton), 1879–1944, short-story writer, novelist, essayist, b. Brockton, Mass., third child and only da. of Julia (Ball) and the Rev. Bradford Morton F. Educ. Boston and France, in 1900 she graduated from Radcliffe College, taking an MA a year later, when she became reader in English at Bryn Mawr. In 1910, she m. Gordon Hall G., English professor, with whom she moved to Princeton and had a son and daughter. She wrote nearly 50 short stories 1900–30, which were included in a number of collections. She shares with Edith WHARTON an interest in moral choice and relationships doomed by the social code. Her characters make crucial sacrifices, often in the context of a marriage, as in 'The Great Tradition' and 'The Weaker Vessel'. Sometimes, as in 'Vain Oblations' and 'The Knight's Move', the sacrifice demanded is life itself. Her novels and essays do not have the power of her short stories, where sophisticated narrative technique and characterization are matched by a compelling emotional and moral intensity: 'there was a kind of glory in having it hurt to be good' ('The Great Tradition'). More than half her stories remain uncollected. The rest are in *Vain Oblations*, 1914, *The Great Tradition*, 1915, and *Valiant Dust*, 1922. Her best novels are *Lost Valley*, 1922, and *The Light that Never Was*, 1931. Her collected essays include *Modes and Morals*, 1920, and *The Aristocratic West*, 1925. KG's work is discussed in Stuart P. Sherman's *Genius of America*, 1924, and Fred B. Millet, *Contemporary American Authors*, 1940.

'Gershon', Karen, Loewenthal, later Tripp, poet, historian, novelist, b. 1923 at Bielefeld, Germany, da. of Selma (Schoenfeld) and architect Paul L. She escaped to England in 1938; her entire family died in concentration camps. She m. Val Tripp, an art teacher, in 1948, and had four children. Her poetry vols. began with 'The Relentless Year' in Edwin Muir, ed., *New Poets*, 1959: repr. alone. In 1965 KG translated

Ludwig Marcuse's *Obscene: The History of an Indignation*. After *Selected Poems*, 1966, she won her first awards, from the Arts Council and the *Jewish Chronicle*. She contributed to recovering her own and others' history in *We Came as Children*, a 'collective autobiography of refugees', 1966, and *Postscript*, a collective account of the lives of Jews in W. Germany since WWII, 1969. Invited to Israel by the government, KG spent four years there; she then returned – although still feeling an exile – to England. Her poems poignantly evoke the links between her dead and living family. *Legacies and Encounters*, 1972, describes her Israeli experience and looks at her children as 'children whom the Germans would have killed'. In *My Daughters, My Sisters*, 1975, she tells how the generations 'in me meet each other', and how, 'with no talent for living, I often wish myself dead, / my single asset is a sense of words.' *Coming Back From Babylon*, 1979, relates Old Testament stories to modern suffering. Of KG's three novels, *Burn Helen*, 1980, centres on a terminally ill woman, *The Bread of Exile*, 1985, on Jewish refugee children in England. *The Fifth Generation*, 1987, about an adolescent boy whose father might be a Jew or Hitler, deals powerfully with responsibility and identity. *Collected Poems*, 1990.

Gerstenberg, Alice, 1885–1972, playwright, novelist, b. in Chicago, da. of Julia (Weischendorff) and Erich G., educ. at Kirkland School and Bryn Mawr. Her first book was *A Little World*, 1908, four plays for Bryn Mawr students; her *Captain Joe* was produced in NYC, 1912. She published two novels, *Unquenched Fire*, 1912, and *The Conscience of Sarah Platt*, 1915, and had a hit with her dramatization of *Alice in Wonderland* and *Through the Looking Glass*, 1915. *Overtones* (one act, Washington Square Players, 1915; in London, 1917, with Lily Langtry; pub. in *Ten One-Act Plays*, 1921; three acts, 1922), pre-dates Eugene O'Neill in use of masks, making four characters of two women. The cultured surface women use small talk for concealment; their alter-egos claw one another verbally: one self telling her other self that their husband doesn't suspect that the calm, suave manner of the one hides the hatred of the other. *The Pot-Boiler*, another in the 1921 volume, satirizes a professional dramatist. A founding member of the Chicago Little Theatre, first in the USA, AG hoped that little theatres would offer playwrights opportunities all over the country; she wrote many one-act plays expressly for them, as well as three-acters for the commercial stage. *Four Plays for Four Women*, 1924, exposes pressures of male traditions on female self-expression; 'The Puppeteer', in *Comedies All*, 1930, shows a dominating grandmother destroying the individuality of her children as society tried to destroy hers. AG also wrote radio drama and articles on Little Theatre. Papers at Syracuse Univ.

Gestefeld, Ursula Newell, 1845–1921, novelist and New Thought leader, b. at Augusta, Maine. Little is known about her early life. She m. Theodore G. and had four children. She became interested in Christian Science and studied with Mary Baker Eddy, though Eddy interpreted UG's *Statement of Christian Science*, 1888, as an attack and had her dismissed from the Church. UG responded with a pamphlet, *Jesuitism and Christian Science*, 1888, highly critical of Eddy's claims to spiritual and scriptural authority. She founded Gestefeld Publishing Company in Pelham, NY, and, publishing a monthly magazine, *Exodus*, 1896–1904, founded the Church of New Thought and the College of the Science of Being. *The Builder and the Plan*, 1901, argues the superiority of reason and logic over the authority of any individual or church. In *The Leprosy of Miriam*, 1894, women represent stages in the personal evolution of Everett Long. Ambitious, intellectual Miriam, 'smitten with the leprosy of scientific materialism' (p. 6), goes mad, while her sister Sarah, combining the rational and intuitive, is the true 'deliverer of men from their own bondage' (p. 219). *The Woman Who Dares*, 1892, presents in a popular novel form coherent, perceptive feminist analyses of issues such as marriage, sexuality, and prostitution: Murva Kroom rails against the sexual subservience of women in marriage, leaves her husband and establishes a women's refuge, 'a halfway station between weakness, pain and crime; and strength, courage and independence' (p. 331). See C. Braden's *Spirits in Rebellion*, 1963.

Gethin, Grace (Norton), Lady, 1676–97, essayist, da. of Lady NORTON. She m. Sir Richard G., an Irish baronet a generation older, and died after eight months (he re-married in a few months more). Her MSS were pub. as *Misery's Virtues Whetstone*, 1699, and as *Reliquiae Gethinianae, or Some Remains of Grace Lady Gethin*, 1700, with a verse compliment by William Congreve. The preface, amid hyperbolical praise, says these prose essays (on topics like friendship, death, gratitude; also a poem written at 11) consist chiefly of hasty 'first Conceptions', published mainly for friends. Her mother later regretted that 'by Mistake' quotations were not footnoted; the work has been dismissed as merely a private anthology lifted from Bacon's *Essays* and elsewhere; but this misinterprets the conventionally large part played by quotation. Though many of GG's topics are inherited, she touches on female concerns, such as the question whether it is worse if a husband has one long-term mistress or 'is continually changing his loves'.

Gibbes, Phebe, d. after 1805, novelist and miscellaneous writer. She told the RLF, 1804, she had pub. 22 novels, plus children's books, translations from French, and pieces for periodicals including the *London Magazine*: many are untraced. She was then a widow with two daughters (a son died in India), near starving after mismanagement by her father-in-law. His family, 'to my unspeakable misfortune', piously condemned 'every species of Literature, except devotional'; she longed to convince them she was not a visionary, just unlucky. Their views and her 'withdrawing turn of temper' had kept her anonymous. Her work has style and wit: having led the hero of *Life and Adventures of Mr Francis Clive* (1764, repr. 1975) through a series of 'genuine scenes' to 'the summit of human felicity' (apparently translatable as wealth), she says she can go no further without 'recourse to fiction'. R. B. Sheridan accepted but then lost a musical drama by her, *c.* 1776. *Friendship in a Nunnery, or The American Fugitive*, 1778 (title and subtitle reversed in repr.), adds the theme of female friendship to that of freedom in marriage choice; the convent option is thoroughly debunked by a young American woman, whose republican opinions offended conservative reviewers. *Hartly House, Calcutta*, 1789 (epistolary, like several of PG's works), was praised in reviews: Elizabeth MONTAGU tried to discover the author; Catherine HUTTON compared it to Frances BROOKE on Canada. PG says she wrote it to combat prejudice against India, to celebrate the country and the actual Hartley family, and to discuss (acutely) literature, courtship, and women's role in society. (Ketaki Kushari DYSON supposes it autobiographical.) Joseph Johnson published PG's *Elfrida, or Paternal Ambition*. Her *Heaven's Best Gift*, 1797, has been ascribed to a Mrs Phillips. In 1799 she offered the RLF 'Two Little Dramas'; in 1804 she sought a grant for copying illegible MSS; in 1805, near death but with 'unsubduable aspiration' to prove 'she has not lived in vain', she was writing a substantial study of the various orders of the poor. The RLF next year listed her claim as 'questionable'.

Gibbons, Stella Dorothea, 1902–89, poet and fiction writer, eldest child of Maud (Williams) and Dr Telford Charles G., whose practice lay in a poor part of North London. Unhappy in childhood, she told 'fantastic romances' to her little brothers before she could read. She was educ. by governesses according to her father's 'eccentric ideas', then from 13 at North London Collegiate School for Girls (where she wrote stories) and from 19 at University College, London (for a then unique two-year JOURNALISM course). She began her ten years in Fleet Street in 1923 as a cable decoder for British United Press; she next wrote for the *Evening Standard*, then *The Lady*, as well as stories and poems. Her work encompasses both romantic and anti-romantic. In *The Mountain Beast*, 1930 (first of three poetry volumes before *Collected Poems*, 1950), she wrote of 'love's cruel wars', of satyrs and dryads, mountains and clouds, African lilies and crocodiles. In *Cold Comfort Farm*, 1932 (her first novel: Femina Vie Heureuse Prize; foreword satirically bewailing 'the meaningless and vulgar bustle of newspaper offices'), a rational, bossy London heroine brings calm and efficiency to her rustic relations the Dooms, demolishing parody versions of the stock-in-trade of earthy regionalists like Thomas Hardy, Mary WEBB, Sheila KAYE-SMITH and D. H. Lawrence. The overblown matriarch Aunt Ada, fixated on having 'seen something nasty in the wood-shed', the devastating sexuality unleashed whenever the sukebind is in flower: such details brought popular success which has swamped the rest of SG's output. She m. actor Allan Bourne Webb in 1933 and had a daughter; she published a children's book, 1935, and five vols. of stories (two using the Cold Comfort name). She planned to issue a posthumous poetry volume, and claimed to see herself as poet, not novelist, to lack interest in people (as opposed to ideas, nature, and 'the possible existence of God'), and to be handicapped for fiction by a distaste for emotional 'scenes'. Irony may lurk in such claims: SG brilliantly depicted distaste for scenes in *The Snow-Woman*, 1969, where a martinet clamped tight since WWI bereavement is shocked into new life and love by discovering an illicit great-nephew (born, to her highly comic outrage, on her sofa). SG's more than 20 novels range from such 'romance' as *Fort of the Bear*, 1953 (in which an earl forsakes London literary society to pursue to the death an obsession with bear-hunting in western Canada), to the sharply naturalistic. Notable female protagonists include pairs of aged London sisters in *A Pink Front Door*, 1959 (Hampstead intelligentsia), and *Starlight*, 1967 (social flotsam in the poverty trap), and a commonsensical housekeeper whose sensibilities remain unplumbed by 'arty' employers (*The Charmers*, 1965). SG has an acute eye for contact between different social groups. MSS at Boston Univ.

Gibbs, Cecilia **May**, 1877–1969, children's writer and illustrator, b. in Sydenham, Kent, da. of Eliza (Emery) and Herbert William G., public servant and artist. In 1881 she arrived in Adelaide, South Australia, with her mother and brothers, then went to Perth, where she attended Amy Best's School for Girls and contributed illustrations and cartoons to newspapers such as the *Western Mail*. After two extended trips back to England, studying art and working e.g. as illustrator for George C. Harrap and Co., in 1913 she settled in Sydney. She m. James Kelly, mining engineer, in 1919, and during the next decade produced some of her best work, including illustrations for publications such as the *Lone Hand* and the *Tatler*, and her long series of famous 'Gumnut' books. The first, *Gumnut Babies*, 1916, was followed by 17 others, including the classics of Australian children's literature, *Snugglepot and Cuddlepie*, 1918, and *Bib and Bub*, 1925. Enormously successful, the beautifully illustrated characters based on native flora have appealed to each generation of Australian children, and the books have never been out of print. She was awarded an MBE in 1955, and from marriage till her death she lived in 'Nutcote', the house she built in Neutral Bay, Sydney.

See Maureen Walsh's 'Mother of the Gumnuts' in *The MG Collection*, 1985. MSS are in the Mitchell Library, Sydney.

Giberne, Agnes, 'A. G.', 1845–1939, novelist and science writer, b. Belgaum, India, da. of Lydia Mary (Wilson) and Major Charles G., of Huguenot descent, whose retirement soon returned the family to England. Educ. at home by masters and sympathetic parents, she began, with her sisters, to write early, at 17 publishing children's stories with the SPCK. Up to *Mignonette*, 1869, she wrote as 'A. G.'; with *The Curate's Home*, also 1869, she began using her full name, going on to produce over 108 titles: tales and stories, historical fiction and pioneering popular science books. *Nigel Browning*, 1890, a small-town family tale of a girl's obsessive unrequited love, has a Christian framework and is aimed at the same readership as the work of Charlotte YONGE. She was best known for her many popular science books 'for beginners of all ages', starting with *Sun, Moon and Stars*, 1879 (admiringly prefaced, unasked, by the Savilian Professor of Astronomy); all are models of lucid explanation.

Gibson, Margaret, also Margaret Gibson Gilboord, writer of short stories and TV scripts, b. 1948 in Toronto, da. of Audrey Elizabeth and H. Dane Gibson. Afflicted from childhood with serious mental illness, she was hospitalized at 15, then spent four years as a voluntary mute: 'I didn't believe I had anything significant to say.' In 1971 she m. S. Gilboord; they had a son, Aaron, and divorced, 1974. Her first collection of stories, *The Butterfly Ward*, 1977, shared the City of Toronto Award with Margaret ATWOOD's *Lady Oracle*. MG has also written short stories (*Considering Her Condition*, 1978) and film and television scripts. She deals with pain, violence, and madness and is especially skilful at capturing the language and speech rhythms of protagonists attempting to cope with harsh reality. Claude Jutra's TV film *Ada*, the story of the lobotomizing of a brilliant woman, comes from her first collection; her story 'Making It' became the successful film *Outrageous*, starring female impersonator Craig Russell, a friend with whom she lived for two years. MG has been compared with Audrey THOMAS and Marie-Claire BLAIS.

Giffard, Martha (Temple), Lady, 1638–1722, memoirist, youngest surviving child of Martha (Hammond) and Sir John T. She acquired solid classical learning and was admired at 15 for her letters. Her husband, Sir Thomas G. of Ireland, died of a fever after only two weeks of marriage, 1662. Her poems include a rendering of Montemayor's early Spanish romance *Diana*. She was a friend of Elizabeth BURNET, and wished that her sister-in-law Dorothy OSBORNE's 'extraordinary' letters could be printed. In 1690 she wrote the life of her brother Sir William T., with whom she had chiefly lived since 1650, then condensed it, probably because another brother found it too domestic and intimate (pub. 1728, further altered; often repr. with Temple's works; full text ed. G. C. Moore, 1930: especially vivid on the plague of 1665). Some surviving letters in Julia G. Longe's life, 1911; angry ones of 1709 to Swift are lost, as are her general family history and account of her nephew's suicide. In 1719–20 she was helping Edward Young with material for a play.

Gilbert, Ann (Taylor), 1782–1866, woman of letters (famous as a CHILDREN's writer), elder sister of Jane TAYLOR. Her verse, written from seven or eight, included ambitious projects like relating events previous to the *Iliad*. Accused of literary vanity in about 1796, she 'made a magnanimous conflagration of all my MSS, and resolved to go humbly all my days'; but soon afterwards came her first work in print (an election song) and in 1799 her first in *The Minor's Pocket-Book*, which she later edited. After the brilliant success of *Original Poems*, 1804–5, she and others of her family did much writing and revising for children. AG edited *The Eclectic Review*, initiated its reviews of novels (by e.g. Jane WEST and Maria EDGEWORTH), and resisted a later plan to re-issue with her 'sentences weakened down to rule'. In 1813 she married the Rev. Joseph G., who approached her because of her writing and urged her to continue even as a busy mother. They lived in Sheffield and Nottingham: she pub. pamphlets on ABOLITION and on drink, and an address from women to the Queen linking poverty with bad legislation; but she opposed votes for women. Her autobiography, pub. 1874 (begun at 66 and set aside to write her husband's life, 1853), reaches her marriage. Until 1838 'never confident, never satisfied' in her faith, she doubted whether a *religious* DIARY could ever be 'honestly done'; she wrote her own secular diary on her last day alive. Poems ed. with her sister's, 1877; for her huge output (and her family's) see bibliography, 1975, by Christina Duff Stewart, also editor of AG's album of verse, pictures, etc., 1978.

Gilbert, Anne (Hart), *c.* 1772–1834, memoirist. B. in Antigua, eldest child of Barry Conyers H., sugar-planter and man of colour, she cared for a large family (her mother died when she was 12) and for blacks on the estate, and (with a sister) became an ardent Methodist. In 1798 she enraged white society by marrying the white John G. (d. 1833). (He wrote that those who abused him for basely degrading himself would have thought he 'acted quite properly' had he seduced and degraded her.) Against opposition, she founded and ran an interracial Sunday School, 1809, other schools, Benevolent Institutions, and a Refuge Society for fallen women. She destroyed, 'no doubt for the best motives', all her MSS about her religious experiences, and never wrote a projected life of her sister, but completed a *Memoir* written by her husband (Liverpool, 1835).

Gilbert, Ruth, poet, b. 1917 at Greytown, NZ, da. of Florence Margaret (Carrington), music teacher, and Henry George G., Presbyterian minister. She trained and worked as a physiotherapist and m. Dr Mackay, physician, 1945. She lives in Wellington, and has pub. three collections: *Lazarus*, 1949, *The Sunlit Hour*, 1955, *The Luthier*, 1966, as well as *Collected Poems*, 1984, and *Early Poems 1938–1944*, 1988. The poems are quiet, lyric, occasional, sometimes slight, about music and biblical stories and places – NY, Samoa, England. But the earliest post-war poems about Lazarus are striking. In a group of moving poems about the events of a woman's life, she writes about birth ('Quickening', 'Justification', 'Still-Born': 'O child who did not cry, you cry forever / Through all my nights'); about woman's need for love, and loss of it; about women's silence ('She Who is Silent', 'By Bread Alone'); and about facing the death of a loved one: 'Death is of the Grass'. See critical study by F. W. Nielsen Wright, 1985.

Gilbert, Sandra (Mortola), poet, critic, scholar, professor of English. B. in 1936 in NYC, da. of Angela (Caruso), an elementary school teacher, and Alexis Joseph M., a civil engineer, she was educ. at Cornell, NY, and Columbia Univs. (PhD, 1968). She m. Elliot G., a professor of English, in 1957; they have three children. Critically prolific, she wrote initially on the canon (dissertation on D. H. Lawrence, pub. 1973, study guides on Shakespeare, Forster, Yeats). In the early 1970s, she shifted ground; in 1979, she and Susan Gubar published their first collaborative volumes, a collection of feminist essays on women poets, *Shakespeare's Sisters*, and *The Madwoman in the Attic*, a ground-breaking work which has permanently altered criticism on the subject its sub-title identifies, *The Woman*

Writer and the Nineteenth-Century Literary Imagination. Its sequel, *No Man's Land*, studies women's writing in the twentieth century: *The War of the Words*, vol. 1, 1988, deals with 'social, literary, and linguistic interactions between men and women from the middle of the nineteenth century to the present'; *Sexchanges*, vol. 2, 1989, treats the period from the 1880s to the 1930s; *Letters from the Front*, vol. 3, is awaited. They also edited *The Female Imagination and the Modernist Aesthetic*, 1986. SG's poetry, her 'core identity', has also shifted radically during its development: W. C. Williams, Auden, and Yeats provide epigraphs for sections of *In the Fourth World*, 1979, but the poems in *The Summer Kitchen*, 1983, evoke her 'Sicilian aunts' and detect a delicate eros in the natural world ('the grapes / that fattened in the arbour', the 'green steam swelling from the cool / root of the kitchen') or a comic force in the edible (as in the tip-toeing army of 'The Brussels Sprouts'). Here a 'supermarket poet', in love with the gorgeously edible, in *Emily's Bread*, 1984 (dedicated to Gubar), SG is literary and historical, turning a sometimes surreal, sometimes domestic gaze to gender imprisonments in the 'forest of symbols' and connecting Emily DICKINSON and Emily BRONTË with their 'womanly' acts ('the bride of yeast, / the wife of the dark of the oven'). Poems in *Blood Pressure*, 1988, move from sensuous childhood memories ('organdy curtains white as milk') to painful sexual awareness ('That's what he hates the most! / More than the mushy breasts, the tender belly, / he hates that swamp inside you, / the moist cleft where flowers quiver'). SG now teaches at the Univ. of Calif. at Davis. See also HISTORICAL FEMINIST CRITICISM.

Gilchrist, Anne (Burrows), 1828–85, literary critic and biographer, b. London, eldest child of Henrietta (Carwardine) and John Parker B., solicitor. She was educ. to age 16 at the Misses Cahusecs' evangelical school (quite advanced for its time), and read Comte, Emerson, Ruskin, Spencer, and also Carlyle, whom she later knew well. In 1851 she m. art critic Alexander G. (d. 1861), and had four children. She wrote on scientific subjects for periodicals, then, with the Rossetti brothers, prepared for publication her husband's *Life of William Blake*, 1862 (revised 1880, with a memoir), and later wrote the *DNB* entry on Blake. Her first major independent work was *An Englishwoman's Estimate of Walt Whitman*, 1870, one of the best contemporary discussions of *Leaves of Grass*, and valuable too as a woman's defence of the notorious 'sex poems'. It expresses her own convictions about the need to accept sexuality without shame. Her *Confession of Faith*, 1885, again celebrates Whitman. After many ardent letters to him (see T. B. Harned, ed., *The Letters of AG and Walt Whitman*, 1919), she spent nearly three years in America but failed to arouse his love. She pub. a life of Mary LAMB, 1883, and 'Three Glimpses of a New England Village', 1884 (*Blackwood's*), praising the educational opportunities for women at Smith College. Whitman later described her as 'a supreme character of whom the world knows too little for its own good'. Life by her son Herbert H. Gilchrist, 1887, includes the Whitman essays and 'Glimpses of a New England Village'.

Gilchrist, Ellen, journalist, short-story writer and novelist, b. 1935 to Aurora 'Bodie' (Alford) and Garth G. Growing up at Hopedale Plantation, Grace, Mississippi, she 'almost never went to school. That's why I'm a writer.' She read hugely, put on plays, and began 'mov[ing] around all of my life' when taken to Indiana during WWII. She edited a high school newspaper at Harrisburg, Ill., ran away at 19 to be married, and had three sons by the first of her four husbands. After a BA from Millsaps College, 1967, she wrote steadily from 1975, edited the *Vieux Carré Courier*, 1976–9, published *The Land Surveyor's Daughter*, 1979 (poems), and adapted Eudora WELTY stories for a broadcast play,

A Season of Dreams. Her first story volume, *In the Land of Dreamy Dreams*, 1981, catches the antics of the 'beautiful spoiled crazy' and often wholly amoral rich. Among many violent or macabre disasters, one narrator says of a public triumph in girlhood: 'Sometimes I think whatever has happened since has been of no real interest to me.' EG variously transforms her early memories in her novel (*The Annunciation*, 1983) and later stories (*Victory over Japan*, 1984, and *Drunk with Love*, 1986), but her sources are richly mixed: one story moves from earthquake and heroic rescue to twin embryos talking in the womb, another from a death-sentence by kidney disease to a fatal accident while liberating trapped sharks. EG's own life features least in *Nine Women*, 1985 (whose cast includes blacks both affluent and struggling), most in *Falling Through Space, The Author's Journals*, 1987, which collects weekly pieces from national public radio, and notes the influence of Edna St Vincent MILLAY and Anne SEXTON. EG has written a play, and worked on screenplays. Latest stories in *The Blue-Eyed Buddhist*, 1990.

Gilding, Elizabeth, poet and essayist. She was orphaned early, educ. wholly at Woolwich near London, and confined to a 'somewhat obscure situation in life', with little leisure; but 'My genius led me to Poetry. I scribbled. It pleased myself.' Publishing poems, with some essays, as *The Breathings of Genius*, 1776, she introduced herself (unlike her 'refined or fawning predecessors') 'with all proper and becoming respect'. The poems, dating from 1759, cover devotion (some hymns, praise of sermons by her local Dissenting minister, Daniel Turner), politics (a fable attacking Lord Bute), social satire, pastoral love, and defence against those who say she cannot have written the poems. A dialogue between 'Honour and its Antagonist' neatly reverses readers' expectations when the antagonist is revealed as death. 'Despair' opens powerfully: 'Moments on moments, still and still succeed; / Arm'd with new points, to make the wretched bleed.' Turner contributed early essays which reveal a mind more conventional than hers.

Giles, Barbara (Atkin), poet and children's writer, b. 1912 in Manchester, da. of Marie (Hanaghan) and John A. She was educ. at Liverpool College for Girls; then, after emigrating to Victoria with her parents in 1923, at Leongatha High School and Melbourne Univ. Poverty forced her to leave; she completed her arts degree in 1968 as a mature-age student. She worked as a school teacher 1931–40 and 1957–77, and in between married and had three sons. The experience of teaching English to migrants prompted her to write her first poem, published in 1967. In 1975 she was a founding editor of the women's literary magazine *Luna*; many of the lyrical and energetic poems in her first collection, *Eve Rejects Apple*, 1978, are, as its title would suggest, strongly feminist. She has also pub. a second collection, *Earth and Solitude*, 1983, and written and ed. many collections of poems and stories for children, such as *My Animal Friends*, 1981, *People and Places*, 1981, and *Bicycles Don't Fly*, 1982.

Gill, Sarah (Prince), 1728–71, Boston Puritan diarist, da. of Deborah (Denny) and Thomas P., preacher at the Old South Church, who owned a copy of Anne BRADSTREET's poems. She began her irregular but persistent diary-keeping in 1743, convinced 'it is my duty to comit to writing my Experiences'. Her first 12 years, she says, were godless; she converted, then in 1742 'fell into decay, became Carnal, and Worldly'. She gave herself to God in October 1743, and her surviving journals (Boston Public Library: those sent to Esther (Edwards) BURR, 1754–7, are lost) record several re-commitments. Well educated, she loved books and left 'many private papers'. She married Moses G., well-to-do republican merchant, in 1759, and ran a large household and women's prayer-meetings. Ten of her meditations (one including verse) and a letter of exhortation 'To all my young Acquaintance, into whose Hands these will come' (written in 1755 but 'Not to be opened 'till after my Death') appeared with her funeral sermon. Reprints under various titles – e.g. Norwich, Conn. [1773], Edinburgh, 1785 – sometimes add a funeral sermon on her sister Deborah, 1723–44, who destroyed most of her own writings.

Gilliam, Florence Edna, journalist and theatre critic. She taught in Columbus, Ohio, published (with Wilbur Henry Siebert) *The Loyalists in Prince Edward Island*, 1911 (a work of history), moved to NYC in 1920, became managing editor of Arthur Moss's magazine *Quill*, married him, and in 1921 migrated to Paris (which she had first visited in 1913). They co-founded *Gargoyle*, 1921–2, which published H. D., BRYHER and Edna St Vincent MILLAY. FG wrote of the theatre for the *Paris Tribune*, *Boulevardier*, *Theatre Magazine* and *Theatre Arts* (both NY); she wrote other columns for the *Paris Herald* and *Paris Times*, and edited a monthly bulletin for the American Women's Club in Paris until 1926. This work remains uncollected. Divorced in 1931, she stayed in Paris until after the German occupation in 1941, and returned in 1945 to direct American Aid. That year she published *France, A Tribute*, 'by an American woman', a warm account of its culture and history. She received the Légion d'Honneur and Médaille de la Reconnaissance Française. She writes more personally in 'My Years with Arthur Moss' (*Lost Generation Journal*, 2 and 3, 1974–5), praising his 'notable gift of treating men and women equally as human beings'. See Benstock, 1987.

Gilliatt, Penelope (Conner), writer of novels, short stories, plays, film and television scripts, an opera libretto, and film and theatre criticism. B. in 1932 in London, da. of Mary (Douglass) and Cyril C., she grew up 'in a background of ancestral Northumberland, of the growth of shipbuilding and coal-mining', also the background for *Mortal Matters*, 1983. Educ. at Queen's Coll., London, and Bennington Coll., Vermont, she is divorced from Prof. R. W. Gilliatt and playwright John Osborne, with whom she has a daughter. A respected film critic on both sides of the Atlantic, PG has written profiles of *Jean Renoir*, 1975, and *Jacques Tati*, 1977, and two books on film and the theatre. She is best known for her Oscar-nominated and award-winning screenplay for *Sunday, Bloody Sunday*, 1971, about a man and woman painfully confronted by middle age when their shared lover goes abroad. Growing old and the past – 'history, therefore still with us' – recurrent themes in her fiction, are treated with 'wit and [a] sense of the absurd' in *Splendid Lives*, 1978, short stories about ageing eccentrics. PG's crisp, economical style and her reliance on dialogue to reveal characters and relationships are exemplified in *The Cutting Edge*, 1979, which explores a remarkable bond between two brothers largely through dialogue and letters. Her six collections of short stories, many of which first appeared in *The New Yorker*, are thought superior to her four novels.

Gillies, Valerie (Simmons), poet. B. 1948 in Edmonton, Alberta, she grew up in Scotland: her grandparents lived on the Lanarks. moors. She went to school in Edinburgh (writing poems by 14 to 'celebrate animal energy'), then Edinburgh Univ.(MA in English, 1970), where she also learned Gaelic, and Mysore Univ., South India (as the only European student), on a Commonwealth Scholarship. (She writes 'India adopted me and I vanished up country', but also 'I am to my country / A leaf on which the likeness of the tree is traced.') Back in Scotland she wrote a thesis, won awards for poetry, m. William G., Professor of Celtic at Edinburgh, and became 'a harassed housewife with no respite'. She has appeared in anthologies (including Rumens and several Scots collections). Her two poetry vols., *Each Bright Eye, Selected Poems 1971–76*, 1977, and *Bed of Stone*, 1984 ('named after the greatest greyhound ever'), treat the birth and growth of her three children, differing cultures, and the poetic process. Indian 'Roadgang Women' take 'a moment / to wipe sweat from around their eyes / with a corner of torn sari'. 'The Old Woman's Reel' pictures an aged Aran Islander spinning 'not on one foot / but on her stick', mimicked by a little girl, a 'pliant offshoot'. 'Marked, maimed, but not yet killed, / the poem shakes a fettered will'; words and whispers are frozen in verse like tussocks of grass. VG has written radio scripts, revues, and notes on Kipling's *Kim*, 1981; she teaches creative writing in schools and admires Elaine Feinstein's translations from Russian.

Gilman, Anne, d. 1686, Quaker minister and pamphleteer, wife of Thomas G., probably of Reading. She pub. *An Epistle to Friends*, 1662, with *A Letter to* [King] *Charles* (whom she directly urges to stop the soldiers breaking up meetings and jailing Quakers), and a broadside, *To the Inhabitants of the Earth* (1663, 2nd ed. 1669), calling the rich and powerful to repentance: 'Let them that reade, understand: for Kings will he bind in Chains. ...'

Gilman, Caroline (**Howard**), 1794–1888, journalist, novelist and poet, da. of Anna Lillie, of the prominent Breck family, and Samuel H., shipwright, who died when she was three. She m. Unitarian pastor Samuel G. in 1819, and moved to Charleston, SC. In 1832 she began the youth journal, *Rose Bud* (later *Southern Rose*), which featured sketches that became *Recollections of a New England Bride*, 1834, a sentimental and humorous (at the expense of the servants) account of a middle-class wife learning to manage a household once the initial bloom of romance has faded, and *Recollections of a Southern Matron*, 1837, which included a justification of slavery. *Love's Progress*, 1840, uneasily conjoins a domestic novel of education to a gothic conclusion. Her collection of poems, *Verses of a Lifetime*, 1849, includes descriptions of the Southern landscape, but mainly consists of romantic ballads and dramatic pieces, verging on the gruesome; in 'Joshua's Courtship' the farm boy Joshua literally casts sheep's eyes at the object of his desire. M. S. Saint-Amand's *A Balcony in Charleston*, 1941, contains a biographical sketch of CHG, some correspondence, and extracts from her work.

Gilman, Charlotte (**Perkins**) Stetson, 1860–1935, novelist, poet, lecturer, artist, economist, feminist theorist, editor, reformer, b. at Hartford, Conn. Her parents, Mary (Westcott) and Frederick Beecher P., separated shortly after her birth. Related to H. B. Stowe; her Beecher aunts provided role models. She was largely self-educated, with her father's help. Spirited and intellectually lively, she espoused dress reform, fresh air, cold baths, weight-lifting, gymnastics, running, lecture clubs, language classes and history–science reading programmes. Like the teenage heroine of her novel *Benigna Machiavelli*, 1914: 'I want to be big – Big – BIG! / I want to know everything ... I want to be strong, skilful'. Intense friendships with women included those with Adeline E. Knapp, with whom she lived for three years in the 1890s, Helen Campbell, and childhood friend Martha Luther, to whom she wrote in 1881: 'why in the name of heaven have we so confounded love with passion that it sounds to our century-tutored ears either wicked or absurd to name it between women?' In 1882 she m. Charles Walter Stetson; severe depression followed the birth of their one daughter in 1885; the rest cure prescribed for 'inappropriate' ambition by Dr S. Weir Mitchell resulted in her well-known tale, 'The Yellow Wall Paper', 1892. In 1888 she moved to California, supporting Nationalist (Utopian socialist) views and feminism;

divorced in 1894, she spent five years in the 1890s on the national lecture circuit speaking on labour and woman's place. In 1900 she m. her cousin George Houghton Gilman. Her political poems on the women's movement, *In This Our World*, appeared in 1903. Other works include *Women and Economics*, 1898, in which she stresses the androcentric nature of the socio-economic world and the need for both sexes to have 'world work'. She accused men of weakening the race by preferring small feeble creatures. In 1909 she founded *Forerunner*, a literary periodical written entirely by her and devoted to contemporary social issues; it published all her novels from *What Diantha Did*, 1910, to *Herland*, 1915, and *With Her in Ourland*, 1916. Politically sophisticated, her fiction is witty, ebullient, unpretentious and positive. *Herland*, a masterpiece of feminist UTOPIAN fiction, celebrates the strength and vigour of a community of women without men. In many of her stories, traditional sex roles are reversed, e.g. 'If I Were A Man' and 'The Widow's Might'. After George G. died (1934), she returned to California, joined by her daughter and her first husband's second wife. Contracting cancer, she committed suicide, leaving her autobiography, *The Living of Charlotte Perkins Gilman*, 1935. See the study by Mary A. Hill, 1980, and Ann J. Lane's introductions to *Herland*, 1979, and the *CPG Reader*, 1980.

Gilman, Dorothy, writer of children's books and mysteries, b. in 1923 in New Brunswick, NJ, da. of Essa (Starkweather) and James Bruce G. She m. teacher Edgar A. Butters in 1945 and had two sons (divorced, 1965). She started her education as an art student in Pennsylvania ('no one knew what else to do with me') but 'scurried over to the University of Pennsylvania once a week to audit writing courses'. Her first attempt at humour, 'Miss Crispin Rides Again', could not find a publisher, and her first books, children's novels, which she wrote under her married name, presented whimsical subjects: puppets, a carnival, an ice-cream caravan. In 1963, she 'rescued herself . . . from a bleak period' by creating 'a brand new reality where outrageous and difficult things would happen' and a DETECTIVE series character, a 'slightly eccentric lady from New Brunswick, New Jersey' who 'travels, has adventures, insists upon living fully and finding herself'. *The Unexpected Mrs. Pollifax*, 1966, was the first of these comic-heroic adventures of the unlikely CIA agent, who has been seen as a 'cross between Miss Marple and Modesty Blaise'. DG's *A New Kind of Country*, 1978, is autobiographical. *Mrs. Pollifax on the China Station*, 1984, researched in China, is richly descriptive. Other DG women are Sister John of *A Nun in the Closet*, 1975; Madame Karitska, the psychic, in *The Clairvoyant Countess*, 1975; Amelia Jones in *The Tightrope Walker*, 1979. See DG on herself in *The Writer*, July 1972, Kathleen Maio in *Wilson Library Bulletin*, Dec. 1983, quoted above, and Patricia Craig and Mary Cadogan, *The Lady Investigates*, 1986.

Gilmore, Mary Jean (Cameron), 1864–1962, poet and journalist, b. near Goulburn, NSW, eldest child of Mary (Beattie) and Donald G., farmer. Educ. at state schools at Wagga Wagga and Downside, from age 12 she worked as a pupil-teacher in country schools and later taught at the mining town of Broken Hill. Increasingly radical, she supported the strikes of the 1890s, and after rejecting a proposal of marriage from writer Henry Lawson, joined William Lane's New Australia Movement, an attempt to found a Utopian community, and sailed for Paraguay in 1895. There she m. fellow colonist William G. in 1897; their only child was born the following year. In 1902, after the failure of the community, they returned to Australia where she began her long editorship (1908–31) of the *Australian Worker*'s women's page. Here she attacked corruption and exploitation, and campaigned for social reform, particularly on issues that concerned women, children, and Aborigines. Her first collection, *Marri'd and other verse*, 1910, attracted considerable attention. Her own marriage became purely nominal from 1912, when she moved to Sydney to further her literary career. She pub. seven further vols. of poetry, including *The Passionate Heart*, 1918, and *Battlefields*, 1939, and some notable reminiscences of pioneering days, *Old Days, Old Ways*, 1934, as well as collections of essays. She accepted a DBE in 1937 and by the time of her death was very much the grand old dame of Australian literature, helping other writers become established. Like Judith WRIGHT, whom she influenced, MG mourns the destruction of Aboriginal tribes and the Australian countryside by white settlers. Her poetry was often strongly nationalistic as in the stirring 'No Foe Shall Gather Our Harvest' (written during WWII) and 'Nationality' (in her final volume, *Fourteen Men*, 1954). MSS are in the National Library of Australia, Canberra, and the Mitchell Library, Sydney. A selection of her letters, 1980, was ed. by W. H. Wilde and T. Inglis Moore. See the recent biography by W. H. Wilde, *Courage A Grace*, 1988.

Gilroy, Beryl, autobiographer, novelist, children's writer, b. 1924 in Berbice, Guyana. After local schools and teacher training, she gained a reputation for her teaching, and also worked for UNICEF. In 1951, eager to learn the newest, child-centred ideas, she left to study education at London Univ. Though qualified and experienced, she had to work as factory clerk and maid before finding her first British primary-school job, 1954, where she found children horrified at her blackness. She m. Pat Gilroy, a British scientist, had two children, and worked at home as journalist, radio reviewer of Caribbean books, publishers' reader and child psychotherapist. Back in teaching, she eventually became the first black headmistress in her north London borough. From 1970 she issued a series of children's stories, then *Black Teacher*, 1976, which relates her fight to improve the self-esteem of West Indian pupils, her commitment to children and to multi-racialism. In the 1980s she finished a PhD in counselling psychology, and became a child psychotherapist and multi-cultural researcher at the Institute of Education, London Univ. After *In For a Penny*, 1982 (stories centred on West Indian teenagers), she published *Frangipani House*, 1985, an adult novel (GLC black literature prize). In it an infirm old Guyanese woman, sent to a rest home by her family, holds on to dignity and freedom, verges on madness, but escapes into a dangerous but vital world of the poor and marginal. (The Institute of Contemporary Arts, London, has a video of BG talking about this work.) *Boy-Sandwich*, 1989, depicts three generations of West Indians in Britain: grandparents confined in a home give their grandson a sense of belonging, a history and a heritage for protection in a racist society.

Gingold, Helene, Baroness Eugenie Alexandra (afterwards Cowen), 1874?–1926, English poet and novelist, about whom little is known. She was often abroad: her second vol. of poems, *Flowers of the Field*, 1903, is dedicated to Carmen Sylva (Queen of Romania and author of several novels transl. into English in the 1890s). HG and her husband, Laurence C., were decorated by the King of Serbia for services to art and literature. Many of her poems, like *A Cycle of Verse*, were written in her teens: whilst some are satirical, most express love enduring through separation. Her novels develop intense, mysterious feelings, as in *Steyneville*, 1885, where a self-effacing male narrator helps to colour a complicated but conventional plot with inwardness and a sense of anxiety. Stories like 'Veritas' in *Seven Stories*, 1893, further dissolve boundaries between inner and outer and move more straightforwardly into fantasy, though the form is more interesting than the trite moral conclusion about sin.

Giovanni, Nikki, poet, b. in 1943 in Knoxville, Tenn., grandda. of 'Book' Watson, a Latin scholar who loved myth, and Louvenia Terrell, whose 'intolerant' response to white aggression required a quick departure from Georgia hidden under a blanket, and da. of middle-class black parents Yolande Cornelia and Jones G. She grew up in Cincinnati and studied history, literature and fine arts at Fisk (which 'released' her because 'her attitudes did not suit those of a Fisk woman'), the Univ. of Pennsylvania and Columbia School of Fine Arts. She has taught at Queens College of City Univ., NY, and at Livingstone College of Rutgers Univ. Active in the Student Nonviolent Coordinating Committee in the late 1960s and early 1970s, she became known for the militancy of her poems: 'Nigger / Can you kill?' (*Black Feeling / Black Talk*, published by her own company, 1968, appearing with *Black Judgement*, 1970). *Re:Creation*, 1970, a shift from violent militancy, uses the rhythm of the blues and the cadence of black speech to celebrate black musicians. Later, 'bored with categories' (*My House*, 1972), NG published collections – *The Women and the Men*, 1975, *Cotton Candy on a Rainy Day*, 1978, and *Those Who Ride the Night Wind*, 1983 – which concentrate on her son, domestic and passionate life, and black community. She has edited an anthology of black women poets, *Night Comes Softly*, 1970, written for juveniles (*Spin a Soft Black Song*, 1971, *Ego Tripping and Other Poems for Young Readers*, 1973, *Vacation Time*, 1979), and made several television appearances and recordings of her poems. A popular performer of her own works, she has won many awards, including Woman of the Year from *Mademoiselle*, 1971, and *Ladies' Home Journal*, 1972. *Gemini*, 1971, contains autobiographical essays and discussions of Phillis WHEATLEY, Lena Horne, and black culture: 'The new Black poetry is in fact just a manifestation of our collective historical needs.' See *A Dialogue: James Baldwin and Nikki Giovanni*, 1972, conversation with Margaret WALKER in *A Poetic Equation*, 1974, and interview in Tate, 1984. Studies by Paula Giddings and William J. Harris in Evans, 1984, and Margaret B. McDowell in Joe Weixlmann and Chester J. Fontenot, eds., *Belief vs. Theory in Black American Literary Criticism*, 1986.

Glasgow, Ellen Anderson Gholson, 1873–1945, novelist, poet, essayist, b. in Richmond, Va., eighth of ten children of Anne Jane (Gholson), of an old Tidewater family, and Francis Thomas G., later managing director of the South's largest foundry and munitions supplier. In her memoir, *The Woman Within*, 1954, EG dramatizes her identification with her mother's fragility and depression and her alienation from her father's Calvinist rigidity. Largely self-educated in the family library, she later ventured into political economy and science. The philosophy of Darwin's *Origin of Species* attracted her, and so did Schopenhauer and Nietzsche's *Thus Spake Zarathustra*. Her first novel, *The Descendant*, 1897, appeared anonymously. She later declared that her career had begun with an inchoate revolt against the South's 'evasive idealism'. EG wrote about many levels of Virginia society, from the poor farming community of *The Miller of Old Church*, 1911, to the milieu of the Southern lady, in *Virginia*, 1913. During these years, she increasingly suffered from a partial deafness, but fell in love, travelled, and lived for a time in NYC before returning to Richmond upon her father's death in 1916. There she became engaged to Henry Watkins A., a lawyer and social climber, but the engagement ended after WWI, although they remained difficult friends for many years, and EG turned with renewed energy and pessimism to her writing. *Barren Ground*, 1925, her own favourite, has a memorable heroine who triumphs over appalling circumstances at the price of stoic suppression. EG then produced *The Romantic Comedians*, 1926, *They Stooped to Folly*, 1929, and *The Sheltered*

Life, 1932, novels which illustrate the tragicomedy of romantic love and the sexual double standard, and the scarcely endurable discontents of traditional family life. Yet her attitude toward modernity and women who, like Milly Burden in *They Stooped to Folly*, assert their right to survive their own 'ruin', is – like the narrative stance of the novels – fundamentally irresolute. Despising sentimentalism, she sometimes falls instead (often via the point of view of an older male character like Asa Timberlake in *This Our Life*, 1941) upon a facile stoic determinism. Her novels prospered in her lifetime. She helped organize the Conference of Southern Writers at the Univ. of Virginia (which holds her papers) in 1931, addressed the MLA in 1936, and was awarded the Pulitzer Prize in 1942. Her reputation has been sustained by Southern and, lately, feminist scholars. See Blair Rouse, ed., selec. letters, 1958, and biography, 1962. *EG Centennial Essays*, 1976, ed. M. Thomas Inge, contains useful bibliography and an essay by Monique Parent Frazee, weighing the complexity of EG's attitudes toward women and sexuality. See also the study by Julius Rowan Raper, 1980.

Glaspell, Susan Keating, 1876–1948, experimental playwright, fiction writer and feminist, b. in Davenport, Iowa, da. of Irish-born Alice (K.) and Elmer S. G. She began writing very young, and on graduating from Drake Univ. in 1899 became a reporter on the *Des Moines News*. She published local-colour stories in *Youth's Companion* in the footsteps of Alice French, and in 1901 became a full-time writer. Her first novel, *The Glory of the Conquered: The Story of a Great Love*, 1909 (which earned enough for a year in Paris), is sentimental; *The Visioning*, 1911, in which a sheltered young woman learns about harsh realities, is less so; some think *Fidelity*, 1915, her finest novel. *Lifted Masks*, 1912, collects stories, though her best date from later. In 1913 SG m. George Cram Cook, and with Mary Heaton Vorse they founded the Provincetown Players (whose name and base later varied), aiming to revolutionize US drama with plays by Djuna Barnes, Edna Ferber, Edna St Vincent Millay, Eugene O'Neill and others. They staged their jointly written *Suppressed Desires*, 1915, a satire on marriage and the cult of Freud. SG was one of the group's leading writers, actors and directors. Among her influential works, *Trifles*, 1916, presents the first of her off-stage protagonists, a wife suspected of murdering a brutal husband and protected by female solidarity; it was recast as a story, 'Jury of her Peers'. (For the two, see Beverly A. Smith in *IJWS*, 5, 1982; Elaine Hedges in *Women's Studies*, 12, 1986.) SG's one-acters were collected in 1920; her first full-length play, *Bernice*, 1919, where people strive to read the character of a woman now dead, was highly successful. Equally ambitious was *The Verge*, 1921, an expressionist drama set in a greenhouse, whose protagonist (to some an admired New Woman, to others a psychotic) transcends the bounds of her own reality by creating new kinds of plants; her family urge her to 'call a halt to this nonsense and be the woman you were meant to be'. SG lived for two years with Cook at Delphi in Greece; he died there in 1924, and she paid tribute to him in *The Road to the Temple*, 1926, a memoir and collage of his personal writings. In 1925 she married Norman Matson (divorced 1932), with whom she wrote *The Comic Artist*, staged 1927. Her last play, *Alison's House*, 1930, suggested by Genevieve Taggard's life of Emily Dickinson, won a Pulitzer Prize. SG returned to fiction (of more conventional mode than her plays) with *Brook Evans*, 1928. Her last four novels, set in her native Midwest, focus increasingly on women's struggle to retain their idealism. On her plays, ed. C. W. E. Bigsby, 1987, see Christine Dymkowski in *Modern Drama*, 31, 1988; general study by Arthur Waterman, 1966; Linda Ben-Zvi in Enoch Baxter, ed., *Feminine Focus, The New Women*

Playwrights, 1989. Some papers in NY Public Library.

Glass, Joanna (McClelland), playwright, novelist, short-story writer, b. in 1936 in Saskatoon, Sask., da. of Kate (Switzer) and Morrell MacKenzie M. She wrote advertising copy for a local radio station, later moved into TV in Calgary, then into acting, and studied on scholarship at the Pasadena Playhouse. She m. physicist Alexander G. in 1959 (divorced, 1975), had three children, and became a US citizen. Motherhood, she said, gave her a fruitful 'distance' from the frustration she had early wanted to express, and when she turned to writing in the late 1960s, she felt 'a strong need to write dialogue. I see life in terms of speech.' Her full-length play, *Santacqua*, 1969, and the one-acters *Jewish Strawberries*, 1971, and *Trying*, 1971, deal with contemporary characters in emotional trouble. *Canadian Gothic* and *American Modern*, 1973, which opened together at the Manhattan Theatre Club, dramatize radically different unhappy domestic situations: the characters in the first (a mother, father, daughter, and Cree Indian) act out clashes between classes and races. In the second, the female protagonist tells her husband of visits to a psychoanalyst and of scavenging in the gutters of Long Island. In JG's much-admired novel *Reflections on a Mountain Summer*, 1974, a middle-aged male narrator recalls his mother's affair in the mountains when he was 14. The comedy *Artichoke*, 1975, deals with adultery and a disintegrating relationship, breaking the monotony of life on a prairie farm with the addled child of a young enchanted girl. *The Last Chalice*, 1977, which was adapted from her short story, 'At the King Edward Hotel', examines the effects of alcoholism in a prairie home. JG's screenplays include an adaptation of Margaret ATWOOD's *Surfacing*. *To Grandmother's House We Go*, 1981, set in Connecticut, where she now lives, treats inter-generational conflict. *Woman Wanted* was published in 1985. See Hetty Clews in *Atlantis*, 4, 1978, and John Parr, *JCF*, 20, 1977. Some papers at the Univ. of Calgary.

Glasse, Hannah (Allgood), 1708–70, COOKERY writer, b. in London, eldest child of Hannah (Clark) and Isaac A. She m. Peter G. by 1725; most of her nine children died or went abroad. Her *Compleat Confectioner*, Dublin 1742, draws on experience and MS sources. Her *Art of Cookery made Plain and Easy, Which far exceeds any Thing of the Kind ever yet Printed*, by 'a Lady' (mostly female subscribers, 1747: facs. 1983), came to dominate its field (with her facsimile signature from 1751). Her preface hopes to 'gain the good Opinion of my own Sex', disclaims 'the high polite Stile', but promises to teach good cooking to 'every Servant who can but read'. Ann COOK attacked her on just those points – experience, practicality and economy – which she boasted; London publishers believed the real author was a man. *The Servant's Directory, or House-Keeper's Companion* (aristocratic subscribers), 1760, is padded with blank pages for account-keeping; its actual advice is lively and revealing.

Gluck, Louise, poet. B. in 1943 in NYC, da. of Beatrice (Grosby) and Daniel G., she studied at Sarah Lawrence College and Columbia Univ. Divorced from Charles Hertz, by whom she has one son, she m. writer and co-founder of the New England Culinary Institute, John Dranow, 1977. She has been Visiting Poet/Professor at many US colleges and universities and is now Scott Professor of Poetry at Williams College. Her first collection, *First Born*, 1968, contains the interwoven themes of sex, birth, death, and the passage of time which mark all her work. In 'The Wound' the speaker is a pregnant woman deeply depressed over the imminent birth of her child; in 'Bridal Piece' a woman recalls her wedding day and her resulting loss of innocence. The poems collected in *The House on Marshland*, 1975, cluster thematically around mourning for things lost: childhood, innocence, love ('There is always something to be made of pain'). *Descending Figure*, 1980, centres on love and death ('It begins quietly / in certain female children: / the fear of death, taking as its form / dedication to hunger, because a woman's body *is* a grave'). *The Triumph of Achilles*, 1985, presents further lyrical explorations of the troubled family relationships and difficulties between lovers ('Once we were happy, we had no memories. / For all the repetition, nothing happened twice') which are the habitual markers of LG's poetic landscape. Among the many awards her poetry has won is the Eunice Tietjens Prize.

Glyn, Elinor (Sutherland), 1864–1943, novelist, b. Jersey, younger da. of Elinor (Saunders) and Douglas S., civil engineer. Her childhood was spent in Canada (where her father died of typhoid fever shortly after her birth), Scotland and Jersey. Educ. at home, in her teens she lived in London and Paris. In 1892 she m. Clayton G., a landowner, who gambled and drank. Highly successful and prolific, EG became a writer of romances partly to support her husband and two daughters. Her first book, *The Visits of Elizabeth*, 1900, was based on her journal. Her most famous novel, *Three Weeks*, 1907, glorifies a brief affair which also leads to the wife's murder by her brutal husband. Beneath the fantasies of the romance genre, the novels often deal with darker elements such as transgressive sexuality and pain within marriage, as in *Beyond the Rocks*, 1906, and *The Sequence 1905–12*, 1913. In *The Reason Why*, 1911, the woman is rewarded for her suffering with a more satisfying relationship, while *The Career of Katherine Bush*, 1916, plots the social success of a secretary who eventually marries a duke who loves her even more when she is honest enough to confess a previous affair. She also wrote *This Passion Called Love*, 1925, a guidebook with chapters like 'How to Attract the Man You Desire'. Her most interesting work is her autobiography, *Romantic Adventure*, 1936, which explores a more problematic subjectivity. She writes of her carelessness with writing and the hostility she faced as 'the first society woman to become a novelist' (p. 130). In retrospect she regrets opposing votes for women, but sees herself as nevertheless 'a member of the band of pioneers in the cause of feminine emancipation' (p. 130). See the life by Anthony Glyn, 1968.

Godden, Margaret **Rumer**, novelist, children's writer, poet, b. 1907 at Eastbourne, Sussex, da. of Katherine (Hingley) and Arthur G. Her sister Jan G. is an artist and author of nine novels: they co-authored *Two Under the Indian Sun*, 1966 (about their childhood in India, which they felt they knew better than most adult Anglo-Indians), and *Shiva's Pigeons*, 1972. Taken to India as a baby, brought back for education in 1920, RG soon borrowed £15 from her mother to publish poems with a vanity press (copies 'lost or thrown away, thankfully'). Moira House, Eastbourne, provided rigorous drill in writing; back in India she found Katherine Mansfield's journals 'a revelation and a springboard'. She studied ballet on another English visit, 1927, and published poems (fantasy with 'a certain crispness') in the *London Illustrated News*, 1929, then opened a dancing school in Calcutta. She m. Laurence Foster, 1934, because she was pregnant; that baby died, but she had two daughters. Two novels (the first, *Gok*, written before marriage) were rejected; the fanciful vein continues in *Chinese Puzzle*, 1936 (the 'life stories' of a Pekinese dog, an ancient mandarin reincarnated), and *Lady and the Unicorn*, 1938; *Black Narcissus*, 1939, her first success, returns to the real, historic world of *Gok*, with nuns working to found a mission in the Himalayas. The profits went towards her husband's stock-exchange debts; he left her in 1941. Her diary of the next months on a tea estate near Darjeeling was popular as *Rungli-Runglior*, 1943, repr. as *Thus Far and No Further*. Constantly reprinted, RG has published 22 novels (to *The Dark Horse*, 1981, charming on an Irish racehorse, stable-lad and nun in 1930s India), almost as many children's books (from *The Doll's House*, 1943), and short stories, poetry, translations and non-fiction. She often quarries her life for fiction and often adopts a child's perspective, most famously in *The Greengage Summer*, 1958, typically atmospheric and delicate. For this, as for other novels, she co-wrote a filmscript: *Loss of Innocence*, 1961. She sometimes experiments with time: *A Fugue in Time*, 1945 (*Take Three Tenses* in the USA), began in WWII as a story, then an unacted play, then an 'unrecognizable' film (*Enchantment*, 1948). Back in England after WWII, she m. James Haynes-Dixon in 1949 and lived from 1968 at Henry James's house in Rye, Sussex. She evokes her 'life as a young writer' in *A Time to Dance, No Time to Weep*, 1987. In 1989 she completed a novel about the Coromandel Coast. Study by Hassell A. Simpson, 1973.

'Godfrey, Elizabeth', Jessie Bedford, 1854?–1918, English novelist and historian, about whom little is known. Her history books include *Home Life Under the Stuarts 1603–1649*, 1903, and *English Children in the Olden Time*, 1907. In the novel *Cornish Diamonds*, 1895, Jennifer Lyon is a violinist who eventually gives up a promising career to marry the man she loves, whilst *A Stolen Idea*, 1899, reveals deep anxiety about female authorship in its concern with a woman writer who steals an idea and writes a successful novel, eventually marrying the man she stole it from. Others, such as *The Winding Road*, 1902, explore the pain of separation. Using the popular novel form, these works treat the conflict for creative women between a career and love, but are disappointingly trite.

Godley, Charlotte (Wynne), 1821–1907, letter writer, b. in North Wales, da. of Sara (Hildyard) and Charles Griffith W., MP. She m. John Robert G., a director of the NZ Company, in 1845 and had four das. and one son. She went to NZ in 1849, returning in 1852. Her *Letters from Early New Zealand* (printed for private circulation in 1936; repr. 1951) record life in the South Island, with nursemaid, manservant, and one child. She comments on prices, rents, colonial etiquette and the problems of getting maidservants. She expresses approval of Maori chiefs who have adopted European life-styles and names, and concern for would-be governesses and for pregnant women – 'the babies almost always die'. She has a pleasantly satirical tone; her values are those of her class and race.

Godolphin, Margaret (Blagge), Lady, 1652–78, religious writer, da. of Mary (North) and Thomas B., an ex-courtier who sent her as a child to France. Here she became a Maid of Honour, resisted Henrietta Maria's attempts to make her a Catholic, perseveringly struggled to 'benefit my soule' in private discipline, and gave pleasure by her acting and conversational skills. Her admiring mentor John Evelyn sent her florid letters; hers are the opposite: 'I love a good plain honest leter.' In 1675, not telling Evelyn, she broke her resolve of Christian virginity to marry Sidney, Baron (later Earl) G., after a long courtship – and discovered the joy of having 'my time my owne, my house quiat'. She died after bearing a child, leaving her husband a touching farewell letter. Evelyn wrote her life with passages from the letters and diaries he preserved (now at Christ Church, Oxford): ed. Harriet Sampson, 1939. Study by W. G. Hiscock, 1951.

Godwin, Gail, novelist, short-story writer, b. 1937 in Birmingham, Ala., da. of Kathleen (Krahenbuhl) and Mose Winston G. Educ. at Peace Junior College, Raleigh, and the Univ. of North Carolina (BA in journalism, 1959), she worked for the *Miami Herald*, m. Douglas Kennedy in

1960, and had two sons. After working in London, 1962–5, and another brief marriage, she attended the Univ. of Iowa (MA and PhD, 1971, in English), and held many teaching posts. Her first two novels, *The Perfectionists*, 1970, and *Glass People*, 1972, treat women who accept the mould into which their husbands pressure them; the heroine of *The Odd Woman*, 1974 (an admirer of George ELIOT), denies the need for marriage and rejects an inadequate relationship, making her own life in teaching and research, but feels 'I shall always be a stranger and alone.' The protagonist of *Violet Clay*, 1978, follows a similar course; *A Mother and Two Daughters*, 1982, is again concerned with different routes to independence. *The Finishing School*, 1985, examines a 14-year-old girl's attraction to her mentor, whose room 'seemed a kind of tabernacle devoted to the life I wanted: music, art, travel', who offers support in trouble and a hint of sexual attraction, but who finally must be 'absorbed', outgrown and, even cruelly, rejected. *A Southern Family*, 1987, presents a woman's odyssey home to bury her brother. GG's short stories, collected in *Dream Children*, 1977, and *Mr Bedford and the Muses*, 1983, sound the same theme of decision-making and the pursuit of self-realization if not of happiness. She has also written librettos for musicals, 1975–81. See Anne Z. Mickelson in *Reaching Out: Sensitivity and Order in Recent American Fiction by Women*, 1979; Mickey Pearlman, ed., *American Women Writing Fiction*, 1990.

Goldman, Emma, 1869–1940, anarchist activist, platform lecturer, writer, editor, and publisher of radical literature, b. in Kovno (Kaunas, in Lithuania), da. of orthodox Jews, Taube (Binowitz), philanthropist and community worker, and Abraham G., a small businessman and patriarch. EG was educated in Königsberg and St Petersburg, leaving school in 1882 to work in a factory. By 1885, rising anti-Semitism and oppressive family circumstances forced her to emigrate to the USA. She lived in Rochester (where she m. fellow immigrant Jacob Kershner, later divorced) and New Haven, moving to NYC's Lower East Side in 1889. She joined the radical front, won notoriety as lover of Alexander Berkman, and gained a reputation for political agitation, serving her first prison term, 1893–4, for 'inciting a riot'. She began nursing in prison and on release travelled to Vienna to study midwifery, meeting notable anarchists en route and lecturing in London, Glasgow, Edinburgh, and Maybole. Addressing immigrant workers and American intellectuals alike, EG rallied against capitalism, militarism, and bureaucracy, advocating civil disobedience and free love. She began cross-country lecture touring in 1897 and continued to appear before massive audiences until driven undercover following assassination of President McKinley by a Polish immigrant claiming to have acted on her behalf. In 1908 EG began a second important love-affair, with her tour manager, doctor Ben Reitman. In 1906 she founded *Mother Earth*, for nine years the country's major anarchist journal: it circulated works of notable past and present activists, including Mary WOLLSTONECRAFT, Charlotte Perkins GILMAN, Olive SCHREINER, and Gertrude Nafe. Mother Earth Publishing Association issued works by Ibsen and Wilde, by Kropotkin and Bakunin, and books on sex and birth-control. EG's books exhibit literary and feminist interests: *The Social Significance of the Modern Drama*, 1914, is didactic, designed to awaken US readers to the social and political dimensions of theatre. EG found friends and admirers among literary radicals, including Margaret ANDERSON and Mabel DODGE. *Anarchism and Other Essays*, 1910, foregrounds sexual politics, condemns marriage as a coercive institution, denounces capitalism's 'traffic in women' and forcing of women into prostitution as the only viable alternative to the impossible wages and conditions of 'legitimate' labour, and attacks the hypocritical legal system for prosecuting the prostitute but not her clients. Not always progressive, EG elevates motherhood above woman's individual ambition, arguing that the 'emancipated' woman must liberate herself from male-identified, self-centred careerism to be true to her 'love instinct', 'mother instinct', 'woman's soul', and natural impulse 'to give of oneself boundlessly'. She campaigned for birth-control and was arrested and sentenced. For speaking against conscription and the war effort, she was imprisoned and deported to Russia. She m. Welshman James Colton, 1925, to get British citizenship, later lived in France, England, and finally Canada, where she campaigned for the Spanish loyalists and where she died. See her autobiography, *Living My Life*, 2 vols., 1931. Selected works are printed in Alix Kates Shulman, ed., *Red Emma Speaks* (in UK *Dancing in the Revolution*), 1983, and *Traffic in Women and Other Essays on Feminism*, 1971 (also ed. Shulman), and *Woman Without a Country and Other Essays*, 1980. Critical biography by Alice Wexler, 1984, 1989. Studies by Candace Falk, *Love, Anarchy, and EG*, 1984, and Shulman, in *Socialist Review*, 61, March–April, 1982.

Goldsmith, Margaret, journalist, biographer, novelist. B. in either 1894 or 1897 in either Milwaukee, Wisconsin or Chicago, Ill., to businessman Bernard G., she was educ. in the USA and Germany, attending Univs. of Illinois and Berlin (BA, MA). She left an economic advisory career – working first in Washington, DC, for the War Industries Board during WWI, and as foreign trade expert for American Chamber of Commerce, and later in Europe at the International Chamber of Commerce, Paris, and as first woman Assistant Trade Commissioner at the US Embassy in Berlin – in 1927 to become Berlin correspondent for the *New York Evening Post* (a position she left in a year). Also while in Berlin she m. *Manchester Guardian* foreign correspondent Frederick Voigt in 1926, met Vita Sackville-West (with whom she had a brief affair), and acted as literary agent for English authors, hoping to arrange the publication of Virginia Woolf in Germany. Writing first in Berlin and later in London, MG published translations from German, 1928–55, biographies (among them of Florence Nightingale, 1937, Madame de Staël, 1938, and Sappho, 1938), and a number of non-fictional studies of women: *Seven Women Against the World*, 1935, discusses women revolutionaries; *Women at War*, 1943, documents wartime involvement; and *Women and the Future*, 1946, considers the implications of women's new-found independence 'due to the war' as well as the difficulties of child-care for working women. The first of MG's two novels, *Karin's Mother*, 1928, set in Germany, describes the troubled personal relationships of a promising woman medical student forced to break with her lover when his conventional demand for marriage conflicts with her commitment to her career and independence. *Belated Adventure*, 1929, treats the marriage of an 'independent . . . modern' US woman practising law in London and a British professor of Slavic languages who goes away with his wife's closest friend (a character Vita thought based on herself). The novel disparages the Bloomsbury Group as 'parlour-adventurers, who sit about analysing their emotions, picking them to pieces and then putting the pieces together again into patterns'. Almost nothing is known of MG after her 1935 divorce.

Goldstein, Vida, 1869–1949, journalist and feminist activist, b. Portland, Victoria, da. of Isabella (Hawkins) and Jacob G., an anti-suffragist who nevertheless encouraged his four daughters to be independent and well educated. VG attended the Presbyterian Ladies' College, Melbourne, then Melbourne Univ., and later ran a school with her sister Bella. In the early 1890s she collected signatures for the Woman Suffrage Petition and campaigned for political reforms. The acknowledged leader of the radical women's movement in Victoria, she travelled to the USA in 1902 to speak at the International Woman Suffrage Conference. She became the first woman in the British Empire to stand for national parliamentary elections; defeat convinced her that women voters needed to be better organized and informed. She helped found periodicals and organizations, including the feminist *Woman's Sphere*, 1900–1905, and *Woman Voter*, 1909–19, and wrote for many Australian and overseas journals. She also pub. *Woman Suffrage in Australia* [1913], and made four further attempts to enter parliament. She represented Australia at a Women's Peace Conference in Zürich (1919) and devoted most of her energies to promoting pacifism and international sisterhood. Her papers are in the Fawcett Library, London. See the life by L. M. Henderson, 1973.

Gom, Leona, poet and novelist. B. in 1946 in Fairview, Alberta, da. of Mary (Baron) and Tony G., homesteaders near Hines Creek, Alberta, LG grew up on their isolated farm and started writing at ten 'to pass the time'. She was educ. at the Univ. of Alberta, Edmonton (BEd, 1968, MA, 1972). She has taught creative writing and English in Surrey, BC, since 1973, and has been poetry editor, then editor, of *Event*, a literary magazine. Widely anthologized, she received the Canadian Authors Association Award for Best Book of Poetry for *Land of the Peace*, 1980. Through a parodic inversion of the pastoral mode, this, like her other collections (*Kindling*, 1972, *The Singletree*, 1975, and *Northbound*, 1984), explores 'All this romantic bullshit / about growing up on farms': 'my mother in the morning / chasing for miles across the fields / a hawk with a chicken / heavy in its talons / . . . A day so rich in implications: / I wait for the connection, / the pulse across the synapse, / but the images seal shut like seeds, / fact impervious to symbol.' Inspired by Margaret LAURENCE, LG writes about rural Canadian life in anecdotal and abstract language, 'tidy wit and gentle humour'. Her novel, *Housebroken*, 1986, and her poems show concern with the place and popular images of women ('right away you see you don't fit / in': *Private Properties*, 1986), a concern originated in her reading of Kate MILLETT, her first, most important feminist influence. Author of two CBC radio dramas – 'The Inheritance' and 'Sour Air' – LG is working on a new novel, *Zero Avenue*, and has plans for a third. See Robert Eady in *Arc*, 10, 1983, and Paul Hjartarson in *JCP*, 1, 1986.

Gomeldon, Jane (Middleton), d. 1780, Newcastle essayist, da. of Joshua M., of Quaker extraction, well educ. (languages, science, philosophy). At an early age she m. Capt. Francis G. (d. 1751, friend of Lady STRATHMORE's father), left him, and to escape his pursuit fled in male dress to France, where various exploits are ascribed to her; she returned at his death. Nearly 500 subscribers to her *The Medley*, 1766 (31 essays), raised £53 10s 7d for the Newcastle lying-in hospital. She assumes a male persona to rejoice in the enlarged sphere of women. Gentlemen now need improvement 'to render them fit to be their Companions': 'Attend also ye Beaux to this important Lesson: Beaux soon grow old!' Influenced by Pope, citing Richardson and T. C. PHILLIPS, anticipating Byron, resolving 'not to play the Prude', she cheerfully and ironically takes up the unbroached subject of female adultery – 'though polite, though spirited not sufferable'. She discusses Homer, Milton, cross-dressing, and the education of daughters, and creates a range of lively fictive characters. *Maxims*, Newcastle, 1779, put traditional wisdom into a form like irregular verse: 'The Illiberal despise not the Poor for / Their Poverty, / More than they fear them for their / Importunity.' See P. M. Horsley in *Heaton Works Journal*, 6, 1951.

Gomersall, Ann, *c.* 1751–after 1834, novelist. Having settled at Leeds, she pub. *Eleonora* [1789], with a poem to her now distant mother, whose 'hand alone did dress the soil'; Lady STRATHMORE, Lady HAWKE, and many residents of Jamaica subscribed. The resilient, down-to-earth, highly class-conscious heroine tells in retrospective letters how, orphaned young and in poverty, she worked as a governess until her happy and pious marriage. Dialect is well used, and Leeds unfavourably compared with Bristol: its labouring men are 'scarce humanized' drunkards and nine in ten brides are pregnant. Reviews praised the simple plot and Yorkshire humour. *The Citizen*, 1790, makes more complex use of letters to contrast bourgeois and genteel attitudes. A young man escapes a siren who charms by flattering his ego (she dies a prostitute) and grows to respect, and marry the daughter of, the merchant he had scorned. *The Disappointed Heir, or Memoirs of the Ormond Family*, 1796, covers two generations of fighting in America, with West Indian episodes. AG began applying for aid to the RLF in 1818, from Newport, Isle of Wight; widowed after 33 years, having lived by manual work for eight, and suffered a stroke and partial blindness, she resumed her 'lyre neglected, out of tune the chords' and pub. by subscription a long poem in couplets, *The Creation*, 1824 (500 copies, all sold).

Gonne, Maud, [1865]–1953, political campaigner, autobiographer, journalist. B. in Tongham, Surrey, da. of Edith Frith (Cook) and Thomas G., she spent her childhood in Ireland, London and Paris, attributing 'most of the little education I possess' to her French governess, 'a strong Republican' of egalitarian and philanthropic sympathies. Attached to French patriot Lucien Millevoie, father of her two daughters (Georgette, who d. 1891, and Iseult), she became passionately devoted to the cause of Irish Republicanism. Best known for having inspired the passion and poetry of W. B. Yeats, she also worked to house evicted tenant farmers during the Land League period, and campaigned for adequate feeding of school-children and improved conditions for political prisoners. Since 'None of the parties in Ireland want women,' she said, 'I have to work all by my lone, till I can form a woman's organization'. In 1900 she founded the Daughters of Erin (Inghinidhe na hEireann) to promote women's participation in nationalist activities. It established classes for children in Irish history and language, music and dancing, and undermined recruitment to the British army by encouraging girls to avoid soldiers. It established, 1908, the first Irish women's magazine to urge complete national independence, *Bean na hEireann* (Woman of Ireland), which also promoted feminist ideas, urging 'Freedom for our Nation and the complete removal of all disabilities to our sex'. MG played Yeats's *Cathleen ni Houlihan* in the Irish National Theatre's production, 1902, becoming a symbol of the nation; her own play, *Dawn*, about the Great Famine of the 1840s, was never produced. She m. Irish patriot John MacBride, 1903, and had a son, Sean, but the marriage ended in 1905. MG was repeatedly imprisoned for her open activities after 1918 when all major patriotic organizations were proscribed, including the Women's Prisoners' Defence League, of which she was secretary. *A Servant of the Queen*, 1938, is 'my own record of the historic events with which I have been associated' to 1903. The account gives the flavour of a woman whose robust engagement was with history itself. Life by Samuel Levenson, 1976.

Gooch, Elizabeth Sarah (Villa-Real), b. 1756, novelist, poet, autobiographer and courtesan, da. of William V.–R., a Portuguese Jew who died when she was three, and Elizabeth (Hutchinson), who had disliked him and quickly remarried. She grew up in Scotland and northern England, with three years at a Chelsea boarding school. After a thwarted sentimental love-affair conducted at Fountains Abbey, she passively accepted, in 1775, marriage for her money with William G., who also had a mistress. Not yet 21, with two children, disapproved of by her father's and husband's families, she was accused – falsely, she says – of infidelity and carried off to exile in France, where in isolation she fell at last into 'the most unfortunate class of human beings!' Working up the social scale of lovers, always seeing herself as victim, she shuttled between France and England seeking family or marital money; she acted, pawned goods, reproached the Almighty, met Grace ELLIOTT, and as mistress of a military prince rode at the head of his regiment dressed in its uniform. She pub. an *Appeal to the Public*, written in the Fleet prison, 1788; a highly coloured *Life*, 1792, as 'an oppressed individual' lacking (in echo of Sarah FIELDING's *David Simple*) '*one real friend*'; egotistical *Poems*, 1793; the essay–fiction blend *Wanderings of the Imagination*, written 1795; five novels in which sensitive victims attain eventual felicity, 1794–1804; a poem on her mother's death, 1797 (*Monthly Mirror*); and a life of Thomas Bellamy in his *Beggar Boy*, 1800 (finished by her), which shows close knowledge of the world of JOURNALISM.

Goodhue, Sarah (Whipple), 1641–81, religious writer of Ipswich, Mass., youngest da. of Elder W. She m. Joseph G. *c.* 1641. Late in pregnancy, with eight children alive, fearing it might 'please the Lord to make a sudden change in thy family', she wrote and left her husband 'infolded among thy papers something that I have to say to thee and others'. She bore the twins she had guessed at, and died three days later. Her letter (with snatches of verse) advises her parents and cousins to take some of her children; everyone to 'prepare your selves for that swift and sudden messenger of death'; her children to consider their worthlessness and the worth of Christ, to learn to read their father's handwritten sermons and to remember his love and care. 'O dear husband of all my best bosom friends, if by sudden death I must part from thee, let not thy trouble and cares that are on thee make thee turn aside from the right way.' Pub. 1661, it was repr. as late as 1850.

Goodison, Lorna, poet and artist, b. 1947 and brought up in the ghetto of West Kingston, Jamaica (cut off by a gully bridge from wealthier districts). After St Hugh's High School she studied art in Kingston and at the Art Students' League, NYC. She has worked in Jamaica as art teacher, advertising copywriter and scriptwriter, and has exhibited in Jamaica and Guyana. She began placing poems in journals like *The Gleaner* and *Savacou*, appeared in anthologies (from Neville Dawes and Anthony McNeill, eds., *The Caribbean Poem*, 1976), and illustrated books like Mervyn Morris, *On Holy Week*, 1976, and her own first volume, *Tamarind Season*, 1980. This dwells on early memories ('The railings on the bridge / parallel spell equal still / what is now curfew zone / was then just home') and on her parents (as remembered, and as lovers). LG places herself in her family and in wider culture and history: 'so how black, black man like you and me / name Goodison and Montgomery?' She writes of S. African police raiding the Mandela home: 'They and their friends are working / to arrest the dreams in our head'. A long poem, 'For My Mother (May I Inherit Half Her Strength)', celebrates 'the figure / who sat at the first thing I learned to read: "SINGER"'; next came *I Am Becoming My Mother*, 1986 (cassette, New Beacon Books, of LG reading from this in both patois and standard English). In 'Songs For My Son', birth opens personal consciousness wide to history. 'The midwife / tie-head African woman' brings an ancient heritage; ancestors gather: 'great grandmother Rebecca of the healing hands / Tata Edward, Bucky and Brownman / my father's lost mother Maria'. LG writes much of women, actual and imagined: 'Mulatta', a powerful persona who refuses to fulfil cultural assumptions, rewrites European myth in 'The Mulatta as Penelope' and 'The Mulatta and the Minotaur'. *Hearts-ease*, 1988, continues to seek through poetry an 'organic perception' of the past; LG calls poetry 'a dominating intensive tyrant', 'a wicked force'. She has been a writer in residence in the West Indies and the USA, and has read her work in Jamaica and London. Interview in the *Guardian*, 22 March 1985.

Goodwin, Maud (Wilder), 1856–1935, novelist, biographer, historical writer, b. Ballston Spa, NY, da. of Delia and John W. In 1879 she m. Almon G. Her career, begun in 1889, spanned 30 years. Her histories include the four-vol. *Historic New York*, 1898, which she ed., and *Dutch and English on the Hudson*, 1919, an elaborate descriptive narrative of NY's history. *The Colonial Cavalier*, 1894, sketches of pre-Revolutionary Southern culture, shows her ability to grasp the mood of an era. Her historical novels, conscientiously authentic, make a clumsy attempt at archaic language: 'I grieve the more over your inhospitable mood that I find myself compelled to intrude ...' (*White Aprons*, 1896). Her contemporary novels, *Four Roads to Paradise*, 1904, and *Claims and Counterclaims*, 1905, are more sophisticated. Most interesting is her biography of Dolly MADISON, 1896. She pub. 12 works, which include *The Head of a Hundred*, 1895 and *Veronica Playfair*, 1909.

Gooneratne, Yasmine (Bandaranaike), poet, biographer, critic. B. in 1935 in Colombo, Sri Lanka, da. of Samuel J. F. Dias B. and Esther Mary (Ramkeesoon), she migrated to Australia, 1972, with her physician and historian husband Brendon G. (m. 1962) and their son and daughter, Devika, now also a poet. She teaches English literature at Macquarie Univ., NSW. Born into a family that produced two prime ministers of independent Sri Lanka, including the world's first woman prime minister, YG studied at a private girls' school in Colombo, later at the Univs. of Ceylon (BA, 1959) and Cambridge (PhD, 1962). She writes about her family's place in Sri Lanka's pre- and post-colonial history. *Relative Merits: A Personal Memoir of the Bandaranaike Family of Sri Lanka*, 1986, probes affectionately yet critically the role of a class that adopted the names as well as the life-style of the colonial masters. YG's deeply self-conscious, ironic poetry explores her place in Sri Lankan society as a privileged woman, juxtaposing this with history, culture, and recent ethnic and class violence. In poems moulding English to native Sri Lankan forms like *sandesa* and *baila*, she writes poignantly about herself and both her original and her adopted countries. Anthologized in Australian and Sri Lankan collections, she has published three volumes of poetry – *Word, Bird, Motif*, 1971, *The Lizard's Cry and Other Poems*, 1972, and *6,000 Ft Death Dive*, 1981 – and critical studies of *English Literature in Ceylon*, 1968, Pope, 1976, AUSTEN, 1970, Ruth Prawer JHABVALA, 1983, Commonwealth Literature, 1980. A co-founder and editor of *New Ceylon Writing*, she also edited *Poems from India, Sri Lanka, Malaysia & Singapore*, and *Stories from Sri Lanka*, both 1979. See Ryhana Raheem and Sinomi Fernando in *WLWE*, 17, 1978.

Gordimer, Nadine, novelist and short-story writer. B. in 1923 in Springs, S. Africa, da. of Nan (Meyers) and Isidore G., a jeweller, she was educ. at a convent school until she was ten, then (after a heart ailment was diagnosed) by tutors until 15 or 16. She began to write at nine, feeling solitary: 'those who didn't share my tastes acted as a stimulus to make me express myself privately – on paper'. She published a short story, 'Come again tomorrow', at 15. Barred by lack of formal education from taking a degree, she attended the Univ. of Witwatersrand for a year at 21.

She had a daughter in a first marriage, and a son with Reinhold Cassirer (m. 1954). Her partly autobiographical first novel, *The Lying Days*, 1953, won immediate acclaim abroad. Eight novels followed, including *A World of Strangers*, 1958, and *Occasion for Loving*, 1963. Her short stories, printed early in *The New Yorker*, *The Yale Review*, and elsewhere, have appeared in eight collections, from *Friday's Footprint*, 1960, to *Something Out There*, 1985, and in *Selected Stories*, 1975. They were made into a film series, 1985. Writing under (and about) Apartheid, NG aims at 'the integrity Chekhov demanded: "to describe a situation so truthfully ... that the reader can no longer evade it".' She deals with inter-racial love, discriminatory labour and strike laws, teenage pregnancy, mother-daughter bitterness, post-colonial hangovers. The emotional and intellectual dilemma of Apartheid traps her characters, like Liz, in *The Late Bourgeois World*, 1966, who grapples with inevitable changes in women's role after marrying and separating from a radical activist. NG gives the private or quotidian its full burden of significance. Her prose is carefully wrought, concise, elegant. Had she lived elsewhere, she writes, her work might have remained apolitical, but, electing to stay in S. Africa, she has become increasingly committed to speaking out. *Burger's Daughter*, 1979, following the Soweto riots, was banned. (An extract appeared in *Pour Nelson Mandela*, 1986.) *July's People*, 1981, a fictional forecast of black majority takeover, shows the coup through the eyes of a sensitive white woman. *A Sport of Nature*, 1987, is a new departure in scope, length, number of characters and in the broad geographical diversity of its settings (most of Africa and the USA). It treats various African political movements through the personal experiences of its heroine, Hillela, who becomes an emblem of hope for a united Africa: 'with her it was already one world; what could be'. NG has published a study of black South African writers (*The Black Interpreters*, 1973), introduced a TV film, *Maids and Madams*, stressing interaction between black and white women in South Africa, and written and directed, with Hugo Cassirer, a film about Allan Boesak. There are 23 essays published in Stephen Clingman, ed., *The Essential Gesture (Writing, Politics and Places)*, 1988. See Jean MARQUARD in *DR*, 59, 1979, Lewis Nkosi in *The New African*, 4, 1986, and M. Trump in *Research in African Literatures*, 17, 1986, Study by Clingman, 1986.

Gordon, Caroline, 1895–1981, novelist, short-story writer, critic. She was b. on her mother's family farm in Todd County, Kentucky, da. of Nancy (Meriwether) and James Morris G.: educ. by her father at home, then at his classical school for boys, before going to high school. After Bethany College (AB 1916) she was a high-school teacher, then reporter on the *Chattanooga News*. Besides reviewing the Fugitive poets, she met the Agrarians, and took up their anti-urban, anti-technological ideals. In 1924 she m. Allen Tate, poet and critic: they had a daughter, and divorced (for the second time) in 1959. After some years in penury in New York and two long stays in France (each in turn on a Guggenheim Fellowship), they lived at Benfolly Farm near CG's birthplace, 1933–8. Entertaining writers was a stimulus and a burden. CG's first novel, *Penhally*, begun in Paris in 1928 (when she also published her first short story), appeared in 1931, with encouragement from Ford Madox Ford, with whom she worked on the *Transatlantic Review*, and of whom she published a study in 1963. Her early novels focus on the decline of antebellum Southern culture, seen through Agrarian eyes: the protagonist of *Aleck Maury, Sportsman*, 1934 (repr. with her afterword, 1980; *The Pastimes of Aleck Maury* ... in UK), is based on her father. She taught at many institutions, beginning with a joint post with Tate at the Women's College of the Univ. of NC, 1938. As a proponent of the New Criticism she wrote

How to Read a Novel, 1957 (which argues against Gertrude STEIN), and edited with Tate the important short-story collection *The House of Fiction*, 1950. Her conversion to Roman Catholicism, 1947, influenced her later fiction towards exploring the workings of grace. She based a character in the anti-Freudian *The Malefactors*, 1956, on Dorothy DAY of the Catholic Worker movement (and others on herself and Tate). The Univ. of Dallas (Catholic) gave her a chair in creative writing, 1973. *The Glory of Hera*, 1972, a Jungian and proto-Christian version of the labours of Hercules (who was named after Hera), treats the usually maligned goddess sympathetically. CG projected – and published parts of – historical and autobiographical works (the 'upper pattern') related to this mythic tale, which Rose Ann C. Fraistat sees as serving 'as the "lower pattern" for all her work'. Flannery O'CONNOR praised her 'real masterly doing'. CG spent her last years in Mexico. Her stories were collected posthumously, 1981 (T. H. Landess ed. a *Symposium* on them, 1972); Robert C. Golden and Mary C. Sullivan compiled *A Reference Guide* to O'Connor and CG, 1977; letters to Sally Wood appeared as *The Southern Mandarins*, 1984; many of her novels have been reprinted. See also W. J. Stuckey, 1972, Fraistat, 1984 (quoted above); Janet LEWIS in *Sewanee Review*, 81, 1973; *SoQ* special issue, spring 1990. MSS at Princeton.

Gordon, Lucie Duff (Austin), 1821–69, translator and travel writer, b. London, only child of Sarah (Taylor) AUSTIN and John A., jurist. Her mother wished her to be financially and mentally independent rather than conventionally 'accomplished' (young Lucie kept a pet snake), and taught her Latin and sent her briefly to Dr Biber's co-ed. school at Hampstead to learn Greek. She learned German when the family visited Bonn in 1826 and later (1836–8) attended Miss Shepherd's school at Bromley. In 1840 she m. Sir Alexander Duff G. (Commissioner for Inland Revenue from 1856), with whom she had three children. LDG soon became part of a distinguished literary and artistic circle which included Landseer, Macaulay, Dickens, Thackeray, Meredith, and Caroline NORTON, while Tennyson reputedly had her beauty and erudition in mind in *The Princess*, 1847. This erudition was evident in her TRANSLATIONS from German and French, including Barthold Niebuhr's children's book *Stories of the Gods and Heroes of Greece* (1842, under Sarah Austin's name), Wilhelm Meinhold's *Mary Schweidler, the Amber Witch*, 1844, P. J. A. von Feuerbach's *Narrative of Remarkable Criminal Trials*, 1846, Ranke's *Memoirs of the House of Brandenburg* (1849, with her husband), *Ferdinand I and Maximilian II of Austria*, 1853, and de Wailly's version of Swift's romantic entanglements, *Stella and Vanessa*, 1850. Her most popular works were *Letters from the Cape*, 1864, *Letters from Egypt, 1863–65*, 1865, and *Last Letters from Egypt*, 1875. Here she criticized Europeans' intolerant, patronizing attitudes towards other races and creeds (observing, for example, that Islam's notoriously polygamous marriage customs actually offered women more rights and greater equality with men than did English law). Her strictures against the brutal, oppressive Turkish rule in Egypt meant that she was spied on and some letters 'lost'. Much loved, she died in Cairo and was buried there 'among my own people'. See her daughter Janet Ross's *Three Generations of Englishwomen*, 1888, vol. II, and G. Waterfield, *LDG in England, South Africa, and Egypt*, 1937.

Gordon, Mary Catherine, novelist, b. 1949 on Long Island, NY, da. of David G., a Jewish convert to Catholicism who d. when she was eight, and Anna (Gagliano), who then supported the family as a legal secretary. MG was educ. at Barnard College (BA 1971) and Syracuse Univ. (MA 1973) and has taught college English at Poughkeepsie and Amherst. She m. James Brain, anthropologist, in 1974, then Arthur Cash, professor of English, in 1979; they have two children. Her novels reflect her Catholicism. In *Final Payments*, 1978, a young woman has to remake her life after caring for her terminally ill father. *The Company of Women*, 1980, deals in part with 'the female habit of abdicating responsibility for their inner lives to men'. It studies the influence of an ultra-conservative priest on devoted women and the daughter of one of them; he teaches her to 'not be womanish'; the 'opposite of womanish was orthodox'. *Men and Angels* focuses on relations between women: an art-historian whose husband is away on sabbatical, an inspiringly 'daring' artist whom she is researching, and a girl she employs for childcare (emotionally deprived and unbalanced, believing herself 'God's chosen'). Short stories collected in *Temporary Shelter*, 1987. *The Other Side*, 1989, treats Irish immigrants to the US. See S. Gilead in *Critique*, 27, 1986; Diana Cooper-Clark, ed., *Interviews with Contemporary Novelists*, 1986, quoted above.

'Gordon', Ruth (Ruth Gordon Jones), 1896–1985, actress, dramatist, screenwriter. She was b. at Wollaston, Mass., da. of Annie Tapley (Ziegler), 'who dreamed I would take piano and dancing lessons ... be a good girl ... marry a good man', and Clinton J., factory foreman. She enrolled in the American Academy of Dramatic Art, NY, 1914, made both Broadway and silent-movie debuts in 1915, then pursued a long and successful US and international stage career. In 1921 she m. actor Gregory Kelly, who died in 1927; she had a son by Jed Harris in 1929. Her play *Over Twenty-One* (in which women manage 'the home front' while men go to war), was staged 1940, pub. 1944, filmed 1945; later plays include *A Very Rich Woman* (adapted: produced 1965). In 1942 she m. Garson Kanin, with whom she wrote, 1948–52, screenplays directed by George Cukor: *A Double Life*, *Pat and Mike*, *The Marrying Kind*, and most famously *Adam's Rib*, 1949, pub. 1972, with Katharine Hepburn and Spencer Tracy as married lawyers confronting each other in court: 'Lots of things a man can do and in society's eyes it's all hunky dory. A woman does the same thing – the same, mind you, and she's an outcast.' 'I don't like being married to what's known as the *new* woman ... I want a wife – not a competitor.' (For the collaboration see P. Houston in *Sight and Sound*, spring 1955: Kanin in *Tracy and Hepburn*, 1971.) RG's own *The Actress*, 1953, from her autobiographical play *Years Ago*, 1947, is another fine example of the same genre. After a few more film roles, 1940–3, she returned to the screen in the mid-1960s, playing a gallery of defiantly outrageous, sometimes frightening old women. Her anecdotal memoirs, *Myself Among Others*, 1971, *My Side*, 1976, and *An Open Book*, 1980, bring out her likeness to the Hepburn character in her movies: 'It's been a ball, it's been sad, it's been lonely, it's been hard work, it's come out right.' Her novel *Shady Lady*, 1983, presents the reminiscences of a down-and-out ex-Ziegfield girl.

Gore, Catherine Grace Frances (Moody), 1799–1861, novelist and dramatist, b. East Retford, Notts., da. of a wine merchant. After her father's death, her mother remarried and moved to London. Educ. mostly at home, she was nicknamed 'The Poetess', and her unpub. poems were warmly commended by Joanna BAILLIE. In 1823 she m. Capt. Charles Arthur G. and had ten children (two survived her), supporting the family by writing when they moved to France in 1832. A substantial inheritance was embezzled by her ex-guardian. She wrote with wit and flair some 70 very successful novels, usually pub. anon. Most were 'silver fork' romances set in the Regency period, extolling the virtues of male domination and female submissiveness (though avoiding excessive female helplessness). Their popularity has been attributed to their domestic detail: 'the minutiae of feminine existence'. She was an astute social observer, but she disparaged her work: 'I was a reader of rubbish long before I became a writer of it' (cited Anderson, 407). In 1827 she had success as a composer: her music for Burns' 'And ye shall walk in silk attire'; the Highland song, 'Welcome, welcome'; and the ballad 'Three Long Years' were particularly popular. She was also a successful playwright, beginning in 1831 with 'The School for Coquettes', which had a long run at the Haymarket. Several dramas followed and in 1843 she won a £500 prize for her comedy, *Quid Pro Quo*. She also wrote poetry, translated, and edited. In later years she returned to England where blindness forced her into complete retirement. See B. Anderson's article in the *Journal of Popular Culture*, 10 (1976).

Gore-Booth, Eva Selena, 1870–1926, poet, dramatist, feminist, b. at Lissadell, Co. Sligo, da. of Anglo-Irish landowners, Georgina (Hill) and Sir Henry G-B. Her sister Constance, 1868–1927, later Countess Markievicz, is famous as an Irish patriot (also an artist and the first woman MP); see lives of her by Seán O'Faoláin, 1934, repr. 1967; Anne Haverty, 1988. EG-B was educ. by governesses; her fragment 'The Inner Life of a Child' mentions 'the visions that surrounded one in the enchanted forests of childhood before the hemlock grew'. She met her lifelong friend Esther Roper in Italy in 1896, and went to live with her in Manchester doing political and social work for women. She edited the *Woman's Labour News*; ran a reading class, dramatic society, and debating society; and befriended and influenced Christabel PANKHURST, 1901–5, though never herself a militant. She published her first poetry book in 1898; poems and prose in journals from the *New Ireland Review* and *The Yellow Book* to *The Common Cause*; pamphlets like *Women's Right to Work* and *Women Workers and Parliamentary Representation*; more poetry volumes (*The One and the Many*, 1904, contains her best-known lyric, 'The Little Waves of Breffny'); a study of St John's Gospel, 1923; and plays in verse (e.g. *The Triumph of Maeve*, 1905) and prose (e.g. *The Sword of Justice*, 1918). *Cuculan* was acted at the Abbey Theatre, Dublin, and *The Sorrowful Princess*, 1907, by a girls' school. In 1913 EG-B's illness caused the friends to move south; she worked for the Women's Peace Crusade, then from 1916 for the cause of Irish independence. Her letters to her sister in prison (each 'a little work of art' exactly fitting the permitted single page) were destroyed by accident; Constance's to her ed. Roper, 1934, repr. 1970. Of Easter Week EG-B wrote, 'Cruelty, bloodshed and hate / Rule the night and the day, / The whole earth is desolate, / To what God shall one pray?' After WWI she campaigned against capital punishment, despite encroaching ill health; she spent 1920–1 in Italy. She left many MSS, most ed. by Roper: poems (a vol. with intro. by Evelyn UNDERHILL, 1926; complete poems with memoir by Roper, 1929); essays and addresses, *The Inner Kingdom*, 1926; dialogues of the dead, *The World's Pilgrim*, 1927; a play, *The Buried Life of Deirdre*, 1930; and an unfinished novel. Called 'equally at home in philosophy and in politics', she gave her writing increasingly to mysticism: 'love is the heart's wall, love the soul's array, / There is nothing living left out in the cold.' W. B. Yeats's elegy ignores the political forces against which both sisters strove, to assert that 'The innocent and the beautiful / Have no enemy but time.' Study by Lewis Gifford, 1988.

Gorst, Nina Cecilia Francesca (Kennedy), 1869–1926, English novelist. Her father, E. R. K., came of an academic family. Educ. at home, she m. Harold G., journalist and author, and published her first novel, *Possessed of Devils*, in 1897, told mainly in diaries and letters. Its heroine marries to escape the squalor of life with her father, but ends by shooting the husband she hates. NG then turned to realistic novels about the life of the London poor, in which female characters are emphasized. *This Our Sister*, 1905, her first success, mixed the reality of male violence against women with a grim Cockney humour. *The Light*, 1906, described as a 'Cockney *Aurora Leigh*', studies a servant girl's spiritual progress, while *The Soul of Milly Green*, 1907, ironically dedicated 'to the average respectable man', charts another girl's descent. *The Thief on the Cross*, 1908, also marked by unremitting naturalism, details women's bondings and betrayals in the face of male violence. Her autobiography, *The Night is Far Spent*, 1919, is unavailable in major libraries, and may have been privately printed.

Gotherson, Dorothea (Scott), later Hogben, 1611–*c*.1680, Quaker minister. B. to a royalist, gentry family at Egerton, Kent, she m., *c*. 1635, Daniel G. (later a major in Cromwell's army). They had five daughters and a son, and left the Church of England for the Quakers by 1660, as she tells in *To all that are Unregenerated*, 1661, a tiny 128-page book, partly in verse, addressed to the king. She admonishes him not to 'think it below him to read that which many think above me to write, in respect of my sex', and rebukes ladies 'who walk with stretched-out necks, and wanton eyes, mincing as you go'. Widowed in 1666, she married after a year or so Joseph H., also of Kent; she emigrated with him, but died soon afterwards on Long Island, NY.

Gothic, a style which became widespread in the late eighteenth century, descended from the heroic ROMANCE, using a stylized version of the middle ages as setting for sensational fiction. Many of its themes and symbols have particular resonance for women: the flow of blood, caves, spirits without body, guilt, imprisonment, physical terror, hunted virgins, stolen inheritance, and discrepancy between authority and the evidence of one's own senses. Women were prominent among its practitioners, from Sarah FIELDING's decaying but not alarming castle in *The History of Ophelia*, 1760 (earlier than Horace Walpole's *Otranto*). Sophia LEE's *The Recess*, 1783–5, contains the most influential of all symbolic wombs. Ann RADCLIFFE (writing terror not horror: suspected apparitions not mouldering corpses) was the central writer of the form's first golden age, and Mary SHELLEY the most original; dozens of their contemporaries use major or minor gothic elements. A popular development in the 1860s and 1870s, supposed to have originated in the USA, was the sensation novel, a sub-genre particularly suited to appropriation by women wanting to subvert the sentimental tradition by exploiting its excesses. Women readers appear to have enjoyed the anti-social impulse of fiction in which crimes are always passionate and often stem from insanity. Caroline CLIVE's anonymous *Paul Ferroll*, 1855, was an early example. Female bigamy is common and murder not unknown in the works of M. E. BRADDON and Ellen WOOD (most famous for *East Lynne*); a keynote is the detailed domestic realism of the settings. Other practitioners included Amelia EDWARDS, Florence MARRYAT, and Louisa ALCOTT. Margaret OLIPHANT deplored the sensation genre, blaming Charlotte BRONTË. See P. D. Edwards, *Some Mid-Victorian Thrillers: The Sensation Novel, Its Friends and Its Foes*, 1971; Winifred Hughes, *The Maniac in the Cellar: Sensation Novels of the 1860s*, 1980; Jane Tompkins, *Sensational Designs*, 1985; Eugenia C. Delamotte, *Perils of the Night, A Feminist Study of Nineteenth-Century Gothic*, 1990. Leslie Fiedler's attempt to reclaim the gothic as masculine has been sufficiently refuted. 'Female gothic', first discussed by Ellen Moers in *Literary Women*, 1963, is typically set in an isolated ancestral home directly descended from innumerable eighteenth-century castles; it involves the pervasive threat to an innocent and passive heroine (owing something to *Jane Eyre* and more to Daphne DU MAURIER's *Rebecca*) of violence and evil from powerful and mysterious male figures close to her. It is a near relation of commercial ROMANCE, and like it was associated early in its history with a particular publisher (Ace Books). It has been variously read as family romance (adolescent-modelled heroine trying to oust a powerful older female figure and win the love of a mysterious patriarchal male), as voicing inarticulate female fears of male violence (or of motherhood, or sexual response), as combining the thrill of adventure with the reassurance of a passive-victim heroine, or as subversively protesting against the feminine mystique and gendered allocation of power. Juliann E. Fleenor, ed., *The Female Gothic*, 1983, divides its essays under the headings Mystique, Madness, Monsters, Maternity. It includes useful studies of Radcliffe, Shelley, Emily BRONTË, Charlotte Perkins GILMAN, 'Victoria Holt' ('Jean PLAIDY'), Christina STEAD, Isak DINESEN, Flannery O'CONNOR and Margaret ATWOOD; and Joanna RUSS's witty, incisive 'Somebody's Trying to Kill Me and I Think It's My Husband; The Modern Gothic'. Russ classifies the Super-Male (whose harsh exterior masks the perfect lover) and Shadow-Male (whose apparent sympathy masks an often violent misogynist), stresses the heroine's passivity, and concludes that the genre is designed to keep housewives compliant. Other works in this volume, however, demonstrate the manifold uses of the gothic tradition to women seeking to depict emotional tyrants, to express gendered rage, terror or self-hatred as either mad or monstrous, and to probe the psychological roots of constructed femininity. For the disturbing 'new gothic', see e.g. Shirley JACKSON; see also Tania Modleski, *Loving With a Vengeance*, 1982.

Gotlieb, Phyllis Fay (Bloom), poet, novelist and short-story writer. Da. of Mary (Kates) and theatre manager Leo B., she was b. in 1926 in Toronto, where she attended the Univ. of Toronto (BA 1948, MA 1950) and m. computer scientist Calvin Carl G., with whom she had three children. Initially recognized as a poet, PG is also respected for her SCIENCE FICTIONS, two of which have been widely translated. *Ordinary, Moving*, 1969, hailed by Louis Martz as 'one of the liveliest and most original volumes of poetry ... in several years', is 'a celebration and lament for all the world's children, ourselves'. Its formal versatility and collage of rhythms and allusions, together with the cultural and mythic wealth of PG's Jewish heritage, speak of the innocent and sinister worlds of children, worlds also explored in the science-fiction context of *Sunburst*, 1964. This first novel is narrated by a bright, self-educated 13-year-old who overturns the revolt of mutant children in a society plagued by sinister twists of history and biology. Precision of colloquial and narrative voice, strong speculations about the future, and psychological acuteness are similarly displayed in *O Master Caliban*, 1976, a novel which, structured around a chess game, explores a father–son relationship and the world of 'ergs' (semi-human machines and genetics). *A Judgement of Dragons*, 1980, *Emperors, Swords, Pentacles*, 1982, and *The Kingdom of the Cats*, 1985, is a trilogy dealing with cats which manage to possess the secrets of the past and of the future. PG's poetry and short stories have been collected: *Works*, 1978, and *Son of the Morning*, 1983. With Douglas Barbour, she has edited *Tesseracts*^{2}, 1987, an anthology of Canadian science fiction. See Barbour in *JCF*, 3, 1974.

Gott, Dorothy (Newberry), religious writer and visionary, b. among Quakers. She learned religion from her mother, but hardly to read and never, she says, to write. Coming from the country to London at about 17, she planned to be a mantua-maker and a minister, but after severe smallpox she became, she says, an exploited servant in a Quaker family. The Friends disowned her in 1773 for marriage 'out', some years before, to a footman with whom she ran a milliner's and haberdasher's, a liquor shop, then a public house. His death in 1785 left her in debt; she lived as maid to a sick sister and increasingly saw visions and heard voices. Involvement with a young Scotsman, John Murray, apparently disturbed her badly. She identified him and his scientific interests with 'the spirit of darkness', yet kept supplying him (to her sister's anger) with money – seeking, it seems, some kind of spiritual conquest. At God's command she sat naked at a window from night till broad daylight; others thought her mad, including a doctor at Bedlam. She relates all this, and prints letters to Murray, 1786–7, in *The Midnight Cry*, 1788. In *Christ the Standard of Truth* [c. 1796] and *The Noon-Day Sun*, 1798, she strongly urges on bishops and other authorities the need for a female voice in religion. The first says that unlike the QUAKERS, 'by rejecting the experience of the women the outward church hath been very dark'; it ends with 'A Call to all Women, under every name, tongue or people'. If women 'were properly encouraged by the men to plead with the Lord', says the second, 'great things would be done for us, that have not yet entered the heart of man'.

Goudge, Elizabeth, 1900–84, popular novelist and CHILDREN'S writer. Da. of Ida de Beauchamp (Collenette) and the Rev. Henry Leighton G., she was b. at Wells, Somerset, and later lived at Ely, Cambs., where her father was a Canon, and Oxford, where he was Regius Professor of Divinity. (Her fiction lovingly re-creates a cathedral close and several versions of an idyllic relationship between vague, scholarly, benevolent male and caring, practical, energetic female.) After two years at Reading University School of Art, EG lived with her parents, teaching design and handicrafts, 1922–32. She first wrote not very successful plays (one on the BRONTËS); her novels began with *Island Magic*, 1934; her 40 titles include children's books (notably *The Little White Horse*, 1946, set in the seventeenth century), short stories, and non-fiction reflecting her religious faith: anthologies, lives of Christ and St Francis. Her 15 novels include historical settings, with appearances by e.g. ELIZABETH I and Sir Philip Sidney. In *Green Dolphin Country*, 1944, her highest-selling work, one female character persistently chafes against the restrictions of her gender; but sensitivity and moral heroism are shown as able to redeem all sorrows of love or marriage. See EG's autobiography, *The Joy of the Snow*, 1974; anthology of her work ed. Muriel Grainger, 1978.

Gould, Hannah Flagg, 1789–1865, poet, b. Lancaster, Mass., da. of Griselda Apthorp (Flagg) and Benjamin G. The family moved in 1808 to Newburyport, where HG spent the rest of her life, keeping house for her father after her mother's death. Her first book, *Poems*, 1832, a collection of her fugitive pieces and previously unpub. work, was surprisingly successful and was repub. 1833, 1835 and 1836, when a second vol. was added. Ten other vols. of poetry, many for children, were pub. between 1844 and her posthumous *Poems for Children*, 1870. Her children's poems are didactic and moral, influenced by Blake and L. H. SIGOURNEY. Her most famous poem, 'The Rising Monument', 1840, which commemorates the Battle of Bunker Hill, is one of her many historical poems, others of which are coll. in *Gathered Leaves*, 1846, and *New Poems*, 1850. In her lifetime her work was reviewed by Poe in the *Southern Literary Messenger*, 1836, and S. J. HALE in the *Woman's Record*, 1853.

Govier, Katherine, novelist, short-story writer, journalist. B. in Edmonton, Alberta, in 1948, da. of Doris E. (Kempt), a teacher, and George G., an engineer and businessman, she was educ. there and in Calgary, then at the Univs. of Alberta (BA, 1970) and York (MA, 1972). She has taught creative writing in Toronto, and been a journalist in Canada, England and the USA. Twice married – 1971, 1981 – she has two children. Her novels depict women finding the voices, words and relationships through which, as the protagonist of *Going Through the Motions*, 1982, says, 'Lives can come together without warning – and fragments make sense.' In *Random Descent*, 1979, after leaving her unfaithful husband and aborting his child, Jennifer sorts out all that she can learn or infer about her 'breeding' through six generations, emphasizing the strengths of her grandmother and great-great-great-grandmother, then returns to 'the present tense' to find her own solutions. The final story of *Fables of Brunswick Avenue*, 1985, 'Palm Beach', ends when its narrator realizes that her triumphant struggle with the crest of an ocean wave is a metaphor for power: 'She gains her feet as the world slips backward under her and comes out on top'. KG began her latest novel, *Between Men*, 1987, before her first child was born, 1981: novels now take 'the kind of time it is very hard to get' and demand a frightening expense of psychic energy for a mother. *Before and After*, 1989, treats her student experiences. Interview in *Books in Canada*, 16, 6, 1987.

Gowan, Elsie Park (Young), playwright, b. Helensburgh, Scotland, in 1905 and brought to Canada in 1912. Studying history at the Univ. of Alberta, she took the lead in its dramatic and literary life. Graduating with first-class honours in 1930, she wrote the first of her 20 plays, *Homestead*, in 1931 (adapted and staged as *God Made the Country*, 1935, about a wife who feels 'chained to a homestead like a dumb beast'). In 1933 she m. Dr Edward Hunter G., a physicist and 'the only man I had ever met who was willing to let me go as far as I could'. A leading figure at the Edmonton Little Theatre, 1933–48, and with Gwen RINGWOOD a foremost prairie dramatist, she sought to make drama 'mirror our environment', not someone else's. She wrote about 250 scripts for radio, a medium which, she said, 'goes back to the minstrels and ballad singers of castle halls and poor men's cottages'. In 1935 and 1940 she crossed swords with critics denigrating either Canadian drama in general or its element of 'kitchen stoves' and 'old ladies sitting in rocking chairs'. *The Giant-Killer*, 1934, deals with militarism and pacifism, *Back to the Kitchen, Woman!*, 1941, with the issues implied, and *One Who Looks at the Stars*, *c.* 1946, with interracial marriage. EPG was denied public credit for her part in *You Can't Do That*, 1936 (written with William Irvine), a satirical farce about a prime minister's niece staging a coup and reforming political life. In *The Last Caveman*, staged 1938 and often adapted (radio version 1950), a family of shack-dwelling hicks defend their land rights, while more educated characters move from contempt to respect. EPG taught at an Edmonton high-school, 1959–69, and from the 1950s to the 1970s produced outdoor historical pageants. See Anton Wagner in *Theatre History in Canada*, 8, 1987 (quoted above), with text of *The Last Caveman*. Some papers in Univ. of Alberta archives.

Grace, Patricia (Gunson), Maori novelist and short-story writer, b. Wellington, NZ, da. of Joyce (of Irish descent) and Edward G. of Ngati Toa, Ngati Raukawa and Te Ati Awa descent, stationery manufacturer. Educ. at St Anne's Primary School, St Mary's College and Wellington Teachers College, she m. Karehi Waiariki G., and for about 20 years they taught in mainly country schools. She taught English as a second language at Porirua College, Wellington, and had seven children. *Waiariki*, 1975, was the first collection of short stories by a Maori woman writer. She received the first Maori Purposes Fund Board writers' grant in 1974, followed by a grant from the NZ Literary Fund. She has been involved in the NZ Book Council's Writers in Schools scheme and the Maori Artists' and Writers' huis (gatherings). Her 1978 novel *Mutuwhenua* is a moving account of a young Maori girl's growing-up, marrying a pakeha, and discovering her need for and her roots in her family and land. It is a sympathetic portrayal of the problems of a mixed marriage. *Potiki*, 1986, is set in a small rural Maori community, threatened by developers. These, and her next collections of short stories, *The Dream Sleepers*, 1980, and *Electric City*, 1987, are the best literary portrayals yet of Maori life. She has also written the texts of children's books, pub. in both Maori and English, and of *Wahine Toa: Women of Maori Myth*, 1984, with illustrations by the Maori woman artist Robyn Kahukiwa. She has written full-time since 1985, when she was Writer-in-Residence at Victoria Univ., Wellington. Asked why so few Maori women wrote, she said: 'They were too busy surviving'.

Grafton, Sue, screen and thriller writer, b. 1940 in Louisville, Ky, da. of Vivian (Harnsberger) and Chip G., attorney and mystery writer. She received a BA from the Univ. of Louisville, 1961. Her first works were non-crime novels (*Keziah Dane*, 1967, and *The Lolly-Madonna War*, 1969), a movie screenplay from the latter, and more than a half-dozen TV screenplays. In 1978 she m. writer Steven F. Humphrey, with whom she co-authored an award-winning pilot for the CBS TV series *Seven Brides for Seven Brothers*. They have three children. SG's thrillers provide a female critique of the long male-dominated DECTECTIVE genre. *'A' is for Alibi*, 1982, introduces her 'strong woman' detective, Kinsey Milhone, an orphan 'raised by a wonderfully unconventional aunt': 32, twice divorced, without ties (her 'own mystery, unplumbed, undetected'), who fears sexual or emotional involvement but likes women. In *'A'* she sleeps with a man later revealed as a murderer who tries to make her his third female victim: she kills him. *'B' is for Burglar*, 1985 (Private Eye Writers of America award, Bouchercon award), makes acknowledgement to Marcia MULLER; it uses SG's characteristic spare style, but takes a sideswipe at the 'rude words' style of Mickey Spillane. Sequels follow the pattern, with Milhone not unfeeling or unanxious about her violent trade. In *'E' is for Evidence*, 1988, which 'turns on ugly family secrets', she finds her always reluctantly-used gun a less effective weapon than a 'handbag and a toilet tank lid'. See Maureen T. Reddy, *Sisters in Crime*, 1988 (quoted above); Kathleen Gregory Klein, *The Woman Dectective*, 1988.

Graham, Gwethalyn (Erichsen-Brown), 1913–65, novelist, short-story writer, journalist. She was b. in Toronto, second of four children. Her mother, a MacCurdy, was a graduate in Classics from the Univ. of Toronto, a strong supporter of women's suffrage, and an advocate of Canadian music and art. Her father was interested in painting; the family possessed a library of several thousand books. 'I grew up on Ibsen, Shaw, Sudermann, Hauptmann, Dickens, Plato and Sinclair Lewis.' GG was educ. in Toronto at Rosedale Public School and Havergal College, then in Switzerland and at Smith College, Mass. At 19 she m. a much older man, later married again and lived in Virginia. Twice divorced, she m. philosopher David Yalden-Thomas in 1947. She had one son. Her first novel, *Swiss Sonata*, 1938, set in a Swiss boarding school just before WWII, won the Governor-General's Award, as did her second, best-known book, *Earth and High Heaven*, 1944 (repr. 1960 with intro. by Eli Mandel). Set in Montréal during WWII, it treats anti-semitism in the story of the love of an upper-class white Protestant and a Jewish officer. A critical and popular success, it was translated into ten languages. With Solange Chaput-Rolland, GG published *Dear Enemy*, 1963, a series of letters between two intelligent, articulate women, one English-Canadian and one French-Canadian, concerning French-English problems of the time.

Graham, Isabella (Marshall), 1742–1814, religious writer and philanthropist. B. in

Lanarkshire, da. of Janet (Hamilton) and John M., a committed Church of Scotland member from her teens, she had seven years at boarding school from a grandfather's legacy. In 1765 she m. John G., army doctor, and travelled to Montréal, Fort Niagara (her happiest years: lacking a church, she spent Sundays in the woods with her Bible), then to Antigua, where he died, leaving her with three small daughters and a posthumous son. Refusing to raise money by selling her Indian servants, she came home to live by school-teaching at Paisley and Edinburgh. In NYC from 1789, she founded and ran charitable institutions, many for women. Her letters, diary-like 'Devotional Exercises', and public addresses, pub. cumulatively in 1817, 1838, 1839, range from vivid early travel-letters, through analysis of her collapse and slow recovery after her husband's death, to intensely pious meditation and measured, earnest social statement.

Graham, Jorie (Pepper), poet, b. 1951 in NYC, da. of Beverley (Stoll) and Curtis Bell P., to whom she dedicated her first book. She took a BFA at NY Univ., 1973, and an MFA at the Univ. of Iowa, 1978, m., and began univ. teaching in Kentucky, then Calif. Her work appeared in journals, then in three books: *Hybrids of Plants and of Ghosts*, 1980 (title from Nietzsche), *Erosion*, 1983, and *The End of Beauty*, 1987. She teases out complex cerebral meanings from both natural and human things: a skein of geese, a pine forest, children at play, cooking (live bodies become meat). On fresh snow she muses, 'Such solitary work / this breaking ground / that will only reclaim itself', on needlework (a frequent topic) 'Passion is work / that retrieves us, / lost stitches. It makes a pattern of us, / it fastens us / to sturdier stuff / no doubt'; on a 'Whore's Bath' 'The clean // is such a steady garment, such a perfected argument. / Where does it unfasten?' JG writes often of Italy; literary and cultural allusions abound. Time, losses, and the nature of humanity feature in the title-piece of *Erosions* and in her latest book, which scatters among other poems a series of 'Self-Portraits', some 'as' famous pairs (Apollo and Daphne, Demeter and Persephone), some whose mythological allusion lies in the sub-title: 'Self-Portrait As the Gesture Between Them' (Adam and Eve), 'As Both Parties' (Orpheus and Eurydice), 'As Hurry and Delay' (Penelope). These dwell on moments of choice or non-choice, of suspension of time between action and inaction or death and life.

Grahn, Judy Rae, poet, publisher, editor, fiction writer, playwright, critic, cultural historian. B. 1940 in Chicago, da. of Vera Doris, a photographer's assistant, and Elmer August, a cook, she grew up in New Mexico, wrote as a child and until leaving home, beginning again at 26 after serious illness. At 21 she was expelled from the Air Force for being lesbian. She attended six colleges, became immersed in poetry and publishing, and completed her BA at San Francisco State Univ., 1984. She has taught gay and lesbian studies, and women's writing. In 1969, she founded with artist Wendy Cadden the Women's Press Collective in Oakland, California, and, with Susan GRIFFIN, Pat PARKER, and ALTA, led a West Coast women's poetry renaissance in the early 1970s, which 'nurtured' Ntozake SHANGE's *For Colored Girls....* Because 'the traditional European sonnet was not enough to want' for her subjects, she invented an 'American sonnet' for 'The Common Woman' sequence in *Edward the Dyke and Other Poems*, 1971, celebrations of women's differences, commonness, commonality and strength. This, with the experimental *She Who*, 1972, suggestive of feminist scripture, and *A Woman is Talking to Death*, 1974, is collected with later poems in *The Work of A Common Woman*, 1978, intro. by Adrienne RICH. *The Queen of Wands*, 1982, first of a projected four-part *Chronicle of Queens* (Cups and Diamonds to come) recalls H. D.: here, the archetypal Helen is abducted, her powers stolen to create civilization; in *The Queen of Swords*, 1987, Helen encounters Ereshkigal, queen of the underworld. *Another Mother Tongue*, 1984, partly autobiographical, also comprises a chapter of gay cultural history. *The Highest Apple*, 1985, outlines a lesbian poetic tradition from SAPPHO. Common women powerfully voice their experiences in *True to Life Adventure Stories*, ed. JG, two vols., 1981, 1983. Her novel, *Mundane's World*, 1988, depicts in fable-like, linguistically playful episodes, its protagonist Ernesta's passage to womanhood in an interdependent gynocentric society; another novel, *The Motherlords*, is in progress. Her anthology with essays, *Really Reading Gertrude STEIN*, 1989, is 'an expression of my great love'. See Marilyn Yalom, ed., *Women Writers of the West Coast*, 1983, Mary J. Carruthers, *Hudson Review*, 36, 1983, and Sue Ellen Case in *Studies in the Literary Imagination*, 21, 1988.

'Grand, Sarah', Frances Elizabeth (Clarke) (later McFall), 1854–1943, novelist and feminist, b. Donaghadee, Co. Down, fourth of five children of Margaret Bell (Sherwood) and Edward John Bellenden C., naval officer and coastguard. The family moved to Yorkshire after his death when SG was seven. Educ. at home and, unhappily, at two girls' boarding schools, at 16 she m. Surgeon-Major David McFall. Her early experience of life with an alcoholic father, then marriage to a doctor who serviced an institution for the incarceration of prostitutes with venereal disease, is fictionalized in *The Beth Book*, 1897. After travelling to Hong Kong and the Far East they lived first in Norwich, then Warrington. She started publishing stories in magazines, and her first successful novel, *Ideala*, 1888 (pub. anon.), combining conventional romantic and domestic detail with discussion of contemporary social issues, gave her enough money to leave her husband and son and move to London. *The Heavenly Twins*, 1893, dealing with women's desire for emancipation, with double sexual standards and, especially, with knowledge gained by her support of Josephine BUTLER's crusade to repeal the Contagious Diseases Act, caused a sensation, selling 20,000 copies in one year. For the next 20 years, she was a frequent lecturer on women's topics, campaigning, among other things, for rational dress. A member of the Women Writer's SUFFRAGE League, she was Vice President of the Women's Suffrage Society and, after moving to Tunbridge Wells in 1898, President of the local branch of the National Council of Women. In 1920 she moved to Bath, where she was Lady Mayoress for six years. After *The Beth Book*, which attacks men for seeing 'but one side of a social question, and that is their own', her fiction became less polemical. See Gilliam Kersley, *Darling Madame*, 1983, and Joan Huddleston's bibliography, *VFRG* 1, 1979.

Grant, Anne (Macvicar), 1755–1838, poet, letter-writer and historian. Da. of Catherine (Mackenzie) and Duncan M., army officer, she was taken from Glasgow for formative years, 1758–68, in Albany, NY, a society she later depicted in *Memoirs of an American Lady*, 1808 (planned since 1773; facs. 1970; popular re-writing by James Kirke Paulding, *c.* 1831). This ranks high as biography (of local matriarch Catalina Schuyler), autobiography (developing relationship with her previously unknown father; her passion, at seven, for 'my treasure, Milton and the ragged dictionary'), and as history, with both detail and elegiac feeling about colonial life, especially the 'distinguished race' of Mohawks. Back in Britain, she married, 1779, the Rev. James G. of Laggan, a remote Highland parish where she farmed, and reared her children to speak Gaelic. Four of 12 died before he did (1801); only one survived her. In 1803, with an impressive subscribers' list, she issued what she called a 'tiresome collection' of *Poems*: the best are least formal, like 'The Bluebells of Scotland' and a bustling tale of homecoming. *Letters from* *the Mountains*, written 1773–1806, mainly to women friends, pub. 1807, discuss books, Highland people, family joys and grief. In 1794 she responded to what she acknowledged as Mary WOLLSTONECRAFT's 'considerable powers', 'feeling' and 'rectitude of intention' with a tirade deploying high ability to prove women's ability normally inferior. In Edinburgh from 1810, she enjoyed wide literary acquaintance. More letters, pub. with an autobiographical fragment, 1844, are rich in acute comment on women writers; others followed in 1896 (on Highland history) and 1901. AG's long poems are *The Highlanders*, 1808, and *1813*, 1814, which uses ELIZABETH I and Queen Anne to foretell a glorious female reign for Princess Charlotte of Wales. She wrote *Essays on ... the Highlanders*, 1811, and an advice-book for 'the Sons and Daughters of Industry', 1815; but not Mary Ann G.'s *Sketches*, 1810, or, probably, the evangelical *Touchstone*, 1842 (listed as hers). Her conservatism and self-deprecation have somewhat obscured her quiet feminism and remarkable mind. Life by 'George PASTON', 1896.

Grant, Elizabeth of Rothiemurchus, later Smith, 1797–1885, AUTOBIOGRAPHER and miscellaneous writer, eldest child of Jane (Ironside) and advocate John Peter G.: great-great-aunt of Julia STRACHEY. (Her grandmother, Elizabeth (Raper) G. wrote a lively diary and creative recipes, pub. 1924.) B. in Edinburgh, EG grew up with winters in London (fashion, dress, gossip), summers in the Highlands (feudal self-sufficiency), with gruelling journeys in between. At less than 18 months she 'tried to make away with' her baby brother; in 1816 she renounced a passionate love, because of violent personal hatred between the fathers. She describes this 'pretty Romeo and Juliet business' which 'changed all things in life to me' as vividly and straightforwardly as her outer life. Her earnings (with her sister Mary) from *Fraser's* and *The Inspector* for 'essays, short tales, and at length a novel' (not traced) saved the family from financial ruin in 1826–7. Her bankrupt father was made a judge in Bengal, where in 1829 EG m. Irish Col. Henry Smith, 'my new master'. She had three children, hectored and served the poor on his estates, and ran a non-sectarian school at Baltiboys; she wrote 'for bread' (mainly for others) during the Irish famine (*Chambers*, 1845ff). Her *Memoirs*, 1845–54, written for her children and a niece, finish: 'a husband – a baby – an end indeed of Eliza Grant' (selection ed. by her granddaughter Jane Maria Strachey, 1897; complete, 1988; as Grant); her *Irish Journals*, 1840–50, as Smith, selection ed. David Thomson and Moyra McGusty, 1980. Another EG (of Carron, *c.*1745–1828) wrote the song 'Roy's Wife o' Aldivalloch', praised by Burns.

Grant, Lilias (Murray), d. ?1644, ?poet, second da. of Catherine (Drummond) and Sir John M., later Earl of Tullibardine. James VI of Scotland attended her marriage, 1591, to John Grant of Freuchie. She had five children; John Taylor the water poet noted her beauty and wit, 1618. She left a catalogue of her library, 1630 (28 pious books including the recent published Dorothy LEIGH), and copies of two poems probably by herself: a happy love-song for a woman ('He is my joy and my veillfair') and a gloomy one for a man ('fanssies fleittein to and fro / My martret mynd do so molest').

Grant, Maria, novelist, b. *c.* 1845, da. of a writer to the Signet and descendant of the old house of Glenmoriston, Inverness. She spent her first 14 years by the River Ness, educ. by her brothers' tutors and later a German governess. The family then moved to Edinburgh, where she studied at the Scottish School of Art, later moving between London, the Highlands, and the Continent. Her first novel, *Artiste*, 1871, treats of a half-Indian girl orphan, who becomes a famous Parisian tragic actress, giving all to her art (until her marriage). Her most successful was *Lescar, the Universalist*, 1874 (repr. 1875 as *Victor Lescar*), a powerful and controversial story of the French Commune and the Franco-Prussian war, anonymous and taken to be by a man. The 'exotic woman of Art' theme recurs in later novels: *The Sun-Maid*, 1876 and *Prince Hugo*, 1880. Her last was *Cara Roma*, 1885.

Grau, Shirley Ann, novelist, short-story writer, b. 1929 in New Orleans, da. of the elderly Katherine (Onions) and Dr Adolph Eugene G. She attended the old-world Booth School for girls (Montgomery, Ala), the Catholic Ursuline Academy, New Orleans (though a Protestant), and took a BA in English, 1950, from Tulane Univ. (the women's college, Sophie Newcomb, whose inferiority she notes). There she helped edit a journal which printed her poems and stories; she 'made up her mind to be a writer', did some graduate work, and was first commercially published in 1953. A story volume, *The Black Prince*, 1954, was acclaimed for lyricism; it uses Southern settings and speech-rhythms, deals with mixed-race issues, and develops elaborate biblical parallels. In 1955 SAG married James Kern Feibleman, a philosophy professor 26 years her senior; they had four children. *The Hard Blue Sky*, 1958, a novel of Cajun island fishermen, uses a young girl as focus for varied episodes: 'Things happened ... and they went on past you.' *The House on Coliseum Street*, 1961, set in New Orleans, deals with a woman caught between two men, having and regretting an abortion, hating the body's power and the 'stupid silly mark of a man', reacting against the mother who gave her four younger sisters by different fathers. SAG's next three novels each present a long-dominant patriarch who joins lust for power to lust for sex; the last two each grew from a short story. In *The Keepers of the House*, 1964 (Pulitzer Prize), a granddaughter dismantles the family heritage from which the black second wife's children were barred; the protagonist of *The Condor Passes*, 1971, seeks a blood or non-blood heir; that of *Evidence of Love*, 1977, narrates the birth he has 'often thought' he remembers, and his (self-administered) death. SAG says that in stories 'the bones are more visible'; her versatility appears in those of *The Wind Shifting West*, 1973, including several on Vietnam deaths and damage. She has taught creative writing at Tulane. See Ann B. Pearson in *Critique*, 17, 1975; interview (among several) in *Cimarron Review*, 43, 1978; bibliog. by Joseph A. Grau (no relation) and Paul Schlueter, 1981. Schlueter's study is both inaccurate and grudging.

Graves, Clo., Clotilde Inez Mary, 'Richard Dehan', 1863–1932, short-story writer, novelist and dramatist, b. at Buttevant Barracks, Co. Cork, third da. of Antoinette (Deane) and Major W. H. G. Largely self-educ., she studied at the Royal Female School of Art, Bloomsbury, and later illustrated her writing, acted in travelling companies, and was known for adoption of male dress. She supported herself by journalism and writing stories for papers like *The World*, *Punch*, and *Hood's Comic Annual*. In 1888 she published an entertaining spoof on R. L. Stevenson: *The Pirate's Hand* ('by the author of "Knee-capped"'). Her plays (staged in London, many unpub.) began with a blank-verse tragedy, 1887, and included light comedies, a version of *The Rape of the Lock*, and a pantomime; most successful was *A Mother of Three*, Comedy Theatre, 1896, a lively farce hingeing on the unreliability of men. Her 20 novels and story volumes embrace feminism, melodrama, and sentimental comedy; *A Well-Meaning Woman*, 1896 (repr. as *The Gilded Vanity*, 1916), treats a young woman's unhappiness in a socially ambitious marriage. With *The Dop Doctor*, 1911, CG began to publish large historical works as 'Richard Dehan', whose identity was for some time an intriguing puzzle. It uses the Boer War as backdrop to the romance of an orphaned rape victim and a reformed drunkard who gradually reconciles her to sexual contact. *Between Two Thieves*, 1912, is set in the Crimean War, and *The Man of Iron*, 1915, in the Franco-Prussian War. CG became a Catholic in 1896 and retired to a convent after her health failed in 1928.

Gray, Christian, poet, b. 1772 at Aberdalgie, Perth, to Janet (McDonald) and George G., who were 'not rich, but respected'. Blinded as a child (probably by smallpox), she would knit stockings while 'walking about in the open air', and compose lines which she then repeated 'to the first amanuensis that turned up'. Her *Tales, Letters, and other Pieces in Verse*, Edinburgh, 1808 – mostly standard English – deal in fiction and in her thoughts and feelings on love, war, emigration, family love, and her blindness; they also versify Ossian. Her farming family was ruined in the drought years 1816–26. Many of CG's *New Selection of Miscellaneous Pieces*, Perth, 1821, are religious; many are requests, or thanks, for help. She wrote a reply to Lady NAIRNE's 'The Land o' the Leal', and answered a Scots courtship song with a cheerful rejection ('For aft a wife maun thole the wrang, / And I sic scaith will never dree').

'Gray', Dulcie, b. 1920, actress and novelist, b. Dulcie Winifred Catherine in Kuala Lumpur, Malaya, to Kate Edith Clulow (G.) and Arnold Savage Bailey, CBE, lawyer, judge and politician. After education in England and Malaya (some teaching in Malaya, too), she m. actor Michael Denison, 1939, and embarked on her two careers: five decades of acting (theatre, film, TV) and writing popular novels. She wrote first a play, *Love Affair*, produced 1956, using her experience as an art student; then conventional murder mysteries, like *Murder on the Stairs*, 1957; character studies of the criminal, like *Murder in Mind*, 1963; suspense novels, like the disturbing *Ride on a Tiger*, 1975, in which political involvement brings death to an actress; and, more lately, non-crime novels which focus on their heroines' turbulent personal lives. She has also written non-fiction: *Butterflies on my Mind*, 1978, won the Times Educational Supplement Information Book Award. She was made CBE, 1983. Her husband's *Overture and Beginners*, 1973, describes her childhood and his, their marriage, and her acting career.

Gray, Francine (du Plessix), novelist, journalist, social critic, b. 1930 in the French Embassy in Warsaw, da. of Tatiana (Jacovieff), eminent hat designer, and Bertrand du P., diplomat, businessman, and later Resistance hero. Her early languages were French and Russian; she learned English when brought to the US at 11. She was educ. at the Spence School, then Bryn Mawr, 1948–50, Black Mountain College (summers, 1951–2) and Barnard (BA in philosophy, 1952). She was deeply influenced by the Christian pacifism of Nikolai Berdyayeu, who taught that evil and social ills come from 'potential unfulfilled'. She worked as a journalist in New York and – socializing wildly – in Paris; convalescing from mononucleosis in the Swiss Alps in 1956 she 'began to feel a very feminist rage' at the censoring imposed on women over sexual topics: she 'wished, some day to write a very erotic book'. Journals from this time 'set the tone for many passages' of *Lovers and Tyrants*, 1976: 'The most tyrannical despots can be those who love us the most.' FdPG married painter Cleve G. in 1957 and has two sons. Of other novels, *World Without End*, 1981, deals with friendship, *October Blood*, 1985, with overlapping spheres of fashion, asceticism, and social activism. A character says she will stay with her exasperating family because 'unless we're saints or monsters there truly isn't that much else'. But FdPG's religion, philosophy and political activism have served her for non-fiction like *Divine Disobedience: Profiles* *in Catholic Radicalism*, 1970. *Hawaii: The Sugar-Coated Fortress*, 1972, examines the American economic takeover by entrepreneurial descendants of missionaries, but points out how ancient structures were already being destroyed in the early nineteenth century as Hawaiian women of the chieftain class revolted against rigidly restrictive taboos. For 'When Memory Goes', an award-winning two-part article on Klaus Barbie (and Beata Klarsfield's part in bringing him to justice), she drew on childhood memories of wartime France; researching this essay, FdPG learned how her father died (pub. in *Vanity Fair*, 1983). Her writings make sophisticated use of her immigrant experience and an idiosyncratic world-view which combines thirst for justice with worldly wisdom and allegiance to family; her journalism and fiction is alive to precedents and possibilities for sanctity and martyrdom. She has written art criticism (having considered painting as a métier) and held teaching posts, and looked at 'officially emancipated' *Soviet Women: Walking the Tightrope*, 1990.

Gray, Mary Anne (Browne), 1812–45, poet (not, despite rumours, sister of Felicia HEMANS), b. at Maidenhead, Berks. She invented her own alphabet while her parents thought her too young to learn to read, 'could not recollect when she was not clothing her thoughts in verse', and pub. her first volume, *Mont Blanc*, in 1827 (title poem in rich, dignified Spenserian stanzas; another defends Woman against charges of evil and unreason by stressing nurturing and dependence). *Ada*, 1828, dedicated to her father, praised in *Blackwood's*, makes much of female friendship amid Byronic Greek islands; *Repentance*, 1829, cites or praises her mother, grandmother, and women writers. In Liverpool from 1836, she worked (to keep her brother at university) as a district visitor and found in German literature 'new domains in the realm of thought'. She pub. further volumes before and after marrying James G., nephew of poet James Hogg, in 1842 and settling – still poor, as she wrote to the RLF – at Cork. From 1839 she published in the *Dublin University Magazine*, which justifiably put her among 'the first of living poetesses', 1841: prose and many poems, some posthumous; the last prefaced by advice to women to 'Prefer the domestic to the literary career'. She is both lyrical and thoughtful; her *Sketches from the Antique*, 1844, treats SAPPHO, Penelope, and girl athletes ('Alas! that time's dark stream hath not brought down / The invigorating race, and olive crown!'). 'The Embroideress at Midnight' toils at a 'stinted price' for her sick mother; sage Queen Damaris in a fairy tale is made to burn her books.

'Gray, Maxwell', Mary Gleed Tuttiet, 1847–1923, novelist and poet, b. Newport, Isle of Wight, only da. of Eliza (Gleed) and F. B. T. She became well known through her novel *The Silence of Dean Maitland*, 1886, a powerful and interesting story of the hidden sin of a charismatic young minister. Whilst tracing both his amazing popularity and success, and the consequences over 20 years of his youthful seduction of a young woman, the narrative displays clear sympathy for the victim and notes society's harsh condemnation of 'fallen' women. Although her later work never equalled this early success, she pub. several other novels, including *In the Heart of the Storm*, 1891, and *Sweethearts and Friends*, 1897, which deal with women's rights; and collections of competent but derivative poetry such as *The Forest Chapel*, 1899, dedicated to Queen VICTORIA, and *England's Sun*, 1919.

Gray, Oriel (Bennett), playwright, scriptwriter, b. 1920 in Sydney, NSW, younger da. of Ida Mary (Sheehan) and Benjamin Holland B.; she was educ. at St George Girls' High School. Influenced by her father's Labour politics (her mother died when she was six), at 17 she joined the left-wing New Theatre in Sydney, and later, the Communist Party. She was m. for six years to John G., then had a de facto relationship (1945–68) with journalist John Hepworth; she has three sons. During the 1940s and 1950s the New Theatre produced all of her plays. Notable are 'Lawson' (produced 1943), based on Henry Lawson's stories; 'The Torrents' (produced 1954) which shared first prize with Ray Lawler's now legendary *Summer of the Seventeenth Doll* in the Playwrights' Advisory Board Competition of that year, and 'Burst of Summer' (produced 1959), winner of a J. C. Williamson's award. Some later plays, mainly for children, appeared in the 1960s. OG also wrote scripts for radio and television, such as the long-running ABC serial, *Bellbird*. Details of her interesting, sometimes controversial, and often amusing life are recounted in her autobiography, *Exit Left, Memoirs of a Scarlet Woman*, 1985.

Green, Anna Katherine, later Rohlfs, 1846–1935, first US woman to write a best-selling mystery, variously called 'mother', 'godmother', and 'grandmother' of the genre. She was born in Brooklyn, da. of Catherine Ann (Whitney) and James Wilson G., a prominent criminal lawyer and descendant of Mayflower pilgrim John Howland. Her mother died when she was three, and her father married Grace Hollister, who encouraged her early attempts at writing. She joined the literary society at Ripley Female College, Poultney, Vermont (BA, 1866), and met Ralph Waldo Emerson. At 38, she m. Charles Rohlfs, an actor with Edwin Booth, later a successful furniture designer. They settled in Buffalo, NY, where she died. Of their three children, only Roland, who was associated with the Wright brothers, survived the parents. Originally wishing to be a poet, AKG published *The Defense of the Bridge and Other Poems*, 1882, and *Risifi's Daughter*, a poetic drama, 1887. When she launched her mystery career, American mainstream fiction was well defined, but 'the mystery sweepstakes remained to be won'. *The Leavenworth Case*, immediately a best-seller, was the first of more than 35 novels written between 1878 and 1923. It preceded Conan Doyle's first work and introduced NY police detective Ebenezer Gryce, who sleuths through 11 novels and 2 short stories (pre-dating Sherlock Holmes by 9 years). AKG's reputation in American popular fiction has rested almost entirely on this first book, which has been praised for its legal accuracy, used in a Yale Univ. course to illustrate the fallacy of circumstantial evidence, dramatized by its author (her husband acting the leading role), filmed in both a silent and sound version, 1923, 1936, and recognized as a landmark in the development of the genre. It brought wide readership and respectability to the genre and introduced many devices later standard in DETECTIVE FICTION, such as the coroner's inquest, clues, suspects, and expert testimony. She also created two other important detective prototypes. From Amelia Butterworth, 'the first really credible woman detective', introduced in *That Affair Next Door*, 1897, came 'such elderly female amateur detectives as Mary Roberts RINEHART's Miss Rachel Innes, Agatha CHRISTIE's Miss Marple, Patricia WENTWORTH's Miss Silver, and Stuart Palmer's Hildegarde Withers'; from Violet Strange, of *The Golden Slipper*, 1915, came 'Nancy Drew, Mignon EBERHART's Susan Dare, and other young women with crime-detecting on their minds'. See Barrie Hayne in Bargainnier, 1981, Michael Slung's introduction to *The Leavenworth Case*, 1981, both quoted above, also Alma E. Murch, *The Development of the Detective Novel*, 1958.

Green, Anne, novelist, b. 1899 in Savannah, Georgia, da. of Mary (Hartridge) and Edward Moon G., taken as a baby to Paris, where she has mostly lived. Educ. at the Lycée Molière, she drove ambulances during WWI, spent some time afterwards in the USA, and wrote for newspapers. Her brother Julian, with whom she re-occupied her parents' old flat in Paris, was a novelist before her. Her first book, *The Selbys*, 1930, is notable for a character she calls a portrait from life of her mother. Her *Reader, I Married Him*, 1931, is also a novel. She spent WWII in the USA, became a Catholic in 1947, did some translation (both solo and with her brother), and published an AUTOBIOGRAPHY, *With Much Love*, 1948, which reveals the degree to which her fiction had been interrelated with her life. After some dozen novels in English (dealing with French and bi-cultural families), she began to publish (as her brother had always done) in French; the tone of her work was little changed. In *Adeline*, 1956, one of her earlier French novels, the heroine delineates the development of two cultures (the dream-soaked Paris of her youth, the brittle, cruel Paris of *entre deux guerres*; the silent ancestral home in S. Carolina), and of her emotional life, immersed in marriage to a man whom at the close of her self-conscious narrative she accuses herself of having ungenerously misrepresented. AG's last book was *La Porte des songes*, 1969.

Green, Rayna (Burns), poet, short-story writer and folklorist, b. 1942, of Cherokee heritage, da. of Ann Naomi (Gillingham) and Floyd Franklin Burns. Born in Dallas, Texas, she was educ. at Southern Methodist Univ. (MA, 1966) and Indiana Univ. (PhD thesis 1973, on *The Image of the Indian in Vernacular American Culture: The Only Good Indian*). She has taught English and folklore in various colleges, including Amherst and Dartmouth, and held awards and positions as folklorist; she is programme director with the Smithsonian Institution. Her work on Native Indian traditional science and women appears in a wide range of science, folklore and feminist journals. She also writes poetry and stories, some evoking Indian women heroes like Cherokee Nanye'hi, who is 'plotting the return of the women / plotting the power of the women / making the women all come home', some presenting everyday women of mixed blood, 'dancing the stories / that made us dream over her / shattered breath'. Her story 'High Cotton' presents wry, sometimes comic, storytelling grandmothers. Editor and contributor to *That's What She Said: A Collection of Poetry and Fiction by Contemporary Native American Women*, 1984, RG has also compiled bibliographies on *Native American Women* and *Native American Tradition Science, Medicine and Technology*, 1983. Her 'Diary of a Native American Feminist' (*Ms*, July, 1982) and her essay in Robin Morgan's *Sisterhood is Global*, 1983, analyse the complexities and possibilities of Indian women's feminism.

Green, Sarah, novelist and miscellaneous writer publishing in London, whose more than 20 titles begin with *Charles Henly, or The Fugitive Restored*, 1790. *Mental Improvement for a Young Lady*, 1793, written for a niece, urges chastity, piety and meekness, and approves no novels but Frances BURNEY; SG later tends to satire and even feminism, with some excursions into GOTHIC. *The Private History of the Court of England*, 1808, thinly disguises the Prince of Wales's love-life with a fifteenth-century setting. (Mary ROBINSON appears talented, sincere, and oppressed: her husband says, 'if I chuse to SELL you I can, and will'.) *Tales of the Manor*, 1809, purports to be from a romantically concealed *modern* MS; *The Reformist!!!*, 1810, debunks various modern trends. In 1810–11 SG pub. a 'Spanish Romance' and a 'Historical Romance', attacked ROMANCE in her preface (part repr. in R. B. Johnson's *Novelists on Novels*, 1928) to *Romance Readers and Romance Writers*, and began to pub. with her name. In *Gretna Green Weddings, or The Nieces*, 1823, the humourless, misogynist Mr Proser turns out to be an actual villain. *Scotch Novel Reading, or Modern Quackery*, 1824, 'By a Cockney', presents in Charlotte LENNOX's manner the distortion of the world by novels: a father who has survived crazes for Fanny BURNEY, Ann RADCLIFFE, Sydney MORGAN and Charlotte DACRE, recounts his daughter's gradual cure from Walter Scott (an elder daughter was Byronic). SG also translated from German.

Greene, Sarah Pratt (McLean), 1856–1935, novelist, b. Simsbury, Conn., da. of Mary (Payne) and Dudley Bestor M.: one of five children. Educ. at local schools, she proceeded to Mount Holyoke College, and in 1874 went to Cape Cod as a school-teacher. This experience provided material for her first book, *Cape Cod Folks*, 1881, which numbered 11 impressions by the end of 1882: its portrayal of local characters was not wholly fictional and court cases resulted. In 1887, she m. Franklin Lynde G. Their twin sons died in infancy. Her novels, of which the best are set in New England, are often narrated by a male character and treat typically of love thwarted, without necessarily offering the palliative happy ending. She shows a keen eye for character and a sense of the absurd, heightened by skilful rendering of regional dialect. The landscape of coastal New England, with its nautical communities, provides her strongest imagery: Vesty Kirtland, flushed and excited, hauling in her catch, offers also a haven for her lover: 'I must have a Basin for my wife, calm, strong, sweet' (*Vesty of the Basins*, 1892). Her other works include *Some Other Folks*, 1884, *Flood-Tide*, 1901, and *Power Lot*, 1906. See J. W. HOWE's *Representative Women of New England*, 1904.

Greenwell, Dora, 1821–82, poet and essayist, b. Greenwell Ford, Lanchester, only da. of Dorothy (Smales) and William Thomas G., magistrate and Deputy Lieutenant of the county. For five years she was taught by a governess, but then taught herself, studying philosophy, political economy and languages. After the loss of Greenwell Ford the family moved to Ovingham in Northumberland, where DG taught local girls and pub. *Poems*, 1848. In 1850 the family settled at Golbourne, Lancs., where DG's favourite brother Alan was a cleric. Here she became friendly with Josephine BUTLER and supported her work. After the death of her father and her brother's resignation in 1854, DG and her tyrannical, invalid mother settled in Durham. This was the period of her greatest intellectual achievement and she met many literary celebrities including Jean INGELOW and Christina ROSSETTI. Her best-known essays are 'On the Education of the Imbecile', 1868, and 'Our Single Women', 1862, a plea for the more extensive education of intelligent women. Constance Maynard (in *DG*, 1926) greatly admired DG's theology, reflected in both her essays and volumes of poetry such as *Carmina Crucis*, 1869, *Songs of Salvation*, 1873, and *The Soul's Legend*, 1873. She settled in London in 1874 and supported the struggle for women's franchise. In later years she became addicted to opium; in 1881 she suffered a near-fatal accident. See William Dorling's *Memoirs of DG*, 1885.

'Greenwood, Grace', Sara Jane (Clarke) Lippincott, 1823–1904, journalist and feminist activist, b. Pompey, NY, da. of Deborah (Baker) and Thaddeus C.; descendant of Sarah and Jonathan EDWARDS. She was twelve when the family moved to Rochester, NY, where she attended school. They moved to New Brighton, Penn., in 1843. Her first pub. works were poems in Rochester newspapers and in the *New Mirror* magazine. Her short 'letters' to magazines were collected as *Greenwood Leaves* in 1850. After one year as editorial assistant for *Godey's Lady's Book*, she wrote for the anti-slavery *National Era* and the *Saturday Evening Post*. By 1850 she had become an advocate for the women's rights movement, and in 1851 she responded to a male essayist who had excepted her from his satire of literary women: 'I stand in the ranks. . . . I will not be received as an exception, where full justice is not done to the class to which I belong' (*Greenwood Leaves*, second series). In the same year she pub. her coll. *Poems* as well as *History of My Pets*, the first of many books for children. In 1853 she m. Leander K. L. and they began *Little Pilgrim*, one of the first American CHILDREN's magazines. In 1852–3 she pub. *Haps and Mishaps of a Tour in Europe*, 1854, which went through a number of eds. During the 1850s she lectured on topics such as prison reform, and throughout the Civil War she helped raise money and lectured on patriotic themes. After the war she lived in Washington, DC, and wrote for various newspapers including the *New York Times* as well as magazines such as the *Ladies' Home Journal*. In 1873 she pub. *New Life in New Lands*, essays about the Rocky Mountains. In the 1880s she lived in NYC and Washington and wrote a column for the *Independent*. During her final years she lived with her daughter in New Rochelle, NY. Her letters and papers are at Henry Huntington Library and Harvard.

Greer, Germaine, critic, reviewer, journalist, broadcaster, b. 1939 in Melbourne, Victoria, da. of Margaret May (Lafrank) and Eric Reginald G. She was educ. at Star of the Sea Convent, Melbourne and the Univs. of Melbourne (BA 1959), Sydney (MA 1962) and Cambridge (PhD 1967), and lectured in English at Warwick Univ. From the late 1960s she contributed regularly to newspapers and journals such as the *Listener*, the *Spectator*, *Oz* and *Rolling Stone* and was a regular columnist with the *Sunday Times* 1971–3. She became a famous personality following the appearance in the USA in 1971 of the influential feminist study, *The Female Eunuch*, 1970. An original, outspoken analysis of female conditioning and sexual stereotypes, it achieved massive sales, was trans. into 12 languages and became a landmark of the women's liberation movement. Since its appearance, she has spent little time in Australia, living in the USA, where she was Founding Director of the Tulsa Center for the Study of Women's Literature at the Univ. of Tulsa, Oklahoma, 1979–82; in Southern Tuscany, Italy; and in England, where she presently resides. She has also pub. other feminist non-fiction, *The Obstacle Race*, 1979, a history of women and painting, and *Sex and Destiny, The Politics of Human Fertility*, 1984, showing a development of her views upon feminism although seen by some critics as regressive. Other works are *Darling Say You Love Me*, 1965, *The Revolting Garden*, 1979 (pub. under the pseudonym 'Rose Blight'), *Slade Women*, 1979, *Shakespeare*, 1981, *The Madwoman's Underclothes: Essays and Occasional Writing 1968–85*, 1986, and an important chapter, 'Women and Power in Cuba' in the book examining the state of women ten years after International Women's Year, *Women: A World Report*, 1985. Her recent *Daddy: We Hardly Knew You*, 1989, charts her search for her father's hidden identity. Her Stump Cross books are eds. of early women writers like BEHN.

Gregory, Isabella **Augusta** (Persse), Lady, 1852–1932, dramatist, translator, biographer, collector of folklore. B. in Roxborough House, near Coole, Co. Galway, da. of Frances (Barry) and Dudley P., she was educ. privately, much influenced by her Irish-speaking nurse, Mary Sheridan, whose telling of fairy stories and local folklore taught her to know and care for Irish myth and legend and the 'beautiful rhythmic sentences' of the local dialect. She m. Sir William G. of Coole, MP, former governor of Ceylon, 1881, and travelled widely with him, interesting herself in the Egyptian nationalist Arabi Bey as well as in her husband's Irish nationalism. AG began to write as early as 1882. Her affair with W. S. Blunt, discovered only after his secret journals were opened, produced her 12 poems titled 'A Woman's Sonnets'. These were altered by Blunt and printed as his in the Kelmscott edition of his poetry, 1892. (See James Pethica and Elizabeth Longford in Saddlemeyer and Smythe, cited below.) After her husband's death, 1892, she edited his journals. Her continuing interest in biography produced the *Life* of her nephew Hugh Lane, 1921, and her own autobiography, *Seventy Years* (ed. C. Smythe, 1974). Her son's death in WWI, 1918, occasioned Yeats's elegy 'In Memory of Major Robert Gregory'. Her nationalism promoted interest in the Gaelic League, and meetings with W. B. Yeats and Edward Martyn, 1896–8, involved her in the creation of the Abbey Theatre; she became, with Yeats and Synge, a director. She saw the Theatre as part of a movement 'for keeping the Irish language a spoken one . . . the discovery, the disclosure of the folk-learning, the folk-poetry, the folk-tradition', specifically aiming 'to *create* a fine drama . . . for the dignity of Ireland'. She translated four Molière plays and collaborated with Yeats and Douglas Hyde. AG wrote numerous successful plays: comedies dramatizing the fables and folk-histories of her region and country (*The Jackdaw*, produced 1907, *The Rising of the Moon*, produced 1907, *The Workhouse Ward*, produced 1908), later more sophisticated tragedies (*Kincora*, produced 1905 and revised 1909, *Devorgilla*, produced 1907, *Grania*, published 1912) and morality plays (*The Story Brought by Brigit*, produced 1924, *Dave*, produced 1927) imaging the struggles of Ireland. Political battles and bloody fighting were recurrent in AG's lifetime and she engaged in polemic journalism and civic campaigns; but throughout she celebrated 'our incorrigible genius for mythmaking, the faculty that makes un-traditional history a perpetual joy, because it is, like the Sidhe, an eternal shape-changer'. This is most purely evident in her collections of Irish folklore and retellings of the heroic cycles of Irish legend (including *Cuchulain of Muirthemne*, 1902, *Gods and Fighting Men*, 1904, *A Book of Saints and Wonders*, 1906, *Visions and Beliefs in the West of Ireland*, 1920). Her autobiography chronicles contemporary history, rendering anecdotally the life, thought and manners of the gentry and aristocracy in Ireland. See Elizabeth Coxhead, 1961, Ann Saddlemeyer, 1966, quoted above, and Saddlemeyer and Colin Smythe, eds, 1987 (includes checklist).

Grenville, Kate, Catherine Elizabeth Gee, novelist, short-story writer, b. 1950 in Sydney, NSW, da. of Isobel Nancy (Russell) and Kenneth Grenville Gee. She graduated (BA Hons, 1972) from Sydney Univ., spent four years in Europe, then in 1982 received her MA in creative writing from the Univ. of Colorado. Following a volume of short stories, *Bearded Ladies*, 1984, she pub. three novels; the Australian Vogel Award winner, *Lilian's Story*, 1985, *Dreamhouse* (her first), 1986, and *Joan Makes History*, 1988. *Dreamhouse* is a pessimistic view of a decaying relationship between the female narrator and her academic husband. In deliberate contrast to this is the wonderfully affirmative and adventurous *Lilian's Story*. Loosely based on the life of the legendary Sydney eccentric, Bea Miles, it celebrates the central character's refusal to conform to prevailing images of femininity, her life-long fight to maintain an individual identity, and her notoriety. *Joan Makes History* (written as a Bicentennial project), retells the history of Australia's colonization from a female viewpoint. Joan, in her imagination, is present at various crucial points in Australia's past, remapping historical landmarks. See P. Gilbert, *Coming Out from Under: Contemporary Australian Women Writers*, 1988.

Greville, Frances (Macartney), 1726?–89, poet. Da. of Catharine (Coote) and wealthy Irish landowner James M., she grew up in London, noted for her beauty, and eloped in 1748 with the spendthrift and later tyrannical Fulke G. She had seven children, and lived for years abroad. Her 'Prayer for [or 'Ode to'] Indifference' (written probably after a son's death in 1756) was much admired in MS: a friend claimed in 1767 to have taken and circulated 40 copies, though the poem had been published in 1759 and reprinted in many places.

Its theme was often voiced and often contested by women poets. Answerers include Lady CARLISLE and Lady TUITE. FG was thought to have helped write Fulke G.'s *Maxims, Characters, and Reflections*, 1756. Frances BURNEY (her god-daughter) may have sketched her as Mrs Selwyn in *Evelina*. In her daughter's album, 1783, FG wrote 'My pipe is broke, my muse is flown'. Descendants have her own poetry album and an unfinished novel left to Burney, who declined to complete it, finding in it gaiety, humour, pathos, and knowledge of human nature, but a structure inferior to its episodes. Other scattered MSS survive.

Grey, Elizabeth Caroline (Duncan), 'Mrs Grey', 1798–1869, POPULAR novelist, niece of actress Maria D. She kept a girls' school with her sister in a fashionable part of London and was for many years secretary and editor to publisher Edward Lloyd, for whom she wrote several action-packed 'penny dreadfuls', notably *The Ordeal by Touch*, 1846 (see M. Summers, *A Gothic Bibliography*, 1941). A prolific and very popular writer, from 1828 to 1864 she produced some 30 novels as well as contributing to the *London Journal* and other periodicals. (Her husband was a reporter for the *Morning Chronicle*.) *The Daughters*, 1847, *Mary Seaham*, 1852, *The Opera-Singer's Wife*, 1861, and *The Autobiography of Frank*, 1861, were reissued in the 1880s. Her plots focus on courtship and marriage, sometimes criticizing women who lean on the 'broken reed' of their own understandings rather than live in their 'natural element' of affection and 'feminine submissiveness'. In spite of occasionally competent characterization, as in *De Lisle, or The Sensitive Man*, 1828, and *The Way of the World*, 1831, her work is often marred by high-flown sentiment and trite pretentious moralizing. Sin is punished in melodramatic fashion and at tedious length.

Grey, Lady **Jane**, 1537–54, scholar and martyr. Her parents, royal-blooded Frances (Brandon) and Henry G., later Duke of Suffolk, saw her as a stake in power politics: 'whatsoever I do els but learning, is ful of grief, trouble, feare, and whole misliking unto me'. Her learning was accordingly exceptional; her keen Protestantism was fostered by Katharine PARR. At 13 she wrote a gospel-preaching letter to a learned male backslider to Catholicism. At 15 she was m. (after, it was said, actual violence from her father) to Lord Guildford Dudley, seven weeks later proclaimed queen, and at once deposed by Mary. Her father's fresh rebellion caused her execution ten months later. Her writings (prayers, letters, a dying speech) began to appear that year: expanded in Foxe's *Book of Martyrs*, 1563, fully ed. 1825, often repr., they had influence disproportionate to their amount. Her diatribes on her enemies ('deformed imp of the devil', 'unshamefaced paramour of Antichrist'), plain speaking to her father and sister, and wrestling with her faith, belie the later legend of her as meek and passive: lives by Hester W. Chapman, 1962, Alison Plowden, 1986.

Grey, Maria Georgina (Shirreff), 1816–1906, educationalist and novelist, b. London, younger sister of Emily SHIRREFF. She was educ. by a Swiss/French governess and then through her own extensive reading. In *Thoughts on Self-Culture, Addressed to Women*, 1850, she and her sister Emily argued for mental cultivation in women. Their novel *Passion and Principle*, 1841, shows a well-educated, clear-sighted woman rejecting an attractive but morally reprehensible suitor, and MG's later novel, *Love's Sacrifice*, 1868, possibly reflects the trying experience of nursing her ailing husband, William G. (d. 1864). From the 1870s she was actively involved in promoting better secondary EDUCATION for girls, launching in 1871 the Women's Education Union, and in 1879 establishing the MG Training College for secondary school teachers. With her sister, she was involved in the kindergarten movement. Her pamphlets and articles attacked conventional conceptions of femininity, and argued vigorously for female SUFFRAGE and wider career opportunities for women. Religious issues were discussed in her three *Modern Review* articles. She became an invalid in 1888 and wrote little more, except for a memoir of her sister, 1897.

'Grier, Sydney C.', Hilda Caroline Gregg, 1868–1933, novelist, b. North Cerney, Glos., eldest child of Sarah Caroline Frances (French) and the Rev. John Robert G.; her sister Katherine was one of the first woman doctors. SG was educ. at home and at a private school, and was an honorary MA of London Univ. Initially a teacher, she began writing steadily in 1881, publishing her first story in 1886. Showing signs of consumption (her father died of it in 1882), she moved with her family to Eastbourne. Her first novel, *In Furthest Ind*, 1894, is a fictional memoir of a seventeenth-century Englishman's adventures in India. Several others were serialized in *Blackwood's*, beginning with *An Uncrowned King* (Dec. 1895–Sept. 1896). Praised for their realism, her novels take place in exotic locales, including Mesopotamia (*His Excellency's English Governess*, 1896), the Balkans (*The Crowned Queen*, 1898), Afghanistan (*The Warden of the Marches*, 1901), and Sicily (*One Crowded Hour*, 1912). She nursed her mother (d. 1913) in their Eastbourne home where she herself died. Details of the family are in George Seaver's life of her brother John, Archbishop of Armagh, 1963.

Grierson, Constantia (Crawley), *c.* 1704–32, poet and scholar, b. to 'poor illiterate Country People', probably in Co. Kilkenny. Later recognized for expertise in Latin and Greek, she studied midwifery with Laetitia PILKINGTON's father (early 1720s) and acquired skill in history, theology, philosophy and mathematics. By 1721 she was working for George G., whose second wife she became about 1726. He owed his later position as King's Printer in Ireland at least partly to her talents as 'corrector of the press', shown in modest-format editions of Virgil, 1724, Terence, 1727, and Tacitus, 1730 (extravagantly praised in 1775). Only one of her children – also a noted scholar – survived. Her friends included Jonathan Swift, Mary BARBER, and Mary DELANY's future husband. Barber says CG undervalued her poems and took no steps to preserve them, and mentions her (unpub.) short history of England. Further short pieces printed anonymously may yet be identified, as a poem of 1730 has recently been. After CG's death Barber (who hoped to raise subscribers for an edition) and Pilkington added a few more poems. A MS volume discovered in 1984 doubles the number known, and adds a few prose pieces (copy at Univ. of Penna). CG writes mostly in flowing iambic couplets, more formal than Barber's, with 'directness and strength of feeling': on love, friendship, faith, the theatre, aspirations of women (citing Mary ASTELL), and her grief for a child overlaid by his nurse. See A. C. Elias, Jr, in *Swift Studies*, 2, 1987.

Griffen, Vanessa, contemporary Fijian short-story writer. Educ. at the Univ. of the South Pacific, she began to publish in the early 1970s, and many of her stories are now set texts in Fijian schools. Some are extremely short, with a lyrical style and a strong but carefully controlled subjective element. 'Marama' describes an afternoon in the life of a Fijian grandmother unable to feed her family from her fishing. 'The Visitors' similarly recounts the realities of everyday life, this time a housewife's day in which the high points are the interaction with a neighbour friend, and the notion of buying oranges as treats for the children. Her work centres on the role of women, with an underlying awareness of the nature of oppression. There is an account of her work in Subramani's *South Pacific Literature*, 1985. Recently she has turned to other writing, living in Sydney and producing education manuals and work on women and technology.

Griffin, Susan, writer of poetry and prose, b. 1943 in Los Angeles, Calif., da. of Sarah (Colvin) and Walden G. She attended UCLA at Berkeley, 1960–3, and San Francisco State Univ. (BA, 1965, MA, 1973), and has since worked at various jobs, including teaching drama, English and women's studies in the early seventies. She m. John Levy in 1966 (divorced 1970). Her most recent collection of poems, *Unremembered Country*, 1987, is dedicated to their daughter, 'Chloe Levy / who has read to me / from the Book of Life'. *Like the Iris of an Eye*, 1976, collects SG's poems from 1967: most of these speak the trials and triumphs of 'being born human and a woman' both in her own life ('This is the story of the day in the life of a woman trying / to be a writer and her child got sick') and in the lives of other women, giving voice to her who 'cannot be here to speak / for herself'. Language, speaking, story-telling, the development and birth of discourse is central to her work. *Let Them Be Said*, 1973, turns to the experiences of women in patriarchy: 'let them be said, / but happen no more'. In *Voices*, a radio drama (pub. 1975 with an intro. by Adrienne RICH), five women of different ages and backgrounds tell their unique histories and discover a common experience; in the essay 'On Wanting to be the Mother I Wanted' (*Ms*, Jan. 1977), SG's discussion of feminism and motherhood invokes the voices of many others, including Tillie OLSEN, Margaret SANGER, Virginia WOOLF and ALTA. The long prose poem', *Woman and Nature: The Roaring Inside Her*, 1977, expands on women's connection with Earth, pitting the 'voice of woman and nature' against the voice of patriarchy and authority: a magnificent convocation of voices, it 'dramatizes the movement of women into a discourse of their own'. *Rape: the Power of Consciousness*, 1979 (revised as *Rape: the Politics of Consciousness*, 1986), examines the deeply rooted physical and psychological control in a sexually 'schizophrenic' male society. *Pornography and Silence: Culture's Revenge Against Nature*, 1981, is a brilliant and provocative study of the pornographic 'mind of our culture'. SG depicts the history of the rigid split between nature and culture, Eros and pornography, the 'other' and the chauvinist, choosing six lives (including Kate CHOPIN, Anne Frank, and Marilyn Monroe) to illustrate the tragic damage. The watching, listening poems of *Unremembered Country* explore talk and touch, writing and body: 'This is knowledge of the body, / how holding is like being held / how being held is like holding.' Interviews in Marilyn Yalom, *Women Writers of the West Coast*, 1983, and Janet Sternburg, ed., *The Writer on Her Work*, 1980. Studies by OSTRIKER, 1986, and Diane Middlebrook in *Kenyon Review*, 2, 1980 (quoted above).

'Griffith, Cecil', Mrs S. Beckett, d. by 1891, novelist. Her earliest novel in the BL is *Victory Deane*, third ed. 1867, which treats the theme of marriage of gentleman to peasant girl with some originality. *Valentine Forde*, 1870, a rather faded sensation story, *Nor Love Nor Lands*, 1873, and *The Uttermost Farthing*, n.d., are all three-vol. romances. More interesting is the posthumously published *Corinthia Marazion*, 1892 [1891], which depicts a strong-minded woman fighting the circumscription of social imperatives, although romance triumphs at last.

Griffith, Elizabeth (Griffith), 'Frances', 1727–93, writer in many genres, b. probably at Dublin, da. of Jane (Foxcroft) and actor Thomas G. Having acted in Dublin 1749–51, she secretly married Richard G. in 1751; their actual courtship letters, pub. 1757 as *Letters Between Henry and Frances* (further vols 1976, 1770) were so popular that they used the nicknames for both themselves and their children. Her 'sense and worth' brought him to a marriage he did not at first intend; tension between plain speaking and current ideals of sentiment gives the letters bite and humour. She acted in London 1753ff, visited Paris in the 1760s, and published, out of need, *c.* 24 works. Her *Amana: A Dramatic Poem*, 1764, and satirical comedy *The Platonic Wife*, 1765, were badly received, and later years saw some failures; but *The Double Mistake* (women much less active and independent), 1766, *The School for Rakes*, 1769 (from Beaumarchais, whose *Barber of Seville* she rendered in 1776), and her last play, *The Times*, from Goldoni, 1779 (despite a cabal against it) did well on stage. She and her husband exploited their public fame in an epistolary novel each in 1769: hers, *The Delicate Distress*, preceded the similar *Lady Barton*, 1771, and *Lady Juliana Harley*, 1776, in which wives behave impeccably, at great personal cost, to unworthy husbands. EG also wrote translations from French, moralistic commentary on Shakespeare, 1775 (facs. 1971), and ADVICE to young ladies (pious, domestic-centred), 1782; she edited (with criticism) vols. of fiction, 1777 (including Penelope AUBIN and Marie de LA FAYETTE) and 1780 (largely her own); her letters and novels are the best. She stopped writing after a son returned rich from India. See studies by J. M. S. Tompkins, 1938, Dorothy Hughes Eshelman, 1949; J. E. Norton in *Book Collector*, 8, 1959.

Griffitts, Hannah, 'Fidelia', 1727–1817, Quaker poet, da. of Mary (Norris) and Thomas G., mayor of Philadelphia: cousin of Deborah LOGAN (educ. like her at Anthony Benezet's school), correspondent of Elizabeth FERGUSON. Writing poetry from the age of ten, she declined to publish, and her large canon is still uncertain, but she was a considerable poet with a sharp critical mind; her prose is mainly religious. She regularly marked the anniversary of her mother's death – 2 February 1750 – with a poem; she was still writing in 1808, her hand illegible with rheumatism. She wrote elegies on Susanna WRIGHT (with whom she exchanged poems) and Jane HOSKENS: 'Till fainting Nature Sigh'd to be undrest, / And drew the Curtain of her evening rest.' Her political verse manages to be patriotic, conservative, and also subversive. 'The Glorious fourth of July – over again' notes that one distant master has merely been exchanged for many; she calls Tom Paine 'the Coldest fibber / I ever knew'; and concludes after evoking the desolation left by the armies that Britain and America 'share and share alike' the blame. The *Friends' Miscellany* printed some poems after her death. MSS, many carefully revised, at Philadelphia Library Company.

Grimké, Angelina Emily, 1805–79, and **Sarah Moore**, 1792–1873, essayists and reformers, b. Charleston, S. Carolina, youngest and sixth, respectively, of thirteen children of Mary (Smith) and Judge John Faucheraud G., wealthy slaveholders. SMG attended a fashionable girls' school but learned more from her secret reading of forbidden subjects such as Latin and law. AEG, after refusing Episcopalian confirmation, and being expelled from her congregation, went to Philadelphia, where SMG had become a Quaker minister, advocating ABOLITION and women's rights. In *Epistle to the Clergy of the Southern States*, 1836, SMG argued the incompatibility of slavery and Christianity; and *Letters on the Equality of the Sexes and the Condition of Woman*, 1838, contests the Biblical justification of women's inequality. AEG's pamphlet *Appeal to Christian Women of the South*, 1836, urges women to take action against slavery. In 1836 the sisters went to work for the New York Anti-Slavery Society, the first American women to publicly address mixed audiences. AEG appears to have been the more effective speaker, and handled political and organizational issues, while SMG took up moral and theological arguments. For the Anti-Slavery Convention of American Women in NYC, AEG wrote *An Appeal to the Women of the Nominally Free States*, 1837, in which she first made the connection between women and slaves. Amidst growing opposition, they toured Boston, and AEG's *Letters to Catharine E. Beecher*, 1838, is the single most effective statement of her belief that moral division of labour is untenable, even 'anti-Christian'. In 1838 AEG m. Theodore Dwight Weld, and together with Sarah who lived and worked with them, compiled *American Society As It Is*, 1859, a powerful documentation of the effects and conditions of slavery. See G. Lerner, *The Grimké Sisters from South Carolina*, 1967.

Grimké, Angelina Weld, 1880–1958, poet and playwright, b. in Boston, Mass., only child of Sarah (Stanley), who was white, and of Archibald Henry G. (lawyer and NAACP vice-president, son of a black slave and of a brother of Angelina and Sarah Grimké): AWG, named for one, celebrated the other in verse. Her mother, who later wrote tracts, left her father when she was small; AWG lived with him from 1887, and wrote of him in *Opportunity*, 3, 1925. She was publishing poems by 1893, and attended liberal schools including Carleton Academy (Northfield, Minn.), Cushing Academy (Ashburnham, Mass.), and Boston Latin School and Normal School of Gymnastics. She took summer classes at Harvard while teaching English in Washington, DC, from 1902. She is best known for her protest play, *Rachel*, staged in Washington in 1916, published 1920, repr. 1969. Like her story 'The Closing Door', 1919 (about a pregnant black woman hearing of her brother's lynching), it fervently expresses the conviction that black children ought not to be brought into so painful and racially divided a world. Many of AWG's poems (like 'To the Dunbar High School', *Crisis*, 1917, and 'The Black Finger', 1923) share these concerns; some express fierce anger; others are delicate and sad love lyrics of unfulfilled longing and the sense of frustration created by her lesbianism. She has affinities both with the Imagist poetry of H. D., Edna St Vincent Millay and Amy Lowell and with black poets like Jessie Redmon Fauset and Georgia Douglas Johnson. While she has been much anthologized, from the 1920s (by leading Harlem Renaissance figures like Alain Locke in *The New Negro*, 1925, and Countee Cullen in *Caroling Dusk*, 1927) to recent years, her work remains uncollected and mostly unpublished. She planned a volume but never published it, and seems to have stopped writing after her father d. in 1930. MSS at Howard Univ., Washington, include diaries, letters, and an unfinished play, 'Mara'. See Gloria T. Hull, *Color, Sex, & Poetry, Three Women Writers of the Harlem Renaissance*, 1987.

Grimké, Charlotte L. **(Forten)**, 1837–1914, diarist, journalist and poet, b. Philadelphia, da. of Mary Virginia (Wood) and Robert Bridges F. Her grandfather, James F., a successful black businessman, was a financial backer of William Lloyd Garrison's *Liberator*. After her mother d. in 1840, CFG spent her childhood on her grandfather's estate and with her uncle Robert Purvis, President of the American Anti-Slavery Society. She was educ. at home until 1854 when she entered Higginson Grammar School, Salem, Mass., graduating in 1855. She became active in the Salem Female Antislavery Society, and began her journal, which she kept until 1864 (selec. pub. 1953; complete 1989). It combines an engaging day-to-day account of a genteel young woman's education with an unsparing awareness of the evils of slavery and the insults to which she and other free blacks were subject in the North: 'Oh! it is hard to go through life meeting contempt with contempt, hatred with hatred, fearing with too good reason, to love and trust hardly anyone whose skin is white' (12 Sept. 1855). She taught 1856–8 at Epes Grammar School, and in 1862 she volunteered to go as a teacher to the newly freed slaves of Port Royal, South Carolina, describing her experiences in two articles in the *Atlantic Monthly* in May and June 1864. She worked for the Freedman's Society and in 1878 she m. the Rev. Francis James G., brother of Angelina Weld GRIMKÉ's, father and spent most of her remaining life in Washington, DC. Her work includes poems, essays on art, racial issues and the 1876 Philadelphia Exposition. See Anna Julia COOPER, 1951, for her life and writings; also Jean R. Sherman, *Invisible Poets*, 1974.

Grossmann, Edith Howitt (Searle), 1863–1931, novelist, teacher and political activist. B. at Beechworth, Victoria, da. of Mary Anne (Beeby) and George Smales S., she moved to NZ in 1878 and was educ. at Invercargill Grammar School, Christchurch Girls' High and Canterbury College, Univ. of NZ, graduating MA in 1886. She became headmistress of Wellington Girls' High School before marrying Prof. Joseph Penfound G. of Canterbury College in 1890. She was a founding member of the Canterbury Women's Institute, and had one son. *Angela: A Messenger*, 1890, reflects her critical vision of NZ society and provides a vehicle for her prohibition sympathies. Her particular concern with the effects upon women of male alcohol abuse leads to the more overtly feminist stance of *In Revolt*, 1893, its sequel, *Hermione: A Knight of the Holy Ghost*, 1907, and a life of Helen Macmillan Brown, first British woman honours graduate, 1905. The novels, centring on injustices to women, earned EG the reputation of a hysterical feminist lacking in imaginative vision or critical value, although she never advocated the overthrow of the corner-stones of male dominance. Active and vocal in the struggle for women's emancipation, she saw it as including elevation of the traditional female role, and re-establishing respect for 'female values' such as moral purity. Both *In Revolt* and *Hermione* (with its picture of US feminism and an Australian female commune) advocate curtailing male immorality rather than throwing off women's shackles. *The Heart of the Bush*, 1910, her last novel, focuses less on women's emancipation than on the struggle for antipodean identity: this has led to its acclaim as by far her best novel.

Grymeston, Elizabeth (Bernye), Lady, before 1563–1602/3, first woman essayist. Da. of Margaret (Flint) and Martin B. of Norfolk, she m. Christopher G. of Smeeton, Yorks., by 1584 – probably in secret, since his later fellowship of Caius College, Cambridge, forbade marriage. She was a Roman Catholic. She complains of 'un-deserved wrath' from her mother, fail-ing health, and anxieties which made her 'a dead woman among the living'; eight of her nine children died. *Miscelanea. Meditations. Memoratives*, 1604, with her name, quotes from Latin and Greek, both Christian and pagan texts: she admits borrowing and says she admires both spider (self-generating) and bee (collecting). Thomas Chaffyn made MS extracts, 1606; 4 eds. with varying titles add six more essays by 1618; nineteenth-century books reprint some passages. The dedication (repr. 1874, in W. C. Hazlitt, *Prefaces* ...) offers advice to her surviving son. Her learning was 'almost unique in her [post-RENAISSANCE] generation'. See Ruth Hughey and Philip Hereford in *The Library*, xv, 1934; Elaine V. Beilin, 1987.

Guest, Barbara (Pinson), poet, playwright, novelist and scholar, b. 1920 at Wilmington, NC, da. of Ann (Hetzel) and James Harvey P., raised in Calif. She took her BA at the Univ. of Calif., (Berkeley) in 1943, and m. Stephen G. (Lord Stephen Haden-Guest) in 1948, divorced in 1954 and that year m. military historian Trumbull Higgins. She has two children, has travelled widely, and lives in NYC and on Long Island. Her plays include *The Ladies' Choice*, 1953 (staged by NY Artists' Theatre), and *Port*, 1965. Linked with the NY school of poets, she has published poems in many journals and anthologies, and in ten volumes, from *The*

Location of Things, 1960 (which emphasizes colours and textures). Painting has been an important influence on her work; she edited *Art News*, 1951–4, and co-authored a biography of painter Robert Goodnough in 1962. *I Ching: Poems and Lithographs* (with Sheila Isham), 1969, experiments with concrete poetry; *Biography*, 1980, is a sequence of nine poems exploring the 'itch / the width of an elbow / an urge / really to "know" / when the flies entered the garment / anemones / where were they picked?' Her laconic, concentrated poems deploy sight, sound and idea, exploring subjectivities and ideologies of language and meaning. Her experimental novel, *Seeking Air*, 1978, deals with creativity. Time, place and voice shift constantly; chapters shrink to as little as five (quoted) words. The opening sentences oppose the ideas of 'telling . . . everything' and 'say[ing] less and less'; a character voices BG's own interest in 'a marvelous, such an extraordinary circumference around what I might or might not tell'. Prefacing her critical life of H. D., 1984, she recalls conversion while at school to Imagism and to H. D.'s 'impeccable' poetry. BG's latest collection is *Musicality*, 1988. MSS at Univ. of Kentucky, NY Univ., and State Univ. of NY, Buffalo.

Guiney, Louise Imogen, 1861–1920, poet, scholar, essayist and short-story writer, b. Roxbury, Mass., da. of Irish Catholics Janet Margaret (Doyle) and Patrick Robert G., lawyer, Civil War brigadier-general and politician. She was educ. at Elmhurst Sacred Heart Convent, Providence, R.I. Her father d. when she was 16, and she wrote to support herself and her mother. Through her first collections of poetry, *Songs at the Start*, 1884, and essays, *Goose Quill Papers*, 1885, she met S. O. Jewett and Annie Fields, and joined the Boston literary circle. Appointed postmistress of Auburndale, Mass., in 1894, she was forced to resign due to protests probably aimed at her sex, as well as her Irish Catholicism; she suffered two nervous breakdowns (1896 and 1897) and from 1899 to 1901 worked in the Boston Public Library. In 1901 she migrated to England, settling in Oxford. Her one fictional work, *Lovers' Saint Ruth and Three Other Tales*, 1895, includes 'The Provider', an understated story of an Irish slum family whose 12-year-old son, the sole income earner, commits suicide to allow more for the other family members; the idea was taken from a Dublin news report. Her poetry, notable for its restraint as well as its fin-de-siècle melancholy, includes *A Roadside Harp*, 1893, and *Happy Ending*, 1909. LG often used the sonnet form, as in 'Astraea' (*Happy Ending*), a powerful poem about the rise and decline of creative ambition. 'Tarpeia' (*The White Sail*, 1887), although having an overtly classical subject, deals by implication with issues of prostitution and sexual politics. *Patrins: A Collection of Essays*, 1897, was well regarded critically, as were her religious lyrics. She also wrote biographies, the best-known being *Robert Emmett*, 1904, and *Blessed Edmund Campion*, 1908; her *Recusant Poets*, an anthology of Roman Catholic poets from Thomas More to Pope, was pub. posthumously in 1938. Her letters are at Dinand Library, Holy Cross College, Worcester, Mass., and at the Library of Congress; 2 vols were pub. 1926. See E. M. Tenison, 1923, and H. G. Fairbanks, 1973, for her life; Emily Stipes Watts, *The Poetry of American Women*, 1977, and Cheryl Walker, *The Nightingale's Burden*, 1982, for critical discussion.

Gulbadan, Princess, *c.* 1523–1603, historian, da. of Dildar and of Moghul Emperor Babur: sister of Humayun, Akbar, Jehangir, Shah Jehan and Aurangzeb, all emperors of India. She was, unusually even for her rank, educated; she m. Khizr Khwaja Khan, and is said to have written poetry, collected books, and acted unobtrusively as court adviser. In her mid-sixties she wrote, on the order of Akbar, a work called *Humayun-nama*, stories of the reign of Humayun, in which Court ladies' lives are interestingly glimpsed. A. S. Beveridge translated it from the courtly Persian as *The History of Humayun*, 1902; Rumer GODDEN drew on it in her life of Gulbadan, 1980.

Gunn, Jeannie (Taylor), 'Mrs Aeneas Gunn', 1870–1961, novelist, b. Melbourne, Victoria, da. of Anna (Lush) and Thomas T., a Baptist minister. Educ. by her mother, she opened a school with her sister in 1889. She m. Aeneas G. in 1901 and left for Elsey Station in the Northern Territory, which he was to manage. Following his death shortly afterwards, she returned to Melbourne where she wrote the two famous books based on her outback experiences, *The Little Black Princess*, 1905, and *We of the Never-Never*, 1908, which sold over half a million copies. A film adaptation appeared in 1982. MSS are in the National Library, Canberra.

Gunnars, Kristjana, poet, short-story writer, essayist, translator and publisher. B. in 1948, in Reykjavik, Iceland, as Gunnarsdottir, da. of a Danish mother, Tove (Christensen), and Icelandic father, Gunnar Bodvarsson, she did not learn English until her family emigrated to Oregon in 1964. She studied English (BA, Oregon State Univ., 1974), m. Charles Kang in 1967, had a son, and separated, 1980. Still an Icelandic citizen, she moved to Vancouver in 1969, then became a landed immigrant. She has lived in many Canadian cities, including Regina (MA, Univ. of Regina, 1977) and Winnipeg (where she taught at the Univ. of Manitoba and studied towards a PhD). KG's imagination remains deeply rooted in Iceland, where she lives periodically. In 1985 she undertook the official translation of Stephan G. Stephanson's selected poetry (pub. 1988). Her belief in the cultural necessity for TRANSLATION led her, with others, to found Gunnars and Campbell, a publishing house wholly devoted to it. She was 'sandpapered with Nordic mythology' as a child; Icelandic words and folklore, and stories about the stoic life of the Icelandic immigrants in Manitoba, recur persistently in her five poetry books and collection of short stories. Caught in a 'cultural bind', not wanting to be seen as an 'ethnic' writer, yet immersing herself in the Icelandic 'voices locked up in old manuscripts and diaries', KG's *Settlement Poems (1 and 2)*, 1980, evoke an unsettling 'primitivism' – 'how to win love; dry / a pigeon's heart & hang it'. Having 'a hard time accepting the limitations of gender', KG writes mostly in first-person male voices. Yet *Wake-Pick Poems*, 1981, are named from a 'device made from a small stick of wood with a slit on one side' used to keep open the eyelids of old Icelandic women when they 'had to stay up nights turning out the quota of knitting required to survive'. *The Prowler*, 1989, autobiographical and writerly, is KG's first novel. Echoing Marguerite DURAS's lucidity and simplicity of perception and language, it recalls a child's deprivation in occupied Iceland. She has also edited a collection of essays on Margaret LAURENCE, 1988. Interview in *CV/II*, 8, 1984. See M. Travis LANE in *CanL*, 105, 1985.

Gunning, Elizabeth, later Plunkett, 1769–1823, novelist and translator, da. of Susannah GUNNING, cousin of Lady Charlotte BURY. At 21 she became a major scandal by opposing her father's choice of suitor; accused of pursuing a reluctant nobleman and of the serious crime of forging letters, she was disowned by her father but supported by her mother and aunt. Later she apparently averted total disinheritance of them all. Her work has been confused with her mother's (they both use melodrama, sentiment, pastoral idyll, allegory, personification, and arch address – apology or apparent fluster – to the reader), though both regularly pub. by name. The nobility dominate plots including a few sentimentalized humble figures in *The Packet*, 1794, *The Orphans of Snowdon*, 1797, and *The Gipsy Countess* (stolen as a child), 1799. *Family Stories*, 1802, are vivid magic tales for CHILDREN.

Married to the Irish Major J. Plunkett, 1803, with a large family, EG kept on writing. In *The Exile of Erin*, 1808, she disclaims, as a woman, all knowledge of politics; this time her usual pastoral retreat is American. *The Man of Fashion*, 1815, dedicated to Princess Charlotte, exposes the evils of primogeniture. She also wrote a rejected opera and translations from German and French (novels, drama, and popular science).

Gunning, Susannah (Minifie), 1740?–1800, novelist, da. of the Rev. James M. of Staplegrove, Som. She wrote at first jointly with her sister, Margaret MINIFIE, later and better alone. Their *Histories of Lady Frances S— and Lady Caroline S—*, by subscription, 1763, mixing satire and pathos, presents one daughter lost as a child, another unjustly driven from her father's house (a motif in which their art anticipated life). Her anonymous *Family Pictures*, 1764 (like the joint *The Picture*, 1766, claiming to depict reality), focuses on middle-class life though it promises 'Persons of Fashion': a preface blasts inadequate female education. In 1768 SG m. John G. (whose two beautiful sisters married dukes) and stopped publishing. (*Combe Wood*, 1783, is her sister's.) In 1791 John G. turned her out for opposing his choice of son-in-law; she stated her version of the case in novelistic style in a *Letter* to a ducal brother-in-law. The trauma re-appears in later works: in *Anecdotes of the Delborough Family*, 1792 (but as an episode in vol. i, allegedly written 20 years before); in the dedication (to Supreme Fashion) and fierce allegorical coda to her narrative poem *Virginius and Virginia* [1792]; and in *Memoirs of Mary*, 1793 (story changed, emotional configuration based on life). Her last works – including *Fashionable Involvements*, 1800 (broad satire), and *The Heir Apparent*, finished by her daughter, 1802 – bear fewer scars; but she often attacks malice and scandal. See Janet Todd in *The Sign of Angellica*, 1989.

Gurney, Anna, 1795–1857, scholar, youngest da. of Rachel (Hanbury) and Richard G. Paralysed by illness at ten months, she could never stand or move alone, but was educ. by an elder sister, then a tutor who could hardly keep up with her in Latin, Greek, Hebrew, and Old English. (Scandinavian languages followed.) Her *Literal Translation of the Saxon Chronicle* appeared privately in a 'very limited impression' 1819; the Rev. James Ingram used it in his ed. collated from MSS, 1823, praising her as 'the ELSTOB of her age'. She lived with a woman friend on the Norfolk coast at Cromer and pioneered advances in lifeboat management. Her pamphlet *On the Means of Assistance in Cases of Shipwreck* (Norwich, 1825) advocated new technology which she often supervised herself on stormy beaches; she corrected in MS a phrase ('all men on board') which concealed the deaths of two women (Bodleian copy). AG travelled to Rome and Athens, 1845, became the first woman member of the British Archaeology Association and wrote for its journal.

Guy, Rosa (Cuthbert), novelist and writer for young adults, b. 1925 in Trinidad, da. of Audrey (Gonzales) and Henry C., brought to Harlem, NYC, in 1932. Her mother died; her father became 'a tyrant . . . terrified of raising two girls amid the corruption of big-city life'. In 1941, just before Pearl Harbor, RG m. Warner Guy, a black American. She had a son, worked in a garment factory, joined the American Negro Theatre, studied (including drama) at NY Univ., began writing (stories and plays, in which she sometimes acted; *Venetian Blinds* was produced, 1954) in response to limited opportunities for black actors, and co-founded the Harlem Writers' Guild. (With Maya ANGELOU and Paule MARSHALL, RG staged a Guild UN sit-in after Patrice Lumumba's assassination, 1961; she became Guild President.) In the late 1940s she was active in the Committee for the Negro in the Arts. In her first book,

Bird at my Window, 1966, a once promising young black man, straitjacketed in a NY hospital prison ward, looks back at his life in the South and in Harlem, at his near-escapes from oppression and violent responses, at the gaps in his memory. In 1970 RG edited *Children of Longing*, interviews with young blacks around the USA at the time of the civil rights marches and the killings of Martin Luther King and Malcolm X. In the early 1970s she left her husband and lived for a time in Trinidad and Haiti. Her interviewing, her own early life, and West Indian speech and memories, went into two trilogies for young people: one about Ruby Cathy, a West Indian transplanted to Harlem, 1973–9, one about Imamu Jones, who has a father dead in Vietnam and an alcoholic mother, 1978–86. RG has travelled widely; her *Mother Crocodile*, for children, 1981, is a Senegalese tale translated from French. Her interest in social pressures on personal development animates more books for the young (*Mirror of her Own*, 1981, focuses, unusually, on a white family) and an ambitious adult novel, *A Measure of Time*, 1983, whose hard-shelled, kind-hearted heroine (disapproved of by some critics) moves from 1920s Alabama to Harlem, from life as prostitute and high-class shoplifter to success as a businesswoman. RG's work has been much reprinted; see Judith Wilson in *Essence*, 14, 1979.

Gwynn, Albinia, d. 1791, novelist, da. of Col. Leonard G. Frances BOSCAWEN, Hannah MORE, and Susannah GUNNING's husband subscribed to her *History of the Honourable Edward Mortimer*, 1785, a 'first essay' dedicated, from Bath, to Georgiana DEVONSHIRE. Its old-soldier hero and a wealthy, benevolent widow upstage its younger figures. Prefacing her epistolary *The Rencontre, or Transition of a Moment*, Dublin, 1785, AG says, 'though I thus wrap myself up in obscurity ... yet I sigh for fame'. She exempts from human inconsistency 'the men – wise souls!' who are '*always* ... consistent, reasonable, &c. &c.', and hints that she knows them so well because unmarried. She then presents a Cinderella-heroine who returns her cruel mother good for evil and is barely rescued by the hero from squalid death. AG died of apoplexy at Wrington, Somerset.

H

'H. D.' Hilda Doolittle, 1886–1961, poet, novelist, autobiographer, film-maker, b. in Bethlehem, Pa. The Moravian faith of her mother, amateur painter and musician Helen (Wolle), and the esoteric symbology of her father, astronomer Charles D., were early encouragement for her quest for 'hermetic definition'. A contemporary of Marianne MOORE at Bryn Mawr, 1904–6, H. D. was also pupil (and, briefly, fiancée) of Ezra Pound, and intimate of Frances Josepha Gregg, with whom she travelled to Europe before setting out alone to London. There, she was named and promoted by Pound as 'H. D., Imagiste'. *Sea Garden*, 1916, her first collection of short, decentred, *vers libre* lyrics, reflects her philhellenism. She reworked the newly discovered SAPPHO fragments and anthropological descriptions of the Goddess cults, and made lyric translations of Euripides. She m. Richard Aldington, 1913, gave birth to a stillborn child, 1915, and took Aldington's place, when he went to fight in France, 1916, as co-editor, with T. S. Eliot, of *The Egoist*. By the end of WWI, both marriage and Imagist movement had collapsed; in 1919, H. D. nearly died in labour. She was rescued by BRYHER, who became her emotional and financial support, lover and life-long friend, and subsequently her daughter Perdita's adoptive mother, *Hymen*, 1921, is dedicated to them. With Bryher's backing, H. D. explored film, psychoanalysis and autobiography as media of self-re(dis)covery. Together they travelled (to the Scilly Isles – where H. D. composed her aesthetic manifesto, her 'yonic' *Notes on Thought and Vision*, pub. 1982 – Greece, Egypt, and the USA), helped to set up POOL Films, producing 'Wing Beat', 'Foothills', and 'Borderline', and wrote for the avant-garde *Close up*, H. D.'s *Collected Poems* appeared in 1925, her experimental first novel, *Palimpsest*, in 1926. In Vienna, 1933–4, she entered her crucial and transforming analysis with Freud, which, ten years later, she was able to translate into 'autobiographical fantasy'. She had experimented with AUTOBIOGRAPHY in 'Paint it Today' (written 1921, unpub.), 'Asphodel' (written 1921–2, unpub.), and *Her* (written 1927, pub. 1981), and with psychobiography in the anti-Oedipal Hellenistic comedy *Hedylus* (written 1926, pub. 1928, repr. 1980) and other works, but *The Gift* (written 1941–3, pub. 1969) masterfully appropriates the Freudian techniques of self-analysis through dream interpretation, childhood reminiscence, recollection, and free association which gave H. D. the elements of her 're-visionary poetics'. *Tribute to Freud* (written 1944, pub. 1954), presented as an unwritten 'chapter' to his *Autobiographical Study*, describes their 'collaborative' research into occult phenomena and maternal/matriarchal prehistory. *Bid Me to Live* (written, literally at Freud's bidding, in 1939 and 1943, pub. 1960, repr. 1983) and *End to Torment* (written 1958, pub. 1979) chronicle H. D.'s attachments to and disaffection from Lawrence and Pound, her (tor)mentors. Her major long poems, written during and after WWII, enact the command of her Freudian muse to 'write, write, or die'. *Trilogy*, 1944–6, repr. 1973, offers, for a modernity otherwise devoted to death-wish and extinction, a vision of heaven (as figured matriarchal prehistory and the redeeming, if uncanny, return of a pre-biblical Mary of Magdala). H. D.'s experiments with surrealism and 'dream syntheses', 1940–55, include the unpublished novels,

'Magic Ring', 'The Sword Went Out to Sea', 'White Rose and the Red', and 'Magic Mirror'. *By Avon River*, 1949, celebrates Elizabethan literary genius. *Helen in Egypt* (written 1952–6, pub. 1961) uses the 'necromantic' medium of auto(psycho) biography to 'see' into the modern woman poet's Egypto-hermetic, pre-Hel(l)enic, genealogical beginnings. *Hermetic Definition*, written in the last year of her life, pub. 1972, traces the 'incubation' and growth of a love poem dedicated to the articulation of a feminine 'Eros' capable of encompassing / transcending 'Death' and (phallic) desire. See lives by Janice Robinson, 1982, and Barbara GUEST, 1984, studies by Susan Stanford Friedman, 1981, Rachel Blau DuPlessis, 1986, Dianne Chisholm, forthcoming. See also the biannual *H. D. Newsletter*, ed. Eileen Gregory. Collection of essays by Michael King, 1987, includes bibliography. Papers at Yale; film fragments at Eastman House Archives, Rochester.

Hacker, Marilyn, poet and editor. B. 1942 in NYC, da. of Hilda (Rosengarten) and Albert Abraham H., she was educ. at Bronx High School of Science, NY Univ. (BA 1964) and the Art Students League. She m. science-fiction writer Samuel Delany in 1961 (separated 1974, divorced 1980) and has a daughter. She edited two magazines, 1967–70, and (jointly with her husband) *Quark*, 1970–1, a speculative fiction quarterly. After two volumes privately printed (one jointly), she won the National Book Award for *Presentation Piece*, 1974 (much on the relation of words to speech and joy to pain): other poetry volumes are *Separations*, 1976 (ancient stories used to articulate the present state of poetry), *Taking Notice*, 1980, *Assumptions*, 1985, *Love, Death, and the Changing of the Seasons*, 1986, and *The Hang-Glider's Daughter*, 1990. In 1982 she edited *Woman Poet: The East*. She has been a teacher, and for four years an antiquarian bookseller in London. Notably gifted with the sonnet and sonnet sequence, she makes arresting use of challenging forms – sestina, pantoum canzone, villanelle, rondeau – to express lesbian and maternal love: 'Was any witch's youngest daughter / golden and bold as you?' Her often witty style has been called 'the colloquial sublime': 'Unloved and underpaid, tonight untold / women will click our failings off, each bead / inflating to a bathysphere'. She writes of friends, lovers, food, NYC, England and France (where she often lives), in images from art ('I'm the lady left of you, who'd like / to peer into your missal, where the writ- / ing (legible Gothic) lauds in Latin poetry / the Lady at the centre') and from crude life: 'I eat a thick soup of pain . . . wake up swollen and sore / as a flaming jaw of impacted teeth.' Since 1982 MH has been editor-in-chief of *13th Moon*, a feminist literary magazine; interview in *Frontiers*, 3, 1980.

Haec-Vir [Latin noun for *man* preceded by feminine pronoun], *or the Womanish Man*, 1620, pamphlet dialogue *perhaps* by a woman, answering the conservative, anti-feminist *Hic Mulier*, part of an on-going controversy about gender roles and costume. Its speakers are one of each sex dressed more like the other: the woman welcomes change, makes radical claims ('I was created free, born free, and live free'), and even feels superior to males. Probably, however, the writer counts on the reader to disagree. A third pamphlet, *Muld Sacke*, presents a submissive female speaker: repr. in *Three Pamphlets*, 1978, and Henderson and McManus, 1985 (see DEFENCES); see Sandra Clark in *SP*, 82, 1985.

Hahn, Emily, writer of travels, fiction, and journalism, b. 1905 at St Louis, Missouri, da. of Hannah (Schoen) and Isaac Newton H. To rebel against her family ('all readers'), she entered the Univ. of Wisconsin as its first woman mining engineer (BS 1926). She soon quit her first job for 'as near drifting as a middle-class, well-brought-up young woman can achieve' (including study at Columbia Univ. and teaching at

Hunter College. NY). Need for money drove her to write for newspapers and publish *Seductio Ad Absurdum: Principles and Practices of Seduction*, 1930, a parody treatise mocking gender roles and cliché situations. She worked for the Red Cross in the Belgian Congo and lived among pygmies (the 'soft, insistent pull' of her mother's anxiety brought her home in 1932): described in *Congo Solo*, 1933. After a first novel, *With Naked Foot*, 1934, she studied at Oxford Univ., 1934–5, and went as a reporter to China, teaching, researching, and helping to edit and write a monthly, *T'ieu Hsia*. She made a marriage 'of convenience' to Zau Sinmay, and bore a daughter to Charles Boxer, whom she m. in 1945. *The Soong Sisters*, 1941, charts the course of the Chinese revolution through the careers of the US-educated sisters who married its moderate, radical, and conservative leaders, Kung Hsiang-Hsi, Sun Yat Sen, and Chiang Kai-shek. After WWII (for her the Japanese invasion and Reign of Terror), EH settled in England: *China to Me*, 1944, repr. 1987, was joined by *England to Me*, 1949, and *Africa to Me*, 1964. Her fiction draws on her TRAVELS: China in *Mr Pan*, 1943, and *Miss Jill*, 1947 (about a Shanghai prostitute, repr. as *House in Shanghai*, 1958), South Africa in *Diamond*, 1956. Of about 40 post-war titles, *Love Conquers Nothing: A New Look at Old Romances*, 1952, takes a sceptical female look at 'great love-stories'. Lives of Frances BURNEY, 1950, Aphra BEHN, 1951, the women in D. H. Lawrence's life, 1975, and Mabel Dodge LUHAN, 1977, are romantic and popular with some feminist tincture. *Once Upon a Pedestal: An Informal History of Women's Lib*, 1974, relates the progress of US women from 1607 to 1966 (the founding of NOW).

'Hale, Katherine', Amelia Beers Warnock, 1878–1956, poet, literary and music critic, travel writer, local historian, musician. B. in Galt, Ont. da. of Katherine Hale (Bayard) and James W., she went to school in Toronto, NYC, and Europe, and was a schoolgirl friend of Mazo DE LA ROCHE. She m. critic and journalist John W. Garvin and, after a time giving recitals as a soprano in London and in major US and Canadian cities, she turned to journalism. She was on the editorial staff of the Toronto *Mail and Empire* for some years and contributed poetry and prose to many periodicals. She published six volumes of poetry, several books of local and social history, and a book on Isabella Valancy CRAWFORD. *Canadian Cities of Romance*, 1928, described as the Canadian version of 'the viewpoint of the new woman', gives lively, informal comments on the history, architecture, and culture of Canadian cities. *The White Comrade*, 1916, and *The New Joan*, 1917, 'songs of women's work', are war poems, patriotic and religious; *Morning in the West*, 1923, has wider range.

Hale, Lucretia Peabody, 1820–1900, short-story, prose and children's writer, b. Boston, one of seven surviving children of Sarah Preston (Everett) and Nathan H., publisher. Educ. at Elizabeth PEABODY's School and the George B. Emerson School, she was one of the first women elected to the Boston school board, 1874. She was a deeply religious Unitarian. Her first independent vol. was *Seven Stormy Sundays*, 1858, a book of devotions linked by narrative. After her father's death in 1863, she supported herself primarily by writing, publishing numerous short stories and 18 vols. of prose, including four on needle-work. Her sense of humour is evident in works such as *An Uncloseted Skeleton*, 1887 (with E. L. Bynner), a ghoulish but light-hearted tale of a brain transplant; and her best-known collection, *The Peterkin Papers*, absurdist CHILDREN'S stories featuring the hapless Peterkin family, saved by the common sense of 'The Lady from Philadelphia', which have been in print since they first appeared in various magazines, 1868–89. See E. D. Hale's 'LPH', June 1925 (*The Bookman*) and E. O.

White's 'LPH', Sept.–Oct. 1940 (*The Horn Book*).

Hale, Martha (Rigby), d. 1803, poet. Da. of Richard R. of Mistley Hall, Essex, she m., 1750, army officer Bernard H., and from 1773 lived at Chelsea Hospital, where he was Lt-Governor; in 1791–2 the BURNEY family noted her wit and humour but found her hard and pretentious. Elizabeth of ANSPACH, Georgiana DEVONSHIRE and Hannah MORE subscribed (for charity) to her *Poetical Attempts*, 1800. Besides love-poetry and family verse, 'The Infant's Petition To Be Nursed at Home', and poignant laments for a dead son, she deplores the 'British spoiler' of India and Africa, congratulates an archbishop's wife for bearing the first-ever baby at Lambeth Palace (her cries astounded the portraits of archbishops hanging in the next room), and urges the future Maria Theresa KEMBLE to emulate Elizabeth INCHBALD by adding the 'nobler' literary achievement to her acting fame.

Hale, Nancy, novelist, short-story writer, biographer, b. 1908 in Boston, da. of Lilian (Westcott) and Philip L. Hale, both painters: great-niece of Lucretia HALE and H. B. STOWE. She acquired a printing press at seven (to run a family paper) and submitted a story to the *Boston Herald* at 11. After Winsor School (graduated 1926) she planned to be a painter and attended the Boston Museum School. On her first marriage, 1928, she moved to NYC, where she worked on *Vogue*, then *Vanity Fair*, 1933–4, then (from 1935, after unemployment and financial struggle) was the *NY Times*'s first woman reporter. Meanwhile she wrote a novel, *The Young Die Good*, 1932, which casts a satiric eye on NY society, and stories for magazines. 'To the Invader', 1933, broaches her favourite themes of conflict between male and female, and US North and South; it won the O. Henry award (repr. with others in *The Earliest Dreams*, 1936). After five gruelling years in the writing (divorce, remarriage, a second son, a second divorce), her third novel, *The Prodigal Women*, 1942 (regional and gender tensions: three richly drawn female characters), was a best-seller. That year she m. bibliographer Fredson Bowers; they have lived (with a WWII spell in Washington, DC) at Charlottesville: the Univ. of Virginia staged two plays by NH, 1952 and 1953. The story volumes *The Empress's Ring*, 1955 (in which autobiography creeps into her fiction), and *Heaven and Hardpan Farm*, 1957 (women's comical, touching relations with their psychiatrist), show the range of her subjects and technique. *Black Summer*, 1963, treats her favourite North–South, male–female themes: a wife who learns to trust her own perceptions, not her husband's, is 'filled with a sense of power so unaccustomed as to feel eerie'. NH explores her own past in delicate linked sketches in *A New England Girlhood*, 1958 (title adapting one by her grandfather), *The Life in the Studio*, 1969 (on artists and their lives, especially her mother), *Secrets*, 1971 (her own growth, thinly disguised portraits of friends and neighbours). Besides other fiction, she has published works on New England, *The Realities of Fiction*, 1962 (lectures given at the Breadloaf Writers' Conference), lives of painter Mary Cassatt, 1975, and sculptor Cathe Wallendahl, 1977, and a children's book, 1978, and planned a fictional life of her great-uncle Charles H. MSS at Smith College and Univ. of Va.

Hale, Sarah Josepha (Buell), 1788–1879, editor, novelist, poet, essayist, b. Newport, NH, third of four children of Martha (Whittlesey) and Capt. Gordon B. Educ. by her mother and brother, she ran a private school from 1806 till 1813 when she m. David H., who died in 1822, leaving her and five children penniless. She turned to writing with *The Genius of Oblivion*, 1823, poems about domestic fulfilment, and the award-winning novel, *Northwood*, 1827 (rev. 1852), filled with moral homilies and quiet, obedient women. From 1828 she edited the new *Ladies' Magazine*, which Godey bought in 1837 and incorporated with his *Lady's Book*; she remained editor till 1877. She advocated female educational reforms and opportunities as well as property rights for women, but was against woman suffrage. *Godey's Lady's Book* became one of the leading periodicals of the nineteenth century, circulation increasing from 10,000 in 1837 to 150,000 in 1860, publishing early works by H. B. STOWE but nothing controversial (the Civil War was never mentioned). Editor or author of some 50 books including housekeeping, children's (she wrote 'Mary had a Little Lamb'), poetry and biography, one of her most valuable contributions was *Woman's Record*, 1854, a mammoth 2500-entry encyclopaedia of 'distinguished women' from 'the creation to A.D. 1854'. It covers women from all walks of life. In the entry on Eve, she argues woman's superiority as the last step in the ascending scale of creation, and sees woman's role as teacher of moral values.

Hales, Ada Matilda Mary, 1878–1957, novelist, da. of a Brighton clergyman, educ. at the Villa Lehman, Montreux, and St Hugh's College, Oxford, graduating in English, 1904. Besides two children's books (prose stories from Chaucer, 1911, a Siamese cat story [1934]), she published three novels. *Leslie*, 1913, and *The Hamlet on the Hill*, 1927, trace sensitive male protagonists through emotional vicissitudes to – respectively – desolate accidental death and literary success. *The Puritan's Progress*, 1920, stands out. Its female narrator looks back over 20 years at a stifling religious upbringing and two daring commitments: to artistic, intellectual, bohemian life with another woman (who dies in a car crash) and to a long, passionate affair with an unhappily married man. Leaving him at last so as 'to stand alone', she salutes these two people, whom she loved 'more than life itself'.

Halkett, Anne (Murray), Lady, 1623–99, autobiographer, religious writer, b. in London. Her Scottish parents, Jane (Drummond) and Thomas M. (who died when she was a baby), both had posts teaching James I's children. She studied French, music, sewing, religion – and medicine and surgery – and started young women buying their own theatre tickets instead of being taken by men. She began marriage negotiations with the impecunious Thomas Howard; her mother's outrage lasted for months, until she found her unhappy daughter was seeking a Protestant nunnery to enter. In 1648 AH helped Col. Joseph Bampfield to engineer the future James II's escape from England; she was closely and painfully involved for years with Bampfield, who posed to her as a widower. She lived in northern Scotland practising medicine, 1650–2, and at Dunfermline from 1656, after her marriage to Sir James H. (a genuine widower). During her first pregnancy she wrote a lost 'Mother's Will to her Unborn Child'. Widowed in 1670, she lived by teaching till James II pensioned her. She left about 50 MS volumes and leaflets, written 1644–99, mostly of religious meditations. Two of these, a life, and *Instructions for Youth* were pub. 1701 at Edinburgh; her memoirs, remarkable for emotional freedom and psychological insight, written 1677–8, ed. John Loftis, 1979.

Hall, Anna Maria, 'Mrs S. C. Hall' (Fielding), 1800–81, novelist and journalist. B. Dublin into a family of Huguenot origin, she grew up in Bannow, Co. Wexford, and came to England with widowed mother Sarah Elizabeth, 1815. She m. 1824 Samuel Carter H., littérateur, journalist, and something of a Pecksniffian charlatan, who managed his wife's literary salon from their London home. She helped many young writers, including Dinah CRAIK and Margaret OLIPHANT. Her own works, numbering over 100 items with many published in periodicals, include Irish tales (earliest are

Sketches of Irish Character, 1829) reminiscent of EDGEWORTH's and MITFORD's stories and attempting an objective view of Irish character and society; three dramas; children's stories; and fiction concerning problems particular to women. These include *The Old Governess*, 1858, and *Tales of Women's Trials*, 1835, dealing with the sufferings of governesses, the situation of spinsters, and the agonies of wives married to ne'er-do-well husbands. Though unsympathetic to women's rights, she helped to found the Governesses' Institute, the Home for Decayed Gentlewomen, and the Nightingale Fund, donating much of her literary profit to these. She was awarded a Queen's Pension in 1868. Without literary sophistication, she earnestly depicted women's wrongs while also upholding an essentially conservative image of female resignation and self-sacrifice. Her husband's view of her can be found in his *Book of Memories*, 1876, and *Retrospect of a Long Life*, 1883; the autobiographies of Mary HOWITT, 1889, and M. Oliphant, 1899, give additional information from friends of her own sex.

Hall, Louisa Jane (Park), 1802–92, poet and novelist, b. Newburyport, Mass. and later moved to Boston where her father, John P., opened a School for Young Ladies. He directed her education, first at home and later at his school, and generally encouraged her literary efforts, helping her during her periods of strained eyesight. She began publishing poetry (anon.) in the 1820s, and did her major work between 1830 and 1840, when she m. Edward B. H. Contemporary sources stress that after her marriage, writing was no longer a priority. Most praised are her historical fictions such as the verse-novel *Miriam*, 1837 (rev. 1838, repr. 1843, 1849, and 1850); her poetry, occasionally humorous, was more often sentimental and/or religious-didactic. Other works include *Alfred*, 1836, *The Sheaves of Love*, 1861, *Joanna of Naples*, 1838, and *A Dramatic Fragment*. Her *Memoir of Elizabeth CARTER*, and a book of religious verse, *The Cross and the Anchor*, appeared in 1844, and she pub. two more books of verse in the final years of her life.

'Hall, Radclyffe', Marguerite Radclyffe-Hall, 'John', 1880–1943, poet and novelist. She was b. near Bournemouth, Hants., to parents on the verge of divorce: American Marie (Diehl) and playboy Radclyffe R-H. Likeness to her father drew physical abuse from her mother, who m., 1883, Alberto Visetti, a London music teacher. RH wrote verse from 'earliest childhood', later setting it to music. Her father died in 1898 leaving her a fortune: she spent a year at King's College, London, toured the USA, and at 21 left home to live with her grandmother, who funded *'Twixt Earth and Stars*, 1906, first of five poetry books as Marguerite R-H. RH called herself 'Peter', later 'John'; she rode, travelled, had love-affairs with women, then in 1907 settled with the much older Mabel Veronica Batten ('Ladye'), and became a Roman Catholic. Her poems express love for girls, in idioms from popular song ('If you were a Rose and I were the Sun', 1906), rustic ballad ('My girl and me', 1913), or decadence ('Regret, the all unbidden guest / Pale faced and silent entereth, / To sit at Love's most sacred feast, / Reproaching those who fain would eat', 1915). A publisher, offered short stories in 1913, advised RH to write a novel. Left guilty at Ladye's death in 1916, she strengthened her new relationship with Una (Taylor), Lady Troubridge (later translator of COLETTE), who was to enable and cherish her work; she also took up SPIRITUALISM. Her first-written novel, *The Unlit Lamp* (conceived in 1920 as *Octopi*), had ten rejections before appearing in 1924. Its protagonist is a daughter erotically and emotionally drained by her mother; she misses her one chance of escape, with an inspiring woman friend, and ends as paid nurse to an aged male 'baby'. *The Forge*, 1924 (written later, pub. first), and *A*

Saturday Life, 1925, make sparkling marital comedies of efforts to reconcile creativity and stability in life. *Adam's Breed*, 1926 (James Tait Black Award and Prix Femina), traces an orphan Italian boy from Soho through growing disgust with every aspect of life to an eleventh-hour discovery of God within his heart. *The Well of Loneliness*, 1928, explicit study of a lesbian writer, moved the *Sunday Express* to pronounce it better to 'give a healthy boy or a healthy girl a phial of prussic acid than this novel'. Its prosecution as an obscene libel rallied writers on its side, but vainly (historical study by Vera BRITTAIN, 1968). RH was much shaken; though she had linked her heroine's suffering with that of Christ, a cartoon of herself crucified made her offer 'amends' in *The Master of the House*, 1932, whose French hero becomes fully a type of Christ on deserting in WWI. *Miss Ogilvy Finds Herself*, 1934, collects stories written over ten years: the title piece ('nucleus' of the *Well*) concerns an unacknowledged, male-oriented, victimized lesbian. *The Sixth Beatitude*, 1936, celebrates a heroic heterosexual working-class woman. In 1933 RH fell in love with Evguenia Souline, a younger nurse, who brought her stimulation but much suffering in an uneasy *ménage à trois* till 1942. Her novels are wordy and often over-explicit, but centred on powerfully realized social and psychological dilemmas. Several recent reprints (one of poems); lives by Troubridge, 1961 (written 1945) and Michael Baker, 1985 (using MSS at Ottawa, Texas, and in private hands); critical study by Claudia Stillman Franks, 1986.

Hall, Sarah (Ewing), 1761–1830, Philadelphia essayist, da. of Hannah (Sargeant) and the Rev. John E., Provost of the Univ. of Pennsylvania. Besides housekeeping from her mother, she learned astronomy, history and literature, and sat in on her brothers' Greek and Latin lessons (though she later argued against classics for girls). She m. John H. in 1782. Returning to Philadelphia after eight years on a Maryland estate, she continued her self-education despite a family of 11 children by regularly sitting up till midnight, often till 2 or 3 a.m. American women, she wrote, 'are the most devoted wives, and mothers, and housekeepers, but every moment given to a book, is stolen'. As 'a lady of Philadelphia' she 'often presume[d] to patch up an essay for a Journal or Newspaper', particularly the *Port Folio* from its birth in 1800 (a son was later editor). Her one book, *Conversations on the Bible* (between a mother and daughters), 1818, begun at past 50, was a huge success. *Selections* from her works, 1833, include a life and reviews of Mary BRUNTON, Maria EDGEWORTH, and Anne GRANT. Always attentive to women's position and influence, she believed in a separate feminine sphere and the mission of wifehood.

Halligan, Marion (Crothall), novelist, short-story writer, b. 1940 in Newcastle, NSW, to Mildred Alice (Cogan) and Arthur James C. Educ. at Newcastle Girls' High School and the Univ. of Newcastle, she has worked as a school teacher, but is now writing full time. Her first novel, *Self Possession*, 1987, set in Canberra during the 1970s, deals with the blossoming of Angela Mayhew, scholastically brilliant but socially inept, with assistance from the, often satirically portrayed, local academic community. There are strong parallels with the Pygmalion legend, though these are denied at the end when, as the title suggests, Angela becomes her own woman. 'Thrift', a story in MH's first collection, *The Living Hothouse*, 1988, deals with similar material; others are set in France, where she lived for some time; many, like the title story, reflect her interest in gastronomy and are not to be read while dieting. The Canberra settings, concentration on women's experiences, and interest in good food and wine recur in her second collection, *The Hanged Man in the Garden*, 1989. This, however, is a group of interrelated stories, focusing on the lives of two sisters, Martha and Frances, but extending also to other relatives and friends. Halligan's wry humour, compassion and elegant handling of the short-story form are well displayed here. Numerous other stories have appeared in magazines and anthologies, including a collection by seven Canberra women, *Canberra Tales*, 1988. Another novel, *Spider Cup*, will be published in 1990. MH is currently working on a third and on a collection of essays, *Eat My Words*, related to the historical, etymological, social and personal aspects of food.

Ham, Elizabeth, 1783–after 1852, autobiographer, poet, novelist and miscellaneous writer, b. to a yeoman family at North Perrott, Somerset. Living away from them for much of her childhood (partly because she insisted on staying at – an inadequate – school), she felt uncouth and excluded when back at home. She began at 66 to 'trace out the influences that were most active in forming the present individual *Me* out of the little neglected girl of my earliest remembrance'. Eric Gillett, who ed. selecs. 1945, claims to have excised self-pitying passages, but what appears is early capacity for enjoyment, emotional honesty ('he thought he loved me, but he loved excitement and change better') and courage under increasing harassment. Her father lost money: as family dependant, she relates financial shifts, life in Ireland 1804–9, West Country village quarrels, a typhus epidemic, attempts at running a school, an escape from work as a milliner, the quandary of a marriage proposal (unwanted but possibly prudent to accept), thoughts of suicide, writing for magazines, work for the poor (making soup, not schemes), leaning towards the QUAKERS and joining the Unitarians, ending as a governess in the 1820s. Her 'Historical Poem' *Elgiva, or The Monks*, with minor pieces, 1824, dedicated to Margaret HOLFORD, Jr, shows talent; her lost *Infants' Grammar*, Dorchester [1820–2] had 30 years in print. Her novel, *The Ford Family in Ireland*, begun 1809, pub. 1845, draws on her own observation and on reports given 'as mere every day events' by those in 'the ranks of the oppressors'. Its English heroine ends like many others, striving successfully to improve an Irish microcosm; unlike others she has made political speeches, shielded a traitor from gunfire with her body, and seen her radical husband executed. The novel looks forward to the future glad tidings 'that, *at last*, "JUSTICE HAS BEEN DONE TO IRELAND!"'

'Hamilton, Cicely', Cicely Mary Hammill, 1872–1952, novelist, playwright, actress and suffragist, b. London, eldest of four children of an Irish mother and Anglo-Scots father who commanded a Highland regiment. She was educ. at school in Malvern, then Homburg, Germany. Declining family fortunes meant she had to support herself from an early age; she worked as student teacher in the Midlands, then as actress in provincial theatre. The author of 20 plays, she is best remembered as a theorist, and much of her work was concerned with the examination of marriage, as in her first successful play, *Diana of Dobsons*, 1908, and her famous polemic, *Marriage as a Trade*, 1909 (repr. Women's Press, 1981). CH saw marriage as the only trade women are trained for; it becomes therefore an economic necessity. Women can win independence through work, but this requires a hard fight against their socialization. Her novel *Just to Get Married*, 1911, explores the degrading scheming of the financially precarious heroine to ensnare a man, though when she confesses this she is rewarded with love and marriage. The war marked a decisive break for CM. In her novel *William an Englishman*, 1919, she depicts the SUFFRAGE campaign as trivial beside the suffering of war; her youthful, idealistic hero and heroine are brutally destroyed by it. Her novel *Theodore Savage*, 1922, also comes from her pessimistic vision of war; there she imagines the future waste of civilization. Though involved in the suffrage campaign she saw herself as feminist rather than suffragist, more interested in 'weakening the tradition of the "normal woman"' than votes, as she writes in her autobiography, *Life Errant*, 1935 (p. 65). Resolutely unmarried, she had a strong belief in her individuality which guided all her thinking and made her resistant to political organizations of all kinds.

Hamilton, Elizabeth, 1758–1816, woman of letters. B. in Belfast, youngest child of well-born but poor parents, Katherine (Mackay) and Charles H., she was orphaned and brought up by a Scots aunt and uncle. She wrote early 'by stealth': an unpub. novel about Arbella STUART, a travel journal which a magazine got hold of, and letters to her brother in India (from 1772). Her first voluntary publication was an essay in *The Lounger*, 1785. A poem of this time pictures her future self as 'one cheerful, pleased, old maid'. When her long-cared-for uncle died, she came south, 1790, and, despite encroaching rheumatism, enjoyed London literary society. *Translation of the Letters of a Hindoo Rajah*, 1796, actually original fiction, commemorates her recently dead brother as the man whose talk of Britain (especially the astounding equality of women) sends the Rajah to see for himself. Its 'Preliminary Dissertation' on Hindu culture is learned, ambitious, and remarkably open-minded; its satirized philosophers and scientists include Mr Vapour, who looks forward to an 'age of reason' in which 'we shall not be troubled with women'; 'the world shall contain only a race of men!!' *Memoirs of Modern Philosophers*, Bath, 1800, a satire on hopes of perfectibility, is best known for attacking Mary HAYS, but it praises Mary WOLLSTONECRAFT's handling of Rousseau. Its heroine, Julia, is tragically destroyed by trying to oppose sexual injustice; the injustice remains untouched. *Letters on Education*, 1801–2, began a series of such works, continued after EH settled at Edinburgh, 1804, with a royal pension: for the nobility, 1806 (after a six-month spell as tutor), for 'the lowest class' at the Female House of Industry in which she concerned herself, 1809, for patrons and directors of public schools, 1815, following Pestalozzi. *A Series of Popular Essays*, 1813, is an ambitious attempt to make 'the science of mind' accessible. Most loved in their day were the song 'My Ain Fireside' and *The Cottagers of Glenburnie: A Tale for the Farmer's Inglenook*, 1808, with its community-managing spinster. EH's plan for a series of historical lives, begun with *Agrippina*, 1804, was dropped in illness, and taken up by her friend E. O. BENGER, who pub. *Memoirs* of her, 1818, with unpub. essays, poems, letters, pious writings and an autobiographical fragment.

Hamilton, Helen, feminist and miscellaneous writer, b. in the tropical 'magic East', probably of Scots descent. She based *My Husband Still: A Working Woman's Story*, 1914, which reads like a novel, on an actual working-class wife's account of her appalling marriage: it makes a powerful implicit plea for divorce. After a play, *The Modern Mother Goose*, 1916, HH issued two startling works in 1917. *The Compleat Schoolmarm: A Story of Promise and Fulfilment*, a long, vivid, irregular poem, aims to make EDUCATION 'more human'; its protagonist is scared at kindergarten, toils at school, loses all originality at a leading women's college, and reaches her peak as a headmistress, imaginatively dead and deadening. *The Iconoclast* is titled after a supposedly feminist journal, propagandist for free love, which briefly tempts the teacher-heroine away from her domestic life with a woman, to a male suitor whom she then rejects. *Napoo! A book of war Bêtes-Noires*, 1918, collects rousing satires in snappy metres on the attitudes of such as the 'strange old ghouls' gloating over casualty lists, the 'Dear Patient Ass' whose 'fine, blind loyalty' accepts any mismanagement – and lastly

'The Scold', HH herself. *Mountain Madness*, 1922, dedicated to her mother, relates her adventures climbing in the French Alps and the Lake District. Her later work is more conventional: *Great Meddow*, 1924 (whimsical, rather patronizing sketches of village life), and two books of poems: *Hope*, 1924, and *the Vision of Fra Bartolo*, 1932, which deal with nature (often Scottish), love (mostly lost), religion, and finally illness.

Hamilton, Janet (Thomson), 1795–1873, poet and essayist, b. Carskill, Lanarkshire, one of two children of Mary (Brownlee) and (?) Thomson, shoemaker. Her parents moved to Langloan in 1802 to work as farm labourers, while seven-year-old JH kept house and worked at the spinning wheel. Her mother taught her to read with the Bible. She m. John H. in 1809, producing ten children. An avid reader, she borrowed copies of *Blackwood's* which she hid in a hole in the wall of her cottage. Although she taught all her children to read and spell she was unable to write, and memorized her verse to be dictated to her husband or son. After the birth of her third child she did not compose poetry again till she was 54. Then she devised an individual style of handwriting and wrote poems in dialect and on social questions, e.g. 'There's been an unco tauk an' fyke / 'Boot weemen's wark, an' things sic like' (*Poems*, 1863). She contributed to Cassell's *Working Man's Friend* and *Good Words* and wrote many TEMPERANCE poems. Volumes include *Poems and Essays*, 1863, which contains a marvellous poem ridiculing the crinoline fashion, *Poems of Purpose and Sketches in Prose*, 1865, and *Poems and Ballads*, 1868, prefaced with a biographical sketch by the Rev. George Gilfillan. Several eminent men sent a memorial of JH to Disraeli, which resulted in a grant of £50 from the Royal Bounty Fund. She started a small CIRCULATING LIBRARY which failed because the books were not returned. An invalid for many years, she was blind for the last 18 years of her life. At her death she had never travelled more than 10 or 20 miles from home. A fountain was erected at Langloan in her memory. See *Pictures in Prose and Verse*, personal recollections by John Young, 1877.

Hamilton, Lillias, d. 1925, novelist and doctor, b. NSW, of an Australian mother (da. of George Innes[?], of Yarrow) and Hugh H. of Ayrshire. Educ. at Cheltenham Ladies' College, she was inspired by Miss Beale to choose a medical career, and braved opposition to train at the Liverpool Infirmary as a nurse, then as a doctor (Edinburgh and the London School of Medicine for Women), qualifying in 1890. She went to Calcutta, and by 1894 was physician in charge of the Dufferin Hospital. After contracting cholera, she moved to Afghanistan, where she became 'Court Physician to Abdur Rahman, Amir of Afghanistan' as she describes herself on the title page of her novel, *A Vizier's Daughter: A Tale of the Hazara War*, 1900. A lurid story of a rebellious girl who bravely resists degradations imposed by a man she refuses to marry, it paints a grim picture of Afghan life. *A Nurse's Bequest*, 1907, is the story of a girl who learns nursing the hard way, in a workhouse; a sub-theme is the support of a scheme to remove British children from their drunken slum-dwelling mothers and raise them on Canadian farms. From 1908 LH was Warden of Studley Horticultural and Agricultural College for Women. See *Times* obit., 9 Jan. 1925.

Hamilton, Lady **Mary** (Leslie), also Walker, 1739–after 1818, didactic novelist, b. Edinburgh, youngest da. of Elizabeth (Monypenny) and Alexander L., Earl of Leven and Melville. In 1762 she married Dr James W., who abandoned her with four young children: to support them she turned her writing from solace to income with *Letters from the Duchess de Crui and Others, On Subjects Moral and Entertaining. Where the Character of the Female Sex, with* *their Rank, Importance, and Consequence, is Stated, and their Relative Duties in Life are Enforced*, 1776, written 'in her nursery', dedicated to 'the Public'. It sets the tone for four more novels. She regrets women's imposed ignorance, wants to inspire them to self-education, but believes 'that *home* is the theatre for female action'. The plot includes a poisoning and ends with weddings and a pious deathbed; more important is wide-ranging discussion of history, culture, sexual morality, second marriages, and especially education. Characters draw on their commonplace-books; learned footnotes abound, as well as unmarked passages from e.g. Hester CHAPONE. The heroine of MH's best-known work, *Munster Village*, 1778, repr. 1987, refuses marriage until she has used her money to found a UTOPIAN academy (200 male scholars, 20 young ladies). MH re-married Robert H. and lived in France. The *Monthly Review*, 1780, remarks on her following in the footsteps of Catharine MACAULAY with a pamphlet on Burke. Widowed again, she visited Jamaica in 1815 to set to rights an estate she owned there; she enjoyed the voyage, the place, but not the (white) people. Two letters in William Fraser's book on the Leslies, 1890.

Hamilton, Mary Agnes (Adamson), CBE, 'Iconoclast', 1884–1962, Scottish novelist, journalist, memoirist and politician. B. in Manchester, eldest da. of ex-teacher Daisy (Duncan), called Margaret after marriage, and Robert A., Professor of Logic at Glasgow, she was educ. by her father, then at Aberdeen Girls' High School, Glasgow Secondary School, and, as Mathilda Blind Scholar, at Newnham, Cambridge (first-class honours in classics, history and economics). In 1905 she began a brief, unhappy and childless marriage to economist C. J. H. She earned her living by writing prolifically: journalism, translations, books on politics, history, and classical culture. Her biography of Ramsay Macdonald, 1923, was much admired; those of Margaret Bonfield, 1924, and Mary Macarthur, 1925, make gender part of their treatment of their political subjects. Her novels (unusual and notable despite sometimes stilted style) present relations between the sexes in an explicitly political context, as in *Dead Yesterday*, 1916, which contrasts strong female opposition to war with male fascination for it, or *Special Providence*, 1930, a powerful depiction of love distorted by a background of WWI violence. *Yes*, 1914, and *Folly's Handbook*, 1927, focus on the anguish of lovers' misunderstandings. *The Last Fortnight*, 1920, in which a young wife kills herself to escape a marriage in which she is helplessly dominated by her husband and mother-in-law, draws on memories of MH's own marriage. She was a Labour MP, 1929–31, and an influential committee woman and office-holder, dealing with industry, the civil service, the post office, and the League of Nations. (*Sydney and Beatrice* WEBB, 1933, draws on this experience.) *Newnham: An Informal Biography*, 1936, rejoices in women's new opportunities and recalls the struggle for access to university EDUCATION. *Women at Work*, 1941, is her guide for women to the trade unions. Her memoirs, *Remembering My Good Friends*, 1944, and *Up-hill All the Way*, 1953, offer valuable comment on her era.

Hamnet, Nina, 1890–1956, most remembered as a 'bohemian' and memoirist, also an artist and book-illustrator. Da. of Mary (Archdeacon), whose father was a surveyor of Western Australia, and George H., a soldier, she was b. in Tenby, South Wales, on St Valentine's day: 'Everyone was furious ... I was furious too, at having been born a girl; I have since discovered that it has certain advantages.' She attended a co-ed school in Belfast, later art school in Portsmouth and the London School of Art ('paradise'). She rented a room in Grafton Street and soon made a wide acquaintance among the avant-garde: reading Murry's and MANSFIELD's *Rhythm*, for instance, she discovered Henri Gaudier-Brzeska's drawings, then the sculptor himself, who sculpted her from a stolen piece of marble. She showed her work for the first time in 1913, and the next year m. artist Edgar De Bergen. They both worked at the Omega Workshops (she was subsequently close to Roger Fry). The marriage was 'the one thing she always regretted', and after Bergen was deported to France, she never saw him again. Gaudier's sculpture provides the title for the best-selling *Laughing Torso*, 1932, NH's witty, anecdotal account of life in Paris and London with Aleister Crowley (who sued her for comments about his black magic), Mark Gertler, CARRINGTON, Nancy CUNARD, Edith SITWELL, Ezra Pound, Apollinaire, Modigliani, and others. *Is She a Lady? A Problem in Autobiography*, 1955, follows, with reminiscences of Yeats, Havelock Ellis, Anna WICKHAM, and others. A successful artist, though not on a grand scale (she exhibited at the Royal Academy and frequently in Paris and London), NH illustrated books by Osbert Sitwell and Seymour Leslie. Life by Denise Hooker, 1986, includes list of exhibition catalogues. Some letters at the Univ. of Texas at Austin.

Hampton, Susan (Mackie), poet, editor, part-time academic, b. 1949 at Inverell, NSW, da. of June (McLean) and Cliff M. She has been married, has one son, and now identifies herself as a lesbian writer. She was educ. at Newcastle Teachers' College, Macquarie Univ. and the Univ. of Sydney. Her poetry was first pub. in *Sisters Poets I* (with Joyce Lee, Kate LLEWELLYN and Anne Lloyd), 1979. Two collections have appeared: *Costumes*, 1981 (poems and prose), and *White Dog Sonnets*, 1987. Most notable are her poems frankly exploring the female experience, such as 'The Power of the/Red Queen', with its strong images of the divided self, the dual roles of female personality. Others evoke adolescent memories, or offer images of city life (as in the title poem of *Costumes*); some explore the connections between childhood and old age. Her language is vigorous, tense, and can be abrupt and uncompromising; her prose tends to be smoother and colloquial. SH also co-edited the major ANTHOLOGY, *The Penguin Book of Australian Women Poets*, 1986 (with Kate Llewellyn), and pub. *About Literature*, 1984 (with Sue Woolfe), an English textbook. See *Poetry and Gender: Issues in Australian Women's Poetry*, 1989 (ed. Brenda Walker and David Brooks), for SH's poet's statement.

Hanagan, Eva Helen (Ross), novelist, b. 1923 and brought up in the Scottish Highlands, da. of Janet Alice (Fraser) and James MacDonald R. Educ. at Inverness Royal Academy and College, she was an avid reader of British and European classic fiction. She worked for the Board of Trade in Inverness till 1945, then for the Foreign Office in Vienna. She m. John H., army officer, in 1947, had two sons, and travelled to Egypt and elsewhere. Settled in southern England, she spent eight years caring for her mother, an Alzheimer's victim, then went back to work and began to write. The Arts Council published 'The Ghost in the Ark' in *New Stories*, 1976. Her compelling novels dwell on often lonely lives in houses with large gardens and countryside beyond: the old, damaged or innocent face mystery, terror and acts of violence. *In Thrall*, 1977 (dedicated to her father's memory), depicts the growth of an elderly woman's obsession with beings which the reader must see as malevolent fairies. *Playmates*, 1978, opens on two aged sisters maimed at birth, one in face and one in mind, and the survivor's gallant struggle to continue alone. The heroine of *The Upas Tree*, 1979, learns (with 'red, jagged, steaming anger') the extent of her recently-dead mother's crime against her, and her Calvinist grandfather's crime against his children, and belatedly essays a life of her own; that of *Holding On*, 1980, is a disquieting schoolgirl with pallid parents and a monster grandfather. In *A knock at the door*, 1982, a crassly do-gooding

Englishwoman brings disaster on a Holocaust survivor who lives in tormented expectation of anti-semitism reborn. EH taught creative writing in prison, 1979–85. Since 1982 she has had two novels rejected, and has published only booklets on writing, 1989. She admires Muriel SPARK, Anita DESAI, and Alice Thomas ELLIS.

Handl, Irene, 1901–87, comic actress (stage, film and TV), novelist. B. in Maida Vale, London, da. of Frenchwoman Marie (Schuepp) and Viennese banker Frederick H. She attended Maida Vale Girls' High School sporadically until 14, but called herself 'practically uneducatable'. Her mother died early of cancer; after that her father (whose house she kept till his death, at 86) encouraged her into a career. After a year at the Embassy School of Acting she went on stage, at 37. She was a success from her first role, and became both distinguished and beloved. Her first novel, *The Sioux*, begun at 14 and continued in Paris in the 1920s after an unhappy love affair, was finished in her early sixties as diversion after a long stage run. Published in 1965 (repr. 1986), it is a sophisticated, original study of the doomed relationship between a fascinated Englishman and a fabulously rich, amoral, passionately tribal French family, 'the Sioux'. Its compellingly iniquitous Marguerite and her son Georges reappear in *The Gold Tip Pfitzer*, 1973 (repr. 1985), where he dies of leukaemia. Margaret DRABBLE has called these very funny books 'oddly haunting'. IH also wrote for radio.

Hands, Elizabeth, poet, many years a servant to the Huddesfords of Allesley near Coventry. She pub. some pieces as 'Daphne' in *Jopson's Coventry Mercury*. By 1785 she m. a blacksmith near Rugby: by 1788 masters at Rugby School were seeking subscribers (including Harriet BOWDLER's mother, Anne DAMER, Anna SEWARD) for *The Death of Amnon*, with her name, Coventry, 1789. Her less formal pieces are even more interesting than her ambitious title poem (blank verse on the biblical, incestuous rape of a sister and revenge by another brother). In two satires on her future readers, she slightly tempers snobbery ('I suppose we shall see / An Ode on a Dishclout'; 'One can't make acquaintance with servants, you know') with encouragement from Miss Rhymer; her imaginary Rector closes with pompous faint praise, which the *Monthly Review* quoted as its own verdict. In EH's pastorals, nymphs rather than shepherds, 'Alike ambitious to excel in song', contend over the value of their lovers, their feelings and their verse. In courtship tales Lob and Roger are decisively rejected by independent girls. EH laments exile from the countryside, rejoices at the birth of a daughter (1785), and brilliantly catches the styles of great poets in 'Critical Fragments'. See Donna Landry in *The Muses of Resistance*, 1990.

Hanrahan, Barbara, novelist, short-story writer, b. 1939 in Adelaide, South Australia, da. of Ronda (Goodridge) and William H., who died young. Brought up by female relatives, she was educ. at Thebarton Technical School, South Australian School of Art, and later Central School of Art, London. A painter and printmaker of international reputation, she taught and exhibited in Australia and London. Since 1966 she has lived with sculptor Jo Steele. Her first novel, *The Scent of Eucalyptus*, 1973, is based on her childhood memories of Adelaide in the 1950s and was followed by *Sea-Green*, 1974, a semi-autobiographical work about a young Adelaide artist who goes to London to study. Following these, BH shifted to a mode of gothic fantasy. *The Albatross Muff*, 1977, *Where the Queens All Strayed*, 1978, *The Peach Groves*, 1979, and *The Frangipani Gardens*, 1980, contrast the prim conventions of Victorian and Edwardian society with its sinister, unacknowledged shadow life, frequently using the naïve viewpoint of the child. Her central characters are often artists or figures who find fulfilment through the discovery or mastery of their creative abilities. Her most recent works are *Dove*, 1982, a volume of autobiography, *Kewpie Doll*, 1984, *Annie Magdalene*, 1985, a collection of stories, *Dream People*, 1987, and *A Chelsea Girl*, 1988. Her artwork is discussed in detail in Alison Carroll's study, 1987. See also P. Gilbert, *Coming Out from Under: Contemporary Australian Women Writers*, 1988.

Hansberry, Lorraine Vivian, 1930–65, playwright and activist, b. in Chicago, da. of Nannie (Perry) and Carl Augustus H., realtor and NAACP supporter. When she was eight he bought a house in 'a white neighborhood'; they were harassed, vandalized, evicted, then upheld in the Supreme Court. LH used the experience in *A Raisin in the Sun*, Best Play of 1959, which made her the first black woman writer on Broadway. She studied from 1948 at the Univ. of Wisconsin, in Mexico, and in NYC: at the New School and (under W. E. B. Du Bois) the Jefferson School of Social Science. She did not take a degree. From 1951 to 1953 she worked on Paul Robeson's *Freedom* (for which Alice CHILDRESS wrote a column), as part of a campaign she described in *The Movement: Documentary of a Struggle for Equality*, 1964 (*A Matter of Colour* ... in Britain). She lost her passport, 1952, for speaking on behalf of Robeson. She m. future song writer and publisher Robert Nemiroff in 1953, worked at various jobs, and wrote stories and unfinished plays. The title of her first completed work, *Raisin*, alludes to a Langston Hughes poem on 'a dream deferred': she wrote to her mother that it 'tells the truth'. A young black man dreams of success in terms of saying 'Hello, Jefferson' to a gardener who will say 'Good evening, Mr Younger'; his mother says (citing her husband): 'being any kind of a servant wasn't a fit thing for a man to have to be'. (One of these scenes was cut in stage production, the other from the film, 1960.) *The Sign in Sydney Brustein's Window*, on 'the Western intellectual poised in hesitation before the flames of involvement', was staged in 1964; cancer prevented LH from revising in rehearsal; the theatre wanted to close it after a week, but donations kept it running. LH's husband (divorced in 1964) followed her intentions in finishing *Les Blancs* (about a post-colonial, European-influenced African), produced 1970, ed. by him both alone and in *Last Plays*, 1972. This also contained *What Use Are Flowers?*, about a post-nuclear hermit striving to hand on 'knowledge of the remnants of civilization', and *The Drinking Gourd*, commissioned by NBC for the Civil War centenary in 1960, then rejected (see Elizabeth Brown-Guillory in *Griot*, 4, 1985): LH called this a non-propaganda 'serious treatment of family relationships by a slave-owning family and their slaves'. Nemiroff also wrote *To Be Young, Gifted and Black: LH in Her Own Words* (from her minor writings including poems; seen off-Broadway in 1968, pub. 1969), and a bibliog. in *Freedomways* special issue, 1979, and ed. *Raisin* and *Sign* with critical essays, 1987. LH left much unpub. and unfinished: essays, a musical, a novel, a work on Toussaint L'Ouverture. Study by Anne Cheney, 1984; Margaret Wilkerson (see *Theatre Journal*, 38, 1986) is working on a critical biography ('Excerpts' in *Mass. Review*, 28, 1987).

Hanson, Elizabeth, New England CAPTIVITY-NARRATOR. Her husband, John H. of Dover, NH, and other men were away when in August 1724 Indians killed two of her eight children, and abducted her with four others (including a two-week-old baby) and a maid. Weak from the birth, she was kept walking through the woods for 24 days to an Indian fort, then sold to a French purchaser for 600 livres. After five months with the Indians and one with the French, she was found and brought home by her husband, who d. in 1727 while searching for one of the lost daughters. Her story, told to Samuel Bownas, pub. as

God's Mercy Surmounting Man's Cruelty, 1728, was often repr. in versions 'improved' with sentimental meditation and anti-French feeling: ed. Richard VanDerBeets, 1973, from London ed., 1760. EH noted the kindness of Indian women, who advised on feeding her baby and protected a small son from male violence.

'Han Suyin' [pseudonym alluding to the gamble for liberty], Rosalie (Chou) Comber (sometimes wrongly called Elizabeth), novelist, autobiographer, cultural commentator. B. 1917 in Sinyang, China, da. of Belgian Marguerite (Denis) and Chinese Y. T. Chou, she learned to talk in French and Chinese (in 1920s Peking she went daily to two schools, one in each language). Despite family opposition and ridicule she attended the Univs. of Yenching and Brussels (studying medicine). Back in China in 1938, during the Sino-Japanese war, she married Pao H. Tang, later a Kuomintang officer; they had a child. She wrote of this marriage and 'the turmoil of war-time China' in *Destination Chungking*, 1942, revised to catch US interest and sympathy by Marian Manly, a missionary doctor under whom HS trained as a midwife. Her husband was posted to London, but then killed. She completed medical studies at London Univ., 1944–8. *A Many-Splendoured Thing*, 1942 (adapted for film, 1955, and TV, 1967), is a first-person narrative of a Chinese woman doctor in communist-run Hong Kong. HS m. publisher L. F. Comber in 1952. *And the Rain My Drink*, 1956, whose fractured narrative reflects an uneasily mixed society, is set against the early independence movement in Malaya, *The Mountain is Young*, 1958, in Khatmandu, *Cast But One Shadow*, 1962 (based on an actual incident, written entirely in dialogue), and *The Four Faces* (in thriller genre), 1963, in Cambodia. These all deal with love-affairs across racial and cultural divides; *Winter Love* (companion novella to *Cast But One Shadow*: jointly titled *Two Loves* in the USA) shows a troubled lesbian affair in London of WWII, and the general predicaments and insecurities of women. HS writes of her personal struggles and those of China (from 1920s war-lords to the Red Army) in *The Crippled Tree*, 1965 (her parents' families; her childhood), *A Mortal Flower*, 1966, and *Birdless Summer*, 1968, blending warm response to the picturesque or moving in age-old China with sharp perception of the need for change, first-person narration with other voices. She has lectured on Asian culture, and continued to visit and to write on Communist China (on the 1966 revolution, 1967, Mao Tse Tung, 2 vols., 1972, 1976, *China*, 1987), as well as autobiography (*My House Has Two Doors*, 1980), and fiction (e.g. *Till Morning Comes*, 1982, *The Enchantress*, 1985). Western critics have accused her of hostility to western values. Many recent reprints. See Radio Canada interview pub. 1969; Esme Lyon in *WLWE*, 17, 1978.

Hanway, Mary Ann, novelist of Blackheath, London, friend of Jane PORTER and niece by marriage of the philanthropist Josiah H. An anonymous *Journey to the Highlands of Scotland*, 1775, which emulates Lady Mary Wortley MONTAGU and takes issue with Samuel Johnson, is said to be hers. *Ellinor, or The World as It Is*, MINERVA, 1798 (facs. 1974), was written (for female readers) as therapy for calamity and sickness, and well reviewed. A preface deplores recent monstrous and charnel-house fiction, though its own effects are sometimes crude. Its heroine loves books and sensibility, is censured as 'a female philosopher in the egg-shell', discovers her unknown parents and marries happily. It shares its moral ('TO BE GOOD IS TO BE HAPPY') with *Andrew Stuart, or The Northern Wanderer*, 1800 (family impoverished by Jacobite allegiance), and the 'long protracted' *Falconbridge Abbey, A Devonshire Story* [1808]. *Christabelle, The Maid of Rouen ... Founded on Facts*, 1814 (which earned only about £4), has a heroine brought up (after an unusually convincing birth-of-mysterious-baby scene) English-speaking in pre-revolutionary France. MAH deplores 'the present masculine system of female education', and favours emancipation of blacks and Catholics.

Harcourt, Mary (Danby), later Countess, *c.* 1750–1833, memoirist and war correspondent. Eldest da. of Mary (Affleck) and the Rev. William D. of Yorks., she m. in 1772 Thomas Lockhart, a Scot, who d. 1775, then in 1778 the distinguished soldier William H. (an earl from 1809). (Her sister-in-law Elizabeth (Vernon) H., 1746–1826, also wrote a court memoir, 1788–9, and poems admired by Horace Walpole.) The Philobiblon Soc. pub. MH's court diary, 1789–91 (selec.), 1872; the *Harcourt Papers* [1880–1905] pub. her letters, 1792–5, from her husband's Low Countries command of the British army (IV, ii). Her evocation of war is unmatched: the plight of refugees and of 'our poor sick men' (especially veterans), the heroism of a five-year-old, an execution by firing squad, gruesome three-week-old traces of a battle. 'It is wonderful how use enables me to bear things that at first seemed tremendous'; 'I begin to think this retreating a pretty kind of thing (don't tell). ... Even a bad peace is better than war'; 'I am told that I am half a democrat, because I wish that this country may in time be free'; 'I cannot tell you how strongly it strikes me that we must have been wrong; that we had no right ... to spread the calamity of war.' She ends on attending Princess Caroline to England to be married. She later corresponded with Frances BURNEY.

Harding, Anne Raikes, 1781–1858, novelist, b. at Bath. She m. Bristol merchant Thomas H., who died young and intestate, 1805. She ran a school for 35 years and from 1818 published seven anonymous novels (with strong Christian purpose: she often quotes Hannah MORE), 'Numerous Tracts and Papers for Periodicals', *Little Sermons*, 1840, and *An Epitome of Universal History*, 1848. Her early 'high-minded, lofty, imperious' heroines tend to need redemption through suffering (done with tact, energy, and humour); later works reward good girls. She often claims to relate fact. In *Correction*, 1818, one heroine grows up in India as a 'violent despot'; the other twice loves passionately and in vain. That of *Decision*, 1819, sets out among Catholic father, rationalist brother, and Quaker uncle, reading Voltaire and wishing to study for herself; that of *Refugees, An Irish Tale*, 1822, moves from a sheltered childhood to work among the Irish poor (who are amenable to reform, kindness, and honesty, but not to 'slavish fear, and the bayonet's point'). ARH presents *Realities*, 1825, as '*Not* a Novel', *Dissipation*, 1827, as by a widow haunted by children's medical bills. She retired when her children (except a mentally handicapped daughter) were settled. Two years later a lawyer decamped with her capital of about £1,000. She opened a high-class London boarding house, applied to the RLF, and from 1853 lived at Boulogne.

Harding, Elizabeth, miscellaneous writer, Roman Catholic wife of London merchant William H. (d. 1729), with whom she spent some time in France. She signed the dedication (to Queen Anne's favourite Anne Masham) of *Innocentia Patefacta*, 1711, a pamphlet perhaps by herself, about the wrongful execution of a man accused of burglary. Her *Masterpiece of Imposture*, 1734, promising 'the Reality of a History, and the Amusement of a Romance', counters the anti-Papist *Memoirs*, 1734, of John Gordon, ex-Catholic priest, whom she calls a swindler. It has been repr., 1973, as fiction, but reads as typical pamphlet polemic.

Hardwick, Elizabeth, essayist, critic, and author of three novels. She was b. 1916, at Lexington, Kentucky, da. of Mary (Ramsey) and Eugene Allen H., who had a central-heating business. After the Univ. of Kentucky (BA in 1938, MA in English 1939), she went to NYC to study at Columbia (till 1941). Her reputation as an essayist began with writings for *Partisan Review* (also one of the periodicals to publish her short stories). Her first novel, *The Ghostly Lover*, 1945 (repr. 1982 and, with her afterword, 1986), delineates relations between a white woman (who feels herself and her 'heritage were held up like hooked fish with the wild eye exposed') and her black servant during segregation. In 1949 she m. the poet Robert Lowell (previously Jean STAFFORD's husband; he and EH divorced 1972), and lived with him in Europe, the Midwest, and Boston. She was 40 when her daughter was born. Her second novel, *The Simple Truth*, 1955, examines prejudice, truth perception, and the legal and judiciary systems. She was a founding editor of the *New York Review of Books*, 1963, and the first woman to win the George Jean Nathan Award for drama criticism; she aims to give her essays 'everything and more than would be required of fiction', since she sees them as 'examples of imaginative writing': collected in *A View of My Own*, 1962, *Seduction and Betrayal: Women and Literature*, 1974, and *Bartleby in Manhattan*, 1983. Her emphasis on moral values and observed human nature recalls essayists of earlier periods; of the BRONTËS she writes, 'The sisters seized upon the development of their talents as an honorable way of life and in this they were heroic.' After letters by William James, 1961, she edited 18 vols of *Rediscovered Fiction by American Women: A Personal Selection*, 1977 (including, for its 'intensity of remembered autobiography' L. M. ALCOTT's *Work*, and for its rendering of 'the great pulling tides of ambition' C. C. HARRISON's *The Anglomaniacs*). Her experimental *Sleepless Nights*, 1979, offers 'a shattered meditation' (Joan DIDION) on her life: 'If only one knew what to remember or pretend to remember'; 'profound changes and removals along the line split the spirit apart'; 'Store clerks and waitresses are the heroines of my memories.' The Reagan era's 'creeping development of . . . Conservative Realism' reminds EH of 'the intellectual follies of Social Realism'. See D. Pinckney in *Paris Review: Writers at Work*, 7th series, 1986.

Hardy, Mary Anne Duffus (McDowell), Lady, 'Addlestone Hill', 1825?–91, novelist, b. London, da. of Eliza and Charles McD., and second wife of Sir Thomas D. H. Her daughter (stepdaughter, says Wolff), Iza D. H., was also a novelist. MDH pub. 15 titles, starting with *War Notes from the Crimea*, 1855. *A Hero's Work*, 1868, is a subversive romance in which the hero, lauded and unscathed after Crimea, gradually reveals his mean contempt for the lower classes and for women. *Beryl Fortescue*, 1881, is more conventional, though still perceptive on the bonds and tensions linking women. Her last was *A Buried Sin*, 1894. Iza was more prolific than her mother, producing over 25 novels between 1872 and 1910, mostly light romances, with titles like *Not Easily Jealous*, 1872, *Friend and Lover*, 1880, and *A New Othello*, 1890. All were published anonymously. She also wrote two books on US travel, and a biographical note on Annie French HECTOR.

Hare, Maria (Leycester), 1798–1870, diarist and religious writer. B. near Knutsford, Cheshire, da. of Mary (Johnson) and the Rev. Oswald L., sister of Catherine STANLEY, she was educ. by various family members, with a year at school and early reading of Sarah TRIMMER. She visited the ladies of LLANGOLLEN, Europe, and the Highlands. An early suitor died in India: in 1829 she m. the Rev. Augustus William H., whose work at Alton Barnes, Hants., she helped by planning education for house-bound mothers and 'writing a sermon to be ready for Augustus's return . . . partly done in his style, which is rather that of plain talking than of preaching'. Shattered at his talking than of preaching'. Shattered at his death in 1834, she began writing 'Memorials' of their shared life, and next year adopted as her own a nephew born just after his death. Pious motives made her treat him harshly, but as writer Augustus J. C. Hare he devotedly edited her diary, letters, and thoughts 'On the Hidden Life' as the hugely popular *Memorials of a Quiet Life*, 1872.

Harford, Lesbia (Keogh), 1891–1927, poet and novelist, b. Melbourne, Victoria, da. of Helen (Moore) and Edmund K., financial agent. Educ. at Catholic convents, she graduated (LLB) from the Univ. of Melbourne in 1916, but her interest in social research led her to work in a clothing factory rather than practise law. She became involved in radical and union politics and joined the IWW, where she was a charismatic figure. A believer in free love, she had many lovers including Katie Lush, a philosophy tutor she met at univ., and the writer Guido Baracchi. In 1918 she moved to Sydney and two years later m. Pat H., artist and fellow IWW worker. Within a few years they had separated; she returned to Melbourne, resumed her legal training, but died soon after. Her poems – remarkable for both their radical and feminist themes and their modern, simple style – first began appearing in 1921. Only a handful were pub. in her lifetime since she did not actively seek publication: 'I take my poetry seriously, and am in no hurry to be read'. She did, however, attempt unsuccessfully to find a publisher for her novel *The Invaluable Mystery*, dealing with radicals in Sydney during WWI: it finally appeared in 1987. Nettie PALMER edited a posthumous collection of her poems, 1941; Drusilla Modjeska and Marjorie Piser a more recent and fuller one, 1985.

Harjo, Joy (Foster), poet and scriptwriter. B. 1951 in Tulsa, Oklahoma into the Creek tribe, she is da. of Wynema (Baker) and Allen W. Foster, and mother of two. She studied creative writing at the Univ. of New Mexico (BA, 1976) and Iowa (MFA, 1978), and film-making at the College of Santa Fe, 1982. She has since taught, been a consultant for Native groups, and served on the board of directors for the National Association of Third World Writers. She started to write poetry at the Univ. of New Mexico about the time her child was born. Identifying as influences in her poetry Simon Ortiz, Leslie SILKO, Flannery O'CONNOR, black writers and African writers, she aimed at 'another way of seeing language and another way of using it that wasn't white European male'. Her poems, widely anthologized, appear frequently in feminist literary journals including *Conditions*. Rayna GREEN, ed., *That's What She Said*, 1984, and Dexter Fisher, ed., *The Third Woman*, 1980, print substantial selections. Her poems – *The Last Song*, 1975, *What Moon Drove Me to This?* 1980, and *She Had Some Horses*, 1983 – record the landscapes of transition marking the lives of contemporary Native Indian women, the all-night drives, long-distance phone calls, resistance to fear, and search for 'visions' in 'winestains / in the snow'. JH's film scripts are 'Origin of Apache Crown Dance', 1985, and (co-author) 'The Beginning': they were released by Native American Broadcasting Consortium. JH is working on an anthology of first nation women writers from North, Central and South America, *Reinventing Ourselves in the Enemy's Language*. See Linda Koolish in Merle Harris and Kathaleen Aguero, eds., *A Gift of Tongues*, 1987, Paula Gunn ALLEN in *The Sacred Hoop*, 1986, and interview in Joseph Bruchac, *Survival This Way: Interviews with American Indian Poets*, 1987.

Harkness, Margaret Elise, 'John Law', *c.* 1861–1921, novelist of whom little is known, a child of 'clerical and conventional' parents, who emancipated herself by doing 'literary piecework' while living near the BM (this from her cousin and – until a quarrel in 1891 – close friend,

Beatrice WEBB). Her early novels embark on a radical critique of religious institutions from a socialist and feminist perspective. Engels praised her first, *A City Girl*, 1887, for 'truthfulness of presentation', but thought it not realistic enough; she hovers between conservatism and radicalism, but many of her East End slum observations are striking. *Out of Work*, 1887, incorporates the Trafalgar Square riots of that year, while *Captain Loke*, 1889, focuses (not uncritically, despite a preface by Booth) on the Salvation Army. A friend of Eleanor Marx and Olive SCHREINER from her early days in London, in later years she became disenchanted with radical causes, and the last of her East End novels, *George Eastmont: Wanderer*, 1905, is dedicated to Cardinal Manning. Her feminism was never militant, but her fiction respects strong and independent women from all classes. See article by Eileen Sypher, *Turn-of-the-Century Women* 1, 2, 1984.

'Harland, Marion', Mary Virginia Terhune (Hawes), 1830–1922, novelist, miscellaneous writer b. Dennisville, Va., da. of Judith Anna (Smith) and Samuel Pierce H., merchant, magistrate and politician. Initially educ. at home as her father considered the local schools inadequate, later she attended Hampden-Sydney College and a Presbyterian school in Richmond. She began writing as a teenager; in 1853 her 'Kate Harper' won a prize for a story on a TEMPERANCE topic, and was pub. in *Southern Era*. In 1856 she pub. her popular novels *Alone* and *The Hidden Path*. Also in 1856 she m. Edward Payson T., a Presbyterian minister, and they moved to Newark, NJ, where her six children were born. She continued writing, producing both novels and collections of short stories such as *Husbands and Homes*, 1864. Her work is generally melodramatic and didactic, although one sketch, 'Might-Have-Been', with its heroine whose sentimental writings 'gave no evidence of her changed life', may suggest similar hidden qualities in its author. In the 1870s, after a bout of TB, she turned to the more practical and realistic genre of household books of ADVICE, beginning with *Common Sense in the Household*, 1871. She pub. 25 such books, edited two magazines on homemaking, *Home-Maker*, 1888–90, and the *Housekeeper's Weekly*, and wrote syndicated columns for the Philadelphia *North American* and the *Chicago Tribune* which were reprinted in 25 other dailies. From 1891 to 1894 she lectured for the Chautauqua Association on topics such as 'The Kitchen as a Moral Agency'. Although she condemned feminism, she did support education for women, believing that every woman should have a trade or profession to support herself if necessary. She also wrote books of travel, history and biography, such as *The Story of Mary Washington*, 1892, and *Some Colonial Homesteads and their Stories*, 1897, and was the first woman member of the Virginia Historical Society. *Looking Westward*, 1914, is a statement of her personal philosophy. Her last novel, *The Carringtons of High Street*, was pub. in 1919. See *MH's Autobiography*, 1910, for her life, and Nina Baym, 1978.

Harley, Brilliana (Conway), Lady, *c.* 1600–43, letter-writer, b. in Holland, da. of Dorothy (Tracy) and Sir Edward C. In 1623 she became the third wife of Sir Robert H., about 20 years her senior; she had seven children and made Brampton Castle, Herefordshire, into a centre of Puritanism in a royalist district. Her letters (selec. ed. Thomas Taylor Lewis, 1854) begin in 1625 to her husband; most pleasing is the loving 'paper discourse' with her eldest son, from his going to study at Oxford, 1638, to the end of her life. The month after telling him 'I am confident you will hate all plundering and unmercifulness', she was holding her castle against a savagely conducted six-week siege. More letters on deposit in the BL.

Harley, Martha, later Hugill, d. 1797, author of six novels published in London.

Georgiana DEVONSHIRE subscribed to her first, *St. Bernard's Priory, An Old English Tale*, 1786: repr. as *The Priory of St Bernard*, 1789; facs. 1977. The plot is confused, episodic, and historically shaky (the priory is a private estate 400 years before the dissolution of the monasteries), with interesting sexual politics: the hero's father rejected his mother and sisters (not him); they grew up in a cave influenced by Sophia LEE; one, 'the most intrepid of her sex', is loved and killed by the villain; the hero vainly loves a supposed Muslim actually fathered by Richard Coeur de Lion. The *Critical Review* noted its improbability and luxuriant fancy, but readers approved. *The Castle of Mowbray*, 1788, with self-deprecating dedication to the public, sets its disputed inheritance in Stephen's reign. *Juliana Ormeston, or The Fraternal Victim*, 1793, is modern, epistolary and tragic (the father of 'Virtue's Favourite Child' causes her death by a forced marriage and further cruelty). *The Prince of Leon*, 1794, and *Isadora of Gallicia*, 1797–8 (pub. after MH's marriage), are both set in Spain.

Harper, Frances Ellen Watkins, 1825–1911, poet, novelist, lecturer and reformer, b. Baltimore, Maryland. Her parents, both free blacks, died when she was three; she was raised by an uncle and attended his school for free blacks until she was 14. No copy survives of her first book of poetry and prose, *Forest Leaves* (also called *Autumn Leaves*), 1845. Active in the ABOLITIONIST movement and Underground Railroad, she gave her first anti-slavery lecture in 1854, and is credited with writing the first short story by a black American ('The Two Offers', 1859). Except during her marriage (1860–4), she lectured until her death on TEMPERANCE, black EDUCATION, and civil rights, also publishing three more books of poems, *Moses*, 1854 (20 eds. by 1871); *Sketches of Southern Life*, 1872; and *The Master of Alabama*, 1894. Her *Iola Leary: or Shadows Uplifted*, 1892, was long thought to be the first novel by a black American woman, but recent scholarship has suggested that Harriet E. WILSON's *Our Nig*, 1859, is a novel, not autobiography as previously thought. Her poems, traditional in form, centre upon slavery, motherhood and Christianity – themes also explored in *Iola Leary*, but in the novel extended to the position of a mulatto in society, the role of a married woman, and the justifiable anger at racial prejudice. In 1893 she became a director of the American Association of Colored Youth and in 1896 vice-president of the National Association of Colored Women. American blacks, she said, are 'homeless in the land of our birth and worse than strangers in the land of our nativity'. See Elizabeth Ammons in *Legacy* (Fall 1985); Barbara Christian, *Black Women Novelists*, 1980; Joan R. Sherman, *Invisible Poets*, 1974; and William Still, *The Underground Railroad*, 1872; repr. 1968.

Harper, Ida (Husted), 1851–1931, journalist and biographer, b. near Brooksville, Indiana, da. of Cassandra (Stoddard) and John Arthur H. Educ. at Indiana State Univ., in 1871 she m. Thomas Winans H., lawyer. She spent a year as principal of the Peru, Ind., high school before beginning her journalistic career, when her posts included managing editor of the Terre Haute *Daily News*, 1888, and editorial writer on the Indianapolis *News*, 1891–2. In 1884 she pub. *Poems on Miscellaneous Subjects*. She supported women's suffrage; her column 'Votes for Women' in *Harper's* noted the progress of legislation and told women how to educate themselves on the issues. She was also chairman of the press committee of the International Council for Women. Her *Life and Work of Susan B. ANTHONY, 1898–1908*, tells of Anthony's campaigns for women's rights, tracing her transition from shy young Quaker girl to reformer and orator. Though deliberately excluding 'personal controversies', it provides an indispensable documentary account of Anthony's life.

Harraden, Beatrice, 1864–1936, novelist and suffragist, b. London, youngest da. of Rosalie (Lindstedt) and Samuel H., musical instrument importer, and ward of Eliza Lynn LINTON. She was educ. in Dresden, then at Cheltenham Ladies' College, Queen's College and Bedford College, graduating from London Univ. She began to write early, publishing her first stories in *Blackwood's Magazine*. Her work is often sentimental, as in her children's book, *Things Will Take A Turn*, 1889, about a little girl who lives with her grandfather and befriends an invalid child. The bestseller, *Ships that Pass in the Night*, 1893, is set in a sanatorium. Bernadine, who has had a 'cheerless childhood', falls in love but dies tragically in a road accident. *Katharine Frensham*, 1903, also sets love and hope against despair; whilst the man finds love again, his wife commits suicide. *Out of the Wreck I Rise*, 1912, again ends in suicide, but before he dies the hero sees his life clearly for the first time. Other novels include *Hilda Strafford*, 1897, *The Fowler*, 1899, *Interplay*, 1908, and *The Scholar's Daughter*, 1906. BH was a member of the WSPU and wrote a book about SUFFRAGE, *Our Warrior Women*, 1916. She worked for Belgian relief during the war and visited refugee camps. Her life and her friends' memories of her suggest a more interesting woman than her novels, which explore love and loss and never engage with feminist issues.

Harris, Bernice (Kelly), 'Bernice Kelly', 1893–1973, playwright, novelist, b. at Mt Moriah, NC, da. of farmers Rosa (Poole) and William [illegible] K. Her earliest writings were poems; she wrote stories for student publications at Meredith College, Raleigh. She took a course in writing folk-plays and taught high-school English and drama before marrying Herbert H., 1926. She then wrote for newspapers and magazines (her husband's opposition melted when he found 'how much was paid for so little'), and formed groups for acting and writing plays. She edited such work as *Folk Plays of Eastern Carolina*, 1940, and *Strange Things Happen*, 1971 (from a local Writing Group and Writers' Conference). During the Depression she worked for the Federal Writers' Project; her interviews in *These Are Our Lives*, 1939 (with an owner-farmer, two tenant farmers, and a doctor), show an ear for dialect and a sympathy with rural problems. These people's vernacular stories, she says, 'were distilled into my fiction': regional stories and seven novels. The second, *Portulaca*, 1948, is more realistic than *Purslane*, 1939 (nostalgic, well received). *Hearthstones*, 1948, traces a family of sisters from the Civil War to WWI, focusing on the eldest and her feeling for their Island home. See life and bibliog. by Richard Walser, 1953; BKH's autobiography, *Southern Savory*, 1964.

Harris, Bertha, novelist, b. 1937 in Fayetteville, NC, da. of Mary (Jones) and salesman John Holmes H. After a BA in English from Women's College of the Univ. of NC, 1959, she moved to NYC, where she did clerical jobs for five years; married in 1963, she divorced a year later. She edited and proofread to support her daughter and wrote a novel, *Catching Saradove*, 1969, which earned her a MFA from the Univ. of NC. Its protagonist (like its author) has a Southern childhood, bitterly discordant lower-class parents, and Greenwich Village relationships with lesbians and a radical young man whose child she bears and raises. Many of BH's recurring themes and techniques appear: marginalized women, manipulation of chronology, dislocations of plot and language. *Confessions of Cherubino*, 1972, called by *The New Yorker* 'ultra-violent comedy', centres on a Southern college student: cross-dressing (as Mozartian page-boy, as dead father) focuses her exhilarations, desolations, and confusions. *Lover*, 1976, a demanding, experimental novel, begins each chapter with a story of female saints, counterpointing the voices of a community of different generations, mothers and daughters; but beginnings here are multiple, on 'all sides at once', and characters have many aspects, or merge into each other, as do 'I' and 'she'. *Lover* was greeted as an 'archive of lesbian experience and values', of times and places 'where women know themselves without reference to men', and by Catharine STIMPSON as 'polymorphic, amorphic, transmorphic, and orphic'. *The Joy of Lesbian Sex*, 1977, co-written with Emily L. Sisley, was the first commercially published book on its topic, subtitled as 'tender and liberated', but restricted to adult purchasers. Alphabetical entries treat 'pleasures and problems' with openness, partisanship and wit; female eroticism is celebrated. BH has taught at East Carolina Univ., the Univ. of NC at Charlotte (as head of creative writing) and the College of Staten Island of the City Univ. of NY (co-ordinator of women's studies), and edited for the feminist press Daughters, Inc., whose writers include Rita Mae BROWN. 1975.

Harris, Claire, poet and editor, b. in 1937 in Trinidad, da. of Gladys Claire (Cardinal) and Conrad K. H. She studied at St Joseph's Convent, Port of Spain, at Univ. College, Dublin (BA in English 1961), UWI (Post-graduate Diploma in Education 1983) and the Univ. of Nigeria, Lagos (Diploma in Mass Media and Communications 1975). She migrated to Canada, 1966, taught school in Calgary (cf. Farida KARODIA), edited a set of posters, *Poetry Goes Public*, 1976–9, and became poetry editor of *Dandelion*, 1981, and a founding editor of *Blue Buffalo*. She sees Afro-Canadian writers as 'working without a net' in an ethnocentric society: she is herself 'deeply embedded in the black earth of the West Indies' and much influenced by West Indian folk tales, Spanish surrealists, and Adrienne RICH. *Fables from the Women's Quarters*, 1984, her first book, won the Commonwealth Prize for the Americas area: its prose and short-lined long poems are often double-voiced. 'Where the Sky is a Pitiful Tent' juxtaposes sensuous tropical lyrics and the brutal oral testimony of Guatemalan revolutionary Rigoberta Menchú. The poems in *Translation into Fiction*, also 1984, search for a 'new naming' to counteract her representation 'in films and books / [where I ...]find myself / always here / stripped to skin and sex'; those in *Travelling to find a remedy*, 1986, 'test the frail bridge of words / [which] anchors us / islands / in our separateness'. *The Conception of Winter*, 1988, resolves to invent passion 'beyond / the circling of tongues As the cold rage / which changes something'. CH is anthologized in *The Penguin Book of Caribbean Verse in English*, 1986, and *Poetry by Canadian Women Poets*, 1989. See her essay in Neuman and Kamboureli, 1986.

Harris, Corra (White), 1869–1935, novelist and journalist, b. Farm Hill, Georgia, da. of Mary (Mat[t]hews) and Tinsley W. She was educ. at home and at the Elberton Female Academy, Ga., and a small school in Old Salem, Va. While teaching there, in 1886 she m. Lundy Howard H., a Methodist divinity student and later professor of classics at Emory College (d. 1910). In 1899 her husband's mental state deteriorated and she returned to teaching. The same year, as a lifelong defender of lynching, she wrote a denunciation of black men to the *New York Independent* and was hired as a book reviewer and invited to submit similar articles on black women and children. Her first novel, *The Jessica Letters*, written jointly with Paul Elmer More, was serialized in 1903. This was followed in 1910 by *A Circuit Rider's Wife*, based on her own early experiences, which appeared in the *Saturday Evening Post* and achieved immediate and enormous success. A recurrent theme is the problem of the weak or unfaithful husband, as in *Eve's Second Husband*, 1911 (in which patient loyalty, not divorce, is offered as the solution), while other novels, such as *Making Her His Wife*, 1918, deal with the young woman 'tamed' to marriage. She also wrote satirical novels such as *The Co-Citizens*, 1915, in which feminists are main targets. Altogether she wrote 14 novels, two collaborations, several vols. of autobiography and travel writing and hundreds of articles and columns. Her conservative moral code and traditional rhetoric of womanhood and religion brought her great popularity. See John E. Talmadge, 1968, for her life.

Harris, Emily Marion, 1844?–1900, novelist and children's writer, one of the large family of Aaron Lascelles H. She lived in London (a friend of the Rothschild family and of Robert Browning), but her pictures of Jewish life in a cathedral city suggest some autobiographical element. In *Echoes*, 1872, the narrator relates tales of her childhood and earlier generations; EMH often writes of music, and of the eighteenth century. The protagonist of *Mercer's Gardens*, 1876, is seen with loving irony as an ambitious schoolgirl poet (some of her efforts printed here reappear in EMH's *Verses*, 1881) before achieving independence through journalism. EMH wrote of her faith in *Estelle*, 1878, and *Benedictus*, 1887, whose heroine gets into trouble in her Jewish family over her photos of Renaissance madonnas: she realizes her ambition to be a painter, but dies young, mourned by the Gentile lover who had 'readily consoled' himself elsewhere. *The Lieutenant: A Story of the Tower*, 1882, spans several generations in presenting friendships of older with younger; *Lady Dobbs*, 1890, is an effective and credible portrait of a dislikeable woman. *Within a Circle*, 1880, contains essays on London Jewry; *The Narrative of the Holy Bible* [or Old Testament], 1889, composed with rabbinical advice, follows a long tradition (cf. Adelaide O'KEEFFE) of novelistic treatment of scripture. *Rosalind, The Story of the Three Parrots*, 1895, is a delightful, non-moralizing novel for children. EMH often published with her initials; the BL catalogue wrongly gives her a highly Christian work of 1854 by a different E. M. H.

Harris, Miriam (Coles), Mrs Sidney S. Harris, 1834–1925, novelist, b. Dosorrs Island near Glen Love, NY, da. of Julia Ann (Weekes) and Butler C. Educ. at religious and private schools, she initially wrote for periodicals. Her bestseller, *Rutledge*, 1860, was the first fully developed US 'GOTHIC romance' (N. Baym, 1978). The novel reinforces patriarchal values and presents the young, unnamed female narrator as the chattel of the older man, Rutledge. To link them eternally, he locks her into a bracelet. '"I don't altogether like the idea", I said, obeying him nevertheless, and arranging the key on his chain. "You should have thought of that before", he said with a laugh. "It is too late to retreat."' (p. 104). Other popular novels such as *Louie's Last Term at St. Mary's*, 1860, *Frank Warrington*, 1863, *A Perfect Adonis*, 1875, present similar abnegating heroines experiencing powerlessness and masochism. Of literary interest are *The Sutherlands*, 1862, an early pro-slavery novel, and *Richard Vandermarck*, 1871, one of the earliest portrayals of the Wall Street businessman hero, while *Happy-Go-Lucky*, 1881, examines lower-class poverty and prejudice against Irish immigrants. Her last three novels also treat social and topical issues such as extra-marital sex. After her husband's death in 1892, she spent her remaining years in Europe, producing a book on her travels in Spain.

Harrison, Constance (Cary), 1843–1920, novelist, journalist and short-story writer, b. Lexington, Ky, da. of Monimia (Fairfax) and Archibald C., lawyer and schoolmaster. His mother, Virginia Randolph C., also pub. at least two books. CH was educ. at Miss Jane Kenah's School, Cumberland, Md., and studied Latin with the local rector. After her father died in 1854, the family lived at Vaucluse, near Arlington, Va., her maternal grandfather's estate, where she had a French governess and later attended the school of Hubert Lefebre in Richmond, Va. Although the Vaucluse slaves had been freed, the family sympathized with the Confederacy. CH pub. her first work, a fictional 'Blockade Correspondence', in the *Southern Illustrated News*, 1864. In 1867 she m. Burton Norvell H., a lawyer who had been Jefferson Davis's private secretary, and they settled in NYC, where CH took part in amateur theatricals and served as a hospital volunteer. Her first short story, 'A Little Centennial Lady', was pub. in 1876 in *Scribner's Monthly*, to which she also contributed articles for the series 'Battles and Leaders of the Civil War'. From 1890 to 1920 she pub. a variety of works, including novels and short stories dealing with the South, such as *Flower de Hundred: the Story of a Virginia Plantation*, 1890, and *A Daughter of the South, and Shorter Stories*, 1892; a novel gently satirizing New York society, *The Anglomaniacs*, 1890; a translation from the French, *Short Comedies for Amateur Players*, 1889; and a work on decorative art, *Woman's Handiwork in Modern Homes*, 1891. She also wrote *Externals of Modern New York*, 1896, a supplementary volume to Martha J. Lamb's *History of the City of New York*. Her etiquette book *The Well-Bred Girl in Society* appeared in 1898. In 1911 she pub. her *Recollections Grave and Gay*, which gives a valuable historical account of life in Richmond during the Civil War. The Harrison family papers are held at the Library of Congress.

Harrison, Elizabeth, miscellaneous London writer. Having seen and enjoyed John Gay's tragedy *The Captives*, she pub. with her name *A Letter* praising it, 1724, with critical comment on characters, plot, sentiments, etc., and a poem to its patron the Princess of Wales. She favourably contrasts Gay's women, both good and bad, with those of other playwrights, and seems to hope for a reply. She may be the teacher who wrote *The Friendly Instructor*, 1741, moral dialogues for children, prefaced by Philip Doddridge (friend of Elizabeth SCOTT of Norwich), long highly popular. In 1756 she collected and pub., to raise money for her ailing old mother, *Miscellanies on Moral and Religious Subjects, in Prose and Verse*. Its tales and letters mix wit, moralizing, and allegory. Samuel Johnson, who subscribed, reviewed it well and likened it to work by Elizabeth ROWE. It advertised EH's similar-sounding *Meditations*, untraced.

Harrison, Jane Ellen, 1850–1928, classical scholar and social anthropologist, b. at Cottingham, Yorks., third da. of Elizabeth Hawksley (Nelson), who died 'almost at my birth', and Charles H., a merchant trading with Russia. Educ. till 17 by governesses (one soon became her stepmother), she learned Felicia HEMANS by heart and made a cult of Lady Jane GREY. At Cheltenham Ladies' College she earned three guineas from the RTS for a tract, 'Praying for Rain'. She studied classics at Newnham Hall, Cambridge, 1874–9: a visit by George ELIOT to her room made her 'almost senseless with excitement'. She then lived in London, studied Greek art at the BM, and lectured there and in boys' schools. *The Myths of the Odyssey in Art and Literature*, 1882, uses vases and engraved gems to supplement the evidence of texts. Gilbert Murray judged that *Mythology and Monuments in Ancient Athens*, 1890 (written after a visit there), was 'her first really important book', while *Prolegomena to the Study of Greek Religion*, 1903, and *Themis, A Study of the Social Origins of Greek Religion*, 1912 (especially disliked by the orthodox), 'transformed the whole approach' to their subject. From 1898 (already eminent, with honorary degrees) to 1922 JH lectured at Newnham. Many of her pamphlets (addresses to the Heretics Club; *Homo Sum, Being a Letter to an Anti-Suffragist from an Anthropologist* [1913], identifying women's claim to full humanity as the secret 'of the whole controversy'; *Peace with Patriotism*, 1915) are coll. in *Alpha and Omega*, 1915. She left England during WWI. By 1926 she felt she had softened her 'intemperate antipathy to the Olympians' and that her one-time heresies ('that gods and religious ideas generally reflect the social activities of the worshipper; that the food-supply is of primary importance for religion; that the *daimon* precedes the full-blown god; that the Great Mother is prior to the masculine divinities') had won acceptance. She influenced Virginia WOOLF (who sketched her as the great scholar Miss Umphleby in *Jacob's Room* and published her *Reminiscences of a Student's Life*, 1925), T. S. Eliot, and D. H. Lawrence (see Keith Sagar, *D. H. Lawrence: Life into Art*, 1985). She lived latterly with Hope MIRRLEES, novelist; they translated works from Russian (a passion with JH) in 1924 and 1926. Several recent reprints; vividly creative letters to Murray (now at Newnham), ed. with linking narrative by Jessie Stewart, 1959.

Harrison, Susan Frances (Riley), 'Medusa', 'Gilbert King', 'Seranus', 1859–1935, poet, journalist, novelist, short-story writer, musician. She was educ. in Toronto, where she was born, and Montréal, where she developed an interest in Québec history, folklore, and culture, becoming a specialist on old French-Canadian folk songs. She began publishing at 16. In 1879 she m. John W. F. H., a musician, with whom she had two children, and lived in Ottawa until 1887, then Toronto, where for 20 years she was principal of the Rosedale Branch of the Conservatory of Music. Her poems, reviews, stories, and essays appeared widely. She was correspondent for the *Detroit Free Press* and the Toronto *Globe*, editor of the *Week*, and for several years editor of the Toronto *Conservatory Monthly*. *Crowded Out! and Other Sketches*, 1886, stories reflecting Edgar Allan Poe's influence, are often set in French Canada, as are SH's two novels, *The Forest of Bourg-Marie*, 1898, and *Ringfield*, 1914. *Pine, Rose, and Fleur de Lis*, 1891, her first volume of poems, includes a sequence of Quebec travel poems and a monody on Isabella Valancy CRAWFORD. She also wrote words and music for several songs and an opera. Well known in late nineteenth-century Canada and well received internationally, SH is valued today for her mastery of the villanelle and for her part in the post-Confederation search for an authentic Canadian voice and themes.

Harrison, Susanna, 1752–84, religious, labouring-class poet. B. to poor parents near Ipswich, she taught herself to write and worked in service from the age of 16 until struck at 20 by undiagnosed illness expected to be fatal. *Songs in the Night* (title from the Book of Job), 1780, were pub. anonymously as sung at her mother's house while awaiting death; an unascribed preface explains her financial need. SH expresses conventional sentiments in vigorous, musical, hymn-like movement. Later eds. (15 by 1823) added more poems and a recommendation to 'those whose circumstances in life do not admit of much reading besides the Bible'.

Harrod, Frances (Forbes-Robertson), 1866–1956, novelist, b. London, youngest of 11 children of Frances (Cott) and John F-R., art critic. Brought up in a household where visitors included Rossetti, Swinburne and Madox Brown, she trained at the Royal Academy, the Slade School and with Frank Brangwyn. She went on the stage in 1873 to earn money since the family was in financial difficulties. In 1900 she m. H. D. H., and had one son, the economist Roy H. She pub. short stories and long fiction from 1888: her novels, including *The Potentate*, 1898, *The Taming of the Brute*, 1905, *The Wanton*, 1909, and *The Triumphant Rider*, 1925, usually historical romances, include spirited, independent heroines 'of hot blood and changing moods'. Her most powerful work, *The Hidden Model*, 1901, gives a picture of the Tite Street studio of the painter G. P. Jacomb-Hood, and tells of an artist who conceals a beautiful mistress.

Harrower, Elizabeth, novelist and short-story writer, b. 1928 in Sydney, NSW, da.

of Margaret (Hughes) and Francis Sharp H. She had a turbulent childhood, growing up in the industrial city of Newcastle, as reflected in her novel *The Long Prospect*, 1958. At the age of 12 she returned to Sydney, completed her educ. and worked as a clerk before travelling to Britain where she lived 1951–7. Intending to study psychology, instead she began writing. After returning to Sydney she has worked for the ABC, as a book reviewer and in a publishing firm but has not pub. much further fiction. EH's four novels are intense studies of psychological conflict, usually between men and women. *Down in the City*, 1957, charts the unsuccessful marriage of an upper-class woman and a working-class man. *The Long Prospect* deals with the struggle of a young, intelligent girl to progress beyond her philistine environment and relatives. *The Catherine Wheel*, 1960, set in London, deals with the destructive power of love and has been compared with H. H. RICHARDSON's *Maurice Guest*. In *The Watch Tower*, 1977, the evil character is again male, something of a suburban Bluebeard. For discussions of her work see Carole Ferrier in Shirley Walker, ed., *Who is She?* 1983, and Frances McInherney in *Hecate*, 1983.

Hart, Julia Catherine (Beckwith), 1796–1867, first Canadian-born novelist. She was b. in Fredericton, NB, da. of Julie-Louise (LeBrun Duplessis) – whose father, Jean, had been on Montcalm's staff – second wife of Nehemiah B., a loyalist who became prosperous in shipping and shipbuilding. JCH wrote her first novel at 17, moved to Kingston, Upper Canada, to live with an aunt, 1820, and there, 1822, m. George Henry H., an English bookbinder with whom she had six children. For two years she ran a girls' boarding school. By 1925 the Harts had moved to Rochester, NY, and by 1831 to Fredericton, where he was employed by the New Brunswick Crown Lands Office and she continued to write, contributing short fiction to the *New Brunswick Reporter and Fredericton Advertiser*. Her mother adopted her husband's Wesleyan Methodism, but had a Roman Catholic, French-Canadian background which provided the basis for JCH's *St Ursula's Convent*, published by Hugh C. Thomson, Kingston, 1824, first novel published in British North America. The story of a nun eventually united with her long-lost husband and children, it is, in the manner of the day, episodic, with a complicated, melodramatic, highly coincidental plot, and shifting scenes. Québec, where JCH often visited her mother's relatives, is well realized; France and England, which she knew only through reading, are frailer. Like JCH's second novel, *Tonnewonte; or, the adopted son of America*, 1824–5, which contrasts the inequality of the old world with the freedom of the new, it is highly moral in tone and evinces an interest in both history and nature. In the preface to *St Ursula's Convent*, JCH views her fiction as part of a literary awakening, urging the new country to 'cherish native genius in its humblest beginnings' so that encouragement of such works as hers 'may elicit others of real and intrinsic merit'. A third novel, 'Edith; or, the doom', was never published.

Hartog, Diana, poet, freelance carpenter and electrician's helper. Da. of Robin (Lane) and Charles H., she was born in 1942 in Palo Alto, California, and brought up in the Sierra Nevada mountains: 'the one true gift – after my birth – that my mother gave, taking her children from the city to the mountains to live'. M. in 1969 and divorced in 1982, DH has lived since 1971 in New Denver, BC, where she built her own house, with her daughter Selena. The forests of British Columbia, her 'proper place', figure prominently in her poetry. She was educ. at San Francisco State Univ., in creative writing (BA, 1965) and Interdisciplinary Studies (MA, 1974). Her thesis, 'The Structure of Insight:

Towards a Common Genealogy of Knowledge and Being', supervised by her influential teacher, Matthew Hudson, shows the effect on her thinking of Thomas Kuhn's *The Structure of Scientific Revolutions*. Although influenced by Hermann Hesse, Thomas Mann, Wallace Stevens, D. H. Lawrence – 'I took his scolding to heart as a woman, and cowered under it; now I realize that he was in truth talking to himself, as we all do' – and Phyllis WEBB, DH has displayed a distinctive poetic signature since the publication of her first book, *Matinee Light*, 1983, which established her reputation as a new poet already technically accomplished, 'unafraid of the lyrical and the imaginary', whose vision 'cuts across categories, even genres'. *Candy from Strangers*, 1986, solidified her presence as one of the strongest, most original female lyrical poets in Canada. History (personal and public) and aesthetics ('You handle rain beautifully. / Your shape reminds me of flesh, an organ / pressured into odd angles'), irony and humour ('I like to think we're God's slippers: / every time we decide to make love / He's already slipped his feet into the two of us') inform both her lyric and prose poems. Although she 'certainly would never call [her]self a feminist' ('My mind is not a feminist mind. I accept the fact that language is a tyrant and most probably male in gender. But I don't believe that tools dictate what I can build'), DH subtly deconstructs patriarchy by asserting her power while accepting the traditional female fear of the male. See Smaro Kamboureli and Brian Edwards in *Malahat Review*, 83, 1988, and Lola Lemire TOSTEVIN, *Brick*, 19, 1987.

Harvey, Jane, b. 1776, Tyneside poet and novelist, da. of Elizabeth and Lawrance H. of Barnard Castle. She pub. by subscription at Newcastle *A Sentimental Tour* of that city by 'a Young Lady', 1794 (sections like 'The Theatre Royal', 'Merchants' Court', 'Tea', 'Supper', with sprightly talk on topics including women and politics), and *Poems on Various Subjects*, 1797, ranging from a sentimental ballad written at the age of 15, to praise of Anna SEWARD, Charlotte SMITH and Helen Maria WILLIAMS, and romantic Spenserian stanzas about her childhood. Her dozen anonymous novels, mostly pub. at London, are well-told tales rich in unusual detail. *Minerva Castle*, 1802, and some others, were pub. by MINERVA. *The Castle of Tynemouth*, 1806, set in the fifteenth century, includes the narrow escape of a woman who detests witchcraft from being burnt for it. *Memoirs of an Author*, Gainsborough, 1812, closes as the hero publishes, by her dying wish, his admired aunt's massive work on 'Zingis Khan' and all the Eastern empires. *Brougham Castle*, 1816, contrasts the gendered discourse of a pedantic husband (hard words and Greek military history) and down-to-earth wife (dialect and local gossip): he abuses women's ignorance when she calls Cyrus, the hero, Ceres. After *The Ambassador's Secretary*, 1828, and little volumes of verse and tales for children, JH ended with *Fugitive Pieces*, 1841, which mixes charming friendship poems, tough political support for striking Tyneside keelmen and exploited female tailors, a witty and comical welcome to 'the railroad', and an elegiac 'Conclusion' of 1840. She was probably related to Margaret H., who ran a boarding school at Bishopswearmouth, and pub. a long poem and melodrama (1814, 1822) on the sixteenth-century history of the Percy family.

Harwood, Gwen (Foster), poet, librettist, b. 1920 in Taringa, Queensland, da. of Agnes (Jaggard) and Joseph F. Educ. at Brisbane Girls' Grammar School, she studied and later taught music. She moved to Tasmania following her marriage to linguistics professor William H. in 1945 and a new career as a housewife and mother of four children. Her frustrations are reflected in many of her poems, such as the well-known 'Suburban Sonnet' and 'In the Park', chilling testaments to the annihilation of women's creative energies under the grind of domestic cares. GH began writing poetry in her late 30s, when ill in hospital. Her first collection, *Poems*, 1963, was followed by *Poems: Volume Two*, 1968, *Selected Poems*, 1975, *The Lion's Bride*, 1981, and *Bone Scan*, 1989. Themes of music and philosophy dominate her poetry, in which the belief in order through art is constantly implied; her lyrics are disciplined and restrained. Many of GH's poems were originally pub. under male pseudonyms and she has written a number centred on two male characters, the ageing nuclear physicist Professor Eisenbart and the alcoholic expatriate musician Professor Krote. Such masks contribute to the apparent impersonality of her poetic vision. GH has also written five opera librettos for the Australian composer Larry Sitsky and has collaborated on pieces with other composers. Her poetry has attracted various important awards; helpful discussions of her work may be found in Jennifer Strauss, *Meanjin*, 1979, and Elizabeth Lawson, *Southerly*, 1983. See also R. Sellick, ed., *GH*, 1987.

Harwood, Isabella Neil, 'Miss I. H.', 'Ross Neil', 1838?–88, novelist and dramatist, da. of Philip H., editor of the *Saturday Review*. Her mother was a Neil. Presumably born in Scotland, she spent most of her life in England, living with her father till his death in 1887. She produced a series of successful novels anonymously, including *Abbot's Cleve*, 1864, *Carleton Grange*, 1866, *Kathleen*, 1869 and *Raymond's Heroine*, 1867. *Carlton Grange*, absurdly plotted, centres on swapped identities; at one point the heroine's 'father', lover and real grandfather all exclaim 'Mine!' simultaneously. *The Heir Expectant*, 1870, set in the 1840s, is better written but still clichéd, though it has an interesting spinster heiress character, and argues for the superiority of a brother's love over a husband's. IH later turned to verse drama and wrote 14 plays under the name 'Ross Neil'. These include *Lady Jane Grey*, 1871, *Lord and Lady Russell*, 1876, and *Andrea the Painter*, *Claudia's Choice*, *Pandora*, all 1883. *Elfinella* was produced at the Princess's, Edinburgh, 1875, and then at Princess's, London, 6 June 1878; *Inez* at the Gaiety Theatre, 1887 as 'Loyal Love'. IH died at Hastings.

Hatch, Mary R. (Platt), 1848–1935, novelist, short-story writer and playwright, b. New Hampshire, da. of Mary R. (Blake) and Charles Grandison P., farmer. She was educ. at home and at the Stratford, NH, public schools, and the Lancaster, NH, Academy. She first published in her teens, as 'Mabel Percy'. In 1871 she m. Antipas Morton H., a farmer. Besides contributing numerous TEMPERANCE tales and romances to popular magazines such as *Frank Leslie's Illustrated Newspaper*, she also wrote mystery novels. *The Strange Disappearance of Eugene Comstocks*, 1895, was the most popular, despite a negative review in the *New York Times*. Its heroine is a captivating villainess who finds female roles insupportable and so becomes 'Eugene Comstocks' or 'Captain Dandy'. Much of MH's fiction is set in the New England countryside and includes believable rural characters. She moved to Boston and attended a playwriting workshop at Radcliffe. Her last published works were two plays, *Mademoiselle Viviane* and *Mrs Bright's Visitor*, both written in 1927. She also wrote some screenplays.

Hatton, Ann Julia (Kemble), also Curtis, 'Ann [or Anne] of Swansea', 1764–1838, novelist, da. of the Protestant Sarah (Ward) and Catholic Roger K.: younger sister of Sarah Siddons. She taught herself to write; her father's theatrical company in Brecon acted a play she penned at 11; but (because, she felt, of her squint and limp) her family mocked her as 'the Genius', and apprenticed her to a mantua-maker. M. in 1783 to an actor named Curtis, she soon found him to be a bigamist: she earned by lecturing on women in society for the quack James Graham (not, it seems, as his nude 'Goddess of Health'), and also began publicly advertising her poverty and her relations' wealth. That year she pub. with her name *Poems on Miscellaneous Subjects*, dedicated to Georgiana Devonshire, with strong subscription list: mostly sentimental or gothic, some written at 14. She attempted suicide in Westminster Abbey, and was shot accidentally in the face in a bagnio, 1789: newspaper reports (perhaps by her) mentioned her immoral avocation and her 'uncommon intellect' and 'proud and strong mind'. In 1792 she married William H.; next year they went to New York, where he made musical instruments and she wrote librettos for *Needs Must*, 1793, and *Tammany, or The Indian Chief*, 1794 (a hit: songs often repr.), and met M. V. Faugeres, to whom she later dedicated *Woman's a Riddle*, 1814. Settled in Swansea about 1800, widowed in 1806, she wrote 14 novels, mostly for Minerva, between [1810] and 1831, and *Poetic Trifles*, 1811. She turned out good examples of every popular line: gothic nuns, social satire, moral progress, and every female stereotype (bossy wife, doting mother, crabbed old maid). Peter Haining prints as hers 'The Unknown, or The Knight of the Blood Red Plume' (*Great British Tales of Terror*, 1972). Unrealized literary projects mostly centred on family memoirs: MSS at the Folger Library.

Hauser, Gwen, poet and activist, b. 1944 at Medicine Hat, Alberta. Her volumes include *Poems from the Sun-Dance & Other Tribes*, 1972, *Hands Get Lonely Sometimes*, 1974, and *Danger, Women at Work*, 1979. She has worked in factories producing coffee, crisps and Canada Dry. Her work throbs with political anger and indictment of 'maleculture', 'male show-winism', rejecting orthodox political discourse: 'you read Marx and colonize / the bodies of women'; 'too bad Karl Marx wasn't a woman' to know 'the exchange value of sex'. The title-figure of *The Ordinary Invisible Woman*, 1978, living 'in a world of nowoman / (there are only "girls" / and someone's "old lady")', is 'your ordinary dyke', not pretty, not nice, not warm, besieged by the yelling and whistling of men, dreaming at night 'that she is huge / & men are invisible'; 'poem for Inez Garcia' (who killed a white rapist) relates her sentencing by judge and all-white jury 'for being a chicano a woman & angry'; 'poem for a liberal' complains, 'you raise & lower / your consciousness / like an elevator' while condemning hippies and people on welfare; 'woman-chant' begins 'i am at war there will be no mercy.' GH celebrates Alta (reading her in a laundrette instead of 'taking / the Laundry Ritual / SERIooOUSLY') and 'Jill Johnston & Kate Millett' (seen riding by with Wonder Woman).

Haven, Alice B., Emily (Bradley) Neal, later Haven, 1827–63, children's writer, b. in Hudson, NY, da. of Sarah (Brown) and George B. One of four children, she was adopted in 1833 by her uncle, a Baptist minister. Her education at a New Hampshire seminary was disrupted by bouts of total blindness. Her first story, pub. under the pseudonym 'Alice G. Lee', while she was at school, appeared in *Neal's Saturday Gazette*. She m. its editor, Joseph C. N., in 1846. Apart from *The Gossips of Rivertown*, 1850, witty sketches of human frailty, her work is didactic. Using the penname 'Cousin Alice', she brought out *Home Books*, a series of moral tales for children, including *No Such Word as Fail*, 1852, *Nothing Venture, Nothing Have*, 1855. Neal having died, she m. Samuel L. H. in 1853. They had four children, at whose request her *Home Stories* were posthumously pub. in 1869. She pub. 13 works, fusing domesticity and Christian virtue: a sick child is going 'home ... all the home such little boys as we can have. Did you know I am going to die?' (*Patient Waiting no Loss*, 1853). 'Cousin Alice's' life is by Cornelia H. B. Richards, 1865.

Havergal, Frances Ridley, 1836–79, poet and hymnist, b. at Astley, Worcs., youngest of six children of Jane (Head) and William Henry H., rector of Astley. She was taught by her mother, then by her eldest sister Jane Miriam (later Mrs Crane). Intellectually precocious (she began writing verse at the age of seven), she was a delicate child, and strenuous study was discouraged. Nevertheless FRH devoted herself to study and the spiritual life. She went to school in England and Germany and continued studying French, German, Greek and Hebrew, as well as contributing to various pocket books under the names 'Sabrina' and 'Zoide' (donating the proceeds to the Church Missionary Society). She taught Sunday School and in 1861 went to live with Jane to teach her two youngest children. She refused several offers of marriage because of her religious devotion. Her first pub. volume was *The Ministry of Song*, 1869. Her poetry and hymns were popular in evangelical circles. When her father died, 1870, she prepared his *Havergal's Psalmody* for press. She contracted typhoid fever in 1874 but eventually recovered. Her only piece of political literature was an anonymous leaflet published in response to the suggestion that the Bible be banished from Board schools. Two years before her death she wrote: 'I am not one of those terrible "strong-minded women", I think we have quite "rights" enough in proportion to our powers and position'. Her close friend Frances A. Shaw put out several vols. of her sel. poems. See the *Memorials of FRH* (including her 1859 autobiography and some letters) by her sister Maria H., 1880, and the rather patronizing memoir by T. H. Darlow, *FRH: A Saint of God*, 1927.

Hawke, Cassandra (Turner), Lady, 1746–1813, novelist, da. of Cassandra (Leigh), who was first cousin to Cassandra COOKE and to AUSTEN's mother, and of Sir Edward T. (called by Dean Swift 'friend of Apollo and the Muses'). She m., 1771, Martin Bladen H., later Baron H., and had six children. Frances BURNEY in 1782 found her 'extremely languishing, delicate, and pathetic': keenly admired by her family for a highflown, exclamatory MS novel; denying authorship of a play by Elizabeth GRIFFITH's husband. Pub. as *Julia de Gramont*, 1788, the novel was, said Burney, 'all love, love, love, unmixed and unadulterated with any more worldly materials'; it offers a meeting in a mausoleum, eager self-sacrifice to extremest paternal tyranny, and sentiment mocked by Elizabeth HERVEY's half-brother.

Hawkins, Laetitia-Matilda, 1759–1835, novelist and memoirist, b. in London, da. of heiress Sidney (Storer) and musical and biographical writer Sir John H., who, she says, brought up his children to think themselves valueless. With her brothers at school she was 'not *educated*, but *broke*' to family secretarial work for token payment. In her teens, knowing no '*honest* means' to raise money for 'a whim of girlish patronage', she pub. an anonymous novel (untraced, like others which followed, also unowned). Her conservative riposte to H. M. WILLIAMS, *Letters on the Female Mind*, 1793, was again anonymous. She used the novel-publishing incident in *The Countess and Gertrude, or Modes of Discipline*, pub. with her name, 1811, dedicated to H. M. BOWDLER as friend of Elizabeth SMITH. Its conservative-feminist preface expresses concern at the lack of employment for women; its story, slowed by much essay-like matter, traces the heroine from dirty child to young woman 'gasping for knowledge', scraping sustenance for her brain, and rejecting her first, noble suitor. In *Rosanne, or A Father's Labour Lost*, 1814, the heroine gradually makes a Christian of her atheist father. With her brother Henry, LMH wrote *Sermonets*, 1814, which *DNB* gives to him. Her *Heraline, or Opposite Proceedings*, 1821, is outstandingly rich and wide-ranging; *Annaline, or Motive-Hunting*, 1824, is unusual and provoking if not successful. Anne GRANT and Jane AUSTEN found her remarkable. *Anecdotes, Biographical Sketches,* *and Memoirs*, 1823 (begun in convalescence, ridiculed by Thomas De Quincey), and its sequel, *Memoirs* ..., 1824 (selecs. repr., 1926, 1978), though pedantic and rambling, comment acutely on many topics including some women writers. She pub. a translation from German, 1806 (good critical preface), and a devotional compilation, 1823, and left a MS book of her English travels.

Hawley, Beatrice, 1944–85, poet and social activist, eldest of three sisters. Her father was in the US consular service; childhood homes included Tuscany, Connecticut, Virginia, Rome, Trieste: 'I love to write in Italian and French and English, because they are all so different.' After TB as a child, she suffered emotional breakdowns in her teens and twenties (recorded with courageous perception in her diaries), later from systemic lupus, and lastly from cancer. Married early, she was twice divorced. Settled in Boston from the 1970s, re-married, she worked vigorously for social, political and peace causes. Among her surviving prose writing is the remark: 'Working out the hope for a few good poems (if I am very lucky and very very attentive) is the major focus of my conscious and unconscious work-life.' In *Making the House Fall Down*, 1977, 'The Cleaning Lady Thinks of Lizzie Borden' and 'Rules for the Cleaning Lady' recall her cooking and cleaning jobs held as a graduate student and then as a teacher. She often evokes the charged world of children (her own, her son's): 'We move back / and see the ring of trees / which keeps the wolves away.' *Nothing is Lost*, 1979, celebrates many women (Joan of Arc, Sylvia PLATH, women who weave and knit, women in prison, BH's two daughters who died as babies) and her Christian faith: 'Women priests, two-headed calves, / looking together at twice as many stars'; 'No one has seen an angel for years. / They are away, dancing and not dancing.' The first of 50 unpublished pieces in *Collected Poems*, 1989, describes BH's 'not harmonious' dealings with her muse; the editor, Denise LEVERTOV, a personal friend, notes the influence of Emily DICKINSON on BH's concrete images freighted with metaphysical meaning, her 'etheriality winged with honest-to-goodness feathers'.

Hawthorne, Elizabeth Manning, 1802–83, pedagogic writer, b. Salem, Mass., elder da. of Elizabeth (Manning) and Nathaniel H.; sister of the novelist NH. Virtually self-educated, she was 'a great genius', according to Elizabeth PEABODY. Although a recluse who spent all her life in or near Salem, she was well versed in current events. This is shown in her family correspondence and in her only two pub. works, both anonymous, the *American Magazine of Useful and Entertaining Knowledge*, 1836, and *Peter Parley's Universal History on the Basis of Geography*, 1837. Co-author with her brother, she probably did most of the writing. The latter was a great success, running to countless editions, but provided no remuneration for EH. Her 1850–1 TRANSLATIONS of Cervantes remained unpub. Her greatest monument lies in her LETTERS, where intelligent sensitivity to literature and the natural world is blended with a keen humour. An edition is to be pub. Material on her life may be found in Rose LATHROP's and Julian Hawthorne's biographies of Nathaniel, 1897 and 1885 respectively.

Hawtrey, Valentina, novelist, friend of Vernon LEE, whom she visited in Florence in 1900. Her novella *A Ne'er-do-well* (Pseudonym Library, 1903, as 'Valentine Caryl') features a musician brought up mute in solitude by his deaf and dumb mother. Next year she translated *The Life of Saint Mary Magdalene*, a fourteenth-century Italian work, called 'exquisite' by Lee, which presents Mary as unconventional, not promiscuous. *Perronelle*, also 1905, and *Suzanne*, 1906, first of seven novels proper, deal with the slavery of marriage and penalties of sexuality in late medieval France: an illegitimate child grows up imbued with his mother's sense of guilt; a young heir centres the varying bitterness of his grandmother, mother, betrothed and illicit wife. VH's sense of the varied predicaments of women grows richer and deeper in more recent settings: *Rodwell*, 1908, opens on the return home of a pregnant girl, and depicts a land-owning family as parasitical on wives taken for money; *In the Shade*, 1909, opens yet more arrestingly on a woman undeservedly acquitted of her husband's murder, who then marries an ex-swindler and adopts a stifling respectability from which their daughter at last escapes. Perhaps most powerful is *Heritage*, 1912, centred on the marriage, for an heir to his estate, of a violent misogynist. *In a Desert Land*, 1915, traces a Catholic family from Edward II's reign to the early eighteenth century; in an epilogue a modern descendant is about to become a nun.

Hayes, Alice, also Smith, 1657–1720, Quaker autobiographer, b. at Rickmansworth, Herts., brought up Anglican. When she was ill her 'tender affectionate' mother prayed that God might take her life for her child's, and then died. At 16, loving 'Dancing, Singing, telling idle Stories', AH went into service to get away from her stepmother; she was deeply but briefly moved by a Quaker woman preacher. After 18 months married to Daniel Smith, severe illness plunged her into spiritual distress: 'constant I was in resorting to the Steeple-House, but sorrowful I went in, and so I came out, Week after Week, Month after Month, seeking the Living LORD among the dead Forms and Shadows, who is not to be found there'. Her joining the QUAKERS brought anger, mockery, and abuse from her husband, in-laws, and priest, but after long firmness 'my dear Husband's Love returned again'. In 1696, after much thought, she challenged and routed this priest in his church. Widowed with five children, she refused to pay farm tithes and was jailed for 13 weeks: she expounds the legal niceties of the case with skill. Her life-story, mostly written in 1708 'for the Encouragement of the Young in Years to Faithfulness', does not mention her second husband (Thomas H., m. 1697, d. 1699) or her preaching travels in Europe. Pub. 1723 as *A Legacy, or Widow's Mite*, often repr.: see Catherine Blecki in *Quaker History*, 65, 1976.

'Hayes, Henry', Ellen Warner (Olney) Kirk, 1842–1928, novelist, essayist and short-story writer, b. Southington, Connecticut, da. of Elizabeth (Barnes) of the publishing family, and Jesse O., writer and geographer. Educ. privately, she wrote early, but she only began publishing after her father's death, with the widely acclaimed *Love in Idleness*, serialized by *Lippincott's* in 1876. In 1879 she m. *Lippincott's* editor, John Foster K. As well as essays and short stories, 28 more novels appeared, including her most successful, *The Story of Margaret Kent*, 1886, an account of a woman torn between love and duty. (It has been suggested that this is a fictional biography of Sherwood BONNER.) A recurrent theme in HH's work is the way money matters affect middle-class life, and both *Queen Money*, 1888, and *A Daughter of Eve*, 1889, were applauded for their examination of the influence of greed on contemporary society. Her characters were praised as 'true to life', but she believed 'Absolute realism ... to be out of the question' (*NY Times*, 29 April 1889), opting instead for romanticized characters and unoriginal plots.

Hayes, Catherine **'Kate' E.**, 'Mary Markwell', 'Yukon Bill', 1856–1945, poet, journalist, dramatist, local historian. She was b. at Dalhousie, NB. Her mother had been a teacher; her father, Patrick H., also a teacher, took the family to Prince Albert, North West Territories, 1879. KEH m. C. Bowman Simpson, 1882 (separated, 1889).

She moved to Regina, 1885, became the first woman to write for the *Regina Leader*, was Librarian to the Territorial Legislature, and worked to establish a library and a musical society. She moved to the *Manitoba Free Press*, 1889, and later worked for the *Ottawa Free Press*. In 1904 she was co-founder, with Kit COLEMAN, of the Canadian Women's Press Club, and its first president. As a result of her ardent support for women's SUFFRAGE, her common-law husband, Nicholas Flood Davin, introduced a motion in favour of it in the House of Commons in Ottawa, 8 May 1895. Her *Prairie Potpourri*, 1895, prose and poetry, was the first such work published by a North West Territories Press. The ribaldry of her *Darby Day at the Yukon* won Robert W. Service's admiration. She died on Vancouver Island.

Hayley, Eliza (Ball), 1750–97, translator and essayist, da. of Margaret and of Thomas Ball, Dean of Chichester. Her husband said her mother conceived her when crazy with selfless suppression of grief over the deaths of earlier children. After boarding school at Chelsea, she m. William H., the poet, in 1769, having negotiated on his behalf in an earlier, failed courtship. His *Memoirs*, 1823, facs. 1971, depict her as frigid, unstable, and manic depressive from about 1786; they separated three years later, but kept in touch; he had a son by another woman, 1790. E. O. BENGER admired her essays translated from Anne Thérèse de LAMBERT, 1780, with feminist preface; Charlotte SMITH wrote a poem to her; Anna SEWARD praised her literary and scientific interests. Her *Triumph of Acquaintance over Friendship, An Essay for the Times*, 1796, urges from a woman's viewpoint the value of 'common civility'.

Haynes, C. D., later Golland, MINERVA novelist. Her father, D. F. H., also published a gothic novel. Her first, *Castle Le Blanc*, is untraced; six long works survive. *The Foundling of Devonshire, or 'Who Is She?'*, 1818, sets her tone with a humble moralizing preface and heroine who suffers much (a minor character notes midway that she ought to be written about) before aristocratic marriage and reclaimed parents (through a birthmark): Pope's 'whatever is, is right' closes the tale. The opening of *Augustus and Adeline, or The Monk of St. Barnardine*, 1819, unites the key elements of 'horrid mystery': a veiled female form gliding among remote Italian ruins, with 'faint blue flame' and thrice-waved hand. In *Eleanor, or The Spectre of St Michael's*, 1821, set in Scotland, the heroine's 'fallen' mother dies on rediscovery. CDH m. before *The Ruins of Ruthven Abbey*, 1827 (misrepresented as parody in Frederick S. Frank's GOTHIC bibliog., 1987). It opens in a genteel Bloomsbury boarding-house where author Monimia Beauville reads passages from a romance-in-progress; CDH's married heroine, whose honour is unjustly impugned, has some 'straight' gothic experiences, like finding among the ruins texts relating to herself; Hannah MORE is quoted at the end. CDH became wordier in *The Maid of Padua, or Past Times*, 1835 (much quoting from Byron), and *The Witch of Aysgarth*, 1841.

Hays, Mary, 1760–1843, feminist and radical, da. of Rational Dissenters, b. in Southwark, London. With little education, she applied herself passionately to learning by letter from John Eccles. His death, 1780, threw her into 'widowhood': still reading avidly, she wrote memorial poems and fiction. In *Cursory Remarks*, 1791, by 'Eusebia', 'pursuing and embracing truth without partiality or prejudice, wherever it may be found', she argues for public worship but against an established church: she also wrote sermons for a dissenting minister. She met Mary WOLLSTONECRAFT in 1792. *Letters and Essays*, 1793, repr. 1974 (some coll. from journals; many moral fictions; two by her sister Eliza), treat materialism, Necessity, and feminist ideas, noting that women are more often liberal in politics than men. That year she left her mother's house to live by writing; letters reflect the intoxication of work and independence. Godwin provided epistolary counselling as she worked on *Memoirs of Emma Courtney*, 1796 (repr. 1974, 1987). Her heroine pursues knowledge, recognizes oppression, approaches and is rejected by the man she loves; her second-best marriage plunges her in melodramatic suffering, and leaves her longing to escape the tyranny of passion and to live by reason. MH's views and her depiction of her own unrequited love for William Frend made her a favourite target for savage reactionary abuse: from S. T. Coleridge, Charles Lloyd (another unattained lover), the *Anti-Jacobin*, Richard Polwhele, and Elizabeth HAMILTON. She defended Godwin in the *Monthly Magazine*, 1796–7 (see Burton R. Pollin in *Etudes anglaises*, 24, 1971). Her anonymous *Appeal to the Men of Great Britain in Behalf of the Women*, 1798, repr. 1974, deplores 'perpetual babyism' and urges vocational (though not professional) training and financial independence. In *A Victim of Prejudice*, 1799, another ideological novel, the heroine (whose mother was hanged for a crime of passion) refuses to marry a reformed rapist. *Female Biography*, 1803 (owned by Jane AUSTEN's sister-in-law), treats heroines before Wollstonecraft, whom MH tended on her death-bed and praised in obituaries. She taught, and pub. religious tracts, pedagogic fiction, and *Memoirs of Queens* (unfinished, 1821). MSS in the Pforzheimer Library (letters to Eccles and from Eliza FENWICK, ed. Annie F. Wedd, 1925, 1927). See Gina M. Luria in *Signs*, 3, 1977–8.

Hays, Matilda M., 1820–*c*. 1866, novelist, translator of George SAND, editor and feminist. Little is known of her life, but she was in the circle of radical thinkers surrounding the painter Samuel Laurence. Her first novel, *Helen Stanley*, 1846, is a plea for a woman's right to earn a living rather than prostitute herself into marriage. G. H. Lewes suggested she translate George Sand, to whom she was recommended by both Charles Macready and Giuseppe Mazzini. Six vols. appeared in 1847, ed. by MH and transl. with Eliza Ashurst, but the series ended abruptly due to inadequate support. During 1848–50 MH contributed to *Ainsworth's Magazine*, and in 1851 she travelled to the USA as the companion of actress Charlotte Cushman. There she met sculptor Harriet Hosmer, with whom she lived in Rome from 1852. In Italy she met Isa BLAGDEN, Sara LIPPINCOTT and E. B. BROWNING, who described MH as dressing like a man in jacket and waistcoat, and living in a house of 'emancipated women'. 'She is a peculiar person altogether, decided, direct, truthful' (EBB: *Letters to her Sister*, ed. Huxley, p. 196). MH returned to England in 1858, where she and Bessie Rayner PARKES jointly ed. the *English Woman's Journal*, to which she also contributed many articles, including one on Hosmer and one on Florence NIGHTINGALE. Another close friend from this time was Adelaide PROCTER. In 1865 her second novel appeared (postdated 1866). *Adrienne Hope: The Story of a Life*, draws upon her years in Italy and her social concerns about issues of women's work and property, treating the exploitation of a woman who unwisely contracts a secret marriage to a man who later marries another publicly. After his death the two mistreated wives sustain one another.

Hayward, Amey, religious verse-writer, of Lymington, Hants. *The Females Legacy*, 1699, 'Commended to all Godly Women', bears her name and a 'Panegyrick' by 'the Person who'll Protect her Poetry', B. H., probably a relative. She addresses the issues of salvation in quaint style: 'Help me to cleanse my Lamp about / from all the stinking Snuffs, / So that it may not Wiffer out / with any windy Puffs.' Many pieces (including the longest: 112 stanzas) are in dialogue; most speakers are male, but she twice addresses her own sex, who, she fears, may feel exempt from religious requirements. Closing stanzas disown another little book 'Publisht in my Name', but mostly not hers.

Haywood, Eliza (Fowler), 1690?–?1756, prose-fiction writer, dramatist, and journalist, whose life and some ascriptions (among nearly 70 works) are still obscure. Da. of a London shopkeeper, she says she lacked 'those Advantages of Education which the other Sex enjoy'; but she had more than most women. She m. the Rev. Valentine H. (at least 15 years her senior) and had a son; whether or not still married, she was acting in Dublin in 1714–17. She had a popular triumph with *Love in Excess, or The Fatal Enquiry* (three parts, 1719–20; six eds., by 1725), and in [1720] pub. *Letters from a Lady of Quality to a Chevalier* (transl.; her only work by subscription; one of many with postdated title-page). In 1721 she was disowned by her husband and revised a harem tragedy, *The Fair Captive* (her dedication says women writers must expect 'raillery'). In 1722 she issued two novels, the Penelope AUBIN-style *British Recluse* (two women betrayed by one man settle down together) and *The Injur'd Husband*, from a projected collection; the rest followed next year, with her comedy *A Wife to be Lett* and the first three volumes of her *Works*. In 1724 she hit her stride: ten titles, including *Works* iv (poems) and vol. i of *Memoirs of a Certain Island Adjacent to ... Utopia*. (She pursued the scandal chronicle in *The Court of Caramania*, 1727, which opens wittily on George II's alleged popularity and inexperience in love; the remarkable *Eovaai*, 1736, a princess's education in ugly political reality, mainly about Robert Walpole; and *The Invisible Spy*, 1755.) She compiled a life of Mary Queen of Scots, using 14 or 15 French works, 1725. Coarsely lampooned in 1727–8 in Swift's Corinna portrait (meant for her not Delarivier MANLEY) and Pope's *Dunciad*, she counter-attacked with a piece in *The Female Dunciad*, 1729, and *Some Memoirs of the Amours and Intrigues of a Certain Irish Dean*, 1728; but she was less prolific in the next decade and began newly to choose anonymity. She acted again in the 1730s, with Charlotte CHARKE in Henry Fielding's company. She exploited hits by others in (probably) *The Court of Lilliput*, 1727, *Anti-Pamela, or Feign'd Innocence Detected*, 1741, and adaptations of Fielding (his drama), 1733, and of Marivaux, 1742. *Life's Progress through the Passions, or The Adventures of Natura*, 1748, is an allegory. Responsive to the literary climate, she moved from erotic adventure to bourgeois morality. At first women are victims, 'loving, always loving' (Virginia WOOLF) or mouthpieces for legitimate anger (Mary Anne Schofield, studies, 1982, 1985). Later they are subjects for education: *The Female Spectator*, 1744–6 (part repr. 1929; see Helene Koon in *HLQ*, 42, 1978), *The Fortunate Foundlings*, 1744 (romance), *Miss Betsy Thoughtless*, 1751, and *Jemmy and Jenny Jessamy*, 1753 ('histories'), and *The Wife* and *The Husband*, 1756 (ADVICE). Always alert to the market, EH is still always intelligent and inventive. She learned well: her last works are probably her best. See life by George Frisbie Whicher, 1915; recent facsimiles and criticism.

Hazzard, Shirley, novelist, short-story writer, b. 1931 in Sydney, NSW, da. of Catherine (Stein) and Reginald H., a government official. She was educ. at Queenwood College, Sydney, then worked for British Intelligence in Hong Kong and at the British High Commission in Wellington, NZ, before moving to NY where she worked at the UN, 1952–62, serving in Italy in 1957. Married to the US critic and biographer Francis Steegmuller, she is now a US citizen. She has pub. many short stories, particularly in the *New Yorker*; some were collected in *Cliffs of Fall*, 1963. Two of her first three novels, *The Evening of the Holiday*, 1966, and *The Bay of Noon*, 1970, are set in Italy and deal with unhappy love affairs. She drew on her experiences at the UN for her second novel, the more satirical *People in Glass Houses*, 1967, and has also written a highly critical analysis of the UN's weaknesses, *Defeat of an Ideal*, 1973. Her reputation rests on her ambitious fourth novel, *The Transit of Venus*, 1980, which won the National Book Critics Circle Award and became a bestseller. It follows the fortunes of two Australian sisters as they travel to Europe, have affairs, work and marry, though definitely not from a feminist perspective. For a bibliography see *Texas Studies in Language and Literature*, 1983; feminist analyses of the reception and marketing of *Transit of Venus* are given by Delys Bird in *Westerly*, 1985, and Bronwen Levy in Carole Ferrier, ed., *Gender, Politics and Fiction*, 1985.

Head, Bessie (Emery), 1937–86, novelist and short-story writer. She was b. in Pietermaritzburg, South Africa, in the mental hospital where her Scottish mother, Bessie Emery, da. of a wealthy racehorse owner, was confined until her death, 1943, for becoming pregnant by a Zulu stable worker. Taken from her mother at birth, BH was brought up by a coloured foster family until she was 13, then given secondary education and teacher training in a Durban mission orphanage. She m. journalist Harold H., became active in African Nationalist circles, then left him and took her son into Botswana, 1964. She worked briefly as a journalist, for *Drum*, taught, and worked with other political refugees in the village garden co-op in Serowe, where she settled to write. She wrote her internationally successful first novel, *When Rain Clouds Gather*, 1969, with the support of a small grant from the World Council of Churches. Its plot reflects her experience: a South African refugee joins forces in a Botswana village with a strong local woman and a British agricultural expert to push back the desert, overturn a corrupt traditional establishment, and find peace of mind in an agrarian communal life. BH intended *Maru*, 1971, which portrays Margaret Cadmore, light-skinned like BH and despised because of her Masarwan (Bushman) origin, to be 'beautiful, like a fairytale, about an ugly subject, racism'. That year, BH suffered a massive mental breakdown. Her third novel, *A Question of Power*, 1973, 'my only truly autobiographical work', figures 'two worlds – the innocent and the consciously evil'. In the mental anguish of her protagonist – who hallucinates the men in her life as rapists, saviours, tormentors, and even Africa itself – surviving by her own power of will, BH represents 'the sufferings of rejected humanity'. *Ms* magazine published two stories, 'Witchcraft', 1975, and 'The Collector of Treasures', 1977, which includes several Botswana sketches. *Serowe: Village of the Rain Wind*, 1981, thought by Agnes Sam (*Kunapipi*, 1986) to be a guide to BH's work, is composed of local histories and personal interviews with 100 villagers. *A Bewitched Crossroad: an African Saga*, 1984, contrasts the narrated history of the great Botswana chief, Khama, with its modern setting: its teller, in the oral tradition of dignity and worth of the past, is the tribe's memory personified. When she died of hepatitis, BH was working on her autobiography. She has had great impact: 'in her concern for women and madness [she] has almost singlehandedly brought about the inward turning of the African novel' (Charles Lawson, *Books Abroad*, summer 1974). 1976 interview in Lee Nichols, *Conversations with African Writers*, 1981. See Taiwo, 1984 (quoted above), which is dedicated to her and Micere MUGO, Grace OGOT, and Buchi EMECHETA; and Charles P. Sarvan, in *Women in African Literature Today*, 1987. Commemorative volume, ed. Cecil Abrahams, forthcoming.

Heap, Jane, 1887–1964, editor, critic and painter, b. in Chicago, where she graduated from the Art Institute, 1905, and studied jewellery design at the Lewis Institute; she also studied painting in Germany. In 1916 she became Margaret ANDERSON's lover and co-editor of the *Little Review*. (JH was a cross-dresser, called 'male-identified'.) The *Little Review* (and its *Anthology*, 1953) contains her writings, but her contribution to it and to the 1920s literary renaissance remains inadequately explored. Though identified for readers only as 'jh' until 1922, she not only modernized its design and commissioned illustrations but also conceived its formula ('To express the emotions of life is to live. / To express the life of emotions is to make art'). Anderson gave her credit for its editorial policy and success. When in 1918 Harriet MONROE alleged that it was 'under the dictatorship of Ezra Pound', JH defended Pound and 'the interest and value of an intellectual communication between Europe and America'. JH visited Paris with Anderson in 1924, took over the now irregular *Little Review*, made it 'the American mouthpiece for all the new systems of art' (like Dadaism and Surrealism), and published the work of artists she exhibited at her NY gallery. She organized an International Theatre Exposition, 1926, and the Machine Age Exposition, 1927, calling the machine 'the inevitable expression of a splendid new art conforming to present-day achievements'. She then moved the magazine to Paris, where she studied with George I. Gurdjieff; in 1929 it ceased publication and she founded a Gurdjieff group in London, where she died relatively obscure. Anderson's appreciative autobiographies, 1930, 1951, 1962 (dedicated to JH), 1969, are the main source of information about her; studies of her milieu give her some mention (e.g. Benstock, 1986). Papers at the Library of Congress.

Hearne, Mary, novelist, perhaps pseudonymous, of Edmund Curll's stable. All 'her' works, from *The German Atalantis*, 1715, alluding to Delarivier MANLEY, seek to ally themselves with others' successes. *The Lover's Week, or The Six Days Adventures of Philander and Amaryllis*, 1718, and its sequel *The Female Deserters*, 1719 (adapted in 1720 as part of a novel collection: facs. of originals with Jane BARKER's *Love Intrigues*, 1973), are pornographic fantasy: a prefatory poem by the invented 'Joseph Gay' relishes the effect on the (male) reader. The heroines (transparently fictional despite the letter form and dropping of actual names; quite unlike such scandal-autobiographers as Manley or Laetitia PILKINGTON) reject brilliant marriages for illicit love, and can hardly endure a moment's absence from their men. Curll at first guessed that the statuesque woman offered as a prize in Pope's *Dunciad*, 1728, was meant as MH (rather than Eliza HAYWOOD).

Hébert, Anne, novelist, poet, short-story writer, playwright. She was b. in 1916 at Sainte-Catherine-de-Fossambault, Québec, da. of Marguerite Marie (Taché) and Maurice H., a literary critic and poet who encouraged his daughter to write, and cousin of poet Saint-Denys Garneau. As an adolescent, she studied in Québec City at the colleges of Notre-Dame-de-Bellevue and Mérici. Later she worked for Radio Canada and the National Film Board. Since the early 1950s she has lived in Paris. One of Québec's most celebrated authors and recipient of many awards, including the Prix Femina for her novel *Les Fous de bassan*, 1982 (*In the Shadow of the Wind*, 1983), AH first gained international acclaim with *Kamouraska*, 1970, now translated into several languages. Both have been filmed. Lyrical and gothic at once, they tell stories of passion, and violence, probing the inner recesses of the mind with stream of consciousness. In four decades of writing, from publication of her first poems, *Les Songes en équilibre*, 1942, AH has published six novels, two collections of poems (*Poèmes*, 1960, transl. 1975, and *Le Torrent*, 1963, transl. 1973), a volume of short stories, a collection of plays, a dialogue on TRANSLATION (with Frank Scott, 1970, preface by Northrop Frye), and many writings in various journals. Iconoclastic from the outset, she breaks the constraints of realistic discourse, contesting social and religious structures. Her novels and poems, which heralded a new writing in Québec, are intensely poetic, often marked by biblical undertones. Her prose speaks of the difficulty of women's relationships with fathers, husbands or lovers. See Delbert Russell, 1983, Janet Paterson, 1985, and Kathryn Slotte and Annabelle M. Rea in *Québec Studies*, 4, 1986.

Hedges, Doris (Ryde), poet and journalist. B. 1900 at Lachine, Montréal, da. of Edith and William Dawes R., she was educ. in Montréal, Switzerland, England and France. She served with the Red Cross and St John's Ambulance in WWI, and was decorated for distinguished overseas service. During WWII, while her husband (Geoffrey H., m. 1926) was overseas, she gave a series of radio broadcasts in Canada called, 'Wives Across the Waves'. She began her career with publication of a short story in the *London Graphic*, and went on to publish essays, short stories and poems in Canadian, US and English periodicals and newspapers. She published three works of fiction, *Dumb Spirit: A Novel of Montreal*, 1952, *Elixir*, 1954, and *Robin*, 1957, and at least five volumes of poems, from *Flower in the Dusk*, 1946, to *Inside Out*, 1971.

Heilbrun, Carolyn (Gold), 'Amanda Cross', novelist and critic, was 'born a feminist' in 1926 in East Orange, NJ, the 'absolutely unplanned-for' only child of Estelle (Roemer) and Archibald G., Jewish immigrants from Russia. She was educ. in private schools, then at Wellesley College, which later she recognized as 'in the nicest way, anti-Semitic' and 'for a women's college . . . marvelously uncommitted to the problems of women', then at Columbia Univ. (MA, 1951, PhD, 1959), where she is now Professor of English. In 1943 she married James H., a professor of economics; she had three children. Since the 1970s her critical work has focused on gender, marriage, the woman as hero, sex roles, and feminist re-evaluation of the canon, but she began as a student of literary modernism, publishing *The Garnett Family*, 1961, about the British literary family which includes Constance GARNETT, and books on Christopher Isherwood, 1976, and Lady Ottoline MORRELL, 1971. *Towards a Recognition of Androgyny*, 1973, launches her dismantling of ideas of 'masculine' and 'feminine', examining the androgynous ideal in writing from classical times to Bloomsbury. *Re-inventing Womanhood*, 1979 (quoted above), links her analytical task with personal experience. Female heroism is central to her, and the re-invention she looks for will come from telling the stories of heroic women. With Margaret Higonnet she edited *The Representation of Women in Fiction*, 1983. As 'Amanda Cross', CH has written eight mystery novels, which she describes as social comedies in the line of Dorothy SAYERS. Their protagonist is handsome, clever, possibly rich, certainly feminist Kate Fansler, professor of literature and amateur DETECTIVE, imaginative construct for 'reinventing womanhood'. Both 'ambitious and female', Fansler 'maps out . . . stages in a feminist negotiation of the canon'. The books in which she figures are learned, literary, political; *In the Last Analysis*, 1964, uses Freud to solve its mystery, and both *The James Joyce Murder*, 1967, which plays with reference to *Dubliners*, and *Poetic Justice*, 1970, her 'Auden book', hide solutions in embedded texts. Feminocentric texts appear in *The Theban Mysteries*, 1971 ('too much *Antigone* and a visit to Dorothy Sayers' Oxford') and *A Question of Max*, 1976, which vividly describes May SARTON's house by the sea. *Death in a Tenured Position*, 1981, dramatizes misogyny at Harvard; *Sweet Death, Kind Death*, 1984, and *No Word from Winifred*, 1986, ostensibly about a suicide and a missing woman, reveal 'women's changing social position and women's relationships with each other'. Interview in Cooper Clark, ed., *Designs of Darkness*, 1983. See

Helena Michi in *Mass. Studies in English*, 9, 1984, Jeanne Roberts in *Clues*, 6, 1985, and M. Reddy in *WRB*, 4, 3, 1986; also Reddy, *Sisters in Crime*, 1988.

Hellman, Lillian, 1905–84, playwright, memoirist, only da. of Julia (Newhouse) and Max H. Born in New Orleans, she grew up there and in NYC ('shabby poor until my father finally settled for a life as a successful travelling salesman'), had two years at NY Univ., and worked briefly for publisher Horace Liveright. After a short-lived marriage to Arthur Kober, she lived with detective novelist Dashiell Hammett until his death in 1961. She did scriptwriting for Samuel Goldwyn in the 1930s and 1940s (see B. F. Dick, *Hellman in Hollywood*, 1982). Her first play, *The Children's Hour*, 1934, based on a nineteenth-century case of two girls' school mistresses ruined when pupils accuse them of lesbianism, was a hit. Almost all LH's plays were filmed; this had two versions: 1936, as *These Three*, and 1962. After the poor showing of *Days to Come*, 1936, about labour struggles in an Ohio town, LH 'was so scared I wrote' *Little Foxes*, 1939, 'nine times'. It made her name (opera, *Regina*, 1949) with its vivid portrayal of greed and sibling rivalry among the Hubbard family of Alabama. After *Watch on the Rhine*, 1941 (her only play 'that came out in one piece'), and *The Searching Wind*, 1944, she went back to the Hubbards' childhood in *Another Part of the Forest*, 1947 (directed by herself), to 'make clear that I had meant the first play as a kind of satire'. *The Autumn Garden*, 1951, was her own favourite; *Toys in the Attic*, 1960, was much acclaimed. She also adapted works by Robles, 1949, Anouilh, 1955, Blechman (as *My Mother, My Father and Me*, 1963), and Voltaire (Leonard Bernstein's *Candide* operetta, 1956). She edited letters by Chekhov, 1955, and short fiction by Hammett, 1966, and held professorial posts. Her four volumes of memoirs notoriously circle the problems of memory, of ways of seeing the truth, reconstructing the past, and refracting the self through others. *An Unfinished Woman*, 1969 (National Book Award), describes her childhood, film work, travel in Spain during the Civil War, friendship with Dorothy PARKER, and Hammett's 'long last days'. *Pentimento*, 1973, 'A Book of Portraits', includes the story of 'Julia' (filmed in 1977), a childhood friend and anti-fascist (whose existence has been questioned), asking LH to smuggle $50,000 into Berlin in 1937. *Scoundrel Time*, 1976, on LH's confrontation with the 1950s House Committee on Un-American Activities, was also denounced as falsified. (LH responded to Mary MCCARTHY's charge of intellectual dishonesty with a $2,225,000 lawsuit: untried at her death.) *Maybe, A Story*, 1980, acknowledges fictionality. LH's *Collected Plays* appeared in 1972; reference guide to them by Mark W. Estrin, 1980; bibliog. by Mary Marguerite Riordan, 1980. Among much debate over her memoirs, see Martha GELLHORN in *Paris Review*, 79, 1981, Linda W. Wagner in *Southern Review*, 19, 1983, Anita Susan Grossman in *Clio*, 14, 1985. William Wright's life, 1987, is hostile, researched without LH's approval. *Conversations* with her ed. Jackson R. Bryer, 1986. Papers at Univ. of Texas.

Helme, Elizabeth, d. 1810 (not 1813 as usually said), teacher, translator, leading MINERVA novelist but published by others as well. She was b. near Durham; soon afterwards her father died, and she was brought to London, where she was educated. She m. William H. at 17 and had five children; he lost his money and became a schoolmaster at Brentford near London. EH is sometimes confused with her daughter, Elizabeth later Somerville, d. 1821, who succeeded her as head of the Brentford school and wrote children's books, beginning with *James Manners, Little John, and their Dog Bluff*, 1799. The elder's first sentimental romance, *Louisa, or The Cottage on the Moor* (rejected by the first publisher she tried) had five editions in

1787; of three titles in the same genre, *The Farmer of Inglewood Forest*, 1797 (seduction and betrayal of an innocent girl) was equally popular, reprinted into the nineteenth century. Though not primarily a GOTHIC novelist, she follows Ann RADCLIFFE into the middle ages in *St Margaret's Cave, or The Nun's Story*, 1801, facs. NY 1977, and later works. Her interest centres in personal morality and its relationship with class and wealth; her women are often spirited and independent-minded. Her many translations include lives of explorers and travel books, as well as Plutarch's *Lives*, 1795; her moral and educational works include histories of England and Scotland written as a 'father'. She sought aid from the RLF, 1801–9, and died in debt. Blagdon's *Flowers of Literature* gave a sketch of her in 1805.

Héloïse, 1100/1?–1163/4, French LETTER-WRITER (in Latin) and abbess. Taught first by nuns, then by the theologian Peter Abelard, she was said to know some Greek and even Hebrew. She became Abelard's lover, but wished to remain single and agreed to secret marriage only at his urgent demand. Her uncle's servants attacked and castrated Abelard, who entered a monastery in 1119; she also, in suicidal mood, took nun's vows. Soon after 1132, by now abbess of the Paraclete convent, she saw a copy of Abelard's autobiographical *Story of Calamities*, and began writing him her well-known letters. At first she voices undying love and demands re-examination of the past; in face of his sternly professional attitude, she asks for religious advice and a Rule designed for women. (His reply became the basis of a set of rules perhaps by her.) The letters (pub. Paris, 1616, London, 1718; fictionalized in French, 1687; further adapted in English, 1713; accurately transl. Betty Radice, 1974) were hugely popular, praised by CHRISTINE DE PIZAN and Marie de SÉVIGNÉ. H's changing myth (quite distinct from the actual, if shadowy, woman) informs Pope's poem, 1717; Judith MADAN's reply; Rousseau's *Julie, ou la nouvelle HÉLOÏSE*, englished as *Eloise*, 1761; a sketch by Anna SEWARD, 1805, novel by Helen WADDELL, 1933, study by Peggy Kamuf, 1982. Life by Enid McLeod, 1938, 2nd ed. 1971.

Hemans (pronounced Hemmans), **Felicia** Dorothea (Browne), 1793–1835, poet, b. in Liverpool, with Irish, German and Italian blood, da. of Felicity Dorethea (Wagner) and George B., merchant. In North Wales from 1800, she learned Latin, drawing, and (from her mother) modern languages; her memory was phenomenal. At 14 she pub. *Poems* (harshly received) and *England and Spain, or Valour and Patriotism*, a poem inspired by her two brothers in the Peninsular War. She declined to correspond with the young Shelley, but later did so with Joanna BAILLIE and Mary Russell MITFORD. In 1812, after publishing *The Domestic Affections*, she m. Capt. Alfred H., an Irish ex-soldier. After five sons and two more vols. of poems, he left her and went abroad, 1818. She put out a volume a year while bringing up (and supporting) her sons, wrote on foreign literature for the *Edinburgh Review*, 1820, and won poetry prizes. One of her tragedies was staged, 1823. Highly popular in the USA, where her poems appeared in 1825, she refused an editorship offered to her in Boston. She moved to Liverpool, 1828, and, in failing health, to Dublin, 1831, where she died after publishing *National Lyrics and Songs for Music* and *Scenes and Hymns of Life* (dedicated to Wordsworth), both 1834. The *Edinburgh Review*, calling *Records of Woman*, 1828, 'female poetry, infinitely sweet, elegant and tender', stressed the lyric and ignored the heroic, exotic, even violent: the celebration of Arbella STUART, Mary TIGHE, and vengeful, tragic heroines of European history, Indian and North American legend. FH's range took in flower poems and Welsh nationalism. Wordsworth mourned 'that holy spirit, / Sweet as the spring, as ocean deep'; George ELIOT admired her;

Rose LAWRENCE, 1836, and FH's sister (1839, in her *Works*) pub. memoirs. See *Poetical Works*, 1914; booklet by P. W. Trinder, 1984.

Heney, Helen, novelist, historian, social worker, b. 1907 in Sydney, NSW, da. of Amy Florence (Gullett) and Thomas William H., a prominent journalist. She was educ. at various private schools and the Univ. of Sydney (Dip. Ed. 1929, MA Hons. 1937), and obtained a dip. in social work in 1939. Whilst living in Poland 1929–35 she taught English, worked as a translator and for the British Embassy. During and after WWII she worked for the Red Cross and as a social worker in Australia and Europe before returning to Sydney to work for the Department of Education from 1948 to 1967. She has written an authoritative biography of the explorer Strzelecki, *In A Dark Glass*, 1961, and novels: *The Chinese Camellia*, 1950, *The Proud Lady*, 1951, *Dark Moon*, 1953, and *This Quiet Dust*, 1956, all portraying forceful or influential women and all distinguished by psychological insight. However, HH considers her most useful contribution to Australian literature to be in the area of social history with an emphasis upon women, as in the collection *Dear Fanny, Letters from Australian Women*, 1985, and her substantial earlier study of women between 1788 and 1822, *Australia's Founding Mothers*, 1978. MSS are in the Mitchell Library, Sydney.

Henley, Beth, Elizabeth Becker Henley, actress, playwright, screenwriter, b. in 1952 in Jackson, Mississippi, one of four das. of Elizabeth (Becker), and Mississippi State Senator and lawyer Charles Boyce H. As a child, BH watched her actress mother's rehearsals, played in Tennessee Williams's *Summer and Smoke* in the fifth grade, and wrote her first play in the sixth. She did a BFA at Southern Methodist Univ., 1974, and a year of graduate study in acting at the Univ. of Illinois, 1975–6. She wrote the one-act *Am I Blue* (produced 1982, anthologized 1983) as a sophomore, under the pseudonym 'Amy Peach'. In 1976 BH moved to Los Angeles, abandoned an acting career and, with the encouragement of friends, especially Stephen Tobolowsky, with whom she lives and who has directed her plays and co-authored screenplays with her, devoted herself entirely to playwriting. *Crimes of the Heart*, produced at the Actors' Theatre of Louisville in 1979, on Broadway in 1981, and filmed, 1986, won a Pulitzer Prize. It depicts the moving, comic, sometimes grotesque reunion of three sisters who, in kitchen-table conversation, reveal their feelings and predicaments and whose humour and affection for each other help them to cope with violence and despair. In *The Miss Firecracker Contest*, produced 1980, *Wake of Jamey Foster*, produced 1982, and *The Debutante Ball*, produced 1985, BH explores an unresolved mother-daughter relationship and registers the impact of Southern social rituals, from beauty contests to funerals. BH, who was early cast as 'Southern GOTHIC', looks in her characters for 'their strange mixture of primitive instincts, intellect and spiritual confusion'. *The Lucky Spot*, produced 1986, sets its comic characters in a rural dance palace. Interviews in John Griffin Jones, ed., *Mississippi Writers Talking*, 1982, and Betsko and Koenig, 1987 (quoted above); studies by Billy J. Harbin and Lisa J. McDonnell in *SoQ*, 25, 1987.

Henniker, Florence Ellen Hungerford (Milnes), the Hon. Mrs Arthur H., 1855–1923, novelist, b. London, da. of Annabella (Hungerford) and Richard Monckton M., later Lord Houghton, friend of Tennyson and editor of Keats. Educ. at home, she showed early literary ability. In 1882 she m. Hon. Arthur Henry H.-Major, an army Major-General. Her first novel, *Sir George*, 1891, about an uncle's doomed love for his nephew's fiancée, suggests the unpredictability of the future. Her themes are always pessimistic; in *Foiled*, 1893, a brutal husband kills himself when he learns of his wife's love for another and in *Second Fiddle*, 1912, a woman lives miserably first with her guardian then with her husband. FH frequently dwells on the transience and pointlessness of life, as in *Sowing the Sand*, 1898: 'Life passes – vain, obscure and dream-like'. She wrote two other novels, *Bid me Goodbye*, 1892, and *Our Fatal Shadows*, 1907, as well as three collections of short stories: *Outlines*, 1894, *In Scarlet and Grey*, 1896, *Contrasts*, 1903. The second of these contains the story she wrote with Thomas Hardy, 'The Spectre of the Real', which is about a romance between noble lady and poor officer. Her relationship with Hardy is treated extensively by R. L. Purdy, *Thomas Hardy: A Bibliographical Study*, 1954.

Henning, Rachel (later Taylor), 1826–1914, letterwriter, b. Bristol, England, eldest child of Rachel (Biddulph) and the Rev. Charles H. Left responsible for four younger children after her mother's death in 1845, in 1854 she went to Australia with her brother, Biddulph, and two sisters, but soon returned, homesick, to England. She returned to Australia in 1861 and the next year she and her sister Annie moved to their brother's Queensland station. She m. his overseer, Deighton T., ten years her junior, in 1866 and lived at various farms in NSW. The delightful letters to her sisters Etty and Amy, written between 1853 and 1882, were never intended for publication. As revealing of RH as they are of colonial life, particularly of rural Queensland, they first appeared in the *Bulletin* in 1951–2 and, as *The Letters of Rachel Henning* (ed. David Adams and illustrated by Norman Lindsay), 1969, are now regarded as classics of Australian non-fiction.

Henry, Alice, 1857–1943, feminist and journalist, b. Melbourne, Victoria, da. of Margaret (Walker), seamstress, and Charles H., accountant. Educ. by her mother and at Melbourne's Educational Institute for Ladies, she became a teacher and later a journalist. She wrote for leading Melbourne papers, 1884–1904, under her own name and pseudonyms, concentrating on social and political reforms. She worked for women's SUFFRAGE and many other radical causes, and was a friend of Catherine SPENCE and Vida GOLDSTEIN. In 1905 she visited England and the USA, where she was invited to lecture for the National Women's Trade Union League of America. She wrote *The Trade Union Woman*, 1915, and *Women and the Labour Movement*, 1923, and for eight years edited the League's official journal, *Life and Labour*, with the assistance of Miles FRANKLIN. In 1933 she returned to Australia, where her literary activities included the compilation in 1937 of a bibliography of Australian women writers. Her *Memoirs* were ed. by Nettie PALMER, 1944; her papers are in the National Library, Canberra.

Hensley, Sophia Margaretta (Almon) 'Gordon Hart', 'Almon Hensley', 1866–1946, poet, novelist. She is not, as has been thought, 'J. Trye-Davies'. B. at Bridgetown, Nova Scotia, a direct descendant of Cotton Mather, and da. of Sarah Frances (DeWolfe) and Henry Pryor A., she was educ. and travelled in England, France and the USA. She was an officer in the Women's Press Club of NYC, 1899. She had three children. Encouraged in her writing by Charles G. D. Roberts, under whom she studied, she published journalism, short stories, and novels in US, British, and Canadian periodicals. Her several vols. of poetry are graceful, well-crafted, unpretentious nature lyrics. *A Woman's Love Letters*, 1895, deals with a wide range of feelings; *Poems*, 1899, was privately printed. She returned to Nova Scotia, 1929. See Carole Gerson and Carol McIver in *CNQ*, forthcoming.

Hentz, Caroline Lee (Whiting), 1800–56, poet, dramatist, short-story writer and novelist, b. Lancaster, Mass., da. of Orphah (Danforth) and John W. She began writing in girlhood and as 'Mob Cap' for the *American Courier*. In 1824 she m. Nicolas Marcellus H., whose unsteady academic career and ill-health prompted her novel-writing. Her first novel, *Lovell's Folly*, 1833, was suppressed by her family as libellous; however, her poem addressed to President Jackson, 1836, achieved greater success and her prize-winning five-act play, *DeLara; or, the Moorish Bride*, 1843, was an instant hit. Her reputation was fully established with *Aunt Patty's Scrap Bag*, 1846. Aunt Patty is a striking exception among fictional heroines; aged, with a withered arm and numerous warts and moles, she reappears in *The Lost Daughter*, 1857. *Linda; or the Young Pilot of the Belle Creole. A Tale of Southern Life*, 1850, became an anti-abolitionist best-seller. Linda, motherless at eight, witness to terrifying scenes of violence and under constant pressure to marry her wild stepbrother, Robert, finds love, loyalty and trust with the black slaves and Indians who take care of her. The highly-praised *Eoline; or Magnolia Vale*, 1852, is a strong critique of marriages of 'compulsion', and Eoline discovers the bonds of 'sisterhood' with a severe headmistress (nicknamed 'The Colonel') in a ladies' seminary. *Helen and Arthur; or Miss Thusa's Spinning Wheel*, 1853, celebrates Miss Thusa, counsellor, sage and helpmeet, idol of children and dedicated spinster: 'I never saw the man I wanted to live with ... I must have my own way ... and there was never a man created that didn't want to have his'. CLH belonged to the same literary group, the Semi-Colons, as H. B. STOWE, and *The Planter's Northern Bride*, 1854, written in response to *Uncle Tom's Cabin*, defends plantation slavery, while *The Banished Son*, 1856, expresses CLH's view that 'Woman is appointed by God to trace the first characters on man's unwritten mind'.

Herbert, Dorothea, 1770–1829, Irish autobiographer, b. in the tower of Kilkenny, eldest child of the well-born Martha (Cuffe) and the Rev. Nicholas H. Three of her MS albums, 'The Orphan Plays and Various Poems and Novels', are lost; *Retrospections of an Outcast* was pub. 1929–30 with some of her own water-colours (vol. i reviewed by Virginia WOOLF). In a childhood full of fun and mischief, DH began learning to write in March 1772 and soon grew 'Book Mad'; at 'about the Size of a Small Monkey' she was 'grave and oracular as an Ancient Sybil'. From 1789 to 1795 she was alternately wooed and slighted by the enigmatic John Roe: an early exchange of looks in public was 'that black Instant' of rejection meeting despair, which 'united us in ... an Eternal Union sacred and sure'. Though he later m. another (whom she roundly abuses) she signs 'Dorothea Roe'. In 1795 her mainly comic poems were read by 'all the Literati' of Cashel; but by 1806, when her tale ends, she was confined and maltreated by her mother and some of her always-violent family. Her 'principal Solace' was writing: dirges for her dead father and eldest brother mention 'Flashes of Madness – Phrenzies wild ... Unhappy lucid Intervals between'.

Herbert, Lady **Lucy**, 1669–1744, devotional writer and prioress, da. of the Catholics William H., later Duke of Powis, and Elizabeth (Somerset), who wrote ballads (one certainly, one probably) on the 1679 plot involving her friend Elizabeth CELLIER. LH entered the English Augustinian convent at Bruges (chosen for its lack of family connections), made her profession in 1693, and became Superior in 1709. She published at Bruges several devotional compilations, beginning in 1722: ed. John Morris, 1873. 'Meditations' advise, 'Lastly endeavour to bribe the porters of heaven, which Saint Justinian says are the poor; give them large Alms, according to your abilities.' Her books bear the mark of her mind: thoughtful, dignified, serene, with no sense of female inferiority. LH persuaded her sister Lady NITHSDALE to write down her famous story.

Herbert, Mary Eliza, *c.* 1832–72, poet, novelist, essayist. B. in Halifax, Nova Scotia, da. of Catherine and Nicholas H., Irish immigrants, she began her career as a writer of romantic and commemorative verse. A strong supporter of regional writing, particularly women's, she founded the woman's literary periodical, *The Mayflower; or, Ladies' Acadian Newspaper* (which published her poetry, as well as her two novellas, *Emily Linwood; or the Bow of Promise*, 1851, and *Ambrose Mandeville*, 1852, before stopping publication in 1852. They described with considerable sentiment the pursuits of devout, honest female characters. The three subsequent published novels, also romantic and sentimental, persistently demonstrated the importance of women's purity. Though in her fiction and half-sister Sara HERBERT's 'the characters are drawn in too unresolved whites and blacks to be convincing, and moral earnestness is never leavened by humour', a novel such as *Belinda Dalton; or, Scenes in the Life of a Halifax Belle*, 1859 gives considerable detail on the financial difficulties of women in Victorian society, and some insight into the details of living in mid-nineteenth-century Halifax. A staunch Nova Scotia Methodist, MEH drew literary attention to church activity in Halifax by promoting and writing for *The Provincial Wesleyan*, 1840–70.

Herbert, Sarah, 1824–46, poet and novelist, half-sister of Mary Eliza HERBERT. B. in Ireland and raised in Halifax, NS, she was a Methodist and, through her short life, a campaigner for temperance. In 1843 she was running a school in Halifax, and the following year became editor of the temperance newspaper, *The Olive Branch*. Her first poetry was published in the *Morning Herald* and the *Novascotian*. Predominantly religious and didactic, it was well received in the Maritimes where 'Sarah' was briefly idolized. Her first novel, *Agnes Maitland*, 1843, describes a woman's descent into alcholism. Her second (published in *The Olive Branch*), *The History of a Halifax Belle*, 1844, illustrates, with much instruction, the domestic life of a mid-Victorian woman. SH died a Victorian death, a young woman with TB, and was celebrated partly because of this fate. Two decades later, some of her poems were collected and published as *Flowers by the Wayside*, 1865. Like her half-sister, SH is occasionally linked with other Maritime Irish writers.

Herberts, Mary, obscure fiction-writer who signs the preface to *The Adventures of Proteus, &c., A Sett of Novels*, London, 1727. Educ. above the female norm ('I can make a piece of Latin much better than a Holland Shirt'), she is now reduced to working as a (favoured) servant, and hopes by publishing 'to divert my Readers, and get Money my self'. She imitates, she says, English, French, and Arabian Nights tales; if encouraged, she will print her own life 'wrought into a Novel'. This, however, is not known. *Proteus* sets an eponymous traveller to relate tales grouped around two pairs of courtly lovers, a woman writer (the Countess Brillante), and an ineffectual Don Juan figure. The lovers undergo unlikely vicissitudes and debate various controversial topics; their eventual happiness is rudely broken by death. The Countess is mocked for vanity and a bombastic, involuntarily comic style. Yet some characters suspect she merely 'condescends to the reigning Taste'; and she is credited with writing the book's later, racier part, a series of slapstick punishments zestfully inflicted on the would-be rake by mostly middle-class women.

Herbst, Josephine Frey, 1892–1969, novelist and journalist, b. in Sioux City, Iowa, third of four das. of Mary (Frey) and William Benton H., who sold farm machinery. She read Frances BURNEY at 16, and took her BA in English at the Univ. of Calif., Berkeley, in 1918, after attending three other colleges with jobs between times. She then moved to NYC to pursue early literary ambitions ('I'd rather fail in story writing than succeed in anything else', she declared in 1913). After an abortion following her brief affair with Maxwell Anderson, and her closest sister's death from *her* abortion, JH moved to Berlin, where she worked on an unpublished novel, and a story printed in H. L. Mencken's *The Smart Set*, 1923. In Paris she met US writer John Herrmann, whom she m. in 1926. Her first two published novels, *Nothing Is Sacred*, 1928, and *Money For Love*, 1929, were enthusiastically reviewed by, among others, Katherine Anne PORTER and Ernest Hemingway. Her trilogy, *Pity is Not Enough*, 1933, *The Executioner Waits*, 1934, and *Rope of Gold*, 1939, repr. 1984, is an ambitious survey of the disintegrating effects of capitalism on a middle-class family (drawn from her own) and the historical events, from the Civil War to the 1930s, which structure lives and relationships. JH's political journalism increased in tempo in the thirties; for periodicals like *New Masses* and *Scribner's* she reported on the regimes of the USSR and Germany, on revolutionary struggles in Cuba and Spain, and on strikes in several states of the USA. By 1935 her marriage collapsed (the divorce was 1940), owing to her growing fame, her husband's Communism, and her lesbian passion for artist Marion Greenwood (which she had vainly tried to make a threesome of people 'very unusual and wise even for danger'). Porter was one of those laying political misinformation against JH in 1942 (resulting in dismissal from a government job). JH's later novels, the low-key *Satan's Sergeants*, 1941, and ambitious, philosophical *Somewhere the Tempest Fell*, 1947, are less remembered than *New Green World*, 1954, a celebration of pre-revolutionary naturalists John and William Bartram (London ed. introduced by Vita SACKVILLE-WEST). JH died of cancer, leaving unfinished multiple projected memoirs and fictions about writers she had known (who ranged from Porter and Genevieve TAGGARD to Jean GARRIGUE), with other MSS used by Elinor Langer in her life, 1984 (packed with information and some imaginative colouring). Sections appeared in *Noble Savage*, 1 and 3, 1960, 1961, and *New American Review*, 3, 1968. Largest archive at Yale Univ. (with bibliog. by Martha Pickering, 1968).

Heron, Mary, novelist and poet or poets. Living at Durham, MH pub. at Newcastle, 1786, with her name, *Sketches of Poetry* (preface pleading youth and 'confined education' to excuse inferiority to Thomson, Pope, 'or a ROWE *of my own sex*') and *Miscellaneous Poems*, which retains the preface but adds more pieces. The conventional poems, dating back to 1781, include nature-description, compliments, politics (she deplores Cornwallis's 'Capitulation in America') and an 'Address to Sensibility' ('A female softness is a female's praise'). *The Conflict*, Newcastle, 1790, an epistolary novel full of refined feelings and description, was repr. London 1793; in *Odes*, Newcastle, 1792, she apologizes for presuming to express (conservative) political views. It was presumably a different MH who set her name to *The Mandan Chief. A Tale in Verse* (London, undated; after George Catlin's *North American Indians*, 1841). This remarkable, ambitious work (not in *NUC*) opens by the Missouri, celebrating freedom; it thoughtfully idealizes the Indians, likening them to 'Homer's heroes'. '"The Elk"'s Musings' include 'The Red man filled, as its vast woods, the plain; / The whirlwinds rushed across, and few remain. / They were, – as massive white clouds on the sky; / Earth shadows of those clouds, their graves here lie.'

Herring, Frances Elizabeth (Clarke), 1851–1916, journalist, writer of fiction and non-fiction. B. at King's Lynn, Norfolk, da. of Harriet and John J. H. Clarke, she was educ. at King's Lynn and Reading, Berks. In 1874 she m. A. M. H., of New

Westminster, BC, and in 1876 became the first woman to obtain a Class A teacher's certificate in British Columbia. She worked for local journals, editing the *Home Circle* magazine and writing for *The Commonwealth*, and also for the Toronto *Globe* and other periodicals. Much of her writing consists of non-fictional or fictionalized accounts of life in western Canada. *Canadian Camp Life*, 1900, is an entertaining, at times melodramatic, fictionalized account of a camping group on the British Columbia coast, and *Among the People of British Columbia: Red, White, Yellow and Brown*, 1903, is based on personal experience of fisherfolk, northern Indians, Japanese and Chinese immigrants, and Indian missions.

Herschberger, Ruth Margaret, 'Josephine Langstaff', essayist, poet, playwright. She was b. 1917 at Philipse Manor, NY, da. of Grace Josephine (Eberhart) and Clarence Bertram H., educ. at the Univ. of Chicago, 1935–8, Black Mountain College, 1938–9, and the Univ. of Michigan, and studied play-writing at the New School for Social Research, NY. In 1948 she published *A Way of Happening* (poems) and *Adam's Rib* (humorously feminist essays, as 'Josephine Langstaff'). 'Women as Something Special' asserts that 'women are weary of being custom-shrunk' to fit male specifications, and asks of child-bearing, 'Must a woman cultivate only that uniqueness which distinguishes her from man? or is she to be allowed to exhibit some purely human characteristics as well?' She wrote feminist lyrics to J. W. HOWE's 'Battle Hymn of the Republic', stories for little magazines, radio plays and film scripts. She had two plays, *A Ferocious Incident* and *Andrew Jackson*, jointly produced in Chicago, 1953. Her second poetry volume, *Nature and Love Poems*, 1969, was reviewed as a 'bizarre amalgam of archaism and vernacular': 'I hear no spirit but the spirit of speech / Endeavouring to sing; if not, to teach.' Her 'Is Rape a Myth?' in Betty and Theodore Roszak, eds., *Masculine and Feminine*, 1970, argues that the crime (seen by men as act, by women as relationship) is 'actively and invisibly supported' by 'the legend of man's natural sexual aggression toward women'. Her play about abortion, *The Decision*, was produced in NYC, 1971. She has staged readings, received grants from writers' colonies, and tried to counter 'anti-verbalists' in the film world by combining her poetry with her film/video work.

Herschel, Caroline Lucretia, 1750–1848, astronomer and memoirist, b. at Hanover, Germany, eighth of ten children of Anna Ilse (Moritzen) and Isaac H., musician. With her schooling went much 'drudgery of the scullery'; more so after 1767, when her father, who had favoured self-improvement, died. In 1772 she was grudgingly allowed to join her elder brother William in Bath, England, where she trained her voice for oratorios and did the hated housework and every possible and unlikely task of 'assistant astronomer', as his hobby took over their lives. In 1782 he was offered a private post by George III; they gave up music and settled near Windsor. Selflessly devoted to *his* work, she found time to write a diary, 'Book of Work Done', and 'Sweep-books' recording her nightly scanning for comets. She discovered eight, and pub. a brief *Account* of 'the first lady's comet' (Frances BURNEY) in 1787, the year she was granted £50 p.a. as William's assistant: 'the first money in all my lifetime I ever thought myself at liberty to spend to my own liking'. In 1788 William m.: she later destroyed the next nine years of her diary. The Royal Society published her *Index* [really an updating] *to Flamsteed's ... Fixed Stars*, 1798: on this she admitted to vanity, although 'among gentlemen the commodity is generally stiled ambition'. Other honours included the Astronomical Society's gold medal, 1828, for her *Catalogue of ... Star Clusters and Nebulae* (unpub. but immensely valuable to astronomers). Desolated at William's death, 1822, she moved back to her remaining family in

Hanover, where she wrote letters, 'Recollections', another unfinished memoir (begun 1842), and her own epitaph in German. Selecs. pub. 1876; ed. Constance A. Lubbock, 1933.

Hertford, Frances Seymour (Thynne), Countess of, 1699–1754, later Duchess of Somerset, poet, letter-writer and patron. Elder da. of Grace (Strode) and Henry T., she grew up at Longleat House and in Dorset, 'well versed' in history, divinity, and romances, great-niece of Anne FINCH, friend of the future Lady LUXBOROUGH and of Elizabeth ROWE (who wanted her poems published, and whose editor she became). She m., 1715, Algernon Seymour, Earl of H. and from 1748 Duke of Somerset; her father-in-law hated her and her only son died, 1744. In 1728 she was writing 'Meditations and Prayers for the Time of Sickness'; later poems include addresses to the east wind, autumn, and frost, as well as a merry love-song to a river, and two poems on Yarico, Richard Steele's Indian girl betrayed by her white lover, 1738. A few were pub. alone or in anthologies; so were some letters, notably those to Lady POMFRET, 1805. Deeply pious in her view of literature, FH admired Elizabeth SCOTT, Marie de SÉVIGNÉ, and Catherine TALBOT. MSS at Alnwick Castle; life by Helen Sard Hughes, 1940. As Duchess of Northumberland her daughter Elizabeth, 1716–76, wrote occasional verse, a *Short Tour* of the Netherlands in 1771 (pub. 1775) and letters (selec. pub. 1926).

Hervey, Elizabeth (March), c. 1748–?1820, novelist, da. of Maria (Hamilton) and Francis M.: elder half-sister of the eccentric writer William Beckford. His tutor thought her in her teens a 'prodigy' who wrote more than some undergraduates read. She m. Col. William Thomas H. in 1774 and had two sons. They were abroad because of his debts when he died, 1778; she had just drafted *Melissa and Marcia, or The Sisters*, pub. anonymously in 1788, a sprightly, predictable story of one vain and one wiser twin (good sketch of their early life with miserly, misogynist father). The ideal heroine of *Louisa* [1789], bullied by her foolish mother, Lady Roseville, shows selfless devotion to her future husband's illegitimate baby. EH's brother, who had outlived his early feeling for her, hits at *Louisa* with 'Arabella Bloomville' in his *Modern Novel Writing* by 'Lady Harriet Marlow', 1796. But his equation of women and sentiment – here and in *Azemia* by 'Jacquetta Agneta Mariana Jenks', dedicated to 'Lady Harriet Marlow', 1797: both facs, 1970 – fits EH less well than those he names: Mary CHAMPION DE CRESPIGNY, the GUNNINGS, Lady HAWKE, Hannah MORE, Mary ROBINSON. (He annotated works by Elizabeth BENGER and Mary SHELLEY with misogynist gibes.) Rumour has it that EH was much upset. She wrote at least four more not especially sentimental novels (MS of *Julia*, 1803, at Yale), dedicating the last, *Amabel* [1813], with her name, to the queen.

Hesketh, Phoebe (Rayner), poet and journalist. B. in 1909 at Preston, Lancs., into 'a world of maids, culture, riding and a conformity that bred rebellion and eccentricity', da. of Amy Gertrude (Fielding) and Arthur Ernest R., pioneer radiologist, she left Cheltenham Ladies' College in 1926 to attend her dying mother. In 1931 she m. Bolton mill-owner Aubrey H. and moved to Rivington, Lancs. (which she elegized in a village history, 1972). She has three children. After publishing *Poems*, Manchester, 1939, she edited the women's page of the *Bolton Evening News*, 1942–5, moved into freelance journalism, and wrote radio plays and documentaries. Her early poems, deeply influenced by the romantics, include pantheistic hymns to nature and cameos of northern rural life: many appeared in *Country Life* magazine. Best known is 'The Fox', much anthologized. Collections which appeared every few years, from *Lean Forward, Spring!* 1948, were selected in *The Eighth Day*, 1980. PH has held lecturing posts since 1967. Besides journal articles, her prose includes a life of her suffragette aunt, Edith Rigby, 1966, and *What Can the Matter Be?*, 1985, an account of her growing up. Later poems turn a philosophic eye on personal experiences of bereavement, age and loneliness. *Over the Brook*, 1986, economically and powerfully employs free-verse techniques. MSS at Univ. of NY, Buffalo.

Hewett, Dorothy, playwright, poet, novelist, critic, b. 1923 in Perth, Western Australia, da. of Doris (Coade) and Arthur H. She grew up on an isolated wheat farm, where she began writing plays, taking lessons by correspondence until she was 12. She then attended Perth Girls' School, Perth College and the Univ. of WA, finally completing an Arts degree in 1961. She joined the Communist Party at 19, attempted suicide a year later and, at 21, m. for the first time. After the death of her son and the breakdown of her marriage (1944) to Communist writer and lawyer Lloyd Davies, she moved to Sydney in 1949; she lived in an inner-city working-class area and worked in factories. She drew on these experiences for her only novel, *Bobbin Up*, 1959, and her first play, *This Old Man Comes Rolling Home*, 1976. During the 1950s she was heavily involved with Communist Party activities in Sydney. She lived with another member of the Party, Les Flood, with whom she had three sons. In 1960 she returned to Perth and m. a seaman, Merv Lilley, and had two daughters. She taught English and Australian Literature at the Univ. of WA and in 1974 moved to Sydney to write full-time. She pub. six collections of poetry: *What About the People!*, 1961 (with Merv Lilley), *Windmill Country*, 1968, *Rapunzel in Suburbia*, 1975, *Greenhouse*, 1979, *Journeys*, 1982, and *Alice in Wormland*, 1987. Her poetry is characterized by her use of personal experiences and the presentation of controversial subjects through the medium of myth and fantasy. These also feature strongly in her plays, most of which incorporate song lyrics. Her combination of tough subject matter – *Bon-Bons and Roses for Dolly*, 1976, provoked a riot in Perth by depicting menstruation on stage – and non-naturalistic style, for many years slowed recognition and professional production of her plays. She has written at least 15, many unpub., and finally achieved popular success with *The Man from Mukinupin*, 1979, a celebration of the dark and light sides of Australian history, written for the 150th anniversary of Western Australia. Her early plays are often strongly feminist, particularly *The Chapel Perilous*, showing a woman questing for self-fulfilment, *Bon-Bons and Roses*, *The Golden Oldies*, 1976, and *The Tatty Hollow Story*, 1976. DH is the first Australian woman playwright to have won widespread recognition and production of her plays. MSS are in the Hanger Collection, Univ. of Queensland Library, and in the Fisher Library, Univ. of Sydney. There is a forthcoming bibliography.

Heyer, Georgette, 1902–74, POPULAR novelist. She was b. Wimbledon near London, da. of Sylvia (Watkins) and George H., a formative influence, like the heroine's father in *Helen*, 1928, one of four contemporary novels GH later suppressed. She was educ. at (not beyond) 'various day schools' (her words), and wrote her first book at 17 to amuse an ailing brother. As *The Black Moth*, 1921, it set her tone, with love between a titled highwayman and the pretty aristocrat he rescues. GH published her third novel, *The Transformation of Philip Jettan*, 1923, as 'Stella Martin'. In 1925 she m. George Rougier, mining engineer, with whom she had a son, and spent a few years abroad. He was later a barrister in London, and was said to have invented the plots for her 12 thrillers. These too have strong love interest. But GH's reputation (established with *These Old Shades*, 1926) rests on the genre of Regency ROMANCE, which she virtually created. (Of her 40 romances, those set in the Elizabethan and Stuart ages were less successful. *The Corinthian*, 1940, was *Beau Wyndham* in the US ed., 1941.) She gleaned authentic detail from first-hand sources (Jane AUSTEN's letters as well as novels), presented it with verve and style, delighted in duels, gambling, disguise, rescue, and the peerage, set her lovers to overcome initial dislike or misunderstanding, and indulged in cautious explorations of gender (some boyish heroines, some effeminate heroes). She declared (of *Friday's Child*, 1944), 'I think myself I ought to be shot for writing such nonsense, but it's unquestionably good escapist literature'. The fruits of a long-running, unfinished research project appeared as *My Lord John*, 1975. Jane Aiken HODGE's life of GH, 1984, says 'She wrote mainly for women, but lived all her life among men, whom she preferred.' See also Harmony Raine, *The GH Compendium*, 1984.

Heyrick, Elizabeth (Coltman), 1769–1831, activist, elder da. of John Coltman and of Elizabeth (Cartwright), an intellectual who while single had pub. journalism and poems (see Catherine HUTTON in *Ainsworth's Magazine*, 1844; book by Catherine Hutton Beale, 1895). EH's sister, Mary Ann, also wrote. EH married John H. in 1789; after his death, 1797, she kept a diary, joined the Quakers, and began publishing, often anonymously at Leicester, where she lived. *The Warning* [1805], an eloquent attack on warmongering, is probably hers. She combated cruelty to animals, 1809 and 1823 (the new act against it, she says, hopes to empty a river by extracting drops). *Family Letters Addressed to Children and Young Persons*, 1811, aimed, she says, at a humbler class than Hester CHAPONE or Hannah MORE, covers many topics with clarity and fervour. She believes in different spheres for the sexes, but urges better job opportunities for women. The best-known of her *c.* 20 works call for ABOLITION of slavery. *Immediate, Not Gradual, Abolition*, 1824, and *Appeal to the Hearts and Consciences of British Women*, 1828, make confident, feeling use of facts and statistics, and stress the power of individual action. Her 'very numerous MS. remains' included 'essays, sermons, prayers'. See anon. life, 1862; Kenneth Corfield in Gail Malmgreen, ed., 1986.

Hickey, Emily Henrietta, 1845–1924, poet, b. Macmine Castle, Co. Wexford, home of her maternal Stewart ancestors. Her mother was a Newton-King and her father the Rev. John Stewart H. of Goresbridge, Co. Carlow. At school EH's Protestant education banned the reading of 'frivolous' books including Shakespeare. After discovering E. B. BROWNING in her late teens she wrote many narrative poems, sending them to Macmillans, with whom she stayed when she first went to London. Here she 'meant to carve her way to fame' (Dennis, p. 20) and undertook teaching, companioning and secretarial work. Through the latter she met Louisa Brough and others advocating higher EDUCATION for women. She attended lectures at University College, London, gained her Cambridge Certificate and for 18 years was lecturer in English Literature at the Collegiate School for Girls under Miss Buss. With Furnivall she founded the Browning Society, 1881, and was Hon. Sec. for many years, in 1884 editing *Strafford* with Robert Browning's collaboration. Her first two vols. of poetry, 1881 and 1889, were well received. A verse-novel on contemporary social problems, *Michael Villiers, Idealist*, 1891, features the philanthropic idealist Lucy Vere, who disproves the scoffing male view of women's powers. Later, as a result of her growing commitment to Anglicanism, she destroyed *Michael Villiers*. By the time *Poems* was published, 1896, EH was in poor health. In 1901 she became a Catholic, a decision possibly influenced by her friend Eleanor Hamilton KING. (Another friend was Emily PFEIFFER.) She was awarded a Civil List pension and became blind two years before her death but continued to write. At her request her poem 'At Eventide' was published in *Catholic World* as a memorial after her death. See life by Enid Dennis, 1927?

Hickman, Rose (Locke), *c.* 1527–1613, memoirist, only child by his second marriage of Sir William L., London merchant; Anne LOCKE m. RH's older half-brother. Educated as a Protestant by her mother, 'very privately for feare of troble', RH in 1543 m. Anthony H., a rich merchant venturer. Persecuted by Mary for harbouring clergy, she fled to near Oxford, then to join her husband at Antwerp till ELIZABETH succeeded, 1558; at each place she agonized over securing correct baptism for a child. Widowed in 1573, she m. Sir Simon Throckmorton of Hunts. About 1610 she wrote brief reminiscences for her children (copies in BL; pub. in *Bulletin of the Institute for Hist. Research*, 1982–3).

Higginson, Ella (Rhoads), *c.* 1860–1940, poet, short-story writer, novelist, journalist, b. at Council Grove, Kansas, da. of Mary Ann and Charles R., the youngest of three children. Moving to Oregon, she was educ. briefly at schools in Oregon City, where she began to write poems and submit them to the local paper. EH m. Russell Carden H., a druggist from NY, c. 1880 and moved with him to Bellingham, Washington, where she ed. the literary department of the *Seattle Sunday Times* for several years. EH pub. short stories in *McClure's*, *Harper's Weekly*, *Lippincott's*, and other national magazines, and collected them in *The Flower that Grew in the Sand*, 1896, *A Forest Orchid*, 1897, *From the Land of the Snow-Pearls*, 1897. *Mariella, or Out West*, 1904, was her only pub. novel. Her short fiction is characterized by a strong sense of Northwestern local colour, plausible domestic and romantic plotting, and realistic dialogue. *When The Birds Go North Again*, 1898, a collection of poems, testifies to EH's love of her Northwestern 'Arcadie', for which she was named Washington's poet laureate in 1931. Her papers are at the Oregon Historical Society, Portland, Oregon. Alfred Powers' chapter on EH in *History of Oregon Lit.*, 1935, is fulsome and imprecise, but has a bibliography.

Highsmith, Mary **Patricia**, 'Claire Morgan', novelist (she rejects the term 'suspense novelist') and short-story writer, b. 1921 at Fort Worth, Texas. Da. of commercial artists Mary (Coates) and Jay Bernard Plangman, who separated before her birth, she took the name of her stepfather, Stanley H. Educ. at Barnard College (BA 1942), she tried drawing and painting, then settled to writing: comic books as well as stories for magazines. Her first book, *Strangers on a Train*, 1950, had an instant success; Alfred Hitchcock filmed it (as others did later works). It presented PH's hallmark, the inverted mystery, in which a good man may murder and an evil one be innocent of technical criminality. The Ripley stories, from *The Talented Mr Ripley*, 1955, give this idea a different twist with an unstable, paranoid charmer who retains some sympathy and interest even when he kills. PH is interested less in crime than in justice, guilt, and the springs of terror; her 20 or so novels depict many intense, often ill-assorted male relationships. She has lived in France and England (where she is more admired than in the USA) since 1963; she has won several crime-writers' awards. She published *The Price of Salt*, 1952, as Claire Morgan, and has also written a children's book (jointly), 1958, and *Plotting and Writing Suspense Fiction*, 1966, repr. 1983. *Little Tales of Misogyny*, 1977 (first pub. in German, 1974; repr. 1986), presents caricatures – 'The Breeder', 'The Mobile Bed-Object' – (and women's complicity in them) in a flat, detached tone with outbreaks of violence: a suitor for a daughter's hand in marriage receives the hand in a box. In *The Animal-Lover's Book of Beastly Murder*, 1975 (also short stories), creatures exact revenge for human cruelty. PH's sense of the macabre is reflected in *Edith's Diary*, 1977 (about a woman who retreats into private creation from an indifferent husband, parasitic son and aged uncle-by-marriage, and violent, corrupt world), *People Who Knock on the Door*, 1983, about pharisaical religious enthusiasts, and *Tales of Natural and Unnatural Catastrophes*, 1988. Brigid BROPHY ranks PH's work very high (*Don't Never Forget*); Franz Cavigelli and Fritz Senn have ed. a book of criticism in German, 1980.

Hill, Ernestine (Hemmings), 1899–1972, journalist, travel writer, novelist, b. Rockhampton, Queensland, da. of Margaret Foster (Lynam) and Robert Hemmings, factory manager. She worked briefly for the ABC and as a public servant, but early began a career of wandering and travel that she pursued virtually full time after 1933. Making her way around and across the continent several times, she provided herself with abundant material for several well-known publications, notably *Flying Doctor Calling*, 1947, an account of the Australian Inland Mission and John Flynn's medical services to remote regions of Australia, and *The Territory*, 1951, an anecdotal history and geography of an extraordinary area and its people. She also wrote *The Great Australian Loneliness*, 1937 (pub. in the USA as *Australian Frontier*, 1942), *Water into Gold*, 1937, an account of the Murray River region, the posthumous *Kabbarli, a Personal Memoir of Daisy Bates*, 1973, and an early book of verse in collaboration with four others: *Peter Pan Land*, 1916. She also wrote a number of radio plays, of which only one was pub.: *Santa Claus of Christmas Creek*, 1946 (in *Australian Radio Plays*). She is chiefly remembered for the best-selling novel, *My Love Must Wait*, 1941, a popular fictionalized biography of navigator Matthew Flinders. She has also contributed to various magazines, in particular the travel and geographical monthly, *Walkabout*. See Meaghan Morris's article, 'Panorama', in Paul Foss, ed., *Island in the Stream*, 1988.

Hill, Isabel, 1800–42, poet, playwright, novelist and translator. B. at Bristol, she began writing early, encouraged in ambition by her parents and elder brother, Benson Earle H., though to her regret she was not able to study Greek or Latin. Ill at 15, she went to live with her brother, by then serving at Dover as a soldier, and they continued to live together and support one another in literary effort. In 1818 her first poem appeared in the *Pocket Magazine*, signed 'Edward'. Her first play, *The Poet's Child*, 1820, was encouraged by Covent Garden Theatre, but not produced. In 1823 two stories appeared, *Zaphna or The Amulet* and *Constance*, and she pub. a number of poems from 1823 to 1828 in local newspapers and London magazines, including the *Athenaeum*, and later contributed to *Hood's Comic Annual* and *The Monthly Magazine*, among others. *Holiday Dreams; or Light Reading in Poetry and Prose*, 1829, is a collection of poems, stories and essays including 'An Indefinite Article', which speaks frankly of IH's professional difficulties as a woman writer: '*we* are sure to be disgraced and spoiled by success, and shunned even if we fail.... Such is the lot of scribbling spinsters, which I discovered too late'. The poems are light, amusing and clever. IH felt isolation as a woman writer, knowing no other professional women until she met the editor Lady Wyatt (L. H. Sheridan) and the actress Helen Faucit. She pub. one novel, *Brother Tragedians*, in 1834 and had two works performed: 'My Own Twin Brother' (a farce written with her brother) and 'West Country Wooing', a monodrama. For money, she translated Germaine DE STAEL's *Corinne*, 1833, and Chateaubriand's *The Last of the Abencerages*, 1835. In 1839 she began a work on female EDUCATION, but died before completing it. Her last work, a tragedy, *Brian, the Probationer: or the Red Hand*, 1842, was pub. with a memoir by her brother.

Hill, Phillippina (Burton), miscellaneous writer and adventurer. She came, she asserts, of good family, and acted at 16 at Brighton; two works have all male subscribers, and all a flirtatious tone; later ones complain of extreme poverty, social snubs, and female fear of authorship. Her *Miscellaneous Poems*, 'by a Lady', 1768 (same title, ascription, and date as a work by Elizabeth ROLT), open her career of self-publicizing: she will either go on printing annually by subscription or retire to a convent; a rare 2nd and 3rd volumes are covertly autobiographical. *A Rhapsody*, 1769, on love, in prose tending towards blank verse rhythms, bears her birth name. In 1770 she played the lead in her own comedy, *Fashion Displayed*, at the Haymarket (unpub.; MS at Huntington). A report of her bankruptcy, 1772, says she is aka Patience Yandall, milliner. She says she had three years courtship and nearly seven years idyllic marriage to Ensign Hill before reappearing at Brighton about 1785, a destitute widow awaiting the outcome of a Chancery suit. She pub. in her married name *A Novel and Genuine Display on...the Human Mind* (four prose and verse vehicles for histrionic recital, dedicated to Georgiana DEVONSHIRE), *Portraits...of the Present Fashionable World*, which spreads innuendo and flatters society beauties (names half-concealed), and her *Apology* [1787], which laments a disastrous stage appearance in a male role, a bid for patronage from the Prince of Wales.

Hill, Selima (Wood), poet, b. 1945 in London, da. of Elisabeth (Robertson), painter, and James W., painter, writer, and Persian scholar. She was educ. at a Hampstead convent school (though not a Catholic), boarding school, and New Hall, Cambridge, where she changed from Moral Science (finding herself the only woman on an intimidatingly male-oriented course) to English. When she m. painter Rod H., 1968, her 'identity as a writer shrank further inside of itself like a snail inside its shell'. She took on care of an autistic child, had three children herself, ran adventure playgrounds, a creche and a children's rights workshop, and worked for the National Childbirth Trust (also in a bookshop). Her poetry is collected in *Saying Hello at the Station*, 1984 (Cholmondeley Award, 1986), *My Darling Camel*, 1988, and *The Accumulation of Small Acts of Kindness*, 1989 (a long poem about mental breakdown). Her work uses fragments of speech, letters and myth to capture the external world and 'the weighing of the heart'. SH lives in Dorset, teaches creative writing, and is working on the diaries (at Magdalene College, Cambridge) of Dorothy Eleanor (Pilley) Richards, wife of critic I. A. Richards. She appears in anthologies by RUMENS, 1985, and ALLNUTT et al, 1988.

Hill, Susan Elizabeth, novelist and writer of short stories, radio plays and children's books, b. in 1942 at Scarborough, Yorks. (whose traces are visible in her fiction), only child of Doris and R. H. H. She was educ. at a convent school, a grammar school in Coventry, and London Univ. (BA in English, 1963). Having already gained some reputation with *The Enclosure*, 1961, she had five years as book-review editor for the Coventry *Evening Telegraph* before turning full-time to fiction. *I'm the King of the Castle*, 1970, *The Albatross and Other Stories*, 1971, and *The Bird of Night*, 1972, are spare, striking presentations of violence, cruelty and suffering. Their protagonists are eccentric, or impaired emotionally, intellectually or physically, too isolated in pain and despair to see any possibility of escape. SH puts forward no protest, proposal for improvement, or analysis of entrapping political or economic conditions, painting a world reflected in the title *The Cold Country*, 1975 (five radio plays, with her account of how she came to write this genre). *In the Springtime of the Year*, 1974, however, shows a young woman moving – at Easter – beyond dependence and grief at her husband's death into spiritual recovery. SH m. Shakespeare scholar Stanley Wells in 1975, and soon afterwards said she would write no more novels. But her output has not slackened. It has included journalism, works for children, autobiographical sketches, 1982, and edited volumes (e.g. *People: Essays and Poems*, 1983, whose contributors include Iris MURDOCH and Margaret DRABBLE). In *Family*, 1989, she poignantly relates her violent desire for a second child, fulfilled after several miscarriages, and the short, agonizing life of a baby born at just 25 weeks. In *The Woman in Black*, 1983 (TV play, 1989), a ghost woman takes revenge for her child's death by killing other children. See Rosemary Jackson in Staley, 1982.

Hincks, Elizabeth, Quaker apologist, who calls herself 'a Woman of the South' in her long poem, *The Poor Widows Mite*, 1671. She presents the Society of Friends as the true Body of Christ, a female body rejecting the trappings of the Popish Whore of Babylon. Extending the common image of God's children as babies at the breast, she mentions the mother's relief as well as the child's: 'And when the Child has suckt its fill, the Breast likewise is eas'd, / The Child then it is satisfi'd, and Mother also pleas'd.'

Historical feminist criticism may be said to have begun with Mary WOLLSTONECRAFT's revisionist readings of Milton and Rousseau in 1792, or even with seventeenth-century women's trenchant re-readings of biblical texts; it now extends to 'the reappraisal of the whole body of texts that make up our literary heritage' (Elaine Showalter, introducing her collection *The New Feminist Criticism*, 1985, quoted below) and to major new enterprises in BIOGRAPHY and scholarly reprinting of 'lost' texts. Virginia WOOLF set out to answer some crucial questions about women's relation to writing, by investigating the circumstances in which women have written, in *A Room of One's Own*, 1928. Woolf's study provided immeasurable food for feminist thought: it supplies the epigraph, opening words, or title of, for instance, enquiries into English women fiction-writers of 1621–1744 (by B. G. MacCarthy, 1944) and into the influence of past heroines on present readers (Rachel M. Brownstein, 1982), and of an essay collection (*Shakespeare's Sisters*, 1979) and an ANTHOLOGY (the Norton, 1985) by Sandra M. GILBERT and Susan Gubar. It also outlines what has since been understood as the female tradition.

Meanwhile a new era in feminist interrogation of old texts was inaugurated by Simone de BEAUVOIR in *The Second Sex*, 1949, translated into English, 1953, Mary Ellman in *Thinking About Women*, 1968, and Kate MILLETT in *Sexual Politics*, 1970. Adrienne RICH's powerfully influential essay, 'When We Dead Awaken: Writing as Re-Vision', 1971 ('Re-vision – the act of looking back, of seeing with fresh eyes, of entering an old text from a new critical direction – is for women more than a chapter in a cultural history; it is an act of survival') examined ways in which 'our language has trapped as well as liberated us', and her essays on Anne BRADSTREET, Emily DICKINSON, and Anne SEXTON pointed to new directions in studies of female authors. So did Tillie OLSEN's *Silences*, 1972, whose title essay, originally a talk of 1962, saw 'Literary history and the present [as] dark with silences' of censorship and self-suppression. Ellen Moers's important *Literary Women*, 1976, documented the existence of a women's literary tradition, outlined a critical history of 'the major women writers', and provided a dictionary. Showalter's *A Literature of Their Own: British Women Novelists from Brontë to Lessing*, 1977, marked a new period of historical inquiry into women's writing: detecting 'problems of sexual bias or projection in literary history', it tracks the British tradition through phases called 'feminine' ('from the appearance of the male pseudonym in the 1840s to the death of George ELIOT in 1880'), 'feminist' ('1880–1920, or the winning of the vote'), and 'female' ('1920 to the present, but entering a new stage of self-awareness about 1960'): she argues, crucially, that women's writing must be seen in its relationship to a women's 'subculture within the framework of a larger society.' The significant rewriting of a literary history both exclusive and gender-blind has been continued by dozens of feminist scholars, including, for example, Jane Spencer, *The Rise of the Woman Novelist*, 1986, Shari Benstock, *Women of the Left Bank, Paris, 1900–1940*, 1986, and Gilbert and Gubar, *The Madwoman in the Attic: the Woman Writer and the Nineteenth Century Literary Imagination*, 1979, and *No Man's Land: the Place of the Woman Writer in the Twentieth Century*, two vols., 1988, 1989 (a third volume planned).

Louise Bernikow wrote in 1974, 'What is commonly called literary history is actually a record of choices': new choices were made by Bernikow in the anthology which this remark introduces, *The World Split Open: Women Poets 1552–1950*, 1974 (1979 in England), by Gilbert and Gubar, and by many valuable critical and biographical works and reprinted or newly published texts from the past. The ideological freight both of canonized texts and of the canonizing process, as practised by traditionally masculine-oriented critics, has been exposed; stereotypes both misogynistic and manipulative have been critiqued; women writers emerging from obscurity have been enjoyed, admired, and examined. Sensitive to the issues of class–specificity raised by SOCIALIST-FEMINIST CRITICISM, historical critics nevertheless argue that significant (sometimes surprising) parallels in thinking about matters of gender are evident in women writing at widely separated periods of time: these parallels, together with the irreducible differences of class, race, and period, make the study of literary 'foremothers' relevant to feminist as well as literary-historical concerns. Rediscovered women writers have to be more than singly relocated (either in their own context or in ours); feminist scholars are learning to read diachronically, alert both to continuity and discontinuity. Gilbert's 'revisionary imperative' is necessarily historical, since the value-judgements of literary critics have been and are likely to continue to be, in Annette Kolodny's words, 'historically determined'. Dominant culture often takes a cosy attitude towards the past, painting its otherness as attractive and exciting; to look at the past as a woman, and far more as a black, ethnic-minority, or lesbian woman, painfully reveals literature's frequent complicity with 'brutally complex systems of oppression', as well as its heartening capacities to record and to create irony, humour, rebellion, and pleasure.

The new historicism has provoked mixed responses from feminist critics. Jane Marcus sees its Foucauldian desire to treat history as discourse as disabling cultural critique, and Judith Lowder Newton observes that new-historicist critical practices are 'intensely familiar' to feminists because its '"post-modernist" assumptions ... were partly generated by the theoretical breaks of the second wave of the women's movement, by feminist criticism of male-centred knowledges for their assumptions of "objectivity," by feminist assertion of the political and historically specific nature of knowledge itself, and by feminist analyses of their cultural construction of female identity' (both in H. Aram Veeser, ed., 1989). Ellen Pollak sees in the 'effort to establish a dialectic between history and literary theory with the aim of simultaneously historicizing textuality and textualizing historiography' (*The Eighteenth Century*, 29, 1988) the possibility of significant common ground between feminism and new historicism, and Mary Poovey's *The Proper Lady and the Woman Writer*, 1984, and *Uneven Developments: The Ideological Work of Gender in Mid-Victorian England*, 1989, bring new-historicist methods to the project of recognizing gender in history. Denise LEVERTOV writes, 'The books of the dead / shake their leaves, / word-seeds fly and / lodge in the black earth.' See also Janet Todd, *Feminist Literary History*, 1988; see also HISTORY.

History of women by women was written in French by CHRISTINE de Pizan and in English by seventeenth-century NUNS. Ann DOWRICHE and Eleanor DOUGLAS represent early approaches, epic and personal, to history. Women with first-hand knowledge of seventeenth-century upheavals, like Lucy HUTCHINSON and Ann FANSHAWE, wrote to relate their experience to a broader canvas. The scandal-novel, on the borders of fiction and history, became a female genre through the work of Delarivier MANLEY and Eliza HAYWOOD, continued a century later by Sarah Draper, 1796, and Sarah GREEN. While Catharine MACAULAY achieved fame in mainstream, national, scholarly history, from 1763 (followed by Annabel (Yorke) Hume, Countess de Grey, 1797), Charlotte Cowley's *Ladies History of England*, 1780, declared the aim (hardly fulfilled) of restoring women's place in broader history. Nineteenth-century historical writing centred on the lives of prominent women. E. O. BENGER and Lucy AIKIN sought to make the historical memoir a new genre, especially fitted to female writers and female subjects. Agnes and Elizabeth STRICKLAND wrote lives of queens and princesses; Mary Anne Everett (Wood) Green edited early letter-writers. Interest became broader in mid-century, stimulated by the advent of the women's movement. Hannah Lawrance's *History of Woman in England*, vol. i, 1843, petered out in the time of Henry I, but Lydia Maria CHILD's *History of the Condition of Women in Various Ages and Nations*, 1835, and Elizabeth ELLET's *Women of the American Revolution*, 3 vols., 1848, 1850, were important. The *English Woman's Journal* and *Victoria Magazine* published many articles on the achievement of women artists, writers, and political and religious figures; leading feminists wrote historical biographies of great women, like Millicent FAWCETT on Joan of Arc and Josephine BUTLER on Catherine of Siena. Many were also concerned to write the history of the women's movement, notably the monumental *History of Woman Suffrage*, eds., Elizabeth Cady STANTON, Susan B. ANTHONY and Matilda Joslyn GAGE, 6 vols., 1881–1922. The development of labour history in the later nineteenth and early twentieth centuries brought new interest in the history of women's work and wages: see B. L. Hutchins and Amy Harrison, *A History of Factory Legislation*, 1903; Alice Clark, *Working Life of Women in the Seventeenth Century*, 1919. Groups like the Fabian Women's Group ran lectures on the history of women's work. Since the 1970s, women's history has expanded to produce courses and study groups both inside and outside universities, the periodicals *Women in History* (US) and *History Workshop*, 'a journal of socialist and feminist historians' (UK), and an International Conference on Women's History, 1986 (see Arina Angerman et al., eds., 1989). Joan Kelly argued in 'The Social Relations of the Sexes: Methodological Implications of Women's History' (*Signs*, 1, 1976), a revolutionary manifesto, that women's history must radically alter the methods of historiography. (See also her *Women, History, and Theory*, 1984.) A revolution in thinking created by broad-ranging works (like Gerda Lerner, *The Majority Finds Its Past, Placing Women in History*, 1979, and *The Creation of Patriarchy*, 1986, Leonore Davidoff, ed., essays in 'the new women's history', 1981, and Rosalind Miles, *The Women's History of the World*, 1988) has also produced specialist works on the fortunes of female sexuality (e.g. Harriet Gilbert and Christine Roche, 1989), childbirth (e.g. Ann OAKLEY, Jenny Carter and Thérèse Duriez, 1986), breast-feeding (e.g. Valerie Fildes, 1986), cross-dressing (e.g. Julie Wainwright, 1988), women and work (e.g. Caroline Davidson, 1982, Ruth Milkman, ed., 1985, Davidoff and Belinda Westover, eds., 1986, and Bridget Hill, 1989), women and science (e.g. Margaret Alic, 1986), women in the family (e.g. Carol N. Degler, 1980, Davidoff and Catherine Hall, 1987, Steven Mintz and Susan Kellogg, 1989), women and culture (e.g. Lillian Robinson, 1978, Elaine Showalter on women and madness in England, 1987, Carroll Smith-Rosenberg on the nineteenth-century USA, 1985), and the history of feminism (e.g. Jane Rendall, 1985, Alice Echols, 1989). See also Sheila Rowbotham, *Hidden from History: Rediscovering Women ...*, 1973, Natalie Zemon DAVIS in *Beyond their Sex*, ed. Patricia H. Labalme, 1980; Joan Thirsk in *Women in English Society 1500–1800*, ed. Mary Prior, 1985. See also HISTORICAL FEMINIST CRITICISM.

Hobart, Alice (Nourse), 'Alice Tisdale', 1882–1967, novelist, travel writer, b. at Lockport, NY, da. of Harriett Augusta (Beaman) – 'Gusty', 'the axis around which we all revolved' – and musician Edwin Henry N., descended from Rebecca Nurse of Salem, who, charged with witchcraft (and hanged, 1692), replied, 'I will not belie myself.' ANH's sister Mary wrote books on the Orient and a brother on economics. Stricken with spinal meningitis as a child, ANH remained frail; she left Northwestern Univ. and the Univ. of Chicago (1904–7) without a degree. In 1914, on a long-term visit to her sister in China, she m. US businessman Earle Tisdale H.; she lived in China with him as a company wife ('as inconspicuous as possible, making no demands on the company') until 1927, escaping from Nanking during the Nationalist revolution that year. She developed her sense of a separate self through her writing: 'Gradually, as I accepted the discipline involved in writing, I perceived that an authentic personality entirely my own was emerging.' The first white woman to see some areas of Manchuria, she overcame extreme shyness ('nothing short of physical torture', from which she felt girls needed to liberate themselves) and ill health (without which 'I might have missed the finest thing that's come to me – the creative world of writing'). Following her first story, 'The Adventure with the Red Beards' (in *Atlantic Monthly*, as Alice Tisdale in case of offending her husband's company, Standard Oil), she expanded articles and letters into three non-fiction books on China, 1917, 1926, and 1928. Her first novel, *Pidgin Cargo*, 1929 (later *River Supreme*), and her biggest success, *Oil for the Lamps of China*, 1933 (twice filmed), depict Americans struggling to integrate US business methods with Asian culture. *Yang and Yin*, 1936, a 'philosophical' novel, depicts a Chinese-American friendship. Her first California novel, *Their Own Country*, 1940, uses the couple from *Oil Lamps* to relate the problems of China to those of the US. Living in Mexico from 1941 (her husband in India on war service), ANH wrote *The Peacock Sheds His Tail*, 1945, a novel of international marriage based on knowledge acquired from friendship with a young Mexican-American woman. *The Cup and the Sword*, 1942, and *The Cleft Rock*, 1949, also about California, develop relationships between people and environment. Her autobiography, *Gusty's Child*, 1959, describes how, having returned to the US, she wished to write about Rebecca Nurse, but on visiting Salem decided to 'Let her lie in peace under the great pines. Her contribution had been made to defeat hysteria in her own generation.' *The Serpent-Wreathed Staff*, 1963, fictionalizes the debate about the topical, contentious issue of financing medical care. *The Innocent Dreamers*, 1963, set against a broad background of twentieth-century Chinese history, deals with the possibility of 'greater understanding between East and West'.

'Hobbes, John Oliver', Pearl Mary-Teresa (Richards) Craigie, 1867–1906, novelist and dramatist, b. Chelsea, Mass., eldest of three children of Laura Hortense (Arnold) and John Morgan R. Brought up in London, she was educ. at boarding school, private day schools, and in Paris, and University College, London. At nine she pub. her first stories, and began writing regular drama and art columns soon after her marriage to Reginald Walpole C., wealthy Bank of England clerk, in 1887. Her first novel, *Some Emotions and a Moral*, 1891, was an immediate success, establishing her as a clever and caustic writer. As well as ten novels, including the idealized fictional portrait of Disraeli, *Robert Orange*. 1902, she wrote several successful plays, sketches and travel essays (many collected as *Imperial India*, 1903), an Encyclopaedia Britannica entry on George ELIOT, 1901, and a critical essay on George SAND, 1902. She headed the Society of Women Journalists, 1895–6. Her success persisted despite a mild form of epilepsy, her 1892 conversion to Catholicism, a highly publicized divorce (1895), and rumours of romantic entanglements (some spread by George Moore, with whom she collaborated on verse plays). Other works include *Osberne and Ursyne*, 1898, a verse tragedy, and *Letters from a Silent Study*, 1904, an essay collection. Whilst she hoped to be considered a serious writer, she was known instead as a witty epigrammatist and often mocked by other writers. Modern readers, however, may find her novels overwritten and dull, although *The Dream and the Business*, 1906, contains some hint of the 'clever' woman's predicament. See the life by John Morgan Richard, 1911. Many of her letters and papers are in the Berg Collection, NYPL.

Hobhouse, Mary Violet (McNeill), 1864–1901, novelist and poet. Her father was Deputy Lieutenant of Co. Antrim. At about 20 she was writing nature poetry: 'ye free winds that blow / Over this cruel shore'. She was an Irish patriot, supporting Union but campaigning against Home Rule: her poems include translations from Irish and a rousing 'Song of the Union': 'Rise, South and North! / Comrades, come forth, / Erin's your country. Defend her.' She married the Rev. Walter H. in 1887; several of her children died young. Her novels, *An Unknown Quantity, A Sad Story of Modern Life*, 1898, and *Warp and Weft, A Story of the North of Ireland*, 1899, are rich in Northern Irish local colour. Her husband edited posthumous *Speculum Animae, Poems and Verses*. 1902, mostly from MSS.

Hobson, Laura (Zametkin), 1900–86, novelist, journalist, b. on Long Island, da. of Russian immigrants Adella (Kean), columnist, and Michael Z., labour leader and editor of a liberal Yiddish newspaper. From Hunter College she transferred, 'in profound disappointment' at its lack of challenge, to Cornell Univ. (BA 1921). She worked as advertising copy-writer and reporter (on the NY *Evening Post*), began getting magazine articles published, and in 1930 m. publisher Thayer H., with whom she co-authored two westerns as 'Peter Field'. They divorced in 1935; LZH later adopted two sons. She wrote freelance journalism and held jobs with *Time, Life*, and other periodicals until her 1947 success enabled her to concentrate on fiction. Besides magazine stories and two children's novels (on dog-owning, 1941, and pregnancy, 1967), she wrote accessible realist fiction on social and political issues, often foregrounding strong women whose committed idealism threatens their personal relationships. The heroine of *The Trespassers*, 1943, opposes immigration quotas on behalf of a family from Germany. LZH's expectation that 'magazines will never look at, the movies won't touch and the public won't buy' *Gentleman's Agreement*, 1947, were confounded by a *Cosmopolitan* serial, award-winning film, and sales of over two million. Its hero adopts temporary Jewish identity to unmask covert US anti-semitism. *First Papers*, 1964, depicts a Russian immigrant immersing himself in Americanism, *Over and Above*, 1979, an agnostic intellectual coming to terms with her Jewishness, *The Tenth Month*, 1971, a 40-year-old, voluntarily single, expectant mother. *Consenting Adult*, 1975, draws on

LZH's own experience with a homosexual son to affirm the need for solidarity with those whom society penalizes. Her unfinished autobiography, *Laura Z.* (a volume on early years, 1983, and one on 'Years of Fulfilment', 1986), was repr. together, 1987.

Hoby, Margaret (Dakins), Lady, 1571–1633, earliest woman to write a surviving DIARY in English. Da. and heiress of Thomasine (Guy) and Arthur D., she grew up in the house of the Puritan Lady Huntingdon and was three times married: 1589, to Walter Devereux (brother of the Earl of Essex); four months after his death (1591) to Thomas Sidney (brother of Lady PEMBROKE); and the year after his death (1596) to Thomas Posthumous H., son of Elizabeth, Lady RUSSELL. MH's diary, written mostly in Yorks., 1599–1605, began as a religious exercise in which with time she grew slacker: most days begin with 'privat praier' (public comes later). She records little emotion or opinion, but sewing, pious reading and writing, walking, fishing, and playing bowls. She trained well-born girls in housekeeping and practised medicine: 'dressed my patients', attended births, and operated (unsuccessfully) on a baby born without an anus. Diary in BL; Dorothy M. Meads, ed., 1930.

Hodge, Jane (Aiken), novelist and biographer, b. 1917 in Watertown, Mass., sister of Joan AIKEN. She was taken to England at three and educ. at Hayes Court, Kent, Somerville College, Oxford (BA 1938), and Radcliffe College, Mass. (AM 1939). She worked in the USA 1941–7: for British organizations in Washington and NYC, then for *Time*, and in London, 1947–8, for *Life*. She m. Alan Hodge (later editor of *History Today*: d. 1979) in 1948, and had two daughters. She has written about 20 novels (beginning in 1964 with *Maulever Hall*), chiefly historical (1775–1832), with brief forays into the twentieth century in detective novels. She regularly introduces important historical events, 'as accurate as I can make them', and sometimes historical characters, quoting their own words when possible, but allowing herself some latitude of interpretation, and adding love interest. Of recent novels, *Wide is the Water*, 1981, moves back and forth between Philadelphia and London at the time of the struggle for American independence, and *Polonaise*, 1987, all across Napoleonic Europe. JAH has also written lives of Jane AUSTEN, 1972, and Georgette HEYER, 1984 (a work attempting to 'redress the balance' of contempt directed at good writing in a POPULAR mode).

Hodge, Merle, novelist and essayist, b. 1944 in Trinidad, one of four das. of immigration officer Ray H. She was educ. at Bishop Anstey's High School, then Univ. College, London: BA in French, 1965, MPhil on the French Guyanese poet Leon Damas, 1967, whom she has also translated. She taught, travelled widely in Europe, and lived for a while in Senegal and Gambia. Her novel, *Crick, Crack Monkey*, 1970, presents, through the narrator's eyes and her own, a Caribbean youngster (her father absent in England) caught between exuberant, patois-speaking Tantie and formal, exacting Aunt Beatrice, determined to 'haul me out of what she termed alternately my ordinaryness and my niggeryness'. Working for a scholarship (like her creator) she is drawn away from the folk-culture world till it shames and almost repels her. (See Roy Narinesingh, intro. to 1981 repr.) In 1970 MH went home to teach at a Port of Spain high school, lecture in French Caribbean and African literature at the Univ. of the West Indies, Kingston, and teach and work as Director of Curriculum Development in Grenada (till the US invasion, 1983). She has engaged in educational controversy (e.g. 'Close Down the Libraries Says This Teacher', interview in Trinidad *Sunday Guardian*, 1 November 1970), and published in Caribbean scholarly journals on the historical oppression of West Indian women (e.g. 'The Shadow of the Whip: A Comment on Male–Female Relations', in Orde Coombs, ed., *Is Massa Day Dead?*, 1974). She wrote the intro. to Erna BRODBER, ed., *Perceptions of Caribbean Women*, 1982.

Hodgman, Helen (Willes), novelist, b. 1945 in Aberdeen, only child of Martha and of John W., gas-fitter. After a village school and Colchester High School, she was taken to Hobart, Tasmania, in 1958; at 15 she went to work in a bank, then taught for a year, and studied two years at Teachers' College, Hobart. She married Roger H., had a daughter, and opened a gallery of contemporary art. Moving to London, she did odd jobs (cleaner, bookmaker's clerk), then wrote the grimly funny *Blue Skies*, 1976. In it a young mother in a Tasmanian seaside suburb, a 'nature-reserve for females', rejects all the 'placebos prescribed to sugar-coat time', opts for two limited friendships with men who are struck by fearful disasters, then kills her next-door neighbour. The tale is haunted by the memory of exterminated Aborigines. The heroine of *Jack and Jill*, 1978 (repr. 1989 with *Blue Skies*), 'coo[s] her first words into the chill, waxy ear' of her mother, who has just died in the outback in her father's absence; she marries a cripple, becomes famous for her books about fantasized ideal childhood, and ends ecstatically supervising another woman's bearing of her husband's son, her intended ideal. Margaret Crosland (1981) ranks HH's housewife portraits above Margaret DRABBLE's. In 1977 HH moved to Vancouver, where she left her husband, worked as editor of an arts-centre journal, and had produced a one-act play, *Oh Mother, Is It With It?*, 1981: daughter (traced from babyhood to marriage) rejects her mother's views. She then migrated to Sydney, where she writes for films and TV. *Broken Words*, 1989, is a novel of lesbian couples and other marginal South London people, written with scalpel-like wit in short, clipped scenes: broken words, broken lives, broken dreams, yet ultimately hopeful.

Hoey, Frances Sarah, 'Mrs Cashel Hoey' (Johnston), 1830–1908, novelist, translator, journalist, b. Bushy Park, Co. Dublin, one of eight children of Charlotte Jane (Shaw: half-sister to G. B. Shaw's mother) and Charles Bolton J., secretary and registrar of Mt Jerome cemetery. She was educ. at home, chiefly by her own efforts. At 16 she m. Adam Murray Stewart, with whom she had two daughters, and from 1853 began to contribute art reviews and articles to *Freeman's Journal* and the *Nation*. When he died in 1855 she went to London with an introduction to Thackeray, wrote for the *Morning Post*, and after 1870 for the *Spectator*. She m. Cashel H., a well-known Dublin journalist and member of the Young Ireland Party, and adopted Catholicism. From 1865 she contributed regularly to *Chambers' Journal*, including two serial novels, *A Golden Sorrow*, 1872, and *The Blossoming of an Aloe*, 1874. Though *A House of Cards*, 1868, was the first novel pub. under her own name, it has been claimed that she was largely responsible for five novels of Edmund Yates (see Edwards, 1982). She was sole author of *A Righted Wrong*, 1870, which uses the familiar plot device of unintentional bigamy but centres on the consequently illegitimate daughter, and subsequently published other sensation novels, some of which give evidence of suppressed feminist feeling. A frequent visitor to Paris, she returned in 1871 with news of the Commune, 'Red Paris on Easter Sunday', appearing in the *Spectator* and *St. Paul's Magazine*, May 1871. Generous and charitable, but chronically short of money, she translated from French and Italian, often in collaboration with John Lillie, worked as a publisher's reader and for more than twenty years sent a fortnightly 'Lady's Letter' to an Australian paper. In 1892 she was granted a Civil List pension. See P. D. Edwards, bibliog., *VFRG* 8, 1982.

Hofland, Barbara (Wreaks), also Hoole, 1770–1844, poet and highly prolific and popular novelist, da. of Sheffield manufacturer Robert W. He d. when she was a baby; after her mother's remarriage an aunt brought her up. The *Sheffield Courant* published her 'Characteristics of Some Leading Inhabitants', 1793–6. In 1796 she m. merchant Thomas Bradshawe Hoole, who died two years later leaving her a baby son and no money. Her interesting *Poems*, 1805 (ballads, personal lyrics, natural description), first of her 60-odd works, brought several hundred pounds from 2,000 subscribers; she then opened a boarding school in Harrogate. There she wrote *The Clergyman's Widow*, 1812, first of several novels of bereaved women achieving self-respect, financial independence and model children. It sold 17,000 copies. In 1808, against advice, she m. the struggling young artist Thomas Christopher Hofland. His art took first place while she 'chiefly wrote at night' to support them: her friend Anna HALL calls her 'wishful to set herself aside, that his value only might appear in a strong light'. He must have modelled for the self-regarding painter in BH's *Son of a Genius*, 1812, written to teach her son that 'a great mind *can* take in petty cares, an aspiring genius stoop to petty details' (a parallel *Daughter of*... followed in 1823). Moving to London, 1811, increased her output: five titles one year (children's and adult), 'Letters to Kinfolk' for provincial papers (whose gossip, with names supplied, gave offence), unsigned pieces in 'magazines, annuals, and reviews' (including criticism), actual letters (notably to M. R. MITFORD), and poems private and public (she celebrated Queen VICTORIA). Her work for children includes imaginative textbooks (she centres both histories and travels on invented young people). Some simplified moral judgements apart, it is intelligent and readable. Depth and variety is added in adult works like *Iwanowa, or The Maid of Moscow*, 1813 (Richardsonian letters; clash of armies and cultures), *Katherine*, 1828 (delicate psychological analysis of misunderstandings in love), *The Captives in India*, 1834 (effective use of Eliza FAY), and *The King's Son*, 1843 (fictional vindication of Richard III). Life by Thomas Ramsay, 1849.

Holcroft, Frances, 1778/83–1844, novelist, da. of Thomas H., radical writer, and his unnamed third wife (of four), who d. 1790. She published an abolitionist poem in the *Monthly Magazine*, Oct. 1797, lived in Europe 1799–1803, and composed music for Thomas H.'s drama *The Lady of the Rock*, 1805, on a story from Sarah MURRAY's guide to Scotland. By now she was working as his amanuensis, skirting starvation, an extra target for his attackers. She translated seven plays (from Italian, Spanish and German, including Calderón and Lessing) for her father's *Theatrical Recorder*, 1805, and the Prince de Condé's life of his great seventeenth-century ancestor (with her name, 1807). On Thomas H.'s death, 1809, she sought help from the RLF to open a school, and turned to novels with *The Wife and the Lover*, 1813. *Fortitude and Frailty*, 1817, set in French revolutionary times, includes lines to his memory: she may have drawn on him for her brave, virtuous, impetuous hero, who loses the philanthropic heroine (she falls for a villain before marrying the book's second most eligible bachelor) and selflessly exchanges places with a hunted émigré. FH self-consciously guides readers to proper insights into characters in various states of fortitude and extreme vulnerability; she comments with horror on revolutionary excess and suggests that pure-hearted individuals will get nearly though not exactly what they want.

Holdsworth, Annie E., later Lee-Hamilton, b. *c.* 1857, novelist, story writer, feminist, b. Kingston, Jamaica, da. of Elizabeth (Hall), of Scottish descent, and the Rev. William H. (1817–92), a Yorkshire Methodist missionary among the emancipated slaves,

1846–71. AH's mother was a great reader and socially concerned, but found the return to England with five children difficult; only the boys went to school. AH began publishing in the 1890s, co-edited *The Woman's Signal*, and probably used the pseudonym 'Max Beresford' (*BLC* says this was A. S. Holdsworth). If so, she wrote *Bonnie Dundee*, 1890, and *Belhaven*, 1892; otherwise, she first published some short stories in *Belgravia* and the *English Illustrated*, and *Spindle and Oars*, 1893, set in a Scottish fishing village. The novel that made her name was *Joanna Traill, Spinster*, 1894 (in Heinemann's Pioneer Series). Joanna inherits a house and income in her late thirties and temporarily escapes the domination of her two disagreeable married sisters, taking in a girl from a brothel, first as servant, then as daughter. In 1896 [1895] AH pub. *The Years that the Locust Hath Eaten*, also well received; in 1898 she m. Eugene Lee-H. (1845-1907: *DNB*), poet and ex invalid half-brother of Vernon LEE. They lived in Italy, where in 1902 a daughter was born (d. 1904). AH continued writing until at least 1913 (*The Book of Anna*), producing novels and collections such as *A Garden of Spinsters*, 1904, fictional stories of different unmarried women. Her ideas deserve better than her cloyingly sentimental style. She died abroad: hence no death-date.

Holford, Margaret (Wrench), *c.* 1761–1834, novelist, poet and playwright, da. of William W. of Chester, wife of Allen H. (d. 1788) of Davenham, Cheshire: mother of Margaret HOLFORD junior. Her first novel, *Fanny*, 1785, opens with a letter from a rake ('Preach away! – I defy thee! – I am proverb proof!'), who after painful remorse (and changing his name on his father's death) *does* become a model husband to the lively heroine. In *Selima, or The Village Tale*, 6 vols., Chester and London, 1798 (well done though too long), an 'orphan' finds a father, title and husband (she is saved from abduction by a maid eavesdropping 'as she was brushing the stairs'). This has been wrongly given to Harriet Ventum (author of the epistolary, didactic *Selina*, 1800), and recorded as a 'ghost' *Fanny and Selima*. MH also pub. in 1798 *Calaf* (a Persian tale written at 17), and *Gresford Vale*, whose title poem, about an estate on the River Dee, compliments Anna SEWARD. MH had several reviews in the *Monthly Mirror*, 1798, so the poem it prints 'to her stammering tongue' is more likely hers than her daughter's. Her Restoration-style comedy, *Neither's the Man*, staged 1798 at Chester and printed there [1799], has a 'capricious, giddy, whimsical, coquettish, dear, angelic' heroine and some stale female butts; its epilogue says that wit, extinct 'in the male line', survives in ladies. *The Way to Win Her*, rejected for the stage but pub. 1814, has lively if crude satire on society marriage and gambling: naïve yet acute heroine, benevolently plotting hero, ridiculous learned lady, and a straying wife converted. MH is credited with another novel, *First Impressions, or The Portrait* [1800].

Holford, Margaret, later Hodson, 1778–1852, poet and novelist, eldest da. of Margaret (Wrench) HOLFORD. Her anonymous 'metrical romance' *Wallace, or The Fight of Falkirk*, 1809, was a hit, though it was said not to ape Scott's *Marmion* but to '*marmoset*' it. Scott wrote to her politely when nudged by Joanna BAILLIE. Highly romantic *Poems*, 1811, dedicated to her mother, bore her name: they include an ode to Anna SEWARD, 1802. In 1813 she quarrelled with Sarah Siddons; she was called 'tenacious of reputation', with a remarkable, bold, plain face. She offered *Margaret of Anjou*, 1816, to her mother in gratitude for her inherited gift. *The Past, &c*, 1819 (short poems), includes 'Weaning': 'the earliest task of woe / Our nature struggles with below'. *Warbeck of Wolfstein*, 1820, is a medieval novel influenced by P. B. Shelley; she turned prose tales from Italian, 1823. By 1826, when she sought help in financial trouble from Scott and became second wife of the Rev. Septimus Hodson, she was an invalid, but still writing tales and translations.

Holland, Catherine, 1637–1720, religious memoirist, the rebellious one among 11 children of a Catholic, Alethea (Panton), and a 'severe father' and 'earnest Protestant', Sir John H.: brought up in Holland during the Civil War. Her parents disagreed over her education; her father, whom she both feared and loved, sought to break her will; she chose her mother's faith without knowing what was in it, though her mother seemed too meek and mild to help. At about ten she attempted suicide; later she sometimes pursued pleasure (dancing, 'Carding', music) and sometimes stole away for 'discoursing with my self: What am I? Why am I?' She dreaded 'the Slavery of Marriage'. About 1661 she told her father, by letter, that reading history had convinced her the Catholic church was right. For two more years he kept her temporizing, scorning equally (as lukewarm) the 'pretended' Bishop of Winchester and a Jesuit Provincial. The high point in her story, written in 1664 as a new NUN (pub. in Catherine S. Durrant's study of English Catholics in Holland, 1925), is the joy and triumph of her escape from London to St Monica's, Louvain. Here she lived, noted for 'high spirit and quick wit' and her efforts to control them, for 'merry conceits and jeasts', for 'genius to poetry' and for putting pious French and Dutch works into English.

Holland, Elizabeth Vassall, Lady, 1771–1845, also Webster, diarist, only child of the American Mary (Clarke) and Richard V.: heiress to Jamaican estates for which both her husbands took her surname. After a gloomy, repressed childhood she discovered learning at 13, then at 15 was m., unhappily, to the 49-year-old Sir Godfrey Webster. She began her diary (which runs to 1811), in impersonal guide-book style, after persuading him to take her abroad in 1791. She delighted in Italy, met the 3rd Lord H. in 1794 and fell in love. In 1796, pregnant by him and expecting to be divorced, she kidnapped her daughter by staging her 'death' (she handed her over six years later). She married H. in 1797, the month of the divorce, took up politics, made Holland House a Whig nerve-centre, wielded a strong will and sharp mind, and admired Napoleon. Lady Caroline LAMB satirized her as the Princess of Madagascar in *Glenarvon*, 1816. MSS at the BL: diary pub. 1908 (reviewed by WOOLF), 1910; letters 1946; life by Sonia Keppel, 1974.

Hollar, Constance, 1880–1945, poet, b. at Port Royal, Jamaica, and well educ. there (a sister, Anna H., was locally influential as a classics teacher). CH was probably the first black woman to attend lectures at London Univ. Back at home, she opened a Kingston kindergarten and was active in the Jamaican Poetry League (founded 1923 as a branch of the Empire Poetry League, later linked with independence movements). Her work, reflecting the League's largely 'Caribbean Georgian' style and subject-matter, appeared in an early Jamaican anthology (J. E. Clare McFarlane, ed., *Voices from Summerland*, London, 1929); her own anthology is *Songs of Empire*, Kingston, 1932. Her one solo vol., *Flaming June*, Kingston, 1941, gathers poems from 25 years; some repr. in later anthologies. With intense feeling she protests human cruelty (e.g. 'The Caged Mongoose'), celebrates tropical fauna and flora, hints, sometimes, at a distinctive Jamaican presence in the landscape or Jamaican identity for herself, and uses imagination to join earth and heaven for those who, like her, have 'seen the green light in the trees'. Often heavily European ('She has tied the blue-bells of the sea / With silver ribbons: and each tree / Draped with Gobelin tapestry'), she can be simple and vivid: 'I shall drink deep of the noontide; my cup all red / And coral bright / Shall glisten in the strong white blaze . . .'. Memoirs by McFarlane in *A Literature in the*

Making, 1956; see Chapter 1 of Lloyd W. Brown, *West Indian Poetry*, 1978.

Holley, Marietta, 'Samantha Allen', 'Josiah Allen's Wife', 'Jemyma', 1836–1926, essayist, poet, humorist, b. Jefferson Co., NY, youngest of seven children of Mary (Taber) and John Milton H. She was educ. at district school, then forced to teach the piano. Encouraged by Lydia H. SIGOURNEY and Oliver Wendell Holmes, she initially published pious, sentimental verse, but it was *My Opinions and Betsey Bobbet's*, 1873, that won her national fame as a humorist and popularizer of 'wimmen's rites'. It consists of loosely connected episodes in the life of Josiah Allen's wife Samantha, who expounds feminist views with vernacular humour. Her foils are the genteel spinster Betsey Bobbet, who believes woman's only 'spear' is marriage, and her husband who feebly opposes women's SUFFRAGE. Though he thinks farming is 'so strengthenin' and stimulatin' to wimmin, . . . when it comes to droppin' a little slip of clean paper into a small . . . box, once a year in a shady room, you are afraid it is goin' to break down a woman's constitution' (p. 92). Eventually Samantha goes to NYC and presents her views to E. C. STANTON, Victoria WOODHULL, and S. B. ANTHONY, who invited MH to the 1878 National Woman Suffrage Convention, and sent her material for *Sweet Cicely*, 1885, which deals with the legal system, and women married to intemperate men. Her most popular work, *Samantha at Saratoga: or Racin' after Fashion*, 1887, pokes fun at genteel values. In her 20 vols, MH covered a wide range of topical issues including racism, US imperialism, prostitution, TEMPERANCE and women's rights, as seen in her last volume, *Josiah Allen on the* WOMAN QUESTION. Her autobiography appeared posthumously in *Watertown (NY) Times*, 1931. Jane Curry's *Samantha Rastles*, 1983, is an anthology of MH's feminist writings. See also Kate H. Winter's 1984 study.

Holme, Constance, later Punchard, 1880–1955, novelist and playwright, youngest of 14 children of Elizabeth (Cartmel) and land-agent John H. Born at Milnthorpe, South Westmorland, near which her whole life was spent, she was a story-teller at school (at Birkenhead and Blackheath, London). Her *Hugh of Hughsdale* was a serial in the *Kendal Mercury and Times*, 1909; a novel of 1912 was unpublished. *Crump Folk Going Home*, 1913, set in county society, shows her intimate understanding of her district and interest in the bearing on life of books and dreams and female consciousness: 'I leave Voltaire and Shaw and the PANKHURSTS about . . . but he doesn't see them – he's too busy collecting me.' *The Lonely Plough*, 1913 (see booklet by Norman T. Carrington [1963]), deals in tradition and change, both social and practical (a new sea wall fatally gives way). In *The Old Road from Spain*, 1916 (*The Homecoming* in the US), CH uses her mother's alleged Spanish-armada blood and an ancient superstition she newly invented. That year she m. Frederick Burt Punchard, also a land-agent, and moved to Kirkby Lonsdale (where Margaret Llewelyn Davies was running the Women's Co-operative Guild). The shadow of WWI lies on CH's four 'Greek novels', each narrating a single decisive day, building personal pasts in flashback. *Beautiful End*, 1918, shares the plot of 'The House of Vision' (dialect play acted by Edith CRAIG's Pioneer Society, in CH's *Four One-Act Plays* [1932]): an old man rejects loving care in his changed old home for grim exile with memory of it as unchanged. Other renunciations are explored in *The Splendid Fairing*, 1919 (Femina-Vie Heureuse Award), *The Trumpet in the Dust*, 1921 (about a retired charwoman and almhouse-dwellers), and *The Things Which Belong*, 1925. *I Want!* (staged 1931, anthologized 1933) is a comedy set in a smart tennis club, where class-conscious shells skilfully cloak desiring selves. *He-Who-Came?*, 1930, carries the lore of a farmer's wife over the verge of the occult. All CH's eight novels were repr. as World's Classics, 1930–5. *The Wisdom of the Simple*, 1937, collects stories in many voices and 'poems in prose', some very brief, some mystical, some sharply observed: two male speakers objectify their wives as a tree and a horse. Meagre archive at Kent State Univ. 'That's Easy' appeared in *Serif*, 1, 1964; CH left *The Jasper Sea* unfinished. See Glen Cavaliero in *The Rural Tradition*, 1977: Margaret Crosland, 1981.

Holmes, Mary Jane (Hawes) 1825–1907, novelist, b. Brookfield, Mass., da. of Fanny (Olds) and Preston H. She was educ. at public schools in Mass. and taught from age 13. Two years later she began publishing articles and short stories and in 1849 she m. Daniel H. Her first novel, *Tempest and Sunshine*, 1854, was an immediate success. *The English Orphans*, portraying life in a county poorhouse and at Mt Holyoke Seminary, followed in 1855. Her novels adapted favourite fairytale plots to the standard themes of mid-nineteenth-century women's fiction, and in *Lena Rivers*, 1856, her most popular, the Cinderella story is almost directly retold. A 'wicked' aunt and her two daughters make life difficult for Lena, while a kindly grandmother provides comfort and a 'prince' supplies the love interest. *Meadowbrook*, 1857, is a semi-autobiographical novel in which MJH's own ideas about marriage and authorship may be discerned. Although her heroines must be 'purified by suffering' and achieve their happy endings through perseverance, high moral character and intelligence, the didactic message is lightened by social comedy. See Nina Baym, 1978.

Holmes, Sarah Katherine (Stone), 1841–1908, DIARIST, b. Hinds County, Miss., da. of Amanda (Ragan) and William S. The oldest daughter of seven children, SH graduated from the Nashville Female Academy and later was intermittently tutored at Brokenburn, the Louisiana plantation her mother bought and ran after her father's death. SH began keeping a journal when the Civil War broke out. She left a lively record of her family's straits on the plantation and as refugees in Texas. Despite – or because of – her remoteness from the scenes of political power, SH's journal conveys something of the Confederacy's political, social and geographical diversity. In 1867 she m. Henry Bry H. and settled in Tallulah, La., where she had four children. She transcribed her journal, adding an introduction in 1900; it was pub. in 1955 as *Brokenburn: The Journal of Kate Stone, 1861–8*, ed. with an introduction by John Q. Anderson.

Holtby, Winifred, 1898–1935, novelist, journalist, social reformer. B. in Rudstone, East Riding of Yorkshire, da. of Alice (Winn) and David Holtby, she was educ. at Queen Margaret's School, Scarborough. In 1917 she went to Somerville College, Oxford, which she left, 1918, for war service in France as a WAAC, returning to Somerville, 1919, where she met Vera BRITTAIN and took a degree in History, 1921. In 1922 she went to live in London with Vera and began lecturing for the Six Point Group (a women's rights organization founded by Margaret Haig, Lady RHONDDA) and the League of Nations Union. She wrote extensively on pacifism and feminism for a variety of journals, including the feminist weekly *Time and Tide*, of which she became a director, 1926. Her first novel, *Anderby Wold*, 1923, is set in the farming community of her youth; the next, *The Crowded Street*, 1924, vividly exposes the trivial lives of provincial middle-class women. Her other novels – *The Land of Green Ginger*, 1927, *Poor Caroline*, 1931, *Mandoa, Mandoa!*, 1933, and *South Riding*, 1936 – her poems and short stories, her anti-fascist play *Take Back Your Freedom* (published posthumously in 1939), and her non-fiction work, including *Virginia Woolf*, 1932 (discussed by Marion Shaw in M.

Monteith, ed., *Women's Writing*, 1986) and *Women in a Changing Civilization*, 1934, increasingly competed for time with her other activities, especially her involvement in the unionization of black workers in South Africa, where she visited in 1926: 'I shall never quite make up my mind whether to be a reformer-sort-of-person or a writer-sort-of-person'. In 1931 she developed symptoms of renal failure. Often very ill thereafter, she continued to write, lecture, and collect funds for the South African scheme. She died one month after completing *South Riding*. A letter to her mother, 1933, summarizes WH's attitudes: 'I want there to be no more wars: I want people to recognize the human claims of Negroes and Jews and women and all oppressed and humiliated creatures. I want a sort of bloodless revolution.' *South Riding*, a novel about local government, illustrates her belief in the need for corporate action to combat poverty, illness and ignorance. Like all her novels, it is also staunchly feminist in its use of a strong woman as the central protagonist. It won the James Tait Black Prize, 1937, and has never gone out of print. It became a film, 1937, and has been twice serialized for TV. Her other novels have recently been reprinted by Virago, along with Vera Brittain's biography, *Testament of Friendship*, 1940. Her correspondence with Brittain, various manuscripts, including one of *South Riding*, and much miscellaneous material, are located in the Holtby Collection, Hull Central Library. Study on her relationship with Brittain by Jean E. Kennard, 1989.

Hooper, Lucy, 1816–41, poet and short-story writer, b. Newburyport, Mass., da. of Joseph H., who taught her botany, chemistry, languages and English literature. After his death in 1831 the family moved to Brooklyn, where LH contributed to the Long Island *Star* and the *New Yorker*. Her prize-winning essay 'Domestic Happiness', with two other pieces, was included in Dunning's collection *Domestic Happiness Portrayed*, 1831. Her romantic verses, such as 'The Lock of Hair' and 'The Turquoise Ring' are obsessed with such fetishes of memory and love. Of more interest is her religious poetry, particularly 'The Daughter of Herodias', the monologue of Salome presenting the head of John the Baptist to her mother. This poem, which illustrates the 'feminization' of US theology and the mortuary cult of 'poetic remains', was included in William Cullen Bryant's vol. of US poetry. Her prose tales, collected in *Scenes from Real Life*, 1841, are mostly predictable and didactic, though 'Reminiscences of a Clergyman' sympathetically depicts the dilemma of a mysterious wanderer, thought to be lost at sea, who returns to find his wife happily married to his brother. Her *Poetical Remains*, 1842, has a memoir by John Keese.

Hooper, Lucy Hamilton (Jones), 1835–93, poet, journalist, novelist and playwright, b. Philadelphia, da. of Bataile Muse J., prominent city merchant. She m. Robert E. H., 1854, and pub. *Poems: with Translations from the German*, 1864. Writing for money, she was both a contributor to and assistant editor of *Lippincott's*, 1868 to 1870. *Poems*, 1871, consists mainly of mortuary verse, patriotic set-pieces and domestic sentimentalism. However, her poems of mourning and memory are interesting, 'Winter Dirge' being reminiscent of Emily BRONTË's Gondal poems. Her male survivors are treated with a certain vengefulness, as in 'A Winter Tale', in which two mysterious women tell 'Of woman's faith and of man's faithlessness'; their vow to avenge each other results in one man committing suicide while the other 'lives and longs to die!' 'The Duel' is a Browningesque dramatic monologue in which the husband, having survived a duel, takes the wife's concern to be for him. In 1874, LHH's husband was appointed vice-consul general in Paris. Their house became a centre for literary, artistic and intellectual circles, and for nearly 20 years LHH was Paris correspondent for the Philadelphia *Evening Telegraph.* Her novel *The Tsar's Widow*, 1881, describes nineteenth-century Russian life, as from the journal of Dorris Romilly, an intelligent, independent heroine who typifies the American girl abroad. LHH also wrote two plays, *Her Living Image*, 1886, with French dramatist Laurencin, and *Helen's Inheritance*, 1888.

Hooton, Elizabeth, 1600?–70, Quaker missionary and pamphleteer, wife of Oliver H. (d. 1652). Possibly the first person to join Margaret FELL's future husband, *c.* 1646, she preached widely in the 1650s. Often in jail, she wrote *False Prophets and False Teachers Described*, 1652, with Mary FISHER and four others, while in York prison. In 1661 she made two voyages to America, the second to Boston with her daughter to preach against persecution of QUAKERS. Despite the king's written permission to buy land, she was whipped and turned naked into the snow, then rescued by American Indians. In 1670 she delivered the king a petition pub. at the end of Thomas Taylor's *To the King* [1671], arguing that impoverishment of charitable Quakers would ruin the kingdom. She died on board ship, having sailed with George Fox and others for Jamaica. Study by Emily Manners, 1914; but Quaker historians have largely ignored her importance.

'Hope, Laurence', Adela Florence Nicolson (Cory), 1865–1904, poet, b. at Stoke Bishop, Glos., da. of Fanny Elizabeth (Griffin) and Arthur C., colonel in the Indian Army, and sister of Vivian, later the novelist 'Victoria CROSSE'. Educ. at school in Richmond, she joined her parents in India and then m. Col. Malcolm Hassels N., a linguist and Queen VICTORIA's ADC, in 1889 and settled at Madras. LH's first book was *The Garden of Kama and Other Love Lyrics from India*, 1901, which went immediately into second and third editions and was reviewed as the work of a man. Exotic Eastern settings heighten the poems' passionate intensity, considered SAPPHIC in their expression of female desire. Some poems deal with the controversial subject of cross-cultural love, English and Indian, while later books attack racial prejudice directly in aphoristic verse. Set to music, some of the poems were equally popular as songs, e.g. 'Pale Hands I Loved Beside the Shalimar'. It is not clear whether any or all of the poems were translations. Two more vols. followed, *Stars of the Desert*, 1903, and *Indian Love*, 1905, the last pub. posthumously. Her husband died in 1904, and LH committed suicide two months later by taking perchloride of mercury.

Hopkins, Anne (Yale), d. 1698, mute, inglorious writer, wife of Edward H., governor of Connecticut. Governor John Winthrop wrote of her in April 1645 as a talented, 'godly young woman', gone insane as a result of 'giving herself wholly to reading and writing . . . many books'; she would have been safe if she had kept to 'her household affairs, and such things as belong to women'. We do not know what she wrote.

Hopkins, Pauline Elizabeth, 1859–1930, novelist, playwright, actress and short-story writer, b. Portland, Maine, da. of Sarah (Allen), descendant of a founding Baptist family. Her father Northrup apparently migrated north from Virginia. She was educ. at Boston public schools and Girls' High School. At 15 her essay 'Evils of Intemperance and Their Remedies' won a Congregational Publishing Society contest. Her first play, *Slaves' Escape: or the Underground Railroad*, was performed in Boston in 1880 with PH, her mother and stepfather (William H.) in the cast. For the next ten years she toured with a family performing group as 'Boston's Favorite Soprano', wrote another play, *One Scene from the Drama of Early Days*, and worked as a stenographer for the Bureau of Statistics.

Her story 'The Mystery Within Us' was pub. in the first issue of *Colored American*, 1890, and the same year her first novel, *Contending Forces: A Romance Illustrative of Negro Life North and South*, was written with the aim of advancing her people. It explores such issues as the victimization of women and the problems of blacks during Reconstruction, while also celebrating the black women's club movement. Until 1904 she was Women's Editor and Literary Editor of *Colored American*, which pub. two more of her stories in 1900, and in 1901 serialized her novels *Hagar's Daughter, A Story of Southern Caste Prejudice* (under her mother's name) and *A Dash For Liberty*. Besides a fourth novel, *Winona: A Tale of Negro Life in the South and Southwest*, 1902, she wrote a series of articles, 'Famous Men of the Negro Race' and 'Famous Women of the Negro Race', for *Colored American*, 1901–2, followed by 'The Dark Races of the Twentieth Century', in *Voice of the Negro*, 1905; her last work, the novella 'Topsy Templeton', was pub. in *New Era*, 1916. Her papers are at Fisk University Library, Nashville, Tenn. See articles by Ann Allen Shockley in *Phylon* 33, 1972, and Claudia Tate in *Conjuring*, ed. M. Pryse and H. Spillers, 1985; also Hazel V. Carby, *Reconstructing Womanhood*, 1987.

Hopkins, Sarah Winnemucca, 1844?–91, writer and campaigner for Indian rights, b. Nevada, da. of Tuboitone and 'Old Winnemucca', northern Paiutes. She left conflicting statements about her schooling, but learned to read and write English and to speak Spanish and at least two Indian languages. While living with whites in the 1850s she changed her name from Thocmetony to Sarah. She m. Edward C. Bartlett, 1871, but divorced him in 1876, and entered into an Indian marriage with an unknown man in the 1870s. Her marriage to Joseph Satwaller, 1878, also ended in divorce, and she subsequently m. Lewis H. H. in 1881. SH was a mediator between the Paiutes and the Federal government, acting as translator and scout for whites in the West and frequently writing to Washington on behalf of Paiute concerns. Her book, *Life among the Paiutes*, 1883, although somewhat rambling and contradictory, amply illustrates the Paiute situation and bears out her contention that 'Everyone knows what a woman must suffer who undertakes to act against bad men'. It was hailed as 'the first book of Indian literature' by Elizabeth PEABODY, who helped publish it and who supported SWH in her often discouraging work of trying to ameliorate the Paiutes' condition. Her husband's gambling addiction drained her resources and she ended her life teaching both Paiute and white culture at her school in Lovelock, Nevada. See Gae Whitney Canfield, 1983, for a detailed biography.

Hopper, Nora (later Chesson), 1871–1906, poet, b. in Exeter, da. of Capt. Harman Baillie H., 31st Bengal Native Infantry, and Caroline Augusta (Francis) to whom she dedicated *Ballads in Prose*, 1894, drawn from Irish folklore. Educ. at school in London, she began early to publish in journals, including *The Yellow Book*. She is chiefly a Celtic revivalist poet, but *Under Quicken Boughs*, 1896, regarded as her best work, also shows classical inspiration. In 1901 she m. novelist and critic Wilfred Hugh C. Two of their three children feature in her poems: Ann Caroline Spry (*Sunday*, xxxiv, 3) and Hugh, who died very young, in 'To a Child' (*Aquamarines*, 1902, which also contains some art movement poems). She also pub. a novel, *The Bell and The Arrow*, 1905 (by Mrs W. H. C.). *Father Felix's Chronicles*, 1907 (poems, ed. W.H. Chesson; written 1895?) claims that NH 'dreamed' the death of her child and seems to have regarded 'Pain as an evocation of Love and Courage' (see Introduction).

Hoppus, Mary Anne Martha (later Mrs Alfred Marks), 1843–1916, English novelist, who also wrote short stories, sonnets and popular history. Extracts from letters and journals of her mother Martha (Devenish; an old west country family), d. 1853, were pub. as *Memorials of a Wife*, 1856, by MH's father, John H., professor of mental and moral philosophy at University College, London (d. 1875). He wanted to show her strong religious sense, but her cheerfulness and love of her sisters also comes through. MH grew up in Camden Town, where undergraduates (e.g. W. Bagehot) boarded with them; many kept in touch with her. Her father taught her Latin, French and mathematics. Her first novel *Five-Chimney Farm*, 1877, realistically told, takes its half-French heroine from her Sussex farm home to Paris, where her brother is one of the insurgents killed in the 1848 revolution. MH wrote 12 books, novels and stories, between 1877 and 1894, including *Miss Montizambart*, 1885, a strong sombre story of a woman with an illegitimate son, brought up as her brother's child and uneasy with her intense love for him. Ruskin found her novel of the time of Domitian, *Masters of the World*, 1888, 'clever and splendid'; *Dr Willoghby Smith*, 1892, is a story of murder committed by a doctor. She also wrote a sonnet sequence on scientific knowledge, free will and necessity, *The Tree of Knowledge* (printed for priv. circulation 1896, pub. 1906 with additions), and two vols. of US and English popular history, 1907 and 1908.

Hopton, Susanna (Harvey), 1627–1709, devotional and theological writer. From a wealthy Anglican Staffordshire family, she m. Richard H., and after the Restoration gathered at Kington, Hereford, a religious circle perhaps including Thomas Traherne (who dedicated his *Centuries of Meditation* to her). In 1661 she abandoned the Catholicism she had embraced on Charles I's execution, and 'gave her Reasons' in a letter: 'long and learned', said Elizabeth ELSTOB, whose patron George Hickes published it in his *Second ... Controversial Letters*, 1710. *Daily Devotions*, by 'an Humble Penitent', 1673 (several later eds.), have been ascribed to Traherne, but those parts not extracted are probably hers. She 'Reformed' a liturgical work by the Catholic John Austin as *Devotions in the Ancient Way of Offices*, 1701: Hickes strongly recommended her version. Elizabeth THOMAS's 'Pylades' mentioned her 'several anonymous Books' in 1705. *A Collection ...*, 1717, reprinted her *Daily Devotions* with 'Meditations and Devotions on the Life of Christ' (which *may* be hers) and 'Meditations on the Creation' (which *may* be Traherne's). See George Robert Geoffrey's introduction to this, 1966; Gladys I. Wade, life of Traherne, 1944; Catherine A. Owen in *MLR*, lvi, 1961: investigation continues.

Hopwood, D. Caroline (Skene), Quaker autobiographer, da. of an able, educated mother and a Scots army officer. In 1781 she began writing, chiefly for her children, an *Account* of her life, finished 1788: pub. 1801 with some meditations and verse, part repr. 1907. She grew up an Anglican, less 'noticed' than her elder sister, 'naturally of a high spirit, proud and passionate'. At about 12 'I often looked at the Priests, and wondered why they were not like the Apostle Paul'; 'the more I saw of them, the worse I liked them'. She became worldly, 'dressed gay', then fell on hard times and worked as a housekeeper; her husband's business 'not answering', she ran a school and taught needlework, drawing and pastry. She tried the Presbyterians and Methodists, and was deeply troubled by cruelty, war and slavey. 'I had many ups and downs, my chariot wheels went on heavily', yet 'the seals were gradually opened in me, and the trumpets sounded in my soul'. The QUAKERS first asked her not to speak at meetings, then permitted her to join but 'rejected' the few words she spoke, then reproved her for staying away and condemned her book as 'not quite sound'.

Horovitz, Frances Margaret (Hooker), 1938–83, poet and reader. Da. of F. E. Hooker (a poem conjures his past as a 'ragged boy'), she grew up at Walthamstow, London, and went to Bristol Univ. (BA in drama and English, 1959) and the Royal Academy of Dramatic Art. She acted in repertory, films, and on TV, m. poet Michael H. in 1964, published in *New Departures* (a journal he edited), and issued *Poems* (12 pieces), 1967. Working for the BBC and Open Univ., she became known for readings of contemporary poets including Russian women; her work as a Poet in Schools was filmed for TV in 1981. Her friends included Anne STEVENSON and Kathleen RAINE. A 'severe judge of her own work', she wrote 'sparely and sparingly', making inanimate things – old silk, bone, glass, water – pregnant with implications of human meaning. *The High Tower*, 1970, deals with intense experiences of engagement and of distance and isolation, both in love and in nature. FH bore a son in 1971, and welcomed 'two extra in our household – / a butterfly / clings to the green curtain / he stays for the winter only / the new child / a guest for many seasons'. Her 'first substantial collection', *Water Over Stone*, 1980 (reprinting, as was her habit, a few earlier poems), voices response to her child both new and growing, to her father's death, to landscape, ancient history and pre-history. *Snow Light, Water Light*, 1983, is centred on a Roman fort near Hadrian's Wall, where she moved from Glos. in late 1980 with fellow-poet Roger Garfitt; in 1981–2 she appeared with him and others in *Wall*, 1981 (poems and drawings), *Presences of Nature*, and *Rowlstone Haiku*. Settled in Herefordshire, she and Garfitt m. shortly before her death from cancer of the ear. He edited her *Collected Poems*, 1985, incorporating her unfinished *Voices Returning* and some other MSS. In 'Flowers' she wrote 'only myself / almost a ghost upon the road / without accoutrement, / holding the flowers / as torch and talisman / against the coming dark'; her last-written line makes rain on a window 'glass beads flung on glass'. She is commemorated in *PN Review*, 35, and Michael H., ed., *Celebration*, 1985.

Horsfield, Debbie, playwright, b. 1955, eldest of five das. in a working-class Manchester family. She was educ. at Eccles Grammar School and Newcastle Univ. (BA in English, 1978). Leaving home, and a later return to stay while she worked nearby, were both experiences which strengthened her hold on her background as the central material of her work. Having devised an Edinburgh Festival Play (the germ of *Red Devils*) as a student, she began writing seriously in 1978, while working at the Gulbenkian Studio Theatre, Newcastle. Her *Arrangements*, for radio, 1981 (teenage pregnancy and shotgun marriage), was followed by a stage play, *Out on the Floor*, Stratford East, London, 1981. She was with the Royal Shakespeare Company, 1980–3, and wrote *Away from It All*, 1982, and *All You Deserve*, 1983. *The Red Devils Trilogy*, pub. 1986, her most successful work, traces the friendship of four young Manchester women: 'disillusion, despair and defeat' as well as 'loyalty, humour and tenacity'. In *Red Devils*, aged 18, they are passionate football supporters: 'God, give us a goal – give us two and I'll give up biting me nails.' In *Truth Dare Kiss* and *Command or Promise* they move on to scarce jobs and problematic relations with men: 'Now that I do root perms for Lou Macari, it's hardly decent for me to be screaming meself hoarse every week. I'm past all that sort of thing.' But in a harshly pressured world their past connection remains emotionally life-giving. In Liverpool, 1983, *Red Devils* was seen as a slice-of-life; in London, 1984–5, the plays seemed explicitly and emphatically political. DH says that character and personal relations take priority in her work over any political message. She has since had staged *Touch and Go*, 1984, and *Revelations*, 1985. Her TV series *Making Out*, 1989, deals with the female workforce of an electronics manufacturing firm. DH has a child and lives in London. Interview in *Plays International*, 1, 1985.

Hosain, Attia, short-story writer, novelist, broadcaster. B. in 1913 in Lucknow, India, into one of the oldest Muslim landowning families of Oudh, called *Taluqdars*, she was educ. in La Martinère, an exclusive school, and by an English governess, both marks of her family's privileged position in British India. She then became the first woman from a Taluqdar family to graduate from Isabella Thorburn College, Lucknow. She has written and broadcast short stories and plays in Urdu and English, on both All-India Radio and the BBC Overseas Service. Her most recognized work, her novel, *Sunlight on a Broken Column*, 1961, semi-autobiographical, graphically describes women's restricted life behind the *purdah* in an aristocratic Muslim household in pre-British India. AH depicts a 40-year-period in India's history through the eyes of a Muslim woman so chained by patriarchy that even the most crucial decisions of her life must be taken by male family members. She forestalls easy answers, complicating gender oppression with class and national oppression. While the narrator and the women of her family are 'sentenced to a life of luxurious incarceration', their only role that of 'symbol of others' desires', poor Muslim women are doubly oppressed, by sexual exploitation by upper-class Muslim men and by the extreme poverty of their men. 'Better to be my father's mule that sometimes digs in its heels and will not move even when it is beaten, than to be poor and a woman', says an outspoken female servant. *Phoenix Fled*, 1953, is a collection of short stories about the lives of Muslim women and the partition of India. AH has been neglected by critics, though her novel attracts a devoted following and though there is so little written on Muslim women in India and so few Muslim women writers. See profile by well-known Indo-Anglian novelist Mulk Raj Anand in *Sunlight*, 1979.

Hoskens or Hoskins, **Jane** (Fenn), 1693-*c.* 1770, Quaker autobiographer and preacher, b. in London. A severe illness at 15 broke into her taste for 'singing and dancing', awaking a sense of sin and of a divine mission to go to Pennsylvania. Her father forbade this ('his will was as a law to me'), but opposition reawakened her desire to go. She landed at Philadelphia in 1712, and was indentured (she calls it 'purchase') as a teacher in Plymouth. She loved the work and the Quaker religion: 'Oh! the calm, the peace, comfort and satisfaction wherewith my mind was cloathed, like a child enjoying his father's favour.' A call to preach dismayed her (she has 'spoken much against womens appearing in that manner'), till she came to accept that 'fear of a forward spirit' had made her 'guilty of the sin of omission'; her first halting words spoken at meeting heralded a remarkable preaching career: all over America, in Barbados (twice), England, and Ireland (twice). She married in 1738, but her *Life and Spiritual Sufferings*, Philadelphia, 1771, says little of her husband. Hannah GRIFFITTS commemorated her 'living language' in a poem. She has been confused with Elizabeth ASHBRIDGE.

Hospital, Janette (Turner), novelist, short-story writer, b. 1942 in Melbourne, Victoria, da. of Elsie (Morgan) and lay-pastor Adrian T. Brought up in Brisbane, she graduated from the Univ. of Queensland in 1965 to become a secondary school teacher, m. the Rev. Clifford H., professor of comparative religion, that year, lived in England, India and the US, had two children, and since 1971 has been based in Kingston, Ontario. She took an MA in medieval English literature at Queen's Univ., 1973, and has lectured in English at various tertiary institutions, and been a writer-in-residence in the US and Australia. She became a full-time writer on winning the Seal Award for her first novel, *The Ivory Swing*, 1982. *The Tiger in the Tiger Pit*, 1983, focuses on estrangement and tensions in a family whose parents approach their fiftieth wedding anniversary. In *Borderline*, 1985, the lives of three strangers simultaneously crossing the Canadian-US border become inexplicably enmeshed. Both these are peopled with self-conscious characters: the piano-tuner narrator of *Borderline* deftly writes into existence evanescent Felicity, muse figure and artist of life alike. JTH's almost compulsive use of literary allusion adds to her characters' complexity but often suggests contrived authorial intrusion. The title of *Dislocations*, 1986 (stories: winner of the Fellowship of Australian Writers Award), identifies themes which persist throughout her fiction: she is 'very conscious of . . . belonging nowhere. . . . All my characters are always caught between worlds or between cultures or between subcultures.' She pub. *Charades* in 1988. See John Moss, *A Reader's Guide to the Canadian Novel*, 2nd ed., 1987; Coral Ann Howells, *Private and Fictional Worlds*, 1987.

Hoult, Norah, 1898–1984, novelist and short-story writer. B. in Dublin, da. of Margaret (O'Shaughnessy) and Powis H., she was orphaned early. Educ. in English boarding schools, she then worked as a journalist in Sheffield and London, and returned to Dublin in 1931. She lived in NYC before WWII, returning to London, then, finally, to Dublin; she m., and the marriage was later dissolved. Her first of nearly 30 books, *Poor Woman!* 1928, collects stories of women in different lines of life: most admired was 'Bridget Kiernan', about a young Irishwoman working as a domestic servant in England. (NH's last work, *Two Girls in the Big Smoke*, 1977, returns to the topic of Irishwomen in England, here sisters in London.) *Time Gentlemen! Time!* 1929, dedicated to the 'gay memory' of her mother, naturalistically depicts masculine pub culture and the financial and emotional problems of marriage to an alcoholic. Dublin supplied the material for *Holy Ireland*, 1935, and its sequel, *Coming From the Fair*, 1937, which follow family life, and the ravages of religious prejudice, from the late nineteenth century to 1916. NH has sometimes chosen settings further afield, like the American South. She favours realistic, sometimes harsh, detail and dialogue rather than narrative rapidity. Critics have found her work feminist in tone, but she believed (in 1955) that feminism had done 'more harm than good to the true welfare of women'.

House, Amelia Pegram, '**Blossom**', South African poet, short-story writer, scholar. B. in Wynberg, Cape, she studied at Hewat Training College and the Univ. of Cape Town (BA, 1961), then taught in Cape Town, using the code name 'Blossom' for her work in the underground. She moved to London, a virtual exile, 1963, and studied drama at the Guildhall School of Music and Drama, acting on stage, TV and radio. In 1972 she m. a man named House and moved to Kentucky. She has a daughter. Divorced, she taught at Fort Knox public schools while studying for a PhD. She received an MA from the Univ. of Louisville, 1977, for several short fiction pieces. She compiled the first *Checklist of Black South African Women Writers in English*, 1980. Published by the Program on Women at Northwestern Univ., it gives brief biographies of 37 writers, and interviews with Manoko Nchwe and Fatima Dike. AH has published poems, stories, and scholarly articles in several journals, including *Présence Africaine*, *Callaloo*, *The Gar*, and *Essence*. Her fiction treats the South African punitive laws on mixed marriage, street drugs, children in poverty, mothers and fathers in detention. 'Awakening', a story about police brutality, published in *Staffrider*, 1979, was banned. *Deliverance*, a collection of poetry 'for South Africa', 1986, takes its title from the lines: 'Like a woman gone / beyond her time, / My country / you amble on / We can no longer / wait for nature's course / We must deliver / You / with force'. AH puts poetry with percussion and dance. Her latest drama, 'You've Struck a Rock', 'a multimedia presentation she directed', commemorates six South African women activists 'of all colors and varied walks of life who worked together and suffered for freedom': Rosa Parks, Fannie Lou Hamer, Helen Joseph, Ruth FIRST, Albertine Sisulu, and Lilian Ngoya.

Housman, H. (Pearsall), d. 1735, religious diarist, eldest of her family, living at Kidderminster, Worcs. She wrote from at least 1710, dwelling constantly on death, especially after her marriage, 1715. 'God hath been exercising me with children, in giving and taking; in raising my hopes, and then disappointing ... if it should please God to ... make me the living mother of a living child, my earnest desire is, to resign it to the Lord, to be his.' Her surviving daughter, 'the delight of our eyes, and joy of our hearts', had many narrow escapes, 'But yet I would not forget she is a dying creature, death is still in pursuit of her.' In 1729, 'Blessed be God, we are yet a family', not, like so many, 'broken up by death' or other causes. Her pious effusions are often tedious, but the emotional struggle to submit is gripping. Selecs. pub. as *The Power and Pleasure of the Divine Life*, 1744, enlarged ed. 1832, not in order but arranged under religious topics.

Houston, Elizabeth Maynard, **'Libby'**, poet and broadcaster, b. in 1941 in North London, da. of Mary Frances (Gillan), a former singer, and Alexander Millar H., a civil servant turned bomber pilot who d. in 1943. While at primary school she had a poem read on radio Children's Hour. She attended Westonbirt Girls' School, Glos., and Lady Margaret Hall, Oxford (BA in English, 1963): she says these facts have little relevance to her life. She found Oxford disenchanting, joined a blues band as a singer, and gave cellar readings of poems (with others) at the 1961 Edinburgh Festival. She lived in Holloway, London, from 1963, as an often unemployed typist, with poetry and poverty as the constants in her life. In 1966 she m. Malcolm Dean, working-class artist and jazz trumpeter, and next year (while working for the publisher) issued *A Stained Glass Raree Show*, illustrated by her husband. She had two children; Dean died of cancer in 1974. She published *Plain Clothes*, 1971, began reading poems for children on radio in 1973, and became an Arvon Foundation poetry tutor. A brief second marriage took her to Clevedon, near Bristol, in 1979. She co-founded a group called Practising Poets, 1983 (bringing closer contact with other women writers), took a certificate in biology at Bristol Univ., 1986, and published a botanical study. *At the Mercy*, 1981, extends her poetic range in content, style and form. She reads – and sings – her work widely, uses assonantal effects learned from Anglo-Saxon poetry, and exploits musical potential: 'syllables might scurry past, for instance, as quavers against the crotchet beat'. She draws on personal experience, from her love of rock-climbing to her husband's death. See her piece in WANDOR, ed., *On Gender and Writing*, 1983.

Houstoun, Matilda Charlotte (Jesse), *c.* 1815–92, novelist. Her mother was the da. of a wealthy Welsh baronet, Sir John Norris. MH was the younger da. of author Edward J., Deputy Surveyor of Royal Parks and Palaces, and was educ. by a Welsh governess whom she loathed for not allowing her to read novels. At 17 she m. the Rev. George Fraser, had a son, and was widowed in less than a year: in 1837 m. William H., captain of Hussars. She lived for a year on their yacht and became known through her travel adventures, *A Yacht Voyage to Texas and the Gulf of Mexico*, 1844, and *Hesperos: or, Travels in the West*, 1850. They settled at Dhulough Lodge, Co. Sligo, a remote estate among the Connaught Mountains, where in 'sheer weariness of spirit' she began to write. She financed her very successful anonymous first novel, *Recommended to Mercy*, 1862, about a woman who lives with a man but refuses to marry him, thus preserving her independence, and wrote over 20 more. *Records of a Stormy Life*, 1888, autobiographical in tone, tells of the marriage of a high-spirited girl to a reckless army colonel who causes her, through loneliness and worry, to lose all vivacity and moral courage. *Twenty Years in the Wild West*, 1879, and *A Woman's Memories of World-Known Men*, 1883, give her impressions of life in Ireland and reveal her gift for anecdote. Her family was close to the Sheridans (Caroline NORTON's family). *Only a Woman's Life*, 1889, is an account of the trial and conviction of Frances Stallard for child murder in 1877; MH was convinced of her innocence and on its publication Stallard was released.

Howard, Anne and **Mary Matilda** (1804–93), sisters who both wrote Broad Church tales for young people, pub. anon. Living in Lincolnshire, Mary spent time at Hastings from 1842 for her health, staying with Dr James Mackness, whose *Memoirs* she pub. 1851 and who urged her to write *Brampton Rectory, or the Lesson of Life*, 1849, to counter religious extremism. Dedicated to Thomas Arnold, with a priggish clergyman hero devoted to good works, it became famous. She also wrote *Compton Merivale: Another Leaf from the Lesson of Life*, 1850, and *The Youth and Womanhood of Helen Tyrrel*, 1854, plus several Handbooks (to Hastings, to Ocean Flowers, to Wild Flowers). Anne pub. three anti-Tractarian novels, two of which are subtitled 'Tale for the Times' (1844, 1845), while the third is *Philip and Susan; or, Twenty Years Ago*, 1851 (repr. 1852).

Howard, Elizabeth Jane, novelist, b. 1923 in London, to Katherine M. and David Liddon H. Educ. at home and at the London Mask Theatre School, she acted briefly at Stratford-on-Avon and in repertory, then worked in TV and modelling. She m. Peter Scott in 1942, had a daughter, and in 1947 left the theatre to be a secretary (later becoming an editor, reviewer, and festival organizer: Cheltenham and Salisbury). Her first novel, *The Beautiful Visit*, 1950 (John Llewellyn Rhys Prize), traces in part diary, part first-person narrative, the maturing of a spirited young girl before and after WWI: chafing to escape her restrictive family and to write, though 'desperately sorry' for her mother as she leaves to go round the world with a woman friend. Its wide and lasting appeal has been matched by most of EJH's later works. *The Long View*, 1956, opens with the break-up of a marriage (then traced back through significant moments to a first meeting 24 years before). In 1959 EJH m. James Douglas-Henry, and published *Sea Change*, about a young actress; in 1965 she m. novelist Kingsley Amis (divorced 1983). *After Julius*, 1965, charts, through one weekend, the lasting effects (on widow, daughters and others) of a man's patriotic death 20 years before in the Dunkirk evacuation; *Something in Disguise*, 1969, made up of three episodes within a year, shows a widow marrying a man who is after her money: EJH wrote a series of TV plays from each of these novels. Later works continue to centre on marriage and other tangled relationships: *Mr Wrong*, 1975, is short stories; *Getting It Right*, 1982, her latest novel (filmed 1985), about a late-developing male hairdresser, is a gallery of satirically observed women ending with true love.

Howarth, Anna, 1854?–1943, novelist and poet, b. in London. When her clergyman father died she was sent to Cape Colony, South Africa. There she trained as a nurse and lived many years with Selina Kirkman, whose family introduced her to S. African farm life. The central figure in her first book, *Jan: An Afrikander*, 1897, is actually the son of an English gentleman and a black chief's daughter: seen through the increasingly admiring eyes of prejudiced whites, he takes up his English heritage with perfect ease, but (violent and tragic as well as noble) kills himself for what is seen as good cause, leaving his brother unconscious that he is Sir Mbangwe Fairbank. *Katrina, A Tale of the Karoo*, 1898, opens in a smallpox epidemic of 1859, *Sword and Assegai*, 1899, in a war between colonists and tribesmen in 1834; *Nora Lester*, 1902, opens in an English orphanage but soon moves its two heroes to the Boer War. Each deals with a small group of family and friends, kept or brought together by coincidence as necessary; each approaches the female characters via their menfolk. *Stray Thoughts in Verse*, Cape Town [1923], includes WWI laments, and some good lines on S. African landscape. AH returned to England in 1935, after Kirkman died.

Howe, Julia (Ward), 1819–1910, poet, biographer and reformer, b. NYC, fourth of seven children of Julia Rush (Cutler) and Samuel W., Wall Street banker. She was educ. by governesses and at young ladies' schools, and tutored by Cogswell, later head of Astor Library. In 1843 she m. Samuel Gridley H., head of the Perkins Institute for the Blind, who fiercely opposed married women entering public life. In *Passion Flowers*, 1854, JWH depicts her husband thinly disguised as 'Thunder' and 'Vulcan'. Many of her poems are about conflict, disappointment and inadequacy, and in her play *Leonora*, 1857, condemned as immoral and closed after one week, the heroine is unable to kill the lover who has abandoned her and kills herself instead. Despite her husband's opposition, JWH persisted with her writing, gaining renown with the 'Battle Hymn of the Republic', 1862. She became a leader of the American Woman Suffrage Association. Her *Reminiscences*, 1899, contrast the condition of the emancipated slave, 'endowed with the full dignity of citizenship', with that of women who had worked for emancipation yet were themselves denied the vote. In 1870 JWH founded and edited the weekly *Woman's Journal*. She lectured to women's groups and was a preacher with the Unitarian Church, and also initiated campaigns for world peace. Her husband died in 1876. JWH was the first woman to be elected to the American Academy of Arts and Letters, 1908. In her *Reminiscences*, she concludes that her greatest successes were 'to plead for the slave when he was a slave, to help initiate the women's movement in many states and to stand with the illustrious champions of justice and freedom for woman SUFFRAGE when to do so was a thankless office involving public ridicule and private avoidance'. Life by Laura E. RICHARDS, her daughter, and Maud Howe ELLIOTT, 1915. Much of her best work remains in MSS at Harvard and Radcliffe.

Howe, Tina, playwright, b. in 1937 in NYC, da. of painter Mary (Post) and radio and TV newsman Quincy H., related through him to Julia Ward HOWE. Writing was in her cultivated, well-off family: she typed for years on a machine on which her father had written eight books; his father was a Pulitzer Prize-winning poet and biographer who published more than 50 books; her aunt Helen H. was a celebrated monologuist in the thirties and forties; and TH 'was defined as a writer before I was defined as a woman'. She was educ. in 'an elitist private girls' school', later at Sarah Lawrence College (BA, 1959). A successful student production of her one-act play *Closing Time*, written to 'save face' when she was not doing well in a short-story writing course, and a year in Paris, made her a serious writer. She did graduate work at Columbia Univ., attended the Chicago Teachers' College, and wrote one-act plays while teaching English and drama in Maine and Wisconsin high schools in the 1960s. She m. novelist Norman Levy, 1961; they have two children. *The Nest*, produced 1970, her first off-Broadway play, closed in one night. It was produced by, among others, Honor MOORE, who also published

In Birth and After Birth in her important anthology, *The New Women's Theatre*, 1970. This still unproduced play identifies the nuclear family as a central subject, exposing the brutality and suppression in US family ritual by unexpected, superbly comic, juxtapositions with other tribal rituals. TH calls it 'absurdist' and says that she wrote it for 'the suburban woman with no exit from her kitchen and a four-year-old seven feet tall'. TH observes precisely the eccentric behaviour of wealthy white Americans in settings she shifts from ordinary to exotic: a gallery show in *Museum*, produced 1978, a restaurant in *The Art of Dining*, produced 1979, a beach in *Coastal Disturbances*, produced 1986. *Painting Churches*, 1983 ('probably my deepest play') depicts an upper-class couple in declining circumstances whose successful daughter returns to paint their portrait, hoping to preserve the past. It was directed by Carole Rothman, with whom TH has worked since. In *Approaching Zanzibar*, 1989, a family confronts the death of its elder members and a sense of renewal in the young: it is a comedy. TH teaches playwriting at New York Univ. Interview in Betsko and Koenig, 1987, quoted above. See Janet Brown, *Feminist Drama*, 1979, Keyssar, 1984, Judith Barlow in Enoch Baxter, ed., *Feminine Focus, The New Women Playwrights*, 1989.

Howell, Ann (Hilditch), leading MINERVA author of perhaps nine novels (her canon, like her life, is obscure), many set in bygone Europe. *Rosa de Montmorien*, 1787, was influenced by Sophia LEE's *Recess*. The *Monthly Review*, calling it well written but trifling and obscure, predicted improvement; but it made fun of her *Mount Pelham*, 1789. *Rosenberg*, also 1789, ends with a 'scene of humiliation – of forgiveness – of explication – of joy . . . which, despairing to exhibit . . . I throw my pen into the fire, only saying. . . .' AH probably married at about this time; she was living in Portsmouth in 1791, according to Elizabeth BENGER, who mentions her otherwise unknown poems. *Mortimore Castle* was advertised with her married name in 1794. *Georgina, or The Advantages of Grand Connections*, 1796, has been confused with 'Georgina Bouverie's' *Georgina, or Memoirs of the Bellmour Family*, 1787. The heroine of *Anzoletta Zadoski*, 1796, is 'the adored child of a murdered mother'.

Howes, Barbara, poet and editor, b. 1914 in NYC, da. of Mildred (Cox) and stockbroker Osborne H. Important early influences, she says, were her mother's reading aloud and her own chance discovery of old compilations of poetic forms. She was educ. until fourth grade in an aunt's small school of six to eight cousins, at Beaver Country Day School, and Bennington College, where Genevieve TAGGARD taught her (BA 1937). She spent summers at Tennessee mountain work camps run by the American Friends' Service Committee, at an integrated co-operative farm in segregated Miss., and at a School of the Arts in Cummington, Mass., where she met R. P. Blackmur and Allen Tate. In 1943, living in NYC, she took over from drafted male friends the editorship of *Chimera* (started by Princeton students of Blackmur): she ran it until 1947, when she m. poet William Jay Smith, with whom she lived in Oxford and then for two years near Florence. They had two sons, and later divorced. BH established a long, valuable connection with Cary F. Baynes, analyst, translator (of Jung and the *I Ching*) and mother of a college friend. BH edited modern short stories, 1963, writings from the Caribbean (where she travelled extensively) as *From the Green Antilles*, 1966, repr. 1980, stories for children (with her son), 1970, and Latin American short stories as *The Eye of the Heart*, 1973. This includes Nobel Prize-winner Gabriela MISTRAL, and Clarice LISPECTOR, transl. Elizabeth BISHOP. BH's poetry, often beneficent in tone, can blend pity and indignation: 'Horns hook out over a headlight, / Nostrils drip / Blood on the fender, eyeballs bulge / At death. The male emblem is red. / Does that car not bear / Sorry insignia: brown / On a field of pastel, / A stag dormant, antlered?' Poetry volumes include *A Private Signal, Poems New and Collected*, 1977, and *Moving*, 1983; stories are collected in *The Road Commissioner*, 1983. Papers at Yale. See Louise BOGAN in *Selected Criticism*, 1955.

Howgill, Mary, Quaker writer and minister (called by contemporaries an 'unsuitable' one), sister of the prolific Francis H. of Westmorland. Jailed at Kendal, 1653, and Exeter, 1656, she told Cromwell in *A Remarkable Letter*, 1657, 'thou hast denied the Lord God, and thy own law with the pride of the heart'. She complains of his soldiers breaking up Quaker meetings, and later rails against Dover Baptists. *The Vision of the Lord of Hosts*, 1662, records a vision she had in 1660 of 'the dark, horrible and miserable estate that would come on this Land of England'.

Howitt, Mary (Botham), 1799–1888, writer, translator, b. Staffs., da. of Ann (Wood; descendant of the William Wood ruined by Swift), a governess and companion before her marriage to MH's father, Samuel B., land-surveyor. Growing up in the country, Mary and her elder sister Anna had a severe Quaker education, but their nurse taught them whist, scandal and oaths. Mary went to school at nine, and was mortified by her odd attire. Later she learned Latin, mathematics and geography, then taught herself and her younger siblings. In 1821 she m. William H., a less strict Quaker. From 1822 they lived at Nottingham and began their literary collaboration in 1823 with poems, *The Forest Minstrel*. In 1824 they had a daughter, Anna. MH wrote for Keepsakes and ANNUALS 'to bring in a little cash' (*Autob.*, 1889, ed. by da. Margaret), but regarded her collection of dramatic sketches, *The Seven Temptations*, 1834, as her best and most original work, though it owes much to Joanna BAILLIE's *Plays on the Passions*, and was damned by critics. Her fiction *Wood Leighton; or, A Year in the Country*, 1836, clearly modelled on M. R. MITFORD's *Our Village*, had some success, but her TRANSLATIONS of Frederika Bremer's novels brought wide acclaim. From 1836 they lived in Surrey, then for three years in Heidelberg. With William, she encouraged Elizabeth GASKELL with *Mary Barton*; Gaskell and Eliza METEYARD first pub. in *Howitt's Journal*. She was a friend of Felicia HEMANS and Anna JAMESON; and L. E. L.'s novel *Romance and Reality* gives a sketch of MH. Her 1847 collection of *Poems and Ballads* had a great vogue. MH converted to Roman Catholicism in 1882, aged 83. 'George PASTON' wrote a useful essay on her; see also the life of both Howitts by Amice Lee, 1955.

Howland, Marie (Stevens), 1836–1921, journalist, novelist and architect, b. Lebanon, NH. She worked in the Lowell mills in her teens, but after a normal-school education, in 1857 she became a school principal and m. radical lawyer Lyman W. Case. She joined the campaign for free love and the 'combined household' advocated by Charles Fourier, which aimed to reduce and collectivize domestic work through architectural reform. During the 1860s she lived for a year with Edward H. at the Familistère or Social Palace established by Fourierists in Guise, France. She returned to the US in 1866 to promote collective housekeeping, and in 1873 translated Godin's *Social Solutions*, which set out the political and philosophical principles on which the Guise Social Palace was founded. She wrote essays and short stories on utopian socialism for *Harper's, Galaxy, Lippincott's* and the *Overland Monthly*. Her only novel, *Papa's Own Girl*, 1874 (repr. 1918, 1975 as *The Familistère*), describes the establishment of a Social Palace in the US. During the 1870s and 1880s MH worked to organize the Pacific Colony, a self-sufficient co-operative community in Topolobampo, Mexico. She lived there for several years, but hostility to various aspects of her feminism, particularly her views on free love, caused her to move to a single-tax community in Fairhope, Alabama, where she worked as community librarian until 1921. Her plans for co-operative colonies influenced C. P. GILMAN. See Dolores Hayden's article, *Signs*, Winter 1978.

Hoyland, Barbara (Wheeler), 1764–1829, Quaker minister and aubobiographer, b. in London, da. of pious Anglicans Sarah and William W. (a wine-merchant), who both died while she was in her teens. After a period as a sceptic (induced by reading) she married William H., Sheffield silver-plate manufacturer and Quaker; the Society disowned him on marriage. She found him and his family repressive; he did not try to convert her, but she feared pressure from a Quaker sister-in-law. She first attended a meeting (without him) during her third pregnancy, after two stillbirths; she felt first disturbed by the silence, fearful of death, then calm, then penitent: 'The tears flowed from my eyes and dropped upon my hands.' She became a Friend in 1792 and a minister in 1793. She bore her twelfth child after William W. died, moved to Bradford to run a business in 1812, and had to fight poverty and illness. She wrote her life for her children after 1811: extracts in the Friends' Hist. Soc. *Journal*, iii, 1906, are more constrained in tone than most.

Hoyt, Helen, 1887–1972, poet, editor. B. in Norwalk, Conn. to Georgiana (Baird) and Gould H., she attended Miss Baird's School for Girls, and received an AB from Barnard College in 1909. She published widely in little magazines throughout the 1910s, including the *Little Review*, *The Egoist*, and Harriet MONROE's *Poetry*, where she also worked from 1913, first as office staff alongside Eunice TIETJENS, then as associate editor, 1918–19. She edited a special 'Woman's Number' of *Others*, Sept. 1916, in which she asked 'woman' to 'tell of herself' since 'most of what we know, or think we know, of women has been found out by men' and many of her poems explore different aspects of women's experience. Her first collection, *Apples Here in My Basket*, 1924, is a series of love poems (which Harriet Monroe called a 'frank and complete expression of connubial rapture in the full flow and ebb of its overwhelming tides'). *Poems of Amis*, 1946, are about motherhood (HH's son Amis was born two years after her 1921 marriage to William Whittingham Lyman): 'I also am one just born. / Out of the nine months of waiting / I, too, had to come forth, / To wake out of dormance, / To find new birth and beginning / In a new world.' Other collections are *Leaves of Wild Grape*, 1929, *The Name of a Rose*, 1931, and *A Girl in the City*, 1970. Lyman's unpub. memoirs are in the Bancroft Library, Berkeley.

Hubback, Catherine Anne (Austen), fl. 1842–67, novelist, da. of Mary (Gibson) and Admiral Francis William A.: niece of Jane AUSTEN. In 1842 she m. John H., barrister; one of their sons, John, mentions her in *Cross Currents in a Long Life*, priv. printed 1935. CH and her sister were brought up on their aunt's novels, and CH's first literary venture was a completion from memory of *The Watsons*, re-titled *The Younger Sister*, 1850. The close adherence of the early part to Jane Austen's MS, which she had not seen for seven years, is remarkable. She wrote ten novels between 1850 and 1863, and though contemporary reviews were favourable, she made no more than £200 or £300 by her writing. Other titles include *The Wife's Sister*, 1851, *May and December*, 1855, *The Old Vicarage*, 1856, *The Stage and the Company*, 1858, and *The Mistakes of a Life*, 1863. Dramatic, even melodramatic, speeches and incidents occur in what are essentially domestic novels centring on young girls' choices in matrimony. She imbibed many of her aunt's views but none of her economy and fine point. Occasional touches of humour and successful characterization hint at a creative spark too often stifled by moral or novelistic convention. Sometimes a secondary heroine makes a successful life of her own, but CH makes it clear she is writing about the days before women claimed the right to be strong-minded and independent.

Huddart, Elinor Louisa, 'Elinor Hume', 'Louisa Ronile', 1853–1902, novelist, b. Festiniog, Wales, da. of Eleanor and George Augustus H. She spent her childhood in Wales, where her father was the only surviving son of Sir Joseph H. (knighted 'for nothing', according to EH); then the family moved to Hampshire and father to London. After his death in 1885, she and her sister lived in Surbiton. She was an early correspondent of G. B. Shaw, suggesting to him that he should write plays. He in turn encouraged her 'fervently-imaginative' writing. She wrote at least six books, all published anonymously or pseudonymously. *Cheer or Kill*, 1878, pleased an aunt so much that she paid for publication of *Via Crucis*, 1882, while *My Heart and I*, 1883, pub. Bentley, paid for itself: it treats two sisters driven apart by a man (one dies; the other rejects him). Bentley declined *Commonplace Sinners*, 1885 ('too wicked for his moral firm'), which was followed by *A Modern Milkmaid*, ?1887, and *Leslie*, 1891. This last has material taken from EH's own experience of love for her mother and grief at her agonizing death, as well as hatred for a rich and selfish father. But all of her plots are fantastic, with unreal characters and settings used to show heroines suffering every extreme of pain, passion and guilt. Although not feminist, her works do raise women's questions. Her side of the Shaw correspondence (1878–91) is in the BL.

Hughes, Anne, novelist and dramatist, publishing at London. Her *Poems*, 1784 (pastorals, landscape, compliment), her early, sympathetic 'Description of the Tomb of Werter' (*GM*, 1785), and her *Moral Dramas Intended for Private Representation*, 1790 (blank-verse tragedies named after their heroines and observing the unities) are rather stiffly conventional; her four well-reviewed novels are better. *Zoraida, or Village Annals*, 1786, opens with a doctor being summoned to the mysterious orphan heroine, who is thought to be dying of too much learning, *Henry and Isabella, or A Traite through Life*, 1788, with two bachelor brothers weighing the respective advantages of marriage or a new housekeeper. AH presents a complex social world, the problem for women of unwanted suitors, and opposition of fashionable to rural life. A 'diary' for 1796–7, pub. serially in 1937, repr. 1981, as by a farmer's wife named AH, is part or chiefly modern.

Hughes, Dorothy Belle (Flanagan), writer of DETECTIVE fiction, biographer, critic. B. in 1904 in Kansas City, Missouri, da. of Calla (Haley) and Frank S. F., she 'always wrote' (poetry and stories from six through high school). She studied at the Univs. of Miss. (BJ, 1924), Columbia and New Mexico, and m. Levi Allen H., 1932. Her only book of poems, *Dark Certainty* (as Flanagan), 1931, rejected one year, won a Yale Younger Poets Award the next. She turned to mystery writing when her 'straight' novels failed to find publishers, and with the help of her editor, Marie Fried Rodell, revised the sprawling manuscript of *The So Blue Marble*, 1940, while pregnant with her first child (of three). Much admired, it made Mignon G. EBERHART experience 'the true frisson of terror'. From then until 1962, when she gave up writing because of her family, DH wrote 14 novels, 11 in the forties. Three became Hollywood *films noirs* (*The Fallen Sparrow*, 1943, *Ride the Pink Horse*, 1946, and *In a Lonely Place*, 1947, the last with Humphrey Bogart). Others, including *Dread Journey*, 1945, and *The Expendable Man*, 1963, represent black characters in key roles. DH's style is haunting, grim, sometimes gory; her action sometimes 'hard-boiled'; her settings, especially when Southwest US, realistic; and her characters tailored precisely to plot. A prolific reviewer of detective fiction (for which she won an Edgar, 1950), DH also wrote a life of Erle Stanley Gardner, 1978. She was a 1978 Grand Master of the Mystery Writers of America, with Ngaio MARSH and Daphne du MAURIER. See Dilys Winn, *Murderess Ink*, 1978, and interview in *PW*, 13 March 1978.

'Hull, Edith Maude' (Edith Maud Winstanley), 'the queen of desert romance' and travel writer. Little is known of her life: her *nom de plume* preserved family anonymity. Married to a gentleman farmer, EMH lived in Derbyshire. An early writer of desert travels, in the line of Freya STARK and Joan Rosita FORBES, EMH wrote her first, hugely popular, desert ROMANCE, *The Sheik*, 1919, while her husband was away at war, perhaps to help support her family and perhaps without having seen the desert, though her later travel-book, *Camping in the Sahara*, 1926, claims that she visited Algeria as a child. The trip which produced *Camping* was taken with a woman friend. The sexual politics of the desert romances are melodramatically ambivalent: the aristocratic English heroine of *The Sheik* sets out assertive and fearless, having refused marriage offers, and travelling alone in the desert she feels 'scornful wonder' at the 'degrading intimacy and fettered existence' of Arab wives; when, however, she is caught and raped by the sheik, she grows to enjoy her situation, and accepts marriage, submission and servility. This (better remembered as a Hollywood vehicle for Rudolph Valentino), *The Sons of the Sheik*, 1925, and *The Lion-Tamer*, 1928, were later abridged by Barbara CARTLAND; five of EMH's titles have recent reprints. She was much imitated (by, e.g., 'Kathlyn Rhodes') and parodied (by, e.g., 'Joan Conquest'). See Nicola Beauman, 1983. Billie Melman, *Women in the Popular Imagination in the Twenties*, 1988 (quoted above), construes both the geographical and sexual adventuring in Hull and other travel writers of the time as bids for freedom and suggests that EH's and others' desert romances offended by being 'obscene novels *for women*'.

Hull, Helen Rose, 1888–1971, novelist, teacher, b. at Albion, Mich., da. of Louise (McGill) and Warren C. H., teacher and schools superintendent. Her first publication, at eight, was thanks to her newspaper-owning grandfather. She was educ. at Albion public schools, Michigan State College, and the Univs. of Michigan and Chicago (PhB 1912). Believing that 'Writers are better off for having another job', she taught English and creative writing at Wellesley and Barnard Colleges and from 1916 at Columbia, where Carson MCCULLERS was her pupil. She and Louise Robinson, a colleague with whom she lived, published *The Art of Writing Prose*, 1930, and *Creative Writing*, 1932. HRH's nearly 20 novels deal largely with women's competing allegiance to themselves, husbands, children, careers and a wider society. The first, *Quest*, 1922, like *Heat Lightning*, 1932, and *Through the House Door*, 1940, examines women's achievement of independence and self-worth. In *Islanders*, 1927, a woman entrapped and cheated by the men in her family emerges self-possessed enough to help her suffragist niece achieve both strength and love. In *The Asking Price*, 1930, a wife nearly destroys her husband by suppressing his creative talent. *Uncommon People*, 1936, collects stories of revelatory moments in women's lives: in 'Waiting' Anne realizes both that her newly dead mother was 'a woman of passion and force caught in too narrow an orbit' and that she herself has tried to prevent her daughter from widening her world. HRH also published stories in magazines, and jointly ed. *Writer's Roundtable*, 1959. *A Tapping on the Wall*, 1960, was an award-winning mystery. *Close Her Pale Blue Eyes*, 1963, is a thriller in which a husband's guilt over his infidelity to his fatally ill patroness-of-the-arts wife drives him to madness. Bibliography in C.A. Andrews, *Great Lakes*, 6, 1979.

Hulme, Keri, short-story writer, novelist, poet and artist, b. 1947 in Christchurch, NZ, da. of Mary Ann Lillian (Miller) and John William H.; of Ngai Tahu: hapu Ngaterangiamoa, Ngaiteruahikihiki descent. After a public school education, she spent four terms at Canterbury Univ. 'training to become a consummate doodler'. She became a postwoman, moving to a remote West Coast settlement and retiring at 25 to paint, write and fish. During the 1970s her short stories appeared in a number of NZ magazines – *The New Zealand Listener, Islands, Te Kara, Broadsheet* – and won awards. However her first volume published was poetry, *The Silences Between (Moeraki Conversations)*, 1982; some poems were also anthologized. In 1984, after numerous rejections by publishers, Spiral, a feminist collective, pub. *The Bone People*, which won local awards and the 1985 Booker Prize. Two short stories appear in a collection ed. by M. McLeod and L. Wevers, 1985, and since the success of *The Bone People* her stories have been collected as *Te Kaihau*, 1986. *The Bone People* is something new in NZ writing, a mixture of autobiography, realism, fantasy and myth. KH creates a protagonist who in many ways resembles herself, a strong eccentric artist, living alone, who struggles to find ways of relating to a deaf, battered pakeha child and his Maori foster-father. She rejects conventional women's roles, and refuses to enter into a couple relationship. The novel fuses pakeha (European) and Maori tradition, ending in a vision of togetherness in the whanau – the possible harmony of another people who would come out of 'the bone people' (the beginning people).

Hume, Anna, Scots translator and scholar. Her versions of Latin poems by her father, David H. of Godscroft, d. 1630?, are lost. She translated Petrarch (as had ELIZABETH I and the Countess of PEMBROKE) from the original. Her *Triumphs of Love, Chastitie, Death*, Edinburgh, 1644, says that success would make her 'turn' his other Triumphs; these are not known. (Instead she made some badly needed money by editing her father's *History of ... Douglas and Angus*, 1644, despite protests from some families treated in it.) Her vigorous, elegant Petrarch was called in 1967 the finest version before this century (mostly repr. by Bohn, 1859, with work by Anne BANNERMAN and Charlotte SMITH). AH's notes comprise pithy summaries of ancient myth and history: Clytemnestra had Agamemnon killed 'as hee was searching for a place to put forth his head' from 'a shirt close at top'; SAPPHO was 'a better Poetesse than a woman'; Aegeria 'had a good hand in' writing the laws of Rome.

Hume, Mary Catherine (later Rothery; then Hume-Rothery), 1824–85, novelist, poet and political campaigner. B. Bryanston Square, London, youngest but one of the seven children of Radical MP Joseph Hume and his wife, a da. of wealthy East India proprietor Mr Burnley. In 1850 she pub. a brief life of Charles Augustus Tulk, d. 1849, friend and colleague of her father's, whom she first met in 1843, later often staying with the Tulks and studying Swedenborg with him. She pub. *The Bridesmaid, Count Stephen, and Other Poems* in 1853, and in 1857 *Normiton: A Dramatic Poem*, and her most popular work, *The Wedding Guests*, a novel about the marriage market. It examines women's role, encouraging female knowledge and independence as justification for love-matches. In 1858 she spent several months in Florence with Tulk's daughter, the Countess Cottrell, later publishing Swedenborgian versions of scripture texts, 1861, and children's stories, 1863, as well as *Sappho*, 1862, a plea for intelligence and knowledge for women. In 1864 she m. the Rev. William R. of St

Bees, Cumberland, a New Churchman. In 1866, after the birth of their son, he changed his name by deed-poll to incorporate hers. In 1870 she pub. a pamphlet protesting to the Queen 'against a system of legalized prostitution' (the Contagious Diseases Acts) and in 1872 an essay on the same theme, *Women and Doctors or Medical Despotism in England*. In 1873 she settled in Cheltenham, in 1876 publishing a pamphlet, *Anti-Mourning*, then collaborating with her husband in *The Divine Unity, Trinity, and At-one-ment*, in 1878, on the New Church scheme of salvation.

Hume, Sophia (Wigington), 1702–74, Quaker pamphleteer, b. in Charleston, SC, da. of prominent Anglican Henry W. and of Susanna (Bayley), a daughter of Mary FISHER. M. to Robert H. in 1721, widowed 1737, she says that assemblies, concerts, playhouses, and corrupting books 'were hastening the Destruction of my Soul', when a smallpox attack awakened her, and she joined the QUAKERS, 1741. This was in England; *An Exhortation to the Inhabitants of...South-Carolina*, Philadelphia, 1747, pub. on a missionary visit home, anticipates ridicule 'on such a novel and uncommon Occasion, as a Woman's appearing on the Behalf of God and Religion': her children apparently disapproved. She attacks theatre-going and women's follies (she is less feminist than many Quakers), and urges breast-feeding. Her other works include an *Epistle* to the same audience, 1754, *A Caution to Such as observe Days and Times*, 1763, a Quaker anthology, 1766, *Remarks on the Practice of Inoculation for the Smallpox*, 2nd ed. 1767 (she condemns inoculation as 'to dishonour God, by taking a privilege out of his hands', mentioning Lady Mary Wortley MONTAGU yet believing the inventor was a devil), and a broadside to 'Handicraftsmen, Labourers', etc. [1769]. She travelled in Holland, 1757, with Catharine, later PHILLIPS. Her work was much repr. in America and at London, where she died: letters in John Kendall's collection, 1802–5.

Hungerford, Margaret Wolfe (Hamilton), 'The Duchess', 1855?–97, popular novelist, b. Ross, Co. Cork, eldest da. of Canon Fitzjohn Hamilton. At school she won composition prizes and wrote stories to entertain friends. In 1872 she m. Edward Argles (d. 1878), solicitor, by whom she had three daughters; then, 1883, Thomas Hungerford, landowner, with whom she had two sons and a da. Her first novel, *Phyllis* (pub. 1877; written at 18), sold well, and was followed by her most successful: *Molly Bawn*, 1878, which deals with the love life of a lively, coquettish Irish girl. The Irish are presented favourably in her works, with an occasional aside on the Land League agitation. Often writing on commission, she produced over 40 best-selling novels and collections of short stories in 20 years, as well as many newspaper articles. Other successful novels include *Mrs Geoffrey*, 1881, *Portia*, 1882, *Rossmoyne*, 1883, *Undercurrents*, 1888, *A Born Coquette*, 1890, *A Life's Remorse*, 1890, *A Conquering Heroine*, 1892, and *The Professor's Experiment*, 1895. Though overwritten, her fiction was popular for its often witty portrayal of courtship in fashionable society, and its treatment of mutual love between husband and wife after initial misunderstandings or the wife's immaturity. See Helen Black, *Notable Women Authors*, 1893.

Hunt, Margaret, 'Mrs Alfred Hunt' (Raine), 'Averil Beaumont', 1831–1912, novelist. B. Durham, da. of Margaret (Peacock), a clergyman's daughter, and the Rev. James R., antiquarian and topographer. Only her first three novels appeared under her pseudonym; her remaining large output of lightweight fiction was either pub. anon. or under her married name. In 1851 she m. landscape painter Alfred William Hunt; she drew upon her knowledge of a painter's life in *Thornicroft's Model*, 1873, dedicated 'with the most respectful admiration' to Robert Browning. Rather a silly story, told in a muddle, it is partly redeemed by the attempt to convey the real passion for his art of the painter-hero (but he neglects his noble young wife until it is too late). Her last novel, *The Governess*, was finished by her daughter, Violet HUNT, and pub. posthumously, 1912, with a preface by Ford Madox Hueffer (who claims D. G. Rossetti as the hero of *Thornicroft*). Violet writes about her mother in *The Flurried Years*, 1926.

Hunt, Isobel **Violet**, 1866–1942, novelist, b. Durham, da. of Margaret (Raine) HUNT, novelist, and Alfred William H., painter; their house was a literary and artistic centre for the Pre-Raphaelites and figures like Oscar Wilde and John Ruskin. VH's early poems were read by Christina ROSSETTI; but, intended by her father for a painter, she studied at South Kensington Art School. She never married, though she had several publicized affairs, and lived with Ford Madox Ford for 10 years, 1908–18. Seen as a typical NEW WOMAN, she was an active supporter of women's SUFFRAGE. Her seventeen novels are all concerned with the sexual politics of relationships, though only the first, *The Maiden's Progress*, 1894, panders to conventional wish-fulfilment. Notorious for their sexual frankness and perverse and 'frigid' heroines, novels such as *Unkist, Unkind!*, 1897, and later short-story collections like *Tales of the Uneasy*, 1911, express the psychological consequences of sexual frustration. Others such as *A Hard Woman*, 1895, use an experimental format and inventive dialogue for which she was widely acclaimed. In novels like *Sooner or Later*, 1904, and *The Celebrity at Home*, 1904, as well as in her autobiographical memoirs, *The Flurried Years*, 1926, and the biography *The Wife of Rossetti*, 1932, she drew directly on early personal experiences. *White Rose of Weary Leaf*, 1908, considered her best novel, exposes the inability of social convention to deal with the complexities of individuals or their relationships. VH also worked with Ford on *The English Review* and contributed a weekly column to the *Pall Mall Gazette*. Her work was admired by James, Lawrence, Rebecca WEST and May SINCLAIR (see her article on VH in *English Review* 36 (Feb. 1922)). In later years this lively, witty woman lived in virtual seclusion, suffering the symptoms of advanced syphilis. See Marie Secor's study in *English Lit. in Transition*, 19 (1976); also M. and R. Secor, *F. M. Ford and V. Hunt's 1917 Diary*, 1983.

Hunter, Anne (Hume), 1742–1821, poet, eldest da. of Mary (Hutchison) and Robert Hume of Berwickshire, army surgeon and uncle of Joanna BAILLIE (whose brother restored an estate forfeited when AH's parents married for love). AH's 'Adieu! ye streams', written at 22 (another version of 'The Flowers of the Forest': see Alison COCKBURN), was pub. in *The Lark*, Edinburgh, 1765. From her marriage, 1771, to distinguished anatomist John Hunter, she lived in London. Her *Poems*, 1802, dedicated to her son, mentions three already published; it includes poems to Mary DELANY and Elizabeth CARTER, and fine plaintive lyrics like 'My mother bids me bind my hair' (famous with music by Joseph Haydn, a friend) and 'Dear to my heart as life's warm streams' (on her daughter's wedding). Her *Sports of the Genii*, 1804, written in 1797 'for the amusement of some young people', was pub. for the sake of its illustrations. William Beloe thought her a principal BLUESTOCKING hostess. She lived in poverty from her husband's death, 1793, till Parliament bought the Hunterian Collection, 1799.

Hunter, Kristin Elaine (Eggleston), writer of adult and juvenile fiction, b. in Philadelphia, Penna., 1931, to pharmacist and teacher Mabel Lucretia (Manigault) and school principal and US Army colonel George Lorenzo E., who believed so strongly that children should be seen and not heard that she 'never got to finish a sentence.' She studied education at the Univ. of Pennsylvania (BS, 1951) and married (Joseph H., 1952), both at her father's insistence, then taught elementary school. Encouraged to write by her aunt (Myrtle Stratton), she took a series of newspaper jobs and was a writer on the *Pittsburgh Courier*, 1946–52. Her documentary television script, *A Minority of One*, 1955, about the integration of an all-black school, won a CBS competition, but the script was revised to portray the introduction of a foreigner into an all-white school. *God Bless the Child*, 1964, shows the failure of an ambitious young black woman to work her way into a secure life: a 'negation' of the American Dream. *The Landlord*, 1966, adapted for film, 1970, is based on KH's encounter with a reform-minded white man who does not realize his black tenants are 'running a game on him'. *The Lakestown Rebellion*, 1978, uses the trickster spirit of Zora Neale HURSTON, together with the Georgia stories of KH's writer husband (John Lattany, m. 1968) to present a black community resisting white encroachment. KH sometimes finds 'humor and satire more effective techniques for expressing social statements than direct statement'. Other works include *The Survivors*, 1975, a novel in which a 13-year-old street kid teaches a middle-aged newcomer to the inner city how to survive. KH's juvenile writing, including *The Soul Brothers and Sister Lou*, 1968, *Boss Cat*, 1971, *Lou in the Limelight*, 1981, and a collection of stories, *Guests in the Promised Land*, 1973, nominated for the National Book Award, tries to show 'some of the positive values existing in the so-called ghetto' and attempts 'to confirm young black people in their frail but growing belief in their own self worth.' KH teaches English at the Univ. of Pennsylvania. Interview in Tate, 1983. See Trudier Harris, *From Mammies to Militants: Domestics in Black American Literature*, 1982.

Hunter, Rachel, 1754–1813, novelist living and publishing at Norwich, notable for ingenious role-playing critical prefaces and for entering as author among her characters. She began writing 'at an advanced period of my life', and meant her moral *Letters from Mrs. Palmerstone to her Daughter* to appear first; but unforeseen obstacles set it behind *Letitia, or The Castle without a Spectre*, 1801 (preface on GOTHIC and moral fiction; mixed Welsh–Black marriage), and *The History of the Grubthorpe Family, or The Old Bachelor and his Sister Penelope*, 1802 (comic preface; bourgeois values withstanding the genteel). *Mrs. Palmerstone* appeared that year, dedicated to the 'child of her affection', headed by a dialogue with the carping Mr Not-At-All (named after his favourite phrase). Its tales wrap layer within layer of fiction. In the preface to *The Unexpected Legacy*, 1804, novels are eloquently attacked by a male friend of the fictitious author. In *Lady Maclairn, The Victim of Villainy*, 1806, the 'author', self-defined as merely an editor of letters, ends as governess to the heroine's promising little half-black, illegitimate brothers. The heroine of *Family Annals*, 1808, nearly remains a maiden aunt; that of *The Schoolmistress*, 1811, actually chooses spinsterhood and poverty. RH was known and joked about by Jane AUSTEN. She has been confused with Maria H., actress and novelist, whose *Fitzroy, or Impulse of the Moment*, 1792, and *Ella, or He's Always in the Way*, 1798, mix classical learning, satire and sentiment (and who has been confused in turn with Maria Susanna COOPER).

Huntington, Susan (Mansfield), 1791–1823, religious writer, youngest child of Sarah and the Rev. Achilles M. of Killingworth, Conn. She recalled 'a solemn consultation in her mind' at about three on becoming a Christian, which she did at about five. As 'the mere child of fiction, and romance', she longed 'to distinguish myself by poetizing, and shining as an authoress'; after marriage, 1809, to the Rev. Joshua H. of Boston, and 'some sharp lessons', she wished only to be 'a good, plain, common-sense' wife, mother and Christian. She destroyed her early DIARY; her *Memoirs* (Boston, 1826, often repr.) use one begun

1812, letters, and a few poems, two from the *Boston Recorder* (which also pub. a letter of 1818 defending women from an attack, accepting submission but not subjection or 'slavery'). She pub., 1820, another letter (with the American Tract Society) and *Little Lucy*, for children. A serious reader and thinker (on educational issues especially), she is open and attentive to all forms of the inner life as well as to sin and preparation for death (she lost her parents, husband, and two children, one a much-loved mentally defective girl).

Hurst, Fannie, 1887?–1968, author of 17 novels, over 300 short stories, and many film and radio scripts, articles and civil-rights pamphlets. Only surviving da. of Rose (Koppel) and shoe-manufacturer Samuel H., both American Jews of German descent, she was b. at Hamilton, Ohio, raised in St Louis, and educ. at Washington and Columbia Univs. She then did part-time jobs in NYC. For five years no one but her family knew of her defiant marriage, 1915, to musician Jacques Danielson, an East European Jew: they lived apart, and she could write uninterrupted. Her first books were short-story volumes: *Just Around the Corner*, 1914, *Every Soul Hath Its Song*, 1916, *Gaslight Sonata*, 1918, *Humoresque*, 1919 (whose title-story she dramatized in 1923), and others. The heroines of her novels echo an ambivalence disclosed in her autobiography, *Anatomy of Me: A Wonderer* [sic] *in Search of Herself*, 1958: 'To write was the be-all, the end-all.... Marriage was not for me, yet nothing short of marriage with Jack would be bearable.' While the 'American Girl' heroine of *Star-Dust*, 1921, extracts herself from a claustrophobic marriage to pursue a singing career (saying 'women can fight back at the world with something besides their sex. I intend to prove it'), successful professional women in both *Imitation of Life*, 1933 (filmed 1934, 1959), and *Lonely Parade*, 1942, feel unfulfilled without husbands and children. *Lummox*, 1923, about a semi-inarticulate Polish immigrant domestic worker, was FH's own favourite: *Back Street*, 1931 (three film versions), about the heroine's 20-year sexual and emotional exploitation by a married man, was the most popular; *God Must Be Sad*, 1961, advocating religious toleration and mixed marriages, was controversial. Described in 1931 by journalist Dorothy Roe as 'our great American Success Story', FH was the country's highest-earning fiction-writer throughout the 1920s and 1930s. She was also an ardent, respected reformer (named by a Woodrow Wilson aide as suitable for a high government post), friend and fellow campaigner of Eleanor ROOSEVELT, and supporter of women's, blacks' and workers' rights. Always critical of US anti-intellectualism, she left the bulk of her estate to Washington and Brandeis Univs. Study by Mary Rose Shaughnessy, 1980; Gay Wilentz on her correspondence with Zora Neale HURSTON in *Library Chronicle of the Univ. of Texas*, 35, 1986; selec. of stories and book of critical essays expected from Susan Koppleman.

Hurston, Zora Neale, 1891/1901?–1960, novelist, short-story writer, anthropologist, b. and reared in Eatonville, Fla, the first incorporated black town in the US, until when she was nine her mother, Lucy Ann (Potts), died and her father, John H., a Baptist preacher and three times mayor, remarried. A fiercely independent child, she embarked on a 'series of wanderings', with jobs and occasional schooling; she found and devoured *Paradise Lost*, and learned Gray's 'Elegy in a Country Churchyard' overnight in case she never met it again. After Baltimore's Morgan Academy she attended, from 1918, Howard Univ. in Washington, DC, where she published her first story. In NYC from 1925, she worked as Fannie HURST's secretary and studied cultural anthropology at Barnard College with Franz Boas and Ruth BENEDICT, graduating in 1928. She made the first of two brief marriages in 1927, and elicited support from 'Godmother', Mrs Mason, for four years' folklore research in the South (including Eatonville). She used this material in *The Great Day* (a revue, 1932), Nancy CUNARD's *Negro*, 1934, two scholarly articles, and most fully in *Mules and Men*, 1935 (tales, songs, talk, sermons, hoodoo practices, linked by narration). Her first novel, *Jonah's Gourd Vine*, 1934, is a version of the story of her parents' marriage. In *Their Eyes Were Watching God*, 1937, the protagonist's search for fulfilment is that of a woman rather than a black. Yet the folksy political analysis is acute: the white man, 'de ruler of everything ... throw down de load and tell de nigger man tuh pick it up. He pick it up because he have to, but he don't tote it. He hand it to his womenfolks.' *Tell My Horse*, 1938 (*Voodoo Gods ...* in the UK), records fieldwork done in the Caribbean. *Moses, Man of the Mountain*, 1939, makes the Jewish prophet into an Afro-American voodoo leader. ZNH moved back South, taught, and worked as a librarian and, again, as a maid. Though central to the Harlem Renaissance, she was at odds with the (male) black mainstream. 'How It Feels to Be Colored Me', 1928, insists, 'I am not tragically colored'; she crossed swords with Langston Hughes over their joint work on a play, *Mule Bone*, 1931; her autobiography, *Dust Tracks on a Road*, 1942, remarks that she 'did not know how to be humble'; her work neither idealizes blacks nor depicts their relation with whites; her last novel, *Seraph on the Suwanee*, 1948, explores the dilemmas of a white Southern woman. Her growing conservatism alienated many. A year after 'What White Publishers won't Print' (*Negro Digest*, April 1950), she denounced Communism in the *American Legion Magazine*; like Anne SPENCER, she opposed the Supreme Court's 1954 ruling against segregated schools. An unfounded libel in 1948 was taken up by black papers; her *Life of Herod the Great*, rejected 1955, was resubmitted in 1959; she died in poverty. Today's black women writers love her for work centred on 'Blacklove'. Many reprints and articles; life by Robert Hemenway, 1977; *I Love Myself When I Am Laughing And Then Again When I Am Looking Mean and Impressive, A ZNH Reader*, ed. Alice WALKER, 1979; bibliog. of secondary sources by Bonnie Crarey Ryan in *Bulletin of Bibliog.*, 45, 1988; study of ZNH's texts by Karla F. C. Holloway, 1987; Walker, *In Search of Our Mothers' Gardens*, 1984; *The ZNH Forum*, 1986ff. MSS mostly at the Univs of Florida and Yale.

Hutchinson, Lucy (Apsley), 1620–after 1675, woman of letters, da. of Lucy (St John) and Sir Allen A., Lieutenant of the Tower of London. Having three sons, her mother was overjoyed at her birth: in pregnancy she had dreamed of 'a daughter of some extraordinary eminency'. Lucy could read at four, got some medical learning from Sir Walter Raleigh and other prisoners, and spurned music, dancing and sewing for adult talk and books (even 'wittie songs and amorous sonnetts'); her autobiographical fragment ends with worsting her brothers at Latin. Her father, who furthered all this, died when she was ten; her mother thought her 'too serious' and came to prefer a younger daughter. In 1638 she m. John H., who loved her studiousness and her verses; from 1640 they lived near Nottingham. They read theology together while she was pregnant with twins: she went on bearing children till 1662, and turned Lucretius into vigorous, expressive English verse in the schoolroom, 'number[ing] the sillables ... by the threds of the canvas I wrought in'. (By 1675 she was 'painfully deprecatory' of this work.) Her acute and learned *On the Principles of the Christian Religion*, for her daughter, and *Of* [pagan] *Theology*, with her own verse renderings, were pub. together, 1817. John H. was a key parliamentary officer in the Civil War; she became a Baptist in 1646, perhaps wrote *A Petition of Women*, 1648, kept a notebook of military events, and quelled a royalist mob in 1660. At the Restoration she displeased her husband by writing a petition for mercy in his name: he was arrested in 1663 and died in prison, 1664. To inform her younger children, to obey his hard 'command not to grieve att the common rate of desolate woemen', and perhaps to match Margaret NEWCASTLE's similar project, she began her famous life of him about 1665: first pub. 1806 (Catharine MACAULAY had tried to bring it out); ed. James Sutherland, 1973. MSS in BL; some poems and her *Aeneid* translation now lost.

Hutton, Catherine, 1756–1846, novelist and miscellaneous writer, da. of Sarah (Cock) and of William H., who rose from poverty to a fortune in bookselling and fine house near Birmingham (burned down by a 'Church and King', anti-Dissenting mob in 1791). An early reader and keen letter-writer, she went to school at her own wish but left at 14. Despite severe lung trouble, she published 60 periodical articles; collected material for a unique history of costume ('the greatest of my works', but too expensive to publish); updated her father's autobiography and his 1781 history of Birmingham (pub. 1816 and 1819); collected 2,000 autographs including women writers (described by her in *La Belle Assemblée*, 1827, part exhibited 1873); and wrote *The Tour of Africa* (male persona: pub. 1819–21), family memoirs ('And why not my mother's family?' – pub. [1869]), and an unpub. history of English queens. The 'prose run mad' of Sydney MORGAN's *Wild Irish Girl* started her writing *Oakwood Hall* (one vol. in print 1812; magazine extracts; the whole 1819) and the unusual *Miser Married*, 1813, admired by S. H. BURNEY. Its newly-poor heroine ('I still want employment . . . something I will do; if it be to write a Dictionary or a Herbal') sees her ladylike mother pursue and marry their rich, crude, near-paranoid landlord. *The Welsh Mountaineer* [a female character], 1817, was much interrupted by tending William H.'s old age. *Oakwood* has a central figure based on Elizabeth HEYRICK's mother (a close friend), who praises Mary WOLLSTONECRAFT and places Eliza HAYWOOD among parents of the novel. Birmingham Public Library has some letters: selecs. pub. 1875, 1891, 1895.

Hutton (or Huldon?), **Lucy**, d. 1788, biblical writer. After her death there appeared at Kendal her *Six Sermonicles* [title designed 'to keep in view the pre-eminence of men' . . . *on the Punishment of Eve*; its title-page refers to her 19 *Letters on the Antediluvian Females* (untraced) and bears the motto 'En Droit Devant'. She preaches as a 'Sister' (name in MS on BL copy), addressing her sisters or her sex from an 'obscure retreat', all on the text which curses Eve with painful childbirth and submission to her husband – only 'husband', says LH, 'now conveys an idea of power, of leadership. . . . Adam was then Eve's partner.' She argues strongly for equality up to the fall: when Milton posits Eve's inferiority he 'contradicts my whole habit of thinking from infancy'; his 'phanatical genius could wrest scripture strangely'. But (though the story of Atlanta is a 'trumped up . . . old affront') that of Eve is to be taken to heart and learned from. There *was*, says LH, sex in Paradise; 'woman had her passions'; Eve may have been pregnant when she fell; 'our sex is of the utmost consequence in the scale of creation', and should influence men for good. She ends thinking of death but planning another work.

Huxley, Elspeth Josceline (Grant), writer of novels, short stories, detective fiction, biography and autobiography, travel and other non-fiction. B. in 1907 in London, da. of Eleanor Lillian (Grosvenor) and Major Josceline G., from the age of five she lived in a Kenya emerging painfully from the colonial experience which, as she records in the native family saga *Red Strangers*, 1939, had itself so transformed an ancient way of life as to make it as uninterpretable to 'the young educated Kikuyu' as to a white observer. She attended European school in Nairobi: her African childhood is the subject of her popular first two volumes of autobiography, *The Flame Trees of Thika*, 1959, and *The Mottled Lizard* (US title, *On the Edge of the Rift*), 1962. The third, *Love Among the Daughters*, 1968, recalling her studies at Reading Univ. and Cornell in the 1920s, is shrewdly sensitive to social distinctions and the behaviour and opinions that go with them. So are her African fictions, which set against or amongst each other groups within the European and native societies in East Africa, and *Back Street New Worlds*, 1964, which investigates immigrant society in Britain. Tensions within native societies and the conflicting motives of European settlers lend subtlety to EH's presentation of cultural differences and emergent struggles between the communities in fictions such as *The Walled City*, 1948, and *A Thing to Love*, 1954. The unfamiliarity of Kikuyu custom and belief itself lends mystery to experiences which become violent or uncanny as in *A Thing to Love*, or *The Red Rock Wilderness*, 1957, in the context of political, tribal or social conflict. These fictions, and the more conventional detective stories such as *Murder on Safari*, 1938, reflect EH's awareness that 'no person of one race and culture can truly interpret events from the angle of individuals belonging to ... different race and culture'. So does her historical non-fiction, from *White Man's Country: Lord Delamere and the Making of Kenya*, 1935, through *Race and Politics in Kenya* (with Margery Perham), 1944, and *Livingstone and His African Journeys*, 1974. Assistant press officer at the Empire Marketing Board in London, 1929–32, EH m. Gervas H., 1931, with whom she continued to travel widely. They had one son. She served as a member of the Monkton Advisory Commission on Central Africa, 1959. A broadcaster, she was also a member of the BBC Advisory Council, 1952–9. Her continuing interest in biography produced *The Kingsleys*, 1973, *Florence* NIGHTINGALE, 1975, and *Scott of the Antarctic*, 1977. She returns to her Africa in *Out of the Midday Sun*, 1985.

'Hyde, Robin', Iris Guiver Wilkinson, 1906–39, NZ novelist, poet and journalist, b. in Cape Town and brought to Wellington shortly after. Second child of Adelaide (Butler) and Edward W., she was educ. at Wellington Girls' College where she won literary prizes and had poems pub. in the school magazine. She later became a journalist on the *Dominion*, 1923, and parliamentary reporter. After a long depressive illness she became permanently lame with an occasional dependency on drugs. In 1926 a brief affair resulted in the birth of a stillborn child, named Robin Hyde, in Sydney. She then worked as a reporter on the Christchurch *Sun*, and the *Wanganui Chronicle*. Her first vol. of poetry, *The Desolate Star*, was pub. 1929, followed by *The Conquerors*, 1935, and *Persephone in Winter*, 1937. The posthumous *Houses by the Sea*, her best, re-creates her childhood in Wellington, as does her autobiographical novel, *The Godwits Fly*, 1938, an account of growing up unhappily far from her cultural heritage in England. She left Wanganui to have a son, the result of another brief affair, and moved to Auckland as 'lady's editor' on the *New Zealand Observer*. In 1933 after a suicide attempt she became a voluntary inmate of the Auckland psychiatric hospital, where, encouraged by her doctor to write, between 1934 and 1936 she produced *Journalese*, essays on her life as a journalist, and the novels *Passport to Hell*, *Check to Your King*, and *Wednesday's Children*, a fantasy. She pub. *Nor the Years Condemn* in 1938, the year she sailed for England and visited the Eastern front in China where she was captured by the Japanese. Her experiences are recorded in *Dragon Rampant*, 1939. RH was one of the few women journalists writing for a living in the 1930s. She was a pacifist whose journalism shows an awareness of Maori rights. She wrote: 'Perhaps the over-wrought, over-taut vision of the woman writer, at her best, touches a humanity and an insight which the serene male has not.' Poorly reviewed, RH committed suicide in London. In *At Home in This World*, autobiographical fragments written after she left the psychiatric hospital, and pub. by her son in 1984, she writes: 'It seems to me now that I am caught in the hinge of a slowly-opening door, between one age and another. Between the tradition of respectability, which was very strong in my household and had cut me off from all family love the moment I infringed it, and the new age.'

Hymns, often anonymous though designed for public hearing, were a popular genre for women in the eighteenth century. Their authors, often Dissenters, probably did not know of the prominence of women among the earliest, Moravian, hymn-writers and the writers of metrical psalms (see Lady PEMBROKE). They ranged from the well-known (Elizabeth ROWE, Anne STEELE) to the obscure (Anne DUTTON). Communities like the Ephrata Cloister of Pennsylvania, founded 1732, produced hymns communally. Bridget (Richardson) Fletcher, 1726–70, included some about women in her posthumous volume, 1773, a landmark in American hymns. Mrs Voke of Gosport, Hants., whose work centres on the birth of the Missionary Society, 1795, is an unusual, near-apocalyptic voice: 'No more shall plunder, war, and death, / Be sanctioned by the Christian name' (anon. *Poems*, Southampton, 1796). The genre was increasingly popular with women in the next century. Harriet Auber pub. her *Spirit of the Psalms*, 1829, as 'A Clergyman of the Church of England'; 'Our Blest Redeemer', which she gives unascribed, may be hers. Anna L. WARING's *Hymns and Meditations*, 1850, ran to nearly 20 eds. Tractarians like C. F. ALEXANDER, famous for 'All Things Bright and Beautiful' and other children's hymns, soon joined the boom following Evangelicals and Non-conformists like S. F. ADAMS. Charlotte ELLIOTT, and Mary Anne Hearne, 1834–1909, a Kent schoolteacher. In the US Elizabeth CHANDLER's poems became anti-slavery hymns; Penina MOISE wrote Jewish hymns; J. W. HOWE wrote the 'Battle Hymn of the Republic'. Catherine Winkworth (friend of Charlotte BRONTË, Harriet MARTINEAU and Elizabeth GASKELL) was one of many women who translated German hymns. See Susan Tamke, *Make a Joyful Noise unto the Lord*, 1978; Samuel Rogal, *Sisters of Sacred Song*, 1981; Margaret Maison in Gail Malmgreen, ed., 1986.

I

Iliff, Maria (Palmer), poet, novelist and actress. Her mother, housekeeper to an actress, started her in children's roles by 1767. She m. an actor, Edward Henry I., in 1785, and continued performing till 1816. His radical politics had caused a separation by 1808, when her preface to *Poems upon Several Subjects*, by subscription, mentions her concern to educate her children and says she 'has not laid aside her Needle' in sometimes taking up her pen. She opens with 'An Apology for Writing Poetry' (the Muse 'stole me from my nurse's arms' and garlands her with wild flowers if not laurels) and closes with a charming expression of reluctance to publish. She describes life with her children, defends the stage, and opposes cruelty to animals. British people in Malta and Corfu subscribed to a second ed., Valletta, 1818, which adds observant, history-conscious poems about both places, and translations from Maltese. A novel, *The Prior Claim*, MINERVA, 1813, is also ascribed to her.

Inchbald, Elizabeth (Simpson), 1753–1821, actress, playwright, novelist. B. near Bury St Edmunds, Suffolk, penultimate child of farming Catholics Mary (Rushbrook) and John S., she had no formal education but could spell better than her brother George, who had seven years of it. She ran away to London to go on stage, like him, at 18 (her second attempt), and in two months married Joseph I., an actor twice her age. Till his sudden death in 1779 they toured the provinces together. She then made her London stage debut, 1780, and writing debut, 1784, acting in her *Mogul Tale, or The Descent of the Balloon*, a topical farce submitted under the pseudonym 'Mrs Woodley', pub. 1788. She quickly won success, and in 21 years wrote 20 plays: comedies, farces, and works from French and German, including the version of Kotzebue's *Lovers' Vows*, 1798, used in Jane AUSTEN's *Mansfield Park*. Friends included Sarah Siddons, J. P. Kemble (whom she loved), Thomas Holcroft and William Godwin. Her novel *A Simple Story* (first part begun 1777, rejected 1779) was unpub. till 1791, when her plays were well known. It pursues through two generations the themes of the Catholic church's dealings with women, of female infidelity and moral education through suffering: ed. J. M. S. Tompkins, 1967. *Nature and Art*, 1796, is a Rousseau-like fable: Nature proves superior; the double sexual standard is savagely applied. EI wrote magazine criticism and prefaces to plays in *The British Theatre*, 25 vols., 1806ff.; she chose *A Collection of Farces*, 7 vols., 1809, and *The Modern Theatre*, 10 vols., 1811 (including her own work): all repr. 1968–70. She lived frugally, left her earned fortune to relatives, and destroyed on her confessor's advice most of the letters and journals of 50 years. See James Boaden's *Memoirs* of her, 1833; study by W. McKee, 1935; bibliog. by G. L. Joughin in *SEL*, 14, 1934; surviving diary and some letters (Folger); plays ed. Paula R. Backscheider, 1980, 1983.

Ingelow, Jean, 1820–97, poet, children's writer and novelist, b. Boston, Lincs., eldest child of Jean (Kilgour) and William I., banker. She was educ. at home by her mother and her brothers' masters. The family moved to London where her first volume, *A Rhyming Chronicle of Thoughts and Feelings*, 1850, was published (ed. Edward Harston; JI's name does not appear). Her first novel was *Allerton and Dreux*, 1851, and five others followed. She joined a small literary group, 'The Portfolio', whose members included Adelaide PROCTER, and edited the evangelical *Youth's Magazine* for a year, contributing as 'Orris'. Her contributions were later collected in *Studies for Stories*, 1864, *Stories told to a Child*, 1865, and *A Sister's Bye-Hours*, 1868. *Poems*, 1863, which went through three editions in a year and contained the popular 'Divided' and 'The High Tide on the Coast of Lincolnshire', established her literary reputation. She knew Tennyson, Browning and Christina ROSSETTI and was a friend of Dora GREENWELL and Jane and Ann TAYLOR. Very popular in England and the USA, setting a fashion for doves, milking pails, daisies, etc., her poems reveal little feminism. She 'resolutely shrank from the women's movement' (*Times* obit., 21 July 1897), but a late novel, *Sarah de Berenger*, 1879, concerns Hannah Dill, a poor woman who inherits money from her uncle. Though the money legally belongs to her husband, a convicted criminal, she is determined to use it to free herself from him. 'He may claim me, but he shall never get me. Rather than that, I'll spend every shilling to get free' (I,83). JI's *Poems*, 1885, were not as successful. However, this did not stop a group of American authors petitioning Queen VICTORIA to make JI Poet Laureate, though 'Sarah TYTLER' thought her prose tales, though 'whimsical and eccentric', much better than her verse (*Three Generations*). In 1896 her health failed. See *Some Recollections of JI*, London, 1901 (anon.), and Alice MEYNELL's 1908 edition of her poems; there is a life by Maureen Peters, 1972.

Iremonger, Lucille (Parks), novelist, folklorist, autobiographer and biographer, b. 1919 near Port Royal, Jamaica, descended on both sides from slave-owning planters: her mother's family fled the French Revolution. LI learned to read very young from her overbearing but intellectually stimulating father, and attended Wolmer's Girls' School and St Hugh's College, Oxford (BA in English). She m. Thomas Lascelles I., an English colonial officer, later a Lloyds' underwriter and MP; they were evacuated from the remote Ellice Islands during the Japanese invasion. She bore a daughter, and revisited the Caribbean after WWII: her autobiography, *Yes, My Darling Daughter*, runs to this point. Back in Britain, she began broadcasting for the BBC. Her first book, *It's a Bigger Life*, 1948, won the Society of Women Journalists' Vera BRITTAIN trophy; her second, *Creole*, 1950, a novel based on her youth, was, said Esther CHAPMAN, 'fiercely repudiated by the class of Jamaicans it portrays'. LI used a Caribbean setting in several more novels, published young people's travel books on the South Seas and the West Indies, 1952, and appeared in the *Caribbean Anthology of Short Stories*, 1953, and Jamaican *Independence Anthology*, 1962. Her *Anansi Stories*, 1956, is an important collection of West Indian folk tales. From 1957 she turned increasingly to biography: she wrote on English princesses, 1958 and 1982, and E. B. BROWNING and her husband (fictionalized), 1976. Holding two medals for contributions to Jamaican writing, she lives in Chelsea, London, writes for newspapers, and is active in Conservative politics.

Irigaray, Luce, French feminist, psychoanalyst, and philosopher, b. 1939. Her first book, *Le Langage des déments*, 1973, studies linguistic disintegration in senile dementia and provides groundwork for her investigation of the language of female hysteria. *Speculum de l'autre femme*, 1974 (*Speculum of the Other Woman*, 1985), discloses the problematic relation between women as speaking subjects and language as a patriarchal institution, arguing that Western man-centred history and culture force women to mime masculine discursive practices, masquerade as objects of masculine desire, and repress their specific needs and desires. *Speculum* deconstructs the rhetoric of sexual opposition in psychoanalytical and philosophical discourse, exposing and denouncing the masculinist ideology it inscribes. It unveils a pernicious 'Logic of the Same' which designates 'woman' as the negative, subordinate, Other of the binary opposition 'Man / woman' inherent to all 'master discourses' of Western metaphysics. LI extends Derrida's critique of 'phallogocentrism' in the 'progressive' psychoanalytic writings of Lacan, where 'feminine sexuality' is cast as 'lacking' the phallus and where 'woman' is represented as 'minus' the means with which to signify her subjection to the patriarchal symbolic order and the social contract ('castration'). After publication of *Speculum*, LI was expelled from l'Ecole Freudienne. In subsequent works, LI supplements her 'mimetic' strategy of foregrounding and belying the Father's censorious Voice in so-called 'objective' discourse, with a utopian poetics which attempts to draw out a specifically female 'imaginary' from the repressed female unconscious. *Ce Sexe qui n'en est pas un*, 1977 (*This Sex Which Is Not One*, 1985), derives a writing style and metaphorics from an 'isomorphism' or parallelism between women's speech and female sexual morphology. Such writing/speaking attempts to reverse and displace the dominant phallocentric discursive forms which, she argues, 'shows isomorphism with masculine sexuality'. *Ce Sexe* features a 'parler femme' and a 'parler entre elles' in the image of 'two lips' whose dialogical and fluid speech disperses the firm, authoritative, first-person singular monologue of the self identified masculine subject. *Et l'Une ne bouge pas sans l'autre*, 1979 (*And the One Does Not Stir Without the Other*, 1981), is a lyrical (re)construction of mother/daughter relations which displaces and subverts Freud's Oedipal complex. LI supplements her psychoanalytic enterprises with feminist intervention in the reading of Marx's writings on commodity fetishism, calling for a 'tactical' separation, to be enacted 'long enough [for] women to learn to defend their desire [and] forge for themselves a social status that compels recognition'. Her proposed tetralogy relies metaphorically on the four elements: she analyses Nietzsche under the theme of water, 1980, Heidegger and phenomenology under the theme of air, 1983. *Passions élémentaires*, 1982, considers feminine figures in Greek mythology. The fourth, projected but unwritten text would have analysed Marx under the element of fire. In *L'Ethique de la différence sexuelle*, 1984, she turns away from the question of sexual difference to that of sexual exchange between sexual beings recognized in their independence and autonomy. See Sarah Kofman, *The Enigma of Woman*, 1980, Toril Moi, *Sexual/Textual Politics*, 1985, and Elizabeth Grosz, *Sexual Subversions*, 1989. See also *Parler n'est jamais neutre*, 1985, and *Sexes et parents*, 1987.

Irwin, Anne Ingram (Howard), Viscountess, before 1696–1764, poet, da. of Anne (Capell) and of Charles H., Earl of Carlisle, who encouraged her writing (letters to him in *Carlisle MSS*, 1897; unpub. ones about her continental travels). Lady Mary Wortley MONTAGU called her vain but good-hearted; they argued in verse about AI's fidelity to the memory of her first husband (5th Viscount Irwin, who died in 1721, less than four years married). AI pub. *Castle-Howard* [1732] in praise of her father's estate, dedicated to him with a wealth of learned reference; in 1736 the *GM* printed her epistolary riposte to Pope's 'Of the Characters of Women'. It argues effectively that women's ambition is just the same, in a more restricted sphere, as men's: 'In education all the diff'rence lies; / Women, if taught, would be as bold and wise / As haughty man.' AI was given a Court post that year, and in 1737 defied her family to marry Col. William Douglas, d. 1748. Only a few more poems reached print. AI's elder sister Elizabeth, d. 1739, widow of Lord Lechmere, also wrote: her second husband,

Sir Thomas Robinson, was painted proudly displaying two MS vols. of her poems.

Irwin, Grace Lillian, Toronto novelist and biographer, b. 1907. Da. of Martha (Fortune) and John I., she received classics degrees from the Univ. of Toronto (MA, 1932), taught at Humberside Collegiate Institute, 1931–69, and retired to write full time. She became a Congregational minister, 1974. Her novels reflect evangelical interest. *Least of All Saints*, 1952, treats a young man taking up the ministry and his conflicts of intellect and faith; *Andrew Connington*, 1954, tells of a young minister's struggle as he moves from a prosperous suburban parish to a small undenominational mission. GI has published two biographical fictions: *Servant of Slaves*, 1961, on preacher and former slave-trader John Newton, and *The Seventh Earl*, 1976, on the Victorian reforming Earl of Shaftesbury. She has called this (with extensive use of letters, diaries, and documents) 'dramatized biography'. Her work has been translated into German, Norwegian, Swedish and Chinese.

Irwin, Inez (Haynes), 1873–1970, suffragist, novelist and writer for the young, b. at Rio de Janeiro to Americans Emma Jane (Hopkins) and the elderly Gideon H. She had an old-fashioned, formal upbringing and a short-lived marriage, 1897, to Rufus Hamilton Gillmore, attended Radcliffe College, 1897–1900, and lived in NYC. Early among her nearly 30 titles came *June Jeopardy*, 1908 (for girls), the first of her *Maida* series for children, 1910, *Angel Island*, 1914, repr. 1978, *The Californiacs*, 1916 (travel book), and *Lady of Kingdoms*, 1917, a novel about small-town women, one married and one a single mother, in NYC. IHI m. writer Will Irwin in 1916 and wrote for magazines from wartime France, England and Italy, 1916–18. Co-founder of the National Collegiate Equal SUFFRAGE League, she wrote *The Story of the Women's Party*, 1921 (repr. as *Up Hill With Banners Flying*, 1964, and by original title, 1971). *Out of the Air*, 1923, is a novel about an ex-flyer in postwar NYC, researching a haunting but, it seems at last, beneficent woman writer of the past. The heroine of *Gertrude Haviland's Divorce*, 1925, who feels like a nonentity in marriage, crumbles when it ends, but later finds new ability, public work, and new love. *Gideon*, 1927, centres on a young man growing up in New England, *P.D.F.R.*, 1931, on a young woman in NYC. *Youth Must Laugh*, 1932, and *Strange Harvest*, 1934, make up a saga of six sisters through the later nineteenth century; the same period looms large in the history *Angels and Amazons, A Hundred Years of American Women*, 1933, repr. 1974. IHI also wrote murder mysteries (in *The Women Swore Revenge*, 1948, five women are instrumental in solving the murder of a sixth) and an autobiography, *Adventures of Yesterday*, 1973.

Isdell, Sarah, Dublin novelist and playwright. Her father held a government post; his death left her destitute. In her anonymous *Vale of Louisiana, an American Tale*, Dublin 1805 (based, she said, on fact), an English emigrant family suffer the horrors of war, Indian captivity, abduction by the villain St Pierre (who convincingly mimics the supernatural), shipwreck, and even the effects of novel-reading; at last rational England offers refuge from 'savage', exciting America. *The Irish Recluse, or A Breakfast at the Rotunda*, London, 1809 (with her name), adds fear of the guillotine to disguise, betrayal, and coincidence. Marriage is discussed, Mary WOLLSTONECRAFT berated for undervaluing it, Hannah MORE recommended instead. Encouraged by good reception so far, SI took her epistolary *Faulkner* (untraced) and two plays to London that year, and was at once in trouble, 'dallied with' for more than five months before rejection by publishers and managers. The RLF paid her five guineas to get home; in 1811 she scored a success in Dublin with *The Poor Gentleman*, comedy.

J

Jabavu, Noni (Helen Nontan-O), novelist. She was b. in ?1919 in Cape Province, South Africa, da. of Nolwandle and Davidson Don Tengo, members of a Xhosa family of statesmen, journalists, and innovative educators. Her grandfather, John Tengo, who herded cattle until he started school at ten, was a learned and prolific journalist who worked to establish colleges for blacks and founded and edited the newspaper, *Opinion of the Blacks*, which he passed on to NJ's father. At 14, she went to London to study music at the Royal Academy, later became a film technician, and m. English cinematographer Michael Cadberry Crossfield. They travelled extensively in Mozambique, Kenya, Uganda and South Africa, but settled in England. NJ's frequent use of Xhosa in her English texts is linked with her grandfather's Xhosa newspaper and her father's Xhosa scholarship, her focus on family cultural history with her father's biography of his father. Her first novel, *Drawn in Colour: African Contrasts*, 1962, depicts her early life in Xhosa culture and her visit to her sister in Uganda. It describes NJ's rejection of a 'woman's place' and her differences from her more compliant 'feminine' sister, who was suffering from an uncongenial marriage. *The Ochre People, Scenes from South African Life*, 1963, depicts three regional cultures and includes three family visits: to her family home in Middledrip; to an uncle's farm in Pondoland; and to her Aunt Daisy in Johannesburg, 'Big Mother', a brilliant professional journalist who gave NJ insight into women in her family, many of whom died in childbirth. Carole Boyce Davies sees her works as combining 'family/cultural history, autobiography, and travelogue', permeated by a sense of loss, and beginning 'the modern period of South African women's writing' (*Current Bibliography of African Affairs*, 19, 1986–7).

Jacker, Corinne (Litvin), playwright and director, b. 1933 in Chicago to Jewish parents, Theresa (Bellak), who represented all that CJ later 'disliked about women', and Thomas Henry L., a plumbing contractor. She wrote a play at nine, adapted Chekhov to a local setting at 11, and directed professionally (with 'fear and timidity') at 18. She went to public school ('so I was never subjected to a real "education"') and Stanford and Northwestern Univs (BS 1954, MA in theatre, 1956, though as a woman she was discouraged from directing). That year she m. Richard J. (later divorced). Her version of Katherine Anne PORTER's *Pale Horse, Pale Rider*, staged in NYC, 1958, drew anti-feminist criticism; after one play off-Broadway and one on TV in 1959, she abandoned drama (distrusting her power to invent acceptable male viewpoints, fearing 'the awful confrontation with the man') for publishing jobs and popular writing on science, 1964–71. Commissioned for TV scripts about men, she later returned to the stage with *Seditious Acts*, produced 1969. Her TV programme on Virginia WOOLF, 1972, won a CINE award. Believing she had a terminal disease, she wrote *Bits and Pieces* (staged 1973, pub. with *Breakfast, Lunch, Dinner* as *Two Plays*, 1975), which makes something topical, surreal and mordantly comic of the Egyptian myth of Isis and her piecemeal retrieval of her husband from the dead (the modern 'Iris' has to learn to 'go on' without hers). This and *Harry Outside*, 1975 (about an architect), both won Obies. In 1976 came a musical, *Travelers*, at Cincinnati.

CJ gave 'my problems' to the protagonist of *My Life*, staged 1977, a successful male WASP physicist (a woman physicist would have been 'peculiar'); *Later*, staged and pub. 1979, has three women similarly engaged in coming to terms with the past. CJ worked with Janet Sternburg on a play from the writings of Louise BOGAN. She strove to make the soap-opera *Another World* 'rich and moving', 1981–2, and won two Film Festival awards with *Overdrawn at the Memory Bank*, TV 1983. Discussing the history and current status of women dramatists in Betty Justice and Renate Pose, eds., *Toward the Second Decade: The Impact of the Women's Movement on American Institutions*, 1981, CJ finds that a female approach 'inevitably results in the making of another form'. See Betsko and Koenig, 1987.

Jackowska, Nicki (Tester), poet, actor, publisher, novelist, b. 1942 at Brighton, Sussex, da. of Elsie Louise (Lucas) and George Matthew T., an accountant. She began writing at 17, took a diploma at Brighton School of Music and Drama, 1965, ran her own company, Tower of Babel, in Cornwall, 1969–70, and founded Poetry St Ives, 1969. In 1970 she m. Andrzej Aleksander Jackowski, who illustrated the first of her many poetry volumes and booklets, *Nightride* and *The King Rises*, both 1973: they have a daughter. She worked for the Arts Council, 1974–8, gave poetry readings (some on radio), took a BA, 1977, and MA, 1978, at the Univ. of Sussex, and taught creative writing at various institutions. The five poems in *The Knot Garden*, 1981, treat the only partly integrated internal and external worlds: 'you cannot mend / your double'. Those in *Letters to Superman*, 1984, deal with issues like the environment, nuclear war, and women as objects of exchange: 'a word-merchant . . . hunted / the voices among my bones', and by naming her female 'is making / literature out of me'. She suspects 'absolute clarity' in poetry is impossible; poems 'extend inwards as well as down the page'; she writes of a dimension of experience 'that is part of being fully human for either sex', but which men find harder to explore than women do. Of her three novels, *Dr Marbles and Marianne*, a surreal 'romance', 1982, deals with 'domination – epistemological, conceptual, sexual' and 'the mutual dependence of male and female'; in *The Islanders*, 1987, a girl growing up finds that sexual relationships may fail or disappoint, while political activity is essential but terrifying. A Labour Party and CND member, NJ has ed. *Voices from the Arts for Labour*, 1985, received various awards and appeared in anthologies. See Nicci GERRARD in *Women's Review*, Dec. 1985.

Jackson, Helen Hunt (Fiske), 1830–85, novelist, poet, essayist, Indian rights crusader, b. Amherst, Mass., second child of Deborah Waterman (Vinal) and Prof. Nathan Welby F. She lived with her aunt after the death of her parents (whose narrow Puritanism she rejected), and was educ. at private schools. Emily DICKINSON was a lifelong friend (*Mercy Philbrick's Choice*, 1876, is purportedly a fictional study of her). After the death of her first husband, Lieut. Edward Bissell Hunt, and her two sons, she was encouraged to write by T. W. Higginson. Emerson overpraised her as 'America's greatest woman poet' (preface to *Parnassus*, 1874). She wrote hundreds of articles and book reviews for the New York *Independent* and other leading journals, using pseudonyms such as 'H. H.', 'Saxe Holm', and 'Rip Van Winkle'. Though unsympathetic to the women's rights movement, she refused as second husband William Sharpless J. till he allowed her complete freedom for self-development. Her greatest achievement was her pioneering work for Indian rights. After hearing the Ponca chief, Standing Bear, speak about the dispossessed Plains Indians, she vowed to write an exposé of government maltreatment of Indians. Her months of research in the Astor Library, NY, resulted in *A Century of Dishonor*, 1881 (repr. 1965, ed. A. F. Rolle), a copy of which she presented to every US Congressman. This is an impassioned account of the various tribes since white contact, beginning with a discussion on the rights of sovereignty and occupancy, and ending with massacres of Indians. It shocked the public and within a year the powerful Indian Rights Assoc. was born, followed by the Dawes Act in 1887. Her novel, *Ramona*, 1884, was intended to fictionalize the Indians' plight, as her friend H. B. STOWE had done for the negro, but its popularity (over 300 reprints) was due to the romantic sugar coating. See the life by R. Odell, 1939; critical discussion in Emily Stipes Watts, *The Poetry of American Women*, 1977.

Jackson, Rebecca (Cox), 1795–1871, Shaker preacher, visionary, writer, b. just outside Philadelphia, a free black seamstress, brought up first by her grandmother, then her mother (d. 1808). She and her husband, Samuel J., lived with her preacher brother's family; in 1830, during a violent thunderstorm, RCJ underwent religious 'awakening'. She felt deeply shamed by her illiteracy; her husband failed to keep his promise to teach her to read (she later taught herself). In 1836 she left home and became an itinerant preacher before joining the Shakers (who believed in the Motherhood as well as the Fatherhood of God). She knew Jarena LEE. Pairing with another preacher, Rebecca Perot, with whom she lived until her death, the 'two Rebeccas' toured successfully, and from c. 1843 RCJ was persuaded to write her memoirs. These include extraordinarily vivid accounts of her dream visions, and were treasured within the Shaker community until their publication in 1981 as *Gifts of Power*, ed. Jean McMahon Humez. 'I am only a pen in his hand', she wrote; but her dreams are conveyed very personally, often involving homely topics like cooking and washing. See the life by Richard Williams, ed. 1981 by Cheryl Dorschner, and a fine essay in Alice WALKER's *In Search of Our Mother's Gardens*, 1981.

Jackson, Shirley, 1919–65, novelist, short-story, children's and screen writer, essayist, humourist. B. in San Fransisco, da. of Geraldine (Bugbee) and Leslie H. J., she began writing as a child and through most of her adolescence kept a record of her progress. She was educ. at Rochester (leaving because of depression) and Syracuse Univs. (BA, 1940). In 1940 she m. critic Stanley Edgar Hyman, with whom she had founded the literary magazine *The Spectre* in 1939. They had four children. SJ wrote six novels, prose and drama for children, and numerous short stories. These frequently centre on women characters alienated from the community by their introspective recognition of their difference from the surface presented by the community, who, under the pressure of ostracism, experience a rite of passage, often emerging with a tentative grasp of a new social and psychic order. SJ's use of the gothic lies primarily in her identification of her protagonists' psyches with the landscapes which entrap them: these produce and symbolize the repressed, with which her heroines are in conflict. She is best known for her much-anthologized, calmly brutal story, 'The Lottery', 1948, in which an unnamed, down-home community chooses its yearly scapegoat (who has considerately done the dishes before arriving at the sacrificial scene). Writing in a flat, affectless tone, SJ reveals the violence underlying the 'normal', of which, as other stories such as 'Elizabeth' and 'The Demon Lover' show, women are the guardians, though they are themselves particularly susceptible to the horror which may disrupt domestic routines. SJ's novels develop these themes and techniques, often within the scenario of the 'new GOTHIC'. The protagonist of *Hangsaman*, 1951, critical of the community and in particular of the family, withdraws into a world of violent fantasies, finally completing her initiation into 'normal' adulthood by rejecting her subversive other. In *The Bird's Nest*, 1954, SJ represents the psychic fragmentation of a lonely, alienated young woman, and her passage through a series of identities uses the multiple voices of its central disturbed young woman as structure. In *The Sundial*, 1958, *The Haunting of Hill House*, 1960, and *We Have Always Lived in the Castle*, 1962, houses become emblems of the isolation of their inhabitants. In the last, Merricat, who wants to be a werewolf, intensifies the mental disturbance of earlier protagonists. More horrifying than her, however, are the villagers, who embody SJ's loathing of prejudice and narrow-mindedness. 'A meticulous storyteller,' wrote Ihab Hassan, 'her work moves on the invisible shadow line between fantasy and verisimilitude; it also hovers between innocence and dark knowledge' (*NYTBR*, 23 September 1962). SJ wrote, with Hyman, *Life Among the Savages*, 1953, and *Raising Demons*, 1957, popular, light-hearted accounts of family life. Critical study by Lenemaja Friedman, 1975, John G. Parks (on her gothic) in *TCL* 30, 1984, and Lynette Carpenter (on her women and power) in *Frontiers* 8, 1984.

Jacob, Naomi Ellington, 1884–1964, 'Ellington Gray', actress, popular novelist, autobiographer, b. Ripon, Yorks. Her mother, Nina Ellington (Collinson), wrote novels as Nina Abbott. Lack of funds made NJ leave Middlesborough High School early; she taught at a church school, was employed by an actress, went on stage herself, and became an 'ardent suffragette' and a Roman Catholic. In WWI she joined the Women's Legion and worked in a munitions factory. Her stage career then prospered, but was interrupted for months in a TB sanatorium. Her play, *The Dawn*, was staged in 1923. Her first novel, *Jacob Ussher*, 1925 (based on a play by Henry Esmond), was followed by nearly 80 more books (two pub. on her 80th birthday). Her novels included *The Beloved Physician*, 1930 (more on the love-life than the profession of its doctor-heroine), and the seven-book saga of 'The House of Gollantz' (scattered through as many countries as the Rothschilds, or, at a humbler level, NJ's father's forebears): the fourth of these, *Four Generations*, 1934, brought her greatest success. Her books of memoirs, essays, commonplaces and advice run from *Me: A Chronicle about Other People*, 1933, and *Me – in the Kitchen*, 1935, to *Me – Thinking Things Over*, 1964 (which gallantly denies fear of age or death). In 1930 she moved to Italy for her health; she wrote women's magazine serials, a life of Marie Lloyd, 1936, a book on Italian opera (jointly) in 1948, and one on Italy itself in 1952. During WWII she worked for the British Overseas Service and also acted in London. She dressed in men's clothes as 'more practical and more economical'. Study by James Norbury, 1965.

Jacobs, Harriet, 'Linda Brent', 1818–96, autobiographer, was b. a slave near Edenton, NC, but learned early to read and spell from her mistress, on whose death she was sold to a licentious master. She soon had two children by another white man, then ran away to the home of her grandmother, a freed slave, and in 1842 escaped North, where she found a job in NYC and re-established contact with her son and daughter. In 1849 she moved to Rochester, NY, where Frederick Douglass was publishing the *North Star*, where the Women's Rights Convention had recently met, and where she became friends with Amy Post, Quaker feminist and abolitionist, at whose urging she wrote her autobiography, *Incidents in the Life of a Slave Girl*, 1861. Pub. as by 'Linda Brent', it was ed. by L. M. CHILD (repr. with intro. by Valerie Smith, 1988, Schomburg Library Series). It is notable for its explicit condemnation of the sexual exploitation of women slaves. The rest of her life was devoted to helping blacks, including Union soldiers and newly freed slaves in Georgia. See Jean Yellin's article in *Am. Lit.* 53, 1981, 479–86, and Hazel V. Carby, *Reconstructing Womanhood: The Emergence of the Afro-American Woman Novelist*, 1987.

Jacobsen, Josephine (Boylan), poet, short-story writer, critic. She was born prematurely in 1908, in Cobourg, Ont., where her US parents, Octavia (Winder) and physician Joseph Edward B., were vacationing. Her father died when she was five; her mother took her travelling until she was 14 ('a series of ephemeral governesses taught me nothing'), then settled in Baltimore and sent her to Roland Park Country School. Intent on a theatre career, she acted in Baltimore's Vagabond Theater, which played experimental and European work. Having written poetry 'as far back as I can remember', she published her first poem in *St Nicholas Magazine*, 1928. After marriage, 1932, to Eric J., and birth of a child, she gave up acting. 'Much too involved in my domestic life to think of myself as a professional writer,' she was amazed when Harriet MONROE published some of her sonnets in *Poetry*. *Let Each Man Remember*, 1940, was followed by five other collections during the next 40 years. During her husband's absence in WWII, she was encouraged by Mary Owings Miller, editor of the Contemporary Poetry series, and wrote the poems of *For the Unlost*, 1946. Unable because of family commitments to write full time, as she desired, she reviewed for the Baltimore *Sun*, and later wrote, with William Mueller, a book on Beckett and one on Ionesco and Genet. At nearly 60, she won recognition for *The Animal Inside*, 1966. In 1971 she became the first woman since Elizabeth BISHOP to be named Poetry Consultant to the Library of Congress: her 1973 lecture, 'From Anne to Marianne: Some American Women Poets', is published. *The Chinese Insomniacs*, 1981, reveals her satiric wit and sense of isolation and displacement: 'I learned, / at secret length, / that any pain, or any love, reminded me: / a leopard-nurser's is a *métier* / by which a child nurses a dangerous beast / to strength' ('The Leopard-Nurser'). JJ began to write fiction in her sixties. Many of the Baltimore stories in *A Walk with Raschid*, 1978, show women facing danger and injustice in an everyday world: their reversals, and the tension they establish between setting and their characters' inner life, give them a suspenseful tautness. Mrs Mayberry in 'The Taxi' faces the cab driver she has found menacing, exorcizing him by understanding his fear; Violet in 'Help' is robbed in her employer's home. Interview in John Wakeman, ed., *World Authors, 1970–75*, 1980, quoted above.

Jaeger, Muriel, novelist and social critic, b. *c.* 1893. She took a degree in English at Somerville College, Oxford, in 1916, and worked as a reviewer and publishers' reader. Her novels (the first two published by Leonard and Virginia WOOLF) deal with issues facing society. *The Question Mark*, 1926, is set in a socialist future: the author explains that she can swallow socialist utopias but not utopians: her male protagonist, a visitor from the unideal present, is left satisfied with neither period. *The Man with Six Senses*, 1927, features an uneducated man with the power of perceiving objects beyond the range of sight, and the woman who alone understands the potential value of his gift. In *Hermes Speaks*, 1933, a spiritualist mass-movement is built on exploitation of a mathematical genius. MJ wrote plays and radio plays, and had the 'curious and painful experience' of a company trying to make 'something different' of what she had written: *The Sanderson Spirit*, staged 1933, pub. 1934, amusingly presents a family's (failed) industrial strike against its patriarch. Her other works include brief studies of psychology, 1929, Nazism, 1942, and *Liberty versus Equality*, 1943 (silent on gender issues). *Experimental Lives* [*Adventures in Living* in the USA] *from Cato to George Sand*,

1932, takes SAND as mapping the limits of possible personal freedom; *Before VICTORIA*, 1956, a social history of England for 50 years to 1837, draws on Hannah MORE, Sarah TRIMMER, and women letter-writers; *Shepherd's Trade*, 1965, includes literary comment and advice on writing. See Susan J. Leonardi, *Dangerous by Degrees: Women at Oxford and the Somerville College Novelists*, 1989.

James, Alice, 1848–92, diarist and letter-writer, b. NYC, fifth child and only da. of Mary Robertson (Walsh) and Henry J. Educ. haphazardly in private schools and by governesses, she spent long periods of her childhood travelling in Europe with her family before they settled in Newport and, later, Cambridge. Devoted to her elder brothers Henry (the novelist) and William (the psychologist), she suffered in adolescence from violent hysteria and suicidal impulses, leading to a complete breakdown in the late 1860s. In 1879 or 1880, while working for charity, she met the warm and energetic Katharine Peabody Loring, and formed an immediate and lasting friendship. In 1881 they visited England and Scotland together, and in 1884 AJ accompanied Katharine and her sickly sister Louisa Loring to England, where Alice withdrew gradually into total invalidism, tended by Katharine, with whom she set up house. In 1889 she began to write her DIARY, remarkable for its detached humour, fervent sense of social justice for the poor and for the Irish, and acerbic comments on British habits and society. Her honesty is startling: 'When will women begin to have the first glimmer that above all other loyalties is the loyalty to Truth, i.e. to yourself, that husband, children, friends and country are as nothing to that.' After her death Katharine Loring published four copies for family distribution, much to the distress of Henry, who felt bound to destroy his, despite his admiration of his sister's style – 'H., by the way, has embedded in his pages many pearls fallen from my lips, which he steals in the most unblushing way, saying, simply, that he knew they had been said by the family, so it did not matter.' It was not republished until Anna Robeson BURR's edition (with a brief life), 1934, followed by Leon Edel's complete edition, 1964. Most letters are in the Houghton Library, Harvard: see Ruth B. Yeazell's selecs., 1981.

James, Elinor, pamphleteer and printer, wife of London printer Thomas J., mother of five children. From 1681 to 1715 she pub. pamphlet and (mostly) broadside salvoes supporting the Church of England and the Stuarts, with her name. She writes with total conviction and reliance on her status as public institution, and recounts personal visits and counsel to several monarchs. She warned James II against Catholicism in [?1685]. Her *Vindication of the Church of England*, 1687, says, 'I know you will say, *I am a Woman, and why should I trouble my self?*' She defends ELIZABETH I's reputation and her own: she has acted in the fear of God for 20 years, been a faithful wife, loved 'Peace and Unity' and 'never made Gain of any thing that ever I did'. A reply, sarcastically proffering the Church's thanks, likens her to Semiramis and Joan of Arc; she was sent to Newgate, 1689. Having shared in her husband's business, she took it over on his death, 1711. She pub. a prayer for Queen Anne, 1710, verses on Charles II, 1712, and an address to the House of Lords, 1715 (reminiscence of James II and cutting advice to George I). The sale of 13 of her broadsides fetched $650 in 1984.

'James, Marian', Emily Jolly, *c.* 1822–1900, English novelist and story-writer, da. of a Bath JP. She always pub. anonymously or as MJ, contributing stories to periodicals like *Blackwood's, Cornhill* and *Household Words*, where Dickens printed several, including the early 'Wife's Story', 1855, for which he suggested a sentimental ending instead of her 'unnecessarily painful' one. This story gave the title to her collection pub. 1875. Her first novel, *Mr Arle*, 1856, with a heroine who writes to support father and brothers, stresses the social undesirability of her role: females should prefer 'homely ministration'. (Her later story, 'My First and Last Novel', coll. 1875, treats the theme more richly.) *A Lord of the Creation*, 1857, gives the heroine an interesting female mentor. *Caste*, also 1857, was probably her most successful novel, since subsequent titles were listed as by its author. *Cumworth House*, 1864, is a very strange story of love and intrigue within a family, where the submissive heroine finds her attempts at intimacy with other women sternly suppressed, and male characters lecture her on woman's place: 'A woman of genius ... is less, rather than more, than a woman. ... A woman's life should be something suffered' (1, 293–4). EJ wrote fourteen works of fiction, and in 1878 she ed. *The Life and Letters of Sydney Dobell*, her last publication.

James, P. D., Phyllis Dorothy, detective novelist. Youngest of three das. of Dorothy and Sidney J., b. in 1920 in Oxford and educ. in Cambridge, she regularly came first in English and once won a short-story prize, but she left school to start a tax office job at 16. In 1941 she m. a doctor, Connor Bantry White, whose WWII experiences damaged him mentally (he died in 1964). PDJ became sole supporter of their two daughters. She joined the Civil Service in 1949, first in hospital administration, then the Home Office, 1968–72, then the Criminal Policy Division of the Home Office, 1972–9, specializing in juvenile delinquency. She wrote her first novel in the early mornings, *Cover Her Face*, 1962: the day her agent phoned to say it had been accepted 'was the most exciting day of my life'. Set in the stereotypical country house, it undermines expectations through its victim, a supposedly 'grateful' unmarried mother who returns resentment and revenge for patronage. With equal attention to police procedure and psychology, PDJ chooses as her first protagonist Commander Adam Dalgliesh, poet and solitary, who has lost wife and son in childbirth. PDJ's hospital knowledge becomes obvious in the 1970s: the institutions playing host to her crimes take on morbidity; questioning of their inmates reveals isolation and lack of privacy. A demonstration of intragastric feeding in a teaching hospital becomes an exercise in murder (*Shroud for a Nightingale*, 1971). Murder moves into a forensic laboratory (*Death of an Expert Witness*, 1977). A new detective, young, amateurish, even romantic Cordelia Grey, appeared in *An Unsuitable Job for a Woman*, 1972. *A Taste for Death*, 1986, however, presents solid, efficient Inspector Kate Miskin, number two to Inspector Dalgliesh, grappling with all the forces frustrating ambition in a woman. Investigating the murders of a minister and a vagrant in a dilapidated church, this is PDJ's darkest novel to date, concerned as before with the psychological and moral implications of murder and detection, their impact on precarious human relations. Latest is *Devices and Desires*, 1989. See Norma Siebenheller's study and Nancy Carol Joyner in Bargainnier, both 1981, also Erlene Hubly in *MFS*, 29, 1983, Sandra Pla in *Caliban*, 1986, and interview in *Clues*, 1985.

Jameson, Anna Brownell (Murphy), 1794–1860, essayist, travel writer, biographer, literary and art critic, b. Dublin, eldest of five daughters of Denis Brownell M., Irish miniature painter, and his English wife. The family moved to England in 1798 and eventually settled in London. AJ was educ. at home, and at 16 became a governess, continuing intermittently until she m. lawyer Robert J. in 1825. They separated in 1829 and she made her first visit to Germany, conceiving there a passion for German art and literature. In 1836 she briefly joined her husband in Toronto (he was about to become Vice-Chancellor of

Upper Canada), but returned alone after eight months and devoted her life to writing, chiefly to support her parents and sisters. She had passionate relationships with Lady Byron and Ottilie von Goethe, and her many friends included the BROWNINGS, Catherine SEDGWICK, Jane CARLYLE, George ELIOT, Fanny KEMBLE, Harriet MARTINEAU, M. R. MITFORD, and particularly Elizabeth GASKELL, to whom AJ was a great source of comfort during the furore over Gaskell's *Ruth*. Her opinion on revisions to *North and South* was highly valued. AJ was deeply concerned with the legal and educational lot of women. Her first publication, *A Lady's Diary*, 1825 (repub. as *Diary of an Ennuyée*, 1826, influenced by Germaine de STAEL's *Corinne*, 1807), is the fictional travel-autobiography of a broken-hearted young governess. In other TRAVEL writings, like *Winter Studies and Summer Rambles in Canada*, 1838, and *Pictures of the Social Life of Germany*, 1840, she discusses female roles and responses. The former describes pioneer and native women, and adventures of her own which have been called 'feminist picaresque'. In her much-acclaimed art and literary criticism she expands the aesthetic context to propound her views on womanhood. She wrote of women celebrated in poetry, 1829, female sovereigns, 1831, and Restoration beauties, 1832. *Characteristics of Women*, 1832, ostensibly a study of Shakespearean heroines, calls for redress of female grievances. She pub. six books on art collections and legends in art, [1842]–1864: completed by her friend Lady Eastlake (Elizabeth RIGBY). Her financial need (and that of her relations) remained acute, though from 1851 she had a Civil List pension. In later writings she treats the plight of governesses and the need for wider female employment opportunities. Her celebrated lectures, pub. as *Sisters of Charity: Catholic and Protestant*, 1855, and *The Communion of Labour: Social Employments of Women*, 1856, focus on the pressing controversy over 'Superabundant Women' and praise the good work and courage demonstrated by women united in communities, while strongly rejecting any separatist ethic. Partly spurred by a sense of injustice on being omitted from her husband's will in 1854, AJ actively supported a group of younger reformers and educational pioneers including Adelaide PROCTER, Emily FAITHFULL and Barbara BODICHON; with Bessie PARKES she helped initiate the *English Woman's Journal*. Life by Clara Thomas, 1967; Pauline Nestor, *Female Friendships and Communities*, 1985; Bina Friewald in Neuman and Kamboureli, 1986. Papers at Weimar, Germany (Goethe Collection), Yale, Harvard, and elsewhere.

Jameson, Margaret **Storm,** 1891–1986, novelist and woman of letters. B. at Whitby, N. Yorks., da. of Hannah Margaret (Gallilee) and William Storm J., a sea-captain, she was educ. at home, private school, and Scarborough Municipal School. She was Leeds Univ.'s first woman BA in English (first class, 1912), and published her MA thesis (King's College, London), *Modern Drama in Europe*, 1920. She m. Charles Douglas Clarke ('K') in 1913, had a son in 1915, divorced 'K' in 1925 and began a 'happy difficult second marriage' to historian Guy Chapman in 1926. She edited *New Commonwealth*, 1919–21. *The Pot Boils*, 1919, began a prolific output of novels including two family-chronicle trilogies: *The Lovely Ship*, 1927, *The Voyage Home*, 1930, and *A Richer Dust*, 1931, about a Whitby shipbuilding community; and (repr. 1982–4) *Company Parade*, 1934, *Love in Winter*, 1935, and *None Turn Back*, 1936, about a provincial 'new woman', Mary Hervey Russell, who reflects herself. SJ published three books of 1937–8 as 'James Hill' or 'William Lamb'. Early aware that human beings are 'wilfully, coldly, matter-of-factly cruel to each other', she later worked (as president of English PEN during WWII) for European refugee writers and intellectuals. Her travels led to three novels about European political life between the wars: *Europe to Let*, 1940, *Cloudless May*, 1943, and the one she thought most highly of as an 'honest book ... an organism, not ... a construction', *Cousin Honoré*, 1940. Her vigorous anti-war and anti-fascist writings include the pamphlet 'The End of This War', 1941, *The Fort*, 1941 (a play which became a novel), and *The Writer's Situation*, 1947. She also wrote for TV. Her fine autobiography, *Journey From the North*, 2 vols., 1969–70, repr. 1984, testifies to her fierce northern pride, emotional intensity, and intellectual integrity. Last writings include *Parthian Words*, 1970 (attacking modern fiction), and *Speaking of Stendhal*, 1979 (voicing her love of French culture). Recent reprints include her excellent trio of stories, *Women Against Men*, 1933, repr. 1982, with intro. by Elaine Feinstein. MSS at Univ. of Texas (Austin) and Wellesley College.

Janeway, Elizabeth (Hall), novelist, children's writer, social critic, b. 1913 in Brooklyn, NYC, da. of Jeanette F. (Searle) and Charles H. She was educ. at Swarthmore and Barnard Colleges (BA 1935), m. economist Eliot J. in 1938 and had two children. In seven novels over two decades she examined women's place in family groups. *The Walsh Girls*, 1943, uses stream of consciousness to contrast the lives of two middle-class New England sisters: one single, one twice married and widowed. *The Third Choice*, 1959, looks at motherhood and marriage in the lives of an aunt and niece, questioning the existence of a further alternative. *Accident on Route 37*, 1964, chooses an arresting moment to focus a male narrator's reflections on relationships between people trapped in social roles. EJ published two children's books: *The Vikings*, 1951, and *Ivanov Seven*, 1963, a folkloric tale of a boy in the Caucasus growing from childhood through army life to marriage 'happily ever after'. During the 1960s she felt her fiction unable to deal with the strains on women's lives; she turned to lecturing and to social criticism, to charting 'the social context of change which has produced the women's movement'. *Man's World, Woman's Place: A Study in Social Mythology*, 1971 (praised by Margaret Mead as ironic, lively and important), shows how woman-in-the-home is seen as dependent, yet as exercising control through dispensing solace and favours. In *Women on Campus: The Unfinished Liberation*, 1975, EJ notes that equality of opportunity 'is still a hopeful dream', and calls for 'women's experience' to 'refresh and extend the curriculum'. These themes are pursued in *Between Myth and Morning: Women's Awakening*, 1974, *Powers of the Weak*, 1980, and *Cross Sections from a Decade of Change*, 1982. *Improper Behaviour*, 1987, looks at the ways authority imposes definitions and prescriptions. EJ sees literature as at last ceasing to exclude 'women's experience, which is now perceived as humanly, "universally" valuable'.

Jay, Harriett, 'Charles Marlowe', 1857–1932, novelist and actress, b. London, da. of Richard Jay, engineer. Adopted by her sister Mary and her husband, the poet Robert Buchanan, she thereafter considered her sister as mother. Mary's dying wish (1882) was that HJ remain with Buchanan. She began writing poetry but later turned to fiction. Her first novel, *The Queen of Connaught*, 1876, was well received and many thought it the work of Charles Reade. Buchanan rewrote the novel as a play in which HJ appeared in the title role at the Crystal Palace, 1880. She also performed in Buchanan's 'The Nine Day Queen' but was more successful as a writer. In a prefatory note to *My Connaught Cousins*, 1883, Buchanan, at HJ's request, counters the charge that HJ was 'an enemy to Irish nationality', explaining that she wrote out of sympathy for the people. HJ and Buchanan collaborated on a melodrama, 'Alone in London', produced in the USA, 1884, and London, 1885, with considerable success. As 'Charles Marlowe' she collaborated with him on at least eight plays, a three-act farce, *The Strange Adventures of Miss Brown*, 1895, having the longest run (256 performances). She remained with Buchanan till his death in 1901, writing little thereafter. However, her own farce *When Knights were Bold* ('Charles Marlowe'), first performed at Nottingham, 1906, had 579 performances in London 1907–8 and was revived annually for many years. HJ died in Ilford after a long illness.

Jebb, Ann (Torkington), 1735–1812, radical writer. Eldest da. of Lady Dorothy Sherard and the Rev. James T., she grew up in Hunts., educated at home, shy and delicate. After her marriage, 1772, to the Rev. John J., Arian lecturer at Cambridge, her reputation grew in university circles. (She later befriended Anne PLUMPTRE.) She wrote mostly in letter form: as 'Priscilla' she forcefully addressed individual theologians in the *London Chronicle* from 1772 (the publisher was advised to drop the series 'for it was only Jebb's wife'); in the *Whitehall Evening Post* and in a tract she advocated annual examinations at Cambridge (an issue over which her husband resigned, 1775); in witty, down-to-earth pamphlets to John Bull from his brother, 1792 and 1793, she exposed repression of radicals; excerpts from her personal correspondence appeared in the *Monthly Repository*, 1812. 'Unfetter the mind, and let it enquire freely', she wrote. Living in London from 1776, she supported American independence, religious toleration, ABOLITION of slavery, the French Revolution, and universal male suffrage, but never raised the issue of women's rights.

Jefferis, Barbara, novelist, journalist, b. 1917 in Adelaide, South Australia, da. of Lucy Barbara Ingoldsby (Smythe) and Tarlton J. She was educ. at Riverside, SA, before moving to Sydney, where she worked in journalism and as a radio scriptwriter for the ABC. She m. John Hinde, well-known film reviewer, in 1939 and has one da. A book critic and reviewer, she is also active in the Australian Society of Authors, its first woman president 1973–6, and pub. for the society *Australian Book Contracts*, 1983. Her nine novels are often characterized by a sense of mystery and psychological interest. They include *Contango Day*, 1953, which relates via flashback the sad past of a middle-aged woman; *Beloved Lady*, 1955, an historical novel set in fifteenth-century England; *The Wild Grapes*, 1963, concerning the tensions within a strange family as they reject the fiancée of one of their members; *Time of the Unicorn*, 1974, set in the time of the Crusades and centring upon six characters shipwrecked off the African coast; and *The Tall One*, 1977, the first-person narrative of a medieval English woman. She has also pub. *Three of a Kind*, 1982, the biographies of three remarkable but forgotten Australian women: the successful actor Susan Wooldridge, her daughter Harriet, and her granddaughter Mary Card, a world-renowned lace crochet designer; and a feminist reworking of Henry Lawson's famous story 'The Drover's Wife', which appeared in the *Bulletin*'s centenary edition.

Jellicoe, Patricia **Ann,** playwright and director, b. in 1927 in Middlesbrough, Yorks. Da. of Frances Jackson (Henderson) and John Andrew J., she wanted at four to be in theatre. After Polam Hall School, Darlington, and Queen Margaret's School, Castle Howard, Yorks., she went to the Central School of Speech and Drama (where she returned to teach, 1953), emerging in 1947 into an essentially pre-war theatre. She m. C. E. Inight Clarke, 1950 (divorced, 1961), and Roger Mayne, 1962, with whom she had two children and pub. a book on Devon, 1975. She founded the Cockpit Theatre Club to Experiment with the Open Stage in 1951. *The Sport of My Mad Mother*, 1956, established her reputation for ritualized, absurdist, and avant-garde plays. In *The Rising Generation*, commissioned but quickly rejected by the Girl Guides Association, 1960, AJ produced a neo-carnivalesque spectacular which 'draws on a long and buried tradition of pageants created by and for women' to satirize both the tradition of pamphlet misogyny and the 'monstrous regiment' itself. *The Knack,* staged 1961, pub. 1962 (filmed 1965, and repr. with *Mad Mother,* 1985), wittily interrogates heterosexual male notions of sexual prowess. *Shelley, or the Idealist,* 1965, dramatizes the eponymous poet's life; *The Giveaway,* staged Edinburgh 1968, pub. 1970, is a farce on consumerism. AJ was manager of the experimental Royal Court Theatre, London, 1973–5, which early promoted the work of Edward Bond, Arnold Wesker and John Osborne. In 1974 she left London for Lyme Regis; in 1978 the first of her successful community plays, *The Reckoning,* was performed at her local comprehensive school. This led to establishment of the Colway Theatre Trust and production of *The Tide,* performed in the Axe Valley, 1980, and *The Western Women,* Lyme Regis, 1984, plays about historical events which involve large, community casts. (See AJ, *Community Plays: How to put them on,* 1987: all of hers deal with local moments in national history, give prominence to women and involve interaction between the community and the professionals.) AJ has also translated classic European plays, including Ibsen's *Rosmersholm,* 1952, and Chekhov's *The Seagull,* 1964, and has pub. *3 Jelliplays,* 1975, for children. See Keyssar, 1984 (quoted above), and WANDOR, 1987.

Jemmat, Catherine (Yeo), 1714–66, autobiographer and anthologist, b. at Exeter, brought up at Plymouth, da. of Admiral John Y. (superannuated from 1747, d. 1756), whom she calls a mediocre sailor and a domestic tyrant. Her mother died when she was five; he grieved loudly but (like Shakespeare's Richard III, she says) m. again in nine weeks. Clever, wild, keen to learn and also to flirt (often in verse and letters), she gave her hand to the 'wretch' and 'monster' Mr J., a Plymouth mercer, to escape her father's cruelty. She found him poorer than expected (his house a 'hog-sty') and as jealous as Othello: 'night after night, like a poor submissive slave have I laid my lordly master in his bed, intoxicated and insensible: Day after day have I received blows and bruises for my reward.' Her *Memoirs,* 1762 (classy subscription list), relate all this, note its likeness to fiction, and add some poems (one by Lady Mary Wortley MONTAGU). *Miscellanies in Prose and Verse,* 1766, dedicated to the Queen, gathers work by various hands, some of it repr., much from Ireland: in 'Essay in Vindication of the Female Sex' a prostitute attacks the double standard. No particular piece here can be safely ascribed to CJ herself.

Jenkin, Henrietta Camilla (Jackson), 1807 (8?)–85, novelist, b. Jamaica, only da. of Susan (Campbell) and Robert Jackson, chief JP in Kingston. In 1832 she m. Charles Jenkin, later Commander, RN. She began to write under pressure of poverty; her first novel, *Violet Bank,* 1858, had little success. Next came *Cousin Stella: or, Conflict,* 1859, set in the late 1820s, with slavery a key issue. Written with penetration and verve, it has graphic scenes of white male brutality as well as sharp depictions of women's familial relationships, and made HJ's reputation. Her next novel, *Who Breaks, Pays,* 1861, also very successful, is a rather silly romance set in Italy in the 1840s. HJ had lived in Genoa from 1848 to 1851, supporting liberal movements. She also encouraged Vernon LEE's early publications. She wrote five more novels up to 1874, and from 1868 lived in Edinburgh, where her son held a professorship. She died three days after her husband.

Jenkins, Margaret **Elizabeth** Heald, novelist, biographer, b. 1915 at Hitchin, Herts., da.

of Theodora (Caldicott Ingram) and James Heald J. She was educ. at St Christopher's, Letchworth, then Newnham, Cambridge (English and history, 1924–7). She taught English at King Alfred's School, 1929–39, worked for the Civil Service during WWII, then became a full-time writer. Many of her dozen novels depict female passive submission. In *Harriet,* 1934 (Femina Vie Heureuse prize), an educationally subnormal woman married for her money is confined to an attic until she and her baby die (paralleling a story by Elizabeth HAM). *The Tortoise and the Hare,* 1954, repr. 1983, portrays an abandoned wife whose dislike of being seen as pitiful gives her a belated, saving recognition that 'There is a very great deal to be done'. EJ wrote of more self-determining women in lives of Lady Caroline LAMB, 1932, Jane AUSTEN, 1938, and ELIZABETH I, 1958. Her biographies also include *Six Criminal Women,* 1949, *Ten Fascinating Women,* 1955, and *Dr Gully,* 1972, carefully researched though fictionalized, on Gully's affair with a patient forty years his junior. Many works currently in print.

Jennings, Elizabeth Joan (Cecil), poet, translator, critic, anthologist, children's writer, b. 1926 at Boston, Lincs., da. of Dr Henry C. She grew up in Oxford, went to Oxford High School and St Anne's College (BA in English, 1949). A cradle Catholic, she began at 13 or 14 to ask questions about her faith and to write free-verse poems (very bad, she says). She worked for Oxford City Library, a London publisher, as a lecturer (Columbia Univ., NY, 1961), then as a freelance writer in Oxford. Her work reflects her opinions that 'poetry is always a search for order' and that 'deeply held belief is bound to influence ... all that you write', even when her topics are love and human relations. After publishing in periodicals and issuing *Poems,* 1953, she received the Somerset Maugham Award for *A Way of Looking,* 1955, and with it made a journey to Rome which, she says, delivered her from English puritanical fear and released her imagination. EJ is prolific: in 1961 she translated Michelangelo's sonnets, discussed mystical poetry in *Every Changing Shape,* and published *Song for a Birth or Death. The Mind Has Mountains,* 1966, deals with a mental breakdown and hospital experience: 'There are no lifebelts here on which to fasten.' The tone of her poems has deepened (some early ones 'seem no longer to be any part of me'), whether celebrating life, confronting loss and suffering, or holding a fine balance between trust and doubt, affirmation and despair. She prays, 'Clarify me, please, / God of the galaxies, / Make me a meteor, / Or else a metaphor // So lively'. 'The One Drawback' says 'I should expect dark to be given when / I have such lights, some are tall as the sun, / Others are hearths which friends will sit around. / When these lights have gone / I am drawn underground.' EJ thinks as well as feels in verse: 'No determinism has / Power to hold us long. We pass / Into every element, / Come and gone but never spent.' Praised by Robert Conquest and Philip Larkin, EJ uses a variety of forms with fluency. Her many volumes include *Collected Poems,* 1967 and 1986, *Selected Poems,* 1979, and *Tributes,* 1989. See Lawrence Sail in *Poetry Review,* 76, 1986.

Jennings, Gertrude Eleanor, d. 1958, English dramatist. Most of her 50 published plays had one act and a short cast-list, often all-female. Typical of their appeal to amateur groups is *Between the Soup and the Savoury,* where a cook and parlour maid, during their employers' dinner, tease the downtrodden ugly kitchen maid about her pretended love-affair: London première 1910. Servants – seen from above – abound in GJ's work. Untypical is *A Woman's Influence,* Actresses' Franchise League [1913], which idealizes campaigners for SUFFRAGE and reform of sweatshops; the heroine's husband improbably embraces the cause in reaction after manipulation by an old-fashioned feminine woman. *Poached Eggs and Pearls,* pub. 1917, shows a duchess and young ladies (all in love with soldiers) running a canteen in wartime, *'Me and My Diary'*, 1921, a female author of scandalous society memoirs, *The Bride,* 1931, a wedding nearly prevented by the spinster aunt of a rejected suitor. GJ wrote children's plays (*Hearts to Sell,* 1922, is a pastoral in couplets), pantomimes, and longer comedies (*Family Affairs,* 1934, centres on a matriarch, *The Olympian*, 1955, on the young housekeeper of an aged male tyrant).

Jerauld, Charlotte Ann (Fillebrown), 1820–45, poet and story writer, b. Old Cambridge, Mass., da. of working-class parents Charlotte and Richard F. She was educ. at Boston common schools, leaving at 14 to work in a bookbindery. She read widely, being familiar with the canonical English poets, and published poetry and prose in the Unitarian *Ladies' Repository* as 'Charlotte'. She also wrote many letters to her close friend and confidant, Sarah C. Edgarton Mayo. In 1843 she m. J. W. J. The birth of her son in 1845 was followed by severe depression and she died soon afterwards. Her *Poetry and Prose* was pub. in 1850 with a vague and wordy memoir by her editor, Henry Bacon. CJ's poetry is mostly on religious themes and includes a series of devotional sonnets. Several poems such as 'The Old Well' and 'The Wood-Path' combine a Wordsworthian naturalism and focus on childhood recollections, with religious didacticism. Although she wrote few pieces directly reflecting on her literary ambitions, in 'The Minstrel Bride', an example of the 'Corinne' lyric, she regrets having 'bartered *peace* for *fame*'. CJ's prose tales, although melodramatic, have an attractive narrative presence that grows more relaxed and expansive as the tales progress.

Jesse, Fryniwyd **Tennyson,** 'Fryn', (Wynifried Margaret), 1888–1958, novelist, journalist, playwright and crime writer, b. at Chislehurst, Kent. da. of Edith Louisa (James) and the Rev. Eustace Tennyson d'Eyncourt Jesse: great-niece of the poet Tennyson. As a child she travelled to South Africa, Naples, Paris, at 19 studied painting at the Newlyn School, Cornwall. There she wrote 'The Book of Fryniwyd Tennyson Jesse': 'What if I become great and want to write a novel round my life and have forgotten?' In 1911 she turned to journalism (*The Times, Daily Mail*), book reviewing (*TLS*), and short-story writing (*The English Review*). Readers speculated that 'The Mask', 1912, was by Frank Harris. Its success led to swift publication of her first novel, *The Milky Way,* 1913, which she thought a 'very bad book'. She was one of the few women war-correspondents, whose presence at the front 'was not considered decent'. Her *Sword of Deborah: First-hand Impressions of the British Women's Army in France,* lives of WAACs, FANYs and VADs, was released by the Ministry of Information only after the war, 1919. Her other publications include short-story volumes, 1915, 1928, a translation from French, 1920, verse, 1920, 1951, and seven plays (notably *Billeted,* 1917, and *The Pelican,* 1924) plus others jointly with her playwright husband, H. M. Harwood, 'Tottie', married secretly in 1918. Joseph Conrad called *The White Riband, or A Young Female's Folly,* 1921, a 'jewel in a casket'. FTJ edited several cases for the Notable British Trials Series; in *Murder and Its Motives,* 1924, she suggests the existence of 'born victims' as well as perpetrators. Her powerful *A Pin to See the Peep Show* (1934, repr. 1979; dramatized 1951 with Harwood, televised 1972) is based on a famous 1922 murder (study by René Weis, 1988). Its heroine seeks financial independence and a self-determined life, but lives imaginatively in rare encounters with a lover; he eventually kills her husband; both are sentenced to die, but only she does so. FTJ suggests that the woman whose experience provides her tale, Edith Thompson, died not for murder but for adultery. Ethel MANNIN compared the book to Dreiser's *An American Tragedy* 'for dramatic power and as a social document'. *Moonraker,* 1927, repr. 1981, subverts the 'masculine' adventure-story genre with a female pirate captain (in disguise). *Lacquer Lady,* 1929, repr. 1979, a historical novel set in Burma, and *The Story of Burma,* 1946, draw on FTJ's wide travel. She 'was a skilful, amusing, clandestine sort of feminist, never tired of getting in an adroit plea for the dignity and independence of womankind'. Rebecca WEST's obituary remembers her as 'ideally beautiful'; she was also addicted to drugs, possibly as a consequence of an early painful accident to her hand. Life by her secretary Joanna Colenbrander, 1984.

Jesserson, Susanna, Mrs, pamphleteer known only by this name on *A Bargain for Bachelors, or The Best Wife in the World for a Penny ... To Young-men for Directing their Choice, and to Maids for their Imitation,* 1675. She aims to surprise readers expecting 'some old decayed Procuress' and 'a pretty handsome bit of temptation out of the Country', by her praise of the ideal, home-loving, economical wife, 'guardian of her husbands honour', who prefers *The Practice of Piety* and divine history to Madeleine de SCUDÉRY and 'tickling comedy'.

Jevon, Rachel, poet, da. of a royalist clergyman at Worcester. She welcomed the Restoration in a verse broadside (most unusually in Latin as well as English), *Exultationis Carmen,* calling it 'these first unworthy Fruits ... / Of my dead Muse', rejoicing in Charles II as a 'Terrestrial God'. Publication may have been in hopes of employment in the royal household: in 1662 she petitioned the king 'for the place of one of the meanest servants about the Queen'.

Jevons, Mary Ann (Roscoe), 1795–1845, Liverpool poet, da. of Jane (Griffies) and William R. (historian, children's writer and reformer), whose large, affectionate family grew up busily writing. She edited some results in *Poems for Youth, By a Family Circle,* 1821–2. She m. a fellow Unitarian, iron-master Thomas J., in 1825, and had 11 children. Her modest little ANNUAL, *The Sacred Offering,* appearing 1831–8, printed (anonymously) Mary Anne Browne, later GRAY, Isabella LICKBARROW, Harriet MARTINEAU, Lydia SIGOURNEY, herself, and others. Collected as *Sonnets, and other Poems, Chiefly Devotional,* 1845, her work has charm and character: among hymns, poems of family love, and vignettes from the Bible, occur protests against 'oppression's power' in England, Ireland and Poland, and praise of the USA as a land of liberty. Her sister Jane Elizabeth Hornblower also published poems, 1821 and 1843. MSS, including journals, at Liverpool City Library.

Jewett, Sarah Orne, 1849–1909, novelist, short-story writer and naturalist, b. South Berwick, Maine, da. of Caroline Frances (Perry), a distant descendant of Anne BRADSTREET, and Theodore J., country physician. She was educ. at girls' schools and Berwick Academy, but primarily by her father, whom she accompanied on calls. She formed intense emotional ties with women throughout her life and was a member of an artistic community of women artists which included Celia THAXTER and Louise GUINEY. Her wide circle of literary correspondents included H. B. STOWE, M. W. FREEMAN, and Willa CATHER. She formed a 30-year 'Boston marriage' – a life-long monogamous relationship between two women – with Annie FIELDS, after the death of James T. Fields. The couple visited Europe several times, meeting literary figures like Tennyson, Dickens and Christina ROSSETTI. SOJ wrote realist fiction, but was a visionary of the quiet but extraordinary transformations of common life in its 'everyday aspects', both in nature and in people. She espoused what she called 'imaginative realism'. Her sketches and stories of rural life and of community in decline focus on the lives of women – the strong, the old, the isolated, the self-reliant. *Deephaven,* 1877, figures the relationship between two women who wish to copy the lives of the ladies of LLANGOLLEN. Her stories *Old Friends and New,* 1879, feature many of SOJ's artist spinster figures, precise descriptions of the local flora, the rural/urban contrast and the supernatural. *A Country Doctor,* 1884, concerns a young woman who wishes to be a doctor and the problems she encounters in her quest, including that of gender and role confusion, the conflicting needs of love and work and of rural and city life. *Country Byways,* 1881, *The Mate of the Daylight* and *Friends Ashore,* 1884, and *A White Heron,* 1886, contain stories dealing with role reversal ('Stolen Pleasures', 'Tom's Husband') and New England spinsters ('Miss Becky's Pilgrimage', 'Mary and Martha'). 'A White Heron', perhaps her best-known tale, celebrates Sylvia's relationship with nature symbolized by her refusal to reveal the heron's whereabouts to the young ornithologist. *The Country of the Pointed Firs,* 1896, is considered her masterpiece; realistic in style and innovative in form, it pursues the matriarchal theme explored in much of her work. Three of her best stories – 'The Green Bowl', 'Aunt Cynthy Dallet' and 'Martha's Lady' – were written in the following years, and her popular historical novel *The Tory Lover* appeared in 1901. Seriously injured in a carriage accident in 1904, she wrote no more fiction. See the life by John E. Frost, 1960; Josephine Donovan's study, 1980, and Judith Roman, ed., *Critical Essays on SOJ,* 1984.

Jewsbury, Geraldine Endsor, 1812–80, novelist, b. Measham, Derbyshire, fourth of six children of Maria (Smith) and Thomas J., millowner. The family moved to Manchester in 1818. GJ was brought up by her sister Maria JEWSBURY after her mother's death in 1819. She attended the Miss Darbys' boarding school near Tamworth and went to London in 1830 to perfect her languages and drawing. She nursed her father till his death in 1840, then ran her brother Frank's household till his marriage in 1853. The house became a social and intellectual centre of Manchester. Her friends included the Kingsleys, the Rossettis, F. P. COBBE, Helena Faucit, Ruskin, Huxley, Froude and Bright. In 1854 she moved to Chelsea to be near her close friend, Jane Welsh CARLYLE (see their corresp. ed. Mrs A. Ireland, 1892). Her first book, *Zoë,* 1845, is one of the earliest Victorian novels to explore religious scepticism. The importance of finding a vocation for women is a major theme of *The Half Sisters,* 1848, which contrasts the independent purposeful life of an actress with the futile existence of a manufacturer's wife, and argues that women should be brought up to be strong and rational rather than dependent and feeble-minded. *Marian Withers,* 1851, is interesting for its treatment of industrialism and the rise of a self-made man; GJ had been influenced by Saint-Simonian ideas, even proposing (unsuccessfully) to the doyen of the movement, Charles Lambert, in 1847. She pub. three more novels, *Constance Herbert,* 1855, *The Sorrows of Gentility,* 1856, and *Right or Wrong?,* 1859, and two children's stories, *The History of an Adopted Child,* 1853, and *Angelo; or, the Pine Forest in the Alps,* 1857, as well as co-editing *Lady* MORGAN's *Memoirs,* 1862 (with W. H. Dixon). From 1849 she wrote over 1600 reviews for the *Athenaeum,* while from 1858 till her death she was a reader for Bentley's, the only woman in such an influential position, and scored an early success by accepting *East Lynne,* 1860, although rejecting works by M. E. BRADDON and OUIDA. There is a life by Susanne Howe, 1935.

Jewsbury, Maria Jane (later Fletcher), 1800–33, poet, essayist and fiction-writer; eldest sister of Geraldine JEWSBURY, b. Measham, Derbyshire. She was educ. at the

Miss Adams' school, Shenstone, until 14. The family moved to Manchester in 1818. She published verse in local papers while still in her teens, and with Alaric Watts' encouragement contributed regularly to the *Manchester Gazette* from 1821. Although burdened by domestic and child-rearing duties after her mother's death in 1819, she read systematically and pub. prose sketches in periodicals. Her volume of poems and prose sketches, *Phantasmagoria,* 1825 (dedicated to Wordsworth, whose daughter Dora became a close friend), satirizes fashionable tastes and contemporary writers and critics: partly repr. as *Occasional Papers,* 1932 (ed. with a memoir by Eric Gillett). Her *Letters to the Young,* 1828, adapted from correspondence with Geraldine, reflects the renewed religious faith following her near-fatal illness of 1826, as do *The Three Histories,* 1830, including an early fictional treatment of religious doubt, and the story of the difficulties faced by a talented woman writer. She dedicated a poetry collection, *Lays of Leisure Hours,* 1829, to her friend Felicia HEMANS, and contributed to ANNUALS and to the *Athenaeum,* 1830–32 (including the first-known article by a woman writer on Jane AUSTEN, 27 August 1831). In 1832 she m. the Rev. William F.; and after sailing with him to India, died at Poona of cholera. See M. C. Fryckstedt in *Bulletin of the John Rylands Library,* 66 and 67.

Jhabvala, Ruth (Prawer), novelist, short-story writer and scriptwriter. She was b. 1927 in Cologne of Jewish parents, German Eleonora (Cohn) and lawyer Marcus P., from Poland. She was educ. in the separate Jewish schools of Nazi Germany (till her parents fled to England in 1939), schools at Coventry and Hendon, near London, and Queen Mary College. London Univ. (BA, MA 1951 with thesis covering early women's fiction). Naturalized British in 1948, she m. a Parsi architect, Cyrus S. J., in 1951, and till 1975 lived chiefly in India. This and 'an Indian family' (three daughters) makes her, she says, neither fully insider nor outsider. Having written since childhood, she filled her first published works with Indian urban upper and lower-middle classes, and meetings (both sad and hilarious) of east and west in these circles. *Esmond in India,* 1958, explores India through western, often prejudiced, characters; *Get Ready for Battle,* 1962, may be read as an attack on post-colonial social problems: layers of venality and hypocrisy, shallow western veneer. *Heat and Dust,* 1975 (Booker Prize), is another view from the outside. But RPJ's film-script for *The Householder* (Merchant– Ivory productions, 1963) treats the emotional blossoming of an arranged Hindu marriage with an insider's intimacy and humour. In 'Myself in India', which prefaces two story collections (*An Experience of India,* 1971, and *Out of India,* 1986, which selects from earlier volumes), she describes her love and hate for the country, 'alone in my room with the blinds drawn and the air-conditioner on'. She has received more attention outside India (especially in the USA) than inside: critics note AUSTEN-like cool analysis and ironic detachment. She won international fame as a script-writer with James Ivory's *Shakespeare Wallah* (written 1964, released 1965), a nostalgic film about a British theatre troupe lingering in independent India and a doomed east-west romance. Further films include her own *Heat and Dust,* 1983, others on displacement themes by Henry James and E. M. Forster, and the adaptation of Bernice RUBENS's *Madame Sousatska.* For a dozen years RPJ has been based in NYC. Her German–Polish–Jewish roots preoccupy her; her TV plays include *Jane Austen in Manhattan,* 1980; her novel *In Search of Love and Beauty,* 1983, deals with wealthy European expatriates in NY, whose search for personal identity, like that of earlier characters, often includes the particularly female. In *Three Continents,* 1987, bogus Eastern mysticism meets morally bankrupt Western wealth, disastrously for the naïve

US narrator and her twin brother. Much critical comment includes study by Yasmine GOONERATNE, 1983; D. Rubin in *Modern Fiction Studies,* 30, 1984; H. Summerfield in *Ariel,* 17, 1986.

Jin, Meiling, poet and children's writer, b. 1956 in Guyana to Chinese parents, who in 1964 fled the politically unstable situation (see MJ, 'Racism and Early Childhood', in *The Funky Black Women's Journal,* 1, May 1985) for London, where 'I did not speak for days.' The family lived seven in one room, then with five more relations in a maisonette. MJ found the 'real squash' comforting; school was 'a solitary and unsupervised life' of indiscipline and racist attacks; she was 'saved' by the public library. She read omnivorously, making 'a strange and sudden leap' from the children's section 'to Coleridge, Bernard Shaw and Wordsworth'. Later she had to fight against their poetic voices, till discovering writers like Maya ANGELOU, Maxine Hong KINGSTON, Audre LORDE and Kitty TSUI, helped her 'call a truce with the Gwei lo [white ghost; male poet] and with the English language'. MJ worked at various jobs, joined the London Black Women's Writing Group, and published in magazines, especially the *Funky*. . . . In *Gifts from My Grandmother,* 1985, she confronts racism in Britain and remembered in Guyana, and celebrates strength and the grounding of a Chinese, female, lesbian identity. She writes of visiting China, 1981, of her barely remembered grandmother, and in 'A long over-due poem to my eyes' of 'Poor brown slit eyes / You cause me so much pain / But for you, I would be / Totally invisible. . . . In story books. / Her big blue eyes opened wide. / But you, you narrowed into slits. . . . Soft brown eyes / Windows of the soul / I can see you staring back / Frank, open, lovely.' MJ appears in Rhonda Cobham and Merle COLLINS, eds., *Watchers and Seekers,* and *Black Women Talk Poetry,* both 1987.

Jinner, Sarah, almanac-maker publishing in 1658–64, who probably pre-dated Aphra BEHN in making her living by her pen (as astrological physician). Her prophecies include one of a month when heterosexual intercourse will be painful: women should 'make much of yourselves, let your Husbands pay for it'. All her books include medical remedies (especially for sexual problems). The scurrilous *Womans Almanac,* 1659, by 'Sarah Ginnor' was presumably pub. to deride her.

Jocelin, Elizabeth (Brooke), *c.* 1595–1622, moral writer, only child of Sir Richard B. of Chester (who left when she was a baby) and Joan (Chaderton), who d. when she was six. Her grandfather, Master of Queens' College, Cambridge (d. 1608), taught her religion, languages and history; she had a good memory for poetry and left 'ingenious', 'chaste and modest' poems; after marrying Tourell J., *c.* 1615, she gradually narrowed her studies to divinity. She died nine days after bearing her only child, whom she named Theodora, gift of God. Her unfinished *Mothers Legacie, To Her Unborne Childe,* written by stages in pregnancy and ended in a shaky hand (MS in BL), was pub. 1624 with a moving letter to her husband, and often repr. Herself excessively modest, she desires humility above all in a child of either sex: 'Dearest, I am so fearefull to bringe thee a proud high minded childe' (as 'little children' will be if parents praise their wit). She hopes a son will be a minister; for a daughter she will not advise education like her own: housewifery and the Bible are enough – unless her husband wishes. She says she will explain why she will not feel she has 'lost her labour' if her child is female, but does not. See Elaine V. Beilin, 1987.

Jocelyn, Ada Maria, 'Mrs Robert Jocelyn' (Jenyns), 1860–1931, sporting novelist. Eldest da. of Rita (da. of H. S. Thompson) and Col. Soames Gambier Jenyns, she m. Robert Orde Jocelyn (1845–1915) in 1882;

he was seventh earl of Roden from 1910, and from 1915 she was Dowager Countess. She wrote around 20 novels between 1888 and 1901, mostly sporting. Her first, *£100,000 Versus Ghosts,* 1888, tells of a girl who inherits that sum on condition she live in a haunted house for at least a year: she succeeds. Others include *A Distracting Quest,* 1889, carelessly written but amusing, with a flirtatious heroine named Gladys; and *Run to Ground,* 1894, a dashing account of riding and racing. *Miss Rayburn's Diamonds,* 1898, is an adventure story with an interesting alliance between the heroine and her maid. Lightly written, with conventionally happy endings, her novels are unusual only in their subject-matter.

Johnson, Amryl, poet, b. in Tunapuna, Trinidad, who is chary of giving biographical detail, as irrelevant to her writing. She was brought up by her grandmother, sent to her parents in Britain at 11, and took a degree in African and Caribbean studies at the Univ. of Kent. Her writing is well known from her readings, workshops, lectures and talks in schools. While she writes from personal impulse, she sees her work as a collective voice of a people. She uses standard English to make her people's experiences (like the sufferings of the slave trade) widely available, and Creole to convey untranslatable experiences. Performance techniques, Calypso rhythms, and carnival atmosphere help her Creole poetry cross the language barrier. She published two distinct collections entitled *Long Road to Nowhere:* 22 poems, Sable Publications, Oxford, 1982, and a collection reprinting only one of the same poems, Virago, 1985. The 1982 collection includes 'Circle of Thorns': 'So / when they ask / For whom the bell tolls? / Tell them / Male black aged nineteen / Female black aged seventeen / Two faces / in / a storm'. Her poems are anthologized in James Berry, ed., *News for Babylon* (West Indian British poetry), 1984, and Rhonda Cobham and Merle COLLINS, eds., *Watchers and Seekers* (creative writing by black women in Britain), 1987. AJ's *Sequins for a Ragged Hem,* 1988 (sequins for 'colour and sparkle' on the damage of slavery), describes visits back to the Caribbean, where she feels alienated yet involved in 'a complex learning process'. She teaches arts education at Warwick Univ. Autobiographical comment and criticism in Lauretta NGCOBO, *Let It Be Told, Black Women Writers in Britain,* 1988.

Johnson, Diane (Lain), novelist, critic, biographer, b. 1934 in Moline, Ill., da. of Frances (Elder) and Delph L. She had a 'bookish childhood' and at about ten wrote a novel influenced by H. S. ADAMS's *The Bobbsey Twins.* She attended Stephens College, but left in 1953 to marry Lamar J., Jr., 'which was the fashion then'. She had four children, two born in 1956 as she completed her BA at the Univ. of Utah. Her friend Alison LURIE's example was valuable in producing her first novels, *Fair Game,* 1965, and *Loving Hands at Home,* 1968, which draws on her 'discontented housewife state'. She moved to UCLA for her MA, 1966, and PhD, 1968 (the year she m. John Frederic Murray, professor of medicine, and began teaching at the Univ. of Calif., Davis). Her novels, like *Burning,* and *The Shadow Knows,* 1974, and *Lying Low,* 1978, tend to view California through Midwestern eyes and with Midwestern values, to observe an American clash between culture and violence. *The True History of the First Mrs Meredith and Other Lesser Lives,* 1972, a biography with explicitly speculative elements, is 'a little down on' the novelist George Meredith. Her life of Dashiell Hammett, 1983, was authorized by his family and by Lillian HELLMAN. DJ's novels often examine lives of women scrambling for survival and dealing with fear day by day; she questions fad therapies aimed at total self-consciousness but favours traditional Western and Eastern encouragements to submerge the self 'in mystical reflection or collective action'. She co-authored with Stanley Kubrick a screenplay of Stephen King's *The Shining,* 1980; her *Terrorists and Novelists,* 1982, collects essays from periodicals. *Persian Nights,* 1986, presents her theme of social instability in intense form, as a recently arrived, acutely intelligent American woman observes Iran on the brink of the Shi'ite revolution. DJ has said she values great books 'no matter by whom they were written': women write literature, not 'women's literature'; with 'different subjects', they do not 'write any differently'. 'Sometimes I wonder if I am that sinister thing, the male-identified woman.' Yet she admires many women novelists, and calls herself a feminist: 'I don't see how another attitude is possible to any serious person' (interview with Janet Todd in *Women Writers Talking,* 1983).

Johnson, Elizabeth, feminist, of Kensington, London. Like Elizabeth Singer, later ROWE, she wrote for John Dunton (see JOURNALISM), who calls her 'gay and witty' and (in 1704) unmarried. She helped persuade Rowe to publish *Poems,* 1696, and wrote a preface hailing her as her sex's champion against 'Violations on the Liberties of Freeborn English Women', worthy successor to SAPPHO, Anna Maria van SCHURMAN, Aphra BEHN, and Katherine PHILIPS.

Johnson, Georgia Blanche **Douglas** (Camp), 1880–1966, poet, playwright, and feminist, b. in Atlanta, Georgia, of English, Indian and Black descent, da. of Laura (Jackson) and George C. After schools in Rome, Ga., and Atlanta, she attended Atlanta Univ. Normal School (graduating 1896), taught for some years, and studied music at Oberlin (Ohio) and Cleveland. She taught, married Henry Lincoln J., prominent Washington lawyer and politician, in 1903, and had two sons. Her first published poem, 'Omnipresence', appeared in *Voice of the Negro,* 1905; regular contributions to *Opportunity* and *Crisis* followed. She also held government jobs and worked in women's organizations. Encouraged by Jessie FAUSET, she published her first book, *The Heart of a Woman and other poems,* 1918: its short lyrics (titles like 'Pent', 'Despair', 'Foredoom') express a sadness ('Her soul, a bud, – that never bloomed') which can be linked with her race and sex. GDJ's racially conscious poems in *Bronze,* 1922, were much praised; she writes of black women refusing motherhood under slavery, and of tragic mixed-race women: 'fretted fabric of a dual dynasty'. After her husband's death in 1925 she became closer to the New Negro movement, to Angelina GRIMKÉ and Gwendolyn BENNETT, She returned with new force to romantic themes in *An Autumn Love Cycle,* 1928, dedicated to Zona GALE: 'There's nothing certain, nothing sure / Save sorrow'. One of the few to praise the book was Anne SPENCER. Gloria T. Hull suspects irony in 'I am a woman / Which means / I am insufficient'. GDJ won prizes from *Opportunity* with social-protest plays in 1926 and 1927. Much of her drama is lost. The Federal Theatre Project of the 1930s rejected at least five pieces (evidently as too stark and radical): *Frederick Douglass* and *William and Ellen Craft* (both about escaping slaves: anthologized by Willis Richardson and May MILLER, 1935), and *Blue-eyed Black Boy, Safe,* and *A Sunday Morning in the Country,* all dealing with lynching and rape. In the 1930s GDJ wrote for black newspapers and printed poetry in journals, published as 'Paul Tremaine' and perhaps by other pseudonyms, and vainly sought awards, fellowships and steady jobs. She published a last poetry volume, *Share My World,* 1962. Her unfinished or unpublished works include stories, a life of her husband, a book on racial mixing called *White Men's Children.* See Gloria T. Hull, *Color, Sex, & Poetry, Three Women Writers of the Harlem Renaissance,* 1987; Ann Allen SHOCKLEY, 1988; unpub. plays at George Mason Univ.

Johnson, Josephine Winslow, novelist, poet, and prose-writer, b. 1910 in Kirkwood, Missouri, da. of well-to-do farmers Ethel (Franklin) and Benjamin H. J. She wrote a three-line poem on the end of WWI and 'found my niche in life'. Her educ. ran from a one-teacher private school to Washington Univ., St Louis. She won a Pulitzer Prize for her first novel, *Now in November,* 1934, which celebrates farming life and condemns modern dehumanizing developments. That year too her short story 'Genacht' was included in the O. Henry Memorial volume: repr. in *The Winter Orchard,* 1935. Her next novel, *Jordanstown,* 1937, repr. 1976, about a small-town newspaper editor and community organizer, linked her with proletarian novelists of the time. She also published a volume of poetry, *Year's End,* 1939. In 1942 she married Grant G. Cannon, ex-Mormon, Labor Relations worker, later editor of *Farm Quarterly*: they had two children. She taught at the Univ. of Iowa, 1942–5. Her later novels, *Wildwood,* 1947, and *The Dark Traveler,* 1963, with female and male protagonist respectively, again display her descriptive talents and the darkness of her vision. She writes with imaginative insight of the land, of country living and its implications for what is humanly desirable in *The Sorcerer's Son,* 1965 (stories), and *Inland Island,* 1969 (essays: repr. 1987; see John Fleischman in *Audubon,* 88, 1986), of childhood and nature in *Seven Houses, A Memoir of Time and Places,* 1973, and of a different place and age in her life of Florence FARR, 1975. MSS at Washington Univ.

Johnson, Pamela Hansford, 1912–81, novelist, b. in Clapham, London, da. of Amy (Howson), an actress, and Reginald Kenneth J., a colonial officer usually away in what is now Ghana. Seven when a sister was born and died, she could not feel sorry: 'It was the beginning of guilt.' Her father died before she was ten, leaving debts; her mother, grandmother and aunt took in lodgers; she left Clapham County Secondary School at 16 and became a secretary in a bank. She published stories and verse (including the prize-winning 'Chelsea Reach'), but judged herself no poet, and during WWII burned the remaining copies of her collection *Symphony for Full Orchestra,* 1934. An illness gave her time (two months) to write a novel, *This Bed Thy Centre,* 1935, reissued 1961 with her preface. The misleading title was chosen by Dylan Thomas, currently a romantic interest. (Her diaries and letters concerning him are at Buffalo, NY.) The book presents a girl drifting into marriage in 'ignorance and unpreparedness'; its relative openness about sexuality won praise and undesired notoriety. In 1936 PHJ m. Neil Stewart, a French-educated Australian; they had two children, and divorced after 14 years. Her five novels to 1939 (while she was in left-wing politics, editing the weekly cyclostyled *Chelsea Democrat*) chart the temper of the time with various social classes 'arbitrarily linked' by plot. The trilogy *Too Dear for My Possessing,* 1940, *An Avenue of Stone,* 1947, and *A Summer to Decide,* 1949, is full of mismatched, tormenting lovers; it grew from the desire to depict a passionate woman – chiefly through male eyes, firstly those of her lover's son. *Winter Quarters,* 1943, uses some of the same characters. PHJ married novelist C. P. Snow in 1950: they had a son, and later co-authored plays. In 1951 she wrote a booklet on Ivy COMPTON-BURNETT, although 'I grated on her, she grated on me'. *Catherine Carter,* 1952, set in the Victorian theatre world, uses family traditions; PHJ drew herself as the novelist-narrator of *An Impossible Marriage,* 1954, and *The Last Resort* (titled from a marriage, not the narrator's, to a homosexual: *The Sea and the Wedding* in USA), 1956. After a play, *Corinth House,* 1954, she wrote on Proust ('one of the greatest of all writers') in 1956. *Six Proust Reconstructions* (for radio: *Proust Recaptured* in US), 1958, moves some of his characters onwards to WWII. A note of savage satire emerged in *The Unspeakable Skipton,* 1959, *Night and Silence Who is Here,* 1962, and *Cork Street, next to the Hatter's,* 1965, all centred on an earth-mother poet-dramatist whose works (parodic texts are given) carry 'long, admiring prefaces by herself': the publisher, oddly, feared this (not PHJ's only caricatured female portrait) would be taken as libel on Edith SITWELL. An account of migraine in *The Humbler Creation,* 1959, led to the founding of the Migraine Trust. *An Error of Judgement,* 1962 (repr. 1987 with intro. by A. S. BYATT), disturbingly anatomizes an act of gratuitous evil; *On Iniquity,* 1967, non-fiction developed from a report for the *Sunday Telegraph* of the Moors murder trial, makes a case against the permissive society and the theatre of cruelty. *The Survival of the Fittest,* 1968, deals with the left-wing 1930s, *The Honours Board,* 1970, with a boys' prep school. *Important to Me: Personalia,* 1974, comments on events in PHJ's life, on 'Women' (for women priests; against degrading pornography, giving women's names to hurricanes, and the stirring up of sexual hatred), and on DETECTIVE FICTION (praise of Agatha CHRISTIE and other women). PHJ's friends included Olivia MANNING. Studies by Isabel Quigley, 1968 (admiring her freedom from 'a specifically feminine point of view'), Ishrat Lindblad, 1982; secondary bibliog. by Mildred Miles Franks in *Bulletin of Bibliog.,* 40, 1983; interview with John Halperin in his *C. P. Snow,* 1983.

Johnson, Emily **Pauline,** 1861–1913, poet, novelist, lecturer. She was b. on the Six Nations Reserve near Brantford, Ont., to an English mother, Emily Susanna (Howells), a relative of William Dean Howells, and a Mohawk father, George Henry Martin J. Later she adopted the name Tekahionwake. From her mother's side of the family she learned the nineteenth-century English Romantic poetic tradition; from her father's side, particularly her paternal grandfather, she heard Indian tales and legends, an ORAL influence important in her writing. She was educated at the Brantford model school. Her early sketch, 'A Red Girl's Reasoning', took a prize in the *Canadian Magazine.* Her poems first appeared in a NY magazine, *Gems of Poetry,* 1884; two were included in W. P. Lighthall's *Songs of the Great Dominion,* 1889. Because she rapidly developed a reputation as an authentic North American Indian, she began to do public readings in Indian dress and became a famous performer, touring Canada, the USA and Britain, 1892–1909. Her first volume of poetry, *The White Wampum,* 1895, was published in England, where her public readings aroused much interest in her writing. *Canadian Born,* 1903, and *Flint and Feather,* 1912, include much idealized narrative verse about Indian life in North America. After retiring from public life, she published *Legends of Vancouver,* 1911, short tales and legends heard from an Indian friend. *The Shagganappi* and *The Mocassin Maker,* short fictions published after her death in 1913, are didactic and sentimental, less well known and less interesting than her poetry, though they reveal her ambiguity about her Indian heritage. Her story 'As It Was in the Beginning' is printed in Paula Gunn ALLEN, ed., *Spider Woman's Granddaughters,* 1989. She died in Vancouver. See Walter McRaye, 1947, Betty Keller, 1981 (contains unpublished poems), and Norman Shrive in *CanL,* 13, 1962.

Johnson, Susannah (Willard), later Hastings, 1730–1810, captivity-narrator, b. in Mass., da. of James W. She m. James J. in 1747 and settled in the frontier area of Charlestown, NH. Seized by Indians in August 1754, with her husband, three children, and 14-year-old sister, she next day gave birth 'in the open wilderness, rendered cold by a rainy day'. They reached Lake Champlain in nine days' forced 'munch', lived some time in an Indian village, were taken in turn to be sold at Montréal, and (her husband having inadvertently broken parole) spent years in jail there and at Québec. In 1757 she sailed for England, from there to New York, and was briefly reunited with her husband before he was killed at Ticonderoga. In

1762 she m. John Hastings. Her *Narrative*, Walpole, NH, 1796, opens with a historical sketch and ends with musing on time ('My aged mother says to me . . . your daughter's daughter, has got a daughter'). It shows remarkable forbearance about the Indians, narrative flair and authentic-sounding detail: 'On viewing myself, I found that I too was naked'; 'A horse came in sight, known to us all by the name of Scoggin' (and plays a vital role, first as transport and then as food). Later eds. add material by others, and some claimed as hers.

Johnston, Dorothy Margaret, novelist, short-story writer, b. 1948 in Geelong, Victoria, da. of Ivy Margaret (Dorman) and Eric Somerville J. After university (Melbourne, 1966–9), she taught high school, worked at the Australian Council for Educational Research and in a women's refuge, before leaving full-time paid employment in 1982 for writing and mothering. She and her de facto husband, William Malone, journalist, now have two children. She lives in Canberra and is known as one of the 'Canberra writers', a group of women including Marion HALLIGAN. She wrote stories for *Canberra Tales,* 1988, but is chiefly a novelist, displaying wit and imagination in her first short novel, *Tunnel Vision,* 1984, set in a massage parlour. *Ruth,* 1986, the story of a woman seeking refuge from various demands, displays a quiet beauty, and less of DJ's former quirky, comic imagery. *Maralinga, My Love,* 1988, is quite different. It focuses on an ex-soldier, forever afflicted by the atomic experiments in South Australia following WWII. Both bleak and tender, with a spare, documentary quality, this novel was one of the few serious Australian political novels to emerge in the late 1980s.

Johnston, Jennifer, novelist. B. in Dublin, 1930, da. of the actress Shelagh Richards and playwright Denis J., she was educ. at Park House School and Trinity College, Dublin. Her first marriage, to lawyer Ian Smyth, took her to Paris and London and produced four children. She began writing in her mid-thirties, publishing her first novel, *The Captains and the Kings,* in 1972, which won three awards. After her divorce JJ m. solicitor David Gilliland, with whom, and five stepchildren, she lives only about a mile from the Londonderry border, next to the River Foyle. *The Gates,* 1973, illustrates the preoccupation with the Anglo-Irish connection (or disconnection) which permeates all her writing. Fascinated by 'seemingly inexplicable relationships', she focuses on the class and religious differences which are the source of Ireland's Troubles. Most of her novels deal with the difficult passage from childhood to adulthood framed within the Irish context. *How Many Miles to Babylon?* 1974, with its gripping descriptions of life in the trenches of Flanders in 1915, is an account of the tragic loss of innocence as the two childhood friends at opposite ends of the social scale confront the horrors of war. *Shadows on Our Skin,* 1977 (short-listed for the Booker Prize and made into a TV film), tells the story of young Joe Logan, a Londonderry Catholic schoolboy who dreams of being a poet, his brother Brendan returned from England to seek out glory as a Provo, and Kathleen Doherty, Joe's teacher from Wicklow, who is engaged to a British soldier. The tragic consequences of this triangular relationship sharply illustrate the tensions in JJ's work between past and present, Irish and English, safety and change. Subsequent novels (*The Old Jest,* 1979, filmed 1988, *The Railway Station Man,* 1984, and *Fool's Sanctuary,* 1987) again juxtapose personal lives with political struggle and bloodshed. JJ has also won success as a playwright. See Joseph Connelly in *Eire* 21, 1986; very hostile article by Rüdiger Imhof in *Etudes Irlandaises,* 10, 1985.

Johnston, Jill, dancer, critic, activist and autobiographer, b. 1929 in London to

Olive Marjorie Crowe, an American nurse from a family of weak men and 'strong but embarrassing women', and Cyril Frederick J., an Englishman who did not marry her. After five years travelling in Europe and the US, JJ and her mother settled at Little Neck, Long Island; her grandmother raised her while her mother worked; at boarding school she 'was a boy'; on graduating in 1947 from St Mary's, Peekskill (run by Episcopalian nuns), she became 'a failed girl'. She studied in Boston and Minnesota, had affairs with female and male mentors, and 'was delivered over to culture, the great realm of paper and performance where our ancestors have taken up immortal residence'. In NYC from 1953 to study at Columbia, dance, and work at odd jobs in 'the female slave market', she had an abortion, married Richard John Lanham in 1958 'because it was the thing to do and I had no idea what else to do at the time', and had two children. Writing for *Village Voice* ('Dance Journal', from 1959, selec. as *Marmalade Me,* 1971) and *Art News,* she found that 'my ambition was extensive'. Divorced in 1964, anarchic and insolvent, she produced and performed in dance concerts and happenings, had another abortion, and lived with a woman. She dropped dance criticism once her mother accepted it, and in two years made 'a double hairpin turn in slow motion around myself': see *Mother Bound,* 1983, first volume of *Autobiography in Search of a Father.* Its sequel, *Paper Daughter,* 1985, charts her search for and invention of fathers: a 'Christian delusion', stay in a 'mental slammer', and discovery of feminism. *Lesbian Nation: The Feminist Solution,* 1973 (essays and diary entries), is 'a picture of an evolving political revolutionary consciousness'. *Village Voice* pieces in *Gullible's Travels,* 1974 (the year she recorded, with others, *A Feminist-Lesbian Dialogue*), punningly re-create 'adventures and misdemeanours': 'one's upon a thyme'. She has written as F. J. Crowe.

Johnston, Mary, 1870–1936, novelist, b. in Buchanan, Va., eldest of Elizabeth (Alexander) and John J.'s six children. Of frail health, MJ received most of her education at home and through travel in Europe and the Middle East. She wrote her first novel, *Prisoners of Hope,* 1898, to help the family finances. Her greatest success, *To Have and to Hold,* 1900, sold more than half a million copies, enabling MJ to build a large country house in Virginia where she lived with three sisters and a brother. The novel, set in seventeenth-century Virginia, is the fast-moving story of a disguised woman in flight from England who is literally sold into marriage. Of her 23 novels, MJ's most successful were the historical romances, mostly set in Virginia, where, despite some clumsy verbosity, she provided well-researched historical detail. Her most interesting novel is *Hagar,* 1913: the heroine, a Southern feminist at variance with her family, becomes a successful writer, financially independent. Her fiancé must accept that 'I shall work on through life for the fairer social order ... The Woman Movement has me for keeps.' An enthusiastic feminist, MJ claimed that woman's best weapon is not '"indirect influence", the indirection of which is extreme indeed', but the vote (*Atlantic Monthly,* 1910). Her papers are at the Univ. of Virginia. Her work is discussed in E. Wagenknecht's 'The World of MJ', *Sewanee Review,* 1936, and G. Longest's *Three Virginia Writers,* 1978; also Ann Goodwyn Jones, *Tomorrow is Another Day,* 1981.

Johnstone, Christian Isobel, 1781–1857, novelist and journalist, b. in Fife. Divorced from a Mr McLeish, she m. John J., then a teacher, *c.* 1812. Her *Clan-Albin, A National Tale* (anonymous, pub. London 1815; but part in print, she says, before Scott's *Waverley,* 1814; repr. 1853) is both gripping and humorous; her preface disclaims moralizing or preaching for the 'very good purpose' of 'mere amusement'. Modern renaissance comes to a West Highland clan (though few emigrants accept a call home: the 'pride of Highland descent was grafted on the vigorous stem of American independence'). Two matriarchs retain benevolent sway: the highborn 'mighty spirit' Lady Augusta (revealed as the hero's grandmother), and the 'wise woman' Moome ('nurse'), finest storyteller and Gaelic poet 'in a glen where all were poets'. CIJ pub. a lasting bestseller in *The Cook and Housewife's Manual,* 1826 (as 'Margaret Dods' of Scott's *St Ronan's Well*); her only other major novel, *Elizabeth de Bruce,* 1827; pleasing juvenile books (fiction, history, science, reading texts, 1823–42), some as 'Aunt Jane'; and *Tales of the Irish Peasantry,* 2nd ed. 1836, using evidence before the Poor Law Commission to stir the 'deadness of the British people to the ... wrongs of Ireland'. With John J., she edited the *Inverness Courier,* then the *Edinburgh Chronicle* and *The Schoolmaster,* which became *Johnstone's Edinburgh Magazine,* 1833–4, then merged with *Tait's.* Favouring literary content, good reviews and low price, she introduced Scotland's first cheap books. She reprinted work by herself and others in *The Edinburgh Tales,* 1845–6.

Jolas, Maria (McDonald), 1893–1987, editor and TRANSLATOR, b. in Louisville, Ky., of a wealthy Virginia family who laughed both at women writers and at her scholarship offer from the Univ. of Chicago. She studied singing in Berlin before WWI, and in 1926 m. Eugene J. (d. 1952), an Alsatian poet. They had two daughters, and founded the important *transition,* 1927–38, 'an international quarterly for creative experiment'. This, unusually, published not only work by mostly male rising stars (including drafts of the future *Finnegans Wake*), but also (as Benstock, 1986, points out) many women, e.g. BRYHER, H. D., Laura RIDING, Emily Holmes COLEMAN, Solita SOLANO, Caresse CROSBY, and Genevieve TAGGARD. MJ began her translating career here, but wrote, she said, only one article. The Jolas house at Colombey-les-deux-églises, bought by Charles de Gaulle when they left France in 1939, is now a national monument. As Joyce's chief benefactor for over 20 years and the salvager of his papers after WWII, MJ edited *A James Joyce Yearbook,* 1949, and wrote 'The Joyce I Knew and the Women around Him' (*Crane Bag,* 4, 1980), and an interview about Nora (Barnacle) Joyce (*James Joyce Quarterly,* 20, 1982). She rendered into English all Nathalie Sarraute's highly experimental books, winning the Scott–Moncrieff prize in 1970, and was a lifelong campaigner for radical causes.

Jolley, Elizabeth (Knight), novelist and short-story writer, b. 1923 in Birmingham, England, da. of Austrian Margarethe Johanna Caroline (von Fehr) and Charles Wilfred K. This mixed inheritance is reflected in much of EJ's fiction, as is the theme of the displaced person. Educ. at home by French, Swiss and German governesses until 11, then as a boarder at the Friends' School, Sibford, she trained as a nurse at St Thomas's Hospital, Birmingham. She migrated to Australia in 1959 when her husband, Leonard J., was appointed librarian of the Univ. of Western Australia Library. From the mid 1960s she had stories broadcast on radio and pub. in journals and anthologies. She has also written numerous radio plays, including the Augie winner 'Two Men Running' (broadcast 1981). Her first book was *Five Acre Virgin and other stories,* 1976. It was followed by another collection, *The Travelling Entertainer,* 1979: both repub. as *Stories,* 1984. Her first novel, *Palomino,* 1980, won little recognition for its sensitive portrayal of a lesbian relationship. Such relationships, as well as incestuous ones, have also been a feature of her later novels. Her zany, often black, humour and her tendency to re-use themes and characters became more apparent in her next two novels, *The Newspaper of Claremont Street,* 1981, and *Mr Scobie's Riddle,* 1982. The latter, set in an old people's home, won the

Age Book of the Year Award and first attracted wide attention to EJ's work. Themes and settings from *Palomino* are reworked in the wonderfully comic *Miss Peabody's Inheritance,* 1983, and in the more gothic *The Well,* 1986, winner of the Miles FRANKLIN Award. Another prize-winning novel, *Milk and Honey,* 1984, has, unusually for EJ, a male central character and examines the tensions between old and new lifestyles. The title story of her third collection, *Woman in a Lampshade,* 1983, focuses on a woman writer; another woman writer is central to *Foxybaby,* 1985, which, like *The Well,* explores the interconnection of life and story-telling. *The Sugar Mother,* 1988, introduces new characters and the theme of surrogate motherhood. *My Father's Moon,* 1989, draws on EJ's own experiences at boarding school and as a nurse during WWII, in a discontinuous narrative. Useful articles in a special issue of *Westerly,* July 1986. Christina Wilcox has made a film of EJ's life and work, *The Nights Belong to the Novelist.* See also P. Gilbert, 1988, and H. Daniel, 1988. MSS in the Mitchell Library, Sydney.

Jones, Alice, 'Alix John', 1853–1933, novelist, essayist, short-story writer. B. and educ. in Halifax, Novia Scotia, da. of Margaret Wiseman (Stairs) and Alfred Gilpin J., a wealthy businessman later Lieutenant-Governor of Nova Scotia, she travelled widely in England, France and Italy, studying languages abroad, and in 1905 moved to France, where she died. Her social situation and European experience are reflected in her five novels, her travel essays and short stories. These use international settings effectively, develop the theme of the innocent abroad, and treat the theme of art. *Bubbles We Buy,* 1903, begins with a Novia Scotia family which made a fortune in the age of sail with trade to the West Indies and South America, then shifts to Boston, an English country estate, Florence, and Paris. Its protagonist, a talented painter, is one of AJ's characteristically strong women characters.

Jones, Amanda Theodocia, 1835–1914, journalist, poet, spiritualist and inventor, b. East Bloomfield, NY, da. of Mary Alma (Mott) and Henry J., master weaver. She was educ. at the local district school and when the family moved to Black Rock, near Buffalo, NY, she attended the East Aurora Academy. She began teaching at 15 but gave it up when her poems were accepted by the *Ladies' Repository.* By 1854 she believed herself to be a medium with healing powers (which she wrote about in her *Psychic Autobiography,* 1910), but in 1859 she developed TB, and never fully recovered. Her first volume of poetry, *Ulah,* was pub. 1861. The title poem, based on an Indian legend, describes the romantically incestuous love of Ocanee, a noble Indian, for Ulah, an Indian maiden who reminds him of his dead sister. *Poems,* 1867, includes patriotic attempts to come to terms with the Civil War. 'Atlantis', a semi-epic, presents the war as a mythical combat between Athens and the denizens of Atlantis, and credits victory to a female agency, namely the goddess Athena and her nymphs. In 1869 ATJ became associate editor of the Chicago *Universe,* and the following year editor of *The Bright Side,* a juvenile periodical. *A Prairie Idyll,* 1882, contains the poem 'From Saurian to Seraph', which questions the impact of the Civil War on domestic life and popular theology. Other poems, together with her *Rubaiyat of Solomon,* 1905, draw on her extensive knowledge of midwestern flora and fauna. She also established a working women's home and founded the Woman's Canning and Preserving Company.

Jones, E. B. C., Emily Beatrice Coursolles (Jones) Lucas, 'Topsy', 1893–1966, poet and novelist, b. in England of Canadian parents, both from eminent legal families. She began to write at seven, attended English and European schools, and knew the Bloomsbury group. While working for the Food Control Ministry during WWI she shared a flat with Romer WILSON, whose work she published while assistant editor of *Woman's Leader,* 1918–19. She published books of poetry – *Windows,* 1917 (with Christopher Johnson), *Songs for Sale,* 1918 (an anthology), and *Singing Captives,* 1921. She reviewed Virginia WOOLF's *Night and Day* for *The Cambridge Magazine,* 1919. Katherine MANSFIELD thought her *Quiet Interior,* 1920, 'remarkably well constructed' for a first novel. She m. Cambridge scholar F. L. Lucas, 1921: Woolf, who liked 'her spruce shining mind', thought her more experienced, sadder and more strained than he was. They separated in 1929: later divorced. Her four further novels reflect her interest in science and metaphysics. In *Helen & Felicia,* the sisters, 'introspective, keenly aware of their own inner lives, and detached from themselves in a way of which those who looked only outwards were quite incapable', make radically different choices. Helen rejects university, wanting instead to be 'the Newnham sort of person' through marriage to a worldly sophisticate, but finds that they belong 'to different branches of humanity'. Felicia, seeing Helen's world as unattainable, seeks 'some sort of life of my own' in a seedy dancing school. The three are left together living under Helen's dictum: 'we must take what pleasure we can'. EBCJ's last novel, *Morning and Cloud,* 1931, presents another marriage of non-communication between the cerebral and philosophic Cedric and a wife of whom his lover wonders how 'that dullness, and that sense of evasion ... should translate themselves into order, serenity and formal beauty'.

Jones, Gayl Amanda, novelist, poet, b. 1949 in Lexington, Ky., da. of Lucille (Wilson) and Franklin J., a cook. Her grandmother wrote plays for church production; her mother wrote stories which she read to her children; GJ says 'the women I'm descended from', and also the ORAL TRADITION, have special significance for her. She began writing by age eight, at a segregated school she attended until tenth grade; she took a BA in English at Connecticut College (where she received poetry and fiction awards and wrote 'poetic journals' which later led to storytelling poems), and studied creative writing at Brown Univ. (MA 1973, DA 1975). At 19 she wrote her 'first Kentucky-oriented story'. Her play *Chile Woman* was staged in 1974. Her novels treat women doubly oppressed by racism and sexism. Toni MORRISON, at Random House, edited the first, *Corregidora,* 1975 ('sort of song' in its first version), whose heroine, a brutally abused blues singer (granddaughter of a Portuguese slave-trader), struggles to preserve the stories of her mother, grandmother, and Great Gram. The protagonist of *Eva's Man,* 1976, murderer of her lover, in a hospital for the criminally insane, becomes increasingly incoherent about her history; she maintains autonomy, says GJ, by 'controlling what she will and will not tell' and by silences. (June JORDAN wrote that the book offered 'sinister misinformation about women', especially black and molested women.) *White Rat,* 1977 (stories), includes persuasive renderings of male viewpoints. GJ's long mythical poems, *Song for Anninho,* 1981 ('adapted from my novel *Palmares*'), and *Xarque,* 1985, recount the stories of Almeyda (survivor of a destroyed settlement of Brazilian slaves) and her descendants; *The Hermit-Woman,* 1983, is also poetry. GJ taught at the Univ. of Michigan, 1975–83. *Callaloo,* 5, 1982, prints stories and poems by GJ, articles, and an interview. See also Tate, 1983, Evans, 1984, and bibliog. in *Callaloo,* 7, 1984.

Jones, Marion, Patrick, later O'Callaghan, novelist and social anthropologist, b. 1934 in Trinidad. She was educ. at St Joseph's Convent, Port-of-Spain, and from 1950 the Imperial College of Agriculture (one of the first two women there). She worked for a year in Brooklyn, NYC, at a ceramics factory in the mid-1950s, qualified as a chartered librarian in Trinidad (while working at the Carnegie Free Library) and took a BSc in social anthropology at University College, London, 1962. She wrote a thesis, 'The Chinese Community in Trinidad', and was a founder member of the Campaign Against Racial Discrimination. In 1973 she went to work for UNESCO in Paris. Her two novels look back at the post-war rise of a Trinidadian middle class, its failure to question working-class dispossession, the rigidity of inherited systems, and low national self-image. *Pan Beat*, 1973, focuses on a teenage steel band and what happens to them in later life (their black parents had feared 'low class steelband people', wishing their offspring to be more like whites who learn the violin). *J'Ouvert Morning*, 1976, follows the fortunes of three generations with different survival tactics, different planned escape-routes, different compromises. MPJ has published books about Namibia and the then Southern Rhodesia, both Paris, 1977, in her married name of O'C. See Harold Barratt in *WLWE*, 19, 1980.

Jones, Mary, d. 1778, Oxford poet and letter-writer, sister of the Rev. Oliver J. of Christ Church. She translated Italian songs into English verse at 15; her mother (*née* Penn) worried about the proverb that one tongue is enough for a woman. In 1732 she mentioned writing poetry as relief for madness, in 1734 her dread of male disapproval of female wit, in 1736 her hopes of publication. That year she was 'highly delighted' at the handsome look of Mary BARBER's *Poems*. She had university and aristocratic friends, made visits to London and Windsor Forest, and corresponded with Charlotte LENNOX. Busy with household duties by day, she read – or skipped – and wrote when 'other People are a bed and asleep'. She published anonymously: memorial verse tributes and a ballad, 'The Lass of the Hill', 1742, which sold 'special well', becoming 'the Fashion of the Town'. A letter of comic reproof to her neighbour Dr Pitt about his decaying garden wall was published behind her back. Dons, royalty, and BLUESTOCKINGS subscribed to (and Samuel Johnson owned) her *Miscellanies in Prose and Verse*, Oxford, 1750, printed in two formats, more and less grand. Her poems are colloquial, sinewy, satirical, sometimes risqué; her letters to women confront their situation both bleakly and playfully. Her 'dearest and best of mothers' died just before the book appeared. In 1761 she declined an offer from Isabella Griffiths's husband (see JOURNALISM) to review for the *Monthly*.

Jones, Sarah, Quaker pamphleteer, probably of Bristol, a dyer's wife. She pub. *To Sions Lovers*, 1644, and *This is the Lights Appearance* [1650?], which calls on people to look within themselves to find God's will, and presents herself in a motherly role, wishing freely to 'breath forth the measure of life that I have received, to do the least babes good'.

Jones, Susan (Morrow), 'S. Carleton', 'S. Carleton Jones', 1864?–1926, novelist. B. and educ. in Halifax, Nova Scotia, da. of Helen (Stairs) and Robert M., she m. Guy Carleton J., later Director-General of the Canadian Army Medical Services. Sister-in-law and cousin of Alice JONES, she contributed to periodicals such as *Atlantic Monthly, Smart Set*, and *Lippincott's Magazine*. Recent research indicates that works ascribed to SJ as 'Helen Milecete' were likely written by her sister, Helen Morrow (m. first to a man called Pask, 1889, then to Major Edward John Duffus). Works by 'Carleton-Milecete' may have been collaborative. 'Helen Milecete's' *A Detached Pirate*, 1903, reminiscent of Frances BROOKE's *Emily Montague*, is a witty, well-crafted novel composed of letters to a friend from a recently divorced protagonist. It has considerable feminist interest, its plot an allegory of desired freedom: the 'lover' who caused the protagonist's divorce turns out to have been herself cross-dressed for the purpose of wandering freely in the city. *The La Chance Mine Mystery,* 1920, concerns romance and mystery at a gold mine in the Laurentians north of Montréal.

Jong, Erica (Mann), poet, novelist, b. 1942 in NYC, one of three das. of Eda (Mirsky), designer in ceramics, and Seymour M., musician and businessman. She was educ. at Barnard College (BA, 1963) and Columbia (MA in eighteenth-century English literature, 1965), and taught English at various colleges beginning with CUNY, from 1964. Allan J., child psychiatrist (m. in 1966), was the second of three husbands; now divorced, EJ has one daughter. From 'my very first collection of verse' she saw her task as writing 'out of a naked female consciousness for a culture that has too often presumed the noun "poet" to be of the male gender'. Her poetry, beginning with *Fruits & Vegetables,* 1971, was selected in 1977 and 1980, continued in *Ordinary Miracles,* 1983. She became known, especially for sexual frankness, with her novel *Fear of Flying,* 1973, and its sequel, *How to save your own life,* 1977. In her bawdy, pastiche eighteenth-century *Fanny: Being The True History of the Adventures of Fanny Hackabout-Jones,* 1980, her witches 'owe as much to the fairy tale as they do to anthropology', but she acknowledges a debt to 'the crucial anthropological work of ... Dr Margaret A. Murray'. This material is treated again in *Witches* (essay and poetry: marred by illustrations of tortured alluring women), 1981. In *Serenissima, A Novel of Venice,* 1987, a US film actress, playing in a version of *The Merchant of Venice,* enters the body of Shakespeare's Jessica, beds the author (who speaks in quotations) and his patron, and helps him rescue a baby boy, 'neither his nor mine', with whom she re-enters the twentieth century. EJ packs her funny, shrewd prose with literary allusion; her first heroine longs to be a 'female Chaucer'; she has edited eighteenth-century novels, 1982; she invokes the tradition of women's writing ('Alcestis on the Poetry Circuit' is dedicated to the memory of 'Marina TSVETAYEVA, Anna WICKHAM, Sylvia PLATH, Shakespeare's sister, etc., etc.') and attacks the painful interlace under patriarchy of 'female psychology' and cultural history ('If she's an artist / & comes close to genius, / the very fact of her gift / should cause her such pain / that she will take her own life / rather than best us'). *Parachutes & Kisses,* 1984, shows how 'Being an artist demands a cut umbilicus (which often bleeds); being a daughter demands the cord intact (a bloodless but confining fate).' *Megan's Book of Divorce,* 1984, is a frivolous 'Kid's Book for Adults'. She has discussed her work in Janet Sternburg, ed., *The Woman Writer on Her Work,* 1980, and Janet Todd, ed., *Women Writers Talking,* 1983.

Jordan, June, poet and essayist. B. in 1936 in Harlem, NYC, da. of nurse Mildren Maude (Fisher) and postal clerk Granville Ivanhoe J., she grew up in Bedford-Stuyvesant, NYC, and started writing poetry at seven. She dropped out after two years at Barnard College, 1953–5: 'No one ever presented me with a single black author, poet, historian, personage or idea ... Nor ... a single woman to study'. She m. Michael Meyer (1955, divorced 1965) and has a son. (Until 1969, she published in periodicals as June Meyer.) A civil rights activist, JJ was assistant producer of *The Cool World,* 1963–4, a film about the police murder of a black boy in New York which triggered the 1964 Harlem riots, and she directed the SEEK (Search for Education, Elevation and Knowledge) program for inner city students, 1967–9. A freelance journalist after *Cool World,* she has written 'The Black Poet Speaks of Poetry' in the *American Poetry Review* since 1974. She has taught English at various colleges and Afro-American studies at Yale, 1974–5. In 1964 she collaborated with Buckminster Fuller on a plan to redesign Harlem, later won the Prix de Rome in Environmental Design, 1970–1, for her first novel, *His Own Where,* 1971 (nominated for the National Book Award), written to 'familiarize kids with ... activist habits of response to environment'. *Who Look at Me,* 1969, her first volume of poetry, was followed by *Some Changes,* 1971, *New Days: Poems of Exile and Return,* 1973, *Things I Do in the Dark* (selecs.), 1977, and *Passion: New Poems, 1977–1980,* 1980. She was a contributing editor for the black journal *First World* and the feminist journal *Chrysalis,* 1977. Influenced by Walt Whitman, Alice WALKER, Adrienne RICH, and Audre LORDE, her poetry combines street and, often ironically, literary idiom as it protests the violence of an anti-black, anti-female society and affirms the necessity of solidarity among people, as in 'Poem for South African Women', 1980: 'And who will join this standing up / and the ones who stood without sweet company / will sing and sing'. She defends her use of black English as containing 'elements of the spirit that have provided for our survival' and sees feminism as 'an inseparable part of a world-wide struggle against all forms of domination'. Speaking out against Israeli bombing of Lebanon, 1982, brought death threats, and rejection by the *NY Times.* Her other writing includes several books for juveniles, a biography of *Fannie Lou Hamer,* 1972, and a collection of personal essays, *Civil Wars,* 1981, from the Harlem riots of 1964 to the Miami riot of 1980. On *Living Room,* poems, and *On Call: Political Essays,* 1986, see Dorothy Abbott in *WRB,* June 1986. *Naming Our Destiny,* 1989, prints new and selected poems. Parallel essays by JJ and Angela DAVIS in *WRB,* July/Aug. 1987, examine the dynamics of Afro-American poetry and politics. See Peter Erickson in *Callaloo,* 9, 1986.

Jordan, Kate (later Vermilye) 1862–1926, novelist, playwright, b. Dublin, Eire, da. of Katherine and Michael J., professor. KJ was taken to NYC aged three and was educ. at home. Always determined to be a writer, she was 12 when her first story appeared. Her first success was *The Kiss of Gold,* 1892. In 1897 she m. Frederic V., NYC broker. KJ's extensive travel is reflected in some of her writing, such as *The Next Corner,* 1921, set in France. Her novels powerfully portray the suffering of women who find themselves trapped in unsatisfactory marriages or social roles. KJ skilfully depicts NYC's unglamorous side, especially for the women striving for financial independence, as in *The Creeping Tides,* 1913, and *Against the Winds,* 1919. Her plots move fast but rely heavily on sudden dramatic twists of a not unpredictable nature. One of her best, *Time the Comedian,* 1905, remorselessly portrays the effects of age and unhappiness on one whose beauty has been destroyed: 'Lotions and powders were futile while her cheeks had hollows in them picked out by the wrath of a hungry heart'. Her last novel, *Trouble-The-House,* 1921, which uncharacteristically concentrates on childhood experience, is partly autobiographical. Her plays, unpub., include 'A Luncheon at Nick's', 1903, and 'Mrs Dakon', 1909. After her husband's death, KJ, ill and unable to finish her current novel, committed suicide. Discussion of her work is in the *Bookman,* June 1913.

Joseph, Jenny, poet, journalist, children's writer, b. 1932 in Birmingham to Jewish parents, Florence and Louis J. She grew up in Bucks., 'in a household that liked books, but even more, words', and dreamed of writing lines that would be anonymously known, like folksongs, to 'any Tom Dick or Harry, Liz Joan or Mary'. Evacuated from Bristol to Devon during WWII, she took a BA in English, 1953, at St Hilda's College, Oxford. After lecturing in adult education, she was a reporter in Bedford, then South Africa, returning under threat of expulsion. She m. Tony Coles in 1961; they have three children, and ran a London pub 1969–72. JJ's first two poetry volumes, *The Unlooked-for Season,* 1960, and *Rose in the*

Afternoon, 1974, received awards. They present complex series of images with delicate detail: 'Women at Streatham Hill' contrasts 'giggling creamy beauties' with women 'Weighted with shopping, spreading hands and feet, / Trunk gnarling, weatherworn'. Philip Larkin chose for *The Oxford Book of Twentieth Century English Verse* her 'Warning': 'When I am an old woman I shall wear purple. ... And make up for the sobriety of my youth'. After six children's books (two jointly) and more poetry (*The Thinking Heart,* 1978, and *Beyond Descartes,* 1983) came *Persephone,* 1986, a prose-and-verse work which JJ calls a novel. It interweaves myth with present-day teenage sexuality, rites of passage, an inner underworld ('Come down, / You who turn from things, / Into my blank domain where the silence would suit you'), and an upper world of fertility and energy ('There stands your wheat. ... Persephone's moist breath in the rising corn'). JJ enjoys 'the variety of modes in English literature', finds translation 'good training', and plays down 'self-expression' and 'identity' in poetry; she likes to use 'the weather, seasons and daily circumstances' as universally meaingful. Resenting the label 'domestic' poet, she grants it is hard for women to 'ruthlessly pursue the quarry of the artefact across the terrain of life'. She teaches, broadcasts and has written of her feminism in *Bananas,* April 1980.

Joudry, Patricia, playwright, novelist, memoirist, b. 1921 in Spirit River, Alberta, to Beth and Clifford J., Catholics who moved to Montréal in 1925. At school, with 'what is known as a strong sense of self', she was 'the first girl ever to get the strap', and wrote and acted in plays. At 18, working as an elevator girl, she wrote a successful radio play, *Going Up Please.* She played the lead in her radio comedy series *Penny's Diary,* 1940–3, co-authored a US radio sitcom, *The Aldrich Family,* in NYC, 1945–9, m. Delmar Dinsdale, had two daughters, and divorced, 1952. After another series, *Affectionately, Jenny,* 1951–2, she added 'serious writing' to her 6 TV and 30 radio dramas (including adaptations from Lucy Maud MONTGOMERY). She m. photographer (later producer) John Steele and wrote an article on the 'Old-Fashioned' birth of her next daughter. Her first stage play, *Teach Me How to Cry,* written in pregnancy, was performed in 1955 (in London, 1958, it was *Noon Has No Shadows*), *The Sand Castle* in 1955, and *Three Rings for Michelle* (contrasting a stuffy conventional family and open, loving orphan) in 1956. PJ and Steele moved to England in 1962, educating their three daughters at home in defiance of various authorities, as told in *And the Children Played,* 1975. Plays from these years included *Walk Alone Together,* staged 1960, 'a spoof on our method of child raising'; *Semi-Detached,* which flopped on Broadway that year when film rights had been sold for $250,000; *Years of Your Father,* 'a sort of religious comedy thriller', one of several plays PJ claimed to have received as spirit messages, some from George Bernard Shaw; and *Think Again,* satirical farce involving a brain transplant to a baboon (pub. in *Canadian Theatre Review,* 23, 1979, with biographical checklist). Back in Canada from 1973, PJ wrote three novels, beginning with *The Dweller on the Threshold,* 1973 (dramatized as *My Lady Shiva;* its male protagonist loves a mysterious cousin based on one of PJ's daughters), *Spirit River to Angels Roost, religions I have loved and left,* 1977 (a part-facetious account of a continuing spiritual search), and *A Very Modest Orgy,* 1981, a comedy pointing the nuclear family's ability to accommodate innovation and eccentricity.

Journalism (see also MAGAZINES) by women began with almanacs (see Sarah JINNER), which were in turn connected with MEDICAL WRITING. John Dunton, 1659–1732, sought female readers and promoted a female voice in his *Athenian* ventures from 1689 and in the *Ladies' Mercury* from 1693 (see

Bertha-Monica Stearns in *MP*, 28, 1930–1; Kathryn Shevelow in *Genre*, 19, 1986; study by Gilbert D. McEwen, 1972). He claimed nearly 30 female contributors, including Mary ASTELL, Damaris MASHAM and the future Elizabeth ROWE. Ladies' journals spread widely (Dublin in 1727, Kent in 1773). The original *Female Tatler*, 1709–10, perhaps by Delarivier MANLEY, was more political than Steele's *Tatler*; Eliza HAYWOOD's *Female Spectator*, 1744–6, discussed women's EDUCATION and relied heavily on fiction. The first magazine proper, 1731, was quickly followed by others aimed partly or wholly at women. The *Reading Mercury* was owned by three generations of women (see Elizabeth LE NOIR); Mrs E. Johnson invented the Sunday newspaper in 1779. (For women in journalism to about 1830 see Alison Adburgham, 1972). In the nineteenth century Eliza Lynn LINTON and Margaret OLIPHANT in England, Margaret FULLER in the USA were among the most influential literary journalists; George ELIOT edited a leading intellectual journal, *The Westminster Review*, 1851–4. Elizabeth COCHRANE in the 1880s was one of the earliest US women newspaper reporters; Elizabeth BANKS was also a daring 'scoop'-hunter. Flamboyant English heiress Rachel Beer, 1859–1927, edited *The Observer* (owned by her husband's family) and *The Sunday Times* intermittently during the 1890s; she scooped Esterházy's confession in the Dreyfus case. Flora SHAW was a distinguished foreign correspondent for *The Times* of London in the 1890s. Florence MARRYAT ran a school of journalism in London.

During this century, journalism specifically by and for women has remained lively from *Votes for Women*, founded 1907, to the *Women's Review of Books*. Women in the profession have inevitably met prejudice and the attempt to restrict their activity to closely defined domestic or personal areas: bodies like The Society of Women Writers and Journalists (UK) have sought to protect and advance professional aims. Women's establishment in previously all-male departments has speeded up as the fields of journalism have multiplied. Sara Jeanette DUNCAN, Solita SOLANO and Anne O'Hare MCCORMICK were pathbreakers in Canada and the USA. WWI produced a crop of women war correspondents, like Mildred ALDRICH, who had already, early in the century, supported herself in Europe as a journalist, and Louise MACK, the first Australian woman war correspondent. Their successors in WWII are discussed in a study by Lilya Wagner, 1989, and those of the Vietnam War, 1961–75, by Virginia Elwood-Akers, 1988; their tradition is upheld today by women like the British award-winner Kate Adie. Photo-journalism, a relatively recent genre, was pioneered by women like Berenice Abbott in Europe and the USA (see study by Hank O'Neal, 1982) and Grace Robertson in 1940s and 50s Britain (see collection with her commentary, 1989). Literary journalism has also remained a valuable market for women writers. Reviewing played an important part in the early creative development of WOOLF as it did in that of WOLLSTONECRAFT; even better known as reviewers are Dorothy PARKER and Pauline KAEL. Djuna BARNES wrote pieces on New York, widely scattered through newspapers and journals, 1911–31, which have only recently been collected. Women have written hard news of every kind, as well as columns on everything from gardening (Vita SACKVILLE-WEST, to an enthusiastic public) to etiquette (Mary Lee SETTLE, under cover of a pseudonym): Ada LEVERSON had already parodied such columns. Settle rejected commiseration from Rosamond LEHMANN on having to work at journalism, and calls it 'the best training in the world' in observation, fluency and professionalism. Ann PETRY is another who attributes the growth of her novelistic skills to her training as a reporter. Many have begun, like Dawn POWELL, by working on school and college papers; Jamaican poet Louise BENNETT trained as a columnist for the *Sunday*

Gleaner and her younger compatriate Christine CRAIG on the *Guardian* in London. It has become usual to combine newspaper journalism with work in other media, like radio (e.g. Marghanita LASKI in England), publicity work (e.g. Mabel SEGUN in Nigeria), TV presentation and interviewing (e.g. Pamela MORDECAI in Jamaica), left-wing activism (Vera LYSENKO in the USA, Emma GOLDMAN in many places), peace campaigning (Vera BRITTAIN in England), or promotional activity (Mabel Dodge LUHAN in the USA). Women have been centrally associated with particular newspapers, like Brittain, Winifred HOLTBY and Mary STOTT with the then *Manchester Guardian*. Stott, who followed both her parents into journalism and was followed by her daughter, and Martha GELLHORN, are good examples of women whose lifelong newspaper careers have been shaped by serious concerns with issues affecting the status of women and the health of public life in general. Gellhorn's fiction is closely linked with her journalism; the same could be said of many others, including Brittain, and also Christine BROOKE-ROSE, theorist and critic, whose journalistic writing has little in common with theirs. See M. Melzolf, *Up from the Footnote: A History of Women Journalists*, 1977.

Judson, Ann (Hasseltine), 1789–1826, missionary and travel-writer. B. in Bradford, Mass., educ. at Bradford Academy, converted at 17, a schoolteacher at 18, she m., 1812, Adoniram J., who was about to sail to Burma as a Congregational missionary. She saw herself as the first American lady 'to carry the Gospel to the distant benighted heathen'. In Calcutta they paused long enough to become Baptists. In Rangoon (where women were 'held in the lowest esteem' and sold as slaves in case of financial need) she studied the language and ran the household ('I have many more interruptions than Mr Judson'), grieved for her first baby's death, taught and ministered to women, and sent home gripping letters for magazine publication. In 1822 ill health drove her home via Britain; on the Atlantic she began writing, in letters to an Englishman, her account of their mission, pub. 1823, at London and Washington, to raise money for freeing and educating Burmese women. The parts written on the spot (by her husband too) are best; a 2nd ed., 1827, tells of her return to Burma and imprisonment at the British invasion, 1824. Posthumous fame linked her with Adoniram J.'s two later wives, Sarah (Hall), widow of his fellow-missionary Boardman, and Emily (Chubbuck) JUDSON (study by Joan J. Brumberg, 1981).

Judson, Emily (Chubbuck), 'Fanny Forester', 1817–54, writer, missionary, b. Eaton, NY, youngest da. in Lavinia (Richards) and Charles C.'s large family. Family poverty obliged her to work in a wool factory, which provided material for her fiction. Self-educ., she taught locally 1832–40, until she won a free place at Utica Female Seminary, where she taught composition 1841–6. Her first successes were didactic children's books, including *Charles Linn*, 1841, and *Allen Lucas*, 1843, which depict destitute children who, through virtue and industry, achieve happiness. A skilled storyteller, EJ addresses her young readers with confiding directness. As 'Fanny Forester' she wrote for an adult audience gracefully witty sketches about an imaginary village, first pub. in the *New Mirror* and collected in 1846 in *Lilias Fane, Trippings in Author-Land* and – most popular – *Alderbrook*: 'from the time when mother Eve fixed her anxious heart on improving her condition, and crushed a world at a single bound, . . . [man] has never lacked a hobby'. She m. the Rev. Adoniram J., missionary, in 1846, and accompanied him and two of her stepchildren to Burma, where her daughter was b. in 1847 and son d. in infancy in 1850. Her main work from this period is her biography of J.'s second wife, *Memoir of Sarah B. Judson*, 1849 –

a popular defence of missionary work. Contrast has been drawn between the ironical 'Fanny Forester' and the earnest Mrs Judson, but throughout her work she promotes the same values, as personified in Sarah Judson, whose true life story conformed to EJ's idealized fictional types. See lives by A. C. Kendrick, 1860 and W. N. Wyeth, 1890.

Julian of Norwich, *c.* 1343–after 1413, visionary and recluse, probably b. at Norwich, where she ended her life as an anchoress attached to the church of St Julian and St Edward, Conisford, from which she took her name. Little is known of her (see P. Molinari, 1958): unusually well educated, and a reader of Latin, she was probably a nun for a time, perhaps in the Benedictine house of Carrow, upon which depended the church where she was eventually enclosed. In May 1373, at the climax of a serious illness, she experienced a series of 16 mystical 'shewings' which provided the substance of her *Revelations of Divine Love*. The 'short version' (ed. Edmund Colledge and James Walsh, 1978; modernized Anna Maria Reynolds, 1958) simply records the facts. The 'longer version' (also ed. Colledge and Walsh; modernized Walsh, 1961, and C. Wolters, 1966) sets them in the context of 20 years of prayer and reflection, linking the visions of Christ's physical sufferings and of the bliss of heaven to thoughts on the nature of sin and the love of God (whom she sees as mother as well as father). Her reputation spread quickly; she was visited by Marjery KEMPE, and was named in wills by several local citizens. Later her writings were copied and read abroad by English recusants; they have influenced moderns like T. S. Eliot and Iris MURDOCH; she is currently claimed as patron by widely varying political and religious groups. See study by Jennifer P. Heimmel, 1982.

Justice, Elizabeth (Surby), 1703–52, TRAVEL writer and autobiographer, b. in London, eldest child of Ann (Ellis) and Dorset S. In *Amelia, or The Distressed Wife,* 1751, she tells, with much gossipy detail, of an unappreciated childhood (stepsisters on each side, learning from her favoured brother's tutor), and reluctant marriage at 16 to a pressing suitor, lawyer Henry J. He left her much alone with small children and no money; when he struck her she arranged a separation ('Dear Sir, do not imagine that all Law centres in you'), but legal and financial wrangles continued. In 1734 she travelled to St Petersburg as governess to an English family, but returned in 1737 (Henry J. having been transported for seven years for stealing rare books from Cambridge libraries). Her *Voyage to Russia,* York, 1739, an unpretentious, observant little book, brought good profit from nearly 600 subscribers: heavily apologetic for attempting to outgo 'Female Abilities'. A 2nd ed., 1746, drops some extraneous padding and adds four – racier – letters from Russia, which Edmund Curll had pub. among Pope's, 1736. EJ worked as a lady's companion, and published *Amelia* only after she dreamed a recently dead male friend commanded (like the ghost in *Hamlet*), 'Write, write'.

K

Kael, Pauline, film critic, b. 1919 in Sonoma Co., Calif., da. of Judith (Friedman) and Isaac Paul K., a farmer. She saw her first movie at four, majored in philosophy at the Univ. of Calif. (Berkeley), 1936–40, was alive to women's issues by her early twenties, worked at various jobs and wrote in various genres. She reached print with a piece on movies in *City Lights,* San Francisco; she broadcast on the same topic and wrote 'short descriptions for theatres and colleges'. She moved to NYC in 1965 and wrote for *Life, McCall's,* and *New Republic,* joining *The New Yorker* in 1968. From it came *I Lost It at the Movies,* 1965, and most of her later books. (*The Citizen Kane Book,* 1971, gives blockbuster treatment to a famous film; *5001 Nights at the Movies, An A–Z Guide for Cinema, TV and Video Viewers,* 1982, gives snappy evaluations of works going back to the earliest.) *Deeper into Movies,* 1973 (National Book Award), stresses the moviegoer's need to know books and the other arts for a 'sense of the range of possibilities and pleasures'. PK praises her daughter as 'the hardest to satisfy and hence my ideal reader'; notoriously hard to satisfy herself, she can be equally witty, analytic and magisterial in approval (e.g. of *Sunday Bloody Sunday* by Penelope GILLIATT, with whom she alternated on *The New Yorker*). She writes with a strong sense of the bearing of film on US society and modern culture generally. *State of the Art,* 1987, represents 'a deliberate break with my sexually tinged titles'.

Kantaris (or Kantarizis), **Sylvia** (Mosley), poet. B. in 1936 in the Peak District, Derbyshire, da. of Minnie (Yates) and John Thomas M., she was educ. at Lady Manners School, Bakewell, and Bristol Univ. (BA in French, 1957). She m. Emmanuel K. in 1958, and taught in Bristol. In 1962 they travelled overland to Australia. In ten years SK had two children, taught French at Queensland Univ., and wrote two theses on French surrealist literature. As an academic (not, as once intended, a painter), she turned her imaginative energy to poetry after the birth of her son, 1965. She published widely in Australian journals, returned to England, 1972, and settled in Cornwall, 1974. Her first book, *Time and Motion,* Sydney, 1975, repr. Cornwall 1986, as Kantarizis, includes a series of exuberant, even extravagant free-verse love poems; it enjoys a cult following. SK taught modern poetry for the Open University, 1974–83 (a founder member). She collaborated with D. M. Thomas in *News from the Front,* 1983, a verse analysis of polarities in gender and politics through a violent heterosexual relationship. Her own *Tenth Muse,* 1983, interrogates (with wit and humour) gender, Christianity, and environmental policies. *The Sea at the Door,* 1985, includes poems on Cornish landscape and translations from French; it develops favourite themes with increasing technical dexterity. *The Air Mines of Mistila,* 1988, records a unique exchange of letters with Philip Gross, each in turn adding to their imagined mountain plateau, peopling it with a 'gipsy commuter', a 'no-nonsense strongwoman', 'the wife of the chief of police', replacing 'hard labour' mining air with tourism and a uranium mine, having sometimes, says SK, to 'murder my darlings' to accommodate her collaborator. The title piece of *Dirty Washing: New and Selected Poems,* 1989, runs through a woman's week in '7 Rinses +

Final Spin'. See SK on 'female writing' in *Stand,* Summer 1987.

Karodia, Farida, novelist and short-story writer, b. 1942 in Aliwal North, South Africa, da. of Mary and Ebrahim K. She had a basic small-town educ.; a strong mother and grandmother 'were positive influences'. She taught for four years, m., and left South Africa in 1966, shortly after her divorce. After teaching in Zambia and visiting her mother in Swaziland, she reached Canada, 1969, with a baby daughter and no idea what to do next. She wrote radio plays while 'upgrading' her teaching certificate to BEd at the Univ. of Calgary, battled both as 'a woman and a non-white' for a teaching job, and three years later turned to full-time writing. She has revisited South Africa only once (1981), but sets her fiction in its rural societies, which are patriarchal but where women 'are the dominant forces'. Her first novel, *Daughters of the Twilight,* 1986, praised by Buchi EMECHETA and Michelene WANDOR, reflects her background and a seldom-noticed facet of apartheid. In a cross-cultural family in the 1950s the eldest daughter, classified as 'Indian', receives a prestigious if costly education; after the Group Areas Act, the younger daughter, for any education at all, must accept the restrictive, 'inferior' designation 'Coloured'. *Coming Home and Other Stories,* 1988, presents rural dilemmas through the eyes of a Boer girl, an Indian grandmother, a black teacher, and others, leaving authorial colour and sex in doubt. FK's next novel will treat Mozambique under Portuguese rule.

Kaufman, Shirley (Pincus), poet, b. 1923 in Seattle, to Nellie (Freeman) and business-man Joseph P. After a BA at UCLA, 1944, she m. Bernard K., Jr., in 1946 and had three daughters. She took an MA at San Francisco State College (now Univ.) in 1967, pub. poems in journals, in *The Floor Keeps Turning,* 1970, and *Gold Country,* 1973. Next year she divorced, m. Hillel Matthew Daleski, and became a visiting lecturer at the Univ. of Mass. Her *Looking at Henry Moore's Elephant Skull Etchings in Jerusalem During the War* was taped in 1976, printed in a limited ed. with the Moore etchings in 1977. The last poem in the sequence runs: 'The elephants come after us / in herds now // they will roll over us / like tanks // we are too sad to move // our skulls / much smaller than theirs.' *From One Life to Another,* 1979, delicately sketches the implications of SK's move with her husband to Jerusalem: she writes of crabs at Ossabaw Island, of her father's death, of divorce ('Old intricate lives / we are so delicately stitched // peritoneum / three layers of muscle / subcutaneous tissue / skin // each layer / sutured tightly / over the wounds // would you undo that?' The last section is 'Starting Over'; the last poem, written on Rosh Hashana 5738, celebrates 'the past we never break out of . . . stories told over and over / that finally matter'. As well as publishing *Claims,* 1984, SK has translated Hebrew poets Abba Kovner, Amir Gilboa and Judith Herzberg, notably Kovner's *My Little Sister and Selected Poems,* 1986. Her introduction mentions other acts of brutality and says 'the Nazi Holocaust remains the type of man's inhumanity to man'.

'Kavan, Anna', Helen (Woods) Ferguson, 1901–68, novelist and short-story writer, b. in Cannes to wealthy Helen (Bright) and C. C. W. She grew up in many countries with her mother (remarried to a South African), and in Calif. and England after her mother's death. She m. Scotsman Donald F., lived with him in Burma, and had a son; divorced, she m. painter Stuart Edmonds. She began to write in Burma. Even the first of her six 'Helen Ferguson' novels, *A Charmed Circle,* 1929, is mildly disturbing, with sisters who turn from enemies to allies in failing to escape their stifling family. *Let Me Alone,* 1930, voices violent personal anguish and feminist protest. Its orphan heroine (whose name AK later wrote under and took by deed poll) is bullied into rejecting a place at Oxford Univ. for conventional marriage with a man who takes her to the tropics, torments and rapes her. Left still battling his will, mourning the loss of a 'rare, fine self', she reappears in *A Stranger Still,* 1935, for an affair which is precious to her lover, desolating to her. By WWII AK was a heroin addict and mental-hospital habituée. The title-story of *Asylum Piece*, 1940, is of a wife committed against her will; this and ten more books as 'AK' (especially the stories published after her suicide) all draw more or less on experience of breakdown: actual ill-treatment and fantasies of destruction and self-destruction. *Who Are You?*, 1963, is a surrealistic, nightmare reworking of the plot of *Let Me Alone,* its unnamed central figures 'the girl' and 'Mr Dog Head' (who likes killing rats with a tennis racquet). In *Ice,* 1967, praised by Brian Aldiss as science fiction, an encroaching ice age is backdrop to the male narrator's obsessive pursuit of a woman who 'demanded victimization and terror'; it closes in to foil a hint of a happy ending. After her second divorce AK lived in London working as an interor decorator, and was assistant editor of *Horizon* from 1942. Anaïs NIN, who had admired her since 1959, compares her to Kafka as a writer of night terrors, non-reason, and the divided self (*The Novel of the Future,* 1968). Stories in *Julia and the Bazooka,* 1970, and *My Soul is in China,* 1975, give varying histories (in one she is hooked on heroin by a tennis coach before she marries) to a woman trapped in self-created 'violence, isolation and cruelty', with an unloved childhood and unresolvable feelings about the splendour and savagery of men; some deal in future worlds, revolutions, and sky-soaring superwomen. See Gunther Stuhlmann and AK's publisher, Peter Owen, in *Anais,* 3, 1985; *My Madness* (selec. writings), 1990.

Kavanagh, Julia, 1824–77, novelist and essayist, b. Thurles, Ireland, only child of Morgan Peter K., eccentric writer of romances and philological works. Her childhood was spent in London and France with her parents, who eventually settled in Paris. JK took up literature as a profession in London from 1844, providing for herself and her mother, her father having apparently abandoned them. Her main productions were studies of famous women and romantic novels, the success of which encouraged her father to try to pass off one of his own feeble tales as hers, an act which involved her in painful public disclaimers. A major concern in all her work is the way in which women can express themselves in the face of restrictive and false conventions: in her *English Women of Letters,* 1862, and *French Women of Letters,* 1862, she criticizes idealized and sickly depictions of romantic relationships, and in her novels she looks critically at women's sufferings below the surface ideology of matrimonial bliss. Her best-known novel, *Nathalie,* 1850, was much admired by Charlotte BRONTË, who first became acquainted with JK when the latter wrote to her praising *Jane Eyre,* and who, when she met her in 1850, was struck by her intelligence and courage. Though the influence of Brontë's work is clear in *Nathalie,* some of its elements may have proved suggestive for *Villette.* JK's novel portrays the stormy romance of its passionate, independent-minded heroine with an older man, finally culminating in a union based on mutual respect and self-knowledge. Though never wholly free of sexual stereotypes, her subsequent fiction continued to question the sacrifice of womanly freedom in marriage, most successfully in *Adele,* 1858, and *Beatrice,* 1865.

Kaye-Smith, Sheila, 1887–1956, Sussex novelist, b. in Hastings. Her mother was *née* de la Condamine; her father was Dr Edward K.-S. She was educ. at Hastings and St Leonard's Ladies' College, 1896–1905. She wrote from childhood; her first publication was *The Tramping Methodist,*

1908. She became an Anglo-Catholic in 1918, m. the Rev. T. Penrose Fry in 1924, lived in London for some years, and with him converted to Roman Catholicism in 1929. They became farmers working their own Sussex land, where they built a chapel to St Thérèse de Lisieux. SK-S published three vols. of poetry and three of autobiography: *Three Ways Home,* 1937, gives an account of her conversion; *Kitchen Fugue,* 1945, collects anecdotes linked by the subject of food; *All the Books of My Life,* 1956, is structured around her reading at significant moments. (Her friend Gladys STERN, with whom she wrote *Talking of Jane* AUSTEN, 1943, and *More Talk* ..., 1950, named the 'three ways home' as 'writing, the country, and her religion'.) *Sussex Gorse,* 1916, best-known of SK-S's 31 novels, about a farmer sacrificing his family life to ambition, has been often reprinted. *Joanna Godden,* 1922 (repr. 1983, intro. by Rachel Anderson; filmed 1947), has a strong, unconventional heroine who inherits her father's farm, runs it herself, but leaves it rather than marry the father of her child, whom she does not love. *The History of Susan Spray the Female Preacher,* 1931 (repr. 1983, intro. by Janet Montefiore), tracks its protagonist's increasing self-deception. *Quartet in Heaven,* 1952, relates the lives of four women saints. See critical biography by Dorothea Walker, 1980.

Kazantzis, Judith, 'poet and feminist' (better separated, she says, than as 'feminist poet'), artist, short-story writer. B. 1940 in Oxford, she began writng at seven. She m. in the early 1960s and has two children. She published two school history kits, 1968 (one on the history of women's emancipation), and during the 1970s worked for the first Women's Liberation Workshop in London, where she teaches, is a member of the Women's Literature Collective, and reviews poetry for *Spare Rib* and other journals. She has published five volumes of poetry, from *Minefield,* 1977, and her work appears with that of Michèle ROBERTS and Michelene WANDOR in *Touch Papers,* 1982. Marion Shaw calls the poems in *Let's Pretend,* 1984, 'intellectually ambitious and demanding', ranging 'freely over a confidently controlled diversity of material'. In one, describing an evening walk in Virginia WOOLF's Sussex, the speaker considers 'a deep and obedient pool' in the Ouse, and concludes 'I run my finger along my arm, for dust.' JK calls herself 'anti-militarist, anti-establishment'; with the aim of changing society, she says, she re-examines the roles of women in myths and fairy-tales, seeing God as 'a rich myth figure through which to have at patriarchal arrogance', and redrafts Clytemnestra 'not as a crazy bitch, but as a human being with strong passions and good reasons' (essay on herself in Wandor, ed., *On Gender and Writing,* 1983). *Flame Tree,* 1988, continues the strong political statement of *A Poem for Guatemala,* 1986, pays homage to the ladies of LLANGOLLEN and reflects winters at Key West, USA.

Keane, 'Molly', 'M. J. Farrell', Mary Nesta (Skrine), novelist and playwright. She was b. 1904 at Ballyrankin, in Co. Kildare, da. of Agnes Shakespeare (Higginson), who wrote poetry as 'Moira O'Neill', and Walter Clarmont S., landowner. She had governesses, and briefly attended a French school at Bray near Dublin. An alleged first novel, *The Knight of the Cheerful Countenance,* begun at 17 when she thought it 'pure Shakespeare', is elusive. She pub. *Young Entry* (a foxhunting term), 1928, and succeeding novels pseudonymously, since she frequented hunting circles which considered reading and writing dubious pursuits; she has claimed she wrote to relieve boredom when suspected tuberculosis dictated bed-rest, or to augment her dress allowance. In 1938 appeared *Spring Meeting,* first of her plays written jointly with John Perry, all successful till the last. That year she m. Robert K.; she had two children. Sorrow at his sudden death, 1946, and family demands, caused her to publish nothing after *Treasure Hunt,* 1952 (a rewriting of a 1949 play), until *Good Behaviour,* 1981, which, first turned down by Collins, was later short-listed for the Booker Prize. This and *Time After Time,* 1983, have been successfully televised. MK's later and earlier works (many recently repr.) bear the same hallmarks. *The Rising Tide,* 1937, repr. 1984, formulates a recurrent theme: 'They had never escaped their youth. They would never all their lives be free of it.' But the comedy grows blacker and the psychological portraits more complex. Characters (based, she says, on real people) are cruel, selfish, obsessive: families are hierarchies of tyranny. The first-person narrator of *Good Behaviour,* in her assured superiority to and incurious insulation from the outside world, and the protagonist of *Loving and Giving,* 1988, with her 'pitiless unknowing complacency and contempt of the young', focus MK's depiction of the class to which she belonged: privileged, decaying, hunting, gardening, adoring their repellent dogs, and (if female) gorging on food or practising painful abstinence. (MK writes of food and childhood memories in her preface to *Nursery Cooking,* 1985.) Interviewed by Polly Devlin in Mary Chamberlaine, ed., *Writing Lives,* 1988. See Bridget O'Toole in Gerald Dawe and Edna Longley, eds., *Across a Roaring Hill: the Protestant Imagination in Modern Ireland,* 1985.

Keary, Annie, 1825–79, novelist and children's writer, b. Bilton, Yorks., sixth child of Lucy (Plumer) and William K., an Irish clergyman. She was educ. at dame school, by governesses, and at boarding school. Many of her children's stories, including *Sidney Grey,* 1857, and *Little Wanderlin,* 1865 (with her sister Eliza), were written for her brother's children, whom she looked after for six years. After breaking off her engagement, she moved to Kensington in 1854 to nurse her father, and after his death (1856) finished her first novel, *Through the Shadows,* 1859. In failing health, AK spent the winter of 1858 in Egypt and subsequently wrote *An Early Egyptian History for the Young,* 1861 (again with Eliza), and *The Nations Around* (Palestine), 1870. During the next ten years, while nursing her mother, she published *Janet's Home,* 1863, *Clemency Franklyn,* 1866, and *Oldbury,* 1869, which was compared to GASKELL's *Cranford.* After her mother's death, AK went to France and began *Castle Daly,* 1875, which, with its sympathetic and exciting account of Irish life during the Famine, brought her recognition. On her return to London she lived with her sister and worked in an East End children's hospital, and a home for unemployed servant girls, the latter inspiring *A York and a Lancaster Rose,* 1876. Her last works were *Father Phim,* 1879 (repr. 1962, ed. Gillian Avery), and *A Doubting Heart,* 1879, a novel depicting the shared life of two sisters. It was left to Kathleen MACQUOID to complete as AK knew she was dying. See Eliza K.'s memoir of her sister, 1882.

Keckley, Elizabeth, *c.* 1818–1907, also known by the 'slave names' Elizabeth Hobbs and Lizzie Garland, autobiographer, dressmaker. B. a slave at Dinwiddie, Va., she m. another black slave, James K., *c.* 1850, after bearing a half 'Anglo-Saxon' son. Freed in 1855 with the help of friends, she dissolved her marriage in 1860 and moved to Washington, DC, where, as an expert dressmaker, she became by 1861 the confidante of Mary Lincoln. The work she is known for, *Behind the Scenes, or Thirty Years a Slave, and Four Years in the White House,* 1868, contains her autobiography and an account of Mrs Lincoln's life and opinions of men in high government positions. Although very likely ghost-written, it is a valuable historical source. It recounts EK's ecstasy upon her manumission – 'Free! the earth wore a brighter look, and the very stars seemed to sing with joy' – but it destroyed her business, and she died in poverty. See Ruth Painter

Randall, *Mary Lincoln,* 1953, and John E. Washington, *They Knew Lincoln,* 1942.

Keesing, Nancy, poet, non-fiction writer, critic, b. 1923 in Sydney, NSW, da. of Margery Isabel Rahel (Hart) and Gordon Samuel K. Educ. at private schools and the Univ. of Sydney, in 1955 she m. A. M. Hertzberg; she had a daughter and son. During WWII she worked as a clerk in the Department of the Navy, later as a social worker, then from 1951 as a freelance writer, editor, and active member of various literary organizations such as the Literature Board of the Australia Council, which she chaired 1974–7, and the Australian Society of Authors, whose journal she edited 1971–4. She has written four vols., of poetry, *Imminent Summer,* 1951, *Three Men and Sydney,* 1955, *Showground Sketchbook,* 1968, and *Hails and Farewells,* 1977, but is probably best known as an editor of Australian poetry and fiction. She has ed. three colls. of bush poetry, in collaboration with poet Douglas Stewart, 1955–67, *The White Chrysanthemum,* 1977, and seven other works, including a collection of writings on Australian motherhood, *Shalom: Australian Jewish Short Stories,* 1978, and *Lily on the Dustbin: Slang of Australian Women and Families,* 1982. She has also pub. six critical and biographical books such as *Elsie Carew, Australian Primitive Poet,* 1965, *Douglas Stewart,* 1965, and *John Lang and 'The Forger's Wife',* 1979. Other publications are two children's books; short stories in the *Bulletin, Quadrant* and *Southerly,* and the autobiographical *Riding the Elephant,* 1988. NK received the Order of Australia, 1979, for services to literature. MSS are in the Mitchell Library, Sydney.

Kefala, Antigone, poet, novelist, arts administrator, b. 1934 in Braila, Romania, to Greeks Anastasia (Babinsky) and Kimon Pandely K. She attended schools in Romania and Greece before migrating to NZ, where she studied arts at Victoria Univ. (MA, 1960). Later she settled in Sydney, Australia. Her poetry, which has appeared in three vols., *The Alien,* 1973, *Thirsty Weather,* 1978, and *European Notebook,* 1988, reflects the richness and conflict of her cross-cultural life; the migrant experience is an essential (but not exclusive) feature of her poetry. AK's fiction, fragmentary and impressionistic (and very poetic), is similarly concerned with personal identity within cultural disorientation. *The First Journey,* 1974, is written from the perspective of a young music student in Bucharest, while *The Boarding House,* 1974, concerns a young Greek woman, Melina, apparently alone and alienated in Sydney. This character reappears in *The Island,* 1984. AK's short novels are powerful documents of the dislocated female self within modern life. *Alexia, A Tale of Two Cultures,* 1984, is a children's novel which also addresses the migrant experience. Important critical comment on AK can be found in Sneja Gunew's articles in *Arena,* 76, 1986 and in Carole Ferrier, ed., *Gender, Politics and Fiction,* 1985.

Keir, Elizabeth (Harvey), sentimental novelist publishing at Edinburgh and London, wife of doctor William K. (d. 1783). Her novels have till recently been ascribed to Susanna (Harvey) K., wife of scientist James K. *Interesting Memoirs,* 1785, dedicated to the queen, punctuates a love-story (rich Henry and poor Louisa) with letters and improving sentiments. *The History of Miss Greville,* 1787, is fully epistolary: cruel parents separate Rivers and his Julia, making each believe the other to be faithless; she marries another, discovers the deception and nearly dies; everyone behaves impeccably, and the married pair attain happiness while Rivers courts and finds a soldier's death in America. Reviewers, otherwise enthusiastic, doubted that first love could be so outlived.

Kelley, Edith (**Summers**), 1884–1956, novelist, b. in Toronto, da. of Isabella

(Johnstone) and George S. She graduated from the Univ. of Toronto, 1903, and moved to NYC, where she worked for Upton Sinclair at Helicon Hall, his socialist commune inspired by Charlotte Perkins GILMAN's ideas. Briefly engaged to Sinclair Lewis, she m. Allan Updegraff in 1908 and supported him and their two children by teaching and writing magazine stories ('stuff that I am not proud of, frothy and inconsequential'). From 1914 she was common-law wife of sculptor C. Fred K.; since there 'wasn't any money in art', they struggled with a tobacco farm Ky., farm with summer boarders (NJ), and alfalfa and chicken ranches (Imperial Valley and San Diego, Calif.), and boot-legging whisky. ESK wrote *Weeds,* 1923 (repr. 1972, 1982), 'at the rate of about three hours every morning after the children had been packed off to school'. A naturalistic novel about tenant tobacco-farmers, it centres on a woman with 'too much life', who scorns the traditional female role until brutalized by pregnancies and poverty. Though well reviewed, it sold badly: see Charlotte Goodman in Emily Toth, ed., 1985; Barbara Lootens in *Women's Studies,* 13, 1986. Always poor (a cleaner in 1937), ESK kept writing poems and stories. From 1946 she lived at Los Gatos, Calif. *The Devil's Hand* appeared in 1974, 'The Old House' in *Women's Studies,* 10, 1983. Each a criticism of marriage through the defeat of a once vibrant woman, they use alfalfa-raising and eastern-farmhouse backgrounds. Papers at Southern Illinois Univ. (Carbondale), letters at Indiana Univ.

Kelley, Emma Dunham (sometimes Kelley-Hawkins), Afro-American novelist of whom little is known. Her husband's name was Hawkins. She dedicated *Megda,* 1891 (repr. 1892) to her widowed mother. A conventional story of a merry, defiant girl's gradual humiliation and submission into true Christian womanhood, it has a suppressed undercurrent emphasizing colour. *Four Girls at Cottage City,* 1898, dedicated to 'Dear Aunt Lottie ... my "Second Mother"' again focuses on the female spiritual life and the huge importance of mother-love and emotional links between girls, and reveals the same anxiety about colour. Both are reprinted in the Schomburg Library Series, 1988.

Kelly, Gwen (Smith), 'Nita Heath', novelist, short-story writer, poet, b. 1922 at Thornleigh, Sydney, NSW, da. of Mary Ann (Heath) and George Rupert S. She attended Fort Street Girls' High School and graduated from Sydney Univ., 1944, with first-class honours in English and philosophy. She was awarded a Teachers' Certificate after lecturing for four years at Armidale Teachers' College, and since the 1950s has combined teaching with writing. She has written six novels, *There is No Refuge,* 1961, *The Red Boat,* 1968, *The Middle Aged Maidens,* 1976, *Always Afternoon,* 1981, and *Arrows of Rain,* 1988, and award-winning stories, coll. in *The Happy People and Others,* 1988. She has also pub. a collection of poetry (with A. J. Bennett), *Fossils and Stray Cats,* 1980. Her work, partly influenced by travels with her husband Maurice K., is chiefly concerned with marital and family relationships. *Always Afternoon,* set in 1915, is the story of an escaped German prisoner of war and his affair with a local girl. It was made into a film in 1987.

Kelly, Isabella (Fordyce), also Hedgeland, *c.* 1758–1857, poet and leading MINERVA novelist. She was b. in a Highland castle, da. of the runaway match of Elizabeth (Fraser) and William Fordyce, who held a commission and then a court post: related to Elizabeth Isabella SPENCE. She m., 1789, Robert K., a spendthrift cavalry officer. Her *Collection of Poems and Fables,* 1794, 2nd ed., 1807, was well subscribed; its preface says some were written very early, and 1 mentions a child's death and other troubles. The poems include personal pathos and social comedy: she writes (in fear of death) to an unborn child, praises her 'exemplary' mother, and uses fable to lampoon enemies and flatter patrons; she later called her poems 'too personal to please in general'. Her novels began that year with *Madeleine, or The Castle of Montgomery.* They cater to popular taste with seemingly haunted abbeys, ancient MSS, cross-dressing for disguise, and the fruits of unchastity (in *A Modern Incident in Domestic Life,* 1803, the mistress's children die while the wife's survive). *The Abbey of St Asaph,* 1795, facs. NY, 1977, moves from the anguish of a soldier's wife ('I have none on earth but thee – father, brothers, friends – the sword hath taken all') into melodrama and revelations of concealed parentage. Capt. K. died in Trinidad leaving her with three children; she was m. to Mr Hedgeland 'one short year' before 'Speculation lost his fortune and broke his heart'. She taught her own daughters (one of them later wrote) and was proud to support her family by her exertions. She lived briefly with Henrietta, widow of Dr James F., and pub. a life of her, 1823. She told the RLF, 1832, she had written ten novels, pedagogical works, and part of a new historical novel she knew (as 'last survivor of all the authoresses' of her era) to be outdated. Another Mrs K. wrote *The Matron of Erin, A National Tale,* 1816 (exemplary heroine survives husband's wickedness), and *The Fatalists,* 1821, set in the Napoleonic wars, which inculcates faith in providence.

Kelty, Mary Ann, 1789–1873, novelist, religious writer and AUTOBIOGRAPHER, b. in Cambridge, youngest child of a 'vivacious' Irish surgeon whose harshness, her mother told her, had been worst before her birth. His jealousy of her intellectual gifts and university friends made her inwardly estranged, angry and increasingly unhappy. She thought her early introspections unique till she read Margaret FULLER; she loved hopelessly and resolved against marriage. Having published two hastily written, unnoticed 'little tales', she worked hard over *The Favourite of Nature,* 1821, dedicated to Joanna BAILLIE and strongly marked by Jane AUSTEN, though its thoughtless, impetuous, talented heroine ruins her life and dies piously. It brought money and (anonymous) praise; reviewers ascribed it to Lady DACRE. MAK's parents read it; both died before she could confess authorship. A 'hateful appetite' for earning drove her through *Osmond,* 1822 (dedicated to Dacre), *Trials,* 1824, and *The Story of Isabel,* 1826. Then, her 'latent bitterness' meeting another's 'fiery Calvinism', she embarked on a lengthy religious quest, renouncing pleasures (she *nearly* burned her piano), furiously championing meekness, trying many sects, as far as healers and speakers in tongues, writing only on evangelical topics: a history of the Reformation, 1830; a failed novel; *Religious Thoughts,* condemned by her mentor who said a woman must not 'legislate for herself in the kingdom of thought'. Having plumbed 'unmitigated, helpless, hopeless woe', MAK evolved her own Quaker-like faith: reliance on inner light, not external guides. After two years of total seclusion, 1832–4, she moved via a country cottage to Peckham near London, resumed writing, and accumulated over 30 titles: lives of women including writers, 1839, and of Quakers, 1844; *Visiting my Relations,* 1851 (Cambridge local colour and nostalgia: reviewers thought the author, like the narrator, male); one more novel, *Alice Rivers,* 1852; *Reminiscences,* 1852; devotional diaries; attractive essay-like musings. Account by Mona Wilson in essays, 1924.

Kemble, Adelaide (later Sartoris), 1816–79, singer and writer, b. Covent Garden Chambers, London, youngest of four children of Maria Theresa (de Camp) KEMBLE: niece of celebrated actors Sarah Siddons and John Philip K., and sister of Fanny KEMBLE. AK's early education was directed by her aunt, Adelaide de Camp; she later studied singing in Paris and

Bologna and had a successful career as an operatic soprano in Europe (esp. Italy), 1838–41, and England, 1841–2. Her performances, discussed by Anna Jameson in her *Memoirs and Essays,* 1846, were notable for her acting and intelligence as much as for her singing. In 1842 AK m. Edward Sartoris, with whom she had a da. and two sons. They spent much time in Rome, entertaining the 'best company', according to AK's friend E. B. Browning. AK's continuing preoccupation with music is evident in the stories written years after her retirement: the otherwise slight efforts in *Medusa, and Other Tales,* 1868 (repr. 1880 as *Past Hours*), and the more complex *A Week in a French Country House,* 1867. The latter, which reveals what Henry James saw as AK's 'flexible, subtly ironic, winningly observant mind', focuses particularly on the ambiguous social status of the artist and the difficulties faced by women performers in their challenge to feminine stereotypes.

Kemble, Fanny (Frances Anne), 1809–1903, actress, writer, abolitionist, b. London, eldest da. of Maria Theresa (de Camp) Kemble, to whom she pays tribute in *Notes on some of Shakespeare's Plays,* 1882: sister of Adelaide Kemble. Brought up by her spinster aunt, Adelaide de Camp, she was educ. in France and through reading partly directed by her brother's schoolmaster, Dr Malkin. She began writing in 1827 with a verse melodrama, *Francis I,* and made a triumphant Covent Garden debut as Juliet in 1829, saving her father's company from bankruptcy. In 1832 she toured the USA, meeting Dr William Channing, who influenced her, and Catherine and Elizabeth Sedgwick, who became close friends, and subsequently published her outspoken *Journal of a Residence in America,* 1835, to provide for her ailing aunt. In 1834, still in the USA, she m. Pierce Butler, a rich plantation owner, but her work for slave women strained her uneasy marriage, and her *Journal* of 1838–9 was not published until 1863. Butler opposed US publication of *An English Tragedy,* written in 1838, and did all he could, including withholding her two daughters, to keep her in check. Undaunted, in 1844 she sold her *Poems* to buy back a favourite horse, and in 1845 sailed for England alone. She spent some time in Rome with her sister, publishing *A Year of Consolation* in 1847 and divorcing in 1848. Returning to the stage, for 20 years she gave Shakespearean readings, mostly in America. Two more vols. of *Poems* appeared (1865, 1883), as well as further reminiscences (1878, 1882, 1890) based on a 50-year correspondence with her friend Harriet St Leger. In her eightieth year (1889), she published a satirical farce, *The Adventures of John Timothy Homespun in Switzerland,* and her first novel, *Far Away and Long Ago.* See life by Dorothy Marshall, 1977, and selection ed. E. Ransome, 1978. Her daughter, Sarah (Butler) Wister, ed. with Agnes Irwin, *Worthy Women of Our First Century,* 1877.

Kemble, Maria Theresa (De Camp), 1775–1838, performer and dramatist, b. in Vienna, eldest child of Jeanne Adrienne (Dufour) and George Louis De C. Brought to England in 1777, she was poorly educ. and slow to learn English, but danced on stage at eight and had a success acting Macheath in 1792. Her comedy *First Faults,* 1799 (eagerly welcomed by Martha Hale), stayed unpub. and led to disputes about plagiarism with William Earle; some other ascriptions remain unclear. She both acted in and published her very popular *Personation, or Fairly Taken In* (farce, 1805), *The Day after the Wedding, or The Wife's First Lesson* (interlude on shrew-taming, 1808), and *The Widow's Stratagem* (comedy with spirited heroine, 1815). Described (by a woman) as 'lively, free, commanding, and self-assured', she was assaulted by John Philip K., then in 1806 married Charles K. against his family's wishes. Retired in 1819, she came back ten years later to play her daughter Fanny Kemble's mother at her debut.

Kempe, Marjery, *c.* 1373-after 1439, mystic, traveller, and first autobiographer in English. B. in Lynn, Norfolk, where her father John Brunham was mayor, she m. John K. about 1393 and bore at least one son, who d. before her. Her *Book* (ed. Sanford B. Meech and Hope Emily Allen, 1940; modernized B. Windeatt, 1985) was dictated to two amanuenses in turn (the first possibly her son, the second a priest) and survives in a single copy by a third scribe, not identified till 1934. It tells how her life was shattered by some sort of spiritual and nervous crisis in 1413. Having agreed with her husband on a life of chastity, she set out to travel, visiting English bishops and religious (including JULIAN of Norwich) and making pilgrimages to the Holy Land, Italy, Compostella and Germany, where her experiences brought on acute outbursts of the shrieking and crying for which she became famed. She was tried for Lollardy at Leicester, 1417, but released as orthodox; by the early sixteenth century she was respected enough for Wynkyn de Worde to publish extracts from her *Book* in his *Short Treatyse of Contemplacyon.* Opinion differs about her work: either rambling, naively egocentric, and lacking in spiritual depth, or valuable as a uniquely lively record of her eccentric, extreme suggestibility and energy. See study by Clarissa W. Atkinson, 1983.

Kendall, 'May', Emma Goldworth, 1861–?1931, poet, reformer and satirist, b. in Bridlington, Yorks., da. of Eliza (Goldworth Level) and James K., Wesleyan minister. She collaborated with Andrew Lang on *That Very Mab,* 1885, satirical essays and verses on contemporary society, politics and science. Her first volume of verse (dedicated to her parents) was *Dreams to Sell,* 1887, which reprinted some poems from magazines like *Punch* and *Longman's.* Notable in it are 'The Lay of the Trilobite', condemning the 'advance' of civilization, and some poems of social criticism: 'Legend of the Crossing-Sweeper', 'Legend of the Maid of all Work' and 'Woman's Future' – 'Alas, is it woolwork you take for your mission'. Her first novel, *From a Garret,* appeared the same year, followed by *'Such is Life'*, 1889, a tart social satire on romantic love doomed to fail, and *White Poppies,* 1893. Her second volume of poems, *Songs from Dreamland,* 1894, includes a portrait of a complacent churchman, 'A Fossil'. *Turkish Bonds,* 1898, consists of stories written against the Turks at the time of the Armenian massacres. She helped B. Seebohm Rowntree with his study, *How the Labourer Lives,* 1913, and his work on the minimum wage, *The Human Needs of Labour,* 1918, by making his statistics into readable anecdotes, work for which she declined a fee. She contributed some later poems, mainly reformist, to the *Cornhill.*

Kenealy, Mary **Annesley** Flood, journalist, novelist and suffragist lecturer. b. 1861 in Portslade, Sussex, elder sister of Arabella and da. of Elizabeth (Nicklin) and E. V. K., a lawyer wrecked by his defence of the Tichborne claimant. Trained in nursing, she published *Care of the Sick* in 1893 while lecturing on the staff of the National Health Society. She was later successful as a journalist, for some time on the editorial staff of the *Daily Mail,* and special correspondent for the *Morning Post* and *Daily Graphic.* She published *Thus Saith Mrs Grundy* in 1911. In this novel 'the woman pays most of old Adam's debts . . . a convenient arrangement for Adam'; yet the style is cloying, and the concern with sacred motherhood obsessional. AK suggested the 'Votes for Woman Novels' series, of which her *Poodle-Woman,* 1913, is the pioneer volume. Sharply written and dedicated to 'my friend Jean Grieve and the immortal feminist cause', it shows the folly of trusting that men will behave like gentlemen when the law is on their side. *A 'Water-Fly's' Wooing,* 1914, is a racist and eugenicist story about the evil results of mixed marriages and 'negroid blood-taint', and is dedicated to 'my sister Henrietta whose unfailing affection has been one of the best things of my life'.

Kenealy, Arabella, 1864–1938, novelist, doctor, writer. Educ. at home and at the London School of Medicine for Women, she practised in London and in Watford 1888–94. Her first novel, *Dr Janet of Harley Street,* 1893, is an eccentric story about a woman doctor's concern for her young female protégée: 'Good looks ... are the greatest of all obstacles to a woman's success ... I won't have any man make love to her – I want her for myself.' AK was sister of Annesley, whom she does not mention in her *Memoirs* of their father, 1908; but to whom her second novel, *Molly and her Man of War,* also 1893, is dedicated. AK had retired from practice after severe diphtheria, but later published medical and scientific works such as *The Mother's Manual,* 1905, *Beauty Through Hygiene,* 1905, *The Failure of Vivisection and the Future of Medical Research,* 1909, and *Feminism and Sex-Extinction,* 1920. She also wrote 24 novels and collections of stories. *The Marriage Yoke,* 1904, has some splendid minor female character portraits, but an absurd central romance, while *The Mating of Anthea,* 1911, seeks to give women importance through eugenics, and *The Hon. Mrs Spoor* (n.d.), treats an ex-prostitute. For AK, women should at all times retain their femininity; her books often have a pretty portrait of the author as frontispiece.

Kennard, Mary Eliza (Faber), 'Mrs Edward Kennard', d. 1936, sporting novelist, da. of Mary (Beckett) and Charles Wilson F. (*not* Samuel Laing, as sometimes claimed) of Northaw, Herts. Educ. by governesses (who considered her 'a dunce'), at 15 she was sent to a private establishment at St Germain, and shortly after her return m. Edward K. (b. 1842), JP for Northamptonshire, and a draughtsman who engraved sporting subjects. He shared her family passion for hunting, and they both rode dashingly to hounds, living in Market Harborough, Leics. She wrote over 30 sporting novels, mostly on hunting, and was widely read in the 1880s, with titles such as *Straight as a Die,* 1885, *The Girl in the Brown Habit,* 1886, *A Crack Country,* 1888, and *Matron or Maid,* 1889. Her style is racy and jocular, with touches of didactic liberalism. A volume of sketches, *Our Friends in the Hunting Field,* 1889, was regarded as savage satire of characters too easily recognizable. As well as hunting, she also cycled, fished and drove cars and motor tricycles, publishing *A Guide Book for Lady Cyclists,* 1896, and *The Motor Maniac,* 1902. She died at a 'very advanced age' (*Times* obit.), having spent her last widowed years blind and practically a cripple from a hunting accident.

Kennard, 'Nina', Anne Homan (Homan-Mulock), 1844–1926, novelist and biographer, b. Bellair, King's Co., eleventh of 15 children of Frances Sophia (Berry) and Thomas Homan Mulock Molloy (later Homan-Mulock). In 1866 she m. Arthur Challis K., of Eaton Place; she had four children. She wrote a number of rather wooden novels, peopled mainly by aristocrats, from *There's Rue for You,* 1880, whose romantic heroine writes poetry, to *Second Lady Delcombe,* 1900, about a US heiress who reforms a rake. NK also contributed volumes on Rachel and on Sarah Siddons to the Eminent Women series, and wrote a life of Lafcadio Hearn, 1912, springing from her friendship with Hearn's half-sister, Mrs Atkinson.

Kennedy, Adrienne Lita (Hawkins), dramatist and screenwriter, b. 1931 in Pittsburgh, Pa., da. of Etta (Haugabook), a teacher and 'terrific storyteller', and YMCA secretary Cornell Wallace H. After public schools in Cleveland, Ohio, she found the social structure of Ohio State Univ. (where she took a BA in education, 1953) hostile to her as a black. She began writing there; early poems imitate Edith SITWELL. She first tried drama while her husband, Joseph C. K. (m. 1953; they had two sons) was in Korea with the army. She studied creative writing at Columbia Univ., NY, 1954–6, and wrote stories and a novel (rejected). Travel in Europe and living in Ghana, 1960–1, 'totally changed my writing'. *Funny-house of a Negro* (staged by Edward Albee's workshop, 1962; Obie 1964, pub. 1969) presents a woman talking in her mind with her 'selves' – white Queen Victoria and a duchess, black Patrice Lumumba and Jesus – dramatizing divisions in her personality, her anxiety over her gender and denial of her race in a world 'where black is evil and white is good' (and is culture). It bore the fruit of five years' thinking (AK notes down dreams and ideas, and calls her work 'a growth of images'), and was instantly controversial. AK says the protagonist of *The Owl Answers* (staged 1963, linked with *A Beast's Story* under the joint title *Cities in Bezique,* pub. 1969), who recalls her first heroine in unstable identities, is a composite of herself, her mother, and a clever, tormented, mixed-race aunt. *A Rat's Mass* (staged 1965, pub. in William Couch, ed., *New Black Playwrights,* 1968) came from a dream she had on a train between Paris and Rome, of 'being pursued by red, bloodied rats'. After divorce, AK had three years in London, where *The Lennon Play: In His Own Write* (1967, credit shared with John Lennon and Victor Spinelli) and *Sun* (1969, inspired by Malcolm X's death and dedicated to her father) were staged. In *Sun,* a 'poem-play' (brief like all AK's works), the one actor, male, speaks in front of changing symbols: moon, sun of various colours, human head and body, all blotted with blood and disintegrating. *Evening with Dead Essex,* 1973, deals with a deranged gunman. AK likes to treat inner experience in poetic, rhythmic, repetitious language (likened to Gertrude STEIN), 'elusive multi-layered images' and material symbols. These are multiple: blood stands for menstruation, fear of soiling, the Mass, racist violence. She has taught at Yale, Princeton, Brown and Budapest. Her plays for children include *A Lancashire Lad* (about Charlie Chaplin), and *Black Children's Day,* both produced in 1980. Her *People Who Led to My Plays,* 1987, expands earlier statements about her life and work, e.g. Betsko and Koenig, 1987. She takes up a new genre, novel-autobiography, in *Deadly Triplets, A Theatre Mystery and Journal,* set in 1960s London, due in 1990. Collected plays forthcoming.

Kennedy, Margaret Moore, 1896–1967, novelist, playwright, critic and screen-writer, eldest da. of Elinor (Marwood) and barrister Charles Moore K., b. at Hyde Park Gate, London. Writing from child-hood, she was educ. by governesses, at Cheltenham Ladies' College, Glos. (from nearly 16), and Somerville, Oxford (BA in history, 1919). She published a scholarly book on modern European history, 1922, then (the first work she felt pleased with) *The Ladies of Lyndon,* 1923, dedicated to her mother. It concerns two misfits in county society: the open ending clearly implies that the woman will not manage, like her artist brother-in-law, to seize her freedom. Next of 16 novels, *The Constant Nymph,* 1924, again concerns bohemia: its child-heroine, daughter of one towering musical genius, passionately loves another, flees with him from his also passionate, but respectable and possessive wife, and dies with shocking abruptness. The studies of the two women are deeper than the plot (which made it the best-seller of its decade and lastingly coloured MK's reputation) would suggest. She adapted it for stage and screen, opening two new careers: four more plays include *Escape Me Never!,* 1934, on the marriage of another male genius. MK m. barrister (later judge) David Davies in 1925; they were rich enough to ensure that their three children did not impede her writing. Her 1930s titles are markedly romantic, but each book takes a new course. *Together and Apart,* 1936, set in her own social milieu, treats divorce with humour and insight: the outrage of parents, the resilience of children growing towards social idealism and romantic love; on the margins, Jewish refugees from Europe are unenthusiastically helped. MK kept a diary 1937–9, which ends on the king and queen carrying gas masks in St Paul's Cathedral. Her critical works (*The Mechanized Muse,* 1942, on writing for films, *Jane* AUSTEN, 1950, and *Outlaws on Parnassus,* 1958, on the novel) are perceptive and independent-minded; she gave a paper on Harriet MOZLEY in the early 1960s. In *Troy Chimneys,* 1953 (James Tait Black Memorial Prize), she uses the shocked comments of Victorian descendants to frame a Regency gentleman's incomplete account of his divided mind and actions. *Not in the Calendar,* 1964, and *Women at Work* 1966 (two novellas), foreground female friendship, relating a triumph over congenital deafness, and the deflation of an arrogant husband (who learns) and son (who does not). MK's friends included Elizabeth BOWEN, Marghanita LASKI, Elizabeth JENKINS and Lettice COOPER. Life by Violet Powell, 1983; Anita BROOKNER introduces two of four recent reprints. Billie Melman, *Women and the Popular Imagination in the Twenties,* 1988, prints passages from MK's own previously unpublished comment on *The Constant Nymph,* still, Melman says, 'the most penetrating comment'.

Kenney, Annie, 1879–1953, suffragette and autobiographer, b. in Springhead, Lancs., one of 12 children of Ann (Wood) and Horatio Nelson K., a cotton-mill hand. Despite eight years at village schools 'my school knowledge was nil . . . the only thing I liked was poetry'; 'I hated study and loved play and fun.' These included walking the moors ('the open road was our friend') and acting obstreperous servant roles in plays at her Sunday-school teacher's house. At five she day-dreamed of God every night; her mother (to whom 'I owe all that I have ever been') encouraged free discussion of every topic. A millhand half-time from 10 and full-time from 13, AK at 20 was learning labour organization and reading Robert Blatchford in the *Clarion*: he – with Christabel PANKHURST the great influence on her adult life – later advised her to be a professional writer. In 1905 her mother died; she met the Pankhursts, was jailed for the first time (three days for 'obstruction' at a Manchester street meeting after Winston Churchill refused Liberal support for women's SUFFRAGE), started a correspondence course from Ruskin College, and began travelling for the cause. Her 'Prison Faces' (*Labour Record and Review,* 1907) drew on further prison terms for a vivid account of 'wrong done to women' by 'the wicked law', 'man-made law'. She went on hunger-strike, and used disguises to avoid re-arrest under the 'Cat and Mouse Act'. During WWI she lectured in the USA and Australia; by 1917 she was suffering from nervous exhaustion; after the first general election with women voters she left the Movement and travelled to Italy; she m. James Taylor, civil servant, in 1920, had a son, and became a theosophist. Her *Memories of a Militant,* 1924, closes with thoughts on women's use of the vote.

Ker, Anne (Phillips), *c.* 1766–after 1820, author of six novels, da. of John P., a surveyor of canals. In *The Heiress di Montaldo, or The Castle of Bezanto,* pub. by subscription, 1799, a first-person English narrator describes contemporary love-affairs, torrid yet noble, among Italian castles. She uses the south of France here and in *Adeline St Julian, or The Midnight Hour* (written c. 1797, she says, dated 1800). Its preface argues that earlier periods 'afford a bolder and more free scope for invention and imagery' and for strongly depicted 'trials of the human heart'; but her grasp on psychology, language, and period (as in *Edric the Forester, or The Mysteries of the Haunted Chamber,* 1817, repr. 1841, supposedly

Norman) is shaky. The preface to *Emmeline, or The Happy Discovery,* 1801, rebukes 'contemptuous open-mouthed devouring' and no doubt venial reviewers, especially the *Anti-Jacobin,* 'whose principles, to a civilized nation, are a well known shame'. She appealed to the RLF in 1820 from Stoke Newington, London: she had gout and a breast abscess; her husband was ill; she lacked money to pursue a promised teaching job.

Ker, Louisa Theresa Bellenden, novelist, dramatist; she seems to have left no trace but the sad tale she told the RLF, 1819–36. Her Irish father, Dr Lewis K., librarian to the Royal College of Physicians 1773–87, brought her up to expect an inheritance, but received charity in 1792 and died early, leaving her destitute. She m., *c.* 1817, St Aubyn, a Catholic army officer, who deserted her. She wrote translations from French but could not get them published, and dramatic pieces but had them stolen (though several did well on stage, some at Jane SCOTT's theatre). She opened a school which failed, 1833–5; she writes of 'withering in distraction', unable to afford legal action while her alleged relations wasted 'in all the excesses of luxury, property legally mine'. The many titles she claims include versions of Bernardin de St Pierre, N. A. Pluche, and Choderlos de Laclos; *The Swiss Emigrants,* usually listed as the prolific Hugh Murray's; plays ascribed to J. R. Planché (himself a notorious 'lifter') or Henry Milner, to Samuel Birch and to Charles Kemble; and the preposterous, horrific, powerful *Manfroné, or The One-Handed Monk,* 1809 (many eds.; facs. NY 1972), unconvincingly ascribed to M. A. RADCLIFFE. The RLF dropped LTBK in 1836 when her 'uncle' Charles Henry B. K. denied knowledge of her.

Kerr, Jean (Collins), playwright and humorist, b. 1923 at Scranton, Pa., da. of Kitty (O'Neill) and Thomas J. C., educ. at Marywood College (BA 1943) and Catholic Univ. (MFA 1945), where she met and m., 1943, drama critic Walter K. Her first plays were acted by his students. They collaborated on *The Song of Bernadette* (pub. 1944; produced, NYC, 1946), *Jenny Kissed Me* (produced, NYC, 1948), and *Thank You, Just Looking* (unpub., produced NYC as *Touch and Go,* 1949). Her longest-running play, *Mary, Mary,* 1961, puts her heroine through much comic anxiety before reconciling her with her husband. JCK's volumes of comic pieces about her family (four sons) are less reliant on gender-stereotyping than earlier domestic humour (e.g. Phyllis MCGINLEY). After *The Snake has All the Lines,* 1960, came a bestseller, *Please Don't Eat the Daisies,* 1957 (film 1963, TV series 1965–7), whose only bad review came from one of the sons. *How I Got to be Perfect* followed in 1978. *Lunch Hour* was produced on Broadway, 1980, pub. 1982.

Kidman, Fiona (Eakin), b. 1940, novelist, short-story writer and poet, b. at Hawera, NZ, da. of Flora (Small) and Hugh E. Educ. in small rural schools in Northland, she trained as a librarian at Rotorua Public Library 1959–61, and was Librarian at Rotorua Boys' High 1961–2. She m. Ian K., school teacher, 1960. In 1964 she began freelance writing, and in 1970 moved to Wellington, wrote radio and TV plays and pub. two vols. of poetry, *Honey and Bitters,* 1975, and *On the Tight Rope,* 1978. In her first novel, *A Breed of Women,* 1979, a 40-year-old woman looks back on her progression from a repressive farm childhood, through two marriages, children, suburbia, a later career in TV in the city, and a not-very-satisfactory love affair with a younger man. *Mandarin Summer,* 1981, is an account of a young girl, after WWII, on a remote Northland orchard, confronting adult sexuality. In *Paddy's Puzzle,* 1983, FK describes a young woman growing up in the respectable provincial town of Hamilton and moving to wartime Auckland, and the seedy underside of prostitution, the black market and American marines. A prolific writer, FK has taught creative writing courses, been a weekly columnist for *The Listener* (Bookmarks), has twice held the NZ Scholarship in Letters, and in 1987 was Writer-in-Residence at Victoria Univ., Wellington, and received the OBE. In 1988 her historical novel, *The Book of Secrets,* 1987, tracing the lives of three generations of women from Scotland to Novia Scotia and NZ, won the NZ National Book Award.

Kilham, Hannah (Spurr), 1774–1832, diarist, TRAVEL writer and linguist, da. of 'respectable tradespeople' Hannah (Brittleband) and Peter S. of Sheffield. She was an Anglican, a dispenser of charity, and a diarist at ten; took on the household at her mother's death, 1786; learned so well at boarding school (from 14 to 16) that her teacher blamed her for 'overstepping the bounds of the female province'. Deeply in love in her early 20s, a Methodist from 1794, she began in 1796 a shorthand journal: 'This morning I have given myself to God.' In April 1798 she became second wife of Alexander K., founder of the Methodist New Connection; in December he died. She bore a daughter (who died young), joined the Quakers, 1803, ran a boarding school, 1805–21, published maxims and pedagogy, 1813ff., and campaigned for the poor and old. In Ireland in 1823 on famine relief work, she set her hitherto humdrum, pious diary (pub. 1837) to depict, and prescribe remedies for, struggle and destitution as fearful, she says, as in Africa: spending power for labourers would fuel the economy; work for the poor would make them 'agents of their own improvement'. From 1820 she studied African languages: her 'full and analytical' pamphlets urge teaching in native tongues (a cause 'nearer my heart than language can describe'), training at a London Institute for African teachers, and an end to whites' arrogance, 'high tones and repelling manner'. On three trips to Africa, 1823–4, 1827–8, and from 1830, she taught ex-slave girls and eagerly recorded the place and the life. She died at sea between Sierra Leone and Liberia. See P. E. H. Hair, bibliog. (*Journal of the Friends' Hist. Soc.*, 49, 1960), and study of African languages, 1962; life by Mona Dickson, 1980.

Killigrew, Anne, *c.* 1660–85, poet, da. of Judith and of royal chaplain Henry K., herself (with Anne FINCH) Maid of Honour to the Duchess of York. The year after her death from smallpox, her father pub. her *Poems* (facs. 1967) with Dryden's poetic eulogy of her painting, verse, and virtue. Her poetry turns from early involvement with military themes ('Alexandreis' includes a joyful description of Amazons) to rejection of female involvement with state affairs and advocacy of pious withdrawal. Like Jane BARKER and 'EPHELIA' she explores and rejects courtly love, advising women 'Remember when you Love, from that same hour / Your Peace you put into your Lover's Power: / From that same hour from him you Laws receive, / And as he shall ordain, you Joy, or Grieve, / Hope, Fear, Laugh, Weep; Reason aloof does stand, / Disabl'd both to Act, and to Command.' 'Upon the saying that my Verses were made by another' laments that 'What ought t'have brought me Honour, brought me shame!' See Ann Messenger, 1986.

Killin, or Killam, **Margaret** (Aldam), d. 1672, English Quaker minister and pamphleteer. 'Convinced' by Margaret FELL's future husband, she travelled widely and was often in prison. She wrote the first section of the otherwise anonymous and collective *A Warning from the Lord to the Teachers and People of Plimouth,* 1655. This, like Hester BIDDLE and other early radical QUAKERS, rebukes the rich and presents God's angry voice and the prophet's as the same. She tells church ministers 'because ye have departed out of my counsel, I wil spread dung on your faces, yea I have cast dung on your faces already'.

Kimenye, Barbara, novelist, short-story writer, writer of children's literature, b. *c.* 1940 in Uganda. She worked in the government of the Kabaka of Buganda, then as a journalist for the *Uganda Nation*, and, in Nairobi, for the *Daily Nation.* Her short stories about Ugandan village life, in *Kalasanda,* 1965, and *Kalasanda Revisited,* 1966, are often satirical treatments of the conflict of traditional and modern values. Her story, 'The Winner', a delightful spoof in which a remotely related widow intervenes to save a lottery winner from his avaricious cousins, is often anthologized. BK's substantial list of works for children includes the Moses series, about an irrepressible Ugandan schoolboy (whether 'On the Move', 'In a Muddle', 'Kidnapped', or with a 'Ghost') whose stories of fun and travel captivate the young reader. See Nancy Schmidt in *Bulletin of the Southern Association of Africanists,* 4, 1976, and *African Studies Review* 19, 1976.

Kincaid, Jamaica, novelist, journalist, short-story writer, b. 1949 at St John's, Antigua. Her mother, Annie Richardson, a Carib-Indian from Dominica, encouraged her wide reading and her writing; she will not speak of her father. After local girls' schools she was apprenticed as a seamstress, then migrated to the USA in 1966. She attended college in NH, began 'real writing' in 1973, was a *New Yorker* staff writer from 1976, and lived with her husband, composer, pianist and professor Allen Shawn, in NYC before settling at North Bennington, Vt. She has children. Her stories appeared in the *Paris Review, New Yorker* and elsewhere: collected in *At the Bottom of the River,* 1983, which won an American Academy Zabel award. Her autobiographical novel, *Annie John,* 1985, deals with the passage out of childhood: fantasy, partial knowledge, secure reliance on a strong mother, are eagerly left behind (her 'heart could have burst open with joy'); but the conventional and paradisally abundant island is displaced by other complex realities. (On debate as to the book's genre – autobiography or fiction – see Bryant Mangum in Daryl Cumber Dance, ed., *Fifty Caribbean Writers,* bio-bibliography, 1986; on teaching it to teenagers see Muriel Lynn Rubin in *Wasafiri,* 8, spring 1988.) JK's long essay *A Small Place,* 1988, is a passionately argued indictment of Antigua's colonial past and present tourist development. She is working on another novel.

Kindersley, Jemima (Wicksteed), 1741?–1809, travel writer and translator. Of 'very humble birth', with 'native energy of mind' but no education, she m. Nathaniel K., artillery officer, at Great Yarmouth in 1762, and travelled in 1764, via Tenerife, Brazil, and the Cape of Good Hope, to many different parts of India. She left for home with ruined health in 1769; her husband died a few months later. She pub. her TRAVEL *Letters* in 1770, not mentioning him or her baby son but relating plainly and pungently what she sees of foreigners' everyday lives (women's wherever possible), of labour and harsh government. Often scathing about other races, she refuses to adjudge intellectual superiority to whites (see Ketaki Kushari DYSON, 1978). The Rev. Henry Hodgson attacked her (letters in the *London Chronicle,* repr. 1778) for some good words (among many bad) about Roman Catholicism; Anne PLUMPTRE used her in *The Rector's Son.* Coming on A. L. Thomas's French *Essay on ... Women* and preferring it to a similar project of her own, she translated it with two fragments by herself, 1781. (It notes how women are always, everywhere 'adored and oppressed', and how they need courage and independence to write.) Her son was the first to translate from Tamil into English.

King, Alice, 1839–94, novelist and religious writer, b. Cutcombe, Som., da. of the Rev. John Myers K. Though blind from the age of seven, she learned several languages, conducted classes in her father's parish, wrote for magazines, typing her work, and produced several novels. These include *Queen of Herself*, 1870, *The Woman with a Secret*, 1872, *Fettered Yet Free*, 1883, and *A Strange Tangle*, 1887. Plots, when protracted through three volumes, are at best agreeably teasing in their suspense, at worst improbable substitutes for in-depth exploration. Yet serious themes emerge, with the role of women as the focus. Young heroines mature to a fuller understanding of love and matrimony, and are depicted as lively, independent career women, or as pillars, not only of home, but of the community. Men find initial difficulty in accepting women as equals, but may even acknowledge them as superiors. The characters are credible, neither paragons nor fiends, and the writing shows perception and a touch of humour, sometimes directed at 'Amazons' and 'naughty, new-fashioned ideas about female education'. Overall is the basic message of doing one's duty and trusting in God.

King, Grace Elizabeth, 1851/3?–1932, novelist, short-story writer and historian, b. in New Orleans, da. of Sarah Ann (Miller) and William Woodson K., lawyer. She was educ. by her mother and grandmother and at the *Institut St Louis* and at a school established by Madame Cenas, whose daughter, Heloise, encouraged her writing. She read widely in French, German and Spanish. In 1885 she spoke on 'Heroines of Fiction' at a meeting of the Pan-Gnostic Society during the New Orleans Cotton Centennial Exposition. Her first story, 'Monsieur Motte', written as a result of her dissatisfaction with George W. Cable's depiction of Creole life, appeared in the *New Princeton Review*, 1886. Concentrating on Creole life in an earlier period, she pub. her stories in journals such as *Harper's* and *Century Magazine* and then collected them in three volumes: *Monsieur Motte*, 1888, *Tales of a Time and Place*, 1892, and *Balcony Stories*, 1893. Her best stories, such as 'A Crippled Hope' and 'La Grande Demoiselle', transcend the 'local color' movement to capture the Creole community (see W. D. Howells, *Harper's*, June 1892). Her novel *Earthlings* was serialized in *Lippincott's*, 1888, and was followed by two other novels, *The Pleasant Ways of St Medard*, 1916, and *La Dame de Saint Hermine*, 1924. She also wrote historical studies, including *Jean Baptiste Le Moyne, Sieur de Bienville*, 1892, for the Makers of America series; *New Orleans, the Place and the People*, 1895; *Creole Families of New Orleans*, 1921; *The History of Mt Vernon on the Potomac*, 1929; and, with John R. Ficklen, *A History of Louisiana*, 1893, and *Stories from Louisiana History*, 1905. She helped run the Louisiana Historical Society and its *Quarterly*. She received an honorary LL.D from Tulane Univ. and was elected as a Fellow of the Royal Society of Arts and Sciences (England) and an Officier de l'Instruction Publique (France). GEK reported in her *Memories of a Southern Woman of Letters*, 1932, that Isabella Beecher Hooker 'talked to me about "Woman's Rights" and converted me to her point of view'. Robert Bush ed. her selec. works, 1973. MSS are at Louisiana State Univ. and Tulane, as well as Duke, Yale and the NYPL. See also David Kirby's study, 1980; Ann Goodwyn Jones, *Tomorrow is Another Day*, 1981.

King, Harriet Eleanor (Baillie **Hamilton**), 1840–1920, poet, da. of Lady Harriet and Admiral William Alexander B. H. At 17 she read Farini's *History of the Roman State, 1820–50*, which initiated her enthusiasm for Italian nationalism and passionate devotion to Mazzini (with whom she corresponded from 1862). At 18 HHK began work on her apologia for Felice Orsini, would-be assassin of Napoleon III, which she considered her finest poem; first printed privately in 1862 by publisher and banker Henry Samuel King, whom she m. in 1863, and subsequently in her *Aspromonte and Other Poems*, 1869. The title poem (an account of Garibaldi's capture) was first pub. in the *Observer*, 15 November 1862, as

'Garibaldi at Varignano'. *The Disciples,* 1873, written after Mazzini's death, celebrates the heroic self-sacrifice of four of his followers (she gleaned details from the *Times'* account of their trial). Part of the longest section (about Ugo Bassi, the Bolognese priest who was executed after Garibaldi's flight from Rome) was pub. separately and circulated in hospitals. The poem was very popular, going rapidly through four editions, and was loved by Cardinal Manning, to whom she dedicated *The Prophecy of Westminster,* 1895. She became a Catholic and continued to write ballads and religious verse (1889; 1902). Her husband d. 1878, leaving her with seven children. Her most impressive collection, *A Book of Dreams,* 1883, explores memory and loss, with sensuous, disconcerting fantasy. Her *Letters and Recollections of Mazzini* was pub. in 1912, but she was too ill to see it through the press; it was ed. by G. M. Trevelyan.

King, Sophia, later Fortnum, b. *c.* 1782, novelist and poet, sister of Charlotte DACRE, with whom in 1798 she pub. verse dedicated to their disgraced father. Her own *Waldorf, or The Dangers of Philosophy* (same year; repr. NY, 1974) is awkward, melodramatic, heavily moralized: the views of the sceptic Hardi Lok cause multiple deaths, lastly his own. In *Cordelia, or The Romance of Real Life,* MINERVA 1799, the heroine suffers her wicked father's defection, drudgery for a foolish woman writer, and doomed love, before settling for religion and her uninspiring mother and siblings. After *The Victim of Friendship,* 1800, came *The Fatal Secret, or Unknown Warrior,* 1801: the unknown destroys his lover morally and physically, and turns out to be the devil; SK's spirited preface mocks her own extremes; her sister contributed poems. SK m. Charles F. in 1801, wrote newspaper verse as 'SAPPHO', and pub. *Poems,* 1804 (many repr. from 1798), with 'Remarks' on the place of fantasy alongside good taste. *The Adventures of Victor Allen,* 1805, anticipates *Frankenstein* with a hero made cruel (especially to women) by persecution.

Kingsford, Anna, baptized Annie (Bonus) 1846–88, doctor, religious writer, woman of letters, b. Stratford, Essex, da. of an Irish–German woman (Schröder) and John B., shipowner. Educ. by tutors and at finishing school in Brighton, in 1867 she m. her cousin Algernon Godfrey K., vicar of Atcham, Shropshire, and three years later converted to Catholicism. She studied in Paris and in 1880 received her MD. A successful women's doctor, she wrote sometimes controversially on anti-vivisection, vegetarianism, women's SUFFRAGE, and beauty aids. President of the Theosophical Society, 1883, and founder of the Hermetic Society in 1884, she demonstrated her religious preoccupation in works such as *The Perfect Way,* 1882 (with Edward Maitland), and *Rosamunda the Princess,* 1875. The stories in this collection show scholarship rather than creative originality, with a sameness of situation but well-drawn historical settings ranging from ancient Greece to fifteenth-century Venice. True art, AK felt, must be unsentimental, religious in spirit, and in tune with the universe. She also wrote stories (signed Ninon Kingsford or Mrs Algernon Kingsford) for magazines, and owned and edited *The Lady's Own Paper,* 1872–3. She died of consumption, after catching cold visiting Pasteur's lab., leaving one daughter.

Kingsley, Mary Henrietta, 1862–1900, travel writer, ethnologist, naturalist, navigator, b. Islington, London, da. of Mary (Bailey) and Dr George Henry K. Apart from formal tuition in German (intended to improve her usefulness as her father's research assistant), she was self-educ. in anthropology, entomology, and ichthyology. The death of her parents and her brother's departure freed her for travel in West Africa where she collected fish (a number were named after her) and insects, and information on tribal customs and religions. Despite her commitment to imperialism, she was a more sympathetic observer of African life than many of her contemporaries, and in lectures in England maintained that good government involved 'pater-maternal duty' to the natives. *Travels in West Africa,* 1897, is a lively book with amusing anecdotes and the more tedious scholarly details wisely saved for the appendices. She was proudest of two achievements, her fishes and her skill in a canoe, and saw herself as a 'humble member' of the great school of African travellers. She died in South Africa of a fever caught nursing Boer prisoners of war and, in accordance with her wishes, was buried at sea. Her LETTERS are quoted by her many biographers, including Stephen Gwynn, 1933, and Katherine Frank, 1986.

Kingston, Maxine Ting Ting **Hong,** writer of imaginative history, fiction, and essays, and teacher, b. in 1940 in Stockton, Calif., da. of Ying Lan (Chew) and Tom Hong. As a child she worked in her parents' laundry and went to 'American school' in the daytime and to 'Chinese school' in the evenings. She took an AB in English, 1962, and a certificate in education, 1965, from the Univ. of Calif. (Berkeley). She m. Earll K., an actor, 1962, and has one son. She taught English and mathematics at high schools and a business college in California and Hawaii, and in 1977 became visiting professor at the Univ. of Hawaii. Her first book, *The Woman Warrior: Memoirs of a Girlhood Among Ghosts,* 1976, winner of a National Book Critics' Circle award, combines myth, from 'the peasant talk-story Cantonese tradition' with autobiography and the biographies of women relatives: of, among others, her mother, Brave Orchid, a successful doctor in China, and her 'no-name' aunt who committed suicide by jumping into the well with her newly born illegitimate child. MHK embroiders threads of her own spinning to fill in the spaces of those lives. *China Men,* 1980, applies the same technique to her father and other male relatives, though with more invention because of her father's silence. In Hawaii, 'talk-story' includes gossip and chitchat and party conversation, but it is 'not only improvisational, not only modern': storytellers use it to remember mythic chants and 'to hand down mythology the way Homer did'. The language to describe Hawaii, MHK insists, is 'the chants to Pele, goddess of the volcano'. But in a work in progress, a perhaps archetypal Book that she once envisioned as a Book of No, balancing Joyce's *Ulysses,* the 'book of Yes', MHK uses a 'first-person narrator and the Chinese-American heroines who have interested [her] may disappear'. See interviews in Janet Sternburg, ed., *The Writer on Her Work,* 1980, and *Contemporary Authors,* article in *Vis a Vis* (June 1987), all quoted above, and Leslie W. Rabine in *Signs,* 12, 1987.

Kinney, Elizabeth Clementine (Dodge), 1810–89, poet and essayist, b. NYC, da. of Sarah (Cleveland) and David D. In 1830 she m. Edmund Burke Stedman. Their son was Edmund Clarence Stedman, poet and critic. After her husband's death in 1835, EK contributed poems and articles to magazines including *Graham's* and the *Knickerbocker.* In 1841 she m. William Burnet K., newspaper editor. In 1850 they went for three years to Turin, while EK worked as chargé d'affaires in Sardinia. They then lived in Florence until 1865. EK's first book, *Felicità,* 1855, a historical narrative in verse, is virtually unreadable: 'in time this silence seemed to jar / Love's concord in Felicità'. Neither do her *Poems,* 1867, repay scrutiny. Her third and final publication, *Bianca Capello,* 1873, is a blank verse drama set in Italy in the second half of the sixteenth century. A well-researched tale of intrigue, violence and illicit love, it is a nineteenth-century imitation of Jacobean tragedy. Her most interesting work is her unpub. 'Journal' and 'Personal Reminiscences', which describe her acquaintances in Italy, including the BROWNINGS. The MSS are in the Univ. of Columbia Library, NYC.

Kinzie, Juliette Augusta (Magill), 1806–70, writer and civic leader, b. Connecticut, da. of Frances (Wollcott) and Arthur M. She was educ. at home, at a local boarding school, and at Emma WILLARD's school in Troy, NY. In 1830 she m. John Harris K. and moved west to Wisconsin and then Chicago, where she helped establish hospitals and churches. In 1844 she pub. a brief narrative of the great Chicago massacre of 1812. Her first and most successful full-length work was *'Wau-bun', The Early Day in the Northwest,* 1848, a semi-autobiographical account of her experiences when her husband worked as an Indian agent in Wisconsin. This book shows a respect for the Indians whose way of life it describes, and it achieved popularity with the public and praise from historians. JK wrote two other novels, *Walter Ogilby,* 1869, and *Mark Logan,* 1871. Her grand-daughter, Juliette Low, founded the Girl Scouts of America.

Kirkland, Caroline Matilda (Stansbury), 'Mrs Mary Clavers', 1801–64, essayist, short-story writer and editor, b. NYC, da. of Eliza (Alexander) and Samuel S., clerk and bookseller: grand-daughter of Joseph S., loyalist poet. She was educ. by a Quaker aunt, Lydia Stansbury Mott, who conducted girls' schools in NYC and provided an excellent classical education. In 1828 she m. William K., tutor in Classics at Hamilton College, Clinton, NY; their son was Joseph K., the novelist. They conducted schools at Geneva, NY and Detroit, then in 1836 left to pioneer the village of Pinckney. CMK's letters to friends were pub. in 1839 under 'Mrs Mary Clavers' as *A New Home – Who'll Follow? or Glimpses of Western Life,* a series of sketches tracing the development of a Western settlement and praised by Poe for 'truth and novelty'. Her second book, the didactic *Forest Life,* 1842, pub. under her own name, lacks the earlier work's ironic, self-mocking style. In 1843, on returning to NYC, she conducted a girls' school and continued to write about the West in *Western Clearings,* 1845. After her husband d. in 1846 she took over editorship of *The Christian Enquirer* and also the literary *Union Magazine.* She ed. Spenser's *Faerie Queene,* 1847, and pub. *Holidays Abroad,* 1849. During the 1850s she wrote a life of Washington and a number of gift books, one of which, *Autumn Hours,* 1854, contained her 'Women of the Revolution': 'No one will question that the women of the revolution bore a far larger share of its actual hardships and sufferings than men.' See the study by William Osborne, 1972.

Kizer, Carolyn, poet, translator, b. in 1925 at Spokane, Washington. Da. of scientist Mabel (Ashley) and lawyer Benjamin Hamilton K., she says of her mother: 'I wrote the poems for her. I still do.' She was educ. at Sarah Lawrence College, NYC (BA 1945), Columbia Univ., and the Univ. of Washington, Seattle. She m. Charles Stimpson Bullitt in 1948 and had three children (divorced 1954). In 1959 she published *Poems* (Portland, Ore., Art Museum) and founded *Poetry Northwest,* which she edited until 1965. In *The Ungrateful Garden,* 1961, her polished, versatile voice emerges, speaking of impartial nature, of mythology, of childhood ('Walking through the worms / After a rain, / Trying not to wound / Anything alive'), in imitations of Japanese, and debate with poets living and dead. In 1964–5 she taught in Pakistan at Kinnaird College for Women; writer-in-residence and univ. posts followed. *Knock Upon Silence,* 1965, contains Chinese imitations and translations, and her well-known 'Pro Femina' (inspired, says CK, by Simone de BEAUVOIR), a poem merciless to the failings of women writers but jaunty, ironic, and hopeful: 'While men have politely debated free will, we have howled for it / Howl still, pacing the centuries, tragedy heroines.' *Midnight* *was my Cry*, 1971, like later volumes, reprints already-seen work. CK directed literary programmes for the National Endowment for the Arts, 1966–70, and m. John Marshall Woodbridge in 1975. In *Mermaids in the Basement: Poems for Women*, 1984, dedicated to 'some of my muses', she writes of love, children, friendship and myth. Persephone muses, 'No clutch of summer holds me here. / I know, I know. I've gone before.' *Yin*, 1984, won a Pulitzer Prize. *The Nearness of You*, 1986, treats relations with men: sometimes light, sometimes obliquely romantic; she 'almost' forgives her 'authoritarian and severe' father. Her translations include Urdu poetry and *Carrying Over: Translations from Various Tongues*, 1985. Interview in *Webster Review*, 11, 1986.

Klepfisz, Irene, poet, b. 1941 in Warsaw, da. of Rose (Perczykow) K., and a socialist father who had hoped for a boy. He 'believed in resistance', and d. in the Warsaw Ghetto uprising, 1943. IK was sheltered by nuns and unwilling peasants: her mother got her to the USA in 1949. Raised in NYC, she fed her 'passion for words and literature' at City College of NY (BA) and the Univ. of Chicago (PhD in English), where in 1964 she felt isolated and wary in her first non-Jewish milieu. She did clerical and publishing jobs, and taught remedial English, Yiddish, women's studies and women's poetry workshops. *Periods of Stress*, 1975 (poems), treats the death camps, personal memories, making love, living alone: 'please don't touch me / wait a moment / just wait one moment / until i'm not so cold.' She was a founder-editor of *Conditions* magazine, 1976–81, and wrote essays on women alone (repr. in *Why Children?*, 1980). 'Anti-Semitism in the Lesbian/Feminist Movement' and 'Resisting and Surviving America' (in *Nice Jewish Girls: a lesbian anthology*, 1982), and 'The Distances Between Us: Feminism, Sisterhood and the Girls at the Office' (*Sinister Wisdom*, 28, 1985). *Different Enclosures*, 1985, includes: poems from her first book; the prose 'Journal of Rachel Robotnik [Polish for *worker*]', telling a kind of truth which its creator cannot fit into her acclaimed stories (the daily 'plug[ging] myself into the machine', job, food, cleaning, talk, jokes, lesbian lover and family anxieties); and, repr., *Keeper of Accounts*, 1982 (poems on the horrors of prison as lived by female monkeys in a zoo, on dreams and their relinquishing). At the end IK has 'discarded all patterns / and blueprints'. She edited with Malanie Kaye/Kantrowitz *Sinister Wisdom* 29/30, on Jewish women's identity, and *The Tribe of Dina: A Jewish Women's Anthology*, 1986. She says her Jewish and lesbian-feminist consciousness are akin: 'Alienated. Threatened. Individual. Defiant.'

Klickmann, Flora, 1867–1958, journalist and memoirist, b. in London, da. of ex-teacher Frances (Warne) and Rudolph Friedrich Auguste K., a German immigrant who encouraged his children's writing. Three of FK's five siblings died young, two of them within two days. She had a BM reading ticket at 17 and studied at Trinity College of Music and the Royal College of Organists. At 21 her health broke down; she dropped her concert ambitions for writing articles on music, co-founded *The Windsor Magazine*, 1895, and *The Foreign Field*, 1904 (Wesleyan missionary journal); she pub. the first of several novels in 1905. From 1908 to 1930 she edited the hugely popular *Girl's Own Paper*, pub. by the RTS (study of its earlier years by Wendy Forrester, 1980), and wrote under its auspices many books on needlework, cooking, etc. Her Wye Valley cottage features in a series (to 1948: selec. ed. Brian Kinglake, Mills and Boon, 1960) begun with *The Flower-Patch Among the Hills*, 1913. Sweetly humorous (except for an outburst on the loneliness and poverty of London working girls), it moves from female friendship and faintly bohemian domesticity to two events of 1913: another breakdown, and marriage to Ebenezer

Henderson Smith of *The Boy's Own Paper*, called 'the Head of Affairs', from whom the handyman now reckons to take his orders. FK wrote from just after WWII against 'the indiscriminate spoliation of our land, for military, industrial and other schemes'. She destroyed her memoirs after a publisher rejected them; but David Lazell's leaflet, 1976, draws on MS material.

Knatchbull, Lady **Lucy**, 1584–1629, spiritual autobiographer. Born Elizabeth, da. of Ann (Crispe) and Reynold K. of Kent, she felt called by God at 17, and after a long struggle with worldly ambition became a postulant, 1604, at a Benedictine convent in Brussels. While still 'deeply oppressed' by the 'solitary life, which had ever been hateful to me', she received her first vision, of a star-like light. Renewed darkness (feeling her soul 'extremely poor and beggarly', or that she would go mad), and frequent illness alternated with mystical experiences like 'the perfect savour of Violets' driving away devils. She noted her faults as talking too much and wanting to be esteemed wise. Tobie Matthews used her 'exact Relation' of her visions (written by command before her election, 1624, as Abbess of a new convent at Ghent) and later 'letters and Papers' for his life of her, pub. 1931; other writings had been burned 'through her humility' or else 'lent and so lost'. She had four nieces in the convent.

Knight, Ellis Cornelia, 1758–1837, novelist, poet, and diarist, da. of Sir Joseph K. and Phillipina (Deane), who wrote an unpublished novel, letters pub. 1905, notes on Boswell's Johnson (quoting Anne FINCH) and personal memoirs of Frances REYNOLDS and Anna WILLIAMS. ECK became a classical scholar; after her father's death in 1775 she went abroad with her mother for economy. After seeing Paris, Toulouse, Rome, and Naples (meeting Hester PIOZZI), she pub. at Genoa her highly popular *Dinarbas*, 1790, romantic sequel and riposte to Johnson's *Rasselas*: prince and princess marry a sister and brother and attain happiness (see Ann Messenger in essays, 1986). In Rome again, ECK completed *Marcus Flaminius*, 1791, an epistolary novel about frontier and metropolitan life under the Roman empire, well researched and widely admired but financially disappointing. In Naples again, she wrote poems about love, patriotism, and Nelson (being linked with his notorious love-affair later embarrassed her). Returning as a refugee to England, she published *Latium*, 1805, a cultivated tourist's guide to Rome and its environs, with her own fine etchings. She held court posts with the Queen (publishing, 1809–12, brief histories of Spain and France, poems and translations) and Princess Charlotte; loyalty to the latter through all emotional vagaries brought dismissal. She lived mostly abroad from 1816, and died in Paris; a medieval novel, *Sir Guy de Lusignan*, 1837, reiterates earlier opinions on women's necessary self-effacement. 'Autobiography' based on her diary, 1861, selec. 1960; life by Barbara Luttrell, 1965.

Knight, Sarah (Kemble), 1666–1727, travel diarist, b. at Boston, Mass., da. of Elizabeth (Trerice) and merchant Thomas Kemble. She m. Richard Knight before 1689 and had one daughter; as a widow she was shopkeeper, landowner, innkeeper and perhaps legal scrivener. She died rich. Her journal of a business trip to New York, 1704–5, acutely observes the hardships of the road and the social customs of other towns. She recreates dialogue convincingly, drops sometimes into verse ('my old way of composing my Resentments'), and deploys vivid images both traditional and idiosyncratic: the sun may be 'the Glorious Luminary, with his swift Coursers', but unsociable drinkers are 'tyed by the Lipps to a pewter engine' and in an unstable canoe she dares not 'so much as to lodg my tongue a hair's breadth more on one side of my mouth then tother.' Pub. 1825, her journal aroused the interest of Hannah CROCKER; latest ed., David R. Godine's, 1972.

Knowles, Mary (Morris), 1733–1807, poet and Quaker apologist, eldest da. of Alice and Moses M. of Staffs. In verse controversy with a Rev. Mr Rand she dismissed baptism as (like circumcision and foot-washing) an outmoded symbol: pub. as *A Compendium of a Controversy on Water-Baptism*, *c.* 1776. She married Thomas K., medical writer, travelled with him in Europe, had one child, and was left a rich widow in 1784. She crossed swords with Samuel Johnson over women's equality and in 1778 over a girl's right to choose her own religion (Quakerism); in her account (as in that by her correspondent Anna SEWARD) she emerges clear victor. Boswell having rejected it, she published it in the *GM*, 1791: repr. 1799. *The Lady's Monthly Museum*, 1803, mentions her widely-known embroidered portraits and her writings 'philosophical, theological, and poetical', some published with her name but more anonymous; Seward mentions her interest in 'the female right to literature and science', and her story of a stagecoach ride, which mocks a pompous doctor.

Knox, Lucy (Spring Rice), the Hon. Mrs O. H. Knox, b. 1845, poet, da. of Ellen (Frere) and the Hon. Stephen Edmond S. R., a Cambridge friend of Alfred Tennyson. In 1866 she m. Octavius Henry K. In 1872 her first volume of poems was privately printed in London and sold by the author through Foynes in Ireland. Among a variety of religious and 'social' poems on the condition of the poor, 'Sonnet: A Cry to Men' and 'Out of the Fulness of the Heart' discuss the postition of women. In 1876 Smith, Elder, pub. an expanded version of this volume with the same title. Extra poems included 'Woman's Future' ('Look in her face O England, this is she, / Aspirant womanhood, whom thou art wont / To scorn, to silence and repudiate'). Her other collection, *Four Pictures from a Life*, 1884, dedicated to her 'most faithful friend and sister' Alice S. R., included some political poems and translations from Italian and German.

Kogawa, Joy (Nakayama), poet, novelist, b. 1935 in Vancouver, da. of Lois (Yao) and the Rev. Gordon Goichi N. She was educ. in an internment camp at Slocan, BC; at Coaldale, Alberta (still, after WWII, barred from living at the coast); at the Univ. of Alberta, Toronto Conservatory of Music and Anglican Women's Training College, and the Univ. of Saskatchewan. She married David K. in 1957 and had two children (divorced 1968). In her first book, *The Splintered Moon*, 1964, she calls herself 'someone who's been / Lost by love'. *A Choice of Dreams*, 1974, records a problematic visit to Japan ('Home is where the heart is, I feel / Which is an open question / These wounding times'; 'I ... Walk the haunted city streets / Lady Macbeth, graduate tourist'), the scars of childhood ('I prayed to the God who loves / All the children in his sight / That I might be white'), and (longest piece in the book, most impassioned and widest-ranging in reference) an abortion of 1971. In *Jericho Road*, 1977, 'Poems for my Enemies' includes 'I will talk about love ... until the words cease / until the wounding ends'; 'The Wedlocked' group moves from a 'measured / step down the aisle' to the 'burial day' of divorce. JK's austerely haunting novel, *Obasan*, 1981 (which she re-wrote for children as *Naomi's Road*, 1986), picks up themes from her poetry as a Nisei woman in Canada hesitantly pursues the traces of her past: the hybrid linguistic forms of words and names; Japanese traditional mourning for her uncle; the long-buried facts about her mother's death; the habitual silence of the aunt who raised her; the writings and newspaper clippings of a younger aunt, the 'word warrior' who urges her to 'Write the vision and make it plain'. JK plans in another novel to continue to voice 'the untold tales that wait for the telling'. *Woman in the Woods*, 1985, again holds a delicate balance of opposing moods, cultures, and elements: its first poem, 'Bird Song', tells of body and spirit ('Flung from our nests ... ordered to fly / or die we are / weaned to the air; unformed bones / and tiny beaks // that sing / inaudible songs'), the last, 'Water Song', of Christ 'who once on singing / water walked'. See JK's essays on cultural themes in *Canadian Forum*, 63, March 1984, and *Toronto Life*, Dec. 1985; interview in *Univ. of Toronto Review*, Spring 1985; on *Obasan*, P. Merivale (linking her with Anne HÉBERT) and A. Lynne Magnusson in *Canadian Literature*, 116, Spring 1988.

Kortright, Fanny (Frances) **Aikin**, 'Berkley Aikin', 1821–1900, novelist, journalist, b. London, da. of Nicholas Berkley K., Commander RN, an American by birth. She wrote leading articles for a country newspaper from 1838 and contributed serials to the *Family Herald*. In 1848 she pub. *Dreams of My Youth: Poems* as Fanny K., but used 'Berkley Aikin' for her first novel, *Anne Sherwood*, 1857, which deals evocatively with the privations of governesses and their dependence on female friendship. Then came *The Dean, or the Popular Preacher*, 1859, *The Old, Old Story*, 1862 (LCC has presentation copy to Hawthorne, whom she knew: he found the heroine 'noble'), and other novels under her own name, including *Dr Vanhomrigh*, 1870 and *A Bohemian Love Story*, 1888. Between 1868 and 1870 she edited (and mostly wrote) *The Court Suburb Magazine*, intended for the inhabitants of Kensington and containing serials, articles on e.g. wild plants of the suburb, and a strong theme of anti-feminism, dismissing Women's Rights as 'a ludicrous subject'. She expounded this theme in *Pro Aris et Focis*, 1870, pub. anon., wrongly attrib. to R. H. DAVIS. Allibone misspells her 'Kortwright'.

Kostash, Myrna, b. 1944, journalist, writer of 'creative documentary' and fiction. Da. of Ukrainian parents Mary (Maksymiuk) and William K., both teachers, she was educ. at univs. in Edmonton (where she was born and raised), Seattle and Toronto (where she took a PhD in Russian literature, 1968). She travelled in Europe for two-and-a-half years, then returned to Toronto to become a free-lance journalist, writing for *Chateleine* and *Maclean's* (a column on 'Women', 1974–5). *Her Own Woman*, 1975, repr. 1984, prints profiles of Canadian women. *All of Baba's Children*, 1977, about Ukrainian Canadians, launched her project of cultural recovery, continued in her film script, *Teach Me to Dance*, 1978, and she settled in Edmonton to 'live a Ukrainian-Canadian life'. *Long Way From Home*, 1980, examines the failure of the New Left and the 1960s generation in Canada, and *No Kidding*, 1987, based on interviews, investigates the condition of young women in a culture seeking to exploit them. See Sharon Batt in *Quill and Quire*, June 1980, and Brian Fawcett, *Books in Canada*, Oct. 1987.

Kristeva, Julia, French theorist and psychoanalyst, b. in 1941 and educ. in Bulgaria. Although intending a career in astronomy or physics, she worked as a journalist, later took up doctoral studies in Paris with Claude Lévi-Strauss, Tzvetan Todorov, Roland Barthes and Lucien Goldmann. With her novelist husband, Philippe Sollers (now divorced), she worked on the avant-garde, Maoist journal, *Tel Quel*. Her contribution to FEMINIST THEORY, though significant, is not clearly feminist. Her notion of 'the feminine' as unrepresentable, material *négativité* which traverses the limits of subject positionality, law and patriarchy, is closer to avant-garde notions of 'excess' and 'jouissance' than to feminism's historical struggle for women to achieve political equality or autonomy. But JK's 'feminine' also signifies a disruptive, transformative 'force' deriving from a biological and cultural conjunction in the maternal body. This creates a 'semiotic *Chora*' and mobilizes and spatializes the child's drive energies into a pre-linguistic organization she terms 'the semiotic', which needs to be an ordering agency, regulated by the law-like functioning of 'the symbolic'. Eventually repressed, the polymorphous semiotic resurges in poetic language. JK's analysis of avant-garde poetry distinguishes between men's and women's writing: women's proximity to the mother tongue disables rather than enables a 'revolution' in poetic language. Since woman is neither as repressed nor as securely positioned in the symbolic order as man, she risks losing her precarious hold on identity and communal language when she attempts, through writing, to recover the maternal semiotic. JK reads Maria TSVETAYEVA, Virginia WOOLF and Sylvia PLATH as 'psychotic'. Her 'semanalyses' cannot accommodate the 'semiotic motility' of women's modernist writing, dismissing it as hysterically symptomatic, on the one hand, and as anarchic, overly revolutionary, on the other. Though she champions male writers of the avant-garde, JK designates a post-feminist project for women: the 'heretical' activity of voicing the silenced experience of motherhood. *L'Hérétique (Her-ethics)* marks woman's specific socio-symbolic contract, her unique self-sacrifice or 'castration' – the bearing, birthing, nurturing of an Other – and her sublimation of maternal *'jouissance' in writing*. See JK's *La Revolution du langage poétique*, 1974 (*Revolution in Poetic Language*, 1984), *Des Chinoises*, 1974 (*About Chinese Women*, 1977), *Desire in Language*, 1980, *Pouvoirs de l'horreur*, 1980 (*Powers of Horror*, 1980), *Histoires d'amour*, 1983 (*Tales of Love*, 1987) and *Soleil noir: dépression et mélancholie*, 1987. Selection in Toril Moi, ed., *The Kristeva Reader*, 1986. Comment in Moi's introduction; also by Ann Rosalind Jones in *FR*, 18, 1984, rebutted by Jacqueline Rose in *Sexuality in the Field of Vision*, 1986. See also Elizabeth Grosz, *Sexual Subversions*, 1989.

Kumin, Maxine (Winokur), poet, novelist and writer for children. B. in 1925 in Philadelphia, da. of Doll (Simon) and pawnbroker Peter W., she attended convent school (nuns 'instilled in me tremendous anxiety' about her soul) and later received her BA, 1946, and MA, 1948, from Radcliffe College. She m. engineer Victor K. in 1946, and had three children. In 1958 she began lecturing in English, and has taught writing at several univs., including Tufts, Princeton and Columbia. *Halfway*, 1961, introduces a personal poetic voice also heard in *The Privilege*, 1965 (about her Jewish background), and *The Nightmare Factory*, 1970, written to exorcize 'a series of bad dreams about my recently dead father'. MK won a Pulitzer Prize for *Up Country*, 1972, a quiet, unsentimental celebration of her rural New England life. In *House, Bridge, Fountain, Gate*, 1975 (in memory of her friend Anne SEXTON, with whom she co-authored children's books), the everyday comfort of the title contains poems about isolation as a Jew, about death and torture: 'Let the joists of this house endure their dry rot. / Let termites push under them in their blind tunnels / thoughtfully chewing.' MK mourns Sexton in *The Retrieval System*, 1978: 'I will be years gathering up our words, / fishing out letters, snapshots, stains, / leaning my ribs against this durable cloth / to put on the dumb blue blazer of your death.' *Our Ground Time Here Will Be Brief*, 1982, addresses the pain of loss and consolation of nature. *The Long Approach*, 1985, rehearses possible scenarios of global disaster; *Nurture*, 1989, voices concern for threatened animal species. MK says that the more complex her emotion, the more strictly formal the poem must be; she enjoys being 'twitted with the epithet "Roberta Frost"'. MK has also published novels including *Through Dooms of Love*, 1965 (an adolescent girl's conflict with her father: autobiographical elements), and *The Designated Heir*, 1974 (another young heroine, raised by eccentric female relations), short stories (*Why Can't We Live Together Like Civilized Human Beings?*, 1982) and essays on poetry (*To*

Make a Prairie, 1979, and *In Deep*, 1987, a journal of rural life: 'the impulse for poems is here for me, in the vivid turn of the seasons, in the dailiness of growing things ... '). See Elaine Showalter and Carol Smith in *Women's Studies* 4, 1976; Alicia OSTRIKER, 1986. MSS at Boston Univ.

Kuzwayo, Ellen Kate (Serasengine), South African activist, 'disgruntled teacher' and autobiographer. B. 1914 on an ancestral farm in the Orange Free State, da. of Emma Mutsi (Merafe) and Phillip S., she went to a rural missionary school, then to boarding school in Natal, then to Adams College, Durban, graduating as a primary school teacher. She m. Ernest Moloto, 1941, had two sons, and divorced, 1947, marrying, 1950, Godfrey K., with whom she had a son, 1951. She studied social work, 1953–5, at the Jan Hofmeyr School of Social Work, and in 1976 accepted a post in the School of Social Work, Univ. of Witwatersrand. Active in Soweto, she was elected president of the Black Consumer Union of South Africa and twice nominated by the Johannesburg *Star* as Woman of the Year. Detained for five months on unspecified charges under the Terrorist Act, 1976, she was appointed consultant to Zamani Soweto Sisters Council, an umbrella body of Soweto women's self-help groups, 1978. A feature speaker at a 1985 Michigan conference on 'Black Women of the Diaspora', EK also helped make two films, *Awake from the Mourning*, and *Tsiamelo: A Place of Goodness*. Her autobiography, *Call Me Woman*, 1985 (preface by Nadine GORDIMER and foreword by Bessie HEAD), records changing times under Apartheid. See Carole Boyce Davies in *A Current Bibliography of African Affairs*, 19, 1986–7.

L

'L. E. L.', Letitia Elizabeth Landon, 1802–38, poet and novelist, b. London. Her mother was of the Bishop family, of Welsh extraction; her father was John L., a traveller in his youth, then partner in an army agency. She was educ. at the same Chelsea school as M. R. MITFORD and Lady Caroline LAMB. Her first poem, 'Rome', heralding a lifelong attachment to Italy, was pub. 1820 in William Jerdan's *Literary Gazette*. She soon took over the *Gazette*'s reviewing, as well as publishing increasingly ambitious poems in her collections *The Fate of Adelaide*, 1821, *The Improvisatrice*, 1824 (6 eds. by 1825), *The Troubadour*, 1825, *The Golden Violet*, 1827. Her poetry is closer to French romanticism than English, and although there are poems about the woman poet, 'a soul of romance', women generally are figured as pure, disempowered, doomed: 'Alas! that man should ever win / So sweet a shrine to shame and sin / As woman's heart!' Her contributions to albums and ANNUALS were extremely popular; she ed. *The Drawing Room Scrap Book*, but also wrote anon. for learned publications. Her friend Anna Maria HALL encouraged her to try fiction, and she pub. *Romance and Reality*, 1831, a lively rag-bag of a novel, containing set pieces on London literary society (including portraits of Edward and Rosina Bulwer LYTTON). This was followed by *Francesca Carrera*, 1834, *Ethel Churchill*, 1837, and *Duty and Inclination*, 1838. Her considerable earnings went to support her impoverished family; she lived in London among female friends, including Emma ROBERTS, and moved in literary circles. Her reputation was besmirched by rumours of an abortion; her engagement to Dickens's friend, John Forster, broken off; and in 1838 she m. George Maclean, Governor of Cape Coast Castle, travelling with him back to the Gold Coast, where she died mysteriously four months later, allegedly from taking prussic acid. Her coll. poems were pub. 1850 and 1873; her letters are uncollected. There is a *Life and Lit. Remains*, 1841, by S. Laman Blanchard, a memoir by Emma Roberts prefacing *The Zenana*, 1839; and a useful article by Germaine GREER in *TSWL*, 1 (Spring 1982).

La Fayette, Marie Madeleine Pioche de la Vergne, comtesse de, 1634–93, author of the first important novel in French. B. in Paris, da. of Elisabeth (Péna) and Marc P. de la V. (who knew Madeleine de SCUDÉRY), she studied Latin with the future Marie de SÉVIGNÉ, and learned some Hebrew. In 1655 she was married to François Mottier, comte de La F. In five years at his Auvergnat estate she bore two sons, wrote a great deal, and pub. a 'character' of Mme de Sévigné, her only work to bear her name. After that she lived mainly at Paris without her husband, often in ill health; François de La Rochefoucauld was probably her lover. She was famous in England for *The Princess of Montpensier* (1662, transl. 1666 as a true story), *The Princess of Cleves* (1678, a landmark of fiction, transl. 1679 as 'by the greatest Wits of France', 1777 by Elizabeth GRIFFITH, and 1950 by Nancy MITFORD), letters, court memoirs of 1688–9 (probably from a lost diary), and a life of Charles I's youngest daughter (begun 1664, pub. 1720, transl. 1722 by Ann Floyd). Much useful comment includes studies by Stirling Haig, 1970, and Anne Green, 1987.

Laffan, May, fl. 1874–87, Irish novelist and essayist, maternally descended from

Gerald Fitzgibbon, Master of Chancery in Ireland. She was the elder da. of Michael L., Custom House officer of Blackrock, Co. Dublin. She attacked her convent school education in her first publication, an essay in *Fraser's* (June 1874). She supported non-sectarian education, and her first novel, *Hogan M. P.*, assumed to be by a man, showed Catholics handicapped by their poor education. *The Hon. Miss Ferrard*, 1877, addressed through characters' dialogue 'educated, interested English criticism' of Home Rule and Irish attitudes to work and culture. Her most highly regarded work, *Flitters, Tatters and the Counsellor*, 1879, realistic tales of the day-to-day survival of Dublin 'street' children, ran through three Irish editions before publication in England. The 1881 Tauchnitz edition has three extra stories, including 'The Game Hen', showing women's vindictive and supportive treatment of one another in a very poor community. Her novel *Christy Carew*, 1880, implies her refusal to accept Catholic discouragement of mixed marriages. In 1882 she married Dr Walter Noel Hartley, chemistry professor at the Royal College of Science, Dublin, knighted 1911. Her story 'Katty the Flash', *Temple Bar*, June 1883, concerns two habitual Dublin prisoners, a mother and daughter whose refusal of the final act of contrition is treated sympathetically. Her last novel, *Ismay's Children*, 1887, treating Irish life, character and politics, consolidated her reputation.

Laing, Dilys (Bennett), 1906–60, poet, novelist, translator, b. in Pwllheli, North Wales, da. of Eve and civil engineer Alfred James B., whose work made her a young traveller. Because of this and her serious illnesses (she had polio at two and a mastoid infection which left her partly deaf at 12), she was educ. privately. She played talking in rhyme to her mother at two, contributed poems to newspapers at 12; from 14 to 16 she was editor of the children's page of the *Vancouver Daily Sun*. (Her family moved to Vancouver in 1915.) She studied at the Slade School of Art, London, 1926–8, then moved to Seattle. In 1936 she married poet Alexander L., settled in Vermont and chafed at domesticity: 'I'd rather be a writer than what I must be. House work exasperates me.' Some of her writing is sharply witty: 'Let us not disparage / marriage. / Even Saint Paul / after all / held that it was better to be tied / than fried'; some (more as time went on) is deeply personal and political. She became a US citizen in 1941, the year she protested, in *Another England*, the horrors and herd-instinct of war. She excoriates human cruelty, waste and homage to inhumane technologies in *Birth is Farewell*, 1944, and devises a metaphor for 'the schizophrenia of her era' (East/West Germany, North/ South Korea) in the two-headed birth in an unpublished, many-times-rewritten novel, *Corazón*. Her only published novel, *The Great Year*, 1948, counters her sense of contemporary society in an imagined unity of humanity with nature; in *Walk Through Two Landscapes*, 1949, she writes that Wordsworth 'tainted the innocent flora with an ethic, / until we know creation through a mind / weary with thought'. In 1950 DL and her husband set up 'The Responsibles' (manifesto in *The Nation*), to oppose the intensifying Cold War. A trip to Mexico, 1951, left its mark on her later poetry, broke her publishing relationship with *The New Yorker*, and generated a novel (unfinished) about the clash of Spanish and Aztec cultures. *Poems from a Cage*, 1961, contains her riposte to St Paul: 'In human need / of the familiar / I see God / woman-shaped // for God created / woman in Her own image / and I have my Pauline pride.' (She was interested both in Christianity and in eastern religions.) Previously unpublished work in *Collected Poems*, 1967 (with memoir by her son), includes feminist thought. She reproves Anne FINCH gently as 'a Sister in Error': 'To be a woman and a writer / is double mischief.... Lost lady! Gentle fighter! / Separate in time, we mutiny together.' 'Grief of the Trojan Women' ends: 'women! despair / of man's intent. / No more lament. / War on war.' MSS at Brown Univ. and elsewhere.

Lamb, Lady **Caroline** (Ponsonby), 1785–1828, novelist and poet. Da. of Henrietta Frances (sister of Georgiana DEVONSHIRE) and Frederick P., 3rd Earl of Bessborough, brought up in cultured, bohemian circles and taught by Frances ROWDEN, she said she 'ought to have been a soldier'; her mother, who had sons and wanted a feminine daughter, worried over her wild passions and self-will. In 1805 she m. William Lamb, later Lord Melbourne, an early sweetheart; her one surviving child was retarded. She melodramatized her notorious affair with Byron (begun in 1812) in the wildly popular *Glenarvon* (1816; facs. NY 1972; repr. [1865] as *The Fatal Passion*: see Joseph Garver in *Irish Univ. Rev.*, 10, 1980). Lady HOLLAND (a victim, along with all her family) accurately called it a farrago. Other writings (all anonymous except the lyrics pub. by Isaac Nathan with Byron's *Fugitive Pieces*, 1829) have more merit: her *New Canto* to Byron's *Don Juan*, 1819, fizzes with verbal inventiveness, as do her letters. *Graham Hamilton* (written 1820, pub. 1822) looks with realism and feeling at an obsessive fine-lady gambler (who shares her married name with Frances BURNEY's first heroine), through the dazzled eyes of a middle-class admirer. *Ada Reis*, 1823, moving from the Mediterranean to South America, invests the struggle of good and evil with genuine exotic awe. CL was a friend of Sydney MORGAN and Elizabeth BENGER. Lives by Elizabeth JENKINS, 1932, Henry Blyth, 1972; see also family letters and works on the men in her life, including Rosina LYTTON's husband.

Lamb, Mary Anne, 1764–1847, CHILDREN'S writer, b. in the Temple, London, da. of Elizabeth (Field) and John L., both of labouring-class origin. After leaving school she learned the trade of dressmaking. In 1796 a quarrel involving an apprentice revealed her instability: she stabbed and killed her crippled mother, whose nursing had long confined her to home. Her younger brother Charles managed to limit her asylum incarceration to three years and some later periods; between times she was sane, witty, and sociable. They lived together and jointly wrote the well-known *Tales from Shakespeare*, 1807 (all Mary's but the tragedies, though by error of the publisher, WOLLSTONECRAFT's widower Godwin, only Charles's name appeared); *Mrs. Leicester's School* [1808] (seven of the tales ML's, some movingly based on life), and *Poetry for Children*, 1809. ML's 'On Needle-Work' (*British Ladies' Magazine*, 1815) voices muted protest about both working and genteel women's lives (see Jane Aaron in *Prose Studies*, 10, 1987–8). Other poems (in periodicals and in Charles's *Works*, 1818), listed in Claude A. Prance, *Companion to Charles Lamb*, 1983. Most studies make her a footnote to Charles: see Ernest Ross, 1940; their letters ed. Edwin W. Marrs, Jr, 1975–8.

Lamb, Myrna Lila, actress and playwright, b. 1930 in Newark, NJ, to working-class parents, Minna Pansy (Feldman) and Melvin Adolph Aaron L., a band musician and sergeant in the National Guard. She wrote a play at eight and a column for the *NJ Herald* at 15, was 'married at seventeen, pregnant at eighteen and a mother at nineteen'. She began her acting career at 20, worked at other jobs, joined the peace and civil rights movements, and took classes at the New School for Social Research and Rutgers Univ. ML (who, says Megan TERRY, 'had never written a play before she saw *Viet Rock*', 1966) then helped the emergence of the New Feminist Repertory Theatre, which encouraged and produced her early short plays. The six collected as *The Mod Donna and Scyklon Z: Plays of Women's Liberation*, 1971, include *But What Have You Done for Me Lately* (produced for abortion and socialist groups, 1969 and 1970) in which a pregnant man begs a woman doctor for an abortion. ML says this 'piece of agit-prop' grew from an experience with her teenage daughter. *Mod Donna*, staged 1970, parodies daytime TV, with commercials and a soap-opera of corrupt marital sex and a female scapegoat, to comment from a chorus of feminists and a closing cry of 'Liberation'. One of the earliest high-profile feminist plays, it aroused much controversy. *I Lost a Pair of Gloves Yesterday*, a brief monologue by a woman scarred by her father's death, is pub. in Honor Moore, ed., *The New Women's Theatre*, 1977. Among ML's musicals, *Apple Pie*, staged 1976, depicts the trial of a Jewish woman (whose 'crime' in an anti-semitic and sexist society is her very existence). Women's Interart Theatre have put on several of her plays, including *Crab Quadrille* (comedy), 1976, *Olympic Park* ('memory play'), 1978, and *Yesterday is Over* (musical), 1980. See Vivian Patraka in *Women and Performance*, 1984.

Lambert, Anne Thérèse de Marguenat de Courcelles, marquise de, 1647–1733, French ADVICE writer, b. in Paris, da. of Monique (Passart) and finance minister de C., who d. during her childhood. Educated by her step-father, she m., 1666, Henri L., whose death in 1686 plunged her in lawsuits on behalf of her children. Financially secure from 1710, she ran a distinguished Paris salon and was the intimate friend of Fontenelle. Her works circulated in MS; she feared contempt as a woman writer and was said to deplore her first publication, 1727. This was her essay on the 'Fair Sex', englished in 1729, as were her letters of advice to son and daughter. Her English *Works*, 1769, include more essays, letters, characters, guardedly feminist opinions, and a short novel, 'The Fair Solitary, or Female Hermit' (who gives up the world after her secretly favoured lover perishes in a duel). Their fame was at its height when Jane AUSTEN owned them; translators include Eliza HAYLEY.

Lambert, Betty (Lee), also Elizabeth, Minnie, 1933–83, writer of children's and adults' plays, novelist. B. in Calgary, Alberta, da. of Bessie Mildred (Cooper) and Christopher Thomas Lee, she m. Frank L. in 1952 (divorced 1960) and had a daughter. As 'Betty Lee' she started publishing poetry at 13. Offered a scholarship for a short story ('The Unloved', 1950), she attended the summer creative writing programme of the Banff School of Fine Arts, Alberta, and in 1956 she received the Macmillan Publishers, Canada, award for the short story 'A Woman in Love'. She attended the Univ. of British Columbia (BA in philosophy, 1957), then travelled extensively through England, Mexico and France, and studied ancient Greek theatre in Epidaurus, Greece. Upon her return to Canada and until her death from cancer, she wrote over 30 plays for radio, TV and the stage, most produced by CBC from 1958. From 1965 until her death, she taught English at Simon Fraser Univ., BC. *Crossings*, 1979 (repr. in the US as *Bring Down the Sun*, 1980), a self-reflexive novel, portrays the physical and sexual abuse of a woman writer: 'I come to this now, like a lover. Guiltily, as if it were sinful. The book'. This same racy quality is displayed in many of her plays, such as *Sqrieux-de-Dieu*, 1976, where a housewife with four children swaps places with her husband's mistress. Other published plays include *Song of the Serpent*, 1973, a children's play, *Clouds of Glory*, 1979, a philosophical comedy, and *Jennie's Story*, 1981. See Aritha VAN HERK in Smaro Kamboureli and Shirley Neuman, eds., *A Mazing Space*, 1986.

'Lancaster, G.B.', Edith Joan Lyttleton, 1874–1925, novelist and short-story writer. B. in Tasmania, da. of Emily and Westcott McNab L., she was brought to NZ, 1878, and educ. in Canterbury. Her *Sons o'*

Men, 1904, *The Spur to Smite*, 1905, and *The Tracks We Tread*, 1907, set on South Island sheep stations, are tales of male endurance and courage, brutality and drunkenness, influenced by Kipling. With delicate feminine heroines worthy of male worship on their periphery, they show no sign of a woman author, but they are vivid and realistic in their portrayal and acceptance of the physical brutality, viciousness and degradation of the 'cowboy' life. *Altar Stairs*, 1908, is set in New Caledonia – a tale of white men's brutality to the Kanak, and the usurpation of the land, but told with a complete acceptance of imperialism and lack of racial awareness: 'the fight's the thing' is the only standard. In 1910 she went to England, and travelled through north-west Canada, the Yukon, Cuba and Australia, setting further novels in wild frontier areas. *Pageant*, 1933, set in Tasmania, and *Promenade*, 1938, set in NZ, are historical novels. Popular at the time, several were filmed in the 1920s. See life by F. A. de la Mare, 1945 (for private circulation).

Lancaster, Lydia (Rawlinson), 1683–1761, 'living, clear, and powerful' Quaker preacher, b. at Graithwaite, Lancs, da. of QUAKERS, Dorothy (Hutton) and Thomas R. She was early pious, but at 14 'withstood' a call to speak at a meeting, causing ten years' bitter suffering 'by my exceedng unwillingness to be what I should be'. In 1708 she 'came forth in public' and 'it was all got over, and I got peace'. She travelled to America, 1718, and all over Britain, although this 'was sometimes pretty trying, not having such care taken at home in my absence as might have been desired'. Her marriage (1706, to Brian L.) was said to be unhappy. Her farewell sermon was pub. *c.* 1738, and extracts of her letters, 1840. Loving solitude all her life, she found her old age at Lancaster peaceful and blessed. She desired the advance of women and (even more) that of Truth; she was at Penrith Yearly Meeting, 1757 (having 'felt the strong cords of his drawing') when it removed local objections to women's PREACHING.

Lane, Elinor (Macartney), 1864–1909, novelist, editor and short-story writer, b. Maryland, da. of Elizabeth (Kirkpatrick) and Nicholas M. She was educ. at Washington High School and Washington Normal School. She began writing at 16, principally short stories of Southern life. In 1891 she m. Dr Francis Ransom L. In 1901 she started the *Trifler Magazine* and wrote her first historical novel, *Mills of God* (which received excellent reviews). Its heroine, Elinor Delany, a woman of passionate temperament and strong intellect who 'fears no man', is disillusioned with her marriage to an ageing husband. Sexually awakened by the dashing young Lord Henry Bedford, to whom she bears a son, Elinor sustains her wrong marriage and her love bond. In *Nancy Stair*, 1904, EL's adoption of a male narrator (Nancy's father) allows the full force of her heroine's male-dominated world to be felt. While Nancy's father believes in the efficacy of a 'man's education' for inculcating male virtues of 'bravery, honesty, self-knowledge' and self-responsibility, his opponents claim that 'you can't educate a woman, can't give her any sense of abstract right or wrong . . . women are not intended to be civilised'. Nancy acts as a self-appointed advocate, defending a destitute widow-mother, and thereby enforcing on men a very clear sense of right and wrong. In *Katrine*, 1909, the gifted and unconventional Katrine Dulany becomes a celebrated opera star, but she is finally presented, like Nancy Stair, as the orthodox romantic heroine who 'threw a world away' for love.

Lane, Millicent (**Travis**), poet and critic. B. in 1934 in San Antonio, Texas, da. of Elsie (Ward) and William T. , she became a Canadian citizen, 1973, and now lives in Fredericton, NB, with her professor husband Lauriat Lane, Jr. (m. 1957), and their two children. Educ. at Vassar (BA 1956) and Cornell (MA 1957, PhD 1967), she has taught English at Cornell and at the Univ. of New Brunswick. Widely anthologized, beginning with her publication in *Five Poets: Cornell 1960*, MTL has received the Pat LOWTHER Prize (1980). Called a 'magnificent reminder of what words can do', *An Inch or So of Garden*, 1969, and *Poems 1968–1972*, 1973, often wittily composed in traditional rhythms and rhymes, express a strong humanistic vision informed by a mythic consciousness and subtle religious tone. The pastoral world she evokes is permeated by her contemporary sensibility – 'For me no antiquated stars. / My radar's mystic: all is green. / The sea noise deafens. Shall I make / sea-anchor in unsounded seas? The echoes break / the echo-graph'. It is often grounded in her maritime landscape. In *Homecomings*, 1977, narrative poems craftily rewrite old myths. 'The Witch of the Inner Wood' (*Reckonings*, 1988) situates the poet in relation to nature's transformations. MTL's publications also include numerous essays on Canadian literature.

Lane, Rose (Wilder), 1887?–1968, novelist, short-story writer, journalist. Da. of pioneers Laura (Ingalls) WILDER and Almanzo W., she was b. in De Smet, S. Dakota, and raised near Mansfield in the Ozark Mountains, setting of many of her novels. Educ. at a one-room school and high-school at Crowley, La, she worked as a telegraph operator in Kansas City, m. Gillette L. in 1909 in San Francisco, and ran a real-estate business with him until 1915. She then worked as a reporter on the SF *Bulletin*, divorced in 1918, and published lives of Henry Ford, 1917, and Herbert Hoover, 1920. She wrote about her travels in Europe and the Near East, 1920ff., for the Red Cross, in newspaper articles and *The Peaks of Shala*, 1922. *Travels with Zenobia*, written jointly with Helen Dore BOYLSTON, pub. 1983, reports their trip to Albania by model T Ford in 1926. RWL's short stories 'Innocence', 1922, 'Yarbwoman', 1927 (both with Southern settings), and 'Old Maid', 1933, won awards or anthology printing. She began writing about the Ozarks in *Hill-Billy*, 1925. *Let the Hurricane Roar*, 1933, and *Free Land*, 1938 (novels), stress the courage of Dakota pioneers facing intolerable conditions, while stories collected in *Old Home Town*, 1935 (notably the overtly feminist 'Immoral Woman'), dwell on midwest women's stultifying small-town existence. RWL also encouraged and organized the career of her mother. RWL's growing conservatism and opposition to the New Deal led her away from fiction to books like *Give Me Liberty*, 1936, and *The Discovery of Freedom*, 1943, and to journalism jobs. For *Woman's Day* she wrote a book on needlework as female art, 1963, and reported the Vietnam war, 1965. She spent her last years on a farm at Danbury, Conn. Roger Lea MacBride has ed. letters of hers and her mothers, 1973 and 1974, and her 'fictionalized autobiography', *Her Story*, 1977. Other letters at West Branch (Iowa), Syracuse Univ., and Berkeley. Several works in recent reprints.

Langer, Susanne Katharine (Knauth), 1895–1985, philosopher, b. NYC, da. of Else (Uhlich) and lawyer Antonio K., educ. at Radcliffe College (AB 1920, AM 1924, PhD 1926). In 1921 she m. William L. Langer and began a year's study at the Univ. of Vienna; she had two sons and later divorced. Her *Cruise of the Little Dipper* [1923] is a fairy-tale book. She taught at Radcliffe, 1927–42, then at other univs., and had several honorary degrees. After *The Practice of Philosophy*, 1930, she published *Introduction to Symbolic Logic*, 1937 (dedicated to her mother), as a guide to 'a relatively new subject'. Her *Philosophy in a New Key, A Study in the Symbolism of Reason, Rite, and Art*, 1942, declares her interest in topics so far neglected. It quotes Jane HARRISON and respectfully contradicts Mary KINGSLEY about primitive people's speech. It became the prelude to *Feeling and Form, A Theory of Art*, 1953; SL became a mother of semiotics. Whether translating Ernst Cassirer's *Language and Myth*, 1946, editing her own and others' essays, or writing *Problems of Art*, 1957, and *Philosophical Sketches*, 1962, dedicated to her sister, she dwells on sign and symbol, and stresses the importance of art and feeling ('emotion and abstraction'), in shaping human individuality. Her massive *Mind: An Essay on Human Feeling*, 3 vols., 1967–82, dedicated to her grandchildren in hopes of 'the great World Peace', completed despite increasng blindness, discusses with great learning beasts and humans, science, magic and death. Several recent reprints; study by Ranjan K. Ghosh, 1979.

Langley, Eve, 1908–74, novelist, b. near Forbes, NSW, da. of Mira (Davidson) and Arthur L. She was educ. mainly near Forbes, although the family moved throughout Victoria before going to NZ. EL went to NZ in 1932 where she m. art teacher Hilary Clark and had three children. After unsuccessful attempts at bean and pea growing, she worked as a proof-reader, freelance journalist, and a librarian, and began publishing verse and short stories. In 1942 she was placed in an Auckland psychiatric hospital where she remained for seven years. Returning to Australia, she played an active part in the Sydney literary scene before becoming a recluse in the Blue Mountains. An eccentric who believed herself to be a reincarnation of Oscar Wilde, her habits during this latter period include adopting male dress, wearing a white topi and carrying a sheath knife. Her two pub. novels are *The Pea Pickers*, 1941, and *White Topi*, 1954. *The Pea Pickers*, which shared the *Bulletin*'s S. H. Prior Prize, is a picaresque account of the adventures of Steve and her sister, Blue, two women who wander the Victorian countryside dressed as labourers. The novel is chiefly concerned with the conflict between Steve's desire for intellectual fulfilment and her desire to be loved, issues which are taken up again in *White Topi*. Biography by Joy Thwaite, 1989; MSS are in the Mitchell Library, Sydney.

Langton, Anne, 1805–93, diarist, letter-writer, painter, pioneer. B. in England, the da. of Ellen (Currer) and Thomas L., a merchant, she was educ. at home and in Switzerland and studied painting in Rome. In 1837 she migrated, with her parents and a maternal aunt, to Canada, joining her brother John, later Canada's Auditor-General, in the backwoods north of Peterborough, Ont. Her father died within a year. She wrote her letters and journals (*A Gentlewoman in Upper Canada*, ed. H. H. Langton, 1950), for a brother in England. They form an important, lively record of the courage, intelligence, initative, and good humour of three pioneer women. With matter-of-fact acceptance, they describe daily life (soap-and candle-making, washing, baking, butchery, gardening, sewing, repairing screens; failing in spite of a constant roaring fire to keep the bedroom temperature above 8°F.; preparing dinner for 26 in primitive conditions). Occasionally, AL protests: 'perhaps you would think my feminine manners in danger if you were to see me steering a boat for my gentleman rowers ... but don't be alarmed ... my woman's avocations will always, I think, more than counterbalance. ... I have caught myself wishing an old long-forgotten wish that I had been born of the rougher sex'. AL describes the developing community spirit as the settlement expands. In 1839 she began to teach children three days a week. After the deaths of her mother and aunt in 1846 she visited England for three years, then rejoined John's family, moving with them to Toronto, Québec and Ottawa.

Langton, Jane (Gillson), writer and illustrator of mysteries and children's books. She was b. in 1922 in Boston, da. of Grace (Brown) and Joseph Lincoln G. She went to Wellesley College, took a BS in astronomy at the Univ. of Michigan, 1944, then an MA in art history there, 1945, and also at Radcliffe College, 1948, before going on to graduate study at the Boston Museum of Art, 1958–9. In 1943, she m. William L., a physicist, with whom she has three sons. Claiming inspirarion from Dorothy SAYERS, she writes in a classic tradition involving tight plots, witty urbane investigators and villains, and richly informative subject-matter. Her first mystery, *The Minuteman Murder* (originally *The Transcendental Murder*, 1964), deals with the lives of Henry David Thoreau and Emily DICKINSON (on whose poems she wrote an 'appreciation', 1980). *Dark Nantucket Noon*, 1975, explores the natural history of the island; *The Memorial Hall Murder*, 1978, involves a rehearsal of Handel's *Messiah*; and *Natural Enemy*, 1982, treats ecology and the desecration of nature. Her series characters, Homer Kelly, who comes into the first novel fresh from writing a book on Emerson, and Mary Morgan, are, by the second novel, married and co-authoring a book on Thoreau. In *Emily Dickinson is Dead*, 1984, JL returns to her earliest interest. JL's first book, *The Majesty of Grace*, 1961, initiated a sequence of nine children's novels, one of which, *The Fledgling*, 1980, earned a Newbery Award. She has taught writing for children, reviews it in the *New York Times Book Review* and elsewhere, and continues to illustrate her books with her own pen and ink drawings. Interview in John C. Carr, *Craft of Crime*, 1983.

Lansdell, Sarah, c. 1778–after 1816, novelist, of Tenterden, Kent. At 18, despite 'confined education' and awe at the excellent works 'of RADCLIFFE's [sic], SMITH's, BENNETT's [later struck out] and BURNEY's', she 'almost by stealth completed in 12 days' *Manfredi, Baron St Osmund, An Old English Romance*, MINERVA, 1796, with illustrations. Ignorance of the world set her 'under the necessity of laying her scene in the days of old, when murder stalked abroad' and superstition was rife. In 1809 she struck out her place of residence and added a MS apology for the 'puerile work' (Bodlein copy). *The Tower, or The Romance of Ruthyne*, 1798, deploys almost every possible GOTHIC motif including an imprisoned wife and a mysterious poem, in female handwriting, testifying grief and despair. It was charged with plagiarism from John Palmer's *Mystery of the Black Tower*, 1796, one of the same sub-genre. SL promised she would write better than this in time; but no more works are known.

Lanyer, Aemilia (Bassano), 1569–1645, poet, da. of Margaret (Johnson) and an Italian musician, Baptista B., who d. when she was seven. Well educ. in a noble household, she became mistress to Lord Hunsdon, Shakespeare's patron; when pregnant in 1592 she married another musician, Alfonso L. (d. 1613), who 'consumed her goods'. She consulted Simon Forman, astrologer, in 1597. In 1611 she pub. with her name, clearly to raise funds, *Salve Deus Rex Judaeorum* ('Hail God, King of the Jews'). Her bold and sensitive central poem on Christ's death is flanked by shorter poems to great ladies (several of them writers), a strongly feminist prose address to the reader, and the earliest known English country-house poem, about the loss, rather than ownership, of Cookham, estate of Lady Anne CLIFFORD's mother. *Salve* depicts Adam and Pilate each misusing his masculine prerogative; Pilate's wife's vain attempt to forestall disaster introduces spirited defence of Eve (as bearing much blame properly deserved by Adam). Christ, done to death by men, is comforted by women, his human sufferings movingly depicted. AL ran a school for children of the gentry and nobility, 1617–19. A. L. Rowse, who thinks she was Shakespeare's 'dark lady', ed. her poems, 1978. See Barbara K. Lewalski in Margaret P. Hannay, ed., 1985; Elaine V. Beilin, 1987.

Lanyon, Carla Lanyon, 1906–71, poet, novelist, painter, b. in Co. Down, Northern Ireland, da. of Helen (Redfern), who published a volume of verse about Ireland, and Charles James L., a flax broker. She was privately educ. *The Wanderer*, 1926, introduces elements which recur in her later poetry volumes: archaic language, traditional forms, rural settings with nature as catalyst for the poet's memories and emotions, conflict between wanderlust and duty, Christian belief (Anglican) sometimes held with difficulty and sometimes related to a quest motif, and human mutability. She m. Edward Sidney Hacker, a lecturer and later a brigadier, in 1927, lived in England, had three children, and exhibited flower paintings at a Paris Salon and her own London exhibition, 1934. Her novel *Penelope*, 1942, is a mother's journal (written for her prisoner-of-war husband) of unchosen wartime independence, isolation and domestic hardship. *Salt Harvest: The Autobiography of an Englishman*, 1947, is a first-person narrative poem. CLL won the Greenwood poetry prize, 1961. *Uncompromising Gladness*, 1968, has poems on mortality ('each man, at the last / Lets slip his spar and goes to death by drowning'), the environment ('Housing Schemes'), the gender gap ('He moves about the room / Dignified, calm'; she 'knows that, intimately, / The act of love is neither calm nor dignified'). It also includes a one-act play, 'The Commiserators', in which a recent widow receives advice 'cluttered by clichés and plastered with platitudes', and learns that in society 'women are acceptable with any husband / Except a dead one.'

Larcom, Lucy, 1824–93, poet, critic, teacher and mill girl, b. at Beverly, Mass. Her merchant sea-captain father died early, leaving ten children nearly impoverished. His widow, Lois Barrett L., moved the family to Lowell to become a supervisor in a dormitory for mill girls. After grade school, from age 11, LL worked for ten years in the Lowell mills. In 1846 she went to the Illinois prairies as a teacher and then attended Monticello Seminary in Godfrey, Ill., 1849–52. In 1854 she returned east to teach at Wheaton Seminary, Norton, Mass., for eight years, before beginning a career of magazine editing (*Our Young Folks*, 1865–73), publishing anthologies of verse, four vols. of her own verse from 1867, and a critical book, *Landscape of American Poetry*, 1879. Neither a feminist nor a women's rights reformer, LL thought of herself primarily as a poet: 'My "must-have" was poetry. From the first, life meant that to me' (*Girlhood*, 1889). LL's verse emphasizes nature, religion, and domestic incidents. She wrote of her early mill experience in *An Idyl* [sic] *of Work*, 1875; 'Among Lowell Mill-Girls', *Atlantic Monthly*, 1881; and *A New England Girlhood*, 1889. See Daniel Dudley Addison, *Lucy Larcom: Life, Letters and Diary*, 1894; life by Shirley Marchalonis, 1989.

Larpent, Anna Margaretta (Porter), diarist, da. of Sir James P. (a diplomat: not brother of the novelist PORTERS). She began at 15 to note daily events: 'I observed much, talked little .... As I grew older I wrote better, judged better – the Employment delighted me, and gave a Spirit to all my occupations'. In 1782, becoming second wife of John L., Examiner of plays, she dedicated to him and her sister a 'Methodized' version of her journal, inviting him: 'Live over my life in this book ... praise me where you can. Condemn me where you must: But *love* me every where if you can.' She continued 'at any odd moment' to record her routine and wide reading (many women, including Lady Rachel RUSSELL). A penetrating, outspoken theatre critic, she admired Elizabeth INCHBALD, saw not 'the least Immorality' in *Lovers' Vows*, but disapproved amateur actresses as indelicate. The diary (carefully indexed) ends in 1830, after John L.'s death, on her disposal of his collection of play MSS (now, with the DIARY, in the Huntington Library). L. W.

Conolly's study of John L., 1976, reveals her as 'practically a Deputy Examiner', who licensed, censored, sometimes initialled.

Larsen, Nella Marian, 1891?–1964, novelist, b. in Chicago to a Danish mother and West Indian father. He d. when she was two; she had a white stepfather and half-sister. She studied at a white private school, Fisk Univ., Tenn. (education), the Univ. of Copenhagen, and the Lincoln School for Nurses, NYC (graduating 1915); nursed in Tuskegee, Ala., and NYC; then became a librarian. In 1919 she married a noted black university scientist, Elmer Samuel Imes. In 1926 *The Brownies' Book*, i, printed her two pseudonymous stories about white characters; an autobiographical sketch she wrote them omits her parents' names. Her first novel, *Quicksand*, 1928 (written at speed), was a hit: its heroine re-enacts NL's own movement between opposing forces and places, beginning in 'a surge of hot anger and seething resentment' at a black congregation's tame complicity in a white preacher's praise of their moderation, ending in 'deep and contemptuous hatred' of her Southern black preacher husband, whose fifth child she is about to bear. *Passing*, 1929, gives two mixed-race women (each ambivalent about her sexuality and her black roots) an ending of rage and violence. NL's story 'Sanctuary' (*Forum*, Jan. 1930) was charged with plagiarism from Sheila KAYE-SMITH; she defended herself in *Forum* in April. That year she had a Guggenheim award to write a novel about blacks in Europe and the USA; it and later works, including a joint project with a young white man, 1933, were unfinished. Divorced that year, she went back to nursing in 1941 when Imes' death ended her alimony. See Hortense E. Thornton, Mary Mabel Youman, in *CLA Journal*, 16, 18, 1973, 1974; novels ed. Deborah E. McDowell, 1986.

Laski, Marghanita, 1915–88, socialist, journalist, novelist and broadcaster, da. of Phina (Gaster) and Neville G. L. (a judge): niece of writer Harold L., and granddaughter of a Chief Rabbi of Portuguese and Spanish Jews in England. She was educ. in Manchester (Ladybarn House School), London (St Paul's Girls' School, from 13 to 16), and studied fashion design before going to Somerville, Oxford (BA in English, 1936, specializing in Anglo-Saxon). She became a journalist, m. publisher John E. Howard, and during WWII had several jobs and two children. Her novels, *Love on the Supertax*, 1944, *To Bed with Grand Music*, 1948 (as 'Sarah Russell'), and *Tory Heaven*, 1948, present middle- and upper-class women leading lives determined by their relations with men, in a society whose class structure disallows any viable moral code. *Victorian Tales for Girls*, 1947, comments sympathetically and perceptively on a now alien habit of idealization. ML published several children's books. Her treatments of authors – including Juliana EWING, Mary Louisa MOLESWORTH and Frances Hodgson BURNETT, 1950, repr. 1976, Jane AUSTEN, 1969, repr. 1986, George ELIOT, 1973, and Rudyard Kipling, 1974 – focus on the emotional and social. Her anti-nuclear play, *The Offshore Island*, 1959, anatomizes British society, as do two further novels; two studies of the phenomenon of ecstasy, 1961 and 1980, approach both religious and secular experiences in a spirit of quasi-scientific investigation. An expert witness in the *Lady Chatterley's Lover* trial of 1959, ML wrote for *The Times* and *TLS*, broadcast frequently, chaired Arts Council and other committees, and wielded influence over public funding of literature and the arts in Britain. She sent in more than 250,000 wordslips to the editors of the *OED*.

'Lathen, Emma', Martha Hennissart and Mary J. Latsis, also 'R. B. Dominic', mystery writers, ML, b. in 1927 in Oak Park, Ill., finished a graduate degree in economics at Harvard, where she met MH, a law student. They identified a shared admiration for 'classic' DETECTIVE FICTION (Agatha CHRISTIE, Dorothy SAYERS Josephine TEY), decided to be 'classics in our own time', made a pen-name from their own, staked their territory as 'white-collar homicide' or business crime and invented John Putnam Thatcher, a chief trust officer of Sloan Bank on Wall Street. For years they gulled the world: C. P. Snow's admiration of EL as 'the best living writer of American detective stories' is widely quoted. Now they have won satisfied complicity from critics, who speak of the fictional EL as one, real person. Since *Banking on Death*, 1961, they have collaborated on more than 25 mysteries, writing alternate chapters: first devising major points of plot (including corpses and perpetrators), then roughly outlining, then revising for inconsistencies. They mix satire (sometimes fierce, as in *A Stitch in Time*, 1968, about medical malpractice), and expert knowledge. *Murder to Go*, 1969, is about the fast-food industry; *Murder Without Icing*, 1972, about ice-hockey; *The Longer the Thread*, 1971, about the garment industry; *Sweet and Low*, 1974, about duplicity in the cocoa futures market. *Green Grow the Dollars*, 1982, is the most recent EL. In a second series, as by 'R. B. Dominic', Ohio Congressman Ben Stafford deals with criminal mayhem in government and politics: see *A Flaw in the System*, 1982, and *Unexpected Developments*, 1984. *Murder Against the Grain*, 1966, thought EL's 'wittiest and most compassionate book', dealing with grain trade between the USA and the USSR, won an Edgar award. Jane Bakerman thinks EL 'the best social critic and ironist this country has produced since Edith WHARTON' (*Armchair Detective*, 9, 1976); C. P. Snow's comparison with Balzac is germane. Both conducted independent professional careers; asked whether, when they started, women had a harder time getting higher pay and promotions, ML replied, 'Did you just think these were fancies in someone's mind?' On the mostly male population of EL novels, MH said, 'Using a male protagonist was an accurate observation of the world as it existed. None of the vice-presidents of the Chase Manhattan were female.' Interview in John C. Carr, *The Craft of Crime*, 1983; see Jeanne F. Bedell in Bargainnier, 1981.

Lathrop, Rose (Hawthorne) 'Mother Alphonsa', 1851–1926, writer, philanthropist, b. Lenox, Mass., third and youngest child of Sophia (Peabody) and novelist Nathaniel H. Educ. mainly by parents and at art schools in Dresden and London, in 1871 she m. writer George Parsons L. Their only child d. in 1881 aged four. They became Roman Catholics in 1891 but in 1895 they separated, and she devoted herself to the care of destitute cancer patients. She joined the Dominican Order where, in 1901, she became Mother Alphonsa, running two hospices in NY State and City. Her one vol. of poetry, *Along the Shore*, 1888, is unspectacular and morbid. Less conventional are *A Story of Courage*, 1894, a history of the Georgetown Convent which she wrote with her husband, the magazine recording her work with cancer patients, *Christ's Poor*, 1901–4, and *Reports of the Servants of Relief for Incurable Cancer*, 1908–22. Her best work, *Memories of Hawthorne*, 1897, displays her sensitivity in summoning up a personality, especially her father's: 'he had a delicate way of throwing himself into the scrimmage of laughter . . .' Her biography is by Katherine Burton in *Sorrow Built a Bridge*, 1938; also T. Maynard, *A Fire Was Lighted*, 1948, and J.J. Walsh, *Mother Alphonsa*, 1930.

La Tourette, Aileen, novelist, short-story writer, playwright, b. 1946 at Somerville, NJ, eldest of seven in a Catholic family. Her education included a year at Oxford; she migrated to London in 1968 and became a journalist. She married in 1970, had two sons and worked as a waitress, lecturer and script-writer; she lives with a lesbian partner. She has written radio plays (*Dial-a-Poem, The Elephant and the Panda*, and *Down to Earth*); *Risking Night, Testing Dreams* was staged in Bristol, 1982. Her work appears in Jo Garcia and Sara MAITLAND, eds., *Walking on the Water*, 1983, in Adam Mars-Jones, ed., *Mae West is Dead*, 1983 (lesbian and gay fiction), and *Weddings and Funerals*, 1984. This volume (with Maitland) opens and closes with 'The Triangular Eye', in which ALT relates an abortive wedding and a death in the voices of the bride (later the dying woman), the ex-lover (female) who attends the reception and abducts her, and the photographer (female) who records. *Nuns and Mothers*, 1984, is a first-person, part-autobiographical novel of lesbian love and parting, and family relations (nuns cherish female children when mothers reject them). *Cry Wolf*, 1988, takes place after a nuclear disaster which five women tried to prevent by telling stories to the military: the last of them, daughter of a Greenham Common martyr, foster-daughter of a social outcast, professor of theology in the new, ignorant world, at last consents to reveal the untold history she has witnessed.

Latter, Mary, 1722–77, miscellaneous writer, da. of Mary and George L. (an attorney), b. at Frilsham, Berks., living and publishing at Reading. At 18 she denied, in verse in the *Reading Mercury* (see LE NOIR), writing satire on local ladies. In [1759] she pub. by name *Miscellaneous Works in Prose and Verse*; letters, an essay after Henry Fielding, poetic 'Soliloquies on Temporal Indigence' and a free-verse piece on material and spiritual poverty which resolves to accept the will of heaven. From 17 years earlier come tales and discussions of love; she is now immersed in business and debt, 'wishing Jupiter to rain me a Shower of Gold; sometimes madly hoping to gain a Competency; sometimes justly fearing Dungeons and Distress!' *A Miscellaneous Poetical Essay*, with 100 subscribers, 1761, relates her happy, poetry-reading youth, her being 'Plunder'd and stript' by 'Legal fraud', her hope for Content. John Rich of Covent Garden liked her tragedy *The Siege of Jerusalem*, advised revision, invited her to London to get to know the stage and to do writing jobs for him. His death prevented production; the play failed at Reading and was later rejected by Garrick; pub. 1763, with an angry preface on critics, managers, and the slavery a woman finds in writing for bread. ML's spirited burlesque poem *Liberty and Interest*, 1764, was widely praised (part repr. in the *GM*); *Pro and Con, or the Opinionists*, 1771 (which says it will not imitate Sterne, but does, satirically and defensively), was badly reviewed.

Laurence, Jean **Margaret** (Wemyss), 1926–87, novelist, short-story writer, essayist, political activist. B. in Neepawa, Man., the town that inspired her fictional Manawaka, to Verna (Simpson) and solicitor Robert Harrison W., she lost both parents early and was raised by an aunt, Margaret Campbell Simpson. She was writing as a child: private stories and pieces in school magazines. She graduated from United College (now the Univ. of Winnipeg) in 1947 and became a journalist on the socialist *Winnipeg Citizen*. That year she married engineer Jack L.; they moved to England, 1949, and soon afterwards to Somalia and Ghana, where they lived until 1957. She translated a volume of Somali poetry and prose (*A Tree for Poverty*, 1954) and wrote an African novel (*This Side Jordan*, 1960), African stories (*The Tomorrow-Tamer*), and a memoir of her time in Somaliland (*The Prophet's Camel Bell*), both 1963. Separated from her husband (divorced 1969), she lived in Vancouver, then (1962–73) at Great Missenden, Bucks., England, where she wrote her first Canadian novel, *The Stone Angel*, 1964. This monologue of an unbending, infuriating, 90-year-old Manawaka matriarch ends unpunctuated at the speaker's death. It made an immediate critical impression, and was followed by four more books about the same community. In the paired novels *A Jest of God*, 1966 (reissued as *Rachel,*

Rachel, title of the film version), and *The Fire-Dwellers*, 1969, the two daughters of the town's undertaker (spinster teacher and housewife mother) each learns to name and confront the terms of her own unfreedom. *A Bird in the House*, 1970, a volume of linked stories, was, said ML, based on her own youth. After settling at Lakefield, Ont., she published *The Diviners*, 1974, a spacious novel which translates experience into art by various formal devices including the admonitory voice of Catherine Parr TRAILL. The narrator, brought up by Manawaka's most marginal couple, explores a web of painful connectedness among Canadian individuals (Scots, French, Native) and their competing national myths. Its unfudged depiction of abortion and of a casual, frightening sexual encounter provoked its banning from Ontario public schools, a painful irony to a writer calling herself both moral and Christian. ML also published children's stories, a study of Nigerian writing (and its relation to national identity), 1971, and a volume of essays both personal and literary, *The Heart of a Stranger*, 1976. She held university posts (as writer-in-residence, and Chancellor of Trent), won the Governor General's Award twice (and served on the Awards Committee), and was a Companion of the Order of Canada. She saw her anti-colonial views as related 'to my growing awareness of the dilemma and powerlessness of women'; she embraced the artist's 'moral responsibility, to work aganst the nuclear arms race'. In 1984 she was said to be writing fiction again. Her memoir, *Dance On The Earth*, 1989, completed by her daughter, includes letters to Adele WISEMAN, and poems. See special issues of *JCS*, 13, 1978, *JCF*, 27, 1980, and *Canadian Woman Studies/Cahiers de la Femme*, 18, 1987; also essays ed. Kristjana GUNNARS, 1988, and studies by Clara Thomas, 1975, Patricia Morley, 1981. Bibliography by Susan J. Warwick, 1979.

Laut, Agnes Christina, 1871–1936, journalist, novelist, historical and travel writer. Da. of Eliza (George) and John L. (and granddaughter of a Queen's Univ. principal), she was b. at Stanley, Ont., but grew up in Winnipeg. Her studies at the Univ. of Manitoba were interrupted by ill health. Her writing career began with political editorials for the *Manitoba Free Press*, and she contributed to many Canadian, US and British newspapers and periodicals. She took an active role in women's organizations. A summer in the mountains of BC (for her health) set her gathering material for her first novel, *Lords of the North*, 1900; *Heralds of Empire*, 1902, adds voyageurs to fur traders. Her imagination was fired by the opening up of Canada's west and north. Even after moving to New York State, she centred most of her fiction and prolific, well-documented nonfiction on Canadian history. With documentation drawn from oral as well as written sources, shaping her genre to serve her interests, she covered explorers, early traders, the gold rush, and the controversial ethics of fur trapping, as well as earlier European pirates and US pioneer experience in many regions.

Laverty, Maura (Kelly), 1907–66, novelist and cookery writer. B. at Rathangan, Co. Kildare, to dressmaker Mary Ann (Treacy) and farmer Michael K., and educ. at the Brigidine Convent in Tullow, Co. Carlow, she went to Spain as a governess, 1925, and became secretary to the writer Princess Bibesco, then worked for a bank and a Madrid newspaper. Returning to Ireland, 1928, she m. journalist James L. and had three children. She published poems, stories and articles, broadcast an advice programme, and edited a women's magazine. Her *Flour Economy*, 1941 (on overcoming wartime shortages), and other recipe books were very popular; her first novel, *Never No More*, 1942, repr. 1985, grew out of memories evoked by an Irish country COOKERY book. ML's novels are strongly autobiographical, sentimental, rich in detail and chacterization. *Never No More* and *No More than Human*, 1944, repr. 1986, share an independent-minded heroine growing up in an Irish rural community with her grandmother, then working in Spain. *Alone We Embark*, 1943 (*Touched by the Thorn* in the USA), was briefly banned in Ireland (as were two more ML novels) for sexual and political 'candour', but received the Irish Woman Writer's award. Of ML's two children's books, *The Cottage in the Bog*, 1945, was *Gold of Glanaree* in the USA. Her last novel, *Lift Up Your Gates*, 1947, about the Dublin slums during WWII, was adapted in the 1950s as a series of plays under its US title, *Liffey Lane*, and in the 1980s as the TV series *Tolka Row*. Maeve BINCHY has written prefaces to the reprints.

Lavery, Bryony, London playwright and director. Her 'But will men like it? ...' opens, 'I was never going to be a writer'; its last page opens, 'I am a lesbian feminist writer' (Susan Todd, ed., *Women and Theatre, Calling the Shots*, 1984). At school BL learned 'Beginner's Reality, Intermediate Boundaries and Advanced Narrow Thinking'. (Her plays for schools typically combat regimentation, like the two in Dan Garrett, ed., *Drama Workshop Plays*, 1984.) She 'did what school told me' and became a teacher in the 1960s (drama at a comprehensive), later a publicity assistant in industry. She began writing as a student with *Of All Living*: early plays (of nearly 30) reflected 'life as I knew it', and gave most and best parts to men. With two actors she formed the feminist theatre group Les Oeufs Malades, 1975, touring with work by her including *I Was Too Young at the Time to Understand Why My Mother Was Crying/Sharing*, 1975, *Bag*, 1979 (camping, sex, and not getting on in the Scottish Highlands), and *Family Album*, 1980 (children at play in a bedroom). She learned that 'just writing isn't enough': you need a whole range of skills to get plays put on. By now she wrote more female parts than male, but not as an avowed feminist. Her plays for Monstrous Regiment include a rescripting of Anita LOOS' *Gentlemen Prefer Blondes*, 1980, *Calamity*, 1984 (about Calamity Jane and other heroines), and *Origin of the Species*, 1984, a version 'not riddled with male chauvinism' of 'The Entire History of the World, The Universe and Womankind From The Dawn of Time Until The Present Day', all for two actors, a present-day woman and the four-million-year-old foremother she digs up (in Mary Remnant, ed., *Plays by Women*, 6, 1987). Plays for the Women's THEATRE GROUP include *Witchcraze*, 1985 (three theatre cleaners play 19 historical parts). BL set up the four-woman Female Trouble 'to present a positive female statement' in unscripted reviews, 1981–2; other satiric reviews include the *Wandsworth Warmers* series, and *Floorshow* (with Caryl CHURCHILL and Michelene WANDOR), 1977. She has written for the TV series *Revolting Women*, and with Patrick Barlow for the National Theatre of Brent (e.g. *Zulu* and *Gotterdammerung*), and been a resident writer for children. *Wicked*, staged 1990, was written for women in prison.

Lavin, Mary, short-story writer and novelist, b. 1912 at East Walpole, Mass., only child of Irish parents, Nora (Mahon) and Tom L., who returned home when she was nine. She was educ. at Loreto Convent and University College, Dublin (BA 1934, MA with thesis on Jane AUSTEN, 1936). Working on a PhD on Virginia WOOLF in 1938, she suddenly grasped that literature was written not, as she had assumed, 'by the dead', but at the present moment, and she abandoned research for writing fiction (and a few poems). Her interest in Woolf marks 'Miss Holland', 1938, 'A Story with a Pattern' (written 1939, pub. 1951, about her own art, discusssed between female and male speakers), and 'The Becker Wives', 1946 (in which the stolid and unimaginative observe with delight a brilliance later revealed as madness and loss of identity). ML m. lawyer William Walsh in 1942 and had three daughters.

Widowed in 1954, she m. Australian, ex-Jesuit Michael McDonald Scott in 1969. Her novels, *The House in Clewe Street* (pub. serially; complete 1945; repr. 1987) and *Mary O'Grady* (1950, repr. 1986), are outshone by her short stories, pub. in many volumes, in journals like *The New Yorker*; selec. 1959 (with ML's critical preface) and 1981; collec. 1964–85. Whether treating family relationships, love and its distortions, catastrophic shipwreck, Irish politics (very obliquely), or making a living from dung, her powerful, restrained stories hold to the end their readiness to surprise and move. They have brought ML many honours, including presidency of the Irish Academy of Letters, 1971–3. Papers at Univ. of Southern Illinois (Carbondale), Boston Univ., and State Univ. of NY (Binghamton); studies by Richard F. Peterson, 1978, and A. A. Kelly, 1980 (who examines ML's revisions of her work); check-list by Ruth Krawschak, Berlin, 1979.

Lawless, Hon. **Emily**, 1845–1913, poet and novelist, eldest of eight children of Elizabeth (Kirwan), famous beauty and sportswoman, and Edward L., third Baron Cloncurry, of Lyons House, Co. Kildare. EL, who loved riding, swimming and science, was educ. at home. Her father died when she was 14. Much time was spent at her mother's home of Castlehacket, Co. Galway, which shaped her love for the west of Ireland. She began writing for natural history journals and her first novels, *A Chelsea Householder*, 1882, and *A Millionaire's Cousin*, 1885, were pub. anonymously. Her first Irish novel, *Hurrish*, 1886, under her own name and dedicated to her friend Margaret OLIPHANT, was a great success, as was her second, *Grania*, 1892 (though less liked in Ireland). Her Irish history, 1887, was 'clear and temperate' (*Spectator*). *With Essex in Ireland*, 1890, convinced Gladstone it was the diary of one of Essex's followers. *Traits and Confidences*, 1898, includes childhood glimpses. In 1901 she published a gentle and reflective *Garden Diary*; in 1902 her poems *With the Wild Geese* were pub. at the instigation of Stopford Brooke, who wrote an introduction. She wrote a life of Maria EDGEWORTH, 1904, and in 1905 was awarded an honorary D. Litt by the Univ. of Dublin. Her friends included Mary WARD and Edith SICHEL, to whom she dedicated *The Point of View*, 1909 (privately printed for the benefit of the Galway fishermen). This vol. contains strong sinewy poems: some to friends; some about old age and death; contained yet moving. She spent her last years living in Surrey with her devoted friend, Lady Sarah Spencer. Her coll. poems, ed. Padraic Fallon, 1965, contains an appreciative criticism.

Lawrence, Margery H., 1896–1969, novelist and short-story writer. B. in Shropshire, da. of Grace (Banks) and Richard John L., a barrister of the Inner Temple, she was educ. privately at home and abroad, then m. civil servant Arthur Edward Towle, later CBE. She published a book of poems at 16; later she moved to various popular fictional forms. Her novels often ensnare women in difficult or impossible situations involving money, class, social convention and opportunity. Female sexuality is a major issue. *Miss Brandt: Adventuress*, 1923, describes subversive adventures: a female 'Fly by Night' wronged in love takes revenge on 'Society' as a variously disguised jewel thief pursued around Europe by an English police officer, with whom, after allowing him to identify her, she runs away. *Bohemian Glass*, 1928, a novel of sexual and artistic awakening, caused a pre-publication scandal which is scorned in ML's challenging 'Foreword'. Her deep interest in spiritualism, from the 1920s (see her *What is This Spiritualism?*, 1946), is importantly reflected in her novels, sometimes as psychology. In *The Madonna of Seven Moons*, 1931, a daughter searches for her mother who has a split personality (a repressed, conservative upper-class wife; a passionate, powerful low-life thief) attributed to her youthful revulsion on witnessing her father make love to a servant. The hero of *Madame Holle*, 1934, rescues an innocent orphan from sexual servitude and murder at the hands of Madame Holle and her sado-masochistic son. Later novels move more deeply into the SPIRITUALIST subject-matter: *Bride of Darkness*, 1967, about a man who marries a modern witch, casts the (female) sexual instincts as 'evil', opposed to the maternal; *A Residence Afresh*, 1969, is told by a man who has left the earth and is 'living on the other side'. Speaking through a medium, the spirit narrator of *The Tomorrow of Yesterday*, 1966 (not, ML says, science-fiction), describes his Martian past in which sexual difference did not exist, attributes its existence on earth to the forces of darkness in a sexually active woman, and proposes a utopian earth future to be achieved by infusion of the psychically male essence into mating earthlings. Other late, non-spiritualist, novels continue to foreground female sexuality: *Autumn Rose*, 1971, makes the sexual inhibitions of a 40-year old central: they derive from an attempted rape when she was nine. In *Skivvy*, 1961, a Victorian servant-girl raped by the butler makes her child the family heir by deft substitution.

Lawrence, Rose (D'Aguilar), miscellaneous writer, da. of army officer Joseph D'A. She translated anonymously Goethe's *Gortz* [sic] *of Berlingen* [1799] and Gessner's *Works*, 1802, each with critical preface; she finds Mary COLLYER's Gessner 'forced and unnatural' in style. Translations from old and modern German, Italian and Spanish feature in *The Last Autumn at a Favourite Residence, with other poems*, 2nd ed. 1829. The title poem laments the imminent loss of Wavertree Hall near Liverpool, a family estate; an edition of 1836 adds memoirs of Felicia HEMANS, an old friend, on whose behalf RL had contacted the RLF the previous year. In 1831 she pub. with her name two children's anthologies of poems, sequels to the *Poetical Primer*: one on ancient mythology (dedicated to Lady DACRE), one scriptural and historical (dedicated to one of her sons; including work by several women).

Lawson, Jessie (Kerr), *c.* 1838–1917, poet, novelist, journalist. She came to Canada in middle age, returned to Scotland, where she had been born (in Fife), and m. William L., then settled in Canada, 1911. A journalist in both Toronto and Dundee, she also published eight novels and a volume of poems and had eight children. *The Epistles o' Hugh Airlie*, 1888, an epistolary novel in the Scottish dialect of its immigrant namesake, looks humorously at cross-cultural misunderstandings. *The Harvest of Moloch*, 1908, set in Scotland, is a TEMPERANCE novel whose action figures the widespread unhappiness alcoholism causes in both women and men. *Lays and Lyrics*, 1913, including some 'in the Scottish Dialect', are philosophical and reflective. The book opens on 'The Evolution of Women', a revisionist interpretation of the creation of Eve: not made of Adam's rib, she is 'an angel strayed / From heaven's estate', with the result that 'Truth, Grace, Wisdom', God decides, 'shall feminine be'.

Lawson, Louisa (Albury), 1848–1920, poet, story-writer, publisher, editor, pioneer feminist, b. in Guntawang, near Mudgee, NSW, da. of Harriet (Wynn) and Henry A. Educ. at Mudgee National School, where she was encouraged to write poetry and invited to become a pupil-teacher, she was forced to leave to help at home. She m. Niels (Peter) Larsen, a Norwegian sailor turned gold-digger, in 1866, and had five children, the eldest being the writer Henry Lawson. In 1883 LL and the children moved to Sydney where she was soon active in radical and feminist circles, purchasing and editing the nationalist monthly, *The Republican*, in 1887. In 1888 she founded *Dawn*, the first Australian feminist journal, running it successfully until 1905. She initially called herself 'Dora Falconer'. By 1889 she was employing ten women, including some as printers, despite threats from the printers' unions which refused membership to women. The Dawn Club, a reform club for women, was also established; LL was one of the pioneers of the Australian women's SUFFRAGE movement. Besides many uncollected articles, editorials, poems and stories, she pub. a Christmas book, *'Dert' and 'Do'*, [1904], and a collection of poems, *The Lonely Crossing*, 1905. Dominant themes in her poetry are of love, death and loneliness, as well as praise of her native land. A rather slight biography has been pub. by Lorna Ollif, 1978; an unconventional but much more scholarly and informative one by Brian Matthews, 1987. See also E. Zinkhan in D. Adelaide, ed., *A Bright and Fiery Troop*, 1988. A coll. of her journalism has been ed. by her great-granddaughter Olive Lawson, 1989.

Lawson, Mary Jane (Katzmann), 'Mrs William Lawson', 'M.J.K.L.', 1828–90, poet, editor, local historian: first Nova Scotia woman to achieve literary recognition. She was b. at Preston, NS, da. of Martha (Prescott) and Christian Conrad K., a retired military officer. She contributed prose and poetry to a number of periodicals. A woman of initiative, in her early twenties she began *The Provincial, or Halifax Monthly* (24 issues from Jan. 1852 to Dec. 1853), thought the most original Maritime magazine of its time. It included reviews of Susanna MOODIE and Thomas Haliburton, essays on science and social conditions, contributions from numerous literary figures, and MJKL's own chatty historical accounts of the Dartmouth area of Nova Scotia. A long essay re-using some of this material won the Akins Prize in 1887 and appeared as *History of the Townships of Dartmouth, Preston and Laurencetown*, ed. Harry Piers, 1893. After the demise of *The Provincial*, MJKL successfully operated a bookstore in Halifax. Her marriage, 1868, to William L., a merchant ten years her junior, with whom she had a daughter, startled Halifax society. The poetry she wrote after marriage was conventional, religious, and occasional: collected in *Frankincense and Myrrh*, ed. Harry Piers and Constance Fairbanks, 1893. See Lois Kernaghan in *Nova Scotia Historical Quarterly*, 5, 1975. Papers in Nova Scotia Archives, together with C. Mullane's biographical notes.

Lazarus, Emma, 1849–87, poet and translator, b. NYC of Sephardic Jewish parents. Educ. at home in a wealthy and cultured environment, she first pub. poems in a private edition in 1866. She became a friend of Emerson and much of her early poetry was derivative. Her second book, *Admetus, and Other Poems*, 1871, received critical attention, as did her novel *Alide: An Episode of Goethe's Life*, 1874. She also pub. translations of Hebrew poetry of medieval Spain and of Heinrich Heine's poems and ballads, and her tragedy, *The Spagnoletto*, was pub. privately in 1876. Her early work is perhaps best characterized by a line from her poem 'Echoes', 1880, in which she complained that 'Late-born and woman-souled I dare not hope'. In later poems, such as 'A Degenerate Age', she dismissed American poetry as 'a cackling of ravens'. Her later work displays originality and a spirit of social concern, apparently inspired by a protest rally against Jewish pogroms in Russia. *Songs of a Semite*, 1882, contains translations of ancient Hebrew poems, and her play *The Dance to Death* concerns persecution of Jews in Thuringia in 1349. In articles in *Century Magazine* and *American Hebrew* in 1882 and 1883 she urged the establishment of a Jewish homeland in Palestine, as well as education for the many Russian Jews who had fled to America. She helped found the NY Hebrew Technical Institute. Her best-known poem is the sonnet 'The New Colossus', 1883, the final five lines of which are inscribed on the pedestal of the Statue of Liberty. Her last pub. work was a prose poem, perhaps the first written by an American, 'By the Waters of Babylon', in *The Century*, 1887. Her coll. poems were pub. 1889; her letters 1868–85 and selec. writings, ed. Morris U. Schappes, 3rd ed., 1967. See Eve Merriam, 1956 and Dan Vogel, 1980, for her life; Emily Stipes Watts, *The Poetry of American Women*, 1977, for a critical discussion.

Lead, Jane (Ward), 1624–1704, mystic, poet, and spiritual autobiographer, b. in Norfolk, da. of an Anglican, Schildnap W. At 18, after three years' inner struggle, she had her salvation experience; at 21 she married William L., a cousin. After 27 years of marriage she had a vision of a woman clothed with the sun (Sophia, the 'Wonder Woman', or divine wisdom), adopted a life of 'Spiritual Virginity' and began to record her visions and warn that 'all Formal Worships set up by Man . . . as a Shadow must pass away'. In 1674 she joined John Pordage's sectarian household in London. She pub. *The Heavenly Cloud New Breaking*, 1681, *The Revelation of Revelations*, 1683, *The Enochian Walks with God*, 1694 (issued from charitable refuge in Stepney), and a dozen later works including her diary for 1670–86 (*A Fountain of Gardens*, 1697–1701), and *The Wars of David*, 1700 (with account of 'her own Experience'). She was composing and dictating just before her death. Her fame grew more quickly in continental Europe (through translations) than in England. She founded the Philadelphian Society in 1694, with Francis Lee, later her son-in-law. Its men highly valued women's visions and pub. several accounts of her, but omitted or revised many of her poems in eds. after she became blind, about 1695. See Catherine F. Smith in Sandra M. GILBERT and Susan Gubar, eds., 1979.

Leadbeater, Mary (Shackleton), 1758–1826, Quaker woman of letters, da. of Elizabeth (Carleton) and schoolmaster Richard S. Well educ., a diarist from ten years old, she lived at Ballitore, Co. Kildare, and published mostly at Dublin, firstly in Joshua Edkins's *Collection of Poems*, ii, 1790. Next year she married William L., farmer; she brought up a family and ran the village post-office. After *Extracts and Original Anecdotes for the Improvement of Youth*, 1794, she set her name to her works. *Poems*, 1808, includes a translation of a fifteenth-century sequel to the *Aeneid*, with verse on family, friends (a ballad speaks for a widow with no voice of her own), and her patron Edmund Burke (including 'The Negro', against slavery). *Cottage Dialogues Among the Irish Peasantry*, 1811, comic, observant and endearing, with notes by Maria EDGEWORTH, trace prudent Rose and harum-scarum Nancy from childhood via 'The Pig', 'Manure', etc., to 'Death'. Moralizing has freer rein in a second and third series (about men), in *The Landlord's Friend*, 1813 (higher ranks), *Tales for Cottagers*, 1814 (jointly with her mother, including a play, *Honesty is the Best Policy*), and *The Pedlars*, 1826. ML ed. her parents' letters, 1822 (with her mother's early memoirs); pub. lives (cottagers, 1822, repr. 1987; Irish Quakers, 1823); and left *Annals of Ballitore* (repr. 1987) and correspondence with George Crabbe, Melesina TRENCH and others (BL: selecs. as *L. Papers*, 1862). Her daughter Lydia Jane, later Fisher, also wrote. See Clara L. Gandy in *Women and Lit.*, 3, 1975.

Leakey, Caroline, 'Oline Keese', 1827–81, novelist and poet, b. Exeter, England, sixth child of James L., an artist. Poor health restricted her educ., but she was an avid reader, particularly of poetry. In 1847 she arrived in Hobart to help her sister Eliza but, continuing ill, returned to England in 1853. While in Tasmania she had written many of the poems in *Lyra Australis, or Attempts to Sing in a Strange Land*, 1854. She also gathered much of the material for *The Broad Arrow*, 1859 (pub. under her pseudonym and repr. 1988). This was one of the earliest novels about the Australian penal system and the first to centre on a woman convict. Its indictment of the system influenced Marcus Clarke's classic, *For the Term of His Natural Life*. Like all her works, and her life, it was strongly religious in tone. A memoir, *Clear Shining Light*, 1882, was written by her sister Emily. See J. Poole, *Southerly*, 2, 1966; L. Hergenhan, *Southerly*, 12, 1976; S. Walker in D. Adelaide, ed., *A Bright and Fiery Troop*, 1988.

Leapor, Mary or Molly, 1722–46, labouring-class poet. B. at Marston St Lawrence, Northants., da. of Ann and Philip L. (a gardener, later of Brackley), she read and wrote poetry from childhood (to her parents' disquiet); her few books included Dryden, Pope and plays. She attracted as patron Bridget Fremantle, who prefaced vol. ii of her *Poems upon Several Occasions* (pub. after her death from measles, for her father's benefit, 1748 and 1751; an inscribed copy remains at Weston Hall, where she worked as kitchen-maid). Mary DELANY, Stephen Duck, Ladies HERTFORD and POMFRET subscribed in 1748, Elizabeth MONTAGU, Sarah Scott and Mrs CUTTS in 1751; the future Susanna DUNCOMBE offered a prefatory sonnet. ML writes much of and to women, of the discrepancy of her sex and class with her poetic urge. Her poems ('only a Parcel of chequer'd Thoughts', written as 'Mira' or 'Myra') excel in the satire which she called idle and whimsical (of chilly patrons and upper-class marriage, for example). 'An Essay on Woman' is strongly feminist. Her 'Will' (cf. Isabella WHITNEY) bequeaths 'my Patience to compose the Lives / Of slighted Virgins and neglected Wives' and expects to be mourned by 'shrewd Instructors, who themselves are wrong'. She dreams of books and pictures but wakes 'to Business and to Woes,/ To sweep her Kitchen, and to mend her Clothes'. Her blank-verse tragedy, *The Unhappy Father* (whose staging was under discussion when she died), makes a wronged wife comment acutely on how enforced obedience stunts girls as independent moral agents. Her second play is unfinished. See Richard Greene, PhD thesis, Oxford 1989.

Leaton, Anne, novelist, short-story writer, poet and playwright, b. 1932 in Texas, da. of Margaret (Clark) and Clyde Sparkman L. (d. 1940). She has written stories ever since she can remember, at 12 reading to female classmates each day a new chapter in a romantic novel; she wrote poems, too, at Texas Christian Univ. (BA 1954) and Technological Univ. (MA 1959). She also studied at Berlin, Perugia and Vienna (1960–1, 'writing verse drama in the manner of T. S. Eliot'). After 17 years in Europe, Turkey, S. Africa and Canada (usually teaching, always writing) she settled at Fort Worth. Since the 1960s her poems, stories, and TV and radio plays have appeared in several countries: *My Name is Bird McKai*, heard in the USA and UK, 1976, about the pull exerted on a young white woman by Indian life and the Arizona desert, and *Happiness*, 1981, USA, S. Africa, Spain, UK, were much praised. Of AL's novels, *Good Friends, Just*, 1983, is savagely funny about gender and international relations: US women teaching in Turkey excel respectively at bi-sexual teasing and at wise-cracking ('you'd really like to go to bed with me, if you could only be somewhere else at the time'), Turkish women are insecurely westernized, Turkish men both threatening and ridiculous: 'I do not always understand what you say, sweetling. But this will not make a problem for me, I think. I understand you as a woman.' *Mayakovsky, My Love*, 1984, collects five stories of madness (living rapport with the dead, cheerfully matter-of-fact murder, Turkish lives ravaged by pathological US naïvety), and alienation (a German woman in Ireland invents, to please her English neighbours, a tragic political past which then engulfs her). *Pearl*, 1985, is a historical novel: the heroine's mother, 'Bandit Queen' Belle Starr, tells her that fathers are bastards who would sell you for a pony 'if it wasn't for your mother hovering there in the shadows with a shotgun of her own'. The two novellas in *Blackbird, Bye Bye*, 1989, centre on people achieving, at great cost, eccentricity enough to move them from small-town USA. AL admires Flannery O'CONNOR. Not an overtly feminist writer, she says she has been 'a subversive feminist since the early 50s . . . I like whenever possible to set small night fires under the male institutional edifice, leaving a little soot on the sweetly white portals.'

Leavis, Q. D., Queenie Dorothy (Roth), 1906–81, scholar and critic, b. in London to poor orthodox Jews, Jane (Davis) and Morris R., educ. at Latymer School and Girton College, Cambridge (first-class honours, 1928). Her parents disowned her when she married, 1929, her teacher and fellow-critic F. R. L. Her PhD thesis became the important *Fiction and the Reading Public*, 1932, repr. 1979. She had three children, taught Cambridge students for many years but held no university post or college fellowship, suffered various illnesses beginning with cancer in her early forties, and became famous for making enemies. She was a major contributor, trenchant and often satirical, to *Scrutiny*, 1932–53; Muriel Bradbrook finds it 'odd' that she was never named as joint editor (*Cambridge Review*, Nov. 1981). QDL said of her husband's *The Great Tradition*, 1948, 'I wrote a good deal of it myself' and of other collaboration 'He was very grateful of course'; the gratitude was expressed parenthetically but increasingly. Volume i of her *Collected Essays*, ed. G. B. Singh, 1983, is almost entirely devoted to nineteenth-century women writers; she shaped new readings of Margaret OLIPHANT and Jane AUSTEN, and held, Robertson judges, an 'idea of the great tradition of women novelists'. She argued cogently for recognition of specific female artistic achievements. However (as shown in what Virginia WOOLF called her 'drubbing and scourging' of *Three Guineas*), she tended to equate feminism with 'sex-hostility'; 'quite a number of women', in her view, shared 'masculine' intellectual virtues. See P. J. M. Robertson in *Novel*, 16, 1983, and study of both Leavises, 1981; Denys Thompson, ed., various people's memoirs of both, 1984, M. D. Kinch's *Appreciation* of QDL, 1982 (with bibliography).

Lee, Eliza (Buckminster), *c.* 1788–1864, writer and translator, b. Portsmouth, NH, da. of Sarah (Stevens) and Joseph B., Calvinist minister. After the death of her mother, EL was raised by her father who, with her brothers, was responsible for her educ. In 1827 she m. Thomas L., whose wealth enabled her to continue her studies and to write. Her first publication, *Sketches of a New England Village*, 1838, was followed by *Delusion*, 1840, which tells of a woman falsely accused in the Salem witch trials of 1692. She turned to translation in her *Life of Jean Paul Richter*, 1842. Her interest in history is reflected here and in her best novel, *Naomi*, 1848. Set in 1660 Boston, its declared aim is 'to present the limited views ... and the stern justice' of the Puritans and the 'audacity . . . the spiritual pride' of their Quaker victims. Its Quaker heroine's inner serenity is contrasted with the bigotry and hypocrisy of her masculine prosecutors. The triumphant intelligence of EL's female protagonists may stem from the low status granted to women in the household of her father and brother, whose lives she recorded in *Memoirs*, 1849. She pub. ten works. Admired by Carlyle, EL has shrunk into obscurity, but her work deserves attention as a watershed in New England tastes.

'Lee, Gypsy Rose', Rose Louise Hovick, 1914?–70, striptease artist and writer, da. of Rose (Thompson) and journalist John H., who divorced just before her first stage appearance, at four. She and her younger sister, later the actress June Havoc, never went to school; managed by their mother, they toured the USA in vaudeville acts like

'Rose Louise and Her Hollywood Blondes'. (June eloped at 13) GRL made her debut as a stripper at 15 in Toledo, Ohio, became a star of Minsky's, then with the Zeigfeld Follies. 'Her' best-selling semi-autobiographical mystery, *The G-String Murders*, 1941, repr. 1984, praised by Janet FLANNER for its 'decolleté' style and 'mascara language', was ghosted by GRL's friend Craig RICE; so was *Mother Finds A Body*, 1942. GRL's play, *The Naked Genius*, 1943, was filmed as *Doll Face*, 1945, starring herself; her magazine articles and cultural *bons mots* were famous; as a hostess she entertained writers like Carson MCCULLERS. Her great hit, *Gypsy: A Memoir*, 1957 (musical 1959, film 1962, repr. 1986), fondly recalls 1920s and 1930s vaudeville and burlesque, with her mother bullying managers and harrassing her girls' rivals. Her first film ventures, as Louise Hovick, 1937–8, were less successful than those of the 1940s. Three times divorced, she had a son, Erik Lee Premiger, who pub. a memoir of her in 1984. She died of lung cancer in Los Angeles.

Lee, Hannah Farnham (Sawyer), 1780–1865, novelist and historical writer, b. Newburyport, Mass., da. of Micajah S., physician, one of three sisters whose mother d. when they were young. In 1807 she m. George Gardner L., naval officer, who d. in 1816. HL concentrated on bringing up her three daughters until 1832 when, aged 52, she began to write for money. Her major writings are a series of didactic works, of which the most successful was *Three Experiments of Living*, 1837, which reached 30 US eds. Divided into three parts, 'Living Within the Means', 'Living Up to the Means' and 'Living Beyond the Means', this slim volume tells of the Fulton family who move from frugality and 'honest independence' to a more extravagant lifestyle, culminating in their financial collapse on the eve of their daughter Elinor's coming-out ball. In *Elinor Fulton*, 1837, it is the women of the household who raise the family from disaster. Elinor's success articulates nineteenth-century American women's desire to prove their abilities, especially in managing finance. The book ran to 11 editions, possibly because of its relevance to the 1837 Panic. HL's next writing phase was educational, producing historical works on, for example, Luther, Cranmer and Toussaint. She pub. nearly 20 books, but was quickly forgotten. Information may be found in Nina Baym, *Woman's Fiction*, 1978.

Lee, Harriet, 1757–1851, novelist and playwright, sister of Sophia LEE. Her epistolary, anonymous *The Errors of Innocence*, 1786, gives one heroine a good husband, her devoted friend a bad one, whose death produces joy all round. Her comedy *The New Peerage, or Our Eyes may Deceive Us*, acted and pub. 1787 despite fears of female inadequacy in 'deep Observation of Life', makes old points: young men swap identities, an old maid is mocked. *The Mysterious Marriage, or The Heirship of Roselva*, an unacted verse-and-prose drama set in Transylvania, was finished 1795, pub. 1798, the year HL politely declined the hand of WOLLSTONECRAFT's widower. Her *Canterbury Tales for the Year 1797*, 1797, opens with Sophia's comic frame story of a male poet (fleeing bailiffs, needing copy), coaxing snowbound fellow-travellers into narrative. The frame is then mostly ignored till the series' end in 1805 (5 vols., 12 tales, two by Sophia; rev. 1832, facs. 1978, repr. 1989). The tales use the Lees' only intermittently realistic style to treat heightened situations and passions, unworthy parents, and feminist ideas: one is GOTHIC, one dwells on the French Revolution's daily 'sacrifice of human blood'; *Kruitzer, The German's Tale*, 1801, often separately repr., has a strong heroine caught between her husband's inadequacy and the resulting full-blown wickedness of her proto-Byronic son. Byron read and admired it at about 14 and dramatized it as *Werner*, pub. [1821];

HL's own stage version, *The Three Strangers* (written soon after the novel, unacted till 1825), was less successful.

'Lee, Holme', Harriet Parr, 1828–1900, novelist, b. in York, da. of Mary (Grandage) and William P., traveller in fine cloth. She resolved on a literary profession at an early age, devoting herself mainly to fiction and producing some 30 novels between 1854 and 1882. Her interest in women's history also led to her publication of *The Life and Death of Jeanne D'Arc*, 1866. Many of her novels are concerned with the problems of women, including *Sylvan Holt's Daughter*, 1858, *Annie Warleigh's Fortunes*, 1863, and *Katherine's Trial*, 1873. The earliest, *Maud Talbot*, 1854, interweaves the stories of three heroines from different social classes, arguing for mutual female support, and challenges the current view of the fallen woman as victim. *Gilbert Massenger*, 1855, was much admired by Dickens, who considered it for publication in *Household Words*. *Kathie Brande*, 1856, claimed to be 'a life-history, not a romance'; it deals with a high-minded heroine who gives up her fiancé in order to support her family, finally marrying him years later. Concerned with single women's employment when marriage is impossible, the novel also implicitly criticizes exaggerated notions of self-sacrifice, which threaten the female personality.

Lee, Jarena, 1783–after 1837, preacher and autobiographer, b. at Cape May, NJ, of apparently free black parents, 'deprived of the advantages of education, measurably a self-taught person', at seven a servant 60 miles from home. Taught religion at work, she was 'gloriously converted' when she managed to forgive someone who had injured her. After four or five years' spiritual struggle, with temptations to suicide, she heard a voice bidding her preach the gospel. So delighted that she 'preached in her sleep', she approached the African Methodist Episcopalian Richard Allen, who told her women might not preach. She acquiesced, even with relief, but noted in her journal that she felt her 'holy energy ... smothered', that Christ (a whole, not a half Saviour) died for women too, and that his rising was *first* preached by Mary Magdalen. In 1811 JL married pastor Joseph L.; once when they disagreed, she had a vision telling her to submit. Widowed in 1817, with two small children, she took over from a dispirited preacher with a fiery address about her own failure to preach: Allen, hearing her, at once believed her called. She spoke to her husband's congregation from his pulpit, travelled widely (2325 miles in 1827) and published tracts. A strong supporter of her sex and race, she loved to convince educated whites. Selecs. from her journal pub. 'for the author' in *Life and Religious Experience*, Philadelphia, 1836 (repr. 1849); Schomburg Library, 1988.

Lee, Mary Elizabeth, 1813–49, poet and prose writer, b. Charleston, South Carolina, da. of Elizabeth and William L., and niece of Judge Thomas L. A delicate child, she did not go to school till ten, when she displayed a great aptitude for languages. From age 20, she pub. poems in several journals, including Caroline GILMAN's *The Rose Bud*. MEL's first volume, *Social Evenings*, pub. by the Mass. School Library Assn. about 1833, contains rosy tales intended for the enlightenment of youth. Her blank verse narratives have potential, e.g., the enchanting Corinna figure in 'A Sketch From Life', though her best known poem, 'The Blind Negro Communicant', is an apology for slavery, with no acknowledgment that 'this dark prison-house' is man-made. Despite illness and a paralysed right hand, MEL continued contributing to periodicals till her health failed completely. Her *Poetical Remains*, 1851, has a memoir by S. Gilman.

Lee, Sophia, 1750–1824, novelist and playwright. B. in London, da. of actors

Anna Sophia and John L., she ran the family from her mother's death, 1770, and accompanied her father (who was given to quarrels) in the King's Bench prison, 1772. Her comedy *The Chapter of Accidents* brings its heroine to happy marriage despite earlier seduction; at first rejected, wrongly said to be borrowed from Diderot, it did well on stage and in print, 1780. John L. died next year, and she invested her profits in a school at Bath (whose theatre he had managed, 1778–9); she and her sister Harriet LEE ran it till 1803, making friends who included the PORTERS and the future Ann RADCLIFFE. SL broke new ground in historical fiction in *The Recess, or A Tale of Other Times*, 1783–5 (5 eds. by 1804; facs. NY 1972; see Bette B. Roberts in *Mass. Studies in English*, 6, 1979). Its heroines, daughters of Mary Queen of Scots by a secret marriage, at first hidden from the world in a cave/mansion and later playing their parts unnoticed among the famous, suggest women's invisible role in history. It overshadows SL's other works, which include *The Life of a Lover* (epistolary, early, unpub. till 1804); *A Hermit's Tale* (ballad), 1787; *Almeyda*, 1796 (tragedy dedicated to its star, Sarah Siddons); and unpub. comedy, *The Assignation*, 1807. One of her *Canterbury Tales* (ii. 1798) presents elaborately paired women (good/sensitive, bad/energetic), the other (iii. 1799) an 'almost unnaturally noble' hero kidnapped in childhood.

'Lee, Vernon', Violet Paget, 1856–1935, novelist, critic and aesthetician, b. near Boulogne, France, only da. of Matilda (Adams) of a Welsh landowning family (previously West India slave-owners), and Henry Ferguson P., a Polish emigré who adopted the family name of his first wife. VL had a half-brother from her mother's previous marriage: Eugene Lee-Hamilton, poet and professional invalid, who m. Annie HOLDSWORTH. Educ. in art and literature by her mother and Eugene, she spent her childhood travelling in Europe. She began using her pseudonym in her teens, believing that no-one would read her seriously as a woman. She pub. historical sketches at 14 and her most famous book, *Studies of the Eighteenth Century in Italy*, in 1880. Her versatility as a writer is seen in her novel *Miss Brown*, 1884, which satirizes aestheticism, the fantasy, *A Phantom Lover*, 1886, as well as the stories collected in *Hauntings*, 1890, which develop powerful emotions of fear, recognition and loss. See Irene Cooper Willis's edition of the *Supernatural Tales*, 1955. Using her knowledge of European (particularly eighteenth-century) culture, she wrote convincing historical novels such as *Ottilie*, 1883, *Penelope Brandling*, 1903, and *Louis Norbert*, 1914, and numerous TRAVEL books including *Genius Loci*, 1899, *The Spirit of Rome*, 1906, and *The Sentimental Traveller*, 1908. Her most significant writing, however, is on aesthetics. With her friend Kit Anstruther-Thomson she developed an interest in the psychological effects of beauty in *The Beautiful*, 1913. She applied these ideas to literary texts in *The Handling of Words*, 1923, where she sees the craft of the writer as dependent on an ability to 'manipulate the contents of the reader's mind'. The impact of these ideas on other writers and critics has yet to be fully recognized. She was a passionate pacifist as her drama *Satan the Waster*, 1920, demonstrates and these unpopular views together with the specialized nature of her knowledge and her difficult personality made her an increasingly isolated figure. Her friend Ethel SMYTH considered that her tragedy lay in her refusal to acknowledge her lesbian nature. See the dated but still informative study by Burdett Gardner, 1987 (repr. from 1952 diss.), the life by Peter Gunn, 1964, and article by Phyllis F. Mannochi in *Eng. Lit. in Transition* 26, 1983.

Lefanu, Alicia, *c.* 1795–*c.* 1826, novelist and biographer. B. into two prolific clans of writers, female and male, she was eldest da. of Elizabeth 'Betsy' (Sheridan) and naval captain Henry L.: granddaughter to Frances SHERIDAN. From fairy story (*The Flowers, or The Sylphid Queen*, 1809), she moved through verse fables for young women inculcating generally traditional virtues (*Rosara's Chain, or The Choice of Life*, 1812), novels set in contemporary England, Spain and Ireland, either realist or Byronically romantic, to her last, historical novel, *Henry IV of France*, 1826. Politically conservative, she attacks aristocratic frivolity, especially in relation to the starving Irish peasantry, whom she patronizes as 'half-savage' but 'affectionate'. Despite her comic talent, and despite presenting many strong or learned women (feminists, founders of schools and 'manufactures' for the poor, or patriot soldiers in male dress), her endings reward submission or docility: the hero chooses not 'the Amazonian maid – the bright and terrible Constantia – but the pale spotless form of a novice, weighed down with feminine fear'. AL's life of Frances Sheridan stresses subordination of the secret writer to the wife and mother. AL died poor: see family memoir by Philip L., 1924.

Le Gallienne, Eva, US actress, director, translator, autobiographer, b. 1899 in London, da. of journalist Julie (Noerregard) and Richard Le G., poet and editor. She was educ. in Paris and at the future Royal Academy of Dramatic Art in London. With a passion for the theatre aroused, she said, by seeing Sarah Bernhardt act, she first appeared on stage in London in 1914 and next year on Broadway. She settled in the USA, founded the Civic Repertory Company in 1926, and published *ELG's Civic Repertory Plays*, 1928, with lavish annotations designed to convey the flavour of her productions. She had a joint adaptation of *Alice in Wonderland* staged and pub., 1932, and later translated and adapted many works by Ibsen and Hans Christian Andersen. Her first autobiographical volume, *At 33*, 1934, sticks closely to her career; *With a Quiet Heart*, 1953, is somewhat more personal. She has also written a book about Eleonora Duse, 1966, children's books, and journalism.

Legge, Margaret, author of seven novels pub. in London, 1912–29, dealing with women's place in society. In the first, *A Semi-Detached Marriage*, a naïve heroine discovers the oppressive nature of marriage, leaves her husband, becomes a successful journalist involved with women's suffrage, and returns years later only when he acknowledges her equal status. In *The Rebellion of Esther*, 1914, a writer-heroine rejects marriage to an aspiring politician in order to retain her own identity. In *The Wane of Uxenden*, 1917, a journalist is enabled by her knowledge of men to save a friend from destruction at the hands of a psychic: 'She had seen men ... as they are, rather than as they like it to be thought they are ... not always the chivalrous knights that women are taught to expect.' *The Spell of Atlantis*, 1927, and *The Crystal Rabbit* 1929, set in Brazil, treat psychic phenomena as well as female friendship triumphing over convention.

Le Guin, Ursula (Kroeber), science-fiction and fantasy writer, essayist and poet, b. 1929 in Berkeley, Calif., da. of writer Theodora (Kracaw) and anthropologist Alfred K. His story-telling, she says, sparked her interest in myth and inner explanations; reading Lord Dunsany at 12 was also crucial: 'I had discovered my native country.' She was educ. at Radcliffe College (BA 1951) and Columbia (MA 1952). She began PhD studies in French and Italian Renaissance literature, married historian Charles A. Le G. in 1953 and had three children. The other worlds of her award-winning fiction reflect the preoccupations and problems of our own. The Hainish universe, in *Rocannon's World*, 1966, and four more novels to *The Word for World is Forest*, 1976, reflects interest in anthropology and holistic ecology. In writing *A Wizard of Earthsea*, 1968 – first of a young-adult trilogy which uses the journey metaphor and Jungian theory to describe adolescent self-awareness and sexuality: see Edward Blishen, ed., *The Thorny Paradise*, 1975 – and *The Left Hand of Darkness*, 1969 (Hainish), she finally separated, she says, her pure fantasy from her SCIENCE-FICTION vein. *The Dispossessed: An Ambiguous Utopia*, 1974, has a male protagonist presenting views about anarchism. *In the Red Zone*, 1983, contains verse. *Always Coming Home*, 1985, a multimedia work of narration, poetry, illustration and music, introduces a race of the future through the voice of the woman Stone Telling. Sarah Lefanu (1988) finds in ULG a reliance on binaries like male/female, 'dreary male heroes', and few and limited female characters, but concludes that her appeal for feminist readers and critics lies in her seriousness in tackling 'questions of a sexual-political nature', her 'wealth of ideas' and 'lucidity and grace'. ULG's essays on her attitudes to feminism and on her notorious publishing in *Playboy*, are published in *The Language of the Night*, 1979; on her narrative mode and on women writers including her mother in *Dancing at the Edge of the World*, 1989. Special issues of *Extrapolation*, 21, 1980, and *Science-Fiction Studies*, November 1975; study by Charlotte Spivack, 1984.

Lehmann, Rosamond Nina, 1901–90, novelist, translator, memoirist, b. at Bourne End, Bucks., da of Alice Marie (Davis), a New Englander, and Rudolph Chambers L., an athlete, MP, and literary figure. At eight she was 'going to be a great poetess', writing worthless verse (she says) at breakneck speed. She was educ. privately, then at Girton, Cambridge, and m. Leslie Runciman in 1922. Her first, best-selling novel, *Dusty Answer*, 1927, 'uncorked a torrent of . . . literally hundreds of letters', with its account of a young woman's sexual awakening and unlearning of 'the weakness, the fatal obsession of depending on other people'; even Cambridge, she realizes, 'had disliked and distrusted her and all other females'. RL found herself, though 'by temperament and upbringing fervently disposed towards' traditional marriage, unhappily longing for divorce, and famous as 'a frank outspeaker upon unpleasant subjects'. Knowing of no female writer but May SINCLAIR, embarrassed and scared by success, she felt 'sisterly in suffering' with her Victorian 'great ancestresses'. In 1928 she married artist Wogan Phillips; they had two children. Her fiction, often called 'female', is notable for insight into the inner lives of women and children, the dynamics of family and social class, and the often destructive power of sexual feeling, and for narrative and chronological complexity, unobtrusive symbolism, and rich but economical prose style. Her male characters (who have been adversely criticized) are often physically or spiritually impaired, disabled from decision-making, commitment or caring. She questions not only human relatedness but the meaning of life itself in *Letter to a Sister*, pub. by Leonard and Virginia WOOLF as Hogarth Letter 3, 1931. She uses girl narrators in *Invitation to the Waltz*, 1932, and *The Ballad and the Source*, 1954, whose young Rebecca Landon (perhaps an *alter ego*) reports the career of a towering matriarch who sometimes inflicts, but cannot suffer, pain or damage. This novel began as a story following from 'The Gipsy's Baby' and 'The Red-Haired Miss Daintreys', which were written during WWII at the behest of RL's brother John, drawing on early memories, and pub. in *The Gipsy's Baby*, 1946. RL also wrote a play, *No More Music*, 1939 (about social disintegration on the eve of war) and translations from Jacques Lemarchance, 1947, and Jean Cocteau, 1955. Her husband left her for the Spanish Civil War and a more political partner; divorced in 1942, she had a nine-year affair with the married poet C. Day Lewis. Her life, she writes, 'has gone, in various intricate disguises, and transmuted almost beyond my own recognition, into my novels'; love triangles figure in *The Weather in the Streets*, 1936, and *The Echoing Grove*, 1953, which traces a rapprochement between sisters who have loved the same man and feel 'distaste for [the] mental picture of Women without Men, cosily resigned'. RL's daughter died suddenly in 1958; violent grief was succeeded by a 'personal discovery that death does not extinguish life'. RL sketched 'this mystical experience' in the journal of the College of Psychic Studies, 1962, and enlarged it in her memoir, *The Swan in the Evening: Fragments of an Inner Life*, 1967. *A Sea-Grape Tree*, 1976, sequel to *The Ballad and the Source*, draws on these beliefs. RL bids 'Reader, farewell' in her 1985 *Album* of captioned photographs with outline of a further, unwritten novel sequel. Many recent reprints. See John L.'s memoirs, 1955 and 1960; bibliog. by Margaret Gustafson in *Twentieth Century Literature*, 4, 1959; studies by Diane E. LeStourgeon, 1965, and Gillian Tindall, 1985.

Leigh, Dorothy (Kemp or Kempe), ADVICE-writer. Her father and husband have been variously identified. As a widow who felt she was dying, she prepared to publish *The Mothers Blessing*, a volume of 'Godly Counsel' for the maturity of her three young sons: pub. 1616 though only its many reprints (up to 1718) are known. To blunt censure for upsetting 'the usual order of Women' by printing, she seeks protection from Elizabeth of Bohemia, a dedicatee along with the sons. After a poem about bees gathering honey, she opens on parental care ('Will she not bless it every time it sucks on her breast, when she feels the blood come from her heart to nourish it?'); writes humanely and imaginatively on Christ, repentance, salvation and prayer; judges her sons favoured as males to whom the 'seven liberal sciences' lie open; urges them to choose wives they can fully love, selects their future children's names, and advises them to spread the skill of reading in English to all they can reach, male and female. One became, as she had wished, a clergyman. See Elaine V. Beilin, 1987.

Leigh, Helen or Ellen, poet, d. by 1795, perhaps *née* Baxter. Wife of George L., curate at Middlewich, Cheshire, with seven children living, she pub. by subscription *Miscellaneous Poems*, Manchester, 1788. The opening poem rigidly opposes exempla of virtue and vice, but most of her topics are more inventive: pleas against duelling, against war (in an epistle to 'Achmet, an Eastern Monarch' from a shepherdess) and for compassion towards 'The Natural Child'; humorously moral anecdotes (one fashionable lady would rather die than give up lead make-up) and beast-fables; ballads of the battle of Agincourt (traditional, rousing) and of a noble Spanish lady who cuts out and tramples the heart of her seducer, murdered at her behest. HL manages various styles and metres with aplomb. Her husband had married again by 1795.

Leighton, Marie Flora Barbara (Connor), *c.* 1876–1941, POPULAR novelist. B. at Clifton, Glos., da. of Elizabeth (Trelawney) and Capt. James Nenon C., she had aristocratic pretensions. Educ. mainly in France, she was, says her daughter, an 'ardent suffragette', yet said she approved only marriage for women, not university or careers. She herself went on stage at 15, published a novel in 1891 (*The Lady of Balmerino*), and married Robert L. at 17 after submitting poems to a magazine he edited. She wrote, at first jointly with him, sensational newspaper serials ('Convict 99', book form, 1898; 'Blackmail') for Alfred Harmsworth, later Lord Northcliffe, whose life she related in *A Napoleon of the Press*, 1900. She slaved away, she said, on more than 60 'potboilers' (they brought in more than her husband's stories for boys), lacking 'time to write the *real* literature and the poems that are inside of me'. Some of her 40 thrillers feature heroines like *Joan Mar, Detective*, 1910, and *Lucile Dare, Detective*, 1919. In *The Bride of Dutton Market*, 1911, a lord's hand is rejected for 'my profession .... I do not want to be a great lady. I want to be a great detective.' After the death of her son Roland (Vera BRITTAIN's fiancé) ML wrote an anonymous memoir of him, *Boy of My Heart*, 1917. *The Baked Bread*, 1917, also deals with WWI: the heroine, courted by stepbrothers (one good, one bad), is left asking 'Will there be any marriage tomorrow?' ML's daughter Clare L. catches her erratic brilliance in *Tempestuous Petticoat*, 1948, repr. 1984.

Lennox, Charlotte (Ramsay), 1729/30–1804, novelist and woman of letters. Da. of James R. (army officer but not, as she said, governor of NY), she composed verse while still learning to read. She spent 1738–42 at Albany, NY, and was then sent to England, where she sought patrons and published *Poems on Several Occasions* 'by a Young Lady', 1747. That year she married Alexander L., who worked for publisher William Strahan; in 1748–50 she appeared on stage. Samuel Johnson's friendship brought her years of literary advice and career support. L. M. HAWKINS's father disapproved of Johnson's celebration (with all-night party, laurel crown, and ceremonies invoking the Muses) of her 'first literary child'. *The Life of Harriot Stuart* [1750]. The precocious, talented, romantic heroine of this first-person narrative (besieged by suitors, one of whom engineers her CAPTIVITY by Indians in America) sets the themes for CL's fiction. In *The Female Quixote*, 1752 (best-selling if not her best: ed. Margaret Dalziel, 1969; dedication by Johnson: much discussed), Arabella has to be taught she is not, as in ROMANCE, a focus of adulatory interest. Apparently childless till 1765 but supporting her husband, CL worked at much besides her next novel, *Henrietta*, 1758. She translated from several languages the first-ever collection of source-material, *Shakespear Illustrated*, 1753–4, with 'Critical Remarks' rather rigidly requiring poetic justice and consistency of character. Other translations include *Memoirs* of the Duke of Sully [1755] (a great hit), of the Countess of Berci, 1756, and of Mme de Maintenon, 1757, and (with others) plays by Euripides and Sophocles from French as *The Greek Theatre*, 1759. CL abandoned a history of ELIZABETH I but, despite ill health and a bankrupt publisher, edited *The Lady's Museum*, 1760–1 (information on many subjects; essays; 'On the Education of Daughters'; *The History of Harriot and Sophia*, rev. 1762 as *Sophia*). She probably wrote *The History of Eliza*, 1766; quarried *Henrietta* for *The Sister*, 1769, a well-turned but unsuccessful comedy of intrigue; and adapted Ben Jonson and others in *Old City Manners*, 1775. Her last-printed novel, the epistolary *Euphemia*, 1790, 'sketched out some years ago', presents friendship between two (unideally) married heroines: American episodes include, again, an Indian captivity. Always seeking work and wrestling with poverty, CL sometimes took in girls to educate, 1761–73; in 1793 she needed funds to send her son to the USA away from his 'most unnatural father'; she seems to have been unacceptable to the BLUESTOCKING circle. Life by Miriam Rossiter Small, 1935; new facts from Duncan Isles in *Harvard Library Bulletin*, 18, 19, 1970, 1971.

Le Noir, Elizabeth Anne (Smart), 1754–1841, poet and novelist, b. at Islington, London, da. of the Catholic Anna Maria (Carnan) and the poet Christopher S.: educ. at a Boulogne convent. On her father's insanity and incarceration the family returned, 1762, to Reading, Berks., to the printing firm owned by her step-grandfather John Newbery and the *Reading Mercury*, ed. in turn by her grandmother, mother and sister. In 1795 she married the

French émigré Jean Baptiste Le N. de la Brosse: he and her stepdaughter M. A. Le N. published in French. Despite her mother's discouragement, her novels (with poems interspersed, set in restricted, charming backgrounds) were admired by e.g., Mary Russell MITFORD: *Village Annals*, 1803, *Village Anecdotes* in letters from a wife to a distant sailor husband, 1804 (pub. under the aegis of Frances BURNEY's father; 2nd ed. [1807] with verse dedication to him and subscriptions from Elizabeth CARTER and Walter Scott), and *Clara de Montfier*, 1808, about a 'patriarchal' pre-revolutionary family in La Vendée, whose daughter marries an Englishman. *Conversations ... with Poems*, 1812 (for children), was followd by *Miscellaneous Poems*, 1825; excerpts from EALN's epistolary reminiscence pub. in Arthur Sherbo's life of her father, 1967.

'Leonowens, Anna', Ann Harriett (Edwards), 1831–1914, teacher and TRAVEL writer. She was (contrary to her own story) b. at Ahmednugger, India, younger da. of the perhaps Eurasian Mary Anne (Glasscock) and sergeant Thomas E., who d. three months before her birth. Two months after it her mother married corporal Patrick Donoughey (later demoted to private). Probably brought up by grandparents in England, AL spent three years, from 1846, touring the Middle East with a clergyman. She married, at Poona in 1849, Thomas Leon Owens, a clerk who died at Penang in 1859, leaving her with two children. She ran a small school till 1862, then became, till 1867, governess to the 82 children of King Mongcut, the fairly enlightened ruler of Siam (now Thailand) whom AL called 'morally mad'. Having moved to the USA, she published *The English Governess at the Siamese Court*, 1870. This largely fabricated account of her life (ancient Welsh blood, private education, a husband dead in a tiger hunt) and of the court (a city of women, with dungeons and human sacrifice) was a sensation. Writers like Emerson and Harriet Beecher STOWE were eager to meet AL; she became a successful lecturer and published *The Romance of the Harem*, 1873 (repr. 1952 as *Siamese Harem Life*, with intro. by Freya STARK), and *Life and Travel in India*, 1884, written, she says, 'as a young girl fresh from school'. She settled in Halifax, Nova Scotia, in 1876, and later in Montréal, travelled to New York (to help set up a school) and Russia (as a reporter), was active in the women's suffrage campaign, and helped found the Nova Scotia College of Art. Her fictionalized story, fed by Margaret Landon's retelling, 1944, two films, and the musical *The King and I*, 1951, was exploded in books by A. B. Griswold, 1961 (on Mongcut), and W. S. Bristowe, 1976 (on AL's son Louis and his career in Siam).

Leprohon, Rosanna Ellen (Mullins), 1829–79, novelist and poet. B. in Montréal, da. of Rosanna (Connelly) and Francis M., an Irish immigrant who prospered as a merchant, she was educ. at the Convent of the Congregation of Notre Dame. She began publishing fiction at 17, serializing five novels in *The Literary Garland* (Montréal), 1847–51. All set in upper-class British society, they focus on courtship, with surprising plot twists and lively dialogue. *The Stepmother*, 1847, introduces an intruder in the family circle. In 1851 she m. Jean-Lukin L., a descendent of an old French Canadian family, army surgeon and publisher of one of the earliest Canadian medical journals. Eight of their 13 children survived to adulthood. She began publishing again with an evangelical Roman Catholic story, 'Eveleen' (Boston *Pilot*, 1859). Then came her three most important works: *The Manor House of de Villerai*, 1860, set in Québec during the English-French war of 100 years earlier, *Antoinette de Mirecourt; or Secret Marrying and Secret Sorrowing*, 1864, dealing with relations between the French and English of the same period, and *Armand Durand; or, a Promise Fulfilled*, 1868, a story of marital relations through two generations of a rural Québec family. Bilingual and bicultural, wishing to contribute to 'an essentially Canadian literature,' RL successfully conveyed the French-Canadian viewpoint to her English-Canadian audience in imaginative romances marked by local colour and carefully researched historical detail: immediately popular, too, in French translations. She turned to English Canada for her last stories and novels: tales of upper-middle-class society except *Ada Dunsmore: or a Memorable Christmas Eve*, 1869, set in Ontario, which describes a life very different from RL's own. Always moralistic, she moved beyond the courtship plot (sometimes implying that to dream of the ideal man was illusory), to treat her protagonists' inner problems and their maturation. Her weaker women win protecting males; her strong characters refuse to marry, or marry unhappily, or marry someone weak and selfish. The protagonist of *The Manor House* hopes that her childhood fiancé, chosen by her parents, does not 'share the vulgar error, that an unmarried woman must necessarily be unhappy' and tells him her 'unalterable resolution . . . that though I may eventually marry, if I chance to meet one of your sex whom I may learn to love and respect, I certainly will never marry to please them, and to escape the dreaded appellation of old maid'. RL's *Poetical Works*, compiled by John Reade, appeared in Montréal, 1881. See Carole Gerson in *CWW*, Fiction Series, I, 1983, and J.R. Surfleet's introduction to *Manor House* in *JCF*, 34 (1983).

Lesbian feminist criticism. Like other feminist critics, lesbians began by uncovering and claiming literary foremothers. Jeannette Foster's *Sex Variant Women in Literature*, 1956 (repr. 1975, 1985), rapidly surveys lesbian writers from SAPPHO to this century, and representations of lesbians throughout European and North American literature. Jane RULE's discussion of specific writers in *Lesbian Images*, 1975, enabled lesbian critics, challenged heterosexual critics, and informed both. Barbara Grier, writing as 'Gene Damon', documented contemporary work in her 'Lesbiana' column in *The Ladder* from soon after its inception, 1956, to its demise, 1972: selected in Grier, *Lesbiana*, 1976. Other feminist journals have gradually increased and deepened coverage of lesbian writing, but none so systematically. Grier also provided critics with their major bibliographic tool: *The Lesbian in Literature*, 3 eds., 1967, 1975, 1981. Other such resources include Marie Kuda, *Women Loving Women*, 1974, Lyn Paleo and Eric Garber, *Uranian Worlds*, 1982, and J. R. Roberts, *Black Lesbians*, 1981. By the mid-70s this first phase in consolidating a 'self-conscious literary tradition' (Bonnie Zimmerman) had been complicated by the still persisting problem of definition. Adrienne RICH famously defined a lesbian as a woman-identified woman and asserted a lesbian continuum of 'woman-identified experience'. Two influential scholarly critics helped to give these concepts historical and cultural validity: Blanche Wiesen Cook situated early twentieth-century lesbian writers of Paris and London in the context of 'cultural tradition' ('Women Alone Stir My Imagination', 1979); Lilian Faderman analysed affective relationships between women writers and women characters from the Renaissance to the present in terms of changing definitions and expectations, and argued that 'lesbianism' was a construct of modern sexologists (*Surpassing the Love of Men*, 1981). This last has proved a useful approach to Radclyffe HALL and charges of obscenity; the 'lesbian continuum' concept has been applied to the issue of women adopting male 'disguise' (like Willa CATHER). Other critics like Catharine STIMPSON and Teresa de Lauretis, interested in the representation of the female body, insist that sexuality defines lesbianism. Claudie Lesselier has identified a 'tension' between 'claiming' the category *lesbian* and 'subverting the whole system of categorization' in the name of feminist inclusiveness. Lesbian criticism early inscribed its exclusion from heterosexual feminist criticism; a second exclusion has concerned lesbians of colour. Among attempts to counter the first exclusion were special issues of *Margins* in 1975 and of *Sinister Wisdom* in 1976 and 1980, and Elly Bulkin's 'Heterosexism and Women's Studies', 1981. The second exclusion (marked in the small proportion of space given in lesbian debates to women of colour) was addressed by Barbara Smith in 'Towards a Black Feminist Criticism' (*Conditions: Two*, 1977, acknowledging a 'near nonexistence' of black overtly lesbian literature), by the special issue co-edited by Smith and Lorraine Bethel, *Conditions: Five*, 1979 (containing Ann SHOCKLEY's overview of 'The Black Lesbian in American Literature'), and Gloria Hull's *Color, Sex and Poetry*, 1987 (which cites Alice DUNBAR-NELSON and Angelina Weld GRIMKÉ to suggest that a black lesbian tradition is suppressed rather than non-existent), and Barbara Christian in *Conjuring*, 1985, discussing the 'overt exploration of lesbian relationships' in 'radical fiction' by black women in the 1980s. By the late 1970s, lesbian feminist criticism had voices in the lesbian press, feminist alternative press, academic feminist journals, and, increasingly, the academic mainstream. Lesbian/feminist presses issued important work on new lesbian poetry (Elly Bulkin's 'Kissing / Against the Light', 1978; Judy GRAHN's *The Highest Apple*, 1985), as well as Margaret Cruikshank, ed., *Lesbian Studies*, 1982, which addresses essential pedagogical – and racial – issues in lesbian studies. Academic feminist journals tended to print studies of individual lesbian writers or critical 'overviews' like Bonnie Zimmerman's much reprinted 'What Has Never Been', 1981, which surveys trends, raises issues of lesbian separatism and heterosexism, and urges historical and cultural specificity and work on stylistics. The essays in *Signs* 1985 *Lesbian Issue* typify recent preoccupations: the historical significance of Hall's Stephen Gordon, 'masquerade' writing, the lesbian tradition from Sappho to modernist to contemporary poets, Monique WITTIG's lesbianizing of phallocratic discourse, and a theory of reading which would ensure lesbians non-exclusion from any text. Mainstream academic publishing has produced Elaine Marks's reading of Wittig and the female body ('Lesbian Intertextuality', 1979), Jane Marcus's analysis of Virginia WOOLF's *A Room of One's Own*, as a 'narration of lesbian seduction', 1987, Zimmerman's discussion of the lesbian novel of development (*The Voyage In*, 1983), and Stimpson's readings of Gertrude STEIN, 1977, 1985, of Rich, 1985, and of romantic and realistic lesbian modes ('Zero Degree Deviancy', 1981). These critics make it clear that in lesbian contexts the boundaries between criticism and theory are unstable. Rich has exerted greater influence here by discussing heterosexual and lesbian culture than by discussing writers; also powerful for lesbian critics have been Mary DALY, Audre LORDE, Wittig, and the Combahee River Collective's 'A Feminist Statement'. As their work has engaged with mainstream cultural and literary theories of psychoanalysis, deconstruction, reader-response, and semiotics, a lesbian feminist literary-theoretical enquiry has emerged. One manifestation is Québec fiction/theory, notably Nicole BROSSARD's efforts through the *process* of writing fiction to stage a theory of the lesbian subject and of her representation. Another is feminist semiotics: de Lauretis challenging the limitations of a theory of sexual and gender difference (*Technologies of Gender*, 1987) and arguing that feminist theories of gender difference may inscribe an 'indifference' to lesbian sexuality and make it impossible to 'see' the '(self-)representation' of the lesbian (*Theatre Journal*, 1988). See bibliography in Cruikshank, ed., *New Lesbian Writing*, 1984.

Lessing, Doris May (Tayler), 'Jane Somers', novelist, short-story writer, dramatist, b.

1919 in Kermanshah, Iran, first child of Emily Maude (McVeagh) and her ex-patient Alfred Cook T., amputee from WWI. They took her at five to a lonely unprosperous homestead in Rhodesia (now Zimbabwe), which gave her an expansive, formative physical freedom. She began writing at nine, educ. herself by reading, and early perceived racial inequality and despised her mother's hankering for English middle-class values. Having endured schooling (a convent school in Salisbury, now Harare) she left at 14 to work as an *au pair*, taught herself secretarial skills and wrote two (unpublished) novels. At 19 she m. Frank Charles Wisdom; at 22 she left him and two children; in 1945 she m. Gottfried Anton L., a German-Jewish communist exile. While married she worked both for the Rhodesian government (as a secretary) and for a small Marxist group seeking black liberation. In 1949 she moved to England with husband and son, then divorced. Next year she made her name with *The Grass is Singing*, a novel of a white farmer's wife crumbling in the isolation of the African veld. Next came short-story volumes (*This Was the Old Chief's Country*, 1951 – title re-used in 1973 – and *Five: Short Novels*, 1953) and the five-vol. Martha Quest series, *Children of Violence*, 1952–69. The books move from Africa to England, charting emotional distress both personal and political (left-wing faith undermined by Stalinism); they combine a traditional, 'scrupulous' realism with fantastic prophecy of communal catastrophe and 'attendant madness' (Joyce Carol OATES). 'Being Prohibited' records a painful trip 'home', 1956. DL had several plays staged and two printed: *Each to His Own Wilderness*, 1959, and *Play with a Tiger*, 1962. The protagonist of *The Golden Notebook*, 1962, composing her identity in its various facets between variously-coloured covers, is the first of many experiments with form. DL notes that 'what many women were thinking, feeling, experiencing, came as a great surprise', as well as how passages which caused her anxiety as 'hopelessly private' (e.g. about menstruation) proved precisely those that 'spoke for other people'. She published more stories in 1963, 1964, and 1966: collected in two vols. (African), 1973, and two vols. (general), 1978. In the late 1960s she moved away from socialism towards mystical Sufism; in a profoundly disordered society, characters' psychological collapse can signal a hope for new perceptions. Otherworldy hints in *Briefing for a Descent into Hell*, 1971, *The Summer Before the Dark*, 1973, and *The Memoirs of a Survivor*, 1974, are developed in the controversial 'speculative' or fantasy series, *Canopus in Argus: Archives*, five vols., 1979–85 (DL adapted an opera libretto, *The Making of the Representative for Planet 8*, 1988). These novels abandon history and 'character', as cosmic forces and vastly superior Canopeans contend with human problems of disharmony and destructiveness. In 1983, hoping to 'be reviewed on merit', outside her reputation's 'cage of associations', or else to expose inequities in the system, DL published (after two rejections) as 'Jane Somers' *The Diary of a Good Neighbour*, and *If the Old Could ...* (repr. as by DL, 1984), on a fashion-magazine editor's entanglement with an old, poor, sick woman. In *The Good Terrorist*, 1985, and *The Fifth Child*, 1988, DL creates situations of moral complexity in which revolutionary idealism and glorification of the family are respectively questioned. DL is a weighty, disquieting prophet about the world's future; Lisa ALTHER says that 'almost every woman writer I know acknowledges a debt' to her. Essay volumes ed. by Eve Bertelsen, 1985, by Claire Sprague and Virginia Tiger, both 1986, and by Carey Kaplan and Ellen Cronan Ross, 1988; study by Sprague, 1987.

Le Sueur, Meridel, poet, novelist, short-story writer, journalist, political activist. B. 1900 in Murray, Iowa, da. of Marian Lucy and William Winston Wharton, she took the name of her step-father, socialist lawyer Arthur Le S., and has passed it to her two daughters. Farm and Indian women were her chosen family: in 'The Ancient People and the Newly Come' she calls them storytellers and poets who changed her life. She dropped out of high school, became a political radical, spent several years as an actress and stunt-woman, and found herself on the fringes of society among unemployed women. She has often found it hard to publish her prolific writings, which include political philosophy and voluminous unpublished journals. She married Harry Rice in the 1920s, but rarely lived with him; she responded to the execution of Sacco and Vanzetti by conceiving a child as her gift to a 'dead and closed' world; *Annunciation* (limited ed. 1935) began as a journal during pregnancy. She published stories (coll. in *Salute to Spring*, 1940) and reportage in the 1930s: 'Women on the Breadlines', 1932, and 'Women are Hungry', 1934, capture poverty and pain but also celebrate survival. *The Girl* (finished 1939, unpub. till 1978) follows the life of a young every-woman, protected from intrusive social workers by other vagrant women, bearing a child with 'the tiny face of my mother. Like in a mirror.' *North Star Country*, 1945, reflects MLS's abiding concern with the history of her native Midwest. She wrote several historical books for children, aiming to show 'what kind of people we are when we are together building and not destroying'. Her life of her parents, *Crusaders*, 1955 (repr. 1984 with her intro.), describes her grandmother, a pioneer and militant TEMPERANCE worker, and her mother, a radical feminist who opposed railroad monopolies and was a leader in workers' education in Kansas. MLS described her travelling, writing, and working for women's causes, in 'Eroded Woman' [1948] and 'The Dark of the Time'. Her poems in *Rites of Ancient Ripening*, 1975, seek an alternative to male language (which describes landscape, as it does a woman, as an object to possess). They blend 'woman talk', with its 'different rhythm and tempo', with Native, particularly Mandan, songs, tales and images as a voice of women's communal experience, seeking to place Indian experience in a feminist context; MLS has been charged with appropriation. *Harvest and Song for my Time*, 1977, collects stories; *Ripening*, 1982, ed. Elaine Hedges, selects from 53 years' work. See autobiographical essay in Chester G. Anderson, ed., *Growing Up in Minnesota*, 1976; Blanche H. Gelfant in *Women Writing in America*, 1984; L. R. Pratt in *Women's Studies*, 14, 1988. MLS has given several interviews and had a film made of her work by the Women's Film Collective of Minnesota.

Letters. To Virginia WOOLF 'the unpublished works of women' were *personal* letters; but most surviving ones by medieval and Tudor women (dictated to male scribes) deal with business: Joan Lady Pelham from a besieged castle, 1399 (L. Lyell, *A Medieval Postbag*, 1934), Elizabeth Lady Zouche about errands like choice of fabric, 1402 (E. Rickert, *RES*, 8, 1932). Notable are Elizabeth (Croke) Stonor (d. 1479: family papers ed. 1919) and Margaret (Mautby) Paston (d. 1484). In her circle (Norman Davis, ed., 1971, 1976) some ladies penned their own notes; Margery (Brews) Paston dictated a Valentine poem for her future husband. Katherine (Knyvett), Lady Paston, 1578–1629, wrote (like her predecessors) on business, and also sympathetic advice to a son at Cabridge (Ruth Hughey, ed., 1941). Many RENAISSANCE ladies, mostly ROYALTY (like Margaret TUDOR) or of powerful families, expressed themselves forcefully by letter (Mary Anne Everett Wood, ed., 1846). More often than their male relations, they combine effective despatch of business or politics with genuinely personal expression, notably Honor Lady Lisle in the 1530s (M. St Clare Byrne, ed., 1981, selec. 1983) and Katherine, Duchess of SUFFOLK. A volume of letters allegedly all by ladies, ed. Du Bosque, appeared in English in 1638; soon women were widely judged the best letter-writers. Dorothy OSBORNE, Marie de SÉVIGNÉ, and Lady Mary Wortley MONTAGU made the familiar letter self-revealing, witty, and creative, as novelists from Aphra BEHN and Eliza HAYWOOD made it a favourite vehicle for fiction; later Mary HAYS, Clara REEVE and many others made letter-essays equally popular. Still good reading are Hill Boothby (1708–56: earnest exhortations to Samuel Johnson, pub. 1805); Mary (Lepel), Lady Hervey (1700–68: J. W. Croker, ed., 1821); and whole families like the Lennox sisters: Lady Caroline, 1723–74, later Lady Holland; Lady Emily, 1731–1814, later Duchess of Leinster; and Lady Sarah, 1745–1826, later Bunbury and Napier. Valuable historical detail is given by Ann Brodbelt writing from Jamaica, 1788–96 (Geraldine Mozley, ed., 1938). Mary Russell MITFORD, Emily DICKINSON and Alice JAMES all conducted their literary lives by letter; so did Elizabeth HAWTHORNE and (before her marriage) Elizabeth Barrett BROWNING. Florence NIGHTINGALE also conducted a massive correspondence from her couch. Notable among travellers' letters are Mary KINGSLEY's, Elizabeth RIGBY's and Lucie Duff GORDON's; Charlotte BRONTË's friend Mary TAYLOR wrote from New Zealand, Rachel HENNING and Elizabeth MACARTHUR from Australia, Dolly MADISON from the White House (which she named) in Washington, DC. Ada M. Ingpen ed. a general anthology of women's letters, 1909, but there has still been comparatively little attention given to women's letters across the span of history (studies of the early period by Ruth Perry and Janet Todd, both 1980, see bibliog.). Attention to women's epistolarity is focusing on exchanges between women, e.g. Vera BRITTAIN and Winifred HOLTBY, pub. 1960, Reneé VIVIEN and Natalie Clifford BARNEY, 1983 (in French), Virginia WOOLF and Vita SACKVILLE-WEST, 1985. See Cheryl Cline, *Women's Diaries, Journals, and Letters, An Annotated Bibliography* (of printed correspondences), 1989.

Leverson, Ada (Beddington), 1862–1933, novelist, journalist, one of eight children of Zillah (Simon), amateur pianist, and Samuel B., wealthy London property owner. She was educ. at home in French, German, and (by a Girton College graduate) Classics, and m. Ernest L. at 19 against her father's wish. Her son died in childhood. Unhappy in her marriage by 1891, she wrote to George Moore of her 'weak terror' of scandal or divorce; she had by then submitted to publishers a 'little sketch' and was working on a novel. Next year she met Oscar Wilde, who praised her wit and and called her 'the Sphinx'. In the first of her four Wilde parodies, Lady Windermere and Salome, each speaking in her own style, attend 'An Afternoon Party' with an opera heroine, Ibsen's Nora, and others. *Punch* followed this (1893) with her parodies of Beerbohm and Kipling; *The Yellow Book* took two stories, 1895–6. She gave sanctuary to Wilde during his trials. Her 113 women's columns for the weekly *Referee*, 1903–5, as 'Elaine', include parody of advice-writers. In 1905 Ernest L., always a gambler, migrated to Canada after a financial crash; left with reduced means, AL began *The Twelfth Hour*, 1907. Its heroine takes 'a cool sportsmanlike pleasure' in being a beauty, and makes her second appearance carrying hyacinths. AL's manner hangs on dialogue and authorial wit: 'feminine intuition, a quality perhaps even rarer in women than in men'. Three of five more novels trace a marriage clearly based on her own: in *Love's Shadow*, 1908, the wife's amused tolerance of her monstrously egotistical mate (besides the courtship of a girl called Hyacinth, loved by many men and a remarkable woman); in *Tenterhooks*, 1912, the anguish of illicit passion; in *Love at Second Sight*, 1916 (her last novel), happiness reached only when the husband leaves for the USA ('Thank heaven') with a vulgar caricature of a woman who will 'look after him – he'll be all right' (all three repr. as *The Little Ottleys*, 1962, 1982). AL prefaced an anonymous astrology book, 1915, parodied free verse and free-verse critics (*The English Review*, 1919), and commemorated Wilde (*Criterion*, Jan. 1926; expanded with his letters to her, 1930, repr. in life by her daughter, Violet Wyndham, 1963). Her friends ran from Violet Hunt to Edith Sitwell (to whom she sent a laurel crown). She left unfinished after 40 years a comedy from French, *The Triflers*. Reprinting her novels began in 1950: study by Charles Burkhart, 1973.

Levertov, Denise, US poet, essayist, translator and activist, b. in 1923 in Ilford, Essex, to Beatrice (Spooner-Jones), descendant of Welsh mystic Angel Jones, and Paul Phillip L., a Russian Jew converted to Christianity. She received no formal education, but grew up in a passionately intellectual, artistic and political environment, her home a centre for Jews escaping Nazism. She became a nurse in WWII, married American writer Mitchell Goodman (divorced, 1972), emigrated to the USA, 1948, and had a son, 1949. Her first, 'neo-romantic', volume of poems, *The Double Image*, 1946, was published in England; her subsequent writing, thought very American, is deeply influenced by the directness of speech and immediacy of experience in the work of W. C. Williams, H.D., and the Black Mountain poets, most apparently in her early US publications, *Here and Now*, 1957, *Jacob's Ladder* 1961, and *O Taste and See*, 1964. In the mid 1960s, DL protested US involvement in Vietnam and travelled in South-East Asia ('we need poems ... to help us *live* the revolution'). *The Sorrow Dance*, 1967, and *Relearning the Alphabet*, 1970, address racism, poverty and war, as well as DL's grief at the death of her sister Olga. The war poems in *To Stay Alive*, 1971, 'record ... one person's inner/outer experience of America during the '60's'. Later volumes, such as *The Freeing of the Dust*, 1975, *Life in the Forest*, 1978, and *Candles in Babylon*, 1982, refocus on interior experience, exploring the specifically female: 'When I am woman – O, when I am / a woman, / my wells of salt brim and brim, / poems force the lock of my throat' ('Canción', 1975). DL's essays on poetry, travel, and politics are collected in *The Poet in the World*, 1973; Linda Wagner, ed., *DL: In Her Own Province*, 1979; and *Light Up the Cave*, 1981. She has translated *In Praise of Krishna: Songs From the Bengali* (with Edward Dincock), 1967, and *Selected Poems*, by Eugene Guillevic, 1969. More recent poems, *Oblique Prayers: New Poems with Fourteen Translations*, 1984, and *Breathing the Water*, 1987, suggest a spiritual or mystical sensibility that finds its power in nature, the body, and her self. See Rachel Blau DuPlessis in Gilbert and Gubar, eds., 1979, Diana Surman in *CritQ*, 22, 1980, Lorrie Smith in *CanL*, 27, 1986, and *Ostriker*, 1986.

Levy, Amy, 1861–89, poet and novelist, second da. of Isabelle (Levin) and Lewis L., editor. B. at Clapham, she was educ. at Brighton, where her parents moved in 1876. AL pub. her first poem at 13, in *The Pelican*, a feminist journal. She studied at Newnham as the first Jewish student, and pub. another poem in *The Pelican* and a story in *Temple Bar* during her first term. At 18, she pub. a letter in the *Jewish Chronicle* on 'Jewish Women and Women's Rights' (7 February 1879). She contributed to Wilde's *Women's World*, and pub. *Xantippe*, a defence of Socrates' maligned wife, in 1881. Subsequently she is supposed to have worked in a factory, lived in a garrett and taught in London, but her close friend Clementina Black maintains that 'she never left her father's house otherwise than on visits to friends or on holiday journeys'. (*Athenaeum*, 5 October 1889). Such journeys included travels in Europe and visits to her friend Vernon Lee. She also knew Olive SCHREINER. *A Minor Poet and Other Verse* was pub. in 1884 (much of it from *Xantippe*). This was followed by three novels: *The Romance of a Shop*, 1888, about four sisters who set up a photographic studio; *Reuben Sachs*, 1888, a satire on the conservatism, materialism and repression of women in the Anglo-Jewish community (possibly in reply to ELIOT's *Daniel Deronda*); and *Miss Meredith*, 1889, about an independent woman who works in Italy as a governess. She corrected proofs for her last poems, *A London Plane Tree*, 1889, a week before she died. These poems are direct, simple narratives, more melancholy than her novels; she recognizes herself as a specifically urban poet. She committed suicide at her parents' home in Endsleigh Gardens, London. See Edward Wagenknecht, *Daughters of the Covenant*, 1983, and Freema Gottlieb, *Jewish Chronicle Lit. Supp.*, 24 December 1976.

Levy, Deborah, b. 1959, poet, short-story writer. Brought to England from S. Africa at nine, she was educ. at many schools as her family moved about, later in theatre language at the Dartington College of Arts in Devon. She has written short stories and read her poetry in England and Europe, but is best known for her plays. Striving to find a dramatic language 'both political and poetic', she often takes her themes from existing literature and world history, seeking a feminist response to what she sees as the spiritual wastelands of our century. Her visually imaginative plays often draw on collaboration with artists and other theatre workers. *Pax* is an anti-nuclear play commissioned by the Women's THEATRE GROUP, 1984, pub. 1987, which represents twentieth-century Europe in archetypes of history, the future, the present and 'The Domesticated Woman' who is both present and past. Other plays include *Clam*, pub. in *Peace Plays*, 1985; *Heresies* (Royal Shakespeare Co., 1986, pub. 1987); *Our Lady* (Women's Theatre Group, 1986). In her volume of short stories, *Ophelia and the Great Idea*, 1988, the title piece is a witty and unnerving fable about the nuclear family and nuclear society; 'A Little Treatise on Sex and Politics in the 1980s' uses verse, lists, dramatic dialogue and contrasted type-faces.

Lewis, Alethea (Brereton), 'Eugenia De Acton', 1750–1827, didactic novelist, b. at Framlingham, Suffolk. Her mother d. when she was four. At 17 she was proud of her learning. She and her fiancé, William Springal Levett (d. 1774), introduced George Crabbe (who wrote to her as 'Stella') to his future wife. In 1788 she m. Augustus L., surgeon and former transported felon, and after trying the USA (perhaps) and Lancs. they settled at Preston Hall, Penkridge, Staffs. Mary MEEKE subscribed to her epistolary *Vicissitudes in Genteel Life* (anon., 1794), which ranges skilfully in style from the aphoristic to the exclamatory. Always intelligent, but too fond of ideal exemplars, AL stayed anonymous in *Plain Sense*, MINERVA, 1795, *Disobedience*, 1797, and *The Microcosm*, 1801. Here a critical preface places the novel in a long tradition of moral writing, and regrets her inability to revise: 'My first copy has always been my last.' The educational, conservative *Essays on the Art of Being Happy*, 1803, first use her PSEUDONYM. A dedication 'To the Gentlemen Reviewers' quotes their praise lavishly but also takes them to task for misreadings. Women, she says, are naturally quick to learn; wives have a 'conciliatory office'; sexual difference needs emphasis more than equality. Six more novels progressively develop in scene-setting and plot; four pub. also in the USA. *The Nuns of the Desert, or The Woodland Witches*, 1805, carries the GOTHIC to extremes with oppressed nuns and (separately) three capriciously powerful sybils. *Things by their Right Names*, 1812, dedicated 'To the Dethroned Sovéreign Truth', is written as by a nameless male who hopes by authorship to emulate women's usefulness. Maria EDGEWORTH ascribed AL's *Rhoda*, 1816, to Frances Margaretta Jackson or Jacson, 1754–1842, whose sister Maria Elizabeth published books on botany, 1797–1816.

Lewis, Janet, poet, novelist, writer of short stories, opera libretti, and children's books, b. in 1899 in Chicago, da. of Elizabeth (Taylor) and novelist and poet Edwin Herbert L. She was educ. at the Lewis Institute, Chicago (AA, 1918), and the Univ. of Chicago (PhD, 1920), where she met Elizabeth Madox ROBERTS. She was a passport clerk in Paris, a proofreader for *Redbook*, and a teacher at the Lewis Institute. After three years in Santa Fe bedridden with tuberculosis, she married poet Yvor Winters in 1926. Her first poems appeared in *Poetry* in 1920; *The Indians in the Woods*, 1922, is the first of her six collections. Her poems are formally traditional, moral in tone, seeking serenity and wholeness of being; they are marked by quiet nostalgia for times when the self was fused more closely with the order of nature, as in Indian culture, ancient cultures, childhood, and moments of stillness in her own past. See *Poems Old and New*, 1981. She bore a daughter in 1931 and wrote the first of her historical novels, *The Invasion*, 1932: it portrays the Ojibway Indians' gradual acceptance of the English presence after invasion in 1759, weaving public and personal histories together. *The Wife of Martin Guerre*, 1941, focuses on the question of why Bertrande, Guerre's wife, chooses to uphold an order which runs counter to her desire: 'More than ever she understood her position in the household, part of a structure that reached backward in time towards ancestors of whose renown one was proud and forward to a future in which ... children were to grow tall and maintain ... the prosperity and honor of the family.' *The Trial of Sören Qvist*, 1947, treats a tale of injustice in seventeenth-century Jutland, examining characters who, dealing with complex moral issues, are inexorably trapped by their dogged belief in a moral order outside themselves. *The Ghost of Monsieur Scarron*, 1959, is also based on a case history; *Against a Darkening Sky*, 1943, has a contemporary setting. JL published an article on Izak DINESEN in *SoR*, 2, 1966. Interviews in *SoR*, 10, 1974, and 18, 1982; studies by Ellen Killoh in *SoR*, 10, and Helen Trimpi in *SoR*, 18. Papers at Stanford Univ., where JL has taught.

Libbey, Laura Jean, 1862–1925, popular novelist, b. Brooklyn, NY, da. of Elizabeth (Nelson) and Thomas H. L., educ. privately. She began writing in her teens, contributing regularly to the *Ledger*, the *Fireside Companion*, and the *Family Story Paper*; from 1891 to 1894 she ed. *Fashion Bazaar*. She wrote over 60 novels in the 1880s and 1890s, with titles like *True Love's Reward or, Cast upon the Wicked World*, all pointing the same moral of the most virtuous girl winning the richest husband and with him, happiness and love. Aimed successfully at working-class girl readers, her novels earned her $50,000 a year. As perceived by LJL, the only cause for hope in her readers' lives lay in the romanticized idea of marriage as a deliverance from the physical and spiritual exhaustion of their daily work. Her preface to *That Pretty Young Girl*, n.d., typically argues for the avoidance of realism and the preservation of girls' 'day-dreams' of 'the roseate future': 'It is not pleasant to think of white doves coming to the muddy pool to drink'. In 1898 she m. Van Mater Stillwell, lawyer, following the death of her domineering mother who would not allow her to marry. After her marriage, LJL ceased writing; nine years later she turned to drama but there is no record of her plays being performed or published. She left her fortune to her sister.

Lickbarrow, Isabella, poet, b. in humble life at Kendal in the Lake District, self-educated, orphaned young with her sisters.

She wrote poetry from an early age and to raise money pub. *Poetical Effusions*, Kendal, 1814, with her name: Wordsworth and Southey subscribed. Her work is versatile and thoughtful: descriptions of local scenery; celebrations of Elizabeth SMITH, 1776–1806, and of Thomas Chatterton; response to Anne GRANT's letters; tender lyrics, love-songs, an 'Invocation to Peace', and comic poems mocking authorial dignity. In 1818 she pub. at Liverpool a masque-like *Lament* for Princess Charlotte (mourners number shepherdesses and shepherds, sea- and wood-nymphs with appropriate offerings, and a stranger calling up 'the shades of Anglo-Saxon kings'); in a companion piece a patriotic young poet sees a vision of Alfred, and prays for the birth of a new Alfred to save and bless the land. IL's work also appeared in anthologies and magazines.

Liddiard, J. (or **I.**) **S. Anna** (Wilkinson), Irish poet, da. of Sir Henry W. She dedicated her *Poems*, Dublin, 1810, to her husband, the Rev. William L., poet and ex-army officer. They spent 1811–13 at Bath, where she pub. a 2nd ed., 1811, titled *The Sgelaighe, or A Tale of Old* from a story said to come from an old Irish MS. Among poems added, 'Addressed to Albion' blames the 'Queen of Wealth, and Fame' for insult to her sister-kingdom. When *The Monthly Review* called JSAL too fond of personification, she diagnosed prejudice against her pro-Irish feeling. She castigated reviewers (quoting Anna SEWARD) in her preface to *Kenilworth and Farley Castle*, Dublin, 1813, dedicated to the Ladies of LLANGOLLEN, whom she had visited. The title poems present a masque before ELIZABETH I (expanded in 2nd ed., 1815) and a tale told by a 'Phantom Knight'; others record her return from Bath to Ireland. In 1816 appeared together her husband's *Mont St Jean*, describing the battle of Waterloo, and her *Theodore and Laura*, subtitled 'Evening after the Battle', in which a heroic wife seeks her husband among the heaps of corpses, finds him dying, and goes mad: not the dead, she says, but the bereaved, should be wept for. *Mount Leinster*, 1819, ascribed to her, is probably William L.'s.

Lim, Catherine, novelist, short-story writer, of Chinese descent. She was b. in 1943 in a small Malaysian village, educ. in English, then moved, 1970, with her businessman husband and two children to Singapore, where she taught at a Catholic Junior College until 1978. She works now in curriculum planning with the Ministry of Education. Described as 'the best writer in Singapore' (*Asiaweek*, 17 July 1981), she has published four collections of short stories – *Little Ironies: Stories of Singapore*, 1978 (originally intended for juvenile readers), *Or Else, The Lightning God & Other Stories*, 1980, *They Do Burn*, 1983, *The Shadow of a Dream*, 1987 – and a novel, *The Serpent's Tooth*, 1982, a brief, deceptively simple tale of personal relationships in a Chinese extended family in Singapore. CL's work explores personal and social subjects – westernization, class attitudes, the plight of the old and the poor and of women and girls in Singapore society. For their irony and clarity her stories have been compared to Maupassant's and Daudet's. See Robert Yeo in *Commentary*, 5, 1982.

Lincoln, Elizabeth Clinton (Knyvett), Countess of, 1574?–?1630, advice-writer. Da. of Elizabeth (Stumpe) and Sir Henry K. of Charlton, Wilts., she was married to the future 3rd Earl of Lincoln in 1584, and by his death, 1618, had 18 children (the younger ones grew up with the future Anne BRADSTREET). She did not suckle them herself: 'partly I was over-ruled by another's Authority, and partly deceived by some ill Counsel, and partly I had not so well considered of my Duty in this Motherly Office.' It was the nurses' fault, she feared, that two babies died. Remorsefully, she published *The Countess of Lincoln's Nursery*, 1622 (repr. *Harleian Misc.*, 1745), addressed to her breast-feeding daughter-in-law ('this lovely Action of yours'). Some of her views are harsh and punitive, some timeless. Meeting complaints 'that it is troublesome; that it is noisome to one's Cloaths, that it makes one look old, &c.', she argues that this 'express Ordinance of God' bonds mother and baby, that a wet-nurse must be exploited (bidden to 'unlove her own to love yours'), and that a sucking baby symbolizes all human beings as God's 'new-born Babes'.

Lindbergh, Anne (Morrow), novelist, poet, memoirist and aviator, b. 1906 in NJ, da. of Elizabeth (Cutter), poet, children's writer, and acting President of Smith College, and of Dwight Whitney M., businessman and ambassador. Shy despite her literary ability, she was educ. at Miss Chapin's School, NYC, and at Smith. Her 1929 engagement to eligible Charles L. was proclaimed 'an argument . . . for old-fashioned femininity' – a comment belied by her activities as aviator, navigator and radio operator. The diffident, retiring couple were driven from the USA by frenzied publicity around the kidnapping and murder of their first son, 1932, the trial and the birth of a second son, 1935, and continuing death threats. Travels in Europe brought contact with leading figures; after the birth of a third son, 1937, they were fêted at the Munich Air Show and toasted by Goering. War pressures forced their return in 1939. Blamed for her political writings (especially *The Wave of the Future*, 1940, espousing pacificism and isolation to advance 'our civilization, our way of life, and our democracy' in face of the threat of war), AL was praised for her works as a two-career woman, 'a flier and writer'. Phrases like 'girlish charm', 'the girl can write', greeted tales of exploration and aviation like *North to the Orient*, 1935, and *Listen! the Wind*, 1938. AL's public life is outranked in interest by her autobiographical novels, memoirs, and poems. Five volumes of adult letters and diaries show her using writing as personal exploration. Essays in *Gift from the Sea*, 1955, probe the continual struggle of a modern woman for self-identity. Being a housewife is 'a circus act we women perform every day of our lives'; an ideal relationship is 'the meeting of two whole fully developed people as persons'. *The Unicorn, and Other Poems*, 1956, treats nature, metaphysics and gender relations: in a wedding photo AL's mother is 'Pretending to be girl, although so strong, / Playing the role of wife ("Here I belong")'. *Dearly Beloved*, 1962, a novel about a wedding, makes each person 'a lens for rays of past and future . . . human hates, loves and histories'. AL's mannered style has dated more than her concern with identity, purpose and personal freedom. See study of the L. case by Ludovic Kennedy, 1985; life (for young readers) by Roxanne Chadwick, 1987.

Lindsay, Caroline Blanche Elizabeth, Lady, 1844–1912, poet, novelist and painter, da. of Hannah Mayer (Rothschild) and Henry Fitzroy, MP. Educ. in France and London, she studied painting at Heatherley's, Newman Street, and m. Sir Coutts L. (d. 1913) in 1864; they separated in the early 1880s. Her first pub. work, *Caroline*, 1888, was followed by a selection of songs, facts and legends called *About Robins*, 1889. Her first major work, the rather flowery *Lyrics and Other Poems*, 1890, was reprinted the same year. Her next collection, *The King's Last Vigil*, 1894, included 'Love or Fame' (the woman poet's choice), 'Of a Dead Poetess' and the much-anthologized 'To My Own Face'. *The Flower-Seller*, 1896, contained a narrative poem sequence, 'Lucinda's Letters'. Among later volumes were *From a Venetian Balcony*, 1903 (illustrated by Clara Montalba), and *Poems of Love and Death*, 1907. She also wrote verses for children, some plays and a patriotic Boer War poem, *For England*, 1900. Her prose works include *Bertha's Earl*, 1891, and *A Tangled Web*, 1892, about a Scottish heiress who masquerades as an ignorant Australian in order to see the world (but meets and loves – her own cousin); and, more seriously, a pamphlet on *The Art of Poetry with Regard to Women Writers*, 1899. Herself a skilful musician, CL had friends who were artists (Watts, Millais, Alma-Tadema, Burne-Jones) and writers (Browning, Lecky, Bret Harte).

Lindsay, Joan (à Beckett Weigall), 1896–1984, novelist, b. Melbourne, Victoria, da. of Anne (Hamilton) and Theyre à B. W., barrister. After Clyde Girls' Grammar, she studied art at the National Gallery in Melbourne and in 1922 m. Sir Daryl L. Her first book, *Through Darkest Pondelayo*, 1936 (pub. as by 'Serena Livingstone-Stanley'), is a whacky parody of gentility, British colonialism, and exploration accounts. Her next two works were largely autobiographical. *Time Without Clocks*, 1962, is concerned with the period of her early married life, while *Facts Soft and Hard*, 1964, is an account of a visit to the USA. Her best-known work is *Picnic at Hanging Rock*, 1967 (film 1975). This recounts the intriguing disappearance of three schoolgirls and their teacher from a picnic in the Mt Macedon area on St Valentine's Day, 1900. The work has a mythic quality and develops her earlier preoccupations with questions of time, in particular, tensions between mechanical time, natural time, and time of the mind. A previously unpub. final chapter was included when the novel was reissued, 1986. JL also wrote a children's book, *Syd Sixpence*, 1982.

Linington, Barbara **Elizabeth**, 'Anne Blaisdell', 'Lesley Egan', 'Egan O'Neill', 'Dell Shannon', historical novelist and thriller writer. Her PSEUDONYMS are all, in one way or another, derived from her grandmothers' names: 'Egan O'Neill', under which she wrote the historical novel *The Anglophile*, 1957 (*The Pretender* in the UK), 'honors' them both. B. in 1921 in Aurora, Ill., da. of Ruth (Biggam) and musician Byron G. L., she was educ. at Glendale Jr. College (AB, 1942). She is a life member of the John Birch Society. Her career began with 'historicals': after *The Proud Man*, 1955, she wrote four more, 1956–8. Her police procedurals feature ethnic detectives: Mexican-American Lt. Luis Mendoza of the Los Angeles Police Department (about whom she writes as Shannon), Jewish Jesse Falkenstein, her 'one non-cop' (as Egan), Italian-American Vic Vatallo (as Linington), and Welsh Sergeant Ivor Maddox. She sees her genre as 'the morality play of the twentieth century' because 'about 99 per cent [of DETECTIVE books] are on the side of the angels'. Her more than 70 fictions (including, recently, *Strange Felony*, 1986, and *Murder by the Tale*, 1987) engage 'the basics': 'truth versus lie, law and order versus anarchy, a moral code versus amorality': 'I try to involve the reader *from the police viewpoint*. For I believe that this is no more than the duty of those of us who have taken sides, as it were, in the never-ending struggle between good and evil.' Her police figures, unsurprisingly, are idealized. See her articles (as Shannon) in *The Writer*, March 1967, quoted above, and October 1970.

Linton, Eliza (**Lynn**), 1822–98, novelist and journalist, b. Crosthwaite, Cumberland, sixth da. and twelfth child of Charlotte (Goodenough), who died in ELL's early infancy, and Rev. James Lynn. Self-educ., she rebelled against her conservative background and in 1845 went to live in London, where she contributed to newspapers and journals, including Dickens's *Household Words*, and pub. her first novel, *Azeth the Egyptian*, 1846, an erudite historical romance. A life-long agnostic, she shows her youthful radicalism in her earlier novels: *Anymone*, 1848, portrays a learned and independent Greek woman, whilst *Realities*, 1850, attacks double sexual standards, urges relaxation of divorce laws, and argues for learned women gaining entry into the male professions. However, a later essay, 'The Higher EDUCATION of Women', 1886, argues against 'education carried to excess, and [the] exhausting anxieties of professional life'. In 1858 she m. writer and engraver William James Linton, largely in compliance with his late wife's request that she look after his seven children. The couple lived apart from 1864. Her later fiction, like her periodical writings, shows an increasingly reactionary attitude towards women's rights. Most notorious are her articles on the 'WOMAN QUESTION' in the *Saturday Review*, 1866–8 (repr. 1883 as *The Girl of the Period*), where she attacks the 'NEW WOMAN' for unfeminine aggressiveness and the 'Shrieking Sisterhood' for 'the hysterical parade they make about their wants and intentions'. She was devoted to W. S. Landor, knew George and Agnes Lewes, John Chapman, and George ELIOT, and was friends with Beatrice HARRADEN, Annie Hector ('Mrs ALEXANDER') and other writers. Two years before her death she was made a member of the Society of Authors, and was the first woman invited to serve on its committee. Biographical details are in several of her novels, especially *The Autobiography of Chistopher Kirkland*, 1885, and in *My Literary Life*, 1899 (pub. posthumously). There are lives by G. S. Layard, 1901, and Nancy Fix Anderson, 1987, and a study by Herbert van Thal, 1979; several of her novels were reprinted in the 1970s.

Lispector, Clarice, 1925–77, novelist, translator, writer of short stories and children's literature. B. in the Ukraine, she migrated to Brazil as an infant, later took a degree in law without intending to practise, married lawyer and diplomat Mauri Gurgel Valente and published her first novel. She travelled to Europe and the USA, then, separated, returned with two children to Rio de Janeiro. She has published nine novels, seven collections of short stories, and four books for children. Hélène CIXOUS describes her writing as 'feminine', in mediative terms: 'she affirms life in a pure affirmation'. *A hora da estrela*, 1977 (*The Hour of the Star*, 1986), announces itself as 'a narrative ... from which blood surging with life might flow'; *Lacos de Familia*, 1960 (*Family Ties*, 1972), short stories, parodies colonialism in an absurd account of an anthropologist's discovery of 'The Smallest Woman in the World'. *A maco no escuro*, 1961 (*The Apple in the Dark*, 1967), traces its wandering anti-hero Martin's 'only awareness of who he was' in 'the sensation he felt in himself of the movements he himself was making'. In *Uma Aprendizagem ou O Livro dos Prazeres*, 1969 (*An Apprenticeship or The Book of Delights*, 1986), a love story of existential and mystical longing, the heroine learns 'how to live through pleasure' and that 'being alive' is more than 'living through pain'. Influenced by existentialism, CL's narratives became increasingly fluid in structure as she explored the interior workings of consciousness, power, and agency: 'Since one feels obliged to write, let it be without obscuring the space between the lines with words.' Barbara HOWES is among those who have anthologized her work, Elizabeth BISHOP among her translators. CL herself transl. Oscar Wilde's *The Picture of Dorian Gray*, 1974. In 1976 she was awarded first prize in the Tenth National Library Competition for her contribution to Brazilian literature and represented Brazil at the World Witchcraft Congress in Bogotá, Columbia. See Naomi Lindstrom in *Chasqui*, 8, 1978, and Regina Helena de Oliveira Machado in Susan Sellers, ed., *Writing Differences: Reading from the Seminar of Hélène Cixous*, 1988. Study by Cixous due in 1990

Lister, Anne, 1791–1840, diarist, businesswoman and traveller. Eldest child of Rebecca (Battle) and Jeremy L., but living with an aunt and uncle, she steadily pursued self-education from practical subjects to classical literature. From 1817 she kept a detailed journal written up from notes: two million words, partly (family matters; lesbian affairs, secrets and fantasies, venereal disease, the search for a lifelong lover found at last in Anne Hunter) in code or foreign languages. Writing it was a solace to her feelings, perhaps also to 'my wish for a name in the world'; though she snobbishly disliked learned ladies, she dreamed of publishing on TRAVEL, politics, religion, or antiquities. Living at Shibden Hall, Halifax, inheriting it in 1826 (her four brothers had died), she described her estate management, coal-mining, Luddites, railways and the Reform Bill. Her travels expanded from visiting France or the Ladies of LLANGOLLEN to the Pyrenees, Scandinavia and Russia. Having survived pot-holing and mountaineering in a dress held at knee-level by strings and loops, she died of plague in Georgia. MS in Halifax Central Libary: see *Transacs. of Halifax Antiquarian Soc.* from 1929, esp. Violet Ingham, 1969, and Phyllis M. Ramsden, 1970; selecs. to 1824 ed. Helena Whitbread, 1988; more awaited.

Little, Janet, 'the Scotch Milkmaid', 1759–1813, poet. Da. of George L. of Nether Bogside, Dumfries, uneducated but for her own reading, she worked as chamber-maid to Frances Anna Dunlop, then in her daughter's dairy. Her *Poetical Works*, pub. by subscription, with name and nickname, Ayr, 1792, brought her £50. Conventional love, courtship, and pastoral poems mix with sinewy, colloquial, intellectually confident work in both English and Scots. She calls herself 'a crazy scribbling lass', prefers Elizabeth ROWE's letters to Lady Mary Wortley MONTAGU's, and repeatedly relishes the indignation which literary arbiters like 'Sam [Johnson], that critic most severe' would feel at the social class of Burns and herself. She addresses poems to 'my Aunty' (on her fear of 'Voratious critics ... Like eagles, watching for their prey') and to 'a poor old wandering woman'. The last poem in the book renounces poetry. Mrs Dunlop, who had encouraged JL to address Burns in verse in 1789, stingingly rebuked him in 1793 for his contemptuous response. By then JL had married John Richmond, a labourer 20 years her senior, with five children; she continued to write poems, many religious.

Little, Flora **Jean** (Llewellyn), teacher and novelist. B. in 1932 in Taiwan, Formosa, da. of physicians Flora (Gauls) and John L., she was educ. at the Univ. of Toronto. Herself handicapped with partial vision, she has specialized in teaching crippled children. The first of her more than 12 books, *Mine for Keeps*, 1961, relates how a cerebral palsied child adjusts to a regular classroom. *From Anna*, 1972, concerns a partially sighted German child living in Toronto during WWII. The more recent of her perceptive novels explore the complexities of adults' relationships to and influences on children: *Mama's Going to Buy You a Mockingbird*, 1984, is a moving study of friendship between a boy whose father has died of cancer and a girl who has never known her mother. JL's work has been translated into French, German, Dutch, Danish, Japanese and Braille.

Little, Sophia Louisa (Robbins), poet and novelist. B. at Newport, Rhode Island, 1799, da. of Asher R. She m. William L. in 1824. Little else is known of SL's life. Her poetry and novels were privately printed; they reflect her strong ABOLITIONIST views and Christian faith. *Thrice Through the Furnace: A Tale of The Times of the Iron Hoof*, 1852, was written in response to passage of the Fugitive Slave Act and shows 'how slavery uproots the domestic affections, and destroys all that purity of attachment between the sexes, which is the boast and the safeguard of Christian civilization'. In addition to the usual plots of attempted rape, seduction and escape, the novel incorporates several apocalyptic visions of the nation's future and some overtly allegorical characters; SL aims at no simple realism, however unconvincing the conventional romantic happy ending. Her long religious poem, *The Birth, Last Days,* *and Resurrection of Jesus*, 1841, sets out the biblical narrative in modestly skilful, mainly Spenserian stanzas.

Lively, Penelope Margaret (Low), novelist, children's writer, b. in 1933 in Cairo, Egypt, da. of Vera (Greer) and Roger Low. She lived in Egypt until she was 12, then spent five unhappy years in English boarding school, later read History at St Anne's College, Oxford. She m. Jack Lively, 1957, and had two children. The link between her 7 books for adults and more than 15 novels and collections of stories for children is her preoccupation with time and place. Time, she says in the adult novel, *Judgement Day*, 1980, 'has juggled the order of things'; *The Presence of the Past; An Introduction to Landscape History*, 1976, insists that the land tells a story. PL's most successful stories deal with the creative, often imaginative, integration of the past in an enriched present. Physical settings, as well as bizarre conjunctions of people and things, are catalysts for narrative development. The Jacobean sorcerer of *The Ghost of Thomas Kempe*, 1973, like a 'malevolent spider, hatching destruction', disturbs the peace of contemporary Ledsham; the heroine of *A Stitch in Time*, 1976, discovers strange correspondences between herself and the child who over 100 years before stitched the sampler hanging in her parents' Lyme Regis summer house; *The House in Norham Gardens*, 1974, contains the relics preserved by 14-year-old Clare's anthropologist great-grandfather. PL also has a knack for unexpected animation, as with the chatty, proprietary spirits in *Uninvited Ghosts*, 1985, and the cannily observant animals who roam London in her extended satire *The Voyage of QV66*, 1978. *Pack of Cards*, 1986, collects short stories. *Moon Tiger*, 1987 Booker Prize winner, makes the last rites of Claudia Hampton a scene of recollection: she desires a complete retrospective of her life; she is able to achieve 'my self in the awful context of time and place: everything and nothing'. *Passing On*, 1989, is about three middle-aged siblings coming to terms with the death of their emotionally ruthless and autocratic mother.

Livesay, Dorothy Kathleen May, poet, editor, teacher, lecturer. B. in 1909 in Winnipeg, Man., she was radicalized and encouraged by her journalist parents, Florence LIVESAY (who helped DL publish her first work) and John Frederick L. (who took her to Emma GOLDMAN's lecture in Toronto in 1926). She attended Glen Mawr private girls' school, the Univ. of Toronto (BA, 1931), where she undertook private study of H.D., Emily DICKINSON and Katherine MANSFIELD, and the Sorbonne (Diplome d'études supérieures in comparative literature, 1932). *Green Pitcher*, 1928, and *Signpost*, 1932, reflected her imagistic skills, but DL soon outgrew this mode of writing by becoming political. In 1932 she joined the Communist Party and entered the School of Social Work, Univ. of Toronto (Diploma, 1934). In 1937 she married Duncan Cameron McNair (d. 1959); she had two children. *Right Hand Left Hand*, 1977, poems and essays, conveys DL's sense of 'struggling alone to make a woman's voice heard'. It covers the time of the Depression and the Spanish Civil War and her discovery of C. Day Lewis, Auden and Spender, which led her away from lyricism to agit-prop plays and poetry overtly opposed to the political climate of the 1930s. *Day and Night*, 1944, and *Poems for People*, 1947, both received Governor General's Awards. Although DL withdrew from left-wing politics in 1939, replacing her political aesthetic with a freer, more abstract yet intimate language, she has never lost sight of the social: 'The real poems are being written in outports / on backwoods farms / in passageways where pantries still exist / or where geraniums / nail light to the window'. Her great formal range reflects the 'miracle of changed feeling, changed thinking'. A more pensive but equally powerful voice characterizes *Ice Age*, 1975, and *The Woman I Am*, 1978. Acknowledging the lack of informed poetry criticism in Canada, she founded in 1944, and edited for years, the influential *CV/II*. Womanhood and female sexuality figure prominently in many of her books, such as *The Unquiet Bed*, 1967, and *Plainsongs*, 1971. Despite her doubt that 'love [is] the only gateway to maturity', DL writes in *The Phases of Love*, 1983, and *Feeling the Worlds*, 1984, about woman loving as mother, daughter, grandmother, lover, artist, with equal depth and humorous irony: 'I seek more / than skin, flesh, blood / I seek the coursing / heaving heart / for my soul's food'. As editor, DL presented neglected works by women in *Forty Women Poets of Canada*, with S. Kayne, 1971, and *Women's Eye: 12 BC Poets*, 1974. She lives on Galliano Island, BC. Awarded the Lorne Pierce Gold Medal, 1947, the Queen's Medal, 1977, and several other honours, she was made a member of the Order of Canada, 1987. *Winnipeg Childhood*, 1973, revised as *Beginnings*, 1989, includes short stories and memoirs. Interviews in *Canadian Forum*, 40, 1975, and Twigg, 1981; special issue of *Room of One's Own*, 5, 1979. See Lorraine M. York in *CP*, 12, 1983, Lee Briscoe Thompson, 1987, and Dennis Cooley, in his *The Vernacular Muse*, 1987. Papers at the Univ. of Manitoba.

Livesay, Florence Hamilton (Randal), 1874–1953, poet, journalist, translator, b. at Compton, Québec, to Mary Louisa (Andrews) and Stephen R., who d. when she was 14, after the family had moved to Florida for his health. Educ. at Compton Ladies' College (now King's Hall), FL taught from age 17 at Sequin School, NYC, and from 1893 (French and Latin) at Buckingham School, Montréal. She pub. sketches and poetry in *Massey's Magazine*, Toronto, edited society columns of the *Ottawa Journal*, and wrote up there and in the *Winnipeg Telegram* her experience of teaching Boer children in a concentration camp near Johannesburg, 1903. She married J. F. B. (John) L. in 1908; one of their two daughters was Dorothy LIVESAY. As a freelance journalist FL ran a column of children's writing and began exchanging vocabulary with mostly Ukrainian 'mother's helpers' (who sang as they worked), then collecting and translating their folk-tales, legends and songs. Her *Songs of Ukraina*, 1916, includes celebrations of the mother-daughter bond, and laments for its breaking when a daughter is given in marriage to a mother-in-law's 'slanders – cruel words ... "useless the bride as a rotten tree!"'. In Clarkson, Ont., from 1920, FL continued her work for Ukrainian literature and cultural studies. In 1927 appeared *Savour of Salt*, and in 1940 *Marusia* (finished in 1930), a translated tale of a peasant girl whose parents strive to keep her from the hard, sad lot of a soldier's wife. Other projects failed to find publishers, but Louisa Loeb, ed., *Down Singing Centuries*, 1981, is a good sampling, with critical and biographical sketch. Papers in the Canadian Museum of Civilization, Hull, Québec.

Livingstone, Dinah, English poet, b. abroad in 1940, brought up in Britain from 1942. She studied at London Univ., the Sorbonne, and Innsbruck Univ. (theology), and has lived in Camden Town, London, since 1966. She has three children. Her *Beginning*, 1967, was the first of nine booklets of verse, including *Holy City of London*, 1970, and *Love in Time*, 1983. After *Saving Grace: New and Selected Poems*, 1987, came *Keeping Heart*, 1989, collecting work from 22 years. She has translated from many languages, notably the Spanish of Latin America, and has performed widely in Britain, Europe and Nicaragua. She teaches poetry at the Camden Institute. Her outlook is always politically radical, whether she states her principles ('It is not right / this house should ride on backs – / one uncosied member thought – of excluded humans crawling'), or describes inner-city or peasant lives (especially women's), or celebrates the 'peculiar raucous animality' of a 'Revolutionary Singer' or more broadly the 'Glimpse of the glory / when the species / finds fulfilment'. She uses violently striking comparisons, erotic images, emphatic rhythms. Her work has figured on the radio, in periodicals, and in anthologies of radical and Labour poetry.

Lizars, Kathleen MacFarlane, d. 1931, novelist, writer of local history. She was b. and d. at Stratford, Ont., da. of Esther (Longworth) and Judge Daniel Home Lizars. Educ. in Toronto and Scotland, she was for some years private secretary to John Robson, Premier of BC, with whom she travelled to England. With her sister Robina (who married Robert Smith and d. in Toronto, 1918), she wrote lively historical accounts of south-western Ontario, based on extensive research in original documents, newspaper and magazine files and personal interviews. The first of these, and best known, *In the Days of the Canada Company, 1825–1850*, 1896, is a 'good-natured sketch-cum-novel' celebrating the memory of William 'Tiger' Dunlop (1792–1848), journalist, doctor, and pioneer. *Humours of '37, Grave, Gay, and Grim*, 1897, about the Rebellion of 1837, has been called a 'slapstick of the times'. *Committed to His Charge*, 1900, is a novel of small-town life. KL was sole author of *The Valley of the Humber 1615–1913*, 1913, and of many unsigned articles in newspapers and periodicals. See Klinck, *Literary History of Canada*, 1967, quoted above.

Llangollen, Ladies of, nickname of Lady Eleanor Butler, 1739–1829, and Sarah Ponsonby, 1755–1831, both of distinguished Irish families. In 1778, after a friendship of nearly ten years, they eloped together (under pressure, respectively, to enter a convent and to accept the advances of a married man who expected his wife to die soon). At Plas Newydd, Llangollen, from 1780, they shared a cultured and studious life rather like that in Sarah SCOTT's *Millennium Hall*. They corresponded with writers; Lady Eleanor began in 1785 the journal she called 'short and simple annals of the poor' (selec. with others in *Hamwood Papers*, 1930, reselec. Elizabeth Mavor, 1984) which, like Dorothy WORDSWORTH's, reflects both practical and romantic response to the natural world. They and the rural ideal they embodied became famous, admired, an object of pilgrimage; they were pained and outraged by journalistic speculation about their sex-life. Lives include Mary GORDON (fictional), 1936, Mavor, 1971.

Llewellyn, Kate (Brinkworth), poet and prose writer, b. 1940 at Tumby Bay, South Australia, da. of Tommy (Shemmald) and Ronald B. She received a Diploma of Nursing from Royal Adelaide Hospital, and later a BA from Adelaide Univ. Her work first appeared in *Sisters Poets 1*, 1979 (with Joyce Lee, Susan HAMPTON, and Anne Lloyd). This was followed by *Trader Kate and the Elephants*, 1982, and *Luxury*, 1985. After moving to the Blue Mountains area near Sydney, she pub. her first long prose work, *The Waterlily: A Blue Mountains Journal*, 1987. This was followed by a volume of poetry, *Honey*, 1988 and *Dear You*, 1988, a series of letters to a departed lover, which lyrically weaves the minutiae of daily life with nature imagery and an examination of love: 'Let us do what the parents of the baby Moses did. Let us take our love, put it back ... into this small ark I have made ... There it goes. Back to the water.' Her poetry has been widely published in newspapers and literary journals as well as being regularly anthologized. She co-edited (with Susan Hampton) a major ANTHOLOGY, *The Penguin Book of Australian Women Poets*, 1986.

Lochhead, Liz, poet, playwright, performer, b. 1947 at Motherwell, Lanarks., da. of Margaret (Forrest) and John L., a local-government official. After a diploma at

Glasgow School of Art, 1970, she taught art for eight years while establishing herself as a writer. In 1972 came a screenplay, *Now and Then*, and a poetry collection, *Memo for Spring*, which won a Scottish Arts Council award. The year her revue *Sugar and Spite* was performed, 1978, she also published *Islands* (poems), was the subject of a National Book League pamphlet, travelled to Canada on a Writers' Exchange Fellowship, and became a full-time writer. On one of several writerships-in-residence (Dundee, *c.* 1979), she wrote *Goodstyle*, 'a history of art revue'. She reworked fairy-tales in *The Grimm Sisters*, 1981 (poems), to highlight the deceptions and self-deceptions of male-female relationships. She calls her *Mary and the Monster*, 1981, about Mary SHELLEY, her 'first try at a real play'; it later became *Blood and Ice*, produced in 1982, and in a new version 1984, the year of *Dreaming Frankenstein and Collected Poems*. The title-poem of this volume muses on the monster patriarchy under the skin: 'getting him out again / would be agony fit to quarter her, / unstitching everything.' LL has several times collaborated with others (e.g. *Tickly Mince*, 1982, *The Pie of Damocles*, 1983). She has written for radio and TV (*Sweet Nothings*, 1984). A clear line cannot be drawn between her plays and her revues, material from which appears in *True Confessions and New Clichés*, 1985 (*True Confessions* was the title of a work of 1981). LL translated Molière's *Tartuffe* into vernacular Scots (performed 1986, pub. 1987). *Mary Queen of Scots Got Her Head Chopped Off* (pub. with *Dracula*, 1989) looks at 'men and women, Catholic and Protestant, Scotland and England'. *Jock Tamson's Bairns*, staged in Glasgow, 1990, probes a Scottish 'collective sub-conscious'. Recently married, LL performs herself on stage and TV, sometimes in aid of causes like the Rape Crisis Centre and women's refuges. A brilliant mimic, in drama and poems she can be tough and cutting, or ironically sensitive to the poet's voyeuristic stance.

Locke, Anne (Vaughan), later Prowse, b. *c.* 1530, Protestant translator from French, elder da. of London merchant Stephen V. (d. 1549/50) and his 'witty and housewifely' first wife (d. 1545). Her stepmother was strongly Protestant. She m. Henry L. (Rose HICKMAN's half-brother); in 1552/3 she became a friend of John Knox, who later corresponded with her. In 1557 she fled Marian persecution to Geneva (one of her two babies died on arrival). On return to London she pub. with her initials, at New Year 1560, English versions of Calvin's four sermons on Isaiah 38 (the song of Hezekiah), with a meditation, and metrical version of Psalm 51 (BL copy inscribed to her husband). Widowed in 1571, she married Edward Dering, a rising preacher about ten years her junior; he died after five years, and by 1583 she married Richard Prowse, draper and mayor of Exeter. Her translation from Jean Taffin, *Of the Markes of the Children of God*, with her name, 1590 (repr. 1608, 1634), is modestly dedicated: 'great things by reason of my sex, I may not doo ... I have according to my duetie, brought my poore basket of stones' to strengthen Jerusalem's walls. See Patrick Collinson in *Godly People*, 1983.

Locke, Jane Erminia (**Starkweather**), 1805–59, poet and journalist, b. Worthington, Mass., da. of Deborah (Brown) and Charles S., deacon. She m. John Goodwin L. in 1829 and they moved to NYC shortly afterwards, later living in Lowell and Boston. JSL raised seven children while pursuing her literary interests. Her first collection, *Miscellaneous Poems*, was pub. in 1842 with a dedication in which JSL feels the need to explain why poetry became woman's work in the Locke household, her husband being employed in 'hard toil for others' welfare'. JSL's domestic sentiments are conventional, but her language has dignity, though her next work, *Rachael, or The Little Mourner*, 1844, is marred by bathos. *Boston*, 1846 (anon.), celebrates that city as the ideal mercantile republic in which, however, women still take second place: 'She may not struggle for ambition's crown, / She may not strive for honour or renown'. From 1830 to 1854 JSL worked as a newspaper correspondent for the Boston *Journal* and the *Daily Atlas*, and wrote prefaces for the James Monroe Publishing Company's American editions. Her final collection, *The Recalled*, 1854, offers a half-ambitious, half-humble apology to her 'Brother Bards' for her presumption, but insists that poetry is her 'very life and breath / And to quench it would be death'. Of particular inteest are her two visionary poems, 'Midnight Shadows' and 'The Sisters of Avon' – the latter possibly a response to Shelley's 'Triumph of Life' – weighing romantic love as a problem in philosophy and in poetic tradition for women.

Locke, Sumner Helena, 1881–1917, novelist, playwright, b. Sandgate, near Brisbane, Queensland, da. of Annie (Seddon) and William L., Anglican clergyman. Brought up in Melbourne, she travelled to England in 1912 where she pub. freelance articles and stories, returning to Australia three years later where she m. Henry Logan Elliot in 1916. After travelling in America the following year she returned again to Sydney but died the day after giving birth to her son, writer Sumner Locke Elliot, whose novel, *Careful He Might Hear You*, 1963, is dedicated to and evokes his mother. Success as a writer came with the appearance of *Mum Dawson 'Boss'*, 1911, humorous stories of a set of rustic selectors dominated by the battling 'Mum'. Earlier, however, SHL had pub. stories in journals such as the *Bulletin* and the *Native Companion* and seen two of her plays produced in Melbourne and Sydney: 'The Vicissitudes of Vivienne', 1908, and 'A Martyr to Principle', 1909. The Dawson characters appeared in two further vols., *The Dawsons' Uncle George*, 1912, and *Skeeter Farm Takes a Spell*, 1915, while her last novel, *Samaritan Mary*, 1916, took rural America (which she visited during WWI) as its setting. Tributes to her by various authors appear *In Memoriam Sumner Locke*, 1921.

Lockett, Mary, b. 1872, one of Jamaica's first novelists and poets. Very little is known of her. Her odd religious-didactic novel, *Christopher*, NY, 1902, calls her 'The Princess' as well as by her name. Its Italian hero, Christopher Columbus, grows up in a US household whose most pious member is the black servant Uncle Sunday, and ends as a missionary to the East India heathen. She contributed to the first *Treasury of Jamaican Poetry*. John Figuerola, ed., *Voices*, 1966, reprints her 'Weather in Action': 'Calm weather is for calm souls; / But the soul of the outcast / Gathers wild weather into itself / And rides the rim of the world.'

Lofts, Norah (Robinson), also 'Juliet Astley' and 'Peter Curtis', 1904–83, historical and crime novelist. B. to a farming family of Shipdham, Norfolk, da. of Ethel (Garner) and Isaac R., she began writing as a child. She was educ. at West Suffolk County School and Norwich Training College (teaching diploma, 1925) and taught English and history at a girls' school till 1936, then wrote full time. In 1933 she married Geoffrey L. (d. 1948); she had a son. She married Dr Robert Jorisch in 1949. After a short-story volume, *I Met a Gypsy*, 1935, came her first historical work, on Walter Raleigh, 1936. Others deal with Ann Boleyn, 1963, and Katherine of Aragon, 1969; they are well researched and mostly well constructed, weaving private lives into political intrigue. She wrote several crime novels as 'Peter Curtis': *Death March in Six Keys*, 1940, involves a switch of identities. Some of NL's works, like the Suffolk Trilogy, 1959–63, follow a family or a house through generations, creating atmosphere with GOTHIC elements like curses, haunted rooms and exorcism. A strong, ambitious, widowed Victorian businesswoman and mother presides in *Gad's Hall*, 1977, and *Haunted House*, 1978; of her doomed family only one daughter, a 'lady novelist', inherits her strength. As 'Julia Astley' NL wrote *Fall of Midas*, 1975, and *Copsi Castle*, 1978.

Logan, Deborah (Norris), 1761–1839, Philadelphia Quaker poet and historian. Da. of Mary (Parker) and the wealthy Charles N., cousin of Hannah GRIFFITTS, she was b. at, grew up at, and later inherited Stenton, the house 'My Honoured Father' built, with fine grounds and the first willows in America. She lovingly described it in prose and verse: 'alas the stamp of evanescence is upon every being and object of this lower world!' (booklet, Philadelphia, 1867). She married, 1781, George L., gentleman farmer, senator and French revolutionary sympathizer, who wanted Pennsylvania to have sovereign independence. She kept a diary from 1815, exchanged verse with Susanna WRIGHT and wrote her life, contributed to *The National Gazette*, and researched family letters (pub. 1870–2). She preserved those in which Hannah (Callowhill) Penn, 1671–1726, deals with the management of a household and later a province (selec. in life by Sophie Hutchinson Drinker, 1958), which others thought 'too homely'. After the deaths of two children and her husband, 1821, she began a private *Memoir* of his life, as service to religion and to posterity. Finished 1822, pub. 1899, it is an effective informal account of the shapers of history, with herself as source of opinion though not as agent; it ends with 'Recollections', a long poem written in 1820. See Terri L. Premo in *PMHB*, 1983; the Hist. Soc. of Penn. (whose first woman member she was) has her MSS.

Logan, Olive, 1839–1909, US actress, lecturer, writer, da. of Eliza (Akeley) and Cornelius Ambrosius L., who was prominent in the theatre. Both Olive and her older sister Celia acted in his company before their independent theatrical and literary careers. Educ. in Cincinnati, Ohio, at the Wesleyan Female Seminary and the Academy of the Sacred Heart, and elsewhere, OL began acting in Philadelphia in 1854. She m. Henry A. Delille, 1857, divorced 1865; m. William Wirt Sikes, 1872, widowed, 1883; m. James O'Neill, 1892, deserted. From 1857 she spent five years in Europe, where she published two books, *Chateau Frissac* and *Photographs of Paris* (both 1860). On returning to the USA, she wrote and took the title role in *Evelene*. Later plays she wrote were unsuccessful, and she left acting in 1868, but continued on stage as a popular lecturer on women's rights. Until 1882 she continued to write and publish: reminiscences of the theatre, essays, and novels. Her writing is energetic and clear, though prone to digression. Her topics range from love to SUFFRAGE, from Christmas stories to life in Paris, from women's hats to nudity on the stage. Her later life was troubled by the unfortunate marriage to O'Neill and finally by madness. She died in obscurity in England. Little has been written on OL; see J. Robert Wills' life (diss., 1971).

Longworth, Maria Theresa, Thérèse Yelverton, Countess Avonmore, 1832?–81, traveller and writer, b. Cheetwood, near Manchester, youngest child of Thomas L., silk manufacturer. Her mother died early and MTL was sent to an Ursuline convent school in France. In 1852 she met William Charles Y., 4th Viscount Avonmore. In 1855 he appeared as a patient when she was nursing the wounded of the Crimean War, and in 1857 he wed her by reading the service at her home followed by a Catholic service in Ireland. In 1858 he declared the marriage illegal and m. a widow named Mrs Forbes. MTL sued but her petition was dismissed and in 1862 a Scottish court annulled the marriage as did the House of Lords in 1864. She continued her appeals until 1868. A ballad was composed about her plight and in

Manchester a public subscription was raised on her behalf. Her novel *Martyrs to Circumstances*, 1861, is a tale of nuns, female self-sacrifice, military prowess and, unsurprisingly, a marriage gone awry with the aid of the lawyers Tangleweb and Quibble. After her inheritance was exhausted by her legal battles MTL began to TRAVEL. *Teresina Peregrina, or 50,000 Miles of Travel*, 1874, is an amusing account of her travels round the world. She takes a particular interest in the condition of women especially within marriage, but is hostile to women who waste their time arguing their right to wear 'bifurcated integuments' (trousers). She describes the age as 'barbarously masculine' but saves her greatest loathing for lawyers and for helpful men who give advice, 'immediately a man prefaces his speech with "I tell you as a friend", I put myself on the defensive, buckle on my armour of determined indifference, and allow him to waste his breath'. She also wrote *Teresina in America*, 1875, and *Zanita; a tale of the Yo-Semite*, 1872. She died in Pietermaritzburg, Natal.

Loos, Corinne **Anita**, 1888–1981, novelist, screenwriter, satirist, b. in Sissons (now Mt Shasta), Calif., da. of Minnie (Smith) and newspaper editor and theatre producer R. Beers L., who put her on stage at five. She was raised in San Francisco and San Diego, and won writing prizes while at high school. Her movie scenario *The Road to Plaindale*, *c.* 1911 (not *The New York Hat*, 1912), was the first of many; 100, she claimed, before she left Frank Pallma (soon after their wedding in 1915) and moved to Hollywood, and almost as many later: for Biograph, MGM and others. She married director John Emerson in 1920; their many collaborations are chiefly by her. A friend of H. L. Mencken, AL satirized his taste for dumb blondes with the creation of Lorelei Lee, the fluffy-sounding 'professional lady', 'a symbol of our nation's lowest possible mentality'. Originally serialized in *Harper's Bazaar* ('where', Mencken claimed, 'it'll be lost among the ads and won't offend anybody'), *Gentlemen Prefer Blondes*, 1925, became a bestseller in many languages, was several times adapted for stage and cinema (later versions starring Carol Channing and Marilyn Monroe, respectively) and made AL one of the few living writers in *The Oxford Book of Quotations*, 1950. Such phenomenal success eluded her sequel, *But Gentlemen Marry Brunettes*, 1928, and further satirical versions of female stereotypes, like *No Mother to Guide Her*, 1961, about a self-destructive star. Her screenplays included *San Francisco*, 1936 (pub. 1979), and Clare Boothe LUCE's *The Women*, 1939. Her plays, like *Happy Birthday*, 1946, and adaptations of COLETTE's *Gigi*, 1951, and *Chéri*, 1959, were Broadway hits. She wrote of Hollywood in *The Talmadge Girls*, 1978, of NYC in *Twice Over Lightly* (with her close friend Helen Hayes), 1972, and of her own career in *A Girl Like I*, 1966, *Kiss Hollywood Good-by*, 1974, and *Cast of Thousands*, 1977. Life by Gary Carey, 1988.

Lord, Gabrielle (Butler), novelist and screenwriter, b. 1946 in Sydney, NSW, da. of Gwendoline June (Craig) and Dr John B. She has been married and has a da. Educ. at several private Catholic schools in Sydney, later the Univ. of New England, Armidale (BA Hons), she has also had informal training as a market gardener and beer brewer. She has pub. three novels: *Fortress*, 1980, based on an actual kidnapping of a country school teacher and her class (which was filmed in 1986), *Tooth and Claw*, 1982, concerning a woman's fight for survival on a remote farm, and *Jumbo*, 1986, set in Sydney's western suburbs and dramatizing the plight of the young unemployed. Suspense and horror are the trademarks of GL's novels, usually described as 'thrillers'. Women, and, in *Fortress*, children, are victims, but also the agents of often violent retribution; central in her fiction is the inevitability of women's complicity in repaying their male torturers. GL acknowledges the moral influence of her Catholic upbringing, with its emphasis on cruelty and victimization, and the literary influence of Graham Greene. She has also had several stories pub. in newspapers and anthologies and is the co-author of the humorous *Growing Up Catholic*, 1986.

Lorde, Audre, 'Rey Domini', black lesbian feminist poet and essayist. B. in Harlem in 1934 to Grenadan parents, Linda (Belmar) and 'Bee' L., she was educ. at Hunter College, NY (BA, 1959), and Columbia (MLS, 1960). Her earliest poems appeared in journals, sometimes as by 'Rey Domini'; she was head librarian at CUNY until 1968, when she published her first volume, *The First Cities*. Since then she has been writer in residence, English teacher, and winner of various awards and fellowships, including the National Book Award for 1974, which she accepted, on behalf of women, with Adrienne Rich and Alice Walker. Her writing concentrates on love between women, racism in the women's movement, and sexism and heterosexism in black communities. Acutely sensitive to language, AL warns that 'the master's tools will not dismantle the master's house', looking to her sensuality, to traditional African myths and to contemporary African writing for affirmation and inspiration. Her poetry, in *Cables to Rage*, 1970, *New York Head Shop and Museum*, 1975, *Coal*, 1976 *The Black Unicorn*, 1978, and *Chosen Poems*, 1982, reflects in increasingly direct language her passionate love for women and her anguish and rage at the effects of white racism. *Our Dead Behind Us: Poems*, 1986, draws both strength and grief from her African allegiances. Her autobiographical works, *The Cancer Journals*, 1980, and *Zami: A New Spelling of My Name*, 1982 (which she calls 'biomythography'), detail her struggle with breast cancer in the context of a lesbian feminist community. Her essays, including the influential 'Uses of the Erotic: The Erotic as Power', are collected in *Sister/Outsider*, 1984, and *A Burst of Light*, 1988, which contains a detailed journal account of her discovery of and battle with liver cancer in 1984. She counsels young black women 'not to be afraid to feel and not to be afraid to write about it. Even if you are afraid, do it anyway'. Interview in Tate, 1983. See Evans, 1984, Amitai F. Avi-Ram in *Callaloo*, 9, 1986, and Jeanne Perreault in *Auto/Biography Studies*, 4, 1988.

'Lothian, Roxburghe', Elizabeth (Kerr) Coulson, *c*. 1818–76, historical novelist. She grew up in Jersey, da. of Elizabeth (Ker) and Robert Kerr, army officer and descendant of the house of Lothian from which she took her pseudonym. Her tutor Dr Giglio (who appears in her 'autobiographical romance', *Lizzie Lothian*, 1877) first interested her in Italy and its history, and she became an ardent supporter of Italian unity and freedom. Hoping it might further the cause, by its evocation of past glory, she wrote *Dante and Beatrice from 1282 to 1290: A Romance*, 1876, dedicated to the city of Florence. This presents the events and relationship from which the *Divina Commedia* was later to evolve. Though no-one suspected its author was a woman, it was criticised by Catholic reviewers because of its unsympathetic portrayal of the priesthood and its Protestant bias. She married twice: Thomas Colville (d. 1851) and in 1853, her cousin Edward Foster Coulson, who wrote the biographical introduction to her memoir.

Love, Mary, writer of PETITIONS repeatedly calling on Parliament to revoke its death-sentence for treason passed on her husband, Christopher L., a church minister. She won a delay till the birth of their third surviving child; after that he was executed, August 1651. She then pub. her petitions in *Loves Name Lives* (re-issued as an appeal to Charles II in 1660), with various letters, some between them: hers urge him to accept death as God's will, adding, 'My Deer, by what I write unto thee, I do not hereby undertake to teach thee; for these comforts I have received by the Lord from thee.'

Lowell, Amy, 1874–1925, poet and critic, b. at Brookline, Mass., much youngest child of Katherine Bigelow (Lawrence) and Augustus Lowell Her family were aristocrats of New England, of which she wrote, 'I speak to it of itself / And sing of it with my own voice / Since certainly it is mine.' She was raised on a large estate, Sevenels, which she bought after her parents died. She had eight years' formal educ. at Boston and Brookline private schools, and wrote her first book, *Dream Drops, or Stories from Fairyland*, by 'a Dreamer', with her mother's help, for charity, 1887. After years of society life, travel, and volunteer work (educational and civic), she began writing poetry in 1902. In 1910 she published a sonnet, 'A Fixed Idea', in *The Atlantic Monthly*; three more followed. She translated a Musset play, produced at a Boston little theatre she had helped to found. Her first poetry volume, *A Dome of Many-Coloured Glass*, 1912, was non-experimental. In January 1913 she took as a revelation the signature 'H. D., Imagiste' in Harriet MONROE's *Poetry*. From 1914 she drew confidence from a lifelong, loving, literary association with actress Ada (Dwyer) Russell, which elicited much of her finest poetry. On visits to England, 1913 and 1914, she met H. D., Richard Aldington, Ezra Pound (who printed one of her new poems in *Des Imagistes*, 1914) and J. G. Fletcher (who praised her in the special Imagist number of *The Egoist*, 1915). After Pound broke with the movement, she edited three annual Imagist anthologies, 1915–17. Margaret ANDERSON refused her offer of money for the *Little Review*, fearing strings were attached. AL's own work appeared regularly in *Poetry*, in little and mainstream magazines, and in volumes: *Sword Blades and Poppy Seed*, 1914, *Men, Women and Ghosts*, 1916, *Can Grande's Castle*, 1918, *Pictures of the Floating World*, 1919, and *Legends*, 1921. Both contents and prefaces detail the development of her poetics: 'precision of language, clearness of vision, concentration of thought', all combined 'in a dominant image'. She was crucial to the US Imagist campaign, though Pound later held that 'Amygisme' was a debased form. Her privileged background, domineering manner, perhaps her weight problem, encouraged slights from contemporaries (and later literary historians), but her critical books, *Six French Poets*, 1915, and *Tendencies in Modern American Poetry*, 1917, were influential. Her life of Keats, 1925, based largely on MS material, challenged existing biographical conventions. *What's O'Clock*, 1925 (poems), won a posthumous Pulitzer Prize. 'The Sisters' muses, 'Taking us by and large, we're a queer lot / We women who write poetry.' There followed *East Wind*, 1926, *Ballads for Sale*, 1927, and *Complete Poetical Works*, ed. Louis Untermeyer, 1955. AL's correspondence with Florence AYSCOUGH, about their translations from Chinese, was ed. Harley F. MacNair, 1945. BRYHER, who met H. D.'s work in *Tendencies*, wrote *AL: A Critical Appreciation*, 1918. Lives include S. Foster Damon, 1935, Horace Gregory, 1958, and Jean Gould, 1975. See too Hanscombe and Smyers, 1987; Claire Healey in *New England Quarterly*, 46, 1973; Lillian Faderman in *Gay Books Bulletin*, 1, 1979. Papers at the Houghton Library, Harvard.

Lowther, Pat (Tinmuth), 1935–75, poet. Her mother, Virginia, was da. of a union organizer, her father, Arthur T., a caretaker and early member of the CCF party. B. in Vancouver, where she spent her life, she could read – and wrote poetry – at four, and at ten won a *Vancouver Sun* poetry competition. She left school at 16 to take a job as a keypunch operator, but threw her energies into poetry, its promotion, publication in small magazines, and connection with politics. Married to Bill Domphousse, 1953, she separated from him, 1957, took their two children to live in her parents' basement suite, and read at coffee houses and political gatherings. In 1963 she married Roy L., a teacher dismissed for his radical politics, and had, as the title of one of her poems has it, 'Two Babies in Two Years'. Her marriage and poverty made her situation 'desperately difficult'. Her husband, convicted of her murder, died in prison, 1985. PL published in Canadian journals – *Fiddlehead*, *Canadian Forum*, *Tamarack Review* and *Canadian Poetry* – and in four volumes: *This Difficult Flowering*, 1968, *The Age of the Bird*, 1972, *Milk Stone*, 1974, and *A Stone Diary*, 1977. Her early work deals with motherhood and poetic birth, the emotional ambiguity of domestic relationships and socialism, her later work with landscape, human spirit and poetic energy against the deadening power of technology. 'Often now I forget how to make love, but I think I am ready to learn politics', she wrote. At her death her friend Dorothy LIVESAY said, 'She has for 10 years been producing, I felt, the most stirring, lyrical, meaningful and committed poetry of any written by man or woman in Canada'. The League of Canadian Poets, which PL co-chaired the year of her death, awards a memorial prize. Previously unpublished poems in *West Coast Review*, Fall, 1980. See Paul Grescoe in *Canadian Magazine* (supplement to the *Ottawa Citizen*, 5 June 1976), Fred Cogswell in *Fiddlehead*, 108, 1976, quoted above, and Sean Ryan in *CanL*, 74, 1977.

Loy, Mina (Mina Gertrude Lowy), 1882–1966, modernist poet, satirist, painter, and playwright. B. in London, da. of Julia (Brian) and tailor Sigmund Lowy, she studied art in Munich, 1899, London (with Augustus John), 1901–2, and Paris, where she shortened her family name to Loy and married English painter Stephen Haweis, 1903, with whom she had three children. Elected to the Salon d'Automne, 1906, she moved to Florence, became a Christian Scientist, met Mabel Dodge LUHAN (later godmother to her son), and by 1913, the Futurists, whose energies she turned to her feminist purposes. 'Aphorisms on Futurism', printed by Alfred Stieglitz in *Camera Work*, 1914, attacks a confining 'feminine' and conventional sexual attitudes. The unpublished 'Feminist Manifesto' (counterpointing Marinetti's 'Futurist Manifesto', 1909) exhorts women to 'leave off looking to men to find out what you are *not* – seek within yourselves to find out what you *are*' and calls for '*unconditional* surgical *destruction of virginity* throughout the female population at puberty' to release women from the marriage-market and give emotional independence. ML rejected the movement when it became fascist: her unpublished play, *The Pamperers*, satirizes its swaggering, paranoid masculinism. Her poetry ('Love Songs', 1915, expanded as 'Songs to Jannes', 1917 spearheaded Alfred Kreymborg's revolt in *Others* against the dominance of Harriet MONROE's *Poetry*. In 1916, ML moved to NYC, joined the Provincetown Players (cf. Djuna BARNES), exibited at the Independent Artists' Exhibition, published poetry in journals, and became the *New York Sun's* 'Modern Woman'. Divorced in 1917, she married proto-Dadaist, 'fugitive, forger, and master of disguise' Arthur Cravan in 1918: he disappeared at the end of that year; she bore his daughter, 1919, and returned to NYC to search for him, 1920. In 1921, Haweis kidnapped her son. In Paris, 1923–36, ML manufactured lampshades and frequented both STEIN's and BARNEY's salons. Robert McAlmon's Contact Press published her *Lunar Baedecker[sic]*, 1923: bold accounts of female experience – like 'Parturition' – which were found pornographic by US customs. Part of *Anglo-Mongrels and the Rose* was printed as work in progress, 1925. In the 1920s and 1930s ML concentrated on her art business and her prose (including the unfinished novel, *Insel*). In NYC, 1936–53, she wrote and painted but published little, withdrew steadily from people and things, and 'engaged in a metaphorical quest to find

Christ in the Bowery' which produced her late, fine destitution poems. From 1953, she lived in Aspen, Col. Widely admired in the time of high modernism – by Pound, T. S. Eliot, W. C. Williams and Yvor Winters – ML became, like H. D., one of its lost voices. Some works – 'strewn like the limbs of Osiris in little magazines and correspondence' were gathered by Jonathan Williams in *Lunar Baedeker & Time-Tables*, 1958; Roger Conover, ed., says that *The Last Lunar Baedeker*, 1982, is 'the closest we will ever get to the *Collected*'. Feminist studies by Carolyn Burke in *Women's Studies*, 7, 1980; Virginia M. Kouidis, 1980 (quoted above), with list of writings; Benstock, 1986; Hanscombe and Smyers, 1987. MSS at Yale and owned by ML's daughters.

Lucan, Margaret Bingham (Smith), Lady, d. 1814, illustrator and poet. Da. and coheiress of Grace and James S. of Canons Leigh, Devon, she m., 1760, Sir Charles B. (who became Baron and then Earl of L.). Living in Ireland led her to publish *Verses on the Present State of Ireland*, Dublin 1768, 'to raise compassion in the breast of power' at a time of concessions made to America, hoping to reach the king but directly addressing the queen. Her vigorous couplets pin the blame for Irish misery squarely on England and ask 'What free born souls will such oppression bear?'; an inset tale exposes the results of religious oppression; prose footnotes supply political and economic chapter and verse. Thereafter she copied miniatures and illustrated Shakespeare, but left nothing more reflecting her literary ability, though Horace Walpole was sent verse by her and noted her 'turn towards poetry' as well as 'prodigious vivacity'. She travelled in Europe, knew Hester PIOZZI, and was, oddly, attacked in a 1794 pamphlet for low birth.

Lucas, Margaret (Brindley), 1701–69, Quaker autobiographer. B. in London, youngest of 14 children of shopkeeper Joseph B., she lost her mother at one and a half and father at about seven. First her guardian's housekeeper, then an uncle and aunt at Leek, Staffs., brought her up to revere the Anglican clergy: 'if I had been a boy I would have been of their cloth'. At 16 living by the churchyard made her think much of death. She ran both a shop (bought her by her uncle) and a school, but increasing interest in the QUAKERS brought threats to her life from her uncle and battering from her aunt. She felt 'an extacy of joy' on first calling herself a Quaker; two years of patience achieved family reconciliation; she married Samuel L. in 1725 and had seven children. Internal combat with her 'great aversion to women's preaching', fiercer than that of her conversion, brought her to the brink of natural death or suicide, 'wishing myself any other creature' or 'that I had never been born'. Managing to stand and speak a few words in meeting 'produced a blessed change'. Her *Account of the Convincement and Call to the Ministry* (not of her ministry itself) was written to a friend and pub. 1797.

Luce, Clare (Boothe), 1903–87, playwright, journalist, politician and diplomat, b. in NYC, da. of Ann Clare (Snyder) and William P. B. Educ. at private schools in NY, she m. George Brokaw in 1923 (divorced 1929, one daughter), and held editorial posts on *Vogue* and *Vanity Fair* which she resigned to write plays. In 1935 she married Henry R. L., publisher of *Time*, and had a short run with *Abide With Me*. She won fame with *The Women*, 1936 (MGM film 1939, less successful musical as *The Opposite Sex*, 1956), a vitriolic comedy about the idle, rich, bridge-playing, much-divorced set 'native to the Park Avenues of America' (see Susan L. Carlson in *Modern Drama*, 27, 1984). Anita LOOS, collaborating on the screen-play, added jokes on 'the ordinary bitchiness of women' to replace blue-pencilled jokes about sex. *Kiss the Boys Goodbye*, 1938, satirises Hollywood's search for an unknown to play Scarlett O'Hara; the anti-Nazi *Margin for Error*, 1940, sets a NY Jewish policeman to guard a Nazi official. Active in the Republican party in the 1940s, CBL was a Congresswoman, 1943–7, and Ambassador to Italy, 1953–7. She wrote of her conversion to Catholicism in a series of articles in *McCall's*, 1947, and her sixth play, *Child of the Morning*, 1951. She edited *Saints For Now*, 1952 (essays by Sister Mary MADELEVA, Kathleen NORRIS, Kate O'BRIEN, Rebecca WEST and others). Her other works include *Stuffed Shirts*, 1931 (lampooning sketches of NY high society), *Europe in the Spring*, 1940 (on experience as a WWII correspondent), and a play called first *A Doll's House*, 1970, then *Slam the Door Softly*, 1971, which voices her consistently feminist views. Journalistic life by Wilfrid Sheed, 1982.

Luckham, Claire, playwright. B. in Kenya in 1944, she was sent early to English boarding-school, staying with aunts in the holidays. She m. Chris Bond in about 1965, and spent her child-rearing years reading. She had no idea that women wrote plays, 'novels, yes, but not plays'. In 1976 they moved to Liverpool (Bond to direct the Everyman Theatre) and co-authored *Scum: Death, Destruction and Dirty Washing*, the first play done by the feminist THEATRE GROUP Monstrous Regiment, set in a Paris laundry during the commune, 1870–1. CL's first solo effort, *Yatesy and the Whale*, 1977, was not 'a great success'. But the Everyman had a new policy of equal roles for both sexes: CL thought of writing about a female wrestler, and made it a life-story set in a wrestling ring, expressing 'what I felt it was like to be a woman'. The rebellious heroine spars with her Mum (who wanted a boy), her Dad (who wants her sweet and pretty), a school psychiatrist, and her husband, who becomes 'the gallant loser' to her champ. As *Tuebrook Tanzi, The Venus Flytrap*, this played in Liverpool pubs and was filmed for the BBC, 1978; it played as *Tugby Tanzi* in Leicester, 1980, and as *Trafford Tanzi* in Manchester, Edinburgh and London, 1981. Michelene WANDOR (1986) admired its mix 'of the bourgeois and the radical feminist', of working-class experience and popular culture. CL continues fertile in ideas and in dramatic use of music in *Aladdin* (pantomime), 1978, *Finishing School*, 1982, *Walking on Water*, 1983, and an adaptation of Defoe's *Moll Flanders*, 1986.

Luhan, Mabel Dodge (Ganson), 1879–1962, patron, journalist, memoirist. B. in Buffalo, NY, only child of wealthy but distant parents, Sarah (Cook) and Charles G., she was privately educ. there, in NYC and at Chevy Chase, Md. She m. Karl Evans, broke down after his accidental death in 1902 (leaving her a son), and went to Europe to recover. (Several later love-affairs led to suicide attempts.) In 1904 she m. Edwin Dodge, a Boston architect, settled in Florence, discovered art, and entertained European and American notables including Gertrude STEIN. Back in NYC in 1912, MDL left Dodge, and set up a famous salon at 23 Fifth Avenue, renowned as hotbed of ideas on anarchism, modernism, art and sexuality. She promoted Stein, cultivated artists and radicals like Emma GOLDMAN, Margaret SANGER, Max Eastman, wrote a newspaper column on Freudian psychology, published poems and stories, and donated much inherited wealth to political causes. In 1913 she was involved in the Amory exhibition of international art and the (not finally successful) Madison Square Garden pageant in aid of striking NJ silk workers. When her very public affair with John Reed ended, she retreated from radical politics. Unhappy in her next marriage, to artist Maurice Sterne, she moved to Taos, New Mexico, and in 1923 married Antonio (Tony) Lujan, a Pueblo Indian. MDL believed that the Pueblo way of life could redeem a bankrupt white culture. She fought for land reform and medical benefits for Indians, and encouraged celebration of the region by artists like Georgia O'Keeffe, Leopold Stokowski, Mary AUSTIN, Willa CATHER and D. H. Lawrence (with whom she described a heated relationship in *Lorenzo in Taos*, 1932). Her own finest celebration was the lyrical *Winter in Taos*, 1935; also her four-volume *Intimate Memories* (her best-known work, begun 1924 as an exercise in psychotherapy) and *Taos and Its Artists*, 1947. The *Memories (Background*, 1933, *European Experiences*, 1935, *Movers and Shakers*, 1936, and *Edge of Taos Desert*, 1937) trace her attempts to create utopian communities, lastly the artists' colony at Taos, and read her life as metaphor for the decline and hoped-for rebirth of US culture. MSS at Yale (largest of several collections: catalogue by Donald Gallup in *Yale Univ. Library Gazette*, 37, 1963) include 23 autobiographical volumes and two unpub. novels. MDL has been much written about; apart from Emily HAHN, see lives by Lois Palken Rudnick and by Winifred L. Frazer, both 1984.

Lumpkin, Grace, novelist, b. 1903?, in Milledgeville, Georgia, da. of Annette (Morris) and William Wallace L., raised near Columbia, SC. She worked as a teacher, wrote stories for school magazines, and was an industrial secretary for the YWCA. At 25 she moved to NYC to take classes at Columbia Univ. and write, and also (since she was robbed on her third day there, cf. Carson MCCULLERS) to work in offices and as a chambermaid. She moved in radical political and literary circles, married, and published short stories, firstly in *New Masses*. Loans from Grace Hutchins and Anna Rochester, prominent figures in the Communist Party, financed her first novel, *To Make My Bread*, 1932 (see Joseph R. Urgo in *the minnesota review*, 24, 1985). This story of exploited NC textile mill workers won the Maxim Gorky award for labour novels and was dramatized by Albert Bein: staged in NYC as *Let Freedom Ring*, 1935–6. *A Sign for Cain*, 1935, another proletarian novel, raised the possibility of political alliance between black and white Georgia share-croppers. After 'The Bridesmaids Carried Lilies' (*North American Review*, 1937), an electrifying tale of sex, race, and cool violence by proxy, *The Wedding*, 1939 (repr. 1976: afterword by Lillian Barnard Gilkes), examines the personal lives of a white, middle-class Columbia family. GL reputedly moved away from Communism in 1941; in 1953, now a devout Christian, she was investigated for *Cain*, and testified before the Senate Permanent Investigating Subcommittee that she 'had written Communist propaganda' into it under threat of Communist reviewers ruining her literary career. *Full Circle*, 1962, describes her brush with 'international Communist "conspiracy."' Depositing her papers at the Univ. of SC in 1971, GL insisted that 'there are two distinct "phases" to consider. First, the Communist, and second, the return to God'. In 1975 she was working on two novels, one to be called *God and a Garden*.

Lumley, Jane or **Joanna** (Fitzalan), Lady, *c.* 1537–76, translator, da. and co-heiress of Katherine (Grey) and Henry F., 12th Earl of Arundel: cousin of Lady Jane GREY. She was married by 1550 to the not much older orphan John, 1st Baron L.; both, with her younger sister Mary, used to present scholarly exercises as New Year gifts to her father, formidable and ambitious owner of the finest library in England. Mary (later Duchess of Norfolk) left only a few Latin MSS; she has been confused with her stepmother or other female Arundels. Jane produced, soon after marriage, the earliest extant English version of a Greek tragedy (ELIZABETH I's being lost): Euripides' *Iphigeneia*, evidently done from Latin. Her heroine elects to die bravely to save her country rather than be saved herself. The goddess Diana rescues her from her ruthless but later penitent father, after everyone is 'wonderfullye astonied at the stoutenes of her minde': MS in BL; ed.

Harold H. Child, 1909, as *Iphigenia at Aulis*. JL's three babies all died.

Lurie, Alison, novelist, b. 1926 in Chicago, da. of Bernice (Stewart) and Harry L., who encouraged her at six or seven to be a writer. She was educ. at Radcliffe College (AB 1947), married Jonathan Peale Bishop, a professor, in 1948, and has three sons (divorced 1985). Her first novel, *Love and Friendship*, 1962 (heroine named Emmy), reflects her leaning towards AUSTEN. She published three more before in 1969 beginning to teach at Cornell Univ. (like her husband, but at first part-time). She teaches children's literature, and has co-edited reprints of children's classics. In 1980 she published, for children, *The Heavenly Zoo* and *Clever Gretchen* (retold 'forgotten' fairy tales with 'strong, brave, resourceful heroines', created, she says, by active, working women with a feminism which nineteenth-century male compilers obscured). Of her novels, *Only Children*, 1979, is told from the point of view of children; in *The War Between the Tates*, 1974 (which made her name; filmed 1976), hostilities between generations precede those between the sexes (with an interfused frame of protest against the Vietnam War). *The Language of Clothes*, 1981, is an incisive look at female and male fashion, for political and sociological as well as aesthetic implications. (AL's attention to such detail appears throughout her novels; a betrayed wife puts on a purple bra for her first assignation.) AL drops New England academics into alien environments like Los Angeles or London, and topples not only characters' pretensions but also novelistic conventions of romance and sex. In *Foreign Affairs*, 1984 (Pulitzer Prize), the ominiscient narrator addresses the topic of sex in middle age; the 54-year-old heroine has an imaginary canine 'familiar demon ... representing self-pity', who shrinks during the story but does not disappear. *The Truth about Lorin Jones*, 1988, treats an academic biographer's struggle to capture the 'multiple, discontinuous identities' of her subject, who resists stock readings including the feminist. AL's comic mode has been faulted for uncaringness towards her characters (Gore Vidal called her 'the Queen Herod' of modern fiction; Elizabeth Fox-Genovese notes 'her merciless eye for the deadly detail that strips poor mortals of their shreds of self-image'); but she examines with acuity the position of the powerless (like domestically-based women). AL pub. a study of 'subversive' children's books, 1990. MSS at Radcliffe College. See Janet Todd, ed., 1983 (quoted above); interview with M. Satz in *Southwest Review*, 71, 1986; Fox-Genovese (quoted above) in *Nation*, 21 Nov. 1981.

Lutz, Alma,1890–1973, biographer and journalist, b. at Jamestown, N. Dakota, da. of Matilda (Bauer) and George L., educ. at Emma Willard School, Vassar College (AB 1912), and Boston Univ. School of Business Administration. Her first book reflects her enduring feminist concerns: a life of Emma WILLARD, 1929, rev. 1964 with the subtitle *Pioneer Educator of American Women* (each version recently repr.). AL worked for the suffrage movement, 1913–18, and, believing that 'Every woman who cherishes freedom owes a debt of gratitude to Elizabeth Cady STANTON', published a life of her in 1940, repr. 1973. She also co-authored the *Memoirs* of Stanton's daughter, Harriet Stanton Blatch, 1940. During the 1930s and 1940s AL worked for the National Women's Party, writing pamphlets and editing its journal, *Equal Rights*; she held many other public posts. She edited *With Love, Jane*, 1945: letters of women fighting in WWII, 'indicative of the spirit and patriotism which animate our young women'. Her biography of Susan B. ANTHONY, 1959, repr. 1976, was inspired by Anthony's and Stanton's joint, fruitless campaign to get Republicans to add the word 'sex' to the phrase 'race, color, or previous condition of servitude' in the Fifteenth Amendment. Russell Sage

College, ND, gave her a DLitt for her biographies of US women in 1959. *Crusade for Freedom: Women of the Antislavery Movement*, 1968, celebrates women's 'outstanding contributions to the abolition of slavery', at a time when their 'participation . . . in public reform movements was frowned upon'.

Luxborough, Henrietta Knight (St John), Lady, 1700?–56, letter and verse-writer, da. of Angelica Magdalen (Pellisary) and Henry, Viscount St J.: much younger half-sister of statesman Lord Bolingbroke, who helped with her education. She married, 1727, Robert K., later (1745) Lord L., and spent time in France hostessing for her father-in-law. A friend of Lady HERTFORD from about 17, she exchanged letters and verse with her and Elizabeth ROWE (MSS at BL and Alnwick; some in 1940 life of Hertford). In 1736 dubious allegations of an affair with Hertford's son's tutor brought a veto on this friendship, separation from husband and children, and virtual confinement at Barrells, Warwicks. The poet William Shenstone found her letters to him (more formal than those to Hertford) unequalled in 'Ease, Politeness, and Vivacity' and in criticism of 'all the Sister Arts': selec. pub. 1775, well reviewed though abused by Horace Walpole. HL thought 'poetess' a 'reproachful name', but four poems appeared in Dodsley's *Collection*, iv, 1755. Walter Sichel's life of Bolingbroke, 1901, briefly relates hers.

'Lyall, Edna', Ada Ellen Bayly, 1857–1903, novelist, b. Brighton, youngest child of Mary (Winter) and Robert B., barrister of the Inner Temple. Devoted to her father, she was educ. at home till orphaned, then at her uncle's (where she began writing stories) and at private schools in Brighton. She later lived with married sisters. Her first novel, *Won by Waiting*, 1879, the life of heroine Esperance, was followed by 17 others. Her own liberal Unitarian background combined with a powerful storytelling technique emerges in her treatment of religious tolerance and political practice in *Donovan*, 1882, and its enormously successful sequel, *We Two*, 1884, loosely based on politician Charles Bradlaugh (whose attempt to take his seat in the House of Commons – he was excluded because he refused to swear on oath – she supported financially). *Derrick Vaughan, Novelist*, 1889, has an autobiographical element; English injustice in Ireland features in *Doreen*, 1894; Turkish oppression in Armenia in *Autobiography of a Truth*, 1896 (profits went to the Armenian Relief Fund); and the immorality of the Boer War in her last novel, *The Hinderers*, 1902. With a strong sense of the past linked with knowledge of her own family history, she wrote *The Burges Letters*, 1902, based on her country childhood. A committed Christian and Gladstonian liberal, she supported women's SUFFRAGE. See life by J. M. Escreet, 1904.

Lynam, Margaret (Ridge), Quaker pamphleteer. Her *For the Parliament Sitting at Westminster* (the restored Rump), 1659, calls on them to end the persecution of Friends in England and New England. She says she 'suffered much in joyning with this Parliament in this late warr, for it was said to be for liberty of conscience, whereby I was free to part with much that I then did enjoy'. Her *Warning from the Lord Unto All Informers* (n.d., probably early 1660s) threatens 'Wo from the Lord God unto you all is now proclaimed, and sore Calamity shall come upon you bloody-minded men.' Some letters survive from her visit to northern Ireland about 1660. She m. John L. by 1670 (when they migrated to Pennsylvania); they wrote part each of *The Controversie of the Lord against the Priests of the Nations*, 1676.

Lynch, Hannah, 1859–1904, novelist, journalist, b. in Dublin, living abroad most of her life: as convent-schoolgirl, as governess, and later as writer. Da. of a Fenian, she grew up with her sisters in a cultivated literary and political household, described by Katherine TYNAN in *Twenty-five Years*, 1913. She was associated with Anna Parnell in the Irish Land League, carrying type to Paris to issue the suppressed *United Ireland*, 1881–2. Charles Parnell cut off funds from the 'Ladies' Land League' in 1882: his sister never spoke to him again. HL's early novel, *Through Troubled Waters*, [n.d.], dedicated to George Meredith, portrays a male mentor educating a simple Irish girl. Her study of Meredith, 1891, is dedicated to translator Rosamond Venning, whom she met in Athens, while *Denis D'Auvrillac*, 1896, is dedicated to Mary Darmesteter (formerly ROBINSON). Her later novels are more strongly feminist: *Rosni Harvey*, 1892, plays mercilessly with romance convention and sharply observed sexual politics; *Autobiography of a Child*, 1899, recounts a fictional unhappy childhood. HL died in Paris, where she had been correspondent of the *Academy*.

Lynd, Sylvia (Dryhurst), 1888–1952, poet, novelist. B. in Hampstead, London, to N. F. (Robinson) and A. R. D., she was educ. at King Alfred's School, the Slade School of Art, and Academy of Dramatic Art, London. In 1909 she m. Robert L. (with whom she had two daughters) and began to write poetry and prose for magazines. Pieces in *The Thrush and the Jay*, 1916, include 'A Day in Town', about a brief interlude of freedom for a young wife 'given in charge' by her parents to her husband. Her two novels, *The Chorus*, 1915, and *The Swallow Dive*, 1921, set the life of the modern girl against a backdrop of more conventional lives: an independent young artist, observing an affair between her employer and a young friend, is troubled most by its secrecy and hypocrisy; a girl decides to live with her journalist mother and to be an actress, despite her mother's fear that she may 'lose her beautiful self in the worldly maze' and a respectable aunt's advice that she should 'teach, or go into the Post Office, or learn typewriting'. Further volumes of poems are lyrical, descriptive, often nostalgic (including *Selected Poems*, 1928, and *Collected Poems*, 1945). Short fiction appears in *The Mulberry Bush*, 1925, work for children in *The Children's Omnibus*, 1932, and later volumes. *English Children*, 1942, is a popular illustrated historical account. SL was many years literary editor of the *News Chronicle*.

Lyon, Agnes (L'Amy), 1762–1840, poet. B. in Dundee, da. of John Ramsay L'A., she m., 1786, the Rev. James Lyon of Glamis; most of her ten children died before her. She left her daughter-in-law four volumes of MS poetry, from early in her marriage to near her death, with a request not to publish unless in need of money: 'Written off-hand, as one may say, / Perhaps upon a rainy day, / Perhaps while at the cradle rocking, / Instead of knitting at a stocking, / She'd catch a paper, pen, and ink', never neglecting the children to do so. A song of 1799–1800, 'Neil Gow's Farewell to Whisky', became well-known, though later abused as unfair to Gow's character; a few more in Charles Rogers, *The Modern Scottish Minstrel*, i, 1855.

Lyon, Lilian Bowes, 1895–1949, poet, da. of Lady Anne Catherine Sybille Lindsay and Frances Bowes-Lyon and cousin of the Queen Mother, she was born and grew up at Ridley Hall, Northumberland, where she learned to love the country life that is the subject of observation and delight in her early poems. In 1942 she moved into a small flat in the bomb-torn East End of London, where, though increasingly crippled by arthritis, she worked night and day, clearing bomb sites and tending to the wounded. In these years, she sent children from the East End to a country house in Northants., adopted two Polish refugees and used her influence (with the Queen Mother and Anthony Eden in particular) to underline the plight of East Londoners. She wrote when she could, and her early lyrics of several kinds (comic observation, ballads, sonnets) give place to poems about war's violations. Her only novel, *The Buried Stream*, 1929, treats post-war despair and the century's failure to confront the real power of subsconscious feeling. Intensely literary (it refers to Proust, Joyce, Flaubert, Baudelaire, and many others), it is oddly passionate and unresolved. She published her poems in many journals, including *Time and Tide*, and in five volumes between 1934 and 1946. The last, *A Rough Walk Home*, composed under 'double attack' (from the bombing and her arthritis), was admired by C. Day Lewis, who wrote the introduction to her *Collected Poems*, 1948, in which he detects the influence of Christina Rossetti, Emily Dickinson, and G. M. Hopkins. Formally accomplished, her poetry is both gentle and satiric (often sharpening phrases of Christian consolation into ironic bite). Her *Uncollected Poems*, written after she had lost both legs and the use of her hands, were not published until 1981: these are searing, direct accounts of pain. Her papers are in the William Plomer collection at the University of Durham; some poems are published in Louise Bernikow, *The World Split Open*, 1984; James Wentworth Day gives some biographical detail in *The Queen Mother's Family Story*, 1967. Studies by Margaret Willy in *Essays and Studies*, 1952, and Anne Treneer in *Poetry R*, 55, 1964.

'Lysenko, Vera', Vera Lesik, 1910–75, novelist, social historian, journalist, playwright, poet, translator, social activist: the first Ukrainian-Canadian to write in English. She was b. in Winnipeg, Man., da. of Anna (Mowchan) and Andrew Lesik, Ukrainian Stundists who fled persecution in Tarashcha, a small city south of Kiev, and emigrated to Canada in 1903. VL graduated from St John's Technical High School in 1925 at the age of 14, and became one of the first Ukrainian-Canadian women to complete a university degree (BA in English, Univ. of Manitoba, 1930). She developed her leftist politics and social conscience in a multi-ethnic, immigrant, working-class neighbourhood in Winnipeg; her work at various jobs (including nurse and teacher in Alberta, and saleswoman, domestic servant, and factory worker in Eastern Canada, where she moved in 1936) gave her experience, political insight, and bite. 'The Girl Behind that "Bargain"' (pub. as Vera Lesik) in *Chatelaine*, 1936, aimed to arouse public awareness of the garment industry's huge profits and starvation wages for its female workers. Other articles appeared under various pseudonyms, including 'Luba Novack', in the leftist *The Clarion*, *Ukrainian Life* and the *Globe and Mail*. VL was also a reporter for the *Windsor Star* and wrote synopses of French novels for *Magazine Digest*. From 1943, she researched her first book, finally titled *Men in Sheepskin Coats: A Study in Assimilation*, 1947, the first English-language history of the Ukrainians in Canada to be written by a Ukrainian-Canadian, a fact VL emphasized by taking the distinctively Ukrainian name 'Lysenko'. Although the book was tightly controlled by its sponsors, members of the Association of United Ukrainian-Canadians, who changed its title and content, it retains VL's feminist outlook. It was attacked by Watson Kirkconnell, a noted academic: VL, devastated, published nothing further for several years. Her fiction represented her view that Canadian culture would come of age only when it embraced 'in its entirety the manifold life of all the national groups which constitute its entity', and her novels present strong ethnic characters, often women who pass on tradition and the cultural heritage. *Yellow Boots*, 1954, her first novel, treats a talented, successful daughter of Ukrainian immigrants; *Westerly Wild*, 1956, presents a heroine in the Saskatchewan dust-bowl of the 1930s who initiates inter-ethnic relations. VL's radio play about Ukrainian poet Ivan Franko was aired on the CBC in 1957, about the time she became reclusive, continuing to write but not publishing. Extensive collection of papers in the National Archives of Canada.

Lytton, Rosina Bulwer (Wheeler), Lady, 1802–82, novelist, b. in Ireland, younger of two surviving das. of Anna WHEELER (Doyle), feminist, and Francis W., of Ballywire, near Limerick, who m. in their teens and separated in 1812. Closer to her alcoholic father than her philosophical mother, who made France her home, RBL spent her teens between Guernsey and London, living with elderly uncle Sir John Doyle. In London she made friends with the bohemian set around L. E. L. and Lady Caroline LAMB, and in 1827 m. Edward Bulwer, later politician and novelist. After a scandalous separation in 1836 (in which he had the mistress but she got the blame), she pub. her first novel, *Cheveley, or the Man of Honour*, 1839, a thinly-disguised satire of him. Her subsequent efforts to write for a living were hampered by his retaliatory injunctions, but she wrote at least ten novels. *The Budget of the Bubble Family*, 1840, dedicated to Frances TROLLOPE in praise of her unwavering integrity, has a typically lively breathless style with glimpses of real wit among rather heavy-handed humour. *Miriam Sedley*, 1851, is largely autobiographical, with some romantic transpositions. It is less satirical than *Very Successful*, 1856, which, like most others, is prefaced by a spirited vilification of her husband. Its 2nd ed. contained a further 'Short Appeal' to the public, outlining her chief grievances (including the death of her neglected 20-year old daughter Emily, whom she had not been allowed to see for ten years). This Appeal was reprinted twice in 1857 by public demand, and in 1858, after her denunciation of him ('Sir Liar') at the hustings in his electorate, he had her forcibly committed to a lunatic asylum. Released upon public outcry, RBL was nonetheless labelled as mad, a myth perpetuated into this century by apologists of Edward. Her life, including autobiographical fragments, was pub. in 1887 by Louisa Devey. See critical article by Lucille P. Shores in *Mass. Studies in English* 6 (1978).

M

McAlpine, Rachel, (Taylor), NZ poet, playwright and novelist, b. 1940 at Fairlie South, Canterbury, da. of Celia Muriel (Twyneham) and the Rev. David Mortimer T. Educ. at small country schools and Christchurch Girls' High, she later took her BA Hons and Dip. Ed. She became a secondary-school teacher, then a clerk at the British Consulate. She was m. to Grant Wallace McA., civil engineer, 1959–78, and had four children. Her 1977 collection of poetry, *Stay at the Dinner Party*, particularly the 'Sheila and the Honorable Member' and 'A Chat with God the Mother' sections, has a bitter, humorous cynicism that make them among the few successful NZ feminist poems. 'Birdwoman' in *Fancy Dress*, 1979, could become the classic NZ feminist poem. After four vols. of poetry she wrote *The Stationary Sixth Form Poetry Trip*, 1980, a verse drama about an English lesson on Kubla Khan in a co-ed school classroom. It explores how and why adolescents read poetry, and the effect of gender on that reading. In 1980 she also pub. *Song in the Satchel*, a research monograph on poetry in the high school. Her next vol. of poetry was *Recording Angel*, 1983. Her first novel, *A Piece of Green*, 1986, is a witty fable with a heroine who creates songs out of plant, fish, and natural noises, communicates with snails, writes music that cures illnesses and saves 'the sleeping isles' (NZ) from destruction by nuclear pollution. It was followed by *Running Away From Home*, 1987, and *Selec. Poems*, 1989. She has been Writer-in-Residence at Victoria Univ., Wellington, and Macquarie Univ., Sydney.

Macarthur, Elizabeth (Veale), 1769–1850, letter writer, founder of the Australian wool industry, b. Devon, England, da. of Grace (Hatherley) and Richard V., farmer. After her father's early death and mother's remarriage, she was brought up by her grandfather. Her letters suggest she received a good educ., probably in part from the Rev. John Kingdon, father of her close friend Bridget. She m. John M. in 1788 and accompanied him to Sydney with the NSW Corps in 1790. Her letters written during the voyage are outstanding historical and personal documents. As the first educated free woman to reach Sydney she was for years at the centre of its social life, while bearing seven children and continuing to write her delightful letters to those back in England. In 1794 the Macarthurs moved to their new home, still standing, at Elizabeth Farm, Parramatta. During her husband's lengthy absence from Australia, 1809–17, following the rebellion against Governor Bligh, EM managed his Camden Park estate and nurtured its valuable merino sheep. By the time of his return, Australia was established as a wool-growing centre. Her later years were saddened by her husband's growing madness, including his belief that she had been unfaithful. Her *Journals and Letters 1789–1798*, ed. Joy N. Hughes, were pub. in 1984. The best account of her life is by Hazel King, 1986.

Macaulay, Catharine (Sawbridge), later Graham, 1731–91, radical historian and polemicist, b. at Wye, Kent, da. of Elizabeth (Wanley), who d. when she was two, and landowner John S. She read Roman history in his library with her younger brother John (also a radical), and struck Elizabeth CARTER as fashionable but learned. In 1760 she married Scottish obstetrician George M., 15 years her senior; she settled in London, bore a daughter and was widowed in 1766. In 1763 appeared, with her name, vol. i of her *History of England from ... James I ...*, written to chart the ongoing national struggle against the oppressions of monarchy. She planned to reach the Hanoverians; but after ending vol. v, 1771, on the Restoration (the nation, 'in a fit of passion and despair', plunging 'headlong into a state of hopeless servitude'), she altered her title to read *To the Revolution* [1688], which took her three more volumes, 1781–3. One of the first and finest works of the new radical school, it grows steadily in authority, and records public-spirited female action with 'infinite pleasure'. CM's sometimes anonymous minor works deal with Hobbes (*Loose Remarks*, a title later derided, with a letter to Paoli on democracy which raises the issue of women's education), 1767; copyright law, 1774 (the year she moved to Bath); the American crisis (answering Johnson), 1775; medical practice, 1777; later English history, 1778 (she also projected works on the Tudors and earlier); and the French Revolution (answering Burke), 1791. A book on natural religion, 1783, became part of *Letters on Education*, 1790 (repr. NY 1974), a reflective, original, feminist work which influenced WOLLSTONECRAFT. Married women, it says, 'have hardly a civil right'. Her views brought her 'long and malevolent persecution', often focusing on her looks and her sex, especially after her marriage, 1778, to the much younger William Graham. Admired in France and America, she visited both, and corresponded with George Washington and Mercy Otis WARREN. First woman admitted to read in the British Museum, she was accused of vandalizing a MS she disagreed with. Among some good recent comment, see Florence and William Boos in *IJWS*, 3, 1980. Study by Bridget Hill forthcoming.

Macaulay, Emilie **Rose**, 1881–1958, DBE, poet, novelist, travel writer, and critic. Da. of Grace Mary (Conybeare) and George M., scholar and later Cambridge lecturer, she was b. at Rugby, Warwicks., where he was then teaching. They lived in Italy, 1887–94; RM then attended Oxford High School and Somerville College (modern history; aegrotat degree, 1903). The first of her 23 novels was *Abbots Verney*, 1906; first to make an impact were *Views and Vagabonds*, 1912, and *The Lee Shore*, 1913, which trace the decline of male protagonists, one idealistic, one charming and initially rich. She published volumes of poetry (less successful than her prose) in 1914 and 1919. During WWI she worked as a civil servant (*What Not: A Prophetic Comedy*, 1918, draws on this experience), and began a relationship with the married Gerald O'Donovan, a novelist, which lasted till his death in 1942 and barred her from communion with the Anglican church. She satirized the popular press in *Potterism*, 1920, won the Femina Vie Heureuse prize for *Dangerous Ages*, 1921, and experimented with period speech in *They Were Defeated*, 1932, a historical novel about Cambridge monarchists (including the poet Robert Herrick) facing the oncoming shadow of civil war. *Told by an Idiot*, 1923, has been compared with *Orlando* (Virginia WOOLF was a friend of RM). *And No Man's Wit*, 1940, was set in civil-war Spain; *The World My Wilderness*, 1950, set in post-war London, has a young heroine marked by the 'moral chaos of occupied France'. In RM's final, best-known novel, *The Towers of Trebizond*, 1956, a narrator unhappily estranged from the church describes her aunt's heroic and comic campaign to liberate Moslem women into high Anglicanism. RM also published critical studies (on Milton, 1934, and E. M. Forster, another friend, in 1938) and TRAVEL books (on British travellers in Portugal, 1946, on Spain and the Algarve, 1949, and *Pleasure of Ruins*, 1953, on the splendour and transience of the past). Many works recently repr.; RM's cousin Constance Babington Smith has written her life, 1972, and ed. her letters: to a male religious mentor,

1961, 1962; to her sister, 1964. Study by Alice R. Bensen, 1969.

MacBeth, Madge Hamilton (Lyons), 'Gilbert Knox', 'W. S. Dill', 1881?–1965, novelist, playwright, travel writer, historian. She was b. in Philadelphia, da. of Bessie (Maffit) and Hayman Hart L., and educ. in London, Ont., at Hellmuth Ladies' College. Shortly after graduating she m. Charles M., an engineer. She began writing as a young widow to support her two children. A prolific writer, she travelled widely (see *Over the Gangplank to Spain*, 1931), but lived mostly in Ottawa. Her *Over My Shoulder*, 1953, and *Boulevard Career*, 1957, are informal, chatty reminiscences of her experiences and of Ottawa society, a subject treated satirically in her novels *The Land of Afternoon*, 1925, and *The Kinder Bees*, 1935. *Kleath*, 1917, is a fictional account of Dawson City during the 1890s' Gold Rush, a subject to which MHM returns in the nonfictional *The Long Day*, 1926. Her foreword to *Shackles*, 1926, discusses women's cultural transition and the dilemma created by vacillation between traditional, domestic subservience and worldly career; the novel figures these antitheses in two men, a self-righteous, insensitive husband of 12 years, and a man who supports not only the protagonist's desire to make a writing career but also the general principle of women's rights. This remarkable romance deals openly with its protagonist's sexual dissatisfaction and rejected complicity, comparing a woman who accepts the sexual advances of a husband she dislikes to a prostitute. MM wrote two plays (*Curiosity Rewarded*, 1926, and *The Goose's Sauce*, 1935), a history of the Lady Stanley Institute for Trained Nurses, 1959, and three books jointly with E. L. M. Burns. See *Canadian Author and Bookman*, December 1947.

McCarthy, Charlotte, Irish poet and religious writer. She calls her father a gentleman, and mentions her parents' deaths. In 1745, after several years in London, she pub., as 'a Gentlewoman', *The Fair Moralist, Or Love and Virtue*, which in highflown prose conducts Melissa from pastoral life 'into the welcome Chains of Matrimony'. With it are spirited poems treating love between women, London localities, and political events. A 2nd ed., 1746 (repr. NY 1974), added her name, more poems, and an essay of advice to women (sharp moral and social comment). In 1749 she was selling theatre tickets in Twickenham and Richmond. Her ambitious *Justice and Reason, Faithful Guides to Truth* was advertised in her jaunty verse *News from Parnassus, or Political Advice from the Nine Muses*, Dublin, 1757, but met opposition including, she says, a Jesuit plot on her life (problems she dramatized in *The Author and Bookseller*, 1765, now rare). *Justice* appeared at London, 1767 (subscribers mostly merchants, in whom she finds more virtue than in others), dedicated to George III. It takes an unusual view of religion, sympathetic to Catholics but not Methodists, widely speculative (how God *felt* when about to create man), with personal and supernatural anecdotes; attached fictional letters include one from a devil relating a failed tempting venture; a poem addresses the still innocent – because infant – Prince of Wales. Her *Letter* to the Bishop of London [?1767] is written as by 'Prudentia Homespun' (cf. Jane WEST); it deals with poverty (especially women's), morality, and the Church.

McCarthy, Mary Therese, 1912–89, novelist, essayist, short-story writer, b. in Seattle, Washington, da. of Therese (Preston) and Roy W. M., who both died of 'flu in 1918. At age eight she won a state prize for an essay on the Irish in the USA. She attended mainly private schools in Minneapolis, Seattle, and Tacoma (described in *Paris Review*, 100, 1986) then Vassar, where she knew Elizabeth BISHOP, Eleanor CLARK and Muriel RUKEYSER. In 1933 she graduated, began writing reviews, and made the first of four marriages, to actor Harold Johnsrud. Her second husband, author Edmund Wilson (m. 1938, one son), urged her to write fiction; she published seven novels (though sceptical about the generic label). She began with satire: *The Company She Keeps*, 1942, on upwardly mobile young New Yorkers; *The Oasis*, 1949 (*Source of Embarrassment*, 1950, in UK), on the failure of liberalism. She also did some college teaching and published stories (collected 1950, 1963), essays, and art-history books on Venice and Florence, 1956 and 1959. Better-known is *Memories of a Catholic Girlhood*, 1957, recalling her early quest for goodness, and her respectable but cruel relatives. Her preface to *Sights and Spectacles*, 1956 (collected drama reviews), describes her early career. She admitted fictionalizing actual people, as in the best-selling, *The Group*, 1963, on a circle of friends made at Vassar, 'conceived as a kind of mock-chronicle novel. ... The idea of progress seen in the female sphere ... the loss of faith in progress.' (Stevie SMITH recoiled from the portrayal of daily work in the poorish film version, 1966.) MM's strong political stands are recorded in *On the Contrary*, 1961 (essays), *Vietnam*, 1967, *Hanoi*, 1968 (fruit of a trip of which she said 'I could not bear to see my country disfigure itself so, when I might do something to stop it. It had surprised me to find that I cared enough about America to risk being hit by a US bomb for its sake'), and *The Mask of State*, 1975 (on Watergate). After her fourth marriage, 1961, to James West, she lived partly in Paris. Her later novels, *Birds of America*, 1971, and *Cannibals and Missionaries*, 1979, deal with political material, the *angst* of liberals and humanitarians in face of violent activists and terrorists. Other writings on politics and literature include an essay on Hannah ARENDT in *Partisan Review*, 51–2, 1984–5. See Elizabeth HARDWICK in *A View of My Own*, 1962; interview by Elisabeth Niebuhr in *Paris Review*, 1962; life by Doris Grumbach, 1967; bibliog. by Sherli Goldman, 1968; study by Willene Schaefer Hardy, 1981.

McCauley, Sue (McGibbon), novelist, b. in 1941 at Dannevirke, NZ, da. of Violet Irene (Montgomery), teacher, and James Dougal McGibbon, sheepfarmer. Her mother died at her birth. She wrote poems and a short (Western) novel while at school. In 1962 she m. Denis John McC., then a journalist; she had two children. She married again in 1979, to Patrick Leslie Hammond, labourer/musician. She has been a full-time writer 'for about the last 20 years', working as a journalist, publishing short stories and writing plays for radio and TV. In 1986 she was Writer-in-Residence at Auckland Univ. Of her two novels, *Other Halves*, 1982, and *Then Again*, 1986, the first (since filmed) is the account of a 32-year-old pakeha suburban housewife's breakdown, and her growing relationship with a 16-year-old Maori street kid. The novel movingly records their problems and compromises, ending with her rejection of pakeha, western values and with the possibility of the lasting success of their relationship.

McClung, Nellie Letitia (Mooney), 1873–1951, Canadian feminist, novelist, short-story writer, public speaker, reformer, legislator, broadcaster. B. on a farm near Chatsworth, Ont., youngest of six children of Letitia (McCurdy) and John Mooney, she moved, 1880, to a Manitoba homestead in a district without a school. An early 'scribbler', she gave up novels for poetry, which could be written before her mother called her to housework. At ten she began formal schooling, attended Normal School in Winnipeg, 1889–90 (returning there to high school, 1893–5), then taught, largely in Manitou, Manitoba, where she 'had to declare my allegiance to the Cause' and began her work with the WCTM (Women's Christian Temperance Movement). She m. pharmacist Wesley McClung, 1896, and had five children. At 17, inspired by

Dickens, she had decided to use her writing for social change. A contest short story became the opening chapter of *Sowing Seeds in Danny*, 1908, the first of her humorous, punchy Pearl Watson novels, which went through 17 editions, selling 100,000 copies. Its heroine, an independent girl, becomes an independent woman and a suffragist in subsequent novels, *The Second Chance*, 1910 (which sold out in a day), and *Purple Springs*, 1921 (which takes its background from the Manitoba struggle for the vote). NM moved to Winnipeg, 1911, became a member of the Canadian Women's Press Club, broadened her sense of the injustice experienced by prairie women with studies of women's rights in Winnipeg garment factories, politics, dower rights and family law, and engaged fully in the 'bonny fight – a knock-down and drag-out fight' for the vote. With others, she organized the Political Equality League, 1912, which staged a Mock Parliament, and produced in 1914 *How the Vote Was Won*, by Cicely HAMILTON and Christopher ST JOHN. Both were, she said, 'a great factor in turning public sentiment in favour of the enfranchisement of women', won in Manitoba in January 1916. *In Times Like These*, 1915, essays, is 'a classic formula of the feminist position'. NM moved to Edmonton, 1914, was elected to the provincial legislature, 1921–6, and afterwards wrote a short story a week (*Be Good to Yourself*, 1930, *Flowers for the Living*, 1931). She joined Emily MURPHY's legal fight in the famous 'Persons Case'. She was League of Nations delegate for Canada, 1938. Unwell in her last decade, she concentrated on broadcasting and her autobiographies, *Clearing in the West; My Own Story*, 1935, and *The Stream Runs Fast*, 1945. *Leaves From Lantern Lane*, 1936, and *More Leaves*, 1937, collect her newspaper columns. Veronica Strong-Boag's introduction to *In Times Like These*, 1973, quoted above, appreciates NM's achievement, comic spirit and acerbic wit. See Candace Savage, 1979 (includes bibliography).

McCord, Louisa Susannah (Cheves), 1810–79, poet, Southern propagandist, b. Charleston, SC, second da. of Mary Elizabeth (Dulles) and Langdon C. Educ. in Philadelphia and by French refugees, she was strongly influenced by her father, a bank president. She managed a cotton plantation, inherited 1830. In 1839, she m. David James M., lawyer and politician, a widower with ten children. They produced three more children, of whom the eldest, Langdon, was killed in the Civil War. Her blank verse tragedy, *Caius Gracchus*, 1851, articulates her desire to fulfil her political ambitions through her son. Gracchus' mentor, his mother Cornelia, wielding her influence from the sidelines, recommends to women 'A quiet comeliness'; their 'noble thoughts' will be effected through men. LM's other books are a translation of F. Basiat's free trade polemic *Sophisms of Protection*, 1848, and *My Dreams*, 1848, a collection of poetry. She pub. articles defending ante-bellum traditions, including slavery, in the *Southern Quarterly Review* and *Southern Literary Messenger*. See also Jessie M. Fraser, in *Bulletin of Univ. of S. C.* No. 91 (1920).

McCormick, Anne Elizabeth (**O'Hare**), 1880–1954, journalist, da. of Teresa Beatrice (Berry) and Thomas J. O., b. in Wakefield, Yorks., and taken to the USA as a baby. She was educ. in Ohio private schools, graduating from St Mary of the Springs in 1898. Deserted by her father, she and her mother went to work for the *Catholic Universe Bulletin*. In 1910 she m. Francis J. McCormick, engineer and importer; they travelled widely in Europe after WWI, and she 'talked with and wrote about people and princes, and events and their meaning, wherever she went'. As early as 1921 she noted a speech by Mussolini as 'a little swaggering, but caustic, powerful and telling'. She published in the *NY Times* from that year, despite a general ban on female reporters (she was the first woman on its editorial board).

Her column 'Abroad' measured the rise of totalitarianism in Europe, protesting 'whenever freedom is interfered with in any part of the world'. She published poetry in magazines, but often declined commissions for books in favour of reporting. However, *The Hammer and the Scythe: Soviet Russia Enters the Second Decade*, 1928, was influential. She won a Pulitzer Prize for her foreign reporting (1937), held various public offices, and lectured widely. Her friend Marion Turner Sheehan published two posthumous volumes of her work: *The World at Home*, 1956 (the USA in the Depression and WWII; perceptive remarks on Franklin and Eleanor ROOSEVELT and on 'a new political generation' of women), and *Vatican Journal*, 1957 (the place of the Church in the twentieth century). Papers at NYPL.

McCrackin, Josephine (Woempner), also Clifford, 1838–1920, conservationist, journalist and short-story writer, b. in Germany, da. of Charlotte (Hartman) and Georg W. She emigrated to St Louis, Missouri, as a child and was educ. privately and in convent schools. In 1864 she m. James Clifford and lived in various army posts in the Southwest, until his mental problems ended the marriage, after which she taught German in San Francisco schools. Her first publication, on the 'Dead Letter Office' based in Washington, DC, appeared in the *Overland Monthly*, 1869, beginning her long association with that magazine and its editor, Bret Harte. She began to write fiction and travel pieces, translations of German tales and accounts of her experiences as an army wife. In 1882 she m. Jackson M. Her first book of short stories, *Overland Tales*, was pub. in 1877 and three more collections followed by 1899. Some of her stories, like 'A Lady in Camp', were melodramatic and sentimentally romantic, her strength being in the more factual pieces based on her own experiences. After 1899 she focused on conservation issues. She was an effective agitator; impassioned appeals such as that in *Overland Monthly*, August, 1900, were largely responsible for the preservation of the Californian Redwood forests. In 1899 her home was destroyed in a forest fire, and after her husband's death four years later she was forced back into writing to earn her living. She continued to write newspaper columns into her seventies, dealing with conservation issues.

McCullers, Lula **Carson** (Smith), 1917–67, novelist, short-story writer, b. at Columbus, Ga, da. of Marguerite (Waters) and Lamar S. She aimed to be a pianist, then after rheumatic fever at 15 wrote several plays, a novel and some poetry 'that nobody could make out, including the author'. She went to NYC to study music (her mother's idea) at the Juillard School and creative writing at Columbia Univ.; after losing all her money on the subway she opted for night classes, work (e.g., dog-walking), and writing. She published her first story in 1936. Next year she married Reeves M., an aspiring writer with whom she led a hectic life, moving from place to place, drinking, splitting up and reuniting. CM felt her nature also 'demanded, craved, a reciprocal love relationship with a woman'. Her *The Heart is a Lonely Hunter*, 1940, features outsiders (grotesques by society's standards), with a pain and intensity typical of her later work: a musical, unloved adolescent boy and two deaf-mutes. It brought her fame which her husband found hard to take: they first separated three months after publication, and divorced in 1941. *Reflections in a Golden Eye*, 1941, set in an army camp in the US South, treats a range of festering smothered passions: male homosexuality, a woman who 'cut off the tender nipples of her breasts with the garden shears', an old corporal who writes a journal-letter every night to Shirley Temple. *The Member of the Wedding*, 1946, embodies in a teenage girl protagonist the loneliness which CM saw as common to all humans. It became one of her two plays, 1950, and one of several fine movies from her works, 1952. That year saw her *Collected Short Stories* and *The Ballad of the Sad Cafe*, featuring a hunchback and a once powerful woman vulnerable to love: 'Once you have lived with another, it is a great torture to have to live alone.... It is better to take in your mortal enemy than face the terror of living alone.' CM remarried her ex-husband in 1945, after he was wounded in WWII. At 30 (after her pneumonia, before her cancer) she was temporarily paralysed by her second stroke. During another brief separation, 1948, she attempted suicide; but she refused the double suicide he urged before killing himself in 1953. *Clock Without Hands*, 1957, embodies black/white, young/old polarities around a premature death from leukaemia. CM kept travelling, with some lecturing, as long as she could; when too ill for 'real' work she wrote children's verse: *Sweet as a Pickle, Clean as a Pig*, 1964. Her important female friends included writers: Muriel RUKEYSER, Isak DINESEN, whom she fell 'in love with' in 1937, Elizabeth BOWEN, whom she visited in Ireland in 1950, and Edith SITWELL, whose 75th birthday took her to England in 1962, the year of her mastectomy, when she was mostly wheelchair-bound. A journal work (tentatively titled *Illuminations and Night Glare*) remained unfinished. MSS at the Univ. of Texas. Life by Virginia Spencer Carr, 1975; studies by Margaret B. McDowell, 1980, and Louise Westling, 1985 (on CM and the struggle against female identity); bibliogs. by George Bixby (*American Book Collector*, 1984) and (of criticism) Adrian M. Shapiro et al., 1980.

McCulloch, Catharine (Waugh), 1862–1945, author and suffragist, b. Ransomville, NY, da. of Susan (Gouger) and Abraham Miller W., educ. at Rockford College, Ill., and Northwestern Univ. Law School. She was admitted to the Bar, and to the Supreme Court of Illinois, 1886 (and to the US Supreme Court, 1898). She wrote *Woman's Wages*, 1887, and practised law until 1890 when she m. Frank Hathorn M, becoming a joint partner in their legal firm. A member of the Equal Suffrage Association and vice president and legal adviser of the National American Women Suffrage Association, she addressed the Illinois Senate and House of Representatives on the SUFFRAGE question in 1892. Author of numerous pamphlets on women's legal position – including *The Bible on Women Voting*, which offers a feminist interpretation of the Bible in support of woman's claims to equality – she wrote, in *Mr Lex and the Legal Status of Mother and Child*, 1899, a fictionalized account of the 'injustices which result from laws which make fathers sole guardians and custodians of their children'. Mr Lex enforces upon his family his every matrimonial legal entitlement, from appropriating his wife's income to depriving her of her children, before being finally committed to an asylum. Mrs Lex emerges from her long-suffering subordination to confront the laws that 'ought to be changed, but I don't believe they will until the majority of women ... demand changes'. CWM also wrote a play, *Bridget's Sisters*. Twice elected Justice of the Peace, she was the first woman to hold judicial office in the USA, and played a leading part in securing the franchise for women in Illinois in 1913.

McCullough, Colleen, novelist, b. 1937 in Wellington, NSW. She was educ. at convent school and the Univ. of Sydney, then worked briefly as a teacher, librarian and journalist before practising as a neurophysiologist in Sydney, London and at Yale Univ., USA. In 1976 she began writing full-time following the success of her first novel, *Tim*, 1974. Since the extraordinary sales of her second novel, *The Thorn Birds*, 1977, an ambitious saga of an Irish-Catholic family in pastoral NSW, she has been internationally recognized. She now lives on Norfolk Island where she m. plantation owner Ric Robinson in 1984. While her novels, all pub. in the USA, have brought commercial success and have wide popular appeal, they have rarely aroused the enthusiasm of critics and reviewers. Other novels are: *An Indecent Obsession*, 1981, set in a 'troppo' ward during WWII, the futuristic *A Creed for the Third Millennium*, 1985, and *The Ladies of Missalonghi*, 1987, controversial because of accusations of plagiarism. She has also pub. a cookery book, 1982. Her first three books have all been filmed, *The Thorn Birds* as a TV series, 1983. She did not wish to appear in the present volume.

MacDonald, Betty, Anne Elizabeth Campbell (Bard), 1908–58, humourist-autobiographer and children's writer, da. of Dutch-descended easterner Elsie (Sanderson) and Darsie B., mining engineer. B. at Boulder, Col., she lived in Mexico, an Idaho mining camp, Butte (Mont.), then, 'pioneering days ... over', in Seattle: in a large, warm family with an eccentric, angry, prophet-of-doom grandmother. Her father died when she was 12. In 1927 she dropped out of the Univ. of Washington to marry a man who persuaded her to 'dive head first into' chicken rearing in the primitive Olympic Mountains. In 1931 she left him and took her two daughters back to Seattle to poverty and office jobs; seven years later a fellow-worker gave her tuberculosis. She kept a diary of her stay in a sanatorium, 1938–9. Married to Donald C. M. in 1941, living on Vashon Island, working as a secretary, having written nothing for adults but 'a couple of punk short stories', she was inveigled by her sister into meeting a publisher. Four books of sparkling memoirs resulted: *The Egg and I*, 1945 ('a sort of rebuttal to ... I-love-life books by female good sports whose husbands had forced them to live in the country without lights or running water'), *The Plague and I*, 1948, *Anybody Can Do Anything*, 1950 (about the office years before her illness), and *Onions in the Stew*, 1955. Often repr., they were abridged together as *Who Me?*, 1959. BM also wrote children's stories of Mrs Piggle-Wiggle, from 1947; her sister, Mary Bard, followed her in writing humorous books about her own life.

MacDonald, Jane **Elizabeth** Gostwycke (Roberts), 1864–1922, poet and short-story writer. The sister of poet Sir Charles G. D. Roberts and da. of Emma (Bliss) and the Rev. G. Goodridge R., she was b. at Westcock, NB, and educ. at Fredericton Collegiate and the Univ. of NB. She taught briefly at the School for the Blind, then in 1896 married her cousin Samuel Archibald Roberts M., with whom she went to Western Canada, 1912, and from whom she separated, 1915, rejoining her family in Ottawa. Her poems and short fictions appeared in Canadian and US periodicals. *Poems*, 1885, was printed privately; *Northland Lyrics*, 1899, was co-authored with her brothers William Carman and Theodore, 'selected and arranged' by Sir Charles G. D. R. *Dream Verses and Others*, 1906, like the others, are unpretentious nature poems and love lyrics; *Our Little Canadian Cousin*, 1904, is fiction.

McElroy, Colleen (Johnson), poet, b. 1935 in St Louis, Missouri, to Ruth (Long) and Jesse O. J., a soldier who 'gut-kicked a trooper. ... Lost his eagle / All for a chance to die equal'. After noisy, dusty, smelly high school later poignantly revisited while 'standing wet / and poetic in the rain', she attended a number of univs. and colleges; degrees include a BS from Kansas State Univ., 1958, and PhD from the Univ. of Washington, 1973. She was a speech therapist in Kansas City from 1963, a professor of English at various univs. from 1966; she married writer David F. M. in 1968, had two children, and is now divorced. In 1972 she published a book on child language development, and her first book of poems, *The Mules Done Long Since Gone* (titled from her grandmother's remark on seeing CJM's newborn son). *Music from Home*, 1976, opens with the child CJM eavesdropping on aunts retailing family history: 'Subjects of sin are whispered, / But my ears are large / Under the shroud of legs.' She writes about bodies sexual or suffering, about history open and covert, about being black in the USA. Her tightly woven imagery draws on anatomy, surgery, vintage cars and day glo socks. Particular moments open resonant implications: 'I rise like an aging lizard / back gone bad / eyes glued with yesterday's sins. . . . 2000 years from now / Anthro students will dig / their spades into my cheeks'; 'sold to the highest bidder for three / hundred dollars, all of my grandma's / life put on the block.' Often humorous, she is seldom optimistic: 'A Poem For My Old Age' anticipates telling sceptical grandchildren 'take off your glasses / your three dimensional rose colored glasses / the world is full of enchanted frogs'; a painfully graphic poem about lynching ends with a warning to remember 'how these acts are inhumanly / possible in your own century – / and how no circumstance should force / you to accept the payoff / in scenery'. *Jesus and Fat Tuesday* is a book of stories. Several poems in *Queen of the Ebony Isles*, 1984 (Before Columbus Association award), feature the 'Dragon Lady', related in one to 'washerwomen full of primordial defiance'. CJM says the poems in *Bone Flames*, 1987, her seventh collection, 'celebrate, shout, glory in' turning 50; she spent 1987–8 in Yugoslavia on a Fulbright Fellowship.

MacEwen, Gwendolyn, 1941–87, poet, novelist, playwright, short-story writer, da. of Elsie Doris (Mitchell) and Alick James M., b. in Toronto. She left high school at 18 to become a writer and did not attend university: 'I didn't want to spend a whole lot of time having to learn what literature was all *about*. I simply wanted to make it myself.' With Al Purdy and Milton Acorn (to whom she was briefly married), she edited the journal *Moment*, 1960–2. Two privately published collections of poetry, 1961, were followed by eight substantial volumes, 1963–82. The 'informing myth' of GM's poetry, writes Margaret ATWOOD, is 'that of the Muse, author and inspirer of language and therefore of the ordered verbal cosmos, the poet's universe' (*Second Words*, 1982); Mary DI MICHELE reads her 'You Held Out the Light', from *The Shadow-Maker*, 1969, winner of the Governor General's Award, as a love affair 'with language itself, with poetry, the Muse'. Twenty years after visiting Tiberias, GM wrote *The T. E. Lawrence Poems*, 1982, remarkable articulations of his experience in which she is 'not so much the inventor as the interpreter'. *Armies of the Moon*, 1973, won the A. J. M. Smith award. GM had completed three novels before publishing *Julian the Magician*, 1963. This, with *King of Egypt, King of Dreams*, 1971, and her collection of short stories, *Noman*, 1972, concentrates on eastern mysteries. In 1971, she married Greek singer Nikos Tsingos (divorced, 1978) with whom, for a time, she ran a coffee house in Toronto, The Trojan Horse. Her play, *The Trojan Women: a New Version*, performed in Toronto, 1978, captures 'what feminist critics seek to achieve theoretically as the revision the androcentric canon'. The inter-related stories of *Noman's Land*, 1986, dedicated to 'all the strangers in Kanada', reflects Canadian culture through the eyes of the stranger and central character, Noman. *Mermaids and Icons*, 1978, is memoirs of Greece. GM wrote two children's stories, *The Chocolate Moose*, 1979, and *The Honey Drum*, 1983, and poems, *Dragon Sandwiches*, 1987, and *Afterworlds*, 1987, which won her second Governor-General's Award. Critical study by Jan Bartley, 1983, essay by Shelagh Wilkinson in *CWS*, 8, 1987.

McGinley, Phyllis, 1905–78, poet, humourist, essayist, children's writer. B. at Ontario, Oregon, da. of Roman Catholics Julia (Kiesel) and Daniel M., she wrote poems as a child. Educ. at the Univs. of Southern California and of Utah (graduating in 1927), she wrote verse for magazines while teaching school in Utah and New York State, and doing odd jobs in NYC. She was poetry editor of *Town and Country*, and turned to light verse at *The New Yorker* editor's suggestion. Her first three collections, *On the Contrary*, 1934, *One More Manhattan*, 1937, and *A Pocketful of Wry*, 1940, show the developing humourist. In 1937 she married Charles L. Hayden, the 'Oliver Ames' of her poetry; she had two daughters. Most of her poems, like 'Why, Some of My Best Friends are Women', are what she termed 'domestic', dealing with suburban married life. *Husbands are Difficult, or The Book of Oliver Ames*, 1941, mocks male foibles. Among many honours, *Love Letters*, 1954, won the Edna St Vincent MILLAY Memorial Award; *Times Three*, 1960, was the first book of light verse to win the Pulitzer Prize. PM's essay volumes take women's sphere more seriously than her poems: *The Province of the Heart*, 1959, and *Sixpence in Her Shoe*, 1964, mount a (sometimes repetitious) case against 'the writers of those feminist books' (implicitly, Betty FRIEDAN) and for 'the true glory of being a woman – sacrifice, containment, pride, and pleasure in our natural accomplishments'. PM published 17 children's books, 1944–67, and a book of saints, 1969. Study by Linda Welshimer Wagner, 1971, has bibliog.

Macgoye, Marjorie (King) Oludhe, Kenyan poet and novelist, b. in 1928 in Southampton, England, da. of R. T. and D. M. A. K., who sent her to local schools. She studied at the Univ. of London (BA, MA), then went to Kenya as a missionary bookseller, 1954. She married D. G. W. Oludhe M., a medical assistant, 1960. They have four children. She took Kenyan citizenship, 1964, immediately after independence: 'I am so much enmeshed in my Luo family and community I am not afraid of writing from within it either.' One of her poems, 'Letter to a Friend', begins, 'Why should I be ashamed / Not to be black?' *Growing up at Lima School*, 1970, is a work for children; *Murder in Majengo*, 1972, an adult novel; *Song of Nyarloka*, 1977, lyric poems. Winner of the BBC Arts and Africa Poetry Award, MM is frequently anthologized. The ironic 'Freedom Song' is a lament for a 14-year-old girl, exploited by her relatives, dead of childbirth, mourned at a funeral more lavish than any gift she ever had. 'For Miriam' is a grandmother's monologue. MM's novel, *Coming to Birth*, 1986, awarded the Sinclair Prize for a prose work 'of very special social and political importance', deals with the development of its female protagonist between 1956 and 1978. Her struggles are set against headlines of events of which she is hardly aware: Ghana's independence, Mboya's assassination, the Nigerian Emergency, the Uhuru demonstrations, the Entebbe Raid. MM draws an ordinary woman with restraint and sensitivity, and at the same time shows 'parallels between the emergence of a new type of woman and the emergence of a new nation'. In *The Present Moment*, 1987, elderly women from different tribes, now in a home, tell one another about their lives and about being caught between the old, rural Africa and the new. *The Story of Kenya*, 1986, is non-fiction.

MacGregor, Mary Esther (Miller), 'Marian Keith', 1876–1961, novelist, writer of short stories. Born in Rugby, Ont., da. of Mary (McIan) and John Miller, she was educ. at Toronto Normal School, then taught at Orillia, and in 1909 married the Rev. Donald C. M., the town's presbyterian minister, and spent most of her life there. She wrote 16 novels, religious biography, some essays, and a travel book (*Under the Grey Olives*, 1927, about a trip to the Holy Land). Her novels – moralistic, humorous, sentimental idylls – deal with the Scottish settlements in Oro township, often with the life of the Manse. The religious biographies include one on the boyhood of Jesus, 1935, and one on missionary George Leslie Mackay of Formosa, 1912. With Lucy Maud MONTGOMERY and Mabel Burns McKinley, she published, as 'Marian Keith', *Courageous Women: Essays and Speeches*, 1934.

McGuckian, Medbh (McCaughan), poet, b. 1950 in Belfast, da. of Margaret (Fergus) and Hugh Albert McCaughan, headmaster. She was educ. at a Dominican convent school and Queen's Univ., Belfast (BA 1972, MA in Anglo-Irish literature, 1974, diploma in education). She taught English in a Catholic boys' school, married John M., also a teacher, in 1977, and has three sons. Although interested in the civil rights movement since 1968, she does not write directly about politics. She won the National Poetry Competition with 'The Flitting', 1979. After *Single Ladies* and *Portrait of Joanna*, both 1980 (pamphlets), and inclusion in *Trio Poetry 2*, 1981, more awards greeted her full volume *The Flower Master*, 1982, which draws on post-natal breakdown: 'Tricks you might guess from this unfastened button, / A pen mislaid, a word misread, / My hair coming down in the middle of a conversation.' (See *Cyphers*, 18, 1983.) MM edited *Venus and the Rain*, 1984, and poems by young Northern Irish people as *The Big Striped Golfing Umbrella*, 1985. Her work transforms personal, public and religious elements into a richly textured, allusive and elusive poetry. Edna Longley has noted her 'teasing, unorthodox feminism – sexual, womb-centred, fertile in imagery'. MM thinks modern readers lazy, expecting poetry to soothe and sedate: she therefore favours 'a construction of substantial bricks', using language 'in a very thick consistency'. Writing for women, she says, 'You don't need to explain anything'; so she addresses primarily male readers, feeling like 'John the Baptist or someone ... a pioneer for my particular society' (quoted by Catherine BYRON, *Women's Review*, 19, May 1987). MM has been writer-in-residence at Queen's. *On Ballycastle Beach*, 1988, uses the voices of troubled women: 'I joined my elbows / To hide my breasts. ... I gathered my limbs / Under me, to suppress my shadow.'

Machar, Agnes Maule, 'Fidelis', 1837–1927, novelist, poet, journalist, feminist, 'ardent literary nationalist', social reformer, b. in Kingston, Ont., da. of John M., Presbyterian minister and principal of Queen's University, 1846–54. He believed in higher education for women, and educ. her at home in Latin, Greek, French, Italian, and German. Widely read, she knew many prominent Canadians, including Pauline JOHNSON. She began writing in childhood, under so many PSEUDONYMS that little is known about her early period. Her prose and poetry was published widely in British, US and Canadian journals, frequently in *The Canadian Monthly and National Review*, 1872–8, *Rose-Belford's Canadian Monthly*, 1878–82, and *The Week*, 1883–96. Her work embodies her 'creed of Empire' and 'sense of mission'. Her strongly nationalist poetry, like that in *Lays of the 'True North' and Other Canadian Poems*, 1899, celebrates nature; her eight novels (several for juveniles), history and biography embody her moral and political vision. A leading Canadian social critic of her day, AMM defended liberal Christianity, and the social gospel, and saw women as leaders in social reform. Her concerns include poverty, TEMPERANCE (she viewed alcoholism as a disease) and higher education for women. She was 'clear-eyed' about poverty as the source of 'women's special inequality in the industrial system', and she saw the need for workers to organize to obtain justice. The hero of her 'Novel of Our Time', *Roland Graeme, Knight*, 1892, who becomes a radical journalist, exemplifies her Christian social gospel. She worked with the National Council of Women and in her will provided for the Agnes Maule Machar home for aged women. See M. Vipond in *JCS*, 10, 1975, Ruth Compton Brower in *JCS*, 20, 1985 (quoted above), and *CHR*, 65, 1984, and Ramsay Cook *The Regenerators*, 1985 (quoted above).

McIlwraith, Jean Newton,'Jean Forsyth', 1859–1938, historical novelist, critic, biographer. Da. of Scottish immigrants Mary

(Park) and Thomas M., a well-known ornithologist, she was b. in Hamilton, Ont., and educ. there at the Ladies' College and through the correspondence programme in modern literature of Glasgow Univ. After working for several years in NYC as a publisher's reader, she returned to Canada, 1922, to devote herself to writing. She published short stories (in *Harper's, Atlantic Monthly, Cornhill Magazine*), literary criticism for young people (on Shakespeare, Longfellow), a much-praised biography of *Sir Frederick Haldimand*, 1904, and well-documented, lively, historical novels which contributed to the popularity of the form, including *The Span o'Life: a Tale of Louisburg and Quebec*, 1899, co-authored with William McLennan; *The Curious Career of Roderick Campbell*, 1901, about three Scottish families who migrate to Canada; and *Kinsmen at War*, 1927, a Canadian-American romance set during the 1812 war between the two countries. She also wrote a comic opera, *Ptarmigan*, performed in Hamilton, 1894, published 1895.

MacInnes, Helen, 1907–85, writer of spy stories. B. in Glasgow, educ. at its Girls' High School and Univ. (MA, 1928), and at the Univ. of London, she worked as a librarian there and in Dunbartonshire. In 1932 she married classical scholar Gilbert Highet (d. 1978). They had one son, migrated to NYC in 1937, and became US citizens in 1951. HM began her career as a prodigiously best-selling writer (20 spy novels, in 22 languages, US sales in the millions) with *Above Suspicion*, 1941 (immediately filmed, MGM, 1943, with Joan Crawford). Based on experiences during a honeymoon trip to Bavaria, it pictures sinister Nazi Germany and a light-hearted Oxford couple caught up in trailing an endangered English agent. Her novels are carefully researched, her women often innocents abroad: in *The Snare of the Hunter*, 1974, the daughter of a Czech writer carries secret notebooks to the West; in *Ride a Pale Horse*, 1984, her last book, a journalist at a Prague Peace Conference becomes carrier of secret documents and potential victim in a game of espionage. In *Prelude to Terror*, 1978, an amateur projected into danger adapts speedily to kidnappings, shoot-outs, and speaking in code: a widowed art dealer foils a Communist plot to fund international terrorism by selling stolen treasures. Patricia Craig and Mary Cadogan, in *The Lady Investigates*, 1981, discuss her interlace of realism and romance.

McIntosh, Maria Jane, 'Aunt Kitty', 1803–78, novelist and children's writer, b. Sunbury, Ga., da. of Mary Moore (Maxwell) and Lachlan M. Educ. at home by her mother, MM proceeded to two academies, returning home in 1823 to run the family estate on her widowed mother's death. She sold the property and moved to NY in 1835; but the 1837 Panic destroyed her fortunes, so she started writing to earn money. Her first book, *Blind Alice*, 1841, and the four which followed during the next two years, were didactic children's stories, pub. under the pseudonym 'Aunt Kitty'. The moralizing tone continues in her adult fiction, for which (from 1846 onwards) she used her real name. *Conquest and Self-Conquest*, 1844, and *Two Lives*, 1847, both trace the parallel development of a pair of contrasting young people. MM's most successful work, *Charms and Counter-Charms*, 1848, which sold 100,000 copies, promotes the ideal of women's emotional independence, while *The Lofty and the Lowly*, 1853, is MM's riposte to *Uncle Tom's Cabin* and a showcase for the beneficial effects of slavery. Her non-fiction work, *Woman in America*, 1850, identifies a public role for women: 'May not we ... mould our social life by our intelligent convictions into a form which shall make it the fit handmaid of our political life?' MM's work is discussed in *Woman's Fiction*, 1978, by Nina Baym.

Mack, Elsie Frances (Wilson), 'Frances Sarah Moore', 1909–67, popular novelist.

B. in Aylmer, Ont., and educ. at the Univ. of Toronto, she lived in Ontario, England, and Saskatchewan, then, after marrying Norman M., in small villages in various areas of Canada, and in London, Ont.. She pub. at least 20 romantic novels (including *Deborah*, 1951, *The Right Girl*, 1956, *Legacy of Love*, 1957) mostly in New York and London, many in paperback, some in magazines like *Redbook*. Often set in both contemporary Canada and the US, her 'light romances', as she called them, provide sufficient action and intrigue to maintain interest. *A Woman of Jerusalem*, 1962, is different: set in the time of Christ, it centres on the woman whose stoning for adultery Christ prevented. See *Canadian Author & Bookman*, December 1947.

Mack, Louise (later Creed and Layland), 1870–1935, novelist, short-story writer, poet and journalist, b. Hobart, Tasmania to Jemima (James) and Hans Hamilton M., a Wesleyan minister: sister of the children's writer Amy Mack (1876–1939). She was educ. by her mother, a governess and at Sydney Girls' High School, where she ed. a magazine in rivalry with one ed. by Ethel TURNER. Twice married, she survived both husbands. She pub. short stories in the Sydney *Bulletin*, where she was a staff member from 1898, writing the 'Woman's Letter'. In 1901 she left her husband to travel to Europe alone. Her first novel, *The World is Round*, 1896, was a story of girlhood. Her best-known ones, *Teens: A Story of Australian School Girls*, 1897, and its sequels *Girls Together*, 1898, and *Teens Triumphant*, 1933, are based on her school experiences. She pub. a further 11 novels, most of them light romances written to make money, such as *The Marriage of Edward*, 1913, one of four titles pub. by Mills and Boon. She also wrote poetry, *Dreams in Flower*, 1901, and two autobiographical works, *An Australian Girl in London*, 1902, and *A Woman's Experiences in the Great War*, 1915. She was the first Australian woman war correspondent.

MacKay, Isabel Ecclestone (Macpherson), 1875–1928, poet, novelist, dramatist, short-story writer, a friend of Marjorie PICKTHALL and Pauline JOHNSON. She was b. and educ. in Woodstock, Ont., da. of Priscilla (Ecclestone) and Donald McLeod Macpherson. She m. Peter MacKay, a court stenographer, 1895, moving with him to Vancouver, 1909, where she was active in the Canadian Women's Press Club and the Canadian Authors' Association. Her poems and stories appeared widely in Canadian, British and US journals, including *Harper's*, *Scribner's*, *McClure's*. She published several volumes of poems, mostly love and nature lyrics (including *The Shining Ship and Other Verse for Children*, 1918, and *Fires of Driftwood*, 1922), at least five novels, ten plays, and a book of folklore. Her novels address women's condition: *The House of Windows*, 1912, treats wages and working conditions; *Blencarrow*, 1926, the attempts of a woman to protect her children against a drunken father.

Mackay, Jessie, 1864–1938, poet and journalist, b. at Rakaia Gorge, Canterbury, NZ, da. of Elizabeth and Robert M., shepherd and sheep-station manager, educ. at home and at Christchurch Normal School and College. She became a teacher and pub. *The Spirit of the Rangatira*, 1889, *The Sitter on the Rail*, 1891, *From The Maori Sea*, 1908, *Land of the Morning*, 1909, *Bride of the Rivers*, 1926, and *Vigil*, 1935 (all vols. of poetry). An idealist, romantic and vegetarian, a defender of oppressed minorities and of women, she argued in her journalism for Irish and Scottish home rule and the Women's Franchise Bill. As 'Lady Editor' (there was a 'real' editor) of the *Canterbury Times* she wrote for prohibition, equal pay, women police, penal reform, nationalism and internationalism. She was widely acclaimed in her lifetime as NZ's leading poet, but today her poems seem slight, very much of the 1890s. Few have a NZ setting, though some Maori 'ballads' are interspersed amidst the Celtic and Gaelic. Her journalistic feminism found no poetic voice. See life by Nellie MacLeod, 1955.

Mackay, Shena, fiction writer, b. 1945 in Edinburgh, educ. at an English grammar and a comprehensive school (Tonbridge and Kidbrooke). Already writing, she left at 16 for jobs in a library, factory, and antique shop, and wrote her first books at 17: two short novels, *Dust Falls on Eugene Schlumburger* and *Toddler on the Run*, 1964 (the toddler is actually a housebreaking dwarf). Both feature teenage girls in drifting, isolated affairs with older men, and graphic descriptions of eccentric violence. SM married Robin Brown and had three daughters. Her work is not for the squeamish. The protagonist of *Music Upstairs*, 1965 (repr. as a Virago Modern Classic, 1989), set in London flats and bedsitters, has simultaneous affairs with a husband and wife; that of *Old Crow*, 1967, dies in an accident (surviving an earlier one, she *thought* she saw her severed head – actually a cabbage – rolling before her); that of *An Advent Calendar*, 1971, eats bits of a human finger severed in a mincing machine and is haunted by guilt, but the novel's eviscerated 'young mothers swung by their feet from hooks' are cows. Some of SM's later surrealism is gentler: in *Redhill Rococo*, 1986 (Fawcett Society prize), a teenager holding up a post office with a toy gun is overpowered by pensioners. SM's stories appear in journals and in *Babies in Rhinestones*, 1983 (title piece about decaying 'artists' brought together by kittens), and *Dreams of Dead Women's Handbags*, 1987. She lives in London, supports animal rights, and has taught creative writing. Her seventh novel, *Dunedin*, is expected in 1990.

Mackellar Isobel Marion **Dorothea**, 1885–1968, poet, novelist, b. Sydney, da. of Marion (Buckland) and Sir Charles Kinnaird M., doctor. She was educ. at home and at Sydney Univ. before travelling to Europe where she became proficient in several languages, later including translations from European verse in her poetry. Her first book, *The Closed Door and Other Verses*, 1911, included the emotive 'My Country' (originally pub. in the London *Spectator*, 1908, as 'Core of My Heart'), one of the best-known Australian poems. This colourful lyric, praising the cruelly beautiful Australian landscape in contrast with the tame and insipid English countryside, has continued to appeal to nationalist sentiment. She pub. five other collections, including *The Witch Maid*, 1914, and *Dreamharbour*, 1923, and three novels, *The Little Blue Devil*, 1912, *Two's Company*, 1914 (both with Ruth Bedford), and *Outlaw's Luck*, 1913. She was awarded the OBE in 1968. She virtually gave up writing some forty years before her death. See her collected poems, 1971.

McKemmish, Jan (Jannette) Anne, Australian novelist and short-story writer, b. 1950 at Tongala, Vic., da. of Marjorie Amelia (Hunter) and Reginald M. She graduated (BA, Dip. Ed.) from La Trobe Univ. Her most important publication to date is an experimental feminist spy thriller, *A Gap in the Records*, 1985, an intelligent and innovative novel, in which women form a spy collective instead of playing traditional roles of victim or sex object. Its structural subversion draws attention to the traditional thriller narrative as a male construct. She has also had stories pub. in the anthologies *Frictions*, 1982 (ed. A. Gibbs and A. Tilson), and *Writers in the Park*, 1986 (ed. C. Christie and K. O'Brien) and has co-written for theatre with Pamela BROWN.

Mackenzie, Anna Maria (Wight), also Johnson, 'Ellen of Exeter', d. after 1816, leading MINERVA novelist, of 'confined education'. Her first husband, a Mr Cox, lost money and died 'a victim of sorrow', leaving her with four children. Need and an 'ardent love of writing' produced the epistolary *Burton-Wood*, Dublin, 1783 (jealous rival nearly ruins heroine's marriage; women's education limitedly and coyly endorsed). Though claiming some independence 'from the beaten track of novel-writing', it typifies her cautious attitudes and stilted style. She often deplores the effect of much fiction while exempting a few authors, some female; reviewers were usually kind to her. Still anonymous in *The Gamesters*, 1786 (heroine's husband, led astray by wicked brother, reforms to exemplary, patriotic benevolence), she re-married and set her name as Mrs Johnson to *Calista*, 1789 (a different Mrs Johnson pub. the Fieldingesque *Francis*, 1786, and two more). *Monmouth*, 1790, based on Restoration history, is perhaps her best work. *Slavery, or The Times*, 1792, gives its princely (half-)African hero a natural, impetuous gallantry (quite unlike the common run of slaves) and the heroine's hand. She pub. as Mackenzie in 1795 (preface, on ROMANCE, to the gothic *Mysteries Elucidated*) and as 'Ellen of Exeter' in 1796 (*The Neapolitan, or The Test of Integrity*); she claimed 16 novels.

Mackie, Pauline Bradford, b. 1874, novelist, known also as Mrs Herbert Müller Hopkins and Mrs Harry Cavendish, b. Fairfield, Conn. Her best novel is *The Washingtonians*, 1899, a closely-wrought tableau of the Washington social élite during the Civil War. Its heroine, wife of an army general and daughter of a Presidential candidate, is 'the most beautiful woman in Washington ... an unthroned but imperious queen' at the centre of a dazzling political circle, which includes Lincoln himself. A skilful portrayer of character and dialogue, PBM is more interested in political intrigue than political theory. Other works include *Ye Little Salem Maide*, 1898, *The Voice in the Desert*, 1903, *The Girl and the Kaiser*, 1904, and *The Moving House*, 1920, a children's story.

Mackworth, Cecily, biographer, travel writer, journalist, poet, novelist, b. 1911 at Llantilio, Wales, da. of Dorothy (Lascelles) and army officer Francis Julian M. Privately educ., she m. Leon Donckier de Donceel in 1936 and had two children. He died in 1939. She has lived chiefly in Paris; her personal fascination with French life, poetry and art shows in work for journals in English and French. Nancy CUNARD published her in *Poems for France*, 1944; her *Eleven Poems* were published in Paris in 1938. When the Germans occupied France, 1940, she came to Britain (describing her Armistice experiences in *I Came out of France*, 1941), where she wrote for *Horizon* and other journals, lectured to troops, and wrote two works pub. 1947: a life of François Villon (whose era she likens to her own) and *A Mirror for French Poetry 1840–1940* (poems in versions by English poets, with her critical views of TRANSLATION). She was in France briefly in 1946, then in 1947 left for Palestine as correspondent for *Paris Presse*. Her experience there is related in *The Mouth of the Sword*, 1949. Next year she travelled in Algeria and the Sahara to research her deeply involved *Destiny of Isabelle Eberhardt* (1951, repr. 1985; cf. Timberlake WERTENBAKER). CM stresses Eberhardt's mysticism and her conversion to Islam and resulting fatalism, and admires her nonconformity, independence, and cross-dressing. CM's novel, the accomplished *Spring's Green Shadow*, 1952, is about a young Welshwoman who, in reaction against her parents' restricted lives and unhappy marriage, chooses an independent writer's life in Paris. In 1956 CM married the Marquis de Chabannes la Palice. Her *Guillaume Apollinaire and the Cubist Tradition*, 1961, takes the artist as representative of his time; the more popular *English Interludes*, 1974, is a view of England, especially London, 'absorbed and transmuted' into poetry by Mallarmé, Verlaine, Valéry, and Larbaud, who saw it while young. CM is reticent about her own life. *Ends of the World*, 1987, on her travels 1937–60 (with brief diary from London in WWII), says an autobiography would be 'another book, which it is unlikely I shall ever write'.

M'Lehose, Agnes 'Nancy' (Craig), 'Clarinda', 1759–1841, Scots letter-writer and poet, da. of Andrew Craig. Her mother d. when she was eight. In 1776, fresh from boarding school, she married against her family's will a ne'er-do-well lawyer, James M., whom she left in 1780, just before bearing her fourth child. In 1787 she fell in love with Robert Burns, but probably declined to become his mistress. Her family interposed; Burns married; when she sailed for Jamaica in 1792 to attempt reconciliation with her husband, Burns wrote a touching farewell, 'Ae fond kiss'; her journal remembered him in 1831. Among several eds. of their 'Clarinda' and 'Sylvander' letters, with her few poems, see Raymond Lamont Brown, 1968. Though she disclaims any 'poetic merit' and regrets she has vivacity instead of the 'softness' she sees as 'the first female ornament', her poems thrive on her sharp perceptions and powers of analysis. Burns extravagantly praised the one that calls love her enemy ('He bound me in an iron chain, and plunged me deep in woe'), yet altered it freely for print, 1788, adding a stanza to soften the sexual rebuff. His reply to her refrain that he loved because 'you'd nothing else to do' is frothy and evasive. Marital reconciliation failed; AM spent the rest of her life in Edinburgh.

M'Leod, E. H., later P----, novelist for the firm succeeding MINERVA, who began under her birth name and reverted to it in her last work. Her subtitles all employ the word 'fashionable'; the satirical element becomes more marked with time. Her preface to *Tales of Ton* (three series – 12 vols., – 1821–2) admits to basing some characters on actual high-life figures; in 1826 she disclaims personal allusion. The mostly moralistic, socially well-observed tales include a few with real or apparent uncanny touches. Her first narrator models himself on the heroes of Ann RADCLIFFE and Caroline LAMB; EHM makes points through literary reference, and inserts poems here and there. Writing at Norwich, she dedicated *Principle!*, 1824, to Walter Scott. Its thoughtless heroine, wrongly suspected by her husband of infidelity, nearly dies in a madhouse; marital dramas also dominate *Geraldine Murray*, 1826 (after EHM's marriage and move to Fingringhoe Hall, Essex), and *Belmont's Daughter*, 1830.

Macmanus, L. (Charlotte), *c.* 1850–1941, novelist and story writer, b. on her mother's family estate at Killeaden, Co. Mayo, third of 17 children (seven reared) of Charlotte (Strong) and James M., ex-sugar planter. Educ. at home by an English governess and then at Torquay, she always loved military history; but her life was transformed when she was over 40 by reading Irish history. She joined the Gaelic League, learnt Irish and joined the Irish literary revival (she knew Moore, Synge, Yeats and Lady GREGORY). She pub. 18 books, novels and story collections, mainly nationalist historical fiction, between 1893 and 1914. Her first success was *Silk of the Kine*, 1896, on the slave traffic carried on in seventeenth-century Ireland by Bristol merchants. *In Sarsfield's Days* convincingly narrates a fast-moving story of the 1690 siege of Limerick from an officer's viewpoint. Her involvement in the Anglo-Irish war and her diary of the 1916 Easter Rising form the second part of her reminiscences, *White Light and Flame*, 1929. See her niece, Emily M., *Matron of Guy's*, 1956, for family information.

MacMurchy, Marjory, later Lady Willison, poet, essayist, feminist, and one of Canada's earliest (cf. J. J. DUNCAN) and best-known journalists. She was b. in Toronto, educ. there at the Collegiate Institute and Univ. of Toronto, da. of Marjory Jardine (Ramsay) and Archibald M. She wrote for many Canadian and US publications, including *Harper's Bazaar*, New York *Bookman*, and the *Canadian Magazine*; she was a regular contributor to *Saturday Night* and the Toronto *Mail and Empire*: weekly articles on 'Politics for Women', 1921–2. Widely known for her support for and generosity to other women writers, MM was Canadian correspondent for *Common Cause*, and President of the Canadian Women's Press Club, 1909–13. Her books include *The Woman – Bless Her. Not as Amiable a Book as it Sounds*, 1916, and *Women of Today and Tomorrow*, and *The Canadian Girl at Work*, both 1919. MM examines women's roles, emphasizing home-making, urging adequate training and education for both paid and unpaid employment; she examines the increase in job opportunities for women after WW1. Her husband, Sir John W., died in 1927, a year after their marriage.

MacNaughtan, Sarah Broom, 1864–1916, novelist and war nurse, b. Scotland, da. of Peter M., JP. Educ. at home, she travelled in her early life to South America, the USA, Canada, Palestine, Egypt, India, Kashmir and Burma, among other places. She experienced the bombardment of Rio de Janeiro and, a trained nurse, tended victims of the Balkan atrocities and worked for the Red Cross in the Boer War. Her fiction, such as *The Fortune of Christina McNab*, 1901, *A Lame Dog's Diary*, 1905 (which contains an interesting picture of a reading society largely run by women), and *The Expensive Miss Du Cane*, 1907, presenting studies of society types, was popular but unremarkable: her most notable publication was *A Woman's Diary of the War*, 1915, describing her experiences during the siege of Antwerp and in the soup kitchen she started at Furnes, before carrying out similar work elsewhere in Belgium and in Russia. War, as she told munitions workers in addresses on her return from Flanders, 'is not a merry picnic'. Her health had been undermined by her experiences, and she died after a period of illness.

McNeill, Janet, b. 1907, novelist, dramatist, and children's writer. B. in Dublin, da. of Jeannie P. (Hogg) and the Rev. William McN., she was educ. at Birkenhead School, Cheshire, and the Univ. of St Andrews (MA 1929). She went to work for the Belfast *Telegraph* and in 1933 married Robert P. Alexander, a civil engineer who died in 1971. She has four children. Her play *Gospel Truth*, 1951, carries a feminist message: the heroine's clergyman father educates her like a son and encourages freedom of choice, but a career is still felt to clash with moral duties. JM's many children's books (*My Friend Specs McCann*, 1955, was the first of a successful series) bend a vivid imagination towards helping children cope with a complex world. She has also written plays and an opera libretto (*Finn and the Black Hag*, 1962) for the young. Her adult novels focus mainly on the stuff of women's lives, including efforts directed into often exhausted marriages. *A Child in the House* (1955, later filmed and televised) concentrates on generational problems, *The Maiden Dinosaur* (1964, after six more titles) on women 'fading, creasing, ageing, dulling, thickening', *The Belfast Friends*, 1966, on a group of women who stay in touch from childhood, especially on Sarah's unspoken love for another member of the group, and *The Small Widow*, 1967, on an unqualified woman left high and dry by her children's departure. *Tea at Four O'Clock*, 1956, is reprinted, with an introduction by Janet Madden-Simpson, 1988. JM has worked in Belfast broadcasting, written about 20 radio plays and another libretto, and lives in Bristol.

McPherson, Heather, poet, b. 1942, at Tauranga, NZ, da. of Mavis Isabel (Hutchinson) and Archibald Frederick M., painter-decorator then war-disabled pensioner. She took her Primary Teacher's Certificate in 1961 and her BA at Canterbury, 1971. A solo mother since 1973, she has been teacher, library assistant, clerk, announcer, proofreader, laundry-worker, kiwifruit packer and tutor in community women's studies courses. She began publishing in literary magazines in the late 1960s and in feminist magazines from the early 1970s. She was involved in the Wellington Women's Gallery, and *Spiral*, a feminist publishing collective. She lives in Matata, Bay of Plenty, with her son – 'survival demands still tend to take precedence over writing'. Her two collections of poems, both produced by small presses, *A Figurehead, A Face*, 1982, and *The Third Myth*, 1986, have received little recognition. They are intelligent, energetic, accessible, personal and consider the implications of being a woman, a feminist and a lesbian here and now in NZ. Something like the later poetry of Adrienne RICH, they are openly lesbian and political – 'Having seen past the gods, their power, we make a goddess, ours . . .'.

Macpherson, Jay, poet and critic, b. in 1931 in London, England, da. of Dorothy (Hall) and James Ewan M. Her family migrated to St John's, Newfoundland, 1940, and settled in Ottawa, 1944. She was educ. at Carleton Univ. (BA, 1951), McGill Univ. (1953), Univ. of Toronto (MA, 1955, PhD, 1964). She is now professor of English at Victoria College, Univ. of Toronto. Her first book, *Nineteen Poems*, 1952, was published by Robert Graves' Seizen Press in Mallorca. Emblem Books (1954–63, 'tiny little booklets put out by JM with covers by Laurence Hyde') published her second book, *O Earth Return*, 1954. *The Boatman*, 1957, dedicated to Northrop and Helen Frye, and winner of the Governor General's Award, established her reputation. Reprinted five times, it was hailed as 'the most beautifully coherent and lyrical book of recent years'. *Welcoming Disaster*, 1974, is her latest collection. Her poetry, called 'Parnassian (Robert Graves-like)', bears the mythic signature of Northrop Frye's 'anagogic phase' of literature. Through its 'strict meters and small frames', it consciously explores the complexities of the world of myth, as in 'Ark Articulate': 'If you repent again / And turn and unmake me, / How shall I rock my pain / In the arms of a tree?' JM's critical study, *The Spirit of Solitude: Conventions and Continuities in Late Romance*, 1982, reflects her involvement with mythical paradigms and pastoralism. Its 'Epilogue' is a strong but problematic reading of the romance motif in Canadian literature. Although major studies of modern Canadian poetry refer to JM, there are few articles: see James Reaney in *CanL*, 3, 1960, Suniti NAMJOSHI in *CanL*, 79, 1978, Lorraine Weir in Barbara Godard, ed., *Gynocritics*, 1986.

McQueen, Cilla, NZ poet, b. 1949 in Birmingham, England, da. of Marion Constance (Going), MA, teacher, and Evan Garth M., Professor of Pharmacology, Otago Medical School: second of four children. She took an MA (Hons) in French at Otago Univ. and taught French full-time in Dunedin secondary schools before being awarded a writer's fellowship (1985 and 1986) and becoming a full-time poet. She began writing regularly in 1978 when she took a year off to travel in Europe. She m. Ralph Hotere, artist (since divorced) and had a daughter, 1969. Of her several vols. of poetry, *Homing In*, 1983, has poems about her daily life: 'Timepiece', surreally satirical about housework, 'The Shopping', 'Living Here', about being a New Zealander, 'Song for a Far Island', about her ancestors from St Kilda. *Anti-Gravity*, 1984, and *Wild Sweets*, 1986, are humorous, witty, in a seemingly casual, colloquial style. It is performance poetry, a sophisticated descendant of Roger McGough: 'poetry is a shock / it wide eyes & spreadeagles you.' Her later vols. include *Benzina*, 1988, and *Two Lovers Dissolve into Birdsong*, 1989.

Macquoid, Katharine Sarah (Thomas), 1824–1917, novelist, b. London, da. of a merchant of Welsh descent, educ. privately at home and in France: dubbed 'The Authoress' by her siblings. She m. Thomas R. Macquoid, artist, who illustrated many of her books, notably her travel guides to

Normandy and Brittany. She pub. in all some 60 works, mostly novels of the 'wholesome' variety. After early success with her first novel, *A Bad Beginning: a Story of a French Marriage*, pub. anon., 1862, often repr., and other titles such as *By The Sea*, 1864, she lost her market, eventually regaining it with the successful *Patty*, 1871, featuring a wilful, pretty heroine particularly admired by male readers. *Doris Barugh*, 1878, is dedicated to her friend Annie KEARY, who supplied the Yorkshire legend of the story. *Louisa*, 1885, set in Italy, unusually features a husband who dies after wrongfully believing his wife unfaithful.

M'Taggart, Ann (Hamilton), *c.* 1753–1834, playwright and autobiographer, eldest da. of a naval officer. Her mother d. when she was ten and she was sent to live with an uncle and aunt, to whom she read many books aloud; her aunt d. when she was 17 and she ran the household (at Exeter); her uncle's re-marriage sent her back to her father (London, then Bristol). She painted seriously, published a newspaper essay on secrecy in 1788, was 'guilty of writing a little poetry now and then', and kept a journal of European travel, 1788–9. In Holland she began writing plays; she read them to friends, lent them to the royal family, and sent at least two to John Kemble, who never replied. Four (repr. 1832) were pub. in John Galt's *New British Theatre*, 1814–15; she issued the rest by subscription, 1824. The blank-verse tragedies or dramas include *Constantia*, from a Mme de GENLIS tale, *Theodora*, which has confused her with Sophia BURRELL, and *Hortensia*, whose heroine Galt found more purely evil than Lady Macbeth. *A Search after Perfection* bases its characters on life (herself as Mrs Rational) and pokes fun at educational theorists like Hannah MORE. Her *Memoirs*, 1830, by 'a Gentlewoman of the Old School', celebrate strong-minded women and end with comic treatment of her unromantic elderly marriage.

Madan, Judith (Cowper), 1702–81, poet, da. of Pennington (Goodere) and Judge Spencer C.: niece of Mary, Lady COWPER (whom she addressed in verse in 1718). The whole family wrote: her poems of 1720–8 (BL MS) include some satires; others, and letters, in Herts. Record Office. She m. Martin M., 'Lysander' in her MSS, in 1723, but hated the separations his army career imposed, and had several breakdowns; of nine children, three survived. A few poems, mostly modest and unassuming, appeared anonymously from 1721: wryly mocking her brother's legal studies, praising work by John Hughes and her friend Pope. 'Abelard to Eloisa', 1720 (pub. in William Pattison's works, 1728), follows Pope closely and gives Abelard a sensibility ('this trembling, this offending Frame') like Eloisa's (cf. HELOISE). 'The Progress of Poetry' (pub. in *The Flower-Piece*, 1731, praised by Susanna DUNCOMBE's husband), rehearses the literary canon. Elizabeth BENGER admired JM. Letters *to* her were pub. anonymously, 1769. Her daughter, Maria Frances Cecilia, who married a Cowper cousin and shared her mother's intense piety, pub. in 1792 a volume including verses in her memory; a son also wrote. See Falconer M., 1933, for M. family; Valerie Rumbold, 1989, for JCM and Pope.

Madeleva, Sister **Mary**, Mary Evaline Wolff, 1887–1964, nun, poet, educator, b. at Cumberland, Wis., only da. of Catholic schoolteacher Lucy (Arntz) and Lutheran harness-maker August Frederick W. After a year at the Univ. of Wisconsin she transferred to St Mary's College at Notre Dame, Ind., run by the Holy Cross Sisters; Sister Rita Heffernan encouraged her religious and literary vocations. There she entered the novitiate, 1908, took her BA and began teaching, 1909. She received an MA (Notre Dame, 1918) and PhD (Berkeley, 1925); in 1925 she published *Chaucer's Nuns and Other Essays* and a study of the *Pearl* poet. She taught and headed communities at Ogden, Utah, 1919–22, Salt Lake City, 1926–33, and St Mary's, 1934–61; facilitated the first US Catholic graduate theology programme open to women (St Mary's, 1943); re-organized the national Catholic Education Association to serve women teachers better, 1948; and wrote of women's education in *Conversations with Cassandra*, 1961. *Knights-Errant*, 1925, made her known as first of the modern US 'nun-poets'; *Penelope*, 1927, drew controversy and praise with 'The King's Secret', remarkably erotic, begging the divine lover to 'Absorb, consume, encompass and confound me'. She seeks God in natural beauty, in 'gray rock, austere and high' and 'Indian paintbrush … half flame, half feather'. Further volumes (selec. 1938, collec. 1947, 1959) comprise some 200 pieces, 'at least one poem a month' for 15 or 20 years, more at times of convalescence from overwork and exhaustion: each for immediate publication in often secular journals. *My First Seventy Years*, 1959, says that students' 'womanhood is measured by, and uplifted to the womanhood of Mary'. Life by Barbara C. Jencks, 1961; papers at St Mary's.

Madison, Dolly (Payne), 1768–1849, Washington hostess and correspondent, also known as Dolley and Dorothea, b. New Garden, NC, eldest in Mary (Coles) and John P.'s family of nine. Educ. at a Quaker school in Virginia and later, when her father had freed his slaves, in Philadelphia. In 1790 she m. John Todd, lawyer, who, along with their younger child, d. in 1793. In 1794 she m. James M. It was a childless but happy marriage. Her outgoing personality undoubtedly helped his political career. When he became Secretary of State under Jefferson, DM acted as First Lady for the widower President. In 1809, M. became President and DM continued as an accomplished hostess. Her only pub. work is her *Letters*, ed., with a Life, by A. C. Clark, 1914. Domestic and personal, they reveal a vivid personality, who set the tone of hospitality at the White House (the name is her invention): 'I have always been an advocate for fighting when assailed, though a Quaker. I therefore keep the old Tunisian sabre within reach,' she wrote of the 1812 War. The best life is by Maud W. GOODWIN, 1896. Her papers are at Lib. of Congress; Univ. of Va.; DC Lib.

Magazines. The pioneering, mainstream *Gentleman's*, from 1731, printed much writing by and about women; yet Isabella Griffiths, *c.* 1712–64, was savaged by Tobias Smollett in 1758 for her part in *The Monthly Review*, especially judgement of works by men; Christian JOHNSTONE gave her husband all the credit for their joint magazine ventures. *The Lady's Magazine*, 1770 ff (by no means the first of its name) was especially strong in fiction, and extended the number and social class of female subscribers (see Jean Hunter in Donovan H. Bond and W. Reynolds McLeod, eds., 1977). *The Monthly Mirror* carried 'SK's' remarkable 'Series of Select Poems by Ladies', 1799 ff, with texts by and comment on early writers still obscure today. *The Columbian Magazine*, Philadelphia, dealt in women's issues from 1786, with work by Elizabeth Graeme FERGUSON, Ann Young SMITH, and many unidentified women. The Philadelphia *Lady's Magazine* began strikingly in 1792 on 'Rights of Woman' and excerpts from WOLLSTONECRAFT's *Vindication*. Longmans' 1816 plan for a London literary journal conducted by women came to nothing. *Eliza Cook's Journal*, 1849–54, (see Eliza COOK) both domestic and literary, began reporting women's rights issues (though from an anti-SUFFRAGE standpoint), taken up after 1858 by the much more radical *English Woman's Journal*, ed. Bessie PARKES. It also included some housewifery; but Samuel Beeton's *Englishwoman's Domestic Magazine*, begun 1852, was the most successful in this field. Jessie BOUCHERETT founded and edited the *Englishwoman's Review*, 1866–71. Emily FAITHFULL's *Victoria Magazine* ran from 1863 to 1880, *The British Workwoman* from 1863 to 1896. Charlotte YONGE held sway over the successful *Monthly Packet*, for girls, for 40 years. Ann STEPHENS, Ellen WOOD, and M. E. BRADDON all edited influential fiction magazines; periodical publication remained a common form of debut for novels. In the US, Margaret FULLER edited the transcendentalist *Dial* in the early 1840s (from Boston: Marianne MOORE was assistant editor on the Chicago *Dial*, 1925–9). Amelia BLOOMER's feminist *Lily* began in 1849 as a TEMPERANCE journal, competing with conservative magazines like the hugely popular *Godey's Lady's Book*, ed. S. J. HALE. Victoria WOODHULL and her sister ran the radically feminist *Woodhull and Claflin's Weekly*, 1870–6. Mormon feminist Emmeline WELLS promoted polygamy as well as equal rights as editor of *Women's Exponent*, 1877–1914. Eliza CUSHING from 1838 and Mary Jane LAWSON in 1852–3 each broke new ground in Canadian magazine publishing. In Australia Louisa LAWSON founded the first feminist journal, *The Dawn*, in 1888.

In the UK, periodicals for women became a rapidly expanding industry between 1885 and 1910: by 1900 most women's magazines were underwritten by advertising. *The Lady's Own*, 1898, aimed 'to find favour with the fair ones and to secure a corner in every household'. 'Quality' magazines proliferated: *The Ladies' Field, The Lady, The Lady's Realm, The Lady's Pictorial, The Ladies' Gazette*, to name a few. *My Weekly*, begun in 1910, for working-class women, exemplified the modern classic formula: 'romantic fiction, household hints, cookery and dress-making, a children's feature, and advice on personal problems, interspersed with interesting titbits of news and gossip and introduced with a "plain talk" from the Editor' (Cynthia White, 1970). See also Brian Braithwaite and Joan Barrell, 1979.

During this century women have moved increasingly into both political magazines and literary and little magazines. Political journals supported the Suffrage cause, which was so inaccurately reported by the mainstream press that Helena Swanwick thought 'It will be impossible for any future historian to write an adequate account of the Suffrage movement by reference only to the Public Press.' Charlotte Perkins GILMAN wrote every word of *The Forerunner*, 1909–16, much of whose material (critical articles, editorials, reviews, fiction, and verse) dealt with the rights of women and socialism. *Time and Tide*, a political and literary journal founded in London in 1920 by Lady RHONDDA, emerged from the suffrage struggle: it assessed the government of the day in terms of the promises it made to women, and published, among others, Rebecca WEST, Elizabeth ROBINS, and Cicely HAMILTON. Benstock, 1986, and Hanscombe and Smyers, 1987, describe the role of women's PUBLISHING in the development of literary modernism. In London, Dora Marsden's *The Freewoman*, 1911, became *The New Freewoman*, 1913, under Harriet Shaw Weaver's editorship, then *The Egoist*, 1914; it published H. D., Dorothy RICHARDSON, Ezra Pound, T. S. Eliot, and May SINCLAIR, and became the English home of the developing Imagist movement. Harriet MONROE founded *Poetry* (Chicago) in 1911, out of her frustration at failing to gain access to the few existing outlets for verse: she published the Imagists, Eliot's *Prufrock*, and, in 1922 and 1926, two all-woman issues, as well as 'literally hundreds' of women poets. Margaret ANDERSON's *Little Review*, founded in 1914, charged with obscenity for publishing James Joyce's *Ulysses*, also published Helen HOYT, Eunice TIETJENS, Mina LOY, Djuna BARNES, and many others. Ethel Moorhead, a Scot who had been a suffragette, financed *The Quarter*, which ran 1925–32; BRYHER financed and assisted in the editing of *Close-Up: An International Magazine Devoted to Film Art*, 1927–33.

In the thirties, US feminist and leftist Martha Foley and her husband Whit Burnett founded *Story*, 1931, as a platform for proletarian writers, including Tess SLESINGER, Elizabeth JANEWAY, Meridel LESUEUR, and Dorothy Canfield FISHER. *The Ladder*, edited by Barbara Grier ('Gene Damon') was founded in San Francisco by the Daughters of Bilitis in 1956, as the first US lesbian magazine: until 1972 it published articles, some fiction and verse, and reviews of lesbian writing, including work by Marion Zimmer BRADLEY, Jane RULE, Myrna LAMB, Rita Mae BROWN, and Judy GRAHN. (See *Lesbiana: Book Reviews from The Ladder*, ed. Barbara Grier, 1976.) The 'second wave' produced a renaissance of women's publishing: *Aphra*, founded in 1969, 'the first national [US] literary magazine birthed by the movement', published excerpts from Monique WITTIG, works by Audre LORDE, Marge PIERCY, and many others. Other journals of the sixties and early seventies are *Amazon Quarterly, A Lesbian-Feminist Art Journal, Earth's Daughters, Chomo-Uri, 13th Moon, Chrysalis, Calyx, Sinister Wisdom*; *Spare Rib*; literary and scholarly journals include *Feminist Studies, IJWS* and *TSWL*. See Mary Biggs in *13th Moon*, 8, 1984, quoted above; E. M. Palmegiano, *Women and British Periodicals 1832–1867*, 1976; David Doughan and Denise Sanchez, eds., *Feminist Periodicals 1855–1984*, 1987; Mary Kelley, *Private Woman, Public Stage*, 1984 (for contributions of writers like Fanny FERN and Caroline GILMAN).

Mahy, Margaret, writer of children's fiction, b. 1936 at Whakatane, NZ, eldest da. of May (Penlington) and Frank M., bridge builder, educ. at the Univs. of Auckland and Canterbury (BA) and Wellington Library School. In the early 1960s she had two daughters; by 1967 was children's librarian at Canterbury Public Library. She was rejected by NZ publishers until an American publishing house, Franklin Watts, pub. five of her stories in 1969. In 1980 she resigned to write full-time. She won the Carnegie Medal for *The Haunting*, 1983, and *The Changeover*, 1985, and NZ's Ester Glen award for CHILDREN'S LITERATURE four times. She has written 22 picture books, 11 collections of stories, five junior novels, five novels for older children and many books for emergent readers. Her books have an international circulation. Many of her picture books have women in strong and positive roles: *The Man whose Mother was a Pirate*, and *Jam*, where the mother is an astro-physicist and the father stays at home. Her novels often focus on the supernatural and 'what if?'. In *The Haunting* the girl narrator, who wants to be a writer, finds out that, even though the family tradition has been that only boys can be magicians, it's not her brother who is one, but her older sister. In *The Tricksters* the narrator tells of a supernatural return of a previous inhabitant of her family's beach house. In *The Changeover* the girl saves her younger brother from a deadly possession, by accepting the witch potential that is within her. See Betty Gilderdale's study, 1982.

Maiden, Jennifer , poet, novelist, b. 1949 at Penrith, NSW, da. of Marjorie Joan (Butler) and Alfred Edward M. She left school early to work in a factory and later returned to studies, graduating from Macquarie Univ., 1974, the same year she m. Cecil Philliponi. Since then she has been a professional writer, a tutor of writing, and has pub. seven collections of poems and ed. several others. She m. David Toohey in 1984 and has a daughter. Her works are *Tactics*, 1974, *The Problem of Evil*, 1975, *The Occupying Forces*, 1975, *Birthstones*, 1978, *The Border Loss*, 1979, *For the Left Hand*, 1981, and *The Trust*, 1987. Her distinctively subtle and ambiguous poetry has brought her to the forefront of contemporary Australian poets. She has also written two collections of poetry and prose, *Mortal Details*, 1977, and *The Warm Thing*, 1983, and a novel, *The Terms*, 1982. She has won several awards including the Harri Jones Memorial Prize, 1973, and the Grenfell Henry Lawson Award, 1979.

Maillart, Ella Kini, travel writer, b. in 1903 in Geneva, Switzerland, to Dagmar Marie (Kliim) and Paul M., a furrier. In youth she played hockey, sailed (the only woman in the Swiss Olympic team, 1924, later in an all-woman crew on a voyage from France to Greece) and skied (for Switzerland, 1931–4). Leaving school at 17, she taught French (in Wales, London, and Berlin), acted in Paris, and worked as a deck-hand. Her trip to Moscow to study Russian film, 1930, launched her on more extensive TRAVELS. She described her experiences in French works which were quickly translated into English: *Turkestan Solo*, 1934, describes her journey from Moscow to Russian Turkestan (now Soviet Central Asia), *Forbidden Journey*, 1937, repr. 1983, her trip from Peking to Northern India. (She had gone to China as a newspaper correspondent, 1934.) *The Cruel Way*, 1947, repr. 1986, her first book in English, is an account of a journey as much spiritual as physical, from Paris to Afghanistan in 1939. Travelling by car with a woman friend who was battling drug addiction, EKM hoped to describe Europe (under the threat of war) 'from a new vantage-point in order to understand the deepest cause of our craziness,' to 'acquire self-mastery and to save my friend from herself'. She spent WWII in India (see *Ti–Puss*, 1951), where she wrote the autobiographical *Cruises & Caravans* and *Gypsy Afloat*, reminiscences of her sailing experiences, both pub. 1942. *The Land of the Sherpas*, 1955, is based on a trip to Nepal. Now settled in Geneva, EKM still travels extensively. See Mary Russell's introduction to *The Cruel Way*, 1986.

Maillet, Antonine, novelist and playwright, b. 1929 in the folkloric village of Bouctouche, NB, da. of teachers Virginie (Cormier) and Léonide M., for whom she concocted her first dramatic sketches. She went to religious schools, colleges at Memramcook and Moncton (BA 1950), and the Univ. of Moncton (MA 1959); she holds doctorates from Montréal and Laval. She has taught at colleges and univs. in NB and Québec, and worked for Radio-Canada. In 1958 she won a prize for her play *Poire-Acre* and published her first novel, *Pointe-aux-Coques*, the saga of a village. International recognition came with *La Sagouine* (written in 1968, produced on radio, stage version 1971, TV adaptation 1975, English translation with same title, 1979), a series of dramatic monologues in Acadien (close to sixteenth-century French) by a 72-year-old scrubwoman and ex-prostitute. This work is typical of AM in its strong, sceptical, life-scarred heroine and its validation of ORAL culture and links with the past. Her carnival of discourses (archaic, dialect, literary, paratactical) reaches a peak in the novel *Don l'Original*, 1972 (English version as *The Tale of . . .* , 1978). *Rabelais et les traditions populaires en Acadie*, 1972 (from her doctoral thesis), catalogues traces of archaic French still current on the Canadian seaboard, which she celebrates in *L'Acadie pour quasiment rien*, 1973. *Mariaágélas*, appearing as both play and novel in 1973, has a bootlegging Depression heroine who fights 'joyously against the sea, customs men, fishermen, priests, gossips'. *Evangéline Deusse* (written 1973, pub. 1975, staged 1976) dramatizes a favourite legend from the 1755 expulsion of Acadians by the British: its protagonist not the pathetic girl in love but the old woman looking back, 'philosophe sans le savoir'. AM returns to this era in the best-selling novel *Pélagie-la-Charrette*, 1979 (Prix Goncourt winner; englished as *Pélagie: The Return to a Homeland*, 1982), in which a woman leads a band of fugitives from Georgia, USA, on the epic journey homewards. AM gave a baby born in this story the name of her mother, the book's dedicatee. (See Michèle Lacombe in *Canadian Literature*, 116, 1988.) *Cent ans* *dans les bois*, 1981 (*La Gribouille* in Paris ed., 1982), continues *Pélagie*'s historical narrative. MA's latest novel is *Le Huitième Jour*, 1986 (*On the Eighth Day*, 1989). Interview in Donald Smith, *Voices of Deliverance*, 1986. See Marjorie A. Fitzpatrick on her heroines in Paula Gilbert Lewis, ed., *Traditionalism, Nationalism and Feminism: Women Writers of Quebec*, 1985; René Le Blanc on her 'oralité' in *Revue d'histoire littéraire du Québec et du Canada Français*, 12, 1986; dossier de presse compiled by Claude Pelletier, 1986.

Maitland, Sara, novelist, short-story writer, journalist and feminist historian. B. in 1950 in London, da. of Hope (Fraser-Campbell) and Adam M., she moved to south-west Scotland when her father changed from printing-press manager to hereditary land-owner; his beloved classical and Old Testament myths became for her 'tools of my thinking and working ever since'. She was educ. 'excessively well' at boarding schools and St Anne's College, Oxford (BA in English, 1971), and discovered feminism, socialism, friendship, and Christianity. In 1972 she married Donald Lee (now a vicar); they share 'two children and a passionate commitment to extreme Anglo-Catholicism'. She published much journalism (sermons as well as essays and reviews), and a novel, *Daughter of Jerusalem*, 1978, which suggests the Bible's feminist relevance by interweaving Old Testament re-tellings with a modern woman's experience of infertility. She also formed, with Zoë FAIRBAIRNS, Valerie MINER, Michèle ROBERTS and Michelene WANDOR, a Feminist Writers' Group which produced the collective *Tales I Tell My Mother*, 1978. In 1983 she edited, with Jo Garcia, a volume of essays by women on spirituality, and published *A Map of the New Country: Women and Christianity* (claiming that feminism offers, as well as a way forward, a way back to the Christian truth of ideals including 'renunciation of power through love') and *Telling Tales*, a collection of explosive power (myths reshaped around female protagonists; modern themes like the celebration of lesbian love). The novel *Virgin Territory*, 1984, presents a nun in crisis when her love for another woman makes her reassess her faith and vows. In 1986 SM published a life of Vesta Tilley, famous music-hall cross-dresser; in 1987 a short-story volume (*A Book of Spells*) and a novel, *Arky Types* (with Wandor), probing the social construction of gender; in 1988, *Very Heaven. Looking Back at the 1960s*, essays by women; in 1990, *Three Times Table*, novel. SM has written of herself in Ursula Owen, ed., *Fathers: Reflections by Daughters* and Wandor, ed., *On Gender and Writing*, both 1983.

Major, Elizabeth, English poet. Her mother died early, her father brought her up; left lame by a severe illness in her mid-twenties, she had to accept this (after vain expenditure in search of a cure) as the will of God, and her consequent writings as his blessing. She tells this in a prose preface to her prose-and-verse *Honey on the Rod, or a Comfortable Contemplation for One in Affliction*, 1656. Like An COLLINS and 'ELIZA', she calls her book her 'babe', which it is her Christian duty to make public. She often images herself as an erring child or poor scholar, God as father and teacher; the last three poems, structured round her name, present her as a model sinner saved, recommending humility, passivity and modesty as a sure route to salvation (which must also have helped to produce a commendatory note by the censor Joseph Caryl). See Elaine Hobby, 1988.

Makin, Bathsua (Reynolds), b. 1600, poet and educator, da. of linguist and schoolmaster Henry R.: sister-in-law (not sister, as commonly thought) of mathematician John Pell. She was said to be a noted, multilingual teacher at 14, and later to be known as 'a good Chymist', with medical skills. Her *Musa Virginea*, 1616, is a collection of poems to royal persons in Greek, French, Hebrew, German and

Spanish; *Index Radiographer*, soon thereafter, is a guide to her own shorthand system, dedicated to queen Anne. She married Richard M. in 1622 and had two children. In the early 1640s she was tutor (usually a male post) to Princess Elizabeth; another poem was pub. 1664. *An Essay To Revive the Antient Education of Gentlewomen, In Religion, Manners, Arts & Tongues*, 1673, repr. 1980, is dedicated 'To all Ingenious and Vertuous Ladies' and the future Mary II. Purportedly by a man, but almost certainly hers, it advertises her girls' school at Tottenham High Cross, and opens by attacking 'the Barbarous custom to breed Women Low': 'A Learned Woman is thought to be a Comet, that bodes Mischief, when ever it appears.' It argues that better education for girls can return through setting up schools for the well-born ones to study maths, languages, politics, medicine, grammar, rhetoric and logic. This will not bring female rebellion, but better wives and also more competitive boys. Her list of models includes Margaret NEWCASTLE and BM's correspondent Anna Maria van SCHURMAN: 'If Women have been good Poets, Men injure them exceedingly, to account them giddy-headed Gossips, fit only to discourse of their Hens, Ducks, and Geese.' See Mitzi Myers in *Studies in Eighteenth-Century Culture*, 14, 1985; Vivian Salmon in mostly German essays ed. Brigitte Asbach-Schnitker and Johannes Roggenhofer, 1987. The ascription to BM of *The Malady and Remedy of ... Unjust Arrests and Actions*, 1646, is speculative.

'Malet, Lucas', Mary St Leger Harrison (Kingsley), 1852–1931, novelist, b. Eversley, Hants., youngest da. of Frances (Grenfell) and the Rev. Charles K., novelist, and aunt of Mary KINGSLEY, travel-writer. After London art school (the Slade) she travelled on the Continent, in the USA and in the East before marrying the Rev. William H. of Devon. Her marriage was unhappy and ended some years before his death in 1897. LM wrote 18 novels, the second, *Colonel Enderby's Wife*, 1885, earning success while the later *History of Sir Richard Calmady*, 1901, was seen as sensationalist for its frank compassionate treatment of the 'nasty' subject of congenital deformity, as well as its forthright discussion of sex. In 1916 she pub. her revised and completed version of her father's unpub. novel, *The Tutor's Story*. LM's own work often centred on strong females in conventional roles. In 1902 she became a Catholic and rewrote some of her earlier work. Several novels contain bizarre dreams and hauntings: *The Carissima*, 1896, *The Gateless Barrier*, 1900, and *Adrian Savage*, 1911. Her last, *The Private Life of Mr Justice Syme*, 1932, was completed after her death by her cousin and adopted daughter, Gabrielle Vallings.

Malkiel, Theresa Serber, 1874–1949, author, editor and women's rights activist, b. Bar, Russia, emigrated with her family to the USA in 1891. She began her political activities as a member of the Russian Workingman's Club, and upon arrival in NYC bcame a Union organizer (first president of the National Woman's Infant Cloak Makers' Union, 1892), a member of the Socialist Party and the National Woman's Committee, a delegate to the Knights of Labor and to the first convention of the Socialist Trade and Labor Alliance, and organizer of the Women's Progressive Society of Yonkers, 1907. She m. Leon A. M. in 1900. A prolific writer of articles in journals such as *Socialist Women*, and editor of the women's column in the *Jewish Daily News*, TSM argued the necessity of combining socialist and feminist goals: women entering the workforce must seek new self-definition and equal rights in sexual and class terms (see *Women of Yesterday and Today* and *Women and Freedom*, 1915). Her motto, 'Get Involved', underscores her riveting fictionalized account in *The Diary of a Shirtwaist Striker*, 1910, of a young sewing-machine operator whose politicization through the strike of six thousand 'girls' transforms her into a militant leader. Initially bemused by her new-found role, she suffers the ridicule of her fiancé and father, the abuse of men who treat picketeers as whores, and police brutality. This results in a growing awareness of sex and class double standards, of sisterhood bonds: the 'feeling of kinship among us . . . amazes even me at times – we feel with and suffer for one another', and of women's courage, 'as brave as the Revolutionary fathers themselves'.

Mallette, Gertrude Ethel, 'Alan Gregg', 'Pedar Larssen', writer of juvenile fiction, journalist, b. 1887 in Victoria, BC, da. of Mary (Johnson) and Charles E. M. Her studies at Washington State Univ. included postgraduate journalism, and she began freelance writing there. Later she taught and worked as a journalist in Alaska, then in NYC. She studied the craft of juvenile fiction at Columbia Univ., 1933–5; her first novel, *For Keeps*, 1936, and several others were Junior Literary Guild selections. As 'Alan Gregg', she published boys' adventure stories. Her stories of the nurse, medical student, photgrapher, art student and defence worker present, positively, the professionally successful young woman. The protagonist of *Inside Out*, 1942, who wants to study art, compromises by attending college as her parents advise and taking art lessons on Saturdays; the fourth-year medical student in *Single Stone*, 1946, helps her physician father with research which leads to an important discovery. Usually of comfortable middle-class background, often daughter of a physician, with loving, supporting parents, the GM protagonist at times finds added interest in romance and mystery.

Malpede, Karen Sophia, playwright, theatre historian, b. 1945 at Wichita Falls, Texas, da. of Doris Jane (Liebschultz) and Joseph James M., accountant: of Italian descent, she calls herself 'a city person'. She took a BS at the Univ. of Wisconsin, 1967, MFA at Columbia Univ., 1971, was briefly married and had a daughter. She has taught and worked with THEATRE GROUPS: she ed. plays from the Open Theater, 1974, co-founded the New Cycle Theater, Brooklyn, in 1976 and was nine years its resident playwright, and worked with At the Foot of the Mountain. She pub. *People's Theater in Amerika*, 1972, as Karen Taylor. Her first-written play, *A Lament for Three Women*, produced 1974, shows women recovering from past abuse of love, mothering and strengthening each other, and reflects how winter lays bare the contour and meaning of landscape concealed by summer richness: KM recalls solemnly locking herself up to write it. Other plays, some pub. in anthologies, include *Making Peace: A Fantasy*, produced 1979, set in the 1840s, which uses dance, miracles, ecstasy, to celebrate heroism but sanction vulnerability; it features escaped slaves like Harriet Tubman and spirits including Mother Ann Lee and Mary WOLLSTONECRAFT. *Women in Theatre: Compassion and Hope*, 1983, is 'a journey through a contemporary past', telling the young 'of a brave heritage' from women who 'created or envisioned entire theatres . . . outside a commercial mainstream'; writings of e.g., Fanny KEMBLE, Ellen TERRY, Emma GOLDMAN, Augusta GREGORY (an unpub. essay), Gertrude STEIN, Lorraine HANSBERRY are sensitively presented. *A Monster has Stolen the Sun* (produced in part, 1981, in full 1988) was pub. 1987 with *Sappho and Aphrodite* (produced 1984) and *The End of War* (shaped partly in rehearsal, produced 1976, privately printed 1977, which shows how choices can be made in hope and love, not despair, violence and hostility). KM is a peace activist. Interview in Kathleen Betsko and Rachel Koenig, eds., 1987.

Man, Judith, b. *c.* 1622, translator, probably da. of Peter M., confidential lawyer to the Wentworth family for years before JM's birth. She travelled with her parents in France and was educ. with the daughters of Thomas Wentworth, Lord Strafford (a possible link with Alice THORNTON). To the elder of them she dedicated *An Epitome of the History of Faire Argenis and Polyarchus*, 1640, englished from Nicholas Coeffeteau's French abridgement, 1628, of John Barclay's Latin novel (whose two English versions were to be joined later by Clara REEVE's). JM's book, now very rare, is well written; her preface voices female modesty but cites the precedent of Lady Mary WROTH.

Mandel, Miriam (Minovitch), 1930–82, poet. B. in Rockglen, Sask., da. of Fanny (Friedman) and Oscar Peter M., she lived in Moose Jaw, Regina, and Saskatoon (BA, Univ. of Saskatchewan), where she met and m., in 1949, poet and critic Eli Mandel. MM was hospitalized for post-partum depression following the birth of a daughter, 1955, and a son, 1959 (though warned not to have more children). Many suicide attempts followed. The most serious, 1967, after her divorce, led to her first major commitment to an asylum, and then, 1969, to writing. Preoccupied with images of suffering such as Michelangelo's Pietà, she saw her life as 'a / rather funny book / with / the last few chapters missing'. Poems from *Lions at her Face*, 1973 (winner of the Governor-General's Award), *Station 14*, 1977, and *Where Have You Been*, 1980, were collected posthumously, with unpublished poetry, and edited by Sheila WATSON, 1984. Watson, instrumental in encouraging MM to write and in publishing her work, sees her poetry as a 'serial poem ... of enclosure and of exclusion ... of implication in a textual death'. Through her ongoing psychoanalysis, perhaps the most important influence on her poetry, and her love for music and prairie painting, MM developed a personal vision which transformed 'the clutter / of life' into an uncluttered poetic world of stark images, crisp, slender lines, and confessional narratives of 'a God-like dignity'.

Mander, Jane (Mary Jane), 1877–1949, novelist, journalist and teacher. B. at Ramarama, near Drury, Auckland, da. of Janet (Kerr) and Francis M., she grew up in the remote Northland, was educ. at numerous primary schools and as a pupil teacher. She became a school teacher and then from 1902 a journalist. She spent ten years from 1912 in NY, studying at Columbia Univ. School of Journalism, and in 1915 campaigned for a NY State referendum on the women's franchise. She wrote three novels there, all set in Northland. *The Story of a New Zealand River*, 1920, vividly portrays two generations of women. A lonely, educated, refined wife in a remote milling settlement clings to strict, life-denying moral and social standards; her daughter, Asia, grows up free from artificial constraints, goes to Sydney to earn her living, and lives with her lover without marriage. *The Passionate Puritan*, 1921, also explores the 'free love' question, while *The Strange Attraction*, 1922, describes the sexual relationship between a male writer and a female journalist and the problems of maintaining independence within marriage. Her later novels were written in London, where she moved in 1923, although *Allen Adair*, 1925, repeats the NZ setting of her childhood. Largely ignored elsewhere, JM was attacked in NZ for her focus on 'sex problems'. She set her last novels, *The Besieging City*, 1926, and *Pins and Pinnacles*, 1928, in NY and London. In 1932 she returned to Auckland to spend ten years caring for her invalid father, and stopped writing altogether, except for occasional journalism. See life by Dorothea Turner, 1972.

Manley, Delarivier, *c.* 1663–1724, often wrongly called Mary, playwright, scandal-novelist, and Tory polemicist, b. in Holland to a Dutch mother and a royalist soldier and writer, Sir Roger M. (d. 1687). She lost a Maid of Honour's post, she says, at James II's flight. Persuaded to marry her older cousin John M., she found him a bigamist and her son, b. 1691, illegitimate. She lived briefly with the Duchess of Cleveland, royal mistress, then in the west country (d'AULNOY-like letters written on the road pub. 1696). As an avowed feminist she celebrated (probably) the recently-dead BEHN and, in 1695, Catharine TROTTER; but her comedy *The Lost Lover* (written, she said, in seven days in 1694; failed on stage, 1696) mocks a lecherous aging woman and 'Orinda, an Affected Poetess'. In 1696 she made female lust and ambition hateful and splendid in *The Royal Mischief* (famous for a wife's lament over gory bits of her husband, shot alive from a cannon: repr. in Fidelis Morgan, ed., 1981), and was attacked in *The Female Wits*. She collected her own and other women's poems in *The NINE MUSES*, 1700, was savaged in 1702 as leader of 'Petticoat Authors', and turned to non-literary business schemes with her lover John Tilly. She returned to drama with *Almyna, or The Arabian Vow*, staged 1706 (learned and virtuous heroine converts wife-murdering Sultan), the tragedy *Lucius, the First Christian King of Britain*, 1717 (repr. Los Angeles, 1988), and two MS plays lost after her death. (*The Court Legacy*, pub. 1733, is probably not hers.) She found her métier in the *roman à clef*: probably in *The Secret History of Queen Zarah* [Duchess of MARLBOROUGH] *and the Zarazians*, allegedly from Italian, 1705. Its important critical preface (from French: repr. 1952) urges psychological realism in fiction and distinguishes the author's voice from the characters'. *Secret Memoirs ... of ... the New Atalantis*, 1709 (including some autobiography, much scandal, and tribute to Anne FINCH), outdid *Zarah* in popularity (7 eds. at least by 1736). A spell in prison for reflecting on 'persons of quality' did not deter DM from publishing a companion piece, *Memoirs of Europe*, 1710, or revamping her *Lady's Pacquet of Letters*, 1707, as *Court Intrigues ... of the New Atalantis*, 1711. That year she issued several political pamphlets and succeeded Swift as editor of *The Examiner* (she had already written for it, and perhaps run *The Female Tatler*, as 'Mrs Crackenthorpe', 1709). Her AUTOBIOGRAPHICAL *Rivella*, 1714, repr. 1976, constructs herself as writer through male eyes, castigates the sexual double standard, and mixes titillation with serious self-defence. *The Power of Love: in Seven Novels*, 1720, adapts inherited tales. See Patricia Köster, ed., repr. *Novels*, 1971, and in *Eighteenth-Century Life*, 3, 1977; life (DM's text with actual names supplied and comment interpolated) by Morgan, 1986.

Mann, Emily, playwright and director, b. in 1952 in Boston, Mass., da. of reading specialist Sylvia and American history professor Arthur M. Her interest in documentary theatre was inspired by her father's oral history project on the holocaust. This is reflected in her first play, *Annulla Allen: the Autobiography of a Survivor*, 1977, which is based on the life of a Central European Jew who died in 1977 and whom EM interviewed in London in 1974. She began writing short stories at six and as a teenager acted and directed productions at the Univ. of Chicago Laboratory Schools. She was educ. at Harvard (BA in English, 1974) and the Univ. of Minnesota (BFA in Directing, 1976). She married actor and playwright Gerry Bamman in 1981; they have one child. *Still Life*, 1980, winner of several Obie awards, was staged as part of the Women's Project at the American Place Theatre. The result of conversations with a Vietnam veteran, his wife, and his woman friend, it is part of EM's 'theatre of testimony', a documentary style which probes and exposes the violence of American culture. In *Execution of Justice*, 1984, EM explores the effects on the community of the violent murder of Mayor George Muscone and homosexual City Supervisor Harvey Milk in San Francisco in 1978: 'what was on trial became ... the liberal ethic versus the conservative church, family and bedrock values' (EM in *New York Times*, 9 March 1986). EM worked from the trial transcript and interviews: 'Most of what I know about human experience comes from listening.' With *Execution*, she was the first woman to direct her own play on Broadway. EM has recently collaborated with Ntozake SHANGE on a 'rhythm and blues opera', *Betsy Brown*. Interview in Betsko and Koenig, 1987, quoted above.

Mannes, Marya, 'Sec', journalist, novelist, b. 1904 in NYC, da. of Clara (Damrosch) and David M., both professional musicians, who took her often to Europe. After the Veltin School, NYC, she had a year in London studying sculpture and writing; her early plays had no success on stage. Married and divorced three times, she had a son by her second marriage. She worked for *Vogue* (1933–8, ending as editor) and *Mademoiselle,* and wrote for a wide range of periodicals, besides sculpting. During WWII she did government intelligence work, partly abroad; she later worked for TV as well as magazines, and urged more visible authority for women in the new medium. Her first novel, *Message from a Stranger,* 1948, uses a woman poet as narrator, largely from beyond the grave. *More in Anger,* 1958, and *But Will It Sell?*, 1964, collect essays from *The Reporter,* criticizing aspects of the contemporary US including its failure to reward brains or talents in women. 'Letter to a Girl' tells an imaginary daughter: 'You would have a rough time if you lived today ... unless you kept all [your] attitudes to yourself.' 'Female Intelligence: Who Wants It?' challenges men who 'need a constant reassurance of their superiority in one field at least, that of creative intelligence'. In 1959 came *The New York I Know,* addressing many of the same issues, and, as 'Sec', the satirical, political *Subverse: Rhymes for Our Times.* MM's second novel, *They,* 1968, is about ageing characters' regret for a lost, better world; *Last Rights,* 1974, advocates euthanasia. Her autobiography, *Out of My Time,* 1971, says of herself: 'The adventurer stretched, the woman made love with no thought of bonds, the writer coiled for another spring.'

Mannin, Ethel, 1900–84, novelist, travel, short-story, children's and non-fiction writer, b. in London, da. of Edith (Gray) and Robert M. She went to work as a stenographer at 15 (so meeting her first husband, J. A. Porteous, m. 1919), then went on to editing and freelance writing of 'woman's page articles' and 'thirty-thousand-word novelettes at a guinea a thousand'. EM wrote almost 100 books, about 50 of them novels. These are socially and politically conscious works, alert to women's oppression. The first, *Martha,* 1923, elaborately plots the life of the 'love-child' of an unmarried woman and 'the price the child has to pay for the sins of the parents'; *Sounding Brass,* 1925, attacks the advertising world; *Julie, the Story of a Dance-Hostess,* 1940, is about a girl born in the workhouse; the last, *The Late Miss Guthrie,* 1976, is a hard-hitting treatment of a woman's working-class life. An atheist and member of the Independent Labour Party in the thirties, EM later moved to anarchism and pacifism. *Red Rose,* 1941, is a novel based on Emma GOLDMAN's life. *Women and the Revolution,* 1938, a long polemic, identifies as enemy 'the capitalist state, which exploits Man and Woman alike'. EM lived in Europe for several years, travelling extensively, often alone, both before and after the death in 1958 of her second husband, writer Reginald Reynolds (m. 1938) to Moscow, Burma, Samarkand, Lapland, and Japan, each trip producing a TRAVEL book. Before writing *Women Also Dream,* 1937, she made, she says, long notes on 'the story of an Ella-MAILLART-Freya-STARK-Amelia-Earhart sort of woman, who, like her creator, could not rest from travel'. Her children's books were written to teach about foreign countries (e.g., *Anne and Peter in Sweden,* 1959, in Japan, 1960, in Austria, 1962). EM wrote the first of seven AUTOBIOGRAPHIES at 29: *Confessions and Impressions,* 1930, *Privileged Spectator,* 1939, *Brief Voices,* 1959, treat her childhood, the 1930s, and the 1940s and 1950s. In *Young in the Twenties,* 1971, she describes herself as 'an emancipated, rebellious, and Angry Young Woman' who fought against the banning of books like *Ulysses* or Radclyffe HALL's *The Well of Loneliness,* whose friends included Daphne DU MAURIER, who met Anna WICKHAM, Nina HAMNETT, Kay BOYLE. Among many other non-fiction works are *Practitioners of Love,* 1969, about literary treatments of love, and *A Lance for the Arabs,* 1963, which argues for the Palestinian cause. *Women and the Revolution,* 1938, argues that 'feminist' aims will be met by the post-revolutionary classless society.

Manning, Anne, 1807–79, novelist and historian, b. London, da. of Joan (Whatmore) and William Oke M., Lloyds' insurance broker. She was educ. by her mother, an accomplished scholar, and her father, in languages, painting, science and history. She taught her brothers and sisters and wrote her earliest work, *A Sister's Gift: conversations on sacred subjects,* 1826, for them. Her first major publication, *The Maiden and Married Life of Mary Powell, Afterwards Mistress Milton,* 1849, pub. anon., purports to be the journal of Milton's first wife from courtship to early marriage. It explores the shattering of her 'gay visions' of matrimony, her boredom with Milton's pompous religiosity and her resentment at being ordered to return after she had fled back to her family. *The Household of Sir Thomas More,* 1851, told from the point of view of Margaret ROPER, also explores feminist topics, such as women's EDUCATION, the attractiveness of single life contrasted with the limitations of marriage, and the superiority of 'the moral courage of women'. Always popular, she wrote over fifty other works, mostly biographies and historical novels including one about Anne ASKEW, 1866. Her *Passages in an Authoress's Life,* 1872, though incomplete, provides autobiographical reminiscences.

Manning, Olivia, 1908–80, novelist, short-story writer, b. at Portsmouth, Hants. Da. of Anglo-Irish Olivia (Morrow) and naval commander Oliver M., she grew up mostly in Ireland but said she felt she belonged nowhere. As a 16-year-old schoolgirl she sold 'four lurid serials' to an agency at £12 each, as 'Jacob Morrow'. She studied art at Portsmouth Technical College, moved to various jobs and acute poverty in London, and wrote novels (rejected). First of her 19 titles was *The Wind Changes,* 1937, repr. 1988, on a young woman's involvement with Irish nationalists and fragile personal relationships. In 1939 OM m. Reginald Donald Smith, British Council lecturer and later professor; her friend Stevie SMITH was bridesmaid. She spent WWII working as press officer in Bucharest, Athens, Cairo and Jerusalem (her husband's postings). Back in England in 1945, she wrote reviews, history, travel, and adapted plays for radio. *Growing Up,* 1948, is a short-story volume, *School for Love,* 1951, a novel from the viewpoint of an orphaned English boy in callous wartime Jerusalem. *A Different Face,* 1953, deals with the sense of estrangement felt by a man returning to his home town after years away. OM wrote comic sketches for *Punch* (collected as *My Husband Cartwright,* 1956) of a bumbling, sometimes dangerously naif husband, widely identified as her own. Life-experience also informs her best-known works. The Balkan Trilogy (*The Great Fortune,* 1960, *The Spoilt City,* 1962, *Friends and Heroes,* 1965) and the Levant Trilogy (*The Danger Tree,* 1977, *The Battle Lost and Won,* 1978, *The Sum of Things,* 1980) juxtapose the political dissolution and chaos of WWII, vividly realized in place and time, with personal pain. The heroine's husband inhabits 'a contained self-sufficient world of men', who are more important to him than she is; what she learns is 'making do with what one had chosen'. *The Play Room,* 1969 (US title *The Camperlea Girls*; repr. 1984, screenplay 1970), a disturbing novel featuring a room full of life-size pornographic dolls, reputedly portrays OM's family: sharp-tongued mother, elderly ineffectual father, gallingly favoured brother, and naive heroine, bullied about her highbrow reading, attempting friendship with a more sophisticated girl who is raped and murdered. *The Rain Forest,* 1974, has a more 'hopeful' ending: unhappily married writers (he resents her greater success) move closer together through compassion and anxiety when, on an Indian island, she loses her unborn child and he narrowly escapes an explosion. OM's stories also present, sometimes with humour, weak men and dependent, destructive, or inconclusive relationships.

Manning, Rosemary, 'Sarah Davys', 'Mary Voyle', 1911–88, novelist, children's writer, autobiographer, b. in Weymouth, Dorset, da. of Mary Ann (Coles), 'a late nineteenth-century career woman' who for a short time did social work among London's East End prostitutes, later nursed, and doctor Thomas Davys M. She was educ. at a number of day schools and at the West Country boarding school she fictionalized as 'Bampfield', later went to Royal Holloway College (BA in Classics, 1933). She worked as a shop clerk and a secretary before settling reluctantly on what would turn out to be a teaching career of 35 years. In 1943 she established, with another teacher, a preparatory school in Herts., in 1950 one in London. In the 1950s, she experienced a surge of creativity (attributed partly to the 'benign catalyst' of Rilke). As 'Mary Voyle' she published *Remaining a Stranger,* 1953, and *A Change of Direction,* 1955, both novels she later dismissed. *Look, Stranger,* 1960 *(The Shape of Innocence,* 1961, in the US), and *The Chinese Garden,* 1962, appeared under her own name. The first examines narrow-minded community oppression of the outsider, an epileptic who has lost a hand, a drunken artist, a schoolteacher hounded to suicide by rumours of his homosexuality. The second treats sensitive autobiographical territory in its tale of lesbianism, hypocrisy and betrayal in a girls' boarding school. A lesbian, but secretly, from an early age, RM had attempted suicide when left by her lover, Elizabeth, in 1962. In *Man on a Tower,* 1965, identifying with her artist-hero George (she 'did not feel free to write as a woman'), she explores the idea that the artistic impulse is destructive to personal happiness. *A Time and a Time,* published as 'Sarah Davys', 1971, a move against the oppression of secrecy, is an account of her love for Elizabeth, her suicide attempt, and her new relationship with a younger woman. RM 'came out' on an ITV program in 1980. *Open the Door,* 1983, embodies its theme in its title (cf. Catherine CARSWELL); its five characters are required to confront their suffering and face loss. For RM, who called herself 'a very autobiographical writer', self-confrontation is crucial and Rilke's 'profitable loss' a goal. *Corridor of Mirrors,* 1987, describes the growth of her identity as a woman, a lesbian, and an artist. Wonderfully witty, it titles its first chapter 'Truth Will Out' and begins: 'To come out at the age of seventy. ...' RM wrote several stories and two reference books for children.

Manning-Sanders, Ruth (Vernon), 1888–1988, poet, novelist, children's writer and folklorist, youngest da. of a Unitarian minister. B. in Swansea, she grew up in Sheffield and Manchester with summers in the Highlands: the family were great readers and performed their own plays. From 14 she boarded at Channing House School, Highgate, London; serious illness ended her study of English at Manchester Univ. After convalescing in Italy and planning to go on stage, she m. painter George M-S (later a novelist); they did two seasons with Rosaire's Circus, living in a horse-drawn caravan, before settling in Cornwall. They had two children. After *The Pedlar, and Other Poems,* 1919, Virginia WOOLF found her long poem *Karn* 'rather exciting and altogether unexpected', and published it, 1922, and *Martha Wish-You-Ill,* 1926. *The City,* 1927 (Blindman International Poetry Prize), relates the redemption of a poor woman ('Sakes alive – / What's come to Moll? She's in a fit, poor thing') by direct intervention of Jesus (at home in the modern world, as in medieval tales, he arrives at a London night-club riding an ass). But RM-S's poems sold poorly, and for money she turned to novels with *The Twelve Saints,* 1925. She issued 13 more adult novels (to 1957), a life of Hans Christian Andersen, 1949, works on British topography, and *The English Circus,* 1952, but is better known for her 70 CHILDREN's books, especially legends and folk-tales, whether original or re-told. The format *A Book of . . . [Witches* or *Mermaids* or *Magic Horses* or *Princes and Princesses,* etc.] ran from 1962 to 1988. Magic, folk themes, and delight in a romantic past of Cornish seafarers, travelling people and entertainers (as in *Circus Boy,* 1960) are central in her own poetry and fiction, and vital in her highly personal re-creations.

Mansfield, Katherine (Kathleen Beauchamp), later Murry, 1888–1923, short-story writer, da. of Annie Burrel (Dyer) and Harold B., businessman, director and chairman of the Bank of New Zealand. Third child of six, she was educ. at Wellington Girls' High, where she wrote her first stories, and the élite Miss Swainson's School. From 1903–6 she went with two sisters to Queen's College, London, where she met her lifelong friend Ida Baker (LM). In 1908 she attended Wellington Technical College to learn typing and bookkeeping, then returned to England. She wrote of NZ: 'Here there is really no scope for development, no intellectual society, no hope of finding any.' Pregnant to another, she m. George Bowden 1909, left him after a day, and had a still-born child in Bavaria. She began publishing stories in Orage's *New Age,* 1910, and met J. Middleton Murry with whom she lived for six years before marrying him in 1918. Her first vol. of stories, *In a German Pension,* 1911, focuses on sexual relationships and the biological helplessness of women. They, and the stories written for the *New Age,* are the most openly feminist of her stories. In NZ the most discussed are the childhood stories set there: *Prelude,* 1918, and *The Garden Party,* 1922. In 'At the Bay' the mother is described as: 'broken, made weak, her courage gone through child-bearing. And what made it doubly hard to bear was, she did not love the children. It was no use pretending. Even if she had had the strength she would never have nursed and played with the little girls.' They are based on KM's own childhood and family. Although they often focus on male–female relationships, there is no overt political or feminist analysis. From 1918 she spent the winters in the south of France in an attempt to defeat the TB which finally killed her. Virginia WOOLF wrote after her death: 'I was jealous of her writing – the only writing I have ever been jealous of. – Probably we had something in common which I shall never find in anybody else.' Middleton Murry ed. and pub. *The Doves Nest,* 1923, *Something Childish,* 1924, *Poems,* 1924, extracts from her journals, 1927, and selected letters, 1928, which often reveal KM at her most intensely creative moments: 'I think to watch the moon rise is one of the most *mysterious* pleasures in life' (letter to Elizabeth VON ARNIM). See lives by Anthony Alpers, 1979, Claire Tomalin, 1987; study by Cherry Hankin, 1983; Vincent O'Sullivan, ed., *Poems,* 1989 (some newly pub.); bibliog. by B. J. Kirkpatrick, 1990, includes unpub. material.

Manvill, P. D., Mrs, memoirist or novelist. Her *Lucinda, or The Mountain Mourner,* Johnstown, NY, 1807 (5 reprs. in 4 different towns), purports to tell, in letters to her sister, 'authentic facts', with names and dates. Its preface says the 'tears of sensibility' should not be for fiction alone. As a widow with one child, the writer m. the widower Elias F. M., a poor retired teacher whose six children were mostly away. Among the idyllic NY hills she supported the family by sewing. When his daughter

Lucinda came home pregnant by Melvin Brown, who had promised marriage, PDM loved and supported her, recorded her story, and urged her to read Hannah FOSTER's *Coquette*. All blame lies squarely on Brown, who raped Lucinda (and later won her complicity) out of pique at her initial refusal. Lucinda dies after childbirth. The 2nd ed., 1810, adds a letter about PDM's growing 'grand-daughter' and a testimony of (empty) sympathy from the local magistrates who had tried to expel Lucinda from the community to save expense.

Marcet, Jane (Haldimand), 1769–1858, writer of elementary books of instruction (especially science) and children's books. B. in London to wealthy Swiss parents, Jane and Anthony Francis H., she m. Alexander M., Swiss-born physician and chemist, in 1799, had three children, and lived in London and Geneva. Her *Conversations* were the early nineteenth-century's best-known introductory science texts for women and young people, widely used in English and American schools, and translated into French: *On Chemistry*, 1805 (16th ed. 1853), *On Political Economy*, 1816 (6th ed. 1827), *On Natural Philosophy*, 1819 (14th ed. 1872), and *On Vegetable Physiology*, 1829. JM found this format – dialogues between Mrs B. (a teacher) and two girls – especially helpful for 'the female sex, whose education is seldom calculated to prepare their minds for abstract ideas, or 1scientific language'. Her popular CHILDREN's books, like *Bertha's Visit to her Uncle in England*, 1830 (6th ed. 1846), and *Stories for very young Children*, 1832 (7th ed. 1861), combine information about the natural world with religious topics. She was friends with Mary SOMERVILLE, Harriet MARTINEAU, and Maria EDGEWORTH, who praised her for accurate information and clear narration, for bestowing 'pleasure and benefit ... without the least ostentation or mock humility'. Title pages do not bear her name but many prefaces mention her sex.

Marchant, Bessie, 1862–1941, adventure writer, b. in Petham, Kent, da. of Jane (Goucher) and William M. She was educ. privately, then married clergyman Jabez Ambrose Comfort, 1899. They had a daughter. Although no evidence exists that she ever travelled far from her home in Charlbury, Oxon., she wrote over 100 full-length adventure stories for girls, featuring plucky heroines like Di the Dauntless, Laurel the Leader and Marta the Mainstay, set in every corner of the globe, from China to Australia, Uruguay to Athabasca. Through reversing the conventional, house-bound roles of girls in adventure stories, she has been called the female Henty. Geographical descriptions are marked by postcard picturesqueness, for BM's real interest lies in rapid-paced action in which, true to her anglophile bias, an English girl makes her mark, or fills the breach, or wins through in a strange land.

Marchessault, Jovette, b. 1938, painter, sculptor, novelist, playwright, lesbian feminist. Da. of Alice and Roger M., she grew up in working-class Montréal after a traumatic move from the country. Self-educated, she draws on the cultural heritage of her matriarchal Native lineage and a wide range of work experience (in the textile industry and with Grolier Encyclopedia) and travel (in Mexico, the US, Canada and Europe). Her first solo sculpture exhibition at the Maison des Arts la Sauvegarde in Montréal, 1970, was followed by others in Québec, Paris, New York, Toronto, and Brussels. She began a trilogy of novels in 1975 with *Comme une enfant de la terre*, 1975, which won the Prix France-Québec, 1976. Her second novel, the autobiographical *Mère des Herbes*, 1980, ends with the death of her inspiring grandmother. *Des cailloux blancs pour les forêts obscures*, 1987, completes the trilogy with a mythopoetic story of two healing women, an aviator and a writer. *Tryptique lesbienne*, 1980 (*Lesbian Triptych*, 1985), takes on Québec's patriarchal stronghold, the Catholic church, and compulsory heterosexuality. JM began writing plays with the popular *Vaches de Nuit (Night Cows,* 1979). *La Terre est trop courte, Violette Leduc,* 1982, and *Alice & Gertrude, Natalie & Renée et ce cher Ernest,* 1984, like JM's biographical prose work, *Lettre de Californie,* 1982, celebrate the lives of women. In *La Saga des Pouilles Mouillées,* 1981 (*Saga of the Wet Hens,* 1983), JM brings together Laure CONAN, Anne HÉBERT, Gabrielle ROY, and Germaine Guèvremont, Québec writers from different periods, to discuss women's erasure under patriarchy and 'vow to end their colossal night of anonymity and inconsolability through mutual acknowledgement and rebirth': 'Le grand livre des femmes': 'Je veux les rencontrer Louise Labé, pis les amazones ... Calamity Jane, Lucy Stone ... Emily DICKINSON, Louise Michel, Gertrude STEIN, Madeleine de Verchères, Natalie BARNEY, Georges SAND, Marguerite de NAVARRE.' *Anais, dans la queue de la comète,* 1985, sends up the patriarchal virtue of feminine self-sacrifice. See Gloria Orenstein in Barbara Godard, ed., 1987 (quoted above) and Godard in *Lesbian Triptych,* transl. Yvonne Klein, 1985.

Margaret Tudor, 1489–1541, Queen of Scots, letter-writer and patron, eldest da. of Elizabeth of York and Henry VII, granddaughter of Margaret of RICHMOND. Her desolate letter to her father after marriage, 1503, to James IV of Scotland, has a postscript in her own hand. She continued to write for herself, fluently and forcefully. Many letters are lost; publication of the impressive remainder began in 1732: see especially those in M. A. Everett Green, ed., 1846. After James was killed at Flodden, 1513, leaving her two surviving sons, MT picked her own second and third husbands (each a disappointment). Agnes STRICKLAND's life, 1850, judges her harshly for her aggressive political will; Patricia Hill Buchanan's, 1985, notes her 'pivotal importance in the establishment of the United Kingdom'.

Marie de France, earliest known French woman poet, whose work was much used by later English writers. Her identity is obscure, but she must have been French-born, living in England, and acquainted with royalty; she knew English and Latin, but wrote in French; she may be the Marie who became Abbess of Shaftesbury in 1181. She wrote, before 1189, twelve *Lais,* short narrative poems of love and marvellous adventure dedicated to 'the King', perhaps Henry II (ed. Jean Rychner, 1966; transl. Eugene Mason, 1911) and a collection of 102 Aesopic *Fables,* dedicated to a 'Count William' (ed. H. U. Gumbrecht, 1973); and, after 1189, *L'Espurgatoire Seint Patrice,* a saint's life (ed. T. A. Jenkins, 1894). Her story of the abandoned twin *Le Fresne* had a fourteenth-century Middle English version; her *lai* of *Lanval,* about a knight's liaison with a fairy mistress, had two. She appears in H. M. BETHAM, 1816, and Ann Radcliffe, 1822. Bibliog., 1977, and study, 1988, by Glyn S. Burgess.

Mario, Jessie White, 1832–1906, newspaper journalist, biographer, field nurse and spy, b. near Portsmouth, Hants. Da. of Jane (Meriton) of American descent, and Thomas White, shipyard owner, she was raised from age two by a stepmother. An early rebel in her father's narrowly Congregationalist household, she was educ. first by a governess, then at school in Portsmouth, Reading, London and Birmingham, where she met Eliza METEYARD and pub. two stories with workingmen heroes in Eliza COOK's *Journal* in 1853. Studying at the Sorbonne in 1854, she travelled to Italy and met Garibaldi, thus beginning her lifelong commitment to the cause of Italian liberation. She made friends with E. B. BROWNING (they later quarreled over politics) and Barbara BODICHON, and returned to London determined to train as a doctor. Refused entry by 14 London hospitals, in 1856 she pub. her TRANSLATION of Fabrice Orsini's graphic *Austrian Dungeons in Italy,* and in

1856–57 toured northern England as a lecturer for Mazzini's fund-raising. She met Emilie Venturi, d. 1893, painter and writer, Mazzini's English translator. Feted on her return to Italy in 1857, she was then imprisoned for espionage, and met Alberto Mario, Italian scholar and fellow liberationist, whom she married in Portsmouth upon her release in late 1857. They lectured in the USA in 1858, meeting sympathizer Lucretia MOTT. From 1866 until her death, JWM was Italian affairs correspondent to the newly founded *Nation*. An inexhaustible traveller, she also acted as field nurse in four of Garibaldi's campaigns. In the 1880s she published biographies of many Italian figures, including Garibaldi and Mazzini, which remained important source books for many years. In Italy she was known affectionately as 'Miss Urigano' (Miss Hurricane), and she died in Florence. Her papers are at the Museo Centrale del Risorgimento, Rome. See excellent life by Elizabeth Adams Daniels, 1972: includes abstracts of all JWM's *Nation* contributions.

'Marion, Frances', Marion Benson (Owens), 1886–1973, screenwriter, novelist, artist, b. in San Fransisco, da. of pianist Minnie (Hall) and advertising man Len Douglas O. She attended Hamilton Grammar School, St Margaret's Hall (Burlingame), the Univ. of California (Berkeley) and the Mark Hopkins Art School. Two early marriages ended in divorce. After working briefly on the *San Francisco Examiner* she went to Hollywood, 1913, as an illustrator. Her career, there and in NYC, as an extremely prolific screenwriter ran from *The Foundling,* 1916, to *Green Hell,* 1940, including a documentary on women's activities during WWI (when FM was a foreign correspondent), and E. M. HULL's *The Son of the Sheik,* 1926. She had two sons by her third marriage, 1920, to Fred Thomson, who acted in westerns she wrote and directed; after he died she married again (briefly) in 1930, the year of *Anna Christie,* with Garbo, her first talkie script. She won two Oscars. Of her six novels, *Minnie Flynn,* 1926, describes a successful but unhappy film-star, 'always the victim' of power-wielding men; *Valley Peoples,* 1935, the best known, has a successful woman narrate the mostly unhappy fates of old friends in her home town; *Molly, Bless Her,* 1937, depicts an out-of-work actress falling on her feet. FM also published short stories, *How to Write and Sell Film Stories,* 1937, and a sentimental, amusing autobiography, *Off With Their Heads!,* 1972. De Witt Bodeen records the help her career received from women (*Films in Review,* Feb.–March 1969). Papers at the Univ. of Southern Calif.; *Reminiscences,* 1958, in the Oral History Collection, Columbia Univ.; some scripts at Museum of Modern Art, NYC.

Marishall, Jean, Scots writer in several genres. A keen and early reader (unlike her mother, who also did not know women authors existed), she thought she could improve on the CIRCULATING LIBRARIES, and on a visit to London wrote, in three intensely pleasurable months but secretly, for fear of contempt, the epistolary *History of Miss Clarinda Cathcart and Miss Fanny Renton,* whose lively, appealing, clothes-conscious heroine professes severe doubts about marriage. Noble, shown a sample, offered a 'very genteel price', which turned out to be a paltry five guineas where JM had expected 100; after much anxiety and cost of binding she achieved a dedication to the Queen; the work appeared in 1766. Disagreeable lobbying did make her 100 guineas by subscribers to *The History of Alicia Montague,* 1767 (again well-written but weak in plot). Good reviews of both novels encouraged her to write a play, *Sir Harry Gaylove, or Comedy in Embryo,* pub. at Edinburgh, 1772, with a preface detailing three years of London and Edinburgh managers' broken promises to stage it. During sad years of family illnesses and deaths she educated children privately, tried running a periodical, then pub. *A*

Series of Letters, Edinburgh, 1788, which embraces moral advice to an ex-pupil, astringent comment on life (old maids are unhappy not for lack of a mate but from poverty which would drive most men to suicide; women's education has improved, in the teeth of opposition), and an unrivalled personal account of the emotional and economic minefield of female authorship.

'Markandaya, Kamala', Kamala (Purnaiya) Taylor, journalist and novelist, b. 1924 to Brahmin parents in India. She read history at Madras Univ., and took up journalism, then fiction. She migrated to London in 1948, married an Englishman, has a daughter, and is published and well received in India, the UK and the USA. Her writing is analytical in a western mould, with characters increasingly anglicized in speech and thought-patterns; she 'explains' her Indian settings for Western readers more than, say, Anita DESAI. She pursues moral themes (notably abuse of money or power) through description, analogy, sensitive character-creation and memorable prose (at first in formal narrative style). Her ten novels (to *Pleasure City,* 1982) treat the interaction of urban and rural, of different classes, Hindu and British, pre- and post-independence. In *Nectar in a Sieve,* 1954 (her third written, first published), a rural South Indian wife narrates her hardships and tragic suffering; urbanized peasants struggle in *A Handful of Rice,* 1960. In *Some Inner Fury,* 1956, a romance between an Indian woman and an Englishman ends in the wartime turmoil of 1942; in *Possession,* 1962, an Englishwoman tries to 'possess' an illiterate boy painter; in *A Silence of Desire,* 1965, a modern Hindu couple try to conceal their feelings from each other. *The Coffer Dams,* 1969, about construction workers, attains immediacy by using the present tense, jerky, often unfinished sentences, and newly economical dialogue. In *The Nowhere Man,* 1972, an elderly Hindu widower in London faces the racial hatred and oppression from which he fled before independence. *Two Virgins,* 1974, and *The Golden Honeycomb,* 1977, set in India, oppose old and new values, and different social worlds. Studies by Margaret P. Joseph, 1980; Susheela N. Rao in *Journal of Indian Writing in English,* 14, 1986.

Marlatt, Daphne (Buckle), poet, novelist, autobiographer, b. in 1942 in Melbourne, Australia, da. of Edrys (Lupprian), who gave her Dickens 'when most kids were reading romances', and Arthur C. B. They moved to Penang, Malaysia, 1945, then migrated to Vancouver, 1951. 'In the Month of Hungry Ghosts', 1979, journal entries, letters and poems, records DM's 1976 return to Penang, reliving childhood memories through her present. She studied English and creative writing with Earle Birney at the Univ. of British Columbia (BA, 1964), then, with husband Alan (m. 1963), pursued graduate work at Bloomington, Ind. (MA, 1968). After reading Jung on fairytales, she began *Frames of a story,* 1968, written in prose and poetry, announcing her major thematic and formal concerns as AUTOBIOGRAPHY, the physical 'body of language' and the blurring of generic boundaries accomplished by her long poetic line. Her son was born in 1969. Active during the 1960s in the West Coast poetry movement, she became an editor of *Tish Magazine,* 1963. The Black Mountain poets 'opened up the whole activity of writing' for her. *leaf leaf/s,* 1968, which evokes the imagism of H. D., shows her careful listening to the making of speech. *Rings,* 1971, a long poem later expanded as *What Matters: Writing 1968–1970,* 1980, records DM's experience of motherhood and her attempts to 'articulate' what remained 'inarticulate' in her strained marriage. The long *Vancouver Poems,* 1972, incorporates Kwakiutl mythology in its sensuous rendering of the city's flow. During the 1970s she taught at Capilano College, was poetry editor for *The Capilano Review,* and co-founder and co-editor of *Periodics,* a magazine of innovative prose;

she lived with painter and poet Roy Kiyooka, 1975–82. *Our Lives,* 1975, is a narrative about living in a communal house. *Steveston,* 1974, with photographs by Robert Minden, presents the town of its title as an open site inscribed by the poet's inquisitive gaze, the human habitat and the story it tells of itself merging with the maze of DM's language. *Steveston Recollected: A Japanese–Canadian History,* 1975, and *Opening Doors: Vancouver's East End,* ed. with Carole Itter, 1979, are 'aural' histories. DM also published *Zocalo,* a novel, and *The Story, She Said,* both 1977. Close to women writers in Québec, DM has collaborated with Nicole BROSSARD on two 'transformances': *Mauve,* 1985, and *Character,* 1986. She was a contributing editor of *Island,* 1981–4, and co-edits *Tessera,* a bilingual magazine of feminist theory. *How Hug a Stone,* 1983, a narrative of her search for her dead mother, tests 'the limit of the old story'. Since 1982 DM has lived with poet Betsy WARLAND; together they wrote *Double Negative,* 1988, about their journey to Australia. *Touch to my Tongue,* 1984, a prose poem woven around, but confusing, the roles of Demeter and Persephone, celebrates lesbian love and her ongoing search for the mothertongue. 'Musing with Mothertongue', its accompanying essay, is her most succint comment on language, 'a living body we enter at birth'. *Ana Historic,* 1988, DM's second novel, brilliantly deconstructs the domestic and official history of nineteenth- and twentieth-century women in BC. Selections, ed. Fred Wah, 1980. See Christine Cole in *Open Letter,* 6, 1985, Barbara Godard in *ARCS,* 15, 1985, and special issue of *Line,* 1989.

Marlborough, Sarah Churchill (Jennings or Jenyns), Duchess of, 1660–1744, memoirist and letter writer, da. of Frances (Thornhurst) and Richard J. She met the future Queen Anne in childhood, was a Maid of Honour at about 13, and m. John C. in 1678. As Anne's intimate friend, adviser, and from 1683 Lady of the Bedchamber, she came into a fine clutch of offices in 1702 and wielded political influence independent of her husband's; but as his military triumphs grew her power waned. She drew up her first political self-vindication for Elizabeth BURNET in 1704, and two more on being ousted from her posts by Abigail Hill (later Masham) in 1711. Persuaded not to publish at once, she worked with various collaborators the rest of her life (through exile from England, 1713–14, family quarrels, the building of Blenheim Palace, and the purchase of 30 estates during her 22-year widowhood) on what became her *Account of the Conduct ...,* 1742, and *Memoirs,* 1930 (multiple MS versions in BL: see Frances Harris in *BL Journal,* 8, 1982). Her claim to be 'a kind of author' is backed by vivid personal and political letters (some pub. 1875, 1943; those to her husband lost; 1838 vol. mostly *to* her); *Opinions* of 1736–42, pub. 1788 ('Women signify nothing unless they are the mistress of a Prince or a First Minister'); and, jointly with Arthur Maynwaring, *Advice to the Electors of Great Britain,* 1708. Delarivier MANLEY helped launch the paper wars around SM; among many studies, see Iris Butler, 1967.

Marquard, Jean, 1942–84, South African critic, poet and short-story writer, educ. at Stellenbosch Univ. (BA 1961, MA 1966) and St Anne's College, Oxford (BPhil, 1969). She taught at a school and three universities: Witwatersrand from 1971, where she also did her PhD. Twice married, she had a son from each marriage. Her lectures and articles were much concerned with South African women writers (Olive SCHREINER, Pauline SMITH, Doris LESSING, Nadine GORDIMER, Bessie HEAD): 'Women come into contact with the whole world, including men, so one should not expect them to write only about women or their so-called world', she said. 'It just happens that women have produced some of the best prose fiction to have appeared in southern Africa.' She edited *A Century of South African Literature,* 1978, and published stories (and poems) of her own, notably 'Regina's Baby', dealing with the maid/madam relationship and the death of feeling (in Paul Scanlon, ed., *A Web of Feelings,* 1982). At her death from cancer she had written nine stories for a projected vol. of 12. Gordimer praised her intellectual honesty and 'uncompromising ... loathing of oppression'.

Marriott, Joyce Anne, poet, radio scriptwriter, journalist. B. 1913 in Victoria, BC, da. of Catherine Eleanor (Heley) and Edward Guy M., she was educ. at private schools, then took creative writing at UBC and a correspondence course from the London School of Journalism. She m. Gerald Jerome McLellan, now deceased, in 1947 and had three children. A founder of *Contemporary Verse,* 1941, she has also been a poetry columnist for the Victoria *Daily Times,* 1943–4, script editor for the National Film Board, 1945–9, assistant editor of *Canadian Poetry Magazine,* 1946–8, and Women's Editor of the Prince George *Citizen,* 1950–3. She has written radio school broadcasts and conducted poetry workshops for children. After publishing poetry during the late 1930s and early 1940s, she broke a 25-year silence with *The Circular Coast,* 1981 (her best earlier and some new poems). *Calling Adventurers,* 1941, won the Governor General's Award. She writes on a wide range of subjects. 'The Wind, Our Enemy' (title poem of her first volume, 1939, a narrative about the drought-ridden prairies), remains her most admired poem. *Sandstone and Other Poems,* 1945, is her best-known book.

Marryat, Florence (later Church), 1838–99, novelist, dramatist, actress, singer, lecturer, editor, manager of a school of journalism. B. at Brighton, Sussex, tenth da. of Catherine (Shairp) and Capt. Marryat, novelist, she was educ. by a governess, her own voracious reading, and her father's unconventional attitudes (e.g. nothing to be locked away from the children). Her sister Emilia Norris, 1835–75, wrote boys' adventure stories, some illustrated by a third sister, Augusta. She was married twice: in 1854, aged 16, at Penang, to T. Ross Church, with whom she had eight children; in 1890, to Col. Francis Lean. Both army men, the first took her all over India with him. Her first novel, *Love's Conflict,* 1865, was written for distraction while nursing children with scarlet fever. Then followed some 75 works, mostly sensational romances like *Veronique,* 1869, *Her Father's Name,* 1876, and *A Scarlet Sin,* 1890, all marked by a forthright style. Some, like *At Heart a Rake,* 1895, tackled seriously questions of female emancipation. She also ventured into SPIRITUALISM, with *The Risen Dead,* 1893, *The Spirit World,* 1894, and others. FM edited a monthly, *London Society,* 1872–6, and wrote sketches of her father's life, 1872, of India, 1868, and of America, 1886, where she toured eight months performing her musical and dramatic monologue *Love Letters.* An excellent businesswoman, she believed women to be especially gifted for fiction 'because they really know more about men than men do about women' (interview: *Annie Swan's Magazine,* 1897, 191).

Marsh, Anne (later Marsh-Caldwell), 1791–1874, novelist, b. Newcastle-under-Lyme, da. of Elizabeth (Stamford) and James Caldwell, JP and deputy-lieutenant of the county. In 1817 she m. Arthur Cuthbert M., London banker. She began writing fiction for amusement at an early age but only pub. her first novel, *Two Old Men's Tales,* 1834, with the encouragement of her friend Harriet MARTINEAU. At least 18 other popular novels followed, as well as two historical works concerning the Huguenots, all anonymous, several with male narrators. Titles include *Angela, or the Captain's Daughter,* 1848, *Mordaunt Hall,* 1849, and *The Rose of Ashurst,* 1867. The best-known is *Emilia Wyndham,* 1846 (mocked by Charlotte YONGE for its melodramatic incidents), which, for all its pious moralizing, contains some astute and acidic observations on matrimony and masculine deficiencies therein. The novel attacks the harsh economic circumstances that force women into undesired marriage and the male myopia which selfishly idolizes female attractions without ever seeing the real woman. In 1858, on succeeding to the family estate, AM changed her name to Marsh-Caldwell. She d. in Staffordshire.

Marsh, Edith **Ngaio**, 1899–1982, detective novelist, Shakespeare director, b. Christchurch, NZ, only child of Rose Elizabeth (Seager) and Henry Edmund M., bank clerk. Educ. at a dame school, by governess, and then at St Margaret's private school (run by Anglo-Catholic nuns) and the Canterbury School of Art, in 1920 she acted and produced with the Allan Wilkie Shakespeare players. After three years in London from 1928, she pub. her first murder mystery in 1933. She went on to earn her living by writing, while directing Shakespeare productions, her first love, for over 20 years in NZ, receiving many awards, including DBE in 1966 and the Grand Master Award from the Mystery Soc. of America, 1978. Of her 32 DETECTIVE novels, four are set in NZ (*Vintage Murder,* 1937; *Colour Scheme,* 1943; *Died in the Wool,* 1944; *Photo-Finish,* 1980). Most others solve murder in upper-class English settings and feature tall, handsome Roderick Alleyn, CID, who quotes Shakespeare, and occasionally his wife 'Troy', a painter with her own career. Class and gender are otherwise conventionally portrayed. NM also pub. some short stories, two NZ travel books, and an impersonal autobiography, *Black Beech and Honeydew,* 1966 (rev. 1981). Her private life remains enigmatic.

Marshall, Emma (Martin), 1830–99, novelist, b. near Cromer, Norfolk, youngest da. of Harriet (RANSOME), a Quaker, and Simon Martin, banker. Educ. privately in Norwich, at 16 she went to live with her mother in Bristol, where she met, and in 1854 m., Hugh Graham M., financier. They lived in Wells, Exeter and Gloucester, where she organized evening lectures for women. EM wrote mildly didactic Christian fiction from 1861, when her children were young, and pub. over 200 works, mostly historical novels. After the failure of her husband's bank in 1878, her writing supported the family. Many of her novels centred on some local celebrity: *Under Salisbury Spire,* 1890, focuses on George Herbert, *Penshurst Castle,* 1894, on Sir Philip Sidney. These, together with *Winchester Mead,* 1891, and *Life's Aftermath,* 1876, were her most popular works. Her work invariably carried an optimistic message: 'Shall we not hold to the faith that a golden thread runs through our lives, however dark the woof may be?' See the biographical sketch by her da., Beatrice Marshall, 1900, who also pub. stories for children and translations from German.

Marshall, Joyce, b. 1913, short-story writer, novelist, editor, translator. Da. of Ruth Winnifred (Chambers) and William W. M., she was b. and educ. in Montréal, lived briefly in Scandinavia, now lives in Toronto. She won her first short-story prize (of several) the year she took her BA (McGill, 1935), subsequently revising the story as her first novel, *Presently Tomorrow,* 1946, which, like *Lovers and Strangers,* 1957, won praise for its perceptive treatment of character. *A Private Place,* 1975 (short stories), includes impressive studies of women in urban communities. JM also transl. three works by Gabrielle ROY and *The Word from France: the Letters of Marie de l'Incarnation,* 1967.

Marshall, Paule (Burke), novelist, short-story writer, b. 1929 in Brooklyn, NY, to Barbadian immigrants Ada and Samuel B. She says her mother and other Barbadian women taught her 'my first lessons in the narrative art'. They trained her ear and set a standard of excellence; she likes to attribute the best of her work to them and their rich legacy of language and culture. A trip 'home' at nine confirmed this legacy (honoured in the story 'To Da-Duh [grandmother], In Memoriam', 1964). She m. Kenneth M. (divorced 1963), graduated from Brooklyn College in 1953, did graduate work at Hunter College, and worked as librarian and as the only female staff member on *Our World*, 1953–6. She has since lectured on black literature and creative writing at many universities. *Browngirl, Brownstones,* 1959, initiates its heroine into conflict between the Barbadian immigrant community and that of white NYC; rejecting the white world which sees her only as an oddity, moving beyond the gender relations of her childhood world, she seeks to find herself. Her mother (with whom her relationship is critical) gives her 'both a dismissal and a benediction' ('G' long! You always was too much woman for me anyway, soul'); she decides she must seek understanding in Barbados. Barbara Christian wrote that PM 'cracks the stereotype of the black matriarch'. *Soul Clap Hands and Sing,* 1961, written after the birth of her son, collects tales of old men; they are named from black, international cultural settings, like 'Brooklyn', 'Brazil'. *The Chosen Place, The Timeless People,* 1969, a novel set in a Caribbean island, explores possibilities of reconciliation for divided natures and communities. PM married Nourry Menard in 1970. She wrote of 'Shaping the World of my Art' in *New Letters,* 40, 1973. In 1983 she published *Reena* (collected stories) and *Praisesong for the Widow,* whose heroine leaves a Caribbean cruise to join a local festival, remembers early love and hardships in Harlem, realizes how much she and her husband had 'foolishly handed over in exchange' for material success, and goes home to relay her African heritage to the younger generations. See Barbara Christian, 1980 and 1985; interview with Alexis de Veaux in *Essence,* 10, 1979.

Marsin, or **Mercen, M.**, writer of tracts. Struck by signs of the imminent Second Coming, she 'did dare do no other then leave and venture the little concern I had, and come above a Hundred Miles' to London, where in 1696 she began publishing her dozen treatises, one dedicated to the king. With lengthy titles offering *All the Chief Points* or *A Full and Clear Account* of various knotty issues, 'Laying Scripture to Scripture', they question 'Mans Scholastick Learning' and the notion of God as 'an old Man with a corporeal Substance'. They hope for the conversion of the Jews, and stress that 'God has often imployed Women in declaring his truth.' *Good News to the Good Women, and to the Bad Women too that will Grow Better,* 1701, puts women, unusually it says, 'in the first place'. Beginning with Noah's 'She Dove', and listing admirable women in the Bible (including Egyptian midwives), MM argues that Christ, born of woman, delivers her from Eve's 'Bondage, which some has [sic] found intollerable'. She disposes of St Paul as confused and inconsistent with other scripture, ends with exhortation to both sexes and promises more publications.

Marson, Una, 1905–65, poet, playwright and journalist, important foremother for black writers. B. in Jamaica, educ. on a scholarship at the Hampton School, Malvern, lastingly scarred by her mother's early death, she wrote poetry from very young and joined the Jamaican Poetry League (founded 1923). Her first volume, *Tropic Reveries,* Kingston, 1930, won an Institute of Jamaica medal; between it and *Heights and Depths,* 1932, she moved away from Georgian influence towards writing of black (usually female) experience. A working journalist, she founded and edited, from 1929, *The Cosmopolitan.* Her first play, *At What a Price,* was staged at Kingston in 1932, the year she left for London. She worked as secretary to the League of Coloured Peoples, then to the exiled emperor Haile Selassie, and was active in movements for colonial independence, in bodies like the Women's

International League for Peace and Freedom, and in Britain's first black THEATRE COMPANY. Life in England sharpened her sense of herself as a black woman. Back in Jamaica in 1936, UM founded the Kingston Readers' and Writers' Club, a branch of the Save the Children Fund, a journal (the *Jamaica Standard*) and a progressive weekly paper (*Public Opinion*). She published *The Moth and the Star,* 1937 (poems), and had two more plays produced: *London Calling,* 1937, and *Pocomania,* 1938 (a hit). In 1938 she returned to London to work for the BBC: she launched and presented, from 1942, the influential 'Caribbean Voices'. *Towards the Stars,* 1945, mainly collects reprinted poems. After WWII, based in Jamaica with some visits to the US (she was influenced by the Harlem Renaissance), she remained active in journalism, social work, and printing (in the Pioneer Press, which published her last work, *Poetry for Children by Poets of Jamaica,* 1958). Her marriage, 1960, to an American widower, was a failure. UM sometimes experiments with Jamaican patwah and Afro-American blues rhythms. She writes of rural poverty (sudden death in the fields from overwork), of racial alienation ('White, white, white / And they all seem the same / As they say that Negroes seem'), of stereotyping ('I must not laugh too much, / They say black folk can only laugh. / I must not weep too much, / They say black folk weep always'), and of building black identity. In 'Cinema Eyes' she swears off film-going till 'black beauties' are stars. The speaker in 'Kinky Hair Blues' feels insecure ('Hate dat ironed hair / and dat bleaching skin. / But I'll be all alone / If I don't fall in'); that of 'Black is Fancy' has learned to be proud of her looks. UM has been much anthologized. See the Kingston *Sunday Gleaner,* 9 May 1965, 22 December 1974; J. E. Clare McFarlane in *A Literature in the Making,* 1956.

Martens, Mary E., author of two novels published in London, concerned with the position of women in S. African society. *A Woman of Small Account: A South African Social Picture,* 1911, dedicated to MEM's husband, tells of a strong-minded woman who feels 'like a caged bird ... I beat my limbs against bars that seem to hold and pin me down': rejecting her husband's call to obedience, she leaves him to become a successful novelist championing the cause of women. *A Daughter of Sin: A Simple Story,* 1915, dedicated to 'Those women of Natal who have suffered under an unjust, one-sided and most iniquitous law', explores the conflicting interests of the black, Boer and English communities, with their differing political and religious life-styles. A reactionary attitude towards black culture is coupled with radical criticism of white patriarchal control of women and brutal punishment for transgression of the norm. The white masters 'go free and honoured and happy, though they have sinned a thousandfold. I who am but a woman have taken one false step and I must expiate my shame to the uttermost.' The double standard applies with especial force to inter-racial sexual relations.

Martin, Mrs, 'Helen of Herefordshire', obscure author of five intelligent, various, stylish MINERVA novels (not Sarah M., author of a 1795 cookery book; or Sarah Catherine M., author-illustrator of the rhyme of Old Mother Hubbard, pub. 1804; or the minor-novelist great-aunt of Mary MARTIN). She planned *Deloraine,* 1798, on country rambles, and wrote it in secret, to beguile solitude and misfortune; it weighs 'sentiment' against true feeling; after marriage the hero and heroine retain 'the obsolete custom' of mutual frankness. Essay-chapters open each volume of *Melbourne,* also 1798 (criticism of novels in general; ingenious similes for her own); the hero as student, struggling on inadequate income, is well drawn. *Reginald, or The House of Mirandola, A Romance,* 1799, praises and follows, without hoping to rival, Ann RADCLIFFE.

The Enchantress, or Where Shall I Find Her?, 1801, defends novels, quotes Coleridge, and voices scepticism about historians (she hopes ladies' maids will join their ranks). Here the heroine answers, with 'fire and spirit', the hero's advertisement beginning 'A Man wants a wife' (cf. Sarah GARDNER).

Martin, Catherine (Mackay), 1847–1937, novelist, poet, journalist, b. Isle of Skye, seventh child of Janet (MacKinnon) and Samuel Mackay, a crofter; taken to South Australia with her family in 1855. Little is known of her education, but it was clearly extensive, with good knowledge of German language and literature. She worked as a teacher and later as a clerk in the Education Department. In 1882 she m. Frederick Martin; they travelled widely in Europe, 1890–1904. She pub. poems and translations in local newspapers from at least 1872; some were collected in *The Explorers and Other Poems,* 1874. Her first novel, *An Australian Girl,* 1890 (repr. 1988), won wide attention and acclaim from Catherine SPENCE. Anonymous (like all her work), it is a wide-ranging, erudite novel of cosmopolitan scope. Stella Courtland is a complex heroine of cultivated tastes and inquisitive intelligence; her character challenges the sterotypical romantic heroine, even though this novel is, largely, a 'romance'. With little regard for the intricacies of plot, CM's strengths are original and interesting characters, convincing dialogue and a sharp eye for the foibles and follies of her time. She also pub. *The Silent Sea,* 1892, *The Old Roof-Tree: Letters of Ishbel to her Half-Brother Mark Latimer,* 1906, and an outstanding book, *The Incredible Journey,* 1923 (repr. 1987), concerning two black women's journey across the Australian desert in search of a stolen child, told from the viewpoint of Aboriginal people. At least two other serialized novels appeared, 'The Moated Grange', 1877, and 'At a Crisis', 1900, and many stories, poems and articles remain uncollected. Recent reprints of *An Australian Girl* and *The Incredible Journey* contain useful introductions to her work. See also M. Allen in D. Adelaide, ed., *A Bright and Fiery Troop,* 1988.

'Martin, Claire' (Claire Montreuil), autobiographer, novelist, short-story writer, playwright, b. in 1914 in Québec, da. of Alice (Martin) and Ovila Montreuil. She studied with the Ursulines in Québec and the Sisters of Notre-Dame in Beauport, had a brief career in radio in Québec and Montréal, and m. Roland Faucher, with whom she lived in France, 1972–82. Her early fiction, *Avec ou sans amour,* 1958, and *Doux-amer,* 1960 (*Best man,* 1983), treats love, duplicity, and the fictional stereotyping of male and female: 'It displeases me greatly that so many novelists inscribe their heroines in a so-called femininity and their heroes in a would-be virility that one rarely meets in life.' Her autobiographical *Dans un gant de fer,* 1965, and *La Joue droite,* 1968 (translated in one volume, 1968, later separately, as *In an Iron Glove,* 1973, and *The Right Cheek,* 1975), won the Governor General's Award, 1967, and gained CM the reputation of a key agent in the social liberation of Québec. In a cruel and sombre depiction of family life and of her traumatic childhood and adolescence, both denounce the oppressive power of her father and patriarchal institutions and criticize women for the complicity of weakness and silence. CM became President of the Société des écrivains canadiens-français, 1962, was writer-in-residence at the Univ. of Ottawa, 1972, and translated Margaret LAURENCE's *The Stone Angel* (*L'Ange de pierre,* 1976). See Robert Vigneault, 1975, and M. J. Green in *Yale French Studies,* 65, 1983.

'Martin, George Madden', Georgia May Madden, 1866–1946, short-story writer, novelist and dramatist, b. Louisville, Ky, da. of Anne Louise (McKenzie) and Frank Madden, and educ. by private tutors. Beginning with 'Teckla's Lilies' (*Harper's*

Weekly, 1895), she drew upon her earlier teaching experiences at Wellesley School to write *Emmy Lou; her book and heart*, 1902. GMM adopts a child's perspective on life in a junior school of the 1880s, while retaining an adult narrator for sympathetic observations on the trials of women teachers, including outmoded schooling systems and traditional female roles. In *The House of Fulfilment*, 1904, she imprints an air of autobiographical intimacy upon the experiences of young Alexina, caught between the opposing temperaments of her Northern, Calvinistic Aunt Harriet Blair and her pleasure-loving Southern mother. GMM pub. nine novels, including *Selina, Her Hopeful Efforts and Her Livelier Failures*, 1914, which questions the failure of women to break free from patriarchal attitudes. She also pub. a children's biography of Shakespeare's youth, *A Warwickshire Lad*, 1916, and a play, *Lion's Mouth*, 1921. Perhaps her finest and most popular work is *Children in the Mist*, 1920, a collection of short stories based on her personal experiences in the South and dealing with racial issues. She took office on the Board of the Committee on Interracial Co-operation and the Association of Southern Women for the Prevention of Lynching. *March On*, 1921, an experimental novel set during WWI, features suffragist Lucy Wing and her grandmother who forcefully advocates woman's greater involvement in government. See also GMM's articles in the *Atlantic Monthly*, 1924–5, and *Made in America*, 1935.

Martin, Helen (Reimensnyder), 1868–1939, novelist, b. Lancaster, Penna., da. of Henrietta (Thurman) and Cornelius R., immigrant German clergyman. Educ. at Swarthmore and Radcliffe Colleges, she taught in a NY school, marrying Frederick M. in 1899 and settling in Harrisburg, Pa. She had two children. Between 1896 and 1939, HM pub. 38 works, of which three became films. The most successful (beginning with *Tillie*, 1904) were about the Pennsylvania Dutch, whose customs HM depicts with detailed accuracy. An advocate of women's SUFFRAGE and a socialist, HM produced her most interesting work when considering women's financial dependence on men. The mercenary nature of marriage is explored in novels such as *Emmy Untamed*, 1937, and *Her Husband's Purse*, 1916, whose heroine has 'avidly read every classic drama in the English and French languages' and, beginning to tire of mending laundry and wrestling with Henry James, marries a bigoted but wealthy man to release herself from dependence on her brother-in-law. HM's work is discussed by Beverly Seaton in *PMHB*, 1980.

Martin, Mary (Letitia), 'Mrs Martin Bell', 1815–50, novelist, only child of Julia (Kirwan) and Thomas Barnewall M., MP, of Ballynahinch Castle, Co. Galway: granddaughter of Richard M., 'Humanity Dick', founder of the RSPCA. Her aunt Harriet Letitia Martin, 1801–91, published *Canvassing*, 1835 (with a work by John and Michael Banim), and *The Changeling*, 1848. MM was widely lauded for work among the peasantry during famine. In 1847 she m. Col. Arthur Gonne B., of Brookhill, Co. Mayo; he took her name, but she returned the compliment for publishing purposes. Her father died that year 'of famine fever caught while visiting his tenants', having broken the entail to leave her an estate heavily burdened with debt; she kept borrowing, for the sake of her tenants, and was bankrupted. She moved with her husband to Belgium (where she is said to have written for French journals), then to the US; she died ten days after reaching NY, after premature childbirth on shipboard. Her *Julia Howard*, 1850, set in Connemara, is written from intimate knowledge of Irish life. A novel called *St Etienne* may or may not be hers; works by 'M. M. Bell' published years after her death are probably not.

Martineau, Harriet, 1802–76, essayist, popular educator, novelist, b. Norwich, sixth of eight children of Elizabeth (Rankin) and Thomas M., cloth manufacturer of Huguenot ancestry, d. 1826. An unhappy childhood, vividly described in her *Autobiography* (written 1855; pub. 1877; repr. 1983), was further shadowed by increasing deafness. Educ. by her Unitarian parents, at a local school and at a Bristol boarding school, she also read systematically and in 1821 pub. her first article, 'Female Writers of Practical Divinity', in the *Monthly Repository*, to which she became a regular contributor (see e.g. 'On Female Education', 1822). In 1829 the family firm failed, and, unable to teach because of deafness, HM supported the family by writing. Her original popularizing serial, *Illustrations of Political Economy*, 1832–3, brought celebrity and a move to London. She travelled in America 1834–6, and in 1837 pub. *Society in America*, outspoken in its condemnation of slavery and its criticism of repressive chivalry (see the chapter 'Political Non-Existence of Women'). In 1839 she published *Deerbrook* (repr. 1983), her first and best novel, in which women's intellectual aspirations and bonds with each other are alike taken seriously. It was followed by a second novel, *The Hour and the Man*, 1841, before increasing illness interrupted her work. In 1844 her 'Letter on Mesmerism' in the *Athenaeum*, describing her cure, caused a furore; in 1845 she moved to the Lake District where she designed and built her own house, living there for the rest of her life, and visited by the Wordsworths, the Arnolds, Charlotte BRONTE, George ELIOT and many others. In 1848 she lectured to Ambleside working men and helped them form a building society. She translated her own abridgement of Comte's *Positive Philosophy*, 1851, and wrote leading articles for the London *Daily News* 1852–69, supporting divorce reform and firing 'the first round' (Josephine BUTLER) in the battle against the Contagious Diseases Acts. She also wrote for the *Edinburgh Review* and for Dickens's *Household Words* until they fell out over his views on women. Her output includes biographical sketches, histories and essays on a wide range of topical subjects. Believing EDUCATION to be the key to equality, she yet supported women's SUFFRAGE movements in England and America. Often ridiculed as a 'Malthusian old maid', her principled forthrightness and indefatigable powers of argument also earned respect: 'There was something that I wanted to say, and I said it. That was all.' She left her American friend Maria Weston Chapman to update her *Autobiography*. The best recent critical biography is by Valerie Pichanick, 1980. See also HM's essays on women, ed. Gayle Graham Yates, 1985. Her house is now a museum.

Mary Agnes, Sister, poet, b. 1928 at Lynton, Devon. She studied art and drama, then philosophy and literature at the Sorbonne. In 1950 she became a Catholic and entered a Poor Clare convent (an enclosed, contemplative, largely silent order). Her three poetry volumes, *Daffodils in Ice*, 1972, with foreword by Elizabeth GOUDGE, *No Ordinary Lover*, 1973, and *A World of Stillnesses*, 1976, belong to the tradition of female spirituality. The experience of isolation imbues her poems: a woman alone at night sensuously imagines reunion with a lover, or embodied state of mind or 'presence', suffers intensely at his departure, yet resents the dawning sun and waking birds which dispel the clarity of night. Goudge usefully compares AM to Emily BRONTË.

Masham, Damaris (Cudworth), Lady, 1658–1708, religious and educational writer and poet, b. at Cambridge, da. of Damaris (Cradock) and Platonist theologian Ralph Cudworth, who gave her some educ. Her sparkling, playful, philosophical letters as 'Philoclea' to John Locke, from 1682 (BL; Bod; his *Corresp.*), include poetry and trenchant comment on women's lives; he praised her 'inlightend and enlarged mind', more learned than most male scholars. She m. the widower Sir Francis M., 1685, added one son to nine step-children, and gathered an intellectual circle at Oates, Essex, where Locke chiefly lived from 1691. Having had Mary ASTELL's *Serious Proposal* ascribed to her, she 'level'd against' Astell and John Norris an anonymous *Discourse Concerning the Love of God,* 1696, which calls them visionary and abstruse, and argues that love of God must not displace love of our neighbour: 'Mankind is designed for a Sociable Life'; 'the most inlightned Reason' is that which 'feels its weakness and dependency'. Astell's *Christian Religion* provoked DM to further defence of herself and Locke, in *Occasional Thoughts in Reference to a Vertuous or Christian Life,* 1705, written some years before. This full and carefully structured essay ends a debate between two women who never name each other. Opening and closing on the shocking neglect of women's EDUCATION, it covers the mother's role, the sexual double standard, the colonial activities of 'exterminators (calling themselves Christians)', the relation of reason to religion, and learning through play. DM wrote Locke's life (MS at Amsterdam Univ.). See Sheryl O'Donnell in Ruth Perry and Martine W. Brownley, ed., essays 1984.

Masters, Mary, 1694?–1771, poet and feminist. Her father, a poor Norwich schoolmaster, thought women should learn 'nothing but common Houshold Affairs'; her 'Genius to Poetry' (at six or seven she wept over the story of David and Jonathan) was 'always brow-beat and discountenanc'd'. Having made well-to-do friends for subscribers, she pub. with her name, to earn money, *Poems on Several Occasions,* 1733, which gathers at least ten years' worth of philosophical and religious pieces, praise of friends, and love-poems written for men. Attacked by the *London Magazine* in 1738, she replied in the *GM,* 1739. In the early 1750s she divided her time between London households: Edward Cave, Elizabeth CARTER (who sometimes read her work in MS), and the future Catharine MACAULAY. Her friendship with Samuel Johnson awoke suspicion that he made revisions to her *Familiar Letters and Poems on Several Occasions* (1755, in press by 1752: all new material); he, Mary JONES, Hester CHAPONE and Anna WILLIAMS subscribed. The letters mostly treat love topics; but a few added late in the day, to a woman inclined to accept female inferiority, praise Mary ASTELL, Elizabeth ROWE and Catharine TROTTER, argue the intellectual parity of the sexes, and call for liberation through education for 'Free-born Maids', 'Equal Woman'. MM lived in Derbyshire, 1755–7.

Masters, Olga (Lawler), 1919–86, prose writer, playwright, short-story writer, journalist, b. Pambula, NSW, da. of Dorcas (Robinson) and Leo L. Educ. at schools in Cobargo, NSW, to Intermediate Certificate Level, she then moved to Sydney where she began a long and successful career as a journalist. She maintained this career while raising seven children, and only began writing fiction when in her late fifties. Publication of her work continued after her sudden death and quickly brought her to the forefront of contemporary Australian writing. She wrote mainly about the experience of rural life, especially from the perspective of women. *The Home Girls,* 1982, a collection of stories, was her first book and a winner of the National Book Council Award in 1983. *Loving Daughters,* 1984, set in a small pastoral township in the late 1900s, explores the tensions within a family when a new, young clergyman comes to court the daughters of a patriarchal widower. *A Long Time Dying,* 1985, is a novel which, through a series of chapters focusing on various families, offers a cumulative picture of a dull, seemingly timeless town in the 1930s. *Amy's Children,* 1987, was pub. posthumously. *The Rose Fancier,* 1988, another collection of stories, was prepared for publication by four of

OM's children. Her fiction is noted for its grim humour, its careful verisimilitude, its preoccupation with the intricacies of relationships, and its meticulous observation of the commonplace. OM's plays were not pub. in her lifetime, but a vol. of them is forthcoming from the Univ. of Queensland Press, and *A Working Man's Castle* was pub. in 1988.

'Mathers, Helen', Ellen Mathews, 'David Lyall', 1853–1920, novelist, b. Misterton, Somerset, in the house described in her first novel, *Comin' Thro' the Rye,* 1875, da. of Maria (Buckingham) and Thomas Mathews, landowner. One of 12 children, she was educ. at home until 13, when she attended the Chantry school until her health broke down, causing lifelong deafness. Her first novel was her most popular, notable for its portrayal of destructive male sexuality (based on her father): Nell, the heroine, cannot understand 'how people can like being married', nor 'what fathers were invented for'. In 1875 HM m. Henry Reeves, a distinguished orthopaedic surgeon: they had one son. She pub. 18 further novels and novelettes, of which the best received were *Cherry Ripe,* 1877, and *Bam Wildfire,* 1897.

Matheson, Annie, 1853–1924, poet, essayist, b. at Blackheath, nr London, da. of Elizabeth (Cripps) and James M., a Congregationalist minister. Her first volume, mainly religious poems, was *Love's Music,* 1894, followed by *Love Triumphant,* 1898, which acknowledges encouragement from Mr and Mrs G. F. Watts, and is inscribed to 'the sorrowful, the downtrodden, the oppressed . . .' It includes the curious poem 'Ecce Homo. After Looking at Effeminate Modern Pictures of the Christ'. The title poem of *The Religion of Humanity,* 1890, addresses theological questions, even though AM acknowledges, and regrets, Ruskin's dictum that 'There *is* one dangerous science for women . . . that of theology' (*Sesame and Lilies,* 1865). 'A Song for Women', describing her sympathy for the sempstress, was later pub. as a leaflet by the Women's Protective and Provident League. Her essays on social questions ranging from the influence of E. B. BROWNING to Children's Invalid Aid and women's emigration, first pub. in periodicals like the *Contemporary Review, Athenaeum, Guardian* and *Weekly Sun,* were collected in 1912 as *Leaves of Prose.* She also wrote introductions for George ELIOT's novels, lives of Florence NIGHTINGALE, 1913, and Elizabeth Fry, 1920, and several books for children. Her last work was her selected poems, *Roses, Loaves and Old Rhymes,* 1899.

Mathews, Eliza Kirkham (Strong), 1772–1802, novelist. B. at Exeter, da. of Mary and Dr George S., she published *Poems* there by subscription, with her birth name, 1796: many dwell sadly on the deaths of her parents and other relatives. She was living as a teacher at Swansea (and publishing in the *Monthly Mirror*) when in 1797 she met and married comic actor Charles M. Her husband's second wife, Anne (Johnson) M., in her life of him, 1838–9, condescends to EKM's writing, believing it stemmed only from pathetically misguided wifely concern. Early, anonymous works are doubtfully ascribed: *Constance,* 1785, a genteel 'first literary attempt of a young lady' who boasts of her family's status; *The Pharos,* 1787, in literary-periodical form; *Argus: The House-Dog at Eadlip,* 1789, about a love-affair across class boundaries and a pair of switched babies; Scottish and German tales offering capable heroines, one disguised as a man. Another Mrs Mathews (before EKM's marriage) pub. *Simple Facts, or The History of an Orphan,* 1793 (the heroine tricks an abductor by agreeing to 'go to church with him', then rejects him at the altar), and *Perplexities, or The Fortunate Elopement,* 1794. EKM's later works (most in her married name) appeared while Charles M. played York and the northern circuit and she warred with tuberculosis and debts; some were posthumous. A number of tiny, improving children's books (some illustrated by Bewick), another feeble novel, a stage adaptation, and more *Poems*, 1802, are outshone by *What Has Been* [1801], a clumsy, intense tale of a much-suffering heroine, last of her line, hiding in the derelict maternal mansion and finding a MS left by a persecuted ancestress, disappointed in her dreams that her novel will earn enough to support her unemployed husband and coming baby. Virginia WOOLF wrote of EKM, 1925.

Maughan, Janet Leith, later Story, 1828–1926, novelist, b. Bombay, da. of Elizabeth (Arnott), a Scotswoman, and Capt. Philip Maughan, East India Co. She grew up in Edinburgh and went to school from age five, already reading fluently. When father lost his money in a Bombay bank crash, her mother (who had pleaded with him to remove it earlier) became 'a very good manager'. A spinster aunt sent JM to a finishing school in Hampstead at 15 and her mother died soon after her return. Musically gifted, JM could sing 700 songs from memory in almost every European language. In 1860 she pub. anon. the highly successful *Charley Nugent; or, Passages in the Life of a Sub.*, having applied to Thackeray for help. She had kept her writing a secret while carefully researching military details, for which she won the respect of her astonished father. Lively and well-written in picaresque style, it contains sharper observations than she allowed herself after she m. Robert Herbert Story, DD, vicar of Rosneath and later principal of Glasgow University. *The St Aubyns of St Aubyn,* 1862, and *Richard Langdon; or, Foreshadowed,* 1863, both well-constructed, were followed by several others marred by increasingly absurd plots. *The Co-Heiress,* 1866, tells of a wicked sister's death after murdering the good, with an ending in which their fiancés marry a fresh pair of sisters. *Kitty Fisher, the Orange Girl,* 1881, was a children's story. In 1911, aged 83, JM published her lively *Early Reminiscences,* followed in 1913 by *Later Reminiscences,* which reveal she knew Margaret OLIPHANT, Isabella BIRD and Mrs Gordon Cumming.

Mayer, Gerda Kamilla (Stein), poet, b. 1927 at Karlovy Vary, Czechoslovakia (formerly German Carlsbad), da. of Jewish parents, Erna (Eisenberger) and shopkeeper Arnold S. She came to England in 1939, the year Hitler invaded Czechoslovakia. She attended several schools there and in England, worked on the land, 1945–6, then as a secretary. She m. businessman Adolf M. in 1949 and became a British subject. In 1963, she took a BA at Bedford College, London Univ. Her books include *Oddments,* 1970 (privately printed), *GM's Library Folder,* 1972, *The Knockabout Show* (for children), 1978, *Monkey on the Analyst's Couch,* 1980 (Poetry Book Society recommendation and other critical praise), and *March Post Man,* 1985. She makes ingenious use of nursery rhymes and jingles (straight or starkly disrupted), deceptively simple forms, and naive points of view to present cruelties or ironies of experience: 'They photograph me / they show me to their students // *And here's a monkey / deprived of love / he has nowhere to flee to / except his own arms*' (from *Monkey*). She has also appeared with Daniel Halpern and Florence Elon in *Treble Poets 2,* 1975; with Frank Flynn and Norman Nicholson in *The Candy Floss Tree,* 1984; in Carol RUMENS, ed., *Making for the Open,* 1985; and in The Raving Beauties, eds., *No Holds Barred,* 1985.

Mayer, Gertrude Mary **Townshend** (Dalby), 1839–1932, miscellaneous writer and editor, b. Amersham, Bucks., da. of Anne (Loathis), who wrote verse, and John Watson D., writer. In 1868 she m. prolific author Samuel Ralph Townshend M. (d. 1880). Her volumes include *Sir Hubert's Marriage,* 1876, a conventional incident-packed tale; *The Fatal Inheritance and Other Stories,* 1878;

and the novelette *Belmore,* 1880. In 1894 she collected a series of articles on the lives of women writers (from Margaret, Duchess of NEWCASTLE, to Lucie Duff GORDON) into *Women of Letters,* based on memoirs and correspondence (including unpub. letters from Mary SHELLEY to the Leigh Hunts). These, as well as her *Temple Bar* articles on early nineteenth-century figures such as Lady Hester STANHOPE, Washington Irving, B. R. Haydon, Sydney Smith, Hood and Croker, are generally crisp, lucid and entertaining. In 1898 Macmillans, for whom GTM had long worked as a reader, took over *Temple Bar* and she edited the periodical till it ceased publication in 1906.

Mayo, Isabella (Fyvie), 'Edward Garrett', 1843–1914, novelist and essayist, b. at her Scots parents' London bakery, one of eight children (five died) of Margaret (Thomson) and George F. who died bankrupt, 1851. Educ. at a private school, she pub. stories and verse in her 'teens, and her first serial, *The Secret Drawer,* in 1867. In a 'life and death fight' to pay inherited debts, she toiled as secretary and 'law writer' 1860–9, including a stint at Bessie PARKES' Office for the Employment of Women. Her first, best-known novel, *Occupations of a Retired Life,* 1867, is an evangelical story of an elderly sister and brother, Ruth and Edward Garrett, whence her pseudonym. In 1870 she m. John Ryall M., solicitor. Among her many novels are *By Still Waters,* 1874, *The Capel Girls,* 1876, *Family Fortunes,* 1881, and *Her Object in Life,* 1881? This last, about a woman's struggles with her selfish brother, implicitly challenges the ideal of female self-sacrifice. She also ed. a collection of Aesop's fables, 1877, and two collections of sayings and stories from Great Britain and the near East, 1910 and 1911. She taught Russian and TRANSLATED several works by Tolstoy, wrote reviews, articles on history and travel, and biographical essays for a variety of magazines. Her *Recollections,* 1910, is a chronicle of her experiences, particularly in London in the 1850s when she was looking for work, but including literary gossip, stories of scandalous murders and mysterious coincidences, and descriptions of her travels throughout the world.

Mayor, Flora Macdonald, 'Mary Strafford', 1872–1932, novelist. B. at Kingston-on-Thames, Surrey, a twin da. of linguist and musician Jessie (Grote), who had translated the Icelandic sagas into English, and the Rev. Joseph M., Professor of Classics and later Moral Philosophy at King's College, London, she was educ. at Surbiton High School and Newnham College, Cambridge. There her third-class qualification, 1896, was blamed on sacrificing study to socializing. As 'Mary Strafford' she both described an adult's view of childhood's world in *Mrs Hammond's Children* [1901], and pursued a tenuous acting career despite ill-health and family opposition, 1901–3. Her fiancé's death in India, 1903, plunged her into long and severe depression. Her novels explore hidden lives. *The Third Miss Symons,* 1913, repr., with intro by Susan HILL, 1980, is a 'clinical study of spinsterhood', the sensitive account of middle-class family trammels for an unmarried daughter, a book to arouse both pity and anger. *The Free Church Suffrage Times* serialized her 'Miss Browne's Friend – The Story of Two Women', 1914–15. Leonard and Virginia WOOLF published *The Rector's Daughter,* 1924, repr. 1987. Its heroine, like her home, Dedmayne Rectory, is in 'decline', her lively imagination and intellect divided between her scholarly father and a man who cherishes a lingering regard for her but marries someone young and beautiful. Woolf (with whom FMM's relations were uneasy), Rebecca WEST and E. M. Forster praised it. *The Squire's Daughter,* 1929, repr. 1987, elegizes a world that FMM saw as moribund after WWI. *The Room Opposite,* 1935, collects 'Tales of Mystery and Imagination'. See life by Sybil Oldfield, 1984, study by Merrin Williams, who thinks her 'of all distinguished English novelists . . . perhaps . . . the least valued', in *Six Women Novelists,* 1987, quoted above.

Mead, Margaret, 1901–78, ethnologist and anthropologist, b. in Philadelphia, eldest child of social scientists Emily (Fogg) and Edward Sherwood M. She grew up in 60 different homes; a grandmother was 'the most decisive influence in my life'; she became a Christian (Episcopalian) at nearly 11. A diarist at nine, she worked on the Doylestown, Pa., *Intelligencer* in 1916, and at school and college wrote poems, essays, stories, plays and pageants. In 1920 she moved from DePauw Univ. to Barnard College, NYC, where Ruth BENEDICT taught her and became a friend. She chose 'anthropology as a profession because I felt the research was urgent and the application to current social problems was visible and compelling': *Coming of Age in Samoa,* 1928, the best-selling fruit of her first South Pacific trip, ends with comparative comment on the education of American girls. Three times divorced, MM strongly influenced all her husbands: her first, Luther Cressman, moved from the Lutheran to the Episcopalian church before they married in 1923, and defended her in print in 1983; in 1933 she made an emotionally painful field trip with both her second and third, anthropologists Reo Fortune and Gregory Bateson (with whom she had a daughter). Her huge output (bibliog. by Joan Gordon, 1976: intro. by MM), includes *Growing up in New Guinea,* 1930, and *Sex and Temperament in Three Primitive Societies,* 1935 (again on the shaping of gender roles), *The Changing Culture of an Indian Tribe,* 1932 (about the Omahas), *People and Places,* 1959 (anthropology for children), *Anthropologists and What They Do,* 1965, *A Rap on Race,* 1968 (with James Baldwin), *Blackberry Winter,* 1972 (on her early life), and *Letters from the Field,* 1977. She edited Benedict's writings, 1959, and wrote of her in 1974; years of writing for *Redbook,* a magazine for young women, were selec. as *Some Personal Views,* 1979, and *Aspects of the Present,* 1980, both ed. Rhoda Metraux; MM enjoyed the role of guru over issues like those of gender, race, and nuclear development. Derek Freeman (who, broadly, ascribes more to biology and less to culture than MM) attacked her in *MM and Samoa: The Making and Unmaking of a Myth,* 1983, unleashing furious dispute both academic and popular. Lives by Jane Howard, 1984 (scholarly but readable), Phyllis Grosskurth, 1989 (unsympathetic).

Meade, L. T. (Elizabeth ('Lillie') Thomasina) (later Toulmin Smith), 1854–1914, novelist, editor and children's writer, b. Bandon, Co. Cork, da. of the Rev. R. T. M. Writing her first book at 17, in 1879, she m. Toulmin S. and moved to London, having three children. Her writing head-quarters was the BM, where she collaborated on 12 books with several men, including R. K. Douglas, Keeper of Oriental Printed Books and MSS. LTM produced some 280 other novels, mostly for girls and young women. One of her most famous, in the school story genre she popularized, was *A World of Girls,* 1886, but despite their celebration of increased access for women to the education system, her stories reproduce traditional stereotypes, tom-boyish girls invariably being transformed into young ladies. Equally conservative were her adventure and medical novels, such as *The Medicine Lady,* 1892, set among the East London poor. For six years she also ed. *Atalanta,* 1887–98, a girls' magazine with such contributors as Rider Haggard, M. L. MOLESWORTH and R. L. Stevenson; she contributed widely to other journals.

Meades, Anna, novelist, 'a little turn'd of twenty' but long familiar with London and Bath society when in 1757 she issued an anonymous, 'inoffencive unexceptionable', but exotic ROMANCE, *The History of Cleanthes, An Englishman of the Highest Quality, and Celemene, The Illustrious Amazonian Princess.* That year she humbly, flatteringly approached Samuel Richardson (who thought *Cleanthes* lacked 'Nature and Probability') for help in revising and publishing her next work (though, she said, not needing the money). Richardson sent her only some of his comments; *The History of Sir William Harrington*, in minutely detailed letters, appeared in 1771 with his name (as reviser), but not hers. Long ascribed to Thomas Hull, repr. 1974 among 'Richardsoniana', it depicts three sisters making ideal marriages, while their dissolute brother and his friend are reformed by marrying another pair of exemplary sisters. See T. C. Duncan Eaves and Ben D. Kimpel in *Papers on Language and Literature*, 4, 1968.

Mears, 'Madge', Marjorie, 1886–1930, author of four feminist novels published in London, 1915–18. B. in Tynemouth, she wrote in North Shields and died in London. In *The Jealous Goddess*, 1915, an artist wife, unable to reconcile the conflicting demands of motherhood and career, gives her baby away and leaves her husband till he acknowledges the error of his ways. In *The Sheltered Sex*, 1916, a modern heroine, handicapped by inadequate education, runs away to London, and glories despite hardship and want in discovering 'The knowledge of her own soul'. In *The Candid Courtship*, 1917, a suffragette with 'decided views ... concerning the advisability of honourable employment and economic independence for every young woman' sacrifices 'feminine companionship and confidence' to provide an example of marital equality, because 'someone has got to do it'. *The Flapper's Mother*, 1918, portrays the effects of social pressure on sexual relations: a mother's personal happiness is sacrificed to save her daughter's reputation. MM stopped writing after her last book was turned down. MSS at Univ. of Texas, Austin.

Medical Writing, early. A fifteenth-century version of a Latin treatise on women's health, probably by Trotula, has been modernized by Beryl Rowland, 1981. From at least the seventeenth century, Margaret HOBY, Lady HALKETT, Jane BARKER and others wrote of their amateur work as healers. Elizabeth Grey, Countess of Kent, 1581–1651, included a recipe for abortion among those she 'collected and practised', pub. as *A Choice Manuall, Or Rare and Select Secrets in Physick and Chirurgery*, 1653, and long linked with her name. The Wellcome Institute, London, has many MS collections of women's remedies. Hannah WOLLEY published in the same popular genre. Practising for a livelihood drew many to write. Almanac-makers covered health: Sarah JINNER and Mary Holden (midwife, of Sudbury, Suffolk, a conservative in astrology who claims to cure as well as foretell disease, and advertises a female apothecary's wares, 1688–9) are unusual only for giving their names. Midwives were often articulate feminists, from Anne Hutchinson in America (see PREACHING) and Louise Bourgeois, 1563–1638, in France. Her *Observations diverses*, 1609, incorporated in Thomas Chamberlayne's *Complete Midwives Practice* (1656, many later eds.) comments in detail on techniques and case-histories, and urges women to prefer the female practitioners whom it carefully and humanely advises: it influenced Jane SHARP. An alleged midwives' petition against war (1643, 1646) is almost certainly spurious; but Elizabeth CELLIER, Sarah STONE, Elizabeth NIHELL, and, less forcefully, the late-eighteenth-century Martha Mears, wrote as practising midwives to claim recognition and status for their sex. For the USA see Martha Ballard (life by L. T. Ulrich, 1990). Elizabeth Blackwell's five-vol. Latin *Herbal*, 1750, brings up-to-date science to an old tradition.

Meeke, Mary, 'Gabrielli', d. 1816, best-selling MINERVA novelist, well-read wife of the Rev. Francis M., of Johnson Hall, Eccleshall, Staffs. (d. 1801): friend of Alethea LEWIS. Beginning with *Count St Blancard, or The Prejudiced Judge*, 1795 (well reviewed: facs. NY 1977), she published about 34 works mostly subtitled 'A Novel' (first anonymous, then with name or pseudonym, peaking with six in 1804), besides four translations from French (two of women) and, in 1811, the rest of Klopstock's *Messiah* (begun by Mary COLLYER). Her contrived plots mostly turn on a young man's discovery of his – always socially dazzling – identity (though in *What Shall Be, Shall Be*, 1823, only one of two heroes becomes, reluctantly, a peer). She writes grippingly, especially in dramatic or low-life openings (spunging house, accoucheurs' practice) before the nobility appear. *Harcourt*, 1799, leaves its female villain undefeated; *The Midnight Weddings*, 1802, opens with remarks on marketing skills: one should consult one's publisher on public taste, since unsold work is wasted labour. MM likes school scenes, European episodes, poetic justice, and alluring titles: *Which is the Man?*, 1801 (set in Scotland); *The Old Wife and Young Husband*, 1804; *There's a Secret, Find It Out*, 1808; *The Veiled Protectress, or The Mysterious Mother*, 1819 (opening as a deluded wife, hearing her marriage is not legal, organizes a female plot to protect her son's future). Thomas Babington Macaulay knew MM almost by heart; Mary Russell MITFORD admired her. Last of several posthumous works was a children's story-book [1825?].

Mehta, Gita, social commentator and novelist, b. in Delhi to wealthy parents, educ. at Bombay and Cambridge univs. She is married, with a son, lives in India, London, and NYC, and has worked on TV films. Her *Karma Cola: Marketing the Mystic East*, 1979 (praised by e.g., Dervla MURPHY) hilariously depicts the results of the West's historic pressure on and current infatuation with India. Delhi hosts, all at once, a World Conference on the Future of Mankind, a swami's seven-week seminar, and a Pacific Area Travel Association Conference; a tourist cries for 'quality control on gurus'; the narrator wisecracks tirelessly ('They had promised us Arpège and given us patchouli'; 'selling our birthright for a mess of pot'). She cites 'the great Indian patriot Sarojini NAIDU' in tracing Indian anglophones' progress from 'the dilatory obliqueness of English' to the 'explosive shorthand of America'. GM makes a stylistic regression in *Raj*, 1989, a historical novel whose heroine, born to regal pomp, lives through several distinct cultures. Her brother dies in WWI ('FELL GLORIOUSLY AT THE HEAD OF HIS BALMER LANCERS', says a telegram from Allenby); her husband (married for two years without seeing her) finds her insufficiently Europeanized ('I'm afraid you won't do, Princess. You really won't do at all'); her mother moves from nearly choosing suttee to admiring Gandhi. We leave her after independence, laughing uproariously at her own standing for election.

Melvill, Elizabeth, Presbyterian poet, da. of Christina (Boswell) and Sir James M. of Halhill, Scotland, courtier and diplomat (whose *Memoirs*, pub. 1683, were well-known). She m. by 1598 John Colville of Culross; her eldest son, b. 1603, became a scholar and Episcopalian priest. She must be the 'M.M.' [Mistress Melvill] on the title-page of *Ane Godlie Dreame, Compylit in Scottish Meter*, Edinburgh, 1603 (later anglicized, as e.g., 'Eliz. Melvil, Lady Culros, yonger': reprs. to 1895). Whatever was meant by a ballad-writer who mentioned her 'wild shrieking dreme', the 60-stanza printed poem is elegant as well as strenuous. The speaker (who is told by God 'I am thy spous ... uhom thou sold faine colours', but again 'Now play the man, thou neids not trimbill so') suffers deep distress at the sinful state of the world, then dreams of being divinely led on a pilgrimage among mountains, rivers, wild beasts, and into a smoking pit among damned souls. Awakened, s/he/ ends by urging readers to courage. EM also left letters and a sonnet; her pious behaviour was reported in 1630 (see Germaine Greer et al., eds., 1988).

Menken, Adah Isaacs (Theodore), 1839?–68, actress and poet: her early life is very obscure, as she gave different versions. Probably she was b. in New Orleans, elder da. of Magdaleine (Janneaux) and Auguste T.; m. four (possibly five) husbands, at least one bigamously, bore two sons who d. in infancy, and had affairs with Dumas *père* and Swinburne. She was known in America and, from 1864, in England and France, as a performer of titillating 'trouser' roles, especially in the title part of Henry Milner's *Mazeppa* (based on Byron's poem), in which, almost nude, she rode across the stage tied to the back of the horse. She wrote for US papers and magazines, and defended her mentor Walt Whitman in the *Sunday Mercury* as a fellow rebel and champion of liberty and humanity. In 1867, with both health and theatrical career in decline, AIM devoted herself to preparing for publication *Infelicia*, a collection of 31 of her poems. Dedicated to Dickens, most are in free verse, and lament lost love or the thwarted aspirations of a woman forced to 'think, and speak, and act, not for my pleasure, / But others,' ('My Heritage') – sometimes coming across as passionate *cris de coeur* and sometimes as overwrought, unfocused self-dramatizations. AIM's private life and the obvious Whitman influence on the poems meant that reviews were damning, but W. M. Rossetti thought they had 'touches of genius'. Their author had died in Paris a week before publication, feeling as if she had 'lived more than a woman of a hundred years of age'. For her life see W. Mankowitz, *Mazeppa*, 1982, which includes some of her poetry.

Meredith, Gertrude Gouverneur (Ogden), 1777–1828, Philadelphia letter writer and essayist. B. in Newark, NJ, da. of Euphemia (Morris) and Samuel O., she was well educ. and wrote as a child. She m. William M., lawyer and banker, at 18, had 12 children and knew all the local élite. She used various pseudonyms and wrote ten mildly satirical pieces for the *Port Folio*, 1801–4. Her letters, many to husband and son, one to Sarah HALL, touch on politics and literature. Exalted as a female ideal 'who wielded her pen without the least ambition or pride of authorship', she calls her children when small 'dear little Cherubs' and later signs letters to them 'M' for Mother. Yet she says men 'monopolize the privilege of writing', and, in 1824, that women, still under the yoke, cannot share male patriotism. Sympathetic to the fallen on the other side, she twice writes to her son 'your country'. MSS at Hist. Soc. of Penn.

Meredith, Gwen (Gwenyth) Valma, playwright, b. 1907 at Orange, NSW, da. of Florence (Broome) and George M. She attended Sydney Girls' High School and graduated from the Univ. of Sydney. She m. Ainsworth Harrison in 1938. Contracted to the Australian Broadcasting Commission from the early 1940s to the 1970s, she wrote numerous radio plays and is remembered for two serials, 'The Lawsons', broadcast 1943–9, and the highly popular 'Blue Hills' which ran for nearly three decades, 1949–76. With its bush setting and portrayal of the lives of ordinary and familiar types, 'Blue Hills' fostered a wide and loyal audience and made its creator an Australian household name. Her only pub. plays were 'Great Inheritance' in *Australian Radio Plays*, 1946, and *Wives Have Their Uses*, 1949. Her success inspired the novels *The Lawsons*, 1948, *Blue Hills*, 1950, *Beyond Blue Hills*, 1953, and *Into the Sun*, 1961, insipid by comparison with the original radio dramas. She also pub. the travel book *Inns and Outs*, 1955 (with Ainsworth Harrison). She received the MBE, 1967, and OBE, 1977, for her contribution to drama.

'Meredith, Isabel', pseudonym of sisters Olivia Frances Maddox (Rossetti) Agresti, 1875–1960, and Helen Maria Madox Rossetti (later Angeli), 1879–1969, b. Endsleigh Gardens, London. Their mother Lucy was the da. of painter Ford Madox Brown; their father was William Michael

R., brother of Christina ROSSETTI. In 1903 IM published *Girl Among the Anarchists*, with a Preface by Morley Roberts (novelist and journalist, 1857–1942). An autobiographical novel, it tells of the eccentric upbringing of a motherless girl and her brother by a father of advanced ideas, and her subsequent self-education as a Socialist, then an Anarchist, journalist; and her emergence as a strong and independent woman alone. WMR called it 'a genuine account' of his daughters' experiences (*Reminiscences*, 1906, 2, 450). None of his children were raised as Christians; Olivia and Helen had no formal schooling, but were kept in their parents' company, and learnt French and German from their foreign nursery governesses. Olivia, Helen, and brother Gabriel Arthur all became anarchists for a time. Olivia also married one (1897: Antonio A., Florentine writer and journalist) and lived in Rome, publishing among other works, *David Lubin, A Study in Practical Idealism*, Boston, 1922, *Not Invaders but Liberators*, 1936? (on the Italians in Abyssinia), and, with M. Missiroli, *The Organization of the Arts and Professions in the Fascist Guild State*, 1938. Helen travelled with her father before her brief marriage to Gastone Angeli in 1903 (d. 1904). She painted miniatures, and wrote on Dante Gabriel R. (1902, 1906, 1949), and on Shelley; she translated T. Silliani, *What is Fascism and Why?*, 1931.

Meredith, Louisa Anne (Twamley), 1812–95, writer, artist, naturalist, actress, b. Birmingham, England, only child of Louisa (Meredith) and Thomas T. Educ. by a governess and her mother, she m. her cousin Charles M. in 1839, and settled in Tasmania in 1840. She began writing early and by 1829 was exhibiting her paintings; she illustrated many of her later books. Poems and reviews appeared in the *Birmingham Journal* from 1832; some were collected in *Poems*, 1835, which was extensively and favourably reviewed. Before leaving England she pub. four other books: three of flower paintings and poems and a scenic travel book, *An Autumn Ramble by the Wye*, 1839, praised by Leigh Hunt. Her arrival in Australia, however, produced her most enduring work, *Notes and Sketches of New South Wales*, 1844. This was followed by two other delightful accounts of her life and travels, *My Home in Tasmania*, 1852, and *Over the Straits: A Visit to Victoria*, 1861. Her two novels, *Phoebe's Mother*, 1869, and *Nellie: or, Seeking Goodly Pearls*, 1882, are more stilted and conventional. She also pub. three children's books and several illustrated accounts of Tasmanian scenes, flora and fauna, and produced and performed in numerous plays, masques, concerts and poetry readings in Hobart. See the excellent biography by Vivienne Ellis, *LAM: A Tigress in Exile*, 1979.

Meriwether, Elizabeth (Avery), 1824–1917, reformer, novelist and autobiographer, b. Bolivar, Tenn., da. of Rebecca and Nathan A. The family moved to Memphis when EAM was 11. After her parents' death, she became a teacher and m. Minor M., a civil engineer. Memphis was occupied by the Union army in 1862, and EAM sought refuge in Alabama where she resumed her childhood interest in writing. Her story, 'The Refugee', based partly on her own experiences, won a prize of $500 from the Selma *Daily Mississippi* for the best story dealing with the war. In 1872 she edited and published *The Tablet*, a weekly newspaper, and her first novel, *The Master of Red Leaf*, was pub. in London, after rejection at home, where however it soon attracted praise for its analysis of the economic differences between North and South as a factor in the war. The novel's convoluted plot, leaning notably on the BRONTËS, depicts the Northern occupation and Emancipation as aspects of the 'war on women'. EAM strongly supported women's SUFFRAGE and corresponded with leading feminists. In 1881 she joined E. C. STANTON and S. B. ANTHONY on a speaking tour of New England, where she met Henry

George and became a supporter of his economic theories. In 1853 she pub. *Black and White,* a novel offering a complex picture of Southern life and condemning the laws depriving married women of their property. Her *Recollections of Ninety-Two Years,* 1916 (repr. 1968), is largely about the horrors of Reconstruction and the nobility of the Ku Klux Klan.

'Merril, Judith', Josephine Juliet (Grossman), science-fiction writer and anthologist, b. 1923 in New York, da. of Ethel (Hurwitch) and writer Schlomo S. G., who d. when she was young (at four she staked a claim to half his desk to write on). She wrote for a high-school paper and a Trotskyist paper, but left City College of NY in 1940 after a year to marry Daniel A. Zissman (she is three times divorced, with two daughters). She worked as research assistant, ghostwriter and editor, and in 1949 m. Frederick Pohl, a prolific science-fiction writer. Her early magazine writings include the well-known 'That Only a Mother', on radiation scarring. Her first novel, *Shadow on the Hearth,* 1950, follows a mother and two daughters through an atomic attack. Disbelief that 'any nation would *use* it' is answered, '*We* did'; in the end the 'enemy concede[s]'; son and husband return safe. JM wrote two books as 'Cyril Judd', jointly with Cyril Kornbluth (she has used other pseudonyms in magazines). Her novellas make fine use of a female viewpoint. 'Daughters of Earth', 1952, about a space-travelling dynasty, begins 'Martha begat Joan, and Joan begat Ariadne. Ariadne lived and died at home on Pluto'; in 'Project Nursemaid', 1954, the army collects babies for acclimatizing to 'low-grav conditions'; in 'Homecalling', 1956, an eight-year-old girl integrates herself and her baby brother into the society of bug-like, mind-reading beings on the planet where her parents have crashed in flames: repr. together as *Daughters . . .,* 1968. From 1951 JM edited 20 SCIENCE-FICTION anthologies: *Beyond the Barriers of Space and Time,* 1955, reprints Agatha CHRISTIE and Rhoda BROUGHTON. In 1968 JM settled in Toronto, where she has taught, written for radio, co-translated from Japanese, worked for the Writers' Union of Canada and the peace movement, pub. *The Best of JM,* 1976, and ed. *The Unknown: Writings by Ontario Women in International Women's Year,* 1975. *Tesseracts,* 1985, titled from a 'four-dimensional cube', is a Canadian anthology which confronts 'the idea that there might not *be* a future': its message is, 'We have met the Alien and it *is* us.'

Meteyard, Eliza, 'Silverpen', 1816–79, novelist, b. Liverpool, da. of Mary (Beckham) and William M., army surgeon. The family moved to Shrewsbury, and in 1842, after her father's death, EM settled in London. She had begun literary work in 1833, helping her brother, a tithe commissioner, prepare his reports relating to the eastern counties. Subsequently, she was a regular contributor of fiction and socially concerned articles to such periodicals as *Eliza* COOK*'s Journal* and *Household Words.* When she contributed the leading article to the first number of *Douglas Jerrold's Weekly Newspaper,* the editor signed it 'Silverpen', which became her pseudonym. Her first novel, *Struggles for Fame,* 1845, deals with problems faced by an aspiring woman writer forced to choose between marriage and career. Her fiction shows an intelligent awareness of women's oppression as well as class issues. She pub. some eight novels, the most popular of which were *Mainstone's Housekeeper,* 1860, and *Lady Herbert's Gentlewoman,* 1862, about a servant girl whose illegitimate child brings its father to repentance, as well as stories for children. She also wrote on the Wedgwood family and Wedgwood pottery. There is a useful discussion of her work in Sally Mitchell, *The Fallen Angel,* 1981.

Mew, Charlotte, 1869–1928, poet, b. in Bloomsbury, London, da. of Anna Maria Marden (Kendall) and architect Frederick

M. Three siblings died young; two (one a much-loved elder brother, d. 1901) were institutionalized for insanity and were a secret drain on family finances; CM lived in London with her remaining sister, Anne (artist and furniture restorer), and her mother till they died. She attended Lucy Harrison's School for Girls, and lectures at Univ. College, London, holidaying with her father's family in the Isle of Wight. She mentions 'pathetically laboured MSS' written in childhood; in 1894 *The Yellow Book* published her 'Passed', a highly-wrought story of moral paralysis and guilt set in the squalid parts of 'this glorious and guilty city'. Much of CM's poetry deals with her family, but she conceals actual facts. They were not well off after her father's death, 1898: she earned money by magazine prose and poems until WWI, with early encouragement from Catherine Amy Dawson-Scott. Rejected by *Poetry,* she was printed by *The Egoist,* through the support of May SINCLAIR. Alida Monro admired 'The Farmer's Bride' ('When us was wed, she turned afraid / Of love and me and all things human': *The Nation,* 1914), and urged on the Poetry Bookshop's ed. of 17 poems with that title, 1916. Anthologies took CM up, but her productivity had already dropped: though a 2nd ed., 1921 (*Saturday Market* in the US), added 11 poems, and *The Rambling Sailor,* 1929, printed 26 more, they mostly date from earlier. Her mother died in 1923 and her sister in 1927, each after long illness; nine months after Anne M.'s death, CM, in a nursing home, killed herself by drinking disinfectant. Her prose includes personal memoirs, acute social comment on London and France, women's HISTORY and literary criticism (on the BRONTËS and, as writers on Mary Queen of Scots, Eliza HAYWOOD, Sophia LEE, Charlotte YONGE and Harriet MARTINEAU). Her poems dwell on lost childhood, dead lovers, passion and renunciation. (Her inclinations seem to have been lesbian, and fear of insanity counselled against marriage.) She encompasses a range of viewpoints through dramatic monologue (the reader feels for the farmer as well as his bride). She said the last stanza of 'In Nunhead Cemetery' (where her brother was buried) was vital as a 'lapse from the sanity and self-control of what precedes it'. 'Madeleine in Church', her longest poem, shows a woman torn between strong sensual, sexual and religious feeling, as much a rebel as the penitent her name suggests: 'His arms are full of broken things. // But I shall not be in them. Let Him take / The finer ones, the easier to break.' This poem in MS shocked the printer as blasphemous. CM claimed 'stacks of MSS. salted away in trunks'; probably she destroyed them; surviving MSS in BL and elsewhere. Viola MEYNELL ed. her letters to Sydney Cockerell of the Fitzwilliam Museum, Cambridge. See *Collected Poems and Prose,* ed. Val WARNER, 1982 (including her play, *The China Bowl,* rejected for the stage but broadcast on radio, 1953); Warner, *Poetry Nation,* 4, 1975; and life by Penelope FITZGERALD, 1984.

Meyer, Annie (Nathan), 1867–1951, novelist and playwright, da. of Anne Augusta (Florence) and Robert Weeks N., members of the Sephardic Jewish community of NYC that included her cousin, the poet Emma LAZARUS. Her childhood was spent partly in the Midwest and partly in NYC. She was educ. at home until she entered the Columbia College extension programme for women in 1885. In 1887 she m. Alfred M. Her first novel, *Helen Brent, M.D.,* was pub. anon., 1892. A very active anti-suffragist (she wanted the franchise linked to EDUCATION and denied suffragist claims that women would 'purify' American politics), AM's writings focus on the problems of women's lives, particularly the difficulties of combining marriage and career. In *The New Way,* produced on stage and radio in 1923, she offers an unusual solution for an unhappily married couple – 'marriage under two roofs', an idea also suggested by Crystal Eastman in her

Cosmopolitan essay the same year. AM later became interested in the problem of racial equality and her play *Black Souls,* 1925, explores interracial sexual attraction, offers an exposé of lynching and portrays the situation of black intellectuals. AM's most lasting achievement was the organization of Barnard College and her work on its board of trustees. Her autobiography, *It's Been Fun,* was pub. in 1951.

Meynell, Alice Christiana Gertrude (Thompson), 1847–1922, poet, essayist and journalist, b. Barnes, Surrey, second da. of Christiana (Weller), concert pianist and painter, and Thomas James T. With her sister Elizabeth, later Lady Butler, well-known painter, AM spent most of her childhood in Italy and Switzerland, educ. by her father. In 1872 she converted to Catholicism. Her first book of poetry, *Preludes,* 1875, was lavishly praised by Ruskin, W. M. Rossetti and ELIOT; in 1877 she m. Wilfrid M., journalist, with whom she co-ed. several journals and had eight children. One was Viola MEYNELL, poet and novelist, who wrote a memoir of her mother in 1929. AM produced seven vols. of poems in the ten years from 1893, all of which (excluding the privately printed *Ten Poems* of 1915) were favourably reviewed, and in 1895 she was nominated for the Poet Laureateship. Her subtle, meditative style looks back to aspects of Christina ROSSETTI and forward to Elizabeth JENNINGS. Late work includes poetry on WWI. Her equally successful essays were pub. over the same period, her first notable collection being *The Rhythm of Life,* 1893. She disliked praise of her writing as 'feminine', and wanted the word to be used 'not as a grace but as a force ... an energy standing sufficiently alone'. Particularly drawn to seventeenth-century writing, she wrote a fine essay on Lucy HUTCHINSON. A staunch supporter not only of women's SUFFRAGE but also of other social reforms, AM pub. in 1889 *The Poor Sisters of Nazareth,* a record of life at Nazareth House, Hammersmith, while in 'Women and Books' in her 1914 essays and in the meditation *Mary, the Mother of Jesus,* 1923, she questioned women's social status. The Meynells are credited with 'discovering' Francis Thompson, but Coventry Patmore and George Meredith were her closest literary friends. AM wrote introductions to the works of many writers, including Jean INGELOW, Christina ROSSETTI and Charlotte YONGE as well as Blake and Shakespeare. Her prose reached a wide audience as journalism in the *Spectator, Saturday Review, Daily Chronicle,* and elsewhere, and she also ed. a selection of poetry for children, *The School of Poetry,* 1923. See life by June Badeni, 1981, and article by Beverly Ann Schlack, *Women's Studies,* 7, 1980.

Meynell, Viola, 1886–1956, short-story writer, novelist, poet and memoirist, one of three das. of Alice MEYNELL. Their home was a cultural centre for Roman Catholics; she grew up close to her parents' publishing activities; her writing repeatedly expresses a sense of having been overshadowed by them. She began early to publish prose and verse, and produced 20 volumes, as well as editing several (the first being selecs. from George ELIOT, 1913). *Cross-in-Hand Farm* appeared in 1911, and poems in journals and in *Eyes of Youth,* an anthology, 1912. In 1922 she m. John Dallyn; she had a son. Her talent shows to great effect in her understated stories, often of intensely feeling but voiceless women, like the disparate pair who open *Young Mrs Cruse,* 1925: a sheltered young wife, afraid of solitude, longing for her husband's daily return from the very moment of his departure, and desperate to prolong her mother's visit; and a farm girl passively resisting her parents' order to write to her absent lover, telling him of her pregnancy and demanding support, whose eventual letter expresses none of this, but only love and longing. VM's stories were collected in 1957. Her novels have rich emotional texture, slight attention to plot. Her poems are often haunted by sorrow: 'I was afraid of people, and afraid / Of everything' ('The Dream'); 'I am your Colony where you have dispatched / What your own selves could spare' ('Child to Parents'). 'A Daughter to her Mother in Illness' says 'You were not very ill, / And yet with cold quiet will, / Standing beside your bed, / I wished you dead' – in order to escape some future 'pitiless terror and agony'. VM is best remembered for her evocative memoirs of her mother, 1929, and father, 1952.

Michael, Julia Warner, obscure poet, b. 1879, whose 'stay' at Nassau, Bahamas, produced some of the first local verse, pub. in the beautifully decorated *Native Nassau, A Memory of New Providence Island,* Lockport, NY, 1904 (some repr. in Jack Culmer, ed., *A Book of Bahamian Verse,* 1930). She takes a tourist viewpoint in 'Chuck a Copper, Boss', 'A Nassau Menu' and 'The Market Woman', where the 'darky' is pictured with 'A face of ebony's polished hue / With gleam of mother-of-pearl, inlaid, / Where pinkish lips part, smiling at you; / The turban, crimson, yellow, and brown'. Her use of dialect is sometimes stereotyped ('hush-a-by, yo' mammy's chile'), but can be vivid, as in 'A Drive in Nassau' where a carriage-driver complacently enumerates the tourist sights going back to 'ole slabe time'. She included black sayings or proverbs.

Middlemass, Jean (Mary Jane), 1834–1919, novelist, da. of Robert Hume M., of East Lothian, Scotland, b. in the family's London house at Regent's Park. She began to write as a child; her father, besides teaching her Latin and Greek, started a magazine for private circulation to which she, her brothers, and other Harrow boys contributed. Presented at court at 18, she had two London seasons before her father's death (?1854). She then moved to Brighton where she joined amateur theatrical groups. She began to write seriously after her mother's death (*c.* 1865), and during the 1870s became one of the most prolific writers of POPULAR FICTION deemed 'suitable for the young': exciting but not improper, beginning with *Lil,* 1872. She preferred writing about middle- or lower-class life: 'I often pick up ideas of lower London life from standing about here and there to listen' (see Helen Black, *Notable Women Authors,* 1893). Her greatest success was *Dandy,* 1881. Other titles included *Wild Georgie,* 1873, slightly daring in having its heroine actually marry the wrong man before attaining the right; *Vaia's Lord,* 1888, a rather silly aristocratic story with some good bits; and *Two False Moves,* 1890.

Middleton, Elizabeth, British poet. Her long work in six-line stanzas, 'The Death and Passion of our Lord Jesus Christ; As it was Acted by the Bloodye Jewes, & Registred by The Blessed Evangelists', with her name, occupies the middle of a finely ornamented MS volume dated 1637, between a Calvinist prose homily against despair and an incomplete version of a poem written by William Austin by 1628 (Bodleian). She dedicates her poem as a 'free guifte' to Mrs Sara Edmondes (with an acrostic on her dedicatee's name), quotes at length from the Catholic poet Robert Southwell, and stresses that Christ 'chose to Dye, Though thay did Act the Deede'. Her narrative is vividly realized, her comment ('Awake, my Soule, Runne forth with Joye, and Dread / Into this Garden, where thy Saviour lyes') is both feeling and ingenious. Judas ('First luckles lambe, that stray'd from Christes deere folde ... Blynde Reprobate') made a bad bargain, purchasing hell fire for a miserly fee. Selecs. in Germaine Greer et al., eds., 1988, who think EM likely one of the prominent Denbighshire Middletons.

Mildmay, Grace (Sherrington), Lady, *c.* 1552–1620, Puritan memoirist, co-heiress of Sir Henry S., of Lacock Abbey, Wilts., who d. when she was a baby. Often beaten by her mother, she was taught by a poor cousin skilled in surgery and in critical judgement to write letters and moral satire in verse: 'she sent me furnished into the world'. Married in 1567 to Anthony M., later a knight, GM lived 20 years with his parents. He was usually away; she worked at pious reading, music and creative needlework: 'God did put into my mynde many good delights.' Later she ran a complex household at Apethorpe, Northants., leaving account books and a 'Book of Simples' (including medical prescriptions) with which she was painted, 1613. In age she wrote for her daughter, b. 1582, a 1,000-page AUTOBIOGRAPHY-cum-journal: its preface recommends a Christian education, but also the teachings of heathen philosophers. Parents, she says, must seek to fit their children for eternal life; better to be active doing good than to sit 'with a dumme pair of cards in our hands'. She left money to Emmanuel College, Cambridge, founded by her father-in-law. Her journal (Northants. Public Library) ends on her husband's death, 1617; see Rachel Weigall in *Quarterly Review,* 1911.

Miles, Josephine Louise, 1911–85, poet, scholar, critic. B. in Chicago, da. of Josephine (Lackner) and insurance man Reginald O. M., taken to California at five, she led an active life although confined to a wheelchair because of rheumatoid arthritis contracted in childhood. She was educ. at the Univ. of California (BA, 1932, at Los Angeles, MA, 1934, and PhD, 1938, at Berkeley). After publishing in the *New Republic* (ed. Malcolm Cowley) and in an anthology, she issued her first volume of poetry, *Lines at Intersection,* in 1939. She taught at Berkeley from 1940, won tenure in 1947, and was for many years the only tenured woman in English. After retiring in 1979 she taught in the MFA programme at Columbia. The dominant voice in her poems is sadly ironic as she writes of Berkeley, political and ecological movements, friends and students, including those who drove and carried her to the campus and to social gatherings. JM's short lines, sometimes rhyming, often evoke the eighteenth century. 'Vote' recalls going to 'door after opened door' as a child with her mother (who lived long and cared for her in their small house with sheltered garden), hearing her say 'Once we've the vote, war will cease'. 'Still the ladies in the sunny neighbor air / Register faithfully, do they not, their care / For no more war?' Of her mother's death she writes: 'Death did not come to my mother / Like an old friend. / She was a mother, and she must / Conceive him. / Up and down the bed she fought crying / Help me, but death / Was a slow child / Heavy. He / waited.' Now Death 'has my mother's features. / He can go among strangers / To save lives'. Besides many poetry volumes and a play (*House and Home,* produced at Berkeley, 1960, pub. 1965), JM did much scholarly work. Her interpretative, quantitative studies deal in precise illuminations: for instance, *The Continuity of Poetic Language,* which traces changing language-patterns from the 1540s to the 1940s, *Eras & Modes in English Poetry,* 1957, and *Style and Proportion,* 1967, which treats 'art's intensifying patterns' in prose as well as poetry. Her *Collected Poems 1930–1983,* 1983, won the Lenore Marshall *Nation* Poetry Prize. She left memoirs, posthumously released; MSS at SUNY (Buffalo), Washington Univ. (St Louis) and Berkeley. See interview in *SoR,* 19, 1983, Julia Randall in *Hollins Critic,* 17, 1980.

'Miles, Susan,' Ursula (Wyllie) Roberts, 1887–1970, poet, novelist, memoirist, da. of an 'ardent Conservative', Lt-Col. R. J. H. W. She broke away from her family's faith; as an idealistic agnostic, she says, she became 'child-wife' of socialist, pacifist Rev. William Corbett R., 1909. She set her name to *The Cause of Purity and Women's Suffrage* [1912], a tough-minded pamphlet on prostitution which confronts low wages and child abuse; later works are pseudonymous (no connection with the medium UR, author of spiritualist books, 1950–73). At Crick, Northants, an old-style rural parish, her street selling of *Votes for Women* caused scandal; her husband helped her in suffrage work; weedkiller was poured on their plants. She 'revelled in' a spell in Delhi, 1915–16, though it put her in hospital. For the free-verse sketches in *Dunch,* 1918 (her name for Crick: dedicated to her recently-dead mother), she was called 'an artist – with a scalpel'; she pictures herself as a knife being told 'God never meant you to cut.' Later poems (in journals, *Annotations,* 1922, *Little Mirrors* [1924], and *The Hares,* 1924) include delightful character-sketch ballads, epigrams, love-poems, and free verse on problematics like childlessness and being born to wealth or poverty. These themes reappear in her fiction. *Blind Men Crossing a Bridge,* 1934, dedicated to Katherine MANSFIELD, seeks, over-ambitiously, to 'make shapes and patterns' of a country parish over several generations. *Rabboni,* 1942, dedicated to Storm JAMESON, opens as a pastoral idyll at a Welsh farm which at the end is bombed; a central experimental section uses dramatic dialogue and verse. SM published a warm, funny, loving memoir of her late husband, 1955, then the verse-novel *Lettice Delmer,* 1958: an odd, powerful story of an outcast orphan boy who makes good and an ignorant, sheltered girl who goes through rape, abortion, attempted suicide, venereal disease and religious conversion.

Millar, Margaret (Sturm), b. 1915, mystery novelist, da. of Lavinia (Ferrier) and Henry W. S., a coalyard operator who was twice mayor of Kitchener, Ont., where she was born and educ. MM studied classics and became interested in archaeology, music and psychiatry at the Univ. of Toronto, 1933–6. There she wrote for the literary magazine and resumed acquaintance with husband Kenneth M. (mystery writer 'Ross Macdonald'). They had one child. MM claims to have known 'quite a bit about murder by the time she was 10' from reading her brother's hidden copies of *Black Mask* and *Detective Fiction Weekly.* Bedbound with a heart ailment, she drafted her first novel, *The Invisible Worm,* 1941, in 15 days. The next year, she wrote two more, these featuring psychiatrist and amateur sleuth Dr Paul Prye, *The Weak-Eyed Bat* and *The Devil Loves Me.* Since 1958, she has lived in Santa Barbara, Calif., where she used to write her more than 25 books longhand, sitting in an old maple chair. Now, legally blind, she touch-types her manuscripts, proofreading from closed-circuit television. Her work has won admiration for its thorough-going revision of the DETECTIVE genre narrative, for its complexities of plot, wit, effective imagery and convincing studies of abnormal psychology. After 1950, MM's novels, mostly set in California, treated a range of subjects: family entanglements, the position of Mexican-Americans in South California, failed marriage. President of the Mystery Writers of America, 1957–8, MM twice received the Edgar Award, for *Beast in View* in 1955 and *Banshee* in 1983, and the Grand Master Award, 1983. A screen-writer for Warner Brothers, 1945–6, she has also written short stories. See the autobiographical *The Birds and the Beasts Were There,* 1968, for accounts of MM's and her husband's interest in environment and natural history. See interview in *Designs of Darkness,* ed. Diana Cooper-Clark, 1983, and Bargainnier, 1981.

Millay, Edna St Vincent, 'Nancy Boyd', 1892–1950, poet and playwright, b. at Rockland, Maine. Her parents, Cora Lounella (Buzzelle), a nurse, and Henry Tolman M., a schoolteacher, divorced when she was about eight; 'Vincent' stayed with her mother. In 1917 she graduated from Vassar, published *Renascence and other poems* (the title piece had won her recognition in 1912), and took the lead at Vassar in her *The Princess Marries the Page* (pub. 1932). She played in it again and directed it for the Provincetown Players in Greenwich

Village, 1918, who also did her *Aria da Capo,* 1919, and *Two Slatterns and a King,* 1921. Meanwhile she earned her living with pseudonymous magazine sketches, collected in *Distressing Dialogues,* 1924. With the frank and cynical love poetry of *A Few Figs from Thistles,* 1920 ('My candle burns at both ends; / It will not last the night: / But ah, my foes, and oh, my friends – / It gives a lovely light!'), and *Second April,* 1921, ESVM was hailed as the voice of her generation, embodiment of the NEW WOMAN. After two years in Europe as correspondent for *Vanity Fair,* she married Eugen Jan Boissevain, 1923; she had dedicated a sonnet to the memory of his first wife, her suffragist idol Inez Milholland. That year she became first woman to receive a Pulitzer Prize for poetry, for *Ballad of the Harp-Weaver* (later *The Harp-Weaver and other poems).* At the height of her popularity she joined a writers' crusade to stay the execution of Sacco and Vanzetti in 1927; she commemorated their end in five poems, 'Justice Denied in Massachusetts', 'Hangman's Oak', 'The Anguish', 'To Those Without Pity' and 'Wine From These Grapes' (collected in *The Buck in the Snow,* 1928). After more volumes of lyrics came a joint translation of Baudelaire's *Fleurs du mal,* 1936; *Conversation at Midnight,* 1937, a dramatic verse colloquoy showing her increasing political awareness; and *Huntsman, What quarry?*, 1939 (six elegiac poems to her close friend Elinor WYLIE, d. 1928). ESVM served in women's and other societies: *Make Bright the Arrows: 1940 Notebook,* 1940, consisted of 'poems for a world at war'; *The Murder of Lidice,* 1942, radio play, was done for the Writers' War Board. Collections of *Lyrics,* of *Sonnets,* and *Poems* appeared in 1939, 1941, and 1956, her letters (at Vassar and elsewhere) in 1952. See studies by Jean Gould, 1969, Norman A. Brittin, 1982; P. M. Jones in *Women's Studies,* 10, 1983; D. Fried in *TCL,* 32, 1986.

Miller, Alice (**Duer**), 1874–1942, popular novelist and poet, b. in New York City to Elizabeth (Meads) and James Gore King D. When his private bank failed, she supported her studies (mathematics and astronomy, Barnard College, BA 1899) by tutoring and publishing stories and verse (*Poems,* with her sister Caroline, 1896). In 1899 she graduated and married Henry Wise M., stockbroker. She kept writing journalism while travelling with him in Costa Rica. Back in NYC in 1903, she bore a son and taught English and math; from 1907 she wrote full-time, becoming a high earner. She worked and lectured for women's SUFFRAGE and ridiculed its opponents in verse in *Are Women People?* 1915 (also the title of her *New York Tribune* column, 1914–17), and *Women are People!* 1917. Several of her novels (like her first great success, *Come Out of the Kitchen,* 1916) began as magazine serials (she was a regular contributor to *The Saturday Evening Post*) and were later adapted as plays, films, and (*Gowns by Roberta,* 1933) a Kerns-Harbach musical; she also wrote film scripts, a comedy (*The Springboard,* produced 1927, pub. 1928) and stories (gathered in *Are Parents People?* 1924, and *Come Out of the Pantry,* 1933). In each genre she enlivens love themes with sharp observation of the wealthy: in *Manslaughter,* 1921, privilege fails to shield a culpable heroine. After *Forsaking All Others,* 1931, wartime sentiment ensured immense popularity for ADM's second 'novel in verse', *The White Cliffs,* 1940, about love between an American girl and a representatively heroic English soldier.

Miller, Anne (Riggs), Lady, 1741–81, patron, poet and travel writer. Da. of Margaret (Pigott) and Edward R. (d. 1748), heiress of her Irish grandfather, she m., 1765, John M., Irish officer. Having overspent in building a villa at Batheaston near Bath, they took their family to France and Italy in 1770 for economy. Once home she instituted, in 1773, her fortnightly poetical assemblies: guests cast their verses (in forms or on topics prescribed) into an antique vase brought back from Frascati, once Tusculum; each paper was drawn and read, and the adjudged victor crowned with a myrtle wreath. Anna SEWARD began writing this way; but Frances BURNEY was gently, and Horace Walpole sweepingly, satirical. AM published some of the results in *Poetical Amusements at a Villa near Bath,* 1775–81, leaving a fifth vol. unfinished. Her guide-book-like *Letters from Italy* to her mother were pub. 1776–7. John M. became a baronet in 1778 and took the name of Riggs-Miller in 1780. Study by Ruth Avaline Hesselgrave, 1927.

Miller, Betty Bergson (Spiro), 1910–65, novelist, b. in Cork, da. of Sara (Bergson), a Polish-descended teacher from Sweden, and Lithuanian shopkeeper Simon S. She began writing at seven. Her father, a Justice of the Peace, received IRA death-threats; her family moved to Sweden, 1920, and London, 1922; she attended St Paul's School, a boarding-school at Boulogne, and Univ. College, London (diploma in journalism, 1930). Her first novel, *The Mere Living,* 1933, opens with a house waking up, and associates times of day (meals) with different characters. Inanimate objects have their life; interior monologues reflect a family's 'latent spiritual disruption'. The style is lush, sometimes wordy, with Joycean overtones and a strong psychological interest. That year she married psychiatrist Emmanuel M.: one of her two children is writer and director Jonathan M. After *Sunday,* 1934 (reviewed as unusually sensuous), and *Portrait of the Bride,* 1935 (reviewed as 'tear-jerking stuff for the femmes'), *Farewell Leicester Square* (about 'the social and psychological conflicts of a Jew in the modern world') was rejected before publication in 1941. This drove her towards short stories (for *John O'London's Weekly*) and plays (unpub.). She wrote in her husband's absence, submerging her writer's self under that of wifehood. *A Room in Regent's Park,* 1942, deals with medical institutions where children 'are treated as a species of contraband', *On the Side of the Angels,* 1945 (repr. 1985 with her daughter's intro.), with the relation of members and spouses to the army at war. BM returned to her Irish roots in her last novel, *The Death of the Nightingale,* 1949; her literary and scholarly work includes Victorian lives (for magazines) and editing letters from E. Barrett BROWNING, to M. R. MITFORD, 1954. BM's friends included Olivia MANNING, Rosamond LEHMANN, and Stevie SMITH. For her piece in *Twentieth Century*'s special number on women, 1958, see Jane Miller in *London Review of Books,* 6 Nov. 1986.

Miller, Caroline (Pafford), author of two Georgia novels, b. 1903 at Waycross, Ga., da. of Levy (Zan) and Elias P. She m. her high-school English teacher, William D. M., immediately on graduating; divorced in 1936, with three sons, she m. Clyde Ray in 1937 and had two more children. In *Lamb in His Bosom,* 1933 (Pulitzer Prize, Prix Femina), frontier woman Cean Carver Smith O'Connor recounts her passage from girl to twice-married woman. 'Cean Carver learned of her mother how to keep a house and how to tend a child and gave her knowledge to Lonzo Smith's wife. Cean Smith learned of God almighty how to bear grief without complaining, and passed that knowledge, like a secret gift, to the woman that married Dermid O'Connor.' *Lebanon,* 1944, centres on another brave frontier woman, shunned for being a 'Frencher', alone after the deaths of husband and son. Accused of murder, she loses the girl she has adopted, and is saved from hanging only when the preacher attests to her good name and offers her marriage. 'I would for a little wish myself a man. . . . Strange it is a man never wished himself a woman. . . . A man never envies a woman's garments or features or manners.'

Miller, Mary Britton, 'Isabel Bolton', 1883–1975, poet and novelist, b. an identical twin at New London, Conn., youngest child of Grace (Rumrill) and wealthy lawyer Charles P. M. They died within an hour when she was three; her twin was drowned at 13. Raised in Springfield, Mass., MBM began to write poetry during a year at boarding school. She travelled in Europe and lived in Greenwich Village, NYC, where she did volunteer work. She began publishing in 1928 with *Songs of Infancy* and *Menagerie*; these and later volumes of poems (some for children) express a religious sense of the divine in nature; *The Crucifixion*, 1944, is a long poem. Her autobiographical novel, *In the Days of Thy Youth*, 1943, was begun in 1930. Thereafter she published as 'Isabel Bolton': stories for *The New Yorker* and other journals ('Ruth and Irma', 1947, set in St Tropez, places itself with mention of Radclyffe HALL and COLETTE), four more novels and a memoir. *Do I Wake or Sleep*, 1946, was praised by critics: Edmund Wilson noted WOOLF's influence in MBM's rendering of inner consciousness. In *The Christmas Tree*, 1949, and *Many Mansions*, 1953, old women look back, the first a disastrously possessive mother. *The Whirligig of Time*, 1971, because of failing sight, was dictated. *Under Gemini: A Memoir*, 1966 (which shares its title with a disturbing story of 1949), again centres on MBM's feeling of special communion with her twin.

Miller, May, later Sullivan, prolific playwright, b. 1899 in Washington, DC, da. of Annie May (Butler), Normal School teacher, and Prof. Kelly M., a prolific writer on race issues. She was educ. at Howard (BA), American and Columbia univs., m. John S., and taught speech and drama at a Baltimore high school before moving into univ. posts. The New Negro Movement's *Opportunity* gave awards to her plays *The Bog Guide*, 1925, and *The Cuss'd Thing*, 1926. She published stories in journals and anthologies, poems there and in *Into the Clearing*, 1959, and *Poems*, 1962. Of her four one-acters in *Negro History in Thirteen Plays*, 1935, which she ed. with Willis Richardson, three centre on women: daughters of King Christophe of Haiti, heroically facing an uprising in 1820; Harriet Tubman saved by a 'smart girl' from a mercenary informer; Sojourner TRUTH exerting influence for good on male white vandals. *Graven Images*, 1929 (in James V. Hatch, ed., *Black Theater, U.S.A.*, 1974), shows Miriam, sister of the prophet Moses, struck with (white) leprosy when she denies that his son by a black woman is made in the image of God. Without such black history plays for children and others, MM said in 1972, 'We would have had no Lorraine HANSBERRY.' She co-ordinated and contributed to a project arranging readings by poets. Not to be confused with May (Merrill) Miller, author of novels, 1938 and [1944], and a poem, 1949, about Californian history.

Millett, Kate, Katherine, (Murray), feminist critic and activist, autobiographer, sculptor, painter. She was b. in 1934 in St Paul, Minnesota, da. of Helen (Feely), who supported three daughters after the departure of James M. She attended the Univ. of Minnesota (BA, 1956) and St Hilda's College, Oxford (BA, 1958). Supporting herself by teaching, she sculpted and painted in NYC, then spent two years in Japan, 1961–3, where she had her first one-woman show. Back in NY, she married sculptor Fumio Yoshimura, 1965 (divorced, 1984) and became active in the Civil Rights and anti-war movements. Her first work, *Token Learning*, 1967, a criticism of curricula in women's colleges, was published by NOW, of which KM was an early member. Her later Columbia PhD dissertation, which became the feminist classic *Sexual Politics*, 1970, marks the beginning of radical analysis in the history of FEMINIST literary criticism. Attacking the canon, it establishes the view that 'sexual distinctions are political definitions'. The same year, KM directed an all-woman film crew in the making of the experimental documentary

Three Lives, which allows three women to speak their own lives on film. Similarly, *The Prostitution Papers,* 1971, KM's edition of prostitutes' ORAL narratives, gives an insightful analysis of the ongoing conflict between feminists and prostitutes. KM's intense and exhaustively detailed autobiographical *Flying,* 1974, makes immediate her passionate relationships with politics, art, her friends and her lovers. This deeply personal account provides an extraordinary history of lesbian-feminist politics in the first intensity of this wave of the women's liberation movement. Her formal experiments extend the possibilities for AUTOBIOGRAPHICAL writing as political history. After *Sita,* 1977, a painful account of her loss of a lover, and her gradual return to strength after the breakdown of her marriage and her incarceration in a mental hospital (the basis of *The Looney Bin Trip,* forthcoming), KM turned to a project that had obsessed her for a decade during which she had sculpted only cages: writing about the torture-murder of 16-year-old Sylvia Likens. *The Basement,* 1979, is a study in the sexual politics of female identity: 'I was Sylvia Likens . . . she was what happens to girls.' *Going to Iran,* 1982, documents KM's experiences in Iran, where she went after the deposition of the Shah at the invitation of the Committee to Defend Women's Rights. KM runs the Millett Farm, a tree farm and feminist artists' colony in NY. Essays by Susan Juhasz and Annette Kolodny in Estelle Jelinek, ed., *Women's Autobiography,* 1980.

Milne, Christian (Ross), 1773–after 1816, labouring-class poet, b. at Inverness, da. of Mary (Gordon), who died soon after her birth, and cabinet-maker Thomas R. She had six months at 'writing school' at Auchentoul, and took to copying poetry 'by stealth' (her stepmother would hide the inkstand). She began to compose her own while in her first job, at about 14; she destroyed most of it but kept a sharply resentful poem about her mistress. Her father fell into debt and had to be cared for; her brother was lost at sea; at 18 she developed consumption. During another illness she admitted her writing habit to her current employers. She married Peter M., a journeyman ship's-carpenter, about 1796. Her *Simple Poems on Simple Subjects,* by subscription, 1805, brought her £100, which she laid away in case of widowhood; but when E. I. SPENCE met her in 1816 she had just invested it in a sixteenth share in a ship. She had eight children living, was usually bedridden in winter, and spoke of encouragement from patrons but embittering 'ridicule and contempt' from her neighbours (*Blackwood's* joined in, in reviewing Spence, 1818). Locals supposed a poet must be idle; CM vividly described the juggling of composition with family work. Her verse dwells much on shipwreck and quayside partings.

Miner, Valerie, novelist, short-story writer, essayist. B. in 1947 in NYC, da. of restaurant hostess Mary (McKenzie) and sailor John Daniel M., she attended the Univs. of California, Berkeley (BA, 1969, MJ, 1970, MA, 1970), Edinburgh, 1968, and London, 1974–5. A newspaper reporter in the sixties, she has published stories, reviews, and articles, and is a founding member of the Feminist Writers Guild. In Toronto, she co-authored *Her Own Woman,* 1975, profiles of Canadian women; in London, she produced, with four other feminists and socialists, Zoë FAIRBAIRNS, Sara MAITLAND, Michèle ROBERTS and Michelene WANDOR, *Tales I Tell My Mother,* 1978, and *More Tales,* 1988, short stories. *Competition: A Feminist Taboo?* co-edited, 1987, with Helen Longino, describes feminist writing circles as 'co-operative competition' and sees fiction as the result of 'an imaginative collectivity of writers and readers'. VM's five novels, from *Blood Sisters,* 1982, to *All Good Women,* 1987, make conventional forms address feminist issues: in *Murder in the English Department,* 1983, a feminist professor is accused of murdering a sexual harrasser.

Most formally innovative, *Movement*, 1982, emphasizes women's heterogeneity by interspersing its protagonist's story with resonant vignettes of other women's lives. *Trespass*, 1989, is also stories. VM has taught at the Univ. of California, Berkeley, since 1977.

Minerva Press, publishing house set up in Leadenhall Street, London, 1790, by William Lane, 1746?–1814, who had begun publishing in 1773 with *The Ladies Museum*. Serving 'ladies and gentlemen', with CIRCULATING LIBRARY attached, it issued twice as many novels by women as men, with peak output in 1787–90. Though usually identified with sensational rubbish, it printed (and reprinted) many good novels. Lane's apprentice Anthony King Newman took on the firm early in the nineteenth century and changed its name in 1820. Study by Dorothy Blakey, 1939.

Minifie, Margaret, novelist, sister of Susannah GUNNING, brought up at Fairwater, Somerset. While her sister and niece pub. by name, she identifies herself only as author of earlier novels. After two joint works she wrote *Barford Abbey*, 1768 (repr. 1974 as her sister's), *The Cottage*, 1769, *The Count of Poland*, 1780, and *Combe Wood*, 1783, all epistolary and sentimental. In depicting aristocratic life, scars inflicted in the marriage market, disputed inheritance, the malign power of detractors, and the angelic superiority of usually victimized women, she recalls her relatives' work and also their real-life drama (in which she figured as 'Auntie Peg'). Janet Todd discusses *Combe Wood* as Susannah Gunning's in *The Sign of Angellica*, 1989.

Mira Bai, 'the earliest poetess known by name in Hindi literature', b. around 1498. What is related about her life comes through legend, such as the story that she merged into a statue of Lord Krishna instead of dying a natural death. What is certain is that she was born into a princely Rajasthani family in north-western India, was married to Prince Bhojraj of Mewar around 1516, and became a widow soon after. The legend and her own poetry suggest that she began flouting family traditions and codes of womanly behaviour by consorting with holy men and singing and dancing publicly. Although ecstatic dancing and singing in the name of Lord Krishna was a popular religious practice at this time, known as the *Bhakti* movement, MB's behaviour was thought scandalous, ruinous to family honour because of her high birth. Many of her songs record her flouting of conventions for the sake of her lover, Lord Krishna: one tells that she laughingly drank a cup of poison sent by her in-laws – continuing, of course, to dance. Her poetry falls within the tradition of *Bhakti*, or devotional poetry, addressed by a supplicant to her/his lord, Krishna or Rama, and its uniqueness lies in MB's abandonment of well-worn themes (Krishna's and Rama's childhoods, values) in favour of an urgent, passionate personal note. She sings of a passionate lover aspiring for physical union with an inaccessible, unpredictable lover, or, most poignantly, dreaming of her lover's arrival, then waking to the harsh reality of abandonment. MB's songs travelled over India in many manuscript versions and orally, though scholars today doubt that all the songs attributed to her are actually by her. They still enjoy a tremendous popularity all over northern India, among literates and illiterates, and have been recorded by well-known singers such as M. S. Subbalakshmi, Juthika Ray and Lata Mangeshkar. Several critical and biographical studies exist. In English, see A. J. Alston, 1980.

Mirrlees, Helen **Hope**, 1887–1978, poet and novelist, da. of Emily (Moncrieff) and W. J. M., a rich sugar merchant. After dropping an ambition to go on the stage, she studied classics at Newnham College, Cambridge, with Jane HARRISON, with whom she later lived. They were learning Russian in Paris in 1915; HM wrote covertly of their relationship in her first novel, *Madeleine, One of Love's Jansenists*, 1919 (after some years in writing and several rejections), set in the seventeenth century, which involves its eponymous heroine with de SCUDÉRY. Virginia WOOLF reviewed it with respect but thought it 'full of affectations and preciosities'. She felt HM's 'taste for the beautiful and elaborate in literature' matched her 'aristocratic and conservative tendency in opinion', but found her poem, *Paris*, 'very obscure, indecent, and brilliant'. It was one of the first book publications of the Hogarth Press [1920]; in 1923 Woolf asked HM for a play, apparently promised, which never appeared. HM's two more novels, *The Counterplot*, 1924, and *Lud-in-the-Mist*, 1926, are fantastical in plot and style. With Harrison she translated from Russian *The Life of the Archpriest Avvakum*, 1924, and 21 tales as *The Book of the Bear*, 1926. Last came a life of Sir Robert Bruce Cotton, 'romantic antiquary', 1962, and *Moods and Tensions, Seventeen Poems* (privately printed, n.d., after 1961).

Mitchell, Elma, poet, translator and miscellaneous writer, b. 1919 in Airdrie, Lanarks. She attended Prior's Field School, studied English at Somerville College, Oxford, and worked in London in journalism, broadcasting, publishing and libraries. She began to be known after appearing in the PEN anthology, 1967; 'Eighteen ways of being a woman' (unpub.) was runner-up in the Camden Poetry Book Prize, 1968. 'Thoughts after Ruskin', in her first collection, *The Poor Man in the Flesh*, 1976, challenges his view of femininity: 'safe at home, the tender and the gentle / Are killing tiny mice, dead snap by the neck, / Asphyxiating flies, evicting spiders ... Mopping up vomit, stabbing cloth with needles.' *The Human Cage*, 1979, points out the 'silent woman' who 'has walked for centuries / carrying the sacred / Fire, bread, water / And never found words / to put them down'. *Furnished Rooms*, 1983, draws on bedsitter life. 'A small space full of unspilt tranquillity. / A life lived like a rite, without haste or pursuit. / To require little, and be insignificant – hardly / A pledge for a manifesto. Perhaps a passport / To a clear land, flattish but unassailable' ('Territory'). *People Etcetera: Poems New and Selected*, 1987, is often sharply witty and satirical on theology (Mary Magdalen's story retold) and politics. EM now lives in Somerset.

Mitchell, Margaret Munnerlyn, 1900–49, novelist famous for one book, *Gone With the Wind*, 1935. She was b. in Atlanta, Ga., youngest da. of prominent suffragist Maybelle (Stephens) and lawyer Eugene Muse Mitchell, of a family local for five generations. She was educ. at Washington Seminary but left Smith College, 1919, to look after her widowed father (letters 1919–21 ed. Jane Bonner Peacock as *A Dynamo Going to Waste*, 1985). In 1922 she m. Berrien K. Upshaw, became a feature writer on the *Atlanta Journal Sunday Magazine*, and began writing 'Jazz Age' stories (rejected by H. L. Mencken's *Smart Set*) and an autobiographical novel (abandoned). In 1925 she married public relations man John Marsh, and next year (having gradually given up journalism) began a romantic historical novel based on her grandmother's stories of chivalrous plantation culture. She wanted to show the Civil War from the viewpoint of 'those Southern women who had refused to accept defeat'. Far advanced in 1929, it remained unpub. until Macmillan's expressed interest in 1935. At 1037 pages and three dollars, billed as 'a complete vacation's reading', it was an undreamed-of hit, headed the US bestseller list for almost two years, won a Pulitzer Prize, and was translated into 27 languages, much pirated, and memorably filmed with Vivien Leigh as the tough and uninhibited Scarlett O'Hara. Ellen GLASGOW and Storm JAMESON praised it; *Publisher's Weekly* called it 'very possibly the greatest American novel'. Its message at a grim time combined the glamour of the past and the grit of Scarlett's 'I'm going to live through this ... as God is my witness, I'm never going to go hungry again.' With her husband as business manager MM won a battle to improve the tax position of authors. Holding an unfashionably low opinion of her own work, she wrote no more, but sold war bonds and worked in the Red Cross during WWII, then raised money for a black hospital in Atlanta. She died after a car accident. Her secretary (at her husband's behest) destroyed most of her papers: survivors at the MM Library, Fayetteville, Ga., and elsewhere, include a few pp. of her book's MS, retained to prove authenticity. Life by Anne Edwards, 1983; Elizabeth Fox-Genovese in *AmQ*, 33, 1981; Blanche Gelfant in *Southern Literary Journal*, 13, 1988; study by Helen Taylor, 1989.

Mitchison, Naomi (Haldane), novelist, poet, writer of children's literature, woman of letters, b. in 1897 in Edinburgh, da. of Kathleen Louise (Trotter), a suffragist whose memoir, *Friends and Kindred*, NM edited, and John Scott Haldane, the philosopher and physiologist. She was educ. with her brother, J. B. S. Haldane, the geneticist, at the Dragon (boys') School, Oxford, until she started to menstruate, then at home with a governess, 'worriedly aware of how far I had slipped behind my old school contemporaries'. (Jack was sent to Eton.) She began a degree in science as a Home Student in Oxford, but left to become a VAD nurse. In 1916, she married Dick M. They had four children: the eldest, Geoffrey, died in 1927. NM has been active in the women's movement, the peace movement, and the Labour Movement. The 'blood and pain' of her first book, *The Conquered*, 1923, conveys her experience of the war, and 'the shadow of Hitler' darkens her work of the 'thirties. Her historical novels – best known are *Cloud Cuckoo Land*, 1925, and *The Corn King and the Spring Queen*, 1931, both recently reprinted – explore contemporary concerns. A member of the committee of the first birth-control clinic to be established after Marie STOPES's own, NM gave a paper at the World League for Sex Reform Congress, 1929 (published 1930). *We Have Been Warned*, 1935, which abandons the mask of history and includes 'a seduction, a rape, much intimate marital chat, an abortion scene' and open reference to birth control, was censored by its publishers. *The Home*, 1934, identifies an idea of woman as property as basic to western patriarchy from the time of Plato. In 1937, NM returned to Scotland and became engaged in local and national politics; in the late 'fifties, she became tribal mother to the Bakgatla of Botswana. Since beginning with poems and plays at sixteen, she has published more than eighty books, including poetry, short fiction, biography, travel writing, children's literature, and collaborations with Lewis Gielgud, Richard Crossman, and Wyndham Lewis. Her autobiography (*Small Talk*, 1973, *All Change Here*, 1975, *You May Well Ask*, 1979) is supplemented by published diaries (*Vienna Diary*, 1934, *Among You Taking Notes*, 1985). Her later novels are science fiction (*Memoirs of a Spacewoman*, 1962, reprinted 1985, *Not by Bread Alone*, 1983). *Solution Three*, 1975, a post-nuclear fantasy, links human sexual behaviour, aggression, and totalitarianism. *Mucking Around*, 1981, describes her travels from the 'twenties onwards. In 1989 NM was writing about the radical mid-seventeenth century. 'So long as I can hold a pencil, let me go on.' Edinburgh Central Library has some family letters. See Beauman, 1983, Leonie Caldecott, *Women of our Century*, 1984, Isobel Murry's ed. of NM's *Beyond This Limit*, 1986, and Elizabeth Longford's intro. to *Travel Light*, 1985.

Mitford, Mary Russell, 1786–1855, sketch-writer, letter-writer, dramatist, poet, b. at Alresford, Hants., only da. of Mary (Russell), heiress, d. 1830, and George M., who trained as a doctor but never worked (he was an excellent whist-player but unlucky gambler),

d. 1842. Educ. at home and (thanks to her own early sweepstake win) at the Hans Place, London, school later attended by L.E.L., MRM never married, preferring to remain with her parents near Reading. She first published poetry, *Miscellaneous Poems*, 1810, *Christina, the Maid of the South Seas*, 1811, and *Narrative Poems on the Female Character*, 1813, but then wrote plays to rescue her family from pressing poverty: *Julian*, 1823, *Foscari*, 1826, and *Rienzi*, 1828, were all performed in London. In 1854 she pub. her collected plays (two vols.), with an autobiographical introduction. But she remains best known for her enormously popular sketches of village life, down-to-earth, sympathetic and humorous. These were collected in *Our Village* (five vols. 1824–32) and followed by similar works, *Belford Regis*, 1834, *Country Stories*, 1837, and *Atherton*, 1854. MRM's village stories were influential, though sometimes mocked, as in Marianne Croker's *My Village versus 'Our Village'*, 1833. She overcame the isolation of country living by sustaining numerous friendships through correspondence, her letters containing some of her best writing, and, particularly those to female friends, her most unguarded moments. She knew Harriet MARTINEAU, Felicia HEMANS, Amelia OPIE, and was especially close to E. B. BROWNING, who affectionately called her 'a sort of prose Crabbe in the sun'. After 1832 her output decreased as her health deteriorated, although she toiled on at the hackwork of almanacs, anthologies and translations to support her adored father's continuing profligacy. Rightly maligned by her biographers, he nonetheless loved literature and took her intellect seriously. In 1857 she pub. *Recollections of a Literary Life*, interspersing quotations from her favourite authors with autobiographical glimpses. Her letters have often been selected, beginning with the 'life in letters', ed. A. G. l'Estrange, three vols., 1870. For a recent critical account, see P. D. Edwards, *Idyllic Realism from MRM to Hardy*, 1988.

Mitford, Nancy, 1904–73, novelist, b. in London, da. of Sydney (Bowles) and David Freeman-M., 2nd Baron Redesdale. She grew up in the Cotswold hills, educ., she thought badly, at home. Of her five sisters, Jessica M., memoirist and social critic, moved to the US in 1939 and published an early autobiography, *Hons and Rebels (Daughters and Rebels* in US ed.), 1960, *The American Way of Death*, 1963, and works on Dr Spock, the penal system, Philip Toynbee, and Grace Darling. Unity M. was notoriously involved with Fascism. Their only brother went to Eton. NM married Peter Rodd in 1933 (divorced 1958). She became a socialist after contact with Spanish refugees in 1939, published four novels by 1940, and lived in France after 1945. Her witty comedies of manners focus on upper-class family lives, reflecting her own. Her protagonists, intelligent women, often eccentric, often unhappily married, tell their own stories. She became popular with *The Pursuit of Love*, 1945 (heroine rejects authoritarian father, makes two reckless, unsuitable marriages, loses a lover to politics and dies in childbirth), *Love in a Cold Climate*, 1949 (again, the instability of love), *The Blessing*, 1951 (MGM film, 1959: scheming child keeps parents together), and *Don't Tell Alfred*, 1960 (diplomatic-service life). NM also edited letters of her Stanley relations (1967, 1968: cf. Catherine STANLEY), translated from French (including Marie de LA FAYETTE's *The Princess of Cleves*), and wrote for the *Sunday Times* 'an insider's views of the fashionable and intellectual life' of Paris. Her essay 'The English Aristocracy' in *Encounter* magazine, Sept. 1955, examines the peerage with tongue in cheek but serious undertones; it provoked heated debate on 'U [upper-class] and non-U' speech-patterns: repr. with essays by others in *Noblesse Oblige*, 1956, which NM co-edited. She wrote the lives of Mme de Pompadour, 1953, Voltaire, 1957, Frederick the Great, 1970, and Louis XIV, 1966, and jointly adapted a successful West End play, 1950. Her essays and reviews are collected in *The Water Beetle*, 1962, and Charlotte Mosley, ed., *Talent to Annoy*, 1986. She was awarded the Légion d'Honneur, 1972. See life by Selina Hastings, 1985.

Mixer, Elizabeth, visionary writer. Da. of a deacon in the church of Ashford, Mass., she wrote for her acceptance into the congregation *An Account of Some Spiritual Experiences and Raptures*, 1736. She vividly recounts her conversion experience, which, unusually, included three visions of Christ: in the Heavenly City, in her own bedroom, and presiding at the Last Judgement.

Moffat, Gwen, mountaineer, autobiographer, novelist. B. in 1924 in Brighton, Sussex, she was educ. at Hove Grammar School, and served in the Auxiliary Territorial Service during WWII. Married to Gordon M., 1948, she had a daughter; in 1956 she married John Lees. She was the first woman mountain guide certificated by both British and Scottish climbing authorities, 1953 and 1957. She turned to writing and broadcasting when guiding (not full-time because of ill health), youth hostel jobs, etc., proved financially inadequate. *Space below My Feet*, 1961, describes early hardships and her passion for climbing. A trip in the footsteps of US early pioneers produced *Hard Road West: Alone on the California Trail*, 1981. Its fictional counterpart, *The Buckskin Girl*, 1982, follows a small group of wagon owners. In spare, unemotional narrative it emphasizes their need for unity: the heroine slowly realizes her talents as natural leader. GM's DETECTIVE novels mostly focus on Miss Melinda Pink, a middle-aged JP, novelist, amateur detective and mountain fanatic: she confronts murder in splendid natural settings in Scotland (*Miss Pink at the Edge of the World*, 1975), the California and Nevada deserts (*Last Chance Country*, 1983), and the Rockies (*Grizzly Trail*, 1984).

Moggach, Deborah (Hough), novelist, journalist and critic. She was b. in 1948 in the Lake District, da. of Charlotte (Woodyat), children's author and illustrator, and Richard H., author of over 60 books. After a BA in English at Bristol Univ., she started writing while living in Pakistan after marrying Anthony M., a publisher, 1971. Her work catches the flavour of particular domestic habitats with accuracy and wit. Her first novel *You Must Be Sisters*, 1978, draws on her own life; so does *Close to Home*, 1979, which she wrote after the birth of her son and daughter, wanting to capture the closed-in world of small babies 'very exactly before I forgot it – the intense joys as well as the frustrations'. Marriages comically shaken by cross-purposes, random coincidence and apparently uncanny events are apparently restored at the end. In *A Quiet Drink*, 1980, such relationships are dissolved, not repaired. *Hot Water Man*, 1982, is set in Pakistan. *Porky*, 1983, is the story of a man's incestuous relationship with his narrator daughter, whose pain and alienation grows until she revenges it on an unusually generous lover, an Indian, 'the only person I've ever been able to hurt'. *To Have And To Hold*, 1986, dramatized as a TV series, treats surrogate motherhood; *Smile*, 1987, collects stories; *Driving in the Dark*, 1988, is narrated by a father seeking the 11-year-old son he has never known.

Moise, Penina, 1797–1880, Jewish poet and hymn-writer, b. Charleston, SC, da. of Sarah and Abraham M. Her father d. when she was 12, forcing her to take up lace-making and embroidery to support the family, but she still managed to study and to write. In 1833 she pub. *Fancy's Sketch Book*, which contains both pious and satiric poems. She also wrote verses for the Charleston *Courier*, many on Jewish themes, and contributed to other journals including *Godey's* and Jewish periodicals. From 1842 PM was superintendent of Beth Elohim, a religious school, and after the war, despite increasing blindness, she founded a school for girls, making up historical and geographical rhymes and riddles for the students. PM is best known for her HYMNS, many of which are still in use amongst US Jewish congregations. See her (selec.) *Works*, 1911; C. Reznikoff, *The Jews of Charleston*, 1950.

Molesworth, Mary Louisa (Stewart), 1839–1921, novelist and children's writer, b. to Scots parents, Agnes Janet (Wilson) and Charles Augustus S., merchant; in Manchester from 1841. Educ. at home and a Swiss boarding school, and by Elizabeth GASKELL's husband, she pub. magazine pieces in her teens and m., 1861, Capt. Richard M. (who had a head wound from the Crimea). They separated, 1879.) Her first book, *Lover and Husband*, 1870, followed the deaths of her eldest and youngest child: till *The Cuckoo Clock*, 1877 (her seventh title, third juvenile, first masterpiece), she pub. as 'Ennis Graham', from an actual female friend who d. in Africa. Her 100 works all draw on phases of her own life, often mixed with fairytale; magazines pub. her poems and essays (four about herself). Some modern reprs. See Marghanita LASKI, 1950, Roger Lancelyn Green, 1961.

Molinaro, Ursule, experimental, bilingual poet, fiction-writer, playwright, translator. Educ. at the univs. of London, Florence, and the Sorbonne, she was a fashion journalist in Paris and multilingual United Nations proof-reader, 1946–51. She has translated authors like Nathalie Sarraute and Christa WOLF, and film sub-titles from many languages. Her first books were *Petit Manuel pour la circulation dans le néant*, 1953, *Rimes et raisons*, 1954 (poems in French), and *Mirrors for Small Beasts*, 1960 (poems in English). *The Borrower: An Alchemical Novel* was drafted in English, but followed its French version (*L'Un pour l'autre*), into print, both 1964. *Green Lights Are Blue: A Pornosophic Novel*, 1967 (with passages of dialogue and stage-directions), and *Sounds of a Drunken Summer*, 1969 (with spoof dedication to dozens of implied lovers of both sexes), each presents several consciousnesses impressionistically: tangled family and sexual relations, short, jerky sentences and sections, graphic and detailed erotic or violent scenes. *The Autobiography of Cassandra, Princess & Prophetess of Troy*, relates, says UM, the end of the era when 'women were wise, men muscled, and all children legitimate'. *Positions with White Roses*, 1983, 'A Novel in the Form of a Cross', centres on twin daughters (one 'normal', one 'deformed; formidable') of an aged, composite, conventional Dad-Mother from a gothic-style Jewish-Italian family migrated to California. UM's journal output is prolific; of many plays seen off- and off-off-Broadway, few are in print. *Breakfast Past Noon* (staged 1971, pub. in Honor MOORE, ed., *The New Women's Theatre*, 1977), presents an interfering mother and middle-aged daughter, surrealistically lodged in harp-cases. Finally a squabble over a cigarette becomes mutual strangulation. UM calls it 'prototypical rather than autobiographical'; one night she played the mother. Her nonfiction includes books on zodiac signs, 1969, numerology, 1971, and *Analects of Self-Contempt: Sweet Cheat of Freedom*, 1983. She lives in NYC, has taught creative writing and translation at its Ecole libre des Hautes Etudes, 1972–3, and recently pub. are *Needlepoint: A Dialogue*, 1987, and *Thirteen*, 1989.

Molisa, Grace Mera, South Pacific poet, b. 1946? in Vanuatu. She went to a mission school from age ten, then to secondary school in NZ, and was the first Ni-Vanuatu woman to obtain a university degree (1977). Her first collection, *Black Stone*, 1983, is politically aware and highly polemical, consciously breaking with the eurocentric tradition of her education. In 'Custom' she rewrites that word to show it as a 'corpse / conveniently / recalled / to intimidate / woman'. 'Marriage' shows the institution specifically serving male interest; 'Pregnant Blues' is about unsupported women. Her second collection, *Colonized People*, 1987, is even more fiercely feminist. Now working in the Prime Minister's department, she was the first and only woman member of the National Constitution Committee and a Signatory to the Constitution of the Republic of Vanuatu, 1979.

Mollineux, Mary (Southworth). *c.* 1651–95, English poet. As weak eyes hindered her sewing as a child, her father taught her Latin, Greek, maths, science, medicine and surgery. She wrote letters in prose and verse (chiefly to a much-loved female cousin), heroic couplets and stanzas; her topics, all religious, include friendship and marriage, the power of words, and need for modesty in both sexes; her vivid images include that of a sucking child. (The earliest date given a poem is 1662.) Urged to print, she felt 'not free' to seek human praise. She met Quaker author Henry M. when they were both imprisoned in Lancaster Castle, 1684, and married him on release, 1685/6: both served further jail terms. After coming off with honour in debate with a bishop and other dignitaries, 1691, she was said to have 'so much Learning, it makes her mad'. She wrote Latin poems to her husband, and in her last illness spoke Latin to him when not alone; she left two 'little Lads'. Her *Fruits of Retirement: or Miscellaneous Poems, Moral and Divine*, 1702 (many British and American reprints) says she lived at Liverpool.

Monck, Mary (Molesworth), *c.* 1680–1715. Irish translator and poet, one of 17 children of Laetitia (Coote) and Robert, later Viscount Molesworth: wife of the sometimes mentally unstable George Monck After her death her father dedicated to the future Queen Caroline the fruits of her 'Remote Country Retirement' with a good library: *Marinda: Poems and Translations upon Several Occasions*, 1716. Original work (epigrams, madrigals, pastoral love-poems which are often ironic, a landscape poem to a brother) is outnumbered by well-turned renderings from Italian, Spanish and French, with many compliments *to* her. The poem best known as hers (dying wife's words to husband) was differently ascribed on first printing, in the *GM*, 1750, after much MS circulation; the *European Magazine*, 1800, gave that and an unpub. piece by her as from MSS.

Monk, Thymol (probably a pseudonym), published *An Altar of Earth*, 1894, in Heinemann's Pioneer Series. Nothing else is known of her. A remarkable short novel, it tells of two women friends from Newnham College (Cambridge) days, Socialists, living together without men. One woman wants motherhood, without a man's 'seal of ownership'; the other, terminally ill, wants to save their unspoilt country retreat from developers, 'for the people'. Reviewed by the *Athenaeum*, which assumed TM to be a man, and saw Beelzebub the bulldog as 'the most humane character ... of this neurotic novelette'. The *Saturday Review* recognized a woman's hand of much promise, but felt she must 'learn to see men as they really are ... that power comes only through love'. (Both reviews 12 Jan. 1895.)

Monroe, Harriet, 1860–1936, poet, playwright, editor, da. of Martha (Mitchell) and lawyer Henry Stanton M., whose fortunes failed after the great Chicago fire, 1871. She was b. in Chicago and educ. there and (though a Protestant) at a convent in Washington, DC. An unhappy adolescent, probably because of her parents' unhappy marriage, she joined a Chicago women's literary club in 1879, and made strong, useful friendships with writers like Margaret Sullivan and Eugene Field. In the 1880s she corresponded with R. L. Stevenson and began serious writing, supporting herself as art, drama and music critic (for the *Chicago Tribune* and elsewhere). In 1890 she visited Europe; on return she lost her *Tribune* job, fell ill, and experienced her second nervous collapse. Having published *Valeria* (a verse play with poems) privately,

1891, she drew limelight when her 'Columbian Ode' was performed at a Chicago world's fair, 1892. HM won $5,000 damages from the *NY World*, which printed it without permission (see Ann Massa in *Journal of American Studies*, 20, 1986). She began a habit of world travel, and published a life of her architect brother-in-law, 1896, and *Literary Women and the Higher Education* (pamphlet), 1905. Only 'perfunctory praise' greeted her five verse plays (*The Passing Show*, 1903) and several long poems (including 'The Dance of the Seasons', 1908, in *The Fortnightly Review*, and 'The Hotel', 1909, and 'The Turbine', 1910, in *The Atlantic*). In London in 1910, she met May SINCLAIR, H. D., Marianne MOORE, Pound and Eliot; then, bemoaning the cold response to all poetry that 'stepped out of the beaten tracks laid down by Victorian practice and prejudice', HM set out to advance its cause. She raised funds from 1911 (the year *The Dance of the Seasons* appeared as a book), and in Oct. 1912 founded *Poetry: A Magazine of Verse*: first of its kind, the major forum for debate on Imagism and free verse, 1914–17. HM wrote for virtually every issue under her 24-year editorship, supported feminism, and resisted takeover by Pound. With Alice Corbin Henderson, Eunice TIETJENS and Helen HOYT, in turn, as associate editors, she printed early work of Robert Frost, Wallace Stevens, Moore, H. D. and Amy LOWELL, and the first mature work of Eliot (including 'Prufrock'), Yeats, Lawrence, Williams and Pound. She also published her own poetry volumes (from *You and I*, 1914, to *Chosen Poems*, 1935) and edited, with Henderson, *The New Poetry: An Anthology*, 1917, rev. 1932 (both versions repr.: see Craig S. Abbott in *Journal of Modern Literature*, 11, 1984), and, with Morton Zabel, *A Book of Poems for Every Mood*, 1933, repr. 1977. She travelled widely: Europe in 1923, Mexico 1929, China (her second trip) 1934. She died after a cerebral haemorrhage at Arequipa, Peru, returning from the PEN Congress in Buenos Aires, where she was US delegate. Her autobiography appeared as *A Poet's Life*, 1938, repr. 1969. Life by Daniel J. Cahill, 1973, study by Ellen Williams, 1977; see Hanscombe and Smyers, 1987. The Univ. of Chicago has HM's papers and controls, under her will, the HM Poetry Award.

Montagu, Elizabeth (Robinson), 1720–1800, BLUESTOCKING, letter writer, critic, and patron. Elder da. of Elizabeth (Drake) and Matthew R., land-owner, she was well educ. with her brothers. In youth she was far from conforming totally to masculine ideals (as Rebecca WEST later said she did), though she wished she were a boy. Some of her sparkling, irreverent, inventive letters (as 'Fidget') to the future Duchess of Portland went via Elizabeth ELSTOB; those to her sister, later Sarah SCOTT, sometimes mock their step-grandfather, Cambridge scholar Conyers Middleton. Later she hated Sarah's husband and admired her books. In 1742 she married wealthy Edward M., nearly 30 years her senior; her only child died a baby. Her three anonymous contributions to Lord Lyttelton's *Dialogues of the Dead*, 1760, satirize modern life (social and literary) and endorse classical seriousness. Her famous *Essay on Shakespear*, 1769, facs. 1966, compares him with the Greeks and magisterially rebukes Voltaire's denigration. She lived chiefly in London and at Sandleford, Berks. (beside Greenham Common), travelling in Scotland and Europe. Her husband died in 1775. EM thought of writing on ELIZABETH I, but decided to leave that to (male) 'high Mightinesses'. Her activities as builder, businesswoman and 'female Maecenas' (notably to chimney-sweep children and women writers), and her fame for benevolent power increased; so did the formality and dignity of her letters (at the Huntington and elsewhere). Selecs. ed. by her nephew and heir, 1810 and 1813, and (with narrative) by Emily J. Climenson, 1906, and Reginald Blunt, 1923.

Montagu, Lady **Mary Wortley** (Pierrepont), 1689–1762, letter writer, poet and essayist, eldest child of Lady Mary (Fielding), who d. when she was about four, and Evelyn P., later Duke of Kingston: she had two remarkable grandmothers. As a girl she secretly 'stole the Latin language' in her father's library, and wrote under male and female pseudonyms, grandly heading a MS of pastoral poems her 'Entire Works' but adding a humble preface. She eloped with Edward W. M. in 1712 after two years' vacillating correspondence, just escaping forced marriage to another. In London from 1714, she met Alexander Pope and John Gay, and wrote satirical town eclogues and a sketch of the court. She travelled to Turkey with her husband's embassy, 1716–18, producing her famous TRAVEL-letters (Mary ASTELL wrote a MS preface) and a meditative poem just before her daughter's birth. In the 1720s, while boldly campaigning to establish smallpox inoculation in England, she wrote brilliant, cynical LETTERS of social comment to her sister, and poems on marriage, divorce, and literary quarrels with Pope and later Swift. Her own political journal. *The Nonsense of Common-Sense*, appeared 1737–8, anonymous like all her publications. She left England in 1739, ostensibly for her health, actually hoping to live with the young Francesco Algarotti. But her love was unreciprocated: she lived in Venice, Rome (dazzling English tourists), Avignon, rural northern Italy (where she began her confidential, reflective letters to her daughter), and Venice again (enduring British harrassment as a learned lady) till her husband's death, 1761; she died in London of breast cancer. Horace Walpole, who hated her for befriending his father's mistress, pub. the first selection of her poems, 1747. Life by Robert Halsband, 1956: letters, 1965–7; essays and poems, 1977.

Montague, Mary Seymour, possibly pseudonymous author of *An Original Essay on Woman*, London, 1771: four verse epistles which rehearse and refute charges against women, praise famous women (especially writers), and discuss marriage. (Francis Bacon Lee wrote an 'Editor's Advertisement'.) MSM says she is 'fired with an honest Indignation' at the 'epidemical' habit of satirizing women in an age when 'female Education is so extremely confined'. Arguing that 'Concerning Woman, Women reason best' and that 'stronger Females should assist the Weak', she 'boldly stands forth the Champion of the Fair', in fine confident verse which curiously blends feminism with submission. 'In most Male Systems Women are bely'd'; 'Men hate an Equal'; yet woman is 'a softer Man', who must accept 'Decency's Controul' and hope to find happiness in an 'easy, ductile, unambitious Mind'. She especially admires Catharine MACAULAY ('Summon your male Historians, lordly Man, / Then search the Group, and match her if you can') and Lady Mary Wortley MONTAGU, who 'alone could cope / With our arch Enemy, satyric Pope', whose *Essay on Man* she aims to rival.

Montgomery, Sophia **Florence** (Leslie), 1843–1923, English novelist, probably b. Donegal, eldest da. of Caroline Rose (Campbell) and Admiral Sir Alexander L. Best known for her studies of children and family relationships, she began by telling stories to her younger sisters. Whyte Melville induced her to publish a story written for the village Industrial exhibition, 'A Very Simple Story', 1867. Her most successful work was *Misunderstood*, first pub. 1869; edition illustrated by Du Maurier in 1873. Its Preface says it is intended not for children, but for those interested in them, and its realistic descriptions are sentimentalized at the death-bed end. *Thrown Together*, 1872, about two sets of cousins, is rather better, but her later works, such as *Seaforth*, 1878, and *Colonel Norton*, 1895, have vapid plots and characters.

'Montgomery, K. L.', Kathleen, 1863?–1960, and Letitia, d. 1930, novelists and translators. B. in Dublin, das. of Robert Hobart M., with maternal connections to Oliver Goldsmith, they were educ. in England and lived in Oxford. Together they wrote eight novels, many elaborately plotted in carefully evoked historical settings. *Major Weir*, 1904, and *Colonel Kate*, 1908 (dedicated to Sir Walter Scott), draw on Scottish history and dialect: Kate is a Jacobite supporter compelled to marry to fulfil the terms of her uncle's will (she wishes to use the inheritance to support the Cause), who unknowingly weds a Hanovarian supporter. Fiamma Bonaventuri, heroine of *The Cardinal's Pawn*, 1904, uses her skills at fencing and other traditional male accomplishments to masquerade as a man, and so involves herself in the Medici family's intrigues. *Maids of Salem*, 1915, is set in Puritan New England. *Love in the Lists*, 1905, is a contemporary love story. An 'old-fashioned girl' who doesn't 'believe women are meant to race men neck and crop, through the colleges and professions' unsuccessfully tries to blacken the reputation of her rival, a 'girl-graduate' (who improvises a limerick to 'rebuff ... wooers': 'It's a question of colour! / I'm *blue* – and he's not *read* enough'). They also translated works of European history by Henri Bremond, 1928–36, and Eduard Reut-Nicolussi, 1930.

Montgomery, Lucy **M**aud, OBE, 1874–1942, writer of novels, short stories, juvenile fiction and autobiography. She was b. at Clifton, Prince Edward Island, da. of Clara Woolner (McNeill) who d. when LMM was 21 months old, and Hugh John M. She was raised by her maternal grandparents in Cavendish, PEI, spending a year with her father in Prince Albert, Sask. She went to Cavendish public schools, then took a teacher-training course in Charlottetown, 1893, and attended Dalhousie Univ., 1895–6. Her first published poem appeared in the Charlottetown *Patriot* when she was 15. Still writing, she taught until her grandfather's death, 1898, then stayed at Cavendish, except for a brief stint with the Halifax *Daily Echo*, 1901–2, until her grandmother's death, 1911, when she married Presbyterian minister Ewan Macdonald and moved to rural Ontario. They had three sons, one of whom lived only a day. Canadian and American publications accepted a growing number of her stories. *Anne of Green Gables*, 1908, with its lively orphan heroine, was an instant success. Written for adolescent girls, it appealed to a much broader audience, including Mark Twain. LMM's full-length stories directed to a young female audience included several *Anne* sequels. Most interesting of her new characters is Emily, the would-be writer, introduced in *Emily of New Moon*, 1923. '*New Moon*', she wrote in her diary, was 'in some respects but not all my own old home and *Emily*'s inner life was my own, though outwardly most of the events and incidents were fictitious.' LMM mythologized PEI, childhood, and adolescence with her enormously popular stories, whose idyllic settings and attractive bright young heroines captivated an international audience. Widely translated, her novels are especially popular today in Japan and Poland. *Anne of Green Gables* became a musical (annually staged in Charlottetown) a film, and a TV mini-series. On her husband's retirement, 1935, LMM moved to Toronto. Her letters to Ephraim Weber, ed. Wilfrid Eggleston, were pub. 1960; those to G. B. MacMillan, eds. Francis Bolger and Elizabeth Epperly, 1980. Mary Rubio and Elizabeth Waterston, eds., *Selected Journals*, 2 vols., 1985, 1988, have fuelled scholarly interest. Life by Mary Rubio, forthcoming; critical study by Mollie Gillen, 1975; bibliography by Ruth Webber Russell et al, 1986.

Montrésor, F. F., Frances Frederica, 1843–1923, novelist, b. in Kent, da. of an admiral: she dedicated books to several sisters. Her fiction covers a wide range of characters, relationships, and social settings, often observed from the margins. In *One Who Looked On* (one of her first two novels, both 1895) intense emotional events among tightly controlled, intellectually or socially distinguished English people (and the clash of two strong-willed males, one of them a small boy) are seen through the eyes of a naive unmarried Irishwoman, maternally devoted to the lives of others: the narrator finds her more interesting than those on whom the spotlight falls. The title story in *Worth While*, 1896, concerns a former workhouse boy who writes letters all his life to an imaginary mother. In *The Alien: A Story of Middle Age*, 1901, a quiet woman in her late thirties discovers the stormy past of her foster-mother when a passionately-loved illegitimate son is produced to take the place and heritage of the dead, unloved offspring of marriage. In *The Strictly Trained Mother*, 1913, another family friend describes relations between a Victorian patriarch's gentle little widow and her strong-minded anti-SUFFRAGE daughters and rebel granddaughter.

Moodie, Susanna (Strickland), 1803–85, poet, writer of fiction and non-fiction, b. in Bungay, Suffolk, da. of Elizabeth (Homer) and Thomas S., sister of Catherine Parr TRAILL and Agnes and Elizabeth STRICKLAND. After their father's death, the daughters wrote to supplement family income. SM published sketches of rural life influenced by Mary Russell MITFORD and contributed poems to annuals (collected in *Enthusiasm*, 1831). Pursuing a literary career, she moved to London, 1831 (see Mary PRINCE), but married half-pay officer John Wedderburn Dunbar M. and reluctantly, because of finances, migrated with him to Canada, 1832, following her sister Catherine and a brother. They had seven children. They farmed near Port Hope, Ont., then moved to the backwoods north of Peterborough. Dunbar kept the family going by military service, 1837–9, then, 1840, abandoned farming to become, until 1863, Sheriff of Belleville. After his death, 1869, SM lived mainly with a son in Toronto. In the 1830s she supplemented the family income by publishing poetry and prose in magazines, including *Canadian Literary Magazine*, *Albion* (NY), *Lady's Magazine* (London), and, during the whole of its existence, 1838–52, Canada's most prestigious journal, *The Literary Garland* (see Eliza CUSHING). Moving to Belleville gave her more time to write. She and Dunbar edited and wrote for the *Victoria Magazine*, 1847–8. Six sketches in *The Garland*, 1847, became chapters of her most enduring work, *Roughing it in the Bush*, 1852 (first of several books pub. by Bentley's, London; Margaret ATWOOD introduces one of several recent eds., 1987). SM here fictionalized her experience in sketches unified by herself as central figure. They stress the harsh climate and difficulties for the inexperienced pioneer farmer, disapprove of Yankee neighbours, but also convey SM's delight in nature. *Life in the Clearing, versus the Bush*, 1853, describes small-town society. SM's several sentimental novels began as *Garland* serials: *Mark Hurdlestone*, 1853, *Matrimonial Speculations*, 1854, and *Flora Lyndsay*, 1854, a fictionalized account of her voyage across the Atlantic. Though conventional about gender roles, SM makes her women strong, courageous, and initiating, her men weak and dependent. (She had herself worked in the fields and been responsible for her husband's appointment with the militia and, perhaps, as Sheriff.) The Ballstadt, Hopkins, Peterman edition of her letters, 1985, also includes much biographical material. See also Carol SHIELDS, *Voice and Vision* 1977; Marian Fowler, *The Embroidered Tent*, 1982.

Moody, Elizabeth (Greenly), d. 1814, poet living near London. She wrote from at least 1760, and pub. some poems anonymously (like Noah's dove, she said, reconnoitring the land); earliest identified, 1780. Verse reproofs (as Miss G.) to her friend Edward Lovibond appeared in his posthumous poems, 1785. She m. the Rev. Christopher Lake M., and wrote about 26 reviews for the *Monthly Review*, 1789–1808, chiefly on novels. 'Anna's Complaint, or The Miseries of War', 1794 (pub. in a polemic by George Miller, 1796), bore her name: so did her *Poetic Trifles*, 1798. Though she felt the time was one for war and pamphlets, not poetry, she shows good sense and imagination (praised by the *Critical*), wit, energy, and interest in science and politics: in epigrams, dialogues, 'The Housewife, or The Muse Learning to Ride the Great Horse Heroic' (blank verse); on a child's death, on friends, and public figures like Samuel Johnson, Sarah TROTTER, Joseph Priestley, Danton and Robespierre. The *GM* (which had printed her verse) had an obituary eulogizing her prose, comparing her letters to Marie de SÉVIGNÉ's and calling her 'young to the last' in her brilliant faculties.

Moore, Edith Mary, feminist novelist publishing in London, 1909–35. Her first novel (of seven), *The Lure of Eve*, 1909, exposes a dogmatic husband who believes that 'the hope for social and personal honour and purity lies with women', and a wife who sees 'herself the figure in the foreground made famous by his work'. Unable to met the financial needs which are her primary requirement of a husband, he writes a successful book ironically titled *Woman and Destiny* to provide money to support her. Her sixth, *The Blind Marksman*, 1920, attacks the social restrictions placed on women, the lack of any 'career' but marriage, and the institution of marriage itself. Jane, seeking a 'comrade' or 'sharer in the problems and adventures life might offer' finds instead a man with 'no urgent need in his composition' for either; her upbringing, which insisted on woman's 'service to a man's arrangements, had blinded her to the resources of her own life'. Leaving her husband, she finds, is the only way not to 'lose sense of any rightness and sincerity in anything'. *The Defeat of Woman*, 1935, is a non-fictional treatise on women and society. EMM seeks to improve understanding between women and men and also amongst women themselves: 'When woman is no longer regarded as a difficult enigma or an aggravating doll. . . . The jealous feuds among women will cease . . . and . . . the long history of her exploitation and subjection will come to an end.'

Moore, Elizabeth, d. 1657, Baptist author of *Evidences for Heaven*, pub. as part of Edmund Calamy's *The Godly Man's Ark*, 1657 (often repr.: '17th ed.' 1693). Calamy presents her as a model for forbearance, obedience, and recording her experiences of God's grace. She lists her reasons for believing herself one of the Elect, comparing the stages of her conversion with others'. She ends 'The desire of my soul is, that God may have all the glory.'

Moore, Frances, *c.* 1789–1881, novelist and historian, da. of Sarah (Webb *or* Richmond) and Peter M., politician. Not to be confused with Frances (Moore) BROOKE, she published anonymously except (as 'Madame Panache'). Her second novel, *Manners*. 1817, shows off her learning, comments on novelists including women, and sharply outlines social distinctions in an English village and in Ireland. *A Year and a Day*, 1818, presents two heroic women: one shy, self-sacrificing yet strong; one a dazzling young countess (once a poor curate's daughter) whose grand marriage, unconventionality, and goodness combine to destroy her. Both were quickly issued in the USA. FM's *Historical Life of Joanna of Sicily*, 1824 (still controversial), seeks the facts about a woman ruler both lauded and vilified, whom she compares to Mary Queen of Scots. She pursues questions of history and biography in prefacing her translation of part of Carlo Botta's *History* *of* [Napoleonic] *Italy*, 1828. She died at Exeter.

Moore, Honor, poet, dramatist and anthologist, b. 1945 in NYC, to Jenny (McKean) and Bishop Paul M.: her large family includes five sisters. At ten, working with her class on a play about ancient Egypt, she became obsessed with the theatre. After Radcliffe College (BA 1967), she studied theatre administration at Yale School of Drama. A message learned there ('Women should not be playwrights'), reinforced by the reception of a woman's play which was her first (joint) production in NYC, made her 'turn my full energy to writing poetry', of which she gave readings. With her mother dying of cancer, pained by a sense of the gulf between her inner feelings and the indifferent people around her, she began a journal with 'Ladies and gentlemen, my mother is dying'. This grew into a series of poems, then a play, *Mourning Pictures* (title from an early nineteenth-century, largely female art-form, depicting mourners at a graveside). In it a mother's fatal illness is set against a background of hospital (various doctors and healers to be played by the same actor) and of the love and inadequacy (both emotional and verbal) of her family, especially her namesake daughter. Flat everyday language alternates with lyric: 'What will she leave me ... A ring or two, / The painting on the stairs / Her mother did / Of her asleep at three / that looks a lot like me – / Will she leave me that?' The chiefly hostile reviews of this intensely moving play, staged 1974, spurred HM to look at the past record and reception of women playwrights, and compile an ANTHOLOGY, *The New Women's Theatre: Ten Plays by Contemporary American Women*, 1977 (including *Mourning Pictures*), with historical introduction: it presents the 'spirit of the new women's theatre ... excellence, variety'. HM's poems appear in journals and anthologies, on a long-playing record ('A Sign I Was Not Alone') and in Claudia Weill's film *Girlfriends* (both 1978), and in *Leaving and Coming Back*, 1979 (chapbook). Her play *Years* (tracing a friendship between two creative women in their thirties) had a staged reading in 1979. She has also written about her painter grandmother; *Memoir* appeared in 1988.

Moore, Jane Elizabeth (Gobeil), b. 1738, autobiographer and poet, born of French parents, living in Britain. Her mother (tricked into marriage, she says) died of grief about 1741; an early reader in French and English, cared for by female relations, JEM disliked her unsuccessful manufacturer father, who wanted a son. She married ('sealed my unfortunate fate') in 1761; her babies died young. Travel around Britain aided her 'search after knowledge in the trading line'; she was in business by *c.* 1766. After her husband died, 1781, she was arrested for his debts; released, she wrote poems to the royal family and stylistically clumsy *Genuine Memoirs* [1786], also called a 'Sentimental Journey' and 'treatise on ... trade, manufactures, laws, and police'. (Essays on such subjects follow her story.) The *Monthly Review* panned it. In Dublin in 1795, pursuing business and publication, she met Henrietta BATTIER, and Tom Moore (no relation), who saw her as a comic Cockney. The *Sentimental and Masonic Magazine* that August pub. her verse 'Request to the Society of Freemasons' to admit women. *Miscellaneous Poems on Various Subjects*, Dublin 1796, by subscription, dedicated to 'the Public', and better than her prose, includes defences of women, comment on Irish affairs, a 'Prayer for Resignation' and songs from her lost opera, *The Female Hermit*.

Moore, Marianne Craig, 1887–1972, poet, critic and editor, younger child of Mary (Warner), later a teacher, and John Milton M., b. at Kirkwood, Missouri, and educ. at Bryn Mawr (BA 1908; she was already writing poems), and Carlisle Commercial College, 1909–10. She worked on a revision of the Dewey Decimal Index, visited England in 1911, and taught three years at a US Industrial Indian School at Carlisle, Penn., before moving to the NY area, settling in Greenwich Village. In 1915 Harriet MONROE's *Poetry* printed her five poems then called 'Pouters and Fantails', and *The Egoist* her 'To a Man Working His Way Through the Crowd' and 'To the Soul of Progress'. 'Poetry', printed in *Others*, 1919 (later several times revised), opens with a prosaic statement of dislike, even 'perfect contempt' for poetry ('all this fiddle'), but adds, 'one discovers that there is in it after all, a place for the genuine', – which in turn she famously defines as 'imaginary gardens with real toads in them'. Her verse is indeed marked by precise observation (she had sketched from nature for years) and surprising zoological metaphors. Admired by Eliot and Pound, MM aimed at literary success and for close relations contented herself with family. She wrote to BRYHER in 1921 that Bryn Mawr 'gave me security in my determination to have what I want', and in 'Marriage', 1923, of the 'amalgamation which can never be more / than an interesting impossibility'. 'H. D. and Mr. and Mrs. [Bryher] Robert McAlmon' selected 24 of her poems for issue, unknown to her, by the Egoist Press, London, 1921; she added 'Marriage' and other poems in re-issuing this as *Observations*, NY, 1924. It brought her the *Dial* award and editorship of that journal until its demise in 1929 (after which she lived by her own writing). Her friendship with Elizabeth BISHOP (see Bonnie Costello in *TCL*, 30, 1984) dates from the early 1930s. Eliot introduced her *Selected Poems*, 1935, praising her as 'the greatest living master' of light rhyme, and 'one of those few who have done the language some service in my lifetime'. MM continued to issue little books of poems until *Tell Me, Tell Me*, 1966. *Collected Poems*, 1951 (Pulitzer Prize), was dedicated to her mother, recently dead, who had lived with her and whose influence, she had said, extended often to 'actual phrases'. *Predilections*, 1955, gathers essays on writers and artists like Louise BOGAN, Ezra Pound and Anna Pavlova. MM translated La Fontaine's fables, 1954, dramatized Maria EDGEWORTH's *The Absentee*, 1962, and re-told Perrault fairy tales, 1963. *A MM Reader*, 1961 (poems and prose), includes an interview. She was a poet of charisma in her lifetime, also a baseball fan. See *Complete Poems*, 1967, repr. 1982 (whose epigraph, 'Omissions are not accidents', points to considered policy); *Complete Prose*, 1986; concordance to 1967 poems by Gary Lane, 1972; bibliog., 1977, and reference guide, 1980, by Craig S. Abbott. MSS at the Rosenbach Museum, Philadelphia (which issues a *MM Newsletter*), include notebooks kept from 1916 and an unfinished memoir. Much comment includes life by Elizabeth Philips, 1982, studies by Costello, 1981, and Taffy Martin, 1986, feminist views in Juhasz, 1976, and Barbara Herrnstein Smith, *On the Margins of Discourse*, 1978.

Moore, Milcah Martha (Hill), 1740–1829, poet, teacher and anthologist, last of 12 children of Deborah (Moore) and Dr Richard H., slave-holding planter of South River, Md: sister of Margaret MORRIS, cousin of Hannah GRIFFITTS. She was b., and grew up till nearly ten, at Madeira. On marrying her first cousin Dr Charles M., 1767, she was disowned by the Philadelphia Quakers. In 1769 the *Pennsylvania Chronicle* printed her poem of 1768, 'The Female Patriots': it calls 'the Daughters of Liberty' to 'point out their duty to men' by boycotting taxables, even though they lack any 'voice but a negative here'. Living at Montgomery Square from 1776, MMM ran a charity girls' school. She kept perhaps several commonplace-books, begun as a child and lent to friends in MS. One, pub. as *Miscellanies, Moral and Instructive*, Philadelphia, 1787, with a puff from Benjamin Franklin, contains mainly moral passages from e.g., Anne FINCH, Pope, and Johnson: many eds., some at

London and Dublin. Widowed in 1801, she was readmitted by the Quakers in 1811.

Moorehead, Finola, poet and prose writer, b. 1947 in Melbourne, da. of Leslie Mary (White) and Arthur Francis M. She identifies as a lesbian writer. Educ. at the University of Tasmania (BA, 1968), since 1973 she has worked as a full-time writer, publishing until the mid 1980s in journals, newspapers and magazines, and in anthologies such as *Mother I'm Rooted* (ed. Kate Jennings), 1975, and *Frictions* (ed. A. Gibbs and A. Tilson), 1982. Her first collection, *Quilt*, appeared in 1985; these are prose pieces, chiefly conversational, interspersed with authorial statements about the nature and purpose of feminist writing. Shortly afterwards followed *A Handwritten Modern Classic*, 1985 (which actually is handwritten), a collection of polemical prose: not entirely readable. *Remember the Tarantella*, 1987, is a longer ambitious novel with 26 female characters (one for each letter of the alphabet). Highly symbolic, carefully constructed like a web, and a challenge to read, it breaks new ground in fiction. All FM's work evades conventional categorization and demonstrates her commitment to experimental feminist writing.

Moorhead, Sarah (Parsons), polemical poet. She m. the Rev. John M. of Boston in 1730 and had three children. In the ferment of the Great Awakening she recommended a degree of restraint to three fiery ministers. The *New England Weekly Journal*, 17 March 1741, pub. with her initials lines to 'dear sacred' Gilbert Tennent. Two poems printed together at Boston, 1742, repr. 1819, address the controversial James Davenport and Andrew Crosswell. With vigorous imagery and fine turn of phrase, she conjures a vision of Davenport in a paradisal garden setting, admonished by angels to be charitable ('Success is not confin'd, dear Man, to you'), feeling shame, weeping, and repenting. She addresses Crosswell lovingly and personally, 'on bended Knees, with flowing Tears', yet authoritatively, bidding him to recognize his own imperfections.

'Mordaunt, Elinor' or 'Eleanor', Evelyn May (Clowes), 1877–1942, popular novelist and travel writer, b. at Cotsgrove Place, Notts., da. of Elizabeth (Bingham) and St John Legh C. She had a 'perfectly futile' educ. from governesses, and after two months of art lessons in London went to Mauritius (the Terracine of her novels) in 1897. An unhappy marriage to a planter (probably named Wiehe, not Mordaunt), malaria, and two still-births started her writing 'a series of letters to no one in particular', pub. as *The Garden of Contentment*, 1901. After returning alone to England she left by sailing ship for Australia (a voyage treated in *The Ship of Solace*, 1911). There she bore a son and supported them both for seven and a half years by odd jobs and writing stories and articles. She returned to England, but continued to travel widely: Africa, the Far East, Central and South America. These provided material for TRAVEL writing like *The Venture Book* and *The Further Venture Book*, 1926, *Hobby Horse*, 1940, and newspaper articles, as well as settings for over 40 novels, and short-story volumes like *The Tales of EM*, 1934. *The Park Wall*, 1916, describes the social ostracism and financial hardships of a young woman back in England with her son after an unhappy marriage in the West Indies, a divorce devised by her husband with trickery and deceit, and her relief 'to be free'. 'I don't think any man can ever realise how a woman can be shamed by her husband and all he has in his power to do to her.' The heroine of *Lu of the Ranges*, 1913, after a brutal and miserable childhood, gains independence by success as a dance-hall girl; when her son's father reappears after 12 years, she fiercely defends her right to the child: 'You did not care to give me your name, or the pretence of your name, or your protection, or your care.' *Full Circle*,

1931 (in US as *Gin and Bitters* by 'A. Riposte'), charts the morally and spiritually empty life of a lionized author. EM married Robert Rawnsley Bowles, probably in 1933 (date disputed). She also published non-fiction (*Here Too is Valour*, 1941, describes East London in the blitz) and for children (*To Sea! To Sea!*, 1943). See *Sinabada* (autobiography), 1937.

Mordaunt, Elizabeth (Carey), Viscountess, 1632/3–79, diarist and writer of prayers, da. of Margaret (Smith) and Thomas C.: friend of Margaret GODOLPHIN. In 1656, about the time she married her fellow-royalist John M. (created Viscount in 1659), she recorded an experience of spiritual joy in a large, handsome volume which became her 'Private Diarie' of prayers and meditations. For some weeks in 1657 she revealingly lists daily 'occasions' of thanksgiving or penitence (e.g., gossip, reading a foolish play, failing to discourage men, 'having bin weded to my owne opinion, and not yelding' to her husband). Notable among events recorded is his arrest for treason against the Commonwealth government, 1658. Lord Clarendon, approving his 'honourable' conduct, records how her resource and energy secured a narrow – and unusual – acquittal, which angered Cromwell. The DIARY, concerned almost wholly with spiritual implications, yet notes the Restoration, plague and Great Fire, as well as births (11 children). MS in BL: selecs. pub. by an anonymous woman, 1810, as *Anecdotes*, for example to less pious ladies; privately printed 1856.

Mordecai, Pamela, poet and editor, b. 1942 in Jamaica, educ. at local schools, in the USA and at the Univ. of the West Indies. She has taught English in schools and as senior lecturer at Mico Teachers' Training College; her media work includes TV presenting and interviewing. Active in developing a specifically Carribbean curriculum, Publications Officer at the School of Education, UWI, she is author or co-author of many school anthologies and textbooks at every level. She edits *The Caribbean Journal of Education* and the literary-scholarly *Caribbean Quarterly*, and has worked on adult poetry anthologies: *The Caribbean Poem* and *Ambakaila*, both 1976, and, with Mervyn Morris, the important *Jamaica Woman*, 1980. Her own poems appear there and in journals and later collections: her first solo volume, *Shooting the Horses*, is expected. PM depicts poems as mysterious, 'and we who write them down / make pictures intermittently / (sweet silhouettes ...) but the bright light / that makes these darknesses / moves always beyond mastery'. She is strongly concerned in social, political, and especially sexual issues. 'Wednesday Chronicle' details the imprisoning routines of a suburban housewife; 'Tell Me' wryly describes the woman's indefatigable contribution to a relationship and demands 'So tell me brother, / what have you to give?' But the speaker in 'Family Story' ascribes her strength to her father: 'He never kiss ass / never owe money / never cuss / never give less / than a day's work / for a day's pay / all of his life. / Careful, then, / how you cross me.'

More, Agnes, Dame, b. 1563/72, translator, b. Grace More, da. of Mary (Scrope) and Thomas M.: aunt of Gertrude MORE, whose associate she was. A Cambrai nun, probably AM, published *Delicious Entertainments of the Soule*. Douai, 1632 (facs. 1974), from the *Entretiens Spirituels* of Francis de Sales (a work written for nuns, whom it judges capable of 'the Apostolicall office' though not of apostolic dignity). A preface apologizes for her sketchy knowledge of French, and says 'God and her superiors' have made her publish what she wrote only for herself and her sisters. Yet she is eager to make this 'praised, prized, and practised' work available to lay people ('especially of the devout sex') and even hopes to teach anti-Catholics to 'leave to detract and deride'. Her style is fluent, unforced but forceful.

More, Gertrude, Dame, 1606?–33, formerly Helen, autobiographical and devotional writer, b. at Leyton near London, da. of Elizabeth (Gage), who d. in 1618, and Cresacre M., who educ. her, and wrote the life of her great-great-grandfather Sir Thomas. In 1623 she sailed for Europe with eight other women, and founded the Benedictine convent at Cambrai where she then lived. Seeking to establish an autonomous contemplative or spiritual life, she endured nearly five years' 'inconveniences and miseries' from a confessor who was apt 'to take al I said and did in another sense then I meant it', till with the support of Dom Augustine Baker she learned 'not to be daunted with my sins' and not to rely too heavily on others' advice. She died of smallpox. Her collection of writings by Baker and others was pub. as *The Holy Practises of a Devine Lover, or The Sainctly Ideots Devotions*, Paris, 1657 (repr. in varying forms, 1669, 1873, 1909, 1937). (Such 'Ideots' are those with simple, fervent and unintellectual desire after God.) Her own *Spiritual Exercises* followed in 1658, dedicated to her sister Bridget M., prioress; an 'Advertisement' tells her own story and discusses convent life (obedience, factions, 'strange friendships'). Baker's life of her, pub. [1937], uses her 'Apology' for him and herself. See Marion Norman in *Recusant History*, 13, 1975–6.

More, Hannah, 1745–1833, dramatist, poet, Christian moralist and pioneer of universal education, b. near Bristol, fourth of five das. of Mary (Grace) and schoolmaster Jacob M. He taught her Latin but refused maths as unfeminine; from 12 she attended the school her sisters set up in Bristol and ran till 1790. She wrote social verse while very young, and at 15 *The Search after Happiness*, pub. 1773, an improving pastoral play for girls' schools, which also celebrates women writers. A middle-aged suitor, William Turner, wavered lengthily and withdrew, but compensated her in money. Her tragedy *The Inflexible Captive*, from Metastasio, was pub. 1774 and later acted at Bath. A visit to London, 1773–4, introduced her, probably through Frances REYNOLDS, to Elizabeth MONTAGU, Samuel Johnson (who praised her poems) and David Garrick (who called her 'Nine' after the Muses, and on whose behalf she attacked Frances BROOKE in print). She published several poems, from the ballad *Sir Eldred of the Bower*, 1775. Vivid letters to her sisters retail heady success: triumph on stage and in print in 1777 with *Percy* (model heroine misjudged and done to death by jealous husband) and *Essays ... for Young Ladies*. Her prologue to another tragedy, *The Fatal Falsehood*, 1779, defends 'domestic woes' as closer to audiences' lives than 'ruin'd empires'. Hannah COWLEY, however, accused it of plagiarism. HM then gave up the London stage, judging it inimical to Christianity: *Sacred Dramas ... for Young Persons*, 1782 (facs. 1990), represented an alternative. She built a cottage, retired with her sisters, supported ABOLITION, boycotted sugar and had BEHN's *Oroonoko* staged. *Thoughts on the Importance of the Manners of the Great to General Society*, 1788 (another best-seller) was anonymous, from humility not caution; after her next critique of the fashionable classes, 1791, schoolboys burned her in effigy. She turned from rich to poor in *Village Politics* by 'Will Chip', 1792, and the series *Cheap Repository Tracts*, 1795–8, helped by three sisters, Hester CHAPONE and Sarah TRIMMER. Deplored by radicals since William Cobbett, lately reassessed by feminist scholars, they sold two million copies a year for charitable distribution, and led to the founding of the Religious Tract Society. From 1789 (see Martha H.'s journal, pub. 1859) the sisters set up Sunday Schools to fight illiteracy and poverty near Cheddar, seeing, said HM, more misery in a week than most people know of in the world. She was vilified during a dispute over Anglican-Methodist relations – ironically, for she hated 'little narrowing names' of sects. Her deeply held orthodox faith often overcame her equal respect for authority (not, however, as regards Ann YEARSLEY). She treated women's education constructively, though conservatively, in *Strictures* ..., 1799, and *Hints* ..., 1805 (which, anonymous and politically acute, aimed at plans for Princess Charlotte, was at first thought to be a man's). The hero of her heavily didactic novel, *Coelebs in Search of a Wife*, 1808 (hugely popular in the USA), picks his ideal from among other gently satirized women. With *Works*, 1801, more penny tracts, 1817–18, and religious titles up to 1825, HM was 'almost ashamed' to 'have made over £30,000 by my books'. She influenced the Victorians through Gladstone and T. B. Macaulay (who met her as children). Her letters, 1834, are mangled and incomplete; life by Mary Gwladys Jones, 1952, repr. 1968.

More, Mary, d. 1713/15, feminist. She had two children by her first husband, named Waller, and m. her second, More, by 1674. She says she had no disputes with either husband, who wisely saw their interests and hers as one. While her daughter, b. *c.* 1663, was little, she wrote *The Womans Right or Her Power in a Greater Equality to her Husband proved than is allowed or practised in England.* She notes the harm done by men's unwarrantable claim to 'a Power over their Wives', which is backed by unjust laws: 'Men always held the Parliament and have enacted their own wills.' A woman must act before marriage to secure her own estate to herself, choose a husband who loves her (on her choice depends 'all worldly Comfort'); if he turns out badly, she must submit, hide her troubles, and outdo him in virtue. The bible, rightly understood, proves that Eve was created Adam's equal: like 'all or most women ever since ... of a finer mould and metall than most men are'. MM mentions famous women (Anna Maria van SCHURMAN, Lady Jane GREY, ELIZABETH I) and prefers the Geneva Bible to the misogynist Authorized Version. Robert Whitehall, an Oxford don, attacked her work but also preserved it: printed in Margaret J. M. Ezell, *The Patriarch's Wife*, 1987.

Morey, Dewans, *c.* 1644–84, Quaker pamphleteer. Her *True and Faithful Warning* [1666], written while fasting, tries to reawaken the Friends' old radical fervour. She calls on Charles II to 'come down from his Throne and sit in the Dust' and to release imprisoned radicals. Having addressed nobles and church ministers, she then rebukes her fellow-believers for trying to 'limit the Spirit of the living God' and reminds them of their former egalitarianism.

Morgan, Elaine (Floyd), science writer, journalist and (chiefly TV) playwright. B. in 1920 at Pontypridd, Wales, da. of Olive (Neville) and mineworker William F., she was educ. at Pontypridd Girls' School and Lady Margaret Hall, Oxford (BA in English, 1942). She married Morien M. in 1945 and has three sons. Her plays and TV scripts include *The Waiting Room* (for women), 1958, *Teli'r Teulu* (in Welsh, with Jean Scott Rogers), 1960, and work on the award-winning screening of Vera BRITTAIN's *Testament of Youth*, 1980. She became internationally known with *The Descent of Woman*, 1972, which argues, from a controversial theory of Prof. Alister Hardy, that many characteristics differentiating humans from other primates result from a prehistoric period of aquatic adaptation. Feminists welcomed her stress on the shaping influence of the needs of females and young, as a challenge to older established theories leaning towards a notion of 'man the hunter'. In *The Aquatic Ape*, 1982, EM pursued a point-by-point comparison with such theories. She has also examined 'cleaner and greener' alternatives to declining urban civilization (*Falling Apart*, 1976) and the future of the South Wales valleys, 1977.

Morgan, Robin, feminist theorist, poet, journalist, b. in 1941 in Lake Worth, Fla., da. of Faith Berkely M. A student at Columbia Univ., RM became an anti-war activist and freelance writer urging the New Left ('the boys' movement') to see Women's Liberation as a necessary part of a necessary social revolution. In 1970 she co-edited with Charlotte Bunch and Joanne Cooke *The New Women*, and herself edited the influential anthology *Sisterhood is Powerful: An Anthology of Writings from the Women's Liberation Movement*, which addresses questions of race, class, lesbianism and cultural representation, and includes historic women's movement documents (the Bill of Rights, the SCUM Manifesto, and WITCH Documents). *Going Too Far: The Personal Chronicles of a Feminist*, 1977 (RM's writings, 1962–77), including letters to her husband (married 1962), poet Kenneth Pitchford, provides a history of the US women's movement from within as RM traces her shift from sixties radical ('conforming to the dogma of non-conformity') to a transformative feminist consciousness. *Sisterhood is Global: The International Women's Movement Anthology*, 1984, collects facts about the condition of women (divorce, economics, abortion) in 70 countries with an essay from a citizen of each. *The Anatomy of Freedom: Feminism, Physics, and Global Politics*, 1984, a personal and poetic exposition of contemporary consciousness from RM's inclusive feminist stance, describes her invention, with her husband, of what became the logo for the women's movement (a clenched fist within the universal sign of female): 'that a woman and man together ... were able to offer this gift to her people as a tool – isn't this actually a sign of hope?' A contributing editor and frequent contributor to *Ms*, RM has published poems: *Monster*, 1972, *Lady of the Beasts*, 1976, and *Depth Perception*, 1982, in which 'something alive before / only in Anywoman's dreamings / begins to stretch, arch, unfold', and *Upstairs in the Garden: Selected and New Poems, 1969–89*. *The Demon Lover: On the Sexuality of Terrorism*, 1989, analyses the Middle East conflict and interviews women in the Gaza Strip and the West Bank from the perspective of an 'apostatic Jew' and feminist. Interview in *Off Our Backs*, April 1989.

Morgan, Sydney (Owenson), Lady, 1776–1859, novelist and Irish nationalist. Probably b. on board ship in the Irish Sea, da. of English Jane (Mill) and actor Robert O. (*né* MacOwen), and sister of Olivia CLARKE, she read Shakespeare and Irish legends while at Protestant boarding schools. In 1801 she pub. *Poems* and in 1803 *St. Clair*, a novel of sensibility with lively heroine, which romanticizes the Irish past. Taken up by society, she left her governess job and revealed her ambivalent feminism in the stated aim to be 'every inch a woman'. *The Novice of St Dominick*, 1806, a well-researched historical novel whose heroine crosses France as a troubadour, attacked religious and political oppression. The famous *Wild Irish Girl*, also 1806, was savaged by J. W. Croker (always her enemy), but with *Patriotic Sketches of Ireland* and *The Lay of an Irish Harp* (collected ballads as sung by herself), 1807, it made both her and romantic Ireland the fashion. *Ida of Athens*, 1809, with a learned heroine, was seen as feminist, yet ends 'it is for men to perform great actions, for women to inspire them'; *The Missionary*, 1811, set in India, inspired Byron, Shelley, and Moore. In 1812 she married the surgeon Charles M., who was then knighted. *O'Donnel*, 1814, *Florence Macarthy*, 1818 (which also satirizes Croker), *Absenteeism*, 1825, and *The O'Briens and the O'Flahertys*, 1827, repr. 1988, expressed radicalism about Ireland, England and America which brought violent attack as well as later praise (as 'chivalrous' from O'Connell. *France*, 1817 (written after a visit to Paris and meeting with STAËL, 1816). *Italy*, 1821, and *Salvator Rosa*, 1824, continue her assault on reactionary regimes. She was the first woman to receive a pension, 1837, 'for services to the world of letters'; Geraldine JEWSBURY became her friend and amanuensis. *The Book of the*

Boudoir, 1829, and *Pages from my Autobiography*, 1859, are trivial hotch-potches. *Woman and Her Master*, 1840, a fascinating historical quest (covering the Bible, Asian and African sources) for the deeds of 'this Pariah of the species, this alien to law, this dupe of fictions and subject of force', concludes that her role is one of 'spiritual and affectionate activity'. Lives by A. L. Stevenson, 1936, Mary Campbell, 1988.

'Morley, Susan', Sarah Frances Spedding, 1836–1921, novelist, b. Newcastle-on-Tyne, second of four children of Jane (Headlam) and John S. (d. 1839), whose brother was James S., Bacon scholar and friend of Tennyson. Little is known of her life, but she published at least five novels. The first, *Aileen Ferrers*, 1874, has good northern and class conflict scenes, turning on a niece adopted into a well-to-do family. *Throstlethwaite*, 1875, and *Margaret Chetwynd*, 1877, are ordinary tales of romance, but *Corbie's Pool*, 1882, and *Dolly Loraine*, 1888, contain interesting 'bad girls', and reveal a sharpness about the position of women as writers and intellectuals. She always used her pseudonym, never married, and died at Sweet Haws Grange, Crowborough, Sussex.

Morrell, Lady **Ottoline** Anne Violet (Bentinck), 1873–1938, memoirist, hostess, b. in London, youngest child of Augusta Mary Elizabeth (Brown), later in her own right Lady Bolsover, and Lt-Gen. Arthur Cavendish-Bentinck. OM's title came to her by special favour of Queen Victoria when her half-brother became Duke of Portland. She was educ. by her mother at Welbeck Abbey, the family seat, and later studied for admission to St Andrews Univ. (but did not attend) and, briefly, at Somerville, Oxford. She married solicitor Philip M., for many years an MP and, like her, an ardent pacifist, in 1902. Of their twins, b. 1906, one survived. OM launched her reputation as a society and literary hostess at 44 Bedford Square, London. Her memoirs (two vols., ed. Robert Gathorne-Hardy, 1963, 1974) remember the luminaries she entertained there and, after 1913, at her farm at Garsington, near Oxford. Here, during WWI, she harboured conscientious objectors; her husband argued their case in parliament. Garsington came to seem 'home' to D. H. Lawrence (who nevertheless drew a cruel portrait of her in *Women in Love*), and many others visited – Carrington, Lytton Strachey, Maynard Keynes, Katherine Mansfield, Mark Gertler, T. S. Eliot, Aldous Huxley. OM's memoirs recall these in sometimes lavish detail. She quarrelled famously with Roger Fry, and was lover of both Augustus John and Bertrand Russell. Called by Lord David Cecil in his *DNB* account 'a character of Elizabethan extravagance and force', she figures in the memoirs of others: see Woolf's letters and diaries, Russell's memoirs, 1968, Michael Holroyd's life of Lytton Strachey, 1979, Frieda Lawrence's memoirs, 1961 and 1964. Life by Sandra Johnson Darroch, 1975.

Morrer, Lizelia Augusta (Jenkins), Afro-American poet about whom little is known. Her 1907 volume, *Prejudice Unveiled*, is unique in its strong protest against the treatment of her race in the turn-of-the-century period of increased violent racism and segregation. Her poems appear in vol. 3 of *Collected Black Women's Poetry*, Schomburg Library series, 1988.

Morris, Margaret (Hill), 1737–1816, Quaker diarist and letter writer, sister of Milcah Martha Moore. In 1758 she married William M. (d. 1766); three of her six children died as babies. Her journal covering the War of Independence in Burlington, NJ, written for Moore, privately printed 1836, presents herself as a helpless, yet wily and intrepid, widow. She concealed a hunted Tory, doctored the sick 'according to art', and effectively fixed a broken swingletree with ribbons and garters. See 1949 ed.: also repr. in *Letters* of her father and family, 1854, with a religious diary, 1751–71, and letters during the yellow fever epidemic at Philadelphia, 1793. When widowed she dreamed six lines of verse spoken to her by her husband; in another dream a prophetess (later identified as the Church) led her 'safe home' and blessed her children.

Morris, Myra Evelyn, 1873–1966, novelist, short-story writer, poet, b. Boort, Victoria, da. of Bessie Lily (Sydenham) and Charles William M., grocer. She was educ. at Rochester Brigidine Convent, and pub. her early verse in the *Bulletin*. Upon leaving school she became a freelance writer, publishing poems, stories and a children's novel, *Us Five*, 1922, before moving to Melbourne, then Frankston in 1927. She contributed to many journals and anthologies and pub. two other novels, *The Wind on the Water*, 1938, and *Dark Tumult*, 1939, plus a collection of short stories, *The Township*, 1947. Her poetry appeared in *England and Other Verses*, 1911, *The Little Track* (with others), 1922, and *White Magic*, 1929. MM's talent as a writer is seen at its best in her stories, with their spare and sharp characterizations tempered with sympathy for the problems of relationships. Her work had wide popularity, appeared in numerous newspapers and magazines, was broadcast on radio and transl. into several languages.

Morrison, Toni (Chloe Anthony Wofford), novelist, b. in 1931 in Lorain, Ohio, da. of Ramah (Willis) and George W. in a family in which 'signs, visitations, and ways of knowing that transcended concrete reality' were commonplace. She grew up in a racially mixed working-class neighbourhood, the setting for her early novels. Educ. at Howard Univ. (BA 1953) and Cornell (MA for a thesis on WOOLF and Faulkner, 1955), she taught English and creative writing at Texas Southern Univ., Howard, and later at Columbia and Yale. She holds the Albert Schweitzer Chair in the Humanities at the State Univ. of New York. At Howard, she married Jamaican architect Harold M. and had two sons. They separated; she went to New York with her children, 1964, eventually becoming a senior editor at Random House. (She edits, among others, Toni Cade BAMBARA, Angela DAVIS and Gayl JONES.) She wrote *The Bluest Eye*, 1970, 'in a corner', 'alone with two children in a town where I didn't know anybody'; as she wrote, she 'reclaimed my self and the world – a real revelation. I named it. I described it. I listed it. I identified it. I recreated it.' In the novel, the tough little black girl Claudia, trying to make sense of her world, tells the story of Pecola Breedlove, raped by her father, possessed of the belief that she has magically acquired the blue eyes that will make her lovable. 'I was Pecola,' says TM, 'Claudia, everybody'. *Sula*, 1973, named for the main character ('like any artist with no art form, she became dangerous'), shatters black female stereotypes in its Peace women and the friendship of Sula and Nel. *Song of Solomon*, 1977 (National Book Critics Award and first Book-of-the-Month Club choice by a black author since *Native Son*, 1940), centres on Milkman Dead, named for his adolescent habit of nursing at his mother's breast. TM says that having sons has given her insight into a 'male view of the world'. *Tar Baby*, 1981, TM's only novel to show much relationship between blacks and whites, treats the encounter of a sophisticated black model with a Sorbonne education financed by wealthy white employers and an unsophisticated southern country man. *Beloved*, 1987, based on the murder of her children by a woman who refuses to have them returned to slavery, blurs lines of history, psychology and magic as the mysterious Beloved appears full grown to take up life with the mother who cut her throat. TM says, 'I am not interested in indulging myself in some private exercise of my imagination ... which is to say, yes, the work must be political.' See interviews in Tate, 1983, and in *Time*, 22 May 1989; 'biracial and bicultural' study by Karla F. C. Holloway and Stephanie A. Demetrakopoulos, *New Dimensions of Spirituality*, 1987; critical essays ed. Nellie Y. McKay, 1988; and extended conversation with Gloria NAYLOR in *SoR*, 21, 1985. See also Ronda Glickin, *Black American Women in Literature: A Bibliography, 1976 through 1987*, 1989.

Mortimer, Penelope Ruth (Fletcher), also Dimont, 'Ann Temple', novelist, b. in 1918 at Rhyl, North Wales, da. of Amy Caroline (Maggs) and the 'highly eccentric' Rev. Arthur Forbes F. She was educ. at private schools as her father 'changed theories and residences'. She spent a year at London Univ., then gave up her first secretarial position after three weeks, and married journalist Charles Dimont in 1937. Divorced, she married writer John M. in 1949 (divorced, 1972). She wrote her first novel, *Johanna*, 1947, as 'Penelope Dimont' and a lonely hearts column for the London *Daily Mail* as 'Ann Temple'. She has collaborated with her second husband on a travel book, *With Love and Lizards*, 1957, has written TV plays and screenplays, including a TV adaptation of COLETTE's *Ripening Seed*. Her fiction includes *A Villa in Summer*, 1954, *The Bright Prison*, 1956, *Daddy's Gone A-Hunting*, 1958, *Saturday Lunch with the Brownings*, 1960, *My Friend Says It's Bullet Proof*, 1967, *The Home*, 1971, and *Long Distance*, 1974. *The Pumpkin Eater*, 1962, is about a woman, often perceived by male characters as insane, who is 'obsessed' with pregnancy: to her it is power and purpose. Her husband persuades her to have an abortion and sterilization: 'anyone would think the emancipation of women had never happened'. It was filmed, with a script by Harold Pinter, 1964. Other works focus intensely on women's experience of married and family life among the English professional classes. The central character of *The Handyman*, 1983, is a recently widowed woman confronted with the frightening potential of freedom. PM has four children from her first marriage and two from her second, lectured at the New School for Social Research and Boston Univ., 1975–6, and is a fellow of the Royal Society of Literature.

Morton, Martha, 1865–1925, dramatist, b. NYC, of English parentage. She was educ. in England and then NY, at public schools and the Normal College. Encouraged by her mother, she began writing while still in school, stories that were published in newspapers and magazines, then plays, the first self-produced. *The Merchant*, 1891, won $5,000 in the *New York World* play contest. She reportedly earned more than a million dollars in the years that followed. She wrote, directed and produced 35 plays; an original novel, *Val Sinistre*, 1924, was published just before her death. MM was widely recognized as the 'first successful woman playwright' in America. She wrote many romantic comedies for particular players. Her least successful but most serious play, *On the Eve*, 1909, is about 'the woman of today, the universal woman seeking her work and finding it'. The public much preferred her light plays, including *A Fool of Fortune*, 1896, *Her Lord and Master*, 1912, and *A Bachelor's Romance*, 1896, for which she earned more than $125,000 in royalties. More important than any of her writings was MM's work to get professional recognition for women playwrights. Excluded from membership in the American Dramatists Club, MM founded the Society of Dramatic Authors in January 1907. It was open to all, and its success led to a merger of the two organizations with full membership for women and men. See Rosemary Gipson, 'MM, America's First Professional Woman Playwright', *Theatre Survey* 23, 2 (Nov. 1982).

Morton, Sarah Wentworth (Apthorp), 'Philenia', 1759–1846, poet. One of 11 children of loyalists Sarah (Wentworth) and James A., of Boston, Mass., she was well educ. and proud of her ancestry; her poems were admired in MS before her marriage, 1781, to Perez M., lawyer, orator, and patriot. In 1784 he bought her family home, on which they centred a busy social life. In 1788 her sister Fanny killed herself, having borne Perez M. a child; SWM apparently held him less to blame than her father. (From 1860 *The Power of Sympathy*, William Hill Brown's novel about this affair, which her family tried to suppress, was, oddly, ascribed to her.) She published in the *Massachusetts Magazine* from its founding, 1789 (at first as 'Constantia', then, realizing the prior claim of Judith Sargent MURRAY, as 'Philenia'), and was the only woman in Elihu Smith's first American anthology, 1793. Her work dwells on pain, loss and fidelity. Author of sonnets (then rare in the USA) and hymns for several denominations, she favoured ABOLITION but not, like Perez M., the French Revolution. They both backed Boston's first theatre, 1795. In *Ouâbi, or The Virtues of Nature*, 1790, an Indian chief cedes his wife to the European hero; *Beacon Hill*, first (and only) part, 1797, glorifies war heroes but says an author has 'no sex'; *The Virtues of Society*, 1799, celebrates a real-life heroine. A friend of John and Abigail ADAMS (relying much on male mentors), SWM praised Mercy WARREN and was praised by Sarah WOOD. From about 1811 her great reputation declined; her husband and six children died before her. Her last work, *My Mind and Its Thoughts*, 1823, was the first to bear her name; her self-analysis, she says, stems from sorrow. Life by Emily Pendleton and Milton Ellis, 1931; MSS in Huntington.

Mosse, Henrietta (Rouviere), d. 1835, novelist, b. in Ireland but writing in London, for MINERVA (ten titles known; others mentioned). She began anonymously, for pleasure, with *Lussington Abbey*, 1804. *Heirs of Villeroy* [1805], with her name, was well reviewed. She had already begun research in the BM and was gathering subscribers for *A Peep at our Ancestors*, set in the twelfth century; but factors including her mother's illness delayed it till 1807. Its heroine rides to war with her husband (for Matilda against Stephen). As often in HRM's work, letters occur in the narrative and female friendship is stressed. She married businessman Isaac M. by 1812, when she published *Arrivals from India*; by 1822 he was reduced, by paralytic strokes, fraud and commercial loss, to 'second childhood': her writing (done while he slept) became their support. *A Father's Love, and a Woman's Friendship*, 1825, pursues the courtships of four lively sisters, and their mother's past history (in letters) of marriage against her rich father's will, and brutal rejection as 'other people's property'. *Gratitude, and Other Tales*, 1826, is prefaced with a tirade against modern luxury; *Woman's Wit, and Man's Wisdom*, 1827, has a pathetic preface and opens at a deathbed; the heroine of *The Blandfords*, 1829 (which earned £30), is briefly a downtrodden governess; yet some humour and high spirits remain. In 1830 HRM was planning a short work on 'Distresses of Women', but doubted she had the drive to get anything done with her several dramatic pieces. The RLF made her many payments, but denied funeral expenses; she died in a 'miserable attic'.

Mott, Lucretia (Coffin), 1793–1880, Quaker minister, woman's-rights advocate, and ABOLITIONIST, was b. in Nantucket, Mass., the da. of Anna (Folger) and Thomas C., a sea captain and merchant. She first attended the Nantucket Quaker School, then public and private schools in Boston. In 1806, she entered Nine Partners, a co-ed. Friends' school near Poughkeepsie, NY, where she soon became an assistant teacher. Noting the discrepancy between men's and women's salaries, she vowed to gain for women 'all that an impartial Creator had bestowed'. In 1811, she m. James M., a fellow teacher who had begun to work in her father's store in Philadelphia. They had six children. In 1818, she made her first appearance as a minister, and in 1821 she was recorded as a minister of the Society of Friends. Because of her friendship with William Lloyd Garrison, she attended the organizational convention in 1833 for the American Anti-Slavery Society and, in 1837, the Anti-Slavery Convention of American Women. Chosen in 1840 as a delegate to the World's Antislavery Convention in London, she discovered that women were not to be seated at the Convention. At this time, LM met Elizabeth Cady STANTON, and the two decided to form a woman's rights group. In 1848, they and Martha Coffin Wright, LM's sister, called the first Woman's Rights Convention in Seneca Falls, NY. LM delivered the opening and closing addresses, although her husband presided as chair. The Declaration of Sentiments of the convention, which LM co-authored, stated 'We hold these truths to be self-evident, that all men and women are created equal.' During this period, LM pub. two articles, 'Diversities', 1844, and 'What Is Anti-Slavery Work', 1846, both in *The Liberty Bell*. In 1849 (pub. 1850), she argued in the *Discourse on Women* that women were 'inferior' because of historical repressions, and declared: 'we deny that the present position of woman is her true sphere of usefulness'. In 1866 she was elected president of the first convention of the American Equal Rights Association. Although she remained a lifelong Quaker (see, especially, *A Sermon to the Medical Students*, 1849), she helped found the Free Religous Association in 1867. Her letters and papers are in the Mott Manuscript Collection, Friends' Historical Library at Swarthmore College and the Garrison Family Papers, the Sophia Smith Collection at Smith College. The DIARY of her 1840 trip to the World's Antislavery Convention has been pub. as *Slavery and 'The WOMAN QUESTION'*, 1952, ed. Frederick B. Tolles. D. Greene collected and ed. her extant sermons and speeches as *LM: Her Complete Speeches and Sermons*, 1981. *James and Lucretia Mott*, 1884, by Anna Davis Hallowell, their granddaughter, is still valuable, as is Otelia Cromwell's 1958 study. Margaret Hope Bacon's life, 1980, contains a bibliography.

Moulton, Louise (Chandler), 1835–1908, poet, sketch writer and novelist, b. near Pomfret, Conn., da. of Louise Rebecca (Clark) and Lucius Lemuel Chandler, farmer. She was educ. at the Rev. Roswell Park's School (Christ Church Hall) and later at Emma WILLARD's Troy, NY, Female Seminary. She pub. her first poem at 15, and in 1853 she ed. *The Book of the Boudoir: or, A Memento of Friendship* and *The Waverley Garland: A Present for All Seasons*. Her first book, *This, That and the Other*, 1854, pub. under 'Ellen Louise', contained both poems and sketches. In 1855 she m. William Upham M., publisher of *The True Flag*, in which her work had appeared, and the same year she pub. a novel, *June Clifford: A Tale*. For the next 20 years she contributed sketches to journals such as *Godey's, Atlantic Monthly* and *Youth's Companion*. Her children's stories were collected in 1873; her narrative sketches in 1874 as *Some Women's Hearts*, and in 1877 a collection of poems, *Swallow Flights*, appeared. From 1870–6 she was a reviewer for the *New York Tribune* and, from 1887–91, for the *Boston Sunday Herald*. Beginning soon after her marriage, she held a Friday salon which attracted such writers as Longfellow, Emerson, Whittier and Lowell. In 1876 she made her first trip to England where she became acquainted with Swinburne, the Rossettis, Wilde, and later Yeats and Pound. She helped the pre-Raphaelites to gain recognition in the USA, editing Philip Bourke Marston, 1887, 1891 and 1892, and writing a study of Arthur O'Shaughnessy, 1894. A second collection of her poems, *In the Garden of Dreams*, appeared in 1889. Her poems, appealing more to British than American readers, are delicate and fragile, with an undercurrent of lost love, lost youth, and contemplations of death. 'A Woman's Knowledge' proves to be only that she is 'a moment's pleasure' for the man, who is her 'sun-god'. Her later sketches, more realistic, often send young American women to Europe for wooing: the heroine from the title story of *Miss Eyre from Boston and Others*, 1889, is a Daisy Miller who survives to return to America and her true love. She left a valuable collection of 900 volumes to the Boston Public Library. Her friend Harriett Prescott SPOFFORD provided biographical information in several works, including *A Little Book of Friends*, 1919, and her intro. to LCM's coll. poems, 1909. The only full-length study is by Lilian Whiting, 1910. Her papers are in the Library of Congress and at the American Antiquarian Society, Worcester, Mass.

Mountain Wolf Woman, oral autobiographer, b. in 1884 in Wisconsin, of the Winnebego nation. She was given a Wolf Clan name when her mother gave the sick child as an honorary gift to an old lady who in return gave the child both her longevity and her name. *Mountain Wolf Woman: The Autobiography of a Winnebego Indian*, 1961, was edited by Nancy Oestreich Lurie, MWW's adopted niece, an ethnologist whose specialized knowledge and personal relationship with MWW provides helpful information about Winnebego traditions and MWW's attitudes. MWW's father, as a member of the Thunder Clan, had no interest in reserved homestead land from the government when the Winnebego were 'relocated': 'I do not belong to the Earth'. Her mother, however, though from the Eagle Clan, also detached from the Earth, insisted on taking the forty acres, where her father built a log house. The family did not long settle and moved readily from state to state. MWW bitterly resented being given in marriage to a man to whom her brother had an obligation, but was told, '"this matter cannot be helped. When you are older ... you can marry whomever you yourself think that you want to marry." Mother said that to me and I did not forget it.' MWW's autonomy, her economic and marital independence, her mobility and assertivenss in learning the traditional medicine she wished to understand and her ability to integrate her Christian beliefs with her Peyote spiritual practices are presented in her own words. Her ORAL autobiography, first taped in Winnebego, was translated by MWW herself, with other bilingual aid when necessary. Her life incorporates the transition from independent traditional communities to the contemporary Indian existence. MWW had eleven children and raised several grandchildren as alcohol and dispersion dislocated family life. She describes plainly shifts in her life as she and her second husband struggled to stay free. 'Who is our boss?' precedes each decision MWW makes before moving on, often to be close to some family member. See Gretchen M. Bataille and Kathleen Mullen Sands, *American Indian Women: Telling Their Lives*, 1984. Brief critical discussion by Helen Carr in Bella Brodzki and Celeste Schenk, eds., *Life/Lines: Theorizing Women's Autobiography*, 1988.

Mouré, Erin, poet. B. in 1953 in Calgary, Alberta, da. of Mary Irene (Grendys) and William Benedict M., she studied briefly at the Univs. of Calgary and BC, moving to Vancouver in 1974. Education for her is 'talking' with other women, such as Montréal writer Gail SCOTT. She has worked for VIA Rail since 1978, in management since moving to Montréal, 1984. A student of Al Purdy's in 1973 in Banff, she appears in his poetry anthology *Storm Warning 2*, 1976. In *Empire York Street*, 1979 and *The Whisky Vigil*, 1981, the predominantly female voice of her poems speaks of work experience, social issues and the complexity of relationships, especially those of women but also among poet, persona and audience. *Wanted Alive*, 1983, written in the vernacular ('The short

& bumpy sentences of the heart'), situates language and writing, two recurring themes, in the physical world ('The words stay silent on the page, their usual selves, / picking lice from under their collars'). In *Domestic Fuel*, 1985, about marriage, divorce (she has been married once) and loving women, the incisive imagery and line-breaks speak of the body of language and love ('Oh alphabet, your secret nest is harboured in my tongue ... As if it were nature / I could kiss any *man* & pretend it's you'). *Furious*, 1988, poems 'Combining the colloquial expression with the words of the intellect' and 'furious' about 'the way people use language', won the Governor-General's Medal for Poetry. See her statement on poetics, *Quarry*, 32, 1983, and interviews in *BC*, April 1981, and *Rubicon*, Summer 1984.

Mourning Dove (Hum-ishu-ma), Christal Quintasket, 1888–1936, folklorist and author of the first known novel by a Native American woman. B. near Bonner's Ferry, Idaho, she was the da. of Lucy (Stukin), a full-blood Scho-yel-pi or Colville, and Joseph Quintasket, whose Irish father had not honoured his tribal marriage ceremony. Like her character Cogewea, she was a 'breed! – the socially ostracized of two races.' At seven and 13 she went to the Sacred Heart Convent in Ward, Washington, where she was educated to the third grade level, but was both times called home to care for younger siblings. From her maternal grandmother, Soma-how-atqu, who appears in *Cogawea* (pub. 1927) as the Stemteema, and from a group of women story-tellers, she learned the ORAL traditions and rituals of her tribe. A renowned rider, MD took part in 'squaw' races and often rode into the mountains to hunt and camp. From 17 to 21, she attended government Indian schools (as unpaid matron for 60 to 70 girls). To facilitate her work with Okanogan folkloric materials and the novel she was writing, MD studied English and typing at a Calgary business school, 1912–13. In 1914 she met ethnographer, writer and defender of the Indian cause, Lucullus V. McWhorter, who encouraged her in her folklore work and her novel, *Cogewea the Half-Blood: A Depiction of the Great Montana Cattle Range*, which she finished in 1916. His help unfortunately included much rewriting, in a pompous, stilted style quite unlike hers. Some critics conclude that he had written the entire work and, because of its departure from MD's own 'knowledge of how an Okanogan story should go' (meandering 'gracefully from event to event', unified by 'the relationship of the tale to the ritual life of the tribe'), Paula Gunn ALLEN sees *Cogewea* as a 'martyred' book. Not finally published until 1927, and then only with MD's own financial support, the novel blends tribal narrative and western romance. Married briefly to Hector McLeod, a Flathead Indian, MD married Fred Galler, a Wenatchee, in 1919. MD spent years as a migrant agricultural labourer, continuing her literary work despite poverty and fatigue. Her 'folklores', gathered with difficulty from suspicious Indians who had been paid for stories by another collector, were printed in *Coyote Stories*, 1933, repr. with deleted chapters restored, forthcoming 1990. See Dexter Fisher's introduction to *Cogewea*, 1981, which includes McWhorter's biographical 'To the Reader'; Allen, *The Sacred Hoop*, 1986; MD's fragmentary autobiography ed. Jay Miller, 1990.

Mowatt, Anna Cora (Ogden), later Ritchie, 1819–70, US playwright, novelist, journalist and actress, b. in Bordeaux, France, ninth child of Eliza (Lewis) and Samuel Gouverneur O.'s 14 children. Educ. chiefly at home, in 1834 she eloped with James M., NY lawyer. Childless, they adopted three orphans. In 1841, his poor health and loss of fortune led her to begin writing and to give public poetry readings. 1845 saw her acting debut in NY, initiating a successful career across the USA and England, and an acclaimed production of her first play,

Fashion; or Life in New York. Stressing the corruptness of city life, it is an incisive sketch of NY manners. Strongly influenced by R. B. Sheridan, it has been called the first truly native American drama (but cf. M. O. WARREN). She wrote novels about NY society, notably *The Fortune Hunter*, 1844, and *Evelyn*, 1845. In 1851, M. died; in 1854, AM m. William R., journalist. In her novels about the theatre, she advocates that women be allowed to develop their abilities in order to earn a living: 'To what end has Heaven gifted me with equal talents, if I am not to use them?' (*Mimic Life*, 1856). *Twin Roses*, 1857, presents women before and behind the curtain, striving for financial independence. In addition to 12 works of fiction, she wrote biography and magazine articles on domestic subjects. Her *Autobiography of an Actress*, 1854, a frank, engaging testimony to the life of a remarkable woman, was admired by Hawthorne. Edgar Allan Poe saw in her novels 'glimpses ... of a genius.' Her life, *The Lady of Fashion*, 1954, is by Eric W. Barnes; also some MSS at the Schlesinger Library, Radcliffe.

Moyes, Patricia (Pakenham-Walsh), crime novelist. Da. of Marion (Boyd) and Ernst Pakenham-Walsh, an Indian colonial judge, she was b. in 1923 in Bray, Co. Wicklow, Ireland, and educ. at Overstone School, Northampton. She was a Flight Officer (WAAF) during WWII, m. photographer John M. in 1951 (divorced, 1959), and worked as secretary to a film company, then as assistant editor of *Vogue*, 1954–8. She published *Dead Men Don't Ski* in 1959, the year of her divorce. In 1962 she m. John S. Haszard, later an official of the International Court of Justice; living in the Netherlands, Switzerland, the USA and the West Indies, as well as her sporting hobbies, have fuelled her novels. These, centred on Scotland Yard man Henry Tibbett and his wife Emmy, represent a return to the classic DETECTIVE FICTION: well-plotted, lighthearted puzzles, a game between author and reader with a fair display of clues. PM's strong first novel sets its victim creepily in a ski-lift; *Murder à la Mode*, 1963, takes place in the fashion industry, *Falling Star*, 1964, in the film world. PM has written more than 20 novels, most recently *Six Letter Word for Death*, 1983, and *Night Ferry to Death*, 1985. Her adaptation of Jean Anouilh's play *Time Remembered* was produced in London in 1954 and in NYC in 1957.

Mozley, Anne, 1809–91, poet, critic and essayist, b. Gainsborough, Lincs., da. of Jane and Henry M., bookseller and publisher. She was one of 11 children; James Bowling M. (Regius Professor of Divinity at Oxford) and Thomas M. (clergyman and journalist) were her brothers. In 1815 the family moved to Derby. Educ. at home (the sisters had a mathematics master), AM spent most of her life there. Her early publications included the children's stories, *The Captive Maiden*, a tale of the third century, and *Female Heroism*, a collection of real-life incidents. She wrote three vols. of poetry : *Church Poetry*, 1843, *Days and Seasons or Church Poetry for the Year*, 1845, and *Poetry Past and Present*, 1849, all pub. by the family firm. *Essays on Social Subjects* from the *Saturday Review*, 1864, written 'from the point of view of a single writer's personal experience', includes essays on moral issues such as prejudice. AM also contributed to *Blackwood's*, *Saturday Review* and *Bentley's Quarterly*, in which her review of George ELIOT's *Adam Bede*, concluding that the author must be a woman, appeared and was described by Eliot as 'on the whole the best we have seen'. She wrote anonymously, adopting an authoritative male persona. No-one outside the family knew that she wrote. In 1867 her mother died, and she went to live with her sister Elizabeth at Barrow-on-Trent. She ed. her brother James's sermons, essays and letters, and the letters of Cardinal Newman, whose two sisters were her sisters-in-law. She also designed church embroideries from medieval patterns. AM went blind at the end of her life. There is a memoir by F. Mozley in *Essays from Blackwood*, 1892.

Mozley, Harriet (Newman), 1803–52, writer of novels and tales for young people, b. London, da. of Jemima (Fourdrinier) and John N., banker (bankrupted 1821). Educ. with her sisters at home and at her aunt's school, all learned Latin. HM was closest to her elder brother John (later Cardinal N.), who feared her first novel, *The Fairy Bower*, 1840, was 'too brilliant'. It is a realistic, witty and uncondescending narrative of the interrelations of a group of children one Christmas holiday: children and adults alike enjoyed it. 1840 also saw the birth of her only child (she had m. Tom M. in 1836, the year her mother died). In 1841 she pub. a sequel, *The Lost Brooch*, and in 1842 her only adult novel, *Louisa*, unusual at that date for its realistic depiction of middle-class life. It figures a young girl with wider knowledge and usefulness, coming to terms with her early married life; its composition was affected by HM's increasing ill-health, and by her distress at her brother's progress towards the RC church. In 1852 her story coll., *Family Adventures*, appeared: written ten years earlier, most were based on her childhood. Charlotte YONGE acknowledged a debt to HM. Her amusing, intelligent letters are sel. in Dorothea Mozley, ed., *Newman Family Letters*, 1962. See also Kathleen Tillotson's splendid essay in G. and K. Tillotson, *Mid-Victorian Studies*, 1965.

Mudd, Ann, b. *c.* 1613, pamphleteer, of Rickmansworth, Herts. Having left the Quakers, with her husband Thomas, in support of John and Mary PENNYMAN, she pub. *A Cry, A Cry*, 1678, recording their decision to leave and calling on Quakers to 'arise from your self-conceitness'. 'O you that are fat and full, and very rich too, I must tell you, that it is the Meek and Lowly that shall inherit the Kingdom, and not You.' John Pennyman's autobiography, 1696, prints some of her letters from 1670 to 1693, when she said she was 'hasting to the Grave'.

Mugo, Micere M. Githae, poet, playwright, scholar, b. in 1942 in Baricho, in the Kirinyaga District of Kenya, of teacher parents who insisted on equal education for their ten children, making their daughters 'feel as important as any male child'. Named 'Madeleine' by her parents, she changed her name to a version of her mother's. 'Privileged', she acted in school plays at Kangaru Girls' School, studied drama under Rebeka NJAU at Alliance Girls' High School, and won the best actress award at the Uganda Drama Festival at Makerere Univ., where she took an Honours BA in English, 1966. The first African 'allowed' to study at an all-white school, she spent two terms at Limuru, 1961–2, venting her frustration in poetry. In 1955, at Alliance, influenced by the English curriculum, she wrote a praise poem to her dormitory in Elizabethan style. At Makerere, she published poetry expressing her own convictions and a short story in *Penpoint*. Impressed by Okot p'Bitek's collections of Ugandan folk poetry, she showed her own poetry on local themes to Chinua Achebe and Eldred Jones, who encouraged her. MM studied at the Univ. of New Brunswick, Canada, 1969–73, receiving her MA for her play *The Long Illness of Ex-Chief Kiti*, in which an extended Kenyan family suffers the bitterness of divided loyalties in war-time: pub. 1976, with her radio play, 'Disillusioned', in which a Kenyan nun leaves the convent because of the white mother superior's racism. MM's PhD dissertation became *Visions of Africa: The Fiction of Chinua Achebe, Margaret* LAURENCE, *Elspeth* HUXLEY *and Ngugi Wa Thiong'o*, 1978. MM's poems, printed in *Okike* and *Fiddlehead* and broadcast on the BBC, are collected in *Daughter of My People, Sing!*, 1976. Ironic, passionate, and sometimes bitter, they express concern for people divided by post-colonial 'commercialism, calculated opportunism, cut-throat materialism' and belief in women's strength: 'I see warriors / me Katilili / Mary Muthoni Nyabjiru / Rosa Parks / Angela DAVIS.' She collaborated with Ngugi on a play in Swahili and *The Trial of Dedan Kimathi*, 1976, which is in print in both Swahili and English. Since the mid 1970s, MM has been at the Univ. of Nairobi, Senior Lecturer in English, then Dean. Interviews with Nancy Owano in *Africa Woman* 6, 1976, and Brenda Berrian in *WLWE* 21, 1982.

Mugot, Hazel (deSilva), East African novelist and poet. B. ?1947 in Nairobi, her mother a Seychelles school teacher, her father a Sri Lankan accountant, she was educ. in Kenyan schools, then studied liberal arts in the US and social sciences in the UK. She returned to Kenya to work as a professional model while teaching at the Univ. of Nairobi, then moved to Mahe, Seychelles, where she writes, paints, and works with batiks and ceramics – aspects of 'traditional Seychelles life now nearly non-existent'. She has many siblings – in Kenya, Canada, Australia and the US – and a son. Her journalist sister, Enid deSilva Burke, encourages her writing. HM's first novel, *black night of quiloa*, 1971, depicts a cross-cultural marriage between an islander and a British anthropologist who takes Hima to the 'cold, cold world' of London, where he treats her more like a case study than a wife. HM, inspired by her own return home, writes of Hima, 'It was her island that kept her mind at peace', and 'which linked her to her heritage, traditions, background, and family ... after the clash of two cultures and the breakdown of her intercultural marriage'. HM sees writing as 'the only escape from the bondage most women are in mentally'. *Makonga, the Hyena* is a novel set in East Africa. In *Sega of the Seychelles*, 1983, which she wrote as deSilva, she splices couplets and phrases from the traditional *sega* (ORAL love laments) into her own poetic narrative. HM asserts that the role of women, still dominated by the slave-master relationship, is complicated by 'casual to lasting relationships, and always the problem of bringing up the children ... which is done mainly by the women, because, inevitably the man has other mistresses and leaves his wife'. HM is most at home with a poetic prose and traditional, folkloric themes in modern settings. See Taiwo, 1984.

Muir, Willa, Wilhelmina Johnstone (Anderson), 'Agnes Neill Scott', 1890–1970, poet, novelist, translator. Her parents came from the island of Unst, Shetland. She grew up 'among legends, fairy stories and Bible stories' at Montrose, Angus, where her father was a draper. She could speak several dialects at four, attended board school and Montrose Academy, but refused a scholarship to St Andrews Univ. to avoid separation from 'my rugby player' fiancé. In London from 1915, she was forced to resign as lecturer and vice-principal of a training college because her new fiancé, Edwin M., then an office clerk, '*doesn't believe in God*'. He also refused the role of dominant male; they married in 1919. WM taught in Glasgow; in 1921 they left for Europe, living in Prague, Dresden, Hellerau (where they ran a school with experimental educator A. S. Neill, 'living in a bright little world of our own, quite unaware that the climate outside was darkening'), Italy, Austria and the south of France. WM added to her store of languages, and they became 'a sort of TRANSLATION factory'. In 1925 Leonard and Virginia WOOLF published her *Women: an Inquiry* as Hogarth essay no. 10, on the 'more or less unconscious inheritance of militant patriarchal feeling' in Britain; WM accepts biological difference but addresses social assumptions. She and Edwin M. returned to England in 1927 (the year their son was born), and in 1935 to Scotland. WM translated over 40 books, mostly 1924–40, some as 'Agnes Neill Scott', some in her own name, some with her husband: from Kafka they translated six books and (for the *New Statesman*) diary excerpts. The two heroines of WM's first novel, *Imagined Corners*, 1931, share a name (through marriage) and pressure to be 'the guardians of decorum'; by the end, they have left their constricting marriages and are heading for Italy by train. Its sexual frankness and humour (to quell laughter Elizabeth says to herself 'I'm not me. I'm a wife, a woman') is matched in *Mrs. Ritchie*, 1933. *Mrs. Grundy in Scotland*, 1936, applies the flyting style to 'the new and bewildering attacks of the English philanthropists' on Scotland. WM lived in Prague again, 1945–9, and the US, 1955–6; she helped edit her husband's *Collected Poems*, 1960 (the year after his death). Her *Living with* BALLADS, 1965, stresses 'the underworld of feeling' in ORAL poetry. *Laconics, Jingles, and Other Verses*, 1969, includes 'Ballad of the Dominant Male'. See her memoir, *Belonging*, 1968, and books by and about Edwin M.

Mukherjee, Bharati, novelist, short-story writer, essayist, educator, b. in 1940 in Calcutta, the da. of Bina (Chatterjee) and Sudhir Lal, Brahmin Bengali chemist and businessman. Fostered by her father's ambition, her mother's determination to 'make sure that her daughters would be well-educated so no one can make them suffer' and two powerfully story-telling grandmothers, she was educ. at an Anglicized Bengali school in Ballgunge, 1944–8, where she read AUSTEN, Dickens and Forster, then in England and Switzerland, 1948–51. She became perfectly bilingual in English and Bengali but came to see herself as a 'shadow person'. Returning to Calcutta, 1951–9, she studied at Loreto House, and at the Univs. of Calcutta (BA, 1959), Baroda (MA, 1961), Iowa (MFA, 1963, PhD, 1969). She married Canadian writer Clark Blaise, 1963, had two children, and lived in Montréal, 1966–80. *The Tiger's Daughter*, 1972, *Wife*, 1975, and *Days and Nights in Calcutta*, 1977 (written jointly with her husband, about their 14-month stay in India), transmute BM's personal experiences and observations of 'lives ... sacrificed to notions of propriety and obedience', concluding that she can tell her own and other women's lives best through a voice that will 'astonish, even ... shock'. A citizen in 1971, she nevertheless refused to set her work in Canada, where 'to be a Third World woman writer' was 'to confine oneself to a narrow, airless, tightly roofed arena'. She emigrated to the US, 1980: 'I see myself as an American writer in the tradition of other American writers whose parents or grandparents had passed through Ellis Island. Indianness is now a metaphor'. The stories in *Darkness*, 1985, explore all the contributing streams of her literary consciousness, Bengali, expatriate, and immigrant. With Blaise, she wrote about the Air India tragedy, 1987. Stories in *The Middleman*, 1988, centre on upwardly mobile migrants from the Third World in the USA. Interviews in *Saturday Night*, March 1981, and *CFM*, 59, 1987, both quoted above. See Peter Nazareth in *CanL*, 110, 1986.

Mulford, Wendy (Rawlinson), poet, essayist, editor, b. 1941 at Woking, Surrey, da. of Clarice Russell (Clarke), cellist, and Gerald R. They divorced; her mother remarried; she grew up in Wales, partly on her grandmother's farm near Abergavenny. She was educ. at Newnham, Cambridge (BA in English, 1959, after changing from archaeology and anthropology). She m. Jeremy M. in 1962, divorced, and married poet John James in 1967; they have a daughter. She taught in schools, 1966–8, then in higher education, from 1971 for the Open Univ.: women's writing, women's HISTORY and feminist criticism. When she began to write, she says, she wondered 'what was speaking me?' 'How far did the illusion of selfhood, that most intimate and precious possession, reach? How could the lie of culture be broken up if the lie of the self made by that culture remained intact? And how could the lie of capitalist society be broken if the lie of culture were not broken?' A Marxist-feminist, belonging to the Communist Party and Women's Peace Movement, she has published in the journal *Red Letters*, 1976ff. As poetry editor with Cambridge Street, 1972–80, she published Veronica FORREST-THOMSON, Alice NOTLEY, and Denise RILEY, with whom she co-authored *No Fee: A Line or Two for Free*, 1978, and *Some Poems: 1968–1978*, 1982. Her own poetry volumes include *Bravo to Girls and Heroes*, 1977 (in which she attempts to 'reclaim the language' as a woman), *Reactions to Sunsets*, 1980, and *Late Spring Next Year*, 1987; her poems enfold puns, prose, and 'found' material. She took a degree in architecture at Cambridge in 1985, and has a special interest in co-operative housing, with which she does voluntary work. In WANDOR, ed., *On Gender and Writing*, 1983 (quoted above), she says 'I have been concerned to *produce* meaning *across* and in defiance of the repressive codes of everyday, communication-ready language.' She appeared in Sylvia Paskin, et al., eds., *Angels of Fire*, 1986, and has published a study of Sylvia Townsend WARNER and Valentine ACKLAND, 1988.

Mulholland, Rosa, Lady Gilbert, 1841–1921, Irish novelist, poet, children's writer, second da. of Dr Joseph Stevenson M., b. Belfast and educ. at home. An early comic story, 'Mrs Archie', *Cornhill*, Aug. 1863, was incorporated into *Eldergowan; or twelve months of my life: and other tales*, 1874. Her first novel, *Dunmara*, 1864, was later reissued as *The Story of Ellen*, 1907, under the name 'Ruth Murray'. Encouraged by Dickens, she wrote *Hester's History*, 1869, which he much admired, under her own name. She spent some years in the remote west of Ireland, and began to write children's stories and poetry such as *Vagrant Verses*, 1886. Her most interesting novels are set in Ireland and deal with Fenianism, the Land League, the evils of landlordism and the use of informers' evidence in the prosecution of nationalists: *Marcella Grace*, 1886, *A Fair Emigrant*, 1888, *Nanno*, 1899 (which she thought her best and which provoked some workhouse reform), and *Onora*, 1900 (repub. as *Norah of Waterford*, 1915). In 1891 she m. the historian John G. (knighted 1897, d. 1898). *The Tragedy of Chris*, 1903, a rather sensational story of a destitute woman's search for her young friend, a Dublin flower-seller decoyed to London, focuses unusually on the relations between women. In later life she tended to concentrate on stories (like 'The Lady Tantivy', *Temple Bar*, Jan. 1898), aimed at and about young women, several of which were reissued after her death.

Muller, Marcia, mystery writer, editor, and critic, b. 1944 in Detroit, da. of Kathryn (Minke) and Henry J. M. She was educated at the Univ. of Michigan (BA in English, 1966; MA in Journalism, 1971). In 1967, she m. Frederick T. Gilson, Jr. (divorced, 1981). She wrote freelance feature articles, worked in the merchandizing department of *Sunset* magazine, and published her first mystery, *Edwin of the Iron Shoes*, 1977, while working part-time. In its series character, Sharon McCone, MM was 'attempting to portray a contemporary American woman who happens also to be a private investigator ... not a superwoman, but a person with day-to-day problems'. McCone, who has appeared in *Ask the Cards a Question*, 1982, *The Cheshire Cat's Eye*, 1983, *Games to Keep the Dark Away*, 1984, and others, occupies a significant place in American DETECTIVE FICTION. (See MM, 'Creating a Female Sleuth', *The Writer*, Oct. 1978.) MM followed her, in *The Tree of Death*, 1983, and *The Legend of the Slain Soldiers*, 1985, with Chicana Elena Oliverez, curator of Mexican art museum in Santa Barbara. Some McCones also deal with ethnic community concerns: *There's Nothing to be Afraid Of*, 1985, is set in the Vietnamese refugee community in San Francisco. *Beyond the Grave* appeared in 1986. With Bill Pronzini she has written *The Lighthouse*, 1987, and compiled *1001 Midnights*, 1986, reviews of crime books. She has edited several anthologies, including, with Pronzini, *The Web She Weaves: An Anthology of Mystery and Suspense Stories by Women*, 1983. See her articles in *The Writer*, Dec. 1983, and June 1987, and Pronzini, *The Ethnic Detectives*, 1985.

Muller, Mary Ann (Wilson), also Griffiths, 1820–1900, NZ journalist and pamphleteer. B. in England, she m. James Whitney G. in 1842 and had two sons. Divorced, she emigrated to NZ in 1850 and in 1851 m. Stephen Lunn M., doctor and resident magistrate at Nelson. She wrote as 'Femina' for the enfranchisement of women, in the *Nelson Examiner*. Her pamphlet *An Appeal to the Men of New Zealand*, 1869, proclaimed: 'Women are now educated thinking beings, very different from the females of the darker ages . . . Let the laws be fitted for the people and times . . . Permit them to take as their right an interest, and some small part in the government of their adopted land . . . Our women are brave and strong, with an amount of self-reliance and freedom from conventionalities eminently calculated to form a great nation.' This evoked an encouraging letter from J. S. Mill. Her husband never knew of her writing, which she kept secret till after his death in 1890.

'Munda, Constantia', polemical answerer of Joseph Swetnam's ATTACK on women, who claims to be female (citing the precedent of Esther SOWERNAM and Rachel SPEGHT), and very likely is. *The Worming of a mad Dogge, or A Soppe for Cerberus the Jaylor of Hell*, 1617, opens with verses: to her mother, 'Prudentia Munda', thanking her for the 'second birth of education' (demonstrated in marginal glosses and new-coined Latinate terms) and to the writer whose 'barren-idle-donghill braine' is mad enough to 'call that bad / Which God calls good'. Prose follows: women are 'the second edition of the Epitome of the whole world', not to be dismissed because they are not warlike; Swetnam is further violently abused for confusing respectable wives and charitable patronesses with loose women. Reprs. 1985.

Munro, Alice (Laidlaw), short-story writer, novelist, B. in 1931 in Wingham, Ont., da. of Anne Clarke (Chamney) and Robert Eric L., she grew up on the impoverished farm where her father raised silver foxes and turkeys. In his seventies he wrote a novel, *The McGregors*, 1979, published posthumously after revisions made on his daughter's advice. She studied at the Univ. of Western Ontario (BA, 1952), m. James M. in 1951 (divorced 1976) and moved to Vancouver, where he worked for the T. Eaton Company, then on to Victoria, BC, where he opened a bookstore. AM wrote during her teens, selling her first story to the CBC at 18. She encountered difficulties while raising her three daughters, but continued with the encouragement of her husband, who 'believ[ed she] was a writer'. Her first collection of short stories, *Dance of the Happy Shades*, 1968, won the Governor-General's Award, but only *Lives of Girls and Women*, 1971, which also won the award – sometimes called a *kunstlerroman*, sometimes a collection of interlinked stories – brough her high reputation for her craft. These books established her fictional terrain: the rural world of southwestern Ontario, the value conflicts between small towns and big cities, ordinary protagonists, subtle but poignantly awkward and embarrassed situations. 'In general, sympathetic' to feminism, though 'not particularly active' in any 'political' sense, AM writes predominantly about female characters (some artists) and their quest for recognition and autonomy. *Something I've Been Meaning to Tell You*, 1974, *Who Do You Think You Are?* 1978, *The Moons of Jupiter*, 1982, *Progress of Love*, 1986, and *Friend of My Youth*, 1990, show her delight in 'the surfaces and textures' of her material and her ability to 'make strange', to evoke the extraordinariness of familiar circumstances through control of the deceptively linear narrative grammar of her stories. Influenced by writers of the American South (Eudora WELTY, Flannery O'CONNOR, Carson MCCULLERS and Reynolds Price), she writes as a regionalist, dealing, paradoxically, with the local human drama to show the universal condition. She has an international audience; her books are widely translated. She received the Canada-Australia Prize, 1974. She lives in Clinton, Ont., with her second husband, Gerald Fremlin (m. 1976). See Louis K. MacKendrick, 1983, Judith Miller, ed., 1984, W. R. Martin, 1987, Ildiko de Papp Carrington, 1989. Interview in Twigg, 1981. Papers at the Univ. of Calgary.

Munro, Georgina C., fl. 1842–53, English novelist of whose life nothing is known. She wrote five 'silver-fork' novels, unusual in having male narrators. The first, *De Montfort, or, the Old English Nobleman*, 1842, was pub. anon. with a preface referring to the author as 'he', and is told by a debauched earl. The preface to *The Voyage of Life*, 1844, promises 'the most improbable occurrences' – lion-hunts and a scene at Niagara – in volumes 'strictly in accordance with the truth'.

Murdoch, Jean **Iris**, DBE, novelist, poet, philosopher, literary critic, playwright. B. in 1919 in Dublin, da. of Irene Alice (Richardson) and Wills John Hughes M., she attended the Froebel Educational Institute and Badminton School, Somerville College, Oxford (BA 1942) and Newnham College, Cambridge, 1947–8. She worked at the British Treasury, 1942–4, and for the UN Relief and Rehabilitation Administration, 1944–6, as fellow and tutor in Philosophy at St Anne's College, Oxford, 1948–63, and as lecturer at the Royal College of Art, 1963–7. She m. J. O. Bayley, 1956. Her earliest writings, *Sartre, Romantic Realist*, 1953, and *Under the Net*, 1954, signal linked interests in philosophy and fiction. IM sees existentialism's self-absorbed human creature as one seeking an absolute – goodness, love or a right decision – in an accidental, even absurd world. The essays on fiction-writing, 'The Sublime and the Beautiful Revisited', 1960, and 'Against Dryness', 1961, defend humanist-realist fiction mirroring the plenitude and contingency of experience and discovering value as opposed to 'the consolations of form, the clear crystalline work, the simplified fantasy-myth'. It has been argued that IM's novels themselves are peopled by types, rather than the 'real people' she urges. But the recurrent plot in which a protagonist creates a personal Wittgensteinian 'net' (a role to play, rules or theories to live by, a quest – see *A Fairly Honourable Defeat*, 1970, *The Good Apprentice*, 1985, and others) to define her or his life only to find reality altering its shape, is itself a subversive structure. Deconstructing their protagonists' strategies for security, these fictions call attention to their own arbitrary, often exaggerated patternedness (*A Severed Head*, 1961, *An Accidental Man*, 1971, *A Word Child*, 1975, and numerous others) as yet another fragile net beyond which the collaborative reader catches glimpses of a desired freedom, a fertile potentiality, a possible location of truth. Responsibility urges us to dismantle the pattern, to discover the process which throws up, randomly, meaning and absurdity, likeness and incompatibility, and to hear 'the unvoiced possibilities in the dominant discourse'. These fictions consider the oppressive elements of language itself – of grammatical logic, of cliché, correctness, or convention, the distortions of illusion (*The Flight from the Enchanter*, 1956) or the enchantment of allusion (*The Black Prince*, 1973, *Bruno's Dream*, 1969, and *The Sea, The Sea*, 1978), the dictatorial powers of men, the word-masters. They teach, too, language's liberating potential as multiple signifier, demystifier, and pointer to the crucial elements beyond the sign: meaning and silence. Deborah Johnson detects in IM's novels 'a dialogue', epitomized in *The*

Bell, 1958, 'between the public "male" philosophical voice' (often the voice of the narrator) 'and the "private" female poetic voice', which allies itself with the unexpected, the particular, the elusive 'real' (and may be assigned to the implied author). In IM's verse play, *The One Alone*, a female prisoner of conscience in an unnamed state is told that 'people will know nothing about her. But', says IM, 'you can't count on your protest being of use – and you can't *know* that it's not.' See A. S. BYATT, *Degrees of Freedom*, 1965, Elizabeth Dipple, 1982, and Johnson's feminist account, 1987, quoted above.

Murfree, Mary Noailles, 'Charles Egbert Craddock', 1850–1922, novelist and short-story writer, b. Murfreesboro, Tenn., da. of Fanny Priscilla (Dickinson) and William Law M., lawyer, plantation owner and revolutionary officer. She was educ. at Nashville Female Academy and Chegaray Institute, a French boarding school in Philadelphia. A childhood illness left her permanently lame. Her pseudonym was adopted (and universally believed) because her themes were not thought to be 'feminine'. The disclosure of her identity when she visited Boston in 1885 received wide publicity, and for over a decade no story of hers was rejected. After her parents' deaths, her sister remained her lifelong companion. Her books were the first to depict life in the southern mountains, and she is important as a local colourist. MNM's greatest work is *In the Tennessee Mountains*, 1884 (repr. 1970), a collection of stories about the lives and frustrations of the mountain dwellers, a theme continued in her novel *The Despot of Broomsedge Cove*, 1889. Here she takes a sardonic look at religion in her description of Parson Donnard who 'drove a hard bargain in salvation', and the candidate for baptism who plunged headlong into the river so as not to 'miss his chance o' gittin' glory'. The novel's heroine, Marcella Strobe, emerges as a strong character 'worth any ten men', who saves her lover, wrongly accused of murder, from the mountain vigilantes. See Edd Winfield Parks, 1941, for her life; Richard Cary, 1967, for a critical study. Her papers are scattered: the most important are at the Houghton Library, Harvard.

Murphy, 'Dervla', Dervilla Maria TRAVEL-writer and AUTOBIOGRAPHER, b. 1931 at Cappoquin, Co. Waterford, only child of Fergus M., county librarian and would-be novelist, and Kathleen (Rochfort-Dowling), who walked 15 miles the day before DM's birth but was crippled with rheumatoid arthritis within two years. At four DM meant to be a writer; at about seven she wrote adventure stories for her parents, inscribed her name on others' title-pages, told herself, with tumultuous joy, stories of 'magic animals and omnipotent teddy-bears', and set herself physical 'endurance tests'; at 12 she won a *Cork Weekly Examiner* essay prize five times running; at 14 she sent an adventure novel to a publisher, and left her second convent school to nurse her helpless mother. *Hibernia* printed her three long pieces on Stratford, London and Oxford (visited by bicycle in 1951); next year she wrote a novel (rejected) about an illegitimate Irish girl. 1959–62 were years of nervous breakdown, the death of her long-time lover, her father, and her once 'heroine-worshipped', now tyrannical mother. Freed, she left by bicycle for India, an ambition for 20 years. She wrote *Full Tilt*, 1965, first of eight travel books so far, 'as an obligation to my parents': dedicated 'To the peoples of Afghanistan and Pakistan' just as *A Place Apart*, 1978, is dedicated 'To the Northern Irish'. DM took her daughter to India at five (in 1973) and to the Andes at ten. She has pub. an autobiography (*Wheels within Wheels*, 1979), a clear-headed, informative survey by 'an avowed anti-nuke' (*Race to the Finish? The Nuclear Stakes*, 1981), 'a personal record of daily life' and feelings in deprived, multi-racial, urban England (*Tales from Two Cities: Travels of*

Another Sort, 1987), and a selec. of Lady Mary Wortley MONTAGU, 1988.

Murphy, Emily Gowan (Ferguson) 'Janey Canuck', 1868–1933, journalist, essayist, the first woman magistrate in the British Empire. B. in Cookstown, Ont., da. of Emily (Gowan) and Isaac F., she was educ. at Bishop Strachan School, Toronto. She m. minister Arthur M. in 1887 and had two daughters. When his health failed, they moved west, to Swan River, Manitoba, then to Edmonton, 1907. An active reformer, EM organized support for the Dower Act (passed by the Provincial Legislature, 1911), which ensured to a wife a third of her husband's property, and was prominent in the SUFFRAGE movement and a president of the Canadian Women's Press Club, 1913–20. She was also the first national president of the Federated Women's Institutes, president of the Edmonton branch of the National Council of Women, and a member of many other organizations. Her writing issued from her reformist concerns: she published widely in journals and newspapers under various pseudonyms, and was the literary editor of the Winnipeg *Telegram* and the Edmonton *Journal*. She was instrumental in the establishment of the women's court, later family court, in Edmonton. Her appointment as magistrate in this court was challenged (women, it was argued, were not 'persons' in respect of rights and privileges) and overruled, but the argument revived when, with Nellie MCCLUNG and others, EM worked for appointment of a woman to the Senate and petitioned Parliament for an interpretation of the word 'persons' in the British North America Act (the Canadian constitution of the time): a Canadian Supreme Court ruling (that women were not persons) was overturned in 1929 by the British Privy Council. As 'Janey Canuck', EM wrote a number of popular books: *The Impressions of JC Abroad*, 1901, worked up from diaries, sees England and Germany through the reformist focus of her Canadian experience; *JC in the West*, 1910, *Open Trails*, 1912, and *Seeds of Pine*, [1914], sketch life in Manitoba and Alberta. *The Black Candle*, 1922, pub. as 'Judge Murphy', collects articles written against the use and trade of narcotics. It has been noted that EM was born to privilege, that she criticized Emmeline PANKHURST for 'putting ungenteel and forward ideas in the heads of women', and that she saw marriage as the lynchpin of civilization. Lives by Byrne Hope Saunders, 1945, and Christine Mander, 1985 (hostilely, interestingly reviewed by Janice McGinnis in *CHR*, 68, 1987).

Murray, Eunice Guthrie, 1878–1960, MBE, novelist and historian, b. at Cardross, Dumbarton, da. of Frances Porter (Stoddart), suffragist, lecturer and poet, and of lawyer David M. Educ. at St Leonard's School, St Andrews, 1890–2, she became an active suffrage writer and lecturer, president of the Women's Freedom League in Scotland. She was arrested in 1913 for speaking at a Downing Street meeting. During WWI she spoke for the War Savings Association and campaigned on behalf of industrial workers; in 1918 she stood for election in Bridgeton, Glasgow. Her novels deal with women's experience: *The Hidden Tragedy*, 1917, with the violence met by militant suffragettes (the college-educated heroine uses her inheritance to train women as lawyers, 'to plead for and advise their fellow sisters', and will marry only 'a suffragist and a believer in the Women's Cause'); *The Lass He Left Behind*, 1918, with working-class women's battle against poverty, bad housing and bad sanitation. Her memoir of her mother, 1920, celebrates a pioneer of the women's cause and remembers her own childhood. EGM wrote a book about Palestine, 1932, several on the community of Cardross, and one on costume: *Scottish Homespun*, 1947. In *Scottish Women in Bygone Days*, 1930, and *A Gallery of Scottish Women*, 1935, she focuses on past subjection and on women who rebelled, including Margaret CALDERWOOD, Joanna BAILLIE, Anne GRANT and Margaret OLIPHANT.

Murray, Grisell or **Griselda** (Baillie), Lady, 1692–1759, memoirist, da. of Lady Grisell BAILLIE. In 1710 she m. Alexander M., later a baronet, whose violent jealousy caused a legal separation in 1714. In 1721 a rape attempt on her by one of her father's footmen brought her unpleasant publicity, including a poem by her erstwhile friend Lady Mary Wortley MONTAGU. In 1739 she set down 'Plain Facts' about her father's life; in 1749, although the task brought on great 'concern and agitation of mind', she wrote a longer and more emotional account of her mother: both pub. as *Memoirs*, Edinburgh, 1822.

Murray, Judith (Sargent), 'Constantia', 1751–1820, poet, essayist, feminist, and playwright. Eldest child of Judith (Saunders) and Winthrop S., merchant and politician of Gloucester, Mass., she shared her brother's pre-Harvard education. In 1769 she married ship's captain John Stevens. Universalist ideas (universal salvation) acquired soon afterwards from the preacher John Murray had her and her family suspended from their church in 1778. She published *Some Deductions from ... Divine Revelation*, 1782, and a poem on the value of self-esteem, especially for women, in 1784. (Besides verse she had already written an 'Essay on the Equality of the Sexes', 1779, before WOLLSTONECRAFT but unpub. till 1790.) In 1788, two years after John Stevens fled from debt to die in the West Indies, she married John M., and soon began appearing in the *Massachusetts Magazine*: poems as 'Constantia' and essays from 1792 as 'The Gleaner', a 'plain man' whose womenfolk mock his solemnity. *The Gleaner* is her major work: repr. to raise money in 1798, with her two plays, it drew most of her famous contemporaries to subscribe. It includes a novella about the Gleaner's adopted daughter Margaretta, 'sketches of celebrated women', and discussion of e.g. Ann YEARSLEY and Mercy WARREN. A woman of ideas, JSM urges her sex to 'a new era in female history'. Thirsting for fame, she wrote as a man to escape the contempt visited on women's works. (*The Medium, or Virtue Triumphant*, 1795, first American play staged in Boston, and *The Traveller Returned*, 1796, had both failed.) John M. had a stroke in 1809; she ed. his letters and sermons, 1812–13, and completed his autobiography, 1816. She died at her daughter's at Natchez, Miss.; most of her MSS mouldered away. Letters of 1790–1 from Philadelphia and NYC in *Universalist Quarterly*, 1881–2; life by Vena Bernadette Field, 1933, is singularly grudging.

Murray, Louisa, 1818–94, poet, novelist, journalist, b. at Carisbrooke in the Isle of Wight, da. of Louisa Rose (Lyons) and Edward M., both from military families, and educ. in Wicklow, Ireland, where she spent her youth with her father's family. She moved with her family to Canada, 1844, first to Wolfe Island, near Kingston, where, according to her niece Mary Louisa M., she 'encountered most of the hardships and privations which the early settlers in the backwoods of Canada had to endure', then to Stamford, where she died. LM sent her first novella, *Fauna; or, The Red Flower of Leafy Hollow*, to the *Victoria Magazine*, edited in Belleville by Susanna MOODIE, who sent it on to the *Literary Garland*, where it was serialized, 1851, running alongside a novel by Rosanna LEPROHON. It was reprinted several times, in New York and Belfast. It unfurls a complex, at times melodramatic, plot (a secret marriage, fraud, intrigue, several complicated romances) of elaborate cross-cultural interest. It shifts from England to North America and back and involves a significant exchange of kinds of knowledge among the English immigrant Helen Blachford, the German immigrant Madame von Werfenstein, and the North American Indian girl Fauna.

Fauna, who reads Keats, teaches Helen how to fend for herself in nature, and, as Judith Zelmanovits shows, Madame von W. teaches the reader how to perceive as a problem the exclusion of women from the realms of knowledge: 'Learning and genius in a woman! Oh! acme of iniquity – the horror of one sex, the dread of the other and the never failing sign of a predestined old maid!' LM followed this with several more novels, all published in periodicals and never, it seems, in book form. She also contributed criticism, essays, and poetry to a number of Canada's most widely-known journals, including the *Nation*, the *Week*, and the *Canadian Monthly*, and to *Once a Week* (London). Her solidly researched article on the Niagara District, for instance, in *Picturesque Canada*, 1882, draws not only on philology, linguistics, history and geology, but also on early explorers' diaries, letters, legend, and *GM*, 1857. It also presents its material dramatically, as in its account of Laura Secord's heroic walk. LM corresponded with Agnes Maule MACHAR, Susan HARRISON, and Ethelwyn WETHERALD, who called her 'a born story-teller'. Her 'Scraps about "Writing Women"' appeared in the *Nation*, 1875. Her niece Mary Louisa M. wrote two sketches, 1923, on LM and her father: unpublished, but generously presented by Zelmanovits in *CWS*, 7, 1986.

Murray, Melissa, playwright, b. 1954, brought up in London, living in Devon. She won the Gregory Poetry Award for *The Falling Sickness*, 1977. She began writing drama in the late 1970s, and has worked with several (mainly feminist) THEATRE GROUPS, like Pirate Jenny (*Bouncing back with Benyon*, 1977, a satire on the anti-abortion lobby, and *Belisha Beacon*, 1978), the Women's Theatre Group (*Hot Spot*, 1978, with Eileen Fairweather), Hormone Imbalance (*Ophelia*, 1979, in which *Hamlet* is reversed and Ophelia falls in love with her maid), Monstrous Regiment (*The Execution*, 1982), and the Avon Touring Company (*The Crooked Scythe*, 1983). *The Admission* was staged and adapted for radio in 1982. Her award-winning *Coming Apart*, 1984, presents this process in a middle-aged woman living in Berlin. *Body Cell* (produced 1986, while MM was writer-in-residence at the Soho Poly Theatre, London) traces a female political prisoner's gradual loss of integrity and sanity. *Changelings*, 1988, collects ten short stories: a few employ fantasy, and several present imagination at odds with actuality.

Murray, Pauli, poet, lawyer, biographer, and Episcopal priest, b. 1910 in Baltimore, da. of Agnes Georgianna (Fitzgerald) and William Henry M., reared by grandparents at Durham, NC, after her mother died. She took a BA at Hunter College, NYC, 1933, taught in NY, and had her first poem published by Nancy CUNARD in 1934, but set aside a writing career to work for blacks through the legal system. Barred as a non-white from the Univ. of North Carolina (to which her ancestors were benefactors) and as a woman from Harvard, she took her law degrees at Howard Univ., 1944, and the Univ. of Calif. at Berkeley, 1945. She was admitted to the Bar in Calif. and NY, practised, published, lectured (in the USA and Ghana), and held many government posts. *Proud Shoes: The Story of an American Family*, 1956, repr. 1978 (the shoes are those of her grandfather, a Union soldier, compelling her to bravery), celebrates her 'near-white' family, outsiders to every group: her respected schoolmistress aunts and hell-raising grandmother (daughter of a part-Cherokee slave raped by her master's son), the family land encroached on by a cemetery for whites. Always 'too much my own person' for subordination or traditional marriage, PM believed the revitalized women's liberation movement 'had a revolutionary potential greater that the Black Revolt because it affected a literal majority of the population'. She published poems in anthologies and in *Dark Testament*, 1970, whose long title-poem deals with the interrelation of black and white. She wrote of US racism and sexism as 'so deeply intertwined' in institutions that the outcome of one struggle 'will depend in large part' on that of the other (essay in Mary Lou Thompson, ed., *Voices of the New Feminism,* 1970). She applied for appointment to the Supreme Court in 1971, to disprove the popular misconception that no suitable women were available. In 1977, as one of the first women ordained in the USA, she became its first black female priest. See her 'Black, Feminist Theologies: Links, Parallels and Tensions' (*Christianity and Crisis,* 40, 1980); Barbaralee Diamonstein in *Open Secrets,* 1972.

Murray, Rona, poet, playwright, short-story writer, b. 1924 in London, da. of Enid (Gregory) and Major Robin M. After infancy in India, she was taken to Canada in 1932; she attended the Univs. of Victoria, BC, and (for a PhD) Kent. She married Walter Dexter, a potter (with whom she compiled *The Art of Earth,* 1979, a wide-ranging anthology of pottery images and words), and had three children by 1951. From 1961 she taught English and creative writing at universites and schools in BC; her poems and stories appeared in magazines and anthologies (e.g., Dorothy LIVESAY's *Forty Women Poets of Canada,* 1972). Of her plays, *Blue Duck's Feather and Eagledown,* was printed, 1958; others, from *My Love is Dead* to *Creatures,* produced 1980, are unpub. Her *Selected Poems,* 1974 (mostly short-lined, succinct, often surrealistic), draw on three volumes, from *The Enchanted Adder,* 1965, to *Ootischenie,* 1974, which seeks to interpret the experience of the Doukhobor sect of western Canada. RM is mythic and metaphysical on 'the halls of the dead', precise and detailed on the natural world, often preoccupied with the infliction of pain. 'In this white wood / cat humped snow lies gentle on / branch and branch and now and then / a humped cat falls.' *Journey,* 1981 (short poems), opens by invoking W. B. Yeats and an aged female Native American shaman 'dying into song'. *Adam and Eve in Middle Age,* 1984, the dialogue of a long-married couple, uses contemporary images of machines to seek a human response to the message that 'time is short'. *The Indigo Dress,* 1986 (stories, the title piece narrated by a young, male, unrequited lover), uses domestic and local settings for fables of human limitation, the losses of age and the promise of renewal.

Murray, Sarah (Mease or Maese), later Aust, 1744–1811, education and travel writer. Patronized by Elizabeth MONTAGU, she was said later to have saved £8000 from her schools at Bath (from 1764) and Kensington. *The School,* 1766–72, 3 vols. of letters mostly from a girl to her mother, has a preface disparaging novels. Summaries of lessons (Assyrian kings, Semiramis, Carthage) alternate with but are kept separate from moral tales of school life. In 1783 SM married Captain William M., a nobly-connected Scot who died three years later. In 1796, with a man, maid, carriage and good pair of horses, she made a Scottish tour of nearly 2000 miles, and in 1799 published a *Companion and Useful Guide* to Scotland, the Lakes, and Craven, anonymous, dedicated to the literary review editors but designed for the pocket or chaise, not the bookshelf. She begins with detailed advice on equipment, and keeps her 'Guide' (mileages, state of roads and inns) separate from her 'Description', a circumstantial, racy tale of intrepid travel. History, folklore, names, the weather, occasional complaint all get their turn. Volume ii, 1803, as 'Lady Murray' (although she had married George Aust of the foreign office in 1802), covers the Hebrides, fruit of four more journeys; eds. of 1805 and 1810 are again updated; a repr., Hawick, 1982, includes Scotland only, 'Description' only. A Lady Murray privately printed journals of art-gallery tours in Holland [1823?] and Italy [1836?], and Sarah Maria (Hay) Murray, bishop's wife, pub. an account of riots in the Isle of Man [1825].

Murry, Ann, writer of instruction books for young people, especially women. Da. of a London wine merchant, she became a private tutor when family fortunes changed, and by 1791 was Preceptress in the royal nursery. Her first book, written for her pupils and dedicated to the Princess Royal, was *Mentoria* [no connection with Susanna ROWSON's work of the same title], *or The Young Ladies Instructor*, 1778, in the form of dialogues between a governess and two aristocratic pupils. It ranges over grammar, politeness, geography, arithmetic, history – all within the framework of Christian virtues. Its mix of information and rules for conduct was very popular (12th ed. 1823). Its *Sequel*, 1799, employs the same characters in dialogues on astronomy and science as a basis for moral reflections and orthodox Christian teachings. AM's *Poems on Various Subjects*, 1779, by subscription, include piety, social satire, and several poems to her sisters. She further instructed 'Young Minds' in *Concise History of the Kingdoms of Israel and Judah*, 1783, and an abridged *History of France*, 1818. *Mentorian Lectures*, 1809, are also ascribed to her. Though critical of 'The Modern Female's idle, useless state', she recommends only Female Virtue and revealed religion as her way to improvement.

Musgrave, Agnes, novelist whose first work, *Cicely, or The Rose of Raby, An Historic Novel*, anonymous (pub. 1795, two years after she submitted it) was a MINERVA best-seller: reprints up to 1874. A preface offers curious 'daughters of our grandmother Eve' an elaborate account of a MS descending into the M. family through female hands (once purloined by a married woman from her father's heir) till [AM] finds it, learns to read it, tries to check its facts at castles from Cumberland to France and Portugal (some by proxy) and modernizes its 'antique dress'. Its purported author, granddaughter to John of Gaunt, grandmother of Elizabeth of York, relates strong scenes in a preposterous plot: much detail about her own story ('even when a mere child I was plunged into adventures that might have appalled the stoutest'), then an accelerated dash through later history. *Edmund of the Forest*, 1797, is also anonymous and historical. *The Solemn Injunction*, 1798 (by name, tepidly reviewed), is a modern family saga: several generations of mystery, evil, incarceration, bloody suicide, faked ghosts, and incest, with a happy ending. *The Confession*, 1801, by name, is titled from the heroine's mother's deathbed revelation of her daughter's previously unsuspected identity.

Musgrave, Susan, poet, novelist, writer of children's literature. She was b. in 1951 in Santa Cruz, Calif., to Canadian parents Judith B. (Stevens) and Edward L. M. Her family moved to Sidney, BC, in 1954. Although a 'straight A student until about grade seven', she left school at grade ten out of 'Boredom', and 'ran away from home' hoping 'to be a writer'. Encouraged by Robin Skelton, she published her first poems at 16 in *The Malahat Review*. She went back to California, 1967–9, and lived in Ireland and England, 1970–2, where she began writing *Grave-Dirt and Selected Strawberries*, 1973: '*out of all strawberries proceeds / either an owl or a devil*'. She was m. to lawyer Jeffrey Green, 1976–80, then to entrepreneur and international drug smuggler Paul Nelson, 1980, with whom she lived for awhile in Panama City. SM now lives near Sidney with her daughter and third husband (m. 1986), Stephen Reid, former bankrobber, now novelist, whom she met at Millhaven penitentiary while she was writer-in-residence at the Univ. of Waterloo, 1983–5. She 'feel[s] most at home' in the Queen Charlotte Islands, BC, where she lived 1972–4. Her ten volumes of poetry, 'populated by embalmers, executioners, vampires, tarts, muggers, and outlaws', have been praised by critics for their craft, and fascinate or repel their readers with their parodic morbidity and bleakness. Herself fascinated with North American, especially Canadian, West Coast Indian mythology, she treats James Frazer's *Golden Bough* satirically and displays a strong affinity with nature and the magic of transformation: 'In the night's past time / I am red rock cut in the vulture's eye'. Influenced by Stevie SMITH ('She's my hero') and compared to Sylvia PLATH, Anne SEXTON and Margaret ATWOOD, SM writes of death and desire, rhythmically, as in *The Impstone*, 1976 – 'we are / making blood / our bodies disguise the / dance / where love is / impossible to / hide' – or through 'black comedy', as in her novel, *The Charcoal Burners*, 1980, where a young woman is victimized by a group of radical Californian feminists and abused and killed, to be eaten by a group of male outlaws. SM acknowledges women's social inequality, but is 'not a feminist at all' because she has 'never had any problems with men'; yet many of her poems, especially those in *A Man to Marry, a Man to Bury*, 1979, affirm the female power of ancient rites. She published some poems, with Sean Virgo, as the invented Indian, 'Moses Bruce': repr. under her name. See Dennis Brown in *CanL*, 79, 1978, Sharon McMillan in *Malahat Review*, 45, 1978. Interview in Twigg, 1981. Papers at McMaster Univ.

Mvungi, Martha, novelist, short-story writer, scholar. B. in Kidugala, Njombe, in Southern Tanzania, she had her early schooling in Ilula and Balali among the Hehe. She loved the communal story-telling village evenings and was fascinated by the several versions she heard of some stories. Later, when her parents moved among the Bena, her own ethnic group, she recognized common plots and variations. After university study in Edinburgh and Dar es Salaam, she taught in Tanzania and heard more stories from her pupils. She values the ORAL TRADITION because it embodies 'social relationships, economic lives, institutions, values and norms'. She collected folk tales from the elders in her immediate environment, from her parents and her grandmother, and her English versions of Hehe and Bena folk tales appear in *Three Solid Stones*, 1975. She has published a novel in Swahili, *Hana Hatia*.

N

Naden, Constance Caroline Woodhill, 1858–89, poet, b. Edgbaston, Birmingham, da. of Caroline Anne (Woodhill), d. 1858, and Thomas N., architect. CN, a 'meditative and silent child', was brought up by her mother's parents, this period being described in her poem 'Six Years Old'. From eight she attended a private day school. She was a talented painter, one of her pictures being accepted by the Birmingham Society of Artists. She attended the Birmingham and Midland Institute and Mason College, studying French, German, Latin, Greek and science. In 1881 she visited Europe and pub. *Songs and Sonnets of Springtime*. She delivered three addresses on evolution, also writing for the *Journal of Science, Agnostic Annual* and others. She inherited her grandmother's fortune in 1887, published *A Modern Apostle, The Elixir of Life*, 1887 and *The Story of Clarice*, and stopped writing poetry – a 'mere amusement'. She travelled extensively with her friend Mrs Daniell, contracting fever in India. On returning to London in 1888 CN became a member of the Aristotelian Society and the Royal Institution and planned to establish an Evolution Society. She was a friend of Elizabeth Garrett Anderson, assisting with the new Hospital for Women in the Marylebone Road. A member of the Somerville Club for women, she lectured in favour of women's SUFFRAGE 'in a mature and commanding style of oratory'. Gladstone drew fresh attention to her poetry (*Spectator*, 11 January 1890) and her complete poems were pub. 1894. These range from long earnest pieces about duty replacing faith ('A Modern Apostle'), through TRANSLATIONS from Schiller and other German poets, which show a lyric gift, to humorous and clever verses in the section called 'Evolutional Erotics'. For her life, see memoir by W. R. Hughes, 1890.

Naidu, Sarojini (Chattopadhyaya), 1879–1949, poet and Gandhian nationalist politician, b. at Hyderabad to Bengali Brahmins, Varada Sundari, who wrote juvenile poems and was a noted singer, and Aghorenath C., PhD (Edinburgh), politician, founder of two colleges, one for women. In 1895 her parents sent her to England, partly out of disquiet at her plan to marry Govindarjulu N., a doctor of different caste. She studied at King's College, London, and Girton College, Cambridge, wrote poetry, and was advised by Edmund Gosse to use Indian topics and settings. In 1898 she returned to India and married N.; she had four children. She used her fine ear for English in archaic mode: 'Lightly, O lightly, we bear her along, / She sways like a flower in the wind of our song; / She skims like a bird on the foam of a stream / She floats like a laugh on the lips of a dream.' Despite the pressure of active public life, she published *The Golden Threshold*, 1905 (containing outmoded images of self-sacrificial women, e.g., 'Suttee'), *The Bird of Time*, 1912, *The Broken Wing*, 1917 (including the well-known 'To a Buddha seated on a Lotus', in mystic vein heightened by one of her many illnesses, and 'The Sanctuary', strikingly erotic), *The Sceptred Flute*, 1928, ofter repr. (whose last poem strikes a new note: 'Take my flesh to feed your dogs if you choose. / Water your garden trees with my blood if you will . . . O Love'), and *Select Poems*, 1930 (various reissues). *The Feather of the Dawn*, 1961, prints poems written in July-August 1927. She met Mohandas Gandhi in 1914 and became his close associate; she began her career by speaking on women's education, then the right to vote and serve on political bodies; she became the first woman to hold each of many key positions. Elected President of the Indian National Congress in 1925, she at once pressed for a women's section of it. She made the first of several visits to Africa in 1924, travelled North America in 1928–9, attended the London Round Table Conference in 1931, and served her longest prison term, 1942–3. Chairing the important Asian Relations Conference, 1947, made her 'the chosen leader for Asia, not only India'. On independence she became governor of India's largest province, Uttar Pradesh. See life by Padmini Sengupta, 1966, study by P. V. Rajyalakshmi, 1977; Meena Alexander in *Ariel*, 4, 1986.

Nairne, Carolina (Oliphant), Baroness, 1766–1845, song writer. Her parents, Margaret (Robertson), who wrote verse and d. when she was eight, and Laurence O. of Gask, Perth, were devoted Jacobites; she was tutored by a clergyman. Quick to admire Burns, she began writing to replace coarse, traditional versions of songs; hers were popular (her brother first sang one in public) for years before the author was known. She ranges through Jacobitism ('Charlie is my darling'), nostalgia ('The Auld Hoose'), pathos ('The Land o' the Leal'), and satire ('The Laird o' Cockpen': a later version, probably by Susan FERRIER, revokes the poor woman's snubbing of the vain laird). In 1806 (after a long engagement for lack of funds) CN married her cousin Major William Murray N., whose attainted barony was restored in 1824, and moved to Edinburgh. Her son was largely educated by herself. In 1821 she assumed the name 'Mrs Bogan of Bogan' for her part in a joint collection, *The Scottish Minstrel*. Widowed in 1830, she lived in Ireland and Europe, but died at Gask, after writing at 75 'Would you be young again? / So would not I.' Her *Life and Songs*' 1869, ed. Charles Rogers, prints a few fine, plaintive lyrics by her niece Caroline Oliphant, 1807–31, and regrets that others remain unpub.

Namjoshi, Suniti, poet, writer of fiction, critic, b. in 1941 in Bombay, da. of Sarojini (Naik Nimbalkar) and Manohar N. She was educ. in an American boarding school and at Rishi Valley, an experimental school founded by J. Krishnamurthi. After graduating from the Univ. of Poona (BA, 1961, MA, 1963), she became an officer in the Indian Administrative Service, 1964–9. Bored with the civil service, she attended the Univ. of Missouri (MS in Business Administration, 1969) and McGill (PhD in English, 1972). Since 1972 she has taught at the Univ. of Toronto. Her first poems were published by the Writers Workshop, Calcutta: *Poems*, 1967, *More Poems*, 1970, *Cyclone in Pakistan*, 1977, and *The Jackass and the Lady*, 1980. With her mother, she translated *Poems of Govindagrao* from the Marathi, 1968, new ed. 1976. SN began to think about being lesbian as early as 11 or 12, and declared her sexual orientation 'in print and at work' in 1979. Prior to this 'Turning my back on unpleasantness and hostility had become a habit, as had the making of a distinction between a private world and a public one.' Her books after coming out are qualitatively different, presenting an artist who has found her own voice. *Feminist Fables*, 1981, successfully reinscribes in prose the traditional, misogynist wisdoms of classical, biblical and eastern fables into a remarkably accessible, hilariously funny, feminist parodic idiom. Her ironic wit and extemely unconventional imagery mark the next two collections of poetry, *The Authentic Lie*, 1982, and *From the Bedside Book of Nightmares*, 1984. *The Conversations of Cow*, 1985, wittily examines the fascination of certain western feminists with goddess religions. Bhadravati, an Indian lesbian cow, manifests herself to SN and takes her on a journey of discovery during which she changes into many guises: male, female, animal. SN's *Flesh and Paper*, 1986, a poetic collaboration with lesbian poet Gillian Hanscombe, evinces a celebratory mood: 'the awareness of ... a lesbian audience' makes them 'able' and gives them 'authority' to 'invent who we are'. *Aditi and the One-Eyed Monkey*, 1986, is a children's story, written for her niece, Aditi: in it Aditi, an Indian princess, first vanquishes a monster then helps him to become friendly and morally responsible. *Because of India*, 1989, selects poems and fables, with essays on the circumstances of SN's writing. Interview in *Pink Ink*, 1: 5, 1984.

Napier, Elma (Gordon-Cumming), 'Elizabeth Garner', 1892–before 1975, short-story writer, novelist, autobiographer, b. in Scotland, da. of Florence Josephine (Garner) and Sir William Gordon G-C. of Altyre and Gordonstoun, who had recently been disgraced for allegedly cheating at cards. EN grew up chiefly in Scotland, Europe and North Africa, educ. by governesses with brief spells at boarding schools. In 1910 she was launched on the debutante husband-hunt, which she loathed. She was later ashamed 'that I did nothing for votes for women. Secretly, I admired the militants ... but wherever I went they were execrated. ... Something desperately important passed me by.' After the near-scandal of love for a married man, she m., 1912, the aristocratic Maurice Gibbs, and had two children. He was posted to Australia in 1914; during nine years there (punctuated by long-distance travel) EN 'escaped into vast freedoms', 'grew up' and began writing; the *Australasian*, 1920, printed her first story, already rich in wry humour, about a dentist's receptionist. In 1923 she left her husband (who scorned her writing); once divorced, she m. Manchester businessman Lennox Pelham N. They had two children, travelled, and worked in socialist politics. EN wrote for the *Manchester Guardian*, and published *Nothing So Blue* (travel sketches), 1927. During the 1930s they migrated to Dominica, where EN set her pseudonymous novels, *Duet in Discord*, 1936, and *A Flying Fish Whispered*, 1938: about a love affair, 'neither indecent nor ridiculous', between an older woman and younger man, and another killed by the man's pride in possessions and in 'his hold over the lives of others'. Increasingly active in politics, EN was the first woman elected to a West Indian Legislative Council, 1940; she pioneered Village Boards and co-operative ventures, and published stories in journals like *BIM* into the early 1950s. Her autobiographical *Youth Is a Blunder*, 1948, and *Winter is in July*, 1949, end on her father's death in 1930. Her grandson Lennox Honychurch dedicated *The Dominica Story*, 1975, to her memory.

Native feminist criticism. Little of the now substantial criticism on writing by North American natives is devoted to women's work. This is partly because the native ORAL TRADITION makes ascription of work to women difficult, particularly when it is transcribed by anthropologists whose own culture and attitudes to women frequently limit *what* they are able to hear and colour *how* they hear it. Early women writers undertaking such 'bi-cultural' presentations of native oral traditions, often heard from women informants, are discussed by Helen Howard in *American Indian Poetry*, 1979. Particularly damaging in these ungendered discussions has been interpreters' inability to recognize the importance of the matriarchal tradition of the Grandmother Gods in native culture. 'Recovering the feminine in American Indian traditions' is the project of Paula Gunn ALLEN in *The Sacred Hoop*, 1986, while Helen Bannan discusses rituals of initiation and kinship in Southwestern US native literature (Davidson and BRONER on mothers and daughters in literature, 1980).

Occasionally native women themselves mediated between cultures by transcribing tribal oral literature for white audiences. In *American Indian Autobiography*, 1988, H.

David Brumble III reads Sarah Winnemucca's *Life among the Piutes*, 1883, as deriving from a 'pre-literate' tradition of Indian narrative and a 'tribal sense of self'. But in the work of Zitkala Sa, an early twentieth-century native collector of material for a white audience, Dexter Fisher finds a 'conflict between tradition and acculturation' (*American Indian Quarterly*, 1979). And Charles Larson, in *American Indian Fiction*, 1978, suggests that the author's 'ambivalent stance towards her Indian subject' and the 'obfuscation within the narrative voice' in *Cogewea: The Half-Blood*, 1927, by Hum-ishu-ma ('MOURNING DOVE') is the result of interference amounting to original writing by her editor. Feminist critic Mary Dearborn argues that Hum-ishu-ma in fact makes an emancipatory space for herself within this colonized narrative by introducing figures who lie to collectors of Indian lore and 'epigrams and chapter titles ... which ... militate ... against the contents of the chapters' in strategies by which she, a trickster-author, 'inserts her own voice into [?] McWhorter's didactic narrative, and creates an alternative text available to the insider' (*Pocahontas's Daughters*, 1986).

Only in the last twenty years has a vigorous written literature by native women grown up. Beth Brant's introduction to *A Gathering of Spirit*, 1984, emphasizes community among women writers, while Rayna GREEN's introduction to *That's What She Said*, 1984, and Dexter Fisher's to *The Third Woman*, 1980, both emphasize contemporary writers' reliance on the oral 'tradition of their grandmothers'. In their major study, *American Indian Women Telling Their Lives*, 1984, Gretchen Bataille and Kathleen Sands trace the development of AUTOBIOGRAPHY in relationship to native narrative traditions in the work of Maria Chona, Maria CAMPBELL, MOUNTAIN WOLF WOMAN, Anna Moore Shaw, and Helen Sekaquaptewa. Jim Ruppert speaks of 'meaning in the ... state of connectedness to ... mythic space' in the poetry of Allen and of Joy HARJO (*AIQ* 1983). In *Studies in American Indian Literature* (ed. Allen, 1983) Bataille traces changes in autobiography in terms and tradition, and Susan Scarberry writes about the figure of 'Grandmother Spider or Thought Woman' in the poetry of Allen and Leslie SILKO. Kenneth Lincoln sums up this critical approach in his survey of seventies native poets, including women, as presenting '*re*visions of Indian ways' (*AICRJ*, 1982).

Whereas critics find a 'conflict' between being native and speaking to whites in the work of earlier women writers, they document an active resistance to white culture in contemporary writers. As Allen puts it, Indian women write as 'tribal singers' facing genocide and the question, 'how does one survive in the face of a collective death?' (*AICJR* 1982). Rebecca Tsosie finds in Roberta Whiteman and Joy Harjo poets of cultural resistance whose themes correlate with the resistance of spirituals and 'blues' music (*AICJR* 1986), while Patricia Smith addresses the theme of breakdown in traditional family and female kinship patterns in poetry by Marnie Walsh and nila northSun (Allen, ed., 1983). The most important collection to take up the question of contemporary writing as 'political mobilization' is Bob Scholer, ed., *Coyote Was Here*, 1984. Particularly noteworthy in it are Carol Hunter's interview with Wendy ROSE, the essays by Mary Stout on Zitkala Sa, by Kate Vangen on Silko's 'Storyteller', and Allen's essay on the 'spiritual foundations' of her own poetry and that of Harjo, Rose, Linda Hogan, Mary Tallmountain, and Carol Lee Sanchez.

In this emerging criticism, Silko's novel *Ceremony*, 1977, has received the most attention, including a special issue of *American Indian Quarterly*, 1979. Jarold Ramsey discusses the novel in the final chapter of *Reading the Fire* (1983); and each of Larson (*American Indian Fiction*), Alan Velie (*Four American Indian Literary Masters*, 1982), Allen (*Studies in American Indian*

Literature), and Kenneth Lincoln (*Native American Renaissance*, 1983) devote a chapter to the place of native spiritual and storytelling traditions in the novel. Allen, for example, reads the novel as a 'feminine landscape' in which there are two types of women, those who 'belong to the earth and live in harmony with her' and those who are 'of human mechanism'. Per Seyersted's *Leslie Marmon Silko*, 1980, discusses *Storyteller* and the poetry as well as *Ceremony*. On other writers and texts, as well as the essays already cited, one should note Joseph Bruchac's brief comments on Wendy Rose and Louise ERDRICH, Koolish's on Harjo, Rose, Allen and Yellowbird, and interviews in which Allen and Harjo discuss the effects on their work of being of mixed blood (all in Harris and Aguero, eds., *A Gift of Tongues*, 1987). Also important are Colonese and Owen's discussion of women (*American Indian Novelists*, 1985), Lincoln's reading of Allen's work (Houston A. Baker Jr., ed. *Three American Literatures*, 1982), and Barbara Godard's of Canadian native women's writing (Neuman and Kamboureli, 1986). Although the work of Inuit women has been anthologized, there is no criticism about it. *Survival This Way* (Joseph Bruchac, 1987) includes interviews with several women poets. Allen's *Studies in American Indian Literature* gives designs for courses on women's writing. Its bibliography is useful, as is that in Bataille and Sands.

Navarre, Marguerite de (d'Angoulême), Queen of, 1492–1549, poet and storywriter, political and religious force in the French Renaissance (not her daughter-in-law Marguerite de Valois, 1553–1615, who wrote poems and letters). Sister of François I, M de N m. the duc d'Alençon, 1509, then the King of Navarre, 1527. During the 1520s and 1530s she wrote religious poetry in many genres, expressing a near-Protestant view of the Bible and of salvation by faith: the soul in her allegory *Le Miroir de l'âme pécheresse*, pub. 1531, ed. Joseph L. Alleine, 1972 (condemned but later vindicated by the Sorbonne), is significantly, as well as grammatically, female. Her influence in England began with its translation by the future ELIZABETH I, pub. 1548. Other poems appeared as *Marguerites de la Marguerite des princesses*, 1547. At her death she was working on another allegory, *Prisons*. Her collection of chiefly prose tales, *Heptameron*, first anonymously pub. 1558 (transl. Paul A. Chilton, 1984), embodies a debate between female and male storytellers. Ladies Anne, Margaret and Jane Seymour wrote a sequence of 104 Latin couplet epigrams on her, pub. Paris, 1551, with versions in Greek, French and Italian by various hands. See Celeste M. Schenck in *TSWL*, 5, 1986.

Naylor, Gloria, novelist, b. 1950 in NYC, da. of Alberta (McAlpin) and Roosevelt N. From grade school she 'felt most complete when expressing myself through the written word'; she 'wrote because I had no choice' and hid it all away. She worked as a telephone operator (like her mother) and in 1968–75 travelled in N. Carolina, NY and Florida as a Jehovah's Witness missionary. At Brooklyn College, CUNY (BA 1981), she read Toni MORRISON's *The Bluest Eye*, which was crucial in assuring her of authority to write and turning her from poetry to prose. *The Women of Brewster Place*, 1982, is a novel in seven stories about the lives of black women in a run-down, dead-end urban ghetto street. They have suffered loss, many at the hands of men ('I bent over backwards not to have a negative message come through about the men'), but they keep the community alive by helping each other. The present-day anguish of an abandoned mother over her dead baby recalls 'the spilled brains of Senegalese infants whose mothers had dashed them on the wooden sides of slave ships'. On her publisher's advance for this, GN travelled to Europe, but found herself as a woman not free to 'roam the streets' safely. She began *Linden Hills* in Cadiz, married at 30 and was startled to find she 'felt as if I needed to ask permission' for her actions. She took an MA in Afro-American Studies at Yale, 1983. Symbology of place remains vital in *Linden Hills*, 1985, as it is in Ann PETRY: GN thought of Dante's *Inferno* as she created her middle-class black suburb, the reward of 'making it'. Her heroine, wife of the local mortician and landlord, has to deal with his oppression in a dehumanized environment with no supportive community. *Mama Day*, 1988, explores the tradition and culture of the rural black US south. Its heroine (descendant of 'a slave woman who *took* her freedom in 1823', by killing her master, father of her seven children) is a skilled herbal folk-doctor provoked by her neighbours' hate into using magic powers. GN publishes stories in periodicals and has written a column in the *NY Times*, held writer-in-residence posts, and lectured in the US and India. It is in writing, she says, that she sometimes reaches a 'spiritual center'. See Christian, 1985, and conversation with Toni MORRISON in *SoR*, 21, 1985.

Neale, Henrietta, d. 1798, religious writer, b. in London. Her widowed mother brought her family up piously at Bromley, then Northampton; HN was writing about her sins at 17. In 1789 she moved to Luton, and taught in her widowed sister's boarding school and at Sunday school. She published anonymously for the young: *Amusement Hall*, 1794 (promising 'Useful Knowledge' but offering more about behaviour), *Sacred History*, 4 vols. 1796, (Old and New Testament, with the history of the Jews from Nehemiah to Vespasian, in dialogues and letters; her brother edited a companion vol. of hymns), and *Britannus and Africus*, for a missionary society, 1797. Here a Sierra Leone chief's son, who has lost a sister to the slave trade but whose family makes a profit from it, meets a Briton. From remarks like 'What! white man love black man! surely you are the first!' and disapproval of Freetown as subverting African customs, he quickly comes to accept the gospel. That year HN wrote in her diary (selecs. pub. 1803), 'I know not how to resign the pen for the needle', and later 'The Lord has delivered me, by making me willing to resign my pen, and contented with it.' Her sister was dying: she wrote her life in the *Evangelical Magazine*, Oct. 1798.

Needell, Mary Anne, 'Mrs John Hodder N.' (Lupton), 1830–1922, English novelist, of whose life nothing is known beyond the fact of her marriage. She wrote at least 12 novels, beginning with *Ada Gresham: An Autobiography*, 1853, which has an odd unlikeable heroine and is interesting on birth and supporting a child alone. *Lucia, Hugh and Another*, 1884, also published in the USA, tells of an 'ideal marriage' which becomes a painful trap. *Unequally Yoked*, 1891, marries a young rector with a mission to a slum girl who grows in stature to match his spirit. A number of her works were signed Lupton; many were clearly influenced by Charlotte BRONTË.

Nesbit, Edith, 1858–1924, 'the first modern writer for children', b. in London, da. of Sarah and John Collis N., an agricultural chemist. In her reminiscences, *Long Ago When I Was Young*, 1966, she says she would have 'preferred a penal settlement' to her boarding schools in England, France and Germany, but she rhapsodizes about family holidays and 'a little room of my own' where she wrote at a mahogany bookcase and dreamed of becoming 'a great poet, like Shakespeare, or Christina ROSSETTI'. In 1880 she m. Hubert Bland (d. 1914), a political journalist whose rigid views strongly influenced hers: though she knew Olive SCHREINER and Charlotte Perkins GILMAN, she saw no need for the vote, and 'The Pretenderette' of *The Magic City*, 1910, may have been intended as 'a mocking allusion to the suffragettes'. With Bland, EN led a Bohemian life, took young lovers herself and looked after, besides her own three children, two her husband fathered on others. EN and Bland were founding members of the Fabian Society, friends of Sydney and Beatrice WEBB, G. B. Shaw, and H. G Wells. She supported the family, initially by decorating and writing verses for greeting cards, and from 1893 by more than 40 books for children. She cherished ambition for her verse, like *Ballads & Lyrics of Socialism*, 1908, praising the labourer's honest sweat 'that others' ease may abound' and pitying the slum child; or later, like *Many Voices*, 1922, reflecting sentimental patriotism about the soldier's sacrifice 'for the sake of the Hope of the World'. She wrote for a wide range of periodicals, and several plays (most unpublished). EN's enduring accomplishment, however, is her work for CHILDREN, especially the two trilogies. *The Treasure Seekers*, 1899, *The Wouldbegoods*, 1901, and *The New Treasure Seekers*, 1904, feature the entirely believable Bastable family; *Five Children and It*, 1902, *The Phoenix and the Carpet*, 1904, and *The Story of the Amulet*, 1907, spotlight mythical creatures like the psammead, a grouchy, ancient sand-fairy. In each, suspenseful yet often humorous action is combined with complex relations among girls and boys. Parents may be absent, preoccupied or (as in *The Railway Children*, 1906, filmed 1970) imprisoned, but the children are essentially secure and also free to roam. After Bland's death, EN married Thomas Terry Tucker, a marine engineer, in 1917. See Julia Briggs, 1987 (quoted above).

Newcastle, Margaret Cavendish (Lucas), Duchess of, 1623–73, woman of letters, youngest child of Elizabeth (Leighton) and Thomas L. (d. 1625) of Colchester, Essex. When war broke out she accompanied Queen Henrietta Maria to France, where in 1645 she met and m. William C., Marquess, later Duke, of N., father of Jane and Elizabeth CAVENDISH. Back in England in 1651 to try to reclaim part of his sequestered estate, she wrote and sent for publication *Poems and Fancies*, 1st ed. 1653, and *Philosophicall Fancies*, 1653 (revised as part of *Philosophical and Physical Opinions*, 1655, 1663, and as *Grounds of Natural Philosophy*, 1668). These texts indicate much of her later range. Her scientific works invent explanations for natural phenomena like the motion of the sea, analyse the workings of language and medicine, and dispute other scientists' theories and methodologies. (She made a famous visit to the Royal Society, 1667.) Her poems include a theory of atoms (which she later rejected), a first version of autobiography ('Similizing a young lady to a Ship'), and many from the point of view of the oppressed (the Earth, birds, a hunted stag, a besieged castle). She explores women's oppression in volumes of plays, 1662 and 1668, *Nature's Pictures*, 1656 (with autobiography), and *The New Blazing World*, 1668. These self-consciously original, rule-defying works offer images of publicly lauded women (intellectual, martial, or conventionally suffering), and fantastic strategies for combatting the restrictions of femininity. Her preface dedicating *Philosophical and Physical Opinions* to the two universities openly attacks 'the overweening conceit men have of themselves' and says women 'are become like birds in cages to hop up and down in our houses'. But often (as in *The Worlds Olio*, 1655, parts of *Orations*, 1662, and *Sociable Letters*, 1664) she expresses contempt not just for the despised lower classes but for other women, with anger at radicals intervening in state affairs. Her work is riddled with contradiction between belief in the general benefit that education would give women, and her desire for personal fame: 'to be the highest on Fortunes Wheele, and to hold the wheele from turning, if I can'. Till recently she was chiefly known for her last published work, the adulatory life of her husband, 1667. See life by Douglas Grant, 1957; Elaine Hobby, 1988.

Newcome Susannah (Squire), 1685–1763, theological writer, youngest da. of Mary and the Rev. Samuel S. of Durnford near Salisbury; other male relations published in the same field. Her anonymous *Enquiry into the Evidence of the Christian Religion*, Cambridge [1727], is confident and philosophical in tone. Between preface and text come 'Definitions' of evidence, happiness, etc., and 'Propositions', notably that it is 'highly irrational not to examine whether [Christianity] be true or not'. The work moves from Lockean reason and natural religion to consider revelation, free will, miracles and prophecies, backed with biblical texts. Soon afterwards she became second wife of John N., Cambridge professor of theology and later Dean of Rochester. The 'improved' second edition, 1732 ('By a Lady' on some title-pages only), sets out to prove humanity is destined to eternal happiness. In 1737–8 SN pub. two parts of a long letter to Bishop Hoadly, taking issue, in friendly but authoritative tone, with his demystifying *Plain Account of . . . the Lord's Supper*. She is said to have written notes for Zachary Grey's ed. of *Hudibras*, 1744, to which she and relations subscribed. Samuel Denne praised her because 'her modesty and humility always strove to conceal' her learning and power of mind. Horace Walpole acquired a print of her from her admirer William Cole.

Newman, Frances, 1883–1928, novelist, b. in Atlanta, Georgia, youngest child of Frances Percy (Alexander) and William Truslow N., the city attorney. She was ten when embarrassment stopped her writing a 'novel'. She attended various private schools, the Univ. of Tennessee, and the Carnegie Library School (Atlanta); in 1923 she studied at the Sorbonne. She worked as a librarian in Tallahassee, then in Atlanta at the Carnegie and the Georgia Institute of Technology; she signalled nonconformity by dressing in purple and having lovers. Encouraged by H. L. Mencken, who admired the biting wit of her book reviews in local and NY papers, she submitted a story, 'Rachel and Her Children', to *The American Mercury* in 1924 and won an O. Henry Award. She called *The Hard-Boiled Virgin*, 1926 (which succeeded an unpublished novel), the first 'in which a woman ever told the truth about how women feel'. Difficult and experimental in style, it was famously banned in Boston for its sexual frankness (after some agonizing, the heroine comes to search for a lover who will rid her of Southern gentility as well as her virginity). In *Dead Lovers are Faithful Lovers*, 1928, an adulterous husband dies before he is discovered. Its violet binding, FN insisted, 'suits the triumphant widow idea of the book'. Both were repr. 1977. Her research in Europe towards a 'history of sophistication' was cut short by eye trouble; she returned and died of an overdose. Her translated and edited volume of Jules LaForgue, 1928 (following an idiosyncratic story anthology, 1924) was posthumous. She left plans for 'There's A Certain Elegance About Celibacy' (novel). Some letters ed. Hansell Baugh, 1929; others at Harvard and the Univ. of Virginia. See Fay M. Blake in *Journal of Library History*, 16, 1981; Marjorie Smelstor in *SoQ*, 18, 1982.

Newmarch, Rosa Harriet, 1857–1940, poet, translator, music essayist, b. Leamington, Warwicks., da. of Sophie (Kenney; da. of James Kenney, playwright) and Samuel Jeaffreson, MD. Educ. chiefly at home, she visited Russia and studied under art critic Vladimir Stassov. In 1883 she m. Henry Charles N. Music was her chief love, and she published mainly music-related works, such as studies of Borodin and Liszt, 1889, Tchaikovsky, 1900, *The Russian Opera*, 1914, and many more. She also published two volumes of verse, *Horae Amoris*, 1903, a sonnet sequence, often on themes of religious love, and *Songs to a Singer*, 1906, which includes 'My Birthday' wherein the female speaker expresses her dejection which is only relieved by the arrival of her woman friend. Many poems have musical or operatic themes or employ musical forms or metaphors.

'New Woman' was a term coined in 1894 during a debate between pro- and anti-feminists, Sarah GRAND and OUIDA, to describe an emergent social and literary type which had challenged traditional representations of women since at least the 1880s. Although identified by her conservative critics variously with feminism, mannishness, promiscuity and decadence, her literary construction was marked more uniformly by her assumption that she was entitled to sexual autonomy than by her hostility to men, her espousal of free love, or her opposition to motherhood. This assumption, coupled with any number of outward manifestations of 'fast' behaviour (smoking, drinking, swearing, birth control), was what counted in Grant Allen's nastily anti-feminist *The Woman Who Did*, 1895, as well as in the ripostes to it by women; best known are *The Woman Who Didn't*, by Victoria CROSSE, and *The Woman Who Wouldn't*, by Lucas CLEEVE, both 1895. Usually presented, however sympathetically, as neurotic by male writers (e.g. Hardy's Sue Bridehead, Gissing's Rhoda Nunn), the New Woman in any manifestation outraged some women (e.g. Margaret OLIPHANT, Mabel BIRCHENOUGH) and inspired others (e.g. George EGERTON, Mona CAIRD, George PASTON). Associated issues remained important until after WWI, and markedly changed the development of the novel. The best full-length discussion is Gail Cunningham's, 1978; useful articles are by Linda Dowling, *NCF* 33, 1979, and Ellen Jordan, *The Victorian Newsletter*, 63, Spring 1983. Patricia Mark's *Bicycles, Bangs, and Bloomers, The New Woman in the Popular Press*, forthcoming 1990, draws on original sources which record satirical and other reactions.

Ngcobo, Lauretta, exiled South African novelist, b. in 1931 in Ixopo, Natal, the first girl in a family of four. Her mother, Rosa Fisekile (Cele) became the family's sole support after LN's father, Simon Shukwana Gwina, died when she was eight. Influenced by the family tradition of story-telling, and by her grandmother, who composed family poetry – a special composition to each child – LN has 'scribbled' since she was a little girl. Despite feeling marginalized as a girl throughout her education in Webbstown, Nokweja and Dumisa Schools, Inanda Seminary, and finally at Fort Hare Univ., where the ratio was 35 women to 500 men, LN received her BA in Education. Writing throughout this time, she discarded her writings each time she moved, feeling that her sex made publication or appreciation impossible. Stifled by repressive laws and persecution of writers in her homeland ('our society was muzzled breathless'), she left with her husband and four children, *c.* 1966, settling in London after a brief period in Swaziland. Because, as a woman, 'I was born into and have always kept on the periphery of life', and because the South African protest she was portraying was credibly male, LN spoke through a male activist character in her first novel, *Cross of Gold*, 1981. 'Looking into the future I wonder if it will prove to have been easier to fight the oppression of Apartheid than it will ever be to set women free in our societies. Writing in the mid 1980s, and watching the black neighbourhoods burning down in South Africa, and our people dying in large numbers, this is a very serious assertion I am making. Male domination does not "burn down".' She has written on women writers and edited *Let It Be Told, Black Women Writers in Britain*, 1987, a collection of autobiographical comments, with criticism (quoted above). LN's novel on rural black South African women is forthcoming 1990 as *And They Didn't Die*. See Carol Boyce Davies in *A Current Bibliography of African Affairs* 19, 1986–7, quoted above.

Nichols, Grace, poet, novelist, and children's writer, b. 1950 at Georgetown, Guyana, educ. at St Stephen's Scots School, the PPI High School and the Univ. of Guyana. She taught, 1967–70, and worked for the Georgetown *Chronicle*, 1971–3, and government information services: besides poetry and prose in the staff journal, she published a story before migrating to Britain in 1977. She is married to poet John Agard and has a daughter. She has published for children, especially for girls; books of stories rich in multi-cultural folk-tale and legend, like *Trust You, Wriggly!*, 1981, *Leslyn in London*, 1984 (novel), and *Come On Into My Tropical Garden*, 1988 (poetry anthology). *I Is a Long Memoried Woman*, 1983 (Commonwealth Poetry Prize), is a sequence of poems forming a psychic history of Caribbean womanhood, its protagonist a 'Child of the middle passage Womb', condemned to slavery: 'Sun shine / with as bright a flame / here ... but where're our shrines? / where're our stools? / How shall I worship?' 'Sugar Cane' presents the symbiotic or erotic bond of cane and slave: 'slowly / pain- / fully / he comes / to learn ... the / crimes / committed / in / his / name.' *The Fat Black Woman's Poems*, 1984, makes intermittent use of its persona, who denies the stereotypes of white beauty, female victim, and down-trodden immigrant. Powerful, clever, sexual, she 'remembers her Mama / and them days of playing / the jovial Jemima .... But this fat black woman ain't no Jemima / Sure thing Honey / Yeah'; she 'see through politicians / like snake sees through rat'; 'my thighs are twin seals / fat slick pups.' GN takes a new persona in *Lazy Thoughts of a Lazy Woman*, 1989. In both patois and standard English, she resists ideology and draws on many cultures. In *A Whole of a Morning Sky*, 1986, a novel based on her youth, a child thrives on the political turmoil of an island capital while her parents each regret their rural past. GN's work appears in journals and anthologies; she gives readings and broadcasts, and has commented on her life and work in Lauretta Ngcobo, ed., *Let It Be Told, Black Women Writers in Britain*, 1987, and in *Wasafiri*, 8, 1988.

Nichols, Mary Sargent (Neal) Gove, 'Mary Orme', 1810–84, writer and health reformer, b. Goffstown, NH, da. of Rebecca N. and William A. Neal. Her disastrous first marriage to hatter Hiram Gove, 1831, ended in divorce and forced her into teaching and sewing to support the family. Four abortive pregnancies and general ill-health led her to an interest in medicine, particularly the ideas of Sylvester Graham and the emerging hydropathy ('water-cure') movement. While working as a health practitioner and running a boarding house she pub. two novels and several short stories and sketches. Her work was praised by Poe as 'remarkable for its luminousness and precision – two qualities rare with her sex'. In her pioneering physiology lectures, she campaigned against women's 'unconditional obedience' and for married women's property rights and education for women. She wrote openly about sexual matters including vigorous defences of 'free love'. In 1848 she m. Thomas Low N., writer and newspaper editor. In 1855 she pub. the autobiographical *Mary Lyndon*, reviewed as 'the American Jane Eyre', in which the heroine discards a vicious husband, travels with men unchaperoned and finally contemplates a free union with her lover. Recognized as a polemic, the novel was denounced in the *NY Daily Times*, but reprinted in 1860. After converting to Catholicism and moving to England in 1861, MN wrote two more novels with less provocative themes. Her non-fiction focused on general health issues.

Ní Chuilleanáin, Eiléan, poet, editor, born 1942 at Cork, da. of novelist Eilis (Dillon) and Cormac O'Cuilleanain, professor of literature in Irish at Univ. College, Cork. She was educ. there (BA, MA in English 1964) and at Lady Margaret Hall, Oxford, then taught at Trinity College, Dublin. She pub. *Acts and Monuments*, 1972 (Patrick Kavanagh award), and *Site of Ambush*, 1975. *Cork*, 1977, vividly describes varying Irish lifestyles. In *The Second Voyage*, 1977, repr. 1986, a mythical figure says 'I plan to swallow the universe like a raw egg / After that there will be no more complaining'; in *The Rose Geranium*, 1981, a sequence about Ireland and the Irish uses similar surreal, magical, physical images. (See Douglas Sealy in *Poetry Ireland*, 4, 1982.) ENC married writer Macdara Woods, 1978, and with him edits *Cyphers*, a magazine aiming to counteract literary 'subservience to English'. She writes (as a socialist-feminist) in English, with rhythmical complexity drawn from traditions of Irish, French and Italian verse. 'The Absent Girl' treats women's social invisibility, 'Swineherd' (with a male persona) Irish national issues. In 'More Islands' she writes, 'A child afraid of islands, their dry / Moonlit shoulders, sees in a deep gutter / A stone, a knot in the stream. / She feels the gasping of wrecks, / Cormorants and lighthouses,' She is a friend of Eavan BOLAND and Leland BARDWELL, and has an essay on writers before Maria EDGEWORTH in *Irish Women: Image and Achievement*, 1985. Her work appears in the *Penguin Book of Irish Verse*, 1970, and Carol RUMENS, ed., *Making for the Open*, 1985.

Nightingale, Florence, 1820–1910, nursing and public health reformer, b. in Florence, da. of Frances (Smith) and William Edward N., country gentleman. Educ. at home, in the family's two houses in Derbyshire and Hampshire, with broad classical educ. from her father, she also studied Italian, French and German. When 16, she had a 'call from God' to work for humanity and found fashionable life increasingly stultifying. *Cassandra*, 1852, demonstrates her frustration: 'Passion, intellect, moral activity – these three have never been satisfied in a woman'. After much parental opposition, in 1851 she spent three months nursing with the Protestant Deaconesses at Kaiserswerth on the Rhine. From 1845 onwards, various influential friends had sided with FN, so by 1853, when she was offered the Superintendency of the Hospital for Gentlewomen in London, her parents reluctantly yielded. Here she began to effect hospital and nursing reform. When the Crimean War broke out, FN's close friend Sidney Herbert, as Secretary at War, invited her to lead a group of nurses to Turkey, where she saw the inept hospital administration of the British Army. Returning to England in 1856, she was influential in initiating the Royal Commission on the Sanitary State of the Army. FN worked incessantly in preparing this Report, visiting hospitals and barracks by day and compiling evidence at night: she collapsed in August 1857. She retired from public life, but continued to supervise the publication of the Report from her bed, and also initiated the subsequent Royal Commission on the Sanitary State of the Indian Army, 1859–63. The Nightingale School for Nurses, which opened at St Thomas's Hospital in 1860, sent nurses all over the world to establish training schools. FN was one reformer of a number, but was called the founder of modern nursing because she raised it to the status of a trained profession. FN involved herself in numerous issues of public concern. See the standard life by Sir Edward Cook, 1913, and C. Woodham-Smith, 1950, and *Selected Writings*, 1954, compiled by Lady Ridgely Seymer. See also her selceted letters, eds. M. Vicinus and B. Nergaard, 1990.

Nihell, Elizabeth, London midwife and polemicist. Trained, unusually for a Protestant, by the women of the Hôtel Dieu in Paris, wife of a surgeon-apothecary and a mother herself, she practised for years, and issued a work on medical use of water, 1759. The spread of men-midwives (and writings of Dr William Smellie) moved her 'unsuppressible indignation' at their 'errors and pernicious innovations' to publish a substantial *Treatise on the Art of*

Midwifery, 1760. Men are interested, she says, merely in money (her husband's business has no relation to her work); their next move could be to annex infant care and boost 'pap' and 'water-gruel' instead of mother's milk. Though glad of 'that divine invention the forceps', she details grisly stories of 'polite murder' by instruments which make 'an art-military' of birth. Though learned herself, she judges reading and dissection less vital than experience: inadequate midwives must be trained, not replaced. Echoing Sarah STONE, she bids women: 'assume liberty enough of mind to shake off the dangerous yoke'; 'cease to be the dupes' of 'scientific jargon'; choose cherishing and heartening by the trained hands of women.

Nin, Anaïs, 1903–77, diarist, critic, novelist, b. in Neuilly, Paris, da. of Rosa (Culmel), a French-Danish singer, and Joaquin N., a Spanish composer. They separated, and at 11, on a boat to NY, she began writing her diary in the form of letters – never sent – to her father (early diaries, 1914–27 so far pub., the first in translation: 1978–86). She left public school in 1919 (reputedly when her writing style was criticized), read philosophy, danced, modelled, and at 20 married Hugh P. Guiler (also known as Ian Hugo), artist (he illustrated much of her work), film-maker (she acted in his films) and banker. They moved back to near Paris. AN's first book *D. H. Lawrence, An Unprofessional Study*, 1932, is a defence of experimentalism which led on, via a preface to Henry Miller's *Tropic of Cancer*, 1934, 'Realism and Reality', 1946, and 'On Writing', 1947, to her 'exploratory' *The Novel of the Future*, 1968. She trained as a psychoanalyst (but hardly practised) before her first fictions, *House of Incest*, 1936, (a 'prose-poem' about a mutilated dancer's escape from nightmare subjectivity), and *Winter of Artifice*, 1939 (three novellas). Back in NYC during WWII and unable to find a publisher there, she bought a press to republish these two and add *Under a Glass Bell* (stories), 1944 and later small works. Erotica written this decade appeared posthumously as *Delta of Venus*, 1977, and *Little Birds*, 1979 (see Smaro Kamboureli in *Journal of Modern Literature*, 11, 1984). *This Hunger*, 1945, was the beginning of a *roman fleuve* or 'continuous novel': with *Bread and the Wafer* it became *Ladders to Fire*, 1946, which with four more parts became *Cities of the Interior*, 1959. *Seduction of the Minotaur*, 1961, an 'outgrowth' of this work, features the AN heroine who goes furthest in self-discovery, in escape out of unfree into free sensuousness and human relatedness. *Nuances*, 1970, comments on all these works and on *Collages*, 1964, a novel about fantasies. AN felt that publication in 1966 of the first volume of her DIARY (from 1931: a period she now saw as historical) made it a correspondence, a collaborative 'universal work'. In vol. vi she wrote, 'It is my thousand years of womanhood I am recording'; the self was 'merely an instrument of awareness'. The late vols. record a continuing dialogue with feminism, and one between the teaching and the confessional functions of the diary. About 3300 pages were in print by 1984. Her lectures, seminars and interviews were ed. Evelyn J. Hinz as *A Woman Speaks*, 1975. Recent reprints; among much comment see Maxine Molyneux and Julia Casterton in *minnesota review*, 18, 1982 (on what makes AN problematic); the journal *Anais*, 1983– .; short study by Nancy Scholar, 1984; Sharon Spencer, ed., *Essays*, 1986. Bibliog. by Benjamin Franklin V, 1973; reference guide by Rose Marie Cutting [1978]; letters to Henry Miller, pub. 1987. Diaries (not accessible) at UCLA.

Nine Muses, The, 1700, a volume of elegies in which each Muse laments John Dryden's death, written not as its title-page says by *nine* 'severall Ladies', but by Susanna CENTLIVRE (perhaps), Sarah FYGE, Delarivier MANLEY (the editor), Lady PIERS, Mary PIX, and Catharine TROTTER. See Ruth Salvaggio in *JPC*, 21, 1987.

Nithsdale, Winifrede Maxwell (Herbert), Countess of, 1672–1749, letter-writer and memoirist, sister of Lady Lucy HERBERT. In 1699 she m., at Paris, her fellow-Catholic William M., Earl of N. When he was arrested in 1715 for his part in the Jacobite rebellion, she rode to Scotland to bury key family papers, rode back to London (despite her pregnancy and girth-deep snow), petitioned 'the Elector' in vain for his release from the Tower, then planned and executed a daring escape on what her husband fully expected to be his last night. Once he was safe she returned for the papers. During these events she wrote letters, chiefly about money, property and arrangements; later she wrote from the Continent about their poverty and his habit of scrounging money behind her back. After 1721, however, she wrote for her prioress sister a justly famous, grippingly tense narrative of her adventure. Copies multiplied (the Ladies of LLANGOLLEN owned one); pub. 1816, 1827; her own text with other letters in life by Henrietta Tayler [1939]. It was fictionalized in *Tales of the Peerage* . . . , ed. Barbarina DACRE, 1835.

Njau, Rebeka, 'Marina Gashe', novelist, short-story writer, playwright, teacher, b. in 1932 in Kanyariri, Kenya, she was educ. at Alliance Girls' High School and Makerere Univ. (diploma in education). She later taught at both institutions, then became Headmistress of Nairobi Girls' Secondary School and married Tanzanian artist Elimo N., with whom she had two children. Her plays, *In A Round Chain*, performed 1964, and the prize-winning *The Scar*, 1965, reflect her childhood desire to be an actress. Her first, unpub. novel, *Alone With the Fig Tree*, won the East African Writing Committee Prize. *The Hypocrite*, short stories, appeared in 1980. Her novel *Ripples in the Pool*, 1975, dramatizes a conflict in post-independence Kenya between the mysterious clan pool and encroaching westernism, engaging its readers not in themes of social reform, but in violence, madness, lust, and magic, dealing also, obliquely, with lesbianism, a subject rarely broached by African writers. See Abiseh M. Porter in *Ariel*, 12, 1981, Mineke Schipper, *Theatre and Society in Africa*, 1982, and Jean F. O'Barr in Jones, ed., 1987.

Noel, 'Mrs John Vavasour N.', 1815–73, novelist and short-story writer. B. in Ireland, she migrated to America in 1832, ran a seminary for young ladies in Savannah, Georgia, for a number of years, moved to Canada in 1847 or 48, and she died in Kingston, Ont. She published her stories and serial novels in American and Canadian periodicals. Several of her novels – sentimental, at times gothic or adventurous – were also published as books. *The Abbey of Rathmore, and Other Tales*, 1859, contains three short novels, one set on the west coast of Ireland during a rebellion; one whose action entails realistic descriptions of England, Scotland, and Ireland; and one which recounts the affairs of a young Irish immigrant to the US in the 1840s and gives a realistically grim picture of the American South in the time of slavery. 'Moonlight Thoughts' is by her daughter, Ellen.

Noonuccal, Oodgeroo, Kath (Ruska) Walker, Aboriginal poet, story-teller, actor and activist, b. 1920 in Brisbane, Queensland, da. of Lucy (McCulloch) and Edward R. She left school at 13 to work as a domestic, but continued to educate herself, and served in the Australian Women's Army, 1941–4. She m. Bruce W., waterside worker, and had two sons; they divorced after 12 years. She became involved with the Aboriginal rights movement in the 1960s, serving as secretary of the Queensland State Council for the Advancement of Aboriginals and Torres Strait Islanders, 1961–70. In 1972 she established the Noonuccal-Nughie Education and Cultural Centre at her home, North Stradbroke Island, in order to teach people, especially children, of all races about traditional Aboriginal culture. Encouraged to publish her poetry by Mary GILMORE and others, ON was the first Aboriginal writing in English to establish a wide readership. Much of her poetic expression reflects Aboriginal narrative and ORAL story-telling patterns. She is best known for her first collection, *We Are Going*, 1964, whose title poem warns of the destruction and possible extinction of Aboriginal culture; others protest against white intolerance and cruelty. Other vols. are *The Dawn is at Hand*, 1966, winner of the 1967 Jessie Litchfield Award, *My People*, 1970, and a collection of stories, *Stradbroke Dreamtime*, 1972. An MBE, in 1987 she took the Aboriginal name Oodgeroo Noonuccal in protest against the treatment of Aboriginals since 1788.

Nooth, Charlotte, poet and novelist, da. of a successful London surgeon, to whom after his probably recent death she dedicated her *Original Poems*, 1815. These include many genres and translations from several languages, praise of Germaine de STAËL (the 'treasure of thy mighty mind'), dialect BALLADS written in Northern Ireland in 1807, and a vigorous, melodramatic prose-and-verse play called *Clara, or The Nuns of Charity*, whose heroine is plagued by family mystery and unjust accusation. Next year came *Eglantine, or The Family of Fortescue*, a novel written at Kew, whose preface interestingly combines homage to 'co-temporary female pens' with acceptance of the handicap of 'situations of comparative sameness and seclusion' and 'very limited opportunities for witnessing human nature under its most striking forms'. The novel, with domestic humour and social satire, a sympathetic young officer hero, and a charming incorrigible con-man as the heroine's father, suggests no cramped imagination.

Norman, Marsha (Williams), playwright and novelist, b. in 1947 in Louisville, Ky., da. of religious fundamentalists Bertha and Billie W. She spent much time with her aunt Bubbie (who read to her), started writing at five, studied the piano seriously, and thought of composing as a career (and now thinks of her play structures as musical). She attended school in Louisville, then Agnes Scott College in Georgia (BA in philosophy, 1969) and the Univ. of Louisville (MA 1971). Twice married, twice divorced, she worked two years with emotionally disturbed and gifted children: 'perhaps the most valuable work I ever did. What you cannot escape seeing is that we are all disturbed kids.' Through a contact at the Actors Theatre of Louisville, she was encouraged to write *Getting Out*, produced 1977, pub. 1980, which is based on her work at Kentucky Central State Hospital. It depicts a character doubly represented as Arlie/Arlene, released from prison after serving a term for murder: the exchange between the two reveals her history of physical and emotional abuse and her struggle for identity. MN wrote her next three plays – *Third and Oak: The Laundromat*, produced 1978, pub. 1980, *Circus Valentine*, produced 1979, and *The Holdup*, produced 1983 – while playwright-in-residence at the Actors Theatre. She moved with her second husband to NYC in the early 1980s. There she wrote the Pulitzer Prize winning play *'night Mother*, first produced 1982, pub. 1983. A 'kind of final submission to the naturalistic form', says MN, it examines the relationship between a woman who contemplates and commits suicide, and her mother. *The Holdup* was produced in 1983, *Traveler in the Dark* in 1984. MN's novel, *The Fortune Teller*, 1987, deals with the politics of abortion and again centres on the mother-daughter relationship. Interview in Betsko and Koenig, 1987, criticism by Keyssar, 1984, Lynda Hart in *SoQ*, 25, 1987, and Jenny S. Spencer in *MD*, 30, 1987. See also 'Women Playwrights: New Voices in the Theater', *NY Times Magazine*, 1 May 1983, and the response to this from some feminist dramatists, 'The "Woman" Playwright Issue', *Performing Arts Journal*, 21, 1983.

Norris, Kathleen (Thompson), 1880–1966, popular novelist, journalist and short-story writer, b. in San Francisco, second of six children. She went to work – as clerk, bookkeeper, saleswoman – to support her family when her parents, Josephine E. (Moroney) and bank manager James Alden T., both died in 1899. She briefly attended the Univ. of California, 1905, then worked as a reporter and social-column editor. In 1909 she married editor and novelist Charles N. They lived in NYC and had a son; twin daughters died at birth. KN's first stories appeared in the NY *Telegram* and *Atlantic Monthly*. Her first novel, *Mother*, 1911, a saga of family life, draws on her own family; most of her settings are Californian, her families Irish Catholic, and the struggle of working girls is a favourite theme. *The Rich Mrs Burgoyne*, 1913, first of several works that began as magazine serials, was written in six weeks. Among mostly frivolous romances, *Certain People of Importance*, 1922, announces its scope with a title from Robert Browning, a 100-year span, and attention to history's seamy side. *Noon*, 1925, is autobiographical; *Through a Glass Darkly*, 1957, presents a utopian, caring society free of war; *Family Gathering*, 1959, is another personal memoir. KN belonged to the Women's International League for Peace and Freedom, and wrote *What Price Peace? A Handbook of Peace for American Women*, 1928; she was prohibitionist, isolationist, anti-capital-punishment, and, after WWII, anti-nuclear. Her voluminous works include a poetry volume, 1942, and radio soap opera, 1945. Papers at Stanford Univ.; also Univ. of Calif. (Berkeley) and Calif. State Library (Sacramento).

North, Jessica Nelson, 1894–1988, poet, novelist, editor, b. in Madison, Wis., to Elizabeth (Nelson) and David Willard North. She grew up on a farm, educ. by her mother, at a country school, and at Lawrence College, Appleton, Wis. (graduated 1917, after her mother's death). She cared for her father and brother until 1920, when she moved to Chicago. There she did graduate work at the Univ. of Chicago, 1921–2, edited the Art Institute *Bulletin*, 1923–5, and (encouraged by Harriet MONROE) began publishing poems (in *Poetry*, *The Dial*, and other journals), and essays on art. She was acting editor of *Poetry* in 1929. She married Reed Innes MacDonald in 1921 and had two children. Eunice TIETJENS praises as 'capable of many moods' – sensitive, humorous – her poetry volume *Prayer Rug*, 1923. The title of the equally well-received *The Long Leash*, 1928, alludes to the male–female relationships it powerfully examines. That year began JNN's 20 years as assistant editor, then editor, of *Poetry*; she taught poetry workshops and was, like Monroe, an enabling force for young poets. In *Dinner Party*, 1942, poems about women's lives range from satire ('Daughter, observe the anchored flower / That sure and steadfast waits its hour. / The world's a-hum, / Sit, sweet and dumb, / And take whatever bee may come') to mournful: 'the incredulous despair / Of women growing older'. Her first novel, *Arden Acres*, 1935, is loosely based on her knowledge of Chicago suburbs during the depression: 'To say [our neighbours] were angry would be stating it mildly.' *Morning in the Land*, 1941, draws on her father's memory to depict English immigrants to Wisconsin in the mid nineteenth century: the hero marries a French girl raised by Indians.

Northampton, Margaret Compton (Clephane), Marchioness of, 1793–1830, poet, eldest da. of Mariane (Maclean) – a friend of Anna SEWARD – and William Clephane (d. 1803). It was probably her mother 'whose praise my verse did first expand': she sent Walter Scott in 1809 a translation from Gaelic; she also set songs to music. Scott introduced her, in 1813, to her future husband, Spencer J. A. Compton, scientist and later (1828) Marquess of N.; he also negotiated (not easily) the marriage contract. He arranged probably her first printing (inaccurately, from memory, 1816) in a collection, and praised her sister Jane's unpub. comedy. MN and her husband lived in Italy, 1817–18, and again from 1820: she died there in childbirth. In 1833 her husband printed her poems headed with the six-canto *Irene*, which uses the *Don Juan* stanza to admirable effect both for beauty (fairy-tale action in Mediterranean setting) and mockery ('reverend parents, guardians, uncles, tutors' are urged to protect their charges from 'that disorder'd baggage call'd the Muse'). Princess Irene and her Florio are supernaturally tested for constancy: she passes the test and dies; he fails, but inherits her throne, a 'right legitimate as e'er was known'. Other poems include 'The Idiot Boy', in unWordsworthian couplets: repr. in her husband's anthology *The Tribute*, 1837 – which also contains a poem by Wordsworth.

Norton, Caroline Elizabeth Sarah (Sheridan), 1808–77, poet, novelist, b. London, da. of Henrietta (Callander), a Scotswoman and author of three novels, and Tom S., erratic son of playwright R. B. S.; grandson of Francis S. In 1809 the family fortune was lost in the Drury Lane Theatre fire, and her parents left the children in Scotland from 1813 and went to the Cape for her father's health (d. 1817). CN grew up with Scottish aunts, educ. by tutors, and from 1817 at school in Surrey, where she met George N., who persuaded her to marry him in 1827. She had always written poems and stories, publishing 'The Dandies' Rout' while still a child. Her first poems, *The Sorrows of Rosalie*, appeared in 1829, and in 1831 she became editor of a court magazine and then of the *English* ANNUAL, 1834–8. Two stories, *The Wife* and *Woman's Reward*, were pub. together in 1835: closely based on personal experience, the book was not a popular success. After the disastrous breakdown of her marriage, CN battled for custody of her three sons. Her pamphlet *A Plain Letter* influenced the passing of the Infant Custody Bill in 1839, while later pamphlets, *English Laws for Women*, 1854, and *A Letter to the Queen*, 1855, supported the Divorce Bill and the Married Women's Property Bill after her husband claimed her copyrights. She also published novels: *Stuart of Dunleath*, 1851, *Lost and Saved*, 1863, with a heroine based on her own character, and a rather scandalous theme of illicit love, and *Old Sir Douglas*, 1867. As well as songs, stories and poems for periodicals, she published long narrative poems, from *A Voice from the Factories*, 1836, to *The Lady of La Garaye*, 1862. The latter tells of a French countess, injured in a hunting accident, who builds and works in a hospital for the poor. Based on a true story, it is interesting in its long justification of the lady's right to enjoy horse-riding: 'Why should the sweet elastic sense of joy / Presage a fault?' In 1869 she wrote an article on her friend Lucie Duff GORDON. In 1877 she m. Sir William Stirling Maxwell, but died after a few months. See life by Jane Gray Perkins, 1909, and Alice Acland, 1948. Her eldest sister, Helen Selina Blackwood, then Hay, later Lady Dufferin, and finally Countess of Gifford, 1807–67, pub. prose and occasional verse, mostly sentimental songs, as well as one play, *Finesse*. All appeared anon.; she did not even attend the 1863 performance of her play, a bustling farcical comedy. Her poem 'The Charming Woman', satirizing would-be learned women, was particularly popular, as was 'The Irish Emigrant', set to music by Charlotte BARNARD. See the posthumous *Songs, Poems and Verses*, 1894.

Norton, Frances (Freke), Lady, 1640–1731, essayist, sister of Elizabeth FREKE, with whom she exchanged verse. She m. Sir George N. of Abbots Leigh, Somerset, but later left him. The last survivor of her three children was Grace GETHIN, whose essays FN had printed posthumously, 1699. In 1705 she set her own name to her handsome vol. in two parts: *The Applause of Virtue* (short essays) and *Memento Mori* (meditations on mortality, with a frontispiece showing her daughter's deathbed), each dedicated to a bereaved female relation (re-issued 1725). She wrote, she says, over some months 'for my Melancholy Divertisement', and did not wish 'to seem wise by making use of another Man's labours': she identifies quotations from a range of ancient philosophers and Church fathers, which reflect her belief that 'Of all others a Studious Life is the least tiresome.' She says that unhappy marriage is 'to tear each others Flesh, and gnaw their Bones'; but as a widow she married Col. Ambrose N., her first husband's cousin, 1718, and then William Jones in 1724. She also pub. at Bristol, 1714, a *Miscellany* of her own poems written to embroider on chairbacks etc., now very rare.

Notley, Alice Elizabeth, poet, b. 1945 at Bisbee, Ariz., and raised at Needles, Calif., a desert town evoked in *Tell Me Again*, 1982, a brief childhood autobiography. She warmly portrays her father, who worked in a garage, and mother, a southerner with alleged Indian blood, who raised her on the Bible. AN was baptized at 14 or 15 as a preliminary to leaving the church. She attended Barnard College, NYC (BA, 1967) and the Univ. of Iowa (MFA, 1969), married Ted Berrigan (d. 1982), settled in New York and had two sons: 'now three irrevocably / I'm wife I'm mother I'm / myself and him and I'm myself and him and him.' After experimental work in magazines came a stream of books from small presses (13 by 1985), from *165 Meeting House Lane*, 1971. Of *Phoebe Light* and *Incidentals in the Day World*, both 1973, the first title-poem reads 'The great cosmetic / Strangeness of the normal deep person'; the second is nine pages long. AN builds haunting, unreal images on close observation ('telephone wires the / luminous lines of the world / on which I walk / bare feet in fog / foggy-footed spider See / the spider toe-dance on its / tender tendril legs across / my hand') or lets the sound of words supplant meaning: 'Scansion / Stamina / Tammany / Amenable.' *For Frank O'Hara's Birthday*, pub. in England, 1976, includes poems about the experience of living there. Her first hardbound book, *Alice Ordered Me To Be Made*, 1976, drew comparison with Gertrude STEIN. *How Spring Comes* and *Waltzing Matilda*, both 1981, use many voices (not all female or human), letters and dialogue (several between Anonymous and Adviser); they dislocate language and syntax, mix the personal with the topical; 'A California Girlhood' lists women writers with loving humour. AN has also ed. *Chicago* poetry magazine, and written 'My being a poet completely coincides with me, there's not other.'

Notley, Frances Eliza Millett (Thomas), 'Francis Derrick', 1820–1912, novelist, b. Landager, near Liskeard, Cornwall. Da. of William Millett T., she was educ. in England and France and in 1843 m. George N. of Combe, Sydenham, Somerset. She began writing in the 1850s, probably after her husband's death (1855), producing a number of stories and novels, mostly anonymous. Her most successful was *Olive Varcoe*, 1868, which first appeared in the *Family Herald* (penny serial literature), and was later translated into several languages, and dramatized three times, but not performed. Signed 'Francis Derrick', the 1872 ed. adds a portrait of Mrs Notley. Olive, the child of an Englishman and a slave girl, is brought up by a great aunt in Cornwall. Ungovernable and fierce, she is wrongly suspected of murdering her rival in love. Other novels, such as *Family Pride*, 1871, also devise sensation plots around the stereotyped theme of female rivalries.

Nott, Kathleen Cecilia, philosphical critic, poet and novelist, b. in London in ?1909, da. of Ellen and Philip N. She attended Mary Datchelor School, King's College, London, and Somerville College, Oxford, graduating in philosophy, politics and economics. She m. scientist Christopher Bailey in 1929 (divorced 1960). After social work in poor areas of London she described these communities in a novel, *Mile End*, 1938. After war work in army education, she pub. three books in 1947: *The Dry Deluge* (a topical, fantastical satire), a translation from Lucien Chauvet (two from Riccardo Bacchelli followed in 1956 and 1958), and *Landscapes and Departures*, first of four volumes of abstract, philosphical poems, concerned with making sense of life and death: 'the lives, / the little lives that pulse in the hand, / happy to hang head downwards, happy like grapes / with their own heaviness; 'A life is a fear that flits.' A traditionalist in literature ('Poetry is a hardwon craft'), she developed her anti-modernist position in *The Emperor's Clothes*, 1953. *Poems from the North*, 1956, includes evocations of the timelessness of nature. *Creatures and Emblems*, 1960, develops a satiric edge: 'So deep we had been walking talking oh my love / (Of love) so long we had been wont to dally, / We had no time nor eyes for what went on above, / We had failed to note we were in rubbish-valley.' KN's latest novel was *An Elderly Retired Man*, 1963, a sober account of an ex-civil servant's progress towards self-discovery. Non-fictional prose includes a book on Sweden, 1960, *A Soul in the Quad*, 1969 (an autobiographical examination of the relations of poetry to philosophy and ethics), and works on philosphy, 1970, and liberalism, 1977. *Elegies*, 1981, voices 'bad temper (and some sour grapes) at the contemporary poetic scene' as preface to sonnets: 'Only asleep I do not think of death / But practise there for your unpeopled night.' KN has been president of the Progressive League and the British PEN club.

Novel, early. Recent scholarship has confirmed that women took the lead among the earliest novelists (see studies by Paul Salzman, Jane Spencer, Dale Spender, all 1986). Aphra BEHN marks an English transition from ROMANCE to novel, as does Marie Madeleine de LA FAYETTE in France. Behn wrote short novels (which we should call novellas) as well as a longer work in the epistolary mode which (as private, personal, emotional and amatory writing) was seen as particularly female. Her immediate successors, Delarivier MANLEY, Mary DAVYS, Jane BARKER and Eliza HAYWOOD, each brought novelty and experiment to the genre. By the date of Haywood's last novels, Samuel Richardson and Henry Fielding had brought a male dominance comparable to that of other forms.

Nugent, Maria (Skinner), Lady, 1771–1834, travel-diarist, one of 12 children of New Jersey loyalists Elizabeth (Kearney) and Brigadier-General Cortlandt S. In 1797, at Belfast, she m. George N. (later a baronet); she began her diary, 1801, 'sick, tired, and disgusted' after the Irish rebellion. On his appointment to govern Jamaica she wrote '*we* are soldiers, and must have no will of our own'. She stayed in Jamaica till 1805 and bore two children there. She despised the social and eating habits of the planters, and angered some of her own class by her – relatively – humane, friendly treatment of the 'blackies'. (The servants' laziness, she decides, is the *result* of slavery.) She continued her diary in England, 1805–11 (banal), and India, 1811–15, with verse on e.g. leaving her children or seeing the Taj Mahal: the whole privately printed, 1839; Jamaican part with other excerpts, 1907; Jamaica only, ed. Philip Wright, Kingston, 1966.

Nuns. English medieval nuns included a few creative translators: twelfth-century Clemence of Barking turned a Latin life of St Catherine into Anglo-Norman. Alexandra A. T. Barratt ascribes the thirteenth-century *Owl and the Nightingale* to a Shaftesbury nun (*UTQ*, 56, 1987) and explores the critical implications of female authorship of the fifteenth-century *Flower and the Leaf* and *The Assembly of Ladies* (*PQ*, 66, 1987: two poems ed. Derek Pearsall, 1962).

JULIAN of Norwich was an anchorite or solitary, not a nun. After the Reformation, Flanders nunneries for Englishwomen produced not only devotional works (e.g. by Gertrude MORE) and translations (e.g. by Agnes MORE) but also fine biographies and auto-biographies (e.g. by Anne or Mary CARY, Catherine HOLLAND, Elizabeth SHIRLEY) and convent chronicles like that written perhaps by Winefrid THIMELBY. These present tales of their members' former years (courage under persecution, often learned from mothers and other female relations), their convent life (emphasis on the domestic and on women's solidarity), and pious deaths (engagingly human, sometimes humorous, without hankering for superhuman sanctity). See Isobel Grundy in Grundy and Susan Wiseman, eds., 1990. A chronicle of very different, dramatic years (the French Revolution, semi-tolerated exile in England, 1794–1802), written by Mary Augustina More (seven generations removed from Margaret ROPER), is quoted in Catherine S. Durrant's study, 1925. For modern US 'nun-poets' see Sister Mary MADELEVA.

Nwapa, Flora Nwanzuruaha, public servant, publisher, short-story writer, writer of children's literature, Nigeria's first woman novelist and the first black African woman to gain an international reputation. Her parents were both teachers, though her mother retired to become a housewife. She was b. in 1931 in Oguta, Nigeria, and educ. at Archdeacon Crowther's Memorial Girls' School, near Port Harcourt, CMS Girls' School, Enugu, and the Univs. of Ibadan (BA 1957) and Edinburgh. She m. Gogo Nwakuche, an industrialist, 1977, and has three children. She has been much involved in education and public service – at the Univ. of Lagos, 1962–7, with the Executive Council of the East Central State, 1970, and as Minister for Health and Social Welfare of the East Central State, 1970–5. After a military coup, her children's books became politically suspect, and they were banned from school reading lists. In 1977 she established Flora Nwapa and Co., which publishes juvenile literature, and Tana Press, for adult fiction. Her long, productive career records changes in women's roles, and her novels take a women's point of view. The first two, *Efuru*, 1966, and *Edu*, 1970, show traditional village women, proud of their heritage but confined by their role. *This is Lagos and Other Stories*, 1971, deals with polygamy, infidelity and drug trafficking for children. *Wives at War and Other Stories*, 1980, like FN's personal narrative, *Never Again*, 1975, treats domestic hardships and atrocities of war in Biafra. *One is Enough*, 1981, examines the drastic changes for Nigerian women in the last 20 years. After one failed marriage, its protagonist decides to go it alone, to be a single parent and make a career by herself, because one husband is enough to put up with. *Women Are Different*, 1986, dramatizes African women's changing needs. A frequent speaker at international conferences, FN aims to provide suitable fiction for Nigerian children, to write about African children for western children, and 'to inform and educate women all over the world, especially Feminists (both with a capital F and small 'f') about the role of women in Nigeria, their economic independence, their relationship with their husbands and children, their traditional beliefs and their status in the community as a whole'. See Taiwo, 1984, Anna Githaiga, *Notes on Flora Nwapa's Efuru*, 1979, Naana Banyiwa-Horne and Carole Boyce Davies in Davies and Graves, 1986, and interviews in *Africa Woman*, August 1977, and on radio (taped) by Charlotte and David Bruner.

Oakes Smith, Elizabeth (Prince), 'Mrs Seba Smith', 'Ernest Helfenstein', 1806–93, poet, novelist and feminist, b. North Yarmouth, Maine, da. of Sophia (Blanchard) and David P., ship's captain, who d. when she was two. The family moved to Portland where she was educ. at Mrs Rachel Neal's school; she was then persuaded by her mother to marry Seba S., editor of the Portland *Eastern Argus*, in 1823. She found her husband 'most exacting', and when sons were born instead of daughters was 'glad not to add to the number of human beings who must be . . . curtailed of so much that was desirable in life' (*Autobiography*, 1924). She assisted him with his editorial duties, and wrote her first essays, poems and stories for the *Eastern Argus* in the 1830s. In 1837, after her husband's bankruptcy, she wrote for magazines. Her first novel, *Riches Without Wings*, 1838, was pub. under 'Mrs Seba Smith', but after 1843 she assumed the names Oakes Smith and changed her children's name legally to Oaksmith. Her narrative poem, 'The Sinless Child', accorded critical acclaim, presents her view of woman as Madonna figure, but later poems like 'The Wife' are more subversive. She gave up poetry, finding it too 'disquieting'. Her major novel, *Bertha and Lily*, 1854, is about Bertha, the intellectual 'NEW WOMAN' who, after being seduced, bears an illegitimate child: 'It is vain to appeal to our brothers. Women ... must learn to uphold each other'. In 1851 EOS became the first woman to lecture on the lyceum circuit, and wrote a series of feminist articles for the *New York Tribune*, collected as *Woman and her Needs*, which expanded on the ideas of Lydia Maria CHILD and Margaret FULLER. In the 1860s she wrote dime novels to make money; she was a charter member of New York's first women's club, Sorosis, in 1868, and in 1877 was pastor of the Independent Church, Canastota, NY. *Selections from the Autobiography of EOS* was pub. in 1924.

Oakley, Ann (Titmuss), feminist sociologist, b. in London, 1944, only child of Kathleen (Miller), social worker, and Richard T., 'academic pundit and social critic'. She despised the spinster teachers at the private school where she was scared and teased; at Chelsea Technical Coll. she wrote 'Socialism and Me' for its bulletin. Deeply influenced by her father, she felt expected to be a caring, family-oriented woman and have a male 'brilliantly successful career'. She had a minor breakdown in 1962, studied philosophy, politics and economics at Somerville College, Oxford, married Robin O. (later an academic) in 1964, and took her BA in 1965. In the next 16 months she wrote 14 short stories, six articles, an unfinished children's history book, and two rejected novels (*Eyelight*, in which a graduate finds happiness as wife and mother, and *The Unborn Child*, in which an infertile wife goes mad); in the next 16 months she had two babies. Taking this plunge, eyes 'completely closed', brought depression, despite doing market research and writing TV scripts for children. In 1969 she began a PhD at Bedford College, London, on the 'laughable' topic of housework, which produced *Sex, Gender and Society*, 1972 (written in six weeks), *Housewife* (centred on four case-studies) and the fuller *Sociology of Housework*, both 1974. The next three years brought an ectopic pregnancy, a miscarriage, another child, and cancer of the tongue, which she wrote of in the *British Medical Journal*, 1979. Her marriage developed gradually from traditional to egalitarian. Other works (blending professional expertise with personal witness) include two books of feminist essays ed. with Juliet Mitchell, 1976 and 1986; *Women Confined*, 1980 (on the medicalization of childbirth); *Subject Women*, 1981 (on 'the profit men make out of women's subordination'); *Taking It Like a Woman*, 1984 (an autobiography built of 'Scenes', 'Chronologies', dreams, poems, and passages of reflection); *Telling the Truth about Jerusalem*, 1986 (essays and poems, their occasions detailed, their imagery arresting: 'love, the appalling joke / standing there in its own bleached halo / like some wet angel a dog found in a park'); and *The Men's Room*, 1988 (title alluding to women's lack of territory), a novel about a long-lived extramarital affair whose heroine outlives belief in a promise that 'I'll never lie to *you*. You're different from other women.' *Matilda's Mistake* followed in 1990.

Oates, Joyce Carol, exceptionally prolific writer of novels, stories, poetry, plays, and essays, b. in 1938, da. of Caroline (Bush) and Frederic James O., a tool and die designer. She was raised in rural New York State, an area similar to her fictional Eden County. She wrote a novel each semester as she earned a BA in English and philosophy at Syracuse Univ., 1960, and an MA from Wisconsin, 1961, where she met and married Raymond Smith, 1961. She had begun work on a PhD in English literature when, discovering one of her short stories listed in Martha Foley's *Best American Short Stories*, 1961, she withdrew, thinking, 'Maybe I could be a writer'. She taught English at the Univ. of Detroit, 1961–7, then at the Univ. of Windsor, Ont., until 1977. With her husband, JCO runs the Ontario Review Press, publishing the *Ontario Review*, from Princeton, where she is a Writer-in-Residence. A 'romantic in the tradition of Stendhal and Flaubert', she was influenced by Faulkner, Kafka, Freud, Nietzsche, Mann and Dostoevsky. She has produced more than 55 books since her first collection of stories, *By The North Gate*, 1963. Madness, violence and lust in bizarre forms appear in her characters, like the 19-year-old matricidal narrator of *Expensive People*, 1968, who plans to commit suicide by eating till he bursts, and Love, the fiercely protective spider riding on the shoulder of the heroine of *Bellefleur*, 1980. From realism, to gothic-horror, to metafiction, or to parody of any form, her attention is on 'the utterly uncontrollable emotions that determine our lives' and her writing evokes 'our own emotional or moral dilemmas and allegiances'. The themes of male violence and female passivity appear in 'Where Are You Going, Where Have You Been', from *The Wheel of Love*, 1970, and other earlier works; and her more recent writing, like *The Bloodsmoor Romance*, 1982, a comic-tragic parody of a nineteenth-century GOTHIC novel about five sisters, reveals a complex feminist consciousness. She calls her poetry 'shorthand'; critics call her plays 'academic', 'untheatrical'. Collections of her stories include *The Goddess and Other Women*, 1974, *The Seduction and Other Stories*, 1975, *Crossing the Border*, 1977. Describing literary criticism as 'the most ingenious form storytelling can take', JCO's collections of essays are *Contraries*, 1981, and *The Profane Art*, 1983. *On Boxing*, 1987, reflects a lifelong interest. *Kindred Passions*, 1987, is a thriller written as 'Rosamond Smith'. Her many awards include Guggenheim and Rosenthal fellow-ships and the National Book Award, for *them*, 1969, which is based on the recollections of one of her students and set in Detroit, 1937–66. See critical essays ed. Linda Wagner, 1979, Katherine Baston, 1983, Harold Bloom, 1987. Bibliography by Francine Lercangée, 1986.

O'Brien, Charlotte Grace, 1845–1909, Irish social reformer, novelist, prose writer and poet. B. Cahirmoyle, Co. Limerick, da. of Lucy Caroline (Gabbett) and William Smith O'B., the exiled Young Ireland leader, she was educ. by a governess. A supporter of Parnell and the Land League, she pub. 'The Irish Poor Man' in *Nineteenth Century*, Dec. 1880, and she worked for Irish female emigrants. As well as contributing articles and letters to the *Pall Mall Gazette* and *Fortnightly*, 1881, and lecturing in the USA, she set up a lodging-house in Queenstown, and visited the ships with medical officers. A Protestant, she worked strenuously to enlist Catholic Church support. Her fiction includes *Dominick's Trials*, 1870, a religious tract, and *Light and Shade*, 1878, a novel about the Fenian rising. Though over-simplified, it shows the sufferings of the Irish peasants and their consequent resentment. Footnotes testify to her personal knowledge and the work merits consideration as a social-problem novel. Her prose sketches include 'The Feminine Animal', exhorting women to develop their responsibilities with their increasing freedom: these humorous yet sensitive sketches of local life and her unpretentious sonnets of Cahirmoyle are amongst her most appealing writings. They were pub. posthumously by her nephew, Stephen Gwynn, 1909.

O'Brien, Edna, writer of novels, short stories, plays, children's fiction, screenplays, non-fiction. B. in 1932 in Tuamgraney, Ireland, da. of Lena (Cleary), who exercised 'lonely stoicism' in 'the male-dominated world of an Irish farm', and Michael O'B., she attended the National School at Scariff, the Convent of Mercy at Loughrea (Co. Galway) and the Pharmaceutical College of Ireland. In 1952 she m. Ernest Gebler, a writer; the marriage was dissolved in 1964. She has two sons. EO'B worked in London as a manuscript reader. Her first novel, *The Country Girls*, 1960, was followed by *The Lonely Girl*, 1962 (dramatized as *The Girl with Green Eyes*, 1964), and *Girls in Their Married Bliss*, 1964, which complete a trilogy autobiographical in inspiration, but employing humour, shrewd observation and contrasting characters to examine with a spare realism the sensibility of women in exile from, or even within, families, communities, or traditions, for whom experience is baffling and defeat recurrent. In *Night*, 1970, the reminiscing female narrator comments, 'You have separateness thrust upon you', an observation which signals the several aspects of EO'B's view of women's condition: with independence comes loneliness, with dream or desire comes frustration, with naivety comes exclusion from understanding and with sophistication comes exploitation. This separateness is not growth-room, but incompleteness. EO'B's women have consciousness not raised by critical understanding, but saddened, embittered, or numbed by the experiences of conflict, deprivation or ignorance in the family, the society or in sexual relationships. *The High Road*, 1988, discovers in a Spanish setting a mature image of woman as exile in a world where friendship is exploitive, loneliness exploited, and violence inseparable from tenderness. Female narratives – moving from the declarative style of the early works to recollection (*A Pagan Place*, 1973), interior monologue (*Night*, 1972), and lyricism (*Johnny I Hardly Knew You*, 1977) – define a limited viewpoint on a world of limitation. In her short stories (*Mrs Reinhard and Other Stories*, 1978, *Returning*, 1982, and others up to *Lantern Slides*, 1990) generic limitation provokes fine, subtle and detailed realism. Her plays, beginning with a *A Cheap Bunch of Nice Flowers*, produced 1962, include *Virginia* (from WOOLF's diaries, produced 1980, rev. ed., 1985) and *Madame Bovary*, 1987. She has also pub. children's books, *James and Nora*, 1981 (on the Joyce marriage), and Irish folk and fairy tales, 1986. *Mother Ireland*, 1976, is an autobiographical essay about the land which formed EO'B's attitudes, affections and antagonisms, as well as providing the material for some of her best writings. (Several of her books are banned there.) Grace Eckley discusses EO'B's debated relation to feminism in *Edna O'Brien*, 1974;

interview in *Paris Review* 92, 1984. Nell Dunn published an interview in *Talking to Women*, 1965.

O'Brien, Kate, 1897–1974, novelist, playwright, journalist, essayist, travel writer and biographer, b. in Limerick, da. of Catherine (Thornhill) and Thomas O'B. She was educ. at Laurel Hill Convent and University College, Dublin. Her childhood was informed by a still-unchanged Victorian Ireland (pony-traps, doormen in top hats, rich mahogany furnishings) and by a 'simple, free and sociable seaside life' of vacations at Kilkee, Co. Clare. The Proustian memories which render her childhood in *My Ireland*, 1962, are the foundation of her style of careful observation and rich evocation which exploits comparisons between places and cultures to unfold searching awareness of human likeness within cultural difference. Childhood observation became involvement as the 'well-instructed school-child' who watched with admiration the flirtatious 'married women of Limerick' and was 'often troubled for her favourite beautiful ladies', became the chronicler of the landed Irish in a wider European context and of tensions between sexual expression, personal choice, and spiritual growth. She worked briefly on the *Manchester Guardian*, in the US, as a teacher in London, and 1922–3 as a governess in Spain. Marriage in 1923 to Dutch journalist Gustaaf Renier lasted a year. She began her writing career as a playwright, with *Distinguished Villa*, 1926, and *The Bridge*, 1927. Two of her novels were later dramatized (*The Ante-Room*, 1934, and *That Lady*, 1946). Her first pub. novel, *Without My Cloak*, 1931 (James Tait Black and Hawthornden prizes), a family saga, established the interests of much of her fiction – the Irish upper-middle class, and an extreme Catholicism which in her third novel, *Mary Lavelle*, 1936, gives rise to conflicts in a Spanish setting, and again informs *The Land of Spices*, 1941 (both the latter declared immoral by the Irish Censorship Board). KO'B's love of Spain led to travel writing (*Farewell Spain*, 1937), biography (*Teresa of Avila*, 1951), and her best-known novel, *That Lady*, 1946 (*For One Sweet Grape* in the USA), a presentation of a woman's meditative self-consciousness and integrity amidst the religious, political and emotional tensions in the court of Philip II. The firm, tactful engagement with sexual commitment and conviction of sin evident in her early novels, searching in *That Lady*, persists in the exploration of a lesbian relationship in *As Music and Splendour*, 1958. Other novels are *Pray for the Wanderer*, 1938, *The Last of Summer*, 1943, and *The Flower of May*, 1953. KO'B's non-fiction works include *English Diaries and Journals*, 1943, and *Presentation Parlour*, 1956. After early success, KO'B died in relative obscurity, but the firm commitment of her fictions to female choice and hard-won self-understanding has provoked recognition in numerous Virago reprints with thoughtful and informative introductions. Study by Lorna Reynolds, 1986.

O'Brien, Mary, Irish patriotic writer, wife of Patrick O'B. While in London (where she clearly stayed through 1788) she pub. *The Pious Incendiaries, or Fanaticism Display'd*, by 'a lady', 1785 (a hudibrastic account of the Gordon riots), and short poems (repr. Dublin, 1790, with her name, as *The Political Monitor, or Regent's Friend*). Both lavishly praise the royal family: many poems treat the Regency crisis; her 'Ode to Milton' is repr. in Joseph Wittreich, *Feminist Milton*, 1987. She says she was only induced to print her 'first Essay' out of fear of fresh outrages from Gordon, that 'needy lord, whose low finances, / Exceeds knight errants, in romances'. It nicely catches the tone of rabble-rousing Protestant fervour (which Ireland, unlike London, resists). Her best short poems are satires which scourge 'hireling advocates', 'mean and suspicious measures', give a vivid picture of John Bull, and make Paddy address Pitt in ballad stanzas as 'Billy' and 'my dear jewel'.

Her comedy *The Fallen Patriot*, Dublin [1790], enlivens a stock love-story with satire on those who barter Ireland's rights for a title; some good fun is had over the status of surnames beginning with 'O'. Her (presumably) novel *Charles Henley* seems not to have survived; the BL has her MS opera *The Temple of Virtue*, set in Rome with Vestal Virgins.

O'Connor Mary **Flannery**, 1925–64, short-story writer, novelist, b. at Savannah, Ga., only child of Regina (Cline) and Edward Francis O'C. They moved to Milledgeville when her father was diagnosed as having lupus erythematosus, which struck her too at 25 and finally killed her. Her Roman Catholic faith deepened with his illness. She was educ. at Peabody High School, Georgia State College for Women (now Georgia College), Milledgeville (BA 1945), and the Univ. of Iowa (MFA 1947). Her fiction treats people financially, emotionally and physically damaged, raising issues of faith and grace in fundamentalists as well as Catholics, since 'I'm not interested in the sects as sects; I'm concerned with the religious individual'. She pub. two short novels, *Wise Blood*, 1952 (Rinehart Iowa Prize), and *The Violent Bear It Away*, 1960, and two vols. of stories. *A Good Man is Hard to Find*, 1955, which deals, she said, with 'original sin', has a title piece about a family massacred by the psychopathic 'Misfit': at its climax the grandmother sees him as 'one of my own children'; he 'sprang back as if a snake had bitten him and shot her three times through the chest'. FO'C complained to her long-time friend and correspondent Caroline GORDON that readers misunderstood her stories, most finding them 'brutal and sarcastic', but said, 'Our age not only does not have a very sharp eye for the almost imperceptible intrusions of grace, it no longer has much feeling for the nature of the violences which precede and follow them.' Her last book, *Everything that Rises Must Converge*, 1965, pursues the theme of 'the action of grace on a character who is not very willing to support it'. *Collected Stories*, 1971, includes these and previously unpub. work. Lisa ALTHER finds FO'C's stories filled with indomitable women. See FO'C's essays on literature, ed. Sally and Robert Fitzgerald as *Mystery and Manners*, 1962; letters ed. S. Fitzgerald as *The Habit of Being*, 1979, more ed. by C. Ralph Stephens, 1986; book reviews, ed. Carter W. Martin and Leo J. Zuber as *The Presence of Grace*, 1983; *Conversations* with FO'C, ed. Rosemary M. Magee, 1987. Papers at Georgia College (catalogue in *FO'C Bulletin*, 14, 1985). Among much comment, see Claire Kahane in Juliane Fleenor, ed., *The Female Gothic*, 1983; essays ed. Melvin J. Freidman and Beverly Lyon Clark, 1985; Mary L. Morton in *SoQ*, 23, 1985; life by Harold Flickett and Douglas R. Gilbert, 1986.

O'Donnell, Lillian (Udvrady), DETECTIVE writer, b. in 1920 in Trieste, Italy, da. of Maria (Basutti) and Zoltan D. U. She attended school in Trieste, then NYC. After studying at the American Academy of Dramatic Arts, she worked as an actress and dancer, eventually as a director and producer from 1940 until marriage, 1954, to J. Leonard O'D. During the course of writing more than 20 mystery novels, she has evolved from a romantic to a 'champion of women', from an entertainer to one 'deeply concerned with the state of the world'. Her first nine books, from *Death on the Grass*, 1960, are GOTHIC romances in which sleuths are male and main characters female. But she turned to the police procedural with her series character Norah Mulcahaney: she makes her appearance in *The Phone Calls*, 1972, a novel 'conceived on the night of the first big blackout in New York City' (where many of LO'D's novels are set). Though not intended as 'a spokesman for women's lib', Norah was intended as 'part of the real world', and she deals at work with cases of violence or prejudice against women (e.g. in *Dial 577 R-A-P-E*, 1974, or *No Business Being A Cop*, 1979, about job discrimination and murder) and at home with the attempt to balance husband, adopted child, extended family, and job. LO'D invented Mici Anhalt, her second female series protagonist, in *Aftershock*, 1977. 'Once a professional dancer', 'unmarried', with 'no desire to tie herself down', she is 'not as morally rigid as Norah'. But in spite of Mici's more light-heartedly sexy existence, Norah continued in indignation, as in *Children's Zoo*, 1981, about juvenile crime. Interview in *The Armchair Detective*, 14, 1981; articles by LO'D in *The Writer*, Feb. 1978, Dec. 1982 (quoted above). See Neysa Chouteau and Martha Alderson in Jane S. Bakerman, *And Then There Were Nine? More Women of Mystery*, 1985 (quoted above).

O'Donoghue, Nannie Power (Lambert), sporting writer. Little is known of her life; she was youngest da. of Charles L. of Castle Ellen, Co. Galway, and grandda. of Commodore Irwin, a prominent figure on the Irish turf. Wolff gives 1858 as birthdate, but she pub. a novel, *The Knave of Clubs*, as Nannie Lambert in 1868. She m. William Power O'D., Professor of Music in Dublin, and pub. two more novels, *Unfairly Won*, 1882 (repr. 1939), a racing book with a spirited heroine, written in a masculine, important tone, and *A Beggar on Horseback*, 1884, an amusing and sharply written picture of provincial society. More popular were her manuals of instruction for lady riders, 1881 and 1887, interspersed with hints and anecdotes, and constantly reprinted.

O'Faolain, Julia, Irish novelist and short-story writer, b. in London, 1932, da. of writers Eileen Gould and Sean O'F. She was educ. at a Dublin convent school, University College, Dublin (BA and MA), Univ. of Rome and the Sorbonne. In 1957, she married American historian Lauro Martines, with whom she has lived in Florence, California, and London. They have one child. Her powerful, often comic fiction engages with women's alternating passivity and obsessive action, in domestic or public spheres. The title story of *Man in the Cellar*, 1974, portrays a woman who almost by accident glides from a fantasy to really chaining her abusive husband to a bed, imagining at the outset that she would 'make him *see* how intolerable it can be to be always on the losing side, the weak partner, the one who must submit', subsequently exulting in the fact that he had to start 'learning the techniques of the underdog'. Her fictional recreation of the founding of a convent in sixth-century Gaul, *Women in the Wall*, 1975, repr. 1985, explores connections between madness and mystical experience, fanaticism and faith; it also suggest the inevitability of political involvement, as the nuns' acts of charity draw them into the wars and intrigues of the outside world. *No Country for Young Men*, 1980, treats Irish nationalism and women's and men's relationships in that climate of political obsession. In *The Obedient Wife*, 1982, Carla abandons an affair with an ex-priest to return to her husband and family: 'I like keeping things together – we have to do that, you know, those of us who believe only in the temporal world.' The title story of *Daughters of Passion*, 1982, addresses the Irish situation: a woman on hunger-strike in prison, demanding political status, remembers the mixed personal, religious and social sources of her decision to kill a policeman. 'Legend for a Painting', a sharply satiric fairy-tale from the same collection, figures a knight who insists on rescuing a lady from a dragon she would have preferred to keep. *The Irish Signorina*, 1984, provides a cross-section of types of political involvement through the relationships of Anna, daughter of a wealthy Italian family's former *au par*, with a wealthy lawyer and his more revolutionary son. With her husband, JO'F compiled and edited *Not in God's Image: Women in History*, 1973. As Julia Martines, she has taught language and interpretation and has pub. two translations from Italian.

Offord, Lenore (Glen), mystery novelist, b. 1905 at Spokane, Washington, da. of Laura (Dell), piano-teacher, and Robert Alexander G., newspaper editor. She took a BA at Mills College, Oakland, 1925, did some graduate work, m. Harold R. O. of the US Forest Service, 1929, and had a daughter. Her books, set in imaginatively various west-coast communities, present ordinary middle-class young women who keep their wits and their nerve when plunged in danger and bafflement. The first, in *Murder on Russian Hill*, 1938 (*Murder before Breakfast*, in UK), is about to leave work because pregnant when her boss is shot and she develops a 'career as a little helper to the police'. In *Skeleton Key*, 1943, a young widow solves a wartime murder among Berkeley eccentrics and has a romance with a detective. These two and their spouses reappear in later books; in LGO's last, *Walking Shadow*, 1959, the latter's daughter makes her stage debut at an Oregon Shakespeare festival. LGO also wrote science-fiction reviews (Edgar Allen Poe award, 1951), magazine stories, light verse, two collaborations (*The Marble Forest*, 1951 – repr. as *The Big Fear*, 1953 – as 'Theo Durrant', and *The Girl in the Belfry*, 1957), a children's book (*Enchanted August*, 1956), and two non-mysteries: *Cloth of Silver*, 1939, and *Angels Unaware*, 1940 (*Distinguished Visitors* in UK). Here the middle-aged heroine has her marriage put under strain and under the microscope by a visit from a bohemian old friend: it emerges triumphant.

Ogilvy, Eliza Anne Harris (Dick), 1822–1912, poet, b. in Perth of an old Scottish family, da. of Louisa (Wintle) and Abercromby D. In 1833 she travelled with her sister Charlotte to India, where their grandfather was a surgeon, and returned in 1843, the year she m. David O. (1813–79). Her eldest child (of seven), Rose, died in infancy and EO privatedly printed in 1845 a small collection of poems about this experience. In 1846 she pub. *A Book of Highland Minstrelsy*, Scottish poems prefaced by anecdotes derived from legend, history, or personal observation. The family lived abroad 1848–52, spending time in Florence, where they first met the Brownings, and in Paris. *Traditions of tuscany*, 1851, dedicated to EO's sister, includes a number of poems on women in Italian history and folklore. *Poems of Ten Years*, 1856, shows the influence of Elizabeth Barrett BROWNING (of whose 'undemocratic ideal' of high-minded poetry she did not approve: see 'To the Poets of the New Generation'), for it included political poems and proclaims their authenticity as the product of personal experience: 'Written in the passion of the living struggle'. Some interesting poems on motherhood appear in this vol. She also wrote stories for *Chambers Edinburgh Journal*, *Sunday Acrostics*, 1867 (a collection of poetic religious puzzles), and a Memoir of E. B. Browning for an ed., of her *Poems*, 1893.

Ogilvy, Ellen **Maud**, 1890s poet, novelist, journalist and biographer. Da of Ellen (Glassnett), and John O., she was educ. in Montreal, where she was b. and also in England. She wrote biographies of men (*Sir Donald A. Smith*, 1891, and Smith and J. C. Abbott in *Men of the Day*, 1892). Her novel *Marie Gourdon*, 1890, concerns Scottish and French interrelationships in the lower St Lawrence area, and it gives an early treatment of the art and exile theme in Canadian writng. Marie becomes a London prima donna and meets Eugène Lacroix, a renowned Paris artist; the two marry (she giving up her career for his) and settle in London to pursue their artistic lives, returning for summers to Canada. MO was one of several English Canadian writers of her time to turn to French Canadian life for a sense of the national tradition – as in *The Keeper of Bic Light house*, 1891. She pub. her poems, *A Christmas Song*, 1913, and, with Frederick C. Emerson, collected *Gold and Silver*, poems and maxims, subtitled *The Best Twenty Poems and Thoughts Extant, Selected with some approach to analytical certainty*.

Ogle, Anne Charlotte, 'Ashford Owen', 1832–1918, novelist, b. at Bedlington, Northumberland, one of large family of Sophia (Ogle, da. of Sir Charles O.) and her cousin Edward Ogle, vicar of Bedlington. Timid and retiring as a girl, she began writing early, and spent most of her life in Northumberland, eventually living with her sister, Mrs Clayton, at Chester, North Tyneside. Her first novel, *A Lost Love*, 1854, pub. pseudonymously, is in part an autobiographical portrait of her own isolated and restricted youth, with a heroine, 'Georgy Sandon', named in compliment to George SAND. It was a popular success, being translated into French (as *Un Amour Perdu* and *Georgy Sandon*, 1860), pirated in the USA (as *Georgy* – AO's original choice of title), and reissued in England in 1862, 1883, and 1920. As a result, AO became friendly with the BROWNINGS, the CARLYLES, Tennyson and Thackeray. She travelled in Europe with her family, visiting Italy, 1858–9, and later staying with Lady Louisa Ashburton at Mentone. She contributed the tale, 'An Old Woman's Story', set in a Northumberland fishing village, to Adelaide PROCTER's *Victoria Regia* anthology in 1861. She pub. one other novel, *The Story of Catherine*, 1885, as bleak and unsparing as her first in describing lack of parental responsibility and the pressure of conventional notions of woman's place and freedom.

Ogot, Grace Emily (Akinyi), journalist, novelist, writer of short stories, stateswoman. She was b. in 1930 at Butere, near Kisuma, Central Nyanza District, Kenya, da. of a prominent Luo father, a teacher: educ. at Maseno Junior School, N'giya Girls' School, and Butere Girls' High School. She later took nurse's training in Uganda at Mengo, 1949–53, and studied at St Thomas's Hospital for Mothers and Babies in London. She was Midwifery Tutor and Nursing Sister at Maseno Hospital, 1958–9, then, back in London, an announcer for BBC Radio. Returning to Africa in 1960, she was Community Development Officer and Principal of the Woman's Training Centre at Kismu, Kenya, then, 1963–4, at Makerere Univ. She married Bethwell O. in 1959 and has four children. She has seen much change for women since the time her brideprice was 25 head of cattle. She has engaged in several kinds of communications activities: community work, Kenyan radio and television, journalism, public relations. Prominent in politics and diplomacy, as delegate to the UN General Assembly, 1975, member of UNESCO, 1976, and member of parliament, she feels that modern women must contribute to public life. GO's fiction draws on her experience, often on her nursing: it poses conflicts between alternative medical systems in East Africa, bases plots on illness and calamity due, as the reader chooses, to coincidence or witchcraft. Her short stories have appeared in *Black Orpheus*, *Transition*, *Présence Africaine*, and *East Africa Journal*, and in collections: *Land Without Thunder*, 1968, *The Other Woman and Other Stories*, 1976, and *The Island of Tears*, 1980. In her novel, *The Promised Land*, 1966, the Luo bride reluctantly migrates with her husband to Tanzania, and is ultimately driven back home by a malevolent neighbour's use of witchcraft. The female protagonist of *The Graduate*, 1980, like GO a cabinet minister, seeks to stop the educational brain drain. The first woman to have fiction published by the East African Publishing House, GO was founder and chair of the Writers' Association of Kenya 1975–80. She has taught the Luo language on radio, joined the controversy about literature in local languages, and written a book of short stories, *Till*, and two novels, *Miaha* and *Simbi Nyaima*, in Luo. See interview in *Africa Report*, July-Aug. 1972, and Taiwo, 1984.

Ogundipe-Leslie, Omolara, Nigerian poet and lecturer, who took a BA at the Univ. of London, 1977, and now lectures in English at the Univ. of Ibadan, Nigeria. She has published numerous critical articles on both British and African writers. Her poetry – lyric, satiric, mythic, socially critical – is collected in *Sew the Old Days and Other Poems*, 1985, which takes its title from an Awoonor poem: 'Do you ask why India grieves? / . . . Do you tie . . . / The gracious receivings, promenades / and tea-soaked evenings to mother's hard palms, her meatless dishes, / Grandfather's goitre and our madness at history's noontime?' Her academic interest in Women's Studies has an international focus on figures such as Simone de BEAUVOIR, George SAND, the BRONTË sisters, and Harriet Beecher STOWE and the writing of African women such as Bessie HEAD, Ama Ata AIDOO, Efua SUTHERLAND and Micere MUGO. She decries the stereotyping of African women as mother or houri, urban prostitute or rural throw-back. She claims that the African woman who writes must commit herself to art, womanhood, and citizenship in the Third World. She expands on her Marxist and feminist views in interviews pub. in *West Africa*, 16 and 23 April 1984. Her article 'The Female Writer and Her Commitment' appears in Jones, 1987; 'African Women, Culture and Another Development' in *Présence Africaine*, 141, 1987 (special issue on black women). See Berrian (who calls her the 'leading feminist critic in Africa today'), 1985.

O'Keeffe, Adelaide, 1776–1865, novelist and children's writer, da. of the Protestant Mary (Heaphy) and Catholic John O'K., both Dublin actors. She says she 'never experienced a mother's care'; her father visited her at nurse and 'was her first object of love'. The marriage broke down; John O'K. left for London. He sent his children to school there in 1782, but shipped them to France when he heard his wife had secretly visited them. After educ. in a convent, 'to her supreme horror and surprise', till 1788, AO'K set to work as amanuensis to her father, by then nearly blind but hugely popular as a dramatist. Her first novel, *Llewellin* (written 1795; pub. anon. 1799), poses as the life-story of Piers Gaveston's son, told to Chaucer as material for a work by him. *Patriarchal Times*, expanding the story of 25 chapters of *Genesis*, was pub. in 1811 after hawking round seven firms, but written in 1798, the year her father retired and money ran short (her brother's education cost over £200 p.a.). It drew much praise, including a letter from Jane PORTER. *Zenobia*, 1814, treats similarly an ancient heroic queen. Most famous were AO'K's verses in the TAYLORS' *Original Poems for Infant Minds*, 1804–5. These, and children's poems of 1808, 1818, 1819 (*A Trip to the Coast*) and [1849], blend heavy admonition with charm and fun: far the best are *National Characters Exhibited*, 1818, dramatic monologues from many lands, with African kings and Jamaican slaves sharply, uncondescendingly individuated. AO'K lived in many places on the south coast of England, sometimes as a governess. Her verses have unjustly eclipsed her other work. The epistolary novel *Dudley*, 1819, treats the topic of bereavement with a range of sentiment and exasperated humour; in *The Broken Sword*, 1854 (set in 1777), children suffer from parents' melodramatic estrangement. About 1830 she estimated her entire literary earnings as £243. She pub. anecdotes of her father in the *New Monthly Magazine*, 1833 (the year he died), then a loving memoir in his poems, ed. as *O'Keeffe's Legacy to his Daughter*, 1834. In 1840 she wrote to the RLF calling her royal pension of £50 p.a. 'this wretched pittance' and detailing the reasons for rewarding authors not casually but by regular annual grants, publicly announced.

Okoye, Ifeoma, novelist and writer of children's stories and secondary-school texts. B. in Umanachi, Nigeria, da. of Victoria and James Okeke, she attended St Monica Teachers' College at Ogbunike and the Univ. of Nigeria, Nsukka (BA in English, 1977). Married with four daughters and a son, she lectures at the Institute of Management and Technology in Enugu. She won the Macmillan Children's Literature Prize for *Village Boy*, 1978, and has since written six children's books and several English texts for children. Her first adult novel, *Behind the Clouds*, 1982, is based on the plight of a childless Nigerian couple. Her second, *Men Without Ears*, 1984, winner of the Nigerian Best Fiction Award, comments on present Nigerian scandals and corruption. Like EMECHETA's *Niara Power*, it concludes with an exposé of the trafficking in human organs obtained from ritual murders. Asked to supply her birth date, IO wrote 'ageless', but her concern is with today's Nigeria caught in problems of technological change and waning traditional values. As a writer and a woman, she hopes to help 'the oppressed, the under-privileged, and those discriminated against, whether male or female'. Works listed in Berrian, 1985.

Olds, Sharon, poet, b. 1942 in San Francisco, and educ. at Stanford Univ. and at Columbia, NY (PhD, 1972). She is married, with a daughter and son. Her teaching career began at the Theodor Herzl Institute, 1976; she has held a chair at Brandeis Univ. since 1986. Various journals have published her work, which she has also read in public. Her first collection, *Satan Says*, 1980 (usefully reviewed by Carolyne Wright in *13th Moon*, 6, 1982), draws on a decade's writing and revising. *The Dead and the Living*, 1984, gives to childhood horrors (alcoholic and abusive relations) a macrocosmic dimension by juxtaposing photographs of (especially) political atrocities. Both these books won awards. *The Gold Cell*, 1987, examines NYC life and suggests ancient patterns, particularly of violence behind the quotidian. SO's poetry is sturdily heterosexual in its pervasive eroticism, reflecting the 'qualities of courage, self-knowledge, determination and, yes, sense of humor' required of the artist / wife / mother. See Diane WAKOSKI in *WRB*, Sept. 1987.

O'Leary, Ellen, 1831–89, poet, b. in Tipperary, Ireland, da. of Margaret (Ryan), who died early, and John O'L., well-to-do shopkeeper. Upon their father's remarriage, the three children were brought up by an aunt. When he died in 1849, they inherited a modest income, and while her brothers studied in Ireland, London and Paris, Ellen acted as housekeeper in their 'bohemian' establishment. At 20, she began writing poems: many appeared in *The Commercial Journal*, *The Irishman*, and, particularly, *The Irish People*, the Fenian organ. She and her brother John (1830–1907) were closely involved with the Irish Revolutionary Brotherhood, and she was frequently employed during the 1860s as messenger and agent, assisting revolutionaries to escape. John spent five years in prison from 1865, and 15 years in exile in Paris, while Ellen visited him frequently from Tipperary. After his return in 1885 they lived together in Dublin at the centre of a nationalist and literary group, which included W. B. Yeats. Her verse volume, *Lays of Country, Home and Friends*, 1889, was pub. posthumously with an intro. by T. W. Rolleston and a verse tribute, 'A Celtic Singer', by Sir Charles Gavan Duffy. Her BALLAD forms were warmly praised by Yeats.

Oliphant, Margaret (Wilson), 1828–97, novelist, biographer, historical writer, critic, b. near Musselburgh, Lothian, da. of Margaret (O.) and Francis W., customs officer. She had no formal educ., but social and religious issues were discussed freely at home, and her mother's constant story-telling affected her profoundly. Her first work, *Passages in the Life of Mrs Margaret Maitland*, 1849, followed by *Caleb Field* and *Merkland*, 1851, pre-dated her marriage to her artist cousin, Francis O., in 1852. He died in 1859; and their two surviving sons (the loss of her eldest child and only daughter in 1864 was a major sorrow), along with several indigent relatives, remained even in their adulthood a financial burden. MO pub. almost 100 novels, of which the best known are her Carlingford series, affectionately satiric tales of country-town life, from *The Rector and the Doctor's Family*, 1863, through *Miss Marjoribanks*, 1866, to *Phoebe Junior*, 1876, and although MO's hard circumstances and professional attitude have often been blamed for her failure to produce a 'masterpiece', novels like *The Doctor's Family* amply repay a feminist rereading. Concerned lest women be regarded as lesser men, MO was not an overt supporter of female equality, but her novels shrewdly record the stresses and compromises of women's lives. Although dismissive of women's unrest over sexual freedom, from the 1880s she took a stronger stand on the right to a full professional life, and her writing grew more acerbic. Apart from fiction, MO wrote biographies, socio-historical studies of cities, art criticism, historical sketches, literary histories and two fragmented and revealing autobiographies (1868 and 1899) (1990 ed. less full than that of Annie Louise WALKER): 'I don't think I have ever had two hours uninterrupted ... during the whole of my literary life.' She also wrote several vols. of stories and over 200 articles for magazines such as *Blackwoods* and *The Cornhill*, besides editing the prestigious Blackwoods Foreign Classics series, for which she wrote *Dante*, 1877, and *Cervantes*, 1880. Her ability to put both sides of a question made her a respected as well as an influential reviewer. She knew many major writers and was particularly close to the CARLYLES and to A. T. RITCHIE, but took little part in literary society. A number of her novels have been repr. since 1980, and Margaret K. Gray has ed. a selection of her supernatural stories, 1985. Critical biography by Merryn Williams, 1986, and bibliog. by John Stock Clarke, *VFRG*, 11, 1986. MSS in NLS.

Olsen, Tillie (Lerner), poet, novelist, short-story writer, critic, teacher, activist, b. 1913 in Omaha, Neb., da. of Ida (Beber) and Samuel L., labourer and secretary of the Nebraska Socialist Party. Her parents fled Russia after the failed revolution of 1905. She grew up poor, leaving school to work after the eleventh grade, but continued to read widely in public libraries and private collections. As a teenager she kept a journal and wrote skits and musicals for the Young People's Socialist League. At 17 she joined the Young Communist League, initiating in these years an enduring political commitment. She was jailed, 1932, for handing out pamphlets to packing-house workers. Her poems, at first 'the effusions of an intense, imaginative young woman as influenced by the romantic traditions of nineteenth-century poetry', later became political. At 19 she wrote her first novel, *Yonnondio*: title an American Indian word meaning 'lament for the lost'. It combines powerful awareness of ruling social forces and sensitivity to individual aspirations. In the early 1930s, TO developed lung disease and was threatened with tuberculosis. From 1936 she lived with Jack O., a printer and union man, whom she married in 1943. She bore four daughters and did not write again until the mid-fifties. *Silences*, given as a talk in 1962, grew to a book, 1965, a moving blend of personal memories and historical observation, which comments on the 'thwarting' of women's and men's voices by societal pressures and on TO's own experiences of the 'triple life' of family, job, and writing. Her few stories – 'Requa I', 1970, and four others, 'serenely beautiful but still politically impassioned', collected in *Tell Me a Riddle*, 1961 – have appeared in over 50 ANTHOLOGIES; several have been adapted for performance. In 1972 she wrote an introduction for Rebecca Harding DAVIS's *Life in the Iron Mills*, 1861, the Feminist Press's first reprint, and published an essay, 'One out of Twelve: Women Who Are Writers in Our Century': these are incorporated in the 1978 ed. of *Silences*. Her *Mother to Daughter, Daughter to Mother*, 1984, is a collection of women's writings. Her work, which issues from her sensitivity to the politics of class and gender, has inspired a generation of writers and scholars. Among those who have written about her are Ellen Moers, Margaret ATWOOD, Adrienne RICH, Catharine STIMPSON, Maxine Hong KINGSTON, and Katherine Anne PORTER. See Selma Burkom and Margaret Williams in *San José Studies*, 2, 1976; Deborah Rosenfelt (quoted above, written with TO's advice and access to her MSS) in Judith Newton and Rosenfelt, eds., *Feminist Criticism and Social Change*, 1985. Parts of the *Yonnondio* MS in the Berg Collection, NY Public Library.

Oman, Carola Anima, Lady Lenanton, CBE, 1897–1978, historical writer, b. at Oxford, da. of university historian Charles William Chadwick O. and Mary Mabel (Maclagen), who helped in her husband's research and insisted at CO's birth that she had not wanted a son. CO learned to read at four, wrote her first story ('Coral and the Bear', a six-sentence gem of drama and wit) soon afterwards, and made a magic wish to write a book. Her early reading included M. M. SHERWOOD and Charlotte YONGE. At the future Wychwood School in Oxford, she met the CANNAN sisters, wrote a play, *Joanne de Beaufort*, and a magazine, and submitted poems (vainly) to periodicals. She nursed in Oxford and France, 1916–19, then worked at and wrote for *The Oxford Magazine*. Her poetry vol., *The Menin Road*, 1919, describes wartime France in fine, spare, precise language, and expresses the grief, shock and blankness the fighting has left. In 1922 she m. Sir Gerald Lenanton, a businessman whose frequent absence left ample time for writing. She pub. nine carefully researched historical novels (from *Royal Road*, 1924; one on E. B. BROWNING, 1929), a 'straight' history book (*Britain Against Napoleon*, 1942), children's lives of figures like King Alfred and Robin Hood, and – the best-known – richly woven, sensitive but sternly objective, historical biographies including three queens. CO nursed again in WWII. *An Oxford Childhood 1892–1914*, 1976, moves from her parents' wedding through the 'beautiful innocence or ignorance' of her upbringing.

O'Meara, Kathleen, 'Grace Ramsay', 1839–88, biographer and novelist, b. Dublin, da. of Dennis O'M. of Tipperary (son of Barry Edward O'M., surgeon to Napoleon I). She went to Paris with her parents at an early age and probably never returned to Ireland. She wrote rather pious Roman Catholic books, some history and biography, the most interesting probably a lively but unreliable study of the Paris salon circle of Mme Mohl (i.e. Mary Clarke), 1885. Not prolific, she pub. her novels as 'Grace Ramsay'. *A Woman's Trials*, 1867, tells of a young English girl's schooling in Paris; the account of poverty, the school itself and its ruthless head, are vivid, but the girl is a cipher. *Are You My Wife?*, 1878, an inconsequential romance, is lent interest by a variation on the 'mad wife' theme.

omowale [= 'the child has returned home'] **maxwell, marina ama** (Archibald-Crichlow), playwright, poet, media-woman and producer, b. 1934 in San Fernando, Trinidad, da. of Beryl May (Methodist soprano, first woman mayor in the West Indies) and Felix A. C. (writer-musician-physician). At Naparima Girls' High School she planned to be a lawyer until she had a story broadcast by the BBC. At the Univ. of the West Indies in Jamaica (BA in English, history and economics, 1959), she produced her surrealist play, *Cane Arrowing*, 1957; she later wrote for the *Daily Gleaner*. She married Jamaican journalist John M., started the Canboulay Singers (of Afro-Caribbean music), then left her husband and took her daughter to Trinidad, then London. There she worked for the BBC and was secretary of the Caribbean Artists Movement. Back in Jamaica, 1969, she began the Yard Theatre, for experiments in dramatic use of black history, patwah and urban proletarian arts.

Her many plays include *Consciousness I*, 1969 (six Spirit Mothers in painted masks present work by Caribbean poets), *Play Mas* and *Hounsi Kanzo* (pub. 1976), and *Woman Veves* (two pieces for women, 1989). From 1976 MAOM has lectured in communications and worked in drama at Cipriani Labor College, Trinidad. Her interviews of African writers were pub. as *About Our Own Business*, 1981. At Carifesta that year she spoke of women 'officiating at our own birth'. Manager of her own video production company (launched 1982), a founder of the Writers' Union of Trinidad and Tobago, 1981, she has been active for women and writers in many countries and organizations (including the Schomburg Center, NYC). Her 'best book', the novel-poem *Chopstix in Mauby*, is expected soon. Yet unpub. are *Conversations with Adam* (essays) and *Decade to Ama* (poems: mourning for deaths in Guyana, 1980, celebrating relatives and self-birth: 'brush the eggshells from your Afro ... eat / your yolk (and apple) / whole').

O'Neill, Frances (Carroll), poet. 'Born with a mind / To write inclin'd', she was at Dublin in 1789 writing of nearby Leixlip, but then came to London, where her poetic schemes were 'overthrown'. Once, she says, she lived well, by pen and needle; now, near starving, she works in freezing 'public Shops'. She wrote verse compliments (many acrostics) for theatre and other notabilities (praising Lady Anne Barnard as superior to Anne Dacier or Elizabeth Montagu; carelessly calling Hurdis, Oxford Professor of Poetry, John instead of James). When her pension requests were rejected ('My humble Muse I soon sent in, / While I stood propp'd against the wall') FO'N responded outrageously: the name of Sir Joseph Banks, naturalist, stands as refrain in a rousing, scatalogical attack. She also burlesques a pompous male servant and colleague; but her *Poetical Essays, Being a Collection of Satirical Poems, Songs and Acrostics*, 1802, also includes contemplation of nature and comment on politics and patriotism.

O'Neill, Henrietta (Boyle), 1758–93, poet, only da. of Susanna (Hoare) and Charles B., Viscount Dungarvan. Very little of her work survives. In 1777 she m. John O'N. (of royal Irish descent; made a viscount just after her death); with him she set up a private theatre at Shane's Castle, Co. Antrim, launched with her prologue and epilogue, 1780. She perhaps provided a verse address to open the Rosemary Lane Theatre, Belfast, 1784; she wrote and spoke a highly Popeian epilogue at Shane's Castle next year in the role of a sylph. Generous patron to Sarah Siddons and Charlotte Smith, she was repaid by Smith's printing two of her poems: the justly famous lyric 'Ode to the Poppy' (begging oblivion to cure a broken heart) in *Desmond*, 1792, with an additional poem on her two sons at play (much indebted to Thomas Gray on Eton schoolboys) in Smith's *Sonnets*, vol. ii, 1797. The BL has a MS poem describing a young man: 'Ambrosia breathes in every sigh.'

Opie, Amelia (Alderson), 1769–1853, poet and novelist, b. at Norwich, only child of Amelia (Briggs) and physician James A. With little formal educ., she learnt French and had her musical and literary talent fostered. She published *The Dangers of Coquetry*, anonymously, 1790, and acted privately with the Plumptres in her tragedy *Adelaide*, 1791. Visits to London began in 1794: she was impressed by William Godwin, Elizabeth Inchbald and Mary Wollstonecraft (met only in 1796). She married the divorced, fashionable 'peasant' painter John O. in 1798, and later distanced herself from the radicals. Her first signed work, *The Father and Daughter*, 1801, sold 9500 copies in 35 years (daughter's seduction sends father mad; she dies). *Poems*, 1802, facs. 1978, dwell on love and death. The heroine of *Adeline Mowbray, or The Mother and Daughter*, 1804 (repr. 1986), lives to repent (painfully if illogically) her rejection of marriage. After early poverty with John O. (d. 1807), AO lived as a lady in Norwich, on a good income (see correspondence with her publisher, Longman) from these and a steady stream of fiction (chiefly 'tales'), poetry, and didactic works. Mary Russell MITFORD said their ingredients were as usual as 'a plum pudding'. AO's memoir of her husband appeared with his lectures, 1809. Having pub. her last novel, *Madeline*, in 1822, and joined the Quakers at the time of her father's death, 1825, she devoted herself to charity. Her collected works had several US eds. from 1827: facs. 1974; lives by Cecilia Brightwell, 1854 (including letters and diaries), and Margaret Eliot Macgregor, 1932.

Oral traditions. Some remarkable 'writers', like Marjery KEMPE and Mary PRINCE, have depended on scribes to take down their words. A more fully oral tradition is that of PREACHING or prophesying women (Anna TRAPNEL, Hannah WHARTON). The tradition of oral song that emerged in the British BALLADS was very largely female. Sojourner TRUTH was one of the many Black preachers whose genius as orators inspired others to transcribe their words. Different awareness of oral tradition was shown by women like Mary FRERE and Mary OWEN, who collected Indian (Native American) folk tales, Catherine L. PARKER, who collected Australian Aboriginal legends, and Willa CATHER, who said 'her first teacher in narration' was an old illiterate Virginia mountain woman. Gretchen M. Bataille (*American Indian Women, Telling Their Lives*, 1984), sees the oral tradition – 'myths, songs and chants, curing rites, prayers, oratory, tales, lullabies, jokes, personal narratives, and stories of bravery or vision' – as a model for Indian women's autobiographies, equal in importance to that of Euro-American autobiographical writing. Stephen E. Henderson ('Introduction' to Mari Evans, ed., *Black Women Writers (1950-1980: A Critical Examination*, 1984) sees black American literature as founded on the oral tradition, 'where the basis of the literature rests on the work songs and the spirituals . . . And certainly the prototype of the love song is the lullabye.' Today the oral traditions of areas like Africa and the Caribbean lend vital elements to experimental writing, and to life-stories like those of Miriam Makeba, entertainer and 'Mama Africa' (*Makeba My Story*, dictated to James Hall, 1987), and Winnie Mandela, controversial 'Mother of the nation' (*Part of My Soul Went With Him*, dictated to Anne Benjamin and published in England, 1985). See also NATIVE FEMINIST CRITICISM.

Orczy, Emma Magdalena Rosalia Maria Josefa Barbara, Baroness, 1865–1947, novelist, b. in Tarna-Eörs, Hungary, only child of Emma (Wass) and Baron Felix O., composer and conductor. Wagner, Liszt, Gounod and Massenet were frequent visitors. She was educ. in Brussels, Paris and at the Heatherley School of Art, London, where she met her husband, Montagu Barstow, an artist; they had one son. She started her career as an illustrator and artist, exhibiting at the Royal Academy. In the late 1890s, she began writing short stories for magazines, and in 1905, wrote the novel which made her name, *The Scarlet Pimpernel*. She followed this success with a whole string of 'Pimpernel' stories about the foppish Sir Percy Blakeney's daring deeds during the French Revolution, including *I Will Repay*, 1906, *The Elusive Pimpernel*, 1908, and *Eldorado*, 1913; and other historical romances, mostly with a continental setting. *The Old Man in the Corner*, 1909, has been regarded as an early example of armchair detective fiction, and she also created a female detective, *Lady Molly of Scotland Yard*, 1910. In 1920, she moved to Monte Carlo. See her autobiography, *Links in the Chain of Life*, 1947.

Orvis, Marianne (Dwight), 1816–1901, letter writer, painter and Utopian reformer.

B. Boston, da. of Mary (Corey) and John D., religious free-thinker and physician, with whom she moved to Brook Farm in 1843, after teaching at a Boston High School for Young Ladies. She had a passionate friendship with *Harbinger* essayist Anna Q. T. Parsons, who founded the Boston Women's Associative Union and maintained a co-operative house run on Brook Farm principles. MO wrote the bulk of her celebrated *Letters from Brook Farm 1844–1847*, ed. Amy Reed, 1928, to Parsons: 'You and yours are to me all Boston, – are more than all Boston. Were you here, I do believe I should be entirely happy – I mean as happy as it is in my nature to be whilst on this unbeautified and ill treated earth.' The letters are a valuable first-hand account of daily life at Brook Farm: the division of labour by gender ('Men complain of having to wash and hang up ladie's night caps'); the farm's financial difficulties, the burning of the phalanstery and the gradual departure of its members; but also her disaffection with the 'conventional life of isolated houses' and her growing sense of women's condition ('Why do people marry and belong to ONE?'). She records the visits of people such as William Channing and Bronson Alcott, from whom she hoped for support in women's struggles for true equality and independence, upon which 'the whole aspect of society will be changed'. She writes of the beauty around her ('We walked on beds of diamonds, and diamonds blazed over our heads'), and of her own 'passional attraction', paintings of birds and wild flowers to be gathered into a fund raising book for the community. The quality of OM's attachment to Anna Parsons and the sensuous dailiness of life at Brook Farm are notable features. In 1846 she m. John Orvis at Brook Farm; they had two daughters.

Osborn, Sarah (Byng), 1693–1775, letter writer, b. at Southill, Beds., eldest child of Margaret (Master) and Admiral George B., later Viscount Torrington. In 1710 she m. John O, of nearby Chicksands, descendant of Dorothy OSBORNE. His death and that of her father-in-law (1719 and 1720) left her to run the estate till her surviving son came of age. In 1726 she understatedly admitted to more business experience 'than many women of my age'. Her daughter-in-law's and son's deaths (1743 and 1753) put her back in charge. Her letters (ed. [1890] and 1930) display lively interest in farming, politics, marriages, literature, education, and the cost of living. Her style can be caustic: 'a poor woman is made nothing off [by the court of Chancery], she may live upon air seven year if she can'; 'I shall kill Bailis if the Tables do not come next Thursday.' When her brother John B. was court-martialed in 1757 (for not engaging a far stronger French fleet), she wrote and probably herself pub. a letter to the Lords of the Admiralty; though to a duke she pleaded female distress, she here employs icy and damaging logic. She later composed and displayed her brother's epitaph, 'To the Perpetual Disgrace of Publick Justice'.

Osborn, Sarah (Hagger), 1714–96, religious writer, b. in London but taken to America in 1722. At Newport, RI, from 1729, she disobeyed her parents in 1731 to marry a sailor; he drowned after two years, leaving her with a son. She became a Congregationalist in 1737, and ran a school which failed in 1741. Next year she married Henry O., a widower with three sons, who soon became bankrupt and infirm. A new school, opened 1744, kept the family going though often in debt. Of her many writings there survive diaries (Newport Public Library) and letters (AAS). One written 'in great Privacy' in 1753 appeared anonymously with her reluctant permission as *The Nature, Certainty, and Evidence of True Christianity*, Boston, 1755 (the basis of Samuel Hopkins's *Memoir* of her, 1799). With orthodox humility ('worthless Worm', 'poor nothing Creature') and sensitivity to her friend's religious anxiety, she confidently relates the working of grace in her life for 11 years: 'Tell [Satan] from me, *He is a Liar*.' In 1767 SO wrote a defence of her charismatic work with local blacks: 'Would you advise me to shut up my Mouth and doors and creep into obscurity?' Teaching, even several nights a week, when the 'throng' increased to over 500 and drew adverse comment, was her 'Sweet refreshing Evenings my resting reaping times'. See Mary Beth Norton in *Signs*, 2, 1976. Her correspondence with Susanna Anthony, pub. 1807, and Anthony's writings (extracts 1796), were well received; SO seems far the more interesting today.

Osborne, Dorothy, later Lady Temple, 1627–95, letter writer, youngest da. of Dorothy (Danvers) and Sir Peter O. of Chicksands, Beds. She wrote her well-known letters (often reissued since their discovery in the nineteenth century; ed. Kenneth Parker, 1987) to William Temple in 1652–4. They explore the attractions and dangers of romantic love, construct and maintain a relationship against family opposition, evoke feeling (melancholy or merry), and detail the concerns of a royalist young woman of wealthy family. She says 'I could be infinitely better satisfied with a husband that had never loved me in the hope he might, than with one that began to love me less than he had done.' Married at Christmas 1654 after losing her beauty by smallpox, she lived in London, Ireland, Brussels, the Hague, and Surrey. Dismayed at Margaret NEWCASTLE's publications, she admired Katherine PHILIPS, corresponding with her and Mary II. She lost many children 'in their cradle': the last survivor killed himself in 1689. Life by Lord David Cecil, 1948; see Genie S. Lerch-Davis in *Texas Studies in Literature and Language*, 20, 1978.

Osgood, Frances Sargent (Locke), 1811–50, poet, b. Boston, Mass., da. of Mary Ingersoll (Foster) and Joseph L., merchant. Educ. at home, she had pub. in *Juvenile Miscellany* by 1825. She lived in England for two years, publishing two vols. of verse, *The Casket of Fate* and *A Wreath of Wild Flowers from New England*, 1838, and a lyric drama, *Elfrida*, after marrying, in 1835, the artist Samuel Stillman O. During this time she established friendships with Caroline NORTON, Harriet MARTINEAU and Lady BLESSINGTON. After her return to NYC, she contributed to leading journals and periodicals, editing *Ladies' Companion* and publishing six books 1841–9. In 1845 she began a year's 'literary courtship' with Edgar Allan Poe, who praised her work. Melville borrowed from her *Poetry of Flowers and the Flowers of Poetry*, 1841, for *Mardi*, and Hawthorne contributed a story to her *Memorial*, 1850, ed. Mary E. Hewitt. From 1847 she suffered from tuberculosis. In *Poems*, 1850, she wrote that women 'still / Must veil the shrine', but she looked forward in this last vol. (dedicated to her literary executor, Rufus Wilmot Griswold) to the day when the 'woodbird' could reveal her 'tone'. Griswold (*Memorial*, 1850) and Arthur Hobson Quinn (*Life* of Poe, 1941) discussed her work, but her wit, grace and originality are only now beginning to be recognized. See Emily Stipes Watts, 1977.

Ostenso, Martha, 1900–63, novelist. She was b. near Bergen, Norway, da. of Lena (Tungeland) and Sigurd Brigt O. In 1902 the family migrated to South Dakota and Minnesota where, for 'eighty cents a column', she contributed to the Junior Page of the Minneapolis *Journal*. At 15 she moved to Brandon, Man., where she attended the Collegiate, and later to Winnipeg, where she went to Kelvin Technical High School and briefly to the Univ. of Manitoba. She taught school for one semester, 1918, at Hayland, near Lake Manitoba (this experience fed the highly acclaimed *Wild Geese*, 1925), and worked as a reporter for the *Winnipeg Free Press*, 1920. More 'conscious of form, technique, and design than the average Canadian writers in the early twenties', MO was taught by Canadian novelist Douglas Durkin at Columbia Univ., 1921–2. In NYC with him, MO was a social worker with the Bureau of Charities, Brooklyn, 1920–3. They moved to Gull Lake, Minnesota, in 1931, married 1944, and moved to Seattle, 1963. MO wrote one book of verse, *The Far Land*, 1924, and 16 novels in the gothic and romantic modes which show European influence (Ibsen, Emily BRONTË, Conrad, Scandinavian sagas). Of these, two are set in Canada: *Prologue to Love*, 1932, in Kamloops, BC, and *Wild Geese* (two British eds. titled *The Passionate Flight*) in Manitoba. Whether romantic or prototype of Canadian prairie realism, *Wild Geese* is judged by David Arnason MO's best (1989 repr.): it would be 'impossible and fruitless to disentangle' her husband's contribution to her other fiction. See Margot Northey, *The Haunted Wilderness*, 1976; Dick Harrison, *Unnamed Country*, 1977.

Ostriker, Alicia (Suskin), poet and critic, b. 1937 in NYC, da. of Beatrice (Linnick) and David S. She was educ. at Brandeis Univ. (BA, 1959) and the Univ. of Wisconsin (MA, 1961, PhD, 1964) and since 1965 has taught English at Rutgers Univ. She m. astrophysics professor Jeremiah O., 1958; they have three children. After her *Vision and Verse in William Blake*, 1965, and her ed. of his *Complete Poems*, 1977, she read women poets in earnest. *Writing Like a Woman*, 1983, includes readings of H. D., Sylvia PLATH, Anne SEXTON, May SWENSON, and Adrienne RICH, 'brave women and strong writers from whom I have learned and with whom I have wrestled', plus two essays on her own poetic process. *Stealing the Language: The Emergence of Women's Poetry in America*, 1986, less a study of individual achievement than an evocation of 'the powerful collective voice' of women poets since the 1960s, considers a literary movement 'comparable to romanticism or modernism' which will transform literary history. Beginning with *Songs*, 1969, AO has pub. six vols. of poetry and prose poems. *The Mother/Child Papers*, 1980, considered by Maxine KUMIN 'an essential part of our history', unsentimentally celebrate maternity in the context of Kent State, Cambodia and Vietnam, a world in which '*All that is weak invites the brute.*' In 'The Exchange' in *A Woman Under the Surface*, 1982, a canoeist envisions trading places with a magnificent 'Wet, wordless' woman, 'bits of sunlight / Glittering on her pubic fur', who will strangle her children and husband, 'once for each insult // Endured.' *The Imaginary Lover*, 1986, continues AO's exploration of motherhood and other relationships, reflections on art and life, and witty transformations of male myths.

'Ouida', Louise de la Ramée, 1839–1908, novelist, story-writer and essayist, b. Bury St Edmunds, Suffolk, da. of Susan (Sutton) and Louis Ramée, French teacher and rumoured Bonaparte agent. A precocious reader and writer, she was educ. at local schools and by her father, who encouraged her interest in history, liberal politics, Balzac and Stendhal. She recorded her visits to France with him in a childhood diary: 'I must study or I shall know nothing when I am a woman.' Her first pub. work, 'Dashwood's Drag; or the Derby and What Came of It', was serialized in *Bentley's Magazine*, in 1859; from then until 1862 every issue contained one of her stories. In 1863 her successful first novel, *Held in Bondage*, popularized a new kind of stiff-upper-lip hero. This was followed by *Strathmore*, 1865, *Chandos*, 1866, and the enormously successful *Under Two Flags*, 1867, with its unconventional tomboy heroine, Cigarette. *Idalia*, 1867 (later dramatized), had an aristocratic and revolutionary heroine; but most female characters in her 47 books were conventional and her novels were generally melodramatic tales of love and intrigue which won her a loyal readership into the 1880s. Some works, like *Moths*, 1880, and *A Village Commune*, 1881, dealt with contemporary social issues, and she also pub.

several vols. of stories, a pamphlet opposing vivisection, *The New Priesthood*, 1893, and numerous essays for the *Fortnightly Review, Nineteenth Century* and *North American Review*, later coll. (1895 and 1900). Of her novels, many were set in her beloved Florence, where she lived from 1871; others incorporated inaccuracies which exasperated readers. By 1893, when her mother died, the extravagant and now eccentric 'Ouida', alone but for adored dogs (for whom she suffered eviction and hunger), was in dire financial need. But she detested Marie CORELLI's fund-raising efforts on her behalf, and died penniless in Lucca in 1908. See Monica Stirling, 1957, for her life.

Overton, Gwendolen, novelist, b. 1876 in Fort Hays, Kansas, da. of Jane Dyson (Watkins) and Capt. Gilbert O. She was educ. at Kansas public schools and private schools in France and Switzerland. GO began her life of continuous travelling with army troops at one month old. A close reflection of her experiences is found in her major work, *The Heritage of Unrest*, 1901, set in Arizona in the 1870s. This starkly realistic tale recounts with subtle irony the exploits of Felipa Cabot, a 'strong tumultuous' frontier woman (part Apache) caught between warring Indian tribes and the US army. Felipa marries her guardian, Captain Landers, who, fearing her 'tainted' blood, wishes to endow her with respectability and status, and she remains loyal to him despite her love for an Apache sympathizer. Thrilled by her daring and challenged by her sharp intelligence and 'unfeminine' earthy animalism, men regard her with admiration and horror. The conventional women in the novel pale beside this ferocious antithesis of the womanly stereotype. GO, while denouncing US action against the Indians, remains unsympathetic to the atrocities, graphically portrayed, committed by Indian raiders. *Anne Carmel*, 1903, has as heroine a sexually assertive woman who fearlessly defies convention, and *The Golden Chain*, 1903, deals with life on the frontier with equal force. GO's other works include *Captains of the World*, 1904, and *The Captain's Daughters*, 1903, and reflect her preference for 'people of action' and 'that part of the West that either breeds self-reliance or kills'.

Owen, Jane, Roman Catholic writer, of Godstow, Oxon., probably also a poet in Latin: eldest of six granddaughters of Dr George O. She recommends good works as *An Antidote against Purgatory*, supporting her argument with her own translations from Latin authors like Bellarmine. Her book, dedicated to 'Worthy and Constant' – especially rich – English Catholics, was posthumously pub. with her name and praise of her learning, 1634 (facs. 1973), probably on the Continent. She advises against luxury and putting one's children before one's own soul, composes a dialogue between soul and dying body, and remembers Christ's mercy to women. Money is urgently needed to educate poor (Catholic) scholars abroad and to enable young women to enter convents. She aims to 'gentle, and in part soften my style' for her own sex, though she is 'the more bold to speake freely' to them, and 'let a Woman once preach to Women': 'though you be weake in Nature, yet knowe your owne strength'. She instances a young woman who gave away £300 of her portion before she would 'enthrall' herself and remaining money 'to the will of a stranger'.

Owen, Mary Alicia, 1858–1935, folklorist and short-story writer, b. St Joseph, Missouri, da. of Agnes Jeannette (Cargill) and James Alfred O., lawyer and finance writer, educ. in private schools and at Vassar College. Her first pub. works were poetry, reviews and travel sketches in a St Joseph weekly newspaper, of which she becme literary editor. As 'Julia Scott' she contributed short stories to journals such as *Century, Overland Monthly, Peterson's Magazine* and *Frank Leslie's Illustrated*

Newspaper. At the same time she was recording stories and myths of various ethnic groups in Missouri, including the Musquakie (Sac) Indians (who made her an honorary tribal member in 1892), emancipated African blacks, and European gypsies. She wrote papers on the culture of blacks in Missouri and on voodoo practices of ex-slaves. Her first book, *Voo Doo Tales, as Told among the Negroes of the Southwest, Collected from Original Sources*, was pub. in 1893 and reissued in 1898 as *Old Rabbit's Plantation Stories*. *The Daughters of Alouette*, 1896, deals with gypsy tribes. The Musquakie Indians form the subject of much of her later writing, including *Folk-Lore of the Musquakie Indians in North America*, 1894, and *The Sacred Council Hills: a Folk-Lore Drama*, 1909.

Owens, Rochelle (Bass), playwright and poet, b. in 1936 in Brooklyn, NYC, da. of Jewish parents Molly (Adler) and Maxwell B. She was educ. in NYC Public Schools, later at the Herbert Berghof Studio and the New School for Social Research. As a child she read Mary Crawford DAVIES' play, *The Slave With Two Faces*, and was 'very moved'; at nine she discovered the 'strong', 'sad', 'protofeminist' poetry of Eliza COOK. In Greenwich Village, she worked as a clerk and typist and wrote experimental poetry – 'as if I was a chemist, an alchemist, mixing and playing around with fluids' – which appeared in her *Not Be Essence that Cannot Be*, 1961, and *Four Young Lady Poets*, 1962. She m. George Economou, poet and professor at Univ. of Oklahoma, 1962. With Adrienne KENNEDY, Megan TERRY, Irene FORNÈS and Rosalyn DREXLER, she was a pioneer of the early Off Off Broadway movement in the 1960s. Her early plays present 'a world of outraged female protagonists'. *Futz*, written 1958, produced 1965, Obie Award 1967, filmed 1969, is a fable – it has been called Artaudian – about a 'gentle sick man' who loves his sow, Amanda. It treats 'sexual imperialism' and 'the hypocrisy of a society which continually needs to find scapegoats'. A fellow at the Yale School of Drama, 1967–8, RO wrote *Beclch*, 1967, out of interest in 'mythm ritual and social conventions' and because of reading Arnold Toynbee. Its title character, though 'not a stick figure Amazonian', is 'feminist rage incarnate', an update in this respect of Mary SHELLEY's *Frankenstein*. *He Wants Shih!*, produced 1968, pub. 1975, explores 'the psyche of men who hate women'. *Spontaneous Combustion*, ed. RO, 1972, collects plays by RO, Kennedy, Terry, and others. *The Karl Marx Play*, produced 1973, pub. 1971, 1974, which evolved from research on 'circumstances and events, factual and imaginary' and from RO's wish to show Marx's 'extreme humanness', won the ASCAP award, 1973, and was widely produced in the USA and Europe. It mixes musical and historical commentary, past and present, Marx's family and Engels and 'Leadbelly', a voice for the oppressed. *Emma Instigated Me*, pub. 1976, casts a playwright and the anarchist, whose diary prompted the work: 'I identified with Emma GOLDMAN because she is as contradictory as I am.' RO had written more than a dozen plays and several books of acutely political, theatrical poems. These explore her Jewish heritage and repression. *I am the Babe of Joseph Stalin's Daughter: Poems 1961–71*, 1972, addresses power and racial exploitation. *The Joe 82 Creation Poems*, 1974, *The Joe Chronicles Part 2*, 1979, and *Shemuel*, 1979, represent 'the tragic, joyous and complicated journey of a mystical consciousness through the world and time'. Keenly aware of discrimination in theatre criticism – a critic said that *Beclch* was 'the work of a housewife who writes plays' – RO nevertheless writes 'To tell the truth. To feel the joy. To risk.' Her plays are collected in *Futz and What Came After*, 1968, and *The Karl Marx Play and Others*, 1974. Interview in Betsko and Koenig, 1987 (quoted above); chapter in Bonnie Marranca and Gautam Dasgupta, *American Playwrights: A Critical Survey*, I, 1981. Papers at

Univs. of Boston, California at Davis, and Oklahoma; also the Lincoln Center, NYC.

Oxlie, or Oxley, **Mary**, Scottish poet living at Morpeth, Northumberland. Her 'Encomium' on her friend William Drummond, d. 1649, was pub. with his poems, 1656. Even more interesting than her elegy (in four-stress couplets) is her self-deprecating preface: 'Perfection in a woman's work is rare; / From an untroubled mind should verses flow, / My discontents make mine too muddy show, / And hoarse encumbrances of household care; / Where these remain, the Muses ne'er repair.' Edward Phillips, who ed. this vol., mentioned in 1675 her 'many other things in Poetry', not now known. Broadsides of [1670] and [1684], attributed to her in *Various Pieces of Fugitive Scotish Poetry*, 1852, were re-ascribed in 1853.

Ozick, Cynthia, fiction writer, literary and cultural critic, translator and poet, b. 1928 in NYC, second child of Celia (Regelson) and William O., pharmacist and scholar of Yiddishized Hebrew: niece of Hebrew poet Abraham Regelson. Her parents owned a pharmacy in the Bronx where she also worked. She attended Public School 71, Hunter College, New York Univ. (BA 1949), Ohio State Univ. (MA 1950), married Bernard Hallote, a lawyer, in 1952 and has a daughter, b. 1965. After a spell as an advertising copywriter she became 'an unnatural writing-beast'; she later taught one year at New York Univ. She worked seven years on a 'philosophical novel' (an answer to the neo-Thomists, later abandoned) and six and a half on *Trust*, 1966, a paean to as well as an analysis of the bookish girl who 'went out like an explorer – not to find a destination, but a route'. She published poems in *Judaism* magazine. Her stories and essays define the role of the Jewish writer in 'pagan' society: notably 'Envy; or Yiddish in America' (*Commentary*, 1969), intended as 'a great lamentation for the murder of Yiddish, the mother-tongue of a thousand years, by the Nazis' (misunderstood and condemned by Yiddish writers, so that CO felt as if her 'mother and father had broken her skull'); 'Usurpation', 1974; the controversial 'America: Towards Yaveh', presented in Israel, 1970; and 'All the World Wants Jews Dead', 1974. *The Pagan Rabbi and Other Stories*, 1971, won awards from the Jewish Book Council and B'nai B'rith; Ruth R. Wisse judged CO a leader in US literary use of Judaism in 1976 (*Commentary*, 61). CO is not solipsistic: on a cartoonish self-portrait she typed 'ego is not interesting'. She insists that the artist has an ethical function. Her novels *The Cannibal Galaxy*, 1983, and *The Messiah of Stockholm*, 1987, delight in the imagination, anticipating her recent repudiation of her former position that storytelling is 'idol-making'; she now hopes to 'figure out a connection between' its work and that 'of monotheism-imagining'. The response to her reading, at Yale Medical School, of her story 'The Sewing Harems' (which surrealistically dissects physical and emotional aspects of motherhood) provoked her essay arguing that metaphor, 'one of the chief agents of our moral nature', 'belongs less to inspiration than ... to memory and pity'. In 'The Shawl' a baby is thrown on an electrified fence by a Nazi soldier; her mother stuffs into her own mouth the shawl which was the baby's milk-tasting emotional sustenance, 'swallowing up the wolf's screech ... and tasting the cinnamon and almond depth of Magda's saliva ... until it dried'. Article by Tom Teicholz in *Paris Review*, 102, 1987, study by Joseph Lowin, 1988, feminist dissertation by Naomi Liron, 1988.

P

Pagan, Isobel, *c.* 1742–1821, Scots poet and alehouse-keeper. She was lame, she squinted, and was deserted early by her parents. 'My learning it can soon be told, / Ten weeks when I was seven years old. ... But a' the whole tract of my time, / I found myself inclin'd to rhyme.' Her 'good, religious' teacher did not shape her personality. She lived alone, sold illicit spirits in a rent-free hovel, and entertained gentry and peasantry with impromptu songs 'of mirth and glee', dramatic monologues, and versions of older pieces. Often drunk, always satirical, openly unchaste, she was to an old clergyman 'the most perfect realization of a witch or hag that I ever saw'. Though a mocker of religion, she knew much of the Bible by heart; though unable to write her name, she dictated to a friend and pub. *A Collection of Songs and Poems on Several Occasions*, Glasgow, 1805: on hunting, local work, scandal and sharp practice, and herself. Burns, who added some stanzas to 'Ca' the yowes to the knowes', does not mention her claim to authorship. Her songs were still heard in 1840.

Page, Dorothy Myra (Gary), 'Dorothy Markey', novelist and journalist. B. in 1899 in Newport News, Va., da. of Willie Alberta (Barham) and Benjamin Roscoe G., a general practitioner, she resented being dissuaded from becoming a doctor whilst her brother was encouraged to do so. Her sense of sexual injustice combined with a hatred of class oppression and, after graduating from Westhampton College, Richmond, and studying political science at Columbia Univ., she worked for the YWCA (as an industrial secretary: cf. Grace LUMPKIN), and the Amalgamated Clothing Workers' Union in Philadelphia, St Louis and Chicago. At the Univ. of Minnesota in 1928 she married a fellow graduate student, John Markey. A writer since early childhood, now a member of the Revolutionary Writers' Federation (as well as labour organizations), she pub. her PhD thesis, *Southern Cotton Mills and Labor*, in 1929, and wrote regularly for *The Nation*, *The Daily Worker*, and *New Masses*. Her first novel, *Gathering Storm: A Story of the Black Belt*, 1932, is a Communist interpretation of the southern textile industry, focusing on the problems of women and black workers (see Joseph R. Urgo in *minnesota review*, 24, 1985). Having visited the USSR in the early 1930s, DP used it as setting for *Soviet Main Street*, 1933, and *Moscow Yankee*, 1935 (the latter dramatizes changing gender roles in post-revolutionary times). Continuity of interest can be seen in *With Sun in Our Blood*, 1950 (repr. as *Daughter of the Hills*, 1986, with intro. by Deborah Rosenfelt), a novel about women of the Tennessee coal-mining community. Blacklisted by publishers in the 1950s, DP used her married name on lives (for young people) of two US scientists, Steinmetz and Pupin. She has been working on two vols. of autobiography, *Soundings* and *Mainstream*.

Page, Louise, playwright. B. in 1955 in London, of 'a very strong mother', she was brought up with close ties to Sheffield. At five, she wanted to be an 'author', by ten was writing 'wonderfully long, extraordinary novels in which nobody did anything other than kiss passionately'. At senior school she worked an hour every night on a novel labelled, 'Please Burn When I Die'. She took a degree at

Birmingham Univ., where she has taught, and a post-graduate degree in theatre at Cardiff – (which gave her her first experience of discrimination against women in the theatre. A radical feminist early in her career ('By radical feminism, I mean any sort of separatist politics'), she later described herself as a socialist feminist. ('Some people would call that a tame sort of feminism, but I think what's needed is a liberation of all people from preinformed ideology.') Her first play was *Want-Ad*, 1977. *Tissue*, 1978, approached 'the way women saw their bodies' through the tough topic of breast cancer. LP arrived with her eighth play, *Salonika*, 1982 (commissioned by the Royal Court, London, about old age: she did most of the research for it on trains talking to 'old ladies travelling'). Its theme (the slaughter and waste of war) extends through the collaborative *Falkland sound/Voces de Malvinas*, 1983, constructed from actual letters and interviews, to *Goat*, 1986, on nuclear war. LP thinks it impossible to 'be a woman in present day society *without* being a feminist', but is wary of the label 'woman writer' and wants to write 'about the things which affect both men and women'. *Real Estate*, 1984, tackles not only mother–daughter relations but also desire for fatherhood. She looks at assertiveness here and ambition ('rather a dirty word in this society' for females) in *Golden Girls* (Royal Shakespeare Co., 1984) about women athletes. *Beauty and the Beast* (Women's Playhouse Trust, 1985) finds in myth 'a happy end for a change'. LP has written for radio and television. Interviews in *Plays and Players*, 353 (Feb. 1983), *Drama*, 3, 1985, and Betsko and Koenig, 1987 (quoted above).

Page, Patricia **K.** (P. K. Irwin), poet, painter, non-fiction writer. B. in 1916, in Swanage, Dorset, she migrated to Canada in 1919 with her parents, Rose Laura (Whitehouse) and Major-General Lionel Frank P., spending her early years in Calgary, Winnipeg, and Saint John, New Brunswick. While working there as a sales clerk and radio actress, she wrote a novel (published years later as *The Sun and the Moon*, 1944, under the pseudonym 'Judith Cape', since she had 'outgrown it'). With Margaret ATWOOD's encouragement and brief introduction, it reappeared, with eight short stories, 1973, under PKP's real name. PKP began writing in her teens when it 'wasn't quite decent', and was later one of the fine Canadian poets launched by Alan Crawley, editor of *Contemporary Verse*. She worked in Montréal as a filing clerk and historical researcher. 'In the pause between the first draft and the carbon / they glimpse the smooth hours when they were children' ('The Stenographers' in *As Ten, as Twenty*, 1946). There, in 1942, with F. R. Scott, A. M. Klein and Patrick Anderson, PKP ed. *Preview*, a 'little MAGAZINE' that contributed to the beginning of modernist poetry in Canada. It created the climate for a rival, *First Statement*; the two merged in the influential *Northern Review*. PKP's poetry of those years, which reflects the new intellectual and aesthetic direction of Canadian poetry, won the Oscar Blumenthal Award from *Poetry* (Chicago), 1944. The language of *The Metal and the Flower* (Governor-General's Award, 1954) is characteristically precise and loquacious: 'Consider a new habit – classical, / and trees espaliered on the wall like candelabra. / ... Who am I / or who am I become, that walking here / I am observer, other, Gemini, / starred for a green garden of cinema?' Influenced by Auden, Rilke, and A. M. Klein, PKP's poetry balances out dream and reality – 'an alphabet the eye / lifts from the air / as if by ear' (*Cry Ararat!*, 1967) – and often insinuates a sinister element into her recurring motif of the green innocence of childhood: 'refracting, like a globe, / its edges bending, sides distorted' (*The Glass Air*, 1985). PKP was a script writer for the National Film Board in Montréal, 1946–50, married W. Arthur Irwin, 1950, and left for Australia when he became Canadian Ambassador there.

Later, posted in Brazil, 1957–9, PKP had 'the real geographical experience of my life'. Her *Brazilian Journal*, 1987, describes 'this beautiful, tropical, golden, dream' and the elegant intricacies of ambassadorial protocol. Unable to write, she started making 'elaborate', 'detailed' drawings, studied art, and continued to draw and paint in Mexico, her husband's next posting. Her artwork, widely shown under her married name, is represented in leading Canadian galleries. *Evening Dance of the Gray Flies*, 1981, retains her visual sensuousness and fluid language, but now PKP's style is crisper, her poetic vision more magical and liberating, a sign, perhaps, of her deep interest in Sufi writers. Included in all important anthologies of Canadian poetry, PKP, who lives with her husband in Victoria, BC, is an Officer of the Order of Canada. See Constance Rooke, in *Malahat Review*, 45, 1978, and Rosemary Sullivan, in *CanL*, 79, 1978.

Pakington, Dorothy (Coventry), Lady, d. 1679, reputed devotional writer. Da. of Elizabeth (Aldersley) and Thomas Lord C. (Keeper of the Great Seal to Charles I), she had a learned educ.; her two brothers were eminent in Restoration politics. About 1648 she married Sir John P. of Westwood, Worcs., and became the centre of an important circle of Anglican thinkers. DP's identity as a writer rests on MSS left at her death, and on the word of her daughter Elizabeth, wife of Anthony Eyre of Rampton (herself author of a bold and learned *Letter from a Person of Quality in the North*, 1689, repr. with her name, 1710, on the Church and 'passive obedience'). Also in 1689, Elizabeth Eyre publicly named DP as author of *The Whole Duty of Man*, 1659, and *Causes of the Decay of Christian Piety*, 1667 (pub. as by the same hand). The immensely influential *Whole Duty*, addressed 'to the very meanest Readers', is warm, appealing, immediate, yet firmly rational; both books end with prayers; both were pub. by T. Garthwaite, London. There followed (besides other books hinting a link with these) four pub. at Oxford as by the same hand, beginning with *The Ladies Calling*, 1673: these were not included in DP's daughter's claim. Bishop John Fell reissued the whole set as *Works* of a (male) author he described without naming. DP's claim was accepted by Mary ASTELL, George Ballard, E. O. BENGER, and M. M. BETHAM; most scholars since John Nichols, 1812, favour Richard Allestree as author of the *Whole Duty*, arguing that DP probably transcribed his unpub. MSS for her own use. Her MSS and letters at Hereford and Worcester Record Office and at the Bodleian have no apparent overlap with her ascribed printed works.

Paley, Grace (Goodside), short-story writer, b. 1922 in the Bronx, NYC, youngest child of Jewish socialist immigrants Mary (Ridnyik) and Isaac G., doctor and painter: reared in an extended family. She 'always knew I would write and I did', despite poor high-school grades (she was writing poetry and thinking about boys) and leaving her college educ. (Hunter and NY Univ.) unfinished. She m. cameraman Jess P. at 19 and had two children. In her mid-thirties she knew her poems ('a couple' pub.) to be derivative; she started on stories and 'Suddenly, I heard the voices.' Publication was slowed by the feeling (which she then shared) that her daily-life material was trivial: the great literary theme then was WWII. Only three stories appeared before *The Little Disturbances of Man: Stories of Men and Women* [she intended it to be *Women and Men*] *at Love*, 1959. Several characters, notably Faith (an alter-ego created on a whim, thinking of a 'family called Faith, Hope, and Charlie'), reappear in later books, giving GP's world a dense texture. From about this time she moved from 'municipal' politics into the Women's Pentagon Action and steadily expanding international anti-war activism: GP has written a story about Americans in China and (jointly) a 1988 peace calendar, *Three*

Hundred Sixty Five Reasons Not to Have Another War. In the 1960s she worked on a novel 'because people said I should' (parts pub. in journals), but threw it out. A finished plot, she says, takes away the human dignity of openness to possibility. In 1972 she married writer Robert Nichols. Later books are *Enormous Changes at the Last Minute*, 1974, and *Later the Same Day*, 1985. Her much-praised humour, wisecracking in face of pain, depends on character and context, undercurrents between families or friends. She excels too at extreme, unsimple starkness, as in 'Samuel', about a boy killed in larking around on subway-car platforms. She has taught at several univs., latterly at Sarah Lawrence College, NYC, spending half her time in Vermont. She has given several interviews. Criticism includes Kathleen A. Coppula in *Mid-American Review*, 7, 1986.

Palmer, Alicia Tindal, 1763–*c*. 1822, novelist and biographer living at Bath, da. of actors Hannah Mary (Pritchard) and John Palmer. Her father and grandmother (the famous tragedian) died in 1768: her mother (re-married the next year) became well-off. *The Husband and Lover, An Historical Moral Romance*, 1809, was well received; *The Daughters of Isenberg, A Bavarian Romance*, 1810, was insultingly panned by Gifford in the *Quarterly* (with a story that she had tried to bribe him). Using the novel as moral vehicle, she admires her heroine's 'bewitching timidity' and ridicules a female pedant, yet talks of women's 'natural wit and sense, which no want of education could prevent from shining forth', and looks back to a time when women participated in 'poetry and philosophy'. In *The Sons of Altringham*, 1811, three loosely linked stories blend humour with romance: writing to raise money for a deaf and dumb boy, AP includes such a boy as a minor character. *The Authentic Memoirs of . . . John Sobieski, King of Poland*, 1815 (to which Byron subscribed), unquestioningly praises military courage and patriotism, and deplores the hero's over-indulgence of his queen. The RLF paid ATP £65, 1824–8.

Palmer, Charlotte, *c*. 1762–after 1834, teacher and miscellaneous writer. Her preface to *Female Stability, or The History of Miss Belville*, 1780, explains that it is not hers, but juvenile work by a sister now dead. Its heroine rejects marriage in favour of eternal grief for a dead lover (her closest friend marries to do good). In 1782 CP visited Bath, Bristol, and Stourhead; with another sister she ran schools near London, teaching writing and incidentally grammar. In 1792 she pub. *Integrity and Content: An Allegory* and *It Is and It Is Not a Novel*, in which a female mentor quotes Susannah DOBSON, and hardship makes even the less sentimental heroine 'amiable and truly feminine'. A review mocked the title (which reflected debate with a male friend). In 1797 CP pub. by subscription *A Newly-Invented Copybook* (chiefly blank pages headed by maxims or parts of speech in copper-plate print, with a self-abasing and pedantic preface on capitalization, grammar, and how to differentiate notes from letters), and *Letters . . . from a Preceptress* to ex-pupils, which inculcates dutiful morality and closes with a poem by Jane WEST. In 1805 her school was in debt for over £200; in prison at suit of 'one relentless Creditor', she wrote humbly to the RLF (which for years made her small payments), listing proposed pedagogical works. Released, she published some of them and ran a little day-school and a private stall in a bonnet-shop.

Palmer, Mary (Reynolds), 1716–94, dialect author, eldest da. of Theophila (Potter) and Samuel R.: sister of Frances REYNOLDS and the future Sir Joshua, who was early influenced by her drawing talent. In 1740 she married John Palmer, gentleman, of Great Torrington, Devon. Some years later she composed *A Devonshire Dialogue*, called by the *DNB* 'the best piece of literature' in the local vernacular, which presents with spirit and humour the gossip of Rab and Bet: Bet's love of reading, her harsh 'Measter' and lovable 'Dame', deaths which balance the approaching marriage. Excerpts were soon copied and printed; a sample appeared anonymously in 1837 and the full text in 1839, repr. [1869].

Palmer, Nettie, Janet Gertrude (Higgins), 1885–1964, critic, journalist and poet, b. Bendigo, Victoria, da. of Katherine (McDonald) and John H., accountant. She was educ. at Presbyterian Ladies' College and Melbourne Univ., continued her Classics studies in Paris and London, then returned to Melbourne to graduate as MA, 1912. In 1914 she m. writer Vance P. in London; she had two daughters, Aileen and Helen, both writers. She published two early vols. of poetry, *The South Wind*, 1914, and *Shadow Paths*, 1915, but by the 1920s had become an influential literary journalist. She lectured, reviewed, and pub. articles arguing the value of Australian writers in a period when literary talent struggled to assert itself against the prevailing 'cultural cringe'. She wrote about (and to) Henry Handel Richardson, Miles Franklin, Frank Dalby Davidson, Katharine Susannah Prichard, Marjorie Barnard, Barbara Baynton, Martin Boyd, and many others. She also knew Christina Stead, André Gide, Paul Eluard, André Malraux, and E. M. Forster. As well as researching her husband's work, she pub. 13 books, including *Modern Australian Literature 1900–1923*, 1923, the anthology, *An Australian Story Book*, 1928, the memoirs, *Fourteen Years*, 1948, biographical and critical studies, and political commentary on the Spanish Civil War, 1937. Much of her journalism, distinguished by a cosmopolitan attitude and a wide-ranging intelligence, appeared in the *Argus*, *Brisbane Courier*, *Bulletin*, and the *Illustrated Tasmanian Mail*. Her papers, in the Vance and Nettie Palmer collection (National Library of Australia), also contain extensive prose works. A recent portable *Nettie Palmer*, 1988, contains journal extracts, poems, reviews and essays. Her autobiography remained uncompleted due to ill-health. See Drusilla Modjeska's significant *Exiles at Home*, 1981; Vivian Smith's biography, 1975, and ed. of letters, 1977.

Pankhurst, Christabel, 1880–1958, DBE, suffragette and religious writer, b. in Manchester, eldest da. of Emmeline Pankhurst and sister of Sylvia. She early met people like William Morris and Annie Besant. After her father's death, 1898, she supported and came to influence her mother. Like him she studied law at Manchester Univ. (LLB 1906), where she met Eva Gore-Booth: applying to follow him to Lincoln's Inn, she was, as a woman, rejected. A founder member of the Women's Social and Political Union, 1903, she chose its name, wrote for its papers *Votes for Women* and *The Suffragette* (which she edited 1912–14 in Paris to avoid further arrest), and was prime mover in its dashing and forceful tactics. She befriended Annie Kenney from 1905, and wrote a chapter on women and law for F. J. Shaw's suffrage vol., 1907. Her own books began with *The Militant Methods of the N.W.S.P.U.*, 1908, and *The Great Scourge* [venereal disease], *and How to End It*, 1913 (see Sheila Jeffreys in *Women's Studies International*, 5, 1982). WWI deflected CP's militancy from the suffrage into patriotic nationalism. She stood for parliament in 1918 (the first election for which women were eligible), and polled high, but not the highest. She adopted 'war babies', speaking of this as a duty of childless women. The war helped shape her religious belief in an imminent Second Coming. Of several books on this topic, *The World's Unrest: Visions of the Dawn*, 1926, typically turns from men's and women's wisdom to God's. 'The Bible has disclosed the future.' After much time in North America, she settled in the USA in 1940, and died in Santa Monica, Calif. Her *Unshackled. The Story of How We Won the Vote*, 1959, is autobiographical as well as historical. David Mitchell's life, 1977, is hostile; Elizabeth Sarah in Dale Spender, ed., *Feminist Theorists*, 1983, combats this but mentions neither Sylvia P. nor CP's life after 1914. See Carol Lavin on CP and Sylvia in *Women: A Journal of Liberation*, 6, 1978.

Pankhurst, Emmeline (Goulden), 1858–1928, suffragette, b. in Manchester, da. of radicals Sophia Jane (Craine) and Robert G., who ran a textile works, was a founder member of the first Women's Suffrage Committee, 1865, yet shocked her by wishing she had been 'born a lad'. Though her mother brought her up on the works of Harriet Beecher STOWE, and took her to a suffrage meeting at 14, the family took boys' education more seriously than girls'. From a 'ladylike' Manchester school she went at 15 to that of Mlle Marchef-Girard in Paris, a leader in female higher education. She m., 1879, the older Richard Marsden P., d. 1898, reforming barrister and friend of John Stuart Mill. (He drafted the Married Women's Property Bill, 1882.) They had three daughters and two sons (one died very young). Active with him in the International Labour Party, she founded, with her daughters Christabel and Sylvia, the WSPU, 1903. She contributed to *The Case for Woman's Suffrage*, ed. Frederick John Shaw, 1907, to *Votes for Women* and *The Suffragette*, and pub. *The Importance of the Vote*, 1912. A rousing public speaker, she printed addresses in *Suffrage Speeches from the Dock* and *Why We Are Militant* (delivered in NYC), both 1913. Hailed for her leadership, often in jail, she vividly relates in *My Own Story*, 1914 (facs. 1979 with intro. by Jill Craigie), the exhilarating, disturbing impact on a middle-class sensibility of involvement in violence and sabotage: 'Our battles are practically over', she says. WWI led EP to call a truce over the vote (maintained during 1916–18, when others were active) and turn to army recruitment. She went to Canada in 1920 to resettle 'war babies'; back in England in 1926, she stood for parliament as a Conservative. For her effect in the USA see John C. Zacharis in *Speech Monographs*, 38, 1971; for links with Elizabeth ROBINS see Jane Marcus in *Signs*, 3, 1978. Numerous lives run from Sylvia P., 1935, to Linda Hoy, 1985; SUFFRAGE archives in the Fawcett Library, London.

Pankhurst, Estelle **Sylvia** 1882–1960, suffragette, activist and social historian, middle da. of Emmeline PANKHURST and sister of Christabel. Educ. at Manchester High School for Girls, Manchester School of Art, and the Royal College of Art, she visited Italy on a travel scholarship, supported herself as a freelance artist in London, and regretted the squeezing out of her visual work by politics. A lifelong socialist, she attended International Labour Party meetings from an early age; she was deeply influenced by her father and by Keir Hardie (she was his lover, *c.* 1904–12). A founder member of the WSPU, she designed the cover of *Votes for Women*, wrote for *The Suffragette* from 1910, and pub. *Suffragette, The History of the Women's Militant Suffrage Movement*, 1911 (preface by Emmeline P.; repr. 1970), which conveys a sense of exaltation and gallantry with a firm grasp on factual detail. Having founded the more democratic and largely working-class East London Federation of the WSPU, she ed. its *Women's Dreadnought* (later, 1914–21, *The Workers' Dreadnought*). In WWI she worked for many causes: a fair deal for women munitions workers, 'The Mother's Arms' centre for their deprived children, and an end to the shooting of teenage deserters. Remembering her family's anti-Boer-war stance, she heard a pro-war speech by Christabel P. 'with grief': 'An impenetrable barrier lay between us.' A keen internationalist, she wrote books on Soviet Russia, 1921, India, 1926, and an international language, 1927, and was an early critic of Mussolini. *Writ on a Cold Slate* (poems), 1922, describes prison experiences: the title refers to lack of paper.

She was joint translator of Rumanian poet M. Eminescu, 1930. Repudiated by her mother, SP never ceased to work for women as well as men. After *Save the Mothers, A Plea for Measures to Prevent the Annual Toll* (pamphlet), 1930, came two exact and dramatic historical-autobiographical works, *The Suffrage Movement, An Intimate Account of Persons and Ideals*, 1931, and *The Home Front, A Mirror to Life in England during the World War*, 1932; repr. 1977 and 1987 with introductions by SP's son Richard P. They vividly evoke the feel of mass meetings, force-feeding in prison, poor people's resilience, and female solidarity. She saw the vote as a means rather than an end: *The Suffrage Movement* concludes, 'great is the work which remains to be accomplished'. Her life of her mother, 1935, repr. 1969, strives for fairness. From *c.* 1925 SP lived with Silvio Corio, a socialist exile from Italy, with whom she collaborated in journalism and publishing. Their son (joint-author of the second of her books on Somalia, Eritrea and Ethiopia, 1951, 1953, and 1955) later recalled waking to find her at her desk, where she had worked all night. She died in Addis Ababa. Long undervalued by admirers of Emmeline and Christabel, she is now receiving her due: lives by Richard P., 1979, Silvia Franchini, 1980, and Patricia W. Romero, 1987. Her younger sister Adela, 1885–1961, also a radical, migrated to Australia, pub. *Put Up the Sword*, and was active in political causes.

Panter-Downes, Mollie Patricia, novelist, journalist, b. 1906 in London to Kathleen (Cowley) and Maj. Edward P-D (d. 1914). She was educ. at Brighton schools and Heathfield House, Horsham. She began writing at six, and pub. verse in *Poetry Review* at 12 and a novel, *The Shoreless Sea* (written at 16), 1923. She later disowned this tale of a (reconciled) love triangle, and also *The Chase*, 1925 (about a self-made man), *Storm Bird*, 1929, and *My Husband Simon*, 1931 (conflict between marriage and work: a young writer decides to part from her husband to concentrate on her next novel). MP-D m. civil servant Clare Robinson in 1927 and had two children. She wrote a *New Yorker* 'Letter from London', 1939–84. Those written during WWII, on 'the average man, patiently and courageously getting on with the job' (coll. in *Letter from England*, 1940, and *London War Notes 1939–1945*, 1971) share a theme with *One Fine Day*, 1947 (repr. 1985 with intro. by Nicola Beauman). Beauman calls this 'almost a hymn of praise to ... the ordinary Englishwoman who did not fight in the war but lived through it as acutely as any soldier'. It is, MP-D says, 'her only novel'. Its style and substance is markedly new: an impressionistic day-in-the-life of a 'perfectly happy married woman, simply getting a little greyer, duller, more tired than I should be getting, because my easier sort of life has come to an end'. MD-P has pub. a children's book, 1943, and non-fiction: *Ooty Preserved: A Victorian Hill Station in India*, 1967, and a work on Swinburne and Watts-Dunton, 1971.

Panton, Jane Ellen (Frith), 1848–1923, journalist and novelist, b. in London into the large family of Isabelle (Baker) and the painter William Powell F. Governesses, she says, taught her little, but literary and artistic circles taught her much. As a girl in short frocks she reviewed a Royal Academy exhibition for the *Bayswater Chronicle*. She m. James P. in 1869, had five children, and wrote for several markets. *Country Sketches in Black and White*, 1882, led to other books of sketches. *Homes of Taste*, 1890, advice on decorating and furnishing, led to similar titles, e.g. *Suburban Residences*, 1896 (how to circumvent 'death traps, cold-givers and misery-makers'). *From Kitchen to Garret*, on house-keeping (7 eds. in 1890), had its own sequels. JEP also advised invalids and carers, 1893, and parents, 1896, and pub. poems for children, n. d. *Leaves from a Life*, 1908 (chatty autobiographical anecdotes), led to further vols. of 'leaves'. Her novels give lively form to problem issues: sibling rivalry between sisters in *Jane Caldecott*, dedicated to her father, 1882, whose heroine sets out 'more bent on reforming the world than on matrimony'; a father's malign power in *A Tangled Chain*, 1887 (his daughter greets his death with 'I have lost my gaoler'; the knowledge that she killed him is long withheld); a wife's embroilment in political journalism in *Having and Holding*, 1890 (her reforming husband is right; she, a diehard, has to learn that she is wrong); and civilization sharply satirized through a complete outsider in *The Cannibal Crusader, An Allegory for the Times*, 1908.

Pardoe, Julia S. H., 1806–82, novelist, biographer, TRAVEL and short-story writer, b. Beverley, Yorks. second da. of Major Thomas P. She showed literary tastes and talents at an early age, publishing a book of poetry at 13. She produced several popular accounts of her travels, including trips to Portugal, 1833, and Turkey, 1837. Her *City of the Magyar*, 1840, was remarkable for its comprehensive research into Hungarian political and economic life, while her somewhat florid books on the East are sympathetic to unfamiliar customs and beliefs. Her unremitting study and literary work, undertaken partly to support poor relations, told on her health, and from 1842 she lived with her parents outside London. Though of uneven quality, her many novels and short stories are at their best in their sharp observation of the greed and affectations of both fashionable and middle-class circles, as in the popular novels *Confessions of a Pretty Woman*, 1846, *The Jealous Wife*, 1847, *The Rival Beauties*, 1848, and *Reginald Lyle*, 1854. More durable were her histories of French court life, including *Louis XIV*, 1847, and *Francis The First*, 1849 (by far the most comprehensive work on his reign). Her very diffuse treatment of Marie de Medici, 1852, combats other historians' critical and unsympathetic portrayal. JP received a Civil List pension in 1860. There is a brief memoir in the 1887 ed. of *Francis the First*.

Paretsky, Sara, mystery writer, b. in 1947 in Eudora, Kan., into a 'family where girls became secretaries and wives, and boys became professionals'. In her early fantasy her parents were space aliens. She went to a two-room country school (playing third base on the baseball team) and the Univs. of Kansas (BA in political science, 1967) and Chicago (MBA, PhD in history, both 1977). She lives with her physicist husband, Courtney Wright, in Chicago, where she worked first in a research firm, then as an insurance company executive. She started writing at six, later devoured mysteries (24 the month she took her PhD orals), finally resolving, on New Year's Day 1979, to write a book 'or die trying'. She produced V. I. Warshawski, a tough, fit, gun-packing political feminist who appears in SP's six DETECTIVE novels from *Indemnity Only*, 1982. In *Deadlock*, 1984, she avenges the murder of a hockey-star cousin, Boom Boom, and uncovers a shipping insurance fraud; in *Toxic Shock*, 1988 (outsold by *Burn Marks*, 1990), she investigates criminal machinations in a chemical company. SP helped to set up Sisters in Crime, a woman's caucus of the Mystery Writers of America, to combat inequities in publishing, reviewing and distributing women's fiction and with violence against women in crime writing. Increasingly political, she is active in the National Abortion Rights Action League. Interview in *Ms*, Jan. 1988.

Park, Ruth, novelist, children's writer, b. 1922 in Auckland, educ. at Auckland University. She began contributing to children's pages in newspapers at the age of 11 and worked as a journalist before coming to Australia in 1942. She m. writer D'Arcy Niland and had two sons and three daughters, two of the latter being writers and artists. Her first novel, *The Harp in the South*, 1948, winner of the *Sydney Morning Herald* Literary Prize, was inspired by a period spent living in Surry Hills, then a Sydney slum. It was followed by a sequel, *Poor Man's Orange*, 1949. These novels of working-class life remain among her best-known works and were recently filmed for TV, which inspired a 'prequel' – describing the earlier lives of her characters – *Missus*, 1985. Prominent amongst RP's other six novels for adults is *Swords and Crowns and Rings*, 1977, winner of the Miles FRANKLIN Award. It follows the fortunes of its hero, Jackie Hanna, a dwarf, from 1907 to 1930 and combines elements of myth and fable with realistic portraits of life in Australia during the Depression. Since 1961 RP has also written much fiction for children, including the prize-winning *Playing Beatie Bow*, 1980 (filmed 1986), in which an adolescent girl travels back in time to nineteenth-century Sydney and discovers much about life and love. For younger children, RP created the character of the Muddle-Headed Wombat, star of radio and TV programmes and of 14 books published 1962–81. She has also written much non-fiction, many short stories and plays for radio and TV. MSS in the Mitchell Library, Sydney.

Parker, Catherine Langloh, 'Mrs K. Langloh Parker', Catherine Eliza Somerville (Field), 1856–1940, collector of Aboriginal legends, b. Encounter Bay, S. Australia, da. of Sophia (Newland) and Henry F. She was brought up on her father's stations in Queensland where she had many Aboriginal friends. After marriage to K. Langloh P., she lived on his properties in northern NSW and Queensland; after his death she m. Percival Stow. She collected Aboriginal legends and stories and published *Australian Legendary Tales*, 1896 (as by Mrs K. Langloh Parker). Other works include *More Australian Legendary Tales*, 1898, and an anthropological study, *The Euahlayi Tribe*, 1905. A selection of her work, *Australian Legendary Tales*, 1953, won the Children's Book of the Year Award the following year. The previously unpub. *My Bush Book*, 1982 (ed. Marcie Muir), includes a biography. MSS in the Mitchell Library, Sydney.

Parker, Dorothy (Rothschild), 'The Constant Reader', 1893–1967, short-story writer, poet, critic and central figure of the celebrated Algonquin Hotel Round Table. Da. of Eliza A. (Marston), who d. in DP's infancy, and wealthy garment manufacturer Henry R., she was b. at West End, NJ, and educ. there and (at a convent school) in NYC. In 1916 she sold some poems to *Vogue* and began writing fashion-picture captions. In 1917 she became drama critic of *Vanity Fair* and married Edwin Pond Parker II (divorced 1928). Her first volume of poetry, *Enough Rope*, 1926, was a bestseller, re-issued in 1936 with two further vols., as *Not So Deep as a Well*. Her self-mocking humour prevails in each: 'I shudder at the thought of men . . . / I'm due to fall in love again'; 'Once you went out, my heart fell, broken. / (Nevertheless, a girl must live.)' Her famous sharp-tongued wit appears again in *New Yorker* book reviews (as the 'Constant Reader') and stories (volumes of 1930 and 1933, collected in *Here Lies*, 1939). Her tone is at once ironic and tender in a study of an alcoholic ('Big Blonde': O. Henry Award, 1929), a woman's heart-rending monologue ('A Telephone Call'), and a girl's gravely constructed fantasy about spending $1 million ('The Standard of Living'). Tragedy lurks beneath the acerbic lucidities: every one of DP's titles refers to death; her poems began with 'Threnody' ('Lips that taste of tears, they say, / Are the best for kissing') and ended with 'War Song', 1944, urging a soldier husband not to be faithful ('Take her smile and lift her hand – / Have no guilt of me.') She married actor-writer Alan Campbell in 1933 and went to Hollywood, where her work included the screen version, 1941, of *The Little Foxes* by Lillian HELLMAN, a friend who wrote of DP in *An Unfinished Woman*. She had a miscarriage in 1935. Her political activism jeopardized her and her husband's positions in Hollywood. He was away during WWII; they divorced in 1947 but remarried in 1950 and survived a later separation. She went on reviewing books, and called her second stage collaboration, *The Ladies of the Corridor* (with Arnaud d'Usseau), staged 1954, 'the only thing I ever did I was proud of'. She died four years after Campbell, alone in a Manhattan hotel room, having suggested for her tombstone 'This is on me.' Her stories were collected 1942, poetry 1944, essays 1970; overall selec. 1944, repr. 1973; others 1977, 1985. Lives by L. R. Frewin, 1986, Marion Meade, 1987; feminist essays by Suzanne L. Bunkers in *Regionalism and the Female Imagination*, 4, 1978, and Paula A. Treichler in *Language and Style*, 13, 1980.

Parker, Elizabeth Mary, domestic servant and author of a novel, b. in 1849? in Bucks., da. of an innkeeper. *The Rose of Avondale*, 1872, is conventional in both narrative and description (the heroine 'carrolling like the gladsome birds', the hero 'a true gentleman in every sense of the word'). Their courtship runs few serious hazards, though the heroine develops acute lack of confidence after losing her money. Arthur J. Munby, connoisseur of books and servant girls, tracked EMP on publication to her London place of work, but nothing is known of her later life.

Parker, Emma, novelist, probably Welsh. Publishing, she said, because her family had little money though plenty of gentility, she began as 'Emma De Lisle', with *A Soldier's Offspring, or The Sisters*, MINERVA, 1810, a slight courtship novel dedicated to her mother. A jaunty preface about truth to human nature, and a conclusion about the joy of writing, hint at greater potential – realized in the longer *Elfrida, Heiress of Belgrove*, with her own name, 1811. Here both heroines and heroes learn through love: one develops from a young officer who 'could not blind himself to the beauties of his own person' and exaggerates a wound for sympathy. An energetic digression rebukes 'violent philippics' by novelists against novels and calls for a league to 'fight their cause to the very last drop of our ink'. Reviewers praised this and her five later novels. *Fitz-Edward, or The Cambrians* (also 1811, containing some poetry) would have been called *Eva of Cambria* if Amelia BEAUCLERC had not beaten EP to that title. *Self-Deception*, 1816, is epistolary, since, says EP, it turns on character rather than incident. Related love stories include French–English (Catholic-Protestant) and that of a French couple who marry from filial duty, each loving elsewhere, and grow to hate before they learn to love. *Important Trifles*, 1817, is a volume of essays on Christian morals and social conduct, strong-minded and well-informed.

Parker, Mary Ann, English travel writer, da. of a doctor. Having seen France, Italy and Spain with her mother, she accepted a last-minute invitation to sail to NSW, 1791, with her husband, Capt. John P., and Anna (Coombe) King, new wife of the governor of Norfolk Island (a hellhole in the making). After 'a fortnight's seasoning and buffeting in the channel, I began to enjoy the voyage'; 'we glided over many a watery grave with peace of mind'. She records storms, crossing-the-line rituals, wild life and human life at Santa Cruz and the Cape, the horrors of transport ships, the feasibility of an Australian whale fishery, the convict settlement at Parramatta, and her acquisition of a prayer-book once owned by a convict and found in a shark's belly. Her account of Aboriginals leads her into an anti-racist plea. She came home, heavily pregnant, to money troubles, later increased by John P.'s death of yellow fever at Martinique. From her journal she wrote (often with her latest baby cradled in her left arm) *A Voyage Round the World in the Gorgon Man of War*, 1793. Frances BOSCAWEN and Hannah MORE subscribed. Between 1796 and 1804 (in which year she was in debtors' prison with her daughters) the RLF gave her 20 guineas. MAP is not to be confused with Mary Elizabeth P., author of two novels, 1795 (by subscription) and 1802.

Parker, Pat (Cook), black lesbian feminist poet. B. in 1944 and raised in 'a giant vacuum called Texas', da. of domestic worker Marie Louise (Anderson) and tire retreader Earnest Nathaniel C., she began writing as a child and later studied journalism and creative writing at Los Angeles City College and San Francisco State College. Formerly married to Ed Bullins, 1962, and Robert P., 1966, she lives in Pleasant Hill, Calif., with her lover and two children. PP has had various jobs, including waitress, clerk, and creative-writing instructor. From 1978 she directed the Oakland Feminist Women's Health Center. *Child of Myself*, 1972, includes the daring, influential autobiographical poem 'Goat Child'. Her voice is direct, colloquial, challenging – 'SISTER! your foot's smaller / but it's still on my neck' (*Pit Stop*, 1973) – often funny, tender and erotic, but always, says Audre LORDE, 'with an iron echo'. PP's sister was murdered by her husband, who was jailed for one year: 'Men cannot kill their wives. / They passion them to death.' PP took the 'love poem' *Womanslaughter*, 1978, to the International Tribunal on Crimes Against Women. *Movement in Black*, 1978 (intro. by Judy GRAHN), collects her poetry 1961–78. In *Jonestown and Other Madness*, 1985, she continues her visionary commitment to 'speak out loudly before the madness consumes us all'. She was a founder, 1980, of the Black Women's Revolutionary Council in Oakland. Recorded readings include *Where Would I Be Without You*, 1975, with Grahn.

Parkes, Bessie Rayner (Belloc), 1829–1925, feminist activist, educationalist, journalist, b. Birmingham, da. of Elizabeth (Priestley) and Joseph P., radical lawyer, and a founder of the Reform Club. The family moved to London when BRP was still a child. She taught herself to read, then attended school in Warwicks., and had ambitions of making her name as a poet. (She pub. three vols. of verse 1852, 1854, 1856, coll. 1904 as *In Fifty Years*.) From early childhood, she was a close friend of Barbara BODICHON, and they made an unchaperoned visit to the Continent together in 1850. Both were prominent members of the committee which drew up the petition for the Married Women's Property Bill. Other friends included Elizabeth GASKELL, George ELIOT, Anna JAMESON, Matilda HAYS, Adelaide PROCTER, and Isa CRAIG. In 1854, she pub. anon. *Remarks on the Education of Girls*, complaining about its restrictive nature. In 1858 she and Bodichon set up the *English Woman's Journal*, run by women for women, and concentrating on their employment possibilities and on profiles of famous and successful women. Her editorial tone was somewhat cautious, in order to avoid alienating potential sympathizers (see Jane Rendall's essay in her *Equal or Different? Women's Politics, 1800–1914*, 1987). The magazine also contained poems, stories, book reviews, and an 'Open Council' column, for readers' views. Brought up a Unitarian, BRP moved to agnosticism, then Catholicism in 1864, becoming increasingly devout. In 1867, she m. Louis Belloc, a semi-invalid from an artistic family, and lived mostly in France until his death in 1872, from which she never fully recovered. They had two children, Hilaire B. and Marie Belloc-Lowndes, whose 1941 autobiography provides a portrait of her mother during her marriage.

Parr, Katharine, 1512–48, sixth wife of Henry VIII, one of eight Englishwomen to publish between 1486 and 1548. Her father, Sir Thomas P., d. in 1517; her mother, Maud (Greene), lived at Court; KP was taught by Ludovicus Vives, pioneer of serious EDUCATION for girls. She was twice widowed before marrying the king in 1543. Strongly interested in the new Protestantism, she protected the universities and oversaw the education of the future monarchs Edward and ELIZABETH (whose writing she encouraged). She arranged the englishing of Erasmus's Latin paraphrase (or commentary) on the New Testament, persuading Mary Tudor to translate St John's gospel and let it bear her name to posterity. Her group of bible-studying ladies grew radical over Anne ASKEW's trial. KP probably saved her head by a show of wifely submission to Henry, with whom she had often held religious debate; she finally changed his ideas on the Mass. Despite her own learning (Latin and some Greek) she urged Cambridge University men to use 'our vulgar tongue'. Her collection of *Prayers and Medytacions*, 1545 (feeling and personal in tone), had 15 eds. by 1608. She wrote a 'classic of Tudor devotional literature', *Lamentacion of a Sinner*, pub. 1547, the year of Henry's death and her marriage to Thomas, Lord Seymour. She d. in childbirth. See life by Anthony Martienssen, 1973.

Parr, Louisa (Taylor), d. 1903, novelist, b. London, only child of Matthew T., RN. She was educ. and grew up at Plymouth, Hants. Her writing career began in 1868 with the publication of a short story, 'How it all happened', by 'Mrs Olinthus Lobb', in *Good Words*, where it attracted attention and was translated into French and German. In 1869 she m. Dr George P. and moved to London. In 1870 she published *Dorothy Fox*, a Quaker novel, more appreciated in the USA than at home, and in 1880 her best-known work, *Adam and Eve*. It revolves around the *femme fatale* figure of Eve, but its interest chiefly lies in the picture of Cornish society and the Cornish dialogue in which much of it is written. Her next, *Loyalty George*, 1888 (serialized 1887–8 in *Temple Bar*), has the same setting with a more unusual heroine. Five more novels followed, as well as some tales (e.g. 'Miss Hazel', in Rosa PRAED (ed.), *For Their Sakes*, 1884). Essays include a series on 'The Follies of Fashion' in the *Pall Mall*, and one on Dinah Mulock CRAIK in *Women Novelists of Queen Victoria's Reign*, 1897. This is pointed and well written, appreciative, but critical of attitudes to women which ignore the circumstances of their oppression.

Parr, Susanna, religious apologist, living at Exeter. When she left her Baptist church for another, its elders attacked her and tried to have her excommunicated. She defended herself in *Susanna's Apologie against the Elders*, 1659: she relates in fine ironic style how her disputes with the minister (he ostensibly occupying the more 'radical' position) became increasingly angry, and how, when he found she spoke up in disagreement, he swiftly reversed his requirement that women speak in church. A bereavement confirmed her conviction that separation from the national church was wrong: 'when I considered the breach the Lord had made in my family, I beheld how terrible it was to make a breach in his family'.

Parry, Catherine, of Montgomeryshire, N. Wales, author of one epistolary novel, *Eden Vale*, 1784. She began it *c.* 1777 (though, she says, deploring the 'pernicious' wares of CIRCULATING LIBRARIES) to record a true tale: that of a woman whose new husband, visiting America, joined the revolutionary army and died in battle at her brother's hand. (The remorse-stricken brother throws his life away; the woman is left railing against the 'obdurate', 'bloody-minded' Americans.) This is inset in a novel endorsing sentiment, though its sentimental heroine undergoes (ennobling) tragedy while her flighty sister survives to happiness.

Parsons, Eliza (Phelp), d. 1811, novelist, brought up in 'Affluence' at Plymouth, married young to a Devon merchant. He suffered losses in the American war, then (after moving to Bow, London) a disastrous warehouse fire and a stroke, then a 'lingering decay'; he died about 1790. Left destitute with eight surviving children dependent on her 'needle and Pen', EP obeyed not her choice but 'the taste of the age' in producing the epistolary *History of*

Miss Meredith, 1790. Its two heroines, or anti-heroines, marry unhappily, each against the other's advice. BLUESTOCKINGS and fellow-novelists subscribed; a preface voices fear of following 'a BURNEY, a SMITH, a REEVE, a BENNET'. This and three more novels enabled EP to start three daughters teaching or mantua-making, two sons in the navy (which figures in her work), and the rest at school: *Woman as She Should Be*, 1793, was written in bed with a painful compound fracture of the leg. The RLF gave her 45 guineas between 1793 and 1803; she also held a post in the royal wardrobe. In 1794 a sudden call for £12 threatened her with debtors' prison (in *Murray House*, 1804, disaster is a call for £4000). EP's large output (19 multi-vol. titles) makes her quality uneven. Her publishers included MINERVA, Longman and, from 1800, Norbury in Brentwood. In every genre – letters or narrative, satire or pathos, historical or modern, and most famously GOTHIC – her conclusions assert that only the good can be lastingly happy. The Northanger set, ed. Devendra P. Varma, 1968, reprints her *Castle of Wolfenbach*, 1793, and *The Mysterious Warning*, 1796 (see Bette B. Roberts in *Journal of Popular Culture*, 12, 1978). She also translated Molière, *The Intrigues of a Morning*, acted and pub. 1792, and ed. tales from La Fontaine, 1804. She died at Leytonstone near London.

Pastan, Linda (Olenik), poet, b. 1932 in NYC, da. of Bess (Schwartz) and Jacob L. O., a physician. At Radcliffe College (BA 1954) she won the *Mademoiselle* poetry prize when Sylvia PLATH was runner-up. In 1953 she married scientist Ira P.; she had three children. She took an MLS at Simmons College, 1955, and MA at Brandeis Univ., 1957; abandonment of writing for 'kids and the clean floor bit' was followed by its resumption, she says, at her husband's urging. Her first volume, *A Perfect Circle of Sun*, 1971, follows the seasons of the year: for winter she writes of the relation of writers to death, for spring of various small resurrections, for summer chiefly of losses ('Summer is only camouflage'), for autumn both of death and of new energies, for each season of the subtleties and contradictions of family relationships. Death and the problematics of love continue to permeate LP's later work: *Aspects of Eve*, 1975, and *The Five Stages of Grief*, 1978, are again divided into sections, the latter a gradual progress from denial to acceptance. *Waiting for My Life*, 1981, alludes to her postponement of her own goals: it is dailiness which wins 'The War between Desire and Dailiness'; the 'household Gods / are jealous Gods'; 'I know the window shuts me in, / that when I open it / the garden smells will make me restless.' *PM/AM*, 1983, offers new and selected poems. *A Fraction of Darkness*, 1985, can be either solemn or jaunty about death: 'Yesterday I feared / the darkness / of the earth I must become'; 'They seemed to all take off / at once: Aunt Grace / whose kidneys closed shop . . .' LP's latest title, *The Imperfect Paradise*, 1988, recalls a highly ambivalent poem about Eden in her 1975 volume, with epigraph from Emily DICKINSON. Sandra M. GILBERT offers rather muted praise (*Parnassus*, 11, 1983).

'Paston, George', Emily Morse Symonds, 1860–1936, novelist, playwright, biographer, cousin of John Addington S. (whose work she did not care for) and da. of Emily (Evans) and the Rev. Henry Symonds, precentor of Norwich Cathedral. After her father's death, she lived comfortably with her mother in South Kensington, London, and began her writing career. *At John Murray's: Records of a Literary Circle*, 1892, was followed by her first novel, *A Modern Amazon*, 1894, which explores the theme of celibate marriage. *A Bread and Butter Miss* and *A Study in Prejudices* followed in 1895; *The Career of Candida*, toughly and stylishly written, appeared in 1896. Candida is raised by her father as a boy and becomes a gym instructor, to the horror of her mother ('Biceps!') but marries an effete young man who needs her. *A Writer of Books*, 1898, deals with the struggles of a self-possessed young woman writer in London. GP next turned her talents to biography, producing studies of the eighteenth century (1901), for which she had a passion, and of the nineteenth (1902), as well as lives of Mary DELANY, 1900, and George Romney, 1903. In 1907 she wrote *Lady Mary Wortley MONTAGU and Her Times*. Her first play, *The Pharisee's Wife*, was produced in London in 1904, followed by *Nobody's Daughter*, 1910 (185 performances): both had feminist themes. Later she turned to frothier subjects, though her successful *Clothes and the Woman*, three acts, 1922, still has an ironic touch. Arnold Bennett knew her in the 1890s and found her 'the most advanced and intellectually-fearless woman I have met' (Journal, 1896).

Paterson, Isabel (Bowler), 1885–1961, novelist and literary journalist. B. on Manitoulin Island, Ont., da. of Margaret (Batty) and Francis Bowler, she spent her childhood on the family cattle ranch in Alberta. Her only formal educ. was two-and-a-half years in a log-cabin country school. She m. Kenneth Birrell P. and worked with the Canadian Pacific Railway in Calgary, then with investment bankers, subsequently on the Spokane *Inland Herald*, the *Vancouver World and Province* and, 1922–49, the *New York Herald Tribune*, becoming known for her reviews and literary column, 'Turns with a Bookworm', 1926–49. She retired to Princeton, NJ, 1949. Her popular novels, 1916–43, include *The Shadow Riders*, 1916, and *The Magpie's Nest*, 1917, whose romance, intrigue, and politics are set in Alberta. *The Singing Season*, 1924, set among the religious and nobility of France and Spain, and *The Fourth Queen*, 1926, set in Elizabethan England, are stilted and stereotypical; LP was more successful with contemporary settings. *Never Ask the End*, 1933, was praised by the *NYTBR* for 'much wit and much good writing'. *The Golden Vanity*, 1934, set in NYC and Europe at the time of the stock market crash, was thought to be a witty, intelligent commentary on life, and *If It Prove Fair Weather*, 1940, was termed 'a flinty and entertaining comedy of manners'. Last came *The God of the Machine*, 1943, a political and economic study. See Isabel Ross, *Ladies of the Press*, 1936.

Paterson, Katherine (Womeldorf), teacher and children's novelist, b. in 1932 in Tsing-Tsiang pu, China, da. of Mary (Goetchius) and missionary George Raymond W. Educ. in Tennessee, Virginia and at Union Theological Seminary, NY (MRE, 1962), she has worked as a public-school teacher (1954–5), a missionary in Japan (1957–62) and a teacher at Pennington (Boys') School, NJ. She married a clergyman and had four children. Her novels for the young, set in nineteenth-century China, feudal Japan, and the contemporary US, deal feelingly and perceptively with various quests for identity and community. *Rebels of the Heavenly Kingdom*, 1983, recounts adventures of a secret, fiercely patriotic anti-Manchu society, with excerpts from the psalms and hopes for literate girl children with unbound feet. Among adventures set in feudal Japan, *The Sign of the Chrysanthemum*, 1973, and *Of Nightingales that Weep*, 1974, centre on a son and a daughter of samurai fathers. *The Great Gilly Hopkins*, 1978, features an eleven-year-old foster-child, clever, manipulative, love-starved. Trenchantly observant of family life from childhood to adulthood, the first-person narrator of *Jacob I Have Loved*, 1981, perceives a parallel connecting herself and her cossetted younger twin to biblical Esau and Jacob.

Patmore, 'Brigit', Ethel Elizabeth (Morrison-Scott), 1882–1965, fiction writer, translator, memoirist, b. in Dublin to Ulster parents, educ. at home except for serious piano study. She m. John Deighton P., grandson of poet Coventry P., had two sons, and met Violet HUNT, Alice MEYNELL Ezra Pound, D. H. Lawrence (*The London Mag*. pub. her memoirs of him, 1957), and H. D. (to whom, as reconciler of 'tenderness and terror', she dedicated her stories *This Impassioned Onlooker*, 1926). She left her husband in 1924, and lived abroad, where Nancy CUNARD was a close friend and Richard Aldington her lover. Her novel, *No Tomorrow*, was pub. in the USA, 1929, two transls. from French in 1930 and 1954, and her memoirs (of her marriage, its aftermath, and writing friends) ed. by her son Derek P., 1968. MSS at Univ. of Texas.

Patrick, Mrs **F. C.**, Irish patriot, officer's wife, author of three novels published by MINERVA. *The Irish Heiress*, 1797, a self-conscious first-person narrative by a funny, spirited, resolutely Catholic, rejected daughter of an Irish squire and English mother, pre-dates Sydney MORGAN's patriotic novels. It constantly attacks the English in Ireland as wilfully ignorant, prejudiced, cold and snobbish. The heroine survives the Terror in Paris, attempted seduction, rescue from prison by a despised kept woman, and her husband's bloody murder, to set about improving her Irish tenants' lot with the help of two priests. The preface of FCP's burlesque *More Ghosts!*, 1798, quickly repr. in the USA, makes fun of a claim to have unearthed old MSS (gentlemen have greater opportunities for such finds) and vividly paints the hardships of military families. *The Jesuit, or The History of Anthony Babington Esq*., 1799, deals with an actual sixteenth-century Catholic martyr.

Patronage. Male RENAISSANCE writers relied heavily on patronage by ladies: 773 women (less than half of them noble) received nearly 1800 dedications before 1641; leaders were the Countesses of Bedford and PEMBROKE (Franklin B. Williams in *N & Q*, 207, 1962; David M. Bergeron in Guy Fitch and Stephen Orgel, eds., 1981). For women patrons of Restoration drama see David Roberts, 1989. Later female patronage was mainly communal, through subscription – even that sometimes cloaked under the names of male relations. Elizabeth MONTAGU, Georgiana DEVONSHIRE, and others made a point of helping their own sex. Despite the sad example of Ann YEARSLEY, patronage remained enabling for many women writers through the early nineteenth century. Posts in the Church or public service (traditional rewards for male authors) were not available to women; elementary teaching was the only plan put forward for such remarkable talents at Elizabeth ELSTOB and Elizabeth CARTER.

Patterson, Mrs, author of a single hugely popular US novelette, *The Unfortunate Lovers and Cruel Parents*, subtitled 'A Very Interesting Tale, Founded on Fact' (the latter being *de rigueur* for American fiction at the time). The earliest known copy, 1797, is a '17th ed.'. A preface observes acutely that 'Parents are either the dupes or tyrants of their children'; they 'will not allow them to love for themselves, but they must love for them'; decent desire to conceal our faults in public gives them free rein at home. The tale which follows is naive and crude. A betrothal in infancy is broken when one of the fathers loses his money; Nancy hopes that 'as property is the cause of our separation' her lover will come home richer than her cruel father; he duly inherits £30,000 from a French noblewoman and returns in the nick of time.

Peabody, Elizabeth Palmer, 1804–94, educational reformer, publisher, essayist, da. of Elizabeth (Palmer) and Nathaniel Peabody. B. at Billerica, Mass., eldest of seven, she was educ. at home (her father taught her Latin) and at her mother's Salem school, where she also later taught. She then opened a school in Brookline, Mass., with her sister Mary, and began her intellectual friendship with William E. Channing. She assisted Bronson Alcott in his Transcendentalist school (described in her *Record of a School*, 1835). In 1837, with Margaret FULLER, she became a founding member of the Transcendentalist Club, but Alcott's notoriety damaged her career, and after a period of unemployment, during which she met and championed Nathaniel Hawthorne, she opened a Boston bookstore, where Fuller held evening conversations, and from which she also ran a publishing business, issuing the philosophical journal, *The Dial*, 1842–3. EDUCATION remained her passion; from 1859, influenced by Friedrich Froebel, she wrote and lectured on kindergarten education: 'To be a kindergartner is the perfect development of womanliness' (*Lectures*, 1893). In 1865 she pub. her *Chronological History of the United States*. Her distrust of romantic individualism, evident in essays coll. in *Last Evening with Allson*, 1886, coloured her attitude towards proponents of women's rights, despite her remarkable friendships with intellectual and radical women (see Bruce Ronda's ed. of her *Letters*, 1984). Life by R. M. Baylor, 1965.

Peabody, Josephine Preston, 1874–1922, poet and playwright, b. Brooklyn, NY, second da. of Susan (Morrill) and Charles Kilham Peabody. Educ. at Girls' Latin School in Boston and Radcliffe College, JP taught English at Wellesley College, 1901–3, and m. Lionel S. Marks, professor of engineering at Harvard, in 1906; they had a daughter and a son. Her first collection of poetry, *The Wayfarers*, 1898, was well received. Poems in subsequent collections treat more overtly political topics. *The Singing Man*, 1911, describes 'the portion of labor', and in *Harvest Moon*, 1917, 'A Woman confronts the world at war': 'I only know / This dark is still the world. / And I must dare.' The best-known of JP's verse plays are *Marlowe*, 1901, and *The Piper*, 1909, which won the Stratford Play Competition in 1910. Her last play, *Portrait of Mrs W.*, 1922, presents Mary WOLLSTONECRAFT's relationship with William Godwin and her death in childbirth. In it Wollstonecraft is less a woman of ideas than the heroine of a sentimental domestic drama.

Pearce, Ann **Philippa**, novelist for children. B. in 1921 at Great Shelford, Cambs., da. of corn merchant Gertrude Alice (Ramsden) and miller Ernest Alexander P., she was educ. at Girton College, Cambridge (MA, 1942), and has worked as a radio scriptwriter and producer and publisher's editor. In 1963 she m. Martin Christie (d. 1965); she has a daughter. Her dozen books convey sympathy with the inner life of lonely children. *Tom's Midnight Garden*, 1958, is a haunting account of friendship between a modern boy and a ghostly yet credible Victorian girl. *A Dog So Small*, 1963, and *The Battle of Bubble and Squeak*, 1978, each concerns a struggle to achieve pet-ownership. With no traces of whimsy or embroidery, PP's touch is deft in vivid settings and intense, direct feelings.

Peard, Frances Mary, 1835–1923, novelist and short-story writer, b. Exminster, Devon, younger da. of Frances (Ellicombe) and Captain (later Commander) George P., naval officer and half-brother of John Whitehead P., 'Garibaldi's Englishman'. Educ. by her mother and elder sister, she was a voracious reader. Possessing 'a sturdy independence of spirit' and an interest in new ideas, she travelled to Europe, Egypt, Palestine, India and Japan, and several of her works are set in foreign countries, notably France. From 1864 FMP was based with her mother in Torquay, where she was part of a literary circle which included her closest friend, Christabel COLERIDGE, and was under the aegis of Charlotte YONGE, to whose *Monthly Packet* FMP regularly contributed. Between 1867 and 1909 she pub. over 40 books. Her adult fiction consists mainly of unpretentious novels of domestic life, lucidly written and with talent for description and characterization: her most popular efforts included *Unawares*, 1870, *The Rose Garden* (1872, repr. 1903), *Mother Molly* (1880, repr. 1914), *Contradictions*, 1883, *Near Neighbours*, 1885, and

Alicia Tennant, 1886. She also wrote for the (Anglican) National Society several historical stories for adolescents, and for the SPCK a *History of the Prayer-Book*, n.d., from a High Church viewpoint. She died having outlived her fame; she was however remembered in a *Cornhill Magazine* article by Stanley J. Weyman (April 1924) and in Mary J. Y. Harris's *Memoirs of FMP*, 1930.

Pearse, Gabriela, poet, b. 1963 in Bogota, Colombia, to a Trinidadian mother and English father. She grew up, 'Tumbled around classes', in Chile, Grenada, Trinidad, and Switzerland, attended Warwick Univ., and settled in London, where she does community research in women's jobs and training. She pub. poetry in magazines, became active in collective writing and publishing (with Black Womentalk), and wrote a play, with her mother, for the Theatre of Black Women. Her poems appear with those of Grace NICHOLS and two others in Pratibha Parmar and Sonia Osman, eds., *A Dangerous Knowing*, 1985, and *Black Women Talk, Poetry*, 1987, which she co-edited. Feeling 'a passion for humanity', she aims to use 'connections, differences' for empowerment, not conflict; her poems work through 'the hundreds of contradictions that arise daily out of being a Black / Third World Feminist', committed to every kind of social change. She writes of her mixed heritage: 'My shade not stridently offensive, / my features not uncomfortably "native"'; 'I am to be the brown bridge / that builds / a trust.' 'Sistahs' paints the exuberance of truthful talk among 'different coloured black / women gathered together': 'We were so loud / we laughed / slapped thighs / hooted and chortled / into the night'; their mothers watched, 'slightly bewildered ... but smiling in their hearts'.

Pearson, Emma Maria, *c.* 1828–93, novelist, da. of Capt. Charles P., RN, of Great Yarmouth. She first pub. a TRAVEL book, *From Rome to Mentana*, in 1868. In 1870 she went with the Red Cross to nurse the sick during the Franco–Prussian war, and, with Louisa Elizabeth Maclaughlin, pub. *Our Adventures During the War*, 1870, which she followed with *Under the Red Cross*, 1872, and *Service in Servia*, 1877. A frequent contributor to *St James's Magazine* and *Temple Bar*, she also wrote two novels, *One Love in a Life*, 1874, and *His Little Cousin*, 1875. A staunch anti-feminist, she shows in *One Love* that good women overcome their problems without women's rights, while the rest cannot organize themselves owing to petty rivalries. Nonetheless, she was clearly drawn to associations of women in clubs and other groups.

Pearson, Jane (Sibson), 1734–1816, Quaker memoirist and 'plain, powerful' minister, b. at Newtown near Carlisle, da. of Jane and Jonathan S. (who died early). Piously educ., she feared death as a child, loved bible-reading, and underwent inner strife before her marriage for love, 1757, to the equally religious John P. For a year 'I swimmed as in an ocean of pleasure'; then into her mind 'was darted, as quick as lightning: "There is no God!"' She had never read of such temptations, and told no-one, but wished 'that my troubles were written with an iron pen', well-told enough to help 'some poor, tossed, afflicted, disconsolate, tempted, bewildered mind'. At last 'in the Lord's own time he gave access to his throne'; after nine more months of conflict and delay she overcame her 'natural timidity' enough to 'open my mouth in public'. Then came peace and joy, vividly imaged as 'melody in my heart' in place of dragons and owls, cormorants and bitterns. JP suffered the deaths of her seven children (the first two of smallpox, her faith making her not 'free to inoculate for it') and husband (to whom she writes a moving testimony). She travelled widely, wrote her life (and some poems) by the 1780s, and kept till near her death a DIARY which describes her faith in terms of baking or washing: in a 'most comforting' vision a 'middle-aged grave matron' assures her that her work in the heavenly household is accepted: pub. as *Sketches of Piety*, York, 1817.

Pearson, Susanna, obscure poet and novelist. She was living at Sheffield when she pub. there *Poems*, 1790, with many local and many Channel Island subscribers. It contains chiefly sonnets (one each to Anna SEWARD and Sarah Siddons) and ballads, with strong comment on the Bastille and other prisons, and on the exploitation of Africa. Her unusual, now very rare, novel, *The Medallion*, London, 1794, has a patriotic dedication to the Prince of Wales and supposedly 'trembling' address to reviewers. The medallion (at first a Volscian bracelet) passes from warrior to senator to courtesan, from Caesar to Cleopatra to Tiberius (recast), to Addison; to the heroine of the novel's courtship plot; at last to SP herself. Of her *Poems on Various Subjects*, 1800, to which Elizabeth CARTER subscribed, some employ the supernatural and some mock it; one defends Ann RADCLIFFE. SP refused an invitation to travel to India. Probably – not certainly – the same pen produced all these works; evangelical writings by Susanna (Flinders) Pearson, 1779–1827, were pub. at Ipswich, 1827 and 1829.

Peattie, Elia (Wilkinson) 1862–1935, novelist, poet, playwright, journalist and short-story writer, b. Kalamazoo, Mich., da. of Amanda (Cahill) and Frederick W. In 1883 she m. Robert Burns P. Their only da. d. in infancy: three sons all became writers. In 1884 she began her writing career as first 'girl reporter' on the *Chicago Tribune* (later literary critic, 1901–17), and in 1888 she became editorial writer for the *Omaha World Herald*. She was active in women's clubs and societies, forming her own 'salon'. Her 'pot-boiler' history, *The Story of America*, 1889, was followed by a prolific output of stories featuring romantic incidents, historical themes and domestic life. They include *With Scrip and Staff*, 1891, *A Mountain Woman*, 1896, in which the proud, strong Judith, 'forever shouting and singing', rejects married life in polite society and returns to the mountains – followed by her husband; *Pippins and Cheese*, 1897, *The Shape of Fear*, 1898, tales of the supernatural; and *Ickery Anne*, 1899, children's stories. *Times and Manners*, 1918, and *The Wander-Weed*, 1923, one-act plays, treat of myth and magic and the transformative powers of women, while *The Judge*, 1890, and *The Precipice*, 1914, touch on issues of patriarchal domination. EP adopted an equivocal stand on gender roles; feminist issues in her work barely survive her genteel romancer's sensibility.

Peck, Frances, Irish officer's wife, author of six novels. Her first, *The Maid of Avon, A Novel for the Haut Ton*, was pub. by MINERVA, 1807. The hero of *The Welch Peasant Boy*, 1808, is really no peasant: the opening (mysterious baby deposited with humble foster-parents) is hackneyed; a nice touch here is that no-one expects him to live. The heroine's mother has once, amazingly, 'supported herself by writing for the press'. Low-life scenes are genuinely comic and original, but sketchy melodrama and expansive sentiment prevail. FP was living at Dublin when she pub. an 'Irish Historical Romance', *The Bard of the West; commonly called Eman ac Knuck, or Ned of the Hills*, 1818 (varying titles on reprints). This tells a seventh-century story from, she says, Gaelic sources, and aims to kindle the pure patriotism of older times; prefaces and notes refer to Charlotte BROOKE and MSS at Trinity College, Dublin. The hero saves Ireland from the Danes, but the idiom is modern: 'O delicacy! have I rudely rent thy magic veil?' FP's last fictional scene was modern: *Napoleon, or the Mysteries of the Hundred Days*, 1826.

Peck, Winifred Frances (Knox), Lady, 1882–1962, novelist and autobiographer, b. in Oxford, da. of Ellen Penelope (French) and the Rev. Edmund Arbuthnott

K., then Fellow of Merton College. She sharpened her wits early in complicated verse games with brothers whose work she later ranked above her own – Cardinal, Anglican Canon, WWII cipher-breaker, and editor. (Neither she nor her sister receives serious notice in her niece Penelope FITZGERALD's *The Knox Brothers.*) WP's *A Little Learning, or A Victorian Childhood*, 1952, describes her education: governesses, dayschools; forward-looking Wycombe Abbey and St Leonard's School; Lady Margaret Hall, Oxford (BA, first-class, in history, 1905). Her study of Louis XI of France, 1909, reflects her interest in history and religion. She m., 1912, Sir James P., Scottish Education Secretary, lived in Edinburgh and London, had three sons, and wrote over 25 books in 45 years. Her novels – like *Tranquillity*, 1944, *Veiled Destinies*, 1948, and *A Clear Dawn*, 1949 – are rich in literary allusion. They deal with moral and social change, showing women as flexible, resilient, and reliant on God, self and men, usually in that order. WP's somewhat class-determined attitudes include commitment to the welfare state, qualified admiration for the toughness of the new 'shadowed' generation, and advocacy of work and Christianity as holding answers to modern dilemmas. *Home for the Holidays*, 1955, is also autobiographical.

Peddle, M., moral writer. Living at Yeovil, Somerset, she pub. at Sherborne *The Life of Jacob*, 1785: mainly local subscribers included Mary SCOTT and Anne STEELE. This prose work, which aims at sublimity through a blend of novel and epic techniques, is probably the one which Clara REEVE contrasted unfavourably with Elizabeth ROWE's verse *Joseph*. (MP deals largely with Joseph once her Jacob has related his early life for his children's edification; Adelaide O'KEEFFE was to have great success in the same form.) MP's *Rudiments of Taste*, London, 1789 (widely repr.), uses a plainer style in ADVICE-letters to her daughters, signed 'Cornelia' after the Roman matron whose children were her jewels. Classical influence blends with Christian: she urges 'steady rational piety' and the 'habit of devotion', and recommends reading ancient and modern history, travels, biography, science and *good* poetry, not novels, which leave their readers incapable 'of relishing any thing superior'.

Peisley, Mary, later Neale, 1717–57, Quaker minister, b. at Ballymore, Co. Kildare, da. of Quaker cottagers Rachel and Richard P. She lived many years 'in disobedience', repeatedly hardening her heart, till a riding fall nearly broke her neck: 'as soon as I rose on my feet and recovered my senses, the Lord ... showed me clearly that I was not in a fit condition to meet him.' Transformed from a governess into a minister, she travelled and preached, despite recurrent illness, in Ulster, England, and in 1753–6 with Catharine PHILLIPS in America, where 'sometimes at our first entrance they would look strangely at us, because they understood not the lawfulness of women's preaching.' She develops an extended comparison of wilderness travel with 'my pilgrimage through the world'. She is pained by Friends' keeping slaves, and cautiously approves of withholding taxes intended for waging war. She wrote an 'Epistle' to Virginia Friends, 1754. Back in Ireland, she preached on her wedding day, 'clear and sweet in the delivery'; two days later she died of violent stomach pains. Her widower, Samuel N., who had been converted by her preaching at Cork seven years before, pub. an *Account* from her own writings (chiefly letters), 1795.

Pembroke, Mary Herbert (**Sidney**), Countess of, 1561–1621, poet and patron, da. of Lady Mary (Dudley) and Sir Henry S. Educ. by tutors (in modern languages, probably Latin but not Hebrew), she was briefly Maid of Honour to ELIZABETH I, and at 15 became third wife of Henry H.,

2nd Earl of Pembroke, 25 years her senior: she had four children. She made Wilton House near Salisbury a centre of bounty to poets. When her elder brother Sir Philip S. died famously in 1586, he had completed (perhaps with her involvement) only 43 of a projected set of metrical psalms; desire to finish his work gave her 'a poet's self-education'. MSS (widely scattered) of the 150 psalms show her revising over perhaps 15 years, developing flexibility, intensity, liberty and formal inventiveness, adding dedications to the queen, 1599, and her brother, 1600. Unpub. for 200 years, the psalms were known to Ben Jonson and other poets, praised by Donne, and influenced George Herbert; Sir John Harington thought them not hers alone, as beyond 'a woman's skill'; later praise has sometimes supposed them Sir Philip's: ed. R. C. A. Rathmell, 1963. Other work may have perished in a fire at Wilton, 1648, or lie unidentified in MS, but what is known proves great industry and purpose. In 1590 MP composed a Senecan tragedy, *Antonie* (from Robert Garnier's French), and a version of Philippe de Mornay's Stoic discourses on life and death; she published them (unheard-of for her sex and class) in 1592. *Antonie*, which began a spate of Senecan works, is ed. Alice Luce, 1897, and Geoffrey Bullough (as an 'analogue' in *Sources of Shakespeare*, v, 1964). MP has been wildly called mistress of Shakespeare or part-author of his works. She issued corrected editions of her brother's work, 1591 and 1595, and revised and completed (from midway in book iii) his romance *Arcadia*, 1593. 'Thenot and Piers in Praise of Astraea', a pastoral dialogue for a royal visit, was pub. in the popular anthology *A Poetical Rhapsody*, 1602. She translated Petrarch's *Triumph of Death* (where Laura, now dead, speaks at last). Her elegy for her brother is both pious and courtly. She seems to have stopped writing on her husband's death, 1601. Often in Europe for her health, 1613–16, she d. of smallpox. Poems ed. G. F. Waller, 1977; study by Waller, 1979; good recent articles; Margaret P. Hannay's biography, 1990, is the first since 1912; complete works also expected.

Pendered, Mary Lucy, 1858–1940, novelist, essayist, story writer and biographer, b. London, probably a Quaker, da. of Elizabeth (Hill) and Thomas P., merchant's clerk. Educ. at Wellingborough, Northants., she lived there until 1906 and after 1916. She began by writing short stories, then a serial in a Yorkshire paper based on M. K. Melford's melodrama, *Sins of the Father*. Her first novels, some pub. anon., some collaboratively, are not in major libraries: the earliest in the BL Catalogue is *Dust and Laurels*, 1893, dedicated 'To that Hybrid Complication, the Woman of To-day'. It traces the friendship of two young women at Oxford and their disappointing marriages: Sylvia admits to her husband: '"if [Vera] had been a man I should never have married you"'. Other novels of this period, *A Pastoral Played Out*, 1895, and *An Englishman*, 1899, were followed by numerous children's fairy stories and light popular fiction up to 1936. She pub. biographies of the Quaker Hannah Lightfoot, 1910, and the painter John Martin, 1923, as well as a play *William Penn*, 1923.

Penington, Mary (Proude), 1623–82, English Quaker memoirist: orphan and heiress from 1628, da. of Anne (Fagge) and Sir John Proude. Superstitious terrors attacked her at about eight; soon she felt passionate concern about how to pray, writing prayers when she could 'scarcely join my letters', rejecting set forms, and walking miles each week to hear a Puritan preacher. In 1642 she married Sir William Springett, who shared her views; in 1644, late in her second pregnancy, she was present at his harrowing death on army service. After this she 'ran from one notion into another', from great zeal and secret praying aloud to 'recreations as they are called', which left her heart 'constantly sad'.

She married Isaac P. in 1654 because he shared her sceptical disillusion; together they rapidly progressed from mocking to respecting the QUAKERS, to pain and distress, then conversion and joy. Holding a meeting at their house in Chalfont St Peter, Bucks., MP felt enabled 'to swim in the life which overcame me'. She wrote her story thus far (with several expressive dreams) for her eldest daughter by 1668 (part in a pamphlet ed. Martha ROUTH, Philadelphia, 1797). The Chalfont estate was forfeited; Isaac P. spent years in jail. On his death MP wrote his testimony, 1680 (in his *Works*, 1681), at night by a sick child's bedside. Pages she added to her own story that year, and to her son John's *Complaint against William Rogers*, 1681, address charges that she tried 'to shun or fly' either prison or fines. Also about 1680 she wrote for a grandson of her first husband (detail on his death, unbroached before) and his mother (who practised medicine and surgery). *Some Account* ... 1821, variously titled later (repr. 1911), includes both sets of memoirs.

Pennell, Elizabeth Robins, 1855–1936, journalist, critic, TRAVEL writer, b. Philadelphia. In 1882 her uncle, Charles Leland, suggested she write the text to accompany Joseph P.'s drawings of Philadelphia. Two years later she m. the artist, and their many collaborations began. They cycled, walked, trained and boated through Europe, producing a dozen travel volumes, many of them following the routes of writers like Sterne and Johnson. Settling in London she wrote for a range of papers and periodicals, adding columns on food and art criticism and a sentimental novel to her output. She criticized women who starve themselves in public only to gorge in private, as a denial of the sensual: 'accept the gospel of good living and the sexual problem will be solved'. She wrote a biography of Mary WOLLSTONECRAFT, whom she considered 'much-maligned', and collaborated with her husband on the authorized biography of the painter Whistler. They entertained many leading artists and writers. *Nights: Rome, Venice in the aesthetic eighties; London, Paris in the fighting nineties*, 1916, and *Our House and the People In It*, 1910, include impressions of her contemporaries, though the most notable portraits in *Our House* are of her female servants. She is appalled by the Scottish crofters' impoverished lives and enraged by the English landlords, whilst her greatest affinities are for gypsies (she learnt Romany). She said of her own long, happy and rambling marriage: 'our freedom would begin where that of most men and women ceases'. They returned to the USA after WWI; Joseph died there in 1926. 'If I have reached the time for looking back, I have my compensations in the invigorating glow, for all its sadness, that I get from my new occupation.'

Pennington, Elizabeth, 1732–59, poet, da. of Elizabeth and the Rev. John P. of Huntingdon, often linked with a friend descended from the FERRAR family. Best-known of her scanty extant work is 'The Copper Farthing', after John Philips's 'Splendid Shilling', which makes a schoolboy the centre of some rather strained mock-heroic, and ends in a simile of devastating volcanic cruption (pub. in Fawkes and Woty's anthology, 1763). John Duncombe and Mary SCOTT praised her, 1754, 1774. Frances SHERIDAN grieved at her death. A few more poems trickled into print to mark her 'once an admired star in the literary hemisphere'.

Pennington, Sarah, Lady, d. 1783, advice writer. Married for 12 years to Sir Joseph P. of Yorks., mother of several children, she paid, she says, insufficient heed to 'the Public Voice' and acted imprudently. What this means is unclear. Her husband then cut her off from her children and her inheritance. She wrote to repay debts, 'to undeceive the Minds of my Children, and justify to them, who are so nearly concerned, my injured Character', and to influence their education. *An Unfortunate Mother's Advice to her Absent Daughters* (1761, 3 eds. that year, praised by Sarah TRIMMER in 1802) moves from self-defence to conduct-manual rules. Its heavy reading-list includes only two women, Elizabeth ROWE and Eliza HAYWOOD's *Female Spectator*. More than mental improvement, religion, philanthropy, etc., SP stresses careful choice of a husband and ADVICE on putting up with one 'of morose and tyrannical temper'. ('When once embarked in the matrimonial voyage, the fewer faults you discover in your partner, the better: – never search after what it will give you no pleasure to find.') She told the publishers to sign each copy to ensure authenticity. The 8th ed., 1817, dropped 'Unfortunate' from the title and added SP's humane, Lockean *Letter to Miss Louisa on the Management of Infant Children*. Her *Letters on Different Subjects*, 1766, includes earlier ones to 'Miss Louisa', fiction, auto-biography, and grievance-filled prefaces threatening to publish memoirs by subscription. *The Child's Conductor*, 1776, sets orthodox Christian belief in dialogue format 'For the Use of her Grandchildren'. SP's story was well known, and the *GM* obituary very sympathetic.

Penny, Anne (Hughes), 1731–84, poet, da. of the Rev. Owen H. of Bangor, Wales. In 1746 she married naval captain Thomas Christian, d. 1751; their son became an admiral. Her second husband, customs official Peter P., was French and had altered his name from Penné. In 1761, as 'a lady', she published a versified *Rambler* story inscribed to Samuel Johnson, *Anningait and Ajutt: A Greenland Tale*. Next year came pastoral poems from a new English prose version of Gessner's *Idyllen*. Her *Poems* ... [1771] reprint these, with a 'dramatic entertainment' called 'The Birth Day', verse on many public occasions, and praise of Elizabeth MONTAGU – who subscribed, with Johnson and Elizabeth CARTER. Her husband's death left AP in 1779 in 'great distress': Frances BOSCAWEN, Georgiana DEVONSHIRE (addressed in verses to the Genius of Britain), Horace Walpole and many others subscribed to *Poems*, 1780, which adds new work to old.

Penny, Fanny Emily (Farr), 1847–1939, novelist and TRAVEL writer, da. of Emily Caroline (Cobbold) and the Rev. John F., Rector of Gillingham, Norfolk. She m. the Rev. Frank P. in 1877, then lived in India till 1901. Her two TRAVEL books and almost all of her score of novels, from *Fickle Future in Ceylon*, 1887, through *Dark Corners*, 1908, to *Desire and Delight*, 1919, owe their inspiration and setting to that country. Although some of her novels feature Indians who have romantic friendships with English characters, she quotes Kipling's 'east is east and west is west' and persistently reminds her readers that miscegenation can only lead to tragedy. Her travel books rarely progress beyond the level of 'India is a land of contrasts' and she never understands protests against Britain's 'benevolent' rule. Her novels follow the conventions of the popular romance with strong silent men (one hero even has his tongue cut out) and adoring women. However, the heroines emerge as competent, fit and sporty, courageous, educated, sometimes even gainfully employed, with a sense of humour and a discreet amount of sexual assertiveness. Her animated and outspoken heroines almost redeem the novels, but as one of them confesses: 'those who have never tried it can have no notion of the difficulty a soft-voiced, refined woman finds in making a noise which is worthy of the name shouting.'

Pennyman, Mary (Heron), 1630–1701, polemicist, one of ten children of Edmund H. (says John P.), who lost a 'good Estate' partly in the royalist cause. She m. Henry Boreham, a Quaker whose death in Newgate, 1662, left her three children and a city business. She tells how in the Great Fire, 1666, she relied on God to protect her honest dealing, and refused to move – the fire stopped: 'if I should forget these Mercies, the Stones in the Street might rise up in Judgement against me'. In 1671 God 'made' the cantankerous John P. take her as his third wife, having previously no such 'Inclination (but rather the contrary)'; hostile Quakers intruded, he said, on their elaborately godly celebration. (MP had leanings towards Jane LEAD's sect.) After 40 days they 'gave forth' a public statement, *The Ark Is begun to be Opened*, including her reasons, written a year before, for leaving city trade. Her later pieces include letters to Anne MUDD, personal reminiscence, vituperative calls to repent, and an account of leaving the Friends ('That my Conscience might not be inslav'd, or kept in Bondage, by any Man or Men'; she threw down the gauntlet by wearing lace on her head). John P. (opposed to women's PREACHING, but not writing) pub. some of these at once, more in his *Short Account* of his own life, 1696, most in a coll. of MP's work, 1702.

Perrin, Alice (Robinson), 1867–1934, novelist and short-story writer, da. of Gen. John Innes R., of the Bengal Cavalry. In 1886 she m. Charles P., of the Indian Public Works Department, with whom she travelled all over the country and gained her varied experience of British life in India. Her first book, *East of Suez*, 1901, contains stories which were compared to Kipling's by contemporaries. She treats Indian and Anglo-Indian characters with knowledge and affection, but preaches against intermarriage. Her novel *Into Temptation*, 1894, is the first-person narrative of an Anglo-Indian woman; it reflects her candid, even blunt, personality in its down-to-earth dialogue and rejection of 'civilized' convention. Other novels include *Free Solitude*, 1907, which paints a detailed and convincing picture of a Eurasian family joined by a young English girl; *Idolatry*, 1909, about missionaries; and *The Anglo-Indians*, 1912, a very readable account of the plight of hard-up Anglo-Indians returned to England. The best stories in *Tales that are Told*, 1917, also draw on Indian experiences, sharply observing British prejudices and insularity. She and her husband retired to Switzerland in the 1920s: he d. in 1931. Her *Times* obit. (15 February 1934) refers to her courage in 'private sorrows of no ordinary kind'.

Perry, Grace, 1927–87, poet, editor, publisher and physician, b. Melbourne, Victoria, da. of Grace (Symes) and R. R. P., journalist. She studied medicine at the Univ. of Sydney. In 1951 she m. Harry Kronenberg; she had two daughters and a son. She worked in medical practice from 1953 to 1972, specializing in paediatrics and living in Berrima, NSW, where she ran her practice, bred livestock and operated the publishing company South Head Press. She founded, 1964, and ed. *Poetry Australia*, the journal for which she was best known. Its contribution towards the fostering of Australian poets and poetry led to her special recognition at the NSW Premier's Literary Awards in 1985. She pub. eight vols. of poetry, including *Red Scarf*, 1964, and *Frozen Section*, 1967, which contain verse based upon her medical experiences, then *Black Swans at Berrima*, 1972, and *Berrima Winter*, 1974, the historical *Journal of a Surgeon's Wife and Other Poems*, 1974, and *Snow in Summer*, 1980; the following year she pub. (with John Millet) a play, *Last Bride at Longsleep*. Her poetry is distinguished by a wide range of subjects and a quiet, almost incantatory tone. See the articles by J. Tulip in *Southerly*, 1973, and *Poetry Australia*, 1980.

'Pesotta, Rose', Rachelle Peisoty, 1896–1965, labour organizer and autobiographer. B. and raised a Jew in the rural Czarist Ukraine, da. of Masya and Itsaak Peisoty, she was educ. at a private school and by tutors. Seeing no future there but 'to marry some young man', she left in 1913 for NYC where a working single life was feasible. Like most female Jewish immigrants she entered a garment factory. She joined the

International Ladies' Garment Workers' Union (ILGWU) and became an office-holder and an advocate for Sacco and Vanzetti. After a summer school for working women at Bryn Mawr, she studied at Brookwood Labor College, 1924–6. She became a full-time organizer with a trip to Los Angeles, 1933; after ten years as the only woman vice-president of the ILGWU, she resigned in 1944 because the union refused to allow more than one woman on the Executive to represent 85 per cent of the members. She writes about rank-and-file women in the labour movement and about her career as an organizer of women – in South America and Canada as well as the USA – in *Bread Upon the Waters*, 1944 (ed. John Beffel, 1987, intro. by Ann Schofield), but little about her anarchist politics or her personal life. In *Days of Our Lives*, 1958, she continues the story and chronicles her childhood. See Alice Kessler-Harris in *Labor History*, 17, 1976. Papers in NYC: Jewish Bund Archives; Public Library (letters and diaries), and NY Univ. (drafts of first book).

Peterkin, Julia (Mood), 1880–1961, novelist and short-story writer, b. in Laurens County, S. Carolina, da. of Alma (Archer), who d. shortly after her birth, and physician Julius Andrew M. She learned Gullah patois, legend and folklore from her black nurse-maid, her 'Mauma'. She attended Converse College, Spartanburg, SC (BA and MA), taught at Fort Motte, married plantation-owner William P. in 1903, and had a son. She began writing in her forties, publishing stories and sketches of plantation life in *The Reviewer, The Smart Set, Poetry*, and *American Mercury*. While her own life was quiet and domestic, typifying that of her sex and class, her characters bear babies out of wedlock, dream of becoming strippers in Harlem cabarets, burn down plantation mansions, gamble and fight. Unsurprisingly damned in the South, her work, notably *Black April*, 1927, was highly praised by radical black writers, influenced William Faulkner, and attracted wide readership in the North. *Scarlet Sister Mary*, 1928, a novel about Gullah Negroes, won the Pulitzer Prize; her depictions of them and their dialect remain arguably the truest written. After a third novel, *Bright Skin*, 1932, stories (collected 1970, ed. Frank Durham), reviews and articles, JMP devoted herself chiefly, from 1936, to caring for her grandson after his mother's suicide; she died in obscurity, and her works are hard to find. MSS at the Univ. of Indiana, NY Public Library, and Clemson Univ., SC; unpub. MA thesis by Marilyn Price Maddox (Univ. of Georgia, 1956); forthcoming feminist critical biography by Michele Barale.

Pethick-Lawrence, Emmeline, 1867–1954, suffragette, b. at Bristol, eldest surviving child of evangelicals. Her father, Henry P., moved away from his faith; her mother was *née* Collen; a family cook, EP-L says, was an important early influence. She was educ. at private schools at Devizes and Weston-super-Mare, 'finished' there, in France, and at Wiesbaden: then, with a sister, she worked two years in the West London Mission's Sisterhood, and in 1895 founded a girls' club. Her 'Working Girls' Clubs' was pub. in W. Reason, ed., *University and Social Settlements*, 1898. In 1901 she married Frederick William L., barrister and Labour MP (later a baron); they combined their names. She joined the Suffrage Society early, and the PANKHURSTS' WSPU in 1906, year of the first of her six prison sentences: in *Why I Went to Prison*, 1909, she wrote 'the power that has shaped my whole life led me there step by step'. (Speeches from the dock were pub., microfiche in BL.) With her husband she co-founded *Votes for Women* in 1907; she published SUFFRAGE tracts from *The New Crusade*, 1907, to *In Women's Shoes*, 1913. In 1912 she judged the democracy-seeking WSPU had become a 'dictatorship' and left; she joined the United Suffragists in 1914. In the first election open to women, 1918, she stood unsuccessfully for a Manchester seat. Her travels included S. Africa (first in 1905; Olive SCHREINER was a friend), Zürich for the Women's International League, 1919, Ireland, 1921 (the *Daily News*, 27 April, printed her report on British soldiers' atrocities including rape), and India, 1926–7; she kept working for women and peace, but supported WWII. See her memoirs, 1938 (for her family and the suffrage struggle); Vera BRITTAIN's life of Frederick P-L., 1963.

Petitions. A direct form of address to higher authority much used by British women in the seventeenth and by American women in the eighteenth century. Many broadside petitions of the mid-seventeenth century bear the names of individual women. Large groups petitioned Parliament in 1642 (claiming 'an equal share and interest with men in the Commonwealth', but not equality 'either in authority or wisdom'), 1643, 1649 (see Katherine CHIDLEY: powerful reasoned rhetoric; female authorship previously denied), 1653 (two petitions, the second asserting the equal concern of women to that of Members of Parliament in 'what is done or intended against ... common right') and 1659 (see Mary FORSTER). Early American revolutionary governments received many women's petitions (for financial help or leave to cross military lines) and ignored most of them. In 1865 Susan B. ANTHONY and Elizabeth Cady STANTON petitioned the US Congress for woman SUFFRAGE for the first time; similar petitions soon spread world-wide. Helen TAYLOR drafted one in England, signed by 1,499 women, and presented to the House of Commons by Emily DAVIES and Elizabeth Garrett in June 1866. It was followed in 1867 by one much longer, and by others including one organized by Clementina BLACK in 1906. The Actresses' Franchise League petitioned the House of Commons in 1913 to be permitted to appear for the debate on the vote: 'While adding to the gaiety of the nation the actresses have themselves been suffering from great wrongs arising out of sex disability ... the actresses do ... ask to be allowed to ... lay before the Commons at first hand their reasons for claiming equality with men in the state' (quoted in Julia Holledge, *Innocent Flowers*, 1981).

Petry, Ann (Lane), journalist, short-story writer, novelist, children's writer. She was b. 1911 at Old Saybrook, Conn., da. of Bertha (James) and Peter Clark L., black pharmacists in a mainly white community. She took a pharmacy degree at the Univ. of Connecticut, and worked in the family drugstores until she married George D. P. in 1938 and moved to Harlem, NY. Having acquired a reporter's-eye-view of the community while writing for the *Amsterdam News* and the *People's Voice*, she studied creative writing at Columbia Univ., 1943–4, and pub. her first story, 'On Saturday the Siren Sounded at Noon', in *The Crisis*, 1943. She also joined the American Negro Theatre and wrote children's plays (she had one daughter). In 1946 she published 'Like a Winding Sheet' (a story chosen for anthologizing); 'My Most Humiliating Jim Crow Experience' in *Negro Digest*, 4 (about racial humiliation at seven – 'here in America they teach us when we are very young'); and *The Street* (her first novel, finished on a Houghton Mifflin fellowship: repr. 1986). Admired from the outset as part of the US black naturalist tradition, and frequently compared to Richard Wright's *Native Son*, 1941, it casts a Harlem street as the equivalent of a lynch mob, 'used to keep Negroes in their place'. Lutie Johnson's rebellion against a life in the slums and against humiliations delivered to her, as female and as black, by both black and white men, ends in murder. It 'marks a change in setting and tone in the literature of the black woman': now 'the black city woman could not be forgotten' (Christian, 1985). *The Country Place*, 1947, depicts a small, stagnant, largely white town. *The Narrows*, 1953, much admired now and too much neglected since its publication, deals with black history and the tension created by interracial love in a mixed Connecticut community. *Miss Muriel and Other Stories*, 1971, includes the novella 'In Darkness and Confusion', 1947, about the Harlem riot of 1943 and the movement of its central character from inarticulate, unconscious passivity to aggressive rage. AP's essays include 'The Novel as Social Criticism' (in Helen Hull, ed., *The Writer's Book*, 1950); her children's books include two lives of strong women unbowed by slavery: *Harriet Tubman, Conductor on the Underground Railway*, 1955 (*The Girl Called Moses* in UK), and *Tituba of Salem Village*, 1964. 'Because I was born black and female', AP says, 'I write for survivors (especially when I write for children).' She returned from NY to Old Saybrook, and has taught at several univs. and been executive secretary of Negro Women Incorporated, a civic watchdog body. See Vernon E. Lattin and Margaret B. McDowell, both in *Black American Literature Forum* (12, 1978; and 14, 1980), Hortense J. Spillers, ed., *Conjuring: Black Women, Fiction and Literary Tradition*, 1985; also Gladys J. Washington on AP's short fiction in *College Language Association Journal*, 30, 1986. MSS at Boston Univ.

Pfeiffer, Emily Jane (Davis), 1827–90, English poet. Her mother was a Tilsley of Milford Hall, Montgomery; her father was R. D., army officer and Oxon. landowner, who lost much of his wealth when his father-in-law's bank failed. As a result, EJP had little formal education, though her parents encouraged her early literary pursuits. She was 'delicate' and subject to fits of depression. Her first production was *The Holly Branch: An Album for 1843*, consisting of her own tales, legends, melodies and illustrations. In 1853 she met and married Jurgen Edward P. (d. 1889), German merchant living in London, and began again to write poetry. *Valisneria: or a Midsummer Day's Dream*, 1857, is a prose tale; *Margaret; or, The Motherless*, 1861, is a long narrative poem dedicated to her mother. From the 1870s she produced a number of vols., both long poems and colls. of shorter works, such as *Gerard's Monument*, 1873, *Glan-Anarch: His Silence and his Song*, 1878, *Songs and Sonnets*, 1880, *The Wynnes of Wynhavod: A Drama of Modern Life*, 1881, and *Flowers of the Night*, 1889. Many poems demonstrate her deep interest in women's EDUCATION and the condition of the working woman: 'Outlawed: A Rhyme for the Time' inveighs against that process which made the legal guardian of children 'not the woman ... but the man who frames the law by which the case between parents ... is adjudged'. She wrote *Women and Work: An Essay Treating on the Relation to Health and Physical Development of the Higher Education of Girls*, 1888, and articles like 'The Tyranny of Fashion' and 'The Suffrage for Women' for the *Contemporary Review* (1878–85). Her *Flying Leaves from East and West*, 1885, is an account of her travels in the Near East and North America. She left a large sum towards women's higher education.

Phelan, Nancy (Creagh), novelist and travel writer, b. 1913 in Sydney, Australia, da. of Florence Amelia (Mack) and William John C., solicitor; her aunts were Louise and Amy MACK. Educ. at the Sydney Conservatorium of Music and the Univ. of Sydney, in 1938 she travelled overseas and lived in England until the end of WWII. In 1939 she m. Raymond P. and had a da. She returned to join the South Pacific Commission Social Development Section in 1951, working as an assistant organizer in Island literature, but since 1956 has been a full-time writer, with three novels, eight autobiographical and travel books, and stories, articles and reviews in several newspapers and journals. The novel *The Voice Beyond the Trees* won a *Sydney Morning Herald* prize in 1950 but was not pub. until 1985. *A Kingdom by the Sea*, 1967, tells of her childhood in Sydney. The travel narrative, *Some Came Early, Some Came Late*, 1970, describes characters met in Australia, and other TRAVEL books are set all over the world, in the Pacific, Turkey, Japan, Chile and Morocco. *The Swift Foot of Time*, 1983, describing NP's early experiences in England, won the Braille Book of the Year Award in 1984. Her most recent publication is *Home is the Sailor and the Best of Intentions*, 1987.

Phelps, Elizabeth Stuart (later Ward), 'Mary Gray', 1844–1911, novelist, da. of novelist Elizabeth Wooster (Stuart) PHELPS, who died when her daughter was eight. ESP was strongly influenced by her mother, whom she described as having been 'torn by the civil war of the dual nature which can be given to women only'. She was educ. at Abbott Academy and Mrs Edwards' School. When the Andover student she loved died in the Civil War, she vowed never to marry. She had pub. stories in journals since she was 13, but it was her first novel, *The Gates Ajar*, 1868, about notions of Heaven, that brought her success. Its theme is women's right to self-fulfilment, and the need of female support in gaining such fulfilment. In it she feminizes religion, providing for a more compassionate sisterhood. More realistic novels followed, including *Hedged In*, 1870, which deals with factory girls. *The Story of Avis*, 1877, based on her mother's life, shows the devastating effect of marriage on a woman's artistic potential: reviewers expressed concern about the detrimental effect this book would have on young women. In the 1870s she pub. a series of articles in the *Independent* advocating women's rights, SUFFRAGE and dress reform, and protesting domestic confinement. She also lectured on TEMPERANCE issues, explored in her novel *A Singular Life*, 1895. In 1888 she m. Herbert Dickinson Ward, 17 years her junior; they collaborated on religious romances such as *A Lost Hero*, 1891, but the marriage was never happy. Her autobiography, *Chapters from a Life*, appeared in 1896, and her memoir of her father, *Austin Phelps*, was pub. in 1891. See Carol F. Kessler, 1982, for her life. Recent articles include Judith Fetterley's in *Legacy*, Fall 1986. Lori Duin Kelly pub. a full-length study in 1983.

Phelps, Elizabeth Wooster (Stuart), 1815–52, novelist, was born in Andover, Mass. Her father Moses S., a Congregational minister, was a professor at Andover Theological Seminary. Her mother, Abigail (Clark), was an invalid. As a child, EWP wrote stories for her brothers and sisters. In 1831 she attended Mount Vernon School in Boston, living with the family of the Rev. Jacob Abbott. Under his direction, she made her public confession of faith in 1834 and began to write articles for religious magazines as 'H. Trusta'. In 1842 she m. the Rev. Austin P., from 1848 a professor at Andover. They had three children, of whom the oldest was the novelist Elizabeth Stuart PHELPS. EWP's first novel, *The Sunny Side; or, The Country Minister's Wife*, pub. in 1851, sold 40,000 copies in four months and was repub. in Edinburgh as *The Manse of Sunnyside*; it was translated into French and German. Based on EWP's own life and journals, some chapters are labelled 'From the Journal'. As she wrote of her heroine, Emily Edwards, 'Her practice of journalizing and writing occasionally had contributed to ... give her command of language.' Her second novel, *A Peep at "Number Five"; or, A Chapter in the Life of a City Pastor*, 1852, reveals that life was especially difficult for a minister's wife, whether they lived in the city or country. *The Angel Over the Right Shoulder; or, the Beginning of a New Year*, 1852, a long short story, advances the theme of domestic conflict for women. Soon after the birth of her third child she died in November 1852. Three books were pub. posthumously: *The Tell-tale; or Home Secrets Told by Old Travellers*, 1853; *The Last Leaf from Sunnyside*, 1853, a collection of short stories, with a memoir by Austin Phelps; and *Little Mary; or, Talks and Tales* *for Children*, 1854. See also her daughter's *Austin Phelps, A Memoir*, 1891, and *Chapters from a Life*, 1896. Recent interest in her work is reflected by Carol Farley Kessler in 'A Literary Legacy: ESP, Mother and Daughter', *Frontiers*, Fall 1980.

Philips, Katherine (Fowler), 'the matchless Orinda', 1632–64, poet, translator and letter writer, b. in London, da. of Katherine (Oxenbridge), whose brothers were leading Parliamentarians, and of wealthy merchant John F., d. 1642. Mrs Salmon's school at Hackney probably fostered her strong royalist views. In 1646 she moved to Wales to marry 54-year-old James P., MP and relative of her mother's new husband. She exchanged poems with her neighbour Henry Vaughan and published verse praise of 'my much valu'd friend' William Cartwright in his posthumous plays, 1651. During the 1650s her work circulated in MS among the Society of Friendship; Jeremy Taylor dedicated to her his *Discourse of Friendship*, 1657. Visiting Ireland in 1662, she wrote a translation of Corneille's *Pompée*, which drew great applause in Dublin and London, and was pub. anonymously, 1663. (She left a version of *Horace* unfinished.) She discussed translation – and anxiety for her parliamentary husband at the Restoration – in letters to Sir Charles Cotterell, pub. 1705 as *Letters from Orinda to Poliarchus*. She also corresponded with Dorothy OSBORNE. Her verse topics include science, royalty, and her son's death; best remembered are passionate poems to 'Rosania' (Mary Aubrey) and 'Lucasia' (Anne Owen), which evoke female love and equality in terms reworked from Donne especially. To Rosania she writes, 'Thus our twin-souls in one shall grow, / And teach the world new love, / Redeem the age and sex, and show / A flame fate dares not move.' Keats praised a poem to Lucasia calling her 'My Joy, my Life, my Rest': 'I am not thine, but thee.' KP died of smallpox, having gone to London to suppress a 'stolen' edition of her *Poems* which followed *Pompey*. She posed as 'so far from expecting applause for anything I scribble, that I can hardly expect pardon'; her improved *Poems*, 1667 (1678 ed. repr. by George Saintsbury, 1905), carry laudatory poems including one by an accomplished writer and outspoken Irish feminist, 'Philo-philippa'. Later hailed by others like Aphra BEHN and Anne KILLIGREW, KP was also used as a restrictive ideal of 'modesty'. Life by Philip W. Souers, 1931, repr. 1968; Elaine Hobby, 1988; MSS at National Library of Wales.

Phillips, Catharine (Payton), 1727–94, Quaker autobiographer and pamphleteer, b. at Dudley, Worcs., da. of Quakers Ann (Fowler) and Henry Payton: her *Memoirs* (1797, with letters) open with praise of her mother and close with praise of her husband. As a child she feared she had sinned against the Holy Ghost, but delighted in 'plays and romances'. At 16 she attended boarding school in London, then underwent conversion and prayed to become a minister. She wrote a verse 'Prayer for Wisdom' at 18 and then began a series of British and Irish preaching tours. Setting out in 1753 with her 'dear friend' Mary PEISLEY, she 'visited almost all the meetings of Friends on the continent of America', covering 'upwards of 8750 miles'. She graphically describes storms at sea and preaching to 'the sailors in steerage' against the captain's and priest's advice. She notes good relations between Indians and Quakers, and (always alert to women's part in the ministry) the caution young female preachers must observe towards single men. She visited Holland with Sophia HUME, 1757, and kept travelling in Britain even after she m., 1772, the widower William Phillips (d. 1785) of Cornwall, whom she had met in 1749 but refused out of 'that superior love, which bound me to the service appointed me'. To a letter to Irish Friends, 1776, she added in 1791–3 (despite encroaching rheumatism) pieces on Cornish mining, grain prices, Methodists and missions to negroes, the lower classes and the French Revolution. Her 'sacred poem', *The Happy King*, 1794 (written 1791), calls on George III to oppose war and slavery, and support missions. More discourses and letters appeared in colls., 1803 and 1805.

Phillips, Janet, 'Mrs Alfred Phillips', fl. 1851–92, British novelist and playwright of whom little is known. She wrote at least six novels and four plays. *Caught in his Own Trap*, 1851, is a comedietta in one act, about a woman who cheats a man into marrying her. *An Organic Affection*, [1850], is a one-act farce. Her novels came later: *Benedicta*, 1878, is predictably romantic and conventional, concluding that 'woman's highest joys' are domestic; but *Man Proposes*, 1884, has a good portrait of a loyal daughter defying her noble husband to go to her dying mother. In *A Rude Awakening*, 1891, which contains some discussion of female SUFFRAGE, the heroine discovers she is the result of her mother's adultery. *A Spinster's Diary*, 1892, is the journal of a woman living with her mother's second family. It is sensitively written, with nice domestic detail, and ends with a choice between marrying a man she hates in order to support her mother, or publishing her diary.

Phillips, Jayne Anne, fiction writer, b. in 1952 in Buckhannon, W. Va., where she grew up, da. of Martha Jane (Thornhill) and Russell R. P. She was educ. at W. Va. Univ. (BA 1974) and the Univ. of Iowa (MFA 1978), and has taught English at several univs. Her first book, *Sweethearts*, 1976, evokes in brief, lapidary pieces of poetic prose (influenced by early poetry writing) a set of family relations as seen by a child in rural W. Va. JAP often returns to this material: moments of 'natural', sexual and psychological violence created here recur in later works institutionalized in pornography, the sex industry and politics. *Counting*, 1978 (again fragments), presents quotidian details (often of parting and loss) in an urban scene. In *Black Tickets*, 1979 (fully developed stories), JAP experiments with different voices articulating the experience of the marginalized; short pieces from *Sweethearts* reappear inwoven in the interior monologues of urban grotesques; a daughter painfully visits a dying or aged parent. In *Machine Dreams*, 1984 (a novel), family memories of W. Va. life from the Depression to Vietnam are evoked through a kaleidoscope of dreams, fantasies and images from popular culture; memory becomes a burdensome legacy. *Fast Lanes*, 1984 (stories), caused JAP to be called 'a poet of the modern American nightmare', and likened to PLATH. It draws on JAP's own experience on the road in the early 1970s, the fear and self-destructiveness of the drifter in search of 'the floater's only fix: I was free'. She married Mark Brian Stockman in 1985 and has a son and two stepsons. Interview in *Croton Review*, 9, 1986.

Phillips, Jennifer, London playwright and novelist, b. in 1942. Educ. at boarding school (till 16) and the Royal Academy of Music, London (drama department), she had written from an early age before her acting interest turned her to drama. In 1969 came her first radio play, the award-winning comedy *Fault on the Line*, and first stage play, *The Backhanded Kiss*, at Leicester. Britain's first woman TV comedy scriptwriter, JP achieved her own television series in *Wink to Me Only*. Further TV and radio comedy series followed, some co-authored with Jill Hyem. In 1973 JP's satiric *Instrument for Love* was given at the first-ever Women's Theatre Festival (Almost Free Theatre). She has written over 40 radio and TV plays. In her best-known stage piece, the tragi-comedy *Daughters of Men*, 1979 (also in *Best Radio Plays*, 1978), a separated couple dispute custody of their only child. Her novel, *Bombshell*, 1985, engages a 'bored housewife' in a plot to extort funds by planting a bomb on an aircraft. JP has a daughter.

Phillips, Teresia Constantia, also Muilman, 1709–65, courtesan and (probably) autobiographer. She claims that her father, Thomas P., lost his army commission when she was four; her godmother the Duchess of Bolton had charge of her briefly; her mother died; at 13 she ran away from a cruel stepmother; villains female and male procured her 'Ruin'. Living as a mistress, overspending on credit, she followed advice to save herself by a bigamous marriage, 1722. (A wife's debts belonged to her husband.) Dutch merchant Henry Muilman married her, 1723, allegedly knowing her past; when his family found out, they and he sought to annul the marriage. There followed a string of lovers, court cases and spells in debtors' prison. Threats aimed to deter the serial printing of *An Apology* for TCP's conduct, 1748–9, and the furore later, stemmed largely from her charges against Lord Chesterfield. Jeremy Bentham, who was deeply affected in youth by the *Apology*'s exposé of legal chicanery, said the satirist Paul Whitehead ghost-wrote it (he was said, too, to have been paid 'in kind'). Most readers took it as TCP's, despite its third-person form and claim that the narrator, commissioned to relate chiefly 'Litigations', feels unqualified to handle love or romance. Irony complicates its lavish moral sententiae, its vilification of her husband, sentimental portrait of herself, and play at concealing and revealing the names of lovers. In 1748 appeared an anonymous *Defence* of Chesterfield and an 'Oxford Scholar's' *Parallel* between TCP and Laetitia PILKINGTON; 1750 added a *Letter* to Chesterfield (signed TCP, calling her 'a Writer', sharing the *Apology* style and voicing moral and semi-feminist as well as provokingly outrageous views), and an answer by Sarah CHAPONE. The *Letter* deplores novel-reading, women's flimsy education, the sexual double standard, and the trouble beauty brings. In 1752 Elizabeth CARTER heard that TCP was keeping a boarding-school in Jamaica; gossip after her death reported her snaring and exploiting rich husbands, wasting her money, dying unlamented.

Piatt, Sarah Morgan (Bryan), 1836–1919, poet, b. Lexington, Ky., da. of Talbot B. and Mary (Spiers) who d. in 1844, after which SMP lived at various times with her maternal grandmother, her stepmother and her aunt. She was educ. at Henry Female College, New Castle, Ky., and her first poems, influenced by the English Romantics, were pub. in newspapers such as the *Louisville Journal*. In 1861 she m. John James P., author and friend of William Dean Howells, with whom he had written a book of poems. They spent time in Ireland, 1892–3, where he served as US Consul at Cork. SMP, the mother of seven children, produced 17 vols. of poetry: her collected *Poems* were pub. 1874. She varied lyric and dramatic forms within each volume and generally used a plain diction. Though her early poems are often for and about children, they are substantial enough to interest an adult. In *Poems in Company with Children*, 1877, she displays a pessimism unusual in children's verse, as in her poem 'If I Had Made the World', while she introduces her children to communism in *A Voyage to the Fortunate Isles*, 1874. Two volumes of poems were written with her husband, a much more conventional and derivative poet: *The Nests at Washington*, 1864, and *The Children Out-of-Doors*, 1885; he also advised her concerning three later vols.: *An Irish Wildflower*, 1891, *An Enchanted Castle*, 1893, and *Pictures, Portraits and People in Ireland*, 1893.

Pickering, Amelia, poet, author of *The Sorrows of Werter*, 1788, a notable example of female response to Goethe: nearly 1000 subscribers included other respondents like Charlotte SMITH and Mary ROBINSON. AP hopes her well-turned Petrarchan quatrains will teach readers to 'curb impatience; better hopes impart'. She gives to Charlotte a voice, if rather weakly moralistic, and to Werter suffering which is acute, credible and unhysterical (see Syndy M. Conger in *Goethe Yearbook*, 3, 1986). Reviewers, though, were unfriendly. AP has no connection with the blind Priscilla (Pointon, or Poynton) Pickering, 1750–1801, friend of Anna SEWARD, who pub. two vols. of poems, 1770 and [1794], with subscribers chiefly from the Midlands.

Pickthall, Marjorie Lowry Christie, 1883–1922, poet, short-story writer and novelist. She was b. at Gunnersbury, Middx, England, da. of Helen (Mallard) and Arthur C. P., who took her to Toronto in 1889. There (between bouts of illness) she attended Bishop Strachan School, and began writing early. She sold her first story for print in 1898, and pub. a children's novel in 1905, but gave up writing for a time when devastated by her mother's death in 1910. Already a librarian, she held several such jobs in Canada and (1919–20) in England; during WWI (despite continuing ill health), she drove an ambulance and did farm work. Lorne Pierce's *Marjorie Pickthall: A Book of Remembrance*, 1925, uses her diary, and lists stories and poems in journals, 1903–22. MP won several literary competitions, wrote novels (those for adults include English and Canadian settings: one uncompleted), and had her verse-drama, *The Wood-Cutter's Wife*, acted in Montréal in 1920 (pub. 1922). But her fame rests on her poems. At times religious or mystical (High Anglican), drawing on knowledge of folklore of many nations, she seeks to mirror spiritual beauty in the earthly. She makes haunting use of colour, and of rhythm and verbal music (she strove not to 'form a rigid scheme of construction and melody'). Moods of loneliness, grief or world-weariness are pervasive. She died in Vancouver of an embolus following surgery. Posthumous publications include *Angels' Shoes* (stories), 1923, and *Complete Poems*, 1925 (enlarged 2nd ed., 1936; election ed., Pierce, 1957). See Clara Thomas in *Canadian Novelists*, 1946; Janice Williamson in Neuman and Kamboureli, 1986.

Piercy, Marge, novelist, poet, political activist, da. of Bert Bernice Bunnin (Badonya), who was given a man's name because her father resented a third daughter, and Robert D. P. Born 1936 in a working-class section of Detroit, raised as a Jew by her mother and grandmother, she is 'passionately interested in the female lunar side of Judaism'. Scholarships and fellowships took her to the Univ. of Michigan (BA, 1957), and Northwestern Univ. (MA, 1958). In Greece, France, NYC and Chicago in the late 1950s and 1960s, she wrote many novels 'too feminist and too political' to be pub. A political activist in NYC, she was gassed at demonstrations, dragged by a car, and beaten by US Nazis. This affected her health, and she moved to Cape Cod, where she lives with her third husband, writer Ira Wood, and is active in the Feminist Writers' Guild and the National Organization of Women. *Going Down Fast*, 1969, like *Dance the Eagle to Sleep*, 1971, and *Vida*, 1980, address the exhilaration and exhaustion of politically radical and sexually unconventional characters attempting to change society and evade the authorities. In *Woman on the Edge of Time*, 1976, a Chicana woman incarcerated in a mental hospital is taken by a time-traveller to visit a utopian but gritty society which is dismantling sexism, heterosexism and racism. Other experiments in form include the autobiographical *Braided Lives*, 1982, and a feminist romance, *Fly Away Home*, 1984. *Gone to Soldiers*, 1987, is a hugely complex novel set in WWII, structured by the lives of characters representative of virtually every group touched by this war. MP's poetry, more than a dozen vols. since *Breaking Camp*, 1968, speaks the many languages of a radical feminist, from rage ('Rape fattens on the fantasies of the normal male / like a maggot in garbage') to female memory ('Before we make a fire of / our bodies I braid my black / hair and I am Grandmother braiding / her greystreaked chestnut hair'). Including *Hard Loving*, 1969, *Living in the Open*, 1976, *The*

Twelve-Spoked Wheel Flashing, 1978, *The Moon is Always Female*, 1980, *My Mother's Body*, 1985, and *Available Light*, 1988, has been called 'compulsive, visceral, full of conviction and bright metaphorical energy, wry, luscious and prepared to take risks'. She has written a play with Ira Wood, *The Last White Class*, 1979, and essays, *The Grand Coolie Dam*, 1970, and *Parti-Colored Blocks for a Quilt*, 1982. She is the editor of *Early Ripening; American Women's Poetry Now*, 1988. See Susan Kress in Marleen Bar, ed., *Future Females*, 1981, and Sue Walker and Eugenie Hamner, eds., *Critical Essays on MP*, 1984.

Piers, Sarah (Roydon), Lady, poet, da. of Sir Matthew R., and wife of Sir George P. (d. 1720) of Stonepit, Kent, an officer with Marlborough. She corresponded with Catharine TROTTER from 1697 (letters in BL with a printed, untitled poem by SP, 1708). Her fervent verse praise appeared with Trotter's *Fatal Friendship*, 1698, and *Unhappy Penitent*, 1701, likening her to Katherine PHILIPS and, with reservations, Aphra BEHN. (Delarivier MANLEY hinted that the friendship was lesbian.) After modest hesitation SP contributed to *THE NINE MUSES*, 1700. Living in the country, teaching her children, she welcomed the new king in *George for Britain*, 1714, a poem pub. with her name in two formats, one lavish. Here she praises England (like James Thomson later) for its landscape, climate, and system of government. She prefers 'The Subject's Right, and Crown's Prerogative' to democracy, republics, or aristocracy, stresses the need for vigilance against rebellion, and invokes Anne, Marlborough, and (male) poets.

Pigott, Harriet, 1775–1846, miscellaneous writer, often confused with Harriet (Pigott) THOMSON. Much youngest da. of Arabella (Mytton), who d. *c.* 1779, and the Rev. William P. of Chetwynd, Shropshire, she grew up unhappily, away from her family, romanticizing its glorious past. She wished 'to make myself at home amongst ... foreigners', and spent years on the Continent. She corresponded with the ladies of LLANGOLLEN, Charlotte BURY, Marguerite BLESSINGTON, Catherine STEPNEY, and Elizabeth STRICKLAND. She left diaries with few gaps from 1812 to her 'Invasion of the Territories of her Ancestors; after thirty years of banishment', 1845. Elaborate, gossipy letters of 1814–16 appeared as *The Private Correspondence of a Woman of Fashion*, 1832 (early reminiscence, Brussels at the time of Waterloo, eulogy of Anne DAMER, satire on H. M. WILLIAMS). By 1838, when she moved to Helensburgh on the Clyde, she was writing for ALBUMS and periodicals. She worked on a life of John Galt, got him to edit her letters of 1817–33 (*Records of Real Life in the Palace and the Cottage*, 1839), and wrote a preface for his posthumous *Demon of Destiny* [1840]. Her *Three Springs of Beauty*, 1844, is a fantasy of magical preservation for the beauty of women descended from fairies. She left voluminous MSS to the Bodleian.

Pike, Mary Hayden (Green), 1824–1908, novelist and abolitionist, b. Eastport, Maine, da. of Hannah Claflin (Hayden) and Elijah Dix G., Baptist deacon, bank director and militia officer in Calais, Maine. At 12 she formally joined the Baptist church. She was educ. at local schools in Calais, Maine, and at the Charlestown Female Seminary in Mass., graduating in 1843. In 1845 she m. Frederick Augustus P., lawyer and member of Congress during the Civil War. Her spirited ABOLITIONIST sentiments found expression in her first novel, *Ida May*, 1854 (written as by 'Mary Langdon'), a melodramatic story of a white child sold into slavery. This was followed in 1856 by *Caste* (written as 'Sydney A. Story, Jr.'), which argues forcefully against racial discrimination. *Agnes*, 1858, combines a realistic portrayal of the American Indian with a chronicle of the War of Independence. MP lived in Washington, DC, 1861–9 and then, after a trip to Europe, returned to Calais, where she lived until her husband's death in 1886. She spent most of her remaining years with her adopted daughter in Plainfield, NJ.

Pilkington, Miss or Mrs, obscure author of four anonymous MINERVA novels, which intelligently reconcile – just – humour and wit with sentimental anguish: often confused with Mary PILKINGTON. In the anonymous, epistolary *Delia, A Pathetic and Interesting Tale*, 1790, set largely in Ireland, faulty mothers and eccentric older relations are rendered credible; so are two heroines, patterns of friendship and other virtues. Women's abilities and education are discussed. Delia's sense of fun survives the malicious breaking of her first love affair; but her lover's return and violent reproaches on her marriage kill her: 'I have seen the equanimity of Socrates emulated by a girl.' In the non-epistolary *Rosina*, 1793, financial problems, unsatisfactory marriage, battles for independence, and some boisterous humour, precede a happiness carefully distinguished from perfection. *The Subterranean Cavern, or Memoirs of Antoinette de Montflorance* (epistolary), 1798, and *The Accusing Spirit or De Courcy and Eglantine* (narrative), 1802, are both set in revolutionary France. The latter ends with a fervent plea to philosophers to keep their dangerous notions to themselves and enjoy toleration without disturbing society.

Pilkington, Laetitia (Van Lewen), *c.* 1706–50, poet and autobiographer, b. in Dublin, first surviving child of obstetrician John Van L. She taught herself to read at five despite her mother's prohibition, and 'from a Reader I quickly became a Writer'. Her *Memoirs*, three vols., 1748–54 (racy and delightful poems at the end; repr. 1928; ed. by A. C. Elias, Jr, forthcoming) tell a breathless tale of survival: fending off starvation and illicit sex, living in poverty as 'muse and secretary', jester, bard, and flirt, to noblemen and bishops. Her style is larded with quotations (often wittily applied), her reportage of famous figures revealing, her tone self-defensive. She says her parents pushed her into early marriage, 1725, with the poor scribbling clergyman Matthew P., who naggingly resented her writing talents and favour with Swift (to whom she says she suggested the dialogue form of *Polite Conversation*). She followed Matthew P. to London in 1733, but returned when he urged her to profitable adultery. He caused her to quarrel with her adored father, who then died horribly after an accident; her youngest child died too. Having at last managed to catch her with a man (reading, she says), he divorced her in 1738. She returned to London to live mostly as 'Mrs Meade' (her grandmother's name) and to seek subscribers for her poems. *The Statues, or The Trial of Constancy* appeared in 1739. She was accused of plagiarism from her husband and jailed for debt, 1742; she set up as a professional letter-writer, opened a pamphlet shop, and sheltered her children from paternal persecution; her daughter got pregnant, 1745, and used her mother's writings for laying fires. LP is cool about female writers and sceptical (after being cold-shouldered) of female friendship, but keenly admires Constantia GRIERSON. Her unpub. comedy, *The Turkish Court, or The London Prentice*, was acted at Dublin, 1748; her tragedy, *The Roman Father*, was unfinished. Her son John Carteret P. concluded her *Memoirs* and pub. letters in his *Real Story*, 1760. Wordsworth admired her poems, which are chiefly occasional and include spirited satires; WOOLF wrote on her in 'Lives of the Obscure', 1923.

Pilkington, Mary (Hopkins), 1766–1839, miscellaneous writer, da. of a Cambridge surgeon, educ. to expect an income which went to a male heir when she was 15, sending her mother insane. In 1786 she married a man 'totally devoid of worldly Prudence'. He became a naval surgeon and she a governess: hence her prolific works for children and the young. These teach traditional virtues and the education of women as agreeable companions for men; but *Miscellaneous Poems*, 1796 (by 'Mrs J. Pilkington', probably MP), includes spirited poems of mock-humility: towards male reviewers, Apollo (who denies women the laurels), bullying husbands, or the god Hymen. These and the more conventional *Original Poems*, 1811, contain many amusing or touching pieces on children, women friends, and domesticities: calling-cards and chamber-lamps. *Memoirs of Celebrated Female Characters*, 1811, praises both learning and physical courage. MP is shocked by Charlotte CHARKE dressing as a man; she reproves yet appreciates Aphra BEHN, Mary ROBINSON and Mary WOLLSTONECRAFT. Her novels for adults (1809–15, one as 'Matthew Moral, Esq.') do not equal those of the obscure Miss PILKINGTON. To the RLF, which helped her 1811–25, she mentioned 22 works, illness, and loss when the publisher Hughes went bankrupt.

Pinchard, Elizabeth, novelist and children's writer. She m. lawyer John P., settled at Taunton, Somerset, *c.* 1794, and had five children. In 'early youth' she wrote *The Blind Child, or Anecdotes of the Wyndham Family*, pub. 1791 as 'By a Lady', to combat 'false' sensibility (on which she quotes Hannah MORE). Emily's lessons on life include keeping calm enough – just – to help her younger sister undergo an operation to restore her sight. A preface praises those like Mme de GENLIS and A. L. BARBAULD who set great talent to serving children. EP's *Dramatic Dialogues*, 1792, and three more moral tales, 1794–1830, are all for the young. Her first adult novel, *Mystery and Confidence*, 1814, depicts (from life, she says) a farmer's daughter marrying an earl. The heroine's mental growth, minor female characters, social and emotional minutiae, are finely handled despite a melodramatic backdrop (hero falsely accused of murdering his first wife). *The Ward of Delamere*, 1815, endorses, not implausibly, female submission, depicting survival of gothic confinement, a mother disgraced and dead, and a grandfather impossibly tyrannical.

Pinckney, Eliza or Elizabeth (**Lucas**), 1722?–93, letter writer and agriculturalist, elder da. of Lt.-Col. George P. Educ. in England, brought to S. Carolina in 1739, she kept a letter-book: some pub. 1850; ed. Elise P., 1972. She ran three plantations, pioneered the growing of indigo, taught French to her sister and reading to 'a parcel of little Negroes', warned her soldier relations against 'false notions of honour', indulged her fitful 'poetic vein' on a mocking-bird while 'laceing my stays', and commented with critical acumen on Richardson's *Pamela*. Having said at 18 'a single life is my only Choice', she married, 1744, the older Charles P. of Charleston (widower of a friend); her sons had notable careers in politics. In England 1752–8, she loved the theatre and sightseeing but not card-playing. Her husband died on their return, leaving her mourning but always busy. She keenly supported American independence; the British sacked and looted her estates, and by 1782 she was ruined. Life by Frances Leigh Williams, 1967; later letters unpub., the last known, of 1787, urging interest in the USA on a grandson living in France (SC Historical Society and elsewhere).

Piozzi, Hester Lynch (Salusbury), also **Thrale**, 1741–1821, woman of letters, only child of Hester Maria (Cotton) and John S., both of ancient, impoverished Welsh lineage. B. at Bodvel, Caernarvonshire, she was variously educ. in London and on an uncle's estate in Herts. 'till I was half a Prodigy'. In her teens she wrote a diary and remarkable poems and translations, learned Latin from Jane COLLIER's brother, pub. pseudonymously in newspapers, and drew verse praise from Sarah FIELDING. In

1762 her father died; next year, pressured by her mother, she married Henry Thrale, a wealthy brewer uninterested in her talents. She met Samuel Johnson in 1765 and was soon translating Boethius with him; her youthful verse MSS bear his notes. Of her journals, 'The Children's Book' (in Mary Hyde, *Thrales*, 1977) records education and illnesses (only four of 12 grew up); *Thraliana* (ed. Katharine C. Balderston, 1942) records sparkling Streatham talk both intellectual and trivial (also detailed by Frances BURNEY) as well as her husband's public infidelity, business crises (and his shame when she saved the day), pregnancies, deaths, historical detail, and her own poems. She pub. in newspapers and in Anna WILLIAMS's book. For two years after Henry T.'s death she reasoned out her right to love the Italian musician Gabriel P.: in 1784 she married him, to outrage from daughters, BLUESTOCKINGS, and other friends. In Italy for three years, she wrote poems and preface for *The Florence Miscellany*, 1785, and her penetrating, non-reverent *Anecdotes of Johnson*, 1786, which brought charges of having exploited and exposed him. Back in England she issued two more controversial works: Johnson's letters, 1788, and her appreciative, colloquial *Observations and Reflections* on Italy, 1789. Later writings – *British Synonymy*, 1794 (professedly aimed to help foreigners like her husband), *Retrospection*, 1801 (world history, damned by critics), the unpub. *Lyford Redivivus* (on place-names), and political polemics, both pub. and unpub., reflect many facets of her originality. She paid poetic tribute to Elizabeth CARTER. After Gabriel P.'s painful death from gout at their Welsh home, 1809, she settled in Bath, copied out three MS vols. of her poetry for her adopted heir, and kept writing to the end. Many unpub. MSS; life by J. L. Clifford, 1941, repr. 1968; study by William McCarthy, 1985; Edward A. and Lillian D. Bloom, eds., *Letters*, 1989– .

Pitt, Marie Elizabeth Josephine (McKeown), 1869–1948, poet, journalist, b. at Bulumwaal in the Gippsland region of Victoria, first of seven children of Mary Stuart McIver (Dawson), a former schoolteacher, and Edward M., goldminer and selector. Educ. intermittently, she spent much of her childhood working on the family farm at Doherty's Corner. She m. gold miner William Henry P. in Tasmania, 1892, had two daughters and a son, and lived for 12 years in remote mining settlements in Tasmania, becoming involved in Labor politics and the union movement. After her husband contracted phthisis (from which he died in 1912), they settled in Melbourne in 1905. Here she worked in a number of jobs to support her family, joined the Victorian Socialist Party and met other political and literary figures including Vance and Nettie PALMER, Louis Esson, and the poet Bernard O'Dowd, with whom she lived from 1920 until her death. She began writing as a girl and had some early work pub. in the *Bairnsdale Advertiser* in the 1890s and the *Bulletin Reciter*, 1901; her first collection of poems, *Horses of the Hill*, appeared in 1911. She wrote feminist and socialist articles for newspapers and for journals such as the *Socialist* (which she edited for some years). She became well known as a champion of the poor and disadvantaged. Her poetry, which appeared in a second volume, *Bairnsdale*, 1922, and two collections, 1925 and 1944, while still uncompromisingly political, was often distinguished by the influences of her bush childhood and the affinity she felt with the natural environment, in particular the landscape of the Tasmanian west coast. Unfortunately she is remembered more for her lyricism than for her political vision. Colleen BURKE's biography, *Doherty's Corner*, 1985, does much to redress this imbalance and has included most of MP's poems.

Pitter, Ruth, CBE, artist and poet, b. 1897 at Ilford, Essex, da. of poetry-loving schoolteachers Louisa R. (Murrell), who 'dabbled in fancy religions', and Fabian agnostic George P. RP wrote her first poem at about five. Educ. at Coburn School in Bow, East London, a Christian charity school, she published a poem at 13 in the socialist weekly *New Age*. She worked as a War Office clerk in WWI, then making and painting pottery, gifts and furniture, first in Suffolk, then from 1930 at the Chelsea craft-workshop she established with her lifelong companion Kathleen O'Hara. 'By commercial slavery and continual anxiety I have avoided patronage and the meal-ticket marriage, and am (as a writer) independent of politics, publishers, and jobbery.' *First Poems*, 1920, was followed by many volumes including *Persephone in Hades*, 1931, and *A Mad Lady's Garland*, 1934. RP was admired by Elizabeth JENNINGS and Kathleen RAINE, who saw in her formal archaic language, inversion and strict metre an alternative to modernism. She was confirmed an Anglican in her forties, worked in WWII in a crucible factory and elsewhere, did popular journalism and broadcasting, and settled at Long Crendon, Bucks., in the 1950s. Among many honours, she was the first woman to receive the Queen's Gold Medal for poetry (personally presented), 1955. Broad or affectionate humour animates poems like 'Maternal Love Triumphant, or Song of the Virtuous Female Spider' (who has eaten her mate 'with streaming eyes', and desires nothing but 'first an honest matron's name, / Than which there is none higher; / And then my pretty children's good'), and books on gardening, 1941 ('I lurk in undergrowth'), and cats, 1947. Late works continue to reflect RP's Christian optimism and concern for the underdog; they deal in dreams, quests for spiritual meaning, and homely images (arum lilies are 'little lavatory basins'). *Urania*, 1950, *Poems 1926–1966* (with her preface), 1968, and *Collected Poems*, 1969, were followed by *End of Drought*, 1975, and *A Heaven to Find*, 1987. See special RP issue of *Poetry Northwest*, 1960; Arthur Russell, ed., *Homage to a Poet*, 1969 (personal tributes from e.g. Raine, Ngaio MARSH, Carolyn KIZER).

Pix, Mary (Griffith), 1666–1709, dramatist, da. of Lucy (Berriman) and the Rev. Roger G. of Nettlebed, Oxon.; she had from childhood an 'Inclination to Poetry'. She m., 1685, George P., a London merchant tailor; her one child died in 1690. After a commendatory poem for *SYLVIA'S REVENGE*, 1688, her career took off in 1696 with her one, highly-coloured novel, *The Inhumane Cardinal, or Innocence Betrayed* (now very rare: facs. of interesting critical introduction, 1984), and two plays: *The Spanish Wives*, a farce with sentiment, and *Ibrahim the Thirteenth* [error for twelfth], *Emperour of the Turks*, a blood-and-lust tragedy. W. M.'s *Female Wits*, also 1696, satirized her quite gently, choosing the perennial target of her fatness. The next ten years brought ten more plays (more than any previous woman but BEHN; more popular with audiences than critics) and a long poem from Boccaccio (*Violenta, or The Rewards of Virtue*, 1704). Her tragedies are fashionably hyperbolical; unlike other women she includes rape in her harrowing plots, on which *The Double Distress*, 1701, grafts a rare happy ending. Her comedies teem with good-humoured fun, sharp observation, and positive pictures of the merchant class usually mocked on stage. *The Deceiver Deceived* and *The Innocent Mistress*, both acted 1697, deal unrigorously with extramarital love; George Powell's plagiarism of her plan for the former led to a paper war which she was seen to have won. She befriended Susanna CENTLIVRE and Catharine TROTTER and wrote for *THE NINE MUSES*, 1700, and Sarah FYGE's poems [1703]. Her death left her family destitute. Plays repr. with Trotter's, 1982; study (with MANLEY and Trotter) by Constance Clark, 1986.

Pixner, Stef, poet, artist and song-writer, b. 1945 in London of working-class parents. Her mother, a communist, worked in an office and taught shorthand-typing in the evenings; her father never returned from WWII. She grew up in Parliament Hill Fields in 'temporary' council flats (sharing a kitchen) till 1959, attended a comprehensive school, and joined the Young Communist League. In 1959 her mother became slightly better off as a political secretary; SP went to Leeds Univ. and the London School of Economics, and became a polytechnic lecturer (sociology, psychology, women's studies). She has also been a gardener, waitress, and feminist therapist. She has contributed poems, stories, songs (which she also performs), drawings and reviews to *Spare Rib* and other journals. She has written of her childhood in Liz Heron, ed., *Truth Dare or Promise*, 1985, and has appeared in poetry anthologies from *Licking the Bed Clean*, 1978 (produced by a women's group she joined the previous year), to Illona Linthwaite, ed., *Ain't I a Woman*, 1987. Her own volume, *Sawdust and White Spirit*, 1985, shows her generally sharp, succinct, vernacular, in poems ranging from dream experience ('high heeled sneakers' describes a meeting with Simone de BEAUVOIR and a surreal juggling of various female roles) to the daily and particular. 'I like being pregnant / I like my breasts / that have soared / from hill to mountain . . . returning to this city / so choked, so spacious . . . I look up information / about "termination".'

'Plaidy, Jean', Eleanor Alice (Burford) Hibbert, novelist, also published as 'Victoria Holt', 'Philippa Carr', 'Ellalice Tate', 'Elbur Ford' and 'Kathleen Kellow'. B. in 1906 in London, da. of Alice (Tate) and Joseph B., she was educ. privately, but often kept from school by illness; she read avidly and became 'fascinated by history'. She married G. P. H., but wrote initially under her birth name (30 novels, from 1941, after beginning with short stories). *Together They Ride*, 1945, was first of more than 80 titles as JP, who is regarded as a leading British historical novelist. They range from the Norman conquest to Victoria's reign, centring on the lives of women (often royal), using third- and (recently) first-person narrative, 'highlighting the drama and the comedy although not diverging from the known facts'. They include 12 separate series, focusing on, e.g., the Tudors, whom JP calls 'special', or Lucrezia Borgia. (One of her five non-fiction works deals with Cesare Borgia.) She launched 'Elbur Ford' in 1950 (four novels), 'Kathleen Kellow' in 1952 (eight novels) and 'Ellalice Tate' in 1956 (five novels). 'Victoria Holt' began in 1961 with *The Mistress of Mellyn*, which sold over a million copies, and launched a 'boom in GOTHIC sales'. Her two dozen novels are romances with historical settings and fictitious plots. 'Philippa Carr' began (in *The Miracle at St Bruno's*, 1972) on 14 family-saga 'historical gothics', a genre which 'falls into place between Jean Plaidy and Victoria Holt'.

Plantin, Arabella, English fiction-writer. In 1727 Edmund Curll included her two short 'novels', 'The Ingrateful, or The Just Revenge' and 'Love led Astray, or Mutual Inconstancy', with their own title-page, in his ragbag *Whartoniana*, centred on a MS once owned by Anne WHARTON (re-issued [1732] as *Poetical Works* of Philip Duke of Wharton). In one tale a lady living in Arcadia offers her spendthrift lover bottomless supplies of cash; when he jilts her she kills him and herself, to applause for revenging the wrongs of her sex. In the other, two pairs of pastoral lovers change partners, led partly by the deities Love and Apollo, partly by their own dabbling in disguise, and mostly by both sexes' irresistible delight in rescue of a woman by a man: 'their Love, by changing the Object, lost nothing of its original Strength'; they exemplify love as well as princes could.

Plath, Sylvia, 1932–63, poet and novelist, b. in Jamaica Plain, Mass., to an American-Austrian mother, Aurelia

(Schober), who encouraged her early interest in writing, and a German father, Otto P., professor of entomology, who d. when she was eight. Her mother then supported the family by teaching. SP had a strong drive to succeed: in high school and at Smith College, 1950– 5, she published poems and stories in magazines, even *Harper's* and *The Nation* (and was paid). As a student guest editor on *Mademoiselle* magazine, 1953, she interviewed Marianne MOORE and Elizabeth BOWEN; soon afterwards she had a breakdown, and attempted suicide. (She was befriended then and earlier by writer Olive Higgins Prouty, whose novel *Stella Dallas*, 1923, was repr. and re-filmed 1990.) This experience was powerfully transmuted in the novel *The Bell Jar* (pub. 1963 as by 'Victoria Lucas', filmed 1979), 'the most complex account of schizophrenia as a protest against the feminine mystique of the 1950s'. On graduating, SP went on a Fulbright scholarship to Newnham College, Cambridge, where she met and married, 1956, poet Ted Hughes; each was an important influence on the other's work. They spent 1957–9 in the USA: SP taught at Smith for a year and attended a poetry workshop with Robert Lowell at Boston. Back in England in 1960, she published her first book of poems, *The Colossus*, and bore a daughter. Next came a miscarriage, then a son, 1962, the year of her radio play, *Three Women: A Monologue for Three Voices*, about the divided self. Living in an old house in Devon, often alone and having discovered her husband was having an affair, SP made a bonfire of MSS, hers and his. She took her children to London, where, at a time of intense cold and furious creative activity, she gassed herself. (Anne SEXTON, a friend, wrote 'I know at the news of your death, / a terrible taste for it, like salt.') SP's *Ariel*, 1965, caused controversy with its brilliant, bitter, angry but controlled treatments of male domination. SP equates sexual and personal politics with wider historical processes and breaks silences concerning women's feelings of alienation and barrenness, and the negative, devouring aspects of motherhood. During her last seven years, and especially at the very end, SP developed amazingly in technique, intensity, and complexity: from the fluency of 'how but most glad / could be this adam's woman / when all earth his words do summon / leaps to laud such man's blood!' to the spareness of 'Each dead child coiled, a white serpent, / One at each little // Pitcher of milk, now empty.' After further volumes of poems, Hughes ed. her short stories and diary excerpts, 1979, *Collected Poems*, 1981, *Journals*, 1982 (he destroyed the last), and *Selected Poems*, 1985. A second novel provisionally called *Double Exposure* disappeared in MS, 1970. Lives (controversial) by Linda Wagner-Martin, 1987, and Anne STEVENSON, 1989. Bibliog. by Stephen Tabor, 1987; concordance by R. M. Matovich, 1986; critical essays ed. Linda W. Wagner, 1984, Paul Alexander, 1985; Critical Heritage vol., ed. Linda W. Wagner, 1988. See also Elaine Showalter, *The Female Malady*, 1985 (quoted above). Remaining MSS at Smith College and Indiana Univ., and owned by Ted Hughes.

Plumptre or Plumtre, **Anne** or Anna, 1760–1818, and **Annabella** or **'Bell'**, 1761–1838, translators, novelists, and miscellaneous writers, daughters of Anna (Newcombe), schoolmaster's daughter, and Robert P., President of Queens' College, Cambridge, Prebendary of Norwich, their usual home: both well educ., especially in modern languages. Anne is said to have begun by writing for periodicals; Bell's 'Ode to Moderation' (*The Cabinet*, Norwich, 1795) rejects that quality for fierce indignation as response to the plight of the poor. Each is credited with an anonymous MINERVA novel of 1796: Anne with *Antoinette* (well reviewed; *Antoinette Percival* in Philadelphia ed., 1800), a two-generation tale with illegitimate heroine, whose author hopes a female philosopher will soon be too common to be a prodigy; Bell with *Montgomery, or Scenes in Wales*. In 1798 Bell published *The Mountain Cottager* (from German) and Anne *The Rector's Son* (less well received), whose hero battles with poverty and succumbs to temptation to think ill of the heroine. In the next few years both were busy TRANSLATING from German: like Elizabeth INCHBALD, they translated Kotzebue. Anne did seven plays by him (A. M. LARPENT's husband refused *La Perouse* a licence on political grounds), a life of him, and two travel books; Bell did W. A. Iffland's play *The Foresters*, 1799, *Domestic Stories* for children, 1800 (prescriptive, from several authors), and (probably) Kotzebue's *The Guardian Angel*, 1802. By 1799 both were living in London, friends of Eliza FENWICK. Original works of 1801 were Bell's (attributed) *The Western Mail*, purporting to be letters robbed from a postbag, and Anne's *Something New*, a novel about 'An ugly heroine – Is't not SOMETHING NEW?' Anne, a friend of H. M. WILLIAMS, travelled to France with Amelia OPIE in 1802 and stayed three years: her *Narrative* of this time, 1810, is part travel book and part sympathetic account of Napoleon and post-Revolutionary France. Bell did some teaching; her *Stories for Children*, 1804, was meant to open a series designed gradually to amuse and instruct. Approved by Sarah TRIMMER, based on everyday life like those of A. L. BARBAULD and others, the tales emphasize domestic good-heartedness rather than intellect. Her *Domestic Management, or the Healthful Cookery Book*, as 'a Lady', dates from the same year. Anne perhaps put personal experience into *History of Myself and My Friends*, 1813, a story of complex Cambridge-based life, as she did into *Narrative*, 1817, of summer trips to Ireland (comments on culture, politics, mineralogy). Joint *Tales of Wonder, of Humour, and of Sentiments*, 1818, are lively, unpredictable, philosophical, often exotic.

Plumptre, Constance Eliza Maria Fanny, 1847?–1929, philosophical and RELIGIOUS writer, b. into a branch of the same old Notts. family as Anne and Bell PLUMPTRE: da. of Caroline (Colmer) and Charles John P., barrister. An avowed agnostic, she was interested in the continual challenge of scientific discovery to traditional Christian belief and committed to the principle of liberty of conscience. Her works include *A General Sketch of the History of Pantheism*, 1878, *Giordano Bruno: A tale of the Sixteenth Century*, 1884, *Natural Causation: An Essay in Four Parts*, 1888, and *Studies in Little Known Subjects*, 1898, which expresses her unease at the 'moral timidity' of agnostics reluctant to declare their views. Although advocating 'higher secularism' (increased happiness in this life), and perceiving the importance of an accurate census for social reform, her political writing is fundamentally conservative and shows little awareness of actual living conditions. There is scant evidence of the woman's perspective in *On the Progress of Liberty of Thought during Queen Victoria's Reign*, 1902.

Pogson, Patricia (Godsell), poet and teacher. B. in 1944 at Rosyth, Scotland, da. of Isabell (Anderson) and William G., she attended grammar schools in several English towns, leaving at 16 for Preston and Oxford Colleges of Art (National Diploma in Design, 1964). She married John P. in 1963 and had two children. After two years as a draughtswoman at the Ashmolean Museum, Oxford, PP travelled in India, Australia and Canada. Her early poetry was inspired by a journal she began in 1976. Divorced in 1977, she married the poet Geoffrey Holloway, and lives in Cumbria: the Cumbrian Poetry Society (based at Charlotte Mason College, Ambleside, where she trained as a teacher, 1968–71) has encouraged her work. Besides appearing widely in poetry journals, she has published *Before the Roadshow*, 1983, and a pamphlet, *Snakeskin Belladonna*, 1986. PP experiments with traditional and free-verse techniques. Her concisely written poems examine (often from a distinctively female viewpoint) the tensions implicit in sexual and filial relationships, or catch, in networks of detail, the essence of people and places. Illness and death often provide her starting points. She has been anthologized in *Purple and Green*, 1985, and *No Holds Barred*, 1985. Her third coll., *A Rough Estate*, is forthcoming.

Pollard, Velma, poet, critic and short-story writer, b. in Jamaica in the 1940s, sister of Erna BRODBER. A senior lecturer at the Univ. of the West Indies, Kingston, she is known for stories and scholarly articles in periodicals like *Jamaica Journal*, and poems there and in Mervyn Morris and Pamela MORDECAI, eds., *Jamaica Woman*, 1980, and Morris, ed., *Focus*, 1983. She edited *West Indian Poets*, 1980, and, with Jean D'COSTA, *Over Our Way* (stories for children), 1981. Her own volumes are *Crown Point*, 1988 (poems), and *Considering Woman*, 1989 (stories). She sometimes varies her standard English with patwah, as when retelling in verse an Anansi story in which the female poet becomes a fly in a cobweb. Celebrations of her family are often negotiations with death. She writes of her father's taciturnity towards her mother, and of his love for his drums, which keeps his voice alive: 'then drums my love / will sweeten all this hill / and hark my father's spirit / home from fruitless wanderings'. The everyday 'clutter' of the poet's life cannot cancel the memory of her comfort-creating, religious grandmother, and beyond her 'mi great grandfather / jumping hopscotch and playing marble'. But her grandmother's orderliness contrasts with rationalization of the graveyard by 'some well-intentioned / madman with his spade' seen on a visit after years like 'jumbie chain-links / ages long'. VP's stories focus, with stylistically varied clarity, on the ordinary struggles and triumphs of Caribbean women, vividly particularized yet rendered universal in their historical, social and gender roles: a possessive mother finding renewed energy as she learns to let go of her son, a wife realizing she must leave a secure but uninspiring marriage, a grandmother taking up responsibility once again for a young child.

Pollock, Sharon (Chalmers), playwright, director, actress. B. in 1936 in Fredericton, New Brunswick, da. of physician and provincial politican Everett C., she was raised in Québec's Eastern Townships, attended the Univ. of New Brunswick and now resides in Calgary. She 'crept with [her] children, into the night', after a violent marriage, 1954, later remarried, to actor Michael Ball, and is now divorced. She has six children. An amateur actor at university, she later toured with Prairie Players and won a Dominion Drama Festival Best Actress Award, 1966. Since her first comedy, *A Compulsory Option*, produced 1972, she has written dozens of plays, widely staged in Canada and elsewhere, including pieces for children, collective works, and radio and TV scripts. Like Carol BOLT's, her early work draws on Brechtian epic-documentary theatre. Plays such as *Walsh*, produced 1973, deal with the effects of political institutions and ideologies on private lives, particularly those of oppressed groups: *The Komagata Maru Incident*, produced 1976, links sexual politics and racism by making a Sikh mother sole representative of a group of immigrants refused entry by Canadian authorities in 1914. In 1976 SP wrote and appeared in a college production, *My Name is Lisabeth*, rewritten as *Blood Relations*, produced 1980; it won the first Governor-General's Award for Drama for its interrogation of identity, culpability, and the docu-drama form as Lizzie Borden's actress lover, coached by Lizzie, enacts events preceding the murder ten years before. (Collec., with *One Tiger to a Hill*, an indictment of Canadian penitentiaries, and *Generations*, about an Alberta farm family, in *Blood Relations and Other Plays*, 1981.) SP's growing concern with domestic politics is also reflected in *Whiskey Six Cadenza*, produced 1983, and the autobiographical

Doc, produced 1984, winner of a second Governor-General's Award. Although critics have distinguished her early work as 'political', her later as 'personal', all SB's plays affirm her conviction that 'Until we recognize our past, we cannot change our future'. See Dianne Bessai in Neuman and Kamboureli, 1986, and Madonne Miner in *Literature in Performance* 6, 1986.

Polwhele, Elizabeth, 1651?–?91, playwright predating BEHN, perhaps the da. of Theophilus P., vicar of Tiverton, Devon; that EP m. the Rev. Stephen Lob 1675 and had five children. *The Frolicks*, acted by the Duke's Company, 1671, dedicated to Prince Rupert, refers to her two earlier plays, *Elysium* (lost) and *The Faythfull Virgins* (verse tragedy, MS in Bodleian, in which two women form a lifelong bond while competing in ritual mourning over the same man). EP calls herself 'an unfortunate young woman ... haunted with poetic devils' and says she writes 'by nature, not by art'. *The Frolicks* presents a courtship with high humour and sound grasp of dramatic technique. Marriage is inevitable but lamentable: Clarabell would have been wise to stay true to her first perception of Rightwit: 'I fear I shall be fool enough, and madwoman together, to fall in love with him. But I will resist it with an Amazonian courage. Love is but a swinish thing at best.' Ed. Judith Milhous and Robert D. Hume, 1977, it is her first play to reach print.

Pomfret, Henrietta Louisa Fermor (Jeffreys), Countess of, *c.* 1700–61, letter writer. Descended from Lady PEMBROKE, da. of Lady Charlotte (Herbert) and John Lord J., she m., 1720, Thomas F., later Earl of P., and had ten children. The death in 1737 of Queen Caroline, by whom she and her husband were employed, sent them on four years' European travel, which saved money and suited her 'rambling disposition'. Her travel-letters to Lady HERTFORD, pub. 1803, show a self-consciousness sometimes hampering, sometimes pleasing ('This humbly knocks at your dressing-room door'). Besides detail of places seen, she sent personal musings, some in verse. She met Lady NITHSDALE and Lady Mary Wortley MONTAGU in Italy, corresponded with Lady Mary, and was mocked as a learned lady. She donated the Arundel Marbles to Oxford Univ.

Ponsonby, Lady **Mary Emily** (Emily Charlotte Mary), 1817–77, novelist, da. of Lady Maria (Fane: da. of John F., tenth earl of Westmorland) and John P., fourth earl of Bessborough. She never married, and published many of her novels anonymously. Her first, *The Discipline of Life*, 1848, deals with two sisters in 'the trials and temptations of common life' (Preface), and in an attractive, easy style puts its moral of self-sacrifice for women. A sequel came out in 1850, *Pride and Irresolution*, followed by other titles such as *The Young Lord*, 1856, and *Katherine and Her Sisters*, 1861, a standard Cinderella tale of three sisters. Her next novel, *Mary Lyndsay*, 1863, was signed, as were her remaining four; the style remains gently didactic, with beautiful heroines and happy endings. She was at one time part of Vernon LEE's circle.

Ponsot, Marie (Birmingham), poet and translator, b. in NYC, da. of Marie (Candee) and William B. Educ. at St Joseph's College for Women, Brooklyn (BA 1940) and Columbia Univ. (MA 1941), she worked for a publisher of children's books after WWII and married French artist Claude P. in 1948. They had a daughter and six sons. During some years at Paris she studied at the Sorbonne and was an archivist with UNESCO, then lived in North Africa and China before returning to teach at City Univ. of NY. Her first slim volume, *True Minds*, 1956, speaks cerebrally and passionately of love ('Let no word with its thinking threat / Thrust between our kissing touch'), of her fifth childbirth ('Loud with surprise / Thrown sprung back wide the blithe body lies / Exultant and wise. The born child cries') and her Catholic faith (sometimes recalling G. M. Hopkins): 'o good world, God's work, turn, turn, turn in place / Wide in the wild eternal air of His embrace.' She likes her words to pack in several meanings. After versions of fairy tales and fables by Grimm, Perrault and La Fontaine, 1957, she went on to Andersen, 1960, and tales from China, 1960, Russia and India, 1961, and Africa, 1963. MP won the Eunice TIETJENS Award, 1960, for work in *Poetry* magazine, and awards for both her TV and radio adaptations of Paul Claudel's 'The Death of Judas', 1962–3. She has translated MARIE DE FRANCE into verse, and written, with Rosemary Deen, two books on how to write, 1981 and 1985. *Admit Impediment*, 1981, and *The Green Dark*, 1988, confirm her 'formal prowess' in many metres and her headlong, ear-catching imagery. Of women of the past (a stunt-performer's 'dreadful ease, its immense self-reference ... hand-span skill and address', a scholar's bringing 'her virgin mind to bear / stretched across nine languages'), she notes that she, the poet, has created them. See *WRB*, July 1989.

Poole, Elizabeth, sectary and prophet. On 29 December 1648 and 4 January 1649 she argued before the General Council of the Army the case she stated in her *A Vision*, 1648: that though they were right to arrest King Charles they must not execute him, just as 'You never heard that a wife might put away her husband, as he is the head of her body, but for the Lords sake suffereth his terror to her flesh.' This was expanded after his execution as *A Prophesie Touching the Death of King Charles* and *An Alarum of War* (both 1649). These two pamphlets include a prefatory letter from T. P. of Abingdon (probably Thomasina Pendarves, wife of a prominent Baptist and Fifth Monarchist) to William Kiffin's Baptist church, which had excommunicated EP. Pendarves had intercepted a copy (meant for her husband) of their attack on EP, and warns them that their defaming EP will deprive her of the livelihood 'she earns by her hands'. She calls on them to send a retraction via the printer, Giles Calvert. It may be the same EP who in 1668 was renting a London room to Calvert's wife, who kept a printing press there.

Pope, Mary, royalist prophet. In 1647 she pub. *A Treatise of Magistracy*, dedicated to King Charles, 'Gods Vice-regent on earth', and arguing at length, with detailed scripture reference, that Presbyterians and Independency are against God's will. This book also includes PETITIONS she presented to Parliament. Two years later, in *Behold, Here is a Word*, she attacked the army for arresting Charles, telling them 'the King, which is supream is not to give an account to any man on earth of any of this matters; but to God that is in heaven: for he onely is higher than the highest.' Both works give a clear narrative of civil war events.

Popular fiction. Before widespread literacy, it was a sophisticated readership which sustained the long popularity of writers like Madeleine de SCUDÉRY, while works connected with the people were limited to chiefly anonymous genres like BALLADS, broadsides (single sheets, prose or verse), and chapbooks (pedlars' wares), in which female input cannot usually be distinguished. Of the three fiction best-sellers before Richardson's *Pamela* (HAYWOOD'S *Love in Excess*, Bunyan's *The Pilgrim's Progress*, Defoe's *Robinson Crusoe*), Haywood is the only one no longer current. By the late eighteenth century popular fiction was well established as a field in which women could make a living, whether in legitimate novels (like A. M. MACKENZIE) or cheap abridgements (S. S. WILKINSON). By the end of the nineteenth, it had become possible for women to amass handsome fortunes from writing aimed at the largest cross-section of the market. Business acumen was a necessary ingredient in such success: while M. E. BRADDON became a shrewd businesswoman in the publishing world, Ellen WOOD failed to retain copyright of *East Lynne*, 1861, which sold half a million by 1900 and was pirated in an even more successful stage version. It became common, especially in the US, for writers to profit from the production of a series following an initial best-seller. Martha FINLEY's hugely successful Elsie Dinsmore series, aimed at adolescent girls, is typical of many. Ann STEPHENS's *Malaeska* was reissued in 1860 as the first 'dime novel', making a fortune for its publishers. Marjorie BOWEN's *The Viper of Milan*, 1906, launched her on a career which produced about 150 titles under at least four PSEUDONYMS and made her feel exploited, by her publisher, her mother, her husband. In the 1920s, Margaret KENNEDY's *The Constant Nymph*, 1926, sold prodigiously, to rave reviews; Elinor GLYN, whose works had a wide market, published *The Elinor Glyn System of Writing*, 1922 ('Anyone, anywhere is welcome to the profession. For years the mistaken idea prevailed that you had to have a special knack in order to write'), and E. M. HULL's *The Sheik*, 1919, filmed in 1921 with Rudolph Valentino, produced the sub-genre of 'desert romance'. Much popular fiction appeared in MAGAZINES: *Eve's Own Stories*, 1919–26, *Forget-Me-Not Novels*, 1919–26, *Marry Magazine*, 1924–30, and many others. (See Billie Melman, *Women and the Popular Imagination in the Twenties*, 1988.) In the 1920s and 1930s, B. M. BOWER wrote about 60 extremely popular westerns; Margaret MITCHELL's *Gone With the Wind*, 1935, widely translated, is still popular as the Clark Gable and Vivien Leigh film. Contemporary feminists, seizing the 'heroinizing' advice of Carolyn HEILBRUN, have moved powerfully, wittily into the genres of popular writing: see DETECTIVE FICTION, GOTHIC, SCIENCE FICTION, ROMANCE, CIRCULATING LIBRARIES and MINERVA PRESS. Since Barthes, the subject has commanded much scholarly attention: see Tania Modleski, *Loving With a Vengeance: Mass-produced Fantasies for Women*, 1982; and Susannah Radstone, ed., *Sweet Dreams, Sexuality, Gender and Popular Fiction*, 1988. Betty Rosenberg, *Genreflecting: A Guide to Reading Interests in Genre Fiction*, 1982, gives bibliography and overview.

Porden, Eleanor Anne, later Franklin, 1795–1825, poet and letter writer, da. of Mary and of William P., successful self-made London architect. By ten she was attending Royal Society lectures and reciting her own poems to guests; she wrote 'I early woo'd the Nine – my infant days / Were fed with flattery, surfeited on praise.' She ran a literary society and was planning a periodical in 1815 when her long poem *The Veils, or The Triumph of Constancy*, written at 16, appeared. This fabric of mythology, medievalism and science, all founded on a tiny actual incident, was crowned by the Institut de France. *The Arctic Expeditions*, 1818, treats, she says, a long-held interest; so does the epic *Coeur de Lion*, 1822 (thought by Alexander Dyce her best work). That year her elderly parents died. Last of many suitors came the Arctic explorer John F.; his frequent absences, she said, would justify her writing. Her life-style and religion ('I believe I love my Creator almost too well to fear Him') worried his straitlaced family; she patiently explained herself, asking 'full indulgence of my literary pursuits', not as a favour but as a parallel to his work. When he lapsed into sudden 'abhorrence for seeing the name of anyone connected with himself in print' she refused to be 'degraded' by ceasing to publish, and rejected marriage for her art – out of loyalty to her father, she said, whose life she planned to write. Yet she married Franklin, 1823, bore a 'fat, fair and funny' daughter, and d. of tuberculosis six days after he left on a voyage from which she would not let him withdraw. See life by Edith Mary Gell, 1930, with letters; Desmond King-Hele, *Erasmus Darwin and the Romantic Poets*, 1986.

Porter, Anna Maria, 1780–1832, novelist, b. in Durham, youngest child of Jane

(Blenkinsop) and William P., army surgeon, who d. before her birth. They moved to Edinburgh, where she went to school, to London by the 1790s (she pub. verse in the *Universal Magazine*, 1795), and to Surrey, 1804. After her juvenile *Artless Tales*, 1793, with her name, she published the brief courtship novel *Walsh Colville*, 1797 (facs. NY 1974), anonymously. With her sister Jane PORTER and brother Robert, later a historical painter and traveller, she that year projected a literary periodical, *The Quiz*. She then returned to using her name. *The Hungarian Brothers*, 1807, approaches the genre of historical romance, describing a European situation which a couple of years' war had rendered distant, and playing to fears of Napoleonic invasion. This favourite form brought success: of her nearly 30 works totalling 54 vols., many were published in the USA and quickly translated into French. She does not focus on women: in *The Knight of St John*, 1817, a bond of friendship forged between heirs of feuding families eclipses all the book's male–female or other relationships. She ranges widely in European history and geography but, stressing sentiment and morality, makes national events a backcloth to private crises and intrigues. A highly effective story-writer, she also wrote *Ballad Romances and Other Poems*, 1811, humanitarian *Tales of Pity on Fishing, Shooting and Hunting*, 1814, and a share with Jane P. in collections of tales. Last before her death from typhus came *The Barony*, 1830.

Porter, Jane, 1776–1850, novelist, sister of Anna Maria PORTER, friend of Hannah MORE, Anna Laetitia BARBAULD, artists and of military men. Her *Thaddeus of Warsaw*, 1803, drew on eye-witness accounts from Polish refugees of the doomed independence struggle of the 1790s (her brother Robert had met General Kosciusko). It expressed British response to European events, and had ten eds. by 1819. Her *Sketch of the Campaigns of Count Alexander Suwarrow Rymnikski*, 1804, is historical, written to go with Robert's painting of Suwarrow defeating the French; she often worked in co-operation with him. *The Scottish Chiefs*, 1810, about William Wallace, was highly popular (French version banned by Napoleon) four years before Walter Scott, a childhood friend, 'did [her] the honour to adopt' her 'biographical romance' method of uniting 'real history with the illustrative machinery of the imagination' (patronizing essay by A. D. Hook, *Clio*, 5, 1976). (Sophia LEE had united more romance with less history.) JP repeated her mixture in three dramas between 1817 and 1822 (less effective), and in the novels *The Pastor's Fireside*, 1817 (on the later Stuarts), *Duke Christian of Luneberg*, 1824 (subject suggested by George IV), and *Sir Edward Seaward's Narrative of his Shipwreck*, 1831. With her more prolific sister she wrote *Tales round a Winter Hearth*, 1826, and *Coming Out*, and *The Field of Forty Footsteps*, both 1828. She was visiting her brother in St Petersburg in 1842 when he died: his MSS are in Kansas and Caracas, Venezuela; hers at the Folger Library include poems, letters, and personal diaries.

Porter, Katherine Anne, 1890–1980, short-story writer and novelist. She was b. 'on a failing farm' at Indian Creek, Texas, da. of Mary Alice (Jones), who d. when she was two, and Harrison Boone P.; she was raised by her grandmother. At 16 she married John Henry Koontz. She became a Catholic during the marriage, which, it seems, lasted seven years, longer than those to Ernest Stock, 1925, Eugene Dove Pressly, 1933, or Albert Russel Erskine, 1938. (Her own words about her past are often inconsistent; she wrote 'My life has been incredible. I don't believe a word of it.') She went to Chicago as a journalist, and by the 1920s was a film publicist, feature-writer and reviewer in Greenwich Village, NYC. She made several long stays in Mexico, publishing in 1922 a book on its popular arts and crafts, and her first story, 'Maria

Concepción', in which, as often in her work, a primitive character represents the passion, directness and moral certainty denied to others. KAP left her life of seventeenth-century theologian Cotton Mather unfinished; in 1930 appeared her short-story collection *Flowering Judas* (expanded 1935 to include *Hacienda*, 1934), including an ambitious portrayal of post-revolutionary Mexico as both feudal and sleazily modern. *Pale Horse, Pale Rider: Three Short Novels*, 1939, movingly depicts the death-threat of the 1918 flu epidemic. KAP writes often of her native South, of children under pressure (including herself as 'Miranda'), and of adults trapped in bad relationships. With her third husband she lived during the 1930s in Berlin, then Paris, where she knew many women writers (commenting tartly in her 'Gertrude STEIN: A Self-Portrait', 1947). After Hollywood in the 1940s she ended in Washington, DC, a frequent visitor to the White House. She held teaching and writer-in-residence posts, and received many awards culminating in the Pulitzer Prize for *Collected Stories*, 1965. Her sole, much-heralded novel, *Ship of Fools*, 1962, an allegorical voyage from Mexico to Germany on the eve of Hitler's rise to power, was received with enthusiasm but later fiercely attacked. It brought her a million dollars. Writers owning a debt to her include Kay BOYLE, Tillie OLSEN and Eudora WELTY; Elizabeth HARDWICK, introducing KAP's *Collected Stories*, 1985, says, 'The extraordinary simplicity and freshness, the perfection of her stories was hard work.' An earlier collection of stories appeared in 1965, essays in 1970. Papers at the Univ. of Maryland, letters at Princeton Univ. and the Univ. of Texas. See life by Joan Givner, 1982; J. K. DeMouy, *KAP's Women*, 1983; Blanche H. Gelfant in *Women Writing*, 1984; study by Darlene Harbour Unrue, 1985 (with bibliog.); Anne Goodwyn Jones on KAP and William Faulkner in *Women's Studies*, 13, 1986; Givner, ed., *Katherine Anne Porter: Conversations*, 1987.

Porter, Rose, 1845–1906, poet and novelist, b. NYC, da. of Rose Anne (Hardy) and David P. She was educ. at private schools in NYC and spent a short time in her mother's native England before returning to a reclusive life with her mother in New Haven, Conn. Her first book, *Summer Driftwood for the Winter Fire*, 1870, received warm reviews in the USA and was pub. in England and in French and German translations. She was prolific, writing over 70 titles in all. Her prose, although pious and too sentimental for modern taste, was praised by her contemporaries for its freedom from sentimentality. Many of her volumes are collections of poetry and miscellaneous quotations, often arranged as daybooks, with space for sketches, notes and pressed flowers. They include *Thoughts for Women from Famous Women*, 1893, *About Men: What Women Have Said*, 1895 (featuring both positive and negative comments from European and US writers), and *Shakespeare's Men and Women*, 1898.

Porter, Sarah (Martyn), d. 1831, poet of Plymouth, NH, who m. physician John P. in 1767 and had five children. Her two highly accomplished poems were pub. together at Concord, 1791: *The Royal Penitent. In Three Parts* and subsidiary *David's Lamentation over Saul and Jonathan*. She quotes Pope on her title-page, and writes in stylish heroic couplets, presenting biblical events through eighteenth-century heroic spectacles. David appears amid parterres and orange-trees; when he prays 'Swift to the skies the wing'd petition flew, / And from above, a radiant Seraph drew; / A sudden light dispels the sable gloom.' Like Dryden, she turns a deliberately anachronistic tone to political ends. David's sin of having Bathsheba's husband killed for his lust is made to comment on American leaders' lust for power and wealth; the *Lamentation* calls to mind fallen Revolutionary heroes.

Potter, Helen **Beatrix**, later Heelis, 1866–1943, author–illustrator, sheep-breeder. B.

in London, da. of Helen (Leech) and Rupert P., wealthy but staid and protective, she was educ. at home, in her 'unloved birthplace' in Bolton Gardens. Her solitary childhood, with few toys and access only to Scott and Maria EDGEWORTH as reading, was enlivened by the pet mice, rabbit and hedgehog she secretly raised in her third-floor nursery world. Her delight in scientific study and drawing of plant and animal life, painstakingly accurate as well as whimsically anthropomorphic, was a buffer against the strict monotony of her life. Her brief engagement to Norman Warne, when both were nearing 40, was opposed by her parents; she surprised them doubly by recovering from Warne's death through the purchase of Hill Top Farm in Sawrey, where her greatest artistic period began. In eight years she wrote and illustrated 13 books, creating such nursery favourites as Jeremy Fisher, Tom Kitten, Jemima Puddle-Duck, Mrs Tittlemouse, Tabitha Twitchit and Miss Moppet. Hers is the perfectly realized yet gently ironic world of the bucolic miniaturist in which, although tragedy is averted, anthropomorphism exists alongside a truthful respect for animal nature. She admitted 'a jealous appreciation' for the work of 'the pioneers', Walter Crane and Randolph Caldecott, yet dismissed Kate Greenaway as someone who 'could not draw'. Her 1913 marriage to country solicitor, William Heelis, her adviser on land purchases, signalled the end of this creative outpouring but also the start of her real contentment. She became a good farmer and an expert breeder of sheep, being elected President of the Herdwick Association, and worked tirelessly for the National Trust to preserve the natural beauty of the Lake District. See her code journal transcribed and ed. Leslie Linder, 1989; selected letters, ed. Judy Taylor, 1989; memoir by Ulla Hyde Parker, 1981; life by Margaret Lane, 1946; study by Linder, 1971; critical biography by Ruth MacDonald, 1986.

Pound, Louise, 1872–1958, scholar, teacher and athlete. She was b. at Lincoln, Neb., da. of Laura (Biddlecombe) and Stephen Bosworth P., judge and senator. With two siblings, she was educ. by her mother (finder of many previously unidentified prairie wildflowers) before entering the Univ. of Nebraska's preparatory Latin School by examination in 1886, then the univ. itself. She became a friend of Willa CATHER, was class orator and poet, and earned a man's varsity letter as tennis champion in men's singles and doubles. She taught at Nebraska, 1894–1945, receiving her MA in 1895 (Neb.), and PhD in 1900 (Heidelberg, where she finished in two semesters a degree which normally took seven). She also won fame for long-distance bicycling and basketball. In many articles and collections, and by example, she pioneered the extension of academic study to include American literature, language, and especially BALLADS. Her *Poetic Origins and the Ballad*, 1921, and *American Ballads and Songs*, 1922, were both groundbreakers. She strove to improve women's opportunities in univs. and in competitive sports, by lecturing to women's groups throughout Nebraska as well as by institutional office-holding. In 1954–5 she was elected first woman president of the MLA and also first woman in the Nebraska Sports Hall of Fame. Some autobiographical material was pub. in the *Nebraska Alumnus*, 1942, and short pieces in *Selected Writings*, 1949, and *Nebraska Folklore*, 1959. Papers at the Nebraska State Hist. Soc. and Univ. of Neb. (Lincoln). See Evelyn Haller in *The Nebraska Humanist*, 7, 1984.

Powell, Dawn, 1897–1965, novelist and journalist, b. at Mount Gilead, Ohio, one of three das. of Hattie B. (Sherman) and Roy K. P. Her mother d. early; DP was raised by various farming and urban working-class relations. She wrote stories very early: when she was 12 her hated new stepmother burned her writings and she ran away to live with an aunt and attend high school at

Shelby, Ohio, where she edited the school magazine and worked for a local paper. With a BA from Lake Erie College, 1918 (where she founded a 'secret paper', and edited the college magazine), she moved to NYC for a brief spell in the US Naval Reserve, married Joseph Roebuck Gousha, an advertising man, and had a son. She published a novel, *Whither*, in 1924, but later disliked it, and called *She Walks in Beauty*, 1928 (pub. after 36 rejections), her first. She wrote plays (*Big Night*, staged 1933, *Jig Saw*, staged and pub. 1934; *Lady Comes Across*, a musical, staged 1941, and later collaborative work), radio, TV, and film scripts, and stories. *Angels on Toast*, 1940, was revised as *A Man's Affair*, 1956. *Sunday, Monday and Always*, 1952 (pieces from *The New Yorker* and elsewhere), juxtaposes one male narrator self-deluded about his power over an old flame, with another whose old love, ceremonially visited, is dead. Her nearly 20 novels draw on varied childhood experience (directly autobiographical in *My Home is Far Away*, 1944; not so in, e.g., *The Story of a Country Boy*, 1934, where a businessman idealizes his distant rural roots until forced by the depression to return to them); on NYC life in *Turn, Magic Wheel*, 1936 (male novelist protagonist), and *The Locusts Have No King*, 1948 (pursuit of success); and on both in *A Time to be Born*, 1942 (three women from Ohio surviving in the city), and *The Golden Spur*, 1962 (young man from Ohio tracing his mother's NY career). Likened to Muriel SPARK, DP is widely seen as a biting satirist of the middle class, though she herself saw her work as realistically observed. See Matthew Josephson in *SoR*, 9, 1973; Gore Vidal in *NYRB*, 34, 5 November 1987.

Powys, Caroline (Girle), 1738–1817, diarist, only child of Barbara (Slaney) and well-to-do London physician John G. (d. 1761). Her letter-journals to him, full of the detail he requested, began on a trip to Norfolk in 1756 and continued on annual travels around England; she describes 'the dreaded coronation' of 1761. Fearing 'rusticity' and tedium, she yet hoped to gain with practice 'the honorary title of an expert journalist'. Men's laziness and dread of being outshone, she suggested, kept women from 'being made acquainted with various subjects they are now ignorant of'. After 1762, when she and Philip Lybbe P. of Hardwick Hall, Oxon., 'agreed – he to love, and I to love and obey', her diary entries grew briefer; but she remained a good observer, especially of country houses and social life: selecs. of diaries and letters, in several private hands, ed. Emily J. Climenson, 1899.

Poyntz, Anne B., English letter writer whose gender must be taken on trust (no connection with Anna Maria (Mordaunt) P., d. 1771, dedicatee of Sarah FIELDING's *The Governess*). She says she had meant proposals for her *Je Ne Scai Quoi, or A Collection of Letters, Odes &c*, 1769 (by subscription), to call her 'a Woman', not 'a Lady' (as the printer did), in hopes to escape censure for female follies and even amorousness. Her title-page adapts Pope on the poet and 'her' muse; her dedication, as 'The Authorling, Parnassus Valley, April 1, 1768', 'To the Greatest and most Universal of Country, Court or City Patrons', is printed in red 'as an emblem of those blushes I hourly wear, for the crimson guilt of publishing such mere, mere trifles'. The letters, from many places around London, are strenuously vivacious, packed with literary and dramatic quotations (even comparing textual variants of *Macbeth*) and semi-feminist asides ('the fates oppose our unfortunate sex from the cradle'; men 'love subjection in a woman, even though we only *make believe*'). She longs for the 'golden days' of 'a BEHN, a CENTLIVRE', but is not sorry to have seen 'a Con. PHIL[L]IPS, a PILKINGTON'. She calls her reputation 'singed', to a man admits her love of love, and to a recent bride hints obliquely at being debarred that 'happy lot'. The poems are few but accomplished.

Praed, Rosa (Murray-Prior), 1851–1935, novelist and dramatist, b. near Ipswich, Queensland, da. of Matilda (Harpur; niece of poet Charles H.) and Thomas M-P., later Postmaster-General of Queensland. Educ. briefly at a Brisbane school, by governesses and by her own extensive reading, she began writing at age ten. She m. Arthur Campbell P. in 1872, spent three years on Curtis Island, Qld, then settled in England. Of her four children, two died in accidents, one in a mental asylum, and one committed suicide. She attributed these tragedies to karmic retribution. Her marriage ended in 1899. She then lived with Nancy Harward, whom she believed to be the reincarnation of a slave from ancient Rome (and herself a priestess) as expounded in *Nyria*, 1904, and *The Soul of Nyria*, 1931, her last novel; other novels also dealt with occult subjects. She published three political works (with Justin McCarthy) and memoirs, *Australian Life: Black and White*, 1885, and *My Australian Girlhood*, 1902. *An Australian Heroine*, 1880, was the first of over 40 (mostly romantic) novels, of which half have Australian settings. Among the most successful was her second, *Policy and Passion*, 1881, with a mix of outback scenes and political intrigues, and a heroine forced to choose between a sexually magnetic but unprincipled Englishman and a dull but chivalrous Australian. Others, set in Europe, contained portraits of figures such as Oscar Wilde (Esme Colquhoun in *Affinities*, 1886). She adapted some for the stage, including 'Ariane' (performed 1888), based on *The Bond of Wedlock*, 1887 (repr. 1987), an exposé of the constraints of marriage. Marriage as a system of barter again comes under scrutiny in *Lady Bridget in the Never-Never Land*, 1915 (repr. 1987). Using the three central characters as separate narrators, RP formulates the ideal marriage based on the Australian male ethos of 'mateship'. See the intros. to 1987 reprints, and D. Spender in D. Adelaide, ed., *A Bright and Fiery Troop*, 1988. There is a bibliography by Chris Tiffin in *VFRG*, 15, 1989. RP's MSS are in the Oxley Library, Brisbane.

Preaching. Several seventeenth-century radical sects nurtured female preachers. QUAKERS included leading women who established from the outset their equal right and duty to preach. For many later-revered women ministers their first public speech was a more gruelling test than conversion itself. The issue of women's preaching underlay attacks on Elizabeth Barton, 'the Maid of Kent', 1525 (study by Alan Neame, 1971) and Anne Hutchinson, New England settler and charismatic leader, 1636 (studies by Selma R. Williams, 1981, Amy Schrager Lang, 1987); it remained a rock of offence from a sensational pamphlet of 1641 to Samuel Johnson in 1763. Women who pub. 'Sermons', like Mary DEVERELL and R. ROBERTS, were making a point, remote as they were from prophets like Hannah WHARTON. Methodist women like Mary FLETCHER did preach; John Wesley (introduced to Mary ASTELL's work by Sarah CHAPONE) often authorized individuals to do so (e.g. 1761, 1791), but only as exceptions. He advised Sarah Crosby (who found herself preaching when 200 turned up for a class) to 'just nakedly tell ... whatever is in your breast': a woman must be modest, careful of offending, and must not compete with 'a preacher'; the Wesleyans banned female preaching in 1803. Dinah Morris, in George ELIOT's *Adam Bede*, 1859, is probably the best-known fictional rendition of a female Methodist preacher. In the USA women preached both with and without a church's blessing, and the tradition of women preachers evolved naturally into secular preaching (e.g. for women's rights: see Lucretia MOTT). Antoinette BLACKWELL was the first ordained woman Unitarian (1853); she was followed by Julia Ward HOWE. Jarena LEE shows the opposition a woman might arouse, even in a black radical church. Nonetheless, she was soon joined by other black evangelists. Amanda

Smith, d. 1915, was 'called' in 1870, but her popularity with white congregations told against her; she took her preaching to Burma and India. Returning, poor, in 1890, she opened a school for black orphans and wrote her *Story of the Lord's Dealings with Mrs Amanda Smith the Colored Evangelist*, 1893 (repr. 1988). Anna SHAW was ordained in 1880 as the first American woman Methodist minister. In Australia, Catherine Helen SPENCE preached as a Unitarian in the 1880s. See Olive Anderson in *Historical Journal*, 12, 1969; Rosemary Ruether and Eleanor McLaughlin, *Women of Spirit: Female Leadership in the Jewish and Christian Traditions*, 1979; E. M. Williams in *Feminist Studies*, 8, 1982; study by Deborah M. Valenze, 1985 (including lives).

Prescod, Marsha, poet, brought to live and work in London by her West Indian parents in the 1950s. As a child she 'was always joining in and listening in to big women's conversations'. The Brixton writers' workshop, Black Ink, helped her poetry flourish from 1980; the Brent Black Music Workshop did the same for her performances of it. Her first book, *Land of Rope and Tory*, 1985, is full of wry political humour, like the second poem she wrote, still her favourite, 'Death by Self Neglect' (title from a coroner's verdict on a death in police custody). In it an international 'group a bigshot whitemen' claim to be 'nat'rally upset, / "Why dese darkies so wicked?" dey cry. / "We've tried so much good kindness for four hundred years, / An dey still go and selfishly die."' 'Womanist Blues' looks dubiously at inter-racial sisterhood ('We're gonna grab the Power, / You from your man, me from mine, / You'll get the wealth, technology, / Whilst I'll get a damn hard time') in keeping with MP's view that 'we've always caught hell as Black people, and then a little extra hell as women'. Caribbean culture, she says, makes art integral to everyday life, 'not highbrow, or obscure, or only for an elite': 'For us to be free / we have to know we / don't let anyone "ethnicize" us.' MP comments on her work in *City Limits*, 1 August 1985, and Lauretta NGCOBO, ed., *Let It Be Told: Black Women Writers in Britain*, 1988.

'Prescott, E. Livingston', Edith Katharine Spicer Jay, d. 1901, British military novelist, da. of Elizabeth Maria (Spicer) and Samuel J. Coming from an army family, though her father was a barrister, she knew military life very well. She wrote some 17 novels, chiefly military romances, others pub. by the RTS. Her first, *The Apotheosis of Mr Tyrawley*, 1896 [1895], which casts the heroine merely as moral inspiration, was followed by titles like *The Rip's Redemption. A Trooper's Story*, 1897. Too male-identified to be a feminist, she was Hon. Lady Superintendent of the London Soldiers' Home and Guards' Home until incapacitated by ill-health. Her pamphlet, *Flogging Not Abolished in the British Army*, 1897, was backed up in the novel *Scarlet and Steel*, 1897, which also describes flogging graphically. Her last three novels were pub. posthumously, up to 1904.

Preston, Harriet Waters, 1836–1911, translator and novelist, b. Danvers, Mass., da. of Lydia (Proctor) and Samuel P. As a young woman, she travelled to Europe, where she lived most of her life. Her first works were TRANSLATIONS: Saint-Beuve's *Portraits of Celebrated Women*, 1868, *The Writings of Madame Swetching*, ed. Count de Falloux, 1870, and Saint-Beuve's *Memoirs of Madame Desbordes-Valmore*, 1872. In 1871 she pub. her first creative work, *Aspendale*, followed by *Love in the Nineteenth Century; A Fragment*, 1873, both written in the form of 'essays' and letters, emphasizing social issues, criticism of other authors and feminism. Thus, for example, Clara, the heroine of *Love in the Nineteenth Century*, denies the claim that women act irrationally on instinct: 'What you clumsily call instinct in a woman is nothing more nor less than reasoning so rapid that you cannot count its steps ...'. Her three other novels are more conventional: *Is That All?*, 1876, pub. in No Name Series; *A Year in Eden*, a 'New World romance', 1887 and *The Guardians*, 1888, written with her niece Louise Preston Dodge. An acknowledged expert on Provençal literature, she translated *Mireio: A Provençal Poem* by F. Mistral in 1872, and *Troubadores and Trouveres: New and Old* in 1876. *The Georgics of Virgil* appeared in her translation in 1881, and with Dodge she wrote *The Private Life of the Romans*, 1893. She also contributed to the *Atlantic Monthly* and other journals. Her final work was an edition of E. B. BROWNING, 1900, with M. Le Baron Goddard. She returned to New England late in her life and died in Cambridge, Mass.

Preston, Margaret (Junkin), 1820–97, poet and fiction writer, b. Milton, Pa., first of eight children of Julia Rush (Miller) and George J. She was educ. in Latin, Greek and English literature by her father, and later by tutors from Lafayette College at Easton. Her first novel, *Silverwood*, 1856, was pub. anon. In 1857 she m. John T. L. P., professor of Latin at Virginia Military Institute; she had two sons. Siding with the Confederacy during the Civil War, MJP next pub. *Beechenbrook: A Rhyme of the War*, 1865, about a Southern wife's travails. *Old Song and New*, 1870, and *Cartoons*, 1875, for the most part treat Biblical, classical and sentimental themes. Her dramatic monologues, many of them conceived from paintings, reflect her admiration for Robert and E. B. BROWNING's poetry. In 'Errina's Spinning', the speaker chafes against her mother's advice to 'rend thy scrolls, and keep thee to thy spinning'; like young Aurora Leigh, she prefers her father's classical learning and her own poetic ambitions to 'matron dignities'. MJP's step-daughter, Elizabeth Preston Allan, printed MJP's diary of the war years in *The Life and Letters of MJP*, 1903. The Univ. of NC holds a collection of her papers.

Prichard, Katharine Susannah, 1883–1969, novelist, short-story writer and political activist, b. Levuka, Fiji, da. of Edith Isabel (Fraser), governess, and Tom Henry P., then ed. of the *Fiji Times*. She was educ. at home in Melbourne, Victoria, and at South Melbourne College, where the headmaster, poet J. B. O'Hara, encouraged her to write; she pub. her first story at 16. Too poor to attend university, she worked as a governess on large country properties and later as a teacher and journalist, and edited the women's page of the Melbourne *Herald*. She worked in London and Europe, writing her first novel, *The Pioneers*, 1915 (filmed the following year), which won an English publisher's competition. In 1919 she married war hero Hugo Throssell and moved to his home near Perth, Western Australia, the setting for many of her later novels, including two of her finest, *Working Bullocks*, 1926, and *Coonardoo*, 1929, controversial for its frank portrayal of sexual relations between Aboriginal women and white men. *Brumby Innes*, a play dealing with the same material, won an award in 1927 (pub. only 1940, staged only 1972). In 1920 she became a founding member of the Communist Party of Australia and in 1933 visited the Soviet Union, as recorded in *The Real Russia*, 1934. While she was away, her husband, suffering business losses, committed suicide. Fearing he had read the draft of her novel *Intimate Strangers*, 1937, which originally ended with the husband's suicide, she changed the ending to one of reconciliation. A Nobel Prize nominee, she pub. 12 novels, five collections of stories, two vols. of poetry, an autobiography, *Child of the Hurricane*, 1963, and political pamphlets and articles, some of which have been coll. in *Straight Left*, 1982. Her trilogy dealing with workers in the goldfields of Western Australia and the growth of the mining industry – *The Roaring Nineties*, 1946, *Golden Wings*, 1948, and *Winged Seeds*, 1950 – was highly praised. Her last novel, *Subtle Flame*, 1967, deals with the nuclear issue.

Her son, Ric Throssell, has ed. *Tribute, Sel. Stories of KSP*, 1988. Her MSS, including some fine unpub. plays, are in the National Library, Canberra. There is a monograph by Henrietta DRAKE-BROCKMAN, 1967, a non-committal biography by Ric Throssell, 1975, and some helpful articles, 1985 (ed. Carole Ferrier).

Primrose, Diana, poet, and 'Noble Lady' who dedicated to 'All Noble Ladies, and Gentle-women' *A Chaine of Pearle*, 1630, in memory of ELIZABETH I, with prefatory verse praise by the otherwise unknown Dorothy Berry. Her 'Pearly-Rowes' are poems on Religion ('Shee bang'd the Pope'), Chastity, Prudence (a gift 'rarely incident / To our weake Sex'), Temperance, Clemency, Justice, Fortitude (praise of the queen's speech at Tilbury), Science or intellectual ability (more praise of her speeches), Patience and Bounty. DP displays knowledge of history and of Latin. Her opinion of women in general is not high; her praise of Elizabeth implies contrast with Charles I. John Nichols in 1823 ascribed her work to Lady Anne CLIFFORD.

Prince, Mary, *c.* 1788–after 1833, slave and autobiographer. Da. of slaves (a house-servant and a sawyer), she was b. at Brackish Pond, Bermuda. With her mother and younger siblings, she was shielded from the worst of slavery by her owner's wife and daughter till she was 11, when he suddenly sold them, not together. A new 'savage mistress' hung MP up naked by the wrists for flogging. With housework and fieldwork, there 'was no end to my toils – no end to my blows ... my heavy lot to weep, weep, weep, and that for years'. She wished to die; when she ran away her father unwillingly returned her. Ten years in the Turk Island salt pans, from *c.* 1806, were equally cruel. Back in Bermuda MP was probably sexually abused, though she mentions only being made to wash her master in his bath. In Antigua, although crippled with rheumatism, she traded for earnings to buy her freedom. Methodists converted her (with 'the first prayers I ever understood'); she learned to read. In 1826 she m. Daniel Jones, a free black carpenter, but, as a slave, had not 'much happiness in my marriage'. Her owners (still refusing to sell her, apparently enraged by her independence of mind) took her to London and threw her out after a row about washing. She was befriended by Moravians, the Anti-Slavery Society, the future Susanna MOODIE (her amanuensis and witness of her scars), and Thomas Pringle, who employed her, submitted her petition to parliament, and ed. and pub. her work, 1831, as a plea for emancipation (repr. 1987, ed. Moira Ferguson). With failing health and sight, MP was attacked by James Macqueen in *Blackwood's*, 1833.

Prince, Nancy (Gardener), TRAVEL writer, b. free in 1799 of mixed African-Indian ancestry, in Newburyport, Mass. She went into service at eight, but aspired to be a teacher, author and humanitarian. At 14 she went to work in Salem, but became ill, then religious. In 1824 she m. a Mr Prince, servant of a Russian princess in the Czar's court. They sailed to Russia; she began a successful business making baby linen, and learned modern Greek, French and 'high' English. After nine years she returned alone to the USA and her husband died before he could rejoin her. She met Lucretia MOTT and became involved in ABOLITION, and pub. *A Narrative of the Life and Travels of Mrs Nancy Prince*, which included an account of her visit to Jamaica in 1850, repr. in *Collected Black Women's Narratives*, Schomburg Library Series, 1988. See Ann Shockley, *Afro-American Women Writers*, 1988, for her life; also Hazel V. Carby, *Reconstructing Womanhood*, 1987.

Procter, Adelaide Anne, 1825–64, English poet, eldest da. of Anne Benson (Skepper) and Bryan Waller P. ('Barry Cornwall', 1787–1874), who encouraged her in languages, mathematics, art and music.

Her first pub. poem was 'Ministering Angels', which appeared in Heath's *Book of Beauty* in 1843. In 1851 she became a Roman Catholic and in 1853 paid an extended visit to her aunt, Emily de Viry, at the Turin court, where she became interested in the Piedmontese people and dialects. In 1853–4 she had poems pub. under the name 'Miss Mary Berwick' in Dickens's *Household Words*. Her first collection, *Legends and Lyrics*, 1858, was dedicated to Matilda HAYS whom she met doing work for the employment of women. She then became involved with the work of Emily FAITHFULL, editing for the VICTORIA PRESS the ANTHOLOGY of verse and prose, *Victoria Regia*, 1861, designed to display the skills of women. Her only other pub. work was *A Chaplet of Verse*, 1861, pub. for the benefit of the Providence Row Night Refuge for Homeless Women and Children, and including her well-known poem 'Homeless', which ironically contrasts the comparative comfort of criminals with that of the destitute child. Her best poems are in *Legends and Lyrics*, introduced by Charles Dickens, and reprinted regularly up to WWI, and including 'A Woman's Question', asking how much a man concedes in marriage, 'A Lost Chord' and 'A Woman's Answer'. Her excellent narrative poems include 'The Wayside Inn', 'The Sailor Boy', 'A New Mother', 'Philip and Mildred', 'Three Evenings in a Life' and 'The Legend of Provence', which deals very boldly with the idea of the 'fallen' woman. She d. at home after a long illness.

Pseudonyms. Real and assumed names are often, from Jane ANGER writing in 1588, hard to distinguish. Despite intense vigilance, this book probably also treats a few fictitious individuals as accurately named. Some celebrated enigmas ('EPHELIA', 'SOPHIA') *may* be well known under other names. Women were probably early users of witty polemical names (Esther SOWERNAM); inhibition against public appearance (see also ANON) made romance names popular. 'Orinda', self-chosen by Katherine PHILIPS, is of the same type as 'Stella', bestowed by Sir Philip Sidney; for probably the most widely used of these, see 'FIDELIA'. Mary ASTELL used six different title-page designations (not so much names as descriptions), and Mary ROBINSON, 1758–1800, at least nine separate names. One of Astell's was the discreet, conciliating 'A Lady', much used for over two centuries by poets, novelists, and other writers. It was appropriated for camouflage by men, like philosopher George Berkeley for *The Ladies Library* (an ADVICE collection), 1714, and, less predictably, for *Maxims on Patriotism*, 1751. Some names came from entrepreneurs, not writers. The fly-by-night Edmund Curll claimed to publish women like Mary HEARNE, whose reality remains dubious; he gave his 'Lady Margaret Pennyman', 1740, some attributes which prove her non-existence. Women's names had particular drawing-power for pornography (seldom a female genre): they include 'Dorothy Noake', 1735, 'Mrs E. Slade', 1743, and 'Sarah Paul', 1760. Some novelists of this time, like Alethea LEWIS, had a regular *nom de plume*, often exotic-sounding, sometimes alternating with their own; others used a pseudonym once and never again. While men assumed female gender to exploit a market (Oliver Goldsmith as 'Mrs Stanhope' in *The Lady's Magazine* from 1759), or in blatant mockery (William Beckford as 'Jacqueta Agneta Mariana Jenks', 1797), women sought the authority conferred by masculinity, most famously the BRONTËS and George ELIOT. US women of this period rarely adopted male pseudonyms, but were often fanciful, e.g. 'Fanny FERN', 'Grace GREENWOOD' and 'PANSY'. Magazine contributors, female and male, frequently wrote pseudonymously, often to disguise their ubiquity. Attribution, already problematic with women writers, is often rendered more complicated by this habit. Collaborative writers sometimes chose a single name, e.g. 'Michael FIELD'. In the twentieth century a pseudonym sometimes implies a second identity. Germaine GREER writes novels as 'Rose Blight', Carolyn HEILBRUN as 'Amanda Cross' (because, she says, 'Secrecy is power'). Joyce Carol OATES has written a thriller, 1987, as 'Rosamond Smith'. Scandal has been caused by Doris LESSING writing as 'Jane Somers' and the Rev. Toby Forward writing as 'Rahila Khan'. Alice SHELDON, writing as 'James Tiptree, Jr.', was described by a critic as 'ineluctably masculine'. 'Rosamund Clay', author of *Only Angels Forget*, Virago 1990, is identified only as 'a well-known woman writer'. 'Jean PLAIDY' can use half-a-dozen or more names, each one carefully matched to a slightly different image: gothic, family saga, historical romance, etc. Women often choose mothers' or grandmothers' names; Rebecca WEST and ANNA LIVIA chose names from the creations of admired male authors. Self-naming offers the chance to achieve uniqueness – COLETTE, Genêt (Janet FLANNER), BRYHER – or to shed a historically imposed racial or patriarchal association: Ntozake SHANGE, Louky BERSIANIK. Alice Kahler Marshall, *Pennames of Women Writers*, 1985, should be used with caution.

Psychoanalytic feminist criticism in the Anglo-American tradition follows a period of resistance, spearheaded in the US by Kate MILLETT, Betty FRIEDAN, and others, and in the UK by Eva FIGES and Germaine GREER. Like their French sisters, Anglo-American feminists reassess Simone de BEAUVOIR's humanistic and existentialist critique of Freud's representation of women as incomplete men who, lacking phallic autonomy, cannot fully exist as self-determining individuals nor enter the dialectic of history. Disillusioned with de Beauvoir's Hegelian aim of dispensing with the notion of sexual difference by extending to women the transcendental conditions of Man, neo-Freudian feminists have sought to recover a (post)-structuralist, psychoanalytic theory to account for the psycho-genesis of sexual difference in language and society. Anglo-American feminism first came to psychoanalysis through the influence of Lacanian readings of Freud. Juliet Mitchell introduced British socialist feminists to the radical materialist critique of bourgeois patriarchal culture afforded by psychoanalysis. Mitchell was herself a socialist feminist for some time before entertaining psychoanalysis as a necessary theoretical supplement for interpreting and transforming sexual relations. Inspired by Althusser's incorporation of Lacanian psychoanalysis in his Marxist reading of the unconscious as the site of bourgeois ideology, she extends his analytical model to feminism. *Psychoanalysis and Feminism*, 1977, represents and champions Lacan's/Freud's theorization of the Oedipal unconscious as a radical 'critique' of identity and a disclosure of the economic and symbolic structuring of the patriarchal family. From this materialist perspective she sees the family as the site of the production and reproduction of a repressive female psychology manifested in society as the largest class of oppressed and alienated labourers – women. *Women: the Longest Revolution*, 1984, carries Mitchell's Marxist-psychoanalytic-feminist reading of the socio-symbolic order into literary criticism. In her campaign to redirect feminist anti-Freudians, Mitchell is supported by Jacqueline Rose, who champions (the feminist use of) Lacan against feminist rejections of psychoanalytic notions of the unconscious. Both present psychoanalysis as feminism's most plausible theory by which to interpret the ideological and material conditions governing the formation (and possible transformation) of the feminine subject. Their *Feminine Sexuality*, 1982, prints some of Lacan's essays, which they hail as a breakthrough reconceptualization of sexual difference as the differential 'desire for the phallus as master signifier'. In *Sexuality in the Field of Vision*, 1986, Rose advances a Freudian-Lacanian reading of 'Femininity and its Discontents'.

Shoshana Felman and Jane Gallop are also indebted to Lacan, but they differ in making their allegiance to him explicit and primary, feminism being a 'secondary' allegiance. Felman's feminist criticism, limited to two influential articles, is tangential to her primary purpose of introducing Lacan's/Freud's theory and practice of reading to critical audiences. In 'Women and Madness: the Critical Phallacy', 1975, and 'Re-reading Femininity', 1981, Felman reads 'specimen texts' for an 'uncanny' or ambiguous inscription of femininity which rhetorically undermines and undoes the (masculine) reading and writing subject. Though she extends the psychoanalytic reading list to include Henry James and Honoré de Balzac as well as Freud's Hoffman and Lacan's Poe, she does not venture to apply her Freudian reading lesson to women's writing. Gallop's *The Daughter's Seduction: Feminism and Psychoanalysis*, 1982, foregrounds the problematical interplay between the two (discursive) practices whose smooth conjunction Mitchell's earlier work had sought to promote. She stages French feminism's (IRIGARAY's, KRISTEVA's, CIXOUS's, Catherine Clément's, Michèle Montrelay's, Eugénie Lemoine-Luccioni's) different and somewhat conflicting readings of Lacan. Her concern here, as in *Reading Lacan*, 1987, is not to disclose means by which feminism might derive variant textual strategies from psychoanalysis, but to expose its ineffectual divergence from the master craftsman. Peggy Kamuf's *Fictions of Feminine Desire*, 1982, exemplifies feminist appropriation of psychoanalysis for the production of reading strategies to disclose the figure of (excessively) desiring woman, inscribed in the (con)textual, patriarchal enclosures. Mary Jacobus's *Reading Woman*, and Margaret Homans's *Bearing the Word*, both 1986, exemplify recent Anglo-American applications of Lacanian-based feminist theory. Jacobus adapts Felman's 'uncanny' to her reading of the critical difference in women's writing (notably George ELIOT and Charlotte BRONTË). For Felman the figure of (woman's) 'madness' in men's writing is the crucial site of textual undoing where phallic discourse collapses; for Jacobus it is, in women's writing, the site signifying 'emergence' of the Other (non-phallic, non-definable) woman. Jacobus reconsiders Felman's 'uncanny' in the light of Mitchell's, Irigaray's and Kristeva's (discourse of the) 'hysteric', advocating the reading of woman's 'lunacy' (as exemplified by Eliot's 'The Lifted Veil' and Charlotte Perkins GILMAN's *The Yellow Wallpaper*) not as a symptom of unnerving, phallic instability but as a sign of revolutionary rupture in the prison-house of language. Informed by Lacan and Kristeva as seen through the lens of Nancy Chodorow's 'feminized' object-relations theory, Homans focuses on textual sites where narrative discourse gives way to poetic, solipsistic musings, and displays 'the articulation of non-symbolic mother–daughter language'. She revises Kristeva's notion of the 'semiotic', not as a symptom of woman's 'psychotic' denial of symbolic castration but as evidence of women's capacity to 'speak in two languages at once', and she claims that this 'non-symbolic mother–daughter language' is produced not by constitutional repression but by institutional 'suppression and silencing'. The prevalence of the semiotic in women's writing indicates that the pre-Oedipal, mother–daughter relationship survives into adulthood, that women are not 'castrated' to the degree men are, that their allegiance to the phallus and to figurative language is not the same as men's, that women writers take pleasure in making literal representations of this primary, imaginary dyad (whereas men flee from the literal in fear of losing their identity). Homans implicitly aligns her approach with Sandra GILBERT's and Susan Gubar's 'madwoman-in-the-attic' thesis that women's literary language is as much a symptom of suppression as it is a sign of protest. American psychoanalytical feminist criticism owes much to the innovative, interventionist readings of Freud by Nancy Chodorow and Dorothy Dinnerstein. Chodorow's *The Reproduction of Mothering*, 1975, borrows from object-relations theory (D. W. Winnicot, Robert Stollers) to interpret clinical experience of mother–daughter relations. She attributes women's greater (men's lesser) sense of communion with others to an enduring memory of the mother–infant relationship and to the daughter's evasion of 'castration' (though she cannot, as Hester Eisenstein points out, account for why women turn to heterosexuality and childbearing as opposed to lesbianism). In *The Mermaid and the Minotaur*, 1975, Dinnerstein critiques the popular myth of gender 'symbiosis' (the 'natural' view which identifies woman with undifferentiated, primal matter or some mermaid-like manifestation of the pre-Oedipal mother, and which identifies man with the minotaur's beastly struggle against the maternal 'cosmos' to become a separate entity). Dinnerstein sees this myth as culturally devastating, attributing it not to essential, archetypal differences but to society's assignment of mothering exclusively to women. For other interventionist readings of Freud's 'femininity', see Sarah Kofman's deconstructive analysis, *The Enigma of Women* (French ed., 1980, transl. 1985), Catherine Clément's post-Lacanian 'The Guilty One' in *The Newly Born Woman*, French ed., 1975, transl. 1986, and *The Weary Sons of Freud*, French ed., 1978, transl. 1987, and Juliet Flower-MacCannell, *Figuring Lacan*, 1986. For critical surveys of the theoretical field which see beyond the unhappy marriage of psychoanalysis and feminism, see Toril Moi, *Sexual/Textual Politics*, 1985, Alice Jardine, *Gynesis*, 1985, Naomi Schor, '"Female Paranoia"; the Case for a Psychoanalytic Feminist Criticism', *Yale French Studies*, 62, 1981. Psychoanalytic feminism has made its impact on feminist FILM THEORY: see Laura Mulvey in *Screen* 16, 1975. Teresa de Lauretis, *Alice Doesn't*, 1984, *Technologies of Gender*, 1987, and Kaja Silverman, *The Acoustic Mirror*, 1988. Shirley Nelson Garner, et al., eds., *The (M)other Tongue*, 1985, collects feminist-psychoanalytic readings of Freud, patriarchal texts, and women's writing (of woman).

Publishing. The first English woman printer was probably Elizabeth (Pickering) Redman in 1539. Like other trades, this one was often successfully taken over by widows (like the writer Elinor JAMES) from their husbands. For women in the English book trade in the seventeenth and eighteenth centuries see Judith E. Gardner in *Gutenberg Jahrbuch*, 1978, Margaret Hunt in *Women in History*, 9, 1984. The first press in North America was landed at Boston by Elizabeth (Harris) Glover after her husband died at sea (see Frances Hamill in *PBSA*, 49, 1955; Madelon Golden Schilpp and Sharon M. Murphy on American women printers, 1983). During the eighteenth and nineteenth centuries several British women writers (Mary BRYAN, Ann FISHER) ran publishing firms. Many women, especially writers of 'improving' fiction aimed at girls, published with the SPCK or RTS in England (both exploiters of their authors), or the ASSU in the US. Later, female publishers took positive action towards making women's voices heard. In England Emily FAITHFULL founded the VICTORIA PRESS in 1860. With Emma Anne Paterson she launched the Women's Printing Society in 1876 to pursue feminist goals. Paterson began the *Woman's Union Journal* the same year. In the US Austin Holyoake established the Female Printing Office in 1860. Geraldine JEWSBURY wielded influence as a publisher's reader for Bentley's in the 1860s and 70s. Much publishing activity was generated by the SUFFRAGE movement. Emmeline PETHICK-LAWRENCE and her husband started *Votes for Women* in 1907 ('to all women all over the world of whatever race or creed or calling'), and while police hunted Christabel PANKHURST it remained her means of keeping 'the trumpet sounding'. The

Woman's Press (fl. 1910s) published works by members of the Women's Freedom League, including Mary GAWTHORPE's *Votes for Women* and C. C. STOPES's *The Constitutional Basis of Women's Suffrage*. The (later 'International') Suffrage Shop published e.g. Christopher ST JOHN and Charlotte DESPARD. The Women Writers' Suffrage League, founded in June 1908 by Cicely HAMILTON and Bessie Hatton, published a number of pamphlets by members and others, including May SINCLAIR's *Feminism*, 1912. (See Stanley Paul, *The Suffrage Annual and Women's Who's Who*, 1913.) At the same time, women were making powerful literary MAGAZINES and, having won a substantial place in commercial publication (see POPULAR FICTION), were seeking access to the less welcoming organs of 'high art' publishing. Benstock, 1986, documents the significance to writers in the twenties and thirties of the small press movement: Nancy CUNARD, Alice TOKLAS, BRYHER, Caresse CROSBY, engaged in the development of publishing outlets; H. D., STEIN, Djuna BARNES, and many others were given a voice by these. The Hogarth Press, established by Leonard and Virginia WOOLF, made her, she said, 'the only woman in England free to write what I like', and also brought to notice many other women, and several books on women's issues.

Feminist publishing has flourished since the 1960s. The Feminist Press, founded in New York by Florence Howe, 1970, has since moved to the State Univ. of NY at Old Westbury: its publishing programme (rediscovered texts, such as Rebecca Harding DAVIS, *Life in the Iron Mills*, women's studies texts, biographies, and, for six years from 1974, the *Women's Studies Newsletter*) has reflected and reinforced the lines of inquiry taken by women's studies. In the UK, Virago, The Women's Press, and Pandora (now owned by Routledge Kegan Paul) have made available a wide range of novels, poems, plays, biographies, autobiographies, letters, critical studies by women (some reprinted), and have opened the possibility of transformed curricula in literary studies. The women's publishing movement is richly international, multi-vocal: The Women's Press in Toronto, founded 1972, has focused on economic and social matters; a South African Press, Seriti sa Sechaba Publishers, puts out a women's fiction series; Kali for Women, India's first feminist publishing house, founded 1984, publishes Indian women's writing in many languages and books on women's issues; Flora NWAPA's Tana Press in Nigeria publishes work for children, including hers; the Redress Press and Sybylla Press are among a number of radical women's presses in Australia; the Attic Press, Dublin, is a women's press publishing poetry, fiction, pamphlets and handbooks. In the US, the lesbian-feminist Naiad Press – founded by Gene Damon (Barbara Grier) and Jeannette Foster, who edited *The Ladder*, a magazine of lesbian fiction, 1956–72 – has published bibliographies, ANTHOLOGIES, collections of reviews, and novels; Garland reprinted early novels by women during the 1970s; Out-and-Out Books, 1975, founded by Joan Larkin, has published Jan CLAUSEN, Irene KLEPFISZ, and Elly Bulkin's and Larkin's anthology of lesbian writing; The Shameless Hussy Press, founded by ALTA and Susan GRIFFIN, has also published lesbian writers; The Kitchen Table Women of Color Press (of Albany, NY) is committed to publishing and distributing the writing of 'Third World women of all racial/cultural heritages, sexualities and classes'. In the UK, Onlywomen, the sole radical lesbian press, publishes ANNA LIVIA, among others; Stramullion Press, Edinburgh, publishes work by and about Scottish women; the Sheba Press publishes works by many nationalities, races, ages; the Black Womantalk Collective publishes works by black women. The Women in Publishing group serves employees of every kind of firm. See Polly Joan and Andrea Chapman, *Guide to Women's*

Publishing, 1978, and Leah Fritz in *WRB*, Feb. and Sept. 1986.

Pugh, Sheenagh, poet, translator, b. 1950 in Birmingham of Irish and Welsh parents. She studied Russian and German at Bristol Univ., settled in Wales in 1971 and worked at the Welsh Office. She is married with two children. She began publishing with initials only, to conceal her sex. Her five volumes of poetry are *Crowded by Shadows*, 1977, *What a Place to Grow Flowers*, 1980, *Earth Studies and other Voyages*, 1982 (which looks back, from the vantage point of space, at our planet with affection and regret, and at earlier travellers like the Norsemen with sensitive particularity), *Prisoners of Transience*, 1982 (from French and German), and *Beware Falling Tortoises*, 1987. 'Literature' declares, 'I like minor voices, / semi-precious stones'; 'In memory 2: A matter of scale' tells how 'Even on his own planet / the most people did not know him; / in his own country, his own town, / his loss was a small matter. // Only in a few lives / is a void left, wider / than a town could fill, or a planet, / or the great sun Aldebaran.' SP deploys felicitous images: 'What is become of the dark bats flaking / like ash off the evening' ('Biology 2'); 'The crops' patchwork on the slopes, the weather-whorls / etched in the faces' ('Saga patterns'). Directly political poems (like 'Because', contributed to the Welsh anthology *Poets Against Apartheid*, 1986) focus their message by repetition and the immediacy of song; perhaps most successful are those that deal with language itself, like 'A shipwrecked Inuit learns Gaelic from a Hebridean'. In *Poetry Wales*, 23, 1987, she argues strongly that minds (and poems) do not 'have genders', but transcend 'sex, race, culture and even death': 'A poet, of all people, should be above putting people in categories, judging them as a group rather than as individuals.'

Purbeck, Elizabeth and **Jane**, sisters and joint novelists publishing at London. They began in 1789 with *Honoria Sommerville*, an entertaining, effective heroine's progress from foundling babyhood, via reunion with her mother (who had nurtured an unworthy changeling), to 'that real happiness so seldom experienced by humanity' – though the good are sure of it hereafter. The hero of *William Thornborough, The Benevolent Quixote*, 1791, a would-be Sir Charles Grandison, is mainly a linking device for disparate episodes; that of the very gently satirical *History of Sir George Warrington, or The Political Quixote*, 2nd ed., 1797 (often misascribed to Charlotte Lennox), takes up with Tom Paine and the French Revolution but is distracted by falling in love, and learns from English social snobbery that equality is impracticable. They used epistolary form for *Raynsford Park*, 1790, *Matilda and Elizabeth*, 1796 (one sister is marriageable, one thinks herself widowed until her lost husband resurfaces from the American war), and *Neville Castle*, 1802 (publication delayed some years by illness and melancholy; its qualified sympathy for the French Revolution dates from before the Terror). It interestingly discusses novelists, notably Sophia Lee and Frances Burney, who is preferred to Richardson or Fielding.

Purcell, Sally, poet and translator, b. 1944 at Stockport, Cheshire, da. of Hilda May (Ingram) and Robert Joseph P. She was educ. at Lady Margaret Hall, Oxford (BA in medieval French, 1966). She also learned Greek, Latin, Old and Middle English, and modern mediterranean languages. While working in bars, offices, and orchards, she has translated from Charles d'Orléans (poet, 1391–1465), 1968; from French Provençal troubadours, including women, 1969; from Hélène Cixous (*The Exile of James Joyce*), 1972; from Greek (pieces in Peter Jay's Penguin anthology, 1973; from Nikos Gatsos, 1980); from Dante, 1981. She has edited (with Libby Purves) *The Happy Unicorns*, 1971 (including poems by Sara Maitland and Val Warner); *Monarchs and the Muse*, 1972 (going back to

ELIZABETH I); and D. G. Rossetti's English versions of Italian poets, 1981. Her poetry volumes from *The Devil's Dancing Hour*, 1968, deal with medieval and classical themes. Elusiveness is evoked in moments of past or future, dream states and half-lights: 'My withered shadow runs before the wind.' In *The Holly Queen*, 1971, she writes, 'Bale-fires on the dark moor / light your journey' to 'find the making place / in the wood whence all things grow'. *Dark of Day*. 1977, and *By the Clear Fountain*, 1980, pursue the themes of love, belief, and quests for 'frontiers of place or time / where Both and Neither are true'.

Putnam, Mary Traill Spence (Lowell), 1810–98, journalist, playwright and biographer, b. Boston, Mass., da. of Harriet Brackett (Spence) and the Rev. Charles L., and older sister of James Russell Lowell. With a gift for languages, MTP was probably educ. at home. In 1832 she m. Samuel R. P., and they moved to Boston. Her first pub. work appears to be a TRANSLATION of Bremer's Swedish play *The Bondmaid*, 1844. She contributed articles on Polish and Hungarian literature to the *North American Review* 1848–50, but then broke sharply with its editor, Francis Bowen, for his articles critical of the Magyar Revolution. She supported the Magyars in two articles which appeared in the *Christian Examiner*, 1850–51 (repr. as *The North American Review on Hungary*). In the 1860s she pub. anon. four works which advocated an ABOLITIONIST position and suggested the double burden of the woman slave. These works form a series centring upon the fictional Edward Colvil, a New England farmer living in the South. *Records of an Obscure Man*, 1861, and *Fifteen Days: An Extract from Edward Colvil's Journal*, 1866, examine African history and Black music and preaching. The two verse plays, *The Tragedy of Errors* and *The Tragedy of Success*, both 1862, dramatize women in slavery, 'The task of woman will not be accomplished, / Until, throughout the world, the law of love / Supplant the law of force ...'. Her *Memoir of William Lowell Putnam*, 1862, is a biographical tribute to her son who died in the Civil War; she also wrote a biography of her father, 1885.

Pye, Jael Henrietta (Mendez), also Campbell, 1736?–82, occasional writer whose London Jewish background is obscure. From youth, she says, her passions were poetry and being admired. Her *Short Account* of 'Seats and Gardens' near Twickenham, 1760 (twice repr.), calls such places a woman's only permitted travels or art education, but is too short to be worth much. After a brief first marriage, her second, in 1766, to Robert Hampden P., made her sister-in-law to an uninspiring Poet Laureate. His daughter Mary's sentimental, melancholy poems have been taken for JHP's, which are fluent, ingenious, usually topical: anonymous, 1767 and (some added) 1771. She endorses Frances GREVILLE on indifference, seeks subscribers for Elizabeth GRIFFITH, laments various aspects of women's lot; her ballad 'Earl Walter' ('Childe Waters' adapted and tidied), admired in its day, reads flatly now. Her farce, *The Capricious Lady* (acted 1771, unpub.), centres on a bossy mother. In France 1774–9 with financial and marital worries, JHP kept writing, and advised Pierre Le Tourneur on translating Shakespeare. English newspapers maligned her (to Marie-Jeanne RICCOBONI's initial horror); she maligned Frances BROOKE to Garrick. Her epistolary 'Mary and Francis Gray', pub. 1786 as *Theodosius and Arabella*, features lovers who wrongly think they are incestuous (having been lost as children in the American revolution, in which JHP's husband fought).

Pym, Barbara Mary Crampton, 1913–80, novelist. B. at Oswestry, Shropshire, da. of Irena (Thomas) and solicitor Frederic Crampton P., she was educ. at Liverpool College, Huyton (an Anglican boarding school), and St Hilda's College, Oxford

(BA in English, 1934). She had written a first, unpublished novel, *Young Men in Fancy Dress*, at 16. During WWII she had a love affair with Gordon George, worked for the Bristol censorship office, 1941–3, then went to Naples with the WRNS (women's navy). She then worked on the journal *Africa* (International African Institute), as assistant, then (till retirement, 1974) assistant editor. She lived with her sister Hilary in Bristol, then London, then Oxon. *Some Tame Gazelle* (written in 1934, rejected by publishers, revised and pub. 1950) is a comedy of manners about two middle-aged sisters: village life, circumscribed, old-fashioned, focused with eager devotion on the church. The fine, assured irony of *Excellent Women*, 1952 (on similar themes), was recognized by a BBC serial and Book Society choice. Jane of *Jane and Prudence*, 1953, was patterned on BP's mother. Publishers thought her seam was worked out in three more explorations of the domestic lives of genteel, under-used women on the edges of academia, anthropology, or the Anglican church, of which the last, *No Fond Return of Love* (1961, BBC serial 1965) opens: 'There are various ways of mending a broken heart, but perhaps going to a learned conference is one of the more unusual.' The next (pub. as *An Unsuitable Attachment*, 1982), was rejected. During 16 so-called 'silent years' she sought, vainly, to publish as 'Tom Crampton', and had a disillusioning relationship with a younger man. In 1977 both Philip Larkin and Lord David Cecil cited her as their most underrated author in a *TLS* questionnaire, and she passed from neglect to cult status. *Quartet in Autumn* appeared that year, *The Sweet Dove Died* and her first US eds. in 1978, three novels posthumously (lastly the early-written *Crampton Hodnet*, 1985), and her diaries and letters as *A Very Private Eye*, 1984. She had a mastectomy in 1971, a slight stroke in 1974. She has been seen as a miniaturist and likened to AUSTEN; but Penelope LIVELY writes: 'what is going on is not tart observation of social manoeuvrings but a devastating, sublimely unfair, wonderfully funny and ultimately fatalistic analysis of the relations between men and women.' Joyce Carol OATES finds her autobiographical writings 'perhaps as good' as the best fiction. Checklist by Lorna Peterson in *BB*, 41, 1984; list of secondary sources by Judy Berndt in *BB*, 43, 1986. See Hortense CALISTER in *New Criticism*, 1, 1982; studies by Robert Emmet Long, 1986, and Diana Benet, 1986; essays ed. Dale Salwak, 1987. Janice Rossen, *The World of BP*, 1987, draws on private papers and friends' accounts.

Q

Quakers (Society of Friends), radical sect begun in the late 1640s by George Fox, who was soon joined by Elizabeth HOOTON and others. A decision in 1672 to preserve all Quaker writings makes them a major source of women's texts. Early pamphlets (often written from prison; often of multiple authorship) express fury at church and state, prophesy a great overturning and justify women's right to PREACHING and activism. Members travelled widely: to New England, the West Indies (Joan VOKINS), Turkey (Mary FISHER), and Malta (Katherine EVANS). After the Restoration many were imprisoned; most surviving radicals fell silent or left the sect. A bureaucratic reorganization of Friends after 1672 produced writings more reactionary in tone, notably by Margaret FELL, Dorcas DOLE, and Rebecca TRAVERS. These appeal to women to accept a more quiescent role confined to Women's Meetings, and reassert the hierarchies of class and family structure earlier rejected by the sect. By the 1670s a major source of Quaker women's writing was collective testimonials to the memory of dead Friends. Their traditions of biography, AUTOBIOGRAPHY, polemic, and preaching lived through the eighteenth century (e.g. Catharine PHILLIPS) to the early nineteenth (Elizabeth CHANDLER, Mary LEADBEATER, Elizabeth HEYRICK, Martha ROUTH, Lucretia MOTT); female Quaker ministers then became less visible. Studies by William Braithwaite, 1912, Mabel Brailsford, 1915, Richard Vann, 1969; Barry Reay in *History*, 63, 1978; Thomas O'Malley in *The Journal of Ecclesiastical History*, 33, 1982; Phyllis Mack in *Feminist Studies*, 8, 1982; Margaret Hope Bacon, *Mothers of Feminism: the story of Quaker women in America*, 1986; Elizabeth Potts Brown and Susan Mosher Stuard, *Witnesses for Change: Quaker Women over Three Centuries*, 1989. This century Jessamyn WEST's work continues the line of Quaker story-tellers.

Quin, Ann Marie, 1936–73, experimental novelist, b. at Brighton, Sussex, da. of Ann Reid and Nicholas Montague, a former opera singer who left when she was ten. Though not a Catholic, she went to a convent school which interested her in sin, death, and evil; she later believed in a God of 'many visions, many signs'. WOOLF and Dostoievsky started her writing at 14. She worked as assistant stage manager (briefly), secretary and publisher's reader, and won a small poetry prize. Two novels (about a male homosexual, then a man who kills his monster child) were rejected; while writing the second she had a serious breakdown. The four she pub. are difficult, influenced by Francis Bacon's painting and *nouvelle vague* film. *Berg*, 1964, repr. 1977, dedicated to her mother, is a fierce, surreal, often farcical tale of a man's efforts to kill the father who deserted him. He kills or seems to kill a cat, a budgie, and a tailor's dummy, seduces or seems to seduce his father in female dress, and ends up with his father's mistress: his mother's relations with each remain unresolved. *Berg* brought AQ critical notice and two scholarships: she travelled in Europe and in 1965 to the US for some years. *Three*, 1966, studies mutual alienation: a married couple, whose visiting friend drowns, perhaps a suicide, confront her tape-recorded and written journals: 'Impressions stain. Spread. Recollections.' 'Mouths. Theirs. She talks to the cat. Theirs.' *Passages*, 1969, again alternates voices: a woman combing Mediterranean towns for her perhaps dead brother speaks in present and past tenses, in the first and third person, with paragraph-breaks in mid-sentence; her male companion writes a diary ('I am on the verge of discovering my own demoniac possibilities'); marginalia include quotations from Jane HARRISON's *Prolegomena*. In *Tripticks*, 1972, another male travelling narrator comments savagely on US culture. *The Unmapped Country* (unfinished) presents mental-hospital experience: 'Patient confronted psychiatrist. Woman and man. . . . Those tentacles crept out of his ears' (chapter i in Giles Gordon, ed., *Beyond Words*, 1975). AQ wrote TV plays and published some short stories; she had won a univ. place but was caring for her ill and homeless mother when she was found drowned. Her friends included Frances HOROVITZ. Papers at Univ. of Indiana, Bloomington. Brocard Sewell in *Like Black Swans*, 1982, prints some letters.

Quincy, Eliza **Susan**, 1798–1884, Maria **Sophia**, b. 1805, **Margaret** Morton, later Greene, b. 1806, and **Anna** Cabot Lowell, later Waterston, 1812–99, diarists, das. of Eliza Susan (Morton) and Josiah Q. of Quincy, Mass. (President of Harvard from 1829): friends of the aged Abigail ADAMS, whose place, said Susan, 'is in History'. Susan made drawings, corresponded with EDGEWORTH, collected poems by e.g. SIGOURNEY and HEMANS, and obtained from AUSTEN's brother a sample of her handwriting. She and Anna wrote poems and historical work, some pub.: MSS at Harvard include Anna's autobiographical notes. Susan's memoirs of her grandfather appeared under her father's name, 1825, enlarged and repr. [1874], those of her mother with writing by her mother, 1861, and of her father co-written with her brother Edmnund, 1867. Anna (who m. the Rev. Robert C. W., 1840) pub. *Verses* as 'A. C. L. W.', 1863; the first stanza of her elegy for Col. Robert Gould Shaw is on his monument in Boston; her poem on the black woman who sculptured him was pub. 1883. M. A. De Wolfe Howe (who owned – and destined for the Mass. Hist. Soc. – the journal-letters they 'reciprocally' wrote in youth and later edited) pub. selecs in 1946. Margaret, who travelled to Cuba on marrying Dr Benjamin G. in 1826, writes of assassinations and of prudently concealing knowledge that a recent acquaintance was a brothel-keeper; in Charleston, SC, she noted the indignation of slaves at owners 'ridiculing their manner of speaking, etc., etc.' Sophia 'looked over a foul coppy' of P. D. MANVILL's book at Stillwater on the Hudson, NY, in 1829. Anna relates being deeply moved by Fanny KEMBLE on stage in 1833, and shrewdly noted the incongruity of Kemble's offstage role as 'delicate, gentle, subdued, *shadowy* creature'.

R

Radcliffe, Ann (Ward), 1764–1823, GOTHIC novelist and poet, da. of Ann (Oates) and Holborn merchant William W. She grew up in London and Bath, well-connected but only averagely educated; as a child she met Elizabeth MONTAGU and the future Hester PIOZZI; Sophia LEE's *The Recess* struck her deeply. In 1787 she married journalist and later magazine proprietor William R., and reputedly began writing as a pastime for evenings when he worked late. Her short novel *The Castles of Athlin and Dunbayne, A Highland Story*, 1789, already depicts rugged landscapes enfolding picturesque oases; *A Sicilian Romance*, 1790, moves to Catholic Europe and makes a heroine the focus of lust and oppression. With *The Romance of the Forest*, 1791 (poems interspersed), AR reached her biggest success and her mature format. Terrified heroines hold on to their religion and reason; natural laws are never infringed; human imagination creates the apparent supernatural. Audio-visual effects are important (AR was a keen opera-goer). *The Mysteries of Udolpho*, 1794, brought her £500, and *The Italian*, 1797, though shorter, £800; she published no more novels. She described in *A Journey* . . . , 1795, a trip with her husband to the Rhine and the Lake District in 1794; later tours kept to southern England. *Poems*, 1815, was pirated. In 1826 appeared *Gaston de Blondeville*, with the long 'St Alban's Abbey' and other poems. Part of the engaging frame story, in which two tourists discover an ancient MS, appeared that year in the *New Monthly Magazine* as 'On the Supernatural in Poetry'. The MS is a monkish account of a visit of Henry III to Kenilworth: MARIE DE FRANCE is praised. AR's sudden silence has been variously ascribed to money inherited from her father, 1798, recoil from her own fame, disgust at the tone of other GOTHIC writers, or unadmitted unease on William R.'s part. She died of an asthma attack, having already been rumoured dead or mad as a result of her perilous trade. Her work became instantly canonical; about 20 titles were falsely ascribed to her. All novels in modern eds. or facs.; critics in several languages include John Garrett, 1980, looking at her relation to imitators (Elizabeth HELME, Isabella KELLY, Mary MEEKE, Eliza PARSONS, Regina Maria ROCHE).

Radcliffe, Mary Ann, *c*. 1746–after 1810, Scots feminist, autobiographer and possibly novelist, only child of a Catholic mother and much older Anglican father who d. when she was two. At 14, a furtively Protestant heiress fresh from a convent, she was inveigled into secret marriage by the 35-year-old Catholic Joseph R.: 'Well! all this seemed vastly like a novel.' Initial happiness ebbed as she bore eight children (two died) and discovered 'my poor husband's *penchant* for parting with money', for drink and inactivity. He left her as an inexperienced 26-year-old to wind up the first failed business. Difficult years followed: shuttling between London and Scotland, taking lodgers, sewing, housekeeping. After 1781, when she was governess to an old schoolfriend, Lady Traquair, she lived chiefly apart from her husband; her children's needs for money and backing increased. About 1792 she began her plea against women's 'unremitted oppression', finished and pub. 1799 (she had just exchanged, for her granddaughters' sake, a shoe-shop for a school at Kennington near London) as *The Female Advocate, or An Attempt to Recover the Rights of Women* *from Male Usurpation* (excerpts in Moira Ferguson, 1985; repr. NY 1980). Cautiously respectful of WOLLSTONECRAFT, she writes from knowledge of declining job prospects for women, and quotes Sarah FIELDING and reprints Hester CHAPONE on the snares of prostitution. This and her *Memoirs*, 1810, where it is revised, bore her name, which later figured on various fictions she never claims as hers. She might have desired secrecy, or had an obscure namesake; but probably publishers stole her name (later purposely confused with Ann RADCLIFFE: see D. K. Adams in *Mystery and Detective Annual*, i, 1972) as they did those of BURNEY and EDGEWORTH. The anon. *Fate of Velina de Guidova* (violent emotion, not terror) and *Radzivil* (which alleges a Russian author, editor, and translator, all male), both 1790, were not listed as hers till 1802, the year of *Radcliffe's New Novelist's Pocket Magazine*. By the date of the blood-chilling *Manfroné*, 1809, (ascribed to her but claimed by L. T. KER), MAR was living on charity in Edinburgh, writing her *Memoirs* in letters to a female friend: 'my every labour seemed like Penelope's web – no sooner put together but as quickly undone again'.

Raffald, Elizabeth (Whitaker), 1733–81, domestic writer. B. at Doncaster, Yorks., well educ. (including French), she was 15 years a housekeeper 'in great and worthy families', married John R., gardener and seedsman, in 1763, and set up business in Manchester. She had 16 daughters (three survived her), ran a confectionery shop and two inns, taught catering, founded a school, and crucially supported two local newspapers. In 1769 she pub. 'for the service of my sex', with 800 subscribers, *The Experienced English Housekeeper*, 'not glossed over with hard names, or words of high stile, but wrote in my own plain language'. (She remarks that cooking standards are low, yet such works elicit 'contempt'.) Many eds. followed (1782, facs. 1970); she reputedly sold the copyright for £1400. She produced the first directory of Manchester, 1772. Her last work, a MS treatise on midwifery, taken to London by her husband after her death, is untraced (Chetham Soc. pubs. 1867).

'Raine, Allen', Anna Adaliza Puddicombe (Evans), 1836–1908, novelist, b. Newcastle-Emlyn, Carmarthens., Wales, eldest of the four children of Letitia Grace (Morgan) and solicitor, Benjamin E. She went to school at Cheltenham and Southfields, and in 1872 m. Benyon P. Interested in story-telling from childhood, AR did not begin serious writing till the 1890s, winning a prize at the 1894 Eisteddfod for the best serial story about Welsh life. All of her work dealt with ancient or modern Wales, including her first and most famous novel, *A Welsh Singer*, 1897, which ran to more than 14 eds. This tells the story of an illiterate girl's rise to fame as a singer, and her eventual reunion with a childhood love. Other books include *Torn Sails*, 1898; *A Welsh Witch*, 1901, set in wilder parts of Wales and utilizing dialect, but with an over-elaborate plot; and the posthumous *Under the Thatch*, 1910, which deals with cancer, from which she died. See Sally R. Jones, *Allen Raine*, 1979.

Raine, Kathleen Jessie, poet, critic, translator. B. in 1908 at Ilford near London, da. of Jessie (Wilkie), a Scot, and George R., she spent part of her childhood as a WWI evacuee in Northumberland (to which she remained passionately attached). She was educ. latterly at the high school where her father taught, then after a 'disastrous' year studying psychology, took a BA in natural sciences at Girton College, Cambridge, 1929. She was the youngest and only female member of the Cambridge Poets, with Charles Madge (later her second husband), Frances CORNFORD's son John, Virginia WOOLF's nephew Julian Bell, and William Empson, who published her work in the magazine *Experiment*. KR calls her writing a Scottish maternal inheritance ('the poet in me is my mother's daughter'), but she learned 'for the first time, and with surprise', from hearing Woolf's paper which later became *A Room of One's Own*, that problems different from a man's were 'supposed' to confront a woman writer. KR's two marriages (the first to Hugh Sykes Davies) were dissolved; she had two children. She was converted to Catholicism, briefly, in 1944. *Stone and Flower*, 1944 (poems from 1935; illustrated by Barbara Hepworth), reveals her neoplatonic mysticism, anti-materialism, and gift for natural observation. Deeply committed to the idea of a traditional symbolic language, KR has developed and articulated her introspective examination of the relation between humanity and cosmos in a dozen vols. of mostly free verse, and in prose spiritual autobiography: *Farewell Happy Fields*, 1973, *The Land Unknown*, 1975, and *The Lion's Mouth*, 1977. Her critical studies – of Blake, Coleridge, Yeats, David Jones – and translations of Balzac are highly regarded. *Collected Poems* appeared in 1981, the year she founded and became co-editor of *Temenos*, a magazine devoted to re-affirming the 'sacred dimensions' of the arts. See Erika Duncan in *Unless Soul Clap Its Hands*, 1984; B. Aubrey in *Studia Mystica*, 19, 1986. MSS at BL and several North American universities.

Ramsay, Martha (Laurens), 1759–1811, diarist and letter writer, b. at Charleston, SC, da. of Eleanor (Ball), who d. when she was ten, and Henry L., a French Huguenot. A daring, active child, preferring 'excesses of the wildest play ... to stagnant life', she could read at four, learned geography, geometry and French, and dedicated herself to God in writing at 14, when she left the Anglicans for the Independents. Sailing in 1775 for England (where her father had spent four years educating her brother) and in 1778 for France, made her destroy most of her MSS. Her father was imprisoned and brother killed in the war. Returning home in 1785, she married writer David R. in 1787, and had 11 children in 16 years (eight survived). Her DIARY follows their growth and education, her religion, studies and help with her husband's medical practice. She admired Elizabeth ROWE, Elizabeth CARTER and Elizabeth SMITH, saw sense in Mary WOLLSTONECRAFT but believed strongly in wifely obedience. She kept her journal of 'Religious Exercises' secret till three days before her death, then asked her family to save it: pub. by David R. with letters, in *Memoirs*, 1811: many reprs.

Ranasinghe, Anne (Katz), poet and writer of stories and radio plays. Da. of a Jewish family, AR was b. in 1925 in Essen, Ruhr, Germany. She left for England, 1939, but her parents and most of her family circle died in Nazi concentration camps. She began her education at Jawne, the only Jewish High School still functioning then in her part of Germany, and she completed it at Parkstone Girls' Grammar School in Britain, later training as a nurse in London. She also holds a Diploma in journalism. Following marriage, 1939, to a Sri Lankan physician, she settled in Colombo; she has three children. She began writing poetry in 1968. Her work, pub. in six vols. from *Poems*, 1971, to *Against Eternity and Darkness*, 1985, has been translated into several languages and won several awards. It is, says Pieter Keuneman in the foreword to AR's *Plead Mercy*, 1976, 'increasingly obsessed with the question of remembering – because she knows what it means for the Germans to forget; because it is through remembering that she creatively interprets her presence in Sri Lanka'. Her remembering of the past bears pointedly on her Sri Lankan present and on her treatment of the insurgency of 1971. Michael Lentz made a film on her work for West Deutschen Rundfunk TV, 1987. See L. de Lanerolle's foreword to her *With Words*, 1972.

Rapoport, Janis, poet, playwright, editor. B. in 1946 in Toronto, Ont., da. of Roslyn

(Cohen) and lawyer Maxwell Lewis R., she was educ. in Neuchâtel, Switzerland, and at the Univ. of Toronto (BA, 1967). She married David J. Seager, 1966 (divorced 1980), with whom she had three children. In 1980 she married publisher Douglas F. Donegani; they had another daughter. Fluent in French and Russian, JR worked in different editorial capacities in London, England and Toronto. Editor from 1983 of *Ethos*, a literary and cultural magazine, she has also taught creative writing. She 'believe[s] in the moral – that is, life affirming – value of art' and credits Dave Godfrey, her creative-writing instructor at the Univ. of Toronto, for her becoming a writer. Of her three books of poetry, *Jeremy's Dream*, 1974, is strongest, in both its unity – a desire to filter a lover's and a mother's experiences 'through layers of porcelain and glass' – and its diversity: – scenes from her Jewish life mixed with images of abortion and birth ('no breath / to reverse the darkness of the blood / prelude to your birth'). JR has had three plays produced, 'And She Could Eat No Lean' (Tarragon Theatre, Toronto, 1975, where she was playwright-in-residence, 1974–5), 'Gilgamesh' (University College Playhouse, Toronto, 1976), and *Dreamgirls*, 1979 (Théâtre Passe-Muraille, 1979), a play of all-female characters about a 'Halfway Home' for women.

Rathbone, Eleanor Florence, 1872–1946, feminist and social reformer who published books on most of the causes for which she campaigned. She was b. in London, da. of Emily Acheson (Lyle) and William R., of a famous Liberal, Quaker family of Liverpool shipowners. After educ. chiefly at home, she attended Somerville College, Oxford, 1893–6, where philosophy was an important part of her studies. She involved herself in her father's charity work till his death in 1902; about then she met Elizabeth Macadam, a social worker who became her life-long companion. Her feminist work began as Parliamentary Secretary to the Liverpool Women's Suffrage Society, 1897, and her writing with a report on labour conditions at the Liverpool docks, 1904, and a life of her father, 1905. She stated her feminist views in Victor Gollancz, ed., *The Making of Women*, 1917, and Ray STRACHEY, ed., *Our Freedom and its Results*, pub. Leonard and Virginia WOOLF, 1936. She succeeded Millicent FAWCETT as President of NUWSS in 1919 as it became the National Union of Societies for Equal Citizenship. Her 'new feminism' – aiming to demand not 'what men have got' but 'what women need' – inspired her famous campaign for family allowances: powerfully advocated in *The Disinherited Family*, 1924 (repr. 1985, 1986), and other works, achieved in 1945. Defeated at the 1922 election, she became the first woman Independent MP in 1929. She worked for the cause of women in India (*Child Marriage: The Indian Minotaur*, 1934), against female circumcision, for the settlement of refugees and for Zionism (*Falsehoods and Facts about the Jews*, 1944). See life by Mary D. Stocks, 1949.

Rathbone, Hannah Mary (Reynolds), 1798–1878, Quaker novelist and poet, da. of Deborah (Dearman) and Joseph Reynolds of Ketley, Shropshire. She married Richard Rathbone, a cousin, in 1816, lived in and later near Liverpool, and had six children although her health was poor. The editor of diaries by her namesake and mother-in-law, 1905 (with a few letters of HMR's), writes, 'At one time there were five Hannah Mary Rathbones living in Liverpool.' Her first publication, as 'a lady', was a poetry ANTHOLOGY, pub. with different titles in [1840] and 1841: it includes nearly 20 women, including herself (poems chiefly on her family and her faith). She is best known for her *Diary of Lady Willoughby*, 1844, a fiction which simulated in style and publisher's presentation an actual document of the civil war period, and which made this genre briefly popular. HMR also published a diary sequel in 1847, *Life's Sunshine*, 1850 (a pious, aphoristic, domestic novel), and *The Strawberry Girl*, 1858, which adds more poems to those already pub. She is credited with several pleasing little moral tales (one repr. in Boston) – doubtfully, since one of 1849 bears the name of Miss H. M. Rathbone.

Ravel, Aviva, poet, playwright, scriptwriter, writer of short stories. B. in 1928 in Montréal of Eastern European Jewish immigrant parents, she was educ. in NYC, at the Bank Street School of Education, and in Montréal, at Loyola College (BA), Univ. de Montréal and McGill Univ. She taught elementary school for ten years, and now teaches at Concordia Univ. She married Nahum R., 1948, and with him spent ten years on an Israeli kibbutz. Back in North America in 1959, she studied playwriting in NYC, then returned to Canada, 1960. She has five children. She began to write plays, 1965, and has had many one- and two-act works produced, mainly in Montréal and Toronto. One of her earliest, *Mendel Fish*, won the National Playwriting Seminar Award and the Canadian Women's Press Club Award for Humour. *The Twisted Loaf* (produced 1974) is printed in *A Collection of Canadian Plays*, Vol. 3, 1973, and *Dispossessed* (produced 1977) in *Women Write for the Theatre*, Vol. 3, 1976. AR has written for TV, translated plays by Québec writers, and pub. stories in *Canadian Forum*, *Journal of Canadian Fiction*, and elsewhere, and essays in *Fiddlehead* and *ECW*.

Rawlings, Marjorie (Kinnan), 1896–1953, novelist and short-story writer, b. in Washington, DC, to Ida May (Traphagen) and patent attorney Arthur F. K. She moved to Madison, Wis., 1914, graduated from the Univ. of Wisconsin, 1918, m. newspaperman Charles A. R. in 1919, and until 1928 wrote for the Louisville *Courier-Journal* and then the Rochester, NY, *Journal-American*. She had a column, 'Songs of a Housewife', but tried unsuccessfully to place her stories in magazines. She then decided on full-time writing, at an orange grove at Cross Creek, Hawthorne, Fla. *Scribner's* took her sketches of Florida folklore and people, 'Cracker Chidlings', 1930 (a cracker is a country herdsman with whip), and 'Jacob's Ladder', 1931; 'Gal Young Un' (about an exploited older woman) won the O. Henry award, 1933. Her first novel, *South Moon Under*, 1933, features the rafting, hunting, and distilling of moonless nights; *The Yearling*, 1938 (Pulitzer Prize, famous film 1946), a boy and his unmanageably growing fawn. *Golden Apples*, 1935, attempts a tricky problem in depicting sexuality and cruelty between an ignorant local woman and an unfeeling English planter; MKR called it 'interesting trash'. *When a Whippoorwill*, 1930, selects from her stories. *Cross Creek*, 1942, evokes the setting of years which included her divorce, 1933, and marriage to hotel-owner Norton Sandford Baskin, 1941. Like her other books, it includes memorable female portraits. She also published a cookbook, 1942, and children's book, 1955. Her last novel, *The Sojourner*, 1953, leaves Florida for a Hudson Valley farm, opening after the Civil War. Life by Gordon Bigelow, 1966; *Reader*, ed. Julia Scriber Bigham, 1956; papers at the Univ. of Florida, Gainesville.

Read, Harriet Fanning (dates unknown), dramatist and novelist, b. Jamaica Plain, Mass. Her mother and father, publisher and bookseller, encouraged her to pursue a literary career. After his death she and her mother went to live with an uncle, Colonel F., in Washington, DC. She made her acting debut at the Boston Theatre in 1848. She appears to have pub. only two works, *Dramatic Poems*, 1848, and *The Haunted Student: A Romance of the Fourteenth Century*, 1860. In both she emphasizes the theme of an individual freedom which sometimes leads women to poor choices. In her best work, the dramatic poem 'Medea', the myth is rearranged, and Medea echoes nineteenth-century feminism by reminding Jason that she is his 'equal partner', not his 'household slave'.

Read, Martha (Meredith), obscure novelist of Philadelphia, the setting of her only known work, *Monima, or The Beggar Girl . . . Founded on Fact*, 1802. Her dedication, to Dr Hugh M., foresees that 'the man of deep erudition' will find its reality insignificant; the *American Review and Literary Journal*, 1802, duly called it preposterously unlike Philadelphia, as well as turgid and eccentric in diction. The 16-year-old Monima and her aged father have been victimized by a rake in France before they flee to the USA and find it no better than home. Monima's descent from workhouse to Bedlam to GOTHIC country house may be unlikely, but not the less-than-living wage she can earn, or the mob's cruel mockery when she is robbed. Her female American persecutor's death rewards her with the hand of a good French widower. Cathy N. Davidson, 1986, notes how the book was 'pirated, plagiarized, and paraphrased' in and out of periodicals.

Redford or Radford, **Elizabeth**, *c.* 1646–1729, Quaker pamphleteer, author of *The Widow's Mite* [1690], *The Love of God . . .* [*c.* 1690], and two similarly-titled leaflets (each *A Warning . . . in Mercy to the People*), 1695 and 1696. Her *Mite*, on Sabbath observance, bases its views on inner experience as well as Scripture: not set forms but 'my Call and Satisfaction is from the Lord to keep the seventh Day, the Lord's Rest'. She was probably in the Netherlands in 1694, publishing there, while London Friends wanted her home for admonition. On her return she was accused of harshness, or failure in meekness, when she urged non-payment of taxes to be used for war. She warns against war and the stink of camps, 1695 ('the Blood that is shed in the Earth is displeasing the Lord'), mentions the plague, fire, and recent slight earthquake, and expects the violent setting up of Christ's peaceable kingdom. In 1696 she warns: 'let not the dependency of your Happiness be upon Money . . . but be contented to stand still a little, that ye may see every one for themselves the great Salvation of God'.

Reed, Myrtle, 1874–1911, novelist, poet and short-story writer, b. Norwood Park, Illinois. She was the youngest child and only da. of Elizabeth (Armstrong), Oriental and theological scholar, and Hiram Von R., preacher and literary editor. She pub. her first story aged ten. Educ. at West Division High School, she missed college owing to a mental breakdown. Instead, she contributed to magazines such as *Harper's Bazaar*. Her first novel, *Love Letters of a Musician*, was pub. in 1899. Her second, *Lavender and Old Lace*, 1902, repr. 40 times in less than ten years, was adapted as a play, *Arsenic and Old Lace*, 1941, and later filmed. She pub. 32 works, including novels, poetry, short stories, biographies and cookbooks. For her domestic magazine articles she sometimes used the name 'Katherine LaFarge Norton'. She left royalties worth $25,000 a year. In 1906, she m. James McCullough, a real estate agent of literary inclinations. Feeling pressurized, he said, into being the ideal husband of MR's writing, he took to drink, but MR refused a divorce. Heavily dependent on the sedative Veronal, she used it as the means of her suicide. She had just completed *A Weaver of Dreams*, 1911, whose heroine, betrayed by her fiancé, resigns herself at the end to living alone, financially independent. Typical of MR's work, albeit more melodramatic, is *A Spinner in the Sun*, 1906, in which the heroine wears a veil throughout the novel, to disguise the beauty which once attracted a cad: 'For such women as Evelina, the knights of old did battle.' He abandoned her when he thought she had been seriously disfigured by burns. Although her plots are bizarre and her characters lacking in subtlety, MR's work is an excellent example of the type of romantic fiction POPULAR at the beginning of this century. Her life is by Ethel S. Colson and Norma B. Carson, 1911.

Reese, Lizette Woodworth, 1856–1935, poet, b. Waverly, Maryland, twin da. of Louisa Sophia (Gabler) and David R., educ. at St John's Episcopal Parish School and Baltimore public schools. From 1873 to 1921 she taught English literature and composition. Her first pub. poem, 'The Deserted House', appeared in *Southern Magazine*, 1874, and in 1887 her first vol. of poetry, *A Branch of May*, was pub. by subscription. It had an unusual aphoristic spareness. Well received by critics, it was followed by *A Handful of Lavender*, 1891. A writer of consistently good lyric poetry, she pub. nine vols., including *Selected Poems*, 1923, drawing on the village life and orchards of Maryland for imagery. Her famous sonnet, 'Tears' (*Scribner's*, 1899), was written as a series of metaphors expressing the futility of wasting one's life through the 'idleness of tears' and it has been repeatedly anthologized. Her poetic instinct carries into her prose expression in *A Victorian Village*, 1929, and *The York Road*, 1931, reminiscences and stories of her youth which conjure up a leisurely life, close to a benign nature that is unlike the world of the New England local-colorists. She was a close observer of male/female relationships, as in 'Sanctuary' (*The York Road*), in which Nancy leaves her husband after finding that in marriage 'you've got to work harder than ever in your life – and things a man ought to do – and you're nobody'. She wrote two narrative poems, *Little Henrietta*, 1927, and *The Old House in the Country*, 1936, and her autobiographical novel *Worleys* was pub. posthumously. Her poetry marked the change from Victorian conventions to the symbolism and imagery of the Moderns. There is no biography; see the critical discussion in Emily Stipes Watts, *The Poetry of American Women*, 1977; Cheryl Walker, *The Nightingale's Burden*, 1982. A recent study is in *DLB* 54 (1987). Her MSS are at the Univ. of Virginia.

Reeve, Clara, 1729–1807, novelist, b. at Ipswich, Suffolk, eldest da. of Hannah (Smithies) and the Rev. William R., who taught her. After his death, 1755, she moved with mother and sisters to Colchester. Her preface to *Original Poems on Several Occasions*, 1769, notes an increase in admired women writers. Among mostly conventional poems of prudential morality, one deals ironically with sex and writing: a woman poet must hide her genius from envy and jeers; what is honour in men 'in us is shame'. (Her play and oratorio libretto had remained unproduced and unset.) She translated Barclay's *Argenis* (cf. Judith MAN) as *The Phoenix*, 1772, and in 1777 pub. *The Champion of Virtue*, revised 1778 with her name as *The Old English Baron* (repr. 1967), an immensely successful GOTHIC novel modelled on *Otranto*: its women are insignificant. Of five more novels (excluding *Castle Connor, An Irish Story*, lost in MS), only *Memoirs of Sir Roger de Clarendon*, 1793, is medieval. *The Progress of ROMANCE* (1785, with *Charoba*, an Arabian tale about a strong, able queen: facs. 1930) defends the genre as essentially female literature (against learned male preference for epic) and reviews early development of novels, foregrounding women writers but approving 'chivalric' attitudes. *The Two Mentors*, 1783, promotes sensibility and 'social virtues', and features evil aristocrats; *The Exiles*, 1788, has a strongly romantic hero; the enterprising heroine of *The School for Widows*, 1791, rejects her idle aristocratic husband and sets up commercial enterprises and a school, as she writes to a friend trapped in a tyrannical marriage. *Plans of Education*, 1792, framed as a continuation, is reactionary, unsympathetic to anti-slavery agitation and to educating poor girls above their station.

Reeve, Winnifred (Eaton), also Babcock, 'Onoto Watanna', 1877–1954, novelist, short-story writer, dramatist, editor. She was b. in Montréal, seventh of 14 children of a Chinese mother and an English father. Two of her uncles married Japanese women, and (unlike her sister 'SUI SIN FAR', who embraced her Chinese identity) WR took a Japanese identity in her writing, partly to evade the intense anti-Chinese feeling of the late nineteenth and early twentieth centuries. (Her Japanese birth is credited in some reference books.) She published her first story at 14, and at 17 became, briefly, a reporter in Jamaica, and later moved to Chicago and NYC as a freelance writer, an experience remembered wryly in 'Writing and Starving in New York' (*Maclean's Magazine*, 15 October 1922). In NYC, she married journalist Bertrand Whitcomb Babcock, with whom she had three children; in 1917 she married Francis Fournier R., a NY businessman, moving with him to Alberta, where they were involved in ranching, then oil. She worked with Universal Pictures and Metro-Goldwyn-Mayer, 1924–32, writing a number of screenplays and adaptations, including *Phantom of the Opera*. Thereafter she lived in Calgary until her death. Most of her 17 novels are about Japan. The most popular – her second – *A Japanese Nightingale*, 1901, sold over 200,000 copies, was transl. into French, Spanish, Swedish, German, Italian and Japanese, and adapted as play, movie, and opera. An allegorical tale of the meeting of two cultures set as a romance between a Eurasian girl brought up in Japan and an American, it shows the American's attempt to understand his wife, weaving respectful description of Japanese culture into the narrative. The semi-autobiographical *Me, A Book of Remembrance*, 1915, thought shocking, sent up the sales of *Century* magazine, where it first appeared. *Marion: The Story of an Artist's Model*, 1916, was based on the life of one of WR's sisters. She also wrote Alberta adventure stories (e.g. *Cattle*, 1932). She published hundreds of stories in periodicals, including *Scribner's*, *Atlantic Monthly*, *Century*, *Harper's*, *Saturday Evening Post* in the USA and the *Strand* and the *Idler* in England. Her friends included Edith WHARTON, Jean Webster, Anita LOOS, Mark Twain, and Nellie MCCLUNG. See Amy Ling in *Melus*, 11, 1984.

Reeves, Amber, later Blanco White, OBE, 1887–1981, novelist and teacher, b. in London to Fabian Society members Magdalen Stuart (Robinson), feminist, and William Pember Reeves, former Minister to New Zealand. She attended Kensington High School and Newnham College, Cambridge (Moral Sciences), where she met H. G. Wells. He persuaded her while pregnant by him to marry, 1909, Rivers Blanco White, a married lawyer and fellow-Fabian with whom she had two more children. (Wells used the story in *Ann Veronica*, 1909, repr. 1980, about the taming of an idealistic young woman.) AR's first novel, *The Reward of Virtue*, 1911, is a fierce attack on the narrow education and opportunities of women, with marriage 'the only profession where the tolerated standard was low enough'. In her second, *A Lady and Her Husband*, 1914, a well-to-do woman is transformed by doing charity work for the waitresses of her husband's chain of shops, challenges a business plan damaging to them, and realizes: 'she did not care for a fine lady's life. She was an ordinary middle-class woman, who preferred doing practical work to being kept in the house to be beautiful and mysterious and tender and all the rest of it.' AR wrote two more novels (the last, *Give and Take*, 1923, is a political satire) and non-fiction works in her married name, some based on Freudian psychology, e.g. *Worry in Women*, 1941, which considers the 'new responsibilities' brought by emancipation. She was Director of Women's Wages at the Ministry of Munitions, 1916–19, contributed material on women to Wells's *The Work, Wealth and Happiness of Mankind*, 1932, ed. *The Townswoman*, 1933, stood for Parliament twice, and taught at Morley College, London, till 1965.

Reid, Hilda Stewart, 1899–1982, novelist, historian. Da. of Imogen (Beadon) and Sir Arthur Hay Stewart R., a judge in India, she was educ. privately, then went to Somerville College, Oxford, 1917, where she became a friend of Winifred HOLTBY, and read history (taking a year's absence for a serious operation). She spent seven years writing her first novel, *Phillida, or the Reluctant Adventurer*, 1928. Like *Two Soldiers and a Lady*, 1932, it is an intriguing love-and-adventure story set in Stuart times, demonstrating not only accuracy of detail but also HR's sense of the exotic and fantastic. She also wrote *Emily*, 1933, and *Ashley Hammel*, 1939. With Vera BRITTAIN she edited Holtby's short-story volume *Pavements at Anderby*, 1937. She was active in the Red Cross (publishing a history of its London branch, 1948), was an air-raid warden in Chelsea during the blitz in WWII, and contributed to the Civil Defence volume of the official WWII History, 1945–51.

Religious and devotional writing was, with LETTERS, the earliest known by women in English, and remained long predominant. It embraces many genres: translation (much, but not all, biblical), prayers and meditations, visions and prophecies, personal diaries and autobiographies, political polemic, sermons, hymns and many kinds of poetry. After Katherine of Sutton's Latin liturgical plays of *c.* 1363–76, and a couple of extant anonymous vernacular writings, came JULIAN of Norwich and other English mystics influenced by those of continental Europe (see THEOLOGY). Dame Eleanor Hull of St Albans (d. after 1460) translated meditations from French. The Reformation and seventeenth-century religious conflicts prompted women on both sides to produce passionate works (still exciting in both literary and feminist terms) on such unpromising topics as payment of tithes. Later, while religious teaching approached more and more closely to social admonition, the note of extremist prophecy recurs in Elspeth or Elspat (Simpson) Buchan, 1738–91, whose letters (one autobiographical) in a Buchanite volume of 1785 are more simply and directly magisterial than those of her associate the Rev. Hugh White. In the nineteenth century the religious impulse, still powerful, found diverse paths of expression. Christina ROSSETTI and Emily DICKINSON wrote devotional poetry; many of lesser talent wrote HYMNS; Frances HAVERGAL was an Evangelical poet and hymnist. 'Michael FAIRLESS' was influential as a mystic agnostic prose-writer. By late century, religious writing in Britain often came from arch-conservative anti-feminists like Edith Gell (who opposed women's SUFFRAGE and valued the 'Christian wife' more highly than potential female artists or public figures), though Alice MEYNELL wrote fine religious lyrics. So did Louise GUINEY in the US, which also produced interesting and eccentric religious writers like Ursula GESTEFELD. The novel form has a well-documented history of appropriation for sectarian purposes. See also SPIRITUALISM and THEOLOGY. See Gail Malmgreen, ed., 1986; and for the nineteenth century Margaret Maison, *Search Your Soul, Eustace*, 1961; Robert Lee Wolff, *Gains and Losses: Novels of Faith and Doubt in Victorian England*, 1977.

Remick, Martha, 1832–1906, novelist, b. Kittery, Maine, youngest da. of Sally (Cram) and Rufus R., shipwright and farmer. MR's novels treat topical issues but unusually do not moralize. *Agnes Stanhope*, 1862, tells of sisterly betrayal, and a marriage destroyed by a gambling, inebriate husband whose wife is accused (wrongly) of poisoning him. Her best novel, *Millicent Halford. A Tale of the Dark Days of Kentucky in the year 1861*, 1865, about a brother's passion for his future sister-in-law, remains equally non-judgmental but the bitter division between North and South, and the harsh realities of slavery and patriarchal law tell their own story. *Richard Ireton*, 1875, shows the persecution of a Quaker woman by the Puritans, but the story turns into a romantic thriller in which multi-directional plots complicate pace and focus, and a confused nomenclature confounds the reader.

Renaissance. Humanist theories led to extensive classical and academic education being given, for a few generations in the sixteenth century, to some girls of royal, noble, or upper-class families (see studies by Ruth Kelso, 1956, Retha M. Warnicke, 1983). Some parents took pride in their daughters' achievements; others blatantly intended to raise their value in marriage power-brokering. Ladies exercised important PATRONAGE, and a number became TRANSLATORS or original writers, some while very young. Their work is celebrated by Pearl Hogrefe, 1975, but (since they shared the training meant to fit boys for statesmanship, without sharing the career) it is seen as oppression by Hilda L. Smith (in Berenice A. Carroll, ed., 1976) and Joan Kelly (in Renate Bridenthal and Claudia Koon, eds., 1977). For women writers see Margaret P. Hannav, ed., 1985; Betty Travitsky, ed., generous anthology, 1981. Among much work on the period's discourses of sexual difference, see Margaret W. Ferguson, Maureen Quilligan and Nancy J. Vickers, eds., *Rewriting the Renaissance*, 1986.

'Renault, Mary' (Eileen Mary Challans), 1905–83, novelist, chiefly historical. B. in London, da. of Clementine Mary (Baxter) and Dr Frank C., she wanted to be a writer from her youth. She took a BA in English at St Hugh's College, Oxford, 1928, worked on a first novel (unpub.), and qualified as a State Registered Nurse, 1937. Her first printed novel, *Purposes of Love*, 1939 (*Promise of Love* in NY ed.), deals with the struggle to retain independence in an intense heterosexual love where both parties find the heroine's brother attractive. *The Middle Mist*, 1945, was repr. 1984 as *The Friendly Young Ladies*. Despite high literary earnings, MR continued nursing till after WWII, when *Return to Night* brought a lavish MGM prize and financial independence. In 1947 she emigrated to South Africa with Julie Mullard. She opposed apartheid and joined the Progressive Party; she became president of the PEN club of S. Africa in 1961, but later resigned. Radclyffe HALL's *Well of Loneliness* had made MR laugh; in her own fiction, homosexual or bisexual love is generally idealizing or caring as well as passionate. *The Charioteer*, 1953, set in an army hospital in WWII, deals openly with male homosexuality. It depicts love at once physical and spiritual, the heartening memory of ancient Greek acceptance, the misogyny of peripheral gay characters with no interest in love on these terms, and the pain of unrequital. Most famous of MR's many novels are those of ancient Greece, especially on Theseus (*The King Must Die*, 1958, which makes Ariadne a heroic lesbian or bisexual athlete, and *The Bull from the Sea*, 1962) and on Alexander (*Fire from Heaven*, 1969, on his early life, and *The Persian Boy*, 1972, told in the voice of his great love, a Persian noble enslaved and castrated in boyhood). Imaginatively drawn to heroes and their tragic fall, to the mysteries of sexual choice, and to the separate women's cultures that flourished beside brutal dismissiveness in the ancient world, MR strove not to exploit the dead, either for 'sensationalism' or for any 'end preferred to truth'. Her careful research also produced *The Lion in the Gateway*, 1964 (for children, on the battles of Greeks and Persians), and lives of Alexander, 1975, and the poet Simonides, 1978. See study by Peter Wolfe, 1969; Carolyn G. HEILBRUN in Dora B. Weiner and William R. Reylor, eds., *From Parnassus*, 1976.

Rendell, Ruth (Grasemann), 'Barbara Vine', novelist. Da. of teachers Ebba Elise and Arthur G., she was b. in 1930 in London and educ. at Loughton High School. From 1948 to 1952 she was a newspaper reporter and sub-editor. In 1950 she m.

fellow-journalist Donald R.; they have a son. RR's large output and often macabre technique have established her as a major crime writer. She alternates DETECTIVE novels (centred on humane, literary Chief Inspector Reginald Wexford) with non-series novels focusing on aberrant circumstances and deprivations which result in murder. In the police procedurals, a network of friends and family surrounding Wexford forms a normal pole to offset the criminal one. In the first, *From Doon to Death*, 1964, the victim is a decent, impoverished housewife. In *No More Dying Then*, 1971, Wexford's assistant is himself bereaved. In *A Sleeping Life*, 1978, his daughter rejects the housewife role and leaves her husband. (RR and Donald R., divorced in 1977, later remarried.) RR's other, darker, ironic novels compel at least near-sympathy with perpetrators of horror: a mass-murderer of her casual, privileged benefactors in *A Judgement in Stone*, 1977, a rapist in *Live Flesh*, 1986, and distorted parodies of feminists in *Unkindness of Ravens*, 1985. *Heartstones*, 1987, is about a teenage anorexic, her compulsive-eater sister, and her widowed father; *Talking to Strange Men*, 1987, involves a schoolboy game of espionage, a revenge plot and a child molester. RR's *Collected Stories* appeared in 1987. Her first novel as 'Barbara Vine', *A Dark-Adapted Eye*, 1986, though still concerned with murder, moves closer to the mainstream; *House of Stairs*, 1988, is about a murder of lesbian passion. *RR's Suffolk*, 1989, expresses her love of the county where she sets many of her novels. See Jane S. Bakerman in Bargainnier, 1981, and Robert Barnard in *Armchair Detective*, 16, 1983.

Renée, playwright, b. 1929, Napier, NZ, of Ngati Kahungunu descent, da. of Rose Adeline and Stanley George Howard Jones, farm worker, who committed suicide when she was four. She left school at 12 to work, first in a woollen mill, then at bookbinding. M. 1949–81 to Laurie Taylor, shop assistant, she had three sons and also worked during marriage at other jobs. In the 1960s she wrote a weekly column for the *Wairoa Star* and book reviews for the *Hawkes Bay Herald Tribune*, and was active in local amateur dramatic groups. When she was 38 she began a Massey Univ. extramural BA, majoring in English, which she completed in 1979. When she moved to Auckland in 1981 after the breakup of her marriage she 'acknowledged her lesbian identity' and rejected her married name, calling herself simply Renée. In 1981 her first play, *Setting the Table*, appeared. She wrote of it: 'I wanted to write something that showed women as witty and intelligent and hardworking ... And I had debated furiously with friends the use of violence as a weapon, as a strategy, as an action ...' *Secrets*, 1982, is a one-woman show about incest and cleaning toilets, *Dancing*, about the menopause, *Groundwork* about the 1981 Springbok tour conflict. Apart from a policeman in *Setting the Table*, they have all-women casts. *Wednesday to Come*, 1985, her first play to have wide critical acclaim, set in the Depression, is more about class and poverty than feminist issues. It is the first of a trilogy, the second of which, *Pass It On*, set during the 1951 Watersiders' strike, appeared in 1986. In 1982 and 1983 she wrote and directed two touring feminist reviews/road shows, sponsored by *Broadsheet*, NZ's feminist magazine. In 1982 Renée received a government grant to write two plays, and in 1986 she was playwright-in-residence at Auckland's Theatre Corporate. *Finding Ruth*, 1987, is a coll. of semi-autobiographical stories. In 1989 she was writer-in-residence at Otago Univ.

Replansky, Naomi, poet. B. in 1918 in the Bronx, NY, where she still lives, da. of Fannie (Ginsberg) and Sol R., she wrote poetry at ten and published in *Poetry* at 16. She studied geography at Univ. of California, Los Angeles (BA 1956), and lived for two-and-a-half years in France. She has done factory, office, and computer programming work. NR's translations of

German and Yiddish literature have appeared in magazines and anthologies. The poems of *Ring Song*, 1952, nominated for the National Book Award, reveal personal outrage and political commitment: 'In silence is the smell of treachery, and sanction / Of hunger, and therefore I shout.' From NR's concise, probing, ironic lines the post-Holocaust world – 'Death above all / Grown technical' – emerges in motley forms of inhumanity, from racism to the exploitation of woman, whose 'clipped wing leans against / Her eagle of experience'. Her poems have appeared in journals (*The Nation, Missouri Review, Feminist Studies*, and others) and many anthologies (Nancy Hoffman and Florence Howe, eds., *Working Women*, 1979; Diana Scott, ed., *Bread and Roses*, 1983). *Twenty-One Poems*, 1988, drawn from *Ring Song* and the not-yet-published *The Dangerous World*, demonstrates NR's unsentimental evocation of powerful emotional moments: 'I met my Solitude. We two stood glaring. / I had to tremble, meeting him face to face.'

Reynolds, Frances, 1729–1807, painter and theorist, sister of Mary PALMER. She came to London in 1752 to housekeep for her elder brother Joshua, who discouraged her work (history painting as well as miniatures and pastels) and blamed her for 'singularity' and intellectual unrest. Later problems about where to live stemmed from social expectation that she would stay with him. She visited Paris in 1768, and bought a London house when he died, 1792. Her commonplace-book notes her longing for 'some grateful gale of praise to push my bark to sea'. In 1781 Samuel Johnson saw in a draft of her *Enquiry Concerning the Principles of Taste, and the Origin of Our Ideas of Beauty* a 'force of comprehension' and 'nicety of observation' worthy of Locke or Pascal, but also confusion or obscurity. She discussed later versions with him, reluctant to 'stand the sale', but soon printed 250 copies privately, dedicated to Elizabeth MONTAGU, to whom she confided her wish to leave 'a respectable memorial of my existence'. (For their letters see *Princeton Univ. Library Chronicle*, 41, 1980.) Pub. 1789, repr. 1951, FR's book is strong on visual emphasis (a diagram relates Nature, Beauty, Truth, Sublimity, etc.), but weaker on logic. She sharply divides masculine from feminine qualities ('The robust and determined expression of the rigid virtues, justice, fortitude, etc., would be displeasing in a woman'), and prefers 'feminine' flowers to 'the robust, unmeaning, masculine, piony, hollyhock, etc'. Her verse *Melancholy Tale* was pub. 1790, her carefully revised recollections of Johnson (with attention to female contemporaries) not till 1831.

Rhondda, Margaret Haig Thomas, Viscountess, 1883–1958, essayist, autobiographer, suffragette, businesswoman, b. in Llanwern, Mon., da. of Sybil Margaret (Haig) and D. A. Thomas, Viscount Rhondda. 'Until I was thirteen I learnt what trifles I did from governesses', but she was later sent to Notting Hill High School, London, then to St Leonard's School in St Andrews and Somerville College, Oxford, leaving to marry Humphrey Mackworth (divorced after the war). She walked in a Suffrage Procession a month before her marriage and joined the WSPU shortly after, going to jail for burning letters in a pillar box. She wrote weekly articles for the WSPU, then for other journals. She joined her father's business, became an accomplished businesswoman, and, when she inherited his title, instructed counsel to ask the Committee for Privileges to 'deal with a point of law which is involved as to whether her sex disqualifies her from receiving a Writ of Summons to the House of Lords'. (The Sex Disqualification Removal Act had been passed, 1919.) Her petition was dismissed. She was founder of the Six Point Group and of *Time and Tide*, the feminist review, which appeared on 14 May 1920, and gave a platform to Rebecca WEST, Stella BENSON, Virginia WOOLF, E. M. DELAFIELD

Naomi MITCHISON, among others. Virginia and Leonard Woolf published her *Leisured Women*, 1928, a post-Vote polemic arguing that 'the half-way house is always a perilous place.... Women have been given freedom, but they have not been given training, opportunity, or the sense of responsibility that would teach them to use freedom wisely.' R's own selected *Time and Tide* essays are published as *Notes on the Way*, 1937; her autobiographical *This Was My World*, 1933, describes the main events of her life (including a long trip to Alberta in 1919 and the sinking of the *Lusitania*). See Dale Spender, *Time and Tide Wait for No Man*, 1984.

'Rhys, Jean', Ellen Gwendolen Rees Williams, 1890–1979, fiction writer, b. at Roseau, Dominica, to Minna (Lockhart), a white Dominican, and Welsh Dr William Rees W. A lonely child, she grew up in a small white community, was barred by a family quarrel from her grandmother's beloved estate, and attended the local Catholic convent where whites were the minority. Early awareness of conflicts of race, sex, and religion, and fascination with colonial history, were important to her development as a writer. At 16, in 1907, she travelled to England with an aunt to attend the Perse School in Cambridge and briefly, 1909, the Academy of Dramatic Art in London. Her father d. about then (precise facts and dates in her life are often disputed), and she survived by joining a touring company as a chorus girl, then on payments from an older lover, and then in desultory jobs. In 1919 she married Jean Lenglet, a Dutch–French song-writer and journalist; living in Paris and briefly in Vienna, they had a son who died at three weeks and then a daughter. A friend rewrote and fictionalized JR's diary of 1910–19; Ford Madox Ford admired the result (unpub.), gave JR her pseudonym, drew her into a painful triangle with him and his common-law wife, Stella Bowen (Lenglet was away, extradited to Holland), published her 'Vienne' sketches in his *Transatlantic Review*, 1924, and praised the 'passion, hardship, emotions' in her first book, *The Left Bank and Other Stories*, 1927. Her topics include a contest between a Dominican mixed-blood editor and a gentleman planter over rights to the English literary heritage, and the sensations brought on by enforced fasting. JR's *Postures*, 1928 (later *Quartet*: filmed 1981), a novel about the Ford affair (rejected by one publisher as possibly libellous), is a third-person story about a girl seen at first as 'decorative but strangely pathetic', later 'lying huddled. As if there were a spring broken somewhere', at the end knocked out cold by her husband, having told him, untruly but wishing to hurt, that she loves the other man. In 1928 JR's translation from Francis Carco appeared as Ford's: in 1932 she translated Lenglet's own pseudonymous account of the Ford events. Divorced about then, she married publishers' reader Leslie Tilden-Smith. The heroine of *After Leaving Mr Mackenzie*, 1930, is seen drifting through London and Paris on tenuous support from an ex-lover. The next two tell their own stories. In *Voyage in the Dark*, 1934, a white West Indian, chorus girl and later kept mistress, finds England unreal beside memories of her island: 'I always wanted to be black.... Being black is warm and gay, being white is cold and sad'; she is left further alienated by an abortion. This work draws on the diaries mentioned above. In *Good Morning, Midnight*, 1939 (title from Emily DICKINSON), a woman in her forties undergoes much 'rosy, wooden, innocent cruelty'; she ends seeing herself as dead or dying, yet uttering to an unwanted sexual partner a Joycean 'Yes – yes – yes': variously interpreted. In 1945 Tilden-Smith died and JR married his cousin Max Hamer. She was twice rediscovered when supposed dead, each time by BBC plans to dramatize *Good Morning*. In 1949 she felt 'rather tactless being alive', but carefully revised the novel; in 1957 she was traced to Devon, where she and Hamer had retired after he served a jail term for embezzlement. JR got back to work on *Wide Sargasso Sea* (begun before WWII, pub. 1966 to three awards: see Ruth Webb on its MSS in *BL Journal*, 14, 1988), which gives Charlotte BRONTË's Jamaican madwoman in the attic a tragic past and motives for turning from love to hatred. Stories followed: *Tigers are Better-Looking*, 1968 (some repr. from *Left Bank*, some from 1960 on), *My Day*, NY 1975 (brief, autobiographical), and *Sleep It Off, Lady*, 1976. *Smile, Please: An Unfinished Autobiography*, 1979, is vivid on Dominica, thinner on Europe, and ends about 1930; *Collected Short Stories* appeared in 1986. JR's will forbade a biography: David Plante pub. a merciless account of her old age (*Difficult Women*, 1983, repr. from 1979); other studies include Arnold E. Davidson, 1985, Nancy R. Harrison, 1988; see Francis Wyndham and Diana Melly, ed. and selec., *Letters, 1931–1966*, 1984; bibliog. by Elgin W. Mellown, 1984.

Riccoboni, Marie-Jeanne (Laboras de Mezières), 1714–92, French anglophile epistolary novelist. Born of a bigamous union, educ. in a convent, she left her unhappy marriage to an Italian actor and supported herself first on the stage, later by writing. She began with English settings and names: Fanni Butlerd (sic), 1757, was the first of her much-wronged heroines. Frances BROOKE published an English rendering, 1760, of *Juliette Catesby*, 1757, most successful of M-JR's eight novels (repr. 1983), and asked leave to translate the rest. M-JR refused, being a friend of David Garrick (her letters to him, Hume, and Sir Robert Liston ed. James C. Nicholls, 1976); but most of her works were influential in English versions. Elizabeth GRIFFITH and Frances BURNEY admired her. Studies by Joan Hinde Stewart, 1976, and Andrée Demay, 1977.

Rice, Anne (O'Brien), novelist, b. 1941 in New Orleans, da. of Katherine (Allen) and sculptor Howard O'B.: raised as a Roman Catholic, she feels an outsider. She was educ. at Texas Woman's Univ., 1959–60, and what is now San Francisco State Univ. (BA 1964, MA 1971). She married poet Stanley R. in 1961, had two children (one since dead), and worked as waitress, clerk, and usherette. In *Interview with the Vampire*, 1976 (which sold a million and a half copies, and made her a cult figure), the narrator relates his life since becoming a vampire in 1791: 'I fed on strangers. I drew only close enough to see the pulsing beauty, the unique expression, the new and passionate voice, then killed before those feelings of revulsion could be aroused in me, that fear, that sorrow.' The book ends with an initiating, not a killing, bite. *The Vampire Lestat*, 1985, and *Queen of the Damned*, 1988 (on a 6,000-year-old mother of vampires: see *WRB*, April 1989), make up the *Vampire Chronicles* trilogy. AR did ten years' research for *The Feast of All Souls*, 1979, about the nineteenth-century 'free colored' New Orleans community: its male protagonist, a young and cherished dandy, is beaten and humiliated when he tries to make contact with the white father who has supported him; female characters fare even worse. Sex and violence go together in all AR's work. As 'Anne Rampling' she writes books like *Belinda*, 1986, on a painter besotted with a 16-year-old nymphet (a despised 'feminist and antipornography spokesperson' calls his exhibition of pictures of her 'a rape'). AR is 'A. N. Roquelaure' (a masquerade cloak) for the trilogy *The Claiming of Sleeping Beauty*, 1983, *Beauty's Punishment*, 1984, and *Beauty's Release*, 1985, labelled erotic novels 'of discipline, love and surrender, for the enjoyment of men and women', in which straps are freely applied to willing flesh.

'Rice, Craig' (Georgiana Ann Randolph Craig), 'Michael Venning', 'Daphne Saunders', 1908–57, prodigiously popular thriller and short-story writer, b. Chicago, da. of painters Mary (Randolph) and Harry

'Bosco' Moshiem C., who left her first with her grandmother, then with her aunt, Mrs Elton Rice, while they travelled in Europe and the East. Educ. partly by her uncle, who is said to have read Poe to her, and by a Jesuit missionary, she later ran away from Miss Ransome's School in Piedmont, Calif. Married at least four times, she had three children, cast as characters in her tenth mystery, the autobiographical *Home Sweet Homicide*, 1944 (which, like *Trial by Fury*, 1941, was listed in the Haycraft–Queen 'Cornerstones of DETECTIVE FICTION' list). Her first mystery novel, *8 Faces at 3*, 1939, followed years of writing radio scripts and news stories in Chicago. She published 19 more in her lifetime, including one gothic, *Telefair*, 1942, and one book about real-life crime, *45 Murders*, 1952, and more than 60 stories. She created John J. Malone, Jake Justus and Helene Justus, among other sleuths, and some memorable villains. Her comedy – indicated by such titles as *Having a Wonderful Crime*, 1943, and by such inset headlines as 'Murdered Model Model Union Member' – was said by *Time* magazine, whose cover she was the first woman mystery writer to grace, to exemplify 'detective farce', an offshoot of 'the American genre' in detective writing. She ghosted two best-selling detective novels for her friend Gypsy Rose LEE, and, with science-fiction writer Cleve Cartmill, George Sanders's *Crime on My Hands*, 1944. Disguise recurs in the narrative of her life: she dressed for a photograph as 'Michael Venning', for *Who's Who*; the authenticity of some later texts is queried. She died of a muscular disease compounded by alcoholism. Some posthumous publications are co-authored; many short stories are uncollected. See her article in *The Writer*, November 1944, and Peggy Moran in Jane S. Bakerman, *And Then There Were Nine: More Women of Mystery*, 1985.

Rich, Adrienne, poet, essayist, theorist, activist. B. in 1929 in Baltimore, to white southern Protestant Helen (Jones), and Dr Arnold Rice R., 'an "assimilated" Jew in an anti-Semitic world', she was educ. at home until the fourth grade, by her mother, a composer and pianist, and in her father's library. Her first, childhood, publications were plays, *Ariadne: A Play in Three Acts and Poems*, 1939, and *Not I, But Death, A Play in One Act*, 1941. The year she graduated from Radcliffe (1951), she won the Yale Younger Poets Award for *A Change of World*. She married Alfred Conrad, a Harvard economics professor, in 1953, and had three sons within the next six years, publishing only *The Diamond Cutters and Other Poems*, 1955. The title poem of her next volume, *Snapshots of a Daughter-in-Law: Poems, 1954–62*, 1963, marks a shift from controlled irony and formal elegance to a poetry 'informed by conscious sexual politics' whose voice becomes increasingly personal and immediate. In 1966, AR separated from her husband, left Cambridge, and taught in the NY Open Admissions and SEEK Programs, then at Brandeis, Bryn Mawr, Rutgers, and Cornell Univs. She taught in California, 1983–6, and became professor of English and feminist studies at Stanford, 1986. She learned from Yeats that poetry can 'root itself' in politics, and when she began to 'write directly and overtly as a woman out of a woman's body and experience, to take women's existence seriously as theme and source for art ... it did indeed *imply the breakdown of the world as I had always known it, the end of safety*'. (She paraphrases James Baldwin.) *Necessities of Life*, 1966, *Selected Poems*, 1967, *Leaflets*, 1969, and *The Will to Change*, 1971, show her involvement in anti-war protests and black civil rights and an increasing identification with female experience. *Diving into the Wreck*, 1973, winner of the National Book Award, 1974, accepted with Audre LORDE and Alice WALKER, articulates personal anger and political principle. The same feminist intensity informs her first analytic work, *Of Woman Born: Motherhood as Experience and Institution*, 1976, which exposes the most 'natural' of phenomena as ideologically shaped. AR's lesbianism, in *The Dream of a Common Language*, 1978, which includes 'Twenty-One Love Poems', allows her to say, 'I choose to love this time for once / with all my intelligence' (from 'Splitting'). *A Wild Patience Has Taken Me This Far*, 1981, continues her figuration of silenced women. From 1981 to 1983 she edited, with Michelle CLIFF, the influential lesbian feminist journal *Sinister Wisdom*, twice in this time undergoing surgery for rheumatoid arthritis. *Sources*, 1983, an autobiographical sequence, and the new poems in *The Fact of a Doorframe*, 1984, address the weight of verbal privilege and the exhaustion of ongoing struggle: 'the thought that what I must engage / . . . is meant to break my heart and reduce me to silence' (from 'North American Time'). *Your Native Land, Your Life*, 1986, brings together AR's personal and historical sensibilities and examines her ethical position as a white woman, reminding us to 'watch the edges that blur'. These powerful and beautiful poems suggest a new formal rigour, less distanced than the early writing. Read alongside her poems, AR's essays, *On Lies, Secrets, and Silence*, 1979, and *Blood, Bread and Poetry*, 1986, offer a history of contemporary US white FEMINIST THEORY. *Time's Power: Poems 1985–1988*, 1989, continues AR's move 'deeper into the heart of the matter' through personal and political history. See AR on her work in selec. ed. by Barbara Charlesworth Gelpi and Albert Gelpi, 1975, and studies by Wendy Martin, 1984, Myriam Diaz-Diocaretz, 1984 and 1985, and Claire Keyes, 1986.

Richards, Laura Elizabeth (Howe), 1850–1943, US biographer and children's writer, da. of poet Julia (Ward) HOWE, whose life she wrote (with her sister) in 1915, winning the Pulitzer Prize for biography. LER married Henry R., 1871, and had seven children. Her historical romances and parables and stories for children are sometimes pithy (like *The Golden Windows*, 1903 – made a structuring motif in DRABBLE's *Jerusalem the Golden* – and *The Silver Crown*, 1906), often sentimentally moralizing. Her lives of Florence NIGHTINGALE, 1909, Elizabeth Fry, 1916, Abigail ADAMS, 1917, and Joan of Arc, 1919, designed for children's edification, seem florid and sketchy today: 'The Angel of Crimea' fits up a kitchen to feed 800 as if with 'a quiet wave of the wand'. LER's ballads, limericks and jingles (like the well-known *Tirra Lirra*, 1921), still sometimes anthologized, are full of often abrupt and undidactic action and silliness, romping rhythms, spontaneous neologisms, and portmanteau coinages. The elephant uses a 'telephant', the pallid Professor Pendleton never had 'a friendleton'; the greedy giant is 'stuffin' on a muffin' 'when all of a sudden he died'.

Richardson, Dorothy Miller, 1873–1957, novelist and journalist. B. in Abingdon, Berks., third of four daughters of Mary (Miller Taylor) and Charles R., a 'gentleman of no occupation' who 'defined life to my dawning intelligence as perpetual leisure spent in enchanting appreciations', DR was educ. at Southborough House in Putney, where she became head girl. Her father's financial difficulties (he was bankrupt by 1893) caused her briefly to become a pupil-teacher in Hanover, Germany, 1891, and then a governess in England, experiences which convinced her that 'many of the evils besetting the world originated in the enclosed particularist home and in the institutions preparing women for such homes'. After her mother's suicide, 1895, she moved to London as a dentist's receptionist, 1896–1908, living alone in a Bloomsbury attic at £1 a week which, after family life, gave her 'the sense of escaping from a charming imprisonment'. Her brief affair with H. G. Wells during this period formed the basis of a life-long friendship. London life she described as 'a kind of archipelago' of different religious, intellectual and political 'islands', 'the habitation of fascinating secret societies, to each of which I wished to belong and yet was held back, returning to solitude and to nowhere, where alone I could be everywhere at once, hearing all the voices in chorus'. By 1908 she was living a vagrant life with friends and family, writing journalism for *Crank*, later *Saturday Review*, *Adelphi*, *Dental Record* and *Little Review*. She began novel-writing, 1912, in a rented cottage in Cornwall. *Pointed Roofs*, the first of the 13 parts which comprise her four-vol. novel *Pilgrimage*, was published in 1915. She married artist Alan Odle, 1917, caring for this younger, delicate man until his death, 1948, the couple alternating between Cornwall and London. BRYHER, whom she met in 1923, became a friend and financial support. After *Pointed Roofs* came *Backwater*, 1916, *Honeycomb*, 1917, *The Tunnel*, 1919, *Interim*, 1919, *Deadlock*, 1921, *Revolving Lights*, 1923, *The Trap*, 1925, *Oberland*, 1927, *Dawn's Left Hand*, 1931, and *Clear Horizon*, 1935. *Dimple Hill* was included in the collec. edition of *Pilgrimage*, 1938, and *March Moonlight* in the 1967 ed. *Pilgrimage* demonstrates DR's dissatisfaction with the conventional novel: 'The material that moved me would not fit the framework of any novel I had experienced. [Both the realist and the romantic novel] left out certain essentials and dramatized life misleadingly. Horizontally. Assembling their characters, the novelists developed situations, devised events, climax and conclusion. I could not accept their finalities.' *Pilgrimage*'s concern is with the interior and essential life of Miriam Henderson, its autobiographical heroine, from her time as a young teacher in Germany to her meeting with 'a tall skeleton in tattered garments' based on DR's husband. In *Pilgrimage* DR sought to express a 'contemplated reality' which was also an attempt 'to produce a feminine equivalent of the current masculine realism'. May SINCLAIR accurately described this feminized realism as 'moments tense with vibration, moments drawn out fine, almost to snapping-point', 'no drama, no situation, no set scene', 'just life going on and on. ... Miriam Henderson's stream of consciousness going on and on'. Virginia WOOLF wrote that she had 'invented, or, if ... not invented, developed and applied to her own uses, a sentence which we might call the sentence of the feminine gender'. See DR, 'Data for Spanish Publisher', *London Magazine*, June 1959, May Sinclair in *The Egoist*, April 1918, Virginia Woolf in *Nation and Athenaeum*, 19 May 1923. Biographies by Gloria G. Fromm, 1977, and John Rosenberg, 1973; critical study by Gillian E. Hanscombe, 1982. Papers at Yale, NYPL, Princeton, Rice, Penn. and Texas Univs., and BL.

'Richardson, Henry Handel' (Ethel Florence Lindsay Richardson, later Robertson), 1870–1946, novelist and short-story writer, b. Melbourne, Victoria, eldest da. of Mary (Bailey) and Walter Lindsay R., an Irish physician, d. 1879, who came to Victoria during the 1850s gold rushes. Her historical trilogy, *The Fortunes of Richard Mahoney*, 1930, which took 20 years to research and write, attempts to fit her father's life into an explicable pattern. Mary supported her family by working as a postmistress in country towns and was able to send HHR to Presbyterian Ladies' College, then Melbourne's leading girls' school. The five years spent there, including her emotional attachment to a fellow-student, are reflected in her satirical novel, *The Getting of Wisdom*, 1910 (filmed 1977 by Bruce Beresford). From 1888 she studied piano at the Leipzig Conservatorium, but found she was temperamentally unsuited to a career as a concert pianist. In 1895 she m. J. G. Robertson, who encouraged her to read European literature and to write. She read Freud in German and absorbed the major philosophical trends of the time. Her pessimistic world view is tempered by themes of romantic love and her lifelong interest in SPIRITUALISM. She pub. translations, and in 1897 began her first novel, *Maurice Guest*, 1908, based on her student years in Leipzig, and, for its period, remarkably frank in its treatment of both homosexuality and women's sexuality. After her husband became Professor of German at London Univ. in 1903, HHR led a reclusive life, devoting herself to writing. The first two vols. of her trilogy, *Australia Felix,* 1917, and *The Way Home,* 1925, attracted little attention, but *Ultima Thule,* 1929, was a bestseller which, for a time, gave her an international reputation. A Nobel Prize nominee in 1932, she pub. a collection of stories, *The End of Childhood,* 1934, which contains an important sequence, 'Growing Pains', focusing on the problems girls face in regard to sexuality and the human body. The inferior quality of her final novel, *Young Cosima,* 1939, a semi-documentary account of the early life of Cosima Wagner, reflects the devastating loss of her husband (d. 1933). Her autobiography, *Myself When Young,* 1948, was completed by her long-time companion, Olga Roncoroni. MSS and letters are in the National Library, Canberra, and the Mitchell Library, Sydney. See the critical studies by Nettie PALMER, 1950, Dorothy Green, 1973, and Karen McLeod, 1985 and biog. of early years by Axel Clarke, 1990.

Richardson, Sarah (Fawcett), d. 1823/4, miscellaneous writer. Because of what he called 'adverse circumstances' she lived with Joseph R., MP and satirist, for years before 1799, when she married him: her daughters were born out of wedlock. His death in 1803, and the burning of Drury Lane Theatre (whose patent he shared) left her poor. She ed. his *Remains,* 1807, with an anon. life, and exploited her family relation to Isaac Watts with poems for children, 1808 (on a plan she said Watts recommended). Mary CHAMPION DE CRESPIGNY and Amelia OPIE subscribed to her blank-verse tragedies, *Ethelred* [1809] (stress on female friendship) and *Gertrude* [1810] (heroine brings trouble all round by swapping her baby son for a rich, sickly infant which unexpectedly survives). SR translated a novel, *The Exile of Poland,* 1819, and recounted biblical history (Creation to Aaron's rod) in heroic couplets, 1820–2.

Richmond and Derby, **Margaret** (Beaufort), Countess of, 1441–1509, translator and letter-writer. Da. of John Beaumont, 1st Duke of Somerset, who d. when she was two, and Margaret (Beauchamp), who brought her up, she was married in 1455 to Edmund Tudor, Earl of R. He d. in 1456, leaving her pregnant with the future Henry VII. Living privately during the Wars of the Roses, she secured her son's marriage to Elizabeth of York; his throne was secured with a change of sides by her third husband, Lord Stanley, during the battle of Bosworth. She sent him written advice (her letters stand out in M. A. E. Wood, ed., 1846), collected books, patronized works by Caxton and others from 1489, and compiled *Ordinances and Reformations of Apparel for Princes and Estates* (1493, MS in BL). She translated, from French, Thomas à Kempis's *De Imitatione Christi,* book iv (other books transl. William Atkynson, 1504; repr. 1893, 1904), and a Carthusian treatise, *The Mirroure of Golde for the Synfull Soule,* printed *c.* 1505. She separated from Lord Stanley in 1504, taking monastic vows but remaining in her own house; she founded Cambridge colleges, and chairs of divinity there and at Oxford; Lady Margaret Hall, Oxford, a women's college till 1978, bears her name. Life by Enid M. G. Routh, 1924.

Riddell, Charlotte Elizabeth Lawson (Cowan), 'Mrs J. H. Riddell', 'F. G. Trafford', 1832–1906, novelist, b. Carrickfergus, Co. Antrim, youngest da. of Ellen (Kilshaw) and James C., who d. early. She and her mother moved to London, where in 1856 her mother died, and in 1857 she m. J. H. R., civil engineer. He soon lost his money, and she began to write. Her first novel, *Zuriel's Grandchild,* 1856, was followed by *The Moors and the Fens,* 1858. Despite a conventional plot, it is a well-written, sharply observed study of the power and effects of mean-spiritedness. It appeared under 'F. G. Trafford', the name she used up to 1864 (she used her own name and other pseudonyms thereafter). She produced at least 30 titles, and from 1867 edited the *St James's Magazine,* founded by Anna Maria HALL. She also wrote tales for the SPCK and for Christmas ANNUALS; her *Weird Stories* were pub. 1882, and *Collected Ghost Stories* 1977, ed. E. F. Bleiler. But her novels were more successful, particularly *George Geith of Fen Court,* 1864, dramatized in 1883 by Wybert Reeve, *Home Sweet Home,* 1873, a fine study of a musically gifted country girl, and *The Nun's Curse,* 1888. Generous to other writers, she always struggled for her own living, and became the first pensioner of the Society of Authors from 1901. Her novels were often set in the City of London, dealing knowledgeably with themes of commerce. *A Struggle for Fame,* 1883, must be autobiographical in its realistic account of a young girl's determination to become a writer, living in London with an invalid parent, tramping round publishers' offices, and finally achieving success and her own (unshared) country cottage.

Riddell, Maria (Woodley), 1772–1812, miscellaneous writer, youngest da. of Frances (Payne) and William W. She wrote verse at 15 and described, in *Voyages to the Leeward and Caribbean Islands,* Edinburgh, 1792, a trip undertaken with her Governor father in 1788. In 1790 she became second wife of Captain Walter R., with whom she returned to live near Dumfries. Robert Burns flirted, then bitterly quarrelled with her; she sent him a poem of reconciliation in 1795, the year she also wrote in support of press-ganged Irish tinkers, and found herself and her husband short of money. On Burns's death she wrote for the Dumfries *Weekly Journal,* Aug. 1796, a memoir called the best by a contemporary critic: revised for Currie's 1801 ed. Her ANTHOLOGY, *The Metrical Miscellany,* 1802, includes her own poems and others by A. L. BARBAULD,Georgiana DEVONSHIRE, and Mary DARWALL. She wrote love poems, an Edinburgh theatre epilogue, and a defence of sensibility against stoicism. After her husband's death that year, she and her surviving daughter lived as pensioners at Hampton Court; she married Phillips Lloyd Fletcher the year of her death. Letters at Kilmarnock and Liverpool; Hugh S. Gladstone prints diary extracts in *Transactions* of the Dumfriesshire ... Antiquarian Soc., 3rd series iii, 1914–15.

Ridge, 'Lola', Rose Emily, 1873–1941, poet, b. in Dublin, only surviving child of Emma (Reilly) and Joseph Henry Ridge. Her mother took her to New Zealand in 1887; after an unhappy marriage LR moved to Sydney, Australia, where she studied at Trinity College and the Académie Julienne (art). After her mother died she migrated to San Francisco, 1907 (its *Overland Monthly* first published one of her poems), and NYC, 1908, where she worked as factory hand and artist's model, and wrote advertisements, magazine stories and poems for Emma GOLDMAN's *Mother Earth.* She 'identified herself from the beginning with the cause of labor and the workers': *The Ghetto,* 1918 (title poem repr. from *New Republic*), impressed critics with its naturalistic celebration of construction workers and Jewish immigrants in NYC. LR married David Lawson in 1919. *Sun-Up,* 1920, mixes personal evocation of her childhood with poems supporting anarchist causes. During the 1920s she edited and wrote for a range of journals, appearing in *New Masses* and *The Left* as well as *Saturday Review* and *Poetry*, toning down the experimental modernism of *Broom* and rejecting work by Gertrude STEIN. Her *Red Flag* (poems), 1927, includes tributes to Soviet and other revolutionary heroes. Her part (with Edna St Vincent MILLAY and others) in the fruitless campaign to save Sacco and Vanzetti resulted in *Firehead,* 1929, a symbolic retelling of the crucifixion story. Called by Laura BENET's brother William Rose 'one of the most extraordinary poems written by an American', it was planned to go with five more (on ancient Babylon, Renaissance Florence, Montezuma's Mexico, revolutionary France, and post-WWI Manhattan) as a great cycle to be called 'Lightwheel'. Travel and research in the Near East, 1931, and Mexico, 1935–7, failed to complete the project; *Dance of Fire,* 1935, again mystically joins the suffering of Christ to that of resisting proletarians. LR received various poetry awards; one set up in her name after her death (from tuberculosis) ran until 1950. Some juvenilia (she regretted destroying the rest) in the Mitchell Library, Sydney; other papers at Yale and the Univ. of Texas (Austin).

Riding, Laura (Reichenthal), also Gottschalk and Jackson, 'Madeleine Vara', poet, critic, short-story writer and novelist. B. 1901, of New York Jewish Socialist parents, Sarah (Edersheim) and Nathaniel S. Reichenthal, she resented pressure to be 'an American Rosa Luxemburg', and often sniped at the Left in stories like 'Socialist Pleasures', 1933. She was educ. at a Brooklyn high school and Cornell Univ., where in 1920 she married Louis Gottschalk (divorced 1925). By then her poems were appearing in Allen Tate and Robert Penn Warren's *The Fugitive* and Harriet MONROE's *Poetry*; Leonard and Virginia WOOLF pub. her volume, *The Close Chaplet,* 1926. Always marked by repetition, assonance, and unconcern for rhyme, sometimes by humour, her obscure, philosophical, brilliant work remains controversial. She was living in England with Robert Graves and his wife, Nancy Nicholson, when the Woolfs issued her *Voltaire: A Biographical Fantasy,* 1927. She and Graves collaborated on *A Survey of Modernist Poetry,* 1927 (often repr.: denouncing Imagism and Georgianism as 'temporary fads'), *A Pamphlet Against Anthologies,* 1928, and (as 'Barbara Rich') a satirical novel, *No Decency Left,* 1932. They founded the Seizin Press in 1927 and published LR's second poetry volume (*Love as Love, Death as Death,* 1928); for nine years, from 1930, they ran the press in Mallorca. In *Contemporaries and Snobs* and *Anarchism is Not Enough,* both 1928, LR urged poets to write of their own experience, not to programmes. She touched on her 1929 suicide attempt in *Experts are Puzzled,* 1930 (stories); *Four Unposted Letters to Catherine,* Hours Press, Paris, 1930, gently advises Graves's daughter to self-discovery. LR plumbed the poet's solitude in *Laura and Francesca,* 1931 (long poem), and turned to the ancient world in *A Trojan Ending,* 1937 (novel), and *Lives of Wives,* 1939 (marital views of Cyrus, Alexander, Aristotle and Herod). Her journal, *Epilogue,* where she wrote as 'Madeleine Vara', ran 1935–8. *Collected Poems,* 1938, was repr. 1980. She denied writing 'God is a Woman' on her bedroom wall, but maintained (as in *The Telling,* 1972) that women's superior insight would save humanity at last. LR returned to the USA in 1939, married Schuyler Jackson (d. 1970), then poetry editor of *Time,* in 1941, and gave up poetry. She and her husband moved to Florida to grow fruit and work on a still unfinished dictionary and thesaurus. But she has since enlarged and prefaced the collection *Progress of Stories,* 1982, published articles (e.g. criticism of her critic Christopher Norris: *Language and Style,* 11, 19, 1978, 1986), printed a new poem ('Lamenting the Terms of Modern Praise': *Chelsea,* 4, 1988). See study by Joyce Piell Wexler, 1979; article by Jo-Ann Wallace, forthcoming.

Ridler, Anne Borkman (Bradby), poet, dramatist and editor She was b. 1912 at Rugby, Warwicks., to Violet (Milford) and Henry Christopher B., Rugby School housemaster. After educ. at Downe House School, for six months in Italy, and at King's College, London Univ. (diploma in journalism), she worked from 1935 as T. S. Eliot's secretary, then junior publisher's editor. She m. Vivian R., Oxford Univ.

printer, in 1938, and had four children. Her nine slim vols. of poetry, from *Poems,* 1939 (whose paper cover was designed by her husband), to *Dies Natalis,* 1980, with pieces in US journals, quietly celebrate erotic, family, domestic themes in a Christian framework: 'love is one interest, love one capital theme' in often 'occasional' verse. AR uses natural imagery, subtle wordplay, traditional forms, and minor metrical surprises. *The Nine Bright Shiners,* 1943, and *The Golden Bird,* 1951, reflect their wartime composition. The title poem of *A Matter of Life and Death,* 1959, charts a son's growing up and away. *Selected Poems,* 1961, appeared only in NY; *New and Selected Poems,* 1988, adds work dealing with the ambivalent conditions of life ('The flesh that formed us can divide / To form a cancer, and the strength / That held our weakness be dissolved'). Her few critics have praised the delicacy and intelligence of her voice. Her verse dramas (not all pub.) contribute to the revival begun by Eliot; they include *Cain,* 1943, *Henry Bly,* 1947, and *The Trial of Thomas Cranmer,* 1956 (written for the 400th anniversary of his martyrdom, played in the Oxford church where he was tried). She has written opera librettos (translated and original) and ed. past poets (including de la Mare, Charles Williams, James Thomson), Shakespeare criticism, and ghost stories. Her *Little Book of Modern Verse,* 1951, includes works of Marianne MOORE, Kathleen RAINE, and Edith SITWELL. See William V. Sparas in *The Christian Tradition in Modern British Verse Drama,* 1962; Tracey Ware in *Poetry,* 73, 1983.

Rigby, Elizabeth, Lady Eastlake, 1809–93, journalist, art historian, travel writer, b. Norwich, fifth child and fourth daughter of Anne Palgrave and Edward R., physician, d. 1821. Educ. at home, mainly by masters, her awareness of her 'very deficient education' probably accounts for her later interest in women's educational reforms. In 1827, after a debilitating illness, she was taken by her mother with the family to Heidelberg for two years; her earliest pub. work was a criticism of Goethe, *Foreign Quarterly Review,* 1836. In 1838, she paid the first of several visits to her married sister in Russia; LETTERS from this trip, pub. as *A Residence on the Shores of the Baltic,* 1841, brought literary success and began her lifelong association with the publisher John Murray. She moved to Edinburgh in 1842, participating in literary circles and contributing to periodicals. In 1849 she m. Charles Eastlake (knighted 1850), later President of the Royal Academy. They travelled widely on the Continent, seeking pictures for the National Gallery and writing collaborative art histories until his death in 1865. Her often pungently expressed pieces include book reviews, biographical studies, and essays on German and Italian art, children's literature, foreign travel, Ruskin, photography, British cultural institutions and women's EDUCATION. Her scathing attack on *Jane Eyre* in the *Quarterly,* December 1848, is curious, given Eastlake's own independence of thought and sympathy with women's emancipation. She also ed. Anna JAMESON's *History of Our Lord in Art,* 1860, and wrote *Fellowship: letters addressed to my sister mourners,* 1868, a book of consolation for bereaved women based on her own experiences. See also her *Journals and Correspondence,* ed. by her nephew, Charles Eastlake Smith, 1895, and life by Marion Lochhead, 1961.

Riley, Denise, poet, b. in 1948 in Carlisle. She did not know her actual parents, and prefers not to name her adoptive parents, a clerical worker from Tyneside and a shipyard worker's son, later an accountant. She grew up in Glos., educ. at a local convent school until 1952 (though not Catholic) and grammar school (where she read WOOLF and de BEAUVOIR and joined the Abortion Law Reform Society). She says, 'when I try to make my life give me its answers to how I have come to my current concerns, I can't do it without feeling that I am on the edge of a dangerous fiction of self-description'. She transferred from Oxford to Cambridge (BA in philosophy and art history), where she met Wendy MULFORD, who encouraged her writing, pub. her *Marxism for Infants,* 1977, and collaborated with her on *No Fee,* 1978, and *Some Poems,* 1982. In 1968 she attended the first national conference of the Women's Liberation Movement as well as demonstrations against the Vietnam war. She worked as a translator in London, had two children, and did a PhD in philosophy at Sussex Univ. Her research (on contemporary developments in social, political and psychological views of mother and child) led to *War in the Nursery,* 1983. She has written for journals including *Feminist Review* and *Spare Rib.* Her *Dry Air,* 1985, adds new poems to some from earlier vols. In 'Affections must not' she writes, 'the houses are murmuring with many small pockets of emotion / on which spongy ground adults' lives are being erected & paid for daily / while their feet and their children's feet are tangled around like those of fen larks / in the fine steely wires which run to & fro between love & economics // affections must not support the rent // I. neglect. the. house.' *Am I that Name,* 1987, tackles problems of theoretical feminism, over-interpretation, and understanding past feminisms; no one, it says, can be a woman 100 per cent of the time. See her account in Liz Heron, ed., *Truth Dare or Promise,* 1985 (quoted above).

Riley, Joan, novelist, b. 1958 at St Mary, Jamaica, youngest of eight children. Educ. at the Univs. of Sussex (BA, 1979) and London (MA, 1984), she teaches black history and culture in Britain, and works for a drugs advisory agency. On balance opposed to separatism for black women, she supports women's 'organising within the wider framework of Black people's struggle'. She has a daughter, and is active on behalf of single parents. Her first novel, *The Unbelonging*, 1985, centres on an 11-year-old girl summoned from her aunt's house in Kingston to join her father in Britain, facing a quest for identity amid the cold gloom of the inner city, racial hostility and isolation at school, her father's violent, threatening, uncomprehended sexuality, and escapist daydreams of home or of academic success. Blamed by some black readers (e.g. Maud SULTER) for negativity, JR in *Waiting in the Twilight,* 1987, pursues her chronicle of 'the forgotten and unglamorous section of my people': a woman crippled by a stroke looks back at Jamaica and Britain in the 1950s and 60s, the betrayals of husband and lover, the closing down of opportunity; yet memories of failure can also be read as a record of an unending struggle for dignity and self-hood. *Romance,* 1988, treats similar themes in less tragic tone: two sisters, chafing respectively in a tedious though successful job and the servicing routines of a wife and mother, are led to re-think themselves and their lives by a visit of grannies from Jamaica, who offer a feast of folktales and the authority of matriarchal age.

Rinehart, Mary (Roberts), 1876–1958, novelist, short-story writer and journalist, b. at Allegheny, Penna, da. of Cornelia (Gilleland) and Thomas Roberts, a sewing-machine salesman. She trained as a nurse in Pittsburgh, married Dr Stanley Marshall Rinehart, 1896, and had three sons (two founded a publishing house) before she was 25. By 1904, fighting debt, she was publishing 'weird and often horrible' stories and poems in magazines like *Munsey's* and *All-Story.* Her first mystery novel, *The Circular Staircase*, 1908 (originally an *All-Story* serial), began both her line of independent, adventurous woman protagonists and her career as leading US popular writer (until about 1940). Some works drew $65,000 in the 1930s from mass-circulation magazines for serial rights; many were filmed. She held to two maxims: that the initial crime is merely forerunner to others, and that the DETECTIVE plot partly conceals a second story. As well as mysteries, MRR wrote POPULAR romances (like *The Street of Seven Sisters*, 1914, and *'K'*, 1915), three plays with Avery Hopwood, and articles on travel, war, women's role, and her cancer operation, 1947. For nearly 30 years from 1910 *The Saturday Evening Post* carried the hilarious adventures of her intrepid, problem-solving spinster 'Tish'. MRR drew on war-correspondent experience in *The Amazing Interlude*, 1918, and home-front WWI novels. She was dismayed by poor reception of her 'serious' novels, particularly *This Strange Adventure*, 1929, a bleak look at marriage from the wife's angle. Her last full-length mystery, *The Swimming Pool*, 1952, has the last of several partial self-portraits. Though her work raises the issue of female independence, she often denied having a career, and stressed the difficulty of combining one with 'domestic happiness'. She left a MS autobiography (Univ. of Pittsburgh), more intimate and honest than her *My Story*, 1931, new ed. 1948; see Jan Cohn's enlightening life, 1980. Other MSS at NYPL and the Houghton, Harvard.

Ringwood, Gwen (Pharis), 1910–84, playwright. B. in Anatone, Washington, da. of Mary (Bowersock) and Leslie P., she moved with her family to southern Alberta, 1913. Educ. first at home and in public schools, she later attended the Univs. of Montana, Alberta and North Carolina (MA in English and Drama, 1939). She married Dr John Brian R., 1939, and lived thereafter in Alberta farming communities, in northern Saskatchewan and at Williams Lake, BC. They had four children. She worked for five years at the beginning of her career with Elizabeth Sterling Haynes, a pioneering theatre-arts teacher, director, and actress, during that time writing 13 radio plays and her first stage play, *The Dragons of Kent*, which Haynes produced at the Banff School of Fine Arts, 1935. A major figure in the development of Canadian drama, GPR wrote more than 60 comedies, musicals, folk dramas, and children's plays. Most have a strong regional flavour; some concern Canada's native peoples. *Still Stands the House*, 1939, about prairie depression and drought in the 1930s, remains best known. A constant experimenter with technique and dramatic structure, GPR felt the influence of Synge, Lorca and Greek classical drama. Her later work moves from gentle satire to direct criticism of injustice, and from portrayal of merely subordinate women to presentations of strong, independent women. She also wrote novels (*Younger Brothers*, 1959, about growing up in southern Alberta, and *Pascal*), two musicals, and several short stories. See Geraldine Anthony, 1981; *Collected Plays*, ed. Enid Delgatty Rutland, 1982, including a 'foreword' by Margaret LAURENCE. Papers at Univ. of Calgary.

Ripley, Dorothy, 1767–1831, missionary, one of the large family of Dorothy and of William R. (d. 1784) of Whitby, Yorks., master mason and associate of John Wesley; he 'Design'd me a preacher, before I was born'. She felt from very young a 'spiritual union' with him, and from 11 a call to preach to the heathen. Another influence was helping, about 1787, a young prostitute whom a gang of men had stripped, tarred and feathered: 'Why is this not me Lord?' asked DR. She left home in 1802; by 1807 she had travelled 30,000 miles, and by 1819 crossed the Atlantic seven times. Belonging to no sect, fighting sometimes severe ill health, she preached to American Indians and blacks, visiting hospitals, workhouses and prisons in all the major cities. She denied the charge of PREACHING for hire, but often paid travelling expenses by publishing. She pub., in England and the US, letters sent her by 'Several Africans and Indians', 1807 (some Indian women think much like Jarena LEE on Christianity and feminism); *The Extraordinary Conversion...*, 1817; *The Bank of Faith and Works United*, 1819 (letters and diary from 1805, prepared for press six or seven years before, with jaunty verse autobiog.); *An Address to All in Difficulties* [1821]; and her father's *Memoirs*, with her account of his death, and elegy, 1826.

'Rita', Eliza Margaret (Gollan), Mrs W. D. Humphreys, 1850?–1938, novelist, b. Inverness-shire, da. of John Gilbert G., landowner and, later, bank accountant. She was educ. at home in Sydney, Australia, where her parents had emigrated when she was about five. On returning to England, she attended Broughton and Mathers' school. She gave a description of her Australian childhood in her first truly successful novel, *Sheba*, 1889. In 1872 she made an early and short-lived marriage to Karl Otto Edmund Booth, professor of music. Her early romantic novels, such as *The Sinner*, 1897, and *Sâba Macdonald*, 1906 – the latter in part a protest against the unreasonable strictness of Victorian moral codes – praised 'the divine touch of human sympathy'. In 1902 she founded the Writers' Club for Women, but was unsympathetic towards polemical feminism: 'the real helper is the woman of the home, not the yelling fiend of the platform' (*Personal Opinions Publicly Expressed*, 1907). She was best known for her novels of society life such as *Souls*, 1903, which were considered daring. Her second marriage was to W. Desmond H., with whom she spent much time in Co. Cork, and by whom she had a daughter. In later life, she turned increasingly to religion, and wrote an autobiography, *Recollections of a Literary Life*, in 1936.

Ritchie, Anne Isabella **Thackeray** (later Lady Ritchie), 1837–1919, novelist, biographer and essayist, b. London, da. of Isabella (Shawe) and William Makepeace T. Owing to her mother's mental illness she spent her early years with her grandparents in Paris, returning in 1845 to live with her father, for whom she acted as secretary and amanuensis from 1851 until his death in 1863. Her first publication was 'Little Scholars', 1860, a descriptive essay for *The Cornhill*, in which her first novel, *The Story of Elizabeth*, greatly admired by George ELIOT, was serialized, 1862–3. Told in a discreet, comfortable, domestic and moral tone, its subtext reveals the waste of women's lives, strait-jacketed by social conformity. This was followed by others, including *Old Kensington*, 1873; *Miss Angel*, the life story of artist Angelica Kauffmann, serialized in *The Cornhill*, 1874–5; and a novella, *From the Island*, 1875. In 1867 her sister Harriet (Minny) m. Leslie Stephen and ATR lived with them, making many literary friends. After Minny's death in 1875, ATR cared for her two children until 1877 when she m. her cousin Richmond R., civil servant, later knighted. Her last novel, *Mrs Dymond*, was pub. in 1885, by which time, pressed by her friend Margaret OLIPHANT, her interest had moved from fiction to memoir-writing. In 1892 she began her major literary project, the biographical and critical introductions to Thackeray's work, pub. 1894–5, rev. 1911. She also wrote introductions to the work of M. R. MITFORD, Elizabeth GASKELL and Maria EDGEWORTH. Her final essay coll., *From the Porch*, 1913, opens with 'A Discourse on Modern Sybils' about her female predecessors, including ELIOT, Charlotte BRONTË and Gaskell. She remained active well into her seventies, entertaining her stepnieces Virginia and Vanessa Stephen and helping to organize war relief for French evacuees. Her many friends included Julia Cameron, Rhoda BROUGHTON, the CARLYLES, and Swinburne. Virginia WOOLF's *Times* obituary of ATR (6 Mar. 1919) rightly praises her deft touch as a memorialist: '[she writes] as a bird ... picks off the fruit and leaves the husk'; she figured her as Mrs Hilbery in *Night and Day*, 1919. See Winifred Gérin, 1981, for her life; Steven Callow's annotated bibliography is in *VW Quarterly* 2, 1980.

Ritter, Erica, playwright, short-story writer and essayist. B. in Regina, Sask., in 1948, da. of painter Margaret and salesman Peter R., she was educ. at McGill (BA, 1968) and the Univ. of Toronto (MA in drama, 1970). As a student, she m. Christopher Covert, from whom she is now separated. She taught briefly at Loyola College, Montréal, then returned to Toronto to write, joining Tarragon Theatre's playwriting workshop in 1975. She has since written radio and TV scripts and much literary journalism. Her first play, *A Visitor from Charleston*, 1974, focuses on a female character absurdly obsessed with *Gone with the Wind*. Like most of ER's plays, it comments ironically, sometimes wittily, on women's fears and anxieties. *The Splits*, 1978, more self-reflexive and carefully crafted, is a comedy about writing comedies, and *Automatic Pilot*, 1980, which had a long run in Toronto, presents a comedienne who needs to suffer to do her autobiographical comic routine. As always concerned with the roles and ethical problems of women, in *The Passing Scene*, 1982, ER dramatizes the tensions between fact and fiction in a contemporary relationship. *Urban Scrawl*, 1984, collects some essays; more in *Ritter in Residence*, 1987. Interview in Robert Wallace and Cynthia Zimmerman, *The Work: Conversations with English–Canadian Playwrights*, 1982.

Robe, Jane, translator–dramatist, a 'young Lady' or 'Maiden Muse' when her tragedy, *The Fatal Legacy*, from Racine's *La Thébaïde*, ran for three nights at Lincoln's Inn Fields, London, 1723. It raised just over £80 in benefit. Anonymous printing followed, but not a hoped-for revival next season. She changes the ending, displacing emphasis from general destructive ambition to Creon's specific lust for 'Antigona': they both kill themselves on stage, she following her mother's example ('See where she welters in her Blood, and lies / Like Roses strew'd on Snow'), he mad with remorse. JR's blank verse is better than that of most contemporary dramatists.

Roberts, Abigail, 1748–1823, Quaker educationalist and letter writer, one of ten surviving children (three sets of twins were born) of Dorothy (Craven) and George R. of Kyle, Queen's County. She and her mother corresponded with Mary LEADBEATER and her family. With little education, AR could read the Bible by five, overcame a speech impediment to work as a teacher, *c.* 1767–73, then ran local general shops with a sister, becoming the family support in hard times. They prescribed medicines, and acted as an impromptu library. AR pub. in periodicals and for the Kildare Place Education Society, but declined book projects (one for her poems, one jointly with her mother); a posthumous subscription was dropped. Little vols. appeared anonymously at Dublin: *The Entertaining Medley*, 1819, *The Cottage Fire-side*, 1822, *Tim Higgins*, 1823, the *The Schoolmistress*, 1824 (improving, amusing narrative, dialogue, and verse, in Leadbeater's style). Family history by Ethel J. Adair Impey, 1939.

Roberts, Dorothy Mary Gostwick, b. 1906, poet, da. of Frances Seymour (Allen) and Theodore Goodridge R. (a novelist and poet, brother of Canadian poet Charles G. D. Roberts). She travelled extensively with her family, living in England, France, and various places in Canada, then returned to the family home in Fredericton, NB. She went to high school there, and to the Univs. of New Brunswick and Connecticut State. She married August M. Leisner, 1929, and had two children. She has lived in State College, Penna, since shortly after her marriage. Her poems, mainly lyrical treatments of children, nature, and domestic life, have appeared widely (*Hudson Review*, *Yale Review*, *Canadian Forum*, etc.) and in six small vols., beginning with *Songs for Swift Feet*, 1927. *The Self of Loss*, 1976, includes new and selected poems.

Roberts, Elizabeth Madox, 1881–1941, novelist and poet, who wrote 'all my work . . . centers around Kentucky objects'. Second of eight children of Mary Elizabeth (Brent) and Simpson R., she was b. at Perryville, Ky, raised (amid family tales of pioneers) at Springfield, which she called the 'Little Country'. Her ill health (which lasted throughout her life) forced her to leave the State College (now Univ.) of Kentucky after a year, 1901. She taught (partly from her home) until 1910, then moved to Colorado for her tuberculosis; there (already corresponding with Harriet MONROE) she published her first poems, with nature photos: *In the Great Steep's Garden*, 1915. She entered the Univ. of Chicago in 1917, and was president of its Poetry Club; *Poetry* and *Atlantic Monthly* published her work. *Under the Tree*, 1922 (Fiske Poetry Prize), contains poems of old-fashioned rural childhood: she called them autobiographical. Her novels present acute analyses of women's consciousness and women's quests, underlaid with mythical symbolism. The first, *The Time of Man*, 1926, which took four years to write, brought immediate reputation. Its tenant-farmer heroine makes an odyssey of discovery: a 'clod-woman' learning that she has in her 'life itself'. The heroine of *My Heart and My Flesh*, 1927, loses wealth and prospects, makes painful discoveries about her family history (including her father's incestuous desires); at her nadir comes an epiphany of joy and peace. *Jingling in the Wind*, 1928, is a satirical fantasy of modern life. *The Great Meadow*, 1930, relates a pioneering journey by a woman of the Revolution period who desires 'beauty and dignity and ceremony'. EMR's popularity declined with her health: her stories in *The Haunted Mirror*, 1932, and *Not by Strange Gods*, 1941, and poems in *Song in the Meadow*, were poorly received. Her last two novels, *He Sent Forth a Raven*, 1935, and *Black is My Truelove's Hair*, 1938, move 'farther and farther away from realisms into symbolisms'; Jane HARRISON is an influence. EMR left memoirs, notes and unfinished fiction including a novel. Studies include Frederick P. W. McDowell, 1963; many recent reprints; unpub. poems in *Kentucky Poetry Review*, Fall, 1981 ('a vivid moment hangs – clean, un-dim, / A bit of other worldliness'); *Southern Review*, 20, 1984, special issue (including memoir by EMR's friend Janet LEWIS). St Catharine College, Springfield, held a centenary conference in 1981. William H. Slavick is editing her surviving letters (many were destroyed). MSS at Library of Congress.

Roberts, Emma, *c.* 1793–1840, poet and journalist, b. at Methley, near Leeds, of Welsh extraction, posthumous da. of Capt. William R., ex-Russian service, and niece of a General. She was brought up by her mother in Bath, and later undertook research at the British Museum, becoming a great friend of L.E.L.'s. They shared a house with other literary women for a year – 'one of the happiest of my life' (see her intro. to *The Zenana*, 1839). In 1828 she went to India with her married sister, though disliking the dependency. On her sister's death in 1831, she went to Calcutta, where she worked for the *Oriental Observer*, then back to London to continue literary work and journalism, and regain her health. She dedicated to L. E. L., 'as a faint tribute to her genius', a book of poems, *Oriental Scenes, Sketches and Tales*, Calcutta, 1830; London, 1832. The most powerful of these is 'The Rajah's Obsequies', dramatically denouncing suttee as a rite upheld by male priests to enrich themselves. *Scenes and Characteristics of Hindostan, with Sketches of Anglo-Indian Society*, 1835, relates her travels and observations, noting the English capacity for making themselves hated; strongly defending Indian servants, especially their honesty, against prejudiced critics; and remarking on cultural changes, including the debate on 'the question of women's EDUCATION'. In 1839 she revisited India by the arduous overland route, settling in Bombay, editing *The Bombay United Service Gazette*, and organizing a scheme of employment for Indian women.

In the same year she pub. her travel advice compendium, *The East India Voyager*. She d. at Poona after some months' illness, with her *Notes of an Overland Journey to Bombay*, 1841, almost completed.

Roberts, Margaret, 1833–1919, novelist and children's writer, b. Honyngs, North Wales. She was educ. by her stepfather, the Rev. Henry Latham, a former barrister who wrote poetry, was a Sussex vicar from 1833, m. twice, and d. 1866. (His widow Charlotte was possibly her mother.) She lived much of her life in Italy, France and Germany and wrote over 30 books, mostly meticulously researched historical novels, many for children. Highly cultured and an expert linguist, she was also a brilliant and witty conversationalist among friends in F. M. PEARD's circle at Torquay from about 1866, though hating publicity. Her first novel for adults was *Mademoiselle Mori*, 1860 (anonymous, like most of her works). Researched in the Vatican library and originally written in Italian, it tells of a young opera singer's involvement in revolutionary politics in Rome during the times of Pius IX. It is notable for its thorough knowledge of Italy and its refusal of neat endings. *Denise*, 1863, and *On the Edge of the Storm*, 1868, were popular early novels, followed by the very successful *Atelier du Lys*, 1876. Later she concentrated on children's stories like *Stephanie's Children*, 1896, which centres on a young woman in revolutionary France. She also contributed to Charlotte YONGE's *Monthly Packet*. Her study of Saint Catherine of Siena was pub. in 1906. She d. near Montreux, Switzerland.

Roberts, Mary, 'Sister Mary', 1788–1864, biographer and scientific writer, da. of Quakers Ann (Thompson) and Daniel R., London merchant who moved to Painswick, Glos., in 1790. She is often confused with another Mary Roberts, 1763–1828, da. of Elizabeth (Wright) and Samuel R. (Sheffield cutler and reformer), who dedicated to Hannah MORE an ambitious collection of poems, 1822, headed by *The Royal Exile, or Poetical Epistles of Mary, Queen of Scots* (pro-Mary, anti-ELIZABETH); Hannah KILHAM subscribed. MR of Painswick (who on her father's death moved back to London and left the Quakers) was learned in Latin, Greek, Hebrew and natural history. Her *Select Female Biography*, 1821, dedicated to 'the Ladies of Great Britain', aims to catch 'some of the brightest rays of moral and intellectual excellence': writers like Anne ASKEW, Elizabeth ROWE, Rachel RUSSELL and Elizabeth SMITH, 1776–1806, are well served. She issued, with several publishers including the SPCK, a few more works of piety and a dozen of wide-ranging science-education: conchology, 1824; *The Annals of my Village* (a monthly calendar of observations), 1831; domestic animals, 1833; trees and ruins with historical associations [1843]; flowers, 1845 (with verse); molluscs, 1851. Even when writing for young children, 1834, she carefully names her sources.

Roberts, Michèle Brigitte, poet, novelist, b. 1949 at Bushey, Herts., da. of Monique (Caulle), a French Catholic teacher, and Reginald R., an English Protestant. Educ. at a convent school and Somerville College, Oxford (BA, 1970), she had various jobs – in London Univ. library, in Thailand for the British Council, as cook, typist, cleaner, pregnancy counsellor, and poetry editor of *Spare Rib*, 1975–7, and *City Limits*, 1981–3. She teaches creative writing in London, performs her own work, and was writer-in-residence in turn to the boroughs of Lambeth and Bromley, 1981–4. Some of her publishing has been done collectively. She has co-authored four poetry volumes: *Cutlasses and Earrings*, 1976 (with Michelene WANDOR), *Licking the Bed Clean*, 1978, *Smile Smile Smile Smile*, 1980, and *Touch Papers* (with Judith KAZANTZIS and Wandor), 1982. With Valerie MINER and others she ed. two vols of feminist short stories. She looks forward to there being 'male writers and female writers, rather than as at present, female writers and writers (read *real, male*)'. Her novels' concern with religion and female sexuality has made them hotly controversial. *A Piece of the Night*, 1978 (Gay News Literary Award), presents daughters refusing to be scapegoats for the sins of the church Fathers, 'no longer corpses in the church and mouths of men'. *The Visitation*, 1983, delineates a woman's efforts to accept her different sides, 'the masculine and feminine; the productive and the reproductive ... the light and the dark'. *The Wild Girl*, 1984, is the 'not simple ... not single' witness of Mary Magdalene, prostitute and 'one of the instruments of his truth', to Christ's life and death and her own dreams: of Eve and Adam's fall, of witch-burnings, of women's judgement on men's crimes against them, and of the apocalyptic approach to the new Jerusalem. *The Book of Mrs Noah*, 1987, takes place between its protagonist's quarrel with her husband and plunge into a Venetian canal and her awakening next day in bed: with five story-telling companions, the Babble-On Sybil, the Deftly Sybil, et al., she roams through seas, islands, visions, and encoded, complex meanings. MR has contributed to Eileen Phillips, ed., *The Left and the Erotic*, 1983, and to Sarah MAITLAND and Jo Garcia, eds, *Walking on the Water: Women Talk About Spirituality*, 1983. Her powerful poems (in many anthologies and *The Mirror of the Mother: Selected Poems 1975–85*, 1986, dedicated to her parents) reveal a voice increasingly forceful, humorous and daringly erotic. She uses varying textures both musically and dramatically: 'having shown / forth my big belly, my songs // I shall burn for this // I will sing high in the fire / oh let the fierce goddess come' ('Sibyl's Song'). *In the Red Kitchen*, 1990, spans present and remote past.

Roberts, R., d. 1778, translator and miscellaneous writer. She began by translating, as a French exercise, Jean François Marmontel's highflown tales of maternal and marital love: *Select Moral Tales*, 'By a Lady', Gloucester, 1763. She later lived in London with a brother who was High Master of St Paul's School. About 1768 a clergyman friend offered to preach any sermon she might write; though he never did so, she published pithy, conservative *Sermons*, 1770 (repr. Philadelphia, 1777, as *Seven Rational Sermons*). In 'The Cruelty of Slandering Innocent, and Defenceless Women', she disclaims 'vanity in endeavouring to reform mankind', notes that women 'labour under evils sufficient to embitter life', and sympathizes with those who 'fall', although only murder has 'such real bad consequences' as female unchastity. Her version of the Abbé Millot's *History of France*, 1771 (abridged), coincided with that by her friend Frances BROOKE of his *History of England*. RR's version of *Peruvian Letters*, 1774, added a volume: she gives to an Inca princess brought to Europe and dropped by her brother/betrothed (whom Françoise de Graffigny in 1747 left desiring independence, learning and escape from passion) both Christian instruction and love for her Spanish captor. Her translation of Jeanne-Marie Le Prince de Beaumont's novel *The Triumph of Truth, or Memoirs of Mr. De La Villette*, 1775, was written earlier and revised by John Hawkesworth. She turned to verse with *Malcolm*, 1779 (unacted tragedy; happy ending), and *Albert, Edward and Laura* and *The Hermit of Priestland*, 1783, tales of medieval love and jealousy. Edward W. Pitcher credits her with many translated and perhaps some original tales signed R. or R.R. in the *Lady's Magazine*, 1771–82 (*Lit. Research Newsletter*, 5, 1980).

Robertson, Eileen Arnot, 1903–61, novelist, film critic and broadcaster. B. at Holmwood, Surrey, da. of Dr G. A. R., she was educ. at Sherborne Girls' School and in Paris and Switzerland. *Cullum*, 1920, repr. 1989, her first novel, explores, in her characteristic anti-sentimental tone, the narrator's obsessive love for a worthless character. In 1928 EAR married Henry E. Turner, General Secretary of the Empire (later Commonwealth) Press Union; they had one son. Primitive, instinctual passions beneath a civilized, mundane exterior appear in *Three Came Unarmed*, 1929, where a missionary's children leave their Malay jungle home for England and civilization. *Four Frightened People* (1931, repr. 1982; filmed by Cecil B. DeMille, 1934) won popular success with a contrasting plot of civilized people forced to abandon ship and trek through the jungle. *Ordinary Families*, 1933, repr. 1982, dissects the emotional bonds and tensions in a Suffolk boating family. EAR depicts psychological and sexual difficulties with cool detachment, and minor characters with acid, even contemptuous wit. Her female protagonists are tough in mind and body, often enjoying professional parity with men, but her narrators often show intolerance of frivolous or stupid secondary females. *Thames Portrait*, 1937, is a joint photographic record of sailing with her husband. EAR worked as an adviser on films during WWII, and published *Summer's Lease*, 1940 (on a boy growing up in his father's Cornish museum), a children's story set in Canada, 1942, and *The Signpost*, 1943 (a French refugee and English pilot meet in Ireland; setting seems more vital than motive). She then became a radio film critic: her 1946 review of MGM's *Greenfields* led to a battle with MGM in which the House of Lords reversed her libel-suit victory. Her later novels concentrate on rendering 'exotic' locations and people: *Devices and Desires*, 1954 (partisans in war-torn Greece), *Justice of the Heart*, 1959 (journalist heroine travelling Europe, then interviewing a political prisoner in Zanzibar), and *Strangers on My Roof*, pub. 1964 (speech-therapist English heroine amongst Hong Kong Chinese). *Spanish Town Papers*, 1959, is an account of naval documents in Jamaica. EAR killed herself soon after her husband's accidental drowning. See Polly Devlin's introductions to reprints.

Robertson, Eliza Frances, 1771–1805, autobiographical writer, b. in or near London, eldest surviving child of Eliza (Earle), whom she calls unkind and inadequate, and David R., who had secrets in his past and frequent financial problems. She left home at 15 to teach, set up (with his help) a school, which crashed because of his debts, worked as governess, and dreamed of emerging as distant heir to estates forfeited by Jacobitism. While teaching in Cheshire she published children's works 'with some credit': didactic tales, a grammar and sermons. From 1795 she taught with a Miss Sharp at Greenwich. In 1799 she inherited some money, began altering a better house for the school, ran up debts and was accused of large-scale swindling and of being variously a whore, a lesbian and a man in drag. She wrote about her case in *Who Are the Swindlers?* [1801]; *Dividends of Immense Value*, 1801 (from Huntingdon jail, which she makes horrific in prose, almost idyllic in verse); a *Life and Memoirs*, 1802; and *Destiny, or Family Occurrences* [1802], a novel which paints her father luridly as rapist, forger, murderer, blackmail victim, with herself as spotless Cordelia. (It also turns from defending to attacking Miss Sharp, whose devotion wavered long enough to reply in a bitter pamphlet.) *Consolatory Verses*, 1808, including some printed in magazines as 'EFR' or 'Hafiz', musters some eloquence and pathos.

Robertson, Hannah (Swan), 1724–?1800, domestic writer and autobiographer, with little educ. (at six she rejected school to stay at home making things with her hands). As she tells it, her father (d. 1730), an illegitimate son of Charles II, spoiled her with dreams of grandeur; her mother depressed her by confiding the miseries of a second marriage which took them to Scotland. HR endured the deaths of two suitors and narrowly escaped a cannon ball in the 1745 rebellion. Her fiancé, missing presumed dead, returned, 1749, to find her on the brink of a loveless marriage which, from 'a false sense of honour', she went through with. Bearing a child a year, she broke down during her eldest child's fatal illness, but gained courage on her husband's bankruptcy, 1756, for running an inn at Aberdeen (twice burned out), teaching, selling millinery, and enduring accidents and spells in debtors' prison. Her *Young Ladies School of Arts*, Edinburgh 1766, is a COOKERY book whose 2nd ed., 1767, added instruction in 'the nice arts for young ladies' – which include not only filigree and cosmetics, but how to gut a bird with sharp scissors, stuff it and preserve its plumage. She dedicated the 4th ed., York, 1777, to the future Mary HARCOURT. Again near destitute, with dependent grandchildren, she pub. at Derby, 1791, a long autobiographical letter, elaborately titled, appealing for patronage.

Robertson, Margaret Murray, 1821–97, Canadian novelist, b. at Stuartfield, Aberdeen, Scotland, da. of Elizabeth (Murray) and James R., Congregational minister. After her mother died the family migrated in 1832 to Derby, Vermont, then to Sherbrooke, Québec. MMR taught at the Sherbrooke Academy, published her first work (on education) in 1864, then from 1866 issued at least 14 family-chronicle novels, many designed for young readers but often of a substance to appeal to adults. Their tone is sentimental, romantic and religious, their protagonists of Scots origin, their settings Scotland, New England, Montréal and rural Canada. *Shenac's Work at Home: The Story of Canadian Life*, 1868, a popular success set in Glengarry, may have influenced the work of MMR's nephew Charles Gordon ('Ralph Connor'). Shenac, whose father's death puts her (temporarily) in charge of the family farm, is one of several heroines shown maturing into adult or parental roles through hard work, suffering, and faith. MMR presents village and farm life with dialect and local colour; her women often show courage and initiative in their traditional sphere; they include a successful businesswoman (*Two Miss Jean Dawsons*, 1880), another gruff but positively drawn spinster (*The Inglises*, 1872), and a wife who leaves an unsatisfactory marriage, undertaken to help her family (*By a Way she knew Not, The Story of Allison Bain*, [1888]).

Robins, Elizabeth, 'C. E. Raimond', 1862–1952, actor, producer, playwright, novelist and feminist, b. Louisville, Ky, eldest of eight children of Charles E. R., banker. She was educ. at Putnam Female Seminary, Ohio, and in 1887 m. actor George Richmond Parks, who committed suicide the same year. Later she lived for many years with Octavia Wilberforce (Virginia WOOLF's physician), with whom she adopted a son. Moving to England in 1889, she became the foremost English Ibsen actress, e.g. as Hedda Gabler, 1891, and a successful producer and manager. With actress Marion Lea and later with Gertrude BELL's stepmother, she mounted most of the first English productions of Ibsen. She became increasingly critical of men like G. B. Shaw, with whom she had a long antagonistic relationship. Her controversial play *Alan's Wife*, 1893 (written with Florence Bell), examines mercy-killing and a woman's sexual passion. Her first novel, *George Mandeville's Husband*, 1894, a critical portrait of a popular woman novelist (George ELIOT?), sympathetically presents the husband whose painting is sacrificed to his wife's conceit. *The Open Door*, 1898, examines heredity and the ethics of suicide. *The Magnetic North*, 1898, a best-seller set in Alaska, was inspired by her 1900 search for her brother Raymond (whose wife, Margaret Dreier R., founded the National Women's Trade Union). Most memorable of her 14 other novels is *The Convert*, 1907, concerning a woman's conversion from apathy to militant feminism, a fictional version of ER's most famous play, *Votes for Women!*, 1907. Both examine 'the greatest evil in the world – the helplessness of women', and include scenes of SUFFRAGE rallies. Profits were contributed to suffrage organizations, and enabled ER to buy

Backsettown Farm, which she established as a retreat for professional women. She founded the Actresses' Franchise League and the Women Writers' Suffrage League, and joined the militant WSPU in 1906, serving on its board until 1912. *Way Stations*, 1913, a collection of feminist essays and lectures, includes 'Time-Tables' of significant events in the suffrage struggle. *Ancilla's Share*, 1924 (pub. anon.), argues for peace and women's refusal to participate in war-promoting activities. Her memoirs include *Ibsen and the Actress*, 1932, *Theatre and Friendship*, 1932, *Both Sides of the Curtain*, 1940, and *Raymond and I*, 1956. Her papers are in the NY Univ. Library, her stage costumes in the Bath Museum. See the life by Jane Marcus (diss.), and her introduction to *The Convert*, 1980; also article by Joanne E. Gates in *Mass. Studies in English*, 6, 1978.

Robinson, A. Mary F. (Agnes Mary Frances), later Darmesteter, then Duclaux, 1857–1944, poet, biographer and critic, and **F.** (Frances) **Mabel**, b. 1858, novelist, das. of Frances (Sparrow) and George R., archidiaconal architect for Coventry, Warwicks. Their parents entertained writers from Robert Browning to Oscar Wilde. Mary, a delicate child, was educ. in her father's extensive library, then in Brussels (from 1870), Italy, and London (seven years studying Greek literature at Univ. College). She privately printed her poems *A Handful of Honeysuckle*, 1878 (exotic, melancholy, *fin-de-siècle*), written for her close friend Vernon LEE. (Lee's *Ariadne*, 1903, borrows a song from AMFR, opening 'Let us forget we loved each other much.') AMFR's many vols. include *The Crowned Hippolytus*, 1881 (from Euripides), *Emily Brontë*, 1883 (in the 'Eminent Women' series: new MS material), *The New Arcadia*, 1884 (poems: notable is 'Man and Wife'), *Arden: A Novel*, 1883, and several more poetry colls. of which the best is probably *An Italian Garden*, 1886, which includes a number of wistful lyrics. In 1888 she m. James Darmesteter, Jewish-born French rationalist, prof. of Persian at Paris (d. 1894); he translated her poems into French, 1888; she prefaced and translated posthumous work by him. Her Paris salon became a centre for French learning and letters; she sought to put French and English culture in touch with each other. She wrote in both languages (on, e.g., Margaret of NAVARRE, 1886, the BRONTËS and BROWNINGS, 1901), and ed. e.g. Navarre, 1887, and Marie de SÉVIGNÉ, 1914 and 1927. After marrying Emile Duclaux (d. 1904) in 1901, she moved to Olmet in the Cantal region. Her *Collected Poems*, 1902, has a preface making a primary claim for women to the BALLAD and other popular forms. *Images and Meditations*, 1923, is dedicated 'to Mabel Only Sister, Dearest Friend', mirroring the dedication of FMR's novel *Disenchantment: An Everyday Story*, 1886. Mabel wrote six novels, from *Mr Butler's Ward*, 1885, to *Chimaera*, 1895 – this last being a frank account of the life of Joseph Treganna (illegitimate son of a betrayed but respectable woman and a baronet), his affair with and marriage to a servant, sister of a fellow private in the army. As 'William Stephenson Greg' she pub. *Irish History for English Readers*, 1885; she also produced French translations, 1923–8. Some AMFR letters, ed. Daniel Halevy, 1959; poems ed. in French by Sylvaine Marandon, 1967; bibliog. by Ruth Van Zuyle Holmes in *English Literature in Translation*, 19, 1967.

Robinson, Emma, 1814–90, novelist, da. of Joseph R., London bookseller. She first came to public attention in 1844, when, posing as a 'young Oxonian', she had her historical comedy *Richelieu in Love* banned by the Lord Chamberlain's Office for 'bringing church and state into contempt'. (It was licensed and performed in 1852, without success.) The first and most successful of her 'historical romances', *Whitefriars*, 1844, is dedicated to her father and written whilst minding his shop: he insisted on her anonymity and implied he himself was the author. She fostered further speculation about her identity by presenting her next novel, *Whitehall*, 1845, as seventeenth-century MSS given to a German professor by the mysterious 'author of *Whitefriars*'. Her other historical novels (all as by 'the author of *Whitefriars*') include *Caesar Borgia*, 1846, *Owen Tudor*, 1849, *Westminster Abbey*, 1854, *The Maid of Orleans*, 1858, and *Dorothy Firebrace*, 1865. Often melodramatic, they re-create big historical 'scenes' and treat major figures. As well as an epithalamion for the Prince and Princess of Wales, 1863, and a dramatic miscellany, *Christmas at Old Court*, 1864, she wrote several contemporary novels including *The Gold Worshippers*, 1851 (based on 'Railway King' George Hudson), *Mauleverer's Divorce*, 1858, *Which Wins, Love or Money?*, 1862, *Madeleine Graham*, 1864 (based on the Madeleine Smith case), and *The Matrimonial Vanity Fair*, 1868. She is concerned to combat the 'deep-seated and heart-eating malady of the age: the universal craving and thirst after money' (*Athenaeum*, 19 March 1864, p. 407). She received a Civil List pension of £75 in 1862, and died in London County Lunatic Asylum.

Robinson, Harriet Jane (Hanson), 1825–1911, author, feminist, clubwoman and 'mill girl', b. Boston, da. of Harriet (Browne) and William H. After her father's death in 1831, her mother ran a company boarding house in Lowell, Mass. From the age of ten until she was 23, Harriet worked in the mills – an experience about which she wrote a reminiscence, *Loom and Spindle, or Life Among the Early Mill Girls*, 1898, repr. 1976. As a mill girl, she was able to attend local schools three months each year and, later, high school for two full years. In 1848 she m. William Stevens R., an anti-slavery and pro-labour newspaper ed., who pub. as 'Warrington' and founded *The Lowell American*. He later became clerk of the Massachusetts House of Representatives. They had four children. In 1877 she pub. a collection of her husband's articles, with a biography: *'Warrington': Pen Portraits*. HJR had early joined the Concord Anti-Slavery Society and in 1868 the SUFFRAGE movement. She served as president of the Middlesex County Woman Suffrage Association, but in 1881 left the American Woman Suffrage Association to join Elizabeth Cady STANTON and Susan B. ANTHONY in the National Woman Suffrage Association. With her daughter, Harriette R. Shattuck, she founded the NWSA of Massachusetts. She was also an early member of the New England Club for Women, and with her daughters founded in 1878 Old and New, a self-improvement club still in existence. She served on the first boards of directors of the General Federation of Women's Clubs in the 1890s. She wrote two lively woman's-rights plays, *Captain Mary Miller*, 1887, which chronicles the eventually successful attempt of a wife and mother to gain a licence to pilot boats on the Mississippi River, and *The New Pandora*, 1889. Her personal papers are in the Schlesinger Library at Radcliffe College. Claudia L. Bushman, 1981, is the only full-length study.

Robinson, Marilynne, novelist and essayist, b. 1943 at Sandpoint, Idaho, one of several places on the Pacific coast where her father worked in the lumber industry. She was educ. at Brown Univ. (BA) and the Univ. of Washington (PhD). She is married and has two sons. Her award-winning first novel, *Housekeeping*, 1980 (filmed 1987), has been much discussed, notably by Elizabeth A. Meese in *Crossing the Doublecross*, 1986, Joan Kirkby in *TSWL*, 5, 1986, and Thomas Foster in *Signs*, 14, 1988. The novel presents the raising of two sisters (whose mother killed herself) by various female relatives who embody a range of attitudes to traditional women's roles. One opts for a conventional life centred, in one form or another, on home-making; the other (the narrator) throws in her lot with an aunt whose domestic habits are those of 'a transient', and is left with 'no particular reason to stay anywhere, or to leave'. The novel closes with alternative, speculative versions of each sister's later story, with 'negation of certainty and affirmation of possibility'. MR has written for journals like *Paris Review* (a story of a perverse, alarming childhood friend: 100, 1986). Her controversial article on the Sellafield nuclear plant (*Harper's*, Feb. 1985) angered the British government. It voices MR's concern that 'things are encased in the assumptions that you have about them, and they remain unknowable to you', for 'Americans are not intellectually capable of understanding that Britain would do anything crazy'. She has also published *Mother Country*, 1989. Interview in Nicholas O'Connell, ed., *At the Field's End*, 1987.

Robinson, Mary (Darby), 'Perdita', 1758–1800, actress, poet and novelist, b. at Bristol, da. of Mary (Seys) and John D., whaling captain from America. She attended several schools (first that of Hannah MORE's sisters), then taught in her mother's small school (her father had returned to America). In 1774 she married Thomas R., articled clerk: she breast-fed her daughter Maria Elizabeth, and wrote later of the 'raptures of childbirth'. She began writing while in debtors' prison with her husband and child: Georgiana DEVONSHIRE patronized her *Poems*, 1775. Next year she won success on stage at Drury Lane: consciousness of honourable independence, she said, 'is the one true felicity in this world of humiliations!' She had a farce staged in 1778. In 1779–80, acting Perdita, she attracted as lover the Prince of Wales, who left her next year the butt of the grossest satires, with a promised £20,000 unpaid. Other lovers were C. J. Fox (financial saviour) and Col. Banastre Tarleton (a long-term relationship and recipient of many of her poems). Intellectuals, radicals and poets were her friends; Coleridge called her 'an undoubted genius'. She was paralysed from the waist down after a miscarriage in 1783, while pursuing Tarleton (who was in debt and fleeing to France); he left her in 1797. She relied increasingly on writing for money. She began a 'poetical correspondence' with Robert Merry, 1790, supported 'the natural rights of man' and breaking of the Bastille, yet took the part of female suffering in 'Monody to the Queen of France', 1793. 'The Progress of Liberty' in her poems of 1806 condemns tyranny, but also Marat and Robespierre. She wrote for the *Morning Post* as 'Tabitha Bramble' and became its poetry editor in 1799. Her wide-ranging poetic output begins in conventional sensibility, moving to treat her own life, friendship and (like her novels) oppression and slavery. Her sensual sonnets '*SAPPHO* and Phaon', 1796, have footnotes from Ovid; her *Lyrical Tales*, 1800, facs. 1989, made Wordsworth consider changing his own title. Her eight novels set sensitive, virtuous heroines and heroes among corrupt high-life characters and coarse or comic low ones. The GOTHIC *Vancenza, or The Dangers of Credulity*, 1792, is said to have sold out in a day; *Angelina* [1795] praises the medieval barons' resistance to royal tyranny; *Hubert de Sevrac*, 1796, set in France, is anti-Catholic. *Walsingham, or The Pupil of Nature* [1797] gives its outcast hero a brilliant cousin who after receiving a Rousseauvian 'masculine education' is revealed to be female, so adding gentleness to mental energy. MR's satiric comedy on women gamblers, *Nobody*, failed on stage in 1794; *The Sicilian Lover*, 1796, is a gothic verse tragedy. Her *Letter to the Women of England, on the Cruelties of Mental Subordination*, 1799, first appeared earlier that year as *Thoughts on the Condition of Women* by 'Anne Frances Randall'. MR's daughter published a lively epistolary novel, *The Shrine of Bertha*, 1794, completed MR's *Memoirs*, 1801, and ed. *The Wild Wreath* (poetry anthology), 1804 (2nd vol. submitted to Longman 1809, not pub.), and MR's *Poetical Works*, 1806. Life (with that of

Tarleton) by Robert D. Bass, 1957, is researched though novelistic.

Roche, Regina Maria (Dalton), 1764–1845, novelist, b. in Waterford, and brought up in Dublin, da. of Capt. Blundell D. Books were her 'early passion', writing a means 'to give utterance to the workings of my mind' almost before 'I could well guide a pen'. She pub., with her name, 16 novels. *The Vicar of Lansdowne, or Country Quarters*, 1789, earlier of two before marriage, disarmingly begs critics to 'disregard the humble tale'. About 1794 she married Ambrose R. (d. 1829) and moved to England. *The Children of the Abbey*, 1796, published with anxiety after the death of her father (a reassuring critic), was a best-seller: ten eds., by 1825, still in print in 1882; repr. 1968. It is a fashionable mix of a sentimental love-and-marriage plot with intrigue about a lost inheritance, and toughens this by acute critical insights into social mores. Jane AUSTEN mentions it in *Emma* and may have been influenced by it; she satirized *Clermont* (1798, repr. 1968) in *Northanger Abbey*. In 1802–4 RMR and her husband were swindled out of Irish estates by a crooked lawyer; a Chancery suit became 'a millstone round our necks'; her 'horizon once so bright' grew 'clouded with sorrow and disappointment and sickness'. She was a pillar of the MINERVA Press, managing deft transformations from polite decorum to GOTHIC sensationalism in sublime and picturesque settings. Many of her works were quickly translated into French. *London Tales, or Reflective Portraits*, 1814, is a collection; *Contrast*, by subscription, 1828, gives some personal facts in a preface; she gave more in a letter of 1831 to the RLF, which had provided £40. She spent years in retirement on the Mall, Waterford. Articles by Natalie Schroeder cover bibliog. (*PBSA*, 73, 1979), anti-feminist reviews (*Essays in Literature*, 9, 1982), and use of Irish material (*Eire-Ireland*, 19, 1984).

Rodriguez, Judith (Green), poet, critic and artist, b. 1936 in Perth, Western Australia, da. of Dora (Spigl) and Gerald G. She was educ. at Brisbane Girls' Grammar School and the Univs. of Queensland and Cambridge. She has taught at colleges and univs. in Jamaica, London and Australia, and currently lives in Sydney with her second husband, writer Tom Shapcott. She is represented in the collection *Four Poets*, 1962, along with her fellow students at Queensland Univ. – David Malouf, Don Maynard and Rodney Hall. Her first volume, *Nu-plastik Fanfare Red*, 1973, was followed by *Water Life*, 1976, which contained her linocuts as well as poems, as do *Shadow on Glass*, 1978, and the winner of the Golden Jubilee PEN Award, *Mudcrab at Gambaro's*, 1980. Later collections are *Witch Heart*, 1982, *Floridian Poems*, 1986, the product of a writer-in-residency at Rollins College, Fla., and *New and Selected Poems*, 1988. Her poetry is remarkable for its strength, energy and often distinctive imagery. She has ed. several ANTHOLOGIES, including *Mrs Noah and the Minoan Queen*, 1983, for the Australian feminist press Sisters. Poetry editor (1979–82) of the literary journal *Meanjin*, she has also written a poetry column for the *Sydney Morning Herald*.

'Rohan, Criena', Deidre Cash, 1925–63, novelist, b. Melbourne, Victoria, da. of Irish Catholics Valerie Eileen (Walsh) and Leo Ovaristus C., minor poet and Marxist. Her parents separated to pursue their respective careers, leaving CR to be brought up on a farm in South Australia by her grandmother (memorably fictionalized in *Down by the Dockside*), later with her aunts in Melbourne. She was educ. at the Convent of Mercy, Mornington, Victoria, before training as a singer at the Albert Street Conservatorium. She was m. twice, first briefly to a univ. student, and had one son, then worked as a singer and dancer before she married Otto Olsen, a coastal seaman; she had one daughter from this marriage.

Her brief but outstanding career as a writer was cut short by her death from cancer at 38. Both her novels were written while ill or convalescent – the first while she was in hospital in Perth, the second completed as she wore an oxygen mask. She did not live to see its publication. *The Delinquents*, 1962 (repr. 1985), is a lively, humorous novel of heady young love set mostly in Brisbane; Lola and Brownie, 'widgie' and 'bodgie' heroes of city life, are rebels of, and survivors in, 1950s society. *Down by the Dockside*, 1963 (repr. 1985), captures the rawness and vitality of working-class Melbourne through the eyes of Lisha Flynn, growing up in the 1930s and 1940s. Both novels draw upon personal experiences and are remarkable for their vigorous realism. Barrett Reid's foreword to *Down by the Dockside* locates CR in a tradition of urban female writers including Kylie TENNANT (who was one of the first to appreciate CR's abilities), Dymphna CUSACK and Ruth PARK, and also tells us that a third unpub. novel, which the author called 'House with the Golden Door' and claimed as her best, has disappeared.

Roland, Betty (McLean), playwright, novelist, and journalist, b. 1903 at Kaniva, Victoria, da. of Mathilda (Blayney) and Roland M. Educ. at various schools in Victoria, she left at 16 and worked as a journalist for *Tabletalk* and *Sun News-Pictorial*. M. to Ellis Harvey Davies 1923–34, she subsequently lived with prominent left-wing activist, Guido Carlo Baracchi till 1942. Her first play, *The Touch of Silk*, 1942 (produced by Melbourne Repertory Theatre, 1928), concerns the fortunes of Jeanne, a French girl who marries an Australian soldier during WWI and returns with him to his drought-stricken farm. Jeanne emerges as a strong and dramatic figure. In 1933 BR travelled to Russia where she worked as a journalist for 15 months; *Caviar for Breakfast*, 1979, recounts her experiences there. She remained active in the Communist Party, writing political revues and plays, until 1939. From 1942 to 1952, she wrote numerous plays, serials and documentaries, and was the author of the first talking feature film made in Australia, 'The Spur of the Moment' (A. R. Harwood Productions, 1932). Her radio serial, 'A Woman Scorned', became the basis of the TV series *Return to Eden*, 1983. She has also written several children's books, travel accounts and novels, *The Other Side of Sunset*, 1972, *No Ordinary Man*, 1974, and *Beyond Capricorn*, 1976. In 1988 *Touch of Silk* was repub. with another play, *Granite Peak*. Her first vol. of autobiography, *The Eye of the Beholder*, 1985, won the Braille Book of the Year Award, 1985, and was adapted for ABC radio. The third vol., *An Improbable Life*, appeared 1989. MSS in the Mitchell Library, Sydney.

Rolls, Mary (Hillary), 'Mrs Henry Rolls', poet, d. 1832/8. Da. of Hannah (Wynne) and Richard H. (owner of Jamaican estates), she grew up in Westmorland, and pub. her first volume, *Sacred Sketches from Scripture History*, 1815, while her husband, in his early thirties, was both a curate and not yet a graduate of Cambridge. The sketches are leisurely, colourful poems on topics like Belshazzar's feast and Jephtha's daughter (the softer version in which she is dedicated to God, not killed; a long note calls the original too fearful to believe). Well received by critics, MR chose a fearful modern subject in *Moscow*, 1816, which moves from people perishing in the flames, to the broken French army, to the allies' restoration of peace and 'Man's best Rights'. A poem to Byron, 1816, and another on his death, regret his misuse of 'matchless' gifts. *The Home of Love*, 1817, whimsically celebrates the marriage of Princess Charlotte of Wales – belatedly, because the MS first sent to the princess, its dedicatee, was lost. MR returns to her best vein in *Legends of the North, or The Feudal Christmas*, 1825: at fifteenth-century Nappa Hall, near her childhood home, a bard entertains revellers with ancient traditions.

Rolt, Elizabeth, poet, b. 1747 at Bletchley, Bucks., youngest child of Elizabeth and Thomas R. Her *Miscellaneous Poems*, 1768, bear her name and preface dated May 1767. (The shared title and date has confused it with a work by Phillippina HILL.) She says she wrote to divert herself or keep out of mischief. The poems reveal a serious mind with capacity for humour: they dwell on the joy of scientific study (though she later judges moral philosophy superior), and on the competing claims of needle and pen: a broken needle reproaches her for fatal carelessness caused by immersion in 'the rhyming trade'. She warns (in cheerful-sounding metre) of the poverty of poets, uses a search for friendship to pronounce satirically on different classes of people, urges wisdom and the control of passion, but feelingly laments the dead. Reviews were unappreciative. In 1772 she married John Bonnycastle, budding mathematician and astronomer, who married again after her 'untimely' death.

Romance, a prestigious genre during the middle ages and RENAISSANCE: feminized by Lady Mary WROTH; particularly linked with women from the time of Madeleine de SCUDÉRY; later regularly contrasted with the more realistic novel. It was defended by Susannah DOBSON (in a historical context), 1784, and by Clara REEVE (as 'in lofty and elevated language, describ[ing] what never happened nor is likely to happen'), 1785, but attacked by many novelists, notably Sarah GREEN, 1810 (who wrote both romance and historical romance herself). Several of her contemporaries distinguish their fiction by sub-title: 'A Novel' or 'A Romance'. The latter remained common on title-pages in the nineteenth century when it had ceased to be useful as a distinguishing term, since almost all novels carried elements of the genre. Historical romances remained particularly popular with women writers. In the twentieth century the term has come to signify primarily the kind of love-story in which passive woman delightedly submits to masterful man: 'formulaic fiction in which frail flower meets bronzed god'. In its pure form the genre is associated with particular publishers, especially Mills and Boon, and Harlequin, which bought Mills and Boon in 1971 (see Margaret Ann Jensen, *Love's Sweet Return, The Harlequin Story*, 1984, on the romance industry, and Carol Thurston, *The Romance Revolution, Erotic Novels for Women and the Quest for a New Sexual Identity*, 1987, on the way the product changes from year to year, especially in the style of sexual-arousal scenes and the earning power of heroines). These books are alternatively regarded as wish-fulfilment or as 'coercing and stereotyping'. Traditionally the woman is younger, poorer, and socially inferior, and often markedly lacking in obvious or socially approved sex-appeal; this may be read as denial of actuality (offering the reader a better class of man than she is likely to secure in life), or as truth-telling (about non-equal, non-affective processes at work in the selection of wives). Historical romance exemplifies the selective realism of the genre: authentic detail in such matters as dress, travel, or even childbirth is not matched by any corresponding effort to represent prevailing contemporary attitudes to marriage, religion, money-management, or to other class, gender or family issues. Critical debate about formula romance still rages at several levels; traditional pundits blame female romance-readers, as in the seventeenth and eighteenth centuries, for shallow and undiscriminating choice of reading; Marxist feminists see romance as ideological oppression, keeping women in a subordinate or victim position; writers like Tania Modleski and Alison Light point out that romance-readers are both expressing and feeding dissatisfaction with the status quo, and that the typical romance heroine puts up a struggle against the hero's domination right up to the final clinch. Lillian S. Robinson points out that 'A fully feminist reading of women's books must look at *women* as well as at books, and try to understand how this literature actually functions in society.' Rachel Anderson, *The Purple Heart Throbs: The Sub-Literature of Love*, 1974, gives a sympathetic account of the genre's development. See also Robinson, *Sex, Class, and Culture*, 1978; Modleski, *Loving with a Vengeance: Mass-Produced Fantasies for Women*, 1982; Light, 'Returning to Manderley' in *Feminist Review*, 16, 1984; Jean Radford, ed., *The Progress of Romance: The Politics of Popular Fiction*, 1986. Recent critics have also addressed the question of the romance element – the courtship plot, the search for and realization of fulfilling man-woman love – in fiction of greater inventiveness, psychological depth or ambivalence, and linguistic complexity than the formulaic novel. Such criticism responds to the often-stated proposition that the male plot turns on ambition and the female plot on love, as well as to the complicity of fiction with social valorization of marriage. Rachel Blau DuPlessis claims that nineteenth-century novels which interweave quest and romance offer their female characters an ending in which the first is set aside for the second. Feminist critics are exploring the origins of 'stories women tell themselves', and finding them in psychological development and the construction of the female, in an 'unsatisfied need for personal identity', and a fantasy of rediscovering a perfected, nurturing, maternal love. See Janice Radway, *Reading the Romance: Women, Patriarchy, and Popular Literature*, 1984; DuPlessis, *Writing Beyond the Ending: Narrative Strategies of Twentieth-Century Women Writers*, 1985; Suzanne Juhasz, 'Texts to Grow On: Reading Women's Romance Fiction' in *TSWL*, 7, 1988.

Roosevelt, Anna **Eleanor** (Roosevelt), 1884–1962, children's writer, political philosopher, journalist, autobiographer, civil libertarian, diplomat. Da. of Anna (Hall) and Elliot R., she was involved in social work before she m. her distant cousin Franklin Delano R., 1905, being given away by President Theodore R., an uncle. An unfailing support to husband and children, she also pursued public affairs and humanitarian causes while FDR was Governor of NY, from 1929. Her first children's book, *When You Grow Up to Vote*, appeared in 1932, the year he was elected President. *A Trip to Washington with Bobby and Betty*, 1935, and *Christmas, A Story*, 1940, followed. *It's Up to the Women*, 1933, detailed her changing perceptions about herself and women's role. She made the social position of First Lady into a political one in its own right, holding press conferences from 1933 (ed. Maurice Beasley, 1983; discussed by him in *Journalism Quarterly*, 61, 1984), and writing a *Ladies Home Journal* column. This moved from women's issues to human rights when it announced her resignation from the Daughters of the American Revolution. She related her life through 1924 in *This is My Story*, 1937, and collected her newspaper journalism in *My Days*, 1938. *The Moral Basis of Democracy*, 1940, pursuing the larger human and philosophical issues behind the domestic economy and international crises, finally took her beyond her husband's shadow. With his death, in April 1945, her independent public life began. She became a delegate to the UN General Assembly in December and chair of the Commission on Human Rights in 1946. Her magazine columns collected as *If You Ask Me*, 1946, helped make her the 'world's most admired woman'. Her years at the UN prompted her to address the global community in *India and the Awakening East*, 1953, *UN Today and Tomorrow*, 1953, and *Tomorrow is Now*, 1963 ('It is today that we must create the world of the future'). Three further volumes (1949, 1958 and 1960) went into *The Autobiography*, 1961. J. P. Lash has written still the most informative life (2 vols., 1971, 1972) and ed. 2 vols. of letters, 1982, 1984, which foreground her friendships with women;

correspondence with her mother ed. Bernard Asbell, 1982.

Roper, Margaret (More), 1505–44, translator and letter writer, eldest child (two more girls came next) of Sir Thomas M. and Jane (Colt), who d. when she was five and was at once replaced by a stepmother. Her father valued that 'new thing', women's learning, and taught his daughters the full syllabus: classics, science, theology. The 'Whole School' wrote to him in Latin, and Margaret also to Erasmus, whom she corrected politely over a crux in Cyprian. She wrote, mostly in Latin, works now mostly lost, including essays on the Four Last Things (death, judgement, heaven and hell). She married William R. at just 16, bore five children who survived, extended her range of study, and had her work displayed to scholars for astonished praise. She translated, 1524, Erasmus's *Devout Treatise upon the Pater Noster*, pub. 1526 (ed. Richard L. DeMolen in *Erasmus of Rotterdam*, 1971). Her letters to her father in prison (ed., with his, 1947, 1961) use supple, colloquial, expressive English; one, a carefully structured, learned dialogue about his religious-political position, may be by her, him, or both. She saw him executed, preserved his letters, and died a Catholic abroad. Lives by Thomas Stapleton, 1588 (a chapter in life of Sir Thomas), Ernest E. Reynolds, 1960; study by Rita M. Verbrugge in Margaret P. Hannay, ed., 1985; selec. ed. Elizabeth McCutcheon in Katherina M. Wilson, ed., 1987. Anne MANNING pub. an imaginary diary by MR.

'Ros, Amanda McKittrick', Anna Margaret (McKittrick) Ross, 1860–1939, novelist and poet, b. near Ballynahinch, Co. Down, da. of Eliza (Black) and Edward McK., 'rigorous' headmaster of Drumaness High School. She later claimed to have written stories and poems from four, and to have been named Amanda Malvina Fitzalan Anna Margaret McLelland McK. Some of these names come from R. M. ROCHE's *Children of the Abbey*: a favourite book from AMR's childhood, influential along with Marie CORELLI. AMR was an unqualified school monitor at Larne from *c.* 1880, and returned there after training at Marlborough College, Dublin, 1884–6. In 1887 she married Andrew Ross, station-master of Larne, who paid for the Belfast printing of her first novel, *Irene Iddesleigh*, as a tenth anniversary gift. It was probably written 1892–6, though she said she had finished it at 14 or 15. With *Delina Delaney*, 1898, it attracted much notice. She took her writing seriously, aiming at 'a strain all my own', 'wholly different from the common-place everyday novel' or from 'any known writer or organizer of prose'. Her extravagant, patterned, sometimes misused language went with bizarre plots and characters: resilient heroines survive horrendous gothic adventures. Irene, soon to be richly but lovelessly married, cries, 'Great Mercy! Only another week and I shall cease to be a free-thinker!' AMR was called the 'worst novelist in the world', but also became a cult figure for her eccentricity: Aldous Huxley in 'Euphues Redivivus', 1923, called her 'intoxicated with ... artifice'. Her verse, *Poems of Puncture*, 1913, and *Fumes of Formation*, 1933, is increasingly given to scurrilous attacks on particular critics: two WWI broadsheets are anon., one as 'Monica Mayland'. Widowed in 1917, she married prosperous farmer Thomas Rodgers in 1922. Her other works appeared posthumously. *Bayonets of Bastard Sheen*, 1949 (title a term for critics), prints letters, 192[illegible]–39, which offer interesting facts and fantasies about her life and writing, as well as polemic. *St Scandalbags*, 1954, an attack on Wyndham Lewis and others, may come from a much longer, uncompleted work called *Six Months in Hell*. *Donald Dudley, The Bastard Critic*, 1954, and *Helen Huddleston*, 1969, are novels: the last completed by AMR's friend Jack Loudan. See his life of her, 1954, 2nd ed. 1969.

Rose, Wendy, 'Chiron Khanshendel', 'Bronwen Elizabeth Edwards', poet, painter and anthropologist. B. in 1948 in Oakland, Calif., of Hopi, Miwok, and white parentage, she was raised by 'the white half of the family'. A student of anthropology at the Univ. of California, Berkeley (BA, 1976; MA, 1978), she has lectured in Native American Studies at Berkeley, now at Fresno City College, and edited *American Indian Quarterly*. Frustrated by the 'Native Americana' classification of poetry by American Indians who 'are seen as literate fossils more than as living, working artists', WR resists the stereotype of the Indian writer: 'Consider that many of us do not speak our native language, were not raised on our ancestral land', that 'there is no genre of "Indian literature" ... only literature ... written by people who are Indians and who, therefore, infuse their work with their own lives.' WR's first volume of poetry, *Hopi Roadrunner Dancing*, 1973, shows the spiritual impulse that led her to co-found the Light of Dawn Temple, a metaphysical research centre in the San Francisco area. Early poems, addressing with wit and pain her literary and academic life, her hunger for home, and her divided sense of self ('body and heart and soul Hopi, / ... tongue something else') are gathered in *Lost Copper*, 1980. Other volumes, *Long Division, A Tribal History*, 1976, and *Academic Squaw: Reports to the World from the Ivory Tower*, 1977, join a brilliant, tense, personal voice with tribal consciousness: 'I suckle coyotes / and grieve'. *What Happened When the Hopi Hit New York* appeared in 1982; *The Halfbreed Chronicles and Other Poems*, 1985, moves from sharp rage to soft chanting as traditional knowledge confronts genocidal history. In 'Hard Beings Woman', WR traces her lineage to the Hopi genetrix, finding in the rocks of mountains and deserts an imagery of her experience as a mixed-blood woman, and community with other Indian women poets. 'That's the Hopi way. / If the corn doesn't grow / you eat the rocks, / drink the clouds / on the distant plains. / SILKO and ALLEN and HARJO and me: / our teeth are hard / from the rocks we eat'. A painter, WR illustrates her books with drawings of powerful female figures, often floating over or emerging from the earth. Interviews in *Melus*, 10, 1983, and Joseph Bruchac, *Survival this Way*, 1987. Fisher, 1981, prints selected poems with discussion; analysis also in Kenneth Lincoln, *Native American Renaissance*, 1983.

Ross, Mrs, obscure but remarkable author of at least 13 novels and groups of stories, 1811–25, some for MINERVA, many repr. in the USA. Her name is shared by an actress, Anna (Brown) Ross, later Brunton, who wrote a successful comic opera, and also by the unidentified authors of a *Scots Magazine* tale, 1779 (a modern heroine sucks poison from her lover's wound), and of a feminist, patriotic pamphlet, NY 1801. Mrs R's novels of ideas assume some culture in their readers, with a wide range of literary quotation. She likes third-person narrative, strong opening scenes (often in mid-story, followed by flashback), complicated plots (often including exotic scenes), large casts of characters, and vividly caught dialogue. With strong allegiance to sense and reason, she handles romanticism and sensibility extensively and with respect, if sometimes critically. She is not afraid to treat sexual irregularity or the seamy side of life, but can be harshly moralistic as well as satirical. In *The Cousins, or A Woman's Promise and a Lover's Vow*, 1811, an archetypal romantic hero leaves a swathe of destruction behind him; *The Marchioness!!! or 'The Matured Enchantress'*, 1813, has a likeable man quite plausibly corrupted by a siren; *Paired not Matched, or Matrimony in the Nineteenth Century*, 1815, verges on bitterness about marriage; the heroine of *The Balance of Comfort, or The Old Maid and Married Woman*, 1817, blissfully wed at last, still thinks a single life usually the best. *The Physiognomist*, 1820, features a glorious, preposterous virago-prophet; female genius leads to tragedy in one of *Tales of the Imagination*, 1820, and in *The Woman of Genius*, 1821. Mrs R's unnamed daughter (educated, she says, by her father) pub. *The Governess, or Politics in Private Life*, 1836, a heavily didactic novel advocating 'the glorious but simple truths of the gospel' and the treatment of (well-bred) governesses as family equals.

Ross, Ellen Edith Alice (McGregor), d. 1892, novelist. B. in Banff, Scotland, da. of Captain M., she m. a journalist named Stalker, and, after his death, Alexander R., a banker with whom she emigrated to Montréal. On his death, she wrote to support herself, publishing short stories and novels in Canadian and US newspapers and journals. *Violet Keith; or, Convent Life in Canada*, 1868, is a melodramatic story of Violet's youth and young adulthood after being orphaned. It includes descriptions of a Scottish household where she is a governess, and of a Canadian convent where she teaches. A Protestant, Violet finds both good and evil in her convent; ER takes the opportunity to decry such Roman Catholic excesses as worship of the Virgin Mary and belief in the intercession of saints. In a melodramatic conclusion, 60 nuns and their 300 charges die in a convent fire, Violet surviving to be reunited with her Scottish lover and to inherit unexpected wealth. Sentimental and melodramatic, ER's novels nevertheless sustain interest by their local colour.

Ross, Katharine Colace, d. 1697, spiritual autobiographer, schoolmistress and sewing teacher. She was 'religiously educate' [sic] at Edinburgh and converted at 13. She often tabulates mercies or crosses, and anatomizes many later backslidings. God, she says, directed her movements: firstly northwards to 24 years in ungodly, preacherless Tain in Ross and Auldearn near Nairn in Moray. She was 'sworn to the extirpation of Prelacy', an associate of Thomas Hog. She suffered sickness, poverty, 'many Crosses from my nearest Relations', and the deaths of all her 12 children. (She grieved most for a son overlain by his nurse, after others had overruled her fear of this, and, about 1667, a daughter who lived to three and a half, and so 'was guilty of actual Sins ... being very capable to discern between Good and Evil'; other deaths are firmly accepted as for the best.) About 1673 KCR moved to Falkland in Fife, then, unwillingly, to Edinburgh. Her *Memoirs or Spiritual Exercises*, pub. there 1735, end with notes, 1679–80, on the religious state of Scotland, and a 'Speech' on her 'pardoned Condition'.

'Ross, Maggie', Maurine Jewel Lufkin (Bright) Bermange, novelist. She was b. and grew up in Essex and m. playwright Barry Bermange in 1961. Her two novels (her only output besides stories and journalism) were praised on appearance. (It is a different MR, an American living in Oxford, who publishes Christian spiritualist books.) The title of *The Gasteropod*, 1968, means a shelled creature like a snail or limpet. Its precise, withdrawn, self-conscious male narrator is a collector with a passion for inanimate objects and for arresting the flight of time, who minutely records on film his wife's ageing, her dangerous sea bathing, and her long love affair with his best friend; he dreams of actually embalming her. Similar plot-elements and similar suspense appear in *Death by Drowning*, 1977, a little book for foreign learners of English, in which an orchid-growing husband wonders placidly whether his missing wife has been drowned. In *Milena*, 1983, an artist, whose bohemian husband impedes her work and sees women as machines needing lubrication, becomes obsessed with Kafka's mistress Milena Jesenska (an excessive woman in an excessive age, who left no letters where her lover left thousands – and later died in Ravensbrück concentration camp); her longing to right the balance, 'perform an act of tribute', brings complications both rational and fantastic.

Rossetti, Christina Georgina, 1830–94, poet, b. London, da. of Frances (Polidori) and Gabriele R., Italian patriot and professor at King's College: sister of Maria, the poet Dante Gabriel, and the critic William Michael R. She was educ. by her mother, and shared her brothers' intellectual interests but not their bohemian activities, apart from serving as artist's model for DGR. She wrote over 900 poems in English and 60 in Italian: most were religious and devotional, though some were love poems (usually stressing sadness, loss and death, subverting conventional romantic views) or BALLADS (often focusing shrewdly on betrayal). Her first *Verses* were privately printed by her grandfather Gaetano Polidori in 1847. From 1850 her poems came out in *The Germ*, either anon. or as by 'Ellen Alleyn'. In 1862, *Goblin Market and Other Poems* appeared to popular success. Its title poem remains her most famous: apparently a children's rhyme about the evil powers of forbidden fruits, seductively offered to two sisters by goblin men, it has given rise to varied critical interpretation. Later vols. include *The Prince's Progress*, 1866 (which reverses gender conventions), *Sing-Song*, 1872 (children's verses), and *A Pageant*, 1881, containing the famous 'Monna Innominata' sonnet sequence of love poems. These self-consciously give voice to the imaginary 'unnamed ladies' who, though sharing their 'lovers' poetic aptitude', are barred from speech by the courtly love tradition. Two further vols., 1893 and 1896, were pub. posthumously. Her prose works were *Commonplace and Other Short Stories*, 1870, *Annus Domini*, 1874, *Speaking Likenesses*, 1874, and *Seek and Find*, 1879. *Maude*, also pub. posthumously, was written in 1850: it treats the struggles of a young woman poet. She also wrote several works of mixed poetry and prose: *Called to be Saints*, 1881, *Time Flies*, 1885, and *The Face of the Deep*, 1892. CR never married, though she was briefly engaged to the painter James Collinson. Her commitment to the high Anglican church was balanced by her work in the 1860s in a Home for Fallen Women, which led to some of her least commentated poems, such as 'The Iniquity of the Fathers upon the Children', which may have inspired Dora GREENWELL's 'fallen woman' poem, 'Christina'. From 1871 she suffered from Grave's disease, eventually dying of cancer. Rebecca Crump is editing the *Complete Poems* in 3 vols.: vol. 1, 1979; vol. 2, 1986. The best life is by Georgina Battiscombe, 1981. Edna Kotin Charles, 1985, gives a useful survey of criticism up to 1982. Good recent studies are by Dolores Rosenblum, 1986, and Antony Harrison, 1988.

Routh, Martha (Winter), 1743–1817, Quaker minister and autobiographer, b. at Stourbridge, Worcs., youngest of ten children of Jane (d. *c.* 1755) and Henry W. Brought up to be godly, she desired to be a minister from about 13; Catharine Payton later PHILLIPS was her mentor, Frances DODSHON and Dorothy RIPLEY her friends. She taught from about 16, then jointly ran a school. She says she became a minister at 28, after three years' spiritual struggle; also that she married Richard R. of Manchester in 1766, and made short preaching journeys early in her married life. Having visited Wales, Scotland, Ireland and France, she sailed in 1794 for Boston (journal of the passage at Hist. Soc. of Penna.); her first feeling in America was alienation, yet diary entries now replace narrative in her *Memoir*, and the persistent note of anxiety or self-doubt vanishes. In just over three years she travelled 11,000 miles. She felt her mind 'dipped into sympathy with women friends'; dealt 'plainly with the careless ... who might have liked smoother things'; rebuked slave-owners (for which she was publicly cautioned); attended the 1796 Philadelphia meeting which unanimously agreed to admit members without 'distinction of colour'; and edited Friends' writings, 1797. She visited the US again with her husband, intending to settle, but followed him home in 1805. At 70 she began writing her *Memoir*: pub. York, 1822 (often repr.), with personal passages excised.

Rowden, Frances Arabella, later St Quintin, d. *c.* 1840, poet and educator. Her father was a clergyman; her mother was running a school at Henley-on-Thames by 1782. She went (like Jane AUSTEN) to the Reading school of the émigré St Quintin and his British wife, was governess to Lord Bessborough's family, taught with the St Quintins at Hans Place, London (see M. M. SHERWOOD), then headed the school, *c.* 1809–20. Pupils included Lady Caroline LAMB, L. E. L. and Mary MITFORD, who praised her in *Our Village*. Her *Poetical Introduction to the Study of Botany*, 1801, popularizes and bowdlerizes Linnaean taxonomy and plant sexuality, draws moral lessons, and stresses gender qualities like women's 'meek retiring grace'. Greeted as 'a genteel guide' to a suitable subject for young women, it was followed by works on 'heraldry, botany, mineralogy, mythology, and at least half a dozen 'ologies more'. *The Pleasures of Friendship*, 1810, a poem dedicated to Mitford, exalts friendship at the expense of passion or society life; its examples end with a seventeenth-century Scottish tale about two women's 'most romantic' affection. FAR treated classical myth in *A Christian Wreath for the Pagan Deities*, 1820, and classical and modern writers in *A Biographical Sketch*, 1821. In the 1820s she started a school in Paris and became St Quintin's second wife.

Rowe, Elizabeth (Singer), 1674–1737, poet and prose-writer, b. at Ilchester, Somerset, da. of Elizabeth (Portnell) and dissenting minister Walter S., who encouraged her poetry and painting; she said he preferred her sister who died at 20 (her mother also died young). She attended boarding school, and in the 1690s published as 'Philomela' and 'the Pindarick Lady' (see JOURNALISM) and found patrons in the wealthy Thynnes (Anne FINCH's friends, Lady HERTFORD's parents). *Poems on Several Occasions*, 1696, includes juvenilia, HYMNS, pastorals, an imitation of Anne KILLIGREW, love-poetry both feeling and comical, and vehement defence of women's right to poetry: for these she was later 'displeas'd with her self'. Matthew Prior flirted with her; Isaac Watts courted her; she married, 1710, Thomas R., a younger writer, and tried not to 'neglect the less honorable cares' of 'the softer sex in the connubial relation'. He d. in 1715, her father in 1719; she settled at Frome, Somerset, in piety, comparative poverty, and charity, educating local children. Disapproving of plays and novels, she treats religion in rhapsodic style in the fictional *Friendship in Death, in ... Letters from the Dead to the Living*, 1728 (18 eds. by 1800), and *Letters Moral and Entertaining*, three parts, 1729–33 (both facs. 1972). The biblical verse epic *History of Joseph*, 1736, was mostly written years earlier. She left letters for posthumous delivery (like Richardson's Clarissa), and copious MSS (Alnwick Castle; films BL and Library of Congress) from which Watts and Hertford pub. *Devout Exercises of the Heart*, 1737. Her *Miscellaneous Works*, 1739, with a life, omits early poems (which had just been repr. by Edmund Curll, 1737). Praised in verse by Hertford, Elizabeth CARTER, and A. L. BARBAULD, she was long and widely influential: life by Henry Stecher, 1973, study by Madeleine Forell Marshall, 1987.

Rowlandson, Mary (White), *c.* 1635–after 1677, first American woman best-seller. She m., 1656, Joseph R., minister of Lancaster, Mass. He was away when, in Feb. 1676, during King Philip's war, Indians killed most of her family and captured her. She endured with unquenchable spirit 11 weeks on the march, sleeping rough. Her 'one poor, wounded Babe' – a six-year-old girl – 'went moaning all along, I shall dy, I shall dy', and did so. Some Indian women befriended MR. She wrote *The Soveraignty and Goodness of God*, earliest and best-known of the CAPTIVITY-NARRATIVES, 'to be to her a memorandum of God's dealing with her'; it is remarkable for vivid detail (on Indian customs and personal response), strong narrative style and much Biblical reference. Of the first ed., Boston, 1682, only fragments are known; reprints, beginning that year at Boston and London, numbered 30 before modern ones began. Nothing is known of MR after a move to Wethersfield, Conn., 1677.

Rowson, Susanna (Haswell), 1762–1824, arguably America's first professional novelist (seven novels plus tales); poet, actor, playwright, educator and feminist. She was b. at Portsmouth, England, da. of Susanna (Musgrave), who d. at her birth, and William H., naval lieutenant, who fetched her in 1766 to join his new family at Boston, Mass.; overtaken by the horrors of war, they returned to England in 1778. In 1786 SHR published by subscription an epistolary seduction-novel, *Victoria* (dedicated to Georgiana DEVONSHIRE), and m. the feckless musician William R. In 1788 came *The Inquisitor, or Invisible Rambler* (idea from Eliza HAYWOOD or Elizabeth BONHOTE; it begins SHR's habit of prefaces to challenge sometimes 'snarling' critics), and two lost works: *Poems on Various Subjects* and *A Trip to Parnassus* (poetic survey of current drama). *Mentoria*, 1791 (no relation to Ann MURRY's work of that title), aims its didactic letters and tales at women who do not read novels. *Charlotte, A Tale of Truth*, MINERVA, also 1791, was a runaway best-seller (more than 200 eds.; see that by Cathy N. Davidson, 1986; usually as *Charlotte Temple*; sequel pub. 1828), a seduction story which readers insisted on taking as fact. The exemplary though socially 'mean' heroine of *Rebecca, or The Fille de Chambre*, 1792, educates herself at a CIRCULATING LIBRARY and is finally rewarded with every blessing except children. SHR and William R. toured England with an acting company, 1792, joined the Philadelphia New Theatre, 1793, and other companies before retiring from Boston's Federal Street Theater, 1797, to open a school which ran, with several moves, till 1822. She says her pupils 'became to me as my children'; several adopted children included her husband's natural son. *Slaves in Algiers*, Philadelphia, 1794 (a musical, most popular of her seven stage pieces), combines laughter with a feminist and abolitionist message. *Trials of the Human Heart*, Philadelphia, 1795, is an epistolary novel whose preface explains her feeling for her adopted country; the family saga *Reuben and Rachel, or Tales of Old Times*, Boston, 1798 (begun years earlier; very popular), mixes the blood of Christopher Columbus, Lady Jane GREY, American Indians (drawn with sympathy and respect) and QUAKERS. SHR edited *The Boston Weekly Magazine*, 1802–5, and pub. textbooks for pupils. *Miscellaneous Poems*, 1804 (subscribers predominantly female), includes songs, HYMNS, private and public poems, with cautious comment on women's position. *A Present for Young Ladies*, 1811, includes 'Sketches of Female BIOGRAPHY'. See bibliog. by R. W. G. Vail, 1933; lives by Dorothy Weil, 1976, and Patricia Parker, 1986.

Roy, Gabrielle, 1909–83, novelist and short-story writer, b. at Saint-Boniface, Man., youngest of 11 children, da. of Mélina Landry and Léon R. She studied at the Académie Saint-Joseph in Saint-Boniface and the Winnipeg Normal Institute, then taught in several rural Manitoba schools and travelled for two years in England and in France, where she studied drama and published several newspaper articles. Her first novel, *Bonheur d'occasion*, 1945 (*The Tin Flute*, 1947), the first French-Canadian work to win France's prestigious Prix Fémina, 1947, became a landmark. Its detailed, compassionate study of a poverty-stricken Montréal family and sensitive portrayal of a mother and daughter upset the traditional idealism of Québec writing, and its unflinching realism, which revealed woman's precarious role in a church-dominated society, paved the way for other women writers in French Canada. The first woman to be admitted to the Royal Society of Canada, 1947, GR has become one of the country's most widely read writers both in French and in translation. Her other novels, collections of short stories, and stories for children deal mainly with human relationships and the writer's vocation. Several, set in Manitoba, use autobiographical material: *La Petite Poule d'eau*, 1950 (*Where Nests the Water Hen*, 1961); *Rue Deschambault*, 1955 (*Street of Riches*, 1957); *Ces Enfants de ma vie*, 1977 (*Children of My Heart*, 1979). *Fragiles Lumières de la terre*, 1978 (*Fragile Lights of Earth*, 1982), gathers GR's essays. Her autobiography, *La Détresse et l'enchantement*, 1984 (*Enchantment and Sorrow*, 1987), describes the artistic, emotional, and spiritual quest of her early life. Studies by M. G. Hesse and Paula Gilbert Lewis, both 1984.

Royall, Anne (Newport), 1769–1854, travel writer and 'first of our Washington commentators, columnists, muckrakers'. She was b. near Baltimore, Md., elder da. of Mary and William N., loyalists who trekked west in 1772. In frontier Pennsylvania her father died and mother was briefly re-married. At Sweet Springs, now West Va., Major William R., a rationalist, radical, patriot and landowner, became her mother's employer, ANR's teacher, then in 1797 (though about 30 years her senior) her husband. Left a rich widow in 1813, ANR travelled the frontier to invest in new industries, keeping a full diary, till in 1823 Royall's family overthrew his will, and she went to Washington as a pauper seeking a pension. The first of her lively, anecdotal travels, *Sketches of History, Life and Manners, in the United States*, New Haven, 1826, covers the eastern states in 1823 and a meeting with Hannah ADAMS, 'the glory of New-England females'. (ANR had enthused over Sydney MORGAN's *France* in 1818.) *The Tennessean*, 1827 (a brisk, matter-of-fact novel with male narrator), and two plays, 1828, did less well. More travels – *The Black Book* (Washington, 3 vols., 1828–9), *Mrs. Royall's Pennsylvania*, 1829, *Letters from Alabama 1817–1822* (1830; repr. 1969), and *Mrs. Royall's Southern Tour*, 1830–1 – revel in outrageous comment on named individuals and in her own status as public figure. Tried and convicted as a 'common scold' in 1829 (for aggressive investigative reporting of Presbyterians), she is hard on evangelicals (alligators remind her of 'religious robbers') and often on her own sex ('The Lord save us from petticoat government'); she supports states' rights, religious tolerance, and Andrew Jackson. In 1830 she acquired a printing press, and with her friend Sarah Stack began producing pamphlets (which she hawked in the halls of Congress) and the periodicals *Paul Pry*, 1831–6, and *The Huntress*, 1836–54. Not always wholly reliable, she earned John Quincy Adams's label: 'a virago errant in enchanted armour'. Lives by George Stuyvesant Jackson, 1937; Alice S. Maxwell and Marion B. Dunlevy, 1985.

Royalty. Women at the head of British society early learned to use the pen for power and recreation. Surviving lyrics are credited to Elizabeth of York and Margaret of Anjou. MARGARET TUDOR, Queen of Scots, wrote notable letters (like her sister Mary, Queen of France and Duchess of Suffolk). Her sister-in-law Katharine PARR and nieces Mary Tudor and ELIZABETH I wrote translation: her granddaughter Mary Queen of Scots (life by Antonia FRASER, 1970) wrote remarkable prose and poetry, chiefly in French, and became a favourite topic for women writers. James I's daughter, Elizabeth of Bohemia, left letters and verse. Mary II and Anne (whose mother wrote verse and a life of her husband) both wrote good letters (pub. together 1924),

Mary part-French meditations and memoirs (Richard Doebner, ed., Leipzig, 1886), and Anne her own political speeches (pub. 1968). Mary's letters (passionate outpouring to female friends, theological and political argument to her father) are the more interesting; but Anne, regnant in her own right, was a focus and inspiration for women writers. Caroline of Anspach, wife to George II, encouraged various kinds of intellectual endeavour. Women writers kindled to the hope of a good ruler in George IV's daughter Charlotte, more, it seems, than to the actuality of VICTORIA, another personal writer. Victorians like Anna JAMESON, 1831, and M. A. E. Wood, 1846, publicized female royal writing.

Royce, Sarah Eleanor (Bayliss), 1819–91, memoirist. B. at Stratford-on-Avon, Warwicks., da. of Mary T. and Benjamin B. The family moved to Rochester, NY, where SR was educ. at the Albion Female Seminary. She m. Josiah R. around 1847, and in 1848 they began travelling westward, finally jumping off for California from Council Bluffs, Iowa in 1849. During the difficult and almost solitary journey SR kept a diary that became a source for the memoir she later wrote at the request of her son Josiah (then a professor of philosophy at Harvard). Ed. by Ralph H. Gabriel and pub. as *A Frontier Lady: Recollections of the Gold Rush and Early California*, 1932, the early parts of the narrative are a gripping account of hardships and miraculous redemptions. Josiah R. used his mother's memoir as a source for his history *California*, 1886, and dedicated the book to her.

Royden, Agnes **Maude**, 1876–1956, preacher and writer on feminist, pacifist and theological issues. She was b. at Mossley Hill near Liverpool, youngest in the large family of Alice Elizabeth (Dowdall) and Thomas Bland R., later a baronet. A dislocated hip, ignored in childhood as a hysterical complaint, left her lame for life. She was educ. at Cheltenham Ladies' College and Lady Margaret Hall, Oxford (degree equivalent in modern history, 1899), worked at a Women's Settlement in slum-area Liverpool, then from 1903 at South Luffenham, Rutland, as parish worker to the Rev. George William Hudson Shaw. Through his Oxford Univ. Extension link she began lecturing on English literature; she joined Millicent Garrett FAWCETT's National Union of Women's Suffrage Societies in 1908, used her public-speaking skills for it, and edited its journal, *The Common Cause*, 1912–14. She published six pamphlets in 1912, *Extracts* from Mission speeches, 1913, and her first book, *Women and the Church of England*, 1916. Working closely in women's peace organizations with Helena SWANWICK and others, she longed for a broader platform, wished vainly to be an Anglican minister, became in 1917 assistant preacher at the nonconformist City Temple, London (where she had moved with the Shaws), and acquired an interdenominational pulpit in 1920. MR's feeling for Shaw had quickly become enduring and reciprocated love. With his wife, Effie (who suffered from mental disturbance and free-floating phobic anxiety), she lived 40 years in a platonic triangular relationship. She argued against the double sexual standard, and for the expression (marital only) of female sexuality in 'Modern Love. The Future of the Women's Movement' (*The Making of Women, Oxford Essays in Feminism*, 1916), and for prevention of venereal disease in *The Duty of Knowledge*, 1917. She was an early supporter of Marie STOPES, writing of birth-control in *Sex and Common-Sense*, 1922, and later works, and of Eleanor RATHBONE in the campaign for family allowances. Her feminism stressed the gender differences epitomized in maternity; she regretted having no children. She wrote on Joan of Arc in A. W. Pollard, ed., *Messages of the Saints*, 1918, and published many titles such as *Political Christianity*, 1922. Important in the peace movement between the wars, she preached in the US, Australasia, India and China, but finally ceased to be a pacifist in WWII. She married Shaw in 1944 on his wife's death, but he (in his 80s) died two months later. MR detailed the relationship (with other aspects of her life) in *The Threefold Cord*, 1947, a courageous work which exercises gender-consciousness, feeling for others, and self-scrutiny without self-pity. See Jane Lewis in *Maryland Historian*, 6, 1975, Anne Wiltsher, *Most Dangerous Women: Feminist Peace Campaigners of the Great War*, 1985, and Martin Ceadel, *Pacifism in Britain 1914–1945*, 1980.

Royde-Smith, Naomi Gwladys, 1875–1964, novelist, editor, playwright, biographer. B. in Llanwrst, Wales, to Ann Daisy (Williams) and Michael Holroyd Smith, she was educ. at Clapham High School and in Geneva. She was literary editor of the *Westminster Gazette*, 1912–22, and her earliest publications were anthologies: two collections of tales from the *Faerie Queene*, 1905, and two poetry volumes, 1908 and 1924. The first of her almost 40 novels, *The Tortoiseshell Cat*, 1925, relates naive, eccentric Gillian's attempts to establish an identity distinct from her sister Lilac who is destined to be 'a leader of London society in three years'. *The Delicate Situation*, 1931, describes Lena Quibell's decision to condone her niece's clandestine love affair because of her own memories of being 'frustrated and gnawed by unfulfilment' in her youth. *Jane Fairfax*, 1940, whose 'Author's Note' thanks 'the shades of Miss Austen, Miss BURNEY, Miss EDGEWORTH, Mrs SHERWOOD and Mr. W. M. Thackeray', centres on the childhood and love affair of AUSTEN's Jane Fairfax. In 1926 NR-S married actor Ernest Milton, who in 1927 acted in *A Balcony* (one of her four plays). In 1930 she travelled with him to the US, about which she wrote *Pictures and People*, 1930. She wrote a play, 1931, and biography, 1933, about the actress Sarah Siddons, and study of M. M. SHERWOOD, 1946, which praises her as 'a satiric novelist of great accomplishment' requiring 'disinterment'. NR-S's last novel was *Love and a Birdcage*, 1960.

Rubens, Bernice, Jewish novelist and short-story writer, b. 1928 in Cardiff, da. of Dorothy (Cohen) and Eli R. She was educ. at the Univ. of Wales, Cardiff (BA in English, 1944; Fellow 1982). In 1947 she m. novelist Rudi Nassauer; she has two daughters. She taught in schools and directed documentary films for the UN and for charities. Her early books present stereotypical characters with a blend of farcical action and deadpan epigrammatic comment. Her first heroine, in *Set on Edge*, 1960 (repr. in Modern Jewish Classics, 1972), 'covered the narrow limitless range of human unhappiness': born on the doormat because her mother (a routine-obsessed 17-year-old), would not hurry the shopping, dominated and exploited all her life, briefly and ridiculously married, and left cursing her dead mother every night for not being there. *Madame Sousatzka*, 1962, features a piano teacher and her prodigy (screenplay by Ruth Prawer JHABVALA, 1988, shifts interestingly from a Jewish to a Bengali family), *Mate in Three*, 1966 (dedicated to BR's mother), treats marriage between a daughter of warm, stifling *Ostjuden* and a son of cold, rich, assimilated refugees from Germany. *The Elected Member*, 1969, centred on a male drug addict, takes a more overtly serious tone with the inherited burden of Jewish suffering: it won the Booker Prize. BR then turned to gentile settings, and has presented memorable grotesque or marginal protagonists: a male transvestite in *Sunday Best*, 1971, a journal-keeping foetus in *Spring Sonata*, 1981. Women are central in *Go Tell the Lemming*, 1973 (suicidal, using a projection of herself as monitor and confidante), *I Sent a Letter to My Love*, 1975 (writing anonymous love-letters to her once hated brother), *Birds of Passage*, 1981 (widows on a cruise, coping variously with a rapist waiter), and *Our*

Father, 1987 (a female explorer). *Brothers*, 1983, traces four generations of a Jewish family from Odessa to Tel Aviv; *Kingdom Come*, 1990, fictionalizes a seventeenth-century self-appointed Messiah, later a convert to Islam. BR has also written for stage and TV.

Ruck, 'Berta', Amy Roberta, 1878–1978, POPULAR novelist and memoirist, b. in Murree, India, to Elizabeth (West D'Arcy) and Col. Arthur Ashley R. In Wales from the age of two (she celebrated her Welsh blood in four books of anecdotal reminiscences, from *A Smile for the Past*, 1959, to *Ancestral Voices*, 1972), she attended boarding school at Bangor, went to Germany as an *au pair* at 16, then studied at art schools in Lambeth, London (the Slade) and Paris (Colarossi's). From 1905 she contributed illustrations and stories to magazines. In 1909 she married fellow-writer Oliver Onions (later George Oliver). She had two sons, and revised, with his help, a serial for *Home Chat* as a novel, *His Official Fiancée*, 1914: 'an original tinge to the grand old Cinderella motif of the hard-up, come-down, toiling heroine who attracts and finally marries the well-to-do attractive employer'. Having found her 'modest niche as a writer for – and about – young girls', she wrote two novels a year: nearly 80 in all, as well as short stories. 'If I minded stuffy highbrow reviews about "sprightly style" and "popular appeal" and "the usual Ruck" I'd be dead by now.' She used the 'wear-well plot of the girl disguised as a boy' in *Sir or Madam?*, 1923, and the hero's escape from the perils of Baby-Snatcher and Gold-Digger to marry the girl-next-door of childhood in *He Learnt About Women*, 1940. Virginia WOOLF put BR's name on a tombstone in *Jacob's Room*, 1922, and comically described their meeting; BR called Woolf her 'grave-digger': BR's *A Story-Teller Tells the Truth*, 1935, describes her childhood and writing career, as well as discussing a number of contemporary women novelists. Some of her books have been condensed by Barbara CARTLAND.

Rudd, Margaret Caroline (Youngson), also Stewart, *c.* 1745–after 1794, adventuress and memoirist, b. at Lurgan, N. Ireland, da. of Marjorie (Stewart) and Patrick Y., surgeon-apothecary. Allegedly expelled from boarding school for sexual misconduct, she m. at 17 Lt. Valentine R., moved to London, and left him for prostitution under various names. From 1770 she lived with Daniel Perreau, a financial speculator and later (with his brother) a forger. In 1775 she and the brothers were separately tried; she was acquitted on her own defence; they were hanged. Her demeanour and her *Facts, or A Plain and Explicit Narrative*, written in prison [1775], presented her as a submissive *de facto* wife who was violently bullied into forgery; having stressed her three children and female weakness, she let the paper war rage on without her. James Boswell, charmed by her 'choice and fluent' language, was her lover, 1785–6. Jailed for debt again in 1787, she claimed a noble Scots heritage through illegitimate descent, detailing her alleged wrongs in *Mrs. Stewart's Case*, 1789 (with newspaper puff calling it 'a masterpiece' in tone), and *The Belle Widows*, fictionalizing her past with satire on fashionable ladies and expected readers Miss Forward and Lady Languish.

Ruddock, Margot, 1907–51, actress and poet, whose early life is obscure. Her stage name was Collis, from an early marriage to Jack C., who retained custody of their son. In 1932 she married actor Terence Byron; they had a daughter. She began writing to W. B. Yeats in 1934 (letters ed. by Roger McHugh in *Ah, Sweet Dancer*, 1970), sending him poems which he called 'passionate, incoherent improvisations'. He acted as editor for her one collection, *The Lemon Tree*, 1937; she accused him of making 'poetry, my solace and my joy, a bloody grind I hate!' Her prose preface, 'Almost I

Tasted Ecstasy', describes a severe depression: 'It seemed best that I should die but I thought, "if I am a good poet I have the right to live".' Yeats included seven of her poems in *The Oxford Book of Modern Verse*, 1936. They are mystical and metaphysical, reflecting a spiritual anguish. She calls compassion an 'unwelcome child' and 'puny babe', to which she is an 'unwilling mother', and life 'A wanton love / My flesh to feed', taken while 'My soul / Insatiate / Cries out, cries out / For its true mate.' Soon after 1937 MR was committed to a mental institution in Surrey where she died.

Rudet, Jacqueline, playwright. B. *c.* 1962 in East London, sent to Dominica, where, 'surrounded by women and harassed by men', she felt an adult before returning to England at nine. 'I refused to learn in school. It's only now I'm learning by reading.' On a college drama course at 16 she was advised by the head of department to give up, since the stage had no jobs for blacks. She found parts – hookers and druggies – but despised them, so founded the THEATRE GROUP Imani Faith, 1983, to present plays for and by black women. She wrote for it *With Friends Like You*, which did not satisfy her on stage, till a visit to Dominica showed her how to improve it. Meanwhile she wrote *Money to Live*, 'a story about hard times' and women who sell their bodies – as strippers – to live; one is converted from demoralizing, ultra-respectable poverty, to find that self-respect goes with better pay. The play ends more disturbingly on violent pressure to accept sex, not for money. This was staged at the Royal Court Theatre in 1984; the male director, JR says, made it hard for her (Mary Remnant, ed., *Plays by Women*, 5, 1986). Next year the Royal Court gave *God's Second in Command* (fiercely drawn black men – defeated father and peacock son – family break-up, son's rich, older, white male lover), with *Basin*, her first play re-named from a symbol of cleanliness and wifely service, and re-written around the Dominican word 'zammie'. This, says JR, means a close, even physically close female friend, not strictly a lesbian. Her heroine says, 'Yes, we're zammies, but I'm in love with you as well' (in Yvonne Brewster, ed., *Black Plays*, 1987). JR does not want to treat black-white relations, or 'what a problem it is being black – that's been battered to death already'. Interview in *Plays International*, 1, 3, 1985.

Rukeyser, Muriel, 1913–80, poet and political activist. B. in NYC, da. of Jewish parents Myra (Lyons) and Lawrence R., she attended Vassar College and Columbia Univ., 1930–2, then, briefly, researched her first book of poems at Roosevelt Aviation School. *Theory of Flight*, 1935, won a Yale Younger Poets Award. Like her later poems, it speaks passionately of social justice. In the 1930s she reported on the racially charged Scottsboro Trials in Alabama (cf. Nancy CUNARD) and on silicosis in West Virginia miners (in *U.S.1*, 1938), and supported the loyalists in the Spanish Civil War. (Much later she travelled to Hanoi protesting American involvement in the war and to South Korea on behalf of a politically imprisoned poet. *The Gates*, 1976, takes its title from a sequence of 15 poems set in an unnamed country: an American woman stands in the rain at the prison gates where a political poet is held for execution.) MR was jailed for anti-war activities. Divorced from Glyn Collins, she raised her son alone, becoming vice-president of the House of Photography in NYC, 1946–60. At Sarah Lawrence College she influenced Alice WALKER, who says that 'she taught by the courage of her own life' (*In Search of Our Mothers' Gardens*, 1983). Among her 19 books of poetry, *Beast in View*, 1944, *The Green Wave*, 1948, and *Elegies*, 1949, show early influence of T. S. Eliot and Whitman, but belief in liberty and justice and continual experiment with form made her 'the best poet of her exact generation' (Kenneth Rexroth).

Later work, like *The Outer Banks*, 1967, and *Breaking Open*, 1973, won another generation's admiration for its female self-awareness and self-scrutinizing reassessment of earlier writing, as in 'The Poem as Mask', 1968: 'When I wrote of the god, / fragmented exiled from himself, his life, the love gone down with song, / it was myself, split open, unable to speak, in exile from myself'. In 'Käthe Kollwitz', 1968, she asks, 'What would happen if one woman told the truth about her life? / The world would split open'. (This gave the title to a well-known ANTHOLOGY.) MR also wrote children's books, a 'poetic' novel, *The Orgy*, 1965, biographies of Willard Gibbs, 1942, and Wendell Willkie, 1957, and a play, *The Color of the Day*, 1961; she translated works by Octavio Paz, 1963, Gunnar Ekelof, 1967, and Bertolt Brecht. See *Collected Poems*, 1978; essay by Rachel Blau DuPlessis in GILBERT and Gubar, 1979; study by Louise Kertesz, 1980.

Rule, Jane, novelist, short-story writer, essayist. B. in 1931 in Plainfield, NJ, da. of Jane (Hink) and Arthur R. R., she attended school in various regions of the US. Although her apprenticeship to reading was delayed and difficult (dyslexia made her a non-reader until she discovered 'the English language locked up in the matter on the page' at 12), she was educ. at Mills College, Calif., University College, London, 1952–3, and Stanford Univ., with Wallace Stegner. Her 'appetite for every literary device and theory of language, and her obsession with point of view, symbolism and time', though 'discouragingly pretentious', trained her in her art. She moved to Vancouver, 1956, to live with Helen Sonthoff, and for the next 20 years worked at UBC, first at International House, then as a lecturer in English. She set up and taught the first groups for the women's movement at UBC, contributed to women's studies programmes, and was willingly labelled, reviewed and interviewed as a lesbian writer. *Lesbian Images*, 1975, measures her 'own attitudes toward lesbian experiences as ... against those of other women writers'. *The Outlander*, 1981, collects her contributions to the *Body Politic* and lesbian journals; *A Hot-Eyed Moderate*, 1985, essays, expresses impatience with the too slow ebb of bigotry. JR's novels and short stories depict her belief that communities can be founded on voluntary relationships. In *Desert of the Heart*, 1964, filmed by American feminist Donna Deitch as 'a joyful, honest statement', Reno is backdrop and catalyst to the sensuous, self-discovering relationship of two women; *This Is Not for You*, 1970, narrates an austere love letter that its central character will never send to the woman whose love she had deflected. Voluntary communities grow out of friendships, kinships and loves in *Against the Season*, 1971, *The Young in One Another's Arms*, 1977, and *Contract with the World*, 1980 (all in Naiad Press reprints). The narrator of the title story of *Outlander*, who sees social and family conflicts as 'her way to fight free into the human debt and credit' she finally achieves, sums up the largely triumphant discoveries of self, in love, which characterize the stories of *Themes for Diverse Instruments*, 1975, and *Inland Passage*, 1985. *Memory Board*, 1987, places the relationship of Diana and Constance in the context of the losses and gains of ageing. JR lives in BC; she suffers severely from arthritis. *CFM*, 23, 1976, prints an interview, Helen Sonthoff's appreciation of her partner's fiction, and a bibliography to date; more recent interview in Twigg, 1981.

Rumens, Carol (Lumley), poet, novelist, editor, b. 1944 in Lewisham, South London, da. of Marjorie May (Mills) and Arthur L. She was educ. at St Winifrede's convent school and London Univ. (BA in philosophy). She m. David Edward R. in 1965 and has two children. She has been an advertising copywriter, poetry editor (for *Quarto*, then the *Literary Review*), and univ. writer-in-residence. Her poetry volumes are *A Strange Girl in Bright Colours*, 1973 (which treats various dilemmas of married women), *A Necklace of Mirrors*, 1979 (which looks also at women's lives in history), *Unplayed Music*, 1981, *Scenes from the Gingerbread House*, 1982, *Star Whisper*, 1983, *Direct Dialling*, 1985 (including poems about Russia and eastern Europe), and *From Berlin to Heaven*, 1989. 'Revolutionary Women' says 'They'd take a lover only for his secrets, / milk him fast and leave him in his blood.' CR's work has received several awards. She edited *Making for the Open: The Chatto Book of Post-Feminist Poetry, 1964–1984*, 1985, which links a controversial title and short introduction ('Those writers concerned with "the stern art of poetry" as an end in itself have tended to be swamped by the noisy amateurs proclaiming that women, too, have a voice') with a useful selection from 56 women poets. In 1987 CR published *Plato Park* (a novel) and *Selected Poems*. 'Two Women' juxtaposes irreconcilable employed and domestic selves: 'paid thinking / and clean hands' and 'a silent, background face / that's always flushed with work, or swallowed anger'. 'SAPPHO' concludes 'She glitters through the mesh dim Phaon trawls, / naming her girl-friends by an act of choice / as treacherous as talent; in its heat / are fused the stolen verbs; – to love, to write.'

Rundell, Maria Eliza or Maria Farquharson (Ketelby), 1745–1826, domestic writer. Only child of Margaret (Farquharson) and Abel Johnstone K. of Ludlow, Shropshire, she m. eminent jeweller Thomas R. Her first alleged work, *Domestic Happiness*, 1806, is probably a ghost. Her stock of recipes, said to be gathered in widowhood for her married daughters, draws on *A Collection of Above Three Hundred Recipes*, compiled in 1724 by Mary Ketelbey or Kettilby, d. 1728, which Elizabeth ELSTOB praised in notes on famous women. MER's book, *A New System of Domestic Cookery*, 'by a Lady', John Murray, 1808, had staggering success. Its introduction stresses women's influence for good within the home, the wickedness of wasting 'the good things that God has given us for our use, not abuse', and the fact that the author will receive 'no emolument'. A companion *Family Receipt Book*, 1810, covers agriculture, science and building as well as cookery. By 1814 MER was no longer without 'the smallest idea of any return': she pub. *Letters . . . to Two Absent Daughters* (traditional advice written years before, during her girls' education), and she offered her *Cookery* to Longman's. After legal wrangles she received £1000 for her copyright and 'a similar sum' for costs; the book sold *c.* 276,000 copies by 1841 and spawned 'London', 'American', 'Jewish' and account-book offshoots. MER died at Geneva.

Rush, Rebecca, b. *c.* 1779, Philadelphia novelist, one of four das. of Mary (Rench or Wrench) and Jacob Rush: niece of writer Benjamin Rush. Her mother, who had supported her family before marriage by painting miniatures, d. in 1806, the year they moved back from Reading to Philadelphia. Her father became a formidable judge. She received $100 for her *Kelroy*, by 'a Lady of Pennsylvania', 1812. Her idealized, deep-feeling heroine (converse of a 'handsome icicle' sister) dies of grief after being wrongly convinced of her lover's perfidy and marrying another; yet the general tone is of social satire and psychological analysis as their widowed, fiercely ambitious mother gambles on their advancement by marriage, splashing out beyond her means and fighting off duns, to die of a stroke once her aims are achieved. (Similar *noms de plume* have caused Leonora SANSAY's *Laura* to be ascribed to RR.)

Russ, Joanna, science-fiction writer, feminist theorist and essayist. B. in 1937 in NYC, da. of teachers Bertha (Zimmer) and Evarett R., she studied at Cornell (BA, 1957) and the Yale School of Drama (MFA, 1960). While teaching at various universities, finally the Univ. of Washington, Seattle, she developed a radical oeuvre of SCIENCE FICTION stories and novels. She married Albert Amateau, 1963 (divorced, 1967). From her first novel, *Picnic on Paradise*, 1968, with its female hero, Alyx, a survivor by wits, strength and courage (the subject of stories in *Alyx*, 1976, and *The Adventures of Alyx*, 1986), JR resists science fiction clichés, integrating myth, technology, and feminist consciousness. She won the Nebula Award, 1972, for 'When it Changed', describing the appearance of male space explorers on a world happily and productively populated by women, and the Nebula and Hugo Awards, 1983, for the novella *Souls*. In the experimental *The Female Man*, 1975 (repr. 1977, with intro. by Marilyn HACKER), four female consciousnesses from varied realities, including contemporary Western society, encounter each other, providing, with acid humour and some violence, a searing exposure of middle-class misogyny. It was followed by *Kittatinny: A Tale of Magic*, 1978 (a juvenile heroic fantasy), *The Two of Them*, 1978, and *On Strike Against God: A Lesbian Love Story*, 1979. *How to Suppress Women's Writing*, 1983, documents a case against the academic, critical, and publishing institutions. *Magic Momms, Trembling Sisters, Puritans and Perverts*, 1985, collects JR's autobiographical and feminist essays on the uses of power in the women's movement and on pornography: 'Maybe some women can tell the difference between pornography and erotica at a single glance. I can't'. *The Hidden Side of the Moon*, 1987, collects stories 1965–83: 'Sword Blades and Poppy Seed' is an idiosyncratic tribute to women writers. JR's extended conversation with Sam Delaney, Ursula K. LE GUIN, 'James Tiptree Jr' (Alice SHELDON), and others, explores the anti-sexist possibilities of science fiction (*Khatru*, 3 and 4, Nov. 1975). See Samuel Delaney and Thelma Shinn, in Jane B. Weedman, ed., *Women World Walkers*, 1985, and Donald Palumbo, ed., *Erotic Universe*, 1986.

Russell, Dora (Black), 1894–1986, autobiographer, feminist, educationist, peace campaigner. Da. of Sarah Isabella (Davisson) and civil servant Sir Frederick B., she was educ. at Sutton High School (a fee-paying girls' dayschool) and Girton College, Cambridge (first class in modern languages, 1915). After research at University College, London, she became a Junior Fellow at Girton, 1918. In 1920–1 she visited Russia (where she met Alexandra Kollontai), then China with philosopher Bertrand R., whom she married in 1921. They set up a progressive school, Beacon Hill, 1927, which DR continued after her bitter divorce in 1935. During their 'open marriage' she had four children, two by Bertrand R. and two by Griffin Barry. Her second husband was Pat Grace (d. 1949). She was active in the birth-control movement, the Sex Reform League, the labour movement, and lifelong in various peace campaigns. Her books emphasize the importance of nurturing, affection and creativity, qualities she judged neglected in a male-dominated world. They include *Hypatia*, 1925, discussing sexual freedom for women, *The Right to be Happy*, 1927, protesting (like her last book, *The Religion of the Machine Age*, 1983) against unthinking use of technology, and *In Defence of Children*, 1932. She began work for British–Soviet relations during WWII, worked on the paper *British Ally* till 1950, and published *The Soul of Russia and the Body of America*, 1982. In 1983, in a wheelchair, she led a London CND rally, and in 1986 attended a demonstration near her Cornish home. In her autobiography, *The Tamarisk Tree*, 3 vols, 1975–85, she states: 'it is to the cause of women that most of my time and energy has been given'; she wanted not only equality of rights, but 'for the very essence of what [women] represent to count in politics and society'. See Dale Spender in *Women of Ideas and What Men Have Done to Them*, 1982, and foreword to *The Dora Russell Reader*, 1983.

Russell, Elizabeth (Cooke), also Hoby, Lady, 1528–1609, translator and letter-writer, sister of Ann BACON: the sisters were called 'rare Poetesses' in 1622. A Puritan, she m. Sir Thomas H., who d. at Paris in 1566, leaving her, pregnant, to bring his body home. She wrote learned, confident, disputatious letters, many on public affairs: she declares she will 'not whyle I live beggar myself for my Cradell', or prefer her son to 'his poore wronged sistars' (MSS Hatfield House and BL: a few with the diary by her daughter-in-law Margaret HOBY, 1930). In 1574 she married John, Lord R. (d. 1584); she set her name, with his and her father-in-law's, to her version (perhaps from French) of a Latin treatise on the Eucharist by John Poynet, *A Way of Reconciliation of a Good and Learned Man*, 1605. It is dedicated 'as my last Legacie', a 'most precious Jewell to the comfort of your Soule', to her 'most entierly beloved' surviving daughter, printed (exquisitely) only because, having lent her MS, ER feared piracy. She wrote Greek, Latin and English epitaphs for several children and both husbands.

Russell, Lady **Rachel** (Wriothesley), 1636–1723, letter writer, da. of Rachel (de Rouvigny), a French Protestant who died when she was three, and of Thomas W., 4th Earl of Southampton. In 1653 she m. Lord Vaughan (she later calls early marriages 'acceptance rather than choosing'); her one child by him died, as he did in 1667. She married Lord William R. (then a younger son whose estate did not match her own) in 1669; he conspicuously opposed Charles II, and was charged with high treason in 1683. She sat by him in open court, acting as his secretary; on his conviction she led a vain campaign for mercy; she parted from him with heroic 'magnanimity of spirit' and a few days after his beheading wrote to the king, as 'a woman amazed with grief', strongly defending his reputation. Her later letters (anatomy of her grief sent to her father's former chaplain; affectionate advice to her three children and others), pub. 1773, ranked her with William R. as a kind of Protestant martyr. Intimate letters to him were pub. 1819 by Mary BERRY (who had catalogued them in 1815) with an enthusiastic life; more letters added, 1853. RR writes 'in bed, thy pillow at my back; where thy dear head shall lie, I hope, to-morrow night', or 'Boy is asleep, girls sing a-bed.' Life by Lois G. Schwoerer, 1986.

Russell, Sheila (MacKay), novelist. B. in Airdre, Alberta, da. of Catherine (Reid) and William M., she was educ. at Central High School, Calgary, then at Calgary General Hospital (RN, 1942) and the Univ. of Alberta (public health nursing, 1944). She worked as a public health nurse in Alberta, married in 1947, and published short stories, professional articles, and two novels, *A Lamp is Heavy*, 1950, and *The Living Earth*, 1954, both popular successes. The first, warm, humorous and insightful, combines a realistic account of the experiences of a student nurse with the pattern of initiation: its protagonist successfully overcomes difficulties, falls in love, and attains adulthood in a ceremony of graduation in which she takes the Florence NIGHTINGALE oath.

Ryves, Eliza, 1750–97, poet and translator, da. of a long-serving Irish army officer. At his death, lawsuits swallowed her inheritance, and she came to London to petition the king, 1775, and to live by writing. *Poems on Several Occasions*, by subscription, 1777, includes compliment, political idealism, praise of strong queens, pastoral elegies, odes and a comic opera. A proposed vol. II never appeared. *The Debt of Honour*, one of several unacted plays, brought in £100; much magazine work in prose and verse remained unpaid. Later poems vigorously support the Whigs: to William Mason, praising 'the free-born mind', 1780 (he probably gave her five guineas); a dialogue between Caesar and Cato (Cato wins hands down), 1784; humbly-offered paeans which are not, says ER, flattery, to one political peer and the infant heir of another, 1784 and 1787; a squib about Warren Hastings's wife bribing Pitt to bend the law, 1785. ER's public poetry is eloquent in several metres; she continued to improve even printed texts. The heroine of her novel *The Hermit of Snowden, or Memoirs of Albert and Lavinia* (1789, purportedly from a chance-found MS), dies destitute (after ill-paid playwriting) of faithful, constantly doubted love; ER's acquaintance Isaac D'Israeli, who made her a type of female-author victim, called it autobiographical. She learned French to qualify as translator of Rousseau's *Social Contract*, 1791, and controversial political works: ascribed to the Abbé Raynal (1789–91, her version untraced) and by J. V. Delacroix, 1792. She worked in the BM towards translating Froissart. The extent of her part in the *Annual Register* was argued in the *GM*. She died poor. No relation of Mrs F. Ryves of Ryves Castle, who pub. by subscription *Cumbrian Legends* in verse, Edinburgh, 1812 (written *c.* 1806).

S

Sackville, Lady **Margaret**, 1882–1963, poet, b. at Buckhurst, Sussex, da. of Constance (Lamington) and Reginald Windsor, later S., 7th Earl De La Warr. At about six she dictated 'a long Dramatic Poem' of which part was later pub.; at 16 she was 'discovered' by the poet Wilfred Scawen Blunt. She published 21 volumes of verse (from *Poems*, 1901) and prose volumes from *Fairy Tales for Old and Young* [1908] (with Ronald Campbell MacFie). The title piece of *Bertrud and other Dramatic Poems*, 1911, Nordic in spirit, presents a king's mistress destroying the queen with slander and then repenting. (A revised version keeps the story-line but chastens its emotional rhetoric.) Other pieces are Hellenic, like 'The Pythoness': 'I am a woman, flesh, / Mortal and incomplete . . . I live a thousand lives, and yet to live / One life – my own life; that is denied me.' *The Dream Pedlar*, 1914, features a half-wit 'who's always seeing what other people can't'. *The Pageant of War*, 1916, paints War magnificent on horseback, but masked, 'lest seeing / the obscene countenance too near, / The heart of every human being / Should shrink in loathing and in fear'. After *Selected Poems*, 1919, and *Collected Poems*, 1939, came further volumes, including *Return to Song*, 1943; three books of poems written for others' pictures, like *Lyrical Woodlands*, 1945, with descriptions of yew, pine, prunus, etc.; *Miniatures*, 1947 (mostly single-quatrain pieces, some concrete-poetry effects). MS is capable of humour (as in 'The Vicar's Wife and the Faun' or 'The Poet', whom his 'neighbours feared to ask to tea, / Save in a moment of rare charity') or nostalgia ('the quick advancing towns, / The smutty dragons which, obscene, / Lurk each behind his foul smoke-screen'). She lived mostly in Edinburgh. Out of step with her age, she nonetheless had many admirers: see Georgina Somerville, ed., *Aeolian Harp*, 1953.

Sackville-West, Vita, Lady Victoria Mary Sackville-West, 1892–1962, poet, novelist, biographer, historian, travel writer, translator, gardener, b. at Knole, near Sevenoaks, Kent. She was granddaughter of the Spanish dancer Pepita, and Lionel Sackville-West: daughter of Victoria, their illegitimate daughter, with whom she had an intense, troubled relationship, and the third Baron Sackville. She was educ. in London, at Miss Woolff's school, but mainly by governesses at Knole, the palace Queen Elizabeth gave to Thomas Sackville in 1566, which, by the 'technical fault' of her sex, VSW was prevented from inheriting. (Her short novel, *The Heir*, 1922, was a farewell to Knole.) In 1913 she married Harold Nicolson, diplomat, author, politician, publisher. They had two sons. These first facts provide central antitheses in a life VSW thought marked by 'duality': she saw herself as rootedly English but romantically foreign, as inheritor but excluded, as traditional but unorthodox. Emotionally bisexual from youth, she learned after marriage of Nicolson's homosexuality, and soon launched an intense, painful affair with childhood friend Violet (Keppel) Trefusis, eloping with her to Paris in 1920. Persuaded to return, she left Violet, to whom she nevertheless remained passionately attached until old age, conducting thereafter a series of affairs with women. Though 'secrecy was all my passion', her imaginative and historical work reflects the preoccupations of her life. The protagonist of *Heritage*, 1919, enacts the conflicts of 'separate, antagonistic strains in her blood, the southern and the northern legacy'; the setting of *The Edwardians*, 1930, repr. 1983, transcribes Knole in every detail; and *Knole and the Sackvilles*, 1922, gives a detailed account of the house and its inhabitants from the beginning to the nineteenth century. *Challenge*, which she withdrew from the English publisher, deals with her relationship with Violet. The moving autobiographical fragment printed by her son Nigel in his *Portrait of a Marriage*, 1973, confronts her lesbianism directly in a prose beneficially disburdened of secrecy. She met Virginia WOOLF in 1922: their relationship produced VSW's *Seducers in Ecuador*, 1924, written for Woolf and published, as subsequent novels were, by the Hogarth Press, and Woolf's *Orlando*, 1928, a loving, playful, deeply sympathetic restoration to VSW of her beloved Knole. Woolf, who said that Vita had given her much happiness, presented her with the manuscripts of *Orlando* and *Mrs Dalloway*. *All Passion Spent*, 1931, shows the impact of Woolf's *A Room of One's Own* (heard by VSW as Cambridge lectures). In 1930, VSW and Nicolson bought Sissinghurst Castle. She became a passionate gardener, writer of gardening columns for *The New Statesman* and *The Sunday Times*. She published more than 40 books – fiction (some very popular), history, biography, travel, and poetry, which she valued most. *Poems of East and West*, 1917, was her first book. *The Land*, 1926, Hawthornden Prize winner, is deeply traditional in form and substance, as is *The Garden*, 1946. Both are Georgics: 'Small pleasures must correct great tragedies, / Therefore of gardens in the midst of war / I boldly tell.' Some other poems, formally unadventuresome, are covertly bold in substance: *The King's Daughter*, pub. 1929, treats lesbian subjects, as do some of the *Collected Poems*, 1933. She translated Rilke's *Duino Elegies*, 1931. 'Always wary of the word "feminism" but living much of her life according to its principles', VSW wrote lives of her grandmother, Pepita, 1937, repr. 1986 with intro. by Alison Hennegan (quoted above), of Saint Joan, of La Grande Mademoiselle, of Aphra BEHN, and edited Lady Anne CLIFFORD's diary, 1923. Lives by Michael Stevens, 1974, Victoria Glendinning, 1983. See also Harold Nicolson, *Letters and Diaries*, 1966. Letters to actor Andrew Reiber, ed. Nancy MacKnight, 1979, to Woolf, ed. Louise De Salvo and Mitchell Leaska, 1984. Several works reprinted; some remain unpublished. The Lilly Library, Bloomington, Indiana, has some letters and early diaries. Studies by Elizabeth Pomeroy in *TCL*, 28, 1982, Louise De Salvo in Susan Squier, ed., *Women Writers and the City*, 1984, Carol Ames in Jack Biles, ed., *British Novelists Since 1900*, 1987. On Woolf and VSW see Sherron E. Knopp, *PMLA*, 103, 1988.

Sadlier, Anna Teresa, 1854–1932, novelist, religious writer, translator, journalist. B. in Montréal, da. of Mary Anne SADLIER, she moved to NYC in 1860, returning to Montréal with her mother soon after her father's death in 1869. She studied French, Italian and German at convent schools in NYC and Montréal. At her home she met American Catholic literary figures. She began writing at 18 and published her first novel, *Seven Years and Mair*, in 1878. She wrote novels, religious biographies, translations of religious works, over 200 stories (mainly for children), and essays on religious and literary topics, published largely in papers in the US and Canada. ATS was an active Catholic, and her fiction reflects her religious viewpoint. *Pauline Archer*, 1899, demonstrates her central concerns. A young girl growing up in NYC comes, through such experiences as giving up her doll, befriending a poor younger girl, and visiting wealthy cousins, to understand the harshness of poverty and the selfishness and materialism often associated with wealth. The language and theme are simple: the necessity of charity, courtesy, and consideration is revealed. In 1903 ATS moved to Ottawa.

Sadlier, Mary Anne (Madden), 1820–1903, novelist, dramatist, editor and publisher. B. in Cootehill, Co. Cavan, of a merchant father, Francis M., she was educ. at home, and by 18 was contributing poetry to *La Belle Assemblée*, London. At 23, after her father died, she migrated with other family members to Canada, where her contributions to the *Literary Garland* helped support the family. She married, 1845, James S., an Irish immigrant who, with his brother Denis, established the major Catholic publishing firm in America. By 1860, when they moved to New York, their company headquarters, MAS had had six children, published eight books, and become a lifelong friend of Thomas D'Arcy McGee, sharing his nationalism and literary interests. His 1850 serialization in the *American Celt* of her novel *The Blakes and Flanagans: A Tale Illustrative of Irish Life in the United States*, began her popularity with the North American Irish immigrant population. When McGee moved to Canada, 1857, Denis S. purchased the *American Celt*, changing its name to the *Tablet*. MAS became its editor and guided its religious and nationalist direction. Between 1860 and her husband's death in 1869, along with editing the *Tablet*, she published 23 books, mostly immigrant novels and historical romances. Michèle Lacombe singles out as best *Elinor Preston; or, Scenes at Home and Abroad*, 1861, the story of a gentlewoman in exile which has parallels with Susanna MOODIE's *Roughing it in the Bush*. Between 1869 and 1885, MAS continued her publishing company and produced another 12 books, most directed to Catholic schoolchildren. In the 1870s she became involved in social and philanthropic works, starting a Foundling Asylum, a Home for the Aged, and a Home for Friendless Girls. After Denis S.'s death, 1885, she returned to Montréal, with the help of her daughter Anna Teresa SADLIER, running the publishing company for another ten years before losing control of it to a nephew, William, 1895, when she turned again to writing as a source of income. A public-spirited woman, concerned with social and religious issues, especially those affecting Irish immigrants, MAS made fiction a vehicle for her ideas. Her female characters are conscious of their situation as women and she makes immigration 'a metaphor for women's continuing struggles to improve their lot'. See Michèle Lacombe in *ECW*, 29, 1984 (quoted above).

Sahgal, Nayantara (Pandit), novelist and political writer. She was b. 1927 at Allahabad, da. of Vijaya Lakshmi (Nehru) and Ranjit Sitaram P., lawyer and scholar, both active politicians, each several times in prison under the British (he d. in 1944 of an illness contracted there; she became Indian Ambassador – the first – to the USSR and later to the US). NS was educ. at Woodstock, Mussoorie (a co-educational school run by US missionaries), and Wellesley College, Mass. (BA, 1947), as she relates in *Prison and Chocolate Cake*, 1954. She married (by choice, not by arrangement) businessman Gautam S. in 1949, and had three children: *From Fear Set Free*, 1962, describes this personal life and her setting out as a writer. She published two novels, besides magazine stories, before her divorce in 1967. Her fiction (magazine stories as well as novels) deals chiefly with life in the major cities of India. NS is interested in making Hinduism more flexible, and freedom of all kinds more accessible to women: her novels often centre on a woman discovering and trying to fulfil her emotional needs. Leela in *This Time of Morning*, 1965, and Mahdu in *A Situation in New Delhi*, 1977, refuse orthodoxy and commit suicide. In 1973 came the first of NS's several visiting academic posts. Introducing *A Voice for Freedom*, 1977, she tells of the censorship of her writing (especially for the *Indian*

Express) by the Emergency, during which she wrote (chiefly in the US, 1976) her courageous exposé, *Indira Gandhi: Her Road to Power*, 1982. She saw this book as a duty to 'the voices the Emergency had silenced in my country' and to the values of NS's uncle, Indira Gandhi's father. In 1978 NS was a delegate to the UN; in 1979 she married E. N. Mangat Rai, civil servant and writer. In *Rich like Us*, 1983, dedicated 'To The Indo-British Experience and what its sharers have learned from each other', Rose, the vital, vulgar, Cockney wife of monied Ram, is eventually murdered as a misfit. In *Mistaken Identity*, 1988, set in 1929, a rajah's playboy son, in prison through error, becomes politicized and learns to care for the motley throng of political and criminal inmates: 'Let's drink to the losers, judge, and to the rainbow harvest of defeat.' Study by Jasbir Jain, 1978.

St Aubin de Terán, Lisa, novelist, b. 1953 in London, da. of Joanna St A., a four-times-married head of a school for disturbed children and a dazzling, absent S. American father. She left James Allen's Girls' School at 16 to marry Jaime de T., Venezuelan land-owner. After two years in Italy, she ran his sugar-and-avocado estate in the Andes for seven years. Back in England with a daughter, she published privately 'The Streak', 1980, a short poem about 'the streak in you / That grows away from me', m. poet George MacBeth, 1982, and lived in Norfolk. *Keepers of the House*, 1983 (Somerset Maugham Award: in USA *The Long Way Home*), is typically, flamboyantly GOTHIC: a third-person account of an English 17-year-old in the Andes as a bride, hearing family history from an old servant, and fleeing years later, pregnant, with her English dog and ageing husband's corpse. After her mother died and her second marriage ended, LSAdT took her son to Italy, had 'a very big nervous breakdown', 1982–4, but won the Eric Gregory poetry award in 1983. *Slow Train to Milan*, 1984, has a 16-year-old narrator who reaches Venezuela after Italian wanderings: the only name reused from *Keepers* is that of an English dog. *The Tiger*, 1985, traces the life of a German-descended, Venezuelan great lover, spender and killer. *The High Place*, 1985, contains poems about estate workers: 'Their skills were of violence, and / patience, and mastering the / knowing silence of the / sharpened blade.' *The Bay of Silence*, 1986 (written during her breakdown), is spoken in turn by an estranged couple whose past includes the gruesome doing to death of a baby son; *Black Idol*, 1987, is narrated by the lover of Caresse CROSBY's husband, with whom he died. *Off the Rails, Memoirs of a Train Addict*, 1989, reviews LSAdT's use of railways as 'means of truancy'; *The Marble Mountain*, 1989 (cover-portrait by her latest lover), collects stories of death, silences, and surreal horrors. She draws on her mother, grandmother and great-grandmother for *Joanna*, 1990, a three-generation novel.

'St Clair, Rosalia', pseudonymous author of 13 novels, 1819–34, the first few for MINERVA. She writes well on Irish and Scots topics, often includes animals, and several times describes the successful freeing and education of slaves. *The Son of O'Donnel*, 1819, brings together Irish and American, white and black; *The First and Last Years of Married Life*, 1821, reconciles Irish Protestant and Catholic (leaving only ancient rugged Mabel still crying revenge and doom) and praises US government as 'emanating from the people themselves'. *The Pauper Boy, or The Ups and Downs of Life*, 1834, opens with a first-person exposé of the workhouse system, and gives Jewish characters (qualified) approval. Dialect is a feature of *The Highland Castle, and the Lowland Cottage*, 1820, and *Eleanor Ogilvie, The Maid of the Tweed*, 1829 (on the 1715 rebellion). In *The Banker's Daughters of Bristol, or Compliance and Decision*, 1824, the daughters (like some characters elsewhere) are recklessly blackened, while extreme female submissiveness is pitied and female firmness praised. *Ulrica of Saxony*, 1828, is set in late medieval times; *Marston*, 1835, is not, as usually said, RSC's.

'St John, Christopher', Christabel Marshal, *c.*1875–1960, suffragette, playwright, journalist, and co-author with Cicely HAMILTON of *How the Vote Was Won*, 1909 (repr. in Rachel Irma, ed., *A Century of Plays by American Women*, 1978, and Dale Spender and Carole Hayman, eds., 1985), the most influential of the suffrage plays: it played widely in the US and Canada (see, e.g., Emily MURPHY). In 1899, having come down from Oxford to work in London as secretary to Lady Randolph Churchill and her son Winston, she met Edith CRAIG, with whom she lived, at first in London, until Craig's death in 1947. CSJ's autobiographical novel, *Hungerheart, The Story of a Soul* (in progress by 1899, pub. 1915) draws on the relationship. In 1905 CSJ became a suffragette and an active campaigner, working first on behalf of the WSPU, then for the Writers' Franchise League (which she helped to found), the Actresses' Franchise League (acting in *The Pageant of Great Women*, produced by Craig, 1909), and, later, for Craig's Pioneer Players, for which she wrote, adapted and translated about 18 plays, including (jointly with Hamilton), *The Pot and the Kettle*, 1909, and work of the medieval playwright and nun Hrotsvit, pub. 1923. Her own *The First Actress*, 1909, which 'celebrated the struggle of women in the theatre against sex discrimination', was the Company's first presentation. In 1901, CSJ and Craig moved to Small Hythe, Kent, with Ellen Terry, Craig's mother; later they were joined by Clare Atwood. CSJ wrote drama and music criticism which caused Ethel SMYTH to write (in *A Final Burning of Boats*, 1928), 'I am acquainted with no more typical instance of a first-line female intelligence and how it works.' Also, because 'All musicians who know her writing are furious that she is not on the Daily Press', Smyth saw CSJ as 'another case of "white crow"; otherwise the all-maleism of our musical Press is undiluted'. CSJ edited Ellen Terry's correspondence with Bernard Shaw, Ellen Terry's memoirs (with Edy Craig), and her four lectures on Shakespeare, all 1932. She also wrote lives of Dr Christine Murrell, 1935, and of Smyth, 1959. See Eleanor Adlard, *Recollections of Edy Craig*, 1949, and Julia Holledge, *Innocent Flowers*, 1981.

Saint John, Mary, d. *c.* 1830, missionary and poet publishing as 'Mary'. She grew up in Queen's Co., probably at Stradbally, to whose landowners she dedicated her long narrative poem *Ellauna*, Dublin 1815, set in St Bridget's convent in the thirteenth century. After years abroad she pub. this work, dating from her youthful listening 'to the Peasant's ORAL tale', by subscription to raise money for Sierra Leone missions. Her short poems for the *Dublin Examiner*, 1816ff. (a few repr. in *Harmonica*, Cork, 1818) show marked improvement. Her themes are now love and Irish patriotism. She pays tribute to Sydney MORGAN and R. C. Maturin: 'If Persecution's bigot sway / Obscure with gloom they rising day, / If cold Oppression's dead'ning hand / Fall heavy on thy native land'.

'St Leger, Evelyn', Evelyn St Leger (Savile), later Randolph, 1861–1944, novelist, b. in Kensington, London, da. of Margaret Marion (Stevenson) and Edward Bourchier S., Recorder of Okehampton. Educ. at home in London and Devon by governesses and tutors, she m. Joseph Randolph R., KC, in 1895. He was a county court judge: they lived in Oxford, Leeds and Malmesbury. Her first book, *Diaries of Three Women of the Last Century 1821–99*, 1907, is a fictionalized account of changing Victorian attitudes towards women and marriage, and the suppression of creativity. *Dapper*, 1908, deals with religious self-abnegation. *The Shape of the World*, 1911, again looks at married life: where generations of women 'had suffered but never complained, had endured but had never run away', the modern woman achieves a rewarding career as a dramatist, bears a daughter, and cures her husband of his deficiencies through a brain operation. In *The Blackberry Pickers*, 1912, a sculptor finds her work disrupted by her ambitious but inadequate fiancé; she is freed only by his death. *The Tollhouse*, 1915, relating village life to world events, aims to encourage WWI recruitment. ESL also wrote magazine stories and children's books, 1927–33, some as Eve St Leger.

Salverson, Laura (Goodman), 1890–1970, novelist and autobiographer, b. in Winnipeg, Man., da. of Ingiborg (Gudsmundotte) and Larus G., Icelandic parents who continued to migrate between the USA and Canada. LS, whose education was often interrupted because of these moves and her frail health, began learning English when she was ten. After discovering that she could borrow books – 'just for nothing' – from the West Duluth library, Minn., she vowed that 'I too, will write a book ... and I will write it in English, for that is the greatest language in the whole world!' This desire was nourished by her 'papa's statement that to be a maker of books was the greatest destiny'. Although her parents' immigrant otherness and poverty often embarrassed the young LS, they instilled in her an immense pride in her Norse origins which often takes the compensating attitude of 'cultural superiority', as in *The Viking Heart*, 1923, an exploration of the mass immigration of 1400 Icelanders to Canada in 1875. In 1913 in Winnipeg, LS married George S., a railway man from Montana, and they moved around the Canadian west as need demanded. 'There is nothing to say of my baby except that the prospect bored me' is the only direct reference to her motherhood in the autobiographical *Confessions of an Immigrant's Daughter*, 1939, for which she received her second Governor-General's Award (the first for the strongly pacifist *The Dark Weaver*, 1937). *When Sparrows Fall*, 1925, dedicated to her mentor Nellie L. McClung – 'Who has been a voice for the voiceless / The humble women of her land' – gives to the problems of a family of Scandinavian immigrants in a fictionalized Duluth a feminist perspective which also characterizes LS's impressive autobiography. She is known primarily as one of the first Canadian writers to write, in work which mixes epic saga, romance and history, about immigration in the West. See Terrence L. Craig in *SCanL*, 10, 1985, and Kristjana Gunnars in Neuman and Kamboureli, 1986.

Sanborn, Kate, Katherine Abbott, 1839–1917, author, humourist and lecturer, b. in Hanover, NH. She was educ. by her father, Edwin David S., a Latin professor at Dartmouth College. Her mother, Mary Ann (Webster), was the niece of Daniel Webster. She pub. her first work in a local newspaper in 1850. From 1859 she lectured on various topics in rural NH and Vermont: 'I think I was the first woman ever invited to make an address to farmers on farming. ... Insinuated that women need a few days *off* the farm' (*Memories and Anecdotes*). In 1864 she taught at Packer Institute, Brooklyn. At this time she became friends with Ann C. Lynch Botta, attending her 'Saturday Evenings', and beginning to lecture in NYC; her first, 'Spinster Authors of England,' later pub. in *My Favorite Lectures of Long Ago*, 1898, mocked the idea that women need to be married to be happy. In 1868 a series of lectures for young people was pub. as *Home Pictures of English Poets for Fireside and School-Room*. From 1869 to 1872 she contributed essays to *The Youth's Companion*; for this 'boy's' journal, she wrote a series on well-known women such as Grace Greenwood. For the next three years, she taught English Literature at Smith College. A friend of Emma Willard's, KS was selected by Willard herself to write her biography, which appeared in *Our Famous*

Women, 1883. In 1885 KS pub. *The Wit of Women*, an anthology which included representative pieces of humour by over 80 women, including J. W. HOWE, Frances WILLARD, H. B. STOWE, and S. O. JEWETT. KS theorized that women's humour was both 'public' (literary) and 'private' (spontaneous). She herself excelled in both kinds, as in her self-parodying *Adopting An Abandoned Farm*, 1891, and *Abandoning an Adopted Farm*, 1894, concerning her attempts to go 'back to the land' on her farm in Foxboro, Mass. Even a book on a serious topic, *Vanity and Insanity of Genius*, 1885, begins with a humorous preface. *A Truthful Woman in Southern California*, 1893, is a direct and practical travel guide. She also wrote about early American artifacts. Her final work was *Memories and Anecdotes*, 1915. Edwin Webster Sanborn's biography, 1918, remains the primary source. See also Karen Cole, 'Women and the Tradition of American Humour in the Nineteenth Century' (unpub. doctoral diss., Univ. of Illinois, Urbana-Champaign, 1989).

Sanchez, Sonia, poet, playwright and activist, b. 1934 as Wilsonia Driver, in Birmingham, Ala., da. of Lena (Jones), who d. when she was a baby, and Wilson L. D. Raised by various relations, she wrote as a child: an early poem told how her aunt spat in a bus-driver's face when ordered off a bus. At Hunter College, NYC (BA in political science, 1955), she discovered the Schomburg Library of black writers, and told the librarian she would be in it one day. She married poet Etheridge Knight, had three children (later divorced), and taught at colleges and univs. She joined the black studies movement at San Francisco State Univ. in 1966 and was later 'white-balled' for militancy. Her first book of poems, *Homecoming*, 1969, was a landmark. Her plays too are important. *The Bronx is Next* shows 'How people live in Harlem' (in *Drama Review*, Summer 1968; produced 1970); *Sister Son/ji*, a dramatic monologue, traces the growth of a black woman's radical female consciousness: 'She is Harriet Tubman, a woman' (in Ed Bullins, ed., *New Plays from the Black Theatre*, 1969; produced 1971); *Uh Uh; But How Do It Free Us?* looks at violence and mastery in race and gender relations (in Bullins, ed., *The New Lafayette Theatre Presents*, 1974, with intro. by SS). Among her poetry volumes, *We A BaddDDD People*, 1970 (influenced by black chanters and Malcolm X), experiments with words, typography, punctuation, and violence of language, almost unquotable in fragments ('an u got a / re vo lu tion / goin' // like, man, program'); *Love Poems*, 1973, is gentler ('come my love into / this cave that holds no idols / there you may worship'); *A Blues Book for Blue Black Magical Women*, 1974, is fierce and often straightforward: 'i vomited up the stench / of the good ship *Jesus* / sailing to the new world / with Black gold.' It is also marked by SS's time in the Nation of Islam, 1972–6 (she then found it sexist and restrictive, and left). *I've Been a Woman*, 1979, mixes old and new poems; *homegirls & handgrenades*, 1984 (American Book Award), includes poems and prose; *Under a Soprano Sky*, 1987, continues to chart the emergence of black women from oppression with the affirming voice of a collective history. Anthologized by June JORDAN, 1970, and Gwendolyn BROOKS, 1971, SS has herself ed. *Three Hundred and Sixty Degrees of Blackness Comin' At You*, 1971, and *We Be Word Sorcerers*, 1973. She has also written for children. 'I write because I must. ... I probably have not killed anyone in America because I write' (interview in Tate, 1983). See Evans, 1984; Rosmary Curb in Karelisa V. Hartigan, ed., *The Many Forms of Drama*, 1985.

'Sand, George', Amandine-Aurore Lucille Dupin, Baronne Dudevant, 1804–76, French novelist. Prolific and professional, she produced an average of two books annually from 1831–76. The facts of GS's independent life, and the declamatory assertion of her early novels (especially *Indiana*, 1832, *Lelia*, 1833, *Jacques*, 1834, and *Consuelo*, 1842–3), provided a significant model for English women writers and exerted a widespread influence on the traditions of the English novel. Enthusiastic, outspoken, sententious, with a bold manifesto of woman's independence and legitimate claim to emotional and sexual fulfilment, GS was dubbed 'the Anti-Matrimonial novelist' by the *Foreign Quarterly Review*. Other male English reviewers saw her novels as the worst of everything disruptive of the social order: typically 'French'. Other readers were at once appreciative and wary: Jane W. CARLYLE read her avidly but coined 'George Sandism' to convey an idea of excessive sentiment and high-flown morality; E. B. BROWNING, though hero-worshipping the novelist (the poet-heroine of *Aurora Leigh* may have been named for her), could not finish *Lelia*: 'a serpent book both for language-colour and soul-slime'. Other admirers (and imitators) included Geraldine JEWSBURY, Matilda HAYS, Anna OGLE, Eliza L. LINTON and, most notably, Emily and Charlotte BRONTË and George ELIOT. It was Eliot who said of Charlotte Brontë's work: 'Yet what passion, what fire in her! Quite as much as in GS, only the clothing is less voluptuous'. See Patricia Thomson's admirable *GS and the Victorians*, 1977; Paul G. Blount, *GS and the Victorian World*, 1979, studies her reputation rather than her influence.

Sandbach, Margaret (Roscoe), 'Mrs Henry Sandbach', 1812–52, poet and novelist, b. Liverpool, da. of Margaret (Lace) and Edward R., merchant, d. 1834. The Roscoes were a well-known Unitarian intellectual family (see Mary Ann JEVONS): MS's grandfather was William R., the historian; her cousin, W. C. R., poet and critic. In 1832 she m. Henry Robertson S. of Hafodunos, Denbigh (High Sheriff, 1855), and in 1840 pub. her first volume of poems. These were followed by *Giuliano de Medici, a Drama, and Other Poems*, 1842, *The Amidei*, a tragedy in five acts, 1845; and *Aurora and Other Poems*, 1850 (repr. 1856), on classical and mythic subjects, like Antigone or Penthesilea, inspired by artwork of her great friend the sculptor John Gibson. Her verse plays are economically structured, unlike her prose fictions: *Spiritual Alchemy*, 1851, deals too lengthily and schematically with the theme of faith versus reason. Her best is *Hearts in Mortmain*, 1850, told through letters dealing with a melodramatic and semi-incestuous passion. *Cornelia*, in the same volume, suffers from its tangle of relationships surrounding the heroine, a singer. Some of her poetry is very fine, written with a good ear and a real feeling for the countryside of Wales. See *Roscoeana*, and the life of John Gibson by Lady Eastlake (Elizabeth RIGBY), 1870.

'Sandel, Cora', 1880–1974, Norwegian novelist, short-story writer, painter. B. Sara Fabricius in Oslo, she spent her adolescence in northern Norway, studied art for a time in Oslo, and, from 1905, in Paris. There she married, 1913, Anders Jönsson, a Swedish sculptor, with whom she had a son. They divorced in 1926. She left Paris in 1920, after over a decade of painting and publishing a few stories and articles, and settled in Sweden where she wrote her Alberta Trilogy, 1926–39, trans. Elizabeth Rokkan as *Alberta and Jacob*, *Alberta and Freedom*, and *Alberta Alone*, 1962–5 (repr. 1980, 1984). These novels trace Alberta's 'difficult,' unconventional childhood, years of poverty, non-achievement and attempts at self-discovery in Paris, unhappy relationship with an artist, and final confrontation of her desire and fear over writing. The third vol. ends with a bleak pronouncement of independence: 'she had finished groping in a fog for warmth and security.... She would go under or become so bitterly strong that nothing could hurt her any more. She felt something of the power of the complete solitary.' *Krane's Cafe: An Interior With Figures*, 1946 (transl. 1968, repr. 1984, 1985), is the story, written with savage irony from the point of view of gossiping neighbours in a small town, of Mrs Katinka Stordal, who creates a scandal by confiding to a passing male stranger her subversive wish to 'get away from it all'. Other translations include *The Leech*, 1960, and *The Silken Thread: Stories and Sketches*, 1986, by Rokkan, and *Selected Short Stories*, 1986, by Barbara Wilson: most have critical introductions.

Sandoz, Mari (Marie) Susette, 1896–1966, historian and novelist, b. in Sheridan County, Neb., da. of Mary (Fehr) and the 'violent visionary' Jules Ami S., whose Sioux friends figured in her earliest memories. Speaking Swiss German, she did not learn English until he was forced to send his children to school when MS was nearly nine. By 16 she had 'passed the rural teachers' examination and had a school'. She did some teaching while married to Wray Macumber, 1914–19; she already meant to write of the Trans-Missouri region. She moved to Lincoln and studied on and off at the Univ. of Nebraska, 1922–33, supporting herself in various jobs, inspired and encouraged by Louise POUND. (Her father wrote to her, 'You know I consider writers and artists the maggots of society.') She became director of research at the Nebraska State Historical Society; after 13 rejections, her life of her father, *Old Jules*, won a prize on publication, 1935 (often repr.: 50th anniversary ed., 1985). This and other works show that maltreatment of women occurs not only under stresses like settlement but because of male assumptions of natural superiority. Some of MS's novels are allegorical (*Slogum House*, 1937, *The Tom-Walker*, 1947) and anti-fascist (*Capital City*, 1939, modelled on midwestern state capitals, which also explores the uneasy position of the independent working woman). This brought her expected harassment. She moved from Lincoln to Denver in 1940 and to NYC in 1943, closer to research collections and publishers. Her writings on Indians (*Crazy Horse*, 1942, *Cheyenne Autumn*, 1953) are both sympathetic and accurate, drawing on archival research and interviews with old-time survivors. *Miss Morissa: Doctor of the Gold Trail*, 1955, about several women doctors in 1870s Nebraska, reflects MS's feminism. Her Trans-Missouri project was realized in *The Buffalo-Hunters*, 1954, *The Cattlemen*, 1958, and *The Beaver Men*, 1964. She undercuts hero-myths by showing how the frontier draws psychotic personalities; two works for young people, *The Horse-catcher*, 1957, and *The Story Catcher*, 1963, explore non-violent values in the warrior culture of Plains Indians. *Son of the Gamblin' Man*, 1960, is a biographical novel about the painter Robert Henri. MS taught at the Univ. of Wisconsin and elsewhere. She was commissioned to write *The Battle of the Little Bighorn*, 1966. Her short writings were collected as *Hostiles and Friendlies*, 1959, repr. 1976, and *Sandhills Sundays*, 1970; her papers are at the Univ. of Nebraska, Lincoln. Much critical comment includes [Marguerite Young] in *Flair*, 1, 1950; critical biography by Helen Winter Stauffer, 1982; Barbara Rippey in Stauffer and Susan J. Rosowski, eds., *Women and Western American Literature*, 1982; Claire Mattern in *CEA Critic*, 49, 1986–7.

Sanford, Mollie E. (**Dorsey**), 1838–1915, diarist, b. in Rising Sun, Indiana, da. of William D. MDS began keeping her journal in 1857, when she left Indianapolis to settle with her family in the Nebraska Territory. In 1860 she m. Byron S., a blacksmith and teamster; two months later they left for Colorado, where they moved first among the mining camps, and later to military bases while he served in the Federal army. MDS stopped keeping her journal in 1866, shortly after the birth of her second child. She transcribed the DIARY in 1895, presenting it to her grandson; it was later ed. by Donald F. Danker and pub. as *Mollie: The Journal of Mollie Dorsey Sanford in Nebraska and Colorado Territories, 1847–1866*, 1959. An appealing realistic-romantic record of a young woman adapting herself to changing circumstances, the journal bears witness both to MDS's loneliness in the settlements, and to her resourcefulness in sustaining relationships, old and new, through hardships and separation.

Sanger, Margaret (Higgins), 1879–1966, birth-control pioneer, b. at Corning, NY, one of 11 children of Anne (Purcell), who d. when MS was a teenager, and Michael Hennessy H., monumental mason. Educ. in Corning and at Claverack College (a Methodist boarding-school), she taught grade school in NJ, then began nurse's training at White Plains, NJ, where she discovered women's fear and reluctance about constant child-bearing. She married Bill S., architect, *c.* 1902. (Her daughter died at five; her two sons became doctors.) Socialist work on NYC's Lower East Side fed her awareness of the misery caused by over-frequent pregnancy and botched abortions. She began writing pamphlets, though her family resented her increasing absorption in work. Articles for *Call* (including 'What every mother should know', 1912, germ of her first book, *What Every Girl Should Know*, 1914) got the paper banned as obscene. Back in NYC after research in Paris, she founded her own paper, *The Woman Rebel*. She left for London to avoid standing on a charge of printing obscene matter, met Marie STOPES, 1915, and Havelock Ellis, visited Holland to investigate a new, improved diaphragm, and returned to NYC, where her husband had been arrested and her sister jailed. Her overwhelmingly popular NYC clinic was closed after nine days as illegal. She edited the *Birth Control Review* from 1911, and published further titles on family planning and sexual fulfilment (contraception, she felt, was only a starting point). Divorced in 1920, she m. J. Noah Slee, a wealthy businessman and backer, in 1922. That year appeared *The Pivot of Civilization*, which, like her autobiography, 1938, repr. 1971, was 'ghosted'. Her activism and worldwide lecturing continued after her husband's death in 1943. See David Kennedy, *Birth Control in America*, 1970; Margaret Forster, *Significant Sisters*, 1984.

Sangster, Margaret Elizabeth (Munson), 1838–1912, journalist, b. New Rochelle, NY, da. of Margaret (Chisholm) and John M., clerk and real-estate investor. She was educ. at home, then at the Passaic Seminary at Paterson, NJ, later graduating from the French and English School of Monsieur Paul Abadie, Brooklyn, NY. Her first story, 'Little Janey', 1855, was pub. by the Presbyterian Board of Education. In 1858 she m. George S., Union Officer in the Civil War. After his death in 1870 MS had to provide for the family, and wrote for journals such as *Atlantic Monthly*, *Christian Intelligencer*, and *Hearth and Home*, for which she became children's page editor in 1873. Her emphasis was Christian and sentimental. From 1875 she ed. the family page of the *Christian Intelligencer* and from 1889–99 she edited *Harper's Bazaar*. She also pub. books of poetry, such as *Poems of the Household*, 1889, together with other compilations of her magazine writing. In 1904 she joined the editorial staff of the *Woman's Home Companion*. Previously opposed to women's SUFFRAGE, she announced her changed mind in 'My Opinion of Suffrage' in the *Woman's Home Companion*, 1910: 'Whether or not the woman who is safely sheltered in a home of ease and comfort needs the protection of the ballot box, it is certainly becoming clear to many of us that her slaving sister should have this shield.' *An Autobiography: From My Youth Up* was pub. in 1909.

Sansay, Leonora, perhaps *née* Hassall, novelist writing as 'a Lady of Philadelphia', who says she grew up an orphan and went to Santo Domingo, 1802, with a sister married to a Frenchman. *Secret History, or The Horrors of St. Domingo*, 1808, in letters to Aaron Burr (who called her 'too well known'), mixes reportage and fiction, atrocity and frivolity: cruel conflict between planters under Leclerc, Napoleon's brother-in-law, and blacks taught 'knowledge of their own strength' by Toussaint L'Ouverture; 'voluptuous indolence', balls, intrigues, and the break-up of LS's sister's marriage. 'It is Clara's fate to inspire great passions.' LS stayed in Cuba and Jamaica before reaching home. *Laura*, 1809, sometimes wrongly ascribed to Rebecca RUSH, poses as 'a faithful account of real occurrences'. Its isolated, motherless heroine nurses her medical-student lover through yellow fever, and after much suffering is cheated of marriage (when pregnant) by his death in a duel. She survives it all to marry another, from need; 'her mind acquired new brilliancy'; yet 'happiness remained a stranger to her bosom'. LS was well reviewed, but her central message is hard to read.

Sappho, b. *c.* 612 BC, Greek poet, of the isle of Lesbos, who on the renown of her few surviving fragments now stands at the head of the lyric tradition, as Homer stands at the head of the epic. Most of her nine books of poems are lost, read to pieces or destroyed by dark-age monks for their eroticism. She loved several women, married and bore a daughter, was a teacher of girls and a friend of her fellow-poet Alcaeus; she was later said, without evidence, to have killed herself for love of a man. Anne DACIER published a French translation in 1681. English versions (usually with poems by Alcaeus) run from Ambrose Philips, 1713, to Willis Barnstone, 1965. The myth of her as seduced and abandoned was fed by Alexander Pope's poem, 1713. Many writers claimed or were awarded honorific association with her: Madeleine de SCUDÉRY, Katherine PHILIPS, Anne KILLIGREW, Aphra BEHN, Judith MADAN, Sarah CHAPONE, Anna SEWARD, Sophia KING. Derogatory use became commoner after Pope savaged Lady Mary Wortley MONTAGU as S. Nineteenth- and twentieth-century critical readings of her work (e.g. by Denys Page, 1955, repr. 1979) have been coloured by readings of lesbianism; a wealth of literary re-vision includes 'Michael Field', C. A. Dawson SCOTT, Eavan BOLAND, Carol RUMENS. See studies by Anne Pippin Burnett, 1983 Joan DeJean, 1990 ; discussion in *Signs*, 4, 1978–9.

Sarton, May Eleanor, poet, novelist, DIARIST, AUTOBIOGRAPHER, b. 1912 at Wondelgem in Belgium, only child of Eleanor Mabel (Elwes), an English designer and portrait painter, and George A. L. S., a pioneer science historian described in MS's *A World of Light*, 1974. Brought to Cambridge, Mass., at four, she attended Shady Hill School, 1917–26 (with a year in Belgium at 12), and Cambridge High and Latin School. She had sonnets in *Poetry Magazine* at 17, trained at Eva LE GALLIENNE's Civic Repertory Theatre, NYC, 1929–33 (with a year in Paris), then founded the Apprentice Theatre to perform neglected European plays. After its demise, 1936, MS held many teaching jobs; she visited Europe every year until WWII. Publishing *Encounter in April*, 1937 (poems), and *The Single Hound*, 1938 (novel), set her usually alternating pattern, writing novels (and, early on, short stories) to explore her thoughts, poetry (which she has called 'so much more a true work of the soul') to explore her feelings. *I Knew a Phoenix*, 1959, describes visiting England, meeting Virginia WOOLF (whom she commemorated in a strong poem) and becoming a friend of Elizabeth BOWEN. She wrote official documentary film scripts during WWII, 1945–6, published *The Underground River*, first of two unproduced plays, in 1947, and translated Paul Valéry and others from French (sometimes with Louise BOGAN). Her poetry often addresses the experience of writing women, notably in 'My Sisters, O My Sisters', which mourns and celebrates 'DICKINSON, ROSSETTI, SAPPHO' and aspires to travel beyond renunciation 'to the deep place where poet becomes woman'. Her novels (many repr.) persuasively analyse the influence of political reality on private relationships, like *Faithful Are the Wounds*, 1955 (based on the suicide of an eminent Harvard scholar), *The Birth of a Grandfather*, 1957 (a favourite of MS's: about coming to terms with middle age), *The Small Room*, 1961 (about women at a New England college; praised by Carolyn HEILBRUN for being open and serious about 'the never easy student–teacher relationship'), *Crucial Conversations*, 1975 (on a 50-year-old woman leaving a marriage blighted by the Vietnam War), and *Anger*, 1982. MS writes of the nature of inspiration and work in the arts (of 'serving an art rather than using it for one's own ends'), of lesbian experience (see her novel, *Mrs Stevens Hears the Mermaids Singing*, 1965, repr. with introduction by Heilbrun, 1975, and MS in *Writers at Work*, 1986), of old age (*Kinds of Love*, 1970, *As We Are Now*, 1973, *A Reckoning*, 1978), and of animals in relation to lonely and despondent people (*The Fur Person*, 1957, *The Poet and the Donkey*, 1969). Besides memoirs written 'looking back', she has pub. day-to-day journals in which everything 'comes from some painful experience which I then analyze and put into philosophical terms. It's the combination of the concrete detail and thinking about feeling that is my strength', as in *Plant Dreaming Deep*, 1968, *Journal of a Solitude*, 1973, *Recovering*, 1980, and *At Seventy*, 1984. Her poems were collected in 1974, selected in 1978, continued in *Halfway to Silence*, 1980, and in *The Silence Now: New and Uncollected Earlier Poems*, 1989. Many letters at Amherst College, papers at NYPL and Harvard. See bibliog. by Lenora Blouin, 1978, interview in Janet Todd, 1983, *Self-Portrait*, ed. Marita Simpson and Martha Wheelock, 1986; also study by Agnes Sibley, 1972; Jane S. Bakerman in *Critique*, 20, 1978; Marlene Springer in *Frontiers*, 5, 1980.

Saunders, Margaret Marshall, 1861–1947, children's writer, novelist, b. in Milton, Nova Scotia, second of six children of Maria (Freeman) and Edward M. S., a Baptist clergyman, who took her to Halifax in 1867. She spent a year at boarding school in Edinburgh and one studying languages in France, later attended classes at Dalhousie and Boston univs. She taught for several years before publishing short stories. A feminist, she spoke widely and joined various groups concerned with social justice, such as the national Child Labour Committee. Her first novel, *My Spanish Sailor*, 1889, was a sentimental romance, but *Beautiful Joe*, 1893, the story of a maltreated dog, won both first prize in a contest designed to find a sequel to Anna SEWELL's *Black Beauty*, and an American Humane Society Award. Translated into 17 languages, it became an international best seller and launched her on further animal stories, many for children, of which the Beautiful Joe sequel, *Beautiful Joe's Paradise*, 1902, is probably most lively and inventive. Among MMS's adult books, *Rose à Charlitte: an Acadian Romance*, 1898, and *The Girl from Vermont*, 1910, are of most interest to modern readers. The teacher protagonist of the latter fights child abuse and the economic exploitation of children. MMS travelled widely, making lengthy stays in New England and California, and frequently to Britain. After her mother's death, 1913, she moved to Toronto and became increasingly absorbed with animals and birds (see *My Pets*, 1908); in 1916, she built an aviary at her house. Some of her novels show humans from the perspective of their pets. Her last, her own favourite, *Esther de Warren: the Story of a Mid-Victorian Maiden*, 1927, makes a Cinderella fiction out of her own boarding-school diary. After ceasing to write, she continued lecturing for some years. See Karen Saunders' unpublished MA thesis in History, Dalhousie Univ.

Savage, M., author of *Poems on Various Subjects and Occasions*, 2 small vols., London, 1777. She was 'unblest with a learned Education', had 'the care of a large Family... and without being in Trade may properly be called a Woman of Business'. John Hawkesworth pub. 'OEconomy' (one of her humorously moral tales in octosyllabic couplets) in the *GM*, 1763. She also writes stanzas and blank verse, imitates Pope and especially Prior, compliments Anne MILLER, quotes Anne IRWIN, and discusses marriage (acute on ADVICE to women), female friendship, and the sentiment-indifference debate. Often satirical (of a London merchant: 'Success had attended his actions thro' life, / He had married his daughters, and buried his wife'), she mentions her 'old-fashion'd' love-poems to her husband (which do not appear) and has her Muse advise, 'Either follow your genius or let me alone.' Of several delightful verse epistles, one tells how the cat got one of her pet sparrows just as she was planning to use them, like Venus, for an air-borne carriage.

Savage, Sarah (Henry), 1664–1752, religious diarist, eldest da. of Welsh parents: Katherine (Matthews) and the Rev. Philip H., also a diarist, of Broad Oak, Flintshire, who taught her Hebrew at six or seven. In 1686 she began the attempt to record 'the true workings of my heart'. Happy at home (not quite 'swalowed', she later said, by youthful follies), she was 'much perplexed' at the idea of marriage and to her mother 'urged my unfitness'. In 1686 she m. widower John S., who farmed near Nantwich, Cheshire; she later feared God might find their love excessive. After longing for a child (see Patricia Crawford in *Local Population Studies*, 21, 1978) she had nine (with five daughters she hoped she did not 'inordinately' desire a son). Four survived her, the losses becoming progressively harder to submit to; yet 'I think I may say I had my roots watered with wine.' Busy with 'the kitchen and the dairy, the market and the fair', visiting relations and the sick, she also read lives like those of Elizabeth BURY, Elizabeth ROWE and Elizabeth WALKER. Though a Dissenter, she attended her local church, delivered measured rebuke to its parson in 1717, and refused to pressure a daughter's own choice of church. Seeking to be 'spiritually minded', she counted it 'the art of arts' to 'make a ladder out of earthly matters, for the raising of our selves in spirit to heaven'. She moved to West Bromwich in 1736. DIARY at Chester Record Office and Bodleian; excerpts ed. J. B. Williams, 1818, often reprinted. Sarah Savage of the USA, 1785–1837, pub. little moral tales (like Mary LEADBEATER's) for the young and poor (beginning with *The Factory Girl*, Boston 1814, notable for its urban US setting) and advice to servant girls, NY, 1823.

Savi, Ethel Winifred (Bryning), 1865–1954, novelist and autobiographer. B. in Calcutta, da. of Eliza Mary (Tilden) and ship's officer John Goode B., she was privately educ. In 1884 she m. John Angelo S., a planter and later colliery manager, and lived in rural Bengal. She had four children, and wrote short stories for Indian and English journals. In 1909 her husband died *en route* for England, where she settled, with one trip to India, 1928. Her many novels, chiefly set in Bengal, handle in romantic, popular style the interaction of Eastern and Western ways of life, and the efforts of young women in adverse circumstances to achieve financial independence from fathers and husbands and to cope with the duty of supporting others. In *Baba and the Black Sheep*, 1914, the heroine's father's death leaves her to run the plantation and establish protective authority over the admiring locals. The 'advanced' and progressive heroine of *Mistress of Herself*, 1918 (contrasted with a conventional, fashionable sister), was found 'too aggressive' by a reviewer. *A Flat in Town*, 1934, presents two girls trying to earn a living independent of their parents. *The Riddle of the Hill*, 1936, and *The Way Thereof*, 1939, deal with modern India and the rapid change in traditional values and habits. *The House Party*, 1952, is one of several works which contrast India during and after the Raj. *My Own Story*, 1947, is a chatty, detailed autobiography.

Saxton, Josephine (Howard), science-fiction/fantasy writer of novels and short stories. B. 1935 in Halifax, Yorks., to Clarice Lavinia (Crowther) and Ernest H., she attended Clare Hall County Secondary School there. She married artist Geoffrey Banks, 1958, and had one son, then married artist Colin S., 1962, had three children, and divorced, 1983. *The Hieros Gamos of Sam and An Smith*, 1969, is the first of five novels; she has also written short stories since the late 1960s. She uses elements of SCIENCE FICTION and fantasy – often to humorous and satirical effect – to explore feminist and social issues. Jane of *The Travails of Jane Saint*, 1980 (repr. with other stories, 1986), tranquillized in preparation for 'total reprogramming, for the crime of being a revolutionary leader', enters a surreal landscape where she quests 'to change human consciousness so that womankind may be as free as man', and meets comically grotesque barriers to her goal, including the Hierophant whose phallic hat begins to wilt when Jane rejects his status as Wise Old Man. Magdalen of *Queen of the States*, 1986, committed to a mental institution by her husband because she does not 'conform to his idea of what I should be', is taken up for observation in a flying saucer. Whether real or imaginary, this experience helps her to decide to pursue her own life: 'I'm on my own planet, out to lunch, and I like it by myself.' See Sarah Lefanu, *In the Chinks of the World Machine*, 1988.

Sayers, Dorothy Leigh, 1893–1957, poet, novelist, playwright, essayist and translator. B. in Oxford, only child of Helen Mary (Leigh) and the Rev. Henry S., she soon moved with her family to a lonely rectory in Hunts. Educ. at home and briefly at Godolphin School, Salisbury, she won a scholarship to Somerville College, Oxford, 1912, to read medieval French. She waited for her first-class degree until 1920, when women were at last admitted to degrees. She published her poems, *Opus I*, 1916, and edited *Oxford Poetry*, 1917–19. After several jobs she became an advertising copywriter, 1922. She had a son, secretly, 1924, and in 1926 married journalist and crime reporter Capt. Oswold Atherton Fleming, a war veteran with deteriorating health. Her first novel, *Whose Body?*, 1923, was innovatively light-hearted in its treatment of murder and detection. Its suave Lord Peter Wimsey went on, with his manservant Bunter, to investigate murder in a gentlemen's club on Armistice Day (*The Unpleasantness at the Bellona Club*, 1928), a Scottish painters' community (*Five Red Herrings*, 1931), and an advertising agency (*Murder Must Advertise*, 1933). DS tired of Wimsey, and shifted interest towards Harriet Vane, crime writer and 'fallen woman' accused of murder (*Strong Poison*, 1930), but then reshaped Wimsey as more psychologically complex. In *The Nine Tailors*, 1934, he unravels riddles of absurdity and campanology. In the feminist *Gaudy Night*, 1935, he identifies the perpetrator of crazed attacks on women academics, and overcomes Harriet's political objections to marriage. Its sequel, *Busman's Honeymoon*, 1937, with authorial debate on sexuality, began as a play written with Muriel St Clare Byrne, and led DS into theatre and radio writing. She published three volumes of short stories, some about Montague Egg, a wine salesman. DS was a pioneer writer *about* DETECTIVE FICTION (see her anthologies, 1928, 1931, 1934, 1936) and co-founder, then president, of the Detection Club, 1949–57. She chaired St Anne's House, a theological society, and wrote articles and pamphlets (like *Creed or Chaos*, 1947) defending intellectual, broadminded Anglicanism. She also wrote religious drama: *The Zeal of Thy House*, 1937, and *The Devil to Pay*, 1939, were Canterbury Festival plays. Her radio plays about Christ, *The Man Born to Be King*, broadcast 1941–2, published 1943, made great impact. Her translation of Dante, 1949, combined her interests as a popularizer, scholar, and poet. She called him a 'miraculous storyteller'. Lives by Janet Hitchman, 1975, Nancy Tischler, 1980, and James Brabazon, 1981; essay collection by Margaret P. Hannay, 1979; study of her Dante translations by Barbara Reynolds, 1989. See also Patricia Craig and Mary Cadogan, 1981. Extensive collection of papers at Wheaton College, Illinois, and Univ. of Texas.

Sayers, Peig, 1873–1958, storyteller in Irish, b. in Dunquin, Kerry, one of 13 surviving children of Peig (Brosnan) and Tomas S. She went into service at 14. Her marriage to Padraig O Guithin of the Great Blasket Island was arranged; by island custom, she kept her birth name. She bore ten children on the Great Blasket (six survived childhood) and became known as Queen of the Storytellers in that 'crowded nest of Gaelic life and story-telling'. (Its other two great names are men, as storytellers were by tradition: PS had her stories from her father.) Her life story and folktales have become Irish classics: published as *Peig*, 1935 (English transl. 1973), transcribed at a woman friend's persuasion by PS's poet-son Micheal O Guithin (who pub. a sequel, 1969, and memoirs transl. 1982); and tales, 1939 (transl. as *An Old Woman's Reflections*, 1962). Her stories are full of her strong voice, strong faith, and the fairies. *Peig* tells in detail of her childhood and adolescence (less of herself after marriage, very little of her husband), and Island life and her own activities: talking to scholars (who wrote down 375 folktales and 40 songs), for love of the Irish language, the Island, and Ireland. The end of *Peig* mourns the closing of an era as well as of her own life. Her husband dead and children emigrated, she was resettled on the mainland, with other islanders, by the government in 1953, and died at Dingle after some years in hospital.

Schaeffer, Susan (Fromberg), poet, novelist, short-story writer, b. 1941 in Brooklyn, NY, eldest child of Edith (Levine), a teacher, and Irving F., who worked in wholesale clothing. She wrote throughout childhood, attended public schools in NYC, and transferred from Simmons College to the Univ. of Chicago (BA 1961, MA 1963, PhD 1966, with the first-ever thesis on Vladimir Nabokov). She taught English at Wright Junior College, Chicago, from 1963, then from 1967 at Brooklyn College, CUNY, and has published on Charlotte BRONTË, Margaret ATWOOD, and Joyce Carol OATES. In 1970 she married Neil Jerome S., a fellow-professor; they have two children. In 1972 came SFS's first published story and *The Witch and the Weather Report*, first of five volumes of soft-voiced but emotionally forceful poems. *Falling*, 1973, a novel, introduces favourite themes and methods (family fixations and hatreds, wry humour, narrative experiment): a Jewish, female graduate student moves from suicidal depression to marriage and a sense of self-worth. *Anya*, 1974, is a pell-mell yet staccato blockbuster about a Polish holocaust survivor looking back from the USA. She wonders if the dead hate the living, and fears for her grandchildren. 'So many nice people killed, no trace. No trace at all.' *Time in Its Flight*, 1978, is set in nineteenth-century New England, *The Madness of a Seduced Woman*, 1983, a little later. Sparked 20 years before by newspaper reports, it depicts a restless, sensitive, tormented woman who commits murder from jealousy, fails at suicide, and voluntarily returns to spend her last years in a mental asylum. Of SFS's later novels, *Mainland*, 1985, and *The Injured Party*, 1986, treat parallel stories in darker and lighter modes. In each a woman intellectual drops out for a while from career success, marriage and children, to physical and mental collapse and an oddly-chosen lover: one talks constantly to her dead mother and grandmother (who treat her as a child); the other lies catatonic in bed for weeks; both end with hope. See Harold U. Ribelow, ed., *The Tie That Binds: Conversations with Jewish Writers*, 1980 (a label SFS dislikes); bibliog. in Mickey Pearlman, ed., *American Women Writing Fiction*, 1989.

Schaw, Janet, b. *c.* 1737, Edinburgh travel-writer, da. of Anne (Rutherfurd) and Gideon S. (d. 1772). In 1774 she sailed with a family party for St Kitts and N. Carolina (she had relations settled in both). Her journal-letters to an unnamed woman friend set out with a Popeian resolve 'to keep good humour, whatever I lose' and to write according to 'my own immediate feelings'. In vivid detail she relates the hardships of shipboard, her initial revulsion and later sympathy for the exploited poor emigrants; West Indian ease and luxury; inefficient American agriculture and political unrest. A natural Tory, she notes her ominous first use of the word 'Rebels', and on leaving apostrophizes the 'unhappy land, for which my heart bleeds in pity . . . you are devoted to ruin, whoever succeeds.' After stopping in Portugal (noting Catholic abuses and, again, hospitable Scots) she reached home in 1776. She made several copies of her journal, heading one 'Travels in the West Indies and South [sic] Carolina' (BL, now lost): ed. E. W. and C. M. Andrews as *Journal of a Lady of Quality*, 1921, rev. 1939.

Schimmelpenninck, Mary Anne (Galton), 1778–1856, essayist and autobiographer, b. at Birmingham, eldest da. of Lucy (Barclay) and Samuel G., of leading Quaker families. A timid, imaginative child intimidated by her parents, she received intensive modern education (A.L. BARBAULD and Mme de GENLIS; Stoic endurance of a back-brace and other pain; science, Latin, maths). Before her teens she wrote fake Elizabethan MS lives connected with Mary Queen of Scots, buried them with two skulls, and planted oak-trees above to delay discovery for 300 years. In 1791 her mother gave her a writing-case that locked; she spent hours writing, both bitter introspection and discoveries from books. She got to know Barbauld, Elizabeth HAMILTON, Hannah MORE and others, and found religious faith through the Moravians, whom she joined in 1818 after a Methodist period. In 1805 she was writing, against her mother's advice, a pamphlet on the education of the poor. Next year she married Dutch-descended Lambert S., and settled at Bristol. Seeing authorship as a trust from God, she pub. works on ABOLITION, the Port-Royal Jansenists (1813 and 1816, combined in 1829), the Moravians (a philosophical-historical poem, *Asaph*, 1822), and the Bible, 1821–2, 1825. In 1854–6 her niece Christiana C. Hankin took down from dictation her AUTOBIOGRAPHY (to 1793: luminous depiction of self and others); she published it with sequel, 1858; also MAS essay volumes, 1859 (reworking of study on aesthetics, begun *c.* 1798, pub. 1815), and 1860 (including scripturally-based 'On the Destiny of Woman').

Schreiner, Olive Emily Albertina, 1855–1920, novelist, polemicist, feminist and pacifist. She was b. in South Africa, on the border of Basutoland, ninth child of Rebecca (Lyndall), a brilliant, exacting Englishwoman, and Gottlob S., a pious, dreamy, ineffectual German missionary. They lived on an isolated farm. Chronically ill with asthma, OS studied mainly at home, reading extensively. Her mother, a minister's daughter, brought her up in strict biblical tradition, and once beat her for using an Afrikaans word. At 11, she went to live with her headmaster brother and her sister. She worked as governess, 1870–81, completing in her spare time the novels *Undine* (pub. 1928) and *The Story of an African Farm* (pub. 1883) and beginning *From Man to Man or Perhaps Only*, which she worked on for most of her life but never finished (pub. 1926, repr. 1982). In 1881 her siblings helped finance her medical studies in Edinburgh (abandoned because of ill health). Publication in England of her partly autobiographical novel, *The Story of an African Farm*, 'authored' by 'Ralph Iron', prompted her friendship with Havelock Ellis, launched her in the avant-garde, and won her an admiring public throughout the Commonwealth. Its intelligent, sensitive protagonist, Lyndall, grows up on a farm in South Africa, chooses to have a child on her own, rejects marriage, and dies giving birth, expressing eloquently her need for freedom and self-fulfilment. *Dreams*, 1891, a collection of fanciful narratives, maxims, and allegories, affirms a future where women and men will be equal in work, love and freedom. In England OS was a close friend of Karl Pearson, Edward Carpenter, and Havelock Ellis, with whom she discussed, in person and in a vast correspondence, ideas on women's sexual and spiritual needs and their position in a socialist state. She returned to South Africa in 1894, the year she married Samuel Cronwright (who changed his name to Cronwright-Schreiner). Their only daughter died within 24 hours of birth, 1895. They became politically involved in the South African war, working against the racist, imperialist and capitalist policies of the South African leaders. OS also worked with suffrage organizations and women's trade unions, but, as a pacifist, disapproved of Emmeline PANKHURST's militant feminism. Her novel *Trooper Peter Hallet of Mashonaland*, 1897, and her collected essays, including *Women and Labour*, 1911, and *Thoughts on South Africa*, 1923, reflect her concerns with the issues of rental restrictions against families with children, degradation of prostitutes, women in war efforts, equal pay for women, women's sexuality. Often ill, in England 1913–20, she decided to return to South Africa, leaving her husband behind, and died in Winberg. Her husband published a selection of her letters and a biography, both 1924. Cherry Clayton, 1983, prints excerpts from her letters and journals. Life by Ruth FIRST and Ann Scott, 1980; letters, vol. i, 1871–99, ed. Richard Rive, 1988; Joyce Avrech Berkman, *Feminism on the Frontier*, 1979, and *The Healing Imagination of OS*, 1989.

Schurman, Anna Maria van, 1607–78, Dutch polymath, feminist, artist and correspondent of Bathsua MAKIN. Her father educ. her in the reformed religion and warned her on his deathbed against marriage. She became joint leader, with Jean de Labadie, of a religious community which, like the Quakers, rejected all set forms. She declined the dedication of Johannes Beverovicius' *Excellency of the Female Sex*, 1639, saying it would bring her ill-will. She admired ELIZABETH I and Lady Jane GREY; her *De Ingenii muliebris* . . . , 1641, englished by Clement Barksdale as *The Learned Maid, or Whether a Maid may be a Scholar*? (1659, with some letters) was influential. Writing only of Christian women without pressng family commitments, using the dryness that befits a 'Logick Exercise', she depicts a quiet, free life of self-improvement (not public or professional work), and briskly refutes the arguments of 'Adversaries'. At 70 she wrote a fine autobiography. See life by Una Birch (later Pope-Hennessey), 1909; J. Irwin in *Female Scholars*, ed. J. Brink, 1980.

Schütze, Gladys Henrietta (Raphael), 'Henrietta Leslie', 'Gladys Mendl', 1884–1946, novelist, journalist and playwright, b. and resident in London, da. of Marianna Florette (Moses), painter, and Arthur Lewis R., who d. when she was very young. Educ. at home by governesses and masters, she m. Louis Mendl, corn merchant, in 1902, but left him about 1910 (rejecting, she said, the idea that woman's place is in the home). She campaigned for the Liberals in 1906, left them for the Women's Social and Political Union, and worked with the PANKHURSTs and militant suffragettes. She published some 30 novels, 1911–46 (three before her second marriage and change of pen-name). Her friends Olive SCHREINER and Vernon LEE influenced her. In *The Roundabout*, 1911, the unhappily married heroine learns the power of female friendship and the value of a single life: 'I want to grow. I must find freedom again.' In 1913 GHS m. bacteriologist Dr Harry Leslie S. A pacifist in WWI, she was ejected from the Society of Women Journalists and the Literary Club because of his German blood. Plays written during WWI, jointly with John Dymock and Laurie Lister, are unpub.; her novel about being shunned as an alien, *Mrs Fischer's War*, 1930, is her best-known work (dramatized jointly with Joan TEMPLE, 1931). She was a reporter on the socialist *Daily Herald*, 1919–23, and worked and travelled abroad for the Save the Children Fund, 1924–33. *A Mouse with Wings*, 1920, tells of a militant suffragette and a domineering mother united by pacifism but unable to save the foolhardy hero from dying in the war. In *The Road to Damascus*, 1929, a strong-minded woman risks her livelihood to challenge new industrial techniques which destroy the workers' imagination. *After Eight O'Clock*, 1930, and *And Both He Loved*, 1937, detail the conflicting demands of wifehood and career. GHS also pub. three travel books and an autobiography, *More Ha'Pence Than Kicks*, 1943.

Science Fiction as a modern form was invented by Mary SHELLEY in *Frankenstein*, 1818, which she began writing as a ghost story. (Ancient satire had sometimes employed fantasy like voyages to the moon.) Judith MERRIL has enlisted some unexpected women as early examples of the genre. Feminist science fiction, 'a movement that is still going on', covers a tremendous range and quantity of material: associated fields of fantasy, speculative, UTOPIAN and dystopian, even vampire fiction (the last written by e.g. Suzy McKee CHARNAS, Anne RICE and Jody Scott). This family of genres is made more complex and sophisticated by the fact that many of its practitioners, like Joanna RUSS (in e.g. 'The Image of Women in Science Fiction' and *'Amor Vincit Foeminam*: The Battle of the Sexes in Science Fiction') and Ursula LE GUIN (in e.g. 'American Science Fiction and the Other' and 'Is Gender Necessary?') are also critics and theorists of it. Like the feminist DETECTIVE story, it defines itself against the expectations of a form once regarded as masculine, macho, even misogynist, dealing in personal heroic dominance and in technological conquest of a nature perceived as feminine. Remaking these expectations has been claimed as a source of female science fiction's rapidly accelerating vigour and freedom of action. Merril's earlier anthologies are predominantly male. Betty Rosenberg included hardly any women science fictionists in *Genreflecting*, 1982. The only two of her thematic sf categories to include more than one woman were, in confirmation of traditional gender demarcations, 'Extrasensory Perception' and 'Women, Love, Sex'; she omitted popular female themes like utopias, medicine and alternative languages. Yet a symposium by mail on women in science fiction, run by *Khatru* magazine in 1974–5 and ed. Jeffrey D. Smith, had started from the assumption that 'many of the best sf writers are the women on this panel.' Women since Charlotte Perkins GILMAN (in *Herland*) have been quick to exploit the opportunites of fictions which posit an alternative reality. Heroic models have been both mocked and appropriated. Alice SHELDON posed as a male writer before blowing her own disguise. Female space travellers have proliferated since Naomi MITCHISON; so have male space travellers, like Esmé Dodderidge's *The New Gulliver*, 1980, who are aghast to find women in control of territories they 'discover'. Many writers, like Zoe FAIRBAIRNS in *Benefits*, develop a future as criticism of the present. Alternatively, women's HISTORY is explored, sometimes through reincarnation or transmogrification of famous names: Josephine SAXTON's *Jane Saint* and Lorna Mitchell's *The Revolution of Saint Jone*, 1988, both allude to Joan of Arc; Jody Scott's alien protagonist in *Passing for Human*, 1977, assumes the guise of Virginia WOOLF among others for her fruitfully disruptive appearances on earth. Saxton uses humour to combine glorification with mockery; humour is equally important in Scott, in Jane Palmer's *The Planet Dweller*, 1985, and *The Watcher*, 1986, and in Rosaleen Love's *The Total Devotion Machine and Other Stories*, 1989. Women engage in every kind of revolt and transgression in science fiction, notably in the work of Russ (who also, in *We Who Are About To . . .*, questions whether life may be in some circumstances not worth living). The most explosive themes tend to be those which challenge or reverse the ideal of man-dominated nature; they are closely interwoven, so that most books combine more than one, but some strands can be identified. Mary Shelley, confronting human cosmic dominance with a 'betrayed and vengeful Nature', opened a vein which becomes more pressing and relevant as practical fears of the effects of such dominance increase. In the work of Charnas and Sally GEARHART, specifically male aggression, exploitation and pollution threaten a Gaia or a cosmos defended by women. Shelley's work also broached (like that of C. L. Moore: see Susan Gubar in *Science-Fiction Studies*, 7, 1980) the themes of 'the coercive effects of technology on the lives/bodies of women' and of self-identification with 'the monstrous alien'. Of these the first has been taken up in the association of advancing medical technology with escalating mass ill-health (Chelsea Quinn Yarbro in *Time of The Fourth Horseman*, 1976, and Kate WILHELM in several works) or of genetic engineering with questions as to what makes a parent or a human being (Maureen DUFFY in *Gor Saga*). The second leads into studies both of ambiguous sanity or madness (like Saxton's *Queen of the States*) and of conflict or harmony achieved between different races or species (the work of Le Guin and of Octavia E. BUTLER). Women embrace and develop their difference from men through creating language (in Suzette ELGIN's *Native Tongue* and *The Judas Rose*, Marge PIERCY's *Woman on the Edge of Time*) or theology (in Mitchell's Saint Jone). The Women's Press (London) prints or reprints many of these, New Zealander Sandi Hall (*The Godmothers*, 1982), and Jen Green and Sarah Lefanu, eds., *Despatches from the Frontiers of the Female Mind, An Anthology of Original Stories*, 1985. Interesting new work by e.g. Nancy Kress, Sheri Tepper (*The Gate to Women's Country*, 1988). See also *SFS* issue on 'Science Fiction on Women – Science Fiction by Women', 7, 1980; Natalie M. Rosinsky, *Feminist Futures: Contemporary Women's Speculative Fiction*, 1987; Lefanu, 1988.

Scot or Scott, **Elizabeth** (Rutherford), 1729–89, poet, b. in Edinburgh, da. of Alice (Watson) and David R., educ. in Latin and French, a verse-writer at ten. Her Irish fiancé was drowned; years later she m. Walter S. of Wauchope near Jedburgh. She thought Scots poetry should throw off its 'antique garb', and that writing Scotswomen should aim to join Englishwomen in the temple of fame. Her surviving poems are all in standard English except a Scots verse epistle she sent to Burns in Feb. 1787 (having borrowed his MS poems from her aunt Alison COCKBURN, his recent acquaintance), concluding 'proud I am to ca' ye brither.' (He answered warmly but later disliked her 'intrepidity of face and bold critical decision'). Her forte is pathos, both self-expressive and dramatized: she used shipwreck imagery of her lover before his death. She had planned to print her poems; a volume by subscription appeared at London, 1801, titled *Alonzo and Cora* after a tale of doomed interracial love from Marmontel's book on the Incas.

Scott, Alicia Anne (Spottiswood), Lady John Scott, 1810–1900, poet, da. of Helen (Wauchope) and John Spottiswoode of Spottiswoode, Co. Berwick. Carefully educ.

in languages, drawing and music, she also took from her father an interest in botany, geology and archaeology. In 1836 she m. Lord John Douglas Montagu Scott (d. 1860), brother of the Duke of Buccleuch and Queensberry, and nephew of Lady Caroline SCOTT. AS's close-knit family was always more important to her than friends: her sister's death in 1839 remained a permanent grief (she wrote a poem on it). She loved the Scottish countryside, was devoted to the Stuart cause, and studied Scottish songs and legends. Her best-known poem, 'Annie Laurie', for which she wrote the music, was pub. in 1838 without her knowledge, after being copied when she sent her music book for rebinding. The authorship was claimed by others, but proved to be hers when the MS was pub. after Crimea, for soldiers' benefit. Her *Songs and Verses*, with a preface by her grand-niece Margaret Warrender, was pub. in 1904; second ed., enlarged, 1911.

Scott, C. A., Catharine Amy, (**Dawson**), 1865–1934, poet and novelist, founder of PEN, eldest child of Catharine (Armstrong) and Ebenezer D. Educ. at boarding-school, then at Anglo-German day-school, Camberwell, London, from 18 she was private sec. for four years to a scholar who taught her Greek and Logic (her only real education, she said). Afterwards she lived a Bohemian existence as an ardent atheist and feminist in London with her sister Nellie. Violet HUNT was one of her closest friends. She pub. at her own expense her epic poem *Sappho*, 1889; it calls upon women to claim their freedom. *The Idylls of Womanhood* followed three years later. At 30, she m. Horatio S., GP, and moved to the Isle of Wight (which she hated). They later separated. She produced seven novels, beginning with *The Story of Anna Beames*, 1906. During WWI she organized women workers, but became disillusioned with patriotism. She loved the wild parts of Cornwall as much as London literary society, where she flourished, organizing the 'To-Morrow Club' for young writers, then founding PEN (Poets, Playwrights, Essayists, Editors, Novelists), a writers' club inspired by a spirit of post-war internationalism. She worked indefatigably for PEN from 1921 until 1933. See the life by her daughter Marjorie Watts, 1987.

Scott, Lady **Caroline** Lucy (Stewart), 1784–1857, novelist. Eldest of five children of Frances (Scott: da. of the Earl of Dalkeith and sister of the 3rd Duke of Buccleuch) and Archibald Stewart, 1st Baron Douglas after winning the famous 'Douglas Cause'. In 1810 she m. Vice-Admiral Sir George S. Her first novel, *A Marriage in High Life*, 1828, is the supposedly true story of an unhappy union between a poor nobleman and a wealthy merchant's daughter, finally reconciled because of her 'feminine home qualities' and his religious conversion. Equally fraught with melodramatic marital misery and deathbed piety is *Trevelyan*, 1831, but its portrait of the growth towards human contact and sympathy of the hero's embittered 'old maid' sister, makes it the best of her three novels (all pub. anon.). George ELIOT used *The Old Grey Church*, 1856, as the basis of her attack on Evangelical 'white neck-cloth' fiction in 'Silly Novels by Lady Novelists'; she criticizes it for idealizing its Evangelical curate hero, and awkwardly grafting religious issues onto a conventional, sentimental love-intrigue set in the fashionable and aristocratic world. Pub. under CS's own name were *Exposition of Types and Anti-Types of the Old and New Testament*, 1856, *Incentives to Bible Study*, 1860, and *Acrostics, Historical, Geographical and Biographical*, 1863.

Scott, Elizabeth, later Williams, later Smith, 1708?–76, HYMN-writer, brought up at Norwich, England, da. of dissenting minister Thomas S. One brother caused family turmoil by adopting Arian belief; another (Thomas, 1705–75) also wrote hymns. She had written 90 by 1740, when she copied them into a volume dedicated to her father (Yale MS). He called her a 'protestant nun' devoted to good works; she confessed to Philip Doddridge in 1745 'a condemning conscience, a hard unbelieving heart, a frowning God', and in 1742 and 1746 prostrating grief at her mother's and father's deaths ('it seems to me as if I had but lived for him'). She was then teaching children. In 1751 she married Elisha Williams, ex-Rector of Yale, and migrated to Connecticut; after his death she married William Smith of NY. Her work, circulated in MS before she left England, was pub. in *The Christian's Magazine*, 1764, and in anthologies (John Ash and Caleb Evans, eds., Bristol 1769, and many more). It voices consolation, praise, and triumph as well as 'tumultuous sickening Fears'. William John Fitzpatrick pub. a book in 1856 alleging that Elizabeth (MacCulloch) Scott, 1776–1848, and her husband, Sir Walter S.'s brother, wrote most of the early Waverley novels. Yet another Elizabeth Scott (of Kendal) included poems of her own in her *Specimens of British Poetry*, Edinburgh, 1823, an anthology with strong female presence.

Scott, Evelyn, 1893–1963, poet and novelist, b. Elsie Dunn at Clarksville, Tenn., da. of Maude (Thomas), a Southerner, and Seeley D., a Yankee. Raised in small towns in Tenn., then in New Orleans, with private tutors before she attended the Sophie Newcomb School, College and School of Art, she always said she had educ. herself. At 17 she was Secretary of the Louisiana Women's Suffrage party: while most Southern women wanted the vote to bolster white supremacy, she was 'ready to champion the negro, the social outcast, and ... the instant termination of industrial slavery'. In 1913 she ran away with the married Frederick Creighton Wellman, Dean of Tropical Medicine at Tulane Univ. Changing their names to Evelyn and Cyril Kay Scott, they sailed to England, had a son, and endured five years of extreme hardship and poverty in Brazil. Soon after returning to the US, ES published *Precipitations*, 1920, a volume of Imagist poetry; she also wrote poems and criticism for the *Egoist*, the *Dial* and *Poetry*. Eager, authoritative critical recognition greeted her first novel, *The Narrow House*, 1921, which with *Narcissus*, 1922 (*Bewilderment* in the UK), and *The Golden Door*, 1925, comprise a trilogy (first two repr. 1977) most notable for its realistic studies of women ensnared in oppressive roles, absorbed by daily trivia and anxiously dependent on male approval. After *Escapade*, 1923, a book about her Brazilian exile, ES used a second trilogy, *Migrations*, 1927, *The Wave*, 1929, and *A Calendar of Sin*, 1931, to combine intimate, vivid depiction of many personal lives with a broad historical study of US development, through war and western expansion, from 1850 to 1914. She employs straightforward narrative, presentation of characters' consciousness, and the 'calendar' tabulation by date. ES's early praise for William Faulkner's *The Sound and the Fury*, 1929, and its publisher's boast that it 'should place' him 'in company with' her, were vital steps towards his success; he later called her 'pretty good ... for a woman'. A friend of Emma GOLDMAN, Kay BOYLE, Lola RIDGE, Louise BOGAN, and Jean RHYS, ES travelled during the late 1920s in Bermuda, N. Africa and Europe. Divorced in 1928, she married English writer John Metcalfe in 1930, the year she published *The Winter Alone* (poems) and a children's book as 'Ernest Souza'. Later books include *Eva Gay*, 1933, a part-autobiographical novel of a woman's divided love for two men; the controversial *Breathe Upon These Slain*, 1934, *Bread and a Sword*, 1937, and *The Shadow of the Hawk*, 1941, all about the individual's upholding of integrity against political or economic forces; and *Background in Tennessee*, 1937, repr. 1980, an account of her 'personal and cultural matrix'. In her last years she was ill and destitute. MSS of unpub. novels, plays, and poetry at the Univ. of Texas, Austin;

other papers at Smith College and the International Institute of Social History, Amsterdam. Her reputation, long eclipsed, is currently rising: life by D. A. Callard, 1985.

Scott, Gail, novelist, short-story writer, essayist, journalist, b. in Ottawa, da. of Darlene (Ingham) and Henry James S. She lived in Western Canada until she was 8, then until she was 17 near the Quebec border. She went to school in Calgary and eastern Ontario, later attended Teachers' College in Ottawa, Queen's Univ., Kingston (BA in English, 1966), and the Univ. de Grenoble, France, 1967. She worked in Montréal with the Canadian Press, travelled in North Africa, lived in Sweden for a year, had a daughter, 1971, and began writing fiction. One of the first Anglophone writers to translate Québec's national struggle, she is a founding editor of the Québec cultural review *Spirale*, and co-editor of the feminist journal *Tessera*. *Spare Parts*, 1982, surreal picaresque short stories, signals her interest in narrative innovation. *Heroine*, 1987 (trans. into French, 1988), records its narrator's fractured bisexual recollections (in her bath): she wonders how an 'English heroine (of a novel) might look against the background of contemporary Québec', from this vantage point constructing her history, rooting through Québec feminist politics and poetics, and the sexual politics of the left. 'The question is, is it possible to create Paradise in the Strangeness.' *Spaces Like Stairs*, 1989, collects her essays, some pub. first in French: 'the old forms essay novel have moved forward maybe two post-moderns one for women one for men ours circular.' See Barbara Godard in *Border/lines*, 1988.

Scott, Harriett Anne (Shanks), Lady, 1819–94, English novelist, b. Bombay, only da. of Henry Shanks. She m. Sir James Sibbald David Scott, antiquary, in 1844 and had seven children. A contributor to *Queen* and other magazines, she published eight novels, and later *Cottagers' Comforts, and other Recipes in Knitting and Crochet by Grandmother*, 1887. Her witty narrative style, with occasional asides on the weaknesses of the 'stronger sex', comments wryly on upper class life and characters, as in *Hylton House and its Inmates*, 1850 (pub. anon.) and her last novel, *Dream of a Life*, 1862, where daughters reject 'good matches' orchestrated by marriage-broking parents and guardians, and marry for love. However, the dream of married love turns to nightmare, with the heroine finally leaving her husband: 'I have my own dignity to support ... and I will assert it to the last.' Other novels include *The Henpecked Husband*, 1847 (anon.); *The Only Child*, 1852 (later in *Select Library of Fiction*, 1865); and *The Skeleton in the Cupboard*, 1860. She died in Queen's Gate, London.

Scott, Honoria, obscure novelist, probably Scottish, who may be identified with her frequent mouthpiece, a widow forced into Grub Street by poverty. In 1810 she pub. at London a pamphlet and four long novels, often complex and fragmented, with richly detailed settings, assuming the reader's knowledge *à clef*. *A Winter in Edinburgh, or The Russian Brothers* moves from Catherine the Great's court to London and Scotland. *Amatory Tales of Spain, France* ... includes a number of female characters battling spiritedly with assorted problems including the financial constraints of professional authorship. These constraints appear again in *The Castle of Strathmey, or Scenes of the North*, 1814, which satirizes characters like Mrs Twicerefined and Mrs Deputy Dumpling. 'The Authoress', a promised picaresque work on HS's own life, seems not to have appeared.

Scott, Jane M., theatrical writer, da. of John S., London dye manufacturer. For her he built the Sans Pareil theatre (later the Adelphi), where she wrote and performed. She began in 1807 with speeches, songs, etc.; the Huntington library has nine of her unpub. burlettas, 1811–18, some very slight, but all ingeniously deploying dialogue and pantomime, with settings embracing the gothic, Turkish, Irish; smugglers, lawyers and the fashionable Whip Club. The theatre sold for £25,000 in 1819.

Scott, Mary, later Taylor, 1751–93, poet, da. of a well-to-do dissenting linen manufacturer of Milborne Port, Somerset; friend of Anna SEWARD, and of Anne STEELE, to whom she dedicated her poem on women writers, *The Female Advocate* (J. Johnson, 1774; facs. 1984). She adds largely to her forerunner John DUNCOMBE's list, admires Catharine MACAULAY, and hopes that Lucy AIKIN will equal A. L. BARBAULD and that better education will allow female Shakespeares and Newtons. She became a Unitarian, like John T., who then became a Quaker, 1790: he waited a dozen years to marry her in 1788, on her mother's death. They lived at Ilminster, in Elizabeth ROWE's former house, then moved to Bristol. *A Catalogue of . . . Celebrated Authors*, 1788, sneered that the *Advocate* had had 'between two and three admirers'; but *Messiah*, pub. that year to aid the Bath Hospital (cf. H. M. BOWDLER), was found by the *Monthly Review* good though heretical. It side-steps a call by Eliza HAYLEY's husband for a national epic ('Arms, and the men for deeds of arms renown'd . . . Let others fondly sing') to celebrate the 'milder hero', Christ. Besides anthology pieces (perhaps) and a *GM* poem, 1783, MS wrote an elegy on Jonas Hanway, d. 1786, a correspondent. Her family moved to Manchester; her son, John Edward T., founded the *Guardian*; C. P. Scott was a great-nephew. She is not the Mrs Taylor of Manchester who pub. a text-book in 1791; she died at Bristol, late in her third pregnancy. See the *Christian Reformer*, 1844, which mentions her hymns.

Scott, Rose, 1847–1925, feminist and social reformer, b. Glendon, NSW, da. of Anne (Rusden) and Helenus S., pastoralist; her cousin was bibliophile David Scott Mitchell. She grew up on the family property, educ. by her mother, governesses, and her own extensive reading. She attributed her feminism in part to her indignation at *The Taming of the Shrew*, which her mother read to her when she was seven. After her father's death in 1879, she moved to Sydney with her mother. In 1891 she became secretary of the Women's Suffrage League and was active in other reforms for women and children; later she worked for the International League of Women and the Peace Society. She wrote some short stories and poems but was mainly influential as the organizer of one of Sydney's first literary and political salons, and for encouraging Australian art and literature. Her close friends included Catherine SPENCE, Mary GILMORE, and Miles FRANKLIN, who has left a good account of her in *The Peaceful Army*, 1938 (ed. Flora ELDERSHAW). A large coll. of her diaries, letters and papers is in the Mitchell Library, Sydney.

Scott, Sarah (Robinson), 1723–95, novelist and historian writing anonymously; sister and correspondent of Elizabeth MONTAGU. Her letters are often racy and comical; her fiction, from *The History of Cornelia*, 1750 (facs. 1974), is didactic with touches of humour, reasonable with touches of sentiment. She later said that those not 'hurried by necessity should write for the honour of the age', as those writing for money, like her, cannot. Having married George Lewis S. in 1752 and left him in 1753, she pooled resources with Lady Barbara Montagu (no relation to her sister) to set up at Bath Easton, 1754, a pious female community, teaching poor children and employing some disabled servants. Lady Barbara (d. 1765) corresponded with Samuel Richardson, and arranged publication of *Penitents in the Magdalen House*, probably by Sarah FIELDING. SS, hoping to earn £40 p.a. by writing, pub. two works in 1754. In *A Journey Through Every Stage of Life*, a lady tells tales to a forcibly secluded princess: Leonora, in the first and longest, demonstrates that a woman can live independent of men, then marries (to the narrator's chagrin). The heroine of *Agreeable Ugliness, or The Triumph of the Graces*, triumphs through her extreme submissiveness: from the French of Pierre Antoine La Place. The famous *Description of Millenium Hall*, 1762, repr. 1986, is less description than stories: of women who have left the bruising world for a hard-working, fulfilling UTOPIA. Their example converts the male narrator's young friend. Writing it took a month: a guinea a day, SS reckoned. *Sir George Ellison*, 1766, relates that narrator's life (in Jamaica improving the lot of slaves he acquired unwillingly; in England emulating Millenium Hall). *The Test of Filial Duty*, 1772, epistolary, attacking clandestine marriages, contrasts good and bad sisters. SS wrote two scholarly biographies, 1761 (critical preface) and 1772, and a history of the new queen's family, 1762. She settled about 1787 at Catton near Norwich; her papers were destroyed on her orders. Life by Walter Marion Crittenden, 1932.

Scovell, E.J., Edith Joy, poet, b. 1907 in Sheffield, Yorks., educ. in Westmorland (she began writing in 1920) and at Somerville College, Oxford (BA in English, 1930). In 1937 she m. ecologist Charles Elton; she later worked with him in the Caribbean and S. American rain forests. Her first book, *Shadows of Crysanthemums*, came out on wartime austerity paper in 1944. *The Midsummer Meadow*, 1946, drew the admiration of Geoffrey Grigson, who anthologized EJS in 1949. *The River Steamer*, 1956, added new to reprinted poems. That year she wrote of her work, 'I should like the surface to be entirely clear, and thc meaning entirely implicit.' Except in magazines, her next appearance was in *The Space Between*, 1982, titled from its last words: 'It is not the flowers' selves only, webbed in their sheath of green, / It is the depth they grant to sight; it is the space between.' After *Listening to Collared Doves*, 1986, *Poetry Review*, 76, called EJS 'probably the best neglected poet in the country' and urged a revival like that of Barbara PYM. Carol RUMENS discerned a modern sensibility in her 'unemphatic, undeceived and honest observation of *what is*'. EJS writes limpidly of personal relations: in 'The First Year' of mother and child (to a background of war), in 'A Girl To Her Sister': 'A girl said to her sister, late, when their friends had gone: / "I wish there were no men on earth, but we alone. // "The beauty of your body, the beauty of your face – / Which now are greedy flames, and clasp more than themselves in light, / Pierce awake the drowsing air and boast before the night – / Then should be of less account than a dark reed's grace, / All summer growing in river mists, unknown – / The beauty of your body, the beauty of my own."' Metaphysical considerations weave through EJS's observation: 'Yet what quells my mind the most / Is not the loved and known / But the unregarded un-/ Apprehended constantly flowing, // Unless there is God, to waste. ...' See *Collected Poems*, 1988.

Scudéry, Madeleine de, 1607–1701, ROMANCE-writer, b. at Le Havre, living in Paris: hugely popular in England, publishing under the name of her brother Georges, and after his death, 1667, anonymously. Her *Ibrahim, ou l'illustre bassa*, 1641, *Artamène, ou le Grand Cyrus* (with portrait of herself as 'SAPPHO', 1648–52), and *Clélie* (with a history of poetry and an influential 'map of love', 1654–60), all entered English, 1652–72, as his: the admiring Dorothy OSBORNE believed the author's sister had helped by supplying 'littlc Storys'. M de S's ample pages, where sensitive, refined heroines and heroes exchange lengthy flashback narratives among persecutions, imprisonments, disguises, and raptures, provided a rich and long-lasting quarry for English dramatists and novelists. She also wrote poetry and dialogues; *Les Femmes illustres* (englished

1681) is a collection of heroines' speeches. Elizabeth ELSTOB translated her *Essay upon Glory* (which the French Academy had crowned, 1671). Life by Dorothy McDougall, 1938, repr. 1972; study by Nicole Aronson, 1978.

Seacole, Mary Jane, 'Mrs Seacole' (Grant), 1805–81, adventurer, autobiographer and doctor, b. in Kingston, Jamaica, of a free black mother and a Scottish soldier father. In 1836 she m. Edwin Horatio S., who soon died; after her mother's death, MS took over her boarding house for army and naval personnel. Her success in doctoring cholera and yellow fever victims and her enthusiasm for the army led her to volunteer her services at Crimea. Unwanted as an official nurse, she set up at her own expense as a 'setler' (provisioner), soon making a fine name for herself as cook, hostess, expert doctor and herbal healer. Bankrupt in London after Crimea, despite widespread public gratitude and a Grand Military Festival (1857) for her benefit, she wrote her autobiography for money. Pub. as *Wonderful Adventures of Mrs Seacole in Many Lands* in 1857 (repr. 1984, ed. Z. Alexander and A. Dewjee), it is a frank, intelligent, lively account, told in wryly humorous but forthright style: 'I am not ashamed to confess – for the gratification is, after all, a selfish one – that I love to be of service to those who need a woman's help.' Enormously successful, it restored her to prosperity and made her a household name, although in later years she was monopolized by Queen VICTORIA and family (in the 1870s she was unofficial masseuse to the Princess of Wales).

Seawell, Molly Elliot, 'Foxcroft Davis', 'Vera Sapoukhyn', 1860–1916, novelist, short-story writer and columnist, b. Gloucester County, Va., da. of Frances (Jackson) and John Tyler S. Educ. at home on the Va. plantation, MS moved to Washington DC after her father's death, where her writing supported her mother and sister. Her early story, 'Maid Marian', 1891, was successfully adapted for the stage. She produced a succession of regional, historical and romantic novels, as well as boys' adventure books. Representative of MS's favourite genres are *Throckmorton*, 1890, a romance set in post-Civil War Virginia; *The History of the Lady Betty Stair*, 1897, which follows some Bourbon exiles into the Napoleonic Wars; and *The Whirl*, 1909, a novel of Washington society that endorses the sexual double standard. MS's plots favour fallen aristocrats and the dilemmas of a man or woman in love with two suitors at once. With six books to her credit and 30-odd more to come, MS pub. in *The Critic*, 1891, a controversial article 'On the Absence of the Creative Faculty in Women'. She argued against women's SUFFRAGE in *The Ladies Battle*, 1911, maintaining that women's voting would inaugurate an unlooked-for 'general revolution', while reiterating in her novels her belief that women already 'conduct the serious business of life'.

Sedgwick, Anne Douglas, 1873–1935, novelist. B. at Englewood, NJ, eldest da. of Mary (Douglas) and George Stanley S., she grew up in or near New York (until nine), then in London. After private schools, she went to Paris at 18 to study painting, and stayed five years. Her first novel, *The Dull Miss Archinard*, 1898, was one of the stories she 'had always' told her sisters, shown to a publisher by her father. An omnivorous reader of fiction, she felt the Russians (in translation) had influenced her most; critics have found her Jamesian. She aimed at 'a tenderness alternating with gay maliciousness'. She wrote seven novels, chiefly about English life, before marrying English writer Basil de Selincourt in 1908 and becoming a British subject. *Tante*, 1911, the story of pianist-villainess Mercedes Okraska (her first important success), was later a play. *The Encounter*, 1914, brings an American girl into reluctant receipt of admiration from three German philosophers, one modelled on Nietzsche. *Adrienne*

Toner, 1921, repr. 1971, has another American heroine, who wreaks havoc in the conventional British family into which she marries. ADS did hospital work in France during WWI, later Red Cross work with her husband. *The Little French Girl*, 1924 (her most popular work, especially in the US), contrasts English and French society through the heroine's experience. Many of her works, like *Dark Hester*, 1929, explore marriage between socially incompatible partners, and the way that jealous third parties exacerbate the problems. Her complex female characters struggle with modernity, men, and each other. She also pub. short stories – *The Nest*, 1912, and *Christmas Roses*, NY, 1920, facs. 1971 (London ed. as *Autumn Crocuses*) – and memoirs (not her own), 1918. Letters selected by her husband appeared as *A Portrait*, 1936.

Sedgwick, Catharine Maria, 1789–1867, novelist and short-story writer, and sister-in-law of Susan Ann S., *c.* 1798–1867, children's writer. CMS was b. in Stockbridge, Mass. Her father, Theodore S., was Speaker of the House of Representatives during Washington's administration, and her mother, Pamela (Dwight), came from a socially prominent family. She was educ. at district schools, Miss Bell's School in Albany, NY, and Miss Payne's School in Boston, but believed that her real education came from the intellectual stimulation at home. In 1822 she pub. her first book, *A New-England Tale: or, Sketches of New-England Character and Manners*, satirizing Calvinism. Her second novel, *Redwood*, 1824, pub. anon., was praised in both England and America for its local colour, and was trans. into Spanish, Italian, Swedish and French. Her first works for children were *The Travellers*, 1825, and *The Deformed Boy*, 1826. *Hope Leslie*, 1827 (repr. 1987), is considered her best novel. Based on her research into Puritan documents, it depicts a strong American woman. *Clarence*, 1830, a novel of manners, and a number of short stories were followed by *The Linwoods*, 1835, a melodramatic novel of the American Revolution. During the next 20 years, CMS taught briefly at the Lenox School, Mass., wrote popular didactic tales in support of reforms like abolition and women's education, and more children's stories. Her *Letters from Abroad to Kindred at Home*, 1841, chronicling her trip to Europe, was better received in America than Britain. Her final novel, *Married or Single?*, 1857, questions romantic assumptions about happiness. Her last work, a biography of a friend, Joseph Curtis, was pub. 1858. *Life and Letters*, ed. Dewey, 1871, contains CMS's unfinished autobiography. See also E. H. Foster's overview and bibliography, 1974. Susan Ann Sedgwick (Livingston Ridley), who m. CMS's brother Theodore in 1808, wrote eight vols. of short stories (beginning with *The Morals of Pleasure*, 1829) and historical novels for children such as *Allen Prescott: or, The Fortunes of a New England Boy*, 1834, and *The Seven Brothers of Wyoming: or, The Brigands of the Revolution*, 1850.

Seeley, Mabel (Hodenfield), thriller writer, b. in 1903 in Herman, Minn., da. of Alma (Thompson) and Jacob H. In high school at Ellsworth, Wis., she was a reporter for the local paper. On scholarship at the Univ. of Minn., she met Kenneth S., a fellow-editor on the *Minnesota Quarterly*. They married, 1926, and had one child. (In 1956 she married Henry S. Ross.) After graduation, she worked as a copy editor in Chicago. Her first novel, *The Listening House*, 1938, was welcomed by Howard Haycraft as 'revitalising' the 'Mary Roberts RINEHART school of feminine suspense writing'; later novels were less enthusiastically received. The first claims as MS's fictional territory the Minnesota of her youth and its immigrant population. It also identifies a central pattern, whose development carried her away from thrillers to 'straight' novels. Its protagonist, 'ladylike' divorcee Gwynne Dacres, moves into a boarding house run by a bizarre, malevolent landlady pivotal to the plot. This female dyad recurs in MS's fiction in more than one form. Though the books are tied up by romantic endings, their protagonists – town librarian Janet Ruell in *The Crying Sisters*, 1939, Solveig Nayers in *The Whispering Cup*, 1940, Ann Gay in *The Chuckling Fingers*, 1941 – confront female others who need to be either unmasked as evil or rescued from an unjust charge of evil. In *Eleven Came Back*, 1943, Delphine Huddleston Parent is 'as hateful a despoiler as ever came to a violent end' (*NY Times*, 28 March 1943). In *Woman of Property*, 1947, not a thriller, the development of the evil female dominates: the story of Frieda Schelmpke inverts the cultural myth of the rise to riches of the young, pretty, underprivileged girl. Frieda, hurt by underprivilege, grows monstrously hurting. *The Stranger Beside Me*, 1951, examines desire, obsession, and male-female power relations. On the first DETECTIVE novel, see Howard Haycraft, *Murder for Pleasure*, 1941.

Segun, Mabel (Imoukhuende), also Joloaso, broadcaster, journalist, writer of juvenile fiction, poet. B. 1930, in Ondo, Western State, Nigeria, MS studied at the CMS Grammar School, then at the Girls' High School, Lagos, 1942–7, and University College, Ibadan, 1949–53. As a student she edited *Hansard*, the record of the West Nigerian Parliament, and later was in charge of overseas publicity for the Information Services of Western Nigeria. She has published poems in Nigerian, Swiss, and German journals, in American anthologies, and in *Conflict and Other Poems*, 1987. They reflect the conflict she sees in the aftermath of colonialism: 'poised between two civilisations, finding the balance irksome ... I'm tired of hanging in the middle way – but where can I go?' Her own background, as daughter of a Christian father, growing up in a Nigerian parsonage with traditional Yoruba environment, sets the story she wrote for young people, *My Father's Daughter*, 1965. The father – judge, artisan, preacher – provides his daughter with a broad perspective on contemporary Nigerian life. Through the eyes of the eight-year-old girl the reader sees today's problems with traditional practices: bride-price, the felt need to bear many children, women's dependence on male protectors. A strong advocate for juvenile fiction, MS is, in the words of Femi Ojo-Ade, a 'children's literature mentor'. She co-edited *Under the Mango Tree: Songs and Poems for Primary Schools*, 1980. *Friends, Nigerians, Countrymen*, 1977, collects her radio commentaries, 1961–74, satiric descriptions of dash, polygamy, urban traffic, job-hunting, legal problems, and so forth, in a rapidly developing society. *Sorry, No Vacancy*, short stories, appeared in 1984, *Conflict* (poems) in 1987.

Selden, Catherine, probably Irish, author of seven novels, most for MINERVA. Her first three titles, 1797, included *The English Nun* (unusually sympathetic to convent life). *Serena*, 1800, defends Ireland against literary attack, and features bigamy, betrayals, women's plight in unequal arranged marriage, and a benevolent nobleman who supports liberty in America and France but opposes women's education lest it make them less 'docile and agreeable'. *German Letters*, Cork, 1804, poses as a translation of a work like *Werther*, which CS had earlier disapproved. *Villa Santelle, or The Curious Impertinent*, 1817, mingles GOTHIC with comedy: the hero has to be rescued by his lady when he falls over while hiding in a suit of armour, and feels 'veneration' for a girl seen with her illegitimate baby, the eventual result of a course of action begun by 'perpetually outraging custom and propriety by thinking for [her]self'. CS praises Mary ROBINSON and Frances SHERIDAN.

Sellon, Martha Ann, poet, one of eight children of Sarah (Littlehales) and the Rev. William S. of Clerkenwell, London. In her anonymous *The Caledonian Comet Elucidated*, 1811, she 'steps forth' an indignant 'volunteer' to oppose John Taylor the oculist's 'flimsy pamphlet' against Walter Scott: 'A spirit independent, open, free, / Is proud to advocate high minstrelsy.' She finds some humour in conflicting accounts of comets by e.g. Aristotle and Newton. *Individuality, or The Causes of Reciprocal Misapprehension*, 1814, is longer and more solemn. Setting out to account for the irreducible differences caused by both nature and nurture, she gives most space to hostile depiction of Catholic and non-Christian faiths, and to support for missionaries. Oppression of women (unwilling nuns, immolated Indian widows) moves her most. Her niece Priscilla Lydia S. founded a controversial religious sisterhood.

Senior, Olive, poet and short-story writer, b. 1943, in a poor Jamaican village. One of ten children, she was adopted at four by urban relatives and educ. in Jamaica and Canada. She has worked in journalism (editing *Jamaica Journal*, now the *Journal of Afro-Caribbean Studies*), publishing, public relations (for the Univ. of the West Indies) and freelance research; she is now a full-time writer, whose work reflects her movement from ORAL, working-class to educated, middle-class cultures. She began with plays (*Down the Road Again* won a medal at the Jamaican National Festival, 1968) and non-fiction: *The Message is Change*, 1972, on voting patterns, then an *A-Z of Jamaican Heritage*, 1983. Her poems and stories are now better known: in periodicals, in anthologies from Pamela MORDECAI and Mervyn Morris, eds., *Jamaica Woman*, 1980; (poems) in *Talking of Trees*, 1985; (stories) in *Summer Lightning*, 1986, and *The Arrival of the Snake Woman*, 1987 (Commonwealth Writers' Prize). Poems like 'Colonial Girls School' confront the quest for identity: 'Borrowed images / willed our skins pale / muffled our laughter ... One day we'll talk about / how the mirror broke / Who kissed us awake / Who let Anansi from his bag / For isn't it strange how northern eyes / in the brighter world before us now / Pale?' OS honours the past in 'To My Arawak Grandmother' and 'Searching for Grandfather', who was a sacrifice to the building of the Panama Canal. But she shuns sentimentality: 'Last year the child died / we didn't mourn long / and cedar's plentiful / but that was the one / whose navel-string we buried / beneath the tree of life / lord, old superstitions / are such lies.' OS's stories treat the same world, sad, threatening, or exuberantly funny, using the vigour of patwah more than her verse. An old woman's grandson demands her 'burial money' at gunpoint; an aunt says of one of OS's vividly rebellious little girls, 'No pickney suppose to come facety and force-ripe so.' OS is working on a novel. See Liz Gerschel in *Wasafiri*, 8, 1988.

Sergeant, Emily Frances **Adeline**, 1851–1904, poet, novelist, b. Ashbourne, Derbyshire, second da. of Jane (Hall), who as 'Adeline' wrote religious verse and stories, and Richard S., Wesleyan minister. A precocious reader and writer (*Poems*, 1866), she was educ. by her mother and at a variety of schools, including Miss Pipe's Laleham, and Queen's College, London. From a non-conformist background, she became Anglican, agnostic, and finally Roman Catholic. When her father died in 1870, followed shortly by the deaths of her mother and sister, she worked for ten years as governess for Canon Burn-Murdoch's children at Riverhead, Kent. In 1882, *Jacobi's Wife* won a £100 prize offered by the *People's Friend*, to which she contributed for over 20 years. This sensation novel features the strong wife of a man who, after a shipwreck, swims ashore alone, despite his wife's entreaties to take the baby with him: years later, she has her revenge. The strong woman/underhand man theme is repeated in other novels such as *Sir Anthony*, 1892, *The Lady Charlotte*, 1897, and *Mrs Lygon's Husband*, 1905. AS was most successful in her depiction of nonconformist provincial middle-class life, as seen in the autobiographical *Esther Denison*, 1889, while the religious *Story of a Penitent Soul*, 1892 (pub. anon.), is her best known work. Her friends included Prof. and Mrs Sheldon Amos, Jessie King, and Ellen Thorneycroft FOWLER. A contributor to *Women Novelists of Queen Victoria's Reign*, 1897, and author of over 90 novels, she felt solidarity with women of all classes and was a Fabian from 1888. She did rescue work in London and was involved in adult education. See the life by W. Stephens, 1905.

Serres, Olivia (Wilmot), 'Princess Olive', 1772–1834, miscellaneous writer and painter. Brought up as da. of Anne Maria (Barton) and Robert W., a painter (related to the Earl of Warwick), she later claimed to be da. of the Duke of Cumberland by a secret marriage to a da. of her 'uncle' the Rev. James W., her teacher in divinity, philosophy, and law. In 1791 she m. John Thomsa S. (marine painter to George III) and in 1806 became landscape painter to the Prince of Wales; Lawrence noted her 'extraordinary talents'. In 1804 she left her husband; she supported herself and nine children. Her *Flights of Fancy*, 1805 (poems with a three-act opera), includes amid conventional sensibility a poem on breast-feeding ('How joyful she unveils her charms / And gives it food within her arms') and comic attack on an unfeeling, fortune-hunting widower. *St Julian*, 1808, is a Rousseauvian sentimental novel; *Letters of Advice*, 1809, addresses a daughter; several works of 1812 attack royal mistresses, especially Mary Anne Clarke. Her *Life of... Junius*, 1813, claims he was her uncle, using MS evidence and complaining that women lack 'opportunites for research'. *Memoirs of... the Earl of Warwick*, 1822, narrates her financial support for him, 'an unusual task for a lady'. In 1822 she pub. a *Statement to the English Nation* asserting her royal birth, but appeals, claims (and court action by her daughter in 1866) failed to establish it: she was imprisoned for debt and died poor, leaving a long list of unpub. works including science and astrology. See life by Mary L. PENDERED and Justinian Mallet, 1939.

Seton, Anya, 'biographical' novelist, b. ?1904 in NYC, da. of travel writer and leading suffragist Grace (Gallatin) and naturalist and writer Ernest Thompson S. Educ. by tutors, at the Spence School, NYC, and at Oxford Univ. (no degree), she married Hamilton Chase, and had two children; having wanted to be a doctor, she began writing at home for money. She claims that her depth of research makes the label 'historical novelist' misleading. Her first book, *My Theodosia*, 1941, is about Aaron Burr's daughter (see under Esther BURR). *Katherine*, 1954, deals with John of Gaunt's wife, who was, AS notes, very important to English history, though in 'the great historians [she] apparently excited scant interest, perhaps because they gave little space to the women of the period anyway'. Women's historical role is again restored in *The Winthrop Woman*, 1958, an accurate account of unrelenting Puritan repression, of Elizabeth Fones Winthrop (whom her uncle and father-in-law, the famous governor of Massachusetts Bay Colony, tried to reduce to properly negligible housewife status) and of Anne Hutchinson (see PREACHING), who challenged his hegemony. Most of AS's 13 works present historical periods through the eyes of women with little power: Roman Britain in *The Mistletoe and Sword*, 1955, tenth-century Britain in *Avalon*, 1965, in both of which women who love their enemies must try to reconcile their love with politics.

Seton, Elizabeth Ann (Bayley), 1774–1821, nun, saint and memoirist, b. in New York, da. of Catherine (Charlton) and Dr Richard B., eminent surgeon. She was religious as a child (happy despite her mother's early death); miserable later at strife between her adored father and stepmother; tempted to suicide in 1792, though her letters sound sociable and fun-loving. She married merchant William Magee S. in 1794 and had five children. In 1797 she helped Isabella GRAHAM found a charity for widowed mothers. By 1800 she was leaning towards Catholicism, drawn by its symbols, sacraments and emotion. Her husband went bankrupt that year; then her father died, and in 1803 William S. died in Italy (this 'strange but beautiful land') after a harrowing, fruitless journey. After two years of painful suspense and pressure she entered the Catholic church; after four more of struggle to support her family by running schools in NYC and Baltimore, she founded, in 1809, with two sisters-in-law, the teaching and nursing order of Sisters of Charity of St Joseph at Emmitsburg, Md. Her irregularly kept journal (prayers, observations, meditations) has some of the lively warmth of her LETTERS. Selecs. pub. 1817 caused her distress. Later eds. (1869, 1935, etc.); the Sisters have MSS including 'Dear Remembrances' of childhood written *c.* 1820. Life by Joseph I. Dirvin, 1962, repr. 1975, the year of her canonization.

Settle, Mary Lee, novelist and autobiographer, b. 1918 at Charleston, W. Va, da. of Rachel (Tompkins) and Joseph Edward S., coal-mine owner and civil engineer. She had two years at Sweet Briar College (in *The Clam Shell*, 1971, the homesick heroine's mother calls her similar college a 'golden opportunity'). MLS left in 1938, for acting and modelling; in 1939 she married an Englishman, Rodney Weathersbee, and moved to Canada, where she bore a son. Back in the USA in 1941, she read Jan STRUTHER's *Mrs Miniver* and sailed for England in 1942 to join the Women's Auxiliary Air Force. She describes this time in *All the Brave Promises, Memories of Aircraft Woman Second Class 2146391*, 1966, dedicated to all wartime WAAFs 'below the rank of sergeant'. Far removed from the 'officers' war', she lived with cold, dirt and oppression, lost 28 lb, and succumbed to 'signals shock': haunted, even off-duty, by phantom SOS messages. (She remains glad to have 'met the common negative experience of nine-tenths of the world'.) She worked for the Office of War Information from 1943, and for *Harper's Bazaar* in the USA, 1945, and returned to England to write: poetry which she dismisses, journalism for *Woman's Day* and briefly for *Flair*, and six plays (the last became a novel). She found her voice with two novels, 1954 and 1955, about her imagined town of Canona. *The Love Eaters*, 1954, highly praised by Rosamond LEHMANN and others, sets the Phaedra story among modern amateur actors, its Hippolytus 'a little old dream-boy', 'used to being suffered over'. MLS's work includes *Juana la Loca*, a play staged in NYC in 1965, books on flying, 1967, and on the Scopes trial, 1972, and nine more novels. She is best known (but not well enough) for her Beulah series. First to appear, *O Beulah Land*, 1956, researched partly in CAPTIVITY NARRATIVES, depicts West Virginia settlers: hopes, hates, prejudices, the vital discovery of coal. Sequels of 1960 and 1980 focus on calms before storms: the Civil War and a 1912 strike. *Prisons*, 1973 (*The Long Road to Paradise* in the UK), moves back to a 20-year-old ancestor executed by Oliver Cromwell's firing squad in 1649 – MLS's first work, she says, with 'clarity of spirit'. *Fight Night on a Sweet Saturday*, 1964, introduces a woman returning to Canona to seek the buried causes of her brother's violent death, causes locked in the relationships which the whole sequence unfolds. *The Killing Grounds*, 1982, returns, finally, to this woman's probing of the past. It moves from speculation about the non-white founders of Canona 3000 years ago to a dream of the packaging of commodified history, the reverse of MLS's unsparing, compassionate vision. Returning to the USA at her second divorce, 1956, MLS left again for five years when Nixon became President. Experience of Turkey and of US expatriates there went into *Blood Tie*, pub. 1978, the year she married historian William Tazewell. See her 'Recapturing the Past in Fiction' in *NY Times Book Review*, 12 Feb. 1984. Bibliog. in Mickey Pearlman, ed., *American Women Writing Fiction*, 1989.

Sévigné, Marie (de Rabutin-Chantal), marquise de, 1626–96, French letter writer, exceptionally well educ., friend of Marie de LA FAYETTE, Madeleine de SCUDÉRY, and Mme de Maintenon. Her father was killed in battle when she was a baby, her spendthrift, rakish husband in a duel in 1651, leaving her with a daughter and son. From her beloved Brittany estate she took part by letter in the intellectual debates of her age; but her loving, intimate, possessive, introspective LETTERS to her daughter have been most admired: by nearly everyone except Lady Mary Wortley MONTAGU. A few letters having been first pub. in 1696, they were first translated into English in 1727. They were discussed by WOOLF, 1942; definitive ed. by Roger Duchesne, 1972–8, selec. and transl. by Leonard Tancock, 1982.

Seward [pronounced 'seeward'], Anne or **Anna**, the 'Swan of Lichfield', 1742–1809, poet and letter-writer, b. at Eyam, Derbyshire, only surviving child of Elizabeth (Hunter) and the Rev. Thomas S. (also a poet, and Canon of Lichfield from 1754). He started her on Milton at two; she wrote religious verse at 10 or 12; but soon her parents took fright at her growing erudition and began to oppose it. An accident in 1768 left her lame, though still a hearty walker. She drew public notice with elegiac poems on David Garrick and Captain Cook, 1780, Major André, 1781, and Anne MILLER (who had provided a much-needed literary outlet), 1782. (André, once a suitor of her adored Honora Sneyd, who then married Maria EDGEWORTH's father, was hanged in the USA, victim of spy-story skullduggery.) In 1784 appeared four eds. of AS's verse novel *Louisa* (begun at 19, her favourite work, innovative in plan but formal and stilted like all her poetry), and anonymous debunking newspaper comment on the newly dead Samuel Johnson, whom she saw as misogynist. The *GM* carried her versions of Horace's odes, and many controversial letters (as 'Benvolio', 1786–7, and later with her name, on Johnson, Boswell and PIOZZI; to H. M. WILLIAMS, 1793, begging her to leave France). AS cared for her father till he died, 1790. Her local ties were strong, her literary friendships extensive, her interest in female writing broad, her authority both mocked and respected. She published a poem on her friends the ladies of LLANGOLLEN, 1796, sonnets, 1799, and memoirs of Erasmus Darwin, 1804. With negotiations stalled on collected works, she left her MSS to Walter Scott: poems appeared 1810 (facs. 1974), letters (heavily re-written), 1811 (selec. 1936); others, with criticism, journals and sermons, remain unpub. Life by Margaret Ashmun, 1931.

Sewell, Anna, 1820–78, novelist, b. Yarmouth, Norfolk, only da. of Mary (Wright) SEWELL and Isaac S. She was educ. at home with books purchased from her mother's literary earnings. An ankle injury sustained in youth made her semi-crippled for life, though she recovered enough to make several trips to Germany and Spain in the 1850s. The family moved to Old Catton, near Norwich, where her health worsened and she became a permanent invalid. Her literary fame rests on one work, *Black Beauty*, 1877, inspired by the desire to improve treatment of horses; purporting to be the autobiography of a horse, it became immensely popular, both as a children's story and as propaganda against cruelty to animals. See study by Margaret J. Baker, 1956.

Sewell, Elizabeth (Missing), 1815–1906, novelist, educationalist, essayist and children's writer, b. in Newport, Isle of Wight, second da. and seventh child of Jane (Edwardes) and Thomas S., prominent local solicitor and land agent. ES grew up in a male-dominated household which, while not neglecting the girls' education, encouraged the notion of female inferiority. She found it particularly hard to free herself from the influence of her brother William, theologian, Oxford professor and educationalist, who took it upon himself to 'edit' her first four novels. As well as 13 novels and some short stories, she wrote histories of Europe, devotional works, travel books and essays. Female EDUCATION was one of her life-long interests. *Principles of Education*, 1865, argues firmly for better upbringing and education for girls, attacking the prevailing myth of marriage as a woman's sole career. In 1852, she and her elder sister established a small school at their home in Bonchurch and, in 1866, she founded a Church High School for girls in Ventnor. ES's fiction is notable for its depiction of women functioning in the everyday world of family duty and neighbourhood affairs. In almost all her novels, her heroines initiate action and influence others by their sturdy good sense; they are also often incisively contrasted with weak-minded or devious men. In *Margaret Percival*, 1847, and *Katherine Ashton*, 1854, ES enacts her own scepticism about matrimonial beatitudes by portraying the marital unhappiness caused by male selfishness or authoritarianism. The semi-autobiographical *Experience of Life*, 1853, is her most positive statement about the single life; the central character, following the example of her spinster aunt, overcomes ill-health and depression to become the pillar of the family and the director of her own school. *Ursula*, 1858, has a similarly innovative heroine who, although finally settling for marriage, initially takes her life into her own hands and refuses to conform to traditional patterns of female subservience. ES's later novels, all written in the 1860s, show a weakening of narrative ability, but she continued to expound her social and educational ideas concernig women until well into old age. See Shirley Foster's, *Victorian Women's Fiction*, 1985.

Sewell, Mary (Young), poet, da. of Elizabeth (Taylor) and Sir William Y., governor of Dominica and Tobago. Her *Horatio and Amanda*, 1777, vividly if sentimentally depicts war smashing the idyll of love: Amanda finds her lover's body on the battlefield, identifiable only by some of her own needlework. *Innocence, An Allegorical Poem*, 1790, was well reviewed: the central figure (male) pursues Pleasure but is saved from Misery first by Experience, then by Religion. She married George S., rector of Byfleet in Surrey, who died in 1801. Royalty subscribed to her *Poems*, 1803; so did C. M. FANSHAWE, Mary HARCOURT, Elizabeth MONTAGU, Lady TUITE, and Elizabeth CARTER. MS imitates Carter and Lady Mary Wortley MONTAGU, answers Frances GREVILLE, and collects juvenilia, poems published in magazines or submitted to Anne MILLER's urn, fables, epistles, ballads, and riddles; she writes on birthdays, deaths, national occasions and religion. She reprinted this volume with two more, 1805–9, which add more poems and brief religious essays. Sometimes facile, she sometimes nicely hits a mood or idea, as in 'The Contented Spinster', who abjures 'the desirable fetters' and shows her liberty in 'a look that's a little demure'. She is often confused with Maria Julia YOUNG.

Sewell, Mary (Wright), 1797–1884, poet, b. Sutton, Suffolk, da. of Quaker farmer John W. She was educ. at home and m. Isaac S. in 1819. MS worked for some time as a teacher, and did not begin writing verse for young people till the age of 60. The moral didactic tone of her work is evident in the sentimental BALLAD which sold over a million copies, *A Mother's Last Words*, 1860, about two boys' efforts to follow the pious advice of their dying mother. Other works include *Homely Ballads*, 1858; *Our Father's Care*, 1861; *Children of Summerbrook*, 1859; and a prose story, *Patience Hart's First Experience in Service*, 1862. She was mother of Anna SEWELL. Elisabeth Boyd Bayly wrote a memoir in MS's *Poems and Ballads* [1886]; Mary Bayly pub. a *Life and Letters*, 1889.

Sexton, Anne, 1928–74, poet, writer of children's books, and lecturer. She was b. Anne Gray Harvey, in Newton, Mass., to upper-middle-class parents, Mary Gray (Staples) and Ralph Churchill H., whose abuse and its effects figure largely in her later poetry. While attending finishing school in Boston, she eloped with Alfred Mueller S. II ('Kayo'), 1948 (divorced, 1973), and worked as a model and sales-clerk. After the birth of her first daughter, 1953, while her husband was in Korea, she began the suicide attempts that ended in her death by carbon monoxide poisoning. During one of her frequent hospitalizations of the late 1950s, she returned to the poetry writing she had done as a young woman in school: it gave her a 'feeling of purpose ... something to do with my life, no matter how rotten I was'. In an adult education poetry class, she met Sylvia PLATH, with whom she compared suicide fantasies, and Maxine KUMIN, who became an intimate friend and collaborator in poetry and children's books, including *Eggs and Things*, 1963, and *Joey and the Birthday Present*, 1971. AS was quickly recognized as a gifted, disturbing poet. Her first collections, *To Bedlam and Part Way Back*, 1960, *All My Pretty Ones*, 1962 (nominated for a National Book Award), and *Live or Die*, 1966 (Pulitzer Prize, 1967), expose her 'dwarf heart' in conversation with her children, her lover, an evasive God and her self. Awards, fellowships, and constant invitations for her dramatic readings could not overcome her interior horrors or her obsession with death, apparent in the 'death baby' poems in the last collection she published, *The Death Notebooks*, 1974. Feminist critics see AS as one of the earliest disrupters of the genteel silencing of women's experience of menstruation, abortion, domestic rage, and emotional and physical child abuse. Often thought 'confessional', she is consistently experimental in form. Her 13 books of poetry focus on interior pain and conflict. Her hunger for a consoling God is evident in her radical revisions of Genesis, the Psalms, and the Gospels in her later poetry: 'Eve came out of that rib like an angry bird' (*Death Notebooks*). *Transformations*, 1972, the coldly witty rewriting of Grimm's fairy tales, shows her 'private pantheon of demons belonged to everyone' as 'derived from the storehouse of cultural nightmare'. Her daughter Linda edited her posthumous works – *The Awful Rowing Towards God*, 1975, *45 Mercy Street*, 1977, and *Words for Dr. Y: Uncollected Poems with Three Stories*, 1978 – and, with Lois Ames, her letters, 1979. See Kumin's essay in J. D. McClatchy, ed., *AS*, 1978, and her intro. to *Complete Poems*, 1981; OSTRIKER, 1983; Diane Hume George's psychoanalytic study, *Oedipus Anne*, 1987. Two vols., of critical essays, 1989: ed. D. H. George, and ed. Steven E. Colburn. Life by Diane Wood Middlebrook forthcoming.

Seymour, Beatrice Kean (Stapleton), 1885?–1955, novelist. B. in London of parents who saw dancing and theatre-going as worldly, she was educ. at a mixed-sex school and at King's College, then worked as a typist before marrying writer and editor William Kean Seymour. Her (nearly 20) novels, which suggest alertness to both women's literary tradition and their subordinated social position, begin with *Invisible Tides*, 1919. *The Hopeful Journey*, 1923, shows how Charlotte BRONTË's novels first influence a young woman's idealization of, and later power her rebellion against, a husband who, because of her idealism, had supposed her uninfected by 'the new-fangled notions women were beginning to get hold of'. BKS's Sally trilogy, beginning with *Maids and Mistresses*, 1932, focuses observation of upper-middle-class families round the life of a maid. Her study of AUSTEN, 1937, repr. 1974, aims to shake the view of her as conventional and sheltered. *The Unquiet Field*, 1940, criticizes marriage law and women's subjection. In *The Second Mrs. Conford*, 1951, a woman barred from study at Cambridge by lack of money pays her way through London Univ., receives the BA which Cambridge was still denying women, becomes a governess (the only available job), and (reworking *Jane Eyre*) marries her handsome young employer. *The Painted Lath*, 1955, centres on its heroine's problems as a woman in office jobs during WWII.

Shange, Ntozake, Paulette Williams, experimental playwright, poet, novelist, performer, and teacher, b. in 1948 in Trenton, NJ, da. of psychiatric social worker and teacher Eloise and surgeon Paul T. W. She grew up with black leader W. E. B. DuBois, and musicians Miles Davis, Chuck Berry and Dizzy Gillespie as frequent visitors: 'I was raised as if everything was all right. And in fact, once I got out of my house, everything was *not* all right'. She graduated from Barnard College (BA, 1970) and the Univ. of Southern California, Los Angeles (MA in American studies, 1973). In 1971, she took her Zulu name, Ntozake ('she who comes with her own things') and Shange ('she who walks like a lion'). She has acted and danced, and taught women's studies, African American studies, and creative writing at various colleges. Three times married (most recently to John Guess), she has a daughter. Her first work, a 'choreopoem' produced with dancer Paula Moss, *For Colored Girls Who Have Considered Suicide / When the Rainbow is Enuf*, 1975, acclaimed for its rich evocation of black women's lives, 'celebrates women's loyalties to women' (Toni Cade BAMBARA). NS's experimental work is written from within a black culture which she 'refuses to annotate for the European reader'. Her dramatic works include *A Photograph*, 1977, *Boogie Woogie Landscapes*, 1978, *Spell #7*, 1979, and an adaptation of Bertolt Brecht's *Mother Courage*, 1980, set in the post-Civil-War reconstruction period. Her poems appear in *nappy edges*, 1978, *A Daughter's Geography*, 1983, and, with essays, in *Natural Disasters and Other Festive Occasions*, 1977. Her first novel, *Sassafrass, Indigo and Cyprus*, 1982, is about a woman and her three daughters, named in the title, who grapple with drugs, sex, and magic, looking for their own lives. The semi-autobiographical *Betsey Brown*, 1985, lets go of NS's early lyricism and portrays the life of a middle-class girl coming to maturity in the late 1950s, contending with changing values in the black community and the effects of legislated integration. *See No Evil: Pieces, Essays and Accounts 1976–1983*, 1984, affirms NS's continuing formal experiment and commitment to women, third world liberation, and black culture. In *Ridin' the Moon in Texas; Word Paintings*, 1987, each poem and story is a specific response to a painting or photo. See Carol P. Christ's *Diving Deep and Surfacing*, 1980, Keyssar, 1984, Christian, 1985, and Deborah Geis in Enoch Baxter, ed., *Feminine Focus, The New Women Playwrights*, 1989. Interview in Tate, 1983.

Sharp, Evelyn Jane, 1869–1955, novelist, suffragist and journalist, b. London, ninth and youngest child of Jane (Bloyd) and James S., slate merchant. She was educ. at home by her sisters, then attended Miss Spark's school, Strathallan House and, later, Kensington boarding school. In compliance with her parents' wishes, she left school at 16 to lead a 'purposeless existence' waiting for a 'problematic husband'. In 1894 she left home for London, supporting herself by teaching. Here she pub. six stories in *The Yellow Book*, becoming part of its circle; and her first novel, *At the Relton Arms*, 1896. Later, she wrote for the *Manchester Guardian*. Her writing often embodies feminist ideas; in *Nicolette*, 1907, she explores a woman's conflict between an artistic vocation and family and marriage. In *Rebel Women*, 1910, a collection of stories, she fictionalized incidents from her own experiences as a suffragist and was particularly astute about men's mockery of women. She also wrote children's books such as *The Making of a School Girl*, 1897, and the collection *All the Way to Fairyland*, 1898. A member of WSPU from 1906, she was imprisoned in Holloway in 1911 for suffragist activities. She was a pacifist during the war, considering that 'the enfranchisement of women involved greater issues than could be involved in any war'. She did relief work for the Society of Friends in Germany and Russia. Her autobiography, *An Unfinished Adventure*, 1933, reveals her determination to make her own life against all opposition, and gives valuable insight into the SUFFRAGE campaign and its social context. In 1933 she m. Henry Nevinson after a friendship of more than 30 years.

Sharp, Isabella (Oliver), 1771–1843, poet, b. at Cumberland, Penn., da. of Mary (Buchanan) and James O., a well-educated farmer who taught her brothers himself but let her grow up able to read (for which she seized every opportunity), but not write. She married James S. While working she would compose verse (occasional and religious) which she later dictated to others. Her *Poems on Various Subjects* were pub. at Carlisle, Penn., 1805.

Sharp, Jane, feminist and midwife for 'above thirty years' when she addressed *The Midwives Book, or the Whole Art of Midwifery*, 1671, to her 'sisters' the 'Celebrated Midwives of Great Britain and Ireland'. Well read in textbooks (some she paid to have translated from French, Dutch and Italian), she wrote 'as plainly and briefly as possibly I can', to keep the skills in female hands. She maintains the superiority of midwives to male doctors (cf. CELLIER, NIHELL), as more practical and less inclined to merely abstract 'Speculation'. She includes jokes at men's expense, gruesomely detailed exposition of techniques like turning a baby in the womb and treating venereal disease, and descriptions of male and female anatomy. Here she praises the clitoris, which 'makes women lustfull and take delight in Copulation', and speculates on the existence of 'lewd Women' (lesbians) with large organs like penises: they 'have endeavoured to use it as men do'. A 4th ed., *The Complete Midwife's Companion*, 1725, bore her name. See Robert A. Erickson in P.-G. Boucé, ed., essays, 1982.

Shaw, Anna Howard, 1847–1919, feminist, minister and physician, b. in Newcastle upon Tyne, da. of Nicolas (Stott) and Thomas S. Her father, a paperhanger, emigrated to the USA in 1848; the family followed in 1851 to Lawrence, Mass., where AHS attended school. As Unitarians, the family was abolitionist, and their home was a station in the Underground Railroad. Her father joined the Union Army, her mother had mental problems, and the 12-year-old AHS and a younger brother ploughed and made furniture on their land in northern Michigan. She later became a teacher, then moved to Big Rapids, Mich., to earn money for college. However, 'thrilled to the soul' by a visiting Universalist woman minister, the Rev. Marianna Thompson, she prepared for the ministry and preached her first sermon as a Methodist in 1870. In 1873 she entered Albion College and then graduated from Boston Univ. Divinity School. She was refused ordination until 1880, when she became the first woman ordained by the Methodist Protestant Church. Six years later she had earned her MD from Boston Univ. In 1885 she became lecturer and organizer for the Massachusetts SUFFRAGE Association and joined the AWSA. Also active in the TEMPERANCE movement, she was superintendent of the Franchise Department of the WCTU 1888–92. At an 1888 meeting of the International Council of Women, Susan B. ANTHONY recruited her to the NWSA. In 1890, she became national lecturer in the combined NAWSA, and vice president, 1892–1904 (president

1911). She spoke in every state in the union and appeared at Congressional hearings and state conventions. During WWI she was chair of the Woman's Committee of the US Council of National Defense, for which she was awarded the Distinguished Service Medal in 1919. After the War, she lectured nationally on behalf of the League of Nations. Her papers are in the Schlesinger Library, Radcliffe College. See her autobiography, *The Story of a Pioneer*, 1915, with Elizabeth Jordan. Anthony and Harper's *History of Woman's Suffrage*, vols. 4–6 (1920–22) recounts her activities in the national movement. Her speeches, ed. Albert Linkugel (Univ. of Michigan diss., 1960) are available through Michigan Microfilms. See also J. R. McGovern, 'AHS: New Approaches to Feminism,' *Journal of Social History*, Winter 1969.

Shaw, Flora, 1852–1929, children's writer and political journalist, third of 14 children of Marie (de Fontaine: da. of a Governor of Mauritius) and General S. who served in the Crimea. Brought up mainly at her grandfather's house (Sir Frederick S., MP) at Kimmage, near Dublin, she was educ. at home, then through access to the soldiers' library. She was later befriended by John Ruskin, who directed her reading. She injured her spine taking care of younger siblings, became close to her French aunt after her father's remarriage in 1872, and had a long period of religious doubt. She opened a co-operative store to help poorer neighbours. In 1877 she pub. her very successful *Castle Blair*, the best of her children's tales, written to help her beloved elder sister Mimi; but after working for slum children, FS decided to write to change conditions rather than provide solace. In 1883, she moved alone to Abinger, Surrey, lodging in a washerwoman's cottage (which she later bought), writing for the *Pall Mall Gazette* and making literary friends, including neighbour George Meredith. Her breakthrough came with her scoop interview in Gibraltar with the exiled Zabehr Pashe, resuscitating his reputation in the *Gazette* of 28 June, 1887 and the *Contemporary Review*, Sept.–Nov. 1887. For the next 15 years she worked as a highly regarded political journalist and foreign correspondent on the *Manchester Guardian*, then *The Times*. An authority on Mediterranean and African affairs, she would have been appointed Colonial Editor on *The Times* from the 1890s had she not been a woman. Always overworking to support family members, she travelled widely, including wilder regions of Canada and Australia, until ill-health forced her retirement from permanent staff in 1900. She m. her friend Sir Frederick Lugard in 1902, and spent the remainder of her life supporting his career as colonial administrator in Nigeria, then Hong Kong. She felt that any woman who had not borne a child was a failure and her life not worth recording, but there is a good biography by E. Moberly Bell, 1947.

Shaw, Helen, 1913–85, short-story writer and poet, b. Timaru, South Canterbury, NZ, da. of Jessie Helen (Gow) and Walter S. She was a pupil-teacher for a year before going to Christchurch Teachers College, then Univ. of Canterbury (BA in History and English). Married in 1941 to Frank Hofmann, photographer, she had two sons. She taught in Christchurch primary schools, then designed and painted buttons, and later pottery bowls and vases in Auckland. The first of six vols. of poetry was pub. in 1968 when she was 55. Frequently religious meditations, with recurring images of natural elements, her poems aspire to the mystical. In 1971 she ed. the letters of D'Arcy Cresswell, and in 1983 ed. *Dear Lady Ginger*, an exchange of letters between him and Lady Ottoline Morrell. Her short stories *The Orange Tree*, 1957, and *The Gypsies*, 1978, are powerful GOTHIC stories, often about ageing eccentrics. They are unusual in NZ women's writing in not being realist or autobiographical or consciously NZ in setting.

Shaw, Hester, wealthy midwife, money-lender, and pamphleteer of Tower Street, London. Having stored goods, after an accident in 1650, at the house of Mr Clendon, the local church minister, she accused him verbally of stealing them; when he attacked her for 'volubility of tongue, and natural boldnesse, and confidence ... and much impudency' she resorted to print: *A Plaine Relation of my Sufferings* ('in the plain stile of a weak woman') and *Mrs Shaw's Innocency Restored* (with affidavits confirming her account), both 1653. No evidence supports Kate Hurd-Head's assertion, 1938, that she was involved in PETITIONS by midwives in the 1630s.

Shearer, Jill, playwright, b. 1934 in Melbourne, Victoria, da. of Leah (Spiller) and John S. Educ. at Brisbane Girls' Grammar School, she later attended business college and now works as a consular secretary. JS began writing seriously in 1971; her first play, 'But I Won't Wear White', winner of a Brisbane playwriting competition, was produced in 1972. She has since pub. many plays including *Catherine*, 1977, *The Foreman*, 1977, *The Boat*, 1978, and *Echoes and Other Plays* (including 'The Kite', 'Stephen' and 'Nocturne'), 1980. JS has a fondness for the seemingly familiar situation overtaken by the unexpected or bizarre. This is perhaps best seen in her one-act plays with their distinctively simple, evocative settings; *The Boat*, for example, opens onto a conventional living-room in which reposes a yellow boat containing a man fishing. *Catherine*, based on the historical figure Catherine Crowley (mistress of D'Arcy Wentworth and mother of W.C. Wentworth), confronts the general failure among men to understand women, the juxtaposition of past and present implying that little has changed. Unpub. plays include: 'Ships That Pass', 1973, 'Who the Hell Needs Whipbirds', 1974, 'The Trouble with Gillian', 1974, 'The Job', 1974, 'Release Lavinia Stannard', 1975, 'The Expatriate', 1978, and 'Shimada', 1987, produced mainly in Brisbane. JS has won numerous awards including the Townsville Drama Festival Prize, 1973, for *The Foreman*, the Alexander Theatre Playwriting Competition, 1976, for *Catherine*, and the Utah-Cairns Playwriting competition, 1976, for both *The Boat* and 'The Kite'.

Sheldon, Alice (Bradley), 'James Tiptree, Jr.,' also 'Raccoona Sheldon,' 1915–87, science-fiction writer, b. in Chicago to travel writer, novelist and WWII correspondent Mary (Hastings) – who wrote books about AS, *Alice in Jungle Land* 1927, and *in Elephantland*, 1929, to which the child contributed line drawings – and Herbert Edwin B., explorer and naturalist. She travelled with them through Africa and India during her childhood. She went to a Swiss school, then to Sarah Lawrence College and became a painter. She married William Davey in 1934 ('the first boy that asked me'; divorced 1938). In 1942 she joined the Army, the first woman to be trained at the Air Force Intelligence School at Harrisburg, became a photo-intelligence officer, and in 1945 married Col. Huntington Denton S., later of the CIA, for which she also worked in photo-intelligence, 1952–5. She attended half a 1dozen univs., receiving a BA from American Univ., 1959, and a PhD in experimental psychology from George Washington Univ., 1967. Toward 1967 she began writing science-fiction as 'James Tiptree Jr.' (after the jam). The 'camouflage' gulled the critics: Robert Silverberg wrote, now famously, that her style was 'ineluctably masculine' ('lean, muscular, supple, relying heavily on dialogue broken by bursts of stripped-down exposition'). Unmasked in 1977, AS said that '"Tiptree" had shot the stuffing out of male stereotypes of women writers. At the same time, the more vulnerable males decided that "Tiptree" had been much overrated.' AS's three novels – *Up the Walls of the World*, 1978, *Brightness Falls from* the Air, 1985, and *The Starry Rift*, 1986 – use their inter-planetary settings to explore moral issues, often gender-related: oppression, violence, cruelty, the destruction of the planet. Her short stories (four vols. of her own, plus anthologies) are better known: some eloquently, disturbingly observe 'woman's place' in a scheme dominated by an aggressive male sexuality explicitly associated with violence and death. 'The Women Men Don't See', 1973, figures a civil servant and her daughter who leave Earth with aliens from another planet to escape a condition of 'no rights ... except what men allow us.' 'Raccoona Sheldon's' 'The Screwfly Solution' (Nebula Award), 1977, depicts aliens who, wanting to exterminate humanity, identify 'the vulnerable link in the behavioural chain' (a pest-control technique) as 'the close linkage between the behavioural expression of aggression/predation and sexual reproduction in the male' and provoke the widespread slaughter of women by men obeying a cult called 'The Sons of Adam' and wishing to 'purify' themselves of their 'animal part, which is woman'. 'Houston, Houston, Do You Read?', 1976, transports three male astronauts to a future in which an epidemic has killed off all men. Their violence against an all-female space crew is intolerable in the new world: 'we simply have no facilities for people with your emotional problems'. AS died when she shot her husband, increasingly disabled by Alzheimer's disease, and herself. Interview in *Isaac Asimov's Science Fiction Magazine*, April 1983, quoted above. Studies by Carolyn Rhodes in Marleen Barr and Nicholas D. Smith, eds., *Women and Utopia*, 1983, Lillian M. Heldreth in *Extrapolation*, 23, 1982, and Sarah Lefanu, 1988.

Shelley, Mary Wollstonecraft (Godwin), 1797–1851, novelist, da. of William G. and Mary WOLLSTONECRAFT, who died ten days after her birth. With encouragement to write from her father but little instruction, she educ. herself by voracious reading: she knew five ancient and modern languages in 1814, the year she left England with Percy Bysshe S. They married in 1816; despite a series of miscarriages and infant deaths, she wrote four of her works before his drowning in 1822; next year she came back to England. Her first (anon.) published work, 1817, was a travel book, as was her last, 1844. *Frankenstein, or the Modern Prometheus*, 1818, began in a group attempt at ghost stories. Its picture of aspiration and rebellion, its strong critique of myths of Romantic titanism, use male personae but also birth imagery; MS's revision, 1831 (followed by many reprints), stresses the element of sacrilege. *Valperga, or The Life and Adventures of Castruccio, Prince of Lucca*, 1823, and *The Fortunes of Perkin Warbeck*, 1830, are historical romances; in *The Last Man*, 1826, the sole, male, survivor tells of the destruction of humanity by plague. The heroine of *Lodore*, 1835, grows up as a child of nature in Illinois; that of *Falkner*, 1837, reconciles her warring father and lover; *Mathilda*, unpub. till 1929, deals with father–daughter incest. With novels, journalism and editing, MS supported herself and educated her only surviving child at Harrow and Cambridge. She published lives of eminent Europeans, 1835–9, but not her projected life of Percy S. Many works now repr. or ed. MS's letters, ed. Betty T. Bennett, 1980ff., and journals, ed. Paula R. Feldman and Diana Scott-Kilvert, 1987, explore her radical–conformist conflict; *Tales and Stories*, ed. C. Robinson, 1976; life by Janet Horowitz Murray, 1989, study by Anne K. Mellor, 1988 (also Muriel SPARK, 1951, rev. 1988).

Sheppard, Elizabeth Sara, 1830–62, novelist, b. Blackheath, London, da. of an Anglican clergyman whose mother was of Jewish extraction. On his early death, ESS's mother opened a school, where ESS taught music. She was also a fine linguist in Greek, Latin, Hebrew and modern languages. She began her first novel, *Charles Auchester*, about Mendelssohn (as 'Seraphael'), at 16, and sent the MS to Disraeli, whom she always admired. He helped her publish it in 1853 (anon.). Her next novel, *Counterparts: or the Cross of Love*, 1854, emulates his highly intellectual, showy, rather cryptic style, but despite its portentousness, carries a serious and interesting study of an unusually gifted young woman. It is dedicated to Mrs Disraeli. ESS wrote three more novels and some children's tales, *Round the Fire*, 1856, and poems. She also ed. *My First Season*, 1855, by Beatrice Reynolds. She possibly used the pseudonym 'E. Berger', French for her surname.

Sheridan, Clare Consuelo Claire (Frewen), 1885–1970, sculptor, TRAVEL writer, novelist, journalist. B. in London, da. of Clara (Jerome) of NYC and Moreton F., she was educ. by governesses at her father's estates in Sussex and Co. Cork, later at finishing schools in France and Germany. As a child, she spent summers with her aunt Lady Randolph Churchill, who launched her into London society. At 18, 'to atone for being a social failure', she decided to be an author, publishing her first article on country house entertaining. Henry James, George Moore, and Rudyard Kipling encouraged her, though when, in 1910, she married Wilfred S., a descendent of Frances SHERIDAN, Kipling advised her to 'chuck poetry and literature', which 'don't make for married happiness on the she-side'. Her husband was killed in action, 1915, a week after their third child was born. A mainly self-taught sculptor, she also studied at the Royal College of Art and exhibited at the Royal Academy and in NYC. In 1920, she travelled with the Russian Trade Delegation to Moscow, where she modelled Lenin and Trotsky, then published excerpts of her journal in *The Times* of London and that of NY. *Russian Portraits*, 1921 (*Mayfair to Moscow* in the US) was followed by *My American Diary*, 1922, about her stay in the US, where she and her son went camping with Charlie Chaplin. Her articles on Russia, Mexico, and the US, were widely syndicated. Roving Correspondent for the *New York World*, 1922–3, she covered the Irish Civil War, the Turko-Greek War and the evacuation of refugees from Smyrna, and interviewed Kemal Atatürk, Mussolini, King Boris of Bulgaria, and delegates to the Geneva Peace Conference. She lived in the Soviet Union in 1923, writing two articles a week. *Across Europe with Satanella*, 1925, records her motorcycle trip to the USSR. Here, and in *A Turkish Kaleidoscope*, 1926, she writes of the position of women, seeing 'the Russian woman' as 'the most highly evolved feminist in the world'. *In Many Places*, 1923 (*West and East* in the US), collects her articles on post-war Europe; *Nude Veritas*, 1927 (*The Naked Truth* in the US) prints political impressions and interviews. *Arab Interlude*, 1936, describes the home she made for a decade in the desert. After her son Richard died at age 21, she went for solace and sculpture to the Blackfoot Indians in the Rockies, recording her impressions in *Redskin Interlude*, 1938, a plea for the preservation of native culture. Her novels include *Stella Defiant*, 1924, *The Thirteenth*, 1925, *Green Amber*, 1929, *El Caïd*, 1931 (*Substitute Bride* in the USA), and *Genetrix*, 1935. *Without End*, 1939, describes her attempts to communicate with her dead son. See Anita Leslie, *Cousin Clare*, 1976.

Sheridan, Frances (Chamberlaine), 1724–66, novelist and dramatist, b. in Dublin, da. of Anastasia (Whyte), who d. early, and the Rev. Philip C.; he disapproved of her learning to read and write, but her brothers taught her subjects including Latin and botany. At 15 she wrote a romance (*Eugenia and Adelaide*) and two sermons. Her published praise of Thomas S.'s theatrical conduct, 1746, led them to meet and marry, 1747. They moved to London in 1754, where she published (with Richardson's encouragement) the highly successful novel *Memoirs of Miss Sidney*

Bidulph, 1761, repr. 1987. It advocates total obedience to parents, husband, and Providence; a 'female libertine' is a 'monster'; the heroine's sufferings climax in saintly death in the sequel, about the next generation, pub. 1767. FS's comedy *The Discovery*, 1763, sets a submissive mother and witty daughter to reform tyrannical or foolish men: the prologue accuses men of resenting female writers. *The Dupe*, 1764, was less successful; *A Journey to Bath* (written after the family's economizing move to Blois, 1764, unpub. till 1788) includes a forerunner of her son Richard Brinsley S.'s Mrs Malaprop (see FS, *Plays*, ed. Robert Hogan and Jerry C. Beasley, 1984). *The History of Nourjahad*, 1767, an oriental tale, shows 'the deceitfulness of worldly enjoyments' through scenes of exotic luxury. Both her daughters wrote: Alicia, later Lefanu, 1753–1817, made FS's early romance into a comic opera and pub. a patriotic comedy, *Sons of Erin*, 1812 (which Maria EDGEWORTH calls 'pretty bad'); Elizabeth or Betsy, later Lefanu, 1758–1837, mother of Alicia LEFANU, wrote journal-letters (those to her sister ed. 1960, 1986; others unpub., National Library of Ireland). *Memoirs* of FS by her granddaughter Alicia, 1824, stress her domestic role. See Margaret Anne Doody in Schofield and Macheski, eds., *Fetter'd or Free?*, 1986.

Sherwood, Mary Martha (Butt), 1775–1851, novelist, diarist and autobiographer (more than 350 titles, chiefly pious works for the young, on whom she exerted a unique influence), b. Stanford, Worcs., da. of Martha (Sherwood), who wrote down her stories before she could do so herself, and the Rev. George B. He thought her a genius and future author; she feared geniuses were 'slovenly and odd', and wished to be a heroine instead, though her intense imaginative life included endless telling of fairy tales. She learned Latin more quickly than her brother, and was happy despite wearing a backboard daily. She attended the St Quintins' school at Reading, 1790–3, and in 1795 reluctantly published a MINERVA novel, 'yclept "The Traditions"', written at 17, to help the school (see F. A. ROWDEN) in need: its network gathered 740 subscribers, many high-ranking and the majority female (Jane AUSTEN's sister was one). In 1802 MMS earned £40 for *Margarita* (begun 1794, continued in mourning for her father: now lost) and £10 for *Susan Gray* (for her Sunday-school pupils, future servant-girls, in Hannah MORE's vein: a hit). In 1803 she m. her cousin Henry S., an army officer, and in 1805 went to India. Here she ran a series of schools, adopted orphans, published busily (many works harshly evangelical), and cancelled her imminent departure for England when a doctor said that future babies might, unlike those already agonizingly lost, survive the climate. *The Indian Pilgrim*, 1815, adapts Bunyan to another culture; that year MMS found herself famous for *Little Henry and His Bearer*, her sister having sold it to a publisher for £5 (later widely translated). Home in 1816, keen to earn the family's living so that her husband might stay with them, she ran a school and finished works begun in India. Her most famous one, *The Fairchild Family*, 1818–47, moves away from its early obsession with human depravity, as her views gradually moved away from any sect. After 1829 she wrote against Catholicism. She studied biblical typology, and left a 'type dictionary' in progress. She published jointly with both her surviving daughters: one, Sophia Kelly, ed. her AUTOBIOGRAPHY (perceptive on her childhood and on women's lives in India) and DIARY extracts, 1854; different selec. ed. F. J. Harvey Darton, 1910: studies by Naomi ROYDE SMITH, 1946, M. Nancy Cutt, 1974 (her CHILDREN'S books), Ketari Kushari DYSON in *A Various Universe*, 1978.

Shields, Carol (Warner), novelist, poet, short-story writer, b., 1935, and raised near

Chicago, da. of Inez (Selgren) and Robert W. In 1957 she graduated from Hanover College, Ind. (having spent a year at Exeter Univ. in England), and m. Donald S., later a professor of civil engineering. A poem, 'Coming to Canada: age 22', marked her relocation that year. She has five children, lives in Winnipeg, and began writing 'with the kind of book I wanted to read but couldn't find – about women's friendships' and women's inner moral and intellectual lives. As a poet, CS (e.g. in *Others*, 1972, and *Intersect*, 1974) writes of relationships and distances between people: 'Sister' pictures 'the way our mother's / gestures survive in us'. After an MA at the Univ. of Ottawa, 1975, she published a study of Susanna MOODIE, 1976. Her first two novels look at the writing process through heroines who complete 'three generations of paired sisters'. In *Small Ceremonies*, 1976 (Canadian Authors' Association Award), a professor's wife near 40 is flanked by two novelists as she strives to uncover the truth about Moodie in a biography: 'My own life will never be enough for me. It is a congenital condition.' In *The Box Garden*, 1977, her sister Charleen wins literary status despite feeling a timid, inadequate woman and meagre dabbler in verse: 'symbolism is such an impertinence, the sort of thing the "pome people" might contrive'. *Happenstance*, 1980, and *A Fairly Conventional Woman*, 1982, examine marriage through the barely overlapping narratives of husband (a historian racked by comically misplaced academic rivalry with an old flame) and wife (satirically dubbed 'a quilt-maker in her own right'). *Various Miracles* (stories), 1986, creates 'scenes that seem to bloom out of nothing': 'The Metaphor is Dead – Pass it on' reports this death in a *tour-de-force* starburst of metaphors. In *Swann: A Mystery*, 1987, an Ontario farm woman, self-taught poet and marital victim vanishes amid conflicting constructs of her by feminist critic, biographer, librarian, and publisher. CS has written award-winning CBC drama. Her domestic fictional settings have led critics to under-rate her. See special issue of *Room of One's Own*, 13, July 1989.

Shinebourne, Jan, novelist and short-story writer, of Chinese and Indian descent, da. of Marion (Bacchus) and Charles Lowe, b. 1947 in Berbice, Guyana, in the Canje area of forest and old plantations, at a time of unrest among the indentured labourers. She began writing early, with plays performed at her school. She migrated to Britain in 1970, but sets her novels in Guyana. The first, *Timepiece*, begun at 18 and incorporating forest descriptions written at school, was pub. at Leeds, 1986: its young female protagonist moves from a rural cane-growing community to make an identity among the young, educated Guyanese of Georgetown. JS works in London as a lecturer, reviewer and editor; she is a leading contributor to *Wasafiri*, and has written stories for international journals and radio. She has two children. Her second novel, *The Last English Plantation*, 1988, presents the conflicts in the life of a 12-year-old girl: torn between attachment to a Hindu neighbour and the drive of her Christianized Indian mother to de-Hinduize her Chinese father. JS skilfully juxtaposes contrasting speech patterns and styles of domesticity. The Institute of Contemporary Arts, London, holds a video interview with her.

Shipton, Helen, novelist, b. 1857 in Barlow, near Chesterfield, Derbyshire. Da. of the Rev. George S., vicar of Brampton, she became a prolific writer of children's stories as well as a novelist, and pub. a number of little plays for children, many with the SPCK. Part of the circle revolving around Charlotte YONGE, she collaborated with Christabel COLERIDGE on *Ravenstone*, 1896. Better known was *Dagmar*, 1888, a story of concealed identity whose eponymous heroine, 'more child than woman', grows up in 'careless freedom' before the toils of love enclose her: more interesting is her father's cousin, Raymond, 'well skilled in the art of doing nothing gracefully'. *The Herons*, 1895 (first serialized in *Macmillans*), focuses on another such dastardly charmer, a disinherited elder son.

Shirley, Elizabeth, d. 1641, biographer. Da. of Sir John S. of Leics., 'brought up an earnest heretic' till 20, she was converted six years later by an old beggar-woman's tale of a miraculous childbirth intervention by the Virgin, and professed a nun at St Ursula's, Louvain, in 1596. She wrote the life of Margaret Clement, 1540–1612 ('our good grandmother' and 'a firebrand to inkendell me in the love of God'), 'acknowledging freely her own imperfect feelings' but hoping to help and inspire herself and her sisters. She sketches Clement's childhood unworldliness and simplicity, the heroism of her mother, Margaret Giggs (foster-sister of Margaret ROPER), and the mixed response to her aspirations as a young nun, then relates her old age with the warmth and humour of personal knowledge. Clement's director was 'confounded, she being a frail woman', at her 'great courage and magnanimity'. ES showed these qualities herself as first superior of the new St Monica's convent, founded largely through her efforts in 1609, whose chronicle (see THIMELBY, Winefrid), relates her story. MS of her life of Clement at the Priory of Our Lady, Hassocks, Sussex; selec. in John Morris, *The Troubles of our Catholic Forefathers* (sic), I, 1872, repr. 1970.

Shirreff, Emily Anne Eliza, 1814–97, educationalist. Sister of Maria GREY, she was the elder da. of Elizabeth (Murray) and Rear-Admiral William Henry S., who took the family to various postings in Europe, including Gibraltar. She was educ. by a governess at home and briefly at a boarding-school in Paris. When the family returned to England in 1834 she pub. *Letters from Spain and Barbary*, 1835 or '36, and a novel, *Passion and Principle*, 1841, both written jointly with her sister. They later collaborated on *Thoughts on Self-Culture, Addressed to Women*, 1850, where they argued that defective EDUCATION and inactive lives were the main reasons for women's lack of power and that acceptance of the 'degrading error' of marriage as being indispensable to women's happiness prevented self-improvement and independence. ES elaborated her principles and suggested a plan of study for girls educ. at home under their mother's supervision in *Intellectual Education and Its Influence on the Character and Happiness of Women*, 1858. She was for a short time principal of Emily Davies' women's college at Hitchin and helped her sister found the Women's Education Union in 1871. From 1872 to 1896 she was a member of the Council of the Girls' Public Day School Company. She helped establish and from 1875 was President of the Froebel Society, lecturing and writing extensively on the kindergarten system and arguing for the necessity of raising the social status of female teachers. Her articles in *The Contemporary Review* (Aug. 1870, June 1871) and the *Fortnightly Review* (July 1873) stress the connection between higher education and widening the scope of employment for women. E. W. Ellsworth's *Liberators of the Female Mind*, 1979, discusses the work of both sisters.

Shockley, Ann (Allen), novelist and short-story writer, anthologist, librarian, b. in 1927 in Louisville, Ky, da. of Bessie (Lucas) and Henry A., social workers who encouraged her passion for books. She began to write and took her first newspaper job in junior high school. While an undergraduate at Fisk Univ. (BA, 1948) she wrote for the *Louisville Defender* and published her first short stories. She took a degree in library science (Case Western Reserve Univ., 1959), free-lanced for various newspapers and periodicals, then returned to Fisk, 1969, where she worked in the library's Special Negro Collection, becoming associate librarian, university archivist, associate professor, and director of the Black Oral History Program. She is divorced with two children. She has published many important monographs – *A History of Public Library Services to Negroes in the South*, 1960, *The Administration of Special Negro Collections*, 1970, repr. 1974, and *A Manual for the Black Oral History Program*, 1971. She also coedited *Living Black American Authors: A Biographical Directory*, 1973, and *Handbook of Black Librarianship*, 1977. Of her *Afro-American Women Writers, 1746–1933: An Anthology and Critical Guide*, 1988, AAS writes, 'I shared a personal empathy with many of those women whose problems mirrored my own and those of women writers throughout the centuries: the absence of what Virginia WOOLF called "a room of one's own" and the money to support it.' *Loving Her*, 1974, AAS's first novel, is an inter-racial lesbian romance. *The Black and White of It*, 1980, repr. with two new stories, 1987, 'the first collection of short stories about lesbians written by an Afro-American woman', was nominated for the American Library Association Task Force Book Award, 1980. The anxieties of 'the life', loneliness and fear of exposure, are set against the sexual pleasure and emotional nurturance of lesbianism; AAS looks at racism in the women's movement, homophobia in the black community, and self-denial in lesbians. *Say Jesus and Come to Me*, 1982, set in Nashville, where AAS lives, portrays the relationship between an exploitative lesbian evangelist and an inexperienced singer. AAS's stories have been published in journals such as *Feminary*, *Sinister Wisdom*, *Black World*, *Essence*. Her study 'The Black lesbian in American literature: an overview,' appeared in *Conditions*, 5, 1979. Bibliography by Rita B. Dandridge in *Black American Literature Forum*, 21, 1987.

Shore, Arabella, *c.* 1820/3–after 1900, poet, **Louisa Catherine**, 1824–95, poet, **Margaret Emily**, 1819–39, diarist; the daughters of Margaret Anne (Twopeny) and Thomas S., 1793–1863, an independent clergyman who spent most of his life as a schoolmaster. The girls were educ. at home with their two brothers, living in Bedfordshire and, later, the New Forest. In 1838 the family went to Madeira for MES's health; she died there of TB. She wrote poetry, short fictions, essays on natural science for the *Penny Magazine* (1838), and, most notably, a detailed and lively journal of her last eight years, ed. by her sisters as *The Journal of Emily Shore*, 1891. Now back in England, the sisters were encouraged not to 'overwork their minds', and did not begin publishing until the mid 1850s, after the death of their parents and brother. LCS had spent some time from home, in Fulham, where she met Fanny KEMBLE and Sara COLERIDGE, and also in Paris, 1851–3. During the Crimean War, she composed a poem which, unknown to the author, AS titled 'War Music' and sent to *The Spectator*, where it was published. This led to *War Lyrics*, 1855, 'by A. and L.', which included LCS's 'When She Went Forth' on Florence NIGHTINGALE, and 'The Maiden at Home' by AS. 'Gemma of the Isles', 1859, is a long narrative poem by LCS; some of AS's short poems also appear, among them the (autobiographical?) poem 'The Ungifted'. LCS's *Hannibal A Drama*, 1861, was well received, but after their next joint vol., *Fra Dolcino*, 1870 (including AS's crime-of-passion narrative, 'Annette Meyers'), she lost interest in publishing, feeling increasingly that they had no audience. AS, however, persisted to produce several more vols. by one or both 1890–1900. Both sisters were actively interested in social questions concerning the position of women: LCS wrote an article for the *Westminster Review* (July 1874), twice repr. as 'The Citizenship of Women Socially Considered'; while AS wrote 'An Answer to Mr John Bright's Speech on the Women's SUFFRAGE' (July 1877). See the memoir of LCS by AS in *Poems*, 1897.

Shotlander, Sandra, playwright, actor, short-story writer b. 1941 in Melbourne, Victoria, third da. of Mollie (Buckley), accountant, and Lionel S., actuary. After her BA from Melbourne Univ. (1963), she spent one resident year at the National Theatre Drama School (1967) before establishing 'The Plantagenets', a theatre-in-education group which she directed for seven years, and 'Mime and Mumbles', one of Australia's first theatres for the deaf. Since then, she has worked extensively in theatre in England, Australia and the USA. Her first play, *Framework*, written after a year at the Women Writers' Centre in Cazenovia, NY, was a co-winner at the Meridian Gay Theatre (NY) International Playreading Competition; it was produced there in 1984 and at several theatres in Australia. SS then directed the premiere production of *Blind Salome* in Melbourne, 1985, and is now working on a play (*Angels of Power*) about women's alignment over the issue of IVF and new reproductive technologies. Her stories have been pub. in *Ash*, *Compass* and *Imprint* magazines and several anthologies; Wild Iris press (USA) and Yackandandah Press (Australia) have pub. her plays. She has had Australia Council writing grants, and is presently teaching in Melbourne. See Rosemary Curb in Lynda Hart, ed., *Making a Spectacle*, 1988.

Showes, Mrs, novelist for the MINERVA press. The title page of *Statira, or The Mother*, 1798, calls her 'author' of six *Interesting Tales ... from the German*, 1797. Statira, maltreated by her husband, takes 'what she had saved of her last year's pin-money' and leaves him: 'the weaker sex often exceed the stronger in stability and resolution.' Melodrama encroaches on psychological observation as she dons disguise to nurse her children through smallpox and dies of it herself, leaving him remorseful. *The Restless Matron, A Legendary Tale*, 1799, features a family curse entailed by the now ghostly Matron's husband: every girl born causes the death of her mother (for which in later life she is scape-goated) if the mother refuses to give birth in the Matron's room – which, since her reputation is undeservedly evil, they do for generations. At last the wife of another unworthy husband takes the Matron as mentor, lifting the curse. *Agnes de Lilien*, 1801, again 'From the German', has more estimable male characters but touches on similar concerns with the heroine's gradual restoration to her victimized mother: her first-person narrative opens interestingly through the eyes of her older self. More *Interesting Tales* (from French), 1805, have been ascribed to Mrs S.

Shuttle, Penelope Diane, poet, novelist, playwright, b. 1947 at Staines, Middx., da. of Joan (Lipscombe) and Jack Frederick S. She was educ. at a secondary modern (non-academic) school, worked as a shorthand-typist, and suffered from anorexia nervosa and agoraphobia; she had a breakdown at 19. She began publishing with *An Excusable Vengeance* (short novel), in *New Writers*, 6, 1967. Then came poetry, from the pamphlet *Nostalgia Neurosis and other Poems*, 1968, and novels, from *All the Usual Hours of Sleeping*, 1969. She has lived since 1970 with poet and novelist Peter Redgrove; they married in 1980, live in Cornwall, and practise Tantric Yoga, which bases itself on male and female sexual energies. They co-authored *The Hermaphrodite Album*, 1973 (poems individually unascribed, but including her award-winning verse sequence 'Witchskin'), on a 'Romance' and a 'Nautical Romance', 1974 and 1976, and *The Wise Wound: Menstruation and Every-woman*, 1978, a study which draws on PS's own experience of extreme pre-menstrual tension, and argues, says Hermione Lee, that 'the Curse is a blessing', often a time of intense creativity. PS and Redgrove see writing as a tool for examining self and the world, for 'confronting gender, fulfilling it, and transcending it'. She has written radio plays (including *The Girl Who Lost Her*

Glove, 1974, and *The Dauntless Girl*, 1978). She holds that feminism 'has begun to address itself to the task of showing how the two sexes can live in complementary partnership, with the male developing his feminine gifts, and the female developing her masculine ones'. In *The Mirror of the Giant*, 1980 (novel), a second wife learns by acceptance of womanhood and female bonding to exorcise her predecessor's haunting ghost. *The Orchard Upstairs*, 1980 (poems), includes 'Period', 'The Conceiving' ('Now / you are in the ark of my blood / in the river of my bones'), and 'First Foetal Movements of my Daughter, Summer 1976'. *The Lion from Rio*, 1986 (poems), deals with children's uncorrupted vision, their power to confine and liberate: 'Like all mothers / I wiped myself out', until her child's daily embrace rehumanizes the 'calm practical robot'. *Adventures with My Horse*, 1989, were called 'shapely odes to human sexual awareness'. See PS and Redgrove in Michelene WANDOR, ed., *On Gender and Writing*, 1983.

Sidgwick, Cecily Wilhelmine (Ullmann), Mrs Alfred Sidgwick, 'Mrs Andrew Dean', 1854–1934, novelist, b. Islington, London, da. of Wilhelmine Auguste (Flaase) and David U., merchant. In 1883 she m. Alfred S., Berkeley Fellow at Owen's College, Manchester, author of *Fallacies*, 1883, and other works on logic. She was later baptized and confirmed a Christian. Her family was of German–Jewish origin; several works draw on her many visits to and deep knowedge of Germany, especially her notable *Home Life in Germany*, 1908, which gives particular emphasis to women's lives. Her first pub. work was a romanticized BIOGRAPHY of Caroline Schlegel, 1889, followed the same year by a novel, *Isaac Eller's Money*, 'by Mrs Andrew Dean'. This deals wittily but sympathetically with the story of a North London German-Jewish community. Only a few of her 45 novels were pub. pseudonymously. Her titles include: *A Woman with a Future*, 1896, a moral tale of an erring wife where the reader's sympathies are subversively directed to the sinner; *Cynthia's Way*, 1901; *Scenes of Jewish Life*, 1904, which includes some penetrating satire on anti-Semitism; and *Below Stairs*, 1913, the story of a housemaid. In the 1920s she wrote several novels portraying 'strong-minded' women, including *Law and Outlaw*, 1921, *Victorian*, 1922, *The Bride's Prelude*, 1927, and *Cousin Ivo*, 1928. Her last novel, *Maid and Minx*, 1932, concerns a Yorkshire servant married to a gentleman whose family disapproves. When he divorces her, she is assisted in supporting their three children by a Cockney woman neighbour. She also wrote two collaborative works: *The Children's Book of Gardening*, 1909, with Mrs Paynter, and a novel, *The Black Knight*, 1920, with Crosbie Garstin. She died at her home in St Buryan, Cornwall.

Sidgwick, Ethel, 1877–1970, novelist and children's dramatist. B. in Rugby, Warwicks., to Charlotte and Arthur S., she attended Oxford High School and studied music and literature privately. She pub. plays for children throughout her career, beginning with an adaptation of Thackeray, 1909; three collections followed, 1913, 1922, 1926. Her 14 novels, beginning with *Promise*, 1910, usually aim, by presenting a vast array of characters, to portray cross-sections of society. *Jamesie*, 1918, describes the impact of WWI and social change on an aristocratic family, culminating in the title character's death in a wartime Channel crossing. (This epistolary novel includes letters written by Jamesie's suffragette aunt, who refuses to perpetuate her mother's desire for 'worship' from her husband in exchange for having 'filled' his 'nest', instead wanting to 'see things fairer to all women.') In her last novel, *Dorothy's Wedding: A Tale of Two Villages*, 1931, a schoolmistress marries 'with the assistance of the entire population' and amid great scandal. In *A Lady of Leisure*, 1914, the genteel heroine, 'burdened' with 'the terrible inheritance of intellect', finally marries the man she loves after her friend rejects him, her father observing that 'it is generally upon the woman that the burden of judgment must fall'. ES also wrote a biography of her aunt, Eleanor Sidgwick, 1938.

Sidhwa, Bapsi, novelist, b. 1936 in Karachi, now Pakistan, da. of Tehmina and Peshotan Bhandara, whose family has been in business in Lahore for generations. Prevented by childhood polio from attending regular school, BS matriculated as a private student at 13, then, recovering completely, graduated from Kinnaird College for Women, Lahore. Her second husband is Noshir R. S., whose father, R. K. S., played a major role in the Indian freedom struggle. She has three children, and, apart from writing, devotes her time to social work. Her first novel, *The Crow Eaters*, 1978, since translated into Urdu and Russian, gives an intimate, humorous account of the life of a Parsee business family in Lahore during the early twentieth century, shown, in Faredoon Junglewalla, the family patriarch who employs corrupt business practices, rules over his wife and children with an iron hand, but must continually battle with his widowed mother-in-law. *The Bride*, 1983, won the Patras Bokhari Award of the Pakistan Academy of Letters, 1986. It portrays a Muslim woman married off by her foster father into a tribal family in the mountainous areas of the Pakistan frontier, describing in harrowing detail the oppression of tribal women because of male allegiance to notions of family honour and clan loyalty: 'A wife was a symbol of status, the embodiment of a man's honour and the focus of his role as provider. A valuable commodity and dearly bought'. Zaitoon, the bride, chased across the mountains by her Kohistani in-laws, who would rather kill her than let her return to her father, 'had no more control over her destiny than a caged animal'. *Ice-Candy Man*, 1988, set in Lahore at the time of the partition of India, describes difference, division, violence, imagination and political evolution through the eyes of polio-stricken Lenny, a middle-class Parsee girl.

Sigerson, Dora, later Shorter, 1866–1918, poet, painter and sculptor, b. Dublin, da. of Hester (Varian), poet and novelist, and George Sigerson, surgeon and Gaelic scholar. Her younger sister, Hester (Sigerson) Piatt, also became a writer. They were educ. at home in a cultured and fiercely Republican household. DS's first published work appeared in the Catholic *Irish Monthly* and her first book, *Verses*, in 1893. In 1896 she m. Clement Shorter, critic and editor of the *Illustrated London News*, and went to live in London. Although she was active in London literary circles, meeting Meredith, Hardy (who wrote introductions to her work) and Swinburne, she was chronically homesick, writing melancholic and highly patriotic verse. Like her friends Kathleen TYNAN and Alice FURLONG, she used Irish themes and images belonging to the renaissance in Irish literature. She was also close friends with American poet Louise GUINEY. She pub. over twenty volumes of verse, including *The Fairy Changeling*, 1898, *Ballads and Poems*, 1899, and *The Troubadour*, 1910. Her BALLADS, many of which recounted Irish legends, were her most admired achievement. Irish society is also reflected in her sculpture, the best of which is a memorial group to the Easter Rebellion patriots of 1916, now in the Dublin cemetery where she is buried. DS was physically and mentally debilitated by her work for the prisoners and defence after the Rebellion, her responses to which are recorded in *The Tricolour*, posthumously pub. in 1922.

Sigourney, Lydia Howard (Huntley), 1791–1865, poet, b. Norwich, Conn., da. of Zerviah (Wentworth) and Ezekiel H., gardener. Her father's employer, Mrs Daniel Lathrop, introduced her to poetry and arranged for her to be educ. in 'female seminaries' in Hartford. With a friend, she opened a school for young women in Norwich and then one in Hartford, which excluded the 'ornamental branches' and offered an advanced curriculum. She was a lifelong friend of Emma WILLARD. In 1815 her *Moral Pieces* appeared, the first of over 50 published vols. In 1819 she m. Charles S., wealthy businessman. After her marriage she pub. anon., her husband fearing for his reputation if his wife were known as a poet. Many of her poems supported charitable causes such as Greek war relief and Indian missions. In 1822 she pub. *Traits of the Aborigines of America*, Indian tales in blank verse based on the work of Heckewelder and Schoolcraft. Her *Biography of Pious Persons* followed in 1832 and *Letters to Young Ladies*, 1833. Failure of the family finances in the 1830s led her to publish under her own name and her prosperous years began. *Poems*, 1834 (later enlarged as *Select Poems*), contains much of her best work, and she was hailed as a 'female Milton' and the 'Christian Pindar'. She ed. an ANNUAL, *The Religious Souvenir*, in 1839 and 1840, and her name appeared on the title page of *Godey's Lady's Book* from 1840–42. In 1840 she visited Europe and met Maria EDGEWORTH, Wordsworth and Carlyle; and *Pleasant Memories of Pleasant Lands*, 1842, records her travels. She returned to Indian themes in *Pocahontas and Other Poems* 1841. In the 1850s she wrote books on the death of her son Andrew in *The Faded Hope*, 1853, on old age in *Past Meridian*, 1854, and Bible studies in *The Daily Counsellor*, 1850. In her autobiography, *Letters of Life*, pub. posthumously, 1866, she recognized the limitations of her verse: 'If there is a Kitchen in Parnassus, my Muse has surely officiated there as a woman of all work.' See Gordon S. Haight, 1930, for her life; Emily Stipes Watts, *The Poetry of American Women*, 1977, for a critical discussion. There is no modern edition.

Silko, Leslie (Marmon), poet and novelist, b. in 1948 in Albuquerque, New Mexico, of Laguna, Mexican and white heritage, to Virginia and Lee H. M. While her parents worked, LMS was cared for by her grandmother, Lillie Stagner, and her great-grandmother Helen Romero, both of whom cherished stories from the 'old days' and who influenced her identification with Laguna traditions. Raised on a Pueblo Indian Reservation, she commuted from Laguna to school in Albuquerque (a round trip of 100 miles, because her father refused to send the children to Indian residential school) until she was 16, then entered the Univ. of Mexico (BA in English, 1969). She began law school, but withdrew to teach literature and to write. Divorced from John S., she has two sons. Several short stories and a collection of poems, *Laguna Woman*, appeared in 1974. She lived in Alaska for a time, where she wrote *Ceremony*, 1977, a witty, tense novel in which a despairing and homeless WWII veteran of mixed blood encounters ancient tribal rituals modified to contemporary circumstances. The eerily changing landscape of Alaska is setting and character in 'Storyteller', a short story telling in varied narrative modes an old man's dream and a young woman's revenge on the store man who gave her parents poison not alcohol in exchange for their rifle. This story among others, poems, legends, songs, essays and old family photos are gathered in *Storyteller*, 1981, which integrates the rhythm and language of traditional stories with LMS's intense clarity and the 'bitterness of Indian feeling against the thefts and betrayals of white colonialists'. Anne Wright, ed., *Delicacy and Strength of Lace*, 1985, is LMS's correspondence with poet James Wright. Critical biography by Per Seyersted, 1980. See Kate Shanley Vangen in Bob Scholer, ed., *Coyote Was Here*, 1984, and Roberta Rubenstein, *Boundaries of the Self*, 1987.

Simcoe, Elizabeth Posthumous (Gwillim), 1766–1851, diarist. Her mother, Elizabeth

(Spinckes), d. at her birth, her father, Thomas G., seven months earlier. An heiress, brought up by an aunt in Devon to love nature and historical study, she m. in 1782 her uncle's godson John Graves Simcoe, 14 years her senior, later first Lieutenant-Governor of Upper Canada. Sailing with him and two of her six children in 1791, she kept a frontier DIARY for five years at and around Quebec, Niagara and York (now Toronto). A fine mapmaker and artist, she took sketches and notes on the spot and wrote up a narrative rich in data on history, wild life and scenery (no degree of physical hardship could spoil her aesthetic pleasure). She admired Frances BROOKE (as introduction to this life) and Indian council speakers (for 'well expressed fine sentiments' – translated – and for 'reliance on the Great Spirit'). After her return home she bore more children, kept another diary of which little survives, continued to love travel, and dominated her daughters during long widowhood. *Canadian diary* (part pub. 1896) ed. Mary Quayle Innis, 1965; life by Marcus Van Stern, 1968.

Simcox, Edith J., 1844–1901, English journalist and activist, only da. of Jemima (Haslope) and F. George Price S. Soundly educ., she acquired a good knowledge of French and German at school, and taught herself Latin and the rudiments of Greek, later learning Italian and Flemish for her international trade union activities. The range and distinction of her knowledge was extraordinary, covering artistic and literary as well as social and political issues. She was a contributor to the *Academy* for more than 25 years, initially using the pseudonym H. Lawrenny. From 1875 to 1884 she ran a successful shirt and collar manufacturing co-operative in Soho with her friend Mary Hamilton. They employed women under decent conditions in an industry that had become, since the invention of the sewing machine, one of the worst sweated trades. Her account of this experience, 'Eight Years of Co-operative Shirtmaking', appeared in *The Nineteenth Century*, June 1884. She was one of the first women delegates to the Trades Union Congress, Glasgow, 1875, and several times attended international labour congresses, which she reported for the *Manchester Guardian*. Her socialist principles are evident in *Natural Law: An Essay in Ethics*, 1877. As a member of the London School Board, she fought for quality compulsory secular EDUCATION for all children. In the course of writing a review of *Middlemarch* for the *Academy*, she met George ELIOT. Her feelings for the novelist developed into a passionate intensity: her love was 'idolatrous', to use her own word. The unpub. 'Autobiography of a Shirt Maker' is essentially a record of her devotion. After Eliot's death she pub. *Episodes in the Lives of Men, Women and Lovers*, 1882, which, though disguised and set in a fictional framework, expresses her love and grief. See K. A. McKenzie, *ES and George Eliot*, 1961. Her only other major work is *Primitive Civilisations, or Outline of the History of Ownership in Archaic Communities*, 1894.

Sime, Jessie **Georgina**, 1868–1958, novelist, writer of short fiction and essays, lecturer and feminist. B. in Scotland, she was da. of James S., great-niece of Margaret OLIPHANT and Sir Daniel Wilson (a principal of the Univ. of Toronto), both writers. She moved in early childhood to London, and was educ. at home, then briefly at Queen's College, London. She also studied music in Berlin for three years. After a brief singing career she worked with her father as a reader for Macmillan publishers. She wrote reviews for the *Athenaeum*, a column for *Pall Mall*, and short stories, and made translations from French and German. Briefly a reader for Nelson publishers in Edinburgh, she spent some time in France and Germany. In 1907 she moved to Montréal. She published novels, essays, and short stories in British and North

American periodicals, and lectured in Canada and the USA. Active in the Canadian Women's Press Club and as President of the Montréal branch of the Canadian Authors' Association, she also helped to found the Montréal branch of PEN. A realistic writer long before the much heralded Canadian realists Morley Callaghan, Raymond Knister, and Frederick Philip Grove, GS dealt with the harsh realities of working-class life and immigrant experience. *Our Little Life, A Novel of To-day*, 1921, is a moving story of a middle-aged single Irish-Canadian seamstress's love for an upper-class British immigrant who fails in his attempt to make a new life in Canada. It vividly portrays a variety of individuals in a rundown Montréal neighbourhood. *Sister Woman*, 1919, stories and sketches of working women, describes the changing role of women during WWI. 'Munitions' depicts the exhilaration of women for whom domestic service has been the only possible employment before the war, on finding work in a munitions factory. 'An Irregular Union' conveys the conflicting emotions of an independent woman caught up in a longstanding affair with a married colleague and forced by an unwilling separation from him to take stock of her situation, which had seemed, until then, to give her the best of two worlds, love and independence. *Orpheus in Quebec*, 1942, compares the old world and the new and speculates on the future of art in Québec.

Simmonds, or Simmons, **Martha** (Calvert), d. 1665, pamphleteer, sister of Giles C. and wife of Thomas S., both printers. In 1655 she pub. *When the Lord Jesus came to Jerusalem* and *A Lamentation for the Lost Sheep*, which tells of her 14 years of spiritual uncertainty before conversion, and bids her reader 'come out from among these Idoll dumb Shepherds that feed themselves, but not you, and if you put not into their moths they will soon shew violence to you.' That year or the next she collaborated with James Nayler and Hannah Stranger (or Stringer) in *O England, thy time is come*. She is best known for her involvement with Nayler's notorious Bristol re-enactment of Christ's entry into Jerusalem, 1656. She died on her way to Maryland. See Kenneth Carroll in *Journal of the Friends' Hist. Soc.*, 53, 1972.

Simons, Beverley, playwright, fiction-writer, b. 1938 in Flin Flon, Manitoba, and taken to Vancouver at 12. She studied music intensively and while at high-school won an award for the one-act *Twisted Roots*, 1956, pub. in Anthony Frisch, ed., *First Flowering*, 1958. She attended the Banff School of Fine Arts and McGill Univ. (where she joined an experimental THEATRE GROUP and wrote two one-act plays), before taking her BA from the Univ. of BC. Early plays, *My Torah, My Tree* and *The Elephant and the Jewish Question* (unpub., unproduced), reflect her concern with her own heritage. Study in the Far East on a Canada Council grant, 1968, was 'a rich, dense two months, the equivalent of a year'. BS married an attorney and has three children. Because her work is difficult to perform, it is little known. *Crabdance*, 1969 (videotape 1977), is reminiscent of Samuel Beckett: introverted, with few characters, depending heavily on its symbolic setting. *The Green Lawn Rest Home*, 1973, is set in a nursing home where identity seems precarious. *Preparing*, 1975, a trilogy of short pieces ('Prologue', 'Crusader', 'Triangle'), is a formally experimental illustration of different ways of preparing for death. *Leela Means to Play*, 1976, draws on oriental theatre, emphasizing ritual through the use of many symbolic devices. A casebook on BS appears in *Canadian Theatre Review*, Winter 1976. She has since turned to other kinds of writing, for example an unpub. children's story, *The Boy With a Piece of Dark*; a novel, she says, unlike a play, 'will find its audience' once a publisher is found.

Simpson, Helen de Guerry, 1897–1940, novelist, poet, playwright, historical biographer, musician, b. Sydney, NSW, da. of Anne (de Laurent) and E.P.S. Her maternal grandfather was a French marquis who settled in Goulburn in the mid-1800s. Educ. at Rose Bay Convent, Sydney, she left for England in 1913 intending to enrol at Oxford Univ. but joined the WRNS during WWI and, fluent in five languages, worked as a decoder in the Admiralty. Afterwards she studied music at Oxford. She was also an expert on domestic science (and pub. three books on the subject), a good horsewoman and fencer, and maintained an interest in witchcraft and demonology. In England she became a well-known novelist, BBC radio broadcaster and later politician, standing (unsuccessfully) as the Liberal candidate for the Isle of Wight. She m. Denis Browne (nephew of novelist 'Rolf Boldrewood') in 1927, and returned to Australia on several occasions, most notably in 1937 when she gave a series of ABC radio talks. Of her 15 novels, two have Australian content, *Boomerang*, 1932, winner of the James Tait Memorial Prize, and *Under Capricorn*, 1937, while book III of *The Woman on the Beast*, 1933, is set in Australia in 1999. A modern 'Renaissance' woman, HS's remarkably diverse interests and talents extended to her writing. *Boomerang* is a family saga drawing upon HS's own family. It sweeps through history and across countries with a detached, often amused, narrative voice; events and personalities recur like boomerangs. *Under Capricorn*, set in colonial NSW, concerns the marital disruption of a beautiful Irish aristocrat and her ex-convict husband; its subtle, complex psychological dimensions appealed to Alfred Hitchcock, who made it into a film in 1949. HS's work includes a vol. of poetry, *Philosophies in Little*, 1921, and the novels *Acquittal*, 1925, *Cups, Wands and Swords*, 1927, *Mumbudget*, 1928, *The Female Felon*, 1935, *Saraband for Dead Lovers*, 1935, and *Maid No More*, 1940. With Clemence DANE she wrote biographies, including *A Woman Among Wild Men*, 1938, an account of Mary KINGSLEY. She also pub. a translation of French verse, a number of plays including *A Man of His Time*, 1923, about Benvenuto Cellini, and many DETECTIVE stories.

Simpson, Mary, *c.* 1617–47, religious autobiographer, of Norwich. On her deathbed she apparently gave her profession of faith and account of her life to John Collings, her Presbyterian-inclined parish minister, who published it as *Faith and Experience*, 1649. It records the years of uncertainty that preceded her acceptance of an orthodox Calvinism, and the physical illnesses that followed it. 'I lookt upon Christ as a husband, but yet as a husband going a Journey, and hid behind a curtaine, so that my soule was as the spouse restlesse in looking out to inquire after him.' Collings, who preached her funeral sermon (attached) probably edited her account.

Sinclair, Catherine, 1800–64, Evangelical novelist, b. Edinburgh, fourth da. of Diana (Macdonald), who was second wife of Sir John S. CS never married, but acted as secretary to her father from the age of 14 until he died (1835), whereupon she began her own writing, in between her numerous charitable works. Initially she wrote for her nephew, the most popular book being *Holiday House: a series of tales*, 1839, really a conversion-narrative. She wrote books on Shetland, 1840, Scotland, 1840, as well as many more tales for young people and didactic novels like the fiercely anti-Catholic *Beatrice; or, the Unknown Relatives*, 1852. Other novels, such as *Modern Flirtations; or, a Month at Harrowgate*, 1841, and *Cross Purposes*, 1855, are interestingly prefaced by CS's views on the current moral status of fiction-reading (and writing). Despite their 'improving' aim and predictable plotting, her works reveal a lively, intelligent writer of acerbic wit and unusual insight into human motivation.

Sinclair, May, Mary Amelia St Clair Sinclair, 1863–1946, novelist, b. Rock Ferry, Cheshire, only da. and youngest child of Amelia and William S., a wealthy shipowner. When MS was seven her father went bankrupt and her parents separated; she lived with her mother until the latter's death in 1901. She was self-educ. apart from one year at Cheltenham Ladies' College, where Dorothea Beale recognized her talent. Her interest in Idealism and the work of T. H. Green was developed in *A Defence of Idealism*, 1917, and *The New Idealism*, 1922. Working at the Medico-Psychological clinic of London from 1913, she encountered Freud's work. Her first novel, *Audrey Craven*, 1897, features a heroine who is overwhelmed by (rather than able to grow through) love, art, nature and religion because 'she had never really given herself up to any of them'. Though interested in the moral progress of her characters through self-denial, as in the best-seller *The Divine Fire*, 1904, she was also interested in how circumstances or personal weakness can cause defeat. Both *Mr and Mrs Nevill Tyson*, 1897, and *The Helpmate*, 1907, reveal the destructive influence of the Victorian ideal of marriage, particularly for women. A member of the Woman Writers' Suffrage League, she argued for women's SUFFRAGE in her pamphlet 'Feminism', 1912. In *The Creators*, 1910, she exposed the way men denigrate women's creativity and showed the difficulty for a woman of sustaining her art against the demands of family. She worked for the relief forces in Belgium and her *Journal of Impressions in Belgium*, 1915, admits to the excitement for her as a woman in being so exposed to 'reality'. In *The Tree of Heaven*, 1917, she traced the shock of war on the family and society, focusing the ways women were profoundly affected by it. *The Three Sisters*, 1914, which drew on her interest in the BRONTËS – she had pub. a critical study of them in 1911 – marked the beginning of her interest in exploring unconscious motivation, drawing on psycho-analysis, and of her discovery of a form in which to express it. In an enthusiastic review, 1918, of Dorothy RICHARDSON's *Pilgrimage in The Egoist*, she coined the phrase 'stream of consciousness'. Her semi-autobiographical novels, *Mary Olivier*, 1919, and *The Life and Death of Harriet Frean*, 1922, place her with Virginia WOOLF and Richardson as a major modernist writer who saw the connection between experimental writing and her own 'difference' as a woman. Later novels, *Arnold Waterlow*, 1924, *The Rector of Wyck*, 1925, and *The Allinghams*, 1927, are less interesting. In the 1920s she contracted Parkinson's disease and suffered physical and mental deterioration. Generally acknowledged in the 1920s as one of the most important writers of her day, the decline of her reputation is an enigma. See Hrisey Zegger's study, 1976.

Sipolo, Jully, contemporary Solomon Islands poet, from Munda, New Georgia. Her first collection, *Civilized Girl*, 1981, explores the dilemma of the westernized Pacific Islander: 'Who am I? ... / make up your mind'. Her poetry is also alive to the difficulties and conflicting emotions that complicate women's lives, often torn between work and children: 'No time for a cuddle, or play', whilc 'A Man's World' contrasts brother and sisters: 'My brother can sit on the table / I mustn't ... / A brother can make a living out of his sisters'. Her second collection, *Praying Parents*, 1986, illustrated by herself and John Z. Finan, contains poems about nuclear exploitation of the Pacific, and explores the ironies of 'development'. 'You [illegible] my resources / In the name of development'. She has been General Secretary of the Solomon Islands YWCA and is active in the international peace movement. M. with three children, she is the first Solomon Islands woman to have a book of her own poetry published. She has also jointly edited *Mi Mere*, 1983, an ANTHOLOGY of SI women's writing, which carries the note: 'The writers of several works in this book chose to remain anonymous because of the very real constraints on freedom of expression by women which still exist in Solomon Islands societies'.

Sitwell, Edith Louisa, DBE, 1887–1964, poet, critic, anthologist, biographer, autobiographer, b. in Scarborough, Yorks., da. of 18-year-old Lady Ida (Denison) and Sir George S., and sister of Osbert and Sacheverell, later her collaborators in several literary projects. They went to Eton; she was educ. at Renishaw Hall, Derbyshire, by a series of governesses. Childhood, she said, was 'hell': both parents were emotionally difficult; she was forced to wear corrective metal braces (her 'Bastille') for both her back and her nose; she was 'in disgrace for being a female'. In 1903, poet, translator, and music-lover Helen Rootham became her governess and introduced her to serious poetry, both English and French. ES grew up loving Christina ROSSETTI and later thoroughly admired Gertrude STEIN, but as a young woman thought that 'Women's poetry, with the exception of SAPPHO ... and "Goblin Market" and a few deep and concentrated, but fearfully incompetent poems of Emily DICKINSON, is *simply awful*'. She made herself a poet in the classical line, at 17 making a pilgrimage to Swinburne's grave, 'taking with me a bunch of red roses, a laurel wreath, and a jug of milk' for a 'libation' in the classical manner. At 26 she escaped to London, where she and Rootham shared a flat and worked on poetry (Rootham on her translation of Rimbaud's *Illuminations*, pub. with intro. by ES, 1932, later set to music by Benjamin Britten and made into a ballet by Frederick Ashton). ES's poems appeared first in the *Daily Mail*, 1915, shortly in small collections, *The Mother*, 1915, *Clown's Houses*, 1918, *The Wooden Pegasus*, 1920, whose contents, with increasing technical sophistication, claim the territory of childishness in perception and voice. In 1916 she launched, with her brothers, the anthology *Wheels*: anti-war and anti-Georgian, it went through five 'cycles', 1916–21, printing poems by, among others, Aldous Huxley, Nancy CUNARD, Iris TREE, Wilfred Owen. Thought radically anti-establishment, it confirmed ES in the revolutionary note she had drawn from the nineties and the French. *Façade*, 1923, notoriously carried her forward in this: inspired by Cocteau's *Parade*, 1917, she collaborated with composer William Walton on a multi-media performance of a suite of poems of remarkable technical bravado: abstract, rhythmically unorthodox, heavily and satirically coded, imagistically surreal, they frame the Victorian and the contemporary in a radically revisionary light. The press was scandalized; Noel Coward shortly parodied the poet as 'Hernia Whittlebot', 'this juggernautic mite of inspiration'. In the twenties she lived in Paris, frequented Sylvia BEACH's bookshop, and met Stein, 1925. Other post-war works move away from rhythmically exuberant satire: *The Sleeping Beauty*, 1924 (influenced by the Ballets Russes, especially *Petrouchka*), and *Troy Park*, 1925, nostalgically evoke childhood scenes and modulate into permanence her theme of lost innocence. 'Metamorphosis', 1929, develops a darker tone, not now of child, but of seer or prophet. In works following this, notably *Gold Coast Customs*, 1929 (dedicated to Rootham), ES attacks 'The Rotten Alleys where beggars groan' and foretells the day 'When the rich man's gold and the rich man's wheat / Will grow in the street, that the starved may eat'. Much depicted (by Roger Fry, Alvaro Guevara, Cecil Beaton, Wyndham Lewis), as elegant, aesthetic, cosmetic, ES was painted in 1936 by her friend Pavel Tchelitchew (whom she loved, painfully) as a sybil, pale and inward. Her voice of the late 1920s foretells that of the later poems, of the widely admired 'Still Falls the Rain', written in 'The Raids, 1940, Night and Dawn', and of her 'Three Poems for the Atomic Age', including 'Dirge for the New Sunrise (Fifteen minutes past eight o'clock, on the morning of Monday the 6th of August 1945)': 'The eyes that saw, the lips that kissed, are gone / Or black as thunder lie and grin at the murdered Sun. . . . Gone is the heart of Man.' ES wrote her first biography, a much attacked life of Pope, in 1930. Others followed: ELIZABETH I, Queen VICTORIA, Elizabeth again with Mary Queen of Scots, and a novel about Jonathan Swift, *I Live Under a Black Sun*, 1937. *Aspects of Modern Poetry*, 1934, gives her views of several contemporaries; *A Poet's Notebook*, 1943, gives fragments from her favourite and shaping authors. ES published several anthologies; her own *Collected Poems* appeared in 1930, 1954. She was the first poet to be made DBE, 1954. In 1955 she became a convert to Roman Catholicism. See her AUTOBIOGRAPHY, *Taken Care Of*, 1965; memoir by her secretary, Elizabeth Salter, 1967; lives by John Pearson, 1978, Geoffrey Elborn, 1981, Victoria Glendinning, 1981. Selected letters ed. John Lehmann and Derek Parker, 1970. Bibliography by Richard Fifoot, 2nd ed. 1971; studies by J. D. Brophy, 1968, Jean MacVean in *Agenda*, 21, 1983; P. Clements in *Baudelaire and the English Tradition*, 1985. Papers at Univ. of Texas, Yale, NYPL. Letters to Tchelitchew sealed away until AD 2000.

Skeete, Monica (Martineau), poet and short-story writer, b. 1920 in Grenada to Barbadian parents. She grew up in Barbados, where she now teaches history. She began publishing in *BIM*: poetry from vol. 2, 1945, in her birth name, stories from 1960. Her long dialect poem for the poet Frank Collymore on his 80th birthday appeared in *Savacou*, special issue, 1973. Of the five stories in her *Time Out*, 1978, for young people, three deal with teenage boys, two with older women who provoke outbreaks of carnival spirit: one by accepting (to her husband's disgust) the gift of a circus elephant, the other, Tantie Trophine, by resisting compulsory purchase of her house.

Skene, Felicia Mary Francis, 1821–99, poet, essayist, editor, campaigner for prison reform, b. Aix-en-Provence, youngest da. of Jane (Forbes) and James S., of old Scottish families; friends of Walter Scott. Educ. by a governess and at day school at Versailles, she also spent two years at a school in Leamington. She learnt modern Greek when her family moved to Greece in 1838, and pub. *The Isles of Greece and other poems*, 1843. Her first literary success was *Wayfaring Sketches among the Greeks and Turks*, 1847, which describes Athens and her journey back to England. In Oxford, where she settled, she pub. *The Divine Master*, 1852, which went into several editions, and supported the anti-vivisection work of her friend F.P. COBBE. In 1854 she organized home nursing in the cholera epidemic and corresponded with Florence NIGHTINGALE. Many of her short stories appeared in the *Churchman's Companion*, which she ed. 1862–80; she considered *Through the Shadows. A Test of the Truth*, 1888 (pseud. 'Erskine Moir'), and 1897 (pseud. 'Oxoniensis'), her most important religious work. From the 1850s she was a prison visitor, and in 1878 became the first woman officially so appointed. Her enlightened high church advocacy of humane treatment for prisoners and 'fallen women' is seen in such works as the pamphlet *Penitentiaries and Reformatories*, 1865. Her writings were much more various than 'prison issues', but her short sketches of prisoners in *Scenes from a Silent World*, 1889 (originally articles in *Blackwood's*, by 'Francis Scougal', a family name), is regarded as her best work. *Hidden Depths*, 1866, a novel also based on her own experience of prison work, realistically exposes the horrors surrounding prostitution. At her death she was acting editor of *The Argosy*. E. C. Richard's *FS at Oxford*, 1902, is an appreciative memoir.

Skinn, Ann (Masterman), *c.* 1747–89, novelist. Da. of Anne (Dawson) and Thomas M., first cousin of Henrietta SYKES, she m.,

1767, William S., attorney. She left him 16 months later and took a lover; after various wanderings she settled in London, where she published an unusual epistolary novel, *The Old Maid, or History of Miss Emily Ravenscroft* [1770]. She says the hateful old-maid aunt, booby uncle, and her own husband ('the greatest brute in nature') are drawn from life, the few tolerable male characters, perforce, from invention. Her heroine stabs an attacker through the hand with scissors (through the heart, she says, 'would not have signified' had she not cared for his wife); she sees marriage as a grim prospect, but cruelly teases the old maid and finds at last a worshipper to marry. Reviewers disliked the book; William S. secured a divorce and damages. AMS m. Irish officer Nicholas Forster, and is said to have written other works (she had promised one about herself), done needlework and run a day-school before dying in poverty at Margate. See Susan Staves in Schofield and Macheski, eds., essays, 1986.

Skinner, Cornelia Otis, 1901–79, dramatist, essayist, biographer and actress, b. in Chicago, only child of actors Maud (Durbin) and Otis S. After Baldwin School and two years at Bryn Mawr she dropped out to train at the Comédie Française, Paris (and attend lectures at the Sorbonne). She made her NYC debut in 1921, had her first play staged in 1925, and turned to dramatic monologues (including *The Wives of Henry VIII*, *The Loves of Charles II*, and *The Empress Eugenie*), later rewritten as pieces in which she played all the roles. She married Alden S. Blodget in 1928, and had a son. Her journalism included verse and satirical essays, highlighting the ridiculous in both the domestic and social arenas, and tirelessly poking fun at herself. (Jokes about 'things that men won't let us do' – like stirring a fire, tuning a radio, reading a map – are prefaced by reassurance: 'I don't want to do man's work. I don't even want the vote.') Collections are *That's Me All Over*, 1948, and *Bottoms Up*, 1955. With Emily Kimborough, her companion on an early foreign holiday, COS wrote up the trip for laughs in *Our Hearts Were Young and Gay*, 1942 (adapted as a play, by Jean KERR, and a film). She also wrote *Family Circle*, 1948 (both autobiography and family biography), the comedy hit *The Pleasure of His Company* (a joint work, produced 1958), in which she acted, and a life of Sarah Bernhardt, 1967.

Skinner, Mollie (Mary Louisa) 1876–1955, novelist, short-story writer, b. Perth, Western Australia, eldest da. of Jessie (Leake) and James Tierney S., army captain. She was educ. erratically in the UK, owing to the constant moves of her father's military career and her own weak eyesight. A highly qualified nurse, she worked in London and India during WWI: these experiences are described in her first book, *Letters of a V.A.D.*, 1918. She contributed sketches to the London *Daily Mail*, then worked as a journalist for the *West Australian*. She ran private hospitals of her own, including the convalescent-holiday home at Darlington where she met D. H. Lawrence in 1922 and formed the friendship and subsequent collaboration on the book for which she is best remembered, *The Boy in the Bush*, 1924 (adapted for television, 1984). Set in the outback in the late nineteenth century, it concerns the young, disaffected emigrant Jack Grant (originally based on MS's own troubled brother Jack), but was greatly altered by Lawrence, not always to her satisfaction. She pub. six other novels, including *Tucker Sees India*, 1937, *W–X Corporal Smith: A Romance of the A.I.F. in Libya*, 1941, *Where Skies are Blue*, 1946, and the historical novel *Black Swans*, 1925. As well as sketches and articles she wrote the collection of Aboriginal stories, *Men Are We*, 1927, and several unpub. novels, including 'Eve in the Land of Nod', extensively edited by Lawrence, who unfortunately did not encourage its publication. Her autobiography, *The Fifth Sparrow*, 1972, gives details of the collaboration. See Hilary Croxford Simpson's article in *Women's Studies International Quarterly*, 1979.

Slade, Caroline Beach (McCormick), 1886–1975, essayist, novelist, story writer. B. at Minneapolis, da. of William G. M., she was taken as a child to Saratoga Springs, NY, and educ. at Skidmore College. She m. John S., a lawyer who taught there, and later helped to train social-work students there. Her career lay in child welfare and children's courts; she was first director of the Saratoga County Board of Child Welfare. Her stories and half-dozen novels (written chiefly in retirement, after 1933) centre on the invisible US class system, on urban deprivation increased by the Depression, on the plight of women economically and socially trapped and lacking birth control, and the helplessness of social workers in the face of bureaucracy. The hero of *The Triumph of Willie Pond* [1940] (later *'Poor Relief', or ...*) recovers from consumption but decides to kill himself to save his family's welfare cheques. While he lies in a sanatorium the book focuses on his wife's struggles: a supportive women's network urges a daughter into the prostitution 'option'. The heroine of *Lilly Cracknell*, 1943, first met as a 'backward' pregnant 14-year-old, is gradually nudged into this option by poverty, gullibility and wrong-headed interventions. *Margaret*, 1946, exposes the patriarchal roots and wide-ranging personal effects of using sex for money and power: an immigrant father is 'deeply puzzled as he beat his daughter'; another feels dimly guilty when his daughter is raped; cowed mothers teach submission. Often criticized as programmatic, CS has remarkable feminist perception.

Slave narratives. Fugitive slaves pub. their stories as early as 1703 (John Saffin's *Adam Negro's Tryall*): these became a literary genre in the US ABOLITION period, 1830–60: Mary PRINCE was pub. in London, 1831. Men's narratives took the limelight, especially Frederick Douglass, 1845, and Josiah Henson, 1849 (1858 ed. intro. by H. B. STOWE, who modelled Uncle Tom on him). Martha G. BROWNE, ex-slave-owner, faked a slave narrative (pub. anon. 1857) out of concern at the lack of representation of women. Genuine women's narratives now surfacing include William Andrews, ed., *Six Women's Slave Narratives*, 1988, and other vols. in the Schomburg Library series. H. B. JACOBS observes, 'Slavery is ... far more terrible for women' (*Incidents in the Life of a Slave Girl*, 1861). Many narratives were written by amanuenses, yet retain vitality and individuality. Patterns are similar and dramatic: suffering in servitude, flight, then freedom. Most begin in the US South; Sojourner TRUTH's is an exception. Other important examples include Elizabeth KECKLEY's, and Sarah Hopkins Bradford's compilation, *Scenes in the Life of Harriet Tubman*, 1869. Tubman, 1821?–1913, was born a slave in Dorchester Co., Maryland. She worked as a field hand before escaping North in 1849; remarkably brave and resourceful, she is credited with helping more than 300 slaves escape through the Underground Railroad. She worked for the Union Army in roles from cook to spy, and in old age cared for children and the elderly. Harriet WILSON's *Our Nig*, 1859, long thought to be of the genre, is now recognized as the first novel by a black American woman. The narratives' tradition of closing on success is a feature purposefully adopted by Afro–American fiction-writers like Alice WALKER and Toni MORRISON. For recent work see Marjorie Pryse and Hortense J. Spillers, eds., *Conjuring: Black Women, Fiction, and Literary Tradition*. 1985; Minrose C. Gwin, *Black and White Women of the Old South*, 1985; Hazel V. Carby, *Reconstructing Womanhood: The Emergence of the Afro-American Woman Novelist*, 1987.

Sleath, Eleanor, author of six GOTHIC novels, now rare, pub. by MINERVA. Her first,

The Orphan of the Rhine (1798, repr. in Northanger Set, 1968) was called by the *Critical Review* a 'vapid and servile' Ann RADCLIFFE imitation. AUSTEN mocked it; it is often ungrammatical and confusingly written. Set in the seventeenth century, sympathetic towards the Catholic religion, it features disguises, suspected ghosts, desolate castles, and sensitive heroines of two generations persecuted by the same villain, proving at last 'the imbecility of vice' and 'the triumphant power of virtue'. ES improved in technique while repeating many of the same elements. *Who's the Murderer? or The Mysteries of the Forest*, 1802, set in Italy, highlights a body in a sack. *The Bristol Heiress, or The Errors of Education*, 1809, opens on debate over women's education and satire on English high society, but moves to a haunted Cumberland castle. In *The Nocturnal Minstrel, or The Spirit of the Wood*, 1810, facs. NY 1972, a beautiful 'widow', stoutly resisting pressures to re-marry, is saved by her husband's re-appearance in various mysterious disguises; the fifteenth century is convincingly depicted.

Slesinger, Tess, 1905–45, fiction-writer, screen-writer, b. in NYC to Jewish parents, only da. (with three elder brothers) of Augusta (Singer) and Anthony Slesinger. Her father was in the garment industry, her mother the director of a child-guidance clinic and a practising lay analyst, who advocated sexual freedom and self-expression. Educ. at the Ethical Culture School, Swarthmore College and Columbia Univ. (where she was taught by Dorothy SCARBOROUGH), she graduated in 1927. Next year she m. Herbert Solow, assistant editor of the *Menorah Journal* and friend of left-wing intellectuals. From 1930 TS's fiction appeared in journals like *The New Yorker* and *Scribner's*, and was praised for its sensitive, original handling of female sexuality and marital conflict. (Her own marriage was deteriorating.) *Story Magazine*, 1932, broke new ground for a mainstream US journal by printing her fictional account of abortion; it became the ending of her novel, *The Unpossessed*, 1934 (repr. 1984). TS's *Time: The Present*, 1935 (selected stories), was repr. with an extra piece as *On Being Told That Her Second Husband Has Taken His First Love*, 1971. In 1935 she moved to Hollywood, where her many filmscripts (only seven produced) included Pearl BUCK's *The Good Earth*, 1937. She m. Frank Davis, a left-wing producer at MGM, in 1936; their joint work included Betty SMITH's *A Tree Grows in Brooklyn*, 1945. TS had two children, and was active politically. She died of cancer. Twenty of her stories remain uncollected and her Hollywood novel unfinished (see Janet Sharistanian in *Mich. Quarterly Review*, 18, 1979). Papers at the Univ. of Delaware (Newark) and at Indiana, Harvard, and Columbia Univs. See Shirley Biagi in *Antioch Review*, 35, 1977.

Slosson, Annie (Trumbull), 1838–1926, short-story writer, b. Stonington, Conn., da. of Sarah A. and Gurdon T.; she m. Edward S. in 1867. Her stories of New England life were pub. in the *Atlantic*, *Harper's*, and several collections, including *The China Hunter's Club*, 1878, *Seven Dreamers*, 1891, *Dumb Foxglove*, 1893, *Story-Tell Lib*, 1900, and *A Local Colorist*, 1912. She was often compared to other local-colour writers, including S. O. JEWETT and M. W. FREEMAN. Her plots often turn on 'conversion' experiences that constitute a sentimentally psychologized revision of New England Calvinism. In 'Aunt Liefy', 1892, an outcast spinster rejoins the human community after being mistaken for the beloved sister of a dead woman. In 'How Faith Came and Went' (in *Seven Dreamers*), a mysterious young woman from nowhere befriends a doctor and his spinster sister, assuming the name of their dead sister, Faith. These nearly allegorical plots of mistaken identity emphasize AS's anti-Calvinist message that human relations are in themselves a form of grace.

AS's popularity waned with her later collections. Her local moralism became predictable and her use of dialect hardened into an inflexible mannerism, rather than an index of individual character.

Smart, Elizabeth, 1913–86, poet, novelist, critic. B. in Ottawa, da. of Louise (Parr) and Russell S., she attended private schools in Canada and studied drama in England (briefly attending the Univ. of London). Her interest in writing appears in her early journals; by 20 she was writing for the *Ottawa Journal*. Her interest in his poetry led to her meeting with English poet George Barker, the love of her life and father of her four children. She moved to England, 1943, remaining there except for a year as writer-in-residence at the Univ. of Alberta, 1982–3, and a year in Toronto, 1983–4. Her brilliant first novel, *By Grand Central Station I Sat Down and Wept*, 1945, repr. 1978, written in 1941 while she was pregnant with her first child, celebrates the beginning of her affair with Barker. Said by Brigid BROPHY to be 'one of the half-dozen masterpieces of poetic prose in the world', it is a lyrical novel marked by incantatory rhythm, evocative language, paradox, extravagant imagery, and a dense web of literary and classical allusion linking the unnamed protagonist's love with expressions of love throughout time. The book embarrassed ES's family, who attempted to suppress its sale in Canada; it received little public attention until the reissue of an extensively revised edition, 1966. ES made her living by writing, for *Vogue*, *Queen*, and other magazines, and for advertising agencies: she was literary editor of *Queen* for several years in the 1960s. She also wrote one cookbook and co-authored another. Generous and encouraging to younger writers, many of them women, she moved to Suffolk, 1968, to return to her own creative writing. She produced two volumes of poems – elliptical, wry, ironic, and conversational, suggestive of Stevie SMITH, whom ES admired (*Bonus*, 1977, and *Eleven Poems*, 1982) – one of poems and prose pieces (*In the Meantime*, 1984), and *The Assumption of the Rogues & Rascals*, 1978. Less lyrically intense than the first, this novel telescopes time and event: 20 years of working, writing, and bringing up children into a scant, 100-page memorial to life. 'The price of life is pain, since the price of comfort is death and damnation.' From the title of her first novel onward, ES expresses the paradoxical co-existence of the marvellous and the mundane, the sacred and the profane, in original, startling, elliptical language. See *Necessary Secrets*, 1986, journals, ed. Alice van Wart, and *Early Writings*, 1987. Interview with Eleanor Wachtel in *City Woman* (Toronto), summer 1980. Papers at the National Library of Canada.

Smedley, Agnes, 1892–1950, journalist, novelist and feminist, called by Emma GOLDMAN 'an earnest and true rebel'. She was b. in rural Missouri and raised in Trinidad, Col., da. of Sarah (Ralls), who died, worn out, when AS was 18, and Charles S., a hard-drinking, often absent labourer. Her educ. was patchy until, already a teacher, she went to Tempe Normal School, Ariz., in 1911. Though much afraid of having children, she married Ernest Brundin in 1912. She studied and taught at San Diego Normal School, was dismissed for socialism in 1916, divorced, and moved to NYC. Involvement with the nationalist movement of India led to her arrest in 1918, under the Espionage Act. In jail she wrote 'Cell Mates', stories inspired by other women there. She also wrote for *The Call* and Margaret SANGER's *Birth Control Review*. Settling in Germany in 1920, she lived with exiled revolutionary leader Virendranath Chattopadhyaya and helped set up Berlin's first birth-control clinic. She wrote her one, autobiographical novel, *Daughter of Earth*, for therapy when this relationship ended. Serialized in the *Frankfurter Zeitung*, printed as a book in

1929, hailed in *The Nation* as America's 'first feminist-proletarian novel', it asserts economic self-determination for women as the key to independence: an enterprising, probably prostitute aunt saves the family from destitution. In 1928 AS left for China. Travelling with the Red Army as it fought Chiang Kai-shek's Kuomintang, she became internationally known as a correspondent on *The Manchester Guardian* and other papers. Five of her books and most of her 330 known articles deal with the Revolution: *Chinese Destinies: Sketches of Present-Day China*, 1933, and *China's Red Army Marches*, 1934, describe the effects of political upheaval on individual lives, especially women's; *China Fights Back: An American Woman with the Eighth Route Army*, 1938, is based on her journals; *Battle Hymn of China*, 1943, combines history, autobiography and war reporting; her study of the Red Army's peasant commander-in-chief, *The Great Road: The Life and Times of Chu Teh* (Zhu De), 1956, dates back to the 1930s. Having returned to the US in 1941 for reasons of political tactics and chronic ill-health, exiled later by McCarthyism, AS died in England while hoping to return to China. Her ashes, exceptionally for a foreigner, lie in Beijing's Cemetery for Revolutionaries. Her books all have recent reprints. Papers at Chinese History Museum, Beijing, and (with photographic record) at Ariz. State Univ. *Portraits of Chinese Women in Revolution*, 1976, is an AS selec. ed. Janice R. and Stephen R. MacKinnon; lives by Ayako Ishigaki, Tokyo, 1967, and (definitive) by the MacKinnons, 1988.

Smedley, Anne **Constance** (later Armfield), 1881–1941, dramatist, illustrator, novelist, b. in Birmingham, da. of Annie (Duckworth), who had strong interest in things French and held music and literary 'miniature salons' at home, and W.T.S., accountant and company director. With her sister, she was educ. by her mother, then attended King Edward VI High School, and Birmingham School of Art. The family moved to London about 1887 so that CS could further her career as illustrator; she moved largely in the Le Gallienne and American circles. Working as a theatrical designer, she began writing plays under the influence of Mrs Patrick Campbell, whilst also composing and illustrating children's stories. The first of some 20 novels was *An April Princess*, 1903, a great success; and further works of romantic, though not cloyingly sentimental, fiction followed. She also wrote magazine articles and a life of Grace Darling. The polemical *Woman: A Few Shrieks*, 1907, emphasizes woman's need for economic independence, attacking those who believe they do or should live in a 'toybox world'. In 1909, she m. Maxwell A., book illustrator, painter, poet, composer, and theosophist. Together, they ran Greenleaf Theatre Drama School, for which CS wrote plays. In 1914, she founded the London International Lyceum Club, inaugurating worldwide institutions for professional women of limited means. See her autobiography, *Crusaders*, 1929.

Smedley, Menella Bute, 1820–77, poet and novelist, b. London, da. of Mary (Hume), described as intelligent, loving and forceful, and the Rev. Edward S., curate and teacher, who also wrote poetry and educ. the children. His health declined and the family moved to Dulwich. MBS learnt Latin from her father and became his scribe in his illness. Delicate herself, she later lived away at Tenby, and also visited Ireland. Her first pub. story, *The Maiden Aunt*, 1849, was followed by 'A Very Woman', pub. in *Seven Tales by Seven Authors*, 1849, produced to assist an indigent woman author and her young family. These were attributed to 'S.M.', as were *The Uses of Sunshine*, 1852, *Nina, A Tale for the Twilight*, 1853 and *Lays and Ballads of English History* [1856]. As 'M.S.' she pub. *The Story of Queen Isabel*, 1863, a long narrative poem with other verses, including some on Garibaldi and Cavour. First pub. in a magazine, *Twice Lost* appeared in vol. form in 1863. A powerful tale of greed and deception, it concerns a father's attempt to defraud his step-daughter by concealing her true identity, set against a background of intrigue relating to Italian independence. *A Mere Story* followed in 1865. Her *Poems* of 1868 included 'A Contrast', comparing the innocence of the bride with the licence permitted the most unexceptionable of bridegrooms. It also includes a five-act verse drama, 'Lady Grace'. She pub. poems for children as well as other poems and tales for adults. In the 1870s she worked with Mrs Nassau Senior on bettering girls' EDUCATION in Pauper Schools, and editing Mrs Senior's reports, repr. from the 1873–4 Blue Book.

Smith, Anna (Young), 1756–80, Philadelphia poet, da. of Jane (Graeme), who died early, and James Y. Little of her work survives, preserved by the poet Elizabeth FERGUSON, her aunt and foster-mother (Ferguson's album for Annis STOCKTON, Dickinson College). Some appeared as by 'Sylvia' in the *Pennsylvania Magazine* while AS lived, rather more in the *Columbian Magazine* from 1790. She expresses warm personal feelings, indignation at British treatment of America, and 'anger' at Swift's 'rude, severe, unjust' satire on women. She m. Dr William S. in 1775 and died after bearing her third child.

Smith, Betty (Wehner), 1896–1972, playwright and novelist, b. in Brooklyn, NY, da. of Catherine (Hummel) and John C. W. On finishing eighth grade she began working to support her widowed mother and younger siblings. In 1924 she married George S., a lawyer, with whom she had two daughters, and began taking writing classes at the Univ. of Michigan, where she won the Avery Hopwood prize for her plays. She then studied playwriting at Yale and held a fellowship at the Univ. of North Carolina. She wrote over 70 published plays (many for young people) and many unpublished, and edited drama collections; but success came with a novel about her childhood, *A Tree Grows in Brooklyn*, 1943, whose heroine, Francie Nolan, had already been central to a play and short story. Francie is born with a caul, supposedly indicating she is 'set apart to do great things in the world'; her mother asks *her* mother 'what must I do to make a different world for her?' and is told 'the child must have a valuable thing which is called imagination. . . . a secret world in which live things that never were.' This world makes Francie rich. Three more novels, *Tomorrow Will Be Better*, 1948, *Maggie – Now*, 1956, and *Joy in the Morning*, 1963, failed to match this success; each features a daughter of immigrants struggling against heavy odds to find happiness in the USA. Between 1937 and 1940 BS collaborated on over a dozen plays with Robert Finch. Twice divorced, she married him in 1957. Papers at Univ. of N. Carolina, Chapel Hill, include 35 plays.

Smith, Catherine or Catherina, novelist and actress. Her verse dedication of *The Misanthrope Father, or The Guarded Secret*, 1807, to the reviewers, says she writes in rural retirement, 'Well born, and possessing a decent estate'; though the book features a skeleton, purloined inheritance and suspected ghosts, bland young love in Cornwall and Bath occupies its centre. Her next is set in Spain, and last two are also exotic, with painfully stagy dialogue but fast-moving plots. In *The Caledonian Bandit, or The Heir of Duncaethal*, 1811, CS (if it is the same person) mentions acting at the Haymarket theatre and gratitude to the MINERVA press for 'liberal encouragement'. (This has been listed as two separate titles.) In *Barozzi, or The Venetian Sorceress*, 1815, facs. NY 1977 (set in the sixteenth century), the heroine disguises herself as a page to serve the hero through various perils; her mother, presumed dead, disguises herself as a sorceress; heroine and hero turn out to be cousins, children of respectively noble and villainous brothers. In 1826 CS acted in a stage version of Lewis's *The Monk*.

Smith, Charlotte (Turner), 1749–1806, novelist and poet, da. of Anna (Towers), who d. when she was three, and Nicholas T., Sussex landowner and poet. He sent her to boarding schools, encouraged her early writing (a poem on Wolfe's death, 1759), brought her very young into society, then in 1765 (having just re-married himself) married her to Benjamin S., a young merchant. Living over the business in Cheapside, she felt a 'guiltless exile' in 'personal slavery'; her first child died just as her second was born, 1767; later her husband pursued expensive pleasures while she did writing work for (but refused a salaried position from) her father-in-law. She lived 1774–83 on the Hants/Sussex border, but was in debtors' prison with her husband in 1784 when she published *Elegiac Sonnets, and Other Essays* at her own expense, and began to earn. She gradually expanded it; vol. ii, 1797, had 827 subscribers (including BLUESTOCKINGS) and a preface rebutting a charge of 'querulous egotism'. In 1784–5, living cheaply in France, she saw her twelfth child taken forcibly off in deep snow to Catholic baptism. She pub. French translations: *Manon Lescaut*, 1786 (withdrawn on charges of immorality), and *The Romance of Real Life*, 1787 (about newsworthy crimes). That year she left her husband, fearing 'my life was not safe', and began publishing novels almost annually for ten years to meet her family's ever-growing needs. In *Emmeline, The Orphan of the Castle*, 1788, women help each other escape male persecution, and the distressed heroine has her social status restored by an ideal husband. CS wrote poems (*The Emigrants*, 1793, *Beachy Head*, 1807, repr. 1985, unfinished) for pleasure, novels 'by necessity': both in haste. Both deal in landscape and in painful emotion; her poems were influential, but read stiltedly today. Her novels involve sentiment, the GOTHIC (Ann RADCLIFFE learned from her), radical politics (notably *Desmond*, 1792), a bitterly funny sketch of the woman novelist at work under difficulties (*The Banished Man*, 1794), satire on lawyers, who caused her much grief (notably *The Young Philosopher*, 1798), yet she retained the uneasy feeling that novels deal mainly with love. She also wrote a pamphlet on shipwrecks, a comedy (*What is She?*), and a collection of tales (*Letters of a Solitary Wanderer*), all 1799, and works for children, mainly in her last years. Her sister Catherine Anne Dorset wrote charming juvenile tales of animals in human dress, and a memoir of CS (in Walter Scott's *Misc. Works*, 1829). Life by Florence M. A. Hilbish, 1941; six recent reprints; letters ed. Judith Stanton, forthcoming.

Smith, Dorothy Gladys, **'Dodie'**, also 'C. L. Anthony', 'Charles Henry Percy', b. 1896, popular playwright and novelist, children's writer. Da. of Ellen (Furber) and Ernest Walter S., who d. when she was a baby, she acted and wrote plays as a child (at Old Trafford, Manchester). After her mother remarried, 1910, she attended St Paul's Girls' School, London, then the future RADA, where she sold a screenplay, *Schoolgirl Rebels*, as by 'Charles Henry Percy'. She acted (often on tour) till 1922, then worked at Heal's department store. Her *British Talent* was staged privately, 1923, *Autumn Crocus* professionally, 1931, as by 'C. L. Anthony'. Its success turned her to full-time writing. *Call It a Day*, pub. 1936, exemplifies her conservative comic structure. In 1939 she m. Alec Beesley. *Dear Octopus*, her best-known play, a rosy portrait of an extended family, was seen in London in 1938 and in the USA, 1939. There DS spent the war, wrote film scripts and more plays, and published a romantic novel, *I Capture the Castle*, 1948 (loved by adolescents, later a play). She has lived in rural England since the 1950s and written five more novels, preferring a form she could 'live right inside'. Eight of her 12 plays (one adapted from Henry James) bore her name. Her greatest success was *The Hundred and One Dalmations*, 1956, first of three children's books. Her four volumes of autobiography, 1974–85, are all titled *Look Back With. . . .*

Smith, Elizabeth, religious poet, very young and living at Truro in Cornwall in 1755; in 1779 writing a poem on Truro graveyard, pub. as *Life Reviewed*, Exeter, 1780: more than 1000 local subscribers, separate commemorative poem attached. Remembering particular people takes precedence over general meditations on life and death; she writes of her father and (a fine passage) her eldest daughter, who died a baby. Later editions add some devotional poems (pub. Exeter and Ilminster, 1781) and new lists of subscribers centred on Gloucester, 1783, and Birmingham, 1782 (including Mary DARWALL) and 1783. At Birmingham too appeared *The Brethren* (of Joseph), 1787, and *Israel* (Jacob), 1789, each 'earnestly recommended to the attention of the rising generation', making Old Testament stories into high-style poetry. Joseph Priestley and Anna SEWARD joined Darwall's husband as subscribers in 1787. *The Brethren* was written in an 'unfortunate situation', *Israel*'s publication long delayed. Another ES pub. extremely local *Poems on Malvern, and Other Subjects*, Worcester, 1829, 2nd ed. 1834.

Smith, Elizabeth, 1776–1806, scholar and poet. Eldest da. of Juliet (Mott) and banker George S., she was educ. by her mother, a governess, and her father's library; from 13 she was governess to her sisters. Inspired by H. M. BOWDLER's mother, she learned in her lifetime French, Italian, Spanish, Latin, German, Icelandic, Irish, Welsh, Persian, Arabic, Hebrew, Syriac, and Chinese and African dialects: the *DNB* pronounces that 'she was overtaxing every faculty'. Her father's bankruptcy, 1793, took the family to Bath, Ballitore in Ireland (where she met Mary LEADBEATER), and the Lake District. Her poems respond to scenery there, or stem from thirteenth-century Welsh or the Hebrew Bible (Elizabeth CARTER verified her skill in verse-translation); her aphorisms and reflections show a powerful mind. She dreaded 'being called a learned lady' but foresaw that prejudice against women's learning would diminish. She vainly fought chest pains by exercise: harvesting, 1805, and walking. Bowdler (a friend, as was Elizabeth HAMILTON) edited her very popular *Fragments in Prose and Verse*, and *Memoirs of Frederick and Margaret Klopstock* (translated, chiefly their letters), both 1808. In 1810 came her version of *Job* (finished 1803) and in 1814 her amazing *Vocabulary, Hebrew, Arabic, and Persian*, compiled with few scholarly tools.

Smith, Eunice, religious pamphleteer of Ashfield, Mass. She took 'a peculiar pleasure in writing on divine subjects', and allowed publication 'very contrary to my own inclination' in hope of doing good. Her highly popular works urge faith in God's loving-kindness: she often dramatizes her arguments, and moves from prose to verse at climactic moments. *Some Arguments Against Worldly Mindedness ... By way of a Dialogue*, 1791, has Mary suggest to the more practical, less spiritual Martha ways of freeing herself from trouble and care. The many editions vary in appearance and text. In *Practical Language Interpreted*, 1792 (another dialogue, quickly re-issued in several places), a Believer gradually persuades an Unbeliever. *Some of the Exercises of a Believing Soul Described*, 1792, also takes the form of answers to questions. The seven sections of *Some Motives to Engage Those Who Have Professed the Name of the Lord Jesus*, 1798, each end in verse; ten songs or hymns follow. She probably m. Benjamin Randle or Randall in 1792.

Smith, Julia (Barnard), conservative novelist publishing at London. Her *Letters of the*

Swedish Court, 1809, purport to be translated (by a man) from actual ones written by Gustavus III and his queen. An appendix covers his assassination. A dedication to Queen Caroline, attacking George IV, points up the theme of royal reconciliation. In *The Prisoner of Montauban, or Times of Terror, A Reflective Tale*, 1810, a retiring, innocent, but well-educated heroine converts a charming libertine to science and Christianity in the prisons of the Terror; novelists, especially Sydney MORGAN, are condemned. In *The Old School*, 1813, a young woman writes to her aunt praising the local squire's actively benevolent family, inculcating industry and modesty, and deploring modern fashions and independent young women.

Smith, Lee, novelist, b. 1944 at Grundy, Va., da. of Virginia and Ernest Lee S., a businessman. At high school she wrote highly-coloured romantic stories; at Hollins College (BA 1967) she submitted for a Book of the Month Club fellowship a collection of stories and a novel which, like her next two, began as a story. This, *The Last Day the Dogbushes Bloomed*, pub. 1968, has a child narrator who transmutes painful experience into fantasy. Married in 1967 to poet James E. Seay, LS had two sons and worked as a newspaper reporter in Tuscaloosa, Ala. (drawn on in *Fancy Strut*, 1973, whose female reporter likes to embroider the facts). She taught high school in Nashville, Tenn., and Chapel Hill, NC, where she now teaches at NC State Univ. In 1980 came *Cakewalk* (stories, the title piece featuring a virtuoso baker and froster) and *Black Mountain Breakdown*, the story of a woman's retreat from life. *Oral History*, 1983 (about generations dogged by a witch's curse), and *Family Linen*, 1985 (whose skeleton of a lost father resides not in a closet but in a sealed-up well), blend a rich brew of Appalachian folklore, multiple voices, and blended layers of time past. LS's skill grows steadily towards the epistolary *Fair and Tender Ladies*, 1988, whose heroine begins as a 12-year-old on a remote farm, longing to be famous for writing 'of Love'. She loves and loves, through thick and thin, until 'fair wore out with it', writing only her impetuous life in letters to a sister (beloved, deranged, institutionalized, dead); in old age she burns them, realizing that the texts do not matter, only 'the *writing* of them'. Interview in *SoQ*, 5, 1983.

Smith, Lillian Eugenia, 1897–1966, novelist, editor and civil-rights campaigner. She was b. at Jasper, Fla., seventh of nine children of Annie (Simpson) and Calvin Warren S. The family finances collapsed in 1915: they moved to their former summer home in Clayton, Ga. LS's studies (Piedmont College, 1915–16, the Peabody Conservatory, 1917–22) were interrupted first by family needs and again for a year as principal of a rural school. She was director of music at a Methodist school at Huchow, China, 1922–5 (she later lived briefly in Brazil and twice visited India). From 1925 until 1949 she managed Laurel Falls girls' camp (taking over from her parents), where she developed innovative, proto-feminist programmes in arts and social sciences. With Paula Snelling (who helped run the camp) LS founded a little MAGAZINE, *Pseudopodia*, 1936 (twice renamed: *The North Georgia Review* and *South Today*, until 1946), which exercized increasing influence by liberal editorials and by printing work by women and black writers. She lost MS novels in a fire of 1944. Her first published novel, *Strange Fruit*, 1944, skilfully explores a tragic interracial love. It was banned as obscene in many places (and by the US Post Office until Eleanor ROOSEVELT intervened). LS's dramatized version (jointly with her sister Esther), was played in 1945. Her enemies were increased by her articles, speeches, and three more outspoken books: *Killers of the Dream*, 1949, which directly attacks segregation, *The Journey*, 1954, and *Now Is the Time*, 1955, which confronts the South's unwillingness to support the Supreme Court decision to end segregation. Racist arson destroyed important MSS, files and letters in 1955. *One Hour*, 1959, a novel, presents the mental instability of McCarthyite legalized attackers of suspected Communists; *Memory of a Large Christmas*, 1962, evokes LS's loved but prejudiced family; *Our Faces, Our Words*, 1964, deals with the non-violent civil rights movement. LS, who had had surgery for breast cancer in 1953, died leaving deliberately unpublished a 'highly personal' novel, *Julia*, on the topic of gender. See life (with bibliography) by Louise Blackwell and Frances Clay, 1971, and selec. of short pieces edited by Michelle CLIFF and prefaced by Snelling, 1978. Papers, including files of little magazines she edited, at the Univ. of Florida.

Smith, Lucy Toulmin, 1838–1911, scholar and librarian, b. Boston, Mass., eldest of five children of Martha (Kendall) and Joshua Toulmin S., medievalist. In 1842 the family settled in Highgate, London. LTS was educ. at home, and became her father's amanuensis, eventually completing his *English Gilds* for the Early English Text Society after his death in 1869. Both this and her next publication, an edition of *The Maire of Bristowe is Kalendar*, 1872, for the Camden Society, throw much light on late medieval town life. Her most important works were her edition of the York mystery plays from the Ashburnham MS (*York Plays*, 1885), and two further editions for the Camden Society, *Expeditions to Prussia and the Holy Land made by Henry Earl of Derby (afterwards King Henry IV) in the Years 1390–1 and 1392–3*, 1894, and the five-vol. *Itinerary of John Leland*, 1907–10: LTS translated Jusserand's early travel book as *English Wayfaring Life*, 1889. She helped edit *Cursor Mundi*, 1883, and *Les Contes moralises de Nicole Bozon*, 1889 (with Paul Meyer), as well as an enlarged version of C. M. Ingleby's *Shakespeare's Centurie of Prayse*, 1879 (a record of references to Shakespeare between 1591 and 1693). In 1894 she was elected Librarian of Manchester College, Oxford, the first woman in England to be made head of a public library.

Smith, Margaret (Bayard), 1778–1844, social commentator and novelist, b. on a farm on the Schuylkill River near Philadelphia, da. of Margaret (Hodge), who d. when she was two, and Col. John Bubenheim B., an officer with Washington and a politician. She attended the Moravian boarding school, Bethlehem, Pa., and from 1792 lived with her sister's family at Brunswick, NJ. In 1800 she m. her cousin Samuel Harrison S. and moved to Washington, where he established the Jeffersonian *National Intelligencer* and became a bank president. 'Domestic Life! There alone is happiness', she wrote; but as well as a son she had 'my solitary chamber with my books and pen'. Her novels (now rare) are *A Winter in Washington, or Memoirs of the Seymour Family*, 1824, which draws on actual figures including Jefferson, and *What is Gentility?*, 1828, pub. to benefit the Orphan Asylum. This humorously vindicates the plebeian, upwardly mobile McCarty family: a happy ending embraces the pipe-smoking, ungenteel mother, her learned and unlearned sons and their talented but humble wives, and a spectacularly self-made male friend; only a fashionable sister is scapegoated. MBS's notebooks and letters, about the social scene and historic moments like the burning of Washington by the British, 1814, form the basis of *The First Forty Years of Washington Society* (with memoir by her grandson), 1906, repr. 1965. She contributed celebrity lives to Herrick and Longacre's *National Portrait Gallery*, 1834 ff., stories and verse to the *National Intelligencer* and other journals, 1835–57, and a series on presidential inaugurals, *Who is Happy?*, to *Godey's Lady's Book*, 1837. A friend of S. J. HALE, C. M. SEDGWICK, and Harriet MARTINEAU, she told her sister, 'take me for better or worse, folios and quartos, prose or verse, nonsense or much sense, gaiety or dullness.' Papers in the Library of Congress.

Smith, Pauline, 'Janet Tamson', 'Janet Urmson', 1882?–1959, novelist, short-story writer, poet, diarist, letter writer, b. in Oudtshoorn, South Africa, da. of Jessie (Milne), a nurse keenly interested in political and current affairs, and Herbert Hurmson S., a doctor and a prominent member of the community, much involved in local drama groups. Of the Smiths' several children, only PS and her sister Helen lived to adulthood. She was educ. mainly at home by governesses, attending school with her sister only intermittently. The two accompanied their parents to Britain, 1895, attending boarding school in Scotland, then, after their father's death, 1899, in Hertfordshire. Chronically ill, PS did not complete her formal schooling. Her earliest works appeared in Scottish newspapers under her pseudonyms, and by 1904 she had engaged a literary agent. In 1908, she met Arnold Bennett in Switzerland, a meeting initiated by her mother which transformed her career. He recognized the skill of her depictions of Afrikaner peasants at Little Karoo, and encouraged and helped her in her work. Although she spent her life officially in England, frequently travelling to South Africa, PS made Little Karoo the setting of most of her fiction. Her extensive travel journal, *South African Journal 1913–1914* (ed. Harold Scheub, 1983), served as source material. Her vast correspondence includes letters to British writers who were personal friends, Arnold Bennett and Frank Swinnerton among them. (At his request, she destroyed letters from Bennett.) Her writing demonstrates meticulous observation, humour, and concern for the poor, isolated farmers. Her works, well regarded in her own time in both South Africa and Britain, include *The Little Karoo*, short stories with an introduction by Arnold Bennett, 1925; *The Beadle*, 1926, a novel; and *Platkops Children*, 1935 (repr. 1981 with introduction by Sheila Scholten), early studies of the Afrikaner children she grew up with; and *The Last Voyage*, a one-act play, written 1928, produced on BBC radio 1929, published posthumously 1965. She left an unfinished novel, *Winter Sacrament* (pub. in Ernest Deveira and Sheila Scholten, eds., *Miscellaneous Writings*, 1983). Her work is esteemed by contemporary South African writers, including Alan Paton, Herman Bosman, Richard Rive, Jean MARQUARD, and Nadine GORDIMER. Critical study by Geoffrey Haresnape, 1969; essays ed. Dorothy Driver (including bibliography), 1983. Leonie Twentyman Jones, *The Pauline Smith Collection*, 1980, lists holdings at the Univ. of Cape Town Libraries, with brief biographical sketch. PS's memoir of Bennett, 1933, includes autobiographical material, as does 'Why and How I Became an Author', *ESA*, 6, 1963. Biographies in progress. See Marquard in *English Academy Review*, Johannesburg, 1981, and *DR*, 59, 1979.

Smith, 'Stevie', Florence Margaret, 1902–71, poet, novelist, illustrator, performer, da. of Ethel (Spear) and Charles Ward Smith. She was b. at Hull, Yorks., 'a cynical babe' who nearly died at birth. She was three when 'papa ran away to sea' (his export firm had failed), and she came to the 'house of female habitation' at Palmers Green (then outside London) where she lived with her mother, sister, and (till the latter's death in 1968) her 'Lion Aunt', Margaret Annie Spear. In 1908 SS (the nickname, after a jockey, came at 19 or 20) developed 'tubercular peritonitis' and was exiled to convalesce by the sea. After educ. at the local High School and the famous North London Collegiate School for Girls (where she was bored), and doing amateur acting, she became a secretary with a publishing firm. Her journals, 1919–30, record omnivorous reading. She felt marrying 'was the right thing to do . . . the natural thing to do, hey-ho – but I wasn't very keen on it' (later it was 'a chance clutch upon a hen-coop in mid-Atlantic'). She had a romance with Karl Eckinger, a German (over, its 'feelings . . . all nicely worked out', in 1931), and an engagement which soon ended. She began writing poems about 1924 (after a few as a child). Offered for publication (with her inimitable drawings) in 1934, they were rejected as 'neurotic'; a few appeared in the *New Statesman* in 1935. Advised to write a novel, she produced *Novel on Yellow Paper*, which in 1936 was first rejected too, then published to critical acclaim (repr. 1980). Its unusual structure (wry journal jottings by publisher's-secretary Pompey, on topics from Nazism to love, death to child-rearing) and mock-naive style were likened to Laurence Sterne and Gertrude STEIN. Reviews by Naomi MITCHISON and Rosamond LEHMANN led to lasting friendships. (Another close friend, by post, was US poet Naomi REPLANSKY.) Next year came *A Good Time Was Had By All*, poems from ten years 'of illicit office scribbling'. SS published two more part-autobiographical novels (*Over the Frontier*, 1938, repr. 1980, and *The Holiday*, 1949) and nine more poetry volumes (not without further rejections), and first read her poems on radio in 1949. She attempted suicide at the office in 1953, three months after writing her most famous poem: 'Oh, no no no, it was too cold always / (Still the dead one lay moaning) / I was much too far out all my life / And not waving but drowning.' SS resigned, and stepped up her reviewing output. Her radio play *A Turn Outside*, 1959, was, she said, 'romantic about old Death'. With *Selected Poems*, 1962, readers began to love her outrageousness – Sylvia PLATH wrote calling herself an addict – and large public readings from 1965 swelled SS's fame. She received the Queen's Gold Medal for Poetry in 1969 (probably not, as rumoured, wearing a hat from a jumble-sale). In hospital two months before she died she read aloud her poem 'Come, Death (2)'. Jeni COUZYNS locates her 'magic' in 'a kind of daredevil dance with poetic form'. See *Collected Poems*, 1975; *Selection*, ed., Hermione Lee, 1983 (both with drawings); Kay Dick, *Ivy* [COMPTON-BURNETT] *and Stevie* (conversations and reflections), 1971; Eleanor Risteen Gordon in *Modern Poetry Studies*, 11, 1983; Martin Pumphrey in *Critical Quarterly*, 28, 1986. Uncollected writings, ed. Jack Barbera and William McBrien (*Me Again*, 1981); bibliog., 1987, and life, 1985, by Barbera and McBrien; life by Frances Spalding, 1988.

Smither, Elizabeth (Harrington), poet and novelist, b. 1941 at New Plymouth, NZ, da. of Elsie Phyllis Irene (Bowerman) and Edwin Russell H. She undertook part-time univ. study without completing a degree at Massey and Victoria Univs, and qualified as a librarian, 1963, m. Michael S., artist, in 1963; since divorced. She has worked as a librarian, written journalism and a weekly verse column for the Taranaki *Daily News*, and had an Auckland Univ. Literary Fellowship, 1984. Her first of eight colls. of poetry was *Here Come the Clouds*, 1975. She also has two novels, *First Blood*, 1983, and *Brother-love, Sister-love*, 1986, and a story for children, 1983. Her poems are small, witty, ironical – mainly about poets, paintings, literary figures, and intellectual concepts. Some earlier poems use fairy-stories from the woman's perspective – 'The Princess and the Pea at Christmas'. *The Sarah Train*, 1980, is a charming sequence for her daughter.

Smyth, Donna, novelist, short-story writer, playwright, feminist, journalist, peace and environmental activist. B. in 1943 in Kimberley, British Columbia, da. of Ellen (Mackie) and Ivan S., she was educ. at the Univs. of Victoria (BA), Toronto (MA), and London (PhD), and now teaches English literature at Acadia Univ., Wolfville, NS. She is founding editor of *Atlantis: A Woman's Studies Journal*. Her plays include *Susanna* MOODIE, 1976, and *Giant Anna*, 1978–9 (about a Nova Scotian side-show giant), both produced by Mermaid Theatre,

Halifax. Increasingly experimental, her stories have appeared in various periodicals and anthologies, several winning awards. Her 1982 novel about three women and their men makes the *Quilt* of its title the emblem of community. *Subversive Elements*, 1986, a 'docu-drama', interweaves fiction and non-fiction, romance and environmental issues.

Smyth, Ethel Mary, 1858–1944, composer, critic of culture, autobiographer, suffragette. Born in Sidcup, Kent, she was da. of Emma (Struth), who had grown up in Paris, and John Hall S., an artillery officer who adamantly opposed her musical career. Her 'first milestone' was provided by a governess, who, when she was 12, played her classical music. She wrote as a child, both at home and at school in Putney – diaries (which, forbidden to keep, she buried), poems (some of which she published in *Impressions that Remained*, 2 vols., 1919, new ed., 1981), and 'articles for some obscure paper' (helped by Juliana EWING, who declared 'she could make me into a writer'). At 19, she went to study at the Leipzig Conservatorium, and in the years that followed became a passionate mountaineer, met Brahms, Grieg, and others, and, from 1883, began a long, close association with Henry Brewster, who wrote the libretto for her best-known opera, *The Wreckers*, produced in Leipzig in 1906. ES composed in several forms, but her six operas are her major achievement. Having left England, 1908, to escape 'the turmoil of the fight for Votes for Women', which 'seemed incompatible with artistic creation', ES returned in 1911, joined the WSPU, became personally devoted to Emmeline PANKHURST, whom she thought 'more astounding than Joan of Arc', and gave two years exclusively to the Cause. Her imprisonment in Holloway is notorious, partly because of Thomas Beecham's anecdote: visiting, he found her leaning out of a cell conducting with a toothbrush while women in the yard below sang her composition 'The March of the Women' to the words by Cicely HAMILTON. All of ES's writing is to some extent AUTOBIOGRAPHICAL, including her books on Maurice Baring, 1938, and Thomas Beecham, 1935. It is also pointedly feminist: she wrote to show 'how these wretched sex-considerations were really the fashioning factor of my life'. Her work, especially *Streaks of Life*, 1921, *A Final Burning of Boats*, 1928, and *Female Pipings in Eden*, 1933, combines accounts of her personal experience of exclusion from English musical life with analysis of 'the complex of public interest, middlemen, and other conditions that I call the Machine'. It also comprises a personal history of the SUFFRAGE Movement. *Female Pipings* includes a long memoir of Emmeline Pankhurst; elsewhere ES writes of Vernon LEE, Lilian Baylis (who produced her opera *The Boatswain's Mate*, 1922, at the Old Vic), Edith SOMERVILLE, the Empress Eugenie, and Brewster. *A Three-Legged Tour in Greece*, 1927, is a richly witty account of a trip with her great-niece. She was made a DBE, 1922, and in 1926 became the first other than local woman to receive an honorary doctorate from Oxford. Christopher ST JOHN's life, 1959, based on ES's letters and papers, prints essays by Kathleen Dale and Vita SACKVILLE-WEST. Selecs. from her autobiographical writings, ed. R. Crichton, 1987. On her friendship with WOOLF, see Suzanne Raitt in *Critical Quarterly*, 30, 1988.

Smythies, Harriet(te) Maria (Gordon), 'Mrs Yorick S.', later 'Mrs Gordon S.', 1813–83, novelist, poet, b. Margate, Kent, da. of Jane (Halliday) and Edward Lesmoin G. of Sunning Hill. Her brother also wrote. Her first book was a long narrative poem in heroic couplets, *The Bride of Siena*, 1835 (second ed. 1838), which takes a line in Dante as a hint for a woman's undying but excessive, idolatrous love for a man who injures her. This was followed in 1838 by her first novel, *Fitzherbert, or Lovers and Fortune-Hunters*, whose preface praises modern novels and lifelike, unByronic 'commonplace villains' – oddly, since her fiction abounds in those of deepest dye, male and female. *Cousin Geoffrey*, 1840, 'edited' by Theodore Hook (who also offered to edit her next, *The Marrying Man*, 1841), was frequently reprinted. In 1842 she m. the Rev. William Yorick S., and by 1850 had had five children and written six more novels. She was supposedly called 'Queen of the Domestic Novel' by Thomas Campbell (see Nigel Cross, *The Common Writer*, 1985). From this date her sentimental moralistic fictions retained steady popularity, supported by titles like *The Jilt*, 1844, *A Warning to Wives*, 1848, *True to the Last*, 1862, and *Faithful Woman*, 1865. Often published serially in popular journals like *Cassell's* and the *London Journal*, sometimes sensational, and always better on motives and manners than plots, her novels were admired by Edward Bulwer Lytton, among others. She often included topical issues (TEMPERANCE, ragged schools, the Crimean War), and pub. two series of advice columns in the *Ladies Treasury* (1857–8; 1859–60). About this time, she left her husband (hopeless at his job, he had mismanaged their income and undertaken crippling litigation). Her poem *Incurable*, 1863, in aid of the Royal Hospital for Incurables, was inspired by her daughter, who died of TB in 1866. Only one son survived her.

Smythies, Susan, 1721–after 1774, author of three anonymous novels, eldest of the large family of Susan (Puplet), d. 1731, and Palmer S., well-to-do Rector of Colchester, who had more children by a second marriage. Lady Mary Wortley MONTAGU liked the comic grotesques in *The Stage-Coach: Containing the Character of Mr. Manly, and the History of his Fellow-Travellers*, 1753, repr. 1789: Captain Cannon values his own charms ('if a poor silly creature takes it into her head to admire one ... '); country justice Moody claims to love his put-upon daughter 'as I love my life ... I would give a thousand pound that she was a boy.' Manly gives good advice and help where possible. *The Brothers*, 1758, with a preface recording a vain desire to emulate *Sir Charles Grandison*, is less light-hearted. David Garrick and Tobias Smollett subscribed. The heroine escapes attacks on her virtue to achieve happy marriage, but is upstaged by her father's recovery of his estate (usurped by a wicked younger half-brother) and launching a parliamentary campaign to revive national greatness and public virtue.

Socialist-feminist criticism has evolved out of a double engagement: with Marxist social, literary and cultural theory and politics on the one hand, and with feminist theory, praxis, and cultural production on the other. It attempts to articulate the complex relations between textual practices (the text, writing, reading, criticism) and gender, class, and race relations. Unlike much feminist criticism, it does not privilege gender over other categories of oppression, but reads it in the context of political, cultural, and textual strategies, ideologies, and struggles. Underlying socialist-feminist critical practice is commitment to social transformation based on socialist and feminist principles. Although socialist-feminist theory/criticism is not monolithic, the hyphenation generally implies mutually informing and transforming dialectic between socialism and feminism.

Socialist-feminist criticism gives us, Jane Marcus says, 'an aesthetics of political commitment to offer in place of current theories based in psychoanalysis or in formalism' ('Still Practice, A/Wrested Alphabet' (*TSWL*, 3, 1984): she sees Virginia WOOLF as its model. It emerged from different intellectual and political traditions in England and the US, but transatlantic collaboration and exchange have blurred these differences. In England in the sixties and seventies, the institutionalized presence of the left permitted open and political engagement with Marxism, and Marxist-feminist critics focused their attention on finding a site for feminist criticism within Marxism, developing rigorous Marxist analysis of gender and women's oppression and discovering ways of incorporating that analysis into literary theory and criticism – in the context of the intellectual ferment generated by the dissemination of the texts of French structuralism, post-structuralism, and psychoanalysis. An early attempt to integrate French theory, Marxism, and feminist praxis was made by the London-based Marxist-Feminist Literature Collective, who both produced feminist rereadings of classic nineteenth-century women's texts ('Women's Writing: *Jane Eyre, Shirley, Villette, Aurora Leigh*', 1978) and challenged the individualist, academic mode of Marxist and mainstream criticism through their feminist mode of collective work and presentation. The nineteenth century has continued to prove a fruitful period for socialist-feminist critics interested in the intersection of gender, class and text (e.g. Judith Lowder Newton, *Women, Power, and Subversion*, 1981, and Mary Poovey, *The Proper Lady and the Woman Writer*, 1984, and *Uneven Developments: the Ideological Work of Gender in Victorian England*, 1988). Feminist popular-culture critics at the Birmingham Centre for Contemporary Cultural Studies continue feminist collective practice.

The work of Marxist/socialist-feminist theorists such as Juliet Mitchell, Sheila Rowbotham and Michèle Barrett in England, Gayle Rubin, Lillian Robinson, and Heidi Hartmann in the US, and Meaghan Morris and Susan Sheridan in Australia, as well as that of some radical feminist theorists and writers, has been important for literary/cultural critics in articulating the relationships between class and gender, Marxism and feminism, in debating the concept of patriarchy as a system of gender oppression, and in theorizing the construction of the female subject. Socialist-feminist theorists reject essentialist or ahistorical views of gender and women's oppression and insist on the historical specificity of women's lives, which they see as determined not only by gender but also by class and race (attention to race, more recent, is a response to struggles within feminism). Barrett's work on aesthetics (*Women's Oppression Today*, 1980, and 'Feminism and the Definition of Cultural Politics' in Rosalind Brunt and Caroline Rowan, eds., *Feminism, Culture, and Politics*, 1982) importantly theorized the cultural meanings of gender as not simply a matter of difference but also of oppression and inequality. Barrett argued for a theory of representation able to encompass the complex relation between text and social reality, neither 'reading off' from the text the historical conditions in which it was produced (as in a more old-fashioned Marxism), nor severing sign and material referent altogether (as in a contemporary post-structuralism).

In their focus on the relation between textual and sexual/class/racial politics, socialist-feminist critics reject feminist criticism premised on the notion of an unproblematic sisterhood of women and on the linked project of recovering a literary tradition of writing sisters. Barrett, for example, argues that this purely gender-based criticism, which celebrates woman and sisterhood, cannot constitute a viable intervention in cultural politics, and Rosalind COWARD delineates the difference between 'feminist' and 'women's' cultural practices in '"This Novel Changes Lives": Are Women's Novels Feminist Novels?' (*Feminist Review*, 5, 1980) and *Female Desire*, 1984. Socialist-feminist critics generally have been less interested in the search for a female aesthetic or even a female tradition than in the historical specificity of reading and writing and the need for a radical rethinking of the literary canon. In the US this approach was pioneered by Lillian Robinson in *Sex, Class and Culture*, 1978, political essays, 1968–77, which analyse the historical construction of gender through critiques of popular culture as well as literature.

Over the past few years there has been a shift in focus in socialist-feminist criticism from mounting a feminist challenge within Marxism to engaging with the increasingly complex and sophisticated body of feminist theory. For example, Toril Moi's *Sexual/Textual Politics*, 1985, articulates the socialist-feminist critique of 'mainstream' Anglo-American feminist criticism as a variant of liberal humanism, then investigates the radical possibilities and political implications of French feminist theory. Feminist uses of psychoanalysis and post-structuralism have had a transformative impact on socialist-feminist theoretical and critical practice, as seen in the work of Moi, Catherine Belsey, Mary Jacobus and Cora Kaplan. Kaplan (*Sea Changes*, 1986) is one of the few socialist-feminist critics to have integrated a critique of ethnocentrism with analysis of gender and class. But the still predominantly white ethnocentric focus of socalist-feminist criticism has been radically challenged by such critics as Hazel Carby (*Reconstructing Womanhood*, 1987), Susan Willis (*Specifying*, 1987), and Gayatri Chakravorty SPIVAK (*In Other Worlds*, 1988). (See also BLACK FEMINIST CRITICISM.) These works epitomize a socialist-feminist criticism revitalized by feminist theory, yet never losing sight of the politics and history that inform both women's writing and the critic's reading.

Shifts in socialist-feminist criticism have led Judith Newton and Deborah Rosenfelt (eds., *Feminist Criticism and Social Change*, 1985) to rename it 'materialist criticism', recognizing by the more inclusive term the fact that many critical texts contain elements of materialist analysis. This renaming strategically mutes Marxist and socialist politics in a conservative social and political climate, and blurs rigorous distinctions between different feminist politics (socialist, radical, liberal).

Sofola, 'Zulu, Nigerian playwright and director. The da. of Igbo parents, she was b. in 1938 in Issele-Uke in mid-western Nigeria, and attended primary school in Nigeria, then Southern Baptist Seminary in Nashville, Virginia Union Univ. (BA *cum laude* in English), and the Catholic Univ., Washington, DC (MA in drama, 1965, with a thesis on the dramatic features of Igbo ritual). She met and married her Yoruba husband, with whom she has five children, in the US, returning with him to Nigeria, 1966, to teach at the Univ. of Ibadan, he in sociology, she in drama (PhD, 1977). She lectures, writes and produces plays at the university and for TV, and works in amateur theatre. As a member of the Nigerian Television Authority, she helped prepare a series on maternity. Her first play, *Wedlock of the Gods*, was produced at the Univ. of Missouri, 1971, where she received an award from the Black Culture House. It uses proverbs to create traditional dialogue, but does not employ folk music, dance, or song. In other works, ZS uses other styles, other languages (Yoruba, Pidgin, and English together); she works in farce as well as tragedy. Her plays include *Disturbed Peace of Christmas*, 1971, *King Emene*, 1974, *The Wizard of Law*, 1975, *The Sweet Trap*, 1977, *The Operators*, perf. 1979, *Old Wines are Tasty*, 1980, 'Fantasies in the Moonlight', 'Song of a Maiden', and 'The Deer and the Hunter's Pearl', 1969. She deals with social themes – absurd legalism, societal greed, teenage stress, academic snobbery, and crime, as well as with the weight of tradition in women's lives.

Solano, Solita, 1888–1975, novelist and poet. B. in New England, she was in the Philippines surveying and building coral roads when she might have been at college. Back in the USA, she began work in 1914 on the *Boston Herald-Traveler* and soon became the first woman drama editor and critic on a major US daily. She was drama editor on the *NY Herald Tribune*, 1920–1, left for Europe with Janet FLANNER (with whom she lived for 20 years), travelled in Greece, Crete, Turkey and Austria, and in 1922 settled in Paris. She was a valued critic to Flanner, and later called their relationship with Nancy CUNARD 'a fixed triangle ... forty-two years of modern female fidelity'. Other close friends were Sylvia BEACH, Margaret ANDERSON, and Djuna BARNES, who included her in her *Ladies Almanack*, 1928. SS's novels (*The Uncertain Feast*, 1924, *The Happy Failure*, 1925, and *This Way Up*, 1927) all 'had the honor of not pleasing' American critics (except Lillian HELLMAN), as Eugene Jolas wrote in excerpting the last in *transition*; all deal with failing relationships and agonizing marriages. Though SS published in mainstream periodicals in the 1920s, Shari Benstock, 1986, mentions lost work in marginal publications; she also notes that SS's experimentalism was not that of the then dominant categories. After a similarly cool reception for her book of poems, *Statue in a Field*, 1934, SS stopped writing. She expressed reservations about art, though she remained interested in etymology. She became, with Anderson and Georgette Leblanc, a disciple of the mystic George Gurdjieff, and worked for four years as his secretary. She died at Orgeval, Paris. Papers at the Library of Congress. Her interview with Anderson, 1967, is unpub.

'Somerville and Ross', Edith Anne Oenone Somerville, 1858–1949, novelist, essayist, illustrator, painter, and her second cousin and collaborator, Violet Florence Martin, 'Martin Ross', 1862–1915, novelist. ES, b. Corfu, da. of Adelaide and Thomas S., Colonel of the Buffs, grew up at the family seat, Drishane, Co. Cork. Educ. at home by governesses and at Alexandra College, Dublin, she later studied at art colleges in Düsseldorf, Paris and London. Her earliest published work was an illustrated essay on art studios for *Cassel's Magazine of Art*, 1885. VM, b. Ross, Oughterard, West Galway, da. of Anna Selina (Fox) and James Martin, was also part of the wealthy Anglo-Irish ascendancy. She and ES met in 1886; their literary collaboration and close friendship ended only with VM's death in 1915. They pub. novels, often dealing with the decay of the landholding class, beginning with *An Irish Cousin*, 1889, and including their best known, *The Real Charlotte*, 1894, a powerful study of a woman who reverses the 'good and beautiful' female stereotype. They also pub. TRAVEL books, such as *Through Connemara in a Governess Cart*, 1892, and short-story collections, including their comic masterpiece, *Some Experiences of an Irish RM*, 1908 (later televised by the BBC). In 1903 ES became the first female Master of Fox Hounds. She and VM worked for SUFFRAGE in Ireland, ES being elected President of the Munster Women's Franchise League, 1913. However, they rejected the militancy and anti-Home Rule stance of the English suffragists. After VM's death, ES continued writing under their joint pseudonym, believing in VM's continued spirit-connection, and pub. memoirs, travel essays and a biography of their shared great-grandfather, Charles Kendal Bush, Lord Chief Justice of Ireland. She also continued to paint, holding successful exhibitions in London and NYC, and in 1919 met Ethel SMYTH, who became a close friend and travelling companion. She also knew Yeats and Lady GREGORY. In 1941 she was awarded the Gregory Medal by the Irish Academy of Letters of which she was a founding member. See John Cronin, 1972, for both their lives; Hilary Robinson's critical study, 1980; selected letters with foreword by Molly KEANE, 1989.

Somerville, Mary (Fairfax), 1780–1872, writer on science, b. Jedburgh, Scotland, da. of Margaret (Charters) and Vice-Admiral Sir William George F. She was educ. at a fashionable boarding school at Musselburgh and through her own wide reading. In 1804 she m. a cousin, Captain Samuel Greig, who had little sympathy for her studies; they had one son. After Samuel's death in 1807, she lived in Edinburgh until she m. another cousin, Dr William S., who encouraged her to pursue and systematize her study. In London their circle included Brougham, Melbourne, Sir William and Sir John Herschel and the Napiers. Humboldt, Laplace and Gay-Lussac were among her foreign correspondents. In 1826 she presented a paper to the Royal Society on 'The Magnetic Properties of the Violet Rays of the Solar Spectrum': though her ideas were later disproved, it showed her capacity for original deduction. Her description of Laplace's *Le Mécanique Céleste*, 1831, immediately put her in the first rank of scientific writers. *The Connection of the Physical Sciences*, 1834, based on the 'mutual dependence and connection' between various branches of science 'treating of the properties of matter and energy', gave rise to the current meaning of the term 'physics'. The revised ed., 1842, suggesting another planet behind Uranus, allowed Professor Adams to deduce the orbit of Neptune. After 1838, she mostly lived abroad – largely in Italy – due to illness, which delayed publication of her much-praised *Physical Geography*, 1848. Although saddened by the deaths of her husband (1860) and son, she pub. a summary of recent discoveries in chemistry and physics, *Molecular and Microscopic Science*, 1869, the same year the Victoria Gold Medal of the Royal Geographical Society was conferred on her. She had a strong interest in women's EDUCATION and SUFFRAGE: after her death in Naples her name was commemorated in the foundation of Somerville Hall, Oxford. See her daughter Martha S.'s *Personal Recollections*, 1873, and the life, 1979, and study, 1983, by Elizabeth C. Patterson.

Sontag, Susan, essayist, cultural critic, novelist, b. 1933 in NYC to American Jewish parents, a teacher and a travelling salesman. She grew up in Tucson (Ariz.) and Los Angeles, with poor health and 'minimal' family life, dreaming of being a great scientist. At 15 she 'knew I would be a writer', and entered the Univ. of Calif., Berkeley. She married social psychologist Philip Rieff at 17, bore a son in 1952 and divorced in 1959. After a BA from Chicago, 1951, two MAs from Harvard (English and philosophy), and PhD study at Harvard, St Anne's College (Oxford) and the Univ. of Paris, she taught at CCNY, Sarah Lawrence College, Columbia Univ., and elsewhere. She has received fellowships and other awards. Yet, though a doyen of the US academic left, she presents herself as, and strives to be, peripheral, 'a writer who is also an intellectual' in a climate increasingly uncomprehending and unfriendly. Radical yet elitist, SS unweaves the texture of dominant ideology and documents the marginalized areas of culture, 'the sensibility' which in 'Notes on "Camp"' she calls an age's 'most decisive', but also 'most perishable' aspect (*Against Interpretation and Other Essays*, 1966). She uncovers, for instance, disturbing connections between the Nazi era and the present, and exposes hidden thought-patterns in 'On the Pornographic Imagination' (*Styles of Radical Will*, 1969), *Illness as Metaphor*, 1978 (to which *AIDS and Its Metaphors*, 1989, is a kind of sequel), and 'Fascinating Fascism' (*Under the Sign of Saturn*, 1980). 'Support for the emancipation of women stands today approximately where support for the emancipation of slaves stood two centuries ago', she writes in 'The Third World of Women' (not her chosen title: *Partisan Review*, 40, 1973), a subtle, trenchant account of socially assigned masculinity and femininity and of the meaning of women's liberation. Her directly political writing, like *Trip to Hanoi*, 1968, combines a sharply personal style with the stance of a prophet. Her fiction and autobiographical essays take up issues of identity, the 'self's' reliance on and disruptions by practical, political and historical circumstances. Her weighty novels, *The Benefactor*, 1963 (whose male protagonist's dreams invade his waking life), and *Death Kit*, 1967 (whose hero may or may not be a murderer), situate themselves in a European tradition: Thomas Mann, Kafka, Sartre and Camus.

I, etcetera, 1978, collects short stories. Her fiction's concern with the self, psychology and society joins with her interest in the visual as she writes on the film-makers Godard and Bergman. She discusses modernity, 'the way we are now', in the Barthesian *On Photography*, 1976, and has directed and written films from *Duet for Cannibals*, 1969, to *Unguided Tour*, 1983. A furore, and repudiation by many on the US left, greeted her public remark in 1982 (of Poland) that communism was successful fascism, 'fascism with a human face'. SS has edited *Commentary*, 1959, and selections of Antonin Artaud, 1976, and Roland Barthes, 1981; she is a prolific magazine contributor. Crossing swords with Adrienne RICH, 1975, she entered a plea that feminism (which, like 'all capital moral truths' is 'a bit simple-minded') should not divorce mind from feeling. See *A Susan Sontag Reader*, 1983; study by Sohnya Sayres, 1989.

Soper, Grace (Isabell), 1766–1830, religious writer, b. in Cornwall, da. of persecuted early Methodists. Her mother, Ann I., whose life she wrote and published (now lost), influenced her deeply. As a child she loved religious books, prayed to be saved, and arranged her own baptism, but had, she wrote later, no 'new heart'. Between 14 and 17 she was held by 'the snare of worldly society', till 'deep self-abhorrence' overtook her: 'I have felt the avenger of blood at my heels', even 'in the garden at mid-day'. After marriage and years of religious practice, inner conflicts returned; about 1800, 'my heart was disclosed (what shall I say?) as a loathsome den of reptiles.' She neglected her children and household, hated eating, and felt so ugly 'my bonnet was all the day hanging over my face.' She 'loved my little ones to excess': four died. At last she learned to cast her care on God. About 1812, feeling the effects of war and 'our property sweeping away on all sides', they sold up and moved to Portsmouth, where she became an Anglican. In 1821 she began a series of letters to sons in London, recounting from memory, emotionally and with a wealth of imagery, 'the Lord's gracious dealings with' her: *Reminiscences of Past Experience*, 1839.

'Sophia', a 'Person of Quality', author of two strong feminist polemics. Her *Woman Not Inferior to Man, or A Short and Modest Vindication of the Natural Right of the Fair-Sex to a Perfect Equality of Power, Dignity, and Esteem, with the Men*, 1739 (replying to a piece in the government journal *Common Sense*), was answered in *Man Superior to Woman*, 1739, by a 'Gentleman' whose noisy contempt for women *may* be ironically assumed. S expanded her claim in *Woman's Superior Excellence over Man* ... , 1740. Elizabeth CARTER was seeking her identity in 1739; suggestions include Lady Mary Wortley MONTAGU (made on an International Women's Year repr.; unlikely, though she had replied to *Common Sense*: she was living abroad, and admired Elizabeth BURNET's husband, whom S insults), Lady POMFRET's daughter Sophia, later Lady Granville (unlikely: no other writings known), or a man. S says an exemplary peer (first of his family with a title) is or has been her 'guardian'. Her reading includes seventeenth-century European feminists untranslated into English; also, all three pamphlets draw largely on Poulain or Poullain de la Barre's treatise on sexual equality (1673; Eng. trans., 1677; Gerald M. MacLean, ed., 1988). Poulain had answered his own carefully-reasoned pro-woman book (see DEFENCES) in 1675 with a courteous anti-feminist reply; although S too relies on reason and logic (women's alleged inferiority is an outmoded prejudice), and 'A Gentleman' on bluster (women – 'Lovely Creatures' – must not forget their 'Allegiance to us', or that their charms lie in 'pretty Fluency in Nonsense'), it *could* be that all three (jointly repr. as *Beauty's Triumph*, 1751) are by a single hand. S's projected 'parallel History of the most eminent persons of both sexes in past ages, for virtue or vice' is not known.

Sorabji, Cornelia, 1866–1954, barrister, novelist, fiction writer, folklorist, autobiographer, b. in Nasik, W. India, one of nine children, 'brought up English', of Parsi Christian parents: Francina, who was 'adopted' and converted by Cornelia, Lady Ford, and Sorabji Kharshedji Langrana, an ex-Zoroastrian. As the first woman to study law at Oxford Univ., from 1884, CS became a close friend of Dean Jowett and orientalist Max Muller, met leading British academic and political figures, developed a lifelong interest in Indian and British politics, and took up rowing. She became both the first Indian and first British woman barrister, returning home in 1894 to work mainly for women and children, as legal advisor for the Court of Wards in Bihar, Bengal, Orissa and Assam. Founder of Indian units of the National Council for Women and the Federation of University Women, she wrote primarily for British readers, glossing Indian words and explaining cultural norms. Her stories, mainly about Indian women, first appeared in British periodicals: collected in the much-admired *Love and Life Behind the Purdah*, 1901, *Sun-Babies*, 1904 (about children; 2nd series 1920), *Between the Twilights*, 1908, and *Indian Tales of the Great Ones Among Men, Women and Bird-People*, 1916 (from legend and folk-tale). She also published *Social Relations: England and India*, 1908; works on women in purdah, 1917, and a child-mother (fictionalized), 1920; *Gold Mohur: Time to Remember* (a play), 1930; a life of her sister, 1932; and two lively 'books of memories', *India Calling*, 1934, and *India Recalled*, 1936, about her legal work. *Queen Mary's Book of India*, 1943, including work by writers like T. S. Eliot, sold to raise money for Indian war-wounded, was CS's brain-child, though her name is not in it. Papers at the India Office, London.

Southcott, Joanna, 1750–1814, prophet, b. near Ottery St Mary, Devon, da. of Hannah (d. by 1770) and William S., a tenant farmer with whom her relation was stormy. She saw ghosts, and prized a copy of meditations written by an aunt. She was meagrely educ.; her writing and spelling made her works hard to read, and she later preferred dictating. She rejected 'many Lovers' and became a domestic servant. In 1792 she was beset with visions: an aerial battle which she linked with French invasion, and a Spirit (described in sensuous bodily terms) who 'visited her by day and by night'. She identified herself with the woman clothed with the sun in *Revelations*, and began voicing prophecies which brought charges of witchcraft, of causing what she foretold. In 1801 she borrowed money to publish *The Strange Effects of Faith*, and was soon 'constantly employ'd in writing' the Spirit's messages: torrential prose, verse often reworking hymns or folk ballads. Her 65 printed works and unnumbered MSS in many libraries (catalogue for Austin, Texas, by Eugene P. Wright, 1968) include an allegorical reading of Ann RADCLIFFE (see Wright in *Discourse*, 13, 1970). Her disciples (63 per cent women, mostly but not all the poor for whom she claimed to speak) soon became a full-blown millenarian movement; she saw them as the woman's seed bruising the serpent's head. She went to London in 1802, toured the Midlands and North, and 'signed and sealed' thousands (a slip of paper stamped with her seal marked the entry of a name on her scrolls of the Elect). After Christmas 1813, as the movement peaked, she announced her pregnancy by the Spirit with a supernatural son, Shiloh. Out of 21 examining doctors, 17 were convinced; only her death a year later brought disillusion. Study by James K. Hopkins, 1982.

Southerland, Ellease, poet and fiction writer, b. 1943 in Brooklyn, NY, eldest da. and third of 15 children of Ellease

(Dozier) and Monroe Penrose S., baker and Baptist minister. She decided to be a poet at ten, ran a weekly poetry session at her father's church, and edited and wrote for school publications at elementary and high school and Queen's College, CUNY, where she took her BA in English in 1965. She wrote an award-winning novella, *White Shadows*, in 1964, did case-work for the NYC Social Services department, 1966–72, published poems and stories in journals from 1970 (*Black World*, 1971, printed her account of a first trip to Nigeria), and won the Gwendolyn BROOKS poetry award, 1971; she calls Brooks her 'literary mother'. She taught literature from 1973, took her MFA at Columbia Univ. in 1974, became poet in residence at Pace Univ., 1979, and has studied Yoruba and Egyptian. Her slim poetry volume, *The Magic Sun Spins*, 1975, is titled from the opening of a poem which says that the sun is beautiful 'because / Black is'. Other poems bind together fire and water, music and speech, Nigeria, Brooklyn, New Mexico and Vietnam. ES wrote on Zora Neale HURSTON in Roseann P. Bell et al., eds., *Sturdy Black Bridges*, 1979. She took five years to write the short, lyrical, intense *Let the Lion Eat Straw*, 1979, based on her mother's life. It covers idyllic rural poverty in NC, life with an ambitious but untender 'New York mother', deep love for a stepfather who dies, fear of an actual father and rape by an uncle, success as 'the Piano Girl', marriage, 15 children, and early death from cancer. ES's later projected volumes have not yet appeared.

Southwell, Frances (Howard), Lady, 'news'-writer, da. of Catherine (Carey), cousin and favourite of ELIZABETH I, and Charles H., Lord High Admiral. She m. naval officer Sir Robert S. (d. 1598), and was chief lady-in-waiting to Anne, James I's queen, and friend of Cecily BULSTRODE and Lady Anne CLIFFORD. Her 'Certain Edicts from a Parliament in Eutopia' were pub. with Sir Thomas Overbury's *The Wife*, 1615 (repr. ed. James E. Savage, 1968). They address the two sexes alternately with such ADVICE as 'no Lady that silently simpereth for want of wit shall be call'd modest'; FS is said to be author of 'other Characters, or lively descriptions of Persons'.

Southworth, E. D. E. N., Emma Dorothy Eliza (Nevitte), 1819–99, novelist, b. Washington, DC, da. of Susannah (Wailes) and Charles Le Compte N., importer, who d. when she was three. She was educ. at the school founded by her stepfather, Joshua L. Henshaw. Graduating in 1835, she taught until 1840, when she m. Frederick Hamilton S., an inventor, and they moved to Prairie du Chien, Wis., where she taught in Platteville until the birth of her son. She separated from her husband in 1844 and returned with her son to Washington, where a daughter was born. To supplement her teacher's salary, she began to write. 'It was in these darkest days of my *woman's* life, that my *author's* life commenced ...' (Hart, 1854). Her first story was pub. in the *Baltimore Saturday Visitor*, 1846, while her first novel, *Retribution*, was serialized in 1849. Eleven more appeared in *National Era* and *Saturday Evening Post*, later pub. by T. B. Peterson. In 1857 she signed a contract for exclusive serial rights to her novels with the *New York Ledger*, which pub. 30 in all, and she continued to write at a prolific pace into her 70s, as the most POPULAR woman novelist. Although she was never a part of the feminist movement, one of her heroines, Capitola, in *The Hidden Hand*, 1859 (repr. 1988), portrays an aggressive woman who needs no man to rescue her. She dresses as a boy, explaining that 'While all the ragged boys I knew could get little jobs to earn bread, I, because I was a girl, was not allowed to carry a gentleman's parcel ... or do *anything* that *I* could do just as well as *they*.' See studies by Regis Boyle, 1939, and Helen Papashvily, 1956; also A. Habegger, 'A well Hidden Hand', *Novel* (Spring 1981), and Susan K. Harris in *Legacy* (Fall 1987).

'Sowernam' or 'Sowrenam', **'Ester'**, pseudonym on *Ester Hath Hang'd Haman*, 1617, a reply to Joseph Swetnam's 1615 ATTACK on women: it inverts his name (he said 'every sweet hath his sowre') and adds that of the biblical Esther, who hanged Haman, would-be slaughterer of the Jews. Its author may really be a woman, despite keeping legal terms in London and chopping logic in learned style on points from many classical and misogynist texts. 'She' dedicates to the 'vertuously disposed, of the Faeminine Sexe': 'You are women; in Creation, noble; in Redemption, gracious; in use most blessed; be not forgetful of your selves.' Rachel SPEGHT's reply, she says, is insufficient. She deals gravely with Swetnam's charge that women do not offer men the help for which they were created (a charge also against God), but allows herself 'a little libertie' in handling his 'scurril' insults. A concluding poem signed 'Joane Sharp' neatly sums up a loaded situation: 'men doe wrest all things [that women do] the contrary way.' Repr. with other DEFENCES, 1985.

Spark, Muriel Sarah (Camberg), novelist, poet, playwright, writer of short stories and children's books, editor, biographer. B. in 1918 in Edinburgh, da. of Sarah Elizabeth Maud (Uezzell) and Bernard C., she approximates to the heroine of *The Mandelbaum Gate*, 1965: 'a Gentile Jewess, a private-judging Catholic, a shy adventuress'. Her maternal grandmother, Adelaide, participated in Emmeline PANKHURST's Suffragette movement. MS was educ. at James Gillespie's School for Girls, Edinburgh, inspiration for the Marcia Blaine School in her best-known novel, *The Prime of Miss Jean Brodie*, 1961. She lived in southern Africa, 1937–44, an experience reflected in *The Go-Away Bird*, 1958. She m. S. O. Spark, 1937, and had one son. The marriage was soon dissolved. MS worked in the Political Intelligence Department of the British Foreign Office, 1944–5. The work, recalled in *The Hothouse by the East River*, 1973, as 'the propagation of the Allied point of view under the guise of the German point of view . . . a tangled mixture of damaging lies, flattering and plausible truths', suggests her fictions' interest in plots and plotters, surveillance, and the dubious authority of fact. MS held editorial and publicity posts in London, 1946–50, including editorship of the *Poetry Review*, 1947–9. She published *Child of Light*, on Mary Wollstonecraft SHELLEY, 1951, and *My Best Mary*, 1953, and, with Derek Stanford, a succession of critical/biographical works and editions, including *Emily* BRONTË, 1953, *The Brontë Letters*, 1953, and *Letters of John Henry Newman*, 1957. She was received into the Catholic Church, 1954. The experience of an 'odd sort of Catholic' convert writing her first novel provides the substance of *The Comforters*, 1957, whose themes and reflexive techniques are developed and exploited in succeeding novels. Rejecting the 'vulgar chronology' (*Not to Disturb*, 1971) of humanism and realist fiction, MS challenges an illusory tyranny of time by destroying sequence and consequence and readjusting vision to the atemporal perspectives of allegory, subjectivity and faith. The authorial activity which is God's and the novelist's is also the prerogative of a host of 'plotters': artists, blackmailers, con-men and women, who parody divine ordering authority, treading the fine line between diabolic presumption and saintly hope. *The Mandelbaum Gate*, 1965, 'solidly rooted in a very detailed setting', exploring relationship between the spiritual and the historical, was an 'important book' for MS, who afterwards departed from realism to write a series of anti-realist novels exploiting and parodying techniques of the *nouveau roman*. In *The Takeover*, 1976, and *Territorial Rights*, 1979, techniques of comedy and the thriller describe a world whose absurdity is recognized as 'stark realism'. Her latest novels recall her earliest. *Loitering with Intent*, 1981, reintroduces confusion between fiction and reality; *The Only*

Problem, 1984, develops her interest in the Book of Job and earthly suffering. In *A Far Cry from Kensington*, 1988, the Sparkian 'plotter', the 'pisseur de copie' Hector Bartlett, unwittingly becomes the designer of Mrs. Hawkins's success story. Derek Stanford, 1963, 1977, informs, but, according to MS, is 'not to be relied on'. MS is reticent about her life; her autobiographical heroine in *Loitering with Intent* says, 'How wonderful it feels to be an artist and a woman in the twentieth century'. Studies by Peter Kemp, 1974, and Ruth Whittaker, 1982; see William McBrien in Thomas F. Staley, ed., *Twentieth-Century Women Novelists*, 1982.

Speght, Rachel, *c.* 1598–after 1630, polemicist and poet, da. of the Rev. James S. of London (not of Thomas S., known as editor of Chaucer). She was first to answer Joseph Swetnam, in *A Mouzell for Melastomus* [i.e. 'muzzle for Black Mouth']: *The Cynicall* [canine] *Bayter of, and Foule Mouthed Barker against Evahs Sex*, 1617 (repr. 1985 by Shepherd only: see DEFENCES). She appoints herself champion to her dedicatees: all 'of Hevahs sex fearing God, and loving their just reputation'. In her quiet, Christian, scholarly judgement, few women lack traditional female virtues, which are quite consistent with learning. If hesitant about full equality, she emphatically claims respect. Her attached 'Certain Queries to the Bayter of Women' contradict him on specific points. She dedicated her verse *Mortalities Memorandum, with a Dreame Prefix'd, Imaginarie in Manner, Reall in Matter*, 1621, to her godmother and teacher, printing it both to assert her claim to her prose work (ascribed by some to her father) and to do good, not sinfully bury her talent. The allegorical dream relates her quest for Knowledge, helped by Truth and Desire to conquer Disswasion. She, 'SOWERNAM' and 'MUNDA' all combat the 'full fed Beast' Swetnam; RS meets the monster Death, who takes her mother. The main poem drops fiction to argue directly that death, inflicted as a curse, is yet a blessing to the godly, a 'Portal of true Paradise' if only we ponder its necessity, impartiality, and uncertain date. She married William Procter that year, and had two children. See Mary Nyquist in Nyquist and Margaret Ferguson, eds, *Re-membering Milton*, 1987.

Spence, Catherine Helen, 1825–1910, novelist, journalist, critic, and feminist activist, b. Melrose, Scotland, fifth child of Helen (Brodie) and David S., lawyer and banker. Taught by her mother and aunts that 'to make the world pleasant for men' was not woman's only role, she hoped to become a teacher and great writer, but her education was interrupted by her father's financial ruin and the family's move to South Australia in 1839. She became a governess and opened her own school, then began contributing (anon.) to Adelaide newspapers. Her *Clara Morison: A Tale of South Australia During the Gold Fever*, 1854, was the first novel with an Australian setting written in Australia by a woman. Conventionally romantic in structure, it presents in Margaret Elliot a less usual picture of a happily unmarried woman. Other fiction includes *Tender and True*, 1856, *Mr Hogarth's Will*, 1865 (repr. 1988), *The Author's Daughter*, 1868, and the utopian 'A Week in the Future', 1889 (in the *Centennial Magazine*). *Gathered In*, 1977, and *Handfasted* – 'too socialistic' – 1984, ed. Helen Thomson, were not pub. as books during her lifetime. Though CHS won some critical acclaim for her fiction, she believed that she would achieve more through JOURNALISM and public speaking. In the 1870s she contributed to the *South Australian Register*, was the first woman to read papers at the South Australian Institute, and preached for the Unitarian Church. Her early religious doubt and her shift to Unitarianism informs *An Agnostic's Progress from the Known to the Unknown*, 1884. She lectured in the USA and Britain and joined the fight for women's SUFFRAGE, and in

1897 was Australia's first woman political candidate. She died while writing her autobiography, 1910 (completed by her companion Jeanne F. Young, who also pub. an appreciation, 1937). The CHS Prize is awarded annually by Adelaide Univ. for the best female student in economics. See the biography by Susan Magarey, 1985, and Helen Thomson's study, 1987. MSS are held by the State Library of South Australia and the Mitchell Library, Sydney.

Spence, Elizabeth Isabella, 1768–1832, novelist and travel writer, b. at Dunkeld, Tayside, only child of Elizabeth (Fordyce) and Dr James S.: related to Isabella KELLY. They lost money in 1772 on the bank crash of one of her prominent Fordyce uncles. Her mother died in 1777, her father in 1786; EIS went to an aunt and uncle in London, and on their deaths turned her writing from pastime to career. She began anonymously: two novels in 1799, two more by 1807. In 1809 came letters from English and Welsh holiday tours, stiffly edited as *Summer Excursions*. They treat of local life and antiquities: in Bristol she mentions 'misguided' Mary ROBINSON, 'amiable' Marianne CHAMBERS and obscure genius Ann YEARSLEY. Later similar works maintain the interest in women writers: *Sketches* of Scotland, 1811, praises (together) James Fordyce and Catharine MACAULAY as advisers of women. *Letters from the Highlands* (to Jane PORTER), 1816, reporting from personal knowledge on Anne GRANT, Christian JOHNSTONE, and Christian MILNE, was vulgarly mocked as by 'the Travelling Spinster' in *Blackwood's*, 1818. Several of EIS's later works blend fiction with local history (though her dates are sometimes confused); some take a ballad or epitaph as starting-point. In *A Traveller's Tale of the Last Century*, 1819, and *Old Stories*, 1822, male tourist-narrators pick up and retail MSS centring on women's lives: the former names its heroine Deletia. *How to be Rid of a Wife*, 1823 (with another short novel), claims to be a true story of a wife 'bought' from her brutal husband for education and marriage by a Duke of Chandos (in fact or rumour Cassandra CHANDOS's stepson). Its aim is adulation of the nobility rather than exploration of female experience; the BL has a copy bound in velvet from the actual Duchess's funeral gear.

Spence, Sarah (Crompton), poet, probably from near Yarmouth, Norfolk, writing by 1783. (The speaker in 'The Gentleman's Petition', 1784, asks a wife who 'scarcely can read', and is annoyed when Jove advises a reasoner.) She m. widower George S. by about 1790; in 1792 he turned against her for undisclosed reasons and parted her from her baby, who then died. Subscribers to her *Poems and Miscellaneous Pieces*, Bury St Edmunds, 1795, included A. L. BARBAULD, Elizabeth COBBOLD, M. S. COOPER, A. B. CRISTALL, Ann JEBB, Joseph Johnson (who sold the book in London), Capel Lofft (who contributed notes) and William Wilberforce. Chiefly in heroic couplets, it discusses solitude, society, education, creation, prophecy (with biblical notes), social issues (debtors; the Humane Society). SS addresses Quakers (respectfully) about war, 1783, and wrestles with personal issues. Fragments of essays (on war and slavery, some repr. from journals) and letters follow. She published *Musical Catechism* [?1810] (well-reviewed dialogues to instruct beginners), a work on prophecy, and at Colchester, 1821, as a widow, two more poems (forceful blank verse) from 1794–5: 'The Millenium' (on the imminent Second Coming and a world where 'In Symphony with man, creation sings' and distant races salute each other) and 'Poverty, or The Irish in London. A Reverie' (an agonized mother is reconciled through faith to the deaths of her babies; but SS excoriates the rich who see the poor as 'a reptile race / Born to be slaves, and not to *them* allied'). She says she could write facts as well as a reverie 'If Critics would allow Poets to mention bricks, mortar, loaves, coals, blankets, &c.'

Spencer, 'Anne', Annie Bethel (Scales), 1882–1975, poet and prose-writer whose work is largely lost, b. on a Virginia plantation of largely Seminole descent, only child of Sarah Louise S. (b. free but illegitimate) and a slave-born father. They separated when she was little; she grew up in Bramwell, West Va., self-educ. until 11 since her mother scorned free black schools. At 14, at Va. Seminary, Lynchburg, she wrote 'The Sceptic', her first poem, against religion and the threat of hell. In 1899 she gave a defiant valedictory address on the future of the Negro. She taught at Maybeury, W. Va., married Edward S. in 1901 against her mother's will, had four children (one died almost at birth), and wrote. She was influenced by Olive SCHREINER from 1900; from 1919 she made her house in Lynchburg a centre for black intellectuals. She published only two or three prose pieces and less than 30 poems. Her first, 'Before the Feast of Shushan' (*Crisis*, 1920), in which King Ahasuerus voices his possessive, oppressive love for Vashti, was well received; but H. L. Mencken urged her to be less experimental. 'Black Man O' Mine' is a love-poem, 'White Things' a blistering protest poem; 'The Carnival' juxtaposes a dancer ('a quivering female-thing / Gestured assignations') with a 'sausage and garlic booth'. Unpub. prose included 'Madame and Maid', a story about race; 'Popes and Prostitutes'; a novel, a 'quiet, sympathetic satire' on local black snobbery, and 1940s pieces for a projected newspaper column. AS reviewed Georgia Douglas JOHNSON. 'I proudly love being a Negro woman. . . . *We* are the PROBLEM – the great national game of TABOO' (in Countee Cullen, ed., *Caroling Dusk*, 1927). She worked as a librarian, 1924–46 and for the NAACP; she ceased trying to publish after 1938, but wrote much after her husband's death in 1964. A keen reviser and 'scrap paper scribbler in pencil', she lost many MSS when her garden-house was vandalized, and more to well-meaning tidiers in her extreme old age. In 1971 she had nearly finished a long prose piece, inspired by H. B. STOWE and Allen Tate, 'Virginia as Narcissus: In the Best Tradition of Slavery': 'fellow citizens, we cannot escape history in honor or dishonor'. In 1972 she began a projected series of poems on generals from Hannibal to LeRoi Jones: notes remain, with several hundred lines of 'A Dream of John Brown' (whose hanged body swings to the pendulum rhythm of history). J. Lee Greene's life of her, 1971, prints nearly 50 poems; papers at her house, now a museum. Of an autobiographical sketch written in 1922 she later wrote 'Tried a lot of 'em to see which tale sounded best.'

Spencer, Elizabeth, novelist and short-story writer, b. 1921 in Carrollton, Mississippi, da. of Mary (McCain) and James Luther S. At Belhaven College, Jackson (BA in English, 1942), 'already a writer', she sought out Eudora WELTY (while still inclined to scorn women writers). She took an MA in English at Vanderbilt Univ., Nashville, Tenn., 1943, taught at colleges and univs., and was a reporter on the *Nashville Tennessean*, 1945–6. *Fire in the Morning*, 1948, first of her three Mississippi novels, took 'some time' to write, and broaches a favourite theme: its hero uncovers buried wrongs from the past. Its modest proceeds gave ES her first trip to Europe. *This Crooked Way*, 1952 (title from directions for finding Death, in Chaucer's *Pardoner's Tale*), picks up a reference from *Fire*; its hero, raised among religious revivalists, tries to escape his family's manipulation of others, but lives to be arraigned by those closest to him for manipulating in his turn. *The Voice at the Back Door*, 1956 (alluding to the black presence on the margin of a white household), deals with miscegenation, corruption, reprisals against the man seeking to bring justice. In Italy on a Guggenheim award in 1953, ES stayed to marry the English John Rusher in 1956; they settled in Montréal in 1958. She wrote three novellas about Americans in Italy: *The Light in the Piazza*, 1960 (in which a mother, with much trepidation, lets her beloved retarded daughter make a marriage for love: a hit, filmed 1962), *Knights & Dragons*, 1965, and *The Cousins*, 1985; repr. together, 1986. In the last two, middle-aged people look back and re-evaluate youthful experience. The same is true of later novels: *No Place for an Angel*, 1967 (a boldly structured novel of moral compromise), *The Snare*, 1972 ('a study of evil ... my most intensely thought-out book'), and *The Salt Line*, 1985. Only in the last do prevailing betrayals and disillusion yield to something better than 'the happy-happy game ... the Optimist Club': this novel of the hurricane-bewitched Gulf coast, of old friends who hate each other, moves from death, paranoia, and gambling rackets towards oddly-assorted friendships and a birth. In 1957 *The New Yorker* printed ES's 'The Little Brown Girl' (rejected in 1944), in which secret, childish, white fantasy meets equally hidden, black self-interest. It was repr. with nine further memorable pieces in *Ship Island*, 1968, all repr. in *Stories*, 1981 (chronologically ranked, many 'about liberation, and the regret you have when you liberate yourself': foreword by Welty); new work in *Jack of Diamonds*, 1988. See study by Peggy W. Prenshaw, 1985. Interview in *SoR*, 18, 1982; checklist by Laura Barge, *Miss. Quarterly*, 29, 1975–6. MSS at Univ. of Kentucky.

Spender, Emily, 1841–1922, novelist, younger da. of Dr John Cottle S. of Bath, Somerset (1801–65), friend of W. S. Landor. Her brother John m. Lilian (Headland) SPENDER. Her two best-known novels, *Son and Heir*, 1864, and *Restored*, 1871, both anon., are odd mixtures of burgeoning feminist insight and old-fashioned sensation plots. A pioneer suffragist, ES toured the west of England lecturing (often at considerable personal risk) from 1870, and knew M. G. FAWCETT. Her later novels are more soberly feminist: *The Law Breakers*, 1903, has a 50-year-old spinster heroine, whose existence 'was made up of checked endeavours, unfulfilled ambitions, unused capacities'. ES spent her later life in Italy, where she had many friends; a copy of her novel dealing with the freedom of Italy, *A Soldier for a Day*, 1901, was placed in Italian Army mess rooms 'as a special compliment to the authoress'. She and Constance Spender compiled an anthology of patriotic poetry in 1911 (repr. 1915). She continued to write short stories up to her death.

Spender, Lilian (Lily), 'Mrs J. K. Spender' (Headland), 1835–95, English novelist. She wrote for money, first with essays on German poets, then novels, which made £1,600 for her sons' education (she also sent one daughter to Somerville), a holiday fund, and her husband's early retirement. An early novel, *Parted Lives*, 1873, was well reviewed in the *Spectator*. Later works, like *A Strange Temptation*, 1893 and *A Modern Quixote*, 1894 (her last), have leading characters of committed ideals, socialistic or otherwise, whose radicalism and loyalty to friends (male or female) leads them into serious difficulties in forming love relationships. Intelligently written, her novels yet lack craft, falling into ill-fitting banal romance endings. She taught herself Greek (rising early), subscribed to many libraries, and her house was always flooded with the newest English and French books. See the reminiscences of her two sons, Harold S. [1926], and J. A. S., 1927.

'Speranza', Jane Francesca (Elgee) Lady Wilde, 1823?–96, Irish poet, translator and essayist, b. Wexford, da. of Sarah (Kingsbury) and Charles E., solicitor. She was educ. at home, and in 1847 began writing poetry as a convert to nationalism, for the Irish periodical *The Nation*, as 'Speranza': 'I dared not have my name published'. Her article 'Jacta Alea Est' (The Die is Cast), 29 July 1848, caused the suppression of the periodical and contributed to the arrest of its editor, Charles Gavan Duffy, for sedition. Her work for *The Nation* included collections of Irish folklore and TRANSLATIONS from Russian, Turkish, Spanish, German, Italian and Portuguese, alien settings often providing cover for revolutionary sentiments. Her *Poems*, 1864, included Nationalist verse in ringing style. In 1851 she m. Sir William Robert Wills W., Irish antiquary and surgeon (later disgraced), and had two sons, William, a journalist, and Oscar, the poet and dramatist. In Dublin she entertained a large literary and artistic salon, being known for her eccentricity and epigrammatic powers: 'nothing in the world is worth living for except sin'. She was also active in the Women's Rights movement. After her husband died in 1876 she moved to London where her circle included Marie CORELLI, OUIDA, Margaret Raine HUNT and Violet HUNT, and her son Oscar. In 1887 she pub. *Ancient legends, mystic charms and superstitions of Ireland*, followed by *Ancient cures, charms and usages*, 1890. She pub. two books of essays, *Notes on Men, Women and Books*, 1891, and *Social Studies*, 1893. Although she was granted a pension in 1890 'in recognition of her services to literature', she died in poverty. There is a lightweight biography by H. Wyndham, 1951.

Spiritualism and **Theosophy**. Spiritualism began in its modern form in the US; its heyday world-wide was from the 1850s to the 1870s. Although often dismissed as a drawing-room fad, its appeal to women was enhanced by the belief that they made the best mediums; it also offered liberation from outdated creeds and clergymen. Trance lecturer Emma Hardinge Britten made a fine living and travelled extensively. E. B. BROWNING angered Robert by her faith in it; Camilla CROSLAND, Katherine WOODS, OUIDA, H. H. RICHARDSON and Marie CORELLI were among numerous nineteenth-century writers drawn to the occult. The Theosophical Society, claiming ancient oriental origins, was founded in NY in 1875 by Russian-born Helena Petrovna Blavatsky and other dissatisfied spiritualists, to find a more direct approach to God by reviving ancient religious knowledge. Sex distinctions (also those of caste, class, colour) were eschewed. Annie BESANT, second president (from 1907), enhanced its appeal to progressive women like suffragist Charlotte DESPARD. Rosa PRAED was influenced by both spiritualism and theosophy. See Pat Holden, ed., *Women's Religious Experience*, 1983; Marion Meade, *Madame Blavatsky*, 1980; Jill Roe, *Beyond Belief: Theosophy in Australia*, 1986; Alex Owen, *The Darkened Room: Women, Power and Spiritualism in Late Nineteenth Century England*, 1989.

Spivak, Gayatri (**Chakravorty**), critical theorist and translator, b. 1941, da. of Sivani (Majunder) and Pares Chandra C. Educ. in Calcutta (BA, 1959), Cambridge, and Cornell (PhD, 1967), she has taught in various US universities, now at Pittsburg. Author of a study of W. B. Yeats, 1974, she is best known as translator of Jacques Derrida's *Of Grammatology* and for her 'interventionist' deconstructive criticism. She risks staging 'the critic as subject', positioned in the variant discourses of feminism, Marxism and race 'from' where the text can be 'worlded' and the specific political, economic, ideological conditions of its historiography exposed. She campaigns against reduction of deconstruction to an institutional 'method' in the belief that classroom and auditorium can produce a radical reading of the world/text and so cultural transformation. GCS pressures feminist audiences and readers to renew their critical vigilance in view of the post-structuralist drift into post-feminism. Focusing on Derrida's figural use of feminity, she shows both how deconstruction 'doubly displaces' the 'discourse of woman' without consideration for women's needs to designate their specific historicity, and how feminism might stage a recuperation of this discourse for the purposes of launching a radical critique of phallogocentric (imperialist and Marxist) historiographies. Intervening in 'first world feminism's' bourgeois self-containment, GCS points to its complicity with 'third world' women's oppression and exploitation by multi-national capitalism. She has introduced the powerful Bengali writer Mahasweta DEVI to the West. Her TRANSLATION, critical readings, and theoretical speculations appear in Indian, American, French and English journals, in *In Other Worlds, Essays in Cultural Politics*, 1987, and in *The Post-Colonial Critic: Interviews, Strategies, Dialogues*, ed. Sarah Harasym, 1990. *Native Informant, Master Discourse* forthcoming.

Spofford, Harriet Elizabeth (**Prescott**), 1835–1921, novelist, poet, short-story writer, b. Calais, Maine, da. of Sarah Jane (Bridges) and Joseph Newmarch P., lawyer and lumber merchant. She was educ. at Putnam Free School, Newburyport, Mass., and Pinkerton Academy, Derry, NH. HPS began her writing career to support her invalid parents. Her short story 'In a Cellar' (*Atlantic Monthly*, 1859), an instant success, was followed by GOTHIC romances such as *Sir Rohan's Ghost*, 1860, and *Azarian*, 1864, which explore themes of relevance to women. Her story 'Circumstance' (*The Amber Gods*, 1863) compellingly presents the predicament of a woman artist: Emily DICKINSON wrote: 'I read Miss Prescott's "Circumstance" but it followed me in the Dark ... so I avoided her'. In 1865 she m. Richard S., lawyer and poet, and they lived in Washington until 1874; *Old Washington*, 1906, is based on her experiences of life there. On returning to Newburyport, her home became the centre for visiting literary friends such as S. O. JEWETT, R.T. COOKE and L. C. MOULTON, of whom she wrote in *A Little Book of Friends*, 1916. Of interest is her destabilization of the polarized stereotypes, Madonna and Magdalen, notably in 'An Ideal' (*Scarlet Poppy*, 1894), which gives victory to the latter, and 'Wages of Sin' (*Old Madame and Other Tragedies*, 1900), in which Judith Dauntry commits herself to a free-love union with Ellis – married and separated from wife and child – in the face of community vilification and violence. 'I have no voice in making the law, why should I obey it?' In *Three Heroines of New England Romance*, 1894, *A Master Spirit*, 1896, and *An Inheritance*, 1897, HPS treats the domestic novel as an organ of sisterhood and woman's experience – the 'proper study of womankind is woman'. Her vol. of poetry, *Titian's Garden*, was pub. in 1897, and story colls. appeared in 1894, 1900 and 1920. See Elizabeth K. Halbeisen, 1935, for her life; Thelma Shiner in *Turn-of-the-Century Women*, 1, 1984.

Squire, Jane, d. 1743, London mathematician and feminist. In 1731 she printed a *Proposal* for a method of ascertaining longitude. (Parliament had offered a reward of £10,000–£20,000, according to accuracy; nearly 250 rejected claimants, 1714–65, included Anna WILLIAMS's father.) JS, a Catholic, begins with the longitude of Bethlehem taken when 'Christ vouchsafed there to be born for us'; her clock for astral time is to be engraved with the Nativity at its centre and angels in unused spaces; she plans an educational system to teach its use to 'poor Sea-Boys'. She sent or took her Proposal to Lord Torrington (Sarah Byng OSBORN's father) and all the Commissioners; none replied. Her letters assert, with increasing anger, women's right to science. To 'Study the Law of God Day and Night, is my proper Business; Philosophy my Amusement, and Mathematicks my Play-things.' Being 'unlearn'd in their Schools', she is 'unable to bow down to their Idols or subscribe to their first Axioms', but 'a time may come, when what is said may be as much regarded, as who says it.' By 1741 she was sure her ideas (actually non-viable) and instrument had been stolen. In 1742 she reprinted her *Proposal*, in both English and French, with all the letters and a complicated 'Explanation'. She gives new names to all the stars according to their positions, and new names for units of measurement (Milduas, Mins, Minduas, etc.), and proposes a new universal alphabet and universal language on logical principles, which for its 'Facility, and Simplicity' she calls 'Lacinfanta'. The scholar Thomas Rawlins admired her. Nothing of hers remains in the longitude papers (Royal Greenwich Observatory, Cambridge).

Staël, Anne Louise **Germaine** (Necker) **de**, 1766–1817, woman of letters, b. in Paris to the Swiss Suzanne (Churchod), hostess and ex-governess, and Jacques N., banker and political power-broker. Her mother educated her formidably as a prodigy and exemplar (English literature was important; GdeS met Elizabeth MONTAGU in London in 1776). She also encouraged writing (Jacques N. disapproved of it) and taught the rigid suppression of feeling. In 1786 GdeS was married to Swedish diplomat Eric Magnus Staël von Holstein, in a deal which also made him a Count. She hated marriage (her daughter died a baby), but took her role as ambassadress seriously. In 1792, as a constitutional monarchist (like her lover the Count of Narbonne and their friend the future husband of Frances BURNEY) she was exiled to Switzerland and England. After other well-publicized affairs, she m. John Rocca in 1816. Much of her work (in French: coll. 1820) was deeply influential for women writing in English. *Letters on Rousseau*, 1788, was given a bad review by Mary WOLLSTONECRAFT; *On Fiction*, 1795, and *On the Influence of the Passions*, 1796, analyse women's various exclusions; the novels *Delphine*, 1802, and *Corinne*, 1807 (new English transl. 1987), present much-extolled heroines. In London 1813–14, she was both fêted and attacked. Her corresp. with Elizabeth DEVONSHIRE was ed. Victor de Pange, 1980; life by Renée Winegarten, 1985; selec. works ed. and transl. Vivian Folkenflik, 1987.

Stafford, Jean, 1915–79, short-story writer and novelist, b. at Corina, Calif., da. of Mary (McKillop) and John S., writer of westerns; they moved to Colorado in 1921. Early 'unhappy and afraid' (she later recalled 'my grandfather's Sunday punishment room'), she found solace in secret writing. She went to schools in Pueblo, Colorado Springs and Boulder, became a Catholic at 18 (later she 'gave up the Ghost'), took a BA and MA, 1936, at the Univ. of Colorado (where she modelled for life classes), and studied philosophy at Heidelberg. A post at St Stephen's College, Missouri, showed her that teaching was not for her. In 1940 she m. the poet Robert Lowell (whom 'I loved to despair and hated to the point of murder', says her savage fictional memoir 'An Influx of Poets', 1978). *Boston Adventure*, 1944, first of her few novels, sets her characteristic tone: an only daughter of immigrants examines and rejects the paths available to her in wealthier or more genteel society. In *The Mountain Lion*, 1947, repr. 1972, set in her archetype-laden Southwest, a sister retreats into fantasy as her once close brother is initiated into an excluding masculine world (see B. H. Gelfant in *Mass. Review*, 20, 1979; B. A. White in *Essays in Literature*, 9, 1982). Badly injured in a car-crash early in her relationship with Lowell, JS had to have her nose rebuilt, an experience described in 'The Interior Castle', 1946 (title alluding to St Teresa). Divorced, she was hospitalized for mental breakdown, which like most significant events in her life is repeatedly explored in her fiction. She began publishing stories in *The New Yorker*, m. photographer Oliver Jensen in 1950, and won the O. Henry Prize in 1955. *The Catherine Wheel*, 1952, a 'New England GOTHIC tale', reveals 'hidden envy, guilt and remorse' through a 'closed structural system of symbols' centred on a 'poor, lonely, obsessed' woman who spends her life lamenting the loss of the man she loved. JS married writer A. J. Liebling in 1959. Though she explicitly rejected the women's liberation movement in her late non-fiction, her interest in 'the misfit, the outcast' leads her to write mostly of women as 'most clearly represent[ing] the "other"' in a sick post-war age. In 1962 she published a children's book, and in 1966 a study of the mother of murderer Lee Harvey Oswald. Her *Collected Short Stories*, 1969, won the Pulitzer Prize, some years after she had virtually stopped writing fiction. See Jeanette W. Mann in *Critique*, 17, 1975; special JS issue in *Shenandoah*, 30, 1979; bibliog. by Avila Wanda, 1983; study by Maureen Ryan, 1987; life by David Roberts, 1988.

Stanford, Ann, 1916–87, poet and scholar, b. at La Habra, Calif., da. of Rose (Corrigan) and Bruce S., who sold oil-drilling tools. Educ. at Stanford Univ. (BA 1938), she m. Roland Arthur White, an architect, in 1942, and had four children. Her first books of poetry were *In Narrow Bound*, 1943, and *The White Bird*, 1949. In *The Weathercock*, 1966, she says she is 'printed with the earth / Always and always the earth ground into the fingers' ('The Blackberry Thicket'), and makes Pandora (in a poem of that name, later awarded a prize) lament that she 'shall never be rid of' the box she was slow to open: 'The day hung so full, time being happy and short, / No reason to fret over a dusty chest in a corner.' *Magellan*, 1958, is a poem for several voices. AS studied journalism, English and American literature at UCLA (MAs 1958, 1961; PhD 1962), edited the *Uclan Review*, 1961–4, and taught at Calif. State Univ., Northridge, from 1968. 'Before' in her next collection, *The Descent*, 1970, explains her work's concern with time: 'When I lay in my mother's womb / Her heart boomed in the chamber above me / The great clock. / Since then I have been enamored of time / And rivers too and seas / Like the sea in which I floated.' She has held poetry fellowships, translated *The Bhagavad Gita*, 1970, edited (besides Renaissance and early American texts) *The Women Poets in English: An Anthology*, 1972, which notes the involvement of women in composing and preserving their cultures' songs and legends, and written a study of Anne BRADSTREET, 1975. *The Countess of Forli*, 1985, is a play based on the life of Caterina Sforza, who ruled Rome and Forli after the death of her husband in the late fifteenth century.

Stanhope, Eugenia (Peters), *c.* 1730–86, translator and alleged advice-writer. Illegitimate da. of a rich Irish Mr Domvile and a Mrs P., she was well educ., musical, plain and poor. She met the 17-year-old Philip S., illegitimate son of the famous Lord Chesterfield, in Rome in 1750, married him secretly c. 1759, and bore two sons in obscure London lodgings. She met Chesterfield only after Philip, a diplomat, had died in France in 1768. After Chesterfield's death she pub. his letters to his son, 1774, with a preface and her own idiomatic renderings from French; in the 2nd ed. she defended their pessimism and advocacy of extramarital sex; a preface to more letters appeared posthumously, 1787. Paid £1,575 for the MSS, she was accused [1775] of greed and immorality. Also ascribed to her (though its author, the Hon. E. S., says she is old and 'long married') is *The Deportment of a Married Life*, in letters to a niece, 1790, which partly endorses, partly rebuts Chesterfield. It argues that husbands are ordained superior, that wives should be financially dependent and the world conformed to. It is severe on infidelity in women ('monstrous') but also on that of men (intrigue is 'very different from what is represented by some'), and on social tolerance of it; married love, good husbands, and freedom of marriage choice are extolled.

Stanhope, Lady **Hester** Lucy, 1776–1839, traveller, eldest da. of Hester (Pitt) and the future 3rd Earl of S., b. at Chevening, Kent. Active and bossy as a girl, she kept house for her famous uncle William Pitt, 1803–6; he consulted her on politics. After his death and other bereavements, she left

London for Wales (finding her pension of £1200 p.a. inadequate for her standing), then in 1810, for Greece, Turkey, and Jerusalem. In 1814 she settled at Jôon, or Djouni, Mount Lebanon, in Syria. Though 'I am not a lady, but a poor Bedouin', she was a local autocrat who spent hugely, clashed with British consuls and despised the society she had left. Her 'soaring and active mind is no merit of mine. I was endowed with it'; 'I have been thought mad – ridiculed and abused; but it is out of the power of man to change my way of thinking upon any subject.' She evolved her own religion, believed in guardian spirits, and expected a second coming ('God is my friend'). Despising 'the gentler qualities of her own sex' and disliking wives, she estimated female influence high. She doubted whether Lady Charlotte BURY, whom she had known, had written the books ascribed to her, and sent a 'presumptuous epistle' (*DNB*) to Queen VICTORIA. Charles Lewis Meryon's *Memoirs* of her, and her *Travels*, 1845, 1846, repr. Salzburg 1985, 1983; life and letters ed. the Duchess of Cleveland, 1913; several lives.

Stanhope, Louisa Sidney, obscure author of 17 novels, many for MINERVA. (Dorothy Blakey, 1939, comments adversely on her work and suspects a PSEUDONYM.) LSS begins in 1806 in the mode of Rousseauvian sensibility: ideal woman is gentle, sensitive, weak and passive, but also the 'natural slave' of passionate feelings. She attacks the French, frivolous high society, libertinism, and arranged marriages with women as merchandise 'consigned over, passing from vendor to buyer'. Titles include *The Bandit's Bride*, 1807, *The Corsair's Bride*, 1830, and *Rosaline, or the Outlaw's Bride*, 1842. The historical novels (for which she claims diverse chronicle sources) set narrative comment on the lost virtues of subordination, filial obedience, wifely submission, and chivalry, against present-day licence. In *The Crusaders*, 1820, a powerful plea for sexual equality subsides into the usual images of propriety and submission. *Runnemede*, 1825, and *The Seer of Tiviotdale*, 1827, stand out, with strong, active women and some hint of more liberal politics, but LSS retreats into the laager in the 1830s.

Stanley, Catherine (Leycester), 1792–1862, diarist, sister of Maria HARE. By 1809 she was keeping a journal: on the idea of 'soul' and on authors including Anne GRANT. In 1810 she m. Edward S., Rector of Alderley, Cheshire (brother-in-law of Maria Josepha S., whose letters have been variously pub.). CS had five children (valuable DIARY of their development, 1811–20, at Cheshire Record Office). She sketched, and wrote of natural beauty 'Artists, one and all, hide your diminished heads.' Hating to 'glide over the surface of life', she is eager 'to get at truth' about human nature, ideas and beliefs. She savours 'the mere pleasure of using all my faculties of mind and body with no restraint or curb': this includes 'being made miserable by Mrs OPIE's "Father and Daughter"'. Two of her essays appeared in Caroline Fry's *Assistant of Education*, 1823 ff.; other set pieces include 'The Mental World', 'A Country Neighbourhood' (likened to a sketch for a novel) and 'Humbug' (good on lip service to, and actual hindrance of, women's education). In Norwich from 1837 as its bishop's wife, CS did much social and religious work, and deeply influenced Jenny Lind. Husband and two sons died in 1849–50; her surviving son ed. selecs. from her journal and letters, 1879.

Stanley, D., adapter of *Sir Philip Sidney's Arcadia, Moderniz'd*, 1725 (the year of the original's 13th ed.). Her dedication to Queen Caroline mentions her youth, implies social status, and offsets her great boldness (and sanction of an age which no longer bars women from 'the highest Undertaking'), by decrying female vanity and stressing her own humble reliance on Sidney. She puts him into modern dress (like Dryden with Chaucer, Pope with Donne), omitting much imagery and all poems, producing 'a simple story of love's triumph' (Paul Salzman, *English Prose Fiction* . . . , 1986). Antiquarians subscribed to her work; BLUESTOCKING Elizabeth VESEY owned it; Richardson probably found Pamela's name in it; Clara REEVE's study of ROMANCE, 1785, judged that it lost 'more beauties than it gained'.

'Stanley, Elizabeth', alleged translator. Edmund Curll advertised as hers *A History of Prince Titi, A Royal Allegory* (three books, 1736, from Thémiseul de St-Hyacinthe's French, to compete with a rival version perhaps by James Ralph). Her accompanying 'Essay upon Allegoric or Characteristic Writing' adds 'or Woman' to 'Man' and 'or Her' to 'His' in quoting from Pope's letters. It equivocates as to anti-royal-family satire in the *History*, which is really pure fairy-tale (fairy disguised as hag), full of dialogue, action, eroticism and humour. A 'second part' (titled *Ismenia and the Prince*), a 'conclusion' (titled *Pausanias and Aurora*), and *Book the Fourth*, all also ascribed to ES later that year, have no French source and no connection with each other. Parts were re-issued as by the certainly non-existent 'Lady Margaret Pennyman', 1740, and as by 'Joseph Morgan', 1745.

Stanley, Mary, 1919–80, poet, b. Christchurch, NZ, da. of Alice Gertrude (Rowland) and Joseph S. After univ. and teachers' college in Auckland, she became a schoolteacher. In 1946 she m. Kendrick Smithyman, poet and tutor; she had three sons. For many years before her death she suffered severely from crippling arthritis. While her husband was a prolific and recognized poet, MS only pub. one slender collection, *Starveling Year*, 1953. The poems are intellectual, well-crafted, in the mode of Auden. There are love poems, poems to her sons, a complex and moving poem about the mother-daughter relationship, 'For my mother', and 'The Wife Speaks', a powerful, condensed and effective statement – 'Being a woman, I am / not more than man nor less / but answer imperatives / of shape and growth'.

Stanley Wrench, 'Mollie', Violet Louise (Gibbs), 1880–1966, novelist and journalist, and **Margaret**, 1916–74, poet and children's writer. The mother, Mollie, was b. in Banbury, Oxon, da. of John Kennedy G. She was privately educ., and m. engineer and journalist William S. W. in 1902. *Love's Fool*, first of her 19 novels, appeared in 1908. *Ruth of the Rowldrich*, 1912, relates the relationship between a would-be writer (who wants 'to use my brains, my faculties', to 'battle with life') and David, who wants to marry and fight her battles for her. Genius in a woman is identified with loneliness and renunciation; when Ruth's early success flags, she goes back to David. *Divorced Love*, 1927, is a kind of mystery story; the heroine discovers that her innocent husband has only been tricked into appearing unfaithful. Mollie SW was a founder member of PEN and wrote on cookery, folklore and opera. Her daughter, Margaret SW, b. at New Barnet, Herts., was educ. at the Channing School and Somerville College, Oxford (BA 1939), where she won the Newdigate poetry prize for 'The Man in the Moon' and issued her first collection, *News Reel and Other Poems*, 1938. Its title poem, like that of her second volume, *A Tale for the Fall of the Year*, 1959, laments desensitizing to others' sufferings: the second, a ballad, indicts a whole community for the death of an innocent mentally retarded man, 'the outsider who made us kindred, / Who gave our unsteady steps a moment's firmness, / Who shut out the greater dark for an instant'. Other pieces (varied verse forms, some deliberate archaism) include lyrics and dramatic monologues by historical figures. Margaret SW also wrote poems for radio, *The Splendid Burden*, 1954 (a verse play about the death of Christ), children's books (pony stories, historical lives), puppet plays, 1955, and a translation of *Troilus and Criseyde*, 1965. She worked as civil servant, journalist and teacher, and died after long disabling illness.

Stanton, Elizabeth (Cady), 1815–1902, feminist writer and campaigner, b. Johnstown, NY, da. of Margaret (Livingston) and Daniel C., lawyer. Frequently punished for youthful 'tantrums', she later described these as 'justifiable acts of rebellion against the tyranny of those in authority' (*Eighty Years*). In 1826, when her only brother died, her father's expressed regret at her sex fired her to pursue Greek and horseback riding. She was educ. first at home and then at Johnstown Academy and Emma WILLARD's Troy Female Seminary, graduating in 1832. With her cousin Gerrit Smith she joined the ABOLITIONIST and TEMPERANCE movements, and in 1840 she m. the reformist Henry Brewster S. in a ceremony from which the word 'obey' was omitted. Their wedding journey to Europe began with the World's Antislavery Convention in London (from which women were excluded), where she met Lucretia MOTT. For the next eight years ECS and her husband lived in Johnstown, then Boston, where she became friends with L. M. CHILD, Whittier and Frederick Douglass. In 1847 they moved to Seneca Falls, NY. In 1848 the NY legislature passed a limited 'Married Women's Property Act', for which ECS had lobbied, and the same year with Mott she organized a woman's rights convention at Seneca Falls for which she drafted the 'Woman's Declaration of Independence', beginning 'men and women are created equal', and also introduced a resolution advocating SUFFRAGE for women. Among her first pub. works are letters to the *New York Tribune* on women's rights, and articles, under the name of 'Sun Flower', for Amelia BLOOMER's temperance paper *Lily*. Through Bloomer, ECS met Susan B. ANTHONY in 1851 and they campaigned together for suffrage and women's rights during the 1860s and 70s. In 1863 they formed the anti-slavery Women's Loyal National League. In 1868–9 ECS co-edited *Revolution*, a women's rights paper, and in 1869 with Anthony she organized the National Woman Suffrage Association. She was principal author of the 'Woman's Declaration of Rights', 1876, and two years later was instrumental in introducing a federal woman suffrage amendment to the Constitution which was finally adopted in 1920. With Anthony and Matilda Joslyn GAGE she co-authored the first three vols. of *History of Woman Suffrage*, 1881–6, and in 1890 became president of the National American Woman Suffrage Association. Critical of the Church's interpretation of the Bible as an obstacle to woman's rights, she pub. *The Woman's Bible*, 1895. Her autobiography, *Eighty Years and More*, 1898 (repr. 1971), displays her ironic humour and candid observations. Valuable recent biographies are by Mary Ann Oakley, 1972; Lois W. Banner, 1980; and Elisabeth Griffith, 1984. A selection of Stanton-Anthony *Correspondence, Writings, Speeches*, 1981, has been ed. by Ellen Carol Dubois. Her papers are at Vassar College and the Library of Congress.

Stark, Freya Madeline, DBE, autobiographer, travel writer, photographer, essayist, Arabist, adventurer. B. in 1893 in Paris to painters Flora and Robert S., she had no formal schooling until she read history at the Univ. of London, 1912–14, and briefly entered the School of Oriental and African Studies, 1926. Travelling between father's Dartmoor and mother's Piedmont as a child, mountaineering in the Alps as a young woman, and nursing near the front line in WWI inspired her to a life of adventurous travel, mostly solitary and sparsely financed, into remote and rugged places. She lived mostly apart from her husband Stewart Perowne (m. 1947). *Baghdad Sketches*, 1932, begins a series of more than twenty TRAVEL books. Subsequent writings adopt a narrative rather than a journalistic form, often taking the ancients as guides, and historical themes as subject matter elaborated with imaginative detail gathered from first-hand travel in Persia, Southern Arabia, Asia Minor and Sicily. FS photographed persons and places throughout the Near East as yet unseen by European audiences (see *Rivers of Time*, 1982, her photographs), charted unknown country in Luristan, co-organized an archaeological expedition in the Hadhramaut, and aspired to be the only English woman to have mastered Arabic, Persian, Kurdish and Turkish. Undaunted by old age and physical infirmity, she jeeped across Afghanistan with a fellow female septuagenarian, rafted down the Euphrates for a BBC film crew in 1977, and trekked around Annapurna by pony in 1979. That she attributes her strength of character to her matrilineal descent may be seen in the opening chapters, 'Grandmothers', of her celebrated AUTOBIOGRAPHY, much of which she structures around letters to and from her mother. FS mobilized progressive attitudes among Arab and European women in Baghdad, protested against the lack of women's employment opportunities, disparaged Victorian-styled marriage no less than life in the harem, and frequently lamented her lack of female companionship; she nonetheless enjoyed her maverick reputation as the only woman daring enough to venture unescorted into male-dominated territory just as she valued her reception into men's diplomatic, military and intellectual society. See *Perseus in the Wind*, selec. essays, 1948, her autobiographies (*Traveller's Prelude*, 1950, *Beyond Euphrates*, 1951, *The Coast of Incense*, 1953, *Dust in the Lion's Paw*, 1961), and Lucy and Caroline Moorehead, eds., letters, eight vols., 1974–82, for a description of her changing attitudes towards women. Life by Caroline Moorehead, 1985.

Starke, Mariana, 1762?–1838, dramatist and TRAVEL writer, da. of Mary (Hughes) and colonial governor Richard S. She drew on her Indian years in a comedy, *The Sword of Peace, or A Voyage of Love*, staged in London, 1788, and pub. with a preface which laughs at rumours about herself (she is a grocer's daughter, adventuress, mother of six starving children), but concludes that a woman writer must veil her identity in delicate reserve. In the play two sisters from England show up, by their honour and kindness to other races, the low-bred, mercenary Anglo-Indian society. There are two non-white characters: an upright Indian merchant and a freed black slave, effusively grateful. MS is credited with 'The Poor Soldier', 1789, a poem about an American loyalist. She adapted a French tragedy as *The Widow of Malabar*, acted 1790, dealing with suttee, which the censor forbade her to call 'hell-born'. Her dedicatee, Mary CHAMPION, staged MS's lost tragedy *The British Orphan* at her private theatre, 1791; *The Tournament*, from German, was publicly staged in 1800. MS spent 1792–8 in Italy nursing sick relatives: her *Letters from Italy*, 1800, mix lively narrative with well-presented guidebook material. She settled at Exmouth, and pub. poems mostly translated from Carlo Maria Maggi, 1811 (noting that Catherine TALBOT had urged Elizabeth CARTER to english him). When a 4th ed. of *Letters* was requested, she preferred to research a new book. *Travels* (many eds., variously titled), based on extensive trips in 1817–19 and later, are highly practical guides, decreasingly personal: a continuing concern is to scotch potential travellers' ungrounded fears.

Stead, Christina, 1902–83, novelist and short-story writer, b. Rockdale, Sydney, NSW, da. of Ellen (Butters) and David George S., socialist and eminent biologist. She was educ. at St George High School, Sydney Girls' High School and Sydney Teachers' College. Largely raised by her father (her mother d. when she was two), she attributed much of her love of storytelling and what she saw as her naturalist's outlook on life to him. After his remarriage in 1907, she helped raise a large family of half-sisters and brothers. These experiences are fictionalized in one of her best-known novels, *The Man Who Loved Children*, 1940. After graduating from Teachers' College in 1921, CS found that her voice was not strong enough for a teaching career. For several years she worked in an office, saving money for a trip to Europe, experiences reflected in *For Love Alone*, 1944, which also questions conventional notions of love and female sexuality. Her own long and successful partnership with the Marxian banker and writer William Blake, whom she m. in London in 1929, was clearly the basis for her rejection of separatist feminism. After spending 1929–37 in France and Spain, the couple moved to the USA where she worked for a time in Hollywood. She drew on these experiences for a novel, pub. posthumously, *I'm Dying Laughing*, 1987, which traces the decline of an American communist couple. After WWII they returned to Europe and lived in England from 1953 until Blake's death in 1968. Her final years were spent in Australia. Though neglected and out of print for many years, she is now recognized as one of the best novelists writing in English this century. Her 11 novels include *Seven Poor Men of Sydney*, 1934, one of the first Australian modernist novels, *The Beauties and the Furies*, 1936, dealing with student life in Paris, and *The House of All Nations*, 1938, also set in Paris, a mammoth study of the world of international finance. *Letty Fox: Her Luck*, 1946, continues the examination of female sexuality, while two other novels set in the USA, *A Little Tea, A Little Chat*, 1948, and *The People With the Dogs*, 1952, focus on a male egoist and an American family, respectively. Her remaining three novels focus on English characters during the postwar period, giving a devastating portrayal of the effects of poverty in *Cotter's England*, 1966, satirizing English expatriates in Switzerland in *The Little Hotel*, 1973, and, in *Miss Herbert (The Surburban Wife)*, 1976, presenting a study of an Englishwoman. She also pub. a collection of novellas, *The Puzzleheaded Girl*, 1967, and a remarkable early collection of stories, *The Salzburg Tales*, 1934, a series of stories told by a group of people of widely differing ages, occupations and nationalities gathered in Salzburg for the annual festival. Another collection, *Ocean of Story*, 1986, was pub. posthumously. In 1974 she received the Patrick White Award. MSS are in the National Library of Australia, Canberra. See the good introduction to her work by Diana Brydon, 1987, and the studies by Ron Geering, 1969, and Susan Sheridan, 1989. The first full-scale biography is by Chris Williams, 1989.

Steel, Flora Annie (Webster), 1847–1929, novelist, b. Harrow-on-the-Hill, Middx., da. of Isabella (McCallum), heiress of a Jamaican sugar-planter, and George Webster, sheriff-clerk of Forfar. She loved play-acting and was educ. by governesses, at private schools, and in Brussels. In 1867 she m. Henry William S. of the Indian Civil Service and they lived in India 1868–89. She was involved in educational administration, advocating EDUCATION for Indian women, acting as first inspector of girls' schools and, in 1884, working on the Provincial Education board with Rudyard Kipling's father. She wrote 17 novels, many set in the East: *Miss Stuart's Legacy*, 1893, tells of an unconventional young woman in love with an Anglo-Indian officer, while *Mistress of Men*, 1917, is the story of an abandoned girl who becomes empress of seventeenth-century India. Other works, such as *Red Rowans*, 1895, and *The Gift of the Gods*, 1897, are set in Scotland, where FAS had family ties. Her most famous novel, *On the Face of the Waters*, 1896, recounts the Indian Mutiny from both viewpoints, 'scrupulously exact, even to the date, the hour, the scene, the very weather' (Preface), and yet very readable. FAS also pub. several colls. of folk and fairy tales, including *Wide Awake Stories*, 1884, (repr. as *Tales of the Punjab*, 1894), and *English Fairy Tales*, 1918, as well as *India Through the Ages*, 1908, and an Indian COOKERY BOOK. She returned to Britain in 1890, living in North Wales, Worcestershire and finally with her daughter at Springfield, Minchinhampton. She supported women's SUFFRAGE, was a member of the Women Writers Suffrage League and marched in the suffrage demonstration of 1910. Her last work was her autobiography, *The Garden of Fidelity*, 1926, where she rather proudly refers to her life-long sexual frigidity. There is a life by Violet Powell, 1981.

Steele, Anna Caroline (Wood), 1840–?1914, novelist. One of seven surviving children of Lady Emma WOOD and the Rev. Sir John Page W., she m. Lt-Colonel Charles S. in 1858 but returned almost immediately to Rivenhall, her parents' home in Essex, avoiding men thereafter. With her mother, she began to write for money after her father's death in 1866. She wrote at least six novels and several plays, with themes of seduction and betrayal, and some focus on women's position. Her very successful first novel, *Gardenhurst*, 1867, suffers from an absurd plot, but is interesting for its concluding implication that the bond between sisters outlives romantic love. It was dedicated to her younger sister 'Kitty' O'Shea, to whom she was very close until they quarrelled over an aunt's legacy. The protagonist of *Condoned*, 1877, is an independent gypsy girl, while *Lesbia*, 1896, concerns an uxorious husband and a frivolous wife, and demonstrates the stifling effect of men's idealization of women. The French Revolution play, *A Red Republican*, 1874, focuses on a woman who becomes a revolutionary after being betrayed and rejected by a nobleman. At the play's end, however, she sacrifices herself to save him from the guillotine. Other novels include *So Runs the World Away*, 1869; *Broken Toys*, 1872; and *Clove Pink*, 1894. In London AS had been a figure in the literary world (several of Trollope's letters are to her), but spent her last years in Brighton, a recluse who fed her pet monkey on anchovy-paste sandwiches. One of her last printed poems was 'An Old Maid's Thoughts'. For biographical detail see Joyce Marlow's life of Kitty O'Shea, 1975.

Steele, Anne, 'Theodosia', 1717–78, poet and Particular Baptist hymn-writer, b. at Broughton, Hants, da. of Anne (Froude) and William S., minister and timber merchant (d. 1769). Her mother died in 1720; AS was brought up by a stepmother and baptized in 1732. In 1735 she was lamed for life in a riding fall; about 1737 her fiancé drowned just before the wedding. She gave to charity the profits of *Poems on Subjects Chiefly Devotional*, 1760. Her HYMNS (metrically inventive, much anthologized) reflect a delight in nature and acute sympathy with Christ's human pain. She bids the clouds 'His goodness speak, / His praise declare, / As through the air / You shine or break.' Her occasional poems deal with retirement, death, friendship, patriotism, the search for happiness. She writes for both solace and aspiration, but insists that 'the Christian seeks a nobler prize' than worldly fame. She encouraged her friend Mary SCOTT to finish *The Female Advocate*. In 1777, as a 'Young Lady' she dedicated to her late father *Danebury: or The Power of Friendship*, a lavishly descriptive and emotional verse tale set at a local Bronze-Age fort (AS once walked there with Hannah MORE), of heroism by two Saxon ladies in war against the Danes. Her last years were bed-ridden, tended by a niece who contributed 'Elegiac Lines' to *Poems*, 1780 (repr. with additional prose meditations); Boston ed., 1808; brief life by J. R. B. in *Hymns*, repr. 1967.

Stein, Gertrude, 1874–1946, avant-garde writer in many genres, some her invention, b. in Allegheny, Penn., youngest of five surviving children of Jewish parents, Amelia (Keyser) and Daniel S., a businessman who settled in Calif. in 1880. Educ. at Oakland High School, and Harvard Annex /Radcliffe College under William James (AB, 1898), GS was 'bored' at Johns Hopkins School of Medicine, 1897–1901, and failed (deliberately?) her final term. She travelled, did brain research, and was painfully involved in a triangular lesbian affair, described in *Q.E.D.* in 1903 (pub. as *Things As They Are*, 1950). GS joined her brother Leo in Paris in 1904; they bought the work of Cézanne, Matisse, Picasso, and Braque, and started the famous Saturday evenings frequented by the expatriate and French avant-garde. In 1905–06, under the influence of Flaubert's *Trois contes* and Cézanne's method in painting, and while sitting for Picasso's portrait of her, GS wrote *Three Lives*, 1909. The second, 'Melanctha', drawing on her observations of the Afro-American community while delivering babies in Baltimore, and fictionalizing *Q.E.D.* as heterosexual romance, advanced through what she later termed 'insistence,' a repetition-with-variations which created the rhythms of characters' knowing in a 'continuous present'. Its method laid the basis for nearly 500 more works. In 1907 GS fell in love with Alice TOKLAS, who lived with her and Leo from 1910, supporting GS in face of Leo's conviction that her writing could not be 'anything' apart from her powerful personal presence. Brother and sister separated permanently, 1913; Toklas remained GS's lifelong lover, helpmeet and ardent reader. From 1906–11, GS worked at *The Making of Americans*, 1925, begun as her family chronicle, later a typology of 'kinds' of US characters in terms of the ways they repeated themselves. She also began writing portraits in 1908; their rhythms and repetitions created the process of her coming to understand her subjects. This 'experiencing' took over from analysing part way through *The Making of Americans*, thereafter dominating GS's writing. Typical is *Tender Buttons*, written 1910–12, pub. 1914, which describes 'Objects,' 'Food,' and 'Rooms' in poems whose linguistic substitutions subvert language's rationality and revel in its free play. Over the next years GS wrote portraits, plays, poems and descriptions indefatigably, becoming notorious for a style her many detractors would neither publish nor read. Invitations from Cambridge and Oxford, instigated by Edith SITWELL, led to *Composition As Explanation*, 1926, a lecture enacting the principles it explains. This meta-writing informs the more abstruse pieces written 1928–30 and collected in *How to Write*, 1931, one of the 5 vols. of the Plain Edition, 1930–33, in which Toklas published some part of GS's accumulated MSS. By the 1930s GS's US income was sufficiently eroded that, at Toklas's urging and against her own resistance to 'serving Mammon', she undertook a popular book. *The Autobiography of Alice B. Toklas*, 1933, earned her a triumphant US lecture tour, 1934–5, and the première of *Four Saints in Three Acts* (opera by her and Virgil Thomson). It also reawoke the unease Leo's earlier criticism had created: lights on Broadway welcomed GS the personality while newspapers parodied her work as nonsense. GS the celebrity embarked on the lucid self-explanations collected in *Lectures in America* and *Narration*, 1935, and capitalized on her fame with further memoirs. Meanwhile, in *The Geographical History of America*, 1936, GS the 'writer' meditated on the difference between 'identity' (granted by fame) and 'entity' ('a thing in itself' which 'writes what it knows' as an 'immediate existing'). From 1937–40 she struggled to embody the conflict between the two in the twinned title character of *Ida*, 1941. The war removed the source of this conflict: Toklas and GS remained isolated in semi-occupied rural Southern France, protected by villagers and their friend Bernard Fäy's links with Pétain. GS wrote children's stories, foraged for food, and wrote the 'continuous present' of waiting for war to end in *Mrs Reynolds* and *Wars I Have Seen*. She returned to an American subject in 1945–6 in her most explicitly feminist work, the opera *The Mother of Us All*, 1949, about Susan B. ANTHONY. She died of cancer. GS has influenced US and Canadian avant-garde writers, performance artists and feminists 'inventing' a language, such as Nicole BROSSARD. Recent scholarship ranks her with DICKINSON and RICH, and reads her as a precursor of post-structuralist and feminist theories. See life by James R. Mellow, 1974; essays ed. Michael Hoffman, 1986, Bruce Kellner, 1988, and Shirley Neuman and Ira B. Nadel, 1988. Papers at Yale.

Steinem, Gloria, journalist, essayist, editor, activist, lecturer, b. 1934 in Toledo, Ohio, granddaughter of Pauline S., a delegate to the 1908 International Council of Women, and da. of Leo S. and Ruth (Nuneviller), a journalist, who sold 'the only house she had' to educate her. She took a BA at Smith College, 1956, then became Chester Bowles Asian Fellow at the Univs. of Delhi and Calcutta, where she wrote *The Thousand Indias*, a guidebook, for the Indian government. Director of the Independent Research Service, Cambridge, Mass., 1959–60, she was a founding editor and political columnist in *New York*, magazine, 1968–71, and co-founder, in 1972, of *Ms* magazine, which she has edited since. *Ms* has reached a wide audience with often influential articles, fiction, and poetry addressing feminist issues for all races, classes and ages, including a feature titled 'Stories for Free Children'. Its name has led to general acceptance in the USA of the title 'Ms', wich does not reveal marital status. GS's lectures, teamed with a black feminist partner, during 'the four or five years surrounding the birth of *Ms*', led to the formation of countless consciousness-raising groups throughout the USA. Her writing is satiric (as in the *That Was the Week That Was* TV series, 1964–5, or 'If Men Could Menstruate', 1979) and political (as in 'After Black Power, Women's Liberation', 1969, which won a Penney-Missouri Journalism Award). *Marilyn*, 1986, is biographical analysis of the film actress as troubled woman and media construct. *Outrageous Acts and Everyday Rebellions*, 1983, a collection of GS's writings, includes autobiographical material.

Stephens, Ann Sophia (Winterbotham) 1810–86, journalist and novelist, b. Humphreysville (later Seymour), Conn., da. of Ann (Wrigley) and John W., part-owner of a woollen mill. Her mother d. when she was young and she was raised by her father and her aunt, whom he m. after his wife's death. She was educ. at the local dame school and in South Britain, Conn. In 1831 she m. Edward S., merchant, moving to Portland, Maine, where, 1834–6, she ed. the *Portland Magazine*, a literary monthly pub. by her husband to which she contributed her first works, including her poem 'The Polish Boy'. In 1837 they moved to NYC where from 1837–41 she was associate ed. of the *Ladies' Companion*, a staff member of *Graham's Magazine* and editor of *Frank Leslie's Ladies' Gazette of Fashion*, while contributing to the *Columbian Lady's and Gentleman's Magazine* and *The Ladies' Wreath*. In 1843 she pub. *High Life in New York*, which continues the Down East, 'Jonathan Slick' tradition originated by Seba Smith. From 1842–53 she was ed. of *Peterson's Magazine*, and from 1856–8 she edited her own magazine, *Mrs Stephens' Illustrated New Monthly*, which then merged with *Peterson's*. Many of her novels were serialized in these MAGAZINES, as was *Fashion and Famine*, 1854, which concludes with a community of poor women in the house of Ada, a wealthy widow, disillusioned by romantic love. *The Old Homestead*, 1855, is a grim tale of urban and rural poverty and disintegrating families. In her preface she claimed: 'I am not one of those who contend that women should ever become law-makers, save in the household and social life', believing rather in the power of womanly influence. In 1860 her earlier serial *Malaeska: The Indian Wife of the White Hunter* was reprinted as the first dime novel, and between 1860 and 1864 she pub. six others in the series. During the Civil War she compiled a *Pictorial History of the War of the Union*, 1863. Her letters are at the Boston Public Library, Brown Univ. Library, Connecticut Historical Society, Historical Society of Pennsylvania and the NY Historical Society. Her MS scrapbooks are at NYPL. See also James Eastman, MA diss. Columbia Univ., 1952, and Linda Morris, PhD diss., Berkeley, 1978.

Stephenson, Sarah, 1738–1802, Quaker minister and memoirist, b. at Whitehaven, Cumberland, da. of Sarah (Storrs) and rich merchant Daniel Stephenson. They lived in worldly style till her father lost money and she was sent to an aunt at Worcester. Here she met Elizabeth ASHBRIDGE (who regretted 'that child should have a ribbon on her head') and the future Catharine PHILLIPS (a 'nursing mother' to SS). Returning seven years later to her parents (now in the Isle of Man), she felt alienated and lonely. On joining the ministry in 1767 she began preaching tours: round Britain, to Ireland (1784, when she warmed to Mary LEADBEATER's father, and 1799, when she noted that pacifist Quakers escaped attack while other Protestants were killed) and the USA, 1801. She died at Philadelphia. *Memoirs*, 1807, from her 'detached pieces' and letters, rather pedestrian as autobiography, is rich in reference to other Quaker women writers.

Stern, Elizabeth Gertrude (Levin), 'Eleanor Morton', 'Leah Morton', 1889–1954, journalist and novelist, b. in Skidel in Poland, da. of Sarah Leah (Rubenstein) and Aaron L., a rabbi. Her fictionalized memoir says that she alone of his five children resisted him, although 'I was only a girl and knew better than to ask questions.' Brought to the USA as a baby, educ. at public schools, the Univ. of Pittsburg (BA 1910), and the NY School of Philanthropy, she m. Christian penologist Leon Thomas S. in 1911. She had two children, taught and did social work (some of it for immigrants) in NYC, Galveston (Texas), and Philadelphia, where she wrote during WWI for the *Sunday Record*. Under her married name she published her first book, *My Mother and I*, 1917, and novels like *A Marriage Was Made*, 1928, and *Gambler's Wife*, 1931. As Eleanor Morton she wrote for the Philadelphia *Public Ledger* (from 1926) and *Inquirer*, and published essays, 1927, and biographies including her last book, *The Women in Gandhi's Life*, 1953. As 'Leah Morton' she wrote *I Am a Woman – and a Jew*, 1926 (facs. American Immigration Collec., 1969), which finely describes a long love-hate relationship with Judaism. She spoke Hebrew at two, then rejected repressive orthodoxy; by 14 'I had seen a vision of God, and He had been awful'; at marriage she 'was in my heart no longer a Jew'; after reconciling, more or less, motherhood with a writing career, she ends at 35 delighting in the intellectual ascendancy of NY Jews, outraged by covert and overt anti-semitism, and declaring that in her inner self, 'I belong to my people.' In life ES became a Quaker and a member of the Women's International League for Peace, working again for the welfare of refugees during WWII.

Stern, Gladys **B**ertha, 1890–1973, novelist. B. in London to Jewish parents, Elizabeth and Albert S., she later changed 'Bertha' to 'Bronwyn'. She was educ. at Notting Hill High School, German and Swiss Schools and the Academy of Dramatic Art, London. An accomplished story-teller, she published about 40 novels, beginning in 1914 with *Pantomime* and *See-Saw*. Her five well-known volumes about the Rakonitz family ('half truth, half invention') draw on her own: a great-aunt became the matriarch Anastasia, whose power passes to her granddaughter Toni in the first two volumes. (The first, *Tents of Israel*, 1924, was re-issued as *The Matriarch*, 1948, repr. 1987). Toni builds a successful business when the Rakonitz fortune fails; her ambition and sense of family tradition prevent her from abdicating her responsibilities through marriage. The series then moved to other family members, ending with *The Young Matriarch*, 1942. GBS's later works, including *Dogs in an Omnibus*, 1942, which has canine rather than human characters, lack her earlier vibrancy. She wrote short stories, plays (*The Matriarch*, on the Rakonitzes, was produced in 1929), and much non-fiction, including works on Robert Louis Stevenson and (with her friend Sheila KAYE-SMITH) Jane AUSTEN. Her 'ragbag chronicles', five vols. on her life, 1936–53, are rambling; those of 1954 and 1956 on her non-practising Jewish childhood and conversion to Catholicism after WWII are more pointed.

Stevenson, Anne Katharine, poet, critic, b. 1933 at Cambridge, England, to Americans Louise (Destler), who wrote fiction, and philosopher Charles Leslie S. They took her as a baby to New England; after her father was dismissed by Yale for his controversial *Ethics and Language*, they settled in Ann Arbor, Mich. AS attended Univ. High School and the Univ. of Michigan (BA in music and languages, 1954), where she wrote a masque and a libretto. Next year she returned to England to marry; divorced, she took her daughter to the USA in 1960, did an MA in English at Michigan, 1962, and started writing again: 'sad, sometimes cynical poems in the shadow of' Robert Frost and Elizabeth BISHOP'. She published a poetry volume, *Living in America*, 1965, and a study of Bishop, 1966. By then she was teaching at Cambridge, Mass., and m. to Mark Elvin, an academic. With him she had two sons (for whom, grown, she recalls paternal advisers: 'Cicero, Polonius – thistles / preaching their beards to their blown seed'). They moved to England again, then Scotland. *Reversals*, 1969, included her best-known short poem, 'The Mother': 'Of course I love them, they are my children. / That is my daughter and this is my son. / And this is my life I give them to please them. / It has never been used. Keep it safe. Pass it on.' In Glasgow in 1974 AS published *Travelling Behind Glass* (selected poems) and *Correspondences: A Family History in Letters*, a long poem exorcizing family guilt, anger, misery, and 'my confused, poisoned feelings about America itself'. *Enough of Green* 1977, was mostly written at Tayport, Dundee; from a creative-writing fellowship at Lady Margaret Hall, Oxford, AS moved to Hay-on-Wye on the Welsh border with Michael Farley (whom she later married) to open The Poetry Bookshop. They later lived in Sunderland, and now in Co. Durham. *The Fiction-Makers*, 1985, includes elegiac poems for Frances HOROVITZ: 'You carried your love of that rushy place / in the candle of your living face / to set in the dark of your poems.' In COUZYN, ed., *Women Poets*, 1985, AS writes 'No artist can be optimistic in days of spiritual decay, but it is possible to be honest. And joyful.' In Mary Jacobus, ed., *Women Writing and Writing about Women*, 1979, she mentions her refusal to sacrifice 'my life as a woman' to 'a life as a writer', but doubts the need for 'a specifically female language' and stresses that both sexes have to share a world. She has ed. Frances BELLERBY, 1986, and written a life of Sylvia PLATH, 1989. See her *Selected Poems*, 1987, and *The Other House*, 1990. *Poetry Review*, 70, 1980, and 72, 1982 (her memoir of childhood). There is also a US romance-writer named AS.

Stewart, Maria W. (Miller), 1803–79, teacher, orator and writer. B. in Hartford, Conn., da. of free black parents, she was orphaned at five, and put out to a clergyman's family. Leaving them when she was 15, she attended Sabbath Schools, and in 1826 m. James W. S. of Boston (d. 1829). In 1830 she became a Christian, making her profession of faith the following year, and in 1832–3 delivering four fiery addresses to Boston audiences, all printed in William Lloyd Garrison's *Liberator*, and later gathered in the *Productions of Mrs Maria W. Stewart*, 1835. MWS exhorted free blacks, especially women, to work collectively for EDUCATION and political rights. 'How long shall the fair daughters of Africa be compelled to bury their minds and talents beneath a load of iron pots and kettles? Until union, knowledge and love begin to flow among us' (Intro., *Productions*). Under criticism for her public speaking, she delivered her 'Farewell Address' on 21 September 1833. She defended her outspokenness with recourse to Old Testament heroines and learned women of history, but left her audience with an injunction to quietism: 'All that man can say or do can never elevate us, it is a work that must be effected between God and ourselves.' MWS then left Boston for NYC; she taught school in NY, Baltimore and Washington, DC. In 1879, she pub. an expanded coll. of her writings, *Meditations from the Pen of Mrs Maria W. Stewart*, with an autobiographical essay on her wartime experiences. See Marilyn Richardson, ed., *MWS: Essays and Speeches*, 1987.

Stewart, Mary Florence Elinor (Rainbow), Lady, POPULAR novelist, b. 1916 at Sunderland, Co. Durham, da. of Mary Edith (Matthews), New Zealander, and the Rev. Frederick Albert R. She went to boarding school at eight (Eden Hall in Penrith and Skellfield in Ripon), then (since Oxbridge, which had offered her places, was too expensive) Durham Univ.: BA in English, 1938, and teaching diploma. She then lectured at Durham (plus school-teaching and night work during WWII), continuing part-time after her marriage in 1945 to geologist Frederick Henry S. (professor at Edinburgh from 1955, knighted 1974). She began writing after an ectopic pregnancy and operation left her infertile. Publication seemed as terrifying as 'walking naked down the street'; she tried vainly to withdraw her first book, *Madam, Will You Talk?* [1955], at proof stage. A dozen more suspense novels feature love stories in exotic settings (the first is Provence). MS's trilogy about Merlin the magician begins with *The Crystal Cave*, 1970 (based on Geoffrey of Monmouth); *The Wicked Day*, 1983, about Mordred, 'add[s] some saving greys to the portrait of a black villain'. Her three children's books begin with *Ludo and the Star Horse*, 1974. The heroine of *Thornyhold*, 1988, inherits a remote house from her herbalist, wise-woman godmother. MS rewrites each work four times: 'The only thing that's worse than writing is not writing.' She admires Mary RENAULT, but guards against being too much influenced. Her work has sustained consistently best-selling figures.

Stimpson, Catharine (Kate) R., critic, novelist, short-story writer, and editor, b. in 1936 in Bellingham, Wash., da. of Catharine (Watts) and Dr Edward S. She studied at Bryn Mawr (AB, 1958) and Columbia (PhD, 1967). MLA president for 1990, she has taught at Columbia, Barnard, and Rutgers. Founding editor of *Signs*, 1974, CRS has edited two vols. of US Congressional hearings on women's rights, a book series, and collections of feminist scholarship (including, with Ethel Spector Person, *Women: Sex and Sexuality*, 1980). She has written *J. R. R. Tolkien*, 1969, and a wide variety of cultural and literary criticism, on feminist theory, lesbian writing, and authors such as Gertrude STEIN, Virginia WOOLF, Doris LESSING, Tillie OLSEN, and Adrienne RICH (selected essays, 1970–87, in *Where the Meanings Are*, 1988). *Class Notes*, 1979, a lesbian novel of development, portrays Harriet Springer's struggles with 'the baffling imperatives of femininity' of the 1950s and her evolving sexuality, ending with her compelling resolve to 'alone decree that sexuality'. CRS's scholarship and fiction engage wide contexts without sacrificing specificity or complexity.

'Like many of us, I am engaged in an experiment that is trying to write new narratives of love and freedom'. A second novel is in progress. Interviews in *Ms*, July/August, 1982, and *New Orleans Review*, 13, 1986.

Stirling, Mary Alexander (Vanlore), Countess of, d. *c.* 1657, petitioner. Da. of Susan (Beck) and Sir Peter V., she eloped with Henry A., Earl of S., in 1637, causing some stir. They had three children; he died by 1649. From 1652 she repeatedly petitioned Parliament to make over to her the Wiltshire estate of her recently-dead aunt, Lady Mary Powell, whose estranged husband, Sir Edward, had forced her to leave it instead to another niece, Anne Levingston. He had first tried witchcraft, then broken into her house as she was dying, 'guarded and secured' it with armed men, and 'chained up the Doors'. Two of MS's PETITIONS were published in 1654, both including counter–petitions by Anne Levingston, who also pub. a separate *True Narrative*. MS re-married Col. John Blount by 1654; her children won the case after her death.

Stirredge, Elizabeth (Tayler), 1634–1706, Quaker minister and autobiographer, b. at Thornbury, Glos., da. of William T. (a puritan, as was her mother). She suffered religious fears (from nine), later with speechlessness and weeping; at other times she delighted 'in bedecking myself in fine Clothes'. She says God's work in her heart dated from preaching by Anne AUDLAND's first husband, 1654. She m. James S. and in 1670 accepted a divine charge to leave her small children and go to London to hand a testimony to the king about persecution, 'Loss of Goods, Beating and Hurling to and fro'; reprisals followed. That year too she opened a campaign against John Story (who said that women should 'wash their Dishes, and not go about to Preach') and Friends who 'turned their backs in the day of Battle'. ES calls herself 'of a sad Heart, and very subject to be cast down'; trembling reluctance preceded her rousing public utterances, which often made officials waver or even retreat. Jailed in 1683, she cowed and worsted a judge and bishop, as well as issuing a *Salutation* to Bristol (with an address by Dorcas DOLE). *A Faithful Warning* [*c.* 1689] followed. About 1691 she wrote her life for her children as *Strength in Weakness Manifest*: pub. 1711, repr. in England and America.

Stockdale, Mary Ridgway, b. 1769 (sometimes confused with the children's writer Mary Sterndale), poet who also wrote for children, da. of Mary (Ridgway) and John S., both of London publishing families. Sickly in childhood, she had some schooling, with the future Harriette WILSON. She later rose regularly at 3 or 4 a.m., to remedy gaps in her education, since women vitally need 'to enlarge the mind, to expand the intellectual capacity, to form the judgement, to promote the habit of close, not desultory thinking'. One of her few feminist poems is 'Lines to Thought, the Only Right of Women'. In 1798 she dedicated to her mother an educational work translated from French, and to Queen Charlotte *Effusions of the Heart*, poems of sadness and sensibility, apparently autobiographical. *The Mirror of the Mind*, 1810, dedicated to the king and showing that she had eminent friends (e.g. Wordsworth), includes a self-approving autobiography and combines patriotism with concern at social issues like ABOLITION and prisons. In 1811 she printed *The Widow and Her Orphan Family*, an affecting verse tale, to raise money for the people concerned. Others among her separate poems praise and lament Sir Samuel Romilly and Princess Charlotte. Her pornographer brother John Joseph S. printed derogatory remarks about her. A volume of *Miscellaneous Poems* (her MS, newspaper, and separately published pieces), specially bound, 1826, is in the Houghton Library, Harvard.

Stockton, Annis (Boudinot), 1736–1801, poet, b. at Darby, Penn., da. of Catherine (Williams) and Elias B. Well educ., she moved to Princeton in 1756, exchanged verse with Esther BURR and Elizabeth Graeme FERGUSON (a special source of inspiration), and published in periodicals, beginning with a reply to antifeminist satire, written at request of female friends. She married wealthy Richard S. (like her an American patriot), probably late in 1757, had six children, and created a Popean garden at their house, Morven (named from Macpherson's recent *Fingal*). She wrote traditional landscape poems, and love poems which ground her sense of worth on her husband's praise. Many of her MSS were destroyed, with property worth £5000, when the British sacked Morven in 1776; some still at Princeton or (because sent to friends) scattered elsewhere. Her play *The Triumph of Mildness* is untraced. Richard S. died of cancer in 1781 after two gruelling years. She lamented him in poems pub. with his funeral sermon and written annually thereafter; she also wrote a series of eulogies of George Washington. See Alfred Hoyt Bill, *A House Called Morven*, rev. ed., 1978.

Stoddard, Elizabeth Drew (Barstow), 1823–1902, novelist and poet, b. Mattapoisett, Mass., da. of Betsey (Drew) and Wilson B., ship-builder, educ. reluctantly at several schools, including the Wheaton Female Seminary, Norton, Mass., and, more enthusiastically, in the library of a local minister. In 1851 she m. Richard Henry S., poet, who encouraged her to write, and their home became a meeting place for writers. She wrote poems (coll. 1895), stories and sketches for monthly magazines, and in 1862, pub. her first novel, *The Morgesons*, praised by Hawthorne as 'genuine and lifelike'. Unusual and original, it conjures up the tensions and rivalries of family life as well as giving vivid pictorial details of social customs. It was followed by *Two Men*, 1865, and *Temple House*, 1867. Here the very weak construction tells against the working out of promising themes, just as her female characters have independent thoughts which they are unable to put into action. In their revelation of the unglamorous aspects of New England life, her novels point forward to the local colour realism of S. O. JEWETT and M. W. FREEMAN; influenced by Emily BRONTË, her depiction of family tensions, near-incestuous blood ties, alcoholism and decaying households predates Faulkner's similar themes of Southern life. See her husband's *Recollections*, 1903, for her life.

Stone, Elizabeth (Wheeler), b. 1803, novelist and social historian, da. of John W., editor of the *Manchester Chronicle*; two brothers also wrote. She grew up in central Manchester during years of industrial strife. In *The Art of Needlework*, 1840, she traces a 'beautiful and useful' art which lacks its 'due meed of praise and record' – unlike its 'glittering antithesis, the scathing and destroying sword'. *William Langshawe, The Cotton Lord* (drafted *c.* 1839, pub. 1842, set in the 1830s) begins with ironic comment on readers' assumed prejudice against an industrial novel: 'drunken men, reckless women, immoral girls, and squalid children'. Her story includes a union murder, a seduction, and a vacuous speech by the future Sir Robert Peel; statistics and parliamentary reports are used to assert authenticity. *The Young Milliner*, 1843, addresses 'Fashionable ladies, – individually kind and good ... collectively the cause of infinite misery to the young and unprotected of their own sex'. Its heroine, left a poor orphan, dies after her society season of regular all-night sweatshop labour; a typical thoughtless young customer turns out to be her cousin, and daughter to this book's heartless seducer. For these two as condition-of-England novels, see Joseph Kestner in *Bulletin of the John Rylands Library*, 67, 1984–5. ES had GASKELL's *Mary Barton* ascribed to her; but her other novels are less politically aware. She wrote two more books on social history ('Manners, Amusements, Banquets, Costume, &c', 1845, and graveyards, 1858), magazine pieces, and little books of piety in prose and verse.

Stone, Lucy, 1818–93, feminist editor and abolitionist, b. West Brookfield, Mass., da. of Hannah (Matthews) and Francis S., of an old settler family. Denied education rights equal to her brothers, she mostly taught herself at home, and became a schoolteacher at 16. After teaching at Mt Holyoke Female Seminary, in 1843 she enrolled at Oberlin College, where she met Antoinette BLACKWELL and became known for her radical views. Graduating in 1847 as the first Mass. woman to take a degree, she began speaking on women's rights and for the Anti-Slavery Society, travelling the country in the early 1850s. She put women's needs first, saying: 'I was a woman before I was an ABOLITIONIST'. In 1855 she m. reformer Henry Brown Blackwell, retaining her maiden name, and issuing with her husband a statement of the disabilities of women in marriage. She continued her career as influential campaigner, from 1872 financing and editing the *Woman's Journal*, the official SUFFRAGE organ for nearly 50 years. Her more conservative American Women's Suffrage Association broke away from ANTHONY and STANTON's National Women's Suffrage Association in 1870, but was later reunited. Her last lecture was for the World Columbian Exposition in Chicago in 1893; her health then gave out. Her daughter, Alice Stone BLACKWELL, wrote her life in 1930. There is another life by Elinor Rice Hays, 1961. Letters are in the Blackwell Family Papers, Library of Congress and in the Schlesinger Library.

Stone, Ruth (Perkins), poet, b. 1915 at Roanoke, Va., da. of Ruth (Ferguson) and Roger McDowell P., educ. at the Univ. of Illinois and Harvard. She m. Walter B. S., who died in 1960, leaving her with one publication (*In an Iridescent Time*, 1959), three young daughters, no job, little money, and an old farmhouse near Brandon, Vt. She taught English in many univs. from 1965, without tenure. Her later volumes are *Unknown Messages*, 1973, *Cheap, New Poems and Ballads*, 1975 (dedicated to her daughters and 'the countless women I respect and admire'), and *Second-Hand Coat, Poems New and Selected*, 1987. She combines wide range in form, mood and voices, writing as the drummer's daughter or the 'regular mid-west child', even a fish ('My love's eyes are red as the sargasso'). Often amused ('The quick brown poem jumped over the lazy woman. / There it goes flapping like an orange with peeling wings ...', she also evokes ecstasy ('Now that I am married I spend / My hours thinking about my husband .... Attend! The cup is filled with light') and grief, loss, and outrage: 'In the weeds of mourning, / Groaning and gnashing, I display / Myself in malodorous comic wrappings and tatters.' Even despair can be undercut: 'And not only that, / My hair is not the way it was at all.' With an unrivalled eye for quotidian detail (cheap travel, domestic pets, writing letters), RS has the art of imbuing simple statement with reverberations of meaning: 'I will sit here drinking until it snows and then / I'll go in and build a fire.' She has written much more than she has published. She is hailed by Sandra GILBERT as 'a paradigm of the "lost" female writer' and by Tillie OLSEN as 'one of the major poets of her time' (*Iowa Review*, 12, 1981).

Stone, Sarah (Holmes), English midwife. She learned anatomy and observed dissection, but set much higher store by her six years as her mother's deputy. She practised for 35 years in north Somerset, among poor weaver-women, then at fashionable Bristol. In 1736 she and her husband moved to London; in 1737 she published *A Complete Practice of Midwifery*, consisting of accounts (some written years earlier) of 43 difficult cases. Dedicated to the Queen (who unluckily died that year), it is prefaced with denunciation of male encroachment in her profession, not of mature men but 'every boyish Pretender'. Their patients, she says, die by the book, 'for a Man was there, and the Woman-Midwife bears all the blame.' Like Elizabeth NIHELL later, she praises traditional training methods and women's feeling for women; she hopes to enable midwives even 'of the lower class' to manage without calling in male help.

Stopes, Charlotte (Carmichael), 1841–1929, feminist and scholar, b. in Edinburgh, da. of landscape-painter J. F. Carmichael. After schools in Edinburgh and Dieppe, and a certificate from the Edinburgh Normal School, she taught privately. She also wrote stories for Chambers' Juvenile Series (coll. 1861 as *Alice Errol and other tales*) and, as 'Lutea Reseda', articles for *The Attempt* (journal of an Edinburgh women's literary society). From 1867 she attended classes run by concerned members of Edinburgh Univ. for the women it excluded; she was the first woman in Scotland to take a Univ. Certificate. In 1879 she m. Henry S., architect, civil engineer and palaeontologist; but she never ceased to find sex repellent, and inculcated guilt in her daughter Marie STOPES. She campaigned for women's SUFFRAGE and ran intellectual societies, working with Constance Wilde in the Rational Dress Society. She published nine meticulous, rather staid works of Shakespearean scholarship, 1888–1922; *The Making of Shakespeare* (verse), 1916; and vigorous, effective polemics about women: pieces in the *British Freewoman* and elsewhere, and *British Freewomen: Their Historical Privilege of Excercising the Franchise*, 1894. See Frederick S. Boas in *Transactions of the Royal Literary Society*, 1930.

Stopes, Marie Charlotte Carmichael, 1880–1950, scientist, birth-control pioneer and miscellaneous writer, b. in Edinburgh, elder da. of Charlotte STOPES. She was educ. by her mother (whose excessive expectations were a problem) till 1892, then at St George's High School, Edinburgh (founded by suffragists), North London Collegiate School from 1894, Univ. College, London (Honours in botany and geology after only two years), and from 1903 the Botanical Institute of Munich Univ. She became Britain's youngest DSc in 1905, and taught at Manchester Univ., 1904–7. Her first book was *Ancient Plants*, 1910, both authoritative and accessible, inspired, like her academic work in general, by her father's interests. An increasingly passionate but unconsummated relationship with Kenjiro Fujii led to *A Journal from Japan*, 1910, and, as 'G. N. Mortlake', ed., *Love Letters of a Japanese*, 1911. That year, still wholly ignorant of sexuality, MS married Canadian botanist Reginald Ruggles Gates. She left him in 1914 and in 1916 had the marriage annulled for non-consummation. Meeting Margaret SANGER in 1915, while already working on *Married Love*, led her to include a chapter on contraception. This and *Wise Parenthood*, both bestsellers, appeared in 1918, the year MS m. Humphrey Verdon Roe, an early aeroplane manufacturer, who funded her work. She had a stillborn son, published *A Letter to Working Mothers: on how to have healthy children and avoid weakening pregnancies*, 1919, and *Radiant Motherhood*, 1920, opened Britain's first birth-control clinic (Holloway, London) in 1921, and bore another son in 1924. What now appears gushingly lyrical or mystical in her work helped to make acceptable detailed physiological instruction on topics generally taboo. Apart from scientific writings on coal, her works, whether sexological, philosophical, theological, imaginative, or on censorship, share a common inspiration, and most draw on her own life: e.g. *Man*, 1914, plays (including *Don't Tell Timothy*, as 'Mark Arundel', 1925; *Vectia*, autobiographical, banned on stage, pub. 1926), fairy-tales as 'Erica Fay', 1926, the novel *Love's Creation*, as 'Marie Carmichael', 1928, *Love Songs for Young Lovers*, 1939, and *We Burn, Selected*

Poems, 1949. Her film *Marie's Marriage* was made in two weeks in 1923. Aylmer Maude's *Authorized Life*, 1924, was largely dictated by herself. Her edition of letters received, *Mother England*, 1929, made hitherto voiceless women audible to society. See her piece in James Marchant, ed., *If I Had My Time Again*, 1950; Muriel Box, *The Trial of MS*, 1967; bibliog. by Peter Eaton, 1977; life by Ruth Hall, 1977. Voluminous papers in the BL and Wellcome Institute, London.

'Storm, Lesley', Mabel Margaret (Cowie) Clark, 1898–1975, novelist and playwright, b. at Maud, Aberdeenshire, da. of Christian (Ewen) and the Rev. William Cowie. Educ. at Peterhead Academy and Aberdeen Univ. (MA 1920), she m. James Doran Thompson Clark, businessman, in 1921 and had four children. Her work treats sexual morality, unconventional marital relations, and the punishment of female transgression. Of her novels, *Lady What of Life?*, 1927, rewards a pair of adulterous lovers with death; *Just As I Am*, 1933, shows a mother and daughter each confronting a need to escape from inhibiting, stifling relationships; *Robin and Robina*, 1931, asserts the possibility of a union permitting 'personal independence'. Her plays, better known than her fiction, vividly depict the influence of desire on behaviour. In *Black Chiffon*, staged 1949, pub. 1950, a jealous mother shoplifts a sexy nightdress and avoids her son's wedding by choosing to go to jail. *The Long Echo*, staged 1956, pub. 1957, treats betrayal, misplaced patriotism, and the impingement of political propaganda on personal life. *Roar Like a Dove*, staged 1957, pub. 1958, is a comic exposure of patriarchal control over women's bodies: a rebellious wife ('America could teach you plenty. . . . they don't give women the status of rabbits') ends by providing her husband with the son he wants. *The Paper Hat*, staged 1965, pub. 1966, looks at the ambiguous nature of 'truth' and the hidden effects of early sexual experience. LS also wrote short stories collected in *Business Man*, 1934, and film scripts including *The Heart of the Matter*, 1953.

Stott, Charlotte **Mary** (Waddington), OBE, journalist, b. 1907 at Leicester, youngest child of journalists Amalie Maria Christina (Bates) and Robert Guy W.: 'as a small child I told my dolls, "I have some copy to write now."' Her mother, a passionate and effective speaker, took her to Liberal meetings very young. She left Wyggeston Grammar School for Girls in 1923 with the highest possible School Certificate marks, and at nearly 18 became a reporter on the *Leicester Mail*. As a woman she was barred from the Typographical Association or that of Correctors of the Press; she took on the Women's Page reluctantly at 19, longing to be a 'hard news' reporter, and wrote theatre reviews as 'Jacques'. Made redundant in 1931, she moved to the *Bolton Express News*, then the Co-operative Press (women's section), Manchester, 1933–45. For *Women's Outlook*, she wrote a series on historical women like Florence NIGHTINGALE (she particularly admired Millicent Garrett FAWCETT and Ray STRACHEY). She felt 'liberated' by marriage in 1937 to fellow-journalist Kenneth S. (whose name she did not write in until 1957): their daughter was also a journalist. MS was news sub on the *Manchester Evening News*, 1945–50, and editor of the *Manchester Guardian* (later the *Guardian*) Women's Page, 1957–72, where she kept alive the tradition of BRITTAIN and HOLTBY. She moved to London with the paper, and edited a Women's Page anthology in 1987. A founder member of the Women in Media group, 1970, she wrote, edited, or co-edited books on women in the media, 1977, and in public life, 1978, 1980, on ageing, 1981, and widowhood, 1987 (20 years after her husband died). Her autobiographical *Forgetting's No Excuse*, 1973, and *Before I Go*, 1985, are vivid and acute on her relations with her parents and husband, the growth of gender consciousness, and her part in the resurgent women's movement. See Dale Spender, *There's Always Been a Woman's Movement This Century*, 1983, titled from MS's reply when asked why there had not.

Stowe, Harriet (Beecher), 1811–96, novelist, b. Litchfield, Conn., da. of Roxana (Foote), who d. when HBS was four, and Lyman B., Congregationalist minister. She was the seventh child, the eldest being Catharine Esther BEECHER and the eighth Henry Ward Beecher. She was educ. at a district school and Sarah Pierce's School for Young Ladies, and in 1824 entered the Hartford Female Seminary, recently opened by Catharine. In 1832 the sisters accompanied their father to Cincinnati, where Catharine opened the Western Female Institute, at which both sisters taught. In 1834 HBS won a prize for 'A New England Sketch' from the *Western Monthly Magazine*. In 1836 she m. Calvin Ellis S., professor at Lane Theological Seminary, and they had seven children. Though HBS viewed marriage as a sanctification, she soon sought domestic help to escape the role of 'a mere domestic slave'. She began writing to help family finances, and in 1843 pub. *The Mayflower*, a collection of stories. HBS had long been concerned about slavery, having read the autobiographies of Frederick Douglass and Louis Clark, as well as the abolitionist tracts of L. M. CHILD and Theodore Weld, and in 1850, when the Fugitive Slave Act was passed, she began writing *Uncle Tom's Cabin: or life among the lowly*, first serialized in the abolitionist *National Era* and pub. in book form in 1852. An immediate sensation, it sold 300,000 copies in one year. Southern writers quickly produced 'anti-Uncle Tom' books, to which she responded with *A Key to Uncle Tom's Cabin*. Important for its crystallization of Northern sentiment before the Civil War, the novel also displays women's ability to create positive social values and celebrates the peaceful order of a woman-dominated home. In 1854 HBS pub. *Sunny Memories of Foreign Lands*, an account of a trip to England in 1853, and in 1856 her second anti-slavery novel, *Dred: A Tale of the Great Dismal Swamp*, appeared. *The Minister's Wooing*, serialized in the *Atlantic Monthly*, 1958–9, was the first of four historical novels dealing with New England. Her other works include *The Amercan Woman's Home*, 1869, written with her sister Catharine and dedicated 'To the Women of America, in whose hands rest the real destinies of the Republic', and *Lady Byron Vindicated*, 1870, which claimed that Byron committed incest with his half-sister, Augusta Leigh. Her son Charles pub. her life, 1889, and her papers are at the Schlesinger Library, Radcliffe College. See article by Johanna Smith, *ESQ*, 1986; crit. essays ed. Eric Sundquist, 1987, and Thomas F. Gossett's study, 1985. There is an important essay by Jane Tompkins in *Sensational Designs*, 1985.

Strachey, Julia Frances, 1901–79, novelist, short-story writer, b. in India into a remarkable family: da. of German-Swiss Ruby (Mayer), who left when she was a small child and later had, she said, four more children by different men, and of Oliver S. JS was granddaughter of Jane Maria (Grant) S., 1840–1928, friend of Millicent FAWCETT and of George ELIOT, editor of Elizabeth GRANT and of M. M. SHERWOOD's *Fairchild Family*, 1913, author of poems for children, 'An International Song' for women's SUFFRAGE societies, and 'Some Recollections of a Long Life' (excerpts pub. in *Nation and Athenaeum*, 1924). Of JS's aunts, Dorothy S., later Bussy, 1866–1960, translated Gide and published *Olivia* (as by 'Olivia', 1949, repr. 1987), an autobiographical novel in which a sensitive, naive teenage girl plays a marginal role in an unhappy lesbian relationship; Philippa S. wrote suffrage plays and a pamphlet on women's status, 1935; Marjorie S., 1882–1964, wrote lives (her fictional work on Chopin, 1925, was a US bestseller), and fiction (*The Counterfeits*,

1927, depicts a Bloomsbury milieu). Amabel WILLIAMS-ELLIS was a cousin. In 1911 JS's father m. Ray (Costelloe) STRACHEY. JS, sent to England at five to live with a series of relatives, remained unsettled all her life. Her 'Pioneer City', pub. in *New Writing*, 1942–3, draws on her time at Bedales progessive school. She trained as a commercial artist at the Slade School, London, and m. sculptor Stephen Tomlin in 1927 (later divorced). Despite fierce resistance to being edited, she published many stories in *The New Yorker*; 'Can't You Get Me Out Of Here?' wrings acute pain from the incident of leaving a dog in kennels ('Animalia' in England, written, like other pieces, for the Memoir Club; repr. in *Stories from the New Yorker*, 1961). Virginia WOOLF found JS's novella *Cheerful Weather for the Wedding* 'remarkable' and 'acidulated', and published it, 1932 (repr. 1978 with *An Integrated Man*, JS's chosen title for the novel printed in 1951 as *The Man on the Pier*). The first is in comic mode: fussy mother persists in putting a good face on everything as wedding guests are ravaged by drink, tears, and rows. The second is darker, toppling its protagonist from order and serenity into a turmoil of unquenchable, unsatisfiable love: 'the Phoenix on her bonfire in his veins raged triumphantly.' In 1952 JS married the much younger artist Lawrence Gowing, with whom she had lived during WWII (later divorced). He owns her diaries, letters and much unpub., largely autobiographical work, from which Frances Partridge ed. *Julia, A Portrait by Herself*, 1983. The Fawcett Library has many Strachey MSS.

Strachey, Ray, Rachel Mary (Costelloe), 1887–1940, feminist and writer. B. in London, da. of Mary (Pearsall Smith) and Frank C., a barrister her mother left for Bernard Berenson, she was largely brought up by her US grandmother, Hannah (Whitall) Pearsall Smith, 1832–1911, preacher, feminist, and religious writer. She went to Kensington High School, Newnham, Cambridge (where she was sufficiently active in 'The Cause' to acquire only a pass degree in mathematics, 1908), and Bryn Mawr, USA. She m. her cousin Oliver Strachey, 1911, and had two children. She became a SUFFRAGE supporter in 1910, working for the non-militant constitutionalist Millicent FAWCETT, whose biography she published in 1931. Her greatest concern was to extend employment opportunities for women and during WWI she was Chairwoman of the Women's Service Bureau, and in 1936 Secretary of the Women's Employment Federation. As Chairwoman of Save the Children Nursery Schools Committee, 1933–6, she worked to establish nursery schools in depressed areas. She was also active in politics, as (unsuccessful) Independent Parliamentary candidate in 1918, 1922 and 1923, and in 1919 and 1932 as Lady Astor's Political Secretary. Her writing career began with her first novel, *The World at Eighteen*, 1907, and encompassed the editorship of the suffrage paper *The Women's Leader* (previously *The Common Cause*); the writing of historical and feminist works including biographies of her grandmother, *A Quaker Grandmother*, 1914, and her grandmother's friend, *Frances* WILLARD*: Her Life and Work*, 1912, and an excellent short history of the women's movement, *The Cause*, 1928 (repr. 1978 with preface by Barbara Strachey), for which she is best known. She also wrote two more novels, *Marching On*, 1923, and *Shaken by the Wind*, 1927, and edited a 'stock-taking' collection of essays by five women (including herself, Eleanor RATHBONE and Mary Agnes Hamilton), *Our Freedom and Its Results*, 1936, on women's current legal and social position. See her daughter, Barbara Strachey, *Remarkable Relations*, 1980, and Dale Spender, *Women of Ideas and What Men Have Done to Them*, 1982.

Strathmore, Mary Eleanor Bowes, Countess of, 1749–1800, playwright and autobiographer. Carefully educ. only child of George

Bowes and Mary (Gilbert), inheriting huge paternal estates, she gave her family name to two husbands but herself always used the title of John Lyon, 9th Earl of Strathmore, whom she m. in 1767. She had five children (he accused her of preferring the girls), studied botany, and argued in a blank-verse drama, *The Siege of Jerusalem*, 1774, that 'soon or late bright virtue must prevail.' Widowed in 1776, she abandoned another lover, by whom she was pregnant, for Andrew Robinson Stoney, a marital speculator who had already buried one rich, maltreated wife. After marriage, 1777, he forced her to revoke legal deeds that kept her property of *c.* £600,000 in her own hands; he insulted her in public, beat her in private, seduced and raped other women. Before February 1778, evidently still in love, she wrote for him her *Confessions*, a rambling document, perhaps part fantasy but deeply interesting; he threatened to publish it when in prison in 1787; it appeared in 1793, four years after her four-year divorce suit had succeeded. See life by Ralph Arnold, 1957 (repr. 1987).

Stratton-Porter, Gene, 1863–1924, novelist, photographer, illustrator, b. Wabash, Indiana, youngest of 12 children of Mary (Shellobarger) and Mark Stratton, self-educ. Her outdoors childhood with father and brothers developed a life-long interest in natural history. She taught herself photography and illustrated her own books. She worked as photography editor for *Recreation*, and in the natural history dept. of *Outing*. After marrying Charles Darwin Porter, she began her writing career with a love-story, *The Song of the Cardinal*, 1903, followed by her most popular novel, *Freckles*, 1904, about an Indian waif believed orphaned, till reclaimed by a wealthy father. *A Girl of the Limberlost*, 1909, features a similar girl, for whom initiative and effort bring due rewards of wealth and social position. Perhaps the most POPULAR author of her day, GS-P presents what she called true-to-life portraits of people and places vividly coloured by her love of nature, man, and God. Though she deals with marital discord (*At the Foot of the Mountain*, 1907) and the problems facing a child of divorced parents (*The Magic Garden*, 1927), her often capable and self-sufficient heroines remain strictly conventional. In *The White Flag*, 1923, Mahala struggles for self-definition but remains a 'beautiful little lady': Linda in *Her Father's Daughter*, 1921, pays her way through school by writing Aboriginal Cookery articles, but is always 'sanely and healthfully and beautifully right'. She originated her own film company, GS-P Productions, to protect the moralistic tone of her work, and had more than 20 films based on her novels. See Jeanette Meehan (Porter), *The Life and Letters of GSP*, 1972 (first pub. as *The Lady of the Limberlost*, 1928), and Bernard F. Richards, 1982.

Strauss, Jennifer (Wallace), poet and critic, b. 1933 in Heywood, Victoria, da. of Edith (Armstrong) and Herbert W. Educ. at Loreto Convent, Portland, and Melbourne Univ., she pub. poetry while a student, but stopped writing for ten years, during which she married and pursued an academic career at the Univs. of New England, Melbourne, and Monash. A committed feminist, she has taken an active role in univ. politics. She has three sons; her husband died in 1978. Poems from her first collection, *Children and Other Strangers*, 1975, are more traditional in form than many of her later ones, but explore some typical moods and themes in their sensitive treatment of human relationships and ironic glances at female stereotypes. *Winter Driving*, 1981, pub. by the feminist press, Sisters, contains more personal and autobiographical poems, as well as strongly feminist ones such as 'Traffic' and 'Bluebeard Re-Scripted'. Her most recent collection is *Labour Ward*, 1988.

Streatfeild, Noel, OBE, 1895–1986, novelist and children's writer. B. at Frant, Sussex, she was da. of Janet (Venn) and the Rev. William Champion S., great-great-granddaughter of prison reformer Elizabeth Fry. She was educ. at Hastings and St Leonard's Ladies' Academy (where she was taught by Sheila KAYE-SMITH, but was expelled in 1910) and Laleham School, Eastbourne. After hospital and munitions work during WWI, she attended the Academy of Dramatic Art, London, 1919–20. Her stage career began in the chorus and included Shakespeare, leading avant-garde roles, and touring in Britain, South Africa and Australia, as 'Noelle Sonning'. She acquired a lifestyle (smoking, drinking) 'that would have horrified her parents'. She was 'enthralled and terrified' on reading Radclyffe HALL; her closest friendships were with women. After her father's death, 1929, she turned from acting to writing, which quickly brought her financial comfort and critical esteem. Her first novel, *The Whicharts*, 1931, reworked as *Ballet Shoes*, 1936, broke new ground in CHILDREN'S books by presenting the ballet and theatre world – one of serious work and ambition. Some of her fiction for adults was found shocking: she tackles illegitimacy, divorce, prostitution, sexual coldness and homosexuality as features of everyday life in *Caroline England*, 1937, and *The Winter is Past*, 1940. *Aunt Clara*, 1952, on the other hand, epitomizes her continuing esteem for religion and family. Having done child-care work in the 1930s, NS was a London air-raid warden and Women's Voluntary Service organizer in WWII, using the experience in novels like *I Ordered a Table for Six*, 1942. Between 1939 and 1951 she published for money, as 'Susan Scarlett', 12 novels which she later excluded from her extensive bibliography. Besides fiction, she wrote plays for children and adults, radio and TV series, and a critical biography of E. NESBIT, 1958. She edited books of advice for teenagers, short stories, early-twentieth-century memoirs, and a *Ballet Annual*, from 1959. She reviewed children's literature, did charity work for children and writers, and went on publishing after her first slight stroke (e.g. a remarkable life of Tutankhamen for children, 1972). See her fictionalized autobiography, *A Vicarage Family*, 1963, *Away from the Vicarage*, 1965, *Beyond the Vicarage*, 1971; life by Angela Bull, 1984.

'Stretton, Hesba', Sarah Smith, 1832–1911, CHILDREN'S writer, b. Wellington, Shropshire, third da. of Ann (Bakewell), strong evangelical, and Benjamin Smith, bookseller and publisher. She was educ. at a local girls' school, but mainly through father's books. 'Hesba' comes from the initials of her surviving siblings, 'Stretton' from a Shropshire village. She wrote for *Household Words* and *All the Year Round* from 1859; *Fern's Hollow*, 1864, is first of her many stories about children's religious experience. She moved to Manchester with her governess sister (and lifelong companion) Elizabeth. Phenomenal success came with *Jessica's First Prayer*, 1867, which sold more than 1.5 million copies and was translated into many languages. Embodying her personal knowledge of slum conditions, it deals with an ill-treated slum girl who is brought to an understanding of the (evangelical) Christian message and is adopted by a miser, redeemed by her example. Later stories often centre on slum children's growth towards an understanding of Christ's love, and show much insight into children's thought processes. But HS's increasing concern about child abuse is reflected in the darker mood and angrier tone of later novels like *In Prison and Out*, 1879, and *The Lord's Purse-Bearers*, 1883, and also in her involvement in the founding of the London (later Royal) Society for the Prevention of Cruelty to Children. Her life and works are discussed in J.S. Bratton, *The Impact of Victorian Children's Fiction*, 1981.

Stretton, Julia Cecilia (Collinson), 1812–78, novelist, b. Gateshead, Durham, second da. of 15 children of Emily and the Rev. John

C., magistrate. Educ. at home, she m. Walter DeWinton *c.* 1831, then Richard William S. in 1858. After the death of her first husband, she began writing children's books to support her three children. Her first novel, *A Woman's Devotion*, 1855, is the story of the triumph through self-sacrifice of Nest, a young wife burdened with a corrupt and selfish mother-in-law. Despite near impossible odds, including the slow death of her husband, Nest eventually wins the love of her mother-in-law. Two of her novels are autobiographical: *The Valley of a Hundred Fires*, 1860, which describes JS's parents, and *The Queen of the County*, 1864, portraying her experiences of Welsh elections during the Reform period. Other novels include the highly popular *Margaret and Her Bridesmaids*, 1864, a tale of two young women who marry inappropriately, and *Lords and Ladies*, 1866. Although an essay by Charlotte YONGE (in *Women Novelists of Queen Victoria's Reign*, 1897), describes the novels as lively, modern readers are more likely to agree with Yonge's emphasis on their 'fond enshrining of the past', and to wonder at the unwavering goodness of the young heroines.

Strickland, Agnes, 1796–1874, and **Elizabeth**, 1794–1875, BIOGRAPHERS, b. London, eldest of the six daughters of Elizabeth (Horner) and Thomas S., dock manager. Catharine Parr TRAILL, Susanna MOODIE, and Jane Margaret S., 1800–88 (she wrote children's stories), were also writers. Believing girls should be educ. like boys, their father taught them Latin, Greek and mathematics, and encouraged them to write; AS wrote poetry from age nine, later producing several vols. of indifferent verse. They lived in London from about 1818, both producing children's stories. By 1833 they were learning palaeography and history in the British Museum, an enterprise which yielded the great success of their careers, *Lives of the Queens of England from the Norman Conquest* (12 vols, 1840–48; many editions; 1852 ed. repr. 1972, intro. Antonia FRASER). This pioneering work covered the lives of queens regnant and queens consort up to Anne; queens as rulers being important historical agents, and as women, instruments of moral and religious influence. The sisters' motto was 'Facts, Not Opinions,' and they made extensive use of hitherto-unpub. official documents, notably MSS from the State Paper Office, to which, being women, they were only admitted after extensive lobbying of politicians. Since AS courted fame while ES eschewed it, the *Lives* appeared under AS's name alone; this made the fifth vol. (1842) seem rather inconsistent in tone, as it contained AS's celebration of Katharine PARR as 'the nursing mother of the Reformation' and ES's brave and inevitably controversial vindication of the execrated 'Bloody Mary.' The sisters' later collaborations (all pub. as by Agnes) included *Lives of the Queens of Scotland*, 1850–59, *Lives of the Bachelor Kings of England*, 1861, and *Lives of the Seven Bishops Committed to the Tower in 1688*, 1866; the last, *Lives of the Tudor Princesses*, 1868, reveals a decline of AS's assiduousness in research as she became a social celebrity, while her solo effort, *Lives of the Last Four Princesses of the Royal House of Stuart*, 1872, gives rein to the sentimentality which had always distinguished her style from ES's. More valuable is her *Letters of Mary, Queen of Scots* (1842, enlarged, 1848), containing much unpub. material. Una Pope-Hennessy's rather unsympathetic biography of AS (1940) also deals in some detail with ES.

Strong, Anna Louise, 'Anise', 1885–1970, radical journalist, b. at Friend, Neb., eldest da. of Ruth (Tracy) and Congregational minister Sydney Dix S. After high school, a year in Germany, and graduation from Oberlin, 1905, she became the Univ. of Chicago's youngest-ever PhD, 1908: thesis pub. as *The Psychology of Prayer*, 1909. She did various social work (with her father, for the Russell Sage Foundation, and National

Child Labor Committee) and began to acquire notoriety for her writings: a report of the Everett Massacre (NY *Evening Post*, 1917); poems as 'Anise' for the socialist *Union Record* of Seattle, repr. in *Ragged Verse*, 1920; editorials about, and later a history of, the Seattle General Strike. Settling in Moscow in 1921, she taught English to Trotsky, who prefaced her book on Soviet economic policy, *The First Time in History*, 1924; but she remained a US citizen. In 1925 she published a book about a short-lived colony for child famine victims, for which she had raised funds in the USA. She founded the *Moscow Daily News*, 1930. Lincoln Steffens calls her autobiography, *I Change Worlds: the Remaking of an American*, 1935, repr. 1979, 'a triumph'. ALS spent much time 'roving to revolutions, and writing about them for the American press': Mexico, Spain, China, the last in several books from *China's Millions*, 1928, to *The Chinese Conquer China*, 1949. Returning to the USA in 1940, she was 'marooned' there by passport obstacles when her husband, Russian editor Joel Shubin (m. by Soviet-style consent, 1931), died in 1942. She wrote on the New Deal in *My Native Land* (suggested by Eleanor ROOSEVELT), 1940, and defended Russia in *The Soviets Expected It*, 1941. Her one novel, *Wild River*, 1943, depicts a New Woman and her equally idealistic young lover in the war-torn Ukraine. ALS expounded Mao's thought in *Amerasia*, June 1947. Back in the USSR from 1944, she was deported as a spy in 1949, and moved to Beijing in 1958. Her monthly *Letter From China* (begun 1962, repr. in four vols.) covered developments like the Vietnam war. She is buried in the National Cemetery of Revolutionary Martyrs, near Agnes SMEDLEY. 'Much of her best writing focuses on women', says Tracy B. Strong's and Helene Keyssar's life, 1983. Papers at Peking and the Univ. of Washington, Seattle.

Strong, Damaris, probable editor, wife of prominent English Independent minister William S. When he died, 1654, she pub. a broadside, *Having seen a paper printed*, to repudiate *The Saints Communion*, published posthumously with his name. She asserts her possession of his MSS, and her resolve that they 'will all (in Gods due time) come out, word for word as himself wrote them, if I may be allowed to have the dispose thereof'. It is likely that she was involved in their subsequent editing (and that other widows also did such invisible work), though her name does not appear.

'Struther, Jan', Joyce Anstruther, 1901–53, poet, short-story writer, journalist. Her mother, Dame Eva Sudeley, da. of 4th Baron Sudeley, was honoured for WWI service to Empire; her father was Henry Torrens A. She was educ. in London, m. Anthony Maxtone Graham, 1923, and had four children. She first published poetry: *Betsinda Dances*, 1931, *Sycamore Square*, 1932, and two collections for children. Her mostly humorous pieces for journals like *Punch* were collected in *Try Anything Twice*, 1938. She began publishing her 'Mrs Miniver' series in *The Times* in 1937. It became a best-selling collection, 1939 (repr. 1984, filmed 1942, later televised), so popular that the public confused JS's family with her fictional creation. Mrs Miniver, designed to embody plucky English resilience and patriotism, made JS *The Times*'s only female leader-writer, and became the basis of her British War Relief lectures and other propaganda work after she moved in 1940 to the USA. She published *The Glass-Blower* (poems), 1940, and *A Pocketful of Pebbles*, 1946, and – by now divorced – m. NY librarian Adolf Kurt Placzek in 1948.

Strutt, Elizabeth, also **Byron**, novelist and woman of letters. Probably da. of lawyer Thomas Frost, she m. a Hull physician, John B.; when he died in 1805, at 25, she was working on *The Borderers* (pub. 1812), a historically informed fourteenth-century romance with lovers from hostile families, a girl dressed as a page, Moorish woman turned Christian and knight turned hermit. She dedicated to her mother the complex, sensitive, epistolary *Anti-Delphine*, 1806, in which a patient wife redeems her seduced husband. It replies (generally, not specifically) to Germaine de STAËL's adulterous, tragic love-story, and to Choderlos de Laclos with two names echoing *Les Liaisons dangereuses*. *Drelincourt and Rodalvi, or Memoirs of Two Noble Families*, 1807, her third treatment of international love, may also date from 1805. By 1818 she m. the artist Jacob George S. (His friend Ann GILBERT, 1782–1866, admired ES's many literary talents, including 'composition of sermons for languid divines'.) ES presents exemplary heroines in *Genevieve, or The Orphan's Visit*, 1818 (persistent sense of unworthiness, marriage to a guardian-mentor), *Chances and Changes*, 1835 (love for a worldly dazzler, marriage to a childhood admirer), and *The Curate and the Rector*, 1859 (broad satire of the Rev. Mr Plufty). ES's works of piety include a life of a modern hermit, 1823, and selections (with lives) from (all male) mentors, 1824, intellectual achievers born poor, 1827, and Christian Fathers, 1837. Until 1851 she was much abroad (often writing sonnets while her husband sketched): her relaxed and personal travel books begin with *A Spinster's Tour*, 1828, which aims to encourage ladies to travel. *The Feminine Soul*, 1857, argues for spiritual equality (social status, she says, is fixed wholly by male power) but also for a distinctive femininity which biases, for instance, her account of women writers.

Stuart, Lady **Arbella**, later Seymour, 1576–1615, letter writer, da. of Elizabeth (Cavendish) and Charles Stuart, Earl of Lennox: granddaughter of the formidable entrepreneur Bess of Hardwick, cousin of ELIZABETH I. Having some claim to succeed to the throne, she was a political pawn all her life; various aspiring husbands were proposed, then forbidden. She secretly married William Seymour in 1610, and was sent to the Tower 18 days later. Recaptured after an escape that got her halfway to France, she was never at liberty again, despite letters and petitions. Her personal physician was husband of Rachel SPEGHT's godmother. AS seems at last to have starved herself (she had been ill already), though when first in prison she had said she would not be 'guilty of my own [wished-for] death'. She was praised for poetry, which does not survive. Her letters have wit, passion, sense of pace, and much classical allusion; the last calls herself 'the most wretched and unfortunate creature that ever lived'. Many ed. by Elizabeth Cooper, 1866, more by E. T. Bradley, 1889; see Sara Jayne Steen in *ELR*, 18, 1988–9, and larger study forthcoming.

Stuart, Augusta Amelia, author of four novels published at London, beginning with the epistolary *Lodovico's Tale, or The Black Banner of Castle Douglas*, 1808. Posing as compiler, she promises if it does well to find more material 'in an old musty trunk ... some white or black tower, or ... in some corner of my own skull'. In fact her tale, well-realized till overwhelmed in pathos, is modern: the hero wrongs the paragon wife he was pressured to marry, gradually reforms after a period of observing his children incognito, and dies once his penitence is complete. In her preface to *Cava of Toledo, or The Gothic Princess* [1813] AAS notes the difficulty of mixing fictitious with historical characters. The result is an effective GOTHIC story of doomed love: princess Cava passes into fiction as she leaves eighth-century Spain for Moorish territory; eastern style is imitated in e.g. 'His steps are short; he often stops; he tosses his sinewy arms; he is like a cloud in the desart, varying its form to every blast'.

'Stuart, Esmé', Amélie Claire LeRoy, 1851–1934, novelist and children's writer. B. Paris of French parents, she was brought to England at the age of five or six, first settling in the Isle of Man with the family of

Bishop Powis. In her twenties she moved to Winchester, began a lifelong close friendship with Mary BRAMSTON, and became part of the circle of writing churchwomen surrounding Charlotte YONGE. She wrote over 60 books, mainly tales for young people pub. by the Christian Knowledge Society and the Church of England Sunday School Institute, but also some temperately sensational novels. *An Out-of-the-Way Place*, 1884, tells of a pretty and a clever sister and their contrasting experiences. The best known are those in the *Harum Scarum* series, beginning 1896 with a young heroine from Australia giving focus to a critique of the snobbery and restrictions of young ladyhood. Other novels, such as *A Woman of Forty*, 1893, and *Christalla: an Unknown Quantity*, 1901, tend not to sustain their initial promise. ES was talented as a watercolour artist and as an essayist, contributing many essays on French literature to reviews such as the *Fortnightly*, the *Scottish*, *Temple Bar* and *Blackwood's*. She devoted herself as well to causes such as women's EDUCATION and the Girls' Friendly Society.

Stuart, Lady **Louisa**, 1757–1851, memoirist and letter writer, youngest child of John S., Earl of Bute and much hated Prime Minister, and of Mary (herself a writer of poems in youth), daughter of Lady Mary Wortley MONTAGU. LS's grandmother's name was used as bugbear to deter the bookish child who at nine planned a French novel and a play on the Numidian king Jugurtha. Closeness to her mother brought wide social experience, but she was shy, fearful of male scorn for her literary pursuits, and mindful of the conventions of her sex and class. Her verse, biographical notes to others' works (alert to make near-feminist points), and fine letters (wry and snobbish on a BLUESTOCKING party, acute and helpful in pre-publication comment on works by Walter Scott) filtered into print from 1857, ed. by family members and others: W. S. Lewis, 1928, lists her publications. She wrote memoirs of her father's family (in Lady Mary COKE's journals), of Caroline Lucy SCOTT's mother (Jill Rubenstein, ed., 1985) and of her grandmother (begun 1827, pub. by her own wish [1836]). When Scott publicized her ballad 'Ugly Meg', she expressed decorous dismay. She wrote part of his spoof *Private Letters of the Seventeenth Century*, pub. 1947. MSS at Sheffield and Scottish Record Office: see Rubenstein in *Prose Studies*, 9, 1986.

Sturm, J.C., Jacquie Baxter, short-story writer, b. 1927, at Opakune, Taranaki, NZ, da. of Ethel (Burley) and Herbert Charles S. After attending girls' high schools, she spent three years at Otago Univ., one at Canterbury Univ. and three at Victoria Univ., Wellington, doing medical intermediate, followed by an MA Hons. in Philosophy. She m. James Keir B., poet, 1948 (d. 1972). They had three children, for whom for long periods, in a difficult marriage, she had primary responsibility. In the 1940s a number of her poems appeared in student papers and in *Review*. In the 1950s she was active in Maori affars, especially in the Ngati Poneke Maori Club, and Maori Women's Welfare League. She lives in Wellington and is the NZ Room Librarian at the Public Library. Her stories were pub. in the magazines *Numbers* and *Te Ao Hou: The Maori Magazine* in the 1950s, but, like her poetry, received little recognition. They were collected only in 1983, by *Spiral*, a feminist collective, as *The House of the Talking Cat*. These stories evoke the feel of NZ in the 1950s while portraying wisely and sensitively issues of female, Polynesian and working-class experience that are very relevant now. Her husband, acclaimed as NZ's greatest poet, has become a national myth. JCS's work, apart from one story in one anthology, *NZ Short Stories: second series*, 1966, was ignored and she stopped writing.

Suckow, Ruth, 1892–1960, novelist, short-story writer, b. in Hawarden, Iowa, da. of second-generation German immigrants, Anna Mary (Kluckhohn) and Congregational minister William John S. She was educ. (from 1907) at Grinnell College, the Curry School of Expression (Boston), and the Univ. of Denver (MA 1918, thesis on women novelists). She published some poems that year. Six years' bee-keeping in Iowa supported her while she wrote the stories of local life which made her name. *The Smart Set* and other magazines published her from 1921. Her first novel, *Country People*, 1924, began as a *Century* serial. *The Odyssey of a Nice Girl*, 1925, is first of several treatments of midwestern heroines seeking self-expression and development amid traditional family demands. After fine reviews of *Iowa Interiors*, 1926 (collected stories), RS moved briefly to NYC; in 1929 she m. Ferner Nuhn, also an Iowa writer (with whom she lived mostly in the southwest), and began her most ambitious work: *The Folks*, pub. 1934, tracing an Iowa family through the effects of 30 years of social history. *Children and Older People*, 1931, and *Carry-Over*, 1936, collect shorter works. Living at Cedar Falls, Iowa, during WWII, she aided pacifist non-combatants; she later became an active Quaker. Despite encroaching arthritis, she wrote two more novels, *New Hope*, 1942, and *The John Wood Case*, 1959 (more schematic: a utopia failed and a scandal surmounted), besides critical articles. *Some Others and Myself*, 1952, includes a fine 'Memoir'. Praised at first as a major realist (by her close friend Dorothy C. FISHER and others), she has since been dismissively labelled a 'midwestern regionalist'. Studies by Leedice McAnelly Kissane, 1969, Margaret Stewart Omrcanin, 1972 (includes bibliog.); see too Barbara A. White in *Growing Up Female*, 1985. RS's diary was ed. by Nuhn in *The Iowan*, 9, 1960–1. Papers at the Univ. of Iowa (see Frank Paluka in *Books at Iowa*, 1964, 1965) and RS Memorial Library, Earlville, Iowa.

Suffolk, Katherine Brandon (Willoughby), Duchess of, 1520–80, letter writer, da. of Mary (de Salinas), a Spaniard, and the 8th Lord W. Orphaned in 1533, she became, probably in 1534, fourth wife to her guardian Charles B., Duke of S. (d. 1545). A friend of Katharine PARR and a leading Puritan (a target for those who martyred Anne ASKEW), she corresponded with William Cecil from 1547. Her letters (PRO, in her own hand) are ahead of their age in liveliness and familiarity; in 1550 she wrote that parents should allow children to love for themselves; forcing them into marriage would be wicked. In 1551 her young sons died both on the same day. In 1553 she m. her gentleman-usher, Richard Bertie; they had children, and lived abroad in Mary's reign. KS was one of 12 leading women patrons of the RENAISSANCE. Several biographies.

Suffrage. In England in the 1640s and 1650s some groups envisioned a political voice for women; a few women actually voted in isolated local instances. In 1776 Abigail ADAMS wrote to her husband of women's place in the new US republic in terms which could be read to imply the vote. The British Reform Bill of 1832 carefully excluded women by the wording '(male) person'. The 1848 Seneca Falls Convention in the US split on this issue: Elizabeth Cady STANTON's motion for suffrage barely passed, as another of the organizers, Lucretia MOTT, felt it might be too radical. Consequent state-level improvements in women's rights did not include the vote. In 1869 (the year Wyoming Territory granted women suffrage, on the initiative of Esther Slack Morris, 1814–1902), Stanton and Susan B. ANTHONY formed the National Woman Suffrage Association. It drew together white women of various social classes throughout the country: a leader of the Mass. branch was Harriet Jane Hanson Robinson, 1825–1911, ex-mill-girl, whose works of 1883 and 1898 chronicle New England factory-girl life of the 1830s and 40s. The association, however, operated in intense rivalry with the

American Woman Suffrage Association (also founded 1869, descendant of the New England Suffrage Association, led by Julia W. HOWE and Lucy STONE, which wanted to enfranchise black men before women). The split (whose effects are differently read in studies by Eleanor Flexner, 1959, and Ellen Carol DuBois, 1978) lasted until 1872, and was fully resolved only in 1890 with the joint formation of the National American Woman Suffrage Association, with Stanton elected president. (There is some parallel with the situation in Britain when the demand for female suffrage was withdrawn from the Chartists' 1838 petition for fear attention would be deflected from the issue of working men's rights.) Stanton, Anthony, and Matilda GAGE published a massive *History of Woman Suffrage*, 4 vols., 1881–1902. Younger women like Carrie Chapman Catt, 1859–1947, from Iowa, and Ann Howard SHAW, recruited by Anthony from the TEMPERANCE movement, gradually took over the NAWSA and worked 'to promote woman suffrage via an amendment to the federal Constitution'. The more militant, less democratic Congressional Union broke away in 1913; a pressure-group with working-class interests, which attracted social activists like Mary Ritter BEARD, it too focused on the constitution, but sought to mobilize the State votes now possessed by many women to 'punish the party in power'. It in turn produced the Woman's Party in 1916, and National Woman's Party in 1917, and picketed the White House, bringing an escalating process of arrests, imprisonment, hunger-strikes and forced feeding. US women achieved the federal vote in 1919 (ratified by the 36th State in 1920), years after the first victories at state and local levels. See Mari Jo and Paul Buhle, eds., *The Concise History of Woman Suffrage*, 1978, Nancy F. Cott, *The Grounding of Modern Feminism*, 1987 (which draws on oral as well as written sources). In Britain, a history of the women's suffrage struggle by Helen BLACKBURN, 1902, charted progress from the setting up of the first committee (by Emily DAVIES, Barbara BODICHON and Helen TAYLOR) in 1866 after an unsuccessful PETITION to parliament through John Stuart Mill. An ideological split developed between those putting female enfranchisement first and those (like Davies: she and Bodichon pulled out the next year) putting improved female EDUCATION and employment opportunites before the vote. Mary Augusta WARD drummed up signatories to her *Appeal Against Female Suffrage* in *Nineteenth Century*, June 1889; they included Eliza Lynn LINTON, Emily LAWLESS and Beatrice WEBB (who later publicly recanted). British territories were well ahead of the UK (1918). Women achieved suffrage in the Isle of Man in 1880, in the Madras presidency in 1885, in New Zealand in 1893 (after a near-miss in 1891), in Victoria in 1896, and in federal Australia in 1902. In Canada the federal vote was achieved by women over 21 in 1918, after a protracted fight by many organizations, beginning with Dr Emily Howard Stowe's Toronto Women's Suffrage Association, founded 1883. Propertied women had voted freely in municipal elections in Québec from 1809 to 1849 (when the word 'male' was inserted in the Quebec Franchise Act), and in all of Canada by 1900, but this was merely by default: the result of official attention to the property rather than the gender qualification. For the winning of the provincial vote in Manitoba, 1916, see Nellie MCCLUNG; for Canada in general, see Catherine L. Cleverdon, *The Woman Suffrage Movement in Canada*, 1950, repr. 1974. In 1897 in England the National Union of Women's Suffrage Societies was formed (led by Millicent Garrett FAWCETT); but by 1903 Emmeline PANKHURST's group of militant suffragettes, the Women's Social and Political Union, had broken away. While the NUWSS strengthened ties with working-class women and voted to support Labour candidates in 1912, the WSPU moved away from their Labour origins entirely, causing the departure of

Charlotte DESPARD and Teresa Billington-Grieg in 1907 to form the Women's Freedom League, and Sylvia PANKHURST in 1912 to form the East London Federation of Suffragettes. The NUWSS, a democratic organization, was committed to constitutional methods while the WSPU became increasingly autocratic and militant. Many WSPU supporters were jailed; their policy of hunger strikes brought force-feeding and (under the 1912 Cat and Mouse Act) temporary release to allow for recovery of health before re-arrest. The Women Writers' Suffrage League, founded 1908, sought to obtain the vote by means of the pen (see also PUBLISHING). Elizabeth ROBINS (also instrumental in the Actresses' Franchise League, with which it combined to create plays), was the first president. Members included many distinguished authors; men were admitted as Honorary Associates. WWI deflected many but not all suffrage campaigners into patriotism; the vote was gained for women over 30 in 1918 and for women over 21 (i.e. equally with men) in 1928. See Ray STRACHEY, 1928, Sylvia Pankhurst, 1931, Constance Rover, *Women's Suffrage and Party Politics 1866–1914*, 1967: Jill Liddington and Jill Norris, *One Hand Tied Behind Us: The Rise of the Women's Suffrage Movement*, 1978, Les Garner, *Stepping Stones to Women's Liberty: Feminist Ideas in the Women's Suffrage Movement 1900–1918*, 1984, Karmela Belinki, *Women's Fiction and Suffrage in England, 1905–1914*, Helsinki 1984; and Jane Marcus, ed., *Suffrage and the Pankhursts*, 1987. See also 'WOMAN QUESTION'.

'Sui Sin Far', Edith Maud Eaton, 1867–1914, 'first Chinese-American fictionist', short-story writer, memoirist, champion of Eurasian equality. Sister of 'Onoto Watanna' (Winnifred REEVE), she was da. of a Chinese, missionary mother, Grace Trefusius, and an English silk-manufacturer father, Edward E. She was b. in England, at five or six moved with her family to the US, then, in 1874, to Montréal. She worked as a typesetter and stenographer for the Montréal *Star* in the 1880s, then, 'ordered beyond the Rockies by the doctor', moved to San Francisco, where she was hired by a newspaper to enlist subscribers in Chinatown. Keenly aware from childhood of the pain of English, Canadian, and American racism, she learned in Chinatown her difference from those she thought to be of her own race. She did not speak Chinese, and 'the Americanized Chinamen actually laugh in my face when I tell them that I am of their race'. Both her sense of belonging to neither east nor west and her awareness of anti-Chinese prejudice are integral to her writing. Her memoir, 'Leaves from the Mental Portfolio of an Eurasian' (quoted above), in the *Independent*, 21 January 1909, describes her growing awareness of both, and her decision to embrace her Chinese identity not mask it as Mexican or Japanese, as many others, including her sister, did. Her essays and stories appeared in journals like the *Dominion Illustrated*, the *Montreal Witness*, the *Independent*, *Century*, *Good Housekeeping*, and *Ladies' Home Journal*, and others. *Mrs. Spring Fragrance*, 1912, collects 37 of them. A few are set in China, most in the Chinese section of a North-American city. They deal realistically and sympathetically with the problems of coping with two cultures and speak ironically, sometimes angrily, of North America. Several are feminist: 'The Inferior Woman' stresses friendship between women. 'Her Chinese Husband' and 'A White Woman Who Married a Chinaman' treat the different sexual attitudes of Chinese and American men, to the decided advantage of the former. SSF lived in various US cities, including Seattle for ten years, and died in Montréal, where the Chinese community erected a monument at her grave. See S. E. Solbert in *Melus*, 2, 1981 (excellent biographical material and checklist), and Amy Ling in *American Literary Realism*, 16, 1983.

Sulter, Maud, poet and short-story writer, b. 1960 in Glasgow of mixed races. Her white working-class grandfather, who d. during her childhood, made possible her hours writing at the kitchen table while her mother was at work; he is dedicatee of *As A Blackwoman*, 1985. As president of her students' union, MS tasted collective action in 1979 against an anti-abortion bill. She had a reluctant abortion in 1982 (written of in a story, 'On Bleecker', 1985, and in Pearlie McNeill et al., eds., *Through the Break, Women and Personal Struggle*, 1986). In 1984 she drew support from Grace NICHOLS and won the Vera BELL prize for 'As a Blackwoman' (poem) which relates to centuries of rape and persecution the political act of bearing a black child. Her book of the same name was pub. by Akira Press after problems with white-dominated writing and publishing collectives, even those with feminist intentions. MS's work challenges imprisoning labels of colour and gender, celebrates love and desire, but exposes oppressions which are perpetrated in private. She addresses incantations to African female spirits, and uses Glaswegian English in a tribute to a friend dead of an unnecessary hysterectomy. 'Under Attack' uses insistent rhyme to protest 'The stigmata on my smooth / blackskinned thigh', put there 'not by divine intervention / but / at the end / of a pair of / twelve inch shears.' A London journalist, MS is active in various projects for enabling black women writers. Her poems and prose appear in journals like *Spare Rib* and anthologies like Cobham and COLLINS, eds., *Watchers and Seekers*, 1987. She interviewed Alice WALKER in 1985 (in Shabnan Grewal et al., eds., *Charting the Journey: Writings by Black and Third World Women*, 1988), and writes of herself and her work in Lauretta NGCOBO, ed., *Let It Be Told*, 1987.

Sumbel, Leah, also Mary Stephens (Davies) Wells, *c.* 1759–1821/6, much-nicknamed actress, autobiographer and journalist, da. of Thomas D., Birmingham carver and gilder. After his death (bankrupt and insane), she supported her family as a child actor in the provinces; while playing Juliet in Gloucester *c.* 1777, she married her Romeo, Mr Wells, who very soon left her. She made her London début in 1781, and in 1787 was earning £50 a night for sketches of other actresses. Her friends included E. S. GOOCH, Elizabeth INCHBALD and Mary ROBINSON. She had four children by Edward Topham, who launched a newspaper, *The World*, in 1787 to boost her career; she wrote for it as 'Old Kent' (reports on drama and on Warren Hastings's trial), helped manage and edit, and provided elements of Topham's farce *The Fool*, 1786. Her children disowned her as she became increasingly erratic, with many spells in debtors' prison. She m. Joseph S., a rich Moroccan Jew, in the Fleet in 1797, converting first to avoid possible Christian bigamy; he proved jealous and violent, and divorced her next year. She was apparently working by 1799 on her *Memoirs*, pub. 1811, dedicated to her grandchildren and her Jewish brother-in-law (whom, with men in general and her 'unhappy and acute feelings', she blames for all her troubles), in which she hurtles through stage roles, reviews, and emotional bruising from lovers, husband and children.

Sunderland, Dorothy Spencer (**Sidney**), Countess of, 1617–84, letter writer. Niece of Lady Mary WROTH, eldest da. of Dorothy (Percy) and the 2nd Earl of Leicester, she was famously wooed in poetry by Edmund Waller as 'Sacharissa', but married Henry Spencer in 1639. His death in battle at Newbury, 1643, left her with three children. Dorothy OSBORNE was inclined to disapprove her re-marriage, 1652. The few that survive of a huge number of letters (called 'the most eloquent in England') are almost all from her last years: to her brother (pub. with his diary, 1843) and her son-in-law the ADVICE-writer Lord Halifax (pub. by Mary BERRY with Lady Rachel RUSSELL's, 1819). She often says she writes silly stuff; once she calls herself, 'the poor old dolt in the corner'; but her style, whether pithy or expansive, reflects her pleasure in writing, and she handles politics, the court (often in cipher) and family marriage treaties with equal gusto. 'I am old enough to remember the ill consequences of princes being deceived'; Charles II 'smiles, dances, makes love, and hunts'; a niece's new husband 'calls the women all the ill names there are, and meddles with every thing in the kitchen much'. Life by Julia Cartwright, 1893.

Sutcliffe, Alice (Woodhouse), religious writer. Da. of Luke W. of Norfolk, she m. John S. of Mayroid, Yorks., and had a daughter by 1624. She gave her name and his position (Groom of the royal Chamber) on the title-page of *Meditations of Man's Mortalitie, or A Way to True Blessednesse*, probably first pub. 1633, 2nd ed. 1634, with verse praises from men including Ben Jonson and George Withers, all of whom comment on her sex. She dedicated her book to Katherine Duchess of Buckingham, as 'more than a Mother to mee', and as likely to value a woman's work *more* highly; she expects mockery or carping for doing something 'not usuall', but cites the prophet Deborah as precedent. She weaves Bible quotations seamlessly into a style which is lyrical and sensual on heavenly joys as well as earthly horrors: 'before thou wast borne, thou wast filthy and obsceane matter, not worthy to be named; now thou art dung, covered over with snow, and a while after thou shalt be meat for Wormes: why then, shouldest thou bee proud, seeing thy Nativity is sinne, thy Life misery, and thy End putrifaction and corruption'? Lastly, an effective long poem recounts 'our losse by Adam, and our gayne by Christ'. Note by Ruth Hughey, *RES*, 10, 1934.

Sutherland, Efua Theodora (Morgue), poet, dramatist and educator. B. 1924 at Cape Coast, now Ghana, she went to Saint Monica's school in Mampong, Ashanti, graduated from Homerton College, Cambridge, and the School of Oriental and African Studies at London Univ., returning to Ghana, 1951. She m. American William S., 1954, with whom she established a school and an experimental village theatre. They have three children. At independence, 1957, when Nkrumah actively sponsored national arts, ES helped to found the Ghana Drama Studio, for which she wrote and directed plays, and the Ghana Society of Writers. Active in *Okyeame: Ghana's Literary Magazine*, she has, since 1963, taught African literature and drama at the Institute of African Studies at the Univ. of Ghana, where she has established a Writers' Workshop, and set up her own film studio. Her compatriate, Ama Ata Aidoo, who, like her, emphasizes the culturally formative role of women, praises ES's use of 'traditional ... dramatic forms' to show cultural change. Many poems and radio plays – e.g. 'The Pineapple Child' or 'Ananse and the Dwarf Brigade' – incorporate the music, dance and audience participation common to folk tradition. *The Marriage of Anansewa*, 1975, features the legendary trickster hero, Ananse the spider man, marrying off his daughter in today's world; its musical interludes provide for audience participation. *Edufa*, 1966 (produced 1962), ES's version of the Greek Alcestis theme, in which a loving wife offers to die instead of her husband, strengthens the wife's role and embellishes a feminist theme in the comments of the women's chorus. In *Foriwa*, 1967 (produced 1962), an extended dramatic version of ES's narrative poem 'New Life at Kyrefaso', a progessive Queen Mother and her daughter, Foriwa, revise the celebration of the annual river-goddess festival. Refusing a traditonally arranged marriage, Foriwa dances at the festival with Queen Mother's blessing as she prepares to wed an educated Hausa stranger from the north with whom she will bring new prosperity and new technologies to the villages. ES created her *Two Rhythm*

Plays: Vulture! Vulture! and Tahinta, 1968, for school children in both an English and an Akan version. She has also published pictorial essays, *The Roadmakers*, 1961, and *Playtime in Africa*, for children, 1962. 'Kreyfaso' is printed in *Voices of Ghana: Literary Contributions to the Ghana Broadcasting System, 1955–57*, other poems in Kofi Awoonor and G. Adali-Mortty, eds., *Messages*, 1971. 'The Redeemed' shows the new African Eve triumphing over the tempter snake that tries to curse her. Study by Linda Lee Talbert in *WLWE*, 22, 1983.

'Sutherland, Joan', Joan Maisie (Collings) Kelly, 1890–1947, popular novelist and periodical contributor. B. at Bishop's Stortford, Herts., to Hannah (Walker) and Henry C., journalist, she was educ. at Bournemouth and Leicester schools, and studied singing in Paris. In 1913 she published her first novel, *Cavanaugh of Kultana*; in 1914 she made her concert debut in Paris, and m. Richard Cecil K. She had five children. She dropped her music, but during a life frequently abroad (Paris, Canada, the USA, and the Orient), she published prolifically (more than 30 novels), often with Mills and Boon, which was already leaning towards stereotypical romances. Despite many exotic Empire settings, affluent and conventional characters, and melodramatic plots, JS depicts genuine problems of female-male relationships, often set in a wider political context. *Wings of the Morning*, 1919, and *In the Midst of the Years*, 1933, treat domestic British politics, while *Wide Horizon*, 1942, and *The High Hills*, 1948, figure Nazi anti-Semitism in the background. JS's protagonists often brave society's disapproval of divorce, and male characters turn to them after disastrous, lust-based marriages; many novels end with hope for mature love.

Sutherland, Margaret (Mansfield), novelist and short-story writer, b. 1941 in Auckland, NZ, da. of Dorothy Genevieve (Bolton) and William Charles M. Educ. at St Mary's College, Auckland, she became a registered nurse. Separated from her husband, she has three children. Her first novel, *The Fledgling*, 1974, was pub. when her youngest child was seven. Her second, *The Love Contract*, 1976, realistically records ten years of married suburban life, a sad account of the contract women enter into and its consequence when true love fails. MS has pub. a coll. of short stories about contemporary life, *Getting Together*, 1977. In 1980 she was Writer-In-Residence at Auckland Univ. *The Fringe of Heaven*, 1984, is about a fortyish solo mother, her children and what she has made of her eccentric life in an Auckland suburb. It is a positive picture of the possibility of individual freedom, once the love contract has been rejected.

Sutton, Katherine, Baptist autobiographer. She spent parts of her life in Holland (once losing her MSS in a storm at sea), and pub. *A Christian Woman's Experiences of the Glorious Workings of Gods Free Grace* at Rotterdam, 1663. Prefaced with a note by Hanserd Knollys (Anne WENTWORTH's persecutor) defending her 'gift of singing spiritual Songs', her book records the years of doubt, illness and suicide attempts that led up to receiving this 'gift', when she began in the later 1650s to prophesy in verse against the national turn of events. She wryly celebrates her marriage as having been 'a furtherance to heaven' because her husband's lack of real religion drove her closer to God, and describes the grief she felt at the deaths of some of her children.

Swan, Annie S., later Burnett Smith, 'David Lyall', 1859–1943, best-selling romantic novelist, b. Edinburgh, one of seven children of potato merchant Edward S. She was educ. at Queen Street Ladies' College, Edinburgh, but passed much of her youth in the country while her father spent business profits on unsuccessful farms. In 1883, after the death of her much-loved gentle mother and her father's remarriage, she m. James Burnett S. and pub. her first novel, *Aldersyde*, admired by Gladstone for its 'truly living sketches of Scotch character'. It was followed by a stream of serial fiction: more than 250 novels and tales. She also ed. the journal *The Woman at Home* from 1893. Her 'serious and innocuous fiction for the delectation of babes', as she dubbed it in her straightforward and readable autobiography, *My Life*, 1934, was enormously popular in its day, and still reprinted up to the 1950s. A selection of her letters was ed. by Mildred R. Nicoll in 1945.

Swanwick, Anna, 1813–99, translator, educator, and scholar, b. Liverpool, youngest da. of Hannah (Hilditch) and John S. She moved to Berlin in 1839 and there acquired the fluency in Greek and German which led to her highly regarded TRANSLATIONS, including the plays of Schiller and Goethe (particularly her blank-verse version of *Faust*, 1860 and 1878), and Aeschylus, 1865, 1873, and 1890. Other works include *An Utopian Dream*, 1888, concerning the improvement of living conditions of London's poor; *Poets the Interpreters of their Age*, 1892; and *Evolution and the Religion of the Future*, 1894. She supported the campaign against the Contagious Diseases Act, and for women's SUFFRAGE, making her first public speech at a suffrage meeting in 1873. An active promoter of education for both women and the working class, she helped found Somerville College, Oxford, and Girton College, Cambridge; served on the Councils for Queen's and Bedford Colleges, London; and was the first woman elected Visitor to Bedford, 1884. See the memoir by her niece, Mary Bruce, 1903.

Swarton, Hannah, CAPTIVITY-NARRATIVE writer. Seized by American Indians at Casco fort, May 1690, 'hurry'd up and down the wilderness' until February (her husband killed, her captured children inaccessible), she feared this was God's punishment for moving to a frontier area without church services, 'thereby exposing our children to be bred ignorantly like Indians'. Having reached Canada, she feared to be converted to Roman Catholicism, and thought herself in greater danger after ransom by Québecois French than before. Discussion with other Protestant captives kept her loyal; she shipped for Boston in Nov. 1695 with her youngest son, leaving a Catholic daughter in Québec. Cotton Mather incorporated her narrative in works of 1697 and 1702.

Sweat, Margaret Jane (Mussey), novelist, poet and TRAVEL-writer, b. 1823 in Portland, Maine, da. of John M. She was educ. in Portland and Roxbury, Maine, and her first publications appeared in the *North American Review*, 1856, after which she became a frequent contributor. She also translated George SAND. In 1859 she pub. *Highways of Travel: or a Summer in Europe* and *Ethel's Love-Life*, her only novel. Praised in its time for its 'pure, tender and elevated sentiment', it is notable rather as an elaborate female erotic fantasy in which Ethel describes to her fiancé her relationships with rejected suitors, as well as with two women bound to her by 'strange and irrevocable ties'. This device enables the reader to experience a variety of exotic relationships while remaining within the context of a traditional engagement. With its tension between 'correct' rhetoric and Ethel's obvious enjoyment of and interest in her erotic life, the novel points up the contradictions in women's lives. MS pub. *Verses*, 1890, as by 'M.J.M.S.'; many poems express erotic desire for women through a male persona, as in 'Give Me the Night': 'When the night comes it brings me bliss and thee'. She also pub. another travel book, *Hither and Yon by Land and Sea*, 1901.

Swenson, May, poet, b. 1919 at Logan, Utah, eldest of ten children of Mormons Anna Margaret (Hellberg) and Dan Arthur S., who taught mechanical engineering at

Utah State Agricultural College (now Utah State Univ.). MS took a bachelor's degree there, 1934, and worked as a reporter for *Deseret News* and *The Logan Herald* before moving to NYC. She worked as a secretary and placed poems (and a few stories) in periodicals beginning with *The Saturday Review*, and in anthologies: *New Directions in Prose and Poetry*, 1949 and 1950, and *Poets of Today*, i, 1954 (including 'Another Animal: Poems'). She has received many fellowhips and grants. Seven more volumes have followed *A Cage of Spines*, 1958, besides a joint translation of poems by Tomas Tranströmer, 1972. She writes of travel and of the onset of age (e.g. 'How To Be Old') in *To Mix With Time*, 1963. Her experimental play, *The Floor*, was produced 1966, pub. 1967. Many pieces in the children's volumes *Poems to Solve*, 1966, and *More Poems to Solve*, 1971, and all in *Iconographs*, 1970, are concrete or 'shaped poems'. MS, 'the poet of the perceptible', writes of her 'tendency to let each poem "make itself" – to develop, in process of becoming, its own individual physique'. The words of 'Women' are arranged on the page to trace the movement of 'moving / pedestals / . . . / little horses / . . . / ridden / rockingly / ridden until / the restored / egos dismount and the legs stride away'. A passionate love-poem from woman to woman is 'A Trellis for R.' *In Other Words: New Poems*, 1987, includes 'Banyan' (33 pp.), whose monkey narrator 'knuckles' along its limbs and swings through its upper reaches (it is perhaps a world-tree) with Blondi, a cockatoo rescued from a library, who repeatedly recites, like a poem: 'The purpose of life is / To find the purpose of life'. MS's poetry is cerebral but hard-hitting, treating human and other animal bodies with an 'earthy eroticism'. She has taught at several universities. See her comments in Howard Nemerov, ed., *Poets on Poetry*, 1966, and William Packard, ed., *The Poet's Craft*, 1987; Ann STANFORD in *Southern Review*, 5, 1969 (quoted above: with poems); Alicia OSTRIKER in GILBERT and Gubar, eds., *Shakespeare's Sisters*, 1979.

Sykes, Bobbi (Roberta), poet, Aboriginal activist, b. 1943 in Townsville, Queensland. She received minimal educ. in Australia (leaving school at 14) but went on to gain a Doctorate in Education from Harvard. Her debate with Senator Neville Bonner was pub. as *Black Power in Australia*, 1975. She also assisted Shirley Perry, one of the founders of the Aboriginal Medical and Legal Services, to write and pub. her autobiography, *Mum Shirl*, 1981. BS's collection of poetry, *Love Poems and Other Revolutionary Actions*, 1979 (initially rejected by mainstream publishers) contains three sequences, 'The Revolution', 'For Love', and 'Of People'. Unashamedly polemical, these poems display a deep commitment to black affairs, as well as offering a more personal view of a black woman's role within a racist society. BS has also pub. her doctoral thesis, *Incentive, Achievement and Community*, 1986, subtitled and best described as 'an analysis of Black viewpoints on issues relating to Black Australian education'.

Sykes, Henrietta (Masterman), 1766–1823, author of three novels for MINERVA. Da. of Anne (Alcock) and Henry M. of Settrington, Yorks., first cousin of Ann SKINN, she m., 1795, Sir Mark S. of Sledmere, who added her family name to his and was famous for breeding horses. A Reynolds full-length of her remains at Sledmere. In *Morgiana, or Widdrington Tower, A Tale of the Fifteenth Century*, 1808, two sisters suffer fearful perils at the court of Henry IV, where their father hopes they will retrieve his political position. HS turned to the present day for the lively, comic *Sir William Dorien, A Domestic Story*, 1812. Its female characters are either ludicrous or virtuously submissive, its men a vividly satirized gallery of villains and eccentrics; Dickens may have learned from it. *Stories of the Four Nations*, 1813, is set in France, England, Spain and Italy.

The banal *Hymns and Poems on Moral Subjects*, 1815, by subscription, has been wrongly ascribed to her. HS made her will when ill in 1813 (voicing deep love for her husband), but survived ten more years.

Sylvia's Revenge, *or A Satyr against Man*, 1688 (repr. 1697), a furious defence of the female sex against male detractors, with prefatory poem by Mary PIX. Misattributed to Richard Ames because of his use of it in *Sylvia's Complaint*, 1692, it could be by Aphra BEHN. (Its style suggests her, as does its attack on husbands and lovers alike.) It is part of a fierce, prolific exchange for and against women. The ATTACKS perhaps began with *Female Excellence* ... (ironically titled), 1679, which includes the misogynous 'General Satyr on Women' that provoked *SR*; they continued with pamphlets by Robert Gould, 1680 (answered by Sarah FYGE) and 1691 (answering *SR*). DEFENCES included *Triumphs of Female Wit ... or, The Emulation*, 1683, which claims female authors but was mainly or wholly by men (answered by Ames). *SR* asks 'Shall a bold Scribling-Fop whose Head contains, / A Thousand Maggots for One Dram of Brains, / In Doggerel Rime, and much more Doggerel Sence, / Vomit six Pen'worth of Impertinence; / Thrust it abroad, and in a Stile not Common, / Call it forsooth – A Satyr Against Woman?'

Szumigalski, Anne (Davis), poet, translator, scriptwriter, editor. B. in 1922 in London, one of seven children of Molly (Winder) and Major Howard E. D., she grew up in Hampshire. She was educ. at home, later with a small group of girls, especially in art, languages, history and literature. She nursed Belgian refugees in England, and after WWII was an interpreter in Europe. She m. Jane S., a Polish Army officer, in 1945, and migrated to a Saskatchewan farm in 1951, later moving to Saskatoon. She had four children. She has taught writing, been active in writers' groups, and edited several regional journals – *Freelance*, the literary magazine *Grain*, 1970–8, and the poetry section of *NeWest Review*, 1983–7. Anthologized by Al Purdy and Dorothy LIVESAY (*Forty Women Poets of Canada*, 1972), AS has published four volumes of poetry, and co-authored two others and five narrative poems for radio with Terrence Heath. She also composes on tape (to voice 'all the sounds that ever were' which 'are stored in the void around us'). Her titles (*Game of Angels*, 1980, *Doctrine of Signatures*, 1983, *Instar*, 1985, and *Dogstones*, 1986) express her sense that images embody ideas and myth and that poetry discovers transient truths. She speaks French, Dutch, German and Polish, is co-translator of the poems in *Invisible Ladder*, 1975, and co-author of *BOooOms*, 1973, for children. See Kathleen Geminder in *ECW*, 18–19, 1980, and Paul Savoie in *Quarry*, 35, 1986.

T

Tabor, Eliza (later Stephenson), 1835–1914, English novelist, da. of Mary (Holdich), a governess and Methodist, and John T., York Methodist schoolmaster. ET was the second girl: three boys died. Her sister was the scholar; Eliza was regarded as frivolous, but later became so devout that she drove away her fiancé by her insistence on his conversion to Methodism. This broken romance became the subject of her first novel, *All for the Best,* 1862, which was savagely reviewed by the *Athenaeum*; her second, *St Olave's,* 1863, was more successful. It gives a scathing picture of Cathedral city snobbery, and shows her knowledge of Yorkshire people and dialect. It was followed by a string of anonymously published romances with sad endings, such as *Hester's Sacrifice* and *Rachel's Secret,* both 1866, in which women are naturally inferior, and English girls a 'delicious blending of womanhood and childhood'. In 1875 she m. widower John Stephenson, a Bombay chaplain, having already repudiated Methodism. Her best work is probably *Lady Lowater's Companion,* 1884. She wrote 19 novels and some children's stories, and her writing gives a picture of girls' education in provincial middle-class life. She also founded a Ruskin society. See the life by Marjorie S. Broughall, 1961.

Tadema, Laurence Alma, 1864/7–1940, miscellaneous writer, b. in Europe, da. of Marie-Pauline (Girard), of Sancerre, France, who d. 1867, and Dutch painter Lourens or Lawrence A-T, who settled in England in 1870 and had great success. In the 1880s and 1890s she was an important contributor (prose and verse) to *The Yellow Book.* Her fiction presents passionate, suffering women. *Love's Martyr,* 1886, memorably describes intellectual and emotional victimization. A widower writes of his half-French wife, orphaned by the guillotine and reared in England in 'a dense wall of ignorance, neglect and misery against which her darkened soul beats itself to death': she loves the first man to extend sympathy, marries another from gratitude, and dies tragically. *The Wings of Icarus,* 1894, less overwrought in style, finely uses letters and journals to depict another fatal triangle. *The Crucifix,* 1895, collects stories. *One Way of Love,* 1893, a blank verse play, shows a high-born medieval lady consigning a poet who loves her to a 'hedge rose' cottage girl: *Four Plays* followed in 1905. Among six poetry volumes, from 1897, *Songs of Womanhood,* 1903, dwells much on unhappy love: 'my spirit understands / Renouncement.' LAT also issued translations, the monthly *The Herb o' Grace,* 1901 ff, fairy tales, 1906, a rhapsodic 'discourse' on *The Meaning of Happiness,* 1909, and a pamphlet on Poland and Russia in 'this great war of emancipation' [1915]. She was made a CBE for work with Polish refugees in WWI.

Taggard, Genevieve, 1894–1948, poet and scholar. Da. of Alta Gale (Arnold) and James Nelson T., she was b. in Waitsburg, Washington, and raised mostly in Hawaii where her parents were Disciples of Christ missionaries and teachers. (She wrote of this time in a 1934 essay repr. in *Calling Western Union,* 1936.) Working her way through Berkeley, 1914–20, she edited the student literary journal, *Occident,* and took up socialist politics. *Harper's* pub. her first poem, 'An Hour on a Hill', 1919; Max Eastman offered a job which failed to materialize; she worked in NY for B. W.

Huebsch's avant-garde *Freeman*, then helped found and edit *The Measure: A Journal of Poetry*. In 1921 she married writer Robert L. Wolf, and in 1922 bore a daughter and published a volume of lyrics, *For Eager Lovers*. During a year in San Francisco she taught poetry and published *Hawaiian Hilltop*, 1923. In New Preston, Conn., from that year, she edited a contemporary Californian anthology (jointly) and one of radical verse from *The Masses* and *The Liberator*, both 1925; a slim volume of verse by Anne Bremer (d. 1923), 1927; and metaphysical poems from Donne to cummings, 1929. Her *Travelling Standing Still*, 1928, like her previous volume, was much praised; so was her life of Emily DICKINSON, 1930. She taught at Mount Holyoke and Bennington, Vt (with a Guggenheim-supported year in Capri in between), and later at Sarah Lawrence until she retired in 1946. Divorced from her husband (by then in a mental asylum), she married, 1935, Kenneth Durant, employee of the Soviet news agency, Tass. She increasingly involved herself in radical causes, and directed poems towards proletarian audiences. *Collected Poems*, 1938 (drawing on several more volumes), shows a continuity between early Hawaiian imagery, poems of women's experience in love, and later revolutionary themes, reflecting a resolute quest for personal, artistic, social and political freedom. Of further poetry volumes, her favourite was *Slow Music*, 1946. Aaron Copeland and others have set her lyrics to music. Papers at Dartmouth College and the NYPL. *To the Natural World*, 1980, is a selec. by her daughter, Marcia T. Liles. UMI has microformed her *Complete Works* (including early periodical printings), 1988.

Talbot, Catherine, 1721–70, miscellaneous moral writer, poet and BLUESTOCKING, coming of two ecclesiastical families: her father, Edward T., d. before her birth; her mother, Mary (Martyn), lived from 1725 in the house of his colleague Thomas Secker (Bishop in turn of Durham, Bristol, Oxford; Archbishop of Canterbury), who oversaw CT's education in the scriptures, languages and astronomy, and used her as secretary. Her friends included Lady HERTFORD, Elizabeth MONTAGU (sometimes perceived as a rival in her more important relationship with Elizabeth CARTER), and Samuel Richardson (her advice helped shape *Sir Charles Grandison*). Eliza BERKELEY's future husband proposed to her and kept some of her poems. Despite writing from about ten, allowing MSS to circulate, regretting Catharine TROTTER's obscurity, and being urged by Carter, she published little (items in the *Athenian Letters*, 1741, *Rambler* and, probably, *Adventurer*). Her 'green book' of essays, poems, dialogues, etc., stayed in her 'considering drawer'. After years of nursing by her mother, she died of cancer; Carter pub. at her own expense CT's *Reflections on the Seven Days of the Week*, 1770 (25,000 copies by 1809), *Essays on Various Subjects*, 1771, and *Works*, 1771 (7th ed., 1809, with additions and a memoir by Carter's nephew M. Pennington). CT's 'Education, A Fairy Tale', 1752/4, was pub. in John Gregory's *Father's Legacy*, 1882 ed., (see ADVICE). Various MSS in BL. See Sylvia H. Myers, *The Bluestocking Circle*, forthcoming.

'Tasma', Jessie Couvreur (Huybers), 1848–97, novelist and journalist, b. Highgate, London, second child of Charlotte (Ogleby) and James H., Dutch merchant. She went at an early age to Tasmania, where she was largely educ. by her mother. Married at 18 to Charles Fraser, she supported herself through freelance journalism during the ten-year separation before their divorce in 1883. Returning to Europe in 1885, she m. Belgian politician and journalist, Auguste C., whom she succeeded, after his death in 1894, as Brussels correspondent for the London *Times*; she also lectured on Australia in France and Belgium. Her first novel, *Uncle Piper of Piper's Hill*, 1889 (repr. 1987 with a useful intro. by Margaret

Harris), achieved popular and critical success. Sophisticated and witty, it examines the clash between nouveau-riche colonialism and poverty-stricken British upper-class snobbery, set in the prosperous city of Melbourne before the crash of the 1890s. This was followed by a collection of stories, *A Sydney Sovereign,* 1890, and five other novels, all portraying women trapped within unhappy marriages. *In Her Earliest Youth,* 1890, and *Not Counting the Cost,* 1895, reflect wider concerns with nationality and culture. She died in Brussels and was cremated, as she requested, in Paris. Harris's chapter in D. Adelaide, ed., *A Bright and Fiery Troop,* 1988, is the best account of this writer and her work to date.

Tatlock, Eleanor, Evangelical poet, da. of Elizabeth (Smith) and of Richard T., naval surgeon; she may be the Ellen T. who d. at Battersea, London, in 1818, aged 55. From Sandwich, Kent (where her widowed mother died in 1797), she moved to Great Marlow, Bucks. A non-bigoted dissenter, she says, with Anglican links, she diverted loneliness with verse for the *Evangelical* and other magazines (one poem appeared in three). Her major work is 'Thoughts in Solitude': its six books in blank verse range through natural description (she was versed in recent scientific knowledge), historical exposition, meditation on time and flux, and developed fictional examples, many female (notably a generally submissive wife who once converted is firm enough to convert her husband too). It closes on intellectual debate with a deist. Its accomplished level is matched by a range of short pieces: hymns, fables, lively retelling of New Testament stories, addresses to friends, a poem on ABOLITION. Humour appears in 'An Ode to a Tea-Pot', 'To a Crow Quill', and 'A Proposal' for full degree-level education for women (BA will become SA; DD can stand): only if women prove still 'boobies' can 'pre-eminent' men savour solid triumph based on fair trial. ET set her name to *Poems,* 2 vols., 1811.

'Tattle-well, Mary', and **'Joane Hit-him-home'**, alleged spinster authors of *The Womens Sharpe Revenge, or An Answer to Sir Seldome Sober,* 1640, prose reply to John Taylor's two misogynist ATTACKS of 1639, *Divers Crabtree Lectures* and *A Juniper Lecture.* The names *may* cloak a woman, or two women; or quite probably Taylor answering himself. The work takes a personal tone, with abuse, name-calling, and rehearsal of the standard DEFENCES and praises of women. A more thoughtful passage remarks how women are kept down by lack of education, how reading is grudged and sewing promoted, how accomplishments are learned for the benefit of men, not women. Repr. in Henderson and McManus, eds., 1985.

Tautphoeus, Jemima, (Montgomery), Baroness von, 1807–93, novelist, b. Seaview, Donegal, Ireland, da. of Jemima (Glasgow) and James Montgomery, landowner. She was educ. at home. In 1838 she m. Cajetan Josef Friedrich, Baron von T. of Marquarstein, chamberlain to the king of Bavaria. She lived most of her life in Bavaria, her observations of European society forming the basis of her four novels: *The Initials,* 1850, *Cyrilla,* 1853, *Quits,* 1857, and *At Odds,* 1863. Her books combine detailed descriptions of exotic Bavarian scenery and its peasant inhabitants with familiar aristocratic main characters, lively dialogue, and a thwarted romance or love interest which provides a dynamic for the narrative. (*Cyrilla* is based on an actual 'murder for love' case.) Though she displays no great social or political analysis in her novels, she occasionally offers acute observations of social behaviour, particularly towards women. There is an article by Lewis Thorpe, *English Miscellany,* 13, 1962.

Tax, Meredith, historical writer whose mother, Martha T., and other 'women of my family trained my ear'. She gave up an academic thesis for political work, and by 1969 had in progress a book about chiefly

NYC and Chicago women in US labour history. She came to NYC in 1976, a single mother living by clerical jobs; from 1977 she reviewed genre fiction for *Kirkus Reviews*. The book, at first rejected, became *The Rising of the Women, Feminist Solidarity and Class Conflict, 1880–1917*, 1980; MT tells the story of its birthing in Carol Ascher et al., eds., *Between Women*, 1984. 'For women, labor history comes attached to community history and family history and the history of reproduction.' MT weaves her threads deftly; she ends on a socialist and a suffragist in Charlotte Perkins GILMAN being told 'Your work is all the same'. Tired of 'stories I could prove', MT next wrote, 'with passion and high seriousness', a novel on the pre-WWI 'nexus of Jews, politics, the union movement and the women's movement'. Rights for *Rivington Street*, 1982, fetched a large sum at auction, but the *New York Times* called it 'summer-weight fiction'. It opens with a Russian pogrom whose 'carnage was on a scale considered large until the modern era'; the family fleeing to America leaves a 14-year-old daughter raped and killed. Its sequel, *Union Square*, 1988 (*Passionate Women* in the UK – 'airline fiction with political content': *NY Times*), traces some of the same people and issues through the 1920s and 1930s. Relaxed about denigration, proud of her mass readership, MT hopes 'to empower my readers. . . . to raise the level of political education in this country' (*WRB*, July 1989).

Taylor, Eleanor Ashworth (later Towle), 1847–1912, **Ida Ashworth**, 1850–1929, and **Una Ashworth**, 1857–1922; all novelists, b. at East Sheen, Surrey, the daughters of Theodosia Alice (Spring Rice) and Sir Henry T., civil servant and poet, as well as friend of Tennyson, Trollope, Jowett and others. EAT's first novel, *Christina North*, 1872, pub. as by 'E. M. Archer', has a wayward heroine who engages herself to three men in succession, then dies. It was well reviewed in the *Athenaeum*, though a later novel, *My Sister Rosalind*, 1876, dedicated to her cousin Aubrey de Vere, was dismissed as a 'dose of unmitigated affliction'. In 1875 EAT m. Charles Seymour Towle, vicar of St Clement's, Bournemouth. Her strength was character study, and she wrote memoirs of A. H. Makonochie, 1890, John Mason Neale, 1906, and Hartley and Sara COLERIDGE: *A Poet's Children*, 1912. IAT's first novel, *Venus' Doves*, 1884, like most which followed, is a light but amusing and well-written romance. But *Allegiance*, 1886, dedicated to Una, is more impressive, conveying a real sense of the heroine's passion for a man ostracized for embezzlement. From 1902 until 1920 she produced popular historical works, such as *Christina of Sweden*, 1909, *Life of Madame Roland*, 1911, and *Life of Cardinal Manning*, 1920 (she may have become a Catholic). One of her novels, *A Social Heretic*, 1899, was written jointly with UAT. UAT pub. four other novels: her earliest, *Wayfarers*, 1886, treats a deserted orphan who becomes an actress after leaving the young nobleman she married as a girl. Other titles include *The King's Favourite*, 1892, and (for John Lane's Keynote series) *Nets for the Wind*, 1896. She also pub. short stories, *Knight Asrael*, 1889, translations of early Italian love stories, 1899, and a critical study of Maeterlinck, 1914. *Guests and Memories. Annals of a Seaside Villa*, 1924, is a readable account of family and friends, including Lewis Carroll, who met the sisters in 1862.

Taylor, Elizabeth (later Wythens), 'Olinda', d. 1708, poet, da. of Elizabeth (Hall) and Sir Thomas T. of Maidstone, Kent. She was m. in 1685 to the 50-year-old 'voluptuary' Sir Francis W., and ran up large debts, perhaps intentionally to damage him. When he died, 1704, she m. her lover, Sir Thomas Colepepper of Aylesford, Kent. Delarivier MANLEY, reprinting a song by her in 1709, called her the wittiest lady of twenty years before. Aphra BEHN's *Miscellany*, 1685, has three songs by ET, all about the harm women suffer in love. One fears to love and be betrayed, the next nobly offers to help the man she loves to court another, a third describes a man who despises women, 'Or what's worse, love[s] 'em all'. (She is the book's only named woman: 'a Lady of Quality' wrote 'The Female Wits', which denigrates women, and a translation of SAPPHO, through French.) As 'Lady Withens' ET contributed to Henry Playford's *Banquet of Music,* ii. 1688. John Dunton claimed her as a contributor in the 1690s (see JOURNALISM); he mentions an Irish Mrs Taylor who wrote an astonishing juvenile autobiography. A later Eliza (Pierce) T., d. 1776, knew Catherine TALBOT and had letters pub. 1927; another Eliza T. published several MINERVA novels, 1799–1817.

Taylor, Elizabeth (Coles), 1912–75, writer of novels and short stories. B. in Reading, Berks., da. of Elsie (Fewtrell) and Oliver C., she was educ. there, at the Abbey School, where she wrote stories, plays, and novels. Later she worked as a governess and in a library. In 1936 she m. John William Kendall T.; they lived in Penn, Bucks., and had two children. *At Mrs. Lippincote's,* 1945, her first published novel, was, characteristically, shrewdly limited in scope and acute in wit. It was followed by *Palladian,* 1946, *A View of the Harbour,* 1947, *A Wreath of Roses,* 1949, the best-seller *A Game of Hide and Seek,* 1951, *The Sleeping Beauty,* 1953, repr. 1982, and *Angel,* 1957, later named one of the Book Marketing Council's 'Best Novels of Our Time'. Her collections of stories, *Hester Lilly,* 1954, *The Blush,* 1958, *A Dedicated Man,* 1965, and *The Devastating Boys,* 1972, are often considered her most formally accomplished works. ET, who calls attention to the Englishness and womanliness of her books ('Village-life ... seems a better background for a woman novelist'), is readily assigned to a lesser tradition of 'sensibility', 'stylistic grace', excelling in subtle observation of women's lives and the morally significant details of social manners. These elements are self-consciously present, in the works of a novelist who teasingly prefers 'books in which practically nothing ever happens' (attempted and successful suicides, violent death, crime, fade into the continuing ordinary). The uneventfulnesses of deep loneliness, terror and despair in her books become conditions from which we look for rescue to the satisfaction of biting wit, of a prose 'beautiful' and 'precise', and to her rich documentation of the cruelties perpetrated by familiar egoism, self-deceit, or desire. Her books implicate themselves ironically in the escapist world they criticize and batten on the fictions people read and live, adopting the paradigms of ROMANCE, thriller, comedy of manners, devastatingly to subvert them. Repeatedly, in *In a Summer Season,* 1961, repr. 1983, *The Soul of Kindness,* 1964, repr. 1983, *The Wedding Group,* 1968, repr. 1985, *Blaming,* 1976, ET discovers the manipulativeness of generous conduct, the destructiveness of the escapist emotions, 'charm', 'pity', 'nostalgia', and the limits of altruism. 'People who have personal codes do such dreadful things' (*A Wreath of Roses*) is a disturbing, constant awareness in her fictions. 'We haven't changed enough' (*The Sleeping Beauty*) is another, for in ET's books no character impinges on another without effecting change; no pattern of life can be preserved untroubled; each ending glimpses new imperfection; mortality (the unmentionable author of the local discomforts and pretences of old age in *Mrs Palfrey at the Claremont,* 1971, repr. 1982) is finally and finely her theme. Robert Liddell, *Elizabeth and Ivy,* 1986, is an account of his friendships with ET and Ivy COMPTON-BURNETT.

Taylor, Hannah (Harris), 1774–1812, Quaker memoirist. Her father, seaman William H., died on shipboard *c.* 1789 (his coffin was macabrely washed ashore); her mother was left with her and five younger children. She m. Henry T., also a seafarer, who proved 'faithless' and left her to go to war (she later grieved herself by following his career in the navy lists); her only child and beloved little brother died; she feared going mad. Most of this part was cut from her 'tribulated' life-story (written 1799) when it appeared in *Memoir,* York, 1820 (with later irregular diary entries, prayers and verse). Hating her homelessness (she was 'tossed' like 'a wandering bird'), she moved often between northern England (Thirsk and Maryport) and Ireland (Clonmel and Cork, where Sarah STEPHENSON counselled her in 1799). She helped with a sister's school, brought up younger twin sisters and orphaned nieces, endured more bereavements, and struggled against 'self-condemnation'.

Taylor, Harriet (Hardy), later Mill, 1807–58, feminist writer, philosopher and poet, b. London, da. of Harriet (Hurst) and Thomas H., surgeon. In 1826 she m. John T., druggist, who introduced her to the Unitarian *Monthly Repository* circle which included Harriet MARTINEAU, Sarah Flower (later ADAMS) and the Rev. William Fox. In 1832 she began writing book reviews and essays for the *Repository.* Through Fox she met J. S. Mill and the two began a lifelong correspondence and friendship which caused great scandal. Her influence on his work may be seen in issues such as female emancipation, the political education of the working classes and socialism. Mill himself claimed that all of his work after 1840, including *The Principles of Political Economy* and *On Liberty,* was written in collaboration with her: misogynist scholars have blamed her for inconsistencies in his work. Her essay 'The Enfranchisement of Women', pub. in the *Westminster Review,* 1851, and originally attributed to Mill, remains one of the most eloquent analyses of the role of women in society (repr. 1983, intro. Kate Sope). She scorns the notion of 'separate spheres', which turns women into a 'sentimental priesthood', and argues that every career should be open to women, asserting that 'It is neither necessary nor just to make it imperative on women that they shall either be mothers or nothing'. She also supports EDUCATION for women, but not simply in order that they can become better companions for men; as she points out, 'they do not say that men should be educated to be the companions of women'. In 1849 her husband died and in 1851 she m. Mill. The couple lived and worked in virtual retirement until her death at Avignon from pneumonia. See *J. S. Mill and HT,* corresp. with an account of their subsequent marriage, ed. F. A. Hayek, 1951; Michael Packe's life of Mill, 1970.

Taylor, Helen, 1831–1907, editor and women's-rights campaigner, b. London, da. of Harriet TAYLOR. She was educ. by her mother, who was her constant companion. At 25, despite her mother's disapproval, she attempted a career as an 'intellectual' actress, but in 1858, after her mother's death, she became J. S. Mill's secretary and housekeeper. She edited the *Miscellaneous and Posthumous Works of H. T. Buckle,* 1865, which begins with a paper on 'The Influence of Women on Knowledge', and began writing articles on women's SUFFRAGE, arguing that contemporary legislation was antagonistic to women in denying them property rights. She disagreed with the more conservative Emily DAVIES and Barbara BODICHON over married women's franchise. She worked with Mill on *The Subjection of Women,* 1869, and ed. his *Autobiography,* 1873 (see Jack Stillinger, *Victorian Studies* 27, 1983), and essays, later acting as his literary executor, and presenting his library to Somerville College, Oxford, in 1904. Her radical socialist principles were evident throughout her work for educational and land reform, and in her attempt in 1885 to stand as the first woman MP.

Taylor, Jane, 1783–1824, poet and woman of letters, too much identified with her CHILDREN'S books: b. in London, younger sister of the future Ann Gilbert, da. of Isaac T., engraver and later dissenting minister. Their mother, *née* Ann Martin, 1757–1830, heeded advice not to become 'a mere plod' on marriage: having disapproved authorship, she followed her children into it with seven works of moral and religious advice (two of them fictional), 1814–25. At Lavenham, Suffolk, from 1786, Colchester from 1796, and Ongar from 1811, the family produced a constant flow of personal writing. JT wrote stories, plays and verse almost from infancy, creating worlds both private and shared with her sister as 'aunt and niece' or 'two poor women making a hard shift to live'. They worked for pay as engravers, but had each her own study-cubicle. Children's poems by them (and Adelaide O'Keeffe) appeared in 1804–5 as *Original Poems for Infant Minds,* beginning a phenomenally successful publishing run by earning £15. Influenced by A. L. Barbauld, it has a unique charm: simple, steadily moral, yet lively, comic, and nonsensical. The many later, similar works by them and other family members approach but do not equal it. JT's writings for young people and adults blend evangelical Christianity (especially after her time spent in Devon and Cornwall, 1812–16) with satire and sparkle, other-worldliness with unabashed realism. Her letters show her wary of her own literary ambition. In her novel, *Display,* 1814, religion teaches a once vain girl to accept her husband's foolishness and her loss of social rank; *Essays in Rhyme,* 1816, includes some major poems; *Correspondence* ... (with her mother, 1817) is fiction. Her essays for *Youth's Magazine,* 1816–22, were ed. by her brother Isaac, 1824; her poems, with a life, 1825 (expanded, 1867). She died of cancer, her mind 'teeming with unfulfilled projects'. Though never out of print (editors include Edith Sitwell) she has MSS still unpub.: massive family bibliog. by Christina Duff Stewart, 1975.

Taylor, Mary, 1817–93, writer, music teacher, feminist, and friend of Charlotte Brontë, b. at Gomersal, Yorks. da. of Anne (Tickell) and Joshua T. Educ. at a boarding school in Yorks. and a pensionnat near Brussels, she travelled in 1845 to NZ where she kept a draper's shop with her cousin Ellen in Wellington, returning to England in 1863. She pub. *The First Duty of Women,* 1870, articles repr. from the *Victoria Magazine* about women and work; and her only novel, *Miss Miles or a Tale of Yorkshire Life 60 Years Ago,* 1890. In its theme of female friendship, this work polemically reflects the early relationship between MT and Brontë, to whom she always remained loyal, despite their disagreements. She was the model for Rose in Brontë's *Shirley,* of which she wrote to its author: 'You talk of women working. And this first duty, this necessity you seem to think that *some* women may indulge in – if they give up marriage and don't make themselves too disagreeable to the other sex. You are a coward and a traitor. A woman who works is by that alone better than one who does not.' Her life reflected her stated belief in women's duty, as well as right, to be independent. Her *Letters from NZ and Elsewhere* were ed. with biographical material by Joan Stevens, 1972.

Taylor, Phoebe Atwood, 1909–76, also 'Alice Tilton' and 'Freeman Dana', mystery writer. B. in Boston, da. of Josephine (Atwood) and John T., she m. a Boston physician with the same surname. She took her BA from Barnard, 1930, and published her first book, *The Cape Cod Mystery,* 1931. It features her first major hero, detective Asa Mayo, the 'Cape Cod Yankee', who appears in 24 books. He and Leonidas Witherall, the hero of eight 'Alice Tilton' novels, are common-sense sleuths, marked by PAT's sense of humour: they are witty, often farcical, the 'mystery equivalent to Buster Keaton'. 'Freeman Dana's *Murder at the New York World's Fair* presents PAT's only female detective, Mrs Boylston Tower of Boston's Louisburg Square, whose invention, speculates Dilys Winn, is closely related to the recent success of Agatha CHRISTIE's Miss Marple. This novel, commissioned by Bennet Cerf for publication at the opening of the 1938 World's Fair, was selected by him as part of the ten million words interred in the World's Fair time capsule. PAT wrote productively through the 1940s and 1950s, publishing her last novel, *Diplomatic Corpse,* 1951; her novels gained new readers when they were reissued from the late 1960s. Papers at Boston Univ. See Dilys Winn's 'Introduction' and Ellen Nehr's 'Afterword' in *Murder at the New York World's Fair,* 1987.

Taylor, Susie King (Baker), 1848–1912, Afro-American washerwoman, teacher and autobiographer, first of nine children of Hagar and Raymond B., slaves from Savannah, Ga. She was sent to her grandmother to learn to read and write, attended an illegal kitchen school for blacks and was taught in turn by a white schoolgirl and schoolboy. In 1862 she escaped with her family behind Union lines, was put in charge of an impromptu school on St Simon's Island, and married Edward K., sergeant in 'the first black regiment that ever bore arms in defense of freedom on the continent of America'. To share his next posting, she became an army laundress, but did less washing than teaching, reading and writing letters for illiterates, and nursing those 'with their legs off, arm gone, foot off, and wounds of all kinds imaginable'. In 1866 she opened a school in Savannah; left widowed and pregnant that year, she tried further school ventures in Ga., became a servant, moved to Boston, and in 1879 married the Rev. Russell L. T. Her son's death in 1898 was hastened by being barred from segregated facilities; her cogent 'Thoughts on Present Conditions' in her *Reminiscences,* 1902 (the year after her second widowhood), wonders whether 'that terrible war' was 'in vain'. Repr. in Anthony G. Barthelemy, ed., 1988.

Teasdale, Sara (later Filsinger), 1884–1933, poet, b. St Louis, Missouri, da. of Mary Elizabeth (Willard) and John Warren T., food wholesaler. An early reader of poetry, including A. Mary F. ROBINSON's and Christina ROSSETTI's, she was educ. at the Mary Institute and at Hosmer Hall. Her first poems were pub. in *The Potter's Wheel,* a manuscript magazine produced by ST and her friends in St Louis from 1904–07. Her poem 'Guenevere', pub. in *Reedy's Mirror,* 1907, attracted wide attention and was included in her first collection, *Sonnets to Duse,* 1907. Her soliloquies by SAPPHO, Helen, Beatrice and other heroines famous for their nonconforming sexuality were pub. in *Helen of Troy and Other Poems,* 1911, confirming her rare emotional honesty and developing lyric talent. In 1912 she travelled to Europe; on returning to America she was courted by Vachel Lindsay but m. Ernst Filsinger, an exporter. Shortly afterwards she wrote to her sister-in-law: 'The man who wants a woman's brains, soul and body wants a slave. And the woman who wants to give *all* herself doesn't want a lover, but a master'. They moved to New York in 1916 and were divorced in 1929. Other poetry volumes include *Rivers to the Sea,* 1915, *Love Songs,* 1917 (awarded the Columbia Univ. Prize, forerunner of the Pulitzer Prize), *Flame and Shadow,* 1920, *Dark of the Moon,* 1926, and *Stars Tonight,* 1930. *Strange Victory,* 1933, and *Collected Poems,* 1937, were pub. posthumously; *Mirror of the Heart,* ed. W. Drake, 1984, collects unpub. poems and critically selects others. Her lyrics speak to women through the ages, protesting the need to be 'self-complete as a flower or a stone' ('The Solitary'), yet, as in 'The Wind', craving the union of heterosexual love. Her poetry expresses the fragility of human life where the only real certainty and strength comes from nature; stars, sea and wind are recurring metaphors for permanence and immortality. Her friendship with Amy LOWELL was a strong influence. In 1932 she researched a planned biographical study of

Christina Rossetti but, depressed after the suicide of Vachel Lindsay, who had remained a close friend, she died (possibly by suicide) before it was written. See Margaret Haley Carpenter, 1960, and William Drake, 1979, for her life; critical study by Carol B. Schoen, 1986. Some letters are at Rollins College, Fla.; her 1905 TRAVEL diary is at Yale.

Teft, Elizabeth, 'Orinthia', poet, b. 1723 at Rothwell, Lincs., da. of Eliza and Joshua T. The title-page of *Orinthia's Miscellanies, or A Compleat Collection of Poems,* 1747, stresses profit ('Three and Six-pence may be much worse spent'); in the first poem a woman friend urges her to publish both for the glory of God, who gave her talent, and for her 'neglected Self', 'self-robb'd of what's your Due'. Though she claims her poems are 'never before published', two made part of a *GM* exchange in 1741–2. Often writing by request, she has a sharply distinctive voice, scorning, she says, to borrow a thought: hypocrisy is a 'Claret-coloured Crime', snuff-taking an emblem of gradually addicting sin. She praises Pope, discusses marriage, dwells on her own lack of good looks, and says 'my Character secures my Bread' (but not how). She demands why girls are not taught like boys, and celebrates female friendship. Indignant rebuke 'To the Unjust Author of Pamela in High Life' for giving her 'gilded Slavery' as reward seems designed for Richardson, not his imitators. She mixes moral and religious poems with humour, describing now a horrific visit to Bedlam, now a hospitable inn at Cley in Norfolk. The 1745 Jacobite rebellion provoked mixed feelings: patriotic fervour, envy of men's scope for heroism, recognition of lacking, as a woman, any stake in her country ('No Rights, no Privilege, no fertile Land'), and wry conclusion that her love of it is instinctive, like mother-love.

Temperance. Women reformers were active in temperance movements world-wide from the 1830s (many temperance societies had Ladies' Committees), and this activism fed back into the women's movement, particularly in the USA, and spread to Australia and Canada. See Ruth Bordin, *Women and Temperance,* 1980; Lilian L. Shiman, *Crusade Against Drink in Victorian England,* 1988. Prominent figures in the US Women's Christian Temperance Union, such as Frances WILLARD, stressed the connection between women's crusade for temperance and for their own rights. Her friend Isabella Somerset helped broaden the movement in Britain in the 1890s. In 1836 the American Temperance Union formally endorsed 'prose fiction and the products of fancy' as weapons. Some novelists, like Clara BALFOUR, devoted themselves to the theme: Amelia Johnson, black novelist, b. 1858?, constantly inveighed against 'demon' alcohol in her fiction. Others drew on it with more or less emphasis (Amelia BLOOMER and Frances GAGE always linked it with feminism); Metta VICTOR was one of the few who treated it with humour. Some, like 'Marion HARLAND' and E. W. WILCOX, only began their careers as temperance writers.

Temple, Anne Grenville (Chambers), Countess, *c.* 1709–77, poet. Da. of Mary (Berkeley) and Thomas C., heiress of £50,000, she m., 1737, politician Richard Grenville, later Earl T., who was said to treat her with impatience and contempt. Her only child died young. Horace Walpole (who thought her husband stupid and politically mistaken) printed at Strawberry Hill her *Poems* (1764, repr. later). They are pleasantly light in touch: compliments for birthdays and so on, fables (the city mouse becomes 'A Lady Mouse of Berkeley-square'), and verses pressing Apollo, Venus, and their peers into the service of modern flirtation. Walpole likened her to SAPPHO, and printed another of her poems separately.

Temple, Laura Sophia, later Sweetman (1763–after 1820), romantic poet, da. of

Frances and Lt.-Col. T., b. at Chester, brought up in Lincs and Devon. She and her elder sister, who died at 19, were 'philosophers in leading strings', taught by their mother 'to decide with the manliness of truth'. Her three volumes, *Poems,* 1805, *Lyric and Other Poems,* 1808, and *The Siege of Zaragoza and Other Poems,* 1812, are similar in tone: much on the loss of hope and love, self-analysis, oriental pieces, nature poems, ballads, sonnets, dramatic monologues (for Mary Queen of Scots, a blind lover, orphans and outcasts, fallen women and a forsaken husband). She calls for apathy but remains emotional, and dwells increasingly on the passing of time and the horrors of war. Her first preface sets 'simplicity and nature' above art: her second defends poetry as 'the breath, the finer spirit, the unfading bloom, of everything most lovely ... the elegance of science, and the beauty of knowledge'. Coleridge wondered who she was in 1808. F. W. Blagdon's *Flowers of Literature* admired her, wrongly ascribed her a poorish novel of 1806, and printed an account of her, 1810. She married Samuel B. Sweetman, who went bankrupt about 1817 and remained unemployed. By 1820 they were destitute; he conducted dealings with the RLF, which gave them £20 in all; a new long poem he mentions is untraced.

Templeton, Edith, novelist and short-story writer, b. 1916 in Prague. Her parents were from land-owning families, her father a technology PhD. She began writing at four, the year the family returned from Vienna to Prague; there she published a story at ten (in the *Prager Tagblatt*), and went to French Lycée and Medical Univ., 1936–7. Next year she m. William Stockwell T. and moved to Cheltenham in England. She worked there as a medical coder for the US War Office, 1942–5, and in Germany as a British army court and conference interpreter, 1945–6 (she is multilingual). She was divorced in 1947. European in her literary affinities, she uses Baudelaire for a chilling epigraph, and admires Jean RHYS. *Summer in the Country,* 1950 (repr. as *Proper Bohemians,* 1952), *Living on Yesterday,* 1951, and *The Island of Desire,* 1952, depict a vanished, wealthy Czech milieu where servants are vital, enmities and eccentricity thrive (especially on country estates), decor and food are lavishly described. In the first two, young women married to prop the family finances rebel, with aplomb and with shocking results. The third vividly portrays a young girl's rigid social training ('a woman is a poor creature; what can she give but herself?') and obscure erotic impulses. Away from Bohemia (marriage to a loathsome Englishman, sexual awakening in a casual encounter), irony and credibility flag. *The Surprise of Cremona,* 1954, is a highly idiosyncratic travel book. *This Charming Pastime,* 1955, takes an Englishwoman in Sicily through passion, jealousy, and her lover's sudden death. That year ET m. Edmund Roland, cardiologist to the King of Nepal, and moved to India; they have a son. She has published stories in *The New Yorker* and other journals, and lived in many European cities. Edna O'BRIEN thinks of her as 'the great writer'; all her books but the last have recent reprints; Anita BROOKNER introduces the novels, and says more work is on the way.

Tennant, Emma, novelist and journalist, b. 1937 in London, da. of Elizabeth (Powell) and Christopher Grey T., Baron Glenconner, she spent WWII in a Scottish mock-gothic castle (setting for the 'fictional childhood memoir' *Wild Nights,* 1979). After St. Paul's Girls' School (which she hated) and an Oxford finishing school ('the most exciting and informative period of my life'), she studied art history in Paris; 'but I always knew I would write'. A débutante at 17, she later used the experience in the autobiographical, picaresque, mock-period *Adventures of Robina,* 1986, whose heroine resolves 'to lead a Different Life, as soon as this Farce was over'. First married in 1957, ET has three children, one each from her first and third marriages, the youngest from another relationship. Her first novel, *The Colour of Rain,* 1964, as 'Catherine Aydy', portraying the shallowness of the young London upper class and influenced by the work of her father-in-law, Henry Green, was dismissed as 'decadence' by Alberto Moravia. After long silence came further novels, from *The Time of the Crack,* 1973, a science-fiction blend of verisimilitude and absurdity: a geological splitting of London offers opportunity for a group of women to seek 'abandonment of our sex roles'. ET pursued the topic of gender roles in *Hotel de Dream,* 1976, *The Bad Sister,* 1979, *Queen of Stones,* 1982, and *Two Women of London,* 1989, a female Jekyll and Hyde story. Revolutionary governments figure in *The Last of the Country House Murders,* 1974 (offering murder as a tourist attraction), and *Black Marina,* 1985, set on a Caribbean island (with explicit reference to Grenada, implicit reference to Mustique, once owned by ET's brother). *Woman Beware Woman,* 1983, was *The Half-Mother* in US ed., 1985. A series begun in *The House of Hospitalities,* 1987, and *A Wedding of Cousins,* 1988, satirizes 'nobs andsnobs'. ET has written for children and for magazines from *Queen* and *Vogue* in the 1960s; in 1975 she became founder-editor of *Bananas,* a journal of new writing. She also edits Penguin's 'Lives of Modern Women'. Interview in *The Literary Review,* 1983.

Tennant, Kylie, 1912–88, novelist, playwright, critic, b. Sydney, NSW, da. of Kathleen (Tolhurst) and Thomas Walker T. Educ. at Brighton College, Manly, Sydney, she worked variously as a journalist, reviewer, lecturer, and barmaid, often to gain first-hand experience for her novels; to this end she also spent a week in jail. In 1932 she m. Lewis Rodd, teacher and social historian. Her first work, *Tiburon,* 1935, the *Bulletin*'s S. H. Prior Prize winner, concerns the plight of the unemployed and is based on her own experiences during the Depression. This was followed by *Foveaux,* 1939, and *The Battlers,* 1941, which both won the S. H. Prior Prize and the Australian Literature Society's Gold Medal. Other novels include *Ride on Stranger,* 1943, *Time Enough Later,* 1943, *Lost Haven,* 1946, *The Joyful Condemned,* 1953 (pub. in full as *Tell Morning This,* 1967), *The Honey Flow,* 1956, and *Tantavalon,* 1983. Her children's works include *All the Proud Tribesmen,* 1959, winner of the 1960 Children's Book Award. *Tether a Dragon,* 1952, a play about Alfred Deakin, won the 1952 Commonwealth Jubilee Stage Play Competition, and *Ma Jones and the Little White Cannibals,* 1967, is a coll. of short stories. Non-fiction includes *Speak You so Gently,* 1959, an account of Aboriginal co-operatives, *Australia: Her Story,* 1953, a biography of former Australian prime minister, H. V. Evatt, 1970, and her autobiography, *The Missing Heir,* 1986. She also ed. three colls. of short stories, worked as a critic for *The Sydney Morning Herald* (1953–76) and was a member of the Advisory Board of the Commonwealth Literary Fund (1961–72). Her work characteristically deals with marginalized groups in Australian society, portraying the tragedy of the human condition against the natural and urban landscape of Australia, and frequently satirizing the Establishment. In 1980 she was awarded the Order of Australia. See M. Dick, 1966.

Tenney, Tabitha (Gilman), 1763–1837, novelist, b. at Exeter, NH, eldest child of Lydia Robinson (Giddinge) and Samuel Gilman. In 1788 she m. Dr Samuel T., a member of Congress from 1800 to his death in 1816. An edition of Ann FISHER's *Pleasing Instructor,* 1799, has been wrongly ascribed to her. Her *Female Quixotism: Exhibited in the Romantic Opinions and Extravagant Adventures of Dorcasina Sheldon,* Boston 1801 (well reviewed; six eds. by 1841), said to be based on life, is dedicated to 'all Columbian Young Ladies who read Novels & Romances'. With Charlotte LENNOX as starting-point, it treats its heroine more harshly. With intelligence, piety, a good heart and reputedly £1000 a year, she lacks nothing but a mother and a critical faculty about novels. At first she is scorned only by the narrow-minded, and dislikes her first suitor on principle (he owns slaves); at the end she resigns herself with dignity to a charitable, non-cynical, single old age. Her friend Harriet, who never read a novel (though she performed with spirit in male disguise), points out that marriage too has pains. Yet Dorcasina, ready victim to any grotesque adventurer speaking the cant of flattery, bears a disturbing weight of ridicule.

Terry, Lucy, or Luce Bijah, *c.* 1730–1821, earliest recorded black woman to compose in English: b. in Africa, captured and landed at Rhode Island, sold in 1735 to Ebenezer Wells of Deerfield, Mass. Baptized that year, she became a full church member in 1744. She was known as a storyteller by 1746, the date of the Indian ambush related in her apparently only surviving piece. Handed down orally for a century, this as printed (1855) is energetic doggerell: the Indians are 'awful creatures'; the only woman mentioned is tomahawked when her petticoats impede her flight. LT married, 1756, a land-owning free black, Abijah Prince, who apparently bought her freedom; they had six children and settled in Vermont in 1764. LT conducted a successful land case against top lawyers before the Supreme Court, but a losing battle to get a son admitted to white-only Williams College: in each case her public speaking was much admired.

Terry, Megan, playwright. B. as Marguerite Duffy in 1932 in Seattle, da. of Marguerite Cecelia (Henry) and Harold Joseph D., Jr., she named herself 'Megan', the Celtic version of her mother's name, and 'Terry' for the earth and for Ellen Terry. At seven she went to a play at the Seattle Repertory Playhouse and 'fell madly in love' with the theatre. She studied at the Banff School of Fine Arts and the Univ. of Alberta, then took her BEd at the Univ. of Washington, 1956. (Her father refused to support her because she would not join a sorority.) She began to 'write up' her workshop improvisations while teaching at the Cornish School of Allied Arts, 1954–6, then tackled NYC, promising her father to be a success by 35 or quit. She has since written more than 60 plays, including several for radio and TV, and made a reputation as both a founder of the new American theatre and the 'Mother of American Feminist Drama'. She started writing to create roles for women: 'I want to redress the balance! If a Martian came here to vsit our culture, it would think that it was visiting a homosexual society. Men run everything.' *Hothouse* and *Ex-Miss Copper Queen on a Set of Pills* (both written in her early New York years but not produced until the early 1970s) treat three generations of women in the same house ('the positive side of a matriarchal love') and three marginal women on the streets in NYC. In 1963, MT co-founded the Open Theatre, where she developed her experimental, anti-naturalist transformational drama. *Calm Down Mother: a Transformation for Three Women,* 1965, deals with mother-daughter relationships, casting its characters as Woman One ('I'm Margaret FULLER. I know I am because from the time I could speak and go alone, my father addressed me not as a plaything, but as a lively mind'), Woman Two, Woman Three. *Comings and Goings,* 1966, focuses on gender roles and power relationsips. MT's best-known play, the anti-war musical *Viet Rock,* 1966, was a collaborative production of the Open Theatre: picketed by the Directors' Guild, panned by Walter Kerr, and closed in NYC, it was 'translated into every major language', 'proclaimed in every major, and many minor, cities all over the world'. *Approaching Simone* (Obie Award, 1970) emerged from 15 years of research on French ascetic, philosopher and writer Simone Weil. Writer-in-residence at Yale, 1966–7, MT co-founded, in 1972, with Maria Irene FORNES, Rosalyn DREXLER, Julie BOVASSO, and Adrienne KENNEDY, the Women's Theatre Council and its successor, New York Theatre Strategy. In 1974, she moved to Omaha to begin her continuing collaboration with director Jo Ann Schmidmann at the Omaha Magic Theatre, Nebraska, focusing on works by and about women. MT's *Babes in the Bighouse,* 1974, about women in prison, casts men as female characters 'to get men to pay attention to what the play was saying'. *American King's English for Queens,* 1978, exposes violence and sexism in language, including the language of criticism; *Goona Goona,* 1979, which emerged from audience discussion following *King's English,* is about family violence; *Klegger,* 1982, addresses teenage alcoholism. Interviews in Helen Crich Chinoy and Linda Walsh Jenkins, eds., 1981, and Betsko and Koenig, 1987 (quoted above); studies by Kathleen Gregory Klein in *Modern Drama,* 27, 1984, June Schlueter in *Studies in American Drama, 1945–Present,* 2, 1987, and Keyssar, 1984 (quoted above).

Teskey, Adeline Margaret, early 1850s–1924, poet, novelist, short-story writer. B. in Appleton, Ont., da. of Elizabeth (Kerfoot) and Thomas T., she was educ. at Genesee College in Lima, NY, and Boston art schools. She lived most of her life in Welland, Ont., and died in Toronto. She contributed poetry and short fiction to American, British and Canadian journals. Some of her fiction is set in rural and small-town Ontario. *Where the Sugar Maple Grows,* 1901, her first volume, is a series of interlocking tales narrated by a townswoman who travels but returns each summer to the small town which is the stories' subject. The characters she views are gently amusing and mildly eccentric, occasionally affecting. They may have influenced Stephen Leacock's *Sunshine Sketches of a Little Town,* 1912. AMT published seven novels between 1905 and 1913. *The Yellow Pearl,* 1911, is about an orphaned girl, half Chinese and half American, who is taken to live with her racist aunt and uncle. *Candlelight Days,* 1913, treats 'incidents of pioneer life' in Ontario, 'reminiscences of aged friends'. Others relay simple Christian morals.

Texidor, Greville (Foster), 1902–64, NZ short-story writer and novelist, b. Wolverhampton, England, elder da. of Editha Greville (Prideaux), artist, and William Arthur Foster, barrister. Educ. at Cheltenham Ladies' College, she then danced in chorus line in Paris, NYC and on tour. M. in Buenos Aires to a Mr ?Wilson, 1929, she then m., Manuel/Manolo T., Buenos Aires industrialist, had one da., and moved to Spain, 1933. Separated in ?1934, she joined Werner Droescher, a German refugee in an anarchist group in the Spanish Civil War. She married him in 1939. She worked with the English Aid Committee and Quaker Relief schemes in Barcelona and London, and was briefly imprisoned at outbreak of war. She emigrated to NZ in 1940, returned to Spain in 1951. Her marriage broke up in 1961, and she took her life in 1964. Her first short stories were pub. 1942, 1944, in *NZ New Writing, Penguin New Writing* and collections. Her novella *These Dark Glasses* was pub. in NZ in 1949, and is about a woman who has been politically involved in the Spanish Civil War, now alone and desperately unhappy in an expatriate artists' colony on the Costa del Sol. Its atmosphere of rented rooms, uncaring 'friends' and desultory sexual relationships is like that of Jean RHYS's 1930s novels. After this GT pub. nothing more, though some later typescripts appear in *In Fifteen Minutes You Can Say a Lot.,* ed. Kendrick Smithyman, 1987. Some stories are set in Spain – 'Maaree' treats an English ex-chorus woman who is kept by a series of Spanish men. Others are in NZ – 'Goodbye Forever', about a Viennese refugee woman who is seen as alien and incomprehensible in NZ. The stories are sad, perceptive, well-crafted, and tend to focus on the loneliness and emptiness of sexual relations, and on characters who are alone, refugees, unable to fit in and not understood.

'Tey, Josephine', Elizabeth Mackintosh, also 'Gordon Daviot', 1896–1952, playwright, novelist. B. in Inverness, Scotland, eldest da. of ex-teacher Josephine (Horne) and greengrocer Colin M., she was educ. at the Royal Academy, Inverness, and (from 1914) in Birmingham, at the Anstey School of Physical Training (a new discipline). She taught in various schools but came home on her mother's death to keep house. Though she called her mystery fiction 'my yearly knitting', she was a major crime writer of the 'Golden Age'. *The Man in the Queue,* 1929, introduces her gentleman-detective Alan Grant, perplexed by a murder in a theatre queue. She wrote these novels and her plays (psychological portraits in historical settings) as 'Gordon Daviot'. Her play *Richard of Bordeaux,* 1933, with John Gielgud, had a huge success, and *Queen of Scots,* 1934, with Lawrence Olivier, a moderate one. *Shilling for Candles,* 1936, became Hitchcock's favourite among his British films as *Young and Innocent,* 1937. *Laughing Woman,* 1934, a romantic drama about Henri Gaudier and Sophie Brzeska, was unsuccessful. As 'Josephine Tey', she went more deeply into Grant's talents, methods, and moral quandaries: innocents are now carefully portrayed. *The Franchise Affair,* 1948, adapts an eighteenth-century kidnapping mystery to the DETECTIVE genre. *Miss Pym Disposes,* a 'crime story' set in a girls' school, was published in 1946, *To Love and Be Wise* in 1950. JT's most famous and original novel, *The Daughter of Time,* 1951, adapts earlier history. Grant, now in hospital (a true armchair detective), researches the murder of the Princes in the Tower, exonerates Richard III, and accuses the least likely suspect, Henry VII. See Nancy Ellen Talburt in Bargainnier, 1981, and Jessica Man in *Deadlier than the Male,* 1981.

Thaman, Konai Helu, contemporary poet, b. Nuku'alofa, educ. Tonga and NZ (Univ. of Auckland, BA 1967) then Santa Barbara (M. Ed. 1973). She is married, with one child, and teaches education at the Univ. of South Pacific. She has published two collections: *You, the Choice of My Parents,* 1974, followed by *Langakali,* 1981 (repr. 1982, 1983). Her poems explore the status of women both inside and outside marriage. The title poem of her first book comments on the chattel status conferred on women in arranged marriages: 'I fit your plans and schemes for the future. / You cannot see the real me'. *Langakali* is a more lyrical volume, voiced with a mature sureness: 'When was / the first time / birds learnt to fly? / i know it was when I began / to write' ('Take-Off'). An interview, examining her own 'cultural values, beliefs, prejudices', appeared in *WLWE* 17, 1 (April 1978).

Thaxter, Celia (Laighton), 1835–94, poet, b. Portsmouth, NH, da. of Eliza (Rymes) and Thomas B. L., a lighthouse keeper, who also served in the NH legislature and was briefly editor of the *New Hampshire Gazette.* In 1847 the family moved to nearby Appledore Island where in 1848 her father and a partner opened Appledore House, a summer hotel which eventually hosted Emerson, Hawthorne, S. O. JEWETT, Lucy LARCOM, James R. Lowell, Mark Twain and Whittier, among others. CT was educ. at home and attended Mount Washington Female Seminary, South Boston, Mass. from 1849–50. In 1951 she m. her father's partner, Levi Lincoln T., who could not decide on a profession. They settled in Newtonville in 1856 and in 1861 her first poem, 'Land-Locked', was pub. in the *Atlantic Monthly.* She also contributed poems to *Scribner's, Harper's,* the *Independent* and the *Century,* with her children's poems in *St Nicholas* and *Our Young Folks.* Because of her husband's illness, they led separate lives from 1869, with CT returning to Appledore while he went to Florida. Her coll. *Poems* appeared in 1872 and the next year her coll.

prose pieces for the *Atlantic Monthly* were pub. as *Among the Isles of Shoals. Drift-Weed,* 1878, contains children's and adults' poems, often undifferentiated. CT's poetry is derivative of William Cullen Bryant and Henry Wadsworth Longfellow. Her *Letters* were pub. in 1897; others are at the Boston Public Library and the Roland Thaxter Collection, Houghton Library, Harvard. See R. Thaxter, 1963, for her life, and the study by Jane Vallier, *Colby Library Quarterly,* Dec. 1981.

Thayer, Caroline Matilda (Warren), 1787?–1844, novelist and religious writer, raised in 'polite and fashionable' New England. She later blamed WOLLSTONECRAFT, Paine and Voltaire for a teenage period of scepticism and disbelief in damnation. Her preface (Sutton, NH, 1805) to her novel, *The Gamesters, or Ruins of Innocence,* calls her opportunities 'penurious' and education limited, notes that even novelists, with 'the whole regiment of literati', disapprove novels, but suggests they can be beneficial. She portrays a sensitive hero whose academic education neglects 'the culture of the heart', leaving him ripe for a false friend delighting 'in the ruins of innocence' to drag him down to gambling, drink and suicide. She involves her readers directly in a woman's fall, first querying their concern for 'female dignity', then begging leave to 'draw a veil over the succeeding scene'. She quotes Judith MURRAY, Hannah MORE and Elizabeth ROWE, and inserts poems of her own, some from the Worcester *National Aegis.* A London edition, 1806, as *Conrade, or The Gamesters,* changes the hero's name; original repr. 1828. Converted by a Methodist at 19, CMT became a teacher (in Mass.), married and settled in a 'western wilderness' (probably in NY) where her husband and three children died. She chose an ex-pupil as 'the vehicle of my advice to my sex in general' in fervent letters pub., with poems, as *Religion Recommended to Youth,* 1815 (many eds., some additions). As head of the Female Dept of the NYC Wesleyan Seminary, CMT agreed to a salary cut ($400 p.a. to $300), then was fired for joining the New Jerusalem church; her angry *Letter* about this, 1821, was repr. USA, England and Ireland. She edited poems by a friend, Harriet Muzzy, with some of hers from magazines, 1821, and wrote a popular US history, 1823; after further shifts of abode and church, she died in Louisiana.

Theatre groups. Women's theatre groups developed in England in the context of the Lord Chamberlain's power to censor plays, of Ibsen's political drama, of G. B. Shaw's affiliation to the cause of the NEW WOMAN, and, shortly after, of SUFFRAGE politics. They were preceded by some women's move into the previously male role of actor-manager (a role aspired to by Susannah Cibber but denied her by David Garrick). Madame Vestris, who rented the Olympic Theatre in 1830, may have been the first of these; Elizabeth ROBINS and Marion Lea, having 'seen how freedom in the practice of our art ... depended on considerations humiliatingly different from those that confronted the actor', launched on a series of productions beginning with *Hedda Gabler,* 1891. In 1894, Florence FARR produced three plays at the Avenue Theatre, with the support of Annie Horniman, who continued to subsidize the new drama after Farr's departure, and who established the Gaiety Theatre in Manchester, 1907, where she 'laid the foundations of the modern repertory movement' (see Eva LE GALLIENNE) just as Lilian Bayliss later laid the foundations of the National Theatre at the Old Vic. Actresses, including Cecily HAMILTON and Elizabeth Robins, shortly began to write their own plays: when *Votes for Women!* was performed in 1907 the new suffrage theatre was launched. The Actresses' Franchise League, formed 1908 (see ACTING, PETITIONS), established a play department run by actress Inez Bensusan, whose play *The Apple* it staged in 1910. In 1911, Edy CRAIG founded The Pioneer

Players, a company in which all of the functions were dominated by women.

Theatre groups flowered again during the 1960s, when groups of women throughout the anglophone world came together in the context of the women's liberation movement, seeking dramatic enactment of female experience. Grassroots theatre grew from consciousness-raising groups where women discovered language to share hidden and silenced stories: the constraints of adolescent femininity, menstrual taboos, lesbian identity, pregnancy and childbirth, depression and madness, and society's label of obsolescence in age. Voices were found to scream against violation (rape, incest, and the commercial exploitation of women's bodies), rituals performed of connecting women in families and reclaiming earth-rooted spirituality. Collective creations often did not separate performer and role. Individual assertions of power and autonomy were used to create improvisational pieces involving a whole group.

Identity of women's collectives has been fluid, with frequent regrouping. Many groups arose from alternative theatre organizations moving from liberal or humanist to specifically feminist stances. A brochure by one of these (the US women's collective led by Martha BOESING and Phyllis Jane Rose, which formed in 1976 from the mixed troupe At the Foot of the Mountain) could speak for many: 'We struggle to relinquish traditions such as linear plays, proscenium theatre, non-participatory ritual, and seek to reveal theatre that is circular, intuitive, personal, involving. We are a theatre of protest, witnesses to the destructiveness of a society which is alienated from itself, and a theatre of celebration, participants in the prophecy of a new world which is emerging through the rebirth of women's consciousness.'

Despite differences in origins, in approach to feminism, in venue (streets, parks, and places of work, or more conventional buildings), in race and class identity and gender orientation, women's theatre groups do have common elements. Distance decreases between performer and performance, and between the audience and both. Collective creations tend to decentre the subject and to fragment character; actors change roles in mid-performance, or share the representation of a single person. Classic female characters are reinterpreted; women's unnoticed bonding is valorized, while mother-daughter and other love relationships are both interrogated and celebrated.

In Britain, collective work has fed into *Plays by Women,* ed. from 1982 by WANDOR and later by Mary Remnant, and Jill Davis, ed., *Lesbian Plays.* Wandor notes influence of street-theatre demonstrations against the Miss World contest in 1970 and 1971; the Women's Street Theatre Group was succeeded by the Women's Theatre Group, 1973 (later Monstrous Regiment: see under Alison FELL). In 1974 the group co-wrote (after improvising) *My Mother Said I Never Should,* about teenage girls and sex: it played live, then on video to school audiences till withdrawn on newspaper protest in Dec. 1978 (ed. Wandor, with *Strike While the Iron is Hot,* 1980). Pam GEMS worked with the Woman's Company, founded 1974 after a series of women's plays at the Almost Free Theatre; other dramatists, like Caryl CHURCHILL, have kept up their links with women's theatre even after achieving mainstream success. In Canada, Carol BOLT and Sharon POLLOCK have both written collectively. For a study of the Australian project Women and Theatre, Sydney, 1981, see Chris Westwood in *Australasian Drama Studies,* 1, i, 1982.

In the US, ANTHOLOGIES of plays by women have abounded (lesbian collections ed. Kate McDermott, 1985, and written by Sarah Dreher, 1988); but the involvement of recognized female dramatists with women's theatre has been rarer. Feminist theatres like those of Los Angeles, 1969–?78, and the Washington area, 1972–8, have sought to showcase women's work rather than make political statements. Improvisation and collectivity, however, prevailed in It's All Right to Be a Woman, NYC, 1970–6, Greenville, SC, Feminist Theatre, 1973–7, and Circle of the Witch, Minneapolis, 1973–7, and in three groups all deriving from the Open Theatre: the Omaha Magic Theatre, from 1968 (Jo Ann Schmidman and, from 1974, Megan TERRY), the Women's Experimental Theatre, NY, from 1976 (where Roberta Sklar, Sondra Segal and Clare Coss combined their different skills to create clusters of plays about the nuclear family and about body and food), and the Rebeccah Company, 1976, later the New Cycle Theatre, Brooklyn, NY, where Karen MALPEDE and Tina Shepherd focus on global oppression and the drift to genocide.

Academic communities have produced theatre groups in sometimes unexpected locations: Womanshine Productions, 1977–?83 in Indianapolis, and Snapdragon Ozark Feminist Theatre, 1980–5, in Fayetteville, Arkansas. Students' experience of sexism at Brown Univ. led to the founding of Rhode Island Feminist Theatre, 1973.

Multicultural consciousness has been an increasingly important force, shown for instance by Lilith, San Francisco from 1974, and its successor, Mouth of the Wolf, 1986, begun by Terry Baum (Jewish-Lesbian perspectives) and Michele Linfante. Women of colour have been forming collectives since the 1970s to create and present their work. In Calif., Asian–American women have been active, and Las Cucarachas was formed by Latina/Chicana performers from El Teatro Campesino in 1974. Cuna–Rappahannock Indian sisters, activists Muriel and Gloria Miguel and Lisa Mayo, founded Spiderwoman Theatre, NY, 1975, and have performed around the world. From 1978 Black Star Theatre, Cambridge, Mass., has performed work by established playwrights, female and male, black and white, to mixed audiences.

Lesbian creativity has fed into many theatre groups: specifically lesbian issues have been addressed (sometimes for women-only audiences) by Lavender Cellar, Minneapolis, 1973–5, Red Dyke, Atlanta, 1974–?9, Medusa's Revenge, NYC, 1977–?80 (elaborate musical plays), and Split Britches and others at the WOW (Women's One World) cafe, NYC, from 1980 (original satiric pieces with parodic foregrounding of butch-femme roles).

In the US the peak of the movement came in the 1970s: numbers have been estimated at almost 90 (Dinah Leavitt, *Feminist Theatre Groups,* 1980) or more than 160 (Chinoy and Jenkins). In the 80s, increasing numbers of women's theatre festivals bore witness to continuing vitality.

On American and British theatre, see Keyssar, 1984; on British theatre see Julia Holledge, *Innocent Flowers: Women in the Edwardian Theatre,* 1981 (quoted above), Michelene Wandor, *Understudies,* 1981, Catherine Itzin, *Stages in the Revolution, Political Theatre in Britain Since 1968,* 1980, and Janette Reinelt in *Theatre Journal,* 38, 1986. On US theatre see bibliog. by Brenda Coven, 1982; Chinoy and Jenkins, 1981 (overview); studies by Janet Brown, 1980, Elizabeth J. Natalle, 1985, and Sue-Ellen Case, 1988; essays ed. Karen Malpede, 1983, and Lynda Hart, 1989; *Women and Performance; A Journal of Feminist Theory,* from 1982; special issues of *The Drama Review,* June 1980, and *Theatre Journal,* 37, 1985, and 40, 1988. Jill Dolan's study, 1988, distinguishes feminisms (liberal; cultural or radical; and materialist) in the theatre.

Theology. Present-day Judaeo-Christian feminist theologians do not lack foremothers. Mediaeval women approached the science of divine things through visions and critiques firmly rooted in the everyday world. While the scholastic Dominican, Thomas Aquinas, sought to reduce faith to unity, European abbesses, nuns, chantresses, beguines, anchorites and mothers represented and celebrated variety: their incarnational, affective spirituality posits an accessible God of might and tenderness, often revealed not in traditional terms but through underlying dialectic. Their evangelical, prophetic, epistolary, dramatic, poetic and autobiographical works reflect the changes in their time. The tenth-century Canoness Hrotsvit of Gandersheim wrote accolades for virgins. The convent Benedictinism in the essays, visions and hymns of St Hildegard of Bingen (d. 1179) gives way to the Franciscan renunciations of the Blessed Angela Foligno (d. 1309) and the severe asceticism of St Catherine of Siena (d. 1380). Marjery KEMPE reflects the movements towards secular, vernacular writing and reform in the Church; so do Marie Dentière, ex-Augustinian abbess, writing to Marguerite de NAVARRE in 1539 defending women's ability to interpret scripture, Anne ASKEW composing her ballad under sentence of death, Teresa of Avila mixing practicality and transcendence, and Jane LEAD keeping her diary of visions. Many of the Continental works are now available in English, and scholars like Peter Dronke and Caroline Walker Bynum are helping to reverse old attitudes of dismissiveness and condescension. There is a continuity among consciously female approaches to the mystery of Godhead. Hildegard's first book, *Scivias* ('Know the Ways') is linked to the earlier matrological tradition of Macrina, Paula and Melania, while her image of wisdom as joined with God 'in the sweetest embrace in a religious dance of burning love' joins hands with later mystical imagers: Gertrude of Helfta, 1256–1302, Mechthild of Magdeburg, 1207–82, Mechthild of Hackeborn, 1241–98, the thirteenth-century Beguine Hadewijch of Brabant, and JULIAN of Norwich. Reformation and Counter-Reformation have each their female intellectual heroes in England: Askew and Katharine PARR on one hand, Margaret ROPER and Mary WARD on the other, each approaching theological issues in a recognizably 'feminist' spirit. Poets, like Aemilia LANYER and Rachel SPEGHT, addressed these issues too. Most seventeenth-century women's writing has at least some theological content; every radical sect has its thinkers and polemicists (Baptists like Anna TRAPNEL, Quakers from Elizabeth HOOTON onwards, old-style Puritans like Elizabeth WARREN, millenarians as late as M. MARSIN in 1701, even anti-radicals like Mary POPE). Many argue with St Paul, especially over women's preaching; none argues with his saying that in Christ 'there is neither male nor female'. During the eighteenth century an orthodox female theologian like Susannah NEWCOME was a rarity easily overlooked; Susanna WESLEY, whose orthodoxy was spiced with more questioning, lastingly affected, by proxy, one of the main streams. The visionary tradition was prolonged in the US by Ann Lee, mother of the Shakers, and in England by Joanna SOUTHCOTT. In the early nineteenth century those who expounded their theological ideas in detail, like Mary Anne SCHIMMELPENNINCK and Mary Ann KELTY, had often come into bruising conflict with male teachers and orthodoxies. Elizabeth Cady STANTON's *The Woman's Bible* foreshadows current feminist Christian exegesis in spirit if not method. The critical edge in contemporary feminist theologians and hermeneuts is sharp; more often affiliated to the academy than to religious institutions, they are keenly aware of the relativity and plurality of interpretations. In Christianity, Judaism, Islam, and elsewhere, women are deliberately challenging hierarchical, exclusive readings and practices, seeking to rediscover traditional syncretism, to reclaim (again) the imagery of the female divine, and to promote non-sexist, inclusive liturgical language. The task is huge, opposition entrenched, and renewed charges of heresy are often heard. Mary DALY, who denies any saving grace in the Judaeo-Christian legacy, has been labelled a neo-Gnostic. Phyllis Trible puts the revisionist argument that patriarchy has been historically, not theologically determined; her *Texts of Terror*, 1984, retells Old Testament stories, pointing to victimized women and condemning male domination, while Sara MAITLAND's retellings often foreground female power and strength. Mieke Bal opts for a semiotics of reading: she views the biblical texts as 'efficient, ideological weapons', revealing the insecurities in patriarchal heroism and the academic imposition of gender-specific interests. Hermeneuts who emphasize the otherness of the female are Joan Engelsman (*The Feminine Dimension of the Divine,* 1979), Virginia Mollenkott (*The Divine Feminine,* 1983) and Sandra Schneiders (*Women and the Word,* 1986). Julia KRISTEVA's *Powers of Horror,* 1982, is an indictment of Judaism's prohibitions and exclusions. Historical changes within Christianity's view of the female are canvassed in Marina WARNER's *Alone of All Her Sex,* 1973, Pamela Berger's *The Goddess Obscured,* 1985, and Margaret Miles's *Image as Insight,* 1985, and *Immaculate and Powerful,* 1985. Early texts and practices are being re-examined, with different conclusions, by liberation theologians and biblical scholars addressing sexist imbalance: Elaine Pagels reads the Gnostic texts as using 'the principle of equality between men and women' to challenge orthodox Christianity, while Pheme Perkins finds that 'anti-feminism was a common presupposition of ancient ascetic writings'. Susanne Heine uses the practice of Jesus as a criterion for judging early Christianity, rejecting a feminist theology she finds negative. More positive cases for women's leadership in early Christian communities are those of Rosemary Ruether and Elizabeth Schüssler Fiorenza, both on reconceptualizing the language of androcentric scholarship. In 1985 Adela Yarbro Collins and Letty Russell each edited a collection of pertinent scholarship, and in 1988 *Semeia,* an experimental journal of biblical criticism, devoted an issue to 'female wit in a world of male power'.

Théoret, France, b. 1942 in Montréal, poet, novelist, teacher, editor, feminist. Da. of Jeanne (Blais) and Roger T., she was educ. at the Univs. of Montréal (BA, 1968, MA, 1977) and Sherbrooke (PhD in French Studies). She also studied semiotics and psychoanalysis in Paris, 1972–4. She has taught at Ahuntsie CEGEP since 1968. Her feminist influence is registered in the journals, *La Barre du jour, Spirale* (on whose editorial boards she has been a member), and *Les Têtes de pioche* (of which she is a founder). Her own work struggles with the impact of feminism on women's subjectivity. Her first publication, 'L'Enchantillon', a textile worker's monologue, appeared in *La Nef des sorcières,* 1976, a collection of feminist monologues (by Nicole BROSSARD, Marie-Claire BLAIS, and others) performed at Montréal's Théatre du Nouveau Monde. Her poetry is published in *Les Herbes Rouges*: see especially *Bloody Mary,* 45, 1977, and *Nécessairement putain,* 82, 1980. *Transit,* 129, 1984, a performance piece set to music, has links with Julia KRISTEVA. Her novels, *Une voix pour Odile,* 1978, and *Nous parlerons comme on écrit,* 1982, her best-known work, show women trying to understand the tenuous ties between inner consciousness and everyday life, to discover an escape from the arid rigidity of the 'désert de l'Autre'. Interview in Jean Royer, *Ecrivains contemporains: Entretiens,* 1983. See Godard, ed., 1987; Patricia Smart in *Dalhousie French Studies,* special number, 1985, and *Estuaire,* 38, 1986; Gail Scott in Neuman and Kamboureli, 1986.

Thesen, Sharon Gail, poet, editor. B. in 1946 in Tisdale, Sask., da. of Dawn (Martin) and Clarence T., she moved to BC in 1953, settling in 1966 in Vancouver, where she studied English at Simon Fraser Univ. (BA, 1970, MA, 1974). She now teaches at Capilano College. She was married to Brian Fawcett, 1966–72 (with whom she had a son), to Dale Clark, 1980–1, and to Peter Thompson, 1986. Poetry editor of *The Capilano Review,* 1977–87, she edited Phyllis WEBB's *The Vision Tree,* 1982. ST believes 'There is not, at present, a feminine lexicon into which a woman can dip for the words of her writing', but also reminds us of the expressive potential of Emily DICKINSON's dashes. She writes about social issues and the politics of love. The line breaks of *Artemis Hates Romance,* 1980, mark the precise and daring unfolding of her language ('The defoliated / imagination is the end / of all lyric'). The imagery of *Holding the Pose,* 1983, winds out of experience ('the open door / just a kiss away') and into the intricacies of the intellect ('There is no / funny grammar / of love // in Prince George / no one reads / *The Pleasure of the Text*'). In *Confabulations: Poems for Malcolm Lowry,* 1984, she explores the dark ambiguities of Lowry's life and work ('the distant tequila the key / to the day, the beauty / of all things burning / . . . / his open heart / a surgical instrument'). *The Beginning of the Long Dash,* 1987, including a long poem of the same title, 'discover[s] the true newness / of the broken world / of discourse' through ST's sharp perceptiveness. *The Pangs of Sunday,* 1990, ed. Pamela Banting, selects from earlier vols. See her 'Poetry and the Dilemma of Expression', in Neuman and Kamboureli, 1986.

Thicknesse, Ann (Ford), 1737–1824, miscellaneous writer, b. in London, only da. of lawyer Thomas F. She moved in fashionable circles. Her father turned her out for, she said, discouraging an elderly admirer, Lord Jersey, and for performing (privately) as a singer; calling on 'the talents God had given me', she began giving subscription concerts in 1760 (Jersey refused support; her father declared himself dishonoured and called out the Bow Street runners; Gainsborough painted her). In 1761 she published *Instructions for Playing on the Musical Glasses* (a clear, concise guide to a new instrument) and a *Letter* to Jersey, calling her present work '*almost* as reputable' as being his mistress at £800 p.a. In 1762 she became the third wife of writer and adventurer Philip T. (his second, a friend of hers, had just died); she had two children and lived in many places. She addressed a first volume of *Sketches of the Lives and Writings of the Ladies of France,* 1778 (apparently lost), to Elizabeth CARTER – oddly, since the three extant vols., 1780–1, retail many scandals and amours. Dedicated to others, they print excerpts with often minimal lives. AT says Englishwomen have achieved less than French, from vanity as well as poor education. Philip T. died in France in 1792 (on their way to Italy): she was stranded there two years, confined in a convent. *The School for Fashion,* 1800, a novel *à clef* dedicated to 'Fashion Herself', presents him as Mr Tudor, who approves his wife exerting herself in public for a living. Mary CHAMPION subscribed to this and *Sketches.*

Thimelby, Gertrude (Aston), *c.* 1617–68, Roman Catholic poet, sister of Constance FOWLER. She spent a few years in Spain as a child, and about 1645 m. Henry T. of Corby, Lancs. She copied her work into a small unbound quarto volume: pub. in *Tixall Poems,* ed. Arthur Clifford, 1813. With searching wit and metaphysical imagery which make occasional verse into art, she commemorates family weddings, marital love (she and her husband are after five years 'an unrepenting pair'), and deaths (hyperbolic on her father, 1639; self-reproachful on her child). Debating with a brother-in-law who calls her 'faire Self-denyer', she argues that this is usual in women: 'I'me sure you'de finde, / If not mongst [sic] men, most women of this minde.' Bereaved of her husband, 1655, and only child (at 11 months), she asks 'What's then my aime? To hide me in the throng, / My voyce be heard, but not observed my song'. She joined her sister-in-law Winefrid THIMELBY as a nun at Louvain in 1658.

Thimelby, Winefrid, 1618–90, letter writer and prioress, thirteenth child of the persecuted Catholics Mary (Brooksby) and Richard T. of Irnham, Lincs. Wishing from childhood to be a nun, she entered St Monica's, Louvain, in 1634, became prioress in 1668 ('most loved of all the Mothers'), and may have written part of its chronicle (selecs. ed. Dom Adam Hamilton, 1904, 1906). Her vividly expressive letters home from 1656 (most to her sister Katherine ASTON and later to Katherine's widower) are published in *Tixall Letters,* ed. Arthur Clifford, 1815. 'Do not suppose me a well mortifyed nun dead to the world; for alas tis not so, I am alive, and as nearly concern'd for thos I love, as if I had never left them.' Are they, she asks, 'willing to give me a child'? In 1671 she wrote for this niece 24 'Meditations of the principal obligations of a Christian'; later she wished they could be 'put forth for the common use of Christians'. On her niece's death she says, 'She laughs at our fond tears, for God has wyp'd her eyes'.

Thirkell, Angela Margaret (Mackail), 1890–1961, novelist. B. in London, 'just opposite Thackeray's own house', she was da. of Margaret (Burne-Jones: the painter's daughter) and John M., and cousin to Rudyard Kipling and Stanley Baldwin. She attended the Froebel Institute and St Paul's Girls' School. She married James Campbell McInnes, a singer, in 1911, and had two children before divorcing him for cruelty and adultery in 1917. In 1918 she married Capt. George T., and went to Australia with him. Her *Trooper to the Southern Cross* (1934, pub. as 'Leslie Parker', repr. 1985) is a first-person male narrative based partly on this voyage. She returned home in 1929 without her husband though with their son: reportedly she said, 'It's very peaceful with no husbands.' Like her Barchester character Mrs Morland, who makes her first appearance in the autobiographical novel *High Rising,* 1933, AT successfully supported herself by writing. Her first book, *Three Houses* (1931, often repr.: childhood memories of famous Victorians), and *Ankle Deep,* 1933, were also autobiographical, and AT was notorious for unadmittedly depicting actual people in her 33 novels. She also wrote children's stories, and a life of Harriette WILSON, 1936, where her characteristic acerbity nicely fits her subject. Her satire, at first good-humoured, became acid after WWII and the postwar Labour government. Her own preoccupations are revealed in her introductions to others' novels: AUSTEN (on whom she is perceptive), Elizabeth GASKELL (whom she approves for writing without the 'splendid isolation' which AT deemed unnecessary as well as impossible 'for many women'), Anthony Trollope (whose topography she borrowed for her own chronicles of contemporary rural life). She was called both snob and social historian; she became a household name, broadcasting and lecturing in England and the USA. Her last novel, *Three Score and Ten,* 1961, was finished by C. A. Lejeune. Life by Margot Strickland, 1977, gives locations of papers and MSS.

Thomas, Annie Hall (later **Cudlip**), 1838–1918, English novelist (not American, as sometimes claimed), da. of Lieut. George T., b. Aldborough. She took up writing to support herself after her father, a coastguardsman, died in 1856. She wrote more than 60 POPULAR novels and ed. a holiday quarterly, *Ours.* In 1867 she m. the Rev. Pender Cudlip. Margaret OLIPHANT and Charlotte YONGE loathed her books: the latter hoped marriage might improve her moral tone, but was disappointed. Her novel *Essentially Human,* 1897, is a shallow romance in sprightly 'modern' style. The sensitive hero, a fashionable playwright of humble origins, is prevented till the end from union with the bright and pretty heroine by stereotyped female villains: jealous old widow and repressive aunt. *Theo Leigh,* 1867, is another very feeble story, pompously told, and with enough mild spice to keep the pages turning. AT wrote until the 1890s. Her *No Hero, But a*

Man, 1894, shows no change: a remarkably silly story held together by a clever, but slight, trick. According to William Tinsley (*Random Recollections,* 1900), AT could easily turn out a three-vol. novel in six weeks.

Thomas, Audrey Grace (Callahan), writer of novels and short stories, b. 1935 in Binghamton, NY, da. of Frances Waldron (Corbett) and Donald Earle C. She found refuge from tense family life in reading (H. S. ADAMS's *Bobbsey Twins,* Nancy Drew) and writing (prize-winning poetry, 'awful stuff') and at the country place of her maternal grandfather, who encouraged her to read, paint and play the violin. Now at work on a novel based on the Corbetts, AT has imaginatively registered her childhood and adolescence in *Songs My Mother Taught Me,* her first novel, not pub. until 1973. She was educ. at St Mary's Anglican boarding school in NH, where she first read Dostoevsky, the Mary Burnham School, and Smith College (BA in English, 1957). She did her junior year at St Andrews Univ., Scotland, and in Birmingham met sculptor and teacher Ian T., whom she married in 1958 (divorced, 1979). They emigrated to Surrey, BC, in 1959, subsequently moving to Vancouver. AT attended the Univ. of British Columbia while raising her three daughters (MA, 1963); her doctoral dissertation on *Beowulf* was rejected as insufficiently scholarly. In Ghana with her husband, 1964–6, AT had her first story published in *The Atlantic,* 1965; a collection, *Ten Green Bottles,* 1967, followed. The African landscape, together with her traumatic experience of miscarriage there, has since been prominent in the imagistic and symbolic structure of much of her fiction, especially *Mrs. Blood,* 1970, a narrative recounted from pregnant Isobel's double point of view ('Some days my name is Mrs. Blood; some days it's Mrs. Thing'), and in *Blown Figures,* 1974, her most experimental novel. A collage of inner and outer experiences, nursery rhymes and cartoons, in which Isobel returns to Africa (as AT did in 1972) to look for her miscarried baby, *Blown Figures* is 'a sort of mimetic analogue of the psychology of a distressed woman'. An admirer of Patrick White, Doris LESSING, Bruce Chatwin, AT almost never fails to embed *Alice in Wonderland* in her fiction: the protagonist of *Intertidal Life,* 1984 (first winner of the Ethel WILSON award in BC), is Alice's namesake. Her work, for instance the novellas *Munchmeyer and Prospero on the Island,* 1971, and the short story collections *Ladies & Escorts,* 1977, *Real Mothers* 1981, and *Goodbye Harold, Good Luck,* 1986, deals primarily with the complexity of relationships and domestic life: it is also highly intertextual in relation to her own and other writers' work and to her life. The novel *Latakia,* 1979, follows her travels around the Mediterranean, rendering the visited ports and ruins as an exploration of three lovers' psyches. Weary of the impact of French theory on 'bad writing going on under the aegis of some kind of feminist polemic', AT 'resents' the label 'intellectual writer'; the 'passionate intensity' she sees as the source of her writing also characterizes many of her women protagonists/writers. She has written more than 14 plays for the CBC, most on topical issues, and been writer-in-residence in a number of Canadian universities. *The Wild Blue Yonder,* short stories, is forthcoming. Interviews in *Open Letter,* 5, 1979, and *Tessera,* 5, 1988. See studies by Lorna Irvine, *Sub/version,* 1986, and Susan Rudy Dorscht in John Moss, ed., *Future Indicative,* 1987; special issue of *Room of One's Own,* 10, 1985–6.

Thomas, Bertha, 1845–1918, novelist, da. of Maria (Sumner: da. of John Bird S., 1780–1862, Archbishop of Canterbury from 1848; niece and cousin of two other bishops) and the Rev. John Thomas of Glamorganshire, Canon of Canterbury from 1862. Bertha's sister Florence, later Mrs Julian Marshall, wrote a life of Mary SHELLEY. BT never married, nor did she need to write for money. She was a contributor to *Fraser's*, 1874–81, as well as *National Review, Cornhill,* and university magazines. Her first *Fraser's* article, 'Latest Intelligence from Venus' (Dec. 1874), is a clever satire on male attitudes to women's SUFFRAGE. The first pub. of her dozen novels was *Proud Maizie,* 1876. Many were serialized: *The Violin-Player,* 1880, and *Elizabeth's Fortune,* 1887, both appeared first in *London Society.* The latter begins unconventionally, with as first-person narrator an orange-seller who becomes a maid in a clergyman's house, commenting freely on the family: '[Miss Alice] was trying to fancy her life into a three-volume novel, and it wouldn't take the mould'. Her last novel, *Son of the House,* 1900, with a socialist hero confined to a madhouse by his mother, also has flashes of real brilliance but is uneven. In 1912 she pub. her last work, *Picture Tales from the Welsh Hills.* BT wrote a study of George SAND in 1883 for the Eminent Women series.

Thomas, Elean, poet and short-story writer, b. 1947 in St Catherine, Jamaica, da. of 'a quiet, dignified, brave working-class woman who works at anything which can provide a decent and honest living and a boppish, dashing middle-class Preacherman'. Educ. at local schools and the Univ. of the West Indies (BA in political science and history), she works as a journalist and publicist, active in the communist Workers' Party. She first became known as a performing poet, and reached print with 'Ode to Woman' on an International Women's Day greetings card of the Committee of Women for Progress in Jamaica, 1983. Her *Word Rhythms From the Life of a Woman,* 1986 (title chosen to avoid pretentiousness), contains poems (mostly) and stories, prefaced by Carolyn Cooper and Trevor Monroe. ET writes from 'the midst of my people', but addresses world-wide as well as Jamaican political issues. 'A Matter of Words' distinguishes 'Women's Equality' from 'Women's Liberation', rejects 'Equality in poverty / Equality in exploitation', and calls for 'People's Liberation'. She spotlights particular women in poverty, the isolated mother or the elderly supermarket shopper anxiously checking every item, afraid 'we bound fe land up / Out a door / When me can't pay the rent / We bound fe plunge into darkness / When them cut off the light.' ET has performed around the Caribbean and in Czechoslovakia and East Germany.

Thomas, Elizabeth, 'Corinna', 1675–1731, poet and letter writer, da. of teenage Elizabeth (Osborne) and 60-year-old Emmanuel T., eminent London lawyer, who, however, left little when he died, 1677. Her life was never free from want. With minimal teaching, she was as a child 'Covetous ... of Learning to the last Degree', 'for ever a Scribling'. Her mother moved to Bloomsbury from Surrey, and mixed with Revolution statesmen; ET studied French and church Fathers. Her poetic 'Spark was light at mighty Dryden's Flame'. In 1699 she sent him two poems; he praised them, likening her to Katherine PHILIPS and the Greek poet Corinna. Next year *Luctus Britannici* published her poem on his death: Richard Gwinnett admired it, met and courted her, against his father's objections. Their letters over 16 years exchange poems and discuss writers, notably the future Elizabeth ROWE. ET had some years of serious illness from 1711; Gwinnett died just as he had come into money but she had postponed marriage once more since her mother was dying of cancer. He left her £600; legal battles with his family took most of it. ET's *Miscellany Poems,* 1722 (re-titled and re-issued, 1726), contain much compliment, lively satire, and feminist views. She deplores women's being 'still deny'd th'Improvement of our Mind' and when married 'made a Property for Life', praises Mary ASTELL (though her Whiggism kept them apart), and welcomes Mary CHUDLEIGH as a 'free-born Muse with Sense of Wrong inspir'd'. ET's *Metamorphosis of the Town,* 1730 (often repr. with poems by others), amusingly notes changing fashions. Her friend (not lover) Henry Cromwell gave her letters written him by the young Alexander Pope; she sold them to Edmund Curll. Printed in [1726], they drew her a nauseous role in the *Dunciad,* 1728, and a lastingly smutty reputation; Pope believed that she and Curll wrote *Codrus, or The Dunciad Dissected* (pub. while she was in jail for debt, 1728). Her defensive autobiography appeared (infiltrated by fiction not hers) in *Pylades and Corinna,* 1731–2, with letters (some repr. from elsewhere) and other material. See T. R. Steiner in *N and Q,* 1983; Joanna Lipking in *Eighteenth-Century Life,* 12: 2, 1988.

Thomas, Elizabeth (Dobson), 'Mrs Bridget Bluemantle', b. 1771 at Berry, Devon, novelist and poet: of, she says, 'the old school, both in politics and religion ... perfectly satisfied with the "powers that be"' . She married the Rev. Thomas T. of Newland, Glos., and moved in 1802 to nearby Tidenham, where she bore her three last children and published eight novels, mostly for MINERVA, mostly as Bridget Bluemantle, from *The Three Old Maids of the House of Penruddock,* 1806. Her *Claudine, or Pertinacity,* 1817, and *Claudine, or Humility the Basis of all the Virtues,* 1822, by children's writer Maria Elizabeth Budden, have confused the two. ET wrote *The Baron of Falconberg, or Childe Harolde* [sic] *in Prose,* 1815, because she admired Byron's poem 'yet thought it wanted a finish'. She lays little stress on her Baron's 'solitary rambles', more on his poetry (which tends to the cheerfully low-life), most on his loss of a bad woman (eloped) and a good one (died) and his conversion by his best friend (also died). *Purity of Heart, or The Ancient Costume,* 1816, as by 'an old wife of twenty years', answers *Glenarvon* by Caroline LAMB (here as Lady Calantha Limb). Its heroine rejects the Byron-figure as an emotional bully, and continues to hold him off after marrying a worldling whom at last she makes a Christian. Her early feelings are well done; so is the satire on libertinism. Reviewers, however, were shocked. ET defended herself in a preface to her first book of poems, *The Confession,* 1818, dedicated to her children. She printed later verse by name: in *The Georgian, or The Moor of Tripoli,* 1847, a widow leaving her long-term home, she collected some early work she had not dared to issue in days of 'great and mighty' Romantic poets.

Thomas, Elizabeth Frances (Amherst), 1716–79, poet, da. of Elizabeth (Kerrill) and Jeffrey A., living near Sevenoaks, Kent. At 12 she was observing nature and rebuking 'an old Beau for railing at Ladies', in neatly-copied verse (chiefly occasional and social: album in Bodleian). She wrote hymns for funerals, and at about 18 movingly lamented a sister's death, but was also 'rather addicted to Satyr'. At 16 she translated Jean-Baptiste Bellegarde's work on ridicule: if a printed version, *The Polite Tutor,* 1749, is hers, she rendered another of his works too. She exposed plagiarism by a fellow-versifier, and poked fun at the military dignity of a brother. Marrying and not marrying are favourite topics: she hopes a husband will not 'dare to contradict me' and inserts a hint of ambivalence in a requested satire on an old maid. She m. the Rev. John T. of Notgrove, Glos., by 1761, when she sent Shenstone a poem signed 'Cotswouldiana'. Her little *Dramatick Pastoral* about Coronation gifts of wedding portions to deserving poor girls was printed in 1762, and a poem on her father's estate in the *GM,* 1767. In 1771 she wrote verses for Newbold, the estate in Warwicks. where she died.

Thomas, Gladys (Adams), poet, playwright, and short-story writer. She was b. in 1935 in Salt River, Cape Town, South Africa, da. of the inter-racial marriage of Dorothy (Craythorne) and John Adams. After primary school, she went to work in a clothing factory. She m. Alfred T., now counsellor for black students at the Univ. of Capetown, and had a daughter and two sons. She wrote her first poem in 1971 when her family house was bulldozed to make their area into a white suburb: 'I didn't know I could write, but when the Group Areas Act forced our family out of Simon's Town ... I wrote "Fall Tomorrow", in retaliation'. Her poems, *Cry Rage,* 1972, co-ed. with James Matthews, were banned. A member of a local Peninsula Dramatic Society, she wrote five plays. *Now We Are Not Alone* treats of crossing the colour line; *David and Dianne* of the Immorality (or Conspiracy) Act forbidding mixed marriages, and *Men Without Women* of the forced separation of male workers from their families in the homelands. These won first prize in the *World* competition, 1978, just after the newspaper was itself banned. GT's poems and short stories have appeared at home and abroad in newspapers, magazines, anthologies and on radio. Her children's stories reflect her own community work in Ocean View. When Crossroads was bulldozed and burned, she went to a church shelter to talk with the dispossessed children whose stories she wrote down in *Children of the Crossroads,* 1986. Eleven of her poems appear in *Exiles Within: 7 South African Poets,* 1986. GT travelled abroad, 1983, to attend the International Writing Program at the Univ. of Iowa. In 1980 she was named on the Kwanzaa honors list for black South African women writers, Chicago, and commended for 'writing under oppressive conditions'. Known for her strong voice on bulldozing of black and coloured settlements, forced dislocation and breaking up of families, and abuse and imprisonment of children under apartheid, she is also a member of the United Women's Congress and a Patron of the anti-apartheid Congress of South African Writers. The stories in *The Wynberg Seven,* 1987, are based on interviews with families of seven children jailed for public violence. *Spotty Dog,* 1988, is stories 'of and for' township children. Autobiography in progress. See Charlotte Bruner in *WLT,* 61, 1987.

Thomas, Joyce Carol (Haynes), poet, novelist, playwright, b. 1938 at Ponca City, Oklahoma, fifth of nine children of Leona (Thompson), 'the most important influence in my life and writing', and bricklayer Floyd Dave H. As a small child she wrote poetry, worked each year picking cotton, and 'used to straddle baby / Brother on my hip and / Run from the gray pack dogs'. Her writing reflects her family's religious fervour, fondness for gospel music, and story-telling art. After two years of college (and evening jobs), in 1959 she married chemist Gettis L. Withers; she took a BA in Spanish at San Jose State College, 1966, and MA in education (with Spanish emphasis) at Stanford, 1967. Divorced in 1968, with three children, she married Prof. Roy T. Thomas, Jr., and had one more; she is now divorced again. She has taught drama, several languages and literatures, creative writing and black studies, in high schools, colleges and universities, and has read and lectured in Nigeria and Haiti. In 1973 came her first book of poems, *Bittersweet;* three more preceded *Inside the Rainbow,* 1982, which includes new and reprinted work; further volumes have followed. Her poetic themes include the strength and beauty of black women: 'make your daughters / New goddesses and your sons / Young pharaohs.' She had four plays produced in San Francisco between 1976 and 1978. Her first novel, *Marked by Fire,* 1982 (pub. on encouragement from Josephine MILES: American Book Award), draws on childhood memory to present a rich, healing female community, 'midwives-in-common' at the birth of the protagonist, Abyssinia. Though it uses Abyssinia's rape at age ten to make a political point about the link between racism and sexism, this book and its equally tough sequels (from *Bright Shadow,* 1983) are listed as for young adults. So is *The Golden Pasture,* 1986, a tale about a horse which evokes black family history. See Marilyn Yalom, ed., *Women Writers of the West Coast,* 1983.

Thompson, Clara Ann, *c.* 1869–1949, and **Priscilla Jane**, 1871–1942, poets, b. at Rossmoyne, Ohio, das. of the former slaves Clara Jane (Gray), who died young, and John Henry T. They lived with an elder brother, who received dedications from both. Their educ. at public school was supplemented by tutors: only CAT worked for a living (as a teacher), and only for a year. PJT's first book, *Ethiope Lays,* 1900, was pub. and sold by herself to 'picture the real side of my race ... their patience, fortitude and forbearance'. She addresses love-poems to a 'Knight of My Maiden Love' and to women with 'sweet midnight eyes', a prayer to the Muse to develop unfamiliar language for overdue praise of 'slighted, Afric maids', and political exhortation to 'Hold each black brother dear ... rise a man with men.' Her topics include lynching, emancipation, and death from tuberculosis. Dialect features in her *Gleanings of Quiet Hours,* 1907, and in CAT's *Songs from the Wayside,* 1908. CAT, who had wished to write novels, creates an ironic, humorous political commentator in 'Uncle Rube', whose deceptively simple utterance ('de way to solve de problum, / Is, to let de black man be') cloaks acute analysis of the symptoms and the dynamic of racism. CAT pub. another poem, *What Means This Bleating of the Sheep,* singly, 1921, and *A Garland of Poems,* 1926. She died in Cincinnati. See Ann Allen SHOCKLEY, *Afro-American Women Writers,* 1988.

Thompson, Clarissa Minnie, novelist and educator, b. into the black élite of Columbia, SC, eldest child of Eliza Henrietta (Montgomery) and Samuel Benjamin T. She first appeared in print, with essays in the African Methodist *Christian Recorder,* during her educ. at Howard School and the State Normal School. She then held teaching posts in SC. Her melodramatic *Treading the Winepress, or A Mountain of Misfortune,* issued serially in the *Boston Advocate,* 1886–7, was apparently only the second novel by a black woman; the *Recorder* had printed three chapters before deciding that its contents were unsuitable for a church paper. Writing to combat evil influences threatening the progress of her race, CMT seems to have included female sexuality among them. Her heroine loves, unrequitedly, a man who is murdered, possibly by her brother, and ends devoting her life to others' good; her sister, nicknamed 'Gipsy', precipitates many of the family's disasters by eloping. In 1886 CMT went to teach in Texas. She published poems (including support for temperance) and prose (including a novelette, *Only a Flirtation*) in newspapers, sometimes as 'Minnie Myrtle', and contributed to James T. Haley, ed., *Afro-American Encyclopaedia,* 1896. See Ann Allen SHOCKLEY, *Afro-American Women Writers,* 1988.

Thompson, Eloise Alberta Veronica **(Bibb),** 1878–1928, poet, journalist, playwright, b. in New Orleans, da. of well-to-do black Roman Catholics, Catherine Adèle and Charles H. Bibb. Her early *Poems,* 1895, include romantic tales of illicit love (in one a husband is ruthlessly sacrificed to achieve a happy ending), and a tribute to the future Alice DUNBAR-NELSON, fellow member of the Phillis WHEATLEY Club. After educ. at Oberlin College Preparatory Academy, teaching in New Orleans, and further study at Howard Univ., EBT held a pastoral post at Howard until she married, 1911, widower Noah Davis T. They moved to Los Angeles. She wrote articles for black and mainstream periodicals, and plays and stories mostly about New Orleans coloured society. *Caught* was staged in 1920, *Africans* in 1922, and *Cooped Up* in NYC, 1924. *Opportunity* magazine pub. her fiction in 1925 and 1927, and comment on her drama and her life in 1925 and 1928. See Ann Allen SHOCKLEY, *Afro-American Women Writers,* 1988.

Thompson, Flora Jane (Timms), 1876–1947, memoirist, poet, essayist. She was b. in Juniper Hill, Oxon., da. of Emma, whose name appears on FT's birth certificate as Lapper, in census returns as Dipper, and Albert Timms. A sensitive girl, she observed her neighbours and the struggles of rural lives. An assistant postmistress in several country post offices, she worked, from 1897, in the Surrey village of Grayshott, where the library nourished her desire to write: 'I cannot remember the time when I did not wish and mean to write', she said, recalling early verses, essays, stories and diaries. After marrying John Thompson, she continued to read widely, but 'my literary dreams failed for a time' faced with his hostility and the demands of two small children (a third was born when FT was 41). Her prize-winning essay on Jane AUSTEN and several published articles, however, provided economic justification for her writing and, while writing verse for satisfaction, she sold 'small sugared love stories' to earn her children's education. Her accomplished but unremarkable poems, *Bog-myrtle and Peat*, appeared in 1921. In 1922 she began to write Peverel Papers, distinguished nature essays, for *The Catholic Fireside* magazine (selec. pub. 1986). In 1928 the Thompsons moved to Devon, where she began to write the childhood sketches which became the basis for her best-known work, the memoirs *Lark Rise*, 1939, *Over to Candleford*, 1941, and *Candleford Green*, 1943, which were re-issued in one volume as *Lark Rise to Candleford*, 1945. The series chronicles life in rural Oxfordshire in the 1880s and 1890s, focusing its history of hamlet, village and market town on the life of the autobiographical Laura. Memories of a pre-industrial rural England survive to enliven this detailed chronicle of social, economic and cultural change. 'Laura' herself is a register of changed times as the cottagers' child who becomes the memorialist of a community. A further volume, *Heatherley*, was not published until 1976, when it appeared with some nature essays. The posthumously published novel, *Still Glides the Stream*, 1948, fictionalizes the rural scene of her youth again through the eyes of a woman who, like Laura, had 'disappeared from the country scene' and returns, 'but never as herself part of it'. See Margaret Lane, *Flora Thompson*, 1976 (first published in *The Cornhill Magazine*, 1957).

Thomson, Harriet (Pigott), novelist. She was second wife of William T., Scottish miscellaneous writer 20 years her senior, and had children. Her novels are epistolary and didactic. *Excessive Sensibility, or The History of Lady St. Laurence*, 1787, begins with the heroine's wedding; *Fatal Follies, or The History of the Countess of Stanmore*, 1788, makes its bad characters entertaining; *The Labyrinths of Life*, 1791, interweaves multiple stories. Only the last, *Laurette, or The Caprices of Fortune*, MINERVA, 1807, bore her name (and has been ascribed to Katherine Thomson). Though she apologizes for 'want of powerful genius and fancy', she makes good her claim to draw both true and moral pictures. Grief and other emotion often runs high, innocence is maligned till poetic justice intervenes; yet good sense and good writing generally triumph over excess. She is not the same person as Harriet PIGOTT.

Thornton, Alice (Wandesford), 1626–1707, memoirist, b. at Kirklington, Yorks., da. of Alice (Osborne) and Sir Christopher W. Piously reared, she pondered the power of God's creation at five, and at 12 felt humbled by Christ's learning at that age. In 1633 her father (d. 1640) took up a post in Ireland under Thomas Wentworth: educated with his daughters, she may have known Judith MAN. Curing a soldier's wound in the civil war brought her timely warning of a plan to rape her. Advice overcame her reluctance to 'change my free estate' (her only sister had died at 29 of her 16th pregnancy, six still-born); she married, 1651, the 'godly, sober, and discreet' but near-bankrupt William T. of East Newton, Yorks. She suffered violent head and stomach pains on her wedding day, lost her first child (owing, she thought, to an unplanned, taxing downhill climb on foot), and underwent various severe physical problems over eight more births. Three children grew up; her husband died in 1669, leaving her resolved despite poverty and family conflict to find the 'soe prodigious a somme' needed to educate her son. She wrote her life that year to combat slanders on her marital loyalty and business dealings, but includes prayers and meditations, dreams, much medical detail, conversations with children, and accounts of her mother, other relations, and enemies. Selecs., heavily ed., Surtees Soc., 1873. Her separate life of her father (lost) was used in one by her great-grandson Thomas Comber, 1778.

Thynne, Harriet Frances (Bagot), Lady, 1816–81, novelist, eldest da. of Richard B., Bishop of Bath and Wells. She m., 1837, the Rev. Lord Charles T., youngest son of 2nd Marquis of Bath; she and he both converted to Rome in 1852 (influenced by Cardinal Newman, a friend). She pub. eight novels and tales. The first, *Eleanor Morrison; or Home Duties*, 1860, is a romance with a background of Catholicism but restrained in its treatment of religious and moral issues, dealing with the upbringing of a girl by a worldly, snobbish aunt: 'an education of the intellect, not of the heart'. Her latest novel, *Maud Leslie*, 1877, is far bleaker, treating the subject of unhappy marriage as a trap for women, and without noticeable Catholic reference. Its heroine matures to deal with her selfish, egotistical husband, but no reconciliation or other happy solution is offered.

Thynne, Joan (Hayward), 1558–1612, and **Maria**, *c.* 1578–1611, letter writers. Joan m. John T. in 1576, and in 1580 became mistress of Longleat, a brand-new mansion and household of 70 people. Her letters are stiff and practical, hinting at but not elucidating difficult human relations, writing 'Good Mr Thynne' to her husband's 'My good Pug'. She later defended Caus Castle, Shropshire, from rival claimants (sleeping with weapons to hand against attack) and speculated in lead mines. In 1594 Thomas T., the 16-year-old heir, secretly married Maria, daughter of a bitterly hostile family (sister of the future Eleanor DOUGLAS); the Thynnes were slow to forgive, and the story may be a source for *Romeo and Juliet*. Maria writes remarkable letters: to her angry mother-in-law at first carefully submissive, later zestfully antagonistic; to her husband lovingly bawdy in English and Latin; in each case delighting in and exploiting the need for indirection. She died in childbirth, leaving three sons. Their letters are ed. Alison D. Wall, Devizes, 1983.

Tiernan, Frances Christine Fisher, 1846–1920, novelist who used the deliberately androgynous pen-name 'Christian Reid'. She was b. Salisbury, North Carolina, eldest of Elizabeth (Caldwell) and Charles F.'s three children. Orphaned young, FT was brought up by her aunt and educ. chiefly at home. In 1868 she converted to Catholicism. She started writing to earn money and her first novel, *Valerie Aylmer*, appeared in 1870. Between this and her last, *A Secret Bequest*, 1914, FT wrote 45 books. An early success was *The Land of the Sky*, 1876, a lively account of a family touring in the North Carolina mountains. She m. James Marquis T., a mineralogist, in 1887; his work took them to Mexico, the setting for novels such as *Carmela*, 1891, and Santo Domingo, where *The Chase of an Heiress*, 1898, takes place. Here, romance in an exotic setting gives FT scope for an adventurous and resourceful heroine beset by dangers, albeit one-dimensionally drawn. FT's writing makes clear her beliefs: *Under the Southern Cross*, 1900, voices her fervent support of the Confederacy; while the heroine of *Ebb-Tide*,

1872, wants to give her life to her art – 'to study, to work, not to be merely an eccentric young lady who dabbles in oils' – but makes a loveless marriage and dies with the Litany for a Departing Soul sounding, 'Ave Maria' on her lips. FT's Catholic propaganda reduced her popularity but she is an interesting if not unusual specimen of late nineteenth-century romantic fiction. Her life is by Kate H. Becker, 1941.

Tietjens, Eunice Strong (Hammond), 1884–1944, poet and novelist. B. in Chicago, da. of Idea (Strong) and banker William A. H., she was educ. mainly in Europe: the Collège de France, the Sorbonne, and the Froebel Institute of Dresden. She married US composer Paul T. in 1904 and lived in NYC until their separation, 1910. Back in Chicago, she began to move in literary circles and write poems. Harriet MONROE published her in *Poetry*, and she served the journal as 'office girl' from 1913 and associate editor from 1916 until near her death. She received the second job offer while in China, gathering with fascination and horror the material for her first and best-known book, *Profiles from China*, 1917, whose short free-verse narratives Amy LOWELL called 'sharp and beautiful'. Her next collections, *Body and Raiment*, 1919 (written earlier), and *Leaves in Windy Weather*, 1929, drew less praise. She based a novel, *Jake*, 1921, on her experience as war correspondent for the Chicago *Daily News* from 1917. She married playwright Cloyd Head, and wrote with him an undistinguished play, *Arabesque*, 1925. In 1928 she published an anthology, *Poetry of the Orient* (gathered from libraries, magazines, and friends' versions), and the first of her children's books, *Boy of the Desert*, set in Tunisia, which, with *The Romance of Antar*, 1929, an Arabian epic retold, draws on her North African travels and interest. She collaborated with her daughter on *The Jaw-Breaker's Alphabet of Prehistoric Animals*, 1930, and taught at the Univ. of Miami, 1933–5. Her autobiography, *The World at My Shoulder*, 1938, mentions the early deaths of two of her four children.

Tighe, Mary (Blachford), 1772–1810, poet, b. in Dublin, da. of Methodist leader Theodosia (Tighe) and the Rev. William B., a librarian who died in her babyhood. Her mother gave her a strict religious education. By 1789 she was already a poet, and involved with her cousin Henry T.; of their wedding in 1793 she wrote 'My soul draws back in terror and awe.' Her mother judged her 'struggling with a foolish and violent passion', and later not returning her husband's love; she disapproved their life in London, first intensely social, later equally literary. MT linked her unhappiness with giving way to 'the temptations of being admired'. She studied Latin with her husband, and wrote, 1801–3, a six-canto allegory in Spenserian stanzas, privately printed (50 copies) as *Psyche, or the Legend of Love*, 1805. Her preface defends her choice of an erotic, not martial, subject. Her verse is calm and luxurious, splendidly sensuous as Psyche explores Cupid's magic palace or gazes at his sleeping beauty; the poem closes on the fast-fading colours of 'Dreams of Delight'. MT was already ill with consumption. She spent her last years at Dublin and Rosanna, Co. Wicklow; her last poem says 'my coward heart / Still shuddering clings to dust.' *Psyche*, pub. with other poems, 1811, was much, though briefly, admired; many reprs. up to 1978. *Mary, a Series of Reflections during 20 years*, 1811, printed on a private press by her brother-in-law William T. with facsimile poems, is rare; her diary was destroyed, though a cousin copied out extracts. In her autobiographical novel *Selena* (MS in National Library of Ireland), it is the mother, not daughter, who dies of TB: see booklet by Patrick Henchy, 1957; Earle Vonard Weller, study of MT's influence on Keats, 1966. The *DNB* entry is full of errors.

Timbury, Jane, b. *c.* 1749, miscellaneous writer. In *The Story of Le Fevre*, 1787, she makes heroic couplets impose incongruous order on material from *Tristram Shandy*: 'I cannot govern that which governs me.' *The History of Tobit*, also 1787, is scripture versified with other poems: patriotic, moral, and (the best) gently satirical, like 'The Card Party'. Reviewers treated these and her epistolary novel *The Male Coquet*, 1788, with scorn beyond their desert. The novel differs widely from *The Male-Coquette, or The History of the Hon. Edward Astell*, 1770, anonymous. In that, two girls reclaim rakes; JT's central figure dies penitent after his two-timing emerges ('Dormer, gracious Heaven! Dormer ... is no other than the perfidious Belmour'); her heroine deplores 'modern novelists' who write 'florid discourses' on love. In *The Philanthropic Rambler*, 1790 (sequel 1791), the bachelor Benevolus does good to such as a Jew and, at greater length, a prostitute. L. M. HAWKINS subscribed to this and *Tobit*. JT claims as hers *The Triumph of Friendship*: a somewhat clumsy anonymous poem of this name, 1791 (male bonding survives loving the same woman), was repr. with some changes in 1805 and then claimed by William Golden as recently written; he *may* have filched it. From 1788 to 1803, when the RLF gave her five guineas, JT ran a tiny school in Westminster, keeping her mother, d. 1797, and sister.

Tincker, Mary Agnes, 1831–1907, novelist, b. Ellsworth, Maine, da. of Mehitabel (Jellison) and Richard T. Educ. at public schools, she began teaching at 13 and, two years later, started contributing anonymous sketches to local journals. A turning point came in 1851, when MT converted to Catholicism. Her first pub. book, initially serialized in the *Catholic World*, was *The House of Yorke*, 1872, set locally. A long stay in Italy, between 1873 and 1887, meant that the most successful of MT's 11 pub. works, notably *Signor Monaldini's Niece*, 1879, were set in Rome. Her casts of Italian aristrocrats, cardinals and monks, and her scattering of Italian into the dialogue, convey quite skilfully the Roman atmosphere, but strained descriptions of the landscape, simplistic characterization and far-fetched plots make her novels insignificant, although they were commended at the time as imaginative Christian works. MT is at her cloying best in a romantic interlude: 'She could not stir, but only leaned and looked down into his upturned face, her head and heart swimming in a sudden, sweet intoxication of delight.' (*The Jewel in the Lotos*, 1884).

Tindal, Henrietta Euphemia, 'Mrs Acton Tindal' (Harrison), 'Diana Butler', 1818?–79, poet and novelist. The only surviving child of Elizabeth Henrietta (Wollaston) and the Rev. John H. of Ramsey, Essex, and vicar of Dinton, Bucks., she was described as an 'heiress'. Though her education was 'desultory', she had French and Italian and read widely among English poets. Not strong, she lived in retirement, but met M. R. MITFORD, with whom she corresponded. In 1846 she m. Acton T.; she bore three sons and twin daughters (one died, aged nine). She pub. poems in periodicals, then a volume, *Lines and Leaves*, 1850. Many poems are based on historical incidents, such as 'The Infant Bridal' (admired by Mitford), 'The Baptism of the Gypsy Babe' and 'The Burial in London'. She pub. one novel under the pseudonym 'Diana Butler': *The Heirs of Blackridge Manor*, 1856. Well-written, though not well-plotted, it is an aristocratic romance spiced with humour and sharply observed eccentricities: 'We do nothing floral at any season of the year, nothing *aesthetic*', says the vicar. *Rhymes and Legends*, 1879, pub. posthumously with a prefatory memoir, reprints many of her earlier poems and also two complimentary poems to VICTORIA: 'To the Most Illustrious Mourner in the New Year, 1862', and 'On the Hartley Colliery Accident, 16 January 1862'; her narrative poems are her most effective.

Tinsley, Annie (Turner), 1808–85, novelist and poet, b. Preston, Lancs., one of numerous children of (?) (Carruthers), a zealous RC convert, and Thomas Milner Turner. AT was sent 'early' to school, and also educ. by her father, who, when she was eight, decided to become an actor, and moved the family about for many years in unsuccessful pursuit of his dream. Her first volume of poems, *The Children of the Mint*, 1826(7?), was pub. at a loss; AT was arrested for debt (illegally, at her age) and only saved from the Fleet Prison by a solicitor, Charles T., met in the sponging-house, whom she m. 1833. He too proved financially unviable, having, in her words, 'industry, rectitude and worthiest purpose [but] one fatal obstacle – incapacity'. They had six children, and AT had to write fiction to keep them, although her ambition had been to become a poet: 'my married life soon knocked the poetry out of me'. Her first novel, *The Priest of the Nile*, 1840, was followed by many short stories, often pub. in magazines, and several other novels, including *Margaret*, 1853, and *Women as They Are. By One of Them*, 1854. Pub. anon., this last has well-written descriptive passages and rather a turgid plot, full of emotion, but finally static. The first-person narrator recounts her solitary, imaginative childhood. An initial 'Advertisement' rebuts charges against the author of *Margaret*, that that work imitated STOWE's *Uncle Tom* and BRONTË's *Villette*, by asserting it was written before either appeared. Her second vol. of poems, pub. as *Lays for the Thoughtful and the Solitary*, by Mrs Charles Tinsley, 1840, is by far her best work, and takes heart from its theme (in 'Dreams of the Future') that work neglected in the present might live for future readers: 'As our own hearts have thrill'd to the words of the dead'. There is a fine and bitter poem to 'The Grave of L.E.L.': '"Fame", cold cheat of woman still'. The only source for her life is Henry Peet's pamphlet, repr. from the Transactions of the Historical Soc. of Lancs., 1930.

Tipper, Elizabeth, English poet. Unmarried, she spent five years of her youthful prime alone in an 'uncouth Cottage', sometimes speaking to no-one for days, till friends persuaded her to try the city. She wrote for John Dunton in the 1690s (see JOURNALISM), and (probably later) worked on alternate days as teacher (of 'Writing and Accompts' to ladies) and as book-keeper (to a shop). In 1698 she dedicated to Lady COVENTRY *The Pilgrim's Viaticum* [i.e. traveller's supplies], *or The Destitute, but not Forlorn*. This, called on the title-page a divine poem, is actually a collection, emotional but assured in style, with prefatory verses comparing her to SAPPHO and (favourably) Aphra BEHN and Katherine PHILIPS. She says her theme is 'the Oracles of God', higher than hero's deeds or lover's rapture; in fact she joins Epictetus to Elijah, meditations on her own life to those on Christ's, the 'racking Passion' of earthly love to true, divine love. She considers scripture texts, laments dead friends, and invents a blood-chilling speech for Salome with John the Baptist's head. She finds satire sanctioned by Christ and not beyond woman's valour, but contrary to the command to see one's own faults first. On the peace of 1697 she exclaims 'I did not think all Earth could give or find / Such Pleasure to my Pleasure-hating Mind.'

Tlali, Miriam, Soweto novelist, short-story writer, journalist, born in 1933, in Doornfontein, Johannesburg, of a mother who encouraged her writing and a teacher father who died early, leaving her his books. She attended St Cyprian's Anglican School and Madibane High School, then studied for two years at Witwatersrand University. Unable to pursue medical studies there, she went to Roma in Lesotho, but ran out of money and returned home to secretarial school. She is married with two children. Parts of her first novel, *Muriel at Metropolitan*, 1975, depicting her own clerking experience and showing the depressed condition of women as blacks and employees, were banned. (By law, her husband had to sign the contract for her book.) Her second, *Amanda*, 1980, based on the Soweto unrest of 1976, is also banned. MT has also written stories, articles and interviews ('Soweto Speaking') for *Staffrider* and local papers. *Mihloti (Tears)*, 1984, includes stories, journalism, interviews and travelogues. Another collection, *Mehlala Khatamping (Imprints in the Quag)*, is in preparation. MT wrote her first novel during the four years in which she had left her job to nurse a dying mother-in-law. Now she sells kitchen-ware door-to-door and works on a third novel in the evenings. She participated in the International Writing Program in Iowa, 1979, and in a conference on African women and literature at Mainz, 1982, and she spent six months in the Netherlands, 1984. The women in her work 'represent both images, that of mother and of liberated woman.... The problems presented by the combination of militancy and motherhood are an entirely new experience for women in our society.' She was a panellist at the PEN conference in Canada, 1989. See interview in Mineke Schipper, ed., *Unheard Words*, 1984, and MT's account of a night raid on her home and a day-long interrogation in *Index in Censorship*, 17, 1988. She mentions here the unavailability of her two novels in South Africa.

Todd, Mabel (Loomis), 1856–1932, short-story and travel writer, conservationist and editor of Emily DICKINSON's poetry, b. Cambridge, Mass., da. of Mary Alden (Wilder) and Eben Jenks L., mathematician, astronomer and naturalist. The family moved to Washington, DC, when she was ten. She was educ. at private schools in Cambridge and Georgetown, primarily the Georgetown Seminary, and later studied music, German and painting in Boston. In 1879 she m. David Peck T., astronomer, who in 1881 became a faculty member at Amherst College. They were friends of Austin and Susan Dickinson, and by 1882 Austin and MLT had become lovers. That year she first heard several of Emily Dickinson's poems, and though they never met, MLT received notes and poems from her. After Dickinson's death in 1886, the family asked MLT to prepare her poems for publication; they appeared in 1890 with a second series in 1891. MLT also ed. Dickinson's letters in 1894, and a third series of poems in 1896. After Austin died in 1895, her connection with the family ended in a lawsuit over property he left her. MLT's own work included the short story 'Footprints', pub. in the *New York Independent* and the *Amherst Record*, 1883; a work of popular science, *Total Eclipses of the Sun*, 1894; and two travel works, *Corona and Coronet*, 1898, and *Tripoli the Mysterious*, 1912, based on expeditions with her husband. Long active in nature and conservation groups, she wrote *A Cycle of Sunsets*, 1910. In 1917 she moved to Coconut Grove, Fl., where she helped establish Everglades National Park. Her daughter, Millicent Todd Bingham, wrote an account of MLT's role in editing Dickinson's poetry in *Ancestor's Brocades: The Literary Debut of Emily Dickinson*, 1945. However, reluctant to expose what she considered her mother's terrible sin, she omitted any mention of her love affair with Austin Dickinson. MLT's papers are in the Sterling Library, Yale. See Polly Longworth, *Austin and Mabel, 1984*, and in *Legacy*, Spring, 1986.

Todd, Margaret Georgina, 'Graham Travers', 1859–1918, doctor and novelist, da. of a businessman, b. in Scotland and educ. at univs. there and on the Continent. She qualified and worked as a doctor in Edinburgh. After two pseudonymous novels, she set her name to two more, a volume of stories, and a life of Sophia Jex-Blake, 1918. Most popular (15 eds. by 1902) was *Mona Maclean, Medical Student*, 1892, whose heroine, an orphan poised between rich Anglo-Indian and poor Scots relations, achieves 'the duty of self-realisation', a first in physiology (after two failures), marriage for love, and practice in partnership with her husband, treating women. Later heroines are awarded less glittering prizes. That of *Windyhaugh*, 1898, has a puritan upbringing (at seven, though an engaging 'healthy animal', she fears not being one of the elect), sacrifices herself for her father, and overcomes morphine addiction before happy marriage; that of *The Way of Escape*, 1902, denied love and happiness, passionately committed to truth yet carrying secret guilt, dies heroically saving children from a fire; that of *Growth*, 1906, lives on the fringes of Edinburgh debate in theology, philosophy and medicine. The title story of *Fellow Travellers*, 1896, shows a rugged, admirable male country doctor astounded by the success of the woman painter he had pitied as neurotic.

Toklas, Alice Babette, 1877–1967, memoirist, publisher, companion to Gertrude STEIN, b. in San Francisco, Jewish da. of Emma (Levinsky) and merchant Ferdinand T. Educ. in private schools there and in Seattle, in 1893 ABT began to study at the Univ. of Washington Music Conservatory to be a concert pianist. After her mother died, 1897, she kept house for three generations of T. men until 1907, when she left for Paris with journalist Harriet Levy. There she soon fell in love with Gertrude Stein, moving in with her and her brother Leo in 1910. Until Stein's death, the two women were inseparable, ABT playing 'wife' to Stein's 'husband', assuming duties of domestic management, occasional (and famous) cook, gardener, and social secretary, adjudicating Stein's friendships, working Picasso designs in petit-point, and 'sitting with the wives' of the 'geniuses' Stein entertained. While her own taste ran to Henry James, she indefatigably promoted Stein's work: she typed MSS, proof-read, corrected the grammar of Stein's occasional French pieces, collaborated in writing her own portrait, 'Ada', in 1908 (pub. 1922) and *A Novel of Thank You* in 1925 (pub. 1958) and, when the couple's income declined after 1929, pushed Stein to write the best-seller *The Autobiography of Alice B. Toklas*, 1933. If in 1932 she censored a work of Stein's (*Stanzas in Meditation*, 1956) out of sexual jealousy, she also published five of her most abstruse works in Plain Edition, 1930–3. After Stein's death, 1946, ABT devoted herself to promoting her companion's memory. *The Alice B. Cookbook*, 1954, celebrated their circle in a series of recipes donated by friends and framed by witty gossip and reminiscence. *Aromas and Flavors of Past and Present*, 1958, proved less fortunate in its editing. Her reminiscences of life with Stein were published as *What is Remembered*, 1963, and occasional memoirs of the Paris circle appeared in US magazines in the 1950s. Her last years were impoverished and painful. Stein's valuable collection of paintings, from which ABT understood she could make modest sales to meet her needs, were removed by the Stein family with insufficient provision for ABT's support. She joined the Catholic Church in 1957, hoping Stein would be reunited with her in heaven. Suffering from arthritis and cataracts, she lived in Paris and with the Sisters of the Precious Blood in Rome. She lies in Père Lachaise, Paris, head to head with Stein, with whom she shares a single tombstone. Some of her letters in Samuel B. Steward, ed., *Dear Sammy: Letters from Gertrude Stein and Alice B. Toklas*, 1977; those written after Stein's death are edited by Edward Burns, 1973. Biography by Linda Simon, 1977. ABT's astute observations, dry wit and considerable asperity are best captured in Stein's *Autobiography*.

Tollet, Elizabeth, 1694–1754, poet, da. of Elizabeth and naval commissioner George T., educ. in Latin, French, Italian, history, poetry, and music. She grew up in the Tower of London, which left its mark on her work in lines given to Ann Boleyn and Lady Jane GREY. She inherited 'a handsome Fortune' and later lived near London. Her anonymous *Poems on Several Occasions*, 1724, is a wide-ranging volume which includes lively renderings of Ovid, Horace, Virgil, Claudian, and Latin verses by Renaissance women; Latin poems of her own; homage to Congreve, Pope, Anne FINCH and Lady Mary Wortley MONTAGU; personal poems to friends; devotional and theological pieces; lyrics and epigrams. She likens predictably plotted novels to country-dance steps, and modern enforced marriage to the enslavement of Trojan princesses by the conquering Greeks. She often revels in the wonders of creation: her most feminist poem is an impassioned and closely-reasoned plea for women's right to pursue scientific investigation. This she puts into the mouth of her ancient Greek foremother Hypatia, mathematician and philosopher, who was murdered. In 1732 ET wrote that 'Sorrow had untun'd my Voice'; but her last-dated poem is 1753. A nephew published a new edition of her *Poems*, 1755, with her name: additions include many metrical psalms and an oratorio libretto, 'Susanna: or Innocence Preserv'd'.

Tomalin, Ruth, also Leaver, children's writer, novelist, b. in Piltown, County Kilkenny, da. of Elspeth Rutherford (Mitchell) and gardener and writer Thomas Edward T. She was educ. at the Univ. of London (Diploma in Journalism, 1939), then worked as a reporter for various newspapers in England, 1942–65, later at the London Law Courts. She served in the Women's Land Army, 1941–2, and in 1942 m. Vernon Leaver; they had one son. In 1971 she m. journalist William N. Ross. All of RT's work shows strong feeling for victims of aggression and violence: her *Threnody for Dormice and Other Poems*, 1947, makes clear her interest in natural history and wildlife preservation, as do her idiosyncratic essays and portraits of largely natural subjects in *The Day of the Rose*, 1947, and her lives of W. H. Hudson, 1954 and 1982. Her children's stories often set their adventures in the countryside: a boy in *The Garden House*, 1964, and *The Spring House*, 1968, escapes the London Blitz living with an independent country aunt. The children in *Green Wishbone*, 1975, *The Snake Crook*, 1976, *A Summer Ghost*, 1986, reflect RT's concern for wild life, the countryside, independent adventure. Her adult novel, *All Souls*, 1952, told from a child's point of view, presents three parallel cases of persecution – a peace-loving old lady, persecuted as a witch because she did not conform to the narrow village idea of what she should be, a schoolteacher mother of an illegitimate son, an unconventional daughter of the vicar, aspiring to be a playwright – and enacts a revenge not on the ignorant guilty villagers but on those who stood by, for their 'sheer innocence'.

Tomlins, Elizabeth Sophia, 1763–1828, English novelist and poet, da. of solicitor Thomas T. Her first novel, *The Conquests of the Heart*, 1785, fictionalizes an actual friend born in Jamaica. She and her brother exchanged poems as Werter and Charlotte: her epistolary, highly sentimental *The Victim of Fancy*, 1787, aims to draw out Goethe's moral. Theresa Morven longs for education but is excessively affected by what she reads (including Sophia LEE's *The Recess*), and cannot survive the deaths of an aunt and a soldier brother 'for whom I lived, for whom I die'. EST's preface to *Rosalind de Tracey*, 1798, defends novels and says that women's virtues are shown in affliction. *En route* to 'the summit of all human felicity' (happy marriage) the heroine learns how luxuries are 'procured by the miseries of the poor', including governesses and lace-makers (a footnote mentions damp cellars and deformed children) and how profit 'goes to *property* and not to *labour*'. EST also translated from French and wrote for periodicals. Poems published by her brother as *Tributes of Affection*, 1797, include ballads, occasional verse, and 'The

Slave' (slavery tarnishes Europe's glory; her slave protagonist nobly refrains from vengeance within his grasp).

Tonna, Charlotte Elizabeth (Browne), 'Charlotte Elizabeth', 1790–1846, evangelical writer and editor, b. Norwich, da. of Michael B., minor canon. She was encouraged to roam freely with her brother, to read widely (she knew much of Shakespeare by heart) and forbidden to wear restrictive clothing. Her first marriage, 1813, to George Phelan, an army officer in Ireland (d. 1837), was unhappy (he physically abused her). While she felt herself in exile with him in Ireland, she resolved to crusade for factory workers. They separated *c.* 1824, and she lived with her brother near Bristol, where she met Hannah MORE. Fearing the 'pernicious sweets' of romantic fiction, she wrote a first and best-known didactic social-realist novel, *Helen Fleetwood*, 1841, which has been credited with influencing the passing of the 1844 Factory Bill, limiting to 12 hours the working day of factory women. She m. L. H. Tonna in 1841. Passionately anti-Catholic, she wrote popular songs for the Orange cause, pub. a collection of essays and sketches, *The Wrongs of Women*, 1843–4, ed. *The Christian Lady's Magazine* from 1836 and *The Protestant Magazine* 1841–6; and respectfully chided H. MARTINEAU in 1844 for her trust in mesmerism. H. B. STOWE glowingly introduced her coll. works in 1844, particularly the *Personal Recollections*, 1841, written ostensibly to recount CET's conversion, but see article on it by Elizabeth Kowaleski, *TSWL*, 1, 1982.

Tostevin, Lola Lemire, poet. B. in 1937 in Timmins, Ont., of francophone parents Laurette (Séguin) and Achilles Lemire, she was educ. as a convent boarder and at Collège St Thomas d'Aquin (Ottawa), later studied French Literature and Art History at the Univ. de Paris, and French and Comparative Literature at the Univs. of Alberta and Toronto. She married anglophone petroleum engineer William T. ('Jerry'), 1962, and had two children. LLT had 'always written' but, feeling divided by two languages, did not write for publication until her late thirties. *Color of Her Speech*, 1982, inscribes this division 'between // the way I speak / the way I spoke': '4 words french / 1 word english ... 1 word french / 4 words english // "*tu déparles*" / my mother says //; *je déparle* / yes // I unspeak'. Loss of mothertongue and the inability to speak a woman's body are analogous throughout her work. The afterword of *Gyno-Text*, 1983, theorizes her recourse to a KRISTEVAN 'génotexte' to affirm 'becoming of subject ... through process' and to allow women 'to repossess their bodies'. These minimalist poems, dedicated to her daughter, culminate in the female writing subject's simultaneously giving birth and being born into language. *Double Standards*, 1985, reassesses the writer's past '*per* through or by / means of *vers* a line of writing' allowing her 'to misinterpret designedly', to enter language as a writing, desiring subject rather than as the culturally constructed figure of Woman. 're' theorizes a woman subject's 'rereading' which 'reverses to resist resists to reverse the / movement along the curve of return ... / reorient / and continue in a different voice'. '*sophie*, 1987, inscribes the absent woman in philosophy, moves to highly erotic verse addressed to the absent man, concluding in 'song of songs' that 'the muse has learned to write ... body distinct / from the metaphor so I can love you now that I am no longer / spoken for'. *Espaces vers*, 1989, in French, suggests LLT's successful retrieval of her mothertongue through a feminist poetics inscribing the female body/subject. Recently she has turned to fiction. See Neuman and Kamboureli, 1986, and Janice Williamson in *Line*, 9, 1987.

Toulson, Shirley (Dixon), poet, journalist, educator and travel-writer, b. 1924 at

Henley, Oxon, da. of Marjorie (Brown) and Douglas Horsfall D., writer. She was educ. at Birkbeck College, London Univ. (BA 1953). Her poetry volumes and pamphlets began with *Shadows in an Orchard*, 1960. Her three children include one from her marriage to poet Alan Brownjohn, 1960–9. After three years, from 1967, as features editor of *Teacher*, she edited *Child Education*, 1970–4. Her poetry volumes are *Circumcision's Not Such a Bad Thing, After All*, 1970 (ambiguities, psychological probing), *The Fault, Dear Brutus: A Zodiac of Sonnets*, 1972 (12 pieces reflecting her concern both with order and rules and with their incapacity fully to explain), and *Bones and Angels*, 1978 (with John Loveday). In 'The Robot' she writes 'Some day, he vows, he'll turn into a person / He'll find a voice and sing to every music, / Tear up his rules and throw away his diary, / Forget the shapes and numbers of the pattern, / Accept as others do the waves of sorrow.' ST's passion for prehistory led to nine travel books between 1977 and 1985, mostly on ancient tracks of Wales, East Anglia, Derbyshire, the southwest, and Scotland, and to folk history books: *The Winter Solstice*, 1984, and *The Celtic Alternative: A Reminder of the Christianity We Lost*, 1987.

Townsend, Mary Ashley (Van Voorhis), 'Xariffa', 1832–1901, poet, essayist, short-story writer, novelist, b. Galveston, Texas, only child of Catherine (Van Wickle) and James G. Van V., who d. a year after she was born. She attended district school and academy, and in 1850 began writing for the *Daily Delta*. After marrying Gideon T., she moved to New Orleans (1860) where she became poet laureate of the county. Under the names 'Crab Crossbones' and 'Michael O'Quillo', she wrote essays on diverse topics, from millinery to military, and as 'Henry Rip' produced popular moral tales. But it was as 'Xariffa' that she gained renown. Her sensation novel, *The Brother Clerks*, 1857, is perhaps more notable for its dualities than its style or plot. Northern puritanism confronts Southern hedonism, a delicate, swooning brother is juxtaposed with a violent one, while Ella breaks through the veneer of feminine graces to express radical views: 'Young women marry old men so that they can be their own mistresses and have their own way'. MT also touches on miscegenation, slavery and sisterhood. *Xariffa's Poems*, 1870, treat renunciation, memory, time and love. 'A Memory' recalls an idyllic encounter with a maiden 'loved with a madness'. Songs to women also feature in *Down the Bayou*, 1882, notably the title poem, in which the speaker recalls a dreamy, lagoon-idling day with her lover. *Distaff and Spindle*, 1895, is dedicated to MT's three daughters. These sonnets speak of death, poetry and women. LXVIII reverses conventional white-goddess symbolism and observes that unlike the sun, the moon, 'like some great bowl of blood / spills no drop on the horizon's rim'.

Townsend, Sue, Leicester playwright and humourist, b. 1945. She left school at 15 and had many jobs before training for community work in a youth club. She began writing while bringing up four children. Her very funny best-sellers, *The Secret Diary of Adrian Mole Aged 13¾*, 1982, and its sequel, 1984, present a teenage view of adolescence, gender relations, and Thatcher's Britain. They have been translated into 20 languages, and adapted for radio, TV and the stage. ST's first play, *Womberang* (Soho Poly, London, 1979), a comedy set in a gynaecological waiting-room, depicts a young working-class woman's battle with illness and the uncaring attitudes of caring institutions. Other plays use a style related to television sit-com, like *Bazaar and Rummage*, 1982, about women suffering from agoraphobia, and *Groping for Words*, 1983, about the fears and embarrassment of illiteracy. *The Great Celestial Cow* (1984, in collaboration with the THEATRE GROUP Joint Stock) deals with the cultural dilemma of Asian women living in Leicester, and celebrates female strength in a new, less naturalistic form. ST's journalism has appeared in a range of periodicals. In 1989 she published a pro-Welfare-State pamphlet, and *True Confessions* of Adrian Mole and of teenage Margaret Hilda Roberts (later career said to be unknown: the future Mrs Thatcher).

Townsend, Theophila, d. 1692, prominent Quaker and pamphleteer. Her *Testimony* for Jane Whitehead, 1676 (parts written by others), describes Whitehead's sufferings with Ann AUDLAND in Oxfordshire, her marriage and imprisonment at Ilchester, Somerset, having stood trial 'with a young Child sucking at her Breast'. TT offers Whitehead as a role-model and reproves Quaker backsliders. Imprisoned herself in 1681, she became gravely ill before release in 1686; she describes her sufferings and those of other Friends in *A Word of Counsel* [1687/8]. In *An Epistle of Love to Friends in the Womens Meetings in London* (with others, 1686), she laments the death of Anne WHITEHEAD, whom she praises for humility. Here and elsewhere she voices conservative views on women's role.

Traill, Catharine Parr (Strickland), 1802–99, writer of juvenile fiction, sketches, and essays; naturalist. She was the sister of Susanna MOODIE and Agnes and Elizabeth STRICKLAND. Her first works were juvenile stories. *Little Downy; or The History of a Field Mouse. A Moral Tale*, 1822, continues to interest, both as accurate observation of nature and as a 'moral' about female initiative, responsibility, and daring. *The Young Emigrants; or Pictures of Canada Calculated to Amuse and Instruct the Minds of Youth*, 1826, predicts CPT's own positive attitude when, in 1832, she married Lieutenant Thomas T. and migrated with him to the Ontario backwoods, where her brother and sister were already settled. They moved to Peterborough, 1839, to Rice Lake, 1846. When he died, 1859, CPT moved to Lakefield, where she spent the rest of her life. They had seven surviving children. (Her daughter Mary Elizabeth, later Muchall, published two small volumes of poetry: *Step by Step, or The Shadow on a Canadian Home*, 1876, a temperance tale of alcohol's tragic consequences, and *The Stolen Skates*.) In Canada CPT made her published sketches and essays about her experiences as a settler an important source of family income. Unlike her sister, CPT sought to show both the advantages and the hardships of immigrant life: both her *Backwoods of Canada: Being Letters from the Wife of an Emigrant Officer; Illustrative of the Domestic Economy of British America*, 1836 (which describes their voyage, their settling, and the bird and plant life of the new world), and *The Female Emigrant's Guide, and Hints on Canadian Homemaking*, 1854, were popular and successful. *The Canadian Crusoes: A Tale of the Rice Lake Plains*, 1852, for juveniles, makes its pioneer heroes children: lost in the woods, they survive on their own for two years. CPT is increasingly recognized for her skills as a naturalist: *Canadian Wild Flowers*, 1868, with sketches by Agnes Fitzgibbon, a daughter of Susanna Moodie, is an abbreviation of *Studies of Plant Life in Canada; or, Gleanings from Forest, Lake, and Plains*, 1885. Allusion to CPT is an important strand in Margaret LAURENCE's *The Diviners*, 1974.

Translation (For its first English female practitioners, see NUNS.) John Florio, famous for englishing Montaigne, held that 'translations are reputed femalls', because subsidiary to their begetters. Whether or not for this cause, many RENAISSANCE ladies translated: both classical literature and key religious texts, e.g. Ann BACON, Jane LUMLEY, Margaret TYLER. Renderings of Petrarch by Elizabeth Carey or Carew, 1576–1635, later Lady Berkeley, are apparently lost. Katherine PHILIPS wrote in letters about theories of translation. After the Restoration it became and remained a fairly reliable though ill-paid source of earnings, sometimes bringing status to scholars (to Elizabeth CARTER, but not to e.g. Anne FRANCIS), but only bare survival to struggling women like Charlotte FORMAN. Ninety-three per cent of eighteenth-century female translators wrote in other genres as well. Sarah AUSTIN and her daughter, Lucy Duff GORDON, achieved distinction as translators of French and German (male) canonical writings; Mary HOWITT translated works by Swedish feminist novelist Frederika Bremer; Mathilde BLINDE first translated Marie Bashkirtseff's influential diary; Harriet PRESTON began her novelist's career by translating works about women. Ellen CLERKE translated Italian poetry; Emma LAZARUS translated ancient Hebrew poems when disaffected by her own culture. Lady Charlotte Guest, 1812–95, published at Llandovery the first English version of the medieval Welsh *Mabinogion* and *Tale of Taliesin*, 1838–49. Matilda HAYS translated George SAND, as did Margaret SWEAT. Fanny Elizabeth Bunnett, 1832?–75, was a prolific translator from the German, as was Anna SWANWICK (who also, like Augusta WEBSTER, translated Aeschylus). George ELIOT translated Strauss and Feuerbach; her essay on 'Translations and Translators' emphasizes the moral dimensions of the task (patience, fidelity, responsibility). See Margaret Homans, *Bearing the Word*, 1986, for an account of the nineteenth-century feminization of translation. Lady GREGORY's renderings from ancient Irish include some in female voices, like 'Donal Ogue'. Constance GARNETT, Elaine FEINSTEIN and Gayatri SPIVAK are modern examples of translators whose work has transformed literary consciousness by the infusion of new voices. Recent years have seen a rapid increase in the numbers of bilingual women writers – translators of themselves, whether in print, like Ursule MOLINARO, or at a gestatory stage of composition – and of women like Joy KOGAWA whose texts incorporate more than one tongue. Writers like Monique WITTIG (*Lesbian Peoples: Material for a Dictionary*, 1976) and Mary DALY (*Webster's First New Intergalactic Wickedary of the English Language*, 1987) aim to replace the man-made language so far used by both sexes. Suzette Haden ELGIN depicts such a replacement.

Trapnel, Anna, Baptist and Fifth Monarchist prophet, da. of William T., shipwright of Poplar, London. At the trial of Vavasour Powell she fell into an 11-day trance, and many came to hear her prophesy, chiefly about Cromwell's being made Protector. She recorded these pronouncements twice in 1654: briefly in *Strange and Wonderful Newes* and at greater length in *The Cry of a Stone*, with an account of her childhood, adolescence, and conversion after a period of uncertainty. She gives her prophecies in verse; their appeal is radically egalitarian, directly addressing affairs of State. Two more works of the same year, her *Report and Plea* and *A Legacy for Saints*, give further biographical details and cover her later visit to Fifth Monarchist MPs in Cornwall, her arrest on suspicion of being a witch, and imprisonment in Bridewell for PREACHING. Questioned in court about being unmarried, she replied, 'Then having no hindrance, why may not I go where I please, if the Lord so will?' Her *Voice for the King of Saints*, 1658, records another trance and series of verse prophecies (vindicating AT as Christ's spouse and lamenting the betrayal of the revolution); when Quaker men attempted to interrupt her, she drowned them out by her singing. See Elaine Hobby, 1988.

Travel writing. Women were early narrators of distant (Marjery KEMPE) and more homely journeys (Celia FIENNES, Sarah KNIGHT). The problems of the road are a constant theme for missionary QUAKERS. From the eighteenth century, those who left home for family reasons often revelled in reporting what they saw, like Lady Mary Wortley MONTAGU, Eliza FAY, and Mrs Blanckley, whose diary of *Six Years'*

Residence in Algiers during 1806–12 was published by her daughter, 1839. The guidebook also had female pioneers like Sarah MURRAY, Mariana STARKE, and Susanna WATTS. Nineteenth-century female travellers can be divided into three broad categories: daughters, wives or occasionally sisters of men posted overseas in their careers; missionaries; and the 'Globe-Trotteresses' who quested after experience, adventure or curious plants (like Marianne North), fish or butterflies. Many produced mere guidebooks, full of facts and statistics; the best rely on the narrator's character and responses. Travel offered women physical and intellectual challenge, a loosening of convention, and often increased understanding of the nuances of their own culture. Frances TROLLOPE criticized the US, Germany, Paris, Austria and Italy. May French Sheldon found that bureaucratic opposition in East Africa 'developed and tried my metal' (*Sultan to Sultan*, 1892). 'Nelly Bly' (Elizabeth COCHRANE) went *Around the World in 72 Days*, 1880, Kate Marsden *On Sledge and Horseback to Outcast Siberian Lepers*, 1893, and Ethel Brilliana Tweedie *Through Finland in Carts*, 1897. Amelia EDWARDS went *A Thousand Miles up the Nile*, 1877, before establishing London Univ.'s first Chair in Egyptology; Fanny Bullock Workman had herself photographed on a Himalayan mountain holding a 'Votes for Women' poster. Mrs R. M. Coopland made *A Lady's Escape from Gwalior* during mutinies, 1859; Louise Vescalius-Shelden was one of the *Yankee Girls in Zululand*, 1889, Agnes Herbert extolled the pleasure of getting 'to a corner of the world by yourself ... and do[ing] a gallop round, tail in air, just when you like' (*Casuals in the Caucasus*, 1912; her authenticity has recently been questioned). Agnes Deans Cameron went up to the Mackenzie River to explore *The New North*, 1910; Constance Gordon-Cummings (Ceylon, Fiji, Hawaii, the Hebrides, Northern India, Egypt and China) rivalled Isabella BIRD. Joan, Lady LINDSAY, delightfully parodied the genre in *Through Darkest Pondelayo: An Account of Adventures of Two English Ladies on a Cannibal Island*, 1936, as 'Serena Livingstone-Stanley'. Studies by Dorothy Middleton, 1965, Alexandra Allen, 1983, Mary Russell, 1986, Maria Aitken, 1987, and Dea Birkett, 1989. In this century the intrepid tradition has been maintained by e.g. Ella MAILLART, Rosita FORBES, Freya STARK and Dervla MURPHY. The project of interpreting cultures distant either in geography or in ethos has been undertaken by e.g. (for China) 'HAN SUYIN' and Agnes SMEDLEY, (for theatres of war) Martha GELLHORN, Mary MCCARTHY and Susan SONTAG. Many black writers settled in the USA and elsewhere have created vital statements about journeys undertaken in search of their roots in Africa or, like Amryl JOHNSON, in the Caribbean.

'Travers, John', Eva Mary Bell, 1878–1959, novelist, journalist, lecturer, da. of Charlotte (Lewis) and Robert Craigie Hamilton. She was educ. at St Winifred's, Eastbourne, and m. Lieutenant-Colonel G. H. B., of the Indian Army. Her 11 novels (most pub. under her pseudonym) had an Indian setting, such as *Sahib Log*, 1912, *Those Young Married People*, 1922, *Safe Conduct*, 1927, and the historical fiction, *The Foreigner*, 1928. Spending 13 years in the country, EB was a recognized authority on Indian social subjects, especially the lives of Indian soldiers' wives. Editor and part-author of *Indian Women and War*, 1910, she was also very active in informing Indian soldiers and their wives about England, and was the only woman to have lectured at the Staff College, Quetta. She also ed. *The Hamwood Papers*, 1930, about the Ladies of LLANGOLLEN and Caroline Hamilton, and was awarded the OBE and the Kaisar-i-Hind medal.

Travers, P. L., Pamela Lydon, poet, critic, children's writer, b. in Queensland,

Australia, in 1906, of a Scots-Irish mother and Irish father. She moved to England as a teenager and, encouraged by A. E. (George Russell), submitted her first poems, 1924–8, to *The Irish Statesman*. Drama critic for *The New English Weekly* in the 1930s and after her return from the USA at the end of the war, until its demise in 1949, she also gave it poems, travel essays (based on her 1934 trip to Moscow), and some film reviews. Much of her fame today rests on the octet of Mary Poppins books, 1934–88, about a timeless, peremptory, almost-mythical nanny (see Jonathan Cott's interview, *Pipers at the Gates of Dawn*, 1983). In the USA in the early 1940s, she published *I Go By Sea, I Go By Land*, 1941, the diary of a British child evacuee, and a series of privately circulated New Year's gift books, many autobiographical: *Aunt Sass* concerns a crusty but ultimately kind-hearted Australian relative, *Johnny Delaney*, 1944, an Irish jockey employed on a sugar plantation. PLT has lectured widely, at Smith, Radcliffe, and Scripps College, Calif., on the importance and relevance of myth and fairy tale. *Friend Monkey*, 1971, though set in Victorian times, really deals with the Hanuman figure from the *Ramayana*. PLT is currently a Consulting Editor for *Parabola; the Magazine of Myth and Tradition*.

Travers, Rebecca, *c.* 1609–88, prolific QUAKER pamphleteer. Once a Baptist, she was converted by James Nayler; she m. William T., London tobacconist, before 1656, and had a daughter and a son. In 1659 she pub. *Of that Eternal Breath* and *For Those that Meet to Worship*, both recording the fury she met with when speaking out against preachers. *A Testimony Concerning the Light and Life of Jesus*, 1663, counsels Friends to stay faithful and not to be misled by Ranter-like spirits who are the sorceress Jezebel, whose 'witchcrafts and enchantments will multiply', whose offspring is cursed. *This is for All, or Any*, 1664 (part in verse), complains of State persecution of Friends, of families split, of people improverished or even banished. *A Testimony for God's Everlasting Truth*, 1669, is a long, closely-argued refutation of anti-Quaker tracts by Robert Cobbet and Elizabeth ATKINSON. Mary PENNINGTON's husband, too, attacked her. Her many testimonials to Friends includes one to Joan WHITROW's daughter, 1677, and Anne WHITEHEAD, 1686.

Treadwell, Sophie, 1890–1970, journalist, playwright, novelist, b. in Stockton, Calif., da. of Nellie (Fairchild) and Alfred B. T. At the Univ. of California, Berkeley (BA, 1906), she wrote and acted in plays. She worked briefly on the San Francisco *Bulletin*, covering WWI as the first accredited woman correspondent of a US paper. In 1910, she m. William O. McGeehan, a sportwriter and columnist for the NY *Herald Tribune*. For this paper she covered the Carranza revolution in Mexico, getting exclusive interviews with General Obregon and Pancho Villa. Her creative work was much influenced by her JOURNALISM experiences: both *Gringo*, 1922 (a play), and *Lusita*, 1931 (a novel), include characters based on Villa. In the novel (amid acute analysis of US–Mexican relations) a young woman assumed to be in need of rescue from revolutionaries turns out to be their ally. ST's central work, *Machinal*, 1928, evolved from her coverage of the Snyder-Gray murder trial: it asks 'How is it possible for a ... woman ... to be so oppressed by life and by her husband that she kills him?' Technically experimental (episodic structure, telegraphic, sometimes layered, dialogue), it declares deep interest in psychology (Freud, on the one hand, and the court use of 'psychological evidence', on the other). (See Jennifer Parent in *Drama Review*, 26, 1982.) *Ladies Leave*, 1929, is a satire about domestic boredom and psychoanalysts, *Plumes in the Dust*, 1936, a dramatized life of Poe. *Hope for a Harvest* (38 performances, 1941), exposes racism about new immigrants in rural

California, but was blamed by the leftist press for ascribing rural decay to moral failings rather than monopoly control of markets. *One Fierce Hour and Sweet*, 1959, is a novel on the themes of *Ladies Leave*. MSS at the Univ. of Arizona (Tucson).

Tree, Iris, 1897–1968, poet, da. of Maud (Holt), teacher and actress, and actor–manager Herbert Beerbohm T. (who also had another, illegitimate family), younger sister of Viola TREE. She was educ. by governesses, then at Miss Wolff's school where she met and exchanged poems with Nancy CUNARD, then at the Slade School of Art, London. Sharing a studio with Cunard, she delighted in shocking: 'I have had twenty-eight / lovers, some more / some less.' In 1915 Solita SOLANO printed one of her poems in the *Boston Herald-Traveler* (IT was in the USA with her parents); Viola read another ('The days come up like beggars in the street') at the Georgian Poetry Society. In 1916 IT married American painter Curtis Moffat: a poem offers him 'my spilt blood in a goblet'; she was determined that her first child should be a son. She published in *Poetry*, in the *Wheels* anthology, and in two volumes entitled *Poems*, 1917 and 1920. Her letters are brilliant concoctions of fantasy and hyperbole. Having fallen in love with Friedrich Ledebur, high-born Austrian horsebreaker and film actor (whom she married in 1934 and later divorced), IT published *The Traveller, and other poems*, NY, 1927, for much-needed cash: it is rare because the secretary of Max Reinhardt, for whom she had acted, bought up most copies. 'I come from all your margins, from your stress / Of questioning, and I am the dividing guess / Of life to dream. Or just a woman in a dress.' She wandered England, Europe and the USA, 'wrote several plays' in Ireland, and joined experimental theatres in Totnes, Devon, Ridgefield, Conn. (where she wrote *Sing About It*, a play for children), and the Ojai Valley, Calif. (with actor Ford Rainey; theatre opened with her *Second Wind*, created from group improvisations). In Rome she wrote 230 pp. of a novel later abandoned, and published poems in *Botteghe Oscure*. Her melodrama *Strangers' Wharf* was well received in London. She played herself in Fellini's film *La Dolce Vita*, 'For the lolly, of course!' In Switzerland in the early 1960s she worked on an autobiography, though lacking diaries and letters destroyed by others in Calif.; later her car was stolen with 'typescripts of plays, unfinished articles' and the opening of a long poem, some pages of which she rescued from a ditch and the branches of a tree; other pieces vanished with a young man who had undertaken to type fair copies. The poem, *The March Picnic* [1966], with preface by John Betjeman, presents herself as a 'withering lady' choosing a remote site for a utopia with friends: the group quarrels; the place becomes a resort, 'under pavement'. IT died in London after a colon operation; her last poem begins 'Bury me under a tree / Because of my name and ancestry.' Life by Daphne Fielding, 1974, is unscholarly but gripping.

Tree, Viola, 1884–1938, actress, singer, memoirist, b. in London, much older sister of Iris TREE. Her father urged her to act: she attended the Academy of Dramatic Art (founded by him) and from 1908 the Royal College of Music. After a debut as Ariel, 1904, she had many stage successes with him, but turned increasingly to singing till she gave it up to marry, 1912, successful civil servant (and drama critic) Alan Parsons (d. 1933). They had three children. In 1920 she, Iris, and their mother contributed to memoirs of her father, ed. Max Beerbohm. In 1923, jointly with Gerald du Maurier as 'Hubert Parsons', VT wrote a play, *The Dancers*, and adapted it as a novel: 'his story, my writing'. Her own play, *The Swallow*, was unpub.; she wrote for *Vogue* and for newspapers on the stage, interior decor and gardening. Virginia WOOLF, who enjoyed VT's 'great egotism' and 'magnification of self', published her *Castles in the Air. The Story of My Singing Days*, 1926 (which draws on diaries and letters and is revealing on her relations with her father, but did less well than hoped because of the general strike), and *Can I Help You?*, 1937 (an etiquette book based on her Sunday paper column, full of personal memories, parodied by Ada LEVERSON), but drew the line at editing the heterogeneous mass of material which appeared as the memoir-anthology *Alan Parsons' Book*, 1937.

Trefusis, Elizabeth, 'Ella', 1763?–1808, poet and unpublished novelist, da. of Anne (St John) and Robert Cotton T. of Trefusis, Cornwall, who re-married before his death in 1778. William Beloe (a suspect witness) said she became poor from subsidizing young poets, and over-used sleeping potions. He named as her friends Anna SEWARD, H. L. PIOZZI (who referred to her lesbianism in 1794), and (despite ET's strong monarchist views) H. M. WILLIAMS. She lived for a time at Bletsoe, Beds. Her posthumous *Poems and Tales*, 1808, after a jaunty introduction rhyming 'Trefusis' to 'Muses', is chiefly romantic in tone: *vers de société* like an advertisement (in a friend's name) for a wife, but also fables, ballads, lyrics, a poem on the death of her mother ('Too good for earth'), and tale of a heroine in her dead brother's armour challenging her lover to single combat. Some are repr. from magazines; many come from juvenile novels since destroyed ('Claribell' and 'Eudora'), a pastoral romance ('The Cousins') and other works. Rumour suggested, wrongly, that her family might publish some of these; a BL copy of her poems adds eight MS pieces, five unpublished.

Trefusis, Violet (Keppel), 1894–1972, novelist, b. in London, elder da. of Alice (Edmonstone), socialite and mistress to Edward VII, and Col. George K. Educ. by governesses, she grew up partly in France; she wrote four of her seven novels in French. Her early friendship with Vita SACKVILLE-WEST became in 1918 a love-affair; in 1919, only weeks after VT's marriage to Major Denys T. of the Royal Horse Guards, the two 'eloped' abroad together for the second time. The relationship (in which Vita, known as 'Julian', often wore male dress) was described by Vita in *Challenge* (pub. in the US, 1924, after the English ed., was cancelled: repr. 1974), by WOOLF in *Orlando* (VT is the Russian princess, Sasha), and by VT in *Broderie Anglaise*, 1935 (in French: transl. 1985), which casts Vita as a man. By 1921 the affair was over. VT and her husband settled in Paris; her first novel, *Sortie de secours*, appeared in 1929, the year he died. Her charming, witty fiction is peopled, like her life, with the wealthy, talented, and eccentric; houses are sometimes nearly as important as humans. *Echo*, 1931, transl. 1988, depicts the civilizing influence of a young Frenchwoman on rambunctious Scottish twins (VT knew Scotland as her mother's country). *Tandem*, Hogarth Press, 1933, follows the lives of sisters married into 'the whirl of fashionable literary life in Paris and the immovable respectability of the English hunting circle'. *Hunt the Slipper*, 1937, repr. 1983, paints a middle-aged love-affair with comic insight. *Les Causes perdues*, 1941, was VT's last French novel; WWII drove her to England (as related in *Prelude to Misadventure*, 1942), where she published magazine stories and broadcast for Radio Free France; from 1947 she lived part in Paris, part in Florence. She wrote an autobiography, *Don't Look Round*, 1952, and two *jeux d'esprit*: the joint *Memoirs of an* [eighteenth-century] *Armchair*, 1960, and *From Dusk to Dawn*, 1972. Lives of her by Philippe Jullian and John Phillips, 1976, and Henrietta Sharpe, 1981, make less of her writing than of her social life as hostess to such as COLETTE and Nancy MITFORD. Her letters to Vita were pub. 1989.

Tremain, Rose (Thomson), novelist, dramatist, historian, da. of Jane (Dudley) and writer Keith Nicholas Thomson, who left home (importantly for her) when she was ten. B. in 1943 in London, she was educ. at Frances Holland School, the Sorbonne (diploma in literature, 1963), and the Univ. of East Anglia (BA in English, 1967). She taught in London for two years and worked at editing and part-time research before writing full-time. She married Jon Tremain in 1971 and has two children (divorced 1978). Her first two books, carefully researched vehicles for strong opinions, appeared in the USA, not in Britain. *The Fight for Freedom for Women*, 1973, on the SUFFRAGE movement in Britain and the USA, warns that political quiescence could re-institutionalize former inequities. A life of Stalin, 1975, attempts to explain him by reference to his childhood, and denies any possible competence to judge him. RT turned to fiction with *Sadler's Birthday*, 1976. She likes to 'express ideas through characters absolutely unlike myself'; her protagonists are often male. She exposes the emotional thinness of many lives, and the debility of age, but the overall effect is one of strength, humour, and poignancy. People do offer each other shelter and comfort, albeit 'this human race is so sad disaster' (*The Swimming Pool Season*, 1985, which makes complex emotional use of the object of its title). RT teaches creative writing at East Anglia, and has published children's books, criticism, and plays for radio and TV. *Temporary Shelter* appeared in Methuen's *Best Radio Plays of 1984*. *Mother's Day* was staged in London, 1980, *Yoga Class* in Liverpool, 1984. She married Jonathan Dudley in 1982. The title story in the collection *The Garden of the Villa Mollini*, 1987, portrays a monstrously egotistical opera-singer and the succession of wives and mistresses who fail to bear him a son. *Restoration*, 1989, uses the reign of Charles II to figure contemporary Britain.

Trench, Melesina (Chenevix), also St George, 1768–1827, letter writer and poet, b. in Dublin, da. of Mary Elizabeth (Gervais) and Philip C.: orphaned, and reared by a harsh governess and aged grandfather. She m. Richard St George in 1786, a 'pleasing dream' turned to nightmare by his illness: she shipped his corpse from Portugal for Ireland on her 22nd birthday. Her surviving journals, written irregularly on loose sheets, are skimpy on these years, and on fashionable London (which she hated), fuller from 1799. In 1802 she began exchanging letters with Mary LEADBEATER, full of critical comment on books (many by women), with some poems and essays. She also wrote to the ladies of LLANGOLLEN (letters lost) and later to E. D. TUITE. Having married Richard T. in Paris in 1803, she was kept in France by war till 1807. She bore in all eight sons and a daughter, 'almost the only link which connected me strongly with my own sex', who was 'resumed by Heaven' at four, in 1816. As when an earlier son died, MT mourned passionately in prose and verse. Her anonymous slim volumes of poetry, mostly pub. Southampton and Bath, contain tales of past ages (sometimes confused in narrative though fluent in verse) or comment on recent events; *The Assize Ball*, Dorchester, 1820, effectively contrasts the ball and the prison next door. She wished she had had less flattery, more criticism and instruction; her prose (including pamphlets on education, pub. in her lifetime and repr. 1837; the slave trade 'Addressed to English Women'; taxes, and [illegible] children) is vivid and to the point. In 1861 a son ed. a European journal and *Remains* from her MSS.

Trimmer, Sarah (Kirby), 1741–1810, educational and CHILDREN'S writer, b. at Ipswich, da. of Sarah (Bull) and John Joshua K., engraver, who moved to London about 1755 to teach the future George III. As a girl she impressed Samuel Johnson; her diary, begun in 1785, including meditations and prayers, followed his example. In 1762 she m. James T. (whose sister Selina worked for Georgiana DEVONSHIRE and was written about by Virginia WOOLF) and settled at Brentford near London. In this poor area ST's Sunday school was, from 1782, an oasis of self-improvement. *An Easy Introduction to the Knowledge of Nature*, 1780 (following A. L. BARBAULD), teaches reverence for God's creation in a maternal monologue whose unrelenting instructiveness easily palls. Other works, constantly reprinted, some with changes of title, cover Bible study and many other topics; she took from Mme de GENLIS the idea of pictures as teaching aids. She opposed fairy tales and 'unsound books': *Fabulous Histories* (1786, later *The History of the Robins*) features highly bourgeois bird families; *The Servant's Friend*, 1787, tells of a little boy making good. *The Oeconomy of Charity*, 1787, is a handbook on running schools for deprived children, offering 'merely ... to my own sex a few thoughts': personal experience, shrewdness, controlled indignation, concern for immortal souls. Several later books pursue the same subject; ST politicized the issue of EDUCATION. Her *Family Magazine*, 1788–9, for servants and other recent readers, is surprisingly varied. She admired Hester CHAPONE, inspired Hannah MORE, and recognized the 'extraordinary abilities' of Mary WOLLSTONECRAFT. Nine of her 12 children survived her. Life with selected personal writings, 1814.

Trist, Margaret (Lucas), 1914–86, novelist, short-story writer, b. Dalby, Queensland, da. of Edith (Hargraves) and George L., a stock and station agent. At 17 she moved to Sydney where she lived for most of her life. In 1933 she m. Frank T.; she had two children. Her short stories first appeared in the *Bulletin* and later in anthologies such as *Coast to Coast*. Whilst her output and range is limited, her two colls. of short stories, *In the Sun*, 1943, and *What Else is There?*, 1946, and three novels, display skilful, witty reconstructions of small town life. *Now That We're Laughing*, 1945, set in the Blue Mountains of NSW, captures country parochialism. *Daddy*, 1947, concerns a disaffected and self-centred man's relationship with his family, while *Morning in Queensland*, 1958, the story of a girlhood dominated by adult women, deftly evokes the pain of growing up in a country town. R. G. Geering discusses her work in *Southerly*, 1986.

Trollope, Frances Eleanor (Ternan), 1834–1913, novelist, eldest da. of actress and singer Frances Eleanor (Jarman), 1803–73, and Irish actor Thomas T. (d. in Bethnal Green lunatic asylum, 1846). She and her sisters were educ. by their mother and then acted with her during the 1850s. The youngest, Ellen, secretly became Dickens's mistress. FET went to Italy to pursue an operatic career, but in 1866 m. the widowed Thomas Adolphus T. (son of Frances TROLLOPE), to whose daughter she had been companion governess, and then became a successful novelist. Her plots are weak, but she describes life in provincial England and modern Italy with realism and humour. Her knowledge of theatrical touring was put to lively use in *Mabel's Progress*, 1867. *A Charming Fellow*, 1876, takes a sharp look at male self-indulgence.

Trollope, Frances (Milton), 1780–1863, novelist and travel writer, b. Stapleton, nr. Bristol, second da. of the Rev. William M. Her mother d. the following year, the family having moved to Heckfield, Hampshire, and her father remarried. FT was educ. in French and Italian at home. In 1803 she went to live with her brother and elder sister in Bloomsbury, where she met Thomas Anthony T., barrister, whom she m. in 1809. She had five children, including the novelist Anthony, and Cecilia (Mrs John Tilley), 1816–49, who wrote a novel, *Chollerton: A Tale of our own Times*, pub. anon. 1846, to embody her high church principles with some humour and gift for observation. FT's husband's ill-health and financial incompetence forced her to earn for the family, and to this end she went to America to support the Utopian commune in Nashoba founded by her friend Frances WRIGHT and to initiate a commercial venture. The trip, though an economic failure, led to her earliest and most notorious work, *Domestic Manners of the Americans*, 1832, whose acidly patronizing view of the New World foreshadows Dickens's later attacks. Her extensive writings include TRAVEL books, 'society' novels and Evangelical fiction such as *The Vicar of Wrexhill*, 1837, and *Father Eustace*, 1847. Her 'industrial' novels, such as *The Life and Adventures of Michael Armstrong, Factory Boy*, 1840, and *Jessie Phillips*, 1844, were innovative in their portrayal of child labour. Her sharp eye for detail and her satirical observation save even her most conventional fiction from mere romantic orthodoxy. She eventually settled in Florence with her eldest son, Thomas Adolphus, and his wife, and continued writing until she was 76. See Anthony Trollope's *Autobiography*, 1883, *A Memoir of Frances Trollope*, 1895, by her daughter-in-law, Frances Eleanor TROLLOPE, and Thomas Adolphus T., *What I Remember*, 1887, for her life; also Johanna Johnston's 1979 biography.

Trotter, Catharine, later **Cockburn**, 1679–1749, dramatist (as T.), philosophical writer (as Cockburn), intellectual, and defender of women. Da. of David T., Scots naval officer who d. 1684, and Sarah (Bellenden), who brought up two daughters in genteel poverty, she composed extemporary verse, was taught Latin and logic, picked up French, and became (till 1707) a Roman Catholic. At 14 she was in print: complimentary verse and a short novel, *Olinda's Adventures*, in Samuel Briscoe's *Letters . . . Written by Ladies*, 1693: repr. 1718 and 1969. The heroine confides to a male friend the saga of her nine suitors: now 18, kept single by a married admirer, she waits in chaste limbo. As 'a Lady', probably from need, CT wrote moralizing tragedies on extreme love situations: dedicated to nobles, repr. 1982 with plays by Mary PIX. *Agnes de Castro*, acted 1695, pub. 1696, is an old-style Senecan handling of an Aphra BEHN story. *Fatal Friendship* (1698; in Fidelis Morgan, ed., 1981) has psychological penetration as well as much-admired reforming intent. After *The Unhappy Penitent*, 1701, *The Revolution of Sweden*, 1706, presents female heroic patriots like Margaret NEWCASTLE's. CT's didactic comedy, *Love at a Loss*, was acted 1700, pub. 1701; her later revised and retitled version never appeared. She was a target of *The Female Wits* (acted 1696), but probably not of Pope's early *Dunciad*. She contributed to *The Nine Muses* (q.v.), 1700, defended Damaris MASHAM and Elizabeth THOMAS, but fell out with Delarivier MANLEY. Locke praised her anonymous *Defence*, 1702, of his *Human Understanding*. She corresponded with Leibnitz, Elizabeth BURNET, Congreve and Farquhar, and pub. a theological *Discourse*, 1707 and 1728. On marriage, 1708, to the Rev. Patrick Cockburn, she bade 'adieu to the muses', living frugally, 'in a manner dead' (in Northumberland from 1726), till her children were grown. She published more moral and theological works, 1726, 1743, 1747, and a *GM* poem 'in the sex's cause', 1737. Thomas Birch ed. her works with a life, 1751: letters (notable literary ones to a niece from Aberdeen), one play, and essays (including advice to her son on religion, work and women). BLUESTOCKINGS subscribed. See Edmund Gosse, *TRSL*, 1916; Alison Fleming, *Scots Mag.*, 1940. MSS in BL.

Troubetzkoy, Amélie Louise (**Rives**), 1863–1945, novelist, poet, dramatist, b. Richmond, Virginia, da. of Sarah (Macmurdo) and Alfred Landon R., both of old Va. families. Educ. by tutors and governesses and encouraged by grandparents, both writers, she began writing early. She m. John Chanler, divorced 1895, and m. renowned portrait painter Prince Pierre T. in 1896. Her first publication, 'A Brother to Dragons' (*Atlantic*, 1886), a romantic Elizabethan story, was an immediate success. Other stories and poems appeared in *Century, Harper's,* and *Lippincott's*, but notoriety came with *The Quick or the Dead?*, 1888, which sold over 100,000 copies in three years. The sensual descriptions ('Barbara and Dering again devoured one another's rebellious faces with hungry eyes') link ART to the 'Erotic School' which included Gertrude ATHERTON and E. W. WILCOX. *Barbara Dering*, 1893, provided a sequel. *Virginia of Virginia*, 1888, has the heroine, a strong country woman who rides like a man, finally consumed by jealousy and unrequited love. ART's four-year morphine addiction is described realistically in her best novel, *Shadows of Flame*, 1915, one of the first such accounts in American literature. She wrote many other successful novels; poems (*Selene*, 1905, is a long narrative poem); and plays: 'Allegiance', 'The Fear Market' (also a film) and 'Love-in-a-Mist' all had successful Broadway runs. Although part of the Southern literary renaissance (she was a friend of Ellen GLASGOW), her affinities were cosmopolitan and she was one of 'The Souls', an English coterie led by Margot Asquith, Balfour and Curzon. While not dealing overtly with women's issues, she was interested in educational reform and women's suffrage. The largest coll. of her letters is in the Alderman Library at the Univ. of Virginia. See also G. Longest, *Three Virginia Writers*, 1978.

Truth, Sojourner, *c.* 1797–1883, abolitionist and feminist, b. a slave in Hurley, Ulster Co., NY, and brought up speaking Dutch. She escaped to freedom in 1827. With the help of the Van Wagener family, she successfully fought a legal battle for the freedom of her son (one of eight children by a fellow slave). As Isabella Van Wagener she moved to NYC and worked with evangelists to convert prostitutes, had visions, and heard voices that gave her a new name. During the 1850s she toured widely as gospel singer and ABOLITIONIST preacher, attracting huge audiences. Her autobiographical *Narrative of ST*, 1850, transcribed and ed. by Olive Gilbert (ST remained illiterate), shows her fervid commitment to abolish sexism as well as racism: 'Where did your Christ come from? From God and a woman! Man had nothing to do with Him!' See life by H. Pauli, 1962; 1878 ed. of *Narrative* repr. 1968.

Trye, Mary (O'Dowde), physician of Pall Mall, London. Her parents died of the plague in 1665, the year her father, Irishman Thomas O'D., pub. *The Poor Man's Physician.* Her *Medicatrix, or The Woman Physician*, 1675, defends 'chemical physicians' like him and herself against attacks from Henry Stubbe and the College of Physicians, linking their case to the more famous empiricists of the Royal Society. Dedicating to Jane Lane, Lady Fisher, she asserts 'It is little of Novelty to see a Woman in Print'. She writes clearly and contentiously, of herself and of the Society of Chemical Physicians: 'such fine things, as are prettily term'd Philosophical in [Stubbes], will scarce be thought rational in me'. See Elaine Hobby, 1988.

Tsvetayeva, Marina, 1892–1941, poet, b. in Moscow, da. of concert pianist Maria Alexandrovna Mein and art history professor Ivan Vladimirovich Tsvetaev. Educ. by governesses and in boarding schools in Switzerland, Germany, Moscow and Paris, she began to write at six and privately printed verses of her early teens in *Evening Album*, 1910. She was reviewed by established poet Max Voloshin, who introduced her to his celebrated literary boarding house, Kiktebel, where she met poet Sergei Efron (married 1912), to whom she dedicated *The Magic Lantern*, 1912. She had three children. *Mileposts 1*, 1922, celebrates her intense affairs in 1916 with poet Osip Mandelstam and translator and critic

Sophia Parnock. Because of the brutalities of the October Bolshevik coup, which separated her from her husband (who had become a White Officer), MT opposed the Liberal-Democratic Revolution of February, 1917. During the famine, she committed her second daughter to a state orphanage, where she died of malnutrition. During these hardships, MT wrote three books of meticulous, innovative lyric verse and her first epic poem, *Tsar Maiden*, 1922. She also befriended Mayakovsky, Pasternak and Alexander Blok. She migrated to Prague, 1922, to rejoin Efron, then to Paris, 1925. Her husband and son returned to the Soviet Union prior to WWII; under pressure from her son, she went back in 1939 unaware that her husband had been shot and her daughter arrested. In despair, partly because of her son's unceasing contempt, she hanged herself and was buried in an unmarked grave. See selec. poems, 1971, selec. prose, 1980, both trans. by Elaine FEINSTEIN, who also wrote a life, *Captive Lion*, 1987; study by Simon Karlinsky, 1986.

Tucker, Charlotte Maria, 'A. L. O. E.' (A Lady of England), 1821–93, CHILDREN's and religious writer, b. Barnet, Middx; her mother was Scottish and her father, St George T., was chairman of the East India Co. Educ. at home, she began writing verses and plays as a child, but only pub. after her father's death in 1851. She produced one book a year, all under her PSEUDONYM, and contributed the proceeds to charity. Among her highly moral tales for children are *The Claremont Tales*, 1851, *The Rambles of a Rat*, 1854, *The Robber's Cave*, 1863, and *Cyril Ashley*, 1870. Emma MARSHALL in Margaret OLIPHANT's *Women Novelists*, 1897, suggests didacticism often marred these stories but testifies to CMT's dedication and the great mid-century popularity of her books. In fact, many are notably realistic (she worked among the London poor). At 54, she went to India as an unpaid missionary to Punjabi women; she taught herself Hindustani. She continued writing, and at the time of her death in Amritsar had pub. 142 books, including her missionary works. There is a life by Agnes GIBERNE, 1895.

Tuite, Eliza Dorothea (Cobbe), Lady, 1764–1850, da. of Elizabeth Dorothea (Beresford) and Thomas C. of Newbridge, Co. Dublin. She m. Sir Henry T. in 1784. Her *Poems*, 1796, opening with a reply to Frances GREVILLE's 'Prayer for Indifference', include lyrics, tales, ballads, and pastorals, addressing friendship, love, and fluctuating moods. She repeatedly pictures the Muses as refusing her aid, but some pieces, particularly songs and occasional poems, are very pleasing. She attends both to the age's gore and treason, 'by horror stain'd', and also to its social and sexual wrong-doing – treated now seriously and now in a hudibrastic epistle beginning 'My ink was mouldy, hard, and dry, / My pens all spoilt by lying by, / Till rous'd by you, I woke my Muse, / And sent her out to pick up news'. A piece 'Intended for Mrs H. MORE's Cheap Publications' compares God's usage of men with men's of beasts. Her prose *Edwin and Mary*, 1818, for children, is sadly heavy-handed: girls must learn courage, but contempt for non-utilitarian flounces comes first. She pub. *Miscellaneous Poetry* at Bath, 1841.

Turell, Jane (Colman), 1708–35, poet, da. of Jane (Clark) and the Rev. Benjamin C., president of Harvard, who on a visit to England had admired and courted the future Elizabeth ROWE. He taught his daughter from infancy: by 18 she had gone through his classical and English library, and 'spent whole Nights' reading. She was writing verse (about God) at nine, and by 13 a secret diary. This 'filled much faster' after marriage, 1726, to the Rev. Ebenezer T. of Medford, Mass., though she restricted her writing because of her new duties, fearing conflict. Her husband felt that too much learning threatened feminine qualities, though he calls her 'fir'd with a laudable Ambition of raising the honour of her Sex'. She lost three out of four babies almost instantly, and writes of childbirth, 'My Eye-balls start, my Heart strings almost crack'd'. Her extant writings (Boston, 1735, retitled 1741, facs. 1979), framed in funeral sermons and memoirs by father and husband, include her own sketch of her divided mind. She prays the Muse for SAPPHO's fire and the power to rival Rowe and Katherine PHILIPS, yet advises her sister against reading romances and 'idle Poems', and repents reading them herself. The deaths of friends tempt her to blaspheme and despair. She wrote much on her mother's death, but accepted her father's immediate remarriage.

Turner, Ethel (Burwell), later Curlewis, 1872–1958, novelist, CHILDREN's writer, poet, b. Doncaster, England, da. of Sarah Jane (Shaw) and George B., who d. when she was two. Her mother remarried, to George T., and after his death came to Australia with her three daughters. ET was educ. at Sydney Girls' High School where she ed. the magazine *Iris* with her sister Lilian, who was also to become a children's writer. Later they ed. the monthly *Parthenon*. In 1896, ET m. H. R. C., a lawyer and later a judge; she had two children. Her first book, *Seven Little Australians*, 1894, is one of the classics of Australian children's literature, particularly for its tomboy heroine, Judy. Its best known sequel is *The Family at Misrule*, 1895. Altogether she pub. 27 novels, besides many colls. of short stories and poetry. *The Sunshine Family: A Book of Nonsense for Boys and Girls*, 1923, was written with her da., Jean Curlewis, who also wrote other books for children before dying of TB in 1930: after her death ET pub. no more books. MSS are in the National Library of Australia, Canberra, and in the Mitchell Library, Sydney. Selections from the diaries for 1889–1930 have been pub., 1979. The best criticism is by Brenda Niall, 1979.

Turner, Jane, religious autobiographer of Newcastle, Berwick, and London. Her husband (army captain John T.) and the Particular Baptist John Spilsbury introduce her *Choice Experiences*, 1654. She recounts her Presbyterian childhood and young womanhood, her conversion to the BAPTISTS after reading a book her minister falsely maligned (she hopes her own will be of comparable use to others), her brief spell with the QUAKERS, and her decision to leave them (this was answered by Edward Burrough, 1654). A religious conservative in some respects, she nonetheless presents her spiritual identity as clearly separate from her husband's: she counts as one of her blessings 'that the Lord should vouchsafe this mercy [return to the Baptists] to both of us, & that at one & the same time: and that at our return he should manifest such a sweet acceptance of us, melting our hearts into tears of joy, to our mutual comfort in the Lord, and in each other.' See Elaine Hobby, 1988.

Turner, Joanna (Cook), 1732–84, religious memoirist, da. of Honour (Shrapnell), who d. 1742, and John C., clothier, of Trowbridge, Wilts. She 'began to be unhappy very early, through my proud passionate disposition'. At boarding school she loved fine clothes, card-playing, and 'reading romances, novels, plays and other books of the devil's inspiring'; she also tried writing some. After her placid father's death about 1749, she wished to do right, burned her romances, read pious books, made a covenant with God, and felt herself 'a new creature'. Her relations disliked her preference for the poor; she lived alone on £29 a year, often depriving herself to give others a weekly meat meal. A brief autobiography ends here; letters, prayers, poems and journal entries (often exclamatory in style) record later efforts and relapses: 'O, what an ignorant, simple, foolish child am I!' After marrying Thomas T., 1766, she found time amongst shop and counting-house work to set up several new

Independent chapels. She died of breast cancer. Much of her writing in biography by Mary Wells, 1787: several reprints.

Turney, Catherine, screenwriter, playwright, novelist, b. 1906 in Chicago, da. of Elizabeth (Blamer) and George Weber T. Taken to NYC as a baby and to Calif. as a teenager, she studied theatre arts at Columbia School of Journalism, until 1925, and Pasadena Playhouse School of the Theatre, 1930–1, ran a touring company, and married Cyril Armbrister in 1931. She wrote for radio, from 1934; films (MGM, then from 1942 for Warner Brothers); the stage (*Bitter Harvest*, produced in London in 1936, treats the 'tragic' love of Byron for Augusta Leigh); and TV (from 1949). She is best known for her 'women's pictures', presenting Joan Crawford, Bette Davis and others in heroically isolated roles usually said to be angled towards women, but carefully judged to interest men too. After her second divorce, from George Reynolds in 1948, she moved for some time to NYC. Her romantic-toned prose works include *The Other One*, 1952 (a novel filmed in 1956 as *Bring Back the Dead* and repr. in 1968 as *Possessed*), and *Byron's Daughter*, 1972, a biography whose subject's parents are called 'very much a man's man in all ways' and 'a woman not conventionally beautiful but exactly his type'. The NYPL has the typed promptbook of *My Dear Children*, a hit first staged at Princeton in 1939.

Tweeddale, Violet (Chambers), 1862–1936, novelist and SPIRITUALIST, da. of Laura (Anderson), an invalid, and writer Robert C., who was also editor of *Chambers' Weekly*. She received no formal educ. Coming into money on her father's death, she moved to London, 1888, ran a night shelter for women in the East End, and met Muriel Menie DOWIE and Eliza Lynn LINTON. In 1891 she married Clarens T. They lived in Aberdeenshire and then Torquay, and travelled widely in Europe. After an alleged book of poems, untraced, she wrote several novels on politics and women's rights (she supported the SUFFRAGE). *And They Two*, 1897, charts the life of a socialist woman with a feminist view of marriage, who says that 'after loving a woman it is very difficult to love a man'; her husband breaks his promise of a non-sexual union, which causes her wedding-night suicide. The rise of socialism and the corruption of ideals figure in *The Sweets of Office*, 1907, and *Hypocrites and Sinners*, 1910; in *The Veiled Woman*, 1918, a wronged wife takes her brother's place in parliament and effects a women's revolution through disrupting industry and transport, then unveils her gender to shocked MPs. VCT's interest in psychic phenomena and Madame Blavatsky's theosophist circle informs *The House of the Other World*, 1913, *Ghosts I Have Seen*, 1920 (non-fiction which tells little about herself), *Found Dead*, 1928 (short stories), and *The Cosmic Christ*, 1930.

Tweedsmuir, Susan Charlotte (Grosvenor), also Buchan, Lady, 1882–1977, novelist, biographer, autobiographer, writer for children, b. in London of a distinguished and wealthy family. Her father, Norman de L'Aigle G., was a great-nephew of the Duke of Wellington, her mother, Caroline Susan (Wortley), a painter and novelist, friend of Marie Belloc-Lowndes Elizabeth ROBINS, Vernon LEE, and Gertrude BELL. After a childhood at home in London and the country, ST was 'flung into that most difficult of worlds, London society of the early years of this century'. In 1907, she married novelist John Buchan, brother of 'O. Douglas', later 1st Baron Tweedsmuir, and Governor-General of Canada, 1935–40. They had four children, and lived near Oxford, where ST was active in the work of the Women's Institute, in Scotland, London, and Canada, where, during the bleak years of the depression, she established the Lady Tweedsmuir Prairie Library Scheme, a CIRCULATING LIBRARY of some 40,000 volumes. She wrote four novels for children and four plays, two adapted from her husband's books, and biographies of Wellington, 1928, Charlotte of Albany, 1935, and Lady Louisa STUART, 1932. The first of her five adult novels, *The Scent of Water*, 1937, was written when official mourning for George V prevented the Governor-General from accepting engagements. *The Rainbow through the Rain*, 1950, dedicated to Elizabeth BOWEN, brings together ST's English and Canadian worlds. The epistolary *Cousin Harriet*, 1957, sketches sharply separated male and female spheres, dramatizing female sexual and reproductive life as quite 'other' to the public world of authority and official identity. ST's reminiscences, *John Buchan*, 1947 (in which she was assisted by her friend Catherine CARSWELL), *The Lilac and the Rose*, 1952, *A Winter Bouquet*, 1954, and *The Edwardian Lady*, 1966 (quoted above), are incisive, sometimes critical reflections on her life and times.

Twysden, Isabella (Saunder), Lady, 1605–57, diarist, da. of Elizabeth (Blunt) and Sir Nicholas S. of Nonsuch near Ewell in Surrey, who lost his money in a capitalist scheme. By 1632 she was waiting-lady to Lady Anne T. of Roydon Hall, Kent (a woman of learning, who wrote prayers), whose son Sir Roger, legal and historical writer, she married in 1635. Their six children all survived. When he was arrested in 1642 and his estate sequestered, she fought a hostile bureaucracy and made 'great journeys' between London and Kent, riding pillion less than a month before childbirth. Unlike his moving account of her death, her diary is succinct and factual: public life, family finance and movements, births, deaths and portents (1645, 1647–9: MS in BL; ed., for Kent Archaeological Soc., 1939).

Tyler, Anne, novelist, short-story writer. B. in Minneapolis, in 1941, da. of Phyllis (Mahon) and chemist Lloyd T., she grew up in 'an experimental Quaker community in the wilderness,' in Raleigh, NC, and spent her childhood 'sitting behind a book waiting for adulthood to arrive.' She attended Duke Univ. (BA, 1961), where she studied with Reynolds Price, won awards in creative writing, and published her first story, 1959. She followed her Russian degree with graduate work at Columbia, and has worked as a Russian bibliographer and librarian at universities. AT m. Iranian psychiatrist and novelist Taghi Mohammed Modaressi, 1963; they have two daughters. Since 1967 she has lived in Baltimore, Md, the locale of much of her writing. Influenced by Eudora WELTY and other southern regionalists, AT has published 11 novels, plus dozens of short stories in magazines such as *The Southern Review*, *The New Yorker*, *Cosmopolitan*, and *Redbook*. Her novels, from *If Morning Ever Comes*, 1964, in which a law student drifts into marriage during a weekend at home, to *Breathing Lessons*, 1988, which examines the strains and strengths of a 28-year marriage, explore family relationships and domestic transitions. Seen through AT's 'mist of irony', ordinary events and people, such as the determinedly pedestrian travel-writer protagonist of the popular *Accidental Tourist*, 1985 (filmed 1988), become significant, eccentric and even sublime. See AT in Janet Sternberg, ed., *The Writer on Her Work*, 1980, Mary F. Robertson in Rainwater and Scheick, eds., 1985, Joseph C. Voelker, *Art and the Accidental in AT*, 1989, essays ed. C. Ralph Stephens, 1990.

Tyler, Margaret, translator. A dependent of the leading Catholic family of Howard, she had reached 'aged years' by [1578], when she translated and pub. the first book of a Spanish ROMANCE, Diego Ortunez de Calahorra's *The Mirrour of Princely Deedes and Knighthood*. Her preface (repr. in Moira Ferguson, *First Feminists*, 1985) says this work was not chosen but 'put upon me by others'; it hopes these 'exploits of wars' will inspire young men to 'magnanimitie and courage', and discusses the problems of TRANSLATION. She seems to expect readers to disapprove of work written 'to beguile time' (not for religious ends), or at least of women's handling such material: she firmly controverts both positions, and alludes to ladies' exercising PATRONAGE. Her work was repr. with the later books (including ix, 1601, specifically addressed to 'worthy ladies') translated by others. See Tina Krontiris in *ELR*, 18, 1988–9.

Tyler, Mary Hunt (Palmer), 1775–1866, author, b. Boston, Mass., da. of Elizabeth (Hunt) and Joseph P. She was educ. by her mother, and at 19 m. Royall T., later Supreme Court judge and writer of the first American comic-drama. The mother of 11 children, MT wrote the first American child-care manual, *The Maternal Physician*, 1811 (anon., repr. 1972), which advocates loving care and a healthy régime. After nursing her husband through terminal cancer, she outlived him by 40 years, eventually to produce, in her eighties, at the request of her children, *Grandmother Tyler's Book*, 1925 (ed. by Frederick Tupper and Helen Tyler Brown). Initially drawing on her mother's notes on the Revolutionary era, she brings to life Lexington, Bunker Hill, and the Boston Tea Party, recalls her mother's readings in Locke on education, and tells the salutary tale of Aunt Kate, never taught to read or write, who lost her true love because his constant letters never drew any response: 'the first sad fruits of Grandpa's system of education'. MT's own matrimonial history emerges, including her husband's insistence on a secret marriage, and his frequent absenteeism. Hurt and mystified by his punitive treatment, she turns to learning new skills and becomes a well-loved figure in her community: 'The world is full of evidence that our sex (proverbially the weaker) is found strongest in the day of trial.' Her papers are held at the Vermont Historical Society.

Tynan, Katharine (later Hinkson), 1861–1931, poet and novelist, b. Dublin, da. of Elizabeth (O'Reilly) and Andrew Cullen T. She was educ. at the Dominican Convent, Drogheda, and had her first poem pub. in 1878, and her first collection in 1885, the year she became friendly with Yeats. In 1893 she m. Henry Albert H., barrister and writer. They lived in England till 1911 when he was appointed Resident Magistrate for Co. Mayo. She wrote over 100 novels which reflected gradual social change, some of them potboilers. She compiled anthologies and wrote articles on social questions such as the ill-health of poor children and working conditions of shop-girls in *Irish Statesman*, but was most significant as a poet. Yeats saw her as an Irish Christina ROSSETTI, A. E. (George Russell), in his foreword to her *Collected Poems*, 1930, as the herald of the Irish Renaissance. She was most successful writing simple, fresh lyrics on subjects close to her heart. Her best-known poem, 'Sheep and Lambs' (usually called by its opening line: 'All in the April morning') was praised by Yeats for finding beauty even in the most hackneyed symbols. The prose sketch, 'The Exile's Sister', in *The Land of Mist and Mountain*, 1895, praises the sister's courage and endurance in contrast to those 'strong women who would mend all the world but themselves and would begin the work by shattering our old tender faiths and ideals'. Wholesome love stories are seen in works such as *The Dear Irish Girl*, 1899, *She Walks in Beauty*, 1899, and *Betty Carew*, 1910. In *A Union of Hearts*, 1901, and *Her Ladyship*, 1907, schemes for the improvement of conditions for Irish peasants come to the fore. *The Playground*, 1930, testifies to KT's concern for slum children deprived of the country things which were her abiding love. There is a study by Marilyn Gaddis Rose, 1974.

Tyrwhit, Elizabeth (Oxenbridge), Lady, d. 1578, devotional writer, da. of Ann (Fynes) and Sir Goddard O. of Romney Marsh, Sussex. Married by 1546 to Sir Robert T. of Leighton Bromswold, Cambs., she was lady-in-waiting to Katharine PARR, shared her narrow escape from arrest for protestantism (Robert T. called her 'halff a Scrypture Woman'), was present at her deathbed, and left a short account of it. She was appointed governess to the future ELIZABETH I, probably in hope that she would share her husband's role as a spy; but she sided with Elizabeth, and he reported that he had no influence over her views or actions. She pub. in 1574 *Morning and Evening Praiers, with divers Psalms, Himnes & Meditations* (one on her daughter's death, 1567, one on her husband's, 1572), repr. with revisions in Thomas Bentley's ANTHOLOGY, 1582. The BL copy of this tiny book was Queen Elizabeth's, finely bound in gold and enamel, with Solomon on one side and Moses on the other, and rings at the top for hanging it at a woman's girdle.

Tytler, Harriet, 1828–1907, memoirist, b. India, da. of Capt. John Lucas Earle (to whom she remained devoted). From age 11 she was raised by an aunt in Birmingham, who subjected her to beatings, severe cold (with bleeding chilblains) and semi-starvation. She was allowed back to India at 18, but her father died while she was journeying there: on arrival, her mother announced her own departure to England with the other children, but insisted HT stay on alone in order to legitimate her own widow's pension. Feeling abandoned, HT travelled 900 miles overland to her nearest relative, an uncle. At 19 she m. Capt. Robert T., who in 1859 pub. an account of the outbreak of the Mutiny at Delhi. She managed to escape Delhi during the seige, but not before giving birth in a bullock-cart, an event for which she became famous. She bore ten children, eight of whom lived, and founded an orphanage, following vows taken as a child upon witnessing starving peasants. These experiences and her adventures travelling overland and by sea with her husband's regiment (he d. 1872) are narrated in her courageous, lively, generous style in memoirs (ed. Anthony Sattin, 1986) written 1903–6, when HT was 75–77. Of mothers, she wrote: 'I do think as a rule [they] are hard on their girls where a darling son is concerned, engendering selfishness in men in after-life, especially towards their daughters and wives.'

'Tytler, Sarah', Henrietta Keddie, 1826?–1914, Scottish novelist and story writer, b. in Fife, da. of a mine-owner, who just missed finding the ironstone seam that would have retrieved the family fortunes. With her two sisters, ST ran a school, but in the 1850s began writing for money. Her first novel, *The Kinnears*, 1853?, was followed by *Phenine Millar*, 1854. Most of her subsequent prolific output (five columns in *BLC*) was pub. as by ST, but some was either anon. or under her own name. In 1869 she left Scotland for England, where she came to know many literary women, including Margaret OLIPHANT, Dinah CRAIK (whom she knew well), Jean INGELOW (whose prose she preferred to her poetry) and Dora GREENWELL. In 1884 she went to live abroad with friends and her adopted daughter; later she became a well-known figure in Oxford. There she spent more than 20 years, initially sharing a house with 'Leslie Keith' (Grace Johnston), d. 1929, a prolific fiction writer also of Scottish background, who, while remaining single herself, none the less venerated marriage and wrote consistently against freedom for women. Later, ST took lodgers herself, and met North American writers Kate Douglas WIGGIN and Lily DOUGAL; she also knew the heads of the women's colleges. She wrote many historical tales for adolescent girls, such as *Citoyenne Jacqueline: a Woman's Lot in the Great French Revolution*, 1865, where despite a conservative viewpoint, a serious interest in different 'kinds' of women emerges. This trait is reinforced in her adult fiction; *Sapphira*, 1890, explores the mother/daughter relationship with unusual respect for their identity apart from these roles. She wrote a life of Queen VICTORIA, 2 vols., 1883, and in 1911 pub. a book about her own family, *Three Generations*.

U

Uhnak, Dorothy, New York police officer and writer of mysteries, b. 1933 in the Bronx – 'I'm half Jewish and half Irish. My maiden name was Goldstein and my mother's name was O'Brien.' She attended City College of New York and John Jay College of Criminal Justice (BS, 1968), and married Tony U., an electrical engineer with whom she has a daughter. An officer and a detective with the NYC Transit Police Force, 1953–67, she was honoured in 1955 with the Outstanding Police Duty Medal for disarming and capturing a rapist-mugger. Her first book, *Policewoman: A Young Woman's Initiation into the Realities of Justice*, 1964, is a semi-autobiographical account of her experiences. Her first police procedural, *The Bait*, 1968, won a Mystery Writers of America Edgar for Best First Novel and introduced series character DETECTIVE Christine Opara, a heroine who 'faces the world on her own terms and puts up with nonsense from no one'. *False Witness*, 1981, introduces Assistant District Attorney Lynne Jacobi, bureau chief of the Violent Sex Crimes Division, who investigates a rape and who is DU's 'best heroine yet ... politically wise ... determined ... tough ... but not without humor or vulnerability'. DU has written seven crime novels, noted for accuracy of police procedure and unstereotyped portraits of women and minority characters, most recently *Victims*, 1986. Papers at Boston Univ. See Bill Pronzini and Marcia MULLER, *1001 Midnights*, 1986 (quoted above), and P. I. Mitterling in *Journal of Popular Culture*, 16, 1982.

Ulasi, Adaora Lily, Nigerian journalist and novelist, b. 1932 in Aba, Eastern Nigeria, the daughter of an Igbo chief from the Royal House of Nnewi, fond of telling his children anecdotes of his experiences as a district court judge. ALU saw as a little girl ironies in the administration of colonial justice. Educated first at several girls' schools in Nigeria, she studied journalism in the USA, at Pepperdine College and the Univ. of Southern California (BA, 1954). Returning to Nigeria, she edited the Woman's Page of the *Daily Times* and the *Sunday Times*, married, accompanied her husband to England, and had three children. Divorced 1972, she returned to Nigeria to edit the magazine *Woman's World*. Since 1976 she has lived in England, writing fiction, newspaper articles, book reviews and verse. Four of her novels, *Many Thing You No Understand*, 1970, *Many Thing Begin For Change*, 1971, *The Man from Sagama*, 1979, and *Who is Jonah*, 1978, set in the colonized Igbo area of her childhood, contrast local people and the expatriate colonial officers and agents as they attempt to solve local crimes. She derives their humour from the earthy wisdom and pidgin of the local speakers (a convention for which she has been criticized). Her novels portray the combined forces of male and colonial power-domination in the pre-independence period, and their sequential plots emphasize greater freedom for women. ALU argues that the Press is vital to social change. *The Night Harry Died*, 1974, a departure, is set in the Southern USA and abandons dialect. See Brown, 1981, and Taiwo, 1984.

Underhill, Evelyn, 1875–1941, mystical and devotional writer, b. at Wolverhampton, only child of cultured, non-religious parents, Lucy (Ironmonger) and solicitor

Arthur U. (later barrister and knight). She went to boarding school at ten, studied arts and sciences at King's College, London, and lived most of her life in Kensington. After being confirmed at school, at almost 17 she was a socialist, admired Caroline HERSCHEL, and wished to be an author. She won a short-story prize in 1892. After years of atheism she became a theist and briefly joined the Golden Dawn (cf. Florence FARR). She mocked legal jargon in free-verse and other poetic styles (*A Bar-Lamb's Ballad Book*, 1902), then turned to experimental symbolic fiction: four stories in *The Horlicks Magazine* (mostly on 'Dorian-Gray'-like portrait themes), 1904, and *The Grey World*, 1904, *The Lost Word*, 1907, and *The Column of Dust*, whose protagonists grope towards vision. The laws of the physical world are sometimes broken, especially as to survival after death: but social comedy and sureness of narrative carry conviction. EU translated miracles of the Virgin from Latin and Old French, 1905, nearly became a Catholic, and married Hubert Stuart Moore (barrister and childhood friend) in 1907. In 1911 she published her first overtly religious book (one of two as by 'John Cordelier'; it never satisfied her), and *Mysticism*, which a 1960 reprint calls 'never superseded'. It mentions JULIAN of Norwich, 'a seer, a lover, and a poet', and Marjery KEMPE, of whom almost nothing was then known. EU's thought became gradually more Christ-centred; she was a practising Anglican by 1921. Baron Friedrich von Hugel was her mentor, May SINCLAIR a friend. Her nearly 40 books include two poetry volumes and many translations (notably Kabir, done with Rabindranath Tagore). She was the first woman invited by Oxford University to lecture, 1921, did editorial work on the *Spectator* and *Time and Tide*, led retreats from 1924, broadcast, and wrote vividly of travel in France and Italy. She was a pacifist in WWII, explaining her reasons clearly and persuasively as always. New selecs. mark her lasting place in Christian thought. *Letters*, 1943; life by Margaret Cropper, 1958 (begun by Lucy Menzies); *An EU Reader*, ed. Thomas S. Kepler, 1962; critical life by Christopher J. R. Armstrong, 1975 (fuller bibliog. than Kepler).

Untermeyer, Jean (Starr), 1886–1970, poet, autobiographer, translator, singer. B. at Zanesville, Ohio, da. of Johanna (Schonfeld) and Abram E.S., she studied music, attended Putnam's Seminary, dreamed of escaping her 'constricting' provincial setting, and formulated a continuing dilemma in 'Dreamers and Doers', an essay written at 12. After Mrs Kohut's School for Girls, NYC, and extension courses at Columbia Univ., she m. poet and editor Louis U. in 1907, a prospect she found 'more exciting than continuing in college. No doubt that too was an education.' When he discovered her secretly-written poems she 'trembl[ed] with fear', but he admired and (once convinced they were hers) sent them to magazines. *Growing Pains*, 1918, first of seven collections, is largely Imagist. JSU made her debut as a lieder singer in 1924, during a two-year stay in Europe. She first left her husband by 1926; in 1927 her only child, a son, killed himself. *Steep Ascent*, 1927, reverberates with bitterness and sorrow about marriage and life: love is a prison 'Where my spirit beat a fevered wing / Against a chosen door.' The marriage was re-attempted, but led to divorces in 1933 ('to retain a shred of my human, not to speak of my womanly, dignity') and 1951. JSU translated Oskar Bie's *Schubert the Man*, 1928, and Hermann Broch's *Death of Virgil*, 1945; she selected from earlier work in *Winged Child*, pub. 1936, the year her varied teaching career began. Of *Later Poems*, 1958, privately printed by her friends Edward and Jule Brousseau Roth, she wrote to Louis U.: 'I hardly expect you to like the poems since it's so long since you have liked what I've written. But others do.' One is a woman's critique of the Norse god Thor: 'Oh, blundering giant, only warmth begets warmth; / You must yield to find yielding. . . . Men make the myths wherein they are heroes; / Women know the measure of truth in them.' She calls *Private Collection*, 1965, 'not the story of my life' but only of its 'pleasanter aspects', and writes warmly of friendship with e.g. Amy LOWELL (who admired her work), BRYHER, Sylvia Townsend WARNER, Valentine ACKLAND. She translated French, German and Hebrew poems in *Re-Creations*, 1970. Louis U.'s *Modern American Poetry*, 1936, praises her early work for relentless self-analysis and middle work for increased assurance.

Upton, Catharine, miscellaneous writer. She grew up (in Nottingham) with a 'love of scribbling', taught in London schools, married an army lieutenant, and wrote lively verse letters home (comment on politics and current events) and an essay intended for the *Lady's Magazine*. She was at Gibraltar with her husband in 1780 when it was blockaded, then shelled; she got out with her two children, and next year (mindful of the discrepancy between army pay and expenses) published *The Siege of Gibraltar*, a vivid prose account of life under siege ('biscuits, full of maggots, a shilling a pound', the despair of women with starving children) and under fire, with a poem on an army promotion. Advertising did not mention her sex ('"What can a Woman say on such a subject?" cries Dapperwit'), but she set her name to this and to *Miscellaneous Pieces in Prose and Verse*, 1784, whose preface claims she has been criticized in ways that a man would not be. (Reviews then declined to comment on a woman seeking to support her family.) By then she was running her own school, and writing on education as well as love, marriage, and bankruptcy. She is better in informal than heroic poems.

Utopias, female. Utopian fiction is imagined in the face of contemporary social realities: women's peculiar oppression thus became the backdrop for a distinctive series of female utopian visions. Ideal communities of women in poetry or fiction are touched on by Katherine PHILIPS, Margaret NEWCASTLE, and Jane BARKER, 1723, and developed by Sarah SCOTT, 1762. Lady Mary HAMILTON makes a woman establish a mixed utopia, 1778, and several other eighteenth-century novels glance at the idea (see B. B. Schnorrenberg in *Women's Studies*, 9, 1982). Interest was roused by Mary ASTELL's *Serious Proposal*, 1694, and focused by the real-life ladies of LLANGOLLEN. Elizabeth CARTER reported a co-operative (failed) in 1770. Mary Edwards Walker founded a US 'Adamless Eden', 1897. The late nineteenth and early twentieth century saw an upsurge of feminist utopian fiction: Marie HOWLAND's *Papa's Own Girl*, 1874, Catherine SPENCE's *Handfasted*, 1984 (written *c.* 1879), Elizabeth CORBETT's *New Amazonia*, 1899, Charlotte P. GILMAN's *Herland*, 1915, and many others. British women utopianists tended to concentrate on their right to enter the dominant order of politics (the public sphere at a national level), Americans on religious or social and communal rather than political transformations. From Gilman onwards, feminist utopias became less a matter of social blueprints and more a matter of fantasy; dystopia (which gained ground rapidly late in the nineteenth century) seems to fit the mood of recent history as utopia did that of Victorian progressivism. Anne K. Mellor argues that since 'a gender-free society has never existed historically, feminist thinking that posits the equality of the sexes is inherently utopian'. By the same token, most feminist narratives about the world as we have it would qualify as dystopian. Novelists like Suzy CHARNAS, Joanna RUSS, and Margaret ATWOOD (in *The Handmaid's Tale*) display positive relish in imaginatively exacerbating problems which are recognizably, in milder form, those of women today. Jean Pfaelzer in *Science-Fiction Studies*, 15, 1988 – arguing that the question raised by women's utopian fiction is not 'What if the world were perfect?' but 'What if the world were feminist?' – traces the way the answers (in Marge PIERCY, Ursula LE GUIN, and Russ) have varied as the women's movement faced different political issues. The weakness of this model of fiction is that it tends towards essentialist assumptions: that competitiveness, delight in wielding power, and the unleashing of deadly inventions are male activities, with women participating only if forced by or colluding with men, while nurturing and community belong to women by birthright. Its strength is its feeding of radical subjectivity by the very act of imagining alternatives to patriarchy, and in the range and ingenuity of the alternatives, both separatist ones and those which construct an equal and loving, or unfettered and carefree, model of gender relations. In *The Female Man*, 1975, says Piercy, Russ creates 'a society where women can do all we now fantasize in closets and kitchens and beds'. See also intro. to Carol Farley Kessler, ed., *Daring to Dream: Utopian Stories by United States Women 1836–1919*, 1984; Nan Bowman Albinski, *Women's Utopias in British and American Fiction*, 1988; Mellor in *Women's Studies*, 9, 1982 (quoted above).

Uttley, 'Alison', Alice Jane (Taylor), 1884–1976, countryside and children's writer. Elder child of ex-lady's-maid Hannah (Dickens) and near-illiterate Henry T., she was b. in a snowstorm at remote Castle Top Farm near Cromford, Derbyshire, which her family had owned 200 years with little change to habits she fiercely loved. Both parents were fine story-tellers; she wrote stories and poems before she went to village school. This, from seven, meant walking four miles a day through scary dark woods; grammar school at Bakewell meant daily milk cart and milk train. She wrote for school and college magazines (she was the second woman to graduate, 1906, in physics from Manchester Univ.) and had precognitive dreams, including one of SAPPHO. After teacher training at Cambridge, 1907, she taught at Fulham, nr. London (science, some English), began writing again on moving into a flat just vacated by Katherine MANSFIELD, went on suffrage marches, and was a friend of Ramsay MacDonald, later Labour Prime Minister. She m. James U. in 1911, settled in Cheshire, and had a son. Wishing to write, she scribbled accounts of French travel, and in 1928 published an essay on children's books and began *The Country Child* (pub. 1931, autobiographical: herself as 'Susan Garland'). James U. called it 'rubbish'; she turned to *The Squirrel, the Hare, and the Little Grey Rabbit*, 1929, first of a delightful series where vain female Squirrel and bumptious male Hare have a 'head of the family' both motherly and clever. Next year James U., a depressive, killed himself. Baffled and grieving, AU took in lodgers, 'replanned my life ... decided to write in earnest' and began a diary in Jan. 1932. Most of her 100 titles are juveniles: fiction (new figures like Moldy Warp the Mole, Fuzzypeg the Hedgehog, Sam Pig and family; supernatural touches in 'Pan, the friend of the animals', and a little girl riding the Great Bear through the night sky; *A Traveller in Time*, 1939, whose modern heroine is taken back into ancestral plots about Mary, Queen of Scots), and the evocative memoirs also loved by adults for 'heritage' reasons. AU hated Enid BLYTON's work. Her two adult novels are mediocre; *The Stuff of Dreams*, 1953 (like her diary), recounts dreams without interpreting. Her relationship with her son, once extremely close, became painful; he destroyed some of her MSS and killed himself in 1978. Surviving papers including the DIARY are at or destined for the John Rylands Library, Manchester; reprints and new selecs. abound; only accurate life by Denis Judd, 1986.

V

Van Duyn, Mona, poet and editor. B. 1921 at Waterloo, Iowa, da. of Lora (Kramer) and businessman Earl George Van D., she was educ. at Iowa State Teachers College (now Univ. of Northern Iowa: BA 1942) and Univ. of Iowa (MA 1943). She m. Jarvis A. Thurston, professor of English, in 1943. In the 1940s she studied and taught at the Univ. of Iowa Writers' Workshop; she has since taught at other universities and at writers' workshops, including Breadloaf. In 1947, with her husband, she founded and became co-editor of the literary quarterly *Perspective*. Her poetry volumes began with *Valentines to the Wide World*, 1959 (including 'Toward a Definition of Marriage'). *A Time of Bees*, 1964, and *To See, To Take*, 1970, both won awards. In *Bedtime Stories*, 1972, she makes her grandmother, speaking a German-toned English, narrator of pioneering journeys and settlement, with Old Country memories. *Merciful Disguises*, 1973, collects earlier poems; *Letters from a Father*, 1982, adds more. Her work examines the long-term marital relationship and other aspects of life from a richly-stored mind. Mindful that women walk on 'the stained and whiskery skin of the world ... but live in our heads, in the sugar and gall / of language', she often writes long poems with long lines, in a cold-eyed but compassionate style, emotionally precise. She describes 'a fight for my life' with Eros: 'There was something obscene about wrestling that baby-faced boy. / Women don't usually wrestle. ... What was dreadful was catching glimpses of freckles and a cute nose, / and dimples at the base of each fat, fierce finger.' MVD is irritated at being called, because female, a domestic poet: 'only about a fourth of my poems are really domestic', she says, although she 'often use[s] domestic imagery to write about everything under the sun'. Besides poems, she has published essays and stories in periodicals.

Van Herk, Aritha, novelist, short-story writer. B. at Wetaskiwin, Alberta, in 1954, da. of Meretje (van Dam) and William H., she grew up on a farm and was educ. at the Univ. of Alberta (BA, 1976, MA, 1978). She m. geologist Robert Sharp, 1974. Her widely-translated first novel, *Judith*, 1978 (written for her MA and winner of the Seal Canadian First Novel Award) sets the subversive pattern: its protagonist, whose career evokes at crucial moments her Biblical ancestress, rejects an urban job and a bland, paternalistic lover to establish a pig farm, expressing her female nature in a symbiotic, growing understanding with her ten pregnant sows and in her acceptance of a female bond with her neighbour and a wholly satisfying relationship with one of the neighbour's sons. *The Tent Peg*, 1981, develops a similar feminist mythic resonance in its story of J. L. (modern daughter of the Biblical Ja-El, tent dweller and peg-staker), a camp cook who confesses and redeems her crew of uranium prospectors, receiving in turn release from her 'detached distance'. *No Fixed Address*, 1986, parodies all tall tales about travelling salesmen (and, of course, the male picaresque) in its tale of Arachne Manteia who, in her cherished old black Mercedes, promotes and sells across Western Canada a line of impeccably tasteless undergarments. AVH's stories, uncollected, have appeared in several Canadian journals. Since 1983, she has taught at the Univ. of Calgary. Interviews in *Kunapipi*, 8, 1986, and *Canadian Woman Studies/les cahiers de la* *femme*, 8, 1987; critical study in Robert Kroetsch and Reingard Nischik, eds., *Gaining Ground*, 1985.

Vanhomrigh, Esther, 'Vanessa', *c.* 1687–1723, letter writer and poet, eldest da. of Hester (Stone) and Bartholomew Van Homrigh, a Dutch immigrant who became Lord Mayor of Dublin. After his death the family moved to London, 1707, and she met Jonathan Swift. By 1712 she was complaining (in jest) of his neglect; in 1714 she moved back to Ireland, and lived at Dublin and nearby Celbridge, seeing Swift seldom but upbraiding him in intense, remarkable letters. Her love, she says, is not of the soul only: 'I was born with violent passions which terminate all in one, that inexpressible passion I have for you.' A few of her poems reached print: a rebus on Swift's name, by 1720; 'To Love' (ascribed to him but probably hers), 1746, which complains of slavery to this 'grand deluder'; two odes in the *GM*, 1767. Letters pub. (from surviving drafts) 1766 (selec.), 1921, and with Swift's. Rumours about her abound (that she bore Swift a son, that she discovered he was married to Stella); by the mid eighteenth century she was read both as 'a miserable example of ... female weakness' and as 'a martyr to love and constancy'. Margaret L. WOODS wrote a novel about her, 1891.

Vardill, Anna Jane, later Niven, 1781–1852, poet, only child of American-born John V., professor and clergyman, who moved to England in 1774 and became a Loyalist spy. She grew up in Galloway (where an uncle lived), London and Lincs. (where John V. became a rector in 1791), wrote her first poem at six, translated from Anacreon at eight, and began at ten a knowledgeable, ambitious, Popean 'Essay on Music' addressed to her mother. After an attack of blindness, she published, as 'a lady', *Poems and Translations*, 1809. Besides juvenilia this includes memorial and charity poems, Scottish landscape sonnets, occasionals, impromptus, and imitations of Persian, Hungarian, medieval, Scots, and other styles. 'The Rights of Woman' cites authorities humorously but with exhaustive learning: woman, it concludes, is prime minister but man is king. *The Pleasures of Human Life*, 1812 (with her name), is weightily, effectively Augustan, ending on heavenly pleasures and a tribute to her father, d. 1811. As 'V', AJV was a leading poetry contributor to the *European Magazine* from 1814. Her exotic verse tales in many voices of the new romanticism include a sequel to Coleridge's 'Christabel' (in print before the original, which she had heard read aloud: see Donald H. Reiman in *The Wordsworth Circle*, 6, 1975). Many emanate from an imaginary hermitage 'seized' in 1816 by a group of spinsters, who 'left less dignified records': often mock-heroic, with satire on both sexes, and ingeniously blended symbolism and modern realism. 'My Godmother's Legacy, or The Art of Consoling', ironically titled prose, 1822, derives from Jane COLLIER on tormenting. AJV married between 1820 and 1826, and returned to Scotland.

'Vase, Gillan', Elizabeth (Palmer), later Palmer Pacht Newton, 1841–1921, novelist, b. Falmouth, Cornwall, da. of Mary Ann (Trewella) and Julius P., shopkeeper, who died when she was two. Partly brought up and educ. in England, she lived so long in Germany that when she pub. *A Great Mystery Solved*, 1878 (a continuation of Dickens's unfinished *Mystery of Edwin Drood*), she felt the need to apologize for the awkwardness of her English expression. Her pen-name is a local variant of the name of a Falmouth beach. Possibly she was adopted by a German family because in 1880, when she m. Richard Newton, a Manchester bristle manufacturer, she was Elizabeth Palmer Pacht, spinster. Her two other works are enigmatic novels with elusive themes, *Through Love to Life*, 1889, and *Under the Linden*, 1900. In each, loveless marriages lead to problem children;

the range and variety of relationships suggests love as a major theme. Men's treatment of women as inferiors is paralleled in *Through Love to Life* with the inequalities between aristocrats and peasants in revolutionary Europe. The novels also point to the duality of good and evil at a deeper level, through character doubling and symbolic description. An unusual writer, GV died in Devon, leaving a son and a daughter.

Veitch, Marion (Fairly), *c.* 1638–1722, memoirist. Brought up at Lanark in Scotland by 'godly parents', she says she early learned to rely not on herself but Christ. After prayer over the choice among her many suitors, she m., 1664, William V., Presbyterian minister and later autobiographer. In 1666 he took up arms for the Covenant and became a fugitive. She was 'greatly molested with parties of troopers' seeking him, joined him in Northumberland, 1671, hid him from a search party, 1677, and wrote of his arrest in 1679: 'I was a stranger in a strange land, and had six small children, and little in the world to look to.' She relates years of 'storms', of 'errands' to God seeking acceptance of his will: when William V. considered emigrating to America, 'at length I got submission to my God, and was content ... but if I went there, I would hang my harp upon the willows when I remembered Scotland.' Back there (Kelso, Peebles, then Dumfries) in William and Mary's reign, she calls her country 'a thorn in the flesh to keep me humble'. Her husband died the day after her. Her *Account of the Lord's Gracious Dealing with Me* ends on the massive effort of prayer by which she has obtained his mercies: MS in NLS; ed. (somewhat tidied), 1825.

Veitch, Sophie Frances Fane, 'J. A. St John Blythe', *c.* 1830s/40s–*c.* 1921/37, novelist and German translator. Da. of Elinor (Rait) and the Rev. William Douglas V. of Eliock in Dumfries. She had two brothers and an elder sister, Zephaniah (or Zepherina) Philadelphia, who wrote a *Handbook for Nurses for the Sick*, 1870. Her father was Principal of the Theological College in Jerusalem, 1843–8. He was also Chaplain to the Anglican Bishop of Jerusalem, 1843–81, and this connection led to the publication of her first book, *Views in Central Abyssinia*, 1868, where she provides text for sketches drawn by a German traveller and presented to the Bishop. Her first novel, *Wise as a Serpent*, 1869, appeared under her pseudonym, as did *Wife or Slave*, 1872, the story of Constance, forced into marriage by her mother, later sustained by her sister Ida. SV's other novels were pub. either under her own name or anonymously. They include: *A Lonely Life*, 1870, *James Hepburn, Free Church Minister*, 1887, *Duncan Moray, Farmer*, 1890, *Margaret Drummond, Millionaire*, 1893, and *A Modern Crusader*, 1895. Her best-known work, *The Dean's Daughter*, 1888, a sensational tale of a woman who perjures herself for her lover, was repr. in 1890 and 1923. She wrote a number of articles for the *Scottish Review* including 'Echoes of the Eighteenth Century', which draws on a collection of Veitch family papers.

Veley, Margaret, 1843–87, poet and novelist, b. at Braintree, Essex, second of four daughters of Sophia (Ludbey) and Augustus Charles V., solicitor, whose family was of Swiss origin. Educ. at home by governesses and masters, with one term at Queen's College, Tufnell Park, London, she began writing verse early and maintained her liberal independence of thought against her family's conservatism. Her first pub. work was a poem, 'Michaelmas Daisies' (*Spectator*, 1870), and her story 'Milly's First Love' appeared in *Blackwood's* the same year. More poems and stories followed in the *Cornhill* (encouraged by Leslie Stephen) and in other journals. Her first and best-known novel was *For Percival*, 1878, about womanly self-sacrifice. Her other prose works included *Damocles*, 1882,

Mitchelhurst Place, 1884, and shorter stories like *Lizzie's Bargain*, 1887. Her work has a dignified, melancholy tone, perceptive characterization, and an intriguing awareness of fictional convention. Her single vol. of poems (selec. by Leslie Stephen), *A Marriage of Shadows*, appeared posthumously in 1888 with a biographical notice. 'A Japanese Fan' and 'Private Theatricals' depict contemporary scenes effectively, while poems like 'One of the Multitude' offer typically evocative but unsentimental meditations on suffering and death.

Venn, Anne, d. before 1658, autobiographer, da. of Margaret (Langley) and John V., well-to-do silk and wool merchant, parliamentary radical, and regicide. The Independents Thomas Weld and Isaac Knight prefaced *A Wise Virgins Lamp Burning*, 1658, a posthumous selection of her writings, with recommendations of her as a role-model. She details the development of her beliefs from early childhood, her attendances at churches in and around London (including those of leading Independents), her search for a like-minded community, and her overwhelming sense of isolation: 'the soule is indeed pained under the sense of its want of inlargedness to Christ, and the like (that it cries out as the infant after the breast) and is not satisfied with any thing without it.'

Vernon, Barbara, 1916–78, playwright, b. Inverell, New South Wales, da. of Constance (Barling) and Murray V. Educ. in Inverell, she worked there as a professional radio announcer and ran her own amateur theatre group. In 1959 she moved to Sydney, where she worked as a freelance writer before joining the ABC Drama Department, writing for radio and later television. Her first major play, *The Multi-Coloured Umbrella*, 1961, came second to Richard Beynon's *The Shifting Heart*, 1960, in the Sydney Journalists' Club competition of 1956. This drama of domestic tensions distinguishes itself by dealing with the preoccupations of the new urban middle class. Other pub. plays are *The Passionate Pianist*, 1958 (part of the trilogy *The Growing Year*, which also includes *The Bishop and the Boxer* and *First Love*), the saga of the Donnelly family, tracing a boy's progression to manhood, and *King Tide Running*, 1967 (with Bruce Beaver). Probably best known of all her work, however, was the TV serial *Bellbird*, which BV originated in 1967. Running into the 1970s, *Bellbird* was set in a country town and concerned the lives of ordinary people; it attracted a devoted following and was the basis for her two novels, *Bellbird: The Story of a Country Town*, 1970, and *A Big Day at Bellbird*, 1972. BV also worked on *Certain Women*, another popular serial of the 1970s. Many of her plays remain unpub.; they include 'Enough to Make a Pair of Sailor's Trousers', 'The Questing Heart', 'Naked Possum', 'Dusty Frangipanis' or 'No Picnic Tomorrow', 'Lancelot and the Lady', 'The Loquat Tree' and 'Silver Bells and Cockle Shells', as well as plays for children.

Vesey, Elizabeth (Vesey), also Handcock, 'the Sylph', 1715?–91, BLUESTOCKING and letter writer. Da. of Mary (Muschamp) and Sir Thomas V., Bishop of Ossory, she m. William H., then by 1746 her cousin Agmondesham V., Anglo-Irish landowner and politician. She knew Elizabeth MONTAGU by 1749. Her London parties had their heyday in 1770–84; Hannah MORE addressed her in 'Bas Bleu' in 1781; her husband's death in 1785 left her poor. Eccentric, unpretentious, widely loved, she collected a good library and left verse (a little) and letters (Huntington: a few pub. in *Bluestocking Letters*, ed. R. Brimley Johnson, 1926). Her pen ('so gauche so diabolical that I should throw it in the fire for ever' but for the answers it brought) ran to whimsical fantasy on dress, gossip, patriotism and the lapse of time: 'Infants I left in their Cradles are now in possession of ... Groves grown into Forest.'

Vickery, Sukey, later Watson, 1779–1821, poet and novelist, b. Leicester, Mass., da. of Susannah (Barter) and Benjamin V., prosperous tailor: educ. at Leicester Academy. As 'Fidelia' she wrote pious, memorial, and political poems for the *Massachusetts Spy*, 1801–3. Plans to publish her epistolary novel, *Emily Hamilton*, 1803, 'Founded on Incidents in Real Life', mostly written 'after the family had retired to rest', gave her hope (of earning money) and anxiety (about remaining anonymous). Her preface argues that novels may do good as well as harm. Emily, steering a course among many suitors, is promised to another when the man she really loves is released from a miserable parentally dictated marriage by his wife's death. Her eventual happiness is set against a range of contrasts: pitfalls and disasters abound, yet one friend emerges strong and angry from being jilted; another comforts a man whose first love has died. SV married Samuel Watson, clothier, in 1804, and had nine children. Only two pages survive from her diary, 1815, recording her teaching of and hopes for her daughters: American Antiquarian Soc. See Cathy N. Davidson, 1986.

Victor, Frances Auretta (Fuller), 1826–1902, and **Metta** Victoria (Fuller), 'Seeley Regester', 1831–85, das. of Lucy (Williams) and Adonijah (or Henry) Fuller. FV was b. in Rome, NY, and MV in Penn. The sisters were educ. in Wooster, Ohio, at the Female Seminary and began writing successfuly while still schoolgirls. In the 1840s they moved to NYC, where their joint *Poems of Sentiment and Imagination*, 1851, brought them wide acclaim from Poe and others. MV became a regular contributor to the *New York Home Journal* as 'Singing Sybil'. In 1853 FV m. Jackson Barritt and moved to Nebraska, but continued to write, contributing to the Beadle Dime Novel series as well as to Western periodicals such as the *Overland Monthly*. Her most lasting contribution to US literature came with her involvement with Bancroft's series *History of the Pacific States*, in which she served as the only woman on the staff from 1878–90. Although receiving no credit at the time, she is now acknowledged to have written several volumes in the series. In 1862 she divorced her husband and m. Henry Clay V., brother of her sister's husband; they separated a few years later. Meanwhile her sister, devoted to 'that branch of literature paying best', achieved financial success with *The Senator's Son*, 1851, a TEMPERANCE tale 'written to order' which had huge sales in Britain and America, and which, together with *Fashionable Dissipation*, 1853, is distinguished by its humour from other temperance fiction. In 1856 she m. Orville James V., editor of the Beadle Dime Novels, and in the same year wrote *Mormon Wives*, a sensational story capitalizing on the topical interest in Mormon polygyny, in which the heroine's husband weds her best friend as his second wife. While the heroine is conventionally portrayed, the best friend, influenced by the writings of 'free lovers' and shown in bold pursuit of the husband, emerges as an interesting character. MV also wrote cookbooks and her novels, mostly written for the Beadle Dime series, range from tales of the West like *Alice Wilde, the Raftsman's Daughter*, 1860, to the humorous *A Bad Boy's Diary*, 1880, and some very early examples of the DETECTIVE novel, including *The Dead Letter*, 1866. Her novel about slavery, *Maum Guinea*, 1860, was very popular with the Union troops: praised by Lincoln.

Victoria, Queen, 1819–1901, grandda. of George III and only child of his fourth son, Edward, Duke of Kent, and his wife (Mary Louisa) Victoria of Saxe Coburg, widow of Prince Ernest Charles of Leiningen; she succeeded to the British throne in 1837, and m., 1840, Prince Albert of Saxe Coburg Gotha, who d. 1861. From childhood until old age she kept a journal, drawn on for her *Leaves from our Life in the Highlands*, 1868, in which she was assisted by Arthur Helps, and *More Leaves*, 1883. Both expressed love of Scotland and knowledge of Highland life and portrayed the happy domesticity of her holidays there with husband and children: they were immediate best-sellers, partly from their very homeliness and naïveté (George ELIOT was touched by the simple and affectionate woman who emerged in *Leaves*). V was an opponent of women's SUFFRAGE and higher EDUCATION; her favourite causes were the RSPCA and anti-vivisection. She was a voluminous letter-writer (five vols., ed. Roger Fulford, 1964–81); it was calculated that she often wrote more than 5000 words a day in journal, letters and official papers. Selections from her correspondence with extracts from her journals (subsequently destroyed) were ed. by A. C. Benson and Viscount Esher, 3 vols. 1907. For her independent-minded beliefs see Walter L. Ashstein in essays ed. Gail Malmgreen, 1986. A good one-vol. biography is by Elizabeth Longford, 1965; Dorothy Thompson's forthcoming, 1990.

Victoria Press. It was founded by Emily FAITHFULL in 1860 to train and employ women compositors: the enterprise was so successful that Queen VICTORIA gave it her personal imprimatur. It published *The English Woman's Journal* and the *Victoria Magazine*. See article by W. E. Fredeman in *The Library*, 29, June 1974.

Vidal, Mary Theresa (Johnson), 1815–69, novelist, b. Torrington, Devon, England, eldest child of Mary (Furse) and William J. She arrived in Australia in 1840 with her husband, an Anglican clergyman. Before they returned to England, she pub. in Sydney *Tales for the Bush*, 1845 (pub. in London as *Tales from the Bush*). Initially printed in eight sixpenny parts and designed for the lower classes, these highly moral little stories were wrongly believed to be the first fiction by a woman pub. in Australia. Ten other works of fiction were pub. in London, including the novels *Cabramatta and Woodleigh Farm*, 1850, and *Bengala*, 1860. There is passing reference to MV in *As Much As I Dare*, 1935, the autobiography of her granddaughter, novelist Faith Compton MacKenzie. See also S. McKernan in D. Adelaide, ed. *A Bright and Fiery Troop*, 1988.

Vigor, Mrs (Goodwin), also Ward and Rondeau, 1699–1783, writer of travel letters, probably da. of Jane (Wainwright) and the Rev. Edward G. of Rawmarsh Hall, Yorks. She became an heiress on her brother's death, married Thomas W., Consul-General to Russia, in 1728, and addressed vivid letters from St Petersburg and Moscow to female friends and relations. She describes Court and private ceremonies (christening, wedding, funeral), human-interest stories, and personalities, mostly though not only of the great. She notes her own propensity to moralize on human foibles, but also her weak judgement; she wants her letters kept private: 'a woman's observations are so ridiculous'. Her husband died after a few years and after some 'wavering' she married his assistant Claudius Rondeau. Widowed again, she returned to England in 1739 and married William Vigor of Taplow, Bucks., a Quaker, who died long before her. She published some letters in 1775, to forestall a pirate edition, cutting personal topics like the fate of probably several children. Second ed. 1775; additional letters, with some contradictory dates [1785].

Viidikas, Vicki, poet and prose writer, b. 1948 in Sydney, New South Wales, da. of an Australian mother and an Estonian violin-maker father. She moved with her mother to Brisbane, Queensland, attending 13 different schools before she left at the age of 15, having nevertheless obtained her Intermediate School Certificate. She began writing poetry as a teenager, and has worked in all kinds of jobs since leaving school, but does not see herself as having any career other than writing. She has pub. four colls. of poetry and prose: *Condition*

Red, 1973, has poems of love and sexuality written in the context of the obsession with self-expression and the difficulties of communication now seen as typical of the early 1970s. These, also, are the preoccupations of her second collection, *Knabel*, 1978, containing passionate images of violence. *Wrappings*, 1974, is a vol. of prose pieces which draws upon VV's travels in India and reflects her interest in mystic religions; its short pieces, like the photos of the author on the cover, are an audacious challenge to our senses, the writing being rich and vibrant. *India Ink*, 1984, contains prose and poetry also inspired by the author's Indian experiences.

Villari, Linda (White), also Mazini, 'M. Dalin', 1836–1915, novelist, essayist, translator, b. London, eldest da. of Mary (Lind) and James W., an alderman and merchant with interests in China, where the family lived for several years from 1841. In her autobiographical novel, *When I was a Child*, 1885, LV describes being 'left behind' and brought up largely by her governess, a friend of her mother's of whom she was very fond, in her great aunt's house. At eleven she was sent to school in Clapham. In 1861 she m. Vincenzo Mazini, with whom she had a daughter. After his death in 1869 she began to write short stories and articles for the *London Academy* and *The Examiner*. Her novels are mainly set in Italy, the first, *In the Golden Shell*, 1872, and the second, *Courtship and a Campaign*, 1873, written as M. Dalin. She married the Italian historian, Professor Pasquale V., in 1876, later translating many of his works. Her novel *In Change Unchanged*, 1877, contains a portrait of Isa BLAGDEN in the generous and lively personality of Miss Whitman, whose home is based on the salon (Villa Bricchieri) frequented by Theodosia Trollope and the Brownings at Bellosguardo, Florence. LV also knew Vernon LEE. She contributed many articles on Italian life and literature to *The National Review, Fraser's*, the *Cornhill, Macmillan's* and the *Contemporary Review*. She translated a Hungarian story, *Life in a Cave*, 1884, by M. Jokai, and also wrote *A Double Bond*, 1882, *On Tuscan Hills and Venetian Waters*, 1884, and *Camilla's Girlhood*, 1885.

'Vivien, Renée', Pauline Mary Tarn, 1877–1909, poet and prose-writer working in French. She was b. in London, da. of Mary Gillet (Bennett), an American, and John T., an Englishman, taken to Paris as a baby, and poorly educ. by an English governess. She wrote stories at six, love-poems at nine, and 'her first serious verse' at 14, when, she said, she 'began to live' after 'a very sad childhood'. Her father died when she was nine and she was taken, perforce, to England by her mother, with whom she got on badly; by 1894 she was suffering psychosomatic ailments. She rejected marriage with a much older French poet and was locked up (in order, she thought, to drive her to suicide). Once of age, she moved to Paris; she wrote in *Une Femme m'apparut*, 1904 (English transl. 1979), a *roman à clef*, of 'the shiver which ran down my spine' when she met Natalie BARNEY, in 1899, and was drawn by the 'charm of peril'. Perceived at once by Barney as a serious author, RV began to write and publish prolifically. They travelled to the USA and to Lesbos; their relationship suffered violent, much-discussed ups and downs before its end in 1904. RV issued her first poetry volume, *Etudes et préludes*, 1901, as 'R. Vivien'; she expanded to the male 'René', then on *Evocations*, 1903, to 'Renée': 'some scandal' greeted the news of her sex. RV's poems mix the joyous sensuality of SAPPHO with the suffering and unfulfilment of the French symbolists. She also published French versions and expansions of Sappho, 1903 and 1904, and prose tales in *Brumes de fjords*, 1902, and *La Dame à la louve*, 1904 (English transl. 1983), which 'rewrite[s] myth and folklore'. Karla Jay, biographer of her and Barney, 1988, doubts that the pseudonym 'Paule Riversdale' indicates RV and her later lover the Baroness de Zuylen de Nyevelt. Before her death (variously ascribed to anorexia or alcohol), RV travelled widely and published six more volumes of poetry. Her *Poèmes,* two vols., 1923, were repr. 1975; letters at the Bibliothèque Nationale; other works repr. in English transl. See Susan Gubar in *Signs*, 10, 1984, Elyse Blankley in Susan Squier, ed., *Women Writers and the City*, 1984, Pamela J. Annas in *Women's Studies*, 13, 1986.

Vokins, Joan (Bunce), d. 1690, Quaker autobiographer. Da. of Thomas B., a prosperous yeoman, she m. Richard V. of West Challow, Berks., and had seven children. Her family opposed her joining the Quakers, but later did so too. In *A Loving Advertisement*, 1671, she justified 'the Sons and Daughters of the Lord' and called their persecutors to repentance with the threat of eternal burning. In 1680 she left her family and set out with women friends to visit meetings in several American colonies and the Caribbean (in the Leeward Islands joining evidently segregated 'Meetings of Negro's or Blacks'); she made a brief return to England that year when the Women's Meetings, last vestige of Quaker female power, looked likely to be abolished. In 1686 she was in Ireland; she died returning home from London. Friends then pub. *God's Mighty Power Magnified: As Manifested and Revealed in His Faithful Handmaid Joan Vokins*, 1691. In it, testimonies (one by Theophila TOWNSEND) precede JV's autobiography and letters: shortly before her death she wrote 'Oh! how many hundred Miles have I travelled in this Land of my Nativity, and thousands elsewhere, in such a condition, not having many well Days in many Years together.'

Von Arnim, 'Elizabeth', Mary Annette (Beauchamp), Countess, also Russell, 1866–1941, novelist, da. of Elizabeth (Lassetter) and shipping merchant Henry B., cousin of Katherine MANSFIELD. B. at her family's holiday home on the west coast of New Zealand, she was taken from Sydney, NSW, via Europe, to London, arriving in 1871. After leaving Queen's College School in 1884, she won a prize for organ-playing at the Royal College of Music. In 1891 she married the Prussian Count von A.-Schiagenthin, whom she had met while travelling in Italy. His Pomeranian estate, where 'there was everything in profusion except money', was the setting for *Elizabeth and her German Garden*, 1898 (whence her nickname), which presents not just her horticultural concerns but her five children, servants, guests, and her husband, 'the Man of Wrath'. Daily shutting herself away to write after performing her household duties, she produced 20-odd works, anonymous except the sentimental, autobiographical *All the Dogs of My Life*, 1936 (as 'Elizabeth'), and *Christine*, 1917 (as 'Anne Cholmondely'). Her first novel, *The Benefactress*, 1902, draws on her husband's imprisonment on a trumped-up charge. Her unpub. play, *Priscilla Runs Away*, was staged in London in 1910. After the Count's death that year her fictions, such as *The Pastor's Wife*, 1914, became more serious. After 1913 she divided her time between Europe and London. She was pursued by H. G. Wells, but married Francis, 2nd Lord Russell (Bertrand Russell's brother), in 1916; they separated in 1919. This marriage provided the basis for *Vera*, 1921, though the heroine, lacking EVA's courage to flee, is left the options of submission or suicide: Rebecca WEST praised its rare success in the macabre. EVA's picture of the French Riviera in *Enchanted April*, 1923, became very popular in the USA, where she moved at the threat of WWII. Sometimes flippant, often caustically witty or eloquently understated, she writes much of women's subjection and need for independent life: her husbands and fathers are often tyrannical (even the comic first-person narrator of *The Caravanners*, 1909), her childbirth scenes powerful. Lives by her daughter Leibet (reticent; as 'Leslie de Charms', from the names of two of EVA's uncles), 1958, Karen Usborne, 1986. Recent reprints; MSS at Huntington.

Von Reich, Momoe Malietoa, contemporary poet from Western Samoa. Educ. in Samoa then New Zealand, she specialized in art, teaching 1966–70 in Western Samoa, and holding successful exhibitions. She is a mother of seven children. In 1979 she pub. a collection of poems, *Solaua, a Secret Embryo*, dedicated 'To my husband who suffered and my children who waited'. Direct, forthright, bitter, many poems explore the imbalances of male/female relationships. In 'My Guest', the wife does not fulfil her husband's expectations in entertaining another, younger, woman; instead, she 'feels like bloody Cinderella'. Women are seen cynically as sex-objects, child-bearers: 'I'm tired of wearing my soul out / For the tall young man / With penis vanity' ('To Keri').

Vorse, Mary Marvin (**Heaton**), 1874–1966, journalist and novelist. B. in NYC, da. of Ellen Cordelia (Blackman) and Hiram H., she grew up in Amherst, Mass., was educ. in Europe, and asserted independence by going to art school. She married writer Albert V. in 1898, sold early humorous sketches and children's stories to *Woman's Home Companion* and *Atlantic Monthly*, and depicted him in her first book, *The Breaking-In of a Yachtsman's Wife*, 1908. She founded the 'A Club' in Greenwich Village, an experimental housing co-operative used by writers, and a Montessori school in Provincetown, Mass., where later she helped set up the well-known Provincetown Players. In 1910 her husband and mother died; next year she based *Autobiography of an Elderly Woman* on her mother and *Stories of the Very Little Person* on her daughter. To support her children she still wrote historical, comic (*I've Come to Stay*, 1919, satirizes Greenwich Village lifestyles) and romantic fiction, but her true work changed from 1912, when she took part in the Lawrence textile strike, met Elizabeth Gurley FLYNN, and married labour reporter Joe O'Brien (d. 1915). A founding member of the *Masses* and foreign correspondent for several journals during WWII (covering the International Congress of Women in Amsterdam and the International Woman Suffrage Convention in Budapest in 1915), she built her professional name with articles and books on labour issues. Her novels based on actual strikes (*Passaic*, 1926, *Strike!*, 1930) stress the centrality of working-class women's often underestimated courage and strength (see Joseph R. Urgo in *minnesota review*, 24, 1985). She had a painful affair with artist Robert Minor and in 1922 a miscarriage which left her a temporary morphine addict. Her other works include *Men and Steel*, 1921, and *Labor's New Millions*, 1938 (labour history), *A Footnote to Folly*, 1935 (an account of her growth in political awareness), and *Time and the Town*, 1942 (a reflective study of Provincetown). Several modern reprs.; Dee Garrison, ed., *Rebel Pen*, 1985, is a selec. of journalism. Papers (on labour history) at Wayne State Univ., Detroit; bibliog. by Rusty Byrne at Radcliffe College; oral reminiscences at Columbia Univ. Life by Garrison, 1989.

Voynich, Ethel Lilian (Boole), 1864–1960, Irish novelist and radical activist, b. Cork, da. of Mary (Everest), feminist philosopher, and George B., eminent mathematician. Educ. at local schools and later in Berlin, she also travelled to Russia. In 1891 she m. Polish patriot Wilfred V., and in 1893 pub. her first TRANSLATION, *Stories from Garshin*, followed by *The Humour of Russia*, 1895, and *Nihilism as it is*, 1895. In 1896 she pub. her first (and best known) original work, *The Gadfly*, a bitterly anti-clerical novel of revolution, set in Italy, whose most admirable character is the minor figure of a young woman revolutionary. *An Interrrupted Friendship*, 1910, develops the obsessive concern with sadism and physical pain evident in earlier works. She translated Chopin's letters, 1931, and, living in New York, pub. her last work, *Put off thy Shoes*, 1945. See Arnold Kettle's article in *Essays in Criticism*, 7, 1957.

Vynne, Nora Eleonora M. S., 1870?–1914, journalist, novelist, dramatic critic and political worker, da. of Charles V., of an old Norfolk family. Educ. at home, she passed the Kensington Local exam. and won a prize. After her father's death, she came to London and took up journalism and literary work, editing *Woman and Progress* and publishing short stories as well as *Women under the Factory Acts*, 1903 (with Helen BLACKBURN and H. W. Allason), and six novels, 1895–1913. The first of these, *A Man and His Womankind*, 1895, portrays a friendly alliance between a mother and daughter-in-law. *The Priest's Marriage*, 1899, is a violent story of an ex-priest's warped, possessive love for a girl who finally learns to defy him. *So It Is With the Damsel*, 1913, treats the white slave trade with grim straightforwardness and a refusal to blame the victim.

Waciuma, Charity, Kenyan writer for children, and autobiographer. Her mother, Wangui wa (Wanjohi), and father both ran away from home to get a Western education, adopted Christianity, and worked consistently for the recognition of women. Her mother became first woman councillor in her district; her father, manager of a government dispensary, tried to reconcile Western alternative medical practices with honoured local practices. Her own education as a teacher was interrupted during the Mau-Mau upheavals in Kenya. *Daughter of Mumbi*, 1969, describes her adolescence during the seven-year Emergency period. It concludes with the death of her father, to whom she dedicated the work, and a note written ten years later when she was married and mother of two. CW writes positively, often humorously, about Kikuyu culture, emphasizes adaptation of traditional cultural values to a modernizing society, and portrays conflicts about medical systems, women's circumcision, and polygyny. Her children's writing (including *Mwenu, the Ostrich Girl*, 1966, *The Golden Feather*, 1966, *Merry-Making*, 1972, *Who's Calling*, 1973, and *Mweru, the Ostrich*) stresses Kikuyu legends and traditions of storytelling, pointing out that girls have a place in folk art and can convey family strength and virtues. See Taiwo, 1984.

Waddell, Helen, 1889–1965, Irish novelist, poet, translator, medievalist, b. in Tokyo, where her father Hugh W., a Presbyterian minister and sinologue, lectured at the Imperial University. After 'an enchanted childhood', she returned to Ulster. Her mother d. when she was two. She was educ. at the Victoria School for Girls in Belfast, then read Latin, French and English at Queen's College. She was examined there by George Saintsbury, who found her brilliant and became a life-long friend. (He wrote the introduction to her translation of *Manon Lescaut*, 1931; she wrote an 'appreciation' of his *Shakespeare*, 1934.) Her writing career mixes scholarship and fancy: she brought the middle ages to the attention of a wide audience with her translations of *Medieval Latin Lyrics*, 1929, and other works, including *The Wandering Scholars*, 1927, a learned account of the Vagantes which made her the first woman to win the A.C. Benson Medal of the Royal Society of Literature, and her novel *Peter Abelard*, 1933, which ran to thirty editions. She translated other works, including Milton's *Epitaphium Damonis*, and letters of a French soldier, 1941. Her *Lyrics from the Chinese*, 1915, poetic versions made from James Legge's prose translations, have been anthologized, with translations by Arthur Waley and Ezra Pound, by David Holbrook, 1968. She published poems and articles in London journals and papers and wrote stories based on Oriental and European legends. During WWII, she was assistant editor of *The Nineteenth Century*. She had several B. Litt. degrees, the first an earned degree for a thesis on Milton. Her letters to her sister form the basis of Monica Blackett's memoir, *The Mark of the Maker*, 1973. Papers ed. M. T. Kelly, 1981; life by F. Corrigan, 1986.

Waddington, Miriam (Dworkin), b. 1917, poet, critic, short-story writer, professor. The Winnipeg home of her Russian-Jewish immigrant parents, Mussia (Dobrusin) and Isidore Dworkin, was a meeting place of socialists and intellectuals: 'Feminism was nothing new to me. ... [P]eople ... en route to lecture tours ... would talk to my mother about women's oppression. And she ... would rebel for the day'. '[N]urtured on a sense of ethics and morality – and indignation', MW, Yiddish speaking, began writing in English at ten. During the depression, the family moved to Ottawa where she attended the Lisgar Collegiate Institute, 1931–6. In the Montréal Yiddish literary salon of Ida Maze, who gave her works by Edna St Vincent MILLAY and Sara TEASDALE, MW was encouraged to 'write a poem about a woman's life. Me, when I was 15!' She studied at the Univ. of Toronto (BA, 1939), married journalist Patrick W., 1939, had two sons, and, with 'no possibility at that time of a woman or a Jew being hired to teach at the University', worked for a year with *Magazine Digest*. She returned to the Univ. of Toronto (School of Social Work, Diploma, 1942), and subsequently attended the Univ. of Pennsylvania (MSW, 1945), then worked with various social agencies in slums and prisons, and taught at the School of Social Work at McGill. In Montréal, poet John Sutherland published her first book, *Green World*, 1945. The 1955 conference on Canadian writing at Queen's Univ., Kingston, Ont., where MW met Phyllis WEBB, Adele WISEMAN and Jay MACPHERSON, was decisive in her 'yearn[ing] to write public poetry' (*The Season's Lovers*, 1958). By 1964, already divorced (1960), MW had won the Borestone Mountain Award for Best Poems (1958, 1964), received a senior Canada Council grant (1962–3), and was teaching Canadian literature at York Univ., Toronto (retired 1983). *A. M. Klein*, 1970, was her revised thesis (Univ. of Toronto, MA, 1968). *The Glass Trumpet*, 1966, bearing the mark of Gertrude STEIN – 'it tells / of maps and sand / and people number-/less on numbered / city streets and / then it tells of / our blind sick-/ness healed and / holds us open-eyed / in pure transparency' – helped her reach 'a new awareness of [her]self as an artist'. Without abandoning social observation, intellectual rigour and her often ironic twist of imagery, MW has displayed in recent poetry (*Say Yes*, 1969, *Dream Telescope*, 1972, *The Visitants*, 1981) a greater attentiveness to language and to the rhythmic and semantic possibilities generated by short lines, sparse punctuation and the breaking down of words and syntax. See L. R. Ricou in *ECW*, 12, 1978, and Peter Stevens, *CWW, Poetry Series*, 5, 1985.

Wade, Rosalind Herschel, OBE, 'Catherine Carr', 1909–89, novelist, b. in London, da. of Kathleen Adelaide (Herschel) and Lt-Col. H. A. L. H. Wade. She was educ. at Glendower School, London, privately abroad, and at Bedford College, London. She was a friend of Pamela Hansford JOHNSON, and married William Kean Seymour (d. 1975), poet and bank manager; they had two sons. She published more than 30 novels in her own name, many reflecting her interest in the disadvantaged and in social work. *Kept Man*, 1933, ends on the problems left unsolved by women in parliament and equality for high-fliers: the dilemma of the unmarried and unexceptional. *Treasure in Heaven*, 1937, about work on a Care Committee, confronts not only the plight of slum dwellers (incest, unwanted pregnancy, 'mothers half-starving themselves to give their children a good meal') but also a rich, middle-aged volunteer forced to reassess her motives when her well-meant bungling leads to a scandal. *Come Fill the Cup*, 1955, looks at the ordeal of alcoholism. *Mrs Jamison's Daughter*, 1957, deals with a woman who gets pregnant while her husband is a prisoner of war. *Mrs Medlend's Private World*, 1973, depicts a mission caring for troubled adolescents, and a woman thought dead, who evades her problems by taking a new identity. RW wrote 11 light romances as 'Catherine Carr' in the 1950s and 60s, taught creative writing with her husband in the 1960s and 1970s, and kept publishing till the early

1980s. Active in public life and literary groups, she chaired the Society of Women Writers and Journalists, 1962–4, and edited *Contemporary Review*, 1970–88, and the *PEN Broadsheet*, 1975–7.

Waite, Mary, of York, Quaker who probably m. Richard W. of Suffolk, and bore a son at Carlisle in 1680. She pub. *A Warning to all Friends* in 1679 after God had saved her from death 'and laid it upon me, to goe warn his people ... to Depart from all filthinesse both of flesh and Spirit'. Designed for reading at Quaker meetings 'whether on this Side, or beyond the Seas', it is far more conservative than earlier tracts, urging 'Masters and Mistresses of Families' to rule over the behaviour of their children, maids and apprentices (repr. as part of the *Epistle* from the women's yearly York meeting, 1688). MW was a signatory of several such official pamphlets.

Waite-Smith, Cicely (Howland), Jamaican dramatist and short-story writer, b. 1913. She began publishing stories in Caribbean journals in the 1930s; in 1943 her *Rain for the Plains* (stories) was published at Kingston, and her first play, *Grandfather Is Dying*, in Edna Manley, ed., *Focus*. In 1948 *Focus* printed CWS's radio play *Storm Signal*. CWS contributed importantly, with at least nine more plays of one or more acts, to ongoing debate between then and 1966 over what constituted a distinctively Jamaican theatre. *The Creatures* (produced 1954, pub. in *Focus*, 1956) looks askance at women as 'hiding, dancing, changing, sulking' and 'sour'; a river is personified as a *femme fatale* who lures a young girl to suicide for love, and a fisherman to shun human (female) company and commune with her and a speaking lizard and bird. *Africa Slingshot*, staged and pub. 1958, written in patwah, shows villagers wildly thrilled by the African word-magic of a glamorous stranger who turns out to be a petty criminal on the run: 'I go a Africa in me mind.' *Return to Paradise* and *The Impossible Situation*, both pub. 1966, are hard-hitting sketches of elderly black women servants and their unfeeling employers. See Henry Fowler in *Jamaica Journal*, 2, 1968.

Wakefield, Priscilla (Bell), 1751–1832, Quaker, natural historian, controversialist, and educationalist, da. of Catharine (Barclay) and Daniel Bell, granddaughter of Robert Barclay the Quaker apologist: b. at Tottenham near London. She m. Edward W. in 1771 and had three children. Her writings, like the savings bank and maternity hospital she founded, aim to improve the state of the world. Though *Juvenile Anecdotes, Founded on Facts* (2 vols., 1795, 1798) advises parents to cut any corrupting pages from their children's books, her works for the young are more tough-minded than most, presenting detailed instruction in botany, entymology, zoology, and the geography of the British Empire, North America, Africa and London. *Reflections on the Present Condition of the Female Sex, with Suggestions for its Improvement*, 1798 (facs. 1974), though, unlike Wollstonecraft, it sees women's sphere as naturally limited, recognizes that women too owe a debt to society, which inadequate education prevents from being paid. Ladies, it says, should promote jobs and equal pay (comparative figures are indignantly cited) for working women. It confronts the issue of prostitution, and praises Hannah More and Sarah Trimmer. PW also wrote essays, stories, and a life of William Penn, 1817.

Wakoski, Diane, poet. B. in 1937 in Whittier, Calif., da. of Marie Elvia (Mengel), who was often ill, and sailor John Joseph W., who was often absent, she later thought of herself as an orphan. She went to a local school 'on a very rural road, amid orange groves, avocado orchards'; in high school, she turned down her Berkeley scholarship to be with the boy she was in love with, became pregnant by, and refused to marry. She had the child in a charitable Home for

Unwed Mothers and gave it up for adoption, 1956. At Berkeley (now working for room and board), she published her first poems, 1958, had a daughter, 1960, also surrendered, and took her BA, 1960. The first of her more than 50 collections of verse, *Coins and Coffins*, 1962, appeared while she was working in a NYC bookstore, and in that year she was published, with Rochelle OWENS, in LeRoi Jones's *Four Young Lady Poets*. She taught high school, 1963–6, then at various colleges, settling at Michigan State Univ, 1976, where she lives with her third husband, Robert Turney (m. 1982). Profoundly influenced by Yeats ('very, very, very, very, very important'), she later used Wallace Stevens and Lorca as models. Charles Olson, Robert Duncan and Robert Creely helped to shape her thought and practice about form and content. Expressly not a political poet, she early developed and continues to elaborate a 'personal mythology' which uses but 'transcends' autobiography, making the 'new' poetry from the premise that 'the work must organically come out of the writer's life', as in the first two parts of her continuing *Greed* series, 1968, though the note of aggression is characteristically her own. *Form is an Extension of Content*, a Breadloaf 'poem lecture' then a Black Sparrow publication, 1972, explores a thought 'so simple as to be almost tautological': 'Do we choose the symbols for our lives / and then write the poems? / Or do the poems write our lives / in ink that stains more than the fingers?' *The Collected Greed, Parts 1–13*, 1984, shows DW's formal development, while her attention to ethics, emotion, and art stays consistent. *The Motorcycle Betrayal Poems*, 1971, *Dancing on the Grave of a Son of a Bitch*, 1973, and *The Fable of the Lion and the Scorpion*, 1973, treat intense, often painful experience in an immediate, direct voice, giving her poems dramatic power. The musical forms and rhythms in *The Man Who Shook Hands*, 1978, *Saturn's Rings*, 1982, and *Why My Mother Likes Liberace: A Musical Selection*, 1985, demonstrate DW's belief that in poetry as in music 'you must hear all the digressions'. After two more volumes, *Emerald Ice*, 1988, selects poems of 1956–87. Alicia OSTRIKER, who calls DW's range of imagery 'wide and wild as any surrealist's, possibly wider and wilder than any other American poet's', finds her work a demonstration of 'the All or Nothing syndrome in female romantic fantasies'. *Toward a New Poetry*, 1979, collects essays, lectures, interviews. Contemporary Authors *Autobiography Series*, 1984, prints a remarkably intimate account of DW's early years. Interview in *DR*, 1961, criticism in Ostriker, 1986, bibliography by Robert Newton, 1987. Papers at Univ. of Arizona.

Walford, Lucy Bethia (Colquhoun), 1845–1915, novelist, b. Edinburgh, seventh child of Frances Sara (Fuller-Maitland) and well-known sportsman John C.; niece of Catherine SINCLAIR. She was educ. at home and began writing when she m. Alfred Sanders W., magistrate. *Mr. Smith, a Part of His Life*, 1874, led to regular contributions to *Blackwood's* and other periodicals, where many of her novels first appeared as serials. This first novel is the story of a charming flirt, Helen Tolleton, and is typical of LW's work in its light-hearted treatment of social and romantic crises. Although her mother's relatives largely disapproved of her novels, Queen VICTORIA was a particular admirer. Other works include *Pauline*, 1877; *The Baby's Grandmother*, 1885; *The Havoc of a Smile*, 1890, the story of a naïve, lonely young man's unrequited love for a glamorous cousin; *The Matchmaker*, 1893, notable as the last three-decker accepted by Mudie's CIRCULATING LIBRARY; *Charlotte*, 1902; and *Leonore Stubbs*, 1908. LW served as London correspondent for the New York *Critic* (1889–93), and pub. 45 books, including *Four Biographies from Blackwood's*, 1888 (lives of Jane TAYLOR, Elizabeth Fry, Hannah MORE, and Mary SOMERVILLE), as well as *Recollections of a Scottish Novelist*, 1910, about her early life, and *Memories of*

Victorian London, 1912, full of literary and social gossip.

Walker, Alice Malsenior, poet, novelist and essayist. B. in 1944 in Eatonton, Georgia, she is the eighth child of sharecroppers Minnie Lue (Grant) and Willie Lee W. Given a typewriter by her mother, and allowed to write rather than do chores, AW sees her mother's passing on her own creativity which she expressed in her flower garden and in the 'urgency' with which she told her stories. AW transferred from Spelman College, Atlanta, to Sarah Lawrence College (BA 1965), where she 'stuffed her poems under Muriel RUKEYSER's door'. Rukeyser sent them to a publisher and *Once: Poems* appeared in 1968. AW received a PhD from Russell Sage College, 1972, married Melvyn R. Leventhal, a civil rights lawyer, in 1967 (divorced 1976) and has a daughter. She has taught and been writer-in-residence at several colleges and universities, including Tougaloo, Wellesley, Yale and the Univ. of California at Berkeley. Her first novel, *The Third Life of Grange Copeland*, 1970, links the necessity of a man's inner development with the outer change in social reality. In 1974 she published a biography of Langston Hughes and became a contributing editor of *Ms.* Her poems, *Revolutionary Petunias*, 1973 (nominated for the National Book Award), *Good Night Willie Lee, I'll See You in the Morning*, 1979, and *Horses Make a Landscape Look More Beautiful*, 1984, celebrate nature, family and community. More complex, her prose is also more forceful. The stories of *In Love and Trouble*, 1973, shift her focus to women, a focus maintained in *You Can't Keep a Good Woman Down*, 1981. The semi-autobiographical novel *Meridian*, 1976, is named for the young woman who makes her way through the violence, hope and disappointments of the civil rights movement of the 1960s. *The Color Purple*, 1982 (adapted for film by Steven Spielberg, 1985), first novel by a black woman to win the Pulitzer Prize, provoked controversy for its portrayal of black male oppression of black women. Its protagonist, Celie, sexually abused by her father, enslaved by her husband, finds joy and community in the love of Shug, the woman her husband moved into their home. Researching voodoo for a story, AW discovered the work of Zora Neale HURSTON, 'one of the most significant unread authors in America'; she edited a Hurston reader, *I Love Myself When I am Laughing, and Then Again When I am Looking Mean and Impressive*, 1979. Her account of this discovery and other autobiographical and literary essays (on Hurston, Flannery O'CONNOR, Jean Tomer, Rebecca Cox JACKSON, as well as on her own life and work) appear in *In Search of Our Mothers' Gardens: Womanist Prose*, 1983, which invites us to imagine the result had singing, like reading and writing, been forbidden to blacks. ('Womanist': 'Loves music. Loves dance. Loves the moon. *Loves* the Spirit. Loves love and food and roundness. Loves struggle. *Loves* the folk. Loves herself. *Regardless*'.) *Living by the Word, 1973–87*, 1988, suggests AW's increasing commitment to nature and its spiritual importance. In *The Temple of My Familiar*, 1989, black women remember their way back through patriarchal history to matriarchal myth. Interview in Tate, 1983. Studies in Pryse and Spillers, 1985, Calvin C. Herton, *The Sexual Mountain and Black Women Writers*, 1987, and Susan Willis, *Specifying: Black Women Writing the American Experience*, 1987. Bibliography by Louis H. Pratt and Darnell D. Pratt, 1988.

Walker, Annie Louisa, 1836–1907, poet and novelist, cousin of Margaret OLIPHANT, later publishing as 'Mrs Henry (or Harry) Coghill'. She was b. in England but brought up in Canada: at Point Levy, Québec, then at Sarnia, Ont., where she and her sisters ran a young ladies' private school. Her *Leaves from the Backwoods*, Montréal, 1861, drew British and American as well as Canadian subscribers. It includes religious, meditative, nature-descriptive, transcendental and narrative verse. Two poems on women's rights are satirical in tone ('husbands, children, what are they?') except when claiming the right to be 'unobtrusive and unnoticed' dispensers of domestic happiness. The hymn 'Work for the night is coming' became well known. In the 1870s, AW returned to England and became housekeeper and confidante to the widowed Margaret Oliphant. Her novel, *A Canadian Heroine*, 1873, set along the St Lawrence River, contrasts the innocent new and the superficial old worlds in a patriotically fantasized plot: its young heroine almost loses her staunch Canadian suitor because of infatuation with an English aristocrat but ends with the best of both when she marries the Canadian who inherits a wealthy English estate. (Her father supplies a gothic element: he is discovered to be a Jesuit-educated Indian from whom her mother escaped when he became drunk and abusive.) ALW married Henry Coghill in 1884 and settled in Staffs., but still called herself 'the one nearest' to Oliphant's circle. She published plays for children, 1876, poetry and prose in journals, and in 1890 *Oak and Maple: English and Canadian Verses*. She edited Oliphant's *Autobiography*, 1899 (repr. 1974, with introduction by Q. D. LEAVIS).

Walker, Elizabeth (Sadler), 1623–90, memoirist, b. in London, eldest child of Elizabeth (Dackum) and John S., well-to-do druggist. She was a delicate baby, later 'of a pensive Nature' but highly capable (she handled the petty cash – £100 or more – for her father's business). She felt lifelong remorse for lying to him at about 14, and depression for six months, *c.* 1642, after a stifled love affair (when she wept steadily and hardly slept or ate). In 1650 she m. the Rev. Anthony W.; she had 11 children (counting three still-births but not miscarriages). Despite dairying and cider-making, mixing medicine for the poor and teaching her servants to read, she wrote much: diary entries, prayers, meditations, letters, memoirs of early life, long accounts of the characters and deaths of children (none survived her), religious advice to them, and notes on events like the plague and fire. When her husband came in she would 'slide her Book or Papers into the Drawer', till he promised not to look. Severe depression and near loss of faith followed her last daughter's death. Anthony W. drew heavily on her writings in his life of her, 1690 (later repr. and abridged); he also wrote on her friend Lady WARWICK.

Walker, Margaret, poet, novelist, biographer, b. in 1915 in Birmingham, Ala., da. of musicologist and teacher Marion (Dozier) and Methodist minister Sigismund W. Enduring poverty so severe that she was often hungry, she took a BA at Northwestern Univ., 1936, worked at various jobs in Chicago, then, hoping to teach, did an MA in English at the Univ. of Iowa, 1940. *For My People*, 1942, made her the first black poet to win the Yale Younger Poets award: these poems speak, in various poetic voices, of her love of her southern home, fear of white violence, indignation at injustice, and of the deep dignity and pain of the past: 'And when I return to Mobile, I shall go by the way of Panama and Bocas del Toro to the littered streets and the one-room shacks of my old poverty, and blazing suns of other lands may struggle then to reconcile the pride and pain in me'. They also celebrate the outrageousness of characters like Kissie Lee ('Every livin' guy get out her way / because Kissie Lee was drawin' her pay'). In 1943 MW m. James Alexander Firnist, who was disabled in the war; they had four children. Though her teaching career in North Carolina, West Virginia, and Mississippi, was fraught with 'conflict, insults, humiliations and disappointments', each successful innovation leading to her being 'immediately replaced by a man', she supported her family by teaching from marriage to retirement, mainly at Jackson

State College, Miss., where she established a Black Studies Program. She returned to Iowa for her PhD, 1965, because 'they could be forced to pay me more money'. Though it was years before she published again, her later works pursue the themes and interests (including black language) of the first. Other collections include *Prophets for a New Day*, 1970, and *October Journey*, 1973. Her best-known work, *Jubilee*, 1966, an historical novel based on the life of her maternal great-grandmother, Margaret Duggans, took thirty years to write. Rich with songs, folk medicine, details of daily life and survival strategies, it is the story of Vyre, born into slavery, who lived through the civil war and reconstruction. Her other work includes an essay published by the Institute of the Black World in Atlanta on *How I Wrote Jubilee*, 1972, as well as *A Poetic Equation: Conversations with Nikki* GIOVANNI, 1974, and a biography, *The Demonic Genius of Richard Wright*, 1987. *This is My Century*, 1989, prints 'New and Collected Poems'. A sequel to *Jubilee – Minna and Jim* – and her autobiography (parts in Tate, 1983) are expected. See MW, essays, 1990; Eugenia Collier and Eleanor Traylor in Evans, 1984, Minrose C. Gwin in Marjorie Pryse and Hortense J. Spillers, eds., *Conjuring*, 1985, and Richard K. Barksdale, in *Black American Poets Between Worlds, 1940–1960*, 1986. Interview in *Frontiers*, 9, 1987.

Wall, Ann, author of an account of systematic abuse by her father: *The Life of Lamenther*, 1771, from its refrain 'Lament Her'. Unlikely as it sounds, its material is unheard-of in contemporary fiction; two duchesses subscribed, and several relations, though they had not wanted it published. Her mother, a substantial merchant's daughter, married against her family's will, and met immediate cruelty. The author bore a permanent scar from a blow at two years old; when her little sister died, and again at four when her mother died, she wished it had been her. She was nearly starved, and beaten more than her tougher elder sister, who was her defender in youth but later a secondary exploiter. An aunt's family gave her six years' respite (and schooling); she writes of her shyness, her fear of being sent back, her recurrent hope that her father might change, her desire to conceal the facts. On her aunt's death he reclaimed her; after another escape, at about 15, she began sewing shirts for a living. Trying to sue him for support only clarified his legal rights over her; in malice he had her led to a prostitutes' den. She ends with no conclusion; a promised *Collection of Miscellaneous Poems* is not known.

Wallace, Bronwen, 1945–89, poet, short-story writer, film-maker, b. in Kingston, Ont., da. of Marguerite (Wagar) and Ferdinand Wallace. She was educ. at Queen's Univ., Kingston (BA in English, 1967, MA, 1969), where she then taught creative writing. She wrote the *Kingston Whig-Standard* feminist column and collaborated with film-maker and social worker Chris Whynot, with whom she raised a son. Her second book of poems, *Signs of the Former Tenant*, 1983, established her focus on women's lives; her next extended the *Common Magic*, 1985, of poetic language, formulating a body consciousness in which 'thought is no different from flesh'. Poems in *The Stubborn Particulars of Grace*, 1987, shift between sexual politics and the dailiness of coming to wisdom. 'Story is an extended metaphor for the voice of discovery and mystery within what happens'. Storytelling which 'tries to explain the fit of things' fascinates the plain speech of the brave gritty friends and family who people her domestic space. Her short stories, *People You'd Trust Your Life To*, appeared in 1990. See Margaret ATWOOD in *JCP*, 2, 1987.

'Wallace, Doreen', Dora Eileen Agnew (Wallace) Rash, novelist, b. 1897 at Lorton, Cumberland, da. of Mary Elizabeth (Peebles) and R. B. Agnew W. After

Malvern Girls' College, she took English Honours at Somerville College, Oxford, in 1919. A close friend of Dorothy SAYERS (later estranged), she published *–Esques*, 1918, with E. F. A. Geach. She taught English at Diss grammar school in Norfolk before marrying farmer Rowland H. Rash in 1922; she had three children, taught part-time for the Workers' Educational Association and kept writing fiction and local journalism into the 1980s. In her first novel, *A Little Learning* [1931], the heroine and her rough farming family are bruised by the sophistication she acquires at Oxford; she finds refuge in a loveless, 'dull and out-of-the-world' marriage. DW has pub. countryside books like *East Anglia*, 1939, the pamphlet *How to Grow Food*, 1940, and the gardening diary *In a Green Shade*, 1950. Her 40 novels observe comic and tragic cross-purposes between different classes, sexes and generations. In *How Little We Know*, 1949, a retired colonel and his wife fail to foresee the threat posed by their genteel tenant to their half-savage proletarian maid; in *Daughters*, 1955, middle-class girls find nothing but tedium in the options open to them; in *Woman with a Mirror*, 1963, the varied, well-meaning society of a little Lake District town combines to destroy and vilify a silly, beautiful flirt; in *Landscape with Figures*, 1976, the old cope gallantly and humorously with change and indignity in a community which the young (recording it in the local paper) find boring. Several books recently repr.; see Susan J. Leonardi, *Dangerous by Degrees: Women at Oxford and the Somerville College Novelists*, 1989.

Wallace, Eglinton (Maxwell), Lady, d. 1803, Scottish dramatist and miscellaneous writer, youngest da. of Magdalen (Blair) and Sir David M. A wild tomboy in childhood, she m., 1770, Thomas Dunlop, who that year became a baronet under the name of W. Having divorced him (easier in Scotland) for infidelity in 1778, she impressed James Boswell with her poems and her 'indelicate effrontery'. She moved from Edinburgh to London, where she pub. *A Letter to a Friend, with ... the Ghost of Werter* (verse) [1787], which with passion and clarity blames Charlotte, stresses the value of female chastity and urges better education (see Syndy M. Conger in *Goethe Yearbook*, 3, 1986). EW's first comedy, *Diamond Cut Diamond*, 1787, was from French; when her second, *The Ton, or Follies of Fashion*, 1788, was damned on stage (unfairly, she says) for indecency, she left for Europe (she was arrested in Paris, 1789, as a British spy). Her tragedy remained unpub.; her last comedy, *The Whim*, was issued with an indignant preface, at Margate, 1795, after Anna Margaretta LARPENT's husband had (unusually) denied it a licence, owing either to subversive, democratic aspects of a day's saturnalia (servants change roles with masters), or else to sniping at the Prince of Wales. EW also published a *Letter* of moral advice to one of her sons, 1792, and political pamphlets in 1793 (relating her own war experience) and 1798 (*A Sermon ... to the People on Peace and Reform*).

Wallace, Ellen, 1815?–94, British novelist of whom little is known. She pub. at least five novels, all anon. *Mr Warrenne The Medical Practitioner*, 1848, is an odd tale with very little to do with its titular character after an initial description of the difficulties of his position as gentleman and pariah of the medical profession: 'Impossible to be more highly educated, impossible to be worse remunerated'. His two daughters and one son are noble and refined, and after tribulations, triumph morally over a spoilt heiress. This was reprinted, still anonymously (by EW's request) in the *Argosy* for 1893. *Lena; or, the Silent Woman*, 1852, has a sophisticated style, especially in dialogue, and again, the most important issue is nuances of gentlemanly behaviour among the moral middle classes: aristocrats gamble and forget their daughters' names.

Wallace, Helen, 'Gordon Roy', Scottish novelist, wrote three novels under her pseudonym 1888–92, nine under her own name 1900–13. *For Her Sake*, 1889, looks at Irish life from the viewpoint of its Scottish heroine, at first highly critical, later sympathetic. *His Cousin Adair*, 1891, set like many of hers, in Scotland, with the humble characters speaking broad Scots, deals in gripping popular style with the love affair of Adair, initially undervalued because of her lack of fragility. *For Better, For Worse*, 1892, her last 'Roy' novel, vividly evokes life in a small bleak east coast Scottish fishing village, and again treats a misunderstood heroine who defies local conventions. Her Wallace novels, such as *The Coming of Isobel*, 1907, are much weaker.

Wallace, Susan J., poet and teacher, b. 1931 at West End, Grand Bahama. She was educ. there and at St John's College (Nassau), Nassau Teacher-Training College, and the Univs. of Exeter (Institute of Education) and Miami (BEd and MEd). She taught English at the Southern Senior School, Nassau, then worked from 1968 for the Bahamas Education Ministry, becoming Assistant Director of Further Education. She is married to Sydney W. of the Department of Civil Aviation (who has illustrated her books), and has five children. Her first volume of poetry, *The Bahamian Scene*, 1970, has been often reprinted. *Island Echoes*, 1973, makes less use of dialect; *Back Home*, 1975, adds stories and short plays to poetry. SJW has also written plays for radio. Her work, addressed to both children and adults, is well known in Bahamian schools and has been anthologized; it deals with distinctively Bahamian or at least Caribbean customs, scenes and attitudes. She hopes to 'express the feeling that comes from a deep sensitivity to [her] environment'. She enjoys comic deflations: at a funeral ('One woman get de Holy Ghos' / In de middle o' my bench, / An' when she did done shake me up, / Ma funeral clothes was drench') or on a visit of school inspectors: 'Billows rolled, boat leapt, / Weight of bodies left the seat, / Boat fell, stomachs rose', till on dry land they 'Puffed their chests and smoothed their hair, / Education men were they.'

Waller, Anne (Paget), Lady, also Harcourt, d. 1662, diarist. Da. of William, 4th Lord Paget, she began her journal in 1649 as widow of the royalist Sir Simon Harcourt (shot in 1642), with resolute optimism, thanking God for her husband's past kindness and reputation, for her hopeful though delicate children, and for the religious feeling planted in her heart 'in my very yong years'. In 1652, struggling with debts and illness, she became third wife of the leading Puritan Sir William W. The diary records childbed, deaths, political vicissitudes, 'my own experience of God's nearness to encouradg and comfort the heart' (despite her 'exorbitant' religious fears), and the way she and her husband surmounted disagreement (here about marrying her son to his daughter) because there is 'soe litle unkindnes between' them. She accompanied him to prison in 1659. Extracts of diary pub. with funeral sermon, 1664.

Waller, Mary Ella, 1855–1938, novelist, translator and poet, b. Boston, Mass., da. of Mary Doane (Hallet) and David W. The early deaths of her father and brother impelled MEW into teaching in an exclusive Boston finishing school, and later at the Brearly School in NY. She founded Miss Waller's School for Girls in Chicago, but poor health forced her to give it up. She began writing children's stories and German verse translations, then scored a hit with *The Woodcarver of 'Lympus*, 1904. Together with *Sanna of the Island Town*, 1905, it ran through over a dozen editions. Here, as in later novels (*The Cry in the Wilderness*, 1912; *Out of the Silences*, 1918), the dominant theme of self-salvation and rescue has underlying motifs of lost parentage, orphanism and illegitimacy. Adopting a male persona in *My Ragpicker*, 1911, a prose poem, MEW depicts a middle-aged artist's unrequited love for a seventeen-year-old orphan girl living in the slum-squalor of Buttes-Chaumont, Paris. As in *Deep in the Hearts of Men*, 1924, set in New Hampshire, loss of love or kin resolves in a kind of psychic recovery through the common bonds of work and fellowship. Communities of women, as in *Sanna*, provide stability and a secure base for exploring the world: the intrepid fatherless heroine is not confined to stereotyped sex roles (see also *A Year out of Life*, 1909). MEW deplored Ibsen's 'morbidity': 'the sex-problem like gravitation ... solves itself' (*From an Island Outpost*, 1914).

Walwicz, Ania, prose writer, poet, playwright, visual and performance artist, community arts worker, b. 1951 in Swidica Slaska, Silesia, Poland, da. of Teresa (Singer-Werk) and Henryk W. She migrated to Australia in 1963, and studied art at the Victorian College of the Arts, Melbourne, and English informally at the Univ. of Melbourne. Her work, not prose, not poetry, but 'Writing', has appeared in anthologies such as *Island in the Sun*, 1981, *Frictions*, 1982, *Difference: Writings by Women*, 1985, and *Off the Record*, 1985 (containing a sound recording of AW reading some of her work). She has also produced a cassette tape, 'Voice Performance of Prose/Poetry Text', 1986, as well as having her work performed in *Girlboytalk* at the Anthill Theatre, Melbourne, 1986. AW is an experimental and wittily innovative writer. Performance is an essential aspect of her work since language is used with such energy. In *Writing*, 1982, her one collection, words and phrases, relentlessly repeated, become a potent weaponry as the poet/artist forces communication with the reader/listener. Her apprehension of images is so crystal clear that at times she becomes the vision she is translating into words (e.g, in 'The Fountain', with its progression from 'I saw a fountain' to 'I was the fountain'). The constant presence of 'I' and 'my' in almost every piece reinforces this sense of the essential solipsism of poetry. The accusatory 'You' found in the piece 'Australia' (in *Island in the Sun*), is thus a shock, embarrassing us into painful recognition.

Walworth, Jeannette Ritchie (Haldermann), 1837–1918, journalist and novelist, b. Philadelphia, da. of Matilda (Norman) and Charles Julius H., German exile and President of Jefferson College in Washington, Miss. She was educ. at home by her father, then worked as governess on a Louisiana plantation until the end of the Civil War, when she pub. newspaper pieces as 'Ann Atom' in New Orleans. After a discouraging start, her novels and stories began to attract attention, and from 1870 until the end of the century she wrote widely for periodicals and had over two dozen books published. Many of her novels are on topical themes, such as *Bar Sinister*, 1885, her popular anti-polygyny novel about the Mormon church. Unlike her other novels, which usually end happily, this one ends with the death of the 'legitimate wife'. JW also wrote several novels based on the Southern experience before and after the war, including *Without Blemish: To-day's Problem*, 1886, which discusses the situation of the freed blacks, though the social comment is secondary to the conventionally romantic narrative involving mistaken (racial) identities.

'Wander, Waif', 'W.W.', Mary Helena (Wilson) Fortune, 1833?–*c*. 1909, short-story writer, mostly of crime, novelist, journalist and poet, b. at Belfast, Ireland, to Eleanor (Atkinson) and George Wilson, civil engineer. Brought up in Canada, she m. Joseph F., surveyor, and travelled to Australia in 1855 with their son George, to join her father on the goldfields. In 1858 she m. Percy Brett, policeman and apparent source for her crime fiction. After their separation, she wrote for a living, contributing prolifically to the popular *Australian Journal*. She is a 'founding mother' of DETECTIVE fiction, she and 'Seeley Regester' (Metta VICTOR) being the earliest known women writers in the genre. Her first crime story, 'The Dead Witness', appeared in January 1866 and her last in 1909; there were hundreds in between. A collection of these tales, *The Detectives Album*, 1871, was her only book publication. She also wrote the memoir 'Twenty Six Years Ago', 1882–3, which mostly describes life (and crime) on the goldfields, and the serials 'Bertha's Legacy', 'Dora Carleton', 'The Secrets of Balbrooke', all 1866, 'Clyzia the Dwarf', 1867, and 'The Bushranger's Autobiography', 1871–2. These, like the rest of her fiction, are lively melodramatic romances, set both in England and Australia. Mystery and crime dominated the stories pub. under the pseudonym 'W.W.'; 'Waif Wander' was more the romancer and poet. See L. Sussex in D. Adelaide, *A Bright and Fiery Troop*, 1988.

Wandor, Michelene (Samuels), b. 1940, prolific feminist playwright, poet, short-story writer and critic. Da. of Russian Jewish emigrés to London, Rosalie (Wander) and Abraham S., she was educ. at Chingford Secondary Modern and High Schools and at Newnham, Cambridge (BA in English, 1962). She m. Edward Victor, had two sons, and divorced in 1975. Involved with the women's liberation movement from 1969, she edited its first English essay collection, *The Body Politic*, 1972. Her reviews and other journalism became influential. Her plays, many for women's THEATRE GROUPS, began with *You Two Can be Ticklish*, produced 1970 (a couple tickle a stranger to death). Most address specific women's issues: *The Day After Yesterday*, produced 1972, on the attitudes behind the Miss World contest, *Mal de Mère* and *Spilt Milk*, produced 1972 and 1973, on traps of motherhood and daughterhood, *Care and Control*, 1977, and *Aid Thy Neighbour*, 1978, on lesbian motherhood. *Future Perfect*, 1981, on utopias, was co-authored with two men. In 1975–6 MW did an MA at Essex Univ. in sociology of literature. She has done much collaborative work, editing and contributing to volumes of essays, poems, and stories (notably with Zoe FAIRBAIRNS, Sara MAITLAND, Valerie MINER and Michèle ROBERTS, 1977, 1978 and 1987). MW has given a lead both in getting feminist plays into print (editing *Strike While the Iron is Hot*, 1980, and *Plays by Women*, 1–4, 1982–5), and in publicizing the women's literary tradition. As well as E. B. BROWNING (*Aurora Leigh* for stage, 1979, radio, 1981), she has dramatized for radio – besides male authors – a dozen women ranging from Jane AUSTEN and Mary Augusta WARD to Antonia WHITE, Radclyffe HALL, Sylvia Townsend WARNER, Dorothy SAYERS, and Catherine COOKSON. She likes radio's scope for the written word, but also works for TV: e.g. adapting plays on Emily DICKINSON, 1987, and Kate CHOPIN, 1988. She has published poems in many anthologies, read them in public herself, and had them peformed in cabaret. *Upbeat*, 1982, includes poems and stories; in *Gardens of Eden*, 1984 (poems), Eve and Lilith rewrite the 'fall'; *Guests in the Body*, 1986 (stories) relates the themes of Jewish identity and gender politics. In *Carry On, Understudies*, 1981, revised 1986, and *Look Back in Gender*, 1987, MW discusses gender aspects of recent British theatre and radical theatre groups; in *Once a Feminist*, 1990, she interviews women at the forefront in the 1960s. Keyssar, 1984, allots her chief credit for 'articulating and supporting the interaction of feminism, theatre, socialism and gay liberation in Britain'.

Ward, Catherine George, later Mason, b. 1787 (in Scotland), poet, novelist, and children's writer, brought up partly in the Isle of Wight, with family connections in Norfolk. She was versifying at ten. She acted at Edinburgh, but later said her writing was her family's sole support from *c.* 1804. Her first little book, by subscription, Edinburgh 1805, contains verse tales and lyrics on love, flowers, beggars and orphans; many reappear in later volumes, Coventry 1812, London 1820 (dedicated to Prince Leopold, with two poems, one repr., on Princess Charlotte's death). She fictionalized the princess's life in the voluminous *Rose of Claremont* [1820]. *The Dandy Family*, illustrated [?1818], is an odd little doggerel satire on the ancestor of the bicycle; *Woman, A Poem*, is untraced. CGW's prose begins with *The Daughter of St. Omar*, 1810: unknown parents, a cruel mother-figure, and happy second marriage for a heroine first compelled to wed a haughty seducer of others. Her style in 20 or so novels is effusive, with long wandering sentences and cardboard characters and plots. *The Widow's Choice*, 1823, is a pamphlet with heavily self-advertising title-page. She could do better, as in *The Eve of St Agnes*, 1831 (no mention of Keats: a Scots version of the legend). Her only child died in 1816 and her tubercular husband in 1824, whereon she was jailed for his debts. She then m. James M. Mason, who also failed in business and in health by 1832. The RLF helped her for years; among unpub. works she mentions two operas and a farce.

Ward, Josephine Mary (Hope), 1864–1932, novelist, middle da. of Lady Victoria Fitzalan (Howard: d. 1870) and James Robert Hope-Scott, QC (d. 1873), of Abbotsford, inherited through his first wife, Walter Scott's granddaughter. JW was brought up from age nine by her maternal grandmother, sharing lessons with her sisters and younger aunts. In 1887 she m. Wilfred W., Newman's biographer, with whom she shared total commitment to Catholicism. The first of her ten novels, *One Poor Scruple*, 1899, deals with an intelligent, worldly woman, brought back to religion at the cost of human happiness: it was a great success. English politics provide the setting for *The Light Behind*, 1903, while *Out of Due Time*, 1906, treats the Modernist controversy through a hero based on her husband. It was attacked from the pulpit by conservative Catholic clergy. Her most polished novel, *The Job Secretary*, 1911, focuses on a young novelist talking over his lifeless characters with three friends, who, unawares, piece together their own story. See Maisie Ward, *The Wilfred Wards*, two vols., 1934, 1937.

Ward, Mary, 1585–1645, religious writer and activist, b. at Ripon, Yorks, eldest child of Catholics Ursula (Wright) and Marmaduke Ward, partly brought up by her mother's mother, who had spent years in jail for her faith. She learned Latin, refused at least four suitors, and campaigned seven years for her father's leave to be a nun. Life with Poor Clares at Gravelines, 1606–9, convinced her that 'the will of God, which *only, only* I desired', lay elsewhere. She visited England, set up at St Omer with seven companions, 1609, and worked for an unenclosed order of women under a rule like that of the Jesuits, not subject to any male order: the active, cosmopolitan, missionary Institute of Mary, also called 'the gallopping girls', was provisionally approved by the Pope in 1616. Travelling on foot across Europe and the Alps, MW founded houses and schools in Cologne, Bratislava, Naples, etc., and was arrested in England in 1619. The order was suppressed in 1628 ff (though papal heresy charges were later dropped) and MW jailed in Munich, 1631. Working in England from 1639, she died in a 'safe home' outside York. Her writings include autobiographical fragments (with fine prayers) in English and Italian, notes, letters, speeches (selec. ed. M. Emmanuel Orchard, 1985). Her order's Augsburg archives have 'Sister Dorothy's' account of her own secret Catholic work in England, 1621–2, and a life of MW in paintings; Manchester has her life by her associates Mary Poyntz and Winefrid Wigmore, *c.* 1650. MSS at the Bar convent, York (now a

MW museum), were thinned by burning in the 1790s (when the nuns first learned of a papal Bull against them of 1749, and the English RC church was moving from family to priestly control). Modern lives began with Sister Mary Catharine Elizabeth Chambers, 1882. See forthcoming study of the Bar convent by Susan O'Brien.

Ward, Mary Augusta, Mrs Humphry Ward (Arnold), 1851–1920, novelist and anti-suffragist, b. Hobart, Tasmania, eldest da. of Julia (Sorell) and Thomas A.: niece of poet Matthew A., sister of Ethel ARNOLD. In 1856 the family moved to England where she was educ. at boarding schools, including one run by Anne Jemima Clough (later first Principal of Newnham). Her first stories appeared in periodicals while she was living in Oxford, where she met and m. Jon and, later, journalist Thomas Humphry W. As early as 1873 she was working to organize lectures for women, and took part in the development of Somerville, the first women's college in Oxford. Untiring in her efforts to improve women's EDUCATION and participation in public service and local government, she also led the movement opposing women's national SUFFRAGE, arguing that it was selfish to demand it and that men's contributions (especially in war) had earned them the vote. She was the moving spirit in the Women's National Anti-Suffrage League, founded 1908. In London from 1881, she began regularly writing reviews and essays. The first of her 28 novels was *Miss Bretherton*, 1884, and she soon became one of the most popular writers of her time, on both sides of the Atlantic. Her most famous and respected novel, *Robert Elsmere*, 1888, so accurately reflected the religious doubt of this period that it became an immediate bestseller. The highly popular *Marcella*, 1894, describes the development of a young woman from unthinking radicalism to informed moderation. Marcella's indignation over the plight of the poor is skilfully evoked, and despite the novel's predictable romantic ending, she never reneges on her commitment to reform. MAW's novel on the WOMAN QUESTION, *Delia Blanchflower*, 1915, has a similar theme. Its portrait of the militant suffrage movement is stinging, and centres on the male guardian's efforts to wean Delia from a romantic friendship with a stereotypically bitter feminist. The novel is typical of MW's warm portrayal of the intense bonds between women. All her works treat social questions seriously. Her autobiography, *A Writer's Recollections*, appeared in 1918. Her papers are held at the Honnold library, Claremont, California; Pusey House, Oxford; University College, London (Arnold family papers); and the Mary Ward Centre, London. Life, 1923, by her da. Janet Penrose Trevelyan; life by John Sutherland, 1990; life in progress by Caryn McTighe Musil; bibliog. by W. B. Thesing and S. Pulsford, *VFRG*, 13, 1987.

'Warden, Florence', Florence Alice (Price) James, 1857–1929, novelist, b. Hanworth, Middlesex, da. of C. W. P. of the London Stock Exchange. Educ. at Brighton and in France, she worked as a 'finishing' governess, 1875–80, and an actress, 1880–5. In 1887 she m. George Edward J. She achieved fame with her second novel, *The House on the Marsh*, 1882, a mystery with echoes of *Jane Eyre*. *Passage Through Bohemia*, 1893 (repr. 1895 as *Strictly Incog.*), is typically composed of mixed comic, pathetic, realistic and sensation elements; it debunks the Pygmalion myth when the hero fails to effect the social transformation of his recalcitrant barmaid wife. FW wrote over 150 novels and tales, most of them mysteries, with titles such as *The Woman With the Diamonds*, 1895, *A Lady in Black*, 1896, and *The Man with the Amber Eyes*, 1907. She regretted that the demand for her mysteries kept her from writing more serious works, and was bitterly disappointed that she failed as a dramatist, though at least two plays were produced. Of particular interest among her non-mystery novels is *A Vagrant Wife*, 1885, which concerns a naïve governess who marries an idle young drunkard, leaves him for a career on the stage, and is eventually reconciled to him when he reforms. An obituary by one of FW's children describes her as 'a staunch conservative patriot'.

Wardlaw, Elizabeth (Halket), Lady, 1677–1727, balladist. Da. of Janet (Murray) and Sir Charles H. of Pitfirrane in Fife, she m., 1696, Sir Henry W. of Pitreavie. Her ballad 'Hardyknute', probably put together from ancient fragments, was printed at Edinburgh, *c.* 1710, expanded in 1719 and in Allan Ramsay's *The Ever Green*, 1724 (as pre-1600), and much reprinted. Scholars accepted it as ancient 'true Sublime' till Thomas Percy told its story in 1765; Walter Scott called it 'the first poem I ever learned, the last I shall ever forget'. Robert Chambers, finding EW's hand in 25 or more of the best-known 'high-class romantic BALLADS of Scotland' in 1859, was at once refuted by Norval Clyne; but EW may have written or revised other pieces, like 'Gilderoy', a sanitized version of an indecent ballad about a robber hanged at Edinburgh in 1638 (new version unpub. in her lifetime).

Warfield, Catherine Ann (Ware), 1816–77, poet and novelist, b. Natchez, Mississippi, da. of Sarah (Percy), who was institutionalized for insanity in 1820, and Nathaniel A. Ware, political economist and amateur scientist. She was educ. at private schools in Philadelphia and Cincinnati, and wrote verse and satire from an early age. In 1833 she m. R. E. Warfield; they lived in Europe for a time, subsequently moving to Galveston, Lexington and Beechmore, near Louisville. With her sister, Eleanor Percy Ware Lee, she pub. *The Wife of Leon, and Other Poems, by Two Sisters of the West*, 1843, followed in 1846 by *The Indian Chamber*. Her first novel, *The Household of Bouverie*, 1860, is considered her best because of her sense of the tensions within the household, especially for a woman. She wrote nine other novels and is viewed as one of the first important woman novelists of the South. Her poetry is generally sentimental. One poem, 'Never, As I Have Loved Thee', concludes that her loyalty and unselfish 'offerings' have left 'my own existence / A bleak, a barren plain'. There is no biographical or critical study.

Waring, Anna Laetitia, 1823–1910, hymn and verse writer, b. Plas-y-Velin, Neath, Glamorgan, Wales, second da. of Deborah and Elijah W. Brought up as a Quaker, ALW converted to Anglicanism in 1842, and was best known for the HYMN 'Father, I know that all my life is portioned out for me', 1846. Books include *Hymns and Meditations*, 1850, which ran to nearly 20 eds.; *Additional Hymns*, 1858; and *Days of Remembrance*, 1886, a calendar of Bible texts. Although she lived most of her life in retirement with her three sisters, she visited Bristol prisoners and worked with the Discharged Prisoners Aid Society. See M. S. Talbot, *In Remembrance of A. L. Waring*, 1911.

Warland, Betsy, poet and editor. B. in 1946 in Fort Dodge, Iowa, da. of Mildred (Hovey) and C. E. W., she studied at Luther College, Decorah, Iowa (BA, 1970), moved to Canada, 1972, and became a citizen, 1981. She was married, 1969–77. She helped develop the Toronto Women's Writing Collective, 1974; this led to many feminist projects, notably Women and Words/Les femmes et les mots, a cross-Canada bilingual conference for women working with the written word (UBC, 1983). BW initiated and co-ordinated it and co-edited its proceedings, 1985. *A Gathering Instinct*, 1981, including some poems she published as 'W. Van Horn', shows her training in painting and her fascination with the strangeness of the familiar ('i have borrowed / your boredom / . . . like a favourite book / its binding broken / from familiarity'). *open is broken*, 1894, interspersed with quotations from writers such as Mary DALY and Hélène CIXOUS, explores women's 'inhertextuality'. Influenced by Daphne MARLATT, with whom BW has lived in Vancouver since 1982, it emphasizes etymology and language. These poems of lesbian desire create the 'semantic space' women inhabit when they move 'from absence to presence' ('i broke in the palm of your hand / *palm*: "planet" drawing my / menses to a new meter'). *serpent write*, 1987, subtitled 'a reader's gloss', is a long non-linear poem also constructed out of a collage of matriarchal and patriarchal voices radicalized by BW's undoing of language and the tradition. Her latest book is *Double Negative*, 1988, co-authored with Marlatt, an exploration of the writing process and perceptions during a stay in Australia ('point of view / night turns the lens around'). Interview with Janice Williamson in *Fuse*, 1985.

Warner, Anne Richmond, later French, 1869–1913, novelist, short-story writer and humourist, b. St Paul, Minn., da. of Anna Elizabeth (Richmond) and William Penn W. She was educ. by her mother, an omnivorous reader and French scholar. At 18 she m. Charles Eltinge F., 25 years her senior, and in 1894 she compiled the genealogy *An American Ancestry* for her son, her family having been early settlers in New England. Travelling with her two children in Europe, where she settled, she pub. *His Story: Their Letters*, 1902, in which the humorous dialogues for which she later became famous centre upon a romantic encounter in France. *A Woman's Will*, 1904, presents a similar light romance, peppered with humour. Her popular Susan Clegg books, in which the raconteur of lively local tales regales a partially deaf audience, constantly falling asleep, were followed by more lightly satiric novels. *The Rejuvenation of Aunt Mary*, 1905, features the partially deaf Aunt Mary with her comic social observations, and the highly popular *Sunshine Jane*, 1913, introduces Aunt Matilda, skilled in malapropisms, who, like Aunt Mary, mishears everything as well as craftily misleading all and sundry. Jane is the New Woman who, as one of the Sunshine Sisterhood, revolutionizes the women's community. She finally marries the reactionary Lorenzo, who would 'smash ladies back to where they belong ...'; however, Jane, we gather, will not be smashed. The stereotypes of *femme fatale* and gay blade recur in AW's fiction, as in *The Tigress*, 1916, where Nina Darling, to whom marriage is a hateful word, sends men to 'perdition' with heartless abandon.

Warner, Marina Sarah, critic of literature and culture, novelist. B. in 1946, da. of Emilia (Terzulli) and Esmond Pelham W., she read Modern Languages at Lady Margaret Hall, Oxford (BA, 1967). Twice married (to William Shawcross, 1972, and John Dewe Mathews, 1981), she has one child. She is best known for her provocative work on representation of the female form and nature. *Alone of All Her Sex; The Myth and Cult of the Virgin Mary*, 1976, traces the history of Marian devotions to show that the Virgin, despite the aesthetic inspiration she may have afforded, cannot be 'the innate archetype' for women because 'the moral code she affirms has been exhausted'. *Joan of Arc; The Image of Female Heroism*, 1981, argues that an acknowledgement of the warrior-maiden's despair and abjuration must be part of a flexible and humane assessment of her virtue. *Monuments and Maidens; The Allegory of the Female Form*, 1985, recognizes that visual representation continues to reify women according to limiting stereotypes; in the use of the female as sign, MW announces the need 'to generate a philosophy of possibilities, not reaction.' Her novels also explore these issues: *In a Dark Wood*, 1977, and *The Skating Party*, 1982, probe forms of sexual power, partly by assessing the continuing force of myth, the first in exploration of differences between Christian and Chinese cultures, the second in patterned variations on relationship, desire, and power, and in juxtaposition of the 'primitive' and the 'civilized'. *The Lost Father*, 1988, a technically ambitious treatment of her grandfather's death for love, was short-listed for the Booker Prize. MW has also written children's stories and a pamphlet on childhood, 1989.

Warner, Susan Bogert, 'Elizabeth Wetherell', 1819–85, novelist, b. NYC, elder da. of Anna (Bartlett, d. 1837) and Henry Whiting W., ruined by 1837. SBW and sister Anna, 1827–1915, also a novelist, had to support themselves, running the household and a small farm. At her aunt's suggestion, SBW wrote *The Wide Wide World*, 1850. One of the most popular nineteenth-century novels, it ran to 13 US editions in two years (repr. 1987, afterword by Jane Tompkins). A devout Presbyterian, she wrote it, according to her sister, 'in closest reliance upon God ... upon her knees.' Its heroine learns to love the God who has brought upon her a sequence of misfortunes, notably the loss of her beloved mother and of a close friend. *Queechy*, 1852, tells of an orphan who is sustained by the words of her late grandfather, 'God will take care of us.' Other works include *The Hills of Shatemuc*, 1856, *Melbourne House*, 1864, *Diana*, 1877, and children's stories. Her novels all deal with powerless young people, often small girls, who through Christian faith overcome a harsh masculine world. Although sentimental, SBW's writing is readable, with a skilful portrayal of rural life and later, of factory work. See Anna W.'s life of her sister, 1909; Nina Baym, *Woman's Fiction*, 1978; Edward Halsey Fester's study, 1978.

Warner, Sylvia Townsend, 1893–1978, FRSL, musicologist, poet, novelist, biographer and short-story writer. B. in Harrow, Middx, da. of Nora (Hudleston) and George T. W., a Harrow history master, she was educ. at home, living in London after her father's death, 1916. She worked in a munitions factory and then, 1922–9, as one of four editors of the ten-volume OUP *Tudor Church Music*. She knew many literary figures including Nancy CUNARD and T. F. Powys, who encouraged and influenced her work and introduced her to poet Valentine ACKLAND, with whom STW lived, mostly in Dorset, from 1932 until Ackland's death in 1969. They went to Spain as Red Cross Volunteers in 1930 and joined the Communist Party in 1935. In 1936, STW was elected to the executive committee of the International Association of Writers for the Defence of Culture. Her first novel, *Lolly Willowes*, 1926, a story of a spinster who becomes a witch, was nominated for the Prix Femina. This was followed by six more novels, ten volumes of short stories, a biography of T. H. White, 1967, and five volumes of poetry, one of them, *Whether A Dove or Seagull*, 1933, with Ackland. Likened as a poet to a 'feminine Thomas Hardy' (although with more range and less plangency), as a fiction writer she is characterized by originality of plot and setting, as in *The Corner That Held Them*, 1948, a novel about medieval nuns, a delicate and sometimes whimsical style, eccentric characters and amazing events. A missionary 'sodomite' falls in love with a convert in *Mr. Fortune's Maggot*, 1927; a woman in the Paris revolution, 1848, becomes the lover of her husband's mistress in *Summer Will Show*, 1936. STW was also a frequent, engaging and witty letter-writer and publication of her letters (ed. William Maxwell, 1982) contributed to the growing respect and affection in which her work and her character are held. *Four In Hand*, 1986, reprints four novels. See Arthur Boaten in *Mass. Studies in English*, 6, 1978; Claire Harman's introduction to *Collected Poems*, 1982; special supplement to *PN Review*, 23, 8, 1981–2; Wendy MULFORD on STW and Ackland, 1988; life by Harman, 1989.

Warner, Val, poet, b. 1946 at Harrow near London, da. of schoolteachers Ivy Miriam

(Robins) and Alister Alfred W. She took her BA at Somerville College, Oxford, in 1968, then taught in London ('the Victorian barracks-like room we locked them in / to "teach" them, then locked them out to stop / them smashing it') and worked as a librarian. She published *These Yellow Photos*, 1971, and *Under the Penthouse*, 1973: poems focusing on significant detail of human activity (packing away, tidying out, suffering a theft from a handbag) or of nature: 'these places / visited by dream, or out of time; polluted now'. She became a full-time writer in 1972, and has held writer-in-residence posts. She translated Tristan Corbière, *Wrecks*, 1973, and edited Charlotte MEW, 1982. Her most recent book is *Before Lunch*, 1986; her contributions to journals include stories as well as poems. Recent poetry often centres on small or older children, and presents interacting perceptions: those of the poet, apprehensive about the world's present and future, with those of a freshly, minutely perceiving child ('a small spider abseiling / down from the lintel'), or those of the older, disruptive, antisocial young with those of their unsympathetic adult observers. Anne STEVENSON finds 'a strangely naked way of facing up to art' in VW's handling of 'half-connections and failed love'.

Warre-Cornish, Mrs **Blanche** (Ritchie), *c.* 1847–1914, novelist, da. of Augusta (Trimmer) and William R., Advocate General in Calcutta. After her father's death, she and her family spent some time living with his cousin William Thackeray, the novelist, some of whose letters she later published (Boston and NY, 1911), 'together with recollections by his kinswoman'. Her first novel, *Alcestis*, 1873, telling of a strange compact made by a composer desperate to have his 'lost' opera performed, and the singer Lisa who loves him, is based on the real story of Josquin Dorioz. This was followed in 1882 by *Northam Cloisters*, *Sunningwell*, 1899, and *Dr Ashford and his Neighbours*, 1914. She was married to the vice-provost of Eton; her daughter, Molly, m. Desmond MacCarthy, and was a friend of Virginia WOOLF.

Warren, Elizabeth, gentlewoman pamphleteer of Woodbridge, Suffolk. Her closely-argued works, replete with detailed Latin marginalia, defend traditional Puritan practices against more radical innovations. *The Old and Good Way Vindicated*, 1646, bears commendations by the censor James Cranford and others, and her own denial that she wrote for publication, being 'consciious [sic] to my mental and Sex-deficiencie'. When her authorship was doubted, a second issue added further male defence, and her assertion that ill health, 'education of youth, and ordinary businesse in governing my family' prevented her writing at greater length. Yet in 1647 appeared *Spiritual Thrift*, which, though she says her meditations are 'produced like abortives in an hour unexpected', is an expansive and analytical attack on both Catholics and sectaries. After Charles I's execution in 1649 she pub. *A Warning-Peece from Heaven*, advising all to fear God's vengeance, and 'mourn for the misery our sin hath contracted'.

Warren, Mercy (Otis), 1728–1814, poet, dramatist, historian and patriot, b. on Cape Cod, eldest da. of Mary (Allyne) and James O., judge and politician. She shared the tutoring (for Harvard) of her elder brother James (a brilliant radical thinker who later suffered brain damage in an assassination attempt). She married his friend James W., gentleman farmer, in 1754, had five sons, and presided over pre-revolutionary gatherings at her Plymouth home. Her poems (many unpub.) discuss 'nature, friendship, philosophy, and religion'. Her satire does not spare women; she 'considered human nature as the same in both sexes'. She was a friend of Abigail ADAMS, and was influenced by Catharine MACAULAY, corresponding with her from the 1760s. Her plays began with *The Adulateur* ('As it is now acted in Upper Servia'), printed in anonymous newspaper instalments, 1772: written with no theatre experience, they are hard-hitting, sometimes rowdy attacks on Tories and the British. She worked from 1775 on her great *History of the ... American Revolution*, published in 1805 (facs. 1970) after much interruption from family troubles. In 1787 she hoped that John Adams might arrange London production for *The Sack of Rome*, one of her two classical blank-verse tragedies featuring heroic patriot Roman matrons. She published pamphlets like *Observations on the New Constitution ...*, 1788; first work to bear her name was *Poems, Dramatic and Miscellaneous*, 1790, with her tragedies and a verse dedication to Elizabeth MONTAGU as a sister fit to 'wrest a female pen' from men's imperious grasp. Her *History* (the only contemporary account which maintains a radical stance throughout, with measured preface asserting women's right to politics) made a breach with John Adams (later healed by Abigail); the letters about this, which MOW wanted destroyed, were pub. in 1878. MSS at Mass. Hist. Soc.; see life by Katharine Anthony, 1958, repr. 1972.

Warton, Jane or Jenny, 1724–1809, miscellaneous writer, b. at Basingstoke, Hants, da. of Elizabeth (Richardson) and Thomas W. the elder: sister of Joseph and Thomas W., friend of the future Hester CHAPONE. Her brothers published her ode on their father's death (in his *Poems*, 1748) and consulted her on their own works. Her *Adventurer* essay (no. 87, 1753) asks how far unusual people should bow to social forms. She worked as a governess both before and after a perhaps crippling 'fever' in 1750. Her conservative *Letters Addressed to Two Young Married Ladies* [ex-pupils], 1782, discusses 'The Importance of Those Accomplishments Most Agreeable to the Husband', but advises firmness in inevitable dependence. The heroines of her epistolary *Peggy and Patty, or The Sisters of Ashdale*, 1783, repr. 1825, leave Cumberland for London at 16 and 17 to earn a living ('Our hands ... disdain not labor'); blocked at every turn, they become prostitutes and die in poverty. 'My name was Summers; it is now – Misery' echoes Richardson's Clarissa. (Their closest woman friend has denied aid under savage pressure from her husband and father.) It was tepidly reviewed; the publisher Dodsley rejected further MSS, now (like JW's admired letters) lost. She wrote about her brother Thomas in the *GM*, 1794 and 1803, and *European Magazine*, 1796. Her niece Mary (Warton) Morgan left a journal of unhappy life in India, 1774–89 (Trinity College, Oxford).

Warwick, Mary Rich (Boyle), Countess of, 1624–78, diarist, autobiographer and author of meditations, b. at Youghal in Ireland, seventh da. and 13th child of Catherine (Fenton), who had links with Katherine PHILIPS and died in 1628, and Richard B., 1st Earl of Cork. Her elder sisters were married to wealthy men (Katherine, Lady Ranelagh, admired for her erudition, to 'the foulest churle in Christendom'). Mary refused her father's first choice of husband, and in 1641 privately married Charles R., later Earl of W. (having engineered paternal consent). In 1647 she promised God to 'become a new Creature'. Her home at Leighs Priory, Essex, became a noted resort of Puritan ministers; her chaplain was Elizabeth WALKER's husband, who published some of her writings with his funeral sermon, 1687. Her two children died before her. Her husband (d. 1673) suffered for his last 20 years from gout; her diaries show her life dominated by his frequent outbursts of violent temper. She attributes her suffering to her disobedient marriage, but also her coming to God to His not letting her find happiness elsewhere: he 'imbitterd the streame that I might com to the fountaine head'. She seems to have found peace only in retired prayer, or meditation under trees which her husband then had cut down. Diary extracts were pub. 1847, her autobiography 1848. Sara Heller Mendelson's life, 1987, uses unpub. MSS.

Wasserstein, Wendy, dramatist, b. 1950 in Brooklyn, NYC. She 'grew up going to the theater', began writing at Calhoun School (using her 'funny' family and 'eccentric' mother as material), transferred from Mount Holyoke College to Smith, where she studied play-writing, and went to Yale Univ. Drama School. Her early, hilarious, parodic plays were put on at New Haven: *Any Woman Can't* (showing the hoops a woman must jump through for a career; she settles for marriage instead), then *Happy Birthday, Montpellier Pizz-zazz*, 1974 (a caricature version of the social lives of college girls), and *When Dinah Shore Ruled the Earth*, 1975 (with Christopher Durang, a spoof of beauty contests). Later, with more rounded characters, WW still seeks to be serious by finding the absurd in the everyday. She sees 'a lot of raw emotion' in her *Uncommon Women and Others* (1975, Obie award; pub. 1979), where five 'Graduates of a Seven Sisters College Six Years Later', confront their life choices and confirm their friendship. (Susan L. Carlson compares it with Clare Boothe LUCE's *The Women* in *Modern Drama*, 27, 1984.) *Isn't It Romantic* (produced in NYC, 1981, pub. 1984) takes some of the same characters a stage further, and, as often, shows women using humour as defence or displacement; WW was glad to see women, often in groups, prominent among the audience. *Tender Offer*, staged 1983, takes an optimistic look at the father-daughter relationship; *The Man in a Case* (staged 1985, pub. 1986) is from Chekhov; *Miami* is a musical. WW has also acted, and written for TV (including *The Sorrows of Gin*, from John Cheever, 1979) and for *New York Woman* magazine. *The Heidi Chronicles*, staged 1988, has a woman professor, still idealistic in a careerist world, looking back at hopes, gains and failures of the women's movement, from consciousness-raising to aerobics. Interview in *Women's Studies*, 15, 1988.

Watson, Jean, novelist, b. 1933 at Mangapai, near Whangarei, NZ, da. of Jane (Struthers) and William Albert W. She was educ. at Mangapai Primary School with one term at Whangarei Girls High, leaving at 15 to help on the family farm. At 19 she went nursing and then worked at 'just about every sort of arse-hole job'. In the 1950s she moved to Auckland and wrote short stories, but aged 22–32 wrote nothing: 'I was tearing about the country after a man, looking for ideal things, ideal existences.' She travelled in Australia, 1962–5, then settled in Wellington, NZ, where she had a son and pub. her first novel, *Stand in the Rain*, 1965. It is a largely autobiographical 'on the road' novel, sparsely and cleanly written, and refreshingly different from tales of marriage and suburbia. In 1975 she pub. *The Balloon Watchers*, a short fantasy allegory about an office worker who learns how to live in the now. Its success led to the publication in 1978 of *The World is an Orange and the Sun*, written ten years earlier, with two other novels rejected by publishers. It is a married woman's objective but wistful account of her neighbour's affair with a younger man. JW's later works, *Flowers from Happyever*, 1980, and *Address to a King*, 1986, have a strong allegorical element and reflect her growing interest in Vedanta and Eastern philosophy, translated into a contemporary NZ context. In 1988 she was writer-in-residence at Auckland Univ.

Watson, Sheila Martin (Doherty), b. 1909, novelist, short-story writer, critic, teacher. She is da. of Elweena (Martin) and Dr Charles D., Superintendent of the Provincial Mental Hospital, New Westminster, BC, on whose grounds (the scene of the story 'Brother Oedipus') the family lived until his death, 1922. She was educ. in convents and at the Univ. of British Columbia (BA 1931, Certificate of Education 1932, MA 1933). She taught 1934–52, in BC and Toronto; 1934–6, in a one-room school in the Cariboo, where, refusing to 'board', she lived in her own 'shack' with dog, horse, and gun. The Cariboo gave her 'images' for writing, beginning with an unpublished novel, *Deep Hollow Creek*. An Ur-story 'And the four animals' (completed by 1952) elliptically symbolizes humans' 'mythic transformation' of gods from Creation, through 'civil gods made tractable by use and useless by custom', to Apocalypse. Fundamental here, as in all SW's work, is the conviction that we become 'human' through the 'mediating rituals' of art, custom, and religion. From 1952–5, SW joined her husband, poet, dramatist and professor Wilfred W. (m. 1941), in Calgary, then Edmonton. Although personally difficult, these years allowed leisure to complete *The Double Hook*, which, finished in 1953, was repeatedly rejected for its unconventional style and not published until 1959. Concerned with the construction of civilization in a place gathering people of diverse origins, it begins with matricide and ends with a birth which calls up in its characters remembered fragments of 'mediating rituals'. Its terse, poetic, resonant speech presents, without sentimentality or judgment, an old mother inescapable even in death, a widow and her illegitimately pregnant daughter, a sterile wife, Angel and her children, and a spinster ('laughed at when no one has come for her, when there's no one to come') whose anger becomes self-directed. Departing radically from the realism dominating Canadian fiction, the novel's elliptic style and structure also eschewed modernist psychologism and stream-of-consciousness. As numerous Canadian writers attest, it made their own (postmodernist) writing possible. In 1956 SW began PhD study (Univ. of Toronto), completing her thesis on Wyndham Lewis under Marshall McLuhan, 1965. (Told by her department chairman she would need to be five times as good as a man, she asked, 'Which man?') The first woman successfully to challenge hiring policies against nepotism, she joined the Univ. of Alberta English Department, 1961–75. A novel about academia, *Landscapes of the Moon*, remained unfinished as she gave unstinting personal and scholarly support to students', her husband's, and younger writers' work, partly through the journal *white pelican*, which she founded, financed, and co-edited, 1970-6, and partly through shaping contributions to the fledgling Canada Council. She moved to Vancouver Island, 1980, and received the Lorne Pierce medal, 1984, for services to Canadian culture. *Five Stories*, 1984, collects her short stories, an *Open Letter* special issue, 1974–5, her essays. See Stephen Scobie, *CWW*, 1985, and Angela Bowering, *Figures Cut in Sacred Ground*, 1988.

Watts, Mary (Stanbery), 1868–1958, novelist and playwright, b. Delaware Co., Ohio, da. of Anna (Martin) and John Rathbone S. She was educ. at the Sacred Heart Convent, Clifton, and gained an MA degree. In 1891 she m. Miles Taylor W., and 17 years later began her writing career. Deeply influenced by her childhood years on an Ohio farm, her first novel, *The Tenants*, 1908, develops richly detailed mid-western settings and themes of class-division and deracination, chronicling the fall from prosperity of the House of Gwynne. Her second novel, *Nathan Burke*, 1910, maps the rise from backwoods obscurity of a young hero in the Mexican war who makes good as a lawyer. *The Rise of Jenny Cushing*, 1914, launches MW's major theme of class-oppression with a sensitive, rebellious child growing up to a free love union with an artist, and work for the suffragettes and an orphanage. MW's struggling heroines are distinguished by their self-possession, dignity, intelligence and quiet power. Well-received for her realism, MW also mocks the literary conventions of her own genre: 'Close the book and let us make believe it ends here, as all well-regulated stories should' (half-way through *The Legacy*, 1911). See also her play within a play, *An Ancient Dance*. See G. OVERTON, *The Women Who Make Our Novels*, 1922, for her life.

Watts, Susanna, 1768–1842, evangelical Baptist poet, prose-writer and artist, only surviving da. of Mary (Halley), 'an uneducated country girl', and John W. of Danett's Hall near Leicester, of a once prosperous and genteel family (that of Alaric W.). A baby when her father died, she taught herself French and Italian, supported her mother by teaching, and translated Tasso's *Jerusalem* (praised by Mary PILKINGTON) and Verri's *Roman Nights*, 1802–3. Neither was pub.: another version forestalled her Verri; parts of her Tasso, with a life, survive in her scrapbook (Leicester City Library, with friends' poems and prints of women writers). Her *Chinese Maxims*, 1784, versified Robert Dodsley's *Oeconomy of Human Life*; her *Original Poems and Translations*, 1802, with 'smaller Pieces' from magazines, was well reviewed. Maria EDGEWORTH, who met SW in 1802, found her comically humble. A relation of SW's friend Elizabeth HEYRICK got £20 for her from the RLF in 1807, mentioning her *Walk through Leicester* (1804, facs. 1967: after Jane HARVEY, a pioneer guide-book to an industrial town), her medal from the Society for Encouragement of the Arts for landscapes composed of feathers, and her mother's insanity (ascribed to fear of the new income tax). SW went on teaching after her mother died, and gathered a female ABOLITIONIST circle: she and Heyrick canvassed all Leicester grocers to open a boycott of West Indian produce. When their Book Society was called 'a set of dragons' SW replied in a poem signed '(for all), the illustrious Name *A Dragon*'. She ed. *The Selector*, Royston, 1823 (verse for the young), and *The Humming-Bird*, 1824–5, in the cause of suffering beasts and humans. *The Insects in Council* (verse), 1828, concerns a petition (*à propos* the new collecting craze) to man not to misuse his power. *The Wonderful Travels of Prince Fan-Feredin, in the Country of Arcadia*, Northampton, n.d., is a ROMANCE self-consciously critical of romances, revealed at last to be a dreamed version of middle-class life. In 1828 SW founded a society 'for the relief of indigent old age'; her *Hymns and Poems*, 1842, have a memoir by 'the child of her adoption'.

Weamys, Anna, author of *A Continuation of Sir Philip Sidney's Arcadia*, 1651, timed to coincide with a new edition and mindful of Sidney's closing invitation to 'some other spirit to exercise his penne' about the minor characters. Calling herself 'a young Gentlewoman', repeatedly decrying her own 'dull capacity', she assumes a thorough knowledge of Sidney, and reckons to capture his spirit in a plainer style, less digressive or expansive. She dedicates to two ladies of the Pierrepont family, and prints laudatory poems by several men, all mesmerized by her sex: 2nd ed., 1690.

Weatherwax, Clara, later Strang, novelist of whom little is known. She was b. and educ. in Aberdeen, Washington, granddaughter of a wealthy mill-owner, and in 1929 went to Stanford Univ. for two years. During the 1930s she became involved in the labour movement; her *Marching! Marching!*, 1935, won the *New Masses*-John Day prize 'for a novel on an American proletarian theme'. Set in a lumber town on the Northwest coast, it describes the mill workers' exploitation, victimization of union leaders, brutality of vigilantes, and, finally, the strikers marching heroically into a confrontation with the armed state militia. It is more experimental and impressionistic than other 1930s proletarian novels, contriving a 'collective' narrative voice instead of using a single protagonist. Granville Hicks thought CW had 'discovered the true poetry of proletarian life and revolutionary struggle'. Mary McCARTHY, however, called the book 'pinched, unhealthy, distorted and incidentally dull', deserving 'a pale green orchid as the Most Neurotic Novel of 1935'. It was repr. in 1976, when CW was said to be living in California with her husband, a composer.

Webb, Beatrice (Potter), 1858–1943, economist, essayist and diarist, b. Standish, Glos., da. of Lawrencina (Heyworth) and Richard P., business entrepreneur. The least favoured of the nine Potter girls, BW had little education. Where the others had governesses, she did not. However, one family friend, Herbert Spencer, encouraged her to read and research. Undergoing a religious crisis in late adolescence, she spent some years trying to work out her beliefs and find an occupation. Assisting her cousin, Charles Booth, in his survey of poverty in London, in 1888 she pub. moving accounts in the *Nineteenth Century* of her investigative experiences in the East End, disguised as a work-girl, followed by 'The docks; the tailoring trade; the Jewish community' in Booth's *Life and Labour of the People in London*, 1889–91. About this time, she joined the Fabian Society. In 1892, she m. Sidney W., civil servant and later London County councillor. (In 1890 she had seen his 'tiny tadpole body . . . Cockney pronunciation, poverty ... self-complacent egotism. ... sensitiveness ... great power' as 'an interesting study'.) They founded the London School of Economics, 1895, and the *New Statesman*, 1912. They worked together on a number of books, beginning with *The History of Trade Unionism*, 1894, and including a massive study of English local government. BW wrote a few small works alone: a series of papers on women and industrial legislation in the 1890s and a long pamphlet on equal wages, 1919. They travelled the world together to observe different political systems and their last major work expressed a particular enthusiasm: *Soviet Communism: a New Civilization*. BW became a major public figure when she was appointed to the Royal Commission on the Poor Law in 1905. She founded the Fabian Research Department in 1913. She pub. two AUTOBIOGRAPHICAL works, *My Apprenticeship*, 1926, in which she explains her search for a creed and a craft, and *Our Partnership*, 1948, which traces her personal and political development during married life. Her DIARIES (pub. microfiche, 1978; sels. 1982–6) are a major source for English social and political history, as well as tracing the conflicts she experienced as a woman wanting to work on an equal level with men. Lives by Deborah Nord, 1985, Lisanne Radice, 1984, Barbara Caine, 1986.

Webb, Elizabeth, *c.* 1663–1726/7, Quaker minister and memoirist. Educ. by an Anglican parson, she at first 'looked on the ministers to be like angels.' She discovered QUAKERS at about 12; at about 14 she became disenchanted with her employer's chaplain and began to think for herself. After a worldly interval, still at 19 'a servant to great persons' whom she feared to offend, she felt that 'the vials of the wrath of an angry father were poured out on the transgressing nature'; 'all other creatures were in their proper places', except herself, till she became a Friend in 1682. In 1697, already a seasoned traveller, married to Richard W., with children, living in Gloucester, she felt a strong call to America. Her husband's dislike of this idea vanished after she fell ill: he gave her leave for seven years; she went back and forth at least five times. In Virginia she found black people strange till a dream informed her that God's call was to them as well. Visiting London in 1712 from Chester Co., Pa., she wrote her story at the request of Anthony William Boehm, chaplain to Queen Anne's consort. Her *Letter* to him, popular in MS, pub. at Philadelphia, 1781, was much repr. She moved to New England in 1724.

Webb, Mary Gladys (Meredith), 1881–1927, novelist and poet. B. at Leighton, Shropshire, da. of Sarah Alice (Scott) and

George Edward M., head of a boys' preparatory school, she was educ. at home, then at a girls' finishing school at Southport, 1895–7. Between 1903 and 1907 (when ill health intervened) she attended Cambridge Univ. Extension lectures. Shy, intense, introspective, devoted to her father (whose death in 1909 affected her deeply), MW was a passionate, almost mystical lover of the Shropshire countryside. She suffered from Graves's disease, which gave her a goitre and staring eyes (disfigurement and responses to it feature in her novels: the heroine of *Precious Bane* (TV version 1989) has a hare lip). MW's marriage, 1912, to teacher Henry Bertram Law W., proved a possessive, finally unhappy relationship. She wrote poetry, short stories, essays and journalism, but is remembered chiefly for her six novels, especially *Gone to Earth*, 1917, *The House in Dormer Forest*, 1920, and *Precious Bane*, 1924. They ignore the contemporary scene, and evoke a rural past of love, violence, beauty and cruelty, of nature's power and mystery, of passionate lives, particularly those of tragic women. In *Gone to Earth* (memorable film version, 1948), the wild, nature-loving heroine dies trying to save her pet fox from the hunt, and herself from conflicting claims: 'body and soul had been put in opposition by belonging to different men'. MW's fame was posthumous, following praise from PM Stanley Baldwin in 1928. Stella GIBBONS's parody, 1932, damaged her credibility, but her narrative and atmospheric power is now again respected. *The Spring of Joy*, 1937, prints poems, miscellaneous prose, and the unfinished novel *Armour Wherein he Trusted*. All her novels have recent reprints; Gladys Mary Coles has ed. *Collected Prose and Poems*, 1977, *Selected Poems*, 1981, and pub. a life, 1978; see Erika Duncan, *Unless Soul Clap Its Hands*, 1984, and M. A. Barale, *Daughters and Lovers*, 1986.

Webb, Phyllis, poet, b. 1927, and brought up in Victoria, BC, da. of Mary (Patton) and Alfred W. She wrote at school, later studied at the Univ. of British Columbia (BA in English and Philosophy, 1949). She read Marx and Engels as a first-year student, then graduated into a provincial election, at 22 the youngest candidate ever to run in Victoria (unsuccessfully, for the CCF party). Earle Birney, F. R. Scott, E. J. Pratt, Dorothy LIVESAY and P. K. PAGE (her 'heroine' at the time) were important influences. In Montréal, 1950–6, she did graduate work in English at McGill, 1952–3, worked as a secretary, and 'began doing the occasional broadcast' for the CBC. She was introduced to American poetry by Louis Dudek and knew Eli Mandel, Miriam WADDINGTON, Jay MACPHERSON and Leonard Cohen. Her first poems, in *Trio*, 1954, announced one of her consistent themes: the 'distress', the 'word', which 'born of the weight of eons / ... skeletons our flesh'. *Even Your Right Eye*, 1956, written during travel in Ireland and England, where she worked briefly as a secretary at the London School of Economics, locates her unique vision in the terrible beauty the poet's eye/I discovers in the world: 'a forest of green angels, / a threat of magnificent beasts.' In Paris for a year and a half, from 1957, she pursued her interest in Marxist and absurdist theatre. Returning, she worked in Toronto in publishing and radio, later lived in San Francisco, and taught at the Univ. of British Columbia, 1960–3. She became Program Organizer in Public Affairs for the CBC, 1964, and producer of its distinguished 'Ideas' programme, 1967–9. She lived in relative isolation on Salt Spring Island, BC, from then until her move to Victoria, 1988. She has taught creative writing or been writer-in-residence at several Canadian universities. Her travels and work experience reflect her restlessness of mind, constant questioning of the self's position in the world, and desire to understand the tentative boundaries of human nature: 'The degree of nothingness / is important: / to sit emptily / in the sun /

receiving fire / that is the way / to mend / an extraordinary world, / sitting perfectly / still / and only / remotely human' (*The Sea is Also a Garden*, 1962). Her *Naked Poems*, 1965, written after UBC's influential 1963 Poetry Conference, are stark and crisp, brief interlinked lyrics touching poetic perfection – 'YOU / took / with so much / gentleness / my dark'. Interested in the anarchist movement, she visited Russia and began work, in 1967, on her 'never completed' 'Kropotkin Poems': 'The infantile ego could not solicit that beautiful anarchist dream poem.' These 'poems of failure', 'remnants' of which appear in *Wilson's Bowl*, 1980, 'signify' in her words, 'the domination of a male power culture in my educational and emotional formation so overpowering that I have, up to now, been denied access to inspiration from the female figures of my intellectual life, my heart, my imagination'. (One such is Adrienne RICH.) *The Vision Tree*, 1982, ed. with an introduction by Sharon THESEN, brings together poems from her earlier seven collections, including *Talking*, 1982, essays, reviews, some broadcasts, and thoughts about the creative process. *Water and Light: Ghazals and Anti-Ghazals*, 1984, reflects how PW works both with and against 'the traditional rules, constraints and pleasures' of the ghazal and lyric: 'Seeing all, all-seeing, even in sleep knows / space (outer, inner, around) tracks freak snows, / slumbering ponies. Love, I am timid / before this oracular seer, opal, apple of my eye.' See Susan Glickman in *CanL*, 115, 1987; Pauline Butling in Neuman and Kamboureli, 1986; John Hulcoop, in *CanL*, 32, 1967.

Webling, Lucy, 'Lucy Betty McRaye', b. *c.* 1870s. Most skilled of theatrical sisters (see Peggy WEBLING), she was a reciter at seven, then 'the original Little Lord Fauntleroy'. She married actor W. J. McRea, 1909. She wrote well-crafted and melodious reflective or nature poems, published in *Poems and Stories* (with Peggy), 1896, and two novels, *One Way Street*, 1933, and *Centre Stage* 1938. Both treat disillusion in marriage; both have a theatrical backdrop.

Webling, Peggy, 'Arthur Weston', b. *c.* 1870–2, journalist, fiction writer. She was b. in London, fifth of six daughters of first cousins Maria (W.) and Robert James W., jeweller and silversmith, and educ. privately, largely at home. With two of her sisters, she began giving recitations at eight, and so met Oscar Wilde, Oliver Wendell Holmes, Edward VII (then Prince of Wales), Ellen Terry, Jerome K. Jerome and John Ruskin, of whom PW later wrote *A Sketch*, 1916. At 18 she stayed a year with cousins in Brantford, Ont., where she sold her first story to the local *Expositor*. Back in England after failing to find theatre work in NYC, she had some success with verses and stories. The three sisters returned again to Canada for three years of theatrical touring, performing in small towns from Toronto to Vancouver, including the gold rush towns of the Kootenay. Back in London, PW began her writing career in earnest, writing for *M.A.P.* (*Mostly About People*, a London journal): English tales under her name and Canadian tales as 'Arthur Weston'. Her first novel, *Blue Jay*, 1905, about an acrobat, uses behind-the-scenes knowledge of the entertainment world. *Poems and Stories*, Toronto, 1896, consists of PW's simple, short, entertaining, unpolished stories, and Lucy WEBLING's poems. PW's *Verses to Men*, 1920, are sometimes satiric, sometimes sentimental; her *Guests of the Heart*, 1917, essays and speeches, are maudlin parables.

Webster, Julia **Augusta** (Davies), 'Cecil Home', 1837–94, feminist poet, translator and dramatist, b. Poole, Dorset, da. of Julia (Hume) and Vice-Admiral George D., educ. at school in Banff and at Cambridge, Paris and Geneva. She m. Thomas W., law lecturer and solicitor, in 1863; they had a daughter. AW began her writing career with the 1860 publication of *Blanche Leslie, and*

Other Poems, followed in 1864 by *Lilian Gray* and a novel, *Lesley's Guardians*. But her 1866 verse TRANSLATION of Aeschylus' *Prometheus Bound* established her as a serious classical translator. In the same year the publication of *Dramatic Studies* brought her attention as a poet, and her work was admired by Christina ROSSETTI. A specialist in the dramatic monologue, AW often used her poetry to explore feminist issues. In 'A Castaway,' 1870, for example, a prostitute defends herself against the Victorian stereotype of the fallen woman. And her unsentimental depiction of motherhood in the posthumous sonnet sequence *Mother and Daughter*, 1895, is a real departure from most of the period's literature. In *A Book of Rhyme*, 1881, AW introduced the Italian verse form *rispetti* into English poetry. Other publications include *A Woman Sold, and Other Poems*, 1867; a transl. of *Medea*, 1868; *A Housewife's Opinions*, 1878, a collection of essays about married women; and pro-SUFFRAGE essays issued as pamphlets by the Women's Suffrage Society. AW's 1887 play, *The Sentence*, a tragedy about Caligula, was considered by some to be her most important work. AW also served on the London School Board, 1879–82 and 1885–8, where she supported the introduction of technical training in elementary schools and worked for better EDUCATION for women.

Weddell, Mrs. obscure dramatist (sometimes using the pronoun 'he'). Her *City Farce*, London 1737, has an appeal 'To the Gentlemen of the Pit' to press for its staging if they enjoy reading it. Writing after the Licensing Act, she hopes the craze for ballad opera may yield to 'the Spirit of our old English Farce', which laughs at follies of 'the Middle Station'. She does this with gusto: trained bands play at soldiers, men edge into traditional women's jobs, products and prices figure largely. She later claims *A Voyage up the Thames*: the known work of this title, 1738, has also been ascribed to Thomas Bryan Richards. Ironically dedicated to the impresario Heidegger, it is a travel burlesque (up-river to Eton instead of abroad), stringing heterogenous material (like a fan-letter from a rejected author to himself) on the thread of an all-male party of London types observing local colour. Her tragedy *Incle and Yarico*, 1742, was printed only after she had failed to get it staged. As far as she can she blurs the stark racial opposition of Richard Steele's story (Englishman sells to slavery the Indian woman who loved and saved him).

Wedgwood, Frances **Julia**, 'Frances Dawson', 1833–1913, novelist and miscellaneous writer, b. Clapham, London, to Frances (Mackintosh) and Hensleigh W., eminent philologist, brother-in-law to Charles Darwin, who admired JW's 1861 criticism of *The Origin of Species*. She pub. two novels in 1858: a repr., 1866, of *An Old Debt* says she aims to leave the value of sacrifice 'an open question'. After 1863 she fell in love with the widower Robert Browning. Of their correspondence (ed. Richard Curle, 1937) her side is open and generous ('I prefer the scorn which falls on those who say too much, to the price . . . paid by those who say too little'), moralistic (his poems plant snowdrops in dunghills), outspokenly perceptive on e.g. *The Ring and the Book*. Lifelong, growing deafness, and her father's ban on fiction-writing, narrowed her life. She supported SUFFRAGE (in essays ed. Josephine BUTLER, 1869) and anti-vivisection (with F. P. COBBE). Later books, like *The Moral Ideal*, 1888, and a life of her great-grandfather Josiah W., 1915, revert to the dutiful.

Wees, Frances Shelley (Johnson), 1902–82, mystery writer. B. at Gresham, Oregon, da. of Rose Emily (Shelley) and Ralph Eaton J., she was educ. in Oregon, then at Saskatoon (Sask.) Normal School. She taught, married Wilfred Rusk W., 1924, and moved to Ontario. Several of the more than fifteen books she wrote, between 1930 and 1960, were chosen as Crime Club Selections; many have been translated into German and Scandinavian languages. Usually set in Canada, often in Toronto, they treat stereotyped characters in upper-middle-class milieux. The protagonist of *The Country of Strangers*, 1960, however, travels to Vancouver, Russia and Vienna in her involvement with drug smugglers.

Weeton, Ellen, later Stock, 1775–?1844, English letter writer, memoirist and feminist, da. of Mary (Rawlinson) and Thomas W., who rose from exploited orphan to slave trader and sea captain before being killed in battle with an American ship, 1782. While poor he had wanted financially viable sons, not daughters who must be 'mop squeezers, or mantua makers'. EW's love of scribbling (she wrote a play at 11) and desire for learning were squelched by her mother (who, cheated of £12,000 prize money, ran a school at Upholland near Wigan, living like a drudge on bread and potatoes); her idolized younger brother attended school and trained as a lawyer. After her mother died, 1797, she kept on scrimping herself for him, to find that 'like all his sex' he 'considered what had been done for him was his right'; yet her letters to him remain loving, inventive, self-mocking. Liking 'a little Nonsense now and then', she poses as 'a universal Genius' courted by royalty and learned men yet retaining 'an amazing share of humility'. She wrote reviews, essays (a sketch on 'contempt of women' and their talents), poems. She was a governess when in 1814 she married Aaron Stock, who turned out 'my terror, my misery', brutal and near-bankrupt; her brother, who recommended him, came into £100 at her marriage. After beatings 'almost to death' and threats of prison or lunatic asylum came legal separation, 1822, and loss of access to her daughter, for whom she wrote an autobiographical sketch (her second). By 1829 they were reunited. EW's surviving journal (memorable on visits to London and Wales, and analysis of the male-biased legal system) and copies of letters at Wigan Public Library: pub. 1936, 1939 (repr. 1969) with selecs. from other MSS. WOOLF quotes her in *Three Guineas*.

Welby, Amelia Bell **(Coppuck)**, 'Amelia', 1819–52, poet, b. St Michael's, Maryland, da. of Mary (Shield) and William C., mason and lighthouse builder. She was educ. in Baltimore. In 1834 the family moved to Louisville, Ky., where she spent the rest of her life. Her first poems, under 'Amelia', appeared in the Louisville *Daily Journal*, 1837. In 1838 she m. George W. and their home became a literary centre. Her *Poems by Amelia*, 1844, went through 14 editions by 1855 and Poe ranked her among the 'literati'. Her work is derivative from Emerson and Longfellow, although her topics, such as Mammoth Cave in Kentucky, are often those of the West. She was unselfish in her admiration of other poets, as well as conscious of herself as a poet, as in her tribute, 'Viola', to fellow poet Laura M. Thurston (d. 1842): 'She has passed like a bird from the minstrel throng, / She has gone to the land where the lovely belong.' AW died soon after bearing her only child.

Weldon, Fay (Birkinshaw), novelist, playwright, critic, b. 1931 at Alvechurch, Worcs., da. of Margaret (Jepson), who had published two novels, and Frank B., a doctor. After her parents' divorce, 1937, she lived with her mother and sister (her early novels include many daughters brought up by mothers alone), attending girls' high schools in Christchurch, NZ, and Hampstead, London. By 1955 she was herself a single mother of a son. After various jobs she became a successful advertising copywriter (like the heroine of *Praxis*, 1978, a typical FW narrator). In 1960 she married Ronald W., an antique dealer; she had three more sons. Her first novel (after rejections), *The Fat Woman's Joke*, 1967, began as a TV play, 1966. Prolific in several media, she has written radio and much TV drama, half-a-dozen stage plays, 14 novels, two short-story volumes, and non-fiction: *Letters to Alice on First Reading Jane Austen*, 1984 (recalling AUSTEN's to her niece), an idiosyncratic and enthusiastic study of Rebecca WEST, 1985, and a manifesto against censorship, 1989. In 1976 FW and her family moved to Somerset, near numinous Glastonbury Tor, which exerts one of several preternatural influences in *Puffball*, 1980, FW's own favourite. Her fiction is marked by succinctness, a characteristic tone of deft ironic understatement and wry appraisal, and an increasingly apocalyptic vision. She delights in weirdness (*Remember Me*, 1976, *Little Sisters*, 1977), in raunchy female sexuality (*Female Friends*, 1975, *Leader of the Band*, 1988), in shock-tactics against society's glossy ideal of woman (*The Life and Loves of a She-Devil*, 1984, televised 1986, with an ugly heroine dedicated to envy and revenge), and in reproductive processes (biological stages of pregnancy counterpointed with human action in *Puffball*, the machinations of a male genetic engineer in *The Cloning of Joanna May*, 1989). Like most of FW's work, this depicts a savage, unstoppable sex war in which women, often cruel to each other, have the moral advantage over men. See Crosland, 1981; Olga Kenyon, *Women Novelists Today*, 1988.

Wellesley, Dorothy (Ashton), later Duchess of Wellington, 1889–1956, poet and autobiographer, b. at Heywood Lodge, Berks., da. of Lucy Cecilia Dunn (Gardner) and Robert A. After her father's death, her mother remarried, to the 10th Earl of Scarborough, and DW grew up in a great house. She was educ. at home, a fact V. SACKVILLE-WEST thought 'unfortunate', since she needed 'the discipline of school and the intellectual stimulus of a university'. She married Gerald W., later 7th Duke of Wellington, in 1914; they had two children, and from an early date lived entirely apart. She wrote from an early age, published *Poems* in 1920, and over the next 35 years nine more books of poetry. She sponsored and edited the Hogarth Press Living Poets series (29 volumes from 1928). In 1928, she bought Penns in the Rocks, her house at Withyham, Sussex, whose dining room was decorated by Vanessa Bell and Duncan Grant. Here she lived with Hilda Matheson ('*amica amicarum*', who resigned her position as director of talks for the BBC when the future Lord Reith refused to let Harold Nicolson praise *Ulysses* on the air), and entertained poets, including W. B. Yeats, who published several of her poems in his *Oxford Book of Modern Verse*, 1936, and prefaced her *Selections from the Poems of Dorothy Wellesley*, 1936. She published his letters to her after his death: a testament to their friendship, *Letters to a Poet*, 1940 (new ed., 1964, with introduction by Kathleen RAINE). This also shows the relation between the lesser poet and the greater and the female and the male. Yeats thought she had 'descriptive genius'; Sackville-West thought her undisciplined. Many of her poems take subjects from nature (some are dedicated to the National Trust); some emerge from her travel (she travelled to Italy, Crete, Egypt, India, and later to Russia, with Vita); some treat the ancient, mythic, prehistoric. 'Matrix', which Yeats admired, figures the generative life of the body and the desire to 'mate with the mould, the Mother, / Who gives nevermore what she gave'. DW's verse is mixed in quality and, deeply, in social attitude. Occasionally at pains to avoid the accusation of thinking well of women, she identifies strongly with other women travellers in her autobiography, *Far have I Travelled*, 1952. *Early Light*, 1955, collects the poems she wished preserved.

Wells, Emmeline Blanche (Woodward), 1828–1921, journalist, suffragist poet, and feminist, b. Petersham, Mass., da. of Deiadama (Hare) and David Woodward. She was educ. in Petersham and New Salem, Mass. In 1843 she m. James H. Harris but he deserted her soon afterwards and she became second wife to Newell K. Whitney in 1845 under Mormon polygyny. After his death she became sixth wife to Daniel H. Wells. As editor and later publisher of the *Women's Exponent*, 1877–1914, she promoted both equal rights for women and Mormon polygyny, and also contributed to the *Exponent* as 'Aunt Em'. From 1874 she was active in national and international feminism, being an early member of the NWSA and National Council for Women: in 1899 a delegate to the International Council of Women's London meeting. With Zina Young Williams she presented a Memorial to the US Congress on the rights of Mormon women, and in 1893 she edited *Charities and Philanthropies. Women's Work in Utah* for the Chicago World's Fair, and *Songs and Flowers of the Wasatch*, a collection of Mormon women's poetry. Her own poetry shows little of her feminist commitment or her deeply held Mormon beliefs, tending rather to follow the sentimental models of her day. *Musings and Memories* was pub. in 1896; a second edition, including later and previously uncollected work, 1915. Papers at Brigham Young Univ., Provo, Utah.

Wells, Helena, later **Whitford**, *c.* 1761–1824, novelist and educationalist. B. in South Carolina, da. of the Scots Mary and Robert Wells (a loyalist publisher), early familiar with writers, she sailed to England in 1774 (not yet 15) and stayed. After a first job interview of comic horror, she and her sister ran a London school from 1789; she had given it up, probably for governessing, when she published *Letters* [to pupils, 1794–9] *on Subjects of Importance to the Happiness of Young Females*, 1799. Her advice is orthodox but robust: against over-sensibility; for reading serious 'ROMANCES' (epic, Tasso, Spenser) rather than novels which heighten reality and invite self-identification (even Frances BURNEY and Charlotte SMITH present implausible heroes). HW's poor heroine in *The Step-Mother*, also 1799, refuses a rich suitor (thereby destroying him) to marry a widower and teach his daughters; that of *Constantia Neville, or The West Indian*, 1800, battles with poverty as an outsider in English society. (Subscribers included Martha L. RAMSAY in Charleston, SC, and many in Berlin and in Hamburg, which features in the story.) HW is a prosy narrator but stimulating commentator: she deplores the misuse of WOLLSTONECRAFT's 'transcendant abilities', says morals will not improve till women glory in 'protecting and supporting each other in what is laudable', and comments on racial prejudice. She already intended a work on women's education, but married in 1801, had four children, and was seriously ill after the last (in 1806, when the RLF, which had helped her in 1801, queried her claim). Her projected *Thoughts and Remarks on Establishing a Protestant Nunnery* changed *Nunnery* to *Institution* just before printing, 1809; Joanna BAILLIE and Anne HUNTER subscribed. Citing *Sir Charles Grandison* but not Mary ASTELL, it proposes a women's teacher-training college (perhaps in Yorkshire, where HW has scouted for potential sites), and analyses current educational abuses and obstacles to women's earning a living. (Cf. Bridget Hill in *Past and Present*, 117, 1987.) Though 'no visionary advocate for the *Rights of Women*', HW is ready 'to censure persons who have not hitherto considered their conduct to be reprehensible', in order to benefit her sex and help to redress its wrongs.

Wells, Mary, didactic poet. Her *Divine Poem.... fit to be learned by all Young Men and Maids, instead of profane Songs and Ballads* (London 1684, 1690) calls on God to 'Let not the love of any sin / Within my heart have place.' Each stanza begins with a successive letter of the alphabet, one with 'Xamine'.

Wells-Barnett, Ida Bell, 1862–1931, b. Holly Springs, Mississippi, da. of Elizabeth (Warrenton) and James Wells, carpenter. Both parents were originally slaves. After their death in an epidemic, IW-B cared for her younger siblings while obtaining her own education in a Methodist-sponsored school in Holly Springs. She taught in the 1880s and began to publish in 1887. She is best known for her courageous exposé of lynching in the American South, in both the black and white press, and in her two books, *Southern Horrors*, 1892, and *A Red Record*, 1895. She argued against the Southern double sexual standard, and repeatedly attacked the charge, irrespective of its source, that black males were raping white women, as seen in her response to Jane Addams, a frequent ally in Chicago. After her marriage to Ferdinand L. Barnett, 1895, her activities centred in Chicago. She was one of the founders of the NAACP and was active in women's clubs and in Chicago politics. She was the first black woman to be named an adult probation officer in Chicago. Her autobiography, *Crusade for Justice*, was begun in 1928 but remained unfinished at her death. It was ed. by her daughter and pub. 1970. See Joanne M. Braxton, *Autobiography by Black American Women*, 1987, diss. Yale Univ.

Welty, Eudora, novelist, short-story writer, b. 1909 in Jackson, Mississippi, da. of schoolteacher Mary Chestina (Andrews), who 'emotionally and imaginatively supported' her 'wish to become a writer' and Christian W. W., who gave her her first dictionary. At Davis School in Jackson she was taught by the indomitable Miss Duling, who 'in some fictional shape or form has stridden into' much of her work. The first story-tellers she knew were the women of Jackson, who visited house to house and *talked*: later she found Chekhov 'kindred' because his people 'are always gathered together and talking and talking'. She went to the Mississippi State College for Women, 1926–7, the Univ. of Wisconsin (BA, 1929), and the Graduate School of Business at Columbia, and worked in NYC, but returned to Jackson during the Depression. As Junior Publicity Agent for the Works Progress Administration she travelled Mississippi, writing stories and taking pictures for local papers. She described the experience and printed the photographs in *One Time, One Place*, 1971. All her work is deeply marked by time and place: 'To my mind, a fiction writer's honesty begins right there, in being true to those two facts. . . . From there, imagination can take him anywhere at all.' She wrote her first stories at 16, about Paris. Soon her Muse recovered the South, whose history, speech and locality preoccupies her whole work. Virginia WOOLF, she said, 'opened the door: When I read *To the Lighthouse*, I felt, Heavens, *what is this?*' Her 'Death of a Traveling Salesman' appeared in *Manuscript* in 1936; soon *Atlantic Monthly, The Hudson Review, Prairie Schooner*, and *Sewanee Review* were regularly printing her stories. Katherine Anne PORTER prefaced her first volume, *A Curtain of Green*, 1941; three more books of new stories followed (*The Bride of the Innisfallen*, 1955, is dedicated to her friend Elizabeth BOWEN), and *Collected Stories* (Presidential Medal of Freedom), 1980. They are technically versatile, sharply individual in perception: grotesque or grim (early work especially), angularly comic (in writing dialogue she 'used to laugh aloud sometimes'), deeply engaged with the Southern past ('First Love'), mythological ('Circe'), or linked in a character-developing sequence (*The Golden Apples*, 1949), always vibrant with the narrator's voice. Power to move the reader resides, says EW, in 'pattern, shape, form ... *the whole*'; fiction cannot 'exhort'. *The Robber Bridegroom*, 1942, first of her five novels, has a pre-revolutionary setting and fairy-tale flavour (EW later disliked historical writing). *Delta Wedding*, 1946, set in a deliberately uneventful year, 1923, is 'about what a family is like'; and so are the rest. High comedy centres in *The Ponder Heart*, 1954, around a trial for alleged murder, in *Losing Battles*, 1970, around release from prison, and in *The Optimist's Daughter*, 1972 (Pulitzer Prize), around a funeral. EW also wrote for

for children (*The Shoe Bird*, 1964), poetry ('A Flock of Guinea Hens Seen From a Car', 1970), much acute criticism selected in *The Eye of the Story*, 1978, and some autobiographical writing, notably *One Writer's Beginnings*, 1984, which describes her 'listening', 'Learning to See' and 'Finding a Voice'. Peggy Whitman Prenshaw, ed., *Conversations with EW*, 1984, gives interviews over 40 years. See also essays ed. Prenshaw, 1979, and Albert J. Devlin, 1987 (with bibliog.); studies by Michael Kreyling, 1980, and Elizabeth Evans, 1981; *The EW Newsletter*, 1977ff. MSS of published works at the Department of Archives and History in Jackson; 'a trunk full of stuff' at home.

Wenman, Agnes (Fermor), Lady, d. 1617, translator. Only surviving da. of Mary (Curson) and Sir George F. of Easton Neston, Northants., she m., *c.* 1595, Richard W., who had estates in Oxon and Bucks. They had eight children; he became a knight in 1596 and a viscount after her death. She was, unlike him, a Catholic, and was interrogated after the Guy Fawkes plot. Her translation (from a French version of 1583) of John Zonaras's Greek *Historyes and Chronicles of the World* got only as far as Cyrus. It calls Judith 'valourous and magnanimous'. Two handsome folio vols. in MS at Cambridge University Library.

Wentworth, Anne, Baptist prophet of London. Her three pamphlets, *A True Account*, 1676, *A Vindication* (of herself), 1677, and *The Revelation of Jesus Christ*, 1679, combine ecstatic verse prophecies with a narrative of the 'cruel and unjust treatment' of her 'Hard-hearted Yoak-Fellow' of 18 years, abetted by members of their church including Hanserd Knollys (see Katherine SUTTON). God, she says, has 'placed the two Spirits in a Man and his Wife, to figure out Zion and Babylon'; He has *forced* her to leave her husband, who is guilty of 'seizing and running away with' her pamphlets, which are not her work but God's, 'written sorely against my own natural mind and will'. Yet her image of herself is Amazonian: 'And in his strength I was by Grace enabled to stand, / Against all my Enemies, with his Battel-ax in my hand, / To wound, kill, amaze, put to flight, and cut them down.' See Elaine Hobby, 1988.

'Wentworth, Patricia', Dora Amy (Elles), 1878–1961, crime novelist. B. in Mussoorie, India, da. of Lt–Gen. Sir Edmund Roche E., educ. privately and at Blackheath High School, she returned to India on marrying Col. George Dillon (d. 1906). As a widow she wrote six historical novels, beginning with *A Marriage under the Terror*, 1910. After remarrying Col. George Oliver Turnbull, 1920, she lived in Surrey, and wrote 65 mysteries, thrillers and DETECTIVE novels of varying quality, from *The Astonishing Adventure of Jane Smith*, 1923. 32 of these, the most popular, feature Miss Maud Silver, who is introduced in the melodramatic *Grey Mask*, 1928. In the mould of Agatha CHRISTIE's Miss Marple, this elderly, dowdy, unmarried ex-governess, of strict morality and striking intelligence, is a professional detective, a 'sleuthess', proud of financial independence, and of supporting a numerous family. Like Marple's, her effectiveness depends upon her female 'unlikeliness' for the role, sometimes on her access to information available to women only. Her knitting suggests the key doubleness: usually a mark of nurturing softness, it is here also an emblem for the inexorable workings of the detecting mind. See Patricia Craig and Mary Cadogan, *The Lady Investigates*, 1981.

Were, Miriam Khamodi, Kenyan novelist and biographer, b. 1940 in Lugale, Kenya. She was educ. in the USA, where she took a BS at the Univ. of Pennsylvania, and in Kenya, studying education at Makerere Univ. and medicine at the Univ. of Nairobi, where she now teaches in the Department of Community Health. A paediatrician, she specializes in maternal and child care. She is married to Humphrey Rapando W.; they have several children. As Kenya's representative to the Nairobi Decade of Women Conference, 1985, she presented papers on health. She has also written on changes for Kenyan women as urbanization occurs. Her four novels are variously thought of as adult or juvenile fiction. The first two follow the English school novel tradition: *The Boy in Between*, 1969, and *The High School Gent*, 1969, track an ambitious, capable boy of humble origin through the successful stages of his schooling, bringing him at the end to the recognition (through his meetings at the Girls' School) that girls can also have brains, determination, success. *The Eighth Wife*, 1972, presents a father-son conflict: the son of the young chief goes through circumcision rites of passage, enters the warrior class, and is fit to succeed his father, who, however, looking for an eighth wife, threatens to take his son's choice. *Your Heart is My Altar*, 1980, like Jane Bakaluba's *Honeymoon for Three*, uses the subject of cross-cultural marriage to expose tribal rivalries, religious antagonisms, and generational differences culminating in violent confrontation. *A Nurse with a Song*, 1978, is a biography of Margaret Owanyoni. See Taiwo, 1984, and Nancy Schmidt in *WLWE*, 17, 1978.

Wertenbaker, Timberlake, playwright, translator, journalist. Da. of Anglo-American parents, brought up in the Basque country of France, bilingual in French and English, she holds a philosophy degree, has worked as a journalist in London and NYC, and lives in London. Her first plays were written and acted in Greece (where she was teaching French). *This is No Place for Tallulah Bankhead* dates from 1978; the comedy *Case to Answer* was produced in 1980 in both London and Ithaca, NY. For the Women's THEATRE GROUP TW wrote *Breaking Through*, also 1980, and *New Anatomies*, 1981, about nineteenth-century adventurer Isabelle Eberhardt (cf. Cecily MACKWORTH). It identifies some key preoccupations – the ideas of 'someone on a quest', of women seeking and changing, 'trying to break the boundaries', and of sex role construction (problematized here by Eberhardt's cross-dressing, in her travels among the Arabs). *Abel's Sister*, 1984, which uses material by Yolande Bourcier, radically alters the biblical tale in casting one of that primal pair as female. The award-winning *Grace of Mary Traverse* (Royal Court, 1985), set in eighteenth-century London, pursues the transgressive theme in a female character who angrily redresses female powerlessness in savagely critical role mimicry. TW has been playwright-in-residence with the group Shared Experience, and the Royal Court Theatre. She won awards for *Our Country's Good*, 1988, which adapts Thomas Keneally's novel set in 1789, about the effect on a group of Australian convicts of putting on a play. *The Love of the Nightingale*, 1988, about, in part, the effects of silence, played in Stratford. TW has translated plays by Marivaux, Jean Anouilh, Ariane Mnouchkine and Lorca (*The House of Bernarda Alba*). *New Anatomies* was produced in a London pub in 1990.

'Wesley, Mary', Mary Aline Farmar, novelist, children's writer, and civil servant. B. in 1912 at Englefield Green, Surrey, da. of Violet (Dalby) and Colonel Harold Mynors F., CMG, DSO, she was educ. by 'about 16 governesses', later attended Queen's College, London, 1928–30, and the London School of Economics, 1931–2. She has been twice married, to Lord Swinfen (Charles Eady), 1937 (they divorced after WWII), and to Eric Siepmann, a writer, 1952. (He died in 1971.) She had three children. Her children's books (*Speaking Terms*, and the apocalyptic *The Sixth Seal*, both 1969; *Haphazard House*, 1983) prefigure her adult fiction in their sophisticated tone and quirky plots: all involve magic or fantasy; animals are prominent. At 70 she began writing novels of manners which gently, humorously upset middle-class sexual values. *Jumping the Queue*, 1983, her first novel, now a film, about a bored widow, a pet goose, and a reluctant matricide, demonstrates MW's talent for macabre humour. Discreet, matter-of-fact celebration of sexuality in its various permutations is a dominant thread in *The Camomile Lawn*, 1984, a superb evocation of personal sunshine filtering through the twentieth century's long shadows of war. *Harnessing Peacocks*, 1985, *The Vacillations of Poppy Carew*, 1986, and *Not That Sort of Girl*, 1987, offer amusing evidence that sexual liberation can be a practical expression of female independence. The darker *Second Fiddle*, 1988, is a tale of intergenerational relationships (centrally between 45-year-old Laura and 23-year-old Claud, an aspiring novelist) among mostly eccentric characters wary of full commitment. *A Sensible Life* appeared in 1990. See Rosemary Stoyle in *Literary Review*, Oct. 1988.

Wesley, Susanna (Annesley), 1669–1742, letter writer and (said her son John) a 'Preacher of righteousness' like her grandfather, father and husband: 25th and youngest child of eminent London dissenter Samuel A. He accepted her reasoned choice, at 12, of the Anglican church which had persecuted him. For her sister Elizabeth Dunton, see under DIARIES. SW married the Rev. Samuel W. and moved to South Ormsby, Lincs., 1690, and Epworth, 1697; ten of her 19 children survived. Her educational 'method' (whence her sons' later title) involved teaching a year-old child 'to fear the rod and cry softly'; *not* to exact total obedience was cruelty. But she rewarded obedience, and taught girls to read first and sew later. She dismayed the curate by reading a sermon publicly, and to her husband defended her taking classes of 200 in his absence, feeling responsible for those souls. They often argued over theology; in 1702 he left her (briefly) when she resisted a move 'to deprive me of my little liberty of conscience'. She left letters, prayers, meditatons, and discourses for her children on points of belief: a *Conference* with a (non-writing) daughter was pub. 1898. To John W. she wrote on church administration, the real presence in the sacrament, zeal and humility, Thomas à Kempis and Jeremy Taylor. Often positive in opinion, she is also open to doubt: 'after many years' search and inquiry, I still continue to pay my devotions to an unknown God'. She narrates family events with verve and wry humour; she had more patience than Samuel, though less than John, with her daughter Mehetabel WRIGHT. John pub. some of her writing in *The Arminian Mag.*, i, 1778. More appeared in works on the family from 1823, and selecs. of her prayers 1955. MSS at Wesley College, Bristol; life by John A. Newton, 1968.

West, Dorothy, 'Mary Christopher', short-story writer, journalist, novelist, b. 1912 in Boston, only child of Rachel (Bensen) and Isaac Christopher W., successful black businessman. Educ. at Girls' Latin School and in writing courses at Boston and Columbia Univs., she joined the Saturday Evening Quill Club, formed in 1925 by 20 black men and women who wanted to write. Her stories appeared in its annual and in the *Boston Post*. 'The Typewriter' made her in 1929 joint winner, with Zora Neale HURSTON, of a prize from the National Urban League. That year she moved to NYC (where she participated with her elders Hurston, Countee Cullen, Langston Hughes and composer Harry T. Burleigh in the Harlem Renaissance), and visited London as an extra in *Porgy*, non-musical forerunner of *Porgy and Bess*. She worked as a relief investigator in Harlem and went on a writers' visit to the Soviet Union in 1932. As 'Mary Christopher' she founded, 1934, financed and wrote for *Challenge* (from 1937 *New Challenge*, opposing fascism and publishing work by 'newer Negroes' like Margaret WALKER), but resisted too strong a Communist presence in it. She worked for the Federal Writers' Project, then in 1938 moved to Martha's Vineyard. Her novel *The Living is Easy*, 1948, has several recent reprints: afterword by Adelaide M. Cromwell, 1982. It vividly portrays complex black Boston society: her Southern heroine 'did not know there was anything she was incapable of doing' to win a place for herself, her daughter and sisters' children. DW wrote twice-weekly stories for the *New York Daily News* until the late 1960s, then a column in the *Vineyard Gazette*. Interview in *A Scholarly Journal on Black Women*, 2, 1985; studies by Gloria Wade-Gayles in *A Scholarly Journal on Black Women*, 1, 1984, and Mary Helen Washington in Ruth Perry and Martine Watson Brownley, eds., *Mothering the Mind: Twelve Studies of Writers and Their Silent Partners*, 1984.

West, Elizabeth, Scots labouring-class autobiographer. Her father was 'nothing but a moral man'; her mother and aunt taught her piety from an age when she thought heaven 'a place, where I would get fine clothes'. She 'satisfied myself with the Pharisee's religion' till after 1688, when she became serious and took the sacrament at Edinburgh, where she lived: later she often walked long distances for it. Her narrative links past diary entries (from 1694), prayers, and accounts of sermons. In her 'journey heavenward, it is up the brae, and down the brae' or again 'like the sun shining on a winter-day, blink up and blink down'. Now she is 'with David singing, my mountain stands strong, I shall never be moved', now in 'grief, trouble and anguish of spirit' about her own unbelief. Reading Francis Spira does her harm; Bunyan's *Grace Abounding* does her good. She took Christ as her spouse in 1696, exhorted her father on his deathbed in 1700, worked as a servant near Dalkeith and briefly, in 1705 or 1706, for Lady Grisell BAILLIE. She became increasingly political, fiercely opposed to 'Prelacy' and to Union with treacherous England. Her work was pub. at Glasgow, 1766: many reprints, most with condescending editorial comment.

West, Jane (Iliffe), 1758–1852, novelist, poet and playwright, b. in London, only child of Jane and John I., who moved to Desborough, Northants., when she was 11. Entirely self-educ., she wrote prolifically in her teens: 'I scorned correction and never blotted'. She married well-to-do yeoman Thomas W. by 1783. Her first collection of *Poems and Plays*, 1791, follows a tragedy and several poetry volumes (but not that ascribed to her of 1780). Her first novel, *The Advantages of Education, or The History of Maria Williams*, 1793 (with anti-sentimental heroine), appeared as by 'Prudentia Homespun'. JW took the name, apparently, from Charlotte MCCARTHY; she used it again on *A Gossip's Story*, written to prove 'the Advantages of Consistency, Fortitude and the Domestic Virtues', and that over-sensitivity may cause undesirable 'female irresolution' (pub. 1797 with *A Legendary Tale*: facs. 1974). The reasonable conservatism of this was admired by Jane AUSTEN – and Mary WOLLSTONECRAFT. The anti-radical *A Tale of the Times*, 1799, pours scorn on mercenary marriage. JW corresponded with Sarah TRIMMER and Bishop Percy, who gave her warm commendation in the *British Critic*, 1801, in response to her plea of need to support her family. Her *Letters to a Young Man*, 1801, are addressed to a son; *Letters to a Young Lady*, 1806, counsel submission in marriage. *The Loyalists*, 1812, and *Alicia de Lacey*, 1814, are historical novels. JW's last novel, *Ringrove, or Old-fashioned Notions*, 1827, which broke a ten-year silence, is as readable as ever. Outliving her husband and three sons, she left her MSS (untraced) to a grandson (see Pamela Lloyd Simmons in *N & Q*, 1984).

West, Mary **Jessamyn**, 1902–84, novelist and memoirist, b. near North Vernon, Ind., da. of Grace Anna (Milhous), a

Quaker, and Eldo Roy W., who had Indian blood. She was taken to California at six, and educ. at Whittier College. In 1923 she took her BA and married Harry Maxwell McPherson, teacher and school administrator; they later adopted a daughter. She taught for four years, studied in England in 1929, then began a doctorate in English at the Univ. of Calif., but was interrupted by a two-year stay (from 1931) in a sanatorium for tuberculosis. When she was pronounced incurable, her mother brought her home; during her first year of recovery, she listened to her mother's tales of rural Indiana, 'the world she had known and the life she had lived and the dreams she had dreamed for my own use'. Her mother, in her final years, thought it was she who had written and published JW's stories drawing on this material: JW let the perception stand. Most notable example is *The Friendly Persuasion*, 1945, which gathers stories of a Quaker farming family at the time of the Civil War. (In *To See the Dream*, 1957, JW describes her involvement in the filming of this work, 1956.) *Except for Me and Thee*, 1969, is a sequel. *The Massacre at Fall Creek*, 1975, on an Indiana event of the 1820s, tells of the first whites executed for killing Indians: also of women's role among the tribes, and the non-violent religion of Handsome Lake (d. 1815). As well, JW writes on lives of twentieth-century California settlers, on motherhood and its transfiguration of women's lives, on relations (and separations) between mothers and daughters, their difficulties and blessings. She shows insight about love between women and men, and the sometimes independent factor of sex. Her several autobiographical works pinpoint certain periods of her life: *The Woman Said Yes*, 1976 (in the UK *Encounters with Death and Life*), tells a story (about the decision of her younger sister, who had cancer, to choose her own time to die) which she had already fictionalized in *A Matter of Time*, 1966. JW has taught at Breadloaf and several universities. Besides novels and memoirs, her prolific output includes stories (the first pub. in 1939; collected, 1986), poems, 1974, science fiction, an operetta and two screenplays. MSS at Whittier College. See study by Alfred S. Shivers, 1972, pamphlet by Ann Dahlstrom Farmer, 1982 (with bibliography).

'West, Rebecca', Cicily Isabel Fairfield, DBE, 1892–1983, novelist, journalist and feminist. B. in London, da. of Isabella (Campbell Mackenzie), a musician, and Charles F., a soldier, then a journalist, she was educ. at George Watson's Ladies' College, Edinburgh, and for a year at the Academy of Dramatic Art, 1910–11, though her acting was not a success. She wrote from childhood, taking up journalism professionally (as 'Rebecca West' after the strong-minded heroine of Ibsen's *Rosmersholm*) in 1911 on the staff of the pro-suffrage *Freewoman* (later the *New Freewoman*) where she established her career as a brilliantly acerbic and versatile left-wing and feminist writer, contributing to the *Clarion*, *Star*, *Daily News*, *New Statesman* and *New Republic* (USA). An irreverent review of H. G. Wells's *Marriage*, 1912, led to their meeting and a ten-year relationship in which a son, Anthony West, was born, 1914. She married Henry Maxwell Andrews, a banker, 1930. A 'woman's war novel', *The Return of the Soldier*, 1918, filmed 1982, about the class-and-marriage-disrupting amnesia of a shell-shocked soldier, and *The Judge*, 1922, were the first of eight novels published during her lifetime, of which the two last, the largely autobiographical *The Fountain Overflows*, 1957, and *The Birds Fall Down*, 1966, a story of pre-WWI espionage and terrorism, are particularly esteemed. Three works were published posthumously: *The Real Night*, 1984, *Cousin Rosamund*, 1985, and *Sunflower*, 1986 (dedicated 'To my Friend G. B. STERN'). Her non-fiction includes a critical study, *Henry James*, 1916, a biography, *St. Augustine*, 1933, a political and historical travelogue, *Black Lamb and*

Grey Falcon: A Journey through Yugoslavia, 1941 (probably her most distinguished and original work), and literary criticism, *The Court and the Castle*, 1957 (1958 in UK). She reported treason trials after WWII, which led to *The Meaning of Treason*, 1947 (revised, 1964, *The New Meaning of Treason*), and *A Train of Powder*, 1955. Latterly she became anti-communist and generally more conservative, writing for the *Daily Telegraph* and *The New Yorker*. This may be a reason for her relative neglect of modern feminists, in addition to her often scathing contempt for dishonesty and ignorance: 'the word "idiot" comes from a Greek root meaning private person. Idiocy is the female defect: intent on their private lives, women follow their fate through a darkness deep as that cast by malformed cells in the brain'. Nevertheless, she remained passionately committed to the cause of women and was one of the great polemical feminists of this century. There are many reprints: see Virago introductions by Victoria Glendinning, Mollie PANTER-DOWNES; selec. with intro. by Jane Marcus, 1982; writings 1911–17, ed. Marcus, 1989; study by Harold Orel, 1986. Glendinning's life, 1987, was written at RW's request. Papers at Yale and Tulsa.

Weston, Mary (Pace), 1712–66, Quaker minister, da. of Anne and Joseph P. of Southwark in London. Her parents, busy in their linen-draper's shop, 'punctual in their Payments and just in their Dealings', neglected their six children's godly education. She made a first, brief preaching journey in 1735; her next reached Scotland. In 1741 she m. Daniel W., a Wapping cooper; four children died young. In 1750 she left husband and daughter to cover nearly 8000 miles in America; her journal breaks off in 1752 (a copy, 94 closely-written folio pages, at Friends' House). She met both interest and antagonism as a woman PREACHING: eminent Bostonians flocked to her 'expecting some great things from a Londoner, but my mind was much shut up amongst them'; at Woodbury, Conn., two hecklers objected that her address, though true and scriptural, was confused and disconnected. She married Jeremiah Waring in 1765. Diary excerpts and loving letters home in *Eliot Papers*, ed. Eliot Howard, ii, 1894, with a thoughtful essay by MW's relation Mariabella Eliot, 1736–69, on (her own) deformity.

Wetherald, Agnes **Ethelwyn**, 'Bel Thistlethwaite', 1857–1940, poet and journalist. B. in Rockwood, Ont., da. of Jemima (Harris) and William W. (founder and principal of Rockwood Academy, later a Quaker minister), she was educ. at home, the Friends' Boarding School, Union Springs, NY, and Pickering College, Ont. Her father became superintendent of Haverford College, near Philadelphia, 1864; a few years later the family moved to a farm near Fenwick, Ont., which remained EW's home for most of her life. She published her first poem in the children's *St. Nicholas Magazine*, but first achieved prominence with her regular Toronto *Globe* contributions, 1887–9, as 'Bel Thistlethwaite' (from her paternal grandmother's maiden name). During these years the Toronto *Week* published her poems and four essays on 'Some Canadian Literary Women'. From 1890 she worked for three years for the London *Advertiser* and was sub-editor of *Wives and Daughters*, a mildly feminist monthly for which she wrote editorials and book reviews and managed 'Selected Poetry' and other departments. In the 1890s, when her friend and mentor E. W. Thomson was its editor, she published much poetry in *Youth's Companion*. Except for brief stints in US publishing centres – as assistant to the editors of the *Ladies' Home Journal*, 1895–6, and *The World's Best Literature* – EW lived at the family home, contributing to various Canadian and US publications. The first of five books of poetry was *The House of the Trees*, 1895; *The Last Robin*, 1907, won favour with Earl Grey, the

Governor-General, and Wilfred Laurier, the Prime Minister. EW also wrote a collection of poems for children. *Lyrics and Sonnets*, ed. John Garvin, 1931, prints all she wished preserved, with her 'Reminiscences'. EW belonged to the Confederation group of writers: Archibald Lampman and E. W. Thomson admired her well-crafted poems on love, death, and nature. She has been compared with Emily DICKINSON.

Wharton, Anne (Lee), 1659–85, poet and dramatist, da. of Anne (Danvers) and Sir Henry L.: an orphan from birth. She says her uncle Lord Rochester taught her 'Infant Muse'. In 1673 she was married to Thomas, later Lord W., who was seldom with her owing to the demands of Whig politics and horse-racing. Elizabeth BURNET's future husband, one of her literary correspondents, showed her work to Edmund Waller and Lord Halifax, but advised against friendship with the 'odious and obscene' Aphra BEHN. AW's unacted tragedy, *Love's Martyr, or Witt Above Crowns*, uses the poet Ovid's love for the emperor's daughter as an allegory of the Exclusion Crisis, 1679–80: blank verse with couplets for high points (MS in BL). From her death her much-admired poems began appearing in collections, often with title-page billing: e.g. *Poems*, ed. Nahum Tate, 1685 (her elegy on Rochester); Edward Young's *Idea of Christian Love*, 1688; *A Collection of Poems*, 1693 (re-issued as *The Temple of Death*, 1695), including her praise of Behn and part of her paraphrase, 1681–2, from the prophet Jeremiah; and *Ovid's Epistles*, 8th ed. 1712 ('Penelope to Ulysses'). Of her Isaiah paraphrase, only a MS fragment remains (Harvard). Often melancholy, AW is too forceful to be plaintive. She compares a storm at sea to the fiercer ones of 'troubl'd Thought', and philosophizes finely on the harsh dilemma of eat or be eaten, victimize or be victimized.

Wharton, Edith Newbold (Jones), 1862–1937, novelist, short-story writer, poet, essayist and translator, b. NYC, da. of Lucretia (Rhinelander) and George Frederick J. She was educ. by governesses and travelled extensively in Europe as a child. Forbidden new fiction, EW spent an intellectually isolated childhood immersed in the classics and 'story-telling fevers'. Her *Verses* were pub. in 1878. She m. Edward W. in 1885 and launched into society-hostessing and visits to Europe, where they lived for half of each year. In 1894, after a nervous breakdown, she entered a sanatorium, where she began a writing career. Early works such as *The Decoration of Houses*, 1897, reflect her interest in domestic architecture, and a lifelong passion for travel inspired such titles as *A Motor-Flight Through France*, 1908, while *Tales of Men and Ghosts*, 1910, enters the realm of the occult. Best known for her novels about high society, she vividly depicted the philistinism of Old New York society in her best-seller *The House of Mirth*, 1905. She divorced after 30 years of passionless marriage, betrayed by his embezzling her funds, and in 1906 settled permanently in France, where she met and fell in love with Morton Fullerton. Their passionate relationship was reflected in her novels *Ethan Frome*, 1911, *The Reef*, 1912, and *Summer*, 1917, which depict the conflict between individual desire and society's dictates. In 1916 she was awarded the Cross of the Legion of Honour for her war-relief work, and she drew on her wartime experiences to write *Fighting France: From Dunkerque to Belfort*, 1915. In 1921 her novel *The Age of Innocence* won the Pulitzer Prize. Her war novel *A Son at the Front* was pub. in 1923, and in the same year she became the first woman to receive an honorary degree of Doctor of Letters from Yale University and the Gold Medal of the National Institute of Arts and Letters, of which she was later a member. A recurrent theme in her novels is the power of social convention and the monstrousness of useless sacrifice. Woman's futile struggle against unendurable reality, often ending in bitter self-renunciation, is a theme pursued in her subtly subversive story 'The Old Maid', from *Tales of Old New York*, 1924 (initially rejected by many magazines), in which the heroine, a stereotypical prim spinster, nevertheless turns out to be the mother of a much-loved illegitimate daughter. EW's wide circle of literary acquaintances included Henry James, 'perhaps the most intimate friend I ever had'. She had only ever longed, she said, to please two people: God and her mother. See R. W. B. Lewis, 1975, for her life, and R. W. B. and Nancy Lewis, 1988, for her *Letters*; critical study by Penelope Vita-Finzi, 1990; and secondary bibliog. by Kristen O. Lauer and Margaret P. Murray, 1990.

Wharton, Hannah, prophet or prophets preaching extempore in 1709–10 (published as *Warnings* 'by the Mouth of' her and Jonathan Taylor, 1711) and again in 1730–1. The addresses from her 'Forty Day Ministration' in London, 1730, were taken down in shorthand, with a foreword and afterword spoken in Birmingham, and pub. that year as *Some Manifestations and Communications of the Spirit*. In 1731 she spoke almost every day for ten weeks at Birmingham, with a call at Worcester: pub. as *Divine Inspiration*, 1732, with testimony from herself and ten others that the Lord would be returning 'suddenly'. As the vehicle of his word she uses 'I' both for him and herself. Her incantatory style is deliberately monotonous (a single word, like 'Righteousness', tolls throughout a whole passage) but fairly coherent, whether in prayer, exhortation or 'Revelation'. Her message is one of comfort: 'Surely the Doctrine I have to preach shall be Joy and Gladness'; 'know yourselves rooted and grounded in the Word of Promise, which is Love, as God is Love.'

'Whateley or **Beck, Anne** or **Elizabeth Anne'**, 1561–1601, alleged poet. 'Wm. Shaxpere' was licensed to marry 'Anna Whateley de Temple Grafton' on 27 Nov. 1582; on 28 Nov. he was licensed to marry 'Anne Hathaway', as he did. Most scholars deduce some mix-up of names, but William Ross, 1939, William J. Fraser Hutcheson [1950], and Margaret B. Graham Morton, 1962, argue that AW (da. of Miss Anne Beck and Capt. Anthony Jenkinson, merchant adventurer, of Market Harborough, Leics.) was a 'concealed poet', 'great unknown genius', who wrote much of Shakespeare's and Spenser's works and others by 'A.B.' or 'A.W.'; they say nothing of her education or of the practical or psychological problems faced by women writers.

Wheathill, Anne, writer of prayers. As an unmarried gentlewoman she published *A handfull of holesome (though homelie) hearbs gathered out of the goodlie garden of Gods most holie word*, London 1584, dedicated 'to all religious Ladies, Gentlewomen, and others'. Her book is rare, her title-page sparing of capitals, her little black-letter pages bordered with flowers. Her preface says she has written to 'avoid idlenes' and please God and her fellow-Christians, 'without the counsell or helpe of anie': the learned may think this 'grose and unwise'. Her herbs are 49 prayers: for morning and evening; for faith, repentance, etc; for troubles and the fear of death; against the tempting devil and the Church's enemies. These, she says, have never been stronger, and God punishes even the elect; yet her tone remains serene. Well versed in the Bible, she turns a lively phrase: 'Christ is the strong rocke, in the which all birds that build doo rest out of jeopardie'; she pours down before him 'my sacke that is full of sinne'. She prays God to hear the complaint of the poor: 'For there was never proud person that pleased thee.'

Wheatley, Phillis, later Peters, 1753?–84, slave and poet. B. in Africa, she was shipped to Boston, Mass., in 1761, aged about seven, and bought for Susannah W. (wife of a rich tailor), who with her teenage daughter took the unusual step of educating her. Writing poems by 1765, publishing one in a newspaper in 1767, she was noticed in society as a curiosity. Proposals for publishing a volume by subscription at Boston in 1772 failed: next year her respiratory complaints caused the W.s to send her on a visit to London; there her *Poems on Various Subjects, Religious and Moral*, appeared in 1773, certified by prominent citizens the unaided work of a 'Negro servant'. She was both lionized as an untaught genius (cf. Ann YEARSLEY) and savaged in the *Public Advertiser* as part of 'a Flood of female Literature'; she kept all her life her copy of *Paradise Lost* given her by the Lord Mayor of London. Her work is fluent, polished, not merely conventional. She expresses fervent Christian piety, celebrates liberty of various kinds, laments a large number of public and private deaths (many of children), and praises a black artist's work. She calls Africa 'land of errors', 'dark abodes', yet paints her father's 'excruciating sorrow' at her capture. Freed on her return, she married in 1778 another free black, John Peters. She published a few more poems, and made vain proposals for another volume, 1779, but sank into poverty (her husband jailed for debt), drudgery, illness, and the birth and death of three babies. *Poems*, ed. Julian D. Mason, 1966, has some errors but is still useful; more information in William S. Robinson, bibliog., 1981, and ed. *Writings*, 1984; *Coll. Works*, ed. John C. Shields, 1988, in Schomburg Library.

Wheeler, christened **Agnes**, usually called Ann (Coward), 1734–1804, miscellaneous and dialect writer, da. of Eleanor and Edward C., b. and educ. at Cartmel, Lancs. She spent 18 years in London, some of it as a gentleman's housekeeper. On the death of her husband (a slave-trading captain), she moved to Arnside in Cumberland. She 'took great delight in writing and making rhymes', and left (in MS but prepared for press) some plays, 'Female Restoration', 'Acco and Ego. A Dialogue', and other pieces. She published *Strictures upon the Inhabitants of a Market Town* (as 'a Citizen of the World'), Kendal 1789, and *The Westmorland Dialect*, 1790, begun on her return north, in three dialogues (cf. Mary PALMER, whose work she is unlikely to have known), and a fourth added in 1802. Her preface foresees that readers may think her 'mitch maar farently' employed in housekeeping than 'tae rite sic Maapment about nae Body knas wha ... a Wark ets fit for nin but Parson et dea'. She vividly renders the lives of countrywomen: one of many reprints, 1839, calls her 'too fond of alluding to female frailty and masculine insinuation'. In the first piece a neighbour called Ann advises, on practical not moral grounds, against leaving a bad husband.

Wheeler, Anna (Doyle), 1785–after 1848, Irish feminist philosopher. She grew up as part of the Anglo-Irish gentry (her father was an archbishop), married at 15, read philosophy, including Mary WOLLSTONECRAFT and French revolutionary thinkers, and left her alcoholic husband (Francis Massy W., d. 1820) as soon as she was free from continuous pregnancies, in 1812, taking their two surviving daughters (one was Rosina, later Bulwer LYTTON). In 1816 she settled in France at Caen, where she was the centre of one of the earliest Saint Simonian circles. She knew Flora Tristan and Charles Fourier, introducing both to Robert Owen. From 1824 she settled in London, involving herself in the Co-operative and feminist movements, a friend of Jeremy Bentham and William Thompson. She contributed regularly to periodicals, including Owen's *Crisis*, and was frequently called upon to lecture. She always opposed religion and marriage, and was respected for her powers of reasoned argument. Thompson's *Appeal of One-Half the Human Race, Women, against the pretensions of the other half, Men, to retain them in political, and thence in civil and domestic, slavery*, 1825, written as a response to James Mill's infamous 'Article on Government', was dedicated to AW. He credits her with the bulk of the text, claiming he acted only as her 'scribe and interpreter'. See the article by Richard Pankhurst, *The Political Quarterly*, 25, 2 (1954), and his intro. to the 1983 repr. of the *Appeal*.

Whipple, Dorothy (Stirrup), 1893–1966, novelist and short-story writer. B. at Blackburn, Lancs., da. of writer Ada (Cunliffe) and architect Walter S., she was a Protestant but educ. at Roman Catholic convents in England and France. She m. Alfred Henry W., 1917. Her earlier autobiographical work, *The Other Day*, 1936, gives childhood anecdotes; the later, *Random Commentary*, 1966, compiled from journals she started to keep in 1925, provides some detail about her career, including publication of her first novel, *Young Anne*, 1927. Of *The Notebooks of a Woman Alone*, DW writes: 'This woman has gathered a fund of quietly bitter wisdom. The sad acceptance of women in their lot is in this book. Though I myself feel a woman, any woman, should *fight*. But the odds are so against the working woman'. Several of her nine novels were bestsellers. DW is preoccupied with women's 'bitter bread of dependence': her novels are structured to make possible the examination of women's relationships, mainly with men. *Greenbanks*, 1932, makes the elderly Louisa its centre, and examines relationships brought into view by her children: a marriage made miserable by a tyrannical husband and father, one made unsatisfactory by money, an unmarried pregnant woman. *They Were Sisters*, 1943, similarly, treats three marriages. *They Knew Mr Knight*, 1934 (*The Great Mr Knight* in the USA), the effects on others of an unscrupulous businessman. (These two were both filmed, 1945; *Mr Knight* reviewed by Winifred HOLTBY.) DW also wrote children's stories.

Whitby, Beatrice Janie, 1855?–1931, novelist, b. Ridgway House, Ottery St Mary, Devon, where she lived 23 years. One of eight children of a Welsh mother (Philipps) and Dr W., she was educ. at home in a family fond of reading and telling each other stories, and later for a year in Hamburg. Her first novel was lost at the publishers; her first published was *The Awakening of Mary Fenwick*, 1889. Lively and well-written, it treats the marriage of an heiress who learns accidentally that she has been wooed for her money: the couple stay together, and gradually fall in love. This was far more enthusiastically received than her more feminist second novel (rewritten from the lost one), *Part of the Property*, 1890, dedicated to BW's sisters. Its heroine is brought up by a devoted governess, then by her grandfather, who wants to arrange her marriage to his stepson. She at first refuses to be 'part of the property', and when her fiancé is killed, she soon recovers, learns estate management, and successfully takes over his role. *One Reason Why*, 1892, takes up the stock Jane Eyre theme, but is perceptive about sexual politics; while *Mary Fenwick's Daughter*, 1894, is a disappointing sequel to her first success. Her later novels, such as *Bequeathed*, 1900, and *The Result of an Accident*, 1908, are increasingly conservative.

Whitcher, Frances Miriam (Berry), 1813–52, satirist and poet, b. at Whitesboro, Oneida Co., NY, one of 11 children of Elizabeth (Wells) and Lewis B., tavern owner. She wrote verse at about five and satirical sketches at the local academy. She became a Presbyterian in 1832, later an Episcopalian. Her sketches of local life, as read to the 'Maeonian Club', appeared in the Rome, NY, *Democratic Sentinel* in 1839, and as by 'Frank' in *Neal's Saturday Gazette* in 1846. Where Ann STEPHENS had used a male narrator, MW uses mostly dislikable female ones to expose the narrowness of would-be gentility, fancy quilting, and fierce blame for women stepping out of line (chiefly the parson's wife). Widow Bedott (called Silly for Priscilly) opens: 'He was a wonderful hand to moralize, husband was, 'specially after he begun to enjoy poor health.' David Ross Locke adapted these pieces for the stage in 1879. In 1847 FMBW married the Rev. Benjamin William W. and moved to Elmira, NY, her Scrabble Hill of 'Aunt Maguire's Experience' in *Godey's Ladies' Book*, 1847–9. *Godey's* sales soared, but the personal allusions (which her husband had vainly hoped to have softened) caused local outrage; he resigned, and fear of her pen made him unemployable in a permanent post. FMBW wrote 'I wish I could be paid as well for more sensible matter'; she published pious poems and hymns in journals, but her 'Mary Elmer', about an exemplary girl living in poverty, lacks the life of her satire. She began another colloquial series, 'Letters from Timberville', but developed TB in 1849 after her daughter's birth. *The Widow Bedott Papers*, 1856, has an intro. by Alice B. Neal (HAVEN), and *Widow Spriggins, Mary Elmer . . .*, 1867, a memoir by her husband's second wife. Some letters and verse at Dunham Public Library (Whitesboro, NY), the Oneida Historical Society (Utica, NY), and the New-York Historical Society; Linda A. Morris in *Women's Studies*, 15, 1988; diss. by Karen Cole, 1989.

'White, Antonia', Eirene Adeline Botting, 1899–1980, novelist, translator and journalist, b. in London, to Christine Julia (White) – who later seemed to AW to 'have no recollection of any . . . female figures in her childhood, only the all-dominating male one of "papa"' – and classical scholar Cecil George B. Expelled from the Convent of the Sacred Heart, Roehampton, for writing a novel about love, AW attended St Paul's Girls' School and the Academy of Dramatic Art, then attempted an acting career, 1920–1. *Frost in May*, 1933, her first novel (all are autobiographical), presents the protagonist's expulsion and rejection by her father. By 1930 she was on her third marriage (to journalist Tom Hopkinson) after two annulled for non-consummation, with a breakdown into madness after the first. She worked as copy-writer, teacher, journalist, and intelligence translator during WWII, broke down again, underwent four years' Freudian analysis, and was reconverted to Catholicism, before writing the Clara Batchelor trilogy: *The Lost Traveller*, 1950, *The Sugar House*, 1952, and *Beyond the Glass*, 1954. These again confront her two poles of patriarchy, her father and the Catholic church; the last deals with her madness. The four novels became a successful TV series, as *Frost in May*, 1982. *The Hound and the Falcon*, 1965, is a collection of letters charting her reconversion. AW translated over 30 French works including Maupassant and much of COLETTE. She also wrote a play, *Three in a Room*, 1947, and two children's stories about cats. *Strangers*, 1981, is a collection of short stories. AW's literary clarity has been criticized as lack of warmth. Lately most of her work has been re-issued: Jeanne A. Flood examines its subversive power of literary imagination in relation to patriarchal ideology in *Critique*, 24, 1983. AW's daughters, Susan Chitty and Lyndall Hopkinson, have publicly voiced strong, mixed, painful feelings about her. Chitty edited AW's early autobiography and other writings (*As Once in May*, 1983); each has published a memoir (Chitty in 1985, Hopkinson in 1988); one or other will continue the psychodrama by editing her explosively plain-speaking DIARIES.

White, Dorothy, 1630?–85, Quaker pamphleteer (most prolific woman in the genre after Margaret FELL) of Weymouth, Dorset. Most of her 20 prophecies were pub. 1659–64; some are incantatory, slipping in and out of verse. They attack England's rulers, threatening 'the Lord God is coming to shake you like a Leaf, & to break down your invented, imagined Laws made by your evil hearts' (*Upon the 22 day*, 1659). Many works of 1661–2 joyfully herald Christ's arrival. *A Call from God Out of Egypt*, 1662, restates Priscilla COTTON's 1655 defence of women's

PREACHING. DW visited London herself in 1662 to present her *Friends, You that are of the Parliament, hear the Word of the Lord*. In *A Diligent Search amongst the Rulers*, 1659, she describes her arrest for repeatedly interrupting a Weymouth church service. Though not then imprisoned ('It did not lie in their power to do it'), she later wrote in jail *The Voice of the Lord saith, Cry*, 1662, and *To all those that Worship*, 1664. In 1684 she broke a 20-year silence with several appeals to QUAKERS against the bureaucratization of their movement: prophets have 'the Word of God written in their Hearts: these must speak, as the Spirit gives Utterance; there is no Limit, nor tye to them'.

White, Elizabeth, *c.* 1637–69, English religious autobiographer. As a child she loved to read plays, 'Histories, and other foolish Books' when supposed to be asleep, and thought herself better than her sisters. (Later she saw 'nothing in my self that makes me more worthy of Salvation than another'.) A month before marrying Thomas W. of Coldecot, Bucks., in 1657, she took the sacrament unworthily, over which a minister aroused her to bitter fear and guilt, and ingenious self-analysis. After childbirth she saw visions (one of failing to get up a ladder to heaven). Having 'let out my Affection in a wonderful Measure to my Child', she feared God might punish this as excess. She wrote out, to be found in her closet after her death (in childbirth, as had been prophesied), her personal 'Principles, and I trust the Lord will so fix me in them, that I may never be tossed too and fro with contrary Winds of Doctrine, as too many in these latter Days are.' Her work was pub. as *The Experiences of God's Gracious Dealing* ..., Glasgow, 1696, often reprinted. A slightly shorter re-issue, Boston, 1741, has made scholars (even Carol Edkins in Estelle C. Jelinek, ed., 1980) wrongly suppose her American, and some to mis-date her.

White, Rhoda Elizabeth (Waterman), 1820?–66, fiction and non-fiction writer, da. of Whitney and Thomas G. Waterman, prominent NY Episcopalians. She converted to Catholicism in 1837 and m. James W. White (of Irish Catholic descent), lawyer and later Supreme Court judge. They had eight children. She began her writing career as 'Uncle Ben of Rouse's Point', who, in *Jane Arlington; or, the Defrauded Heiress. A Tale of Lake Champlain*, 1853, tells of Jane's adventures as a penniless orphan whose ladylike accomplishments ill-fit her to the menial work of housemaid. *Portraits of My Married Friends, or a Peep Into Hymen's Kingdom*, 1858, presents a set of moral tales dealing with marital discord, mismatches, wife-abuse and tenement life. Wry humour offsets moral absolutism, and close domestic detailing (down to rose-adorned lace caps), belies the diffidence of the crusty 'bachelor'-narrator's voice. *Mary Staunton, or The Pupils of Marvel Hall*, 1859, criticizes elitist boarding schools in which 'neglectful parents' leave their young to be bullied and abused into 'empty-headed' simpering doll-women. RW's most notable work is her biography of her daughter, *Memoir and Letters of Jenny C. White del Bal*, 1868. Jenny's LETTERS from Panama during the 1860s revolution, interpolated with RW's commentary, vividly describe the state of the nation under Mosquero's dictatorship, and the unfolding of her own story is a tale of unsung heroism. RW's other works include *From Infancy to Womanhood: A Book of Instruction for Young Mothers*, 1881, and *What Will the World Say? An American Tale of Real Life*, 1885. No biography exists; some sources give RW's birthdate as 1858!

'White, Roma', Blanche (Oram) Winder, 1866–1930, novelist and children's writer, b. at Bury, Lancs., da. of Esther (Allanson) and Henry O. After a successful career in JOURNALISM she turned to fiction (under a pseudonym translating and transposing her birth name) with *Punchinello's Romance*,

1892, an unusual mix of whimsy, sentiment, and advanced ideas. Its heroine begins as a fairy-tale orphan surrounded by comic grotesques; she survives 'wholesale' or 'button-manufactory' education to become a radical, protects rioting mill-hands from the police, finds out her mother's passionate, 'fallen' history, and marries happily. *Moonbeams and Brownies*, 1894, contains fairy-stories. In 1896 came *The Changeling of Brandlesome* (a well-told, first-person, north-country tale of Charles I's reign) and *A Stolen Mask*, perhaps RW's best book. Its heroine's 'untidiness, her excitability, and her general attitude of schism' find their niche in a touring theatre company, drawn warts and all; comedy shifts to tragedy when she advances her career by getting her rival drunk. After marrying Charles Winder, 1897, she also published as RW. *The Island of Seven Shadows*, 1898 (set in modern London, Paris and Brittany), a gardening book, 1900, and two more novels. *Backsheesh*, 1902, and *Moons and Winds of Araby*, 1906, are set in Egypt: an Englishman makes an Islamic marriage, flirts with a mixed-race woman, is widowed, and turns with relief to an English girl ('No evil can live near you'); an English wife writes a lyrical travel book with comic comment on men and domesticity, supposedly while trying to produce a book on household management. RW used her married name for a joint book on wildlife, 1907, stories and a historical novel for children, [1924]–48, and *Trespassers in Paradise*, 1928, and *The Sin-Offering*, 1930, each about the repercussions of socially unacceptable marriages or liaisons.

Whitehead, Anne (Downer), 1624–86, first woman convert to the QUAKERS in London: her family disowned her. She m. in 1662 Benjamin Greenwell, then in 1669 George W., *c.* 1637–1723, who used his acute legal mind to defend Friends. In 1670 she was a signatory (with Mary FORSTER, Rebecca TRAVERS and 33 others) to a PETITION to king and parliament against Friends' imprisonment. Her *Epistle For True Love*, 1680, rebuffs objections to the setting up of separate Women's and Men's Meetings. Like Forster in 1685, she lists the duties of the women's meetings as caring for the poor and sick, and guiding younger women 'to all wholesome things, having their own Husbands and Children, to be Discreet, Chaste, Sober, keeping at Home, that the Word of God we profess be not Blasphemed'. Her death was marked by *Piety Promoted*, 1686, a collection of testimonies mostly by women.

Whitman, Narcissa (Prentiss), 1808–47, diarist and missionary, b. Plattsburg, NY, the third of nine children of Clarissa (Ward) and Stephen P. NW attended public school in Plattsburg, spent a year at Franklin Academy, finished her educ. at a seminary in Troy, NY, and then taught school. In 1834 she applied to the American Board of Missionaries, hoping to teach the Indians beyond the Rocky Mountains. Turned down because she was unmarried, NW in 1835 met Marcus W., another prospective missionary. They married in 1836 and a few weeks later began the trek across the mountains. The journal NW sent to her parents in 1836 grew out of notes taken along the way west. In the tradition of spiritual autobiography, NW marks her journey with references to Bunyan's *Pilgrim's Progress* and the Bible as well as to the natural curiosities – soda springs and basalt columns – encountered on the way. She and her husband established Waiilatpu Mission, on the Walla Walla River, where she had a daughter. In 1847, a band of Cayuse Indians killed NW and her husband along with 11 others. The journal has often been referred to and excerpted; it was recently pub. as *My Journal: 1836, by Narcissa Prentiss Whitman*, 1982, ed. Lawrence L. Dodd. For a guide to her unpub. letters, see Clifford Drury, *Marcus and Narcissa Whitman and the Opening of Oregon*, 1973.

Whitman, Sarah Helen **(Power)**, 1803–78, poet and essayist, b. Providence, Rhode Island, da. of Anna (Marsh) and Nicholas P., merchant, whose business failed after 1812. SPW was initially educ. at home by her mother. While living with an aunt in Jamaica, RI, she attended a Quaker school and later a school in Providence, where she began writing poetry. In 1828 she m. John Winslow W., a writer who had pub. as 'Ichabod' and had ed. the *Boston Spectator and Ladies' Album* (in which SPW pub. her first work as 'Helen') and the *Bachelor's Journal.* They lived in Boston, where she was influenced by the Transcendentalists, especially Bronson Alcott. Here too she began her advocacy of women's rights, and also became interested in mesmerism and SPIRITUALISM. As 'Egeria' she pub. essays praising Shelley, Emerson and Goethe. She returned to Providence after her husband's death in 1833. During 1848 she was engaged briefly to Poe, whose second poem 'Helen' honours her. In 1853 her verses *Hours of Life* appeared, and in 1860 she pub. *Edgar Poe and His Critics* in response to Griswold's damaging biography. Acclaimed as the first literary woman of note to support SUFFRAGE, she became a vice-president of the Rhode Island Suffrage Association in 1868. Her motto was 'Break all bonds'. While her early poems, though graceful, were derivative, her late poems indicate a real sense of lyric art. Her collected *Poems* appeared in 1879. Her MSS are at the Univ. of Virginia, Brown Univ. and the Lilly Library of Indiana Univ. See Caroline Ticknor, 1916, for her life.

Whitney, Isabella (probably later Eldershae), first Englishwoman to publish (as 'Is. W.') a book of poems. She says she was bred in Smithfield, London, though Geoffrey W. from Cheshire, emblem-book writer, was probably one of her brothers. Her *Copy of a Letter ... in Meeter by a Yonge Gentilwoman to her Unconstant Lover* need not be autobiographical. It exists both in broadside and 'Newly joyned' to poems on similar themes (a warning to 'Maids being in Love' and two epistles addressed by men to more or less certainly inconstant women) [1567?]. The first two poems deploy classical allusion to question male values (ancient heroes won fame by falsehood to women); the later two, less ingenious and more accusatory, are probably not IW's. Her next book, *A Sweet Nosegay, or Pleasant Posye Contaynning a Hundred and Ten Phylosophicall Flowers*, 1573, includes metrical versions of maxims from Sir Hugh Platt's *Flours of Philosophie*, 1572. Several poems mark her imminent departure from London (which, she says, like a typical woman, she repays with love for ill-treatment). She plays at unlimited power in her 'Wyll and Testament', which bequeaths the city everything it already has. Unusually, she praises not churches or palaces but commercial products (street by street, lovingly enumerated), bequeathing also, to defray costs, the contents of the Mint. The ungainly 'poulter's measure' cannot damp her charm and verve. She probably pub. other poems in anthologies (e.g. Richard Jones, ed., 1578, 1584). She wrote to a sister that being single kept her from 'household cares', free for her 'bookes and Pen', but by 1600 she probably had a husband and two children. Good selec. in ANTHOLOGY ed. Betty Travitsky, 1981. See Travitsky in *ELR*, 10 and 14, 1981 and 1984; Elaine V. Beilin, 1987.

Whitrow, Joan, pamphleteer, wife of the ungodly Robert W. of Covent Garden, London. Three months before the great plague, 1665, she walked to Bristol to preach in sackcloth and ashes; she did this in London too. Her Quaker testimonies on the successive deaths of her small son (marked to die as God's 'beloved') and 15-year-old daughter, Susanna, appeared in *The Work of God in a Dying Maid*, 1677 (collectively written, prefaced by Rebecca TRAVERS, offering an example to young Friends). JW writes, 'out of the Willingness of my Heart have I offered my Children unto the Lord' though they were 'dear to me as my Life'. Susanna's deathbed speech, taking several days, is the key item: she repents having opposed women's speaking, lavishly praises JW, and wishes, if she might live, they could 'get us into the Country to some little remote Place, amongst the Woods, where none can hear us: O then shall our Crys pierce thro' the Heavens.' Other people praise her virtue and deny a rumour that she died for human love. JW became a solitary and ascetic, of no fixed abode, 'Sect or gathered People'; she spent three years in sackcloth, and as a widow published and presented to the king and queen a series of exhortations, from 1689, attacking the vice and luxury of the rich, calling for repentance, and indignantly lamenting 'empty Bellies, both of Weavers and others'. She quotes Cowley and Marcus Aurelius, and mentions (1694) her 30 years of visions. Seven texts survive; she refers to more.

Whitton, Katherine or Catherine, prominent Yorkshire Quaker, signatory with Judith BOULBIE and Mary WAITE to several official and conservative documents from Women's Meetings in 1686–8, which call on women to be modest and chaste, and not to create factions. Her one solo publication, *An Epistle to Friends Every Where*, 1681, urges Quakers to unite and attend to spiritual 'good Housewifery'.

'Wickham, Anna', Edith Alice Mary (Harper), later Hepburn, 1884–1947, poet, b. at Wimbledon near London. Her parents, the flamboyant Alice (Whelan), teacher, hypnotist and 'character-reader', and Geoffrey Harper, piano-tuner, who encouraged her early writing, took her to Australia at six. She attended schools in several towns there, lastly Sydney, where she and her mother relieved their poverty with remunerative elocution lessons. Two of her children's plays were privately printed there, with her name. She returned to England alone in 1904 and studied singing in London and Paris, but gave up operatic ambitions after a year to marry Patrick Hepburn, London lawyer. She hated bourgeois married life; frustration and erotic energy poured into poetry. In 1907, after bearing the first of four sons (one died at four), she began lecturing on mothercraft. Publication of *Songs*, as 'John Oland' (Women's Printing Society, 1911), caused a violent quarrel with her husband, who 'had no intention of allowing his wife to be a poet': he committed her as insane, and she spent six weeks in an asylum. In 1915 she met D. H. Lawrence. He thought some of her work '*very* good'. She thought his 'a sort of miasma of menace towards women who detach any considerable portion of their energy from their purely sexual function' ('The Spirit of the Lawrence Women'). Alida and Harold Monro of the Poetry Workshop included her work in *Poetry and Drama*, 1914, and issued two of her collections, *The Contemplative Quarry*, 1915, and *The Little Old House*, 1921. These were published together in NY, 1921, with an introduction by Louis Untermeyer. In 1922 AW travelled to Paris, where she met Natalie BARNEY and other writers. Separated from her husband in 1926, she corresponded with Barney for years, expressing passionate love and debating the role and problems of the woman artist. In 1935 she articulated her own experience of these problems in her sparkling and poignant 'Fragment of an Autobiography: Prelude to a Spring Clean' (to the birth of her second son). John Gawsworth anthologized her and included her (as an Edwardian) in his 'Richard's Shilling Selection' series, 1936. With several hundred poems in print, this left over a thousand unpub.; a fire in 1943 destroyed many letters and MSS. AW committed suicide during severe depression. Her best work is epigrammatic, sardonic, experimental (free verse), and charged with exuberant feminist consciousness. It includes scathing, frankly autobiographical critiques of marriage, sex, and middle-class oppression ('I married a man of the Croydon class. . . . And as I sit in his ordered house, / I feel I must sob or shriek, / To force a man of the Croydon class / To live, or to love, or to speak') as well as celebrations of motherhood and passionate love. Harold Monro discusses her briefly in *Some Contemporary Poets*, 1920, but her wide reputation of the 1930s vanished completely till David Garnett's selection, 1971. Her son James Hepburn prefaces her *Writings* (which call her 'Free Woman and Poet'), 1984. An unpublished memoir by Eliot BLISS is in his possession. See Margaret Newlin in *SoR*, 14, 1978, and Myra Stark in *Four Decades of Poetry*, 2, 1978.

Wiggin, Kate Douglas (Smith), later Riggs, 1856–1923, children's writer and educator, b. Philadelphia, da. of Helen Elizabeth (Dyer) and Robert Noah S., lawyer, who d. when she was three. Her mother remarried and the family moved to Hollis, Maine. An avid reader, KDW also kept a journal as a child. She was educ. at a local dame school, Gorham Female Seminary and Morison Academy. In 1871 the family moved to Santa Barbara, Calif. Her first pub. work, written to earn money after her step-father's death, was 'Half a Dozen House-keepers' in *St. Nicholas* magazine. In 1877 she met Caroline M. Severance, who interested her in the kindergarten method, which she then trained in and taught in San Francisco until 1881, when she m. Samuel Bradley W., lawyer. Her first book, *The Story of Patsy*, 1883, was written to help support Silver Street Kindergarten, as was *The Birds' Christmas Carol*, 1887. The royalties allowed her to travel after her husband's death in 1889. She then wrote the popular 'Penelope' series, beginning with *A Cathedral Courtship*, 1893. In 1895 she m. George Christopher Riggs, an importer. Her most famous book, *Rebecca of Sunnybrook Farm*, 1903, was influenced by Wordsworth's ideas of nature and child-hood. She joined with her Scottish friends, the FINDLATER sisters, to write the light-hearted *Affair at the Inn*, 1904. In her auto-biography, *My Garden of Memory*, written with her sister Nora Archibald Smith, 1919–23, she says: 'Nothing but writing rests me; only then do I seem completely myself!' See Nora's memoir, 1925; study by Helen Frances Benner, 1956.

Wight, Sarah, b. 1632, Baptist pamphleteer. As a child she spent four years in spiritual turmoil, frequently trying, with horrific violence, to kill herself, as Henry Jessey reported after the climax – a two-week trance in 1647 – brought her to public notice. In 1656 she published *A Wonderful Pleasant and Profitable Letter* to a friend, which opens: 'A Christian's happiness lies in being emptied of all self, self refined, as well as gross self; and being filled with a full God.' She lengthily amplifies this view, and repeatedly denies any desire for public recognition of her work.

Wijenaike, Punyakante (Kotelawala), poet, writer of fiction. She was educ. at Bishop's College, a private girls' school in Colombo, Sri Lanka, where she was born in 1933. She inherited affluence and leisure from her surgeon grandfather, described in *A Way of Life*, 1987, sketches of her childhood and adolescence in an upper middle-class home in Colombo from the 1930s to the 1950s. As an isolated child, she learned 'I am happiest when I am alone', and her playmates were 'imaginary characters'. The house she grew up in provides the setting for her novel *Giraya*, 1971, though here it is altered, presented as a decaying rural feudal manor-house, an emblem for 'the helplessness of a group of men and women enmeshed in the web of an out-moded social system'. Her work is influenced by Pearl BUCK and informed by a deeply Buddhist and female sensibility. She values simplicity and restraint, examining with a sympathy devoid of shrillness the tensions of family life, especially in the experience of girls and women. Her works also include *The Third Woman*, short stories, 1963; *The*

Waiting Earth, 1966 (transl. into Sinhala as *Uhulana Derana*, 1967), a novel which explores with freedom and insight the inner world of rural Sri Lankan women often hopelessly tied down by custom and ritual, and which has been called 'a classic of contemporary village life'; *The Betel Vine*, a short story published with another, 'Call of the Sea', 1976; and *The Rebel*, short stories, 1979. Between 75 and 100 short stories have appeared in newspapers and journals. For her treatment of provincial female lives, these have been compared to the work of Willa CATHER. See Alastair Niven in *JCL*, 12, 1977, and Siromi Fernando and Ryhana Raheem, 'Women Writers of Sri Lanka', in *WLWE*, 17, 1978.

Wilcox, 'Dora', Mary Theodora Joyce (later Hamelius, then Moore), 1873–1953, poet and playwright. B. at Christchurch, NZ, da. of Mary Elizabeth (Washbourne) and William Henry W., saddler, she was educ. privately and at Canterbury Univ. College, taught in NSW, then travelled to France, Germany and England, where she m. in 1909 Jean Paul H., Professor of English at Liege Univ. Separated, and then widowed, she m. William M., Australian art critic and writer, in 1923 and settled with him in Australia. She pub. *Verses from Maoriland*, 1905, and *Rata and Mistletoe*, 1911. 'After the Honeymoon' and 'Forsaken (A Modern Woman Speaks)' in *Verses from Maoriland* portray woman's dilemma: either crushed and conditioned as 'poor slave to artificiality', or condemned as 'Too bold, too modern, and too free'. She wrote several one-act plays in the 1920s. Her obit. in *Southerly*, 15, 1, said, 'Her most important work was in helping her husband in his *Story of Australian Art*; she was indefatigable in research for this'.

Wilcox, Ella (Wheeler), 1850–1919, poet, b. Johnstown Center, Wisconsin, youngest of four children of Sarah (Pratt) and Marcus Hartwell Wheeler, farmer and ex-teacher of music and dancing. She was educ. at the local public school and the Univ. of Wisconsin, but mainly by her mother, who encouraged EWW to read OUIDA, Mary J. HOLMES and E. D. E. N. SOUTHWORTH. She wrote her first novel at nine, her first essay was pub. by the NY *Mercury* in 1865, and by 18 she was earning substantially from her writing. In 1872 she pub. *Drops of Water*, a collection of TEMPERANCE verses. Her first big success was *Poems of Passion*, 1883, initially rejected by publishers for 'immorality' (celebrating female sexuality), and selling 60,000 copies in two years. In 1884 EWW m. Robert Marius Wilcox, manufacturer of silver art works. Her early views on the WOMAN QUESTION were very conservative: *Men, Women and Emotion*, 1893, asserts that housekeeping is the sacrifice a woman should offer on the altar of love. By 1897, in her long narrative poem *Three Women*, one woman asserts, 'Well I'm done with the role of housewife', while her poem 'To Men' concludes, 'There is no looking down or up / Between us: eye looks straight in eye: / Born equals, so we live and die.' EWW was a very prolific writer, producing thousands of verses which, although often clichéd – 'heart, not art' was her motto – achieved very wide popular appeal. Some of her lesser-known poetry displays much tougher qualities. EWW had a nervous breakdown at the end of her life after touring WWI camps and exhorting soldiers to 'come back clean' from venereal disease. Her autobiography, *The Worlds and I*, was pub. in 1918. See Jenny Ballou, 1940, for her life; Cheryl Walker, *The Nightingale's Burden*, 1982, and Emily Stipes Watts, 1977, for critical discussion. Her papers are at the State Historical Society of Wisconsin, Columbia Univ. and NYPL.

Wilder, Laura (Ingalls), 1867–1957, children's writer, b. in a log cabin in Pepin, Wis., second of four das. of Caroline Lake (Quiner) and Charles Philip Ingalls. Between 16 and 18 she taught near De Smet, SD; then she married Almanzo J. W.

They had two children, Rose, later LANE, and Charles, who d. within 12 days of birth in 1902. They farmed in Mansfield, Missouri, cutting, planing and fitting 'every stick' of their own home at Rocky Ridge. LIW served in the Missouri Home Development Association to assist farmwives and founded the Mansfield Farm Loan Association to offer low-interest loans to Ozark farmers, but she is remembered because of her nine books of Mid-West pioneer life. The best-known are the Little House books (*Little House in the Big Woods*, 1932, *Little House on the Prairie*, 1935, *On the Banks of Plum Creek*, 1937, *By the Shores of Silver Lake*, 1939, *The Long Winter*, 1940, *Little Town on the Prairie*, 1941) which celebrate her homesteading Ma and Pa and the courageous resourcefulness and love surrounding her frontier childhood. LIW had contributed essays to the *Missouri Ruralist*, 1911–1924; her daughter's prompting produced these affecting, direct 'stories of long ago'. In 1954 the American Library Association presented her with the first LIW Award, to be given every five years to an outstanding children's author or illustrator. After her death appeared her diary of migration, 1894, to Missouri, 1962, *The First Four Years*, 1971, and *West from Home: Letters, San Francisco, 1915*, 1974. Life by Daniel Zochert, 1976. Rosa Moore has examined her pencil MSS (edge-to-edge in cheap, lined notebooks) to comment on her artistic restructuring of experience; other studies by Hamida Bosmajian (*Children's Literature*, 11, 1983) and Virginia Wolf (*CLAQ*, 9, 1985).

Wilhelm, Gale, novelist, b. 1908 in Eugene, Ore., da. of Ethel (Brewer) and Wilson Price W. She was educ. in Oregon, Idaho and Washington, moved to San Francisco in 1925 and published several sonnets in *Overland Magazine*. After a brief period in New York she returned to the West coast in 1937 and lived with Helen Hope Randolph Page, editor of the *Stockton Herald*, Oakdale branch, till Page's death in the mid-1950s. Reviewers liked *We Too Are Drifting*, 1935, a novel of lesbian love, for its sexual frankness and freedom from the self-consciousness associated with 1920s and 1930s lesbian writing. Its artist-heroine strives for 'great leanness and simplicity, a pure and definite meaning'. Six more novels followed. *No Letters For the Dead*, 1936, is a heterosexual love-story whose limpid intensity avoids over-sensationalism in handling suicide, imprisonment, and the death of a child. *Torchlight to Valhalla*, 1938, is based on GW's relationship with Page. Honorary membership of the International Mark Twain Society marked GW's 'outstanding contribution in the field of fiction' in 1942. In *The Time Between*, 1942, and *Never Let Me Go*, 1945, she treats love between woman and man, the former complicated by a background of war and the latter by the heroine's sexual problems, springing from her father's 'legal rape' of her mother. After this GW dropped out of sight. Naiad Press, reprinting *We Too* in 1984 (intro. by Barbara Grier), searched vainly for her; they found her, in Berkeley, in time for her to supply a characteristically laconic preface to their re-issue of *Torchlight*, 1985. Her letters to Carl Sandburg are at the Univ. of Illinois (Urbana-Champaign).

Wilhelm, Kate Gertrude (Meredith), novelist and short-story writer, b. 1928 in Toledo, Ohio, da. of Ann (McDowell) and Jesse Thomas M. A voracious reader, she went to high school in Louisville, Ky, married Joseph W. in 1947 (divorced 1962), and after various jobs began publishing in magazines in 1957. Her first books were *More Bitter Than Death* (mystery), 1962, and *The Mile-Long Spaceship* (stories), 1963, repr. 1980. In 1963 she married Damon Knight (with whom she co-authored *Better Than One*, 1980). She has three sons. Prolific in speculative fiction, she defines it in prefacing *The Infinity Box*, 1975 (stories all to do with misuse of special power), as 'realistically' exploring 'worlds that probably never will exist' but that we 'dread or yearn for'. These worlds are richly imagined: here a personal re-evaluation provoked by revisiting the past; a writer's discovery that life imitates his stories; futuristic totalitarian rule by teachers (a few girls escape); and two medical nightmares – a gradual rundown of all curing and caring, and a conspiracy against those incapable of newly-invented immortality. This theme is re-worked in *Welcome, Chaos*, 1983. KW collects more stories in *Somerset Dreams*, 1978, and *Listen, Listen*, 1981 (with 'The Uncertain Edge of Reality', a speech made in 1980, declaring her faith in questioning, for the sake of the world's future, 'the framework of reality we have accepted'). She links literary experiment with interest in advances and controversies in social sciences, medicine, psychology; her protagonists include talented and unorthodox women in these fields who are threatened by malign professional or government systems. In *The Clewiston Test*, 1976, a woman accusing her husband of rape is counter-charged with ingesting the mind-altering drugs she has invented. In *Crazy Time*, 1988, a psychologist has her perception of reality both threatened and denied. *Axolotl*, 1979, is a multimedia fantasy drama. KW has founded, lectured at, and run conferences and workshops for SCIENCE-FICTION writers. MSS at Syracuse Univ., NY.

Wilkinson, Anne (Gibbons), 1910–61, poet and editor. B. in Toronto, where she lived until her death of cancer, AW spent her childhood in London, Ont., and, after the death of her father, in her maternal grandfather's mansion, Craigleigh, Toronto, with periodic stays in Santa Barbara, Calif. She married (1932, divorced 1952) F. R. W.; she had three children. *Lions in the Way*, 1956, a collage of voluminous journals and letters of relatives, traces the history of her mother's (Mary Osler Boyd Gibbons) family, which settled in the backwoods of Ontario in 1837 and had produced distinguished men and women since the eighteenth century. Educ. by private tutors and at 'progressive schools' in England, France and the USA, AW was taught as a child about 'Freud and dreams, and a great deal of minutiae about sex'. Her happy and privileged upbringing is reflected in her two poetry books, 1951 and 1955 (posthumously collec., with MSS fragments, by A. J. M. Smith, 1968). Although acclaimed in the fifties, AW's poetry has received scant critical attention. 'Obsess[ed] with exits' and Empedocles's world of transformation – 'Numberless as clowns / Are my beginnings' – she writes a poetry of natural sensuality 'inscribing the excluded subjective into her poems', where images of women, children and poets figure prominently: 'My woman's eye is weak / And veiled with milk; / ... My woman's iris circles / A blind pupil; / The poet's eye is crystal, / Polished to accept the negative'. AW's 'green' world of nursery rhymes, ballads and postscripts, with the poet imaged as child, has been compared to Blake's and Donne's, to Emily DICKINSON's and Isabella Valancy CRAWFORD's, for its visionary sensibility and its 'erotics of living'. AW also wrote a children's book, *Swann and Daphne*, 1960, and founded and edited *The Tamarack Review*. See Robert Lecker in *SCanL*, 3, 1978, and Douglas Barbour in Neuman and Kamboureli, 1986.

Wilkinson, Eliza (Yonge), letter writer, da. of Francis Y., a Welsh-born slave-owner near Charleston, SC. Married young and widowed after six months, she sent a female friend, a few years after the event, a serial account of her revolutionary war experiences, *c.* 1779 (album at University of SC, most ed., Caroline GILMAN, 1839). She cites Homer, Ovid, the Stoics, Milton, and mocks the notion of ladies as statesmen. For cultural reasons she had expected to think well of the British, but records disillusion at the soldiers' behaviour, growth of American patriotism, and the dawn of parallel feminist feeling, as she finds her favourite authors denying women 'the liberty of thought, and that is all I want'. By 1781, recording a smallpox attack and writing 'a long letter out of nothing', she has reached her present life.

Wilkinson, Elizabeth (Gifford), d. 1654, religious memoirist, da. of Devon gentry Elizabeth (Cottle) and Anthony G. She says she was born in an ignorant place, but soon removed by God to the care of a pious aunt. She was an early diarist, deeply affected at 12 by *The Practice of Piety*; troubled by all kinds of religious fears, she sought answers in wide reading. Not for many years did she find evidence of salvation. She married Dr Henry W. (principal of Magdalen Hall, Oxford, from 1648), practised medicine and charity, was often ill, and died young in childbed leaving three children. Her brief 'Narrative ... of God's gracious dealings' (written for admission to Holy Communion) appeared with Edmund Staunton's funeral sermon and life of her, 1659.

Wilkinson, Jemima, 1752–1810, American preacher and religious leader, b. at Cumberland, RI. One of the large family of Amey (Whipple), who d. in 1764, and Quaker farmer Jeremiah W., she had little formal education. Expelled by Friends, 1776, for involvement in the New Light revival, she suffered a severe fever; on recovery she believed herself actually raised from the dead to preach as the Publick Universal Friend. From converting her sisters she progressed to PREACHING tours which drew the educated and affluent; she went further afield from 1782, when Elizabeth DRINKER found her 'remarkable'. In 1784 she appeared in Hannah ADAMS's *Compendium* of sects, and printed a pamphlet of *Advice*, her only published work. Her sermons and letters are simple and sane despite visionary touches: 'Descend down into thine own heart and there read what thou art and what thou shalt be'; 'Try to be on the Lords side.' She advises celibacy, but is undogmatic, fond of the phrase 'as much as possible'. In 1788 her followers founded a wilderness colony at Seneca Lake, where she settled in 1790. Cheated at the outset by land speculators, they later succumbed to conflict between rich and poor. JW aroused violent hatred, and an early and enduring folk image quite distinct from what evidence suggests. Life by Herbert A. Wisbey, 1964; film of her MSS at Cornell.

Wilkinson, Sarah Scudgell, d. after 1830, novelist and condenser. She says she had early literary ambitions, published her first work, *The Thatched Cottage*, by subscription, and opened a library with the proceeds. Her novels (like *The Fugitive Countess*, 1807, dedicated to Mary CHAMPION DE CRESPIGNY) favour themes like that of women cast out for their own or other's sexual lapses; they are emotionally poignant and stylistically vivid if exaggerated (or stilted in upper-class talk). *The Spectre of Lanmere Abbey*, 1820, jokes about its inclusion of all the ingredients of an Ann RADCLIFFE novel; but the spectre turns out to be a bereft mother in disguise. SSW is better known for the survivors among her 100 easy-read chap-books abridged from other's work (fiction and drama, English, French and German, some the very latest titles). She usually gives her own name and that of her source: Henry Fielding, Matthew Lewis, Amelia OPIE, Jane PORTER, Ann RADCLIFFE, Walter Scott, and (at two removes) Richard Steele and George Lillo. She handles ghosts and priories with necessary succinctness, verve, and a hint of mockery. Some such works claim to be original or 'Founded on facts', like *The History of Crazy Jane* [1817], probably most reprinted and re-titled of all. SSW wrote for periodicals, and also pub. a school textbook, a life of Alfred the Great, and several booklets of witty, pleasing Valentine verses. Widowed and receiving aid from the RLF by 1818, with breast cancer from 1820, she ran schools (when she could afford decent clothes) and a 'parlour shop'; she was writing songs in 1828.

Willard, Emma (Hart), 1787–1870, educational reformer, b. Berlin, Conn., ninth child of Lydia (Hinsdale) and 16th of Samuel Hart. She grew up on a farm in an educated household, and began teaching early. By 1807 she was Head of the Middlebury Female Academy, Vermont: in 1809 she m. Dr John W. and pursued further study, though too early to obtain a degree. In 1814 she opened the Middlebury Female Seminary with a new curriculum including mathematics and philosophy. She pub. her *Plan for Improving Female Education*, 1919, at her own expense. From 1821–38 she ran the Troy Female Seminary and wrote highly successful textbooks on history, science and geography, imaginatively combining moral EDUCATION with factual learning, as in *Temple of Time*, 1844. She travelled, publishing *Journal and Letters from France and Great Britain*, 1833; wrote many poems; remarried; divorced; and campaigned for more public schools and better conditions for woman teachers. She did not campaign for women's rights, but opposed the Anti Women Suffrage Society supported by her sister, Almira Phelps, 1793–1884, educator and science textbook writer, who also pub. three didactic novels for schoolgirls, despite her declared distrust of fiction.

Willard, Frances Elizabeth Caroline, 1839–98, temperance activist and suffrage leader, b. Churchville, NY, da. of Mary Thompson (Hill) and Josiah Flint W. She grew up tomboyishly in Oberlin, Ohio, and on the Wisconsin frontier, later moving to Evanston, Illinois, where she attended college and then based her life. After graduating in 1859, she taught school and college, then travelled to Europe 1868–70. A woman's woman, she never married, and after resigning as Dean of Women and Professor of Aesthetics from Northwestern Univ. in 1873, became President of the Women's Christian Temperance Union (national president from 1879 until her death). Using their journal, *Our Union*, she linked TEMPERANCE issues with other women's issues like SUFFRAGE, arousing nation-wide support. With Mary A. Livermore, she wrote the influential *Woman of the Century*, 1893 (rev. 1897), a heroinizing but also factual collection. Her feminism remained conservative, embracing women's domestic role, while her own professional life was sustained by a series of devoted woman friends, especially Anna Gordon, companion and secretary for more than 20 years. She wrote books on temperance; for girls; on bicycling; on her sister; and her autobiography, *Glimpses of Fifty Years*, 1889 (repr. 1970). See lives by Ray STRACHEY, 1912, and Ruth Bordin, 1986.

Willey, Chloe, b. 1760, visionary writer. Da. of a tradesman of Windham, Conn., disfigured by burns as a baby, she lost her friends and schooling at 12 when her family moved to New Hampshire. She developed religious fears, which ended when one night at prayer she 'had a most shining view of the justice and holiness of God' and experienced dialogue with Christ. She realized she must join the 'poor, despised Baptists', whom pious and learned men disparaged. She married in 1781 and again 'removed into the wilderness', this time with God for companion. In 1788 she dreamed of 'the Highway of Holiness' and was told the millenium was coming; a cloud interposed between her and what she was reading (Isaac Watts) and she went in a two-hour trance 'to the borders of hell'. There followed fasting, prayer, visions of devils and saints; she would not allow people to classify her as sick. Her regular angel-guide 'gave me to understand, that the wheel of my nature was broken, but the inner wheel of grace was good and strong'; he also expounded the symbols of the great flood and the balance or scales, and taught her to know saints from sinners, and to prevent a visiting elder from bullying her. Her *Short Account*..., written in 1807, pub. 1810, ends abruptly with verses on a young man who died in despair.

Williams, Anna, 1706–83, scientist and poet, b. at Rosemarket near Haverfordwest, Wales, da. of Martha and Zachary W. In 1714 her grandfather left her a heifer. In probably 1726 her father (seeking the longitude prize, like Jane SQUIRE) brought her to London. She worked on early electrical experiments with the scientist Stephen Grey, jointly and anonymously translated a French *Life of the Emperor Julian*, 1746, supported her father by sewing, and in 1747 was evicted from his Charterhouse lodging, which allowed no women. (His *True Narrative* of this affair, 1749, includes letters by her.) Blinded by cataract (an operation of 1752 failed), she became a life-long lodger with Samuel Johnson, to whom her 'universal curiosity and comprehensive knowledge' (of French, Latin and English books, besides science) were a mainstay. Her *Miscellanies in Verse and Prose* includes work by others, and her own worthwhile pieces on standard topics (proposals by Johnson 1750; pub. by subscription 1766; the delay gave her much pain). Her hopes of producing a scientific dictionary (with scribal help), 1754, came to nothing. Elizabeth MONTAGU gave her a pension (from 1775); so did some Welsh ladies. She left all she had to a refuge for destitute women; E. C. KNIGHT's mother, a friend, wrote on her in the *European Mag.*, 1799.

Williams, Helen Maria, 1762–1827, radical poet, novelist and historical letter writer, da. of Helen (Hay) and army officer Charles W., b. in London but brought up and educ. by her Scots mother at Berwick-on-Tweed. Back in London in 1781, she next year published *Edwin and Eltruda*, a legendary tale in verse. Further poems and collections profitably followed, including *Peru*, 1784, the famous sonnets, 1786, and *A Poem on ... the Slave Trade*, 1788. A visit that year to a sister in France led her later to settle there. Her novel, *Julia*, 1790, revises Rousseau's *Nouvelle Héloise*, making the triangle one of a man, who dies, and two women, who are left with a child to bring up together. Her various collections of *Letters* from France, pub. from 1790 (facs. of first, 1989) and describing the events of the Revolution as she saw them, were more radical and controversial. Her factual slips as historian and political commentator scarcely mar her spirited, emotional recreation of individual experience. She emphasizes women's 'considerable share' in the Revolution, their various efforts to combat tyranny, their fortitude under hardship (she was herself imprisoned during the Terror). Often badly reviewed on political grounds, she continued to promulgate her views, on Switzerland, 1798, and later French history, 1815 and 1819. Further works include translations from French, and *Poems* (written earlier), 1823. Catherine WILMOT reported her cosmopolitan parties 'of 60 or 70 people, almost all celebrated for something or other'. To the scandal of her politics she added living with the divorced John Hurford Stone; she may have secretly married him in 1794, and was buried with him in Paris. Life in French by Lionel D. Woodward, 1930; Judith Scheffler in *The Wordsworth Circle*, 19, 1988.

Williams, Jane, 'Ysgafell', 1806–85, historian and biographer, b. Chelsea, London, da. of Eleanor and David W. Although she spent much of her life in England, she is known as a Welsh writer and lived for many years in Ysgafell, Wales. With her three brothers and three sisters she created an imaginary world cut out of paper, complete with governments, kings and historical records: she later wrote *The Origin, Rise, and Progress of the Paper People*, 1856, for her friend Mrs Shaw Lefevre. Her *History of Wales*, 1869, is considered one of the best English language histories of that country and she also wrote a memoir of Welsh historian Thomas Price, 1885. Other works include *Miscellaneous Poems*, privately printed 1824; *Celtic Fables, Fairy Tales, and Legends*, 1862, delightfully recounted in rhyming couplets; and *Literary Women of England*, 1861. While this work provides a diligent survey of women writers 1500–1850, JW insists that no artistic gift justifies 'the neglect of even the smallest act of domestic duty'.

Williams, Sarah, 'Sadie', 1841–68, poet, only child of Louisa and Robert W. (whose Welsh extraction she saw as the source of her 'bardic' gift), educ. by governesses and at Queen's College, London. Her family was wealthy: she used the profits from her writing to help the poor. Her poetry was admired by Henrietta Keddie ('Sarah TYTLER'): it was pub. in a posthumous volume as *Twilight Hours. A Legacy of Verse*, ed. and with a memoir by one of her teachers, E. H. Plumptre, 1868. Most striking is 'Sospiri Volate', the series of verse-letters between a pair of self-analysing lovers, although some of the devotional verse is also unusual, and lighter pieces show promise too: 'Marjory gathered the peaches fine, / That dropped in the sun behind the tree. / "Where is your husband to share the feast?"/ "I can eat peaches," said Marjorie' [sic] (from 'Marjory's Wedding'). Never in good health, SW died soon after her father, following an operation.

Williams, Sherley Anne, poet, novelist, critic, b. in 1944 in Bakersfield, Calif., da. of Lena (Silver) and Jessee Winston W. She was first inspired to write because 'We were missing these stories of black women's struggles and their real triumphs'. She wrote short stories while at California State Univ. at Fresno (BA in English, 1966), then studied at Howard Univ., 1966–7, and (while teaching at Federal City College in Washington, DC) at Brown (MA, 1972). She taught at California State, 1972–3, then from 1975 at the Univ. of Calif. at San Diego. *Give Birth to Brightness*, 1972, is a critical analysis of 'neo-black' writers, James Baldwin, LeRoi Jones, and Ernest J. Gaines, who try to 'define themselves and their people in images which grow out of their individual quests and group explorations'. Her interest in the roots of contemporay Afro-American culture affects both her own poetry and fiction and her 'ethnopoetics ... the study of the new forms of poetry which develop as a result of the interfaces or confrontations between different cultures'. In the encounter of blues tradition and 'literary' white writing, she sees a set of transformations also manifested in contemporary Afro-American poetry. For her, the blues offer both 'some kind of philosophy, a way of looking at the world' and 'a basis of historical continuity for black people'. Her funny and sad *Peacock Poems*, 1975, a 'song for our mothers', are 'women's blues' marked by the rhythms of speech, racy, sensuous language, and mournful refrains: 'These is old blues / and I sing em like any woman do.' 'I been the / strong sister, the pretty sister, the one with / no mens. ... Yeah, that's all our stories; that's where we all been'. *Some One Sweet Angel Chile*, 1982, includes a 'New England Negro's' 1867 letters to friends about Emancipation, bluesey poems to Bessie Smith, and contemporary observations on Black Power, pride, and identity. *Dessa Rose*, 1986, SAW's first novel, is loosely based on incidents in Kentucky and North Carolina in 1829–30 (discovered by SAW in an essay by Angela DAVIS): its title character is a slave who awaits both her baby's birth and her own hanging for leading an insurrection. The novel powerfully depicts both racial and sexual violence and a conviction that 'slavery eliminated neither heroism or love'. SAW writes for *Ms* (reviews and articles on, among others, Ann PETRY, Octavia E. BUTLER) and other journals, believing, classically, that 'writing has a purpose: to teach and to delight' and trying, politically, to 'fill in some of those gaps that ought not to be there.' See SAW's own 'The Blues Roots of Contemporary Afro-American Poetry' in *The Mass. Review*, 18, 1977 (with analysis of Lucille CLIFTON's poetry); Tate, 1983.

Williams-Ellis, Amabel (Strachey), 1894–1984, novelist, biographer, children's writer, writer of science fiction, editor, b. at Newlands, near Guildford, Surrey, da. of Henrietta Mary Amy (Simpson) and John St Loe Strachey, later owner of the *Spectator*. Her parents' guests were the powerful and famous; she remembered Mary KINGLSEY as the visitor 'who produced the only really brilliant early impression on me'; later they were visited by Gertrude BELL. AW-E was educ. at home ('but for what? ... especially to please young men'), later was a débutante ('a change of status ... important then for members of our sub-tribe'). In 1913, she wrote a historical pageant, *The Sea-Power of England*, pub. with a chorus by her mother and a note by its producer. A VAD in WWI, she married architect (then also soldier) Clough W.-E. in 1915. With him she wrote *The Tank Corps*, 1919, and *The Pleasures of Architecture*, 1923. As literary editor of the *Spectator*, 1922–3, she published, among others, Edith SITWELL (who dedicated *Troy Park* to her, 1925) and compiled *An Anatomy of Poetry*, 1922 (later repudiated as too 'Georgian'). She had three children. Her first novel, *Noah's Ark*, 1926, emerged from 'something sharp and professionally awake in me [which] caused me to wonder ... why the dickens it was that no one seemed to be writing about the oddities of marriage'. In it, she wanted to 'open the door that hides our old friends Pity and Terror as they show themselves in the business of giving birth'. Much involved in politics (with the United Front and the Communists in the thirties) AW-E travelled in Russia, Berlin and the USA before WWII. *To Tell the Truth*, 1933, third of her five novels, is a political fable about Communist/Capitalist attitudes. In the 1930s, she began to write educational books for children, published her first collection of 'retold' fairy-tales, wrote for *Time and Tide* and the *Left Review*, and was involved in establishing the Left Book Club. *Is Woman's Place in the Home?*, 1946, opposes, with much reference to Margaret MEAD, the idea that sex roles are 'natural'; *Women in War Factories*, 1943, argues for better conditions; and *The Art of Being a Woman*, 1951, attacks the 'undercurrent of contempt of woman' in western societies, urging not adaptation but social change. In 1960, AW-E co-edited the first of some 15 anthologies of SCIENCE FICTION, occasionally including a story of her own. Her autobiography, *All STRACHEYS Are Cousins*, 1983, is fine on 'Edwardian glitter' and 1930s politics, generous in treatment of some aspects of AW-E's life as a woman.

Willis, Lydia (Fish), 1707–67, letter writer, b. at Duxborough, Mass., only da. of Thomas F. Early troubled with ill health, she loved reading 'polite as well as religious' books. In 1734 she left home (reluctantly) to work; her parents both died suddenly in 1736–7, and she felt 'that *her* sins had slain her mother'. In 1738 she married the Rev. Eliakim W. None of her three babies lived; a brother's four children died all within days: another brother had drowned. Of her many MSS, chiefly letters, those printed as *Rachel's Sepulchre* ([?1767], retitled 1788) express almost unrelieved gloom, both religious and human: one says she has no ideas and cannot believe that her 'former lines' were worth anything. But those selected and edited may not be typical: an obituary calls her sociable, with unusual 'vivacity and sprightliness of ... countenance'.

Wilmot, Catherine, *c.* 1773–1824, and **Martha**, later Bradford, 1775–1873, travel-writers. They grew up near Cork, in the large, warm family of Irish Martha (Moore) and English officer Edward W. CW spent 1801–3 seeing Europe with Lord and Lady Mount Cashell (ex-pupil of WOLLSTONECRAFT), sending journal-letters to a brother; though she found the genre heavy, stale, and flat, she was urged to print them in 1812: pub. 1920 as *An Irish Peer on the Continent*. MW meanwhile left in 1803 to visit her 'Russian Mother', Princess

Daschkaw or Dashkova, writer, land-owner and Director of the St Petersburg Academy, who had met her family in Ireland. MW persuaded the princess to write her *Memoirs*, then translated and published them, 1840, with her own retrospective account of Russia, written in 1814, and CW's letters from *her* visit, 1805–7. (MW's own letters appeared with her sister's in 1934.) CW delights in a land 'but in the 12th Century', with a sky 'So vaulted, & so blue; so cloudless & so etherial!' MW, more curious about people than places, visits the Jewish synagogue and the parents of the servant girl given her as her property; she comments on the extremes of society, the financial independence of Russian wives, and the life of a tiny Finnish-speaking island explored on the way home. Most creative are letters of CW's maid Eleanor Cavanagh: 'The inside of me sour'd at the sight of him & there he stud as grand as twopence.... With that they all laugh'd, & I came home and told it all to my Mistress.' MW stayed till war ousted her in 1808; MSS at Royal Irish Academy include hers from Austria and Italy as wife of the Rev. William Bradford.

Wilson, Ethel (Bryant), 1888–1980, novelist, short-story writer. She was b. in Port Elizabeth, South Africa, only child of Eliza Davis (Malkin) and Robert B., a British Methodist missionary. Her mother d. when she was 18 months old, and she returned to England with her father a year later. In 1898, after his death, she joined her maternal grandmother, aunts, and uncles who had migrated to Vancouver, BC. She returned to England, 1902, to spend four years in a school for daughters of Methodist ministers. She taught school for 13 years before marrying William W., a physician, 1921. Her first stories, published in the *New Statesman* (London) in the late 1930s, indicate a long apprenticeship in writing. Her first novel, *Hetty Dorval*, 1947, presents a beautiful, sophisticated, unknowable woman through the eyes of a naive younger woman. *The Innocent Traveller*, 1949, uses EW's own family history to narrate the life of Topaz Edgeworth from a three-year-old in the English Midlands to a centenarian in Vancouver. *The Equations of Love*, 1952, is two novellas: 'Tuesday and Wednesday', about two days in the life of a working-class couple, and 'Lily's Story', about an unmarried working-class woman's struggle to bring up her daughter. The protagonist of EW's best-known novel, *Swamp Angel*, 1954, leaves an impossible marriage to forge a new life for herself among the mountains, lakes and forests of BC, discovering there 'the miraculous interweaving of creation'. In *Love and Salt Water*, 1956, EW's last, darkest novel, the strong, self-reliant protagonist is scarred for life by an accident in which she nearly causes the death of her young nephew. Pain, violence and death, always a part of her writing, obtrude more often and more unexpectedly. In all EW's works, her women protagonists, seeking freedom and security, become aware of their inextricable connection with others and with the universe. Often they acquire awareness of self, others, and God through interaction with the natural world. Yet EW continually reminds her readers that, as *Swamp Angel*'s Maggie Lloyd says, living is like swimming: 'it is done alone'. EW's strong sense of place links her with Canadian regional writers, her independent protagonists with later Canadian feminist writers. Her polished, graceful style is subtle, economical, deceptively simple, unobtrusively imaged; her writing is marked by wit, gentle irony, and whimsical humour. See Lorraine McMullen, ed., *The Ethel Wilson Symposium*, 1982, and selec. stories, essays, and letters, ed. David Stouch, 1987. Papers at Univ. of British Columbia.

Wilson, Eve, Evelyn, 1880s–before 1935, DIARIST. Second da. of a Manchester silk-manufacturer, she left her private school at 17, in the year her mother died. Her father's money went to her brothers, none to her. After three equally unhappy governess jobs, she sank her savings in a stenography course and became a clerk in an agency where she stayed for 21 years, living alone in a small room, with scarcely any money for books or anything personal. Her writing dwells on the lack of opportunities for women, on loneliness, poverty, and oppression from husbands and relatives. She stresses the writer's need for a room of her own, warmth, comfort, financial independence. Yet she maintains 'a woman with brains can make a livelihood' and achieve social standing without marriage. She read widely and collected passages on women's predicament (Charlotte BRONTË, George ELIOT, Thomas Hardy, Joseph Conrad, and Winifred HOLTBY on the frustrated need 'to be used to the full scope of our ability'). She died nine months after leaving her job, unable to find another, leaving eight thick notebooks to an office friend, Geraldine Waife, who wrote the introduction to them as *The Note Books of a Woman Alone*, 1935, ed. M. G. Ostle.

Wilson, Harriet E. (Adams), 'Our Nig', 1807/8?–?70, b. Fredericksburg, Virginia, the first Afro-American to publish a novel in the USA. Little is known of her life: she was self-educated, and in 1831 she m. Thomas W., a sailor, who later deserted her, but with whom she had a son, George, in 1852. He died of fever aged eight. Her only work, *Our Nig: or, Sketches from the life of a Free Black, in a two-storey white house, North. Showing that Slavery's Shadows Fall Even There*, pub. under the ironic pseudonym 'Our Nig' in 1859, became widely known only on reissue with intro. by Henry Gates, Jr., in 1983. It treats interracial marriage between a white woman and a black man, and vividly describes the abusive treatment of a mulatto girl servant in a wealthy household. Its autobiographical element was previously overestimated. Written in a dignified and intelligent style, it offers acute observation of the power structure in a so-called Christian family. HEW's dates given here follow Ann SHOCKLEY, 1988.

Wilson, Harriette (Dubochet), later Rochfort, 1786–1845, courtesan and autobiographer. B. in London, sixth da. of the illegitimate Amelia (Cook) and of Swiss-born John Du Bochet, she was a questioning and self-willed child. At four she puzzled to reconcile the nature of God with sickness and death; at five she was beaten unconscious by her father for obstinacy. After two years at a French convent, and earning her keep from 13 by teaching music (latterly at a prison-like Newcastle boarding-school), she ran away with a son of Elizabeth ANSPACH. Her *Memoirs* famously begin 'I shall not say why and how I became, at the age of fifteen, the mistress of the Earl of Craven.' She later reveals why: her father's severity. She went from man to man, in London and Paris; by 1823 she married, in the Fleet prison, Irish adventurer William Henry Rochfort. (Wilson was an arbitrary choice of name.) They planned the memoirs together as a blackmail tool. HW's later complaint of interpolations by her publisher (Mary STOCKDALE's brother) cast doubt on her authorship of the rest; but her colloquial, quick-witted style is consistent through all her work. The *Memoirs* in instalments, 1825, were followed that year by uproar among ex-lovers, publishers, editors, and moralists; an angry reply by HW's rival Julia Johnstone; a '35th ed.'; and from HW *Paris Lions and London Tigers* (facs. 1973), a *roman à clef* which mentions her own fame and pokes fun at Hannah MORE. Walter Scott praised her dialogue, preferring her to T. C. PHILLIPS and others. Her female-picaresque novel, *Clara Gazul* (title from Prosper Merimée) *or Honi Soit Qui Mal y Pense*, 1830, has been too much despised. Prefaced with early memoirs, it includes London scandal (HW as 'Harriette Memoirs') and grotesque slapstick about European bigwigs like a cardinal. An 1831 ed. of the *Memoirs* added material both her own (old and new; comment on women writers) and extraneous. HW's letters to Byron were pub. in *Cornhill*, 1935; to Lord Chancellor Henry Brougham in 1975; she mentions several other writing projects. *N & Q*, 1987, records a sighting of her as 'a wonderful old hag, who lived on lucifer matches and gin'. *Memoirs*, selec., 1957, repr. 1985. Virginia WOOLF wrote on her in 1925, Angela THIRKELL in 1936.

Wilson, Margaret, 'Elizabeth West', 'An Elderly Spinster', 1882–1973, novelist, short-story writer, missionary. She was b. at Tracer, Iowa, da. of Agnes (McCormack) and West Wilson, and published poems as 'Elizabeth West' in 1894 and 1907. Deeply influenced by her parents' Presbyterianism, she was painfully alert to its flaws. Educ. at the Univ. of Chicago (BPhil, 1904), she published her first story in her own name while serving ('why, I am not altogether able to say') as a missionary in India. She stayed till 1910, formally resigning in 1916 because of ill health and emotional stress. Her six 'Tales of a Polygamous City', by 'An Elderly Spinster', appearing in *Atlantic Monthly*, 1917–21, turn a Christian-feminist spotlight on conflict between individual piety and repressive religious forms. Having already, she said, mislaid 'my American point of view', she settled in England on marrying George Douglas Turner (a penologist she met in India) in 1923, the year of her first novel, *The Able McLaughlins* (Pulitzer Prize), based on historical research. *The Law and the McLaughlins*, 1936, features a social-reforming heroine. In *The Kenworthys*, 1925, Emily is rejected by her fiancé for reading books he disapproves of, but prefers his loss to that of the sense of freedom gained from the books. *Daughters of India*, 1928, and *Trousers of Taffeta* (drawing specifically on an earlier story), 1929, use MW's emotionally rending contact with Indian women valued only as producers of male heirs. *The Crime of Punishment* and *The Dark Duty* (both 1931, non-fiction) examine the US and English penal systems and their shortcomings.

Wilson, Rachel, 1720–75, Quaker preacher of Kendal, Westmorland. Da. of Deborah (Wilson) and John Wilson, whose marriage was witnessed by Lydia LANCASTER, she m., 1740, Isaac Wilson! She had already been a minister for two years. Despite ten children, she made preaching journeys from 1744. In 1768–70 she toured America. Despite an early severe fall from her horse in deep snow, she went on to address blacks, Princeton students (by invitation), and a 'poor creature' under sentence of death. She met Patrick Henry ('a man of great moderation') and Annis STOCKTON. Three of her sermons, from England and America, were printed, 1766 and 1769. Her style, like her delivery, has 'Clearness, Strength, and Solemnity': 'Most men live as if they were never to die.' Extracts from her matter-of-fact journals and letters to Isaac W. (which she calls conversing) in a life of both by John Somervell, 1924.

Wilson, Florence **Romer** Muir, 1891–1930, novelist, da. of Amy Letitia (Dearden) and Arnold Muir W., Sheffield solicitor. After West Heath School (Ham, near London), she studied law at Girton College, Cambridge, and worked for the Ministry of Agriculture, 1917–18. Her novels (several set in Europe) deal with issues of art, love, and contemporaneity. *Martin Schüler* [1918] shows a German would-be composer, once 'a simple dull boy', exploiting a series of women whom he thinks necessary to the procreation of masterpieces as of babies: 'used, inferior, and dismissed, he had no further need of her. She was inferior, she felt inferior – inferior and feminine.' Having repossessed a MS from under a dead friend's mattress, he dies at his moment of triumph: in 1914. The heroine of *If All These Young Men*, 1919, navigates inconclusive love-affairs and friendships in postwar England; in *The Death of Society, Conte de Fée Premier*, 1921, an Englishman is struck with transcendent love for a Norwegian philosopher's wife, and rides away changed for ever. *The Grand Tour*, 1923, presents cosmopolitan, bohemian life in letters from a Parisian sculptor: WOOLF noted its 'romantic power of making us feel the stir and tumult of life as a whole.' RW married Bostonian Edward Joseph H. O'Brien in 1923; she had a son, and later lived in Switzerland. *Dragon's Blood, Conte de Fée Deuxième*, 1926, traces the career of an anti-Semitic German parson's son from his political schemes to 'create an entirely new civilization with new values' to murder of an ex-ally (a prostitute gets the blame) and to a lunatic asylum. *Greenlow*, 1927, is a striking first-person narrative set in Derbyshire uplands, whose heroine loves two men, makes a choice, and finds happiness. RW also wrote novellas (*Latterday Symphony*, 1927, set in London jazz society; *The Hill of Cloves*, 1929, a philosophic tale set in timeless Italy), a play (*The Social Climbers*, 1927, which traces a Russian bourgeois family from affluent intellectual debate in 1912, to beggarly wandering in 1921), short stories, and a life of Emily BRONTË, 1928. She edited several fairy-tale volumes, from *Green Magic*, 1928.

Winslow, Helen Maria, 1851–1938, novelist, poet, feminist editor and publisher, b. Westfield, Vermont, da. of Mary Salome (Newton) and Don Avery W. She was educ. at Westfield Academy, the Vermont Normal School, Johnson, and the New England Conservatory of Music. She began by writing pastoral poems and stories for children's periodicals (as 'Aunt Philury' in *Youth's Companion*, *Wide Awake*, *Cottage and Hearth*, etc.). Actively involved in numerous literary and reformist women's clubs in Boston, where she lived with three sisters, she pub. many articles in *The Arena*, *The Critic* and *The Atlantic Monthly* celebrating the work of club women. She worked on the staff of *The Boston Transcript* and *The Delineator*, 1898–1930, editing the 'Woman's Club' column. Reformist themes feature strongly in her novels *The Shawsheen Mills*, 1882, and *A Bohemian Chapter*, 1886, which portrays a struggling woman artist, while in *Salome Shepard, Reformer*, 1893, a young society woman improves working conditions for women in her father's mills; in *A Woman for Mayor*, 1909, the mayor elect, Gertrude Van Deusen, a Progressive-era reformist, pledges to eliminate corruption. In *Spinster Farm*, 1908, two women renovate a derelict farm, create productive, independent lives for themselves, articulate a preference for self-sufficiency and then, at the last, get married. Most significant is her extensive history, 'The Story of the Woman's Club Movement' (*New England Magazine*, June, Oct., 1908), her *Annual Register and Directory of Women's Clubs in America from 1898–1930*, and *Literary Boston of Today*, 1902: a richly detailed, lightly humorous account (illustrated) of Boston's literati, including some 39 portraits of women and such notables as J. W. HOWE and S. O. JEWETT. See K. Blair, 'The Clubwoman as Feminist' (PhD diss., SUNY at Buffalo, 1976).

'Winter, John Strange', Henrietta Eliza Vaughan (Palmer) Stannard, 1856–1911, novelist, journalist and publisher, b. York, England, da. of Emily Catherine (Cowling) and Rev. Henry Vaughan Palmer, ex-army officer. She was educ. at Bootham House School, York. Her earliest work was pub. under 'Violet Whyte' in the *Family Herald* to which she contributed 42 articles 1874–84. In 1881 she began writing the regimental tales for which she was best known, including *Cavalry Life*, 1881, and *Regimental Legends*, 1883; the *Herald*'s editor refused to publish them under a female name. John Ruskin greatly admired her military portrayals: this early writing was strongly male-identified, with sentimental representation of male comradeship, and women characters divided into 'dearest little women' and 'most worthless little jilts'. In 1884 she m. Arthur Stannard, civil engineer. In 1885, in *The Graphic*, she pub. *Bootles Baby*, which sold two million copies in the first ten years. In all she pub. almost 100 novels and ten books of stories, as well as articles for *The Cornhill* and *Temple Bar*. Between 1891 and 1895 she pub. her own weekly magazine, first called *Golden Gates*, 1891, then *Winter's Weekly*. Her novel *Confessions of a Publisher*, 1892, mocks patronizing male publishers. She was the first president of the Writer's Club, 1892, president of the Society of Women Journalists, 1901–3, and a fellow of the Royal Society of Literature. Her other interests included animals (*A Book of Mortals*, 1905, is devoted to their 'good deeds and good qualities') and women's clothes and appearance. See Helen Black, *Notable Women Authors*, 1893.

Winterson, Jeanette, novelist, b. 1959 in Manchester, adopted da. of Pentecostal Evangelists Constance (Brownrigg), 'missionary on the home front', and John William W., factory worker. She wrote sermons at eight, 'can't remember a time when I didn't preach', and attended Accrington Girls' Grammar School. At 15 she fell in love with a woman, found with surprise this was seen as sin, incompatible with a preaching career, and left home. While at Accrington College of Further Education she did weekend jobs driving an ice-cream van, making up corpses in a funeral parlour, and helping in a mental home. After St Catherine's College, Oxford Univ. (BA in English, 1981) she dogsbodied at the Roundhouse theatre, London, 1981–2, and worked in publishing, 1983–7. She wrote her autobiographical novel, *Oranges Are Not the Only Fruit*, 1985, for money in two months, and adapted it for TV, 1990. It vividly depicts an upbringing in an environment where 'everything in the natural world was a symbol of the Great Struggle between good and evil'. Lesbian identity clashes with absolutist ideology; the narrator rejects 'a book with the words set out' to become another kind of prophet, 'a voice that cries in the wilderness, full of sounds that do not always set into meaning'. *Boating for Beginners*, 1985, grafts modern capitalist and publicizing tactics onto the biblical story of Noah, imbuing it with a feminist meaning. In 1986 JW edited *Passion Fruit: Romantic Fiction with a Twist* and issued *Fit for the Future*, an alternative fitness guide. She has been a full-time writer since 1987, the year of *The Passion* (written in the house of Ruth RENDELL: two awards, at least ten translations). The fantastic, grotesque, futile war machine of Napoleon is juxtaposed with the love ('not so much an emotion as a destiny') of a male army kitchen hand for a bisexual, cross-dressing Venetian woman. He has the larger share in narration; 'Trust me', he says repeatedly when relating the impossible. After a radio play, *Static*, 1988, JW's *Sexing the Cherry*, 1989, set in a fantasy version of the seventeenth century, explores the tenuousness of 'reality'. She says her outsider characters, 'the unlikely, the overlooked', succeed against odds 'in a personal, often socially ambiguous way. My women are always fighters. So am I.' Interview by Joan Feeney in the *Boston Globe Magazine*, 20 Nov. 1988.

Wiseman, Adele, novelist, playwright, essayist, b. in 1928 in Winnipeg, Man., da. of Jewish-Ukrainian parents, Chaika (Rosenberg) and Pesach Waisman. In 1949 she graduated from the Univ. of Manitoba, Winnipeg (BA Hons., English), won the Chancellor's Prize for best story, and began her first novel, *The Sacrifice*, 1956, which received the Governor-General's Award. A resident of Toronto, she lived and worked in London, 1950–1, Rome, 1951–2, Montréal, 1964–9, and NY (on a Guggenheim Fellowship), 1957–60. She met her husband, Dmitry Stone, 1966; their daughter was born in 1969. In 1960, 'aboard a freighter' on an aborted trip to China, she completed *The Lovebound* (of which only an excerpt was published, in the *Journal of Canadian Fiction*, 1981), a play about the ships aboard which Germany sent away Jewish refugees with illegal permits of entry into other countries. AW went to China in 1981 with a Canadian delegation of writers (see *Chinada: Memoirs of the Gang of Seven*, 1982). Writing out of her 'Jewish consciousness' – 'I'm a flower in somebody else's garden. I'm a different flower and my selfhood and my "otherness" I sing about' – she explores the 'life-oriented' drive of Judaism by creating characters like Hoda, the protagonist of *Crackpot*, 1974. A fat whore – 'part-time wife to the whole damn world!' – Hoda embodies the innocence of a 'cracked' morality, but knowingly submits to incest when her abandoned son, who has never known her, visits her for his first sexual experience. *Old Woman at Play*, 1978, celebrates AW's mother's life-long making of dolls, which she enjoyed giving away: an eloquent attempt which 'trace[s] the creative process in this apparently simple manifestation', this book is as much about AW's inspiration from her mother as it is about the social, moral and political implications of 'created worlds' – 'they can be colonized, they can be lost, they can be rediscovered . . . and they can be destroyed. They exist in the same flux as the rest of us, created beings all.' *Memoirs of a Book Molesting Childhood and Other Essays* appeared in 1987; *Kenji and the Cricket*, 1988, is a child's picture book. See Michael Greenstein, 1984, and Marco LoVerso, 1982 and 1984.

Wiseman, Jane, later Holt, dramatist and poet. Abel Boyer's *Letters of Wit . . .*, 1701, print her letters (as 'Daphne') indicating friendship with George Farquhar and the future Susanna CENTLIVRE, and a poem to Aphra BEHN about a woman attracted by two worthless men. Her blank-verse tragedy, *Antiochus the Great, or The Fatal Relapse*, also 1701, flanks its chief male character (unstable, passionately pursuing first one woman and then another) with two faithful women, one lustful and ambitious, one altruistic and self-sacrificing. JW's preface calls it 'first Fruits' of her muse; she admits she has taken advice on revision, but denies critics' charges of earlier reliance on male help. Giles Jacob in 1723 wrote that she was a servant to Mr Wright, Recorder of Oxford; that she began writing after reading plays and romances, married a vintner named Holt and opened a Westminster tavern on her play's proceeds. Despite this, she is likely the Mrs Holt who published *A Fairy Tale, With other Poems*, 1717 (compliment, wit, country retirement and female friendship), who admired Behn and had links with well-connected people including a different Mr Wright, Recorder of Cambridge.

Wister, Sarah or **Sally**, 1761–1804, Quaker diarist of Philadelphia, da. of Lowry (Jones) and Daniel W. She met 'sawcy Debby Norris' later LOGAN, at Anthony Benezet's school; when their correspondence was broken by her family's retreat 15 miles from the city in 1777, she substituted a journal for several months, continued occasionally until 1781. Pub. 1903, it suggests the experimenting of a born writer, in description, narrative, dialogue, and address to her reader. She writes lightly of unlearning her fear of soldiers, and in turn dispelling their bashfulness. She feels even for a horse 'taken from the hospitable quiet barn to plunge into the thickest ranks of war', but recognizes that 'pity is a poor remedy'. This journal ends with a heartfelt contrast of the rainy countryside to the 'smiling scenes' of poets: 'overflow'd meadows board fences, sloppy roads, woods, woods, woods'. SW read Sophia BRISCOE and later Mary PENINGTON (in MS), and often quotes Pope. She kept a devotional journal through a time of spiritual crisis, 1796–7, and wrote an essay on happiness and occasional poems, many to her mother: see Kathryn Zabelle Derounian, ed., 1987.

Wittig, Monique, b. 1935, French lesbian-feminist writer and activist now living in the USA, the first of 'the new French feminists' widely read outside France. For *L'Opoponax*, 1957 (transl. 1964), she was awarded the *prix médicis* and regarded as an up-and-coming writer of the *nouveau roman*. *Les Guérillères*, 1969 (transl. 1971) openly stages a lesbian writing at war with patriarchal discourse. Devoted to the scriptures of their 'feminaries', MW's Amazon armies annihilate the old symbolic order and, with it, practising patriarchs who maintain an allegiance to the phallus as master signifier. *Le Corps lesbien*, 1973 (transl. 1975), deconstructs both the sublimated and fetishized female body of masculine fantasy and the patriarchal body politic. Here MW represents a new class of speaking subject, neither men nor women but lesbian ('the only concept I know of which is beyond the category of sex ... because lesbian societies are not based upon women's oppression and because the designated lesbian subject is not a woman economically, politically, or ideologically'). Her lesbian lovers address each other non-discursively, neither lover alienating the other as the 'object' of her love. The speaking subject, often a lesbianized god or hero of Christian or Greek myth, sings of the painful/joyous de/reconstruction her body-image undergoes 'in love'. *Lesbian Peoples: Material for a Dictionary* (with Sandy Zeig), 1976, provides the forthcoming 'golden age' with a lexicon in which the terms 'mother', 'daughter' and 'wife' appear only as anachronisms, like 'men' and 'women'. Though she has been anthologized along with psychoanalytic feminists KRISTEVA, IRIGARAY, and CIXOUS, MW attacks the psychoanalytic-social contract. Her highly influential essays, 'The Straight Mind' in *Feminist Issues*, 1, 1980, and 'The Mark of Gender' in Nancy K. Miller, ed., *The Poetics of Gender*, 1986, reject both the naturalist assumption of inherent heterosexuality and the idea of a psycho-linguistic structure which 'determines' sexual difference. *Virgile, Non*, 1985 (transl. as *Across the Acheron*, 1987) replaces utopian lesbian futurism with a parody of Dante's *Inferno*, allegorizing 'the hell on earth' of patriarchy today. See also 'One is Not Born a Woman' in *Feminist Issues*, 1, 1982. Critical studies by Namascar Shaktini in *Signs*, 8, 1982, and Helene Vivienne Wenzel in *FS*, 7, 1981.

Wolf, Christa, novelist, short-story writer, essayist, critic, journalist, screenwriter, autobiographer, b. in 1929 in Landsberg, Warthe (now Poland). She was educ. at Jena and Leipzig univs., worked as an editor at the Writers' Union and elsewhere in Berlin. She joined the Communist Party in 1949, married Gerhard Wolf (with whom she worked on film projects and anthologies and had two children) in 1951, and in 1955 made the first of many trips to the Soviet Union. Responding to socialist realist guidelines for writers, CW worked in a factory, 1959–62, to ground her writing in the practical world; since 1962 she has lived on income earned by writing. Her socialist-realist first publication, *Moskauer Novelle*, 1961, she later repudiated as 'a treatise for the propagation of pious views.' Her first novel, *Der geteilte Himmel*, 1963 (*Divided Heaven*, 1964), shifts towards critique of socialist realism in its explorations of the industrial working class and of alienation in a divided Germany. (CW and her husband filmed it.) *Nachdenken über Christa T.*, 1968 (*The Quest for Christa T.*, 1970), a semi-autobiographical novel (also a successful film) brought international recognition: this traces 'the difficulty of saying "I"' and the struggle for independence of women in socialist society. While CW has remained a committed socialist, in 1976 she resigned from the Communist Party in protest against exclusion from the GDR of writer Wolf Biermann. That year, convinced that 'unused memory gets lost, ceases to exist, dissolves into nothing,' she published *Kindheitsmuster*, 1976 (translated 1980 as *A Model Childhood*, and 1984 as *Patterns of Childhood*), about her childhood in a Nazi family in Hitler's Germany. *Kein*

Ort. Nirgends, 1979 (*No Place on Earth*, 1982), fictionalizes an imagined 1804 meeting between poet Karoline von Gunderrode (whose works CW ed. the same year) and Heinrich von Kleist. After tracking a key word, 'Cassandra', CW wrote five 'Lectures on Poetics': the fifth became a draft of her novel *Kassandra*, 1983 (*Cassandra*, 1984); the other four became 'Conditions for a Narrative'. A novel, *Störfall: Nachrichten eines Tages*, 1987 (*Accident: A Day's News*, 1989), exposes a 'disturbing incident', the nuclear meltdown at Chernobyl. In 1990 CW urged people not to leave East Germany. Her critical writing from 1959 is coll. in *Lesen und Schreiben*, 1977 (*The Reader and the Writer: Essays Sketches Memories*, 1977). See *The Fourth Dimension: Interviews with CW* (trans. Hilary Pilkington [Material Word]), 1988 and Anne Herrman on Virginia WOOLF and CW in *New German Critique*, 38, 1986.

Wolf, Emma, b. 1865, novelist. Her place of birth is unknown; she worked and lived in San Francisco. Her novels deal with middle- and upper-class San Francisco Jewish society and its internal conflicts over assimilation. In *Other Things Being Equal*, 1894, EW's heroine finally marries a Christian doctor; however, in *Heirs of Yesterday*, 1900, a young doctor discovers he can never throw off the 'chains' of his Jewish identity. Men are the bearers of Jewish ideas in EW's fiction, while women cope with the emotional contradictions of assimilation.

Wolferstan, Elizabeth Pipe (Jervis), b. 1763, poet, eldest da. of Philip J. of Nether Seile, Leics. In 1796 she became second wife of Samuel P.-W. (d. 1820), land-owner and antiquary, of Statfold, Staffs. In 1823, with 'extreme diffidence', she fulfilled her long-held intention to print *The Enchanted Flute*, a substantial volume (some poems dating from *c.* 1806), with versions of La Fontaine's fables which show her confidence and resourcefulness in wit and metre. In the title-poem (alluding to Mozart) a girl whose 'Poems good, if not surprising, / On Friendship, Death, and Early Rising / Prov'd that she had at least a *turn* / For "thoughts that breathe and words that burn"', is amazed to find that the source of mysterious nocturnal music is a dour footman, a musician who has tried in vain to earn a living by his talent. EPW excels in narrative, encompassing sentiment as well as humour and satire: several tales of quasi-parental relationships (including *Eugenia*, 1824) involve exchange of letters. Prefacing *The Fable of Phaeton*, 1828 (from Ovid, whose Latin text appears with hers), she says she translated the work twice, at 16 and at 61. There followed captivating *Fairy Tales in Verse*, 1830; 'Flora's Fete' and 'Pomona's Fete' (privately printed to raise money for her parish church); and *Golden Rules*, 1841. Her *Conversations on Early Education* (2nd ed. 1839) expounds her method of teaching her [step-]grandchildren through play: with acute critical comment on female CHILDREN'S writers.

Wolley or Woolley, **Hannah**, 1621?–?76, COOKERY and ADVICE-writer. In service to the nobility till 1645, she then m. Benjamin W. (headmaster of Newport Grammar School, Essex, till 1652, then of a school in Hackney, London). From 1661 (when he died and she married Francis Challinor of Westminster, who died by 1669) begin her books on cooking, medicine and household skills. Addressing women, she seeks to keep cookery in female hands despite male professional encroachments; aiming explicitly to attract students, she pre-dates Aphra BEHN in using her pen to live by. *The Ladies Directory*, 1661, was followed by *The Cook's Guide*, 1664, *The Queen-Like Closet*, 1670 (often repr.; German transl. 1674), and *The Ladies Delight*, 1672. As her fluency developed she also included instructions on formal letter-writing. In 1673 the publisher Dorman Newman issued *The Gentlewoman's Companion*, with her name on the title-page and a spurious life of her as a romance heroine (followed by most standard sources). Enraged, she included an autobiography in her *Supplement*, 1674. In 1675 she was living near the Old Bailey with one of her four surviving sons. *The Accomplish'd Ladies Delight*, 1675, and *Compleat Serving Maid*, 1677, are often wrongly ascribed to her. See Elaine Hobby, 1988.

Wollstonecraft, Mary, later Godwin, 1759–97, feminist moral writer and novelist, b. in Spitalfields, London, second child and eldest da. of Elizabeth (Dixon), from Ireland, and Edward John W., an ex-weaver, who took the family from London to a succession of different places. MW had little education. Resenting her brother's favoured status, trying to protect her mother from marital violence, she early developed an idealizing, demanding habit of friendship. She gave up a job (as lady's companion) to cope with her mother's last illness. In 1784 she defied 'all the rules of conduct' to help a sister flee (without her baby) an unhappy marriage. With MW's friend Fanny Blood they set up a school at Newington Green which brought contact with a stimulating circle of Rational Dissenters. In 1785 she went to Lisbon to help the tubercular Fanny at a birth which proved fatal. Returning, MW compelled her ship's captain to rescue French sailors in distress. In 1787 came her first book, *Thoughts on the Education of Daughters* (more attuned to the status quo than later works, but broaching the employment issue), a spell as governess to the Kingsborough family in Ireland, then, more congenially, work for radical London publisher Joseph Johnson. She translated, wrote reviews, a children's book and a novel, *Mary* (both 1788), and compiled *The Female Reader*, 1789. *A Vindication of the Rights of Men*, 1790, composed and issued in a rush to combat Burke on the French Revolution, pre-dates Tom Paine. *A Vindication of the Rights of Woman*, Jan. 1792, was written in equal haste: her dissatisfaction with it was not false modesty. Yet its passion and inclusiveness fully merit its classic status. It makes striking use of literary criticism: of Milton, Pope, Rousseau. Now a focus of both admiration and loathing, MW went to France in December: she fell in love with American literary adventurer Gilbert Imlay, lived through the Terror, reported an earlier phase in *A Historical and Moral View of the French Revolution*, 1794, and bore Imlay's daughter, Fanny. She travelled in Scandinavia with baby and nurse in 1795 (still hoping to hold Imlay), and wrote and published *Letters*, 1796, which blend the personal and political. She made two suicide attempts, one nearly successful, before beginning to recover, to work on her next novel, *Maria, or The Wrongs of Woman*, and re-enter London intellectual society. She began an affair with radical writer William Godwin, but married him (March 1797) only for the sake of her coming baby, the future Mary SHELLEY, ten days after whose birth she died. Godwin began within two weeks on his *Memoirs* of her; pub. 1798 with her *Posthumous Works* (mostly unfinished projects), it increased her notoriety. Essay by WOOLF, 1929; many lives, reprints, selections and scholarly editions; letters ed. Ralph M. Wardle, 1979; bibliog. by Janet Todd, 1976; *Works*, ed. Todd and Marilyn Butler, 1989. Among much good comment see Cora Kaplan, *Sea Changes*, 1986.

'Woman Question'. Term used from about the 1830s to the 1880s (as an alternative to 'women's rights') for the escalating debate over the nature and role(s) of women before the SUFFRAGE issue, and debates about sexual emancipation centred on the NEW WOMAN, became dominant. Key figures in the debate included Lucretia MOTT, Margaret FULLER, Susan B. ANTHONY, Harriet TAYLOR, Caroline NORTON, Frances COBBE, and Eliza LINTON, no two of whom held identical views. In Britain, Harriet MARTINEAU's 1830s essays on women refocused a dispute which had run for centuries before WOLLSTONECRAFT (see e.g. ATTACKS and DEFENCES). She thought US women backward, yet Federalist women like Mercy Otis WARREN and Abigail ADAMS had hoped that both sexes would enjoy the 'inalienable rights' established in the Declaration of Independence. Sarah GRIMKÉ's *Letters on the Equality of the Sexes*, 1838, were followed by *Woman in the Nineteenth Century*, 1845 (first version 1843), by Fuller, who approached the condition of women through the slavery of blacks and destruction of native Americans. The American Anti-Slavery Society (before its aims diverged) and the TEMPERANCE movement provided women with a training-ground in political activism, a sense of the possibility of social progress, and escape from control by the clergy. Demands during the 1840s for improved property and inheritance rights for married women implied equal citizenship. By 1860 NY and 13 other states had responded to lobbying and had reformed laws on married women. Black women's organizations included anti-lynching societies formed by Ida WELLS-BARNETT, and the National Federation of Afro-American Women, founded by Josephine St Pierre Ruffin, 1842–1924, later the National Association of Colored Women. See Catherine Clinton, *The Other Civil War*, 1984. In 1870 and 1882 the important Married Women's Property Acts were passed in Britain. Eleanor Marx, 1855–98, published *The Woman Question* with Edward Aveling in 1886. Writers who treated the Woman Question varied enormously in topics and in standpoint, writing of middle class EDUCATION, marriage, divorce, property laws, and the assumed problem of insultingly labelled 'superfluous' single women (an issue particularly to the fore in the 1840s and 50s and again in the 90s). Elizabeth Helsinger, Robin Sheets and William Veeder, eds., in *The Woman Question 1837–83*, 3 vols., 1983, identify four main positions: those of the Angel in the House, the Angel out of the House (e.g. Florence NIGHTINGALE), the proponent of complete equality (e.g. Taylor, Anthony), the Female Saviour (e.g. S. J. HALE, Fuller). Many writers (e.g. Margaret OLIPHANT) occupied, or spanned, more than one of these at different times. Mary Evans re-used the title for an anthology, *The Woman Question, Readings on the Subordination of Women*, 1982; but her texts span the period not only of the Woman Question but also of the multifarious women's movement of our own century.

Wong, Nellie, poet, prose-writer and feminist, b. in Chinatown, Oakland, Calif., after her parents and three sisters migrated to the USA. She has written since the early 1970s, is active in the Women Writers' Union and in Radical Women, and is married but 'a woman without a man, a woman without children'. She has published in many anthologies, also in *Dreams in Harrison Railroad Park*, 1983, and *The Death of Long Steam Lady*, 1986 (title piece a prose elegy among poems of family love and tensions, of fractured identity and search for lost names, with a tribute to SUI SIN FAR). NW's poems invest her personal past and present with strong political feeling: 'when I was growing up ... to become / a woman, a desirable woman, I began to wear / imaginary pale skin. ... when I was growing up, I felt / dirty. I thought that god / made white people clean'; 'I own no podium. Only the fierceness of fingers / that scratch and type .... Fish cannot fly, but we women can write.' Her essay 'In Search of the Self as Hero: Confetti of Voices on New Year's Night, A Letter to Myself', about NW's identity as Asian American, writer, and feminist, celebrates Ding Ling, China's most prolific woman writer today (then writing again after being silenced for supposedly bourgeois feminism), and tells herself, 'You don't understand why you have this vision, of leaving work, signs and clues, knowledge and art, stones, however rough or polished' (Cherrie Moraga and

Gloria Anzaldúa, eds., 1983). NW teaches and is politically active at the Univ. of Calif., San Francisco. Film about her and Mitsuye YAMADA, 1981.

Wood, Ellen, 'Mrs Henry Wood' (Price), 1814–87, novelist and publisher, b. Worcester, da. of Elizabeth (Evans) and Thomas P., glove manufacturer. She suffered from curvature of the spine. In 1836 she m. Henry W., prominent banker who later lost his money. Most of the next 20 years were spent abroad, mainly in Dauphine, from where she began contributing immensely popular short stories to *Bentley's Miscellany* and the *New Monthly Magazine*. Her first financial success was *Danesbury House*, 1860, a comparatively serious novel which won a prize from the Scottish Temperance League. *East Lynne*, 1861, her second novel, was an enormous POPULAR success. It ran first in the *New Monthly*, was then pub. by Bentley and was afterwards adapted to become a stock melodrama (though owing to the inadequate contemporary copyright laws, she received no royalties from the adaptation). *East Lynne* was in many ways a compendium of the prejudices and desires of the middle classes. It represents EW's extreme political conservatism and religious orthodoxy, in its exhortation to women to bear silently the worst trials of married life and to die rather than lose their good names. Over 30 novels followed, including *Mrs Halliburton's Troubles* and *The Channings*, 1862, as well as six vols. of short stories. In 1856 she returned to England, and in 1867 she launched *The Argosy*, where most of her work, including the *Johnny Ludlow* tales, was pub. before appearing in book form. 1867 also saw *A Life's Secret* pub. anon. in the *Leisure Hour*, the RTS journal. It was an anti-labour story of strikes and trade union practices, which prompted protest action outside the Society's offices. In spite of precarious health, EW supported her family for many years by her writing. Her son Charles W. pub. a memoir of her, 1895; Adeline SERGEANT wrote on her in *Women Novelists of Queen Victoria's Reign*, 1897. See also Jeanne Elliott's article on *East Lynne*, *Victorian Studies*, 19, 1976, and S. Mitchell's intro. to the 1986 reprint.

Wood, Emma Caroline (Michell), Lady, 'C. Sylvester', 1802–79, English novelist. B. in Portugal, da. of Sampson M., English naval officer, she m. Sir John Page W., rector, in 1820. She had six children, including novelist Anna STEELE. Little is known about ECW. Her first novel, *Rosewarn*, 1866, was pub. after her husband's death that year; she then averaged one book a year until her own death. Among the novels are *Sabrina*, 1867; *Seadrift*, 1871; *Up-hill*, 1873; and *Youth on the Prow*, 1879, a pleasant moral tale of young aristocrats' lives and loves. Other books include the anthologies *Leaves from the Poets' Laurels*, 1869, and *Choicest Selections from Modern Poets*, 1870.

Wood, Joanna Ellen, 1867–1927, novelist and short-story writer, b. in Lanark, Scotland, youngest of 11 children of Agnes (Todd) and Robert W., who migrated to the Queenston area of Ontario when she was a small child. She travelled widely in France and England, and spent several winters in the USA; her first stories appeared under pseudonyms in US periodicals. Her first and perhaps her best novel, *The Untempered Wind*, 1894, was highly praised by US critics; it explores the hypocrisy and narrow puritanism of a small town through the story of an unmarried mother. *Judith Moore; or Fashioning a Pipe*, 1898, placed her among leading Canadian novelists: its heroine gives up her triumphant international career as a singer for married life in an Ontario farming community. One of the first writers to anatomize Canadian small-town puritanism and colonialism, JW in her last two novels presents strong, passionate women: *A Daughter of Witches*, 1900, treats romance, revenge, and religious hysteria; *Farden Ha'*,

1901, set on the English-Scottish border, treats unconsummated marriage, illegitimacy, and death. After her mother's death in 1910, JW lived in NYC and Detroit, where she died.

Wood, Sally or **Sarah Sayward** (Barrel), also Keating, 1759–1854, novelist. Eldest of 11 children of well-to-do loyalists Sally (Sayward) and Nathaniel B., an officer with Wolfe, she was b. and grew up at York, Maine. She married Richard K. in 1778, had three children, and began writing after his death, 1783, to ease grief and boredom. She issued *Julia and the Illuminated Baron*, Portsmouth, NH, 1800 (written years earlier), as 'By a Lady of Massachusetts' though she says her identity was known. Her preface and dedication to the public claim 'independence of mind' and praise Sarah MORTON and Judith MURRAY, but argue that both nature and custom have set 'very confined and limited bounds' to female duties. 'I have ever hated female politicians' – but the French Revolution, which supplies her story, concerns piety and morals as well as politics. The novel attributes the Revolution to the sect of *illuminati* and praises American liberty and non-arbitrary government. Its tone is literary (quotation from Anne FINCH and Elizabeth ROWE); its GOTHIC plot of mysterious origins and sexual persecution is strained. *Dorval, or The Speculator*, 1801, set in the US, attacks the rage to get rich quick; *Amelia, or The Influence of Virtue*, 1802, set in France and England, makes a long-suffering wife (understatedly billed as no disciple of Mary WOLLSTONECRAFT) reform her obnoxious mate; *Ferdinand and Elmira*, 1804, set in Russia, brings a villain to flamboyant repentance. The same year SSW married General Abiel W. (d. 1811), stopped writing, and later destroyed her MSS; but in 1827 she published *Tales of the Night* (good Maine scenes).

Woodfall, Sophia, later MacGibbon, d. after 1837, author of two unusual novels, b. into a London family of actors and journalists. Her father, William W., died in 1803, the year she made her own stage debut and published the epistolary *Frederick Montravers, or The Adopted Son*. Its central story is a disturbing one of unreasonable compulsion over marriage, self-sacrificially accepted; among a rich cast of characters, a flighty coquette and a seduced woman are also granted happy marriages. *Rosa, or The Child of the Abbey*, 1805, uses narrative for remarkably open treatment of sexual matters. The pure heroine loves once unhappily before marrying; her father's gambling and duels, and his mistress's progress from rejected bastard child to impenitent murderer, are detailed; the hero's mother was divorced for adultery; the mother of a seduced village girl fears the parson ('not the best christian in the world') will scare her by a 'a long sarment' or penance into fancying she can never 'be made a good and honest woman again' – which however she is. Frederick S. Frank's GOTHIC bibliog., 1987, implausibly alleges plagiarism from R. M. ROCHE's *Children of the Abbey*. SW married and in 1810 moved to the stages of Edinburgh and northern English towns.

Woodfin, Mrs **A.**, novelist. She ran a school off the Strand, London, and published five titles between 1756 and 1764. She uses loosely woven plots full of inset tales: heroines are often unwanted by their families, then cheated and exploited in a world teeming with sex- and money-seekers; low life yields both satire and sympathetic observation. The orphan heroine of *The History of Miss Sally Sable* [1758] is brought up by 70-year-old Goody Heartwell and marries the nephew of her would-be rapist. *The Auction: A Modern Novel*, 1760 (facs. 1975 from 1770 repr.), is titled from a vividly described minor episode in the tale of a minor character. *The History of Miss Harriot Watson*, 1762, first bears AW's name. *The Discovery, or Memoirs of Miss Marianne Middleton*, 1764, uses a dedication to Pythagoras as excuse for a whimsical account of a bird's previous lives (toad, raven, Stoic philosopher, etc.). She says her real heroine is not the usual teenager but the 'little Gentlewoman' who befriends her, 30-year-old Mrs Dubois, who has learned warmth and wisdom after family abuse. The book ends with verses on the lewdness of *Tristram Shandy*.

Woodhull, Victoria (Claflin), 1838–1927, editor, orator, suffragist, b. Homer, Ohio, da. of Roxana (Hummel), itinerant worker, and Reuben Buckman C., tavern keeper. With her sister, Tennessee Celeste Claflin (later Lady Cook), 1846–1923, she had little formal education, but their psychic powers were exploited by the family in a travelling act before the sisters moved to NYC in 1868. VW soon won fame as an outspoken campaigner for causes like free love, SPIRITUALISM, woman SUFFRAGE and workers' rights. Cornelius Vanderbilt set them up as Wall Street stockbrokers (they were very successful); they then founded and published the radical *Woodhull and Claflin's Weekly* (1870–6), where the first American translation of Marx's *Communist Manifesto* appeared in 1872. The split in the suffrage movement between ANTHONY and STANTON, and the more conservative Lucy Stone, was largely due to VW's radical interventions. Following their imprisonment on an obscenity charge for publishing an article attacking Henry Ward Beecher's alleged double life, the sisters left for England, where VW continued to lecture magnetically even after her third marriage, in 1883, to banker John Biddulph Martin; she also became a society hostess. She pub. several volumes and, with her daughter, ran another journal (on eugenics). With her sister, she pub. in 1890 *The Human Body: The Temple of God*, in which they denounce prudery: 'the second chapter of Genesis was written by Moses to mean the body . . . where should the Garden of Eden be found if not within the human body?' There are lives by M. Marberry, 1967, and J. Johnston, 1967. Most of VW's important essays, pamphlets and speeches selec. in Madeleine B. Stern's *VW Reader*, 1974. Her characteristic style on audacious topics is straightforward and plausible.

Woodland, Miss **M.**, of Devon, writer of moral tales 'intended for the use of young ladies' and mothers. Her four-vol. *Tales for Mothers and Daughters*, 1807, contains *A Tale of Warning, or The Victims of Indolence; Bear and Forbear, or The History of Julia Marchmount; Matilda Mortimer, or False Pride*; and *Rose and Agnes, or The Dangers of Partiality*: three were separately pub. in 1809, 1810, 1814. *Histories of Four Young Ladies* (n.d.) may be the same in yet another format. The tales warn parents and guardians 'to early inculcate those qualities which most adorn the daughter, the wife, and the mother', display vices like maternal neglect, 'pernicious apathy' and ROMANCE-reading, and inculcate filial piety, patience, self-command, and 'independence of mind which, should we be overtaken by adversity, will excite us to exert our talents for an honourable support rather than live in splendid dependence'. The last may be a clue about a life otherwise unknown.

Woods, Katherine Pearson, 1853–1923, novelist, short-story writer and suffragist, b. Wheeling, Va., da. of Josephine Augusta (McCabe) and Alexander Quarrier W., who d. when KPW was ten. Educ. by her literary mother and at a private seminary, she entered the Sisters of the Poor at Mt Calvary Episcopalian Church, Baltimore in 1874, but later withdrew. She taught in girls' schools (Wheeling, 1876–86), and began writing short stories about the industrial poor. Her first novel, *Metzerott, Shoemaker*, 1889, anon., was considered her finest work and became required reading in many college sociology courses. Dedicated to 'the clergy and working men of America', it opposes Alice, the 'theorist', to pious Dora, who 'feels strongly' but 'reasons weakly', and synthesizes the conflict between Socialist and Christian ideology and Karl Metzerott's founding of 'Prices' – a co-operative training school for a proposed commune. *A Web of Gold*, 1890, fundamentally a domestic novel, is, like *Metzerott*, profusely peopled with infants and children; it sets the greedy, honest, homely and shrewd to debate issues of capital and labour and the inequities of man-made laws. *From Dusk to Dawn*, 1892, moves into the world of SPIRITUALISM, faith-healing and theosophy. *The Crowning of Candace*, 1895, treats a young woman's self-awakening and conflicts over her art. KW was active in SUFFRAGE work, and her address to the Woman's Literary Club was hailed as 'awakening' Charleston to the suffrage cause. Her last works reflect both her reformist and her missionary zeal. *John: a Tale of the Messiah*, 1896, and *The Son of Ingar*, 1897, are set in Jerusalem at the time of Christ. In *John*, she portrays Magdalen as a proud, wealthy courtesan, and Mary as a woman of sharp intellect whose instinct is to 'pierce to the heart of the truth'.

Woods, Margaret (Hoare), 1748–1821, Quaker diarist of Stoke Newington, London, eldest da. of Grizell and Samuel H. 'Religion took hold of my mind at an early period', she says, and 'I once greatly thirsted after knowledge.' She m. business-man Joseph W. in 1769: one of her sons became an eminent scientist. She bequeathed her MS journal to a daughter and granddaughter: generous extracts from 1771 to near her death were pub. 1829. Her entries often amount to short essays or sermons, with some prayers and letters. She notes that hurry and bustle too often prevent the working through of one's own opinions, and that it takes 'very close and diligent search, to find out the true motives of an action'; but she was impressed by a warning from Catharine PHILLIPS, 1775, against over-indulgence in speculative reasoning. She questions particular opinions of Locke and Johnson, but hesitantly rejects a correspondent's view on sexual equality: wives, surely, ought to obey; women love power and 'often make an improper use of it'. She feels strongly over the plight of the poor, and the tendency of 'benefactors' to grudge them any comfort or enjoyment.

Woods, Margaret Louisa (Bradley), 1856–1945, poet, novelist, essayist and playwright, b. Rugby, Warwicks., da. of Marian (Philpot) and George Granville B., Rugby schoolmaster, later Dean of Westminster. She was educ. at home and at Miss Gawthorp's school, Leamington. In 1879 she m. Henry George W., President of Trinity College, Oxford, d. 1915. Her first publication was *A Village Tragedy*, 1887. She wrote nine novels, several of which explore female characters; *Esther* VANHOMRIGH, 1891, the historical romance based on Swift's life which established her reputation, looks at the psychology of infatuation, while *The Vagabond*, 1894, represents the male response to two conventional female images, the intelligent, conscientious woman and the shallow, frivolous one. Her five vols. of poems, from *Lyrics and Ballads*, 1889, to *Collected Poems*, 1914, contain love lyrics as well as poems devoted to social problems such as prostitution. Other works include *Weeping Ferry and other stories*, 1898, travel essays, in *Pastels under the southern cross*, 1911, and two dramatic poems: *Wild Justice*, 1896, which deals with a woman's attempt to save her children from her violent husband, and *The Princess of Hanover*, 1902. MW contributed essays on biography, literary criticism, Nietzschean philosophy and female aesthetics, to journals such as *Cornhill* and the *Fortnightly Review*. Her essay 'Poetry: And Women As Artists', combines materialist analysis with a perceptive and sympathetic observation of the low status and limited role of women in society.

Woolf, Adeline **Virginia** (Stephen), 1882–1941, novelist, short-story writer, critic, diarist and letter writer. She was b. in Kensington, London, to Julia (Jackson) – who pub. a booklet on amateur nursing, 1883, repr. 1980 – and Leslie S., man of letters: each had offspring from a former marriage. (VW's early recollections in *Moments of Being*, ed. Jeanne Schulkind, 1976). She told stories to her sister and brothers as a small child, wrote a family newspaper, 1891–5, and a first diary in 1896. Her 'History of Women', *c.* 1897, is lost. Educ. at home by both parents, she read hard and took classes at King's College from 1897, but envied her brothers' school and univ. careers. A two-year gap in lessons followed a breakdown, 1895, after 'the greatest disaster that could happen' (her mother's death), her father's frantic mourning, and her elder half-brother's sexual harrassment. In 1904 her father died (as did her half-sister, 1897, and brother Thoby, 1906); despite another breakdown she published a newspaper article on the BRONTËS' home at Haworth. She settled with her sister in Bloomsbury, wrote for periodicals and taught at Morley College. In 1910 she completed a draft of *Melymbrosia*, later *The Voyage Out*, a novel about woman's search for a place in the world and about death (see Louise A. DeSalvo, 1980). In 1912 she married Leonard W., ex-colonial administrator and member of the Cambridge nucleus of Bloomsbury. Severe breakdowns and suicide attempts accompanied the acceptance, 1913, and appearance, 1915, of *The Voyage Out*: the role of Leonard and his devoted care in all this is hotly debated. In 1917 they set up the Hogarth Press, dividing their time between Richmond (then Bloomsbury from 1924) and Sussex (Monk's House, Rodmell, from 1919). VW's next major works are *Night and Day*, 1919 (satire on Victorian ancestor-worship, a courtship dance reminiscent of Shakespearean comedy); a series of highly experimental stories; *Jacob's Room*, 1922 (a collage of fragmentary impressions elegizing the young, male, unknowable dead of WWI); *The Common Reader* (her first book of essays) and *Mrs Dalloway* ('civilization' and madness interlaced with profound psychological exploration in the newly flexible narrative style she called 'tunnelling'), both 1925; *To the Lighthouse*, 1927 (Victorian marriage and gender relations, based on memory of her parents); *Orlando*, 1928 (homage to her love for Vita SACKVILLE-WEST, spoof history of English literature and sexuality); *A Room of One's Own*, 1929 (a definitive essay on women and writing, based on lectures at Girton College, Cambridge); and *The Waves*, 1931 (fully realized stream of consciousness with a complex larger patterning of individual lives). *The Years*, about the evolution of a family from 1880, cost VW unusual travail: pub. 1937, like her key feminist polemic, *Three Guineas*. The pre-war period held terror because of Leonard's anti-war career and Jewish blood: so, later, did living in Sussex beneath the nightly Battle of Britain. She completed *Between the Acts* on 26 Feb. 1941 (pub. in July): it is another startlingly new departure, an intricate paratactic structure relating the present (rendered as both communal and individual) and the past (the pre-historic, the historical, and the deeply-buried personal). A month later she drowned herself. Her husband pub. several vols. of short writings and *A Writer's Diary*, 1953; Nigel Nicolson and Joanne Trautmann ed. her letters, 1975–80; Anne Olivier Bell her diary, 1977–84; Michèle Barrett some essays as *Women and Writing*, 1979; Andrew McNeillie her essays, 1985ff; Susan Dick her shorter fiction, 1986. Bibliog. by B. J. Kirkpatrick, 1957 (3rd ed. 1980); life by VW's nephew Quentin Bell, 1972; Robin Majumdar and Allen McLaurin, eds., *Critical Heritage*, 1975; Thomas Jackson, *VW: A Guide to Research*, 1984; Edward Bishop, *A VW Chronology*, 1989, Gradual realization of VW's importance to literature, modernism and feminism has produced a flood of comment, recently Susan Merrill Squier, 1985, and Mark Hussey, 1986.

James M. Haule and Philip H. Smith, Jr., are making microfilm concordances to the novels. MSS at Univ. of Sussex (also on film) and NYPL. Novel MSS have been pub. 1976, 1983; scholarly editions expected.

Woolsey, 'Gamel', Elizabeth Gammell, 1895–1968, poet and novelist. She was b. in Aiken, S. Carolina, da. of Elizabeth (Gammell) and plantation-owner William Walton Woolsey, after whose death, 1910, the family moved to Charleston. Educ. at Ashley Hall there, she went to NYC in 1921 hoping to act or write; she published a poem next year in the *NY Evening Post*. She based her first novel, *One Way of Love*, on her unhappy marriage, 1923, to NZ writer Rex Hunter: originally, ironically entitled 'Innocence', it is about a young woman's struggle with tuberculosis and a pregnancy she is advised to terminate. She received proofs (now in the BL), for publication by Gollancz in 1932, but they 'took fright' at the prosecution of Radclyffe HALL; GW's book, withdrawn on grounds of sexual explicitness, was unpub. till 1987 (intro. by Shena MACKAY). She had an affair with Llewellyn Powys, then met writer Gerald Brenan in England in 1930 and lived with him the rest of her life, mostly in Spain. She published *Middle Earth*, 1931, repr. 1975 (poems), *Death's Other Kingdom*, 1939 (a novel set in the Spanish Civil War), *Spanish Fairy Stories*, 1944, and *The Spendthrifts*, 1951, transl. from the Spanish of Benito Perez Galdo. She died of cancer in Spain, leaving much unpublished: *Patterns on the Sand* (a novel based on her childhood), sonnets (rejected by T. S. Eliot for Faber in 1956, *Twenty Eight Sonnets* pub. 1977) and other poems pub. as *The Last Leaf Falls*, 1978, *The Search for Demeter*, 1980, *The Weight of Human Hours*, 1980, and *Collected Poems*, 1984, ed. Glen Cavaliero. Kenneth Hopkins has ed. her letters to Powys, 1983, and Bertrand Russell's to her, 1985, and is working on a memoir.

Woolsey, Sarah Chauncey, 'Susan Coolidge', 1835–1905, short-story writer, author of CHILDREN'S novels, poet, editor, b. Cleveland, Ohio, eldest of five children of Jane (Andrews) and John Mumford W. She attended private schools in Cleveland and the Select Family School for Young Ladies in Hanover, New Hampshire, the model for 'The Nunnery' in *What Katy Did at School*, 1873. The family moved to New Haven, Conn., in 1855, where SW befriended H.H. JACKSON. During the Civil War she worked at hospitals in New Haven and Rhode Island. After her father's death in 1870, the family built a house near Jackson's in Newport, Rhode Island, and SW began her writing career with *The New-Year's Bargain*, 1871, a collection of stories for children. Her greatest successes were the 'Katy' books, which take the tall, lively tomboy Katy Carr and her family from her childhood to maturity. In *What Katy Did*, 1872, SW's rambunctious heroine takes a serious fall, after which – tried by pain – she learns to take responsibility for herself and her motherless household. In *What Kady Did at School*, however, Katy wins back a measure of teenage light-heartedness; moral growth is not one-dimensional in the 'Katy' books, nor is maturity equivalent to death. SW disavowed any high ambitions for her meditative *Verses*, 1880, intended for adults. She claimed 'The right to a life of my own, – / Not merely a casual bit / Of the life of somebody else' ('My Rights').

Woolson, Constance Fenimore, 1840–94, short-story writer and novelist, b. Claremont, New Haven, da. of Hannah Cooper (Pomeroy: niece of James Fenimore Cooper), and Charles Jarvis W., manufacturer, who moved the family to Cleveland soon after CFW's birth. She was educ. at Miss Hayden's School, the Cleveland Female Seminary and Mme Chegaray's School, New York (described in her first novel, *Anne*, 1882. repr. 1977). After her father's death in 1869, CFW travelled with her mother throughout eastern and southern America, writing travel sketches for *Harper's*, *Putnam's* and other leading periodicals. Her first volume of regional stories and sketches was *Castle Nowhere: Lake Country Sketches*, 1875. Mostly set on the lake island of Mackinac, the sketches, like JEWETT's and MURFREE's, bring a region to life, but are less convincing in their characterization. The hero of the title story lures ships to their doom so that he can lavish his pseudo-daughter with gifts: many of CFW's characters similarly sacrifice their life for another's. From 1879 CFW lived in Europe with her sister, where, in 1880, she met Henry James, beginning a life-long friendship. Her second collection, *Rodman the Keeper: Southern Sketches*, 1880, treats the post-war South with sympathy and honesty. 'Old Gardiston' compassionately portrays the heroine's proud resistance to her growing love for a Northern officer, while 'In the Cotton Country' tells of a woman's hopeless sufferings from the effects of war. Regional settings and descriptions of pioneer life characterize all her fiction, including her four later novels – *For the Major*, 1883, *East Angels*, 1886, *Jupiter Lights*, 1889, and *Horace Chase*, 1894 – but the short-story form suited her distinctive combination of realism and fantasy rather better. Her Italian stories, *The Front Yard*, 1895, and *Dorothy*, 1896, were pub. posthumously, together with a book of travel sketches, *Mentone, Cairo and Corfu*, 1896. She died in Venice, probably by suicide, while ill and depressed. See John D. Kern, 1934, and Rayburn S. Moore, 1963, for her life, and Cheryl B. Torsney, 1989, for a critical study; see also the coll. of her stories ed. Joan Myers Weimer, 1988.

Worboise, Emma Jane (later Guyton), 1825–87, novelist and editor, b. Birmingham, eldest child of Maria (Lane) and George Baddeley W. She began writing prolifically in her teens, and went on to produce more than 50 vols. of evangelical novels and stories. Her first book was *Alice Cunningham*, 1846. 'Wholesome' as her writings were, they were also very sympathetic towards women. Titles such as *The Wife's Trials*, 1858, *Chrystabel*, 1873, *Husbands and Wives*, 1873, and *A Woman's Patience*, 1879, are typical. She m. Etherington Guyton, of French descent, and sometimes signed herself 'Mrs Guyton'. The heroine of *Labour and Wait*, 1864, is a successful writer, and meets other successful women in her career: but she gives it up when her baby is born. EJW wrote a life of Thomas Arnold, 1859, and was editor of *The Christian World*.

Wordsworth, Dorothy, 1771–1855, diarist, letter writer and poet, da. of Ann (Cookson) and John W., b. in Cumberland. After her mother died, 1778, she grew up with irksomely conventional relations. Reunited in 1794 with her beloved brother William, she chose to live without servants or regular routine, writing and walking long hours in the countryside. Detesting 'the idea of setting myself up as an Author', tirelessly cherishing William and his poems, she also wrote some remarkable ones herself; a few appeared (anonymously, with his) in her lifetime, as did prose passages (some altered) in his *Guide to the Lakes*, 1820. Her DIARIES kept at Alfoxden and in Germany, 1798, and at Grasmere, 1800–3, catch the minutest shades of changing landscapes, the detail of domestic activity, the hardships and tenacity of the poor (the last also in her account of George and Sarah Green, 1808, pub. 1936). She wrote narratives of tours in Scotland and Europe (1803, 1820, 1822). A serious illness in 1829 heralded gradually encroaching arteriosclerosis and premature senility. The caring role passed to William and his family; lucid intervals still produced journal entries, poems, and letters which tell of long struggles and fretting. Letters with her brother's (and selec. 1981); journals 1897, 1941 (selec. 1971); studies by Margaret Homans, 1980, and Susan M. Levin (with texts of poems and 'Mary Jones and her Pet-Lamb'), 1987; life by Robert Gittings and Jo Manton, 1985; MSS at Dove Cottage, Grasmere.

Wright, Frances, later D'Arusmont, 1795–1852, Scots-American radical. B. at Dundee, da. of Camilla (Campbell: great-niece and god-daughter of Elizabeth MONTAGU), and of James W., she was orphaned at two and brought up by an aunt in London, then from 1806 in Devon. Socially conscious from childhood, she wrote poetry and educated herself in the family library. She returned to Scotland with her sister in 1813, and in 1818 sailed for the USA. Here she had her tragedy *Altorf* (about the Swiss freedom struggle) staged and printed, and recorded delighted impressions of the new world (greater freedom for women; distinguished public men democratically at work in the fields) in letters meant for print (to a Scots friend whose sister Margaret Cullen, pub. two intelligent novels, one reformist). Appearing as *Views of Society and Manners in America*, 1821, they provoked much notice and conservative outrage, as did her Epicurean tract, *A Few Days in Athens*, 1822. By then she had been in France and met Lafayette; back in the USA in 1824, she travelled to New Orleans, becoming steadily more critical of the country. She founded a colony of free blacks near Memphis (plan pub. 1825), which acquired notoriety and was dissolved in 1830. She bought a journal which developed in 1829 into the *Free Enquirer* of NY, leading voice of feminism and free thought, and backed it up with lecture tours and organization of workers. Always on the move, she met William Phiquepal D'A. in France in 1830, bore him a daughter, 1831, then married, and divorced him in 1851 after long property battles. She pub. her lectures, 1829, and *Biography*, 1844; life by Celia Morris Eckhardt, 1984.

Wright, Judith, poet, story writer, critic, historian, conservationist, b. 1915 at Armidale, NSW, da. of Ethel (Bigg) and Phillip W. She was educ. at Blackfriar's Correspondence School, New England Girls' School, Armidale, and the Univ. of Sydney. Since 1962 she has been awarded honorary degrees from many Australian univs. A member of one of Australia's pioneering pastoral families, she travelled to England and Europe after univ., then settled in Sydney and began writing and publishing poetry. During WWII she returned to help on the family property in northern NSW, a visit which inspired many of the poems in her first vol., *The Moving Image*, 1946. From 1945–8 she worked as a statistician at the Univ. of Queensland where she met and m. the writer and philosopher, J. P. McKinney. Her second vol., *Woman to Man*, 1949, has as its title poem one of her best known works, a meditation on the mysteries of reproduction and childbirth. Her subsequent vols. of poetry, which include *The Gateway*, 1953, *The Two Fires*, 1955, *Birds*, 1962, *City Sunrise*, 1964, *The Other Half*, 1966, *Fourth Quarter and other poems*, 1976, and *Phantom Dwelling*, 1985, have been less favourably received. Her so-called 'mysticism' has sat uneasily beside the dominant male realism of Australian literature. Her increasingly critical presentation of modern Australian society, particulary of its attitudes to Aboriginal people and women and its exploitation of the environment, in works such as *We Call for a Treaty*, 1985, and *The Coral Battleground*, 1977, has also been greeted with some dismay. Like many other Australian women poets, JW has delighted in challenging patriarchal myths, such as those associated with the Garden of Eden. She is the best-known Australian woman poet, the first to establish an international reputation and to be regularly studied throughout Australia. Other works include a collection of stories, *The Nature of Love*, 1966, a collection of essays, *Because I Was Invited*, 1975, and four books for children. She has also made a valuable contribution to research, teaching and criticism of Australian poetry, especially through her study *Preoccupations in Australian Poetry*, 1964, her monograph on the colonial poet Charles Harpur, 1978, and her editing of poetry anthologies and of selections of J. S. Neilson's poetry. She wrote the history of her family in *The Generations of Men*, 1959, and *The Cry for the Dead*, 1981, which draws attention to the destruction of Aboriginals and their culture. The fullest discussion of her poetry is by Shirley Walker, 1980, who has also pub. a bibliography, 1981.

Wright, Laurali (Appleby), novelist and journalist. B. in 1939 in Saskatoon, Sask., to teachers Evelyn Jane and Sidney A., later an army officer whose career took her to Abbotsford, BC, and West Germany. She started writing as a child, in a hard-covered book labelled *Daily Journal*, given by her father. When he died, she attended secretarial school and took night classes in creative writing. She sold her first article to the Toronto *Globe and Mail* when she was 19, took jobs on a BC newspaper, in California, and in amateur theatre in Vancouver, then married John Wright (separated 1986) and had two children. She took a job with the Saskatoon *Star-Phoenix*, 1968, and in 1976 won a Calgary *Herald* scholarship to the Banff School of Fine Arts, where W. O. Mitchell taught her creative writing. *Neighbours*, 1979, initiates her themes of madness and solitude. Patronized by Toronto critics ('has a certain cachet in cattle country'), it was followed by the more warmly welcomed *The Favorite*, 1982 (about a girl haunted by her loved father), and *Among Friends*, 1984 (three separate but parallel tales of single women of different ages). Always interested in mysteries (one of her characters reads Ruth RENDELL), LW was the first Canadian winner of the Edgar award with *The Suspect*, 1985. Here, the reader quickly becomes attracted to the 80-year-old protagonist, following with concern his relationship with a much younger Cassandra. *Sleep While I Sing*, 1986, continued the DETECTIVE genre, which she finds easier than 'mainstream' writing: 'it's not like writing with your own blood any more'. See Eleanor Wachtel in *Books in Canada*, June-July 1987.

Wright, Mehetabel or Hetty (Wesley), *c.* 1697–1750, poet, da. of Susanna WESLEY. She could read the Greek New Testament at eight, worked as her father's copyist, and may have written the long poem 'Eupolis'. One of her 'gay sportive poems' to a sister refers to a governess post as a 'noisom irksom Den'. After several such jobs she left home in 1725 with a suitor disapproved by her father: he wrote that she was 'not so well as dead'; 'I've had little hopes of her – I consider what I write – since she has been half a year old.' Pregnant, she submitted to marry William Wright, an uneducated plumber of Louth. They moved to London in 1727; he drank heavily, and she suspected it was lead fumes from his work that killed all her babies. A letter begging her father's forgiveness drew a snub from him in 1729. Her poems after marriage express mostly painful emotions with rare directness. She bids her husband 'tell me why I cease to please', prays God for patience, describes the 'hard constraint of seeming much at ease', rages at marriage as 'Thou tyrant, whom I will not name ... Abhorr'd and shunn'd, for different ends, / By angels, Jesuits, beasts, and fiends!', records watching a child die, and repeatedly wishes for death herself. She wrote to John Wesley about her search for God in 1743. Some poems appeared in the *GM*, 1733, the *Christian's Magazine*, 1762, and with poems by her brother Samuel and others; many, sent to her family, are lost. A novel about her by A. T. Quiller-Couch, 1903, had several reprints.

Wright, Susanna, 1697–1784, American colonist, scholar and poet, b. at Warrington, Lancs., eldest child of the Quakers Patience (Gibson) and John W., who settled in Chester, Penn., by 1714. (She perhaps followed a little later.) She ran the family after her mother's death in 1722, from 1728 at Wright's Ferry (a frontier post on the Susquehanna), and became widely known and respected. A linguist (Latin, French, Italian) and practical scientist, she did scribal work for illiterate neighbours, doctored them, and farmed silkworms on a large scale. She wrote 'Directions for the Management of Silk-Worms' (*Philadelphia Medical and Physical Journal*, i, 1804) and (it is said) a pamphlet defending Indians, 1763. Her poems went in letters to Hannah GRIFFITTS and the future Elizabeth FERGUSON and Deborah LOGAN, and may have appeared in magazines; but she kept no copies, so few survive. 'On the Death of a Young Girl', 1737, does not shirk the physical facts of dying. Griffitts praised SW's 'Striking sense and energy of mind', and kept a poem to Logan which analyses the sexual politics by which men's 'soft soothing flattery' draws 'feign'd submission' from women equal in reason. MSS at Hist. Soc. of Penn. and Library Company of Philadelphia.

Wroth, Lady **Mary** (Sidney), 1587?–1651/53, first woman to write a full-length prose fiction and first to write a sonnet sequence in English. Her mother was Barbara (Gamage); her father (Sir Robert S., later Earl of Leicester), uncle (Sir Philip S.) and aunt (Lady PEMBROKE) were poets. She was well educated, travelled abroad, married Sir Robert W. of Loughton, Essex, in 1604, and acted in court masques. Many writers complimented her; Ben Jonson (who also praised the poems of her cousin Lady Rutland) praised hers, and dedicated *The Alchemist*, 1610, to her. Her husband died in 1614; their only child (born just a month earlier) died at two. As a widow in debt MW struggled to run her own finances, and took as lover her cousin William Herbert, 3rd Earl of Pembroke and Montgomery (joint dedicatee of Shakespeare's first folio). They had two children. In 1621 she published a ROMANCE, *The Countesse of Montgomerie's Urania*, addressed to her lover's wife. Its title-page names herself and famous relations; it ends with *Pamphilia to Amphilanthus*, a set of sonnets in three sequences: prose and sonnets have songs interspersed. Only ten copies survive: MW lost her hoped-for earnings when she withdrew the book six months after printing because Lord Denny (later Earl of Norwich) and others objected to her portraits from life. He attacked her in verse as a probably promiscuous monster; her splendid 'Railing Rimes returned upon the Author' matches his charges line by line (see *N & Q*, 1984). *Urania* has, like all its genre, super-abundance of incident: by p. 20 we know that the shepherdess Urania is long-lost sister of Amphilanthus (whose name 'signifieth the lover of two'), heir to the kingdom of Naples; the remaining 538 pages teem with fights (often from the viewpoint of the waiting females), magic, infidelities (more attention to marriage than in her uncle's *Arcadia*), disguises, hiding-places, and the perhaps over-fidelity of Pamphilia. The plot is touched with disillusion, the dialogue with realism. An unfinished sequel (Newberry Library) shows the characters in decline. Some appear also in her pastoral verse play, *Loves Victorie*, partly pub. in 1853. Her metrically varied poems (ed. Josephine A. Roberts, 1983) clearly refer to her love-affair: the female courtly lover is full of complaint but struggles persistently to make love overcome jealousy. Among much useful comment see Roberts in *Tulsa Studies*, 1982; Elaine V. Beilin, 1987.

Wyatt, Edith Franklin, 1873–1958, novelist, short-story writer, poet, essayist and suffragist, b. Tomah, Wisconsin, da. of Marian (La grange) and Franklin Osmon, educ. at Miss Price's Higher School for Girls, Chicago, and Bryn Mawr College, Pa. Her collection of short stories, *Every One His Own Way*, was pub. in 1901, and her first novel, *True Love, a Comedy of the Affections*, in 1903. *The Whole Family, a Novel by Twelve Authors*, 1908, is a collaborative work, numbering Henry James among its authors; and in 1911 she pub., with Sue Ainslie Clark, *Making Both Ends Meet*, a collection of industrial articles depicting the income and outlay of New York working girls. EFW was a Director of Woman's City, 1913–15, and Vice-President of the Illinois Consumers' League, 1921–7, and was a member of the Chicago Woman's Club. Her volume of essays, *Great Companions*, 1917, includes, in 'Nonsense About Women', an attack on the 'manufactured mystification' of women through victimization or idealization; in an essay on P. B. Shelley's friendships with women she writes: 'Perhaps no man was ever less fitted to be a wise liberator of the souls of women'. Her most outstanding essay, 'The Letters of a Woman Homesteader', lauds the self-reliance and creative ingenuity of American farm women, while deploring their impoverished recreation and education. *The Wind in the Corn*, 1917, *The Invisible Gods*, 1923, and *The Satyr's Children*, 1939, range in subject from celebrations of the 'overland spirit' (her song poems of Democracy), to a less optimistic world untouched by the *belle époque* and overshadowed by political corruption and WWI.

Wylie, Elinor Hoyt (Martyn), 1885–1928, poet and novelist, da. of Anne McMichael (Hoyt) and Henry Martyn, later assistant attorney general of the USA. She was b. at Somerville, NJ, and raised at Rosemont, Penn., and Washington, DC, going to private schools in Bryn Mawr (Penn.) and Washington and then travelling in Europe. She married Philip Simmons Hichborn in 1905, and in 1910 scandalized Washington society by eloping to England with Horace Wylie, a married lawyer, leaving her son with an aunt. She later disowned her first book of poems, *Incidental Numbers*, privately printed, London, 1912, telling Harriet MONROE in 1919, 'I have never published anything.' She returned to the USA in 1914, but was able to marry only in 1916, after Horace W.'s divorce and her husband's suicide; she also suffered a series of miscarriages, a stillbirth, and the death of a premature baby. She sent poems to *Poetry* in 1919, and won recognition when Monroe printed four in May 1920. In 1921 she left her husband, settled in NYC, became literary editor of *Vanity Fair*, and published *Nets to Catch the Wind* (Poetry Society prize, praised by Edna St Vincent MILLAY). In 1923 she married William Rose Benét and published, in *Black Armour*, some of her best-known poems. She also wrote four well-researched historical novels. *Jennifer Lorn: A Sedate Extravaganza*, 1923, set in late eighteenth-century India, England and France, and *The Venetian Glass Nephew*, 1925, about a Mephistophelian bargain with a Murano glass-blower, pick up familiar themes of her poetry: disguise, entrapment, women whose husbands construct them as ornaments. The others reflect EW's passion for Percy Bysshe Shelley: *The Orphan Angel*, 1926 (*Mortal Image* in the UK), fantasizes his return to life in the American Mid-west; *Mr Hodge and Mr Hazard*, 1928, depicts his destruction by an alien Victorian age. EW dedicated *Trivial Breath*, 1928 (poems), to Shelley. *Angels and Earthly Creatures*, also 1928, are sonnets written to Henry de Clifford Woodhouse, an Englishman with whom she fell in love. *Collected Poems*, 1932, *Collected Prose*, 1933, and *Last Poems*, 1943, followed her death from a stroke. Lives by Stanley Olson, 1979, and (literary-critical) Judith Farr, 1983; Kathryn Hilt in *BB*, 42, 1985. Among much recent comment, Anna S. Elfenbein and Terence A. Hoagwood (*Women's Studies*, 15, 1988) note 'disturbing undercurrents' in EW's imagery. MSS at the NYPL, Yale Univ., and Smith College.

Wylie, I. A. R. (Ida Alexa Ross), 1885–1959, novelist and short-story writer, b. Melbourne, Australia, da. of Ida Millicent (Ross) and Alexander W., a Scottish barrister. The family returned to England after her birth, where her mother died a little later. At ten, her father supplied her with money and encouraged her to travel all over England and the Continent on her own, which rendered her 'fully capable of managing myself under most usual and a great many unusual circumstances'. With almost no prior formal educ., at 14 she attended a finishing school in Brussels for three years, then Cheltenham Ladies' College. At 19, she went to Karlsruhe, where she wrote her first pub. stories, and stayed with a friend in Germany for eight years; *Towards Morning*, 1918, is based on these years. Returning to England in 1911, IARW became extremely active in the SUFFRAGE movement. In London during WWI, she also carried out war work in France. She visited the USA in 1917, and it subsequently became her home; her works were always better received there than in England. A friend of Una Troubridge and Radclyffe HALL, she introduced the latter to her literary agent, Audrey Heath, and supported her during the trials of *The Well of Loneliness*. The best known of her many novels is *The Daughter of Brahma*, 1912, which, like *The Temple of Dawn*, 1915, and *The Rajah's People*, has an Indian setting; her short stories were even more popular. See her autobiography, *My Life with George*, 1940.

Wymark, Olwen, playwright. She was born in 1929 at Oakland, Calif., da. of English Barbara (Jacobs: da. of the writer W. W. Jacobs) and of American Prof. Philip W. Buck. She studied English at Pomona College and then at Univ. College, London, which she left to marry actor Patrick Wymark, d. 1970. They had four children (all later in theatre or films). OW began writing with *The Unexpected Country*, 1956, for radio. *The Child* appeared in Methuen's Best Radio Plays for 1989. She has also written for TV, but her main interest is the stage, where she began with *Lunchtime Concert*, 1966. She writes subtle, moving, often bizarre studies of human relationships, the strongest parts being usually female. Her plays (widely produced in England and the USA) include *Triple Image* (three one-act plays), 1966, *Speak Now*, 1971 (revised 1975), *Find Me*, 1977, *Loved*, 1978, *Best Friends*, 1981, and *Lessons and Lovers: D. H. Lawrence in New Mexico*, pub. 1986, which features Mabel Dodge LUHAN. OW has held playwright-in-residence posts in London (where she lives) and lectured at Wesleyan Univ., Conn., 1978–9; she teaches at playwriting seminars and lectures. She was drama representative on the Arts Council, 1981–5, resigning in protest over the new financial policy.

Wynter, Sylvia, also Carew, dramatist, novelist and critic, b. *c.* 1930 in Cuba, da. of Jamaicans Lola Maude (Reed) and Percival W. She grew up in Jamaica, educ. at St Andrew's Girls' High School and King's College, London Univ. (BA in modern languages, 1949). She had a year in Madrid on a Spanish government scholarship (few Caribbean Anglophone writers have her fluency in another local language), then did a London MA (by research) on seventeenth-century Spanish drama, 1953. She wrote for London radio and TV, travelled widely in Europe, m. Capt. Isachsen, a Norwegian pilot, and had a daughter, then met and later married Guyanese writer Jan Carew. They co-authored plays (e.g. *The Big Pride*, broadcast 1961, staged in Guyana as *The University of Hunger*, 1966); SW wrote as 'Carew' for some years. Her one novel, *The Hills of Hebron*, 1962, repr. 1984, began as a joint play, *Under the Sun*. Through the story of a Christian preacher whose mother dances in ecstasy at Pocomania meetings, it depicts a crisis in a revivalist community, tensions between religion, magic, and dawning political consciousness, and the Carribean's African roots. SW and Carew returned home via Guyana (where they witnessed riots), hoping to create a Jamaican Theatre Company to perform homegrown plays: their *Miracle in Lime Lane* appeared in

Spanish Town in 1962. Next year they separated (divorced 1971). SW began lecturing in Spanish at the Univ. of the West Indies and writing for *The Daily Gleaner* (till 1980). Further dramatic works include musicals (*Shh, It's a Wedding*, produced 1962, *Maskarade*, produced 1979), plays (*1865 Ballad For a Rebellion* and *Brother Man*, both 1965), and a pantomime, *Rockstone Anancy*, with Alex Gradussov, produced 1970. SW's articles on West Indian writing and folk culture are important: *Jamaica Journal*, 2, 1968; *Caribbean Studies*, Oct. 1972; *New World Quarterly*, 5, 1973; John Hearne, ed., *Carifesta Forum*, 1976. She has written studies of *Jamaican National Heroes*, 1971, Edward Brathwaite (*BIM*, 16, 1977), and Alexander Bustamente (*Daily Gleaner*, 1976). In 1970 she adapted Jan Carew's novel *Black Midas* for children. Active in women's studies, she has held posts at US univs: Michigan, Calif. (San Diego), and Stanford.

Y

Yamada, Mitsuye May (Yasutake), poet and fiction-writer, b. 1925 in Kyushu, Japan, to dressmaker Hide (Shiraki) and interpreter Jack Kaichiro Yasutake, who were already based in the USA. Raised chiefly in Seattle, she was interned during WWII in Idaho, where she wrote in desert sand 'three words: I died here / the winds filed them away.' She did a BA at NY Univ., 1947, MA at the Univ. of Chicago, 1953, and further study at Irvine (Univ. of Calif.). She married Yoshikazu Yamada, had four children, taught from 1966 in colleges in Southern Calif., and became active in women's and Asian-American organizations. Her sharply observed, verbally exquisite poems, full of personal, national and political feeling, appeared in anthologies including *The Japanese American Anthology*, 1976, the year of her first book, *Camp Notes and Other Poems*. In Cherrie Moraga and Gloria Anzaldúa, eds., *This Bridge Called My Back*, 1983, she writes of the determination of Asian Pacific American women to emerge from their invisibility. She co-edited an anthology, *The Webs We Weave*, 1986. Tales in *Desert Run: Poems and Stories*, 1988, focus on Nisei (US-born) women confronting the strangeness of an earlier, Japanese generation (a father's mistress, converse with the dead, tightly decorous child rearing). Poems dwell on paradox: a grandchild called both to conceal and to tell the story of a bitterly oppressed grandmother; the desert, glossy on Christmas cards, hiding the bodies of 'coolie' labourers; the child sent to Japan to become 'less / tomboy American more / ladylike Japanese'; the adult woman visiting Japan and blamed for Hiroshima. PBS showed a film about MY and Nellie Wong in 1981.

Yamamoto, Hisaye, story-writer, b. 1921 at Redondo Beach, Calif., to immigrants from Japan, educ. at Compton Junior College. She got her first rejection slip at 14; teenage work included some as 'Napoleon', some in a Japanese-American newspaper. In WWII she was interned in Poston concentration camp, Ariz. (later a painful 'lump ... in my subconscious'); her contributions to its *Chronicle* included a mystery serial. She worked briefly as a cook, then, 1845–8, for the *Los Angeles Tribune*, a black weekly. Her first stories in literary magazines drew praise from Elizabeth Bishop and Yvor Winters. 'Yoneko's Earthquake' (in which a ten-year-old girl finds and loses faith in God, while tangled adult emotions pass her by) was one of *Best American Short Stories* of 1952; other early stories share its concern with female sexuality and socially inadmissible loves. HY wrote for *The Catholic Worker* in NYC, 1953–5, then married Anthony DeSoto; she has children and grandchildren. *Seventeen Syllables: 5 Stories of Japanese American Life* (title piece about a farm woman whose hard-pressed husband violently objects to her haiku-writing) appeared in Tokyo, 1985; *Seventeen Syllables and Other Stories*, Latham, NY, 1988, has a bibliography listing almost 40 slowly-worked stories from 40 years. HY says 'my output is minimal'; 'Educational Opportunities', 1989, took 20 years to write. She often draws on her own life, notably in 'Having Babies', 1962, 'The Losing of a Language' [Japanese], 1963, and 'Writing', 1968; her variously-named narrators reflect aspects of herself; but her social and national range is broad. She calls her political opinions 'vehement and even revolutionary'. See *WRB*, July 1989.

Yankowitz, Susan, playwright, b. 1941 in Newark, NJ, da. of Ruth (Katz) and Irving N. Y. She wrote fiction while at Sarah Lawrence College, NYC (BA 1963), spent a year in India during which she tried drama, and went to Yale School of Drama (MFA 1968: 'a tremendously valuable and creative period'). *The Cage*, first of her more than 20 plays performed, was seen in 1965. *Terminal* (about society confronting or failing to confront death) was collaboratively written, staged 1969, pub. in Karen MALPEDE, ed., *Three Works by the Open Theatre*, 1974. *Slaughterhouse Play* (about racism and submissiveness to authority) was pub. in *Yale/Theatre*, summer 1969, staged in 1971. *Boxes*, 1972, is about pigeon-holing, with actual boxes as symbols. Following Brecht and Artaud, SY rejects 'naturalistic or linear form'; she uses 'very textured and literary language' with shocking action. Her work polarizes opinion, appealing more to women, she says, than to the men who wield theatrical power. She has written political plays, 'But where are they? In my file drawer.' Her novel, *Silent Witness*, 1976, deals with 'ways of seeing' and 'alternative interpretations of experience'. She married Herbert Liebowitz in 1978 in France, where her *Qui est Anna Marks?* was produced that year. SY's TV writing includes programmes on Charlotte Perkins GILMAN, 1979, and Sylvia PLATH, 1986. Her screenplay *The Amnesiac*, 1980, about a woman with memory loss who re-invents herself, ends with a 'happy' restoration of the status quo which SY did not choose. But she did 'sneak ... in' some irony; such layering interests her. *A Knife in the Heart*, produced 1982, written after her son's birth, looks at the mother of an assassin (a woman who sees 'her worst fears realized'), and refuses to palliate the fear by identifying a cause. *Taking Liberties*, a novel about an actress who puts herself in the power of a charismatic healer, was rejected as 'too bleak'. *Baby*, a musical, was staged in NYC in 1983, *Alarms* in London in 1987. See Betsko and Koenig, 1987.

Yardan, Shana, poet, b. 1942 in Guyana. In the much-anthologized 'Earth is Brown' she addresses her grandfather, brought as a child from India, whose 'dhoti is become a shroud' because his sons are clerks with 'city faces' who don't want to know, while 'you cannot cease / this communion with the smell / of cow-dung at fore-day morning, / or the rustling wail / of yellow-green rice / or the security of / mud between your toes.' She appeared in 1972, year of Carifesta, the Caribbean Festival of the Creative Arts, with Evadne D'OLIVIERA and four other women poets in *Guyana Drums*, then published her own volume, *This Listening of Eyes*, 1976. She writes romantic love poetry ('I learned my name / when first you called it'; 'your kiss is a vision of scarlet flowers / In the month of May when they bloom the best') and Yeatsian political protest: 'Oh, there are notions enough, / Late sittings of Parliament, / Commissions, Trade teams', yet 'those who once fought / Now bear a terrible silence' ('These Desperate Days'). A. J. Seymour, in an anthology and Guyanese literary history, both 1980, recognizes both styles, but stresses her love poetry and femininity: 'perhaps the most important woman poet in Guyana today'.

Yeamans, Isabel (Fell), 1637/41–1704, Quaker pamphleteer, da. of Margaret FELL. She m. William Y. in 1664 and had four children; he died in 1674. With eight others she witnessed Robert Jeckell's deathbed narrative, *A Lively Testimony*, 1676, and with a group of Friends she visited Princess Elizabeth of the Palatinate, 1677. She wrote *An Invitation of Love*, 1679, 'with as much brevity as I could with Clearness, hoping the ponderous Reader, and such whom it chiefly concerns, may not be distasted at the simplicity of the Stile'. Her clear prose draws on biblical stories of women's activities, and counsels all to heed the 'small, still Voice' of Wisdom, for 'she uttereth her Voice in the Streets of the World, and in the midst of the Concourse of the People.' In 1689 IY m. Abraham Morrice of Lincoln.

Yearsley, Ann (Cromartie), 'Lactilla, the Bristol Milkwoman', 1752–1806, poet, playwright, novelist, b. at Clifton Hill near Bristol, da. of John C., labourer, and Ann C., who taught her the milk-round trade and borrowed books for her; a brother taught her to write. In 1774 she m. John Y., who then enjoyed a tiny annual income: they had six children. Hannah MORE (already provider of kitchen scraps for AY's pig) was shown verses by her in 1784, after AY's family had sunk to destitution. She gave her a dictionary and grammar, corrected without radically altering poems, and raised 1000 subscribers for *Poems on Several Occasions*, 1785. AY was at first grateful; but when More, apparently fearing wild spending sprees, put all profits in a trust, advanced money only with insulting 'ungracious admonitions', and had MSS burned, she rebelled. Her 4th ed., 1786, tells how she wanted to be a trustee, to draw her own interest (not capital), and educate her sons – not, it seems, her daughters. (One son grew rich.) She gained her ends after a massive row, and lasting mutual resentment. *Poems on Various Subjects*, 1787, shows growth in power of thought and expression. Her poem on slavery [1788] competes directly with More. Her play, *Earl Goodwin*, acted at Bristol, 1789, was pub. 1791; poems followed on her eldest son's apprenticeship and on an act of cruelty by a landowner, 1790, on the French royal family, 1793, and in *The Rural Lyre*, 1796. She opened a CIRCULATING LIBRARY, 1793, which did well. *The Royal Captives*, 1795 (facs. 1974), purportedly from a seventeenth-century MS, is a gothic tale of prisons and oppression of women and political dissidents. Its preface declares 'I love Fame': authors affecting to despise it are cowards or insincere. See Mary Waldron in *Age of Johnson*, 3; Donna Landry in *The Muses of Resistance*, forthcoming.

Yezierska, Anzia, 1880?–1970, fiction-writer and autobiographer, b. in Plinsk in Russian Poland, da. of Pearl and Baruch Y., who migrated to the USA with their nine children sometime between 1890 and 1895. In New York's Lower East Side, AY worked in sweatshops, learning English at night school. Teacher's College, Columbia Univ., admitted her in 1900 to study domestic science, which, *faute de mieux*, she taught while she sought some outlet, a means to find herself personally. Her orthodox family were unhelpful and her marriages (to attorney Jacob Gordon in 1910, and in 1911 to teacher Arnold Levitas, with whom she had a daughter) short-lived. For her first-published story, 'The Free Vacation House' (*Forum*, 1915), she resumed her name, dropping that given her by immigration officials; she was encouraged by John Dewey (her model for several fictional WASP lovers or teachers). Her books chronicle Jewish immigrant lives, and women's struggles (often her own) to escape drudgery and realize their desires. 'The Fat of The Land' won the O'Brien award in 1919. Samuel Goldwyn paid $10,000 for rights to AY's first book, *Hungry Hearts*, 1920 (repr. with additions, 1985). Suddenly marketable, she was invited to Hollywood but disliked it, returning to write *Salome of the Tenements*, 1922, and *Arrogant Beggar*, 1927 (novels), *Children of Loneliness*, 1923 (stories with essay about her writing), and *Bread Givers*, 1925 (novel depicting her own power struggles with her scholar father: repr. 1975 with intro. by Alice Kessler-Harris). During the thirties AY joined the WPA Writers' Project, but her rate of publication declined. The heroine of *All I Could Never Be*, 1932, doubts she can write again, without going back to the real life of factory work; but AY, though forgotten, kept writing (and publishing in magazines) all her life. See her semi-fictional autobiography, *Red Ribbon on a White Horse*, 1950, and *The Open Cage*, 1979 (some previously unpub. work: afterword by AY's daughter); thesis by

Ralda Sullivan (Berkeley, 1975); study by Carol B. Schoen, 1982; three articles in *Studies in American Jewish Literature*, 3, 1983. MSS at Boston Univ.

Yglesias, Helen (Bassine), novelist, essayist, editor and teacher, b. 1915 in NYC, da. of Kate (Goldstein) and Solomon B., and educ. at NY public schools until 16. She began writing a novel, but money needs pushed her into low-paying jobs instead, several for socialist and communist groups. In 1937 she m. photographer Bernard Cole (two children: their daughter became a playwright), then in 1950 writer Jose Y. (their son became a writer). As literary editor for *The Nation*, 1965–9, HY acquired a formidable knowledge of contemporary fiction: she left to write her first novel, *How She Died*, pub. 1972. This anatomizes the milieu of a left-wing woman who is dying of cancer: it won the Houghton Mifflin award. *Family Feeling*, 1976, recalls HY's own youth in narratives of a brother and (especially) a sister struggling to shed the 'burdens and terrors in sisterhood ... our shared history lying between us like a bed of snakes', to diverge into 'Her divorce. Her politics. Her goy lover' without losing what was good in the past. *Starting: Early, Anew, Over, and Late*, 1978, relates real-life stories of the various changes women have made in their lives; an 'Autobiographical Fragment' discusses her own shift to full-time writing, which she had desired since adolescence. *Sweetsir*, 1981, based on an actual New England woman's killing of her violent husband, disturbingly explores class connections, shared fantasies, and psychological complicities of an abusive relationship: shortly before she kills, the woman thinks, 'It was like making love, this fight.' In 1987 HY published *The Saviors* (in which an elderly political activist struggles with the difficulties of ageing and remembers her idiosyncratic youth among the Universal Society of Brotherhood and affair with an East Indian mystic) and 'Invoking America, A Gitchee-Gumee Memoir' (*NY Times Book Review*, 5 July: from an address given at the Univ. of Mass., Amherst), in which she describes her experience as an immigrant.

Yonge, Charlotte Mary, 1823–1901, novelist, children's writer and educationalist, b. Otterbourne, near Winchester, only da. of Frances Mary (Bargus) and William Crawley Y., ex-army officer and magistrate. She was educ. by her father in languages, classics and mathematics, thus stimulating her belief in wider mental opportunities for women, though also strengthening her acceptance of male authority. CY became deeply involved in Oxford Movement Anglicanism on acquaintance with John Keble, and subsequently dedicated her life to church work and her literary proceeds to Anglican causes. She promoted women's EDUCATION, both at school and university level, though opposed to large institutions and mixed-sex instruction. Her contemporaries greatly admired her; among her friends were Mary A. WARD and Frances PEARD. Her first popular success, *The Heir of Redclyffe*, 1853, attuned to contemporary religious ardour, influenced William Morris and others of the Pre-Raphaelite school, while *Heartsease*, 1854, deeply affected Charles Kingsley. CY pub. over 200 works, including domestic and historical novels, biographies, CHILDREN'S tales, history and language textbooks, and religious manuals. She also ed. a periodical for young women, *The Monthly Packet*, 1851–90. Despite holding hierarchical views on social status and sex roles, in *Womankind*, 1887, she demands better female education and calls for a revised image of singleness. Though essentially conservative, her novels depict women playing positive roles in family and parochial contexts. Ethel May, the unconventional heroine of *The Daisy Chain*, 1856, and *The Trial*, 1864 – perhaps a partial self-portrait – represents the possibilities of a fulfilled unmarried life, while the portrayal of Honora Charlecote in *Hopes and Fears*, 1861, honestly confronts *the consolations as well as the strains of self-reliance. The Clever Woman of the Family*, 1865, though mocking the absurdities of female self-assertion, acknowledges the need for an outlet for women's energies and talents. CY's later novels attempt to come to terms with social change as it affects women – her heroines go to university and ride bicycles – but are less successful. The earliest biography, a *Life and Letters*, was pub. by her friend and editorial colleague, Christabel Coleridge, 1903. See also Ethel Romanes, 1908, Georgina Battiscombe, 1943, and M. Mare and A. Percival, 1948, for her life. There is a CY Society, founded by Lettice Cooper, Elizabeth Jenkins and Marghanita Laski.

Yonge, Juliana, d. after 1806, writer of moral and religious advice. Her *Essays and Letters on the Most Important and Interesting Subjects*, 1783, as 'J. Yonge', conceals her sex, but asserts defensively the liberty of independent thought, and says 'though I enter the world veiled, I tremble every step I take.' She has been writing – her only amusement – for 'a great number of years'. The essays are desultory but commonsensical and attractive, the letters (from Mentor to Euphemia) more obviously conservative. 'Fragments' at the end contain some self-suppressive morality, as well as a nice imitation of Sterne's manner and a verse 'supposed Speech in a supposed Play'. Her *On the Importance of the Baptismal Vow* is untraced; *Practical and Explanatory Commentary on the Holy Bible*, 1787, aims with modest confidence to chart the unity of God's plan from promises to fulfilment: 'I had an interest myself in the subject, a candidate for those mansions whence the angels fell.' She annotated a copy as if for re-issue; a 2nd ed. of *Essays*, 1806, gives her full name (presentation copy, BL).

'Yorke, Stephen', Mary Linskill, 1840–91, novelist and short-story writer, b. Whitby, Yorkshire, eldest of six surviving children of Mary Ann (Tyerman) and Thomas L., watchmaker and later County Court Bailiff. Probably educ. at the local School for Young Ladies, at 16 she was apprenticed as a milliner, and later became a school teacher and governess; then she decided to return to Whitby and earn her living by writing. Some success came with the serialization in *Good Words* of 'Cornborough Vicarage', a discerning tale about an estranged mother and daughter (included in *Tales of the North Riding*, 1871). After the death of her father in 1874, she struggled to support her mother and a younger sister but was increasingly in debt and depressed by continual rejections. Some stories were published, and her first novel *Cleveden*, 1876, but it was *Between the Heather and the Northern Sea*, 1884, that gained her a wide readership. *Haven under the Hill*, 1886, was based partly on her own experience of a community continually threatened by shipwreck and disaster, and a heroine for whom success came too late. Earlier work like *Hagar: A North Yorkshire Pastoral*, 1887, was now in demand but she was turning increasingly to opiates and alcohol to combat neuralgia and sleeplessness. Another coll. of stories, *Robert Holt's Illusion*, appeared in 1888, and 'Vignettes of a Northern Village' in *Good Words*, but her novels only really became popular after her death. See the life by D. Quinlan and A. Humble.

Young, E. H., Emily Hilda, 1880–1949, novelist. B. in Northumberland to Frances Jane and William Michael Y., ship-broker, she attended Gateshead Grammar School and Penrhos College in Wales. In 1902 she m. J. A. H. Daniell, a solicitor. She lived in Bristol (the Radstowe of her novels) until his death in 1917, then in London with her lover, Ralph Henderson, headmaster of Alleyn's School, and his wife. This arrangement, in which EHY was addressed as 'Mrs Daniell', effectively hid their relationship. They lived in Wilts. from 1940 until her death from lung cancer. Her 13 novels, from *A Corn of Wheat*, 1910, are subtle, delicate studies of relationships made complex by class and rigid standards of behaviour. The protagonist of *The Bridge Dividing*, 1922 (reissued as *The Misses Mallett*, 1927), EHY's first novel written in London, marries a man some thirty years after rejecting him in her conviction that 'she was surely meant for something better, harder, demanding greater powers'. *Jenny Wren*, 1932, and its sequel *The Curate's Wife*, 1934, deal with two daughters of a gentleman who married 'beneath' himself. One feels compelled to conceal the 'commonness' of her mother as she perceives it; the other marries 'for friendship' and is distressed when it proves 'difficult to find a friend in a man who so constantly saw himself as a husband'. EHY won the James Tait Black Memorial Prize with *Miss Mole*, 1930. Her final novel, *Chatterton Square*, 1947, presents a satirical portrait of Herbert Blackett, husband, father, and self-appointed arbiter of public morality, scandalized by his new next-door neighbour, an attractive middle-aged woman, separated from her husband, who conducts herself with 'that air of happiness to which he considered she had no right.' Blackett's wife grows towards liberation and criticism: 'Your world is made and entirely occupied by Herbert Blackett and anyone else who sees him as he sees himself.... You have never known the first thing about me. You have never troubled to find out.' EHY wrote two children's books, 1940 and 1942. Six Virago reprints are introduced by John Bayley and by Sally Beauman, who speaks of EHY's 'subversiveness': 'it is with the unconventional that the sympathies of this apparently conventional author lie.'

Young, Marguerite, novelist and poet, b. in 1909 in Indianapolis, Indiana. Da. of Fay (Knight) and Chester Y., she is a collateral descendant of Brigham Young, a direct descendant of John Knox. She grew up believing 'that to be born in Indiana was to be born a poet', with her 'beautiful, gifted, artistic' grandmother, who introduced her to the works of Balzac, Dickens and Anatole France and told her she would be either a writer or the first woman President of the USA. Indiana gave her a strong conviction of being a Middle West writer; her grandmother after a stroke gave her her first observation of a state between dream and reality ('like Lear on the heath'). She was educ. at Indiana and Butler Univs. (BA, 1930), then at the Univ. of Chicago (MA, 1936). Her thesis on the birds and beasts of *Euphues* and her later doctoral research on Elizabethan and Jacobean emblems signalled her writerly fascination with systems of symbols. She dismissed her early poems, *Prismatic Ground*, 1937, as 'a teenage book'; but the philosophic, often playful poems of *Moderate Fable*, 1944, won the American Academy of Arts and Letters Award, 1945. *Angel in the Forest*, also 1945, studies two Utopias, one of married celibates at New Harmony, Indiana, the other, which followed it immediately on the same site, Robert Owen's community of free-lovers and agnostics. As a student, MY read Shakespeare to 'the Opium Lady', 'the most fabulous, single person I had known', who, with Madame Blavatsky, became the model for the leading character in MY's epic novel, *Miss MacIntosh, My Darling* (begun 1947, published in sections from then, complete in 1965). During its writing, MY taught at the New School for Social Research in NYC and at various universities. Called 'one of the few fully integrated syntheses of recent psychological discoveries and archetypal mythologies in our contemporary literature', it has, for its scope, density of metaphorical webbing, ear for the unconscious, and stylistic richness, been compared with Proust and Joyce. A learned 'inquest into the illusions individuals suffer from', it investigates the meaning-making mind: in the quest of Vera Cartwright for her former nursemaid, now presumed dead, MY layers the apparent unity of the 'so usual, down-to-earth' Miss MacIntosh into the multiplicity of 'many moods and many dimensions'. Widely learned, MY sees literature in its relation to other fields, including psychology, philosophy, religion, ornithology. She has spent much of her life in Greenwich Village, where she became a friend of Mari SANDOZ and Anaïs NIN. She wrote a memoir of political reporter Paul Y. Anderson, 1939. Interview in *Paris Rev.*, 18, 1977, and affectionate critical reminiscence by MY's former student Erika Duncan, in *Unless Soul Clap Its Hands*, 1984, both quoted above.

Young, Mary Julia, poet and novelist living in London, educ. by her mother, often confused with Mary (Young) SEWELL. Her 'Voluminous' output mostly went to press uncorrected, sheet by sheet. She issued her first novel, *The Family Party*, MINERVA 1791, anonymously, but poems with her name: *Adelaide and Antonine*, 1793, a sentimental tale of French refugees to England's 'hospitable shore', and *Genius and Fancy*, 1795 (a survey of the London stage, circulated in MS from 1792). Most of *Poems*, 1798, re-appeared as *The Metrical Museum*, part I [1801]. Her novels are well-told though implausibly plotted, good-humouredly disparaging of fashionable society. The heroine of *The East Indian, or Clifford Priory*, 1799, approaches theatre-going seriously and apparent GOTHIC mysteries with gusto; her curmudgeonly great-uncle and a Jewish moneylender (who despises 'the Christian's law' of 'de life for de property') have each a heart of gold. MJY liked best her sentimental *Right and Wrong, or The Kinsmen of Naples*, 1803, opening in Italy and closing in Wales. The melodramatic, racist *Mother and Daughter*, 1804, about settlers in San Domingo, is one of her several translations. The heroine of *Donalda, or The Witches of Glenshiel*, 1805, deals boldly with supposed ghosts and corpses. MJY wrote the life of actress Anna Maria Crouch, 1806. The CIRCULATING LIBRARIES gave her 'a very fair reading'; she applied to the RLF in 1808, after a publisher's bankruptcy, to tide her over till her next work, calling herself the survivor of two large families: last relation of the poet Edward Y., she had outlived six siblings and 25 cousins.

Young, Rida (Johnson), 1875–1926, playwright and songwriter, b. Baltimore, Maryland, da. of Emma (Stuart) and William A. J. She was educ. at public schools and at Wilson College, Chambersberg, Penn. Despite family opposition, she attempted a career in NYC as actress and playwright, initially without success, and also wrote songs, 'Mother Machree' being her best known. She m. James Y. in 1904, but they were later divorced. *Brown of Harvard*, 1906, her first successful play, ran for five years and was filmed in 1925. It was followed by more than two dozen other plays and musicals and over 500 songs. Her comedy *Little Old New York*, 1920, in which various real New Yorkers like Washington Irving and John Jacob Astor are linked to a girl-disguised-as-a-boy plot, was filmed twice and she also wrote a novelized version. It features a spirited young heroine, while *The Lottery Man*, 1909, includes several strong parts for older women. Her plays are uniformly comic rather than realistic, and her formula of 'youth and young love', while not winning critical acclaim, brought her great popular success.

Z

Zaturenska, Marya, 1902–82, poet, b. in Kiev, Russia. Her parents, Johanna (Lupovska) and Avram Alexander Z., migrated to the US in 1909. A US citizen from 1912, she left high school for factory work, but studied at night and attended Valparaiso Univ., 1922–3, and the Univ. of Wisconsin; she graduated in library science in 1925, the year she married poet and critic Horace Gregory. She published in poetry magazines as a student, then became a newspaper feature-writer. Her volumes *Threshold and Hearth*, 1934, *Cold Morning Sky*, 1937 (Pulitzer Prize), and *The Listening Landscape*, 1941, use landscape to explore the psyche: 'Imagination colors all our watching mood.' GOTHIC elements ('The frightened virgin at the burning fountain') represent fear and desire, with its intimations of decay encroaching on innocence: 'In that rich burial ground where the leveled dead / Lie darkened in extinction, I have groped / Through solitudes like death'. Woman appears as elusive object of desire ('Imperceptibly the world became haunted by her white dress. / So the years passed; more fierce in pursuit her image grew; / She became the dream abjured, the ill uncured, the deed undone, / The life one never lived'), or as mirrored, imaged, peering from windows. In later volumes (including *Collected Poems*, 1965, and *The Hidden Waterfall*, 1974) such imagery gradually gives way to Christian symbolism and classical myth. With her husband MZ wrote and edited works including a *History* of modern US poetry, 1946, and a volume of *Religious Verse*, 1957; she wrote a life of Christina ROSSETTI, 1949, and edited the poems of Sara TEASDALE, 1966. Teasdale admired Rossetti; MZ claims lineage from both Rossetti's 'devotional inspiration' and Teasdale's 'inner world', 'personal, lucid, pure, somewhat classical, in the best sense'.

Zins-Penninck or Zinspinning, **Judith**, later Sewel, d. 1664, Quaker pamphleteer of Amsterdam. Da. of Conrad Z., in early life a Baptist, she m. Jacob Williamson S. and with him joined the Quakers in 1657. Well known as a preacher in Holland, she visited England in 1663, the year her *Some Worthy Proverbs*, addressed to English Friends, appeared in London in English (her second work to be translated). It urges 'Hearken then unto the Instructions of thy Father, and forsake not the Command of thy Mother, that thou mayest be freed from the sore servitude.' She died young. Her son William S. published a *History* of Quakers, 1722, with an 'Epistle' she wrote *c.* 1664.

Zugsmith, Leane, 1903–69, novelist, short-story writer, b. in Louisville, Ky., da. of Gertrude (Appel) and Albert Z., who privately printed writing she did at five. She grew up in Atlantic City, NJ, and was educ. at Goucher College, the Univ. of Pennsylvania, and Columbia. After working in pulp magazines, advertising, and (briefly) Hollywood screen-writing, she married journalist Carl Randau, 1940, settled in New York, and wrote special features for the paper *P.M.* Opposed to fascism, including US 'disguised forms', she published six novels (not, she said, 'proletarian novels') which often reflect current political events, ethnic (notably Jewish) radicalism and labour unionism. She researched her facts and cared about fictional technique, admiring Josephine HERBST and learning from Virgina WOOLF. In *All Victories Are Alike*, 1929, a disenchanted journalist tries and fails to make his wife conform to his feminine ideal. In *Goodbye and Tomorrow*, 1931, an elderly woman becomes a patron of the arts. *Never Enough*, 1932, looks cynically at 1920s hedonism; *The Reckoning*, 1934, centres on a boy from NYC slums. *A Time to Remember*, 1936, links women of different backgrounds (working-class immigrant, privileged middle-class Jewish) in a strike of department-store workers. In *The Summer Soldier*, 1938, a group of Northern liberals investigates reported abuses of black workers in the South. *Home is Where You Hang Your Childhood*, 1937, and *Hard Times with Easy Payments*, 1941, are short-story volumes, *L Is for Labor*, 1938, a pamphlet glossary of labour terms. LZ published two books jointly with her husband: *The Setting Sun of Japan*, 1942 (based on travels for *P.M.*), and *The Visitor*, 1944, a mystery story, later a play. She went on printing stories in *The New Yorker* and elsewhere after moving to Madison, Conn., in the 1940s.

Zwicky, Fay (Rosefield), poet, critic, short-story writer, b. 1933 in Melbourne, Victoria, da. of Iris (Rothstadt) and Clifford R. Her European Jewish cultural heritage has enriched her work at many levels. She was educ. at the Church of England Girls' Grammar School, Melbourne, and the Univ. of Melbourne, where she began publishing poems and stories. A talented musician, she toured as a concert pianist for several years. She was a senior lecturer in English at the Univ. of Western Australia until 1987. She first attracted critical attention for her poetry, collected in *Isaac Babel's Fiddle*, 1975, and the prize-winning *Kaddish and other poems*, 1982, which includes the sequence 'Ark Voices'. She has since pub. a collection of stories, *Hostages*, 1983. A dominant concern in her writing has been a metaphysical quest for synthesis of the contemplative and active life. She is a committed humanist, and her work generally endorses patricarchal values, though she defends Sylvia PLATH against Hughes's 'editing' and can surprise with odd flashes of irreverent humour, as when Mrs Noah speaks (in 'Ark Voices'): 'Lord, the cleaning's nothing / What's a pen or two?' An original and forceful critic and lecturer, she has pub. many essays and reviews, some of which have been collected in *The Lyre in the Pawnshop*, 1986. She has also ed. *Quarry: a Selection of Western Australian Poetry*, 1981, *Journeys*, 1982 (an anthology of poems by Judith WRIGHT, Rosemary DOBSON, Gwen HARWOOD and Dorothy HEWETT pub. by the Australian feminist press Sisters), and *Procession: Young Street Poets*, 1987.

List of Works Frequently Cited

The following list includes works much used: those whose frequent appearance makes it economical to give a short form in the body of the text. It includes neither the vast range of sources from which materials for entries have been drawn, nor the standard reference books to which bio-bibliographical researchers must have constant recourse: Allibone's *Dictionary*, 1858, Boase's *Biography*, 1892ff, S. J. Brown's *Irish Fiction, Contemporary Authors, The Dictionary of American Biography, Dictionary of Literary Biography, Dictionary of National Biography*, Kunitz, Mainiero's *American Women Writers*, Miles's *Poets*, repr. 1905–7, Poole's Index, Todd's *Women Writers 1660–1800, Twentieth-Century Authors*, the *Wellesley Index*, etc.

Abel, Elizabeth, ed., *The Voyage In: Fictions of Female Development*, Hanover, NH, 1983.
Adelaide, Debra, ed., *A Bright and Fiery Troop: Australian Women Writers of the Nineteenth Century*, Ringwood, Victoria, 1988.
Auerbach, Nina, *Communities of Women: An Idea in Fiction*, Cambridge, Mass., 1978.
Bakerman, Jane S., *And Then There Were Nine . . . More Women of Mystery*, Bowling Green, Ohio, 1985.
Ballard, George, *Memoirs of Several Ladies of Great Britain Who Have Been Celebrated for Their Writings or Skill in the Learned Languages, Arts and Sciences*, Oxford, 1752: ed. Ruth Perry, Detroit, 1985.
Bargainnier, Earl F., *10 Women of Mystery*, Bowling Green, Ohio, 1985.
Bataille, Gretchen M., and Kathleen Mullen Sands, *American Indian Women: Telling Their Lives*, Lincoln, Neb., 1984.
Baym, Nina, *Women's Fiction: A Guide to Novels by and about Women in America, 1820–1870*, Ithaca and London, 1978.
Beauman, Nicola, *A Very Great Profession: The Women's Novel 1914–39*, London, 1983.
Beilin, Elaine V., *Redeeming Eve: Women Writers of the English Renaissance*, Princeton, 1987.
Bell, Roseann P., ed., *Sturdy Black Bridges: Visions of Black Women in Literature*, Garden City, NY, 1979.
Benstock, Shari, *Women of the Left Bank: Paris, 1900–1940*, Austin, Texas, 1987.
Berrian, Brenda F., *Bibliography of African Women Writers and Journalists*, Washington, DC, 1985.
——, *Bibliography of Women Writers from the Caribbean*, Washington, DC, 1989.
Betsko, Kathleen, and Rachel Koenig, *Interviews with Contemporary Women Playwrights*, New York, 1987.
Black, Helen, *Notable Women Authors of the Day*, Glasgow, 1893; repr. Freeport, NY, 1972.
Brink, J.R., ed., *Female Scholars: A Tradition of Learned Women before 1800*, Montreal, 1980.
Brown, Cheryl L., and Karen Olson, eds., *Feminist Criticism: Essays on Theory, Poetry and Prose*, Metuchen and London, 1976.
Brown, Janet, *Feminist Drama: Definition and Critical Analysis*, Metuchen and London, 1979.
Brown, Lloyd W., *Women Writers in Black Africa*, Westport, Conn., 1981.
Bruchac, Joseph, *Survival This Way: Interviews with American Indian Poets*, Tucson, Ariz., 1987.
Carby, Hazel, *Reconstructing Womanhood: The Emergence of the Afro-American Woman Novelist*, Oxford and New York, 1987.
Chinoy, Helen Krich, and Linda Walsh Jenkins, *Women in American Theatre: Careers, Images, Movements, An Illustrated Sourcebook*, New York, 1981.
Christian, Barbara, *Black Women Novelists: The Development of a Tradition, 1892–1976*, Westport, Conn., 1980.
—— *Black Feminist Criticism*, New York, 1985.
Colby, Vineta, *The Singular Anomaly: Women Novelists of the Nineteenth Century*, New York, 1970.
Cotton, Nancy, *Women Playwrights in England, c. 1363–1750*, Lewisburg, Penn., and London, 1980.
Craig, Patricia, and Mary Cadogan, *The Lady Investigates: Women Detectives and Spies in Fiction*, London, 1981.
Crawford, Patricia, 'Women's Published Writings 1600–1700' in Mary Prior, below.
Crosland, Margaret, *Beyond the Lighthouse: English Women Novelists in the 20th Century*, London, 1981.

Cunningham, Gail, *The New Woman and the Victorian Novel*, London and New York, 1978.
Daims, Diva, and Janet Grimes, *Toward a Feminist Tradition: An Annotated Bibliography of Novels in English by Women, 1891–1920*, New York, 1982.
Dalziel, Margaret, *Popular Fiction 100 Years Ago: An Unexplored Tract of Literary History*, London, 1957.
Dance, Daryl Cumber, ed., *Fifty Caribbean Writers: A Bio-Bibliographical Critical Sourcebook*, New York, 1986.
Davidson, Cathy N., *Revolution and the Word: The Rise of the Novel in America*, New York and Oxford, 1986.
Davies, Carole Boyce, and Anne Adams Graves, *Ngambika: Studies of Women in African Literature*, Trenton, NJ, 1986.
Donovan, Josephine, ed., *Feminist Literary Criticism: Explorations in Theory*, Lexington, Ky, 1975.
Evans, Mari, ed., *Black Women Writers (1950–1980): A Critical Evaluation*, Garden City, NY, 1984.
Ferguson, Moira, *First Feminists: British Women Writers, 1578–1799*, Bloomington, Ind., 1985.
Fisher, Dexter, *The Third Woman: Minority Women Writers of the United States*, Boston, 1980.
France, Rachel, ed., *A Century of Plays by American Women*, New York, 1979.
Freibert, Lucy M., and Barbara A. White, eds., *Hidden Hands: An Anthology of American Women Writers, 1790–1870*, New Brunswick, NJ, 1985.
Gartenberg, Patricia, and Nena Thames Whittemore, 'A Checklist of English Women in Print, 1475–1640', *Bulletin of Bibliography and Magazine Notes*, 34, 1977: 1–13.
Gates, Henry Louis, Jr., gen. ed., The Schomburg Library of Nineteenth-Century Black Women Writers, 30 vols., New York and Oxford, 1988– .
Gelfant, Blanche H., *Women Writers in America: Voices in Collage*, Hanover, NH, 1984.
Gilbert, Pam, *Coming Out from Under: Contemporary Australian Women Writers*, London, 1988.
Gilbert, Sandra M., and Susan Gubar, *The Madwoman in the Attic: The Woman Writer and the Nineteenth-Century Literary Imagination*, New Haven and London, 1979.
——, *Shakespeare's Sisters: Feminist Essays on Women Poets*, Indiana University Press, Bloomington and London, 1979.
Godard, Barbara, *Bibliography of Feminist Literary Criticism – Bibliographie de la critique féministe*, Toronto, 1987.
——, ed., *Gynocritics/Gynocritique: Feminist Approaches to Writing by Canadian and Québécoise Women/Approches Féministes à l'écriture des canadiennes et québécoise*, Toronto, 1987.
Gould, Jean, *Modern American Women Poets, Pioneers of Modern Poetry*, New York, 1984.
Greer, Germaine, Susan Hastings, Jeslyn Medoff, Melinda Sansone, eds., *Kissing the Rod: An Anthology of Seventeenth-Century Women's Verse*, London, 1988.
Hannay, Margaret P., *Silent But For the Word: Tudor Women as Patrons, Translators, and Writers of Religious Works*, Kent, Ohio, 1985.
Hanscombe, Gillian, and Virginia L. Smyers, *Writing for Their Lives: The Modernist Women, 1910–1940*, London, 1987.
Helsinger, Elizabeth, et al., *The Woman Question: Society and Literature in Britain and North America 1837–1883*, 3 vols., New York and London, 1981.
Herrera-Sobek, Maria, ed., *Beyond Stereotypes: The Critical Analysis of Chicana Literature*, Binghamton, NY, 1985.
Highfill, Philip H., Kalman A. Burnim, and Edward A. Langhans, *A Biographical Dictionary of Actors, Actresses ...1660–1800*, Carbondale, Ill., 1973– .
Hobby, Elaine, *Virtue of Necessity: English Women's Writing 1646–1688*, London, 1988.
Homans, Margaret, *Woman Writers and Poetic Identity: Dorothy Wordsworth, Emily Brontë, and Emily Dickinson*, Princeton, 1980.
Itzin, Catherine, *Stages in the Revolution: Political Theatre in Britain Since 1968*, London, 1980.
James, Edward T., et al., eds., *Notable American Women, 1607–1950: A Biographical Dictionary*, Cambridge, Mass., 1971.
Jelinek, Estelle C., ed., *Women's Autobiography: Essays in Criticism*, Bloomington, Ind., 1980.
Jones, Anne Goodwyn, *Tomorrow is Another Day: The Woman Writer in the South, 1859–1936*, Baton Rouge, La., 1981.
Jones, Eldred, *Women in African Literature Today: A Review*, Trenton, NJ, 1987.
Juhasz, Suzanne, *Naked and Fiery Forms: Modern American Poetry by Women, A New Tradition*, New York, 1976.
Kanner, Barbara, ed., *The Women of England from Anglo-Saxon Times to the Present: Interpretive Bibliographical Essays*, Hamdon, Conn., and London, 1979.
Keyssar, Helene, *Feminist Theatre: An Introduction to Plays of Contemporary British and American Women*, London, 1984.
Klein, Kathleen Gregory, *The Woman Detective: Gender and Genre*, Urbana and Chicago, 1988.

Lee, L. L., and Merrill Lewis, eds., *Women, Women Writers, and the West*, Troy, NY, 1979.
Lefanu, Sarah, *In the Chinks of the World Machine: Feminism and Science Fiction*, London, 1988, repr. as *Feminism and Science Fiction*, Bloomington, Ind., 1989.
Malpede, Karen, *Women in Theatre: Compassion and Hope*, New York, 1983.
Marzolf, Marion, *Up from the Footnote: A History of Women Journalists*, New York, 1977.
Melman, Billie, *Women and the Popular Imagination in the Twenties: Flappers and Nymphs*, London, 1988.
Mickelson, Anne Z., *Reaching Out: Sensitivity and Order in Recent American Fiction by Women*, Metuchen, NJ, 1979.
Mitchell, Sally, *The Fallen Angel: Chastity, Class and Women's Reading, 1835–1880*, Bowling Green, Ohio, 1981.
Moers, Ellen, *Literary Women: The Great Writers*, NY, 1976.
Moraga, Cherrie, and Gloria Anzaldúa, eds., *This Bridge Called My Back: Writings by Radical Women of Color*, New York, 1981.
Mordecai, Pamela, and Mervyn Morris, eds., *Jamaica Woman: An Anthology of Poems*, Kingston, Jamaica, and London, 1980.
Moss, John, *A Reader's Guide to the Canadian Novel*, Toronto, 1981: 2nd ed. 1987.
Mussell, Kay, *Women's Gothic and Romantic Fiction: A Reference Guide*, Westport, Conn., 1981.
Natalle, Elizabeth J., *Feminist Theatre: A Study in Persuasion*, Metuchen, NJ, and London, 1985.
Nestor, Pauline, *Female Friendship and Communities: Charlotte Brontë, George Eliot, Elizabeth Gaskell*, Oxford and New York, 1985.
Neuman, Shirley, and Smaro Kamboureli, eds., *A Mazing Space: Writing Canadian Women Writing*, Edmonton, Alberta, 1986.
Olauson, Judith, *The American Woman Playwright: A View of Criticism and Characterization*, Troy, NY, 1981.
Oliphant, Margaret, et al., *Women Novelists of Queen Victoria's Reign*, London, 1897, repr. Folcroft, Penn., 1969.
Ostriker, Alicia, *Writing Like a Woman*, Ann Arbor, Mich., 1983.
——, *Stealing the Language: The Emergence of Women's Poetry in America*, Boston, 1986.
Palmegiano, E.M., *Women and British Periodicals, 1832–1867*, New York and London, 1976.
Perry, Ruth, *Women, Letters and the Novel*, New York, 1980.
Prior, Mary, ed., *Women in English Society, 1500–1800*, London, 1984.
Pryse, Marjorie, and Hortense J. Spillers, eds., *Conjuring: Black Women, Fiction, and Literary Tradition*, Bloomington, Ind., 1985.
Radford, Jean, ed., *The Progress of Romance: The Politics of Popular Fiction*, London and New York, 1986.
Radway, Janice, *Reading the Romance: Women, Patriarchy, and Popular Literature*, Chapel Hill, NC, 1984.
Rainwater, Catherine, and William J. Scheick, eds., *Contemporary American Women Writers: Narrative Strategies*, Lexington, Ky, 1985.
Read, Thomas Buchanan, *The Female Poets of America*, 1848, repr. New York, 1969.
Reardon, Joan, and Kristine Thorsen, *Poetry by American Women, 1900–1975: A Bibliography*, Metuchen, NJ, 1979.
Reddy, Maureen T., *Sisters in Crime: Feminism and the Crime Novel*, New York, 1988.
Reynolds, Myra, *The Learned Lady in England, 1650–1760*, Boston, 1920.
Robinson, Doris, *Women Novelists, 1891–1920: An Index to Biographical and Autobiographical Sources*, New York, 1984.
Rogers, Katharine M., *Feminism in Eighteenth-Century England*, Urbana, Ill., 1982.
Rule, Jane, *Lesbian Images*, Garden City, NY, 1975.
Rumens, Carol, ed., *Making for the Open: The Chatto Book of Post-Feminist Poetry, 1964–1984*, London, 1985.
Schipper, Mineke, *Unheard Words: Women and Literature in Africa, the Arab World, Asia, the Caribbean and Latin America*, London, 1985.
Schofield, Mary Anne, and Cecilia Macheski, eds., *Fetter'd or Free? British Women Novelists, 1670–1815*, Athens, Ohio, and London, 1986.
Schwartz, Narda Lacey, *Articles on Women Writers, 1960–1975: A Bibliography*, Santa Barbara, Calif., and Oxford, 1977.
Shockley, Ann Allen, *Afro-American Women Writers, 1746–1933: An Anthology and Critical Guide*, Boston, 1988.
Showalter, Elaine, *A Literature of Their Own: British Women Novelists from Brontë to Lessing*, London, 1977; rev. 1982.

Spencer, Jane, *The Rise of the Woman Novelist: From Aphra Behn to Jane Austen*, Oxford, 1986.
Spender, Dale, *Writing a New World: Two Centuries of Australian Women Writers*, London and New York, 1988.
Staley, Thomas, ed., *Twentieth-Century Women Novelists*, London, 1982.
Sternburg, Janet, ed., *The Writer on Her Work*, New York, 1980.
Stetson, Erlene, ed., *Black Sisters: Poetry by Black American Women, 1746–1890*, Bloomington, Ind., 1981.
Taiwo, Oladele, *Female Novelists of Modern Africa*, New York and London, 1984.
Tate, Claudia, ed., *Black Women Writers at Work*, New York, 1983.
Todd, Janet, *Women's Friendship in Literature*, New York, 1980.
——, ed., *Women Writers Talking*, New York, 1983.
Tompkins, J.M.S., *The Popular Novel in England, 1770–1800*, London, 1932, repr. 1969.
Toth, Emily, ed., *Regionalism and the Female Imagination, A Collection of Essays*, New York, 1985.
Twigg, Alan, *For Openers: Conversions with 24 Canadian Writers*, Madiera, BC, 1981.
Walker, Cheryl, *The Nightingale's Burden: Women Poets and American Culture before 1900*, Bloomington, Ind., 1983.
Wandor, Michelene, *Carry On, Understudies: Theatre and Sexual Politics*, London and New York, 1981, rev. 1986.
——, *Look Back in Gender: Sexuality and the Family in Post-War British Drama*, London, 1987.
Watts, Emily Stipes, *The Poetry of American Women from 1632 to 1945*, Austin, Texas, and London, 1977.
Westbrook, A.G.R. and P.D., *The Writing Women of New England, 1630–1900: An Anthology*, Metuchen, NJ, 1982.
White, Barbara Anne, *American Women Writers: An Annotated Bibliography of Criticism*, New York, 1977.
White, Cynthia, *Women's Magazines 1693–1968*, London, 1970.
Williams, Merryn, *Six Women Novelists*, London, 1987.
Wolff, Robert Lee. *Nineteenth-Century Fiction: A Bibliographical Catalogue Based on the Collection Formed by*, 5 vols., New York, 1981–6
——, *Gains and Losses: Novels of Faith and Doubt in Victorian England*, New York and London, 1977.

Indexes

Index of Topics

Index of Names (Chronological)

Writers are grouped by birth-date: within a century, then a half-century, then a quarter-century, After each group are listed those whose place there is only probable, with dates of writing or publishing.

Ann Hughes, active 1784–90, Sarah Isdell, active 1805–11, Elizabeth Keir, active 1785–7, Anna Margaretta Larpent, active 1782–1830, Helen Leigh, pub. 1788, Anna Maria Mackenzie, active 1783–1809, E. H. M'Leod, active 1821–30, P. D. Manvill, active 1807–10, Mrs Martin, active 1798–1801, Mary Meeke, active 1795–1816, Ann Murry, active 1778–1818, Agnes Musgrave, active 1795–1801, Henrietta Neale, active 1794–8, Mary O'Brien, active 1785–90, Frances O'Neill, active 1789–1802, Catherine Parry, active 1777–84, Mrs F. C. Patrick, active 1797–9, Mrs Patterson, active ?1797, Susanna Pearson, active 1790–1800, M. Peddle, active 1785–9, Amelia Pickering, pub. 1788, Miss or Mrs Pilkington, active 1790–1802, Elizabeth and Jane Purbeck, active 1789–1802, Martha Meredith Read, pub. 1802, Catherine Selden, active 1797–1817, Mrs Showes, active 1798–?1805, Eleanor Sleath, active 1798–1810, Eunice Smith, active 1791–8, Julia Smith, active 1809–13, Augusta Amelia Stuart, active 1808–[13], Eleanor Tatlock, active *c.* 1800–11, Harriet Thomson, active 1787–1807, Sojourner Truth, active 1850, Catharine Upton, active 1781–4, Eglinton Wallace, active 1787–98, Sarah Scudgell Wilkinson, active 1800?–28, Mary Julia Young, active 1791–1808.

Born 1801–25: Sarah Flower Adams, Grace Aguilar, Annie Alexander, Cecil Frances Alexander, Susan B. Anthony, Delia Salter Bacon, Clara Balfour, Isabella Banks, Charlotte Barnes, Clara Barton, Annie Baxter, Antoinette Blackwell, Isa Blagden, Amelia Jenks Bloomer, Sara Tittle Bolton, Anne Botta, Jessie Boucherett, Sue Bowen, Mary Boyle, Anne, Charlotte and Emily Brontë, Mary Brotherton, Frances Brown(e), Elizabeth Barrett Browning, Selina Bunbury, Anna Maria Bunn, Cecilia Mary Caddell, Jane Welsh Carlyle, Alice and Phoebe Cary, Elizabeth Chandler, Georgiana Chatterton, Ednah Dow Cheney, Caroline Chesebro, Mary Boykin Chesnut, Lydia Maria Child, Caroline Chisholm, Louise Clappe, Mary Clarke, Caroline Clive, Frances Power Cobbe, Sara Coleridge, Mary Colling, Eliza Cook, Susan Fenimore Cooper, Camilla Crosland, Madeleine Dahlgren, Caroline Healey Dall, Lucretia Maria and Margaret M. Davidson, Abby Morton Diaz, Mary Doolittle, Julia Dorr, Anna Dorsey, Eliza Dupuy, Mary Henderson Eastman, Mary Baker Eddy, George Eliot, Elizabeth Ellet, Emma Embury, Anne Evans, Eliza Farnham, Elizabeth Fenton, Fanny Fern, Marjory Fleming, Caroline Fox, Elizabeth Frame, Lucy Virginia French, Margaret Fuller, Lady Georgiana Fullerton, Frances Gage, Elizabeth Gaskell, Margaret Gatty, Charlotte Godley, Lucie Duff Gordon, Mary Anne Gray, Dora Greenwell, Grace Greenwood, Maria Grey, Angelina Emily Grimké, Lucretia Peabody Hale, Louisa Jane Hall, Mary Duffus Hardy, Frances Ellen Watkins Harper, Elizabeth Hawthorne, Matilda Hays, Sarah Herbert, Mary Jane Holmes, Lucy Hooper, Matilda Charlotte Houston, (Anne and) Mary Matilda Howard, Julia Ward Howe, Mary Catherine Hume, Jean Ingelow, Harriet Jacobs, Marian James, Henrietta Camilla Jenkin, Charlotte Ann Jerauld, Geraldine Jewsbury, Emily Judson, Julia Kavanagh, Annie Keary, Elizabeth Keckley, Adelaide Kemble, Fanny Kemble, Elizabeth Kinney, Juliette Augusta Kinzie, Caroline Matilda Kirkland, Fanny Aikin Kortright, L. E. L., Anne Langton, Lucy Larcom, Mary Elizabeth Lee, Eliza Lynn Linton, Jane Starkweather Locke, 'Roxburghe Lothian', Rosina Bulwer Lytton, Louisa McCord, Maria McIntosh, Katharine Macquoid, Anne Manning, Mary Martin, Harriet Martineau, Louisa Meredith, Elizabeth Avery Meriwether, Eliza Meteyard, Susanna Moodie, Anna Mowatt, Anne Mozley, Harriet Mozley, Mary Ann Muller, Louisa Murray, Mary Nichols, Florence Nightingale, Mrs John Vavasour Noel, Caroline Norton, Frances Notley, Elizabeth Oakes Smith, Eliza Ogilvy, Marianne Orvis, Frances Osgood, Julia Pardoe, Elizabeth Palmer Peabody, Elizabeth Wooster Phelps, Mary Pike, Lady Mary Emily Ponsonby, Margaret Junkin Preston, Adelaide Procter, Mary Traill Putnam, Anna, Margaret and Sophia Quincy, Elizabeth Rigby, Margaret Murray Robertson, Emma Robinson, Harriet Jane Robinson, Sarah Royce, Mary Anne Sadlier, George Sand, Margaret Sandbach, Alicia Scott, Harriett Anne Scott, Mary Seacole, Anna Sewell, Elizabeth Sewell, Emily Shirreff, Arabella Shore, Felicia Skene, Menella Bute Smedley, Harriet(te) Smythies, E. D. E. N. Southworth, Catherine Spence, Speranza, Elizabeth Cady Stanton, Ann Sophia Stephens, Maria W. Stewart, Elizabeth Drew Stoddard, Elizabeth Stone, Lucy Stone, Harriet Beecher Stowe, Julia Stretton, Anna Swanwick, Margaret Sweat, Jemima Tautphoeus, Harriet Taylor, Mary Taylor, Harriet Frances Thynne, Henrietta Euphemia Tindal, Annie Tinsley, Catharine Parr Traill, Charlotte Maria Tucker, Queen Victoria, Mary Vidal, Ellen Wallace, Catherine Ann Ware Warfield, Anna Laetitia Waring, Susan Bogert Warner, Amelia Welby, Frances Miriam Berry Whitcher, Rhoda Elizabeth White, Narcissa Whitman, Sarah Helen Power Whitman, Jane Williams, Harriet E. Wilson, Ellen Wood, Emma Wood, Emma Jane Worboise, Charlotte Yonge.

Mrs Robert Cartwright, active 1850–9, Mabel Sharman Crawford, active 1859–64, Anna Drury, active 1840–79, Anne Katharine Elwood, active 1830–43, Catherine Hubback, active 1850–67, Janet Phillips, active 1850–92.

Born 1826–50: Bertha Jane Adams, Louisa May Alcott, Isabella Alden, Elizabeth Akers Allen, Eliza Andrews, C. L. Antrobus, Agatha Armour, Louisa Atkinson, Jane Austin, J. Calder Ayrton, Louisa Baldwin, Mary Anne Barker, Charlotte Barnard, Amelia Barr, Emilie Barrington, Frances Baylor, Lydia Becker, Annie Besant, Matilda Betham-Edwards, L. S. Bevington, Isabella Bird, Helen Blackburn, E. Owens Blackburne, Lillie Devereux Blake, Mathilde Blind, Barbara Bodichon, Sara Knowles Bolton, 'Sherwood Bonner', Mary Louise Booth, Dorothea Boulger, Mary Elizabeth Braddon, Mary Eliza Bramston, Anna Brassey, Emma Frances Brooke, Rhoda Broughton, Mary Edwards Bryan, Frances Hodgson Burnett, Josephine Butler, Bertha Henry Buxton, Jessie Ellen Cadell, Ada Cambridge, Caroline Emily Lovett Cameron, Helen Stuart Campbell, Rosa Nouchette Carey, Sarah Elizabeth Carmichael, Mary Hartwell Catherwood, Charlotte Chanter, Elizabeth Charles, Kate Chopin, 'Lucas Cleeve', Mary Ellen Clerke, Frances Colenso, Christabel Coleridge, Laure Conan, Isabella Valancy Crawford, Rose Terry Cooke, Ina Coolbrith, Katherine Cooper,

Elizabeth Burgoyne Corbett, Isa Craig, Dinah Mulock Craik, B. M. Croker, May Crommelin, Mary Cruger, Hannah Cullwick, Maria Cummins, Sarah Curzon, Elizabeth Bacon Custer, Emily Davies, Rebecca Harding Davis, Charlotte Dempster, Mary Andrews Denison, Charlotte Despard, Emily Dickinson, Alice Diehl, Emilia Frances Dilke, E. A. Dillwyn, Mary Abigail Dodge, Sarah Dorsey, Sarah Doudney, Amanda Douglas, 'George Douglas', Abigail Duniway, Annie Edward(e)s, Amelia Edwards, Lady Charlotte Elliot, Sarah Barnwell Elliott, Ellen E. Ellis, Augusta Jane Evans, Juliana Ewing, Emily Faithfull, Lanoe Falconer, Violet Fane, Millicent Garrett Fawcett, Maria Fetherstonhaugh, Kate Field, Annie Fields, Martha Finley, May Agnes Fleming, Mary Hallock Foote, Mary Hannay Foott, Maud Jeanne Franc, Christiana Fraser-Tytler, Mary Eliza Frere, Maria Amelia Fytche, Matilda Joslyn Gage, Emily Gerard, Ursula Gestefeld, Alice Giberne, Anne Gilchrist, Maria Grant, Maxwell Gray, Anna Katherine Green, Charlotte L. Forten Grimké, Marion Harland, Emily Marion Harris, Miriam Harris, Constance Harrison, Jane Harrison, Isabella Harwood, Mary R. Hatch, Alice B. Haven, Frances Ridley Havergal, 'Henry Hayes', Rachel Henning, Mary Eliza Herbert, Emily Hickey, Frances Sarah Hoey, Marietta Holley, Sarah Holmes, Lucy Hamilton Hooper, Sarah Winnemucca Hopkins, Mary Hoppus, Marie Howland, Margaret Hunt, Helen Hunt Jackson, Alice James, Sarah Orne Jewett, Amanda Theodocia Jones, Nina Kennard, Alice King, Harriet Eleanor King, Anna Kingsford, Lucy Knox, Emily Lawless, Jessie Lawson, Louisa Lawson, Mary Jane Katzmann Lawson, Emma Lazarus, Caroline Leakey, Holme Lee, Anna Leonowens, Rosanna Leprohon, Caroline Lindsay, Olive Logan, Maria Theresa Longworth, Josephine McCrackin, Agnes Maule Machar, L. Macmanus, Jessie White Mario, Florence Marryat, Emma Marshall, Catherine Martin, Janet Maughan, Gertrude Mayer, Isabella Fyvie Mayo, Adah Isaacs Menken, Alice Meynell, Jean Middlemass, Mary Louisa Molesworth, Florence Montgomery, F. F. Montrésor, Susan Morley, Louise Chandler Moulton, Rosa Mulholland, Georgina Munro, Mary Noailles Murfree, Mary Anne Needell, Charlotte O'Brien, Anne Ogle, Ellen O'Leary, Margaret Oliphant, Kathleen O'Meara, Ouida, Jane Ellen Panton, Elizabeth Mary Parker, Bessie Rayner Parkes, Frances Mary Peard, Emma Maria Pearson, Fanny Penny, Emily Jane Pfeiffer, Elizabeth Stuart Phelps, Sarah Morgan Piatt, Constance Plumptre, Rose Porter, Harriet Waters Preston, 'Allen Raine', Martha Remick, Laura Elizabeth Richards, Charlotte Riddell, Rita, Anne Thackeray Ritchie, Margaret Roberts, Christina Rossetti, Kate Sanborn, Mollie Dorsey Sanford, Margaret Sangster, Rose Scott, Anna Howard Shaw, Elizabeth Sheppard, Edith J, Simcox, Annie Slosson, Lucy Toulmin Smith, Emily Spender, Lilian Spender, Harriet Spofford, Flora Annie Steel, Anna Steele, Charlotte Stopes, Hesba Stretton, Eliza Tabor, 'Tasma', Eleanor Ashworth Taylor, Helen Taylor, Susie King Taylor, Celia Thaxter, Annie Thomas, Bertha Thomas, Frances Tiernan, Mary Tincker, Mary Townsend, Frances Eleanor Trollope, Harriet Tytler, Sarah Tytler, Gillan Vase, Sophie Veitch, Margaret Veley, Frances and Metta Victor, Linda Villari, Lucy Walford, Annie Louisa Walker, Jeannette Walworth, Waif Wander, Blanche Warre-Cornish, Augusta Webster, Emmeline Wells, Julia Wedgwood, Ella Wheeler Wilcox, Frances Willard, Sarah Williams, Victoria Woodhull, Sarah Woolsey, Constance Fenimore Woolson, 'Stephen Yorke'.

Emma Willsher Atkinson, active 1858–9, Harriette Bowra, active 1872–7, Martha Griffith Browne, active 1853–5, Marion Clarke, active 1872–87, Deas Cromarty, active 1873–1911, Cecil Griffith, active 1867–91, Mary Eliza Kennard, active 1883–1903, May Laffan, active 1874–87, Nannie Power O'Donoghue, active 1868–87, Louisa Parr, active 1868–97, Harriet Fanning Read, active 1848–60, Ellen Ross, active 1862–88, Helen Wallace, active 1888–1913.

Born 1851–75: Eleanor Abbot, Mildred Aldrich, Mary Andrews, Edith Jessie Archibald, Ethel M. Arnold, Gertrude Atherton, Mary Austin, Florence Ayscough, Alice Mabel Bacon, Temple Bailey, Ella Baker, Louisa Alice Baker, Elizabeth L. Banks, Helen Bannerman, Florence Barclay, Jane Barlow, Katharine Lee Bates, Blanche Baughan, Barbara Baynton, Gertrude Bell, Ursula Bethell, Mary McLeod Bethune, Mabel Birchenough, Clementina Black, Alice Stone Blackwell, Jean Blewett, Geraldine Bonner, B. M. Bower, Grace Boylan, Nina Boyle, Anna Branch, Angela Brazil, Alice Brown, Margaret Brown, J. E. Buckrose, Barbara Burke, Anna Robeson Burr, Olivia Ward Bush, Beatrice Butt, Mrs Julian Byng, Kathleen Caffyn, Emma Marie Caillard, Mona Caird, Emily Carr, Adelaide Casely-Hayford, Willa Cather, Ethel Mary Channon, Mary Cholmondeley, Lucy Clifford, Constance Clyde, Elizabeth Cochrane, Kathleen Coleman, Mary Coleridge, Colette, Katharine St John Conway, Anna Julia Cooper, Marie Corelli, J. E. Courtney, Elizabeth Covey, Edith Craig, Maud Cuney-Hare, 'Frank Danby', Ella D'Arcy, Olive Tilford Dargan, Mary Davis, Voltairine de Cleyre, Margaret Deland, Elizabeth De la Pasture, Mary Dickens, Maud Diver, Lady Florence Dixie, Ella Hepworth Dixon, Catherine Isabel Dodd, Lily Dougall, Menie Muriel Dowie, Alice Dudeney, Alice Dunbar-Nelson, Sara Jeanette Duncan, Toru Dutt, Elaine Goodale Eastman, 'George Egerton', Maud Howe Elliott, Edith Ellis, Edith Escombe, Erminda Rentoul Esler, Evelyn Everett-Green, 'Michael Fairless', Florence Farr, Gertrude Minnie Faulding, 'Michael Field', Mary and Jane Findlater, 'George Fleming', Anne Flexner, Mabel Forrest, Caroline Fothergill, Jessie Fothergill, Ellen Thorneycroft Fowler, M. E. Francis, Mary Fraser, Mary Wilkins Freeman, Elsa Freytag-Loringhoven, Anna Fuller, Mary Fullerton, Zona Gale, Helen Hamilton Gardener, Constance Garnett, Susa Young Gates, Mary Gaunt, Charlotte Perkins Gilman, Mary Gilmore, Helene Gingold, Ellen Glasgow, Elinor Glyn, Elizabeth Godfrey, Emma Goldman, Vida Goldstein, Maud Gonne, Maud Goodwin, Eva Gore-Booth, Nina Gorst, Sarah Grand, Clo. Graves, Sarah Greene, Augusta Gregory, Sydney Grier, Edith Grossman, Louise Guiney, Jeannie Gunn, Cicely Hamilton, Margaret Harkness, Ida Harper, Beatrice Harraden, Corra Harris, Susan Harrison, Frances Harrod, Kate E, Hayes, Florence Henniker, Alice Henry, Sophia Hensley, Frances Elizabeth Herring, Ella Higginson, 'John Oliver

Index of Cross-references